LAW OF PROPERTY
Fourth Edition

Dale A. Whitman

James E. Campbell Missouri Endowed Professor Emeritus of Law
University of Missouri School of Law

Ann M. Burkhart

Curtis Bradbury Kellar Professor of Law and
Distinguished University Teaching Professor
University of Minnesota Law School

R. Wilson Freyermuth

John D. Lawson Professor and Curators' Teaching Professor
University of Missouri School of Law

Troy A. Rule

Professor of Law
Arizona State University, Sandra Day O'Connor College of Law

HORNBOOK SERIES®

WEST
ACADEMIC
PUBLISHING

Hornbook Series is a trademark registered in the U.S. Patent and Trademark Office.

COPYRIGHT © 1984, 1993 By WEST PUBLISHING CO.
COPYRIGHT © 2000 By WEST GROUP
© 2019 LEG, Inc. d/b/a West Academic
     444 Cedar Street, Suite 700
     St. Paul, MN 55101
     1-877-888-1330

West, West Academic Publishing, and West Academic are trademarks of West Publishing Corporation, used under license.

Printed in the United States of America

ISBN: 978-1-64020-237-5

Preface

In its essence, private property is the right of a person or a defined group of persons to use a thing or a parcel of land and to exclude others from interfering with that use. One can barely conceive of a social order without property; every political society must have a system to insure that at any given time all items of land and goods will be in the protected use of identified persons. Even in a nation in which the state "owns" all property, a tractor driver may not own the tractor, as does the American farmer, but he or she has a protected right against others to use it for some period of time. What would be the consequences if some society attempted to abolish all such rights? Theft and vandalism would be legitimized, and no person in the society could make effective use of anything. Investment in property would make no sense in such a regime, and its aggregate wealth would dwindle into insignificance.

This book is about the American system of property law, but our law is descended from England. It began shortly after the Norman conquest of 1066, and English history still exerts a surprisingly strong influence on our system. The principles of property law comprise a very large subject. Anyone familiar with the workings of lawyers' minds and pens must know that nearly a thousand years of development will produce a prodigious body of law! Within one volume of hornbook size, this book surveys the chief areas and more: history and basic concepts; estates in land, present, future, and concurrent; comparable interests in personalty; landlord and tenant law; rights against neighbors and other third persons; easements and profits; running covenants; governmental controls on land use; land contracts; conveyances; titles; and recording systems.

Most people think of property law as unchanging, so stable as to be downright dull. But by small degrees, and occasionally by large leaps, property does advance, and for the most part in ways that better fit it to society's needs. In the nineteen years since this book's previous edition, it is not hard to identify important changes. One might think of the advent in many states of the beneficiary deed (or "transfer on death" deed), of electronic recording, or of statutes requiring notification and time to cure before construction defect litigation can be filed. In the area of land use controls, the Supreme Court has continued to refine the Fifth Amendment "takings" issue. Statutes amending the impact of the Rule Against Perpetuities have continued to proliferate. Many other examples could be cited. Property law turns out to be surprisingly fluid.

It may not be amiss to reflect briefly on this book's history. This is its fourth edition. Work on the first edition began in 1980 and it was published in 1984. Two of its three authors are now deceased. Roger A. Cunningham was the first to conceive of the book. Roger was born in Paxton, Illinois in 1921. He graduated from Harvard College in 1942 and Harvard Law School in 1948, practiced briefly in Boston, and then became a law teacher, first at George Washington University and then at Rutgers University, before joining the University of Michigan law faculty in 1959. He remained there for the rest of his academic career. Roger was a meticulous scholar with interests in all aspects of property law, but was perhaps best known for his work in land use planning law. He was responsible for the roots of the careful and thoughtful explication of estates in land and future interests that appears in all editions of this book, including the present one. Roger was a coauthor of both the first and second editions of this book. The second edition was published in 1993, and Roger died in 1994.

William B. Stoebuck was also an author of all previous editions of this book. Bill was born in Wichita, Kansas in 1929. He received a B.A. from Wichita State University in 1951 and joined the Air Force. During his service he earned an M.S. in history from Indiana University. After his discharge he enrolled in law school at the University of Washington, graduating in 1959. He practiced law in Seattle for five years. Bill then began his law teaching career at the University of Denver in 1964, and in 1967 moved to the faculty of the University of Washington, where he remained for the rest of his career. He received an S.J.D. degree from Harvard in 1973. Bill became the "dean" of Washington property law, but his influence was national as well as statewide.

Bill met Dale Whitman, the third original author of this book, when Dale joined the University of Washington faculty in 1978. The two became close friends, carpooled to work together, and talked endlessly of property law issues. Bill was a gifted writer and a brilliant thinker, with an encyclopedic knowledge of property law. The evidences of some of his best work are still apparent in Chapter 6 of this edition dealing with landlord and tenant law. The third edition of the book, prepared by Bill and Dale, was published in 2000, and Bill died in 2012.

We have divided the work on this edition in the following way. Ann Burkhart of the University of Minnesota prepared the first five chapters, which deal with estates, future interests, and concurrent ownership. Wilson Freyermuth of the University of Missouri was responsible for Chapters 6 and 8, dealing with landlord-tenant law and servitudes. Troy Rule of Arizona State University wrote Chapter 7 on rights incident to possession of land and Chapter 9 on land use controls. Dale Whitman, now an emeritus faculty member at the University of Missouri, prepared Chapters 10 and 11, which deal with conveyancing and titles.

We have endeavored to be as accurate and concise as possible, not a simple task when approaching a topic of this magnitude. We have not been reluctant to express our opinions about the merits of the present state of the law and the directions in which it should be moving, sometimes with the ill-concealed hope that we may nudge the courts in beneficial ways. We hope our writing is insightful, true to the memory of our deceased colleagues, and most of all, helpful to a new generation of law students and lawyers.

We thank our friends at West Academic for entrusting us with this enterprise, and our spouses for putting up with the many hours we spent at our computer keyboards. Our families share in the toll taken by this work, and they share in our hope that for you the reader our work will have been worthwhile.

ANN M. BURKHART
R. WILSON FREYERMUTH
TROY A. RULE
DALE A. WHITMAN

Acknowledgments

A number of authors and publishers have consented to our use of short extracts from their copyrighted materials. Such materials are clearly identified, where they appear in this book, by source and date of publication. Here, we gratefully acknowledge the permissions to reprint those copyrighted materials. In some instances, we were asked to note additional information about a work or to furnish acknowledgment in a particular form, and we are happy to comply with these requests in acknowledging permission to reprint the following materials.

Dunham, Possibility of Reverter and Powers of Termination—Fraternal or Identical Twins?, 20 U.Chi.L.Rev. 215, 219 (1953). Copyright © 1953, University of Chicago. Permission granted by University of Chicago Law Review.

Stoebuck, Running Covenants: An Analytical Primer, 53 Wash.L.Rev. 861 (1977). Copyright © 1977, Washington Law Review. Permission granted by Washington Law Review and Fred B. Rothman Company.

The American Law Institute, Model Land Development Code, Article 4 Commentary at pp. 150, 158. Copyright © 1976 by The American Law Institute. Permission granted by the American Law Institute.

Summary of Contents

Table of Contents

——————

B.   REVERSIONARY FUTURE INTERESTS

C.   NONREVERSIONARY FUTURE INTERESTS

D.   RESTRICTIONS ON CREATION OF NONREVERSIONARY FUTURE INTERESTS

E.   CHARACTERISTICS OF FUTURE INTERESTS

CHAPTER 4. RELATIONS BETWEEN OWNERS OF PRESENT AND FUTURE ESTATES AND INTERESTS

C.   CREATION OF THE LANDLORD-TENANT RELATIONSHIP

D.   TENANT'S RIGHT OF POSSESSION AND ENJOYMENT

E.   INTERFERENCE WITH TENANT'S POSSESSION

F.   CONDITION OF THE PREMISES

G. ANNEXATION OF BUILDINGS AND IMPROVEMENTS

H. RENT AND SECURITY

I. TAXES AND INSURANCE

J. RENEWALS AND EXTENSIONS

K. PURCHASE OPTIONS

L. TRANSFERS BY LANDLORD OR TENANT

M. TERMINATION

LAW OF PROPERTY
Fourth Edition

Chapter 1

INTRODUCTION

Table of Sections

§ 1.1 THE CONCEPT OF PROPERTY AND THE INSTITUTION OF PRIVATE PROPERTY

A layperson typically defines "property" as something that is tangible and is owned by a natural person, a corporation or other legal entity, or the government. However, this response is inaccurate from a lawyer's point of view for at least two reasons: (1) It confuses "property" with the various objects of property; and (2) It fails to recognize that property may be intangible.

For lawyers, property is not a thing, although things are the subject of property law. As Jeremy Bentham said, property is a legally protected "expectation * * * of being able to draw such or such an advantage from the thing" in question, "according to the nature of the case."[1] Bentham conceded that "[t]here have been from the beginning, and there always will be, circumstances in which a man may secure himself, by his own means, in the enjoyment of certain things." But Bentham also correctly noted that "the catalogue of these cases is very limited" and that "a strong and permanent expectation" of being able to draw an advantage from the thing in question "can result only from law."[2] In this book, we adopt Bentham's view of the nature of property, which Felix Cohen summarized as follows: "That is property to which the following label can be attached. To the world: Keep off X unless you have my permission, which I may grant or withhold. Signed: Private citizen[.] Endorsed: The state[.]"[3]

Cohen's statement assumes that private property is the norm. That has certainly been the case in the United States since its founding and in most of western Europe from the end of the Middle Ages to the present, although the institution of private property—private persons' ownership of things—has long been a subject of controversy among philosophers, political scientists, and economists. At least five theories have been

---

1   J. Bentham, Theory of Legislation 112 (C. Ogden ed., 1931).

2   Id. at 112–13.

3   F. Cohen, Dialogue on Private Property, 9 Rutgers L. Rev. 357, 374 (1954).

advanced as justifications for the institution of private property:[4] (1) the "occupation" theory—occupation or possession of a thing justifies legal protection of the occupier's or possessor's claim to it; (2) the "labor" theory—a person has a moral right to own and control the things produced or acquired through his or her labor; (3) the "contract" theory—private property is the result of a contract between individuals and the community; (4) the "natural rights" theory—natural law dictates the recognition of private property; and (5) the "social utility" theory—the law should promote the maximum fulfillment of human needs and aspirations by legally protecting private property.

The institution of private property has, of course, been vigorously criticized in the Western world from very early times. Such eminent philosophers as Plato[5] and Sir Thomas More[6] rejected the concept of private property and argued for communal property. Similarly, Karl Marx and Frederick Engels argued that the State, rather than private persons, should own the "means of production."[7] But even communist countries did not completely abolish private property. For example, the former Soviet Union permitted private ownership of certain property that was intended "for the satisfaction of * * * [citizens'] material and cultural needs."[8] Citizens could "own [their] income from work and [their] savings, a house (or part of a house) and subsidiary household production, and household articles * * * of personal use and convenience."[9] But "[p]roperty under the personal ownership of citizens [could] not be used to derive non-labor income."[10]

A number of American scholars have advanced an economic theory of property. For example, Judge Richard Posner has written that legally protecting property rights serves the important economic function of creating incentives to use resources efficiently, which increases property values. He believes that an efficient system of property rights requires:

      1. *Universality*—all resources should be owned unless they are sufficiently abundant that everyone can consume them without diminishing others' ability to do so;

      2. *Exclusivity*—to give owners an incentive to incur the necessary costs to make efficient use of resources owned by them; and

      3. *Transferability*—to allow resources to be transferred from an owner who is making less productive use of them to an owner who will make more productive use of them.

---

[4]   For discussion of these theories, see C. Rose, Possession as the Origin of Property, 52 U. Chi. L. Rev. 73 (1985); The Rational Basis of Legal Institutions 195–200, 167–84, 314–44, 387–400 (H. Wigmore & A. Kocourek eds., 1923); M. Cohen, Property and Sovereignty, 13 Cornell L. Rev. 8, 15–16 (1927); J. Stone, The Province and Function of Law 529 (1946).

[5]   Plato, Republic.

[6]   T. More, Utopia.

[7]   K. Marx, Das Kapital. For a discussion of socialist property theories, see 2 W. Lecky, Democracy and Liberty 224–361 (1896), excerpts from which are reprinted in The Rational Basis of Legal Institutions, supra note 4, at 232–54.

[8]   Grazhdanskii Kodeks Rossiiskoi Federatsii [GK RF] [Civil Code] art. 105 (Russ.) (transl. W. Gray and R. Stults 1965).

[9]   Id.

[10]   Id.

However, Judge Posner recognizes that these three factors do not operate in a vacuum. Uses of land, for example, can create positive and negative externalities.[11]

Judge Posner's assertion that legal protection of property rights performs the economic function of creating incentives to use resources efficiently is, of course, a normative proposition, rather than a factual description of the way in which the rules of property law actually operate at any given time in a particular legal system. However, although neither the courts nor the legislatures have been consistently articulate on the point, Anglo-American property law has rarely lost sight of this normative proposition.[12]

If property is a legally protected expectation of deriving certain advantages from a thing, property must be comprised of legal relations among persons with respect to things. These legal relations may be of widely varying types. In fact, ownership of a thing can be divided into smaller interests. These interests, which are often analogized to a "bundle of sticks," include a variety of rights, such as title (ownership), the right to possess, the right to crops and other products of the land, the right to damage or harm the land, the right to exclude others, and the right to transfer ownership, including at death. One person may have all these rights, or they may be divided. For example, a landlord has title to leased land, while the tenant has the right to possess it.

European civil law provides an interesting contrast to Anglo-American concepts of property. The civil law adopts a basically unitary view of property that emphasizes ownership, rather than the various separate legal interests that are included in ownership. For example, the Louisiana Civil Code, which is derived from the French Code Napoleon, provides: "Ownership is the right that confers on a person direct, immediate, and exclusive authority over a thing."[13] As we shall see, the Anglo-American law employs a very different approach that places much greater emphasis on the various aggregates of legal interests into which a property title may be divided.[14]

§ 1.2 JUDICIAL REMEDIES FOR PROTECTING PROPERTY AND THE RELATIVITY OF PROPERTY RIGHTS AT COMMON LAW

Property law determines what property rights are legally protected. The mode of protection in the United States was largely determined by the historical evolution of common law civil remedies in England between the twelfth and the sixteenth centuries. These remedies were granted when a person seeking them used the appropriate form of action. These forms of action were very rigid and were mainly designed to protect those who possessed land or chattels from unauthorized interference with their possession.

Common law actions for recovery of land *in specie* developed in England as early as the reign of Henry II (1154–1189). Ulitmately, a wide variety of *real actions* were available to plaintiffs who alleged that they were legally entitled to possession (*seisin*) of land that the defendant wrongfully possessed.[15] However, these real actions did not

---

[11]   R. Posner, Economic Analysis of Law 40–42 (9th ed. 2014).

[12]   See id. at 13–39; R. Coase, The Problem of Social Cost, 3 J.L. & Econ. 1 (1960); H. Demsetz, Toward a Theory of Property Rights, 57 Am. Econ. Rev. 347 (1967).

[13]   La. Civ. Code Ann. art. 477 (1980).

[14]   See infra Chapters 2 through 6, and Chapter 8.

[15]   S. Milsom, Historical Foundations of the Common Law 124–49 (2d ed. 1981) (hereinafter Historical Foundations); T. Plucknett, Concise History of the Common Law 353–62 (5th ed. 1956) (hereinafter Concise

provide a fully satisfactory set of judicial remedies for plaintiffs who sought to recover possession of land. Therefore, when the action of *ejectment* became generally available in the sixteenth century as a specific remedy for plaintiffs who were seeking to recover possession of land wrongfully withheld from them, the older real actions gradually fell into disuse and were practically obsolete by the end of the seventeenth century.[16]

Ejectment was a relatively expeditious method for recovering possession of land and provided a right to a jury trial. It was an offshoot of the ancient action of *trespass*. Trespass was a personal, rather than real, action because a successful plaintiff got a judgment for money damages, rather than restitution of the property.[17] The trespass action originally provided a damage remedy for any direct and tortious interference with possession of land or chattels. But trespass produced many offshoots, including ejectment, that became separate forms of action. Among the other offshoots were *case* (or *trespass on the case*), which provided a damage remedy for indirect or consequential injury to land or chattels resulting from the defendant's intentional or negligent wrongful act,[18] and *trover*, which provided a damage remedy when the defendant converted the plaintiff's chattel to his own use by wrongful seizure, withholding, or disposition.[19]

The usual remedy for wrongful interference with possession of chattels was money damages. In certain cases, the plaintiff could recover possession of chattels by an action for *replevin*[20] or *detinue*.[21] Replevin originated as a remedy for a tenant whose landlord wrongfully *distrained* the tenant's chattels for nonpayment of rent or other breach of duty. In England, the courts seem never to have expanded replevin to cover wrongful seizures other than distraint,[22] and replevin clearly did not provide a remedy for the mere wrongful withholding of possession.[23] Detinue was the proper action in that situation. In detinue, if the defendant wrongfully withheld possession of the plaintiff's chattel, the defendant had the option of returning it or paying its value as damages.[24] If the defendant chose to pay damages, the outcome of the action was similar to the outcome of a successful trover action.

History); E. Morgan, Introduction to the Study of Law 83–88 (2d ed. 1948); F. Maitland, The Forms of Action at Common Law 21–48 (1936).

[16] Historical Foundations, supra note 15, at 152–63; Concise History, supra note 15, at 373–74; Morgan, supra note 15, at 112–15; Maitland, supra note 15, at 56–61. For more detailed discussion, see P. Bordwell, Ejectment Takes Over, 55 Iowa L. Rev. 1089 (1970).

[17] Historical Foundations, supra note 15, at 283–300; Concise History, supra note 15, at 369–71; Morgan, supra note 15, at 102–05; Maitland, supra note 15, at 48–50, 53–55, 65.

[18] Historical Foundations, supra note 15, at 300–13; Concise History, supra note 15, at 372–73; Morgan, supra note 15, at 105–07; Maitland, supra note 15, at 65–68.

[19] Concise History, supra note 15, 374–75; Morgan, supra note 15, at 111–12; Maitland, supra note 15, at 71. See also Historical Foundations, supra note 15, at 366–79.

[20] Concise History, supra note 15, at 367–69; Morgan, supra note 15, at 88–92; Maitland, supra note 15, at 48, 61.

[21] Historical Foundations, supra note 15, at 262–75; Concise History, supra note 15, at 364–65; Morgan, supra note 15, at 96–99; Maitland, supra note 15, at 61–63.

[22] Concise History, supra note 15, at 367–69; Maitland, supra note 15, at 61 ("A few instances of replevin used to recover goods though not taken by way of distress * * * occur late in the day, and are not important in relation to general theory."). But cf. J. Ames, Lectures on Legal History 69–70 (1913).

[23] Mennie v. Blake [1856] 119 Eng. Rep. 1078.

[24] Maitland, supra note 15, at 62; Morgan, supra note 15, at 98. Damages for the detention (loss of use) in addition to the value were awarded.

From an early date in most American jurisdictions, the common law action of ejectment was available to recover possession of land.[25] The other forms of action mentioned above also were available to protect property interests in land and chattels. In most jurisdictions, the scope of replevin was broadened so that it could be used to recover chattels when the defendant was wrongfully withholding them[26] and to recover damages when the defendant had wrongfully disposed of them.[27] Because a plaintiff could recover either possession or damages in an action of replevin or an action of trover, detinue fell into disuse in most American jurisdictions. When a defendant damaged the plaintiff's chattels but did not convert them to the defendant's use, trespass and case provided a damage remedy in all American jurisdictions.[28] Trespass also provided a damage remedy when the defendant invaded the plaintiffs' right to possession but did not dispossess them.[29] An action on the case for *nuisance* gave owners a remedy for non-trespassory interferences with the use and enjoyment of their land.[30]

The forms of action mentioned above, along with others designed to protect personal and contract rights, evolved in the English courts of law. The English Court of Chancery also developed distinctive equitable remedies to protect property interests, such as injunctions against interference with those interests, rescission of property transactions, reformation of instruments, and removal of clouds on land titles.[31] In some cases, Chancery only provided a better remedy to protect legal property interests. In other cases, Chancery protected property interests that the courts of law did not recognize, such as the rights of a trust beneficiary in trust property. Although not all American jurisdictions established separate courts of equity, equitable and legal remedies were generally available in America from an early date.[32]

Today, virtually every American jurisdiction has abolished the common law forms of action, and all forms of legal and equitable relief are available in a single civil action.[33] Nonetheless, the common law forms of action and the equitable remedies that evolved in England continue to have a profound influence on modern property law. For example, in many instances today, possessors of land are entitled to restitution of the land and possessors of chattels are entitled to damages in the amount of the property's value based on prior possession alone; the plaintiffs need not prove that they have title. This rule results from the great importance that the common law placed on possession during the law's formative period. In ejectment, plaintiffs could recover possession of land from a

---

[25]   In the New England states, the action for possession of realty was called a "writ of entry," but it was substantially the same as "ejectment" and was quite different from the old English "writ of entry."

[26]   Concise History, supra note 15, at 367–69. But cf. Morgan, supra note 15, at 91 (orthodox rule in U.S. allowed replevin only when a wrongful taking occurred, but Pennsylvania and Massachusetts extended replevin to all cases of wrongful detention in early cases).

[27]   Although the courts in early English cases allowed the recovery of damages in such cases, the American cases were in conflict in the absence of a governing statute. Morgan, supra note 15, at 91. Most jurisdictions have enacted such statutes.

[28]   Generally, see W. Prosser, Handbook of the Law of Torts §§ 7, 14 (4th ed. 1971).

[29]   See infra § 7.1.

[30]   See infra § 7.2.

[31]   Generally, as to the origin of equity and equitable remedies, see D. Dobbs & C. Roberts, Law of Remedies ch. 2 (3d ed. 2018); H. McClintock, Handbook of the Principles of Equity §§ 1–7 (2d ed. 1948); W. Walsh, A Treatise on Equity chs. 1–83 (1930).

[32]   McClintock, supra note 31, at § 5.

[33]   Id. § 6; Walsh, supra note 31, at § 7; C. Clark, Handbook of the Law of Code Pleading §§ 6–10, 15 (2d ed. 1947); F. James & G. Hazard, Civil Procedure 22–26 (5th ed. 2001).

dispossessor unless the latter could show a better right to possession.[34] Similarly, in trover, plaintiffs could recover the full value of chattels from a dispossessor unless the latter could show a better right to possession.[35] The defendant could not defeat either action by showing that a third party had a better right to possession than the plaintiff.[36] In most jurisdictions, these rules still apply in actions to recover possession of land and in actions to recover damages for conversion of chattels. However, courts are divided as to whether prior possession alone is a sufficient basis for specific recovery of chattels in replevin[37] or for recovery of damages equal to the reduced value of land resulting from trespassory interferences.[38]

Therefore, property rights are generally only relative. In many cases, a mere possessor of land or chattels is entitled to legal or equitable relief. For example, if B wrongfully dispossesses A and C later wrongfully dispossesses B, B may recover from C, and A may recover from B and C solely on the basis of prior possession. In some cases, the plaintiff will try to prove that it is the property owner or that the owner gave it the right to possess. But even if the court determines that the plaintiff owns the land or chattel, that determination is binding only on the parties to the action.[39]

§ 1.3   REAL AND PERSONAL PROPERTY

An initial distinction in property law is between real and personal property. Real property in the common law corresponds with immoveable property in the civil law. It includes land and the things attached to it, such as buildings. Real property is also called real estate or realty. In contrast, personal property in the common law corresponds with moveable property in the civil law. Personal property includes chattels and intangible things, such as claims represented by bank accounts, promissory notes, corporate and government bonds, shares of corporate stock, life insurance policies, annuities,[40] patents, copyrights, trademarks, and the good will of business enterprises.

The classification of property as real or personal does not affect the law that applies, with some exceptions. For example, a deed transfers title to real property, while a bill of sale transfers title to personal property. The distinction between real and personal property is based on the historical development of legal remedies for the protection of property in England. In the medieval period, property interests in land were protected by the real actions in which a plaintiff could recover possession of the land. In contrast, property interests in chattels were generally protected only by personal actions, such as trespass, case, trover, and detinue. A successful plaintiff got a personal judgment for

---

[34]   E.g., Tapscott v. Cobbs, 52 Va. (11 Gratt.) 172 (1854).

[35]   E.g., Anderson v. Gouldberg, 51 Minn. 294, 53 N.W. 636 (1892).

[36]   Supra notes 34, 35. Contra: Russell v. Hill, 125 N.C. 470, 34 S.E. 640 (1899) (identity of true owner was known).

[37]   See J. Macy, Annotation, Mere Possession in Plaintiff as Basis of Action for Wrongfully Taking or Damaging Personal Property, 150 A.L.R. 163, 192 (1944); B. Shipman, Handbook of Common Law Pleading 126 (3d ed. 1923). In a traditional replevin action, a sheriff is directed to seize a chattel and deliver it to the plaintiff before a hearing on the plaintiff's claim. The plaintiff must post a bond to prosecute the action and must return the chattel to the defendant if the judgment goes against the plaintiff. This procedure has encountered constitutional obstacles. See Fuentes v. Shevin, 407 U.S. 67, 92 S.Ct. 1983, 32 L.Ed.2d 556 (1972), reh'g denied, 409 U.S. 902, 93 S.Ct. 177, 34 L.Ed.2d 165 (1972).

[38]   Compare Todd v. Jackson, 26 N.J.L. 525 (1857), and Ill. & St. Louis Rr. & Coal Co. v. Cobb, 94 Ill. 55 (1879), with Winchester v. City of Stevens Point, 58 Wis. 350, 17 N.W. 3 (1883). See generally 6A American Law of Property § 28.14 (1952–54) (hereinafter Am. L. Prop.).

[39]   See Restatement (Second) of Judgments §§ 5, 6, 17, 30 (Am. Law Inst. 1982).

[40]   These intangible subjects of property are often called "choses in action."

damages. For this reason, property interests in land came to be called real property, and property interests in chattels came to be called personal property.[41]

Classifying property interests based on the actions that were available to protect them sometimes produced anomalous results. For example, when land was leased for a definite period of time, the lessee originally had no action to recover possession from one who wrongfully took or withheld it. The lessee had only an action for damages.[42] Therefore, the lessee's interest was classified as personal property. This classification persisted long after the action of ejectment was recognized and was extended in the latter part of the fifteenth century to enable the lessee to recover possession of the leased premises.[43] Many states today still classify the lessee's interest in leased land as personal property.

As previously noted, real property includes interests in things attached to land, as well as land itself. Substantial structures and all natural vegetation, such as trees, perennial shrubs, and grasses (sometimes called *fructus naturales*), are treated as real property for practically all purposes.[44] Interests in cultivated crops (sometimes called *emblements or fructus industriales)*, however, are sometimes treated as real property and sometimes as personal property, depending on the circumstances.[45]

Chattels that are affixed to real property are called *fixtures* and are treated as real property for most purposes.[46] In determining whether a chattel has become a fixture, courts focus on factors such as the intent of the party who affixed the chattel, how firmly affixed the chattel is to the real property, how much harm would be caused by removing the chattel from the real property, and how well the chattel is adapted to the use of the real property. Life tenants and lessees generally have the right to remove fixtures installed by them for trade purposes and sometimes for domestic or ornamental purposes.[47] When the vendor of a chattel that becomes a fixture retains a security interest in it, the vendor can remove the fixture if the purchaser fails to pay the full purchase price, so long as the removal will not unreasonably damage the real property to which the fixture is attached.[48] If a fixture is lawfully removed, it becomes and remains a chattel unless it is again affixed to land or a structure attached to land.

§ 1.4   LEGAL AND EQUITABLE PROPERTY

Due to English legal developments before the founding of the United States, American law still has some separate laws based on the law jurisprudence and the equity jurisprudence of England. These distinctions have survived despite the procedural

---

[41]   See Concise History, supra note 15, at 354–61.

[42]   See 1 Am. L. Prop., supra note 38, at 175–76; Concise History, supra note 15, at 371–72.

[43]   See 2 R. Powell, Powell on Real Property § 16.02 (2018). Cf. 1 Am. L. Prop., supra note 38, at 176 (suggesting that continued classification of the lessee's interest as personal property may be due more to "the fact that leases frequently were used for security purposes," rather than because the remedy was originally only an action for damages).

[44]   See 5 Am. L. Prop., supra note 38, at §§ 19.15–16.

[45]   See id. § 19.16.

[46]   See id. §§ 19.1–14; 8 Powell, supra note 43, at § 57.05.

[47]   5 Am. L. Prop., supra note 38, at § 19.11 (1952); 8 Powell, supra note 43, at § 57.06.

[48]   See U.C.C. § 9–334 (Am. Law. Inst. & Unif. Law Comm'n 1998); 5 Am. L. Prop., supra note 38, at § 19.12 (1952); 8 Powell, supra note 43, at § 57.02[2][b].

reforms of the nineteenth and twentieth centuries that largely merged law and equity.[49] One consequence of the continuing distinction between law and equity is that, in many cases, equitable property interests may be recognized and protected in persons who do not have legal property interests. In most cases, equitable property interests result from the creation of a trust or a specifically enforceable contract.

A trust is created whenever a property owner (the settlor) transfers legal title to land or chattels to a trustee for the benefit of a third party (the beneficiary).[50] Based on the title owner's transfer, law recognizes the trustee as the owner, but the trustee has only bare legal title. The beneficiary is entitled to all the beneficial rights of ownership. Therefore, equity recognizes the beneficiary as the equitable owner and protects the beneficiary's interest in accordance with equitable principles that require the trustee to deal fairly with the beneficiary and to manage the trust property honestly and prudently.

Although the beneficiary is the equitable owner, courts historically regarded the beneficiary's interest as providing only an in personam claim against the trustee, rather than an *in rem* claim. Therefore, in the absence of statutory authority, a court generally does not enforce the beneficiary's rights directly against the trust property, such as by awarding the beneficiary the right to possess, but merely orders the trustee to perform the duties that the trust terms and equitable principles impose. Moreover, as the legal owner of the trust property, the trustee is the proper party to sue third persons to protect it. However, the beneficiary's interest in the property is protected against the trustee's unauthorized transfers of it, unless the transferee paid value for it without actual or constructive notice of the trust.

Courts have extended the trust concept to many situations in which no real trust exists. For example, courts impose a constructive or resulting trust or an equitable lien on property to prevent a wrongdoer's unjust enrichment.[51] When a court imposes a constructive or resulting trust, the court treats the legal owner like a trustee and orders it to transfer legal ownership to the person who is equitably entitled to ownership. A court may grant similar relief when the plaintiff is entitled to the equitable remedy of rescission or reformation of a contract or conveyance.[52] Therefore, a person with an equitable right to rescission or reformation can be described in some cases as the equitable owner of property that is legally owned by another.

Because land is generally deemed to be unique, courts will ordinarily order specific performance of an enforceable contract for the sale of land in favor of either party to the contract.[53] In states that follow the doctrine of equitable conversion, courts hold that an

---

[49] On the historical development of common law and equity jurisprudence in England, with primary emphasis on the common law, see Concise History, supra note 15. For a more detailed treatment of the historical development of equity, see 1 J. Pomeroy, A Treatise on Equity Jurisprudence 14–117 (S. Symons ed., 5th ed. 1941); McClintock, supra note 31, at 1–19; Walsh, supra note 31, at 1–36. "In Anglo-American law, equity means the system of legal materials developed and applied by the court of chancery in England and the courts succeeding to its powers in the British Empire and the United States." McClintock, supra note 31, at 1.

[50] This book will consider the law of trusts only incidentally. The principal multivolume treatises on the law of trusts are A. Scott, The Law of Trusts (4th ed. 1987), and G. & T. Bogert, The Law of Trusts and Trustees (rev. 2d ed. 1977). The best single-volume textbook is G. & T. Bogert, Law of Trusts (6th ed. 1987).

[51] For an extended discussion, see 5 Scott, supra note 52, at §§ 404–552; 1 G. Palmer, The Law of Restitution 9–21, § 6.7 (1978); McClintock, supra note 31, at §§ 85, 120.

[52] See McClintock, supra note 31, at §§ 84, 86, 94–104; Walsh, supra note 31, at §§ 106, 110–11 (1930); 2 Palmer, supra note 53, at §§ 12.6, 13.8–19, 14.25–26 (1978).

[53] See 4 Pomeroy, supra note 49, at §§ 1400–10; McClintock, supra note 31, at §§ 53–78; Walsh, supra note 31, at §§ 58–85.

enforceable land sale contract makes the vendee the equitable owner of the property based on its equitable right to specific performance of the contract. The vendor remains the legal owner until it delivers an effective conveyance to the vendee.[54]

Like a trust beneficiary, the vendee is protected against the vendor's subsequent unauthorized transfer of the land, unless the transferee paid value without notice of the prior land sale contract. Under every state's recording system,[55] recording a written trust instrument or land sale contract gives any subsequent transferee notice of the trust or contract.

As the equitable owner of the property, the contract vendee's interest in it is characterized as a real property interest, while the vendor has only a personal property interest.[56] Therefore, if the vendor dies before the contract is performed, the vendor's claim to the purchase money passes to the vendor's next-of-kin or legatees as personal property. If the vendee dies before the contract is performed, the vendee's claim to the land passes to the vendee's heirs or devisees as real property. The doctrine of equitable conversion also applies when land is devised by will to a trustee with a direction to sell it and distribute the proceeds and when a marriage settlement directs the conversion of land into money or vice versa.

§ 1.5   FROM FEUDAL TENURE TO LAND OWNERSHIP— SOME ENGLISH HISTORY

The Norman Conquest of England resulted in the establishment of a feudal system of landholding.[57] William the Conqueror confiscated all the land held by the Saxon nobles and redistributed most of it among his principal Norman barons, who were called tenants in chief.[58] Most tenants in chief held their land by knight service, which obligated them to furnish a specified number of knights for military service when the king required them.[59] A few tenants in chief held their land by a tenure called serjeanty, which obligated them to fill important offices in the royal household.[60] Religious bodies and ecclesiastical officials held land in frankalmoin ("free alms"), which required them to perform religious duties, such as saying masses or prayers for royal family members.[61]

---

[54]   See McClintock, supra note 31, at §§ 106–17; Walsh, supra note 31, at §§ 86–98 (1930). See also infra § 10.13.

[55]   The recording system is considered in detail, infra § 11.9.

[56]   See infra § 10.13; McClintock, supra note 31, at § 106; Walsh, supra note 31, at § 86.

[57]   On feudal tenures in England, see 1 Am. L. Prop., supra note 38, at §§ 1.2–.4; R. Megarry & H. Wade, The Law of Real Property 22–36 (8th ed. 2012) (hereinafter Real Property); S. Milsom, Legal Framework of English Feudalism (1976) (hereinafter Feudalism); Historical Foundations, supra note 15, at 99–103; C. Moynihan & S. Kurtz, Introduction to the Law of Real Property 1–23 (6th ed. 2015) (hereinafter Introduction to Law); Concise History, supra note 15, at 546–50, 564–74; 1 F. Pollock & F. Maitland, History of English Law 229–406 (2d ed. 1898, reissued 1968) (hereinafter History); A. Simpson, Introduction to the History of the Land Law 1–25, 47–48 (2d ed. 1986) (hereinafter Introduction to History).

[58]   There were probably about 1,500 tenants in chief by 1086 when the Domesday Survey was carried out. Introduction to History, supra note 57, at 4.

[59]   At an early date, the time of service was fixed at forty days each year, and the knights were only required to serve within the kingdom of England. Introduction to History, supra note 57, at 4 n.12.

[60]   E.g., offices such as marshal, constable, chamberlain, and butler.

[61]   Two types of frankalmoin tenure existed: (1) the tenant had only a general obligation to pray for the souls of the donor and his ancestors, which was enforceable only in the ecclesiastical court; and (2) the tenant had an obligation to furnish specified religious services, such as to say ten masses a year, which was enforceable in the king's courts. Introduction to History, supra note 57, at 10–11.

Soon after the Norman Conquest, tenants in chief subinfeudated to provide for their needs. They granted portions of their land to subtenants to be held by knight service, which helped the tenant in chief supply the required quota of knights for service in the king's army,[62] or in serjeanty, frankalmoin, or socage. Socage was any form of tenure other than knight service, sargeanty, or frankalmoin. It often required the tenant to perform agricultural services on the lord's land or, more commonly, to pay a fixed rent in kind or, eventually, in money.[63] Subtenants could create further layers of feudal tenures by further subinfeudation.

Once this system of feudal tenure[64] was established, all the land in England, except the king's demesne land (land reserved by the king for his own use), was held of a lord and, ultimately, of the king in return for service of some kind.[65] Therefore, under the tenurial system, two or more persons had interests of some sort in each parcel of land, except the king's demesne land.[66] However, saying that anyone, other than the king, had full ownership of any parcel of land would have been inaccurate[67] and remained so for as long as feudal tenure played a significant role in English land law.

The king's grants to his tenants in chief and tenants in chiefs' grants to subtenants were for life only.[68] Because feudal tenure involved reciprocal obligations,[69] it terminated when either the lord or the tenant died. If the tenant died first, the land reverted to the lord. If the lord died first, the tenant's interest terminated, and the land reverted to the person who succeeded the decedent as lord.[70] However, tenancies that lasted only as long as the lord and tenant were both alive were an unsatisfactory basis for the complex system of military tenures that extensive subinfeudation caused. Therefore, by the middle of the twelfth century, lords normally accepted the homage of a deceased tenant's eldest son and regranted the land to him,[71] subject only to payment of a "just and lawful relief."[72]

---

[62] The smallest unit allotted to a subtenant was the *knight's fee*, given to a single knight. The term *fee* comes from the Latin *feudum* or *feodum*, which originally simply meant *holding*. The transaction by which a *fee* was granted was a *feoffment*. In the twelfth century, the term *fee* came to designate an inheritable interest in land, rather than a mere life interest. Introduction to History, supra note 57, at 4 n.11.

[63] "Socage was the great residual category of [free] tenure, and its characteristics can only be defined negatively." Introduction to History, supra note 57, at 11–12.

[64] The classification of free tenures used here is that adopted in Introduction to Law, supra note 57, at 10–13. Cf. 1 Am. L. Prop., supra note 38, at 8–9, which mentions only military tenure, frankalmoin tenure, and socage tenure.

[65] This proposition was fully recognized in the Domesday Book (1086).

[66] "An obvious consequence of the tenurial system is that a number of persons have interests of some sort in the same parcel of land . . . at the bottom of the feudal ladder there will be a tenant who has seisin of the land and is called the tenant in demesne, and at the top there is the King. In between there may be a string of mesne [intermediate] lords, who are lords and tenants at the same time." Introduction to History, supra note 57, at 47.

[67] Land held in "demesne" is personally possessed by its owner and is not granted out in tenancy.

[68] Historical Foundations, supra note 15, at 105–06.

[69] Feudalism, supra note 57, at 39.

[70] Thorne, English Feudalism and Estates in Land, 1959 Cambridge L.J. 193, 196–97. Accord Introduction to History, supra note 57, at 49–50.

[71] Thorne, supra note 70, at 198, points out that "no one was likely to be more readily available, or more acceptable to the men of the fief, or (in the great majority of cases) better prepared to undertake the duties required, than the deceased tenant's eldest son."

[72] During the reign of William Rufus, the amount exacted from the deceased tenant's heir was sometimes so large, it seemed, as to amount to a repurchase. But Henry I's Coronation Charter (1100) provided that the heirs of both tenants in chief and of other tenants should "take up" (*relevabit*) their lands "with a just

Undoubtedly, the lord originally had discretion whether to grant the land formerly held by a deceased tenant to his eldest son or other heir, but the practice eventually became customary.[73] As that custom evolved, it also became customary for the lord to grant the land to the new tenant "and his heirs." The term *feodum* or *fee*, which previously had applied to any feudal holding, came to mean a feudal holding that was created by such language and was customarily regranted to a deceased tenant's heir.[74]

During the second half of the twelfth century, the customary claim of a deceased tenant's heir to have the land regranted to him crystallized into a "common law right of inheritance."[75] A grant to a named person "and his heirs" created a property interest of potentially infinite duration that was inheritable by the original grantee's heirs for all succeeding generations. The heirs in that period were a much more limited class than today. Although direct descendants and collateral relatives could be heirs, the decedent's spouse and parents could not be. If a tenant died without heirs, the fee would escheat to his lord.[76]

The principle of primogeniture characterized the inheritance system that evolved for fees held by military tenure. Based on primogeniture, the deceased tenant's eldest male descendant inherited all the tenant's property.[77] Ultimately, primogeniture applied to fees held by any kind of tenure,[78] except in those parts of England where the king's courts continued to apply local customs.[79]

When the custom of regranting a fee to a deceased tenant's heir was crystallizing into a common law rule in the latter part of the twelfth century, a tenant's power to alienate land was clearly restricted. A tenant could not alienate without the lord's consent[80] and had only a limited power to disinherit his heir by alienating the land during his lifetime.[81] However, by the middle of the thirteenth century, the common law

---

and lawful relief," rather than being required to repurchase them. The relief to be paid was subsequently fixed at a definite amount.

[73] Thorne, supra note 70, at 198. Accord, Feudalism, supra note 57, at 180.

[74] See Thorne, supra note 70, at 198.

[75] For a more detailed discussion of the evolution of the heritable fee, see Feudalism, supra note 57, at 154–86, especially at 164–71.

[76] In the case of tenants in chief, the fee would escheat to the king. In all other cases, it would escheat to some *mesne* lord.

[77] See Introduction to Law, supra note 57, at 38–39 n.23. When primogeniture was the rule of inheritance, the eldest son of a deceased tenant would inherit to the exclusion of younger children. If the eldest son predeceased the tenant but left a son who survived the tenant, that surviving son would inherit to the exclusion of younger children of the deceased tenant. If the deceased tenant had no surviving male descendants, the tenant's nearest female descendant or descendants would inherit. If two or more female descendants in the same degree, such as daughters, survived, they would inherit in equal shares as *coparceners*. If no descendant of the deceased tenant survived him, his collateral relatives would inherit, with a preference for male stocks, unless the lands had descended from a female stock. For more detailed discussions of the common rules of inheritance, see Introduction to History, supra note 57, at 56–63; Concise History, supra note 15, at 712–22.

[78] Concise History, supra note 15, at 527–28, 530; Introduction to History, supra note 57, at 51: "[B]y Edward I's time primogeniture had become the common law of all tenures, and exceptions to the rule were treated as anomalous customs in opposition to common right."

[79] For more information on the local variations in inheritance schemes, see Introduction to History, supra note 57, at 20–21.

[80] The lord's consent may not have been essential if the gift was reasonable and did not seriously affect the lord's interests. Introduction to History, supra note 57, at 54. For more detailed discussions, see History, supra note 57, at 329–49; Feudalism, supra note 57, at 103–10.

[81] See Thorne, supra note 70, at 207–08; Feudalism, supra note 57, at 121–22; Concise History, supra note 57, at 526–27 (setting out the text of Glanvil's treatise vii, 1).

became settled that a tenant could alienate without his lord's consent, subject to payment of a fine, and free of any claim by his heir.[82] However, the lords continued to object strongly to the practice of alienating by subinfeudation, which frequently deprived them of the value of the incidents of feudal tenure such as wardship (the lord's right to guardianship of an underage heir and the heir's property with no duty to account for the profits) and marriage (the lord's right to arrange a ward's marriage and receive a payment for doing so).[83]

The Statute of Quia Emptores[84] was enacted in 1290 to settle all questions concerning the alienation of fees granted to a person "and his heirs." Quia Emptores established that: (1) Such fees—then coming to be called fees simple[85]—were freely transferable inter vivos provided that the transferee was substituted for the transferor and that no new tenure was created;[86] (2) No tenant of such a fee could thereafter subinfeudate, unless the king authorized him to do so;[87] and (3) Fines for alienation could not be exacted except when a tenant in chief transferred.[88]

Even after Quia Emptores, lands held in fee simple were not devisable by will,[89] except in localities where courts recognized local customs that permitted it.[90] However,

---

[82] Introduction to History, supra note 57, at 54. The court held in D'Arundel's Case, Bracton's Notebook, case 1054, decided in 1225, that the heir could not recover from the transferee if the transferor had given a warranty on behalf of himself and his heirs, because the heir was bound by the warranty.

[83] When a tenant by knight service or grand sargeanty died leaving a male heir under 21 or a female heir under 14, the lord was entitled to wardship of the heir and the heir's lands. Wardship entitled the lord to the rents and profits of the lands until the heir, if male, reached 21 or, if female, either reached 16 or married. The lord had a duty to provide for and educate his ward but had no duty to account for the rents and profits of the lands. Moreover, the lord had the right to arrange an appropriate marriage for his ward and to keep the amount that the family of the prospective spouse was willing to pay for the match. If the ward refused the marriage, the lord nevertheless was entitled to receive the same amount. If the ward married without the lord's consent, he was entitled to double that amount. By the thirteenth century, the rights of wardship and marriage could be bought and sold, and they remained a significant source of royal revenue into the early seventeenth century. Introduction to Law, supra note 57, at 17–18.

"Suppose, for example, Osbert, who holds of Robert, wishes to alienate his holding to Richard, and does so by subinfeudating. If the alienation takes place on account of a sale, then Osbert will receive the purchase price and grant the lands to Richard to hold of him at a nominal service of, say, a red rose at midsummer. Osbert will be left seised of the seignory [lordship], worth one rose annually, and it is on the value of the seignory that the amount due in incidents to Robert, his lord, will be calculated. Thus if Osbert dies and his heir, a minor, succeeds him, Robert will be entitled to the wardship over a seignory of trivial value; if Osbert commits felony, the seignory and not the land, will come to Robert by escheat." Introduction to History, supra note 57, at 53.

For discussion of the other incidents of feudal tenure, including homage and fealty, relief and primer seisin, aids, fines for alienation, escheats, and forfeitures, see Introduction to Law, supra note 57, at 15–19; Introduction to History, supra note 57, at 15–18, 19–20.

[84] Statute of Quia Emptores 1290, 18 Edw. 1 c.1 (Eng.).

[85] The terms *pure fee* or *fee simple* came into use in the latter part of the thirteenth century to designate an interest inheritable by collateral, as well as lineal, heirs. In contrast, a *fee tail* was inheritable only by lineal heirs ("heirs of the body").

[86] The statute provided: "[F]rom henceforth it shall be lawful to every Freeman to sell at his own pleasure his Lands and Tenements, or part of them; so that the Feoffee shall hold the same Lands and Tenements of the Chief Lord of the same Fee, by such Service and Customs as his Feoffor held before."

[87] Because *Quia Emptores* did not expressly mention the king, he retained the power to create new feudal tenures by virtue of the general rule that the king's rights are unaffected by a statute unless it specifically names him.

[88] Because the statute did not affect the king's rights, he retained the right to exact fines for alienation from his tenants in chief.

[89] See Introduction to History, supra note 57, at 60.

[90] Such local customs existed most frequently with respect to *gavelkind* land in Kent and land held by *burgage* tenure. See Introduction to Law, supra note 57, at 13 n.26.

Chancery's enforcement of *uses* enabled devises of equitable estates in fee simple as early as 1400,[91] and enactment of the Statute of Wills in 1540[92] enabled devises of legal fee simple estates regardless of local custom.[93] Thus, the major characteristics of the fee simple estate were fully established before the middle of the sixteenth century. The tenant could freely transfer the estate, either inter vivos or by will, free of any claim of the transferor's heirs. If the tenant did not make an inter vivos or testamentary transfer, the deceased tenant's lineal or collateral heirs could inherit the estate, generation after generation.[94]

The feudal tenure system established in England after the Norman Conquest had begun to disintegrate even before *Quia Emptores* was enacted. The essential personal tie between lord and tenant could hardly be maintained once land held in fee simple was freely alienable and subinfeudation was prohibited. Moreover, tenure by knight service was no longer an efficient basis for maintaining a royal military force.[95] Tenure by knight service would undoubtedly have disappeared fairly quickly if some of the incidents of such tenure, especially wardship and marriage, had not continued to have substantial value to the king for another three and a half centuries.[96] New frankalmoin tenures could not be created after 1290, except by the king or with his permission,[97] and frankalmoin gradually lost its importance thereafter.[98] Serjeanty tenure became functionally obsolete as it became customary to obtain personal services by paying money wages, and it survived after the fifteenth century only in connection with a few ceremonial offices in the royal household.[99] Socage tenure gradually emerged as the most desirable form of tenure because it was not subject to the burdensome incidents of wardship and marriage and because the money rents fixed when socage tenures were first created became decreasingly burdensome due to inflation and the declining value of money.[100]

When the Statute of Tenures (1660)[101] converted all military and serjeanty tenures into socage tenures and abolished most of the incidents of tenure, feudal tenure ceased

---

[91] The "use" was a medieval device similar to the modern trust. The trustee held legal title, but the trustor could direct by will that the beneficial or equitable ownership was to pass to designated persons at the trustor's death. The Court of Chancery enforced such designations.

[92] Statute of Wills 1540, 32 Hen. 8, c. 1 (Eng.).

[93] The statute was enacted to restore the power to devise after the Statute of Uses (1535), 23 Hen. 8, c. 10 (Eng.), converted uses (beneficial interests) into legal estates, which were not devisable. The Statute of Wills empowered a fee simple owner to devise all his lands held by socage tenure and two-thirds of his land held by military tenure. The Statute of Wills also provided that persons to whom lands were devised should be subject to feudal services as though they took by inheritance. The Statute of Tenures 1660, 12 Car. 2, c. 24 (Eng.) removed all restrictions on the power to devise land.

[94] See T. Plucknett, Legislation of Edward I 79–80 (1949). The Doctrine of Worthier Title evolved to ensure that an inter vivos conveyance or devise to the transferor's heirs would have the same result as passage of the fee by inheritance, which preserved the lord's right to the incidents of feudal tenure. See infra § 3.15.

[95] In the twelfth century, it became clear that a paid professional army was more effective than a feudal levy based on actual knight service. By the time of Edward I (1272–1307), scutage had entirely replaced knight service and, having become a fixed rate, steadily declined in value. Introduction to Law, supra note 57, at 10–11; Concise History, supra note 15, at 532–33.

[96] History, supra note 57, at 276.

[97] That was the effect of the statute *Quia Emptores*, c. 3.

[98] Introduction to Law, supra note 57, at 12; Introduction to History, supra note 57, at 10–11.

[99] Introduction to Law, supra note 57, at 12; Introduction to History, supra note 57, at 9–10.

[100] See Introduction to Law, supra note 57, at 16, 18; Concise History, supra note 15, at 537; Introduction to History, supra note 57, at 11–14.

[101] Statute of Tenures 1660, 12 Car. 2, c. 24 (Eng.), which was retroactive to February 24, 1645, and confirmed a resolution of the Long Parliament that was passed on that date and was previously confirmed under the Commonwealth in 1656.

to have substantial significance in English law. Most tenants in fee simple already held directly of the king as a result of the prohibition of subinfeudation in 1290, except by the king, and the consequent disappearance of mesne lordships through escheat[102] during the intervening centuries. Rent was sometimes still payable by a tenant in fee simple after 1660, but the rent was almost always trifling in amount, and the remaining incidents of socage tenure were not onerous.[103] In substance, the English tenant in fee simple had full ownership of his land after 1660.[104]

§ 1.6 TENURE AND LAND OWNERSHIP IN THE UNITED STATES

When the English king granted land in North America to individual proprietors and proprietary companies in the seventeenth and eighteenth centuries, the grants were made in fee simple, which were held of the king and his heirs "in free and common socage." The proprietors' subsequent grants to settlers were also in fee simple. Although subinfeudation seems to have been authorized in all the colonies, except Massachusetts Bay, Plymouth, Connecticut, and Rhode Island, subinfeudation seems to have been common only in Maryland, Pennsylvania, and New York. In these states, it took the form of grants to settlers in fee simple, subject to the payment of "ground rents" or "quit rents." Elsewhere, grantees in fee simple held of the king.[105]

The American Revolution clearly ended any tenurial relationship between the English king and American landholders.[106] Some of the original thirteen states adopted the view that the state had succeeded to the English king's position as lord and that tenure continued to exist, while other states enacted statutes or constitutional provisions declaring that land ownership was "allodial" (owned absolutely) or otherwise declaring that tenure was abolished.[107] Throughout the rest of the United States, it seems clear that tenure never existed.[108] Even in the states where tenure may theoretically still exist between the state and one who owns land in fee simple, tenure would appear to have little or no practical significance.[109] For all practical purposes, one who owns land in fee simple anywhere in the United States has "complete property" in (full ownership of) the land.[110]

---

[102] When a tenant in fee simple died without heirs, the land escheated to his lord. Over time, the doctrine of escheat eliminated most of the mesne lordships that had been created by subinfeudation before 1290.

[103] Because rents were usually small or nominal, the "relief" of one year's rent that an heir paid when his ancestor died was also usually small or nominal. The Statute of Tenures did not abolish relief. But it made escheat the most valuable incident of tenure.

[104] The growing shortage of agricultural labor in England after the Black Death in the fourteenth century forced most lords to commute the labor services of their villein tenants to money rents. Introduction to History, supra note 57, at 160–61.

[105] See Am. L. Prop., supra note 38, at 57–59.

[106] Id. at 58.

[107] Id.

[108] Most land outside the original thirteen states became part of the public domain of the United States. Land grants by the United States in fee simple were "allodial" and did not create any tenure between the United States and the grantee.

[109] 1 Am. L. Prop., supra note 38, at 58–60. All states have statutes providing that property escheats to the state if the owner dies intestate and without heirs. Although escheat existed in England as an incident of tenure, modern statutory escheat provisions are not based on any theory of tenure between landowners and the state.

[110] See Real Property, supra note 57, at 36, stating that this is also true in England today.

§ 1.7   THE ESTATE CONCEPT—PRESENT AND FUTURE INTERESTS

If the fee simple estate had been the only possessory real property interest recognized in the period after Quia Emptores, Anglo-American law might have developed along the same lines as the civil law of continental Europe, where property in land was viewed in essentially unitary terms. But recognition of the fee simple as an inheritable interest did not eliminate the possibility of creating life estates. Indeed, the courts not only continued to recognize life estates in land, but also held that a conveyance of land to a natural person without adding the words "and his heirs" or "and the heirs of his body" could only create a life estate.[111] Moreover, even before Quia Emptores, courts had recognized inheritable estates in which the right of inheritance was limited to the original donee's direct descendants.[112]

In the early feudal period, gifts of land were often made to the grantee "and the heirs of his [or her] body" with an intent to restrict ownership to the grantee's descendants forever. However, courts resisted this invitation to tie up the land in the grantee's family. Courts came to construe the "heirs of the body" phrase as giving the donee a fee simple on condition that he or she have issue, with full power in the donee to alienate the fee simple if a child was in fact born.[113] In most instances, of course, this construction was contrary to the donor's intent. Landholders' continued protests against the courts' conditional fee construction led to enactment of the Statute De Donis Conditionalibus (1285),[114] which provided that "the Will of the Giver, according to the Form in the Deed of Gift manifestly expressed, shall be from henceforth observed; so that they to whom the Land was given under such Condition, shall have no Power to aliene the Land so given, but that it shall remain unto the Issue of them to whom it was given after their Death, or [shall revert] until the Giver or his Heirs, if Issue fail."

The Statute De Donis Conditionalibus resulted in judicial recognition of a new kind of inheritable estate called a fee tail.[115] Immediately after enactment of the statute, the first tenant in tail clearly could not, by inter vivos conveyance, transfer more than an interest for his own life, whether he had a child or not. In 1311, the tenant's interest was inalienable, except for his lifetime, until the third heir of the body had succeeded as tenant in tail.[116] By 1410, it was settled that a fee tail would endure so long as there were heirs of the body in successive generations.[117] Thus, by the early fifteenth century,

---

[111] "At common law, a freehold estate of inheritance could be created only by a phrase that included the word 'heirs'. An attempt to grant a freehold estate in other terms (as 'to A', or 'to A in fee simple') gave A merely a life estate." Real Property, supra note 57, at 47.

[112] For a more extended discussion of the evolution of such estates, see 1 Am. L. Prop., supra note 38, at 15–18; Real Property, supra note 57, at 71–77; Concise History, supra note 15, at 546–57; Introduction to History, supra note 57, at 63–65, 81–87.

[113] 1 Am. L. Prop., supra note 38, at 15; Real Property, supra note 57, at 71–72; Concise History, supra note 15, at 549–51; Introduction to History, supra note 57, at 66–68.

[114] De Donis Conditionalibus 1285, 13 Edw. 1 c. 1 (Eng.). For a more extended discussion of the statute, see 1 Am. L. Prop., supra note 38, at 15–16 (providing the text of the statute in English translation); Real Property, supra note 57, at 71–72; Concise History, supra note 15, at 551–52 (also setting out the text of the statute); Introduction to History, supra note 57, at 81–82.

[115] A *fee tail* was a fee that was carved or shaped (French, *tailler*) in a particular way; it was also frequently called simply an "estate tail" or an "entailed estate."

[116] Y.B. 5 Edw. II, reprinted in Selden Society, Vol. 31, p. 177, Vol. 33, p. 326.

[117] Y.B. 12 Hen. IV Mich., pl. 15, f. 9 (holding that a *maritagium* (or marriage gift) creates a fee tail that is inalienable in perpetuity). See also Introduction to History, supra note 57, at 84, stating that "[i]n 1346 the

the fee tail was a substantially inalienable interest that might last forever. But when and if the line of descendants ran out, the land would either revert to the original grantor or his heir (immediate or remote) in fee simple or, if the original grant so provided, the land would go to a specified person or his heir (immediate or remote) in fee simple.[118]

Sometime before 1472, English courts sanctioned the use of a collusive action called a "common recovery" to enable a tenant in fee tail to transfer an estate in fee simple, free from the claims of his descendant.[119] In the sixteenth century, the courts held that a common recovery would also bar reversioners and remainder holders who would otherwise be entitled to the land on failure of the original grantee's issue.[120] But the fee tail continued to be an important part of English family settlements until modern times. By making the original conveyance to "A for life, remainder to the eldest son of A and the heirs of his body" and then "resettling" the land when the eldest son of each successive owner reached the age of twenty-one, land continued to be entailed for generation after generation.[121]

Continued judicial recognition of life estates in the thirteenth century, coupled with the development of the fee tail after the Statute De Donis Conditionalibus as "a different sort of fee, * * * a fee which has been cut down, and which is lesser in *quantum* than a fee simple,"[122] ultimately led to judicial formulation of the theory that a fee simple can be divided into at least two smaller estates: (1) a presently possessory estate for life or in fee tail and (2) a future estate, comprising the residue of the fee simple, that would become a possessory estate when the preceding life estate or fee tail terminated. If the grantor did not expressly transfer the residue of the fee simple, the grantor retained it, and it was called a reversion. If the grantor expressly transferred the residue of the fee simple to someone else, that person had an interest called a remainder. Although the English courts later came to recognize future interests other than remainders and reversions, the doctrine of estates in land was established once courts sanctioned the creation of presently possessory interests smaller than a fee simple and began to protect the future interests comprising the residue of the fee simple.[123]

The English scheme of present and future estates in land was brought to the British colonies in North America in the seventeenth century, and the doctrine of estates has developed along roughly parallel lines in England and in the United States. It should be emphasized that a future estate is not merely an interest that will or may come into existence at a future time; it is a presently existing, legally protected interest that may

---

indefinite continuance of the entail seems to be accepted" in cases where the fee tail was not created by a *maritagium.*

[118] The fee tail, which created rights in the original tenant's descendants, could not be prejudiced by forfeiture, "gave to landowners what the common law had always denied to them: the power to create a virtually inalienable estate." Real Property, supra note 57, at 72.

[119] 3 Holdsworth, History of English Law 119 (3d ed.1922).

[120] For a good brief discussion of the operation of the common recovery to convert a fee tail into a fee simple, see 1 Am. L. Prop., supra note 38, at § 2.2.

[121] The Settled Land Act of 1882 and the Settled Land Act of 1925 made it impossible to keep land in the family. See Real Property, supra note 57, at 393–410 for a detailed discussion of these statutes.

[122] Introduction to History, supra note 57, at 86.

[123] "* * * [T]he doctrine [of estates] * * * involves a recognition not simply that the sum of possible interest—the fee simple—may be cut up into slices like a cake and distributed amongst a number of people, but that all of them will obtain present existing interests in the land, though their right to actual enjoyment, to seisin in demesne, may be postponed." Introduction to History, supra note 57, at 86–87.

provide possession to its owner at a future time.[124] In other words, it is possession and not ownership that is deferred. Although the doctrine of estates was confined to real property for several centuries, it was later extended to personal property as well.

§§ 1.8–2.0 ARE RESERVED FOR SUPPLEMENTAL MATERIAL.

---

[124] Introduction to Law, supra note 57, at 133.

Chapter 2

PRESENT ESTATES IN REALTY AND EQUIVALENT INTERESTS IN PERSONALTY

Table of Sections

§ 2.1 PRESENT ESTATES IN LAND—IN GENERAL

Present estates in land carry with them, as their single most salient characteristic, the present right to exclusive possession of a particular parcel of land.[1] Moreover, by the traditional view, this right to exclusive possession extends downward "to the center of the earth,"[2] except where a mineral estate is created by severance of ownership of the subsurface from the surface.[3] Originally, it was also said that the owner of the present estate had an exclusive right to possess that extended indefinitely upward from the

---

[1]   See infra § 7.1.

[2]   E.g., Edwards v. Sims, 232 Ky. 791, 24 S.W.2d 619 (1929). For additional discussion see infra § 7.1.

[3]   E.g., in Texas, a severance of the subsurface oil and gas from the soil may result in a division "into two tracts as if the division had been made by superficial lines, or had been severed vertically by horizontal planes." Humphreys-Mexia Co. v. Gammon, 113 Tex. 247, 254 S.W. 296 (1923). In Pennsylvania, where coal mining has been a major industry, ownership may be divided into three separate estates—the surface estate, the subsurface (mineral) estate, and the support estate (the right to subjacent support of the surface). See, e.g., Patton v. Republic Steel Corp., 342 Pa.Super. 101, 492 A.2d 411 (1985).

surface of the earth.[4] The invention of the airplane and the advent of extensive air travel has, of course, brought about a modification of this ancient maxim. The United States Supreme Court held that the Air Commerce Act of 1926 and the Civil Aeronautics Act of 1938 made the air space above the prescribed minimum altitudes for flight "a public highway." Therefore, the surface owner's rights in the superjacent air space are subject to a public easement for air travel above the minimum altitudes established by the federal statutes and regulations.[5] Additional laws concerning unmanned aircraft systems (drones) may further circumscribe the surface owner's rights.[6]

Ownership of a present estate in land also carries with it substantial privileges of use and enjoyment, subject to important restrictions imposed on all possessors of land by the common law[7] or by statute for the protection of other possessors of land and the public at large.[8] The owners of present estates that are smaller than a fee simple absolute—which constitutes full ownership of land—are also subject to common law rules restricting their use and enjoyment of the land to protect the owners of future interests in the same land.[9] And the owner of any present estate may hold it subject to "servitudes"—easements and covenants—that limit the owner's exclusive right to possession and the usual privileges of use and enjoyment incident to a present estate in land.[10]

Traditionally, present estates have been classified as either freehold or nonfreehold estates. At common law, the former were created by livery of seisin (prescribed procedures for transferring the estate), while the latter were not. And the former were given substantial protection very early in the development of the common law, while the latter were not given substantial protection until much later.[11] The freehold estates include (1) all varieties of the fee simple, both absolute and defeasible, (2) the fee tail and the fee simple conditional, in states that still recognize them, and (3) all kinds of life estates. The nonfreehold estates include the estate for years, the periodic estates, the estate at will, and the estate at sufferance.[12] Because the original reasons for

---

[4]   The old maxim was that ownership and the right to possession extended "ad coelum usque ad infernos."

[5]   United States v. Causby, 328 U.S. 256, 66 S.Ct. 1062, 90 L.Ed. 1206 (1946), superseded by statute, 72 Stat. 739, 49 U.S.C. § 1301(24), 49 U.S.C.A. § 1301(24) (2015) (redefining "navigable airspace"); Griggs v. Allegheny County, 369 U.S. 84, 82 S.Ct. 531, 7 L.Ed.2d 585 (1962), reh'g denied, 369 U.S. 857, 82 S.Ct. 931, 8 L.Ed.2d 16 (1962).

[6]   See L. Donohue, A Tale of Two Sovereigns: Federal and State Use and Regulation of Unmanned Aircraft Systems (2018), https://scholarship.law.georgetown.edu/facpub/1967.

[7]   These common law restrictions include rules forbidding the use of land in such a way as to interfere unreasonably with the use of neighboring land in the possession of others (the law of "nuisance"); rules as to lateral and subjacent support of land in the possession of others; and rules as to the use of streams and lakes, the extraction of underground percolating water, and disposal of diffused surface water. See infra §§ 7.2–.6.

[8]   See infra Chapter 9.

[9]   See infra Chapter 4.

[10]   See infra Chapter 8.

[11]   The various "real actions" could be used to recover seisin (possession) of freehold land only. Seisin of a freehold meant possession of land as tenant in fee simple, fee tail, or for life. 1 American Law of Property 12 (1952–54) (hereinafter Am. L. Prop.).

[12]   Many writers also add an "estate at sufferance." A "tenant at sufferance," however, is merely a wrongful possessor who originally gained possession rightfully as tenant and remained in possession after his or her legal right to possession ended. Thus the "estate" of a "tenant at sufferance" is no more substantial than the interest of any other mere possessor of land whose possession is legally protected as against those who cannot show a better right to possession. See infra § 6.20.

differentiating freehold from nonfreehold estates have been largely eliminated, the distinction is no longer as important.[13] In fact, the Third Restatement of Property expressly rejects the distinction as being "archaic."[14]

Present estates may also be classified as either inheritable or noninheritable. The fee simple, fee tail, and fee simple conditional estates are inheritable. Estates for the life of the tenant are noninheritable, but estates *pur autre vie* (measured by the life of someone other than the life tenant) are inheritable until the measuring life terminates.[15] Estates for years and periodic estates are also inheritable if the tenant dies during the term.[16] Estates at will and at sufferance, however, are never inheritable.[17]

The fee simple absolute is the largest possible estate in land. Therefore, by definition, all the other present estates are smaller. For this reason, when a smaller present estate is carved out of a present fee simple absolute, one or more future interests will exist.[18] A future interest provides possession, if ever, in the future.

At the present time, the most important legal estates in land are undoubtedly the fee simple and the estate for years. These are the only estates that are commercially saleable, although periodic estates are also a significant factor in providing housing. The fee tail has almost completely disappeared in the United States, having been abolished either by statute or by constitutional provision in most states.[19] The fee simple conditional could not be created in England after 1285 because it was abolished by the Statute De Donis Conditionalibus,[20] but—anomalous though it may seem—can still be created in a few American jurisdictions.[21] Legal life estates are not very common today, although equitable life estates in favor of trust beneficiaries are very frequently created.

Any of the present estates in land may be owned either in severalty (by a single person) or concurrently (by two or more persons, each of whom owns an "undivided" fractional interest in the estate). The early common recognized four forms of concurrent ownership—joint tenancy, tenancy by the entirety, coparcenary, and tenancy in common.[22] Coparcenary no long exists in the United States, and most states have eliminated tenancy by the entirety. Some states also have abolished the joint tenancy.[23] In some American jurisdictions, the common law forms of concurrent ownership between spouses have been largely supplanted by a form of concurrent ownership called community property.[24] Where concurrent ownership exists, no single co-owner has the

---

[13] Until well into the nineteenth century, only freeholders could vote in parliamentary elections in England, although the legal remedies provided for protection of the two types of estates had been substantially the same since the seventeenth century.

[14] Restatement (Third) of Property: Wills and Other Donative Transfers § 24.1, cmt. a (2011) (hereinafter Third Restatement of Property).

[15] This was not always the rule. See infra § 2.12.

[16] 2 R. Powell, Powell on Real Property § 16.04[1] (2018).

[17] The estate can only continue so long as both landlord and tenant personally "will" it to continue. The death of either party automatically terminates an estate at will. Restatement of Property (Second) § 1.6, cmt. e (Am. Law Inst. 1977).

[18] For detailed treatment of future estates in land, see infra Chapter 3.

[19] See infra § 2.10. Since 1925, only equitable entailed interests can be created in England.

[20] See supra § 1.7.

[21] See infra § 2.10.

[22] See infra Chapter 5.

[23] Id.

[24] See infra §§ 5.13–.15.

right to exclude the other co-owners, but the co-owners have the right to exclude the rest of the world.

Generally, all the present estates, except the estate at will, are freely alienable by inter vivos conveyance. The present estates are also freely alienable by a will, except the estate at will or at sufferance, fee tail, fee simple conditional, and a life estate owned by the person who is the measuring life. However, if the owners are tenants by the entirety or joint tenants, both of which have a right of survivorship, an individual owner can transfer his or her interest by will only by surviving all the other co-owners.[25] For a tenancy by the entirety, neither owner can transfer his or her interest by inter vivos conveyance unless the other owner joins in the conveyance.[26]

The validity of restraints on the alienation of present estates in land imposed by express provisions in the creating instrument will be considered in connection with the more detailed discussion of each of the present estates in the ensuing sections of this chapter.

§ 2.2   FEE SIMPLE ABSOLUTE

An estate in fee simple absolute provides the greatest possible rights with respect to land. It constitutes full ownership of the land. A fee simple absolute is inheritable by either lineal or collateral heirs, generation after generation, but is also freely transferable, either inter vivos or by will, free of any claim of the transferor's heirs. It is not subject to any legally effective provision for defeasance (termination) on the happening of a stated event. Therefore, a fee simple absolute has a potentially infinite duration, which is the key feature of the Third Restatement's definition of the estate.[27] However, if the owner of a fee simple absolute dies intestate and without heirs, the estate will pass to the state by escheat. In states where tenure still theoretically exists, escheat may be viewed as terminating a fee simple absolute. However, in states where land ownership is allodial, the state merely takes the estate as the "ultimate heir" when it escheats.

Today, any language in a deed or a will that is sufficient to create a fee simple estate will create a fee simple absolute in the absence of a legally effective provision for defeasance on the happening of a stated event. It was settled in the early thirteenth century that the words "and his heirs" in a grant to "A and his heirs" were only "words of limitation" that defined A's estate as a fee simple, rather than "words of purchase" that conveyed an estate to A's heirs.[28] Nevertheless, the rigid common law rule developed in England that a fee simple could not be created in a natural person by inter vivos conveyance unless the word "heirs" was used in the grant.[29] When the Statute of Wills,[30] in 1540, made fee simple estates and other interests in land devisable by will, the courts

---

[25]   See infra §§ 5.5–.6.

[26]   See infra § 5.6.

[27]   "The estate in 'fee simple absolute' is the present interest in land that is unlimited in duration." Third Restatement of Property, supra note 14, at § 24.2.

[28]   This was the consequence of decisions in the early thirteenth century denying the heir any right to recover lands alienated by a tenant in fee during his lifetime. See 1 Am. L. Prop., supra note 11, at 82.

[29]   1 Am. L. Prop., supra note 11, at 82–84 . For an application of the common law rule requiring use of the word "heirs" to create a fee simple, see Ivey v. Peacock, 56 Fla. 440, 47 So. 481 (1908) (conveyance omitting the word "heirs" but purporting to convey "in fee simple forever" created only a life estate).

[30]   Statute of Wills 1540, 32 Hen. 8 c. 1 (Eng.).

refused to apply the rigid common law rule requiring use of the word "heirs." Instead, courts held that a will would transfer a fee simple whenever the testator's language, taken as a whole, manifested that intent.[31]

In England, statutes now provide that "the fee simple or other the whole interest" which a grantor or testator has the power to transfer shall pass by a conveyance or will, unless the instrument affirmatively manifests a contrary intent.[32] Similar statutes are now in force in almost all American jurisdictions, although statutes in a few states are limited either to only wills or inter vivos conveyances.[33]

A strong public policy favoring the alienability (transferability) of fee simple estates has existed since the enactment of the statute of Quia Emptores in 1290. Courts consistently have applied this policy to invalidate almost all attempts to impose restraints on alienability of fee simple absolute estates by means of express deed or will provision. Provisions purporting, without any limitation as to duration or scope, to prohibit the transfer of a fee simple absolute—so-called disabling restraints—or to defeat or terminate what would otherwise be a fee simple absolute upon transfer—so-called forfeiture restraints—are universally held to be void.[34] In the United States, courts always void even disabling restraints that are limited as to duration or scope.[35] Forfeiture restraints thus limited are also generally void,[36] but some authority exists that they are valid.[37] Covenants by the grantee of a fee simple absolute not to alienate—

---

[31] 1 Am. L. Prop., supra note 11, at 89–91; R. Megarry & H. Wade, The Law of Real Property 48 (8th ed. 2012); 1 Powell, supra note 16, § 13.04.

[32] As to conveyances, this rule was established by the Law of Property Act 1925, 15 Geo. 5, § 60(1) (Eng. & Wales). As to wills, this rule was established by the Wills Act 1837, 1 Vict. c. 26, §§ 28, 34 (Eng., Wales & N. Ir.). The Conveyancing Act 1881, 44 & 45 Vict. c. 41 (Eng., Wales & N. Ir.) had provided that, in deeds executed thereafter, the words "in fee simple" would suffice, without the word "heirs."

[33] 1 Am. L. Prop., supra note 11, at § 2.4. The common law rule appears to remain in force for conveyances only in Maine and South Carolina and for wills only in Florida. In South Dakota and perhaps in Pennsylvania, the rule for conveyances is the same as that applied to wills in England between 1540 and 1837—the intent to create a fee simple must be expressed, but words of inheritance are unnecessary. See id. including footnotes.

[34] "Disabling restraints": e.g., Payne v. Hart, 178 Ark. 100, 9 S.W.2d 1059 (1928); Davis v. Geyer, 151 Fla. 362, 9 So. 2d 727 (1942); Nashville, Chattanooga & St. Louis Ry. v. Bell, 162 Tenn. 661, 39 S.W.2d 1026 (1931). Louisiana appears to be an exception; see Mardis v. Brantley, 30,773 (La. Ct. App.); 717 So. 2d 702, writ denied, 98–2488 (La. 1998); 729 So. 2d 563. Restrictions in a trust instrument prohibiting alienation of specific property by the trustee are valid. E.g., Legge v. Canty, 176 Md. 283, 4 A.2d 465 (1939); Matter of Roe, 119 N.Y. 509, 23 N.E. 1063 (1890).

"Forfeiture restraints": e.g., Casey v. Casey, 287 Ark. 395, 700 S.W.2d 46 (1985); Courts v. Courts' Guardian, 230 Ky. 141, 18 S.W.2d 957 (1929) (dictum). However, courts have recognized exceptions when property is conveyed to a charitable trust or to a beneficial association. See Pilgrim Evangelical Lutheran Church v. Lutheran Church-Missouri Synod Found., 661 S.W.2d 833, 839 (Mo. Ct. App. 1983) (charitable trust); National Grange of Order of Patrons of Husbandry v. O'Sullivan Grange, 35 Wash. App. 444, 667 P.2d 1105 (1983) (fraternal order).

[35] E.g., Superior Oil Co. v. Johnson, 161 Kan. 710, 171 P.2d 658 (1946); Mills v. Blakelin, 307 Mass. 542, 30 N.E.2d 873 (1941); Triplett v. Triplett, 332 Mo. 870, 60 S.W.2d 13 (1933); State Bank v. Thiessen, 137 Neb. 426, 289 N.W. 791 (1940); Wrubel Realty Corp. v. Wrubel, 138 N.J. Eq. 466, 48 A.2d 793 (1946); Buckner v. Hawkins, 230 N.C. 99, 52 S.E.2d 16 (1949); Goffe v. Karanyianopoulos, 53 R.I. 313, 166 A. 547 (1933); Barrows v. Ezer, 668 S.W.2d 854 (Tex. Ct. App. 1984).

[36] E.g., Jenne v. Jenne, 271 Ill. 526, 111 N.E. 540 (1916); Douglass v. Stevens, 214 N.C. 688, 200 S.E. 366 (1939); Andrews v. Hall, 156 Neb. 817, 58 N.W.2d 201 (1953); Wise v. Poston, 281 S.C. 574, 316 S.E.2d 412 (1984).

[37] Valid when limited to a "reasonable time": Turner v. Lewis, 189 Ky. 837, 226 S.W. 367 (1920) (life of conveyor); Francis v. Big Sandy Co., 171 Ky. 209, 188 S.W. 345 (1916) (term of years less than 21); Blevins v. Pittman, 189 Ga. 789, 7 S.E.2d 662 (1940) (valid when forfeiture restraints are limited to members of a small

so-called promissory restraints—appear to be void whenever a similar restraint of the forfeiture type would be void.[38]

In recent years, many cases have dealt with the validity of indirect restraints on alienation.[39] A majority of these cases have been concerned with the validity of so-called due-on-sale clauses in mortgages and other security instruments, such as trust deeds. These clauses give the mortgage holder the right to accelerate the mortgage debt and to foreclose on the mortgaged land if the owner transfers without the mortgage holder's consent. Although mortgage holders sometimes use these clauses for protection from transactions that endanger the mortgage security and increase the risk of default, they often also use the clause to force the refinancing of below-market interest rate mortgage loans during periods of rising interest rates.[40] The problems created by state court hostility to due-on-sale clauses have now been resolved by a United States Supreme Court decision[41] and by federal legislation[42] that validated their use.

Courts in a number of cases have considered whether various kinds of preemptive ("first refusal") rights to purchase land are invalid as unreasonable restraints on alienation. Courts generally uphold a preemptive right to purchase at either the owner's asking price, the highest bona fide third party offer, or market value.[43] However, courts generally invalidate preemptive rights of unlimited duration that require the owner to offer land to the preemptioner at a fixed price before selling it to anyone else,[44] though some courts have upheld such rights.[45]

When the statute of Quia Emptores conclusively established the alienability of possessory estates in fee simple, the most prominent feature of English inheritance law

---

group). See also Hutchinson v. Loomis, 244 S.W.2d 751 (Ky. 1951) (discussing standard of "reasonableness"). See generally 6 Am. L. Prop., supra note 11, at §§ 26.19–26, 26.31–34; 10 Powell, supra note 16, at § 77.01.

[38] E.g., Fritz v. Gilbert, 8 Cal. 2d 68, 63 P.2d 291 (1936); Sisters of Mercy v. Lightner, 223 Iowa 1049, 274 N.W. 86 (1937); Winsor v. Mills, 157 Mass. 362, 32 N.E. 352 (1892). See also 6 Am. L. Prop., supra note 11, at § 26.11 n.14; Restatement of Property § 406 (Am. Law Inst. 1936) (hereinafter First Restatement of Property). Ordinarily, a covenant restricting the use of land, as distinguished from its transfer, will not constitute an invalid restraint on alienation. Id. at Introductory Note to Part II. However, courts have invalidated use restrictions that affect marketability of property by unreasonably limiting the class of persons to whom the property may be transferred. Falls City v. Mo. Pac. R.R. Co., 453 F.2d 771 (8th Cir. 1971); Grossman v. Hill, 384 Pa. 590, 122 A.2d 69 (1956).

[39] "An indirect restraint on alienation arises when an attempt is made to accomplish some purpose other than the restraint of alienability, but with the incidental result that the instrument, if valid, would restrain practical alienability." L. Simes & A. Smith, The Law of Future Interests § 1112 (3d ed. 2016).

[40] For a comprehensive treatment of due-on-sale clauses, which are not within the scope of this book, see G. Nelson, D. Whitman, A. Burkhart & R. Freyermuth, Real Estate Finance Law §§ 5.21–26 (6th ed. 2015).

[41] Fidelity Fed. Sav. & Loan Ass'n v. de la Cuesta, 458 U.S. 141, 102 S.Ct. 3014, 73 L.Ed.2d 664 (1982).

[42] Garn-St. Germain Depository Institutions Act of 1982, 12 U.S.C.A. § 1701j–3 (West 2016). For a good discussion of the Act, see Nelson, Whitman, Burkhart & Freyermuth, supra note 40, at § 5.24.

[43] See cases cited in 6 Am. L. Prop., supra note 11, at § 26.67 nn.7–8. See also First Restatement of Property, supra note 38, at § 406; Metro. Transp. Auth. v. Bruken Realty Corp., 67 N.Y.2d 156, 501 N.Y.S.2d 306, 492 N.E.2d 379 (1986). Contra, see Ferrero Constr. Co. v. Dennis Rourke Corp., 311 Md. 560, 536 A.2d 1137 (1988).

[44] Edgar v. Hunt, 218 Mont. 30, 706 P.2d 120 (1985) (price was fixed and was much less than market value).

[45] Lawson v. Redmoor Corp., 37 Wash. App. 351, 679 P.2d 972 (1984); First Restatement of Property, supra note 38, at § 406 (a preemptive right to purchase at a fixed price is valid if the restraint is promissory in nature, allows alienation to some possible alienees, is reasonable under the circumstances, and does not violate the Rule Against Perpetuities). See also cases cited in 6 Am. L. Prop., supra note 11, at § 26.67 n.3.

was primogeniture, by which the oldest son inherited all his parents' property.[46] Primogeniture made the law concerning the inheritance of land very complicated and quite different from the law concerning the distribution of intestate personal property. The Administration of Estates Act (1925)[47] vastly simplified the English law of intestate succession by abolishing primogeniture and eliminating the distinction between intestate succession to real and personal property.

In the United States, the common law of inheritance as to real property has been changed by adoption of intestate succession laws in all jurisdictions.[48] Primogeniture has been abolished everywhere, and the different rules as to real and personal property have been eliminated in almost every state. In a few states in which the distinction between real and personal property still continues, a surviving spouse is still excluded from intestate succession to real property and must rely on dower or curtesy,[49] as at common law. In all other jurisdictions, as in England, a surviving spouse takes by intestate succession under the statute, and, subject to the surviving spouse's right, descendants of the decedent take the property to the exclusion of all ancestors and collateral relatives. Descendants in equal degree take equal shares. In the absence of descendants and subject to the surviving spouse's share, the decedent's parents are next in line in most states, followed by the decedent's siblings, though parents and siblings share the intestate property in some states. The statutes sometimes also make express provision for aunts and uncles, nieces and nephews, and grandparents and their issue, and most statutes provide that failing takers of any expressly designated class, the property shall pass to the decedent's next of kin. Many statutes expressly provide for escheat to the state or make the state the ultimate heir if there are no takers of any expressly designated class. However, in some states, escheat is provided for in a statute other than the intestate succession law.

When the United States transferred most of its public domain during the nineteenth and early twentieth centuries, it almost always granted the land in fee simple absolute.[50] In commercial real estate transactions, the only significant estate, other than the leasehold estate, is the fee simple absolute. When a contract for the sale of land requires the vendor simply to convey described land, the vendor is obligated to convey a fee simple absolute in the absence of additional contract language providing for a smaller estate.[51]

The fee simple estate plays an important role for condominiums. In a condominium building, each unit normally consists of a defined interior space within the building and is separately owned in fee simple absolute by one or more persons.[52] But the exterior

---

[46] See supra § 1.5, at nn. 77–79.

[47] For a discussion of the Administration of Estates Act (1925) and the subsequent changes made by the Intestates' Estates Act (1952), see Megarry & Wade, supra note 31, at 602–10.

[48] For a discussion of the modern intestate succession laws, see T. Atkinson, Law of Wills §§ 14–26 (2d ed. 1953). For a detailed summary of the intestate succession laws of all the states, see 7 W. Page, The Law of Wills ch. 63 (W. Bowe & D. Parker, rev. 3d ed. Supp. 1979–80).

[49] As to dower and curtesy, see infra § 2.13.

[50] See G. Warvelle, A Practical Treatise on Abstracts and Examinations of Title to Real Property §§ 137–59 (4th ed. 1921).

[51] See infra § 10.12.

[52] The earliest condominium statute was Article 664 of the Code Napoleon of 1804, a very brief provision that was later substantially expanded. Code Civil [C. Civ.] [Civil Code] art. 664 (Fr.). Most European and Central and South American nations adopted condominium statutes before any were adopted in the United States.

walls of the building, the hallways and other common areas within the building, and the exterior grounds around the building are owned by all the unit owners as tenants in common. Although condominiums could probably have been created under the common law in some jurisdictions, use of the condominium concept has generally proceeded on the basis of special enabling legislation. Since Puerto Rico enacted the first condominium enabling statute in 1958, all fifty states have enacted them. Many of the first generation condominium statutes were based on the Federal Housing Administration's Model Statute for the Creation of Apartment Ownership.[53] Since then, the Uniform Law Commission has produced two new models for states interested in enacting second generation condominium statutes, the Uniform Condominium Act[54] and the Uniform Common Interest Ownership Act.[55]

The essential elements of a condominium development include:[56]

(1)   Ownership of part of the building or of an interior space in it as an interest in land;

(2)   An effective restraint against partition of the commonly-owned land and of the building;

(3)   An effective restraint against the separation of a unit owner's share in the commonly-owned land from the separately-owned unit;

(4)   Separate assessment of units for taxation; and

(5)   Provision for the use, management, and maintenance of the commonly-owned property.

Among their other provisions, all condominium statutes provide for the execution of an instrument called a "declaration" by which a particular tract of land is "submitted to the provisions" of the statute and provide for the election of a board of directors by the property owner's association and for covenants, by-laws, and administrative regulations to "run with" each unit and bind all successive owners. Chapter 8 of this book examines the concept of covenants running with the land" While most condominiums involve residential buildings and the surrounding grounds, many statutes authorize office building condominiums and townhouse condominiums. The latter can also be constructed, in many states, under local planned unit development ordinances.[57]

---

[53]   This Model Statute was promulgated in 1961 in response to passage of Section 234 of the National Housing Act in 1960, which authorized the Federal Housing Administration to insure mortgage loans on condominium units.

[54]   This act was promulgated in 1977 and was amended in 1980. It is currently in effect in Alabama, Arizona, Kentucky, Maine, Minnesota, Missouri, Nebraska, New Mexico, Pennsylvania, Rhode Island, Texas, Virginia, Washington, and West Virginia.

[55]   This act was promulgated in 1982 and was amended in 1994 and 2008. It makes broad provision for establishment of communities characterized by "common interest ownership," including condominiums and planned unit developments. It currently is in effect in Alaska, Colorado, Connecticut, Delaware, Minnesota, Nevada, Vermont, Washington, and West Virginia.

[56]   This summary is drawn from Note, Condominium: A Reconciliation of Competing Interests?, 18 Vand. L. Rev. 1773, 1775–76 (1965). For the most detailed treatment of condominiums, see J. Rohan & M. Reskin, Condominium Law and Practice: Forms (2017).

[57]   See infra § 9.24.

Full ownership of chattels (tangible subjects of personal property) and intangible personal property is generally analogous to ownership of land in fee simple.[58] Transfer of full ownership of personal property has never required the use of words of inheritance, but it has always been necessary to indicate by express language any intent to transfer less than full ownership, such as a leasehold interest.

§ 2.3   FEE SIMPLE DEFEASIBLE ESTATES—IN GENERAL

Fee simple defeasible estates are created by instruments that contain language sufficient to create a fee simple, coupled with a condition under which the estate will terminate ("to A for so long as the land is used as a park").[59] Often, though not always, the likelihood of defeasance (termination) is uncertain. If defeasance is uncertain, the defeasible estate can last potentially forever, like a fee simple absolute. However, the condition may make defeasance a certainty.[60]

The principal fee simple defeasible estates are (1) fee simple determinable,[61] (2) fee simple subject to condition subsequent,[62] and (3) fee simple subject to executory limitation.[63] When the first two terminate, possession returns to the person who created the defeasible estate.[64] In contrast, the fee simple subject to executory limitation is defeasible in favor of someone else who is specified in the instrument that created the estate ("to A for so long as the land is used as a park, then to B"). The fee simple determinable and the fee simple subject to executory limitation terminate automatically when the specified condition occurs. In contrast, the fee simple subject to condition subsequent does not terminate automatically. Instead, the person who created the

---

[58] The leading general treatise on personal property law, R. Brown, The Law of Personal Property (W. Raushenbush ed., 3d ed. 1975) includes no discussion of the general legal characteristics of "full ownership" of personalty.

[59] See First Restatement of Property, supra note 38, at § 16. Such estates have also been called "qualified fee simple estates." See, e.g., 1 Am. L. Prop., supra note 11, at § 2.6. If it becomes impossible for the event that will terminate the fee to occur, the fee becomes a fee simple absolute; see Willhite v. Masters, 965 S.W.2d 406 (Mo. Ct. App. 1998).

[60] E.g., A, owning Blackacre in fee simple absolute, transfers Blackacre "to B and his heirs from and after one year from the date of this instrument." A retains a fee simple subject to executory limitation. First Restatement of Property, supra note 38, at § 46(1), illus. 2. In this example, the date of termination is certain, but this need not be the case.

[61] Such estates have also been called "base fees," "qualified fees," "estates in fee on limitation," "estates in fee on conditional limitation," and "estates in fee simple on special limitation." The first four terms are ambiguous because they have also been applied to quite different kinds of defeasible fee simple estates. Either "fee simple determinable" or "fee simple on special limitation" is unambiguous, but "fee simple determinable" (or "determinable fee") has the advantage of brevity. The First Restatement of Property adopts this term. Supra note 38, at § 44.

[62] Such estates have also been called "estates in fee on condition," "estates in fee on condition subsequent," "estates in simple subject to a right of entry for breach of condition" (or "condition broken"), and "estates in fee simple subject to a power of termination." All these terms, with the possible exception of the first, are unambiguous. "Fee simple subject to a condition subsequent" is the term adopted in the First Restatement of Property. Supra note 38, at § 45.

[63] Such estates have also been called "estates in fee simple on conditional limitation" or "estates in fee simple subject to a shifting (or springing) use (or devise)." The first term is objectionable, because it is also applied to estates in fee simple determinable. The second term is now practically obsolete. "Fee simple subject to an executory limitation" is the term adopted in the First Restatement of Property. Supra note 38, at § 46.

[64] In all cases, if the person who would take possession upon the expiration of the estate is dead, his or her successors will take instead. In the interest of simplicity, the phrase "or his or her successors in interest" will not be repeated in the text each time it is applicable.

defeasible estate has the power to terminate the defeasible estate, but need not do so, when the condition occurs.

The Third Restatement of Property rejects the common law distinctions among the three types of defeasible fees as being "unnecessarily complex."[65] Instead, the Restatement combines them all into a single "fee simple defeasible." Some scholars agree that the current classification system is overly complicated and that the number of recognized property interests should be reduced.[66] However, no court has yet adopted the Restatement approach. Therefore, this book will focus on the three currently recognized forms of defeasible fee. It also cites the First Restatement of Property, because it restates the accepted common law.

Fee simple defeasible estates generally grant most of the same rights as a fee simple absolute. Thus, the owner of a defeasible fee has the same power as the owner of a fee simple absolute to transfer the entire estate or to create smaller estates. When the defeasible fee owner dies, the estate passes by will or intestate succession in the same manner as a fee simple absolute, though the defeasible fee remains subject to the condition.[67] The rules determining the validity of restraints on alienation of a fee simple absolute also apply to restraints on alienation of a defeasible fee.[68] However, some important differences exist. For example:

(1) Although the owner of a defeasible fee has the same exclusive right to possession, use, and enjoyment of the land as the owner of a fee simple absolute, actions by the defeasible fee owner that substantially reduce the land's value may be enjoined by the person who is entitled to possession of the land if the defeasible estate terminates, so long as a reasonable probability exists that the estate will terminate.[69]

(2) In jurisdictions that still recognize dower and curtesy, the interest that the surviving spouse acquires in the decedent's defeasible fee is generally held to be subject to the same condition or limitation on the defeasible fee, though courts in a few cases have reached a contrary result when the decedent's estate was subject to an executory limitation.[70]

(3) The general rules concerning a concurrent owner's right to compel partition are the same for a defeasible fee as for a fee simple absolute, but defeasibility may substantially alter the result of applying these rules.[71]

---

[65] Third Restatement of Property, supra note 14, at § 24.3 cmt. a and intro. note.

[66] T. Gallanis, The Future of Future Interests, 60 Wash. & Lee L. Rev. 513 (2003); L. Waggoner, Reformulating the Structure of Estates: A Proposal for Legislative Action, 85 Harv. L. Rev. 729 (1972). See also A. Dunham, Possibility of Reverter and Power of Termination—Fraternal or Identical Twins?, U Chi. L. Rev. 215 (1953).

[67] See First Restatement of Property, supra note 38, at §§ 50, 55; Mayor of Rockville v. Walker, 86 Md. App. 691, 587 A.2d 1179 (Md. Ct. Spec. App. 1990) (if the grantee of a defeasible fee mortgages it and the fee terminates because the condition occurs, the mortgage terminates as well).

[68] See supra notes 28–33.

[69] See cases cited in 1 Am. L. Prop., supra note 11, at § 20.23 nn.9–12; cases cited in 8 Powell, supra note 16, at § 56.07 n.7; First Restatement of Property, supra note 38, at §§ 49, 193.

[70] See 1 Am. L. Prop., supra note 11, at §§ 5.26–29, 5.63; 1 Powell, supra note 16, at § 13.06; First Restatement of Property, supra note 38, at § 54.

[71] See 1 Powell, supra note 16, at § 13.06; First Restatement of Property, supra note 38, at §§ 51–53.

Just as personal property ownership can be analogous to fee simple absolute, it can also be analogous to a defeasible fee.[72] In practice, a defeasible fee in personal property is more often a fee simple determinable or fee simple subject to executory limitation, rather than a fee simple subject to condition subsequent. Most such analogous interests are created in intangibles, such as stocks and bonds held in trust, so that such interests are equitable, rather than legal.

Whether the subject matter is real or personal property, courts generally hold that certain kinds of conditions and limitations are illegal and void because they are contrary to public policy. Prominent among these are conditions and limitations that are intended to discourage marriage, encourage divorce or separation, or penalize will contests. Although the law concerning such conditions and limitations is too complex to be readily summarized,[73] its broad outlines may be gathered from a reading of the First Restatement of Property's black-letter provisions.[74]

With respect to conditions and limitations in restraint of marriage or encouraging separation or divorce, the First Restatement broadly asserts that conditions and limitations "designed to prevent the acquisition or retention of an interest in land or in things other than land in the event of any first marriage" are invalid "unless the dominant motive of the conveyor is to provide support until such marriage."[75] But a similar restraint on "some, but not all first marriages, is valid" unless "the circumstances under which a marriage is permitted are such that a permitted marriage is not likely to occur" and "the dominant motive of the conveyor" is not "to provide support until such marriage or in the event of such marriage."[76] Moreover, conditions and limitations "designed to prevent the acquisition or retention" of real or personal property "in the event of remarriage" are valid "where the person restrained is the spouse of the person imposing the restraint" or, where that is not the case, "unless it is found to be unreasonable."[77] But conditions and limitations "designed to permit the acquisition or retention of an interest in land or in things other than land only in the event of a separation or divorce" are invalid "unless the dominant motive of the conveyor is to provide support in the event of such separation or divorce."[78]

The First Restatement further asserts that conditions and limitations "designed to prevent the acquisition or retention" of real or personal property in the event of a contest of the entire will in which the property is devised are invalid unless the contest is "based upon a claim of forgery or * * * subsequent revocation by a later will or codicil, provided there was probable cause for the making of such contest."[79] Moreover, a condition or

---

[72]   See, e.g., Woodard v. Clark, 236 N.C. 190, 72 S.E.2d 433 (1952); N.C. Gen. Stat. §§ 39–62. See also Simes & Smith, supra note 39, at § 7.

[73]   An excellent and very detailed treatment of this topic may be found in 6 Am. L. Prop., supra note 11, at §§ 27.1–23. For an earlier version of much of the same material, see O. Browder, Conditions and Limitations in Restraint of Marriage, 39 Mich. L. Rev. 1288 (1941); O. Browder, Testamentary Conditions Against Contest, 36 Mich. L. Rev. 1066 (1938); O. Browder, Testamentary Conditions Against Contest Re-Examined, 49 Colum. L. Rev. 320 (1949).

[74]   First Restatement of Property, supra note 38, at §§ 424–38. For a parallel treatment with citation of authorities, see 10 Powell, supra note 16, at ch. 78.

[75]   First Restatement of Property, supra note 38, at § 424.

[76]   Id. § 425.

[77]   Id. § 426.

[78]   Id. § 427.

[79]   Id. § 428.

limitation "designed to prevent the acquisition or retention of a devised interest * * * in the event of any attack upon the validity of particular provisions" in a will is valid unless "it applies to an attack which is either successful or, although unsuccessful, is brought by a person having probable cause therefor, and which asserts that the provision attacked (a) violates the social restrictions * * * [embodied in the rule against perpetuities, the rule against restraints on alienation, or the rules against restraints on marriage, etc.] or (b) violates a mortmain statute primarily designed to curb charitable ownership."[80]

In addition to the rules relating to conditions and limitations with respect to marriage, separation, divorce, and will contests, the First Restatement also deals with conditions and limitations imposing miscellaneous restraints concerning the relation of parent and infant, religion, "bad habits," and education or occupation.[81]

It should be noted that the rules as to illegality of conditions and limitations apply to conditions precedent, as well as to conditions subsequent and special and executory limitations.[82] They may also be applied to conditions and limitations attached to life interests and leasehold interests, as well as fee simple estates in land and analogous interests in personalty.

§ 2.4   FEE SIMPLE DETERMINABLE

The fee simple determinable has existed from an early date in England. Two requirements must be satisfied to create it. In the document that creates the determinable estate, the grantor must retain the future interest following it, and the transfer must be subject to a limitation that the estate last only "so long as" a designated state of affairs continues or only "until" the occurrence of a designated event was recognized as a permissible estate. For example, the owner of land in fee simple absolute could convey it to "ABC Church so long as the land shall be used for church purposes" or to "ABC Church until the land shall cease to be used for church purposes." Such qualified fee simple estates may still be created under English and American law.[83]

The estate is created by any words of duration or time. In addition to the terms "so long as" and "until," other words of duration or time include "while" and "during." In both of the above examples, the qualifying language is a "special limitation" ("so long as the land shall be used for church purposes"),[84] and the estate obtained by the church is a fee simple determinable.[85] The estate continues only until the designated limitation is

---

[80]   Id. § 429. See also id. §§ 430–32 as to "restraints on claims," "restraints on intermeddling," and "provisions excluding extra-testamentary acquisition."

[81]   See id. §§ 433–38.

[82]   The effect of valid conditions precedent is explored in subsequent sections of this book dealing with contingent remainders and executory interests.

[83]   For John Chipman Gray's argument that such qualified fee simple estates could not be created after *Quia Emptores* because that statute abolished tenure between feoffor and feoffee when land was conveyed in fee simple and for a refutation of that argument, see 1 Am. L. Prop., supra note 11, at § 2.6, and R. Powell, Determinable Fees, 23 Colum. L. Rev. 207 (1923).

[84]   "The term 'special limitation' denotes that part of the language of a conveyance which causes the created interest automatically to expire upon the occurrence of a stated event, and thus provides for a terminability in addition to that normally characteristic of such interest." First Restatement of Property, supra note 38, at § 23. This definition was approved in Williams v. Watt, 668 P.2d 620 (Wyo. 1983).

[85]   As to use of the term "fee simple determinable" in preference to other terms sometimes employed, see infra note 61. For an excellent, succinct treatment of the fee simple determinable, see J. Harris, Note, Property—Fee Simple Determinables—Distinguishing Characteristics, 71 W. Va. L. Rev. 367 (1969). Cases in

breached, at which time the estate simply expires. This expiration is not deemed to divest or cut short the fee simple determinable.[86]

A fee simple determinable is a smaller estate than a fee simple absolute because the special limitation may cause the fee simple determinable to expire, rather than to continue indefinitely. A fee simple absolute owner who conveys a fee simple determinable retains a future interest called a "possibility of reverter."[87] If the fee simple determinable was created in a will, the testator's heirs will inherit the possibility of reverter.

An express provision for reverter to the grantor or his heirs is often included in the creating instrument,[88] but it normally is unnecessary to create a fee simple determinable if the special limitation language of duration or time is used. If such language is used, the possibility of reverter arises by operation of law.[89] If the creating instrument does not contain appropriate terms of duration or time, a court will still normally find that a fee simple determinable has been created if the document includes an express reverter clause.[90] Without either an express reverter clause or terms of duration or time, a mere statement of the purpose for the property transfer ("to A for use as a hospital") usually transfers a fee simple absolute, rather than a fee simple determinable.[91]

When the limitation on the fee simple determinable is breached, the determinable estate expires by operation of law, without the necessity of any action by the person who owns the possibility of reverter.[92] The owner of the possibility of reverter has an immediate right to possession of the property and may bring an action to recover it. For this reason, the applicable statute of limitations for an action to recover possession of the land begins to run as soon as the limitation is breached.[93]

---

which the court held that the words "so long as" create a fee simple determinable include Lacer v. Navajo Cty., 141 Ariz. 396, 687 P.2d 404 (Ct. App. 1983); Edling v. Stanford Twp., 381 N.W.2d 881 (Minn. Ct. App. 1986).

[86]   Simes & Smith, supra note 39, at § 13.

[87]   See First Restatement of Property, supra note 38, at § 154(3), cmt. g; 2 Simes & Smith, supra note 39, at §§ 13, 281; 1 Am. L. Prop., supra note 11, at § 4.12.

[88]   For example, the owner of a fee simple absolute might convey land "to ABC Church so long as the land shall be used for church purposes, and if the land shall cease to be used for church purposes it shall revert to the grantor or his heirs."

[89]   See, e.g., Staack v. Detterding, 182 Iowa 582, 161 N.W. 44, L.R.A. 1918C, 856 (1917); Bailey v. Eagle Mountain Tel. Co., 202 Tenn. 195, 303 S.W.2d 726 (1957); Edling v. Stanford Twp., 381 N.W.2d 881 (1986).

[90]   E.g., Williams v. Kirby Sch. Dist. No. 32, 207 Ark. 458, 181 S.W.2d 488 (1944) (" 'to be used * * * for School and Church purposes and to revert to me should School and Church be discontinued or moved.' "); Mt. Gilead Church Cemetery v. Woodham, 453 So. 2d 362 (Ala. 1984). Contra Hardman v. Dahlonega-Lumpkin Cty. Chamber of Commerce, 238 Ga. 551, 233 S.E.2d 753 (1977) (the law favors fee simple subject to condition subsequent, rather than fee simple determinable, to avoid a forfeiture when possible).

[91]   See Lacer v. Navajo Cty., 141 Ariz. 396, 687 P.2d 404 (Ct. App. 1983); U.S. Tr. Co. v. New Jersey, 226 N.J.Super. 8, 543 A.2d 457 (App. Div. 1988); Little Miami, Inc. v. Wisecup, 13 Ohio App. 3d 239, 468 N.E.2d 935, 13 Ohio B. 292 (1984); Indigo Realty Co. v. City of Charleston, 281 S.C. 234, 314 S.E.2d 601 (1984). But sometimes the court finds that a charitable trust was created. See Abel v. Girard Tr. Co., 365 Pa. 34, 73 A.2d 682 (1950). In one case, the court held that the deed created an easement, rather than a fee simple estate. Hawk v. Rice, 325 N.W.2d 97 (Iowa 1982).

[92]   E.g., Williams, 181 S.W.2d 488; Valer Oil Co. v. Souza, 182 Cal. App.2d 790, 6 Cal. Rptr. 301 (1960); Caldwell v. Brown, 553 S.W.2d 692 (Ky. 1977); Brown v. Haight, 435 Pa. 12, 255 A.2d 508 (1969); Saletri v. Clark, 13 Wis.2d 325, 108 N.W.2d 548 (1961).

[93]   See Storke v. Penn Mut. Life Ins. Co., 390 Ill. 619, 61 N.E.2d 552 (1945). But see Sch. Dist. Twp. of Richland v. Hanson, 186 Iowa 1314, 173 N.W. 873 (1919). For further discussion of this point and comparison of the fee simple determinable with the fee simple subject to a condition subsequent, see infra § 2.7.

Currently, fee simple determinable estates are almost never created in commercial transactions.[94] They are primarily used when land is given to charitable, educational, religious, or government entities.

§ 2.5   FEE SIMPLE SUBJECT TO CONDITION SUBSEQUENT

English courts have also recognized the fee simple subject to condition subsequent since early in the development of the law of estates in land. Two requirements must be satisfied to create it. In the document that creates the estate, the grantor must retain the future interest following it, and the transfer must be subject to an express condition, such as "to A and his heirs upon the condition that the land hereby conveyed shall be used for no other purpose than as a burying ground."[95] In addition to "upon the condition that," other words sufficient to create a fee simple subject to condition subsequent include "provided that," "however," and "but if."[96]

The grantor's future interest following a fee simple subject to condition subsequent is a "right of entry" (also called a "power of termination"). The right of entry gives the grantor the right to oust the grantee or his successors in interest if a breach of the condition occurs.[97] Upon the grantor's re-entry, the owner of the fee simple subject to condition subsequent is divested of the estate, and the grantor is re-vested with the fee simple absolute. Unlike a fee simple determinable, a mere breach of the condition, without a re-entry by the grantor, does not terminate the fee simple subject to condition subsequent.[98]

According to the English common law, an express reservation of a right to re-enter was unnecessary because that right was held to arise by operation of law from the use of words of condition.[99] In the United States, however, courts have sometimes held that words of condition, standing alone, are ambiguous and that the grantor who omits an express right to re-enter may have transferred title subject only to a personal covenant,[100] real covenant,[101] equitable servitude,[102] easement,[103] equitable charge,[104] or

---

[94]   The principal exception is that oil and gas leases often contain special limitations creating estates in fee simple determinable. See, e.g., Humble Oil & Ref. Co. v. Harrison, 146 Tex. 216, 205 S.W.2d 355 (1947).

[95]   Recognition of estates subject to such conditions reflects the liberality of the courts in giving effect to "the form of the gift" in the thirteenth century. 2 F. Pollock & F. Maitland, History of English Law §§ 25–27 (2d ed. 1898, reissued 1968). See, e.g., Walker v. Lucas Cty. Bd. of Comm'rs, 73 Ohio App. 3d 617, 598 N.E.2d 101 (1991). For a listing of appropriate language to create a fee simple subject to a condition subsequent, see DeHart v. Ritenour Consol. Sch. Dist., 663 S.W.2d 332 (Mo. Ct. App. 1983) ("upon condition that," "upon express condition that," "provided that," "but if," or "if it happens that").

[96]   As to use of the term "fee simple subject to a condition subsequent," in preference to other terms sometimes employed, see supra § 2.3, at note 62.

[97]   The interest retained by the grantor was called a "right of entry for breach of condition broken" or a "right of entry for breach of condition." For a discussion of the legal characteristics of this interest, see infra § 3.5.

[98]   These rules were well settled by the time of Littleton. See T. Littleton, Tenures §§ 325–31 (1825).

[99]   See, e.g., Mary Portington's Case (1614) 10 Co. Rep. 35b, 42a. Of course, the grantor could expressly provide for a right of entry as well.

[100]   E.g., Skinner v. Shepard, 130 Mass. 180 (1881).

[101]   E.g., Post v. Weil, 115 N.Y. 361, 22 N.E. 145 (1889).

[102]   E.g., Queen City Park Ass'n v. Gale, 110 Vt. 110, 3 A.2d 529 (1938).

[103]   E.g., Boston Consol. Gas Co. v. Oakes, 279 Mass. 230, 181 N.E. 225 (1932).

[104]   E.g., Selzer v. Selzer, 146 Kan. 273, 69 P.2d 708 (1937).

trust,[105] rather than a defeasible estate. Indeed, courts in many cases have stated a constructional preference against finding that the grantor intended a defeasible estate.[106] Therefore, to safely create a fee simple subject to condition subsequent, the drafter should expressly provide for re-entry and termination of the estate on breach of the stated condition. When an express right of entry is included in the creating instrument, American courts normally hold that a fee simple subject to a condition subsequent was created,[107] though occasionally a court reaches the opposite conclusion.[108]

Under the old English common law, the term "right of entry for breach of condition" appropriately described the grantor's retained interest because the grantor was required to make an actual entry on the land after breach of the condition, in the presence of witnesses, to terminate the fee simple subject to a condition subsequent.[109] Today, however, a grantor can terminate a fee simple subject to condition subsequent without physically entering the land. In some American jurisdictions, merely initiating an action to recover possession of the land is sufficient.[110] In other jurisdictions, the person entitled to enforce the condition must manifest his or her election to terminate in some appropriate way, such as by giving notice to the holder of the fee simple, before initiating legal action.[111] Under either rule, the term "power of termination," rather than "right of entry," more accurately describes the grantor's retained interest.[112]

In modern real estate practice, estates in fee simple subject to a condition subsequent are rarely created in commercial transactions, but they are still sometimes created when land is given to charitable, religious, educational, or government entities.

---

[105] E.g., MacKenzie v. Trs. of Presbytery of Jersey City, 67 N.J. Eq. 652, 61 A. 1027 (1905).

[106] E.g., Kinney v. Kansas, 238 Kan. 375, 710 P.2d 1290 (1985); In re Congregational Conference Appeal, 352 Pa. 470, 474, 43 A.2d 1, 3 (1945) ("when there is any doubt as to whether a clause in a deed restricting the enjoyment of the land is a condition or merely a covenant, the latter construction is always favored"); 4 Kent, Commentaries on American Law 145 (G. Comstock, ed., 11th ed, 1867) ("If it be doubtful whether a clause in a deed be a covenant or a condition, the courts will incline against the latter construction; for a covenant is far preferable to the tenant"). Contra Forsgren v. Sollie, 659 P.2d 1068 (Utah 1983).

[107] E.g., Lacer v. Navajo Cty., 141 Ariz. 396, 687 P.2d 404 (Ct. App. 1983). However, courts also frequently hold that a fee simple subject to condition subsequent is created by instruments qualifying the estate granted by words such as "forfeit," "revert," or "null and void" in connection with conditional language. See infra § 2.6, particularly notes 115–120; DeHart v. Ritenour Consol. Sch. Dist., 663 S.W.2d 332 (Mo. Ct. App. 1983).

[108] Second Church of Christ, Scientist v. Le Prevost, 67 Ohio App. 101, 35 N.E.2d 1015 (1941); Scaling v. Sutton, 167 S.W.2d 275 (Tex. App. 1942).

[109] See 1 W. Cruise, Digest of the Laws of England 50 (H. White ed., 4th ed. 1835); 1 Simes & Smith, supra note 39, at § 255 n.62.

[110] E.g., Mattox v. North Carolina, 280 N.C. 471, 186 S.E.2d 378 (1972).

[111] E.g., City of New York v. Coney Island Fire Dep't, 285 N.Y. 535, 32 N.E.2d 827 (1941); Emrick v. Bethlehem Twp., 506 Pa. 372, 485 A.2d 736 (1984) ("the power [of termination] could be exercised by a writing with or without previous, simultaneous or subsequent physical possession"). If the grantor exercises the power of termination without taking legal action, a subsequent quiet title action may be required to establish title in the public records if the grantee is unwilling to give the grantor a quitclaim deed. See Forsgren v. Sollie, 659 P.2d 1068 (Utah 1983).

[112] The First Restatement of Property adopted the term "power of termination." Supra note 38, § 155. See 1 Am. L. Prop., supra note 11, at § 2.9 (criticizes the First Restatement's adoption of the term). Most courts seem to have continued to use the term "right of entry."

§ 2.6   DISTINGUISHING A FEE SIMPLE DETERMINABLE FROM A FEE SIMPLE SUBJECT TO CONDITION SUBSEQUENT

In a properly drafted conveyance, determining whether it conveys a fee simple determinable or a fee simple subject to condition subsequent should be easy. If the conveyance includes a special limitation (introduced by words such as "so long as" or "until"), it creates a fee simple determinable.[113] If the instrument includes an express condition (introduced by words such as "on condition that" or "provided that") and an express right to re-enter for breach of the condition, it creates a fee simple subject to condition subsequent.[114] Unfortunately, deeds and wills often fail to employ the appropriate words to create one or the other of these two types of defeasible estates. Instead, deeds and wills often contain a confusing mixture of words appropriate for creation of both types of defeasible estate. Consider the following cases:

1.   A deed provides that the grantor and grantee "covenant and agree that no saloon shall be kept and no intoxicating liquors be sold * * * on said premises herein conveyed * * *; and that in case of breach in these covenants or any of them said premises shall immediately revert to the grantors, and the * * * [grantee] shall forfeit all right, title and interest in and to said premises."[115]

2.   A deed provides: "It is hereby agreed that the said above-described property is to be used for school purposes, and that, whenever it shall cease to be so used, the said property will revert to the grantor herein, his heirs and assigns."[116]

3.   A deed provides: "The conditions of the above gift is that the said * * * School Directors * * * are to erect on the said parcel of land a good and suitable house for the purpose of having taught therein a public free school * * *, the same is to be at all times used but if at any time the same shall cease to be used for said public free school purpose then the title to said * * * parcel of land is to revert back to the said Gregg, his heirs and assigns in as full and ample a manner as if this instrument had never been given."[117]

4.   A deed conveying land to a Baptist church further provides that, as soon as the land ceases to be used as Baptist church ground, "this deed to be null and void."[118]

5.   A deed conveying land to a Baptist church further provides: "This deed is made expressly upon the condition that the said premises granted are to be used exclusively for a [Baptist Church] site * * * and whenever the same shall hereafter cease to be used for such purpose, this deed shall become void and the title shall revert to the grantors herein, their heirs and assigns."[119]

6.   A deed conveying land to a land developer lists a number of "conditions and restrictions," and further provides that "failure to comply with the covenants and

---

[113]   See supra § 2.4, at notes 84–85.

[114]   See supra § 2.5, at note 95.

[115]   Storke v. Penn Mut. Life Ins. Co., 390 Ill. 619, 61 N.E.2d 552 (1945).

[116]   Denver & S. F. Ry. Co. v. Sch. Dist., 14 Colo. 327, 23 P. 978 (1890).

[117]   Pickens v. Daugherty, 217 Tenn. 349, 397 S.W.2d 815 (1965), noted in 33 Tenn. L. Rev. 546 (1966).

[118]   United States v. 2,086 Acres of Land, 46 F.Supp. 411 (W.D.S.C.1942).

[119]   Union Missionary Baptist Church v. Fyke, 179 Okla. 102, 64 P.2d 1203 (1937).

conditions * * * hereof will automatically cause title to all lands to revert to the [grantor]."[120]

What kind of defeasible estate is created in each of these examples? The word "condition" is used in four cases, the phrase "null and void" is used in two cases, and the word "revert" is used in five cases. Indeed, in example 6, the term "automatically revert" is used. Thus, determining the grantor's intent is difficult in any of the six examples. In such cases, it is often said that courts will apply a constructional preference in favor of a fee simple subject to condition subsequent, because it is less likely to cause a forfeiture than a fee simple determinable.[121] In the actual cases on which the six examples are based, the court did hold that a fee simple subject to condition subsequent was created in cases 1,[122] 3,[123] 4,[124] and 6.[125] However, in cases 2[126] and 5,[127] the court held that a fee simple determinable was created. Obviously, the constructional preference for a fee simple subject to condition subsequent is not an infallible guide.[128]

As an alternative to the constructional preference for a fee simple subject to condition subsequent, consider the following test that The American Law of Property suggests: "If the purpose is to compel compliance with a condition by the penalty of forfeiture, an estate on condition arises, but if the intent is to give the land for a stated use, the estate to cease when that * * * use is ended * * * a fee on limitation [fee simple determinable] results."[129] Whether this rule can be applied intelligently is doubtful. Arguably, it would lead to the conclusions reached by the courts in cases 1, 2, 5, and 6

---

[120] Oldfield v. Stoeco Homes, Inc., 26 N.J. 246, 139 A.2d 291 (1958).

[121] This constructional preference is apparently based on the view that "[a]n *optional* forfeiture is less objectionable than an *automatic* forfeiture." 1 Powell, supra note 16, at § 13.05.

[122] Storke v. Penn Mut. Life Ins. Co., 390 Ill. 619, 61 N.E.2d 552 (1945). The court expressly relied on the constructional preference for a fee simple subject to condition subsequent, but the result would have been the same even if the court had found that the ambiguous language created a fee simple determinable, because the statute of limitations would have barred the grantor's heirs). Accord Hardman v. Dahlonega-Lumpkin Cty. Chamber of Commerce, 238 Ga. 551, 233 S.E.2d 753 (1977); Nielsen v. Woods, 687 P.2d 486 (Colo. App. 1984). See infra § 2.7 note 158.

[123] Pickens v. Daugherty, 217 Tenn. 349, 397 S.W.2d 815 (1965) (the court did not mention the constructional preference in concluding that the deed created "an estate upon a condition subsequent" and then applying the common law rule that a right of entry is inalienable).

[124] United States v. 2,086 Acres of Land, 46 F.Supp. 411 (W.D.S.C. 1942) (when U.S. took land by eminent domain and thus prevented further church use, the breach of condition was excused and the church was entitled to the entire condemnation award; court did not mention constructional preference).

[125] Oldfield v. Stoeco Homes Inc., 26 N.J. 246, 139 A.2d 291 (court relied on constructional preference and held that fee simple subject to condition subsequent was created despite use of the phrase "automatically cause title to revert"); Hardman v. Dahlonega-Lumpkin County Chamber of Commerce, 238 Ga. 551, 233 S.E.2d 753 (1977).

[126] Denver & S. F. Ry. Co. v. Sch. Dist., 14 Colo. 327, 23 P. 978 (1890) (the court did not mention constructional preference in holding that the title conveyed was "a qualified fee" and that "[w]henever the event might occur upon which the limitation was based, the estate of appellee would immediately cease.").

[127] Union Missionary Baptist Church v. Fyke, 179 Okla. 102, 64 P.2d 1203 (1937) (court assumed the church had a fee simple determinable, without considering any alternative; but "forfeiture" was not an issue). See also Johnson v. City of Hackensack, 200 N.J.Super. 185, 491 A.2d 14 (App. Div. 1985).

[128] The cases discussed in the text are not necessarily an adequate basis for any definitive judgment. But see 1 Simes & Smith, supra note 39, at § 248 n.35, citing 12 cases as directly supporting the asserted constructional preference and 5 cases under "but see." For a case applying the constructional preference, see Montana v. Berklund, 217 Mont. 218, 704 P.2d 59 (1985).

[129] 1 Am. L. Prop., supra note 11, at § 2.6 nn.15–16. The court relied on the quoted language in Nielsen v. Woods, 687 P.2d 486 (Colo. App. 1984).

but would not lead to the court's conclusions in cases 3 and 4.[130] So this rule of construction, like the one previously suggested, is not infallible.

In many of the cases on which the foregoing examples are based, whether the court construed the defeasance language to create a fee simple determinable or a fee simple subject to condition subsequent apparently made no real difference.[131] Perhaps the only conclusion that can be drawn from these cases is that the courts are not much concerned with the labels they attach to defeasible estates when it makes no practical difference. On the other hand, a careful examination of a much larger group of cases might reveal that, in cases where it does make a practical difference, the courts attach the label that they believe is necessary to achieve a just result.[132] If so, we need to consider carefully what differing results may follow from attaching one label, rather than the other, to language creating a fee simple defeasible. This consideration will be found in the next Section of this book.

Even if a court decides initially that language in a deed or will creates either a fee simple determinable or a fee simple subject to condition subsequent, the nature and scope of the condition or limitation may not be absolutely clear. In general, at least in inter vivos conveyances, courts tend to construe ambiguous language in favor of the grantee to reduce the chance of forfeiture. For example, where land was conveyed to a church upon the "consideration * * * that said premises shall be used for church purposes only and that in case the same is abandoned * * * the title shall be revested in" the grantor, the court held that the execution of an oil lease and the moving of the church building to another part of the premises to make way for a drilling rig did not amount to an abandonment of use "for church purposes only" and did not constitute a breach of condition entitling the grantor's heirs to re-enter.[133] But relatively slight differences in language may produce different results.[134]

Courts not only construe language in favor of grantees, but also require that a breach be clearly proved before enforcing a forfeiture. Courts also refuse to allow a forfeiture when the purpose of the special limitation or condition is still being substantially achieved.[135] Additionally, courts often recognize defenses such as election, waiver, and estoppel in cases in which a grantor fails to terminate a fee simple subject to condition subsequent within a reasonable time after a breach occurs.[136] Courts may

---

[130] See supra notes 115–120. Examples 3 and 4 appear to be indistinguishable from examples 2 and 5, except that example 4 does not include an express reverter clause.

[131] This would seem to be the case in Storke v. Penn Mut. Life Ins. Co., 390 Ill. 619, 61 N.E.2d 552 (1945); Union Missionary Baptist Church, 64 P.2d 1203; United States v. 2,086 Acres of Land, 46 F.Supp. 411 (W.D.S.C. 1942).

[132] See Dunham, supra note 66, at 216–17.

[133] Skipper v. Davis, 59 S.W.2d 454 (Tex. App. 1932) (grantor's heirs could enjoin commission of waste, though not entitled to recover possession of land), overruled by Davis v. Skipper, 125 Tex. 364, 83 S.W.2d 318 (1935). The court construed the language quoted in the text as creating a fee simple subject to condition subsequent, though it referred to the grantor's retained interest as a "right of reverter," a "reverter," and a "right to reversion." The court also said, " 'Reversion' and 'reverter' are synonymous, and denote a vested estate or right," which, of course, is nonsense.

[134] E.g., Union Missionary Baptist Church v. Fyke, 179 Okla. 102, 64 P.2d 1203 (1937).

[135] Johnson v. City of Hackensack, 200 N.J.Super. 185, 491 A.2d 14 (App. Div. 1985); Kinney v. Kansas, 238 Kan. 375, 710 P.2d 1290 (1985).

[136] See infra § 2.7 at notes 158–159.

also grant equitable relief against forfeiture if the grantor "may be made whole otherwise" by awarding damages or an injunction.[137]

§ 2.7   DOES THE DISTINCTION MATTER?

Despite the difficulty of determining whether ambiguous language in a deed or will has created a fee simple determinable or a fee simple subject to condition subsequent, it is commonly said that 91530the distinction is important because, if the former is created, the defeasible estate terminates automatically upon breach, whereas, if the latter is created, a breach does not terminate the estate unless and until the grantor exercises the right to re-enter.[138] But the automatic termination of a fee simple determinable does not immediately dispossess the former owner of that estate and restore possession to the grantor. Indeed, unless possession is voluntarily surrendered, the grantor must sue for possession. Therefore, we must consider the defenses that may be available to the defendant when the grantor brings an action to recover possession, either after the automatic termination of a fee simple determinable or after a breach of a condition subsequent, in order to see what practical differences, if any, exist between the two types of defeasible fees.

1. *Statute of limitations.* The statute of limitations for an action to recover possession of land begins to run immediately upon the breach that automatically terminates a fee simple determinable, because the right to possession automatically vests in the grantor and makes continued possession by the former owner of the determinable fee wrongful.[139] In contrast, continued possession after a breach by the owner of a fee simple subject to condition subsequent is not wrongful unless and until the grantor exercises her right to re-enter by giving notice or starting an action for possession. Therefore, until the right of entry is effectively exercised, the statute of limitations applicable to actions for possession of land should not run. Some courts have so held,[140] thus recognizing an important difference between a fee simple determinable and a fee simple subject to condition subsequent. However, in some states, either by statute[141] or by decision,[142] the applicable statute of limitations begins to run against the owner of a right of entry as soon as a breach occurs. In these jurisdictions, the positions of the owners of either type of defeasible fee would seem to be identical after a breach.[143]

---

[137] See Nielsen v. Woods, 687 P.2d 486 (Colo. App. 1984), and infra § 2.7 at notes 158–159.

[138] E.g., 1 Simes & Smith, supra note 39, at § 282 n.10; Storke v. Penn Mut. Life Ins. Co., 390 Ill. 619, 61 N.E.2d 552 (1945). Also see 1 Powell, supra note 16, at § 13.06; First Restatement of Property, supra note 38, at §§ 23–24, 44–45.

[139] E.g., Storke, 61 N.E.2d 552. Cf. Sch. Dist. v. Hanson, 186 Iowa 1314, 173 N.W. 873 (1919). See infra § 11.7 for a more detailed treatment of statutes of limitation and title by adverse possession.

[140] Mills v. Pennington, 213 Ark. 43, 209 S.W.2d 281 (1948); City of New York v. Coney Island Fire Dep't, 285 N.Y. 535, 32 N.E.2d 827 (1941), aff'g, 259 A.D. 286, 18 N.Y.S.2d 923 (1940) (delay of 41 years did not bar right of entry); Metro. Park Dist. v. Rigney's Unknown Heirs, 65 Wash. 2d 788, 399 P.2d 516 (1965), noted in Power of Termination—Effect of Failure to Exercise Within a Reasonable Time, 40 Wash. L. Rev. 377 (1965).

[141] E.g., Ark. Code Ann. § 18–61–102 (West 2017); Cal. Civ. Proc. § 320 (West 2017); 735 Ill. Comp. Stat. Ann. 5/13–106 (West 2017); Minn. Stat. § 500.20 (West 2017). See also Colo. Rev. Stat. § 38–41–119 (2017) (action to recover possession for violation of any "restriction" must be brought within one year).

[142] E.g., Sanford v. Sims, 192 Va. 644, 66 S.E.2d 495 (1951).

[143] From a policy standpoint, the rule concerning when the statute of limitations begins to run should be the same for both types of defeasible estate. The statute should begin to run when the terminating event occurs for a fee simple determinable and when the condition is breached for a fee simple subject to condition subsequent.

2. *Recovery of mesne profits.* Because continued possession by the former owner of a determinable fee after it has terminated is clearly wrongful, the grantor has a cause of action for mesne profits, which are usually measured by the reasonable rental value of the land, for the period of wrongful possession.[144] In contrast, the owner of a right of entry has no right to mesne profits merely because a breach of condition has occurred in a fee simple subject to condition subsequent. Because the breach alone does not make continued possession by the owner of the defeasible fee wrongful, mesne profits are recoverable only for the period after the right of entry has been exercised.[145] But this difference between the two types of defeasible fee may be minimized in jurisdictions that, either by statute or by decision, limit the recovery of mesne profits or allow set-offs and credits when land is wrongfully possessed by a claimant occupying the land in good faith.[146] The former owner of a fee simple determinable who retains possession after his estate has terminated would generally qualify as an occupying claimant in good faith because of the difficulty of predicting in advance the correct interpretation of the estate and the limitation.

3. *Defenses.* For a fee simple subject to condition subsequent, an owner of the right of entry who does not exercise it within a reasonable time after breach may be barred from asserting it by waiver, election, or estoppel.[147] With respect to waiver and election, which are normally the same in this context,[148] some courts have held that mere silence or inaction will not bar exercise of a right of entry,[149] but other courts have held or said that mere failure to exercise the right within a reasonable time after learning of a breach will bar it.[150] Neither waiver nor election requires a writing,[151] and neither requires proof that the defeasible fee owner detrimentally changed position in justifiable reliance on

---

[144] For a good general discussion of mesne profits, see J. Glenn et al., Corpus Juris Secundum, Ejectment §§ 128–165 (2017).

[145] No cases on point have been found, but both logic and fairness point to the conclusion stated in the text. But note the anomaly of holding that the right to mesne profits accrues only when the right of entry is actually exercised, though the statute of limitations may begin to run against the owner of the right of entry as soon as a breach occurs.

[146] See, e.g., 735 Ill. Comp. Stat. Ann. 5/6–140 (West 2017) ("Occupying Claimants' Act"), which disallows any claim for mesne profits accruing "prior to receipt of actual notice of the adverse claim" by the defendant if he can show a record title and that he is without notice of an adverse record title. Even in the absence of an "occupying claimants' act," courts have allowed the defendant to reduce the amount of the plaintiff's recovery by showing that he held possession under color of title and in good faith. E.g., Simmons v. Holliday, 226 Ala. 630, 148 So. 327 (1933). See also Santmeyer v. Clemmancs, 147 Wash. 354, 266 P. 148 (1928), overruled by Chaplin v. Sanders, 100 Wash. 2d 853, 676 P.2d 431 (1984) (overruling *Simmons* to the extent that it held that subjective intent in the interest in land was relevant).

[147] Generally, see Dunham, supra note 66, at 224–29; 1 Simes & Smith, supra note 39, at § 258; 1 Am. L. Prop., supra note 11, at § 4.9.

[148] Dunham asserts that "it is more proper to say that the owner of the power of termination [i.e., right of entry] has 'elected' not to terminate than to say he 'waived' his power." Dunham, supra note 66, at 225. But courts seem to use the terms interchangeably.

[149] E.g., Cottle v. Tomlinson, 192 Ga. 704, 16 S.E.2d 555 (1941); Rumford Falls Power Co. v. Waishwill, 128 Me. 320, 147 A. 343 (1929); Trs. of Union Coll. v. City of New York, 173 N.Y. 38, 65 N.E. 853 (1903).

[150] E.g., Jeffries v. State, 216 Ark. 657, 226 S.W.2d 810 (1950); Goodman v. S. Pac. Co., 143 Cal. App. 2d 424, 299 P.2d 321 (1956); Burr v. Tierney, 99 Conn. 647, 122 A. 454 (1923) ("laches"); Hale v. Elkhorn Coal Corp., 206 Ky. 629, 268 S.W. 304 (1925); Robinson v. Cannon, 346 Mo. 1126, 145 S.W.2d 146 (1940). What is a "reasonable time" varies with the circumstances and the court's general attitude. In City of New York v. Coney Island Fire Dep't, 285 N.Y. 535, 32 N.E.2d 827 (1941), 41 years was a reasonable time.

[151] See supra notes 149–150.

conduct alleged to amount to a waiver or an election.[152] Moreover, the waiver or election need not even be express; the intent not to exercise a right of entry may be inferred from nonverbal conduct.[153] However, if the waiver of or election is not express, the defeasible fee owner is more likely to avoid forfeiture by showing a substantial detrimental change of position in justifiable reliance on the failure to enforce.[154] When such a change of position is shown, the defeasible fee owner usually also can successfully assert a defense of estoppel.[155]

When the defeasible estate is a fee simple determinable, the estoppel defense should also be available to the defeasible estate owner who substantially and detrimentally changes position in reliance on an express or implied representation by the owners of a possibility of reverter that they do not intend to assert their rights after a breach.[156] But, absent such a change of position, courts are unlikely to accept the defense of waiver or election after a breach has occurred.

Whichever type of defeasible estate is involved, the estate owner may be obtain equitable relief against forfeiture, because courts view forfeiture as a particularly harsh remedy. Courts frequently grant such relief when the owner of a right of entry seeks to recover possession after breach.[157] However, courts are less likely to grant equitable relief after breach of a fee simple determinable because the estate has expired naturally by virtue of its special limitation. For this reason, courts often reason that a forfeiture is not involved when a determinable fee is breached, though some authority exists for granting equitable relief even in such cases.[158] Moreover, some authority suggests that courts tend to grant some kind of relief against forfeiture, including based on the doctrines of waiver, election, and estoppel, if the purpose of the defeasance clause is to penalize noncompliance with a required course of conduct, but to withhold relief if the purpose of the clause is to terminate the defeasible estate when the purpose for which it was created can no longer be realized.[159]

§ 2.8   FEE SIMPLE SUBJECT TO EXECUTORY LIMITATION

A fee simple subject to executory limitation is the third type of defeasible estate. When the limitation on the defeasible fee is violated, the property automatically passes

---

[152] Id.

[153] Id.

[154] See, e.g., Jeffries v. State, 216 Ark. at 659, 226 S.W.2d at 811 ("a waiver of forfeiture will be found more readily when the grantee has created an element of estoppel by changing his position after the grantor's failure to re-enter").

[155] E.g., Storke v. Penn Mut. Life Ins. Co., 390 Ill. 619, 61 N.E.2d 552 (1945).

[156] See, e.g., applying the estoppel doctrine to determinable fees, Humble Oil & Ref. Co. v. Harrison, 146 Tex. 216, 205 S.W.2d 355 (1947). See generally 31 Glenn et al., supra note 144 Estoppel, § 150; J. Ewart, Estoppel by Misrepresentation 251–95 (1900).

[157] See the extensive citation of cases in support of this proposition in 1 Simes & Smith, supra note 39, at § 257 nn.77–79, 81.

[158] Browning v. Weaver, 158 Kan. 255, 146 P.2d 390 (1944). See Fancher, Oil and Gas—Unless Clause—Equitable Relief from Termination for Failure to Make Delay Rental Payment on Time, 22 Miss. L. J. 118 (1950). A court may, of course, construe automatic reverter language as creating a "fee simple subject to right of entry for condition broken" and then grant equitable relief. See Nielsen v. Woods, 687 P.2d 486 (Colo. App. 1984).

[159] Dunham, supra note 66, at 227–28, noting that earlier writers tended to view penalizing for noncompliance as the proper purpose of a condition subsequent and termination when the purpose of the conveyance could no longer be realized as the proper purpose of a special limitation.

to a designated person, other than the person who created the defeasible estate (O conveys "to A for so long as the land is used as a park, and then to B").[160] The defeasible fee owner generally does not care who gets the property when the defeasible estate terminates. However, the distinction was important before enactment of the Statute of Uses in 1535.[161] Before that time, the common law courts consistently held that a fee simple estate could not be made defeasible in favor of anyone other than the grantor, because the law did not sanction conditions in favor of strangers.[162] Yet even before 1535, the court of equity would enforce future uses that defeated present uses when a designated future event occurred. In this way, equity recognized present equitable estates that were defeasible in favor of persons other than the grantor.[163]

An unintended consequence of the enactment of the Statute of Uses in 1535[164] and the Statute of Wills in 1540[165] was that legal estates in fee simple subject to an executory limitation could be created in favor of persons other than the grantor by deed or by will. A common law conveyance or devise "to A and his heirs, but if A shall die leaving no children him surviving, then to B and his heirs," gave A a fee simple subject to executory limitation and gave B a shifting executory interest in fee simple absolute.[166] B's interest is a "shifting" executory limitation because, when the designated event occurred (A's death without leaving any surviving children), the fee simple automatically shifts from A to B.[167] A fee simple also can be subject to a "springing" executory limitation, such as

---

[160] For the reasons for using the term "fee simple subject to an executory limitation," rather than other terms, see supra § 2.3 note 63.

[161] 1536 27 Hen. 8, c. 10 (Eng.).

[162] The reason was that livery of seisin, which was necessary to transfer a freehold estate, could operate only *in praesenti*. See infra text between notes 164–168.

[163] If the legal owner of a fee simple estate, O, enfeoffed "A and his heirs, to the use of B and his heirs, but if B shall die without children him surviving, then to the use of C and his heirs," B acquired a "use" or equitable estate in fee simple, subject to a "shifting use" in favor of C in fee simple. The same result followed from a variety of other methods of creating a use. Although the common law courts refused to recognize that such transactions created any rights in *cestui que use*, the court of equity began to recognize and enforce them early in the fifteenth century. These rights included the right to take the profits of the land and the right to have the legal owner of the fee simple take all necessary proceedings to protect or recover the land.

[164] Because holding a use or equitable estate in land enabled *cestui que use* to evade feudal burdens, to devise the use by will, and to enjoy curtesy and dower, the greater part of the land in England was said to be held in use by the time of the Wars of the Roses. Because the King suffered substantial losses from this evasion of feudal dues, "the Statute of Uses was forced upon an extremely unwilling parliament by an extremely strong-willed king," Henry VIII, in 1536. F. Maitland, Equity 34 (1910). The purposes and major effects of the Statute of Uses were to turn uses into legal estates that were subject to all the usual feudal burdens and to abolish the power to devise land. A by-product of the Statute was the transformation of shifting uses and springing uses into legal interests.

[165] 1540 32 Hen. 8 c. 1. As indicated supra, note 164, one purpose of the Statute of Uses was to abolish the power to devise land by creating a use in favor of A, with a direction that the legal estate should be held after A's death "to such uses as A may by his will devise and appoint." But the attempt to abolish the power to devise was so unpopular that the Statute of Wills was enacted in 1540. The Statute of Wills allowed a testator to devise all land held by him in socage and two-thirds of his land held by knight service. A by-product of the Statute of Wills was that legal shifting and springing interests could be created directly by will, without the necessity of creating uses to be turned into legal interests ("executed") by the Statute of Uses. Shifting and springing future interests created by will were called "executory devises."

[166] Although executory interests came into the law originally in the form of shifting and springing uses that were converted into legal interests by force of the Statute of Uses, employing the machinery of the Statute of Uses is no longer necessary to create executory interests. The term "executory interest" is now employed to designate any future interest formerly called a shifting use, a springing use, or an executory devise.

[167] The shifting executory interest is, in substance, like the pre-1536 shifting use that is discussed supra, note 166.

a conveyance "to A and his heirs, from and after A's marriage to B." Before A and B's marriage, the grantor has the fee simple subject to an executory limitation that will cause the fee simple to spring out of the grantor and automatically vest in A upon marriage.[168]

A fee simple subject to executory limitation shares important characteristics with both the fee simple determinable and the fee simple subject to condition subsequent. Like the former, defeasance is automatic when the terminating event occurs, and the owner of the executory interest acquires the land without having to take any affirmative action.[169] However, like a fee simple subject to condition subsequent, the defeasible fee simple is considered to have been divested or cut off when the terminating event occurs, rather than simply to have expired as is the case with a fee simple determinable.[170]

The specified terminating event in an executory limitation is almost always contingent; it is uncertain whether it will occur. For example, the specified terminating event may be the death of the first taker without surviving issue or without surviving children;[171] the death of the first taker with surviving children;[172] the death of the first taker before reaching a certain age;[173] the marriage or nonmarriage of the first taker;[174] or an educational institution's failure to continue to exist.[175] Executory limitations specifying such terminating events are valid if they are not illegal or against public policy[176] and if the terminating event is not so remote as to violate the Rule Against Perpetuities.[177] If the executory limitation is invalid, the first taker will have a fee simple absolute, rather than a fee simple subject to executory limitation.[178]

Can a grantor create a valid executory limitation with a terminating event that is certain to happen? For example, suppose that O conveys "to A and his heirs, from and after O's death" or "to A and his heirs, from and after B's death." In these cases, O's retained estate cannot longer than O's or B's life, as the case may be. Some courts have held that O retained only a life estate and that A received a vested remainder in fee

---

[168] The springing executory interest is, in substance, like the pre-1536 springing use that is discussed supra note 166.

[169] E.g., Proprietors of Church in Brattle Square v. Grant, 69 Mass. 142, 3 Gray 142 (1855).

[170] E.g., Pearson v. Easterling, 107 S.C. 265, 92 S.E. 619 (1917); Bradford v. Fed. Land Bank of New Orleans, 338 So. 2d 388 (Miss. 1976). See 1 Simes & Smith, supra note 39, at § 228.

[171] E.g., Dickson v. Renfro, 263 Ark. 718, 569 S.W.2d 66 (1978), appeal after remand, 276 Ark. 223, 634 S.W.2d 104 (1982); In re Fleck's Estate, 261 Iowa 434, 154 N.W.2d 865 (1967); Bradford, 338 So. 2d 388; Jernigan v. Lee, 279 N.C. 341, 182 S.E.2d 351 (1971).

[172] E.g., Warrington v. Chester, 294 Ill. 524, 128 N.E. 549 (1920). A grantor normally conveyed such an executory limitation to the first taker's children to ensure that they would get the land at the first taker's death.

[173] E.g., Thomas v. Thomas, 97 Miss. 697, 53 So. 630 (1910); Bailey v. Brannon, 293 Ala. 83, 300 So. 2d 344 (1974).

[174] E.g., Pumroy v. Jenkins, 151 Kan. 466, 99 P.2d 752 (1940); Hinton v. Bowen, 190 Tenn. 463, 230 S.W.2d 965 (1950).

[175] E.g., Lehigh Univ. v. Hower, 159 Pa. Super. 84, 46 A.2d 516 (1946).

[176] The same qualification applies, of course, to conditions subsequent and special limitations. See supra §§ 2.4–5.

[177] The great case establishing the Rule Against Perpetuities involved the validity of an executory limitation. The Duke of Norfolk's Case (1682) 22 Eng. Rep. 931. Cases invalidating executory limitations because they violate the Rule Against Perpetuities are legion. See infra §§ 3.20–21.

[178] E.g., Proprietors of Church in Brattle Square v. Grant, 69 Mass. 142, 3 Gray 142 (1855).

simple absolute.[179] But other courts have held that O retained a fee simple subject to an executory limitation and that A received an executory interest in fee simple absolute.[180] Because O presumably did not intend to limit his or her hitherto extensive rights of use and enjoyment as a fee simple owner, holding that O retained a defeasible fee simple seems reasonable.[181]

A similar problem may arise when, for example, O conveys "to A and his heirs, five years from the date of this conveyance" or "to A and his heirs, then to B and his heirs five years from the date of this conveyance." In the first case, because O's estate can only last for five years, O arguably retains only an estate for years and not a fee simple subject to executory limitation. In the second case, A arguably receives only an estate for years, rather than a fee simple subject to executory limitation. However, as in the examples in the preceding paragraph, O presumably intended to retain his or her hitherto extensive rights of use and enjoyment in the first example. In contrast, in the second example, no reason exists to believe that O intended to confer such extensive rights on A. Consequently, a court should hold that O retained a fee simple subject to executory limitation but that A received only an estate for years.[182] The First Restatement supports this distinction.[183]

Equitable, as well as legal, estates in fee simple subject to executory limitation may be created, and interests analogous to these estates may be created in personal property. Indeed, at the present time, most defeasible estates or interests subject to executory limitation are equitable, because they are beneficial interests under a trust, and the predominant subject matter of such trusts is probably personal property, such as stocks and bonds.

§ 2.9   FEE SIMPLE DETERMINABLE
WITH EXECUTORY LIMITATION

Suppose land is transferred "to A and her heirs until A marries B, and then to B and his heirs." Some authority exists that A has a fee simple determinable by virtue of the express special limitation—"until A marries B"—and that B has an executory interest.[184] If A marries B, the gift over to B precludes any reverter to the transferor. Because the only kind of future interest that a third party can have following fee simple is an executory interest, B's interest must be an executory interest in fee simple absolute.[185] The Property Restatement calls A's estate a "fee simple with an executory

---

[179] E.g., Wise v. Wise, 134 Fla. 553, 184 So. 91 (1938); Scott v. Wilcox, 238 Ga. 184, 232 S.E.2d 59 (1977); Hess v. Jones, 335 Pa. 569, 7 A.2d 299 (1939); Picadura v. Humphrey, 335 S.W.2d 6 (Mo. 1960).

[180] E.g., Abbott v. Holway, 72 Me. 298 (1881). See also Jones v. Caird, 153 Wis. 384, 387, 141 N.W. 228, 229 (1913); Lemen v. McComas, 63 Md. 153 (1885).

[181] Most cases involving limitations of the kind under discussion also contained language to the effect that the conveyance should "not take effect" or "not become absolute" until the grantor's death. The issue in most of the cases was not whether waste had been committed but whether the conveyance was effective at all or was ineffective as an attempted testamentary disposition by deed.

[182] The holding in Thompson v. Thompson, 237 Ga. 509, 228 S.E.2d 886 (1976) supports the result suggested in the first example. No cases dealing with the second example have been found.

[183] First Restatement of Property, supra note 38, at § 46, cmt. i. But, in the second case, "if the language indicates clearly an intention that the first taker shall have a fee simple until the executory interest vests, then it may properly be given effect." 1 Simes & Smith, supra note 39, at § 223.

[184] 1 Powell, supra note 16, at § 13.05[1].

[185] "There can be no remainder after a determinable fee * * *. Hence, if we sustain the future interest in such cases, we must call it an executory interest. Since the executory interest was essentially a type of future

limitation creating an interest which takes effect at the expiration of a prior interest."[186] But this is surely too cumbersome for general use. The term "fee simple determinable with an executory limitation" would clearly be more convenient than, and as descriptive as, the term adopted by the Property Restatement. The Third Restatement of Property rejects all distinctions among the different types of defeasible fees and combines them into one "fee simple defeasible."[187]

Because the distinction between succeeding a prior interest after its natural expiration and divesting or cutting off a prior interest has little current significance, the distinction between a fee simple subject to an executory limitation and a fee simple determinable with an executory limitation is important only when the purported executory limitation is void *ab initio* under some rule of law, such as the Rule Against Perpetuities.[188] If the transfer purports to create a fee simple subject to an executory limitation and the purported executory limitation is void, the first taker is left with a fee simple absolute.[189] On the other hand, if the transfer attempted to create a fee simple determinable with an executory limitation and the purported executory limitation is void, the first taker is left with a fee simple determinable, provided that the special limitation is valid.[190]

§ 2.10 FEE TAIL AND FEE SIMPLE CONDITIONAL IN THE UNITED STATES

Although most American colonies recognized the fee tail estate before the American Revolution,[191] courts and legislatures regarded it with hostility, and most of the original thirteen states abolished it soon after the Revolution. Today, almost all states have legislation that expressly or effectively eliminates the fee tail estate.[192]

---

interest which could not exist prior to the Statute of Uses, it is quite consistent to call the future interest in these cases an executory interest." 1 Simes & Smith, supra note 39, at § 228.

[186] First Restatement of Property, supra note 38, at § 47.

[187] Third Restatement of Property, supra note 14, at § 24.3.

[188] The common law Rule Against Perpetuities will be violated and the executory interest rendered void *ab initio,* whenever the executory limitation can become operative at any time in the future, however remote. See, e.g., Proprietors of Church in Brattle Square v. Grant, 69 Mass. 142, 3 Gray 142 (1855); Inst. for Sav. in Roxbury v. Roxbury Home for Aged Women, 244 Mass. 583, 139 N.E. 301 (1923); City of Klamath Falls v. Bell, 7 Or. App. 330, 490 P.2d 515 (1971).

[189] E.g., Proprietors of Church in Brattle Square, 69 Mass. 142; Cody v. Staples, 80 Conn. 82, 67 A. 1 (1907); Nevitt v. Woodburn, 190 Ill. 283, 60 N.E. 500 (1901); Bunting v. Hromas, 104 Neb. 383, 177 N.W. 190 (1920); City of Klamath Falls, 490 P.2d 515.

[190] E.g., Inst. for Sav. in Roxbury, 139 N.E. 301; Brown v. Indep. Baptist Church, 325 Mass. 645, 91 N.E.2d 922 (1950); Jones v. Burns, 221 Miss. 833, 74 So. 2d 866 (1954).

[191] The common law rules concerning the language necessary to create a fee tail were less rigid than the rules applicable to the fee simple. A fee tail could be created by an inter vivos transfer either to "A and the heirs of his body" or to "A and the heirs of his body, then to B and his heirs." In the first case, the grantor retained a reversion; in the second case, B received a remainder. But a fee tail and a remainder could also be created by an inter vivos transfer to "A and his heirs, but if A should die without issue, then to B and his heirs." In the last example, the words "die without issue" were said to refer to an "indefinite" failure of issue—i.e., the death of a tenant in fee tail without issue, whenever that might occur—and "A and his heirs" was therefore construed to mean "A and the heirs of his body." But the word "heirs" was always necessary for creation of a fee tail by inter vivos conveyance. After 1540, however, a fee tail could be created by will if the will, as a whole, showed the intent to create a fee tail although the words "heirs" or "heirs of the body" were not used.

[192] First Restatement of Property, supra note 38, at ch. 5, intro. note lists the statutes. See also 1 Am. L. Prop., supra note 11, at § 2.13; 1 Powell, supra note 16, at § 13.04. Article 1, § 26 of the Texas Constitution prohibits "entailments," but no Texas statute defines the consequences of this prohibition. In Merrill v. Am.

The most common type of legislation converts what would have been a fee tail under the English common law into a fee simple in the first grantee or devisee named in the deed or will. In about half of these states, the first taker acquires a fee simple absolute.[193] In the other half, statutes of this type also provide, in substance, that any remainder purportedly created to follow the fee tail shall be construed as an executory interest in fee simple absolute to become possessory if the first taker dies without lineal descendants ("without issue").[194] Under such a statute, if O conveys "to A and the heirs of A's body, remainder to B and B's heirs," A acquires a fee simple subject to executory limitation, and B acquires an executory interest in fee simple absolute that will become possessory only if A dies without issue. In those states where the statute makes no reference to purported remainders, A would acquire a fee simple absolute, and B would acquire no interest.

In the next largest group of states, the legislation changes what would be a fee tail under the English common law into a life estate in the first grantee or devisee named in the deed or will, with a remainder in fee simple absolute to the lineal descendants of the first taker.[195] Under statutes of this type, a conveyance by O "to A and the heirs of A's body" will give A a life estate, with a remainder in fee simple absolute to her lineal descendants. The legal authority is divided on whether a child or more remote descendant of A must survive A in order to share in the fee simple absolute.[196]

A third kind of statute provides that the first taker shall acquire a fee tail and that the lineal descendants of the first taker shall acquire a fee simple absolute. Connecticut and Ohio have statutes of this type that apply to both deeds and wills, and Rhode Island has a similar statute that applies only to wills.[197] In cases covered by such a statute, a

---

Baptist Missionary Union, 73 N.H. 414, 62 A. 647 (1905), the court held that the fee tail was inconsistent with New Hampshire's institutions and, therefore, was not included in the reception of English common law in New Hampshire. 2 Powell, supra note 16, at § 14.01, lists Alaska, Idaho, Louisiana, Nevada, Utah, and Washington as having no statutes or decisions recognizing, modifying, or abolishing fees tail. It seems unlikely that any of these states will ever recognize the fee tail and practically certain that it will not be recognized in Louisiana, which is a civil law jurisdiction.

[193] The jurisdictions with legislation of this type include Alabama, Arizona, Colorado, District of Columbia, Georgia, Minnesota, Mississippi, New Jersey, North Carolina, Ohio, Pennsylvania, Tennessee, Vermont, and Wisconsin. The same result has sometimes been reached by judicial decision in Texas, where the state constitution prohibits the fee tail. Generally, see First Restatement of Property, supra note 38, at ch. 5, intro. note; 2 Powell, supra note 16, at §§ 14.06–07.

[194] The states with statutes so providing include California, Indiana, Kentucky, Michigan, Montana, Nebraska, New York, North Dakota, Oklahoma, South Dakota, Virginia, West Virginia, and Wyoming. See First Restatement of Property, supra note 38, at ch. 5, intro. note; 1 Am. L. Prop., supra note 11, at § 2.13 n.4; 2 Powell, supra note 16, at § 14.07[3] nn. 32, 33.

[195] The states with statutes so providing include Arkansas, Florida, Georgia (for only certain types of conveyances), Illinois, Kansas, Missouri, and New Mexico. See First Restatement of Property, supra note 38, at ch. 5, intro. note; 1 Am. L. Prop., supra note 11, at § 2.13 n.5; 2 Powell, supra note 16, at § 14.07[2]. The lineal descendants entitled to take the remainder usually include, by statute, adopted children. See Sides v. Beene, 327 Ark. 401, 938 S.W.2d 840 (1997); Unsel v. Meier, 972 S.W.2d 466 (Mo. Ct. App. 1998), rev'd, 1999 WL 34795421 (Mo. Cir. 1999).

[196] See, e.g., Mitchell v. Mitchell, 208 Ark. 478, 187 S.W.2d 163 (1945) (survival required); Schee v. Boone, 295 Mo. 212, 243 S.W. 882 (1922) (same); Stearns v. Curry, 306 Ill. 94, 137 N.E. 471 (1922) (survival not required).

[197] Conn. Gen. Stat. Ann. § 47–3 (West 2017); Ohio Rev. Code Ann. § 2131.08 (West 2017); R. I. Gen. Laws, § 33–6–10 (2017). From 1939 to 1949, Wyoming also had a statute like those of Connecticut and Ohio, having previously recognized the common law fee tail. In Connecticut and Ohio, a fee tail owner has no power to execute a disentailing conveyance, and the power of the owner's creditors to satisfy their claims from the entailed land is correspondingly restricted. See, e.g., Chesebro v. Palmer, 68 Conn. 207, 36 A. 42 (1896); Wolf

gift "to A and the heirs of A's body" gives A a fee tail, and, at A's death, his surviving descendants have a fee simple absolute. A's estate has the normal characteristics of a fee tail, except that it cannot transfer anything more than an estate for his own life.

Four states—Delaware, Maine, Massachusetts, and Rhode Island (in Rhode Island, only when the estate is created by deed)—recognize the fee tail substantially as it existed in England, except that a tenant in tail has the power to convey an estate in fee simple absolute by an ordinary deed of conveyance and thereby "bar the entail" and all future interests limited to take effect on termination of the fee tail by failure of issue.[198] In addition, a creditor of the tenant in tail (except in Delaware) can subject the debtor's estate to the satisfaction of the creditor's claims as if it were fee simple.[199] However, the tenant in tail cannot dispose of the estate by will. It is unclear whether, on the death of the tenant in tail in these jurisdictions, the estate will descend to all the tenant's descendants in equal shares or whether the old English rule of primogeniture will still be applied.[200]

Rather surprisingly, Iowa, Nebraska, Oregon, and South Carolina all, at one time, held that an estate in fee simple conditional—which could not be created in England after enactment of the Statute De Donis Conditionalibus in 1285—would be created by language that would have created a fee tail in England after 1285.[201] The rationale, except in Oregon, was that De Donis was not part of the common law in these states.[202]

---

v. Stout, 11 W.L.B. 236 (Ohio 1884). The Rhode Island statute, supra, is ambiguously worded, but a court construed it to allow a fee tail created by will to endure only for the life of the first devisee. Wilcox v. Heywood, 12 R.I. 196 (1878). A tenant in tail of Rhode Island land may convert a fee tail created by will into a fee simple by a deed expressing the intent to do so. R. I. Gen. Laws, §§ 34–4–5, 34–4–16–17. Entailed land in Rhode Island may be sold on execution in fee simple to satisfy the claims of creditors of the tenant in tail. R. I. Gen. Laws, § 34–4–14.

[198] See Del. Code Ann. tit. 25, § 302 (applies to both legal and equitable estates and empowers either possessory owner in fee tail or owner of future interest in fee tail to convert fee tail into fee simple); Me. Stat. tit. 33, § 156 (2017) (seemingly applies only to legal estates; possessory fee tail owner, or life tenant and reversioner or remainder holder in fee tail acting together, may convert fee tail into fee simple); Mass. Gen. Laws ch. 183, §§ 45–47 (West 2017) (legal or equitable estates in fee tail may be converted into fee simple estates by deed from possessory owner in fee tail, or from life tenant and reversioner or remainder holder in fee tail acting together); Md. Code Ann., Real Prop. § 2–102; R. I. Gen. Laws, §§ 34–4–15–17 (same as Massachusetts statutes).

[199] See Me. Stat. tit. 14, § 2008 (2017); Mass. Gen. Laws ch. 183, § 4 (West 2017); R. I. Gen. Laws, § 34–4–14.

[200] In a few old cases, courts seemed to recognize the survival of primogeniture with respect to fee tail estates in Delaware, Maine, and Massachusetts. See First Restatement of Property, supra note 38, at § 85, Special Note. But a court today seems unlikely to hold that primogeniture exists, because it has long since been abolished with respect to fee simple estates on the ground that it is inconsistent with American institutions. When the owner of a fee tail dies without having conveyed the land in fee simple and is survived by both a spouse and issue, the issue acquire a fee tail subject to the surviving spouse's dower or curtesy, as the case may be. Id. §§ 84–85. When no issue survive, dower and curtesy will be cut off if they are deemed to be derivative estates, as stated in id. § 84. But see Holden v. Wells, 18 R.I. 802, 31 A. 265 (1895).

[201] See, e.g., Pierson v. Lane, 60 Iowa 60, 14 N.W. 90 (1882); Yates v. Yates, 104 Neb. 678, 178 N.W. 262 (1920) (dictum); Lytle v. Hulen, 128 Or. 483, 275 P. 45 (1929); Blume v. Pearcy, 204 S.C. 409, 29 S.E.2d 673 (1944). For a vigorous critique of such decisions, see 1 Am. L. Prop., supra note 11, at § 2.11.

[202] See Pierson, 14 N.W. 90; Yates, 178 N.W. 262; Blume, 29 S.E.2d 673. In Lytle, 128 Or. 483, 275 P. 45, the court held that the Oregon statute providing that a deed passes the grantor's entire estate, whether the word "heirs" is used, which impliedly repealed De Donis and restored the fee simple conditional.

Nebraska abolished the fee simple conditional by statute in 1941,[203] and this medieval artifact currently has substantial importance only in South Carolina.[204]

As was true in England before 1285, the owner of a fee simple conditional in South Carolina cannot transfer it by will even after the birth of issue.[205] But, after the birth of issue, the owner has the power to convey or mortgage the land in fee simple absolute,[206] and the owner's judgment creditors can satisfy their claims by means of an execution sale of the fee simple absolute.[207] If the owner dies survived by issue before making an inter vivos transfer, the issue will take a fee simple conditional by descent.[208] This means that the condition as to birth of issue must again be satisfied before the estate can be converted into a fee simple absolute by inter vivos transfer.[209]

§ 2.11 LIFE ESTATE—IN GENERAL

As we have seen, in the period immediately following the Norman Conquest of England, estates granted by the king or by lesser lords to feudal tenants were for the tenant's life only.[210] After judicial recognition of the fee simple as an estate of inheritance in the twelfth century, it was still possible to create life estates—estates with a duration measured by the life of a designated person or the survivor of a group of persons. Life estates could be created either by using express language indicating that intent or by omitting any words of limitation, such as "and her heirs."[211] Neither a fee simple nor a fee tail could be created without words of inheritance, such as "and her heirs," because these words were necessary to indicate an intent to transfer an inheritable estate. Therefore, a conveyance by O "to A" would create only an estate for A's life.

Under modern American statutes prescribing, in substance, that every conveyance shall be deemed to convey the grantor's entire estate unless a contrary intent is manifested,[212] the owner of a fee simple estate can create a life estate only by an instrument clearly indicating the intent to create a life estate, rather than to transfer the fee simple, though no particular form of words is required.[213] On the other hand, the owner of a life estate can transfer it to another without using any words of limitation.

---

[203] Neb. Rev. Stat. § 76–110 (2017).

[204] The ultimate basis for holding *De Donis* not part of the common law in South Carolina seems to have been the adoption in 1712 of a decree selecting certain English statutes as "suited to the conditions" of the South Carolina colony and excluding all other English statutes. See T. Cooper, The Statutes at Large of South Carolina 401 (1837). More than a dozen South Carolina cases recognize the existence of the fee simple conditional—called a "fee conditional" or "special fee conditional"—in that state. See 1 Am. L. Prop., supra note 11, at § 2.11 nn.5–11; 2 Powell, supra note 16, at § 14.04 n.1.

[205] E.g., Burriss v. Burriss, 104 S.C. 441, 89 S.E. 405 (1916).

[206] E.g., Holley v. Still, 91 S.C. 487, 74 S.E. 1065 (1912) (issue need not be alive when conveyance is made); Crawford v. Masters, 98 S.C. 458, 82 S.E. 793 (1914) (issue need not be legitimate); Bonds v. Hutchison, 199 S.C. 197, 18 S.E.2d 661 (1942) (mortgage foreclosure transfers absolute fee).

[207] E.g., Williams v. Gause, 83 S.C. 265, 65 S.E. 241 (1909).

[208] E.g., Withers v. Jenkins, 14 S.C. 597 (1881).

[209] Withers, 14 S.C. 597. But see Blume, 29 S.E.2d 673, which can be interpreted as holding that the issue take a fee simple absolute—a clear departure from prior holdings but clearly desirable because it would eliminate all fee simple conditional estates after the existence of only one life.

[210] Supra § 1.7.

[211] Concerning the need for words of inheritance to create a fee simple, see supra § 2.2 at note 28.

[212] Supra § 2.2 at note 33.

[213] First Restatement of Property, supra note 38, at §§ 18, 107–08. For language that will create a life estate, see id. § 107, illus. 6, and § 108, illus. 6–8 (indicating that a transfer to "to A" with a "gift over" to A's

Life estates can be created to last for the life of a single transferee, for the lives of two or more transferees, for the life of the transferor, or until the death of the first to die of two or more designated measuring lives.[214] When the duration of a life estate is measured by the grantee's life, it is an ordinary life estate. If someone other than the grantee is the measuring life, it is a life estate pur autre vie (for the life of another).[215]

Life estates may also arise by operation of law, as occurs with dower and curtesy[216] or when a statute converts an attempted conveyance of a fee tail into a life estate in the first taker.[217] The latter type of life estate is rare, because grantors today rarely try to create a fee tail. Dower and curtesy are still of substantial, though decreasing, importance in the United States and will be given separate consideration in subsequent sections of this book.[218]

As with the fee estates, a life estate, however created, is an aggregate of rights and duties. The most important right of the life estate owner (the "life tenant") is exclusive possession of the land, which is protected by actions at law to recover possession and damages.[219] These actions are available against the world at large, including the owners of future estates that will become possessory when the life estate terminates. If the owner of a future estate injures the land, the life tenant is entitled to recover damages to the extent of her interest in the land, which is the difference between the value of the life estate before and after the injury was inflicted.[220] The weight of authority applies the same measure of damages when a person with no interest in the land injures it.[221] In some states, the life tenant can recover the entire diminution of the land's value, which is the amount that a fee simple owner could recover). However, in that case, the life tenant is accountable to the future interest owners for their share of the damages.[222]

---

children or to a third party will create a life estate in A and a remainder in A's children or the third party, as the case may be). See also Robinson v. King, 68 N.C. App. 86, 314 S.E.2d 768 (1984), review denied, 311 N.C. 762, 321 S.E.2d 144 (1984).

[214] See 2 Powell, supra note 16, at § 15.02. The measuring lives may, of course, include the grantor, the grantee, or both.

[215] For examples, id. at § 15.02 n.4.

[216] At common law, a widow was entitled, by operation of law, to a life estate in one-third of the lands of which her deceased husband was seized in fee simple or fee tail at any time during the marriage. A widower was entitled to a life estate in all the lands of which his deceased wife was seized in fee simple or fee tail at any time during the marriage. For more on dower and curtesy, see infra §§ 2.13–14.

[217] See supra § 2.10.

[218] See infra §§ 2.13–14.

[219] For a discussion of these actions, see supra § 1.2.

[220] See First Restatement of Property, supra note 38, at §§ 117–18. Note, however, that the owner of a future interest in the same land has a right to enter the land during the continuance of the life estate (1) to inspect the premises to determine whether waste has been or is being committed; (2) to demand payment of any rent due; (3) to make repairs that may be necessary to protect the property from damage; (4) to remove timber or other materials that have been severed from the land when the future interest owner is entitled to possession of them; and (5) to take actions necessary to protect the future estate from the effects of a breach of covenant or "conduct on the land" that would cause or accelerate the defeasance of the future interest. Id. § 117, cmt. c.

[221] E.g., Beard v. Hicks, 163 Ala. 329, 50 So. 232 (1909); Brown v. Woodliff, 89 Ga. 413, 15 S.E. 491 (1892); Zimmerman v. Shreeve, 59 Md. 357 (1883); Lee v. Lee, 180 N.C. 86, 104 S.E. 76 (1920). Accord First Restatement of Property, supra note 38, at § 118.

[222] E.g., Cargill v. Sewall, 19 Me. 288 (1841); Austin v. Hudson River R.R. Co., 25 N.Y. 334 (1862); Beck v. Lynch, 306 Ky. 738, 209 S.W.2d 58 (Ct. App. 1947). New York statutorily provides that, when land ownership is divided between present and future estates, the owner of the present estate can recover for injuries to future

In addition to the right of exclusive possession, a life tenant also has rights to use the land and to any rents or profits from its use.[223] Except as against any future interest owners, a life tenant's right to use is the same as that of any other possessor of land.[224] It is subject to restrictions imposed by the common law of nuisance, riparian rights, and rights of support, together with government land use regulations, such as zoning. As against the future interest owners, a life tenant also is subject to the law of waste, which prohibits using the land in a way that injures the future interest owners' rights, such as by diminishing the land's value. In addition, a life tenant has certain affirmative duties with respect to payment of taxes, mortgage interest, and special assessments for the protection of the future interests. The life tenant's duties will be considered in more detail in a later chapter of this book.[225]

Life estates in land, like estates in fee simple and in fee tail, were classified under the English common law as freehold estates because they were created by livery of seisin. The life tenant, unlike the tenant for years, had seisin, as well as possession, of the free tenement.

§ 2.12 CONVENTIONAL LIFE ESTATES— CONSTRUCTIONAL PROBLEMS

Conveyance "to A for life." A conventional life estate is created by a voluntary conveyance, such as by a deed or will, rather than by operation of law, such as dower and curtesy or when a state law changes an attempted fee tail into a life estate in the first taker. An owner who wishes to convey a conventional, ordinary (measured by the grantee's life) life estate can use language such as "to A for her life," "to A to have and to hold during his natural life," "to A for her sole use and benefit during her natural life," or "to A until his death."

But what if the conveyance does not specify that A is the measuring life, but simply transfers "to A for life"? This language could be construed to create either an estate for A's life or an estate for the grantor's life. The Third Restatement of Property indicates that A will receive an ordinary life estate if the grantor had a fee estate.[226] But if the grantor had only an ordinary life estate, most of the cases and the Restatement agree that A acquires an estate for the grantor's life.[227] In the latter case, the grantor cannot convey an estate that will last longer than his or her own life.

Tenancy terminable only by tenant. Courts are split on the proper treatment of a lease that, by its terms, can be terminated at the will of the tenant but not at the will of

---

interests only if all living persons who have interests in the land are joined as parties. N.Y. Real Prop. Acts. § 833.

[223] E.g., Haselwood v. Moore, 100 Colo. 556, 69 P.2d 248 (1937). See also First Restatement of Property, supra note 38, at § 119.

[224] This privilege may, of course, be expressly restricted by the terms of the instrument creating the life estate. E.g., Hair v. Farrell, 21 Tenn. App. 12, 103 S.W.2d 918 (1936) (conveyance to A for support and maintenance during his life; held, A's estate not entitled to retain income from land during A's life that is not used for his support and maintenance).

[225] Infra Chapter 4. See also supra note 219 concerning the future interest owners' right to enter the land to protect their interests while the life tenant is in possession.

[226] Third Restatement of Property, supra note 14, at § 24.5 cmt. a, illus. 1 & cmt. b, illus. 2.

[227] E.g., Turner v. Mo. Pac. Ry. Co., 130 Mo. App. 535, 109 S.W. 101 (1908); Brevoort v. Brevoort, 70 N.Y. 136 (1877). Contra Doe v. Robinson (1828) 108 Eng. Rep. 1053; Third Restatement of Property, supra note 14, at § 24.5 cmt. c, illus. 5.

the landlord. Based on reciprocity of rights, some courts hold that both the landlord and the tenant can terminate the lease despite its language. However, depending on the exact language of the lease, other courts hold that the tenant has a defeasible life estate.[228] For example, the Second Restatement of Property states that a lease of a farm to T "for as long as T desires to stay on the land" creates a determinable life estate.[229]

More than one measuring life. When a conveyance or devise is made "to A for the lives of A, B, and C" or "to A for the lives of B, C, and D," it is unclear whether A's life estate is to continue until the last person dies or only until the first one dies. The result should turn on the intent of the grantor or testator as manifested in the deed or will. In such cases, the tendency has been to find that A's estate is to be measured by the life of the surviving member of the group.[230]

Substitutionary gift. When a conveyance or devise is made with language such as "to A, and at his death to A's children,"[231] "to A, and if A dies, then to B," or "to A, and at A's death to B," another constructional problem may arise. If the instrument contains additional language from which an intent to give A a fee simple can be inferred, courts have held that A acquired a fee simple subject to an executory limitation.[232] Absent such language, courts normally hold that A acquired only a life estate.[233] However, in some cases in which the transfer was by will, courts have held that A acquires a fee simple estate if A survives the testator, with a substitutionary gift to A's children or to B, as the case may be, if A predeceases the testator.[234] Courts have also adopted the substitutionary gift construction in some cases in which the will included a gift over "at the death of A" or "when A dies" and also included additional language indicating that the gift over was included solely to avoid intestacy if A predeceased the testator.[235]

When a conveyance or devise "to A," without express language defining A's estate, is followed by contingent limitations to take effect at A's death,[236] determining whether the stated contingencies exhaust all the fact situations possible at A's death is necessary. If they do,[237] the conveyance or will in substance makes a gift over at A's death, and A

---

[228] 2 Powell, supra note 16, at § 16.05[1]; Restatement (Second) of Prop.: Landlord and Tenant § 1.6 cmt. g, illus. 6 (1976) (hereinafter Second Restatement of Property).

[229] Second Restatement of Property, supra note 228, at § 1.6 cmt. g, illus. 6. See also Gunnison v. Evans, 136 Kan. 791, 18 P.2d 191 (1933) (lessees "might occupy * * * as long as they wish[ ]"); Thompson v. Baxter, 107 Minn. 122, 119 N.W. 797 (1909) (lease to tenant so long as he "shall wish to live in Albert Lea"); Garner v. Gerrish, 63 N.Y.2d 575, 483 N.Y.S.2d 973, 473 N.E.2d 223 (1984) (lessee had the "privilege of termination [sic] this agreement at a date of his own choice").

[230] 2 Powell, supra note 16, at § 15.02[1]; Third Restatement of Property, supra note 14, at § 24.5 cmt. d.

[231] E.g., Lowery v. Madden, 308 Ky. 342, 214 S.W.2d 592 (1948); Flagg v. Badger, 58 Me. 258 (1870); Clark v. Owens, 18 N.Y. 434 (1858).

[232] E.g., Hicks v. Fairbanks' Heirs, 208 Okla. 346, 256 P.2d 169 (1953) (second gift phrased so as to affect what the first taker has not disposed of); Davis v. Davis, 225 Mass. 311, 114 N.E. 309 (1916) (limitation as a whole leads to finding of fee simple).

[233] E.g., Adams v. Eagle, 194 Ark. 171, 106 S.W.2d 192 (1937) (gift over "at" the death of the first taker); Ripley v. Benjamin, 111 Vt. 76, 10 A.2d 205 (1940) (gift over "after" the death of the first taker); Rowe v. Rowe, 95 N.H. 241, 61 A.2d 526 (1948) (gift over "on" the death of the first taker).

[234] E.g., Mitchell v. Snyder, 402 Ill. 279, 83 N.E.2d 680 (1949); Stevenson v. Stearns, 325 Mo. 646, 29 S.W.2d 116 (1929). Cf. Reedy v. Propst, 169 W.Va. 473, 288 S.E.2d 526 (1982).

[235] E.g., O'Reilly v. Irving, 284 Mass. 522, 188 N.E. 253 (1933).

[236] E.g., "to A, and on the death of A survived by children, to such children but on A's death not survived by children, to B."

[237] This is the case in the example given supra note 236.

will generally take a life estate.[238] Even if the stated contingencies do not exhaust all the fact situations possible at A's death,[239] courts will sometimes imply an alternative gift over that, together with the expressed contingencies, exhausts all possible alternatives, and A generally takes a life estate.[240] If the alternative gift over is not implied, A will generally take a fee simple subject to executory limitation.[241]

Implied life estate. If a will devises land "to B to take effect at the death of A," a partial intestacy may occur if a life estate is not implied in A's favor. Moreover, if B is the testator's heir, B will get the land immediately, rather than at the future time intended by the testator. Hence the courts in some English cases[242] and American cases[243] find an implied life estate in favor of A if, and only if, B is the testator's heir.[244] Courts in other American cases find an implied life estate in A even if B is not the testator's heir, provided that the evidence as a whole indicates that the testator intended A to have a life estate.[245]

Internal inconsistencies. Inconsistencies between the granting and habendum clauses in a deed, such as when one clause conveys a fee simple but the other conveys a life estate, may be resolved by a mechanical application of some rule of construction. For example, a court may apply the rule that the granting clause controls the habendum clause[246] or that a deed must be construed in favor of the grantee.[247] But courts in the best-reasoned cases reject these artificial rules of construction and emphasize that the deed is to be construed in its entirety to ascertain the parties' intent.[248]

Power to transfer fee simple. When language in a deed or will conveys a life estate but also purports to give the transferee the power to transfer a fee simple, the prevailing rule is that the transferee has only a life estate despite the added power. The result is the same whether the added power of disposition is unlimited[249] or is exercisable only by

---

[238] E.g., George v. George, 283 Ky. 381, 141 S.W.2d 558 (1940).

[239] E.g., "to A, and on the death of A survived by children, to such children."

[240] E.g., Ware v. Minot, 202 Mass. 512, 88 N.E. 1091 (1909).

[241] E.g., Hill v. Terrell, 123 Ga. 49, 51 S.E. 81 (1905). This assumes, of course, that words of inheritance are unnecessary to create a fee simple.

[242] E.g., Chamberlin v. Springfield (1894) 3 Ch. 603.

[243] E.g., Matter of Keehn, 156 Misc. 259, 281 N.Y.S. 591 (1935), aff'd, 248 A.D. 697, 289 N.Y.S. 819 (1936).

[244] This rule is adopted in the First Restatement of Property, supra note 38, at § 116.

[245] E.g., Phoenix State Bank & Tr. Co. v. Johnson, 132 Conn. 259, 43 A.2d 738 (1945). See also Edwards v. Bradley, 227 Va. 224, 315 S.E.2d 196 (1984).

[246] E.g., Dickson v. Wildman, 183 F. 398 (5th Cir. 1910) (granting clause is essential to the deed while the habendum is not).

[247] E.g., Meacham v. Blaess, 141 Mich. 258, 104 N.W. 579 (1905) (dictum that "a grant of a life estate may by the habendum be enlarged to a fee simple.").

[248] E.g., Boyer v. Murphy, 202 Cal. 23, 259 P. 38 (1927) (including a habendum for life, cutting down fee simple language in granting clause; intent to create only life estate clear from other parts of the deed and attendant circumstances); Luther v. Patman, 200 Ark. 853, 141 S.W.2d 42 (1940); Swearingen v. McGee, 303 Ky. 825, 198 S.W.2d 805 (1946); Robinson v. King, 68 N.C. App. 86, 314 S.E.2d 768 (1984), review denied, 311 N.C. 762, 321 S.E.2d 144 (1984).

[249] E.g., Burlington Cty. Nat'l Bank v. Braddock, 24 N.J.Super. 462, 94 A.2d 868 (Ch. 1953); In re Smythe's Estate, 132 Cal. App. 2d 343, 282 P.2d 141 (1955); St. Joseph Hosp. v. Dwertman, 268 S.W.2d 646 (Ky. 1954); Matter of Martindale's Estate, 423 N.E.2d 662 (Ind. Ct. App. 1981), overruled by Ind. Dep't of State Revenue v. Hungate, 439 N.E.2d 1148 (1982). See First Restatement of Property, supra note 38, at § 111.

deed,[250] only by will,[251] only with a third person's consent,[252] only in favor of designated persons,[253] only on a stated contingency,[254] or only by sale, rather than by gift.[255] However, the courts in four states have departed from the prevailing rule and have held that an unlimited power of disposition in fee simple converts what would otherwise have been a life estate into a fee simple.[256] Of these states, courts in Maine have narrowly defined the situations in which this will occur,[257] and Tennessee, Virginia, and West Virginia have statutorily narrowed this holding.[258]

In contrast, when the language in a deed conveys a fee simple and also gives the transferee an unlimited power to transfer and encumber the land, the provision concerning transferring and encumbering does not prevent the court from finding that a fee simple is created.[259] However, if that language gives the transferee only a limited power of disposition, courts usually hold that the transferor intended to transfer a life estate, rather than a fee simple.[260]

Defeasible life estate. A life estate may be made defeasible by use of a special limitation, condition subsequent, or executory limitation.[261] For example, if O devises Blackacre to O's spouse "during widowhood," "so long as she shall remain a widow," or "so long as he does not remarry," the spouse will acquire a determinable life estate.[262]

Multiple life tenants. A life estate may be transferred to two or more grantees as tenants in common. When land is conveyed to tenants in common for life, surviving cotenants have cross-remainders for life following a deceased cotenant's interest until the remainder becomes possessory at the last cotenant's death. Although implication of cross-remainders is more common when life estates are created by will, substantial authority exists for such implication when the life estate is created by deed.[263]

§ 2.13 MARITAL LIFE ESTATES AT COMMON LAW

From a very early date, the English common law provided for a surviving spouse from the land in which a deceased spouse was seised of an estate of inheritance at any

---

[250] E.g., In re Fahnestock's Estate, 384 Ill. 26, 50 N.E.2d 733 (1943).

[251] E.g., Nelson v. Johnson, 354 Pa. 512, 47 A.2d 650 (1946).

[252] E.g., Jackson v. Robinson, 195 Ark. 431, 112 S.W.2d 417 (1938).

[253] E.g., Roberts v. Randleman, 352 Mo. 980, 180 S.W.2d 674 (1944).

[254] E.g., Owen v. Dumas, 200 Ark. 601, 140 S.W.2d 101 (1940).

[255] E.g., Patch v. Smith, 113 Colo. 186, 155 P.2d 765 (1945).

[256] E.g., Bradley v. Warren, 104 Me. 423, 72 A. 173 (1908); Hair v. Caldwell, 109 Tenn. 148, 70 S.W. 610 (1902); Rolley v. Rolley's Ex'x, 109 Va. 449, 63 S.E. 988 (1909); Swan v. Pople, 118 W.Va. 538, 190 S.E. 902 (1937).

[257] Barry v. Austin, 118 Me. 51, 105 A. 806 (1919) (if language expressly creating life estate is used, it will not be enlarged to a fee simple by addition of unrestricted power of disposition).

[258] See 2 Powell, supra note 16, at § 15.02.

[259] E.g., Luckey v. McCray, 125 Iowa 691, 101 N.W. 516 (1904).

[260] E.g., In re McClure's Will, 136 N.Y. 238, 32 N.E. 758 (1892). See also First Restatement of Property, supra note 38, at § 108, cmt. e.

[261] See infra § 2.15 text accompanying note 330, § 3.4 text accompanying note 37, § 3.5 text accompanying note 52; Edwards v. Bradley, 227 Va. 224, 315 S.E.2d 196 (1984).

[262] E.g., Mouser v. Srygler, 295 Ky. 490, 174 S.W.2d 756 (1943).

[263] See 1 Am. L. Prop., supra note 11, at § 2.15 in text accompanying n. 23.

time during the marriage.[264] In each case, the surviving spouse was given a life estate in such lands or part of them. The widow's life estate, called "dower," consisted of a life estate in one-third of such lands, provided the husband's estate was inheritable by the wife's issue and provided the wife had not released her dower during the marriage.[265] During the spouses' joint lives, the wife had a protected expectancy called inchoate dower. If she survived her husband, her dower became consummate. She was then entitled to have one-third of the lands to which her inchoate dower attached set off to her by metes and bounds, at which time she acquired a present estate in the lands assigned to her.[266] Assignment of dower could be effected by agreement between the widow and the heir of the deceased spouse or by court order.

Inchoate dower could not be defeated by the husband's inter vivos conveyance, by the husband's will (after 1540), or by seizure and sale on execution to satisfy creditors' claims against the husband.[267] However, after enactment of the Statute of Uses, an antenuptial or postnuptial settlement could bar inchoate dower, though a postnuptial settlement did not absolutely bar dower but merely made the widow choose between the benefits of the settlement or dower.[268] By the seventeenth century, a widow also had to elect in equity between dower and her husband's testamentary provision for her if the latter was inconsistent with dower or was expressly declared to be in lieu thereof.[269]

At common law, a surviving wife was entitled to dower only in lands in which her husband had a present estate of inheritance, though the husband need not ever have been in actual possession. Only an immediate right to possession ("seisin in law"), not actual possession ("seisin in deed"), was required.[270] The husband had to have a legal

---

[264] The widow's life estate was called "dower," and the widower's life estate was called "curtesy." While both spouses were alive, the husband also enjoyed the right to control and manage all of his wife's real property *jure uxoris*—"by the marital right."

[265] In the twelfth century, a bridegroom at the time of marriage normally identified specific lands as the dower his wife was to enjoy if she survived him. Although the amount of dower was a matter of bargain between the parties and their kin, a man was not free to marry without naming a dower. By the end of the thirteenth century, "named dowers" had begun to fall into disuse. By the fifteenth century, the common law was settled that dower consisted of one-third of the lands of which the husband was seised of an estate of inheritance (a fee simple or a fee tail) at any time during the marriage. If the husband was seised in fee tail special, the wife was not entitled to dower unless the issue of her marriage might, by possibility, inherit the fee tail. The wife's dower attached both to lands of which her husband was already seised at the time of marriage and land which he subsequently acquired in fee simple or fee tail. See, e.g., Wigginton v. Leech's Adm'x, 285 Ky. 787, 149 S.W.2d 531 (1941).

[266] Until dower was actually set off by metes and bounds, she was not entitled to enter the land, except that she had a right to remain in her husband's principal dwelling house for forty days, which was the right of "quarantine." See J. Park, A Treatise on the Law of Dower 334–62 (1819); 1 R. S. Roper, A Treatise on the Law of Property Arising from the Relation Between Husband and Wife 387 (2d ed. 1826); 2 C. Scribner, A Treatise on the Law of Dower 27 (2d ed. 1883).

[267] E.g., Hamm v. Piper, 105 N.H. 418, 201 A.2d 125 (1964); Thomas v. Thomas, 245 Ala. 607, 18 So. 2d 544 (1944) (dower not subject to claims of husband's creditors). However, a purchase money mortgage given by the husband during marriage was widely regarded as superior to the wife's dower right, whether she joined in the mortgage. E.g., Jones v. Tainter, 15 Minn. 512 (1870).

[268] 1536, 27 Hen. 8 c. 10, §§ 6, 9 (Eng.); see 2 H. Ballantine, Blackstone's Commentaries 138 (1915); 2 Scribner, supra note 266, at 394–408; 1 Am. L. Prop., supra note 11, at § 5.39; 1 Roper, supra note 266, at 488–89.

[269] 2 Scribner, supra note 266, at 439–40; 1 Am. L. Prop., supra note 11, at § 5.41.

[270] Generally, see 1 Am. L. Prop., supra note 11, at § 5.10.

estate, because seisin did not exist for an equitable estate.[271] Therefore, the widow of a trust beneficiary, mortgagor, or land contract purchaser, each of whom had only an equitable estate, was not entitled to dower even if her husband had actual possession of the land during his lifetime.[272] On the other hand, the widow of a trustee, mortgagee, or land vendor was also denied dower because her husband was not beneficially seised of the land.[273]

Dower was recognized at common law only when the claimant's husband had "sole seisin" of an estate of inheritance.[274] When the husband was a tenant in common of an estate of inheritance, his widow was entitled to dower because he was deemed to have sole seisin of his separate undivided interest.[275] But where the husband was a joint tenant, his widow was not entitled to dower for two reasons: (1) Because the undivided interest of a deceased joint tenant passes to the surviving joint tenant or tenants, rather than to the decedent's heirs, a joint tenant does not have an inheritable estate; and (2) A joint tenant is not deemed to be solely seised of his undivided interest.[276] However, the widow of the final surviving joint tenant was entitled to dower because the survivor became solely seised in severalty. Similarly, the widow of one to whom the undivided interest of a joint tenant was transferred had a dower right in that interest because the conveyance severed the joint tenancy and made her husband a tenant in common.[277]

Dower is clearly a derivative estate. Therefore, it should not last longer than the husband's estate, which is its source. But the common law decisions in England are only partly consistent with dower's derivative nature. For example, if the husband had a fee simple that terminated because he died without heirs, his widow nevertheless had dower in the land.[278] Similarly, if the husband had a fee tail estate that terminated because he died without issue, his widow had dower in the land,[279] because, by the fifteenth century, so much English land was entailed that the courts thought it necessary on policy grounds to protect widows of tenants in tail by holding their dower rights to be superior to the rights of remainder holders and reversioners upon termination of the husband's fee tail estate.[280] By analogy to the rule applied when the husband had a fee tail estate, the courts held that a widow was entitled to dower, as against the holder of an executory

---

[271] See generally 1 Am. L. Prop., supra note 11, at §§ 5.10, 5.23. The rule denying dower in equitable estates was finally changed by statute in England. 1833, 3 & 4 Wm. 4 c. 105, § 2 (Eng.).

[272] 1 Am. L. Prop., supra note 11, at §§ 5.23–24.

[273] Id. § 5.11. The widow of a trustee was entitled to dower at common law, but the Court of Chancery would enjoin her from asserting her right if her husband had no beneficial interest under the trust. Noel v. Jevon (1678) 22 Eng. Rep. 1047.

[274] Littleton, supra note 98, § 45; 1 Scribner, supra note 266, at 335–36.

[275] As to the characteristics of tenancies in common, see infra § 5.2.

[276] As to the characteristics of joint tenancies, see infra § 5.3.

[277] As to severance of a joint tenancy by transfer of one joint tenant's interest, see infra § 5.3.

[278] 1 S. Atkinson, The Theory and Practice of Conveyancing 258 (1839); 4 H. de Bracton, De Legibus et Consuetudinibus, fol. 297b (T. Twiss ed., 1881); Kent, supra note 106, at 49; Park, supra note 266, at 158; 1 Scribner, supra note 266, at 286–88. This rule meant that the widow's dower right was superior to the right of escheat of the feudal overlord in England. The same rule was applied here, although the right of escheat accrues to the state in the United States. E.g., Pac. Bank v. Hannah, 90 Fed. 72 (9th Cir. 1898).

[279] E.g., YB 5 Edw. 2 (1311) (Eng.), reprinted in Selden Society 18 (1944); E. Coke, Commentary Upon Littleton ¶ 241a, note (F. Hargrave & C. Butler eds., 1812); Paine's Case (1587) 77 Eng. Rep. 524. The rule was applied whether the husband literally died without issue or his line of descendants became extinct after his death.

[280] First Restatement of Property, supra note 38, at app. 13; 1 Am. L. Prop., supra note 11, at 680 n.19.

interest to which her husband's fee simple estate was subject, when the divesting contingency occurred at the husband's death, which was typically because the husband's fee simple was subject to an executory limitation upon his death without surviving issue.[281]

In contrast, courts have given legal effect to dower's derivative nature by holding that, if the husband has a fee simple determinable or a fee simple subject to condition subsequent, the wife's dower right is extinguished by the occurrence of the special limiting event or exercise of the right of entry for breach of the specified condition.[282] Similarly, if the husband's estate of inheritance is subject to a power of appointment, courts have held that exercise of the power defeats the wife's dower right, even when her husband holds and exercises the power.[283]

Because inchoate dower arose by operation of law from the marital relationship, it existed only if a valid marriage existed.[284] An annulment or absolute divorce extinguished any inchoate dower interest in the lands of the former husband.[285] Moreover, an early English statute provided that, "if a wife willingly leave her husband and go away, and continue with her advouter," her dower was barred unless she reunited with her husband.[286]

The English common law provided more handsomely for a widower than for a widow. During the marriage, the husband had an estate *jure uxoris* (by marital right) in all the lands in which his wife, during the marriage, owned a fee simple, a fee tail, or a life estate.[287] The husband's estate by marital right was, at common law, in substance an estate for the lives of husband and wife, or, with respect to the wife's estates of inheritance, until issue was born capable of inheriting those estates. The husband's marital estate gave him the right to exclusive possession of his wife's freehold lands and to their profits, as well as the power to convey or mortgage such lands for the spouses' joint lives, without any duty to account to his wife for money obtained by their sale or mortgage.[288] The wife's freehold lands were also subject to execution and sale to satisfy

---

[281] The leading case is Moody v. King (1825) 130 Eng. Rep. 378 (CP); see 1 Am. L. Prop., supra note 11, at § 5.29 nn.7–9.

[282] E.g., Moriarta v. McRea, 45 Hun. 564 (N.Y. 1887), aff'd 120 N.Y. 659, 24 N.E. 1103 (1890) (determinable fee); Sullivan v. Sullivan, 139 Iowa 679, 117 N.W. 1086 (1908) (fee subject to condition subsequent); First Restatement of Property, supra note 38, at § 54, app. 3.

[283] E.g., Ray v. Pung (1822) 106 Eng. Rep. 1296 (KB) (power exercised by husband during his lifetime); Thompson v. Vance, 58 Ky. 669 (1858) (power exercised by will).

[284] 1 Am. L. Prop., supra note 11, at §§ 5.7–8.

[285] Id. §§ 5.8–9, 5.36.

[286] Statute of Westminster 1285, 13 Edw. 1 c. 34 (Eng.). This statute is deemed part of the common law in some American jurisdictions, and comparable legislation is fairly common in the United States. See 1 Am. L. Prop., supra note 11, at § 3.35.

[287] The best modern treatment of the husband's estate by the marital right is in 1 Am. L. Prop., supra note 11, at §§ 5.50–56, reprinted substantially from G. Haskins, The Estate by the Marital Right, 97 U. Pa. L. Rev. 345 (1949).

[288] Coke, supra note 279, at ¶ 325b; Eaton v. Whitaker, 18 Conn. 222 (1846). Despite his power to manage and enjoy his wife's lands, the husband could not exclude her from them, except by transferring them to another.

her husband's debts.[289] However, if he predeceased her, her lands were returned to her free from encumbrances.[290]

The husband's marital right underwent substantial modification during the sixteenth and seventeenth centuries.[291] By the beginning of the eighteenth century, the Court of Chancery had established that lands conveyed to trustees for a woman's sole and separate use, either before or after her marriage, were free from her husband's control and from any liability for his debts.[292] The wife could sell or mortgage her separate equitable estate without her husband's consent or joinder.[293]

When a child of the marriage capable of inheriting from the wife was born, the common law gave her husband an estate called curtesy initiate in all the lands she owned in fee simple or fee tail.[294] Like inchoate dower, curtesy initiate was a protected expectancy that the wife could not defeat or diminish by transfer[295] or by mortgage, without her husband's joinder or release,[296] and her creditors could not sell her land to satisfy debts she incurred after marriage.[297] Unlike inchoate dower, the husband's curtesy initiate was a present estate for his life, defeasible if he predeceased his wife, and gave him the sole right to possession, use, and income of the lands to which it attached.[298] Curtesy initiate extended to lands in which the wife had either a legal or equitable estate of inheritance, provided that either spouse acquired seisin in deed during the marriage or, if the wife's estate was equitable, a trustee had given income from the land or something else equivalent to possession of it.[299]

If the husband predeceased his wife, his curtesy initiate terminated. But if he outlived her, he acquired an estate called curtesy consummate in all the lands to which his curtesy initiate previously attached.[300] Curtesy consummate was a present estate for

---

[289] 2 Kent, supra note 106, at 131; Beale v. Knowles, 45 Me. 479 (1858); Nicholls v. O'Neill, 10 N.J. Eq. 88 (Ch. 1854).

[290] Coke, supra note 279, at ¶ 325b; Flagg v. Bean, 25 N.H. 49 (1852).

[291] See 1 Am. L. Prop., supra note 11, at §§ 5.53–54.

[292] See id. § 5.55. Subsequently, courts held that lands could be conveyed to the husband as trustee for his wife's sole and separate use or even directly to the wife, in which case her husband was treated as a trustee. See 2 Scott, The Law of Trusts § 146.1 (4th ed. 1987).

[293] E.g., Forbes v. Lothrop, 137 Mass. 523 (1884).

[294] Coke, supra note 279, at ¶ 30a. The best modern treatment of curtesy is to be found in 1 Am. L. Prop., supra note 11, at §§ 5.57–74, from which the discussion in this Section is largely drawn.

[295] E.g., Farley v. Stacey, 177 Ky. 109, 197 S.W. 636 (1917) (deed).

[296] E.g., Wright v. Pell, 90 N.J. Eq. 11, 105 A. 20 (Ch. 1918). Although no cases in point have been found, in analogous cases involving inchoate dower, the husband's curtesy initiate clearly was subordinate to a purchase money mortgage or vendor's lien given by the wife.

[297] E.g., Myers v. Hansbrough, 202 Mo. 495, 100 S.W. 1137 (1907). Of course, because of the general common law disability of a married woman to enter into contracts, the problem seldom arose.

[298] E.g., Shortall v. Hinckley, 31 Ill. 219 (1863).

[299] Originally, seisin of a legal estate of inheritance was required. Littleton, supra note 98, at § 52; Coke, supra note 279, at ¶¶ 29a, 31a; 2 Ballantine, supra note 268, at 128. It became settled in the eighteenth century that the husband was entitled to curtesy in his wife's equitable estates of inheritance. See 1 Am. L. Prop., supra note 11, at § 5.59 nn. 20–26.

[300] Coke, supra note 279, at ¶ 30a. Legitimate issue, the birth of which was necessary to create the husband's curtesy initiate, need not survive for any length of time. Littleton, supra note 98, at § 35; Coke, supra note 279, at ¶ 30a. Testimony that the baby was heard to cry was generally sufficient. YB 20–21 Edw. 1 Rolls Ser. 1866 38 (1292) (Eng.); Littleton, supra note 98, at § 35; Coke, supra note 279, at ¶¶ 29a, 30a.

the balance of the husband's life. It prevented the wife's heirs or devisees from taking possession until after the husband's death.[301]

If the wife died owning a fee simple or fee tail that terminated for want of heirs or by operation of a special limitation, condition subsequent, or executory limitation, the rules applicable to dower were also applied to curtesy. Curtesy, like dower, was not consistently treated as merely a derivative estate and sometimes survived the termination of the wife's estate.[302]

§ 2.14 MODERN MARITAL LIFE ESTATES

As Professor Richard Powell observed, dower "was a reasonable product of a society in which most wealth consisted of land, and in which there was a desire to provide at least a modest social security * * * for widows,"[303] and a society in which the widow was not an heir under the common law canons of descent. But curtesy seems never to have had any justification other than that it served the interest of males in a male-dominated society. As an increasing proportion of the total wealth in England and the United States came to consist of personal property and as surviving spouses became statutory heirs under new intestate succession laws, it began to seem that neither dower nor curtesy made a great deal of sense, especially because both constituted encumbrances that inhibited the free transfer of land and were often difficult to discover.

Therefore, it is unsurprising that the English Parliament provided in the Dower Act of 1833[304] that a wife could no longer claim dower in any land that her husband disposed of by deed or by will or for which dower was barred by declaration in a deed or will. Moreover, the reforms that the Court of Chancery began in the sixteenth and seventeenth centuries to develop and protect the wife's sole and separate equitable estate[305] were completed in the nineteenth century by enactment of the Married Women's Property Act, which conferred on married women the same control of their real and personal property as was enjoyed by unmarried women. This Act abolished the husband's marital estate and his estate by curtesy initiate. Finally, England completely abolished dower and curtesy in 1925.[306]

In the United States, the enactment of Married Women's Property Acts also abolished a husband's marital estate and, in most states, his estate by curtesy initiate.[307] In most states today, dower and curtesy have been statutorily eliminated.[308] Even where they have not been completely eliminated, they have usually been greatly modified. Thus, in most states where they are recognized, dower and curtesy are both confined to lands that the deceased spouse owned at death, rather than all lands owned during the

---

[301] Because the husband's curtesy consummate applied to all the wife's inheritable estates—unlike the wife's dower consummate—there was no need for any assignment or allocation of specific land as curtesy.

[302] See supra text accompanying notes 278–283.

[303] 2 Powell, supra note 16, at § 15.04.

[304] 1833 3 & 4 Wm. 4 c. 105 (UK). This statute also made dower subject to the husband's debts and extended dower to the husband's equitable estates.

[305] See supra § 2.13 text accompanying notes 291–293.

[306] Administration of Estates Act 1925, 15 & 16 Geo. 5 c. 23 (UK).

[307] See cases collected in Notes, Curtesy as Affected by Conveyance or Mortgage by Wife Without Joining Husband, 14 A.L.R. 355 (1921); Extent and Effect of Exception in Married Women's Acts as to Husband's Right by the Curtesy, 29 A.L.R. 1338 (1924).

[308] See 2 Powell, supra note 16, at § 15.08. Only a handful of states still recognize either dower or curtesy even in modified form.

marriage. These states also generally limit curtesy to the same fraction of the deceased spouse's lands as dower.[309] And, in some states where dower and curtesy have been retained but have been limited to the same fraction of the deceased spouse's lands, the surviving spouse gets a fee simple title, rather than a life estate.[310]

Statutory abolition or modification of dower and curtesy has everywhere been preceded or accompanied by revision of the intestate succession laws to make a surviving spouse an heir who is entitled to a specified share of the decedent's estate in fee simple.[311] In many states, statutes also now allow a surviving spouse to renounce the decedent's will and take a "forced share" of the decedent's estate unless the decedent's will provides a stipulated minimum amount for the survivor.[312] Indeed, many states where dower and curtesy still exist have enacted forced share statutes. Therefore, it is rarely advantageous for a surviving spouse to claim dower or curtesy, because the survivor's intestate share or forced share when there is a will is usually more valuable than the property that might be obtained by electing dower or curtesy. As the Massachusetts court has observed, a claim of dower or curtesy is usually disadvantageous except in two special situations: "(1) if the deceased [spouse] owned real estate, but died insolvent or so nearly so that the bulk of the real estate must be sold to pay the debts and expenses; and (2) if the deceased [spouse] during his or her lifetime conveyed a considerable amount of real estate without procuring a release * * * in the deed."[313]

Where dower and curtesy still exist, a surviving spouse must elect between dower or curtesy and an intestate share if the other spouse died intestate or a forced share if the other spouse died testate.[314] Where dower still exists, a widow does not automatically become entitled to possess any particular portion of her deceased husband's lands but must, as at common law, have her dower assigned either by agreement with the heirs

---

[309] The spouses' shares must be equal to comply with the Equal Protection Clause of the Fourteenth Amendment. See Orr v. Orr, 440 U.S. 268, 99 S.Ct. 1102, 59 L.Ed.2d 306 (1979), on remand 374 So. 2d 895 (Ala. Civ. App. 1979), writ denied, 374 So. 2d 898 (Ala. 1979). See also discussion of gender-based discrimination, infra note 314. And see Jacobs v. Meade, 227 Va. 284, 315 S.E.2d 383 (1984).

[310] E.g., Minn. Stat. §§ 507.02, 525.16(2)–(3) (one-third or, in some cases, one-half, in fee simple). Such statutes give surviving spouses something different than an intestate share because they take free from the deceased spouse's debts.

[311] Atkinson, supra note 48, at § 15.

[312] See, e.g., N.Y. Est. Powers & Trusts § 5–1.1.–17 W. McKinney, McKinney's Consolidated Laws of New York 5–1.1(a) (1916).

[313] Opinion of the Justices, 151 N.E.2d 475, 478, in which the court upheld the constitutionality of a statute that limited dower and curtesy to land owned by the deceased spouse at the time of death.

[314] In general, see 1 Am. L. Prop., supra note 11, at § 5.42.

U.S. Supreme Court decisions have invalidated statutes that produce gender-based discrimination, which has affected statutes providing for such election. For example, in Orr v. Orr, 440 U.S. 268, 99 S.Ct. 1102, 59 L.Ed.2d 306, the Court held that gender-based discrimination violates the Fourteenth Amendment's Equal Protection Clause unless it bears a substantial relationship to an important governmental objective. Applying this standard, the courts in Hall v. McBride, 416 So. 2d 986 (Ala. 1982), and Stokes v. Stokes, 271 Ark. 300, 613 S.W.2d 372 (1981), appeal after remand, 275 Ark. 110, 628 S.W.2d 6 (1982) invalidated statutes that allowed a widow to claim dower against the will of her deceased husband but did not accord a widower an equivalent privilege. But in Beck v. Merritt, 280 Ark. 331, 657 S.W.2d 549 (1983), the court held that the Arkansas dower statute does not constitute unconstitutional gender-based discrimination when a husband dies intestate, because in such case the widow is not "claiming against" the husband's will and her dower right under the statute is the exact equivalent of the curtesy right the husband could have asserted had he survived his wife. Accord Dent v. Rose, 281 Ark. 42, 661 S.W.2d 361 (1983).

or, if agreement cannot be reached, by court order.[315] If curtesy is still recognized but is limited to some fraction of the deceased spouse's lands, a widower must likewise obtain an assignment of his curtesy. In most states where dower and curtesy still exist, the surviving spouse is entitled to have an assignment made by a physical division of the land, unless this is either impossible, such as when the property consists of a single house, or inequitable, in which case the court may award the surviving spouse a gross sum of money or a share of the income produced by the land.[316]

The wife obviously has no inchoate dower interest in a tenancy by the entirety. But where, under modern law, she can release her interest as a tenant by the entirety to her husband, she may acquire inchoate dower in the fee simple of which he is solely seised by virtue of her release.[317]

§ 2.15 LIFE ESTATES—ALIENABILITY

A life estate is freely transferable by deed unless the person who transferred it made it subject to an effective restraint on alienation.[318] Because a life estate, by its nature, is not very saleable, courts have not strictly applied to life estates the common law rule that substantially prohibits restraints on the alienation of fee simple estates.[319] A total forfeiture restraint, unlimited in scope or in time, is therefore valid when applied to a life estate.[320] Presumably, a total promissory restraint would also be valid, but a purported disabling restraint is ineffective unless it can be construed as a forfeiture or promissory restraint.[321] On the other hand, a spendthrift trust provision may impose an effective disabling restraint on the beneficial interest of an equitable life estate. The equitable life tenant under a spendthrift trust cannot transfer the beneficial interest, nor may the beneficiary's creditors subject it to the satisfaction of their claims.[322]

---

[315] See supra § 2.13, at note 266. See also Marino v. Smith, 454 So. 2d 1380 (Ala. 1984); Wilder v. Mixon, 442 So. 2d 922 (Ala. 1983); Devers v. Chateau Corp., 748 F.2d 902 (4th Cir. 1984), appeal after remand, 792 F.2d 1278 (1986), reh'g denied, 802 F.2d 1486 (1986).

[316] See 1 Am. L. Prop., supra note 11, at §§ 5.45–.47.

[317] In re Estate of Del Guercio, 206 N.J. Super. 159, 501 A.2d 1072 (Law Div. 1985). In a sense, a tenancy by the entirety is a marital estate because it can exist only between spouses. It is characterized by an indestructible right of survivorship. See infra § 5.5 for discussion of tenancies by the entirety.

[318] See, e.g., Guilford v. Gardner, 180 Iowa 1210, 162 N.W. 261 (1917) (dictum); Hendley v. Perry, 229 N.C. 15, 47 S.E.2d 480 (1948). Dower, once it is assigned, and curtesy consummate upon the wife's death, in jurisdictions where they still arise by operation of law, are freely transferable by deed.

[319] See First Restatement of Property, supra note 38, at § 409, cmt. a.

[320] See, e.g., Edwards v. Bradley, 227 Va. 224, 315 S.E.2d 196 (1984); Brumsey v. Brumsey, 351 Ill. 414, 184 N.E. 627 (1933).

[321] This rule is generally accepted in the United States. E.g., Grossman v. Hill, 384 Pa. 590, 122 A.2d 69 (1956), overruling recognized by Cent. Delaware Cty. Auth. v. Greyhound Corp., 386 Pa. Super. 423, 436, 563 A.2d 139, 146 (1989); Wise v. Poston, 281 S.C. 574, 316 S.E.2d 412 (1984); Sternberger v. Glenn, 175 Tenn. 644, 137 S.W.2d 269 (1940). The First Restatement of Property, supra note 38, at § 405 adopts the rule that disabling restraints are invalid. Some contrary authority exists. See, e.g., Gray v. Gray, 300 Ky. 265, 188 S.W.2d 440 (1945) (provision allowing transfer only to cotenants valid).

[322] See Domo v. McCarthy, 66 Ohio St. 3d 312, 612 N.E.2d 706 (Ohio 1993). For a brief discussion of spendthrift trusts, see 6 Am. L. Prop., supra note 11, at §§ 26.94–95. For a more extensive discussion, see 2 Scott, supra note 292, at §§ 149–62.

If a life estate is not subject to an effective restraint on alienation, the life tenant may sell, give, or mortgage the entire estate[323] or create lesser estates, such as leasehold estates, or nonpossessory interests, such as easements.[324] On the other hand, a life tenant obviously cannot convey an interest that will last longer than the life estate,[325] unless the grantor of the life estate expressly gave that power.[326]

The tenant of an estate for his or her own life obviously has no power to devise the estate by will, because it terminates at the tenant's death.[327] But the tenant of an estate *pur autre vie* may devise the residue of the estate if the measuring life is still alive.[328] If the tenant of an estate *pur autre vie* does not devise the residue of the estate, it will pass by intestate succession. In those states where the intestate succession laws treat real and personal property differently, the residue of a life estate *pur autre vie* will usually pass as personal property to the decedent's next of kin. In some of these states, however, it will pass as real property to the decedent's heirs as "special occupants" if the instrument creating the estate expressly gave it to the named grantee "and his or her heirs."[329]

It is implicit in the prior discussion of the validity of forfeiture restraints on the alienation of life estates that a life estate may be made defeasible by means of a special limitation, condition subsequent, or executory limitation. In general, the rules for determining what types of special limitations, conditions subsequent, and executory limitations are invalid because they are contrary to public policy or illegal are substantially the same when such limitations or conditions are attached to life estates as when they are attached to fee simple estates.[330]

§ 2.16   LIFE INTERESTS IN PERSONALTY

Today, most life interests are beneficial interests under trusts, the corpus of which consists mainly of personal, rather than real, property. The primary purpose of the trust device is to permit the creation of one or more beneficial life interests that entitle the life tenants to the income produced by the corpus, to preserve the corpus of the trust for distribution to one or more remainder holders after termination of all the life interests, and to permit professional management of the trust corpus for the benefit of both the life tenants and remainder holders. The corpus of the trust may include real property but

---

[323] Recognizing the life tenant's power to mortgage, see Kenwood Tr. & Sav. Bank v. Palmer, 209 Ill. App. 370 (1918), aff'd, 285 Ill. 552, 121 N.E. 186 (1918); Mo. Cent. Bldg. & Loan Ass'n v. Eveler, 237 Mo. 679, 141 S.W. 877 (1911). Of course, mortgages on life estates are not very attractive to most creditors.

[324] This is simply part of the life tenant's general power to alienate the interest in whole or in part. Palman v. Reynolds, 310 Mich. 35, 16 N.W.2d 657 (1944) (life tenant can create estate for years).

[325] This follows from the general rule that one cannot transfer a greater interest than he has. That a mortgage given by a life tenant does not bind owners of future interests in the land, see, e.g., Mid-State Homes, Inc. v. Johnson, 218 Ga. 397, 128 S.E.2d 197 (1962). That a lease given by a life tenant expires when the life estate terminates, see, e.g., Busby v. Thompson, 286 Ark. 159, 689 S.W.2d 572 (1985).

[326] That such a power may, in most states, be added by appropriate language in an instrument purporting to create a life estate without giving the grantee a fee simple, see supra § 2.12 at notes 249–260.

[327] But the life tenant may be given the power to dispose of the fee simple by will. E.g., Powers v. Wells, 244 Ill. 558, 91 N.E. 717 (1910) (power to use and dispose and to distribute to children by gift or by will).

[328] The Statute of Frauds 1677, 29 Car. II c. 3 (Eng. & Wales) first authorized such devises.

[329] The Statute of Frauds (1677) established this rule in England, and several American jurisdictions have adopted it. See First Restatement of Property, supra note 38, at § 151, Special Note.

[330] See supra § 2.3 at notes 73–82.

typically consists mainly of intangible forms of personal property, such as stocks and bonds.[331]

When personal property is given directly to a life tenant, with the remainder to another, or when a trust terminates before the life tenant's death, courts often hold that the life tenant is a trustee or quasi-trustee of the trust property for the remainder holder.[332] This characterization of the life tenant results from the special problems that arise from creating a legal life interest in personalty, including the fact that the law of waste does not adequately protect the remainder holder's interest because personalty is easily transportable, may be perishable, and may require expert management to avoid diminution in value, such as when it consists of stocks and bonds. These special problems and the statutory and judicial efforts to deal with them are discussed in Section 4.11.

§ 2.17 NONFREEHOLD (LEASEHOLD) ESTATES

Even in the heyday of English feudalism, tenants of freehold estates (fee simple, fee tail, or for life) commonly leased land to another for a definite period of time, thus creating a term of years in the lessee.[333] These leases seem originally to have been designed to avoid the ecclesiastical prohibition against usury in connection with loans.[334] The tenant of a freehold estate who borrowed money would give the lender a term of years of sufficient duration to enable him to recover the principal amount of the loan, together with a substantial profit in lieu of interest, out of the revenues from the land. But leases creating terms of years were not used only as a means of avoiding the prohibition against usury. By the late twelfth century, leases were made for a fixed term and at an agreed rent to tenants who farmed the land. These agricultural leases became increasingly common in the centuries that followed.

For reasons that are not entirely clear, a tenant for years was not considered to have a "free tenement" (freehold estate)[335] and, therefore, could not use the assize of novel disseisin to recover possession from one who wrongfully dispossessed him. Although other actions were developed in the thirteenth century to give the tenant for years a means to recover possession from the lessor or one claiming by feoffment from him, the tenant for years was limited to a damage remedy against a stranger who wrongfully dispossessed him or her before 1499.[336] In 1499, in response to the obvious need for a possessory remedy against strangers, the courts finally allowed the tenant for years to

---

[331] Treatment of the law of trusts is generally beyond the scope of this book, but the peculiar characteristics of equitable future interests subject to a trust are briefly considered in Chapter 4.

[332] See, e.g., Farmers' Mut. Fire & Lightning Ins. Co. v. Crowley, 354 Mo. 649, 190 S.W.2d 250 (1945); Comment Note, Life Tenant in Possession as Implied or Quasi Trustee, 137 A.L.R. 1054 (1942).

[333] See generally 1 Am. L. Prop., supra note 11, at § 3.1; T. Plucknett, Concise History of the Common Law 570–74 (5th ed. 1956); F. Pollock & F. Maitland, History of English Law 106–117 (2d ed. 1898, reissued 1968). In the absence of a relevant statute, no limit on the length of a leasehold estate exists. Courts have upheld terms as long as 2,000 years or of 99 years renewable forever. In such cases, the tenant, as a practical matter, has the equivalent of a fee simple estate, except for the added obligation to pay rent, if any. See 1 Am. L. Prop., supra note 11, at § 3.15.

[334] In medieval times, charging any interest on a loan was considered to be usury.

[335] It has sometimes been asserted that the refusal to treat the term of years as a freehold estate was a result of its unsavory reputation as a stratagem to evade the prohibition against usury.

[336] 1 Am. L. Prop., supra note 11, at § 3.1 nn.3–5 and authorities cited.

recover the leased land in the action of trespass *de ejectione firmae*, later called ejectment.[337]

The ejectment action was obviously superior to the real actions available to the tenant of a freehold estate, which soon led freeholders to seek and obtain the right to use ejectment in lieu of the real actions.[338] But the interest of the tenant for years had already been classified as personal, rather than real, property in the fourteenth century.[339] Because the term of years was clearly an interest in land and a tenure relationship existed between the landlord and tenant, the eventual solution was to call the interest of the tenant for years a "chattel real," thus recognizing its anomalous nature.

The term of years, subject to payment of an annual rent, filled a fundamental need for a tenant to obtain the possession and use of land for a fixed period for agriculture, trade, or residence without the capital outlay required to purchase a freehold estate. Although land could be leased to a tenant for life at an annual rent, the term of years had obvious advantages over a life estate from the tenant's viewpoint: (1) It had a definite duration, which could be fixed by the parties' agreement; (2) It could commence in the future, unlike a freehold estate before 1536;[340] (3) Because it was personal property, rather than real, it could be transferred by will, unlike a freehold estate before 1540;[341] (4) It would pass intestate when the tenant died according to the more rational rules governing succession to personal property, rather than the canons of descent applicable to real property;[342] and (5) Before enactment of the Statute of Frauds in 1677, it could be created by a parol agreement followed by the tenant's entry into possession, without either livery of seisin or a written deed of conveyance.[343] The last advantage was, of course, substantially eliminated by the Statute of Frauds,[344] which provided that parol leases, except those "not exceeding the term of three years from the making thereof," created only an estate at will.

The term of years, despite its anomalous classification as a chattel real, has the essential characteristics of an estate in land. The tenant for years has the exclusive right of possession during the term. Like the freehold estates, a term of years may be defeasible by means of an express power of termination (right of entry for breach of condition), special limitation, or executory limitation. And a term of years is freely transferable, except to the extent that transfer is expressly subjected to a forfeiture or promissory restraint.

---

[337] Id. at note 6 and authorities cited.

[338] See infra § 1.2 for development of the ejectment action as an all-purpose remedy for persons wrongfully dispossessed.

[339] It is often said that this resulted from the fact that trespass, and its offspring, ejectment, were classified as "personal actions." 1 Am. L. Prop., supra note 11, at § 3.1 n.10 suggests, however, that it was more a result of the fact that leases creating a term of years were frequently used as security for loans.

[340] See supra § 2.8 note 164 as to the reason for the rule prohibiting creation of freehold estates to commence *in futuro*. Enactment of the Statute of Uses in 1535 abrogated this rule.

[341] The Statute of Wills 1540, 32 Hen. 8 c. 1 (Eng. & Wales) authorized devises of freehold estates by will.

[342] 1 Am. L. Prop., supra note 11, at § 3.1, at 177.

[343] Id.

[344] Statute of Frauds 1677, 29 Car. 2 c. 3 (Eng. & Wales). American versions of the Statute of Frauds generally contain similar provisions. See infra § 6.15.

The term of years (or estate for years) is not the only nonfreehold estate recognized in Anglo-American law. Writing near the end of the fifteenth century, Littleton stated that a tenancy at will would arise whenever person, with the consent of the freehold tenant, occupied land as a tenant under an express or implied agreement that either party could terminate the tenancy at will.[345]

An additional type of nonfreehold estate was recognized in the sixteenth century— the tenancy from year to year, which continued indefinitely unless terminated by proper notice from one party to the other.[346] This became a common form of agricultural tenancy because it had substantial advantages over a tenancy at will for both the landlord and tenant. It entitled the landlord to the agreed rent for at least one year, and it assured to the tenant the right of possession and use of the land for at least one year.[347]

Other periodic tenancies were later recognized, such as tenancies from quarter to quarter, from month to month, and from week to week.[348] The distinguishing feature of these periodic tenancies is that, like a tenancy from year to year, they continue indefinitely unless terminated by proper notice as of the end of some period. Like tenancies for years, tenancies at will and periodic tenancies of all types are now considered to be nonfreehold estates in land, although they are also chattels real.

Many writers also recognize a nonfreehold estate called a tenancy at sufferance. But the so-called tenancy at sufferance is really not an estate. It is simply a term used to describe the status of a tenant who has wrongfully held over after the end of the leasehold estate. The possessory rights of the so-called tenant at sufferance, as against any person other than the landowner, are no greater than the rights of any other wrongful possessor of land. As against the landowner, the tenant at sufferance has no right to possession. But the owner may elect to treat the tenant at sufferance as being bound to a further lease term.[349]

The tenant of any nonfreehold estate has, in general, the same right to exclusive possession and the same privileges of use as a life tenant. The rights and duties of landlords and tenants of nonfreehold estates are largely governed by the express covenants in the lease. Other duties peculiar to landlords and tenants of nonfreehold estates are imposed by law, often in the form of implied covenants. The law that imposes these duties may be either judicially or legislatively created. Whatever their source, the duties of landlords and tenants of nonfreehold estates usually include both affirmative and negative obligations.

The characteristics of the nonfreehold estates and the legal obligations of landlords and tenants will be considered in some detail in Chapter 6 of this book.

§§ 2.18–3.0 ARE RESERVED FOR SUPPLEMENTAL MATERIAL.

---

[345] See infra §§ 6.18–19. For a more detailed discussion, see 1 Am. L. Prop., supra note 11, at §§ 3.28– 31.

[346] See infra §§ 6.16–17. For a more detailed discussion, see 1 Am. L. Prop., supra note 11, at §§ 3.23– 27.

[347] In addition, neither the landlord nor the tenant could terminate a tenancy from year to year except by giving notice at least six months before the end of a yearly period. Thus, both parties had ample time to arrange for a new tenancy if they desired.

[348] See infra §§ 6.16–17. For a more detailed discussion, see 1 Am. L. Prop., supra note 11, at §§ 3.23– 27.

[349] See infra §§ 6.17, 6.20.

Chapter 3

FUTURE ESTATES IN REALTY AND PERSONALTY

Table of Sections

A. GENERAL INTRODUCTION

§ 3.1 FUTURE INTERESTS IN REALTY AND PERSONALTY—IN GENERAL

A future interest is a nonpossessory interest that may become possessory at some time in the future. Future interests are presently existing, legally protected property interests. As applied to such interests, the adjective "future" refers to only one component of property, the right to possess, and does not mean that the future interest will come into existence only at some future time.[1]

When the owner of a possessory estate in land transfers the entire estate without providing for defeasance of the estate on the happening of a stated event, no future interest is created.[2] But the owner of a possessory estate in land may create one or more future interests (1) by transferring less than the owner's entire estate,[3] (2) by dividing the estate into two or more smaller estates and transferring each of them to different people,[4] or (3) by transferring the entire estate subject to defeasance on the happening of a stated event.[5] In the first case, the grantor retains a future interest. In the second case, the transferees of all but the first of the smaller estates receive future interests. In the third case, a future interest is either retained by the transferor or transferred to some third party; this interest will become possessory on defeasance of the possessory estate transferred to the first taker.

As the preceding discussion suggests, two principal kinds of future interests exist— reversionary future interests held by the transferor and nonreversionary future interests transferred to someone other than the transferor. A future interest retained by the transferor is either a reversion,[6] possibility of reverter,[7] or right of entry (also called a power of termination).[8] A future interest that is transferred at the time of its creation to a third party is either a remainder or an executory interests. Different types of

---

[1] "A future interest is an ownership interest in property that does not currently entitle the owner to possession or enjoyment of the property. The owner's right to possession or enjoyment is postponed until sometime in the future and may be contingent or vested." Restatement (Third) of Prop.: Wills and Other Donative Transfers § 25.1 (2011) (hereinafter Third Restatement of Property). See generally 3 R. Powell, Powell on Real Property § 20.01 (2018); L. Simes & A. Smith, 1 The Law of Future Interests § 1 (3d ed. 2018); 1 American Law of Property § 4.1 (1952–54) (hereinafter Am. L. Prop.).

[2] If the transferred estate is less than a fee simple, such as a life estate or estate for years, a future interest comprising the balance of the fee simple will be vested in some person or persons.

[3] For example, the fee simple owner, O, may transfer Blackacre "to A for life." By operation of law, O will retain a future interest in fee simple called a "reversion."

[4] For example, the fee simple owner, O, may transfer Blackacre "to A for life, remainder to B." This will give B a future interest in fee simple absolute called a "remainder."

[5] For example, the fee simple owner, O, may transfer Blackacre "to A, but if A should die without issue surviving him, then to B." B has a future interest called an "executory interest" or "executory limitation."

[6] See supra note 3.

[7] As we have previously seen, O, a fee simple absolute owner, retains a possibility of reverter when she transfers Blackacre "to B so long as the land is not used for other than residential purposes." See supra § 2.4.

[8] As we have previously seen, O, a fee simple absolute owner, retains a right of entry when she transfers Blackacre "to B, but if the land shall ever be used for other than residential purposes, O or her heirs may re-enter and repossess the land." See supra § 2.5.

remainders and executory interests can be created, as will be described later in this chapter.[9]

The doctrine of estates, including future interests, developed as part of the English land law. But the panoply of future interests developed by the common law courts, with some assistance from Parliament, was adopted with modifications by the English Chancellors for application to equitable interests in land.[10] Later, the scheme of future interests, legal and equitable, was applied to certain forms of personal property, such as intangible property and nonconsumable chattels.[11]

When the law of future interests was developing in England, its major purpose was to enable the creation of inter vivos or testamentary arrangements to provide for members of the owner's family in succeeding generations, which was important to members of the English landed gentry and aristocracy.[12] Today, such inter vivos and testamentary family settlements are still the principal setting in which future interests in real and personal property, legal or equitable, are to be found. In addition, future interests are often employed to effect charitable gifts. For example, an owner may transfer property to a charitable organization after the owner or the owner's spouse or other relative has enjoyed the income for life.

In all the hypothetical examples employed in the following sections of this book, assume that the transferor, O, owned the property in fee simple absolute, unless the contrary is expressly stated. Also, the book will use the generic term "transfer," rather than "conveyance" (inter vivos transfer) or "devise" (testamentary transfer), unless it makes a difference in a particular case. Words of inheritance (i.e., "to A *and her heirs*") that were formerly necessary to create an estate in fee have generally been omitted, because they are no longer necessary in virtually any state.

§ 3.2   VESTED AND NONVESTED FUTURE INTERESTS

In determining what future interests are created when a present estate in fee simple absolute is fragmented into smaller estates or made subject to defeasance, the fundamental rule is that the entire fee simple absolute must always be vested, in possession and in interest, in some identifiable group of persons. That is, the various present and vested future interests resulting from a particular transfer must add up to a fee simple absolute. A transfer also may create nonvested future interests that are not considered when accounting for the fee simple absolute.

In view of the fundamental rule stated in the preceding paragraph, distinguishing between vested and nonvested future interests is essential. A future interest is vested if it is transferred to a living person who is identifiable and ready to take possession of the land immediately on the natural expiration of all prior estates. To be vested, no express or implied condition precedent to the future interest's becoming possessory can exist,

---

[9]   See supra notes 4–5.

[10]   Even before enactment of the Statute of Uses in 1535, the Chancellor recognized and protected equitable future interests ("uses").

[11]   In the United States, future interests may be created in personal property. See Third Restatement of Property, supra note 1, at 25.1 cmt. c, indicating that all varieties of future interests may be created in personal property. See, e.g., Johnson v. Swann, 211 Md. 207, 126 A.2d 603 (1956); Woodard v. Clark, 236 N.C. 190, 72 S.E.2d 433 (1952).

[12]   On the family (or marriage) settlement in England, see G. R. Y. Radcliffe, Real Property Law ch. XIV (2d ed. 1938); 7 W. S. Holdsworth, History of English Law 376 (1938).

other than the natural expiration of all prior estates.[13] A future interest is nonvested if it is created in favor of an unborn or otherwise unidentifiable person or if it cannot become possessory before a condition precedent occurs, other than the natural expiration of all prior estates.[14]

The only future interests that can be vested are reversions and remainders. Reversions are always vested.[15] Remainders may be either vested or nonvested.[16] Possibilities of reverter, rights of entry, and executory interests are never vested.[17] Possibilities of reverter, rights of entry, and nonvested remainders are always contingent, because it is uncertain when they are created whether they will satisfy the conditions precedent to become a possessory estate or a vested future interest.[18] Most executory interests also are contingent, but they can be noncontingent, such as when they are given to a living, identifiable person, subject to a condition precedent, such as a lapse of time, that is certain to occur (O conveys "to A for life, then to B one year after A's death").[19]

Future interests in personalty are generally subject to the same classification system as future interests in realty. They are either vested or nonvested, and the present interests and vested future interests must add up to the equivalent of a fee simple absolute. As is the case with future interests in realty, almost all nonvested future interests in personalty are contingent. Reversions are always vested, and possibilities of reverter and rights of entry are always contingent. Remainders may be vested or contingent, and executory interests are always nonvested, though sometimes not contingent.

The distinction between vested and nonvested future interests in land was once extremely important because legal contingent remainders (as distinguished from equitable contingent remainders) were "destructible" in various ways.[20] Moreover, nonvested interests were, at one time, generally held to be inalienable.[21] The destructibility rule has now been almost entirely eliminated and, with minor exceptions,

---

[13] "Vested remainders (or remainders executed, whereby a present interest passes to the party, though to be enjoyed *in futuro*) are where the estate is invariably fixed, to remain to a determinate person, after the particular estate is spent." A contingent interest, on the other hand, involved uncertainty. There was a condition precedent to the taking effect, or the person to take was unascertained. 1 Simes & Smith, supra note 1, at § 65.

If we accept the definition of "vested" set out in the text, the executory interest following a fee simple determinable would be vested if it is certain to become a possessory fee simple, though the date when it will become possessory is uncertain. See Williams v. Watt, 668 P.2d 620 (Wyo. 1983) (Thomas, J., concurring). However, the *Williams* court held that the future interest in that case is a vested remainder in fee simple, rather than an executory interest, because the latter interest is always deemed to be contingent and subject to the Rule Against Perpetuities.

[14] Being born or being ascertained is, of course, a kind of implied condition precedent. The condition precedent need not be one that is uncertain to be satisfied.

[15] Simes & Smith, supra note 1, at § 82.

[16] When remainders are vested, they may be indefeasibly vested, vested subject to complete defeasance, or vested subject to open (i.e., subject to partial defeasance). When remainders is nonvested, it is always contingent. Id. at ch. 5.

[17] Id. § 64.

[18] Id. §§ 65, 281 (possibility of reverter).

[19] See id. § 221; infra §§ 3.11–.12.

[20] See infra § 3.10.

[21] See infra §§ 3.23–.24.

nonvested future interests are alienable if they are held by a living person.[22] But determining whether a future interest is vested or nonvested is still necessary to determine whether it is subject to the Rule Against Perpetuities.[23] In addition, lawyers and courts so commonly use the terms "vested," "nonvested," and "contingent" that understanding their meaning is essential, especially for those who practice estate and trust law.

As with the present interests,[24] the Third Restatement of Property simplifies the classification of future interests. Any future interest retained by the transferor is a reversion. Any future interest created in a transferee is a remainder.[25] Reversions and remainders can be either vested (vested reversion and vested remainder) or contingent (contingent reversion and contingent remainder).[26] The Third Restatement also recognizes vested and contingent remainders subject to open.[27] Though the Restatement classification system provides much needed simplification to a complex system of future interests, no court has adopted it.[28] Therefore, this book will focus on the currently recognized future interests. It also cites the First Restatement of Property, because it restates the accepted common law.

B.   REVERSIONARY FUTURE INTERESTS

§ 3.3   REVERSION

A reversion is the future interest left in a transferor when she transferred less than her entire estate.[29] For example, if O owned the fee simple absolute and transferred "to A for life, then to B for life," O retained a reversion because the two life estates do not add up to a fee simple absolute. For the same reason, if O transfers "to A for ten years, then to B for ten years," O retains a reversion in fee simple absolute.[30] And in jurisdictions where a fee tail may still be created, a transfer by O to A in fee tail, with a remainder to B in fee tail, would leave O with a reversion in fee simple absolute.

---

[22]   Id.

[23]   See infra §§ 3.17–.18.

[24]   See § 2.3, text accompanying notes 69–70.

[25]   Third Restatement of Property, supra note 1, at § 25.2.

[26]   Id. § 25.3. An indefeasibly vested remainder is a vested remainder under the Third Restatement, whereas a remainder vested subject to defeasance and a contingent remainder are both contingent remainders. L Waggoner, What's in the Third and Final Volume of the New Restatement of Property That Estate Planners Should Know About, 38 ACTEC L.J. 23, 30–31 (2012).

[27]   Id. § 25.4.

[28]   "[S]ome ideas propounded in the Restatements have no prospect of ever becoming law. For instance, the Restatement (Third) of Property offers up major revisions of the law of future interests. To my mind, these revisions would make a great deal of sense, yet they could never realistically dislodge the formulations that have remained entrenched in Anglo-American law for centuries on end." A. Hirsch, Teaching Wills and Trusts: The Jurisdictional Problem, 58 St. Louis U. L.J. 681, 684–85 (2014).

[29]   As to reversions generally, see Simes & Smith, supra note 1, at ch. 3; 1 Am. L. Prop., supra note 1, at §§ 4.16–24. For purposes of applying this basic rule, all fee simple estates are regarded as having the same quantum. Therefore, the owner of a possessory fee simple absolute does not retain a reversion after transferring a fee simple determinable, a fee simple subject to a condition subsequent, a fee simple subject to an executory limitation, or a fee simple conditional (where such an estate is recognized), because the estate transferred is not "smaller" than the original estate of the transferor. However, the grantor may retain a possibility of reverter or right of entry.

[30]   Technically, the owner of a freehold estate who leases it retains the fee title subject to the lease, rather than a reversion. However, today the lessor normally is treated as holding a reversion.

Because a reversion arises from a transferor's failure to transfer her entire estate, the transferor need not expressly reserve a reversion. Indeed, a reversion may arise when the transferor's express intent is to transfer the entire estate, but part of the attempted transfer is void. For example, if O's will devises land "to A for life, remainder to B" and B predeceases O, the devise to B lapses and is void if an anti-lapse statute does not apply and O retains a reversion in fee simple absolute.[31]

Therefore, a reversion in fee simple may arise when a transferor creates several successive life estates, several successive estates for years, or (where fee tail estates may still be created), several successive fee tail estates, without expressly transferring the residue of the fee simple.[32] When all the prior estates have expired, the person who then owns the reversion will be entitled to possession as a matter of law. The reversioner's right to possession accrues automatically, without the necessity of making an entry, bringing an action for possession, or giving notice of termination.[33]

In all the examples given above, O's reversion is indefeasibly vested, and O is certain to be entitled to possession at a future time. But a reversion may be vested subject to complete defeasance if, for example, the deed or will creates a possessory life estate followed by a contingent remainder, an executory interest, or a power of appointment. Therefore, O retains a reversion subject to complete defeasance if he transfers land "to A for life, remainder to B's surviving children," "to A for life, and then to B one day after A's death if B survives A," or "to A for life, remainder to such of A's children as A shall appoint."[34]

If O did not have a fee simple absolute before the transfer but, instead, had a defeasible fee, any reversion retained by O after the transfer will be subject to the same possibility of defeasance as O's original possessory estate. Dividing O's possessory estate into two or more estates will not eliminate the special limitation, condition subsequent, or executory limitation to which that possessory estate was originally subject.

Even if a transferor had only a life estate or a fee tail estate before the transfer, transferring less than the entire estate creates a reversion.[35] For example, if O has a fee tail and transfers "to A for life, then to B for life," O retains a reversion in fee tail. If O has only a life estate and transfers "to A for ten years, then to B for ten years," O retains a reversion for life because any estate for years, however long its duration, is deemed to be smaller than a life estate. O's interest is a reversion though O may die before the successive estates for years terminate so that O's reversion never becomes possessory.[36] If O has only an estate for years to begin with, a sublease for a shorter term also leaves O with a reversion.

[31] Simes & Smith, supra note 1, at § 87; 1 Am. L. Prop., supra note 1, at § 4.18.

[32] See examples in text supra § 3.1.

[33] This characteristic is shared with the possibility of reverter and the executory interest. It should be contrasted with the right of entry.

[34] Simes & Smith, supra note 1, at §§ 85, 86, 90; see, e.g., St. George v. Fulton Tr. Co., 273 App. Div. 516, 78 N.Y.S.2d 298 (1948); Whitten v. Whitten, 203 Okla. 196, 219 P.2d 228 (1950); McCready v. Lyon, 167 Va. 103, 187 S.E. 442 (1936).

[35] This is simply another application of the general rule that a transferor retains a reversion if he does not transfer his entire estate.

[36] O has a reversion though the term of years is for longer than the possible life of any human being. See Earl of Derby v. Taylor (1801) 102 Eng. Rep. 193–95; Simes & Smith, supra note 1, at § 89; 1 Am. L. Prop., supra note 1, at § 4.18.

§ 3.4   POSSIBILITY OF REVERTER

A possibility of reverter is the future interest that follows a fee simple determinable, life estate determinable, or any other determinable estate.[37] A possibility of reverter most often is created when a fee simple absolute owner transfers a fee simple determinable and retains the entire future interest following it.[38] However, a possibility of reverter can also be created when a fee simple determinable is followed by an executory interest that does not exhaust the factual possibilities[39] or by a void executory interest.[40] Moreover, if the owner of a life estate transfers it subject to a special limitation, she retains a possibility of reverter for the balance of her life. If a tenant for years transfers the entire leasehold estate subject to a special limitation, he retains a possibility of reverter for the balance of the lease term.

Suppose that the owner of a possessory estate transfers a smaller estate subject to a special limitation. For example, assume that the owner of a fee simple absolute estate, O, transfers land "to A for life, so long as the land is used only for residential purposes." Clearly, A receives a life estate determinable, and O retains a reversion in fee simple absolute. Does O also retain a possibility of reverter? The prevailing view is that he does not because, by definition, the future interest retained by a transferor is a reversion when the quantum of all present and vested future interests expressly created by a transfer, when added together, is less than the quantum of the transferor's original estate.[41] But even if we do not call the transferor's interest a possibility of reverter, O clearly will have the right to possess the fee simple absolute before A dies if the property is used for nonresidential purposes.

Similarly, the future interest retained by a lessor who owns land in fee simple or for life is simply called a reversion when the lessor leases it for a term of years subject to a special limitation, though the lessor may become entitled to possession before the lease term expires.

Although a deed or will often contains an express provision for reverter to the transferor if and when the designated terminating event occurs, the possibility of reverter arises by operation of law whenever the transferee receives a determinable estate.[42] If the transfer is by deed, the grantor retains the possibility of reverter. If the transfer is by will and the will does not dispose of the testator's residual interest, the

---

[37]   This book treats the possibility of reverter as a reversionary interest. First Restatement of Property § 154(3) (Am. L. Inst. 1936) (hereinafter First Restatement of Property).

[38]   For example, O, the owner of Blackacre, transfers it "to A so long as the land is used only for residential purposes." See Emrick v. Bethlehem Twp., 506 Pa. 372, 378, 485 A.2d 736, 739 (1984).

[39]   For example, O, the owner of Blackacre, transfers it "to A so long as it is used only for residential purposes, but if it shall be used for nonresidential purposes during A's lifetime, then to B." B's executory interest is valid, but it will fail if Blackacre is used only for residential purposes during A's lifetime, and O will retain a possibility of reverter that may become a possessory fee simple absolute if Blackacre is used for nonresidential purposes after A's death. See generally 1 Am. L. Prop., supra note 1, at § 4.14; First Restatement of Property, supra note 37, at § 23, cmt. e.

[40]   For example, if O purports to transfer Blackacre "to A so long as the land is used only for residential purposes, and if the land is ever used for nonresidential purposes, then to B," the executory interest limited in favor of B is void under the Rule Against Perpetuities, and O therefore retains a possibility of reverter, which is not subject to the Rule. In support of this proposition See, e.g., Inst. for Sav. v. Roxbury Home for Aged Women, 244 Mass. 583, 139 N.E. 301 (1923); Leonard v. Burr, 18 N.Y. 96 (1858).

[41]   See supra § 3.3.

[42]   E.g., Elmore v. Austin, 232 N.C. 13, 59 S.E.2d 205 (1950).

testator's heirs receive a possibility of reverter by intestate succession. But if the transfer is by will and the will also disposes of the testator's residual interest either by specific devise or by residuary devise, the devisee of the residual interest receives an executory interest, rather than a possibility of reverter.[43]

Because possibilities of reverter are not subject to the common law Rule Against Perpetuities, they can last potentially forever. The event upon which they are to become possessory may be uncertain to occur and may occur at any time in the future, however remote.[44] Therefore, some states statutorily limit how long a possibility of reverter can continue. This type of legislation extinguishes a possibility of reverter and makes the possessory fee simple estate indefeasible when the statutorily prescribed maximum period has expired.[45] Another type of statute provides that special limitations and conditions subsequent are unenforceable if they are no longer of any substantial benefit to the persons otherwise entitled to enforce them. Under this type of statute, a court can extinguish a possibility of reverter if it determines that the special limitation has become "merely nominal,"[46] which normally occurs when changed conditions make it difficult or impossible to achieve the original purpose for the special limitation. For example, if land was transferred "to A for so long as the land is used only for residential purposes," but the area surrounding the land subsequently became used solely for commercial or industrial uses.

§ 3.5   RIGHT OF ENTRY

When an inter vivos conveyance of land is subject to a stated condition subsequent, the English common law courts held that the grantor retained a right of entry for breach of that condition, though the conveyance did not contain an express provision for reentry.[47] In the United States, an express right of entry normally is not essential,[48] but it is good drafting practice to include one, because American courts are prone to hold

---

[43] This is true because a will only operates once, immediately upon the testator's death. It does not operate once to create a fee simple determinable and then a second time to dispose of the testator's residual interest. Cf. Brown v. Indep. Baptist Church of Woburn, 325 Mass. 645, 91 N.E.2d 922 (1950), holding that, where a specific executory devise was void under the Rule Against Perpetuities, a residuary devise to the same beneficiaries was valid because it transferred a possibility of reverter, rather than an executory interest! For telling criticism of the *Brown* decision, see L. Simes, Is the Rule Against Perpetuities Doomed?, 52 Mich. L. Rev. 179 n.4 (1953) ("Of course, under orthodox doctrines, the residuary clause created a void executory interest as well as the prior gift over. For it was created by the same instrument by which the determinable fee was created. The testatrix did not first create a determinable fee and then devise it, for she did not die twice."). Cf. W. B. Leach, Perpetuities in Perspective: Ending the Reign of Terror, 65 Harv. L. Rev. 720, 743.

[44] See infra § 3.18 text accompanying notes 273–274. It has often been said that possibilities of reverter are not subject to the Rule against Perpetuities because they are vested, but this is obviously not true. See First Restatement of Property, supra note 37, at § 154(3); see also Simes & Smith, supra note 1, at § 1239 ("[I]n substance a possibility of reverter is essentially a contingent interest [rather than a vested one]."); Leach, supra note 43, at 740–41.

[45] E.g., Fla. Stat. Ann. § 689.18 (West 2018) (21 years; thereafter, use restrictions can be enforced only as covenants or equitable servitudes); Conn. Gen. Stat. Ann. § 45a–505 (West 2018) (30 years unless contingency is certain to be resolved within the period allowed by the Rule Against Perpetuities); Me. Rev. Stat. Ann. tit. 33, § 103 (same); 765 Ill. Comp. Stat. Ann. 330/4 (West 2018) (40 years). A "marketable record title act" may also have the effect of cutting off a possibility of reverter. See Walton v. City of Red Bluff, 2 Cal. App. 4th 117, 3 Cal. Rptr. 2d 275 (Cal. Ct. App. 1991).

[46] E.g., Mich. Comp. Laws Ann. § 544.46 (West 2018).

[47] Supra § 2.5, at note 99.

[48] Simes & Smith, supra note 1, at 278–79.

that words of condition, standing alone, create a real covenant, equitable servitude, easement, charge, or trust, rather than a condition subsequent.[49]

Although the English common law term for the grantor's future interest following an estate in land subject to a condition subsequent is "right of entry for breach of condition," actual entry is unnecessary. Instead, an ejectment action is an appropriate method of electing to terminate the possessory estate.[50] Therefore, the future interest following an estate subject to complete defeasance is also called a "power of termination." This term is more appropriate than "right of entry" when referring to a transfer of personalty subject to a condition subsequent.[51]

A right of entry can be created by transferring a fee simple, life estate, or leasehold estate subject to a condition subsequent.[52] Leases typically contain a number of covenants that bind the lessee and expressly provide that the lessor may "reenter," "terminate the lease," or "forfeit the lease" if the tenant breaches them.[53] These phrases and equivalent language creates a right of entry in the lessor. When the owner of land in fee simple creates a life estate or a leasehold estate subject to a condition subsequent, the common law rule is that the grantor retains both a reversion and a right of entry for breach of the condition.

Like possibilities of reverter, rights of entry are not subject to the common law Rule Against Perpetuities.[54] But, like possibilities of reverter, some states statutorily limit their duration,[55] and other states statutorily provide for their termination when the conditions upon which they are limited become merely nominal and are no longer of any substantial benefit to the persons otherwise entitled to enforce them.[56]

---

[49]   Supra § 2.5 at notes 100–105.

[50]   E.g., McElvain v. Dorris, 298 Ill. 377, 131 N.E. 608 (1921); Trs. of Union College v. City of N.Y., 173 N.Y. 38, 65 N.E. 853, 93 Am. St. Rp. 569 (1903). Even a suit to quiet title may be sufficient. See Ross v. Sanderson, 63 Okla. 73, 162 P. 709, L.R.A.1917C 879 (1917).

[51]   The term "entry" is obviously inapplicable to personalty. It is also inapplicable to equitable estates in land subject to a trust except, unless the trust beneficiary has possession of the land.

[52]   Supra §§ 2.5, 2.11, 2.17.

[53]   Supra § 2.17.

[54]   See infra § 3.21. Exempting rights of entry from the Rule Against Perpetuities is, if anything, less justified than exempting possibilities of reverter, because rights of entry are even more contingent. See supra § 3.4, note 44.

[55]   See supra § 3.4, at note 45, for examples of such statutes, which apply both to possibilities of reverter and to rights of entry. California has an unusual statute, Cal. Civ. Code § 885.020 (West 2018), that converts all possibilities of reverter into rights of entry. See Walton v. City of Red Bluff, 2 Cal. App. 4th 117, 3 Cal. Rptr. 2d 275 (Cal. Ct. App. 1991), applying the statute and then cutting off the resulting right of entry.

[56]   E.g., Mich. Comp. Laws Ann. § 544.46 (West 2018) (applicable to both possibilities of reverter and rights of entry).

C. NONREVERSIONARY FUTURE INTERESTS

§ 3.6   NONREVERSIONARY FUTURE INTERESTS— REMAINDERS AND EXECUTORY INTERESTS

Future interests created in favor of someone other than the transferor are classified as nonreversionary. The two categories of nonreversionary interests are remainders[57] and executory interests.[58]

A non-reversionary interest is a remainder if (a) it is created simultaneously with a present estate smaller than a fee simple—the "particular estate"; and (b) it is possible for the future interest to become a present estate as soon as all the prior interests created by the transfer have expired naturally. The requirement that a particular estate and all remainders dependent on it must be created simultaneously is satisfied if they are created by the same deed or will, by two deeds delivered simultaneously, or by a will and a codicil thereto.[59] A remainder does not become possessory until all preceding interests created at the same time terminate, and it may not become possessory as a result of defeasance of (divesting) a preceding interest.[60]

B's interest in all the following examples is a remainder:

(1)   "To A for life, then to B" (or "remainder to B");

(2)   "To A for life, then to B for life" (or "remainder to B for life");

(3)   "To A for life, then to B for life, then to C" (or "remainder to B for life, remainder to C").[61]

In contrast, an executory interest (a) need not be created simultaneously with a present estate, though it often is, and (b) as a general rule, becomes either a present or a vested future interest by divesting another's present estate or a vested remainder.[62] B has an executory interest in the following examples:

(4)   "To A, but if A dies without children surviving him, then to B";[63]

---

[57]   The term "remainder" is said to be derived from the Latin word "remanere," signifying that the land was to "remain out," instead of "coming back," to the transferor as occurs when a reversion becomes a possessory estate. 2 Pollock & Maitland, History of English Law 21 (2d ed. 1911).

[58]   The term "executory interest" refers to the effect of the Statute of Uses (1535) in converting ("executing") equitable estates ("uses") into legal estates. See supra § 2.8, at notes 164–166.

[59]   The will and the codicil both would become legally operative on the testator's death.

[60]   Compare the definition in First Restatement of Property, supra note 37, at § 156.

[61]   As the examples in the text indicate, use of the word "remainder" is unnecessary to create a remainder, although it is common practice to do so. On the other hand, interests named "remainders" in a deed or will may, in fact, be executory interests.

[62]   "Thus we may lay it down as a fundamental characteristic of the executory interest that it vests in derogation of a vested estate of freehold, and not at the termination of such estate. To this rule there is one exception, that of the executory interest after the determinable fee or the fee simple conditional." Simes & Smith, supra note 1, at § 228 (footnote omitted).

[63]   In example (4), A's death without surviving children is a condition subsequent to A's present fee simple and a condition precedent to B's executory interest. If the condition occurs, the present fee simple estate "shifts" from A to B. Therefore, B's interest is called a "shifting" executory interest.

(5)   "To B, from and after B's marriage to A";[64]

(6)   "To A for life, then to B one year after A's death."[65]

In each example, all the language following the initial language of gift to A or B is an executory limitation.

The particular estate that precedes a remainder is usually a life estate,[66] but it also can be a fee tail[67] or, under the modern view, an estate for years.[68] The particular estate can be subject to a special limitation that may cause it to terminate before it would normally expire.[69] On the other hand, an executory interest can divest a present fee simple estate created in a transferee as in Example 4, a present fee simple estate retained by the grantor as in Example 5, a reversion in fee simple retained by the grantor as in Example 6, or an estate less than a fee simple.[70] Moreover, for purely historical reasons, any nonreversionary future interest following a fee simple determinable or a fee simple conditional is classified as an executory interest.[71]

To fully describe a future interest, one must state what its duration will be once it becomes possessory. Remainders and executory interests are most often in fee simple,[72] but they can be in fee tail[73] or for life.[74] Strictly speaking, neither remainders nor executory interests in land may be created for a term of years only,[75] but a term of years with the essential characteristics of a remainder or an executory interest can be created.[76]

As subsequent sections of this book will describe in more detail, remainders may be either "vested" or "contingent" (subject to a condition precedent not certain to be

---

[64]   In example (5), the transferor keeps the fee simple unless and until B marries A. B's marriage to A is a condition subsequent to the transferor's fee simple and a condition precedent to B's executory interest, which is called a "springing" executory interest because it "springs out of" the transferor's estate if and when the condition occurs.

[65]   In example (6), the transferor's reversion in fee simple will become a present estate when A dies, but one year later the fee simple will pass to B one year later. B has a "springing" executory interest.

[66]   See examples (1), (2), and (3) in text, supra.

[67]   For example, "to A and the heirs of his body, remainder to B."

[68]   For example, "to A for ten years, remainder to B." In earlier times, B would have a present estate subject to a term of years in A because seisin would pass at once to B. Today, however, B's interest normally would be described as a remainder. See First Restatement of Property, supra note 37, at § 156, illus. 9.

[69]   For example, "to A for life or until remarriage, remainder to B."

[70]   For example, "to A for life, but if A remarries, then to B." This gives A a life estate subject to an executory limitation and gives B a shifting executory interest in fee simple. The transferor may, of course, create both a remainder and an executory interest in B, such as "to A for life, remainder to B, but if A remarries, then immediately to B."

[71]   See supra note 59. Cf. Williams v. Watt, 668 P.2d 620 (Wyo. 1983), distorting this rule to escape application of the Rule Against Perpetuities.

[72]   See examples (1), (3), (4), (5), and (6) supra in text.

[73]   For example, "* * * to A for life, remainder to A and the heirs of his body" (remainder in fee tail); "to A, but if A dies without children him surviving, then to B and the heirs of his body" (executory interest in fee tail).

[74]   For example, "to A for life, remainder to B for life" (remainder for life); "to A, but if A dies without children surviving him, then to B for life" (executory interest for life).

[75]   A term of years, technically, is personal property—a "chattel real"—and the owner of an estate for years cannot have seisin.

[76]   For example, "to A for ten years, then to B for ten years," or "to A for life, then to B for ten years." In both cases, the term of years given to B is similar to a remainder.

fulfilled), and vested remainders are further subdivided into remainders that are "indefeasibly vested," "vested subject to complete defeasance," and "vested subject to open."[77] Executory interests are never deemed to be vested.[78] Usually, they are contingent, but an executory interest may be subject to a condition precedent that is certain to be fulfilled, in which case it is neither vested nor contingent.[79]

No limit exists on the number of remainders that can be simultaneously created, so long as the particular estate and all the vested remainders do not exceed a fee simple absolute.[80] Nor is there a limit on the number of executory interests that may be simultaneously created.

Before enactment of the Statute of Uses in 1535, remainders were the only nonreversionary future interests that English common law courts recognized and protected.[81] However, the Court of Chancery enforced equitable executory interests (then called "uses") during the fifteenth century,[82] and common law courts did so after enactment of the Statute of Uses in 1535.[83] In the United States, executory interests have always been recognized and protected both in equity and at law.[84]

§ 3.7   INDEFEASIBLY VESTED REMAINDER AND VESTED REMAINDER SUBJECT TO COMPLETE DEFEASANCE

An indefeasibly vested remainder is not subject to any express or implied condition precedent or any condition subsequent, special limitation, executory limitation, or power of appointment that may cause the remainder to be completely or partially defeated (prematurely terminated) before it becomes a possessory estate.[85] A remainder that is not subject to a condition precedent[86] but is subject to a condition subsequent, special

---

[77]   See infra §§ 3.8–10.

[78]   "Historically, the concept of 'vestedness' had application only to the future interests evolved by the common law processes as distinguished from the Chancery practice in uses * * * Hence, for historical reasons, executory interests are not thought of as having degrees of 'vestedness,' and the classification of remainders * * * [as to the degree of vestedness] has no exact application to executory interests." First Restatement of Property, supra note 37, at § 158, cmt. b.

[79]   For example, "to A for life, and then to B one year after A's death," in which case B's springing executory interest is certain to become a present estate.

[80]   O might transfer "to A for life, remainder to B for life, remainder to C for life, remainder to D if D shall survive A, B, and C, but if D shall not survive A, B, and C, then to E." In that case, A, B, and C would all have vested remainders for life, while D and E would have alternative contingent remainders in fee simple. Because only vested remainders can be counted as parts of the fee simple absolute, O would retain a reversion in fee simple. Theoretically, there can be any number of alternative contingent remainders in fee simple but only one vested remainder in fee simple.

[81]   Limitational and conditional defeasance provisions in favor of "strangers" (persons other than the transferor and his heirs) were invalid at common law. See examples (4) through (6) supra in text at notes 63–65.

[82]   Supra § 2.8, at note 163.

[83]   Supra § 2.8, at notes 163–164.

[84]   Supra § 2.8, at note 166. Equitable executory interests may still be created when the legal title to property is transferred to a trustee for the benefit of designated beneficiaries.

[85]   Technically, it can be argued that premature termination before the vested remainder becomes a present interest should be termed "divestment," rather than "defeasance," but courts seem to use the terms as synonyms.

[86]   Contingent remainders are discussed in more detail infra §§ 3.9, 3.10, and 3.13. A strong preference exists for construing doubtful language as a vested, rather than a contingent, remainder. McGill v. Johnson, 799 S.W.2d 673 (Tex. 1990).

limitation, executory limitation, or power of appointment that may cause the remainder to be completely defeated is a vested remainder subject to complete defeasance.

In the following examples, the future interests are all indefeasibly vested remainders:[87]

(1) "To A for life, remainder to B";

(2) "To A for life, remainder to B for life, remainder to C";

(3) "To A for twenty-five years, remainder to B."

In earlier times, B's interest in the third example would have been classified as a fee simple subject to a term of years if created in land, but it is today generally classified as a remainder.[88]

In the following examples, B's interest is a vested remainder subject to complete defeasance:[89]

(4) "To A for life, remainder to B, but if the land shall ever be put to nonresidential use, the grantor or his heirs may reenter and terminate the interests hereby created";

(5) "To A for life, remainder to B, so long as the land shall be put to residential use only";

(6) "To A for life, remainder to B, but if B predeceases A, then to C";

(7) "To A for life, remainder as A shall appoint, and in default of appointment to B."

In examples (4) through (6), the remainders are vested subject to complete defeasance by a condition subsequent, a special limitation, and an executory limitation, respectively. In example (7), the strong constructional preference for vested interests causes courts to hold that B's remainder, though apparently subject to a condition precedent, is vested subject to complete defeasance by A's exercise of the power of appointment.[90]

The First Restatement of Property asserts that a vested remainder should be classified as subject to complete defeasance if it can terminate before all the prior estates have terminated even if the future interest is not subject to an express condition or limitation. It states that a conveyance "to B for life, remainder to C for life" transfers a remainder vested subject to complete defeasance, because C may predecease B.[91] If this assertion is logically applied, only a remainder in fee simple absolute should be classified as indefeasibly vested.[92] Vested remainders for life or in fee tail would be vested subject

---

[87] In each of these cases, the transfer exhausts the transferor's property interest, because the present and vested future interests created by the transfer add up to a fee simple absolute.

[88] See discussion in Simes & Smith, supra note 1, at 16; see also First Restatement of Property, supra note 37, at § 156, illus. 9.

[89] The comment supra note 87 is equally applicable here.

[90] See Simes & Smith, supra note 1, at § 150.

[91] First Restatement of Property, supra note 37, at § 157, cmt. p, illus. 11. Accord id. § 157, cmt. f; Simes & Smith, supra note 1, at § 113.

[92] Under the First Restatement of Property's test, even a remainder in fee simple absolute could not be indefeasibly vested unless the state, taking by escheat on the owner's death intestate, is considered to take as ultimate heir of the decedent, because the owner of a remainder in fee simple may die intestate and without any common law heirs or next of kin before termination of all prior interests created by the same instrument.

to complete defeasance because they may expire before all prior interests created by the transfer terminate. Yet the First Restatement further asserts that a remainder in fee tail may be indefeasibly vested because "[t]he element of uncertainty, present because * * * the remainderman and his issue may become extinct before the preceding interests end, is nullified" by the remainderman's power to make a disentailing conveyance in fee simple absolute.[93] However, a remainderman in fee tail does not has the power to make a disentailing conveyance in every state that still recognizes the fee tail. In the states that do not allow disentailing, vested remainders in fee tail would always be subject to complete defeasance under the rule laid down in the First Restatement.[94]

Whether vested remainders for life or in fee tail are classified as indefeasibly vested or vested subject to complete defeasance is not really of great importance.[95] However, a remainder cannot be indefeasibly vested unless it is created in favor of a specific person or a specific group of persons that cannot increase in number. If a vested remainder is created in favor of a group of persons that can increase, the remainder interest of any existing member of the group is subject to partial defeasance in favor of future members of the group. In such case, the remainder is "vested subject to open."[96]

In modern times, remainders vested subject to conditions subsequent or to special limitations are still used on occasion in connection with gifts in remainder to religious, charitable, and educational institutions. On the other hand, remainders vested subject to executory limitations or to powers of appointment are frequently used to control the transmission of family wealth from generation to generation.

Indefeasibly vested remainders and remainders vested subject to complete defeasance are freely alienable by deed[97] or by will,[98] and they can pass to heirs or next-of-kin of the remainder holder by intestate succession.[99] Because these vested remainders are alienable by deed, they are subject to seizure and sale to satisfy creditors' claims.[100] But a remainder vested subject to complete defeasance retains its character as a defeasible estate no matter how often it is transferred by deed, will, or intestate succession or by sale for the satisfaction of creditors' claims.

§ 3.8 REMAINDER VESTED SUBJECT TO OPEN

A remainder is classified as vested subject to open (or subject to partial defeasance) when it is created in favor of a class that may increase in number but only if at least one

---

[93] First Restatement of Property, supra note 37, at § 157, cmt. k (also asserting that a remainder in fee simple conditional may be indefeasibly vested).

[94] See Simes & Smith, supra note 1, at § 113 n.2.

[95] Estates in fee tail or fee simple conditional, whether present or future, are recognized only in only a few states and are rarely created even in those states. Remainders for life not subject to an express condition precedent are simply termed "vested remainders for life" by the courts, without further qualification, because it really makes no practical difference whether they are classified as indefeasibly vested or vested subject to complete defeasance.

[96] For discussion of such remainders, see infra § 3.8.

[97] Simes & Smith, supra note 1, at § 1856 and cases cited.

[98] Id. § 1902 and cases cited.

[99] Id. § 1883 and cases cited.

[100] Id. at ch. 56; Edwards v. Bradley, 227 Va. 224, 315 S.E.2d 196 (1984).

member of the class has satisfied the requirements for having a vested interest. A remainder vested subject to open also can be vested subject to complete defeasance.[101]

To have a vested interest, a class member must be identifiable and must have an interest that is not subject to any condition precedent to becoming a present interest, other than expiration of all prior interests created by the same transfer.[102] For example, if O transfers "to A for life, remainder to A's children," and A has one child, B, at the time of transfer, B receives a vested remainder subject to open in fee simple.[103] If A does not have a child when O transfers, the future interest is a contingent remainder because no class member exists yet.

Whenever an additional member of the designated class of remainder holders[104] acquires a vested interest in the remainder, the interests of the existing remainder holders are partially defeated by being reduced in size. In the preceding example, if a second child, C, is born to A, C will obtain an undivided one-half interest in the vested remainder, and B's interest would be reduced to an undivided one-half. The birth of additional children to A will correspondingly reduce the undivided interests of all children previously born. Because the remainder is in fee simple absolute and the remainder is not subject to the express condition that the children must survive A, the interest of any child who predeceases A transfers to the deceased child's heir by intestate succession, unless the deceased child transferred by deed or by will.[105]

Because B's interest is subject to partial defeasance in favor of A's afterborn children, B will want to know when the class of remainder holders ("A's children") will stop growing (when the class will "close").[106] In the example above, the answer is easy. The class will close at A's death or, if A is a male, within the period of gestation after his death because his wife may be pregnant at his death.[107]

But what if O transfers "to A for life, remainder to B's children," and B is alive? In this type of case, courts generally apply a so-called "rule of convenience." Unless O has expressed a contrary intent, the class closes when any member is entitled to possession or enjoyment of the transferred property. In the example, the class will close at A's death,

---

[101] For example, "to A for life, then to A's children, but if a child of A does not survive A, that child's interest shall go to C." The First Restatement of Property terms the children's interest a remainder subject to complete defeasance on the ground that it lacks one essential element of a remainder vested subject to open— the certainty that the remainder will actually become a present interest. First Restatement of Property, a note 37, § 15t 7, cmt. c. This conclusion is questionable. See § 3.7 of this book, supra.

[102] See generally Simes & Smith, supra note 1, at § 114; First Restatement of Property, supra note 37, at § 157, cmts. l, m.

[103] Cases of this kind are numerous, e.g., Stearns v. Curry, 306 Ill. 94, 137 N.E. 471 (1922); Blanchard v. Ward, 244 N.C. 142, 92 S.E.2d 776 (1956); Mullins v. Simmons, 235 Va. 194, 365 S.E.2d 771 (1988).

[104] The class generally, though not always, consists of the "children" or "grandchildren" of a named person.

[105] A remainder vested subject to open is inheritable and is freely transferable by deed or by will. See infra §§ 3.23–24.

[106] See generally First Restatement of Property, supra note 37, at ch. 22, Topic 3; Simes & Smith, supra note 1, at §§ 632–51; 3 Powell, supra note 1, at § 20.04.

[107] "In the absence of indications of a contrary intent in [the deed or] will children begotten but not born at the time when the class closes will be included in the class if subsequently born." Simes & Smith, supra note 1, at § 650.

because B's living children, if any, are then entitled to possession or enjoyment of the property.[108]

The rule of convenience has a number of advantages. It eliminates the potential claims of persons who may be born after the class closes and makes the property more marketable by identifying all the owners.[109] When personalty is transferred, the rule allows immediate distribution of at least a minimum share to the people who are entitled to possession or enjoyment when the class closes.

If O transfers "to A for life, remainder to A's children who reach the age of 21 years," and A dies with one child who is over 21 and six children who are under 21, the rule of convenience does not require exclusion of the six children who are under 21 at A's death because the maximum class membership is determined at A's death.[110] If the subject matter is realty, the oldest child will take a present estate in fee simple subject to partial defeasance in favor of A's other children who live until the age of 21.[111] If the subject matter is divisible personalty, the oldest child is immediately entitled to one-seventh, and each additional child who reaches 21 will be entitled to an equal share. If a child dies without reaching 21, the other children's shares are proportionately enlarged.

When would the class of remainder holders close if O transfers "to A for life, remainder to B's children who reach the age of 21 years"? The class closes only when two events have occurred: (1) A has died, and (2) B has at least one child who has reached 21.[112] B's children will not be excluded from the class if they are born (or conceived) before the occurrence of both events. B's child will be included in the class if she or he is born or conceived either (1) before A's death but after at least one child of B has reached 21 or (2) after A's death but before any child has reached 21.

§ 3.9 CONTINGENT REMAINDER—IN GENERAL

A remainder is contingent if it is (a) created in favor of unborn or otherwise unidentifiable persons or (b) is subject to a condition precedent (other than expiration of all prior interests created by the same transfer) that must be satisfied before the remainder can vest or become a present interest.[113] All the remainders in the following examples are contingent:

(1) "To A for life, remainder to A's children" (if A has no children);

---

[108] The rule is also based on considerations of expediency and policy, and its application may sometimes result in defeating the transferor's probable general intent to benefit as many potential class members as possible.

[109] See generally Simes & Smith, supra note 1, at § 640 (also pointing out that if B were still alive but had no children at A's death, the class would be held open until B's death, despite the inconvenience attending such a result).

[110] Since the maximum class membership is determined, the minimum share of each member of the class is determined; and in the case of land, the persons who must join in a conveyance in order to convey a marketable title are determined. See Simes & Smith, supra note 1, at § 654; 3 Powell, supra note 1, at § 30.12.

[111] As to classification of the contingent interests of such children, see infra § 3.13. As to the status of the rule that contingent remainders are destroyed by failure to vest before the termination of all supporting life estates, see infra § 3.10.

[112] Simes & Smith, supra note 1, at § 645; 3 Powell, supra note 1, at § 30.12.

[113] Simes & Smith, supra note 1, at § 111 at n. 46 and cases cited. In a sense, the two definitions stated in the text are one. If the taker is unidentifiable, the obvious condition precedent is that the taker must be identifiable before possessing the land. See First Restatement of Property, supra note 37, at § 157(d) and cmts. u–x.

(2) "To A for life, remainder to B's heirs" (if B is alive);

(3) "To A for life, remainder to A's heirs" (if A is alive);

(4) "To A for life, remainder to B if B reaches the age of 21" (if B is under 21);

(5) "To A for life, remainder to B if B survives A" (if A and B are both alive);

(6) "To A for life, remainder to A's children who reach the age of 21" (if A does not have a child who has reached 21);

(7) "To A for life, remainder to A's children who survive her" (if A is alive).

In examples (1) and (2), the remainders are contingent because they are created in favor of unborn or otherwise unidentifiable persons.[114] The same conclusion would probably be reached as to example (3) everywhere except New York,[115] where, from an early date, a statute has provided that a remainder is vested "when there is a person in being, who would have an immediate right to the possession of the property, on the determination of all the intermediate or precedent estates."[116] In the famous case of *Moore v. Littel*,[117] the New York court held that the remainder to "the heirs of A" in a limitation like example (3) was vested in A's heirs presumptive because: "If you can point to a human being and say as to him 'that man or that woman, by virtue of a grant of a remainder, would have an immediate right to the possession of certain lands if the precedent estate of another should now cease,' then the statute says, he or she has a vested remainder." In so holding, the court ignored a further statutory provision that a remainder is contingent "while the person to whom or the event on which it is limited to take effect remains uncertain."[118] Although *Moore v. Littel* was vigorously criticized, no subsequent New York case has directly repudiated it. The doctrine of *Moore v. Littel* is unlikely to be applied in any other state, though a few states have statutory definitions of vested and contingent remainders like those in New York.[119]

In examples (4) through (7), the remainders are contingent because they are subject to express conditions precedent that must be satisfied before they can become a present estate. If A does not have children, the remainders in examples (6) and (7) are also contingent because they are created in favor of unborn persons.

In each of the seven examples above, the only present interest created by the transfer is a life estate, but no vested future interests are created. Therefore, because the present and vested future interests must add up to a fee simple absolute, the transferor has a reversion in fee simple absolute in all the examples. However, the reversion is subject to complete defeasance because the contingency may be resolved in favor of the remainder holders and give them a present estate.

---

[114] In example (2), the remainder holders are unidentifiable because a person's heirs cannot be identified during her lifetime. *Nemo est haeres viventis* (no one is heir of the living). See 2 William Blackstone, Commentaries *208.

[115] See Simes & Smith, supra note 1, at §§ 154–63.

[116] N.Y. Est. Powers & Trusts § 6–4.7 (McKinney 2018).

[117] 2 Hand 66, 41 N.Y. 66 (1869).

[118] Id.

[119] E.g., Idaho Code §§ 55–105, 55–106; Mich. Comp. Laws § 554.13; Minn. Stat. Ann. § 500.12; Mont. Code Ann. §§ 70–1–322 to 70–1–324; N.D. Cent. Code § 47–02–15; S.D. Codified Laws § 43–4–9 to 49–3–11. See Simes & Smith, supra note 1, at §§ 160–63.

§ 3.10   CONTINGENT REMAINDER—
THE DESTRUCTIBILITY RULE

At common law in England, legal contingent remainders in land were destructible. They were destroyed if they failed to vest at or before termination of the last preceding estate created by the same instrument. They would not vest if the remainder holders could not be ascertained or if the express conditions precedent were not satisfied when the remainder was intended to become possessory. For example, if land was transferred "to A for life, remainder to B if B reaches 21" and B was not at least 21 at A's death, the remainder was destroyed.[120]

The destructibility doctrine was based on the medieval English practice of transferring freehold estates by livery of seisin. A remainder could become a possessory estate immediately on expiration of the prior estate because the owner of that estate received seisin both for himself and for the remainder holder. Therefore, no "gap in the seisin" occurred when the prior estate terminated. However, if the prior possessory estate terminated while the remainder was still subject to a condition precedent, seisin re-vested in the reversioner and could not pass automatically to the remainder holder when the condition was later fulfilled.

At common law in England, legal contingent remainders in land were also destroyed by premature termination of the immediately preceding ("particular") estate. Premature termination might occur in two ways—forfeiture or merger. In the last example, if A failed to perform his feudal obligations to his lord or purported to convey a fee simple estate (a "tortious feoffment"), the lord could forfeit A's life estate. If B had not reached 21 at the time of the forfeiture, the remainder was destroyed.[121] Destruction of the remainder by merger occurred if A transferred the life estate to the owner of the reversion in fee simple or the reversion owner transferred it to A. In either case, the life estate would merge in the reversion and extinguish the remainder if B had not yet reached 21.[122]

Even in England, equitable contingent remainders in land were not destructible.[123] If land was transferred to T in trust to pay the income to A for life and then to convey the land to B in fee simple if B should reach 21, B's equitable contingent remainder was not destructible, and T had a duty to convey the land to B whether B reached 21 before or after A's death.[124] If B had not reached 21 at A's death, T would hold the land in a resulting trust for the grantor or his successors in interest until B either reached 21 or

---

[120] E.g., Festing v. Allen (1843) 152 Eng. Rep. 1204; Price v. Hall (1868) L. R. 5 Eq. 399.

[121] E.g., Archer's Case (1597) 76 Eng. Rep. 139; Chudleigh's Case (1220) 76 Eng. Rep. 270. The conveyance was tortious only if effected by feoffment, fine, or common recovery, all of which have long since become obsolete in England and the United States.

[122] E.g., Thompson v. Leach (1696) 92 Eng. Rep. 951; Purefoy v. Rogers (1670) 85 Eng. Rep. 1181; Egerton v. Massey (1857) 140 Eng. Rep. 771.

[123] E.g., Abbiss v. Burney (1880) 17 Ch. 211; Marshall v. Gingell (1882) 21 Ch. 790. "The historical reason is that the seisin is in the holder of the legal title, and therefore there can be no question where it will go on the termination of the estate of freehold preceding the contingent remainder; it simply remains in the trustee." Simes & Smith, supra note 1, at 200.

[124] As in the example, the modern trust ordinarily imposes on the trustee various affirmative duties with respect to the management of the trust property. The trustee's duty mentioned in the text exist whether the trustee had other management duties.

died before attaining that age. If B died before he reached 21, T would be obligated to convey the legal title to the grantor or his or her successors in interest.[125]

When the destructibility doctrine first evolved, estates in personal property were not recognized. Moreover, the concept of seisin, as distinct from possession, did not apply to personal property. Therefore, when courts later came to recognize present and future interests in personal property, no logical or historical basis existed for holding that legal contingent remainders in personal property were destructible.[126] Therefore, courts today are very unlikely to apply the destructibility doctrine to legal contingent remainders in personalty,[127] though courts in a few old cases did so.[128]

England[129] and at least twenty-one American states[130] have statutorily eliminated the destructibility doctrine, and at least four jurisdictions statutorily prevent destruction of contingent remainders by forfeiture or merger but not by natural termination of the preceding estate before the remainder vests.[131] In at least two other states, courts have held that statutes authorizing the creation of freehold estates to commence in the future have eliminated the destructibility doctrine.[132] The destructibility doctrine has been recognized in five states where no legislation exists on the subject,[133] but only two of these states have post-1900 decisions recognizing the doctrine.[134] On the other hand, four states have eliminated the destructibility rule entirely by judicial decision,[135] and

---

[125] The grantor would be entitled to the income so long as the resulting trust continued. See 5 A. Scott, The Law of Trusts § 430 (3d ed. 1967).

[126] See Price v. Price's Adm'r, 23 Ala. 609, 612 (1853) (Chilton, C.J., concurring).

[127] In re Rentz' Estate, 152 So. 2d 480 (Fla. Dist. Ct. App. 1963), so holds.

[128] E.g., Price, 23 Ala. at 612 (tortious sale); Broome v. King, 10 Ala. 819 (1846). Alabama later statutorily abolished the destructibility doctrine. See infra note 130.

[129] Real Property Act 1845, 8 & 9 Vict. C. 106, § 8 (Eng., Wales, Scot. & N. Ir.); Contingent Remainders Act 1877, 40 & 41 Vict. C. 33, § 1 (Eng., Wales, Scot. & N. Ir.).

[130] Ala. Code § 35–4–212 (2018) (contingent remainders take effect as executory interests); Ariz. Rev. Stat. Ann. § 33–228 (2018); Cal. Civ. Code §§ 741, 742 (West 2018); Ga. Code Ann. § 44–6–62 (West 2018); Idaho Code § 55–114 (West 2018); 765 Ill. Comp. Stat. Ann. 340/1 (West 2018); Iowa Code Ann. §§ 557.7, 557.9 (West 2018); Ky. Rev. Stat. Ann. §§ 381.100, 381.110 (West 2018); Md. Code Ann., Est. & Trusts § 11–101 (West 2018); Mass. Gen. Laws Ann. Ch. 184, § 3 (West 2018); Mich. Comp. Laws Ann. §§ 554.32, 554.34 (West 2018); Minn. Stat. Ann. § 500.15 (West 2018); Mont. Code Ann. §§ 70–1–423, 70–1–424 (West 2018); Neb. Rev. Stat. Ann. § 76–116 (West 2018); N.Y. Est. Powers & Trusts § 6–5.11 (McKinney 2018); N.D. Cent. Code Ann. §§ 47–02–30, 47–02–32 (West 2018); Ohio Rev. Code Ann. §§ 2131.05, 2131.06 (West 2018); S.D. Codified Laws §§ 43–3–18, 43–3–19 (2018); Va. Code Ann. §§ 55–15, 55–16 (West 2018); W. Va. Code § 36–1–15 (West 2018); Wis. Stat. Ann. § 700.14 (West 2018).

[131] Miss. Code Ann. § 89–1–17 (West 2018); 34 R.I. Gen. Laws Ann. § 34–4–14 (West 2017); Tex. Prop. Code. Ann. § 5.003; D.C. Code Ann. § 42–514 (West 2018).

[132] See Rouse v. Paidrick, 221 Ind. 517, 49 N.E.2d 528 (1943); Miller v. Miller, 91 Kan. 1, 136 P. 953, L.R.A. 1915A 671 (1913).

[133] Florida, Mississippi (by natural termination of life estate), Oregon, Pennsylvania, and Tennessee. Simes & Smith, supra note 1, § 209.

[134] Florida and Oregon. See Popp v. Bond, 158 Fla. 185, 28 So. 2d 259 (1946); Love v. Lindstedt, 76 Or. 66, 147 P. 935, Am. Ann. Cas. 1917A 898 (1915); see also J. Smith, Destructibility of Contingent Remainders in Florida, 3 U. Fla. L. Rev. 319 (1950); J. Smith & R. Keathley, Future Interests in Florida: A Plea for Judicial Supremacy, 9 U. Fla. L. Rev. 123 (1956); Note, Remainders—Contingent Remainders—Destructibility Doctrine in Oregon, 23 Or. L. Rev. 138 (1944).

[135] Hawaii, Massachusetts, New Hampshire, and New Mexico. See, e.g., Godfrey v. Rowland, 16 Haw. 377 (1905), reh'g denied 16 Haw. 502, overruled in part on other grounds by Parke v. Parke, 25 Haw. 397 (1920); Simonds v. Simonds, 199 Mass. 552, 85 N.E. 860 (1908); Hayward v. Spaulding, 75 N.H. 92, 71 A. 219 (1908); Abo Petroleum Corp. v. Amstutz, 93 N.M. 332, 600 P.2d 278 (1979); Johnson v. Amstutz, 101 N.M. 94,

several other states have cases indicating that courts probably would not recognize the rule.[136] The First Restatement and leading scholars agree.[137]

When most future interests were legal estates in land, the destructibility of contingent remainders made it necessary to distinguish carefully between contingent remainders and executory interests, because the latter were indestructible in England from 1620.[138] Today, the distinction is less important, because most contingent remainders are indestructible either because they are equitable, their subject matter is personal property, or the relevant jurisdiction has eliminated the destructibility doctrine. But distinguishing between vested future interests, such as reversions and some remainders, and nonvested future interests, such as executory interests and contingent remainders, is important in America today because the Rule Against Perpetuities applies only to the latter.

§ 3.11 SHIFTING EXECUTORY INTEREST—IN GENERAL

As previously noted,[139] when a present interest or a vested remainder created in a transferee is subject to complete defeasance by operation of an executory limitation, the future interest that displaces the defeated interest is a shifting executory interest. Today, almost all executory interests are shifting,[140] as in all the following examples:

(1) "To A, but if A marries B, then to B";

(2) "To A, but if A dies without children surviving him, then to B";

(3) "To A, but if A uses the land for nonresidential purposes during his lifetime, then to B";

(4) "To A so long as the land is used only for residential purposes, but if the land is put to nonresidential use during A's lifetime, then to B";

(5) "To A for life, remainder to B, but if B does not survive A, then to C";

(6) "To A for life, remainder to B, but if B dies without children surviving him, then to B's heirs."

In examples (1), (2), and (3), A has a fee simple subject to executory limitation, and B has a shifting executory interest in fee simple absolute. In example (4), A receives a fee simple determinable that is also subject to an executory limitation, the transferor retains a possibility of reverter in fee simple, and B has a shifting executory limitation in fee simple absolute.[141] In examples (5) and (6), A has a life estate, B has a remainder

---

678 P.2d 1169 (1984) ("doctrine has never been the law in New Mexico"); see also Whitten v. Whitten, 203 Okla. 196, 219 P.2d 228 (1950).

[136] E.g., Hughes v. Neely, 332 S.W.2d 1 (Mo. 1960), noted in 25 Mo. L. Rev. 435 (1960); see also H. Hanover & J. Miller, Comment, Destructibility of Contingent Remainders in Missouri, 34 UMKC L. Rev. 342 (1966).

[137] Simes & Smith, supra note 1, at § 209; First Restatement of Property, supra note 37, at § 240 (doctrine is no longer significant in American law).

[138] Pells v. Brown (1620) 79 Eng. Rep. 504.

[139] See supra § 3.6 note 62.

[140] See 3 Powell, supra note 1, at § 20.05.

[141] The possibility of reverter is not subject to the common law Rule Against Perpetuities, but the executory interest is subject to the Rule and would be void unless it would be certain to fail or become a present estate within the perpetuities period. For more on the Rule Against Perpetuities, see infra §§ 3.17–22.

vested subject to complete defeasance in fee simple, and C or B's heirs, respectively, have a shifting executory interest in fee simple absolute.

In example (1), B's executory interest will become a present interest and A's interest will be completely defeated if A marries B. In examples (2) and (3), B's executory interest will become a present interest and A's interest will be completely defeated if the stated condition occurs. In example (4), B's executory interest will become a present interest only if the land is put to nonresidential use during A's lifetime, and the transferor's possibility of reverter will become a present interest only if the land is first put to nonresidential use after A's death. In either event, A's fee simple will be completely defeated.[142]

In example (5), B's vested remainder will become a present estate in fee simple absolute if B survives A, and C's executory interest will fail. But if B predeceases A, B's vested remainder will be completely defeated, and C will have an indefeasibly vested remainder in fee simple absolute that will become a present interest when A dies.[143]

In example (6), B's vested remainder will be completely defeated if B predeceases A and leaves no surviving children. B's heirs can be determined at his death, and their executory interest will become an indefeasibly vested remainder in fee simple absolute, which will become a present interest when A dies. If A predeceases B, B will have a fee simple estate subject to executory limitation. If B dies without surviving children, B's heirs will have fee simple absolute.

None of the shifting executory interests in examples (1) through (6) is vested.[144] Because all of them are subject to a condition precedent that is not certain to occur, all of them are contingent.[145] In the first five examples, the executory interests are all given to living, identifiable persons, but the executory interest in example (6) is given to a class whose membership is unascertainable during B's lifetime. Although shifting executory interests can be created in favor of a class of unborn or otherwise unidentifiable persons, not all types of springing executory interests can be.[146]

Can a shifting executory interest become a present interest at the end of a fixed period of time, such as by a transfer "to A and his heirs, but then to B at the end of ten years"? The First Restatement of Property gives a negative answer, asserting that the transfer would give A only an estate for years, despite the use of words of inheritance, and would give B a vested remainder in fee simple absolute.[147] The First Restatement's rule seems appropriate when the instrument of transfer does not include express words

---

[142] In both examples (3) and (4), the executory interest cannot vest or fail later than the end of A's life and, therefore, is valid under the Rule Against Perpetuities.

[143] In examples (1)–(4), the executory interest "vests in possession" (becomes a present interest) if and when the preceding interest is defeated. However, in example (5), the executory interest only "vests in interest" if B dies before A, because it cannot vest in possession until A's death. Because an executory interest, by definition, cannot be vested in interest, it becomes a vested remainder.

[144] See supra note 143.

[145] This is analogous to the common classification of remainders subject to a condition precedent as "contingent remainders." That most executory interests are contingent in this sense, see supra text between notes 113–114.

[146] See Simes & Smith, supra note 1, at § 227.

[147] First Restatement of Property, supra note 37, at § 46, cmt. i.

of inheritance or otherwise clearly indicate that the first taker is to have a fee simple.[148] In such cases, the transferor would probably want the first taker's use privileges to be limited by the common law of waste. But when the instrument of transfer clearly indicates the transferor's intent to give the first taker a fee simple, it is at least arguable that the transferor intended the first taker to hold without impeachment for legal waste.[149] In any case, the holder of the executory interest would be able to enjoin unconscionable conduct amounting to equitable waste, because the executory interest is certain to become a possessory estate.

A shifting executory interest can displace a prior executory interest when the instrument of transfer contains two or more alternative executory limitations.[150] And, as we have previously noted,[151] any future interest that is created in a third party and that follows a fee simple determinable or a fee simple conditional is classified as a shifting executory interest.

When a transfer creates a remainder vested subject to open and the interests of some class members are still contingent when the preceding estate terminates, classifying those interests as contingent remainders or as executory interests is unimportant if the rule of destructibility of contingent remainders has been abolished.[152] But if the destructibility rule does apply, classifying the interests will be important. Because these contingent interests, if they eventually vest, will partially divest the vested interests of other class members, it seems that such contingent interests should be classified as executory interests, which are not subject to the destructibility rule. A Massachusetts court agreed in the leading case of *Simonds v. Simonds*.[153] However, a leading treatise states that "the opening of such vested remainders to let in subsequent members of the class is a unique process, and should not be described as the vesting of either a contingent remainder or an executory interest" but as "simply a unique characteristic of remainders vested subject to open."[154]

The dispositive clauses in modern wills, even those disposing of relatively modest estates, commonly employ a series of shifting executory limitations. For example, a will might provide: "To my spouse for life, then to my children in equal shares, but the share of any child who predeceases my spouse shall pass to the children of such child, and if any child predeceases my spouse without leaving any surviving children, the share of such child shall pass in equal shares to those of my other children who survive my spouse."

---

[148] If the words of inheritance were omitted, the transfer to A would be qualified by the language "at the end of ten years" and would give A only a term of years.

[149] Accord Simes & Smith, supra note 1, at § 222 n.2; see supra § 2.8 at note 182.

[150] E.g., Lee v. Oates, 171 N.C. 717, 88 S.E. 889 (1916).

[151] See supra § 3.6, note 63, and accompanying text.

[152] See supra § 3.10. The facts are well illustrated by the case in the next footnote.

[153] 199 Mass. 552, 85 N.E. 860, 19 L.R.A.N.S. 686 (1908). A grantor transferred land to his son Charles for life, with "remainder to such of the children of Charles as shall arrive at the age of twenty-one years, their heirs and assigns." When Charles died, he left five children, two of whom had reached 21 and three of who had not. When one of the latter reached 21, the issue was whether she took an interest in the property. The court held that she did. The court reasoned that the gift would fail if classified as a contingent remainder because it did not vest until after the life estate terminated.

[154] Simes & Smith, supra note 1, at § 205; see also id. § 114.

§ 3.12 SPRINGING EXECUTORY INTEREST—IN GENERAL

Springing executory interests are rarely created today. In the following examples, B has a springing executory interest in fee simple absolute.

(1) "To B, from and after B's marriage to A";[155]

(2) "To A for life, then to B one year after A's death";

(3) "To B from and after next January 1."

In examples (1) and (3), the transferor retains a fee simple subject to an executory limitation, and B has a springing executory interest in fee simple absolute. In example (2), A has a life estate, the transferor has a reversion in fee simple subject to an executory limitation, and B has a springing executory interest in fee simple absolute.[156] Example (3) involves a recognized exception to the general rule that a fee simple estate cannot have a fixed duration. Although arguably the transferor in example (3) has only a term of years and B has a present fee simple subject to the term, it seems more probable that the transferor intended to retain the same virtually unlimited use privileges with respect to the property that she had before the transfer.[157] This rationale seems to underlie the First Restatement's assertion that, in cases like example (3), the transferor retains a fee simple subject to a springing executory interest.[158]

In all three examples, the springing executory interests were transferred to identifiable persons. In some cases, courts have held that a springing executory interest cannot be created in favor of unborn or otherwise unascertainable persons if that is the only interest transferred.[159] These decisions deny any legal effect to an inter vivos transfer "to the heirs of A at A's death" or "to the heirs of A 21 years after A's death" when A is alive. The cases seem to be based on the questionable "assumption that in every case of an inter vivos conveyance, whether the interest conveyed be present or future, there must be some grantee in existence at the time of the conveyance."[160] However, some courts have held that such transfers do create a springing executory interest.[161] And a springing executory interest can be created in favor of an unborn or unidentifiable person or a class of unascertainable persons if the transfer also creates a present interest in a transferee,[162] such as "to A for life, and one day after A's death to A's heirs."

---

[155] Formerly in England, such transfers were commonly made in contemplation of the transferee's marriage.

[156] Note that B's executory interest in example (2) is certain to become a present interest, though the time when this will occur is uncertain.

[157] Supra § 2.8, at note 182.

[158] First Restatement of Property, supra note 37, at § 46, cmt. I; see also Simes & Smith, supra note 1, at § 223.

[159] Legout v. Price, 318 Ill. 425, 149 N.E. 427 (1925), noted in 22 Ill. L. Rev. 894 (1928) (deed to "heirs" of a living person void); Hickel v. Starcher, 90 W.Va. 369, 110 S.E. 695, 22 A.L.R. 708 (1922) (same).

[160] See discussion in Simes & Smith, supra note 1, at § 227.

[161] Loats Female Orphan Asylum v. Essom, 220 Md. 11, 150 A.2d 742 (1959); Hayes v. Kershow, 1 Sand. Ch. 258, 7 N.Y. Ch. Ann. 321 (N.Y. Ch. 1844).

[162] Simes & Smith, supra note 1, at § 227.

§ 3.13 ALTERNATIVE CONTINGENT REMAINDER OR VESTED REMAINDER SUBJECT TO EXECUTORY INTEREST?

Classifying two or more nonreversionary future interests can sometimes be difficult. The general rules are that, if the first future interest is a remainder vested subject to complete defeasance, the other future interests will be executory interests, because they will divest the vested remainder. In contrast, if the first future interest is a contingent remainder, the other future interests will also be contingent remainders. Therefore, classifying the first future interest is the key to classifying succeeding future interests. Consider the following examples:

(1)   "To A for life, remainder to B, but if B predeceases A, then to C";

(2)   "To A for life, remainder to such of A's children as survive her, but if no child of A survives her, then to B";

(3)   "To A for life, remainder to B if B reaches 21, but if B dies before 21, then to C."

In example (1), B's remainder is vested subject to complete defeasance. B predeceasing A is a condition subsequent because the words of limitation ("but if B predeceases A") are in a separate clause that follows the words of purchase ("to B"). This construction reflects the transferor's intent that B is to be vested immediately with a remainder but that the remainder will be divested if the condition subsequently occurs. C has a shifting executory interest that will vest only if B's vested remainder is divested because he predeceased A.[163] The transferor does not retain a reversion, because B's vested remainder in fee simple absolute exhausts the fee simple absolute that the transferor formerly owned.

In example (2), the future interest created in favor of "such of A's children as survive her" is a contingent remainder if A does not have children, because they cannot be identified. If A does have children, the interest is still a contingent remainder until A dies because the survival condition is in the same clause as the words of purchase, which indicates that the transferor intended that the condition must occur before the remainder vests.[164] The same intent would be found if the condition was in a separate clause preceding the words of purchase ("to A for life, then if any of A's children survive her, to those children, otherwise to B").

B's future interest is a remainder because, if it becomes possessory, it will not divest A's children. The children's contingent remainder is not a property interest. It is the *possibility* of a property interest. B's remainder is contingent because it is subject to the condition precedent that A die without a surviving child.[165] It is an "alternative" contingent remainder because the two conditions are exact opposites; if one is fulfilled, the other must necessarily fail.

Although both contingent remainders are in fee simple absolute, the transferor retains a reversion in fee simple, because A's life estate is the only present or vested

---

[163] E.g., Witcher v. Witcher, 231 Ga. 49, 200 S.E.2d 110 (1973); Wilson v. Pichon, 162 Md. 199, 159 A. 766 (1932); De Ford v. Coleman, 348 Mass. 299, 203 N.E.2d 686 (1965); Silvester v. Snow, 373 Mich. 384, 129 N.W.2d 382 (1964); Roome v. Phillips, 24 N.Y. 463 (1862); Gist v. Brown, 236 S.C. 31, 113 S.E.2d 75 (1960).

[164] E.g., Morehead v. Goellert, 160 Kan. 598, 164 P.2d 110 (1945); Saulsberry v. Second Nat'l Bank, 400 S.W.2d 506 (Ky. Ct. App. 1966); Buchan v. Buchan, 254 Iowa 566, 118 N.W.2d 611, 100 A.L.R.2d 1063 (1962).

[165] Simes & Smith, supra note 1, at § 149, text accompanying note 18.

§ 3.13

ALTERNATIVE CONTINGENT REMAINDER OR VESTED
REMAINDER SUBJECT TO EXECUTORY INTEREST?

87

future interest that was transferred.[166] In a jurisdiction where merger cannot destroy contingent remainders, the reversion is valueless, because one contingent remainder or the other is certain to become a fee simple absolute, and the reversion is certain to be completely defeated. But in a jurisdiction where merger can destroy contingent remainders, a reversion in land has substantial value because the reversioner and the life tenant can merge the life estate in the reversion and destroy the contingent remainders.[167]

In example (3), most American courts would hold that B has a contingent remainder because B reaching the age of twenty-one is an express condition precedent.[168] However, a few American courts have held that it is a remainder vested subject to complete defeasance by treating the language "if B reaches 21" as surplusage.[169] Courts have justified this result with the constructional preference for vested, rather than contingent, remainders.[170] However, that constructional preference has not caused courts to treat an express condition precedent as surplusage when only one remainder is created ("to A for life, remainder to B if B reaches 21").

(4)   Suppose O transfers "to A for life, remainder to B so long as B, during B's lifetime, does not use the land for any nonresidential purpose; but if B should use the land for any nonresidential purpose, then to C." If the restriction on B's use is construed to apply both while he has a future interest and a possessory interest, B's remainder is vested subject to complete defeasance in a fee simple subject to executory limitation. C has a shifting executory interest.

(5)   Suppose O transfers "to A for life, and if A shall die without leaving surviving children, then to C, remainder to B." If we look at the form alone, C's remainder appears to be contingent, because it is subject to an express condition precedent, and B's remainder appears to be vested, because no condition precedent is expressed in connection with B's remainder. But the old English case, *Loddington v. Kime*,[171] contains dictum that a vested remainder in fee simple cannot follow a contingent remainder in fee simple. Moreover, except for the order in which the two future interests are limited, example (5) is substantially identical with example (1). Therefore, arguably, B has a vested remainder subject to complete defeasance and C has a shifting executory interest.[172] On the other hand, B and C could have alternative contingent remainders if B's future interest is subject to an implied condition precedent that A die with surviving

---

[166]   The alternative contingent remainders do not count as parts of the transferor's original fee simple absolute, because they are just the possibility of a property interest.

[167]   Merger would result from transfer of the life estate to the reversioner, transfer of the reversion to the life tenant, or transfer of both to a third party.

[168]   E.g., Brown v. Andrews, 288 Ala. 111, 257 So. 2d 356 (1972); Fletcher v. Hurdle, 259 Ark. 640, 536 S.W.2d 109 (1976); In re Wehr's Tr., 36 Wis. 2d 154, 152 N.W.2d 868 (1967).

[169]   E.g., Cockey v. Cockey, 141 Md. 373, 118 A. 850 (1922); In re McLoughlin, 507 F.2d 177 (5th Cir. 1975).

[170]   See Phipps v. Ackers (1842) 8 Eng. Rep. 539.

[171]   91 Eng. Rep. 198 (1795).

[172]   This result is consistent with the universally-accepted rule that a gift in default of appointment is vested subject to defeasance by an exercise of the power of appointment. See supra § 3.7, at note 90.

children. Very little case authority exists on the point,[173] and legal scholars are divided, with some supporting each of the three possible views.[174]

§ 3.14   POWER OF APPOINTMENT

The Third Restatement of Property defines a power of appointment as "a power that enables the donee of the power to designate recipients of beneficial ownership interests in or powers of appointment over the appointive property."[175] Historically, the power of appointment was associated with the doctrine of uses and the development of executory interests. Exercise of a power of appointment was viewed as shifting the equitable ownership of land to a transferee by virtue of the provisions of the instrument that created the power.[176] In this way, powers of appointment provided a means of devising land by will before the Statute of Wills (1540) allowed a direct transfer by will.[177]

Powers of appointment may be classified in several ways, including:[178]

(1)(a)   A general power that the donee can exercise in favor of anyone, including the donee or the donee's estate,[179] or (b) a special (also called limited or nongeneral) power that allows the donee to appoint the property only to or within a specified group of people that is not unreasonably large and that does not include the donee;[180]

(2)(a)   A presently exercisable power or (b) a power that the donee can exercise only in the future;

(3)(a)   A power to appoint only by deed, (b) only by will, or (c) by deed and by will;

(4)(a)   A collateral power that exists when the donee has no interest in the property, other than the power, and (b) a power in gross that exists when the donee has an interest in the property in addition to the power, but the power relates to interests he does not own; and

(5)(a)   A power in trust that imposes a duty on the donee, under some circumstances, to exercise the power within a designated time period and (b) a power not in trust.

---

[173] In support of the view that C obtains a contingent remainder and B obtains a vested remainder, see Ringgold v. Carvel, 196 Md. 262, 76 A.2d 327 (1950); In re Herrmann's Estate, 130 N.J. Eq. 273, 22 A.2d 262 (1941), aff'd 132 N.J. Eq. 458, 28 A.2d 517 (1942).

[174] In support of the view that C obtains a contingent remainder and B obtains a vested remainder, see J. Warren, Progress of the Law 1919–1920, 34 Harv. L. Rev. 508, 515–18 (1921); 2 H. T. Tiffany & B. Jones, The Law of Real Property and Other Interests in Land § 333 (3d ed. 1939); see also J. C. Gray & R. Gray, The Rule Against Perpetuities § 113.1 (4th ed. 1942). In support of the view that B obtains a vested remainder and C obtains an executory interest, see A. Kales, Estates, Future Interests and Illegal Conditions and Restraints in Illinois § 95 (1920); 1 R. Preston, An Elementary Treatise on Estates, 84, 502 (1820). In support of the view that C and B obtain alternative contingent remainders, see First Restatement of Property, supra note 37, at § 278, cmt. d.

[175] Third Restatement of Property, supra note 1, at § 17.1; see also Simes & Smith, supra note 1, at §§ 33, 871. For an analysis of the Third Restatement's treatment of powers of appointment, see C. Rounds, Old Doctrine Misunderstood, New Doctrine Misconceived: Deconstructing the Newly-Minted Restatement (Third) of Property's Power of Appointment Sections, 26 Quinnipiac Prob. L.J. 240 (2013).

[176] Simes & Smith, supra note 1, at §§ 33, 872.

[177] Id.

[178] Id. §§ 33, 874–79.

[179] Third Restatement of Property, supra note 1, at § 19.13.

[180] See id. § 19.14.

For most purposes, the exercise of a power of appointment relates back to the creation of the power, so that the property transfer effected by the power is treated as if it had been effected by the instrument that created the power, and the appointee is deemed to take title from the donor, rather than from the donee, of the power.[181] However, courts and legislatures have often disregarded the relation back doctrine when justice or policy requires it. For example, the relation back doctrine is disregarded in applying the Rule Against Perpetuities to general powers of appointment,[182] and modern tax statutes tend to tax the appointment as a transfer from the donee to the appointee, at least when the power is general, rather than special.[183]

Although a prospective appointee might well be viewed as having a property interest substantially like an executory interest, the prevailing view is that a prospective appointee has a mere expectancy, like an heir presumptive, unless the power of appointment is in trust.[184] If the power is in trust, the prospective appointee may be viewed as the beneficiary of a trust with an equitable property interest protected by law.[185]

Some authority exists that the interest of the donee of a power is property.[186] However, the weight of modern authority is that neither the donee's interest nor the interest of a person who has reserved a power is property.[187] In contrast, the term "power of ownership" is now an accepted term in English law,[188] and, in this country, the donee of a general power to appoint by deed and by will certainly has an interest that comes close to full ownership.[189]

D. RESTRICTIONS ON CREATION OF NONREVERSIONARY FUTURE INTERESTS

§ 3.15 DOCTRINE OF WORTHIER TITLE

After the English courts recognized the validity of contingent remainders, they developed a rule of law—the Doctrine of Worthier Title—that precluded the creation of a contingent remainder in favor of the transferor's heirs. The Doctrine applies when the conveyance transfers an interest to someone other than the transferor's heirs, followed

---

[181] E.g., Smith v. Bank of Clearwater, 479 So. 2d 755 (Fla. Dist. Ct. App. 1985). See generally Simes & smith, supra note 1, at §§ 912, 913.

[182] E.g., Appeal of Mifflin, 121 Pa. 205, 15 A. 525 (1888).

[183] 26 U.S.C. § 2041(a)(2) (2012) includes in a decedent's gross estate all property subject to a general power of appointment that the decedent did not exercise, as well as property for which the decedent exercised a general power by a disposition that, if it were a transfer of the decedent's property, would be included in his gross estate. Many state inheritance tax statutes are similar. See Simes & Smith, supra note 1, at § 948.

[184] E.g., In re Vizard's Trusts (1866) 1 Ch. 588; In re Keene's Estate, 221 Pa. 201, 70 A. 706 (1908).

[185] Therefore, if O devises property in trust for A for life, with a power in A to determine by will the shares of his children, A holds the power in trust. If A fails to exercise the power, A's children who are living at his death will share equally in the property. Bridgewater v. Turner, 161 Tenn. 111, 29 S.W.2d 659 (1930).

[186] See L. Berger, The General Power of Appointment as an Interest in Property, 40 Neb. L.R. 104 (1960).

[187] E.g. In re Martindale's Estate, 423 N.E.2d 662 (Ind. Ct. App. 1981), overruled by Ind. Dep't of State Rev. v. Hungate's Estate, 439 N.E.2d 1148 (Ind. 1982).

[188] G. Farwell, A Concise Treatise on Powers 9 (3d ed. 1916); 25 Halsbury's Laws of England 510 (D. Hailsham ed., 2d ed. 1937).

[189] E. B. Sugden, A Practical Treatise of Powers 396 (8th ed. 1861).

by a remainder or executory interest to them.[190] For example, a conveyance from O "to A for life, remainder to O's heirs" is ineffective to create a contingent remainder in O's heirs. Instead of retaining a reversion in fee simple subject to complete defeasance in favor of O's heirs, O retained a reversion in fee simple absolute, which was a marketable and valuable estate.[191] If O devised the land by a will that included the same language, the Doctrine was intended to cause O's heirs to take the future interest by descent (intestate succession), rather than by purchase (by voluntary transfer).[192]

The Doctrine was probably invented to prevent a grantor's heir from acquiring the grantor's land by purchase, which would deprive the grantor's feudal overlord of the valuable rights of wardship and marriage.[193] This reason became completely obsolete in England with the enactment of the Statute of Tenures in 1660,[194] and the Doctrine was finally statutorily abolished in England in 1833.[195]

In the United States, a rational basis for the Doctrine has never existed, but it was generally accepted as part of the American common law in the nineteenth century.[196] At least ten states have now statutorily abolished the Doctrine,[197] and at least one other state has statutorily abolished its application to wills.[198] Judicial decisions in at least three jurisdictions have abolished it.[199] The Doctrine survives in its original form, as a rule of law, in a few states[200] and in modified form as a rule of construction in a larger

---

[190]   Simes & Smith, supra note 1, at § 1606.

[191]   Because O's reversion was alienable, no assurance existed that O's heirs would ultimately acquire the fee simple. Therefore, application of the Doctrine could lead to disinheritance of O's heirs, not merely their taking the fee simple by inheritance (the "worthier title"), rather than by "purchase."

[192]   Again, this reasoning ignores the possibility that another clause in the will, such as the residuary clause, would transfer the future interest to someone other than the testator's heirs.

[193]   See Simes & Smith, supra note 1, at §§ 1602, 1612.

[194]   Tenures Abolition Act 1660, 12 Car. 2 c. 24 (Eng. & Wales).

[195]   Inheritance Act 1833, 3 & 4 Wm. 4 c. 106, § 3.

[196]   E.g., King v. Dunham, 31 Ga. 743 (1861); Harris v. McLaran, 30 Miss. 533 (1855); Robinson v. Blankinship, 116 Tenn. 394, 92 S.W. 854 (1906).

[197]   Cal. Prob. Code § 21108 (West 2018); 765 Ill. Comp. Stat. Ann. 350/1, 350/2 (West 2018); Mass. Gen. Laws Ann. Ch. 190b, § 2–710 (West 2018); Minn. Stat. Ann. § 500.14(4) (West 2018); Neb. Rev. Stat. Ann. §§ 76–114, 76–115 (West 2018); N.Y. Est. Powers & Trusts § 6–5.9 (McKinney 2018); N.C. Gen. Stat. Ann. § 41–6.2 (West 2018); Tex. Prop. Code Ann. § 5.042; Wash. Rev. Code Ann. § 11.12.185 (West 2018); W. Va. Code Ann. § 36–1–14a (West 2018); see D. Kerson, Recent Legislation, Future Interests: Statutory Abolition of the Doctrine of Worthier Title, 47 Cal. L. Rev. 740 (1959).

[198]   Kan. Stat. Ann. § 58–506 (West 2018).

[199]   In re Estate of Kern, 274 N.W.2d 325 (Iowa 1979); Peter v. Peter, 136 Md. 157, 110 A. 211 (1920); Hatch v. Riggs Nat'l Bank, 361 F.2d 559 (D.C. Cir. 1966), noted in 16 Cath. Univ. L. Rev. 239 (1966); 66 Colum. L. Rev. 1552 (1966); 41 N.Y.U. L. Rev. 1228 (1967); 42 Wash. L. Rev. 919 (1967). The abolition of the Doctrine, whether by statute or judicial decision, has often been prospective only, so that it continues to apply to instruments that were effective before the date of abolition. See, e.g., In re Estate of Grulke, 546 N.W.2d 626 (Iowa Ct. App. 1996).

[200]   The Georgia and Mississippi cases cited supra note 196 are quite old. Whether either Georgia or Mississippi would apply the Doctrine in any form today is uncertain. Tennessee apparently has changed the Doctrine into a rule of construction. Cochran v. Frierson, 195 Tenn. 174, 258 S.W.2d 748 (1953). But see Standard Knitting Mills, Inc. v. Allen, 221 Tenn. 90, 424 S.W.2d 796 (1967).

number of states.[201] Some state courts have enlarged the Doctrine's scope by applying it to personal, as well as real, property.[202]

The metamorphosis of the Doctrine into a rule of construction was largely the consequence of Justice Cardozo's opinion in *Doctor v. Hughes*.[203] In that case, the court held that a grantor who expressly conveys a remainder to his heirs should not be presumed to intend to create a remainder unless additional evidence exists of the intent to do so. This decision is ironic because the New York courts had never recognized the Doctrine before *Doctor v. Hughes*.[204] New York has since statutorily abolished the Doctrine.[205]

Despite "some indications" that the Doctrine of Worthier Title retains a "modicum of vitality" as to dispositions by will,[206] most recent cases apply the Doctrine only to inter vivos transfers, usually in trust. In a transfer by will today, no practical difference may exist between a testator's heirs acquiring a future interest by will or by descent, because property often devolves in the same manner in either case.[207]

Even as a rule of construction, the Doctrine of Worthier Title applies only when the dispositive instrument expressly gives a remainder or executory interest to the transferor's "heirs" or "next-of-kin" or uses equivalent technical language to describe the beneficiaries, such as "those persons as would be entitled to receive the settlor's real and personal property in case of intestacy."[208] It does not apply when a future interest is given to a named person who ultimately proves to be the transferor's sole heir or next-of-kin.[209] The Doctrine also does not apply when the future interest is given to the transferor's "children," even if the children prove to be the grantor's heirs or next-of-kin;[210] or when a statute provides that the word "heirs" shall be deemed to mean "children," unless a contrary intent is expressed;[211] or when the future interest is given to the transferor's "heirs" as determined at a date other than the transferor's death or according to the intestate succession laws of a foreign jurisdiction.[212]

Whether held to be a rule of law or a rule of construction, the Doctrine has been applied mainly in the following situations:

---

[201] E.g., Thurman v. Hudson, 280 S.W.2d 507 (Ky. 1955); In re Lichtenstein's Estate, 52 N.J. 553, 247 A.2d 320 (1968); Kohler v. Ichler, 116 Ohio App. 16, 186 N.E.2d 202, 21 O.O.2d 221 (Ohio Ct. App. 1961); Braswell v. Braswell, 195 Va. 971, 81 S.E.2d 560 (1954).

[202] E.g., In re Warren's Estate, 211 Iowa 940, 234 N.W. 835 (1931) (abrogated by 274 N.W.2d 325, which held that the Doctrine of Worthier Title does not apply to the state's antilapse statute); Fidelity & Columbia Tr. Co. v. Williams, 268 Ky. 671, 105 S.W.2d 814 (1937).

[203] Doctor v. Hughes, 225 N.Y. 305, 122 N.E. 221 (1919), noted in 4 Cornell L. Q. 83 (1919), 28 Yale L.J. 713 (1919).

[204] E.g., Genet v. Hunt, 68 Sickels 158, 113 N.Y. 158, 21 N.E. 91 (1889).

[205] Supra note 197.

[206] Simes & Smith, supra note 1, at § 1601 at n.8; see also J. Morris, The Wills Branch of the Worthier Title Doctrine, 54 Mich. L. Rev. 451 (1956).

[207] See First Restatement of Property, supra note 37, at § 314(2) and cmt. j.

[208] Simes & Smith, supra note 1, at §§ 1604, 1606 & 1610.

[209] E.g., Schoellkopf v. Marine Tr. Co., 267 N.Y. 358, 196 N.E. 288 (1935).

[210] First Restatement of Property, supra note 37, at § 314.

[211] See, e.g., Ga. Code Ann. § 44–6–23 (West 2018).

[212] E.g., Robinson v. Blankinship, 116 Tenn. 394, 92 S.W. 854 (1906); Warren-Boynton State Bank v. Wallbaum, 123 Ill. 2d 429, 123 Ill. Dec. 936, 528 N.E.2d 640 (1988) (Doctrine inapplicable when the word "heirs" refers to takers at a time other than the grantor's death).

(1)   When O has conveyed property "to A for life, remainder to my heirs at law," and thereafter purported to convey or devise the entire interest in the property to someone other than O's heirs. If the Doctrine applies, the subsequent grantee or devisee will take the property at A's death, and O's heirs will take nothing.[213]

(2)   When O has conveyed property to a trustee "in trust to pay the income to O for life, and to transfer the property to O's heirs after his death," without expressly reserving the power to revoke the trust. If the Doctrine applies, O is the only person with a beneficial interest in the trust property and can revoke the trust at any time.[214] If the Doctrine does not apply, O generally cannot unilaterally revoke the trust and destroy the heirs' contingent remainder, and O cannot join with them to terminate the trust, because O's heirs cannot be ascertained during O's lifetime.[215]

(3)   When O's creditors or the creditors of O's heirs apparent try to reach and apply their debtor's interest in property transferred by O "to A for life, remainder to my heirs." If the Doctrine applies, O has a reversion that is subject to the creditors' claims,[216] and the heir apparent has no interest in the property that can be subjected to his or her creditors' claims.[217] If the Doctrine does not apply, a contrary result should be reached, at least in jurisdictions where contingent remainders are alienable by deed.[218]

The Doctrine of Worthier Title has been the subject of a good deal of criticism.[219] It can cause unexpected consequences for a transferor who believes that she has disposed of her entire interest in the property. For example, under the federal estate tax law, her estate will include the reversion at her death, unless she re-transferred it inter vivos, and can be taxed for it.[220]

Moreover, as a rule of construction, the Doctrine invites litigation and makes the outcome of cases quite unpredictable. The unpredictability has been increased by some courts' rejection of Justice Cardozo's dictum in *Doctor v. Hughes*[221] that only a clear expression of intent should be sufficient to rebut the presumption against an intent to create a remainder in favor of the transferor's heirs. In New York and elsewhere, the presumption may now be rebutted if a contrary intent can be gathered from the

---

[213]   E.g., Thurman v. Hudson, 280 S.W.2d 507 (Ky. 1955); All Persons v. Buie, 386 So. 2d 1109 (Miss. 1980); Cochran v. Frierson, 31 Beeler 174, 195 Tenn. 174, 258 S.W.2d 748 (1953); Braswell v. Braswell, 195 Va. 971, 81 S.E.2d 560 (1954).

[214]   E.g., Fidelity & Columbia Tr. Co. v. Williams, 268 Ky. 671, 105 S.W.2d 814 (1937); Fidelity Union Tr. Co. v. Parfner, 135 N.J. Eq. 133, 37 A.2d 675 (N.J. Ch. 1944); Scholtz v. Cent. Hanover Bank & Tr. Co., 295 N.Y. 488, 68 N.E.2d 503 (1946).

[215]   E.g., Sutliff v. Aydelott, 373 Ill. 633, 27 N.E.2d 529 (1940); Clark v. Judge, 84 N.J. Super. 35, 200 A.2d 801 (1964), aff'd 44 N.J. 550, 210 A.2d 415 (1965); In re Burchell's Estate, 299 N.Y. 351, 87 N.E.2d 293 (1949).

[216]   E.g., Seguin State Bank & Tr. Co. v. Locke, 129 Tex. 524, 102 S.W.2d 1050 (Tex. Comm'n App. 1937); McKenna v. Seattle-First Nat'l Bank, 35 Wash. 2d 662, 214 P.2d 664, 16 A.L.R.2d 679 (1950).

[217]   Doctor v. Hughes, 225 N.Y. 305, 122 N.E. 221 (1919).

[218]   Although both the contingent remainder and the reversion are alienable, only the contingent remainder should be subject to creditors' claims in such a case, because the contingent remainder is certain to become a present interest and the reversion is certain to be completely defeated (assuming that O has an heir). See infra § 3.25.

[219]   E.g., L. Waggoner, Future Interests in a Nutshell § 11.3 (1981); W. Nossaman, Gift to Heirs— Remainder or Reversion, 24 Cal. St. B. J. 59 (1949); Note, 17 U. Chi. L. Rev. 87 (1949).

[220]   See 26 U.S.C. § 2033 (2012); Bartlett v. United States, 146 F.Supp. 719, 137 Ct. Cl. 38 (1956).

[221]   Doctor v. Hughes, 225 N.Y. 305, 122 N.E. 221.

dispositive instrument as a whole,[222] and the New York courts in particular were quite willing to find such an intent.[223] As a result, Professor Richard Powell has commented that "[i]n New York no case involving a substantial sum could be fairly regarded as closed until it had been carried to the Court of Appeals" and that other states' treatment of the Doctrine as a presumption also cause "wasteful expenditures of money by helpless clients" and "uncertainty in the law."[224]

The Doctrine has been defended mainly on the ground that it promotes alienability.[225] If the transferor's heirs have the future interest, it cannot be conveyed until the transferor is dead and the heirs are ascertained. However, continued application of the Doctrine seems undesirable. The Third Restatement of Property states that the Doctrine is no longer recognized,[226] though the First[227] and Second[228] Restatements recognized it as a rule of construction.

When the transfer to the heirs is made in trust, which is common, legislatures and courts have tools other than the Doctrine of Worthier Title to enable the settlor to revoke the trust and reclaim the future interest despite the failure to reserve that power. For example, New York has statutorily abolished the Doctrine but has enacted legislation providing that, for trust termination purposes only, the settlor's heirs do not acquire any beneficial interest in the trust property.[229] California also statutorily abolished the Doctrine[230] and enacted legislation that makes all inter vivos trusts revocable, unless the settlor expressly provides to the contrary.[231] And a court in the District of Columbia has held that the Doctrine is no longer in force but that courts may appoint a guardian ad litem to consent to premature termination of a trust on behalf of the settlor's unascertained heirs.[232]

In jurisdictions where courts apply the Doctrine of Worthier Title as a rule of law, the only way to avoid its application is to limit the remainder to persons other than the grantor's "heirs" or "next of kin." For example, a grantor might accomplish substantially the same disposition by limiting a remainder to his "children" or "nieces and nephews," with a clear statement that the class is not intended to be the equivalent of "heirs." Similarly, the grantor can transfer the remainder to named persons who are the heirs

---

[222] E.g., Richardson v. Richardson, 298 N.Y. 135, 81 N.E.2d 54 (1948), noted in 62 Harv. L. Rev. 313 (1948), 24 Ind. L.J. 292 (1949); In re Burchell's Estate, 299 N.Y. 351, 87 N.E.2d 293 (1949), noted in 49 Mich. L. Rev. 139 (1950).

[223] Id.

[224] 3 Powell, supra note 1, at § 31.08.

[225] This may have been, at least in part, what Judge Cardozo had in mind when he said "seldom do the living mean to forego the power of disposition during life by the direction that upon death there shall be a transfer to their heirs." Doctor v. Hughes, 225 N.Y. at 313, 122 N.E. at 223 (1919).

[226] Third Restatement of Property, supra note 1, § 16.3. For an analysis of the Third Restatement's approach, see K. Guzman, Worthier for Whom?, 68 Okla. L. Rev. 779 (2016).

[227] First Restatement of Property, supra note 37, at § 314.

[228] Restatement (Second) of Prop.: Donative Transfers § 30.2 (1983) (hereinafter Second Restatement of Property).

[229] N.Y. Est. Powers & Trusts § 7–1.9 (McKinney 2018).

[230] Supra note 197.

[231] Cal. Prob. Code § 15400 (West 2018).

[232] Hatch v. Riggs Nat'l Bank, 361 F.2d 559 (D.C. Cir. 1966).

apparent, without designating them as "heirs," or to the grantor's heirs to be determined at a date other than the grantor's death.[233]

In jurisdictions where courts apply the Doctrine of Worthier Title as a rule of construction, a limitation to the grantor's "heirs" will be legally effective if the grantor clearly indicates an intention to create a remainder or executory interest in their favor. For example, the conveyance can include a clause such as: "It being my intention that those persons, now unascertained, who shall prove to be my heirs, shall by this instrument take a contingent remainder as purchasers."[234]

It goes without saying that the person who drafts a deed or trust instrument should ascertain the grantor's real intention before including a limitation to the grantor's "heirs." The drafter should not include a final limitation to the grantor's "heirs" simply because the grantor has not, in instructions to the drafter, expressly provided for all possibilities.

§ 3.16 RULE IN SHELLEY'S CASE

Another English common law rule relating to contingent remainders in land—the Rule in Shelley's Case[235]—is now practically as moribund as the destructibility rule. England abolished the Rule by the Law of Property Act of 1925,[236] and the great majority of American jurisdiction have statutorily abolished it.[237] Two states have statutorily abolished the Rule for wills only.[238] In two other states, courts have refused to recognize the Rule though it has not been statutorily abolished,[239] and four states have neither a statute nor a judicial decision concerning the Rule.[240] One of the latter is Louisiana, where it seems clear that the Rule is not in force because Louisiana adheres to the civil law, rather than the common law. The Rule is now still in force as to both deeds and wills in only four states.[241]

As developed by the English courts, the Rule in Shelley's Case prescribed that when a deed or will purported to give a remainder to the heirs or the heirs of the body of a

---

[233] See Simes & Smith, supra note 1, at § 1613.

[234] Id.

[235] Wolfe v. Shelley (1581) 76 Eng. Rep. 206 (1581), was not the first case recognizing the Rule, which probably antedated its early application in the Provost of Beverley's Case, YB 40 Edw. 3, f. 9, no. 18 (1366).

[236] Law of Property Act 1925, 15 Geo. 5 c. 20 § 131 (UK).

[237] See Simes & Smith, supra note 1, at § 1563 and statutes cited; N.C. Gen. Stat. Ann. § 41–6.3 (West 2018); Wash. Rev. Code Ann. § 11.12.180 (West 2018); J. Orth, Observation: Requiem for the Rule in Shelley's Case, 67 N.C. L. Rev. 681 (1989). The jurisdictions where the Rule has been completely abrogated are Alabama, Arizona, California, Connecticut, District of Columbia, Florida, Georgia, Idaho, Illinois, Iowa, Kansas, Kentucky, Maine, Maryland, Massachusetts, Michigan, Minnesota, Mississippi, Missouri, Montana, Nebraska, New Jersey, New Mexico, New York, North Carolina, North Dakota, Ohio, Oklahoma, Pennsylvania, Rhode Island, South Carolina, South Dakota, Tennessee, Virginia, Washington, West Virginia, and Wisconsin. Where the rule is abolished, the life tenant grantee or devisee can transfer his or her life estate but not the remainder. See Lusk v. Broyles, 694 So. 2d 4 (Ala. Civ. App. 1997). Statutory abolitions are frequently construed as prospective only, so that the Rule continues to apply to transfers that were effective before the abolition date, See, e.g., City Bank & Tr. Co. v. Morrissey, 118 Ill. App. 3d 640, 73 Ill. Dec. 946, 454 N.E.2d 1195 (1983); Soc. Nat'l Bank v. Jacobson, 54 Ohio St. 3d 15, 560 N.E.2d 217 (1990), reh'g denied 55 Ohio St. 3d 709, 563 N.E.2d 302 (1990).

[238] N.H. Rev. Stat. Ann. § 551:8; Or. Rev. Stat. § 112.345. See Simes & Smith, supra note 1, at § 1563.

[239] Simes & Smith, supra note 1, at § 1563 (Hawaii and Vermont).

[240] Id. (Louisiana, Nevada, Utah, and Wyoming).

[241] Id. (Arkansas, Colorado, Delaware, and Indiana).

person who received a prior freehold estate by the same instrument, that person also took the remainder.[242] The Rule prevented creation of a contingent remainder in the heirs or heirs of the body of a person to whom the same instrument transferred a prior freehold estate. The Rule applied whether the prior freehold estate was possessory or was itself a remainder[243] and whether an intervening estate separated the prior freehold and the purported remainder to the heirs or heirs of the body.[244]

The Rule applied only if both the prior freehold and the remainder were of the same quality. Both had to be legal ("to A for life, then to A's heirs") or both had to be equitable ("to Trustee to hold in trust for A for life and then to hold in trust for A's heirs").[245] Before England abolished the Rule in Shelley's Case, it applied whether the prior freehold estate was a life estate or fee tail.[246] In the United States, the Rule only applies when the prior freehold is a life estate.[247]

Although Sir Edward Coke stated the Rule in Shelley's Case[248] in a form indicating that it would apply only when the word "heirs" denotes "all the heirs (or heirs of the body) which the ancestor might have from generation to generation throughout the future"[249] and the English courts seem generally to have adhered to this definition,[250] most American cases seem to reject it and hold that the Rule applies when the word "heirs" is used to describe the class of persons who would inherit if the ancestor died intestate.[251] However, "it can hardly be said that in any given jurisdiction either doctrine as to the meaning of heirs is consistently followed,"[252] though the Rule clearly does not apply when the remainder is expressly given to the "children" of the person to whom the

---

[242] Sir Edward Coke stated the Rule as follows: "It is a rule of law, when the ancestor by any gift or conveyance takes an estate of freehold, and in the same gift or conveyance an estate is limited either mediately or immediately to his heirs in fee or in tail, that always in such cases, 'the heirs' are words of limitation of the estate, and not words of purchase." Shelley's Case (1581) 76 Eng. Rep. 206. Thus, "to A for life, then to A's heirs," is construed by the Rule as if it read "to A and his/her heirs." The Rule does not apply where a deed merely *reserves* a life estate in the grantor rather than creating a life estate in a third person. Warren-Boynton State Bank v. Wallbaum, 123 Ill. 2d 429, 123 Ill. Dec. 936, 528 N.E.2d 640 (1988).

[243] E.g., Depler v. Dyer, 312 Ill. 537, 144 N.E. 212 (1924); Wright v. Jenks, 124 Kan. 604, 261 P. 840 (1927); Dukes v. Shuler, 185 S.C. 303, 194 S.E. 817 (1938).

[244] E.g., Carpenter v. Hubbard, 263 Ill. 571, 105 N.E. 688 (1914); Hartman v. Flynn, 189 N.C. 452, 127 S.E. 517 (1925).

[245] E.g., Johnson v. Shriver, 121 Colo. 397, 216 P.2d 653 (1950) (rule not applicable where one estate was legal and the other was equitable); Elsasser v. Elsasser, 159 Fla. 696, 32 So. 2d 579 (1947); Harlan v. Manington, 152 Iowa 707, 133 N.W. 367 (1911).

[246] Goodright v. Wright (1717) 24 Eng. Rep. 442 (semble). The Rule is so stated in 1 W. Hayes, An Introduction to Conveyancing, and the New Statutes Concerning Real Property 545 (5th ed. 1840); 1 Preston, supra note 174, at 313; 1 C. Fearne, An Essay on the Learning of Contingent Remainders and Executory Devices ch. XVII (1844).

[247] First Restatement of Property, supra note 37, at § 312, states that the Rule applies only when the ancestor has a life estate.

[248] Supra note 242.

[249] 3 Powell, supra note 1, at § 31.07.

[250] Id.; Simes & Smith, supra note 1, at § 1548.

[251] Cf., e.g., Gordon v. Cadwalader, 164 Cal. 509, 130 P. 18 (1912) (rule inapplicable where "heirs" described persons who would take on the ancestor's death and not those taking in indefinite succession); Ratley v. Oliver, 229 N.C. 120, 47 S.E.2d 703 (1948) (contra).

[252] Simes & Smith, supra note 1, at § 1548.

prior freehold is given[253] or where the word "heirs" is construed to mean "children."[254] Because the Rule in Shelley's Case is a rule of law, rather than a rule of construction, any direction in a deed or will that the Rule shall not apply is completely ineffective.[255]

Assume that the Rule in Shelley's Case is in effect at the time of the following transfers:

(1)　"To A for life, then to A's heirs." The Rule converts this transfer into "to A for life, then to A." Because A owns two consecutive interests in the property, the doctrine of merger combines them, and A has fee simple absolute.[256]

(2)　"To A for life, then to B for life, then to B's heirs." The Rule converts this transfer into "to A for life, then to B for life, then to B." Because B owns two consecutive interests in the property, they merge, and B has an indefeasibly vested remainder in fee simple absolute.[257]

(3)　"To A for life, then to B for life, then to A's heirs." The Rule converts this transfer into "to A for life, then to B for life, then to A." Because B's interest separates A's two interests, they cannot merge.[258] A has a life estate and an indefeasibly vested remainder in fee simple absolute, and B has an indefeasibly vested remainder in a life estate. However, if B predeceases A, A's interests will merge, and A will have fee simple absolute.[259]

(4)　"To A for life, then to A's heirs if A marries B." Although the transfer attempts to give A's heirs a remainder that is subject to a condition precedent, the Rule still applies. However, merger does not occur for so long as the condition precedent remains unsatisfied.[260] Therefore, A has a life estate and a contingent remainder in fee simple absolute, and O retains a reversion in fee simple subject to executory limitation. If A marries B, A will have fee simple absolute.

(5)　"To A for life, then to the heirs of A's body." When the Rule in Shelley's Case and the doctrine of merger are applied, A has a fee tail, rather than fee simple absolute, because "heirs of the body" is the language used to create a fee tail.[261] Of course, A will

---

[253]　E.g., Bowen v. Frank, 179 Ark. 1004, 18 S.W.2d 1037 (1929); Beall v. Beall, 331 Ill. 28, 162 N.E. 152 (1928).

[254]　E.g., Williams v. Johnson, 228 N.C. 732, 47 S.E.2d 24 (1948); Green v. Green, 210 S.C. 391, 42 S.E.2d 884 (1947).

[255]　E.g., Bishop v. Williams, 221 Ark. 617, 255 S.W.2d 171 (1953); Sybert v. Sybert, 250 S.W.2d 271 (Tex. Civ. App. 1952), aff'd 152 Tex. 106, 254 S.W.2d 999 (1953).

[256]　See discussion of this point by Lord MacNaghten in his opinion in Van Grutten v. Foxwell [1897] App. Cas. 658; see also Simes & Smith, supra note 1, at § 1556; 2 Powell, supra note 1, at § 15.03 n.76.

[257]　E.g., Springbitt v. Monaghan, 43 Del. (4 Terry) 501, 50 A.2d 612 (Del. Super. Ct. 1946); Dallmeyer v. Hermann, 437 S.W.2d 367 (Tex. Civ. App. 1969), noted in 22 Baylor L. Rev. 146 (1970).

[258]　E.g., Carpenter v. Hubbard, 263 Ill. 571, 105 N.E. 688 (1914); Harlan v. Manington, 152 Iowa 707, 133 N.W. 367 (1911); Hartman v. Flynn, 189 N.C. 452, 127 S.E. 517 (1925).

[259]　E.g., Rose v. Rose, 219 N.C. 20, 12 S.E.2d 688 (1941); Chappell v. Chappell, 260 N.C. 737, 133 S.E.2d 666 (1963); Burnham v. Balt. Gas & Elec. Co., 217 Md. 507, 144 A.2d 80 (1958).

[260]　E.g., Fed. Land Bank of Balt. v. Walker, 345 Pa. 185, 26 A.2d 436 (1942), noted in 16 Temp. L. Q. 449 (1942); McNeal v. Sherwood, 24 R.I. 314, 53 A. 43 (1902).

[261]　See Coke's statement of the Rule, supra note 242. Where the remainder is to the "heirs of the body" of the person taking the prior freehold, the remainder will be either in fee tail or fee simple conditional if such estates are still recognized in the jurisdiction where the land is situated. E.g., Wayne v. Lawrence, 58 Ga. 15 (1877) (fee tail); Blume v. Pearcy, 204 S.C. 409, 29 S.E.2d 673 (1944) (fee simple conditional).

not have a fee tail in the states that do not recognize it.[262] And the Rule's effect will be completely stymied by a statutory provision that an attempt to transfer a fee tail instead transfers a life estate to the first taker and a remainder in fee simple absolute to the heirs of his body. Under this type of statute, a transfer "to A for life, remainder to the heirs of his body" first creates a fee tail in A through application of the Rule in Shelley's Case and then statutorily converts it into a life estate in A and a contingent remainder in fee simple absolute in the heirs of A's body.

§ 3.17   RULE AGAINST PERPETUITIES

John Chipman Gray wrote the classic statement of the Rule Against Perpetuities, which is the principal common law rule limiting the creation of nonreversionary future interests: "No interest is good unless it must vest, if at all, not later than twenty-one years after some life in being at the creation of the interest."[263]

The Rule Against Perpetuities does not require certainty concerning the period within which a nonvested future interest will either become a present interest or lose its capacity to become a present interest. The certainty required by the Rule relates only to the vesting in interest.[264] Of course, the conveyance language may result in the interest vesting in interest and in possession at the same time.[265]

The common law Rule Against Perpetuities is based on the long-established judicial policy against permitting effective restraints on the alienation of fee simple estates in land and equivalent interests in personalty.[266] This policy also provided the basis both for judicial recognition of the common recovery as a device for converting a fee tail into a fee simple ("barring the entail") and for judicial refusal to enforce any provision for defeasance conditioned on alienation by common recovery. If the English courts had held that a fee simple subject to executory limitation could be converted into a fee simple absolute by resort to an appropriate action, such as a common recovery, the Rule Against

---

[262] Supra § 2.10, at notes 192–197.

[263] J. C. Gray & R. Gray, The Rule Against Perpetuities 191 (4th ed. 1942). Gray's treatise was originally published in 1886. Professor Richard Powell criticized Gray's formulation:

It is preferable to adopt the description of the rule, made by the Restatement, as one that promotes the alienability of property by destroying future interests of two types: (1) those that eliminate the power of alienation for longer than the permissible period; and (2) those that create nonvested future interests that are indestructible, thus lessening the probability of alienation for longer than the permissible period. These two prohibited types of future interests inconveniently fetter property and are socially undesirable.

10 Powell, supra note 1, at § 72.06.

[264] E.g., Matter of Isganaitis, 124 Misc. 2d 1, 475 N.Y.S.2d 699 (Surr. Ct. 1983) (whether interest violates Rule depends on "what might have happened rather than on what actually happened" and "if under any possible chain of events the interest may not vest within the period; it will be deemed invalid"); Sherrod v. Any Child or Children Hereafter Born to Watson N. Sherrod, Jr., 65 N.C. App. 252, 308 S.E.2d 904 (1983), modified and aff'd 312 N.C. 74, 320 S.E.2d 669 (1984).

[265] For example, if O transfers "to A for life, remainder to the children of A who are living at his death, but if no children of A are living at his death, then to B." B's interest is an executory interest that may never vest. But if no child of A is living at A's death, B's executory interest simultaneously vests in interest and vests in possession.

[266] See Simes & Smith, supra note 1, at §§ 1202, 1212; 10 Powell, supra note 1, at ch. 75.

Perpetuities might never have evolved.[267] But in *Pells v. Brown,*[268] the court held that executory interests were indestructible. This holding provided the impetus for judicial development of a new rule to control executory interests and prevent their use in family settlements in a way that would prevent alienation of settled land for an unreasonable period of time.[269]

As the quotation from Professor Gray's famous treatise indicates, the Rule Against Perpetuities, in form, invalidates executory interests and contingent remainders that are not certain to vest or fail within the stated "perpetuities period" of "lives in being," plus twenty-one years. Its purpose is largely to prevent the restraint on alienation that may result from the creation of a series of future interests that might not vest or fail within the perpetuities period. If such future interests were valid, they could prevent anyone from owning a marketable title to the fee simple absolute for an unlimited period of time.[270]

As we shall see, the Rule Against Perpetuities is applicable to executory interests and contingent remainders in both realty and personalty and to both legal and equitable interests.[271] When the Rule is applied to legal executory interests and contingent remainders, its utility in preventing an unreasonable restraint on alienation is clear. But applying the Rule to the equitable interests of trust beneficiaries does not affect the alienability of the property held in trust in the ordinary case in which the trustee has a broad power to alienate the property and replace it with other property. Similarly, when the Rule is applied to nonvested future interests in shares of corporate stock, whether held in trust, the effect on alienability of the corporation's assets is at best minimal, because the corporate management always has broad power to alienate corporate assets. In these cases, the Rule's application must be justified on the grounds suggested by Professor Simes; the Rule is necessary to limit "dead hand" control over property and to "strike[ ] a fair balance between the satisfaction of the wishes of the members of the present generation to tie up their property and those of future generations to do the same."[272]

---

[267] The common law has long had a distaste for restraints on alienation. Therefore, if the courts had held that a fee simple subject to an executory limitation was alienable, the need for the Rule Against Perpetuities might never have developed. See 1 D. Thomas, Thompson on Real Property, Thomas Editions, § 28.02 (2018).

[268] Pells v. Brown (1620) 79 Eng. Rep. 504.

[269] Although contingent remainders were recognized a century before *Pells v. Brown*, their destructibility assured that they would normally be certain to either vest or fail within lives in being when they were created.

[270] Although placing property in trust imposes some restraint on alienation, a trust is not necessarily void because it may last longer than twenty-one years after some life in being at the creation of the trust. Indeed, a charitable trust is valid though it may last forever and is made indestructible by the instrument creating it. Although authority is scant, in most states a private non-charitable trust probably cannot be made indestructible for a period in excess of lives in being plus twenty-one years. If the settlor attempts to make it indestructible for a longer period, the courts most likely would declare the trust to be terminable from its inception. A private, noncharitable trust for an unincorporated association is simply void if, by its terms, it is not terminable within lives in being, plus twenty-one years. See Simes & Smith, supra note 1, at §§ 1392, 1393, 1395.

[271] See infra § 3.18.

[272] Simes & Smith, supra note 1, at § 1117. For fuller development of this thesis, see L. Simes, Public Policy and the Dead Hand (1955).

§ 3.18   INTERESTS SUBJECT TO THE RULE AGAINST PERPETUITIES

As stated by Gray, the Rule Against Perpetuities appears to apply to all nonvested future interests, reversionary and nonreversionary, including possibilities of reverter, rights of entry for breach of condition (powers of termination), contingent remainders, and executory interests. However, American courts have consistently held that possibilities of reverter and rights of entry are not subject to the Rule.[273] The reasons for this exemption are largely historical. Possibilities of reverter and rights of entry were recognized long before the Rule began to evolve. They were somewhat analogous to a feudal lord's right of escheat, which was not deemed to be an objectionable restraint on alienation of land. Moreover, they were often created to assure that property given for charitable purposes would continue to be devoted to those purposes.[274] Therefore, the Rule applies, as a matter of common law, only to nonreversionary future interests.

When the Rule Against Perpetuities began to evolve in the late seventeenth century, it was aimed primarily at executory interests, which the court in *Pells v. Brown* (1620) had held were indestructible.[275] If an executory interest is contingent (subject to a condition precedent that is not certain to be satisfied), which is usual, it is subject to the Rule. An exception can exist if a transfer document conveys both a fee simple subject to executory limitation to a charitable organization and the executory interest following it to another charitable organization.[276]

But an executory interest can be neither vested nor contingent, such as the springing executory interest created by a conveyance "to A, from and after the expiration of 25 years from the date of this conveyance." Although little authority exists,[277] the Rule should not apply to this type of executory interest.[278] In the example, A's executory interest is substantially equivalent to a vested remainder in fee simple absolute following a twenty-five year term, is as easy to value as a vested remainder, and is as readily marketable. However, if a court decided that even this type of executory interest

---

[273] E.g., with respect to possibilities of reverter: Collins v. Church of God of Prophecy, 304 Ark. 37, 800 S.W.2d 418 (Ark. 1990); Commerce Union Bank v. Warren Cty., 707 S.W.2d 854 (Tenn. 1986); Hamman v. Bright & Co., 924 S.W.2d 168 (Tex. App. 1996), vacated in aid of settlement, 938 S.W.2d 718 (Tex. 1997). With respect to powers of termination: Hinton v. Gilbert, 221 Ala. 309, 128 So. 604, 70 A.L.R. 1192 (1930); Dennis v. Bird, 941 S.W.2d 486 (Ky. Ct. App. 1997). See generally Simes & Smith, supra note 1, at §§ 1238, 1239.

[274] Simes & Smith, supra note 1, at § 1170.

[275] Pells v. Brown (1620) 79 Eng. Rep. 504

[276] E.g., Dickenson v. City of Anna, 310 Ill. 222, 141 N.E. 754, 30 A.L.R. 587 (1923); Carson Park Riding Club v. Friendly Home for Children, 421 S.W.2d 832 (Ky. Ct. App. 1967); First Church in Somerville v. Attorney Gen., 375 Mass. 332, 376 N.E.2d 1226 (1978); Hornets Nest Girl Scout Council, Inc. v. Cannon Found., Inc., 79 N.C. App. 187, 339 S.E.2d 26 (1986). The exception for charitable trusts is applicable only when the property is initially given to a charitable organization with a gift over of an executory interest to another charitable organization. Simes & Smith, supra note 1, at § 1280; Lancaster v. Merchs. Nat'l Bank, 752 F.Supp. 886 (W.D. Ark. 1990), rev'd, 961 F.2d 713 (8th Cir. 1992).

[277] See Nicol v. Morton, 332 Ill. 533, 164 N.E. 5 (1928); Mercantile Tr. Co. v. Hammerstein, 380 S.W.2d 287 (Mo. 1964), discussed in Eckhardt, The Rule Against Perpetuities in Missouri, 30 Mo. L. Rev. 27 (1965); Hunt v. Carroll, 157 S.W.2d 429 (Tex. Civ. App. 1941), error dismissed, 140 Tex. 424, 168 S.W.2d 238 (Tex. Comm'n App. 1943).

[278] Simes & Smith, supra note 1, at § 1236; First Restatement of Property, supra note 37, at § 370, cmts. g, h. The Rule is said to apply to noncontingent executory interests in J. C. Gray & R. Gray, The Rule Against Perpetuities § 201 n.3 (4th ed. 1942).

is subject to the Rule Against Perpetuities, the court might construe the conveyance as creating a vested remainder to prevent the Rule from invalidating it.[279]

The Rule Against Perpetuities clearly applies to equitable contingent remainders[280] and to all contingent remainders in personalty, whether legal or equitable.[281] Substantial authority supports the view that the Rule also applies to legal contingent remainders in land.[282] In jurisdictions where the doctrine of destructibility has been completely abolished, legal contingent remainders in land are no longer distinguishable from shifting executory interests, and they clearly should be subject to the Rule.[283] But where legal contingent remainders in land are still destructible if they fail to vest at or before termination of all prior estates created by the same instrument, the Rule would rarely invalidate them because the destructibility rule will assure in most cases that they will either vest or fail within the perpetuities period.[284]

As applied to class gifts, the general rule is that the entire gift is void if the Rule voids a gift to any potential class member because class membership can increase or decrease for longer than the perpetuities period.[285] Two recognized exceptions exist to this harsh rule:

(1) The gift is a specified amount for each class member, such as a bequest of $1,000 for each child of A, whenever born, who attains the age of thirty years. The gift to each class member is treated separately for purposes of the Rule. Therefore, the gift may be valid for some class members but not for others.[286]

(2) The initial gift is to a class the membership of which is certain to be determined within the perpetuities period, with a gift over of each class member's share (or the share from which each class member receives income) to his or her children, issue, heirs, or the like, such as a bequest of personal property in trust to pay the income in equal shares to A's children for their respective lives and, on the death of each child, to distribute the share from which he or she received income to his or her then living issue in equal shares. The gift over to each designated subclass is treated separately for purposes of the Rule,

---

[279] Simes & Smith, supra note 1, at § 1236; see Williams v. Watt, 668 P.2d 620 (Wyo. 1983); supra § 2.9, at note 188.

[280] E.g., Abbiss v. Burney (1880) 17 Ch. 211; Lawrence v. Smith, 163 Ill. 149, 45 N.E. 259 (1896); In re Feeney's Estate, 293 Pa. 273, 142 A. 284 (1928).

[281] E.g., Bull v. Pritchard (1825) 67 Eng. Rep. 1036; Mich. Tr. Co. v. Baker, 226 Mich. 72, 196 N.W. 976 (1924); Norton v. Ga. R.R. Bank & Tr., 253 Ga. 596, 322 S.E.2d 870 (1984). The famous Duke of Norfolk's Case, (1682) 22 Eng. Rep. 931, in which Lord Nottingham first formulated the modern Rule Against Perpetuities, involved contingent equitable future interests in a chattel real.

[282] In re Ashforth (1905) 1 Ch. 535; see also Warren v. Albrecht, 213 Ill. App. 3d 55, 157 Ill. Dec. 160, 571 N.E.2d 1179 (1991); Graham v. Whitridge, 99 Md. 248, 57 A. 609, 66 L.R.A. 408 (1904); Geissler v. Reading Tr. Co., 257 Pa. 329, 101 A. 797 (1917).

[283] Simes & Smith, supra note 1, at §§ 132, 1237.

[284] For example, if O transfers "to A for life, remainder to those children of A living at A's death," the contingent remainder given to A's children would necessarily either vest or fail at the end of a life in being (A's life).

[285] E.g., Keefer v. McCloy, 344 Ill. 454, 176 N.E. 743 (1931); In re Wanamaker's Estate, 335 Pa. 241, 6 A.2d 852 (1939); Crockett v. Scott, 199 Tenn. 90, 284 S.W.2d 289, 56 A.L.R.2d 442 (1955), noted in 24 Tenn. L. Rev. 617 (1956); Merrill v. Wimmer, 453 N.E.2d 356 (Ind. Ct. App. 1983), rev'd on other grounds, 481 N.E.2d 1294 (Ind. 1985). See generally Simes & Smith, supra note 1, at § 1265; W. Leach, The Rule Against Perpetuities and Gifts to Classes, 51 Harv. L. Rev. 1329 (1938).

[286] E.g., In re Helme's Estate, 95 N.J. Eq. 197, 123 A. 43 (N.J. Prerog. Ct. 1923); Storrs v. Benbow, 43 Eng. Rep. 153 (1853).

so that the gift may be valid for some subclasses but void for others.[287] However, if the gift over is per capita, rather than per stirpes, separate subclasses do not exist, and the second exception does not apply.[288]

A class gift is not always valid under the Rule Against Perpetuities when the maximum and minimum class membership is certain to be determined within the perpetuities period. If the entire class gift is subject to a condition precedent that may not be satisfied within the perpetuities period, the entire gift is void.[289]

Although the Rule Against Perpetuities is a rule of property law and not a rule of contract law, an option to purchase real or personal property may be specifically enforceable, which creates a contingent equitable future interest in the property.[290] Courts generally hold that an option "in gross" to purchase land (an option that is not attached to a leasehold or other property interest) is subject to the Rule and is void if it can be exercised beyond the period of perpetuities.[291] An option to purchase personal property that is specifically enforceable because of the property's unique character also is subject to the Rule.[292]

In England, even an option to purchase realty that is attached to a leasehold estate is subject to the Rule.[293] But courts in the United States follow the better view that such options are not subject to the Rule because they do not hinder alienability of the land and because the option promotes tenant land improvements.[294] Therefore, a lessee's option to purchase the fee simple is valid though it may be exercised after the perpetuities period.

Preemptive rights ("rights of first refusal") should be distinguished from options to purchase. An option to purchase grants its holder the power to compel the owners to sell the property even if they do not want to sell. A preemptive right merely requires the owners, when and if they decide to sell, to offer the property first to the preemptive right holder. The holder then can meet a third-party offer or buy at the price specified in the

---

[287] E.g., Shepard v. Union & New Haven Tr. Co., 106 Conn. 627, 138 A. 809 (1927); Lanier v. Lanier, 218 Ga. 137, 126 S.E.2d 776 (1962), noted in 49 Iowa L. Rev. 200 (1963), 14 Mercer L. Rev. 275 (1962); Second Bank-State St. Tr. Co. v. Second Bank-State St. Tr. Co., 335 Mass. 407, 140 N.E.2d 201 (1957); In re Jones' Estate, 410 Pa. 380, 190 A.2d 120 (1963); Indus. Tr. Co. v. Flynn, 74 R.I. 396, 60 A.2d 851 (1948).

[288] E.g., Westport Paper-Board Co. v. Staples, 127 Conn. 115, 15 A.2d 1 (1940); Landrum v. Nat'l City Bank, 210 Ga. 316, 80 S.E.2d 300 (1954); Vickery v. Md. Tr. Co., 188 Md. 178, 52 A.2d 100 (1947).

[289] E.g., Sears v. Putnam, 102 Mass. 5 (1869); In re Lee's Estate, 49 Wash. 2d 254, 299 P.2d 1066 (1956).

[290] See generally 6 Am. L. Prop., supra note 1, at § 24.55 and authorities cited. When a contract for the sale of land contains no date for performance, a reasonable time, which is clearly less than 21 years may be implied. Therefore, the purchaser's equitable contingent future interest will not violate the Rule. Byke Constr. Co. v. Miller, 140 Ariz. 57, 680 P.2d 193 (Ct. App. 1984); Read v. GHDC, Inc., 254 Ga. 706, 334 S.E.2d 165 (1985); see also Estate of Royer v. Wineland Equip., Inc., 444 Pa. Super. 276, 663 A.2d 780 (Pa. Super. Ct. 1995).

[291] Cent. Del. Cty. Auth. v. Greyhound Corp., 527 Pa. 47, 588 A.2d 485 (1991); see also Silvicraft, Inc. v. Se. Timber Co., 34 Ark. App. 17, 805 S.W.2d 84 (1991); Certified Corp. v. GTE Prods. Corp., 392 Mass. 821, 467 N.E.2d 1336 (1984); Hansen v. Stroecker, 699 P.2d 871 (Alaska 1985). See generally 6 Am. L. Prop., supra note 1, at § 24.56.

[292] See generally 6 Am. L. Prop., supra note 1, at § 24.56.

[293] See J. C. Gray & R. Gray, The Rule Against Perpetuities § 230.3 (4th ed. 1942) and authorities cited.

[294] See 6 Am. L. Prop., supra note 1, at § 24.57 and authorities cited; see also Lattimore v. Fisher's Food Shoppe, Inc., 313 N.C. 467, 329 S.E.2d 346 (1985); Camerlo v. Howard Johnson Co., 710 F.2d 987 (3d Cir. 1983).

preemption agreement. If the preemptive right holder decides not to buy, the owners are free to sell to anyone they want.

Courts are divided as to whether the Rule applies to preemptive rights.[295] The courts that have declined to apply the Rule have generally done so on the ground that (1) the preemptive right holder has a vested property interest or (2) the holder has only a contract right, rather than a property interest. Some courts hold that preemptive rights are similar to options in gross and, therefore, subject to the Rule. Commentators have suggested that courts should concede that preemptive rights may create contingent future interests that ordinarily would be subject to the Rule but that their utility in many legal transactions may justify exempting them from the Rule. For example, a preemptive right should be exempted when it encourages the holder, such as a tenant, to develop property by protecting his or her ability to benefit from it.[296]

§ 3.19   PERPETUITIES PERIOD

The basic element of the perpetuities period—"some life in being at the creation of the interest"—was established in 1682 in *The Duke of Norfolk's Case,*[297] in which Lord Nottingham sustained a contingent future interest in a chattel real that was certain to vest or fail within a life in being at the creation of the interest. In later English cases, courts held that several lives can be used to delimit the perpetuities period. The courts also held that the measuring lives need not be the people who acquired an interest under the document in question,[298] so long as the designated "extraneous" lives are "neither so numerous nor so situated that evidence of deaths is likely to be unreasonably difficult to obtain."[299] In most cases, however, the relevant lives in being are the people who receive interests under the instrument creating the contingent future interest and of other persons closely connected with them, such as spouses and children.

The additional twenty-one years included in the perpetuities period seems to have been derived from the period of an actual minority during which a fee tail estate could be made unbarrable at common law.[300] Courts eventually determined that a period of twenty-one years in gross could be added to lives in being regardless of whether an actual

---

[295] Preemptive rights were held to be subject to the Rule in the following recent cases: Morrison v. Piper, 77 N.Y.2d 165, 565 N.Y.S.2d 444, 566 N.E.2d 643 (1990), appeal after remand 171 A.D.2d 958, 567 N.Y.S.2d 903 (N.Y. App. Div. 1991); Ferrero Constr. Co. v. Dennis Rourke Corp., 311 Md. 560, 536 A.2d 1137 (1988); Estate of Johnson v. Carr, 286 Ark. 369, 691 S.W.2d 161 (1985), appeal after remand 288 Ark. 461, 706 S.W.2d 388 (1986). The First Restatement of Property, supra note 37, at § 413 states that preemptive rights are subject to the Rule.

Contra, not applying the Rule to preemptive rights, see Cambridge Co. v. E. Slope Inv. Corp., 700 P.2d 537 (Colo. 1985), superseded by statute, Colo. Rev. Stat. Ann. § 15–11–1102.5 (West 2018), as recognized in Atl. Richfield Co. v. Whiting Oil & Gas Corp., 320 P.3d 1179 (Colo. 2014); Shiver v. Benton, 251 Ga. 284, 304 S.E.2d 903 (1983), appeal after remand 254 Ga. 107, 326 S.E.2d 756 (1985); Cherokee Water Co. v. Forderhause, 641 S.W.2d 522 (Tex. 1982); Robroy Land Co. v. Prather, 95 Wash. 2d 66, 622 P.2d 367 (1980).

[296] Simes & Smith, supra note 1, at § 1154; W. Leach, Perpetuities: New Absurdity, Judicial and Statutory Correctives, 73 Harv. L. Rev. 1318, 1320 (1960).

[297] Duke of Norfolk's Case, (1682) 22 Eng. Rep. 931.

[298] E.g., Low v. Burron (1734) 24 Eng. Rep. 1055; Thellusson v. Woodford (1799) 31 Eng. Rep. 117; Cadell v. Palmer (1833) 131 Eng. Rep. 859; Fitchie v. Brown, 211 U.S. 321, 29 S.Ct. 106, 53 L.Ed. 202 (1908).

[299] First Restatement of Property, supra note 37, § 374 (from which the statement quoted in the text is drawn); see In re Villar (1928) Ch. 471, (1929) 1 Ch. 243 (" 'ending at the expiration of twenty years from the day of the death of the last survivor of all the lineal descendants of Her Late Majesty Queen Victoria' who shall be living at the testator's death" held valid).

[300] Stephens v. Stephens (1736) 25 Eng. Rep. 751; Cole v. Sewell (1848) 9 Eng. Rep. 1062.

minority was involved.[301] Courts also determined that a person was in being for purposes of the Rule if conceived before, though born after, the date when the instrument creating the contingent future interest became operative.[302] However, a nine-month period in gross, unconnected with any actual gestation, could not be added to the perpetuities period.[303]

As indicated in Gray's statement of the Rule,[304] the perpetuities period starts to run in most cases when the contingent future interest is created.[305] But where that interest is subject to a power in any person to create an absolute beneficial interest (a fee simple absolute in realty or an equivalent interest in personalty) in himself, such as when a trust settlor reserves the power to revoke the trust and recover the trust property, the perpetuities period starts to run only upon the power's expiration.[306]

Suppose that, instead of one person having the power to create an absolute beneficial interest in himself, there are persons in being who can join together to transfer a fee simple absolute to a third person. For example, assume that land was transferred "to A, but if the land is ever used for nonresidential purposes, then to B." Acting together, A and B can transfer the fee simple absolute. However, because alienability is still fettered, courts have held that the Rule voids B's interest.[307]

Any power of appointment that is exercisable beyond the perpetuities period is void under the Rule,[308] unless it is a general power of appointment that can be exercised by either deed or will within the perpetuities period.[309] When an appointment is made pursuant to a valid general power to appoint both by deed and by will, the perpetuities period for the contingent future interests created by the appointment starts to run only from when the power is exercised.[310] But when an appointment is made pursuant to a valid special power or a valid general power to appoint only by will, the perpetuities period will run from when the power was created.[311]

---

[301] Cadell v. Palmer (1833) 131 Eng. Rep. 859.

[302] Long v. Blackall (1797) 101 Eng. Rep. 875. The period could include more than one period of gestation, which might come at the end or the beginning of the lives in being as well. See Thellusson v. Woodford (1799) 31 Eng. Rep. 117.

[303] Cadell v. Palmer (1833) 131 Eng. Rep. 859.

[304] Supra § 3.17 at note 263.

[305] For an inter vivos conveyance, the interest is created when the conveyance is delivered. For a will, it is created when the testator dies. E.g., Bradford v. Griffin, 40 S.C. 468, 19 S.E. 76 (1893) (deed); Safe Deposit & Tr. Co. v. Sheehan, 169 Md. 93, 179 A. 536 (1935) (will).

[306] E.g., Cook v. Horn, 214 Ga. 289, 104 S.E.2d 461 (1958); Mfrs. Life Ins. Co. v. Von Hamm-Young Co., 34 Haw. 288 (1937), reh'g denied 34 Haw. 316.

[307] In re Hargreaves (1890) 43 Ch. 401.

[308] In re Estate of Jones, 318 So. 2d 231 (Fla. Dist. Ct. App. 1975), cert. denied 334 So. 2d 606 (Fla. 1976); Camden Safe Deposit & Tr. Co. v. Scott, 121 N.J. Eq. 366, 189 A. 653, 110 A.L.R. 1442 (1937), noted in 36 Mich. L. Rev. 146 (1937); Am. Tr. Co. v. Williamson, 228 N.C. 458, 46 S.E.2d 104 (1948).

[309] E.g., Keville v. Hollister Co., 29 Cal. App. 3d 203, 105 Cal. Rptr. 238 (1972); Robinson v. Speer, 185 So. 2d 730 (Fla. Dist. Ct. App. 1966), cert. denied 192 So. 2d 498 (Fla. 1966); In re Ransom's Estate, 89 N.J. Super. 224, 214 A.2d 521 (1965).

[310] Matter of McMurtry, 68 Misc. 2d 553, 326 N.Y.S.2d 965 (Surr. Ct. 1971); Appeal of Mifflin, 121 Pa. 205, 15 A. 525 (1888); see also Keville v. Hollister, 29 Cal. App. 3d 203, 105 Cal. Rptr. 238 (1972); Restatement (Second) of Property: Donative Transfers § 1.2, cmt. d, illus. 10 (Am. Law Inst. 1983).

[311] E.g., In re Bird's Estate, 225 Cal. App. 2d 196, 37 Cal. Rptr. 288 (1964); Second Nat'l Bank of New Haven v. Harris Tr. & Sav. Bank, 29 Conn. Supp. 275, 283 A.2d 226 (Conn. Super. Ct. 1971).

§ 3.20   RULE AGAINST PERPETUITIES— SELECTED PROBLEMS

Consider the following examples in which the Rule Against Perpetuities invalidates a contingent future interest:

1.   O conveys "to A for so long as the property is used for church purposes, then to B." B's executory interest may not vest or fail within the perpetuities period and, therefore, is void under the Rule.[312] A has a fee simple determinable, and O has a possibility of reverter in fee simple absolute. The possibility of reverter is valid because the Rule does not apply to contingent reversionary future interests.[313] O could have conveyed a valid contingent future interest to B by using two transfers, instead of one. O first could have conveyed "to A so long as the property is used for church purposes," without an executory limitation to B. Then, in a state where possibilities of reverter are alienable, O could have conveyed the possibility of reverter to B by a separate conveyance. Alternatively, O could have transferred the property to B in fee simple absolute, and B could then have transferred a fee simple determinable to A, retaining a valid possibility of reverter.

2.   O conveys "to A, but if the property should ever cease to be used for church purposes, then to B." Again, B's executory interest is void under the Rule because it may not vest or fail within the perpetuities period.[314] However, unlike the previous example, most courts would hold that A has a fee simple absolute. Courts generally will not imply a right of entry.[315] But, as in the previous example, O could have used two conveyances to transfer a valid contingent future interest to B that would become possessory if the property was not used for church purposes. O first could have transferred a fee simple subject to condition subsequent to A. Then, in a state where a right of entry is alienable, O could transfer the right of entry to B by a separate instrument. Alternatively, if B would cooperate, O could have transferred a fee simple absolute to B, and B could then have transferred a fee simple subject to condition subsequent to A and retained the right of entry.

These two examples show that an executory interest is always void under the Rule if the event that will make the executory interest possessory is not subject to a time limit. However, the ease with which the Rule can be avoided by using two transfers strongly suggests that it makes little sense to hold—as American courts traditionally have done—that executory interests are subject to the Rule but that contingent reversionary interests are not.[316]

3.   O conveys "to A for life, remainder to the first child of A, whenever born, who becomes a lawyer." If the remainder is contingent because A does not have a child who

---

[312] E.g., McCrory Sch. Dist. of Woodruff Cty. v. Brogden, 231 Ark. 664, 333 S.W.2d 246 (1960); Brown v. Indep. Baptist Church of Woburn, 325 Mass. 645, 91 N.E.2d 922 (1950); Jones v. Burns, 221 Miss. 833, 74 So. 2d 866 (1954); Donehue v. Nilges, 364 Mo. 705, 266 S.W.2d 553, 45 A.L.R.2d 1150 (1954).

[313] See supra § 3.18, text accompanying note 273.

[314] E.g., McMahon v. Consistory of Saint Paul's Reformed Church at Westminster, 196 Md. 125, 75 A.2d 122 (1950); Betts v. Snyder, 341 Pa. 465, 19 A.2d 82 (1941); Rust v. Rust, 147 Tex. 181, 214 S.W.2d 462 (1948).

[315] Simes & Smith, supra note 1, § 824.

[316] Some American legislatures have enacted statutes that either make contingent reversionary interests subject to the Rule Against Perpetuities or limit their duration to a fixed period of years. See infra § 3.22.

is a lawyer when the transfer occurs and if the contingent remainder is indestructible under state law, the remainder may not vest or fail within the perpetuities period because the only relevant lives in being are A and any child of A who is alive when the transfer occurs. A's first child to become a lawyer, if any, may not do so for more than twenty-one years, plus any actual period of gestation, after the deaths of A and all of A's children who are living when the transfer occurs. Therefore, the remainder is void under the Rule, and O has a reversion in fee simple absolute. However, if state law makes the contingent remainder destructible, it would be valid because it would vest or fail no later than A's death.

4.   O conveys "to A for life, remainder to A's first child to reach twenty-five." If A does not have a child who is at least twenty-five when the transfer occurs and if the contingent remainder is indestructible under state law, the remainder may not vest or fail within the perpetuities period, because the only relevant lives in being are A and any child of A who is alive when the transfer occurs. A's first child to reach twenty-five, if any, may not do so for more than twenty-one years, plus any actual period of gestation, after the deaths of A and all of A's children who are alive when the transfer occurs. As in example 3, the contingent remainder is void under the Rule, and O has a reversion in fee simple absolute. Also as in example 3, if the remainder is destructible under state law, it is valid because it will vest or fail no later than A's death.

5.   O conveys "to A for life, remainder to A's children for life, and upon the death of A's last surviving child, to such of A's grandchildren as are then living." The remainder to A's children includes all children born before or after the transfer takes effect. The remainder is valid because the class members will be determined at A's death, plus any actual period of gestation. But the contingent remainder in favor of A's grandchildren is void under the Rule, because it is not certain to vest or fail within the perpetuities period. The only relevant lives in being are A and any child of A who is living when the transfer takes effect. A's last surviving child may die more than twenty-one years after the deaths of A and all of A's children who were living when the transfer took effect. Because the contingent remainder in favor of A's grandchildren is void, O has a reversion in fee simple absolute.

6.   O conveys "to A for life, remainder to such of A's lineal descendants as are alive on January 1, 2041." If the transfer is effective before January 1, 2020 and if contingent remainders are indestructible under state law, the remainder is void because it may not vest or fail within twenty-one years. The only relevant lives in being are A and any descendants of A who are alive when the transfer occurs, and they are not related to the date for determining the identities of the remainder holders in any legally relevant manner. O has a reversion in fee simple absolute following A's life estate.

7.   O conveys "to A for life, remainder to A's widow for her life, remainder to A's children who are alive at the widow's death." This example involves the "case of the unborn widow." The remainder to A's children is void because they must survive A's widow, and she might not have been born before the transfer occurred and might outlive A and any of A's children who were alive when the transfer occurred by more than twenty-one years.[317] O has a reversion in fee simple absolute that follows the life estates to A and A's widow, if any.

---

[317] E.g., Re Allan's Will Trusts (1958) 1 All E.R. 401; Dickerson v. Union Nat'l Bank of Little Rock, 268 Ark. 292, 595 S.W.2d 677 (1980).

8. O conveys "to A for life, remainder to those of A's grandchildren who reach the age of twenty-one years." The remainder to A's grandchildren is void if contingent remainders are indestructible under state law and if A can have children after the transfer occurs, because the remainder may not vest or fail within twenty-one years after the deaths of A and all of A's children who are alive when the transfer occurs.[318] If A has additional children after the date of the transfer, they will not be lives in being, and they may have children who will not reach twenty-one within twenty-one years after the deaths of A and any children of A who are alive when the transfer occurs. Moreover, courts have generally presumed that A is capable of having additional children regardless of age and sex.[319] In the famous "case of the fertile octogenarian," the court applied this presumption though A was an eighty year old woman.[320] Keep in mind that "grandchildren" can include A's adopted children. However, adoption statutes and procedures often deny adoption to persons of advanced age, and a few states have statutorily eliminated the conclusive presumption of reproductive capacity for perpetuities purposes.[321] At least one state has eliminated the conclusive presumption by judicial decision.[322]

In some cases, the conclusive presumption of reproductive capacity may be avoided by construing language to exclude children who theoretically could be born to the transferee after the transfer. In the last example, if A is an eighty year old woman when the transfer occurs, a court could construe "those of A's grandchildren who reach the age of twenty-one years" as referring only to the children of A's then living children, in which case the remainder would be valid. A few courts have adopted this construction,[323] despite the traditional rule that courts should not construe language to avoid applying the Rule Against Perpetuities.[324]

The common law Rule Against Perpetuities has been subject to vigorous criticism because of (1) "the glaring absurdities of the requirement of absolute certainty from the beginning" that a contingent future interest will vest or fail within the perpetuities period; (2) "the fact that if an interest violates the Rule it is completely defeated instead

---

[318] E.g., Jee v. Audley (1787) 29 Eng. Rep. 1186; First Ala. Bank of Montgomery v. Adams, 382 So. 2d 1104 (Ala. 1980); Conn. Bank & Tr. Co. v. Brody, 174 Conn. 616, 392 A.2d 445 (1978); Nelson v. Mercantile Trust Co., 335 S.W.2d 167 (Mo. 1960); Parker v. Parker, 252 N.C. 399, 113 S.E.2d 899 (1960).

[319] Simes & Smith, supra note 1, § 1229.

[320] Jee v. Audley (1787) 29 Eng. Rep. 1186.

[321] Idaho Code Ann. § 55–111 (West 2018); N.Y. Est. Powers & Trusts § 7–1.9 (McKinney 2018) (presumption limited to males over 14 and females aged 12 to 55, and it may be rebutted by evidence); Tenn. Code Ann. § 24–5–112 (West 2018); see also Perpetuities and Accumulations Act 1964, 13 Eliz. 2 c. 55, § 2 (UK) (same as N.Y. statute, supra).

[322] In re Bassett's Estate, 104 N.H. 504, 190 A.2d 415, 98 A.L.R.2d 1281 (1963), noted in 43 B.U. L. Rev. 562 (1963), 62 Mich. L. Rev. 1099 (1964); see also W. Leach, Perpetuities: New Hampshire Defertilizes the Octogenarians, 77 Harv. L. Rev. 279 (1963). And see Exham v. Beamish (1939) Ir. R. 336, noted in 53 Harv. L. Rev. 490 (1940) (also holding the presumption to be rebuttable).

[323] This conclusion is supported by Worcester Cty. Tr. Co. v. Marble, 316 Mass. 294, 55 N.E.2d 446 (1944); In re Wright's Estate, 284 Pa. 334, 131 A. 188 (1925).

[324] In re Lattouf's Will, 87 N.J. Super. 137, 208 A.2d 411 (N.J. Super. Ct. App. Div. 1965). As to the presumption of reproductive capacity, see generally W. Leach, Perpetuities in the Atomic Age: The Sperm Bank and the Fertile Decedent, 48 A.B.A.J. 942 (1962) (suggesting that it is now possible for a male to beget children after his death); R. Lynn, Raising the Perpetuities Question: Conception, Adoption, "Wait and See," and Cy Pres, 17 Vand. L. Rev. 1391 (1964); C. Sappideen, Life After Death—Sperm Banks, Wills and Perpetuities, 53 Austl. L.J. 311 (1979); W. Schwartz, Mr. Justice Kenison and Creative Continuity in Perpetuities Law, 48 B.U. L. Rev. 207, 219 (1968).

of being remodeled to accommodate itself to the Rule"; (3) "the fact that possibilities of reverter and rights of entry for condition broken are (under American law at least) exempt from the Rule"; and (4) "the fact that vested interests are not subject to the Rule, enabling property to be effectively tied up for over a hundred years."[325] Many states have enacted legislation in response to these criticisms. The most important legislative responses have been the so-called wait and see rule, which tests the validity of contingent future interests on the basis of actual events, rather than on merely possible events, and statutes providing for *cy pres* reformation of limitations that cause an interest to violate the common law Rule. The Uniform Statutory Rule Against Perpetuities incorporates both of these modifications, together with an alternative perpetuities period of 90 years in gross.[326]

Another response to criticisms leveled against the common law Rule is the development of "saving clauses" that are included in instruments creating contingent future interests. The late Professor W. Barton Leach, in cooperation with an estate planning group and counsel for several corporate fiduciaries, drafted a Standard Saving Clause. It gives a corporate fiduciary the power to reform an interest that is challenged as violating the common law Rule "in such manner as will most closely approximate, within permissible limits, the intention of the testator, settlor or appointer" to avoid violating the Rule.[327] Others have prepared additional types of saving clauses.[328] Courts generally appear to uphold saving clauses.[329]

§ 3.21 EARLY STATUTORY MODIFICATIONS OF THE COMMON LAW RULE AGAINST PERPETUITIES

In 1830, New York enacted the first significant statutory modification of the common law Rule Against Perpetuities. The New York legislation prohibited the creation of any future interest that would suspend the absolute power of alienation of real property or "the absolute ownership of personal property" for longer than "two lives in being" when the future interest was created.[330] For real property, the New York statute made an exception if a contingent remainder in fee was "created on a prior remainder in fee, to take effect in the event that the persons to whom the first remainder is limited, shall die under the age of twenty-one years, or upon any other contingency, by which the estate of such persons may be determined before they attain their full age." A similar exception for personal property was added in 1929.[331] Although this legislation expressly prohibited only suspension of the absolute power of ownership, courts held that it invalidated certain contingent future interests that were not certain to vest or fail within

---

[325] Am. L. Prop., supra note 1, at § 24.11 (Supp. 1976, p. 855).

[326] See infra § 3.22 for discussion of all these legislative modifications of the common law Rule Against Perpetuities.

[327] W. Leach & J. Logan, Perpetuities: A Standard Saving Clause to Avoid Violations of the Rule, 74 Harv. L. Rev. 1141 (1961).

[328] E.g., A. Casner, Estate Planning 1251–52 (3d ed. 1961); R. Goldman, Drafting Trust Instruments Revisited, 36 U. Cin. L. Rev. 650, 657–58 (1967); Comment, That "Simple and Clear Rule"—The Common Law Rule Against Perpetuities in Mississippi, 34 Miss. L.J. 63, 80 (1962).

[329] E.g., Norton v. Georgia R.R. Bank & Tr., 253 Ga. 596, 322 S.E.2d 870 (1984); Nelson v. Mercantile Tr. Co., 335 S.W.2d 167 (Mo. 1960); Zweig v. Zweig, 275 S.W.2d 201 (Tex. Civ. App. 1955), error refused n.r.e.; In re Lee's Estate, 49 Wash. 2d 254, 299 P.2d 1066 (1956); Lux v. Lux, 109 R.I. 592, 288 A.2d 701 (1972).

[330] In its current form, this legislation is codified as N.Y. Est. Powers & Trusts § 9–1.1–1.3 (McKinney 2018).

[331] N.Y. Laws 1929, c. 229, § 18.

the statutory two-life period though they did not suspend the power of alienation or ownership for more than two lives.[332]

New York amended the legislation[333] (1) to change the permissible period during which the absolute power of alienation or ownership can be suspended to lives in being when the transfer was made, plus "a term of twenty-one years,"[334] and (2) to enact the common law Rule Against Perpetuities.[335] Therefore, the same perpetuities period now applies to both the prohibition against suspending the absolute power of alienation or ownership and the prohibition against creating future interests that may vest or fail too remotely. In both cases, an actual period of gestation may be added to the statutory period,[336] and measuring lives cannot be "so designated or so numerous as to make proof of their end unreasonably difficult."[337] The current New York rules against suspending the power of alienation and remoteness of vesting are also qualified by a *cy pres* provision that applies to a limitation that a person must reach an age of more than twenty-one years[338] and by rules of construction that tend to prevent invalidation.[339] In addition, New York has codified the common law rules concerning the time from which the statutory perpetuities period is counted to determine the validity of the exercise of a power of appointment.[340]

During the nineteenth century, fourteen other jurisdictions enacted legislation based on the 1830 New York legislation.[341] In one of these jurisdictions, Iowa, the legislation may have been intended merely to codify the common law Rule Against Perpetuities.[342] In the other twelve jurisdictions, subsequent amendments modified the original legislation in various respects, but the basic tenor of the legislation in these states remained very similar to that of the New York legislation until quite recently.[343]

---

[332] Matter of Wilcox, 194 N.Y. 288, 87 N.E. 497 (1909); Walker v. Marcellus & Otisco Lake Ry. Co., 226 N.Y. 347, 123 N.E. 736 (1919).

[333] These amendments were codified in what is now N.Y. Est. Powers & Trusts § 9–1.1–1.3 (McKinney 2018).

[334] Id. § 9–1.1(a)(2).

[335] Id. § 9–1.1(b).

[336] Id. § 9–1.1(a)(2), (b).

[337] Id.

[338] Id. § 9–1.2. For the meaning of *cy pres,* see text infra § 3.22, second paragraph.

[339] Id. § 9–1.3. These rules are designed, inter alia, to prevent invalidation when limitations involve an unborn widow or a fertile octogenarian. See text supra § 3.20.

[340] N.Y. Est. Powers & Trusts §§ 10–8.1, 10–8.3; see Matter of Grunebaum, 122 Misc. 2d 645, 471 N.Y.S.2d 513 (Surr. Ct. 1984) (exercise of power of appointment "suspended illegally the absolute power of alienation and violated the rule against perpetuities"); Accounting of Estate of Isganaitis, 124 Misc. 2d 1, 475 N.Y.S.2d 699 (Surr. Ct. 1983) (testamentary provision must comply with both the remoteness of vesting and the suspension of absolute power of alienation tests of the statutory rule).

[341] These jurisdictions were Arizona, California, the District of Columbia, Idaho, Iowa, Indiana, Kentucky, Michigan, Minnesota, Montana, North Dakota, Oklahoma, South Dakota, and Wisconsin. Simes & Smith, supra note 1, §§ 1415, 1416, 1420, 1424, 1426, 1427, 1429, 1433, 1434, 1437, 1445, 1447, 1452, 1460.

[342] Iowa subsequently amended the legislation and codified the common law Rule Against Perpetuities, as modified by the wait and see and *cy pres* reformation doctrines, in accordance with the Second Restatement of Property, supra note 228. See Iowa Code Ann. § 558.68 (West 2018). See Simes & Smith, supra note 1, §§ 1427, 1429.

[343] Some of the New York-type statutes were amended to provide different permissible periods for suspension of the power of alienation. See Simes & Smith, supra note 1, at ch. 41.

Legislation prohibiting suspension of the power of alienation is incompatible with the Uniform Statutory Rule Against Perpetuities (USRAP).[344] Approximately thirty-two jurisdictions have enacted USRAP (though many have amended it in recent years), and most of them that had legislation prohibiting suspension of the power of alienation repealed it when they adopted USRAP. Only a few jurisdictions still have this legislation for newly-created interests.[345]

§ 3.22   MORE RECENT STATUTORY MODIFICATIONS OF THE COMMON LAW RULE AGAINST PERPETUITIES

Many states have enacted legislation that modifies the common law Rule Against Perpetuities in important respects. One type of modification is wait and see legislation.[346] It provides that the validity of future interests under the Rule is to be determined by actual future events, rather than possible future events. Pennsylvania enacted the first wait and see legislation in 1947.[347] It provided in part:

> Upon the expiration of the period allowed by the common law rule against perpetuities as measured by actual rather than possible events, any interest not then vested and any interest in members of a class the membership of which is then subject to increase shall be void.

Another type of legislation modifies the common law Rule Against Perpetuities by authorizing or directing courts to reform instruments that violate the Rule by applying the equitable doctrine of *cy pres*. For example, a courts may reduce a period of more than twenty-one years in gross or an age contingency of more than twenty-one years to twenty-one years so that an interest that otherwise would be void for remoteness will either vest or fail within the common law perpetuities period.

Some states have legislation that includes both wait and see and *cy pres*,[348] and a few other states have legislation that includes only one or the other of these modifications of the common law Rule.[349] However, the most widespread modification of

---

[344] The USRAP and other legislation that incorporates the wait and see and *cy pres* reforms of the common law Rule are discussed infra § 3.22.

[345] E.g., Alaska Stat. § 34.27.100; N.J. Stat. Ann. § 46:2F–10; S.D. Codified Laws § 43–5–1; Wis. Stat. Ann. § 700.16. J. Dukeminier & J. Krier, The Rise of the Perpetual Trust. 50 UCLA L. Rev. 1303, 1313–14 (2003).

[346] The Second Restatement of Property adopted the wait and see approach, but the Third Restatement has replaced it with a perpetuities period that ends "at the death of the last living measuring life" who can be no more than "two generations younger than the transferor." Second Restatement of Property, supra note 228, § 1.4; Third Restatement of Property, supra note 1, § 27.1. See T. Gallanis, The New Direction of American Trust Law, 97 Iowa L. Rev. 215 (2011); T. Merrill & H. Smith, Why Restate the Bundle?: The Disintegration of the Restatement of Property, 79 Brooklyn L. Rev. 681 (2014).

[347] 20 Pa. Stat. and Cons. Stat. Ann. § 6104 (West 2018) (part of the Pennsylvania Estates Act of 1947). Subsequently, many states have enacted wait and see legislation. Some of this legislation differs in substantial respects from the pioneering Pennsylvania wait and see legislation. While Pennsylvania directs the courts to wait and see for the full common law perpetuities period, some statutes direct the courts to wait and see only until expiration of all life estates created by the instrument in question.

[348] E.g., Iowa Code Ann. § 558.68; Ohio Rev. Code Ann. § 2131.08(C); Vt. Stat. Ann. tit. 27, § 501. See 10 Powell, supra note 1, § 75A.03[1].

[349] See 10 Powell, supra note 1, § 75A.02.

the common law Rule is the Uniform Statutory Rule Against Perpetuities.[350] In its current form, USRAP provides as follows:

Section 1. Statutory Rule Against Perpetuities

(a) [Validity of Nonvested Property Interest.] A nonvested property interest is invalid unless:

(1) when the interest is created, it is certain to vest or terminate no later than 21 years after the death of an individual then alive; or

(2) the interest either vests or terminates within 90 years after its creation.

(b) [Validity of General Power of Appointment Subject to a Condition Precedent.] A general power of appointment not presently exercisable because of a condition precedent is invalid unless:

(1) when the power is created, the condition precedent is certain to be satisfied or becomes impossible to satisfy no later than 21 years after the death of an individual then alive; or

(2) the condition precedent either is satisfied or becomes impossible to satisfy within 90 years after its creation.

(c) [Validity of Nongeneral or Testamentary Power of Appointment.] A nongeneral power of appointment or a general testamentary power of appointment is invalid unless:

(1) when the power is created, it is certain to be irrevocably exercised or otherwise to terminate no later than 21 years after the death of an individual then alive; or

(2) the power is irrevocably exercised or otherwise terminates within 90 years after its creation.

* * *

Section 3. Reformation

Upon the petition of an interested person, a court shall reform a disposition in the manner that most closely approximates the transferor's manifested plan of distribution and is within the 90 years allowed by Section 1(a)(2), 1(b)(2), or 1(c)(2) if:

(1) a nonvested property interest or a power of appointment becomes invalid under Section 1 (statutory rule against perpetuities);

(2) a class gift is not but might become invalid under Section 1 (statutory rule against perpetuities) and the time has arrived when the share of any class member is to take effect in possession or enjoyment; or

---

[350] The text of the USRAP, with the 1990 Amendment, appears in Uniform Laws Annotated as Article II, Pt. 9 of the Uniform Probate Code, and as a freestanding statute, presumably to make it easier for a state that has not adopted the Uniform Probate Code to enact USRAP. Uniform Statutory Rule Against Perpetuities (Unif. Law Comm'n 1986/1990) (hereinafter USRAP).

(3)   a nonvested property interest that is not validated by Section
1(a)(1) can vest but not within 90 years after its creation.

As the quoted provisions show, USRAP incorporates the common law Rule and
supplements it with wait and see, *cy pres*, and an alternative 90-year perpetuities period.
Approximately thirty-two jurisdictions have enacted it.[351]

In general, USRAP applies only to donative and other intrafamily transfers but not
to commercial transactions.[352] Therefore, options and preemptive rights to purchase land
(unless created by gift) are no longer subject to time strictures.[353] USRAP also excludes
from its coverage all transfers in which both the present and future interests are held by
charitable or governmental entities.[354] The statute expressly supersedes the common
law Rule Against Perpetuities and other incompatible state laws, including *cy pres* and
wait and see legislation, in favor of the new statutory rules.[355] The statute applies only
to interests created by transfers occurring after the statute's effective date.[356] However,
if a transfer occurred before USRAP's effective date but is adjudged after that date to
violate the state's preexisting perpetuities law, courts are invited to "reform the
disposition in the manner that most closely approximates the transferor's manifested
plan of distribution and is within the limits of the rule against perpetuities applicable"
at the time of transfer.[357]

The addition of an alternative 90-year perpetuities period is probably the most
significant modification of the common law Rule Against Perpetuities, particularly in
states that had adopted both wait and see and *cy pres*. The Prefatory Note to USRAP
explains the rationale of the 90-year vesting period as follows:[358]

> The   myriad   problems   associated   with   the   actual-measuring-lives
> approach are swept aside by shifting away from actual measuring lives and
> adopting instead a 90-year permissible vesting period as representing a
> reasonable approximation of—a proxy for—the period of time that would, on
> average, be produced by identifying and tracing an actual set of measuring lives

---

[351]   Ala. Code §§ 35–4A–1 to –8; Ariz. Rev. Stat. Ann. §§ 14–2901–07 (West 2018) (eff. Jan. 1, 2009); Ark.
Code Ann. §§ 18–3–101 to –109; Cal. Prob. Code §§ 21200–31 (West 2018) (eff. Jan. 1, 1992); Colo. Rev. Stat.
Ann. §§ 15–11–1101–07 (West 2018) (eff. Jan. 1, 1992); Conn. Gen. Stat. Ann. § 45a–491–501 (West 2018) (eff.
May 2, 1989); D.C. Code §§ 19–901 to –907; Fla. Stat. Ann. § 689.225 (West 2018) (eff. Oct. 1, 1988); Ga. Code
Ann. §§ 44–6–200–06 (West 2018) (eff. May 1, 1990); Haw. Rev. Stat. Ann. § 525–1–6 (West 2017) (eff. June
1992); Ind. Code Ann. §§ 32–1–4.5–1–6 (West 2018) (§§ 32–1–4.5–1–3, 32–1–4.5–5–6 eff. July 1, 1991; § 32–1–
4–4 eff. May 8, 1991); Kan. Stat. Ann. §§ 59–3401–3408 (2018); 33 Me. Rev. Stat. Ann. § 111 (eff. 2018); Mass.
Gen. Laws Ann. Ch. 184A, §§ 1–11 (West 2018) (eff. June 30, 1990); Mich. Comp. Laws Ann. §§ 554.71–78
(West 2018) (eff. Dec. 24, 1988); Minn. Stat. Ann. §§ 501A.01–07 (West 2017) (eff. Jan. 1, 1992); Mont. Code
Ann. §§ 70–1–801–07 (West 2017) (eff. Oct. 1, 1989); Neb. Rev. Stat. Ann. §§ 76–2001–08 (West 2018) (eff.
August 25, 1989); Nev. Rev. Stat. Ann. §§ 111.103–39 (West 2017) (eff. Mar. 17, 1987); N.M. Stat. Ann. §§ 45–
2–1001–07 (West 2018) (eff. Mar. 1992); N.C. Gen. Stat §§ 41–15–22 (West 2017) (eff. Oct. 1, 1995); N.D. Cent.
Code Ann. §§ 47–02–27.1–7.5 (West 2017) (eff. July 1, 1991); Or. Rev. Stat. Ann. §§ 105.950–75 (West 2018)
(eff. Jan. 1, 1990); S.C. Code Ann. §§ 27–6–10–80 (West 2018) (eff. March 12, 1987); Tenn. Code Ann. § 66–1–
201–08 (West 2018) (eff. July 1, 1994); Utah Code Ann. §§ 75–2–1201–08 (West 2017) (eff. July 1, 1998); Va.
Code Ann. § 55–12.1 (eff. 2013); W. Va. Code Ann. §§ 36–1A–1–6 (West 2018) (eff. 1992).

[352]   USRAP, supra note 350, § 4(1).

[353]   See § 3.18 supra; § 10.14 infra.

[354]   USRAP, supra note 350, § 4(5).

[355]   USRAP, supra note 350, § 9.

[356]   USRAP, supra note 350, § 5.

[357]   USRAP, supra note 350, § 5(b).

[358]   USRAP, supra note 350, at Prefatory Note (citations omitted).

and then tacking on a 21-year period following the death of the survivor. The selection of 90 years as the period of time reasonably approximating the period that would be produced, on average, by using the set of actual measuring lives identified in the Restatement (Second) [of Property] or the earlier draft of the Uniform Act is based on a statistical study published in Waggoner, *Perpetuities: A Progress Report on the Draft Uniform Statutory Rule Against Perpetuities*, 20 U. Miami Inst. on Est. Plan. Ch. 7 (1986). This study suggests that the youngest measuring life, on average, is about 6 years old. The remaining life expectancy of a 6-year old is reported as 69.6 years in the U.S. Bureau of the Census, Statistical Abstract of the United States: 1986, Table 108, at p. 69. (In the Statistical Abstract for 1985, 69.3 years was reported.) In the interest of arriving at an end number that is a multiple of five, the Uniform Act utilizes 69 years as an appropriate measure of the remaining life expectancy of a 6-year old, which—with the 21-year tack-on period added—yields a permissible vesting period of 90 years.

The adoption of a flat period of 90 years rather than the use of actual measuring lives is an evolutionary step in the development and refinement of the wait-and-see doctrine. Far from revolutionary, it is well within the tradition of that doctrine. The 90-year period makes wait-and-see simple, fair, and workable. *Aggregate dead-hand control will not be increased beyond that which is already possible by competent drafting under the Common-law Rule.*

Not all commentators have a positive view of USRAP. For example, Professor Jesse Dukeminier has argued that, contrary to the statement from the Prefatory Note quoted above, the 90-year period is a great deal longer than the typical time limitation imposed by the common law Rule and, in effect, guarantees an undesirable 90-year period of dead-hand control.[359] Professor Dukeminier has also suggested that the 90-year period during which the property title will be held in an uncertain manner is undesirably and unnecessarily long. Note that any wait and see system of perpetuities restriction creates this same uncertainty. Finally, he has argued that the common law period is not especially difficult to measure and is much preferable to the USRAP's 90-year period in gross.[360]

Even more radical reform is now afoot—the virtually complete abolition of the Rule. Idaho,[361] South Dakota,[362] and Wisconsin[363] have had statutes for a number of years confirming that the Rule is not in force. More recently, several other states have abolished the Rule or made it optional for property held in trust, provided (in most of

---

[359] J. Dukeminier, The Uniform Statutory Rule Against Perpetuities: Ninety Years in Limbo, 34 UCLA L. Rev. 1023 (1987).

[360] Dukeminier also criticizes the USRAP because it fails to include possibilities of reverter and rights of entry within its scope. See § 3.18 supra.

[361] Idaho Code Ann. § 55–111 (West 2018) (eff. 1957), which prohibits suspension of the power of alienation for a period longer than lives in being, plus 25 years. See Riley v. Rowan, 131 Idaho 831, 965 P.2d 191 (1998).

[362] S.D. Codified Laws §§ 43–5–1 through –8 (West 2018) (eff. 1983), which prohibits suspension of the power of alienation for a period longer than lives in being, plus 30 years.

[363] Wis. Stat. Ann § 700.16 (West 2017) (eff. 1971), which prohibits suspension of the power of alienation for a period longer than lives in being, plus 30 years.

those states) that the trustee has the power to sell the trust assets.[364] Some states also now permit trusts to last for extended periods of time, such as 1,000 years.[365] These approaches do address concerns about the marketability of property, but they do nothing to allay concerns about dead hand control and about perpetuating concentrations of wealth. The principal political objective for these laws seems to have been to attract large dynasty trusts to the states in question.[366] Although banks and other professional trustees may urge the elimination of perpetuities restrictions, doing so is highly questionable public policy, especially if neither the beneficiaries nor the courts have any authority to terminate such trusts.[367]

E. CHARACTERISTICS OF FUTURE INTERESTS

§ 3.23 INHERITABILITY AND DEVISABILITY OF FUTURE INTERESTS

As a general rule, future interests of all types are inheritable and devisable by will in the same manner as present interests in land and in personalty.[368] Contingent future interests limited in favor of an unborn person or persons are obviously neither inheritable nor devisable by will.[369]

Possibilities of reverter and powers of termination are generally inheritable (intestate succession) and devisable (testate succession) in the same manner as present interests in land or personalty.[370] However, in some states, these contingent

---

[364] See, e.g., Del. Code Ann. tit. 25, §§ 501–06; Idaho Code Ann. § 55–111; 765 Ill. Comp. Stat. 305/3 to /4; Ky. Rev. Stat. Ann. § 381.224; Md. Code Ann., Est. & Trusts § 11–102; Mo. Rev. Stat. § 456.025; Neb. Rev. Stat. § 76–2005; N.H. Rev. Stat. Ann. § 564:24; N.J. Stat. Ann. §§ 46:2F–9 to –11; N.C. Gen. Stat. § 41–23(h); Ohio Rev. Code Ann. § 2131.09; Pa. Cons. Stat. § 6107.1; R.I. Gen. Laws § 34–11–38; S.D. Codified Laws § 43–5–8; Va. Code Ann. § 55–13.3; Wis. Stat. § 700.16(5); Third Restatement of Property, supra note 1, ch. 27, intro. n.42; J. Dukeminier & J. Krier, The Rise of the Perpetual Trust, 50 UCLA L. Rev. 1303 (2003); T. Gallanis, The New Direction of American Trust Law, 97 Iowa L. Rev. 215, 231 (2011).

[365] See, e.g. Alaska Stat. § 34.27.051; Ariz. Rev. Stat. Ann. § 14–2901; Colo. Rev. Stat. § 15–11–1102.5; Del. Code Ann. tit. 25, § 503; Fla. Stat. § 689.225; Mich. Comp. Laws Ann. §§ 554.71–.78; Nev. Rev. Stat. § 111.1031; Tenn. Code Ann. § 66 1–202; Utah Code Ann. § 75–2–1203; Wash. Rev. Code §§ 11.98.130–.150; Wyo. Stat. Ann. § 34–1–139; Third Restatement of Property, supra note 1, ch. 27, intro. n.43; T. Gallanis, The New Direction of American Trust Law, 97 Iowa L. Rev. 215, 231–32 (2011).

[366] R. Sitkoff & M. Schanzenbach, Jurisdictional Competition for Trust Funds: An Empirical Analysis of Perpetuities and Taxes, 115 Yale L.J. 356 (2005).

[367] The American Law Institute has stated: "It is the considered opinion of The American Law Institute that the recent statutory movement allowing the creation of perpetual or near-perpetual trusts is ill advised." Third Restatement of Property, supra note 1, ch. 27, intro. note.

[368] Simes & Smith, supra note 1, § 1883, asserting that, although the rule is the result of modern statutes of descent and distribution in the United States, "a court would be justified in reaching that result entirely independent of statute."

[369] As soon as a person answering the description in the contingent limitation is born, the contingent interest vests and becomes inheritable and devisable.

[370] For possibilities of reverter, see, e.g., Sch. Dist. No. Six in Weld Cty. v. Russell, 156 Colo. 75, 396 P.2d 929 (1964), noted in 41 Denver Law Center J. 396 (1964); Willhite v. Masters, 965 S.W.2d 406 (Mo. Ct. App. 1998); City of Wheeling v. Zane, 154 W. Va. 34, 173 S.E.2d 158 (1970), noted in 73 W. Va. L. Rev. 91 (1971). For powers of termination, see, e.g., Watson v. Dalton, 146 Neb. 78, 20 N.W.2d 610 (1945). Accord, First Restatement of Property, supra note 37, § 164. Some states statutorily provide that all future interests or, specifically, that possibilities of reverter and powers of termination are descendible and devisable. E.g., Md. Code Ann., Real Prop. § 6–104 (West 2018); Minn. Stat. Ann. § 500.16 (West 2017); N.Y. Est. Powers & Trusts § 11–a (McKinney 2018). Ironically, a few statutes make possibilities of reverter and powers of termination

reversionary interests pass "by representation," rather than by the usual law of intestate succession.[371] For example, if O conveys land "to A and his heirs for so long as the premises are used only for residential purposes," O retains a possibility of reverter. If O then dies intestate, leaving his son X as his sole heir, X takes the possibility of reverter "by representation" from O, who is the "stock of descent." If X does not transfer the possibility of reverter by deed and dies intestate, the possibility of reverter will pass to the person who would have been O's heir if O had died when X died, because O, not X, is the stock of descent. Therefore, the person who gets the property at X's death may not be his heir. This pattern of descent will continue until either the owner of the possibility of reverter makes an inter vivos transfer or the possibility of reverter becomes a present interest. When the possibility of reverter is transferred inter vivos, the transferee becomes the new stock of descent, and the same rule of succession by representation applies if the transferee dies intestate.[372] In states where possibilities of reverter and powers of termination pass by representation when the owner dies intestate, courts are likely to hold that those interests are not devisable by will.[373]

A remainder for the life of its holder is obviously neither inheritable nor devisable, but a remainder *pur autre vie* is both inheritable and devisable if the owner predeceases the person who is the measuring life.[374]

§ 3.24 ALIENABILITY OF FUTURE INTERESTS INTER VIVOS

Vested future interests. All vested future interests—remainders and reversions—are freely transferable inter vivos, whether the subject matter is land or personalty,[375] unless the future interest is subject to a valid restraint on alienation.[376]

Contingent remainders and executory interests. The inter vivos alienability of contingent future interests is not as clearly established. According to the English common law, a contingent remainder was inalienable because it was merely the

---

non-devisable and non-alienable inter vivos. See Neb. Rev. Stat. Ann. §§ 76–107–299 (West 2018); 765 Ill. Comp. Stat. Ann. 330/1 (West 2018).

[371] For possibilities of reverter, see, e.g., Elmore v. Austin, 232 N.C. 13, 59 S.E.2d 205 (1950); Burnett v. Snoddy, 199 S.C. 399, 405, 19 S.E.2d 904, 906 (1942). For powers of termination, see, e.g., Methodist Protestant Church of Henderson v. Young, 130 N.C. 8, 40 S.E. 691 (1902).

[372] This illustration is drawn from Simes & Smith, supra note 1, § 1882.

[373] Methodist Protestant Church of Henderson, 130 N.C. 8, 40 S.E. 691.

[374] See supra § 2.15 at notes 327–328.

[375] Vested future interests are transferable by deed whether they are legal or equitable and whether they are indefeasibly vested or vested subject to defeasance. E.g., Greer v. Parker, 209 Ark. 553, 191 S.W.2d 584 (1946); Grant v. Nelson, 100 N.H. 220, 122 A.2d 925 (1956). In most American jurisdictions, the transferability of vested future interests in land by deed is confirmed by statutes which expressly provide that "future interests," or "expectant estates"—or, more broadly, "all estates and interests"—may be transferred by deed.

[376] Attempted restraints on the alienation of vested future interests appear to be valid in the United States only to the extent that restraints upon the alienation of present interests of the same quantum are valid. Dep't of Pub. Works & Bldgs. v. Porter, 327 Ill. 28, 158 N.E. 366 (1927) (vested remainder); Ramey v. Ramey, 195 Ky. 673, 243 S.W. 934 (1922) (same); see also Simes & Smith, supra note 1, § 1159. Thus attempted restraints upon the alienation of vested remainders in fee simple or the equivalent interest in personalty are generally void, but forfeiture or promissory restraints upon the alienation of a vested remainder for life are generally valid. As to restraints upon alienation of present fee simple estates, see supra § 2.2. As to restraints upon alienation of life estates, see supra § 2.15.

possibility of acquiring an interest in the future.[377] When legal executory interests were recognized in the sixteenth century, they also seem to have been regarded as inalienable.[378] In any case, a contingent remainder or executory interest in favor of an unborn person or persons is not alienable inter vivos.

Today, contingent remainders and executory interests held by ascertained persons appear to be transferable inter vivos in most American jurisdictions.[379] Many jurisdictions have statutorily provided for their transferability. Some of these statutes expressly make "contingent interests" or "contingent remainders and executory interests" transferable inter vivos.[380] Other statutes are less specific in their terms[381] or do not cover all kinds of contingent future interests.[382] Many statutes appear to apply only to interests in land,[383] and courts have narrowly construed some of them.[384]

Even without a statute that makes contingent remainders and executory interests transferable inter vivos, some state courts have held that they are transferable.[385] However, absent such a statute, other courts have held that they are not transferable inter vivos,[386] unless the transfer falls within one of three well-recognized exceptions: (1) the interest holder releases it by transferring it to the person whose interest would be defeated if the contingent interest vested,[387] (2) the doctrine of estoppel by deed validates

---

[377] See King v. Withers (1735) 24 Eng. Rep. 1125; see also 7 W. Holdsworth, A History of English Law 102 (2d ed. 1937); W. Roberts, Transfer of Future Interests, 30 Mich. L. Rev. 349 (1932).

[378] Like contingent remainders, executory interests were, until fairly recently, deemed to be only possibilities of acquiring an interest at a future time—a view derived from the fundamental idea that only vested estates could constitute the component parts of a fee simple absolute when it was divided into present and future interests.

[379] See First Restatement of Property, supra note 37, § 162, asserting that all remainders and executory interests are alienable by the ordinary deed of conveyance used in the state where the land is situated.

[380] E.g., Ala. Code § 35–4–212 (West 2018); Ariz. Rev. Stat. Ann. § 33–221 (West 2018); Me. Rev. Stat. Ann. tit. 33, § 152 (West 2018); Mass. Gen. Laws Ann. ch. 184, § 2 (West 2018); Mich. Comp. Laws Ann. § 554.35 (West 2018); Minn. Stat. Ann. § 500.15 (West 2017); Ohio Rev. Code Ann. § 2131.04 (West 2018); 34 R.I. Gen. Laws § 34–4–11 (West 2017); Wis. Stat. Ann. § 700.07 (West 2018).

[381] Some statutes declare that "future interests pass by succession, will and transfer in the same manner as present interests." E.g., Cal. Civ. Code § 699 (West 2018); Idaho Code Ann. § 55–109 (West 2018); N.D. Cent. Code § 47–02–18 (West 2017); S.D. Codified Laws § 43–3–20 (West 2018). Other statutes state that "any interest in land may be conveyed," or that "every conveyance of real estate passes all the interest of the grantor therein" unless a contrary intent is manifested. E.g., Iowa Code Ann. § 557.3 (West 2018); Kan. Stat. Ann. § 58–2205; Ky. Rev. Stat. Ann. § 382.010 (West 2018); Miss. Code Ann. § 89–1–1 (West 2018); Mo. Rev. Stat. § 442.020 (West 2017); Tenn. Code Ann. § 66–5–101 (West 2018); Va. Code Ann. § 55–6 (West 2018).

[382] E.g., Del. Code Ann. tit. 25, §§ 101, 302 (West 2018) (estates "in possession, reversion, or remainder"); Okla. Stat. Ann. tit. 60, § 30 (West 2018) ("a remainder * * * may be created and transferred by that name"); 21 Pa. Cons. Stat. Ann. § 3 (West 2018) ("reversions and remainders"); N.M. Stat. Ann. § 47–1–4 (West 2018) ("remainder or reversion").

[383] Most of the statutes cited supra notes 380–382 are contained in subdivisions devoted to real property only.

[384] E.g., Clarke v. Fay, 205 Mass. 228, 91 N.E. 328, 27 L.R.A.N.S. 454 (1910).

[385] E.g., McAdams v. Bailey, 169 Ind. 518, 82 N.E. 1057, 13 L.R.A.N.S. 1003 (1907); Rutherford v. Keith, 444 S.W.2d 546 (Ky. 1969); Granite State Elec. Co. v. Gidley, 114 N.H. 226, 318 A.2d 486 (1974); Jernigan v. Lee, 279 N.C. 341, 182 S.E.2d 351 (1971); Parker v. Blackmon, 553 S.W.2d 623 (Tex. 1977).

[386] Fletcher v. Hurdle, 259 Ark. 640, 536 S.W.2d 109 (1976); Roper v. Finney, 7 Ill. 2d 487, 131 N.E.2d 106 (1955); see also In re Schmidt's Will, 256 Minn. 64, 97 N.W.2d 441 (1959), noted in 37 U. Det. L.J. 411 (1960) (Minnesota statute, supra note 380, applies only to real property.)

[387] E.g., Towns v. Walters, 225 Ga. 293, 168 S.E.2d 144 (1969); Kohl v. Montgomery, 373 Ill. 200, 25 N.E.2d 826 (1940); Bradley Lumber Co. v. Burbridge, 213 Ark. 165, 210 S.W.2d 284 (1948) (release by class member to other members); Rembert v. Evans, 86 S.C. 445, 68 S.E. 659 (1910) (same).

an attempted transfer of the contingent interest if it later vests in the transferor,[388] or (3) the deed is given for adequate consideration and can be treated as a specifically enforceable contract if the interest later vests in the transferor.[389] In short, the minority rule that contingent remainders and executory interests are inalienable by deed actually applies only if the purported transfer is to someone other than a person in whose favor the contingent interest could be released or if the transfer was by quitclaim deed or without adequate consideration.[390]

In some jurisdictions, courts have held that a future interest contingent as to "event" is alienable inter vivos but that a future interest contingent as to "person" is not.[391] In these jurisdictions, courts have sometimes strained to find that contingencies relate to an "event," rather than to a "person."[392] On the other hand, at least a few courts have sustained forfeiture restraints imposed on the alienation of contingent future interests that would have been void if imposed on a present interest or vested future interest of the same quantum.[393] Courts that uphold these restraints may be concerned about the advisability of permitting alienation of contingent remainders and executory interests.[394]

Possibilities of reverter and rights of entry. Some states statutorily provide that possibilities of reverter and rights of entry are alienable inter vivos.[395] Without this type of statute, courts are divided concerning the transferability of these interests.[396] However, even in states where a possibility of reverter is not freely transferable inter

---

[388] E.g., Phelps v. Palmer, 192 Ga. 421, 15 S.E.2d 503 (1941); Byrd v. Allen, 351 Mo. 99, 171 S.W.2d 691 (1942); Hobson v. Hobson, 184 Tenn. 484, 201 S.W.2d 659 (1947). Even a quitclaim deed, if it contains a representation that the grantor has title to a particular interest, will create the necessary estoppel. See infra § 11.5.

[389] E.g., McAdams v. Bailey, 169 Ind. 518, 82 N.E. 1057, 13 L.R.A.N.S. 1003 (1907); Bishop v. Horney, 177 Md. 353, 9 A.2d 597 (1939); Hobson, 184 Tenn. 484, 201 S.W.2d 659.

[390] Waggoner, supra note 219, at 95.

[391] In New Jersey, the statute makes interest contingent "as to the event" alienable, but interests contingent "as to the person" are declared inalienable. N.J. Stat. Ann. § 46:3–7 (West 2018). In other states the same distinction is made in the case law. E.g., Raney v. Smith, 242 Ga. 809, 251 S.E.2d 554 (1979); In re Clayton's Estate, 195 Md. 622, 74 A.2d 1 (1950); Thames v. Goode, 217 N.C. 639, 9 S.E.2d 485 (1940).

[392] E.g., Taylor v. Stewart, 18 A. 456 (N.J. Ch. 1889); Prince v. Barham, 127 Va. 462, 103 S.E. 626 (1920) (remainder to the surviving children of a living person held contingent as to event rather than person). Both Simes and Powell are critical of the distinction. Simes & Smith, supra note 1, § 1859; 2A Powell, supra note 1, ¶ 283 in text around n.18. Cf. Waggoner, supra note 219, at 96–97, arguing that a future interest contingent "as to person" cannot be *truly* alienable even where the interest is "presently owned" by a person capable of making a transfer, such as an heir apparent.

[393] E.g., Sec.-First Nat'l Bank of L.A. v. Rogers, 51 Cal.2d 24, 330 P.2d 811 (1958); Wohlgemuth v. Des Moines Nat'l Bank, 199 Iowa 649, 192 N.W. 248 (1923); Gordon v. Tate, 314 Mo. 508, 284 S.W. 497 (1926).

[394] See Simes & Smith, supra note 1, §§ 1159, 1852.

[395] E.g., Mich. Comp. Laws Ann. § 554.111 (West 2018); Minn. Stat. Ann. § 500.16 (West 2017); N.C. Gen. Stat. Ann. § 39–6.3 (West 2017). In other states, there is broader legislation making all future interests, or all interests in land, alienable. For a comprehensive list of statutes, see First Restatement of Property, supra note 37, § 160, cmt. d.

[396] Finding transferability, see Irby v. Smith, 147 Ga. 329, 93 S.E. 877 (1917); Monroe v. Scott (Tex. Ct. App. 1986); Collette v. Town of Charlotte, 114 Vt. 357, 45 A.2d 203 (1946). Contra, e.g., Pure Oil Co. v. Miller-McFarland Drilling Co., 376 Ill. 486, 34 N.E.2d 854, 135 A.L.R. 567 (1941). The Illinois rule against alienability was later codified; see 765 Ill. Comp. Stat. Ann. 330/1 (West 2018).

vivos, its holder can release it to the owner of the defeasible interest.[397] It also can be transferred by applying the estoppel by deed doctrine[398] or by treating the deed as a specifically enforceable contract to convey.[399]

Absent a statute that makes rights of entry transferable inter vivos, the weight of authority still holds that such interests are not transferable,[400] except by release to the owner of the defeasible interest.[401] Indeed, some authority exists that an invalid attempt to transfer a right of entry inter vivos destroys it.[402] However, if the right of entry is incident to a reversion, it can be transferred with the reversion.[403]

Personality. As previously indicated,[404] most statutes that make future interests alienable inter vivos expressly apply only to interests in land. But, in most jurisdictions, the same alienability rules probably would be applied, as far as possible, to interests in land and in personalty.[405] Even in those states where contingent future interests are not fully alienable, the interest owner should be able to release it to the person whose interest would be defeated if the contingent interest vested. And if the transfer document includes title warranties, the doctrine of estoppel by deed should apply by analogy to personalty transfers. However, an assignment of a contingent future interest in personalty for consideration may be unenforceable as a contract to assign. Because personal property is not normally regarded as being unique, a contract to assign a contingent interest in personalty probably would not be specifically enforceable. However, the difficulty of determining damages for breach of the contract of sale may justify specific enforcement.

§ 3.25 CREDITORS' CLAIMS

Which future interests can be subjected to creditors' claims?[406] The general rule is that creditors can only reach future interests that are fully alienable inter vivos. Reversions and vested remainders in land, whether indefeasibly vested or vested subject to defeasance, or equivalent interests in personalty are generally subject to seizure and

---

[397] E.g., Carden v. LaGrone, 225 Ga. 365, 169 S.E.2d 168 (1969); Application of Mareck, 257 Minn. 222, 100 N.W.2d 758 (1960). 765 Ill. Comp. Stat. Ann. 330/6 (West 2018), expressly permits release of a possibility of reverter.

[398] E.g., Pure Oil Co. v. Miller-McFarland Drilling Co., Inc., 376 Ill. 486, 34 N.E.2d 854, 135 A.L.R. 567 (1941). As to estoppel by deed, see generally infra § 11.5.

[399] Although no cases involving possibilities of reverter have been found, the "enforceable contract" exception would clearly apply to possibilities of reverter, as well as powers of termination, and the "mere expectancy" of a presumptive heir.

[400] E.g., Strothers v. Woodcox, 142 Iowa 648, 121 N.W. 51 (1909); Purvis v. McElveen, 234 S.C. 94, 106 S.E.2d 913 (1959) (dictum); Pickens v. Daugherty, 217 Tenn. 349, 397 S.W.2d 815 (1965), noted in 33 Tenn. L. Rev. 546 (1966).

[401] E.g., 765 Ill. Comp. Stat. Ann. 330/6 (West 2018) (permits the release of a possibility of reverter and a right of entry).

[402] The first case so holding was Rice v. Bos. & Worcester R.R. Corp., 94 Mass. 141 (1866). Accord Wagner v. Wallowa Cty., 76 Or. 453, 148 P. 1140, L.R.A.1916F 303 (1915).

[403] E.g., Trask v. Wheeler, 89 Mass. (7 Allen) 109 (1863). That a right of entry incident to a reversion may be transferred with the reversion was established beyond doubt by Grantees of Reversions Act 1540, 32 Hen. 8 c. 34, § 9 (Eng. & Wales).

[404] Supra note 383.

[405] Sinclair v. Crabtree, 211 Cal. 524, 296 P. 79 (1931); In re Dixon's Will, 280 A.2d 735 (Del. Ch. 1971); Nalley v. First Nat'l Bank of Medford, 135 Or. 409, 293 P. 721, 76 A.L.R. 625 (1930) reh'g denied 135 Or. 409, 296 P. 61, 76 A.L.R. 625 (1931); Old Nat'l Bank v. Campbell, 1 Wash. App. 773, 463 P.2d 656 (1970).

[406] For general discussion of the question, see Simes & Smith, supra note 1, §§ 1922–27.

sale.[407] Contingent remainders, executory interests, possibilities of reverter, and rights of entry are generally subject to the satisfaction of creditors' claims in those jurisdictions where such interests are alienable inter vivos[408] but not where they are inalienable or are alienable only by release, estoppel, or by virtue of the enforceable contract theory.[409]

Even if contingent future interests are fully alienable inter vivos, some courts have refused to allow creditors to seize them and apply them to satisfaction of their claims.[410] Although the language of the opinions differs, the basic rationale is that contingent interests are unlikely to bring a fair price when offered at forced sales, as indicated in the following passage from an opinion of the Oklahoma Supreme Court:[411]

> Where the contingencies are such * * * as to render the interest in specific property a mere remote possibility the difficulty in determining the value of the interest for sale upon execution gives strong practical and legal reasons for denial of the right to so levy. Especially so where sacrifice of the judgment debtor's expectancy is probably without substantial benefit to the judgment creditor.

If the court does allow a creditor to seize the interest in an equitable proceeding, the court may regulate the time and conditions of sale in an attempt to avoid undue prejudice to the debtor.[412] But courts rarely have interfered even to this extent with creditors' rights to reach future interests vested subject to defeasance, though the "prevention of sacrifice" rationale seems to apply equally.[413]

Suppose a contingent interest is not fully alienable inter vivos but is devisable by will. Can creditors of the deceased owner reach and apply it to the satisfaction of their claims? It can be argued that creditors should be able to reach the interest if the contingency that makes it inalienable inter vivos is resolved at the owner's death. Indeed, the same result arguably should be reached when the contingent interest vests after the owner's death but during the course of administering her estate.[414]

§§ 3.26–4.0 ARE RESERVED FOR SUPPLEMENTAL MATERIAL.

---

[407] E.g., King v. Fay, 169 F.Supp. 934 (D.D.C. 1958); Stombaugh v. Morey, 388 Ill. 392, 58 N.E.2d 545, 157 A.L.R. 254 (1944); Koelliker v. Denkinger, 148 Kan. 503, 83 P.2d 703, 119 A.L.R. 1 (1938), modified, 149 Kan. 259, 86 P.2d 740, 119 A.L.R. 1525 (1938); First Nat'l Bank v. Pointer, 174 Tenn. 472, 126 S.W.2d 335 (1939). For additional cases, see Simes & Smith, supra note 1, § 1923.

[408] E.g., State ex rel. Cooper v. Cloyd, 461 S.W.2d 833 (Mo. 1971); Jonas v. Jones, 153 Kan. 108, 109 P.2d 211 (1940) (attachment); Ragan v. Looney, 377 S.W.2d 273 (Mo. 1964); N.C. Nat'l Bank v. C.P. Robinson Co., 319 N.C. 63, 352 S.E.2d 684 (1987), based on N.C. Gen. Stat. § 39–6.3.

[409] E.g., Nat'l Bank of Commerce v. Ritter, 181 Ark. 439, 26 S.W.2d 113 (1930); Kenwood Tr. & Sav. Bank v. Palmer, 285 Ill. 552, 121 N.E. 186 (1918).

[410] Muller v. Cox, 98 N.J. Eq. 188, 130 A. 811 (N.J. Ch. 1925); Bourne v. Farrar, 180 N.C. 135, 137, 104 S.E. 170, 172 (1920), overruled by N.C. Nat'l Bank, 319 N.C. 63, 352 S.E.2d 684; Adams v. Dugan, 196 Okl. 156, 163 P.2d 227 (1945).

[411] Adams v. Dugan, 196 Okl. 156, 163 P.2d 227 (1945).

[412] Mudd v. Durham, 98 Ky. 454, 33 S.W. 1116 (1896); Martin v. Martin, 54 Ohio St. 2d 101, 374 N.E.2d 1384 (1978).

[413] See cases cited supra note 407. Contra Mears v. Lamona, 17 Wash. 148, 49 P. 251 (1897), involving vested equitable interests, where the court merely imposed a lien on the debtor's interest, with the sale of that interest postponed until it should become vested.

[414] See Simes & Smith, supra note 1, § 1927.

Chapter 4

RELATIONS BETWEEN OWNERS OF PRESENT AND FUTURE ESTATES AND INTERESTS

Table of Sections

§ 4.1   IN GENERAL—WASTE

When ownership of land is divided into present and future estates, courts often must decide the extent to which the holders of a possessory estate should be restricted in their use and enjoyment to protect the future interest holders. The rules that the courts have developed, with some legislative assistance, are known as the law of waste.[1] Waste can be "voluntary"—a result of the possessor's deliberate affirmative acts[2]—or

---

[1]   Waste is considered infra in §§ 4.2–4.5. See generally 1 American Law of Property §§ 2.16(e), 4.100–.105, 20.1–.23 (1952) (hereinafter Am. L. Prop.); 4 R. Powell, Powell on Real Property §§ 56.01–.12 (2018); L. Simes & A. Smith, Future Interests §§ 1651–90 (3d ed. Borron ed. 2018); Restatement (Second) of Property: Landlord and Tenant (Am. Law Inst. 1977) (hereinafter Second Restatement of Property); Restatement (First) of Property §§ 138–46, 188–99 (Am. Law Inst. 1936) (hereinafter First Restatement of Property). Waste may also be committed by one cotenant against another. See Cowart v. White, 711 N.E.2d 523 (Ind. 1999), on reh'g 716 N.E.2d 401 (1999); § 5.7 infra. A mortgagor or land contract vendee may be liable for waste to the mortgagee or vendor. See Restatement (Third) of Property: Mortgages § 4.6 (Am. Law Inst. 1997) (hereinafter Third Restatement of Property).

See Vogel v. Pardon, 444 N.W.2d 348 (N.D. 1989); Meyer v. Hansen, 373 N.W.2d 392 (N.D. 1985) (" 'Waste' implies neglect or misconduct resulting in material damage to property, but does not include ordinary depreciation of property due to age and normal use."); McKibben v. Mohawk Oil Co., Ltd., 667 P.2d 1223 (Alaska 1983); In re Estate of Gauch, 308 N.W.2d 88 (Iowa 1981).

[2]   See infra § 4.2. A dispute exists whether conventional tenants for life were liable for waste before the Statute of Marlbridge (1267) if they had not been enjoined against waste in the conveyance creating the possessory estate. All writers agree that tenants for years were not liable for waste at common law. The Statute of Marlbridge, 52 Hen. 3, c. 23, § 2 (Eng.) (1267) clearly imposed liability for waste on tenants for years and any tenants for life who were not already liable for waste at common law.

"permissive"—a result of the possessor's failure to perform an affirmative duty for the future interest owners' benefit.[3]

In the earlier common law, a possessor also was liable to the future interest holders though she was without fault. For example, a tenant for life or for years was liable to the reversioner or remainder holder for a trespasser's permanent damage to the property.[4] The possessor apparently was liable for this "innocent waste" because only she could maintain an action of trespass against the tortfeasor.[5] The possessor could recover damages for the full amount of the property's reduced value in such cases but was accountable to the future interest holders for the amount by which the recovery exceeded the injury to the possessory estate.[6] The possessor's liability was so strict that she was liable to the future interest holders for the injury to their interest even if she did not sue the tortfeasor.[7]

Although development of the action on the case enabled future interest holders to recover directly from a tortfeasor for damaging their interest,[8] the early common law still allowed a possessor to recover full damages from the tortfeasor and still held the possessor liable for the tortfeasor's actions. Today, however, courts normally hold that a possessory interest holder is not liable for the acts of strangers unless the possessor is at fault.[9] As a result, most courts now hold that the possessory interest holder is limited to recovering only for her actual loss and that only the future interest holders can recover for the injury to their interests.

In addition to the law of waste, courts have developed a closely related body of law to assist them in determining how certain burdens, such as payment of property taxes and special assessments, and certain benefits, such as rents, should be apportioned among the holders of successive interests in the same property.[10] The courts also have developed rules for determining when a possessory interest holder can force a sale of the realty in fee simple absolute over the objections of the future interest owners.[11] Similar

---

[3] Because the Statute of Marlbridge, supra note 2, and the Statute of Gloucester, 6 Edw. 1, c. 5 (1278), provided only that certain kinds of tenants should not "make" waste, some doubt initially existed concerning liability for failure to perform affirmative duties. But courts later held that a tenant could "make" waste either by action or by failure to act. Coke, Commentary Upon Littleton, ¶ 53a (F. Hargrave & C. Butler eds. 1812).

[4] Coke, 2 Institutes of the Laws of England, ¶ 145 (E. & R. Brooke 1797).

[5] Coke, supra note 4, at ¶ 303. Also see 1 Am. L. Prop., supra note 1, at § 2.16, at 130; 5 Am. L. Prop., supra note 1, at § 20.13. American law now allows a tenant for life or for years, as owner of a possessory estate, to bring a trespass action whether actually in possession or not, unless the land is adversely possessed by another. See 6A Am. L. Prop., supra note 1, at § 28.12, text accompanying nn. 4–6.

[6] Coke, supra note 3, at ¶ 54a ("The tenant by courtesie, the tenant in dower, the tenant for life, years, etc. shall answer for the waste done by a stranger and shall take their remedy over [against the wrongdoer].").

[7] Having been held liable to the future interest holder, the possessory tenant could still sue the tortfeasor for trespass and recover the full damages, thereby recovering reimbursement for what he had to pay the future interest owner.

[8] The action on the case developed during the fourteenth century, but the future interest owner's right to recover from the tortfeasor in an action on the case apparently was not established until the end of the seventeenth century. See Bedingfield v. Onslow, 3 Lev. 209, 83 Eng. Rep. 654 (1685).

[9] See Rogers v. Atl., Gulf & Pac. Co., 213 N.Y. 246, 107 N.E. 661 (1915). Accord First Restatement of Property, supra note 1, at § 146. All the cases to the contrary are quite old, and courts today are unlikely to follow them.

[10] This body of law is considered infra in §§ 4.6–4.10. See generally 1 Am. L. Prop., supra note 1, at §§ 216, 218–225; 4 Powell, supra note 1, at §§ 58.01–.04, 59.01–.04; Simes & Smith, supra note 1, at §§ 1691–710; First Restatement of Property, supra note 1, at §§ 129–52.

[11] This subject is considered infra § 4.10. See generally 1 Am. L. Prop., supra note 1, at §§ 4.98, 4.99; Powell, supra note 1, at § 21.05; Simes & Smith, supra note 1, at §§ 1921–40; First Restatement of Property, supra note 1, at § 179.

problems may arise concerning personalty, but most judicial rules dealing with these problems are part of the law of trusts, because future interests in personalty are almost always equitable interests in trust property, rather than legal interests.[12]

§ 4.2   VOLUNTARY WASTE

When ownership of realty was divided between presently possessory and future interests, the English law courts held that any affirmative act of a possessor that "injured the inheritance" constituted voluntary waste,[13] absent a provision in the creating instrument that absolved the possessor from liability for waste.[14] Although courts in older English cases often did not articulate their rationale, they clearly proceeded on the assumption that any substantial alteration of the land or the structures on it constituted waste because the future interest holder was legally entitled to possession of the property in substantially the same condition as when the title was divided into successive estates.[15] In many decided cases, the possessor's waste reduced the value of the future interest, but reduction in value was not the determining factor in the court's decision as to whether the possessor had committed waste.[16]

Most English cases dealing with voluntary waste involved either (1) cutting down mature, valuable trees, (2) changing the "course of husbandry" on farm land (the way the land is used), (3) extracting minerals, or (4) demolishing or substantially altering structures. The English law concerning cutting mature, valuable trees was complicated and very strict. Generally, such cutting constituted waste unless the trees were needed for fuel or repairs.[17] But "it was early held in the United States that * * * the cutting of timber * * * to clear up land for cultivation, consonant with good husbandry, was not waste, although such acts would clearly have been waste in England."[18] American courts

---

[12]   The trust property often includes realty as well, in which case the rules dealing with the rights and duties of the owners of successive equitable interests are also part of the law of trusts. The protection of owners of legal future interests in personalty is briefly considered infra in § 4.11.

[13]   "Voluntary waste" is contrasted with "permissive waste," which essentially means failure to perform the tenant's limited duty to keep the property in repair. "Permissive waste" is considered infra in § 4.3.

[14]   If the instrument that created the successive estates in property expressly authorizes a particular use, that use cannot constitute waste. Express provisions concerning permissible uses of the premises are very common in leases. Although they are much less common in instruments creating a life estate, they may provide that the life tenant will hold "without impeachment of waste." From an early time, courts have construed this type of provision as protecting a tenant for life from any legal liability for waste. However, courts of equity have sometimes provided a remedy for "unconscionable" conduct that injures a future interest holder though the life tenant holds "without impeachment for waste." First Restatement of Property, supra note 1, at § 141, cmt. a, illus. 4.

[15]   See 8 Powell, supra note 1, at § 56.05, also suggesting that "[this is] a social judgment in favor of preserving the status quo ante and a rejection of the modern concept of 'reasonable use' in the light of changing circumstances." Cf. 1 Am. L. Prop., supra note 1, at § 2.16; 5 Am. L. Prop., supra note 1, at § 20.1.

[16]   This is illustrated by cases of so-called "meliorating waste," where conduct was held to constitute waste although it increased the value of the property. E.g., City of London v. Greyme, Cro. Jac. 181, 79 Eng. Rep. 158 (1607); Cole v. Green, 1 Lev. 309, 83 Eng. Rep. 422 (1670).

[17]   The rule was a reasonable one in a timber-scarce agricultural society. The prohibition against cutting by a tenant for life or for years applied to oak, ash, and elm, which were "timber trees" everywhere, and to other trees which, by local custom, were classified as "timber trees." It also applied to fruit trees, ornamental trees, and to other trees "beneficial to the inheritance." "Timber trees" could be cut for use as fuel or for necessary repairs, provided there were insufficient dead or inferior trees for these purposes. This privilege was termed the right of "estovers" or "botes." Generally, as to the English common law, see Coke, supra note 3, at ¶ 53a, 53b; 5 Am. L. Prop., supra note 1, at § 20.4, text accompanying nn. 3 and 5.

[18]   Melms v. Pabst Brewing Co., 104 Wis. 7, 79 N.W. 738 (1899). See McGregor v. Brown, 10 N.Y. 114 (1854); Ward v. Sheppard, 3 N.C. 283, 2 Am. Dec. 625 (1803). "In order to make usable the forested wilderness of this country, it was necessary to clear it for the only industry then important, farming. * * * In addition,

generally have substituted the test of "good husbandry" or, more broadly, "reasonable use" for the strict English common law rules.[19]

The English law concerning a change in the course of husbandry was also very strict. Any change in use, such as converting meadow land to arable land, was waste.[20] But even in England this strict rule "was early softened down * * *, and the doctrine of meliorating waste was adopted, which, without changing the definition of waste, still allowed the tenant to change the course of husbandry upon the estate if such change be for the betterment of the estate."[21] Consequently, American courts never adopted the earlier, strict English rule.

The English rule concerning a possessor's mineral extraction was simple. If the mine was open when the possessory interest was created, the possessor was privileged to work the mine to exhaustion. However, if the mine was not open when the possessory interest was created, any mineral extraction was waste.[22] Unless statutorily altered, American law appears to apply the same simple test.[23]

Perhaps the most controversial English voluntary waste cases were those in which the court held that a possessor's demolition or substantial alteration of structures or land was waste, even if the property's value was thereby increased, because it jeopardized the ability to define the land's boundaries.[24] Courts in both England and the United States rejected this doctrine in its strict form by the end of the nineteenth century.[25] The leading American case is *Melms v. Pabst Brewing Co.*,[26] in which the court held that a life tenant could substantially alter the land and demolish a structure "when * * * there has occurred a complete and permanent change of surrounding conditions, which has deprived the property of its value and usefulness." The court also held that the tenant is "not bound by contract to restore the property to the same condition in which he received

---

* * * in a land where timber is very plentiful * * * there could not be much serious objection to the cutting of trees." 5 Am. L. Prop., supra note 1, at § 20.5.

[19] What is "good husbandry" depends on the use to which the land was intended to be put. Thus, in the case of land leased for agriculture, trees could be cut only in furtherance of reasonable agricultural use. "[I]n cases wherein the land was originally acquired for timber, or where it was chiefly valuable as timber land, the tenant was allowed to cut timber for profit, this being a reasonable use in light of the nature of the land." 5 Am. L. Prop., supra note 1, at § 20.2.

[20] Coke, supra note 3, at ¶ 53a.

[21] Melms v. Pabst Brewing Co., 104 Wis. 7, 79 N.W. 738. See also Wyndham Anstis Bewes, The Law of Waste, 134 and cases cited (Sweet & Maxwell 1894).

[22] Coke, supra note 3, at ¶¶ 53b, 54b. The same rule applied to removal of soil, clay, and gravel. Id. at ¶ 53b.

[23] Ward v. Carp River Iron Co., 47 Mich. 65, 10 N.W. 109 (1881); Gaines v. Green Pond Iron Mining Co., 33 N.J. Eq. 603 (1881); Riley v. Riley, 972 S.W.2d 149 (Tex. App. 1998). A tenant is not privileged to open a new mine. See Ohio Oil Co. v. Daughetee, 240 Ill. 361, 88 N.E. 818 (1909); Russell v. Tipton, 193 Ky. 305, 235 S.W. 763 (1921). See also McKibben v. Mohawk Oil Co., 667 P.2d 1223 (Alaska 1983) (unprofessional mining activity was waste). But see Vicars v. First Va. Bank-Mountain Empire, 250 Va. 103, 458 S.E.2d 293 (1995) (mining not waste if plaintiff consented to the mining operation).

[24] See, e.g., Keepers of Harrow Sch. v. Alderton, 2 Bos. & Pul. 86, 126 Eng. Rep. 1170 (C.B. 1800) (argument of Shepherd, Serjt.); Young v. Spencer, 10 B. & C. 145, 109 Eng. Rep. 405 (K.B. 1829).

[25] The leading English case is Doherty v. Allman [1878], 3 App. Cas. 709 (HL) (1878), in which the court refused to enjoin "meliorating waste" consisting of the conversion of rundown, obsolete store buildings into dwelling houses of much greater value. The court specifically rejected the old "impairment of evidence of title" rationale for treating such changes as waste, pointing out that it was no longer persuasive once land descriptions in deeds of conveyance ceased to identify the land by reference to natural monuments or the uses to which the land was put. Id. at 725–726.

[26] 104 Wis. 7, 79 N.W. 738. The *Melms* case contains a good review of the changes in the law of waste in England and the United States during the 19th century.

it."[27] In *Melms,* the trial court had found that the acts alleged to constitute waste—demolition of a large house and grading the land down to street level—"substantially increased" the reversion's value and that the reversioners were "in no way injured thereby."[28] Pursuant to this decision, a life tenant cannot substantially change the property based on changed conditions if the value of the future interests would decrease.

Although the American cases since *Melms* are by no means entirely harmonious, substantial American authority now exists for the view that a possessory interest holder can make extensive alterations or demolish and replace structures to make a reasonable use of the property, provided that such changes do not diminish the value of the future interest.[29] But, of course, reasonable minds can differ on what is a reasonable use.

The First Restatement of Property adopted the following rules, which are consistent with the *Melms* opinion: (1) A life tenant has a duty not to diminish the market value of subsequent interests,[30] and (2) A life tenant "has a duty not to change the premises, as to which the estate for life exists, in such a manner that the owners of the interests limited after the estate for life have a reasonable ground for objection thereto."[31] A literal reading of the second rule suggests that future interest holders may have a reasonable ground to object to changes, even if the value of their interests would not decrease. The commentary, by negative inference, also indicates that a reasonable ground for objection would exist even if the future interest's value is not diminished.

However, the objection will not be reasonable if "a substantial and permanent change in the conditions of the neighborhood in which the land is located has deprived the land in its existent form of reasonable productivity or usefulness; and the proposed alteration or replacement is one which the owner of an estate in fee simple absolute normally would make; and the owners of the interests limited after the estate for life are either not subject to financial liability or are adequately protected against financial liability arising from the proposed construction operations. . . ."[32]

The Restatement's tests for determining the reasonableness of objections to proposed changes are based only in part on *Melms.*[33] They are also based in part on the facts, though not the outcome, in *Brokaw v. Fairchild,*[34] in which the life tenant wanted to demolish a large house and replace it with an apartment building.[35] The facts of the

---

[27]   104 Wis. at 15–16, 79 N.W. at 741.

[28]   See 104 Wis. at 9, 79 N.W. at 738. The facts of the *Melms* case were unusual in that the house, prior to demolition, stood twenty to thirty feet above the level of the street and was surrounded by railroad tracks, factories, and other industrial buildings, with no other dwellings in the neighborhood.

[29]   E.g., J.B. Hill Co. v. Pinque, 179 Cal. 759, 178 P. 952 (1919); Dodds v. Sixteenth Section Dev. Corp., 232 Miss. 524, 99 So. 2d 897 (1958); J.H. Bellows Co. v. Covell, 28 Ohio App. 277, 162 N.E. 621 (1927); Melms, 104 Wis. 7, 79 N.W. 738. Alterations may constitute waste if, although they increase the value of the property, they also increase the burdens (such as taxes) to which the property is subject. E.g., Crewe Corp. v. Feiler, 28 N.J. 316, 146 A.2d 458 (1958).

[30]   First Restatement of Property, supra note 1, at § 138.

[31]   Id. § 140.

[32]   Id. § 140, cmt. f(2).

[33]   104 Wis. 7, 78 N.W. 738.

[34]   135 Misc. 70, 237 N.Y.S. 6 (1929), aff'd without majority opinion (Finch, J., dissenting), 231 App. Div. 704, 245 N.Y.S. 402 (1930), aff'd per curiam without opinion, 256 N.Y. 670, 177 N.E. 186 (1931); noted in 15 Cornell L.Q. 501 (1930), 43 Harv. L. Rev. 506 (1930), and 30 Mich. L. Rev. 784 (1931).

[35]   The plaintiff, the life tenant, was opposed by the owners of the two adjoining townhouses, who had contingent remainders in the subject property that would vest only if the plaintiff outlived his four-year-old daughter and then died without other issue, which seemed highly unlikely.

Brokaw case provide one of the illustrations appended to the commentary,[36] though the commentary does not articulate the life tenant's principal reason for replacing the house in that case.[37] He argued that the home had become too large and expensive to maintain as a single-family residence. It would seem that this kind of financial change, as well as a "substantial and permanent change in the neighborhood," should be sufficient to justify substantial alteration or replacement of a structure. However, the commentary cited only the change in the neighborhood from single-family homes to apartment buildings to justify letting the life tenant build one, too.

Especially in cases like *Brokaw,* in which the future interest holders were likely to demolish the house and build an apartment building if they got possession of the property,[38] the court should not enjoin the life tenant from doing so.[39] This type of case clearly meets the Restatement's tests and should be considered to be nonactionable meliorating waste. On the other hand, if the property is capable of a reasonable use by the future interests owners if and when they get possession and if they object to the life tenant's proposed changes, their objection should be deemed to be reasonable even if the change would not decrease the property's value or even if it would increase the value.

§ 4.3   PERMISSIVE WASTE

Absent contrary provisions in the instrument creating a life estate, the life tenant has a limited duty to make repairs on the property[40] and to pay carrying charges, such as property taxes, mortgage interest, and special assessments for public improvements.[41] Failing to make required repairs constitutes permissive waste, and failing to pay carrying charges is also frequently called permissive waste.[42] But these affirmative duties are subject to the important limitation that the life tenant has no duty to spend more than the income that the land can generate or, if the life tenant personally occupies the land, its rental value.[43] However, the surplus income or rental value from prior years must be applied to current repairs and carrying charges, and surplus current income or

---

[36]   First Restatement of Property, supra note 1, at § 140, illus. 6.

[37]   135 Misc. at 72, 237 N.Y.S. at 10–11.

[38]   Id. Finch, J., dissenting, suggested that the plaintiffs objected to redevelopment of the parcel because they hoped to develop the entire frontage on 79th Street, including the neighboring parcels that they owned, if and when they got possession. 231 App. Div. at 705, 245 N.Y.S. at 404.

[39]   The *Brokaw* decision resulted in the enactment of N.Y. Laws 1937, c. 165, now N. Y. Real Prop. Acts. Law § 803 (McKinney 2018), which excludes liability for waste if the change (1) will not decrease the market value of the future interests, (2) is of the sort that a prudent fee simple owner would make under the circumstances, (3) and does not violate the terms of any agreement or other instrument regulating the conduct of the tenant for life or for years. This statute effectively overrules *Brokaw.*

[40]   E.g., Clark v. Childs, 253 Ga. 493, 321 S.E.2d 727 (1984); Stevens v. Citizens & S. Nat'l Bank, 233 Ga. 612, 212 S.E.2d 792 (1975). However, the instrument creating the life estate may shift these responsibilities entirely to the remainder holders. See In re Estate of Campbell, 87 Wash. App. 506, 942 P.2d 1008 (Wash. App. 1997).

[41]   E.g., Garrett v. Snowden, 226 Ala. 30, 145 So. 493, 87 A.L.R. 216 (1933) (mortgage interest); Hausmann v. Hausmann, 231 Ill. App. 3d 361, 172 Ill. Dec. 937, 596 N.E.2d 216 (1992) (taxes); Beliveau v. Beliveau, 217 Minn. 235, 14 N.W.2d 360 (1944) (taxes); Sherrill v. Board of Equalization, 224 Tenn. 201, 452 S.W.2d 857 (1970) (taxes); Morrow v. Person, 195 Tenn. 370, 259 S.W.2d 665 (1953) (assessment apportioned in ratio of value of life estate to value of future estate).

[42]   "The tendency is to treat failure to carry out these obligations in the same manner as failure to repair, and the cases are consequently discussed together." 5 Am. L. Prop., supra note 1, at § 20.12, at 100.

[43]   E.g., In re Stout's Estate, 151 Or. 411, 50 P.2d 768, 101 A.L.R. 672 (1936) (repairs); Nation v. Green, 188 Ind. 697, 123 N.E. 163 (1919) (taxes).

rental value must be applied to make up any accrued deficits in making repairs or paying carrying charges.[44]

No satisfactory general definition of the life tenant's common law duty to make repairs can be found in the decided cases. However, the cases do make clear that the life tenant need not rebuild a structure that was completely dilapidated when he became entitled to possession or to make general repairs needed at that time.[45] The life tenant also is not required to rebuild a structure that is destroyed by fire, storm, or other casualty, unless the life tenant was responsible,[46] or to eliminate the results of ordinary wear and tear, unless repairs are necessary to prevent further deterioration.[47] But a life tenant has a duty to repaint when exterior surfaces will otherwise be exposed to serious deterioration,[48] to keep roofs in repair,[49] and, more generally, to keep the land and structures in a reasonable state of repair.[50]

A life tenant also has a duty to pay all current general property taxes[51] and the interest periodically accruing on any mortgage or similar consensual encumbrance that constituted a lien on the fee simple estate when the life estate was created.[52] The latter duty dates from a time when mortgages usually had relatively short terms, with the entire principal of the mortgage debt payable in a lump sum at the end of the term. If the entire principal balance of the mortgage comes due during the life tenancy, the life tenant and the future interest owner must each pay their fair shares of the principal, which are determined based on the relative values of the present and future estates.[53] With respect to periodic payments on the mortgage loan, obvious practical difficulties exist in arranging payment by the life tenant and by the future interest holder. If either party pays an entire installment, that person will presumably be entitled to contribution from the other party.[54]

---

[44]   Green, 188 Ind. at 703, 123 N.E. at 165.

[45]   E.g., Sav. Inv. & Tr. Co. v. Little, 135 N.J. Eq. 546, 39 A.2d 392 (1944).

[46]   E.g., id.; In re Stout's Estate, 151 Or. 411, 50 P.2d 768.

[47]   E.g., Keesecker v. Bird, 200 W. Va. 667, 490 S.E.2d 754 (W. Va. 1997).

[48]   E.g., Woolston v. Pullen, 88 N.J. Eq. 35, 102 A. 461 (1917). Compare Staropoli v. Staropoli, 180 A.D.2d 727, 580 N.Y.S.2d 369 (N.Y. App. Div. 1992) (failure to paint exterior of house is not waste if no structural damage results), with Zauner v. Brewer, 220 Conn. 176, 596 A.2d 388 (Conn. 1991) (failure to paint and make ordinary repairs are waste).

[49]   See id.

[50]   First Restatement of Property, supra note 1, at 139. The older authorities all state that "the tenant must keep the premises windtight and watertight," which has "a quaint sound in modern America." 5 Am. L. Prop., supra note 1, at § 20.12, at 101. The duty extends to caring for lawn and shrubs. See Kimbrough v. Reed, 130 Idaho 512, 943 P.2d 1232 (Idaho 1997). Permitting hazardous waste contamination may be waste. See Wright Motors, Inc. v. Marathon Oil Co., 631 N.E.2d 923 (Ind. App. 1994).

[51]   The life tenant has no duty to the future interest holder to pay taxes that are a lien only on the life estate. E.g., Ferguson v. Quinn, 97 Tenn. 46, 36 S.W. 576, 33 L.R.A. 688 (1896). However, taxes ordinarily are a lien on the fee simple and, therefore, the life tenant has a duty to pay them. See Graham v. Vannoy, 1999 WL 89116 (Wash. App. 1999) (unpublished); Simes & Smith, supra note 1, at § 1693; Duties of Legal Life Tenants to Remaindermen in Iowa, Note, 45 Iowa L. Rev. 113 (1959). See also In re Estate of Olsen, 254 Neb. 809, 579 N.W.2d 529 (Neb. 1998) (life tenant has no liability for taxes that do not fall due until after life tenant's death).

[52]   See cases cited supra note 51. The duty does not exist if the mortgage is a lien on only the life estate.

[53]   Murphy v. May, 243 Ala. 94, 8 So. 2d 442 (1942); Garrett v. Snowden, 226 Ala. 30, 145 So. 493, 87 A.L.R. 216 (1933); Thompson v. Watkins, 285 N.C. 616, 207 S.E.2d 740 (1974); Simes & Smith, supra note 1, at § 1697; First Restatement of Property, supra note 1, at § 132.

[54]   The obligation to pay an installment of the mortgage principal should be apportioned on an equitable basis between the life tenant and the future interest owner. See supra note 61 as to apportionment. See also the discussion of apportionment of special assessments, infra in text accompanying nn. 68–72.

When the fee simple was subject to a mortgage before the life estate was created, the amount required to preserve the interests of the life tenant and the future interest holder if default occurs and the mortgagee declares the entire principal amount to be immediately due and payable ("accelerates") should be apportioned between the life tenant and the future interest owner. How should this be done if the instrument creating the successive interests does not prescribe a method? Many courts require the life tenant to pay the amount of interest that would have accrued during the balance of her life, discounted to the present value, and require the future interest owner to pay the balance of the total amount necessary to satisfy the mortgage.[55] Some states statutorily mandate a different method of apportionment.[56] Of course, the life tenant and the future interest owner may agree to a different method of apportionment.[57]

A life tenant has a duty to pay all special assessments levied against the property for public improvements if their estimated life does not exceed the life estate's probable duration.[58] When the estimated life of the public improvement exceeds the life estate's probable duration, the duty to pay special assessments is divided between the life tenant and the future interest owner based on the values of their respective estates.[59] Courts generally hold that a life estate's value is the cost of an annuity equal to the annual income from or rental value of the land for the probable duration of the life estate and that the future interest's value is the difference between the value of the life estate and the value of the fee simple.[60] This formula may result in substantial injustice to the future interest owner when the estimated life of the public local improvement only slightly exceeds the life estate's probable duration. The future interest owner will receive a far smaller benefit, proportionally, from the improvement based on the relative values of the present and future estates.

When land is held in trust for the benefit of a life tenant (life beneficiary), the trustee has a duty to pay the property taxes and all special assessments against the trust property.[61] When the trustee pays a special assessment installment, the trustee must charge the life tenant with the interest component of the installment (deducting it from the income otherwise payable to the life tenant) and charge the future interest owners for the principal component of the installment.[62]

---

[55] E.g., Garrett, 226 Ala. 30, 145 So. 493; Beliveau v. Beliveau, 217 Minn. 235, 14 N.W.2d 360 (1944); In re Daily's Estate, 117 Mont. 194, 159 P.2d 327 (1945); Coughlin v. Kennedy, 132 N.J. Eq. 383, 28 A.2d 417 (1942).

[56] See 9 Powell, supra note 1, at § 59.03.

[57] See, e.g., Burnett v. Quell, 202 S.W.2d 97 (Mo. App. 1947); Kruse v. Meissner, 136 N.J. Eq. 209, 40 A.2d 777 (1945).

[58] E.g., Appeal of Wordin, 71 Conn. 531, 42 A. 659 (1899); Holliday v. Phillips Petroleum Co., 275 F.Supp. 686 (E.D. Ark. 1967).

[59] E.g., Troy v. Protestant Episcopal Church, 174 Ala. 380, 56 So. 982 (1911). Some courts have required the life tenant to pay only the interest on the special assessment and the future interest owner to pay the entire principal amount of the assessment. E.g., Holzhauser v. Iowa St. Tax Comm'n, 245 Iowa 525, 62 N.W.2d 229 (1953) (dictum).

[60] E.g., Troy, 174 Ala. 380, 56 So. 982; Morrow v. Person, 195 Tenn. 370, 259 S.W.2d 665 (1953).

[61] See 2 A. Scott, Trusts § 176 n. 19 (4th ed. 1987); G. Bogert, The Law of Trusts and Trustees § 602 n.81 (2d ed., rev. 1980); Appeal of Wordin, 71 Conn. 531, 42 A. 659 (1899); Orr v. St. Louis Union Tr. Co., 291 Mo. 383, 236 S.W. 642 (1921), overruled on other grounds as recognized by, Steele v. Cross, 366 S.W.2d 434 (Mo. 1963).

[62] E.g., Brown v. Brown, 72 N.J. Eq. 667, 65 A. 739 (1907), superseded by statute as recognized by, Sheridan v. Riley, 133 N.J. Eq. 288, 32 A.2d 93 (1943); Chamberlin v. Gleason, 163 N.Y. 214, 57 N.E. 487 (1900). But see 1 Am. L. Prop., supra note 1, at § 2.21 at p. 157: "It seems clear * * * that a correct

Most courts hold that the life tenant has no duty to maintain insurance on the property for the benefit of the future interest holder, unless the fee simple is subject to a mortgage that requires the mortgagor to maintain insurance or unless the instrument creating the life estate imposes that duty.[63] If the life tenant does have a duty to insure, the insurance premiums are a carrying charge to be paid from the income or rental value of the property.[64] In a few states, courts hold that a life tenant has a duty to insure the property for the future interest owner's benefit as part of the general duty to preserve and protect future interests in the property.[65]

Like the life tenant, the tenant for years was traditionally subject to an ill-defined common law duty to make repairs to prevent serious deterioration of the leased premises[66] but without any limitation based on the value of the benefits that the tenant received in the form of income or imputed rental value.[67] In recent years, however, many residential tenants have been relieved of a common law duty to make repairs as a result of the widespread judicial recognition of an implied warranty of habitability and legislative enactments in many states that require residential landlords to keep the leased premises in habitable condition. Both the judicially implied warranties of habitability and the statutes shift the duty of making repairs from the tenant to the landlord. In many states, the duty cannot be shifted back to the tenant even by an express written agreement.[68]

A tenant has no common law duty to pay property taxes on the leased premises[69] unless (1) the lease is perpetual or for a long term with options in the tenant to renew forever[70] or (2) the tenant has built improvements on the leased premises for his own

---

apportionment requires the payment of such interest [on principal amounts paid by the remainder holder] while the life tenant lives, or an apportionment based on the value of the estate of each * * *."

[63]   E.g., Converse v. Boston Safe Deposit & Tr. Co., 315 Mass. 544, 53 N.E.2d 841 (1944). See also cases cited in Simes & Smith, supra note 1, at § 1695 n.29.

[64]   E.g., Livesay v. Boyd, 164 Va. 528, 180 S.E. 158 (1935).

[65]   E.g., Clark v. Leverett, 159 Ga. 487, 126 S.E. 258, 37 A.L.R. 180 (1924). But see Clark v. Childs, 253 Ga. 493, 321 S.E.2d 727 (1984).

[66]   E.g., Consol. AG of Curry, Inc. v. Rangen, Inc., 128 Idaho 228, 912 P.2d 115 (1996); Suydam v. Jackson, 54 N.Y. 450 (1873). See Coke, supra note 3, at ¶ 53a. Tenants at will were never subject to any such duty. See, e.g., Means v. Cotton, 225 Mass. 313, 114 N.E. 361 (1916).

[67]   See 5 Am. L. Prop., supra note 1, at § 20.12 n.13. In all other respects, the duty is the same as a life tenant's duty to repair. See, e.g., Earle v. Arbogast, 180 Pa. 409, 36 A. 923 (1897); Thalheimer v. Lempert, 49 Hun 606, 1 N.Y.S. 470 (Sup. 1888).

[68]   See infra §§ 6.36–.45.

[69]   E.g., Eckert v. Miller, 57 Ariz. 94, 111 P.2d 60 (1941); Valencia Ctr., Inc. v. Publix Super Markets, Inc., 464 So. 2d 1267 (Fla. Dist. Ct. App. 1985); Deutsch v. Frey, 36 Ohio App. 226, 173 N.E. 40 (1930); W. Crais, Liability as Between Lessor and Lessee, Where Lease does not Specify, for Taxes and Assessments, 88 A.L.R.2d 670, at § 2 (1962).

[70]   In such cases, the tenant is treated as the owner for tax purposes. E.g., Appeal of Reid, 143 N.H. 246, 722 A.2d 489 (1998); Ocean Grove Camp Meeting Ass'n v. Reeves, 79 N.J.L. 334, 75 A. 782 (1910), aff'd 80 N.J.L. 464, 79 A. 1119 (1911); Quill v. R.A. Inv. Corp., 124 Ohio App. 3d 653, 707 N.E.2d 35 (1997); B. Van Arsdale, et al., General Considerations Imposing Tax Obligation on Tenant, 49 Am. Jur. 2d Landlord and Tenant § 360 (June 2018 Update).

benefit.[71] A tenant also generally has no common law duty to pay carrying charges, such as special assessments,[72] insurance premiums,[73] or mortgage payments.[74]

Commercial and agricultural leases, especially for a long term, often include express covenants that require the tenant for years to make all or specified kinds of repairs[75] and to pay specified carrying charges, such as property taxes,[76] special assessments,[77] and insurance premiums.[78] Long-term residential leases may also include these provisions, though implied or statutory warranties of habitability may shift the repair obligation to the landlord. Construction and application of lease covenants concerning repairs and payment of carrying charges are covered in Chapter 6.

§ 4.4   LEGAL REMEDIES FOR WASTE

At least since enactment of the Statute of Marlbridge in 1267,[79] future interest holders can recover compensatory damages for voluntary or permissive waste committed by tenants for life or for years. The Statute of Gloucester, enacted in 1278,[80] provided that the tenant's estate should be forfeited for waste and that the future interest holder should recover treble damages.[81] Although these penalties seem to have been intended to apply to both voluntary and permissive waste, courts eventually held that they applied only to voluntary waste.[82] Neither the Statute of Marlbridge nor the Statute of Gloucester changed the rule that a tenant at will was not liable for permissive waste.

---

[71]   In such cases, the tenant must pay taxes on the improvements. 1108 Ariola, LLC v. Jones, 139 So. 3d 857 (Fla. 2014).

[72]   E.g., De Clercq v. Barber Asphalt Paving Co., 167 Ill. 215, 47 N.E. 367 (1897); Blake, 247 Mich. 73, 225 N.W. 587, 63 A.L.R. 1386.

[73]   E.g., Ingold v. Phoenix Assurance Co., 230 N.C. 142, 52 S.E.2d 366, 8 A.L.R.2d 1439 (1949). See 66 A.L.R. 864 (1930), C. Drechsler, Right to Proceeds, or to Apportionment Thereof, Where Fire Insurance Policy Is Issued Jointly to Lessor and Lessee Covering Destruction of or Damage to Building, 8 A.L.R.2d 1445 (1949).

[74]   The landlord's common law duty to assure the tenant's "quiet enjoyment" of the premises clearly obligates the landlord to protect the tenant from eviction resulting from a default on an outstanding mortgage of the fee simple. E.g., Ganz v. Clark, 252 N.Y. 92, 169 N.E. 100 (1929).

[75]   For example, the tenant may covenant "to keep the premises in repair, reasonable wear and tear excepted," "to maintain and keep the premises in repair," or "to surrender the premises at the expiration of the lease term in as good condition as they were at the beginning of the term, reasonable wear and tear excepted."

[76]   For example, the tenant may covenant "to pay all taxes imposed on the property during the lease term" or "to pay all taxes levied on the property, extraordinary as well as ordinary." A court held that the latter covenant did not create a duty to pay a special assessment for local improvements. Blake v. Metro. Chain Stores, 247 Mich. 73, 225 N.W. 587, 63 A.L.R. 1386 (1929).

[77]   For example, the tenant may covenant "to pay all special assessments on the leased premises imposed during the lease term" or "to pay all installments of any special assessment on the leased premises that become due and payable during the lease term."

[78]   For example, the tenant may covenant "to maintain adequate insurance on the leased premises throughout the term of the lease, the proceeds in the event of any loss covered by the insurance to be used to restore the premises to their former condition."

[79]   52 Hen. 3, c. 23 (1267).

[80]   6 Edw. 1, c. 5 (1278).

[81]   The Statute of Gloucester also created a new writ of waste, which provided both a new remedy and a new procedure. Later, actions on the case for waste were permitted in lieu of actions initiated by a writ of waste.

[82]   In England, courts later held that life tenants had no liability for permissive waste. See, e.g., In re Arbitration Between Parry and Hopkin [1900], 1 Ch. 160 (Eng.).

Although England abolished the forfeiture and treble damages remedies in the nineteenth century,[83] both remedies are still available in the United States.[84] Many jurisdictions statutorily authorize multiple damages for waste.[85] In some of these states, multiple damages are available only when the waste was voluntary, wanton, or malicious.[86] In some states with forfeiture statutes, the wrongdoer's "estate," rather than "the place wasted," is forfeited,[87] and under many of these statutes forfeiture is authorized only when the waste was voluntary or wanton, when the damages equal the value of the wrongdoer's unexpired interest, or when the wrongdoer does not pay the awarded damages.[88]

Compensatory damages and, where statutorily authorized, multiple damages and forfeiture are generally available to the holder of an indefeasibly vested reversion or remainder in fee simple[89] but are generally unavailable to the owner of a contingent remainder, contingent executory interest, possibility of reverter, right of entry (power of termination), or vested remainder or reversion that is subject to defeasance, because it is uncertain whether the interest will ever become possessory.[90] Some courts have awarded damages when the owner of a contingent remainder sues on behalf of all the future interest owners and then impounded the damages until resolution of the contingencies on which the future interests depend.[91] The same rule should apply when a life estate is followed by a remainder vested subject to complete defeasance, if the future interest owner sues on behalf of all the future interest owners.[92] If the possessory estate is a defeasible fee, the future interest owner generally cannot recover damages or obtain other legal relief for waste.[93] However, if the defeasible fee is certain to become a possessory estate ("to A ten years after the date of this transfer"), the future interest owner should be entitled to damages if the fee owner's conduct is so wanton or unconscionable that a court would enjoin it.[94]

----

[83]   3 & 4 Wm. 4, c. 27, § 36 (1833), and Civil Procedure Acts Repeal Act (1879), 42 & 43 Vict., c. 59, which abolished both the writ of waste and the remedies of forfeiture and treble damages.

[84]   McIntyre v. Scarbrough, 266 Ga. 824, 471 S.E.2d 199 (Ga. 1996) (forfeiture ordered for life tenant's nonpayment of taxes). See the detailed summary of the American statutes in case law in 5 Am. L. Prop., supra note 1, at § 20.18.

[85]   5 Am. L. Prop., supra note 1, at § 20.18; Simes & smith, supra note 1, at § 1658.

[86]   5 Am. L. Prop., supra note 1, at § 20.18. Cf. Gammon v. Verrill, 651 A.2d 831 (Me. 1994) (treble damages unavailable against third parties who damaged property).

[87]   5 Am. L. Prop., supra note 1, at § 20.18.

[88]   Id.; Simes & Smith, supra note 1, at § 1659.

[89]   E.g., Ferguson v. Rochford, 84 Conn. 202, 79 A. 177 (1911); Ussery v. Sweet, 137 Ark. 140, 208 S.W. 600 (1919) (reimbursement); Chapman v. Chapman, 526 So. 2d 131 (Fla. App. 1988). See also §§ 4.1–4.3, supra and cases cited.

[90]   E.g., Strickland v. Jackson, 261 N.C. 360, 134 S.E.2d 661 (1964) (contingent remainder); Sermon v. Sullivan, 640 S.W.2d 486 (Mo. App. 1982). But see Pedro v. January, 261 Or. 582, 494 P.2d 868 (1972) (contingent remainder holder who sued alone obtained a damage award that the court impounded until vesting). See J. Bryant, Right of Contingent Remainderman to Maintain Action for Damages for Waste, 56 A.L.R.3d 677 (1974).

[91]   E.g., Watson v. Wolff-Goldman Realty Co., 95 Ark. 18, 128 S.W. 581 (1910) (suit in equity). Accord First Restatement of Property, supra note 1, at § 189(1)(c). See also Louisville Cooperage Co. v. Rudd, 276 Ky. 721, 124 S.W.2d 1063, 144 A.L.R. 763 (1939) (damages awarded against third party tortfeasor).

[92]   See First Restatement of Property, supra note 1, at § 189(1)(c); 1 Am. L. Prop., supra note 1, at §§ 4.103 n.9, 4.104 at 584–85.

[93]   E.g., Abbott v. Holway, 72 Me. 298 (1881) (executory interest).

[94]   See 1 Am. L. Prop., supra note 1, at § 4.104, at 586.

Some jurisdictions statutorily authorize damages for waste to the holder of a remainder for life.[95] Absent such a statute, courts generally deny a legal action for waste to the owner of a vested remainder for life.[96] Because a remainder for life is not certain to become a present estate, recovery of damages should be denied or, if allowed, be impounded until the death of the present estate owner or of the remainder holder for life, whichever occurs first. The remainder holder should receive the damage award only after surviving long enough to get possession.[97]

After the death of a life tenant who has committed waste, a remainder holder whose interest then becomes indefeasibly vested may recover damages from the decedent's estate,[98] though damages were unavailable while the remainder was contingent or vested subject to complete defeasance. Similarly, the owner of an executory interest or a possibility of reverter that becomes possessory should be able to recover damages for waste if the fee simple owner's conduct was wanton, unconscionable, or malicious.[99]

In a legal action to recover damages for waste, the measure of damages is generally the diminution in the property's market value or the cost of restoring the property, whichever is less.[100] However, considerable disagreement exists concerning which of these two measures is preferable.[101]

§ 4.5　EQUITABLE REMEDIES FOR WASTE

Even when a legal remedy for waste is available, courts often grant an injunction as an alternative equitable remedy. Originally, to get an injunction, the plaintiff had to show that the available legal remedies were inadequate because they would necessitate a multiplicity of actions or because the defendant was insolvent.[102] Today, however, courts rarely refuse equitable relief on the ground that legal remedies are adequate, and the plaintiff's usual allegation that legal remedies are inadequate has become, in many jurisdictions, a mere matter of form that is rarely questioned.[103] A court will not grant an injunction, of course, unless the plaintiff can show that the possessor has not only

---

[95]　E.g., Mich. Comp. Laws Ann. § 600.2919(2)(b) (West 2018).

[96]　Mayo v. Feaster, 2 McCord Eq. 137 (S.C. 1827); Peterson v. Clark, 15 Johns. 205 (N.Y. 1818); Williams v. Peabody, 8 Hun 271 (N.Y. 1876). But see contrary dicta in Dickinson v. City of Baltimore, 48 Md. 583, 589, 30 Am. Rep. 492 (1878); Dennett v. Dennett, 43 N.H. 499, 502 (1862); Dozier v. Gregory, 46 N.C. 100, 106 (1853).

[97]　If the remainder holder for life predeceases the owner of the present estate, the impounded damages should be paid to the owner of the remainder or reversion.

[98]　See Rhoda v. County of Alameda, 134 Cal. App. 726, 26 P.2d 691 (1933), noted in 22 Calif. L. Rev. 704 (1934); Fisher's Ex'r v. Haney, 180 Ky. 257, 202 S.W. 495 (1918).

[99]　First Restatement of Property, supra note 1, at § 194(b).

[100]　Smith v. CAP Concrete, Inc., 133 Cal. App. 3d 769, 184 Cal. Rptr. 308 (1982); Duckett v. Whorton, 312 N.W.2d 561 (Iowa 1981); Vogel v. Pardon, 444 N.W.2d 348 (N.D. 1989) (denying replacement cost award).

[101]　Meyer v. Hansen, 373 N.W.2d 392 (N.D. 1985) (plaintiff "has the right to elect the measure [of damages] deemed more accurate and if the defendant disagrees, he has the burden to prove the alternative measure is more appropriate"). Compare Three & One Co. v. Geilfuss, 178 Wis. 2d 400, 504 N.W.2d 393 (Wis. Ct. App. 1993) (cost of repair is preferred method of calculating damages, but tenant may introduce evidence that diminution of value is the lesser, and therefore correct, measure), with Brown v. Midwest Petro. Co., 828 S.W.2d 686 (Mo. Ct. App. 1992) (measure is generally reduction in market value, but cost of repair is the proper measure when it is small in relationship to the property as a whole and when the amount of the repair is easily ascertained).

[102]　See generally 5 Am. L. Prop., supra note 1, at § 20.20, text accompanying nn. 5–6.

[103]　E.g., Wise v. Potomac Nat'l Bank, 393 Ill. 357, 65 N.E.2d 767 (1946). Contra Redwood Hotel Co. v. Korbien, 195 Md. 402, 73 A.2d 468 (1950) (no injunction if plaintiff fails to allege absence of adequate remedy at law).

committed waste in the past but is continuing to do so or has threatened to do so in the future.[104] Once the court has determined that injunctive relief is appropriate, it will also order an accounting for waste already committed.[105] Because a plaintiff can obtain complete relief in the suit for an injunction, the equitable remedy has effectively superseded all legal remedies for waste.[106]

Because mandatory injunctions can be difficult to supervise, courts traditionally have been reluctant to issue them, but some courts have issued them to compel tenants for life or for years to fulfill their obligation to keep the property in repair and to restore it after committing voluntary waste.[107] When a life tenant fails to make necessary repairs or to pay carrying charges, courts in some cases have appointed a receiver to take possession of the property to collect rental income and use it for those purposes.[108]

In some cases, a court has granted injunctive relief, though the plaintiff was not entitled to legal relief. For example, the holder of a contingent remainder, defeasible reversion, or remainder subject to complete defeasance in fee simple generally can enjoin waste by a life tenant.[109] An injunction and accounting for waste already committed may also be available to the holder of a possibility of reverter or executory interest if the defeasible fee owner has committed wanton, unconscionable, or malicious acts that reduce the property's value and if a reasonable probability exists that the plaintiff's future interest will become possessory.[110] A future interest holder can enjoin waste even if she will only have possession, if any, of a life estate.[111] Additionally, if a future interest holder sues on behalf of all the future interest owners, a court will order injunctive relief and an accounting. In that case, the court may impound the damages paid by the defendant for the benefit of those who eventually become entitled to possession.[112] But a court may deny injunctive relief if the future interest is unlikely to become possessory.[113]

A life tenant who holds without impeachment of waste is not liable at law for conduct that would otherwise constitute waste.[114] But if the life tenant's conduct is wanton, unconscionable, or malicious and reduces the property's value, a future interest

---

[104] Hausmann v. Hausmann, 231 Ill. App. 3d 361, 172 Ill. Dec. 937, 596 N.E.2d 216 (Ill. App. 1992) (injunction appropriate remedy for life tenant's refusal to pay taxes); Burns v. Hale, 162 Ga. 336, 133 S.E. 857 (1926); Redwood Hotel Co. v. Korbien, 195 Md. 402, 73 A.2d 468.

[105] E.g., Kimberlin v. Hicks, 150 Kan. 449, 94 P.2d 335 (1939); Watson v. Wolff-Goldman Realty Co., 95 Ark. 18, 128 S.W. 581 (1910).

[106] See Palmer v. Young, 108 Ill. App. 252 (1903).

[107] E.g., Baltimore & Philadelphia Steamboat Co. v. Starr Methodist Protestant Church, 149 Md. 163, 130 A. 46 (1925); Sawyer v. Adams, 140 App. Div. 756, 126 N.Y.S. 128 (1910).

[108] E.g., Chapman v. Chapman, 526 So. 2d 131 (Fla. Dist. Ct. App. 1988). If there is no rental income because the life tenant personally occupies the property, a court will presumably be less willing to appoint a receiver. But see Smith v. Smith, 219 Ark. 304, 241 S.W.2d 113 (1951).

[109] E.g., Peterson v. Ferrell, 127 N.C. 169, 37 S.E. 189 (1900) (contingent remainder); Kollock v. Webb, 113 Ga. 762, 39 S.E. 339 (1901).

[110] E.g., Union Cty. v. Union Cty. Fair Ass'n, 276 Ark. 132, 633 S.W.2d 17 (1982); Elkhorn City Land Co. v. Elkhorn City, 459 S.W.2d 762 (Ky. 1970). Accord First Restatement of Property, supra note 1, at § 193, stating that the rule also applies to powers of termination. See also Frensley v. White, 208 Okla. 209, 254 P.2d 982 (1953), discussed in O. Browder, Defeasible Fees in Oklahoma—An Addendum, 6 Okla. L. Rev. 482 (1953).

[111] E.g., Kane v. Vanderburgh, 1 Johns. Ch. 11 (N.Y. 1814); Williams v. Peabody, 8 Hun 271 (N.Y. 1876). Accord Simes & Smith, supra note 1, at § 1622; First Restatement of Property, supra note 1, at § 192(a).

[112] See supra note 111.

[113] E.g., Brown v. Brown, 89 W. Va. 339, 109 S.E. 815 (1921) (contingent remainder).

[114] E.g., Bowles's Case (1616), 77 Eng. Rep. 1252 (K.B.), 11 Co. Rep. 79b.

holder may get an injunction.[115] In such cases, as well as in cases in which the court grants injunctive relief to a future interest owner, the conduct of the owner of the present estate is characterized as equitable waste.[116]

When a present estate owner has a power, such as a power of appointment, to destroy a future interest, the future interest owner has no rights, either at law or in equity, with respect to conduct that would otherwise constitute waste.[117] However, if the power is conditional or is exercisable only by will, the future interest owner should have a right to enjoin waste under some circumstances.[118]

§ 4.6   PAYMENT OF CARRYING CHARGES— CONTRIBUTION AND SUBROGATION

A future interest holder is entitled to a judgment in an action for reimbursement if she pays property taxes, mortgage interest, or special assessments that the possessor had a duty to pay.[119] The future interest holder also has an equitable lien on the possessory estate that she can foreclose by a court-ordered sale to recover her payments.[120] Additionally, the future interest owner is entitled to the benefit of the equitable doctrine of subrogation. Under subrogation, a person who protects her own interest by paying another's obligation can enforce any security held by the person to whom payment was owed.[121] Therefore, a future interest holder who pays a property carrying charge can enforce the tax lien, mortgage lien, or other security interest of the person to whom it was paid.[122] The possessor can redeem his estate to prevent the foreclosure sale by reimbursing the future interest holder.[123] When a property possessor has paid mortgage principal, special assessments, or other carrying charges that the future interest holder had a duty to pay, the possessor has the same rights of reimbursement, equitable lien enforcement, and subrogation.[124]

---

[115] In Bowles's Case, id., the court held that the phrase "without impeachment for waste" excuses the tenant from all liability for waste, not merely from treble damages and forfeiture. See Camden Tr. Co. v. Handle, 132 N.J. Eq. 97, 26 A.2d 865 (1942). Accord First Restatement of Property, supra note 1, at § 141.

[116] Camden Trust Co. v. Handle, 132 N.J. Eq. 97, 26 A.2d 865. See also 5 Am. L. Prop., supra note 1, at § 20.14; 4 J. Pomeroy, Equity Jurisprudence § 1348 (5th ed. Symons ed. 1941).

[117] See West v. United States, 310 F.Supp. 1289 (N.D. Ga. 1970); Magruder v. Magruder, 525 S.W.2d 400 (Mo. Ct. App. 1975); Dickerson v. Keller, 521 S.W.2d 288 (Tex. Civ. App. 1975). Accord First Restatement of Property, supra note 1, at § 197. But see In re Mitchell's Will, 15 Misc. 2d 651, 181 N.Y.S.2d 436 (Sur. 1959).

[118] See Rudisill v. Hoyle, 254 N.C. 33, 118 S.E.2d 145 (1961); Johnson v. Messer, 437 S.W.2d 643 (Tex. Civ. App. 1969), writ refused n.r.e.

[119] Ussery v. Sweet, 137 Ark. 140, 208 S.W. 600 (1919). At common law, reimbursement was obtained in an action of assumpsit for money paid to the plaintiff's use.

[120] Id. Accord 1 Am. L. Prop., supra note 1, at § 2.24 n.6; First Restatement of Property, supra note 1, at §§ 131, 132. The rights to a personal judgment and a foreclosure sale may be asserted in the same action. E.g., Hancock Fabrics, Inc. v. Ruthven Assocs., No. 2:06cv466, 2007 WL 593573 (E.D. Va. Feb. 20, 2007) (unpublished decision); Waynesboro Nat'l Bank v. Smith, 151 Va. 481, 145 S.E. 302 (1928).

[121] As to subrogation, see generally 4 Pomeroy, supra note 116, at §§ 1211, 1212. See also Restatement (Third) of Property: Mortgages § 7.6 (1997).

[122] E.g., Krebs v. Bezler, 338 Mo. 365, 89 S.W.2d 935, 103 A.L.R. 1177 (1936); Elmora & W. End Bldg. & Loan Ass'n v. Dancy, 108 N.J. Eq. 542, 155 A. 796 (1931).

[123] See 1 Am. L. Prop., supra note 1, at § 2.22, at 158. If the possessor fails to redeem, his estate may be extinguished by foreclosure regardless of any rents and profits that he has received or the value of his actual use and enjoyment.

[124] E.g., Ward v. Chambless, 238 Ala. 165, 189 So. 890 (1939); Boggs v. Boggs, 63 Cal. App. 2d 576, 147 P.2d 116 (1944); Randall's Estate v. McKibben, 191 N.W.2d 693 (Iowa 1971); King v. Rainbolt, 515 P.2d 228 (Okla. 1973).

If the possessor does not pay property taxes or other carrying charges that are his sole obligation and later buys the fee simple absolute title at a tax or foreclosure sale, the possessor does not get the fee simple estate.[125] Rather, the purchase price is treated as payment of the taxes or other carrying charges and leaves the property title unchanged.[126] On the other hand, if the possessor buys at a tax or foreclosure sale when the future interest holder was at least partially responsible for payment, the possessor gets fee simple title, subject to the right of the former owner of the future interest to re-acquire it by contributing, within a reasonable time, a proportionate share of the possessor's payment.[127] If the future interest owner was solely responsible for the carrying charge, the possessor acquires the fee simple, subject to the right of the former owner of the future interest to reacquire the interest by fully reimbursing the possessor within a reasonable time.[128]

Conversely, if the future interest owner buys at a foreclosure or tax sale after failing to pay a carrying charge for which he was solely or partially responsible, he should acquire the fee simple title, subject to the former possessor's right to re-acquire the possessory interest by paying him the amount necessary for proper reimbursement.[129] In either case, the interest holder who buys the land has a quasi-fiduciary relationship with the other holder and acquires the fee simple, subject to a constructive trust in the other's favor.[130]

§ 4.7 RIGHTS TO INSURANCE PROCEEDS

If a possessor buys a property insurance policy in his or her name and has no duty to maintain it for the future interest holder's benefit, only the possessor can recover in the event of loss, unless the policy expressly insures the future interest.[131] Even if the policy purports to insure the entire fee simple estate, the general rule is that an insurance policy is enforceable only to the extent of the insured's actual loss.[132] And even if the insurer fails to invoke this rule, most courts hold that a future interest holder is not entitled to any portion of the insurance proceeds paid to the possessor, even if the possessor is overcompensated as a result.[133] However, some courts hold that the

---

[125] E.g., Wheeler v. Harris, 232 Ark. 469, 339 S.W.2d 99 (1960); Richton Tie & Timber Co. v. Tillman, 233 Miss. 12, 103 So. 2d 139 (1958).

[126] E.g., Rushton v. McLaughlin, 213 Ala. 380, 104 So. 824 (1925); Henderson v. Ellis, 10 Ark. App. 276, 665 S.W.2d 289 (1984); Thompson v. Watkins, 285 N.C. 616, 207 S.E.2d 740 (1974).

[127] E.g., Drane v. Smith, 271 Ala. 54, 122 So. 2d 135 (1960) (right lost after 16 years); Fleming v. Brunner, 224 Md. 97, 166 A.2d 901 (1961) (right barred by laches); Thompson v. Watkins, 285 N.C. 616, 207 S.E.2d 740 (right lost after 19 years). Cf. Scotch v. Hurst, 437 So. 2d 497 (Ala. 1983) (remainder holder's right not barred after 29 years).

[128] The authorities cited supra in notes 126 and 127 state the rule so broadly as to apply even when the future interest owners were solely responsible for the carrying charges.

[129] See Hall v. Hall, 173 Minn. 128, 216 N.W. 798 (1927); Smith v. Kappler, 220 Ark. 10, 245 S.W.2d 809 (1952).

[130] See, e.g., the authorities cited supra in notes 126 and 127.

[131] This is simply an application of ordinary contract principles to the insurance contract. See Carlton v. Wilson, 665 S.W.2d 356 (Mo. Ct. App. 1984).

[132] This rule is based on the theories that (1) the policy would become a "wagering contract" and (2) the "moral risk" would be increased if the policy could be enforced for losses in excess of the insured's interest. See W. Vance, Handbook of the Law of Insurance §§ 28–30 (3d ed. 1951); 1 G. Richards, A Treatise on the Law of Insurance §§ 64–70, 152 (5th ed. 1952).

[133] E.g., Converse v. Boston Safe Deposit & Tr. Co., 315 Mass. 544, 53 N.E.2d 841 (1944) (dictum). Courts find that there a trust relationship does not exist between the life tenant and the future interest owners. See Vance, supra note 132, at § 132.

possessor is a trustee for the future interest holder and can enforce the insurance policy for the full face amount, subject to a duty to account to the future interest holder for its share.[134] Moreover, if the possessor has no duty to insure for the benefit of the future interest holder but nevertheless does so, the future interest owner can ratify the possessor's action, even after a loss occurs, and enforce the policy for his own benefit.[135]

When land or structures are insured for the benefit of both the possessor and the future interest holder,[136] the First Restatement of Property states that, in the event of a loss, a life tenant has "a privilege to use, and a power to compel the use of, the proceeds from such policy for the restoration of the land or structures to its former condition, when such restoration is both practicable and reasonable" and "a privilege to have the use of such proceeds for the duration of his estate" if they are not used for restoration.[137] Use of the proceeds means receiving "the interest earned by such proceeds, periodically, during the continuance of such estate for life."[138] Some states statutorily authorize courts to apportion the proceeds between the life tenant and the future interest owners, so that each receives a portion of the proceeds in a lump sum.[139]

Leases for a term of years often include express contractual provisions concerning required property insurance coverage, payment of insurance premiums, and the use or apportionment of insurance proceeds in the event of loss.[140] In the absence of such provisions, the rules that apply between a life tenant and the future interest owners also should apply between a tenant for years and the landlord.

§ 4.8　APPORTIONMENT OF RENTS

A possessor can lease the property for any use that does not amount to waste and is exclusively entitled to all rents received from lessees.[141] If the possessory interest was transferred subject to an existing lease, the transferee is exclusively entitled to the rents.[142]

As we have already seen, it is waste for a possessor to open and exploit new mines, oil wells, or gas wells or to cut and sell mature timber except in the course of "good husbandry."[143] Consequently, it is also waste to lease the property to a tenant for such uses.[144] However, if mines, oil wells, or gas wells are already open or the land is already

---

[134] E.g., Crisp Cty. Lumber Co. v. Bridges, 187 Ga. 484, 200 S.E. 777 (1939); Sampson v. Grogan, 21 R.I. 174, 42 A. 712, 44 L.R.A. 711 (1899) (dictum).

[135] 1 Am. L. Prop., supra note 1, at § 2.23, at 160.

[136] The insurance proceeds will generally be made payable to the life tenant and the future interest owner "as their interests may appear." See, e.g., Hopkins v. Keazer, 89 Me. 347, 36 A. 615 (1896); Lynch v. Johnson, 196 Va. 516, 84 S.E.2d 419 (1954).

[137] First Restatement of Property, supra note 1, at § 123. As to periodic payments of interest, see Cope v. Ricketts, 130 Kan. 823, 288 P. 591 (1930).

[138] First Restatement of Property, supra note 1, at § 123, cmt. b.

[139] Id.; 9 Powell, supra note 1, at § 59.02.

[140] See infra § 6.60.

[141] As we have already seen, the possessor's personal obligation to keep the property in repair and to pay carrying charges, such as taxes, is limited to the rents she obtains from the property or, if she occupies the property, its fair rental value.

[142] E.g., Redwine v. Ansley, 32 Okla. 317, 122 P. 679 (1912); In re Blodgett's Estate, 254 Pa. 210, 98 A. 876 (1916).

[143] Supra § 4.2.

[144] Moore v. Vines, 474 S.W.2d 437 (Tex. 1971), noted in 8 Houston L. Rev. 753 (1971), 24 Baylor L. Rev. 142 (1972) (opening a new oil or gas well was outside the "open mine" doctrine).

used to produce and sell timber when the possessory interest is created, the possessor can lease the property for such uses.[145] And, of course, the possessor can join with the future interest holder to lease the property to a tenant that will open new mines, oil wells, or gas wells or cut and sell timber. In that case, the lease normally specifies the division of rents or royalties. Absent an express provision to the contrary, the possessor is entitled to the present value of the use of the rents or royalties, computed on the basis of the probable duration of the possessory estate.[146]

An estate for years created before a life estate will continue after the life tenant's death if the term has not expired. The future interest owner becomes the landlord and is entitled to all rents thereafter. Because rent is due, at common law, only on the days fixed by the lease, the entire amount payable on the next rent day after the life tenant's death belongs to the new landlord.[147] This is manifestly unjust and has been changed in England and in some American jurisdictions by statutes that enable the life tenant's personal representative to recover a share of the rent based on the number of days in the rent period that preceded the life tenant's death.[148]

§ 4.9   EMBLEMENTS AND FIXTURES

Any estate of indefinite duration, such as a life estate, carries with it the right of "emblements," which permits the possessor to harvest and remove, after the termination of her estate, any crops that she planted.[149] This special right is an exception to the usual rule that annual crops are part of the realty and pass with it.[150] The right exists only when no act or default of the possessor caused the estate to terminate.[151] When a life estate expires at the life tenant's death, his personal representative can harvest and remove the annual crops that the life tenant planted.[152] The personal representative's right is not affected by the life tenant's exercise of a power to appoint the property in fee

---

[145] Under the "open mine" doctrine, the life possessor or his lessee can work the open mine or wells even to exhaustion. E.g., Ohio Oil Co. v. Daughetee, 240 Ill. 361, 88 N.E. 818, 36 L.R.A. (N.S.) 1108 (1909); Gaines v. Green Pond Iron Mining Co., 33 N.J. Eq. 603 (1881). But the open mine doctrine does not authorize the possessor or his lessee to open additional mines.

[146] E.g., Weekley v. Weekley, 126 W.Va. 90, 27 S.E.2d 591, 150 A.L.R. 689 (1943). First Restatement of Property, supra note 1, at § 119, cmt. b urges that apportionment should apply to all leases or contracts for the removal and sale of minerals or timber. But see Haskell v. Wood, 256 Cal. App. 2d 799, 64 Cal. Rptr. 459 (1967). See generally V. Woerner, Rights of Tenant for Life or for Years and Remaindermen Inter Se in Royalties or Rents Under Oil, Gas, Coal, or Other Mineral Lease, A.L.R.2d 100–79 (1951).

[147] E.g., Peery v. Fletcher, 93 Or. 43, 182 P. 143 (1919); Ex parte Smyth, 1 Swanst. 337, 36 Eng. Rep. 412 (1818).

[148] See Stat. 4 Wm. 4, c. 22 (Eng. 1834); Stat. 2 Geo. 2, c. 19, § 15 (Eng. 1738); First Restatement of Property, supra note 1, § 120, cmt. d, Special Note; Coleman v. Edwards, 70 N.C. App. 206, 318 S.E.2d 899 (1984).

[149] See 1 Am. L. Prop., supra note 1, at § 2.6, at 142–44; 5 id. § 19.16, at 67–68. For the origin of the doctrine, see Coke, supra note 3, at ¶ 55b. See also Lower v. Appel, No. 2–13–1288, 2015 WL 3965909 (Ill. App. Ct. June 29, 2015) (unpublished decision); Leigh v. Lynch, 112 Ill.2d 411, 98 Ill. Dec. 19, 493 N.E.2d 1040 (1986) (right to remove perennial crop did not continue after first harvest season).

[150] See Mitchell v. Martindill, 209 Ark. 66, 189 S.W.2d 662 (1945) (crops pass on conveyance of realty by deed); In re Andersen's Estate, 83 Neb. 8, 118 N.W. 1108 (1908) (crops pass by will). However, for many other purposes, crops are treated as personalty. See 5 Am. L. Prop., supra note 1, at § 19.16 at nn. 4–8.

[151] E.g., Carpenter v. Jones, 63 Ill. 517 (1872); Eckman v. Beihl, 116 N.J.L. 308, 184 A. 430 (1936); Leigh, 112 Ill. 2d 411, 98 Ill. Dec. 19, 493 N.E.2d 1040.

[152] First Restatement of Property, supra note 1, at § 121. The same privilege may be exercised by the life tenant's lessee when the death of the life tenant terminates the lease. E.g., Strand v. Boll, 44 S.D. 228, 183 N.W. 284, 15 A.L.R. 652 (1921). See also First Restatement of Property, supra note 1, at § 121, cmt. a, Special Note.

simple.[153] A tenant for years has no right to remove annual crops under the doctrine of "emblements," because that estate has a definite duration,[154] but a periodic tenant or tenant at will is privileged to do so.[155]

When a tenant for life or for years annexes a chattel to the realty, whether for trade, agricultural, domestic, or ornamental purposes, courts have generally presumed that the tenant does not intend to make a permanent annexation and have allowed the tenant to remove the chattel—commonly called a "fixture"—at or before the end of the tenancy if removal will not cause substantial injury to the realty or substantially destroy the fixture.[156] If the chattel was annexed by a life tenant, her personal representative can remove it within a reasonable time after the life estate terminates.[157] If a tenant for years annexed the chattel, however, the tenant loses the right to remove it when the lease term ends.[158] Most modern cases on removal of a tenant's fixtures involve tenants for years. These cases are discussed in the chapter dealing with the law of landlord and tenant.[159]

§ 4.10   JUDICIAL SALE OF REALTY ENCUMBERED BY FUTURE ESTATES

Dividing land ownership into present and future estates can cause substantial hardship. The law of waste restricts the possessor's use of the property, and the possessor is obligated to pay property taxes and other carrying charges to the extent that they do not exceed the property's actual rental income or, if the possessor personally occupies the property, its rental value.[160] However, renting the property may be difficult because of the uncertainty as to the duration of the estate or the lack of suitable improvements on the land. Even if actual rental income can be obtained, it may be insufficient to pay the property taxes and other carrying charges. Nonpayment of taxes, mortgage interest, or special assessments may result in a sale that will extinguish not only the possessory interest, but also the future interests.

The possessor's financial inability to keep the property in good repair may result in substantial injury to the future interest owners, as well as to the possessor. For that reason, the future interest owners may consent to sell the land in fee simple and to investing the proceeds in trust for the holders of all interests in the land.[161] But, in many

---

[153] E.g., Keays v. Blinn, 234 Ill. 121, 84 N.E. 628 (1908).

[154] E.g., Miller v. Gray, 136 Tex. 196, 149 S.W.2d 582 (1941).

[155] E.g., Harris v. Frink, 49 N.Y. 24 (1872) (tenancy at will).

[156] The modern American rule generally allows removal of tenant fixtures without regard to whether they are trade, agricultural, or ornamental fixtures. See, e.g., Warrington v. Hignutt, 42 Del. 274, 31 A.2d 480 (1943) (oil heaters and outside oil tanks, including connecting copper tubing); Leslie Pontiac, Inc. v. Novak, 202 N.W.2d 114 (Iowa 1972) (steel shell structure on concrete slab, with no insulation or utilities); Old Line Life Ins. Co. of Am. v. Hawn, 225 Wis. 627, 275 N.W. 542 (1937) (furnace and brooder houses).

[157] E.g., Ray v. Young, 160 Iowa 613, 142 N.W. 393, 46 L.R.A.(N.S.) 947 (1913). The same rule applies to a tenant at will, e.g., Henderson v. Robbins, 126 Me. 284, 138 A. 68 (1927), or the owner of a determinable fee simple, e.g., Dickerman v. Town of Pittsford, 116 Vt. 563, 80 A.2d 529 (1951).

[158] E.g., Stout v. Stoppel, 30 Minn. 56, 14 N.W. 268 (1882).

[159] See infra §§ 6.48, 6.49.

[160] See supra §§ 4.2–4.3.

[161] When the rental income or rental value is insufficient to cover the carrying charges, the future interest owner may pay them in full and then sue the possessor for reimbursement and a lien for the amount that she is entitled. The lien will be enforced by an order for sale of the possessory estate. See supra §§ 4.3, 4.4, 4.6. However, selling the entire fee simple estate may be a better solution for the future interest owners because it requires no financial outlay by them and because life estates are not readily salable.

instances, contingent future interests may be limited in favor of unborn or otherwise unascertainable persons who are incapable of consenting to a sale, and consent may not always be forthcoming even if all the future interests are vested.

When selling the fee simple title is necessary to preserve all the interests, the weight of authority is that courts have the inherent power to order a sale, with the sale proceeds to be held in a judicially created trust for the benefit of all the owners.[162] However, some courts refuse to order a sale in fee simple unless it is statutorily authorized.[163] At least half the states have such statutes.[164] Some statutes give courts very broad powers, but others grant the power only in narrowly defined situations.[165]

When courts assert the power to order a sale without statutory authorization, the precise scope of their power is often unclear. Some courts order a sale only if all non-consenting future interest owners are either minors or are unborn or otherwise unascertained.[166] Other courts have ordered a sale even if nonconsenting future interest owners are ascertained and of full age.[167]

Some courts have said that a sale should not be ordered unless the petitioner shows that it is "necessary for the best interest of all the parties."[168] This test is not very useful, because a sale that may be strongly advantageous to one party may be highly undesirable to another. In one significant case, the Mississippi court cited this test and held that it had the power to order a sale, though the property "was not deteriorating" and there was "sufficient rental income to pay taxes," to provide "economic relief" to the aging life tenant whose income from the property was insufficient for her to "live comfortably in view of her age and the infirmities therefrom."[169] The court also held that "the best interest of all the parties would not be served by a judicial sale of the entirety of the property at this time," because it appeared that the land's value would increase from $168,500 to $336,000 within four years.[170] The court further suggested that the life tenant would immediately be entitled to "sale of a part of the burdened land sufficient to provide for her reasonable needs from interest derived from the investment of the

---

[162] E.g., Dunn v. Sanders, 243 Ga. 684, 256 S.E.2d 366 (1979); Baker v. Weedon, 262 So. 2d 641 (Miss. 1972). For the theoretical basis of this judicial power, see Simes & Smith, supra note 1, at § 1941. See also C. Rogers, Removal of Future Interest Encumbrances—Sale of the Fee Simple Estate, 17 Vand. L. Rev. 1437 (1964); 57 A.L.R.3d 1189 (1974).

[163] E.g., Losey v. Stanley, 147 N.Y. 560, 42 N.E. 8 (1895); Brown v. Brown, 83 W. Va. 415, 422, 98 S.E. 428, 431 (1919) (dictum).

[164] See statutes listed in Simes & Smith, supra note 1, at § 1946 n.28.

[165] Some statutes allow a sale upon petition of the owner of any present or future interest. E.g., Mass. Gen. Laws ch. 183, § 49. Other statutes allow a sale upon petition by the owner of any present or specified future interest. E.g., N.H. Rev. Stat. Ann. § 477:39. And some statutes allow sale only on petition by the owners of present interests. E.g., Ohio Rev. Code Ann. §§ 5303.21, 5303.31.

[166] E.g., Bofil v. Fisher, 3 Rich. Eq. (24 S.C. Eq.) 1, 55 Am. Dec. 627 (S.C. 1850).

[167] E.g., Williams v. Colleran, 230 Ga. 56, 195 S.E.2d 413 (1973).

[168] Baker, 262 So. 2d at 643. Accord: Gavin v. Curtin, 171 Ill. 640, 49 N.E. 523, 40 L.R.A. 776 (1898); Cagle v. Schaefer, 115 S.C. 35, 104 S.E. 321 (1920); Soules v. Silver, 118 Or. 96, 245 P. 1069 (1926) (refusing a sale when no proof existed that it would benefit the remainder holder); DeLisi v. Caito, 463 A.2d 167 (R.I. 1983).

[169] Baker, 262 So. 2d 641, 645.

[170] Id. at 643. The court said that an immediate sale of all the land in fee simple "would unjustly impinge upon the vested rights of the remaindermen." Id. at 645. The anticipated appreciation in value was due to the planned construction of a federal highway by-pass.

proceeds" if "the parties cannot unite to hypothecate [mortgage] the land for sufficient funds for the life tenant's reasonable needs."[171]

When a court orders a sale in fee simple of land burdened with future interests, the sale proceeds are held in a judicially-created trust, and the investment income is paid to the former life tenant during the balance of her life. When the life tenant dies, the principal is distributed to the future interest owners.[172] If a court has the power to order a sale of the fee title despite the existence of future interests, the court also should have the power to order that the property be mortgaged, leased, or exchanged, rather than sold.

§ 4.11 PROTECTION OF OWNERS OF LEGAL FUTURE INTERESTS IN PERSONALTY

A donor who wishes to create future interests in personalty is well-advised to use a trust, particularly if the personalty consists mainly of cash, stocks, bonds, or similar intangible forms of property. A trustee holds and manages the property for the benefit of both the present and future interest owners. A life beneficiary of a trust has a right only to the net income of the trust property. The remedies that the present and future interest owners have against each other and against the trustee are governed by the law of trusts, which is beyond the scope of this book.

Suppose a donor divides the ownership of personalty into present and future interests without expressly creating a trust, which is more likely to occur with tangible personalty, such as art works or heirlooms. In that case, the owner of a present interest is entitled to possession of the property, and problems like those considered previously in this chapter may arise. But personalty poses additional problems that do not arise in the case of realty, because personalty is movable and readily saleable and, if it consists of cash, stocks, bonds, or the like, may require expert management to avoid capital loss. Because the law of waste, as developed in connection with the division of ownership of realty into present and future estates, does not afford future interest owners in personalty adequate protection against misappropriation or misuse by the possessory owner, courts have often construed ambiguous language in wills as creating a trust with the executor as trustee.[173] Pennsylvania has statutorily provided, in substance, that the owner of a possessory interest in personalty shall be treated as a trustee even if an express trust was not created.[174] Several other states statutorily require life tenants of personalty to account periodically, as if they were trustees.[175]

---

[171] Id. at 644.

[172] See Smith v. Smith, 600 S.W.2d 666 (Mo. Ct. App. 1980) (life tenant is not entitled to the present value of the life estate in a lump sum when the land is sold in fee simple).

[173] E.g., Mt. Freedom Presbyterian Church v. Osborne, 81 N.J. Super. 441, 195 A.2d 907 (Law Div. 1963). The First Restatement of Property, supra note 1, at § 200, states a constructional preference for finding a trust. See Backer v. Levy, 82 F.2d 270 (2d Cir. 1936), containing dictum in support of the First Restatement.

[174] 20 Pa. Con. Stat. § 6113.

[175] E.g., N.Y. Surr. Ct. Proc. Act § 2201 (McKinney 2018). Under such statutes, a life tenant clearly is entitled to all income derived from the property, but it is not always clear whether the usual trust law rules as to allocation of stock dividends and the like between principal and interest are applicable. See First Restatement of Property, supra note 1, at §§ 119, 120; W. Allen, Rights of Life Tenant and Remaindermen Inter Se Respecting Increase, Gains, and Enhanced Values of the Estate, 76 A.L.R.2d 162 (1961); J. Ludington, Modern Status of Rules Governing Allocation of Stock Dividends or Splits Between Principal and Interest, 81 A.L.R.3d 876 (1977).

If the transfer instrument does not create a trust and the jurisdiction does not statutorily create a trust when ownership of personalty is divided into present and future interests, courts often protect the future interest owners by ordering the possessory owner to give security.[176] If he does not obey the order, the court will appoint a trustee to manage the property.[177] In some states, the probate court is statutorily authorized to require the possessory owner to give security before personalty passing by will is delivered to him.[178] Even without such a statute, some courts, upon petition by a future interest owner, require the possessory owner to give security if she has expressly been given the power to alter the form of the property or has that power by implication because the personalty consists of cash, stocks, bonds, or the like.[179]

In a significant number of states, courts will require security from the possessory owner only on a showing that a substantial danger exists that he will misappropriate or misuse the property.[180] If such a danger is shown, all courts will require the possessory owner to give security, unless she has been given an unrestricted power to consume the property or a power to appoint the property, free of all future interests, to a person other than the future interest owner.[181] If it is reasonably probable that any of the future interests for which protection is sought will become possessory, whether it is indefeasibly vested, vested subject to open, vested subject to complete defeasance, or contingent, is immaterial.[182] Whether the possessory owner has a life interest or an interest analogous to a defeasible fee simple in realty also is largely immaterial.[183]

Although most courts hold that security for protection of future interests in personalty is a matter of right when danger of loss is shown,[184] courts in fact have substantial discretion in determining whether such danger exists. Courts weigh a variety of factors in making the determination, such as whether the possessory owner is

---

[176] E.g., Frye v. Cmty Chest of Birmingham, 241 Ala. 591, 4 So. 2d 140 (1941); Reed v. Reed, 80 Conn. 411, 68 A. 852 (1908); In re Estate of Bozarth, 378 Ill. Dec. 879, 5 N.E.3d 259 (Ill. App. Ct. 2014); Quigley v. Quigley, 370 Ill. 151, 18 N.E.2d 186 (1938); Fewell v. Fewell, 459 S.W.2d 774 (Ky. 1970); Evans v. Adams, 180 S.C. 214, 185 S.E. 57 (1936); Long v. Lea, 177 S.C. 231, 181 S.E. 6 (1935). Cf. Matter of Estate of Jud, 238 Kan. 268, 710 P.2d 1241 (1985). See generally E. Nemmers, The Right of the Owner of a Future Interest in Personalty to Security, 1943 Wis. L. Rev. 229; Comment, Protecting the Remainderman, 33 Chi. Kent L. Rev. 240 (1955).

[177] E.g., Frye, 241 Ala. 591, 4 So. 2d 140; Reed v. Reed, 80 Conn. 411, 68 A. 852; Van Dusen's Appeal, 102 Pa. 224 (1883). See also Koplon v. Koplon, 274 Ala. 214, 148 So. 2d 245 (1962).

[178] See 20 Pa. Con. Stat. § 6113.

[179] E.g., Tripp v. Krauth, 340 Ill. 11, 171 N.E. 919 (1930); In re Blakely's Estate, 115 Kan. 644, 224 P. 65 (1924). In these cases in which the possessory owner had only a life interest, the courts appeared to view the power of changing the form of the property as itself creating a danger of loss. But see Matter of Estate of Jud, 238 Kan. 268, 710 P.2d 1241.

[180] Long v. Lea, 177 S.C. 231, 181 S.E. 6. See also, Busbee v. Haley, 220 Ga. 874, 142 S.E.2d 786 (1965); Holley v. Marks, 535 S.W.2d 861 (Tenn. 1976); Wise v. Hinegardner, 97 W.Va. 587, 125 S.E. 579 (1924).

[181] See cases cited, supra note 180. That an unrestricted power to consume precludes requiring the possessory owner to give security, see In re Hays' Estate, 358 Pa. 38, 55 A.2d 763 (1947). See also Marshall v. Hewett, 156 Fla. 645, 24 So. 2d 1 (1945). Contra Abbott v. Wagner, 108 Neb. 359, 188 N.W. 113 (1922). It is not always easy to decide whether a possessory owner has been given an unrestricted power to consume the property. See, e.g., Phillips v. Lynch, 247 Cal. App. 2d 510, 55 Cal. Rptr. 658 (1966); In re Estate of Perkins, 289 Minn. 53, 182 N.W.2d 881 (1970).

[182] E.g., Security Co. v. Hardenberg, 53 Conn. 169, 2 A. 391 (1885) (contingent remainder); Phipps v. Doak, 235 Mo. App. 659, 145 S.W.2d 167 (1940) (indefeasibly vested remainder).

[183] See Meins v. Pease, 208 Mass. 478, 94 N.E. 845 (1911).

[184] Contra Quigley v. Quigley, 370 Ill. 151, 18 N.E.2d 186 (1938); Heintz v. Parsons, 233 Iowa 984, 9 N.W.2d 355 (1943). See also In re Estate of Jud, 238 Kan. 268, 710 P.2d 1241 (1985). See generally cases cited, supra note 180.

or is likely to become insolvent,[185] reside outside the jurisdiction,[186] or is likely to remove the personalty from the jurisdiction.[187]

Of course, the transferor's expressed intention that possessory owners of personalty shall or shall not be required to give security for the protection of the future interest owners is controlling.[188] Even if the transferor did not express any intent, courts have inferred an intent that security shall not be required from the fact that the possessory interest was given to the transferor's spouse[189] or to the executor of the will, when the will expressly exempts the executor from any requirement to post a performance bond.[190] However, in other cases, courts have required the possessory owner to give security despite such facts.[191]

The future interest owner's ability to compel the possessory owner to give security and to account for the property seems to largely obviate the need for other remedies. But courts have awarded damages for injuries to the property caused by the possessory owner or a third party[192] and have enjoined threatened injuries.[193] The future interest owner also can prevent removal of the property from the jurisdiction by obtaining a writ of *ne exeat*.[194]

§§ 4.12–5.0 ARE RESERVED FOR SUPPLEMENTAL MATERIAL.

---

[185] E.g., Collins v. Barksdale, 23 Ga. 602 (1857).

[186] E.g., Scott v. Scott, 137 Iowa 239, 114 N.W. 881, 23 L.R.A.(N.S.) 716 (1908).

[187] Reed v. Reed, 80 Conn. 411, 68 A. 852 (1908).

[188] E.g., Smith v. Smith, 359 Mo. 44, 220 S.W.2d 10 (1949); Rife v. Rife, 154 Miss. 529, 122 So. 739 (1929). But see In re Sims' Estate, 225 Miss. 311, 83 So. 2d 93 (1955).

[189] E.g., Underwood v. Underwood, 162 Ala. 553, 50 So. 305, 136 Am. St. Rep. 61 (1909).

[190] E.g., Smith v. Smith, 359 Mo. 44, 220 S.W.2d 10

[191] E.g., Scott v. Scott, 137 Iowa 239, 114 N.W. 881, 23 L.R.A.(N.S.) 716; Koplon v. Koplon, 274 Ala. 214, 148 So. 2d 245 (1962); Gahan v. Golden, 330 Ill. 624, 162 N.E. 164 (1928); In re Taylor's Estate, 149 Misc. 705, 268 N.Y.S. 70 (1933), aff'd sub nom Matter of Hurley, 242 App. Div. 608, 271 N.Y.S. 1057 (1934).

[192] E.g., Broome v. King, 10 Ala. 819 (1846) (damages against possessory owner); Wintuska v. Peart, 237 Ky. 666, 36 S.W.2d 50 (1931) (damages against third party).

[193] E.g., Dillen v. Fancher, 193 Ark. 715, 102 S.W.2d 87 (1937); Reed v. Reed, 80 Conn. 411, 68 A. 852 (1908); Brown v. Wilson, 41 N.C. 558 (1850).

[194] E.g., Riddle v. Kellum, 8 Ga. 374 (1850); Swindall v. Bradley, 56 N.C. 353 (1857). Ala. Code § 35–4–171, provides: "The tenant for life in personalty cannot remove it beyond the jurisdiction of this state without the consent of the remainder holder. If he attempts to do so, the remainder holder or reversioner is entitled to the writ of *ne exeat* to restrain him."

Chapter 5

CONCURRENT OWNERSHIP OF REALTY AND PERSONALTY

Table of Sections

§ 5.1   CONCURRENT ESTATES AND INTERESTS IN REALTY AND PERSONALTY—IN GENERAL

From an early date, the English common law has recognized that concurrent, as well as several, estates in property can be created. Concurrent estates exist when two or more persons have a concurrent and equal right to possession and use.[1] Several forms of concurrent estate could be created at common law: joint tenancy, tenancy by the entirety, tenancy in common, tenancy in coparcenary, and tenancy in partnership. Only the first three survive in the United States. They can be created in personal property, as well as in real property. Joint tenancies can still be created in a majority of American jurisdictions, but they are no longer favored as at common law. Many states have abolished tenancies by the entirety. Tenancies in coparcenary have been absorbed into the tenancy in common. All states have now eliminated the tenancy in partnership, which was a modified form of tenancy in common, by adoption of the Uniform Partnership Act.[2] In addition to the common law forms of concurrent ownership, a form of concurrent ownership called "community property," which derives from the civil law,

---

[1]   See generally 2 American Law of Property §§ 6.1–6.26 (1952) (hereinafter Am. L. Prop.); 7 R. Powell, Powell on Real Property § 49.01 (2018).

[2]   Uniform Partnership Act (1997) (amended 2013), 6 pt. 2 U.L.A. 1 (2015).

is recognized and may co-exist with the common law forms in eight western and southern states.[3] Note that the word "cotenant" is used to refer both generically to the owners of all three types of concurrent ownership and specifically to tenants in common.

§ 5.2   TENANCY IN COMMON

The tenancy in common is the most common type of concurrent estate. The English courts appear to have first recognized it in the fourteenth century.[4] At an even earlier date, the English courts recognized the joint tenancy, which differs from the tenancy in common in important respects. A joint tenancy, unlike the tenancy in common,[5] has a right of survivorship. The surviving joint tenant becomes the sole owner of the property in which the joint tenancy formerly existed,[6] but no right of survivorship exists among tenants in common. A joint tenancy exists only when the four unities of time, title, interest, and possession are satisfied. The cotenants must acquire their undivided interests at the same time and by the same instrument, and their undivided interests must be identical as to fractional shares, quality, quantity, and rights of possession and enjoyment.[7] In contrast, a tenancy in common requires only the unity of possession. Each cotenant must have an equal right of possession and enjoyment with respect to the entire property.[8]

The unities of time and title are always satisfied when a single conveyance is made to two or more people, and the unities of interest and possession are presumed when the instrument does not provide to the contrary, such as when the conveyance is "to A and B." But a conveyance to two or more people creates a tenancy in common if it (1) gives each cotenant a specified undivided interest, whether the cotenants' fractional interests are equal or not,[9] (2) gives some cotenants fee simple estates and others an estate for life,[10] or (3) expresses the grantor's intent to create a tenancy in common. A tenancy in common also exists if the cotenants receive their interests at different times by different instruments of transfer.

In the early common law, neither a tenancy in common nor a joint tenancy could be created except by inter vivos conveyance. After 1540, either type of concurrent estate

---

    [3]   See generally 2 Am. L. Prop., supra note 1, at §§ 7.1–7.36; 7 R. Powell, supra note 1, at §§ 53.01–53.09. Community property is discussed, infra §§ 5.13–5.15.

    [4]   See 2 Am. L. Prop., supra note 1, at § 6.1.

    [5]   E.g., Wolfe v. Wolfe, 207 Miss. 480, 42 So. 2d 438 (1949); Burns v. Nolette, 83 N.H. 489, 144 A. 848 (1929), superseded by statute as recognized by Brennan v. Timmins, 104 N.H. 384, 187 A.2d 793 (1963); In re Hoermann's Estate, 234 Wis. 130, 290 N.W. 608, 128 A.L.R. 89 (1940).

    [6]   E.g., Wilken v. Young, 144 Ind. 1, 41 N.E. 68 (1895); In re Peterson's Estate, 182 Wash. 29, 45 P.2d 45 (1935). See infra, § 5.3 at note 46.

    [7]   2 William Blackstone, Commentaries *180. "The requirement of the four unities necessarily arose as a result of the basic concept [of joint tenancy] rather than as prerequisites to the creation of the estate." 2 Am. L. Prop., supra note 1, at § 6.1.

    [8]   2 Blackstone, supra note 7, at *191; 2 Am. L. Prop., supra note 1, at §§ 6.1, 6.5; Clayton v. Clayton, 75 So. 3d 649, 654 (Ala. Civ. App. 2011); Porter v. Porter, 472 So. 2d 630 (Ala. 1985); Mulsow v. Gerber Energy Corp., 237 Kan. 58, 697 P.2d 1269 (1985); LDDC, Inc. v. Pressley, 71 N.C. App. 431, 322 S.E.2d 416 (1984); Rouse v. Glascam Builders, Inc., 101 Wash. 2d 127, 677 P.2d 125 (1984); Osborn v. Warner, 694 P.2d 730 (Wyo. 1985).

    [9]   If the fractional interests were unequal, the unity of interest requirement was violated. Even if the fractional interests were equal, a tenancy in common was created "because the gift was to them as separate individuals and not to them as a unit." 2 Am. L. Prop., supra note 1, at § 6.1.

    [10]   The unity of interest requirement is violated because the quantum of the cotenants' estates is not identical.

could be created by will.[11] A tenancy in coparcenary existed when two or more heirs took real property by descent, such as when female heirs inherited because no male heir survived the deceased owner of the fee simple estate or when male heirs inherited by virtue of the Kentish custom of gavelkind tenure.[12] An estate in coparcenary, like an estate in joint tenancy, was characterized by the unities of time, title, interest, and possession, but no right of survivorship existed among coparceners.[13] The undivided interest of a deceased coparcener passed to his or her heirs by descent. Unlike joint tenants and tenants in common, coparceners could compel partition and thereby obtain separate estates in specific parts of the property.[14] Even after judicial recognition of the tenancy in common in the fourteenth century, a coparcener's power to compel partition originally was an important feature that distinguished tenancy in coparcenary from tenancy in common. However, in 1539, actions at law to partition tenancies in common and joint tenancies were statutorily authorized.[15]

Because the United States has abolished primogeniture and male and female heirs of equal degree inherit equally, tenancy in coparcenary and tenancy in common now seem to be identical for all practical purposes. Very few American cases mention coparcenary as a separate form of concurrent ownership, and, even when they do, it seems substantially the same as tenancy in common.[16] American intestate succession laws often expressly provide that heirs take as tenants in common, but it seems generally to be assumed that heirs take as tenants in common even in the absence of this type of provision.

Today, every American jurisdiction has statutorily created a presumption in favor of a tenancy in common, rather than a joint tenancy.[17] If land is transferred to spouses in a jurisdiction where tenancies by the entirety have been abolished, the statutory presumption in favor of tenancies in common applies. In some jurisdictions that have not abolished tenancies by the entirety, a presumption exists for a tenancy by the entirety when property is conveyed to spouses,[18] but a presumption for tenancy in common exists in other jurisdictions that recognize tenancies by the entirety.[19] However, a conveyance to unmarried persons "as tenants by the entirety" generally creates a tenancy in common even if tenancies by the entirety have not been abolished.[20]

---

[11]　Statute of Wills, 32 Hen. 8, c. 1 (Eng.) (1540).

[12]　E. Coke, Commentary Upon Littleton ¶¶ *163b,*164a; 2 Blackstone, supra note 7, at *187; 4 J. Kent, Commentaries on American Law *366 (1826–30); 2 Am. L. Prop., supra note 1, at §§ 6.1, 6.7.

[13]　E.g., Gilpin v. Hollingsworth, 3 Md. 190 (1852).

[14]　2 H. de Bracton, De Legibus et Consuetudinibus, ff. 72–75 (T. Twiss ed. 1881); 2 Am. L. Prop., supra note 1, at § 6.1.

[15]　31 Hen. 8, c. 1 (Eng.) (1539); 32 Hen. 8, c. 32 (Eng.) (1540). Before 1539, joint tenants and tenants in common could partition by agreement. See infra § 5.11.

[16]　See Graham v. Graham, 22 Ky. (6 T.B. Mon.) 561, 17 Am. Dec. 166 (1828); Donnelly v. Turner, 60 Md. 81 (1882); Gilpin v. Hollingsworth, 3 Md. 190 (1852); Phillips v. Wells, 147 Va. 1030, 133 S.E. 581 (1926).

[17]　See statutes listed in 2 Am. L. Prop., supra note 1, at § 6.3 n.1. Some of these statutes have been in effect since shortly after the American Revolution. The presumption applies whether or not the four unities are present.

[18]　E.g., O'Neal v. Love, 2015 Ark. App. 689, 476 S.W.3d 846 (2015); Underwood v. Bunger, 70 N.E.3d 338 (Ind. 2017); Casse v. Sink & Rise, Inc., 297 P.3d 762 (Wyo. 2013).

[19]　E.g., Carver v. Gilbert, 387 P.2d 928, 32 A.L.R.3d 563 (Alaska 1963).

[20]　See infra § 5.5, note 130.

Because the interest of a tenant in common is generally alienable,[21] a tenant in common can, without his cotenants' consent, transfer his interest by deed[22] or by lease[23] and can mortgage his interest.[24] Moreover, because survivorship is not an incident of tenancy in common, a tenant in common can devise his interest by will or it will pass by intestate succession to his heirs.[25]

Because the unities of time, title, and interest are not required for a tenancy in common,[26] tenants in common need not have acquired their interests at the same time or from the same source.[27] Some can have an interest in fee simple and others only a life estate.[28] Some can have a legal estate and others an equitable estate,[29] and they can have different fractional shares.[30] Only the unity of possession is required. All tenants in common must have equal rights of possession and use, at least when the concurrent interests are "legal."[31]

When a tenancy in common arises by intestate succession, the cotenants' shares are determined by the intestate succession law. A deed or will may, of course, expressly provide that the interests of the cotenants shall be unequal. If the instrument does not specify each cotenant's share, they presumptively take equal undivided interests,[32] but this presumption may be rebutted by proof that, for example, the cotenants contributed unequal amounts toward the purchase price of the property and no evidence exists that those who contributed more intended to make a gift to their cotenants.[33] Although each

---

[21] Restraints on alienation of the interest of a tenant in common are valid to the same extent as restraints upon estates owned individually.

[22] E.g., Moore v. Foshee, 251 Ala. 489, 38 So. 2d 10 (1948); Wilk v. Vencill, 30 Cal. 2d 104, 180 P.2d 351 (1947). A tenant in common cannot, of course, convey more than his own undivided interest, and a deed purporting to convey the entire premises conveys only his undivided interest. E.g., Swindle v. Curry, 218 Ga. 552, 129 S.E.2d 144 (1962); Schank v. N. Am. Royalties, Inc., 201 N.W.2d 419 (N.D. 1972).

[23] E.g., Cahaba Forests, LLC v. Hay, 927 F.Supp.2d 1273 (M.D. Ala. 2013); Sun Oil Co. v. Oswell, 258 Ala. 326, 62 So. 2d 783 (1953); Schank, 201 N.W.2d 419. Such a lease, of course, makes the lessee only a tenant in common for the lease term and does not give the lessee an exclusive right to possess. E.g., Cook v. Hollyday, 186 Md. 42, 45 A.2d 768 (1946); Trowbridge v. Donner, 152 Neb. 206, 40 N.W.2d 655 (1950). See W. W. Allen, Annotation, Effect of Lease Given by Part Only of Cotenants, 49 A.L.R.2d 797 (1956).

[24] E.g., Shreve v. Harvey, 74 N.J. Eq. 336, 70 A. 671 (1908); Z. V. Pate, Inc. v. Kollock, 202 S.C. 522, 25 S.E.2d 728 (1943).

[25] 2 Am. L. Prop., supra note 1, at § 6.10; 4 Thompson on Real Property §§ 32.06, 32.08 (Thomas ed. 2017).

[26] See authorities cited supra note 8.

[27] Therefore, a tenancy in common is created when one joint tenant severs the joint tenancy by conveying his interest. The grantee obtains his interest at a different time and from a different source than the non-conveying joint tenants. For more on severance of joint tenancies, see infra § 5.3.

[28] E.g., Am. Bank & Tr. Co. v. Cont'l Inv. Corp., 202 Okla. 341, 213 P.2d 861 (1949). See 2 Blackstone, supra note 7, at *191.

[29] Comer v. Landrum, 277 S.W. 743 (Tex. Civ. App. 1925).

[30] E.g., Sanders v. Knapp, 674 P.2d 385 (Colo. App. 1983); Van Veen v. Van Veen, 213 Iowa 323, 238 N.W. 718 (1931); Roach v. Roach, 406 S.W.2d 731 (Ky. 1966). See 2 Blackstone, supra note 7, at *191; 2 Am. L. Prop., supra note 1, at § 6.5; H. Challis, Law of Real Property 370 (Charles Sweet ed., 3d ed. 1911). Equal shares will be presumed if the deed or will does not specify otherwise.

[31] See 2 Am. L. Prop., supra note 1, at § 6.5; 2 Blackstone, supra note 7, at *191; Spencer v. Austin, 38 Vt. 258 (1865). See also Taylor v. Millard, 118 N.Y. 244, 23 N.E. 376 (1890). Each tenant in common holds an undivided fractional interest in every part of the common property. Willis v. Peabody Coal Co., 332 S.W.3d 260 (Mo. Ct. App. 2010); State v. Hoskins, 357 Mo. 377, 208 S.W.2d 221 (1948); Succession of LeBlanc, 577 So. 2d 105 (La. Ct. App. 1991).

[32] E.g., Caito v. United Cal. Bank, 20 Cal. 3d 694, 144 Cal. Rptr. 751, 576 P.2d 466 (1978); In re Estate of Anders, 238 Iowa 344, 26 N.W.2d 67 (1947); Hoover v. Haller, 146 Neb. 697, 21 N.W.2d 450 (1946).

[33] People v. Varel, 351 Ill. 96, 184 N.E. 209 (1932); Williams v. Monzingo, 235 Iowa 434, 16 N.W.2d 619, 156 A.L.R. 508 (1944); Taylor v. Taylor, 310 Mich. 541, 17 N.W.2d 745, 157 A.L.R. 559 (1945); Succession of

tenant in common has an equal right to possess and use the entire property without regard to the quantum of their interest,[34] their relative shares must be determined upon transfer of some or all of their interests and when a voluntary or court-ordered partition occurs.

Cotenants who own undivided interests in subsurface minerals, whether in fee simple or for a term of years, are usually tenants in common.[35] However, a person who is not entitled to possession or to a present beneficial interest cannot be a tenant in common.[36] Therefore, future interest holders cannot be a tenant in common either with a life tenant or among themselves.[37] Nevertheless, they may be subject to fiduciary duties among themselves, like tenants in common.[38]

Although survivorship is not an incident of tenancies in common, courts in many cases have stated that a right of survivorship can be annexed to a tenancy in common.[39] For example, an instrument with an express survivorship provision can create a tenancy in common for the cotenants' lives, with a contingent remainder in favor of the surviving cotenant. Courts have so held when the conveyance was "to A and B and to the survivor of them,"[40] though arguably the quoted language should simply create a joint tenancy.[41] Courts have reached the same result when an express attempt to create a joint tenancy is frustrated because joint tenancies have been statutorily abolished or because one of the requisite unities is missing.[42]

LeBlanc, 577 So. 2d 105 (1991). See also Progressive Universal Ins. Co. of Ill. v. Taylor, 375 Ill. App. 3d 495, 874 N.E.2d 910 (2007). But see Miller v. Miller, 101 Or. App. 371, 790 P.2d 1184 (1990) (when cotenants expressly agreed that their shares should be equal, it was immaterial that one cotenant paid two-thirds of the purchase price).

[34]   Supra note 8.

[35]   E.g., Skelly Oil Co. v. Wickham, 202 F.2d 442 (10th Cir. 1953) (fee simple); Dampier v. Polk, 214 Miss. 65, 58 So. 2d 44 (1952) (fee simple); Petroleum Expl. Corp. v. Hensley, 284 S.W.2d 828 (Ky. 1955) (term of years).

[36]   Le Bus v. Le Bus, 269 S.W.2d 506 (Tex. Civ. App. 1954).

[37]   E.g., Givens v. Givens, 387 S.W.2d 851 (Ky. 1965); Cline v. Henry, 239 S.W.2d 205 (Tex. Civ. App. 1951).

[38]   Wilson v. Linder, 21 Idaho 576, 123 P. 487, 42 L.R.A.(N.S.) 242 (1912); Givens v. Givens, 387 S.W.2d 851 (Ky. 1965).

[39]   E.g., Mitchell v. Frederick, 166 Md. 42, 170 A. 733, 92 A.L.R. 1412 (1934) (dictum); Papke v. Pearson, 203 Minn. 130, 134, 280 N.W. 183–85 (1938) (dictum); Anson v. Murphy, 149 Neb. 716, 32 N.W.2d 271 (1948); Burns v. Nolette, 83 N.H. 489, 144 A. 848 (1929) (personalty), superseded by statute as recognized by Brennan v. Timmins, 104 N.H. 384, 187 A.2d 793 (1963); Pope v. Burgess, 230 N.C. 323, 325, 53 S.E.2d 159, 160 (1949). Accord 4 Thompson, supra note 25, § 1793 at n.36, § 1796. But see Hershy v. Clark, 35 Ark. 17, 37 Am. Rep. 1 (1879).

[40]   Bonner v. Pugh, 376 So. 2d 1354 (Ala. 1979); Rowerdink v. Carothers, 334 Mich. 454, 54 N.W.2d 715 (1952), noted, 51 Mich. L. Rev. 756 (1953); Papke v. Pearson, 203 Minn. 130, 134, 280 N.W. 183, 184–185 (dictum); Smith v. Cutler, 366 S.C. 546, 623 S.E.2d 644 (2005); Davis v. Davis, 223 S.C. 182, 75 S.E.2d 46 (1953). See also Hass v. Hass, 248 Wis. 212, 21 N.W.2d 398 (1946), reh'g denied 248 Wis. 212, 22 N.W.2d 151 (1946). But see Wright v. Smith, 257 Ala. 665, 60 So. 2d 688 (1952); Hart v. Kanaye Nagasawa, 218 Cal. 685, 24 P.2d 815 (1933).

[41]   Cf. 2 H. Tiffany, Real Prop. § 424 (3d ed. 2017) ("[W]hen one makes a gift to two or more with the right of survivorship, it appears to be a reasonable conclusion that he has in mind an indestructible right of survivorship. The view that there is in such case a tenancy in common for life with a contingent remainder in favor of the survivor, or even that there is a tenancy in common in fee simple with an executory limitation in favor of the survivor, might seem more in accord with the intention of the grantor or testator.").

[42]   E.g., Erickson v. Erickson, 167 Or. 1, 115 P.2d 172 (1941); Holbrook v. Holbrook, 240 Or. 567, 403 P.2d 12 (1965). See also Hass, 248 Wis. 212, 21 N.W.2d 398. When the grantor expresses the intent to create a joint tenancy, the right of survivorship should be indestructible, because it could be destroyed at common law by a transfer that severed the joint tenancy.

§ 5.3   JOINT TENANCY—IN GENERAL

Courts recognized the joint tenancy as early as the thirteenth century.[43] Joint tenants hold title *"pur my et pur tout,"* which means that, for purposes of tenure and survivorship, each joint tenant is seized of the entire estate in which the joint tenancy existed, whether it is an estate in fee simple, in fee tail, or only for lives.[44] But for purposes of alienation, each joint tenant has only a fractional interest in the entire estate.[45] The joint tenancy was the preferred form of concurrent ownership because one of its inseparable incidents was the right of survivorship—the last surviving joint tenant became the sole owner of the entire estate.[46] The right of survivorship was not a future interest like a reversion or a remainder. The last surviving joint tenant became the sole owner because his original interest in the joint tenancy was the only one remaining after all the other joint tenants died.[47]

Because of this preference for the right of survivorship, earlier common courts presumed that any conveyance or devise to two or more persons, other than a married couple, created a joint tenancy, unless expressly specified otherwise.[48] But a joint tenancy could not arise by inheritance. As previously indicated,[49] when no male heir in closer or equal degree existed, female heirs would take concurrent estates as coparceners, rather than as joint tenants.

---

[43]   2 Am. L. Prop., supra note 1, at § 6.1 at p. 3. For a good summary of the historical origins and characteristics of joint tenancies, see Spessard v. Spessard, 64 Md. App. 83, 494 A.2d 701 (1985).

[44]   Coke, supra note 12, at *186a; Blackstone, supra note 7, at *182; 4 Kent, supra note 12, at *360, note (a); H. Challis, Real Prop. 367 (3d ed. 1911); 2 Am. L. Prop., supra note 1, at § 6.1; 4 Tiffany, supra note 41, at § 418.

[45]   See authorities cited infra note 52.

[46]   Littleton, Tenures § 280 (H. Butterworth ed. 1825); 2 Blackstone, supra note 7, at *183; 4 Kent, supra note 12, at *360; 2 Tiffany, supra note 41, at § 419. See, e.g., Henderson v. Henderson, 59 Ariz. 53, 121 P.2d 437 (1942); McDonald v. Morley, 15 Cal. 2d 409, 101 P.2d 690, 129 A.L.R. 810 (1940); In re Estate of Brose, 416 Pa. 386, 206 A.2d 301 (1965); Porter v. Porter, 472 So. 2d 630 (Ala. 1985); Wiggins v. Parson, 446 So. 2d 169 (Fla. Dist. Ct. App. 1984); Neaderhiser v. Dep't of Soc. & Rehab. Servs., 9 Kan. App. 2d 115, 673 P.2d 462 (1983).

As previously noted in § 5.1, joint tenancies may be created in personalty, as well as in realty. For example, one person may deposit funds in either a savings account or a checking account in his own name and that of another, subject to withdrawal by either party. By the terms of the bank's signature card or certificate of deposit, the account is described as "joint" or the co-creditors are described as "joint tenants." There is also frequently a provision that upon the death of either co-creditor, the balance in the account shall be payable to the survivor. These "joint and survivor" accounts have given rise to an enormous amount of litigation. Detailed treatment of joint bank accounts is beyond the scope of this book. For a discussion of them, see W. Hines, Personal Property Joint Tenancies: More Law, Fact, and Fancy, 54 Minn. L. Rev. 509, 531 (1970). For cases illustrative of the difficulties that courts have had in dealing with these accounts, see Citizens Bank of Batesville v. Estate of Pettyjohn, 282 Ark. 222, 667 S.W.2d 657 (1984); Morton v. McComb, 281 Ark. 125, 662 S.W.2d 471 (1983); In re Estate of Gainer, 466 So. 2d 1055 (Fla. 1985); In re Estate of Steppuhn, 221 Neb. 329, 377 N.W.2d 83 (1985).

[47]   E.g., Kleemann v. Sheridan, 75 Ariz. 311, 256 P.2d 553 (1953); Klajbor v. Klajbor, 406 Ill. 513, 94 N.E.2d 502 (1950); United Tr. Co. v. Pyke, 199 Kan. 1, 427 P.2d 67 (1967), overruled on other grounds by Harper v. Prudential Ins. Co. of Am., 233 Kan. 358, 662 P.2d 1264 (1983); Harms v. Sprague, 105 Ill. 2d 215, 85 Ill. Dec. 331, 473 N.E.2d 930 (1984).

[48]   Coke, supra note 12, at *70b; 2 Blackstone, supra note 7, at *193; 2 Tiffany, supra note 41, at § 421; 2 Am. L. Prop., supra note 1, at § 6.21, at 3. It was unnecessary to say "as joint tenants" or to expressly provide for survivorship.

[49]   See supra § 5.2.

Although joint tenants have individual fractional interests, the essence of a joint tenancy is that the joint tenants as a unit constitute an ownership entity.[50] To create this entity, the four unities of time, title, interest, and possession must be satisfied. All joint tenants must acquire their interests at the same time[51] and by the same instrument (deed or will), and they must have identical fractional shares, quantum of estate,[52] and quality of estate (legal or equitable).[53] For this reason, a grantor's conveyance to himself and another "as joint tenants" or the conveyance of an undivided half interest to another does not create a joint tenancy.[54] In both cases, the unities of time and title are not satisfied because the intended joint tenants, including the grantor, acquired their individual undivided interests at different times and by different instruments. However, courts today sometimes do not require the unities in situations that are not easy to predict.[55]

As noted in the preceding section, all American jurisdictions today presume that a conveyance to two or more persons, without additional qualifying language, creates a tenancy in common, rather than a joint tenancy. Some American states have statutorily abolished the joint tenancy, and many other states have significantly modified it.[56] However, even where the joint tenancy has been abolished, some courts have preserved the right of survivorship by holding that transfers such as "to A and B, and to the

---

[50]　Therefore, when a joint tenant dies, the surviving joint tenants do not take anything from the decedent. Instead, their shares simply increase by the amount of the decedent's share. See 2 Tiffany, supra note 41, at § 419.

[51]　Courts have held that the unity of time is unnecessary when the joint tenants received an executory interest. E. Sugden & G. Gilbert, The Law of Uses and Trusts 135, n.10; C. Fearne, Essay on the Learning of Contingent Remainders and Executory Devices 313 (Robert H. Small ed. 1845).

[52]　Therefore, a joint tenancy cannot be created if one cotenant has a fee simple and another has only a life estate. However, if a life estate is given to joint tenants, with a remainder to one of them in fee simple, and if the one who has the remainder is not the survivor, the survivor will hold the entire property for the balance of his life. At his death, the remainder holder's heirs or devisees will get possession. Coke, supra note 12, at *188a; 2 Blackstone, supra note 7, at *181; 4 Kent, supra note 12, at 357.

[53]　For equitable joint tenancies, see Edmonds v. Comm'r, 90 F.2d 14 (9th Cir. 1937), cert. denied 302 U.S. 713, 58 S.Ct. 32, 82 L.Ed. 551 (1937); Lowry v. Lowry, 541 S.W.2d 128 (Tenn. 1976), noted, 7 Mem. St. L. Rev. 332 (1977). Therefore, a tenancy in common is created when one joint tenant severs the joint tenancy by conveying his interest. The grantee obtains his interest at a different time and from a different source than the non-conveying joint tenants.

[54]　E.g., Pegg v. Pegg, 165 Mich. 228, 130 N.W. 617, 33 L.R.A.(N.S.) 166 (1911); In re Walker's Estate, 340 Pa. 13, 16 A.2d 28, 132 A.L.R. 628 (1940), noted, 83 U. Pa. L. Rev. 681 (1935); Moe v. Krupke, 255 Wis. 33, 37 N.W.2d 865 (1949), superseded by statute, 1947 Wis. Laws, ch. 140, as recognized in Marchel v. Estate of Marchel, 349 Wis. 2d 707, 838 N.W.2d 97 (Wis. Ct. App. 2013).

[55]　See, e.g., Harms v. Sprague, 105 Ill. 2d 215, 85 Ill. Dec. 331, 473 N.E.2d 930 (1985) (four unities are essential). But courts in other cases have held, in particular situations, that the four unities are not essential. For instance, courts have held that an owner can directly convey to himself and another as joint tenants. See, e.g., Miller v. Riegler, 243 Ark. 251, 419 S.W.2d 599 (1967), noted, 23 Ark. L. Rev. 136 (1969) (personal property); Strout v. Burgess, 144 Me. 263, 68 A.2d 241 (1949); Therrien v. Therrien, 94 N.H. 66, 46 A.2d 538 (1946). See also Nunn v. Keith, 289 Ala. 518, 524, 268 So. 2d 792, 797 (1972), followed in Porter v. Porter, 472 So. 2d 630 (Ala. 1985).

[56]　See, e.g., Ariz. Rev. Stat. § 33–431 (abolishes joint tenancies, except for grants or devises in trust, to executors, or to spouses, but also provides that a deed or will may, "by express words, vest the estate in the survivor upon the death of a grantee or devisee"); Ga. Code Ann. § 44–6–190 (transfer creates "interests in common without survivorship," absent express intent to create joint tenancy); 765 Ill. Comp. Stat. 1005/1, 1005/2 (abolishes joint tenancies, except for executors and trustees, or when a will expresses intent to create a joint tenancy in personal property); Ky. Rev. Stat. §§ 381.120, 381.130 (abolishes joint tenancy, except for executors and trustees, or "when it manifestly appears, from the tenor of the instrument, that it was intended that the part of the one dying should belong to the others"); Mass. Gen. Laws ch. 184, § 7 (same as Ga. Code Ann. § 44–6–190); Or. Rev. Stat. § 93.180 (abolishes joint tenancies, but see cases cited infra note 69).

survivor of them"[57] and "to A and B as joint tenants, and to the survivor of them"[58] creates a concurrent estate for the life of the shorter-lived cotenant, with a remainder in fee simple to the survivor.

In many states, statutes do not abolish joint tenancies but provide in substance that a transfer to two or more people in their own right creates a tenancy in common, unless the transferor indicates that they take as joint tenants. These statutes usually declare that such a transfer creates a tenancy in common unless the transferees are "expressly declared to be joint tenants"[59] or are directed to take "as joint tenants and not as tenants in common"[60] or unless the instrument "expressly provides that the property is to be held in joint tenancy,"[61] "jointly with survivorship,"[62] or some combination of these or similar expressions of intent.[63]

When the statute provides several alternatives or indicates that any language showing the intent to create a joint tenancy will be sufficient to overcome the statutory presumption in favor of tenancies in common, the drafter has substantial leeway. Even when the statutory language is rather restrictive, using the exact language generally is unnecessary to create a joint tenancy.[64] But courts have often held that the phrase "to A and B jointly" is insufficient,[65] though some courts have held that it sufficiently demonstrates the intent to convey a joint tenancy.[66] A division of authority also exists when the transfer is "to A and B and the survivor of them." In some cases, courts have held that the survivorship provision shows the intent to create a joint tenancy, because survivorship is its most important characteristic.[67] In other cases, however, the court

---

[57] E.g., Houghton v. Brantingham, 86 Conn. 630, 86 A. 664 (1913); Withers v. Barnes, 95 Kan. 798, 149 P. 69 (1915); Molloy v. Barkley, 219 Ky. 671, 294 S.W. 168 (1927).

[58] E.g., Erickson v. Erickson, 167 Or. 1, 115 P.2d 172 (1941); Holbrook v. Holbrook, 240 Or. 567, 403 P.2d 12 (1965); Gilbert v. Brown, 71 Or. App. 809, 693 P.2d 1330 (1985), rev. denied 300 Or. 367, 712 P.2d 109 (1985). But see In re Marriage of Leversee, 156 Cal. App. 3d 891, 203 Cal. Rptr. 481 (1984) (spouses who took as joint tenants before marriage in community property state remained joint tenants after marriage).

[59] E.g., Ark. Stat. § 18–12–603.

[60] E.g., Del. Code Ann. tit. 25, § 701.

[61] Md. Code Ann., Real Prop. § 2–117; Mont. Code Ann. § 70–1–307 (must "expressly" purport to create "joint tenancy"); Okla. Stat. tit. 60 § 74 (same). See Hill v. Hill, 672 P.2d 1149 (Okla. 1983) (words "joint tenancy" in statute presumed used in common law sense).

[62] Code Ga. Ann. § 44–6–190.

[63] See Ga. Code Ann. § 44–6–190; Kan. Stat. Ann. § 58–501; Mass. Gen. Laws ch. 184, § 7 (1977); Ohio Rev. Code Ann. §§ 5302.17, 5302.20; Va. Code Ann., §§ 55–20, 55–21; Jones v. Conwell, 227 Va. 176, 314 S.E.2d 61 (1984) (interpreting Va. Code Ann. §§ 55–20, 55–21). Many statutes reversing the common law presumption in favor of joint tenancies were originally enacted soon after the American Revolution, because they were regarded as remnants of the feudal system. See 2 Tiffany, supra note 41, at § 424 n.47.

[64] E.g., Blumenthal v. Culver, 116 Iowa 326, 89 N.W. 1116 (1902); Palmer v. Flint, 156 Me. 103, 161 A.2d 837 (1960); Moxley v. Vaughn, 148 Mont. 30, 416 P.2d 536 (1966); Kilgore v. Parrott, 197 Okla. 77, 168 P.2d 886 (1946); Petition of Buzenac, 50 R.I. 429, 148 A. 321 (1930). See also Neb. Rev. Stat. § 76–205, which simply provides that "the true intent of the parties" shall be controlling.

[65] E.g., Porter v. Porter, 472 So. 2d 630 (Ala. 1985); Switzer v. Pratt, 237 Iowa 788, 23 N.W.2d 837 (1946); Cohen v. Herbert, 205 Mo. 537, 104 S.W. 84 (1907); Overheiser v. Lackey, 207 N.Y. 229, 100 N.E. 738 (1913); Weber v. Nedin, 210 Wis. 39, 246 N.W. 307 (1933) (dictum). These decisions seem to rest on the idea that "jointly" is ambiguous and is as likely to be used to create a tenancy in common as a joint tenancy.

[66] E.g., Case v. Owen, 139 Ind. 22, 38 N.E. 395 (1894); Murray v. Kator, 221 Mich. 101, 190 N.W. 667 (1922). But see Taylor v. Taylor, 310 Mich. 541, 17 N.W.2d 745, 157 A.L.R. 559 (1945) (casting doubt on the validity of *Murray*).

[67] E.g., Wood v. Logue, 167 Iowa 436, 149 N.W. 613 (1914); Blaine v. Dow, 111 Me. 480, 89 A. 1126 (1914); Weber v. Nedin, 210 Wis. 39, 246 N.W. 307 (1933). In states that have a statute abolishing joint tenancies, except when survivorship is expressly provided, the transfer presumably would create a joint tenancy. See, e.g., Fla. Stat. § 689.15.

has held that the express survivorship provision conveys a concurrent estate for the life of the first transferee to die, with a remainder in fee simple absolute to the survivor.[68] In several states, courts have reached the same conclusion even when the transfer is "to A and B as joint tenants and to the survivor of them."[69] But the prevailing and better rule is that such language creates a joint tenancy in accordance with the transferor's clearly expressed intent.[70]

Statutes that abolish joint tenancies or create a presumption in favor of tenancy in common generally provide that any concurrent estate vested in executors or trustees shall be held in joint tenancy.[71] Even when the statutes do not expressly provide for trustees and executors to hold in joint tenancy, courts have held that a joint tenancy has been created when land is transferred to multiple executors or trustees.[72] In such cases, a right of survivorship is highly desirable so that the estate or trust may be administered without interruption when one fiduciary dies.

In jurisdictions that have abolished tenancies by the entirety, a transfer to "A and B, a married couple, as joint tenants with right of survivorship" creates a joint tenancy between A and B if it would have done so had they not been married. But in jurisdictions where tenancies by the entirety can still be created, the cases are divided as to whether such a transfer creates a joint tenancy[73] or a tenancy by the entirety.[74]

The old common law rule that a grantor could not create a joint tenancy by conveying to himself and another or by conveying an undivided interest to another, generally has been evaded by conveying the entire estate to a third party "straw person" who, by prearrangement, then conveys the estate back to the entire group of intended joint tenants, including the grantor. In some states, the need to use a straw person has

---

[68] See § 5.2, supra. Cf. Gagnon v. Pronovost, 96 N.H. 154, 71 A.2d 747 (1949) (deed to A and B "and to the survivors of them" created tenancy in common).

[69] E.g., Williams v. Studstill, 251 Ga. 466, 306 S.E.2d 633 (1983); Hunter v. Hunter, 320 S.W.2d 529 (Mo. 1959).

Alabama has had a checkered history on this point. See Bernhard v. Bernhard, 278 Ala. 240, 177 So. 2d 565 (1965) (language that would create joint tenancy at common law instead created tenancy in common with "indestructible contingent remainder"); Nunn v. Keith, 289 Ala. 518, 268 So. 2d 792 (1972) (overruling *Bernhard*); Durant v. Hamrick, 409 So. 2d 731 (Ala. 1981) (*Bernhard* did not apply to a conveyance to two or more persons "as tenants in common, and to the survivor"); Johnson v. Keener, 425 So. 2d 1108 (Ala. 1983), appeal after remand, 447 So. 2d 689 (1984) (*Nunn* should not be applied retroactively, so that *Bernhard* was controlling as to conveyances made before *Nunn*).

[70] E.g., Palmer v. Flint, 156 Me. 103, 161 A.2d 837 (1960). This is the better rule because the policy behind statutes that abolish joint tenancy or create a presumption in favor of tenancy in common is hostility to the right of survivorship. Allowing an indestructible contingent remainder in the survivor violates this policy more than allowing joint tenancy survivorship, because the contingent remainder cannot be destroyed by severance but a joint tenancy survivorship can be.

[71] E.g., Ariz. Rev. Stat. § 33–431; 765 Ill. Comp. Stat. 1005/2; Ky. Rev. Stat. Ann. § 381.130.

[72] E.g., Saunders v. Schmaelzle, 49 Cal. 59 (1874); Stout v. Van Zante, 109 Or. 430, 220 P. 414 (1923); Franklin Inst. for Sav. v. People's Sav. Bank, 14 R.I. 632 (1885).

[73] E.g., Wilken v. Young, 144 Ind. 1, 41 N.E. 68 (1895); Kolker v. Gorn, 193 Md. 391, 67 A.2d 258 (1949); Witzel v. Witzel, 386 P.2d 103 (Wyo. 1963).

[74] E.g., Naler v. Ballew, 81 Ark. 328, 99 S.W. 72 (1907); Kollar v. Kollar, 155 Fla. 705, 21 So. 2d 356 (1945); Fulton v. Katsowney, 342 Mass. 503, 174 N.E.2d 366 (1961); Hoag v. Hoag, 213 Mass. 50, 99 N.E. 521 (1912); Goethe v. Gmelin, 256 Mich. 112, 239 N.W. 347 (1931). But see Fekkes v. Hughes, 354 Mass. 303, 237 N.E.2d 19 (1968); Knight v. Knight, 62 Tenn. App. 70, 458 S.W.2d 803 (1970).

been eliminated by a statute[75] or judicial decision[76] that allows the creation of joint tenancies by direct conveyance. These statutes and decisions effectively eliminate the requirement of the unities of time and title in the creation of a joint tenancy.[77]

As noted earlier, the right of survivorship is the distinguishing feature of the joint tenancy. If there are more than two joint tenants, the death of one increases the individual fractional shares of the survivors, and the ultimate survivor becomes the sole owner.[78] If the ultimate survivor acquires a fee simple estate, she can convey it inter vivos or devise it by will,[79] and it will pass to her heirs if she dies intestate. If the ultimate survivor acquires only a life estate, it will terminate when she dies.

Courts are presented with a terrible conundrum when one joint tenant (or tenant by the entirety; see § 5.5, infra) feloniously kills the other. If the right of survivorship is permitted to operate, the survivor succeeds to sole ownership. Some states statutorily address this problem.[80] Absent a statute, judicial decisions vary a great deal. The California Court of Appeals opinion in *Whitfield v. Flaherty*[81] provides a good summary of the possibilities and cites numerous authorities:

> It has been held that: (1) The killing does not affect the right of the surviving tenant to take the entire interest in the joint tenancy property. (2) The killing destroys the survivorship characteristics of the tenancy and the estate in the

[75]   E.g., Mass. Gen. Laws ch. 184, § 8; Mich. Comp. Laws § 565.49; Ohio Rev. Code Ann. § 5302.18; Wash. Rev. Code § 64.28.010; Wyo. Stat. Ann., § 34–1–140.

[76]   E.g., Miller v. Riegler, 243 Ark. 251, 419 S.W.2d 599 (1967), noted, 23 Ark. L. Rev. 136 (1969) (personal property); Strout v. Burgess, 144 Me. 263, 68 A.2d 241 (1949); Therrien v. Therrien, 94 N.H. 66, 46 A.2d 538 (1946).

[77]   As stated earlier in this section, although courts generally state that the four unities are essential to creating a joint tenancy, courts often have held them to be unnecessary in particular situations. Moreover, courts have frequently held that the unity of possession may exist even though the joint tenants agree that one of them has the exclusive right to possession of and income from the jointly owned property. See, e.g., Miller v. Riegler, 243 Ark. 251, 419 S.W.2d 599 (1967); Tindall v. Yeats, 392 Ill. 502, 64 N.E.2d 903 (1946); Neaderhiser v. Dep't. of Soc. & Rehab. Servs., 9 Kan. App. 2d 115, 673 P.2d 462 (1983); Jones v. Cox, 629 S.W.2d 511 (Mo. Ct. App. 1981). See also Porter v. Porter, 472 So. 2d 630 (Ala. 1985) (wife's exclusive possession pursuant to divorce decree did not sever joint tenancy).

[78]   E.g., Erwin v. Felter, 283 Ill. 36, 119 N.E. 926, L.R.A. 1918E 776 (1918); Switzer v. Pratt, 237 Iowa 788, 23 N.W.2d 837 (1946); Nussbacher v. Manderfeld, 64 Wyo. 55, 186 P.2d 548 (1947). The survivor's right takes precedence over any devise or bequest made by the deceased joint tenant, because the latter has no interest that survives him. E.g., Cranston v. Winters, 238 N.W.2d 647 (N.D. 1976); Bassler v. Rewodlinski, 130 Wis. 26, 109 N.W. 1032, 7 L.R.A.(N.S.) 701 (1906). If joint tenants die simultaneously, the Uniform Simultaneous Death Act provides that the property shall be divided into as many equal shares as there were joint tenants and that each one's share shall be distributed as if he or she had survived the others. Unif. Simultaneous Death Act § 3, 8B U.L.A. 315 (2014). However, authority exists that evidence is admissible to show that, in equity, the shares should be unequal. See In re Strong's Will, 171 Misc. 445, 12 N.Y.S.2d 544 (1939) (tenancy by the entirety; presumption of equal shares may be rebutted by proof of unequal contributions).

[79]   A will executed by the surviving joint tenant during a cotenant's lifetime passes the property that resulted from survivorship, without the need to republish the will after the cotenant's death. Eckardt v. Osborne, 338 Ill. 611, 170 N.E. 774, 75 A.L.R. 509 (1930).

[80]   E.g., Cal. Prob. Code § 25 provides that the wrongful killing "thereby effects a severance of the interest of the decedent so that the share of the decedent passes as the decedent's property and the killer has no rights of survivorship." However, the court interpreted this statute in Estate of Castiglioni, 40 Cal. App. 4th 367, 388, 47 Cal. Rptr. 288, 302 (1995), to require that the decedent's share be calculated "by application of principles of tracing and reimbursement of contributions* * * *." N.C. Gen. Stat. § 31A–5 and Wash. Rev. Code § 11.84.050 both provide that the decedent's estate takes one-half, the surviving killer takes a life estate in half, and the killer's half goes to the decedent's estate when the killer dies. However, courts generally interpret a statute that regulates inheritance or a devise to slayers as not applying to a joint tenant's right of survivorship. See Duncan v. Vassaur, 550 P.2d 929 (Okla. 1976).

[81]   228 Cal. App. 2d 753, 760 n.3, 39 Cal. Rptr. 857, 861 n.3 (1964) (citations omitted).

property reverts to a tenancy in common. In some instances a constructive trust is imposed on a one-half interest in the property to effect this result. (3) The killing does not result in a termination of the joint tenancy; the survivor and the heirs of the victim remain joint tenants. (4) The killing deprived the wrongdoer of all interest in the property. (5) The killing does not interfere with the vesting of title in the survivor but, (a) the killer is chargeable as a constructive trustee of the whole of the property absolutely, or, in some instances, subject to a life estate in himself as to one-half interest therein, or the equivalent of such a life estate. (b) The killing raises a conclusive presumption that in the natural course of events the deceased joint tenant would have survived the killer and a constructive trust is imposed to effect this result. (c) The killing raises a doubt as to who would survive, which should be resolved against the killer and the whole property subjected to a constructive trust. (d) A constructive trust is imposed on the property to the extent the interest of the killer is enlarged by his wrongful act.

The Oklahoma Supreme Court decision in *Duncan v. Vassaur* contains a similar list of possibilities, which mostly overlaps the list in *Whitfield v. Flaherty* but is less complete, differs in some respects, and does not cite supporting authorities.[82]

§ 5.4 JOINT TENANCY—CONVERSION TO TENANCY IN COMMON BY SEVERANCE

As a general rule, the undivided fractional interest of each joint tenant is freely alienable without the other joint tenants' consent.[83] However, the transfer of one joint tenant's interest "severs" it from the joint tenancy and defeats the survivorship right for that share.[84] Therefore, a transfer of the interest of one of two joint tenants to a third party creates a tenancy in common between the transferee and the other (former) joint tenant.[85] If there were originally three or more joint tenants, the transfer makes the

---

[82] 550 P.2d 929, 930–31 (Okla. 1976). Nat'l City Bank of Evansville v. Bledsoe, 237 Ind. 130, 144 N.E.2d 710 (1957), includes a similar listing, which the court relied on in Estate of Grund v. Grund, 648 N.E.2d 1182 (Ind. Ct. App. 1995). In *Grund*, a tenant by the entirety was charged with murdering her spouse. The court held that, if she was convicted, the tenancy by the entirety would be severed. The wife would own half in her own right, as a tenant in common with the deceased spouse's heirs or devisees.

[83] Comm'l Factors of Denver v. Clarke & Waggener, 684 P.2d 261 (Colo. App. 1984) (unless parties are spouses and a written homestead declaration has been recorded); Hall v. Hamilton, 233 Kan. 880, 667 P.2d 350 (1983). Total or partial restraints on alienation are presumably valid only if they would be for individually owned property.

[84] E.g., McLaughlin v. Cooper's Estate, 128 Conn. 557, 24 A.2d 502 (1942); Harms v. Sprague, 105 Ill. 2d 215, 85 Ill. Dec. 331, 473 N.E.2d 930 (1984); Jackson v. Estate of Green, 484 Mich. 209, 771 N.W.2d 675 (2009); Smith v. Smith, 290 Mich. 143, 287 N.W. 411, 124 A.L.R. 215 (1939); Mullikin v. Jones, 71 Nev. 14, 278 P.2d 876 (1955). Severance destroys the unities of time and title and, therefore, also destroys the other joint tenants' survivorship rights. Cf. Albro v. Allen, 434 Mich. 271, 454 N.W.2d 85 (1990) (conveyance to "A and B as joint tenants with right of survivorship" created an estate for their joint lives, with an indestructible remainder to the survivor; conveyance by one does not destroy the contingent remainder).

[85] E.g., Handy v. Shiells, 190 Cal. App. 3d 512, 235 Cal. Rptr. 543 (1987); Porter v. Porter, 381 Ill. 322, 45 N.E.2d 635 (1942); Sathoff v. Sutterer, 373 Ill. App.3d, 869 N.E.2d 354, 311 Ill. Dec. 680 (2007); Wood v. Logue, 167 Iowa 436, 149 N.W. 613 (1914); In re Estate of King, 261 Wis. 266, 52 N.W.2d 885 (1952). See also Minonk St. Bank v. Grassman, 95 Ill. 2d 392, 69 Ill. Dec. 387, 447 N.E.2d 822 (1983) (in a state in which joint tenancies can be created without the use of a straw person, one joint tenant's conveyance to herself as a tenant in common severed her interest); In re Estate of Knickerbocker, 912 P.2d 969 (Utah 1996) (same). But cf. Nettles v. Matthews, 627 So. 2d 870 (Ala. 1993) (one joint tenant's conveyance to the other did not sever).

transferee a tenant in common with the remaining joint tenants, who continue to be joint tenants among themselves.[86]

If there were originally three or more joint tenants and one of them conveys his interest to another joint tenant, the transferee remains a joint tenant as to her original undivided interest but holds the transferred interest as a tenant in common.[87] If there were originally only two joint tenants, the conveyance of the undivided interest of one to the other should extinguish the joint tenancy by merger and give the transferee sole ownership of the estate.[88]

Transferring less than the joint tenant's entire interest also may cause severance. For example, if the joint tenants own the fee simple and one joint tenant conveys his interest for the transferee's life, the joint tenancy will be partially severed.[89] If a joint tenant dies during the life estate, no immediate right of survivorship exists.[90] But when the life estate terminates, the joint tenancy revives,[91] unless only one joint tenant is still living, in which case she has sole ownership.

A joint tenant who purports to lease the entire estate in which the joint tenancy exists cannot bind his cotenants, unless they consent, to give the lessee the exclusive right to possess. The lease is effective but only for the lessor's undivided interest.[92] Whether a lease will sever that interest has been a subject of controversy since the time of Littleton and Coke.[93] In England, a lease appears to completely sever the lessor's interest from the joint tenancy and to destroy the right of survivorship as to that interest,[94] though this result seems inconsistent with the rule concerning the effect of a joint tenant's transfer for the transferee's life. In the United States, courts have reached opposite results concerning the effect of a lease given by one joint tenant.[95] If a lease does not sever the joint tenancy, the lessor's death during the lease term terminates it.

---

[86] E.g., Hammond v. McArthur, 30 Cal. 2d 512, 183 P.2d 1 (1947); Jackson v. O'Connell, 23 Ill. 2d 52, 177 N.E.2d 194 (1961) (dictum); Giles v. Sheridan, 179 Neb. 257, 137 N.W.2d 828 (1965).

[87] E.g., Jackson, 23 Ill. 2d 52, 177 N.E.2d 194; Rendle v. Wiemeyer, 374 Mich. 30, 132 N.W.2d 606 (1965); Leonard v. Boswell, 197 Va. 713, 90 S.E.2d 872 (1956). The conveyance is technically a release.

[88] 2 Tiffany, supra note 41, at § 425. Contra Nettles v. Matthews, 627 So. 2d 870 (Ala. 1993), overruling Isom v. Bledsoe, 488 So. 2d 1356 (Ala. 1986).

[89] Hoover v. El Paso Nat'l Bank, 498 S.W.2d 276 (Tex. Civ. App. 1973). See Littleton, supra note 46, at § 302; Coke, supra note 12, at *191b.

[90] Littleton, supra note 46, at §§ 302, 303. In that case, the deceased joint tenant's share passes to his heirs or devisees until the life estate ends.

[91] Hammond v. McArthur, 30 Cal. 2d 512, 183 P.2d 1 (1947). See Coke, supra note 12, at *193a; 2 R. Preston, Abstracts of Title 59 (2d ed. 1824). But see Comment, 25 Cal. L. Rev. 203, 206 (1937), arguing that total severance should result.

[92] E.g., Swartzbaugh v. Sampson, 11 Cal. App. 2d 451, 54 P.2d 73 (1936).

[93] Compare Coke, supra note 12, at *193a, with 2 Blackstone, supra note 7, at *186. See R. Swenson & R. Degnan, Severance of Joint Tenancies, 38 Minn. L. Rev. 466, 472–74 (1954); 2 Am. L. Prop., supra note 1, at § 6.2; Comment, 61 Cal. L. Rev. 231 (1973); Comment, 25 Cal. L. Rev. 203, 206–09 (1937); Comment, 8 Hastings L.J. 290, 293 (1957); Comment, 21 So. Cal. L. Rev. 295, 297 (1948).

[94] Roe v. Lonsdale (1810) 12 East. 39, 104 Eng. Rep. 16 (K.B.); Napier v. Williams, [1911] 1 Ch. 361. But see Clerk v. Clerk (1694) 2 Vern. 323, 23 Eng. Rep. 809.

[95] E.g., Tenhet v. Boswell, 18 Cal. 3d 150, 133 Cal. Rptr. 10, 554 P.2d 330 (1976) (neither temporary nor permanent severance; when lessor died, lease terminated); Alexander v. Boyer, 253 Md. 511, 253 A.2d 359 (1969) (joint tenancy severed); Chambers v. Cardinal, 177 Md. App. 418, 935 A.2d 502 (2007) (joint tenancy severed).

An executory contract to convey one joint tenant's interest severs that interest from the joint tenancy once the contract becomes specifically enforceable.[96] Courts are divided as to whether severance occurs, entitling each cotenant to a pro rata portion of the purchase money, when all the joint tenants join as vendors in the executory contract.[97]

Granting a mortgage on a joint tenant's interest may sever it from the joint tenancy in jurisdictions that follow the title theory of mortgages and, if the borrower defaults, in jurisdictions that follow the intermediate theory.[98] Discharge of the mortgage will not revive the joint tenancy as to the mortgaged interest. In jurisdictions that follow the lien theory of mortgages,[99] the cases conflict. In some cases, courts hold that no severance occurs when one joint tenant mortgages his undivided interest.[100] Courts in other cases hold that severance occurs to the extent necessary to protect the mortgagee against loss of its security if the mortgagor predeceases the other joint tenants. However, the other joint tenants still take the mortgagor's undivided interest by survivorship.[101] Under the latter view, if another joint tenant predeceases the mortgagor while the mortgage is outstanding, the mortgagor should acquire the deceased joint tenant's interest by right of survivorship.

An involuntary transfer of a joint tenant's interest also may sever it from the joint tenancy, such as by virtue of a sale of the interest in bankruptcy or in execution of a judgment.[102] However, a division of authority exists concerning a mere levy of execution

---

[96] E.g., Kozacik v. Kozacik, 157 Fla. 597, 26 So. 2d 659 (1946); Naiburg v. Hendriksen, 370 Ill. 502, 19 N.E.2d 348 (1939); Kurowski v. Retail Hardware Mut. Fire Ins. Co., 203 Wis. 644, 234 N.W. 900 (1931).

[97] Severance occurs and vendors are entitled to the purchase money as tenants in common: In re Baker's Estate, 247 Iowa 1380, 78 N.W.2d 863 (1956), noted, 42 Iowa L. Rev. 646 (1957), 55 Mich. L. Rev. 1194 (1957); Buford v. Dahlke, 158 Neb. 39, 62 N.W.2d 252 (1954); Yannopoulos v. Sophos, 243 Pa. Super. 454, 365 A.2d 1312 (1976). Severance does not occur: Weise v. Kizer, 435 So. 2d 381 (Fla. Dist. Ct. App. 1983), rev. denied, 444 So. 2d 417 (Fla. 1984) (no severance "unless there is an indication in the contract, or from the circumstances, that the parties intended to sever and terminate the joint tenancy"); Watson v. Watson, 5 Ill. 2d 526, 126 N.E.2d 220 (1955); but see Ill. Pub. Aid Comm'n v. Stille, 14 Ill. 2d 344, 153 N.E.2d 59 (1958). See also Swenson & Degnan, supra note 93; Note, 41 Cornell L.Q. 154 (1955); Note, 34 Neb. L. Rev. 501 (1955); Comment, 24 Mo. L. Rev. 108 (1959). Alexander v. Boyer, 253 Md. 511, 253 A.2d 359 (1969) (unexercised option to buy does not sever).

[98] Under the title theory, the mortgage transfers title to the mortgaged property to the mortgagee. Under the intermediate theory, the mortgagee gets title if and when the borrower defaults. G. Nelson, D. Whitman, A. Burkhart & W. Freyermuth, Real Estate Finance Law § 1.5 (6th ed. 2015). E.g., Hammond v. McArthur, 30 Cal. 2d 512, 183 P.2d 1 (1947) (dictum); Schaefer v. Peoples Heritage Sav. Bank, 669 A.2d 185 (Me. 1996) (severance if mortgage not satisfied; dictum that joint tenancy reestablished if mortgage satisfied); Eder v. Rothamel, 202 Md. 189, 95 A.2d 860 (1953); Hardin v. Wolf, 318 Ill. 48, 148 N.E. 868 (1925) (intermediate theory of mortgages). See 7 Powell, supra note 1, at § 51.04[1][c].

[99] Based on the lien theory, the mortgagee does not get title to the mortgaged property. The mortgagee only has a lien on it. G. Nelson, D. Whitman, A. Burkhart & W. Freyermuth, Real Estate Finance Law § 1.5 (6th ed. 2015).

[100] Brant v. Hargrove, 129 Ariz. 475, 632 P.2d 978 (Ariz. App. 1981) (deed of trust); Hammond v. McArthur, 30 Cal. 2d 512, 183 P.2d 1 (1947); D.A.D., Inc. v. Moring, 218 So. 2d 451 (Fla. 1969); Harms v. Sprague, 105 Ill. 2d 215, 85 Ill. Dec. 331, 473 N.E.2d 930 (1984); American Nat'l Bank & Tr. Co. v. McGinnis, 571 P.2d 1198 (Okla. 1977). See also Coffman v. Adkins, 338 N.W.2d 540 (Iowa Ct. App. 1983) (joint tenancy in certificate of deposit not severed).

[101] Wilken v. Young, 144 Ind. 1, 41 N.E. 68 (1895).

[102] Mangus v. Miller, 317 U.S. 178, 63 S.Ct. 182, 87 L.Ed. 169 (1942), reh'g denied, 317 U.S. 712, 63 S.Ct. 432, 87 L.Ed. 567 (1943); New Haven Trolley & Bus Emps. Credit Union v. Hill, 145 Conn. 332, 142 A.2d 730 (1958); Maniez v. Citibank, F.S.B., 404 Ill. App. 3d 941, 937 N.E.2d 237 (2010); Poulson v. Poulson, 145 Me. 15, 70 A.2d 868, 12 A.L.R.2d 939 (1950), superseded by statute as recognized in Hedges v. Pitcher, 942 A.2d 1217 (2008). Contra Jackson v. Lacey, 408 Ill. 530, 97 N.E.2d 839 (1951). In any case, no severance until the redemption period has expired without redemption having occurred.

or an attachment without sale.[103] Merely docketing or recording a judgment against a joint tenant does not sever her interest.[104] In contrast, a mortgage foreclosure sale of one joint tenant's interest will sever it even in a lien theory state. A divorce decree between spouses who are joint tenants does not sever the joint tenancy if the decree does not dispose of the jointly held property.[105] Because divorced spouses ordinarily do not want the other to have a right of survivorship, their attorneys should address this issue.

The joint tenants' express agreement to hold as tenants in common severs the joint tenancy,[106] as does an agreement that is implied from conduct that is inconsistent with the continuance of a joint tenancy.[107] Although a final judgment for partition terminates a joint tenancy, merely commencing the action, without more, is insufficient because it may be discontinued before entry of a final judgment. Therefore, if a joint tenant dies while the partition action is pending, her interest passes by right of survivorship to the other joint tenants.[108]

§ 5.5 TENANCY BY THE ENTIRETY

At common law, a conveyance or devise to spouses created a tenancy by the entirety with an indestructible right of survivorship, even if the instrument expressly provided that the grantees or devisees were to hold as joint tenants or as tenants in common.[109] A tenancy by the entirety was the only concurrent estate that could be created between a married couple because they were deemed, at common law, to constitute a single person or entity.[110] In the nineteenth century, the single-entity notion was almost wholly eliminated by adoption of the Married Women's Property Acts and the accompanying changes in social attitudes with respect to the relationship of husband and wife. In the United States, most jurisdictions have now abolished tenancies by the entirety.[111] Where

---

[103] Severance: Mangus, 317 U.S. 178, 63 S.Ct. 182, 87 L.Ed. 169; Hammond v. McArthur, 30 Cal. 2d 512, 183 P.2d 1 (1947); Frederick v. Shorman, 259 Iowa 1050, 147 N.W.2d 478 (1966); Ladd v. Oklahoma ex rel. Oklahoma Tax Comm'n, 688 P.2d 59 (Okla. 1984). No severance: In re Rauer's Collection Co., 87 Cal. App. 2d 248, 196 P.2d 803 (1948); Maniez v. Citibank, F.S.B., 404 Ill. App. 3d 941, 937 N.E.2d 237 (2010); Knibb v. Sec. Ins. Co., 121 R.I. 406, 399 A.2d 1214 (1979).

[104] Frederick v. Shorman, 259 Iowa 1050, 147 N.W.2d 478 (1966); Hughes v. Fairfield Lumber & Supply Co., 143 Conn. 427, 123 A.2d 195 (1956); N. St. Bank v. Toal, 69 Wis. 2d 50, 230 N.W.2d 153 (1975).

[105] Porter v. Porter, 472 So. 2d 630 (1985) (no severance though one spouse awarded sole possession); Estate of Layton, 44 Cal. App. 4th 1337, 52 Cal. Rptr. 2d 251 (1996); In re Marriage of Lutzke, 122 Wis. 2d 24, 361 N.W.2d 640 (1985).

[106] E.g., Cal. Tr. Co. v. Anderson, 91 Cal. App. 2d 832, 205 P.2d 1127 (1949).

[107] E.g., Thomas v. Johnson, 12 Ill. App. 3d 302, 297 N.E.2d 712 (1973); Mann v. Bradley, 188 Colo. 392, 535 P.2d 213 (1975); Neaderhiser v. Dep't. of Soc. & Rehab. Servs., 9 Kan. App. 2d 115, 673 P.2d 462 (1983) (dictum); Carson v. Ellis, 186 Kan. 112, 348 P.2d 807 (1960). An agreement to allocate income and possession to one joint tenant does not necessarily sever the joint tenancy. Neaderhiser, 9 Kan. App. 2d 115, 673 P.2d 462.

[108] Allison v. Powell, 333 Pa. Super. 48, 481 A.2d 1215 (1984).

[109] See 2 Blackstone, supra note 7, at *182; 2 Kent, supra note 12, at *132; Heath v. Heath, 189 F.2d 697 (D.C. Cir. 1951); Pineo v. White, 320 Mass. 487, 70 N.E.2d 294 (1946), superseded by statute, Mass Gen. Laws ch. 209, § 1, as recognized by Coraccio v. Lowell Five Cents Savs. Bank, 415 Mass. 145, 612 N.E.2d 650 (1993); Stuckey v. Keefe's Ex'r, 26 Pa. 397 (1856), superseded by statute as recognized by In re Sampath, 314 B.R. 73 (Bankr. E.D. Va. 2004). For a good summary of the historical origin and characteristics of the tenancy by the entirety, see Spessard v. Spessard, 64 Md. App. 83, 494 A.2d 701 (1985).

[110] See 1 Bracton, supra note 14, at f. 416; Littleton, supra note 46, at § 291; 2 Blackstone, supra note 7, at *182. A tenancy by the entirety requires the unities of time, title, interest, possession, and person.

[111] For a list of jurisdictions, see 7 Powell, supra note 1, at § 52.01[3]. In most states in which tenancies by the entirety can no longer be created, courts reasoned that the Married Women's Property Act destroyed the necessary spousal unity, because the Act eliminated married women's common law disabilities. In a few jurisdictions, courts based the holding on a statute that enumerated the permitted kinds of co-tenancies but did not include the tenancy by the entirety. A few courts simply rejected the tenancy by the entirety as

it has been abolished, a conveyance to spouses will create either a tenancy in common, a joint tenancy, or community property in a community property state.

In the jurisdictions that have not abolished tenancies by the entirety, some presume this form of concurrent ownership when property is conveyed to spouses,[112] but a presumption for tenancy in common exists in others.[113] Even in jurisdictions with a presumption for tenancy by the entirety, some courts hold that, when real property passes to spouses by intestate succession, they take as tenants in common, because each spouse takes a separate share that is independent of their marital relationship.[114] Based on a similar rationale, some courts hold that a specific transfer of equal and identical undivided interests to spouses creates a tenancy in common, because the grantor transferred to them as individuals, rather than as an entity.[115]

In jurisdictions where tenancies by the entirety are presumed, courts will give effect to a clearly stated intent that the spouses are to hold as tenants in common or as joint tenants, rather than as tenants by the entirety.[116] But a conflict of authority exists as to whether a transfer to spouses "as joint tenants with right of survivorship and not as tenants in common" will create a joint tenancy or a tenancy by the entirety.[117]

A tenancy by the entirety may be created by a transfer to three or more persons, two of whom are spouses. The spouses can acquire their interest as tenants by the entirety, and others can take as tenants in common or joint tenants with respect to the spouses' interest.[118]

A tenancy by the entirety cannot be created even by a clear expression of intent if the transferees are not actually married, such as when their purported marriage is void

---

"repugnant to our institutions and to the American sense of justice to the heirs, and therefore not the common law." Kerner v. McDonald, 60 Neb. 663, 84 N.W. 92 (1900).

[112] E.g., O'Neal v. Love, 2015 Ark. App. 689, 476 S.W.3d 846 (2015); Underwood v. Bunger, 70 N.E.3d 338 (Ind. 2017); Casse v. Sink & Rise, Inc., 297 P.3d 762 (Wyo. 2013).

[113] E.g., Carver v. Gilbert, 387 P.2d 928, 32 A.L.R.3d 563 (Alaska 1963).

[114] E.g., Knapp v. Windsor, 60 Mass. (6 Cush.) 156 (1850); Brown v. Baraboo, 90 Wis. 151, 62 N.W. 921, 30 L.R.A. 320 (1895). Contra Gillan's Ex'rs v. Dixon, 65 Pa. 395 (1870) (husband and wife, as their child's sole heirs, were tenants by the entirety).

[115] E.g., Highsmith v. Page, 158 N.C. 226, 73 S.E. 998 (1912); Blease v. Anderson, 241 Pa. 198, 88 A. 365 (1913).

[116] E.g., Underwood, 70 N.E.3d 338; Thornburg v. Wiggins, 135 Ind. 178, 34 N.E. 999, 22 L.R.A. 42 (1893); Baker v. Stewart, 40 Kan. 442, 19 P. 904, 2 L.R.A. 434 (1888); Hiles v. Fisher, 144 N.Y. 306, 39 N.E. 337, 30 L.R.A. 305 (1895). See also Carver, 387 P.2d 928, 32 A.L.R.3d 563.

[117] Tenancy by the entirety: Naler v. Ballew, 81 Ark. 328, 99 S.W. 72 (1907); Jurewicz v. Jurewicz, 317 Mass. 512, 58 N.E.2d 832 (1945); Hoag v. Hoag, 213 Mass. 50, 99 N.E. 521 (1912); Goethe v. Gmelin, 256 Mich. 112, 239 N.W. 347 (1931). Joint tenancy: Wilken v. Young, 144 Ind. 1, 41 N.E. 68 (1895); Kolker v. Gorn, 193 Md. 391, 67 A.2d 258 (1949), noted 13 Md. L. Rev. 43 (1949). Courts holding that a tenancy by the entirety was created often find that the quoted language is designed to rebut the presumption in favor of tenancies in common and that language otherwise effective to create a joint tenancy will create a tenancy by the entirety when the grantees are spouses.

[118] E.g., Dennis v. Dennis, 152 Ark. 187, 238 S.W. 15 (1922); W. Chicago Park Comm'rs v. Coleman, 108 Ill. 591 (1884); Bartholomew v. Marshall, 257 A.D. 1060, 13 N.Y.S.2d 568 (1939); Plastipak Packaging, Inc. v. DePasquale, 937 A.2d 1106 (Pa. Super. 2007). See also Heatter v. Lucas, 367 Pa. 296, 80 A.2d 749 (1951); Margarite v. Ewald, 252 Pa. Super. 244, 381 A.2d 480 (1977). In both *Heatter* and *Margarite,* the court said that a conveyance to three parties, two of whom are spouses, will create a tenancy in common with the grantees holding equal shares, unless the grantor clearly indicates that the spouses hold as tenants by the entirety. In both cases, the court held that language identifying one grantee as the "wife" of another grantee clearly showed the intent to create a tenancy by the entirety. Three married couples, as grantees, may hold one-third shares in common, with each share held by a couple as tenants by the entirety. Burt v. Edmonds, 224 Tenn. 403, 456 S.W.2d 342 (1969).

for some reason.[119] If the transferees are not married, they will take as tenants in common or as joint tenants. The modern constructional preference for tenancies in common causes some courts to hold that a tenancy in common has been created.[120] But other courts have held that a joint tenancy was created because it is more like the tenancy by the entirety that the transferor intended to convey.[121]

A good deal of litigation has resulted from one spouse's attempt to create a tenancy by the entirety by conveying an undivided interest to the other spouse or the entire estate to both spouses. In the absence of a statute, courts have most often held that the conveyance created a tenancy in common, though they sometimes hold that it is a joint tenancy.[122] The usual basis for holding that the spouses have a tenancy in common is that the unities of time and title are missing. To create the tenancy by the entirety, the transferring spouse would have to convey the title to a third party straw person who, by prearrangement, would then convey back to the spouses as tenants by the entirety. In some states, a judicial decision[123] or legislation[124] eliminates the need for a straw person and allows one spouse to create a tenancy by the entirety either by conveying an undivided interest to the other spouse or by conveying the entire estate to both spouses. However, a statute that authorizes conveyances by the owner to himself and another as joint tenants may not apply to tenancies by the entirety.[125]

Courts have determined that the Married Women's Property Acts abolish the husband's common law right to exclusive control of land held by the entirety and his right to convey or encumber the entire estate, subject to the wife's right of survivorship, without her consent.[126] Although tenancies by the entirety still cannot be destroyed by

---

[119] Coke, supra note 12, at *187b; Mitchell v. Frederick, 166 Md. 42, 170 A. 733, 92 A.L.R. 1412 (1934) (void marriage); Morris v. McCarty, 158 Mass. 11, 32 N.E. 938 (1893) (same); Emmons v. Sanders, 217 Or. 234, 342 P.2d 125 (1959) (same). See also Lopez v. Lopez, 250 Md. 491, 243 A.2d 588 (1968) (couple not married at time of conveyance).

[120] E.g., Bove v. Bove, 394 Pa. 627, 149 A.2d 67 (1959); Hynes v. Hynes, 28 Wash. 2d 660, 184 P.2d 68 (1947); In re Estate of Kappler, 418 Mich. 237, 341 N.W.2d 113 (1983); Reinhardt v. Diedricks, 439 So. 2d 936 (Fla. Dist. Ct. App. 1983), appeal after remand sub nom Diedricks v. Reinhardt, 466 So. 2d 375 (Fla. Dist. Ct. App. 1985).

[121] E.g., Mitchell v. Frederick, 166 Md. 42, 170 A. 733, 92 A.L.R. 1412 (1934); Morris v. McCarty, 158 Mass. 11, 32 N.E. 938 (1893).

[122] Tenancy in common: Pegg v. Pegg, 165 Mich. 228, 130 N.W. 617, 33 L.R.A. 166 (1911); In re Walker's Estate, 340 Pa. 13, 16 A.2d 28, 132 A.L.R. 628 (1940), noted 7 U. Pitt. L. Rev. 164 (1941). Tenancy in common with right of survivorship: Little River Bank & Tr. Co. v. Eastman, 105 So. 2d 912 (Fla. Dist. Ct. App. 1958). Common law joint tenancy: Tindall v. Yeats, 392 Ill. 502, 64 N.E.2d 903 (1946); Stuehm v. Mikulski, 139 Neb. 374, 297 N.W. 595, 137 A.L.R. 327 (1941); Lawton v. Lawton, 48 R.I. 134, 136 A. 241 (1927). In a few cases, courts have held that one spouse's conveyance to both spouses instead transferred the entire estate to the other spouse. E.g., Hicks v. Sprankle, 149 Tenn. 310, 257 S.W. 1044 (1924); Wright v. Knapp, 183 Mich. 656, 150 N.W. 315 (1915).

[123] E.g., Ebrite v. Brookhyser, 219 Ark. 676, 244 S.W.2d 625 (1951), noted, 51 Mich. L. Rev. 121 (1952); Johnson v. Landefeld, 138 Fla. 511, 189 So. 666 (1939); Fay v. Smiley, 201 Iowa 1290, 207 N.W. 369 (1926); Therrien v. Therrien, 94 N.H. 66, 46 A.2d 538 (1946); Promenade Nursing Home v. Cohen-Fleisher, 41 Misc. 3d 1236(A), 983 N.Y.S.2d 205 (N.Y. Sup. Ct. 2013); Boehringer v. Schmid, 254 N.Y. 355, 173 N.E. 220 (1930); Jameson v. Jameson, 387 So. 2d 351 (Fla. 1980). See also Dutton v. Buckley, 116 Or. 661, 242 P. 626 (1926) (deed from husband to himself and wife as tenants by the entirety gives wife a half interest in fee simple and a remainder in fee simple in the other half interest to become possessory at husband's death).

[124] E.g., N.C. Gen. Stat. § 39–13.3(b) (2018).

[125] E.g., Estate of Lee v. Graber, 170 Colo. 419, 462 P.2d 492 (1969), abrogated by Taylor v. Canterbury, 92 P.3d 961 (Colo. 2004); Ames v. Chandler, 265 Mass. 428, 164 N.E. 616 (1929).

[126] E.g., Cooper v. Maynard, 156 Fla. 534, 23 So. 2d 734 (1945); Hiles v. Fisher, 144 N.Y. 306, 39 N.E. 337, 30 L.R.A. 305 (1895); Shapiro v. Shapiro, 424 Pa. 120, 224 A.2d 164 (1966), overruled on other grounds by Butler v. Butler, 464 Pa. 522, 347 A.2d 477 (1975). Contra Licker v. Gluskin, 265 Mass. 403, 164 N.E. 613, 63 A.L.R. 231 (1929), superseded by statute, Mass. Gen. Laws ch. 209, § 1, as recognized by Coraccio v. Lowell

either spouse's unilateral act, courts have reached different conclusions about the alienability of an interest. Courts in a few states have held that each spouse has an undivided one-half interest that can be conveyed or encumbered and that a creditor can sell to satisfy that spouse's individual debts. However, a conveyance, encumbrance, or involuntary sale cannot deprive the other spouse of his or her right to possess or right of survivorship.[127] In contrast, courts in a larger number of states have held that neither spouse has an interest that can be separately conveyed or encumbered or seized by the creditors of one spouse alone.[128] Even in these states, one spouse can "release" his or her interest to the other spouse.[129]

Tenants by the entirety acting together can convey or mortgage their property, and property held in a tenancy by the entirety may be subjected to the payment of the spouses' joint debts and sold on execution.[130] When one tenant by the entirety dies, the surviving spouse becomes the sole owner of the property,[131] unless he or she previously conveyed the survivorship right or unless it was sold on execution in the few states that permit conveyance or sale.[132]

Five Cents Sav. Bank, 415 Mass. 145, 612 N.E.2d 650 (1993); Arrand v. Graham, 297 Mich. 559, 298 N.W. 281 (1941), reh'g denied, 297 Mich. 559, 300 N.W. 16 (1941); In re Perry's Estate, 256 N.C. 65, 123 S.E.2d 99 (1961); Mass. Gen. Laws, ch. 209, § 1 (husband and wife are equally entitled to the rents, products, income, profits, control, management, and possession of property held by them as tenants by the entirety).

[127] E.g., Coraccio, 415 Mass. 145, 612 N.E.2d 650 (statute equalizing spouses' rights in entireties property did not prohibit one spouse from mortgaging his or her interest without other spouse's consent, subject to other spouse's survivorship right); Schwind v. O'Halloran, 346 Mo. 486, 142 S.W.2d 55 (1940); Zanzonico v. Zanzonico, 24 N.J. Misc. 153, 46 A.2d 565, 166 A.L.R. 964 (1946), overruled in part by King v. Greene, 30 N.J. 395, 153 A.2d 49, 75 A.L.R.2d 1153 (1959), noted, 73 Harv. L. Rev. 792 (1960), 58 Mich. L. Rev. 601 (1960), 14 Rutgers L. Rev. 457 (1960), 5 Vill. L. Rev. 154 (1959) (creditor's interest attaches to the debtor spouse's interest after the other spouse's death); Hiles v. Fisher, 144 N.Y. 306, 39 N.E. 337, 30 L.R.A. 305 (1896). Cf. Stauffer v. Stauffer, 465 Pa. 558, 351 A.2d 236 (1976) (only survivorship right can be unilaterally transferred or seized by creditors); Robinson v. Trousdale Cty., 516 S.W.2d 626 (Tenn. 1974) (same).

[128] E.g., Estate of Chester Lampert v. Estate of Helen Lampert, 896 P.2d 214 (Alaska 1995) (applying Hawaii law); Sawada v. Endo, 57 Haw. 608, 561 P.2d 1291 (1977); Arbesman v. Winer, 298 Md. 282, 468 A.2d 633 (1983) (neither spouse alone can lease); Elko v. Elko, 187 Md. 161, 49 A.2d 441 (1946); Brownley v. Lincoln County, 218 Or. 7, 343 P.2d 529 (1959), noted, 39 Or. L. Rev. 194, 386 (1960); Roberts v. Bailey, 338 S.W.3d 540 (Tenn. Ct. App. 2010); Jones v. Conwell, 227 Va. 176, 314 S.E.2d 61 (1984). Cf. Branch Banking & Tr. Co. v. Wright, 74 N.C. App. 550, 328 S.E.2d 840 (1985), rev. allowed by 314 N.C. 662, appeal withdrawn by 318 N.C. 505; Moehlenkamp v. Shatz, 396 N.E.2d 433 (Ind. Ct. App. 1979). The cited cases recognize exceptions to the stated rule. See also N.J. Stat. Ann. § 46:3–17.4 (one spouse cannot alienate).

[129] E.g., Thornburg v. Wiggins, 135 Ind. 178, 34 N.E. 999, 22 L.R.A. 42 (1893); Backus v. Backus, 464 Pa. 380, 346 A.2d 790 (1975).

A judicial separation decree may also terminate a tenancy by the entirety. In re Estate of Violi, 65 N.Y.2d 392, 492 N.Y.S.2d 550, 482 N.E.2d 29 (1985). The spouses' execution of a contract to sell the land does not terminate a tenancy by the entirety, unless the doctrine of equitable conversion applies. In re Houghton's Estate, 75 N.J. 462, 383 A.2d 713 (1978) (doctrine of equitable conversion inapplicable).

[130] See Arbesman v. Winer, 298 Md. 282, 468 A.2d 633 (1983) (when both spouses executed lease, one alone could not terminate it).

[131] As previously indicated, the right of survivorship is indestructible and inalienable at common law. See, e.g., In re Estate of Que, 26 Misc. 3d 1227(A), 907 N.Y.S.2d 440 (Sur. Ct. 2010). If the spouses die simultaneously, the Uniform Simultaneous Death Act provides that the property shall be distributed one-half as if one spouse had survived, and the other half as if the other spouse had survived. Unif. Simultaneous Death Act § 3, 8B U.L.A. 315 (2014). However, a court may hold that equality of interest is only presumed and that proof of unequal contributions will rebut the presumption. In re Strong's Will, 171 Misc. 445, 12 N.Y.S.2d 544 (1939).

[132] See supra text accompanying note 127, and cited authorities.

Divorce or annulment also generally terminates a tenancy by the entirety and converts it into a tenancy in common.[133] However, some jurisdictions statutorily provide for "equitable distribution of the property * * * which was legally and beneficially acquired by * * * [the spouses] or either of them during the marriage,"[134] in which case the divorce will not necessarily convert a tenancy by the entirety into a tenancy in common. A court also may give effect to an express pre-divorce agreement to preserve the right of survivorship between the parties.[135] Where divorce does convert a tenancy by the entirety into a tenancy in common, either cotenant can compel a partition.[136]

Courts in some jurisdictions still hold that a tenancy by the entirety cannot be created in personal property,[137] though the Married Women's Property Acts have eliminated the basis for such holdings, which was the common law rule that a husband acquired absolute ownership of his wife's personal property.[138] In most jurisdictions, however, a tenancy by the entirety can now be created in personal property.[139] Even in these jurisdictions, creating a tenancy by the entirety in a bank account may be impossible if the bank's rules allow an individual spouse to withdraw funds because that right amounts to a unilateral power to terminate the tenancy, which is inconsistent with its basic nature.[140]

§ 5.6   TRANSFER OF A COTENANT'S UNDIVIDED INTEREST

As we have seen, the individual undivided interests of a tenant in common and a joint tenant are transferable by inter vivos conveyance, but the authorities are divided as to whether a tenant by the entirety can transfer his or her interest. If a tenant by the entirety can transfer, the transfer cannot destroy the other spouse's right of survivorship. In contrast, a joint tenant's conveyance severs that interest from the joint tenancy and destroys the right of survivorship to it.[141]

---

[133] E.g., Sebold v. Sebold, 444 F.2d 864 (D.C. Cir. 1971), superseded by statute, D.C. Code § 16–2901(c), as recognized by Ballard v. Dornic, 140 A.3d 1147 (D.C. 2016); Donegan v. Donegan, 103 Ala. 488, 15 So. 823 (1894); Wild v. Wild, 157 So. 2d 532 (Fla. 1963); Bernatavicius v. Bernatavicius, 259 Mass. 486, 156 N.E. 685, 52 A.L.R. 886 (1927); Rahily v. Guermoudi, N. 15 NISC 000441(HPS), 2016 WL 797118 (Land Ct. Mass. Mar. 1, 2016); Beudert-Richard v. Richard, 894 N.Y.S.2d 22, 72 A.D.3d 101 (N.Y. App. Div. 2010); In re Estate of Violi, 65 N.Y.2d 392, 492 N.Y.S.2d 550, 482 N.E.2d 29 (1985) (separation agreement for future sale of marital home does not convert tenancy by the entirety into tenancy in common); Branch Banking & Tr. Co., 74 N.C. App. 550, 328 S.E.2d 840 (1985); Rogers v. Kelly, 66 N.C. App. 264, 311 S.E.2d 43 (1984); Brown v. Prisel's Estate, 97 Mich. App. 188, 293 N.W.2d 729 (1980); Ark. Code Ann. § 9–12–317; 23 Pa. Cons. Stat. § 3507; Villanova v. Pollock, 264 Ark. 912, 576 S.W.2d 501 (1979); Hubbard v. Hubbard, 251 Ark. 465, 472 S.W.2d 937 (1971); Backus v. Backus, 464 Pa. 380, 346 A.2d 790 (1975).

[134] New Jersey Stat. Ann. § 2A:34–23. Approximately 38 states have similar statutes. Under these statutes, whether one spouse or both spouses have legal title is immaterial. See generally, D. Freed & H. Foster, Divorce in Fifty States: An Overview as of 1978, 13 Family L.Q. 105 (1979).

[135] Heath v. Heath, 189 F.2d 697 (D.C. Cir. 1951), disapproved, Sebold, 444 F.2d 864 (divorce leaves status of former tenancy by the entirety undefined until judicial determination).

[136] E.g., Bernatavicius, 259 Mass. 486, 156 N.E. 685, 52 A.L.R. 886; Jones v. Conwell, 227 Va. 176, 314 S.E.2d 61 (1984).

[137] E.g., Hawthorne v. Hawthorne, 13 N.Y.2d 82, 242 N.Y.S.2d 50, 192 N.E.2d 20 (1963); In re Blumenthal's Estate, 236 N.Y. 448, 141 N.E. 911, 30 A.L.R. 901 (1923); Lovell v. Rowan Mut. Fire Ins. Co., 302 N.C. 150, 274 S.E.2d 170 (1981).

[138] Coke, supra note 12, at *351.

[139] E.g., Carlisle v. Parker, 38 Del. 83, 188 A. 67 (1936); Dodson v. Nat'l Title Ins. Co., 159 Fla. 371, 31 So. 2d 402 (1947); Madden v. Gosztonyi Sav. & Trust Co., 331 Pa. 476, 200 A. 624, 117 A.L.R. 904 (1938).

[140] See W. Allen, Annotation, Estates by Entirety in Personal Property, 64 A.L.R.2d 8, at § 31 (1959).

[141] See §§ 5.3, 5.4, supra; In re Marriage of Lutzke, 122 Wis. 2d 24, 361 N.W.2d 640 (1985) ("A joint tenant, absent some prohibition of specific nature, always has the power to sell his or her interest.").

A cotenant can transfer by an absolute conveyance or by a lease.[142] In either case, the transferee obtains only the transferor's concurrent rights of possession and use,[143] even if the transferor purports to convey or lease the entire property.[144] Any attempt to exclude the other cotenants from possession or to interfere with their use and enjoyment of the entire property is tortious.[145]

If a joint tenant or tenant in common purports to convey or lease a specific portion of the property, the transfer is viewed as a unilateral attempt to partition the property without the other cotenants' consent. Although the transfer is valid between its parties, it is not binding on the other cotenants, except as a transfer of the transferor's undivided interest in the portion of the property that the conveyance describes.[146] If the transferor later acquires sole title to that portion by partition or otherwise, the doctrine of estoppel may automatically transfer it to the transferee.[147] In any cotenant's partition action, the court may allot to the transferor the specific portion that he previously tried to transfer if it will not prejudice the other cotenants.[148] The grantee or lessee can intervene in the partition action to request the court to recognize and protect her interest in the property.[149]

One tenant in common or joint tenant cannot grant an easement that is valid against the other cotenants,[150] because the grant "involves an attempt by one cotenant, not to substitute another as cotenant in his place, as in the case of a conveyance or lease of his interest, but to enable a person, not a cotenant, to interfere, it may be perpetually,

---

[142] Lease of one cotenant's interest is valid, see Swartzbaugh v. Sampson, 11 Cal. App. 2d 451, 54 P.2d 73 (1936) (dictum that he can convey or mortgage it); Kresha v. Kresha, 220 Neb. 598, 371 N.W.2d 280 (1985) (when one cotenant acquires sole ownership, she takes land subject to existing lease executed by other cotenant).

[143] Wash. Ins. Agency, Inc. v. Friedlander, 487 A.2d 599 (D.C. App. 1985) (lessee became tenant in common of non-lessor cotenant when premises were capable of nonexclusive use and was liable to lessor for full lease rent); Burack v. I. Burack, Inc., 128 Misc. 2d 324, 490 N.Y.S.2d 82 (N.Y. City Ct. 1985); Kassover v. Gordon Family Assocs, Inc., 120 Misc. 2d 196, 465 N.Y.S.2d 668 (N.Y. City Civ. Ct. 1983).

[144] See authorities cited infra note 145.

[145] E.g., Swartzbaugh, 11 Cal. App. 2d 451, 54 P.2d 73 (dictum); Miller v. Gemricher, 191 Iowa 992, 183 N.W. 503 (1921); Cook v. Boehl, 188 Md. 581, 53 A.2d 555 (1947); Howard v. Manning, 79 Okla. 165, 192 P. 358, 12 A.L.R. 819 (1920); Rogers v. Kelly, 66 N.C. App. 264, 311 S.E.2d 43 (1984) (lessee liable to non-lessor cotenant for pro rata portion of reasonable rental value when premises were not capable of nonexclusive use). The rule stated in the text is recognized in Dozier v. Wallace, 169 Ga. App. 126, 311 S.E.2d 839 (1983) (consent of one of three cotenants to sublease did not bind the other cotenants, and the latter could "refuse to recognize the right of possession in the sub-tenant and proceed to expel [it] from the rented premises as a mere intruder").

[146] E.g., Russell v. Stylecraft, Inc., 286 Ala. 633, 244 So. 2d 579 (1971); Elmore v. Elmore, 99 So. 2d 265 (Fla. 1957); Davis v. Hinson, 67 So. 3d 1107 (Fla. Dist. Ct. App. 2011); Thompson v. Gaudette, 148 Me. 288, 92 A.2d 342 (1952); Landskroner v. McClure, 107 N.M. 773, 765 P.2d 189 (1988). If recognizing the transfer would prejudice the other cotenants, the transfer may be set aside in equity. Long v. Howard, 311 Ky. 66, 223 S.W.2d 376 (1949).

[147] E.g., Barnes v. Lynch, 151 Mass. 510, 24 N.E. 783, 21 Am. St. Rep. 470 (1890); McElroy v. McLeay, 71 Vt. 396, 45 A. 898 (1899); Worthington v. Staunton, 16 W. Va. 208 (1880).

[148] E.g., O'Neal v. Cooper, 191 Ala. 182, 67 So. 689 (1914); Pellow v. Arctic Mining Co., 164 Mich. 87, 128 N.W. 918, 47 L.R.A. (N.S.) 573 (1910); Young v. Edwards, 33 S.C. 404, 11 S.E. 1066, 10 L.R.A. 55 (1890). Contra Taylor v. Taylor, 243 N.C. 726, 92 S.E.2d 136 (1956), noted 35 N.C. L. Rev. 431 (1957).

[149] E.g., Benedict v. Torrent, 83 Mich. 181, 47 N.W. 129, 11 L.R.A. 278 (1890); Seavey v. Green, 137 Or. 127, 1 P.2d 601, 75 A.L.R. 1451 (1931).

[150] E.g., East Shore Co. v. Richmond Belt Ry., 172 Cal. 174, 155 P. 999 (1916); Burnham v. Baltimore Gas & Elec. Co., 217 Md. 507, 144 A.2d 80 (1958); City Club of Auburn v. McGeer, 198 N.Y. 160, 91 N.E. 539 (1910), reh'g denied, 198 N.Y. 609, 92 N.E. 105 (1910); LDDC, Inc. v. Pressley, 71 N.C. App. 431, 322 S.E.2d 416 (1984). One cotenant cannot authorize the police to search the common property without a warrant if another cotenant is in possession and objects. See Georgia v. Randolph, 547 U.S. 103 (2006); Tompkins v. Superior Court, 59 Cal. 2d 65, 27 Cal. Rptr. 889, 378 P.2d 113 (1963).

with the possession of the other cotenants."[151] But the grant is valid as against the grantor and will be effective by operation of estoppel if the grantor later acquires sole title to the portion of the land that is needed to use the easement.[152]

Direct restraints on alienation of concurrent estates in fee simple are no more effective than direct restraints on alienation of fee simple estates that are owned individually, whether the restraints are of the disabling, the forfeiture, or the promissory type. To avoid the common law rule against restraints on alienation, most condominium bylaws provide that the association has a preemptive right of first refusal when a condominium unit owner wishes to sell or lease his unit,[153] but this provision may create problems under the Rule Against Perpetuities.[154]

§ 5.7 RIGHTS OF COTENANTS INTER SE—POSSESSION AND USE OF THE REALTY—ACCOUNTING

One cotenant's possession and use of concurrently owned property is subject to the other cotenants' equal rights to possess and use. All are entitled to possession of all parts of the property at all times.[155] Therefore, one cotenant's sole possession and use are not tortious or adverse to the others, so long as the possessor does not exclude or oust the others.[156] Exclusion or ouster occurs only when (1) the possessing cotenant refuses to allow another cotenant to share possession after the latter has demanded it,[157] (2) one cotenant purports to convey sole ownership of the land, the grantee enters into sole possession in reliance on the conveyance, and the other cotenants have notice of these facts,[158] or (3) generally, the possessing cotenant asserts a hostile claim of sole ownership and the other cotenants have notice of the claim.[159] Notice is required because, without

---

[151] 2 Tiffany, supra note 41, § 456, at 274.

[152] E.g., White v. Manhattan R. Co., 139 N.Y. 19, 34 N.E. 887 (1893); McElroy, 71 Vt. 396, 45 A. 898 (1899). The non-grantor cotenants may, of course, effectively ratify or consent to the grant of the easement and thus become bound by it. Keller v. Hartman, 175 W. Va. 418, 333 S.E.2d 89 (1985), overruled on other grounds by O'Dell v. Stegall, 226 W. Va. 590, 703 S.E.2d 561 (2010).

[153] 8 Powell, supra note 1, at § 54A.05[4][a].

[154] 10 Powell, supra note 1, at § 72.11[4].

[155] E.g., Zaslow v. Kroenert, 29 Cal. 2d 541, 176 P.2d 1 (Cal. 1946); Watson v. Little, 224 S.C. 359, 79 S.E.2d 384 (S.C. 1953); Coulbourn v. Armstrong, 243 N.C. 663, 91 S.E.2d 912 (N.C. 1956).

[156] E.g., Tarver v. Tarver, 258 Ala. 683, 65 So. 2d 148 (Ala. 1953); Johnson v. James, 237 Ark. 900, 377 S.W.2d 44 (Ark. 1964); Hare v. Chisman, 230 Ind. 333, 101 N.E.2d 268 (Ind. 1951); Bader v. Bader, 207 Okla. 683, 252 P.2d 427 (Okla. 1953); McKnight v. Basilides, 19 Wash. 2d 391, 143 P.2d 307 (Wash. 1943); Diedricks v. Reinhardt, 466 So. 2d 375, 10 Fla. L. Weekly 756 (Fla. Dist. Ct. App. 1985); Evans v. Covington, 795 S.W.2d 806 (Tex. App. 1990).

[157] E.g., Zaslow, 29 Cal. 2d 541, 176 P.2d 1; Cameron v. Chi., Milwaukee & St. Paul Ry. Co., 60 Minn. 100, 61 N.W. 814 (Minn. 1895).

[158] E.g., West v. Evans, 29 Cal. 2d 414, 175 P.2d 219 (Cal. 1946); Whittington v. Cameron, 385 Ill. 99, 52 N.E.2d 134 (Ill. 1943); Witherspoon v. Brummett, 50 N.M. 303, 176 P.2d 187 (N.M. 1946). See Annotation, Possession by One Claiming Under or Through Deed or Mortgage by Cotenant as Adverse to Other Cotenant, 27 A.L.R. 8 (1923); Annotation, Possession by Stranger Claiming Under Conveyance by Cotenant as Adverse to Other Cotenants, 32 A.L.R.2d 1214 (1953).

[159] E.g., Johnson v. James, 237 Ark. 900, 377 S.W.2d 44 (Ark. 1964); Blankenhorn v. Lenox, 123 Iowa 67, 98 N.W. 556 (Iowa 1904); Saucier v. Kremer, 297 Mo. 461, 249 S.W. 640 (Mo. 1923); Diedricks v. Reinhardt, 466 So. 2d 375, 10 Fla. L. Weekly 756 (Fla. Dist. Ct. App. 1985) (cotenant's sole possession deemed adverse to other cotenant after the latter began action to obtain joint possession); Evans v. Covington, 795 S.W.2d 806 (Tex. App. 1990); Sweeney Land Co. v. Kimball, 786 P.2d 760 (Utah 1990); In re Estate of Neil, 152 Vt. 124, 565 A.2d 1309 (Vt. 1989). Cf. Coggan v. Coggan, 239 So. 2d 17 (Fla. 1970) (no ouster when one cotenant sued for partition and the possessing cotenant alleged in answer that plaintiff had no interest in the property).

it, each cotenant is entitled to assume that the other cotenant's possession is consistent with the all the cotenants' rights to concurrent possession and use.[160]

An excluded or ousted cotenant has various remedies, the most important of which is ejectment or its modern equivalent, coupled with a claim for mesne profits.[161] A judgment for the plaintiff does not dispossess the defendant but does restore the plaintiff's concurrent possession with the defendant.[162] The award of mesne profits usually is in the amount of the plaintiff's pro rata share of the reasonable value of the defendant's use and occupation of the land.[163]

At old common law, if one cotenant was in sole possession of property but had not excluded the others, she was not accountable for either the rental value of her use and possession or for the actual net income she received from the property,[164] unless she (1) was the other cotenants' bailiff or agent,[165] (2) is leasing the other cotenants' right to possess,[166] or (3) was the other cotenants' guardian or trustee.[167] But England changed the common law rule by a statute enacted in 1705 that is commonly known as the Statute of Anne.[168] It provided that a cotenant must account, as bailiff, for any rents and profits he received from the property in excess of his just proportion. English courts have narrowly construed this statute to apply only to rents that a cotenant receives from a third person[169] but not to income derived from the cotenant's nontortious use of the property, even if the income was from exploiting mineral or timber resources in a way that permanently reduced the property's value.[170]

---

[160] E.g., Johnson v. James, 237 Ark. 900, 377 S.W.2d 44 (Ark. 1964); Fallon v. Davidson, 137 Colo. 48, 320 P.2d 976 (Colo. 1958); Diedricks v. Reinhardt, 466 So. 2d 375, 10 Fla. L. Weekly 756 (Fla. Dist. Ct. App. 1985); Evans v. Covington, 795 S.W.2d 806 (Tex. App. 1990); Sweeney Land Co. v. Kimball, 786 P.2d 760 (Utah 1990); In re Estate of Neil, 152 Vt. 124, 565 A.2d 1309 (Vt. 1989); Fairchild v. Fairchild, 106 Idaho 147, 676 P.2d 722 (Idaho Ct. App. 1984). Without notice of a hostile claim, a tenant who has acquired an outstanding hostile title is deemed a fiduciary for the benefit of his cotenants and does not hold adversely to them. E.g., Leach v. Hall, 95 Iowa 611, 64 N.W. 790 (Iowa 1895); Woods v. Richardson, 190 Tenn. 662, 231 S.W.2d 340 (Tenn. 1950).

[161] A separate trespass action for mesne profits is unnecessary after recovering possession in ejectment. E.g., Zapp v. Miller, 109 N.Y. 51, 15 N.E. 889 (N.Y. 1888).

[162] E.g., Ewald v. Corbett, 32 Cal. 493 (Cal. 1867); King v. Dickerman, 77 Mass. (11 Gray) 480 (Mass. 1858).

[163] E.g., Lane v. Harrold, 72 Pa. 267 (Pa. 1872); Wait v. Richardson, 33 Vt. 190 (Vt. 1860). But actual net income is sometimes awarded. See, e.g., Edwards v. Lee's Adm'r, 265 Ky. 418, 96 S.W.2d 1028 (Ky. 1936). See also Stylianopoulos v. Stylianopoulos, 17 Mass. App. Ct. 64, 455 N.E.2d 477 (Mass. App. Ct. 1983) (occupying cotenant liable for rental value only if he ousted other cotenants or agreed to pay); Weaver v. Am. Nat'l Bank, 452 So. 2d 469 (Ala. 1984).

[164] E.g., Warner v. Warner, 248 Ala. 556, 28 So. 2d 701 (Ala. 1946); DesRoches v. McCrary, 315 Mich. 611, 24 N.W.2d 511 (Mich. 1946); Arnold v. De Booy, 161 Minn. 255, 201 N.W. 437 (Minn. 1924); Beer v. Beer (1852) 12 C.B. 60, 138 Eng. Rep. 823; Succession of LeBlanc, 577 So. 2d 105 (La. Ct. App. 1991).

[165] Absence an express agreement, the possessing cotenant was neither a bailiff nor an agent. Coke, supra note 12, at *200b.

[166] In such case, the possessing cotenant had to pay the agreed rent or, if no definite rent was fixed, a reasonable rent. See, e.g., Burk v. Burk, 247 Ala. 91, 22 So. 2d 609 (Ala. 1945); Kites v. Church, 142 Mass. 586, 8 N.E. 743 (Mass. 1886); Stylianopoulos, 17 Mass. App. Ct. 64, 455 N.E.2d 477.

[167] The guardian or trustee was accountable for actual net income or the reasonable rental value if there was no actual income. See, e.g., Minion v. Warner, 238 N.Y. 413, 144 N.E. 665 (N.Y. 1924).

[168] Statute 4 Anne, c. 16, § 27 (1705). See, generally, 2 Am. L. Prop., supra note 1, § 6.14, at 59; D. Weible, Accountability of Cotenants, 29 Iowa L. Rev. 558, 559 (1944).

[169] Job v. Potton (1875) L.R. 20 Eq. 84.

[170] E.g., Job v. Potton (1875) L.R. 20 Eq. 84 (one cotenant mining).

Most American jurisdictions have either substantially re-enacted the Statute of Anne[171] or have declared it to be part of their common law.[172] In most of these jurisdictions, the duty to account has been limited almost as narrowly as in England,[173] except that a cotenant who derives income from a nontortious use of the land that permanently reduces its value generally must account to the other cotenants.[174] In a minority of American jurisdictions, the duty to account applies more broadly whenever one cotenant derives any income from sole possession of the property in the form of rents or otherwise.[175] In a few states, a cotenant in sole possession must account for the land's reasonable rental value even if he derives no actual income from it.[176] But no duty to account exists for income produced by improvements that the occupying cotenant made alone.[177] In some jurisdictions, the interest of a cotenant who has a duty to account for income is subject to an equitable lien,[178] but no such lien exists in most jurisdictions.[179]

One cotenant's exclusive use of concurrently owned property may be tortious not only because she has ousted the other cotenants,[180] but also if she has committed waste. In 1285, England authorized an action for waste against a fellow joint tenant or tenant

---

[171] American statutes usually authorize an action both for an accounting and for recovery of "money had and received to the use of the plaintiff." 2 Am. L. Prop., supra note 1, § 6.14, at n.10.

[172] E.g., Flack v. Gosnell, 76 Md. 88, 24 A. 414 (Md. 1892); Brown v. Wellington, 106 Mass. 318 (Mass. 1871); Lancaster v. Flowers, 208 Pa. 199, 57 A. 526 (Pa. 1904). See also Lohmann v. Lohmann, 50 N.J. Super. 37, 141 A.2d 84 (N.J. Super. Ct. App. Div. 1958). But see Pico v. Columbet, 12 Cal. 414 (Cal. 1859). See generally A. Heon, Comment, The Liability of a Cotenant to Other Cotenants for Rents, Profits and Use and Occupation, 42 Marquette L. Rev. 363 (1958); R. Macy, Note, Accountability of a Cotenant for Use and Occupation, 12 Wyo. L.J. 156 (1958).

[173] E.g., Dabney-Johnston Oil Corp. v. Walden, 4 Cal. 2d 637, 52 P.2d 237 (Cal. 1935); Coggan v. Coggan, 239 So. 2d 17 (Fla. 1970); Mastbaum v. Mastbaum, 126 N.J. Eq. 366, 9 A.2d 51 (N.J. Ch. 1939); LeBarron v. Babcock, 122 N.Y. 153, 25 N.E. 253 (N.Y. 1890); Diedricks v. Reinhardt, 466 So. 2d 375, 10 Fla. L. Weekly 756 (Fla. Dist. Ct. App. 1985) (occupying cotenant not accountable for non-rent benefits, absent ouster or adverse possession); Smith v. Smith, 464 So. 2d 1287, 10 Fla. L. Weekly 627 (Fla. Dist. Ct. App. 1985) (occupying cotenant not accountable for his or his tenant's nonexclusive possession). See also Baird v. Moore, 50 N.J. Super. 156, 141 A.2d 324 (N.J. Super. Ct. App. Div. 1958) (equitable considerations led court not to charge possessing tenant for actual rents or rental value). Of course, an occupying cotenant is accountable for rents that he actually received. E.g., Albright v. Albright, 73 Or. App. 410, 699 P.2d 195 (Or. Ct. App. 1985).

[174] McCord v. Oakland Quicksilver Mining Co., 64 Cal. 134, 27 P. 863 (Cal. 1883); Abbey v. Wheeler, 170 N.Y. 122, 62 N.E. 1074 (N.Y. 1901) (called waste, but cotenant was accountable for net profits, rather than for damages); Meeker v. Denver Producing & Refining Co., 199 Okla. 455, 188 P.2d 854 (Okla. 1947); White v. Smyth, 147 Tex. 272, 214 S.W.2d 967 (Tex. 1948) (cotenant who mined and marketed rock asphalt was accountable for net profits from mining, processing, and sale and not merely for value of asphalt in the ground).

[175] E.g., Armstrong v. Rodemacher, 199 Iowa 928, 203 N.W. 23 (Iowa 1925); Lohmann v. Lohmann, 50 N.J. Super. 37, 141 A.2d 84 (N.J. Super. Ct. App. Div. 1958); Griffin v. Griffin, 82 S.C. 256, 64 S.E. 160 (S.C. 1909). In Pennsylvania, a cotenant in possession of mineral estate who develops the minerals has a duty to account to nonoccupying cotenants for the pro rata share of income that he received. Lichtenfels v. Bridgeview Coal Co., 344 Pa. Super. 257, 496 A.2d 782 (Pa. Super. Ct. 1985).

[176] McPherson v. McPherson, 33 N.C. 391 (N.C. 1850); McKnight v. Basilides, 19 Wash. 2d 391, 143 P.2d 307 (Wash. 1943). See also Baird v. Moore, 50 N.J. Super. 156, 141 A.2d 324 (N.J. Super. Ct. App. Div. 1958). In some states, the occupying cotenant is liable for a proportionate share of the land's reasonable rental value by virtue of a statute other than the Statute of Anne. See, e.g., West v. Weyer, 46 Ohio St. 66, 18 N.E. 537 (Ohio 1888); Collins v. Jackson, 34 Ohio App. 3d 101, 517 N.E.2d 269 (Ohio Ct. App. 1986).

[177] E.g., Hannah v. Carver, 121 Ind. 278, 23 N.E. 93 (Ind. 1889); Van Ormer v. Harley, 102 Iowa 150, 71 N.W. 241 (Iowa 1897); Larmon v. Larmon, 173 Ky. 477, 191 S.W. 110 (Ky. 1917). See also Haas v. Haas, 165 F.Supp. 701 (D. Del. 1958).

[178] E.g., New Winder Lumber Co. v. Guest, 182 Ga. 859, 187 S.E. 63 (Ga. 1936); Stevens v. Pels, 191 Iowa 176, 175 N.W. 303 (Iowa 1919); Peets v. Wright, 117 S.C. 409, 109 S.E. 649 (S.C. 1921). See Recent Cases, 27 Harv. L. Rev. 382, 397–98 (1914).

[179] E.g., Griffin v. Ayers, 233 Ala. 389, 171 So. 719 (1936); Whitehurst v. Hinton, 209 N.C. 392, 184 S.E. 66 (1936); Tedder v. Tedder, 123 S.C. 346, 116 S.E. 436 (1923).

[180] See supra text accompanying notes 71–74.

in common,[181] and most American jurisdictions have enacted similar statutes.[182] English courts gave the statute only limited application to cotenants in fee simple, on the ground that they had the same broad privileges of use and enjoyment as the sole owner of a defeasible fee simple estate.[183] A fee simple cotenant was subject to an injunction against waste only if he used the realty in a malicious or unconscionable manner. Thus, a fee simple cotenant was not liable for waste for cutting and selling mature trees that had no special ornamental value[184] or for opening and operating mines or quarries while in sole possession of the property.[185]

The American case law concerning waste is extremely confused. Some courts hold or say that a cotenant is liable for waste if he cuts timber or opens new mines, oil and gas wells, or quarries.[186] Other courts hold that such conduct does not constitute waste.[187] However, even when a court holds a fee simple cotenant liable for waste for such activities, they have not imposed the usual penalties for waste, such as treble damages, but have simply required the defendant to account for the net profits derived from his use of the property.[188] Of course, if the cotenant in sole possession ousts his cotenants and commits waste, the ousted cotenants can recover damages for waste and mesne profits in an ejectment action.[189]

§ 5.8   RIGHTS OF COTENANTS INTER SE—CONTRIBUTION TO CARRYING CHARGES OF COMMON PROPERTY

When one cotenant pays more than her pro rata share of the cost of necessary repairs on the property, she can assert an equitable right to compel the other cotenants to contribute proportionately in an accounting for rents and profits[190] or in the final settlement of accounts between the cotenants on partition.[191] Absent an express or implied agreement that the other cotenants will contribute, courts are divided on

---

[181] Statute of Westminster 1285, 13 Edw. c. 22.

[182] E.g., N.Y. Real Prop. Acts. Law § 817 (McKinney).

[183] E.g., Martyn v. Knollys (1799) 8 T.R. 145, 101 Eng. Rep. 1313; Job v. Potton (1875) LR 20 Eq. 84.

[184] Martyn v. Knollys (1799) 8 T.R. 145, 101 Eng. Rep. 1313.

[185] Job v. Potton (1875) L.R. 20 Eq. 84.

[186] E.g., Clark v. Whitfield, 218 Ala. 593, 119 So. 631 (1928) (mining); Fitzhugh v. Norwood, 153 Ark. 412, 241 S.W. 8 (1922) (timber); Page v. Donnelly, 346 Mass. 768, 193 N.E.2d 682 (1963) (timber); Childs v. Kansas City, St. Joseph & Council Bluffs R.R. Co., 117 Mo. 414, 23 S.W. 373 (1893); Abbey v. Wheeler, 170 N.Y. 122, 62 N.E. 1074 (1901); Cosgriff v. Dewey, 164 N.Y. 1, 58 N.E. 1 (1900); Cecil v. Clark, 49 W. Va. 459, 39 S.E. 202 (1901); Dotson v. Branham, 197 Va. 674, 90 S.E.2d 783 (1956) (mining). See also Green v. Crawford, 662 S.W.2d 123 (Tex. App. 1983); Chosar Corp. v. Owens, 235 Va. 660, 370 S.E.2d 305 (1988).

[187] E.g., McCord v. Oakland Quicksilver Mining Co., 64 Cal. 134, 27 P. 863 (1883); Meeker v. Denver Producing & Refining Co., 199 Okla. 455, 188 P.2d 854 (1947); White v. Smyth, 147 Tex. 272, 214 S.W.2d 967 (1948); Lichtenfels v. Bridgeview Coal Co., 344 Pa. Super. 257, 496 A.2d 782 (1985). In all these cases, the producing cotenant was held accountable for net income but was not liable for waste.

[188] See, e.g., Childs v. Kansas City, St. Joseph & Council Bluffs R.R. Co., 117 Mo. 414, 23 S.W. 373 (1893); Abbey v. Wheeler, 170 N.Y. 122, 62 N.E. 1074 (1901); Cosgriff v. Dewey, 164 N.Y. 1, 58 N.E. 1 (1900); Cecil, 49 W. Va. 459, 39 S.E. 202 .

[189] In some cases in which the court purports to impose liability for waste, the cotenant charged with waste had ousted his cotenants and could also have been liable for mesne profits in an ejectment action.

[190] E.g., Van Veen v. Van Veen, 213 Iowa 323, 236 N.W. 1 (1931), as modified in part by 213 Iowa 323, 238 N.W. 718 (1931); Pickering v. Pickering, 63 N.H. 468, 3 A. 744 (1886); Fassitt v. Seip, 249 Pa. 576, 95 A. 273 (1915); Ward v. Ward's Heirs, 40 W. Va. 611, 21 S.E. 746 (1895).

[191] E.g., In re Cochran's Real Estate, 31 Del. Ch. 545, 66 A.2d 497 (Del. Orphans' Ct. 1949); Larmon v. Larmon, 173 Ky. 477, 191 S.W. 110 (1917); Williams v. Coombs, 88 Me. 183, 33 A. 1073 (1895); Hogan v. McMahon, 115 Md. 195, 80 A. 695 (1911); Stylianopoulos v. Stylianopoulos, 17 Mass. App. Ct. 64, 455 N.E.2d 477 (1983).

whether a cotenant who pays more than her pro rata share of repair costs can maintain an independent contribution action against the others.[192] If one looks only at what the courts say, the prevailing view seems to allow the independent contribution action if the cotenant who made the repairs first notified the other cotenants of the need for them. But many of the opinions that express this view involved an accounting for rents and profits or a partition action, and the courts' statements concerning the availability of an independent action for contribution are only dicta.[193]

Courts distinguish between a cotenant's claims for reimbursement for improvements and for necessary repairs. Courts appear to hold unanimously that a cotenant who pays more than his pro rata share of the cost of improvements to the property can get contribution only in the final accounting incident to a partition, unless the other cotenants agreed to share the cost.[194] Generally, the contribution amount is the lesser of the cost of the improvements or of the value they added to the land. As an alternative remedy in a partition action, a court may award the portion of the land with the improvements to the cotenant who made them, if possible.[195]

A cotenant who is not in sole possession and pays more than her pro rata share of property taxes or mortgage interest and principal may have a right of contribution[196] in

---

[192] Coke, supra note 12, at *300b; Shelangowski v. Schrack, 162 Iowa 176, 143 N.W. 1081 (1913); Calvert v. Aldrich, 99 Mass. 74 (1868); Barry v. Barry, 147 Neb. 1067, 26 N.W.2d 1 (1947); Baird v. Moore, 50 N.J. Super. 156, 141 A.2d 324 (N.J. Super. Ct. App. Div. 1958); Johnson v. Hendrickson, 71 S.D. 392, 24 N.W.2d 914 (1946); Perez v. Hernandez, 658 S.W.2d 697 (Tex. App. 1983) (cotenant who incurs expenses necessary for preservation of property, such as taxes, is entitled to reimbursement from other cotenants). "The law's remedy in all such cases is partition; * * * and in that action he will be credited with * * * expenditures [for reasonable repairs] in the final accounting." 2 Am. L. Prop., supra note 1, § 6.18, at 78. But cf. Hahn v. Hahn, 297 S.W.2d 559 (Mo. 1957).

[193] E.g., Pickering, 63 N.H. 468, 3 A. 744 (1886); Fassitt v. Seip, 249 Pa. 576, 95 A. 273 (Pa. 1915); Larmon, 173 Ky. 477, 191 S.W. 110 (1917); Williams, 88 Me. 183, 33 A. 1073 (1895); Hogan, 115 Md. 195, 80 A. 695 (1911).

[194] E.g., Shelangowski, 162 Iowa 176, 143 N.W. 1081; Barry, 147 Neb. 1067, 26 N.W.2d 1; Baird, 50 N.J. Super. 156, 141 A.2d 324; Fassitt, 249 Pa. 576, 95 A. 273; Ward, 40 W. Va. 611, 21 S.E. 746; Perez, 658 S.W.2d 697 (improving cotenant not entitled to reimbursement in independent action for cost of development of property as a citrus grove). "Improvements made by the voluntary action of one of the cotenants become part of the land and therefore all the cotenants share in their ownership, but in the absence of a contract to pay his share of the cost there is no reason, legal or equitable, why any other tenant should be required to contribute [either in an independent action or in an action for an account of rents and profits]." 2 Am. L. Prop., supra note 1, § 6.18, at 81. Also, see infra § 5.11, text accompanying note 275, and authorities cited. Of course, credit may be awarded to an improving cotenant in the final accounting in a partition action.

[195] 2 Am. L. Prop., supra note 1, § 6.18; 2 H. Tiffany, Real Property § 462 (3d ed. 1939).

[196] Taxes: E.g., Cocks v. Simmons, 55 Ark. 104, 17 S.W. 594 (Ark. 1891); Eads v. Retherford, 114 Ind. 273, 16 N.E. 587 (1888); Hogan, 115 Md. 195, 80 A. 695 (1911); Van Veen v. Van Veen, 213 Iowa 323, 236 N.W. 1, 238 N.W. 718 (1931), as modified in part at 213 Iowa 323, 238 N.W. 718 (1931); Kites v. Church, 142 Mass. 586, 8 N.E. 743 (Mass. 1886); Woolston v. Pullen, 88 N.J. Eq. 35, 102 A. 461 (N.J. Ch. 1917); Fassitt, 249 Pa. 576, 95 A. 273. Mortgage payments: E.g., Kelly v. Carmichael, 221 Ala. 371, 129 So. 81 (Ala. 1930); Scanlon v. Parish, 85 Conn. 379, 82 A. 969 (Conn. 1912); Laura v. Christian, 88 N.M. 127, 537 P.2d 1389 (N.M. 1975); Connell v. Welch, 101 Wis. 8, 76 N.W. 596 (Wis. 1898); Spessard v. Spessard, 64 Md. App. 83, 494 A.2d 701 (1985) (right to contribution recognized). But courts may reject particular contribution claims. See, e.g., Allen v. Allen, 687 S.W.2d 660 (Mo. Ct. App. 1985) (occupying cotenant not entitled to contribution when land's rental value exceeded amount of taxes paid); Albright v. Albright, 73 Or. App. 410, 699 P.2d 195 (Or. Ct. App. 1985) (occupying cotenant not entitled to contribution when charges for some expenses were unjustified and occupying cotenant was liable for other cotenants' pro rata share of rents).

an independent action,[197] an action for an accounting,[198] or a partition action.[199] If the cotenants are personally liable for the property taxes, which usually is not the case, or the mortgage payments, a court can render a personal judgment in an independent action for contribution.[200] If the cotenants are not personally liable, the paying cotenant can recover contribution from the others only by judicial recognition and enforcement of an equitable lien on the property[201] or by subrogation and enforcement of the lien held by the taxing authority or mortgagee, as the case may be.[202] In either case, the ultimate result will be a judicial sale of the property and an equitable distribution of the proceeds, as is frequently the case when the court enters an order for partition.[203]

If a cotenant who is in sole possession of the property, though he has not excluded his cotenants, has paid taxes or made mortgage payments in excess of his pro rata share, he cannot obtain contribution in any form of action if the value of his use and occupation exceeds those payments.[204] A cotenant who has excluded his cotenants and is, therefore, an adverse possessor can never maintain an action for contribution against the cotenants.[205] However, in an action by the cotenants to recover possession and mesne profits, he will be credited with the amounts he paid for property taxes or mortgage payments in excess of his pro rata share.[206]

---

[197] E.g., Eads, 114 Ind. 273, 16 N.E. 587 (1888); Kites, 142 Mass. 586, 8 N.E. 743.

[198] E.g., Hogan, 115 Md. 195, 80 A. 695; Fassitt, 249 Pa. 576, 95 A. 273. See Annotation, Accountability of Cotenants for Rents and Profits or Use and Occupation, 27 A.L.R. 249 (1923).

[199] E.g., Cocks v. Simmons, 55 Ark. 104, 17 S.W. 594 (A1891); Van Veen, 213 Iowa 323, 236 N.W. 1; Hahn v. Hahn, 297 S.W.2d 559 (Mo. 1957); Woolston, 88 N.J. Eq. 35, 102 A. 461; Spessard, 64 Md. App. 83, 494 A.2d 701; Kamin-A-Kalaw v. Dulic, 322 Md. 49, 585 A.2d 216 (Md. 1991).

[200] E.g., Troy v. Protestant Episcopal Church, 174 Ala. 380, 56 So. 982 (Ala. 1911); Dickinson v. Williams, 65 Mass. (11 Cush.) 258 (Mass. 1853) (mortgage was assumed).

[201] E.g., Kelly v. Carmichael, 221 Ala. 371, 129 So. 81 (1930); Eads, 114 Ind. 273, 16 N.E. 587; Kirsch v. Scandia Am. Bank, 160 Minn. 269, 199 N.W. 881 (1924); Hahn, 297 S.W.2d 559 (Mo. 1957); Connell v. Welch, 101 Wis. 8, 76 N.W. 596 (Wis. 1898). But see Kites, 142 Mass. 586, 8 N.E. 743 (money judgment for contribution in suit on "account annexed").

[202] E.g., Scanlon v. Parish, 85 Conn. 379, 82 A. 969 (Conn. 1912); Hansen v. Cerro Gordo State Bank of Clear Lake, 209 Iowa 1352, 230 N.W. 415 (Iowa 1930). See also Baird v. Moore, 50 N.J. Super. 156, 141 A.2d 324 (N.J. Super. Ct. App. Div. 1958). Subrogation to mortgage holder's lien is possible only when the entire indebtedness is discharged. See L. Simpson, Suretyship § 47 (1950).

[203] See infra § 5.12.

[204] Ward v. Pipkin, 181 Ark. 736, 27 S.W.2d 523 (1930); Willmon v. Koyer, 168 Cal. 369, 143 P. 694 (1914); Ellis v. Snyder, 83 Kan. 638, 112 P. 594 (1911); Mastbaum v. Mastbaum, 126 N.J. Eq. 366, 9 A.2d 51 (N.J. Ch. 1939); Roberts v. Roberts, 136 Tex. 255, 150 S.W.2d 236 (1941). In Ward, supra, the court said that the benefits received by the occupying cotenant are presumed to be at least equal to the taxes paid, in the absence of contrary evidence.

[205] E.g., Victoria Copper Mining Co. v. Rich, 193 Fed. 314 (6th Cir. 1911) (conclusive presumption that benefits are at least equal to taxes paid); Appeal of Wistar, 125 Pa. 526, 17 A. 460 (1889). But see Lovin v. Poss, 240 Ga. 848, 242 S.E.2d 609 (1978) (occupying cotenant entitled to contribution in his action for equitable accounting).

[206] E.g., Willmon, 168 Cal. 369, 143 P. 694; Engle v. Terrell, 281 Ky. 88, 134 S.W.2d 980 (1939); Smith v. Mount, 149 Mo. App. 668, 129 S.W. 722 (1910) (credit for taxes but not improvements; independent action after partition); Eaton v. Davis, 165 Va. 313, 182 S.E. 229 (1935) (improvements); Plebuch v. Barnes, 149 Wash. 221, 270 P. 823 (1928) (taxes and assessments). See also Spessard v. Spessard, 64 Md. App. 83, 494 A.2d 701 (1985) (husband's claim for contribution could be considered in determining monetary award to wife in divorce action).

§ 5.9   RIGHTS OF COTENANTS INTER SE—ACQUIRING OUTSTANDING INTERESTS IN COMMON PROPERTY

When cotenants acquire their concurrent interests at the same time, they may be subject to fiduciary duties with respect to their dealings with the common property.[207] A major consequence of a fiduciary relationship among cotenants is that an individual cotenant who acquires a superior title to the property must hold it for the others' benefit if they offer to contribute their pro rata shares of the acquisition cost within a reasonable time.[208] This rule does not apply if a cotenant acquired the superior title before the concurrent estate was created or after it ceased to exist.[209] For example, if A takes a mortgage on Blackacre from the owner and subsequently acquires Blackacre with B and C, A is not required to hold the mortgage for B's and C's benefit and can enforce it as if she were a stranger, rather than a cotenant. Similarly, A has no fiduciary duty to the other cotenants if she buys Blackacre from a third person who purchased Blackacre at a tax sale, mortgage foreclosure sale, or execution sale.[210] However, if A buys Blackacre while it is subject to a statutory right of redemption after the sale or if A redeems the property after the sale, she has acquired it while the concurrent ownership still exists. In this situation, courts are fairly evenly divided on whether A has a fiduciary duty to hold the title for B's and C's benefit.[211]

Some courts that permit the purchasing cotenant to hold the title for his sole benefit state that the other cotenants, if adults, had an equal opportunity to bid at the sale, unless the purchasing cotenant acted fraudulently or otherwise inequitably. Therefore,

---

[207] E.g., Minion v. Warner, 238 N.Y. 413, 144 N.E. 665 (1924); Givens v. Givens, 387 S.W.2d 851 (Ky. 1965) (dictum); Dampier v. Polk, 214 Miss. 65, 58 So. 2d 44 (1952); Foster v. Hudson, 437 So. 2d 528 (Ala. 1983). The requirements for a fiduciary relationship are most easily satisfied in a tenancy by the entirety or a joint tenancy because of the incident of survivorship. Some courts hold that a fiduciary relationship exists between tenants in common simply because of the unity of possession. E.g., Smith v. Borradaile, 30 N.M. 62, 227 P. 602 (1922). Moreover, tenants in common may, by their own conduct, create a fiduciary relationship among themselves, such as when one cotenant is an agent for the others, as in West v. Madansky, 80 Okla. 161, 194 P. 439 (1920).

[208] E.g., Chatman v. Hall, 246 Ala. 403, 20 So. 2d 713 (1945); Fuller v. McBurrows, 229 Ga. 422, 192 S.E.2d 144 (1972); Chapin v. Stewart, 71 Idaho 306, 230 P.2d 998 (1951); Givens, 387 S.W.2d 851; Raker v. G. C. Murphy Co., 358 Pa. 339, 58 A.2d 18 (1948); Cecil v. Dollar, 147 Tex. 541, 218 S.W.2d 448 (1949); Finley v. Bailey, 440 So. 2d 1019 (1983). See Annotation, Right of Cotenant to Acquire and Assert Adverse Title or Interest as Against Other Cotenants, 54 A.L.R. 874 (1928).

[209] E.g., Watson v. Edwards, 105 Cal. 70, 38 P. 527 (1894); Franklin v. Dragoo, 155 Ind. App. 682, 294 N.E.2d 165 (1973); Ford v. Jellico Grocery Co., 194 Ky. 552, 240 S.W. 65 (1922); Fuller v. Dennistoun, 164 Minn. 160, 204 N.W. 958 (1925).

[210] E.g., Hurley v. Hurley, 148 Mass. 444, 19 N.E. 545 (1889); Franklin, 155 Ind. App. 682, 294 N.E.2d 165; Hamilton v. Shaw, 286 S.C. 374, 334 S.E.2d 139 (S.C. Ct. App. 1985) (provided there is no fraud or collusion). Cf. Massey v. Prothero, 664 P.2d 1176 (Utah 1983) (tenant in common purchased at tax sale in his and his wife's name as joint tenants; both held to be fiduciaries for the other tenants in common).

[211] About half the states have a statutory right of redemption. It allows the foreclosed owner and, in some states. junior lienors to redeem the title to the property from the foreclosure sale. Nelson, Whitman, Burkhart & Freyermuth, Real Estate Finance Law § 8.4 (6th ed. 2015). See, e.g., Kuklo v. Starr, 660 So. 2d 979 (Ala. 1995) (cotenant redeemed after tax sale); Wood v. Wood, 51 Ark. App. 47, 908 S.W.2d 96 (1995) (tax sale); Pease v. Snyder, 169 Kan. 628, 220 P.2d 151 (1950) (execution sale); Carpenter v. Carpenter, 131 N.Y. 101, 29 N.E. 1013 (N.Y. 1892) (mortgage foreclosure sale); Rebelo v. Cardoso, 91 R.I. 153, 161 A.2d 806 (1960) (same); Stevahn v. Meidinger, 79 N.D. 323, 57 N.W.2d 1 (1952) (cotenant redeemed after mortgage foreclosure sale); Massey v. Prothero, 664 P.2d 1176 (Utah 1983) (tax sale). See also Foster, 437 So. 2d 528. Contra, Plant v. Plant, 171 Cal. 765, 154 P. 1058 (1916); Wenzel v. O'Neal, 222 S.W. 392 (Mo. 1920); Jackson v. Baird, 148 N.C. 29, 61 S.E. 632 (1908); Davis v. Solari, 132 Tenn. 225, 177 S.W. 939 (1915).

no basis exists to hold that any cotenant has a duty to purchase for the others' benefit.[212] However, this rationale ignores the basic assumption that cotenants who acquire their interests at the same time are subject to fiduciary duties so long as their cotenancy continues.

Some courts that require a cotenant who purchases at a tax sale to hold the title for the other cotenants' benefit reason that all cotenants have a duty to pay the property taxes and that one cotenant, after failing to discharge that duty, cannot "take advantage of his own wrong" and acquire the property for his sole benefit.[213] This argument is not entirely persuasive in jurisdictions where owners are not personally liable for property taxes, so that the government can recover them only by enforcing a lien on the property.[214] It is difficult to see why failing to discharge the tax lien by payment is more wrongful than failing to pay a mortgage when the cotenant is not personally liable for it.[215] The concept of a fiduciary duty provides a better basis for requiring the purchasing cotenant to hold the title acquired at a tax sale for all the cotenants' benefit. That duty provides the usual ground for similar holdings in cases involving one cotenant's purchase at a mortgage foreclosure or execution sale.

If one cotenant purchases the co-owned property at a mortgage foreclosure or execution sale in a jurisdiction that has no statutory right to redeem after the sale, does she acquire the title for the cotenants' benefit or solely for her own benefit? The cases give no clear answer to this question. The purchasing cotenant arguably should acquire the title for her sole benefit because she acquired it after termination of the cotenancy, which is the essential basis for recognizing a fiduciary relationship. However, if the purchasing cotenant persuaded the other cotenants not to bid at the sale by representing that she would protect their interests or if she engaged in other fraudulent or inequitable conduct in connection with the sale, she should take title subject to a constructive trust in favor of the other cotenants.[216] Moreover, when the cotenants are personally liable for a mortgage debt or a judgment, none of them should be allowed to improve their position by defaulting and then purchasing at the mortgage foreclosure or execution sale, because that would permit them to "take advantage of their own wrong."[217]

---

[212] E.g., Plant, 171 Cal. 765, 154 P. 1058; Wenzel, 222 S.W. 392; Jackson, 148 N.C. 29, 61 S.E. 632; Davis, 132 Tenn. 225, 177 S.W. 939.

[213] E.g., Batson v. Etheridge, 239 Ala. 535, 195 So. 873 (1940); Hollaway v. Berenzen, 208 Ark. 849, 188 S.W.2d 298 (1945).

[214] See Hamilton, 286 S.C. 374, 334 S.E.2d 139 (cotenant does not have duty to redeem common property from tax sale absent a contractual duty to do so). The tax lien is enforced by a public sale of the property.

[215] In most litigated cases, the cotenants are not personally obligated to the mortgage holder, because they acquired title by inheritance, devise, or purchase after the land was mortgaged and did not assume the mortgage debt.

[216] E.g., Caldwell v. Caldwell, 173 Ala. 216, 55 So. 515 (1911) (one cotenant fraudulently arranged with others not to bid at sale, representing that he would give them time to redeem); Cohen v. Friedman, 259 Ill. 416, 102 N.E. 815 (1913) (third person bought at sale under agreement with one cotenant to convey to that cotenant after statutory redemption period expired); Mosher v. Van Buskirk, 104 N.J. Eq. 89, 144 A. 446 (N.J. Ch. 1929) (collusion by purchasing cotenants as to infant cotenants); Carpenter, 131 N.Y. 101, 29 N.E. 1013 (foreclosure induced by cotenants in order to buy in and destroy interests of infant cotenants). See also Hamilton, 286 S.C. 374, 334 S.E.2d 139.

[217] E.g., Skolnick v. Skolnick, 131 Conn. 561, 41 A.2d 452 (1945); Hardin v. Council, 200 Ga. 822, 38 S.E.2d 549 (1946); Schilbach v. Schilbach, 171 Md. 405, 189 A. 432 (1937); Jolley v. Corry, 671 P.2d 139 (Utah 1983). A similar rule applies when a grantee assumes both the first and second mortgages, defaults on both, and then buys at the first mortgagee's foreclosure sale. In that case, the purchaser in equity holds title subject to the second mortgage though the second mortgagee's interest was foreclosed at law. See, e.g., Hilton v. Bissell, 1 Sand. Ch. 407 (N.Y. Ch. 1844).

To assert their ownership rights when the purchasing cotenant holds title for them, the other cotenants must, within a reasonable time after notice of the acquisition, either reimburse or offer to reimburse the purchaser for their pro rata shares of the purchase price.[218] The doctrines of repudiation, abandonment, laches, or estoppel will bar the other cotenants' rights if they fail to do so.[219]

If a fiduciary duty rule exists when one cotenant acquires title subject to a statutory right of redemption, any other cotenant can exercise that right within the statutory period. However, statutory redemption requires tender of the entire amount that the purchasing cotenant paid for the property.[220] In contrast, the fiduciary duty rule enables a cotenant to preserve his rights by contributing only his pro rata share of the purchase price,[221] and he generally has more time to do so than is available for statutory redemption.[222]

If one cotenant pays off and discharges an outstanding mortgage on the co-owned property, he has a lien on the property to secure his right to pro rata contributions from the other cotenants.[223] If one cotenant buys the mortgage, rather than the mortgaged land, his position will be substantially the same if a fiduciary relationship exists among the cotenants; he must hold the mortgage for the cotenants' benefit.[224] In either case, the other cotenants can preserve their undivided interests by reimbursing the purchaser within a reasonable time for their pro rata share of the expense.[225] If the buying cotenant brings suit to foreclose the mortgage, it is unclear whether the additional time allowed to the other cotenants for contribution would exceed the usual equitable redemption period before the sale.

Cotenants for a term of years who acquire their interests at the same time may invoke the fiduciary duty rule when one cotenant renews the lease or enters into a new

---

[218] E.g., Draper v. Sewell, 263 Ala. 250, 82 So. 2d 303 (1955); Smith v. Goethe, 159 Cal. 628, 115 P. 223 (1911); Wilson v. Linder, 21 Idaho 576, 123 P. 487 (1912); Mason v. Barrett, 295 Ky. 462, 174 S.W.2d 702 (1943); Toole v. Lawrence, 144 Neb. 779, 14 N.W.2d 607 (1944); Laura v. Christian, 88 N.M. 127, 537 P.2d 1389 (1975); Morris v. Roseberry, 46 W. Va. 24, 32 S.E. 1019 (1899). For additional cases, see Annotation, Right of Cotenant to Acquire and Assert Adverse Title or Interest as Against Other Cotenants, 54 A.L.R. 875, at 910 (1928); Annotation, Right of Cotenant to Acquire and Assert Adverse Title or Interest as Against Other Cotenant, 85 A.L.R. 1535, at 1538 (1933). But see Jolley, 671 P.2d 139 (where purchasing cotenant was only one personally liable for mortgage debt, she was not entitled to contribution).

[219] See cases cited supra note 218.

[220] See, e.g., Iowa Code Ann. § 628.11; Minn. Stat. Ann. § 580.23. For general discussion of statutory redemption from mortgage sales, see G. Nelson, D. Whitman, A. Burkhart & R.W. Freyermuth, Real Estate Finance Law §§ 8.4–8.7 (6th ed. 2015).

[221] See cases cited supra note 218.

[222] The general principle is that delay becomes unreasonable only when there is a change of position or a change in the property's condition that renders it inequitable to enforce the purchasing cotenant's fiduciary duty, such as when the doctrine of laches or estoppel is applicable. See, e.g., Mason, 295 Ky. 462, 174 S.W.2d 702 (more than 20 years' delay not unreasonable when no change of position or change in property's condition). But see Draper, 263 Ala. 250, 82 So. 2d 303 (3 or 4 years' delay is unreasonable); Savage v. Bradley, 149 Ala. 169, 43 So. 20 (1907) (redeeming cotenant has two-year statutory period to redeem).

[223] See supra § 5.8, at note 201; Kelly v. Carmichael, 221 Ala. 371, 129 So. 81 (1930); Eads v. Retherford, 114 Ind. 273, 16 N.E. 587 (1888); Kirsch v. Scandia Am. Bank, Crookston, 160 Minn. 269, 199 N.W. 881 (1924); Hahn v. Hahn, 297 S.W.2d 559 (Mo. 1957); Connell v. Welch, 101 Wis. 8, 76 N.W. 596 (1898).

[224] E.g., McArthur v. Dumaw, 328 Mich. 453, 43 N.W.2d 924 (1950); Jones v. Stanton, 11 Mo. 433 1848). But see Patterson v. Wilson, 203 Okla. 527, 223 P.2d 770 (1950).

[225] Though he owns only a fractional interest in the land, a cotenant who exercises an equitable right to redeem from a mortgage must pay the entire mortgage debt. E.g., Douglass v. Bishop, 27 Iowa 214 (1869); Lamson v. Drake, 105 Mass. 564 (1870); Hamilton v. Dobbs, 19 N.J. Eq. 227 (N.J. Ch. 1868); Wunderle v. Ellis, 212 Pa. 618, 62 A. 106 (1905).

lease, subject to the requirement that they pay their pro rata share of the rent for the new or extended lease.[226] A court also has applied this rule when one cotenant remainder holder acquires a term of years from the life tenant before the remainder becomes possessory.[227] However, this rule does not apply when a cotenant remainder holder acquires the life estate preceding the remainder[228] or when one co-lessee purchases the reversion.[229] In these situations, neither the life estate nor the reversion is a hostile interest vis-a-vis the nonpurchasing cotenant. The fiduciary duty rule also does not apply when one cotenant buys another cotenant's interest, either directly or at a tax, mortgage foreclosure, or execution sale or from a third party who purchased it at the sale.[230]

§ 5.10 PARTITION—IN GENERAL

Any kind of concurrent estate terminates and becomes an individual ownership estate if one person acquires all the undivided interests by conveyance, devise, or inheritance. The undivided interests merge to form a single estate.[231] Most often, however, concurrent estates terminate and convert into individual estates by partition, either voluntary or by court action.[232] A partition can be a physical division of the property (partition in kind) or a sale of the property and a division of the proceeds (partition by sale). A voluntary partition can be effected by an exchange of deeds among the cotenants, with all the cotenants joining in each deed to divide the land into separate parcels.

Before the Statute of Frauds, a parol agreement for partition was valid if each cotenant took exclusive possession of a separate portion of the common property pursuant to the agreement.[233] After enactment of the Statute of Frauds, courts have held that a parol agreement for partition is void at law.[234] However, they have upheld parol agreements for partition based on either part performance or estoppel when the cotenants have taken possession of separate portions of the property pursuant to the

---

[226] E.g., Thayer v. Leggett, 229 N.Y. 152, 128 N.E. 133 (1920); Weaver v. Akin, 48 W. Va. 456, 37 S.E. 600 (1900).

[227] Givens v. Givens, 387 S.W.2d 851 (Ky. 1965).

[228] E.g., Frank v. Frank, 305 Ill. 181, 137 N.E. 151 (1922); McLaughlin v. McLaughlin, 80 Md. 115, 30 A. 607 (1894).

[229] E.g., Ramberg v. Wahlstrom, 140 Ill. 182, 29 N.E. 727 (1892); Kershaw v. Simpson, 46 Wash. 313, 89 P. 889 (1907).

[230] E.g., Brittin v. Handy, 20 Ark. 381 (1859); Ziebarth v. Donaldson, 150 Minn. 308, 185 N.W. 377 (1921); Murray v. Murray, 159 Minn. 111, 198 N.W. 307 (1924); Snell v. Harrison, 104 Mo. 158, 16 S.W. 152 (1891); Colby v. Colby, 96 N.H. 452, 79 A.2d 343 (1951); Douglas v. Jepson, 88 Wash. App. 342, 945 P.2d 244 (1997) (direct purchase); Sharples Corp. v. Sinclair Wyoming Oil Co., 62 Wyo. 341, 167 P.2d 29 (1946). A fortiori, the rule is inapplicable if one cotenant purchases at a sale for nonpayment of taxes assessed only on another cotenant's undivided interest. E.g., Bennet v. North Colorado Springs Land & Improvement Co., 23 Colo. 470, 48 P. 812 (1897); Jesberg v. Klinger, 187 Kan. 582, 358 P.2d 770 (1961).

[231] See 2 Blackstone, supra note 7, at *186, *195; 13 R.C.L. § 1162.

[232] See generally 2 Am. L. Prop., supra note 1, at §§ 6. 19–.26.

[233] Coke, supra note 12, at *169a; Thomas v. Gyles, 2 Vern. 232, 23 Eng. Rep. 750 (1691). The transfer of possession was held to constitute a livery of seisin so as to transfer an interest in severalty.

[234] E.g., Boyers v. Boyers, 310 Ky. 727, 221 S.W.2d 657 (1949); Duncan v. Sylvester, 16 Me. 388 (1839); Ballou v. Hale, 47 N.H. 347 (1867); Miller v. Miller, 34 N.C. App. 209, 237 S.E.2d 552 (1977); Va. Coal & Iron Co. v. Richmond, 128 Va. 258, 104 S.E. 805 (1920). But see, e.g., Shepard v. Rinks, 78 Ill. 188 (1875); Sanger v. Merritt, 120 N.Y. 109, 24 N.E. 386 (1890); Hughes v. Kay, 194 Or. 519, 242 P.2d 788 (1952); Reynolds v. Mangrum, 250 S.W.2d 283 (Tex. App. 1952) (cited with approval in Stradt v. First United Methodist Church of Huntington, 573 S.W.2d 186 (Tex. 1978)).

parol agreement and have made improvements or otherwise materially changed position in reliance on it.[235]

When the common property cannot be divided into equally valuable portions, the cotenants who receive more valuable portions can make money payments, called "owelty," to the other cotenants.[236] Or the cotenants can agree to sell the common property and divide the proceeds.

If cotenants cannot agree on a voluntary partition, any cotenant, except a tenant by the entirety, can bring an action to partition. A court normally will grant partition, unless the cotenants have agreed not to do so.[237] Although a partition action was originally available only to coparceners,[238] a statute of Henry VIII made it available to tenants in common and joint tenants.[239] Thereafter, partition could be at law or in equity,[240] but partition in equity became the exclusive form in England after 1833.[241] In the United States, the old distinction between partitions at law and in equity appears to have little current significance. However, in some states that statutorily authorize partition, equitable partition is still available when special equities require protection.[242] Partition by judicial action will be discussed more fully in the next two sections.

---

[235] E.g., Ellis v. Campbell, 84 Ark. 584, 106 S.W. 939 (1907) (part performance); Duffy v. Duffy, 243 Ill. 476, 90 N.E. 697 (1909) (same); Herrman v. Golden, 93 Ill. App. 3d 937, 49 Ill. Dec. 543, 418 N.E.2d 187 (1981); Cooper v. Davis, 226 Md. 371, 174 A.2d 144 (1961) (same); Martin v. Taylor, 521 S.W.2d 581 (Tenn. 1975) (same). See also Swift v. Swift, 121 Ark. 197, 180 S.W. 742 (1915) (estoppel); Brown v. Wheeler, 17 Conn. 345, 44 Am. Dec. 550 (1845) (same). In some cases in which the court held that a parol partition agreement is valid at law, the court could have based its holding on either part performance or estoppel. E.g., Wood v. Fleet, 36 N.Y. 499 (1867).

[236] Gonzalez v. Gonzalez, 174 Cal. 588, 163 P. 993 (1917); Newsome v. Harrell, 168 N.C. 295, 84 S.E. 337 (1915); Schnell v. Schnell, 346 N.W.2d 713 (N.D. 1984) (by statute); Wright v. Wright, 131 Ill. App. 3d 46, 86 Ill. Dec. 342, 475 N.E.2d 556 (1985). Pronounced "o-el-ty."

[237] E.g., Caruso v. Plunk, 574 So. 2d 1230 (Fla. Dist. Ct. App. 1991) (right to partition is absolute unless waived); Gore v. Beren, 254 Kan. 418, 867 P.2d 330 (1994); Albro v. Allen, 434 Mich. 271, 454 N.W.2d 85 (1990) (life estates in common); Swartz v. Becker, 246 N.J. Super. 406, 587 A.2d 1295 (App. Div. 1991); First Trust Co. v. Holt, 361 N.W.2d 476 (Minn. Ct. App. 1985); Prickett v. Moore, 684 P.2d 1191 (Okla. 1984). In some states, statutes or judicial decisions may limit the right to partition. See, e.g., Unif. Condominium Act § 2–107 (2017) (barring partition of common elements); Mulsow v. Gerber Energy Corp., 237 Kan. 58, 697 P.2d 1269 (1985) (refusing partition if it would cause fraud or oppression); Vincent v. Gustke, 175 W. Va. 521, 336 S.E.2d 33 (1985) (statute). A tenancy by the entirety cannot be judicially partitioned. Jones v. Conwell, 227 Va. 176, 314 S.E.2d 61 (1984). But judicial partition is available after divorce has converted a tenancy by the entirety into a tenancy in common. Butler v. Butler, 122 Mich. App. 361, 332 N.W.2d 488 (1983); cf. Salyers v. Good, 443 So. 2d 152 (Fla. Dist. Ct. App. 1983) (denying partition after divorce when decree gave one spouse possession).

[238] See supra § 5.2.

[239] 31 Hen. 8, cl. 1 (1539); 32 id., cl. 32 (1540).

[240] The English Chancery Court assumed jurisdiction over partitions at an early date when physical division of the property without regard to the parties' special equities would result in injustice. See 1 A. Freeman, Cotenancy and Partition § 432 (2d ed. 1886); 2 J. Story, Commentaries on Equity Jurisprudence § 872 (14th ed. 1918); Hill v. Reno, 112 Ill. 154, 159 (1883).

[241] 3 & 4 Will. 4, c. 27, § 36 (1833).

[242] Partition in equity is "made exclusive by statute in some of the states; and in all of them courts of equity or courts with equitable powers have jurisdiction over partition suits and exercise that jurisdiction to the practical exclusion of the ancient common law action." 2 Am. L. Prop., supra note 1, § 6.21, at 95. See, e.g., Swartz v. Becker, 246 N.J. Super. 406, 587 A.2d 1295 (App. Div. 1991) (allowing partition both statutorily and under equitable power of courts); Lohmiller v. Weidenbaugh, 503 Pa. 329, 469 A.2d 578 (1983) (explaining that statutory action was "neither the sole nor exclusive remedy"). Cf. Eller v. Eller, 168 A.D.2d 414, 562 N.Y.S.2d 540 (App. Div. 1990) (questioning whether equitable defense available in statutory action).

Cotenants in fee simple sometimes expressly or impliedly agree that none of them or their successors will have the right to compel a partition by court action.[243] This agreement imposes a restraint on alienation that would ordinarily be void under the common law rule against restraints on alienation.[244] But a court will uphold an agreement prohibiting judicial partition of a concurrent estate in fee simple if it is enforceable in equity and is limited to a reasonable time, which may be as long as the period permitted by the Rule Against Perpetuities ("lives in being at the creation of the interests, plus a period in gross not exceeding twenty-one years").[245] Courts also have upheld disabling restraints on judicial partition imposed by the creator of a concurrent estate if they are limited to a reasonable time.[246] Indeed, courts sometimes deny partition when it would defeat a purpose of the creator of the concurrent estate.[247] And some states statutorily authorize the creator of a concurrent estate to prohibit judicial partition.[248]

Condominium enabling legislation usually prohibits any action by individual unit owners to compel partition of the common elements of the condominium development.[249] Presumably, statutory prohibitions against partition are valid and are effective to prevent partition while the condominium exists. Some state statutes address the issue of validity by expressly providing that neither the rule against restraints on alienation nor the Rule Against Perpetuities applies to this condominium restriction.[250]

Generally, only concurrent interest owners who have actual possession or an immediate right to possess can bring an action for partition.[251] However, when cotenants have leased their concurrent estate, they can still bring an action to partition their

---

[243] N. N.H. Mental Health & Dev'm'l Servs., Inc. v. Cannell, 134 N.H. 519, 593 A.2d 1161 (1991); Bessen v. Glatt, 170 A.D.2d 924, 566 N.Y.S.2d 750 (App. Div. 1991).

[244] See supra §§ 2.2–2.3.

[245] Ex parte Watts, 130 N.C. 237, 41 S.E. 289 (1902). Other cases in which the court held that the period of the restraint was "reasonable" and, therefore, valid include Condrey v. Condrey, 92 So. 2d 423 (Fla. 1957) (lives in being), superseded in part by Fla. Stat. § 61.075(1)(h) (2018); Rosenberg v. Rosenberg, 413 Ill. 343, 108 N.E.2d 766 (1952) (same); Porter v. Tracey, 179 Iowa 1295, 162 N.W. 800 (1917) (not more than 21 years); Michalski v. Michalski, 50 N.J. Super. 454, 142 A.2d 645 (App. Div. 1958) (lives in being but "changed circumstances" may make agreement unenforceable); Bessen v. Glatt, 170 A.D.2d 924, 566 N.Y.S.2d 750 (App. Div. 1991) (purchase option limited to cotenants' lives). See also Marchetti v. Karpowich, 446 Pa. Super. 509, 667 A.2d 724 (1995) (allowing partition when conditions to agreement limiting partition have not been met); Schultheis v. Schultheis, 36 Wash. App. 588, 675 P.2d 634 (1984) (fixing a "reasonable time" when no time is specified).

[246] E.g., Harvey v. Sessoms, 284 Ga. 75, 663 S.E.2d 210 (2008); Kepley v. Overton, 74 Ind. 448 (1881) ("kept together until a co-tenant reached a stated age"); Freeland v. Andersen, 114 Neb. 822, 211 N.W. 167 (1926) (lives in being); Griffith v. Kirsch, 2005 Pa. Super 361, 886 A.2d 249 (same).

[247] E.g., Carter v. Weowna Beach Cmty. Corp., 71 Wash. 2d 498, 429 P.2d 201 (1967) (dismissing action that would defeat purpose of cotenancy to partition common area in subdivision).

[248] E.g., Ark. Code Ann. § 18–60–413 (2018) (only when created by will); Mo. Ann. Stat. § 528.130 (West 2018).

[249] See, e.g., Unif. Common Interest Ownership Act § 2–107(f) (2008) (as amended in 2014); Unif. Condominium Act § 2–107 (2017) (no partition of common elements); 7 R. Powell, supra note 1, § 50.07[3][c].

[250] E.g., Mo. Ann. Stat. § 448.210 (West 2018); Utah Code Ann. § 57–8–28 (West 2018).

[251] E.g., Bowman v. Bennett, 250 N.W.2d 47 (Iowa 1977), modified by Iowa Code § 557.9; Wagner v. Maskey, 353 N.W.2d 891 (Iowa App. 1984); Baker v. Baker, 97 N.J. Eq. 306, 127 A. 657 (Super. Ct. Ch. Div. 1925); Phillips v. Wells, 147 Va. 1030, 133 S.E. 581 (1926). But a cotenant's creditor is sometimes allowed to bring a partition action. See, e.g., Jones v. Conwell, 227 Va. 176, 314 S.E.2d 61 (1984); Vincent v. Gustke, 175 W. Va. 521, 336 S.E.2d 33 (1985); Harris v. Crowder, 174 W. Va. 83, 322 S.E.2d 854 (1984). A cotenant in a life estate can partition his and the other life tenants' shares but cannot force partition among remainder holders. Peters v. Robinson, 636 A.2d 926 (Del. 1994).

reversion, though they do not have the right to possess.[252] Additionally, some states statutorily provide that future interest owners can partition when a life estate or defeasible fee estate is outstanding.[253] These statutes vary considerably, and some of them include important limitations on the right to compel partition. For example, many statutes authorize partition only if the future interests are indefeasibly vested.[254] Even when a statute does not include this limitation, in no reported decision has a court ordered partition of future interests that are contingent or vested subject to defeasance.

When partition of future interests is statutorily authorized, a life tenant clearly cannot be compelled to accept either a part of the property or a money payment in lieu of his life estate. The partition must be made subject to the life estate, unless the life tenant agrees to participate.[255] A life estate owner who also owns an undivided interest in the reversion or remainder in fee simple can compel partition.[256] If the partition is in kind, the life tenant will get his fractional share in possession in fee simple, and his life estate will continue in the other future interest owners' share. If the partition is by sale, the life tenant's consent to it enables a sale of the entire fee simple and an immediate division of all the proceeds.[257] Based on a statute that authorizes partition between co-owners of future interests, a life tenant who has an undivided interest for life and an undivided interest in the future interest in fee simple can compel a partition in kind or by sale and an immediate division of the proceeds.[258]

§ 5.11 PARTITION ACTIONS—PARTIES AND FINAL ACCOUNTING

In a partition action, all owners whose interest will be affected must be joined either as plaintiffs or defendants.[259] If a cotenant's undivided interest is subject to an executory contract of sale, the vendor is a necessary party[260] and the purchaser is at least a proper party.[261] Some states statutorily require joinder of the contract purchaser.[262]

---

[252] E.g., Watson v. Watson, 150 Mass. 84, 22 N.E. 438 (1889); Swanson v. Swanson, 856 N.W.2d 705 (Minn. 2014); Peterman v. Kingsley, 140 Wis. 666, 123 N.W. 137 (1909). The tenant has no basis to object, because the partition will not affect the leasehold estate.

[253] See 3 R. Powell, supra note 1, § 21.05 for a detailed listing and discussion of these statutes.

[254] For a listing of these statutes, see id. Under these statutes, only indefeasibly vested remainders, reversions in fee simple, and possibly executory interests that are certain to become fee simple absolute can be partitioned. See discussion, id. ¶ 290 at nn.13–19.

[255] E.g., Powe v. Payne, 208 Ala. 527, 94 So. 587 (1922); Tolson v. Bryan, 130 Md. 338, 100 A. 366 (1917); Noyes v. Stewart, 361 Mo. 475, 235 S.W.2d 333 (1950). When the life tenant also owns an undivided interest in the remainder, the other remainder holder does not have the right to partition the life estate unless the right is expressly statutorily conferred. Compare Feiner v. Wolgemuth, 10 A.D. 175, 199 N.Y.S.2d 351 (App. Div. 1960), with Tower v. Tower, 141 Ind. 223, 40 N.E. 747 (1895).

[256] E.g., Chapman v. York, 212 Ala. 540, 103 So. 567 (1925); Shafer v. Covey, 90 Kan. 588, 135 P. 676 (1913).

[257] 3 R. Powell, supra note 1, § 21.05.

[258] E.g., Cottingham v. Love, 211 Ala. 152, 99 So. 907 (1924); Weedon v. Power, 202 Ky. 542, 260 S.W. 385 (1924); Bosley v. Burk, 154 Md. 27, 139 A. 543 (1927). If no such statute exists, only the concurrent life estate can be partitioned. E.g., Brown v. Brown, 67 W. Va. 251, 67 S.E. 596, 28 L.R.A.N.S. 125 (1910).

[259] E.g., Curtis v. Reilly, 188 Iowa 1217, 177 N.W. 535 (1920); Benedict v. Beurmann, 90 Mich. 396, 51 N.W. 461 (1892); Lohmiller v. Weidenbaugh, 503 Pa. 329, 469 A.2d 578 (1983).

[260] E.g., Jones v. Napier, 93 Ga. 582, 20 S.E. 41 (1894); Crippen v. Spies, 255 A.D. 411, 7 N.Y.S.2d 704 (App. Div. 1938).

[261] E.g., Howard v. Morrissey, 71 Misc. 267, 130 N.Y.S. 322 (Cty. Ct. 1911).

[262] See, e.g., Rich v. Smith, 26 Cal. App. 775, 148 P. 545 (1915).

A lessee of a cotenant's undivided interest is a necessary party in a partition action,[263] but a lessee of the entire property is not because the partition will not disturb the leasehold estate.[264] For the same reason, a mortgagee or other lienor is not a necessary party.[265] Statutes often require joinder of the holder of a mortgage or other lien on a single cotenant's interest in the common property.[266] Absent such a statute, the cases are divided on whether the holder of a mortgage or other lien on a single cotenant's interest is a necessary party.[267] The lienor should be a necessary party because the court's order for partition will determine the part of the land to which the lien attaches.

Because partition of a concurrent life estate cannot affect the future interests following it,[268] those future interest owners are not necessary parties, unless a statute expressly requires that they be joined.[269] Owners of contingent interests, such as dower or curtesy, generally need not be joined in a partition action unless required by statute.[270]

In the final accounting incident to every partition action, all the cotenants may be charged for rents and profits that they received in excess of their pro rata share,[271] and, if one cotenant excluded the others, for the mesne profits (usually the fair rental value).[272] Any cotenant may also be charged for waste that he committed.[273] Conversely, each cotenant may get a credit for sums she expended beyond her pro rata share for

---

[263] All persons whose interests in the common property will be affected by partition must be joined, so they will be bound by the court's judgment or decree. But see Lichtenfels v. Bridgeview Coal Co., 344 Pa. Super. 257, 268, 496 A.2d 782, 788 (1985) (requiring notice only if lessee has "sufficient" interest in land).

[264] The order for partition should be made subject to the lease. E.g., McLear v. Balmat, 194 A.D. 827, 186 N.Y.S. 180 (App. Div.), aff'd, 231 N.Y. 548, 132 N.E. 883, appeal withdrawn, 231 N.Y. 599, 132 N.E. 904 (1921); Consol. Gas Supply Corp. v. Riley, 161 W. Va. 782, 247 S.E.2d 712 (1978) (citing W. Va. Code § 37–4–7).

[265] E.g., Graham v. Graham, 202 Ala. 56, 79 So. 450 (1918); Tompkins v. Kyle, 95 W. Va. 584, 122 S.E. 150 (1924). But see, e.g., Neale v. Stamm, 100 N.J. Eq. 35, 135 A. 345 (Super. Ct. Ch. Div. 1926) (mortgagee of entire property, rather than of an undivided interest, not a proper party).

[266] See, e.g., Marx v. State Bank of Chicago, 294 Ill. 568, 128 N.E. 475 (1920) (mortgagee); Metcalf v. Hoopingardner, 45 Iowa 510 (1877) (judgment lienor); cf., e.g., Grogan v. Grogan, 177 S.W. 649 (Mo. 1915) (construing similar statute as making holders of mortgages or other liens at least proper parties).

[267] Compare Bradley v. Fuller, 40 Mass. (23 Pick.) 1 (1839) (necessary) and Whitton v. Whitton, 38 N.H. 127, 135, 75 Am. Dec. 163 (1859) (mortgagee necessary only because partition may "seriously affect or impair his security"), with Graham, 202 Ala. 56, 79 So 450 (unnecessary); Baltzell v. Daniel, 111 Fla. 303, 149 So. 639, 93 A.L.R. 1259 (1933) (same); Baldwin v. Baldwin, 347 Ill. 351, 179 N.E. 859 (1932) (same).

[268] E.g., Jordan v. Walker, 201 Ala. 248, 77 So. 838 (1917); Snapp v. Gallehue, 333 Ill. 138, 164 N.E. 222 (1928); Albro v. Allen, 434 Mich. 271, 454 N.W.2d 85 (1990).

[269] See, e.g., Cal. Civ. Proc. § 872.510 (requiring joinder of all known or reasonably apparent interest claimants); Colo. Rev. Stat. Ann. § 38–28–103 (West 2018) (requiring joinder of "all persons having any interest . . . contingent, or otherwise"); Mo. Rev. Stat. § 528.060 (West 2018) (requiring joinder of all interests).

[270] E.g., Brady v. Paine, 391 Ill. 596, 63 N.E.2d 721 (1945) (dower); Turner v. Turner, 185 Va. 505, 39 S.E.2d 299 (1946) (dower); Hazelbaker v. Reber, 123 Kan. 131, 254 P. 407 (1927) (curtesy); Helmick v. Kraft, 84 W. Va. 159, 99 S.E. 325 (1919) (curtesy). Where curtesy initiate still exists as at common law, the cotenant's husband must be joined. E.g., Appeal of Welch, 126 Pa. 297, 17 A. 623 (1889); Helmick v. Kraft, 84 W. Va. 159, 99 S.E. 325 (1919).

[271] See, § 5.7, supra. Recent cases include England v. Alicea, 827 N.E.2d 555 (Ind. Ct. App. 2005); Hawkins v. Hawkins, 11 Ohio Misc. 2d 18, 464 N.E.2d 199 (Common Pleas. 1984). A court will not order reimbursement if no demand for an accounting is made. Bessen v. Glatt, 170 A.D.2d 924, 566 N.Y.S.2d 750 (1991).

[272] See Stylianopoulos v. Stylianopoulos, 17 Mass. App. Ct. 64, 455 N.E.2d 477 (1983), rev. denied, 390 Mass. 1107, 459 N.E.2d 824 (1984). But see Sanborn v. Johns, 19 Mass. App. Ct. 721, 724, 477 N.E.2d 196, 199 (1985) ("[The] choice of charges to be made . . . varies according to circumstances" and "rent may or may not be deducted from the share of the occupant"). See also supra § 5.2.

[273] See supra § 5.7.

necessary repairs,[274] improvements (to the extent they increased the property's value),[275] property taxes, interest and principal payments on a mortgage or other lien,[276] insurance for the common benefit,[277] or money paid to protect the title.[278] A cotenant is not entitled to credit for the value of his personal services in managing and caring for the property, unless the other cotenants agree.[279] However, in a partition in kind, a cotenant who increased the property's value by making improvements at her own expense will receive the portion of the property with the improvements, if possible.[280]

After the final accounting has established each cotenant's charges and credits, the proceeds from a partition by sale are distributed accordingly.[281] In a partition by kind, a former cotenant's claim for the balance that his cotenants owe him is usually secured by a lien on their parcels.[282] He can get a personal judgment against them only if they were personally liable for the expenses that he paid.[283]

---

[274] See supra § 5.8; Willett v. Clark, 542 N.E.2d 1354 (Ind. Ct. App. 1989); Hawkins v. Hawkins, 11 Ohio Misc. 2d 18, 464 N.E.2d 199 (Common Pleas 1984).

[275] E.g., Staples v. Pearson, 230 Ala. 62, 159 So. 488 (1935); Mastin v. Mastin's Adm'rs, 243 Ky. 830, 50 S.W.2d 77 (1932); Buschmeyer v. Eikermann, 378 S.W.2d 468 (Mo. 1964) (awarding cost or increase in value, whichever is less); Knowlton v. Knowlton, 673 S.W.2d 502 (Mo. App. 1984) (recognizing general rule but limiting recovery by just and equitable considerations). Blue v. Blue, 2018 S.D. 58, 916 N.W.2d 131 (2018); Cleveland v. Milner, 141 Tex. 120, 170 S.W.2d 472 (1943); White v. Pleasants, 227 Va. 508, 317 S.E.2d 489 (1984) (recognizing general rule but denying compensation because improver was lessee with actual notice of an outstanding interest belonging to someone other than the lessor cotenant); Quillen v. Tull, 226 Va. 498, 312 S.E.2d 278 (1984) (preferring enhancement, rather than cost, as basis for compensation); Willett, 542 N.E.2d 1354 (Ind. Ct. App. 1989); see also supra § 5.8.

[276] See supra § 5.8; England v. Alicea, 827 N.E.2d 555 (Ind. Ct. App. 2005); Hawkins v. Hawkins, 11 Ohio Misc.2d 18, 464 N.E.2d 199 (Common Pleas 1984).

[277] Fenton v. Wendell, 116 Mich. 45, 74 N.W. 384 (1898); Clapp v. Hunter, 52 A.D. 253, 65 N.Y.S. 411 (App. Div. 1900).

[278] E.g., Allen v. Allen, 363 S.W.2d 312 (Tex. App. 1962); Blackwell v. McLean, 9 Wash. 301, 37 P. 317 (1894); see also In re Marriage of Leversee, 156 Cal. App. 3d 891, 897, 203 Cal. Rptr. 481, 485 (1984) (allowing "equitable compensatory adjustment to compensate [wife] for her use of separate funds for the down payment on the [community property] residence").

[279] E.g., Goodenow v. Ewer, 16 Cal. 461 (1860) (rental services); Shipman v. Shipman, 65 N.J. Eq. 556, 56 A. 694 (Super. Ct. Ch. Div. 1904) (legal services); Myers v. Bolton, 157 N.Y. 393, 52 N.E. 114 (1898) (rental services), reh'g denied, 158 N.Y. 665, 52 N.E. 1125 (1899); cf. Baird v. Moore, 50 N.J. Super. 156, 174, 141 A.2d 324, 333 (App. Div. 1958) (denying credit for personal services as such but taking them into account as part of the "total factual picture").

[280] E.g., Hall v. Hall, 250 Ala. 702, 35 So. 681 (1948); Farley v. Stacey, 177 Ky. 109, 197 S.W. 636, 1 A.L.R. 1181 (1917); Fair v. Fair, 121 Mass. 559 (1877); Lawrence v. Donovan, 207 Mont. 130, 673 P.2d 130 (1983). Occasionally, if some of the improvements are allotted to cotenants who contributed nothing to their cost, courts require them to pay their pro rata shares of the increased value of the common property to the improving cotenant. E.g., Michael v. Davis, 372 So. 2d 304 (1979) (requiring improving cotenant to have good faith belief that he was sole owner); Swift v. Swift, 121 Ark. 197, 180 S.W. 742 (1915). Courts also can grant additional land to the improving cotenant when the improvements cannot be allotted entirely to him. E.g., Arnold v. De Booy, 161 Minn. 255, 201 N.W. 437 (1924).

[281] E.g., Killmer v. Wuchner, 79 Iowa 722, 45 N.W. 299, 8 L.R.A. 289 (1890) (improvements); Moore v. Thorp, 16 R.I. 655, 19 A. 321, 7 L.R.A. 731 (1889) (same); Ward v. Ward's Heirs, 40 W. Va. 611, 21 S.E. 746, 29 L.R.A. 449 (1895) (same). In the more frequent modern cases in which the property is sold, the adjusting these items is a simple matter of accounting in distributing the proceeds. 2 Am. L. Prop., supra note 1, § 6.26, at 118.

[282] E.g., Kelly v. Carmichael, 221 Ala. 371, 129 So. 81 (1930); Cocks v. Simmons, 55 Ark. 104, 17 S.W. 594 (1891); Hogan v. McMahon, 115 Md. 195, 80 A. 695 (1911); Giles v. Sheridan, 179 Neb. 257, 137 N.W.2d 828 (1965).

[283] E.g., Scanlon v. Parish, 85 Conn. 379, 82 A. 969 (1912). See 2 Am. L. Prop., supra note 1, § 6.17, at 77, § 6.26, at 118. But see Goergen v. Maar, 2 A.D.2d 276, 153 N.Y.S.2d 826 (App. Div. 1956).

§ 5.12 PARTITION ACTIONS—PHYSICAL DIVISION OR SALE AND DIVISION OF PROCEEDS

In a partition action, the court generally first renders an interlocutory judgment that specifies the share of each cotenant[284] and any other party properly joined in the action.[285] The court also determines whether the property should be physically divided or sold and the proceeds divided.

When a deed or will creates a concurrent estate but does not specify each cotenant's share, the presumption is that they have equal undivided interests.[286] If the creating instrument expressly provides for unequal interests, it necessarily creates a tenancy in common, because joint tenancy shares must be equal. If the tenancy in common arises by intestate succession, the cotenants' shares may be equal or unequal, depending on the intestate succession statute and the cotenants' relationships. For example, a surviving spouse and children may take unequal shares. But even when the shares are equal during the continuance of the cotenancy, the presumption of equality may be rebutted in determining the share of each cotenant in a partition action, whether it is a joint tenancy[287] or a tenancy in common.[288]

In earlier times, courts always ordered a partition in kind, unless all the cotenants consented to a sale.[289] Courts still have a preference, often strong, for physical division.[290] But all states now statutorily authorize partition by sale when the property

---

[284] E.g., Stoffer v. Verhellen, 195 Cal. 317, 231 P. 233 (1925); Provident Life & Trust Co. v. Wood, 96 W. Va. 516, 123 S.E. 276, 41 A.L.R. 570 (1924); Daughtrey v. Daughtrey, 474 So. 2d 598 (Miss. 1985) (determining shares unnecessary before order for sale but is better practice). The court may appoint commissioners to determine the shares. E.g., Lawrence v. Donovan, 207 Mont. 130, 673 P.2d 130 (1983).

[285] E.g., Arnold v. Arnold, 308 Ill. 365, 139 N.E. 592 (1923) (leaseholder).

[286] E.g., People v. Varel, 351 Ill. 96, 184 N.E. 209 (1932) (tenancy in common); Schroeder v. Todd, 249 Iowa 139, 86 N.W.2d 101 (1957) (same); Anderson v. Anderson, 137 Kan. 833, 22 P.2d 471 (same), reh'g denied, 138 Kan. 77, 23 P.2d 474 (1933). When the creating instrument clearly indicates that a joint tenancy is intended, the presumption of equality cannot be rebutted while the joint tenancy continues, but it is not controlling when a partition action is begun. See Jezo v. Jezo, 23 Wis. 2d 399, 127 N.W.2d 246, reh'g denied 23 Wis. 2d 399, 129 N.W.2d 195 (1964).

[287] Langevin v. York, 111 Nev. 1481, 907 P.2d 981 (1995) (holding unequal contributions to purchase price may cause unequal partition of joint tenancy); Jezo, 23 Wis. 2d at 406, 127 N.W.2d at 250 (factoring in unequal shares of purchase price or unequal cost of improvements causes unequal partition of joint tenancy); see also Sebold v. Sebold, 444 F.2d 864 (D.C. Cir. 1971) (though tenants by entirety have equal shares, upon dissolution of marriage, distribution is not necessarily equal).

[288] Schroeder v. Todd, 249 Iowa 139, 145, 86 N.W.2d 101, 104 (1957); Clark v. Dady, 131 S.W.3d 382 (Mo. App. 2004). See generally L.S.T., Annotation, Presumption and Proof as to Shares of Respective Grantees or Transferees in Conveyance or Transfer to Two or More Persons as Tenants in Common, Silent in that Regard, 156 A.L.R. 515 (1945).

[289] E.g., Chuck v. Gomes, 56 Haw. 171, 532 P.2d 657 (1975); Bragg v. Lyon, 93 N.C. 151 (1885). See generally 1 A. Freeman, supra note 240, §§ 536–49; 4 J. Pomeroy, Equity Jurisprudence § 1390 (Spencer Symons ed., 5th ed. 1941); 2 H. Tiffany, Real Property § 479, at 324, 325 n.44 (Basil Jones ed., 3d ed. 1939); 2 Am. L. Prop., supra note 1, § 6.26 n.5.

[290] E.g., McNeely v. Bone, 287 Ark. 339, 698 S.W.2d 512 (1985) (expert testimony established that equitable physical division was impossible); Wilcox v. Willard Shopping Ctr. Assocs., 208 Conn. 318, 544 A.2d 1207 (1988) (reiterating strong preference for physical division); Filipetti v. Filipetti, 2 Conn. App. 456, 479 A.2d 1229, cert. denied, 194 Conn. 804, 482 A.2d 709 (1984); Wright v. Wright, 131 Ill. App. 3d 46, 86 Ill. Dec. 342, 475 N.E.2d 556 (1985) (partition by sale proper only when property cannot be divided among cotenants, including an unequal division of property with owelty); Swartz v. Becker, 246 N.J. Super. 406, 587 A.2d 1295 (App. Div. 1991); Chamberlain v. Beam, 63 N.C. App. 377, 304 S.E.2d 770 (1983); Barth v. Barth, 901 P.2d 232 (Okla. App. 1995) (partition in kind with owelty); Lay v. Raymond, 265 Or. App. 488, 336 P.3d 550 (2014); Dickinson v. Killheffer, 497 A.2d 307 (R.I. 1985) (affirming order for physical division despite zoning problems and unequal frontage); Gartner v. Temple, 2014 S.D. 74, 855 N.W.2d 846 (2014) (factors to determine whether partition in kind would result in great prejudice).

cannot be fairly and equitably divided.[291] For example, the common property may be a relatively small parcel of land that is improved with a single structure[292] or an unimproved parcel that would substantially diminish in value if divided.[293] In some cases, inequality in the value of the parcels allocated to the former cotenants can be corrected by money payments, called "owelty," as in cases of voluntary partition.[294] But most partition actions today result in a court order for sale of the entire property and division of the proceeds.[295]

The judgment in a partition action binds all persons who were joined as parties.[296] When the entire property is subject to a mortgage or similar lien, a physical property division leaves each separate portion of the property still encumbered by the security interest.[297] However, if the holder of a mortgage or other lien on the entire property is joined in the partition action, the court may order a sale free and clear of the encumbrance and provide that the security interest will attach to the sale proceeds.

When only one cotenant's undivided interest is subject to a mortgage or similar lien, the results are similar to the results when the security interest covers all the cotenants' shares. For a partition in kind, the mortgage or other lien is not limited to the property that the debtor cotenant receives. For a partition by sale, the entire property remains

[291] E.g., Chuck, 56 Haw. 171, 532 P.2d 657; McConnell v. McConnell, 449 So. 2d 785 (Miss. 1984) (ordering sale when parties admitted physical partition infeasible though reasonable price might not be obtained); Nordhausen v. Christner, 215 Neb. 367, 338 N.W.2d 754 (1983) (determining sale was proper because partition in kind would result in complex settlement that granted parties rights they did not want or could not use); Cavanagh v. Cavanagh, 468 A.2d 286 (R.I. 1983); White v. Pleasants, 227 Va. 508, 317 S.E.2d 489 (1984); Wilkins v. Wilkins, 175 W. Va. 787, 338 S.E.2d 388 (1985), superseded in part by W. Va. Code § 37–4–3. Courts have generally held that they have no power to order one cotenant to sell the concurrently owned land to another cotenant. George v. Tanner, 108 Idaho 40, 696 P.2d 891 (1985); Hay v. Hay, 885 N.E.2d 21 (2008); see also Jolly v. Knopf, 463 So. 2d 150 (Ala. 1985) (expanding statutory private sale to allow plaintiff cotenant to purchase others' shares). But see Andersen v. Andersen, 376 N.W.2d 711 (Minn. App. 1985) (affirming, in part, court order for one cotenant to sell his interest to another in lieu of public sale).

[292] E.g., McGuire v. Owens, 300 S.W.2d 556 (Ky. 1957); Succession of Miller v. Evans, 184 La. 933, 168 So. 106 (1936); Wright, 131 Ill. App. 3d 46, 86 Ill. Dec. 342, 475 N.E.2d 556; McConnell, 449 So. 2d 785 (ordering sale because parties admitted physical partition infeasible). Indeed, the fact that the tract is very small, without more, may justify an order for sale. Swartz, 246 N.J. Super. 406, 587 A.2d 1295. But see Wilcox, 208 Conn. 318, 544 A.2d 1207 (reiterating strong preference for physical division); Marshall & Ilsley Bank v. De Wolf, 268 Wis. 244, 67 N.W.2d 380 (1954) (dividing a city lot with a 3-story building covering entire lot).

[293] E.g., Arnold v. Cesare, 137 Ariz. 48, 668 P.2d 891 (App. 1983); Phillips v. Phillips, 185 Ill. 629, 57 N.E. 796 (1900); Tichenor v. Rock, 140 Ky. 86, 130 S.W. 989 (1910) (affirming sale when each heir had a 1/14 interest in a 90-acre farm); Loupe v. Bybee, 570 So. 2d 31 (La. Ct. App. 1990); Swartz, 246 N.J. Super. 406, 587 A.2d 1295; Halamka v. Halamka, 799 S.W.2d 351 (Tex. App. 1990). When the common property is a farm, physical division is likely to diminish its value and to produce parcels so small as to be unsalable. Physical division of a substantial urban land parcel is also likely to reduce its value, regardless of whether the resulting lots are salable. See discussion in Note, Role of the Judicial Sale in Preventing Uneconomic Parcellation of Inherited Land, 23 U. Chi. L. Rev. 343 (1956).

[294] E.g., Filipetti, 2 Conn. App. 456, 479 A.2d 1229; Cooter v. Dearborn, 115 Ill. 509, 4 N.E. 388 (1886); Robinson's Adm'r v. Alexander, 194 Ky. 494, 239 S.W. 786 (1922); Barth v. Barth, 901 P.2d 232 (Okla. Civ. App. 1995); Blue v. Blue, 2018 S.D. 58, 916 N.W.2d 131; Von Herberg v. Von Herberg, 6 Wash. 2d 100, 106 P.2d 737 (1940); Marshall & Ilsley Bank, 268 Wis. 244, 67 N.W.2d 380. Some statutes specifically authorize equalization by an order for payment of owelty, but courts have the power to order such payment even in the absence of express statutory authorization.

[295] 2 Am. L. Prop., supra note 1, § 6.26, at 114; see, e.g., Cunningham v. Hastings, 556 N.E.2d 12 (Ind. Ct. App. 1990) (denying reimbursement for amount originally paid from purchasing cotenant's funds because proceeds should be divided equally regardless).

[296] E.g., Henslee v. Williams, 253 Ala. 363, 44 So. 2d 763 (1950); Southerland v. Potts, 234 N.C. 268, 67 S.E.2d 51 (1951).

[297] E.g., Schuck v. Schuck, 413 Ill. 390, 108 N.E.2d 905 (1952), appeal transferred, 347 Ill. App. 557, 107 N.E.2d 53 (1952); Washburn v. Washburn, 234 N.C. 370, 67 S.E.2d 264 (1951); Smith v. Smith, 206 Okla. 206, 242 P.2d 436 (1952).

subject to the security interest, unless the sale is made free and clear and the security interest attaches to the debtor cotenant's share of the proceeds.

When all the cotenants have leased the property, neither a physical division nor a sale affects the lessee's estate and right to possess.[298] When only one cotenant has leased her undivided interest, a physical division of the property results in the lessee's estate being limited to the parcel set off to his lessor.[299] But a sale of the entire property should be subject to the lease, which would make the lessee and the purchaser tenants in common for the balance of the lease term. If this situation might chill the bidding at the partition sale because it would be inconvenient for the lessee and the purchaser, a court would be justified in refusing to order a sale.

In a jurisdiction that still recognizes inchoate dower and curtesy, a partition in kind transfers the inchoate interest of a cotenant's spouse to the separate parcel set off to that cotenant.[300] If the court orders a sale of the property, the inchoate dower or curtesy interest of a cotenant's spouse in the common property is cut off, even if the spouse is not joined in the partition action.[301] However, the spouse's interest may attach to that cotenant's share of the sale proceeds.[302]

§ 5.13   COMMUNITY PROPERTY—IN GENERAL

Eight states—Arizona, California, Idaho, Louisiana, Nevada, New Mexico, Texas, and Washington—have a marital property system known as community property. It is a substitute for the common law marital property system of the other states. Community property is a European civil law institution. Its ancient wellsprings are among the Visigoths. In modern times, it is principally associated with the legal systems of France and Spain.[303] American community property law is primarily of Spanish origin, even in French Louisiana.[304] The system was established by the constitutions of California,

---

[298] If the common property is sold, the court should expressly order the sale to be made subject to the lease. E.g., McLear v. Balmat, 194 A.D. 827, 186 N.Y.S. 180 (App. Div. 1921), aff'd, 231 N.Y. 548, 132 N.E. 883 (1921), appeal withdrawn 231 N.Y. 599, 132 N.E. 904 (1921); Consol. Gas Supply Corp. v. Riley, 161 W. Va. 782, 247 S.E.2d 712 (1978).

[299] E.g., Noble v. Beach, 21 Cal. 2d 91, 130 P.2d 426 (1942). The lessee must be made a party to be bound by the partition judgment. See supra § 5.11.

[300] E.g., Colton v. Smith, 28 Mass. (11 Pick.) 311 (1831); Hinds v. Stevens, 45 Mo. 209 (1870), overruled in part by Crosby v. Farmer's Bank, 107 Mo. 436, 17 S.W. 1004 (1891); Lloyd v. Conover, 25 N.J. L. 47 (1855); Shelton v. Shelton, 225 S.C. 502, 83 S.E.2d 176 (1954). The spouse need not be joined in the partition action. Hinds, 45 Mo. 209.

[301] E.g., Cole v. Cole, 292 Ill. 154, 126 N.E. 752, 38 A.L.R. 719 (1920); Frahm v. Seaman, 179 Iowa 144, 159 N.W. 206 (1916); Hazelbaker v. Reber, 123 Kan. 131, 254 P. 407 (1927); Hinds v. Stevens, 45 Mo. 209 (1870), overruled in part by Crosby v. Farmer's Bank, 107 Mo. 436, 17 S.W. 1004 (1891); Shelton v. Shelton, 225 S.C. 502, 83 S.E.2d 176 (1954); Turner v. Turner, 185 Va. 505, 39 S.E.2d 299 (1946). However, some courts require joinder of each cotenant's spouse. E.g., Warren v. Twilley, 10 Md. 39 (1856); Greiner v. Klein, 28 Mich. 12 (1873); Jordan v. Van Epps, 85 N.Y. 427 (1881).

[302] See cases cited supra note 301. In Turner, the partition sale statutorily eliminated the inchoate dower interest of a cotenant's wife, and it did not attach to the husband's share of the sale proceeds, though the wife was not joined in the partition action. Turner v. Turner, 185 Va. 505, 511, 39 S.E.2d 299, 302 (1946).

[303] W. de Funiak & M. Vaughn, Principles of Community Property § 11.1, at 19–36, 37–39 (2d ed. 1971).

[304] Id. at § 37; H. Cross, The Community Property Law in Washington, 49 Wash. L. Rev. 729, 733 (1974). Louisiana's code system of law is mostly adapted from French law, but its community property law seems to be of Spanish origin. When the United States acquired Louisiana from France in 1803–1804, Spain had just returned the territory to France after approximately three decades of Spanish rule.

Nevada, and Texas and by statute in the remaining five community property states.[305] In all the states, community property has a statutory skeleton that is fleshed out with numerous judicial precedents. Civil law sources today play hardly any role in American community property decisions, despite scholarly pleas that lawyers and judges become more familiar with these sources.[306] Common law principles have had an effect on American community property law, as community property principles, such as equality between spouses and marital partnership, have much influenced the entire country's laws.[307] American community property law has become an indigenous system or, more precisely, eight common systems that differ in important details.

Underlying community property is the philosophical premise that spouses are equals. Together in marriage, they form a kind of marital partnership. They may own property in their individual right, called separate property. They own other property together as community property.[308] Therefore, characterizing property as separate or community is the crucial first step in determining the spouses' legal relationships with respect to it. Classification of their contract or tort obligations as community or separate is also important in determining liability. Dissolution of the marriage by death or divorce raises the problem of who is entitled to the community property and who is liable for community obligations. One is sometimes tempted to think of the community as a third entity in the marriage, but we must resist this temptation, because respected sources say it is not.[309]

For a marital community to exist, the couple must be legally married. Under the doctrine of putative marriage, the civil law extends the benefits of community property to one or both spouses if they entered into a ceremonial marriage in good faith that proves to be legally invalid.[310] Louisiana has adopted the principle by statute.[311] In California, where the term "putative marriage" appears in a statute and in some judicial decisions, property may be divided as if it were community property on dissolution of an innocent relationship, but the relationship is not called a marriage.[312] Texas decisions are in disarray, with some seeming to recognize the civil law putative marriage doctrine and others refusing to recognize it.[313] Courts in other states generally have not adopted

---

[305] Cal. Const. art. I, § 21; Nev. Const. art. IV, § 31; Tex. Const. art. XVI, § 15; Ariz. Rev. Stat. Ann. § 25–211; Idaho Code § 32–903; La. Civ. Code Ann, arts. 2325–2327; N.M. Stat. Ann. § 40–3–8; Wash. Rev. Code § 26.16.030. Puerto Rico also has a community property system. P.R. Laws Ann. tit. 31, § 3621.

[306] See de Funiak & Vaughn, supra note 303, at §§ 3–5.

[307] For a discussion of the influence of principles associated with community property, see W. McClanahan, Community Property Law in the United States §§ 14.2, 14.3 (1982) (hereinafter McClanahan).

[308] The concept is that, while the marriage endures, the spouses have equal, undivided shares in the community property. While they may agree to change the character from community to separate and vice versa, any property that is classified as community must be equal, which is not true of business partnership property. E.g., Cal. Civ. Code § 5105; La. Civ. Code Ann. art. 2336; Nev. Rev. Stat. § 123.225; Phillipson v. Bd. of Admin., 3 Cal. 3d 32, 89 Cal. Rptr. 61, 473 P.2d 765 (1970).

[309] See Household Fin. Corp. v. Smith, 70 Wash. 2d 401, 423 P.2d 621 (1967); Bortle v. Osborne, 155 Wash. 585, 285 P. 425 (1930); de Funiak & Vaughn, supra note 303, at § 95.

[310] Barkley v. Dumke, 99 Tex. 150, 87 S.W. 1147 (1905); de Funiak & Vaughn, supra note 303, at § 56.

[311] La. Civ. Code Ann. art. 96.

[312] Cal. Fam. Code § 2251; In re Marriage of Tejeda, 179 Cal. App. 4th 973, 102 Cal. Rptr. 3d 361 (2009); Estate of Vargas, 36 Cal. App. 3d 714, 111 Cal. Rptr. 779 (1974); de Funiak & Vaughn, supra note 303, at § 56.2; W. Reppy & C. Samuel, Community Property in the United States 335–36 (2d ed. 1982).

[313] Lee v. Lee, 112 Tex. 392, 247 S.W. 828 (1923) (putative marriage); Barkley v. Dumke, 99 Tex. 150, 87 S.W. 1147 (1905) (putative marriage); Tex. Emps. Ins. Ass'n v. Grimes, 153 Tex. 357, 269 S.W.2d 332 (1954) (no wrongful death benefits to putative wife); Ft. Worth & Rio Grande Ry. Co. v. Robertson, 103 Tex. 504, 131

the doctrine.[314] Nevertheless, when one or both parties were unaware that they were not married, courts in community property states generally divide property on dissolution of the relationship on a basis that may approximate division of community property, on theories such as equitable division or partnership.[315] When the couple knows that they are unmarried, community property does not exist. However, a court may divide the property between them upon theories of deceit, implied contract, partnership, or restitution.[316]

§ 5.14 COMMUNITY PROPERTY— CHARACTER OF OWNERSHIP

When a marital community exists, spouses own their property as either the separate property of one or the community property of both. Subject to some qualifications that will be noted, each spouse owns separate property in his or her own right, free from the other spouse's claims.[317] All property acquired by either spouse before marriage remains that spouse's separate property, which is the feature that particularly distinguishes the Spanish "ganancial" system from other European community property systems.[318] Property acquired by either one after marriage by gift, devise, bequest, or inheritance also is separate.[319] In other words, donative ("lucrative") acquisitions after marriage, rather than those that result from either spouse's effort, skill, or industry ("onerous"), are separate. The distinction between lucrative and onerous acquisitions is based on the premise that community property is the product of a couple who are working as a team.

If a spouse uses separate property to acquire other property, the newly-acquired property is separate.[320] The income from separate property, such as rents, issues, and profits, is community property in Idaho, Louisiana, and Texas (the civil law or Spanish

---

S.W. 400 (1910), rev'g 55 Tex. Civ. App. 309, 103 Tex. 504, 121 S.W. 202 (1909) (putative wife may not maintain survival action).

[314] Poole v. Schrichte, 39 Wash. 2d 558, 236 P.2d 1044 (1951); de Funiak & Vaughn, supra note 303, at §§ 56–56.8; Cross, supra note 304, at 736.

[315] Estate of Vargas, 36 Cal. App. 3d 714, 111 Cal. Rptr. 779 ("equitable principles"); McGhee v. McGhee, 82 Idaho 367, 353 P.2d 760 (1960) (constructive fraud against innocent party); Poole v. Schrichte, 39 Wash. 2d 558, 236 P.2d 1044 (1951) (partnership; alternative theory); Creasman v. Boyle, 31 Wash. 2d 345, 196 P.2d 835 (1948) (resulting trust), overruled on other grounds, In re Marriage of Lindsey, 101 Wash. 2d 299, 678 P.2d 328 (1984).

[316] Carroll v. Lee, 148 Ariz. 10, 712 P.2d 923 (1986) (contract); Marvin v. Marvin, 18 Cal. 3d 660, 134 Cal. Rptr. 815, 557 P.2d 106 (1976), appeal after remand, 122 Cal. App. 3d 871, 176 Cal. Rptr. 555 (1981); In re Marriage of Cary, 34 Cal. App. 3d 345, 109 Cal. Rptr. 862 (1973), rejected by Marvin, 18 Cal. 3d 660, 134 Cal. Rptr. 815, 557 P.2d 106; Connell v. Francisco, 127 Wash. 2d 339, 898 P.2d 831 (1995) (treated similarly to community property when relationship is of significant duration); In re Marriage of Lindsey, 101 Wash. 2d 299, 678 P.2d 328 ("just and equitable"); In re Estate of Thornton, 81 Wash. 2d 72, 499 P.2d 864 (1972); Poole v. Schrichte, 39 Wash. 2d 558, 236 P.2d 1044 (1951) (alternative approach). See also Soltero v. Wimer, 159 Wash. 2d 428, 150 P.3d 553 (2007).

[317] Ariz. Rev. Stat. Ann. §§ 25–214, 33–451; Cal. Fam. Code § 770; Idaho Code §§ 32–903, 32–904, 15–1–201; La. Civ. Code Ann. art. 2371; Nev. Rev. Stat. §§ 123.060, 123.170; N.M. Stat. Ann. § 40–3–3; Tex. Fam. Code Ann. § 3.101; Wash. Rev. Code §§ 26.16.010, 26.16.020.

[318] Ariz. Rev. Stat. Ann. § 25–213; Cal. Fam. Code § 770; Idaho Code §§ 32–903, 15–1–201; La. Civ. Code Ann. art. 2341; Nev. Rev. Stat. Ann. § 123.130; N.M. Stat. Ann. § 40–3–8; Tex. Fam. Code Ann. § 3.001; Wash. Rev. Code §§ 26.16.010, 26.16.020; de Funiak & Vaughn, supra note 303, at §§ 58, 63, 64, 66; McClanahan, supra note 307, at §§ 6.1–6.3.

[319] See authorities cited supra note 318.

[320] See In re Clark's Estate, 94 Cal. App. 453, 271 P. 542 (1928) (division of estate received in settlement of contested will was separate); de Funiak & Vaughn, supra note 303, at §§ 62, 69; W. Brockelbank, The Community Property Law of Idaho 134–38 (1962). The principle that a previously owned separate asset may impart its character to a present asset is variously discussed as the source doctrine, a tracing, or an exchange.

rule) but is separate property in the other community property states (the American or California rule).[321] When rents, issues, and profits of separate property remain separate, the income may be the result of one or both spouse's "onerous" efforts, especially when the assets are in a going business. In principle, that income should be community property, but judicial formulas differ.[322] A similar and partially overlapping problem arises when a marriage dissolves and the value of separate property has increased in part due to market forces and in part due to spousal efforts, which again creates a complex apportionment problem with various factors to be considered and differing judicial formulas.[323] Joint gifts to spouses are generally community property, at least if no arrangement is made otherwise, in part due to the presumption that assets received after marriage are community property.[324] However, spouses can be tenants in common or, except in Louisiana, joint tenants with each other and thereby own their shares as separate property.[325]

Community property is nearly always described by exclusion. In the typical language of the Texas Family Code: "Community property consists of the property, other than separate property, acquired by either spouse during marriage."[326] Only the Louisiana Civil Code attempts an affirmative definition: "The community property comprises: property acquired during the existence of the legal regime through the effort, skill, or industry of either spouse; property acquired with community things or with community and separate things * * * ; property donated to the spouses jointly; natural and civil fruits of community property; damages awarded for loss or injury to a thing belonging to the community; * * * " but backstops the definition with "and all other property not classified by law as separate property."[327]

Some community property states also recognize a category called quasi-community property. Generally, it is property that a spouse, who resides in a community property

---

[321] Ariz. Rev. Stat. Ann. § 25–213; Cal. Fam. Code § 770; Idaho Code § 32–906(1); La. Civ. Code Ann. art. 2339; Nev. Rev. Stat. § 123.130; N.M. Stat. Ann. § 40–3–8; Wash. Rev. Code §§ 26.16.010, 26.16.020; Frame v. Frame, 120 Tex. 61, 36 S.W.2d 152 (1931). In Idaho, Louisiana, and Texas, spouses can agree that rents, issues, and profits of separate property will be separate. McClanahan, supra note 307, at § 6.12. Cf. Swope v. Swope, 112 Idaho 974, 739 P.2d 273 (1987), appeal after remand, 122 Idaho 296, 834 P.2d 298 (1992) (earnings of separate-property partnership are community).

[322] The two best known formulas are contained in Pereira v. Pereira, 156 Cal. 1, 103 P. 488 (1909), and Van Camp v. Van Camp, 53 Cal. App. 17, 199 P. 885 (1921). See discussion in McClanahan, supra note 1, at § 6.18.

[323] See Cockrill v. Cockrill, 124 Ariz. 50, 601 P.2d 1334 (1979), appeal after remand 139 Ariz. 72, 676 P.2d 1130 (1983); In re Marriage of Brandes, 239 Cal. App. 4th 1461, 192 Cal. Rptr. 3d 1 (2015); Beam v. Bank of Am., 6 Cal. 3d 12, 98 Cal. Rptr. 137, 490 P.2d 257 (1971); Simplot v. Simplot, 96 Idaho 239, 526 P.2d 844 (1974); Speer v. Quinlan, 96 Idaho 119, 525 P.2d 314 (1973); St. Marie v. Roy, 29 So. 3d 708 (La. Ct. App. 2010); Abraham v. Abraham, 230 La. 78, 87 So. 2d 735 (1956); Cord v. Neuhoff, 94 Nev. 21, 573 P.2d 1170 (1978); Jensen v. Jensen, 665 S.W.2d 107 (Tex. 1984) (reimbursement theory); Vallone v. Vallone, 644 S.W.2d 455 (Tex. 1982); Norris v. Vaughan, 152 Tex. 491, 260 S.W.2d 676 (1953); McClanahan, supra note 307, at § 6.18.

[324] Hamilton v. Hamilton, 381 So. 2d 517 (La. Ct. App. 1979) (apparent result); In re Estate of Salvini, 65 Wash. 2d 442, 397 P.2d 811 (1964).

[325] Ariz. Rev. Stat. Ann. § 33–431; Cal. Fam. Code § 750; Idaho Code § 55–104; La. Civ. Code Ann. art. 480 (ownership in "indivision"); Nev. Rev. Stat. § 123.030; N.M. Stat. Ann. § 40–3–2; Tex. Est. Code Ann. § 101.002; Wash. Rev. Code §§ 64.28.010, 64.28.020; de Funiak & Vaughn, supra note 303, at § 134.

[326] Tex. Fam. Code Ann. § 3.002. To similar effect, see Ariz. Rev. Stat. Ann. § 25–211; Cal. Fam. Code § 760; Idaho Code § 32–906(1); Nev. Rev. Stat. § 123.220; N.M. Stat. Ann. § 40–3–8(B); Wash. Rev. Code § 26.16.030.

[327] La. Civ. Code Ann. art. 2338.

state, acquired in another state and that would have been community property if it had been acquired in the community property state.[328]

The characterization of personal injury damages has most severely tested the basic distinction between separate and community property. Originally, community property states classified them as community property, based on statutory provisions that all property acquired after marriage is community property, unless acquired by donative transfer.[329] That united front has broken down in a welter of confusion. Idaho still adheres to the traditional community view, though some question exists whether the rule is weakening.[330] Most of the other seven states now apportion personal injury awards. The portions for loss of earnings and community expenses are community property, while the portions for pain, suffering, and loss of body parts are the injured spouse's separate property. Louisiana, Nevada, and Texas have statutorily adopted this approach.[331] Arizona, New Mexico, and Washington have done so by judicial decision.[332] California, by statute and by judicial decisions before the statute, has a jumbled scheme. A spouse's personal injury damages from a suit against the other spouse are separate, but damages from a suit against a third party are community property but are subject to possible reimbursement between spouses for certain expenses paid from separate funds.[333]

Characterization problems that may be simpler theoretically than personal injury damages can be more complex practically when spouses acquire assets partly with community and partly with separate funds or when property of one kind is improved with funds of the other kind. Property's characterization as separate or community is fixed when it is acquired and does not change.[334] But determining when acquisition occurred is difficult when a spouse acquires property over a period of time that extends before and after marriage, such as purchases by periodic payments on a mortgage, real estate contract, or life insurance policy. Courts use three approaches to resolve these time-of-acquisition problems—inception-of-title (when the credit transaction was

---

[328] The definition of quasi-community property usually also includes property received in exchange for property that would have been community property if the spouse who acquired it had lived in the community property state when it was acquired. Some statutes attempt to make out-of-state realty quasi-community, and some do not. See Cal. Fam. Code § 125 (out-of-state realty included); Idaho Code §§ 15–2–201, 15–2–209 (out-of-state realty not included); N.M. Stat. Ann. § 40–3–8 (out-of-state realty included); Tex. Fam. Code Ann. § 7.002 (out-of-state realty included; words "quasi-community property" do not appear); Wash. Rev. Code § 26.16.220 (quasi-community property of deceased persons; certain out-of-state realty included).

[329] de Funiak & Vaughn, supra note 303, at § 82; McClanahan, supra note 307, at § 6.27.

[330] Hanks v. Sawtelle Rentals, Inc., 133 Idaho 199, 984 P.2d 122 (1999); Evans v. Twin Falls Cty., 118 Idaho 210, 796 P.2d 87 (1990); Rogers v. Yellowstone Park Co., 97 Idaho 14, 539 P.2d 566 (1974); Cross, supra note 304, at 773–76.

[331] La. Civ. Code Ann. art. 2344; Nev. Rev. Stat. § 123.121; Tex. Fam. Code Ann. § 3.001.

[332] Jurek v. Jurek, 124 Ariz. 596, 606 P.2d 812 (1980); Sota v. Vandeventer, 56 N.M. 483, 245 P.2d 826 (1952); In re Marriage of Brown, 100 Wash. 2d 729, 675 P.2d 1207 (1984) (overruling prior decisions); McClanahan, supra note 307, at § 6.27; S. Akers, Blood and Money—Separate or Community Character of Personal Injury Recovery, 9 Texas Tech. L. Rev. 1, 2–14 (1977); P. George, Whose Injury? Whose Property? The Characterization of Personal Injury Settlements Upon Dissolution of Marriage in Community Property States, 32 Idaho L. Rev. 575 (1996).

[333] Cal. Fam. Code §§ 780–82; McClanahan, supra note 307, at § 6.27.

[334] de Funiak & Vaughn, supra note 303, at § 64; McClanahan, supra note 307, at § 6.3; Cross, supra note 304, at 755.

initiated), time-of-vesting (when legal title vested), and pro rata (piecemeal division of ownership).[335]

Even when a court decides that property is entirely separate or entirely community, a claim for reimbursement can arise if funds of the other kind were spent to acquire it. Similarly, when community funds have been used to improve a separate asset or vice versa, a claim for reimbursement can exist.[336] Realistically, establishing a community claim against separate assets is often easier than the other way around, because some jurisdictions presume that separate improvements on community property are intended as a gift.[337] Indeed, the problems discussed in this paragraph are frequently associated with, if not resolved within the framework of, the presumption in favor of community property and the doctrine of tracing and commingling.

A presumption exists, by statute in four community property states and by decision in the other four, that property acquired during marriage is community.[338] Several jurisdictions have an even broader presumption for community property if the only known facts are that people are married and own property.[339] Of course, proof that a particular asset was acquired before marriage or after marriage by gift, devise, bequest, or inheritance rebuts the presumption.[340] This proof may not be too difficult when a separate asset has been segregated and separately maintained, such as a single parcel of real estate, a block of corporate stock, or a scrupulously segregated bank account.

However, extremely complex problems arise in two common situations: (1) when property is not an original separate asset but is allegedly traceable back to it, usually through a series of exchanges, and (2) when separate and community funds or fungible goods have been commingled. Property remains separate if it can be traced back to a source that was separate. However, as more time passes between the source and the present asset and as more tracing steps are required or as community efforts or funds increasingly go into the asset, overcoming the community property presumption becomes progressively more difficult. Commingling occurs when fungible separate and community property are intermixed. The most common example is a bank account into and from which separate and community funds are deposited and withdrawn. If that is the only evidence, the community property presumption prevails unless, according to

---

[335] E.g., Cosey v. Cosey, 364 So. 2d 186 (La. Ct. App. 1978) (time of vesting rule), writ granted 366 So. 2d 570, aff'd, 376 So. 2d 486 (La. 1979); McCurdy v. McCurdy, 372 S.W.2d 381 (Tex. Civ. App. 1963), error refused (inception-of-title rule); Wilson v. Wilson, 35 Wash. 2d 364, 212 P.2d 1022 (1949) (pro rata theory), overruled on other grounds, Francis v. Francis, 89 Wash. 2d 511, 573 P.2d 369 (1978); In re Dougherty's Estate, 27 Wash. 2d 11, 176 P.2d 335 (1947) (inception-of-title rule); Reppy & Samuel, supra note 312, at 80–83.

[336] See Hanrahan v. Sims, 20 Ariz. App. 313, 512 P.2d 617 (1973); In re Marriage of Peterson, 243 Cal. App. 4th 923, 197 Cal. Rptr. 3d 558 (2016); In re Marriage of Moore, 28 Cal. 3d 366, 168 Cal. Rptr. 662, 618 P.2d 208 (1980); Portillo v. Shappie, 97 N.M. 59, 636 P.2d 878 (1981) (value of community lien measured by value added by community labor).

[337] See In re Marriage of Warren, 28 Cal. App. 3d 777, 104 Cal. Rptr. 860 (1972); McClanahan, supra note 307, at § 6.16.

[338] Cal. Fam. Code § 760 (subject to exception of § 761); La. Civ. Code Ann. art. 2340; N.M. Stat. Ann. § 40–3–12(A); Tex. Fam. Code Ann. § 3.003; de Funiak & Vaughn, supra note 303, at §§ 60, 60.1.

[339] In re Marriage of Schwarz, 192 Wash. App. 180, 368 P.3d 173 (2016); State ex rel. Marshall v. Superior Court, 119 Wash. 631, 206 P. 362 (1922); McClanahan, supra note 307, at § 6.5; Cross, supra note 304, at 747.

[340] See, e.g., Duncan v. United States, 247 F.2d 845 (5th Cir. 1957) (Texas law); See v. See, 64 Cal. 2d 778, 51 Cal. Rptr. 888, 415 P.2d 776 (1966), superseded by statute as recognized by Hebbring v. Hebbring, 207 Cal. App. 3d 1260, 255 Cal. Rptr. 488 (1989); de Funiak & Vaughn, supra note 303, at § 60; McClanahan, supra note 307, at § 6.5.

some decisions, the amount of intermingled community property is trifling or negligible.[341]

Uncommingling the property requires tracing. If the spouse who is maintaining the bank account, for example, has kept records of each deposit and withdrawal in sufficient detail to identify its separate or community source or destination, tracing can be accomplished. The less complete the records, the less likely that the party seeking to establish that the property is wholly or partly separate will succeed. Sometimes that party will benefit from the widely recognized family expense presumption that community funds, if available at a given time, are used for community living expenses.[342] Courts are divided whether a party can offset total family expenses against total community income during the marriage (total recapitulation technique) or whether proof must relate to specific transactions.[343]

California and Washington statutorily provide that, when spouses are living "separate and apart," their "earnings and accumulations" are separate property.[344] Courts have had difficulty determining what "separate and apart" means, but it means more than a simple physical separation. A permanent rupture of the marriage must have occurred. Some courts have held that the rupture must be so complete that both spouses have abandoned the marriage.[345] Even absent a statute, courts have held in some cases that assets acquired after separation are not community property. This holding may result from the theory that the spouses had impliedly made a separate property agreement, that the nonacquiring spouse had abandoned the marriage, or that that spouse was estopped to assert a community claim.[346]

"Transmutation" is the spouses' conversion of separate into community property or vice versa, and all community property states allow it to some extent.[347] Transmutations are effected by two legal mechanisms, contractual agreement and gift.

Before marriage, contractual agreements must be written and generally must be acknowledged.[348] After marriage, spouses can contract with each other, with some limitations. One limitation is that they must deal with each other from a position of trust

---

[341] In re Marriage of Mix, 14 Cal. 3d 604, 122 Cal. Rptr. 79, 536 P.2d 479 (1975); See v. See, 64 Cal. 2d 778, 51 Cal. Rptr. 888, 415 P.2d 776 (1966), superseded by statute as recognized by Hebbring, 207 Cal. App. 3d 1260, 255 Cal. Rptr. 488; McClanahan, supra note 307, at § 6.8.

[342] See See v. See, 64 Cal. 2d 778, 51 Cal. Rptr. 888, 415 P.2d 776 (1966); Reppy & Samuel, supra note 312, at 119; Comment, 19 Stan. L. Rev. 661 (1967) (critical of family expense doctrine).

[343] See See v. See, 64 Cal. 2d 778, 51 Cal. Rptr. 888, 415 P.2d 776 ("total recapitulation" not allowed); McClanahan, supra note 307, at § 6.8; Reppy & Samuel, supra note 312, at 119–21.

[344] Cal. Fam. Code § 771; Wash. Rev. Code § 26.16.140.

[345] Marriage of Baragry, 73 Cal. App. 3d 444, 140 Cal. Rptr. 779 (1977); Makeig v. United Sec. Bank & Tr. Co., 112 Cal. App. 138, 296 P. 673 (1931) (no "actual rupture" when living apart was supposedly to save money); Cross, supra note 304, at 750–53. But cf. Loring v. Stuart, 79 Cal. 200, 21 P. 651 (1889) (only husband intended to break the marriage permanently).

[346] Togliatti v. Robertson, 29 Wash. 2d 844, 190 P.2d 575 (1948) (implied contract); McClanahan, supra note 307, at § 6. 19.

[347] As to pre-marital agreements, see Ariz. Rev. Stat. Ann. § 25–201; Cal. Fam. Code §§ 1500–02, 1612; Idaho Code §§ 32–905, 32–916, 32–917; La. Civ. Code Ann. arts. 2328–31, 2370; Nev. Rev. Stat. §§ 123.010, 123.270; N.M. Stat. Ann. §§ 40–2–4, 40–2–7, 40–3–8; Tex. Const. art. XVI, § 15. Washington has no statute providing for pre-marital agreements. As to agreements during marriage, see Ariz. Rev. Stat. Ann. § 25–317 (on separation or dissolution only); Cal. Fam. Code §§ 721, 1620; Idaho Code § 32–906; La. Civ. Code Ann. arts. 2329–31, 2339, 2343; Nev. Rev. Stat. §§ 123.070, 123.080; N.M. Stat. §§ 40–2–2, 40–3–8; Tex. Const. art. XVI, § 15; Tex. Fam. Code Ann. § 4.202; Wash. Rev. Code §§ 26.16.050, 26.16.120, 26.16.210.

[348] See statutes cited supra note 347.

and confidence.[349] Post-marital agreements can transmute a spouse's presently existing or after-acquired separate assets into community property or community assets into separate property. An exchange of assets between the spouses or marriage constitute consideration.[350] The Statute of Frauds governs whether the agreement must be written.

Transmutation of real property must be by a document that satisfies the local requirements for conveyances or contracts to convey.[351] In keeping with a trend in all community property states, Louisiana and Texas impose strict limitations on post-marital transmutations, though they have relaxed the restrictions.[352] An oral transmutation may also be implied from the circumstances, such as spouses treating certain assets as separate or community or from the form in which title is taken, but most jurisdictions probably require evidence sufficient to establish an agreement for transmutation.[353]

Transmutations may also occur by gift between spouses. In most community property states, proving a gift of separate property to the community is easier than the other way around due to the presumption in favor of community property.[354] However, when the alleged gift is an object for the donee spouse's use, such as personal effects or jewelry, proving a gift should be easy.[355] Conceptually, a gift of community property to one spouse as separate property transfers only the other's community interest. Therefore, as some statutes provide, only the donor spouse should have to make the transfer.[356]

[349] See, e.g., Cal. Fam. Code § 721; Nev. Rev. Stat. § 123.070; N.M. Stat. Ann. § 40–2–2; Wash. Rev. Code § 26.16.210 (burden to prove good faith); de Funiak & Vaughn, supra note 303, at § 138.

[350] Woods v. Sec. First Nat'l Bank, 46 Cal. 2d 697, 299 P.2d 657 (1956), superseded on other grounds by Cal. Fam. Code § 761, as recognized by In re Estate of MacDonald, 51 Cal. 3d 262, 272 Cal. Rptr. 153, 794 P.2d 911 (1990); de Funiak & Vaughn, supra note 303, at § 136.

[351] Woods v. Sec. First Nat'l Bank, 46 Cal. 2d 697, 299 P.2d 657 (1956), superseded on other grounds by Cal. Fam. Code § 761, as recognized by In re Estate of MacDonald, 51 Cal. 3d 262, 272 Cal. Rptr. 153, 794 P.2d 911, is a classic example of bootstrapping. The court held an oral agreement that purported to transmute land from separate to community property was outside the Statute of Frauds, apparently because there was an agreement that "the property *had become* community property." All other states seem to require a writing to transmute land. McClanahan, supra note 307, at § 8.16; Reppy & Samuel, supra note 312, at 28.

[352] La. Civ. Code Ann. art. 2329; Tex. Const. art. 16, § 15; McClanahan, supra note 307, at § 8.13.

[353] O'Connor v. Travelers Ins. Co., 169 Cal. App. 2d 763, 337 P.2d 893 (1959) (individually maintained bank accounts; implied separate property agreement); In re Estate of Fletcher, 94 N.M. 572, 613 P.2d 714 (1980), cert. denied 94 N.M. 674, 615 P.2d 991 (1980) (taking title as joint tenants implied separate shares); In re Estate of Olson, 87 Wash. 2d 855, 557 P.2d 302 (1976) (deed from third person to spouses as joint tenants created community property because they did not agree to separate shares by deed); Reppy & Samuel, supra note 312, at 31–32, 37–38.

[354] In re Marriage of Lucas, 27 Cal. 3d 808, 166 Cal. Rptr. 853, 614 P.2d 285 (1980), superseded by statute, Cal. Fam. Code § 850, as recognized by In re Marriage of Valli, 58 Cal. 4th 1396, 171 Cal. Rptr. 3d 454, 324 P.3d 274 (2014); de Funiak & Vaughn, supra note 303, at § 147; Cross, supra note 304, at 813–14. See also Barber v. Bradley, 505 S.W.3d 749 (Ky. 2016); O'Neill v. O'Neill, 600 S.W.2d 493 (Ky. Ct. App. 1980) (presumption in favor of Kentucky marital property).

[355] Johnson v. Dar Denne, 161 Wash. 496, 296 P. 1105 (1931); Cross, supra note 304.

[356] Idaho Code § 32–906; La Civ. Code Ann. art. 2343; Tex. Fam. Code Ann. § 4.102; Wash. Rev. Code § 26.16.050; de Funiak & Vaughn, supra note 303, at § 147.

§ 5.15 COMMUNITY PROPERTY—MANAGEMENT, DISPOSITION, AND DISSOLUTION OF COMMUNITY PROPERTY

In community property states, spouses have full power to manage and dispose of their separate property, as if they were single.[357] The husband historically was the manager of the community property.[358] However, since Washington legislation in 1972, the historic scheme has been much changed. All community property states now vest general powers of management and disposition in each spouse, with exceptions to be noted. Statutes simply provide that spouses have equal management powers or that each has full management powers.[359] Texas gives each spouse powers of management and disposition over "the community property that he or she would have owned if single," which creates a presumption that property in one spouse's name or possession is subject to that one's management.[360]

Exceptions to full individual powers frequently exist for acquisitions or transfers of interests in land and for transfers of household necessities, assets of a business in which both spouses participate, and occasionally for other specified assets. When such exceptions exist, both spouses must join in the transaction.[361] To some extent, one spouse alone may have enhanced powers of management in emergencies, such as when the other has disappeared or is legally incompetent.[362] In this connection, the statutory rule in several states that one spouse's income is separate property when the spouses are living separate and apart, may effectively enhance management powers. A spouse's death dissolves the marital community. In all community property jurisdictions, spouses can dispose by will of their separate property[363] and one-half of the community property.[364]

The effect of community property on a spouse's liabilities to third persons is pervasive and all but incapable of meaningful general restatement.[365] With variations

---

[357] Ariz. Rev. Stat. Ann. §§ 25–214, 33–451; Cal. Fam. Code § 770; Idaho Code §§ 32–904, 32–906(1); La. Civ. Code Ann. art. 2371; Nev. Rev. Stat. § 123.170; N.M. Stat. Ann. § 40–3–13(A); Tex. Fam. Code Ann. § 3.101; Wash. Rev. Code §§ 26.16.010, 26.16.020.

[358] See de Funiak & Vaughn, supra note 303, at §§ 113, 115.1.

[359] Ariz. Rev. Stat. Ann. § 25–214; Cal. Fam. Code § 1100; Idaho Code § 32–912; La. Civ. Code Ann. art. 2346; Nev. Rev. Stat. § 123.230; N.M. Stat. Ann. § 40–3–14; Tex. Fam. Code Ann. § 3.102; Wash. Rev. Code § 26.16.030.

[360] Tex. Fam. Code Ann. §§ 3.101, 3.104.

[361] See statutes cited supra note 359. See also Cal. Fam. Code § 1102; La. Civ. Code Ann. arts. 2347, 2349, 2350, 2351; N.M. Stat. Ann. § 40–3–13.

[362] Cal. Fam. Code § 1103; La. Civ. Code Ann. art. 2355; N.M. Stat. Ann. § 40–3–16; Tex. Fam. Code Ann. §§ 3.301, 3.302. Beyond statutory provisions, there is some thought that a spouse who needs to act in an emergency should have enhanced powers of management and disposition. See McClanahan, supra note 307, at § 9.14; Cross, supra note 304, at 787–88.

[363] E.g. Ariz. Rev. Stat. Ann. § 14–3101(A); Cal. Prob. Code § 6101; Idaho Code § 15–3–101; La. Civ. Code Ann. art. 1470; N.M. Stat. Ann. § 45–3–101(B); Tex. Est. Code Ann. § 58; Wash. Rev. Code § 11.12.010; McClanahan, supra note 307, at § 4.24.

[364] Ariz. Rev. Stat. Ann. § 14–3101(A); Cal. Prob. Code §§ 100, 6101; Idaho Code § 15–3–101; Nev. Rev. Stat. § 123.250(1); N.M. Stat. Ann. §§ 45–2–804(A), 45–2–808; Tex. Prob. Code Ann. § 251.002; Wash. Rev. Code § 11.02.070; McClanahan, supra note 307, at § 4.26.

[365] As evidence of the difficulty of even agreeing on an analytic framework, see the three works from which the present discussion on liabilities is mainly drawn. de Funiak & Vaughn, Chapter 9, after stating some historical and preliminary matters, basically organizes the discussion around the various kinds of liabilities and discusses the peculiarities of the states' doctrines within each of those categories. McClanahan, Chapter 10, was contributed by Professor Frederick M. Hart and is organized similarly. But W. Reppy & C. Samuel, Community Property Law in the United States, Chapter 17, divides its discussion into two principal

from state to state, separate and community liabilities are treated the same as separate and community assets. Courts generally agree that one spouse's premarriage liability is separate. A spouse can incur a separate liability after marriage, but it is less likely than before marriage. This result is due in part to a presumption that debts incurred during marriage are community debts and in part to the broad general concepts that post-marriage contract obligations are on behalf of the community and that even tort liabilities arise during activities that benefit the community.[366] Courts have made a total shambles of their attempts to define separate and community tort liability.[367]

If a spouse has a separate obligation, his or her separate assets clearly are liable to satisfy it, and community assets can be reached for a community obligation.[368] One spouse's separate assets are not liable for the other spouse's separate obligations, except to a limited extent in several states that make the separate estates liable for family necessities.[369] A creditor's right to reach community property for a separate claim exists to some extent in all community property states.[370] Theoretically, if a community is a separate entity, its assets should be insulated from separate claims. But if no entity exists and the spouses simply have a cotenancy in community assets, each one's share should be reachable.[371] Courts might consider whether (1) the obligation arose in contract or tort, (2) whether it arose before or after marriage, (3) whether the community assets to be reached are controlled by the debtor spouse, and (4) whether the assets to be reached are earned income.[372] Some community property states follow the so-called "managerial system," in which the community property that one spouse manages generally is liable for that spouse's separate obligations.

The right of a creditor who holds a community claim to reach separate assets is much clearer than the right of one who holds a separate claim to reach community assets. Under Spanish law and generally in America, the creditor of a community obligation can reach the separate assets of the spouse who incurred the obligation, as well as the community assets.[373] However, some states require the creditor to exhaust community assets before seizing the separate property.[374] If the marriage is dissolved, the spouse

---

parts, one for the states that follow the "managerial system" and the other for those that follow the "community debt system."

[366] See McClanahan, supra note 307, at §§ 10.2–10.4.

[367] See, e.g., Babcock v. Tam, 156 F.2d 116 (9th Cir. 1946); deElche v. Jacobsen, 95 Wash. 2d 237, 622 P.2d 835 (1980).

[368] McClanahan, supra note 307, at §§ 10.6, 10.8.

[369] Cal. Fam. Code §§ 913, 914, 4301; La. Civ. Code art. 2372; Wash. Rev. Code § 26.16.205; McClanahan, supra note 307, at § 10.6.

[370] See A. Carroll, The Superior Position of The Creditor in the Community Property Regime: Has the Community Become a Mere Creditor Collection Device?, 47 Santa Clara L. Rev 1 (2007). See also Cal. Fam. Code § 910(a); La. Civ. Code Ann. art. 2345; Lezeine v. Sec. Pac. Fin. Servs., Inc., 925 P.2d 1002 (Cal. 1996); Action Collec'n Serv., Inc. v. Seele, 69 P.3d 173 (Idaho Ct. App. 2003). But see Ariz. Rev. Stat Ann. § 25–215(B); Nev. Rev. Stat. § 123.050.

[371] For discussion of what are essentially the entity and shares theories, though perhaps couched in slightly different language, see the majority and dissenting opinions in deElche v. Jacobsen, 95 Wash. 2d 237, 622 P.2d 835 (1980).

[372] McClanahan, supra note 307, at § 10.7. See Chase Bank of Ariz. v. Acosta, 179 Ariz. 563, 880 P.2d 1109 (Ariz. Ct. App. 1994).

[373] McClanahan, supra note 307, at § 10.9; Cross, supra note 304, at 820.

[374] Ariz. Rev. Stat. Ann. § 25–215; N.M. Stat. Ann. § 40–3–11.

whose separate assets were used to pay community obligations may have a claim for reimbursement.[375]

A marriage is dissolved by a spouse's death or by divorce or annulment. If a spouse in a community property state dies without a will, the state's statutory plan of descent or succession dictates the distribution of the decedent's separate property. These statutory plans have their origins in the common law and are similar to the comparable statutory schemes of the common law states.[376] As to the intestate decedent's half of the community property, most states provide that the surviving spouse inherits it.[377] In some states, the decedent's children also inherit.[378]

When spouses divorce, the division of their property is affected by whether it is separate or community. In some states, the judge must award separate property to the spouse who owns it. However, statutes in California and Idaho allow alimony or support allowances to one spouse from the other's separate property.[379] The other community property states do not strictly require separate property to be awarded to the owning spouse but instead allow it to be divided on an equitable basis. However, the fact that it is separate generally determines its ownership.[380] As to community property, some states are known as "equal division" states, which require equal division of community property. However, the division only has to be substantially equal, which allows the judge some leeway.[381] Other jurisdictions, which may be called "equitable division" states, allow the judge wide discretion in awarding the community property, with its status as community being one factor.[382]

§ 5.16 UNIFORM MARITAL PROPERTY ACT

The Uniform Marital Property Act (UMPA)[383] is based on community property principles and builds on provisions of the Uniform Probate Code[384] and the Uniform Marriage and Divorce Act,[385] as well as the many statutes providing for equitable apportionment of spousal property on marriage dissolution.[386] The UMPA fills a gap left by the Uniform Probate Code and the equitable apportionment statutes, which protect

---

[375] La. Civ. Code Ann. art. 2365; Reppy & Samuel, supra note 312, at 267.

[376] Ariz. Rev. Stat. Ann. § 14–2101; Cal. Prob Code § 6402; Idaho Code § 15–2–101; Nev. Rev. Stat. §§ 134.030–134.210, N.M. Stat. Ann. §§ 45–2–102, 45–3–101; Tex. Est. Code Ann. §§ 101.001, 101.003, 101.051, 201.001, 201.002, 201.102, 201.103; Wash. Rev. Code § 11.04.015; McClanahan, supra note 307, at § 4.25.

[377] Cal. Prob. Code § 6401; Idaho Code § 15–2–102 (but see § 15–2–201 as to Idaho's quasi-community property); Nev. Rev. Stat. § 123.250(1); N.M. Stat. Ann. § 45–2–102; Wash. Rev. Code § 11.04.015(1).

[378] Ariz. Rev. Stat. Ann. § 14–2102; Tex. Prob. Code Ann. § 201.003.

[379] See, e.g., Ariz. Rev. Stat. Ann. § 25–318; Cal. Fam. Code § 4321; Idaho Code §§ 32–705, 32–708, 32–903; La. Civ. Code Ann. art. 155; Mitchell v. Marklund, 47 Cal. Rptr. 756, 238 Cal. App. 2d 398 (1965); Shill v. Shill, 115 Idaho 115, 765 P.2d 140 (1988); McClanahan, supra note 307, at § 12.3.

[380] See Nev. Rev. Stat. § 125.150; N,M. Stat. Ann. § 40–4–7; Tex. Fam. Code Ann. § 7.002; Wash. Rev. Code §§ 26.09.050, 26.09.080.

[381] E.g., Cal. Fam. Code §§ 2550, 4008, 4338; Idaho Code § 32–712; N.M. Stat. Ann. §§ 40–4–3, 40–4–20; Reppy & Samuel, supra note 312, at 297.

[382] Ariz. Rev. Stat. Ann. § 25–318; Nev. Rev. Stat. § 125.150; Tex. Fam. Code Ann. § 7.002; Wash. Rev. Code § 26.09.080; McClanahan, supra note 307, at §§ 12.6–12.14 (detailed state-by-state analysis); Reppy & Samuel, supra note 312, at 297.

[383] The text of UMPA, along with copious commentary, is in 9A U.L.A. Part I, at 103–58 (1998)).

[384] The text of the Uniform Probate Code is in 9 U.L.A., Parts I and II (1998).

[385] The Uniform Marriage and Divorce Act is in 9A U.L.A., Parts I and II (1998).

[386] See supra § 5.5.

the nonowning spouse in common law jurisdictions only when the owning spouse dies first or the marriage is dissolved. The UMPA creates shared property rights during the marriage for property that is in the "marital property" regime. In this way, property division when the marriage dissolves or a spouse dies is more predictable and less a product of the adversarial process.

Under UMPA:

1.   All of the spouses' property is presumed to be marital property;[387]

2.   Each spouse has a present, undivided one-half interest in the marital property;[388]

3.   Property that a spouse owns at the "determination date" for classification is individual property if acquired (a) by gift or testamentary disposition from a third party, (b) in exchange for or with the proceeds of other individual property, or (c) from appreciation of the spouse's individual property, except to the extent that UMPA classifies the appreciation as marital property;[389]

4.   Ownership and management of marital property are carefully separated, and the right to manage and control marital property does not determine its classification or rebut the presumption that all of the spouses' property is marital property;[390]

5.   A spouse acting alone can manage and control marital property held in that spouse's name alone, not held in either spouse's name, or held in both spouses' names in the alternative,[391] but spouses must act together to manage and control property held in their joint names;[392]

6.   The amount of a spouse's gifts of marital property to a third party in a single year is significantly restricted;[393]

7.   A bona fide purchaser for value who deals with the spouse who has the right to manage and control property takes free of the other spouse's claims;[394]

8.   Special provisions deal with the classification of life insurance policies and proceeds,[395] deferred employment benefits,[396] interspousal remedies,[397] and the effect of a judicial declaration that a purported marriage is invalid;[398]

---

[387] UMPA § 4(b). Unless classified otherwise, all spousal property is marital property. Id. § 4(a).

[388] Id. § 4(c).

[389] Under § 5, the "determination date" is generally the date of the marriage or the date that the parties move to a state that has the Act. Section 14(b) provides for transmutation of individual property of one spouse by, roughly speaking, the other spouse's augmenting its value by his or her effort.

[390] Id. § 5(d).

[391] Id.

[392] Id. § 5(b).

[393] Id. § 6.

[394] Id. § 9.

[395] Id. § 12.

[396] Id. § 13.

[397] Id. § 15.

[398] Id. § 16.

9. When a marriage dissolves, each spouse owns an undivided one-half interest in the marital property as a tenant in common, unless a decree or written consent provides otherwise;[399] and

10. Whether all or only half of the marital property is subject to probate administration when one spouse dies is unclear.

An important feature of UMPA is that spouses can change their property's classification by gift or by written agreement.[400] By agreement, they also can alter their control and management of the property.[401] In this way, they can effectively opt out of UMPA, but they cannot adversely affect the rights of creditors, bona fide purchasers, or a child who is entitled to support.[402] The marital property agreement is enforceable without consideration[403] and may be amended or revoked by a later agreement.[404] A couple who intends to marry can enter into a marital property agreement, but the agreement becomes effective only when they marry.[405] All marital property agreements are unenforceable if the spouse against whom enforcement is sought proves unconscionability, involuntary execution, or lack of fair and reasonable disclosure of the other party's property or financial obligations.[406] If a marital property agreement modifies or eliminates the spousal support right, which causes a spouse to be eligible for public assistance when the marriage is dissolved, the court may require the other spouse to provide support to the extent necessary to eliminate that eligibility, notwithstanding the agreement.[407]

To date, Wisconsin is the only state that has enacted UMPA.[408] In addition to making a number of minor changes in UMPA's language, Wisconsin added a section entitled "Credit transactions with married persons"[409] and made substantial additions to the UMPA section on remedies.[410]

§§ 5.17–6.0 ARE RESERVED FOR SUPPLEMENTAL MATERIAL.

---

[399] Id. § 17.

[400] Id. §§ 7(b), 10(a).

[401] Id. § 10(c).

[402] Id. §§ 10(c), 10(b), 2, 8(e). See 9A U.L.A., Prefatory Note to UMPA 104, 107 (1998).

[403] Id. § 10(a).

[404] Id. § 10(d).

[405] Id. § 10(e).

[406] Id. § 10(f), (g).

[407] Id. § 10(i).

[408] 9A U.L.A., Part I (1998), 1999 Pocket Part, p. 2. The Wisconsin version of UMPA is Wis. Stat. ch. 766, enacted by 1983 Wis. Laws, Act 186, effective Jan. 1, 1986.

[409] Wis. Stat. § 766.56.

[410] Wis. Stat. § 766.70.

Chapter 6

LANDLORD AND TENANT

Table of Sections

A. NATURE AND HISTORY OF LEASEHOLDS

§ 6.1   THE LANDLORD-TENANT RELATION

In medieval English law a "tenant" was anyone who held any estate in land in a tenurial relationship. This implied that another person (the "lord") had previously held the same or a larger estate in the land and had conveyed the tenant's estate to the tenant with the latter having to perform stated duties in return during the tenancy. For instance, the king (ultimate owner of all land) might parcel out some land to one of his nobles in fee simple or for life, in return for which the noble would owe the king military or other service. The king was lord and the noble was tenant. If the noble similarly parceled out a portion of the same land, the process was called "subinfeudation" and created another lord-tenant relation, another rung on the feudal ladder.

One still occasionally sees definitions of "tenant" that are as broad as the description above.[1] However, today we understand and use the phrase "landlord and tenant" in a narrower sense. A tenant is one who holds a possessory estate in land for a determinate period or at will by permission of the landlord, who holds an estate of larger duration in the same land.[2] The word "possessory," though redundant in the sense that all estates are possessory, emphasizes that a leasehold is truly an estate in land, even if not listed

[1]   See, e.g., Urban Inv. & Dev. Co. v. Maurice L. Rothschild & Co., 323 N.E.2d 588 (Ill.App.1975); 1 Am. Law of Prop. § 3.2 (1952).
[2]   See United States v. 15.3 Acres of Land, 154 F.Supp. 770 (M.D.Pa.1957); Chubb Group of Ins. Cos. v. C.F. Murphy & Assocs., Inc., 656 S.W.2d 766 (Mo.App.1983); Port of Coos Bay v. Dept. of Revenue, 691 P.2d 100 (Or.1984); Hughes v. Chehalis Sch. Dist. No. 302, 377 P.2d 642 (Wash.1963).

among the freehold estates. And the requirement that the landlord hold a longer estate than the tenant implies that the landlord has something left over—a reversion—after the end of the tenant's estate.

One may carve a leasehold out of any "larger" estate. For this purpose, all of the freehold estates are larger. A leasehold tenant may also carve another leasehold of shorter duration, called a sublease, out of the primary leasehold. The parties to this new arrangement are sublandlord and subtenant. In fact, the subtenant in turn could create a sub-subtenancy, and so on without theoretical end. A corollary is that the holder of an estate who transfers all of the holder's estate does not create a leasehold, but effects a conveyance (when the transfer is of a freehold) or an assignment (when the estate transferred is a leasehold).

The transaction that creates a leasehold is called a leasing, lease, letting, demise, or renting. In popular parlance the word "lease" often refers to a written leasing document, although some leases may be oral. Leases, particularly written ones, customarily contain a number of contractual covenants, virtually always including a tenant's covenant to pay rent. None of these covenants are necessary to the existence of the leasehold, which could for example be granted as a gift with no covenants by either party. However, because landlords generally expect rent, it is likely that a court would find an implied promise for rent unless the parties had overcome the implication. In addition, once the landlord-tenant relation arises, the parties have those rights and duties with which the relation is surrounded by judge-made and legislative law. That body of law is the bulk of the material in this chapter.

B. LEASEHOLDS DISTINGUISHED FROM OTHER RELATIONSHIPS

§ 6.2 DISTINGUISHED—LICENSE, EASEMENT, OR PROFIT

Courts have sometimes used false bases to distinguish leaseholds from licenses, easements, or profits. Decisions can be found in which a lease was said to be irrevocable and a license revocable.[3] This is a false distinction because, while a license is revocable, so is a tenancy at will (one form of leasehold). Moreover, leases can contain clauses allowing one or both parties to terminate. One may also find courts that purport to distinguish a license on the ground that it is given without consideration, whereas a leasehold is given in consideration of rent.[4] This distinction is also false because rent is not necessary for a leasehold, and the holder of a license may well have paid for it.

The true point of distinction is that a leasehold (being an estate) gives the right of possession or occupation, whereas licenses, easements, and profits involve only rights of use.[5] To be sure, there can be real problems distinguishing possession from use, but these

---

[3]   1 Am. Law of Prop. § 3.3 (1952).

[4]   Siver v. Atl. Union Coll., 154 N.E.2d 360 (Mass.1958); Jewish Child Care Ass'n of N.Y. v. City of N.Y., 129 Misc.2d 871, 493 N.Y.S.2d 936 (Sup.1985) (occupancy without rent not leasehold but license).

[5]   Tanner Cos. v. Ariz. State Land Dept., 688 P.2d 1075 (Ariz.App.1984) (right to remove clay only profit, not leasehold); Clayton Cty. Bd. of Tax Assessors v. City of Atlanta, 298 S.E.2d 544 (Ga.App.1982) (right to operate airport commissary was mere "usufruct" or license, not leasehold); Kiehm v. Adams, 126 P.3d 339 (Haw.2005) (interest of roommate was license, not a leasehold); Hi-Rise Laundry Equip. Corp. v. Matrix Props., Inc., 96 A.D.2d 930, 466 N.Y.S.2d 375 (1983) (right to occupy for 10 years upon rent was leasehold); Todd v. Krolick, 96 A.D.2d 695, 466 N.Y.S.2d 788 (1983), aff'd, 466 N.E.2d 149 (N.Y.1984) (right to install coin laundry equipment was license, not leasehold); Nextel of N.Y., Inc. v. Time Mgmt. Corp., 297 A.D.2d 282, 746 N.Y.S.2d

problems are not peculiar to landlord-tenant law. They occur in other areas, such as in distinguishing adverse possession from adverse use or prescription.

§ 6.3   DISTINGUISHED—SIGNS, BILLBOARDS, AND ANTENNAS

One may obtain the right to place a sign, billboard, or antenna on another's land. The installer may become a tenant by leasing a specified parcel for the purpose. However, in most cases the relationship is not so clear, as when the right is only to erect a free-standing sign on a field or a roof or to paint a message on the landowner's wall. These cases pose a problem of distinguishing easements and licenses from leaseholds. As suggested in the prior section, the question is whether the installer has possession of a defined area or only use. Crucial to this question is the underlying question whether the parties intend the installer to have exclusive control over a defined area.

When the sign is painted on a wall otherwise used by the landowner, the installer likely has only an easement for the sign (and for temporary use of the owner's land for sign maintenance). Sign or antenna structures on roofs pose closer questions, as the installer intrudes more on the landowner's exclusive occupation. However, in most cases, if the dominant function of the roof continues to be to shelter the landowner's building, the sign installer probably has an easement. Free-standing signs or antennas on the ground pose the most difficult questions. If the parties have agreed that the installer is to have exclusive control over a defined plot of ground, a landlord-tenant relation should exist.[6] If this is not clearly agreed, but the structure is large and so built that the landowner can make no substantial use of the area without interfering with the structure, then this would seem to imply a leasehold. Most billboards, supported by a few posts separated by open spaces, probably do not imply a leasehold. The law conventionally allows easements for minor structures, such as utility poles or the improvements upon a road easement. By analogy, most courts would allow easements for fairly substantial billboards.[7]

---

169 (2002) (cell tower agreement was lease, rather than license, because agreement contained many provisions typical of lease and conferred rights well beyond those of licensee or holder of temporary privilege); Riverwood Commercial Park, LLC v. Standard Oil Co., Inc., 698 N.W.2d 478 (N.D.2005) (permit granting permission to "construct, operate, and maintain" a sewer pipeline created easement or license, not leasehold); Weathers v. M.C. Lininger & Sons, Inc., 682 P.2d 770 (Or.App.1984) (agreement was for mineral lease, not license); Restatement (Second) of Property-Landlord & Tenant § 1.2 (1977); 1 Am. Law of Prop. § 3.3 (1952).

One sometimes sees a court describe an easement or profit for so many years as being a leasehold in an easement or profit. E.g., Jordan v. Indianapolis Water Co., 64 N.E. 680 (Ind.1902); Knapp v. Crawford, 48 P. 261 (Wash.1897). One scholar suggested that such an easement or profit should give rise to a landlord-tenant relationship, presumably with the usual incidents of that relationship. Walsh, Licenses and Tenancies for Years, 19 N.Y.U.L.Q.Rev. 333 (1942). This conclusion is both technically and practically unwise. On the technical side, an easement or profit does not fit the historical understanding that a leasehold is a possessory estate with a tenurial relationship. In practical terms, it is awkward to try to impose the incidents of this tenurial estate upon easements and profits. It is preferable to think of an easement or profit for years as an easement or profit and not as a leasehold.

⁶   E.g., Z. Justin Mgmt. Co., Inc. v. Metro Outdoor, LLC, 137 A.D.3d 577, 28 N.Y.S.3d 31 (2016); Trading Fair Houston v. SignAd, Inc., 2005 WL 1691113 (Tex.App.2005).

⁷   See generally 1 Am. Law of Prop. § 3.4 (1952).

§ 6.4 DISTINGUISHED—CONCESSION ON BUSINESS PREMISES

A merchant in general possession of its business premises often contracts with others to carry on certain business activity within part of the premises (e.g., a Starbucks coffee shop operating inside a Target department store). The parties' agreement may be called a "lease," the concessionaire may pay "rent" (often based wholly or partly on sales volume); the concession area is somewhat physically separated from the rest of the premises; employees of the larger business may be privileged to enter the concession area; and the larger business may be able to move the concessionaire around within the general premises. These are key factors in determining whether the concessionaire is a tenant. Other possible legal relationships are grantor and grantee of an easement, employer and employee, and licensor and licensee. The ultimate question should be whether the concessionaire has the right of possession; if so, a tenancy arises. If the right is only of use, then the concessionaire will likely have an easement or a license.[8] If the concessionaire's relationship to the larger business is such that the concessionaire is really an employee, then the concessionaire has no relation to the land that can be called either possession or use (as the use of the premises is only for the employer).

In practice, there is inconsistency among court decisions, with the landlord-tenant issue often being made to turn upon some detail of the parties' relationship.[9] In addition, the key issue before the courts in the concessionaire cases is often not a landlord-tenant issue, but some other question, such as whether the larger business entity must pay employee benefits for the concessionaire or whether the larger entity is liable to the concessionaire's employee in a slip-and-fall case.[10] In such cases, the landlord-tenant issue may not receive thorough attention. In a proper analysis, the ultimate determination is whether the concessionaire has possession on all the facts.

§ 6.5 DISTINGUISHED—CROPPING AGREEMENTS

A "sharecropper" is one who raises crops on land possessed by another, the two of them sharing the crops produced. The sharecropper does not have possession and is not a tenant, but holds a right in the nature of an easement to enter and produce crops. This relationship has much in common with an agricultural tenancy in which the tenant pays rent wholly or partly in crop shares. The key difference once again is who has possession.

Whether the parties stand in a landlord-tenant relationship depends on their agreement and the surrounding circumstances. Important factors in the decisions are whether the parties called their agreement a "lease," whether they used a lease form with customary leasing clauses, whether the alleged tenant has general rights to use the land for purposes beyond raising a crop, who furnishes farming supplies, and the length

8   E.g., Linro Equip. Corp. v. Westage Tower Assocs., 233 A.D.2d 824, 650 N.Y.S.2d 399 (1996) (agreement to install coin-operated laundry machines in condominium in exchange for "rent" payment created only a license; laundry concessionaire did not have exclusive dominion over designated area).

9   Compare Friend v. Gem Int'l, Inc., 476 S.W.2d 134 (Mo.App.1971) (operator of furniture department was tenant of department store), with Wandell v. Ross, 245 S.W.2d 689 (Mo.App.1952) (operator of hat-check stand that sold candy and tobacco was licensee of restaurant). See 1 Am. Law of Prop. § 3.5 (1952). Courts are not precise in distinguishing the words "concession" and "lease" from each other. See South Carolina Pub. Serv. Auth. v. Summers, 318 S.E.2d 113 (S.C.1984) (property "leased" to "concessionaires"); McGary v. Westlake Invs., 661 P.2d 971 (Wash.1983) (parking "concession" was "leased").

10   E.g., Friend v. Gem Int'l, Inc., 476 S.W.2d 134 (Mo.App.1971) (slip-and-fall case); George J. Wolff Co. v. Comm'r, 163 P.2d 179 (Wash.1945) (employee benefits).

of the agreement.[11] If the alleged tenant both resides on the land and farms it under the agreement, this is usually conclusive that a leasehold exists, though living elsewhere does not necessarily negate a leasehold estate.[12] However, residence on the premises hardly is an infallible test, because hired farm hands often are provided housing. The only safe statement is that one must examine the parties' total relationship to determine whether the alleged tenant has possession.

§ 6.6   DISTINGUISHED—LODGING AGREEMENTS

A "guest" is a transient occupant of quarters in a hotel, motel, or inn, while a "lodger" (also called a "roomer" or "boarder") is a more permanent occupant. While the distinction between "guest" and "lodger" may have legal significance, our purpose here is to distinguish both of those relationships from that of a tenant. For our purposes, "lodger" may include "guest," for neither is a tenant.

As with the other non-tenant statuses we have discussed, the basic distinction concerns possession: a tenant has possession, but a lodger does not. The difficulty is to identify those factual circumstances that will lead a court to choose one alternative or the other. Factors have included whether the occupant's stay was short, whether the owner lived in the same building, whether the owner had free access to the room, whether the owner provided services such as maid service, whether the occupant shared bathroom facilities, whether the owner provided meals, whether the room was furnished, and whether the owner holds the premises out to the public as a place for travelers or lodgers. To the extent answers to these questions tend to be "yes," the occupant is likely a lodger and not a tenant.[13] No single factor is determinative. For instance, one can be a tenant for only a few hours,[14] and a lodger (but hardly a "guest") for months or years.[15] The ultimate question is for the trier of fact.

The most frequently litigated consequence of the lodger-tenant distinction is the extent of the landowner's liability to the occupant for the latter's personal injuries. An innkeeper, hotel or motel proprietor, or lodging house operator has greater duties of care for the occupant's personal safety than does a landlord.[16] A similar question is the standard for measuring the owner's liability for the occupant's loss of personalty from theft or casualty.[17] Another question is whether the owner may oust an occupant from the premises without notice (yes, if the occupant is a lodger[18]) or whether prior notice is

---

[11] See Dopheide v. Schoeppner, 163 N.W.2d 360 (Iowa 1968); Davis v. Burton, 246 P.2d 236 (Mont.1952); Hampton v. Struve, 70 N.W.2d 74 (Neb.1955). See also Hofmann v. Hofmann, 446 N.E.2d 499 (Ill.1983) (suggesting sharecropping is less formal and more temporary than leasehold).

[12] 1 Am. Law of Prop. § 3.6 (1952).

[13] See Benham v. Morton & Furbish Agency, 929 A.2d 471 (Me.2007) (vacation rental created license, not lease); Johnson v. Kolibas, 182 A.2d 157 (N.J.Super.1962); Chawla v. Horch, 70 Misc.2d 290, 333 N.Y.S.2d 531 (Sup.1972); Buck v. Del City Apts., Inc., 431 P.2d 360 (Okla.1967); Restatement (Second) of Property-Landlord & Tenant § 1.2 (1977); 1 Am. Law of Prop. § 3.7 (1952).

[14] See Hughes v. Chehalis Sch. Dist. No. 302, 377 P.2d 642 (Wash.1963).

[15] See Marden v. Radford, 84 S.W.2d 947 (Mo.App.1935).

[16] See Marden v. Radford, 84 S.W.2d 947 (Mo.App.1935); Johnson v. Kolibas, 182 A.2d 157 (N.J.Super.1962); Buck v. Del City Apts., Inc., 431 P.2d 360 (Okla.1967).

[17] See Chawla v. Horch, 70 Misc.2d 290, 333 N.Y.S.2d 531 (Sup.1972).

[18] See Dewar v. Minneapolis Lodge, No. 44, B.P.O.E., 192 N.W. 358 (Minn.1923); Fischer v. Taub, 127 Misc.2d 518, 491 N.Y.S.2d 538 (Sup.1984) (residents of adult care home not "tenants," nor was it a "hotel").

required (yes, if the occupant is a periodic tenant).[19] Court decisions make these questions and some others turn on the lodger-tenant distinction, in spite of scholarly criticism that that distinction is not necessarily related to the differing questions presented.[20] Some modern legislation avoids the distinction altogether in certain cases by including lodgers within the definition of a "tenant."[21]

§ 6.7   DISTINGUISHED—OCCUPATION INCIDENTAL TO EMPLOYMENT

One can be a tenant of their employer. However, there are some jobs in which the employee must occupy the employer's premises, not in a separate landlord-tenant relationship but to perform the duties of the job (e.g., a building caretaker). Such persons are not regarded as tenants, with the rights and duties that status would imply, but as employees whose occupancy is in the employer's right and not the employee's possession.[22] In making this determination, courts have focused on whether the occupancy was granted as part of the hiring and whether occupancy was a necessary part of the job or at least for the employer's convenience. New York decisions have held that if the occupant was first a tenant and only later became an employee (e.g., building manager), this was conclusive of a tenancy despite the employment relationship.[23] Other notable decisions involve migrant farm workers who lived in cabins in their employers' company camps. The ultimate question in these cases was whether the workers were tenants who enjoyed easements of access for visitors (e.g., union organizers, attorneys, or doctors); courts often held the workers to be tenants.[24] Employees who reside in a company town will usually be tenants, for even if the site is isolated so that other housing is not available, the housing is for the worker's convenience. In the Uniform Residential Landlord and Tenant Act, employees whose occupancy is "conditioned on employment in and about the premises" are excluded from the act's operation, but no such exclusion appears in the Model Residential Landlord-Tenant Code.[25]

What are the consequences of being an employee occupant instead of a tenant? The primary consequence is that an employee licensee is not entitled to the advance notice

---

[19]   See Hundley v. Milner Hotel Mgmt. Co., 114 F.Supp. 206 (W.D.Ky.1953), aff'd, 216 F.2d 613 (6th Cir.1954). See also Harkins v. Win Corp., 771 A.2d 1025 (D.C.App.2001) (roomer was not "tenant" and thus rooming house operator could use self-help to evict roomer).

[20]   Comment, Tenant, Lodger and Guest: Questionable Categories for Modern Rental Occupants, 64 Yale L.J. 391, 396, 410 (1955).

[21]   These statutes often distinguish between long-term lodgers who are entitled to tenant protections and "transient" guests who are not. See ABF Model Residential Landlord-Tenant Code §§ 1–204, 2–101 (1969) (hereafter "MRLTC"); Uniform Residential Landlord and Tenant Act § 1.301(14), 1.202 (1972) (defining "tenant" and excluding transient occupancy from coverage) (hereafter "URLTA"); Revised Uniform Residential Landlord and Tenant Act §§ 102(34), 103(a)(2), 103(c)(4) (2015) (defining "tenant" and "transient occupancy," and excluding transient occupancy from coverage) (hereafter "RURLTA").

[22]   See generally Restatement (Second) of Property-Landlord & Tenant § 1.2, Illus. 4 (1977); 1 Am. Law of Prop. § 3.8 (1952).

[23]   See Kwong v. Guido, 129 Misc.2d 211, 492 N.Y.S.2d 678 (Sup.1985); Dobson Factors, Inc. v. Dattory, 80 Misc.2d 1054, 364 N.Y.S.2d 723 (Sup.1975).

[24]   Franceschina v. Morgan, 346 F.Supp. 833 (S.D.Ind.1972); Folgueras v. Hassle, 331 F.Supp. 615 (W.D.Mich.1971); State v. Fox, 510 P.2d 230 (Wash.1973). But see De Bruyn Produce Co. v. Romero, 508 N.W.2d 150 (Mich.App.1993) (migrant workers not considered tenants); State v. Shack, 277 A.2d 369 (N.J.1971) (concluding it unnecessary to reach question of whether migrant workers were tenants).

[25]   MRLTC § 2–101 (1969); URLTA § 1.202(5) (1972); RURLTA § 103(c)(5) (2015).

to quit generally allowed periodic tenants.[26] If occupancy is only as an incident to employment, then the only notice to vacate that the employer must give is that notice required to terminate the employment relationship.[27] The fact that the employment relationship is terminable at will does not necessarily mean the occupant is not a tenant, because tenancies at will are terminable without advance notice, unless a statute requires otherwise.[28] Similarly, it is possible for an employee to be a true tenant and for the tenancy to end with the termination of employment if the parties so agree.[29]

§ 6.8   DISTINGUISHED—CONTRACT PURCHASER IN POSSESSION

The modern form of the real estate installment sale contract gives the purchaser possession while the contract is executory, yet the vendor purports to retain legal title until the vendee has made full performance. To be sure, most jurisdictions recognize that the installment purchaser has equitable title during the executory period. This equitable title enables courts generally to conclude that the purchaser's possession is not as tenant of the vendor but as equitable owner in the purchaser's own right,[30] often labeled simply as contract purchaser in possession.[31] There is even authority that if the contract gives the purchaser the right of possession, but the purchaser allows the vendor to remain in possession, the vendor becomes the purchaser's tenant.[32] There are a number of legal consequences which flow from the conclusion that the purchaser is not a tenant. The vendor may not use a statutory scheme for summary possession to evict a defaulting purchaser if the statute applies only to actions between landlords and tenants.[33] In case persons suffer injuries on the premises, the contract vendor's exposure to liability is different from (and generally less than) that of a landlord.[34] A tenant who becomes a contract purchaser may thereby bear the risk of loss of the premises from a casualty such as fire.[35] Finally, one who is in possession as an installment contract purchaser does not owe rent (though of course the purchaser owes the payments due under the contract).[36]

---

[26] See Bennardo v. Searchwell, 54 Misc.3d 924, 43 N.Y.S.3d 878 (Cty.Dist.Ct.2016) (home healthcare aide was not tenant but licensee whose occupancy was incidental to employment); Dobson Factors, Inc. v. Dattory, 80 Misc.2d 1054, 364 N.Y.S.2d 723 (Sup.1975); 1 Am. Law of Prop. § 3.8 (1952).

[27] See De Bruyn Produce Co. v. Romero, 508 N.W.2d 150 (Mich.App.1993); Johnson v. Simpson Oil Co., 394 S.W.2d 91 (Mo.App.1965).

[28] See infra § 6.18.

[29] See Coldiron v. Good Coal Co., 125 S.W.2d 757 (Ky.1939); Najewitz v. City of Seattle, 152 P.2d 722 (Wash.1944).

[30] See generally 1 Am. Law of Prop. § 3.9 (1952); Nelson, Whitman, Burkhart & Freyermuth, Real Estate Finance Law §§ 3.26–3.38 (6th ed.2015).

[31] MacKenna v. Jordan, 182 S.E.2d 550 (Ga.App.1971); Edwards v. Van Skiver, 256 A.D.2d 957, 681 N.Y.S.2d 893 (1998); Shipley v. Bankers Life & Cas. Co., 377 P.2d 571 (Okla.1962); Strengowski v. Gomes, 268 A.2d 749 (Vt.1970); 1 Am. Law of Prop. § 3.9 (1952).

[32] Lasher v. Redev. Auth., 236 A.2d 831 (Pa.Super.1967).

[33] Bemis v. Allen, 93 N.W. 50 (Iowa 1903) (defendant held to be tenant); Kiernan v. Linnehan, 24 N.E. 907 (Mass.1890); Strengowski v. Gomes, 268 A.2d 749 (Vt.1970). For this reason, installment land contracts frequently stipulate that after default, the vendor may terminate the contract and that if the purchaser does not surrender possession, the purchaser retains possession only as a tenant.

[34] See MacKenna v. Jordan, 182 S.E.2d 550 (Ga.App.1971); Shipley v. Bankers Life & Cas. Co., 377 P.2d 571 (Okla.1962).

[35] Ridenour v. France, 442 N.E.2d 716 (Ind.App.1982).

[36] Ankeny v. Clark, 148 U.S. 345, 13 S.Ct. 617, 37 L.Ed. 475 (1893); Barrell v. Britton, 138 N.E. 579 (Mass.1923) (dictum).

§ 6.9   DISTINGUISHED—MORTGAGEE IN POSSESSION

Mortgage law contains a doctrine whereby a mortgagee who goes into possession of the mortgaged premises under certain circumstances is privileged to keep possession until the mortgage debt is paid or the mortgagor's interest is foreclosed. Courts disagree on what "certain circumstances" will allow this privilege. One formula is that the mortgagee has a kind of right, analogous to a pledge, to hold possession as security.[37] Another theory is that the mortgagor expressly or impliedly "consents" to the mortgagee's holding possession for security.[38] Whatever the explanation, it is clear that the mortgagee in possession as *mortgagee* in its own right is not a tenant. In fact, courts have held that if a mortgagee takes possession as a tenant (under a lease), the mortgagee is not a "mortgagee in possession."[39]

While the status of mortgagee in possession is *sui generis* and is not that of a tenant, it is closer to a tenant's position than a contract purchaser in possession. One may think of the mortgagee in possession as a kind of caretaker, with duties of care and management roughly parallel to those of a responsible owner. The mortgagee in possession may lease out the land and collect rent from and deal with new or pre-existing tenants. The mortgagee in possession may apply any rental income to the mortgage debt after paying for necessary expenses, but must strictly account for its dealings. Should the mortgagee in possession use the land for some profitable business of its own, such as farming, it is usually chargeable with the fair rental value. There is little authority to suggest the mortgagee in possession is liable for rental value if it neither rents out the land nor uses it, though some have urged this position.[40]

§ 6.10   CONVEYANCE OR CONTRACT?

When parties enter into a lease, have they executed a conveyance or a contract? The lease conveys a leasehold estate, but also contains contractual undertakings, such as promises to pay rent, make repairs, pay taxes, procure insurance, and so forth. Analytically, it is correct to say a lease is both a conveyance and a contract. But this simple statement masks significant historical tensions involving the remedies that courts have recognized for breach of a lease covenant.

Under modern contract law, covenants in a bilateral contract are mutually dependent; one party's material breach excuses the other party's performance. By the time this principle became established under contract law, however, property law had long characterized the tenant as having a leasehold estate—and thus the landlord-tenant relationship was seen as one deriving from real property law. Property law viewed the essence of the leasehold as an exchange of possession of the land (the tenant's estate) in return for the obligation to pay rent; all other aspects of the landlord-tenant bargain, including any other covenants of the parties, were secondary and independent. Thus, for example, if the lease obligated the tenant to repair damage to the premises but the tenant failed to do so, this failure did not excuse the landlord's obligation to respect the tenant's possession! The landlord would still have a cause of action against the

---

[37] See Spect v. Spect, 26 P. 203 (Cal.1891).

[38] See Barson v. Mulligan, 84 N.E. 75 (N.Y.1908).

[39] Barson v. Mulligan, 84 N.E. 75 (N.Y.1908).

[40] For a detailed discussion of the matters summarized here, see Nelson, Whitman, Burkhart & Freyermuth, Real Estate Finance Law §§ 4.24–4.29 (6th ed.2015).

tenant for damages for breach of its promise to repair, but could not terminate the lease and evict the tenant unless the express terms of the lease so provided.

This caveat—that covenants are dependent if the lease expressly makes them so—reflects that the common law and statutory rules governing the landlord-tenant relationship are primarily background rules or "default" rules, i.e., ones that will apply unless the parties expressly agree to the contrary. Often, a lease agreement explicitly states that if the tenant breaches any of its obligations, the landlord can terminate the lease. The converse is usually not the case, however; only the rare lease agreement will explicitly allow the tenant to terminate the lease if the landlord breaches.

If a lease is not sufficiently explicit, should the law fill the "gap" in the parties' agreement by reference to property law (treating lease covenants as independent) or by reference to contract law (treating them as dependent)? There is a trend in landlord-tenant law that recognizes the increasing influence of contract law. The Restatement (Second) of Property takes the view that either party to a lease may terminate the lease if one party breaches a covenant that deprives the other party of "a significant inducement to the making of the lease."[41] Agreeing with this view, Massachusetts has abolished the doctrine of independence of covenants as a default rule, concluding that a tenant can terminate the lease in response to a significant landlord breach, even if that breach did not amount to a constructive eviction of the tenant.[42] Some courts have also treated certain covenants as dependent in particular factual contexts. For example, some courts have allowed a shopping center tenant to terminate a lease when the landlord breached a clause that gave the tenant the exclusive right to operate the only business of a certain type in the center.[43] Likewise, a few decisions have permitted a tenant to terminate a lease when the landlord breached it by unreasonably refusing to consent to a tenant's proposed assignment or sublease,[44] though the weight of authority remains to the contrary.[45]

Another important consequence of categorizing a lease as a conveyance was to deny tenants the benefits of implied warranties as to the condition of the premises. Contract law governing sales of goods long ago developed implied warranties of fitness of purpose and merchantability, but real property law did not recognize similar warranties. For conveyances, including leases, the traditional rule was rather *caveat emptor,* so that the tenant was generally out of luck if the premises (including buildings) proved defective or unsuitable. Moreover, the tenant generally could not maintain actions for injuries to person or property caused by defective conditions. In the residential lease context, the edifice of *caveat emptor* has largely collapsed since the 1960s. A number of courts

---

[41] Restatement (Second) of Property-Landlord & Tenant § 7.1(1) (1977) (tenant may terminate for landlord's breach), § 13.1(1) (landlord may terminate for tenant's breach). Several courts have cited § 13.1 as authority for the landlord to terminate upon tenant's default, e.g., Grubb v. Wm. Calomiris Invst. Corp., 588 A.2d 1144 (D.C.1991), and Cain Partn., Ltd. v. Pioneer Invst. Servs. Co., 914 S.W.2d 452 (Tenn.1996)—although as noted in the text, most leases expressly grant landlord such a termination right. Arizona has adopted § 7.1 as authority for tenant termination. Terry v. Gaslight Sq. Assocs., 897 P.2d 667 (Ariz.App.1994).

[42] Wesson v. Leone Enters., Inc., 774 N.E.2d 611 (Mass.2002).

[43] See, e.g., Medico-Dental Bldg. Co. v. Horton & Converse, 132 P.2d 457 (Cal.1942); University Club v. Deakin, 106 N.E. 790 (Ill.1914). See also University Props., Inc. v. Moss, 388 P.2d 543 (Wash.1964) (tenant allowed to rescind because landlord breached covenant to expand premises).

[44] See, e.g., Chrysler Capital Corp. v. Lavender, 934 F.2d 290 (11th Cir.1991) (Alabama law); Ringwood Assocs., Ltd. v. Jack's of Route 23, Inc., 398 A.2d 1315 (N.J.Super.1979) (citing Restatement § 7.1).

[45] See, e.g., Rock County Sav. & Trust Co. v. Yost's, Inc., 153 N.W.2d 594 (Wis.1967); Ernst Home Ctr. v. Sato, 910 P.2d 486 (Wash.App.1996).

abolished *caveat emptor* as applied to dwellings and have implied into residential leases warranties of fitness for human habitation. More states have new residential landlord-tenant statutes accomplishing the same result.[46] Nevertheless, *caveat emptor* continues to predominate with respect to commercial leases.[47] We explore these matters in detail later in this Chapter.

Despite the fact that courts have often stated that leases are conveyances, there are significant areas in which pure contract principles govern. One such area is the interpretation of promissory language. For example, if the question is whether a covenant to "insure" the premises requires a policy with extended coverage or a policy for the full value of improvements, cases from the branch of contract law dealing with insurance will control. Another example is the familiar rule that ambiguous language in the lease will be construed against the landlord; this is an application of the contract rule of construing against the drafter (who in the lease context is almost always the landlord). We may also note that, while it is usually descriptive and not decisive, landlord-tenant decisions almost routinely speak of a lease as a contract.

Given the nature of the common law decision-making process, courts will continue to struggle with the significance of the conveyance/contract dichotomy in resolving lease disputes. As one court has honestly acknowledged, "as a result of the dual nature of a lease, neither contract principles nor property principles can be exclusively relied upon to govern the resolution of all issues . . . . Whether contract principles, property principles, or a blend of both control the resolution of a particular case depends largely on the intent of the parties, the interests of society, and the relative fairness of the results to be achieved through selection among the potentially applicable principles."[48]

§ 6.11 NATURE OF TENANT'S PROPERTY INTEREST

A tenant has an estate in land in the strictest sense. The tenant has the right to possession, the hallmark of every estate. Yet for purely historical reasons, real estate law classified this estate not as a freehold estate, but rather as a non-freehold "chattel real," a species of personalty.[49] The freehold-chattel real distinction has lost most of its significance over the centuries, so that today it is generally accurate to think of a leasehold as simply an estate.

---

[46]   See §§ 6.37–6.45 infra.

[47]   Texas courts have held that there is an implied warranty of suitability in the leasing of commercial premises. Davidow v. Inwood N. Prof. Group–Phase I, 747 S.W.2d 373 (Tex.1988).

[48]   Schneiker v. Gordon, 732 P.2d 603 (Colo. 1987).

[49]   See Goff v. State, 875 A.2d 132, 144 n.12 (Md.2005) ("A leasehold estate or tenancy is more than a non-possessory interest in property, yet something less than a present freehold estate."); Wilson v. Fieldgrove, 787 N.W.2d 707 (Neb.2010) (leasehold interest in tenancy for term or periodic tenancy is personal property); In re Estate of Hayes, 342 P.3d 1161 (Wash.App.2015) (same); 2 Pollock & Maitland, History of English Law 106–17 (2d ed. 1898) (tracing the early history of the leasehold).

One area in which the peculiar concept of a chattel real still may be significant is the settlement of decedents' estates. In England before the Statute of Wills in 1540, one could pass personalty by will but not realty. See T. Atkinson, Wills § 3 (2d ed.1953). Persons who took personalty by descent were also different in England from those who inherited land. To a much lesser extent, differences as to wills and between descent and inheritance existed in former times in the American colonies and states. Today, these differences have virtually disappeared, so that it can be said that a leasehold descends by intestacy or may pass by will to the same persons as may take freehold estates. T. Atkinson, Wills § 4 (2d ed.1953). Of course, a lease can provide explicitly that the tenant's death terminates the leasehold estate, in which case the leasehold would not pass by descent or will.

§ 6.12   NATURE OF LANDLORD'S PROPERTY INTEREST

The landlord, having given the tenant a present possessory estate, has retained a reversion that follows the end of the leasehold.[50] If the landlord held the fee simple, the reversion is in fee. It is possible, too, for the landlord's estate to be shorter in duration than a fee, so long as it is longer than the leasehold. For example, the landlord may have a life estate. Even if the landlord is 100 years old and creates a 99-year leasehold, we regard the leasehold conceptually as smaller than the life estate, so that in theory the life tenant has a reversion, however unlikely this is in practice. As another example, a tenant may create a subtenancy for a shorter time than the primary leasehold. The primary tenant becomes also a sub-landlord with a sub-tenant and a reversion in his own primary leasehold; there is now a true second landlord-tenant relationship.

The landlord-tenant relationship is the surviving remnant of the tenurial relationship that dominated medieval English land law. This is not quite correct, for the leasehold did not descend from the medieval freehold; the present freehold estates so descended, but they no longer carry tenure. The essence of tenure is that one person holds an estate of or under another person and owes the other continuing or recurring duties (such as the payment of rent) during the duration of the estate. With some inconsequentially rare exceptions, tenures do not exist in freehold estates in the United States.[51] With the leasehold, not only are the medieval words "lord" and "tenant" used, but the customary covenant to pay rent will make the relationship tenurial.

C.   CREATION OF THE LANDLORD-TENANT RELATIONSHIP

§ 6.13   PRINCIPLES APPLIED TO ALL LEASEHOLDS

All leaseholds must be founded in an agreement between landlord and tenant.[52] Thus, the parties must have the legal capacity to make an agreement.[53] One must understand the concept of "agreement" broadly. A lease "agreement" may arise by implication simply from the circumstance that the holder of an estate permits another to possess the land (this would likely be a tenancy at will).[54] Absence of explicit written

---

[50]   See, e.g., Mobil Oil Corp. v. Phoenix Central Christian Church, 675 P.2d 284 (Ariz.App.1983) (landlord and tenant have separate interests in condemnation award); Wing v. Martin, 688 P.2d 1172 (Idaho 1984) (landlord has right to recover for permanent damage to reversion); Foertsch v. Schaus, 477 N.E.2d 566 (Ind.App.1985) (landowner making oil lease has right to only such oil as remains in ground after end of lease); Lentz Plumbing Co. v. Fee, 679 P.2d 736 (Kan.1984) (tenant has no general right to burden landlord's reversion with mechanic's lien).

[51]   The Statute Quia Emptores, 18 Edw. 1, cc. 1–3 (1290), forbade generally the subsequent creation of new tenures in freehold. However, an exception was allowed for freeholds created by the crown. Tenurial freeholds existed to some extent in some of the American colonies. Whether this has carried over into modern time is a debatable question. See 1 Am. Law of Prop. § 1.41 (1952).

[52]   See, e.g., McCarter v. Uban, 166 N.W.2d 910 (Iowa 1969); Faroldi v. Nungesser, 144 So.2d 568 (La.App.1962); Vic's Parking Corp. v. Nash, 26 Misc.3d 413, 890 N.Y.S.2d 803 (Sup.2009) ("A leasehold is not created when the contract to form a leasehold fails.").

[53]   718 Assocs. v. Banks, 21 A.3d 977 (D.C.App.2011); Tecklenburg v. Washington Gas & Elec. Co., 241 P.2d 1172 (Wash.1952); Restatement (Second) of Property-Landlord & Tenant § 1.3 (1977).

[54]   E.g., Dismuke v. Abbott, 505 S.E.2d 58 (Ga.App.1998) (son who lived in with life tenant mother was implied tenant at will while remaining in possession during estate administration). Compare Faroldi v. Nungesser, 144 So.2d 568 (La.App.1962) (occupancy alone will not imply a leasehold).

covenants, including a covenant for rent, would not defeat the landlord-tenant relationship; the possessor would not be a trespasser or adverse possessor.

When the alleged tenant has not taken possession, the word "agreement" must refer more strictly to a memorialized exchange of undertakings. In the absence of a Statute of Frauds, an oral agreement is as good as a written one.[55] Whatever form the agreement is in, it must be sufficiently definite in its "essential" parts that a court can determine the parties' intent. The question of definiteness seems to be the same as in the law of contracts.[56] As to the "essential" parts of a lease, courts often say that an enforceable lease agreement must cover the identity of the parties,[57] a description of the premises, and a statement of the term and the amount of rent.[58]

The sufficiency of the description of the premises has caused occasional problems for courts. The usual judicial formula is that a description is adequate—even though it is not a formal legal description or even a complete informal one—if it gives a clue that, with extrinsic evidence, identifies the intended premises.[59] Courts have held street addresses and nicknames adequate under this standard.[60] In some jurisdictions, stricter standards may apply, possibly even a formal legal description.[61] An inadequate description is cured if the tenant takes possession.[62]

The duration of a leasehold term must be stated, either explicitly or by reference to a formula by which the term can be computed.[63] If the term cannot be determined, the lease is not sufficiently definite to be enforced.[64] The most crucial point to be fixed is the

---

[55]   Maccarini v. New Haven Trap Rock Co., 148 F.Supp. 271 (S.D.N.Y.1957), aff'd, 249 F.2d 893 (2d Cir.1957); McCarter v. Uban, 166 N.W.2d 910 (Iowa 1969); Mirizio v. Joseph, 4 A.3d 1073 (Pa.Super.2010) (dictum); Restatement (Second) of Property-Landlord & Tenant § 2.1 (1977). Where a state's statute of frauds requires a written lease, parties must take care to ensure that the lease satisfies any peculiar state law requirements for a valid conveyance. E.g., S & I Invsts. v. Payless Flea Market, Inc., 36 So.3d 909 (Fla.App.2010) (commercial lease invalid because it was not signed in presence of two subscribing witnesses); Game Place, L.L.C. v. Fredericksburg 35, LLC, 813 S.E.2d 312 (Va.2018) (purported 15-year lease was unenforceable because it failed to satisfy state's common-law requirement to include a seal).

[56]   See, e.g., In re Wonderfair Stores, Inc., 511 F.2d 1206 (9th Cir.1975); Walker v. Keith, 382 S.W.2d 198 (Ky.1964).

[57]   Where an individual signs a lease on behalf of a business entity like a corporation or limited liability company, the individual signer is not liable for the tenant's obligations unless the lease makes this explicit. See Fairway Mortg. Solutions, Inc. v. Locust Gardens, 988 So.2d 678 (Fla.App.2008).

[58]   See Cook v. Hargis, 435 P.2d 385 (Colo.1967); McCarter v. Uban, 166 N.W.2d 910 (Iowa 1969); Slue v. N.Y.U. Med. Ctr., 409 F.Supp.2d 349 (S.D.N.Y.2006); Smith v. Smith, 308 S.E.2d 504 (N.C.App.1983); Clover Belt Farms v. Rademacher, 699 N.W.2d 253 (Wis.App.2005). Cf. King v. Oxford, 318 S.E.2d 125 (S.C.1984) (purchase option was not essential part of lease). Even the amount of rent may not be material if the parties intend no rent, though this would be rare. Cf. Askinuk Corp v. Lower Yukon Sch. Dist., 214 P.3d 259 (Alaska 2009) ($1/year rent adequate consideration for lease); Mirizio v. Joseph, 4 A.3d 1073 (Pa.Super.2010) ("reservation of rent is not essential to the creation of the landlord and tenant relation").

[59]   Bajrangi v. Magnethel Enters., Inc., 589 So.2d 416 (Fla.App.1991); Peripety Group, Inc. v. Smith, 514 S.E.2d 262 (Ga.App.1999) (lease agreement valid, although it did not identify premises, where guaranty agreement executed by tenant's president did contain sufficient description); Consolidation Coal Co. v. Mineral Coal Co., 126 S.E.2d 194 (W.Va.1962); Soppe v. Breed, 504 P.2d 1077 (Wyo.1973).

[60]   Keck v. Brookfield, 409 P.2d 583 (Ariz.App.1965) (street address); Cook v. Hargis, 435 P.2d 385 (Colo.1967) ("Old Pine Theatre Building").

[61]   See Stoebuck, The Law Between Landlord and Tenant in Washington, 49 Wash.L.Rev. 291, 311–12 (1974).

[62]   E.g., Crown CoCo, Inc. v. Red Fox Restaurant of Royalton, Inc., 409 N.W.2d 919 (Minn.App.1987); McKennon v. Anderson, 298 P.2d 492 (Wash.1956); Soppe v. Breed, 504 P.2d 1077 (Wyo.1973).

[63]   Restatement (Second) of Property-Landlord & Tenant § 1.4 (1977); 1 Am. Law of Prop. § 3.14 (1952).

[64]   E.g., Cypert v. Holmes, 299 P.2d 650 (Ariz.1956); Adams v. Lay, 128 S.E.2d 502 (Ga.1962); Ross v. Ross, 172 A.3d 1069 (N.H.2017); MacThompson Realty v. City of Nashua, 993 A.2d 773 (N.H.2010).

commencement of the term; if this cannot be determined, no kind of tenancy can arise; by contrast, if only the extent of the term is in doubt, a tenancy at will might exist.[65] The term may commence in the future and upon an uncertain event, such as completion of structures on the demised land.[66] Though a lease to commence at a future date is generally unexceptional, a lease to commence on the date of an uncertain event that may not occur within 21 years may violate the Rule Against Perpetuities, at least in jurisdictions that have not enacted perpetuities reform.[67] The drafter can avoid this problem by providing that the lease will fail if the term does not commence within 21 years of its execution. As long as the term commences within the period of the Rule, no perpetuity is created by an extremely long term, even a thousand years.[68] When the lease commences at a future date, the time before commencement is no part of the term, and the future tenant's right during this time is sometimes called *"interesse termini."*[69]

A special problem exists with leases to commence on completion of a commercial structure, such as a store in a shopping center. If the lease contemplates the building of substantial structures before the term commences, this is a sufficiently material condition that the lease is not enforceable unless an agreement describes the structures with some degree of particularity. Some decisions suggest that lease must contain (or incorporate by reference) plans and specifications detailed enough to direct construction.[70] This seems an extreme position, and most courts would probably enforce an agreement that enabled the court to determine the rough design of the buildings.[71] Obviously the parties' agreement and surrounding circumstances have much to do with the specificity required. Sometimes the parties provide that building plans shall be satisfactory to one of them, giving rise to arguments that the agreement is too vague or is illusory. The predictable judicial response is that the party to be satisfied must act in good faith or not unreasonably disapprove, matters into which the court may inquire.[72]

Some decisions deal with whether an agreement is a lease to commence at a future date or instead only a contract to make a lease. The major consequence of this distinction is the measure of damages if the alleged tenant defaults. If the agreement is a lease,

---

[65]   E.g., Providence Land Servs., LLC v. Jones, 353 S.W.3d 538 (Tex.App.2011).

[66]   Cape Oil Delivery, Inc. v. Hayes, 2005 WL 3739861 (Mass.Super.Ct.2005) (term to commence at earlier of expiration of prior tenant's lease or prior tenant's vacation of premises); Carolina Helicopter Corp. v. Cutter Realty Co., 139 S.E.2d 362 (N.C.1964) (term to commence when tenant got business permit); E.I. DuPont de Nemours & Co. v. Zale Corp., 462 S.W.2d 355 (Tex.App.1970) (term to commence when building erected). See also In re Wonderfair Stores, Inc., 511 F.2d 1206 (9th Cir.1975).

[67]   See Wong v. DiGrazia, 386 P.2d 817 (Cal.1963) (lease to commence on uncertain future date was nevertheless valid because lease impliedly obligated developer to complete construction within a reasonable time, which under circumstances was a period less than 21 years). See also Shaver v. Clanton, 26 Cal.App.4th 568, 31 Cal.Rptr.2d 595 (1994) (noting California's adoption of Uniform Statutory Rule Against Perpetuities, which explicitly excludes interests created in commercial transactions from application of RAP).

[68]   1 Am. Law of Prop. § 3.15 (1952).

[69]   See Arthur Treacher's Fish & Chips of Fairfax, Inc. v. Chillum Terrace Ltd. Partn., 327 A.2d 282 (Md.1974); Duane Reade v. I.G. Second Generation Partn., L.P., 280 A.D.2d 410, 721 N.Y.S.2d 42 (2001); E.I. DuPont de Nemours & Co. v. Zale Corp., 462 S.W.2d 355 (Tex.Civ.App.1970).

[70]   See Target Stores, Inc. v. Twin Plaza Co., 153 N.W.2d 832 (Minn.1967).

[71]   Brodsky v. Allen Hayosh Indus., Inc., 137 N.W.2d 771 (Mich.App.1965). See also In re Wonderfair Stores, Inc., 511 F.2d 1206 (9th Cir.1975); S. Jon Kreedman & Co. v. Meyers Bros. Parking-Western Corp., 58 Cal.App.3d 173, 130 Cal.Rptr. 41 (1976).

[72]   In re Wonderfair Stores, Inc., 511 F.2d 1206 (9th Cir.1975); S. Jon Kreedman & Co. v. Meyers Bros. Parking-Western Corp., 58 Cal.App.3d 173, 130 Cal.Rptr. 41 (1976). Cf. Saxon Theatre Corp. v. Sage, 200 N.E.2d 241 (Mass.1964) (agreement for lease held unenforceable when *both* parties were to agree to building plans and other matters).

damages are the unpaid rent; if the agreement is merely a contract to enter into a lease, damages are only the difference between the agreed rent and fair rental value of the premises.[73] Other consequences may flow from the lease/contract-to-lease distinction, such as whether the landowner's trustee in bankruptcy must recognize a leasehold or whether the purported tenant has an interest that is subject to local real estate taxation.[74] Ultimately it is a question of fact whether the parties intended a contract or a lease. Factors may include whether they use the word "lease" or an equivalent, whether they intend to draw up a later agreement, and whether a document contains legally required elements for a lease. The fact that the tenant is not to have possession immediately is of little consequence. Even if the transaction is found to be a purported contract to lease, it may still fail for indefiniteness because an agreement to contract must contain the essential elements of the final agreement for a court to enforce it. Thus, we still face questions similar to those faced with a lease itself, i.e., whether parties, premises, term, etc. are spelled out with adequate specificity.[75]

§ 6.14 TENANCY FOR YEARS—NATURE

The distinguishing characteristic of a tenancy for years is that it is for a definite period, fixed in advance.[76] Leaseholds may commence upon some uncertain future event, but once the tenancy for years begins, its term must be fixed. It is thus sometimes called a fixed-term tenancy. The term need not be literally for a year or multiple of a year; any fixed term—a month, a week, or even a few hours—will suffice.[77]

§ 6.15 TENANCY FOR YEARS—STATUTE OF FRAUDS

State statutes generally provide that leaseholds for over one year, or in some states a longer period, must be created by a written instrument. To be a complete lease, the written document must contain the essential elements discussed in Section 6.13.[78] Most

---

[73] Lee Shops, Inc. v. Schatten-Cypress Co., 350 F.2d 12 (6th Cir.1965) (contract to lease); Handley v. Guasco, 332 P.2d 354 (Cal.App.1958) (contract to lease); Malani v. Clapp, 542 P.2d 1265 (Haw.1975) (contract to lease); Gromelski v. Bruno, 147 N.E.2d 747 (Mass.1958) (lease); Maida v. Main Bldg., 473 S.W.2d 648 (Tex.App.1971) (lease). See also Wright v. Baumann, 398 P.2d 119 (Or.1965).

[74] In re Wonderfair Stores, Inc., 511 F.2d 1206 (9th Cir.1975) (bankruptcy); Motels of Maryland, Inc. v. Baltimore Cty., 223 A.2d 609 (Md.1966) (taxation).

[75] See, e.g., M.N. Landau Stores, Inc. v. Daigle, 170 A.2d 673 (Me.1961); Saxon Theatre Corp. v. Sage, 200 N.E.2d 241 (Mass.1964); GRB Farm v. Christman Ranch, Inc., 108 P.3d 507 (Mont.2005) (agreement that requires parties to agree to material terms in future is not enforceable agreement); Rouzani v. Rapp, 203 A.D.2d 446, 610 N.Y.S.2d 600 (1994); Joseph v. Doraty, 144 N.E.2d 111 (Ohio App.1957); Ski River Dev., Inc. v. McCalla, 167 S.W.3d 121 (Tex.App.2005) (agreement leaving material terms to be agreed upon later is indefinite as to material and essential terms and is therefore unenforceable).

One might obviate the difference between a lease and a contract to lease by arguing that a contract to lease constitutes a lease if it is specifically enforceable. See, e.g., Motels of Maryland, Inc. v. Baltimore Cty., 223 A.2d 609 (Md.1966); Granva Corp. v. Heyder, 139 S.E.2d 77 (Va.1964) (dictum). One might support this view either on the ground that an enforceable agreement to make a contract amounts to the final contract, see 1 A. Corbin, Contracts § 29 (1963), or on the same basis that gives a contract purchaser of land equitable title (i.e., equitable conversion). See 3 Am. Law of Prop. § 11.22 (1952). Williston urged that equitable conversion be applied to leases as well as contracts. 7 S. Williston, Contracts § 945 (3d ed.1963).

[76] E.g., In re Coffey, 339 B.R. 689 (Bankr.N.D.Ind.2006) (monthly payment of rent did not convert fixed-term tenancy into periodic tenancy); Waldrop v. Siebert, 237 So.2d 493 (Ala.1970); F.H. Stoltze Land Co. v. Westberg, 206 P. 407 (Mont.1922). See also Womack v. Hyche, 503 So.2d 832 (Ala.1987) (leasehold ending at uncertain time created tenancy at will); Union Bldg. Materials Corp. v. Kakaako Corp., 682 P.2d 82 (Haw.App.1984) (leasehold stated to end at uncertain time was periodic tenancy, not tenancy for years).

[77] Hughes v. Chehalis Sch. Dist. No. 302, 377 P.2d 642 (Wash.1963).

[78] An exchange of letters signed by the parties or letters aided by other documents may satisfy the requirement of a writing. Satterfield v. Pappas, 312 S.E.2d 511 (N.C.App.1984) (correspondence between

disputes have concerned who must sign the instrument. Statutes sometimes require both parties to sign and sometimes the lessor alone, but the most common requirement is that "the party to be charged" shall sign.[79] "The party to be charged" is the party against whom the lease is sought to be enforced.[80] Thus, each party wants to insure that the other has signed.

A lease that fails to comply with the Statute of Frauds does not by itself create either a leasehold or any duties. If, however, the tenant takes possession with the landowner's permission, some sort of leasehold (at least a tenancy at will) is created. Should the tenant, after entry, pay rent by an agreed period (e.g., $200 per month), this generally implies a periodic tenancy by that period.[81] When such a periodic tenancy does arise, the courts will charge the parties with the provisions of their intended lease (i.e. the lease that did not comply with the Statute of Frauds), except for the agreement on the term.[82] This certainly should be the result, for parties may enter into a periodic tenancy orally and may in that form agree to such contractual matters as rent, repairs, and insurance.

Under the equitable doctrines of part performance and estoppel, an otherwise noncompliant lease may become specifically enforceable. A careful definition of the part performance doctrine is that it allows the enforcement of a noncompliant agreement by a party who has acted under it and whose actions give independent evidence of the existence of the agreement—i.e., the actions are ones a party would not take without an agreement of the sort claimed.[83] With a lease, this typically means a tenant goes into possession and makes substantial improvements of a type the tenant would not make with a periodic or short-term tenancy.[84] Under the estoppel theory, the same sort of fact pattern is said to estop the landlord to deny that a tenant, who relied upon having a valid lease, had one.[85]

The most frequently litigated question is what acts of the tenant are sufficient to excuse the statute, on whichever theory is used. Courts generally agree that possession and payment of rent alone are not sufficient; these acts are as consistent with a short-term as with a long-term leasehold. There must be acts that suggest a long-term leasehold, which almost always means valuable and substantial improvements by the tenant.[86] On principle, it seems that payment of long-term rent (e.g., a lump-sum payment of several years' rent) might suffice, but there is little case authority.

---

parties satisfied statute of frauds); Fuller v. Southland Corp., 290 S.E.2d 754 (N.C.App.1982) (letter from tenant satisfied statute of frauds when ambiguities were clarified by other documents).

[79] E.g., Ala. Code § 8–9–2; Colo.Rev.Stat.Ann. § 4–2.5–201(1); Ga.Code Ann. § 13–5–30. See generally Restatement (Second) of Property-Landlord & Tenant § 2.1 Statutory Note (1977) (compilation of state statutes).

[80] Restatement (Second) of Property-Landlord & Tenant § 2.2, Illus. 6 (1977). But it is possible for the phrase "party to be charged" to be interpreted "grantor," i.e., landlord alone. See Central Bldg. Co. v. Keystone Shares Corp., 56 P.2d 697 (Wash.1936) (lease need not be signed by lessee provided that lessee accepts possession and acts under lease).

[81] E.g., Kent v. Humphries, 281 S.E.2d 43 (N.C.1981); Peoples v. Holley, 908 N.E.2d 517 (Ohio App.2009).

[82] Restatement (Second) of Property-Landlord & Tenant § 2.3 (1977); 1 Am. Law of Prop. § 3.20 (1952).

[83] See Sleeth v. Sampson, 142 N.E. 355 (N.Y.1923).

[84] See Martin v. Jones, 41 N.E.3d 123 (Ohio App.2015); Bennett v. Pratt, 365 P.2d 622 (Or.1961).

[85] See Whitelock v. Leatherman, 460 F.2d 507 (10th Cir.1972); In re Tayfur, 513 B.R. 282 (W.D.Pa.2014); Delfino v. Paul Davies Chevrolet, Inc., 209 N.E.2d 194 (Ohio 1965); Garbrick v. Franz, 125 P.2d 295 (Wash.1942).

[86] See, e.g., Whitelock v. Leatherman, 460 F.2d 507 (10th Cir.1972); Knorr v. Norberg, 844 N.W.2d 919 (N.D.2014) (oral lease with purchase option not enforceable under part performance doctrine; tenant's payment

Typically it is tenants rather than landlords that seek to enforce noncompliant leases. When the landlord seeks enforcement, one would look for acts by the landlord that were peculiarly referable to a long-term leasehold, particularly acts that the landlord would not have performed otherwise. Most commonly, the acts would involve substantial improvements or alterations called for by the noncompliant lease, made at the tenant's request, or of a kind to suit the tenant's use.[87] Whether the tenant had taken possession or paid rent would seem irrelevant, but some courts have considered it.[88]

§ 6.16 PERIODIC TENANCY—NATURE

A periodic tenancy is of indefinite duration. It must have a definite commencement, but after that it continues until one of the parties terminates it by effective notice to the other.[89] To be effective, a termination notice must be given a minimum time before the end of some recurring period.[90] The recurring period—commonly a week, a month, or a year—is fixed by the parties by agreement, express or implied. So, for example, we may speak of a monthly periodic tenancy or a "month-to-month" tenancy. This latter expression is misleading, for it suggests a series of separate successive monthly terms, but that is incorrect; there is only one indefinite term.[91] In practice, the tenant pays rent by the same periods, though there is no reason the parties might not have a year-to-year leasehold with monthly rent if they so agree. However, unless the agreement was clear, a court would be likely to imply a periodic tenancy by the rental periods.

The minimum time of notice to terminate is prescribed by a rule of law. With the original periodic tenancies in England—yearly leaseholds of agricultural land—the period was six months, to ensure the tenant could harvest crops before being evicted.[92] Today statutes prescribe notice periods, running from seven days to one year. The shorter periods are for short-term leaseholds, and the longer periods tend to be for long-term or agricultural leaseholds.[93]

---

of landlord's mortgage obligations, taxes, insurance, utilities, and maintenance expenses were as consistent with a simple lease with no purchase option); Walter C. Pressing Co. v. Hogan, 133 N.E.2d 419 (Ohio App.1954); Bennett v. Pratt, 365 P.2d 622 (Or.1961); 1 Am. Law of Prop. § 3.21 (1952). Compare Losh Family, LLC v. Kertsman, 228 P.3d 793 (Wash.App.2010) (invalid lease enforceable by part performance despite tenant's lack of improvements).

[87]   Annot., 101 A.L.R. 185 (1936).

[88]   See Omak Realty Invst. Co. v. Dewey, 225 P. 236 (Wash.1924); Annot., 101 A.L.R. 185, 188–89 (1936).

[89]   See Woodruff v. Gazebo East Apts., 181 So.3d 1076 (Ala.App.2015); State v. Fin & Feather Club, 316 A.2d 351, 357–58 (Me.1974); Carlo v. Koch-Matthews, 53 Misc.3d 466, 37 N.Y.S.3d 426 (City Ct.2016); Rossow Oil Co., Inc. v. Heiman, 242 N.W.2d 176 (Wis.1976); 1 Am. Law of Prop. § 3.23 (1952). In this respect, the periodic tenancy is like a tenancy at will; indeed, it developed out of the tenancy at will 400 or so years ago.

[90]   The periodic tenancy must terminate at the natural end of the applicable period. Traditionally, courts held that a notice was not effective to terminate a periodic tenancy if the notice identified an improper termination date. E.g., Gill v. Gill, 161 Ill.App. 221 (1911). Today, courts generally hold that as long as the notice was given a sufficient time prior to a permissible termination date, the notice will be effective to terminate the tenancy at the earliest possible termination date—e.g., if the parties had a periodic monthly tenancy that began on May 1, and tenant gave a notice to terminate it on September 20, the tenancy would terminate on October 31. E.g., Foster v. Schwickerath, 780 N.W.2d 746 (Iowa App.2009); S.D.G. v. Inventory Control Co., 429 A.2d 394 (N.J.Super.1981); Restatement (Second) of Property-Landlord & Tenant § 1.5 (1977).

[91]   Janofsky v. Garland, 109 P.2d 750 (Cal.App.1941); Saracino v. Capital Props. Assocs., Inc., 141 A.2d 71 (N.J.Super.1958). But see Berlingo v. Sterling Ocean House, Inc., 497 A.2d 1031 (Conn.App.1985).

[92]   4 Thompson on Real Property § 39.05(b)(3), at 585 (2d ed.2004).

[93]   See Restatement (Second) of Property-Landlord & Tenant § 1.5, Statutory Note (1977).

§ 6.17   PERIODIC TENANCY—METHODS OF CREATION

Landlord and tenant may expressly agree for a periodic tenancy. Phrases such as "month-to-month," "monthly," or "periodic by the month" should suffice. While the parties may use a professionally drafted written lease, experience suggests that a periodic tenancy most commonly arises by a "general letting." This agreement is usually oral and probably largely implied at that. The premises are usually a dwelling and the parties are relatively unsophisticated and casual in their dealings. They may discuss little more than the amount of rent, how often it will be paid, who will pay which utility bills, and possibly something about furnishings and damage to the premises and a damage deposit. For present purposes the crucial—and likely only relevant—fact is that they agreed on a stated period for rent; this is generally sufficient to imply a periodic tenancy by that period. The same implication arises even in the absence of an agreement for periodic rent if rent is actually paid and accepted by some period.[94]

A periodic tenancy may arise when a tenant holds over after the term has expired. The holdover initially enters an ephemeral and temporary status called tenancy at sufferance (addressed further shortly). At this point it is enough to know that the actions of one or both parties may transform the tenant at sufferance into a periodic tenant. Some courts permit the landlord to create a periodic tenancy by giving notice to that effect to the holdover tenant.[95] More commonly, a periodic tenancy will arise because the tenant tenders and the landlord accepts rent for a time beyond the termination date. If the prior tenancy was periodic by periods less than a year, e.g., month-to-month, the new tenancy will be by the same period.[96] But if the prior leasehold was for a term of a year or more, the weight of authority treats the new periodic tenancy as year-to-year.[97]

---

[94] Radvansky v. City of Olmsted Falls, 395 F.3d 291 (6th Cir.2005) (monthly periodic tenancy created by tenant's payment and landlord's acceptance of rent on a monthly basis); Plank v. Bourdon, 326 S.E.2d 571 (Ga.App.1985) (tenant in possession while parties negotiated formal lease was periodic tenant); Ogden v. John Jay Esthetic Salons, Inc., 470 So.2d 521 (La.App.1985) (holdover subtenant became new periodic tenant); Longmier v. Kaufman, 663 S.W.2d 385 (Mo.App.1983) (party who took possession and paid rent during negotiations for five-year lease was periodic tenant); F.H. Stoltze Land Co. v. Westberg, 206 P. 407 (Mont.1922); Harry's Village, Inc. v. Egg Harbor Tp., 446 A.2d 862 (N.J.1982) (tenants who have no written leases but pay monthly rent are month-to-month tenants); Peoples v. Holley, 908 N.E.2d 517 (Ohio App.2009); Restatement (Second) of Property-Landlord & Tenant § 1.5 (1977); 1 Am. Law of Prop. § 3.25 (1952); URLTA § 1.401(d) (1972) and RURLTA § 202(c) (2015) (lease implied by payment and acceptance of rent is periodic weekly tenancy if tenant pays rent weekly, or periodic monthly tenancy otherwise).

[95] David Props., Inc. v. Selk, 151 So.2d 334 (Fla.App.1963); Mabe v. Montague, 615 S.E.2d 435 (Table) (N.C.App.2005) ("When a tenant for a year or longer holds over and is recognized by the landlord without further agreement or other qualifying facts or circumstances, he becomes a tenant from year to year, and is subject to the payment of the rent and other stipulations of the lease as far as the same may be applied to existing conditions."). In some cases, applicable statutes have prevented holdover tenants from becoming periodic tenants. Cf. Bledsoe v. United States, 349 F.2d 605 (10th Cir.1965); Leaders Int'l Jewelry, Inc. v. Board of Cty. Comm'rs, 183 So.2d 242 (Fla.App.1966).

[96] Redevelopment Agency v. Superior Court, 13 Cal.App.3d 561, 91 Cal.Rptr. 886 (1970); Governor Claiborne Apts., Inc. v. Attaldo, 235 So.2d 574 (La.1970); Mid Continent Mgmt. Corp. v. Donnelly, 372 N.W.2d 814 (Minn.App.1985); Kiefer v. First Capitol Sports Ctr., Inc., 684 S.W.2d 483 (Mo.App.1984); Mississippi State Dept. of Public Welfare v. Howie, 449 So.2d 772 (Miss.1984); Mack v. Fennell, 171 A.2d 844 (Pa.Super.1961).

[97] Butz v. Butz, 299 N.E.2d 782 (Ill.App.1973); Donnelly Adv. Corp. v. Flaccomio, 140 A.2d 165 (Md.1958); Mason v. Wierengo's Estate, 71 N.W. 489 (Mich.1897); Zola v. Havivi, 17 Misc.2d 366, 184 N.Y.S.2d 305 (Sup.1959); Williams v. King, 101 S.E.2d 308 (N.C.1958); Bergeron v. Forger, 214 A.2d 85 (Vt.1965); Rottman v. Bluebird Bakery, Inc., 88 N.W.2d 374 (Wis.1958) ("presumption" of year-to-year leasehold). But see Crechale & Polles, Inc. v. Smith, 295 So.2d 275 (Miss.1974) (tenant for years who held over became monthly periodic tenant by payment of monthly rent); Hofmann v. McCanlies, 413 P.2d 697 (N.M.1966) (same).

When the tenant becomes a periodic tenant by holding over, serious issues may arise about the provisions of the new lease, particularly as to rent. If, in electing for the new tenancy, the landlord specifies a new amount of rent and the tenant does not contest it, courts have held the tenant liable for that amount.[98] If the landlord notifies the tenant of a rent increase and the tenant protests it—perhaps verbally or by tendering only the old rent—some decisions say there is no increase, though there seems to be a contrary view.[99] Whether the landlord has power to alter other provisions is a question on which authority seems lacking, but one may argue landlord could do so to the extent landlord would be allowed to raise rent. If the landlord says nothing about new provisions, then the provisions of the former lease will carry over unless they are found to be inconsistent with the new situation.[100]

Another situation in which a periodic tenancy often arises is by the tenant's entry under an invalid lease for years, i.e., one that fails to conform to the Statute of Frauds when no circumstances excuse the statute's operation. Nevertheless, if the tenant enters permissively and pays rent which the landlord accepts, a periodic tenancy arises. The rental periods stated in the informal agreement will be the tenancy periods, provided they do not exceed the maximum length allowed by the Statute of Frauds. Thus, the tenancy will be year-to-year if rent was stated in annual installments[101] and month-to-month if stated monthly.[102] In a few states, however, the periods are fixed by the way rent is actually paid and received.[103] If rent is neither stated nor paid, the tenancy is at will.[104] In a few states, courts have labeled the periodic tenancy as a tenancy at will.[105]

§ 6.18   TENANCY AT WILL—NATURE

As its name suggests, a common-law tenancy at will is terminable at any time by either party. We speak now of tenancy at will as the phrase is traditionally used, not as it is used in a few states that thus label periodic tenancies. The status is considered a leasehold estate, because the tenant does have permissive possession of another's land.[106] Yet, because the permission may be revoked at any time, the possession is a most tenuous one; practically, it is analogous to a license. Owing to its insubstantial nature,

---

[98]   David Props., Inc. v. Selk, 151 So.2d 334 (Fla.App.1963); Bhar Realty Corp. v. Becker, 140 A.2d 756 (N.J.Super.1958). One wonders, however, if courts would not prevent the landlord from raising the rent to an unreasonable amount.

[99]   Compare Moll v. Main Motor Co., 210 S.W.2d 321 (Ark.1948) (protesting tenant who explicitly refuses to pay increase is liable only for reasonable use and occupation for period of holdover) with Bhar Realty Corp. v. Becker, 140 A.2d 756 (N.J.Super.1958) (tenant objected to increased rent and tendered prior rent amount, which landlord accepted after expressly reserving its rights to collect larger demanded amount; tenant held liable for increased amount).

[100]   Barragan v. Munoz, 525 S.W.2d 559 (Tex.Civ.App.1975). See also Butz v. Butz, 299 N.E.2d 782 (Ill.App.1973) (holding that a purchase option did not carry over).

[101]   Amwax Corp. v. Chadwick, 612 A.2d 127 (Conn.App.1992); Darling Shops Delaware Corp. v. Baltimore Ctr. Corp., 60 A.2d 669 (Md.1948); Arbenz v. Exley, Watkins & Co., 50 S.E. 813 (W.Va.1905).

[102]   Luster v. Cohon's Estate, 297 N.E.2d 335 (Ill.App.1973); Delfino v. Paul Davies Chevrolet, Inc., 209 N.E.2d 194 (Ohio 1965); Logan v. Time Oil Co., 437 P.2d 192 (Wash.1968).

[103]   1 Am. Law of Prop. § 3.27 (1952).

[104]   Maccarini v. New Haven Trap Rock Co., 148 F.Supp. 271 (S.D.N.Y.1957), aff'd, 249 F.2d 893 (2d Cir.1957); Parceluk v. Knudtson, 139 N.W.2d 864 (N.D.1966).

[105]   See, e.g., Gower v. Waters, 132 A. 550 (Me.1926); Riedel v. Plymouth Redev. Auth., 241 N.E.2d 852 (Mass.1968).

[106]   See Nicholas v. Howard, 459 A.2d 1039 (D.C.1983) (distinguishing tenant at will from trespasser).

a tenancy at will may not be assigned; an attempt terminates it,[107] as does the tenant's death.[108] The tenant at will should not be entitled to eminent domain compensation, but the decisions show some confusion on the point.[109]

§ 6.19 TENANCY AT WILL—METHODS OF CREATION

Only in unusual circumstances is a tenancy at will accompanied by rent. As we have seen, if rent is payable by a period, this generally implies a periodic tenancy. The parties might expressly agree that a tenancy with rent was at will, but such an agreement is unlikely. Thus, a tenancy at will upon rent ordinarily arises only if the rent is not measured by a period, which practically means some form of rent in kind. This may occur if the tenant takes possession with no agreed term but agrees only to make repairs or pay taxes.[110] An employee at will who is provided a home as part of the employee's pay may be a tenant at will.[111] Obviously a permissive possession without any agreement for a term, money rent, or rent in kind is a tenancy at will.

The tenancy may arise in some situations that may generically be called holdovers. A grantor who remains in possession with the grantee's consent after a conveyance may be a tenant at will.[112] Statutes may declare certain persons tenants at will who normally would occupy another relationship; examples include holdover tenants and even trespassers.[113]

Disagreement exists about a tenant who holds for as long as the tenant "desires" or "wishes." Some courts have held that such an agreement is illusory and creates no valid lease at all.[114] Others hold that a tenancy at will arises, on the reasoning that the holding at tenant's will is by implication also at the landlord's will.[115] However, a few decisions have held that such an arrangement makes the possessor a life tenant.[116]

§ 6.20 TENANCY AT SUFFERANCE

Tenancy at sufferance arises only in one narrow situation: when a tenant in one of the three other tenancies holds over (wrongfully) after the termination of that tenancy. The courts might have treated such a person as a trespasser, but that would produce

---

[107] Bellis v. Morgan Trucking, Inc., 375 F.Supp. 862 (D.Del.1974); Irving Oil Corp. v. Maine Aviation Corp., 704 A.2d 872 (Me.1998); 1 Am. Law of Prop. § 3.28 (1952).

[108] Dean v. Simpson, 108 So.2d 546 (Miss.1959); Paddock v. Clay, 357 P.2d 1 (Mont.1960).

[109] See Lasher v. Redev. Auth., 236 A.2d 831 (Pa.Super.1967) (statute allowed $250 to any tenant); Lee v. Venable, 213 S.E.2d 188 (Ga.App.1975) (tenant at will allowed compensation); 1 Am. Law of Prop. § 3.28 (1952) (no compensation allowed).

[110] See Maccarini v. New Haven Trap Rock Co., 148 F.Supp. 271 (S.D.N.Y.1957), aff'd, 249 F.2d 893 (2d Cir.1957) (repairs); Parceluk v. Knudtson, 139 N.W.2d 864 (N.D.1966) (repairs and taxes).

[111] Najewitz v. City of Seattle, 152 P.2d 722 (Wash.1944).

[112] Lasher v. Redev. Auth., 236 A.2d 831 (Pa.Super.1967).

[113] See Townsend v. Singleton, 183 S.E.2d 893 (S.C.1971).

[114] E.g., Dwyer v. Graham, 457 N.E.2d 1239 (Ill.1983).

[115] E.g., Foley v. Gamester, 170 N.E. 799 (Mass.1930); Nitschke v. Doggett, 489 S.W.2d 335 (Tex.App.1972), vacated on jurisdictional grounds, 498 S.W.2d 339 (Tex.1973); 1 Am. Law of Prop. § 3.30 (1952). But see Philpot v. Fields, 633 S.W.2d 546 (Tex.App. 1982) (lease to run for 20 years and thereafter as long as tenant used premises for certain purpose created valid lease, but was not a tenancy at will terminable by landlord).

[116] Collins v. Shanahan, 539 P.2d 1261 (Colo.1975). See also Restatement of Property § 21, Comment a (1936); Thompson v. Baxter, 119 N.W. 797 (Minn.1909) (strangely holding that a possession upon monthly rent "while [tenant] shall wish to live there" was a life estate, but stating in dictum that possession for as long as the tenant "wishes" would be a tenancy at will).

certain inconveniences (such as making the tenant a possible adverse possessor).[117] Hence, the holdover is called a tenant at sufferance, though it stretches the point to say this possession is permissive. It is regarded as permissive, subject to the landlord's power to make it wrongful *ab initio,* but the tenancy is ephemeral and intended to be temporary.[118]

Ordinarily it is obvious when a tenant is holding over; however, some borderline situations produce litigation. The tenant's merely leaving items of personalty behind is not a holding over, because possession is required.[119] Courts are likely to excuse a holding over for a temporary period, such as for a few hours when the tenant is moving out.[120] It is less clear whether the tenant's serious illness or similar misfortune will excuse a delayed quitting.[121] The Restatement suggests that equitable considerations justify excusing the tenant's brief delay when the tenant does not intend to hold over but does so due to circumstances beyond the tenant's control.[122]

If a tenancy at sufferance exists, the first important consequence is that the landlord has a power to make the tenant either a trespasser or a periodic tenant retroactively to the beginning of the holdover period. Whether this power arises out of intention imputed to the parties or whether it has evolved into a rule of law is in debate,[123] but American courts do not allow the tenant to defeat it. The landlord must exercise the power by making an election within a reasonable time.[124] However, "reasonable" is not well defined, nor is there agreement whether the landlord's failure to act within a reasonable time will result in the tenant's being a trespasser, periodic

---

[117] See Rivera v. Santiago, 495 A.2d 1122 (Conn.App.1985) (tenant who remained in possession after landlord terminated leasehold became tenant at sufferance); St. Regis Pulp & Paper Corp. v. Floyd, 238 So.2d 740 (Miss.1970); Hill v. Dobrowolski, 484 A.2d 1123 (N.H.1984) (tenancy at sufferance was true tenancy, so that landlord-tenant act applied). See also Small Business Inv. Co. v. Cavallo, 449 A.2d 988 (Conn.1982) (mortgagor who wrongfully continued in possession after foreclosure sale became tenant at sufferance).

The status of a tenant who remains in occupation after title has been taken by condemnation is unclear. As condemnation not only transfers title but terminates existing leaseholds, one could argue a new leasehold arises that would be either a tenancy at will or a periodic tenancy. See Redevelopment Agency v. Superior Court, 13 Cal.App.3d 561, 91 Cal.Rptr. 886 (1970). Nevertheless, a former tenant that retains possession after condemnation appears to fit the definition of a holdover tenant. Lowell Hous. Auth. v. Save-Mor Furniture Stores, Inc., 193 N.E.2d 585 (Mass.1963).

[118] For discussions of the nature and basic mechanism of tenancy at sufferance, see David Props., Inc. v. Selk, 151 So.2d 334 (Fla.App.1963); Bradley v. Gallagher, 303 N.E.2d 251 (Ill.App.1973); Warehouse Distribs., Inc. v. Prudential Storage & Van Corp., 161 S.E.2d 86 (Va.1968). But see Rise v. Steckel, 652 P.2d 364 (Or.App.1982) (life tenant who continued in possession when life estate ended upon his marriage was tenant at sufferance for 13 years, not adverse possessor). For an example of how statutes may affect tenancy at sufferance, see Townsend v. Singleton, 183 S.E.2d 893 (S.C.1971).

[119] E.g., Brown v. Music, Inc., 359 P.2d 295 (Alaska 1961); Byrns v. Pierce, 76 Misc. 176, 136 N.Y.S. 293 (1912).

[120] E.g., Commonwealth Bldg. Corp. v. Hirschfield, 30 N.E.2d 790 (Ill.App.1940); Byrns v. Pierce, 76 Misc. 176, 136 N.Y.S. 293 (1912).

[121] The decision in Herter v. Mullen, 53 N.E. 700 (N.Y.1899), held no tenancy at sufferance arose when the critical illness of a member of the tenant's family caused a lengthy delay, but it is not certain other courts would follow this precedent. For a contrary result, see Mason v. Wierengo's Estate, 71 N.W. 489 (Mich.1897). See also Feiges v. Racine Dry Goods, 285 N.W. 799 (Wis.1939) (tenant not liable for treble damages for holdover where tenant's surrender of possession was delayed by threats of violence from striking employees).

[122] Restatement (Second) of Property-Landlord & Tenant § 14.4, Comment i (1977).

[123] Some courts regard the tenant's holdover as an effective offer to enter into a new lease which the landlord might accept. E.g., Stern v. Equitable Trust Co., 144 N.E. 578 (N.Y.1924). Under the weight of authority, however, the landlord's election operates without regard to the tenant's actual intention. E.g., Maniatty v. Carroll Co., 41 A.2d 144 (Vt.1945); Donnelly Adv. Corp. v. Flaccomio, 140 A.2d 165 (Md.1958).

[124] E.g., Millhouse v. Drainage Dist., 304 S.W.2d 54 (Mo.App.1957).

tenant, or tenant at will.[125] Some decisions seem to imply that if the landlord makes no positive election to treat the tenant as having a new term, the tenant is a trespasser.[126]

Although the clearest way for the landlord to elect to treat the tenant as a trespasser would be an express statement, the cases tend to involve implied elections based on conduct that is inconsistent with the creation of a new tenancy. This conduct may include filing a lawsuit to evict the tenant,[127] or leasing the premises to a new tenant.[128] While the landlord's accepting rent from the holdover tenant is likely to constitute an election to create a new tenancy, this may not be the case if the landlord accepted rent as a temporary expedient while the parties were negotiating for a possible new lease.[129] If the landlord elects to treat the holdover tenant as a trespasser, then the landlord does not need to give a notice to terminate the tenancy; an action to recover possession from a trespasser will suffice.[130] At a minimum, the landlord can recover damages equal to the fair rental value of the premises for the period in which the tenant holds over.[131] Statutes in some states may permit the landlord to recover a multiple of the agreed rent or the fair rental value from the holdover tenant so as to discourage holding over.[132] If a commercial lease agreement liquidates the amount of damages in the event of a holdover, the agreement is enforceable unless the amount constitutes a penalty or exceeds any allowed statutory limit.[133]

The landlord's other choice is to treat the holdover tenant as a tenant under a new leasehold. While this election may have harsh consequences for the holdover tenant, one may justify it on the basis that it deters holdovers and thus protects the expectations of

---

[125] See 1 Am. Law of Prop. § 3.33 (1952). The Restatement provides that the landlord's failure to make an election within a reasonable time is a factor in determining whether the landlord has waived the right to bind the holdover to a new term. Restatement (Second) of Property-Landlord & Tenant § 14.4, Comments c, d (1977).

[126] See, e.g., Kilbourne v. Forester, 464 S.W.2d 770 (Mo.App.1970); Rottman v. Bluebird Bakery, Inc., 88 N.W.2d 374 (Wis.1958).

[127] See Bledsoe v. United States, 349 F.2d 605 (10th Cir.1965); Kilbourne v. Forester, 464 S.W.2d 770 (Mo.App.1970). Cf. Gower v. Waters, 132 A. 550 (Me.1926); Baker v. Simonds, 386 P.2d 86 (Nev.1963).

[128] Brown v. Music, Inc., 359 P.2d 295 (Alaska 1961).

[129] Rottman v. Bluebird Bakery, Inc., 88 N.W.2d 374 (1958) (acceptance of rent during negotiations did not constitute binding election to hold tenant to new lease). But see Clairton Corp. v. Geo Con, Inc., 635 A.2d 1058 (Pa.Super.1993) (tenant remained in possession for seven months, paying rent which landlord accepted while negotiations proceeded; court held payment and acceptance of rent created periodic monthly tenancy).

[130] Bledsoe v. United States, 349 F.2d 605 (10th Cir.1965); Vandenbergh v. Davis, 190 Cal.App.2d 694, 12 Cal.Rptr. 222 (1961); Kilbourne v. Forester, 464 S.W.2d 770 (Mo.App.1970). This rule may not apply in states that have adopted statutory notice requirements. E.g., Fisher v. Parkwood, Inc., 213 A.2d 757 (D.C.1965) (statute held to require 30 days' notice). Likewise, a landlord who sends a termination notice but thereafter accepts rent before commencing a possessory action risks voiding the effectiveness of the termination notice, e.g., Rensselaer Hous. Auth. v. Beverly, 59 Misc.3d 534, 72 N.Y.S.3d 322 (City Ct.2018), unless the lease expressly reserved such right to the landlord. E.g., Owens v. Prudential Cooper & Co., Inc., 940 So.2d 1034 (Ala.App.2006).

[131] E.g., Conn.Gen.Stat. § 47a–3c; Mass.Gen.Laws Ann. ch. 186, § 3.

[132] For example, under the Uniform Residential Landlord and Tenant Act, if the tenant's holdover is "willful and not in good faith," the landlord may recover the greater of three month's rent or three times the rental value of the premises. URLTA § 4.301(c) (1972); RURLTA § 802(a) (2015). See also Fla.Stat.Ann. § 83.06 (landlord may demand "double the monthly rent" from holdover); Lorril Co. v. LaCorte, 800 A.2d 245 (N.J.Super.2002) (statutory double rent for holdover tenancy owed only until tenant vacates).

[133] E.g., Carlyle, LLC v. Quik Park Beekman II, LLC, 59 Misc.3d 35, 74 N.Y.S.3d 434 (2018) (upholding commercial parking garage lease clause that liquidated holdover damages at two times agreed rent plus $25,000/mo.); Brunswick Ltd. Partn. v. Feudo, 870 N.E.2d 804 (Ohio App.2007) (upholding clause providing for double the agreed rent during holdover period). In residential leases, a liquidated damages amount presumably could be enforced if it did not exceed any cap imposed by an applicable residential landlord-tenant statute. E.g. URLTA § 4.301(c) (1972); RURLTA § 802(a) (2015).

a potential incoming tenant.[134] Express verbal or written statements are the clearest manner of election, although more frequently the election is implied by the tenant's paying and the landlord's accepting rent after the tenant holds over.[135]

Traditionally, the new tenancy was for a term of years, up to one year in length.[136] In most jurisdictions today, the new lease is regarded as a periodic tenancy.[137] In other respects, the new lease will generally be on the same terms and conditions as the original lease.[138] The landlord can cause the terms to differ by providing notice to the tenant and specifying the additional new terms, although the cases differ somewhat as to whether a tenant who remains on the premises is thereby bound to the new terms.[139]

D. TENANT'S RIGHT OF POSSESSION AND ENJOYMENT

§ 6.21 LANDLORD'S IMPLIED COVENANT TO DELIVER POSSESSION

A lease contains an implied covenant of quiet enjoyment, under which the landlord covenants that the landlord will not personally prevent the tenant's taking or maintaining possession and that no third person with a paramount legal right will do likewise.[140] We focus here, however, on the further question whether the landlord impliedly warrants that there will be no third person wrongfully occupying the premises at the time the lease commences. In other words, is there an implied warranty to deliver

---

[134] E.g., A.H. Fetting Mfg. Jewelry Co. v. Waltz, 152 A. 434 (Md.1930).

[135] Chappell v. Reynolds, 176 S.W.2d 154 (Ark.1943); Multani v. Knight, 23 Cal.App.5th 837, 233 Cal.Rptr.3d 537 (2018); Bellows v. Ziv, 187 N.E.2d 265 (Ill.App.1962); Crechale & Polles, Inc. v. Smith, 295 So.2d 275 (Miss.1974); Bill Swad Chevrolet, Inc. v. Ricart Jeep Eagle, Inc., 718 N.E.2d 470 (Ohio App.1998).

[136] 1 Am. Law of Prop. § 3.35 (1952); Security Life & Accident Ins. Co. v. United States, 357 F.2d 145 (5th Cir.1966); Spiritwood Grain Co. v. Northern Pac. Ry., 179 F.2d 338 (8th Cir.1950).

[137] In some jurisdictions, if the original tenancy was for a year or longer, the new periodic tenancy would be year-to-year. In others, it would be on a month-to-month basis. Under the Restatement, a periodic tenancy would result, with the period determined by how rent was payable under the original lease. Restatement (Second) of Property-Landlord & Tenant § 14.4, Comment f (1977). In some states, the duration of the new tenancy is dictated by statute. E.g., N.Y.Real Prop.Laws § 232–C (month-to-month tenancy arises upon acceptance of rent). In rare cases, courts have found that tenant's continued possession of the premises and payment and acceptance of rent operated as a renewal for a new term despite noncompliance with the renewal provision in the original lease. E.g., Bill Swad Chevrolet, Inc. v. Ricart Jeep Eagle, Inc., 718 N.E.2d 470 (Ohio App.1998).

[138] E.g., Warehouse Distribs., Inc. v. Prudential Storage & Van Corp., 161 S.E.2d 86 (Va.1968); Barragan v. Munoz, 525 S.W.2d 559 (Tex.App.1975).

[139] See, e.g., David Props., Inc. v. Selk, 151 So.2d 334 (Fla.App.1963) (tenant remained in possession but did not expressly agree to pay increased rent and did not actually pay it; tenant held liable); Heckman v. Walker, 92 N.W.2d 548 (Neb.1958) (same); Abrams v. Sherwin, 112 A. 235 (Pa.1920) (tenant not bound absent express agreement); Wilson v. Rodman, 243 Ill.App. 570 (1927) (tenant bound, despite objections, by remaining in possession); Abraham v. Gheens, 265 S.W. 778 (Ky.1924) (tenant bound, despite objections, by remaining in possession and paying increased rent demanded).

[140] Kohl v. PNC Bank, N.A., 912 A.2d 237 (Pa.2006); Hannan v. Dusch, 153 S.E. 824 (Va.1930); Restatement (Second) of Property-Landlord & Tenant § 4.2 (1977). While the covenant of quiet enjoyment is a type of title covenant, it assures only that the tenant's possession will not be interfered with by the landlord or a party holding paramount title. Unlike the common law of covenant of seisin, the covenant of quiet enjoyment is not breached merely because the landlord's title is subject to a defect. E.g., Slater v. Conti, 341 P.2d 395 (Cal.App.1959). A tenant that desired the greater protection afforded by the covenant of seisin (and had the bargaining power to obtain such a covenant) should insist upon an express warranty of the landlord's title. 1 Friedman on Leasing § 2:2, at 2–19 (6th ed.2017).

actual possession to the tenant (not just the legal right to possession)? On this question, American courts are divided.

The weight of authority follows the so-called "English rule."[141] This rule is that the landlord impliedly warrants that the premises will be free from the presence of a former tenant holding over or from some other person wrongfully in possession.[142] This rule is embodied in the Uniform Residential Landlord-Tenant Act and other legislation,[143] as well as the Restatement.[144] This rule presumes that a tenant bargains for actual possession of the premises, not for the possibility of a lawsuit requiring the tenant to evict the wrongful possessor. Advocates of this rule argue that the landlord is typically in a better position than an incoming tenant to know if a prior tenant holds over and to take any needed action against the prior tenant.[145] For breach of the warranty, the tenant may repudiate the lease[146] and may recover expectation damages measured by the difference between the rental value of the premises and the agreed rent over the term of the lease, discounted to present value.[147] If the tenant does not terminate the lease, the tenant may assert the landlord's breach as a defense to an action for rent[148] and may recover damages (again, measured by the difference between the rental value and agreed rent) for the period during which the tenant is denied possession.[149] If the tenant has the legal right to possession, the tenant may also take action to obtain possession.[150]

A minority of states follow the so-called "American rule," under which the landlord does not impliedly warrant that the tenant shall have actual possession.[151] Courts taking this view regard it as unfair to charge the landlord with the wrongful act of a third

---

[141] See Weissenberger, The Landlord's Duty to Deliver Possession: The Overlooked Reform, 46 U.Cinn.L.Rev. 937 (1977).

[142] See King v. Reynolds, 67 Ala. 229 (1880); Hall v. Major, 312 So.2d 169 (La.App.1975); Adrian v. Rabinowitz, 186 A. 29 (N.J.1936); 1 Am. Law of Prop. § 3.37 (1952); Annot., 96 A.L.R.3d 1155 (1979) (collecting decisions).

[143] URLTA § 2.103 (1972); RURLTA § 301 (2015); N.Y. Real Prop. Law § 223–A.

[144] Restatement (Second) of Property-Landlord & Tenant § 6.2 (1977).

[145] See Sloan v. Hart, 63 S.E. 1037 (N.C.1909); Hannan v. Dusch, 153 S.E. 824 (Va.1930).

[146] E.g., Dengler v. Michelssen, 18 P. 138 (Cal.1888); Sloan v. Hart, 63 S.E. 1037 (N.C.1909); Draper Machine Works, Inc. v. Hagberg, 663 P.2d 141 (Wash.App.1983); URLTA § 4.102(a)(1) (1972); RURLTA § 405(a)(1) (2015).

[147] E.g., Foreman & Clark Corp. v. Fallon, 479 P.2d 362 (Cal.1971); Ivy v. Argentieri, 471 P.2d 122 (Wash.App.1970). The tenant could also recover any consequential damages, e.g., relocation or storage costs, or lost profits, that tenant incurred and can prove with sufficient certainty. Compare Fera v. Village Plaza, Inc., 242 N.W.2d 372 (Mich.1976) (jury verdict for $200,000 in lost profits was justified), with Dieffenbach v. McIntyre, 254 P.2d 346 (Okla.1952) (recovery of lost profits denied as too speculative where tenant's business was not strongly established).

[148] E.g., Wallace v. Carter, 299 P. 966 (Kan.1931); Adrian v. Rabinowitz, 186 A. 29 (N.J.1936); URLTA § 4.102(a) (1972); RURLTA § 405(a) (2015). If the new tenant takes possession of part of the premises but is prevented by a third party from taking possession of the rest, the tenant's rent obligation is equitably abated. E.g., Lalekos v. Manset, 47 A.2d 617 (D.C.1946).

[149] E.g., Sloan v. Hart, 63 S.E. 1037 (N.C.1909); Dieffenbach v. McIntyre, 254 P.2d 346 (Okla.1952); 1 Am. Law of Prop. § 3.37 (1952).

[150] URLTA § 4.102(a)(2)(B) (1972); RURLTA § 405(a)(2)(B). Under appropriate circumstances, the tenant may also have a cause of action against a holdover tenant for interference with the tenant's contract rights under the new lease. See Havana Central NY2 LLC v. Lunney's Pub, Inc., 49 A.D.3d 70, 852 N.Y.S.2d 32, 49 A.D.3d 70 (2007).

[151] Reynolds v. McEwen, 244 P.2d 961 (Cal.App.1952); Hannan v. Dusch, 153 S.E. 824 (Va.1930).

person; they also note that the tenant, having a leasehold estate and thus the legal right to possession, can eject the trespasser just as well as the landlord can.[152]

§ 6.22 TENANT'S POSSESSORY INTEREST

A tenant, having an estate in land, has the general and exclusive right of possession during the term. The tenant may exclude third persons and, with few exceptions, the landlord as well.[153] Of course, leases frequently give landlords a privilege to enter for stated purposes, such as to inspect the premises, make repairs, or show the premises to prospective new tenants. If the landlord has a duty to make certain repairs, the landlord generally may enter for that purpose.[154] In the absence of some specific privilege to enter, the landlord may enter to collect rent and to repossess the premises (where that is legally permitted).[155]

The tenant's estate may carry with it implied rights in surrounding areas the landlord owns. This may include such diverse rights as easements over walkways and driveways;[156] the use of halls, stairs, and entrances,[157] the right to a view into windows or skylights,[158] the rights to use utilities and pipes serving the demised premises,[159] and even the right to install vents and ductwork as needed to permit the tenant's permitted use.[160] Much litigation has arisen over the rights of shopping center tenants to use and to prevent alteration of parking areas and other common areas.[161] The theory upon which tenants have such implied rights is akin to the theory of easement by way of necessity or by prior use.[162] A few older decisions contain language suggesting that the tenant has the implied right in the landlord's adjoining areas only if strict necessity exists.[163] But

---

[152] See Hannan v. Dusch, 153 S.E. 824 (Va.1930); Gazzolo v. Chambers, 73 Ill. 75 (1874); Snider v. Deban, 144 N.E. 69 (Mass.1924).

[153] E.g., North Main St. Bagel Corp. v. Duncan, 6 A.D.3d 590, 775 N.Y.S.2d 362 (2004) (landlord's unauthorized entry into possession constituted trespass and wrongful eviction).

[154] The Uniform Residential Landlord and Tenant Act provides that the landlord may enter without the tenant's consent in case of emergency, and that tenant cannot unreasonably withhold consent to the landlord's entry to make necessary or agreed repairs, to provide necessary or agreed services, or to exhibit the premises to prospective tenants. URLTA § 3.103 (1972); RURLTA § 701 (2015).

[155] 1 Am. Law of Prop. § 3.38 (1952).

[156] See, e.g., Owsley v. Hamner, 227 P.2d 263 (Cal.1951); Weigand v. American Stores Co., 29 A.2d 484 (Pa.1943); State v. Fox, 510 P.2d 230 (Wash.1973).

[157] See, e.g., Martel v. Malone, 85 A.2d 246 (Conn.1951); Nyer v. Munoz-Mendoza, 430 N.E.2d 1214 (Mass.1982) (tenant had right to use exterior of door to her apartment and to post signs on it); Tremont Theater Amusement Co. v. Bruno, 114 N.E. 672 (Mass.1917); Konick v. Champneys, 183 P. 75 (Wash.1919).

In the post-9/11 world, many landlords of multi-tenant buildings have adopted security measures (e.g., metal detectors) that some tenants and their guests may find intrusive. It seems likely that reasonable efforts in this regard are unlikely to violate a tenant's rights in building common areas. See, e.g., Cipriani Fifth Ave., LLC v. RCPI Landmark Props., LLC, 4 Misc.3d 850, 782 N.Y.S.2d 522 (landlord did not breach lease of upscale restaurant tenant by installing security measures applicable to tenant's guests after regular building hours).

[158] See, e.g., Owsley v. Hamner, 227 P.2d 263 (Cal.1951); O'Neill v. Breese, 3 Misc. 219, 23 N.Y.S. 526 (Sup.1893).

[159] See, e.g., Tong v. Feldman, 136 A. 822 (Md.1927); Gans v. Hughes, 14 N.Y.S. 930 (City Ct.1891).

[160] E.g., Second on Second Cafe, Inc. v. Hing Sing Trading, Inc., 66 A.D.3d 255, 884 N.Y.S.2d 353 (2009).

[161] LaPointe's, Inc. v. Beri, Inc., 699 P.2d 1173 (Or.App.1985) (shopping center lease interpreted to allow tenant's employees to park in parking lot). Compare Muzzi v. Bel Air Mart, 171 Cal.App.4th 456, 89 Cal.Rptr.3d 632 (2009) (lease allowing use of common areas for "loading and unloading of merchandise" did not permit retailer's long-term use of parking spaces for storage of food racks, pallets and the like).

[162] For discussion of implied easements based on necessity or prior use, see §§ 8.4 and 8.5 infra.

[163] E.g., Julius A. Bauer & Co. v. Chamberlain, 138 N.W. 903 (Iowa 1912); Tong v. Feldman, 136 A. 822 (Md.1927).

most courts generally imply these rights if they are "reasonably necessary" to the use of the premises.[164] Moreover, if an easement or other right exists, it may be used by the tenant's guests and customers.[165]

Unless the lease agreement provides otherwise, the tenant has the right to use the premises for any legal purposes for which they are suited.[166] Limitations on the tenant's rights of use are contained in the rules against waste, nuisance, and negligent damage, to which we now turn.

§ 6.23　TENANT'S MODE OF USE

A tenant, as holder of a present possessory estate followed by a reversion in the landlord, is subject to the doctrine of waste. This doctrine imposes a duty on the holder of the present estate not to act so as to permanently damage the land or improvements on it to the detriment of the reversion. Breach of this duty by a tenant would typically permit the landlord to bring an action for damages, or perhaps to enjoin action that threatened waste.[167]

Cutting standing timber was a classic common-law example of waste, but the prohibition is not absolute: the holder of the present estate has always been allowed to cut timber for building repairs and fences, and to cut at least "small stuff" for firewood. In America, where clearing land for farming was a benefit, most courts have adopted the principle that it is not waste to cut timber to promote "good husbandry."[168] Other activities that may constitute waste are the razing of buildings; serious damage to their component parts; and soil erosion due to improper farming.[169]

Whether removal of minerals, such as coal and gravel, is waste involves a special aspect of the law on the subject. If a tenant leases land that already has ongoing mineral extractive operations and the lease does not prohibit it, the tenant may continue to work

---

[164] See Owsley v. Hamner, 227 P.2d 263 (Cal.1951); Dubin v. Robert Newhall Chesebrough Trust, 96 Cal.App.4th 465, 116 Cal.Rptr.2d 872 (2002); Devlin v. The Phoenix, Inc., 471 So.2d 93 (Fla.App.1985) (restaurant tenant in shopping center had implied easement for access and parking); Weigand v. American Stores Co., 29 A.2d 484 (Pa.1943); Annot., 24 A.L.R.2d 123, 125–29 (1952); Annot., 56 A.L.R.3d 596 (1974).

[165] See Franceschina v. Morgan, 346 F.Supp. 833 (S.D.Ind.1972) (labor union organizer); State v. Fox, 510 P.2d 230 (Wash.1973) (legal services lawyer); Konick v. Champneys, 183 P. 75 (Wash.1919) (grocer making delivery).

[166] Restatement (Second) of Property-Landlord & Tenant § 12.5 (1977).

[167] See Eastwood v. Horse Harbor Found., Inc., 241 P.3d 1256 (Wash.2010) (landlord may recover in tort for waste without regard to existence of lease covenants). But see Avalon Pacific-Santa Ana, L.P. v. HD Supply Repair & Remodel, LLC, 192 Cal.App.4th 1183, 122 Cal.Rptr.3d 417 (2011) (where lease had eight years to run, court refused to allow landlord to recover damages for waste, despite tenant's demolition of office building, while lease remained in effect and rent continued to accrue; court held that "[i]f the waste is remediable, either by repair or passage of time, the waste might be cured by the time the lease expires and the lessor retakes possession").

[168] See Kremer v. Rule, 244 N.W. 596 (Wis.1932); 1 Am. Law of Prop. § 3.39 (1952); 5 Am. Law of Prop. §§ 20.1–20.4 (1952); see also Melms v. Pabst Brewing Co., 79 N.W. 738 (Wis.1899).

[169] See Sigsbee Holding Corp. v. Canavan, 39 Misc.2d 465, 240 N.Y.S.2d 900 (City Ct.1963); Graffell v. Honeysuckle, 191 P.2d 858 (Wash.1948) (damage to building components); Melms v. Pabst Brewing Co., 79 N.W. 738 (Wis.1899) (razing house); 5 Am. Law of Prop. §§ 20.7, 20.9, 20.10 (1952); Niehuss, Alteration or Replacement of Buildings by the Long-term Lessee, 30 Mich.L.Rev. 386 (1932).

the same mines or pits[170]—and perhaps even to expand existing operations[171]—but may not open new mines or pits on the premises unless the lease agreement permits.[172]

Our law of waste also includes the doctrine known as "ameliorating waste." This doctrine is that a permanent harm to the freehold that increases the land's value is not actionable, though it technically constitutes waste.[173] The decisions allowing tenants to clear farmland of timber may be analyzed as ameliorating waste cases, and would be the most common application of the doctrine. Melms v. Pabst Brewing Co.,[174] a leading but unusual case, discussed the doctrine in connection with the razing of a house that increased the land's value. How broadly one applies the doctrine depends largely upon whether one views waste as causing economic rather than physical harm.[175]

In addition to a duty not to act affirmatively to commit waste, a tenant is also under a duty to take reasonable steps to prevent waste, i.e., not to permit it.[176] This means the tenant has a common-law duty to make such repairs as will prevent waste to the land or to its improvements. In practice, this usually means the tenant must keep buildings sealed enough that the elements will not enter and cause waste. It is difficult to give a definition of the duty that has universal application; circumstances shape the duty.[177] This is the only common-law duty that the tenant has to make repairs.

Beyond the duties not to permit or commit waste, the courts have often recognized that a tenant has a duty not to cause specific damage to the premises intentionally or negligently.[178] The duty here is affirmative; in this respect it is like the duty not to commit waste. But, for the landlord to have a cause of action, the harm done need not be (though it may be) as serious as the harm necessary to constitute waste.

Finally, the law of nuisance imposes limitations on the tenant's mode of use. The tenant, like other possessors of land, owes a duty to nearby landowners not to commit nuisances.[179] The tenant also owes a duty to the landlord (implied into the landlord-tenant relation) not to engage in nuisances.[180]

---

[170] Cherokee Constr. Co. v. Harris, 122 S.W. 485 (Ark.1909); Schuylkill Trust Co. v. Schuylkill Mining Co., 57 A.2d 833 (Pa.1948); 5 Am. Law of Prop. § 20.6 (1952).

[171] See Westmoreland Coal Co.'s Appeal, 85 Pa. 344 (1877).

[172] Schuylkill Trust Co. v. Schuylkill Mining Co., 57 A.2d 833 (1948); Westmoreland Coal Co.'s Appeal, 85 Pa. 344 (1877); Kremer v. Rule, 244 N.W. 596 (Wis.1932) (mortgagor).

[173] See Melms v. Pabst Brewing Co., 79 N.W. 738 (Wis.1899); 5 Am. Law of Prop. § 20.11 (1952). The *Melms* case, which involved a life tenant and the holders of a reversion, suggested there would be less reason to apply the ameliorating waste doctrine to a leasehold tenant than to a life tenant. It seems unlikely that the doctrine would be applied to relatively short leaseholds.

[174] 79 N.W. 738 (Wis.1899).

[175] See Niehuss, Alteration or Replacement of Buildings by the Long-term Lessee, 30 Mich.L.Rev. 386 (1932).

[176] Glenn R. Sewell Sheet Metal, Inc. v. Loverde, 451 P.2d 721 (Cal.1969); Hooker v. Goodwin, 99 A. 1059 (Conn.1917) (life tenant); Grimm v. Grimm, 113 S.E. 91 (Ga.1922) (life tenant); Gade v. National Creamery Co., 87 N.E.2d 180 (Mass.1949); 1 Am. Law of Prop. § 3.78 (1952); 5 Am. Law of Prop. § 20.12 (1952).

[177] See 5 Am. Law of Prop. § 20.12 (1952).

[178] United States v. Bostwick, 94 U.S. (4 Otto) 53, 24 L.Ed. 65 (1877); Precisionware, Inc. v. Madison Cty. Tobacco Warehouse, Inc., 411 F.2d 42 (5th Cir.1969); Gade v. National Creamery Co., 87 N.E.2d 180 (Mass.1949); Annot., 10 A.L.R.2d 1012 (1950). See also King v. Cooney-Eckstein Co., 63 So. 659 (Fla.1913).

[179] For further discussion of the law of nuisance, see § 7.2 infra.

[180] Mosby v. Manhattan Oil Co., 52 F.2d 364 (8th Cir.1931); Hall v. Smith-McKenney Co., 172 S.W. 125 (Ky.1915). See also Louisiana Leasing Co. v. Sokolow, 48 Misc.2d 1014, 266 N.Y.S.2d 447 (Sup.1966) (breach of covenant not to disturb); Stroup v. Conant, 520 P.2d 337 (Or.1974).

§ 6.24   COVENANTS LIMITING TENANT'S USE

In addition to the common law limits discussed above, a lease may contain covenants limiting the tenant's use. As a general proposition, such covenants are enforceable.[181] They are restrictive covenants burdening the tenant's leasehold estate which, if they meet the requirements for running covenants, will burden the tenant's assignees. However, because the law does not favor burdens on land and because the language of a lease is usually construed against the landlord, courts tend to limit the scope of such restrictions by a strict or literal reading.[182] For example, a lease clause that authorizes the premises to be used for a stated purpose, or states that the tenant intends to use the premises for a stated purpose, does not prohibit other uses.[183] Thus, a landlord who wishes to limit use of the premises to a specific purpose should insure that the tenant covenants to use the premises "only" for those purposes "and no other purposes."

Traditionally, covenants restricting the tenant's use may arise only by agreement of both parties. Sometimes, however, a lease clause will purport to allow the landlord to take unilateral action to impose or amend rules governing the tenant's use of the premises. Under the Uniform Residential Landlord and Tenant Act and statutes based on it, the landlord may unilaterally impose and amend a rule concerning the tenant's use and enjoyment of the premises,[184] although the landlord cannot enforce such a rule if it substantially modifies the benefit of the tenant's bargain.[185]

§ 6.25   TENANT'S DUTY TO OCCUPY AND USE

As the holder of an estate in land, the tenant has a right of possession. Keeping in mind the distinction between right and duty, American courts have adopted the general rule that the tenant has no duty to take possession of the premises or to make any particular use of them, absent contrary agreement.[186] This is usually true even if the lease specifies an exclusive manner in which the tenant may use the premises, as long as the court does not interpret the lease to require that the tenant to occupy and use the

---

[181] Denecke v. Henry F. Miller & Son, 119 N.W. 380 (Iowa 1909); Dennis & Jimmy's Food Corp. v. Milton Co., 99 A.D.2d 477, 470 N.Y.S.2d 412 (1984), aff'd, 464 N.E.2d 484 (N.Y.1984) (lease clause limiting use solely to delicatessen and grocery did not allow tenant to install video games); Davis v. Driver, 271 S.W. 435 (Tex.Civ.App.1925); 1 Am. Law of Prop. § 3.40 (1952).

[182] Winn-Dixie Stores, Inc. v. Dolgencorp, LLC, 881 F.3d 835 (11th Cir.2018) (Alabama and Florida law); Otting v. Gradsky, 172 S.W.2d 554 (Ky.1943); Mutual Paper Co. v. Hoague-Sprague Corp., 8 N.E.2d 802 (Mass.1937); Town of Beech Mtn. v. Genesis Wildlife Sanctuary, Inc., 786 S.E.2d 335 (N.C.App.2016).

[183] Cox v. Ford Leasing Dev. Co., 316 S.E.2d 182 (Ga.App.1984) (lease recital that tenant intended to use premises for certain business did not prevent other use); Otting v. Gradsky, 172 S.W.2d 554 (Ky.1943); Bennett v. Waffle House, Inc., 771 So.2d 370 (Miss.2000) (lease limiting premises to use as a "standard Waffle House" did not imply or create restriction on seating capacity); Sky Four Realty Co. v. C.F.M. Enters., Inc., 128 A.D.2d 1011, 513 N.Y.S.2d 546 (1987) (lease restricting use to a convenience store did not preclude tenant from selling lottery tickets); Boyd v. Shell Oil Co., 311 A.2d 616 (Pa.1973) (lease for operation of an automobile service station did not preclude tenant from converting one auto bay into a car wash and operating car wash). But see Asa G. Candler v. Georgia Theater Co., 96 S.E. 226 (Ga.1918) (tenant's covenant to use premises for a stated purpose implies a promise not to use them for other purposes); 12 Broadway Realty, LLC v. Lakhani Enters. USA, Corp., 115 A.D.3d 503, 981 N.Y.S.2d 720 (2014) (lease obligating tenant to use premises for Quizno's sandwich shop did not permit tenant to operate a different sandwich shop). Some statutes provide that if the tenant leases the premises for a particular purpose specified in the lease, the tenant must not use the premises for any other purpose. E.g., Cal.Civ.Code § 1930; S.D.Codif.Laws § 43–32–11.

[184] URLTA § 3.102 (1972); RURLTA § 304(b) (2015).

[185] URLTA § 3.102(b) (1972); RURLTA § 304(d) (2015).

[186] Security Builders, Inc. v. Southwest Drug Co., 147 So.2d 635 (Miss.1962); Giessow Restaurants, Inc. v. Richmond Restaurants, Inc., 232 S.W.3d 576 (Mo.App.2007); Davis v. Wickline, 135 S.E.2d 812 (Va.1964); Annot., 40 A.L.R.3d 971, 973–74 (1971); Annot., 46 A.L.R. 1134 (1927).

premises.[187] While some have argued that the tenant's duty not to permit waste should imply a duty to occupy, courts have not agreed.[188]

Courts may make an exception to the general rule in the case of certain commercial leases which provide for rent based on a percentage of sales on the premises. Indeed, if a court will infer a duty, it will be a duty not only to occupy the premises but to conduct the business. The theory is that if rent is based on sales, the parties must have intended that the tenant would operate and make sales. Under the weight of authority, courts have refused to make this inference if the lease provides for more than a nominal fixed minimum rent in addition to the percentage rent.[189] Where courts have implied a duty on the tenant to operate, the lease has typically provided no fixed minimum or only a nominal minimum.[190] While a few courts have been willing to infer an operating covenant when the fixed rent was more than nominal and the tenant was the "anchor" (primary) tenant in a shopping center,[191] not all courts have embraced this view.[192] A landlord who expects the tenant to maintain business operations should bargain for an express operating covenant in the lease.[193] Likewise, a tenant that expects another key tenant to maintain business operations—and wishes to have the right to rescind or

[187] See, e.g., Daniel G. Kamin Kilgore Enters. v. Brookshire Grocery Co., 81 Fed.Appx. 827 (5th Cir.2003); Giessow Restaurants, Inc. v. Richmond Restaurants, Inc., 232 S.W.3d 576 (Mo.App.2007) ("a provision which restricts use of the premises is not identical to a provision which enjoins nonuse of the premises"); Weil v. Ann Lewis Shops, Inc., 281 S.W.2d 651 (Tex.Civ.App.1955); Davis v. Wickline, 135 S.E.2d 812 (Va.1964); Annot., 40 A.L.R.3d 971, 975–77 (1971).

[188] See 1 Am. Law of Prop. § 3.41 (1952). In Asling v. McAllister-Fitzgerald Lumber Co., 244 P.16 (Kan.1926), the court did allow the landlord to terminate the lease based on the tenant's failure to use the premises as a lumber yard, but the tenant's failure to maintain the premises in good repair provided an independent basis on which landlord could terminate the lease.

[189] See Percoff v. Solomon, 67 So.2d 31 (Ala.1953); The College Block v. Atlantic Richfield Co., 206 Cal.App.3d 1376, 254 Cal.Rptr. 179 (1988); Piggly Wiggly Southern, Inc. v. Heard, 405 S.E.2d 478 (Ga.1991); Chicago Title & Trust Co. v. Southland Corp., 443 N.E.2d 294 (Ill.App.1982) (no implied covenant to continue in business); Stop & Shop, Inc. v. Ganem, 200 N.E.2d 248 (Mass.1964); Tuttle v. W.T. Grant Co., 5 A.D.2d 370, 171 N.Y.S.2d 954 (1958), aff'd, 159 N.E.2d 202 (N.Y.1959); Palm v. Mortgage Invst. Co., 229 S.W.2d 869 (Tex.Civ.App. 1950); Bradlees Tidewater, Inc. v. Walnut Hill Inv., Inc., 391 S.E.2d 304 (Va.1990); Thompson-Dev. Inc. v. Kroger Co., 413 S.E.2d 137 (W.Va.1991); Sampson Invs. v. Jondex Corp., 499 N.W.2d 177 (Wis.1993); Annot., 38 A.L.R.2d 1113 (1954); Randolph, "Going Dark Aggressively," 10 Prob. & Prop. (Nov.–Dec. 1996), at 6.

[190] See Sinclair Refining Co. v. Giddens, 187 S.E. 201 (Ga.App.1936); Seggebruch v. Stosor, 33 N.E.2d 159 (Ill.App.1941); East Broadway Corp. v. Taco Bell Corp., 542 N.W.2d 816 (Iowa 1996); Mercury Inv. Co. v. F.W. Woolworth Co., 706 P.2d 523 (Okla.1985); Marvin Drug Co. v. Couch, 134 S.W.2d 356 (Tex.Civ.App.1939). Some of the cases are "gas station cases," such as Giddens and Seggebruch, in which rent was so much per gallon of gasoline the tenant sold, with a nominal fixed rent.

[191] E.g., Ingannamorte v. Kings Super Markets, Inc., 260 A.2d 841 (N.J.1970); Columbia East Assocs. v. Bi-Lo, Inc., 386 S.E.2d 259 (S.C.App.1989).

[192] E.g., Daniel G. Kamin Kilgore Enters. v. Brookshire Grocery Co., 81 Fed.Appx. 827 (5th Cir.2003) ("The parties to this lease had the option of inserting an express provision requiring [the tenant] to operate continuously, but they chose not to do so."); Sampson Invs. v. Jondex Corp., 499 N.W.2d 177 (Wis.1993) ("a commercial lessee is not required to continue operating a business in the absence of a lease which expressly requires continuous operation"). See also Randolph, "Going Dark Aggressively," 10 Prob. & Prop. (Nov.–Dec. 1996), at 6.

[193] If a tenant breaches an express operating covenant, it is unlikely that a court will grant the landlord an injunction. In the typical case, the landlord's damages remedy would be adequate; further, courts are reluctant to supervise a tenant's ongoing operations and to risk ordering a tenant to re-open and continue operating a business that may well have closed due to unprofitability. See, e.g., Summit Town Centre, Inc. v. Shoe Show of Rocky Mount, Inc., 828 A.2d 995 (Pa.2003). Landlords sometimes negotiate liquidated damages clauses where a tenant agrees to open by a certain date but is delayed. Such clauses have been upheld as valid. See, e.g., CPMI, Inc. v. Kolaj, 65 A.3d 605, 885 N.Y.S.2d 496 (2009).

terminate the lease if the key tenant never opens or ceases operations—should negotiate for and obtain a clause specifically granting that right.[194]

§ 6.26   COVENANTS TO PROTECT TENANT'S BUSINESS

In commercial leases, one often finds covenants by the landlord not to conduct or permit stated activities on the landlord's land outside the premises. Typical is a covenant by the landlord of a shopping center providing that a tenant shall have the exclusive right to conduct a described business within the shopping center. Such a clause is popularly called an "exclusive." If the landlord further covenants not to use land located beyond the shopping center perimeter for the described business, the covenant is labeled a "radius clause." Either clause is a restrictive covenant, in which the tenant's premises are the benefitted estate and the landlord's other premises are the burdened estate. Such clauses are generally enforceable, but with some qualifications.[195] Courts frequently say that such covenants, which constitute restraints upon competition and the alienation of the burdened estate, are to be strictly construed.[196] Courts also rarely imply such clauses,[197] though in a few cases courts have found such an implication from the presence of a percentage rent clause.[198]

The common-law policy against restraints on free trade is often raised in support of the argument that a covenant restricting business activities is void. This argument generally fails, because of the exception that allows such private agreements if they are limited in time or place and if the parties find them useful.[199] Likewise, attacks based on state and federal antitrust laws are likely to fail, at least with respect to the typical shopping center exclusive or radius clause.[200]

---

[194] E.g., Chesterfield Exchange, LLC v. Sportsman's Warehouse, Inc., 572 F.Supp.2d 856 (E.D.Mich.2008) (allowing tenant to rescind lease where lease provisions and extrinsic evidence surrounding negotiation made clear that landlord represented that Sam's Club would be a tenant in the development).

[195] For a thorough discussion of these covenants, see 3 Friedman on Leases §§ 28:1 to 28:10 (6th ed.2017).

[196] See, e.g., Marriott Corp. v. Combined Props. Ltd. Partn., 391 S.E.2d 313 (Va.1990) (covenant in restaurant lease prohibiting drive-in restaurant within 2000 feet of premises was not violated by lease for McDonald's restaurant). See also Norwood Shopping Ctr., Inc. v. MKR Corp., 135 So.2d 448 (Fla.App.1961); Crest Commercial, Inc. v. Union-Hall, Inc., 243 N.E.2d 652 (Ill.App.1968).

[197] See Crest Commercial, Inc. v. Union-Hall, Inc., 243 N.E.2d 652 (Ill.App.1968); Horton v. Uptown Partners, L.P., 720 N.W.2d 192 (Table) (Iowa App.2006); Leebron & Robinson Rent A Car, L.L.C. v. City of Monroe, 907 So.2d 875 (La.App.2005); Great Atl. & Pac. Tea Co. v. Bailey, 220 A.2d 1 (Pa.1966).

[198] See Carter v. Adler, 291 P.2d 111 (Cal.App.1955); Tabet v. Sprouse-Reitz Co., 409 P.2d 497 (N.M.1966). These cases reason that because the parties agreed on percentage rent, they must have intended that the landlord would not derogate from the tenant's ability to make sales on which rent was based).

[199] See Goldberg v. Tri-States Theatre Corp., 126 F.2d 26 (8th Cir.1942); Venture Holdings Ltd. v. Carr, 673 A.2d 686 (D.C.1996); Buford-Clairmont Co., Ltd. v. RadioShack Corp., 622 S.E.2d 14 (Ga.App.2005); Colby v. McLaughlin, 310 P.2d 527 (Wash.1957).

[200] Such clauses are subject to "rule of reason" analysis under antitrust law, which involves consideration of factors such as the duration of the restriction, the geographic area covered by the restriction, and whether the party benefitted by the restriction possesses sufficient market power that the restriction can have a serious anticompetitive effect. See Alan M. DiSciullo, Negotiating a Commercial Lease from the Tenant's Perspective, 18 Real Est. L.J. 27 (1989); Baum, Lessors' Covenants Restricting Competition, 1965 U. Ill.L.F. 228. See also Dalmo Sales Co. v. Tysons Corner Regional Shopping Ctr., 308 F.Supp. 988 (D.D.C.1970), aff'd, 429 F.2d 206 (D.C.Cir.1970) (preliminary injunction denied); Savon Gas Stations No. Six, Inc. v. Shell Oil Co., 309 F.2d 306 (4th Cir.1962); Optivision, Inc. v. Syracuse Shopping Ctr. Assocs., 472 F.Supp. 665 (N.D.N.Y.1979); Elida, Inc. v. Harmor Realty Corp., 413 A.2d 1226 (Conn.1979); Amelia Island Restaurant II, Inc. v. Omni Amelia Island, LLC, 164 So.3d 26 (Fla.App.2015).

Some types of "aggravated" forms of tenant exclusive clauses may be more suspect under antitrust laws, such as a clause permitting a major shopping center tenant such as a national "big box" retailer to exercise

What are the tenant's remedies if the landlord breaches or threatens to breach an exclusive or radius clause? Damages are available, though tenants seldom would find this remedy adequate. The usual measure of damages is the difference in rental value between the value of the tenant's leasehold with and without the breach, but the tenant may find it difficult to prove with sufficient certainty the extent to which the breach caused the tenant's lost profits.[201] The tenant would prefer obtaining an injunction against the landlord, and typically can obtain this remedy before the landlord has consummated the competing lease.[202] If the landlord has already executed that lease with another tenant who had no notice of the exclusive clause, however, an injunction against the other tenant is not available.[203] An injunction is allowed against the landlord and a competing tenant who had notice of the exclusive clause.[204] A few decisions have held the landlord's breach of an exclusive clause permits the tenant to terminate the leasehold. One theory is that the breach constitutes a constructive eviction.[205] A second theory—more novel in that it implies the dependency of lease covenants—is that the landlord's breach of the exclusive clause is substantial and gives the tenant a power to rescind the lease.[206]

§ 6.27 ILLEGAL USE—EXISTING AT TIME OF LEASING

If a lease agreement limits the use of the premises to a purpose that is then forbidden by law, the attempted lease is void.[207] All permitted uses must be illegal; if some uses are illegal and some legal, the lease is valid.[208] At work here is the contract

veto powers over the admission of new tenants or their manner of doing business. See In re Tysons Corner Regional Shopping Ctr., 85 F.T.C. 970 (1975) (consent order forbade exercise of such a clause). But see Dalmo Sales Co. v. Tysons Corner Regional Shopping Ctr., 308 F.Supp. 988 (D.D.C.1970), aff'd, 429 F.2d 206 (D.C.Cir.1970).

[201] Fontainbleau Hotel Corp. v. Crossman, 323 F.2d 937 (5th Cir.1963); Parker v. Levin, 188 N.E. 502 (Mass.1934); Annot., 97 A.L.R.2d 4, 111–19 (1964).

[202] E.g., J.C. Penney Co. v. Giant Eagle, Inc., 813 F.Supp. 360 (W.D.Pa.1992); Gastineau v. Summit Realty Co., 652 S.W.2d 711 (Mo.App.1983); 3 Friedman on Leases § 28:6.2 (6th ed.2017) (collecting cases).

[203] See Skaggs v. Jensen, 484 P.2d 728 (Idaho 1971); Meredith Hardware, Inc. v. Belknap Realty Trust, 369 A.2d 204 (N.H.1977); Fratelli's Pizza & Restaurant Corp v. Kayzee Realty Corp., 74 A.D.3d 481, 902 N.Y.S.2d 534 (2010) (exclusive cannot be enforced against competing tenant whose lease predates the lease containing the exclusive); Annot., 97 A.L.R.2d 4, 88–96, 120–22 (1964). Even if the tenant cannot enforce the exclusive clause via injunctive relief, however, the tenant may still recover damages from the landlord if the tenant can show the violation diminished the value of the premises, e.g., Mabros v. Donuts-R-Us, Inc., 536 S.E.2d 215 (Ga.App.2000), or if the lease contains a valid provision liquidating damages, e.g., Valentine's Inc. v. Ngo, 251 S.W.3d 352 (Mo.App.2008).

[204] See Fontainbleau Hotel Corp. v. Crossman, 323 F.2d 937 (5th Cir.1963); Hildebrand v. Stonecrest Corp., 344 P.2d 378 (Cal.App.1959).

[205] See Kulawitz v. Pacific Woodenware & Paper Co., 155 P.2d 24 (Cal.1944).

[206] See Medico-Dental Bldg. Co. v. Horton & Converse, 132 P.2d 457 (Cal.1942); University Club v. Deakin, 106 N.E. 790 (Ill.1914).

[207] Lucky Jacks Entertainment Ctr. LLC v. Jopat Bldg. Corp., 32 So.3d 565 (Ala.2009); Central States Health & Life Co. v. Miracle Hills Ltd. Partn., 456 N.W.2d 474 (Neb.1990); Merry Homes, Inc. v. Chi Hung Luu, 312 S.W.3d 938 (Tex.App.2010). See also Musco v. Torello, 128 A. 645 (Conn.1925); Warshawsky v. American Automotive Prods. Co., 138 N.E.2d 816 (Ill.App.1956); Restatement (Second) of Property-Landlord & Tenant § 12.4 (1977); 1 Am. Law of Prop. § 3.43 (1952).

In the 1960s, the District of Columbia court ruled in Brown v. Southall Realty Co., 237 A.2d 834 (D.C.App.1968), that a lease was void for illegality if the condition of the premises violated a local housing code or statute at the lease's inception. Now that states have adopted judicial or statutory warranties of habitability in residential leases, one rarely encounters illegal lease arguments based on the habitability of the premises. See §§ 6.37–6.39 infra.

[208] Green Cross Medical, Inc. v. Gally, 395 P.3d 302 (Ariz.App.2017) (lease by tenant seeking to open marijuana dispensary was not void for illegality where lease permitted tenant to sublease for other purposes); Warshawsky v. American Automotive Prods. Co., 138 N.E.2d 816 (Ill.App.1956) (alternative ground); Stern

doctrine of illegality, providing an instance in which contract law principles have replaced conveyancing principles in landlord-tenant law. If strict conveyancing theory applied, illegality would not affect the existence of the leasehold estate; the tenant could have the estate without physical possession or use.

There are few cases in which the parties' agreement expressly limits use to an illegal activity. More cases involve a pattern in which the agreement imposes no such limitation on its face, but the tenant in fact intends to make a use that is then illegal. Unless the landlord knows of this intent, the validity of the lease is not affected.[209] If the landlord knows of the intended illegal use, some decisions hold that this would invalidate the lease.[210] Under other decisions, however, the landlord's mere knowledge is not enough; the landlord must in some way participate in the illegality, though it is not clear just what actions amount to participation.[211]

Violations of zoning ordinances present a special situation. In some cases in which the lease is for a purpose that violates zoning, courts have held the lease valid or invalid on the principles stated above, just as for other kinds of illegality.[212] Other courts refuse to do so where, as is usually the case, the zoning ordinance allows for nonconforming uses, variances, special permits, and the like.[213] These courts reason that the parties may have written their lease intending that zoning relief would be obtained, though it would seem to be a question of fact whether they did so. Some courts may simply feel zoning restrictions are different from an ordinance or statute prohibiting prostitution or sales of marijuana. In any event, a tenant who is concerned about zoning should always expressly reserve a power to terminate if the tenant cannot legally make the intended use.

§ 6.28 ILLEGAL USE—SUPERVENING ILLEGALITY

Now suppose that the tenant's intended and actual use of the premises is permitted by law, but becomes illegal by subsequent changes in the law. The consequences of this are discussed more fully in section 6.86, but are briefly summarized here. If the lease

Holding Co. v. O'Connor, 196 A. 432 (N.J.1938); Restatement (Second) of Property-Landlord & Tenant § 12.4 (1977).

[209] E.g., Ashford v. Mace, 146 S.W. 474 (Ark.1912); Harbison v. Shirley, 117 N.W. 963 (Iowa 1908); Restatement (Second) of Property-Landlord & Tenant § 12.5 (1977).

[210] See, e.g., Dougherty v. Seymour, 26 P. 823 (Colo.1891); Musco v. Torello, 128 A. 645 (Conn.1925); Boyd v. Topham, 152 P. 1185 (Utah 1915); Annot., 166 A.L.R. 1353, 1374–79 (1947). But see Green Cross Medical, Inc. v. Gally, 395 P.3d 302 (Ariz.App.2017) (rejecting attempt by landlord to invalidate lease to tenant who planned marijuana dispensary, where lease permitted tenant to sublease for other uses).

[211] See Hoefeld v. Ozello, 125 N.E. 5 (Ill.1919); Bank of Commerce & Trust Co. v. Burke, 185 S.W. 704 (Tenn.1916); Fuchs v. Goe, 163 P.2d 783 (Wyo.1945). See 1 Am. Law of Prop. § 3.43 (1952) (suggesting that majority rule is that landlord's mere knowledge makes lease unenforceable); but see Annot., 166 A.L.R. 1353, 1374–79 (1947) (decisions suggest that mere knowledge is enough in nearly all cases in which prostitution is the illegal activity, but landlord must participate where gambling or illegal liquor sales is the activity).

[212] See Walker v. Southern Trucking Corp., 219 So.2d 379 (Ala.1969); Becerra v. Hochberg, 193 Cal.App.2d 431, 14 Cal.Rptr. 101 (1961); Sippin v. Ellam, 588 A.2d 660 (Conn.App.1991) (both zoning and restrictive covenant prohibited intended use); Central States Health & Life Co. v. Miracle Hills Ltd. Partn., 456 N.W.2d 474 (Neb.1990) (lease invalid when made for a purpose neither party knew was in violation of zoning law); Ober v. Metropolitan Life Ins. Co., 157 Misc. 869, 284 N.Y.S. 966 (1935); Merry Homes, Inc. v. Chi Hung Luu, 312 S.W.3d 938 (Tex.App.2010); Annot., 37 A.L.R.3d 1018, 1031–35 (1971).

[213] See Entrepreneur, Ltd. v. Yasuna, 498 A.2d 1151 (D.C.App.1985); Margolis v. Malesky, 515 So.2d 425 (Fla.App.1987); Warshawsky v. American Automotive Prods. Co., 138 N.E.2d 816 (Ill.App.1956); Shawmut-Canton LLC v. Great Spring Waters of Am., Inc., 816 N.E.2d 545 (Mass.App.2004); Schlesinger v. Levine, 28 Misc.2d 654, 212 N.Y.S.2d 904 (1961); Young v. Texas Co., 331 P.2d 1099 (Utah 1958); Pennsylvania State Shopping Plazas, Inc. v. Olive, 120 S.E.2d 372 (Va.1961).

limits the tenant's use of the premises solely to the use that becomes illegal, the leasehold terminates in most jurisdictions.[214] The same is true if the tenant's main or principal activity becomes illegal, though a minor part remains legal.[215] The corollary seems true; if the part that remains legal is found to be a major part of the activity, the lease remains valid.[216] Some courts, contrary to the weight of authority, do not allow the lease to terminate on account of supervening illegality, reasoning that the tenant should have anticipated the possibility of illegality and have inserted a termination clause in the lease.[217] In cases where the facts are such that the tenant actually should have contemplated that the use might become illegal, courts generally will enforce the lease despite supervening illegality.[218] If the activity is not illegal per se, but the tenant nevertheless cannot obtain a necessary permit or license for the activity, most courts will not set the lease aside for that reason,[219] but some have done so.[220]

E. INTERFERENCE WITH TENANT'S POSSESSION

§ 6.29 IMPLIED COVENANT OF POWER TO LEASE

We begin with the reminder that a lease is a conveyance. Though contractual undertakings usually take up most of the lease agreement, the essential part is the landlord's conveyance of a leasehold estate. Implied in this act of conveyance is a representation that the grantor has legal power to make the conveyance described.[221] This representation is called a "covenant" but, because it is a statement of supposed existing facts and not an undertaking to do something, it is more precisely a "warranty." Observe that the representation is not that the landlord has title, but that the landlord

---

[214] E.g., Greil Bros. Co. v. Mabson, 60 So. 876 (Ala.1912); Lucas Games, Inc. v. Morris AR Assocs., LLC, 197 So.3d 1183 (Fla.App.2016); Brunswick-Balke-Collender Co. v. Seattle Brewing & Malting Co., 167 P. 58 (Wash.1917); 1 Am. Law of Prop. § 3.44 (1952). Many of the older cases involve leases for tenants to operate bar and saloons prior to the eighteenth amendment's adoption of prohibition, or leases for tenants to operate automobile dealerships prior to wartime restrictions on new car sales.

[215] Doherty v. Monroe Eckstein Brewing Co., 115 Misc. 175, 187 N.Y.S. 633 (1921), aff'd, 198 A.D. 708, 191 N.Y.S. 59 (1921); Stratford, Inc. v. Seattle Brewing & Malting Co., 162 P. 31 (Wash.1916). But see O'Byrne v. Henley, 50 So. 83 (Ala.1909) (lease not terminated by prohibition law where tenant could continue to sell nonintoxicants).

[216] E.g., Deibler v. Bernard Bros., Inc., 48 N.E.2d 422 (Ill.App.1943) (tenant operating auto sales showroom could not terminate lease based on severe, but not total, federal wartime restrictions on sales of new automobiles); Mel Frank Tool & Supply, Inc. v. Di-Chem Co., 580 N.W.2d 802 (Iowa 1998) ("The tenant is not relieved from the obligation to pay rent if there is a serviceable use still available consistent with the use provision in the lease."); Standard Brewing Co. v. Weil, 99 A. 661 (Md.1916); Warm Springs Co. v. Salt Lake City, 165 P. 788 (Utah 1917).

[217] See, e.g., Standard Brewing Co. v. Weil, 99 A. 661 (Md.1916); Imbeschied v. Lerner, 135 N.E. 219 (Mass.1922); Annot., 22 A.L.R. 821, 830–34 (1923).

[218] See Nebaco, Inc. v. Riverview Realty Co., 482 P.2d 305 (Nev.1971); North Am. Capital Corp. v. McCants, 510 S.W.2d 901 (Tenn.1974).

[219] E.g., Peek v. Dominguez, 72 S.W.3d 239 (Mo.App.2002) (tenant's failure to obtain occupancy permit for commercial enterprise in building zoned for residential use but used by previous tenants for commercial enterprise via lawful permit); Kosher Konvenience, Inc. v. Ferguson Realty Corp., 171 A.D.2d 650, 567 N.Y.S.2d 131 (1991).

[220] E.g., Weyerhauser Real Estate Co. v. Stoneway Concrete Co., 637 P.2d 647 (Wash.1981) (lease terminated due to practical inability to obtain strip-mining permits).

[221] Restatement (Second) of Property-Landlord & Tenant § 4.2, Comment b (1977) (tenant may rescind lease if there is an outstanding paramount title that could prevent tenant from enjoying contemplated use of the premises); 1 Am. Law of Prop. § 3.46 (1952). See Hannan v. Dusch, 154 Va. 356, 153 S.E. 824 (1930).

has a power to convey a leasehold. In most cases, the landlord has that power as an incident of ownership; however, it would be possible for the landlord to have a power of conveyance beyond any interest landlord has in the land.[222] Because the warranty is as to the existence of this power at the point of leasing, breach will occur only if the landlord lacks a power to convey at that time.

§ 6.30 IMPLIED COVENANT OF QUIET ENJOYMENT

There is implied in every lease a covenant of quiet enjoyment.[223] It is both a covenant and a warranty. The landlord warrants that the tenant will not be disturbed in possession by any other person with a superior legal right to possession. In case of disturbance, the landlord covenants to defend the tenant. Moreover, the landlord covenants not to evict the tenant, actually or constructively. Thus, the covenant is breached only if, during the term, the tenant's possession is disturbed by a third person or by the landlord.

§ 6.31 QUIET ENJOYMENT—INTERFERENCE BY THIRD PERSONS

Interference with the tenant's possession by trespassers or wrongdoers generally does not breach the covenant of quiet enjoyment. To breach the covenant, third-person interference must occur by a person having "paramount title." Under the weight of authority, the covenant is breached only when the third-person interference comes to an actual dispossession of the tenant.[224] Probably the most common manner in which this occurs is foreclosure of a mortgage by a mortgagee who has priority over the tenant, followed by sale and possession by the purchaser.[225] Dispossession or exclusion by a prior tenant whose term has not ended is another example.[226] Likewise, if the holder of a life estate leases for a term but dies before the end of that term, entry by the holder of the future interest breaches the warranty.[227] By contrast, courts have held that a taking of

---

[222] Cf. Lensky v. DiDomenico, 409 P.3d 457 (Colo.App.2016) (putative adverse possessor has, from beginning of time of possession, an interest in the property enforceable against all other parties except the rightful owner, including the right to exclude all persons but the true owner).

[223] Standard Livestock Co. v. Pentz, 269 P. 645 (Cal.1928); Hankins v. Smith, 138 So. 494 (Fla.1931); Kuiken v. Garrett, 51 N.W.2d 149 (Iowa 1952); Dobbins v. Paul, 321 S.E.2d 537 (N.C.App.1984); Kohl v. PNC Bank, N.A., 912 A.2d 237 (Pa.2006); Annot., 41 A.L.R.2d 1414, 1420–22 (1955). The only exception appears to be in New Jersey, where the warranty is not implied merely from the landlord-tenant relationship. Mershon v. Williams, 44 A. 211 (N.J.1899); Adrian v. Rabinowitz, 186 A. 29 (N.J.1936).

[224] E.g., Standard Livestock Co. v. Pentz, 269 P. 645 (Cal.1928); Duck Creek Tire Serv., Inc. v. Goodyear Corners, L.C., 796 N.W.2d 886 (Iowa 2011) (eviction of subtenant by landlord under primary lease following default by sublandlord); Bates v. Smith, 243 N.W. 829 (Mich.1932) (mortgagee's mere threat to foreclose is not a violation); Hyman v. Fischer, 184 Misc. 90, 52 N.Y.S.2d 553 (Sup.1944); 1 Am. Law of Prop. § 3.48 (1952).

[225] E.g., Metropolitan Life Ins. Co. v. Childs Co., 130 N.E. 295 (N.Y.1921). Note that in the wake of the mortgage crisis that began in 2007, Congress enacted a temporary measure, the Protecting Tenants at Foreclosure Act (PTFA), which provided residential tenants with some protection from eviction following a mortgage foreclosure. For discussion of the PTFA, see Nativi v. Deutsche Bank Nat'l Trust Co., 223 Cal.App.4th 261, 167 Cal.Rptr.3d 173 (2014).

[226] See, e.g., Sandall v. Hoskins, 137 P.2d 819 (Utah 1943). Cf. 2401 Pennsylvania Ave. Corp. v. Federation of Jewish Agencies, 489 A.2d 733 (Pa.1985) (landlord breached new tenant's covenant of quiet enjoyment by extending lease of holdover tenant).

[227] See, e.g., Dupree v. Worthen Bank & Trust Co., 543 S.W.2d 465 (Ark.1976); Dwyer v. McCoy, 512 S.E.2d 70 (Ga.App.1999) (lessee unaware of lessor's life estate).

the leased premises by eminent domain does not breach the covenant of quiet enjoyment.[228]

§ 6.32 QUIET ENJOYMENT—ACTUAL EVICTION

In an actual eviction, the landlord physically forces the tenant off the premises or enters and wrongfully excludes the tenant.[229] The tenant has an action for damages for trespass, as well an action to regain possession (by ejectment and likely by forcible entry statutes). More remarkably—and of more interest to most tenants—the eviction empowers the tenant to terminate the lease or at least to suspend paying rent. The reasons for this remarkable remedy and the mechanism by which it operates merit explanation.

Traditionally, English authorities stated that if the landlord wrongfully evicted the tenant, the tenant might suspend paying rent during the period of eviction.[230] In other words, neither the leasehold nor the other lease covenants were terminable; only the covenant to pay rent was suspended, and only while the eviction lasted. The rationale was that rent reserved by a landlord was to be paid by the tenant out of the produce of the land. Therefore, if the tenant was wrongfully ousted, the tenant was denied the source of the rent (and the rent obligation was thus suspended).[231] This was the same concept underlying the common-law rule that rent is not due until the end of the term (i.e., until crops could be harvested). Whether this concept should apply to a modern residential lease is questionable, but applying it avoided the question whether the rule suspending the tenant's duty to pay rent was really an application of the contract law doctrine of dependency of covenants to leases.[232]

American courts, however, have described the rationale in contractual terms, characterizing the tenant's quiet enjoyment of the premises as consideration for, or as a condition to, the tenant's obligation to pay the rent.[233] Indeed, Dyett v. Pendleton,[234] the earliest constructive eviction decision in America (the difference between actual and constructive evictions does not matter here), reads much like a contract case. In

[228] See, e.g., Dolman v. United States Trust Co., 138 N.E.2d 784 (N.Y.1956). Although the government acquires title in a condemnation proceeding, the government's constitutional ability to take property for public purposes is not itself a property interest. Thus, the interference with the tenant's possession as a result of condemnation does not result from a defect in the landlord's title. See 1 Am. Law of Prop. § 3.54 (1952).

[229] See Barash v. Pennsylvania Terminal Real Estate Corp., 256 N.E.2d 707 (N.Y.1970) (court distinguishes actual and constructive evictions); Olin v. Goehler, 694 P.2d 1129 (Wash.App.1985) (landlord breaches implied covenant of quiet enjoyment by wrongfully locking out tenant); 1 Am. Law of Prop. § 3.49 (1952). If the landlord has not lawfully terminated the lease, the landlord's act of changing the locks and refusing to provide tenant with a key constitutes a wrongful eviction. Hinton v. Sealander Brokerage Co., 917 A.2d 95 (D.C.App.2007).

[230] See, e.g., E. Coke, Littleton *148b, *292b; Clun's Case, 10 Co.Rep. 127a, 77 Eng.Rep. 1117 (1614); Collins v. Harding, Cro.Eliz. 606, 78 Eng.Rep. 848 (1598); 7 W. Holdsworth, History of English Law 267–70 (1925).

[231] See, e.g., E. Coke, Littleton *148b, *292b; 7 W. Holdsworth, History of English Law 267–70 (1925). Only occasionally does this rationale appear in American decisions. E.g., Smith v. McEnany, 48 N.E. 781 (Mass.1897).

[232] 6 Williston, Contracts 891 (3d ed.1962).

[233] See, e.g., Kulawitz v. Pacific Woodenware & Paper Co., 155 P.2d 24 (Cal.1944); J.C. Penney Co. v. Birrell, 32 P.2d 805 (Colo.1934); Automobile Supply Co. v. Scene-in-Action Corp., 172 N.E. 35 (Ill.1930); Charles E. Burt, Inc. v. Seven Grand Corp., 163 N.E.2d 4 (Mass.1959); Fifth Ave. Bldg. Corp. v. Kernochan, 117 N.E. 579 (N.Y.1917) ("Eviction as a defense to a claim for rent . . . suspends the obligation of payment either in whole or in part, because it involves a failure of the consideration for which rent is paid."); 1 Am. Law of Prop. § 3.51 (1952).

[234] 8 Cow. 727 (N.Y.1826).

American law, then, the covenant of quiet enjoyment effectively operates as an exception to the traditional doctrine that lease covenants are independent. This supports the conclusion that courts will allow the evicted tenant to terminate its obligations—a result that is essentially rescission in the contract sense.[235]

In some cases, a landlord evicts the tenant from only part of the premises, while the tenant retains possession of the rest. For example, suppose that a lease defines the premises to include both an apartment and a specific parking space for the tenant's exclusive use. If the landlord installs a dumpster on that parking spot which prevents the tenant from parking there—but without any interference with the tenant's possession of the apartment itself—the landlord's conduct is a partial actual eviction. Under the traditional rule, a partial actual eviction suspends the tenant's duty to pay rent in full—every penny![236] Some describe this rule as the "one-inch" rule, reflecting the idea that the landlord cannot collect rent while a partial actual eviction continues, even if the interference with tenant's possession is very small (e.g., one inch).[237]

The rationale—more talismanic than rational—is that the wrongdoing landlord should not be permitted to apportion its wrong. Perhaps a better rationale is that suspension of the full rent is necessary to discourage landlords from interfering with the tenant's right to possession in ways that otherwise will likely go unaddressed. For example, consider the parking hypothetical above; if the parking lot is big enough that tenant can park elsewhere in the lot despite loss of the dedicated space, the tenant's actual damages may be so small that the tenant would not bother to seek damages. Knowing this, the landlord might readily install the dumpster and block the parking space without the tenant's consent; by contrast, if the tenant's obligation to pay rent is suspended in full, the landlord likely will not do so without negotiating for the tenant's consent.[238]

Nevertheless, there is some recent authority suggesting that the tenant cannot obtain a total rent abatement for a de minimis intrusion. For example, in Eastside Exhibition Corp. v. 210 E. 86th St. Corp.,[239] a landlord installed steel crossbeams into a tenant's theater premises—without notice or tenant consent—to enable the landlord to build additional stories onto the building. These crossbeams occupied twelve square feet out of a premises over 16,000 square feet in size. The court held that the landlord's interference was de minimis and did not justify total rent abatement. The court reasoned that for an intrusion to be considered an actual partial eviction, it "must interfere in

---

[235] Indeed, many courts have explicitly justified the tenant's right to terminate in this circumstance on the contract theory of rescission. E.g., University Club v. Deakin, 106 N.E. 790 (Ill.1914); Stifter v. Hartman, 195 N.W. 673 (Mich.1923); Higgins v. Whiting, 131 A. 879 (N.J.1926); Ringwood Assocs., Ltd. v. Jack's of Route 23, Inc., 398 A.2d 1315 (N.J.Super.1979); University Props., Inc. v. Moss, 388 P.2d 543 (Wash.1964); Restatement (Second) of Property-Landlord & Tenant § 7.1 (1977).

[236] E.g., Dolph v. Barry, 148 S.W. 196 (1912); Barash v. Pennsylvania Terminal Real Estate Corp., 256 N.E.2d 707 (N.Y.1970); Fifth Ave. Bldg. v. Kernochan, 117 N.E. 579 (N.Y.1917); E. Coke, Littleton *148b; 7 W. Holdsworth, History of English Law 270 (1925). Note, however, that if the tenant is partially evicted by a third person who has paramount title, rent is apportioned and not fully excused. Fifth Ave. Bldg. Co. v. Kernochan, 117 N.E. 579 (N.Y.1917); E. Coke, Littleton *148a, 148b; 7 W. Holdsworth, History of English Law 267–70 (1925).

[237] 3 Friedman on Leases § 29:2.3, at 29–14 (6th ed.2017).

[238] E.g., Marquardt & Roche/Mediz & Hackett, Inc. v. Riverbend Exec. Ctr., Inc., 812 A.2d 175 (Conn.App.2003) (tenant granted injunction against landlord's appropriation of parking space on ground that the tenant suffered "irreparable harm" by the interference).

[239] 965 N.E.2d 246 (N.Y.2012), cert. denied, 568 U.S. 1028, 133 S.Ct. 654, 184 L.Ed.2d 461 (2012).

some, more than trivial, manner with the tenant's use and enjoyment of the premises."[240] The court suggested that the tenant could have negotiated for a complete rent abatement as a remedy,[241] but there is reason to doubt that even strong and sophisticated commercial tenants could readily obtain an explicit lease clause permitting a complete rent abatement for any physical intrusion by the landlord, no matter how small.

§ 6.33 QUIET ENJOYMENT—CONSTRUCTIVE EVICTION

Both historically and functionally, the doctrine of constructive eviction is an extension of the doctrine of actual eviction. Here the concept is that, because of some wrongful act or omission by the landlord, the premises become uninhabitable ("untenantable") for the intended purposes. The tenant is not physically evicted or excluded, but might as well be. In fact, to invoke the eviction remedy of rent suspension or termination, the tenant must complete the eviction cycle by moving out. Thus, there is an eviction, though "constructive" instead of actual.[242]

For a constructive eviction to occur, the interference must result from a wrong attributable to the landlord.[243] A classic hypothetical instance would be the landlord's removal of all windows and doors in the middle of a hard winter. Sometimes the landlord's acts or wrongful omissions outside the leased premises may release disturbances or substances that invade the premises. Examples are flooding or rodents originating from common areas under the landlord's control[244] or a nuisance emanating from the landlord's nearby brothel.[245] Many decisions go so far as to impute to the landlord nuisances caused by other tenants,[246] but some courts refuse to charge the landlord with another's wrong.[247] Frequently, the landlord's wrong consists of failing to make repairs required by the lease[248] or failure to provide promised utilities or services.[249] It seems that the landlord's failure to make repairs or to provide utilities

---

[240] *Eastside Exhibition Corp.*, 965 N.E.2d at 250. See also Dussin Invst. Co. v. Bloxham, 96 Cal.App.3d 308, 157 Cal.Rptr. 646 (rule will not apply where landlord's intrusion is "inconsequential or insubstantial").

[241] *Eastside Exhibition Corp.*, 965 N.E.2d at 250 ("a commercial lessee is free to negotiate appropriate lease terms").

[242] For general discussion of constructive eviction, see 1 Am. Law of Prop. §§ 3.51, 3.52 (1952); 3 Friedman on Leases § 29:3 (6th ed.2017).

[243] For this reason, where the lease provides no express or implied duty on the landlord to protect the tenant against the interference in question, no constructive eviction arises even from serious interferences. E.g., NYCHA Coney Island Houses v. Ramos, 41 Misc.3d 702, 971 N.Y.S.2d 422 (2013) (tenant not constructively evicted by damage caused by Hurricane Sandy); Charlotte Eastland Mall, L.L.C. v. Sole Survivor, Inc., 608 S.E.2d 70 (N.C.App.2004) (landlord did not have duty to provide security in common areas and thus interference posed by criminal incidents did not constitute constructive eviction).

[244] See, e.g., Village Commons, LLC v. Marion Cty. Prosecutor's Office, 882 N.E.2d 210 (Ind.App.2008) (repeated flooding resulting in mold that in turn resulted in illnesses of tenant's employees); Simon v. Solomon, 431 N.E.2d 556 (Mass.1982) (repeated flooding from adjoining areas); Reste Realty Corp. v. Cooper, 251 A.2d 268 (N.J.1969) (same); Jacobs v. Morand, 59 Misc. 200, 110 N.Y.S. 208 (1908) (bugs).

[245] See Dyett v. Pendleton, 8 Cow. 727 (N.Y.1826).

[246] Milheim v. Baxter, 103 P. 376 (Colo.1909) (brothel); Barton v. Mitchell Co., 507 So.2d 148 (Fla.App.1987) (adjacent tenant, exercise studio); Bocchini v. Gorn Mgmt. Co., 515 A.2d 1179 (Md.App.1986) (noisy tenants in apartment above); QC Corp. v. Maryland Port Admin., 510 A.2d 1101 (Md.App.1986) (adjacent tenant had chrome waste landfill); Phyfe v. Dale, 72 Misc. 383, 130 N.Y.S. 231 (Sup.1911) (brothel); Daftary v. Prestonwood Mkt. Square, Ltd., 404 S.W.3d 807 (Tex.App.2013) (adjacent tenant, dance studio).

[247] E.g., Stewart v. Lawson, 165 N.W. 716 (Mich.1917) (offensive language from other tenants).

[248] See, e.g., Young v. Scott, 700 P.2d 128 (Idaho App.1985); Ridley v. Newsome, 754 S.W.2d 912 (Mo.App.1988); Krieger v. Elkins, 620 P.2d 370 (Nev.1980); Kenyon v. Regan, 826 P.2d 140 (Utah App.1992).

[249] See, e.g., Dimassimo v. City of Clearwater, 805 F.2d 1536 (11th Cir.1986) (water); American Nat'l Bank v. Sound City, U.S.A., Inc., 385 N.E.2d 144 (Ill.App.1979) (heat); Charles E. Burt, Inc. v. Seven Grand Corp., 163 N.E.2d 4 (Mass.1959) (electricity, heat, elevator); Barash v. Pennsylvania Terminal Real Estate

required by statute or ordinance should be the basis for constructive eviction,[250] but some courts have rejected this view.[251] There is even some authority stretching constructive eviction to include the landlord's breach of a covenant giving a tenant the exclusive right to conduct a described business.[252]

Not only must the interference be attributable to the landlord, it must be of such severity that the premises become "untenantable"—i.e., uninhabitable as a residence or unusable for the tenant's business. The cases described in the preceding paragraph give the flavor of what sorts of interferences may cause that condition. In pure form, the concept is that the effect on the tenant is as bad as if the landlord had actually evicted the tenant. In reality, a lesser test satisfies—something like, "Should a tenant be expected to continue to occupy the premises under these conditions?"[253] While the interference cannot be a one-time or isolated occurrence, it need not be literally continuous; an intermittent or recurring problem may suffice.[254] In most situations, there is some interference with the tenant's physical use of the premises, and some decisions suggest this is required.[255] However, the decisions that find constructive eviction in the landlord's breach of an exclusive business clause clearly protect the tenant's economic enjoyment.[256]

No constructive eviction can arise unless the tenant first gives the landlord notice of the problem and a reasonable opportunity to cure it.[257] Further, even if the problem

---

Corp., 256 N.E.2d 707 (N.Y.1970) (air conditioning); Old City Hall LLC v. Pierce Cty. AIDS Found., 329 P.3d 83 (Wash.App.2014) (heating and cooling).

[250] See, e.g., Welsch v. Groat, 897 A.2d 710 (Conn.App.2006); Portal Enters., Inc. v. Cahoon, 715 P.2d 1324 (Nev.1986); Sears, Roebuck & Co. v. 69th St. Retail Mall, L.P., 126 A.3d 959 (Pa.Super.2015); Old City Hall LLC v. Pierce Cty. AIDS Found., 329 P.3d 83 (Wash.App.2014).

[251] See, e.g., Adams v. Woodlands of Nashua, 864 A.2d 322 (N.H.2005) (violation of implied warranty of habitability does not necessarily violate covenant of quiet enjoyment; court refused to allow tenant to recover treble damages authorized by statute for violation of quiet enjoyment); Thompson v. Shoemaker, 173 S.E.2d 627 (N.C.App.1970) (subsequently superseded by statute); Annot., 86 A.L.R.3d 352 (1978). A recent Georgia decision held that the covenant of quiet enjoyment applies only to claims arising from a defect in the landlord's title, and thus does not encompass a non-title-related constructive eviction defense. George v. Hercules Real Estate Servs., Inc., 795 S.E.2d 81 (Ga.App.2016).

[252] In re Consumers World, Inc., 160 F.Supp. 238 (D.Mass.1958); Kulawitz v. Pacific Woodenware & Paper Co., 155 P.2d 24 (Cal.1944).

[253] Sometimes, the court answers "Yes." See, e.g., Longwood Towers Corp. v. Doyle, 166 N.E. 634 (Mass.1929) (failure to make minor repairs); Middagh v. Stanal Sound Ltd., 382 N.W.2d 303 (Neb.1986) (landlord's failure to build promised fence did not make premises untenantable).

[254] See, e.g., Reste Realty Corp. v. Cooper, 251 A.2d 268 (N.J.1969) (periodic flooding); Joylaine Realty Co., LLC v. Samuel, 100 A.D.3d 706, 954 N.Y.S.2d 179 (2012) (repeated flooding); Fidelity Mut. Life Ins. Co v. Kaminsky, 768 S.W.2d 818 (Tex.App.1989) (weekly interference by protestors on date tenant doctor performed abortions).

[255] See, e.g., Griffin Indus., LLC v. Dixie Southland Corp., 162 So.3d 1062 (Fla.App.2015) ("tenant is not entitled to terminate a lease based on a theory of constructive eviction unless the premises are unsafe, unfit, or unsuitable for occupancy for the purposes for which they were leased"). Tenants have sometimes argued constructive eviction based on being sued by the landlord, typically without success. E.g., Trade Winds Hotel, Inc. v. Cochran, 799 P.2d 60 (Haw.App.1990); JS Prop. LLC v. Brown & Filson, Inc., 914 A.2d 297 (N.J.Super.2006) (suggesting that constructive eviction requires physical interference with tenant's use and rejecting argument that landlord's lawsuit for possession constituted constructive eviction where tenant did not vacate and opposed lawsuit). There is some authority, however, that a landlord's improper declaration of default and acceleration of future rent can serve as a basis for constructive eviction. E.g., Kohl v. PNC Bank, N.A., 912 A.2d 237 (Pa.2006); Tenn-Tex Props. v. Brownell-Electro, Inc., 778 S.W.2d 423 (Tenn.1989).

[256] See Kulawitz v. Pacific Woodenware & Paper Co., 155 P.2d 24 (Cal.1944).

[257] E.g., Mason-McDuffie Real Estate, Inc. v. Villa Fiore Dev., LLC, 335 P.3d 211 (Nev.2014); Pague v. Petroleum Prods., Inc. 461 P.2d 317 (Wash.1969); Schaaf v. Nortman, 120 N.W.2d 654 (Wis.1963); Restatement (Second) of Property-Landlord & Tenant § 5.4 (1977).

remains uncured, no constructive eviction can arise unless the vacates the premises.[258] To be sure, even if the tenant remains in possession, the tenant can recover damages, generally in the amount of the diminution in rental value.[259] But the tenant that wishes to terminate must first vacate, and the vacation requirement is a serious stumbling block. First, in residential tenancies of low-quality housing, the tenant likely has little choice of an alternative home, and the alternative may be as rundown as the present one. Second, a tenant who vacates based on the belief that the premises are "untenantable" gambles that a court will agree—a gamble that will result in the tenant having breached if the court does not agree. Maryland and Massachusetts allow the tenant to hedge against that gamble by first maintaining a declaratory judgment action.[260] Other states should follow this sensible procedure.

Not only must the tenant vacate to complete a constructive eviction, but must do so within a reasonable time after the interference justifies it. Certainly, it is too late for the tenant to quit when the leasehold has otherwise come to an end. If the tenant uses the constructive eviction as a defense to paying rent, the defense is not good with respect to rent that came due before the tenant vacated. Nor is the tenant privileged to vacate after the interference has abated.[261] What is a reasonable time to vacate is a question of fact,[262] and may be extended by various factors, such as the tenant's difficulty in finding new premises, difficulty in removing personal items or fixtures, or the tenant's serious illness.[263] If the landlord promises to correct the defective conditions and then delays doing so, this particularly justifies the tenant's delay in vacating.[264]

§ 6.34   INTERFERENCE BY STRANGERS TO TITLE

Interference with the tenant's possession by persons other than the landlord (or the landlord's agents) or holders of paramount title does not breach of the covenant of quiet enjoyment.[265] Such persons are called "strangers to title." They probably are liable to the tenant for trespass or disseisin, but the landlord is not liable. A limitation of sorts on this statement exists in those cases, discussed in the preceding section, in which courts find a constructive eviction from activities carried on by the landlord's other tenants. In

---

[258] Automobile Supply Co. v. Scene-in-Action Corp., 172 N.E. 35 (Ill.1930); JS Props., L.L.C. v. Brown & Filson, Inc., 914 A.2d 297 (N.J.Super.2006); Barash v. Pennsylvania Terminal Real Estate Corp., 256 N.E.2d 707 (N.Y.1970); Thompson v. Shoemaker, 173 S.E.2d 627 (N.C.App.1970).

[259] E.g., Sigsbee v. Swathwood, 419 N.E.2d 789 (Ind.App.1981); Holmes v. P.K. Pipe & Tubing, Inc., 856 S.W.2d 530 (Tex.App.1993).

[260] Stevan v. Brown, 458 A.2d 466 (Md.App.1983); Charles E. Burt, Inc. v. Seven Grand Corp., 163 N.E.2d 4 (Mass.1959).

[261] Gateway Co. v. Charlotte Theatres, Inc., 297 F.2d 483 (1st Cir.1961); Merritt v. Tague, 23 P.2d 340 (Mont.1933).

[262] See Annot., 91 A.L.R.2d 638, 646–51 (1963).

[263] See Greenstein v. Conradi, 201 N.W. 602 (Minn.1924) (delay in finding new premises); Rome v. Johnson, 174 N.E. 716 (Mass.1931) (court lists several factors); Leider v. 80 William St. Co., 22 A.D.2d 952, 255 N.Y.S.2d 999 (1964) (delay in commencement of another leasehold).

[264] See Reste Realty Corp. v. Cooper, 251 A.2d 268 (N.J.1969); Rockrose Assocs. v. Peters, 81 Misc.2d 971, 366 N.Y.S.2d 567 (1975); Annot., 91 A.L.R.2d 638, 655–58 (1963).

[265] E.g., Net Realty Holding Trust v. Nelson, 358 A.2d 365 (Conn.Super.1976); Blomberg v. Evans, 138 S.E. 593 (N.C.1927); Johnson-Lieber Co. v. Berlin Machine Works, 151 P. 778 (Wash.1915); 1 Am. Law of Prop. § 3.53 (1952).

general, though, absent an express covenant to the contrary,[266] the landlord does not warrant against interference by strangers to title.

§ 6.35 CONDEMNATION

The taking of all or part of leased land (or of some interest in it, such as an easement) by a public entity under the power of eminent domain is not a breach of the covenant of quiet enjoyment.[267] Sometimes courts say that the lease contemplated the possibility of condemnation, but it is sufficient to say the condemnation occurs through no fault of the landlord.

Even though there is no breach of the covenant, condemnation impacts upon the landlord-tenant relationship. The most orderly way to approach the subject is to consider two basic fact patterns—one in which all the leased land is taken, and the other in which only a part is taken. If the entire premises is taken by eminent domain, the leasehold and all duties under the lease terminate, including the tenant's duty to pay rent.[268] In some cases, absent contrary agreement, the tenant will be entitled to a share of the compensation award. The nearly universal rule is that the condemnor pays only one award, as if the fee simple title were not subject to the lease; i.e., the leasehold and the reversion are not valued separately.[269] If the tenant has "bonus value" in the lease—i.e., the discounted present value of the sum by which the fair rental value of the premises for the remainder of the term exceeds the tenant's actual rental obligation for that period—the tenant is entitled to share in the condemnation award to this extent unless the lease provides otherwise.[270] The landlord is entitled to the balance of the award.

When only part of the leased premises is taken, the legal situation is more complicated. Logically the tenant's duty to pay rent should abate pro rata,[271] and a few

---

[266] Where the lease contains an express covenant and breach of the covenant contributes to the third-party interference, a constructive eviction can arise. E.g., Fidelity Mut. Life Ins. Co. v. Kaminsky, 768 S.W.2d 818 (Tex.App.1989) (landlord breached duty to provide security on Saturdays, when tenant provided abortions; absence of security resulted in interference by anti-abortion protestors). Even if the lease does not express an affirmative covenant by the landlord to protect against third-party interferences, some courts have implied such a duty in appropriate circumstances, such as where the landlord has the power to control the behavior of other tenants. See, e.g., Eskanos & Supperstein v. Irwin, 637 P.2d 403 (Colo.App.1981); Blackett v. Olanoff, 358 N.E.2d 817 (Mass.1977).

[267] Cornell-Andrews Smelting Co. v. Boston & Providence R.R. Corp., 89 N.E. 118 (Mass.1909); Hockersmith v. Sullivan, 128 P. 222 (Wash.1912); 1 Am. Law of Prop. § 3.54 (1952).

[268] Corrigan v. City of Chicago, 33 N.E. 746 (Ill.1893); Goodyear Shoe Machinery Co. v. Boston Terminal Co., 57 N.E. 214 (Mass.1900); 1 Am. Law of Prop. § 3.54 (1952); 2 P. Nichols, Eminent Domain § 5.06[3] (3d ed.1980); Polasky, The Condemnation of Leasehold Interests, 48 Va.L.Rev. 477 (1962).

[269] J.J. Newberry Co. v. City of E. Chicago, 441 N.E.2d 39 (Ind.App.1982) (total of landlord's and tenant's awards may not exceed market value of fee); Kentucky Dept. of Highways v. Sherrod, 367 S.W.2d 844 (Ky.1963); 4 P. Nichols, Eminent Domain §§ 12.36[1], 12.36[2] (3d ed.1980). However, the existence of a leasehold and the amount of rent may affect the valuation of the fee simple estate. See 4 P. Nichols, Eminent Domain § 12.3122 (3d ed.1980).

[270] Alamo Land & Cattle Co. v. Arizona, 424 U.S. 295, 96 S.Ct. 910, 47 L.Ed.2d 1 (1976); United States v. Petty Motor Co., 327 U.S. 372, 66 S.Ct. 596, 90 L.Ed. 729 (1946); Corrigan v. City of Chicago, 33 N.E. 746 (Ill.1893); J.J. Newberry Co. v. City of E. Chicago, 441 N.E.2d 39 (Ind.App.1982); Annot., 3 A.L.R.2d 286, 290–94 (1949); 1 Am. Law of Prop. § 3.54 (1952); 4 P. Nichols, Eminent Domain § 12.42[3] (3d ed.1980); Restatement (Second) of Property-Landlord & Tenant § 8.2(2)(a) (1977). See also State ex rel. State Highway Comm'n v. St. Charles Cty. Assocs., 698 S.W.2d 34 (Mo.App.1985) (month-to-month tenant not entitled to share in condemnation award).

[271] E.g., 1 Am. Law of Prop. § 3.54 (1952); 2 P. Nichols, Eminent Domain § 5.06[3] (3d ed.1980); Restatement (Second) of Property-Landlord & Tenant §§ 8.1(2)(b), 8.2(2)(b), 11.1 (1977). Nichols and the Restatement also advocate that the taking of so much of the land as significantly to interfere with the tenant's use should terminate the lease.

statutes codify this approach.[272] However, the predominant rule in the courts is that the unless the lease provides otherwise, the tenant must continue to pay the entire rent—including for the portion of the premises of which tenant has lost possession![273] Therefore, the tenant may be entitled to a share of the condemnation award that is comprised of two components. Absent contrary agreement, the tenant will receive an amount equal to the present value of the excess rent the tenant is obliged to pay after the condemnation. In addition, if the tenant has a bonus value in the lease, the tenant will be entitled to a discounted amount equal to the portion of the bonus value allocated to the part of the premises taken.[274] The parties may specifically agree in their lease as to the consequences of condemnation, and courts will generally enforce their agreement.[275] In any long-term lease or one in which condemnation may be anticipated, the parties should (and typically do) include such a clause.

The above apportionment rules apply only when the estate condemned is a fee simple or of greater duration than the remaining time of the leasehold. An entity that has eminent domain power may condemn lesser interests in the land, such as the leasehold alone or even an estate of shorter duration. In such a case, because the reversion is not affected, the landlord has no interest in the condemnation award absent contrary agreement.[276]

F. CONDITION OF THE PREMISES

§ 6.36 FITNESS OF PREMISES FOR INTENDED USE—TRADITIONAL RULES

For clarity's sake, we begin by emphasizing that this section deals *only* with the landlord's or tenant's *contractual* duty to maintain the leased premises—i.e., whether one has a legal right to have the other make repairs to the premises, or whether one has a cause of action for damages or perhaps specific performance on account of the other's failure to make repairs. This section does *not* have anything to do with a landlord's liability *in tort for injuries to the tenant or to any other person*. Section 6.46 addresses a landlord's liability for personal injuries on or about the leased premises, and section 6.47 addresses a landlord's liability for criminal activity against tenants and other persons on or about the premises.

The common law concept of a lease as primarily a conveyance of a leasehold estate resulted in the general application—until recently—of the doctrine of *caveat emptor* with respect to the condition of the leased premises at the inception of a tenancy. Under this doctrine; the landlord did not impliedly warrant that the leased premises were suitable

---

[272] E.g., W.Va.Code § 37–6–29.

[273] See Stubbings v. Village of Evanston, 26 N.E. 577 (Ill.1891); Elliott v. Joseph, 351 S.W.2d 879 (Tex.1961); Olson Land Co. v. Alki Park Co., 115 P. 1083 (Wash.1911).

[274] For a more detailed explanation, see 2 Friedman on Leases § 13.2 (6th ed.2017).

[275] See City of Kansas City v. Manfield, 926 S.W.2d 51 (Mo.App.1996) (enforcing clause allocating entire condemnation award to landlord); State v. Garley, 806 P.2d 32 (N.M.1991) (same). Such provisions are common in commercial leases, because the absence of such a clause may complicate a landlord's ability to obtain mortgage financing.

[276] See Almota Farmers Elevator & Warehouse Co. v. United States, 409 U.S. 470, 93 S.Ct. 791, 35 L.Ed.2d 1 (1973); United States v. General Motors Corp., 323 U.S. 373, 65 S.Ct. 357, 89 L.Ed. 311 (1945); 2 P. Nichols, Eminent Domain § 5.06 (3d ed.1980). Cf. Leonard v. Autocar Sales & Serv. Co., 64 N.E.2d 477 (Ill.1945) (condemnation for time shorter than leasehold does not end it).

for the tenant's intended use.[277] Hence, absent an express warranty of fitness, the tenant generally could not assert the unsuitability of the premises either as a basis to recover damages or as a defense to an action for unpaid rent. *A fortiori,* the tenant could not terminate or "rescind" the lease on the ground that the premises were not suitable for the tenant's use.[278]

Even if the leased premises were suitable for the tenant's use at the beginning of the lease term, the common law did not impose on the landlord any duty to make repairs so as to keep the premises suitable for the tenant's use.[279] Instead, as discussed earlier, the common law imposed on the tenant a minimal duty not to commit waste to buildings, i.e., not to damage them beyond ordinary wear and tear and to keep them sealed against the "wind and weather" to prevent "permissive waste."[280] Of course, a lease is both a conveyance of a leasehold estate and a contract; thus, either party might make an express covenant to make repairs generally or to make specific repairs. It is routine for leases to contain provisions for one or both parties to make repairs; indeed, the repair clauses of a commercial lease are likely to be elaborate.

A "general repair clause" commits the covenanting party to make any and all repairs. A tenant's "redelivery clause" commits the tenant to return the premises to the landlord at the end of the term in some described condition, such as "in good condition" or "in the same condition as when received." When the tenant is the covenanting party, it is important that a repair and redelivery clause "match," i.e., that the undertakings in both are the same. Further, no tenant should sign an unqualified general repair or redelivery clause; at the least, these clauses should exempt the tenant from liability for casualty loss not the fault of the tenant and, unless the tenant is willing to make decorative repairs, from liability for "ordinary wear and tear."[281] The casualty-loss exemption is critical; the traditional common law rule is that, without such an exemption, the tenant not only must repair damage from casualties such as fire and storm, but also rebuild or replace the premises if they are destroyed by such casualties.[282] While this traditional rule is changing, it is still in effect in some jurisdictions.[283]

---

[277] Little Rock Ice Co. v. Consumers' Ice Co., 170 S.W. 241 (Ark.1914); Davidson v. Fischer, 19 P. 652 (Colo.1888); Valin v. Jewell, 90 A. 36 (Conn.1914); Lawler v. Capital City Life Ins. Co., 68 F.2d 438 (D.C.App.1933); Anderson Drive-In Theatre v. Kirkpatrick, 110 N.E.2d 506 (Ind.App.1953); Boyer v. Commercial Bldg. Invst. Co., 81 N.W. 720 (Iowa 1900); Smith v. State, 48 A. 92 (Md.1901); Causey v. Norwood, 156 So. 592 (Miss.1934); Arbuckle Realty Trust v. Rosson, 67 P.2d 444 (Okla.1937).

[278] Even if the lease contained an express warranty of suitability for the tenant's use, the traditional doctrine that lease covenants are "independent" would preclude termination or "rescission" for breach of that warranty. See § 6.10 supra.

[279] E.g., Friedman v. Le Noir, 241 P.2d 779 (Ariz.1952); Chambers v. Lowe, 169 A. 912 (Conn.1933); Duthie v. Haas, 232 P.2d 971 (Idaho 1951); Divines v. Dickinson, 174 N.W. 8 (Iowa 1919); Sipprell v. Merner Motors, 82 N.W.2d 648 (Neb.1957); Harrill v. Sinclair Refining Co., 35 S.E.2d 240 (N.C.1945); Lyman v. Cowen, 31 P.2d 108 (Okla.1934); Irish v. Rosenbaum Co., 34 A.2d 486 (Pa.1943).

[280] See § 6.23 supra.

[281] Courts will tend to construe repair clauses somewhat narrowly. For example, if a lease does not explicitly obligate the tenant to replace a roof and the tenant's own conduct or negligence does not cause the need for replacement, a general repair clause likely will not obligate the tenant to replace an old, dilapidated roof with a new roof at the tenant's expense. See, e.g., ASP Props. Group, L.P. v. Fard, Inc., 133 Cal.App.4th 1257, 35 Cal.Rptr.3d 343 (2005); Miller v. Gammon & Sons, Inc., 67 S.W.3d 613 (Mo.App.2001).

[282] See Chambers v. North River Line, 102 S.E. 198 (N.C.1920) (pier destroyed by ice); Armstrong v. Maybee, 48 P. 737 (Wash.1897) (lumber mill destroyed by fire); 1 Am. Law of Prop. § 3.79 (1952).

[283] For evidence of a change in the traditional rule, see, e.g., Brockett v. Carnes, 416 A.2d 1075 (Pa. Super.1979); Washington Hydroculture, Inc. v. Payne, 635 P.2d 138 (Wash.1981) (contrary to *Armstrong v. Maybee,* cited in preceding note, but refusing to overrule it). See also URLTA § 4.106 (1972) (allowing residential tenants to terminate if the premises are "damaged or destroyed by fire or casualty" to the extent

Another problem for tenants concerns repairs needed because some governmental agency requires the work. Suppose that a commercial tenant has made a general repair covenant and a covenant to comply with applicable laws governing use of the premises; then, during the lease, a local or state governmental agency requires that sprinklers be installed in the building and that the building be structurally retrofitted to withstand earthquakes. Courts may or may not extend the coverage of a tenant's general repair clause or a "compliance with laws" clause to such major governmentally-required repairs, depending upon a number of factors—especially the length of the term, the amount of rent as compared with the cost of repairs, whether the tenant's mode of use somehow contributed to the need for repair, and the relative benefit of the repairs to landlord and tenant. Two decisions from California, *Hadian v. Schwartz*[284] (holding tenant liable for cost of earthquake retrofitting) and *Brown v. Green*[285] (holding tenant not liable for cost of asbestos removal), should be read for a comprehensive listing and discussion of all the relevant factors. The question of repairs required by governmental authorities is serious enough that commercial leases should (and typically do) contain a clause dealing with it; such clauses are customarily enforced (though they may be narrowly construed if ambiguous).

While landlords can covenant to make repairs without limitation, there are in most jurisdictions certain limits on the ability of residential tenants to covenant to make repairs. For example, as to residential premises governed by the Uniform Residential Landlord and Tenant Act, landlords are normally given the duty to comply with building and housing codes and to maintain the premises "in a fit and habitable condition." The Act permits landlords to shift certain repair and maintenance duties to tenants by written agreement, somewhat more so to tenants of "single family" dwellings than to tenants in multi-family buildings, but such agreements cannot relieve a landlord of its obligation to comply with building and housing codes.[286] The Restatement (Second) of Property would allow parties to either residential or commercial leases to apportion maintenance duties by agreement. But in the absence of a contrary agreement, the Restatement would require landlords of all premises to have them suitable for their intended purpose when the term begins (i.e., the rule of caveat emptor would be abolished); to repair casualty losses that occur after the term begins; and, in the case of residential premises, to keep them in safe condition and to comply with health, safety, and housing codes.[287] And in most jurisdictions, housing codes and both judicially-created and statutory warranties of habitability have powerfully shifted repair duties to

---

that enjoyment of the premises is "substantially impaired"); RURLTA § 403(a) (2017) (comparable tenant protections to URLTA).

[284] 884 P.2d 46 (Cal.1994). See also Prudential Ins. Co. v. L.A. Mart, 68 F.3d 370 (9th Cir.1995) (commercial tenant was required, under a general repair clause, to do earthquake proofing that was not ordered by governmental authority); compare Griffith v. New England Tel. & Tel. Co., 649 N.E.2d 766 (Mass.1995) (tenant not liable under general repair clause for cleaning up hazardous waste required by state statute).

[285] 884 P.2d 55 (Cal.1994). See also, e.g., Gaddis v. Consolidated Freightways, Inc., 398 P.2d 749 (Or.1965) (tenant held liable for major elevator repairs); Fresh Cut, Inc. v. Fazli, 650 N.E.2d 1126 (Ind.1995) (tenant's covenant to repair fire sprinkler system that municipal ordinance required "owner" to maintain was not against public policy and was valid).

[286] URLTA § 2.104(a)(1) (1972) and RURLTA § 302(a)(1) (2015) (landlord's duty includes compliance with all applicable code regulations), URLTA § 2.104(d) and RURLTA § 302(d) (landlord and tenant may agree tenant is to perform certain repair or maintenance tasks, but only if work is not necessary to cure landlord's noncompliance with applicable codes).

[287] Restatement (Second) of Property-Landlord & Tenant §§ 5.1–5.6 (1977).

residential landlords. These developments are the subject of the following sections of this book.

Under traditional rules, when the lease contained an express covenant by the landlord to keep the premises in repair, or to make certain specified kinds of repairs, the tenant's remedy for the landlord's breach was to make the required repairs, if minor in character, and then to seek reimbursement by bringing an action against the landlord for breach of the covenant.[288] If the landlord failed to make major repairs required by an express covenant, the tenant could either make the repairs and sue for reimbursement or bring an action for breach of the landlord's covenant.[289] But because the covenants of a lease are independent, the tenant could not withhold the rent because of the landlord's breach, nor could the tenant terminate the lease absent an express provision in the lease authorizing that remedy. As discussed earlier, only a breach of the landlord's covenant of quiet enjoyment—in the form of an actual or constructive eviction—would justify the tenant in withholding rent or terminating the lease.[290]

Moreover, the common law imposed no duty on the landlord to furnish any services in connection with the leasing of realty, regardless of the purpose for which the lease was made. And if the lease contained an express covenant by the landlord to supply services such as water and heat—as might be the case in leases in multi-family buildings—the tenant's remedies for breach were limited to those available for breach of a covenant to repair.

These common law rules may have been reasonable in an agrarian society where multi-family dwelling houses were uncommon, materials required for repairs were simple and easy to obtain, and tenants were generally as capable of carrying out needed repairs as landlords.[291] But as the United States became increasingly urban, courts began to recognize various exceptions to the traditional doctrines. For example, some courts held that a landlord who leased "furnished" premises for a short term had an implied duty to put them in a "habitable" condition before the tenant took possession.[292] Some courts also held that if the tenant signed a lease for premises that were under construction by the landlord, the landlord had an implied duty to put the premises into a condition suitable for its intended use.[293] Courts further extended tenants' rights by recognition and development of the doctrine of "constructive eviction" in the nineteenth

---

[288] E.g., Young v. Berman, 131 S.W. 62 (Ark.1910); Olinger v. Reahard, 70 N.E.2d 436 (Ind.App.1947); Warner Bros. Pictures, Inc. v. Southern Tier Theatre Co., 279 A.D. 309, 109 N.Y.S.2d 781 (1952); Pappas v. Zerwoodis, 153 P.2d 170 (Wash.1944).

[289] Young v. Berman, 131 S.W. 62 (Ark.1910); Borochoff Props., Inc. v. Creative Printing Enters., Inc., 210 S.E.2d 809 (Ga.1974); Charles E. Burt, Inc. v. Seven Grand Corp., 163 N.E.2d 4 (Mass.1959); Parker v. Meadows, 6 S.W. 49 (Tenn.1887). The measure of damages is usually the difference in rental value of the leased premises with and without the repairs. E.g., Williams v. Fenster, 137 A. 406 (N.J.1926); Gordon v. Reinheimer, 29 P.2d 596 (Okla.1934). But cf. Cato Ladies Modes of N.C., Inc. v. Pope, 203 S.E.2d 405 (N.C.App.1974) (damages are the reasonable cost of repairs plus compensation for loss resulting from breach).

[290] See §§ 6.31–6.33 supra.

[291] See T. Quinn & E. Phillips, The Law of Landlord-Tenant: A Critical Evaluation of the Past with Guidelines for the Future, 38 Fordham L.Rev. 225, 231 (1969).

[292] Young v. Povich, 116 A. 26 (Me.1922); Hacker v. Nitschke, 39 N.E.2d 644 (Mass.1942); Pines v. Perssion, 111 N.W.2d 409 (Wis.1961). But see Conley v. Emerald Isle Realty, Inc., 513 S.E.2d 556 (N.C.1999) (rejecting implied duty in rental of vacation cottage), abrogated by N.C.Gen.Stat. § 42A–31 (imposing statutory warranty of habitability in rental of vacation property).

[293] E.g., Woolford v. Electric Appliances, 75 P.2d 112 (Cal.App.1938); J.D. Young Corp. v. McClintic, 26 S.W.2d 460 (Tex.Civ.App.1930); The Hardman Estate v. McNair, 111 P. 1059 (Wash.1910). This exception reflected that a tenant could not be expected to inspect the premises and find them satisfactory prior to leasing them when the premises (the to-be-completed building) did not yet exist.

century. Where a lease contained an express or implied covenant to repair the premises or provide an essential service, courts came to hold that a constructive eviction could arise out of the lessor's breach of that covenant if that breach rendered the premises untenantable.[294]

These changes constituted a nineteenth (and early twentieth) century response to the problems of an increasingly urban society. But these responses were a weak palliative to what became a problem of national dimensions—the problem of rundown housing, especially in tenement-house neighborhoods in America's growing cities. In theory, the tenement dweller *might* obtain a repair covenant from the landlord—but in reality rarely did, thanks to a lack of bargaining power. Moreover, many low-income tenants were month-to-month tenants; if they overly complained of conditions or happened to try to invoke a landlord's repair clause, the landlord would quickly give notice to terminate the lease and evict them.[295] In theory, the tenement dweller might invoke the remedy of constructive eviction if the landlord breached a repair clause, but constructive eviction required the tenant to vacate. To where would the low-income tenant move—another tenement house down the street where the rats were even larger?

§ 6.37 STATUTORY MODIFICATIONS OF THE TRADITIONAL RULES: THE HOUSING CODE APPROACH

Another legislative approach to modification of the traditional rules was the adoption of "tenement house laws" and "housing codes."[296] The ancestor of all modern "housing codes" is the New York Tenement House Law of 1867, which applied only to lodging houses and multiple dwellings located in New York City.[297] Massachusetts enacted a similar statute applicable to Boston in 1868. These early statutes provided the foundation for modern "housing codes," which achieved widespread adoption by the 1960s and which typically arise either by municipal ordinance or state law.[298]

---

[294] See § 6.33 supra. See also Gibbons v. Hoefeld, 132 N.E. 425 (Ill.1921) (covenant to waterproof basement); Kinsey v. Zimmerman, 160 N.E. 155 (Ill.1928) (covenant to mend leaking pipes); Shindler v. Grove Hall Kosher Delicatessen & Lunch, 184 N.E. 673 (Mass.1933) (covenant to supply heat); McCall v. New York Life Ins. Co., 87 N.E. 582 (Mass.1909) (elevator service); Reste Realty Corp. v. Cooper, 251 A.2d 268 (N.J.1969) (oral promise to seal outside driveway and basement wall).

[295] In a summary eviction action, the traditional rule was that affirmative defenses, e.g., the tenant's claiming an offset to rent for the landlord's breach of a repair covenant, were not germane to the action and not allowed. See § 6.78 infra.

[296] See generally, see Grad, Legal Remedies for Housing Code Violations, at 1–6 (Research Report 14, Nat'l Comm'n on Urban Problems, 1968); Friedman, Government and Slum Housing 25–55 (1968); Abbott, Housing Policy, Housing Codes and Tenant Remedies: An Integration, 56 B.U.L.Rev. 1, 40–48 (1976); Cunningham, The New Implied and Statutory Warranties of Habitability in Residential Leases: From Contract to Status, 16 Urban L.Annual 3, 10–51 (1979).

[297] Friedman, Government and Slum Housing 26–27 (1968).

[298] Grad, Legal Remedies for Housing Code Violations, at 2 (Research Report 14, Nat'l Comm'n on Urban Problems, 1968). As Grad points out, the term "housing code" may mean more than a particular municipal ordinance. It may include the entire body of state and local law that prescribes housing standards, including parts of building codes, health codes, plumbing codes, electrical codes, and the like. But, for our purposes, we distinguish the "housing code" from the other types of regulatory ordinances.

There are broad similarities in current housing codes, most of which derive from a number of early model codes. Most arise by municipal ordinance, but there are several state housing codes. Some of the state codes apply statewide; others are applicable only to certain cities or to municipalities falling in certain classifications. Some are "mandatory" but allow municipalities to adopt more stringent requirements; others are "optional"— i.e., municipalities may, but need not, adopt them as local ordinances. See Mood, The Development, Objectives, and Adequacy of Current Housing Code Standards, in Housing Code Standards: Three Critical Studies (Nat'l Comm'n on Urban Problems, Research Rep. No. 19, 1969). For discussion on the significant role that federal

A housing code generally provides minimum standards in regard to four different features of the housing it regulates: (1) structural elements such as walls, roofs, ceilings, floors, windows, and staircases; (2) facilities such as toilets, sinks, bathtubs, radiators or other heating fixtures, stoves, electrical outlets, window screens, and door and window locks; (3) services such as heat, hot and cold water, sanitary sewage disposal, electricity, elevator service, central air conditioning, and repair and maintenance services; and (4) occupancy standards setting limits on the number of occupants per dwelling or per bedroom.[299]

Until relatively recently, tenants had no direct remedies against the landlord when housing code violations occurred. Enforcement of early codes was delegated to local government agencies, both proactively (review on a regular periodic basis) and reactively (review in response to tenant complaints); this continues to be the normal mode of enforcement of modern housing codes.[300] If the issuance of a violation notice and one or more informal or formal administrative hearings do not lead to correction of the violation, the agency can order vacation of the building, followed by an order for demolition if the owner does not correct the violation within a designated time. In some states additional modes of agency enforcement are authorized; these may include a criminal action against the building owner; obtaining an injunction requiring the owner to bring the building into compliance with the housing code; suits to impose a "civil" penalty on the owner; direct agency action to correct code violations by making repairs and improvements; and appointment of a receiver to take over the building and apply its rents to correct code violations.[301]

If the traditional modes of code enforcement had proven effective, perhaps the "revolution" of the 1960s and 1970s in landlord-tenant law would not have occurred. But local governments have been notably unsuccessful in code enforcement.[302] Most agencies are understaffed and underfunded; the public is often unaware of code enforcement problems; local elected officials may not prioritize code enforcement;[303] periodic inspections often do not occur in a timely fashion, and may be compromised by corruption (i.e., housing inspectors taking bribes to supplement their low pay).[304] Even honest housing inspectors may grow discouraged because of the ease with which landlords can

---

housing policy and regulation played in the spread of housing codes, see National Comm'n on Urban Problems, Building the American City, H.R.Doc. No. 91–34, 91st Cong., 1st Sess. 276–77 (1968).

[299] Abbott, Housing Policy, Housing Codes and Tenant Remedies: An Integration, 56 B.U.L.Rev. 1, 40 (1976). For a more extended discussion of the contents of housing codes, see Grad, Hack & McAvoy, Housing Codes and Their Enforcement 195–216 (1966).

[300] Grad, Legal Remedies for Housing Code Violations, at 5 (Research Report 14, Nat'l Comm'n on Urban Problems, 1968).

[301] Grad, Legal Remedies for Housing Code Violations, at 22–61 (Research Report 14, Nat'l Comm'n on Urban Problems, 1968).

[302] The literature is voluminous. See, e.g., M. Teitz & S. Rosenthal, Housing Code Enforcement in New York City (1971); B. Lieberman, Local Administration and Enforcement of Housing Codes: A Survey of 39 Cities (1969); J. Slavet & M. Levin, New Approaches to Housing Code Administration (Research Report 17, National Commission on Urban Problems, 1969); Abbott, Housing Policy, Housing Codes and Tenant Remedies: An Integration, 56 B.U.L.Rev. 1, 49–56 (1976).

[303] Abbott, Housing Policy, Housing Codes and Tenant Remedies: An Integration, 56 B.U.L.Rev. 1, 54–55 (1976).

[304] See J. Slavet & M. Levin, New Approaches to Housing Code Administration 179 (Research Report 17, National Commission on Urban Problems, 1969).

obtain "variances,"[305] and public prosecutors rarely demonstrate much zeal in code enforcement.[306]

Another barrier to code enforcement was the difficulty of obtaining personal jurisdiction over the owner of a non-compliant building. This resulted from the common practice of placing title to the building in a corporation whose officers and offices could not be located and whose agents could not identify their principals.[307] In response, some states began to adopt new legislation authorizing tenants to withhold rent when their landlords failed to correct serious housing code violations which rendered their rental units "uninhabitable," at least while serious code violations persist.[308]

The statutes authorizing tenants to withhold rent because of serious housing code violations do not alter the contractual rights and duties of landlords and tenants. In substance, however, they make the tenant's duty to pay rent conditional on the landlord's compliance with housing code provisions designed to assure that residential premises should be habitable throughout the lease term. Some of these statutes apply to all kinds of rental housing, some apply only to multi-family dwellings, and some have an even more limited application. Many include provisions designed to protect the tenant from retaliatory action by the landlord, and most expressly prohibit any waiver of the tenant's right to withhold rent because of serious housing code violations. Further discussion of these statutes appears in section 6.43.

The "illegal lease" doctrine. In Brown v. Southall Realty Co., the District of Columbia Court of Appeals held that a tenant could avoid liability for unpaid rent by proving the premises were in serious violation of the D.C. housing regulations when the tenancy began—although the regulations did not expressly authorize tenants to assert such violations as a defense to an action for unpaid rent.[309] In that case, the court held the tenant's lease to be "void as an illegal contract"—pointing out that the landlord knew that the violations "existing . . . at the time of the signing of the lease agreement were of

---

[305] Lieberman reported that most code enforcement personnel believed that variance boards act on the basis of political considerations or emotion. Lieberman, Local Administration and Enforcement of Housing Codes: A Survey of 39 Cities 23 (1969).

[306] Few housing code enforcement agencies have legal staffs of their own, and even the ones that do must usually bring prosecutions through the municipality's regular legal department. In the usual course, the municipal law officer or deputies have little experience or knowledge of housing matters and tend to regard housing prosecutions as a very minor, troublesome, and unexciting area for the application of their legal expertise. Grad, Legal Remedies for Housing Code Violations, at 25 (Research Report 14, Nat'l Comm'n on Urban Problems, 1968). See also Philadelphia Housing Ass'n, Impediments to Housing Code Compliance iv (1963); Abbott, Housing Policy, Housing Codes and Tenant Remedies: An Integration, 56 B.U.L.Rev. 1, 53–54 (1976).

[307] Abbott, Housing Policy, Housing Codes and Tenant Remedies: An Integration, 56 B.U.L.Rev. 1, 50 (1976). For a more detailed discussion of the problem, see Grad, Legal Remedies for Housing Code Violations, at Ch. X (Research Report 14, Nat'l Comm'n on Urban Problems, 1968) ("The Phantom Landlord: Finding the Absentee Landlord").

[308] These statutes leave for judicial determination the question whether particular code violations are serious enough to justify withholding of rent. Most require a tenant seeking to withhold rent to show that an official inspection was made and that the inspecting officer reported one or more code violations to the code enforcement agency.

[309] 237 A.2d 834 (D.C.1968). In this holding, the court relied on a section of the regulations which prohibited the renting of "any habitation . . . unless such habitation and its furnishings are in a clean, safe, and sanitary condition, in repair, and free from rodents and vermin," and upon another section which required all "premises accommodating one or more habitations" to "be maintained and kept in repair so as to provide decent living accommodations for the occupants." The latter provision also included a statement that its purpose was to "make a premises or a neighborhood healthy and safe" rather than merely to require "basic repairs and maintenance to keep out the elements."

a nature to make the 'habitation' unsafe and unsanitary."³¹⁰ In Saunders v. First National Realty Corp.,³¹¹ the D.C. Court of Appeals refused to extend the *Brown* "illegal contract" doctrine to cases in which the tenant failed to prove that the alleged housing code violations existed at the beginning of the tenancy. The *Brown* doctrine was later extended to such cases when the "illegal contract" doctrine was incorporated in the D.C. Landlord-Tenant Code, but at least one subsequent case ignored the Code provision and refused to apply the "illegal contract" doctrine in a case where violations only arose "after commencement of the lease."³¹²

A moment's reflection should show why *Brown's* illegal lease doctrine is of little practical use to tenants. If the lease is truly illegal, there is no leasehold—and the tenant has no legal right to possession! To avoid this result, a D.C. court later held (quite illogically) that though the landlord and tenant's lease agreement was void, the tenant was still a "tenant at sufferance" who the landlord could not evict.³¹³ The illegal contract doctrine has gained virtually no recognition;³¹⁴ in practical terms, it is a dead letter.

§ 6.38 THE JUDGE-MADE IMPLIED WARRANTY OF HABITABILITY

A revolution in landlord-tenant law began in the early 1960s. Courts began to abandon *caveat emptor* in residential leases and to impose on landlords an implied warranty that residential premises were fit for human habitation—much as sales law had long imposed a comparable warranty on the seller of goods.³¹⁵ Because courts have not extended the implied warranties to commercial leases (with a few exceptions), we now have a large area in which there really are two bodies of landlord-tenant law. The "revolution" has now pretty much run its course, but the changes it brought have become an established part of our landlord-tenant law.³¹⁶

As early as 1931, the Minnesota Supreme Court held that there was an "implied" warranty of habitability in the leasing of an apartment, whether furnished or not, and whether the lease was for a long or a short term.³¹⁷ But the revolution began in earnest in 1961 with the decision of the Wisconsin Supreme Court in Pines v. Perssion,³¹⁸ where the court rejected the traditional rule of *caveat emptor* and held that a warranty of habitability was implied in every residential lease. The *Pines* court seems to have believed that recognition of an "implied" warranty of habitability would provide an effective if indirect way to enforce state and municipal housing codes. The court reasoned

---

³¹⁰   *Brown*, 237 A.2d at 836.

³¹¹   245 A.2d 836 (D.C.1968), rev'd on other grounds sub nom. Javins v. First Nat'l Realty Corp., 428 F.2d 1071 (D.C.Cir.1970), cert. denied, 400 U.S. 925, 91 S.Ct. 186, 27 L.Ed.2d 185 (1970). For more on the *Javins* case, see § 6.38 supra.

³¹²   Winchester Mgmt. Corp. v. Staten, 361 A.2d 187 (D.C.1976).

³¹³   Robinson v. Diamond Hous. Corp., 463 F.2d 853 (D.C.Cir.1972).

³¹⁴   Missouri recognized the doctrine in King v. Moorehead, 495 S.W.2d 65 (Mo.App.1973), but that case also adopted the implied warranty of habitability and held that a tenant had to elect between those theories in defending an action for rent. The Wisconsin Supreme Court expressly rejected the doctrine in Posnanski v. Hood, 174 N.W.2d 528 (Wis.1970).

³¹⁵   One may debate whether the implied warranty of habitability is closer to the implied warranty of "merchantability" imposed by U.C.C. § 2–314 or the implied warranty of "fitness for a particular purpose" imposed by U.C.C. § 2–315, as it has some of the qualities of both of those warranties.

³¹⁶   See Korngold, Whatever Happened to Landlord-Tenant Law?, 77 Neb.L.Rev. 703–708 (1998).

³¹⁷   Delamater v. Foreman, 239 N.W. 148 (Minn.1931).

³¹⁸   111 N.W.2d 409 (Wis.1961).

that *caveat emptor* was "inconsistent with the current legislative policy concerning housing standards" as exemplified in modern building codes.[319]

Although *Pines* was arguably later overruled,[320] and has in any case been partly superseded by subsequent Wisconsin legislation,[321] courts in nineteen other jurisdictions followed the Wisconsin court's lead in adopting an "implied" warranty of habitability. These jurisdictions are California,[322] D.C.,[323] Hawai'i,[324] Illinois,[325] Indiana,[326] Iowa,[327] Kansas,[328] Massachusetts,[329] Missouri,[330] Mississippi,[331] New Hampshire,[332] New Jersey,[333] New York,[334] Ohio,[335] Pennsylvania,[336] Texas,[337] Vermont,[338] Washington,[339] and West Virginia.[340] In many of these states, the judicial warranty has since been superseded in whole or in part by detailed statutory warranties of habitability.[341] Courts

---

[319] *Pines*, 111 N.W.2d at 412–413.

[320] See Posnanski v. Hood, 174 N.W.2d 528 (Wis.1970). The court rejected the argument that the housing code created a contractual duty on the landlord to comply with the code, reasoning that the legislature had intended "a method of enforcement based entirely upon orders issued by the commissioner of health." Strangely, *Pines* was not cited in *Posnanski* or in any Wisconsin Supreme Court opinion in support of an implied warranty of habitability in residential leases. See Earl Milliken, Inc. v. Allen, 124 N.W.2d 651, 654 n.1 (Wis.1963), and Dickhut v. Norton, 173 N.W.2d 297 (Wis.1970), both of which were decided before *Posnanski*. See also State ex rel. Michalek v. LeGrand, 253 N.W.2d 505, 509 (Wis.1977).

[321] Wis.Stat.Ann. § 704.07.

[322] Green v. Superior Court, 517 P.2d 1168 (Cal.1974).

[323] Javins v. First Nat'l Realty Corp., 428 F.2d 1071 (D.C.Cir.1970), cert. denied, 400 U.S. 925, 91 S.Ct. 186, 27 L.Ed.2d 185 (1970).

[324] Lemle v. Breeden, 462 P.2d 470 (Haw.1969); Lund v. MacArthur, 462 P.2d 482 (Haw.1969).

[325] Jack Spring, Inc. v. Little, 280 N.E.2d 208 (Ill.1972); Pole Realty Co. v. Sorrells, 417 N.E.2d 1297 (Ill.1981).

[326] Johnson v. Scandia Assocs., Inc., 717 N.E.2d 24 (Ind.1999). The *Johnson* decision is curious in that the court held that an implied warranty was not imposed by law on every residential lease, but would be implied in fact based on the parties' agreement as proven "through evidence of the parties' course of dealing or performance and by evidence of ordinary practices in the trade." On the facts, the *Johnson* court held (in a 3–2 decision) that the tenant had failed to establish that her lease implied a warranty that protected her against an electric shock she received when she simultaneously touched two kitchen appliances while cooking.

[327] Mease v. Fox, 200 N.W.2d 791 (Iowa 1972).

[328] Steele v. Latimer, 521 P.2d 304 (Kan.1974).

[329] Boston Hous. Auth. v. Hemingway, 293 N.E.2d 831 (Mass.1973).

[330] Detling v. Edelbrock, 671 S.W.2d 265 (Mo.1984) (adopting the views set forth in King v. Moorehead, 495 S.W.2d 65 (Mo.App.1973)).

[331] O'Cain v. Harvey Freeman & Sons, Inc., 603 So.2d 824 (Miss.1991); Moorman v. Tower Mgmt. Co., 451 F.Supp.2d 846 (S.D.Miss.2006).

[332] Kline v. Burns, 276 A.2d 248 (N.H.1971).

[333] Marini v. Ireland, 265 A.2d 526 (N.J.1970); Berzito v. Gambino, 308 A.2d 17 (N.J.1973).

[334] Tonetti v. Penati, 48 A.D.2d 25, 367 N.Y.S.2d 804 (1975).

[335] Glyco v. Schultz, 289 N.E.2d 919 (Ohio Mun.Ct.1972).

[336] Pugh v. Holmes, 405 A.2d 897 (Pa.1979); Staley v. Bouril, 718 A.2d 283 (Pa.1998) (mobile home park lease).

[337] Kamarath v. Bennett, 568 S.W.2d 658 (Tex.1978).

[338] Hilder v. St. Peter, 478 A.2d 202 (Vt.1984).

[339] Foisy v. Wyman, 515 P.2d 160 (Wash.1973).

[340] Teller v. McCoy, 253 S.E.2d 114 (W.Va.1978) (court held that a common law warranty should be "implied" where case arose after adoption of a statute establishing a warranty of habitability but before the statute became effective).

[341] A comprehensive 50-state memorandum regarding the implied and statutory warranty of habitability, prepared in 2012 for the benefit of the Revised Uniform Residential Landlord and Tenant Act drafting committee, appears on the Uniform Law Commission's website at http://www.uniformlaws.org/shared/docs/residential%20landlord%20and%20tenant/urlta_memo_warrantyofhabitability_021212.pdf.

in several states have rejected the judicially-implied warranty of habitability on the ground that their habitability statutes have covered the field.[342]

The rationales for implying the warranty are reflected in the opinion in the influential Javins v. First National Realty Corp.[343] decision. There, the D.C. Circuit Court of Appeals noted that the factual assumptions underlying *caveat emptor* no longer accurately described the modern residential tenant, who sought not an estate in land but "a well-known package of goods and services . . . [including] adequate heat, light, and ventilation, serviceable plumbing facilities, secure windows and doors, proper sanitation, and proper maintenance."[344] The court further noted that implied warranties of quality had become well-established in contract law, that adopting comparable warranties into the residential tenancy would harmonize landlord-tenant law with modern contract law, and that *caveat emptor* could not "coexist with the obligations imposed on the landlord by a typical modern housing code."[345] Finally, *Javins* relied on policy concerns to justify implication of the warranty, noting both the inequality of bargaining power between residential landlords and tenants and the negative social and public health implications of dilapidated housing.[346]

Tenancies covered. In jurisdictions adopting only the judicial implied warranty, it is not always clear just what rental housing is subject to the warranty. In *Javins*, the court held that the D.C. housing code implied a warranty of habitability in the leasing of all housing covered by the code, and also suggested that a warranty of habitability should be implied into urban dwelling leases as a matter of common law. The latter suggestion was superfluous, because the housing code applied to "any habitation" in the District and all rental housing in the District is clearly "urban." A later decision has interpreted *Javins* as applying only to dwelling units covered by the D.C. housing code.[347] After *Javins,* the highest courts of California, Illinois, Iowa, Massachusetts, New Jersey, Pennsylvania, Washington, and West Virginia held that the warranty was implied in all residential leases;[348] in Iowa, Washington, and West Virginia, this broad coverage was confirmed by later legislation establishing a statutory warranty of habitability.[349] In New Hampshire, the implied warranty is limited to multi-family dwelling units;[350] in

---

[342] Thompson v. Crownover, 368 S.E.2d 170 (Ga.App.1988), rev'd on procedural grounds, 381 S.E.2d 283 (Ga.1989); Worden v. Ordway, 672 P.2d 1049 (Idaho 1983); Conley v. Emerald Isle Realty, Inc., 513 S.E.2d 556 (N.C.1999); Bellikka v. Green, 762 P.2d 997 (Or.1988); Carlie v. Morgan, 922 P.2d 1 (Utah 1996). See also Tex.Ann.Prop. Code §§ 92.061 (statutory warranty supersedes implied warranty); Osborn v. Brown, 361 So.2d 82 (Ala.1978) (declining to adopt implied warranty); Hurst v. Field, 661 S.W.2d 393 (Ark.1983) (same).

[343] 428 F.2d 1071 (D.C.Cir.1970), cert. denied, 400 U.S. 925, 91 S.Ct. 186, 27 L.Ed.2d 185 (1970).

[344] *Javins*, 428 F.2d at 1074.

[345] *Javins*, 428 F.2d at 1076–77. The *Javins* court was on shaky ground to rely on the analogy to the U.C.C. warranties to support its holding that the landlord has a continuing duty to keep the premises in habitable condition during the term. The U.C.C. warranties do not obligate the seller to repair defects arising from deterioration over time. Cunningham, The New Implied and Statutory Warranties of Habitability in Residential Leases: From Contract to Status, 16 Urb.L.Ann. 3, 76 (1979); Abbott, Housing Policy, Housing Codes and Tenant Remedies: An Integration, 56 B.U.L.Rev. 1, 31 (1976).

[346] *Javins*, 428 F.2d at 1079–80.

[347] Winchester Mgmt. Corp. v. Staten, 361 A.2d 187 (D.C.App.1976).

[348] Green v. Superior Court, 517 P.2d 1168 (Cal.1974); Pole Realty Co. v. Sorrells, 417 N.E.2d 1297 (Ill.1981); Mease v. Fox, 200 N.W.2d 791 (Iowa 1972); Marini v. Ireland, 265 A.2d 526 (N.J.1970); Pugh v. Holmes, 405 A.2d 897 (Pa.1979); Kamarath v. Bennett, 568 S.W.2d 658 (Tex.1978); Foisy v. Wyman, 515 P.2d 160 (Wash.1973); Teller v. McCoy, 253 S.E.2d 114 (W.Va.1978).

[349] See § 6.39 infra.

[350] Kline v. Burns, 276 A.2d 248 (N.H.1971).

Kansas, it was originally limited to "urban residential property,"[351] but was later broadened by statute to cover all property leased for residential use.[352]

When is the warranty violated? The relationship between the judicial implied warranty and the standards set out in applicable housing codes is not always clear. In general, the cases indicate that proof of housing code violations having a substantial adverse impact on health or safety is sufficient to establish a breach of the warranty.[353] By contrast, most of the cases recognize that some code violations do not pose any substantial threat to the health or safety of tenants and thus do not violate the warranty;[354] as the court observed in *Javins,* "one or two minor violations standing alone, which do not affect habitability, are *de minimis.*"[355]

Can a breach result if there is no code violation at all? It is not clear what position the *Javins* court would have taken on this question, but the D.C. Court of Appeals subsequently interpreted *Javins* as holding that the implied warranty is measured solely "by the standards set out in the [D.C.] Housing Regulations."[356] In several other jurisdictions, however, courts have defined the implied warranty broadly enough to include all cases where the leased premises are unfit for human habitation because of health or safety hazards, whether or not there is a housing code violation.[357] In these states, whether a violation exists is determined in light of the specific facts and circumstances.[358] One such circumstance is whether the alleged defect violates an

---

[351] Steele v. Latimer, 521 P.2d 304 (Kan.1974).

[352] See Kan.Stat.Ann. §§ 58–2540 to 58–2573 (URLTA as enacted in Kansas).

[353] Javins v. First Nat'l Realty Corp., 428 F.2d 1071 (D.C.Cir.1970); Green v. Superior Court, 517 P.2d 1168 (Cal.1974); Jack Spring, Inc. v. Little, 280 N.E.2d 208 (Ill.1972); Boston Hous. Auth. v. Hemingway, 293 N.E.2d 831 (Mass.1973); King v. Moorehead, 495 S.W.2d 65 (Mo.App.1973); Kline v. Burns, 276 A.2d 248 (N.H.1971); Berzito v. Gambino, 308 A.2d 17 (N.J.1973); Chase v. Pistolese, 190 Misc.2d 477, 739 N.Y.S.2d 250 (City Ct.2002) (presence of lead-based paint); Pugh v. Holmes, 405 A.2d 897 (Pa.1979); Foisy v. Wyman, 515 P.2d 160 (Wash.1973); Teller v. McCoy, 253 S.E.2d 114 (W.Va.1978). By contrast, see Schiernbeck v. Davis, 143 F.3d 434 (8th Cir.1998) (no common law or statutory duty to install smoke detectors); Curry v. 1716 Ave. T Realty, LLC, 89 A.D.3d 978, 933 N.Y.S.2d 342 (2011) (same); Solow v. Wellner, 658 N.E.2d 1005 (N.Y.1995) (amenities for luxury apartment not within warranty of habitability); Weiler v. Hooshiari, 19 A.3d 124 (Vt.2011) (implied warranty not implicated by snow and ice falling from roof and damaging tenant's car).

[354] Javins v. First Nat'l Realty Corp., 428 F.2d 1071 (D.C.Cir.1970); Green v. Superior Court, 517 P.2d 1168 (Cal.1974); Lund v. MacArthur, 462 P.2d 482 (Haw.1969); Boston Hous. Auth. v. Hemingway, 293 N.E.2d 831 (Mass.1973); McAllister v. Boston Hous. Auth., 708 N.E.2d 95 (Mass.1999) (natural accumulation of snow and ice did not violate implied warranty); Fletcher v. Littleton, 859 N.E.2d 882 (Mass.App.2007) (use of now-prohibited combination of wiring and insulation not per se violation of implied warranty where electrical standards did not require existing wiring to be brought into compliance); Chiodini v. Fox, 207 S.W.3d 174 (Mo.App.2006) (exposed wires violated warranty because they posed fire hazard); Berzito v. Gambino, 308 A.2d 17 (N.J.1973); Stikeleather Realty & Invsts. Co. v. Broadway, 775 S.E.2d 373 (N.C.App.2015) (landlord's failure to provide operable smoke and carbon monoxide alarms not a violation of warranty); Foisy v. Wyman, 515 P.2d 160 (Wash.1973). But see Breezewood Mgmt. Co. v. Maltbie, 411 N.E.2d 670 (Ind.App.1980) (evidence that there were "numerous housing code violations" was sufficient to sustain finding of breach).

[355] *Javins,* 428 F.2d at 1082 n.63.

[356] Winchester Mgmt. Corp. v. Staten, 361 A.2d 187, 190 (D.C.1976).

[357] Green v. Superior Court, 517 P.2d 1168 (Cal.1974); Lemle v. Breeden, 462 P.2d 470 (Haw.1969); Glasoe v. Trinkle, 479 N.E.2d 915 (Ill.1985); Mease v. Fox, 200 N.W.2d 791 (Iowa 1972); Old Town Dev. Co. v. Langford, 349 N.E.2d 744 (Ind.App.1976), superseded, 369 N.E.2d 404 (Ind.1977); Boston Hous. Auth. v. Hemingway, 293 N.E.2d 831 (Mass.1973); King v. Moorehead, 495 S.W.2d 65 (Mo.App.1973); Kline v. Burns, 276 A.2d 248 (N.H.1971); Marini v. Ireland, 265 A.2d 526 (N.J.1970); Berzito v. Gambino, 308 A.2d 17 (N.J.1973); Tonetti v. Penati, 48 A.D.2d 25, 367 N.Y.S.2d 804 (1975); Pugh v. Holmes, 405 A.2d 897 (Pa.1979).

[358] E.g., Mease v. Fox, 200 N.W.2d 791 (Iowa 1972); Boston Hous. Auth. v. Hemingway, 293 N.E.2d 831 (Mass.1973); King v. Moorehead, 495 S.W.2d 65 (Mo.App.1973); Kline v. Burns, 276 A.2d 248 (N.H.1971); Marini v. Ireland, 265 A.2d 526 (N.J.1970); Berzito v. Gambino, 308 A.2d 17 (N.J.1973). Many cases emphasize that defects in the premises or failures in provision of services must have "a serious and substantial relationship to the rental value," see Doric Realty Co. v. Union City Rent Leveling Bd., 442 A.2d 652

applicable housing code; other factors include the nature of the defect, its effect on safety and sanitation, the length of time it has persisted, the age of the structure, and the amount of the rent. The implied warranty generally requires the provision of essential services such as hot water, heat, and elevators (in high rise buildings), even if these services are not strictly necessary to protect the tenant's health or safety;[359] where a housing code applies, it will usually require that the landlord provide such services.[360] In one notable decision, a New York court suggested that secondhand smoke from other apartments could, if sufficiently serious, breach the implied warranty of habitability.[361]

"Patent" vs. "latent" defects. In *Pines*,[362] many of the defects that made the premises uninhabitable were "patent," but some were "latent." The court, however, said nothing to suggest any distinction between "patent" and "latent" defects mattered with respect to the implied warranty. Likewise, in Lemle v. Breeden[363] and Lund v. MacArthur,[364] all the defects appear to have been "latent," but the courts did not indicate that this was significant. The *Javins* opinion includes a dictum that the shortage of housing in D.C. compels tenants to accept rental units notwithstanding observable defects;[365] the court's emphasis on the need for effective tenant remedies suggests that the *Javins* court would draw no distinction between "latent" and "patent" defects.[366] In Massachusetts, it is clear that the implied warranty covers both latent and patent defects existing at the beginning of the tenancy.[367]

New Jersey courts, by contrast, have held that the residential landlord impliedly warrants that "at the inception of the lease, there are no *latent* defects in facilities vital to the use of the premises for residential purposes because of original faulty construction or deterioration from age or normal usage."[368] New Hampshire[369] and Iowa[370] courts later adopted this language. But the significance of the "latent" defect limitation is hard to determine, because the Iowa, New Hampshire, and New Jersey courts have all held that the implied warranty also includes a continuing duty to keep the premises in a

---

(N.J.Super.1981), or "be such as to render the premises uninhabitable in the eyes of a reasonable person," see Berzito v. Gambino, 308 A.2d 17 (N.J.1973). See also Allen v. Housing Auth. of Chester County, 683 F.2d 75 (3d Cir.1982) (sewage water in apartment); Hilder v. St. Peter, 478 A.2d 202 (Vt.1984) (parade of horrible conditions).

[359] Permanent Mission of Republic of Estonia v. Thompson, 477 F.Supp.2d 615 (S.D.N.Y.2007) (heat and hot water; irrelevant that lease provided tenant was to provide and pay for heat and hot water); Winchester Mgmt. Corp. v. Staten, 361 A.2d 187, 190 (D.C.App.1976) (hot water, but not air conditioning, is required by housing code and thus by the implied warranty); Marini v. Ireland, 265 A.2d 526 (N.J.1970) ("facilities vital to the use of the premises for residential purposes"); Berzito v. Gambino, 308 A.2d 17 (N.J.1973); Academy Spires, Inc. v. Brown, 268 A.2d 556 (N.J.Super.1970) (garbage disposal, hot water, elevator service); Park Hill Terrace Assocs. v. Glennon, 369 A.2d 938 (N.J.Super.App.Div.1977) (air conditioning); Pugh v. Holmes, 405 A.2d 897 (Pa.1979) (hot water); Foisy v. Wyman, 515 P.2d 160 (Wash.1973) (same).

[360] E.g., Winchester Mgmt. Corp. v. Staten, 361 A.2d 187 (D.C.1976).

[361] Poyck v. Bryant, 13 Misc.3d 699, 820 N.Y.S.2d 774 (City Ct.2006).

[362] 111 N.W.2d 409 (Wis.1961).

[363] 462 P.2d 470 (Haw.1969).

[364] 462 P.2d 482 (Haw.1969).

[365] *Javins*, 428 F.2d at 1079 n.42.

[366] The tenants in *Javins* conceded that the violations had arisen after the term commenced; thus, the court had no reason to discuss whether the warranty would cover patent defects existing at the beginning of the term.

[367] Boston Hous. Auth. v. Hemingway, 293 N.E.2d 831, 843 (Mass.1973).

[368] *Marini*, 265 A.2d at 534 (emphasis added), repeated with approval in *Berzito*, 308 A.2d at 20.

[369] Kline v. Burns, 276 A.2d 248 (N.H.1971).

[370] Mease v. Fox, 200 N.W.2d 791 (Iowa 1972).

habitable condition.[371] This continuing duty probably extends to the repair of patent as well as latent defects.[372]

The warranty as a continuing warranty. The opinion in *Pines*[373] contained no language indicating that there is also a continuing duty of the landlord to maintain the premises in a habitable condition. But in *Javins,*[374] the court explicitly held that the landlord was subject to such a continuing duty. This conclusion is not justified by analogy to the consumer-protection cases relied on by the court,[375] but it does seem justified by the policy underlying the D.C. housing code. Since *Javins,* courts have consistently held that the implied warranty includes a continuing duty to maintain the dwelling unit in a habitable condition.[376] In effect, the implied warranty operates not only as a warranty that the premises are in habitable condition at the commencement of the term but as a continuing covenant to keep them in that condition.[377]

Waiver. Can a residential tenant waive the implied warranty of habitability and, if so, under what conditions? Most courts that have considered the question have generally refused to give effect to even the most explicit waiver by the tenant,[378] though there are a few contrary decisions.[379] The Restatement (Second) of Property takes the position that waivers are permitted if they are not "unconscionable or significantly against public

---

[371] Mease v. Fox, 200 N.W.2d 791 (Iowa 1972); Kline v. Burns, 276 A.2d 248 (N.H.1971); Marini v. Ireland, 265 A.2d 526, 534 (N.J.1970). In Iowa, the implied warranty has been superseded by a statutory warranty of habitability that clearly covers both "latent" and "patent" defects. Iowa Code Ann. § 562A.15 (based on URLTA § 2.104(a) (1972)).

[372] Both Mease v. Fox, 200 N.W.2d 791 (Iowa 1972), and Berzito v. Gambino, 308 A.2d 17 (N.J.1973), say the court should consider whether the tenant knowingly waived defects, which implies that defects may be patently observable. Later New Jersey cases seem to have abandoned the requirement that the warranty extends only to existing latent defects. See, e.g., Trentacost v. Brussel, 412 A.2d 436 (N.J.1980); Chess v. Muhammad, 430 A.2d 928 (N.J.Super.1981).

[373] 111 N.W.2d 409 (Wis.1961).

[374] 428 F.2d 1071 (D.C.Cir.1970), cert. denied, 400 U.S. 925, 91 S.Ct. 186, 27 L.Ed.2d 185 (1970).

[375] *Javins*, 428 F.2d at 1079. Neither the common law warranties of fitness and quality implied in sales of goods nor their modern statutory counterparts under the Uniform Commercial Code include any continuing duty to repair defects arising from the normal use of the goods after acquisition by the buyer. Nor do such implied or statutory warranties cover patent defects discoverable by a reasonable inspection. See, e.g., Remy, Schmidt & Pleissner v. Healy, 126 N.W. 202, 203 (Mich.1910); U.C.C. §§ 2–314 through 2–317.

[376] E.g., Green v. Superior Court, 517 P.2d 1168 (Cal.1974); Jack Spring, Inc. v. Little, 280 N.E.2d 208 (Ill.1972); Boston Hous. Auth. v. Hemingway, 293 N.E.2d 831 (Mass.1973); Marini v. Ireland, 265 A.2d 526, 534 (N.J.1970); Berzito v. Gambino, 308 A.2d 17 (N.J.1973); Pugh v. Holmes, 405 A.2d 897 (Pa.1979); Foisy v. Wyman, 515 P.2d 160 (Wash.1973). None of these opinions limits the landlord's duty of repair to latent conditions at the inception of the tenancy that first become apparent during the term. In Knight v. Hallsthammar, 623 P.2d 268 (Cal.1981), the court expressly rejected any limitation of the implied warranty to latent defects.

[377] In this regard, the implied warranty of habitability represents "a judicial recognition of the largely accomplished fact of the transition of residential lease law from the private law fields of property and contract to an area in which public regulatory law predominates." Glendon, The Transformation of American Landlord-Tenant Law, 23 B.C.L.Rev. 503, 552 (1982).

[378] In *Javins*, 428 F.2d at 1080 n.49, 1082 n.58, the court refused to consider whether the tenant's express covenant to repair constituted a waiver of the implied warranty of habitability. Most cases have followed *Javins* in holding or stating that the implied warranty of habitability cannot be waived. See, e.g., Permanent Mission of Republic of Estonia v. Thompson, 477 F.Supp.2d 615 (S.D.N.Y.2007); Green v. Superior Court, 517 P.2d 1168 (Cal.1974); Moity v. Guillory, 430 So.2d 1243 (La.App.1983); Boston Hous. Auth. v. Hemingway, 293 N.E.2d 831 (Mass.1973); Foisy v. Wyman, 515 P.2d 160 (Wash.1973); Teller v. McCoy, 253 S.E.2d 114 (W.Va.1978). None of the cases dealt with a fact situation like that envisaged by URLTA § 2.104(c), (d), where the parties make a separate written agreement, for an adequate consideration, to shift some of the repair obligations of the landlord to the tenant.

[379] E.g., Lee v. Keller Williams Realty, 247 So.3d 293 (Miss.App.2017) (upholding tenant's waiver of implied warranty as knowing and voluntary).

policy."[380] Adopting this approach, the Utah Supreme Court ruled that a express waiver could be enforceable with respect to specific defects listed as waived.[381] To the extent it may influence courts in common law decisions, the Revised Uniform Residential Landlord and Tenant Act does not permit a blanket waiver in the lease; it does permit the tenant to make a separate, written agreement to perform specified repairs, but only if "the work is not necessary to cure the landlord's noncompliance" with applicable housing or building codes.[382]

Notice/cure. The landlord does not breach the implied warranty unless the landlord fails to make the necessary repairs within a reasonable time after receiving notice of the defective condition—at least where the defective condition only arises, or becomes patent, after the tenancy begins.[383] The implied warranty does not cover conditions resulting from the deliberate or negligent conduct of the tenant or anyone for whose conduct the tenant is responsible.[384]

The Restatement (Second) of Property. The Restatement (Second) of Property includes a comprehensive restatement of the law of landlord and tenant.[385] Sections 5.1 and 5.2 state that there is an implied warranty (without using that term) that property leased for residential use will be suitable for such use both when the lease is made and at the commencement date. The comments state that the leased property "is unsuitable for residential purposes if it would be unsafe or unhealthy for the tenant to enter on the leased property and use it as a residence"; that "[a] significant violation of any controlling building or sanitary code, or similar public regulation, which has a substantial impact upon safety or health, is *conclusive* that the premises are unsafe or unhealthy, but other modes of proof are acceptable"; and that "[t]he premises may not be unsafe or unhealthy to occupy but may [nevertheless] be unsuitable for residential purposes."[386] Section 5.5 creates a separate "obligation of the landlord to keep leased property in repair," which includes, but is not limited to, a duty to keep the leased premises in compliance with applicable housing code provisions. As a whole, these provisions appear largely based on the corresponding sections of the original Uniform Residential Landlord and Tenant Act.[387] It thus more nearly approximated a restatement of the then-current statutory law with respect to these duties than a restatement of the then-current case law.

Commercial leases. Will courts imply a parallel warranty into a commercial lease that the premises will be fit for the tenant's intended purpose? So far there has been little movement in this direction. Because commercial tenants generally have more

---

[380] Restatement (Second) of Property-Landlord & Tenant § 5.6 (1977).

[381] P.H. Inv. v. Oliver, 818 P.2d 1018 (Utah 1991). The New Jersey court indicated a willingness to consider the possibility of waiver in Berzito v. Gambino, 308 A.2d 17 (N.J.1973), but ultimately sustained the trial court's conclusion that the scarcity of available housing for low-income families with children in the area precluded an effective waiver. See also Mease v. Fox, 200 N.W.2d 791 (Iowa 1972).

[382] RURLTA § 302(d)(2) (2015).

[383] E.g., Kolb v. DeVille I Props., LLC, 326 S.W.3d 896 (Mo.App.2010). This is also the rule in cases where the lease contains an express covenant by the landlord to make repairs on the leased premises. E.g., Chambers v. Lindsey, 55 So. 150 (Ala.1911); Bowling v. Carroll, 182 S.W. 514 (Ark.1916); Woodbury Co. v. Williams Tackaberry Co., 148 N.W. 639 (Iowa 1914).

[384] E.g., Wade v. Jobe, 818 P.2d 1006 (Utah 1992); Restatement (Second) of Property-Landlord & Tenant § 5.1 & Comment i (1977).

[385] The first Restatement of Property (1936) did not address the law of landlord and tenant.

[386] Restatement (Second) of Property-Landlord and Tenant § 5.1, Comment e (1977) (emphasis supplied).

[387] See § 6.39 infra.

bargaining power and because there is not perceived to be a pressing national problem with the condition of commercial premises, little pressure has been generated for the implication of commercial warranties. The only jurisdiction clearly to recognize such an implied warranty is Texas, in Davidow v. Inwood North Professional Group–Phase I.[388] As defined by the Texas Supreme Court, this warranty means that at the inception of the lease there are no latent defects in the facilities that are vital to the premises for their intended commercial purposes and that these essential facilities will remain in a suitable condition. Perhaps not surprisingly—given the common assumption that parties to commercial agreements are more sophisticated and bargain at arms-length—the Texas Supreme Court later held that the implied warranty can be waived by appropriate language in the lease agreement.[389] A 1996 Utah decision came close to implying a warranty of fitness to a commercial lease and discussed *Davidow* approvingly, but simply allowed the tenant a rent abatement for the landlord's breach of an express written covenant to repair an elevator.[390] More commonly, courts have rejected the application of the implied warranty to commercial leases generally.[391]

§ 6.39 STATUTORY WARRANTIES OF HABITABILITY IN RESIDENTIAL LEASES

The French civil law in force in Louisiana at the beginning of the nineteenth century imposed on the landlord, absent contrary agreement, a duty to deliver the premises to the tenant in a condition suitable for the tenant's intended use, and to make all major repairs on the premises not made necessary by the tenant's wrongful conduct. Successive revisions of the Louisiana Civil Code have carried forward this duty.[392]

Early in their history, California, Georgia, Montana, and the Dakota Territory enacted the proposed Civil Code drafted by David Dudley Field.[393] As enacted in all these

---

[388] 747 S.W.2d 373 (Tex.1988). The premises in question had been leased for use as a doctor's office, and the defects were serious; the air conditioning did not work, the roof leaked, pests and rodents infested the office, there was no hot water, the parking lot was filled with trash, and the electricity was off for several days because the landlord failed to pay the bill. *Davidow* was followed in Coleman v. Rotana, Inc., 778 S.W.2d 867 (Tex.App.1989), and Kerrville HRH, Inc. v. City of Kerrville, 803 S.W.2d 377 (Tex.App.1990). See Murray, The Evolution of Implied Warranties in Commercial Real Estate Leases, 28 U.Rich.L.Rev. 145 (1993).

[389] See Gym-N-I Playgrounds, Inc. v. Snider, 220 S.W.3d 905 (Tex.2007).

[390] Richard Barton Enters., Inc. v. Tsern, 928 P.2d 368 (Utah 1996).

[391] See Gehrke v. General Theatre Corp., 298 N.W.2d 773 (Neb.1980); Golub v. Colby, 419 A.2d 397 (N.H.1980); B.W.S. Invsts. v. Mid Am Restaurants, Inc., 459 N.W.2d 759 (N.D.1990); Joyce v. Rapp, 660 N.E.2d 542 (Ohio App.1995). A few courts have refused to imply the warranty on the specific facts, while suggesting that an implied warranty might be justified if the facts and circumstances warranted. E.g., Four Seasons Invst. Corp. v. Int'l Hotel Tenants' Ass'n, 81 Cal.App.3d 604, 146 Cal.Rptr. 531 (1978).

[392] La.Civ.Code art. 2684 (lessor must deliver premises "in good condition suitable for the purpose for which it was leased"); art. 2691 (lessor must "make all repairs that become necessary to maintain the thing in a condition suitable for the purpose for its was leased, except those for which the lessee is responsible"); art. 2696 (lessor warrants premises "is suitable for the purpose for which it was leased . . . and free of vices or defects that prevent its use for that purpose"). These duties exist in all Louisiana leases, not just residential ones.

[393] See A. Reppy, The Field Codification Concept, in David Dudley Field Centenary Essays 17, 48 (A. Reppy ed.1949). The Field Code was designed for adoption in New York, but was rejected by the New York legislature.

Georgia's statute draws a peculiar distinction between a lease for five years or longer and one for fewer than five years. Absent contrary agreement, the former creates a common law leasehold while the latter creates a civil law usufruct, under which the landlord has the obligation to keep the premises in good repair. Ga.Code Ann. §§ 44–7–1, 44–7–13, 44–6–105. As the Georgia Supreme Court has said, when a common law leasehold is created, "our Civil Code, . . . following the common law, makes the tenant bound for all repairs or other expense necessary for the preservation and protection of the property . . . ." Mayer v. Morehead, 32 S.E. 349

jurisdictions except Georgia, the Field Code contained provisions that imposed on the landlord of a building intended for human habitation a duty to "put it into a condition fit for such occupation, and to repair all subsequent dilapidations thereof, which render it untenantable." These Field Code provisions were carried over to the subsequently enacted Civil Codes of North and South Dakota and were still later enacted in Oklahoma.[394]

No other American jurisdiction followed the lead of California, Georgia, Montana, the Dakotas, and Oklahoma in adopting these Field Code provisions. In California, the Civil Code details the conditions deemed to make a dwelling untenantable and provides additional protection for residential tenants.[395] North and South Dakota have enacted amendments providing protections comparable to those in California.[396] The Montana and Oklahoma Field Code enactments have been superseded by adoption of new legislation based on the Uniform Residential Landlord and Tenant Act (the URLTA).[397]

The Uniform Law Commission lists 21 states that have adopted the URLTA, which includes detailed provisions that require landlords to have and keep residential premises in habitable condition and that prescribe in detail tenants' remedies for landlords' breach of their duties.[398] Delaware has enacted similar comprehensive legislation based on the American Bar Foundation's Model Residential Landlord-Tenant Code (the MRLTC), which itself influenced both the URLTA and other state statutes.[399] Both the URLTA and the MRLTC provide in substance that every residential lease includes a warranty of habitability coupled with a continuing duty to keep the leased premises in a habitable condition.

Both the URLTA and the MRLTC apply to substantially all residential rental units, not just to rental units in multi-family dwellings or to housing covered by state or local

---

(Ga.1899). See also Thompson v. Crownover, 368 S.E.2d 170 (Ga.App.1988) (with leasehold, no implied warranty of habitability beyond landlord's statutory duty), rev'd on procedural grounds, 381 S.E.2d 283 (Ga.1989). But when the Georgia tenant has a "usufruct" instead of an estate for years, "the civil law is adopted, and the landlord must keep the premises in repair." Mayer v. Morehead, 32 S.E. 349 (Ga.1899). Moreover, the landlord must have the premises in a condition fit for the tenant's intended use at the beginning of the tenancy "if full rent is reserved." E.g., Whittle v. Webster, 55 Ga. 180 (1875); Driver v. Maxwell, 56 Ga. 11 (1876).

[394] Field Civ. Code §§ 990, 991. See, e.g., Cal.Civ. Code §§ 1941, 1942; N.D.Cent.Code §§ 47–16–13, 47–16–13.1; S.D.Codif.Laws §§ 43–32–8, 43–32–9. Montana and Oklahoma enacted comparable provisions but ultimately replaced them by adopting the Uniform Residential Landlord and Tenant Act.

[395] Cal.Civ.Code § 1941.1. In Knight v. Hallsthammar, 623 P.2d 268 (Cal.1981), the court held that the standards set out in § 1941.1 may be relevant to a determination of "uninhabitability," depending on the circumstances, but that § 1941.1 is not controlling as to breach of the implied warranty of habitability.

[396] See N.D.Cent.Code §§ 47–16–13.1 to –14; S.D.Codif.Laws §§ 43–32–8 to –10.

[397] Mont.Code Ann. §§ 70–24–101 to –442; 41 Okla.Stat.Ann. §§ 101 to 135. The URLTA was recommended for adoption by the states in 1972. In 2015, the Commission approved a comprehensive Revised Residential Uniform Landlord and Tenant Act (RURLTA), but RURLTA has not yet been enacted in any state. The full text of both the URLTA and the RURLTA is available at the Uniform Law Commission's website, http://uniformlaws.org.

[398] These states include Alabama, Alaska, Arizona, Connecticut, Florida, Hawaii, Iowa, Kansas, Kentucky, Michigan, Mississippi, Montana, Nebraska, New Mexico, Oklahoma, Oregon, Rhode Island, South Carolina, Tennessee, Virginia, and Washington. Some states enacted the URLTA comprehensively; others enacted portions of it, and the state-by-state enactments include some nonuniform modifications. The precise content of any state's enactment requires consulting the specific statute. A recent and comprehensive 50-state memorandum regarding the implied and statutory warranty of habitability, prepared for the drafting committee for the RURLTA, is available for review on the Uniform Law Commission's website at http://www.uniformlaws.org/shared/docs/residential%20landlord%20and%20tenant/urlta_memo_warrantyofhabitability_021212.pdf.

[399] 25 Del. Code §§ 5501 to 5517.

housing codes.[400] The URLTA imposes on landlords a duty to "comply with the requirements of applicable building and housing codes materially affecting health and safety."[401] They are also required to "make all repairs . . . necessary to put and keep the premises in a fit and habitable condition," to "keep all common areas of the premises in a clean and safe condition," to "maintain in good and safe working order and condition all . . . facilities and appliances . . . supplied or required to be supplied by" the landlord, and to provide adequate waste disposal, water, and heat.[402] If the duty of compliance with the applicable building and housing codes "is greater than any duty imposed by" the specific provisions set out in the URLTA, "the landlord's duty shall be determined by reference to" the building and housing code provisions.[403] The duties imposed on landlords by the MRLTC are similar,[404] although there are important differences in the sections dealing with remedies.[405]

Although the landlord-tenant codes based on the URLTA are generally similar, several states have enacted substantial variations in the coverage of the statute,[406] the scope of the landlord's duty to put and keep the leased premises in a habitable condition,[407] or both. Still, the statutes based on the URLTA impose a greater duty on landlords than do the statutes previously considered in section 6.37. The URLTA does not expressly state that the landlord must have a rented dwelling unit "habitable" at the beginning of the tenancy, but a careful reading of the provisions governing the landlord's duty and the remedies for breach of the duty makes it clear that there is an immediate breach of the landlord's duty if the dwelling unit is not habitable at the start of the tenancy.[408] Neither the URLTA nor the MRLTC makes an explicit distinction between "latent" and "patent" defects.

At least ten other states have enacted a statutory warranty of habitability outside the context of comprehensive residential landlord-tenant legislation. Some of these

---

[400] See URLTA § 1.201 (1972); MRLTC § 1–104 (1969). URLTA § 1.202 excluded the following agreements from coverage: residence at certain public and private institutions such as schools or nursing homes; occupancy by a contract purchaser of land; occupancy by a member of a fraternal or social organization; occupancy by hotel and motel guests; occupancy by an employee as a condition of employment; occupancy by the owner of a condominium or co-operative unit; and occupancy of farm homes. RURLTA contains similar scope provisions. RURLTA § 103(b), (c) (2015).

[401] URLTA § 2.104(a)(1) (1972). RURLTA imposes a comparable duty but has revised the quoted language in ways not material to the discussion here. RURLTA § 302(a)(1) (2015).

[402] URLTA § 2.104(a)(2)–(6) (1972). RURLTA imposes comparable obligations. RURLTA § 302(a) (2015).

[403] URLTA § 2.104(b) (1972); RURLTA § 302(a)(1) (2015).

[404] MRLTC § 2–201 (1969).

[405] See §§ 6.41–6.45 infra.

[406] E.g., Ariz.Rev.Stat. § 33–1308(7) (excluding public housing); Rev.Code Wash.Ann. § 59.18.040(7) (same); Haw.Rev.Stat.Ann. § 521–7(7) (excluding leases for 15 years or more); Neb.Rev.Stat. § 76–1408(8) (excluding leases for 5 years or more); Va.Code § 55–225.01(B)(1) (excluding any single-family residence where landlord owns no more than two such residences and parties expressly contract out of coverage of Virginia statute).

[407] E.g., Wash.Rev.Code Ann. § 59.18.060 (listing specific duties of landlord in addition to general requirement to "keep the premises fit for human habitation"); Okla.Stat.Ann. tit. 41, § 118 (omitting any reference to building or housing codes and expressly limiting the duties of the landlord with respect to "common areas," waste disposal, and supplying heat and water to rental units within a multi-family dwelling).

[408] URLTA §§ 2.104, 4.101, 4.103, 4.104 (1972); MRLTC §§ 2–203 to 2–207 (1969); RURLTA §§ 302, 401 to 404, 407 (2015).

statutes are based on Section 2.104 of the URLTA.[409] Others are not based on the URLTA but impose a comparable duty to provide the tenant with a habitable dwelling.[410]

In many states where the courts first recognized an implied warranty of habitability, subsequent comprehensive legislation of the type discussed in this section has largely, if not entirely, pre-empted the field.[411] By contrast, where the legislature has merely provided new tenant remedies for violation of applicable housing codes, the courts have sometimes also recognized an implied warranty of habitability and allowed additional remedies for breach of the implied warranty.[412] And in California, which adopted the Field Code over a century ago, the courts have recognized an implied warranty of habitability as well, and have allowed remedies for breach of the implied warranty in addition to the statutorily prescribed remedies.[413]

§ 6.40   CAN THE BENEFIT OF THE WARRANTY OF HABITABILITY BE WAIVED?

Most statutes based on the URLTA provide that the lease agreement may not include any provision waiving the tenant's rights or remedies under the statute. The obvious purpose is to prevent landlords from including boilerplate waivers in lease forms.[414] However, the URLTA does allow the lease to require that the tenant will obtain and pay for utility services.[415] In addition, the URLTA allows the parties to agree by a separate agreement (i.e., not in the lease agreement itself) that tenant will perform "specified" repairs or maintenance, but not if the work is necessary to cure defects that violate a housing or building code.[416]

---

[409]   N.C.Gen.Stat. § 42–42; N.D.Cent.Code § 47–16–13.1; Utah Code Ann. § 57–22–4; W.Va.Code § 37–6–30. See generally 5 Thompson on Real Property § 43.05(c)(2) (2d Thomas ed.2007).

[410]   This legislation includes D.C. Landlord-Tenant Regulations § 2902.2 (1970); Idaho Code §§ 6–320 to –323; 14 Me.Rev. Stat.Ann. § 6021; Md. Code Real Prop. § 8–211 et seq.; Mich.Comp.Laws Ann. § 554.139; Minn.Stat.Ann. § 504B.161; N.Y.-McKinney's Real Prop. Law § 235–b; Tex.Prop. Code §§ 92.051 to 92.262; Wis. Stat.Ann. § 704.07. For a summary of the relevant distinctions in these statutes, see 5 Thompson on Real Property § 43.05(c)(2) (2d Thomas ed.2007). A court in New York has ruled that New York's statutory warranty of habitability was not breached by the presence of a registered sex offender, at least where the landlord was statutorily prohibited from removing the offender based solely on that status. Knudsen v. Lax, 17 Misc.3d 350, 842 N.Y.S.2d 341 (Cty.Ct.2007).

[411]   See, e.g., Tex.Prop.Code § 92.061 (expressly providing that the statutory duties of the landlord and the statutory remedies of the tenant "are in lieu of existing common law and other statutory law warranties and duties of landlords for maintenance, repair, security, habitability, and nonretaliation, and remedies of tenants for a violation of those warranties and duties"); Thompson v. Crownover, 368 S.E.2d 170 (Ga.App.1988) (statute pre-empts previous common law implied warranty), rev'd on procedural grounds, 381 S.E.2d 283 (Ga.1989). But for an instance where the implied warranty has broader coverage than the statutory warranty, compare Foisy v. Wyman, 515 P.2d 160 (Wash.1973) with Wash. Rev. Code Ann. § 59.18.040.

[412]   See, e.g., Boston Hous. Auth. v. Hemingway, 293 N.E.2d 831 (Mass.1973).

[413]   Compare Cal.Civ.Code §§ 1941–1942 with Green v. Superior Court, 517 P.2d 1168 (Cal.1974).

[414]   URLTA § 1.403(a)(1), (b) & Comment (1972). RURLTA is comparable. RURLTA § 203(a)(1), (b) (2015).

[415]   URLTA § 2.104(c) (1972); RURLTA § 302(b) (2015).

[416]   URLTA § 2.104(d) (1972); RURLTA § 302(d) (2015). This separate agreement must be in a record signed by the parties. Under the URLTA, the agreement had to be entered in "good faith"; under RURLTA, the agreement must be "supported by adequate consideration" and cannot "affect the obligation of the landlord to other tenants on the premises." RURLTA § 302(d) (2015).

Statutes based on the MRLTC generally prohibit any effective waiver of the tenant's rights but expressly provide for agreements that shift the burden of maintenance to the tenant to a limited extent. MRLTC § 2–203(2), (3) (1969). For example, the Delaware statute requires such an agreement to be placed in a "conspicuous writing independent of the rental agreement" and to be "supported by adequate consideration apart from the

The general anti-waiver section of the URLTA also contains an additional provision that "[i]f a landlord deliberately uses a rental agreement containing provisions known by him to be prohibited, the tenant may recover in addition to his actual damages an amount up to [3] month's periodic rent and reasonable attorney's fees."[417] This punitive approach underlines the importance the drafters attached to the anti-waiver provisions, but one might question the legitimacy of a mandatory statutory penalty on a landlord who had made no effort to enforce the waiver. RURLTA rejected this automatic penalty, and now provides the court with discretion to award a tenant "an amount not to exceed [three times] the periodic rent" if the landlord "seeks to enforce the provision or accepts the tenant's voluntary compliance with the provision."[418]

Of those statutes not based on the URLTA or the MRLTC, waiver rules vary. The Michigan statute authorizes a "modification" of the statutory warranty where the lease has a term of at least one year.[419] The Minnesota statute declares that the parties may not waive or modify the warranty.[420] The Maine statute allows waivers only if they are specific, in writing, and for reduction in rent or other consideration.[421] The New York statute states that any waiver or modification agreement "shall be void as contrary to public policy."[422] The West Virginia statute[423] says nothing about waiver, but a West Virginia court has said that a waiver of either a statutory or judicially implied warranty is against public policy.[424]

As discussed in section 6.38, where courts have implied warranties of habitability independently of statutes, most have followed *Javins*[425] in rejecting the possibility of an effective waiver of the implied warranty.[426] Nevertheless, a few courts have suggested that the tenant can waive the implied warranty by express agreement.[427] In those states where the courts have not yet decided whether a tenant can waive the benefit of the implied warranty of habitability, Section 5.6 of the Restatement (Second) of Property

---

rental agreement." 25 Del. Code Ann. § 5115. By contrast, the Hawaii statute, also based on the MRLTC, omits these requirements for an effective waiver. Haw.Rev.Stat. § 521–42.

[417] URLTA § 1.403(b) (1972).

[418] RURLTA § 203(b) (2015).

[419] Mich.Comp.Laws Ann. § 554.139.

[420] Minn.Stat.Ann. § 504B.161(1)(b).

[421] Me.Rev.Stat.Ann. tit. 14, § 6021(5).

[422] N.Y.-McKinney's Real Prop. Law § 235–b(2).

[423] W.Va. Code § 37–6–30.

[424] Teller v. McCoy, 253 S.E.2d 114 (W.Va.1978) (holding that an implied warranty of habitability identical with the new statutory warranty was already in force prior to enactment of statute).

[425] 428 F.2d 1071, 1080 n.49, 1082 n.58 (D.C.Cir.1970), cert. denied, 400 U.S. 925, 91 S.Ct. 186, 27 L.Ed.2d 185 (1970) (court refused to consider whether tenant's express covenant to repair constituted a waiver of the implied warranty of habitability because any agreement to shift the burden of compliance with the housing code to the tenant would be illegal and unenforceable).

[426] See, e.g., Green v. Superior Court, 517 P.2d 1168, 1173 n.9 (Cal.1974); Boston Hous. Auth. v. Hemingway, 293 N.E.2d 831, 843 (Mass.1973); Foisy v. Wyman, 515 P.2d 160, 164 (Wash.1973); Teller v. McCoy, 253 S.E.2d 114 (W.Va.1978). All of these decisions were handed down in states that have statutory warranties of habitability in addition to judicially implied ones. Therefore, if tenants are able to assert either form of warranty in those states, tenants might choose simply to assert the nonwaivable implied warranty.

[427] E.g., Lee v. Keller Williams Realty, 247 So.3d 293 (Miss.App.2017) (upholding tenant's broad waiver of implied warranty as knowing and voluntary); P.H. Inv. v. Oliver, 818 P.2d 1018 (Utah 1991) (upholding waiver that was express and operated as to specifically identified defects). The New Jersey court indicated a willingness to consider the possibility of waiver in Berzito v. Gambino, 308 A.2d 17 (N.J.1973), but ultimately sustained the trial court's conclusion that the scarcity of available housing for low-income families with children in the area precluded an effective waiver. See also Mease v. Fox, 200 N.W.2d 791 (Iowa 1972).

may influence future judicial decisions on this question. Section 5.6 allows the parties to make an agreement to increase or decrease the scope of the landlord's habitability obligation or to expand or contract what the tenant's remedies for breach of those obligations, provided the agreement is not "unconscionable or significantly against public policy."[428]

§ 6.41 REMEDIES FOR LANDLORD'S BREACH OF DUTY—TERMINATION

Breach of the statutory warranty of habitability gives the tenant the remedy to terminate the tenancy and avoid any further liability for rent. At least where the landlord's breach of duty materially affects the tenant's health and safety and the tenant complies with the stated notice requirements, this remedy exists both in states that have comprehensive landlord-tenant codes based on the URLTA or the MRLTC[429] and in states that have enactments based on the Field Code, other civil codes, or other models.[430] In states that have adopted the warranty by judicial decision, courts generally hold that the landlord's warranty obligation and the tenant's rental obligations are mutually dependent; consequently, the landlord's breach of the implied warranty entitles the tenant to terminate the lease and avoid further rent liability.[431]

Whatever the source of the landlord's duty, the tenant must vacate the premises if the tenant wishes to terminate the tenancy. Here lies the rub: habitability issues usually arise in connection with badly run-down premises occupied by tenants with modest finances and limited bargaining power. These tenants need a remedy that will get their premises fixed, not one that requires them to move to another apartment where the rats are even larger.[432] There may be marginal advantages to termination under a statutory

---

[428] Restatement (Second) of Property-Landlord & Tenant § 5.6 (1977). The comments suggest a wide variety of relevant factors may be indicative of unconscionability or contrary public policy, e.g., that the agreement opposes health and safety regulations; that tenants are of "moderate income"; that premises are multi-family residential; whether the agreement was the result of "conscious negotiations"; whether it was a "boilerplate" provision; whether tenants are financially burdened; and whether both parties were represented by counsel. Id., Comment e. Moreover, the comments to Section 5.3 say that tenants, as a matter of law, may not waive the landlord's liability for defects that are present at the time of entry that would make use of the premises "unsafe or unhealthy." Id. § 5.3, Comment c.

[429] See URLTA § 4.101(a) (1972); RURLTA § 402(a)(1) (2015).

[430] Cal.Civ.Code § 1942; La.Civ.Code art. 2719 (breach may give cause for "dissolution of the lease"); N.D.Cent.Code § 47–16–13; S.D.Codif.Law § 43–32–9.

Some statutes not deriving from URLTA or civil-law informed codes expressly permit termination as a remedy for landlord's breach of the statutory habitability duty. E.g., Wis.Stat.Ann. 704.07. Others do not expressly provide remedies, see, e.g., Mich.Comp.Laws Ann. § 554.139; Minn.Stat.Ann. § 504B.161; N.Y. Real Prop. Law § 235–b. In these states, the tenant presumably has the same option to terminate, as the cases typically note that the tenant's rental obligation is dependent on the landlord's compliance with the warranty. E.g., Bayview Estates, Inc. v. Bayview Estates Mobile Homeowners Ass'n, 508 F.2d 405 (6th Cir.1974) (Michigan law); Fritz v. Warthen, 213 N.W.2d 339 (Minn.1973); Park West Mgmt. Corp. v. Mitchell, 391 N.E.2d 1288 (N.Y.1979).

[431] See Javins v. First Nat'l Realty Corp., 428 F.2d 1071 (D.C.Cir.1970), cert. denied, 400 U.S. 925, 91 S.Ct. 186, 27 L.Ed.2d 185 (1970); Lemle v. Breeden, 462 P.2d 470 (Haw.1969); Lund v. MacArthur, 462 P.2d 482 (Haw.1969); Steele v. Latimer, 521 P.2d 304 (Kan.1974); Boston Hous. Auth. v. Hemingway, 293 N.E.2d 831 (Mass.1973); King v. Moorehead, 495 S.W.2d 65 (Mo.App.1973); Kline v. Burns, 276 A.2d 248 (N.H.1971); Marini v. Ireland, 265 A.2d 526 (N.J.1970); Tonetti v. Penati, 48 A.D.2d 25, 367 N.Y.S.2d 804 (1975); Pugh v. Holmes, 405 A.2d 897 (Pa.1979); Hilder v. St. Peter, 478 A.2d 202 (Vt.1984); Landis & Landis Constr., LLC v. Nation, 286 P.3d 979 (Wash.App.2012) (rodent infestation breached implied warranty and justified rescission); Teller v. McCoy, 253 S.E.2d 114 (W.Va.1978) (material breach gives tenant remedy of rescission). See also Restatement (Second) of Property-Landlord & Tenant §§ 5.1(1), 5.4(1), 5.5(4) (1977).

[432] This explains why courts have refused to follow through with the "illegal lease" theory of Brown v. Southall Realty Co., 237 A.2d 834 (D.C.1968). As explained in § 6.37 supra, it would follow logically from *Brown*

or implied warranty, as compared with constructive eviction, such as not having to vacate within a "reasonable" time. But the tenant's right to terminate still depends in part on tenant's having taken reasonable steps to notify the landlord of the breach and the decision to terminate, and the continuance of the landlord's breach until the time specified for termination.[433] Likewise, the tenant that vacates runs some risk that the landlord could establish that the premises were in fact habitable and thus that the tenant breached the lease by vacating the premises.[434]

Though termination is a remedy of limited use for the vast majority of tenants of uninhabitable premises, some tenants have the finances and bargaining power to terminate and obtain other satisfactory housing. An example would be the tenant of an average or better home in which a serious defect occurs which the landlord refuses to repair. For such a tenant, termination might be the remedy of choice. Judicial decisions say the tenant would be liable for the agreed rent for the period of possession, subject to an offsetting claim for damages for the landlord's breach of the warranty of habitability.[435] The URLTA adopts the same rule.[436] In addition, the tenant should be able to recover any advance rent paid, plus any security deposit, either on a restitutionary theory or as damages.

§ 6.42   REMEDIES FOR LANDLORD'S BREACH OF DUTY—DAMAGES

A breach of the landlord's judicial or statutory duty of habitability entitles the tenant to a damage recovery, whether or not the tenant terminates the lease. The URLTA[437] and comparable statutes expressly authorize the recovery of "actual damages" by the tenant for breach of the landlord's duty to put and keep the premises in a habitable condition, but do not contain a general formula for measuring those damages. Neither the MRLTC nor the state statutes based on it expressly authorize a damage recovery.[438]

Case law treats a breach of the warranty of habitability as a breach of contract, whether the warranty is judicially implied or imposed by statute. But courts have developed three different formulas for measuring the tenant's expectation damages for

---

that, if the lease was truly illegal, there would be no leasehold—and thus the tenant would be a trespasser and would have to move out. But even the D.C. Circuit Court refused to extend *Brown* in this fashion. Robinson v. Diamond Housing Corp., 463 F.2d 853 (D.C.Cir.1972).

[433]   URLTA § 4.101(a) (1972) and RURLTA § 401 (2015) (specifying notice requirements). MRLTC § 2–205 (1969) does not require notice to the landlord if "the condition renders the dwelling unit uninhabitable or poses an imminent threat to the health or safety of any occupant." Restatement (Second) of Property-Landlord & Tenant § 10.1 (1977) requires the tenant to vacate and to take "reasonable steps to assure that the landlord has knowledge of his decision to terminate the lease and the reason therefor."

[434]   E.g., Tulley v. Sheldon, 982 A.2d 954 (N.H.2009) (tenant vacated due to mold, but court later held mold was "relatively minor in nature" and awarded back rent to landlord).

[435]   E.g., Lund v. MacArthur, 462 P.2d 482 (Haw.1969); Mease v. Fox, 200 N.W.2d 791 (Iowa 1972); Berzito v. Gambino, 308 A.2d 17 (N.J.1973). Cf. Pines v. Perssion, 111 N.W.2d 409, 413 (Wis.1961) (court said tenants relieved of liability for agreed rent, but they were liable for reasonable rental value).

[436]   URLTA § 4.101(b), (c) (1972); RURLTA § 402(a)(2) (2015).

[437]   URLTA § 4.101(b) (1972); RURLTA § 402(a)(2)(B) (2015).

[438]   Both the URLTA and the MRLTC supply a special damage formula in sections authorizing the tenant to exercise self-help remedies where the landlord fails (1) to keep leased premises in a safe and sanitary condition, or (2) to provide essential services, as required by the lease and/or any applicable housing code. URLTA § 4.103 (1972) and RURLTA §§ 402(a)(2)(D), 406 (2015) (very limited cost of repairing minor defects); URLTA § 4.104 (1972) and RURLTA §§ 402(a)(2)(E), 407 (2015) (damages measured, under RURLTA, by "actual and reasonable cost" of services); MRLTC §§ 2–206, 2–207 (1969); 25 Del.Code §§ 5306, 5307; Haw.Rev.Stat. § 521–64(b) (but omitting provisions for self-help for nonprovision of essential services).

the landlord's breach of the warranty: (1) damages equal to "the difference between the agreed rent [in the lease] and the fair rental value of the premises as they were during their occupancy by the tenant in the unsafe, unsanitary or unfit condition";[439] (2) damages equal to "the difference between the fair rental value of the premises if they had been as warranted [i.e., fully habitable] and the fair rental value of the premises as they were during the occupancy in the unsafe or unsanitary condition";[440] and (3) damages equal to the agreed rent times the percentage by which the breach compromised the tenant's rightful use and enjoyment of the premises.[441] Presumably, in states where a statute establishes a warranty of habitability but does not explicitly address the calculation of damages, courts may adopt any of these formulas.

Either the first or the second formula is somewhat workable if the dwelling unit complies with the warranty at the beginning of the tenancy but later becomes "uninhabitable;" in this situation, the "agreed rent" and the "fair rental value as warranted" are *prima facie* the same. But suppose visible conditions make the dwelling unit uninhabitable at the beginning of the tenancy—a common situation in low-income housing. In such a situation, the "fair rental value of the premises" should be exactly equal to the "agreed rent," unless the tenant agreed to pay more than the premises were worth. Under the first formula, the tenant will then be unable to prove any damages, at least where the condition of the dwelling unit has not gotten worse during the tenancy. Under the second formula, the tenant theoretically could recover the excess value of the dwelling unit "as warranted" over the "agreed rent," which could produce the absurd result that the landlord would have to pay the tenant for occupying the unit. Finally, because these two damage formulas depend on a determination of "fair rental value," each may depend to some extent on expert testimony—a cost for which few low-income tenants can appreciate the need and even fewer can afford. These difficulties may explain why some courts have rejected these two approaches in favor of the third percentage-diminution formula.[442] This approach also may more effectively regulate landlord compliance by ensuring that the aggrieved tenant always has some damage recovery.[443]

---

[439] Kline v. Burns, 276 A.2d 248, 252 (N.H.1971). See also Glyco v. Schultz, 289 N.E.2d 919, 925 (Ohio Mun.Ct.1972). As the court said in Lane v. Kelley, 643 P.2d 1375 (Or.App.1982), this formula seems to assume that the agreed rent is "the fair rental value of the premises if they had been as warranted." Compare Berzito v. Gambino, 308 A.2d 17, 22 (1973) ("tenant will be charged only with the rental value of the property in its imperfect condition").

[440] Green v. Superior Court, 517 P.2d 1168, 1183 (Cal.1974). See also Breezewood Mgmt. Co. v. Maltbie, 411 N.E.2d 670, 675 (Ind.App.1980); Steele v. Latimer, 521 P.2d 304, 311 (Kan.1974); Love v. Monarch Apts., 771 P.2d 79, 83 (Kan.App.1989); Boston Hous. Auth. v. Hemingway, 293 N.E.2d 831, 845 (Mass.1973).

[441] E.g., Academy Spires, Inc. v. Brown, 268 A.2d 556 (N.J.Cty.Dist.Ct.1970); Morbeth Realty Corp. v. Rosenshine, 67 Misc.2d 325, 323 N.Y.S.2d 363 (N.Y.City Civ.Ct.1971) (20% reduction); Morbeth Realty Corp. v. Velez, 73 Misc.2d 996, 343 N.Y.S.2d 406 (N.Y.City Civ.Ct.1973) (50% reduction); Glyco v. Schultz, 289 N.E.2d 919, 925 (Ohio Mun.Ct.1972) (⅔ reduction). See also Cooks v. Fowler, 455 F.2d 1281 (D.C.Cir.1971) (⅓ reduction).

[442] For example, in McKenna v. Begin, 325 N.E.2d 587 (Mass.App.1975), the court directed the trial judge to abandon the second formula used at trial and instead to adopt the percentage-diminution approach.

[443] See generally Moskovitz, The Implied Warranty of Habitability: A New Doctrine Raising New Issues, 62 Calif.L.Rev. 1444, 1470 (1974) (tenant should be compensated for discomfort and annoyance); Sax & Hiestand, Slumlordism as a Tort, 65 Mich. L.Rev. 869, 875, 913 (1967) (deterrence and punishment should be prime objectives); Abbott, Housing Policy, Housing Codes, and Tenant Remedies: An Integration, 56 B.U.L.Rev. 1, 24 (1976) (under "percentage diminution" formula, "tenant's recovery really amounts to a civil fine levied on the landlord"). In a recent decision in Massachusetts, which has adopted the percentage reduction approach, an appellate court held that the trial court should not have denied rent abatement damages to a tenant complaining of ventilation problems just because the tenant might have been more sensitive than

In a few states, the determination of damages for breach of the implied warranty of habitability has been complicated by decisions adopting a two-tiered formula. In Mease v. Fox,[444] the Iowa Supreme Court held that the first damage formula applied during the tenant's period of occupancy, but the second formula applied during the period after the tenant vacated the premises.[445] The Missouri intermediate appellate court adopted the same two-tiered formula in King v. Moorehead.[446]

In addition to expectation damages, the tenant that remains in possession after breach should be able to recover "consequential" damages that result from losses that were "foreseeable," unless a statute expressly bars such an award.[447] Statutes based on the URLTA and the MRLTC authorize self-help remedies such as "repair-and-deduct" and thus in substance authorize recovery of certain consequential damages.[448] The Maine statute, by contrast, expressly prohibits recovery of consequential damages for breach of the warranty.[449] A number of New York lower courts have held that where breach of the warranty of habitability consists of a failure to provide essential services such as heat and hot water, the measure of damages is either (1) the difference in value of the leased premises with and without such services, (2) the actual monetary loss suffered by the tenant, or (3) some other practical measure of damages fair to both parties.[450]

Section 10.2 of the Restatement (Second) of Property rejects the traditional division of damages between "general" and "special" damages. Rather, it divides damages into those the tenant may recover when the tenant has validly terminated the leasehold and those tenant may recover when the lease remains in effect. As explained in section 6.41, termination often is not a helpful remedy for tenants of "uninhabitable" premises, who usually do not have the money or bargaining power to move to better premises. But if the tenant has terminated, section 10.2 allows two kinds of damages. The first is "the fair market value of the lease on the date [tenant] terminates the lease." This is commonly called "bonus value," i.e., the amount by which the agreed rent is less than the rent the premises would fetch in the marketplace. This remedy is seldom useful to the tenant of uninhabitable residential premises, because it would be a rare case in which the tenant could prove the premises had a market value appreciably above the contract rent. The second form of damages for the terminating tenant is "reasonable relocation costs," which could have value to a tenant willing to move to other premises.

---

someone of "average sensibility." South Boston Elderly Residences, Inc. v. Moynahan, 76 N.E.3d 272 (Mass.App.2017).

[444] 200 N.W.2d 791 (Iowa 1972).

[445] The court's reason for applying the second damage formula after the tenant vacated was that the tenant was no longer affected by the rundown condition of the premises. Mease v. Fox was followed in Roeder v. Nolan, 321 N.W.2d 1, 5 (Iowa 1982).

[446] 495 S.W.2d 65 (Mo.App.1973). In Detling v. Edelbrock, 671 S.W.2d 265 (Mo.1984), the Missouri Supreme Court accepted the implied warranty of habitability theory enunciated in King v. Moorehead, but did not adopt the two-tiered damage formula.

[447] Such damages are within the limits set by Hadley v. Baxendale, 9 Exch. 341 (1854). Consequential damages were awarded in Detling v. Edelbrock, 671 S.W.2d 265 (Mo.1984), and Love v. Monarch Apts., 771 P.2d 79, 83 (Kan.App.1989). Accord: Restatement (Second) of Property-Landlord & Tenant § 10.2(2), (3) & Comments c, d (1977).

[448] URLTA §§ 4.103, 4.104 (1972); RURLTA § 402(a)(2)(D), (E) (2015); MRLTC §§ 2–206, 2–207 (1969).

[449] Me.Rev.Stat.Ann. tit. 14, § 6021(4)(D).

[450] Leris Realty Corp. v. Robbins, 95 Misc.2d 712, 408 N.Y.S.2d 166 (City Ct.1978); Goldner v. Doknovitch, 88 Misc.2d 88, 388 N.Y.S.2d 504 (Sup.1976); Whitehouse Estates, Inc. v. Thomson, 87 Misc.2d 813, 386 N.Y.S.2d 733 (City Ct.1976).

If the tenant has not terminated the lease, section 10.2 allows two kinds of damages—"the reasonable costs incurred by the tenant in eliminating the default" (i.e., making repairs that the landlord should have made), and the "reasonable additional costs of substituted premises incurred by the tenant as a result of the landlord's default while the default continues." These provisions should be compared with the damages remedies under the URLTA, the MRLTC, and by case law enforcing judicially created warranties of habitability, which were discussed in section 6.42. The URLTA allows self-help only for minor defects and in a very limited amount,[451] does not provide a general formula for calculation of damages, and explicitly allows for recovery of the cost of "comparable substitute housing" only for the failure to provide an "essential service."[452] Thus, it is not clear (absent the landlord's failure to provide an essential service) whether the URLTA would allow tenants to recover the Restatement's "reasonable additional costs of substituted premises."[453]

The tenant may assert a claim for damages for breach of the warranty of habitability either by a direct action or by way of counterclaim in an action by the landlord for unpaid rent. The tenant may also assert such a claim as a defense to an action to evict the tenant for nonpayment of rent. In the latter case, courts often speak of an "abatement of the rent" instead of a "counterclaim for damages." This remedy is discussed further in the next section.

Breach of the warranty of habitability may cause of other kinds of injury, such as injury to personal property of the tenant on the premises, physical injury to the tenant or the tenant's family, and injury in the form of emotional distress. Damages for physical injury to the tenant or members of the tenant's family are addressed in section 6.46. Injury to the tenant's personal property would appear to be a reasonably foreseeable consequence of breach of several of the duties generally imposed by both judicial and statutory warranties of habitability.[454] At least one case has allowed recovery for destruction of a tenant's personal property, but others have denied recovery.[455] At least one court has allowed damages for "tangible consequences" of a breach of warranty such as physical illness, medical bills, inability to sleep, and inability to eat or work in one's dwelling. That court, however, denied recovery for "the strain or preoccupation and vexation" resulting from a continuing dispute with the landlord.[456] And a few decisions have allowed recovery of damages for "intentional," "wanton or willful," or "reckless"

---

[451] URLTA § 4.103 (1972); RURLTA § 406 (2015) (reasonable cost to remedy noncompliance cannot exceed one month's periodic rent).

[452] URLTA § 4.104 (1972); RURLTA § 407(a) (2015).

[453] While section 10.2 has been cited in numerous decisions in involving commercial leases, it has had little apparent impact in residential habitability cases after its 1977 promulgation, being cited in only three such cases. See George Washington Univ. v. Weintraub, 458 A.2d 43 (D.C.App.1983) (cited in dissenting opinion); Glasoe v. Trinkle, 479 N.E.2d 915 (Ill.1985) (citing section 10.2 but ultimately remanding for new trial decision on whether implied warranty had been breached); Wade v. Jobe, 818 P.2d 1006 (Utah 1991) (in which court actually adopted the percentage diminution formula).

[454] See generally E. Farnsworth, Contracts § 12.14 (1982).

[455] Miller v. Christian, 958 F.2d 1234 (3d Cir.1992) (landlord liable for personal property damage caused by breach of implied warranty of habitability); Abram v. Litman, 501 N.E.2d 370 (Ill.App.1986) (no award for personal property destroyed by fire caused by faulty wiring, alleged to have made premises uninhabitable); Weiler v. Hooshiari, 19 A.3d 124 (Vt.2011) (implied warranty not implicated by landlord's failure to protect tenant's car from snow and ice falling from building).

[456] Brewer v. Erwin, 600 P.2d 398 (Or.1979).

infliction of "emotional distress" resulting from breach of the warranty of habitability.[457] In most, if not all of these cases, recovery was based on the theory that the landlord's breach of warranty amounted to a tort when it caused "emotional distress" to the tenant.

Although courts generally do not award punitive damages for breach of contract, courts have awarded punitive damages when the breach was in some respect tortious.[458] At least two courts have approved the award of punitive damages when a breach of the warranty of habitability was accompanied by conduct of the landlord characterized by the court as "culpable and demeaning . . . and clearly expressive of a wanton disregard of plaintiff's rights"[459] or as "outrageous."[460]

§ 6.43 REMEDIES FOR LANDLORD'S BREACH OF DUTY—RENT WITHHOLDING—RETALIATORY EVICTION

A habitability dispute may evolve like a game of chess between the landlord and the tenant, where each party makes moves and counter-moves, each hoping to checkmate the other. A tenant who seeks to compel the landlord to make needed repairs has something the landlord wants and needs: the rent. If the tenant holds back the rent, the landlord may move to evict the tenant, typically in a summary eviction action of the kind discussed in section 6.78. But if the tenant could somehow assert the landlord's own breach of the duty to repair as an effective defense in the landlord's action for non-payment, the tenant would have the landlord in check; the tenant would keep possession despite withholding rent. But if the tenancy is a short-term periodic tenancy, the landlord typically can terminate the tenancy—even without asserting nonpayment of rent or any reason—by giving sufficient prior notice to terminate (e.g., 30 days, in a monthly periodic tenancy). If the landlord gives the requisite notice and the tenant still fails to vacate, the landlord could then bring an action for possession in which the tenant's counterclaim for damages would not be a defense to eviction. Has the landlord now achieved checkmate? It appears so—unless there is a statutory or judge-made rule that the landlord may not seek to evict the tenant in "retaliation" for the tenant's attempt to compel repairs.

As suggested above, a tenant may wish to withhold the payment of rent as a lever to compel the landlord to perform repair duties. Rent withholding is of two kinds, which we will call "offset rent withholding" and "escrow rent withholding." The materials below first discuss offset rent withholding, followed by the related subject of retaliatory eviction, and then conclude with a discussion of escrow rent withholding.

Offset Rent Withholding

Offset rent withholding begins by the tenant simply failing to pay rent and waiting for the landlord to commence a statutory summary eviction action for failure to pay rent. [We are assuming that the landlord has failed to place and/or keep the premises in habitable condition.] When the landlord brings the summary eviction action, the tenant answers by admitting the rent default, but pleading affirmatively a counterclaim (or offset) for damages for the landlord's breach of the warranty of habitability. Because

---

[457] Simon v. Solomon, 431 N.E.2d 556 (Mass.1982); Hilder v. St. Peter, 478 A.2d 202 (Vt.1984); Fair v. Negley, 390 A.2d 240 (Pa.Super.1978); Beasley v. Freedman, 389 A.2d 1087 (Pa.Super.1978).

[458] E. Farnsworth, Contracts § 12.8, at 842–843 (1982).

[459] Hilder v. St. Peter, 478 A.2d 202 (Vt.1984).

[460] 49 Prospect St. Tenants Ass'n v. Sheva Gardens, Inc., 547 A.2d 1134 (N.J.Super.1988).

conditions that cause uninhabitability will almost always be extensive and usually long-standing, the amount of the counterclaim will frequently be as large or larger than the rent due. If the court allows the counterclaim and permits the tenant to offset it against the rent due, no rent will be due, and the summary eviction action will be dismissed. The tenant will remain in possession—still not paying rent—and waiting to defeat the landlord's next summary eviction action in the same manner.

For the tenant, the traditional problem with this strategy was that most states did not allow a tenant to interpose affirmative defenses in a summary eviction action. The rationale was that summary eviction statutes were a special form of action—intended to be quick and summary, with limited issues to be decided, for the main purpose of evicting a tenant.[461] But over time, court decisions in a number of jurisdictions have chipped away at the traditional rule and have allowed the tenant to assert counterclaims that would defeat the basis for the summary eviction action. The leading case of Jack Spring, Inc. v. Little[462] is representative of this decisional trend.[463] Likewise, in states that have adopted the URLTA, the MRLTC or similar legislation, statutes have abolished the traditional rule for residential tenants.[464] Thus, in most states today, a residential tenant may counterclaim for damages for the landlord's breach of the warranty of habitability, and may assert that claim in an unlawful detainer action by the landlord.

This strategy works well enough for the tenant holding a fixed-term tenancy. In some cases, however, the tenant occupying uninhabitable premises holds a periodic tenancy, perhaps on a month-to-month basis. Generally, either party may terminate a periodic tenancy by giving notice to quit a certain time before the end of a period; no reason or cause is necessary.[465] Statutes in every state establish the time required for effective notice of termination; a typical time for a month-to-month tenancy is 30 days prior to the end of any period.[466] Suppose a landlord, faced with a tenant withholding rent, chooses to give a general notice to terminate the periodic tenancy instead of a notice to terminate for nonpayment of rent. Traditionally, there was no defense to a general notice to terminate a periodic tenancy, as long as the terminating party gave notice at the time and in the manner required by statute. This would permit the landlord to maintain a summary eviction action for possession, to which the tenant's counterclaim

---

[461] See People ex rel. Tuttle v. Walton, 2 Thompson & Cook 533 (N.Y.Sup.Ct.1874); Class v. Carter, 645 P.2d 536 (Or.1982) (in unlawful detainer action, tenant may not claim offsetting damages for landlord's breach); Sundholm v. Patch, 382 P.2d 262 (Wash.1963); Gibbons, Residential Landlord-Tenant Law: A Survey of Modern Problems with Reference to the Proposed Model Code, 21 Hastings L.J. 369, 372–78 (1970). Lindsey v. Normet, 405 U.S. 56, 92 S.Ct. 862, 31 L.Ed.2d 36 (1972), held the limitation of issues was constitutionally valid. See generally § 6.78 infra.

[462] 280 N.E.2d 208 (Ill.1972).

[463] E.g., Javins v. First Nat'l Realty Corp., 428 F.2d 1071 (D.C.Cir.1970), cert. denied, 400 U.S. 925, 91 S.Ct. 186, 27 L.Ed.2d 185 (1970); Bell v. Tsintolas Realty Co., 430 F.2d 474 (D.C.Cir.1970); Cooks v. Fowler, 455 F.2d 1281 (D.C.Cir.1971); Green v. Superior Court, 517 P.2d 1168 (Cal.1974); Boston Hous. Auth. v. Hemingway, 293 N.E.2d 831 (Mass.1973) (only if statutory withholding procedure is used); Detling v. Edelbrock, 671 S.W.2d 265 (Mo.1984); King v. Moorehead, 495 S.W.2d 65 (Mo.App.1973); Marini v. Ireland, 265 A.2d 526 (N.J.1970); Academy Spires, Inc. v. Brown, 268 A.2d 556 (N.J.Super.1970); Pugh v. Holmes, 405 A.2d 897 (Pa.1979); Foisy v. Wyman, 515 P.2d 160 (Wash.1973); Teller v. McCoy, 253 S.E.2d 114 (W.Va.1978). See generally § 6.78 infra.

[464] URLTA § 4.105 (1972); RURLTA § 408 (2015); MRLTC § 3–210 (1969). See Cunningham, The New Implied and Statutory Warranties of Habitability in Residential Leases: From Contract to Status, 16 Urban L.Ann. 3, 113–26 (1979).

[465] See § 6.16 supra.

[466] See statutes described in Restatement (Second) of Property-Landlord & Tenant § 1.5, Statutory Note (1977).

for breach of warranty would not be relevant. This could effectively prevent the periodic tenant from enjoying the benefits of the warranty. To avoid this result, courts and legislatures have recognized an additional tenant defense of retaliatory eviction.

The Retaliatory Eviction Defense

Under the defense, a landlord may not evict a tenant if the landlord is acting in retaliation for the tenant's attempt to remedy conditions violating the warranty of habitability, such as by reporting housing code complaints or asserting a remedy under a residential landlord-tenant act. This defense exists in several states by judicial decision.[467] It was first recognized in Edwards v. Habib[468] (a 1968 District of Columbia Circuit Court decision), and Dickhut v. Norton[469] (a 1970 decision from the Supreme Court of Wisconsin, which drew heavily on *Edwards*). Both courts held that it was contrary to public policy, as manifested in state residential landlord-tenant acts, for a landlord to evict a tenant in retaliation for making a complaint to public officials that the landlord was violating local housing codes. Because the purpose of such codes was to compel landlords to make repairs, the courts reasoned that it would defeat that purpose if the landlord could use the threat of eviction to discourage or prevent the tenant from using the code's machinery. The same policy would protect a tenant who sought to invoke other remedies allowed by residential landlord-tenant acts or by judicially implied warranties of habitability.

In some states, courts have required a tenant asserting retaliatory eviction to prove that the landlord's action was taken for the "sole purpose" of retaliation.[470] This makes some sense given that it would be very unusual for a court to block someone from taking an action that they are entitled to pursue on independent grounds. However, because a landlord may be able to credibly offer several potential motives for the landlord's conduct, tenants may have a very difficult time meeting this burden of proof. As a result, in other states, the tenant may have to show only that the tenant's protected conduct was the "dominant" or "primary" motive for the landlord's conduct.[471]

About 30 states have adopted residential landlord-tenant statutes that embody versions of the retaliatory eviction principle. Both the URLTA and the MRLTC contain

---

[467] See Schweiger v. Superior Court, 476 P.2d 97 (Cal.1970); Wright v. Brady, 889 P.2d 105 (Idaho App.1995); Building Monitoring Systems, Inc. v. Paxton, 905 P.2d 1215 (Utah 1995) (court adopts retaliatory eviction doctrine, though Utah statute does not provide for it); Annot., 40 A.L.R.3d 753 (1971 and 1991 supp.); Cunningham, The New Implied and Statutory Warranties of Habitability in Residential Leases: From Contract to Status, 16 Urban L.Ann. 3, 135–37 (1979). Contra: Mobilia, Inc. v. Santos, 492 A.2d 544 (Conn.App.1985) (court refused to allow retaliatory eviction defense in summary eviction action against residential tenant). Cf. Custom Parking, Inc. v. Superior Court, 138 Cal.App.3d 90, 187 Cal.Rptr. 674 (1982) (allowing retaliatory eviction defense to *commercial* tenant).

Courts have sometimes struggled to identify whether the tenant's conduct is protected by the doctrine. For example, one court rejected the defense as raised by a tenant evicted for participation in a labor strike, on the ground that the defense has to relate to conduct by the tenant that is incidental to the tenancy itself. Imperial Colliery Co. v. Fout, 373 S.E.2d 489 (W.Va.1988). Likewise, a recent Alaska decision rejected a retaliatory eviction defense as raised by a tenant evicted for demanding compensation after a slip and fall accident on the premises. Helfrich v. Valdez Motel Corp., 207 P.3d 552 (Alaska 2009).

[468] 397 F.2d 687 (D.C.Cir.1968), cert. denied, 393 U.S. 1016, 89 S.Ct. 618, 21 L.Ed.2d 560 (1969).

[469] 173 N.W.2d 297 (Wis.1970).

[470] This was the standard expressed in both *Edwards* and *Dickhut*.

[471] E.g., McQueen v. Druker, 438 F.2d 781 (1st Cir.1971); Cal.Civ.Code § 1942.5. The Restatement adopts the "primarily motivated" standard. Restatement (Second) of Property-Landlord & Tenant § 14.8(4) (1977).

anti-retaliatory eviction provisions.[472] State statutes vary widely, and some statutes are more complete than others. For example, while all of them would forbid the landlord to evict in retaliation, some also prevent other forms of retaliatory conduct, such as increasing rent or decreasing services.[473] Some protect a tenant who joins a tenants' union[474] as well as one who reports housing code violations or pursues remedies under the residential landlord-tenant act.[475] Many of the statutes create a presumption that, if the landlord attempts a listed form of conduct within a certain time (perhaps 90 days to one year) after the tenant's protected action, the landlord's conduct is retaliatory.[476] Exceptions in the landlord's favor exist if the tenant is at fault in certain ways, including being in default in paying rent, which raises some doubt as to the efficacy of the tenant's remedy of rent withholding.[477] Courts have differed as to whether a landlord's refusal to renew a fixed-term tenancy could constitute retaliation;[478] the RURLTA provides that such conduct would be retaliatory.[479]

Escrow Rent Withholding

In "escrow" rent withholding, the tenant actually pays the rent into an escrow account or to some official to hold pending the landlord's compliance with the warranty of habitability. The Restatement (Second) of Property allows the tenant, after notice to the landlord, to deposit withheld rent into escrow "until the default is eliminated or the lease terminates, whichever first occurs."[480] A few decisions have held that a tenant may thus withhold rent as a matter of common law.[481] Several decisions have held that it was proper for a trial court to enter protective orders requiring the tenant to pay the accruing rent into court while the case was pending, and the URLTA concurs.[482] Courts in a significant number of states have statutes that permit or require tenants to pay withheld rent into court during at least some kinds of landlord-tenant litigation.[483] In general, however, a court cannot set up a general escrow withholding system for tenants who are not in litigation before the court; courts, unlike legislative bodies, cannot issue orders to persons who are not before them. Nor would a court have the power to order some public

---

[472] URLTA § 5.101 (1972); RURLTA § 901 (2015); MRLTC § 2–407 (1969).

[473] E.g., URLTA § 5.101(a) (1972); RURLTA § 901(b) (2015).

[474] E.g., URLTA § 5.101(a)(3) (1972); RURLTA § 901(a)(4) (2015).

[475] E.g., URLTA § 5.101(a)(2) (1972); RURLTA § 901(a)(1), (2), (5) (2015).

[476] The time period was one year under URLTA § 5.101(b) (1972), but is reduced to six months under RURLTA § 903(a)(1) (2015).

[477] E.g., URLTA § 5.101(c)(2) (1972); RURLTA § 901(c) (2015).

[478] E.g., Van Buren Apts. v. Adams, 145 Ariz. 325, 701 P.2d 583 (Ct.App.1984) (yes); Frenchtown Villa v. Meadors, 117 Mich.App. 683, 324 N.W.2d 133 (1982) (no).

[479] RURLTA § 901(b)(4) (2015) (retaliation includes "refusing to renew a tenancy for a fixed term under a lease containing a renewal option that is exercisable by the tenant without negotiation with the landlord, for any period after the lease would otherwise terminate.").

[480] Restatement (Second) of Property-Landlord & Tenant § 11.3 (1977).

[481] Both King v. Moorehead, 495 S.W.2d 65 (Mo.App.1973), and Hilder v. St. Peter, 478 A.2d 202 (Vt.1984) suggest escrow withholding is available, but in neither decision was it actually used.

[482] See Green v. Superior Court, 517 P.2d 1168 (Cal.1974); Fritz v. Warthen, 213 N.W.2d 339 (Minn.1973); Teller v. McCoy, 253 S.E.2d 114 (W.Va.1978). URLTA § 4.105(a) (1972) and RURLTA § 408(b) (2015) allow the court to order a tenant in pending litigation to pay accruing rent into court if the tenant is in possession.

[483] E.g., Alaska Stat.Ann. § 34.03.190(a); Ariz.Rev.Stat.Ann. § 33–1365(A); Fla.Stat.Ann. § 83.60(2); Kan.Stat.Ann. § 58–2561(a); Ky.Rev.Stat.Ann. § 383.645(1); Neb.Rev.Stat. § 76–1428(1); Ohio Rev.Code Ann. § 5321.07(B); Or.Rev.Stat. § 90.370(1)(b); 35 Pa.Stat. § 1700–1. Some statutes authorize the court to appoint a receiver to collect rents in cases involving violations of applicable housing codes. E.g., Mich.Comp. Laws Ann. § 125.535; Mo.Rev.Stat. § 441.570(1); N.Y.Mult.Dwell.Law § 309.

official, such as a county treasurer, to establish a general escrow account for tenants who wished to withhold rent.

§ 6.44 REMEDIES FOR LANDLORD'S BREACH OF DUTY—SELF-HELP

The early statutes derived from the civil law all provided the tenant with a self-help remedy for breach of the landlord's habitability obligation—i.e., the authority to make the repairs necessary to put the premises in a habitable condition and to deduct the repair cost from the agreed rent. The Louisiana Civil Code gives the tenant a right to make "necessary" repairs and to deduct their cost from the rent if the landlord fails to make the repairs when asked.[484] The Georgia Civil Code also provides the tenant with a "repair-and-deduct" remedy when the lease creates only a "usufruct" and the landlord fails to keep the premises reasonably fit for its intended purposes.[485] As in Louisiana, the landlord must have received notice of the condition requiring repair before this remedy becomes available to the tenant.[486] California, Montana, Oklahoma, and North and South Dakota also provided tenants with the "repair-and-deduct" remedy when the landlord failed after notice to make repairs to keep the premises "habitable."[487] In California and Montana, however, early amendments limited the amount that could be deducted to one month's rent,[488] which precluded use of the "repair-and-deduct" remedy for major repairs. California limited the remedy further by a 1970 amendment that allowed the tenant to assert the remedy only once in any 12-month period.[489] In Montana and Oklahoma, the original protections have been superseded by comprehensive landlord-tenant legislation based upon the URLTA.[490]

The URLTA allows the tenant to "repair-and-deduct" for repairs the landlord has a duty to make but refuses to make, but places a dollar limit on the amount. This amount varies as set by an adopting state, but typically limits the repairs to very minor ones.[491] The tenant has more significant self-help remedies when the tenant fails to receive an "essential service" such as heat, running water, hot water, electric, or gas. Here, the tenant may recover the "actual and reasonable cost" of procuring replacement services during the period of the landlord's default or the cost of "comparable substitute housing" during that period, in which case the tenant is excused from paying rent for that period.[492] These self-help remedies are available only if the tenant has given the landlord

---

[484] La.Civ.Code art. 2694. The tenant may not withhold rent unless the tenant has made the repairs under the statutory authority. Bruno v. Louisiana School Supply Co., 274 So.2d 710 (La.App.1973); Leggio v. Manion, 172 So.2d 748 (La.App.1965).

[485] E.g., Lewis & Co. v. Chisholm, 68 Ga. 40 (1881); Valdes Hotel Co. v. Ferrell, 86 S.E. 333 (Ga.App.1915).

[486] E.g., Ocean Steamship Co. v. Hamilton, 38 S.E. 204 (Ga.1901); J.P. White & Co. v. Montgomery, 58 Ga. 204 (1877).

[487] Cal.Civ.Code § 1942; Mont.Rev.Code § 42–202 (now repealed); 41 Okla.Stat.Ann. § 31 (now repealed); N.D.Cent.Code § 47–16–13 (also authorizing recovery of the lessee's repair expenditures "in any other lawful manner from the lessor"); S.D.Codif. Laws § 43–32–9.

[488] Cal.Civ.Code § 1942.

[489] Cal.Civ.Code § 1942(a).

[490] Mont. Code Ann. §§ 70–24–101 to 70–24–442; 41 Okla. Stat. Ann. §§ 101 to 135. See § 6.39 supra.

[491] URLTA § 4.103 (1972) (greater of $100 or one-half the periodic rent); RURLTA § 406(b) (2015) (one month's periodic rent). Under RURLTA, the tenant use of the repair-and-deduct remedy is also "limited to one month's periodic rent during any 12-month period." RURLTA § 406(e) (2015).

[492] URLTA § 4.104(a)(1), (3), and (b) (1972); RURLTA § 407(a) (2015).

notice of the need for repairs.[493] Likewise, the tenant must complete the repairs and give the landlord satisfactory evidence of completion.[494]

Although the "repair-and-deduct" remedy is primarily a creature of statute, Wisconsin authorized it by judicial decision in Pines v. Perssion.[495] It was subsequently authorized by Marini v. Ireland[496] in New Jersey and by Jackson v. Rivera in New York.[497] Section 11.2 of the Restatement (Second) of Property could influence courts to recognize the "repair-and-deduct" remedy where no statute provides for it.[498] A tenant who is entitled to pursue the repair-and-deduct remedy may also have damages under Restatement section 10.2, to the extent that the landlord is not in effect required to pay more than once.[499]

§ 6.45 REMEDIES FOR BREACH OF LANDLORD'S DUTY—SPECIFIC PERFORMANCE

In *Javins*, the court stated that "[i]n extending all contract remedies for breach to the parties to a lease, we include an action for specific performance of the landlord's implied warranty of habitability."[500] This statement was dictum; specific performance was neither sought nor granted in *Javins*. Yet specific performance—in this context, a mandatory order to the defaulting landlord to put the premises into habitable condition—is precisely what the tenant needs. In a functional sense, the whole purpose of the implied warranty was to allow the tenant to remain in possession and get the premises repaired. A court order requiring the landlord to satisfy the warranty obligation or face punishment for contempt is likely to be more effective than erratic municipal enforcement of housing codes.

Specific performance has its limitations, however. Some of the factors that make enforcement of housing codes ineffective in practice may also make specific performance ineffective. A court of equity will refuse to enter—because it cannot well enforce—an order that calls for supervision of a complex series of actions over a long period of time. Therefore, a court may be reluctant to order the correction of multiple defects in rental housing, but may limit orders to one or a few serious defects that can be quickly

---

[493] URLTA §§ 4.103(a), 4.104(a) (1972); RURLTA § 401 (2015)

[494] Some of the states that have enacted legislation based on the URLTA have either omitted these self-help provisions or have substantially changed them. For example, Florida, Iowa, and Kansas omitted URLTA § 4.103; Florida, Kansas, and Washington omitted URLTA § 4.104. The MRLTC contains provisions similar to those in the URLTA. MRLTC §§ 2–206, 2–607 (1969); these have been adopted in Delaware, 25 Del.Code §§ 5306, 5307, and (in part) in Hawaii. Haw.Rev.Stat. § 521–64.

[495] 111 N.W.2d 409 (Wis.1961).

[496] 265 A.2d 526, 535 (N.J.1970).

[497] 65 Misc.2d 468, 318 N.Y.S.2d 7 (City Ct.1971). In *Jackson*, the court permitted the tenant to deduct part of the amount claimed, but refused to allow deduction of the remainder of that amount because the tenant failed to prove she had made the expenditures claimed.

[498] Restatement (Second) of Property-Landlord & Tenant § 11.2 (1977). The Restatement allows the tenant to "deduct from [the] rent reasonable costs incurred in eliminating the [landlord's] default" after giving the landlord "proper notice." The comments indicate that "reasonable costs" may not exceed the rent that would be available to be applied and that repairs are limited to ones a "reasonably prudent owner" would make. To date, the Restatement's impact on this point has proven nominal; only one court has cited it as authority for a repair-and-deduct remedy. Pugh v. Holmes, 405 A.2d 897 (Pa.1979).

[499] Restatement (Second) of Property-Landlord & Tenant, Introductory Note to Chap. 11 (1977). See generally section 6.42 supra.

[500] Javins v. First Nat'l Realty Corp., 428 F.2d 1071, 1082 n.61 (D.C.Cir.1970), cert. denied, 400 U.S. 925, 91 S.Ct. 186, 27 L.Ed.2d 185 (1970).

corrected.[501] The financial inability of an owner of slum housing to lay out the money to repair many years of dilapidations imposes a practical limit. If the tenant withholds rent, the landlord cannot make payments on its mortgage debt and may simply abandon the property. Not even the law can get blood out of a turnip. Moreover, tenants of slum housing are sometimes only periodic tenants who are unlikely to be interested in compelling the landlord to make expensive repairs and improvements that will primarily benefit subsequent tenants.

§ 6.46 LANDLORD'S LIABILITY FOR PERSONAL INJURIES

This section considers a subject that lies at the intersection of tort law and property law—the liability of a landlord to the tenant and others for personal injuries they suffer on the leased premises or on common areas associated with the leased premises. It is useful to compare the very general discussion here, written from a property-law perspective, with discussions approached from a tort-law point of view.[502] Landlord tort liability has evolved over time along with changes in landlord repair duties to residential tenants and to shifts in public policy that underlie those changes. Therefore, this section will first discuss the rules governing the landlord's traditionally limited tort liability, then address more recent developments expanding the scope of that liability. Section 6.47 will deal with the landlord's liability for injuries caused by criminal acts of third persons.

The Traditional View

Controlling decisions in most jurisdictions still subscribe to the "traditional view" of the landlord's liability to the tenant and others for personal injuries on or about the leased premises.[503] This view starts with the general proposition that a landlord is not liable, then proceeds to a series of exceptions under which liability may arise. The general rule flows from two traditional principles of landlord-tenant law—the doctrine of *caveat emptor* and the concept that the tenant (as the possessor of an estate in land) is responsible for what happens on the land.

Before we describe the exceptions, we emphasize a principle that (save for one of the exceptions) runs consistently through the law of landlord tort liability. A landlord's liability, if any, is the same to third persons on or about the leased premises with the tenant's permission—i.e., members of the tenant's family and invitees—as it is to the

---

[501] E.g., Pugh v. Holmes, 405 A.2d 897, 908 (Pa.1979) (specific performance is "not available as a matter of course but only in unique situations"); Bartley v. Walentas, 78 A.D.2d 310, 434 N.Y.S.2d 379 (1980) (injunctive relief denied because it would "inject the court into the day-to-day operations and management of this and any other building in which one or more tenants are dissatisfied with the services supplied by the landlord"). See also Abbott, Housing Policy, Housing Codes and Tenant Remedies: An Integration, 56 B.U.L.Rev. 1, 64, 135–136 (1976) (concluding that, despite the difficulties of enforcing them, mandatory injunctions are the remedy of choice when the premises comply with housing codes when the tenancy begins and the landlord fails to maintain them thereafter).

[502] Two useful introductory tort-law discussions are Restatement (Second) of Torts §§ 355–62 (1965), and Dobbs, The Law of Torts § 240 (2000). From a property-law perspective, Restatement (Second) of Property-Landlord & Tenant §§ 17.1–17.7 (1977), generally tracks the Restatement (Second) of Torts, with some significant additions. Another useful introductory discussion is Browder, The Taming of a Duty—The Tort Liability of Landlords, 81 Mich.L.Rev. 99 (1982).

[503] See Borders v. Roseberry, 532 P.2d 1366 (Kan.1975); Restatement (Second) of Property-Landlord & Tenant §§ 17.1–17.7 (1977); Restatement (Second) of Torts §§ 355–62 (1965).

tenant personally. One consequence of this principle is that a defense the landlord would have against the tenant is also available against these third persons.[504]

The first exception is that a landlord is liable to the tenant and others for personal injuries caused by the landlord's failure to use reasonable care in maintaining "common areas."[505] These are areas not within the leased premises but within the landlord's control and that are used in connection with the premises, such as hallways, stairways, walkways, driveways, entrances, and laundry rooms. As these areas are not within the tenant's control, the landlord's liability is more likely.[506] While the "common-area exception" probably accounts for the largest number of personal injury suits by tenants against landlords, it really should not be treated as an exception at all. Common areas are by definition outside the leased premises; they are the landlord's land, just as the front porch of a private home is under the general possession and control of the owner. It is possible for landlords to be liable to tenants for injuries on land beyond the common areas if such land is under the landlord's control.[507] It is quite incidental to the landlord-tenant relationship that a tenant or invitee happens to be injured on a common area; the landlord is equally liable to anyone who has a legitimate reason to be there.

Under the second exception, a landlord may be liable to the tenant and others for injuries caused by "latent" defects that exist on the premises when the leasehold begins. A "latent" defect is one of which the landlord knows (or reasonably should know) but of which the tenant does not know or have reason to know; generally this means a concealed defect.[508] "Latent" also implies that the landlord may avoid liability to the tenant or others by disclosing the defect to the tenant. The Restatements distinguish between a landlord who simply fails to disclose and one who actively conceals a known or knowable latent defect. In the former case, the Restatements provide that the landlord's liability ends after the tenant has had a reasonable opportunity to discover the condition; in the

---

[504] For instance, if the tenant's knowledge of a dangerous condition would give the landlord a defense against the tenant for an injury from that condition, the tenant's knowledge also gives the landlord a defense in a suit by an injured third person. See, e.g., Piccola v. Woodall, 921 P.2d 710 (Ariz.App.1996); Ortega v. Flaim, 902 P.2d 199 (Wyo.1995); Borders v. Roseberry, 532 P.2d 1366 (Kan.1975). The one exception to which this principle does *not* apply is the exception under which the landlord may be liable to third persons on premises leased for admission of members of the public.

[505] Paul v. Sharpe, 352 S.E.2d 626 (Ga.App.1987); Borders v. Roseberry, 532 P.2d 1366 (Kan.1975) (held not applicable on facts); Fipps v. Glenn Miller Constr. Co., Inc., 662 So.2d 594 (Miss.1995) (duty of reasonable care to keep common areas reasonably safe); Kennett v. Yates, 250 P.2d 962 (Wash.1952); Restatement (Second) of Property-Landlord & Tenant § 17.3 (1977); Restatement (Second) of Torts § 361 (1965); Dobbs, The Law of Torts § 240, at 627 (2000); Browder, The Taming of a Duty—The Tort Liability of Landlords, 81 Mich.L.Rev. 99, 102–03 (1982).

[506] This concept is illustrated by several cases of attacks by vicious animals owned by tenants, but that occur within common areas. Courts seem more willing to hold landlords liable when the attack occurs on common areas than when it occurs on the tenant's premises. Compare Allison by Fox v. Page, 545 N.W.2d 281 (Iowa 1996) (landlord not liable for dog attack on premises), and Frobig v. Gordon, 881 P.2d 226 (Wis.1994) (landlord not liable for attack by tenant's tiger on yard leased to tenant) with Matthews v. Amberwood Assocs. Ltd. Partn., 719 A.2d 119 (Md.1998) (landlord liable for attack by tenant's pit bull on common area).

[507] See Alcaraz v. Vece, 929 P.2d 1239 (Cal.1997) (landlord liable to tenant for injury on adjacent city-owned land that landlord controlled); cf. Kuzmicz v. Ivy Hill Park Apts., Inc., 688 A.2d 1018 (N.J.1997) (landlord not liable to tenant for criminal assault on adjacent land that landlord did not own or control).

[508] See Casey v. Estes, 657 S.2d 845 (Ala.1995) (landlord had no duty to inspect faulty gas line); City of Yuma v. Evans, 336 P.2d 135 (Ariz.1959) (longstanding defect); Borders v. Roseberry, 532 P.2d 1366 (Kan.1975) (tenant had actual knowledge); Freitag v. Evenson, 375 P.2d 69 (Or.1962) (landlord had done work that he should have disclosed); Restatement (Second) of Property-Landlord & Tenant § 17.1 (1977); Restatement (Second) of Torts § 358 (1965); Dobbs, The Law of Torts § 240, at 626 (2000).

latter case, they provide that the landlord's liability continues until the tenant actually discovers the condition.[509]

Courts are still divided on the third exception, involving personal injuries on the premises caused by conditions which landlord covenanted, but failed, to repair.[510] Under the majority view, the landlord is liable for such injuries; this is a major area in which landlord tort liability has expanded.[511] The older view is that breach of the covenant to repair gives rise only to an action for breach of contract.[512] Both Restatements, as well as other leading secondary authorities, endorse liability in tort where the landlord has notice of the need for agreed repairs, fails to exercise reasonable care to make them, the disrepair creates an unreasonable risk of harm, and the disrepair causes injury to the tenant or invitees.[513] Unless the lease creates a duty on the landlord to inspect for needed repairs, the landlord's duty to repair does not arise until the landlord has notice that repairs are needed.[514] It is unclear whether a landlord who has not covenanted in the lease to make repairs may impliedly acquire that duty by gratuitously making repairs during the term. The case for implying such a duty seems doubtful;[515] not only is there no contractual consideration for the landlord's gratuitous undertaking,[516] but it would be poor policy to discourage gratuitous repairs by penalizing the landlord for making them.

Under a fourth exception, a landlord may be liable for personal injuries caused by the landlord's negligence in making repairs, even if the landlord had no contractual obligation to make them.[517] The Restatements provide that the landlord is liable only if the attempted repairs make the defective condition more dangerous or create a deceptive appearance of safety, and if the tenant does not know or have reason to know of those facts.[518] Thus, a landlord is not liable if the landlord only partially completes a repair job and leaves the premises in a dangerous condition, but this condition is obvious to the tenant.[519] A number of courts have gone even further, holding that the landlord may be

---

[509] Restatement (Second) of Property-Landlord & Tenant § 17.1 (1977); Restatement (Second) of Torts § 358 (1965).

[510] See Restatement (Second) of Property-Landlord & Tenant § 17.5, Reporter's Note 4 (1977) (exhaustive citation of decisions from American courts).

[511] See, e.g., Williams v. Davis, 362 P.2d 641 (Kan.1961); Kornspan v. Hertzberg, 197 A.D.2d 673, 602 N.Y.S.2d 873 (1993); Teglo v. Porter, 399 P.2d 519 (Wash.1965); Browder, The Taming of a Duty—The Tort Liability of Landlords, 81 Mich.L.Rev. 99, 104 (1982).

[512] E.g., Leavitt v. Twin Cty. Rental Co., 21 S.E.2d 890 (N.C.1942); Dobbs, The Law of Torts § 240, at 626 (2000).

[513] Restatement (Second) of Property-Landlord & Tenant § 17.5 (1977); Restatement (Second) of Torts § 357 (1965); Dobbs, The Law of Torts § 240, at 626.

[514] Dobbs, The Law of Torts, § 240, at 626 & n.13 (2000); Juarez v. Wavecrest Mgmt. Team Ltd., 672 N.E.2d 135 (N.Y.1996). Note the distinction between a lease clause that gives the landlord a positive duty to inspect for defective conditions and a clause that merely gives the landlord a privilege to enter and inspect. See Gourdi v. Berkelo, 930 P.2d 812 (N.M.1996) (mere privilege to enter does not create duty to inspect and to discover defects); Gore v. People's Sav. Bank, 665 A.2d 1341 (Conn.1995) (landlord has no duty to correct defect that violates statutory warranty of habitability when landlord has no knowledge of it).

[515] Flynn v. Pan Am. Hotel Co., 183 S.W.2d 446 (Tex.1944).

[516] See Restatement (Second) of Property-Landlord & Tenant § 17.5, Reporter's Note 6 (1977).

[517] Dobbs, The Law of Torts § 240, at 627 (2000). Traditionally, negligent repairs completed before the lease did not bring the landlord within this exception. E.g., Casey v. Estes, 657 So.2d 845 (Ala.1995).

[518] Restatement (Second) of Property-Landlord & Tenant § 17.7 (1977); Restatement (Second) of Torts § 362 (1965).

[519] Borders v. Roseberry, 532 P.2d 1366 (Kan.1975).

liable for injuries caused by negligent repairs even if the work did not worsen the condition or make it deceptively appear safe.[520]

A landlord who leases premises to be used for admission of the public may be liable to members of the public who are injured by defective conditions that existed on these public areas at the time of leasing. Here the landlord's duty is not to the tenant, but to third persons who enter the premises for the purposes for which they are open to the public.[521] Public areas certainly include such places as stadiums, amusement parks, lecture halls, and hotels. Some early authority limited this exception to places where masses of persons would congregate.[522] Today, by the strong weight of authority, the exception extends to places admitting small numbers of the public—e.g., stores, shops, restaurants, motels, and professional offices—but not to private places such as dwellings or the private portions of commercial premises.[523] The landlord is liable if the landlord knows or reasonably should know of a defective condition that poses an unreasonable risk of harm to the public and fails to act reasonably to repair it. The tenant's mere knowledge of the defect does not relieve the landlord of liability, because the duty is not to the tenant. However, if the tenant promises to repair the condition and not to admit members of the public until it is repaired, this promise relieves the landlord of liability provided the tenant's promise is a credible one in the circumstances.[524]

Earlier sections discussed the judicially-implied and statutory landlord warranties of habitability. Now that such warranties exist in most states, to what extent is a landlord liable in tort for an injury caused by a defective condition that the landlord failed to repair in violation of such a warranty?[525] If a state allows a landlord's tort liability to flow from breach of a repair duty created by contract with the tenant, it is logical to say that such liability might also flow from breach of a repair duty created by an implied or statutory warranty. Court decisions on the question identify three possible answers to the liability question.

One possible result is that no tort liability will attach on account of the landlord's breach of warranty. Leading decisions for this position are Isbell v. Commercial Investment Associates, Inc.[526] and Dapkunas v. Cagle.[527] These decisions refused to

---

[520] Janofsky v. Garland, 109 P.2d 750 (Cal.App.1941); Marks v. Nambil Realty Co., 157 N.E. 129 (N.Y.1927); Restatement (Second) of Property-Landlord & Tenant § 17.7, Reporter's Note 4 (1977).

[521] Dobbs, The Law of Torts § 240, at 627 (2000). Generally, the landlord owes the duty only to persons who enter public areas for purposes for which they are open to the public, not to persons who enter for other purposes. Compare Sherwood Bros. v. Eckard, 105 A.2d 207 (Md.1954), and Van Avery v. Platte Valley Land & Inv. Co., 275 N.W. 288 (Neb.1937) (denying recovery) with Hayes v. Richfield Oil Corp., 240 P.2d 580 (Cal.1952), and Hamilton v. Union Oil Co., 339 P.2d 440 (Or.1959) (allowing recovery).

[522] Restatement of Torts § 359 (1939).

[523] Restatement (Second) of Property-Landlord & Tenant § 17.2, Comment d (1977); Restatement (Second) of Torts § 359, Comment c (1965). However, when part of the premises are public areas and part are private, the landlord is not liable under this exception for injuries that occur on the private areas. See Brenner v. Central Realty Co., 37 A.2d 230 (Conn.1944) (storage room); Wilson v. Dowtin, 2 S.E.2d 576 (N.C.1939) (same).

[524] Maglin v. Peoples City Bank, 14 A.2d 827 (Pa.Super.1940); Restatement (Second) of Property-Landlord & Tenant § 17.2, Illus. 10 (1977). The landlord is not relieved of liability by the tenant's promise to repair if it is apparent that members of the public will be invited before the tenant can make the repairs. See Warner v. Lucey, 207 A.D. 241, 201 N.Y.S. 658 (1923), aff'd, 144 N.E. 924 (N.Y.1924); Folkman v. Lauer, 91 A. 218 (Pa.1914).

[525] For a thorough and thoughtful exploration of developments in this area, see Browder, The Taming of a Duty—The Tort Liability of Landlords, 81 Mich.L.Rev. 99, 109–41 (1982).

[526] 644 S.E.2d 72 (Va.2007).

[527] 356 N.E.2d 575 (Ill.App.1976).

create a new exception to the general common-law rule that landlords are not liable for tort injuries, reasoning that the warranty was not intended to create tort liability.

A second possible result, reflected in the Restatement (Second) of Property, is that the landlord's breach of an implied or statutory warranty gives rise to tort liability if the landlord negligently made or unreasonably failed to make the required repairs.[528] Liability on this basis applies only to residential premises, as implied or statutory warranties generally do not extend to commercial tenants.[529] Dwyer v. Skyline Apartments, Inc.,[530] a 1973 decision from New Jersey, was the first decision for this position, and numerous courts are in agreement.[531] If the landlord is liable only for negligence or lack of reasonable care, this implies that the landlord shall have had notice of the defect that caused the injury and a reasonable opportunity to repair it.[532] A variation on this result appears in a few decisions holding that the landlord is liable in tort for negligently failing to make the repairs required by a residential landlord-tenant statute, with violation of the statute said to be negligence per se.[533] These decisions essentially follow the rule stated in Restatement (Second) of Torts[534] that violation of a safety statute is negligence per se. However, the Restatement imposes so many qualifications on this point that its rule may not work much differently in practice from ordinary negligence.[535]

The third possible result is that a landlord is strictly liable for personal injuries caused by defects the landlord failed to correct in violation of an implied or statutory duty to repair. Kaplan v. Coulston,[536] a decision of the Civil Court of New York City, held there was strict liability under the warranty provisions of the New York Real Property Law, but there is little other authority for that position.[537]

---

[528] Restatement (Second) of Property-Landlord & Tenant § 17.6 (1977).

[529] Texas has extended a judicially implied warranty to commercial tenants, Davidow v. Inwood N. Prof. Group–Phase I, 747 S.W.2d 373 (Tex.1988), though it is not clear whether this would justify implying a commercial landlord's tort liability.

[530] 301 A.2d 463 (N.J.Super.1973), aff'd, 311 A.2d 1 (N.J.1973).

[531] E.g., Newton v. Magill, 872 P.2d 1213 (Alaska 1994) (Alaska's version of URLTA creates general duty to keep premises safe from defects that unreasonably risk injury); Thompson v. Crownover, 381 S.E.2d 283 (Ga.1989); Jackson v. Wood, 726 P.2d 796 (Kan.App.1986); Crowell v. McCaffrey, 386 N.E.2d 1256 (Mass.1979) (alternative ground); Henderson v. W.C. Haas Realty Mgmt., Inc., 561 S.W.2d 382 (Mo.App.1977); Humbert v. Sellars, 708 P.2d 344 (Or.1985); Rivera v. Selfon Home Repairs & Impr. Co., 439 A.2d 739 (Pa.Super.1982); Porter v. Lumbermen's Inv. Corp., 606 S.W.2d 715 (Tex.Civ.App. 1980); Lincoln v. Farnkoff, 613 P.2d 1212 (Wash.App.1980).

[532] See Henderson v. W.C. Haas Realty Mgmt., Inc., 561 S.W.2d 382 (Mo.App.1977); Rivera v. Selfon Home Repairs & Impr. Co., 439 A.2d 739 (Pa.Super.1982); Lincoln v. Farnkoff, 613 P.2d 1212 (Wash.App.1980); Restatement (Second) of Property-Landlord & Tenant § 17.6, Comment c (1977).

[533] See especially Calder v. Anderson, 911 P.2d 1157 (Mont.1996); Shroades v. Rental Homes, Inc., 427 N.E.2d 774 (Ohio 1981), overruling Thrash v. Hill, 407 N.E.2d 495 (Ohio 1980).

[534] Restatement (Second) of Torts § 288A(b) (1965).

[535] See Browder, The Taming of a Duty—The Tort Liability of Landlords, 81 Mich.L.Rev. 99, 132–33 (1982).

[536] 85 Misc.2d 745, 381 N.Y.S.2d 634 (City Ct.1976).

[537] An argument for strict liability is made in Love, Landlord's Liability for Defective Premises: Caveat Lessee, Negligence, or Strict Liability?, 1975 Wis.L.Rev. 19. The argument there is for broader strict liability, not limited to statutory breaches. See also Becker v. IRM Corp., 698 P.2d 116 (Cal.1985), in which the California Supreme Court imposed strict liability on residential landlords on common law grounds. But Becker was explicitly overruled in Peterson v. Superior Court, 899 P.2d 905 (Cal.1995).

Liability Based on Ordinary Negligence Doctrine

As explored above, the traditional approach generally assumed that the landlord was not liable in tort, but then recognized a series of exceptions. In 1973, in Sargent v. Ross,[538] the New Hampshire Supreme Court took a fresh approach, declaring that a landlord is liable to the tenant or others for injuries on or about the premises if the landlord failed to exercise reasonable care in all the circumstances. A guest of the tenant, a small child whom the tenant was baby-sitting, was killed when she fell off an outside stairway leading to the tenant's second-floor apartment. Allegedly, the landlord was negligent because the stairway was too steep and had an inadequate railing. The plaintiff (the child's mother) argued that the stairway was a common area, so as to invoke the common-area exception, while the landlord argued that the stairway was part of the leased premises under the tenant's control. The court announced that the landlord's liability should be based on ordinary negligence rules.[539] The court said that questions of control, hidden defects, and common areas—matters determinative under the traditional exceptions—should be considered only to the extent they "bear on the basic tort issues such as the foreseeability and unreasonableness of the particular risk of harm."[540]

Consistent with *Sargent*, courts in at least ten other jurisdictions now evaluate the landlord's tort liability using general negligence principles.[541] Some decisions basing liability on violation of implied or statutory warranties also contain language suggesting approval of the *Sargent* doctrine.[542] Several courts have rejected the *Sargent* approach, though the grounds for rejection would not necessarily apply in other courts.[543] The *Sargent* court did not extend its ordinary negligence rule to commercial tenancies,[544] and thus the traditional approach may still govern the tort liability of commercial landlords even in states that have adopted *Sargent* in the residential context.

The *Sargent* approach does not mean a plaintiff can recover for any injury caused by defects in the premises. Under ordinary negligence principles, the landlord would

---

[538]   308 A.2d 528 (N.H.1973).

[539]   *Sargent*, 308 A.2d at 534 ("A landlord must act as a reasonable person under all of the circumstances, including the likelihood of injury to others, the probable seriousness of such injuries, and the burden of reducing or avoiding the risk.").

[540]   *Sargent*, 308 A.2d at 534.

[541]   E.g., George Washington Univ. v. Weintraub, 458 A.2d 43 (D.C.1983); Presson v. Mountain States Props., Inc., 501 P.2d 17 (Ariz.App.1972); Swanberg v. O'Mectin, 157 Cal.App.3d 325, 203 Cal.Rptr. 701 (1984); Mansur v. Eubanks, 401 So.2d 1328 (Fla.1981); Stephens v. Stearns, 678 P.2d 41 (Idaho 1984); Young v. Garwacki, 402 N.E.2d 1045 (Mass.1980); Turpel v. Sayles, 692 P.2d 1290 (Nev.1985); Collingwood v. General Elec. Real Estate Equities, Inc., 376 S.E.2d 425 (N.C.1989); Williams v. Melby, 699 P.2d 723 (Utah 1985); Pagelsdorf v. Safeco Ins. Co., 284 N.W.2d 55 (Wis.1979).

[542]   See especially Newton v. Magill, 872 P.2d 1213 (Alaska 1994) (relying on both *Sargent* and Alaska's adoption of URLTA to hold residential landlords have a duty to repair conditions that create unreasonable risk of injury).

[543]   See Murphy v. Hendrix, 500 So.2d 8 (Ala.1986) (rejecting implied warranty of habitability, suggesting legislature should determine whether to enact expanded liability rule); Webster v. Heim, 399 N.E.2d 690 (Ill.App.1980); Broughton v. Maes, 378 N.W.2d 134 (Minn.App.1985) (refusing to adopt broadened rule of liability because no state supreme court decision had done so).

[544]   *Sargent*, 308 A.2d at 533–534 (noting that ordinary negligence standard follows "naturally and inexorably" from New Hampshire's adoption of implied warranty of habitability in residential leases). See also Propst v. McNeill, 932 S.W.2d 766 (Ark.1996) (adhering to traditional rule in lease airplane hanger, and suggesting legislature is appropriate body to consider expansion of landlord liability).

have no liability if there is no duty to protect against the particular risk at issue,[545] if the landlord did not know or have reason to know of the defect,[546] or if the injury was not reasonably foreseeable.[547]

Strict Liability

The California Supreme Court's 1985 decision in Becker v. IRM Corp.[548] generated much attention for a few years, more for the novelty of its position than for its persuasiveness. *Becker* held a landlord of residential premises strictly liable to a tenant for injuries caused by a defect that existed at the time of leasing. The court's rationale was based upon products liability cases from the field of torts. Underlying the decision is a policy to shift the risk of liability for the tenant's injuries—and thus the practical necessity to insure against those risks—to the landlord. In 1995, in *Peterson v. Superior Court,* the California Supreme Court explicitly overruled *Becker.*[549] During its short life, *Becker* brought little reaction from other courts, and mostly negative at that.[550] Before *Peterson* overruled *Becker,* a California appellate court refused to extend it to commercial leases, on the ground that *Becker*'s underlying policies should apply only to residential landlords and tenants.[551] The evidence is that courts are not willing to make landlords insurers that defects in the premises will not injure their tenants.

Louisiana has long had a statutory rule that imposes strict liability on landlords for injuries caused by defects in the premises that exist at the beginning of the lease.[552] Studies disagree upon whether, or how much, strict liability may drive up landlords' insurance rates (and, in turn, tenant rents) in Louisiana.[553] Apparently, however, the rule is not viewed in Louisiana as causing insuperable hardship to landlords.

---

[545] E.g., Garcia v. Paramount Citrus Ass'n, Inc., 164 Cal.App.4th 1448, 80 Cal.Rptr.3d 512 (2008) (no duty to place sign on private road warning of approaching intersection with public road); Brooks v. Eugene Burger Mgmt. Corp., 215 Cal.App.3d 1611, 264 Cal.Rptr. 756 (1989) (no duty to provide fence to keep tenant children away from adjacent street); but see Barnes v. Black, 71 Cal.App.4th 1473, 84 Cal.Rptr.2d 634 (1999) (acknowledging possible duty due to steeply-sloped driveway on premises that allegedly carried tenant's child and his tricycle into busy public street).

[546] E.g. Serrano v. Laurel Hous. Auth., 151 So.3d 256 (Miss.App.2014); Bradley v. Wachovia Bank & Trust Co., 369 S.E.2d 86 (N.C.1988); Stephens v. Covington, 754 S.E.2d 253 (N.C.App.2014) (landlord not liable to plaintiff bitten by tenant's dog where plaintiff failed to show landlord knew dog was dangerous).

[547] There is a substantial body of cases addressing the landlord's potential liability for injuries resulting from poisoning due to exposure to lead-based paint on the premises. While some early decisions held the risks associated with lead-based paint were not foreseeable, Kolojeski v. John Deisher, Inc., 239 A.2d 329 (Pa.1968), more recent decisions have taken the contrary approach. This is not surprising given the greater public awareness of the widespread use of lead-based paint and the dangers associated with lead poisoning. E.g., Antwaun A. v. Heritage Mut. Ins. 596 N.W.2d 456 (Wis.1999).

[548] 698 P.2d 116 (Cal.1985).

[549] 899 P.2d 905 (Cal.1995).

[550] Cases rejecting *Becker* include: Fitzgerald v. Cestari, 569 So.2d 1258 (Fla.1990); Armstrong v. Cione, 738 P.2d 79 (Haw.1987); Young v. Morrissey, 329 S.E.2d 426 (S.C.1985).

One New York court held that strict liability could result where an injury resulted from a condition that breached the landlord's warranty of habitability. Kaplan v. Coulston, 85 Misc.2d 745, 381 N.Y.S.2d 634 (1976). Later New York decisions have not followed *Kaplan*, however. E.g., Segal v. Justice Court Mut. Hous. Co-op., Inc., 105 Misc.2d 453, 432 N.Y.S.2d 463 (Sup.1980) (explicitly rejecting *Kaplan*; "landlords are not in the insurance business and we cannot fairly expect them to be absolute insurers of their property").

[551] Muro v. Superior Court, 184 Cal.App.3d 1089, 229 Cal.Rptr. 383 (1986).

[552] La.Civ.Code arts. 2696, 2697; Entrevia v. Hood, 427 So.2d 1146 (La.1983).

[553] See Browder, The Taming of a Duty—The Tort Liability of Landlords, 81 Mich.L.Rev. 99, 138–41 (1982).

Exculpatory Clauses

Landlords often draft the leases used in routine leasing transactions, and often insert a clause that purports to relieve them from liability for tort injuries. Such "exculpatory clauses" take various forms, but their general import is that the tenant agrees to relieve the landlord from liability or "waives" any claim for injuries on the demised premises or associated common areas. Under the concept of freedom to contract, courts traditionally enforced such clauses.[554] However, because of the imbalance in bargaining power between residential landlords and tenants, courts have been suspicious of the extent to which exculpatory clauses reflected a true "bargain," and often found ways not to enforce them or to construe them narrowly.[555]

In recent years, the trend has run strongly against the enforceability of exculpatory clauses in residential leases. Some judicial decisions have invalidated them wholesale in residential leases on public policy grounds.[556] Others have invalidated clauses to the extent that they exculpated a landlord for "active" negligence,[557] on unconscionability grounds,[558] or upon a showing of an actual inequality in bargaining power.[559] In addition, residential landlord-tenant statutes in many state outlaw such clauses or severely restrict their operation.[560] In sum, exculpatory clauses in residential leases are now of doubtful effect in most jurisdictions. However, except in states in which statutory prohibitions apply to commercial leases as well,[561] exculpatory clauses are likely as enforceable in commercial leases as they traditionally were.

---

[554] See, e.g., O'Callaghan v. Waller & Beckwith Realty Co., 155 N.E.2d 545 (Ill.1958) (later abrogated by statute); Manaster v. Gopin, 116 N.E.2d 134 (Mass.1953); Broderson v. Rainier Nat'l Park Co., 60 P.2d 234 (Wash.1936), overruled in Baker v. City of Seattle, 484 P.2d 405 (Wash.1971); 6 S. Williston, Contracts § 1751C (Rev.ed.1938). Several recent Missouri decisions have upheld explicit exculpatory clauses effective to release the landlord from its own future negligence. E.g., Abbott v. Epic Landscape Productions, L.C., 361 S.W.3d 13 (Mo.App.2011); Milligan v. Chesterfield Village GP, LLC, 239 S.W.3d 613 (Mo.App.2007) (explicit terms of exculpation clause effective to release building owner, but not building manager).

[555] See Taylor v. Leedy & Co., 412 So.2d 763 (Ala.1982) (construing exculpatory clause to waive liability for future acts of negligence, but not for existing latent defects known to landlord); Fuller v. TLC Prop. Mgmt., LLC, 402 S.W.3d 101 (Mo.App.2013) (construing exculpatory clause covering claims "on or about premises" not to include a claim arising in parking lot; "about" was ambiguous and construed narrowly); Jewett v. Rechler, 140 A.D.2d 669, 529 N.Y.S.2d 16 (1988) (construing exculpatory provision to waive liability for property damage but not personal injury). Cf. Industrial Risk Insurers v. Industrial Design & Mfg., Inc., 884 S.W.2d 432 (Mo.App. 1994) (clause requiring tenant to indemnify landlord construed not to require tenant to indemnify landlord against consequences of landlord's own negligence); 6 S. Williston, Contracts § 1751C (Rev.ed.1938).

[556] See Henrioulle v. Marin Ventures, Inc., 573 P.2d 465 (Cal.1978); Stanley v. Creighton Co., 911 P.2d 705 (Colo.App.1996); Ransburg v. Richards, 770 N.E.2d 393 (Ind.2002); Hi-Tec Props., LLC v. Murphy, 14 N.E.3d 767 (Ind.App.2014); Calef v. West, 652 N.W.2d 496 (Mich.App.2002); Cappaert v. Junker, 413 So.2d 378 (Miss.1982); Crawford v. Buckner, 839 S.W.2d 754 (Tenn.1992); McCutcheon v. United Homes Corp., 486 P.2d 1093 (Wash.1971).

[557] E.g., Matthews v. Mountain Lodge Apts., Inc., 388 So.2d 935 (Ala.1980).

[558] E.g., Johnson v. Mobil Oil Corp., 415 F.Supp. 264 (E.D.Mich.1976).

[559] E.g., Weaver v. American Oil Co., 276 N.E.2d 144 (Ind.1971); Cardona v. Eden Realty Co., 288 A.2d 34 (N.J.Super.1972); Galligan v. Arovitch, 219 A.2d 463 (Pa.1966).

[560] URLTA §§ 1.403, 2.104 (1972) (general prohibition of exculpatory clauses); RURLTA § 203(a)(5) (2015) (same). See also Cal.Civ.Code § 1953; Haw.Rev.Stat. § 521–33. Other statutes are reviewed in Browder, The Taming of a Duty—The Tort Liability of Landlords, 81 Mich.L.Rev. 99, 142–43 (1982).

[561] E.g., Md.Real Prop.Code § 8–105; Mass.Gen.Laws Ann. ch.186 § 15; N.Y.Gen.Oblig.Law § 5–321. See also 765 Ill.Comp.Stat.Ann. § 705/1 (invalidating exculpatory clauses in all leases to the extent they exempt landlord from liability for personal injury, but upholding exculpation of landlord as to liability for property damage in commercial leases).

§ 6.47 LANDLORD'S LIABILITY FOR CRIMINAL ACTS

Under traditional landlord-tenant law, landlords were not liable to tenants and others for injuries to their persons or property caused by the criminal acts of third persons on or about the premises. This is consistent with the traditional rule of landlord nonliability discussed in the prior section, as well as the general common law rule that an individual has no affirmative duty to protect others from criminal acts of third persons.[562] While an exception arose where a special relationship existed between the parties, such as an innkeeper-guest or common carrier-passenger relationship,[563] courts in nearly all states have rejected the view that the landlord and tenant stand in such a special relationship.[564]

Today, many courts have retreated from the traditional common law rule, and will impose liability on the landlord for third-party criminal acts if the appropriate facts and circumstances are present. The case that began this evolution was Kline v. 1500 Massachusetts Ave. Apt. Corp.[565] The case involved a tenant who suffered a criminal assault in her apartment house hallway. Even though the landlord knew of prior criminal assaults against other tenants in the common areas, the landlord did not provide additional security (and in fact decreased security measures). The court held the landlord liable for the tenant's personal injuries suffered in the assault, holding that a landlord in a multi-tenant apartment building owed a tenant a duty of reasonable care, including "a duty to take those measures of protection which are within [landlord's] power and capacity to take, and which can reasonably be expected to mitigate the risk of intruders assaulting and robbing tenants."[566]

In many decisions since Kline, courts have held that landlords can have, on one legal basis or another and in appropriate factual circumstances, a duty to exercise reasonable care to provide and maintain security to prevent foreseeable criminal acts by third parties.[567] The following paragraphs address this development, beginning with the

---

[562] See, e.g., Hall v. Rental Mgmt., Inc., 913 S.W.2d 293 (Ark.1996); Walls v. Oxford Mgmt. Co., 633 A.2d 103 (N.H.1993); Tambriz v. P.G.K. Luncheonette, Inc., 124 A.D.3d 626, 2 N.Y.S.3d 150 (2015); Dobbs, The Law of Torts § 322 (2000).

[563] Restatement (Second) of Torts § 314A (duty of common carriers and innkeepers to protect passengers or guests from unreasonable risk of physical harm); Dobbs, The Law of Torts § 323 (2000). In this situation, a duty of protection was justified on the view that the passenger or guest was effectively submitting to the control of common carrier or innkeeper.

[564] E.g., Pippin v. Chicago Hous. Auth., 399 N.E.2d 596 (Ill.1979); Scott v. Watson, 359 A.2d 548 (Md.1976); Feld v. Merriam, 485 A.2d 742 (Pa.1984); Lay v. Dworman, 732 P.2d 455 (Okla.1986); Cramer v. Balcor Prop. Mgmt., Inc., 441 S.E.2d 317 (S.C.1994); Walther v. KPKA Meadowlands Ltd., 581 N.W.2d 527 (S.D.1998); Gulf Reston, Inc. v. Rogers, 207 S.E.2d 841 (Va.1974). At least one Florida decision has articulated the landlord-tenant relationship as a special relationship justifying the imposition of a duty to protect the tenant from reasonably foreseeable criminal conduct. E.g., T.W. v. Regal Trace, Ltd., 908 So.2d 499 (Fla.App.2005).

[565] 439 F.2d 477 (D.C.Cir.1970).

[566] Kline, 439 F.2d at 487.

[567] Because the landlord's liability is based in negligence and not strict liability, the plaintiff must show that the landlord's failure caused the plaintiff's injuries, i.e., that the failure facilitated the commission of the crime. Exactly how much the landlord's failure must facilitate commission of the crime is not clear. Courts have stated that the landlord's failure must be "a substantial factor in bringing about the injury." Nixon v. Mr. Prop. Mgmt. Co., 690 S.W.2d 546 (Tex.1985). In reality, as discussed later in the section, foreseeability has been a more important issue than proximate cause. It is likely sufficient to show that the criminal actor gained entry through the failed system or that the landlord's breach otherwise enabled the criminal to commit the crime, even if the crime might have been committed otherwise. See Duncavage v. Allen, 497 N.E.2d 433 (Ill.1986) (intruder used ladder landlord left out); Scott v. Watson, 359 A.2d 548 (Md.1976) (landlord's neglect in "stream of events" that led to crime); Aaron v. Havens, 758 S.W.2d 446 (Mo.1988) (landlord negligent in

source of the landlord's duty, followed by the standards by which courts have evaluated the foreseeability of criminal conduct, and concluding with a brief discussion of liability for property loss and liability claims in commercial leases.[568]

Source of the Landlord's Duty

To be liable for injuries caused by third-party criminal acts, the landlord must have control over the part of the premises where the crime occurs or over the person (such as a guard or employee) whose failure facilitates the crime.[569] If a court determines that the landlord has a duty to provide devices or systems that will guard against crime—e.g., door or window locks, lighting, alarms, or security guards—at what point will a failure of such devices or systems make the landlord liable for injuries resulting from criminal acts?

As noted above, many cases imposing tort liability involve criminal acts in common areas as to which the landlord failed to take adequate security measures. As in *Kline*, some courts conclude that because tort law already imposes on the landlord a duty of reasonable care to maintain common areas in reasonably safe condition, this duty should apply equally to protect against both physical defects and predictable criminal acts by third parties.[570] The *Kline* court found this extension of the landlord's duty appropriate, particularly as applied to a multi-tenant urban apartment building.[571]

Most courts have refused to go as far as *Kline* to conclude that the landlord has a general duty to provide security activities in common areas to protect against criminal attacks. For example, in Pippin v. Chicago Housing Authority,[572] the Illinois Supreme Court refused to extend a general duty of care to the landlord, rejecting the argument that the landlord and tenant stood in a "special relationship" that justified taking the case outside the traditional rule.[573] *Pippin* also rejected an argument that the landlord's warranty of habitability justified the extension of a duty of care, concluding that the

---

maintaining fire escape in fashion that readily enabled intruder to access windows of tenant's apartment). By contrast, where the evidence suggests that substantial security measures would not have prevented the plaintiff's injuries, causation is lacking. E.g., Davenport v D.M. Rental Props., Inc., 718 S.E.2d 188 (N.C.Ct.App.2011) (security cameras or security guards would not have prevented attack on tenant by drunk, hostile, and delusional attacker who set tenant on fire).

[568] For further background on the landlord's duties with regard to criminal activity in and around the premises, see Dobbs, The Law of Torts § 324 (2000).

[569] E.g., Alcaraz v. Vece, 929 P.2d 1239 (Cal.1997) (landlord could be liable for injury suffered by tenant on adjacent city-owned land over which landlord exercised control); Rosenbaum v. Security Pacific Corp., 43 Cal.App.4th 1084, 50 Cal.Rptr.2d 917 (1996) (landlord owed no duty to protect tenant from attacks occurring off property on land not under landlord's control); Kuzmicz v. Ivy Hill Park Apts., Inc., 688 A.2d 1018 (N.J.1997) (landlord not liable for criminal attack on adjoining vacant lot over which landlord had no control). Cf. J.M. v. Shell Oil Co., 922 S.W.2d 759 (Mo.1996) (jury could find Shell retained enough control over service station franchisee to owe duty to protect customers against criminal attack).

[570] *Kline*, 439 F.2d at 481. See also Scott v. Watson, 359 A.2d 548 (Md.1976); Samson v. Saginaw Professional Bldg., Inc., 224 N.W.2d 843 (Mich.1975).

[571] *Kline*, 439 F.2d at 481 ("The landlord is no insurer of his tenants' safety, but he is certainly no bystander. And where, as here, the landlord has notice of repeated criminal assaults and robberies, has notice that these crimes occurred in portions of the premises exclusively within his control, has every reason to expect like crimes to happen again, and has the exclusive power to take preventive action, it does not seem unfair to place upon the landlord a duty to take those steps which are within his power to minimize the predictable risk to his tenants.").

[572] 399 N.E.2d 596 (Ill.1979).

[573] *Pippin*, 399 N.E.2d at 598.

warranty extended "exclusively to the physical condition of the premises."[574] Similar rejections of *Kline*'s general duty of care appear in numerous other cases.[575]

Still, courts have found other bases to impose a duty on the landlord under appropriate circumstances. The cases tend to fit within one of the exceptions to the traditional rule that an individual has no affirmative duty to protect others from third-party criminal acts. One such exception arises when a person's prior conduct actually creates a condition that involves an unreasonable risk of harm to another.[576] For example, in Aaron v. Havens,[577] a landlord installed a fire escape in a negligent manner, which enabled an intruder to use the fire escape to gain access into tenant's apartment and rape the tenant. The Missouri Supreme Court held that the landlord's failure to take reasonable precautions to deny an intruder easy access to the fire escape provided a sufficient basis for tort liability.[578] Courts have also found liability where the landlord leased property to another person who posed a clear danger to the tenant. For another example, in Estate of Hough ex rel. Lemaster v. Estate of Hough ex rel. Berkeley County Sheriff,[579] the landlord leased a home across the street from the tenant to her estranged husband—against whom she had obtained a protective order—despite landlord's knowledge of the protective order and tenant's fear for her safety. The court held the landlord liable for the tenant's murder by her husband.

A second exception to the traditional rule of landlord nonliability arose where the landlord had undertaken to provide security, either gratuitously or pursuant to a contractual duty. This exception "derives from the general tort principle that one who voluntarily assumes a duty thereafter has a duty to act with reasonable care."[580] In *Pippin*, the Illinois Supreme Court found that the landlord had voluntarily provided guard services through an independent contractor, and could be liable for a tenant's injuries in an assault if the landlord's hiring of the contractor was negligent.[581] Likewise in Feld v. Merriam, the Pennsylvania Supreme Court held that if a landlord undertook to provide security specifically charged to patrol and protect the building, the landlord

[574] *Pippin*, 399 N.E.2d at 599.

[575] E.g., Bartley v. Sweetser, 890 S.W.2d 250 (Ark.1994); Walls v. Oxford Mgmt. Co., Inc., 633 A.2d 103 (N.H.1993); Feld v. Merriam, 485 A.2d 742 (Pa.1984); Gulf Reston, Inc. v. Rogers, 207 S.E.2d 841 (Va.1974).

[576] Restatement (Second) of Torts § 321(1) (1965) ("If the actor does an act, and subsequently realizes or should realize that it has created an unreasonable risk of causing physical harm to another, he is under a duty to exercise reasonable care to prevent the risk from taking effect."); Dobbs, The Law of Torts § 325 (2000).

[577] 758 S.W.2d 446 (Mo.1988)

[578] *Aaron*, 758 S.W.2d at 448. Similarly, in Duncavage v. Allen, 497 N.E.2d 433 (Ill.App.1986). a landlord knew the tenant's apartment had previously been burglarized using a ladder, but left the ladder outside the building, unsecured. The court held the landlord liable for injuries suffered by a tenant who was murdered by an intruder using the same ladder. See also Killebrew v. Sun Trust Banks, Inc., 472 S.E.2d 504 (Ga.App.1996) (bank placed employee who *appeared* to be a security guard in parking lot, but who in fact was acting only to prevent noncustomers from using bank's parking lot; court held bank created misleading appearance that its parking-lot ATM was secure when bank knew it was not).

[579] 455 S.E.2d 821 (W.Va.1999). See also Samson v. Saginaw Prof. Bldg., Inc., 224 N.W.2d 843 (Mich.1975) (landlord liable where it had leased one space to health clinic serving criminal parolees, without warning other tenants, and another tenant suffered attack from clinic patient); Rosales v. Stewart, 113 Cal.App.3d 130, 169 Cal.Rptr. 660 (1980) (landlord liable for failing to control behavior of tenant who commonly shot firearms in yard and, while doing so, shot and killed neighboring child).

[580] Walls v. Oxford Mgmt. Co., Inc., 633 A.2d 103, 106 (N.H.1993) (citing Restatement (Second) of Torts §§ 323, 324 (1965)). See also Hemmings v. Pelham Wood Ltd. Liability Ltd. Partn., 826 A.2d 443 (Md.2003) (landlord that had provided exterior lighting at apartment complex as security measure to deter criminal activity had duty to adequately maintain it).

[581] *Pippin*, 399 N.E.2d at 599–600. See also Rockwell v. Sun Harbor Budget Suites, 925 P.2d 1175 (Nev.1996) (murder committed by apartment complex security guard hired by landlord).

could be liable if the landlord's negligence in carrying out that security caused the tenant to suffer a foreseeable assault.[582]

Another context involving this exception would be a defective lock on the tenant's apartment door or window. Here, a duty of care could not arise based on the landlord's duty to control common areas, but could arise based on an agreement by the landlord to make repairs,[583] by the landlord's voluntary performance of negligent repairs, or by virtue of a statute requiring the landlord to provide specific security measures.[584] This raises another question frequently addressed in these cases—whether a tenant's implied or statutory warranty of habitability itself imposes a duty on the landlord to provide security measures to protect against criminal acts.

Does the implied warranty of habitability include an obligation to provide security services for the tenant? In Trentacost v. Brussel,[585] the New Jersey Supreme Court answered yes, concluding that a landlord that failed to provide a door lock on the entrance to an apartment building was liable for the injuries of a tenant who was attacked in a common stairwell by an intruder who entered the building through the unlocked entrance. The court held that the implied warranty extended to all facilities vital to the residential use of the premises, concluding "an apartment is clearly not habitable unless it provides a reasonable measure of security from the risk of criminal intrusion."[586] Nevertheless, the weight of case authority takes the contrary view that the implied warranty of habitability does not *by itself* impose on the landlord a duty in tort to take affirmative security measures.[587]

---

[582] Feld v. Merriam, 485 A.2d 742, 747 (Pa.1984). See also Carlock v. Kmart Corp., 489 S.E.2d 99 (Ga.App.1997) (shopping center landlord that provided security guard based on prior robberies had duty to provide such security during tenant's full business hours); Sharp v. W.H. Moore, Inc., 796 P.2d 506 (Idaho 1990) (once building owner initiated locked-door policy and employed security service for that purpose, owner was liable for injuries suffered in rape of tenant's employee due to landlord's failure to carry out that policy with reasonable standard of care); see also Phillips v. Chicago Hous. Auth., 431 N.E.2d 1038 (Ill.1982); Hemmings v. Pelham Wood Ltd. Liability Ltd. Partn., 826 A.2d 443 (Md.2003).

Not all courts have been willing to hold that voluntary conduct by the landlord results in the imposition of a duty to protect against third-party criminal activity. See, e.g., Dailey v. Housing Auth. for Birmingham Dist., 639 So.2d 1343 (Ala.1994) (hiring of security guard to patrol housing project did not impose duty on landlord to provide "totally crime-free environment" for tenant shot on her porch during drug transaction on neighboring parcel); Hall v. Rental Mgmt., Inc., 913 S.W.2d 293 (Ark.1996) (landlord had instructed employees to patrol, check lights, and communicate with residents about suspicious activities; court stated "[w]e are reluctant to hold a landlord's use of these modest, conscientious measures imposes a full-blown duty to protect tenants from third party criminal activities"); Bourgonje v. Machev, 841 N.E.2d 96 (Ill.App.2005) (landlord's providing door buzzers and intercom system did not constitute voluntary undertaking to provide broader security measures); Cramer v. Balcor Prop. Mgmt., Inc., 848 F.Supp. 1222 (D.S.C.1994) (landlord did not assume duty by having previously hired a "courtesy officer" to patrol apartment grounds). Perhaps one might better explain these results on other grounds—such as the unforeseeability of the crime in question, lack of causation (e.g., even security patrols might not prevent a drive-by shooting), or a conclusion that the landlord's voluntary actions were carried out reasonably. E.g., Rabel v. Illinois Wesleyan Univ., 514 N.E.2d 552 (Ill.1987) (landlord held to have reasonably carried out voluntary security measures).

[583] E.g., Richmond Medical Supply Co., Inc. v. Clifton, 369 S.E.2d 407 (Va.1988) (failure to satisfy lease obligation to repair defective premises door).

[584] E.g. Paterson v. Deeb, 472 So.2d 1210 (Fla.App.1985) (failure to provide security lock on tenant's door in violation of Florida's residential landlord-tenant statute).

[585] 412 A.2d 436 (N.J.1980).

[586] *Trentacost*, 412 A.2d at 443. See also *Kline*, 439 F.2d 477 (in imposing general duty of care, noting significance of landlord's implied warranty under *Javins*).

[587] E.g., Pippin v. Chicago Hous. Auth., 399 N.E.2d 596 (1979); Doe v. New Bedford Hous. Auth., 630 N.E.2d 248 (Mass.1994); Walls v. Oxford Mgmt. Co., Inc., 633 A.2d 103 (N.H.1993); Timberwalk Apts., Partners, Inc. v. Cain, 972 S.W.2d 749 (Tex.1998); Jack v. Fritts, 457 S.E.2d 431 (W.Va.1995). See also Dailey

Where a statutory warranty generically requires the landlord to keep the premises in "safe" condition, some courts have also been unsympathetic to tenant claims. For example, in Walther v. KPKA Meadowlands Ltd.,[588] the South Dakota Supreme Court held that the state's statutory warranty of habitability—which required that the landlord "shall keep the premises and all common areas in reasonable repair and fit for human habitation and in good and safe working order during the term of the lease"—did "not create a duty on the part of lessors to protect lessees from criminal acts of third persons."[589] By contrast, courts are more likely to find breach of a duty where the landlord fails to provide a security measure that the statute *specifically* imposes, such as door locks,[590] lighting, security guards,[591] or a fire escape.[592]

Foreseeability

For claims of landlord tort liability for third-party criminal acts, the most critical and complicated issue is often whether the action resulting in plaintiff's injury was foreseeable. This is not surprising, given the reluctance of tort law to require defendants to anticipate intervening causes of harm. Crime can occur anywhere, but landlords are not held to anticipate it everywhere; the landlord should have a duty only where the landlord has a sufficient reason to expect crime at the particular location (i.e., on or about the premises or common areas).

Typically, foreseeability is established through evidence of previous criminal activity on the property in question;[593] while there are a few cases of truly isolated crimes being held foreseeable, they are quite rare.[594] Courts have disagreed as to the appropriate standard to measure how much prior criminal activity, and of what type, is needed to justify a duty. Some courts have articulated a "prior similar incidents" or "prior

---

v. Housing Auth. for Birmingham Dist., 639 So.2d 1343 (Ala.1994) (contractual provision in lease obligating landlord to maintain premises in "safe and sanitary condition" did not create duty to hire security patrols).

[588] 581 N.W.2d 527 (S.D.1998).

[589] *Walther*, 581 N.W.2d at 535. Accord: Deem v. Charles E. Smith Mgmt., Inc., 799 F.2d 944 (4th Cir.1986) (Virginia law); Mengel v. Rosen, 735 P.2d 560 (Okla.1987); Cramer v. Balcor Prop. Mgmt., Inc., 441 S.E.2d 317 (S.C.1994); Jack v. Fritts, 457 S.E.2d 431 (W.Va.1995).

[590] E.g., Brock v. Watts Realty Co., Inc., 582 So.2d 438 (Ala.1991); Paterson v. Deeb, 472 So.2d 1210 (Fla.App.1985); Brichacek v. Hiskey, 401 N.W.2d 44 (Iowa 1987) (noting statute required door lock, and ultimately concluding that tenant failed to establish that existing door lock failed to meet standard of reasonable care); Braitman v. Overlook Terrace Corp., 346 A.2d 76 (N.J.1975). Cf. Tex.Prop.Code § 92.153 (requiring door locks and window latches without necessity of tenant request).

[591] Cf. 515 Assocs. v. City of Newark, 623 A.2d 1366 (N.J.1993) (upholding Newark ordinance requiring security guards for public or private housing buildings containing over 100 units).

[592] E.g., Gaines v. Property Servicing Co., 276 S.W.2d 169 (Mo.1955) (landlord liable for injury suffered by tenant who jumped from window to escape fire set by arsonist where landlord failed to provide fire escape as required by statute).

[593] See, e.g., Kline v. 1500 Mass. Ave. Apt. Corp., 439 F.2d 477 (D.C.Cir.1970) (prior crimes on common areas); Holley v. Mt. Zion Terrace Apts., Inc., 382 So.2d 98 (Fla.App.1980) (same); Scott v. Watson, 359 A.2d 548 (Md.1976) (same); Aaron v. Havens, 758 S.W.2d 446 (Mo.1988) (prior attempt to break into premises); Griffin v. West RS, Inc., 984 P.2d 1070 (Wash.1999) (prior break-in to premises).

[594] One such unusual case was Samson v. Saginaw Prof. Bldg., Inc., 224 N.W.2d 843 (Mich.1975), where the court held the owner of an office building liable for an assault by a patient of a mental health clinic located in the building. Though there had been no prior assaults, persons working in the building had repeatedly expressed fears of such an assault to the owner. Another unusual (but understandable) case is Estate of Hough ex rel. Lemaster v. Estate of Hough ex rel. Berkeley County Sheriff, 455 S.E.2d 821 (W.Va.1999), where tenant was murdered by her estranged husband. Although landlord knew tenant had obtained a protective order against her husband—or should have known, based on tenant having repeatedly articulated to the landlord fears for her safety—landlord nevertheless rented a home to the husband directly across the street from the tenant. The landlord had further threatened to evict tenant unless she mowed her front yard, which she was doing when her husband shot and killed her.

similars" rule. For example, in Timberwalk Apartments, Partners, Inc. v. Cain, a case involving a tenant's rape in her apartment, the Texas Supreme Court held that in evaluating foreseeability, courts should "consider whether any criminal conduct previously occurred on or near the property, how recently it occurred, how similar the conduct was to the conduct on the property, and what publicity was given the occurrences to indicate that the landlord knew or should have known about them."[595] Based on these factors, the court concluded that the tenant's rape was not foreseeable, noting that no violent personal crime had occurred in the apartment complex during the prior ten years, and that a few recent property crimes involving cars did not portend an increased likelihood of sexual assault.[596]

Some have criticized the "prior similars" approach as being too narrow and providing the landlord with an insufficient incentive to take preventive measures against known risks until multiple victims have suffered a comparable attack.[597] Likewise, some have criticized this approach as too unpredictable to provide meaningful guidance to landlords—exactly what locations are "proximate," and exactly what prior incidents are "similar"? For example, courts have disagreed as to whether foreseeability requires that prior incidents be on or adjacent to the property, or whether incidents at similar types of properties could establish foreseeability.[598] Likewise, as noted above, several courts have held that a tenant's rape was not foreseeable where there had been no prior sexual assaults on the premises.[599] Other courts, however, have held that a rape

---

[595] Timberwalk Apts., Partners, Inc. v. Cain, 972 S.W.2d 749, 757 (Tex.1998). See also Boren v. Worthen Nat'l Bank, 921 S.W.2d 934 (1996) (considering the "similarity, frequency, location, and proximity in time of the prior incidents"); Jacqueline S. v. City of New York, 614 N.E.2d 723 (N.Y.1993) (analyzing "location, nature and extent" of previous crimes and their "similarity, proximity, or other relationship to the crime in question"); Polomie v. Golub Corp., 226 A.D.2d 979, 640 N.Y.S.2d 700 (1996).

[596] Timberwalk, 972 S.W.2d at 758–59 ("vandalism to automobiles in an apartment complex's parking lot can be a serious concern, but it does not suggest the likelihood of sexual assault"). See also Ann M. v. Pacific Plaza Shopping Ctr., 863 P.2d 207 (Cal.1993) (owner of shopping center had no duty to tenant's employee who was raped on premises to provide security guards in common areas, absent notice of previous assaults); Sharon P. v. Arman, Ltd., 989 P.2d 121 (Cal.1999) (sexual attack was not sufficiently foreseeable to require landlord to provide security guards in underground parking garage absent evidence of prior assaults); Doe v. Prudential-Bache/A.G. Spanos Realty Partners, 492 S.E.2d 865 (Ga.1997) (prior property crimes did not establish foreseeability of tenant's violent sexual assault).

[597] See, e.g., Isaacs v. Huntington Memorial Hospital, 695 P.2d 653 (Cal.1985) ("Surely, a landowner should not get one free assault before he can be held liable for criminal acts which occur on his property."); Killebrew v. Sun Trust Banks, Inc., 472 S.E.2d 504 (Ga.App.1996) (noting that prior similars rule would "create the equivalent of a 'one free bite rule' for premises liability cases").

[598] Compare Boren v. Worthen Nat'l Bank, 921 S.W.2d 934 (Ark.1996) (bank could not be held liable to customer for criminal attack at ATM machine absent proof of prior incidents at that location, despite evidence of robberies at other ATMs operated by bank) with Killebrew v. Sun Trust Banks, Inc., 472 S.E.2d 504, 506 (Ga.App.1996) (suggesting that given well-documented dangers associated with ATMs generally, "it would be difficult to say that a criminal occurrence at an ATM is unforeseeable as a matter of law"). While some decisions say that the landlord must be able to foresee criminal acts on the property and not merely in the "neighborhood," e.g., Scott v. Watson, 359 A.2d 548 (Md.1976), courts do routinely accept evidence of off-premises criminal activity, but only where it is probative of the foreseeability of the crime in question. See, e.g., Paterson v. Deeb, 472 So.2d 1210 (Fla.App.1985) (evidence that neighborhood was experiencing increasing number of break-ins was relevant to foreseeability of sexual attack on tenant); Admiral's Port Condo. Ass'n, Inc. v. Feldman, 426 So.2d 1054 (Fla.App.1983) (evidence of prior crimes committed substantial distances away from the premises not probative of foreseeability); Martinko v. H-N-W Assocs., 393 N.W.2d 320 (Iowa 1986) (experience with criminal activity at defendant's malls in other cities and states not relevant to foreseeability of attack in question).

[599] Ann M. v. Pacific Plaza Shopping Ctr., 863 P.2d 207 (Cal.1993); Doe v. Prudential-Bache/A.G. Spanos Realty Partners, 492 S.E.2d 865 (Ga.1997); Timberwalk Apts., Partners, Inc. v. Cain, 972 S.W.2d 749, 757 (Tex.1998) ("vandalism to automobiles in an apartment complex's parking lot can be a serious concern, but it does not suggest the likelihood of sexual assault"). The Doe case is remarkable, because only a few months earlier, the Georgia Supreme Court held that the landlord's knowledge of prior burglaries in the complex made

could be foreseeable even in the absence of prior violent assaults.[600] For example, in Aaron v. Havens, where the rapist gained access to the tenant's apartment by means of a negligently designed and maintained fire escape, the court held that a jury could find the tenant's rape was foreseeable.[601] For this reason, some courts have articulated what has been called the "totality of the circumstances" test, under which foreseeability might be found from circumstances other than prior acts of the identical type.[602]

As litigation against landlords for criminal attacks exploded in volume, however, the "totality of the circumstances" test also received criticism. Some argued that it was "too broad a standard, effectively imposing an unqualified duty to protect [tenants or customers] in areas experiencing any significant level of criminal activity,"[603] and that it increasingly forced onto landlords costly policing burdens traditionally borne by public officials. Driven by these concerns, some courts have adopted a "balancing test" that "seeks to address the interests of both business proprietors and their customers by balancing the foreseeability of harm against the burden of imposing a duty to protect against the criminal acts of third persons."[604] This approach was articulated by the California Supreme Court in Ann M. v. Pacific Plaza Shopping Center,[605] which involved the rape of a shopping center tenant's employee who alleged that the landlord was negligent in failing to provide security guards in common areas of the center. The court held that "the scope of the duty is determined by balancing the foreseeability of the harm against the burden of the duty to be imposed. In cases where the burden of preventing future harm is great, a high degree of foreseeability may be required. On the other hand, in cases where there are strong policy reasons for preventing the harm, or the harm can be prevented by simple means, a lesser degree of foreseeability may be required."[606] After

---

it reasonable for landlord to anticipate other unauthorized entries, including an intrusion that resulted in the tenant-plaintiff's rape. See Sturbridge Partners. Ltd. v. Walker, 482 S.E.2d 339 (Ga.1997). The *Doe* court acknowledged the ruling in *Sturbridge*, but ruled the prior crimes in *Doe* were only "thefts from automobiles" and "acts of vandalism" that did not suggest the risk of personal injury. *Doe*, 492 S.E.2d at 867. See also Walker v. Harris, 924 S.W.2d 375 (Tex.1996) (stabbing of apartment guest at apartment complex was not foreseeable from four prior incidents of vandalism).

[600] See, e.g., Jardel Co., Inc. v. Hughes, 523 A.2d 518 (Del.1987) (rejecting landlord's view that foreseeability require proof of prior violent assault; noting that property crimes can turn violent, can involve weapons, and thus frequency of criminal activity may be sufficient to place landlord on notice of the risk of personal injury as well as property loss); Galloway v. Bankers Trust Co., 420 N.W.2d 437 (Iowa 1988) (no prior sexual assaults at the mall, but jury was allowed to consider evidence of prior property crimes, several of which had involved weapons, and two of which had involved attacks on mall security guards); Erickson v. Curtis Invst. Co., 447 N.W.2d 165 (Minn.1989) (no prior sexual assault in parking ramp, but "the jury might consider the likelihood of the appreciable increase in criminal activity [in the ramp] breeding crimes of violence"); Aaron v. Havens, 758 S.W.2d 446 (Mo.1988) (discussed in text).

[601] *Aaron*, 758 S.W.2d at 447–48 ("If a private apartment can be entered through a window, injury to the occupants is foreseeable. . . . It is not necessary to allege that past crimes involving entry into unauthorized places are of the same general nature as the one which gives rise to the claim. If a burglar may enter, so may a rapist.").

[602] See, e.g., Isaacs v. Huntington Memorial Hospital, 695 P.2d 653, 659 (Cal.1985) ("foreseeability is determined in light of all the circumstances and not by a rigid application of a mechanical 'prior similars' rule"; only the general nature of the harm must be foreseeable, not "its precise nature or manner of occurrence"); Jardel Co., Inc. v. Hughes, 523 A.2d 518 (Del.1987); Sharp v. W.H. Moore, Inc., 796 P.2d 506 (Idaho 1990); Rowe v. State Bank of Lombard, 531 N.E.2d 1358 (Ill.1988); Galloway v. Bankers Trust Co., 420 N.W.2d 437 (Iowa 1988); Seibert v. Vic Regnier Builders, Inc., 856 P.2d 1332 (Kan.1993); Small v. McKennan Hospital, 403 N.W.2d 410 (S.D.1987).

[603] McClung v. Delta Square Ltd. Partn., 937 S.W.2d 891 (Tenn.1996).

[604] Posecai v. Wal-Mart Stores, Inc., 752 So.2d 762 (La.1999).

[605] 863 P.2d 207 (Cal.1993).

[606] *Ann M.*, 863 P.2d at 215 (citations omitted).

noting the significant expense of security guards and the uncertainty of how much security is necessary to deter criminal activity, the court held:

> [W]e conclude that a high degree of foreseeability is required in order to find that the scope of a landlord's duty of care includes the hiring of security guards. We further conclude that the requisite degree of foreseeability rarely, if ever, can be proven in the absence of prior similar incidents of violent crime on the landowner's premises. To hold otherwise would be to impose an unfair burden upon landlords and, in effect, would force landlords to become the insurers of public safety, contrary to well established policy in this state.[607]

The court held that while the plaintiff had alleged prior assaults and robberies had occurred, she had offered no evidence that the landlord had notice of those assaults, and that the alleged prior incidents were "not similar in nature to the violent assault that she suffered."[608] The court did note, however, that the attack occurred in the tenant's retail store rather than a parking garage or an all-night convenience store—which at least suggests that some locations might be sufficiently inherently dangerous to require security guards, even absent proof of prior similar incidents.[609] Further, while the trial court had allowed the tenant to introduce evidence regarding the presence of transients in the area and crime rates in the surrounding neighborhood, the court held that these were not sufficient to establish the high foreseeability necessary to impose a duty to provide security guards.[610] Courts in several other states have adopted the balancing approach reflected in *Ann M.*[611]

The potentially complicated nature of this balancing is reflected in a subsequent California decision, Castaneda v. Olsher,[612] where a mobile harm park tenant was shot and injured by another tenant who was a gang member. The injured tenant sued the landlord claiming that the landlord had breached its duty not to rent to gang members and to evict gang members that were harassing other residents, and that these breaches were the cause of the tenant's injury. The California Supreme Court upheld the dismissal of the tenant's action, concluding that:

> Landlords, including mobilehome park owners, ordinarily have no duty to reject prospective tenants they believe, or have reason to believe, are gang members. To recognize such a duty would tend to encourage arbitrary housing discrimination and would place landlords in the untenable situation of facing potential liability whichever choice they make about a prospective tenant. With regard to eviction, we agree that a residential tenant's behavior and known

---

[607] *Ann M.*, 863 P.2d at 215–16 (citations omitted).

[608] In this respect, the decision gives new life to the "prior similars" rule. The California Supreme Court had rejected that rule in Isaacs v. Huntington Memorial Hospital, 695 P.2d 653 (Cal.1985), but the *Ann M.* court re-embraced it—stating that *Isaacs* was an inappropriate case to have rejected the rule because the landlord in *Isaacs* knew or should have known of numerous prior violent third-party attacks on the premises. *Ann M.*, 863 P.2d at 215.

[609] *Ann M.*, 863 P.2d at 216 n.8. Six years later, however, in Sharon P. v. Arman, Ltd., 989 P.2d 121 (Cal.1999), the California Supreme Court held that an underground parking structure is not so inherently dangerous so as to impose a duty on the landlord to provide security guards in the absence of prior similar incidents.

[610] *Ann M.*, 863 P.2d at 216.

[611] E.g., Posecai v. Wal-Mart Stores, Inc., 752 So.2d 762 (La.1999); McClung v. Delta Square Ltd. Partn., 937 S.W.2d 891 (Tenn.1996); Krier v. Safeway Stores 46, Inc., 943 P.2d 405 (Wyo.1997).

[612] 162 P.3d 610 (Cal.2007). The court stated that a screening obligation would be warranted only in "circumstances making gang violence extraordinarily foreseeable." 162 P.3d at 618.

criminal associations may, in some circumstances, create such a high level of foreseeable danger to others that the landlord is obliged to take measures to remove the tenant from the premises or bear a portion of the legal responsibility for injuries the tenant subsequently causes. In the present case, however, the facts known to [tenant] did not make a violent gang confrontation involving these tenants so highly foreseeable as to justify imposition of a duty to undertake eviction proceedings.[613]

The court noted that the tenant had introduced evidence of two prior shooting incidents, but only one that was clearly gang-related, and further noted that no one had reported that the shooter or any other resident of the shooter's unit had used, displayed, or possessed a gun on the property.

Other Issues

The vast majority of the criminal-injury cases involve personal injuries or death to tenants or others by assault, rape, and murder. Would the tenant be able to recover for the tenant's loss of property (e.g., property lost due to theft by an intruder who gained access to the premises because of a defective lock)? There is no reason in principle for analyzing the landlord's liability differently for a property loss as compared to a personal injury; many of the reported cases involve robbery as well as assault, and courts have not paid special attention to that fact in determining liability. One California decision holds that a commercial landlord had no duty to protect the tenant's personal property from foreseeable criminal activity,[614] but the decision is dubious,[615] and the weight of case authority suggests that tenants can recover for property loss in appropriate circumstances.[616] If a theft in a tenant's apartment is committed by an employee of the landlord, liability for property loss may also be predicated upon the landlord's position as employer. Courts have tended not to impose liability on the doctrine of respondeat superior, on the ground that acts of thievery are not within the scope of the employment. However, a landlord may be liable if the tenant can show that the landlord was negligent

---

[613] *Castaneda*, 162 P.3d at 613. See also Davenport v. D.M. Rental Props., Inc., 718 S.E.2d 188 (N.C.Ct.App.2011) (landlord did not have duty to tenant assault victim to screen potential tenants or to evict resident who attacked the tenant).

[614] Royal Neckwear Co., Inc. v. Century City, Inc., 205 Cal.App.3d 1146, 252 Cal.Rptr. 810 (1988) (commercial landlord does not owe a duty to its tenant "to safeguard that tenant's property from reasonably foreseeable criminal activity by third parties").

[615] Tenants (especially commercial tenants) will carry insurance against theft risks, but the mere act of carrying insurance does not imply a conscious choice by the tenant to waive the benefit of any legal duty the landlord might owe the tenant. Further, to the extent the landlord did owe and breach such a duty, the tenant's insurer would presumably be subrogated to the tenant's right to pursue a claim for negligence against the landlord. It is more plausible that a court might, in the context of a commercial lease, give effect to a clearly-drafted clause in which the tenant agreed to exculpate the landlord from liability for the tenant's lost property. The clauses commonly used in commercial leases more likely reflect an agreement between landlord and tenant to look to insurance as the exclusive source of recovery due to events such as theft.

[616] See, e.g., Blum v. Kauffman, 297 A.2d 48 (Del.1972); Center Mgmt. Corp. v. Bowman, 526 N.E.2d 228 (Ind.App.1988); Brichacek v. Hiskey, 401 N.W.2d 44 (Iowa 1987) (suggesting tenant could recover for value of stolen property if landlord was in breach of duty to provide adequate locks, but concluding tenant had failed to establish breach on the facts); Peacock's Inc. v. Shreveport Alarm Co., 510 So.2d 387 (La.Ct.App.1987); Vermes v. American Dist. Tel. Co., 251 N.W.2d 101 (Minn.1977); Braitman v. Overlook Terrace Corp., 346 A.2d 76 (N.J.1975); Richmond Medical Supply Co. v. Clifton, 369 S.E.2d 407 (Va.1988) (recognizing possibility of liability and remanding for trial).

Some courts have denied the tenant recovery for property loss on the ground that the theft was not foreseeable. E.g., Hilligoss v. Cross Cos., 228 N.W.2d 585 (Minn.1975). Others have denied the tenant recovery on causation grounds. E.g., Sakhai v. 411 East 57th St. Corp., 272 A.D.2d 231, 707 N.Y.S.2d 630 (2000) (claim that inadequate security measures permitted burglary entailed "speculation").

in hiring, supervising, or retaining an untrustworthy employee or maintained an inadequate policy regarding master keys.[617]

In general, landlords may be liable to commercial tenants (or their employees or customers) as well as to residential tenants for injuries due to foreseeable criminal activity.[618] However, as a practical matter, there are several reasons that these cases more frequently involve residential tenants than commercial tenants. First, courts' special concern for the welfare of residential tenants is well-known and has some effect, though hard to quantify. Second, the implied and statutory warranties of habitability, which have in some cases been the basis for a landlord's duty to secure residential premises against criminal intrusion, are typically not available to commercial tenants. However, commercial tenants may more frequently obtain express landlord repair covenants, which can be the basis for a duty to secure the premises.[619] Finally, in commercial lease agreements, it is more likely that the parties have agreed to (and that a court will enforce) comprehensive clauses involving exculpation of liability, insurance, indemnification, and waivers of subrogation rights. For this reason, many of the cases involving commercial landlords involve claims brought by victims who are employees or customers of tenants (who are nonparties to such agreements).

G. ANNEXATION OF BUILDINGS AND IMPROVEMENTS

§ 6.48   OWNERSHIP AND REMOVAL OF THINGS ANNEXED

During the lease term, the tenant may erect new buildings or other permanent improvements on the premises or install new components or chattels into the existing buildings or improvements. Such additions may be a form of waste if the tenant makes them wrongfully,[620] but we assume here that the lease permits them or the landlord has otherwise consented. Does the tenant now own the additions, so that the tenant may remove them at or before the end of the term? This question involves the subject of fixtures law; here, we explore only those aspects that pertain especially to landlord and tenant. Moreover, we will not consider the effect of lease clauses covering ownership and removal other than to observe that such clauses are common in leases, they generally control when they exist, and any well-drafted lease should address ownership and removal of fixtures explicitly.

By the doctrine of "accession," if one person affixes chattels to land owned by another under such circumstances that the law will not permit their removal, ownership of the chattels passes to the landowner.[621] In these circumstances, the law categorizes

---

[617] E.g., Center Mgmt. Corp. v. Bowman, 526 N.E.2d 228 (Ind.App.1988) (landlord breached duty to protect tenants from wrongful entry by landlord's employees, liable for tenant's property lost in burglary); Annot., 38 A.L.R.4th 240 (1985).

[618] Samson v. Saginaw Professional Bldg., Inc., 224 N.W.2d 843 (Mich.1975) (landlord liable to employee of tenant of office building); Richmond Medical Supply Co. v. Clifton, 235 Va. 584, 369 S.E.2d 407 (1988) (landlord may be liable to commercial tenant for theft; remanded for trial); Annot., 43 A.L.R.3d 331, 363 (1972).

[619] See Richmond Medical Supply Co. v. Clifton, 369 S.E.2d 407 (Va.1988) (express covenant to repair a defective door created duty).

[620] 1 Am. Law of Prop. § 3.39 (1952).

[621] See, e.g., DeAngelo v. Brazauskas, 210 A.D.2d 989, 620 N.Y.S.2d 692 (1994); 5 Am. Law of Prop. §§ 19.1–19.3 (1952). Cf. U.C.C. § 9–102(a)(41) (" 'Fixtures' means goods that have become so related to particular real property than an interest in them arises under real property law.").

the annexed chattels as "fixtures" (not to be confused with a tenant's "trade fixtures"). Courts use a facts-and-circumstances test to determine whether a chattel constitutes a fixture, with the cases focusing on the following elements: (1) the degree to which the chattel is firmly imbedded in or connected to the realty (including the extent to which removal of the chattel would damage it or the realty); (2) the degree to which the chattels are peculiarly adapted or fitted to the particular realty; and (3) the intent of the person annexing the chattel to the land (which is informed to some extent by the nature of the annexor's interest in the realty).[622] Because the parties' actual intent is often unknown or disputed, one must "filter" the other factors, which are the real determinants, through some synthesized intent.

When a tenant installs chattels that may be fixtures upon the premises, the second factors (adaptation) and the third (the tenant's intent) are likely to be crucial to the determination.[623] Traditional English law, and certainly American law, have long been liberal in allowing a tenant to remove so-called "trade fixtures."[624] A trade fixture—strictly speaking an item used by a tenant in a trade or business on the premises[625]—may almost always be removed, up to the point that removal would do serious damage to the realty.[626] Courts have allowed such tenants to remove very substantial items, even buildings and large objects installed in a building.[627] Moreover, courts commonly include under the trade fixture umbrella items that may not strictly be used in a business but that may be for domestic use or only ornamental.[628] Thus, commercial tenants are likely

---

[622] See 5 Am. Law of Prop. §§ 19.1–19.3 (1952); 5 R. Powell, Real Property §§ 651, 652 (rev. ed.1990); 2 H. Tiffany, Real Property §§ 606–611 (3d ed.1939).

[623] As to the adaptation factor, the greater the degree of adaptation of the chattel to the realty, the less likely it is that the annexor could make meaningful use of the chattel elsewhere if removed. As to the intent factor, the leading fixture case, Teaff v. Hewitt, 1 Ohio St. 511 (1853), articulated that the intent of the annexor is to be judged at the time of annexation. While courts customarily follow this statement, it creates some awkwardness given that the intent of contracting parties is customarily judged at the time of contracting—in this context, that would be when the parties entered into the lease, not when the tenant annexed a chattel to the premises. See 5 Thompson on Real Property § 46.02(b)(3) (2d Thomas ed.2007). In any event, in the landlord-tenant context, with the exception of long-term leases, the intent factor militates more or less in favor of removability. The shorter the time the leasehold has to run, the shorter the period in which a tenant could expect to benefit from the fixture—and thus the more likely that the parties would expect for the tenant to be able to remove it at the end of the term.

[624] See Poole's Case, 91 Eng. Rep. 320 (1703); Van Ness v. Pacard, 27 U.S. (2 Pet.) 137, 7 L.Ed. 374 (1829); Curry Invst. Co. v. Santilli, 494 S.W.3d 18 (Mo.App.2016); Handler v. Horns, 65 A.2d 523 (N.J.1949); Ballard v. Alaska Theater Co., 161 P. 478 (Wash.1916); Old Line Life Ins. Co. v. Hawn, 275 N.W. 542 (Wis.1937).

[625] See Poole's Case, 91 Eng. Rep. 320 (1703) (justifying the removal of trade fixtures by the encouragement of industry and the effective use of commercial property).

[626] For example, even wind turbine towers have been treated as trade fixtures. E.g., AUI Constr. Group, LLC v. Vaessen, 67 N.E.3d 500 (Ill.App.2016). If substantial and unrepairable damage would be done to the premises, however, the tenant may not remove even trade fixtures. Jim Walter Window Components v. Turnpike Dist. Center, 642 S.W.2d 3 (Tex.App.1982) (electrical equipment was trade fixture that might be removed when slight damage from removal could be repaired); Connelly v. Art & Gary, Inc., 630 S.W.2d 514 (Tex.App. 1982) (sign was not trade fixture and could not be removed when it would leave concrete footing and iron pipe in ground).

[627] See, e.g., Van Ness v. Pacard, 27 U.S. (2 Pet.) 137, 7 L.Ed. 374 (1829) (house); Alabama Farmers Coop., Inc. v. Jordan, 440 Fed. Appx. 463 (6th Cir. 2011) (greenhouses on farmland); LaFarge Bldg. Materials, Inc. v. Stribling, 880 So.2d 415 (Ala.2003) (structures associated with concrete plant); City of Wichita v. Denton, 294 P.3d 207 (Kan.2013) (billboard structure); Cameron v. Oakland County Gas & Oil Co., 269 N.W. 227 (Mich.1936) (service station buildings); Ballard v. Alaska Theater Co., 161 P. 478 (Wash.1916) (built-in theater pipe organ, etc.); Old Line Life Ins. Co. v. Hawn, 275 N.W. 542 (Wis.1937) (small farm buildings, furnace).

[628] See Old Line Life Ins. Co. v. Hawn, 275 N.W. 542 (Wis.1937) (furnace used in farm home).

to be able to remove chattels they annex.[629] The tenant may not remove ordinary building materials incorporated into an existing structure, such as bricks, nails, and lumber used in repairs.[630] Nor is removal likely if it would cause major irreparable damage to the land. When a tenant is allowed to remove chattels, the tenant must repair physical damage caused by the removal.[631]

Absent a contrary agreement, the tenant must exercise the right to remove any annexations during the lease term; if the tenant does not timely remove, the tenant loses that right.[632] Courts have allowed the tenant to remove after the lease term in cases where the tenant remains in possession,[633] particularly when that possession continues during negotiations for a new lease that was not completed prior to the expiration of the term.[634] Under the weight of modern authority, the tenant may also remove annexations during the period of a renewal lease.[635] Courts have split as to whether the tenant may remove annexations following termination of the lease due to tenant breach; some allow tenant a reasonable period of time for removal,[636] while others hold the tenant loses the right of removal after termination.[637]

§ 6.49 PAYMENT FOR ANNEXATIONS

In some cases, a tenant must leave behind those annexed items that the tenant cannot legally remove under the principles discussed above. Absent a binding promise to do so, the landlord is under no duty to pay for these annexations.[638] The practical implication is that in any lease in which substantial tenant improvements are foreseeable, the lease should include express provisions governing removal, payment, and other details.

---

[629] Further, any ambiguity in the lease with regard to removability of a trade fixture will typically be resolved in the tenant's favor. E.g., H. Allen Holmes, Inc. v. Jim Molter, Inc., 127 So.3d 695 (Fla.App.2013) (presumption in favor of a tenant retaining its trade fixtures could only be overcome by a clear agreement to the contrary).

[630] In this circumstance, the building materials essentially lose their character as chattels as the construction process proceeds. Cf. U.C.C. § 9–334(a) ("A security interest does not exist . . . in ordinary building materials incorporated into an improvement on land.").

[631] The tenant's liability for damages is limited to physical damages to the realty caused by the removal, and does not include any diminution in value to the real estate caused solely by the absence of the affixed chattel. Cf. U.C.C. § 9–604(d).

[632] Wright v. Michelman, 141 N.E. 234 (Mass.1923); Annot., 109 A.L.R.5th 421 (2003).

[633] Restatement (Second) of Property-Landlord & Tenant § 12.3, Reporter's Note 4 (1977).

[634] Blackwell Printing Co. v. Blackwell Wielandy Co., 440 S.W.2d 433 (Mo.1969); Restatement (Second) of Property-Landlord & Tenant § 12.3, Reporter's Note 8 (1977); Annot., 6 A.L.R.2d 322 (1949).

[635] Restatement (Second) of Property-Landlord & Tenant § 12.3, Comment j (1977). At one time, many courts held that if a tenant renewed a lease without expressly reserving the right to remove annexations made during the original term, the new lease resulted in a surrender of the old lease and thus tenant lost the right to remove annexations. E.g., Wadman v. Burke, 81 P. 1012 (Cal.1905); Teddy Rose Enters., Inc. v. Hartford Fire Ins. Co., 427 A.2d 1081 (Md.App.1981); Loughran v. Ross, 45 N.Y. 792 (1871). New York has abrogated this result by statute, N.Y. Real Prop. Law § 226–a, and numerous court decisions permit removal in this situation. E.g., Handler v. Horns, 65 A.2d 523 (N.J.1949).

[636] E.g., Shepard v. Alden, 201 N.W. 537 (Minn.1924). See also Eun Bok Lee v. Ho Chang Lee, 411 S.W.3d 95 (Tex.App.2013) (landlord's retention of trade fixtures despite tenant's objection after termination of lease constituted unjust enrichment of landlord).

[637] E.g., Cabana, Inc. v. Eastern Air Control, Inc., 487 A.2d 1209 (Md.App.1985). The Restatement requires that removal must occur prior to termination due to tenant breach, "unless equitable considerations justify some extension of time." Restatement (Second) of Property-Landlord & Tenant § 12.3(1) & Comment d (1977).

[638] Hughes v. Kershow, 93 P. 1116 (Colo.1908) (by implication); Najewitz v. City of Seattle, 152 P.2d 722 (Wash.1944).

H. RENT AND SECURITY

§ 6.50 DUTY TO PAY RENT

The payment of rent is not essential to the existence of a leasehold, which may (like other estates) arise gratuitously. If the parties agree that the tenant shall pay no rent, none is due.[639] Normally, rent is due upon an express agreement for it, the strongest form of agreement being a covenant to pay and not merely a clause reserving rent.[640] Commercial leases often contain elaborate, lengthy provisions for rent and attendant matters, the interpretation of which has generated volumes of litigation beyond the scope of this treatise. In the absence of any agreement for or against rent, one who permissively occupies another's land generally owes the reasonable value of the occupancy absent circumstances negating such liability.[641] No such rent is owed if the circumstances negate such intent, as where an employee occupies as part of the employee's duties or where a contract purchaser goes into possession prior to closing and the sale later closes.[642] There also is a question whether the owner's recovery should be called "rent" or only "reasonable use value." The Restatement takes the position it is not rent, but some decisions label the recovery "rent," apparently on the theory that the implied agreement is one for rent.[643]

Absent contrary agreement, rent accrues (i.e., becomes payable) at the end of the term (or, in the case of a periodic tenancy, at the end of a period).[644] This means that rent is not apportionable (i.e., it does not accrue day to day) in the event the lease is prematurely terminated. For example, suppose that landlord terminated the lease due to tenant default during the middle of a period—fifteen days after tenant's last payment was due, and fifteen days before the next payment was due. In this situation, the landlord could not prorate and collect rent for the two weeks tenant had possession prior

---

[639] See Altman v. Alaska Truss & Mfg. Co., 677 P.2d 1215 (Alaska 1983) (tenant does not owe rent if parties tacitly agree none is due, but rent becomes due if landlord later demands it); Pinnell v. Woods, 121 S.W.2d 679 (Ky.App.1938); Enslein v. Enslein, 82 N.E.2d 555 (Ohio App.1948); Najewitz v. City of Seattle, 152 P.2d 722 (Wash.1944).

[640] When there exists only a reservation of rent, the tenant's liability for rent arises based purely on privity of estate. By contrast, where there is an express covenant to pay rent, the tenant's liability arises based on privity of contract. If there exists only a reservation of rent and no express covenant to pay rent, courts have held that assignment of the leasehold releases the original tenant from paying rent. See, e.g., Consumers' Ice Co. v. Bixler, 35 A. 1086 (Md.1896).

[641] Restatement (Second) of Property-Landlord & Tenant § 12.1, Comment b & Reporter's Note 4 (1977). There is some question about the mechanism by which this occurs. A 1738 English statute allowed the owner of land to recover reasonable use value from one who occupied it without an express agreement for rent. 11 Geo. 2, c.19, § 14 (1738). Many American states have similar statutes, some based on URLTA § 1.401(b) (1972) ("fair rental value") or MRLTC § 2–301 (1969). 1 Am. Law of Prop. § 3.64, n.2 (1952). In other jurisdictions there is, by judicial rule, an implied contractual duty to pay reasonable use value. See, e.g., Lazarus v. Phelps, 152 U.S. 81, 14 S.Ct. 477, 38 L.Ed. 363 (1894); Gunn v. Scovil, 4 Day 228 (Conn.1810); Webb v. Young, 338 So.2d 767 (La.App.1976); Dwight v. Cutler, 3 Mich. 566 (1855); Enslein v. Enslein, 82 N.E.2d 555 (Ohio App.1948).

[642] See Carpenter v. United States, 84 U.S. (17 Wall.) 489, 21 L.Ed. 680 (1873) (contract purchaser); Najewitz v. City of Seattle, 152 P.2d 722 (Wash.1944) (employee). If a sale fails to close, however, the contract purchaser usually owes reasonable rental value for the period of occupancy. Webb v. Young, 338 So.2d 767 (La.App.1976).

[643] Compare Restatement (Second) of Property-Landlord & Tenant § 12.1, Comment b and Reporter's Note 4 (1977) with Carpenter v. United States, 84 U.S. (17 Wall.) 489, 494, 21 L.Ed. 680 (1873) ("reasonable rent") and Enslein v. Enslein, 82 N.E.2d 555 (Ohio App.1948) ("reasonable rental").

[644] First Nat'l Bank v. Omaha Nat'l Bank, 214 N.W.2d 483 (Neb.1974); Bernard v. Triangle Music Co., 95 P.2d 43 (Wash.1939).

to the termination.[645] However, some courts and the Restatement allow for the apportionment of rent if the lease is terminated prematurely,[646] as does the Uniform Residential Landlord and Tenant Act.[647] Again, a well-drafted lease moots these issues by explicitly addressing the timing of the tenant's payment obligations and the impact of premature termination. Finally, unless the parties agree otherwise, where more than one tenant makes the leasing agreement, each tenant is jointly liable for rent.[648]

§ 6.51   PERCENTAGE RENT CLAUSES

In commercial leases for retail stores, it is common for part (or perhaps all) of the rent to be expressed as a percentage of the tenant's sales on the premises. In this way, the landlord shares in the tenant's good (or bad) fortune. Further, percentage rent gives the landlord a built-in rent adjustment in the form of a hedge against inflation; as the tenant's prices (and thus the dollar value of its sales) increase with a general rise in prices, the rent should increase accordingly. Percentage rental is usually based on the tenant's "gross sales" rather than "net sales"; gross sales is far preferable because the landlord can compute it with greater certainty and less controversy than net sales. The most common formula establishes a fixed minimum rent, plus a percentage on all sales over a stated amount typically called the "breakpoint" (e.g., $25,000 plus 2% of gross sales exceeding $2,000,000"). Not only is a well-drafted percentage rent clause a finely-tuned, sophisticated piece of drafting, it is often accompanied by further clauses designed to protect the landlord's expectations regarding the tenant's sales. These may include covenants requiring the tenant to maintain operations and keep minimum store hours and inventory levels, noncompetition provisions, and provisions allowing the landlord to review (or "audit") the tenant's sales figures.[649]

Percentage rent clauses are unquestionably legally enforceable; courts tend to enforce their language broadly in favor of landlords.[650] Litigation about such clauses is usually over their specific interpretation (e.g., are certain types of transactions included within the tenant's gross sales?)[651] or over the question whether a percentage rent clause

---

[645] E.g., Baker v. Eilers Music Co., 146 P. 1056 (Cal.App.1915).

[646] E.g., Deringer v. Pappas, 164 So.2d 569 (Fla.App.1964); Restatement (Second) of Property-Landlord & Tenant § 12.1, Comment e (1977).

[647] URLTA § 1.401(c) (1972).

[648] E.g., Libby v. Perry, 311 A.2d 527 (Me.1973); Sentliffer v. Jacobs, 86 A. 929 (N.J.1913). This result is explained by the principles governing the obligations of joint contractual promisors. See 4 Corbin, Contracts §§ 925, 926, 928 (1951).

[649] For background on percentage rent, practical tips, and forms, see Berman, 1 Friedman on Leases §§ 6.1–6.14 (6th ed.2017); Colbourn, A Guide to Problems in Shopping Center Leases, 29 Brooklyn L.Rev. 56 (1962); Kranzdorf, Problems of the Developer, 1965 U.Ill.L.F. 173, 187–88, 197–99; Note, 61 Harv.L.Rev. 317 (1948).

[650] See, e.g., Gamble-Skogmo, Inc. v. McNair Realty Co., 98 F.Supp. 440 (D.Mont.1951), aff'd, 193 F.2d 876 (9th Cir.1952); Professional Building of Eureka, Inc. v. Anita Frocks, Inc., 178 Cal.App.2d 276, 2 Cal.Rptr. 914 (1960); Cissna Loan Co. v. Baron, 270 P. 1022 (Wash.1928).

[651] For example, consider the sale of lottery tickets. A store that sells a $1 lottery ticket receives $1 from the ticket buyer, but the store's agreement with the state may require the store to remit 97% of ticket sales to the state; thus, the store only keeps 3%. If the store lease requires percentage rent of 4% of gross sales—and gross sales includes every dollar paid by ticket buyers—the store would lose a penny on every lottery ticket sold. In this situation, a store tenant may negotiate for the lease to define "gross sales" to include only the gross amount retained by the tenant on account of lottery ticket sales. Failure to do so may result in litigation, though the weight of authority in these cases has favored the tenant. See., e.g., In re Circle K Corp., 98 F.3d 484 (9th Cir. 1996) (interpreting "gross sales" to include only tenant's commission on lottery ticket sales); Anest v. Bellino, 503 N.E.2d 576 (Ill.App.1987) (same); Hartig Drug Co. v. Hartig, 602 N.W.2d 794 (Iowa 1999) (same); Cloverland Farms Dairy, Inc. v. Fry, 587 A.2d 527 (Md.App.1991) (same).

implies further covenants in aid of percentage rental. For instance, does the existence of a percentage rent clause imply that the tenant will keep long business hours, not open a nearby competing business, or otherwise conduct the business so as to maximize sales when the lease contains no express undertakings of these kinds? Case law has generally implied an operating covenant on the tenant when the lease provided for *only* percentage rent. or when the fixed minimum rent amount was nominal.[652] But when the lease provides for fixed minimum rent that is more than a nominal sum, the weight of judicial authority refuses to imply further covenants.[653] In a few notorious cases, courts have allowed a tenant to shut down operations and leave its space vacant (while paying only nominal rent) to prevent the landlord from placing a competitor in that space for the duration of the lease term—a practice referred to as "going dark."[654] A landlord that expects the tenant to operate and thereby generate substantial sales volume should not rely on a court to imply an operating covenant in future litigation, but should insist on an express operating covenant.

§ 6.52 RENT ADJUSTMENT CLAUSES

Many commercial leases may run for three to ten years or longer (including renewal or extension periods). A landlord likely will not agree to a fixed rent for such a long period of time without some formula for adjusting the rent upwards during the term to account for the risk of inflation and market changes. This is especially true in nonretail leases, in which percentage rent is not a meaningful option. Rental adjustment formulas are generally enforceable;[655] the problem is in the clear drafting of a formula that is workable and will not produce controversy. Obviously any formula should not depend on the discretion of either or both parties. One technique is to base rent adjustments on independent appraisals of the fair rental value of the premises at stated intervals during the term. This approach may match best with future changes in the local rental market, but it is expensive (often, these provisions require a panel of three professional appraisers) and cumbersome.[656] More frequently, the parties agree to adjust the rent periodically by reference to a generally available price index, such as the Department of Commerce Consumer Price Index. From an accuracy perspective, this is clearly a "second

---

[652] E.g., College Block v. Atlantic Richfield Co., 200 Cal.App.3d 524, 246 Cal.Rptr. 340 (1988); Pequot Spring Water Co. v. Brunelle, 698 A.2d 920 (Conn.App.1997); Sinclair Refining Co. v. Giddens, 187 S.E. 201 (Ga.App.1936); Columbia East Assocs. v. Bi-Lo, Inc., 386 S.E.2d 259 (S.C.App.1989); Ingannamorte v. Kings Super Mkts., Inc., 260 A.2d 841 (N.J.1970); Marvin Drug Co. v. Couch, 134 S.W.2d 356 (Tex.Civ.App.1939); Reeker v. Remour, 244 P.2d 270 (Wash.1952). These cases typically conclude that reasonable parties would have understood that if the tenant was agreeing to pay a rent amount based exclusively or predominantly on gross sales, the tenant impliedly agreed to operate business activity likely to generate gross sales.

[653] E.g., Scot Props., Ltd. v. Wal-Mart Stores, Inc, 138 F.3d 571 (5th Cir.1998) (Texas law); Rothe v. Revco, D.S., Inc., 976 F.Supp. 784 (S.D.Ind.1997); Percoff v. Solomon, 67 So.2d 31 (Ala.1953); Westside Ctr. Assocs. v. Safeway Stores 23, Inc., 42 Cal.App.4th 507, 49 Cal.Rptr.2d 793 (1996); Stop & Shop, Inc. v. Ganem, 200 N.E.2d 248 (Mass.1964); Mercury Inv. Co. v. F.W. Woolworth Co., 706 P.2d 523 (Okla.1985); Nalle v. Taco Bell Corp., 914 S.W.2d 685 (Tex.App.1996).

[654] E.g., Sampson Invs. v. Jondex Corp., 499 N.W.2d 177 (Wis.1993) ("[A] commercial lessee is not required to continue operating a business in the absence of a lease which expressly requires continuous operation."); Patrick A. Randolph, Jr., Going Dark Aggressively, 10 Prob. & Prop. (Nov.–Dec.1986), at 6. Professor Randolph correctly suggested that the trend in the cases favored the tenant, but there are also some landlord-favorable decisions. E.g., Lagrew v. Hooks-SupeRx, Inc., 905 F.Supp. 401 (E.D.Ky.1995); BVT Lebanon Shopping Ctr., Ltd. v. Wal-Mart Stores, Inc., 48 S.W.3d 132 (Tenn.2001).

[655] McMillan v. Great Northern Rwy. Co., 278 P.2d 316 (Wash.1954).

[656] In addition, some landlords and tenants are reluctant to agree to appraisal provisions because of concerns that courts will not engage in any review of the appraisers' decision as erroneous, absent proof of fraud or bad faith. Rice v. Ritz Assocs, Inc., 447 N.E.2d 58 (N.Y.1983).

best" form of adjustment; the CPI is not an index of real estate values but of goods and services generally. Thus, a CPI adjustment may not accurately reflect the market value of the premises at the time of adjustment. However, many parties find use of a CPI adjustment provision superior given the cost and delay inherent in the appraisal method.[657] In other cases, the parties may provide for fixed rental increases (either in fixed dollar amounts or fixed percentage increases) at stated periodic intervals.

§ 6.53   RENT MODIFICATION AGREEMENTS

Like any contracting parties, the parties to a lease may expressly modify their covenants, including the rental covenant. The question is not whether they may do this, but how. Issues may include whether the modification agreement is supported by consideration and whether it must (or does) comply with the Statute of Frauds.

In principle an agreement to modify rent requires fresh consideration.[658] In practice, courts have often stretched to find the necessary consideration. When the agreement is to reduce rent, consideration may be present in the tenant's new promise to occupy the premises, to make repairs or improvements, to surrender a portion of the premises, or to waive an alleged breach of the lease by the landlord.[659] Some decisions even find consideration when the rent reduction is designed to alleviate a tenant's financial difficulties, reasoning it is worth something to the landlord to keep the tenant from abandoning the premises.[660] Other decisions, reasoning that such a tenant incurs no new legal liability, refuse to find consideration in these circumstances.[661] Cases involving rent increases are fewer in number; in these cases, consideration may be found in the landlord's agreement to extend the term, to waive an alleged tenant default, or to permit the tenant to use the land in some manner previously forbidden.[662]

A Statute of Frauds issue may arise if the original lease was in writing but the modification agreement is not. As Corbin noted, modification agreements really have a double aspect: they are both rescissions of part of the original agreement and new agreements for substituted provisions.[663] As to their rescission aspect, the Statute does not apply; absent a contrary provision in the original contract, a formal contract may be rescinded informally.[664] As to the substituted provisions, however, a Statute of Frauds problem can arise. If the original lease was both valid and informal—e.g., an oral lease for a term of one year or less—the parties could orally agree to modify the rent amount, unless the modification also extended the term so as to trigger the Statute. Likewise, even if the original lease was in writing, but the Statute would have allowed an oral lease (e.g., a lease for one year or less), the parties could orally modify the rent amount

---

[657] For further background on the drafting of CPI-based adjustment clauses, see generally 5 Thompson on Real Property § 44.04(c)(2) (2d Thomas ed.2007).

[658] United States v. Bostwick, 94 U.S. (4 Otto) 53, 24 L.Ed. 65 (1876); Green v. Millman Bros., Inc., 151 N.W.2d 860 (Mich.App.1967); Annot., 30 A.L.R.3d 1259, 1262–67 (1970).

[659] E.g., Cohen v. Homonoff, 41 N.E.2d 193 (Mass.1942) (occupancy); Segal v. M.H. Harris, Inc., 10 A.2d 748 (N.J.1940) (partial surrender); Natelsohn v. Reich, 50 Misc. 585, 99 N.Y.S. 327 (1906) (repairs); Annot., 30 A.L.R.3d 1259, 1278–86 (1970).

[660] E.g., William Lindeke Land Co. v. Kalman, 252 N.W. 650 (Minn.1934).

[661] E.g., Green v. Millman Bros., Inc., 151 N.W.2d 860 (Mich.App.1967); Levine v. Blumenthal, 186 A. 457 (N.J.1936), aff'd per curiam, 189 A. 54 (N.J.1937).

[662] E.g., Anderson v. Miller, 133 N.E. 29 (Ind.App.1921) (agreement not to terminate); Jensen v. Anderson, 167 P. 811 (Utah 1917) (increased use permitted). See Annot., 43 A.L.R. 1451, 1477–78 (1926).

[663] 2 Corbin, Contracts § 303 (1950).

[664] 2 Corbin, Contracts § 303 (1950); 4 Williston, Contracts § 592 (3d ed.1961).

absent a contrary agreement in the lease—except for the Statute, an oral and written agreement are of equal dignity.[665] When the Statute required the original lease to be in writing, it becomes critical how long the lease has to run at the date of the modification agreement. If this time is short enough that the Statute would allow an oral lease for that time period, then an oral modification for the balance of the term should be valid (again, absent a contrary provision in the original lease).[666] The cautious drafter will always put the modification agreement in writing any time the original lease was required to be in writing; some decisions make the sweeping statement that this is necessary.[667]

Even when a rent modification agreement falls under the Statute, noncompliance with the Statute may be excused. First, when the tenant has paid and the landlord has accepted modified rent under such an agreement, generally neither party may recover the difference between the amounts paid and the original rent.[668] Second, as to future rental payments under such an agreement, there is the possibility that agreement may be taken out of the Statute's operation by the doctrine of estoppel or part performance.[669]

§ 6.54   RENT ACCELERATION CLAUSES

A rent acceleration clause typically authorizes the landlord to advance the due date of future rent installments if the tenant defaults in the payment of rent or the performance of any other covenant.[670] One reason a landlord would include such a clause is that the contract doctrine of breach by anticipatory repudiation is problematic as applied to landlord and tenant.[671] The main advantage of an acceleration clause, however, is an important practical one. If the tenant is on the verge of default, the

---

[665] See Teal v. Bilby, 123 U.S. 572, 8 S.Ct. 239, 31 L.Ed. 263 (1887); Anderson v. Miller, 133 N.E. 29 (Ind.App.1921); Aris Indus., Inc. v. 1411 Trizechahn-Swig, LLC, 294 A.D.2d 107, 744 N.Y.S.2d 362 (2002); 2 Corbin, Contracts § 301 (1950).

[666] Tashjian v. Karp, 177 N.E. 816 (Mass.1931); Sherman Clay & Co. v. Buffum & Pendleton, Inc., 179 P. 241 (Or.1919); Restatement (Second) of Property-Landlord & Tenant § 2.4, Comment b (1977); 1 Am. Law of Prop. § 3.70 (1952).

[667] E.g., Bonicamp v. Starbuck, 106 P. 839 (Okla.1910); Vance Lumber Co. v. Tall's Travel Shops, Inc., 142 P.2d 904 (Wash.1943). In these decisions the theory, contrary to Corbin's, is that the modified provision is part of an agreement the whole of which is within the Statute.

[668] E.g., Central Sav. Bank v. Fashoda, Inc., 94 A.D.2d 927, 463 N.Y.S.2d 335 (1983), aff'd, 465 N.E.2d 367 (N.Y.1984); Bamberger Co. v. Certified Productions, 48 P.2d 489 (Utah 1935); Oregon & Wash. R.R. Co. v. Elliott Bay Mill & Lumber Co., 126 P. 406 (Wash.1912); Annot., 118 A.L.R. 1511 (1939).

[669] E.g., 3637 Green Rd. Co., Ltd. v. Specialized Component Sales Co., Inc., 69 N.E.3d 1083 (Ohio App.2016). See generally Restatement (Second) of Property-Landlord & Tenant § 2.3 (1977); 2 Corbin, Contracts § 308 (1950).

[670] Most rent acceleration clauses do not provide that acceleration is automatic upon default, but instead merely authorize the landlord to accelerate rent upon default at its option. This is sensible; otherwise, a landlord that accepted installment payments following a tenant's default risks waiving the acceleration clause. Contrast Hardin v. Kirkland Enters., Inc., 939 So.2d 40 (Ala.App.2006) (landlord did not waive right to collected unaccrued rent after eviction where landlord did not make a demand for payment pursuant to optional acceleration clause) with Snyder v. Exum, 315 S.E.2d 216 (Va.1984) (landlord that sued for unpaid installments, despite mandatory acceleration clause, could not later recover remaining unpaid rent balance).

[671] The problem is that if rent only accrues at the end of a term or period, as noted in Section 6.50 supra, a tenant's failure to pay a rent installment would not necessarily constitute a tenant's repudiation of the obligation to make timely payment of future installments. Most American courts now probably apply the anticipatory breach doctrine to leases. See Farmers & Bankers Life Ins. Co. v. St. Regis Paper Co., 456 F.2d 347 (5th Cir.1972); Hawkinson v. Johnston, 122 F.2d 724 (8th Cir.1941); Szabo Assocs., Inc. v. Peachtree Piedmont Assocs, 234 S.E.2d 119 (Ga.App.1977). However, the doctrine was not a traditional part of landlord-tenant law, and some courts have refused to apply it. E.g., Wells v. Twenty-First St. Realty Co., 12 F.2d 237 (6th Cir.1926); People ex rel. Nelson v. West Town State Bank, 25 N.E.2d 509 (Ill.1940).

landlord's threat to accelerate all future rent can be a powerful lever to induce strict compliance with the lease terms or to obtain a favorable modification of those terms.[672]

The potential power of this leverage gives rise to a legal argument against acceleration clauses. Most decisions on the question have upheld the validity of such clauses.[673] These decisions reason that parties have freedom to contract and could have agreed that the entire rent was due at the beginning of the term. A smaller group of decisions conclude that rent acceleration clauses constitute a penalty and refuse to enforce them.[674] The same question arises in testing the validity of a liquidated damages clause; indeed, acceleration clauses are viewed as a form of liquidated damages clause. Therefore, a court that is inclined to question an acceleration clause will be most upset by one that allows acceleration of a large amount of rent for minor breaches.[675] Even courts that generally enforce acceleration clauses will not allow the landlord both to terminate the leasehold and to recover the sum of accelerated rent for the balance of the term.[676]

§ 6.55 GOVERNMENT REGULATION OF RENT

Federal, state, or local governments sometimes legislatively control maximum rents to which residential landlords and tenants may agree. Although early rent control measures were driven by housing shortages during wartime, more modern rent control provisions began in the 1960s and 1970s in response to widespread inflation. Most of these are municipal regulations enacted by local governments under state enabling acts that specifically authorize local governments to enact rent control. In the absence of specific enabling legislation, there is a split of authority over whether local governments

---

[672] A rental acceleration clause can also prove useful in cases of the tenant's death or bankruptcy, which may require the landlord to file a claim against the tenant's intestate estate or bankruptcy estate by a specific date (after which claims would be barred).

[673] Maddox v. Hobbie, 152 So. 222 (Ala.1934); Aurora Bus. Park Assocs., L.P. v. Michael Albert, Inc., 548 N.W.2d 153 (Iowa 1996); Shepard Realty Co. v. United Shoe Stores Co., 190 So. 383 (La.1939); Cummings Props., LLC v. National Communications Corp., 869 N.E.2d 617 (Mass.2007); Belnord Realty Co. v. Levison, 204 A.D. 415, 198 N.Y.S. 184 (1923); Platt v. Johnson, 31 A. 935 (Pa.1895); Annot., 128 A.L.R. 750 (1940).

[674] Ricker v. Rombough, 261 P.2d 328 (Cal.App.1953); Nobles v. Jiffy Market Food Store Corp., 579 S.E.2d 63 (Ga.App.2003); 884 W. End Ave. Corp. v. Pearlman, 201 A.D. 12, 193 N.Y.S. 670 (1922), aff'd per curiam, 138 N.E. 458 (N.Y.1922); Patton v. Milwaukee Com. Bank, 268 N.W. 124 (Wis.1936). Note that there is some conflict in the New York decisions. E.g., Belnord Realty Co. v. Levison, 204 A.D. 415 (1923) (upholding acceleration clause). See also Frey v. Abdo, 441 So.2d 1383 (Miss.1983) (acceleration being harsh remedy, court will not find acceleration clause if language is not clear); Saladino v. Rault Petroleum Corp., 436 So.2d 714 (La.App.1983) (to accelerate, landlord had to comply strictly with notice provisions of lease).

[675] E.g., 172 Van Duzer Realty Corp. v. Globe Alumni Student Assistance Ass'n, Inc., 25 N.E.3d 952 (N.Y.2014) (tenant entitled to hearing as to whether collection of undiscounted accelerated rent was disproportionate to actual damages and thus unenforceable penalty); 884 W. End Ave. Corp. v. Pearlman, 201 A.D. 12, 193 N.Y.S. 670 (1922), aff'd per curiam, 138 N.E. 458 (N.Y.1922) (landlord's recovery of accelerated rent disproportionate to landlord's loss).

[676] See, e.g., 16 Cobalt LLC v. Harrison Career Inst., 590 F.Supp.2d 44 (D.D.C.2008); Maddox v. Hobbie, 152 So. 222 (Ala.1934); Geiger Mut. Agency, Inc. v. Wright, 233 So.2d 444 (Fla.App.1970); Chili Venture LLC v. Stahl, 54 Misc.3d 461, 39 N.Y.S.3d 735 (City Ct.2016) (acceleration clause under which evicted tenant was liable for future rent was unconscionable); Gentry v. Recreation, Inc., 7 S.E.2d 63 (S.C.1940); 1 Am. Law of Prop. § 3.74 (1952); Annot., 128 A.L.R. 750, 755 (1940). The Restatement takes the same position. Restatement (Second) of Property-Landlord & Tenant § 12.1, Comment k (1977). Where the tenant has abandoned the premises, some courts have allowed the landlord to enforce an acceleration clause, but require the landlord to credit the abandoning tenant with any rents collected from reletting the premises. E.g., Aurora Bus. Park Assocs., L.P. v. Michael Albert, Inc., 548 N.W.2d 153 (Iowa 1996); Caplan v. Latter & Blum, Inc., 462 So.2d 229 (La.App.1984), rev'd on other grounds, 468 So.2d 1188 (La.1985).

may adopt rent controls under their general police powers.[677] Rent controls exist today in roughly ten jurisdictions.[678]

In recent years, there has been a trend to abolish or curtail rent controls. In 1995, a California statute effectively prohibited local rent controls for housing units completed after the date of the statute.[679] A 1997 New Jersey statute made permanent a 1987 "experimental program" that had, with certain exceptions, abolished rent controls for newly constructed units for the lesser of 30 years or of the amortization period of mortgages on those units.[680] The Massachusetts "Rent Control Prohibition Act" of 1997 ended rent controls by cities and towns, with some exceptions for publicly owned or assisted housing, as of the end of the year 1996.[681] Effective August 1998, the Illinois legislature prohibited local rent controls.[682] And in New York, the Court of Appeals declared unconstitutional the provision of New York City's rent stabilization ordinance that required owners of rent-stabilized apartments to offer tenants renewal leases.[683]

The constitutionality of federal rent control during wartime was established by the Supreme Court in *Bowles v. Willingham* in 1944.[684] *Block v. Hirsh* upheld the constitutionality of the peacetime controls that existed in the District of Columbia following World War I.[685] There was once a question whether rent controls had to be justified by an emergency and thus had to be temporary.[686] However, the Supreme Court's decision in *Pennell v. City of San Jose* leaves no question that peacetime controls are constitutionally permissible in areas that have housing shortages.[687] The Court has also rejected an argument that the Berkeley, California, rent control ordinance violated the Federal Sherman Antitrust Act.[688] Nevertheless, a given rent control system may be challenged as a taking or perhaps as a denial of due process if it denies a particular landlord profitable use of the land.[689]

---

[677] E.g., Heubeck v. City of Baltimore, 107 A.2d 99 (Md.1954) (yes); Tietjens v. City of St. Louis, 222 S.W.2d 70 (1949) (no); Inganamort v. Borough of Fort Lee, 303 A.2d 298 (N.J.1973) (yes). The legal theories underlying the exercise of municipal powers are beyond the scope of this treatise.

[678] These include Alaska, California, Connecticut, District of Columbia, Florida, Maine, Maryland, Massachusetts, New Jersey, and New York. 5 Thompson on Real Property § 43.04(b)(2), at 411 (2d Thomas ed. 2007); see also Restatement (Second) of Property-Landlord & Tenant § 12.1, Statutory Note 4 (1977) (noting then-existing rent control legislation).

[679] Cal.Civ.Code § 1954.52.

[680] N.J.Stat.Ann. § 2A:42–84.2.

[681] Mass.Gen.Laws Ann. ch. 40P, §§ 1–5.

[682] Ill.Comp.Stat.Ann. ch. 50, § 825/5 (units of local government), § 10 (home rule units).

[683] Manocherian v. Lenox Hill Hospital, 643 N.E.2d 479 (N.Y.1994).

[684] Bowles v. Willingham, 321 U.S. 503, 64 S.Ct. 641, 88 L.Ed. 892 (1944).

[685] Block v. Hirsh, 256 U.S. 135, 41 S.Ct. 458, 65 L.Ed. 865 (1921).

[686] Teeval Co. v. Stern, 93 N.E.2d 884 (N.Y.1950); Meyers v. New York State Div. of Hous. & Community Renewal, 36 A.D.2d 166, 319 N.Y.S.2d 522 (1971).

[687] Pennell v. City of San Jose, 485 U.S. 1, 108 S.Ct. 849, 99 L.Ed.2d 1 (1988).

[688] Fisher v. City of Berkeley, 475 U.S. 260, 106 S.Ct. 1045, 89 L.Ed.2d 206 (1986).

[689] See Nash v. City of Santa Monica, 688 P.2d 894 (Cal.1984) (holding constitutional an ordinance that restricted landlord's ability to evict tenants or to demolish rental units; far-reaching decision); Birkenfeld v. City of Berkeley, 550 P.2d 1001 (1976); Westwinds Mobile Home Park v. City of Escondido, 30 Cal.App.4th 84, 35 Cal.Rptr.2d 315 (1994) (2.78% not fair rate of return); Orange Taxpayers Council, Inc. v. City of Orange, 416 A.2d 353 (N.J.1980) (ordinance valid, even though it allowed rent increase only when premises were in substantial compliance with housing codes); Helmsley v. Borough of Fort Lee, 394 A.2d 65 (N.J.1978) (to extent ordinance did not allow "reasonable return," it was void). For further discussion of when municipal regulation may constitute a taking or a denial of due process, see §§ 9.4 to 9.6 infra.

A different sort of rent regulation exists in states that have adopted residential landlord-tenant statutes with provisions prohibiting "retaliatory eviction." Going back to Edwards v. Habib[690] in 1968, decisions in several jurisdictions concluded it was against public policy for a landlord to attempt to evict a residential tenant to retaliate for the tenant's taking some action to enforce the landlord's duty to keep the premises habitable. A number of jurisdictions have since enacted residential landlord-tenant acts with similar but broader anti-retaliatory sections.[691] Both the Uniform Residential Landlord and Tenant Act and the Model Residential Landlord-Tenant Code contain such provisions.[692] These prohibit not only retaliatory evictions but also other kinds of retaliatory actions, including rent increases. Usually the statutes either create a presumption that a rent increase attempted after the tenant's action is retaliatory or prohibit a rent increase for a stated time after such action, with exceptions for certain bona fide increases.

§ 6.56 ACTIONS FOR RENT—ESTOPPEL TO DENY TITLE

Suppose that tenant takes possession of land pursuant to a lease and enjoys possession for six months, but then refuses to pay further rent because the tenant learns that the landlord lacks valid title to the land. If the landlord sues for rent, can the tenant raise a valid defense by establishing that the landlord's title is invalid? Generally speaking, no; a tenant that actually enjoys the bargained-for possession of the premises is estopped to defend by establishing a title adverse to the landlord's.[693] This statement requires some qualification. First, the estoppel is only as to the landlord's title at the inception of the lease; the tenant may assert that the landlord's title passed to a third person or even to the tenant after the term began.[694] Second, if the tenant is excluded or ousted from possession by someone with paramount title, this breaches the covenant of quiet enjoyment and gives the tenant a valid defense to the payment of rent that would have accrued thereafter.[695] Third, there is no estoppel if the landlord induced the tenant to make the lease by fraud or misrepresentation as to the landlord's title.[696]

§ 6.57 DISTRAINT AND STATUTORY LIENS

Under the ancient common-law right of "distraint" or "distress," the landlord could enter the premises and seize goods found there for the collection of unpaid rent—even goods being sold to the tenant on conditional sale and, with some limited exceptions, goods belonging to third persons![697] The seizure gave the landlord what amounted to a

---

[690] 397 F.2d 687 (D.C.Cir.1968), cert. denied, 393 U.S. 1016, 89 S.Ct. 618, 21 L.Ed.2d 560 (1969). *Edwards* has been followed by a number of other decisions around the country, e.g., Dickhut v. Norton, 173 N.W.2d 297 (Wis.1970).

[691] See Cunningham, The New Implied and Statutory Warranties of Habitability in Residential Leases: From Contract to Status, 16 Urban L.Ann. 3, 126–35 (1979).

[692] URLTA § 5.101 (1972); RURLTA § 901 (2015); MRLTC § 2–407 (1969).

[693] E.g., Merill v. DeMott, 951 P.2d 1040 (Nev.1997); Atlantic & East Carolina Rwy. Co. v. Wheatly Oil Co., Inc., 594 S.E.2d 425 (N.C.App.2004); Lund v. Gray Line Water Tours, Inc., 289 S.E.2d 404 (S.C.1982).

[694] E.g., Seivert v. Powell, 232 P.2d 806 (Or.1951) (conveyance by landlord to third person); Holzer v. Rhodes, 163 P.2d 811 (Wash.1945) (tenant purchased tax title after lease term commenced).

[695] See Section 6.31 supra.

[696] Williams v. Higgason, 53 S.E.2d 473 (Ga.1949); Gray v. Whitla, 174 P. 239 (Okla.1918); Annot., 2 A.L.R. 359 (1919).

[697] 1 Am. Law of Prop. § 9.47 (1952); Annot., 62 A.L.R. 1106, 1107–11 (1929).

common-law holding lien; the landlord could not sell the goods, but could hold them "hostage" until the tenant made up the rent default.[698]

Practically, common-law distraint no longer exists in American jurisdictions. A few jurisdictions never adopted it.[699] Others have refused to apply the doctrine, concluding that it has been expressly or impliedly abolished by statute.[700] Both the Uniform Residential Landlord and Tenant Act and the Model Residential Landlord-Tenant Code expressly abolish distraint.[701] In states where distress still exists, it is generally governed by statutes that more or less modify its common-law form.

Most jurisdictions have codified common-law distraint or replaced it with statutory landlords' liens.[702] Because the lien statutes vary from state to state, one must examine the statutes of a given state. These statutes commonly allow the landlord to assert a lien on growing crops; some allow a lien on the tenant's goods (but not on goods owned by third persons, goods the tenant is purchasing by conditional sale, or items sold to bona fide purchasers). The lien may secure rent or both rent and the tenant's other covenants. As the landlord's interest is limited to a lien, there will be procedures for foreclosure and sale. Some statutes provide for seizure of the tenant's goods by a public officer, by a procedure similar to pre-judgment attachment.

Especially when this last feature is present, there are serious questions about the constitutionality of landlords' lien statutes. The most likely objection is that expressed in Fuentes v. Shevin and Sniadach v. Family Finance Corporation—that seizure by state officers without a hearing deprives the tenant of property without due process of law.[703] Courts have struck down a number of landlords' lien statutes on this ground.[704] Even when the statute provides for seizure by the landlord rather than by state officers, so that state action is harder to find, several lien statutes have been held to deny due process.[705] Another possible constitutional objection is that invasion of the tenant's premises by a public officer, conceivably even by the landlord, amounts to an unreasonable search and seizure. Some courts have adopted this argument in pre-judgment replevin cases; some have rejected it.[706] Other courts have concluded that seizure without a prior hearing was contrary to public policy.[707] Both the Uniform

---

[698] See generally Henderson v. Mayer, 225 U.S. 631, 32 S.Ct. 699, 56 L.Ed. 1233 (1912); Jones v. Ford, 254 F. 645 (8th Cir.1918); Annot., 62 A.L.R. 1106 (1929), 2 Tiffany, Landlord & Tenant §§ 325–46 (1912).

[699] E.g., Jones v. Ford, 254 F. 645 (8th Cir.1918) (Missouri law); Heer v. Johnson, 18 P. 342 (Colo.1888); Howland v. Forlaw, 13 S.E. 173 (N.C.1891); 2 Tiffany, Landlord & Tenant § 325 (1912).

[700] See, e.g., Webb v. Sharp, 80 U.S. (13 Wall.) 14, 20 L.Ed. 478 (1871) (District of Columbia); P.F. Scheidelman & Sons, Inc. v. Webster Basket Co., 143 Misc. 836, 257 N.Y.S. 552 (Sup.1932), aff'd, 236 A.D. 774, 259 N.Y.S. 963 (1932). See also, e.g., Minn.Stat.Ann. § 504B.101; Or.Rev.Stat. § 91.835.

[701] URLTA § 4.205(b); MRLTC § 3–403(2).

[702] For a list of statutes, see Restatement (Second) of Property-Landlord & Tenant § 12.1, Statutory Note 5 (1977) (identifying lien statutes from 28 jurisdictions and noting 16 others with statutes codifying distraint).

[703] Fuentes v. Shevin, 407 U.S. 67, 92 S.Ct. 1983, 32 L.Ed.2d 556 (1972), rehearing denied, 409 U.S. 902, 93 S.Ct. 177, 34 L.Ed.2d 165 (1972) (pre-judgment replevin); Sniadach v. Family Finance Corp., 395 U.S. 337, 89 S.Ct. 1820, 23 L.Ed.2d 349 (1969) (pre-judgment garnishment).

[704] See Annot., 18 A.L.R. Fed. 223, 276–80 (1974); Restatement (Second) of Property-Landlord & Tenant § 12.1, Reporter's Note 12 (1977).

[705] Hall v. Garson, 468 F.2d 845 (5th Cir.1972); Barber v. Rader, 350 F.Supp. 183 (S.D.Fla.1972). See also Gross v. Fox, 349 F.Supp. 1164 (E.D.Pa.1972), vacated, 496 F.2d 1153 (3d Cir.1974) (distraint statute).

[706] See Annot., 18 A.L.R. Fed. 223, 248–50 (1974).

[707] Cf. Bass v. Boetel & Co., 217 N.W.2d 804 (Neb.1974) (lease clause authorizing self-help seizure).

Residential Landlord and Tenant Act and the Model Residential Landlord-Tenant Code forbid the assertion of a statutory rent lien.[708]

§ 6.58 SECURITY AND DAMAGE DEPOSITS

Presumably on the theory of "a bird in the hand," the landlord frequently requires the tenant to deposit a sum of money with the landlord at the beginning of the term, as security for the tenant's lease obligations. A specialized form of security deposit is the so-called "damage deposit," which the landlord holds to cover the cost of repairing physical damage or perhaps extraordinary cleaning costs caused by the tenant's acts. It is common for leases to require one deposit to cover both rent and other damages. Lease clauses for cash security deposits are too varied to cover in detail, but they commonly establish one of three basic mechanisms: (1) the tenant deposits a sum against which the landlord may draw to make up any default or to pay for damage; (2) the tenant deposits a sum which is forfeited if the tenant defaults; or (3) the tenant makes a payment denominated "prepaid rent," usually for one or more rent periods at the end of the leasehold. We discuss each in turn, then take up some problems pertaining to security deposits generally.

The most common mechanism is for the tenant to deposit a sum of money with the understanding that the landlord may draw on that sum to apply against the tenant's obligations in case the tenant defaults and will return all sums not so drawn on at the end of the lease. Courts disagree over the proper characterization of the relationship between landlord and tenant with respect to the fund. Traditionally, most courts considered the deposit to create a "debt." Under this view, unless the lease or a statute provides otherwise, the tenant's deposit essentially constitutes a loan to the landlord—who becomes the owner of the funds, can commingle them with other monies, and can use them for any purposes subject only to the contractual duty to refund the deposit (less any properly withheld damages) at the end of the lease.[709] A few states regard the deposit as a "pledge" whereby the deposit remains the tenant's property.[710] Under the "debt" or "pledge" approaches, the landlord has no obligation to segregate the deposit from landlord's other funds or pay interest on it unless either the lease or a statute so requires.[711] In New York and several other states, by virtue of a statute, the landlord is a trustee of the deposit, which landlord may not commingle with landlord's own funds.[712]

---

[708] URLTA § 4.205(a) (1972); RURLTA § 603 (2015); MRLTC § 3.403(1) (1969). Compare Butters v. Jackson, 917 P.2d 87 (Utah App.1996) (contractual agreement in lease for landlord to have security interest in tenant's personal property was a valid security interest under UCC Article 9, even though the agreement did not satisfy the requirements of state's statutory lien).

[709] Henning & Freyermuth, Article 9 and the Characterization and Treatment of Tenant Security Deposits, 35 UALR L. Rev. 999, 1004–1011 (2013) (collecting, discussing, and criticizing cases following the "debt" approach).

[710] E.g., Rasmussen v. Helen Realty Co., 168 N.E. 717 (Ind.App.1929) (parties agreed deposit was "collateral"); Partington v. Miller, 5 A.2d 468 (N.J.1939).

[711] Under the pledge approach, however, if the landlord does invest the tenant's deposit and earns a return on it, the landlord must account to the tenant for that return. Ingram v. Pantages, 260 P. 395 (Cal.App.1927). Conceptually, the pledge approach is the correct approach—why else would the parties call it a "security" deposit?—and arguably it is codified by Article 9 of the Uniform Commercial Code. For further discussion, see Henning & Freyermuth, Article 9 and the Characterization and Treatment of Tenant Security Deposits, 35 UALR L. Rev. 999, 1004–1011 (2013).

[712] See Mallory Assocs. v. Barving Realty Co., 90 N.E.2d 468 (N.Y.1949); Ga.Code Ann. § 44–7–31; N.H.Rev.Stat.Ann. § 540–A:6; N.Y.Gen.Oblig.Law § 7–103; S.C.Code Ann. § 27–40–210.

Under any of these views, however, the landlord must account to the tenant for any amount that the landlord withdraws from the fund.[713]

A second form of security deposit clause is one that allows the landlord to retain the entire deposit if the tenant breaches in any way.[714] This is a liquidated damages mechanism, and a question arises as to whether such a provision may be declared void as a penalty. Decided cases go both ways on this question.[715] The correct approach, which seems to reconcile most of the decisions, is to begin with the principle that parties may agree for liquidated damages as long as the amount is "reasonable." To test reasonableness, we place ourselves in the position of the parties when they made their agreement and then ask whether, looking ahead, the amount provided for liquidated damages bore a reasonable relationship to actual damages that might have been anticipated. If so, the provision is valid; if not, it is void.[716]

The third form of security device—prepaid rent—is not truly a "deposit." When paid at the commencement of the term, the money becomes the landlord's absolute property.[717] The main legal reason a landlord would include a prepaid rent provision is to avoid the common-law rule that if the landlord re-enters and terminates the lease during the term due to tenant's breach, this terminates the tenant's liability for rent that would have accrued after the termination. When courts have been willing to categorize the sum as prepaid rent, they have generally allowed the landlord to retain it upon re-entry.[718] Though landlords do not commonly use both a traditional deposit and prepaid rent, their functions do not completely overlap and thus there seems no reason why a landlord could not use both absent a contrary statute.

With either kind of true security deposit, a problem arises if the landlord conveys the reversion. Is the grantee of the reversion liable to refund the deposit (or that portion to which the tenant is entitled) to the tenant at the end of the term? The issue is whether the landlord's express or implied promise to refund the deposit is a running covenant, the burden of which runs with the reversion. At the heart of this question is whether such a burden touches and concerns the reversion. The courts that have faced the issue

---

[713] Restatement (Second) of Property-Landlord & Tenant § 12.1, Comment 1 & Reporter's Note 11 (1977).

[714] Questions about commingling, interest, and accounting for this type of deposit should be resolved in the same manner as for the first form of deposit.

[715] See Annot., 106 A.L.R. 292 (1937) (collecting cases); 1 Am. Law of Prop. § 3.73 (1952).

[716] In the residential setting, a landlord runs a serious risk in structuring a deposit this way. A typical deposit is often only the equivalent of one to two months' rent, and unpaid rent and physical damages by a defaulting tenant may significantly exceed that amount. If the clause is structured as a true liquidated damages provision, acceptance and application of the deposit would be the landlord's exclusive remedy and the landlord could not pursue the tenant for additional damages. Further, as discussed later in the text, residential landlord-tenant statutes today commonly limit the landlord's right to withhold amounts from the security deposit, and courts are likely to treat a forfeiture clause as an impermissible waiver of the tenant protections provided by such statutes. E.g., Kaeding v. Auleciems, 886 N.W.2d 658 (Minn.App.2016).

[717] Thus, landlord would be required to include it in that year's income for federal income tax purposes. Hyde Park Realty v. Comm'r, 211 F.2d 462 (2d Cir.1954); Astor Holding Co. v. Comm'r, 135 F.2d 47 (5th Cir. 1943).

[718] E.g., Lochner v. Martin, 147 A.2d 749 (Md.1959); Dutton v. Christie, 115 P. 856 (Wash.1911); Annot., 27 A.L.R.2d 656 (1953) (collecting cases); Restatement (Second) of Property-Landlord & Tenant § 12.1, Reporter's Note 11 (1977). Some courts, however, have had a tendency to interpret loosely drawn clauses as calling for security deposits instead of prepaid rent, and have thus allowed the landlord to retain only actual damages. E.g., Annot., 27 A.L.R.2d 656 (1953) (collecting cases); Restatement (Second) of Property-Landlord & Tenant § 12.1, Reporter's Note 11 (1977); 1 Am. Law of Prop. § 3.73 (1952).

have reached opposite conclusions.[719] If the sum is prepaid rent, the tenant is entitled to have it applied to the agreed rental period, whether or not the landlord has conveyed the reversion.

Today, statutes in most states affect significantly the preceding discussion about security and damage deposits.[720] Likewise, the Uniform Residential Landlord and Tenant Act and the Model Residential Landlord-Tenant Code regulate such deposits. Thus, one must refer to a state's applicable statute for details. These statutes commonly regulate the maximum amount of the deposit,[721] the landlord's duty to segregate the deposit from the landlord's personal funds,[722] the landlord's duty to render an accounting and to give notice of claimed physical damage (and perhaps to provide receipts for repairs necessitated by such damage),[723] collection of attorneys' fees and penalties to a tenant if the landlord fails to reimburse the deposit in a timely manner,[724] the liability of the landlord's grantee to refund deposits, and whether the landlord must pay interest on the tenant's deposit.[725] Most of these statutes apply only to residential leases, and they have spawned a tremendous amount of litigation. In general, such statutes are designed to give tenants protection the common law never afforded, and courts tend to interpret the statutes against landlords.[726] An unresolved question under some of these statutes is whether prepaid rent is a "security deposit" under such statutes.[727]

---

[719] Moskin v. Goldstein, 196 N.W. 415 (Mich.1923) (grantee is bound to refund tenant); Richards v. Browning, 214 A.D. 665, 212 N.Y.S. 738 (1925) (refund obligation is personal to original owner and does not run); Mullendore Theatres, Inc. v. Growth Realty Invs. Co., 691 P.2d 970 (Wash.App.1984) (landlord's covenant to return security deposit personal covenant that did not bind landlord's grantee). See also Vinton v. Demetrion, 473 N.E.2d 207 (Mass.App.1985) (landlord's grantee has statutory duty to return residential tenant's security deposit).

[720] Statutes from 30 states are cited and summarized in Restatement (Second) of Property-Landlord & Tenant § 12.1, Statutory Note 6 (1977).

[721] URLTA § 2.101 (1972); RURLTA § 1201(b) (2015) (no more than two months' rent); MRLTC § 2–401 (1969).

[722] RURLTA § 1203 (2015).

[723] See Garcia v. Thong, 895 P.2d 226 (N.M.1995) (landlord failed to itemize, lost deposit); Mallah v. Barkauskas, 474 N.E.2d 886 (Ill.App.1985) (receipts); Ackerman v. Little, 679 S.W.2d 70 (Tex.App.1984) (itemized list of damages).

[724] Wrongful withholding of a security deposit, whether because there was no ground to hold it or because landlord failed to comply with technical conditions of the statute, may subject the landlord to double or treble damages or to liability for the tenant's attorney fees. See, e.g., Garcia v. Thong, 895 P.2d 226 (N.M.1995) (attorney fees); Rohrbaugh v. Estate of Stern, 505 A.2d 113 (Md.1986) (treble amount wrongfully withheld, plus attorney fees); Mellor v. Berman, 454 N.E.2d 907 (Mass.1983) (treble damages); Mitchell v. Preusse, 358 N.W.2d 511 (N.D.1984) (treble damages); Vardeman v. Llewellyn, 476 N.E.2d 1038 (Ohio 1985) (double damages but only as to amount wrongfully withheld); Ackerman v. Little, 679 S.W.2d 70 (Tex.App.1984) (treble damages); Shands v. Castrovinci, 340 N.W.2d 506 (Wis.1983) (tenant awarded attorney fees though represented by legal services office for free).

[725] The original URLTA did not address whether the landlord was obligated to pay interest on security deposits, although legislatures in some states did impose such a requirement. Henning & Freyermuth, Article 9 and the Characterization and Treatment of Tenant Security Deposits, 35 UALR L. Rev. 999 (2013) (collecting statutes). The RURLTA provides that the landlord need not place the deposit in an interest-bearing account or pay the tenant interest on the deposit unless the lease so requires. RURLTA § 1203(d) (2015).

[726] See, e.g., Mellor v. Berman, 454 N.E.2d 907 (Mass.1983); Mitchell v. Preusse, 358 N.W.2d 511 (N.D.1984); Shands v. Castrovinci, 340 N.W.2d 506 (Wis.1983).

[727] If the sum is clearly prepaid rent—after allowing for the fact that in doubtful cases some courts prefer to describe sums as deposits—perhaps ambiguity over the application of the statute should be resolved in favor of the landlord.

I.   TAXES AND INSURANCE

§ 6.59 TAXES AND ASSESSMENTS

Nothing in the ordinary leasing situation implies a tenant's duty to pay real estate taxes or special assessments on the premises.[728] If the tenant has the duty, it usually arises under an express covenant in the lease. There are a few circumstances in which courts may imply a tenant's duty. For example, the tenant generally has a duty to pay an increase in the taxes caused by the tenant's construction of improvements that tenant will use up or can remove.[729] By some decisions, if the tenant has a leasehold that is perpetual or for a term of 99 years or more, the tenant has a duty to pay taxes on the theory that the tenant owns the fee or its equivalent.[730] Landlords have sometimes argued that a tenant's duty should be implied when the tenant has been voluntarily paying taxes or when the tenant has a purchase option, though courts have been unreceptive to these arguments.[731]

On the landlord's side, still assuming no lease clause governs, the opinions often say the landlord has a "duty" to pay real estate taxes.[732] While the landlord may lose the land if taxes are not paid, it is inaccurate to say the landlord owes the tenant a duty for which the tenant would have an action at law for breach. If the landlord fails to pay the taxes for so long a period that the land is sold at tax sale, a breach of the covenant of quiet enjoyment will result when the tax sale purchaser actually disturbs the tenant's possession.[733]

Commercial leases (and some long-term residential leases) frequently contain clauses requiring the tenant to pay all or some part of the real estate taxes. Especially in a "net" lease, the tenant may be required to pay all real estate taxes and assessments. A more limited form of the clause requires the tenant to pay tax increases that flow from improvements the tenant makes.[734] Many modern commercial leases, especially office leases, contain a so-called "tax stop" clause which requires the tenant to pay increases in real estate taxes that occur during the term.[735] In drafting, landlords should make clear the scope of tenants' duties to pay taxes, as courts are likely to resolve ambiguity

---

[728] In most residential leases and some commercial leases, the landlord essentially builds the expected cost of real estate taxes into the tenant's rent obligation. The tenant is thus paying the taxes, but only indirectly so. In these situations, it is sometimes said that the tenant is paying rent on a "gross" basis.

[729] E.g., Beck v. F.W. Woolworth Co., 111 F.Supp. 824 (N.D.Iowa 1953) (dictum); Wycoff v. Gavriloff Motors, Inc., 107 N.W.2d 820 (Mich.1961); Annot., 86 A.L.R.2d 670, 682–85 (1962).

[730] E.g., Piper v. Town of Meredith, 139 A. 294 (N.H.1927); City of Norfolk v. J.W. Perry Co., 61 S.E. 867 (Va.1908); Annot., 55 A.L.R. 154 (1928).

[731] Annot., 86 A.L.R.2d 670, 681–82 (1962).

[732] E.g., Wycoff v. Gavriloff Motors, Inc., 107 N.W.2d 820 (Mich.1961); City of Norfolk v. J.W. Perry Co., 61 S.E. 867 (Va.1908).

[733] See Barry v. Frankini, 191 N.E. 651 (Mass.1934); Rustin Co. v. Bowen, 30 A.2d 70 (N.J.1943); Restatement (Second) of Property-Landlord & Tenant § 4.3, Reporter's Note 3 (1977).

[734] E.g., Tiara Corp. v. Delta Elec. Co., 424 So.2d 459 (La.App.1982) (lease clause interpreted to require tenant to reimburse landlord for tax increase caused by tenant's improvements).

[735] In such leases, the landlord generally pays the taxes directly, and builds into the base rent the amount of real estate taxes for the year the lease commences. To the extent the taxes increase during the term, the clause obligates the tenant to pay its pro rata share of such increases as "additional rent." For decisions construing such clauses, see Annot., 48 A.L.R.3d 287 (1973).

over such duties in favor of tenants.[736] For example, courts have held that a covenant to pay "taxes" does not impose a duty to pay special assessments.[737]

§ 6.60 INSURANCE

Both parties have insurable interests in the premises—the landlord's being that part of the interest apportionable to the reversion, and the tenant's being the part apportionable to the leasehold. Absent a covenant to do so, however, neither owes a duty to the other to procure fire or casualty insurance.[738] If either party voluntarily insures its own interest in its own name, the other has no control over what the insured does with the proceeds.[739] Even if the voluntary insured takes out insurance in an amount larger than its insurable interest, i.e., over-insures, most courts reach the same result, though a few decisions require the insured to account to the other for a share.[740] However, where the voluntary insured procured a policy payable jointly to both parties, courts have held that they share the proceeds according to their respective interests.[741]

Commercial leases typically contain covenants by one party to procure insurance. In some cases, the tenant covenants to insure directly (often where the tenant has possession of an entire building); in others, the landlord maintains insurance and the tenant reimburses the landlord for tenant's pro rata share of the cost of that insurance. A well-drafted insurance clause should specify the kind of insurance (Fire and other casualty? Earthquake? Terrorism?), the amount (Full insurable value? Deductible amount?[742]), to whom the proceeds are payable (To landlord? To tenant? To both, as their interests shall appear?),[743] and how and by whom proceeds are to be applied. This clause must coordinate carefully with any repair clauses and with clauses providing for

---

[736] See, e.g., First Nat'l Bank of Highland Park v. Mid-Central Food Sales, Inc., 473 N.E.2d 372 (Ill.App.1984) (lease clause requiring tenant to pay taxes when due during lease term only obligated tenant to pay pro rata taxes for last partial year of lease); Beck v. F.W. Woolworth Co., 111 F.Supp. 824 (N.D.Iowa 1953); Gold Medal Stamp Co. v. Carver, 270 N.E.2d 834 (Mass.1971); Annot., 48 A.L.R.3d 287 (1973).

[737] E.g., Crestview Bowl, Inc. v. Womer Constr. Co., 592 P.2d 74 (Kan.1979); G&A, Inc. v. Nahra, 514 N.W.2d 255 (Mich.1994).

[738] Alexander v. Security First Nat'l Bank, 62 P.2d 735 (Cal.1936); Carolina Helicopter Corp. v. Cutter Realty Co., 139 S.E.2d 362 (N.C.1964); Yoshida v. Security Ins. Co., 26 P.2d 1082 (Or.1933); Gebhart v. Huffman, 326 N.W.2d 891 (S.D.1982); Hart v. Hart, 117 Wis. 639, 94 N.W. 890 (1903); 1 Am. Law of Prop. § 3.75 (1952).

[739] Alexander v. Security First Nat'l Bank, 62 P.2d 735 (Cal.1936); Yoshida v. Security Ins. Co., 26 P.2d 1082 (Or.1933); Annot., 66 A.L.R. 864 (1930).

[740] Miller v. Gold Beach Packing Co., 282 P. 764 (Or.1929).

[741] Hale v. Simmons, 139 S.W.2d 696 (Ark.1940); Ingold v. Phoenix Assurance Co., 52 S.E.2d 366 (N.C.1949); Annot., 8 A.L.R.2d 1445 (1949).

[742] E.g., Boston Market Corp. v. Hack, 2007 WL 2349989 (N.J.Super.2007) (where lease did not specify exact deductible amount, court may consider tenant's creditworthiness and other factors bearing on risk of loss in deciding whether high-deductible policy satisfies tenant's insurance obligation under the lease).

[743] For example, suppose that the landlord carries insurance on a residential apartment building. A tenant negligently starts a fire, the building is damaged, and the insurer pays the landlord under the policy. Can the insurer proceed against the tenant for negligence on the ground that it is subrogated to the landlord's rights? While the traditional answer was yes—and still is in some states, e.g., Neubauer v. Hofstetter, 485 N.W.2d 87 (Iowa 1992); Phoenix Ins. Co. v. Stamell, 21 A.D.3d 118, 796 N.Y.S.2d 772 (2005); Winkler v. Appalachian Amusement Co., 79 S.E.2d 185 (N.C.1953)—there is an emerging trend in the case law that absent an express agreement to the contrary, a tenant is a co-insured under the landlord's insurance policy, and the casualty insurer is thus precluded from asserting subrogation rights against the tenant. E.g., Rausch v. Allstate Ins. Co., 882 A.2d 801 (Md.2005); Tri-Par Invsts., LLC v. Sousa, 680 N.W.2d 190 (Neb.2004); Sutton v. Jondahl, 532 P.2d 478 (Okla.App.1975); Dattel Family Ltd. Partn. v. Wintz, 250 S.W.3d 883 (Tenn.App.2007); Union Mut. Fire Ins. Co. v. Joerg, 824 A.2d 586 (Vt.2003). But see Osborne v. Chapman, 574 N.W.2d 64 (Minn.1998) (implied co-insured rule does not protect tenant from liability to landlord for lost rent suffered by landlord in fire caused by tenant's negligence).

termination or alteration of the lease in the event of whole or partial destruction. When one party covenants to insure, that party is liable to the other for the other's share of proceeds, whether or not the policy on its face runs to both parties.[744] If the lease requires insurance proceeds to be applied to repairs ("coupled with" a repair clause), courts agree that the burden of the covenant runs with the estate of the covenanting party so as to bind a grantee or assignee.[745] Due to dictum in the old case of Masury v. Southworth,[746] when the lease does not require proceeds to be applied to repairs (i.e., when it contains a "bare" insurance clause), the courts are split on whether the burden of the covenant to insure runs with the land.[747]

J.   RENEWALS AND EXTENSIONS

§ 6.61   DISTINCTION BETWEEN RENEWALS AND EXTENSIONS

Leases for years may contain clauses giving tenants the power to be tenants for one or more terms beyond the end of the original term. Two mechanisms serve that purpose: a power to renew (i.e., to compel a new lease) and a power to extend the original term. For many purposes, the parties may not care which mechanism they employ, but in a couple of ways there could be significant differences. For example, many courts have held that a renewal (being a new grant) would require the execution of an entirely new lease while an extension (merely continuing the existing term) would not.[748] Further, while the tenant's act of holding over and paying rent may be a sufficient election to extend,[749] something more is required to elect a new lease—probably the tendering of a new lease or at least some notice before the end of the original term.[750]

Parties who wish one of the above arrangements should "watch their language." Use of the word "extend" or "extension" is reasonably safe; courts generally agree that this denotes a continuation of the original term and not a new lease. Unadorned use of the word "renew" or "renewal" is generally not advised, as some courts may interpret such words to refer to a new lease. Increasingly, courts do not give determinative effect to the specific word used, but look to other circumstances to determine if the parties intended an extension or a new lease.[751]

---

[744] See Grand Forks Seed Co. v. Northland Greyhound Lines, Inc., 168 F.Supp. 882 (D.N.D.1959); Cambron v. Carlisle, 435 So.2d 1216 (Ala.1983); Meyer v. Caribbean Interiors Inc., 435 So.2d 936 (Fla.App.1983); Annot., 66 A.L.R. 864, 866–67 (1930).

[745] E.g., Masury v. Southworth, 9 Ohio St. 340 (1859); Burton v. Chesapeake Box & Lumber Corp., 57 S.E.2d 904 (Va.1950); Annot., 18 A.L.R.2d 1051 (1951).

[746] 9 Ohio St. 340 (1859).

[747] Annot., 18 A.L.R.2d 1051 (1951).

[748] See, e.g., Riggs v. United States, 12 F.2d 85 (E.D.S.C.1926); Riverside Land Co. v. Big Rock Stone & Material Co., 40 S.W.2d 423 (Ark.1931); Head v. Scanlon, 367 S.E.2d 546 (Ga.1988); HLM Realty Corp. v. Morreale, 477 N.E.2d 394 (Mass.1985); McClellan v. Britain, 826 P.2d 245 (Wyo.1992); 1 Am. Law of Prop. § 3.85 (1952); Annot., 172 A.L.R. 1205 (1948).

[749] See Berman, 2 Friedman on Leases § 14:3.1, at 14–76 (6th ed.2017) (collecting cases). See also Grand Invst. Corp. v. Connaughton, Boyd & Kenter, 119 S.W.3d 101 (Mo.App.2003) (holding over by tenant and waiver of notice by landlord combine to exercise option to extend on original lease terms).

[750] See Riggs v. United States, 12 F.2d 85 (E.D.S.C.1926) (renewal); Shannon v. Jacobson, 160 N.E. 245 (Mass.1928) (extension); Ahmed v. Scott, 418 N.E.2d 406 (Ohio App.1979); Annot., 172 A.L.R. 1205, 1219–22 (1948).

[751] This evolution is reflected in a series of Massachusetts decisions. See Quereshi v. Fiske Capital Mgmt., 796 N.E.2d 459 (Mass.App.2003) (distinction between extension and renewal is a "legal nicety" that

§ 6.62   OPERATION OF RENEWAL/EXTENSION PROVISIONS

A well-drafted renewal or extension clause specifies how many renewals or extensions the tenant may have and which provisions, if any (e.g., amount of rent or length of term) are to be adjusted. When the language is general or vague as to the number of renewals or extensions, courts usually allow the tenant to have only one.[752] If the clause provides for renewal or extension but does not specify for what term or upon what provisions, the courts imply that it shall be for the same term as the original one[753] and with the same provisions, including the rent.[754] If, however, the renewal or extension clause states that some or all the key provisions—especially rent—shall be determined by the parties' future agreement or words to that effect, courts generally refuse to enforce the clause on the ground it is indefinite.[755] Some decisions have enforced clauses calling for rent to be set by future agreement, the courts being willing to determine a "reasonable" rent.[756] Obviously, the parties are free to provide a formula that fixes the rent for renewal or extension periods through some process or standard such as appraisal, arbitration, or a price index.[757]

Because renewal or extension is at the tenant's election, the tenant must sufficiently act to make the election. There is a split of authority on whether a tenant loses the power to renew when the tenant has breached a material provision in the lease, but the

---

court will disregard in interpreting agreement between nonlawyers); HLM Realty Corp. v. Morreale, 477 N.E.2d 394 (Mass.1985) (critical distinction is whether some additional act is necessary, not whether option is called "renewal" or "extension"); Anderson v. Lissandri, 472 N.E.2d 1365 (Mass.App.1985) (use of word "renewal" not conclusive where circumstances show parties intended extension). See also Blanck v. Kimland Realty Co., 189 A. 176 (Conn.1937); Med-Care Assocs., Inc. v. Noot, 329 N.W.2d 549 (Minn.1983) (legislature's use of word "renewal" held to include extensions); Dubinsky Realty, Inc. v. Vactec, Inc., 637 S.W.2d 190 (Mo.App.1982) (dictum that Missouri courts usually ignore technical distinction between renewals and extensions); Jador Service Co. v. Werbel, 53 A.2d 182 (N.J.1947); Annot., 172 A.L.R. 1205, 1222–25 (1948).

[752] Berman, 2 Friedman on Leases § 14:1, at 14–11 & n.33 (6th ed.2017) (collecting cases). In cases where the lease did not specify the exact number of renewals, courts have limited the tenant to one renewal even when the original lease used the plural term "renewals." Id. In perhaps the most ridiculous example, one court limited the tenant to one renewal term even though the original lease stated that the rent would increase "upon the 3rd or any subsequent renewal"! Geyer v. Lietzan, 103 N.E.2d 199 (Ind.1952).

[753] E.g., Mutual Paper Co. v. Hoague-Sprague Corp., 8 N.E.2d 802 (Mass.1937); Starr v. Holck, 28 N.W.2d 289 (Mich.1947); Annot., 172 A.L.R. 421, 422–24 (1948).

[754] Johnson v. Hudson, 420 So.2d 85 (Ala.1982); Penilla v. Gerstenkorn, 261 P. 488 (Cal.App.1927); Subcarrier Communications, Inc. v. Satra Realty, LLC, 11 A.D.3d 829, 785 N.Y.S.2d 545 (2004); Little Caesar Enters., Inc. v. Bell Canyon Shopping Ctr., L.C., 13 P.3d 600 (Utah App.2000); Annot., 166 A.L.R. 1237, 1243 (1947). See also Bold MLP, LLC v. Smith, 201 So.3d 1261 (Fla.App.2016) (where original lease provided for fixed rent increases of $75/month annually during term, but was silent as to rent during renewal period, fixed rent increases of $75/month annually continued during renewal term).

[755] E.g., Dixieland Food Stores v. Geddert, 505 So.2d 371 (Ala.1987); Lonoke Nursing Home, Inc. v. Wayne & Neil Bennett Family Partn., 676 S.W.2d 461 (Ark.App.1984); Etco Corp. v. Hauer, 161 Cal.App.3d 1154, 208 Cal.Rptr. 118 (1984) (renewal agreement with rent to be fixed "by mutual agreement" too vague to be enforced); Camichos v. Diana Stores Corp., 25 So.2d 864 (Fla.1946); Intrepid, Inc. v. Bennett, 176 So.3d 775 (Miss.2015); State ex rel. Johnson v. Blair, 174 S.W.2d 851 (Mo.1943); R.A.S., Inc. v. Crowley, 351 N.W.2d 414 (Neb.1984); Berman, 2 Friedman on Leases § 14:1.3, at 14–27 & n.86 (6th ed.2017) (collecting cases).

[756] E.g., Edwards v. Tobin, 284 P. 562 (Or.1930); Rainwater v. Hobeika, 38 S.E.2d 495 (S.C.1946); Young v. Nelson, 209 P. 515 (Wash.1922). These cases suggest the willingness of some courts to equate "reasonable" with "fair market value," which might be readily determined by appraisal. See also Robert T. Miner, M.D., Inc. v. Tustin Ave. Invs., LLC, 116 Cal.App.4th 264, 10 Cal.Rptr.3d 178 (2004) (renewal agreement at "reasonable rent" not unenforceable as a matter of law); Hall v. Weatherford, 259 P. 282 (Ariz.1927) (enforcing renewal at rent to be determined "by agreement" on theory that renewal right was bargained for and nonenforcement would deprive tenant of bargain).

[757] Berman, 2 Friedman on Leases § 14:1.3, at 14–24, 14–25 & nn.80–81 (6th ed.2017) (collecting cases).

landlord has not acted to terminate the lease.[758] For this reason, if the landlord expects that a tenant's breach should preclude the tenant from acting to renew or extend the lease, the lease should express this expectation clearly; otherwise, a court may consider the clauses to be independent and conclude that the tenant did not lose the benefit of the renewal or extension clause simply because the tenant breached a different clause.

A well-drafted clause states expressly what notice or other acts the tenant must do, when the tenant must do them, and that the tenant loses the election if the tenant does not exercise it in the manner and within the time specified. The landlord normally should insist that the tenant must make an irrevocable election by an appropriate fixed time before the end of the term, so that the landlord has adequate time to re-let the premises if the tenant does not elect to renew or extend. If the clause is clear, the courts will usually make the tenant's strict compliance a condition precedent to renewal or extension.[759] In some circumstances, involving mistake, unexpected and excusable delay, or landlord's waiver, equity courts may excuse late election, especially if the lease does not make time of the essence.[760] Should the renewal or extension clause require notice but not specify when it must be given, notice by the end of the term is adequate.[761] If written notice is not required, oral notice is as good as written.[762]

§ 6.63 PERPETUAL RENEWALS

Perpetual renewals are allowed and are considered to amount to a conveyance in fee simple.[763] They do not violate the Rule Against Perpetuities because the grantee has a vested possessory estate.[764] However, courts strongly disfavor perpetual renewals and will if possible interpret language so as to avoid their existence.[765]

---

[758] Under the majority view, the tenant can renew or extend while in default. See, e.g., Aickin v. Ocean View Invsts. Co., Inc., 935 P.2d 992 (Haw.1997); Steven W. Barrick & Assocs. v. Witz, 498 N.E.2d 738 (Ill.App.1986); Vice v. Leigh, 670 So.2d 6 (Miss.1995); Hindquarter Corp. v. Property Dev. Corp., 631 P.2d 923 (Wash.1981). Under the minority approach, default deprives the tenant of the power to renew or extend. See, e.g., Reno Realty & Invst. Co. v. Hornstein, 301 P.2d 1051 (Nev.1956); Cowan v. Mervin Mewes, Inc., 546 N.W.2d 104 (S.D.1996).

[759] E.g., La Salle Nat'l Bank v. Graham, 456 N.E.2d 323 (Ill.App.1983); Gurunian v. Grossman, 49 N.W.2d 354 (Mich.1951); Wayside Homes, Inc. v. Purcelli, 104 A.D.2d 650, 480 N.Y.S.2d 29 (1984); Royer v. Honrine, 316 S.E.2d 93 (N.C.App.1984); Jones v. Dexter, 292 P.2d 369 (Wash.1956). See also Hsu v. Marian Manor Apts., Inc., 743 N.W.2d 672 (N.D.2007) (failure to maintain necessary medical license prevented exercise of renewal option).

[760] E.g., R & R of Conn., Inc. v. Stiegler, 493 A.2d 293 (Conn.App.1985); Aickin v. Ocean View Invst. Co., Inc., 935 P.2d 992 (Haw.1997). See also Berman, 2 Friedman on Leases § 14:1.1, at 14–17 & n.50 (6th ed.2017) (collecting cases); Annot., 44 A.L.R.2d 1359 (1955).

[761] See Penilla v. Gerstenkorn, 261 P. 488 (Cal.App.1927); Caito v. Ferri, 116 A. 897 (R.I.1922) (two days after term ended).

[762] E.g., Economy Stores, Inc. v. Moran, 172 So. 865 (Miss.1937); Caito v. Ferri, 116 A. 897 (R.I.1922); Annot., 51 A.L.R.2d 1404, 1412–13 (1957).

[763] Williams v. J.M. High Co., 36 S.E.2d 667 (Ga.1946) (dictum); Department of Natural Resources v. Board of Trustees of Westminster Church, 318 N.W.2d 830 (Mich.App.1982); Burns v. City of N.Y., 108 N.E. 77 (N.Y.1915); Tipton v. North, 92 P.2d 364 (Okla.1939); Annot., 31 A.L.R.2d 607, 622–24 (1953); 1 Am. Law of Prop. § 3.87 (1952).

[764] Rose v. Chandler, 279 S.E.2d 423 (Ga.1981); Bleecker St. Tenants Corp. v. Bleeker Jones LLC, 945 N.E.2d 484 (N.Y.2011); Dixon v. Rivers, 245 S.E.2d 572 (N.C.App.1978).

[765] McLean v. United States, 316 F.Supp. 827 (E.D.Va.1970); Nakdimen v. Atkinson Improvement Co., 233 S.W. 694 (Ark.1921); Lonergan v. Connecticut Food Store, Inc., 357 A.2d 910 (Conn.1975); Schroeder v. Johnson, 696 So.2d 498 (Fla.App.1997); Geyer v. Lietzan, 103 N.E.2d 199 (Ind.1952); Thomas v. Knight, 457 So.2d 1207 (La.App.1984); Lattimore v. Fisher's Food Shoppe, Inc., 329 S.E.2d 346 (N.C.1985); Annot., 31 A.L.R.2d 607, 623–30 (1953). As noted in section 6.62, courts have done this by interpreting a lease to allow only one renewal where the lease does not establish a definite number of permitted renewals.

K.　PURCHASE OPTIONS

§ 6.64　NATURE AND CREATION OF PURCHASE OPTIONS

A lease may grant to the tenant an option to purchase the premises. Two forms of option are in common usage: the "straight option" and the "right of first refusal."[766] With the first form, the tenant has a power to compel the landlord to convey the reversion at a fixed or determinable price at any time during all or a stated portion of the lease term. The second form of option disables the landlord from conveying the reversion to a third person without first offering it to the tenant, usually at the same price the third person has offered. From the tenant's perspective, this second form operates as an option to purchase only if the landlord has received an offer and agreed to sell on the offered terms.

These rights can exist only by virtue of specific language in the lease. An option must be supported by consideration (being a contract of irrevocable offer), but this is no problem in a lease because of the parties' various valuable exchanges. Problems can arise over definiteness of terms, particularly price and mode of payment, as an option has the aspect of a contract to consummate further contractual undertakings. In general, the lease agreement must state the terms of a straight option with the same particularity as would be required of any valid offer.[767] With a right of first refusal, the terms are determined by the third person's offer and are definite enough because they are controlled by an external standard. Much litigation has arisen over whether certain language created a straight option or right of first refusal. Generalizations are difficult. Drafters should be careful not to mix language usually associated with a straight option with customary first refusal language. The word "first," even when connected with "refusal" or "privilege," may be regarded as ambiguous, and provisions for a stated price or for exercise of the optionee's right at anytime within a stated period suggest a straight option.[768] Especially when the parties intend a right of first refusal, the mechanism for its exercise should be carefully spelled out.[769]

§ 6.65　OPERATION AND EXERCISE OF PURCHASE OPTIONS

Leases frequently grant options for only a stated portion of the lease term; long-term commercial leases may contain an elaborate series of options, exercisable during successive stages on differing terms. If the lease does not limit the time when the tenant

---

[766] A third device sometimes encountered is a "right of first offer" or "ROFO." In the lease context, a ROFO would obligate the landlord to negotiate the sale of the reversion to the tenant before offering the reversion for sale to a third party. If the tenant did not purchase the reversion (or the parties could not reach an agreement), the landlord could then offer the property to other parties. See generally Circo, Purchase Options, ROFRs, and ROFOs: Theory and Practice, ACREL Papers (Spring 2016).

[767] A failure to fix the price of an option (or a method for determination of the price) renders the option invalid. E.g., Alaska Fur Gallery, Inc. v. Hwang, 394 P.3d 511 (Alaska 2017); Friedl v. Benson, 609 P.2d 449 (Wash.App.1980). While most courts have upheld options to purchase at the then-current appraised market value at the time of exercise, e.g., Miller v. McCullough, 224 S.E.2d 916 (Ga.1976); Miller v. Bloomberg, 324 N.E.2d 207 (Ill.App.1975); Crow v. Crow's Sports Ctr., 119 So.3d 352 (Miss.App.2012), there are some contrary decisions. E.g., NRC Golf Course v. GMR Golf, LLC, 731 S.E.2d 474 (N.C.App.2012) (option unenforceable where lease failed to identify how third party appraiser would be selected); Connor v. Harless, 626 S.E.2d 755 (N.C.App.2006) (option unenforceable where lease established no means to reconcile discrepancies between the two appraisals it required).

[768] See Berman, 2 Friedman on Leases § 15:6.3 (6th ed.2017) (collecting cases).

[769] See, e.g., Pollack v. Quick Quality Restaurants, Inc., 172 A.3d 568 (N.J.Super.2017) (tenant exercising right of first refusal had no obligation to pay commission to broker that introduced landlord and third-party purchaser).

may exercise the option, it endures during the term plus any extensions or renewals.[770] The fact that a lease has a very long term, or even that it is perpetually renewable, does not void a purchase option; American courts have not applied the Rule Against Perpetuities to invalidate options in leases.[771] As a general rule, termination of the lease terminates the option,[772] but mere breach by the tenant does not prevent the tenant's exercise of an option unless the terms of the lease explicitly so provide.[773] If the tenant assigns the leasehold, the assignee generally may exercise a purchase option or right of first refusal, which is considered a running covenant.[774]

Upon due exercise of a purchase option, the landlord-tenant relation ends; the parties become vendor and vendee.[775] A purchaser of the premises with notice of the tenant's option takes subject to the rights of the tenant optionee, including a right to specific performance.[776] For this reason, landlords should be aware that the existence of a purchase option may hinder the landlord's ability to obtain mortgage financing.[777]

L. TRANSFERS BY LANDLORD OR TENANT

§ 6.66 TENANT'S TRANSFERS IN GENERAL

Absent contrary agreement, the tenant may transfer its leasehold estate or lesser interests carved out of it.[778] Transfers of possession come in two forms, assignments and subleases, discussed in detail in the following sections. A tenant may also create

---

[770] Moiger v. Johnson, 180 F.2d 777 (D.C.Cir.1950) (extension); Hindu Incense Mfg. Co. v. MacKenzie, 403 Ill. 390, 86 N.E.2d 214 (1949) (renewal); Taylor v. Wells, 188 Or. 648, 217 P.2d 236 (1950) (during term); Durepo v. May, 73 R.I. 71, 54 A.2d 15 (1947) (during term); Exxon Corp. v. Pollman, 729 S.W.2d 302 (Tex.App.1986) (during extension). A few courts have made a distinction between extensions and renewals, saying or holding that purchase options do not carry over to renewals. See Seefeldt v. Keske, 111 N.W.2d 574 (Wis.1961). A court, in interpreting disputed language in a lease, may find the parties did not intend a purchase option to continue during extension or renewal. See, e.g., Denver Plastics, Inc. v. Snyder, 416 P.2d 370 (Colo.1966). Where a lease contains both a fixed-price purchase option and a right of first refusal, courts have differed as to whether the tenant may exercise the fixed-price option after being notified that the landlord has received an offer of purchase at a higher price. Compare Texaco, Inc. v. Creel, 314 S.E.2d 506 (N.C.1984), and Amoco Oil Co. v. Snyder, 478 A.2d 795 (Pa.1984) (tenant may exercise fixed-price option) with Tantleff v. Truscelli, 110 A.D.2d 240, 493 N.Y.S.2d 979 (1985), aff'd, 505 N.E.2d 623 (N.Y.1987) (tenant could exercise fixed-price option only until right of first refusal became operative).

[771] The tenant's option would not violate the Rule if the option is exercisable no later than the end of the lease term. Berman, 2 Friedman on Leases § 15:1, at 15–14 (6th ed.2017); Keogh v. Peck, 147 N.E. 266 (Ill.1925); Hollander v. Central Metal & Supply Co., 71 A. 442 (Md.1908).

[772] E.g., Bateman v. 317 Rehoboth Ave., LLC, 878 A.2d 1176 (Del.Ch.2006); Arquette Dev. Corp. v. Hodges, 934 So.2d 556 (Fla.App.2006).

[773] E.g., Creech v. Ranmar Props., 551 S.E.2d 224 (N.C.App.2001); Berman, 2 Friedman on Leases § 15:2, at 15–27 & n.93 (6th ed.2017) (collecting cases).

[774] E.g., Bewick v. Mecham, 156 P.2d 757 (Cal.1945); Moore & McCaleb, Inc. v. Gaines, 489 So.2d 491 (Miss.1986); Randolph v. Koury Corp., 312 S.E.2d 759 (W.Va.1984); Annot., 45 A.L.R.2d 1034 (1956).

[775] Willard v. Tayloe, 75 U.S. (8 Wall.) 557, 19 L.Ed. 501 (1870); Gassert v. Anderson, 276 N.W. 808 (Minn.1937).

[776] Martinez v. Affordable Housing Network, Inc., 123 P.3d 1201 (Colo.2005); Berman, 2 Friedman on Leases § 15:5.1, at 15–58 to 15–59 & n.225 (6th ed.2017) (collecting cases).

[777] If the lease with the purchase option is prior to the mortgage, the tenant exercising the option would take title free of the mortgage. E.g., Savoie v. Southeast Bank, N.A., 529 So.2d 1275 (Fla.App.1988). This would cause a sophisticated mortgage lender to object to the option, or to require the tenant to agree to subordinate its option rights as a condition of the mortgage loan. See, International Council of Shopping Centers, Shopping Center Report No. 13, A Lender's Examination of Shopping Center Leases 8 (1964).

[778] See generally, Annot., 23 A.L.R. 135 (1923), Supp., 70 A.L.R. 486 (1931).

nonpossessory interests, such as easements or licenses, within a leasehold (e.g., a retail tenant might expressly or impliedly grant licenses to its customers).

The general rule of transferability is subject to important qualifications. It is doubtful that a tenant at will has a sufficient interest to be transferred.[779] A more important limitation on transfer arises from the common practice of lease clauses that prohibit or limit assignment or subletting, which we address in Section 6.70.

§ 6.67 ASSIGNMENT AND SUBLEASE DISTINGUISHED

The distinction between assignment and subletting is important and technical. It is important because different legal consequences can follow each transaction—perhaps the most important, as discussed in the next two sections, being whether the landlord may enforce the lease obligations against the transferee. It is technical because courts generally characterize the transaction based on the form of the transaction rather than on the parties' stated intent.[780] A transfer is an assignment if the tenant transfers the right of possession to all or part of the premises for the full time remaining on the term. By contrast, a transfer is a sublease if the tenant transfers the right of possession to all or part of the premises for a period less than the full time remaining. Stated differently, in a sublease, the tenant retains a reversion in the leasehold following the subtenancy; in an assignment, the tenant does not retain a reversion.[781]

Within this formal test, some questions still arise. A minority of courts have held that if the tenant transfers the entire balance of the term but reserves a power of termination (e.g., for the transferee's breach), the transfer is a subletting and not an assignment.[782] A few courts have also held that a transfer for the entire balance of the

---

[779] Several decisions have stated that the transferee from a tenant at will becomes only a trespasser against the landowner. Hunnicutt v. Head, 60 So. 831 (Ala.1912); Ferrigno v. O'Connell, 53 N.E.2d 384 (Mass.1944); Annot., 167 A.L.R. 1040 (1947). But see Public Serv. Co. v. Voudoumas, 151 A. 81 (N.H.1930).

[780] Tidewater Invs., Ltd. v. United Dominion Realty Trust, Inc., 804 F.2d 293 (4th Cir.1986) (transfer of full term is assignment, though parties called it "sublease"); Siragusa v. Park, 913 S.W.2d 915 (Mo.App.1996) ("sublease" of full term is actually an assignment). Some courts have argued that the parties' intent should govern, see Jaber v. Miller, 239 S.W.2d 760 (1951). However, the result in *Jaber* (that the transfer was an assignment) would have been reached under the traditional test.

[781] E.g., Haynes v. Eagle-Picher Co., 295 F.2d 761 (10th Cir.1961), cert. denied, 369 U.S. 828, 82 S.Ct. 846, 7 L.Ed.2d 794 (1962); In re Lafayette Radio Electronics Corp., 9 B.R. 993 (Bankr.E.D.N.Y.1981) (reversion of one day); V.O.B. Co. v. Hang It Up, Inc., 691 P.2d 1157 (Colo.App.1984); Southcross Commerce Ctr., LLP v. Tupy Props., LLC, 766 N.W.2d 704 (Minn.App.2009); Conklin Dev. Corp. v. Acme Markets, Inc., 89 A.D.2d 769, 453 N.Y.S.2d 930 (1982); Christensen v. Tidewater Fibre Corp., 616 S.E.2d 583 (N.C.App.2005); Royalco Oil & Gas Corp. v. Stockhome Trading Corp., 361 S.W.3d 725 (Tex.App.2012); L & M Corp. v. Loader, 688 P.2d 448 (Utah 1984); Anthony Gagliano & Co., Inc. v. Openfirst, LLC, 850 N.W.2d 845 (Wis.2014); 1 Am. Law of Prop. § 5.07(1)(C) (1993). But see City of Pensacola v. Seville Harbour, Inc., 219 So.3d 984 (Fla.App.2017) (holding, somewhat questionably, that tenant's transfer of balance of leasehold estate subject to the retention of an easement over the premises was a sublease).

[782] Hartman Ranch Co. v. Associated Oil Co., 73 P.2d 1163 (Cal.1937); Dunlap v. Bullard, 131 Mass. 161 (1881); American Community Stores Corp. v. Newman, 441 N.W.2d 154 (Neb.1989); Tenet Health Systems Hospitals Dallas, Inc. v. North Texas Hospital Physicians Group, P.A., 438 S.W.3d 190 (Tex.App.2014). For the contrary view that retention of a power of termination alone still creates an assignment, see, e.g., Rocklen, Inc. v. Radulesco, 522 A.2d 846 (Conn.App.1987); Berkeley Dev. Co. v. Great Atl. & Pac. Tea Co., 518 A.2d 790 (N.J.Super.1986); Banque Nationale de Paris v. 1567 Broadway Ownership Assocs., 202 A.D.2d 251, 608 N.Y.S.2d 635 (1994); L. & M. Corp. v. Loader, 688 P.2d 448 (Utah 1984). The minority cases typically characterize the tenant's power of termination as a "contingent reversionary interest" and thus rule that the tenant's retention of such an interest requires characterizing the transfer as a sublease. The majority cases either characterize the tenant's power of termination as being a mere chose in action that is not a reversionary estate, or conclude that it "was not the retention of such reversionary interest as is intended when distinctions are drawn between assignments and subleases." Gillette Bros. v. Aristocrat Restaurant, Inc., 145 N.E. 748, 749 (N.Y.1924).

term nevertheless constitutes a sublease if it involves different terms than the primary lease (such as an increase in rent), on the theory that variations from the original lease indicate that the parties intended to create a separate tenancy.[783] Likewise, a few decisions hold that a transfer for the balance of the term nevertheless constitutes a sublease if the transferee has the right to cancel the lease prior to the end of the original lease term.[784] Under the great weight of authority, a transfer for the full balance of the term, but for only a portion of the premises, is an assignment (and has been called an assignment pro tanto).[785]

§ 6.68 ASSIGNMENTS

The assignee, by acquiring the tenant's entire estate, comes into privity of estate with the landlord. Under both real covenant and equitable servitude theories, the assignee thus becomes liable to the landlord to perform most or all of the tenant's covenants in the lease, including the covenant to pay rent.[786] If assignee A later reassigns to assignee B, assignee A no longer maintains privity of estate with the landlord and owes no further duties to the landlord unless the purported assignment was a sham.[787] Sometimes, however, an assignee may make an express covenant to perform the tenant's duties under the lease—i.e., to "assume" those obligations, as the expression goes in mortgage law. If the assignee assumed the tenant's obligations, then reassignment will not relieve the assignee; the assignee's liability in this situation is not based on privity of estate (which no longer exists with landlord following the reassignment), but on privity of contract (i.e., the landlord can enforce the assumption covenant unless it has since agreed to release that covenant).[788] Along with acquiring the tenant's duties to the

---

[783] D.A.C. Uranium Co. v. Benton, 149 F.Supp. 667 (D.Colo.1956); Morrisville Shopping Ctr. v. Sun Ray Drug Co., 112 A.2d 183 (Pa.1955).

[784] Orchard Shopping Ctr., Inc. v. Campo, 485 N.E.2d 1248 (Ill.App.1985); Indian Refining Co. v. Roberts, 181 N.E. 283 (Ind.App.1932).

[785] E.g., Waller v. Comm'r, 40 F.2d 892 (5th Cir. 1930), cert. denied, 282 U.S. 889, 51 S.Ct. 101, 75 L.Ed. 784 (1930); Kostakes v. Daly, 75 N.W.2d 191 (Minn.1956); Sheridan v. O.E. Doherty, Inc., 181 P. 16 (Wash.1919); Annot., 99 A.L.R. 220 (1935).

[786] Price v. S.S. Fuller, Inc., 639 P.2d 1003 (Alaska 1982); BRE DDR BR Whittwood CA LLC v. Farmers & Merchants Bank of Long Beach, 14 Cal.App.5th 992, 222 Cal.Rptr.3d 435 (2017); Kelly v. Tri-Cities Broadcasting, Inc., 147 Cal.App.3d 666, 195 Cal.Rptr. 303 (1983); Italian Fisherman, Inc. v. Middlemas, 545 A.2d 1 (Md.App.1988); Southcross Commerce Ctr., LLP v. Tupy Props., LLC, 766 N.W.2d 704 (Minn.App.2009); Back Ventures, L.L.C. Series D v. Safeway, Inc., 410 S.W.3d 245 (Mo.App.2013); 718 Assocs., Ltd. v. Sunwest N.O.P., Inc., 1 S.W.3d 355 (Tex.App.1999). As explained in Chapter 8, only those lease covenants that "touch and concern" the premises will run with the land to bind the tenant's assignee; any covenants that are purely personal to the tenant will not bind the assignee. The typical tenant covenants in a lease are of the type that touches and concerns land.

The assignee's liability that arises by privity of estate does not include liability for the tenant's obligations that accrued before the assignment. Thus, if the tenant made an assignment on August 1 but had not paid rent for July, the assignee would become liable for the August rent but not the July rent, e.g., Williams v. Safe Deposit & Trust Co., 175 A. 331 (Md.1934), although the landlord could exercise any right to terminate the lease on account of the default. See Berman, 1 Friedman on Leases § 7:5.1, at 7–106 (6th ed.2017).

[787] Williams v. Safe Deposit & Trust Co., 175 A. 331 (Md.1934); Shoolman v. Wales Mfg. Co., 118 N.E.2d 71 (Mass.1954); Gillette Bros. v. Aristocrat Restaurant, Inc., 145 N.E. 748 (N.Y.1924); A.D. Juilliard & Co. v. American Woolen Co., 69 R.I. 215, 32 A.2d 800 (1943) (sham assignment); OTR v. Flakey Jack's, Inc., 770 P.2d 629 (Wash.1989). See also Childs v. Warner Bros. Southern Theatres, Inc., 156 S.E. 923 (N.C.1931) (reassignment in breach of covenant not to assign). Note, however, that the re-assignment would not relieve the assignee of liability that accrued during the time the assignee was in privity of estate. E.g., Bloor v. Chase Manhattan Mtge. & Realty Trust, 511 F.Supp. 17 (S.D.N.Y.1981).

[788] Studebaker Corp. v. Aetna Sav. & Trust Co., 21 F.2d 385 (7th Cir.1927); Hamlen v. Rednalloh Co., 197 N.E. 149 (Mass.1935); Packard-Bamberger & Co. v. Maloof, 199 A.2d 400 (N.J.Super.1964), rev'd on other

landlord, the assignee also acquires the right to the landlord's performance of all the landlord's covenants the benefit of which run with the leasehold;[789] privity of estate cuts both ways.

Assignment does not relieve the tenant-assignor of the duty to perform tenant's lease covenants.[790] This is because the tenant made contractual promises in the lease and remains liable based on privity of contract until the tenant performs those promises or the landlord releases the tenant. Thus, as to covenants running with the leasehold estate, the landlord can proceed against both the tenant and the assignee, though the landlord can have only one recovery.[791] The landlord may release the tenant from personal liability, but release is not implied based solely on the landlord's consent to the assignment or its acceptance of the assignee's performance.[792] The tenant, who has no further estate in the land, probably cannot enforce the landlord's covenants.[793]

The legal relationship between tenant and assignee is also significant. The assignee has either impliedly (i.e., by privity of estate) or expressly (e.g., by assumption) agreed with the tenant to perform the tenant's running covenants. Thus, as between the tenant and the assignee, the assignee has a primary duty to perform those covenants. As far as the assignee is concerned, it follows that the tenant's concurrent duty to the landlord to perform these same covenants becomes a secondary duty. Out of this primary-secondary order of duties arises a suretyship relationship, with the assignee being the principal and the tenant a surety.[794] This means, for example, that if the landlord compels the tenant to perform one of these duties, the tenant may later recover from the assignee. It should also follow, as a principle of suretyship law, that the landlord's release of the assignee from some major duty or the material alteration of that duty—such as by significantly raising or lowering the rent or postponing due dates—will release the tenant from all duties of which tenant is a surety, if that release or alteration occurs without tenant's consent.[795]

---

grounds, 214 A.2d 45 (N.J.Super.App.Div.1965); A.D. Juilliard & Co. v. American Woolen Co., 69 R.I. 215, 32 A.2d 800 (1943).

The assignee does not assume the tenant's obligations merely by taking possession of the premises, or even by agreeing to take them "subject to" the terms of the lease. An assumption requires clear language indicating the assignee's intention to assume liability on the tenant's obligations. E.g., Coles Trading Co. v. Spiegel, Inc., 187 F.2d 984 (9th Cir.1951); Packard-Bamberger & Co. v. Maloof, 214 A.2d 45 (N.J.Super.1965).

[789] E.g., Infinity Broadcasting Corp. v. Prudential Ins. Co. of Am., 869 F.2d 1073 (7th Cir.1989); Income Props. Inv. Corp. v. Trefethen, 284 P. 782 (Wash.1930).

[790] Peiser v. Mettler, 328 P.2d 953 (Cal.1958); Vallely Invsts. L.P. v. BancAmerica Comm. Corp., 88 Cal.App.4th 816, 106 Cal.Rptr.2d 689 (2001); Net Realty Holding Trust v. Giannini, 432 N.E.2d 120 (Mass.App.1982); Siragusa v. Park, 913 S.W.2d 915 (Mo.App.1996); Gerber v. Pecht, 104 A.2d 41 (N.J.1954); Lincoln Place LLC v. RVP Consulting, Inc., 16 A.D.3d 123, 791 N.Y.S.2d 31 (2005); Hoffman v. Junior Vogue, Inc., 91 A.D.2d 703, 457 N.Y.S.2d 601 (1982); B&G Props. Ltd. Partn. v. OfficeMax, Inc., 3 N.E.3d 774 (Ohio App.2013); Cauble v. Hanson, 249 S.W. 175 (Tex.Com.App.1923).

[791] Berman, 1 Friedman on Leases § 7:5.1, at 7–115 (6th ed.2017).

[792] Gerber v. Pecht, 104 A.2d 41 (N.J.1954); Bird Hill Farms, Inc. v. United States Cargo & Courier Serv., Inc., 845 A.2d 900 (Pa.Super.2004); Cauble v. Hanson, 249 S.W. 175 (Tex.Com.App.1923).

[793] Murray Hill Mello Corp. v. Bonne Bouchee Restaurant, Inc., 113 Misc.2d 683, 449 N.Y.S.2d 870 (1982). See Restatement (Second) of Property-Landlord & Tenant § 16.2 (1977); Stoebuck, Running Covenants: An Analytical Primer, 53 Wash.L.Rev. 861, 887 (1977).

[794] Kendall v. Ernest Pestana, Inc., 709 P.2d 837 (Cal.1985); Lincoln Place v. RVP Consulting, Inc., 16 A.D.3d 123, 791 N.Y.S.2d 31 (2005).

[795] For further discussion of the legal implications of the tenant-assignor's role as a surety, see Berman, 1 Friedman on Leases § 7:5.2 (6th ed.2017).

§ 6.69 SUBLEASES

In a sublease, the tenant retains a reversion within the leasehold. This means that the transferee (the "subtenant" or "sublessee") is neither in privity of estate nor privity of contract with the landlord under the original (or primary) lease. But, being in rightful possession, the subtenant is a tenant with a leasehold estate that is carved out of the primary leasehold. Between the original tenant (the "sublandlord" or "sublessor") and the subtenant there is a true landlord-tenant relationship, governed by the same general rules that govern the primary lease. The sublessee has a direct landlord-tenant relationship with the tenant-sublessor but no direct relationship with the landlord under the primary lease. This is why two tenants who agree between themselves to divide up the premises and the rent—but each of whom gained possession through the landlord—are not tenant and subtenant, but instead co-tenants who each owe the full rent to the landlord.[796]

Lacking privity of estate, a sublessee is not liable to the landlord to pay rent or perform any covenant of the primary lease as a real covenant.[797] This does not mean, however, that the sublessee can act with impunity or disregard the performance of the primary lease covenants. Leases commonly permit the landlord to terminate the leasehold in case of the breach of certain covenants—particularly the covenant to pay rent—and termination of the primary lease results in the termination of the sublease.[798] A subtenant may also be directly liable to the landlord despite lacking privity of estate if the subtenant has expressly assumed the obligations in the primary lease.[799] Finally, a sublessee could be liable to the landlord if the sublessee commits waste or other tortious damage to the premises.[800]

Because termination of the primary lease also terminates the sublessee's estate,[801] any sublessee should make arrangements with the tenant or the landlord under the primary lease for appropriate protections of the sublessee's interest. This might include, for example, ensuring that the sublessee has a right to notice of the tenant's default and an opportunity to cure that default. Courts have concluded that the primary tenant

---

[796] Sentliffer v. Jacobs, 86 A. 929 (N.J.1913).

[797] Bordelon v. Bordelon, 434 So.2d 633 (La.App.1983); American Community Stores Corp. v. Newman, 441 N.W.2d 154 (Neb.1989); LaVack v. National Shoes, Inc., 124 A.D.2d 352, 507 N.Y.S.2d 293 (1986); Neal v. Braun Craig Brown, Inc., 356 S.E.2d 912 (N.C.App.1987); Davis v. Vidal, 105 Tex. 444, 151 S.W. 290 (1912). Likewise, the subtenant cannot enforce against the tenant-sublessor the latter's covenants in the primary lease. Summit Foods, Inc. v. Greyhound Food Mgmt., Inc., 752 F.Supp. 363 (D.Colo.1990).

As discussed in Chapter 8, under equitable servitude theory, no privity is required for a covenant to run with land. Certainly a subtenant would normally have actual knowledge of the primary lease's contents and in some cases constructive notice as well. Could a court of equity compel a subtenant to perform the covenant to pay rent (or other covenants in the primary lease) as an equitable servitude? It is tempting to say that equity will not, because equity will not award damages, but the issue is not that simple. One can argue that equity would be ordering performance of the very thing promised (i.e., paying rent). Further, courts can and do order a contract purchaser of land to pay the purchase price and to accept a deed. D. Dobbs, Remedies § 12.13 (1973). Nevertheless, courts have not used equitable servitude theory to allow the primary landlord to obtain a judgment against a subtenant for unpaid rent.

[798] Precision Dynamics v. Retailers Representatives, 120 Misc. 180, 465 N.Y.S.2d 684 (1983); Cleveland v. A.J. Rose Mfg. Co., 624 N.E.2d 245 (Ohio App.1993).

[799] C.R. Anthony Co. v. Wal-Mart Props., Inc., 54 F.3d 514 (8th Cir.1995); Goldberg v. L.H. Realty Corp., 86 So.2d 326 (Miss.1956).

[800] Some courts have even held that the primary tenant-sublessor is also liable for waste committed on the premises by the sublessee. E.g., Lustig v. U.M.C. Indus., Inc., 637 S.W.2d 55 (Mo.App.1982); Dixie Fire & Cas. Co. v. Esso Standard Oil Co., 265 N.C. 121, 143 S.E.2d 279 (1965).

[801] E.g., Applebee's Northeast, Inc. v. Methuen Invs., Inc., 709 N.E.2d 1143 (Mass.App.1999).

cannot terminate the sublease by voluntarily surrendering the primary lease—at least in the absence of clear language so providing—reasoning that the tenant cannot surrender an interest already conveyed to the sublessee.[802] Under the weight of authority, the primary tenant is not required to exercise options to renew or extend the term for the benefit of the sublessee, absent express language in the sublease or circumstances indicating a contrary expectation.[803]

Because a sublease does not transfer privity of estate to the sublessee, the original tenant remains in both privity of estate and privity of contract with the primary landlord.[804] As the sublease creates a separate landlord-tenant relationship between the tenant-sublessor and the sublessee, the sublessee is obligated to pay the rent reserved in the sublease and to comply with other covenants in the sublease; likewise, the tenant-sublessor can resort to the customary landlord remedies for breaches by the sublessee.[805]

§ 6.70 RESTRICTIONS ON TENANT'S TRANSFER

Nearly all written leases contain clauses restricting the tenant's power to assign or sublease. Sometimes the lease prohibits the tenant from making an assignment or a sublease altogether. More commonly, the lease prohibits an assignment or a sublease without the landlord's prior consent.

Clauses restricting transfer run contrary to the law's general policy against restraints on alienation. However, the policy is not absolute, and permits restraints when they serve good purposes (i.e., when they are "reasonable"). A landlord has many good reasons for concern about the identity of the person occupying the premises; the landlord wants to ensure, for example, that the person can pay the rent, properly maintain the premises, and will not commit waste or use the premises in a fashion for they are not suited. For this reason, courts generally enforce clauses restricting transfer,[806] but will tend to interpret them strictly. Thus, a clause restraining only "assignment" will not be interpreted to prevent subleasing,[807] nor will a clause prohibiting only "subleasing" prevent assignment.[808] Some decisions have stated that a tenant does not violate a no-subleasing clause by subletting only a portion of the

---

[802] E.g., Goldberg v. Tri-States Theatre Corp., 126 F.2d 26 (8th Cir.1942); Byrd v. Peterson, 186 P.2d 955 (Ariz.1947); Warnert v. MGM Props., 362 N.W.2d 364 (Minn.App.1985); Unionport Shoes, Inc. v. Parkchester South Condo., Inc., 205 A.D.2d 385, 613 N.Y.S.2d 605 (1994).

[803] Regional Pacesetters, Inc. v. Eckerd Drugs of Ga., Inc., 358 S.E.2d 481 (Ga.App.1987); Minister, Elders & Deacons of the Reformed Protestant Dutch Church v. 198 Broadway, 451 N.E.2d 164 (N.Y.1983).

[804] Broida v. Hayashi, 464 P.2d 285 (Haw.1970); First Am. Nat'l Bank v. Chicken Systems of Am., Inc., 510 S.W.2d 906 (Tenn.App.1974).

[805] 5 Thompson on Real Property § 42.04(e)(3)(ii), at 336 (2d Thomas ed.2007).

[806] E.g., Kendall v. Ernest Pestana, Inc., 709 P.2d 837 (Cal.1985); Van Sloun v. Agans Bros., Inc, 778 N.W.2d 174 (Iowa 2010); Julian v. Christopher, 575 A.2d 735 (Md.1990); 200 Eighth Ave. Restaurant Corp. v. Daytona Holding Corp., 293 A.D.2d 353, 740 N.Y.S.2d 330 (2002). Note, however, that the clause exists for the protection of the landlord; thus, a subtenant may not use the tenant's failure to obtain the landlord's consent as a defense to payment of rent under the sublease. E.g., Kleyle v. Deogracias, 195 So.3d 234 (Miss.App.2016).

[807] American Community Stores Corp. v. Newman, 441 N.W.2d 154 (Neb.1989); 24 Broad St. Corp. v. Quinn, 87 A.2d 759 (N.J.Super.1952); Burns v. Dufresne, 121 P. 46 (Wash.1912); Restatement (Second) of Property-Landlord & Tenant § 15.2, Reporter's Note 5 (1977). For this reason, landlords ordinarily ensure that the clause expressly restrain both types of transfers. But see Megargel Willbrand & Co., LLC v. Fampat Ltd. Partn., 210 S.W.3d 205 (Mo.App.2006) (clause prohibiting assignment without landlord consent also prohibits assignment of right of first refusal to buy premises contained in the lease).

[808] Cities Service Oil Co. v. Taylor, 45 S.W.2d 1039 (Ky.1932); Krasner v. Transcontinental Equities, Inc., 70 A.D.2d 312, 420 N.Y.S.2d 872 (1979); Willenbrock v. Latulippe, 215 P. 330 (Wash.1923).

premises.[809] Courts have held that nonconsensual transfers and transfers by operation of law, including inheritance and even devises, do not fall within the prohibition of a no-transfer clause unless the clause mentions them explicitly.[810] A tenant's mortgaging of the leasehold does not violate a clause against transfer in a lien theory state (unless the lease explicitly defines "transfer" to include a mortgage), but it may in a title theory state.[811] The granting of a license, such as by an agricultural tenant's granting grazing rights, usually does not breach a clause prohibiting transfer.[812]

The Rule in *Dumpor's Case*[813] is another example of the judicial disfavor for transfer restraints. The rule provides that if a landlord gives consent to one particular assignment without reserving the right to restrict future assignments, the tenant thereafter may make future assignments without the landlord's consent. Though England has abolished the rule[814] and its logic is dubious, it remains the apparent American rule,[815] though courts have refused to apply it to clauses prohibiting subleasing.[816] In any event, the careful landlord can avoid the rule's application by reserving the right to restrict future assignments when giving consent to an assignment. No-transfer clauses commonly state that the giving of consent shall not negate the need for consent to future transfers, and courts have given effect to such language.[817]

As noted above, no-transfer clauses often require the landlord's consent to a proposed assignment or sublease. Sometimes, however, leases are silent regarding what standard governs the landlord's exercise of discretion to withhold consent. In these circumstances, the traditional rule and likely weight of authority is that the landlord may withhold consent in its complete discretion, without having to give a reason.[818] These courts typically reason that because a landlord has the right to select its tenants in the first instance, the landlord likewise should have the same freedom in accepting

---

[809] Drake v. Eggleston, 108 N.E.2d 67 (Ind.App.1952); Denecke v. Henry F. Miller & Son, 119 N.W. 380 (Iowa 1909); Presby v. Benjamin, 62 N.E. 430 (N.Y.1902); Annot., 56 A.L.R.2d 1002 (1957).

[810] Gazlay v. Williams, 210 U.S. 41, 28 S.Ct. 687, 52 L.Ed. 950 (1908) (transfer to bankruptcy trustee); Francis v. Ferguson, 159 N.E. 416 (N.Y.1927) (transfer to and by executors); Powell v. Nichols, 110 P. 762 (Okla.1910) (execution by tenant's creditors); Annot., 46 A.L.R. 847 (1927); Restatement (Second) of Property-Landlord & Tenant § 15.2, Reporter's Note 5 (1977).

[811] Chapman v. Great Western Gypsum Co., 14 P.2d 758 (Cal.1932) (lien theory); Becker v. Werner, 98 Pa. 555 (1881) (title theory).

[812] Annot., 71 A.L.R.3d 780 (1976); Annot. 89 A.L.R. 1325 (1934); Restatement (Second) of Property-Landlord & Tenant § 15.2, Reporter's Note 5 (1977).

[813] 4 Coke 119b, 76 Eng.Rep. 1110 (K.B.1603).

[814] Law of Property Act, 22 & 23 Vict., c. 35, § 1 (1859).

[815] German-American Sav. Bank v. Gollmer, 102 P. 932 (Cal.1909); Reid v. Weissner & Sons Brewing Co., 40 A. 877 (Md.1898); Aste v. Putnam's Hotel Co., 141 N.E. 666 (Mass.1923); Easley Coal Co. v. Brush Creek Coal Co., 91 W.Va. 291, 112 S.E. 512 (1922); Annot., 32 A.L.R. 1080 (1924). Contra Reynolds v. McCullough, 739 S.W.2d 424 (Tex.App.1987); Investors' Guaranty Corp. v. Thomson, 225 P. 590 (Wyo.1924); Restatement (Second) of Property-Landlord & Tenant § 16.1, Comment g (1977). North Carolina has abolished the Rule by statute. N.C.Gen.Stat. § 41–6.4.

[816] German-American Sav. Bank v. Gollmer, 102 P. 932 (Cal.1909); Miller v. Newton-Humphreville Co., 116 A. 325 (N.J.Ch.1920); Annot., 31 A.L.R. 153, 157–59 (1924).

[817] See Merritt v. Kay, 295 F. 973 (D.C.App.1924); Springer v. Chicago Real Estate, Loan & Trust Co., 66 N.E. 850 (Ill.1903); Italian Fisherman, Inc. v. Middlemas, 545 A.2d 1 (Md.App.1988); 1 Am. Law of Prop. § 3.58 (1952).

[818] First Fed. Sav. Bank v. Key Mkts., Inc. 559 N.E.2d 600 (Ind.1990); Gruman v. Investors Diversified Servs., Inc., 78 N.W.2d 377 (Minn.1956); Dress Shirt Sales, Inc. v. Hotel Martinique Assocs., 190 N.E.2d 10 (N.Y.1963); Abrahamson v. Brett, 21 P.2d 229 (Or.1933); Dobyns v. South Carolina Dept. of Parks, Recreation & Tourism, 454 S.E.2d 347 (S.C.App.1995); Coulos v. Desimone, 208 P.2d 105 (Wash.1949); B & R Oil Co. v. Ray's Mobile Homes, Inc., 422 A.2d 1267 (Vt.1980); Annot., 31 A.L.R.2d 831, 831–34 (1953).

assignees or sublessees unless the parties expressly agree to limit that discretion. However, several recent decisions, most notably the California decision in Kendall v. Ernest Pestana, Inc.,[819] have flipped the default rule and hold that the landlord must have a reasonable basis to withhold consent, unless the lease expressly reserves to the landlord absolute discretion.[820] These decisions reason that the landlord's refusal to consent in the absence of objectively reasonable grounds breaches the landlord's duty of good faith and fair dealing in its enforcing its rights under the lease contract, and also renders the exercise of the clause an unreasonable restraint on alienation. These decisions may not yet reflect a majority rule but do reflect a clear modern trend.[821]

In these jurisdictions, landlords commonly negotiate for specific language that permits the landlord to withhold consent for any or for no reason.[822] By contrast, in jurisdictions following the traditional rule, a tenant may negotiate for language requiring that the landlord not "unreasonably" withhold consent. Whether a landlord acts reasonably in withholding consent is a factual question—and thus results tend to vary with the facts and circumstances involved—but some generalizations are possible. The landlord can safely withhold consent because the proposed transferee is uncreditworthy[823] or because of the objectionable nature of the proposed transferee's use.[824] The landlord cannot reasonably withhold consent based on personal taste or

---

[819]   709 P.2d 837 (Cal.1985).

[820]   Kendall v. Ernest Pestana, Inc., 709 P.2d 837 (Cal.1985). Accord: Homa-Goff Interiors, Inc. v. Ceruden, 350 So.2d 1035 (Ala.1977); Tuscan Med. Ctr. v. Zoslau, 712 P.2d 459 (Ariz.1985); Cafeteria Operator, L.P. v. AMCA/Denver Ltd. Partn., 972 P.2d 276 (Colo.App.1998); 1010 Potomac Assocs. v. Grocery Mfrs., 485 A.2d 199 (D.C.1984); Funk v. Funk, 633 P.2d 586 (Idaho 1981); Jack Frost Sales, Inc. v. Harris Trust & Sav. Bank, 433 N.E.2d 941 (Ill.App.1982); Julian v. Christopher, 575 A.2d 735 (Md.1990); Newman v. Hinky-Dinky Omaha-Lincoln, Inc., 427 N.W.2d 50 (Neb.1988); Boss Barbara, Inc. v. Newbill, 638 P.2d 1084 (N.M.1982). The Restatement also adopts this position. Restatement (Second) of Property-Landlord & Tenant § 15.2 (1977).

In some states that follow the traditional rule, the tenant may attempt to surrender the premises if the landlord unreasonably refuses to consent to a proffered assignee, and then argue that the landlord must mitigate damages by re-letting to the proferred assignee or another available substitute tenant. If the jurisdiction requires the landlord to mitigate when the tenant wrongfully surrenders possession, the landlord's refusal to re-let to the proferred assignee (or another available substitute tenant) could result in a termination of the lease and the tenant's liability. See Bert Bidwell Invst. Corp. v. LaSalle & Schiffer, P.C., 797 P.2d 811 (Colo.App.1990). For further discussion of tenant abandonment and whether the landlord has a duty to mitigate, see § 6.81 infra.

[821]   5 Thompson on Real Property § 42.04(b)(3), at 310 (2d Thomas ed.2007) ("[A] clear majority of courts that have addressed the issue in the past 20 years have adopted the minority position, with 14 states following the minority position and only 7 holding to the majority position.").

[822]   See Annot., 31 A.L.R.2d 831, 834–35 (1953); Restatement (Second) of Property-Landlord & Tenant § 15.2 (1977).

[823]   E.g., Riggs v. Murdock, 458 P.2d 115 (Ariz.App.1969); Pakwood Indus., Inc. v. John Galt Assocs., 466 S.E.2d 226 (Ga.App.1995); Jack Frost Sales, Inc. v. Harris Trust & Sav. Bank, 433 N.E.2d 941 (Ill.App.1982); Jonas v. Prutaub Joint Venture, 567 A.2d 230 (N.J.1989). If the landlord objects to a proposed assignee as not financially suitable, courts will evaluate the reasonableness of that decision. E.g., Tollius v. Dutch Inns of America, Inc., 244 So.2d 467 (Fla.App.1979) (landlord's refusal based on financial irresponsibility was unreasonable where original tenant had "nebulous" net worth at time of lease, but proposed transferee's net worth exceeded $3.5 million).

[824]   E.g., Evans v. Waldrop, 220 So.3d 1066 (Ala.App.2016) (proposed sublease for bingo parlor); Pay 'N Pak Stores, Inc. v. Superior Court, 210 Cal.App.3d 1404, 258 Cal.Rptr. 816 (1989) (proposed transferee would have competed with landlord's business operations); Van Sloun v. Agans Bros., Inc., 778 N.W.2d 174 (Iowa 2010) (sublessee would have unduly competed with existing tenants); Newman v. Hinky Dinky Omaha-Lincoln, Inc., 512 N.W.2d 410 (Neb.App.1994) (lease based on percentage rent; sublessee's operations would have generated smaller sales volume); Sayed v. Rapp, 10 A.D.3d 717, 782 N.Y.S.2d 278 (2004) (assignee's proposed use not permitted by original lease and materially differed from original use).

considerations unrelated to operation of the premises.[825] Under the significant weight of authority, the landlord cannot reasonably withhold consent simply to compel the tenant to agree to increase the rent.[826] This issue sometimes arises in the context of long-term leases, where landlords sometimes find that the rental amount due under the original lease has not kept track with market rental values. Courts have rejected efforts by landlords to use their consent power to obtain a readjustment of the rent to market levels, unless the express terms of the lease made it clear that such an adjustment was possible. For this reason, commercial leases often include "recapture clauses." These clauses come in various forms: some expressly permit the landlord to condition its consent upon a readjustment of the rent; others allow the landlord to terminate the lease in the event of a proposed assignment or sublease (thus allowing the landlord to lease the premises to the proposed transferee or another lessee directly at currently prevailing market rents).

Landlords typically ensure that lease agreements couple a no-transfer clause with a power to terminate the leasehold if the tenant attempts a transfer without consent. This is important because a transfer made without the required consent is nevertheless valid;[827] however, if the landlord may terminate the lease for the unauthorized transfer, termination of the lease will terminate the transferee's rights.

§ 6.71   TRANSFERS BY LANDLORD

A landlord may convey the reversion, typically by deed. Generally, the grantee will take subject to the tenant's leasehold.[828] The grantee, as owner of the reversion, comes into privity of estate with the tenant. A few decisions have gone so far as to consider the grantee a substitute landlord, meaning that in every respect the grantee has the right to performance of the tenant's lease covenants and the duty to perform all landlord's

---

[825] E.g., Gelino v. Swannell, 263 Ill.App. 235 (1931) (landlord's refusal to consent based on nationality of assignee and landlord's distaste for chain stores was unreasonable); Stern v. Taft, 361 N.E.2d 279 (Ohio App.1976) (landlord's refusal to consent because transferee was a widow was unreasonable). In one notorious case, American Book Co. v. Yeshiva Univ. Dev. Found., Inc., 59 Misc.2d 31, 297 N.Y.S.2d 156 (1969), the landlord was a religious organization and withheld its consent to a proposed transfer to Planned Parenthood based on its religious objections. The court held that the landlord's withholding of consent was unreasonable because the transferee was creditworthy and its proposed use (office use) was consistent with existing uses in the building. The case should be understood in the context of the fact that the religious organization was not the original landlord, but had acquired the building after the tenant had signed the lease. If the tenant had originally contracted with Yeshiva as its original landlord, the possibility that Yeshiva might have raised a religious objection to the identity of a particular assignee would have been foreseeable. But because the original landlord was an ordinary real estate developer, there would have been no reason for the original tenant to think that assignment decisions would be based on moral grounds rather than financial ones.

[826] E.g., Kendall v. Ernest Pestana, Inc., 709 P.2d 837 (Cal.1985); Funk v. Funk, 633 P.2d 586 (Idaho 1981); Julian v. Christopher, 575 A.2d 735 (Md.1990); D.L. Dev., Inc. v. Nance, 894 S.W.2d 258 (Mo.App.1995); Berman, 1 Friedman on Leases § 7:3.4[D][3], at 7–64 (6th ed.2017) (collecting cases). The *Julian* court suggested that the landlord could reasonably demand additional rent in exchange for its consent if the proposed transferee in some way subjected the landlord to additional risk of expense.

[827] People v. Klopstock, 151 P.2d 641 (Cal.1944); OTR v. Flakey Jake's, Inc. 770 P.2d 629 (Wash.1989). But see Reynolds v. McCullough, 739 S.W.2d 424 (Tex.App.1987) (holding that a landlord has an implied power to terminate if a tenant breaches a clause forbidding assignment).

[828] It is possible—but unlikely—for the grantee to take free of the leasehold by force of a recording act. For this to occur, the following conditions would have to exist: (1) the lease term was long enough to require the lease to be recorded; (2) the lease was unrecorded; (3) the grantee gave value; (4) the grantee had no notice of the tenancy; and (5) the tenant was not in possession, for possession would give the grantee inquiry notice of the unrecorded lease. In states with race-notice recording acts, the grantee would have to have recorded its conveyance while the lease remained unrecorded to qualify for the protection of the recording act. If the landlord had mortgaged the reversion instead of conveying it, the above statements would govern priority between the mortgagee and the tenant. 1 Am. Law of Prop. § 3.59 (1952).

covenants.[829] These decisions go too far; instead, by the correct analysis, the grantee has the right to performance of those tenant covenants—and the duty to perform those landlord covenants—that run with the land.[830] As a practical matter, these include most of the valuable tenant covenants, such as the covenant to pay rent, and most of the landlord's covenants. However, if the grantee and the tenant want to be sure all covenants (even "personal" ones) are binding between them, they must make a new lease or adopt the existing lease contractually. The grantee is not liable for the breach of a landlord's covenant that occurred before the conveyance to the grantee.[831]

Under the original common-law rule, the tenant had to "attorn" to the grantee before rights or duties existed between them. This meant the tenant had to recognize the grantee, usually by paying rent. In England, the Statute of Anne of 1705[832] ended the requirement for attornment. American states have likewise abandoned the attornment requirement, either by statute[833] or by judicial decision.[834]

While the landlord's conveyance of the reversion terminates privity of estate between the landlord and the tenant, the landlord would remain liable on any landlord lease covenants for which landlord was personally liable under privity of contract, absent contrary agreement.[835] For most landlord obligations in the lease, however, a landlord is not likely to agree to remain personally liable following a transfer of the reversion. For example, the original landlord would not expect to be responsible to repair the premises once the landlord no longer had ownership or control over them. In one example, a court held that after a sale of property subject to a restaurant lease, the landlord was no longer liable on a covenant to repair a sewer line servicing the premises.[836]

When acquiring the reversion, a grantee will want to review the lease carefully to confirm the nature of the tenant's interest and duties of each party. As part of this review, the grantee will often require that the tenant execute an "estoppel letter" or "estoppel certificate," in which the tenant confirms the grantee's expectations regarding the lease. This certificate should confirm, among other things, that the lease is valid, the

---

[829] See, e.g., F. Groos & Co. v. Chittim, 100 S.W. 1006 (Tex.Civ.App.1907); Annot., 14 A.L.R. 664, 678 (1921).

[830] E.g., Mrotek Enters., Inc. v. Dryer, 256 A.2d 557 (D.C.App.1969) (covenant to appoint agent for service of process did not run to bind grantee of reversion); P.M.K., Inc. v. Folsom Heights Dev. Co., 692 S.W.2d 395 (Mo.App.1985) (covenant to return security deposit did not run to bind grantee of reversion); Mullendore Theatres, Inc. v. Growth Realty Investors Co., 691 P.2d 970 (Wash.App.1984) (same).

[831] E.g., Bank of N.Y. v. Hirschfeld, 63 A.D.2d 794, 404 N.Y.S.2d 916 (1978); Cal.Civ.Code § 1466 ("No one, merely by reason of having acquired an estate subject to a covenant running with the land, is liable for a breach of the covenant before he acquired the estate. . . .").

[832] 4 Anne, c. 16, §§ 9, 10.

[833] See 5 Thompson on Real Property § 42.03(a), at 288 & n.4 (collecting statutes) (2d Thomas ed.2007).

[834] See Glidden v. Second Ave. Invst. Co., 147 N.W. 658 (Minn.1914); Cooper v. Ratley, 916 S.W.2d 868 (Mo.App.1996); Stasyszyn v. Sutton East Assocs., 213 A.D.2d 337, 623 N.Y.S.2d 879 (1995); Northern Pac. Rwy. Co. v. McClure, 81 N.W. 52 (N.D.1899). It is still common, however, that commercial leases will contain a clause in which the tenant covenants to attorn to the landlord's successor.

[835] E.g., Won's Cards, Inc. v. Samsondale/Haverstraw Equities, Ltd., 165 A.D.2d 157, 566 N.Y.S.2d 412 (1991) (original landlord released following conveyance of reversion by express language in lease).Thus, for example, where the landlord promises to refund a security deposit, but later sells the building, the landlord remains liable to the tenant to refund the security deposit; as discussed in section 6.58 supra, some courts have held that this obligation is personal to the landlord and does not run with the land.

[836] Del Taco, Inc. v. University Real Estate Partn. v. 111 Cal.App.4th 16, 3 Cal.Rptr.3d 311 (2003) ("the nature of the express covenants in the lease do not support a theory that sufficient privity of contract existed to connect these particular express promises to [landlord] as personal to it, or to hold it liable on an ongoing basis to [tenant], past the time of transfer of the leasehold property").

amount of rent due, that the lease has not been amended, that the lease is not in default, and that the tenant has no claims against the landlord or defenses to enforcement of the lease. The document's name explains its purpose—to permit the grantee to interpose an estoppel if the tenant later takes a position inconsistent with the statements in the certificate.[837] Because a landlord could have difficulty transferring or mortgaging its reversion if the tenant does not execute an estoppel certificate, a well-drafted lease will contain a clause obligating the tenant to execute one on the landlord's request.[838]

M. TERMINATION

§ 6.72 NORMAL END OF TERM—TENANCY FOR YEARS

A tenancy for years (or fixed-term tenancy) terminates automatically at the agreed end of the term. Neither party need give notice or do any other act to make it end; the parties' agreement has already limited the leasehold's life.[839] When the agreed period is for some definite calendar period, such as a month or day, the term ends at the end of the last day of that period.[840] If the tenant holds over without the landlord's consent, the tenant becomes a tenant at sufferance, as discussed in section 6.20.

§ 6.73 NORMAL END OF TERM—PERIODIC TENANCY

As explained in section 6.16, a periodic tenancy has a term of indefinite duration that terminates at the end of some rental period by effective notice by one of the parties to the other. Statutes prescribe the length of notice required, the time usually being counted backward from the end of one of the periods of the leasehold. The various statutes prescribe times varying from seven days to one year. A given state may prescribe different times for different kinds of leases (e.g., shorter periods of notice for short-term leaseholds and longer periods for agricultural and long-term leaseholds).[841]

To confirm the proper form of notice and manner of delivery, one must consult the lease and the controlling statute. Notices may be oral unless, as is likely, the lease or the applicable statute requires written notice. A well-drafted notice should identify the sender as landlord or tenant (and the recipient as the other); identify the premises; state that it is a notice to terminate; and expressly designate the day of termination.[842] Length

---

[837] E.g., Plaza Freeway Ltd. Partn. v. First Mtn. Bank, 81 Cal.App.4th 616, 96 Cal.Rptr.2d 865 (2000).

[838] For further background on estoppel certificates and sample certificates, see generally Berman, 3 Friedman on Leases § 36.9 and Appendices A–C (6th ed.2017).

[839] Minor v. Hicks, 180 So. 689 (Ala.1938); Chappell v. Reynolds, 176 S.W.2d 154 (Ark.1943); Tredick v. Birrer, 200 P. 272 (Kan.1921).

[840] Minor v. Hicks, 180 So. 689 (Ala.1938).

[841] See Restatement (Second) of Property-Landlord & Tenant § 1.5, Statutory Note (1977), for a listing and analysis of the many state statutes. For sample discussions of the operation of various notice statutes, see Darling Shops Delaware Corp. v. Baltimore Ctr. Corp., 60 A.2d 669 (Md.1948); 28 Mott St. Co. v. Summit Import Corp., 34 A.D.2d 144, 310 N.Y.S.2d 93 (1970), aff'd, 267 N.E.2d 880 (N.Y.1971); Arbenz v. Exley, Watkins & Co., 50 S.E. 813 (W.Va.1905); Annot., 86 A.L.R. 1346 (1933).

A recent California decision suggests that an implied periodic tenancy that arose following a holdover was terminated by the tenant's failure to pay rent, despite the fact that neither party gave a specific notice of termination. Multani v. Knight, 23 Cal.App.5th 837, 233 Cal.Rptr.3d 537 (2018). This conclusion is dubious, as a tenant's nonpayment of rent might well be motivated by the lack of funds rather than a desire to terminate the leasehold.

[842] Traditionally, courts held that a notice was not effective to terminate a periodic tenancy if the notice identified a termination date other than the natural end of a period. E.g., Gill v. Gill, 161 Ill.App. 221 (1911). Today, courts generally hold that as long as the notice was given a sufficient time prior to a permissible termination date, the notice will be effective to terminate the tenancy at the earliest possible termination date.

of notice is computed by excluding the day of service and including the designated termination day.[843]

Courts have sometimes struggled to interpret what may be called the landlord's "notice in the alternative." Such a notice tells the tenant either to quit the premises on a designated day (i.e., a permitted termination date) or, if not, to render an amended performance that may include an increased rent. Many courts hold the tenant liable for the amended performance if the tenant remains in possession and fails to dispute the proposed amendment.[844] Because the tenant's new liability is based on implied assent to the proposed amendment, the tenant's expressed dissent would presumably prevent the change.[845] By a minority view, the notice in the alternative (being neither fish nor fowl) has no effect, either to amend the lease or to terminate it.[846]

§ 6.74   NORMAL END OF TERM—TENANCY AT WILL

As its name suggests, a tenancy at will extends only so long as both parties desire it. At common law it is instantly terminable by either party giving notice to terminate it, although the courts do allow the tenant a reasonable time to remove possessions.[847] Approximately half of the American states now have statutes requiring advance notice to terminate a tenancy at will. Required notice periods run from three days (Colorado) to as long as three months (Minnesota), with 30 days or one month being the most common period.[848] Such a requirement converts the tenancy at will into a periodic tenancy in effect, if perhaps not in strict theory. Indeed, Massachusetts uses the phrase "tenancy at will" to refer to what has traditionally been known as a periodic tenancy.[849]

§ 6.75   NORMAL END OF TERM—TENANCY AT SUFFERANCE

As noted in Section 6.20, it stretches the imagination to say that a tenant at sufferance (who becomes such by a non-permissive holding over) is truly a tenant. If so, the tenancy does not come to an end in any regular way. The relationship, temporary by nature, usually ends by the tenant's becoming either a trespasser or a tenant under a new lease. The landlord has a power, exercisable for a "reasonable time" after the tenancy at sufferance begins, to transform the holdover into one of these two

---

E.g., Pertillo v. Forest Ridge Ltd., 304 S.E.2d 925 (Ga.App.1983); Foster v. Schwickerath, 780 N.W.2d 746 (Iowa App.2009); Harry's Village, Inc. v. Egg Harbor Township, 446 A.2d 862 (N.J.1982); Restatement (Second) of Property-Landlord & Tenant § 1.5 (1977).

[843] Restatement (Second) of Property-Landlord & Tenant § 1.4, Comment d; § 1.5, Comment e (1977).

[844] Garrity v. United States, 67 F.Supp. 821 (Ct.Cl.1946); Welk v. Bidwell, 73 A.2d 295 (Conn.1950); David Props., Inc. v. Selk, 151 So.2d 334 (Fla.App.1963); Heckman v. Walker, 92 N.W.2d 548 (Neb.1958); Bhar Realty Corp. v. Becker, 140 A.2d 756 (N.J.Super.1958). Cf. Annot., 109 A.L.R. 197 (1937) (addressing cases dealing with landlord notices purporting to amend lease provisions when such notices are not conjoined with a notice to quit).

[845] Moll v. Main Motor Co., 210 S.W.2d 321 (Ark.1948).

[846] Maguire v. Haddad, 91 N.E.2d 769 (Mass.1950).

[847] 1 Am. Law of Prop. § 3.91 (1952); Restatement (Second) of Property-Landlord & Tenant § 1.6 (1977). See also Day v. Kolar, 341 N.W.2d 598 (Neb.1983) (lease that allowed either party to terminate "upon 0 days notice" was tenancy at will that was terminable at any time).

[848] See Colo.Rev.Stat.Ann. § 13–40–107(1)(d); Minn.Stat.Ann. § 504B.135(a) (lesser of three months or the interval between the time rent is due); Restatement (Second) of Property-Landlord & Tenant § 1.6, Statutory Note 3 (1977) (compiling statutes).

[849] See Mass.Gen.Laws Ann. c. 186, § 12; Maguire v. Haddad, 91 N.E.2d 769 (Mass.1950).

relationships. Courts generally have not characterized the holdover tenant as a trespasser until the landlord has ordered the holdover to vacate the premises.[850]

§ 6.76 TENANCY UPON SPECIAL LIMITATION

As discussed in Chapter 3, a fee estate may be created to endure only "so long as" a given state of affairs obtains, e.g., so long as a school is maintained or so long as liquor is not sold. The continuation of the described condition is necessary to support the estate, which is called an estate determinable or upon special limitation. When the necessary state of affairs ceases, the estate terminates automatically, without entry or other act by the holder of the succeeding estate. A leasehold estate could be limited in a similar fashion; in practice, this arises when a lease contains an automatic termination clause. Terminating events depend upon the language of the lease, which may include the tenant's illegal activities on the premises; the tenant's insolvency, bankruptcy, or death; the tenant's vacating of the premises; or the landlord's sale of the reversion. Upon the specified event's happening, the leasehold automatically ends.[851]

Automatic termination clauses are ill-advised, in two senses. First, if the lease terminates automatically upon the tenant's breach, this could permit the tenant to terminate the lease and escape future liability for rent simply by choosing not to perform. As it is hardly conceivable that a landlord would intend such a result, courts have tended to construe such clauses as giving the landlord an option to terminate the lease.[852] Second, the landlord is better served to structure the clause to create an optional right of termination rather than an automatic one. This permits the landlord to consider the circumstances involved at the time of the default and to decide whether termination of the leasehold is in the landlord's best interest at that time.

§ 6.77 POWERS OF TERMINATION

Landlord-tenant law has traditionally held lease covenants to be independent, but has always permitted leases to contain clauses giving one party or the other a power to terminate the leasehold if certain conditions exist. Such clauses are very common; they are sometimes called "forfeiture" clauses, but "power of termination" is more precise. Such a clause could benefit either party, but leases more frequently confer termination powers on the landlord than on the tenant. Unlike automatic termination, a power of termination clause allows the benefited party to elect whether to terminate. A threat of exercise can powerfully restrain the burdened party from breaching the lease.

No termination occurs until the party who has the power exercises it in some unequivocal way.[853] When the landlord holds the power, the landlord may exercise it by

---

[850] The cases sometimes address whether the landlord is liable to the holdover in tort for injuries suffered due to the defective condition of the premises—with the landlord arguing that the holdover is a trespasser to whom no duty is owed. E.g., Selvy v. Beigel, 670 N.E.2d 784 (Ill.App.1996); Slusher v. State, 437 N.E.2d 97 (Ind.App.1982); Brown v. Guerrier, 457 N.E.2d 630 (Mass.1983).

[851] See Remedco Corp. v. Bryn Mawr Hotel Corp., 45 Misc.2d 586, 257 N.Y.S.2d 525 (Civ.Ct.1965); Jamaica Builders Supply Corp. v. Buttelman, 25 Misc.2d 326, 205 N.Y.S.2d 303 (Mun.Ct.1960); Restatement (Second) of Property-Landlord & Tenant § 1.7 (1977).

[852] See Entrepreneur, Ltd. v. Yasuna, 498 A.2d 1151 (D.C.App.1985); Cochran v. Lakota Land & Water Co., 17 P.2d 861 (Wash.1933). Courts tend to construe these clauses to create automatic termination only where the language leaves no doubt that was the parties' intent. E.g., Remedco Corp. v. Bryn Mawr Hotel Corp., 45 Misc.2d 586, 257 N.Y.S.2d 525 (Civ.Ct.1965) ("shall immediately cease and determine" meant automatic termination); Restatement (Second) of Property-Landlord & Tenant § 1.7 (1977).

[853] Padilla v. Sais, 414 P.2d 223 (N.M.1966); Larsen v. Sjogren, 226 P.2d 177 (Wyo.1951).

entry (where the law permits) or by a court action for possession. If the lease permits it, the landlord may exercise the power by giving effective notice, but must comply with any special requirements (such as giving a period of advance notice and allowing any cure period) contained in the lease or other law.[854]

Two particular doctrines impose limits on the exercise of powers of termination: waiver and estoppel. Waiver may occur when the burdened party breaches and triggers a right of termination but, before taking action sufficient to terminate, the benefited party expressly or impliedly recognizes the tenancy as continuing.[855] The most common example is a breach by the tenant that is known to the landlord, followed by the landlord's acceptance of rent due for a period after the breach; in such circumstances, the landlord may not terminate based on that breach.[856] Similarly, if the tenant assigns the leasehold in violation of a no-transfer clause, but the landlord accepts rent from the assignee, the landlord waives the power to terminate based on the assignment.[857] The waiver is only as to breaches that have previously occurred, not for later repetitions of the same breach or for a later period of a continuing breach.[858] Landlords often attempt to protect against assertion of waiver by including broad "anti-waiver" clauses in their leases (i.e., a clause that states, for example, that the landlord's receipt of rent with knowledge of a breach shall not be deemed a waiver of that breach), but courts have disagreed as to the enforceability of such clauses[859] and some courts have found that the landlord's conduct constituted a waiver of the anti-waiver clause.[860]

Waiver is often confused with another equitable doctrine, estoppel. It is possible for a party who has the benefit of a power of termination to be estopped from exercising it,

---

[854] Joseph J. Freed & Assocs., Inc. v. Cassinelli Apparel Corp., 491 N.E.2d 1109 (Ohio 1986); Dang v. Cox Corp., 655 P.2d 658 (Utah 1982); Gray v. Gregory, 218 P.2d 307 (Wash.1950).

Courts have sometimes excused a landlord's noncompliance with termination requirements if compliance would have been futile. E.g., Tkach v. American Sportsman, 316 N.W.2d 785 (N.D.1982) (requirement for notice delivered to tenant's premises not required where tenant had vacated premises). Likewise, some (but not all) courts have excused the landlord's failure to comply with specific notification requirements in the lease where the tenant did receive actual notice of the termination. E.g., Dixon v. American Indus. Leasing Co., 253 S.E.2d 150 (W.Va.1979).

[855] Courts have articulated different rationales for finding waiver in different cases. For example, courts might find a waiver because the finding may advance the law's general policy disfavoring forfeitures. See, e.g., 3A Corbin, Contracts § 754 (1960); C & A Land Co. v. Rudolf Invst. Corp., 296 S.E.2d 149 (Ga.App.1982). Alternatively, courts sometimes articulate that the benefited party has made a binding election not to pursue the termination remedy. 5 Williston, Contracts § 687 (3d ed.1961).

[856] E.g., Riverside Dev. Co. v. Ritchie, 650 P.2d 657 (Idaho 1982); Steven W. Barrick & Assocs. v. Witz, 498 N.E.2d 738 (Ill.App.1986); Woollard v. Schaffer Stores Co., 5 N.E.2d 829 (N.Y.1936); Quinn v. Cardinal Foods, Inc., 485 N.E.2d 741 (Ohio App.1984); C & K Market, Inc. v. Roccasalva, 265 P.3d 81 (Or.App.2011). Waiver does not occur if the landlord accepts payment of rent that accrued prior to the tenant's breach. See, e.g., Connealy v. Mueller, 319 N.W.2d 86 (Neb.1982) (accrued but unpaid rent was "debt" and, in the absence of an agreement to reinstate the tenancy, acceptance of the money did not waive the default); Sherrill v. Harlan Theater Co., 75 S.W.2d 775 (Ky.1934). Likewise, waiver does not occur where the landlord accepts rent without knowledge of the tenant's default. E.g., Weintraub v. Weingart, 277 P. 752 (Cal.1929).

[857] E.g., Buchanan v. Banta, 266 P. 547 (Cal.1928); Johnson v. Hotel Lawrence Corp., 169 N.E. 240 (Ill.1929); Towle v. Comm'r of Banks, 140 N.E. 747 (Mass.1923).

[858] Club Rd. Corp. v. Whitehead, 378 A.2d 110 (Conn.App.1977); Sherrill v. Harlan Theater Co., 75 S.W.2d 775 (Ky.1934); Shepard v. Dye, 242 P. 381 (Wash.1926); Annot., 109 A.L.R. 1267, 1277–79 (1937).

[859] See Berman, 2 Friedman on Leases § 16:5.2, at 16–103 to 16–105 (6th ed.2017) (collecting cases).

[860] See, e.g., Shields L.P. v. Bradberry, 526 S.W.3d 471, 484 (Tex.2017) ("Parties to a contract cannot, even by an express provision in that contract, deprive themselves of the power to alter or vary or discharge it by subsequent agreement. . . . [A] provision that an express condition of a promise or promises in the contract cannot be eliminated by waiver, or by conduct constituting an estoppel, is wholly ineffective. The promisor still has the power to waive the condition, or by his conduct to estop himself from insisting upon it, to the same extent that he would have had the power if there had been no such provision.").

at least to a certain extent. For example, suppose a landlord has a power to terminate for the tenant's breach of a covenant not to alter the premises. The tenant makes forbidden alterations, but the landlord knowingly stands by silently or even assists the tenant in making them. Courts have held that the landlord, having sanctioned the breach, is estopped from terminating on account of that breach.[861] For another example, suppose that the landlord has repeatedly tolerated tenant's late rent payments without objection. In such circumstances, courts have held that the landlord cannot terminate for future late rent payments without first giving tenant effective notice that late performance will no longer be accepted.[862]

Courts have sometimes granted equitable relief from forfeiture in cases where the burdened party's breach is only the failure to pay a sum of money, provided that the money is paid. For example, a Mississippi court refused to permit the landlord to terminate the tenant's lease based on a seven-day delay in the payment of rent where the lease did not suggest that time was of the essence of the contract.[863] Such a remedy being in the court's equitable discretion, a court may refuse to permit termination where "the delay has been slight, the loss to the lessor small, and when not to grant relief would result in such hardship to the tenant as to make it unconscionable to enforce literally the conditions of the lease."[864] The party holding the termination power (typically the landlord) is favored by the opposites of those factors or by a showing that to deny termination will cause a hardship.[865] A court is likely to allow termination when the tenant has repeatedly defaulted in paying rent. At work here is the maxim that equity abhors a forfeiture; the process by which equity intervenes is essentially the same as that by which equity developed the modern mortgage.

Leases frequently contain clauses empowering the landlord or tenant to terminate if the other becomes insolvent or is declared a bankrupt. Under the federal Bankruptcy Code, such a clause is unenforceable.[866]

§ 6.78 SUMMARY EVICTION STATUTES

Every jurisdiction now has some form of statute that allows the landlord to evict a breaching tenant through a special summary proceeding known as summary eviction or unlawful detainer.[867] Each statute specifies the types of breaches that will trigger the

---

[861] See Annot., 76 A.L.R. 304, 317–19 (1932).

[862] E.g., Park Forest of Blackman v. Smith, 316 N.W.2d 442 (Mich.App.1982); Pollock v. Adams, 548 S.W.2d 239 (Mo.App.1977); Berman, 2 Friedman on Leases § 16:5.1, at 16–94 & n.363 (6th ed.2017).

[863] Ladner v. Pigg, 919 So.2d 100 (Miss.App.2005).

[864] Nicoli v. Frouge Corp., 368 A.2d 74 (Conn.1976) (nevertheless permitting landlord to proceed with summary eviction where tenant had assigned lease without landlord's consent and trial court concluded landlord was materially affected by such breach).

[865] E.g., Gamble-Skogmo, Inc. v. McNair Realty Co., 98 F.Supp. 440 (D.Mont.1951), aff'd, 193 F.2d 876 (9th Cir.1952); Humphrey v. Humphrey, 48 So.2d 424 (Ala.1950). See also Entrepreneur, Ltd. v. Yasuna, 498 A.2d 1151 (D.C.App. 1985) (landlord could not terminate for tenant's technical breach of failure to apply for business permit); Dillingham Comm. Co. v. Spears, 641 P.2d 1 (Alaska 1982) (landlord could not terminate for tenant's slight breach of failing to pay real estate taxes); Housing Auth. of City of Mansfield v. Rovig, 676 S.W.2d 314 (Mo.App.1984) (landlord could not terminate for tenant's minor breach of keeping a dog).

[866] 11 U.S.C.A. § 365(e); 3 Collier, Bankruptcy ¶ 365.08 (16th ed.2017).

[867] A complete list of these statutes (as of the late 1970s), with brief descriptions, appears in Restatement (Second) of Property-Landlord & Tenant § 12.1, Statutory Note 1 (1977). A 2012 memorandum covering the particulars of eviction laws in 15 different states, prepared for the benefit of the members of the RURLTA drafting committee, appears on the Uniform Law Commission's website at http://www.uniformlaws.org/shared/docs/Residential%20Landlord%20and%20Tenant/2012sep13_URLTA_Memo_EvictionSurvey.pdf.

statutory remedy. Some statutes allow the remedy only for nonpayment of rent; others may allow it for other kinds of breaches, such as the tenant's illegal use of the premises or commission of waste. A few allow the remedy for the tenant's material breach of any lease covenant. The usual scheme is that the landlord must give the tenant a notice in a prescribed manner, requiring the tenant either to vacate or to cure the breach (if it is curable) within a certain period of time. Times of notice vary from state to state and according to the nature of the breach; from three to ten days' notice is typical for a rent default. If the tenant vacates, the lease terminates; if not, the tenant falls into a status usually called "unlawful detainer."[868] At that point, the landlord has a summary court action for possession and, in most states, for back rent with perhaps a penalty. The statutes typically provide for an accelerated hearing date, perhaps only a few days or weeks after service of the summons on the tenant. In Lindsey v. Normet, the U.S. Supreme Court upheld the constitutionality of the summary form of action.[869]

These statutes provide a streamlined process designed to permit the landlord to avoid the delay and expense associated with the traditional common law remedy of ejectment. For this reason, courts traditionally limited the issues for determination to whether the tenant committed the breach alleged. Most frequently, courts applied this principle to prevent a tenant from presenting evidence of an offset or counterclaim to the tenant's rental obligation; the tenant typically can assert affirmative claims or defenses only in a separate action.[870] Many jurisdictions have modified the traditional rule to permit tenants to raise offsets or counterclaims against unpaid rent in circumstances where a residential tenant claims a breach of the implied warranty of habitability.[871] This allows a form of "rent withholding" by a tenant whose premises do not meet the habitability standard. A number of states that have adopted residential landlord-tenant statutes have accomplished the same result legislatively.[872]

Under a few summary eviction statutes, the landlord's sole remedy is possession. Most statutes also permit recovery of rent due, and some permit even a penalty in a multiple of the agreed rent. When there is a statutory penalty, courts certainly may award it, but they have frequently refused to do so when tenants have had a reasonable excuse for holding over after the statutory notice to quit.[873]

---

[868] Some states refer to the tenant in this circumstance as a tenant at sufferance. See Gower v. Waters, 132 A. 550 (Me.1926); Margosian v. Markarian, 192 N.E. 612 (Mass.1934).

[869] 405 U.S. 56, 92 S.Ct. 862, 31 L.Ed.2d 36 (1972). The Court did strike down a requirement that the tenant post a bond of double the rent owed before the tenant could appeal in a summary eviction action.

[870] E.g., Class v. Carter, 645 P.2d 536 (Or.1982); Sundholm v. Patch, 382 P.2d 262 (Wash.1963). Lindsey v. Normet, 405 U.S. 56, 92 S.Ct. 862, 31 L.Ed.2d 36 (1972), held this limitation of issues constitutional.

[871] Jack Spring, Inc. v. Little, 280 N.E.2d 208 (Ill.1972); Marini v. Ireland, 265 A.2d 526 (N.J.1970); Foisy v. Wyman, 515 P.2d 160 (Wash.1973). See also Javins v. First Nat'l Realty Corp., 428 F.2d 1071 (D.C.Cir.1970), cert. denied, 400 U.S. 925, 91 S.Ct. 186, 27 L.Ed.2d 185 (1970) (offset allowed by court rule). Some decisions take the position that while the tenant may offset damages caused by a breach of an implied warranty of habitability, the tenant may not offset damages for the landlord's breach of an express lease covenant. See Winchester Mgmt. Corp. v. Staten, 361 A.2d 187 (D.C.App.1976); Timber Ridge Town House v. Dietz, 338 A.2d 21 (N.J.Super.1975).

[872] URLTA § 4.105 (1972); RURLTA § 408 (2015); MRLTC § 3–210 (1969). See Cunningham, The New Implied and Statutory Warranties of Habitability in Residential Leases: From Contract to Status, 16 Urban L.Ann. 3, 113–26 (1979).

[873] See Jones v. Taylor, 123 S.W. 326 (Ky.1909) (tenant "in good faith"); Feiges v. Racine Dry Goods Co., 285 N.W. 799 (Wis.1939) (tenant's employees on strike).

§ 6.79   EVICTION BY SELF-HELP

At common law, the landlord could recover possession of the premises from the tenant at the end of the lease, whether the lease expired or was properly terminated. If the tenant voluntarily relinquished possession, the landlord could re-enter. If the tenant did not relinquish possession, however, the landlord's judicial remedy was an action in ejectment. This remedy was slow and expensive, and subjected the landlord to economic risk; the landlord was delayed in renting the property to someone else, and had no guarantee that it could collect from the tenant for the period that the tenant wrongfully retained possession.[874] Because of the inefficient nature of ejectment, landlords often retook possession by self-help, i.e., without judicial process—such as by entering while the tenant was out and changing the locks, or even by entering and forcing out a tenant who was present. To what extent may the landlord lawfully use such self-help?

A brief review of English history informs the answer to this question. In England, the landlord could oust a holdover tenant by any force short of serious injury or death until 1381, when the Statute of Forcible Entry[875] made it a crime for the landlord (or anyone) to enter by self-help except in a "peaceable and easy manner." English courts did not treat a violation of that statute as a trespass to land, reasoning that the landlord could not be liable for trespass if the tenant no longer had the legal right to possess the premises. Nevertheless, courts treated any touching of the person or goods of the tenant as a tort.[876] In effect, then, the landlord was privileged to enter in the tenant's absence, or peaceably in the tenant's presence, but not to use any force whatever to remove the tenant or the tenant's goods. In 1920, however, in Hemmings v. Stoke Poges Golf Club, Ltd.,[877] the King's Bench established the current English rule that the landlord is privileged to use such reasonable force as is necessary to expel the holdover tenant.[878]

Against this backdrop, American courts struggled to address two questions: (1) is it trespass for the landlord to enter by self-help; and (2) what degree of force, if any, is the landlord privileged to use to remove persons or goods? American courts took different and confusing positions on these questions, with the confusion sometimes fostered by the failure of some courts to treat the questions as separate ones. Further, every jurisdiction now has adopted a statutory summary eviction procedure, and many courts take the view that these statutes effected a trade-off of the summary judicial remedy for the self-help remedy.[879] Other states have forcible entry statutes similar to the 1381 English statute or have incorporated the principles of the English statute as a received part of the state's common law, but this does not necessarily preclude a court from disagreeing with the English view and concluding that a landlord's forcible entry is a civil wrong.[880] The different definitions of "forcible" or "peaceable" in the state statutes and court decisions make generalization complicated as well.

---

[874] As discussed in the prior section, all jurisdictions now provide the landlord with a summary judicial process for obtaining possession of the premises following termination of the lease.

[875] 5 Rich. 2, c. 7.

[876] Newton v. Harland, 1 Man. & G. 644, 133 Eng.Rep. 490 (1840).

[877] [1920] 1 K.B. 720.

[878] For further background, see City of Chicago v. Chicago Steamship Lines, 159 N.E. 301 (Ill.1927); Dobbs, The Law of Torts § 80 (2000).

[879] See, e.g., Spencer v. Commercial Co., 71 P. 53 (Wash.1902).

[880] See, e.g., Jordan v. Talbot, 361 P.2d 20 (Cal.1961).

The rule in some jurisdictions is that the landlord cannot enter premises possessed by a holdover tenant. Any entry is a trespass; the landlord may use only legal process.[881] Many courts justify this position based on the legislature's enactment of summary eviction and forcible entry statutes, as well as the policy to avoid breaches of the peace. This rule was traditionally regarded as a minority rule,[882] but there is a clear trend toward this rule in judicial decisions.[883] Further, this rule is adopted by the Restatement (Second) of Property and both the Uniform Residential Landlord and Tenant Act and the Model Residential Landlord-Tenant Code.[884] Given the number of states that have adopted versions of the Uniform Act, the Model Act, or similar legislation, plus those that have adopted the rule by court decision, this rule provides the governing rule—at least as to *residential* leases—in the substantial majority of American jurisdictions.

Even in states that allow the landlord a privilege to re-enter, courts hold that the landlord's entry must be by "peaceable" means; otherwise, it will be an unlawful forcible entry. What is "peaceable" varies so widely from state to state and from case to case that generalizations are dangerous. Entry on open land is likely to be "peaceable." Some courts have ruled that the landlord's actions in unlocking or breaking down a door are peaceable,[885] but many others have ruled such actions as entry by trick, passkey, lockpicking, or even climbing through an open window as a breach of the peace.[886] "Peaceable" entries are usually made in the tenant's absence; any confrontation between landlord and tenant or objection by the tenant makes it more likely that a court will find the entry was a breach of the peace.[887]

Even if the landlord makes a "peaceable" entry, the ensuing exclusion of the tenant may still be wrongful in some jurisdictions. Forcible entry statutes often also prohibit forcible "detainer." The word "detainer" usually refers to a tenant's wrongful possession, but a few states have also held landlords liable for unlawful detainer for wrongfully excluding tenants. Again, there is a variety of judicial opinion about what actions are forcible and what are "peaceable." Decisions have held it wrongful to exclude the tenant by removing doors or windows, terminating utilities, by threatening the tenant, or even

---

[881] E.g., Gorman v. Ratliff, 712 S.W.2d 888 (Ark.1986) (no self-help); Jordan v. Talbot, 361 P.2d 20 (Cal.1961); Spencer v. Commercial Co., 71 P. 53 (Wash.1902).

[882] See Moriarty v. Dziak, 435 So.2d 35 (Ala.1983) (landlord's reentry proper when lease allowed reentry upon default, tenant was in default, and landlord had demanded rent); Annot., 6 A.L.R.3d 177, 186 (1966); 1 Harper, James & Gray, Torts § 1.12 (2d ed.1986); Restatement (Second) of Property-Landlord & Tenant § 14.1, Statutory Note 7, and § 14.2, Reporter's Note 1 (1977).

[883] Annot., 6 A.L.R.3d 177, 186 (1977). See also Gorman v. Ratliff, 289 Ark. 332, 712 S.W.2d 888 (1986); Hinton v. Sealander Brokerage Co., 917 A.2d 95 (D.C.2007).

[884] Restatement (Second) of Property-Landlord & Tenant § 14.2 (1977); URLTA § 4.207 (1972); RURLTA § 605 (2015); MRLTC § 2–408 (1969).

[885] Smith v. Detroit Loan & Bldg. Ass'n, 73 N.W. 395 (Mich.1897) (unlocking door); Mussey v. Scott, 32 Vt. 82 (1859) (breaking down door).

[886] E.g., Karp v. Margolis, 323 P.2d 557 (Cal.App.1958) (lockpicking); Pelavin v. Misner, 217 N.W. 36 (Mich.1928) (trick); Simhiser v. Farber, 71 N.W.2d 412 (Wis.1955) (threat); Bank of Cal. v. Taaffe, 18 P. 781 (Cal.1888) (climbing through open window).

[887] E.g., Spinks v. Taylor, 278 S.E.2d 501 (N.C.1981) (state subsequently enacted statute prohibiting self-help eviction in residential tenancies). Today, most cases addressing breach of the peace involve self-help possession of personal property collateral (e.g., cars) by creditors; under the weight of authority in those cases, a creditor's self-help repossession in the face of a debtor who is present and objecting to the repossession constitutes a breach of the peace. See Lawrence, Henning & Freyermuth, Understanding Secured Transactions § 18.01[A][1] (5th ed.2012).

by changing locks.[888] Indeed, residential landlord-tenant statutes may subject the landlord to severe penalties for cutting off utilities.[889]

If the landlord's entry is privileged, may the landlord use force against the tenant's person or goods? No jurisdiction will allow the landlord to use more force against the tenant or the tenant's goods than is reasonably necessary to evict.[890] A number of states go further and apply the former English rule that the landlord is not privileged to touch the tenant or the tenant's goods at all.[891]

Leases sometimes contain a clause purporting to allow the landlord to use self-help to evict the holdover tenant. A significant number of decisions have enforced such clauses, so as to confer on the landlord privileges of self-help that applicable rules of law would otherwise deny.[892] But these cases tend to be old, and recent decisions treat such clauses as invalid in violation of public policy.[893] The Restatement likewise adopts this view,[894] as does the Uniform Residential Landlord and Tenant Act.[895]

§ 6.80   LEGAL INHIBITIONS ON EVICTIONS

This section discusses several discrete subjects that have no connection, other than that they all involve situations in which the law places restrictions on a landlord's capacity to maintain an action to evict a tenant. Most of the discussion focuses on the doctrine against "retaliatory evictions," followed by a brief discussion of the extent to which the law regulates evictions in particular circumstances, such as when there is public housing or rent control or when the tenant is in military service.

The doctrine of "retaliatory eviction" began to evolve in 1968 with the District of Columbia Circuit's opinion in Edwards v. Habib.[896] After a tenant reported the landlord's housing code violation to public authorities, the landlord gave the tenant a notice to terminate the tenancy and began a summary eviction action. The court held that the tenant had a valid defense if she could prove the landlord had acted in retaliation for her report. The court reasoned on policy grounds that to allow retaliatory eviction would thwart the purpose of a housing code. *Edwards* has been followed in decisions in several states.[897] Presumably this defense would protect a tenant who brought an action to

---

[888] See, e.g., Jordan v. Talbot, 361 P.2d 20 (Cal.1961) (threats); Pelavin v. Misner, 217 N.W. 36 (Mich.1928) (locking tenant out); Whalen v. Taylor, 925 P.2d 462 (Mont.1996) (changing lock).

[889] E.g., URLTA § 4.104 (1972); RURLTA § 407(a) (2015); Kinney v. Vaccari, 612 P.2d 877 (Cal.1980) ($36,000 penalty, plus $7,901 actual damages, plus $5,600 attorney fees).

[890] See Gower v. Waters, 132 A. 550 (Me.1926); Shorter v. Shelton, 33 S.E.2d 643 (Va.1945); Annot., 6 A.L.R.3d 177, 182–86 (1966); 1 Harper, James & Gray, Torts § 3.15 (2d ed.1986); Restatement (Second) of Property-Landlord & Tenant § 14.1, Statutory Note 7, and § 14.2, Reporter's Note (1977).

[891] Maddix v. Gammon, 169 S.W.2d 594 (Ky.1943); Rivers v. Tessitore, 165 So.2d 888 (La.App.1964); Annot., 6 A.L.R.3d 177, 181, 222–37 (1966); Dobbs, The Law of Torts § 80 (2000); Restatement (Second) of Property-Landlord & Tenant § 14.2, Reporter's Note 4 (1977).

[892] E.g., Goshen v. People, 44 P. 503 (Colo.1896); Rucker v. Wynn, 441 S.E.2d 417 (Ga.App.1994); Restatement (Second) of Property-Landlord & Tenant § 14.2, Reporter's Note 5 (1977).

[893] Jordan v. Talbot, 361 P.2d 20 (Cal.1961); Bass v. Boetel & Co., 217 N.W.2d 804 (Neb.1974); Restatement (Second) of Property-Landlord & Tenant § 14.2, Reporter's Note 5 (1977).

[894] Restatement (Second) of Property-Landlord & Tenant § 14.2(2) (1977).

[895] URLTA §§ 1.403(a)(1), 4.207, 4.302(b) (1972); RURLTA §§ 203, 605 (2015).

[896] 397 F.2d 687 (D.C.Cir.1968), cert. denied, 393 U.S. 1016, 89 S.Ct. 618, 21 L.Ed.2d 560 (1969).

[897] Schweiger v. Superior Court, 476 P.2d 97 (Cal.1970); Wright v. Brady, 889 P.2d 105 (Idaho App.1995); Building Monitoring Systems, Inc. v. Paxton, 905 P.2d 1215 (Utah 1995); Dickhut v. Norton, 173 N.W.2d 297 (Wis.1970). Contra: Mobilia, Inc. v. Santos, 492 A.2d 544 (Conn.App.1985) (court refused to allow retaliatory eviction defense in summary eviction action against residential tenant).

enforce the landlord's warranty of habitability and not just one that reported housing code violations.[898] Generally the defense is available only to residential tenants.[899]

Some 30 states have adopted residential landlord-tenant statutes that codify the retaliatory eviction principle, many based on the Uniform Residential Landlord and Tenant Act or the Model Residential Landlord-Tenant Code (which contain anti-retaliatory eviction provisions).[900] State statutes vary widely. Many forbid not only retaliatory eviction, but also other retaliatory actions such as rent increases or refusal to provide services. Some prohibit the landlord from retaliating because the tenant joined a tenants' union or pursued remedies under the landlord-tenant statute. Some of the statutes create a presumption that listed forms of conduct are retaliatory if landlord takes them within a certain period of time after the tenant's protected action. Some create exceptions if the tenant is in default as to payment of rent.[901] Courts have split as to whether a landlord's refusal to renew a fixed-term tenancy can serve as a basis for a retaliation claim.[902]

Several specialized situations exist in which federal or state laws regulate landlords in evicting certain tenants. This is true under regulations of the Department of Housing and Urban Development that pertain to federally assisted publicly owned housing.[903] State statutes or local ordinances and regulations may similarly regulate public housing.[904] On a related subject, whenever there is legislative rent control, one may expect to find restrictions on evictions as a part of the scheme.[905]

The Soldiers' and Sailors' Civil Relief Act of 1940 restricts evictions in some cases. Whenever a dwelling is occupied by the spouse, children, or other dependents of a person in military service and the rent is below a certain statutory maximum per month,

---

[898] Pohlman v. Metropolitan Trailer Park, Inc., 312 A.2d 888 (N.J.Ch.Div.1973) (allowing defense where landlord evicted tenant who opposed landlord's application for rezoning premises). There is some recent authority, however, narrowing the scope of conduct protected by the doctrine. See, e.g., Helfrich v. Valdez Motel Corp., 207 P.3d 552 (Alaska 2009) (Alaska's version of URLTA did not permit retaliatory eviction defense where landlord evicted tenant in response to tenant's assertion of a personal injury action); Central Hous. Assocs., LP v. Olson, 910 N.W.2d 485 (Minn.App.2018) (statute allowing retaliatory eviction defense did not protect tenant who filed discrimination complaint with state civil rights agency; refusing to recognize common law retaliatory eviction defense). See also Hernandez v. Stabach, 145 Cal.App.3d 309, 193 Cal.Rptr. 350 (1983) (court may enjoin landlord from threatened retaliatory eviction or action).

[899] But see Custom Parking, Inc. v. Superior Court, 138 Cal.App.3d 90, 187 Cal.Rptr. 674 (1982) (allowing assertion of defense of retaliatory eviction by a *commercial* tenant).

[900] URLTA § 5.101 (1972); RURLTA § 901 (2015); MRLTC § 2–407 (1969).

[901] For example, Minnesota courts have interpreted its landlord-tenant statute to preclude a retaliatory eviction defense where the tenant is in breach of the lease. Central Hous. Assocs., LP v. Olson, 910 N.W.2d 485 (Minn.App.2018) (interpreting Minn.Stat.Ann. § 504B.285). See generally Cunningham, The New Implied and Statutory Warranties of Habitability in Residential Leases: From Contract to Status, 16 Urban L.Ann. 3, 126–37 (1979).

[902] Compare Van Buren Apts. v. Adams, 701 P.2d 583 (Ariz.App.1984) and E. & E. Newman, Inc. v. Hallock, 281 A.2d 544 (N.J.App.1971) (yes) with Frenchtown Villa v. Meadors, 324 N.W.2d 133 (Mich.App.1982) (no).

[903] The full details of the regulation of eviction in public housing leases is beyond the scope of this treatise, but can be explored in 5 Thompson on Real Property § 45.11 (2d Thomas ed.2007). In general, a federally-assisted public housing lease cannot be terminated except for "serious or repeated violation" of the lease terms or "for other good cause." 42 U.S.C. § 1437d(*l*). See also Thorpe v. Housing Auth., 393 U.S. 268, 89 S.Ct. 518, 21 L.Ed.2d 474 (1969); Caulder v. Durham Housing Auth., 433 F.2d 998 (4th Cir.1970), cert. denied, 401 U.S. 1003, 91 S.Ct. 1228, 28 L.Ed.2d 539 (1971); Housing Auth. v. Mosby, 192 N.W.2d 913 (Wis.1972).

[904] See Escalera v. New York City Hous. Auth., 425 F.2d 853 (2d Cir.1970), cert. denied, 400 U.S. 853, 91 S.Ct. 54, 27 L.Ed.2d 91 (1970); Sanders v. Cruise, 10 Misc.2d 533, 173 N.Y.S.2d 871 (1958).

[905] See Block v. Hirsh, 256 U.S. 135, 41 S.Ct. 458, 65 L.Ed. 865 (1921); 1 Am. Law of Prop. § 3.93 (1952).

eviction may be stayed as long as 90 days.[906] In commencing an eviction action, a landlord who knows of it must disclose the serviceperson's military status. The Act also allows the serviceperson to terminate tenancies commenced before his entry into the armed services where the serviceperson or their family has occupied the premises.[907]

§ 6.81 SURRENDER AND ABANDONMENT

"Surrender" is the early termination of a leasehold, either by the parties' agreement or by the tenant's abandonment of the premises and the landlord's acceptance of that abandonment. Surrender by agreement is simply the modification or cancellation of a contract. Contract law issues may arise, such as whether the parties' words amount to a termination agreement, or whether the agreement must comply with the Statute of Frauds to be enforceable.[908]

The English Statute of Frauds excepted surrenders that occurred "by operation of law" when the tenant abandoned the premises and the landlord accepted them back for the landlord's own account.[909] Here, one might reason that the parties' intent is sufficiently evidenced by non-verbal acts. Some of the cases are ones in which the parties made an oral surrender agreement (perhaps unenforceable as such), but the tenant then abandoned the premises and thereby "executed" the oral agreement.[910]

The tenant's abandonment alone does not work a surrender by operation of law; the landlord must accept the premises back for the landlord's own account to complete the termination. More precisely, at common law, the tenant's abandonment confers on the landlord three choices: (1) to complete surrender and termination by re-entering for the landlord's own account; (2) to do nothing and maintain the leasehold, as well as the tenant's duty to pay rent; or (3) to re-enter and re-let "for the tenant's account," charging to the tenant any difference between the agreed rent and the rent received from the replacement tenant.[911] Today, the question is whether the second option (do nothing) still exists or whether the landlord has only the first (accept the surrender) and third (re-let on the tenant's account) options. If the landlord does not wish to accept surrender, must the landlord make a reasonable attempt to re-let the premises to mitigate the landlord's potential damages from the tenant's abandonment?[912]

---

[906] 50 U.S.C. § 3951(a)(1), (b)(1). When the statute was amended in 2003, the maximum was set at $2,400 per month; the currently applicable maximum is determined by reference to the Consumer Price Index.

[907] 50 U.S.C. § 3955(a).

[908] Some state statutes, patterned after the English Statute of Frauds of 1677, expressly require "surrenders" to be in writing. Such a statute could be construed to require any surrender agreement to be in writing, regardless of the duration of the original lease or how long it had left to run. By contrast, one might construe such a statute to permit an oral surrender if the remaining term is short enough that an oral lease for that duration would be valid. Other state statutes are more explicit. Some do not mention surrenders at all; under statutes of this type, if the original lease did not have to be in writing, a surrender agreement need not be. If the original lease was within the statute, courts have split—some require the surrender agreement to be in writing and others require it only if the time remaining on the lease is so long that a term of that length must be in writing. See 1 Am. Law of Prop. § 3.99 (1952); Annot., 78 A.L.R.2d 933, 941–49 (1961).

[909] See, e.g., Riggs v. Murdock, 458 P.2d 115 (Ariz.App.1969); McGrath v. Shalett, 159 A. 633 (Conn.1932); Liberty Plan Co. v. Adwan, 370 P.2d 928 (Okla.1962).

[910] See Annot., 78 A.L.R.2d 933, 939, n.9 (1961).

[911] In addition to the decisions cited in the next footnote, see Sagamore Corp. v. Willcutt, 120 Conn. 315, 180 A. 464 (1935); Novak v. Fontaine Furniture Co., 84 N.H. 93, 146 A. 525 (1929).

[912] Courts sometimes speak of this in terms of whether the landlord has a "duty" to mitigate. Technically, it is not a duty—the tenant has no affirmative claim for relief if the landlord does not mitigate. However, if the landlord does not mitigate, courts in some states will give the tenant a complete defense to payment of rent, e.g., Finish Line, Inc v. Jakobitz, 557 N.W.2d 914 (Iowa App.1996), or will at least give the tenant a credit for

Traditionally, the contract law doctrine of mitigation did not apply to leases in this context. The Restatement (Second) of Property, which usually does not hesitate to keep up with (or ahead of) trends in landlord-tenant law, adopted this view.[913] At least with respect to commercial leases, it is likely that at least half of American states continue to adhere to this view; even within the past several decades, numerous court decisions have refused to incorporate the mitigation concept into commercial leases.[914] Under this approach, the landlord can allow the premises to sit vacant and can hold the abandoning tenant liable for all rent as it accrues.

By contrast, a strong trend in the case law takes the position that the landlord must mitigate by making reasonable efforts to re-let the premises.[915] Both the Uniform Residential Landlord and Tenant Act and the Model Residential Landlord-Tenant Code adopt this view.[916] Taking into account the states that have adopted these acts, it is likely that by legislation or court decision, a majority of states now impose consequences on residential landlords for failing to mitigate.[917]

In states that require the landlord to mitigate, the landlord must accept a willing and suitable replacement tenant offered by the abandoning tenant, and must otherwise take reasonable steps to find a replacement. In assessing whether the landlord has taken reasonable steps, courts will take into account all of the facts and circumstances.[918] A

---

the sums the landlord could have obtained through reasonable mitigation efforts. E.g., St. George Chicago, Inc. v. George J. Murges & Assocs., 695 N.E.2d 503 (Ill.App.1998). Given such consequences, the landlord may practically view mitigation as a duty.

[913] See Restatement (Second) of Property-Landlord & Tenant § 12.1(3), Comment i, and Reporter's Note 8 (1977).

[914] See, e.g., Bowdoin Sq., LLC v. Winn-Dixie Montgomery, Inc., 873 So2d 1091 (Ala.2003); Brennan Assocs. v. OBGYN Specialty Group, P.C., 15 A.3d 1094 (Conn.App.2011); Marvin Hewatt Enters., Inc. v. Butler Capital Corp., 761 S.E.2d 857 (Ga.App.2014); Mesilla Valley Mall Co. v. Crown Indus., 808 P.2d 633 (N.M.1991); Holy Props. Ltd., L.P. v. Kenneth Cole Prods., Inc., 661 N.E.2d 694 (N.Y.1995); New 24 W. 40th St. LLC v. XE Capital Mgmt., LLC, 104 A.D.3d 513, 961 N.Y.S.2d 139 (2013); Stonehenge Square Ltd. Partn. v. Movie Merchants, 715 A.2d 1082 (Pa.1998). Following the lead of the *Holy Properties* case, at least two New York lower court decisions have refused to apply any mitigation requirement to residential leases. See Whitehouse Estates, Inc. v. Post, 173 Misc.2d 558, 662 N.Y.S.2d 982 (1997); Duda v. Thompson, 169 Misc.2d 649, 647 N.Y.S.2d 401 (1996).

In Volume 2 of the Friedman on Leases treatise, Appendix 16A (6th ed.2017), Professor Berman provides a chart detailing the current status of the mitigation question by jurisdiction. His chart shows at least 17 states where statutes or court decisions have affirmed the continued applicability of the traditional rule, as well as several others where authority is conflicting or no recent authority exists.

[915] Schneiker v. Gordon, 732 P.2d 603 (Colo.1987); Vawter v. McKissick, 159 N.W.2d 538 (Iowa 1968); Miller v. Burnett, 397 P.3d 448 (Kan.App.2017); Hand Cut Steaks Acquisitions, Inc. v. Lone Star Steakhouse & Saloon of Neb., Inc., 905 N.W.2d 644 (Neb.2018); Sommer v. Kridel, 378 A.2d 767 (1977); Frenchtown Square Partn. v. Lemstone, Inc., 791 N.E.2d 417 (Ohio 2003); U.S. Nat'l Bank of Or. v. Homeland, Inc., 631 P.2d 761 (Or.1981); Austin Hill Country Realty, Inc. v. Palisades Plaza, Inc., 948 S.W.2d 293 (Tex.1997). California requires mitigation by statute, Cal.Civ.Code § 1951.4, but allows the landlord to keep the lease alive and recover the rent from the abandoning tenant as it comes due if the lease specifically provides for this remedy. Likewise, some courts have held that a commercial tenant may validly agree in the lease to waive the landlord's obligation to mitigate. E.g., Sylva Shops Ltd. Partn. v. Hibbard, 623 S.E.2d 785 (N.C.App.2006); New Towne L.P. v. Pier 1 Imports (U.S.), Inc., 680 N.E.2d 644 (Ohio App.1996).

[916] URLTA § 4.203(c) (1972); RURLTA § 604(d) (2015); MRLTC § 2–308(4).

[917] See 2 Friedman on Leases Appendix 16A (6th ed.2017); Restatement (Second) of Property-Landlord & Tenant § 12.1, Statutory Note 7 (1977).

[918] For example, the fact that the landlord did not use a broker to identify potential replacements would be relevant, but not necessarily determinative if the landlord made other reasonable marketing efforts. E.g., Ruud v. Larson, 392 N.W.2d 62 (N.D.1986). Likewise, the fact that the landlord re-marketed the premises at a higher rent would not be unreasonable where the evidence shows that prevailing market rents increased. *Ruud*, 392 N.W.2d at 64–65. By contrast, in Vawter v. McKissick, 159 N.W.2d 538 (Iowa 1968), the landlord's only marketing of the premises was a "for rent" sign in the window, and landlord made insubstantial efforts to

question sometimes arises whether the mitigation requirement means the landlord must place a prospective new tenant into the abandoning tenant's premises rather than other similar space that the landlord has available for rent. Properly understood, the answer should be no—the landlord with available similar space is in the position of the "lost volume seller" under contract law. The Revised Uniform Residential Landlord and Tenant Act adopts this position.[919]

A landlord who undertakes to mitigate is in a ticklish position. If the landlord re-enters and re-lets "for the tenant's account," the leasehold remains in effect and the tenant remains liable for any accrued rent that the landlord cannot recover through re-letting. Particularly where mitigation is a legal requirement, the tenant should also be liable for the landlord's reasonable expenses of re-letting.[920] But if the landlord goes too far and acts "for the landlord's own account," then the leasehold will terminate and the tenant's liability for rent that would have accrued under the lease thereafter comes to an end.[921] Whether the landlord's actions cross the line to become an acceptance of surrender is a question of fact, sometimes of degree. Acts such as accepting keys, entering the premises, advertising them for rent, cleaning, and perhaps even some alterations do not necessarily cause termination by surrender, because these acts are also necessary if landlord is re-letting on the tenant's account.[922] But if the landlord makes alterations greater than those required to re-let, this may strengthen the tenant's argument that the landlord has accepted surrender.[923] Where the landlord re-lets for a term longer than the tenant's remaining term, courts generally conclude that surrender has occurred, though again there are contrary decisions.[924] Some states have adopted the rule that to avoid surrender, the landlord who wishes to re-let on the tenant's account must expressly notify the tenant of that purpose.[925] Even where state law does not so require, a well-advised landlord should adhere to this practice anyway, as such a written notification serves as strong evidence of the landlord's intent not to accept surrender.[926]

---

negotiate with the two prospective tenants who responded to the sign. The court held that the landlord failed to establish it had made reasonable effort to re-let the premises.

[919] RURLTA § 604(d)(1) (2015).

[920] See Ross v. Smigelski, 166 N.W.2d 243 (Wis.1969).

[921] For this reason, a landlord who is willing to accept the tenant's surrender should wait to do so until landlord has re-let the premises to a new tenant, so that the abandoning tenant's rent will continue to accrue until a new tenant is secured.

[922] See, e.g., American Nat'l Bank & Trust Co. v. Hoyne Indus., Inc., 738 F.Supp. 297 (N.D.Ill.1990) (landlord may attempt to re-let at higher rent when lease allows this); Dahl v. Comber, 444 A.2d 392 (Me.1982) (landlord did not accept surrender of premises by reletting parts of them for terms not longer than original tenant's term); Windsor Real Estate & Mortg. Co. v. Ruma, 674 S.W.2d 252 (Mo.App.1984) (landlord did not accept surrender of premises by attempting to re-let); Novak v. Fontaine Furniture Co., 146 A. 525 (N.H.1929); Armijo v. Pettit, 259 P. 620 (N.M.1927); Liberty Plan Co. v. Adwan, 370 P.2d 928 (Okla.1962); Washington Securities Co. v. Oppenheimer & Co., 1 P.2d 236 (Wash.1931).

[923] See H.S. Chase & Co. v. Evans, 160 N.W. 346 (Iowa 1916) (evidence of extent of repairs relevant). But see Washington Securities Co. v. Oppenheimer & Co., 1 P.2d 236 (Wash.1931) (argument made unsuccessfully).

[924] Welcome v. Hess, 27 P. 369 (Cal.1891); Michigan Lafayette Bldg. Co. v. Continental Bank, 246 N.W. 53 (Mich.1933); In re Adams' Estate, 149 Misc. 289, 267 N.Y.S. 910 (1933); Casper Nat'l Bank v. Curry, 65 P.2d 1116 (Wyo.1937) (one of several factors). Contra: McGrath v. Shalett, 159 A. 633 (Conn.1932); Armijo v. Pettit, 259 P. 620 (N.M.1927). See also Mesilla Valley Mall Co. v. Crown Indus., 808 P.2d 633 (N.M.1991) (landlord's re-letting rent-free to charitable organization was acceptance of surrender); Temple Bldg. Assocs. v. Somerville, 226 A.D.2d 1103, 642 N.Y.S.2d 140 (1996) (question whether landlord used diligence to obtain best rent possible upon re-letting).

[925] Bernard v. Renard, 165 P. 694 (Cal.1917); Casper Nat'l Bank v. Curry, 65 P.2d 1116 (Wyo.1937).

[926] E.g., Liberty Plan Co. v. Adwan, 370 P.2d 928 (Okla.1962).

Even if the landlord accepts the tenant's surrender, that should only excuse the tenant's obligation for future rent; the landlord properly should retain the ability to recover damages from the abandoning tenant on account of the tenant's breach.[927] Some courts have held that the landlord's acceptance of the tenant's surrender released the tenant from liability for rent or damages.[928] Under the better view, the landlord may recover damages in an amount equal to the present value of the difference between the agreed rent and the fair rental value for the remainder of term.[929] Certainly, the landlord may recover such damages where the lease so provides.

§ 6.82 MERGER

Generally, when a leasehold and the immediately succeeding estate come together in the same person, the leasehold merges into the succeeding estate and terminates.[930] The succeeding estate may be a reversion or remainder in fee or for life or another leasehold of longer duration; any such estate will be "larger" in legal concept than the leasehold in question. No merger will occur unless the leasehold and the following estate are adjoining, as the word "immediately" connotes. Extinction of the leasehold estate also terminates the rights and duties of the parties as landlord and tenant.[931]

Merger does not operate with mechanical absoluteness; courts may refuse to find a merger in certain cases. For example, courts sometimes say that no merger will occur when merger would be contrary to the parties' apparent intent or would defeat the expectations of a third party holding an intervening interest.[932] Another application of particular relevance to leaseholds involves subleases; if the tenant-sublessor surrenders the leasehold to the primary landlord, there will be no merger so as to extinguish the sublease. Rather, the primary landlord is viewed as having acquired the sublessee as a direct tenant.[933]

---

[927] A landlord wishing to maximize its recovery may wish to take care in its re-letting efforts. For a cautionary tale, see Centerline Invst. Co. v. Tri-Cor Indus., Inc., 80 S.W.3d 499 (Mo.App.2002), where the landlord re-let the premises by moving another tenant in the building into the abandoning tenant's space, at a higher rent. When the landlord sued the tenant for damages, the court held that the abandoning tenant was entitled to credit for the higher rent paid by the replacement; the court also held that the landlord could not recover damages for the rent lost on the space previously occupied by the replacement!

[928] E.g., Roosen v. Schaffer, 621 P.2d 33 (Ariz.App.1980); Signal Mgmt. Corp. v. Lamb, 541 N.W.2d 449 (N.D.1995); Maney v. Parker, 1995 WL 577805 (Tenn.App.1995).

[929] E.g., United States Nat'l Bank v. Homeland, Inc., 631 P.2d 761 (Or.1981).

[930] E.g., Clayton v. Clayton, 75 So.3d 649 (Ala.App.2011); In re Rosenstein, 129 A.D.3d 847, 11 N.Y.S.3d 631 (2015); Schmaeling v. Schmaeling, 127 Misc.2d 763, 487 N.Y.S.2d 494 (Sup.1985).

[931] See generally Erving v. Jas. H. Goodman & Co. Bank, 153 P. 945 (Cal.1915); Liebschutz v. Moore, 70 Ind. 142 (1880); Hudson Bros. Commission Co. v. Glencoe Sand & Gravel Co., 41 S.W. 450 (Mo.1897); Hall v. Professional Leasing Assocs., 550 S.W.2d 392 (Tex.App.1977); Tolsma v. Adair, 73 P. 347 (Wash.1903); Restatement of Property § 238, Comment d (1936).

[932] See, e.g., 6424 Corp. v. Commercial Exchange Prop., Ltd., 171 Cal.App.3d 1221, 217 Cal.Rptr. 803 (1985) (leasehold and fee did not merge to invalidate intervening leasehold deed of trust); Telecom Tower Group, LLC v. Honeysuckle Creek Holdings, Inc., 227 So.3d 1170 (Miss.App.2017) (merger did not apply to extinguish creditor's equitable lien on landlord's interest despite tenant's exercise of purchase option); Osman v. Saleh, 27 Misc.3d 223, 893 N.Y.S.2d 750 (City Ct.2010) (tenant exercising purchase option may avoid merger through express declaration of intent in purchase agreement); Mobley v. Harkins, 128 P.2d 289 (Wash.1942); Annot., 143 A.L.R. 93, 107–11 (1943). Some courts have gone further and have held that merger will not occur unless the parties intended for the fee and leasehold estates to merge. E.g., Colopy v. Wilson, 548 N.E.2d 1322 (Ohio App.1989).

[933] Metropolitan Life Ins. Co. v. Hellinger, 246 A.D. 7, 284 N.Y.S. 432 (1935), aff'd, 3 N.E.2d 621 (N.Y.1936); Hessel v. Johnson, 18 A. 754 (Pa.1889).

§ 6.83   EXPIRATION OF LANDLORD'S ESTATE

Because a leasehold is carved out of an estate of longer duration, anything that brings that estate to an end before the agreed termination date of the leasehold will terminate the leasehold. The cases generally follow this principle, and typically are ones in which a life tenant creates a leasehold but dies before the end of the tenancy.[934] Though the leasehold ends, the tenant may be allowed to enter later for certain limited purposes; for example, if the tenant has growing crops, the tenant may enter to cultivate and harvest them.[935] Likewise, if the landlord has mortgaged the premises and landlord's title is extinguished in a foreclosure sale, the sale will also terminate any leasehold estate that was subordinate to the mortgage (i.e., any lease entered into after the mortgage arose or any lease which tenant voluntarily subordinated to the mortgage), unless the mortgagee has made an agreement not to disturb the tenant's possession.[936]

§ 6.84   DEATH OF A PARTY

In a common-law tenancy at will, death of either landlord or tenant terminates the tenancy.[937] But with tenancies for years and periodic tenancies, death of the landlord or of the tenant does not generally work a termination unless the lease or a statute so provides.[938] Thus, the landlord's underlying estate passes to the landlord's heirs or devisees subject to the leasehold;[939] the leasehold estate, viewed as a chattel real, passes as personalty to the tenant's estate. There are occasional decisions in which courts have permitted the tenant's estate to escape continuing obligation under the lease by concluding that the tenant's lease obligations were personal in nature.[940]

---

[934] E.g., Plafcan v. Griggs, 724 S.W.2d 467 (Ark.1987); Good Ol' Days Commissary, Inc. v. Longcrier Family Ltd. Partn. I, 522 S.E.2d 249 (Ga.App.1999); Egbert v. Duck, 32 N.W.2d 404 (Iowa 1948); Estate of Duncan v. Kinsolving, 70 P.3d 1260 (N.M.2003) (lease entered by life tenant-lessor terminates upon lessor's death, absent ratification of lease by remainderman); Haywood v. Briggs, 41 S.E.2d 289 (N.C.1947); Englehart v. Larson, 608 N.W.2d 673 (S.D.2000); Kerns v. Pickett, 287 P.2d 88 (Wash.1955).

[935] E.g., Englehart v. Larson, 608 N.W.2d 673 (S.D.2000) (tenant may re-enter to harvest crops planted before lessor's death). Cf. Olmstead v. Nodland, 828 N.E.2d 338 (Ill.App.2005) (under applicable statute, farmland lease terminated at end of year in which life tenant-lessor died); Ganzer v. Pfab, 360 N.W.2d 754 (Iowa 1985) (when landlord who was contract purchaser of farm land had his contract forfeited after default; held that tenant's leasehold continued for following crop year, to prevent loss of crops).

[936] E.g., Dover Mobile Estates v. Fiber Form Prods., Inc., 220 Cal.App.3d 1494, 270 Cal.Rptr. 183 (1990); Kratovil, Mortgages—Problems in Possession, Rents, and Mortgagee Liability, 11 DePaul L. Rev. 1 (1961).

[937] E.g., Perry v. Veal, 134 S.W. 458 (Ky.1911); Hancock v. Maurer, 229 P. 611 (Okla.1924).

[938] E.g., Kensington Assocs. v. Moss, 426 So.2d 1076 (Fla.App.1983); In re Estate of Conklin, 451 N.E.2d 1382 (Ill.App.1983); In re Lewis' Estate, 492 S.W.2d 385 (Mo.App.1973); Visutton Assocs. v. Fastman, 44 Misc.3d 56, 991 N.Y.S.2d 240 (Sup.2014); Gross v. Peskin, 244 A.2d 692 (N.J.Super.1968); Sherman v. Carlin, 546 N.E.2d 433 (Ohio App.1988); Dobyns v. South Carolina Dept. of Parks, Recreation & Tourism, 480 S.E.2d 81 (S.C.1997); 1 Am. Law of Prop. § 3.102 (1952). The Revised Uniform Residential Landlord and Tenant Act generally allows the representative of a deceased tenant to terminate by giving 30 days' notice (in the case of a fixed-term tenancy) or one period's notice (in the case of a periodic tenancy). RURLTA § 803(b) (2015).

[939] The transfer would occur by intestacy or by the terms of the landlord's valid will, not by the terms of the lease itself. Courts have held that a lease clause that provides that the lessor's interest would be transferred to a nonparty upon the lessor's death was testamentary in nature and thus not enforceable if the lease does not satisfy the applicable will statute. E.g., Estate of Greer v. Ball, 218 So.3d 1136 (Miss.2017).

[940] Goodman v. Jardine, 353 So.2d 896 (Fla.App.1977); Warnecke v. Estate of Rabenau, 367 S.W.2d 15 (Mo.App.1963). See also Schnee v. Jonas Equities, Inc., 103 Misc.2d 625, 426 N.Y.S.2d 431 (1980) (vacancy from tenant's death caused termination "by operation of law").

§ 6.85 DESTRUCTION OF BUILDING

Under the traditional common-law rule, destruction of a building on the premises by a casualty not the fault of either party did not terminate the lease.[941] A leasehold estate is what the tenant rented, and the estate remained despite the casualty. Naturally, the harshness of the rule causes the tenant to insert in any well-drafted lease a clause providing remedies (including, perhaps, a power of termination) for different degrees of destruction of the premises.

The general rule is subject to a sizable common-law exception and some modern statutory limitations. The exception arises when the leasehold is for rooms within a building (such as an apartment) and the building is destroyed; in this case, as the tenant leased only space and has practically lost everything bargained for, the destruction terminates the lease.[942] Statutory limits on the common law rule are of two types. Even before the widespread adoption of residential landlord-tenant statutes, a number of states had adopted statutes reversing or modifying the rule.[943] Further, many modern residential landlord-tenant acts empower the tenant to terminate in case of casualty destruction.[944] A further limitation on the common-law rule must exist where, by residential landlord-tenant acts or court decisions, the landlord has an implied warranty of habitability in residential leases. If the premises are destroyed and the landlord fails to rebuild, this breaches the warranty. The Restatement takes the position that the tenant then has, among other remedies, a power to terminate.[945] In any event, the tenant may achieve the same result by invoking the traditional doctrine of constructive eviction.

§ 6.86 FRUSTRATION OF PURPOSE

In Section 6.28, we noted that if a lease limits the tenant to a certain use of the premises and that use subsequently becomes prohibited by law, in most jurisdictions the tenant's performance is wholly excused. Even if the uses limited do not all become illegal, if the main or principal use is made illegal, most courts excuse the tenant. At work here is a theory adopted from the law of contracts—another of many modern examples of contract law's growing influence in landlord-tenant relations. What is not so clear is whether the theory ought to be called "impossibility of performance" or "frustration of purpose." "Frustration of purpose" or "commercial frustration" seems the accurate description, as most commentators contend.[946] The doctrine of impossibility excuses the promisor's performance of the duty that has become impossible (illegal). That ordinarily does not fit this situation, because the clause limiting use is not a promised performance

---

[941] Chambers v. North River Line, 102 S.E. 198 (N.C.1920); Evco Corp. v. Ross, 528 S.W.2d 20 (Tenn.1975); Gonzalez v. Cavazos, 601 S.W.2d 202 (Tex.Civ.App.1980); Restatement (Second) of Property-Landlord & Tenant § 5.4, Reporter's Note 4 (1977).

[942] Martin Emerich Outfitting Co. v. Siegel, Cooper & Co., 86 N.E. 1104 (Ill.1908); Crow Lumber & Bldg. Materials Co. v. Washington Cty. Library Bd., 428 S.W.2d 758 (Mo.App.1968); Albert M. Greenfield & Co. v. Kolea, 380 A.2d 758 (Pa.1977); Restatement (Second) of Property-Landlord & Tenant § 5.4, Reporter's Note 4 (1977).

[943] A summary of the various statutes existing in the mid-1970s appears in Restatement (Second) of Property-Landlord & Tenant Ch. 5, Statutory Note 2 (1977).

[944] See Restatement (Second) of Property-Landlord & Tenant Ch. 5, Statutory Note 2 (1977); URLTA § 4.106 (1972); RURLTA § 403(a) (2015).

[945] Restatement (Second) of Property-Landlord & Tenant § 5.4(1) & Reporter's Note 9 (1977).

[946] See Lloyd v. Murphy, 153 P.2d 47 (Cal.1944); 6 Corbin, Contracts § 1320 (1962); 18 Williston, Contracts § 1955 (3d ed.1978); Restatement (Second) of Contracts §§ 261 (impracticability), 265 (frustration of purpose) (1981).

by either party. If the tenant has both covenanted to occupy and to use for a stated purpose and to make no other uses, the tenant probably has promised to do so—but the impossibility doctrine would excuse only *that* performance, not the performance of other covenants such as the covenant to pay rent.[947] Rescission is not the theory, for the landlord has breached no duty. Rather, because there has been frustration of an object of the agreement that certainly was fundamental to the tenant—if not to both parties—the law excuses the tenant's whole performance. Because the tenant's performance is excused, the landlord's is likewise excused as the landlord suffers a total failure of consideration.[948]

§§ 6.87–7.0 ARE RESERVED FOR SUPPLEMENTAL MATERIAL.

---

[947] See especially Restatement (Second) of Contracts §§ 261, 264, 265, 267 (1981).

[948] See Restatement (Second) of Contracts § 237 (1981).

Chapter 7

RIGHTS INCIDENT TO POSSESSION OF LAND

Table of Sections

This chapter deals with certain rights enjoyed by one who is entitled to possession of land: property rights that are a consequence of possession, as distinguished from property rights that arise by contract such as easements or restrictive covenants. The rights discussed in this chapter normally come with rightful possession unless the possessor has somehow given them up. In particular, this chapter covers landowners' rights to be free from physical intrusion and nuisance, as well as the rights in lateral and subjacent support, flowing streams, underground water, surface water, and certain other types of natural resources.

Many of the matters discussed in this chapter lie along the boundary between property law and tort law. Because this is a treatise on property law, these matters are examined from the perspective of the possessor—the "rights" side. Tort law primarily views them from the perspective of persons who have "duties" not to invade these rights. In treatises on tort law, some of the subjects discussed in this chapter will be found under the headings of trespass, nuisance, and, to some extent, negligence.

§ 7.1   FREEDOM FROM PHYSICAL INTRUSION

The landowner's right to exclude has long been considered fundamental to any system of property rights. Sir William Blackstone defined the right of property as "that sole and despotic dominion which one man claims and exercises over the external things of the world, in total exclusion of the right of any other individual in the universe."[1] William Pitt similarly declared: "the poorest man may, in his cottage, bid defiance to all the forces of the Crown. It may be frail; its roof may shake; the wind may blow through it; the storm may enter; but the King of England may not enter"[2] To some, "the essence of private property is always the right to exclude others."[3] Indeed, the right to physically exclude others is probably the most foundational of the many property rights that generally flow from ownership or rightful possession of land. However, the right to exclude is not absolute. Not only may others enter with the rightful possessor's

---

[1]   2 William Blackstone, Commentaries *2.

[2]   William Pitt, Speech on the Excise Bill.

[3]   Morris R. Cohen, Property and Sovereignty, 13 Cornell L. Rev. 8, 12 (1927).

permission but, in a few cases, against his will. Still, the United States Supreme Court has on numerous occasions reminded us that property owners may generally insist strictly upon excluding others, without regard to competing interests—a degree of protection that the law does not fully extend to some other property rights.[4]

Unless it is consented to or excused as privileged[5], any knowing entry upon a rightful possessor's land is wrongful and constitutes a trespass. Not only is a trespasser liable for any actual harm done to the property, he is liable for nominal damages even if there is no actual damage. Moreover, a number of courts have held that nominal damages are sufficient to support an award of punitive damages where the trespass is particularly egregious.[6] Continuing or threatened trespasses may also be enjoined. Even an unknowing non-permissive and unprivileged entry is wrongful if it is negligent or the result of extra-hazardous activity.[7]

Trespassory invasions may be committed not only by the trespasser in person but also by instrumentalities under his control. For example, objects placed or left on the plaintiff's land, projectiles or aircraft propelled through owned airspace, and animals allowed to wander can constitute a trespass.[8] At some point the law of trespass shades into the law of nuisance. Trespass applies to physical invasions by tangible objects, such as those just suggested. Nuisance, on the other hand, applies to indirect intrusions that interfere with the owner's use and enjoyment of his land, such as noise, odors, or vibrations. As discussed later in this chapter, substances such as dust and smoke are analyzed under the law of nuisance, even though they do technically have some physical size and weight. An argument can be made, for which there is some authority, that invasions by such substances are trespasses.[9]

---

[4]   See, e.g., Coll. Sav. Bank v. Fla. Prepaid Postsecondary Educ. Expense Bd., 527 U.S. 666, 667, 119 S.Ct. 2219, 2221–22, 144 L.Ed.2d 605 (1999) ("The hallmark of a constitutionally protected property interest is the right to exclude others."); Loretto v. Teleprompter Manhattan CATV Corp., 458 U.S. 419, 102 S.Ct. 3164, 73 L.Ed.2d 868 (1982) ("The power to exclude has traditionally been considered one of the most treasured strands in an owner's bundle of property rights."); Kaiser Aetna v. United States, 444 U.S. 164, 179–80 100 S.Ct. 383, 393 62 L.Ed.2d 332 (1979) (describing the right to exclusive possession as a "universally held . . . fundamental element" of property).

[5]   In addition to being addressed below, permissive entries are covered in parts of this treatise dealing with tenancies, easements, profits, and licenses.

[6]   See, e.g., Downs v. Lyles, 41 So. 3d 86 (Ala. Civ. App. 2009) ("Punitive damages are also available to a plaintiff in a trespass action, even if only nominal damages are awarded."); Rhodes v. Harwood, 273 Or. 903, 544 P.2d 147 (1975) (awarding punitive damages for intentional trespass, explaining that "the law presumes that a plaintiff has been damaged without the necessity of proof of actual damage"); Jacque v. Steenberg Homes, Inc., 209 Wis. 2d 605, 563 N.W.2d 154 (1997) (holding nominal damages can support a punitive damage award in the case of intentional trespass). But see Boring v. Google Inc., 362 F. App'x 273 (3d Cir. 2010) (holding the defendant liable for nominal damages but not punitive damages absent evidence of outrageous conduct).

[7]   6A American Law of Property §§ 28.1, 28.12, 28.17 (A.J. Casner ed. 1954); Restatement (Second) of Torts §§ 158, 162–166 (1965).

[8]   United States v. Causby, 328 U.S. 256, 66 S.Ct. 1062, 90 L.Ed. 1206 (1946) (aircraft); Portsmouth Harbor Land & Hotel Co. v. United States, 260 U.S. 327, 43 S.Ct. 135, 67 L.Ed. 287 (1922) (artillery projectiles); Herrin v. Sutherland, 74 Mont. 587, 241 P. 328 (1925) (shotgun pellets); see also Annot., 42 A.L.R. 945 (1926); 6A American Law of Property §§ 28.2, 28.4 (A.J. Casner ed. 1954); Restatement (Second) of Torts §§ 159–61 (1965).

[9]   See, e.g., Borland v. Sanders Lead Co., 369 So. 2d 523 (Ala. 1979) (holding that damage to land caused by emissions from a smelter constituted a trespass); Martin v. Reynolds Metals Co., 221 Or. 86, 342 P.2d 790 (1959) (holding that "gases and particulates" containing fluoride compounds caused a trespass and speculating that even bright lights might cause trespass). But see Amphitheaters, Inc. v. Portland Meadows, 184 Or. 336, 198 P.2d 847 (1948) (holding bright lights are not a trespass).

Most trespasses occur on the surface of the plaintiff's land. However, they may also occur below the surface because ownership is viewed as extending downward indefinitely.[10] For example, encroaching building foundations, mining tunnels, and entering a cave under another's land may constitute trespasses.[11] To the extent the surface owner owns the airspace above his land, the unauthorized and unprivileged passage through it is also a trespass.[12] With aircraft overflights, it has become clear that landowners do not literally own "to the heavens," as once stated. A landowner is now understood as having property rights in overlying airspace only to the extent necessary to protect his use and enjoyment of his land.[13]

Entry onto land without permission is not wrongful and is not a trespass if it is privileged. There are a surprising number of privileges—so many that the Restatement of Torts devotes an entire chapter to them.[14] A large group of privileges are founded in transactions between the possessor of the land and the entrant. For example, entries by former tenants, licensees, vendors, landlords, and mortgagors to remove property they are entitled to possess are not trespasses.[15] Another large group of privileges do not depend upon any present or former special relationship between possessor and entrant. Instead, they are based on some claim of the entrant's that, in the balance, is stronger than the possessor's right to exclude. Entries by public officers, such as police (with or sometimes even without a warrant), health and fire inspectors, and process servers are examples.[16] Even private individuals may enter in certain situations. For example, a private individual may enter to: retrieve property that has accidentally gone onto

---

[10] This view is reflected in the ad coelum rule, the common law doctrine that the rights of the landowner extend upward to the heavens and downward to the center of the earth. Ad Coelum Doctrine, Black's Law Dictionary (10th ed. 2014); see also W. Virginia Dep't of Transportation v. Veach, 239 W. Va. 1, 799 S.E.2d 78, 93 (2017) (explaining that the starting point of all property law is that "a parcel of land includes all interests and estates therein from the center of the earth to the heavens.")

[11] See Edwards v. Sims, 232 Ky. 791, 24 S.W.2d 619 (1929) (Great Onyx Cave); Marengo Cave Co. v. Ross, 212 Ind. 624, 10 N.E.2d 917 (1937) (cave; dictum), modified by Fraley v. Minger, 829 N.E.2d 476 (Ind. 2005); 6A American Law of Property § 28.3 (A.J. Casner ed. 1954); Restatement of Torts Second § 159(1) (1965). However, a landowner who, by "excusable neglect," builds a building that slightly overlaps a neighbor's boundary may have a defense to the neighbor's action for an equitable order to remove the encroachment, under the "mistaken improver" doctrine. The owner essentially has the equitable defense of balancing the hardships, with the result that the court will award the neighbor damages, but not order the building to be removed. See, e.g., Urban Site Venture II Ltd. P'ship v. Levering Assocs. Ltd. P'ship, 340 Md. 223, 665 A.2d 1062 (1995); Davis v. Westphal, 389 Mont. 251, 405 P.3d 73 (Mont. 2017).

[12] See authorities cited in note 8, supra.

[13] See, e.g., United States v. Causby, 328 U.S. 256, 66 S.Ct. 1062, 90 L.Ed. 1206 (1946); Hinman v. Pac. Air Lines Transp. Corp., 84 F.2d 755 (9th Cir. 1936); Restatement (Second) of Torts § 158 (1965) (stating that there is no trespass from aircraft overflight unless there is an interference with the landowner's actual use of his property).

[14] Restatement (Second) of Torts §§ 167–215 (1965). For an extended discussion of privileged entry, see 6A American Law of Property §§ 28.9–28.11 (A.J. Casner ed. 1954).

[15] See, e.g., Ilderton Oil Co. v. Riggs, 13 N.C. App. 547, 186 S.E.2d 691 (1972) (permitting a former tenant to enter land in order to retrieve chattels); State v. Buckley, 202 Vt. 371, 149 A.3d 928 (2016), reargument denied (July 6, 2016) (noting in dicta that entering land to repose property is not a trespass).

[16] The subject of entry by governmental officers rapidly becomes a constitutional question of search and seizure. For something on this tangled web, see United States v. Jones, 565 U.S. 400, 132 S.Ct. 945, 181 L.Ed.2d 911 (2012); Oliver v. United States, 466 U.S. 170, 104 S.Ct. 1735, 80 L.Ed.2d 214 (1984); Marshall v. Barlow's, Inc., 436 U.S. 307, 98 S.Ct. 1816, 56 L.Ed.2d 305 (1978); Zurcher v. Stanford Daily, 436 U.S. 547, 98 S.Ct. 1970, 56 L.Ed.2d 525 (1978); Colonnade Catering Corp. v. United States, 397 U.S. 72, 90 S.Ct. 774, 25 L.Ed.2d 60 (1970); Camara v. Municipal Court, 387 U.S. 523, 87 S.Ct. 1727, 18 L.Ed.2d 930 (1967) Camara v. Municipal Court, 387 U.S. 523, 87 S.Ct. 1727, 18 L.Ed.2d 930 (1967); See v. City of Seattle, 387 U.S. 541, 87 S.Ct. 1737, 18 L.Ed.2d 943 (1967).

another's land, detour around a blocked public highway, or abate a private nuisance.[17] The United States Supreme Court has also allowed private persons to enter shopping centers to disseminate information in pursuit of their privilege of free speech; however, the parameters of this form of privileged entry are still ill defined.[18]

Examination of the privilege cases highlights some overarching general principals. First, entry may be made only for the limited purposes for which a particular privilege exists. Second, the right to remain is temporary—it lasts only as long as needed to accomplish the privileged purpose. Privileged entrants are immune from liability for minor damage to the premises if the damage was necessary to accomplish the permitted purpose. However, a privileged entrant may be held liable for substantial harm caused to property even if it was done necessarily or unavoidably. Privileged entrants are also liable for harms to the premises caused by negligence or by exceeding the limits of the privilege. Although the examples of privileged entry demonstrate that the possessor's right to exclude is not absolute, the restrictions on the privileges also show that exclusion is the norm.

§ 7.2   FREEDOM FROM NUISANCE

A "nuisance" is perhaps best understood as a particular state of affairs. To conduct a nuisance is a tort. In tort law, the word "nuisance" has had an extremely elastic meaning. Sometimes it is little more than a pejorative term—a weasel word used as a substitute for reasoning.[19] As used in this section, "nuisance" refers only to what seems to be by far the largest branch of the subject: cases in which a defendant substantially interferes with a plaintiff's rights to use and enjoy his land. Put simply, a rightful possessor of land has a right to be free from nuisance.

The general distinction between a nuisance and a trespass is that trespass flows from a physical invasion while nuisance does not. Unfortunately, as mentioned in the preceding section, the physical and non-physical shade together in certain classes of cases.[20] Typical nuisance-causing agents are noise, dust, smoke, odors, other airborne or water-borne contaminants, vermin, insects, and vibration, though that list is not exhaustive.[21]

---

[17]   See, e.g., Gulf Prod. Co. v. Gibson, 234 S.W. 906 (Tex. Civ. App. 1921) ("[I]f a public highway be out of repair and impassable, a traveler may lawfully go over the adjoining land, without being guilty of trespass.") (citation omitted); Sammons v. Am. Auto. Ass'n, 912 P.2d 1103 (Wyo. 1996) (permitting the owner to retrieve his broken-down car off another's property).

[18]   See Marsh v. State of Ala., 326 U.S. 501, 66 S.Ct. 276, 90 L.Ed. 265 (1946) (holding that a state trespassing statute could not be used to prevent the distribution of religious materials in a privately owned company town). But see Lloyd Corp. v. Tanner, 407 U.S. 551, 92 S.Ct. 2219, 33 L.Ed.2d 131 (1972) (holding protestors were not entitled to exercise their free-speech rights on private mall property).

[19]   See W. Prosser and W. Keeton, Torts §§ 86, 87 (5th ed. 1984).

[20]   See Martin v. Reynolds Metals Co., 221 Or. 86, 342 P.2d 790 (1959) (gases and particulate matter); cf. Guttinger v. Calaveras Cement Co., 105 Cal. App. 2d 382, 233 P.2d 914 (1951) (cement dust); Borton v. Forest Hills Country Club, 926 S.W.2d 232 (Mo. Ct. App. 1996) (use of easement to retrieve golf balls beyond scope of easement could be nuisance); Boomer v. Atl. Cement Co., 26 N.Y.2d 219, 257 N.E.2d 870 (1970), on remand 72 Misc.2d 834, 340 N.Y.S.2d 97 (1972), affirmed 42 A.D.2d 496, 349 N.Y.S.2d 199 (1973) (cement dust); Amphitheaters, Inc. v. Portland Meadows, 184 Or. 336, 198 P.2d 847 (1948) (bright lights).

[21]   See, e.g., Spur Indus., Inc. v. Del E. Webb Dev. Co., 108 Ariz. 178, 494 P.2d 700 (1972) (flies and odors); Lancaster v. Monroe, 45 Ga. App. 496, 165 S.E. 302, 302 (1932) (gases and odors); Schlotfelt v. Vinton Farmers' Supply Co., 252 Iowa 1102, 109 N.W.2d 695 (1961) (noise, dust); Pendoley v. Ferreira, 345 Mass. 309, 187 N.E.2d 142 (1963) (smelly piggery); Boomer v. Atl. Cement Co., 26 N.Y.2d 219, 309 N.Y.S.2d 312, 257 N.E.2d 870 (1970), on remand 72 Misc.2d 834, 340 N.Y.S.2d 97 (1972), affirmed 42 A.D.2d 496, 349 N.Y.S.2d

Courts generally define a nuisance as an "unreasonable" activity or condition on the defendant's land that "substantially" or "unreasonably" interferes with the plaintiff's use and enjoyment of his land.[22] The Restatement of Torts calls nuisances thus defined "intentional" nuisances. The Restatement also has another category of "unintentional" nuisances, which it defines as conduct that would be actionable under rules for negligence and extra-hazardous activity.[23] However, none of the decisions discussed in this section are of that sort. The following discussion is therefore organized under the two main elements for "intentional" nuisance: the question of the defendant's "unreasonable" conduct and the question of "substantial" harm to the plaintiff.

Whether a particular defendant's use of his own land is "unreasonable" is, of course, a mixed question of fact and law. Certain kinds of activities constitute a nuisance anywhere, such as malicious designs to harm a neighbor, acts forbidden by statute, and activities openly carried on that a court considers flagrantly against accepted moral standards.[24] When one gets beyond these activities, it may be said that no activity is necessarily a nuisance at all times and places. As Justice Sutherland's famously declared, "[a] nuisance may be merely a right thing in the wrong place,—like a pig in the parlor instead of the barnyard."[25] Since a trier of fact may consider all relevant circumstances an enumeration of them is suggestive only. Factors that often predispose to a finding of nuisance include evidence that: the activity is not customary for or suited to the area; the activity causes observable effects that most of us would find disagreeable, independently of whether they actually harm the plaintiff; the activity is carried on by methods that produce more disturbance than other available methods; the activity is of little value to the defendant; the activity is unimportant to society; or the defendant's activity began after the plaintiff started using his land. Opposites of these factors tend to increase the likelihood of a finding that the defendant's activity is reasonable.[26] However, no single factor is conclusive for all cases. Despite statements in some decisions that an activity permitted by zoning cannot be a nuisance, this too is correctly considered only a factor.[27] There has also sometimes been confusion about whether an activity not originally a nuisance may become one solely because the area in which it is located changes. It clearly may so become, as the courts generally hold.[28] The related question

---

199 (1973) (cement dust); Campbell v. Seaman, 63 N.Y. 568 (1876) (acid fumes); Estancias Dallas Corp. v. Schultz, 500 S.W.2d 217 (Tex. Civ. App. 1973), writ refused NRE (Mar. 13, 1974) (noise, vibration).

[22]   In addition to the cases cited in the preceding note, see Cty. of Westchester v. Town of Greenwich, 76 F.3d 42 (2d Cir. 1996) (growing trees not nuisance though under approach to airport runway); Bove v. Donner-Hanna Coke Corp., 236 App. Div. 37, 258 N.Y.S. 229 (1932); W. Prosser, Torts § 87 (4th ed. 1971); Restatement (Second) of Torts § 822 (1979); see also the definition in Restatement (First) of Torts § 822 (1939), which has probably been cited by the courts more than any other definition of nuisance.

[23]   Restatement (Second) of Torts § 822(b) (1979); Restatement (First) of Torts § 822(d)(ii) (1939).

[24]   Restatement (Second) of Torts § 829 (1979).

[25]   Village of Euclid v. Ambler Realty Co., 272 U.S. 365, 388, 47 S.Ct. 114, 118, 71 L.Ed. 303 (1926).

[26]   Schlotfelt v. Vinton Farmers' Supply Co., 252 Iowa 1102, 109 N.W.2d 695 (1961) (unsuited; plaintiff there first); Pendoley v. Ferreira, 345 Mass. 309, 187 N.E.2d 142 (1963) (unsuited; defendant there first, but area changed); Bove v. Donner-Hanna Coke Corp., 236 App. Div. 37, 258 N.Y.S. 229 (1932) (defendant's use suited to area); Amphitheaters, Inc. v. Portland Meadows, 184 Or. 336, 198 P.2d 847 (1948) (defendant's racetrack suited to area); Estancias Dallas Corp. v. Schultz, 500 S.W.2d 217 (Tex. Civ. App. 1973), writ refused NRE (Mar. 13, 1974) (noise, near homes, severe); W. Prosser and W. Keeton, Torts § 87 (5th ed. 1984); Restatement (Second) of Torts §§ 826–831 (1979).

[27]   Compare Weltshe v. Graf, 323 Mass. 498, 82 N.E.2d 795 (1948) (only a factor); with Bove v. Donner-Hanna Coke Corp., 236 App. Div. 37, 258 N.Y.S. 229 (1932) ("not for the court" to "override" zoning).

[28]   Pendoley v. Ferreira, 345 Mass. 309, 187 N.E.2d 142 (1963); Bove v. Donner-Hanna Coke Corp., 236 App.Div. 37, 258 N.Y.S. 229 (1932); Annot., 42 A.L.R.3d 344, 364–68 (1972).

whether "coming to a nuisance" is a defense will be discussed shortly. Another question that occasionally arises is whether one may commit a nuisance by refusing to alter his land's natural condition, such as by failing to cut weeds or to spray for insects. Despite arguments to the contrary, courts overwhelmingly hold that it is not wrongful to fail to correct a natural condition, though it may be wrongful to fail to abate an artificial one.[29]

An interesting question, upon which there has been some litigation, is whether blockage of light, air, and view can cause a nuisance. As a general rule, plaintiff landowners have no common law right to the unobstructed flow of light or view over adjoining land.[30] And courts have largely refused to consider the economic impact loss of light, air, or view has upon the plaintiff, saying merely that a blocking structure cannot be a nuisance.[31] However, at least two courts have recognized that a landowner may have a cause of action against another landowner who blocks his sunlight and air flow.[32] Perhaps most famously, in Prah v. Maretti, the Wisconsin Supreme Court determined that it might be possible for a defendant to commit and actionable nuisance merely by shading a neighbor's solar energy device given the growing social value of solar energy technologies.[33] Similarly, a few state legislatures have enacted "solar access" statutes that seek to promote rooftop solar panel installations by legally protecting rooftop solar arrays from shading by neighbors.[34] Still, in most states, even landowners with rooftop solar panels have no legal protection against shading of sunlight under statutory or common law.[35]

Even though a defendant's activities may be outrageously unreasonable, they are not actionable as a "private" nuisance unless they cause "substantial" harm to the plaintiff's use and enjoyment of land. Once again, the question of what is "substantial" is a mixed question of fact and law, the resolution of which depends upon consideration of all the circumstances. Factors frequently considered as tending to show substantial harm include evidence that: the plaintiff's loss is financially large; there is observable physical damage to his premises; persons on his land suffer observable physical harm or mental anguish; it would be costly or difficult for the plaintiff to avoid the harm; or the

---

[29]   See Bandy v. Bosie, 132 Ill. App. 3d 832, 477 N.E.2d 840 (1985) (natural trees); Merriam v. McConnell, 31 Ill. App. 2d 241, 175 N.E.2d 293 (1961) (natural condition); Andrews v. Andrews, 242 N.C. 382, 88 S.E.2d 88 (1955) (artificial condition); Annot., 83 A.L.R.2d 936 (1962); Restatement (Second) of Torts § 839 (1979). But see Sprecher v. Adamson Companies, 30 Cal. 3d 358, 636 P.2d 1121 (1981) (holding that a possessor can be liable under the theory of nuisance for a natural condition); Dix W. Noel, Nuisances from Land in its Natural Condition, 56 Harv. L. Rev. 772 (1943) (critical of general rule that landowners are immune from liability from harm caused by natural conditions).

[30]   E.g., Sher v. Leiderman, 181 Cal. App. 3d 867, 226 Cal. Rptr. 698 (1986); Fontainebleau Hotel Corp. v. Forty-Five Twenty-Five, Inc., 114 So. 2d 357 (Fla. Dist. Ct. App. 1959); Blair v. 305–313 East 47th Street Assocs., 123 Misc. 2d 612, 474 N.Y.S.2d 353 (Sup 1983).

[31]   See Wolford v. Thomas, 190 Cal App 3d 347, 235 Cal Rptr 422 (1987); Venuto v. Owens-Corning Fiberglas Corp., 22 Cal. App. 3d 116, 99 Cal. Rptr. 350 (1971); Mohr v. Midas Realty Corp., 431 N.W.2d 380 (Iowa 1988); Bubis v. Kassin, 323 NJ Super 601, 733 A2d 1232 (App. Div. 1999); Cash v. Cincinnati Bd of Zoning Appeals, 117 Ohio App 3d 319, 690 NE2d 593 (1996); Scharlack v. Gulf Oil Corp., 368 S.W.2d 705 (Tex. Civ. App.1963); Collinson v. John L. Scott, Inc., 55 Wash. App. 481, 778 P.2d 534 (1989).

[32]   Tenn v. 889 Assocs., Ltd., 127 N.H. 321, 500 A.2d 366 (1985); Prah v. Maretti, 108 Wis. 2d 223, 321 N.W.2d 182 (1982); cf. Wilson v. Handley, 97 Cal. App. 4th 1301, 119 Cal. Rptr. 2d 263 (2002); Economides v. D.C. Bd. of Zoning Adjustment, 954 A.2d 427 (D.C. 2008); Segars v. Cleland, 255 Ga. App. 293, 564 S.E.2d 874 (2002); Tarlton v. Kaufman, 348 Mont. 178, 199 P.3d 263 (2008); Doin v. Champlain Bluffs Dev. Corp., 68 A.D.3d 1605, 894 N.Y.S.2d 169 (2009).

[33]   See Prah v. Maretti, 108 Wis. 2d 223; 321 N.W.2d 182 (1982).

[34]   See, e.g., WY ST § 34–22–103 (1981); NMSA § 47–3–4.A (1978).

[35]   For a more thorough description and analysis of solar access issues, see generally Troy A. Rule, Shadows on the Cathedral: Solar Access Laws in a Different Light, 2010 U. Ill. L. Rev. 851 (2010).

harm is of long duration or unremitting. Opposites of these factors tend to increase the likelihood of a finding that the harm is not substantial.[36] No single factor is necessarily controlling.

Nuisance defendants sometimes try to defend themselves by showing that the plaintiff acquired possession of his land after the defendant's activity was already established—the so-called "coming to the nuisance" defense. This is generally recognized as one relevant factor, particularly if the plaintiff had full knowledge of the defendant's activities, and it may diminish the plaintiff's chance to get an injunction. However there is hardly any authority for its being an absolute defense.[37]

Whether the interference with the plaintiff is substantial is measured from the viewpoint of a person of ordinary sensitivity who is making an ordinarily sensitive use of land, not from the viewpoint of a particular plaintiff or use.[38] For this reason, defendants have argued that something that causes only mental disturbance, such as a nearby cemetery or funeral home, cannot be a nuisance. However, courts have generally held that such activities may be nuisances if the distress or fear they engender would cause substantial harm to an ordinary person.[39]

So far, these materials have discussed what are known as "private" nuisances, as contrasted with "public" nuisances. The term "public nuisance" played a special role in the history of nuisance law.[40] However, today the difference between a public and private nuisance is chiefly a matter of degree. The basic distinction is that, whereas a private nuisance affects one or a limited number of plaintiffs, a public nuisance is viewed as being so serious that it affects the public generally or at least a large number of the public.[41] Illegal uses of land, such as houses of prostitution or illegal gambling places,

---

[36] Spur Indus., Inc. v. Del E. Webb Dev. Co., 108 Ariz. 178, 494 P.2d 700 (1972) (dwellings out of place in rural area; dictum); Nicholson v. Connecticut Half-Way House, Inc., 153 Conn. 507, 218 A.2d 383 (1966) (vague future harm; loss of value); Schlotfelt v. Vinton Farmers' Supply Co., 252 Iowa 1102, 109 N.W.2d 695 (1961) (plaintiff's home, in suitable area, there first); Pendoley v. Ferreira, 345 Mass. 309, 187 N.E.2d 142 (1963) (plaintiff's home in residential area); Robie v. Lillis, 112 N.H. 492, 299 A.2d 155 (1972) (harm to plaintiffs fairly ordinary for area); Campbell v. Seaman, 63 N.Y. 568 (1876) (irreplaceable trees destroyed); Bove v. Donner-Hanna Coke Corp., 236 App. Div. 37, 258 N.Y.S. 229 (1932) (plaintiff's home in industrial area); Amphitheaters, Inc. v. Portland Meadows, 184 Or. 336, 198 P.2d 847 (1948) (plaintiff's use abnormally sensitive); W. Prosser and W. Keeton, Torts, § 87 (5th ed. 1984); Restatement (Second) of Torts §§ 827, 829, 829A, 831 (1979).

[37] Spur Indus., Inc. v. Del E. Webb Dev. Co., 108 Ariz. 178, 494 P.2d 700 (1972) (defense recognized, but exception found); Schlotfelt v. Vinton Farmers' Supply Co., 252 Iowa 1102, 109 N.W.2d 695 (1961) (priority of occupation a "circumstance"); Patton v. Westwood Country Club Co., 18 Ohio App. 2d 137, 247 N.E.2d 761 (1969) (factor against plaintiff; no injunction); Annot., 42 A.L.R.3d 344 (1972).

[38] Schlotfelt v. Vinton Farmers' Supply Co., 252 Iowa 1102, 109 N.W.2d 695 (1961); Campbell v. Seaman, 63 N.Y. 568 (1876); Amphitheaters, Inc. v. Portland Meadows, 184 Or. 336, 198 P.2d 847 (1948); Jenkins v. CSX Transp., Inc., 906 S.W.2d 460 (Tenn. Ct. App. 1995) (hypersensitive plaintiff; no nuisance); Restatement (Second) of Torts § 827, Cmt. e (1979); see also Poole v. Lowell Dunn Co., 573 So. 2d 51 (Fla. Dist. Ct. App. 3d Dist. 1990) (noting that a plaintiff's hypersensitivity does not necessarily preclude him from recovering).

[39] Powell v. Taylor, 222 Ark. 896, 263 S.W.2d 906 (1954) (funeral home); Jones v. Trawick, 75 So. 2d 785 (Fla.1954) (cemetery); W. Prosser and W. Keeton, Torts, § 87 (5th ed. 1984). But cf. McCaw v. Harrison, 259 S.W.2d 457 (Ky. 1953) (cemetery); Nicholson v. Connecticut Half-Way House, Inc., 153 Conn. 507, 218 A.2d 383 (1966) (halfway house for ex-prisoners).

[40] See W. Prosser and W. Keeton, Torts §§ 86, 90 (5th ed. 1984); Restatement (Second) of Torts § 821B, Cmt. a (1979).

[41] Spur Indus., Inc. v. Del E. Webb Dev. Co., 108 Ariz. 178, 494 P.2d 700 (1972); Robie v. Lillis, 112 N.H. 492, 299 A.2d 155 (1972) (dictum).

are one group of uses that ordinances sometimes declare to be public nuisances.[42] However, not all public nuisances are illegal activities. Many are the same kinds of activities that are private nuisances (indeed, they are both) but have such a pervasive and widespread effect that they harm a large number of the public.[43] Even though a public nuisance affects the public generally, the traditional rule is that the only persons who may maintain a public action are land possessors who are specially affected or a public prosecutor.[44] The Restatement of Torts, however, advocates that any affected member of the public should be able to maintain an abatement action.[45]

The successful plaintiff in a nuisance action may always recover as much damages as he can prove, measured by loss of rental value for a temporary nuisance or by loss of market value for a permanent nuisance.[46] For obvious reasons, plaintiffs also often seek an injunction stopping the offending activity if it is still occurring. Except possibly in a few jurisdictions where injunctions against nuisances are said to be a matter of right, injunctions, being an equitable remedy, are regarded as being within the court's discretion. Thus, in most states various equitable defenses may bar an injunction even though the common law remedy of damages will be given. The particular equitable defense most important in this context is called either "balancing the equities" or "balancing the hardships", although the latter phrase fits this situation better. Roughly stated, the court may refuse to issue an injunction if issuing it would do more harm than good. The court seeks to balance the hardship from the plaintiff's side if the injunction is not issued against the hardship from the defendant's side if it is issued. In assessing these respective hardships, the court generally considers the same factors that were described above when the questions of "unreasonable" use and "substantial" interference were discussed.[47] At this stage, economic and social effects of an injunction *vel non* on the community may be crucial. For instance, a court may refuse to enjoin a commercial enterprise when this would cause much unemployment or otherwise disadvantage the community.[48] Still, if an injunction is issued, equity always tailors it to the case. Rather

---

[42] See, e.g., State ex rel. Fisher v. Reno Hotel, Inc., 95 Ohio App. 3d 67, 641 N.E.2d 1155 (1994) (prostitution in hotel, known to operators, was public nuisance); see generally Donald G. Gifford, Public Nuisance As A Mass Products Liability Tort, 71 U. Cin. L. Rev. 741, 831 (2003) (discussing the link between the tort of public nuisance and real property).

[43] Spur Indus., Inc. v. Del E. Webb Dev. Co., 108 Ariz. 178, 494 P.2d 700 (1972) (cattle feedlot); Hoover v. Durkee, 212 A.D.2d 839, 622 N.Y.S.2d 348 (1995) (noisy auto racetrack); Town of Preble v. Song Mountain, Inc., 62 Misc. 2d 353, 308 N.Y.S.2d 1001 (Sup. Ct. 1970) (rock concert); W. Prosser and W. Keeton, Torts §§ 86, 90 (5th ed. 1984); Restatement (Second) of Torts § 821B (1979).

[44] See, e.g., City of Chicago v. Beretta U.S.A. Corp., 821 N.E.2d 1099 (Ill. 2004).

[45] Restatement (Second) of Torts § 821C (1979).

[46] W. Prosser and W. Keeton, Torts § 89 (5th ed. 1984); see Boomer v. Atl. Cement Co., 26 N.Y.2d 219, 309 N.Y.S.2d 312, 257 N.E.2d 870 (1970), on remand 72 Misc.2d 834, 340 N.Y.S.2d 97 (1972), affirmed 42 A.D.2d 496, 349 N.Y.S.2d 199 (1973); Restatement (Second) of Torts § 822, Cmt. d (1979).

[47] Nicholson v. Connecticut Half-Way House, Inc., 153 Conn. 507, 218 A.2d 383 (1966); Schlotfelt v. Vinton Farmers' Supply Co., 252 Iowa 1102, 109 N.W.2d 695 (1961); Robie v. Lillis, 112 N.H. 492, 299 A.2d 155 (1972) (dictum); Campbell v. Seaman, 63 N.Y. 568 (1876); Smith v. Wallowa County, 145 Ore. App. 341, 929 P.2d 1100 (1996) (asphalt plant enjoined; disturbance outweighed economic loss); Estancias Dallas Corp. v. Schultz, 500 S.W.2d 217 (Tex. Civ. App. 1973), writ refused NRE (Mar. 13, 1974); Mathewson v. Primeau, 64 Wash. 2d 929, 395 P.2d 183 (1964).

[48] City of Harrisonville, Mo. v. W. S. Dickey Clay Mfg. Co., 289 U.S. 334, 53 S.Ct. 602, 77 L.Ed. 1208 (1933); Boomer v. Atl. Cement Co., 26 N.Y.2d 219, 309 N.Y.S.2d 312, 257 N.E.2d 870 (1970), on remand 72 Misc.2d 834, 340 N.Y.S.2d 97 (1972) affirmed 42 A.D.2d 496, 349 N.Y.S.2d 199 (1973) (injunction "granted" but to be "vacated"); W. Prosser and W. Keeton, Torts § 89 (5th ed. 1984).

than enjoin the defendant completely, a court may issue a partial injunction that zeroes in on certain features of the defendant's activities, such as time, manner, and place.[49]

§ 7.3   RIGHT TO SUPPORT

Possessors of land have a common law or "natural" right against other persons for two kinds of support for their land: rights to "lateral support" and "subjacent support." Lateral support is support in a vertical plane from the adjoining lands of other persons. Subjacent support is support in a horizontal plane from underlying strata of earth owned or occupied by other persons. This section focuses on these two important landowner rights.

The right of lateral support is the right to have one's land in its natural condition (i.e., as if it were not burdened by structures or other weighty objects) supported by the adjacent neighbors' land. This right is absolute and is traditionally thought of as a servitude burdening the adjoining land.[50] Therefore, the neighbor is strictly liable for removing support, which usually occurs by excavating on his land.[51] Implicit in this statement is the rule that the neighbor is not strictly liable if the plaintiff's land would have been adequately supported if it had been in its natural condition, unburdened by buildings or other artificial weight.[52] Of course, one's neighbor may well be liable for harm to weight-burdened land on some tort theory, such as negligence or malicious harm that is beyond the scope of this treatise. Since the right-duty is to have and maintain support, the plaintiff has a cause of action as soon as the neighbor removes support, even if no subsidence has yet occurred. However, no action for damages may be maintained until subsidence causes provable damage—though it seems an action for an injunction should be possible.[53]

A defendant whose activities, such as excavating, would cause a loss of lateral support to his neighbor's land may avoid liability by providing artificial support with a retaining wall or some similar installation. He can thereby escape liability so long as the artificial support actually does its intended job. Conversely, if he fails to maintain the artificial support or it otherwise fails to keep lateral support up to the legally required standard, the defendant will then become liable.[54]

---

[49] E.g., Weltshe v. Graf, 323 Mass. 498, 82 N.E.2d 795 (1948) (hours of operation); Pendoley v. Ferreira, 345 Mass. 309, 187 N.E.2d 142 (1963) (injunction granted but delayed); Payne v. Johnson, 20 Wash. 2d 24, 145 P.2d 552 (1944) (manner of operation).

[50] See, e.g., Downs v. Lyles, 41 So. 3d 86 (Ala. Civ. App. 2009); Vikell Inv'rs Pac., Inc. v. Hampden, Ltd., 946 P.2d 589 (Colo. App. 1997); Franc v. Bethel Holding Co., 73 Conn. App. 114, 807 A.2d 519 (2002).

[51] Holtz v. Superior Court, 3 Cal.3d 296, 90 Cal. Rptr. 345, 475 P.2d 441 (1970) (implied); Moellering v. Evans, 121 Ind. 195, 22 N.E. 989 (1889); Levi v. Schwartz, 201 Md. 575, 95 A.2d 322 (1953) (dictum); Prete v. Cray, 49 R.I. 209, 141 A. 609 (1928). See discussion of this and related points in 6A American Law of Property §§ 28.36, 28.39–28.42 (A.J. Casner ed. 1954), and Restatement (Second) of Torts §§ 817–819 (1979). These two treatises may sometimes be drawn upon in this section without further attribution, to save repeated citations; see also Annot., 33 A.L.R.2d 111, 112–20 (1954); Annot., 50 A.L.R. 486, 486–98 (1927), Supp., 59 A.L.R. 1252 (1929).

[52] Moellering v. Evans, 121 Ind. 195, 22 N.E. 989 (1889); Spall v. Janota, 406 N.E.2d 378 (Ind. App. 1980); see generally sources cited supra note 50. It has been held that the plaintiff has the burden to prove that the land would have slipped in its natural condition, i.e., that the weight of the buildings did not contribute to the subsidence. See Vikell Investors Pacific, Inc. v. Kip, 946 P.2d 589 (Colo. App. 1997); Klebs v. Yim, 54 Wash. App. 41, 772 P.2d 523 (1989).

[53] See Restatement (Second) of Torts, Ch. 9, Scope and Introductory Note; §§ 817, Cmt. i, and 936, Cmt. e (1979).

[54] Gorton v. Schofield, 311 Mass. 352, 41 N.E.2d 12 (1942); Restatement (Second) of Torts § 817, Cmt. k (1979).

It is worth noting that, in defining the property right of lateral support, the text above carefully states that it is a right to support from "adjacent" land. There remains some controversy regarding whether the right extends to support from neighboring but non-adjacent land. The Restatement of Torts, Second, states that it does so extend, and American Law of Property apparently advocates it.[55] As to the decided cases, it seems that, while non-adjacent neighbors have sometimes been held liable for causing subsidence, this has nearly always been on a theory of negligence and not of absolute liability.[56] For that reason, lateral support, as a real property right, probably does not extend to a right of support from nonadjacent lands.

A question that sometimes arises is whether a plaintiff may recover for damage to his buildings that happen to be on the land when the defendant is liable for damage to the bare land for destroying lateral support. The question assumes the defendant removed lateral support and the plaintiff's land consequently subsided and would have subsided without the weight of buildings on it. We may assume the defendant is liable for damages for the diminution in value of the bare land. At issue is whether he is also liable for damages for the harm to the building. By the English rule and the very decided weight of American authority, he is.[57] A few decisions that deny damages to the building reason that, since the defendant's duty is only to support the unburdened land, his liability for damages should exist only to the same extent.[58]

Turning now to the subject of subjacent support: it was defined at the beginning of this section as a right to have one's land supported "in a horizontal plane from underlying strata of earth owned and occupied by other persons." This generally implies a severance of one or more estates in layers of underlying earth from the estate in the surface, with the underlying layers being owned, occupied, or used by others than the holder of the surface estate. Potential defendants are thus necessarily limited to such underlying owners or users, and potential plaintiffs are limited to the possessor of the surface or of some layer above the defendant. An exception, in some jurisdictions, exists in cases in which a neighbor removes underground water in such quantities as to drain the water from under the plaintiff's land and to cause the plaintiff's land to subside. The Restatement of Torts, Second, some text writers, and some decisions take the position that the neighbor in that instance should be liable for the loss of subjacent support.[59] It appears, however, that the majority of courts deciding the question have refused to extend liability, on the theory that subjacent support means support from solid substances in the earth and not from underground water.[60]

The right of subjacent support is quite similar to the right to lateral support except that it applies in a horizontal plane. One difference is in the defendant's exposure to liability for failing to support land burdened by weighty structures. With lateral support,

[55] Restatement (Second) of Torts § 817, Cmt. g (1979); 6A American Law of Property § 28.39 (A.J. Casner ed. 1954).

[56] See United States v. Peachy, 36 F. 160 (S.D. Ohio 1888); Puckett v. Sullivan, 190 Cal.App.2d 489, 12 Cal. Rptr. 55 (1961); Annot., 87 A.L.R.2d 710 (1963).

[57] Smith v. Howard, 201 Ky. 249, 256 S.W. 402 (1923); Prete v. Cray, 49 R.I. 209, 141 A. 609 (1928); Annot., 50 A.L.R. 486 (1927), Supp., 59 A.L.R. 1252 (1929).

[58] See Moellering v. Evans, 121 Ind. 195, 22 N.E. 989 (1889); Annot., 50 A.L.R. 486 (1927), Supp., 59 A.L.R. 1252 (1929).

[59] 6A American Law of Property § 28.46 (A.J. Casner ed. 1954); Restatement (Second) of Torts § 818 (1979).

[60] See Finley v. Teeter Stone, Inc., 251 Md. 428, 248 A.2d 106 (1968); Annot., 4 A.L.R. 1104 (1919).

it will be recalled, the duty is only to preserve support for the land as if it were unburdened by structures. Technically, this is also usually stated to be the extent of the defendant's duty to maintain subjacent support.[61] An apparent minority of courts have adopted the rule that the subjacent defendant owes a duty to support the surface with the structures that were on it at the date of severance.[62] There seems to be agreement that the defendant owes no duty to support structures added later. As a practical matter, however, a rule of evidence is likely to cause the defendant to be liable for land burdened by buildings that fall in, whether the buildings were emplaced before or after severance. Courts generally are agreed that the burden of proof is on the defendant to show that the land would not have subsided in its unburdened condition—i.e., that the buildings caused it. Because proof of actual cause is difficult in these cases, the plaintiff is likely to win on this otherwise troublesome point.[63] If the defendant is liable at all, he will be liable for damage to improvements on the overlying land as well as for damage to the land itself.

§ 7.4 RIGHTS TO STREAMS AND LAKES (RIPARIAN RIGHTS)

An owner or possessor of land that abuts a natural stream, pond, or lake is commonly called a "riparian" proprietor. The word "littoral" is technically more correct for an owner on a pond or lake, but the word "riparian" will be used in this section for convenience. Riparian possessors have certain rights to the water that are incident to their rights of possession. These include rights to have the body of water remain in more or less its natural quantity and quality, limited use and consumption, access, and accretion and reliction.[64] However, these rights are not absolute. Unless a given person owns all the riparian land around a pond or lake, others whose land abuts the same stream or body of water have the same claims to riparian rights—competing claims. The public may also have claims to a certain extent to use the water, especially if it is navigable. Accordingly, the study of riparian rights is not only an investigation of the rights of an individual owner; it is a study of competing claims and shared rights in a limited resource.

The English common-law doctrine of riparian rights, applied in many early American cases, is known as the "natural flow" doctrine. Developed mostly with reference to flowing streams, its basic thesis is that the various owners on a body of water have use rights but that, with minor exceptions, none are permitted to actually own the water. The doctrine affords some protection to the lower owners on a stream. Ideally, under the natural flow doctrine the lower owners would receive as much and as

---

[61] Annot., 32 A.L.R.2d 1309, 1310–13 (1953); Restatement (Second) of Torts § 820, Cmt. c (1979); see Platts v. Sacramento Northern Ry., 205 Cal. App. 3d 1025, 253 Cal. Rptr. 269 (1988) (absolute duty to maintain land in natural condition; dictum).

[62] Annot., 32 A.L.R.2d 1309, 1310–18, 1325–29 (1953); 6A American Law of Property § 28.44 (A.J. Casner ed. 1954) (stating the rule to be that the duty is to support buildings that were there at the date of severance).

[63] See Restatement (Second) of Torts § 820, Cmt. d (1979); see also sources cited supra note 61.

[64] Olde Severna Park Improvement Ass'n, Inc. v. Gunby, 402 Md. 317, 936 A.2d 365 (2007); Levene v. City of Salem, 191 Or. 182, 229 P.2d 255 (1951); 1 H. Farnham, Waters and Water Rights 278–347 (1904); Wiel, Running Water, 22 Harv. L. Rev. 190 (1909). On the right of access, see Cmt. Note, 89 A.L.R. 1156 (1934); see also Johnson v. Board of County Comm'rs, 259 Kan. 305, 913 P.2d 119 (1996) (riparian owner has right to flow of water in channel that was established by artificial structure many years ago); Horry County v. Woodward, 282 S.C. 366, 318 S.E.2d 584 (1984) (when stream shifts so far that it cuts into land that never had waterfront, but had fixed upland boundary, then shifts back toward its original location, fixed boundary is restored along its original line and is fixed there once again).

good water as the upper owners. Of course, if the doctrine were applied literally in that way, no owner who was upstream of anyone else could even touch the water because any use of it would in some degree alter the quantity and quality of water downstream. The doctrine permits every owner to consume as much water as needed for "domestic" purposes, which generally means for personal human consumption, drinking, bathing, etc., and for watering domestic animals. Beyond this, riparian owners may use the water for "reasonable" artificial or commercial purposes, subject to the very large proviso that they may not substantially or materially diminish the quantity or quality of water.[65] Certainly, no water may be transported to land beyond the riparian land.

The natural flow doctrine bears the stamp of an agrarian society; it is not designed to promote irrigation or commercial use of water. If any use may be made for those purposes, it is slight. Many old cases applying the doctrine involved some variant of the question of whether a mill owner—usually one with a dam to impound a pond to feed the mill—may temporarily detain water and to some extent use it up in manufacturing processes and by evaporation.[66] As the industrial revolution progressed in America and it became increasingly apparent that the natural flow theory inhibited important developments, courts began to modify the doctrine. Though they were not always explicit about it, their tendency was to move toward—or at least to introduce elements of—the "reasonable use" doctrine discussed below. Courts inched in that direction through such means as expanding the notion of what were "domestic" uses[67] or possibly expanding how much water could be detained or consumed in commercial uses.[68]

Today, most U.S. states located East of the Mississippi River follow some version of the "reasonable use" riparian rights doctrine to allocate surface water rights. States situated West of the Mississippi River generally follow some version of the prior appropriation doctrine, which is described below. A few states have a hybrid or dual system bearing elements of both the prior appropriation doctrine and the reasonable use doctrine. The reasonable use doctrine generally provides that riparian owners may make any and all reasonable uses of the water, so long they do not unreasonably interfere with the other riparian owners' opportunity for reasonable use. An underlying policy of this approach seems to be that, although protecting the natural flow of water in rivers is a legitimate ideal, the law should be flexible enough to allow some water to be used to serve human endeavors. The reasonable use doctrine also avoids the natural flow theory's problematic tendency to favoring the lower owners on a stream at the expense of upper owners.[69]

Determining whether and to what extent a given use is allowed under the reasonable use doctrine requires a weighing of factors on the would-be user's side against similar factors on the side of other riparian owners. No list of such factors is exhaustive

---

[65]   Scranton Gas & Water Co. v. Delaware, Lackawanna & Western Railroad Co., 240 Pa. 604, 88 A. 24 (1913); Filbert v. Dechert, 22 Pa. Super. 362 (1903); 6A American Law of Property §§ 28.56, 28.57 (A.J. Casner ed. 1954); Restatement (Second) of Torts, Ch. 41, Introductory Note on the Nature of Riparian Rights and Legal Theories for Determination of the Rights (1979).

[66]   See, e.g., Evans v. Merriweather, 4 Ill. 492 (1842); Gehlen v. Knorr, 101 Iowa 700, 70 N.W. 757 (1897); Moore v. California Oregon Power Co., 22 Cal. 2d 725, 140 P.2d 798 (1943); Annot., 70 A.L.R. 220 (1931) (listing the many cases involving mills); see also Annot., 9 A.L.R. 1211 (1920) (reporting cases on increased velocity and volume).

[67]   E.g., Filbert v. Dechert, 22 Pa. Super. 362 (1903) (water for 800 hospital inmates "domestic" use).

[68]   E.g., Evans v. Merriweather, 4 Ill. 492 (1842) ("reasonable" use for "artificial" purposes; dictum); Gehlen v. Knorr, 101 Iowa 700, 70 N.W. 757 (1897) (detaining water in pond).

[69]   See Gehlen v. Knorr, 101 Iowa 700, 70 N.W. 757 (1897); Dumont v. Kellogg, 29 Mich. 420 (1874).

because the court will consider all the circumstances that are relevant in a given case.[70] However, factors that frequently are important include the purposes of the various uses, their economic value and importance to the owners and to the community, their social value, how much a given use impinges upon the other riparian owners, how appropriate a use is to the particular body of water, and the cost and practicality of adjusting a given use or the other uses.[71] In theory, no single factor is conclusive. In practice, however, some factors unquestionably get more weight than others. Domestic uses are so favored that they will generally prevail over other uses. Indeed, some courts embrace a two-tiered doctrine—essentially a carryover from the natural flow theory—that recognizes domestic uses as a preferred category and other reasonable uses as a second category.[72] In arid regions of the West, irrigation may be a use favored over all other uses except domestic uses.[73] While the reasonable use doctrine generally permits water to be transported to and used on non-riparian lands, uses there may be in some ways disfavored over uses on riparian lands.[74] The result of all this is that the reasonable use doctrine is flexible, applied with local variations in the states that follow it.

In the seventeen states west of the ninety-eighth meridian, another system of water law, some form of a statutory "appropriation" system, is exclusively or partly in effect. Really, there is not one system but seventeen. In the states of Arizona, Colorado, Idaho, Montana, Nevada, New Mexico, Utah, and Wyoming, forming an arid inner core, an appropriation system is the exclusive system. This is called the "Colorado doctrine." The less arid states on the eastern and western fringes, California, Kansas, Nebraska, North Dakota, Oklahoma, Oregon, South Dakota, Texas, and Washington, follow combinations of both appropriation and reasonable use doctrines. This is known as the "California doctrine."[75]

To anyone who reads the list of states above and who has any familiarity with American geography, it will come as no surprise to learn that the underlying purpose of an appropriation system is to assure that scarce water resources are put to use, rather than being conserved or apportioned among all riparian owners. The basic appropriation principle is that someone—not necessarily a riparian owner—who makes a prior use of water for some "beneficial" purpose may gain the right to continue doing so.[76] Under most systems, the prior appropriator's right is subject to being diminished by a later claimant who can establish a need for water for a preferred beneficial purpose. However, since water rights are viewed as property rights, the diminished prior appropriator must

[70] See Stratton v. Mt. Hermon Boys' Sch., 216 Mass. 83, 103 N.E. 87 (1913); Dumont v. Kellogg, 29 Mich. 420 (1874).

[71] A listing of factors is contained in Restatement (Second) of Torts § 850A (1979).

[72] See Evans v. Merriweather, 4 Ill. 492 (1842) (dictum); Stratton v. Mt. Hermon Boys' Sch., 216 Mass. 83, 103 N.E. 87 (1913) (dictum); 6A American Law of Property § 28.57 (A.J. Casner ed. 1954).

[73] E.g., Herminghaus v. Southern California Edison Co., 200 Cal. 81, 252 P. 607 (1926), superseded by constitutional amendment, Cal. Const. art. X, § 2; 6A American Law of Property § 28.57 (A.J. Casner ed. 1954).

[74] See, e.g., West's Ann. Cal. Water Code § 1254; Anaheim Union Water Co. v. Fuller, 150 Cal. 327, 88 P. 978 (1907); see generally Frank J. Trelease, Coordination of Riparian and Appropriative Rights to the Use of Water, 33 Tex. L .Rev. 24, 41 (1954).

[75] For a standard backgrounds on appropriation systems, of both the California and Colorado types, see Wells Hutchins, Selected Problems in the Law of Water Rights in the West 27–109 (1942); Trelease, supra note 74. These works are the source for much of this material on appropriation systems. For a historical discussion of the appropriation system, tracing it back to the miners' law of the California gold rush, see Justice Field's opinion in Jennison v. Kirk, 98 U.S. 453, 25 L.Ed. 240 (1878).

[76] For a classic discussion of beneficial vs preferred use, see Coffin v. Left Hand Ditch Co., 6 Colo. 443 (1882).

be compensated. Water statutes may list preferred uses, but litigation arises over what is a beneficial or preferred use.[77] The entire appropriation system is generally under the control of a state agency that issues water permits, irons out disputes, and enforces the water code through local officers who have such titles as "stream wardens" or "water masters."[78]

The "California" systems, in which appropriation rights and common-law rights under the reasonable use doctrine are mixed in various ways, seem particularly predisposed to controversy. Of course, the conflicts would be much worse if the Western states still applied the natural flow doctrine, with its insistence that a stream be kept at full flow and that water be used only on riparian land, as California once did.[79] Even with the reasonable use doctrine, serious conflicts can arise between a permit holder who claims by prior appropriation and a riparian owner who comes along later and claims under riparian rights. Or a later appropriator may take rights from a prior riparian owner, who is generally entitled to compensation.[80] Another frequent type of conflict involves water transported for use beyond riparian land, particularly on land beyond the watershed of the stream from which it is diverted.[81]

On navigable waterways, a major limitation on the riparian owner's rights is imposed by what is commonly called the "navigation servitudes" held by the Federal Government and to a much lesser extent by state governments. Under an extension of the commerce clause of the United States Constitution, the Federal Government has the power to regulate and improve navigation.[82] It is well settled that this gives the Government not only the power to regulate water traffic but also to build and license the building of structures in navigable water, which in recent history has significantly included hydroelectric dams. In those few instances in which Congress has not exercised it, states also have this power.[83] The navigation servitude doctrine provides that private riparian rights are held subject to a "servitude" held by the Government to do and license the doing of things under the navigation power. Accordingly, it is no wrong to the riparian owner to interfere with his riparian rights—either those arising at common law or under an appropriation system—if the interference involved activity pursuant to the navigation power because his rights were always subject to the power. Why government should be able to interfere with property rights under the navigation power when it cannot so interfere under other powers has never been satisfactorily explained, and the navigation servitude doctrine has been roundly criticized by legal writers. Nevertheless, it generally remains intact.[84]

---

[77] See, e.g., State, Dep't of Parks v. Idaho Dep't of Water Admin., 96 Idaho 440, 530 P.2d 924 (1974) (addressing whether scenic preservation a beneficial use).

[78] See, e.g., Cal. Water Code §§ 1201–1675 (West); Wash. Rev. Code Ann. chs. 90.03—90.16 (West)

[79] See Lux v. Haggin, 69 Cal. 255, 4 P. 919 (1884), and Lux v. Haggin, 69 Cal. 255, 10 P. 674 (1886).

[80] See Trelease, supra note 74; W.B. Stoebuck, Condemnation of Riparian Rights, a Species of Taking Without Touching, 30 La. L. Rev. 394, 413–16 (1970).

[81] E.g., Anaheim Union Water Co. v. Fuller, 150 Cal. 327, 88 P. 978 (1907) (not beyond the watershed); Trelease, supra note 74; cf. Lowe v. Sun Ref. & Mktg. Co., 73 Ohio App. 3d 563, 597 N.E.2d 1189 (1992).

[82] U.S. Const. Art. I, § 8, cl. 3; Gibbons v. Ogden, 22 U.S. 1, 6 L.Ed. 23 (1824).

[83] United States v. Bellingham Bay Boom Co., 176 U.S. 211, 20 S.Ct. 343, 44 L.Ed. 437 (1900); Colberg, Inc. v. State ex rel. Department of Public Works, 67 Cal.2d 408, 62 Cal. Rptr. 401, 432 P.2d 3 (1967), certiorari denied 390 U.S. 949, 88 S.Ct. 1037, 19 L.Ed.2d 1139 (1968).

[84] This entire discussion of the navigation servitude is based largely upon Stoebuck, supra note 80 at 421–39 (1970).

Under the navigation servitude doctrine, the riparian owner has no redress for loss of riparian rights when the impact falls out beyond the line that divides his upland or fast land from the adjacent water. Such non-compensable impacts may interfere with access to the water, water level (including loss of power-site value), and the right to use the water (port-site value).[85] Even if the upland owner also owns the bed under the water, the bed is subject to the servitude.[86] However, it is clear that the servitude stops at the point where water or bed ends and upland begins.[87] Where that line is seems now to be a matter of state law, though perhaps the Supreme Court still has some work to do to make that entirely clear.[88] It is also believed that the servitude does not burden riparian rights in non-navigable streams,[89] but Supreme Court decisions leave that point in some doubt, too.[90]

In addition to being subject to navigation servitudes, private riparian rights may be subject to the public's right to boat and perhaps to use the water for recreational purposes. This is true on navigable waters, and some courts have extended these public rights to some extent to waters that would not otherwise be considered navigable.[91] And so we return to a point made in the beginning of this section: that the study of riparian rights is in large part a study of competing claims to a limited resource. Riparian rights are not absolute. They are rights shared with those of other riparian owners and even with rights of the public.

§ 7.5   RIGHTS TO UNDERGROUND WATER

Water collects in useful concentrations under the surface of the earth in permeable rock, sand, or gravel, in basins or reservoirs known as "aquifers." From these aquifers, surface possessors may obtain this water through natural springs and pools and from artificial wells. Aquifers generally underly the lands of multiple owners, and withdrawals of water from an aquifer by one person obviously lowers its upper level—known as the "water table"—for all of those owners. Withdrawals by many commercial or municipal users, employing large mechanical pumps, may lower the table a lot, causing other possessors within the aquifer to suffer losses of supply and perhaps to have

---

[85]   United States v. Rands, 389 U.S. 121, 88 S.Ct. 265, 19 L.Ed.2d 329 (1967) (port site); United States v. Twin City Power Co., 350 U.S. 222, 76 S.Ct. 259, 100 L.Ed. 240 (1956), rehearing denied 350 U.S. 1009, 76 S.Ct. 648, 100 L.Ed. 871 (1956) (water level; power site); United States v. Willow River Power Co., 324 U.S. 499, 65 S.Ct. 761, 89 L.Ed. 1101 (1945) (water level; power site); United States v. Chandler-Dunbar Water Power Co., 229 U.S. 53, 33 S.Ct. 667, 57 L.Ed. 1063 (1913) (mostly water level, power site).

[86]   United States v. Cherokee Nation of Oklahoma, 480 U.S. 700, 107 S.Ct. 1487, 94 L.Ed.2d 704 (1987); Lewis Blue Point Oyster Cultivation Co. v. Briggs, 229 U.S. 82, 33 S.Ct. 679, 57 L.Ed. 1083 (1913).

[87]   United States v. Kansas City Life Insurance Co., 339 U.S. 799, 70 S.Ct. 885, 94 L.Ed. 1277 (1950).

[88]   See Oregon ex rel. State Land Board v. Corvallis Sand & Gravel Co., 429 U.S. 363, 97 S.Ct. 582, 50 L.Ed.2d 550 (1977), on remand 283 Or. 147, 582 P.2d 1352 (1978); see also Phillips Petroleum Co. v. Mississippi, 484 U.S. 469, 108 S.Ct. 791, 98 L.Ed.2d 877 (1988), rehearing denied 486 U.S. 1018, 108 S.Ct. 1760, 100 L.Ed.2d 221 (1988) (state owned to tide line, upward of navigation line, when it claimed to that line); Utah Div. of State Lands v. United States, 482 U.S. 193, 107 S.Ct. 2318, 96 L.Ed.2d 162 (1987), on remand 846 F.2d 613 (10th Cir.1988) (state owned lake bed).

[89]   United States v. Cress and United States v. Kelly, 243 U.S. 316, 37 S.Ct. 380, 61 L.Ed. 746 (1917).

[90]   See United States v. Grand River Dam Authority, 363 U.S. 229, 80 S.Ct. 1134, 4 L.Ed.2d 1186 (1960), rehearing denied 364 U.S. 855, 81 S.Ct. 33, 5 L.Ed.2d 79 (1960); United States v. Willow River Power Co., 324 U.S. 499, 65 S.Ct. 761, 89 L.Ed. 1101 (1945).

[91]   See Annot., 6 A.L.R.4th 1030 (1981); see also Anderson v. Bell, 433 So. 2d 1202 (Fla. 1983), reversing 411 So. 2d 948 (Fla. App.1982) (riparian landowner who owned portion of bed of non-navigable artificial lake not allowed to use waters over portion of bed owned by another); Black v. Williams, 417 So. 2d 911 (Miss.1982) (riparian landowner who owned portion of bed of non-navigable lake had right to exclude other riparian owners from water above his portion).

to extend their own wells deeper. Competing claims over this limited common resource have predictably caused disputes over the years that have found their way into the courts. This section deals with the principles of law that attempt to resolve those disputes.

Generally, the first step in analysis of an underground water dispute is to ask whether the water in question flows in a defined underground stream. Most underground water does not do so; most is diffused or "percolating" water that seeps and trickles through the permeable strata. The judicial presumption is that a supply of water is percolating water, meaning that the burden is on the one who claims it to prove the water flows in a stream. Evidence of an underground stream with defined banks and bed could take the form of test borings, observations of the stream appearing from or disappearing into the earth, surface sounds of flowing water, vegetation on the surface, and other signs. When a court determines that underground water is flowing in a stream, it typically applies the same riparian or prior appropriation doctrine it applies to a flowing surface stream. The rules governing riparian and prior appropriation rights outlined in the preceding section generally apply.[92]

If the underground water supply is determined to be percolating rather than a stream, then under the common law in most states disputes are settled under one of three doctrines. The oldest and most traditional of the three is the English doctrine of Acton v. Blundell, sometimes called the "absolute ownership" doctrine.[93] Under this doctrine, a possessor of land may withdraw as much underground water as he wishes, for whatever purposes he wishes, and let his neighbors look somewhere other than to the law for relief. Essentially the only limit on this doctrine is that one may not withdraw water for the malicious purpose of injuring others. The English rule became the traditional, and once prevailing, rule in early American courts, and is still followed in some places.[94] However, for many years the trend of American decisions has been against the English doctrine. It takes second place today to the rule of "reasonable use," which is discussed next.

The "reasonable use" doctrine, sometimes called the "American doctrine" or doctrine of "correlative rights," traces back to dictum in Bassett v. Salisbury Manufacturing Company—an 1862 decision involving surface waters.[95] The court there suggested that the use of underground water should be regulated by a rule of "reasonable use," a

---

[92] Bristor v. Cheatham, 75 Ariz. 227, 255 P.2d 173 (1953); Finley v. Teeter Stone, Inc., 251 Md. 428, 248 A.2d 106 (1968) (dictum); Higday v. Nickolaus, 469 S.W.2d 859 (Mo.App.1971) (dictum); 6A American Law of Property § 28.65 (A.J. Casner ed. 1954); Joseph L. Sax, Water Law, Planning & Policy 459 (1968). A major annotation, covering all the law of underground water, is contained in 55 A.L.R. 1385–1566 (1928) supplemented by Annot., 109 A.L.R. 395–422 (1937). Pages 1487–1501 and 415–16, respectively, deal with underground streams; see also Annot., 29 A.L.R.2d 1354 (1953), on the subject of obstruction and diversion of underground waters. The American Law Institute, in a missionary effort to reform the law of underground water, has adopted rules that, inter alia, abolish the distinction between underground streams and percolating water. Restatement (Second) of Torts § 858 and Introductory Note thereto (1979).

[93] 12 Mees. & W. 324, 152 Eng. Rep. 1223 (Exch.1843). Dickinson v. Grand Junction Canal Co., 7 Exch. 282, 155 Eng. Rep. 953 (1852), seemed to limit and question Acton. But the House of Lords fully reaffirmed Acton v. Blundell in Chasemore v. Richards, 7 H.L.C. 349, 11 Eng. Rep. 140 (1859).

[94] Bristor v. Cheatham, 75 Ariz. 227, 255 P.2d 173 (1953) (dictum); Finley v. Teeter Stone, Inc., 251 Md. 428, 248 A.2d 106 (1968) (dictum); Meeker v. City of E. Orange, 77 N.J.L. 623, 74 A. 379 (1909) (dictum); Higday v. Nickolaus, 469 S.W.2d 859 (Mo. App. 1971) (dictum); City of Corpus Christi v. City of Pleasanton, 154 Tex. 289, 276 S.W.2d 798 (1955) (rule of decision); Annot., 55 A.L.R. 1385, 1390–98 (1928), Supp., 109 A.L.R. 395, 397–99 (1937); Sax, supra note 92 at 460–61.

[95] 43 N.H. 569 (1862); accord, Swett v. Cutts, 50 N.H. 439 (1870).

suggestion that Lord Wensleydale had previously made in Chasemore v. Richards—one of the English decisions that followed Acton v. Blundell.[96] *Bassett's* dictum bore fruit about forty years later, after American courts became disillusioned by the way the absolute ownership rule allowed municipalities to dry up aquifers by transporting huge amounts of water off the overlying lands. Decisions began coming down in which cities were enjoined from this practice on the ground that the right to underground water was only for "reasonable uses."[97] The doctrine as generally applied today provides that all uses of water upon the land from which it is extracted are "reasonable," even if they more or less deplete the supply to the harm of neighbors, unless the purpose is malicious or the water is simply wasted.[98] However, when the question is whether water may be transported off that land for use elsewhere this is usually found "unreasonable," though it has sometimes been permitted. Although authorities on the topic are not all agreed, a principle that seems to harmonize the decisions is that water may be extracted for use elsewhere only up to the point that it begins to injure owners within the aquifer.[99] As already mentioned, the reasonable use doctrine has become the rule of decision in the large majority of American jurisdictions. Its main thrust has been substantially to undo the old English doctrine as to water used on parcels away from where it was extracted, but it has only slightly altered rights to the use of water upon that land.

California has developed a variant of the reasonable use doctrine, known as the "correlative rights" doctrine. This third doctrine does more to alter the rights to use of water upon the land from which extracted. Under the correlative rights doctrine, owners of land within an aquifer are viewed as having equal rights to put the water to beneficial uses upon those lands. However, an owner's rights do not extend to seriously depleting his neighbor's supply, for in the event of a water shortage a court may apportion the supply that is available among all the owners. It is sometimes said that this is an application of the reasonable use doctrine of flowing streams to underground water. In an arid state, where shortages are frequent or chronic, this may produce a practical result significantly different than would the normal reasonable use doctrine. As to uses outside the land from which the water is drawn, for municipal and other uses, the rule is similar to that under the ordinary reasonable use doctrine: water may be transported only if the overlying owners have been fully supplied.[100]

To a greater or lesser extent in various states, statutes have altered the law of underground water. For example, in many states a permit is required for the digging of

---

[96]   7 H.L.C. 349, 11 Eng.Rep. 140 (1859).

[97]   See Katz v. Walkinshaw, 141 Cal. 116, 70 P. 663 (1902), rev'd, 141 Cal. 116, 74 P. 766 (1903) ("reasonable use" and "correlative rights" used interchangeably); Forbell v. City of New York, 164 N.Y. 522, 58 N.E. 644 (1900); see generally Annot., 55 A.L.R. 1385, 1398–1404 (1928), Supp., 109 A.L.R. 395, 399–402 (1937).

[98]   See Farmers Inv. Co. v. Bettwy, 113 Ariz. 520, 558 P.2d 14 (1976) (dictum); 6A American Law of Property § 28.66 (A.J. Casner ed. 1954) Restatement (Second) of Torts, Introductory Note to § 858 (1979); Sax, supra note 92 at 462 (1968); Annot., 55 A.L.R. 1385, 1398–1421 (1928), Supp., 109 A.L.R. 395, 399–405 (1937).

[99]   Farmers Investment Co. v. Bettwy, 113 Ariz. 520, 558 P.2d 14 (1976); Finley v. Teeter Stone, Inc., 251 Md. 428, 248 A.2d 106 (1968) (dictum); Higday v. Nickolaus, 469 S.W.2d 859 (Mo. App. 1971); Meeker v. City of E. Orange, 77 N.J.L. 623, 74 A. 379 (1909); see also sources cited supra note 97 (discussing off-premises use of water somewhat differently).

[100]   City of Pasadena v. City of Alhambra, 33 Cal. 2d 908, 207 P.2d 17 (1949), certiorari denied 339 U.S. 937, 70 S.Ct. 671, 94 L.Ed. 1354 (1950); Katz v. Walkinshaw, 141 Cal. 116, 70 P. 663 (1902), rev'd, 141 Cal. 116, 74 P. 766 (1903); 6A American Law of Property § 28.66 (A.J. Casner ed. 1954); Annot., 109 A.L.R. 395, 399–401 (1937); Restatement (Second) of Torts, Introductory Note to § 858 (1979); Joseph L. Sax, Water Law, Planning & Policy 462–63 (1968); Hutchins, supra note 75.

a new water well. While this requirement may in some states be only a formality that does not change the applicant's substantive rights to take water, it may in other states somewhat alter those rights. Much larger alterations of rights have been wrought in a number of the arid Western states. Historically, underground waters were not placed under the statutory appropriation systems that have long applied to streams and lakes in those states.[101] Today, however, most of the Western states that have statutory appropriation systems for streams and lakes (described in the preceding section) have also adapted the same systems to underground waters. This generally implies a preference for beneficial uses that existed prior to the adoption of the statute, a registration and permit system, and administration by a state agency. It also implies a mixed appropriation-common-law system in states where the so-called "California" doctrine obtains.[102]

§ 7.6   DIFFUSE SURFACE WATER

Diffuse surface water is drainage water from rain, melting snow, and springs that runs over the surface of the earth or perhaps stands in a marsh but does not amount to a stream. The factual situations that give rise to legal disputes over diffuse surface water are usually quite different from those involving stream, lake, or underground water described in the preceding two sections. Those other disputes generally arose because neighbors contended to get ahold of a quantity of water. In contrast, conflicts over diffuse surface water usually arise because owners want to get rid of surface water and, in so doing, cast it upon neighbors who do not want it either. Occasionally, a case comes along in which one neighbor wants to use diffuse surface water and complains that his neighbor wrongfully impounded it first. The rule in such cases is that whoever impounds the water may have all he can get, unless possibly his motive was malicious.[103] Usually, however, an upper owner precipitates a diffuse surface water dispute by doing something on his land that allegedly increases the quantity or force of the surface water as it flows onto a lower neighbor's land. It is also possible for a lower owner to back up the water onto a higher neighbor by damming or filling, but this variation from the usual fact pattern seems to make no difference in the legal principles a court will apply.[104] In the resolution of such disputes, the courts are split among three doctrines: the "common enemy," "civil law," and "reasonable use" doctrines.

The common enemy doctrine is simple in its pristine form: a landowner is privileged to use any and all methods to get rid of surface water and is not liable to his neighbors for flooding them. They in turn may do the same. Surface water is considered an outlaw or common enemy; a high value is placed upon getting rid of it to develop land.[105] States

---

[101] See Annot., 55 A.L.R. 1385, 1450–51 (1928), Supp., 109 A.L.R. 395, 408–12 (1937). Interestingly, an examination of the two A.L.R. annotations suggests that, by the time the supplemental one came along, there was some movement toward subjecting underground water to appropriation systems.

[102] Detailed examination of statutory appropriation systems is beyond the scope of this Hornbook. For support for the statements in this paragraph and for a start on further study, see Supplement to American Law of Property § 28.67 (1977); Hutchins, supra note 75; Sax, supra note 92 at 463–68.

[103] Terry v. Heppner, 59 S.D. 317, 239 N.W. 759 (1931); Restatement (Second) of Torts § 864 (1979); Sax, supra note 92 at 489 (1968).

[104] See Pendergrast v. Aiken, 293 N.C. 201, 236 S.E.2d 787 (1977); Carland v. Aurin, 103 Tenn. 555, 53 S.W. 940 (1899).

[105] For particularly apt descriptions of the common enemy rule, see Keys v. Romley, 64 Cal. 2d 396, 412 P.2d 529 (1966); Yonadi v. Homestead Country Homes, Inc., 35 N.J. Super. 514, 114 A.2d 564 (App. Div. 1955), petition denied 42 N.J. Super. 521, 127 A.2d 198 (1956); Butler v. Bruno, 115 R.I. 264, 341 A.2d 735 (1975); Carland v. Aurin, 103 Tenn. 555, 53 S.W. 940 (1899).

that follow the doctrine generally do so with varying modifications that may considerably soften its seeming harshness. A frequent modification is that landowners may not artificially collect water and expel it in a larger quantity than, or in a place or manner different from, the natural flow.[106] Courts often make a distinction between increased runoff that is incidental to grading or improving land—which is said to be privileged— and increased runoff caused by alterations undertaken merely to deflect water, which may create liability.[107] Sometimes, courts following the common enemy rule consider the landowner's purpose for altering drainage and even suggest he might be liable for increased runoff if that purpose or the manner of alteration is not reasonable.[108]

Subject to the modifications suggested above, it appears some form of the common enemy rule is employed in perhaps ten states.[109] The number was larger decades ago, but since that time several states have replaced it with the reasonable use rule.[110] Several of the states appearing to employ the common enemy doctrine also have decisions containing language appropriate to the civil law rule and perhaps turning on that rule. Moreover, modifications to both the common enemy and civil law doctrines have tended to blur the distinctions between them.[111] While courts still resolve some surface water controversies by asserting the common enemy rule in absolute terms, it would be unsafe to assume that any given court would so apply the rule to all cases.

The civil law rule, as its name suggests, comes from an 1812 Louisiana decision— Orleans Navigation Company v. New Orleans.[112] This rule in its pure form is the opposite of the common enemy rule: it provides that a landowner who interferes with the natural flow of surface water is strictly liable for any harm this causes his neighbors. When the doctrine is cast in property law terms, land is said to be burdened with a servitude in favor of neighboring land that natural drainage will not be altered.[113] The civil law doctrine, like the common enemy doctrine, has been encumbered with significant modifications. Most of these have been appended because, if applied literally, the civil law rule inhibits land development. A modification in some jurisdictions is that the common enemy rule, or at least a civil law rule with "balancing" instead of the strict

---

[106] Butler v. Bruno, 115 R.I. 264, 341 A.2d 735 (1975) (dictum); King Cty. v. Boeing Co., 62 Wash. 2d 545, 384 P.2d 122 (1963); Island Cty. v. Mackie, 36 Wash. App. 385, 675 P.2d 607 (1984) (exception to common enemy rule is that landowner is liable for damage caused by his diverting natural drain onto another's land); Annot., 93 A.L.R.3d 1193, 1203–07 (1979); Annot., 88 A.L.R.4th 891 (1991). But cf. Yonadi v. Homestead Country Homes, Inc., 35 N.J. Super. 514, 114 A.2d 564 (App. Div. 1955) petition denied 42 N.J. Super. 521, 127 A.2d 198 (1956) (increased force permitted).

[107] See Jordan v. St. Paul, M. & M.R. Co., 42 Minn. 172, 43 N.W. 849 (1889); Mason v. Lamb, 189 Va. 348, 53 S.E.2d 7 (1949); Annot., 93 A.L.R.3d 1193, 1203–07 (1979); Annot., 88 A.L.R.4th 891 (1991).

[108] See Morris v. McNicol, 83 Wash. 2d 491, 519 P.2d 7 (1974); Annot., 93 A.L.R.3d 1193, 1203–07 (1979); Annot., 88 A.L.R.4th 891 (1991).

[109] Wendy B. Davis, Reasonable Use Has Become the Common Enemy: An Overview of the Standards Applied to Diffused Surface Water and the Resulting Depletion of Aquifers, 9 Alb. L. Envtl. Outlook J. 1, 9 (2004); see generally Jill M. Fraley, Water, Water, Everywhere: Surface Water Liability, 5 Mich. J. Envtl. & Admin. L. 73, 93 (2015).

[110] Compare the counts that have appeared through the years in Carland v. Aurin, 103 Tenn. 555, 53 S.W. 940 (1899); Yonadi v. Homestead Country Homes, Inc., 35 N.J.Super. 514, 114 A.2d 564 (App. Div. 1955), petition denied 42 N.J.Super. 521, 127 A.2d 198 (1956); Keys v. Romley, 64 Cal. 2d 396, 412 P.2d 529 (1966); Pendergrast v. Aiken, 293 N.C. 201, 236 S.E.2d 787 (1977); and Annot., 93 A.L.R.3d 1193, 1199–1201 (1979).

[111] See Butler v. Bruno, 115 R.I. 264, 341 A.2d 735 (1975); Annot., 93 A.L.R.3d 1193 (1979); Annot., 88 A.L.R.4th 891 (1991).

[112] 2 Mart.(o.s.) 214 (La. Super. 1812).

[113] See discussions in Keys v. Romley, 64 Cal. 2d 396, 412 P.2d 529 (1966); Armstrong v. Francis Corp., 20 N.J. 320, 120 A.2d 4 (1956) (dictum); Pendergrast v. Aiken, 293 N.C. 201, 236 S.E.2d 787 (1977) (dictum); Carland v. Aurin, 103 Tenn. 555, 53 S.W. 940 (1899); Annot., 93 A.L.R.3d 1193, 1207–11 (1979).

civil law rule, will be applied to urban land.[114] Even in rural areas, some courts modify the civil law rule to allow farmers to accelerate the flow of drainage if needed for "good husbandry," so long as they confine the flow to natural channels.[115] These are not the only modifications; there are others and sometimes decisions that contain language suggestive of the reasonable use doctrine.[116]

The civil law doctrine, often modified as indicated, appears to be adopted in more states than the common enemy doctrine—apparently twenty-five or so.[117] In a few of these there are also decisions that suggest or follow the common enemy or reasonable use doctrines. Up until the last few decades, both the civil law and common enemy doctrines gained adherents but the ratio between them seemed not to have varied much.[118] In recent years, however, the reasonable use rule has become more dominant by picking up some uncommitted states and wooing other states away from one of the more traditional doctrines.

The reasonable use doctrine is traced back to the 1870 New Hampshire case of Swett v. Cutts—a decision linked with New Hampshire's slightly earlier decision founding the same doctrine for underground water.[119] The doctrine essentially provides that an owner is privileged to make reasonable use of his land and thereby alter the drainage of surface water up to the point that the alteration causes unreasonable interference with his neighbors' use of their land.[120] Thus, the question of liability is one of mixed fact and law. Factors that often are considered include how necessary it was for the actor to alter the drainage that reaches his neighbor, whether the actor acted with care, whether better methods of drainage are feasible, and the degree of harm to the neighbor. The decision making process is one of balancing the factors.[121] Simply to state the doctrine makes it apparent that its foundations are more in the law of torts than of property. It has been described as the application of nuisance law principles to surface water.[122] Indeed, the Restatement of Torts, Second treats the law governing surface drainage as a branch of the law of nuisance.[123]

The common law has unquestionably been migrating toward the reasonable use rule for the past few decades. Several jurisdictions have expressly departed the common

---

[114] See Keys v. Romley, 64 Cal. 2d 396, 412 P.2d 529 (1966) ("balancing"); Annot., 93 A.L.R.3d 1193, 1212–14 (1979). Some states have rejected the urban-land exception. Carland v. Aurin, 103 Tenn. 555, 53 S.W. 940 (1899); Annot., 93 A.L.R.3d 1193, 1214–15 (1979).

[115] See Butler v. Bruno, 115 R.I. 264, 341 A.2d 735 (1975) (dictum); Annot., 93 A.L.R.3d 1193, 1215–16 (1979).

[116] See Keys v. Romley, 64 Cal. 2d 396, 412 P.2d 529 (1966).

[117] See the "nose counts" in Keys v. Romley, id., and Annot., 93 A.L.R.3d 1193, 1207–11 (1979).

[118] Compare the counts in Carland v. Aurin, 103 Tenn. 555, 53 S.W. 940 (1899), and Annot., 93 A.L.R.3d 1193 (1979).

[119] Swett v. Cutts, 50 N.H. 439 (1870). The earlier decision was Bassett v. Salisbury Mfg. Co., 43 N.H. 569 (1862).

[120] See Enderson v. Kelehan, 226 Minn. 163, 32 N.W.2d 286 (1948); Armstrong v. Francis Corp., 20 N.J. 320, 120 A.2d 4 (1956); Pendergrast v. Aiken, 293 N.C. 201, 236 S.E.2d 787 (1977); Butler v. Bruno, 115 R.I. 264, 341 A.2d 735 (1975); see also Wendy B. Davis, Reasonable Use Has Become the Common Enemy: An Overview of the Standards Applied to Diffused Surface Water and the Resulting Depletion of Aquifers, 9 Alb. L. Envtl. Outlook J. 1, 9 (2004); see generally Jill M. Fraley, Water, Water, Everywhere: Surface Water Liability, 5 Mich. J. Envtl. & Admin. L. 73, 93 (2015).

[121] See Enderson v. Kelehan, 226 Minn. 163, 32 N.W.2d 286 (1948); Butler v. Bruno, 115 R.I. 264, 341 A.2d 735 (1975).

[122] Pendergrast v. Aiken, 293 N.C. 201, 236 S.E.2d 787 (1977).

[123] Restatement (Second) of Torts § 833 (1979).

enemy or civil law rules.[124] The reasonable use rule is now the principal rule of decision in at least twenty-one states.[125] And for the jurisdictions that still follow some form of the common enemy rule or the civil law rules, most have adopted some exceptions or limitations to the two traditional doctrines.[126] Decisions in these states also often contain language imparting the flavor of the reasonable use doctrine.[127]

It is a truism to say the common law in this area is in a period of historical movement because the common law is always evolving. However with the law of diffuse surface waters, this statement is more than truism. It is hardly surprising that two seemingly opposite doctrines—the common enemy and civil law doctrines—would tend to merge over time. In between these two rules is the reasonable use doctrine, which courts seem increasingly declined to embrace. It seems likely that the principle of reasonable use, though now a minority position in a number of states, will increasingly govern the law of surface waters in the near future. Its counterparts already predominate in the law of riparian and underground waters.

§§ 7.7–8.0 ARE RESERVED FOR SUPPLEMENTAL MATERIAL.

---

[124] E.g., Armstrong v. Francis Corp., 20 N.J. 320, 120 A.2d 4 (1956); Pendergrast v. Aiken, 293 N.C. 201, 236 S.E.2d 787 (1977); Butler v. Bruno, 115 R.I. 264, 341 A.2d 735 (1975); see Annot., 93 A.L.R.3d 1193, 1216–21 (1979); Wendy B. Davis, Reasonable Use Has Become the Common Enemy: An Overview of the Standards Applied to Diffused Surface Water and the Resulting Depletion of Aquifers, 9 Alb. L. Envtl. Outlook J. 1, 9 (2004).

[125] See Annot., 93 A.L.R.3d 1193, 1216–21 (1979).

[126] See, e.g., Pruitt v. Douglas Cty., 116 Wash. App. 547, 554, 66 P.3d 1111, 1116 (2003).

[127] See, e.g., Linvill v. Perello, 234 Cal. Rptr. 392, 394–95 (Ct. App. 1987); Sachs v. Chiat, 162 N.W.2d 243, 246–47 (Minn. 1968) (making reference to a reasonableness standard in the common enemy rule).

Chapter 8

SERVITUDES

Table of Sections

A.   EASEMENTS AND PROFITS

B.   RUNNING COVENANTS (CONTRACTUAL SERVITUDES)

A. EASEMENTS AND PROFITS

§ 8.1 NATURE OF EASEMENTS AND PROFITS

Easements and profits, like diamonds, present different facets from different angles. To those who hold them, they are rights or interests in land. To distinguish them from estates in land, they do not give the holder a right of possession but a right to use or to take something from land in which another holds a possessory estate. Viewed from this other person's angle, an easement or profit is a burden—an encumbrance—upon that person's estate. Some of the sticks have been taken from the bundle that comprise the estate and have been transferred to the holder of the easement or profit.

Some sources still refer to easements and profits as "incorporeal hereditaments."[1] In medieval law, the word "hereditament" signified that the interest was inheritable, i.e., a species of real property. The word "incorporeal" denoted that such interests, being non-possessory, were not created or transferred by livery of seisin (as estates were), but granted by a written instrument.[2] Thus, "incorporeal" means simply "non-possessory." Today, however, the word carries inaccurate connotations that easements and profits are non-physical interests, contrasted with physical estates. In the first place, all interests in land are non-physical concepts, i.e., legally protected rights. Second, the holder of a servitude can often make uses which are as physical as the possession that goes with an estate; they are simply different kinds of physical acts.

Today, both servitudes and estates are generally created and transferred by the same kinds of instruments and usually pass under the same statutes of inheritance. Thus, the chief distinction is that servitudes give rights of "use" and estates rights of "possession." Typical easements are for driveways, roads, rail lines, walkways, and pipe and other utility lines. Profits are usually to remove from the soil substances like minerals, gravel, and timber.[3] "Possession" also includes the right to make these uses, but easements and profits are limited rights, whereas possession includes all kinds of use and enjoyment that the law allows. The conveyance of an estate, by words sufficient to make the transfer, carries the full rights. But it would hardly do for the owner of the estate to grant simply an "easement"; its purpose must also be stated, which defines and limits the permitted uses. Possession means exclusive occupation, which means that the possessor may exclude all others from all parts of the land, without having to show they will actually interfere with any aspect of use and enjoyment. By contrast, the holder of

---

[1] E.g., Stanton v. T.L. Herbert & Sons, 141 Tenn. 440, 211 S.W. 353 (1919); Cottrell v. Nurnberger, 131 W.Va. 391, 47 S.E.2d 454 (1948).

[2] Cottrell v. Nurnberger, 131 W.Va. 391, 47 S.E.2d 454 (1948); 2 Am. Law of Prop. §§ 8.15–8.17 (1952).

[3] In most cases, the distinction between an easement and a profit is clear, but there are some situations in which complications occur. One of these is that a profit nearly always is accompanied by easement rights, either expressly spelled out or implied in the grant. A profit to remove any substance must necessarily carry with it access over the burdened land sufficient to reach, work, and remove the substance. These secondary easements may become quite extensive if extraction and removal requires heavy equipment. See, e.g., Callahan v. Martin, 3 Cal.2d 110, 43 P.2d 788 (1935); Kitras v. Town of Aquinnah, 474 Mass. 132, 49 N.E.3d 198 (2016); Wardell v. Watson, 93 Mo. 107, 5 S.W. 605 (1887).

an easement or profit has the right to exclude others only so far as to prevent their interference with the servitude's particular purpose.[4]

Use is difficult to distinguish from possession in some cases. Grantors occasionally create "exclusive" easements or profits. Courts may treat such interests as being or "almost" being possessory estates in the area or substance covered by the easement or profit.[5] At the opposite extreme, there might be only an easement or profit if a deed grants what appears to be an estate but excepts for the grantor such extensive rights that the grantee could exercise only limited uses.[6] Easement and profit rights generally include some right to improve the burdened land—perhaps only the right to gravel a road, but perhaps to erect and maintain more substantial structures such as bridges, pipelines, or even buildings to facilitate use of the easement or profit. The question arises whether at some point the structures become so substantial that we should say the rights are those of occupation or possession and not only use. Can one have an easement for a large office building or even a dwelling house, for instance? To determine if the interest is an estate or servitude, courts look at the total circumstances—not only the labels the parties used, but also the kinds of activities in which the grantee may engage. The existence of permanent, substantial structures militates strongly in favor of an estate.[7]

In some cases, there may be disagreement over whether a right constitutes an easement or profit, particularly where a right allows its holder to enter land to remove things that the landowner may not own, e.g., a right to fish in a stream, hunt for wild animals, or take water from a stream. These involve easements to enter and to move around, but can there be a profit when the landowner does not own the fish, game, or water? The majority of courts agree there can be a profit in fish and game, even though the landowner does not own the wild creatures.[8] Where the landowner does not own the

---

[4]   Restatement of Property § 450, Comment b (1944). See also Howard v. County of Amador, 220 Cal.App.3d 962, 269 Cal.Rptr. 807 (1990) (what parties called "mineral lease" was not possessory estate but only profit); Avery Dev. Corp. v. Village by the Sea Condo. Apts., Inc., 567 So.2d 447 (Fla.App.1990) (easement holder may not use servient land beyond what easement allows); Messer v. Leveson, 23 A.D.2d 834, 259 N.Y.S.2d 662 (1965). See also Gray v. McCormick, 167 Cal.App.4th 1019, 84 Cal.Rptr.3d 777 (2008) (servient owner may not make any use inconsistent with rights of user holding "exclusive" easement); Walton v. Capital Land, Inc., 252 Va. 324, 477 S.E.2d 499 (1996) (same).

[5]   For a good example, see Gray v. McCormick, 167 Cal.App.4th 1019, 84 Cal.Rptr.3d 777 (2008). In that case, the developer of a subdivision created an "exclusive" easement over a portion of one lot to benefit an adjacent lot that would otherwise have been landlocked. Later, the owner of the dominant estate planned to build a driveway and perimeter walls that would have prevented the servient owners from making any use of a significant portion of the easement area. The servient owners objected, arguing that as owners of the servient estate, they could use it in any way that did not interfere with their neighbor's use of the dominant estate. The California Court of Appeal held that because the easement was "exclusive," it not only permitted the easement holder to exclude third parties, but even the owner of the servient estate! The court also rejected an argument that such an "exclusive" easement created the equivalent of a fee and thus was prohibited under California law. The *Gray* case reflects the reality that many land buyers likely would not appreciate the potential legal consequences of an easement being labeled as "exclusive."

[6]   See Deterding v. United States, 69 F.Supp. 214 (Ct.Cl.1947) (deed "for the purpose of widening and straightening" a river, in which grantor reserved right to make any uses that would not interfere with grantee's intended purpose, held to create only easement).

[7]   See Lynch v. Cypert, 227 Ark. 907, 302 S.W.2d 284 (1957) (railroad depot); Standard Oil Co. v. Buchi, 72 N.J.Eq. 492, 66 A. 427 (1907) (underground oil pipeline); Miller v. City of New York, 15 N.Y.2d 34, 255 N.Y.S.2d 78, 203 N.E.2d 478 (1964) (driving range and buildings in city park); Texas & Pac. Rwy. Co. v. Martin, 123 Tex. 383, 71 S.W.2d 867 (1934). Cf. Farnes v. Lane, 281 Minn. 222, 161 N.W.2d 297 (1968) (boat dock may be part of easement).

[8]   E.g., St. Helen Shooting Club v. Mogle, 234 Mich. 60, 207 N.W. 915 (1926); Anderson v. Gipson, 144 S.W.2d 948 (Tex.Civ.App.1940); Annot., 49 A.L.R.2d 1395, 1397–99 (1956); Restatement of Property § 450, Comment g (1944). Note some American decisions rely upon English decisions rendered at a time when English

water in a stream, spring, or lake, the right to take it is generally labeled an easement.[9] If the landowner has reduced fish, animals or water to ownership by capture or impoundment, the landowner certainly may grant a profit in them.[10]

Easements and profits differ from licenses, though they all involve similar kinds of land use. The fundamental difference is that a license is terminable at the will of the creator landowner,[11] whereas easements and profits exist for a determinate time or "perpetually."[12] Easements and profits are interests in land; licenses are not. Licenses may be granted orally; easements and profits are subject to the Statute of Frauds. In difficult cases, when the parties' words and actions are unclear, courts often say that it is a matter of their intent which relationship was meant.[13] There are some cases in which the ultimate conclusion is that the parties simply could not have intended to create a right in land, such as cases involving admission to public places of entertainment.[14] Factors that indicate a relationship is an easement or profit and not a license are that it is for a specified time, that it is for a designated area, that substantial consideration was paid for it, and that the holder is allowed to make improvements and repairs or somehow exercise control vis-à-vis the landowner.[15] Opposites of these factors suggest a license. A finding that the landowner could not terminate the relationship at the landowner's will should be conclusive of an easement or profit.

Some question has existed whether one may have an easement to roam at large over another's land. The question is associated with easements for hunting, fishing, and other recreational pursuits, and arises in part because of statements in English cases that "incidents of a novel kind" should not be allowed.[16] That reason no longer has force. Perhaps also there is some vague notion that a right to wander about, having no fixed

---

landowners did own wild animals on their land. See Hanson v. Fergus Falls Nat'l Bank & Trust Co., 242 Minn. 498, 65 N.W.2d 857 (1954).

[9] Saratoga State Waters Corp. v. Pratt, 227 N.Y. 429, 125 N.E. 834 (1920); Diffendal v. Virginia Midland Rwy. Co., 86 Va. 459, 10 S.E. 536 (1890); 3 H. Tiffany, Real Property § 841 (3d ed.1939).

[10] See Loch Sheldrake Assocs. v. Evans, 306 N.Y. 297, 118 N.E.2d 444 (1954).

[11] In Hohfeldian terminology, while easements and profits are "rights," a license is only a "privilege." Hohfeld, Some Fundamental Legal Conceptions as Applied in Judicial Reasoning, 23 Yale L.J. 16, 43–44 (1913).

[12] Easements and profits that have no express or implied termination date are often called "perpetual." This is not strictly accurate, because they are carved out of estates. Even a fee simple estate may end by escheat.

[13] See, e.g., Hubbard v. Brown, 50 Cal.3d 189, 266 Cal.Rptr. 491, 785 P.2d 1183 (1990) (Forest Service grazing permit was "interest" in land); McCastle v. Scanlon, 337 Mich. 122, 59 N.W.2d 114 (1953); Kansas City Area Transp. Auth. v. Ashley, 485 S.W.2d 641 (Mo.App.1972).

[14] See Marrone v. Washington Jockey Club, 227 U.S. 633, 33 S.Ct. 401, 57 L.Ed. 679 (1913); Soderholm v. Chicago Nat'l League Ball Club, Inc., 225 Ill.App.3d 119, 587 N.E.2d 517 (1992) (season tickets constituted series of revocable licenses rather than an estate).

[15] See, e.g., South Ctr. Dept. Store, Inc. v. South Parkway Bldg. Corp., 19 Ill.App.2d 61, 153 N.E.2d 241 (1958) (no license; owner had general control); Baseball Publishing Co. v. Bruton, 302 Mass. 54, 18 N.E.2d 362 (1938) (agreement for billboard advertising sign created easement); Kansas City Area Transp. Auth. v. Ashley, 485 S.W.2d 641 (Mo.App.1972) (parking rights constituted lease or commercial easement in gross and were assignable); LSP Ass'n v. Town of Gilford, 142 N.H. 369, 702 A.2d 795 (1997) (owners of cottages in park who owned no land had only license to use roads); Standard Oil Co. v. Buchi, 72 N.J.Eq. 492, 66 A. 427 (1907) (deed allowing installation of pipeline not a license revocable at will of grantor); Miller v. City of New York, 15 N.Y.2d 34, 255 N.Y.S.2d 78, 203 N.E.2d 478 (1964) (20-year right to build and operate driving range was lease, not license, and thus beyond authority of park commissioner to grant).

[16] See Keppell v. Bailey, 2 My. & K. 517, 39 Eng.Rep. 1042 (Ch. 1834); Conard, Easement Novelties, 30 Cal.L.Rev. 125 (1942).

locus, is too indefinite. In any event, many American decisions recognize and enforce hunting and fishing easements.[17]

"Negative" easements. The easements and profits discussed above are "affirmative" in the sense that the holder has a right to enter onto and make an affirmative use of the servient estate. By contrast, one could conceptualize a "negative" easement—i.e., one that does not allow the holder to enter onto and make an affirmative use of the servient estate, but instead allows the holder to prevent the servient owner from making a particular use. For example, imagine that Smith, the owner of a parcel of land in the mountains, subdivides it into two parcels. Smith conveys one of the parcels to Jones, but wants to ensure that Jones does not build a structure that will block Smith's view of a nearby mountain. Smith's deed to Jones thus delivers title subject to an easement that purports to allow Smith to prevent Jones from building any structure taller than 20 feet. Is this permissible?

English law recognized only a few kinds of negative easements, including easements to prevent interference with (a) support of a building, (b) the flow of light or air, or (c) the flow of an artificial stream. English courts refused to recognize other types of negative easements, concerned that negative easements would unreasonably burden the alienability of land.[18] Because England originally had no universal system for recording land interests, buyers of land could have had difficulty discovering the existence of negative easements (particularly if such easements could arise by prescription).

Because all American states have adopted recording systems and generally do not recognize negative easements by prescription,[19] one might have expected American courts to recognize express negative easements other than those in the limited catalog of easements permitted by English law. Other than a number of decisions recognizing easements for preserving scenic views,[20] however, American courts generally have not recognized new forms of negative easements.[21] As a result, landowners wishing to acquire negative rights (beyond those recognized historically) typically do so through the use of restrictive covenants running with the land, as discussed beginning in Section 8.13.

Two other developments deserve brief mention. First, most American states have enacted statutes that authorize landowners to create a negative easement known as a "conservation easement." This easement allows a landowner to burden scenic or

---

[17]　See, e.g., St. Helen Shooting Club v. Mogle, 234 Mich. 60, 207 N.W. 915 (1926) (hunting); Anderson v. Gipson, 144 S.W.2d 948 (Tex.Civ.App.1940) (hunting); Cottrell v. Nurnberger, 131 W.Va. 391, 47 S.E.2d 454 (1948) (recreational area); Annot., 49 A.L.R.2d 1395 (1956).

[18]　Sara, Boundaries and Easements 174–176 (1991).

[19]　E.g., Mohr v. Midas Realty Corp., 431 N.W.2d 380 (Iowa 1988) (refusing to use nuisance law to prevent neighbor from building a structure that would block plaintiff's view on theory that this would recognize a prescriptive negative easement); Ceynar v. Barth, 904 N.W.2d 469 (N.D.2017) (same). But see Prah v. Maretti, 321 N.W.2d 182 (Wis.1982) (blocking of neighbor's solar panels constitutes nuisance capable of being enjoined); Tenn v. 889 Assocs., Ltd., 127 N.H. 321, 500 A.2d 366 (1985) (acknowledging, but rejecting, nuisance claim based on deprivation of light and air).

[20]　E.g., 8960 Square Feet, More or Less v. State Dept. of Transp. & Public Facilities, 806 P.2d 843 (Alaska 1991); Petersen v. Friedman, 162 Cal.App.2d 245, 328 P.2d 264 (1958). Cf. Patterson v. Paul, 448 Mass. 658, 863 N.E.2d 527 (2007) (recognizing view easement but characterizing it as affirmative easement because easement granted owner of dominant estate self-help rights to enter servient estate to trim vegetation).

[21]　In a number of states, state legislation has expressly authorized "solar easements," although these likely would have fit within the common law negative easement for light. See, e.g., Ind. Code Ann. § 32–23–4–4; Iowa Code § 564A.7.

historically significant land with an easement to prevent otherwise permissible development, despite the fact that such an easement would not have been valid at common law.[22] Conservation easements have become increasingly common, particularly as federal tax policy allows a landowner who imposes a perpetual conservation easement a substantial charitable tax deduction.[23] Second, as noted above, landowners wishing to acquire negative rights typically do so by creating restrictive covenants. As we will see later in this Chapter, such covenants are common in modern residential condominium and subdivision development, where they create reciprocal burdens and benefits on all lots or units within the development. Some courts have referred to these covenants as creating "negative reciprocal easements,"[24] but these covenants do not create "easements" in the sense used in this section. If these rights actually were easements, then they would not be subject to the special rules that govern the creation and running of covenants.[25] Instead, even where courts have referred to these covenantal rights as "negative easements," courts have governed their enforcement by the rules that govern running covenants, as discussed beginning in Section 8.13.

Easements and restrictive covenants are similar to certain "natural rights" that are incidents of land ownership. They are of the same "stuff," but they differ in that natural rights inhere by law while servitudes exist only when specifically created. Examples of natural rights are riparian rights, lateral and subjacent support, and freedom from nuisances. From the viewpoint of a landowner who enjoys these rights, they are incidents of property and give rights against others—usually neighbors—who have duties not to interfere. From the neighbor's perspective, the duties impose burdens on them in the use of their land that may appear quite similar to the duties arising from servitudes. These natural rights and duties are more or less reciprocal among owners.

§ 8.2   EASEMENTS AND PROFITS APPURTENANT AND IN GROSS

An easement or profit "appurtenant" is one whose benefits serve a parcel of land. More exactly, it serves the owner of that land in a way that is inseparable from the owner's rights in the land; it becomes a right in that land, passes with the title, and cannot be assigned separately from the title to the dominant estate.[26] Typical examples of easements appurtenant are walkways, driveways, and utility lines across Whiteacre, leading to adjoining or nearby Blackacre. Profits appurtenant, though less common, include rights to take timber or some substance from the soil of Whiteacre, for use for

---

[22]   Many of these statutes derive from the Uniform Conservation Easement Act (1981), enacted in 23 jurisdictions. See UCEA § 4 ("A conservation easement is valid even though (1) it is not appurtenant to an interest in real property; . . . (3) it is not of a character that has been recognized traditionally at common law; (4) it imposes a negative burden . . . .").

[23]   Conservation easements today likely affect more than 40 million acres in the United States. See McLaughlin, Perpetual Conservation Easements in the 21st Century: What Have We Learned and Where Should We Go from Here?, 2013 Utah L.Rev. 687.

[24]   See, e.g., Mason Family Trust v. DeVaney, 146 N.M. 199, 207 P.3d 1176 (App.2009); Land Devs., Inc. v. Maxwell, 537 S.W.2d 904 (Tenn.1976).

[25]   See Trustees of Columbia College v. Lynch, 70 N.Y. 440 (1877); Fitzstephens v. Watson, 218 Or. 185, 344 P.2d 221 (1959).

[26]   E.g., Fruth Farms v. Village of Holgate, 442 F.Supp.2d 470 (N.D.Ohio 2006).

some purpose on Blackacre. We speak of the benefited parcel (Blackacre) as the "dominant estate" and of the burdened parcel (Whiteacre) as the "servient estate."[27]

Easements or profits "in gross" are those whose benefits serve their holder only personally, not in connection with ownership or use of any specific parcel of land. Whatever doubt there may be in England about the existence of easements in gross,[28] they exist in the United States and in large numbers. Examples are easements for utility service held by utility companies, street easements, and railroad easements. Profits in gross include rights to remove timber or substances from the soil when the holder of the right is not limited to using them on specific land. Thus, there is no parcel we can call dominant, which in turn means the easement right cannot pass with the title to any land. It is proper to speak of land burdened by an easement or profit in gross as a "servient estate."[29]

Ideally, the document creating an appurtenant easement would both label the easement as appurtenant and identify the benefited parcel of land. Sometimes, however, the language of the document is unclear and, in such cases, whether an easement or profit is appurtenant or in gross depends upon surrounding circumstances. With easements, but probably not with profits, courts generally have a strong preference for construing ambiguous easements as appurtenant.[30] A typical example occurs when the owner of Whiteacre grants the owner of neighboring Blackacre an easement, using such language as "an easement for driveway purposes across the south 18 feet of Whiteacre," but without explicit language indicating that the easement serves Blackacre. If Whiteacre and Blackacre are so situated that an easement in the location serves Blackacre, a court will surely observe that fact and find the easement is appurtenant.[31] Another fact that courts often say indicates appurtenance is that the instrument creating an easement contains words of inheritance.[32] When a court holds an easement to be in gross, it is usually because its holder owned no land that was so situated as to be benefited by the easement.[33] With profits, though authority is slight, by their nature

---

[27]   For discussions of the basic principles in this paragraph, see Martin v. Music, 254 S.W.2d 701 (Ky.1953); Shingleton v. State, 260 N.C. 451, 133 S.E.2d 183 (1963); 2 Am. Law of Prop. §§ 8.6, 8.7 (1952); Restatement of Property §§ 453, 455, 456 (1944); Restatement (Third) of Property-Servitudes § 1.5 (2000).

[28]   See 2 Am. Law of Prop. § 8.9, n.1 (1952).

[29]   For discussions of the general nature of easements and profits in gross, see Stockdale v. Yerden, 220 Mich. 444, 190 N.W. 225 (1922); Standard Oil Co. v. Buchi, 72 N.J.Eq. 492, 66 A. 427 (1907); Loch Sheldrake Assocs. v. Evans, 306 N.Y. 297, 118 N.E.2d 444 (1954); 2 Am. Law of Prop. § 8.9 (1952); Restatement of Property §§ 454, 455 (1944); Restatement (Third) of Property-Servitudes § 1.5 (2000).

[30]   See, e.g., Cushman v. Davis, 80 Cal.App.3d 731, 145 Cal.Rptr. 791 (1978); Martin v. Music, 254 S.W.2d 701 (Ky.1953); French v. Estate of Gutzan, 128 A.3d 657 (Me.2015); Shingleton v. State, 260 N.C. 451, 133 S.E.2d 183 (1963); Newman v. Michel, 224 W.Va. 735, 688 S.E.2d 610 (2009); Baker v. Pike, 41 P.3d 537 (Wyo.2002). But see Tarason v. Wesson Realty, LLC, 40 A.3d 1005 (Me.2012) (easement to "this Grantee" construed to create easement in gross). For a suggestion that the preference for appurtenance does not apply to profits, see Loch Sheldrake Assocs. v. Evans, 306 N.Y. 297, 118 N.E.2d 444 (1954).

[31]   See Wilson v. Brown, 320 Ark. 240, 897 S.W.2d 546 (1995); Moylan v. Dykes, 181 Cal.App.3d 561, 226 Cal.Rptr. 673 (1986); Meade v. Ginn, 159 S.W.3d 314 (Ky.2004); Niceforo v. Haeussler, 276 A.D.2d 949, 714 N.Y.S.2d 788 (2000); Shingleton v. State, 260 N.C. 451, 133 S.E.2d 183 (1963); Siferd v. Stambor, 5 Ohio App.2d 79, 214 N.E.2d 106 (1966); Garza v. Grayson, 255 Or. 413, 467 P.2d 960 (1970); Maranatha Settlement Ass'n, Inc. v. Evans, 385 Pa. 208, 122 A.2d 679 (1956); Alft v. Clayton, 1995 WL 412876 (Tenn.App.1995); Green v. Lupo, 32 Wash.App. 318, 647 P.2d 51 (1982).

[32]   See Siferd v. Stambor, 5 Ohio App.2d 79, 214 N.E.2d 106 (1966); Maranatha Settlement Ass'n, Inc. v. Evans, 385 Pa. 208, 122 A.2d 679 (1956).

[33]   See Baseball Publishing Co. v. Bruton, 302 Mass. 54, 18 N.E.2d 362 (1938) (advertising sign on wall); Johnston v. Michigan Consolidated Gas Co., 337 Mich. 572, 60 N.W.2d 464 (1953) (pipeline easement); Boatman v. Lasley, 23 Ohio St. 614 (1873) (holder owned no land when easement granted); Miller v. Lutheran

they are more likely to be in gross than are easements. The mere fact that the holder of the profit owned adjoining land should not suggest appurtenance; it should take specific language or some peculiarity in the nature of the profit that indicates it is usable only in connection with the other land.[34]

§ 8.3   CREATION OF EASEMENTS AND PROFITS BY EXPRESS ACT

Because easements and profits are interests in land, the drafter should create them in a deed that complies with the Statute of Frauds or a will that complies with the Statute of Wills.[35] It is doubtful that the grant of a "perpetual" easement, one having the duration of a fee simple estate, must contain words of inheritance—laws in most states no longer require that a deed contain words of inheritance to effect a conveyance in fee simple—but drafters often include words of inheritance by customary practice.[36] Because words of inheritance are not required to devise fee simple estates, such words are not necessary to create easements in wills.[37] There are exceptions to the Statute of Frauds by which informal agreements are sometimes saved, but these are for the litigator who must salvage someone else's mistakes, not for careful drafters.

Nevertheless, easements often involve careless drafting. The instrument should say that the grantor or testator "grants" "an easement [or profit] for the purpose of" such and such to the grantee.[38] One should avoid words of grant like "convey and warrant" or "quitclaim and convey," which suggest estates in land.[39] The drafter should describe the interest conveyed as an "easement" or "profit" or, if in doubt, a "right to use," but never as a "strip of land," "right of way," or the like. These latter phrases are very suggestive of an estate and have caused serious interpretive problems, especially in any number of railroad cases.[40] Instruments often fail to describe adequately such matters as the area

---

Conference & Camp Ass'n, 331 Pa. 241, 200 A. 646 (1938) (recreational easement on lake). Railroad easements have presented a problem. They should be classified as easements in gross, as it stretches the facts to say they serve any land owned by the railroad. But, to avoid the question whether easements in gross are alienable, courts sometimes classified railroad easements as sui generis or even as appurtenant to the whole rail system. See Geffine v. Thompson, 76 Ohio App. 64, 62 N.E.2d 590 (1945) (dictum).

[34]   See Loch Sheldrake Assocs. v. Evans, 306 N.Y. 297, 118 N.E.2d 444 (1954); Restatement of Property § 453, Illus. 2 (1944); 3 H. Tiffany, Real Property § 843 (3d ed. 1939).

[35]   Camp v. Milam, 291 Ala. 12, 277 So.2d 95 (1973); Sedor v. Wolicki, 206 A.D.2d 854, 616 N.Y.S.2d 124 (1994) (parol evidence admissible to clear up ambiguity in easement deed); 2 Am. Law of Prop. § 8.20 (1952); Restatement of Property §§ 466, 467, 469 (1944); Restatement (Third) of Property-Servitudes § 2.7 (2000).

[36]   This cautionary practice is explained by cases like Wentworth v. Sebra, 829 A.2d 520 (Me.2003), where the court, interpreting a deed executed in 1917, held that appurtenant easement was not perpetual where deed did not use the term "heirs."

[37]   Restatement of Property § 470 (1944).

[38]   E.g., Thrasher v. Arida, 858 So.2d 1173 (Fla.App.2003) (deed that conveyed a parcel "[t]ogether with a 50-foot strip for ingress and egress" was ambiguous as to whether it conveyed fee in 50-foot strip or merely easement over it; case remanded for evidentiary hearing as to parties' intent).

[39]   See Deterding v. United States, 69 F.Supp. 214 (Ct.Cl.1947); Johnson v. Ocean Shore R.R. Co., 16 Cal.App.3d 429, 94 Cal.Rptr. 68 (1971); Annot., 136 A.L.R. 379 (1942). Indeed, statutes may provide that "convey" transfers an estate; e.g., Midland Valley R.R. Co. v. Arrow Indus. Mfg. Co., 297 P.2d 410 (Okla.1956).

[40]   See, e.g., Chicago Coating Co., LLC v. United States, 892 F.3d 1164 (Fed.Cir.2018) (deed describing "strip of land" conveyed fee and not easement); City of Manhattan Beach v. Superior Court, 13 Cal.4th 232, 52 Cal.Rptr.2d 82, 914 P.2d 160 (1996) (words "right of way" ambiguous; extrinsic evidence admissible); Severns v. Union Pac. R.R. Co., 101 Cal.App.4th 1209, 125 Cal.Rptr.2d 100 (2002) (deed conveying "strip of land" created fee subject to condition subsequent); C&G, Inc. v. Rule, 25 P.3d 76 (Idaho 2001) (deed to railroad that did not contain reversion clause or use restriction, and where words "right of way" appeared only on deed jacket and not in deed itself, conveyed fee title); Hochstetler Living Trust v. Friends of Pumpkinvine Nature Trail, Inc., 947 N.E.2d 928 (Ind.App.2011) ("strip of land" created fee, which in turn railroad conveyed to rail-to-trail

covered by an easement or profit; the easement's purposes; whether and to what extent the easement holder may exclude the servient owner from the easement area or limit the servient owner's use;[41] and secondary but still important issues such as maintenance of the easement, rights to improve the easement area, or the right to relocate the easement area. Courts can "fill the gaps" when the parties do not describe these matters adequately; for example, even when no location is stated, a court will fix a reasonable and convenient location.[42] Nevertheless, the careful drafter should describe the location by metes and bounds so clearly that a surveyor can run out the area from the instrument; in exceptional cases, description by reference to an existing location may have to suffice.

Sometimes the grantor of a parcel of land wishes to have an easement or profit on it after the conveyance, usually when the grantor retains title to an adjoining parcel. In early English law, and to a lesser extent in early American law, there were serious questions about whether and how the grantor could accomplish this.[43] Today it is clear that the grantor may accomplish this by what is properly called a "reservation." The grantor's instrument of conveyance may provide that "grantor reserves" an easement or profit, describing its purposes, location, and duration.[44] "Reservations" are sometimes confused with "exceptions," with deeds often saying that the grantor "excepts" an easement or profit. Properly, an exception is the withholding of title to a piece of a larger parcel of land, e.g., "all of Blackacre except the east 10 feet thereof." Modern courts will attempt to discern the parties' true intent, even if they use "except" instead of "reserve."[45] But drafters should use "reservation," first because it is technically correct, and second because "exception" may create genuine ambiguity when combined with certain other words.[46]

---

nonprofit); Schoenberger v. Missouri Pac. R.R. Co., 26 P.3d 701 (Kan.App.2001) (deed to railroad that did not contain reversion clause or use restriction conveyed fee title); Minneapolis Athletic Club v. Cohler, 287 Minn. 254, 177 N.W.2d 786 (1970) ("right of way"); Midland Valley R.R. Co. v. Arrow Indus. Mfg. Co., 297 P.2d 410 (Okla.1956) ("strip of land for a right of way"). By contrast, see, e.g., Timberlake, Inc. v. O'Brien, 902 N.E.2d 843 (Ind.App.2009) (deed that conveyed "a strip of land . . . forever" to railroad only granted easement where deed was further qualified by expressions of purpose that strip was to be used for right of way for railroad purposes).

[11]   This can create problems between neighbors in the case of access easements. Consistent with the "rule of reason," even if an access easement does not specifically reserve parking rights to the owner of the servient estate, the servient owner nevertheless retains the right to park in the easement area as long as that does not unreasonably interfere with the access rights of the easement holder. E.g., Patterson v. Sharek, 924 A.2d 1005 (D.C.App.2007). But if the easement document describes the easement holder's rights as "exclusive," the court may construe the easement to prevent the servient owner from making any meaningful use of the area covered by the easement. See, e.g., Gray v. McCormick, 167 Cal.App.4th 1019, 84 Cal.Rptr.3d 777 (2008).

[42]   Cox v. Glenbrook Co., 78 Nev. 254, 371 P.2d 647 (1962) (width); Alban v. R.K. Co., 15 Ohio St.2d 229, 239 N.E.2d 22 (1968) (no location stated); Clearwater Realty Co. v. Bouchard, 146 Vt. 359, 505 A.2d 1189 (1985); Cushman Virginia Corp. v. Barnes, 204 Va. 245, 129 S.E.2d 633 (1963) (width); Annot., 110 A.L.R. 174 (1937). If no location is stated in the grant, the owner of the servient tenement may locate it, provided the chosen location is a reasonable one. Alban v. R.K. Co., 15 Ohio St.2d 229, 239 N.E.2d 22 (1968). However, the instrument must at least locate the servient estate. E.g., Berg v. Ting, 125 Wash.2d 544, 886 P.2d 564 (1995) (no easement when servient estate described by reference to plat that never came into existence).

[43]   See generally 2 Am. Law of Prop. §§ 8.24–8.28 (1952); Restatement of Property § 473, Comment a (1944); Madden, Creation of Easements by Exception, 32 W.Va.L.Q. 33 (1925).

[44]   Petersen v. Friedman, 162 Cal.App.2d 245, 328 P.2d 264 (1958); McDermott v. Dodd, 326 Mass. 54, 92 N.E.2d 875 (1950); Mitchell v. Castellaw, 151 Tex. 56, 246 S.W.2d 163 (1952).

[45]   Coon v. Sonoma Magnesite Co., 182 Cal. 597, 189 P. 271 (1920); McDermott v. Dodd, 326 Mass. 54, 92 N.E.2d 875 (1950); Restatement of Property § 473, Comment a (1944).

[46]   See, e.g., Coon v. Sonoma Magnesite Co., 182 Cal. 597, 189 P. 271 (1920) (attempting to interpret phrase "saving and excepting therefrom a strip of land"). See also Annot., 139 A.L.R. 1339 (1942).

Many jurisdictions follow the rule that a grantor may not reserve an easement or profit in favor of a third person.[47] The rationale is that the stranger has no interest in the land conveyed, out of which the stranger might reserve an easement or profit. Legal writers are critical of the rule, and both Restatements have refused to adopt it.[48] Some jurisdictions, probably representing a trend, do allow easements and profits to be created in favor of third persons by language of reservation.[49] They reason either that the intent of the parties to the deed should be followed, or that the reservation operates as a grant from the grantee of the deed. In jurisdictions where there is doubt, the drafter may finesse the problem by having the grantor make separate grants of the estate and of the easement in the same deed, or through the use of two deeds—the first creating the easement by grant, and the second conveying title to the servient estate. A grantor may not reserve an easement in favor of herself or himself, however, as one logically cannot have an easement in one's own land. Thus, an attempted appurtenant easement recorded by a grantor who holds title to both the dominant and servient parcels is void.[50]

§ 8.4   EASEMENTS IMPLIED FROM NECESSITY

In three distinct fact patterns, the law allows the creation of easements by implication. In each pattern, the implication arises in connection with the conveyances of an estate in land; however, in none of these cases is the language of the conveyance determinative. Instead, implication arises out of circumstances surrounding the conveyance, which tend to indicate that the parties intended for an easement to arise without regard to the fact that the deed of conveyance did not expressly create one. Implication of an easement in these cases does not violate the Statute of Frauds; the court is implying the easement into a written instrument of conveyance that itself satisfies the Statute.[51]

The first kind of implied easement is the implied easement of necessity. Its essential elements are: (1) the owner of a parcel of land makes a conveyance of part of that land, retaining the rest;[52] and (2) after severance of the two parcels, one of them is "landlocked," i.e., to reach that parcel, it is "necessary" to pass over the other to reach a public street or road. The implication of an easement of necessity reflects an inference about the intent of the parties to the deed severing the common parcel, i.e., under the

---

[47]   E.g., Benninger v. Derifield, 142 Idaho 486, 129 P.3d 1235 (2006); Estate of Thomson v. Wade, 69 N.Y.2d 570, 509 N.E.2d 309 (1987); Haverhill Sav. Bank v. Griffin, 184 Mass. 419, 68 N.E. 839 (1903); Potter v. Chadaz, 977 P.2d 533 (Utah App.1999); First Nat'l Bank v. Laperle, 117 Vt. 144, 86 A.2d 635 (1952); Pitman v. Sweeney, 34 Wash.App. 321, 661 P.2d 153 (1983); Annot., 88 A.L.R.2d 1199 (1963).

[48]   E.g., 2 Am. Law of Prop. § 8.29 (1952); Restatement of Property § 472, Comment b (1944); Restatement (Third) of Property-Servitudes § 2.6(2) (2000).

[49]   E.g., Willard v. First Church of Christ, Scientist, Pacifica, 7 Cal.3d 473, 102 Cal. Rptr. 739, 498 P.2d 987 (1972); Michael J. Uhes, Ph.D., P.C. Profit Sharing Plan & Trust v. Blake, 892 P.2d 439 (Colo.App.1995); Brademas v. Hartwig, 175 Ind.App. 4, 369 N.E.2d 954 (1977); Townsend v. Cable, 378 S.W.2d 806 (Ky.1964); Garza v. Grayson, 255 Or. 413, 467 P.2d 960 (1970).

[50]   E.g., Collins v. Metro Real Estate Servs. LLC, 72 N.E.3d 1007 (Ind.App.2017); Woodling v. Polk, 473 S.W.3d 233 (Mo.App.2015).

[51]   See Restatement of Property § 475, Comment b (1944). See also Kincaid v. Yount, 9 Ohio App.3d 145, 459 N.E.2d 235 (1983) (implied easement may not be acquired across registered-title land unless it is on register of title).

[52]   Where the owner at the time of severance held full ownership of the would-be servient parcel, but only a fractional cotenancy interest in the landlocked parcel, there is sufficient common ownership for the implication of an easement of necessity. E.g., Burnham v. Kwentus, 174 So.3d 286 (Miss.App.2015).

circumstances (no other means of access), the parties must have intended for an easement to arise to permit the owner of the landlocked parcel to reach it.[53]

Can an easement arise out of necessity for some purpose other than for ingress and egress? For example, might a grantee make out a claim of necessity to run utility lines over the grantor's remaining land? Courts have generally denied easements of necessity for light and air, usually stating that an easement for these purposes may arise only by grant.[54] But if a deed states that the land conveyed is to be used for a certain purpose, such as to operate a particular business, this may imply such easements as are reasonably necessary to conduct that activity.[55] The Restatement of Servitudes provides that "[a] conveyance that would otherwise deprive the land conveyed to the grantee, or land retained by the grantor, of rights necessary to reasonable enjoyment of the land implies the creation of a servitude granting or reserving such rights . . . ."[56] Consistent with this view, there is growing authority for the proposition that an implied easement of necessity may be granted to allow a property access to utilities.[57]

Much litigation on ways of necessity concerns the meaning of the second element that the use be "necessary." Certainly, if the conveyance will result in either the granted or retained parcel being literally without access to the outside world—landlocked—this meets the strictest definition.[58] If the claimant has free access to some part of the parcel, the claimant cannot make out a way of necessity to another part just because it would

---

[53] See, e.g., Murphy v. Burch, 46 Cal.4th 157, 92 Cal.Rptr.3d 381, 205 P.3d 289 (2009) ("strict necessity and common ownership [are] circumstances from which the intent of the parties may be inferred"); Perry v. Nemira, 91 Mass.App. 12, 69 N.E.3d 592 (2017) (noting that when all factors support an easement by necessity, the absence of express right of way was the result of careless drafting rather than the intent of the parties to purposely landlock a parcel).

Where the grantor is a sovereign government, however, courts may be less likely to imply the reservation of an easement. For example, in the *Murphy* case, the two parcels in question were originally conveyed by federal patent deeds. When the owner of the landlocked parcel—which had been conveyed after the other parcel—asserted an implied easement of necessity, the court rejected the claim, concluding that no implied easement of necessity could have arisen in favor of the federal government at the time of the first conveyance. *Murphy*, 205 P.3d at 294–295 (discussing interpretation of sovereign deeds). But see Malulani Group, Ltd. v. Kaupo Ranch, Ltd., 133 Haw. 425, 329 P.3d 330 (App.2014) (unity of ownership requirement for implication of easement could be satisfied by prior government ownership of parcels). Likewise, some courts have concluded that an implied easement of necessity did not arise upon the partition of tribal lands because tribal customs permitting free access to tribe members rebutted any presumption that the grantor had intended an easement by necessity to arise. E.g., Kitras v. Town of Aquinnah, 474 Mass. 132, 49 N.E.3d 198 (2016).

[54] E.g., Fontainebleau Hotel Corp. v. Forty-Five Twenty-Five, Inc., 114 So.2d 357 (Fla.App.1959); Maioriello v. Arlotta, 364 Pa. 557, 73 A.2d 374 (1950).

[55] 3 H. Tiffany, Real Property § 792 (3d ed. 1939).

[56] Restatement (Third) of Property-Servitudes § 2.15 (2000).

[57] E.g., Francini v. Goodspeed Airport, LLC, 164 Conn.App. 279, 134 A.3d 1278 (2016); Fleming v. Napili Kai, Ltd., 50 Haw. 66, 430 P.2d 316 (1967); Brown v. Miller, 140 Idaho 439, 95 P.3d 57 (2004); Gacki v. Bartels, 369 Ill.App.3d 284, 859 N.E.2d 1178 (2006); Stroda v. Joice Holdings, 288 Kan. 718, 207 P.3d 223 (2009). One might also argue that if an easement by necessity arises, the scope of that easement should be understood to permit modern developments such as modern vehicle access and the installation of utility lines. E.g., Ashby v. Maechling, 356 Mont. 68, 229 P.3d 1210 (2010) ("modern vehicle access and utility services may be allowed as part of an easement by necessity even though the easement arose as a legal matter before the general use of such improvements"); Morrell v. Rice, 622 A.2d 1156 (Me.1993); Adams v. Planning Bd., 64 Mass.App. 383, 833 N.E.2d 637 (2005). But see Perdue v. Cruse, 38 So.3d 1235 (La.App.2010) (implied easement of necessity for passage did not permit servient owner to install utilities). We return to the scope of easements later in this Chapter.

[58] See, e.g., Finn v. Williams, 376 Ill. 95, 33 N.E.2d 226 (1941); Collins v. Metro Real Estate Servs. LLC, 72 N.E.3d 1007 (Ind.App.2017); Horner v. Heersche, 202 Kan. 250, 447 P.2d 811 (1968); Soltis v. Miller, 444 Pa. 357, 282 A.2d 369 (1971).

be more convenient.[59] However, some courts may recognize a degree of flexibility in this determination. Some courts have said the claimant is entitled to sufficient access to make "effective use" of the land. This might be lacking if the only established road was, for instance, flooded much of the time.[60]

The required necessity does not exist if the claimant owns other adjacent land over which the claimant has access.[61] Where a stranger owns the adjoining land, the claimant can show the required necessity unless the claimant has an easement across the adjoining land (i.e., a permissive right to cross the adjoining land would not defeat the required necessity).[62] Courts have disagreed on whether access to a navigable body of water will defeat a claim of necessity. Many decisions hold the claim is defeated,[63] but some allow the claim of necessity if the water access does not permit effective use of the dominant estate.[64] The trend is symptomatic of a general tendency toward a flexible understanding of "necessity."

Necessity for the easement must exist at the moment of severance; a necessity arising later will have no effect.[65] Once the easement arises, similarly to a granted easement of general access, its permitted scope is capable of gradual change to keep pace with reasonable changes in uses of the dominant estate.[66] However, if the necessity later ends because the holder acquires an alternative legal means of access, the easement by necessity ends.[67] Location of the route of a way of necessity is more difficult than with

---

[59]   See, e.g., Hereford v. Gingo-Morgan Park, 551 So.2d 918 (Ala.1989); Murphy v. Burch, 46 Cal.4th 157, 92 Cal.Rptr.3d 381, 205 P.3d 289 (2009); Hunt v. Zimmerman, 139 Ind.App. 242, 216 N.E.2d 854 (1966); Wolf v. Owens, 340 Mont. 74, 172 P.3d 124 (Mont.2007).

[60]   See, e.g., Morell v. Rice, 622 A.2d 1156 (Me.1993) (access over marshy tidal flat that would require expensive dredging and often froze did not defeat claim for easement of necessity); Kelly v. Burlington Northern R.R., 279 Mont. 238, 927 P.2d 4 (1996) (land surrounded by mountains on three sides and railroad on fourth); State v. Deal, 191 Or. 661, 233 P.2d 242 (1951); Restatement of Property § 476, Comment g (1944); Restatement (Third) of Property-Servitudes § 2.15, Comment d (2000).

[61]   Bully Hill Copper Mining & Smelting Co. v. Bruson, 4 Cal.App. 180, 87 P. 237 (1906); Harkness v. Butterworth Hunting Club, Inc., 58 So.3d 703 (Miss.App.2011). If the claimant cannot get access over the claimant's adjoining land because of a physical barrier such as a stream or cliff, this will not defeat the claim of necessity. Wiese v. Thien, 279 Mo. 524, 214 S.W. 853 (1919); Annot., 5 A.L.R. 1557 (1920).

[62]   Finn v. Williams, 376 Ill. 95, 33 N.E.2d 226 (1941). Cf. Robertson v. Robertson, 214 Va. 76, 197 S.E.2d 183 (1973).

[63]   E.g., Murch v. Nash, 861 A.2d 645 (Me.2004); Kingsley v. Gouldsborough Land Improvement Co., 86 Me. 279, 29 A. 1074 (1894); Davidson v. Collins, 195 So.3d 825 (Miss.App.2015); Foti v. Noftsier, 72 A.D.3d 1605, 901 N.Y.S.2d 434 (2010); Bauman v. Wagner, 146 A.D. 191, 130 N.Y.S. 1016 (1911).

[64]   E.g., Redman v. Kidwell, 180 So.2d 682 (Fla.App.1965); Hancock v. Henderson, 236 Md. 98, 202 A.2d 599 (1964); Parker v. Putney, 254 Va. 192, 492 S.E.2d 159 (1997).

[65]   See, e.g., Murphy v. Burch, 46 Cal.4th, 92 Cal.Rptr.3d 381, 205 P.3d 289 (2009); Leonard v. Bailwitz, 148 Conn. 8, 166 A.2d 451 (1960); B & J Dev. & Inv., Inc. v. Parsons, 126 Idaho 504, 887 P.2d 49 (Idaho App.1994) (later necessity does not suffice); King v. Gale, 166 So.3d 589 (Miss.App.2015) (same); Kelly v. Burlington Northern R.R., 279 Mont. 238, 927 P.2d 4 (1996) (necessity existed in 1891); Koonce v. J.E. Brite Estate, 663 S.W.2d 451 (Tex.1984) (no way of necessity unless parcels were owned as a unit prior to separation).

There is not a "time limit" on the recognition of an implied easement of necessity. In a 2004 New York case, the court recognized an implied easement of necessity where the dominant and servient parcels had been severed nearly 140 years earlier, in 1866! See Bogart v. Roven, 8 A.D.3d 600, 780 N.Y.S.2d 355 (2004).

[66]   Soltis v. Miller, 444 Pa. 357, 282 A.2d 369 (1971). Thus, the fact that the implied easement arose before development of the automobile would not prohibit the easement holder from making reasonable use of an automobile for access.

[67]   E.g., Murphy v. Burch, 46 Cal.4th 157, 92 Cal.Rptr.3d 381, 205 P.3d 289 (2009); Ballard v. SVF Found., 181 A.3d 27 (R.I.2018); Hamrick v. Ward, 446 S.W.3d 377 (Tex.2014); Bruce & Ely, The Law of Easements and Licenses in Land § 4:12 (2008). Cf. Enzor v. Rasberry, 648 So.2d 788 (Fla.App.1994) (alternative route later acquired did not afford "reasonable and practical" access so as to terminate easement of necessity).

an easement implied from prior use because, by definition, no location is established on the ground. If the parties cannot agree, a court of equity will fix the location, having regard for not only the shortest route but for all other factors that bear upon the most convenient and suitable route.[68]

An implied easement of necessity does not arise merely because a parcel of land becomes landlocked. For an implied easement of necessity to arise, landlocking must result because of the severance of a common parcel. Thus, when part of an owner's parcel becomes landlocked because the state takes a strip of land by eminent domain for an interstate highway and that strip divides the parcel, the owner does not have an implied easement of necessity to cross neighboring parcels.[69] In such a case, many states have statutes that would permit the owner of the landlocked parcel to condemn (and pay for) an easement across a neighboring parcel for access to and from a public road.[70]

§ 8.5   EASEMENTS IMPLIED FROM PRIOR USE

The second kind of implied easement is the "easement implied from prior use." Its essential elements are: (1) the owner of a parcel of land makes a conveyance of part of that land, retaining the rest; (2) before the severance of the parcel, the owner was using one of the parts to benefit the owner's use and enjoyment of the other (i.e., had the two parts been severed, the use could have been the subject of an appurtenant easement benefitting one and burdening the other); (3) the use is "apparent," and (4) the use is to some extent "necessary" to the continued use and enjoyment of the part it would benefit.[71] To provide a mechanism by which implied easements arise, some courts say the grantor conveys the granted parcel together with a pre-existing easement burdening the grantor's retained parcel, or subject to a pre-existing easement benefitting the retained parcel. The question then arises—both parcels were in the grantor's unitary

---

[68] Hancock v. Henderson, 236 Md. 98, 202 A.2d 599 (1964); Higbee Fishing Club v. Atlantic City Elec. Co., 78 N.J.Eq. 434, 79 A. 326 (1911); Annot., 68 A.L.R. 528 (1930).

[69] E.g., Clifton v. Wilkinson, 286 Va. 205, 748 S.E.2d 372 (Va.2013).

[70] E.g., Ala.Code § 18–3–1; Ariz.Rev.Stat. § 12.1202; Miss.Code Ann. § 65–7–201; 36 Pa.Cons.Stat. § 2731; Rev.Code Wash.Ann. § 8.24.010. Courts have disagreed as to whether a landlocked owner can use a private condemnation statute if the owner would qualify for an implied easement of necessity. Compare Bickel v. Hanson, 169 Ariz. 371, 819 P.2d 957 (App.1991) (owner can exercise private condemnation statute only where owner is ineligible for implied easement of necessity) and In re Laying Out and Opening of Private Road in Hazle Township, 41 A.3d 163 (Pa.Cmw.Ct.2012) (potential availability of implied easement of necessity must be considered in determining necessity of private right of way) with Brown v. McAnally, 97 Wash.2d 360, 644 P.2d 1153 (1982) (owner can exercise private condemnation statute even if facts support implied easement). Some courts have held, however, that owners could not show the reasonable necessity required to condemn an easement where the owners had voluntarily landlocked themselves. See, e.g., Graff v. Scanlan, 673 A.2d 1028 (Pa.Cmw.Ct.1996) (self-created landlock defeated finding of necessity); Ruvalcaba v. Kwang Ho Baek, 175 Wash.2d 1, 282 P.3d 1083 (2012) (owners had landlocked themselves 35 years before bringing action).

[71] See, e.g., Capstar Radio Operating Co. v. Lawrence, 160 Idaho 452, 375 P.3d 232 (2016); Granite Props. Ltd. Partn. v. Manns, 117 Ill.2d 425, 512 N.E.2d 1230 (1987); Romanchuk v. Plotkin, 215 Minn. 156, 9 N.W.2d 421 (1943); Hillary Corp. v. U.S. Cold Storage, Inc., 250 Neb. 397, 550 N.W.2d 889 (1996); Boyd v. Bellsouth Telephone Telegraph Co., Inc., 369 S.C. 410, 633 S.E.2d 136 (2006); Westbrook v. Wright, 477 S.W.2d 663 (Tex. Civ.App.1972); Adams v. Cullen, 44 Wash.2d 502, 268 P.2d 451 (1954); 2 Am. Law of Prop. §§ 8.32, 8.37–8.42 (1952); 3 H. Tiffany, § 7.91 (3d ed. 1939); Restatement of Property § 476 (1944); Restatement (Third) of Property-Servitudes § 2.12 (2000). The grantor is sometimes called a "common grantor," which is accurate only if the grantor has conveyed the retained parcel after conveying the first one.

A recent Florida decision held that while Florida law does permit an implied easement of necessity (discussed in the prior section), it does not recognize implied easements from pre-existing use. One Harbor Financial Ltd. Co. v. Hynes Props., LLC, 884 So.2d 1039 (Fla.App.2004). There is a similar implication in Woodling v. Polk, 473 S.W.3d 233 (Mo.App.2015), but that decision ignores a long line of Missouri cases recognizing implied easements based on prior use.

ownership prior to the conveyance, so how could the grantor have held an easement over the grantor's own land? To answer this, courts indulge in the fiction that a "quasi easement" pre-existed.[72] It is sufficient and simpler to say that the easement arises initially by implication in the grantor's conveyance.[73]

The first element—severance of a common parcel[74]—is the same as for the implied easement of necessity discussed in the preceding section. The essential difference is that for the implied easement of necessity, there is no requirement that a pre-existing use of the parcel existed prior to severance.[75] Obviously there will be cases in which both theories could apply, as when a conveyance by the common grantor will landlock one parcel but there is already a pre-existing road in use over the parcels.[76] As with the easement implied by necessity, implication of an easement of prior use reflects an inference about the intent of the parties to the deed severing the common parcel, i.e., given the elements described above, the parties must have intended for an easement to arise to permit the continuation of the prior use.[77]

Most litigation involving these easements involves the "necessary" and "apparent" elements. The word "necessary" covers a broad spectrum. Some courts, at least verbally, cling to the notion that the use must be strictly necessary to the use and enjoyment of the dominant parcel.[78] A more relaxed standard of "reasonable necessity" describes the stance most courts take.[79] Some decisions have found "reasonable necessity" where the

---

[72]   E.g., Harrison v. Heald, 360 Mich. 203, 103 N.W.2d 348 (1960); Romanchuk v. Plotkin, 215 Minn. 156, 9 N.W.2d 421 (1943); Wiesel v. Smira, 49 R.I. 246, 142 A. 148 (1928).

[73]   See, e.g., Wymer v. Dagnillo, 162 N.W.2d 514 (Iowa 1968); Restatement of Property §§ 474, 476, Comment i (1944); Restatement (Third) of Property-Servitudes § 2.12 (2000).

[74]   Sometimes, a "common parcel" may include multiple parcels of land, all owned by the same owner. In such a case, the owner might have granted a mortgage on some, but not all, of the lots. If a foreclosure later occurs and the mortgaged parcel is sold to a third party, could an implied easement based on prior use arise? If there was a visible driveway in use across one parcel to benefit another parcel, the answer should be yes, at least if that use was existing and visible at the time the mortgage was granted. If the foreclosed parcel is benefited by the prior use, the buyer of the foreclosed parcel would no doubt have expected it to continue. By contrast, if the rest of the parcel is benefited, the buyer of the foreclosed parcel would appear to have notice of the visible prior use. There is recent case authority, however, suggesting that the answer is no. See, e.g., In re Eicher, 574 B.R. 659 (Bankr.E.D.Tenn.2017) (implied easement may not arise upon foreclosure of quasi-servient parcel).

[75]   E.g., Hinrichs v. Melton, 11 Cal.App.5th 516, 218 Cal.Rptr.3d 13 (2017) (court may grant implied easement by necessity to landlocked parcel without preexisting use by landowner seeking the easement).

[76]   E.g., Hellberg v. Coffin Sheep Co., 66 Wash.2d 664, 404 P.2d 770 (1965).

[77]   See, e.g., Murphy v. Burch, 46 Cal.4th 157, 92 Cal.Rptr.3d 381, 205 P.3d 289 (2009) ("strict necessity and common ownership [are] circumstances from which the intent of the parties may be inferred"); Perry v. Nemira, 91 Mass.App. 12, 69 N.E.3d 592 (2017) (noting that when all factors support an easement by necessity, the absence of express right of way was the result of careless drafting rather than the intent of the parties to purposely landlock a parcel).

[78]   Wymer v. Dagnillo, 162 N.W.2d 514 (Iowa 1968) ("essential"); Haase v. Zobkiw, 36 A.D.2d 821, 321 N.Y.S.2d 152 (1971); Mitchell v. Castellaw, 151 Tex. 56, 246 S.W.2d 163 (1952); Ward v. Slavecek, 466 S.W.2d 91 (Tex.Civ.App.1971).

[79]   See, e.g., Romanchuk v. Plotkin, 215 Minn. 156, 9 N.W.2d 421 (1943); Van Sandt v. Royster, 148 Kan. 495, 83 P.2d 698 (1938); NAMN, LLC v. Morello, 291 Neb. 462, 867 N.W.2d 545 (2015); Peterson v. Beck, 537 N.W.2d 375 (S.D.1995) (parking lot necessary to use of golf course); Westbrook v. Wright, 477 S.W.2d 663 (Tex.Civ.App.1972); Hellberg v. Coffin Sheep Co., 66 Wash.2d 664, 404 P.2d 770 (1965); 2 Am. Law of Prop. § 8.39 (1952). Even those courts articulating a "reasonable necessity" standard have sometimes rejected claims of implied easement where evidence suggested that the prior use was a "mere convenience." E.g., Mau v. Schusler, 124 A.D.3d 1292, 1 N.Y.S.3d 609 (2015) (prior use of parking turnaround was "mere convenience" because it was used to facilitate ease of on-street parking rather than access to parcel itself).

continued use will be convenient to enjoyment of the dominant estate.[80] What "necessity" means in a given case depends much on the circumstances. Most courts, except those that hold to strict necessity, will find the requirement satisfied if the owner of the dominant estate would be put to appreciable expense to provide a substitute for the claimed easement.

The pre-existing use must be "apparent," so that continuance of the use would be within the grantor's and grantee's contemplation. No difficulty is met in satisfying this element when the use is visible by casual observation, e.g., a well-established roadway or other surface use. Difficult cases are those that involve underground uses, such as sewer or other utility lines. A number of interesting decisions hold that such underground lines are sufficiently "apparent."[81] These decisions reason that, while the underground line is not visible to the casual observer, it is discoverable by inspection of utility connections that are visible. Thus, it can be said that "apparent" includes "reasonably discoverable."[82]

In some older decisions, courts required another factor—that the prior use had to be "continuous." This was critical in roadway and driveway easement cases, for if the use had to be literally continuous, the grantor's prior intermittent use of an access way would not qualify.[83] Such an element has largely disappeared, though it has occasionally surfaced in court decisions.[84] Generally courts either do not mention the element at all,

---

[80]   E.g., Madden v. Scott, 416 Ill.Dec. 264, 83 N.E.3d 1101 (App.2017) (condominium developer built two units separated by vestibule with outside door that provided only access to front doors of each unit; nearly all of vestibule was physically located within one of the two units; held that implied easement over vestibule arose in favor of other unit, even though that unit had four other exterior doors, because use of the vestibule as a means of access to the front door of the unit was both "obvious" and "beneficial to the enjoyment" of the unit). See also, e.g., Romanchuk v. Plotkin, 215 Minn. 156, 9 N.W.2d 421 (1943); Westbrook v. Wright, 477 S.W.2d 663 (Tex.Civ.App.1972) ("necessary for the convenient and quiet enjoyment").

[81]   E.g., Van Sandt v. Royster, 148 Kan. 495, 83 P.2d 698 (1938); Romanchuk v. Plotkin, 215 Minn. 156, 9 N.W.2d 421 (1943); Otero v. Pacheco, 94 N.M. 524, 612 P.2d 1335 (App.1980); Wiesel v. Smira, 49 R.I. 246, 142 A. 148 (1928); Westbrook v. Wright, 477 S.W.2d 663 (Tex. Civ.App.1972); Hansuld v. Lariat Diesel Corp., 245 P.3d 293 (Wyo.2010).

[82]   See Restatement of Property § 476, Comment j (1944) ("within the possibility of their knowledge"). In some decisions, courts appear to have stretched to contemplate that implication might be possible in circumstances even where there was no evidence of apparent use prior to severance. For example, in George v. Goshgarian, 139 Cal.App.3d 856, 189 Cal.Rptr. 94 (1983), the court held that a power line easement for Lot A to a main power line running across the adjoining Lot B could be implied—even though there was no line on Lot A at the moment of severance of the two lots—because given the situation of the two lots, a jury could conclude that a buyer of Lot A would believe that the power line was intended to serve Lot A as well. The *George* decision appears to dispense with the usual requirement that a "quasi easement" be in existence at the moment of severance. Likewise, in Connolly v. Maine Cent. R.R. Co., 969 A.2d 919 (Me.2009), an owner of land conveyed a strip across the parcel to the railroad, but without reserving an express easement to cross the tracks to reach the rest of the parcel. After tracks were constructed, the landowner began crossing the tracks and, when the railroad objected, claimed an implied easement (but without any proof of use prior to construction of the tracks). The court denied summary judgment, remanding for a trial at which evidence might be presented to support an inference that the landowner intended to retain an easement.

In another interesting case, a recorded contract for the purchase and sale of a shopping center outparcel contained a clause under which the seller covenanted to convey an easement for parking and access for the benefit of the outparcel, but the deed to the outparcel did not contain any express easement. The court held that because the deed contained a general appurtenances clause, it was sufficient to convey the easement to a subsequent purchaser of the dominant estate. Franklin Park Plaza, LLC v. V&J Nat'l Enters., LLC, 57 A.D.3d 1450, 870 N.Y.S.2d 193 (2008). It would seem more satisfactory to say that in this circumstance, the court should imply an easement based on the contract language and the fact that the overall shopping center plan showed the outparcel did not otherwise have direct highway access or adequate on-site parking.

[83]   Annot., 34 A.L.R. 233 (1925); Note, 1 Cal.L.Rev. 275 (1913).

[84]   See Milewski v. Wolski, 314 Mich. 445, 22 N.W.2d 831 (1946); Burling v. Leiter, 272 Mich. 448, 262 N.W. 388 (1935) (alternative ground).

find that intermittent use is continuous enough, or treat the element of visible use as the important question (with continuity being only an aspect of visibility).[85]

Some have questioned whether an implied easement may arise in favor of the grantor's retained land, i.e., an implied easement by reservation. Concern arises from the principle that one may not derogate from one's own grant and the companion rule of construction that a deed is construed against the grantor. When an easement is implied in favor of the grantor, this detracts from the estate the deed's words appear to convey. For this reason, some decisions hold that a reserved easement will be implied only when it is strictly necessary to the use of the grantor's retained parcel.[86] However, courts do not always observe the distinction between granted and reserved implied easements, and it appears less pronounced now than a century ago.[87] Still, some courts may be less disposed to find, or to require stronger proof of, a reserved than a granted implied easement. For this reason, if the grantor and grantee expect the pre-existing use to continue after severance of the parcel, the deed severing the parcel should explicitly create the easement under the principles described in Section 8.3.[88]

§ 8.6   EASEMENTS IMPLIED FROM PLAT

A purchaser who acquires a lot in a platted subdivision will, to an extent that varies from state to state, acquire implied private easements to use streets and alleys (and likely parks and playgrounds) shown on the plat. Litigation over such easements seldom arises in states where the act of subdividing automatically dedicates to public use those easements shown on the plat. This is not because the individual lot owners might not also claim private easements, but for the practical reason that they are usually content to exercise the right as members of the public.[89] In other states, where the act of platting does not necessarily dedicate to the public, an individual lot purchaser's claim to a private easement is more likely to be crucial. The purchaser's claim may sound in estoppel, based upon having bought in reliance on the availability of the easements shown on the plat.[90] More likely, the claim will be that easements were implied into the purchase deed because it incorporated by reference the plat showing the easement areas.[91]

---

[85]   2 Am. Law of Prop. § 8.41 (1952).

[86]   E.g., Van Sandt v. Royster, 148 Kan. 495, 83 P.2d 698 (1938); Brown v. Fuller, 165 Mich. 162, 130 N.W. 621 (1911); NAMN, LLC v. Morello, 291 Neb. 462, 867 N.W.2d 545 (2015) (reasonable necessity for easements implied by grant, but strict necessity required for easements implied by reservation); Toothe v. Bryce, 59 N.J.Eq. 589, 25 A. 182 (1892) (dictum, but classic discussion); Wiesel v. Smira, 49 R.I. 246, 142 A. 148 (1928); Annot., 58 A.L.R. 824, 837–42 (1929).

[87]   Compare Harrison v. Heald, 360 Mich. 203, 103 N.W.2d 348 (1960) and Peterson v. Beck, 537 N.W.2d 375 (S.D.1995) with Brown v. Fuller, 165 Mich. 162, 130 N.W. 621 (1911). See Annot., 58 A.L.R. 824, 840–42 (1929).

[88]   See Restatement of Property § 476, Comment c (1944).

[89]   See Scott v. Snyder, 73 Ohio App. 424, 54 N.E.2d 157 (1943); Shertzer v. Hillman Invst. Co., 52 Wash. 492, 100 P. 982 (1909); Annot., 7 A.L.R.2d 607, 608–09 (1949).

[90]   See, e.g., Lindsay v. James, 188 Va. 646, 51 S.E.2d 326 (1949).

[91]   See, e.g., Ross v. Dorsey, 154 Idaho 836, 303 P.3d 195 (2013); Perry v. Nemira, 91 Mass.App. 12, 69 N.E.3d 592 (2017); Yorlum Props. Ltd. v. Lincoln Cty., 372 Mont. 159, 311 P.3d 748 (2013); Gooldy v. Storage Center-Platt Springs, LLC, 422 S.C. 332, 811 S.E.2d 779 (2018) (deed reference to plat sufficient to give rise to implied easement, even though plat was never recorded, where plat was submitted to planning commission for approval).

Courts have held private easements in platted streets and other access ways to exist to some extent in all jurisdictions that have decided the question.[92] The question on which courts have differed is the extent to which the lot owner has easements over the access ways. Courts have expressed three general positions. The first is the so-called "broad" or "unity" rule, that the owner has a private easement over all parts of all ways shown on the plat.[93] Next is the "intermediate," "beneficial," or "full enjoyment" rule, which holds that the owner has private access easements over such platted ways as are reasonably beneficial to the use of the owner's lot. This generally means the owner may not be denied use of any way if the deprivation would diminish the lot's market value.[94] Finally, the "narrow" or "necessary" rule is that the owner has private easements over only his abutting street and such connecting streets as are necessary to give access to the system of public streets and roads.[95] A review of the decisions indicates that the three positions are not as neatly compartmentalized as suggested above. In several jurisdictions there are conflicting decisions, in which courts have applied both the "narrow" rule and one of the broader rules.[96] Some decisions that seem to fall into the "narrow" category are ones in which the courts had no occasion to consider a broader rule, because the facts showed lot owners truly needed to use platted streets to reach public ways. In deciding these cases, courts often use language indicative of both estoppel and implied grant theories. Also, there is a tendency in some opinions to intermix a theory of implied private easement with the doctrine of dedication to public use.

Besides the cases involving platted streets, there are a smaller number that deal with implied private easements for platted parks and playgrounds. In these cases, a lot owner's implication claim may be unsuccessful unless the court adopts the "broad" or "unity" rule of implication. Most of the decisions implying private easements for these purposes do employ the "broad" rule.[97] A few courts, however, have stretched one of the narrower rules to fit the case of parks.[98] Again, as with street easements, one finds implied private easement theory intermixed with doctrines of estoppel and of public dedication.

---

[92]   Annot., 7 A.L.R.2d 607, 612 (1949). Courts have also implied an easement as shown on a map of a planned unit development, even though such a map is not a traditional "plat." E.g., Barry Simon Dev., Inc. v. Hale, 210 S.W.3d 312 (Mo.App.2006). In *Hale*, in fact, the court implied the easement in favor of the developer—even though the developer had sold all of the lots within the development—and concluded that the implied easement also benefited the developer's ownership of adjacent property indicated as such on the map. *Hale*, 210 S.W.3d at 316 (rejecting the "stranger to the deed" doctrine discussed in Section 8.3 supra).

[93]   E.g., Trustees of Schools v. Dassow, 321 Ill. 346, 151 N.E. 896 (1926); Krzewinski v. Eaton Homes, Inc., 108 Ohio App. 175, 161 N.E.2d 88 (1958); Annot., 7 A.L.R.2d 607, 613–33 (1949).

[94]   E.g., Lake Garda Co. v. D'Arche, 135 Conn. 449, 66 A.2d 120 (1949); Lindsay v. James, 188 Va. 646, 51 S.E.2d 326 (1949) (some dependence on estoppel theory); Annot., 7 A.L.R.2d 607, 633–39 (1949).

[95]   E.g., Wellwood v. Havrah Mishna Anshi Sphard Cemetery Corp., 254 Mass. 350, 150 N.E. 203 (1926); In re Wooley Ave., 270 N.Y. 368, 1 N.E.2d 467 (1936); In re East 177th St., 239 N.Y. 119, 145 N.E. 903 (1924); Annot., 7 A.L.R.2d 607, 639–43 (1949).

[96]   See Cashman v. Shutter, 226 A.D.2d 961, 640 N.Y.S.2d 930 (1996); Annot., 7 A.L.R.2d 607, 643–50 (1949).

[97]   E.g., Caffey v. Parris, 186 Ga. 303, 197 S.E. 898 (1938); Ross v. Dorsey, 154 Idaho 836, 303 P.3d 195 (2013) (easement for lakefront beach access); Schurtz v. Wescott, 286 Mich. 691, 282 N.W. 870 (1938); Putnam v. Dickinson, 142 N.W.2d 111 (N.D. 1966) (some estoppel reasoning); Eidelbach v. Davis, 99 S.W.2d 1067 (Tex.Civ.App.1936); Annot., 7 A.L.R.2d 607, 650–51 (1949).

[98]   See Annot., 7 A.L.R.2d 607, 660–67 (1949).

§ 8.7 EASEMENTS BY PRESCRIPTION

This section should be read together with section 11.7, covering adverse possession. Though the history of the two doctrines is much different, American law today largely blends prescription and adverse possession.[99] With some differences noted below, it is accurate enough as a working doctrine to substitute "adverse use" for "prescription," as courts commonly do.[100] The chief distinction is that in adverse possession the claimant occupies or possesses the claimed land, while in prescription the claimant merely makes some easement-like use of it. As with adverse possession, if the prescriptive acts continue for the period of the statute of limitations, the prescriber acquires rights that correspond to the nature of the use. Because an estate carries the right of possession, adverse possession creates an estate; an easement carries the right of use, so adverse use creates an easement. Once created, the easement is as enduring as an easement created by deed; it cannot be revoked or changed by an informal act of the parties.[101]

To consummate the parallel with adverse possession, we may define prescription as the actual, open, notorious, hostile, and continuous use of another's land for the sufficient prescriptive period. Having drawn the parallel, this section highlights the key differences between prescriptive easements and adverse possession. The most basic difference is between "use" and "possession," for that determines whether activities that are adverse will gain an easement or an estate for the claimant. Often it is obvious whether the activity is only use (such as passing over land) or possession (marked by occupation, fencing, or permanent improvements),[102] but there are some situations in which the distinction is difficult. The maintaining of a paved driveway is usually treated as a prescriptive use,[103] but its permanent, continuous, and substantial nature could in appropriate cases lead a court to consider it possessory.[104] In the handful of cases

[99] See Stoebuck, The Fiction of Presumed Grant, 15 Kan.L.Rev. 17 (1966). Some American prescription decisions discuss the doctrine or fiction of "lost grant" or "presumed grant," usually erroneously. Particularly objectionable are those opinions that say the doctrine is the origin of prescription. See, e.g., Romans v. Nadler, 217 Minn. 174, 14 N.W.2d 482 (1944); Hester v. Sawyers, 41 N.M. 497, 71 P.2d 646 (1937); Big Cottonwood Tanner Ditch Co. v. Moyle, 109 Utah 213, 174 P.2d 148 (1946); Shellow v. Hagen, 9 Wis.2d 506, 101 N.W.2d 694 (1960). In fact, the doctrine developed in English law hundreds of years after prescription was established as a means of acquiring easements and related "incorporeal" interests. At that time, and indeed until 1832, English prescription theory depended upon a presumption that the prescriptive use dated back to "time immemorial"—3 September 1189, the day on which Richard I ascended the throne. To assist in establishing that presumption, a second presumption was created, that proof of use of an easement for the period of the statute of limitations raised an inference of a grant, now lost. Lost grant is part of the historical development of American prescription law, but that is all. The blending of prescription and adverse possession, whether right or wrong in history and theory, has in fact made title arise simply by virtue of the running of the applicable statute of limitations. There is no need to presume usage back to 1189, or any other ancient historical date, and no need to presume a lost grant. Except for historical reference, discussion of the lost grant should be irrelevant.

[100] E.g., Truc v. Field, 269 Mass. 524, 169 N.E. 428 (1930); Romans v. Nadler, 217 Minn. 174, 14 N.W.2d 482 (1944); Winterringer v. Price, 370 P.2d 918 (Okla.1961); State ex rel. Shorett v. Blue Ridge Club, Inc., 22 Wash.2d 487, 156 P.2d 667 (1945).

[101] See Glenn v. Grosfield, 274 Mont. 192, 906 P.2d 201 (1995) (parties cannot change location of prescriptive easement by informal consent).

[102] See, e.g., Silacci v. Abramson, 45 Cal. App.4th 558, 53 Cal.Rptr.2d 37 (1996) (fencing in is adverse possession, not prescription). Because California's five-year adverse possession statute requires payment of taxes, some California litigants may try to label what would generally be adverse possession as prescriptive use.

[103] E.g., Shanks v. Floom, 162 Ohio St. 479, 124 N.E.2d 416 (1955); Johnson v. Whelan, 171 Okla. 243, 42 P.2d 882 (1935). See Annot., 27 A.L.R.2d 332 (1953).

[104] See Predham v. Holfester, 32 N.J.Super. 419, 108 A.2d 458 (App.Div.1954) (court held claim was not hostile, but spoke of a driveway as "possession").

involving overhanging house eaves, courts have treated them as use and not possession.[105] The distinction is best understood by reference to the principle that possession implies not only the possessor's use but the exclusion of others, while use involves only limited activities that do not imply or require the exclusion of others.[106] Thus, in distinguishing adverse use from adverse possession, we are not ultimately concerned with the substantiality of physical objects, but with whether the claimant's uses and purposes are inconsistent with other persons' shared uses.

Adverse possession must be "hostile," which means it must be without the record owner's permission. This is also true of prescription; permission granted by the landowner prevents hostile use.[107] With prescription, some peculiar recurring fact patterns introduce special permission problems not found with adverse possession. One example involves cases in which neighbors maintain by oral agreement a common driveway straddling their common boundary. If they had made a written cross-easement agreement that complied with the Statute of Frauds, each would have an easement over the neighbor's portion of the driveway by formal grant. When the agreement is oral, however, whether each acquires a prescriptive easement depends on how a given court characterizes their transaction. Some courts reason that, while the oral agreement fails as a conveyance, it still creates mutual oral licenses, so that each one's use of the neighboring portion of the driveway is permissive and cannot be prescriptive.[108] Other courts regard the oral agreement as a complete nullity—neither conveyance nor license—so that each neighbor's use of the other's land is hostile, without permission.[109]

In many cases, there is no clear evidence of the circumstances under which the use began; these cases tend to turn in significant part on whether the court draws a presumption that one's use of another's land is hostile or instead that it is permissive. If a court presumes that unexplained use is permissive, then the adverse claimant has the burden to go forward with evidence showing hostility.[110] A presumption of permissiveness flows from the concept that prescriptive rights are founded in the owner's "acquiescence," which in turn seems to be connected with mistaken notions about the doctrine of lost grant.[111] Prescriptive rights, like adverse possession title, are today founded in wrongful, hostile, trespassory acts that ripen into title when the statute of limitations bars the owner's action of trespass or ejectment. Moreover, to indulge in a

---

[105] Romans v. Nadler, 217 Minn. 174, 14 N.W.2d 482 (1944); Annot., 58 A.L.R. 1037, 1038–39 (1929).

[106] E.g., Judd v. Bowen, 397 P.3d 686 (Utah App.2017) (recognizing prescriptive easement for access over narrow driveway, but rejecting claim for prescriptive easement to park on the driveway, concluding that under the circumstances, such a right would effectively be equivalent to possession and would deprive the servient owner of use of the driveway in question).

[107] E.g., Burnham v. Kwentus, 174 So.3d 286 (Miss.App.2015) ("if use is based on permission, express or implied, no matter how long, it can never ripen into the hostile use required for a prescriptive easement"); King v. Gale, 166 So.3d 589 (Miss.App.2015) (same); Newman v. Michel, 224 W.Va. 735, 688 S.E.2d 610 (2009).

[108] E.g., Mueller v. Keller, 18 Ill.2d 334, 164 N.E.2d 28 (1960); Sexton v. Holt, 91 Kan. 26, 136 P. 934 (1913); Annot., 27 A.L.R.2d 332, 359–62 (1953).

[109] E.g., Clinger v. Hartshorn, 89 P.3d 462 (Colo.App.2003); Kirby v. Hook, 347 Md. 380, 701 A.2d 397 (1997); Alstad v. Boyer, 228 Minn. 307, 37 N.W.2d 372 (1949); Burciaga Segura v. Van Dien, 344 P.3d 1009 (N.M.App.2014); Shanks v. Floom, 162 Ohio St. 479, 124 N.E.2d 416 (1955); Annot., 27 A.L.R.2d 332 (1953). The Restatement of Servitudes agrees, providing that a prescriptive use is one that is either adverse (hostile) or one that is "made pursuant to the terms of an intended but imperfectly created servitude, or the enjoyment of the benefit of an intended but imperfectly created servitude." Restatement (Third) of Property-Servitudes § 2.16 (2000).

[110] E.g., Mueller v. Keller, 18 Ill.2d 334, 164 N.E.2d 28 (1960); Dartnell v. Bidwell, 115 Me. 227, 98 A. 743 (1916).

[111] See supra note 99.

generalized presumption that an intruder is anything but a trespasser is contrary to the basic principle that the whole world must stay off the owner's land unless the owner affirmatively admits them. The better view is that the unexplained use or occupation of another's land is presumed hostile.[112] If the owner wishes to rebut by showing permission, the owner may do so by proof of specific facts that should be known to the owner or predecessors.

In some circumstances, however, courts may conclude that permission is implied in fact. For example, some courts recognize a presumption that use of unenclosed and unoccupied land is permissive.[113] It is said that, because owners of such land ordinarily allow others to make light, occasional uses, permission is presumed. Perhaps the most complicated situation involves the "common driveway." Suppose that *A* uses a portion of a driveway located on the adjacent parcel owned by *B*, for access to reach *A*'s home. If *A*'s use of the driveway does not meaningfully interfere with *B*'s enjoyment, and *B* does not object, should a court presume that *A*'s use is adverse, or should it instead presume that *A*'s use is permissive—a neighborly accommodation by *B*? The cases are divided. Many courts in this situation presume *A*'s use as permissive,[114] effectively precluding *A* from acquiring a prescriptive easement unless *A* can show facts sufficient to transfer the use from permissive to hostile.[115] Other courts apply the traditional presumption that *A*'s use is hostile, effectively placing the burden on *B* to demonstrate an affirmative grant of permission.[116] The Washington Supreme Court recently held that a presumption of permissiveness applies in any case, such as a shared driveway, in which there is a "reasonable inference of neighborly sufferance or acquiescence."[117] It justified this approach by suggesting that it "incentivizes landowners to allow neighbors to use their roads for the neighbors' convenience"[118]—which it surely does. The court also argued that a presumption of adverseness "punishes a courteous neighbor by taking away his or her property right"[119] and avoids having to require an owner "to adopt a dog-in-the-

---

[112] See, e.g., Celebration Worship Ctr., Inc. v. Tucker, 35 N.E.3d 251 (Ind.2015); Alstad v. Boyer, 228 Minn. 307, 37 N.W.2d 372 (1949); Shanks v. Floom, 162 Ohio St. 479, 124 N.E.2d 416 (1955).

[113] E.g., Warnack v. Coneen Family Trust, 266 Mont. 203, 879 P.2d 715 (1994) (unfenced land; apparent presumption of permission); Greenwalt Family Trust v. Kehler, 267 Mont. 508, 885 P.2d 421 (1994) (local custom to allow neighbors to cross land); Hester v. Sawyers, 41 N.M. 497, 71 P.2d 646 (1937) (dictum); State ex rel. Shorett v. Blue Ridge Club, 22 Wash.2d 487, 156 P.2d 667 (1945); Shellow v. Hagen, 9 Wis.2d 506, 101 N.W.2d 694 (1960) (dictum). But see Harambasic v. Owens, 186 Ariz. 159, 920 P.2d 39 (Ariz.App.1996) (prescriptive easement over open land).

[114] E.g., Simmons v. Perkins, 63 Idaho 136, 118 P.2d 740 (1941); Wilkinson v. Hutzel, 142 Mich. 674, 106 N.W. 207 (1906); Wels v. Hippe, 360 Or. 569, 385 P.3d 1028 (2016); Altieri v. Dolan, 423 A.2d 482 (R.I.1980); Gamboa v. Clark, 183 Wash.2d 38, 348 P.3d 1214 (2015).

[115] E.g., Melendez v. Hintz, 111 Idaho 401, 724 P.2d 137 (App.1986) (claimant built, maintained and used exclusively a spur off of common driveway, with spur being located partially on neighbor's land; this use was beyond neighborly accommodation and thus hostile); Hester v. Sawyers, 41 N.M. 497, 71 P.2d 646 (1937) (claimant stopped using old road over which claimant had permissive right and constructed and maintained new road; claimant acquired prescriptive easement).

[116] E.g., Fischer v. Grinsbergs, 198 Neb. 329, 252 N.W.2d 619 (1977); Czebiniak v. Woloszyn, 159 N.Y.S.2d 632 (Sup.1956), aff'd, 5 A.D.2d 807, 170 N.Y.S.2d 1023 (1958); Myers v. Clodfelter, 786 S.E.2d 777 (N.C.App.2016); Causey v. Lanigan, 208 Va. 587, 159 S.E.2d 655 (1968). See also Judd v. Bowen, 397 P.3d 686 (Utah App.2017) ("Utah courts have differentiated between consent or license and mere acquiescence. Proof of the former—consensual use—rebuts the adversity presumption; proof of the latter—mere acquiescence—does not.").

[117] Gamboa v. Clark, 183 Wash.2d 38, 348 P.3d 1214 (2015).

[118] *Gamboa*, 183 Wash.2d at 48, 348 P.3d at 1219.

[119] *Gamboa*, 183 Wash.2d at 49, 348 P.3d at 1219.

manger attitude" to protect their title.[120] This sounds nice, but is questionable if not misguided. Which neighbor acts in a "courteous" and "neighborly" fashion—one who says *nothing* about the other's use for 20 years before suddenly objecting, or one who promptly starts a conversation with the other person as soon as the use starts, even if that conversation is necessarily somewhat awkward? The better "neighbor"—and the more vigilant owner—is surely the latter.

Now consider the reverse situation: if an adverse claimant begins using the owner's land in a way that is hostile and otherwise prescriptive, how may the use later become permissive? Clearly it may if the parties execute a formal agreement to that effect. But can the owner unilaterally make future use permissive by giving the user a notice to this effect? The slight authority on the question holds that unilateral, unsolicited consent by the owner to the user does not interrupt a period of adverse use already begun.[121] The decisions purport to distinguish "permission" from "consent," which they equate with the "acquiescence" that is supposedly the "foundation" of prescription. As the flaws of the "acquiescence" doctrine were previously noted, the notion that unsolicited consent is not permission rests on a weak theoretical basis. It is also harsh on the landowner who discovers an ongoing prescriptive use, for it leaves the owner with no sure way to stop it short of a lawsuit or a physical confrontation.[122]

Exclusivity is one of the essential elements of adverse possession, meaning that the claimant may not share possession with the owner. Properly understood, this element is not appropriate for a prescriptive easement.[123] In the nature of things, the owner of the servient land may legally make any use of the easement area that does not unreasonably interfere with the easement. The same is true with prescriptive easements.[124] In a different meaning of exclusivity, however, some decisions have adopted the rule that the public at large cannot prescribe.[125] Often these decisions involve public use of unenclosed, unoccupied land, so that courts may also reason the use is impliedly permissive. Prescription by a large but definable group, such as the members of a large organization, is generally allowed.[126] Some courts do allow the public to prescribe, though they seem to require strong proof of hostility, again perhaps because cases often

---

[120] *Gamboa*, 183 Wash.2d at 48, 348 P.3d at 1219.

[121] Naporra v. Weckwerth, 178 Minn. 203, 226 N.W. 569 (1929); Huff v. Northern Pac. Rwy. Co., 38 Wash.2d 103, 228 P.2d 121 (1951)

[122] In some circumstances, the owner may interrupt the running of the prescriptive period by placing some type of barrier sufficient to preclude continued use. E.g., Trask v. Nozisko, 134 P.3d 544 (Colo.App.2006); Pittman v. Lowther, 363 S.C. 47, 610 S.E.2d 479 (2005). But consider the owner of a shopping center, faced with certain individuals who regularly cut through the parking area on their way to and from work. Consent in the form of signboards will have no legal effect; barring access with gates or chains is wholly impractical, as are lawsuits against everyone using the parking lot for unauthorized purposes. Such an owner should be able to "thrust" permission on the wrongdoer, perhaps by giving and recording a notice.

[123] E.g., Brandhorst v. Johnson, 362 Ill.Dec. 198, 12 N.E.3d 198 (App.2014) (properly rejecting argument that prescriptive user had to "altogether deprive" servient owner of use of easement area, and characterizing that argument as setting an "impossibly high standard").

[124] Fowler v. Matthews, 204 S.W.2d 80 (Tex.Civ.App.1947); Shellow v. Hagen, 9 Wis.2d 506, 101 N.W.2d 694 (1960). But see Othen v. Rosier, 148 Tex. 485, 226 S.W.2d 622 (1950).

[125] E.g., State ex rel. Haman v. Fox, 100 Idaho 140, 594 P.2d 1093 (1979); Scoville v. Fisher, 181 Neb. 496, 149 N.W.2d 339 (1967).

[126] See, e.g., Confederated Salish & Kootenai Tribes v. Vulles, 437 F.2d 177 (9th Cir.1971) (Indian tribe); Williams v. Harrsch, 58 Or.App. 301, 648 P.2d 386 (1982) (public, as well as individual claimant, acquired prescriptive easement for recreational purposes); Mountaineers v. Wymer, 56 Wash.2d 721, 355 P.2d 341 (1960) (hiking and climbing club).

involve unenclosed, unoccupied land.[127] Where the public may prescribe, an individual may not obtain a private prescriptive easement by making only the same use the public makes.[128]

The element of continuity is also part of prescription, but with a meaning adapted to the nature of easements. In the typical adverse possession case, even if the claimant is not physically on the land constantly, the claimant often has improvements that stay there. Cases of intermittent occupancy of wild and unenclosed land create division in the courts, though adverse possession is in theory possible.[129] An easement is like that; its holder uses it intermittently, as the user has need. In prescription cases, the courts accept as sufficiently continuous a frequency of use that is normal for the kind of easement claimed.[130] Likewise, use can be sufficiently continuous even when it is carried on by a series of successive users; the respective periods of adverse use may be tacked together to satisfy the prescription period.[131]

Adverse possession elements of "actual," "open," and "notorious" are also prescription elements. Obviously the adverse claimant must make some physical use, and it must have some degree of definiteness.[132] Most prescriptive easements are for walkways, driveways, or roads on the surface, so that if there is use at all, it is open, visible, and confined to a defined area. While slight variations in the line of travel are acceptable, it often is said that the prescriptive use of an access way must follow a definite or ascertainable route.[133] If a jurisdiction permits easements to wander over land for recreational purposes (such as hunting), it should be possible to establish such an easement by prescription, though proof may be difficult.[134] Prescriptive easements for drains, pipes, or sewers pose a special problem. If they are on the surface, the use is

---

[127] E.g., State ex rel. Thornton v. Hay, 254 Or. 584, 462 P.2d 671 (1969) (dictum); Fowler v. Matthews, 204 S.W.2d 80 (Tex.Civ.App.1947); Gray v. McDonald, 46 Wash.2d 574, 283 P.2d 135 (1955).

[128] Pirman v. Confer, 273 N.Y. 357, 7 N.E.2d 262 (1937); Annot., 111 A.L.R. 221 (1937).

[129] Compare Monroe v. Rawlings, 331 Mich. 49, 49 N.W.2d 55 (1951) with Murray v. Bousquet, 154 Wash. 42, 280 P. 935 (1929).

[130] E.g., Confederated Salish & Kootenai Tribes v. Vulles, 437 F.2d 177 (9th Cir.1971) (use "continuous"); Holbrook v. Taylor, 532 S.W.2d 763 (Ky.1976) (not "continuous"); Romans v. Nadler, 217 Minn. 174, 14 N.W.2d 482 (1944) (use twice a year not "continuous"); Brannock v. Lotus Fund, 367 P.3d 888 (N.M.App.2015) (use of road for hiking, driving, and walking once or twice a month consistently for over 30 years held "continuous"); Duke v. Sommer, 205 A.D.2d 1009, 613 N.Y.S.2d 985 (1994) (seasonal use sufficient on recreational land); Shellow v. Hagen, 9 Wis.2d 506, 101 N.W.2d 694 (1960) (use during summers "continuous").

[131] E.g., Marlette Auto Wash, LLC v. Van Dyke SC Props., LLC, 501 Mich. 192, 912 N.W.2d 161 (2018). In *Marlette*, use by customers of an adjoining parking lot for access to a car wash was sufficient to give rise to a prescriptive easement where it continued for 25 years under two different owners of the car wash. At the time of the litigation, the current owner of the car wash had accrued less than 10 years of use, as against a 15-year limitations period. The court recognized a prescriptive easement, even though the prior car wash owner had not taken legal action to claim such an easement.

While courts do typically permit tacking between a series of adverse users, an Oregon court has ruled that a tenant does not have standing to bring an action for a prescriptive appurtenant easement, on the theory that even if a series of tenants had carried on the adverse use, any such appurtenant easement would inure to the benefit of the landlord. 7455 Inc. v. Tuala Northwest, LLC, 274 Or.App. 833, 362 P.3d 1179 (2015).

[132] Shellow v. Hagen, 9 Wis.2d 506, 101 N.W.2d 694 (1960). Cf. Parker & Edgarton v. Foote, 19 Wend. 309 (N.Y.1838) (no prescriptive easement for light and air; no physical use).

[133] Nelms v. Steelhammer, 225 Ark. 429, 283 S.W.2d 118 (1955); Descheemaeker v. Anderson, 131 Mont. 322, 310 P.2d 587 (1957); Othen v. Rosier, 148 Tex. 485, 226 S.W.2d 622 (1950).

[134] Vigil v. Baltzley, 79 N.M. 659, 448 P.2d 171 (1968); State ex rel. Thornton v. Hay, 254 Or. 584, 462 P.2d 671 (1969); Anderson v. Osguthorpe, 29 Utah 2d 32, 504 P.2d 1000 (1972); 4 H. Tiffany, Real Property § 1194 (3d ed. 1975). But see State ex rel. Haman v. Fox, 100 Idaho 140, 594 P.2d 1093 (1979).

usually open and notorious. But if they are concealed beneath the ground, they generally have been held not to be so.[135]

Some states have special statutes of limitation that not only establish a limitation period but list elements of adverse possession. When such statutes list elements not part of the common law, usually color of title or payment of taxes, the question has sometimes arisen whether these elements are required for prescriptive easements. Because of the blending of adverse possession and prescription in America, some courts have required the additional elements.[136] Other courts take the contrary view, that the only part of the statute that applies to prescription is the limitation period.[137] This latter view seems preferable, on the theory that the elements of prescription arose and exist by judge-made law, independent of any statute of limitations. Indeed, the elements developed in the law of prescription first and were in America incorporated into adverse possession. Also, it is unrealistic to require a prescriptive user to pay taxes, because they will not be separately assessed to the user.[138]

Consider one additional situation that does not fit neatly into the analysis described above and in the preceding sections. Suppose that a public road has been used for many years, both by landowners adjoining the road and owners of parcels in the area that are accessible only by other lanes that intersect with the road. The municipality later closes the road, vesting title to the road back in the adjoining landowners. Could they now prevent other area owners from using the road to reach the secondary roads needed to reach their lands? There may well be no "plat" into which an easement could be implied, even if the public road appeared on maps. There is "necessity" and "prior use," but not the prior common ownership of the dominant and servient parcels needed to imply such easements. Finally, it is awkward to describe the prior use of a public road as "hostile." Yet courts have held that such an "abutting" property owner would nevertheless have a right to use the road for access to their property. Some have done so using expectation arguments similar to those seen in implied easement cases;[139] one might also argue that the continued use of the road provides the foundation for the acquisition of a prescriptive easement by abutting owners who continue making use of the road.

§ 8.8   CREATION BY ESTOPPEL OR PART PERFORMANCE

In 1942, Alfred Conard wrote that "[i]n every American jurisdiction except North Carolina, a person may become unconditionally entitled to the use of land through an oral agreement followed by certain types of conduct. . . . Pursuant to the agreement, the licensee must have expended money, property or labor which he would not have spent but for the license, and the licensor must have had reason to anticipate the

---

[135] See Annot., 55 A.L.R.2d 1144 (1957).

[136] Annot., 112 A.L.R. 545 (1938).

[137] Hester v. Sawyers, 41 N.M. 497, 71 P.2d 646 (1937); see also Rutland v. Stewart, 630 So.2d 996 (Miss.1994) (tacking possible with prescription).

[138] E.g., Vieira Enters., Inc. v. McCoy, 8 Cal.App.5th 1057, 214 Cal.Rptr.3d 193 (2017) (payment of taxes requirement for adverse possession does not apply to prescriptive easement unless easement area has been separately assessed for taxation purposes).

[139] See, e.g., Tweedy v. Counts, 73 Ark.App. 163, 40 S.W.3d 238 (2001); Paschall v. Valentine, 45 Tenn.App. 131, 321 S.W.2d 568 (1958).

expenditure."[140] The result on the facts seems clear enough, but courts run into trouble when they attempt to state the theoretical or doctrinal basis for this result.

Courts have used a number of descriptive phrases for the underlying theory. "Irrevocable license" is one, which describes the result but gives little clue to the mechanism at work. All it suggests is that a license, ordinarily not an interest in land and revocable, has been transformed into a corresponding interest in land, i.e., an easement or profit. Alternative phrases, "licenses irrevocable in equity," "easements in equity," and "oral contracts enforceable in equity," suffer from the same shortcoming.[141] Equity has no general rule that all oral conveyances are taken out of the Statute of Frauds, only specific doctrines limited to certain fact patterns.

In these cases, one is taking an oral agreement for an interest in land out of the Statute of Frauds or, as Corbin said, finding facts that block the Statute's application.[142] There are two recognized equitable doctrines to accomplish this: estoppel and part performance. Under one or the other, oral conveyances or agreements to convey interests in land, even the fee simple estate, can be enforced. Surely a doctrine powerful enough to uphold the oral conveyance of a fee estate ought to suffice for the oral conveyance of a lesser interest such as an easement or profit.

Judge Clark argued that estoppel is the true basis for enforcing oral easements.[143] On this theory, one reasons as follows: the oral grantor represented to the grantee that the grantee had an easement or profit upon the grantor's land; in reliance upon the representation, the grantee expended money or labor or made improvements upon or with reference to the easement or profit, i.e., detrimental reliance; and therefore, the grantor became estopped to deny the easement or profit. The theory seems now to be the theory predominantly used in the decisions.[144] Some decisions even suggest that to allow

---

[140] Conard, Unwritten Agreements for the Use of Land, 14 Rocky Mtn.L.Rev. 153–65, 294–314, 313 (1942). North Carolina rejects the theories of equitable estoppel and part performance for the creation of any interest in land. However, the state allows the oral grantee restriction for expenditures. Pickelsimer v. Pickelsimer, 257 N.C. 696, 127 S.E.2d 557 (1962). See generally N.C.Gen.Stat. § 22–2; Sanders v. Wilkerson, 285 N.C. 215, 204 S.E.2d 17 (1974); Hill v. Smith, 51 N.C.App. 670, 277 S.E.2d 542 (1981).

Much more recently, the Michigan Supreme Court has taken a similar position, holding that an oral license for the use of land to allow part of an irrigation system to cross the land could not become irrevocable by estoppel alone, as an irrevocable license would be an "interest in land" that could not be granted orally in compliance with the Statute of Frauds. Kitchen v. Kitchen, 465 Mich. 654, 641 N.W.2d 245 (2002).

[141] E.g., Croasdale v. Lanigan, 129 N.Y. 604, 29 N.E. 824 (1892) ("license . . . irrevocable").

[142] 2 A. Corbin, Contracts § 276 (1950). See, e.g., Richardson v. Franc, 233 Cal.App.4th 744, 182 Cal.Rptr.3d 853 (2015) (driveway easement holder installed substantial landscaping, irrigation and lighting within easement area and maintained it for six years with full knowledge of and without objection from servient owner; held easement holder had acquired irrevocable license); Hay v. Baumgartner, 870 N.E.2d 568 (Ind.App.2007) (neighbor's use of shared driveway is a revocable license; neighbor cannot recover damages absent proof that license was given for valuable consideration or proof of expenditure of money or labor in reliance on license not being revoked).

[143] C. Clark, Real Covenants and Other Interests Which "Run with Land" 59–64 (2d ed. 1947).

[144] E.g., Camp v. Milam, 291 Ala. 12, 277 So.2d 95 (1973); Richardson v. Franc, 233 Cal.App.4th 744, 182 Cal.Rptr.3d 853 (2015) (driveway easement holder installed substantial landscaping, irrigation and lighting within easement area and maintained it for six years with full knowledge of and without objection from servient owner; held easement holder had acquired irrevocable license); Holbrook v. Taylor, 532 S.W.2d 763 (Ky.1976); Cooke v. Ramponi, 38 Cal.2d 282, 239 P.2d 638 (1952) (also discussion of part performance theory); Stoner v. Zucker, 148 Cal. 516, 83 P. 808 (1906); Kephart v. Portmann, 259 Mont. 232, 855 P.2d 120 (1993); Ricenbaw v. Kraus, 157 Neb. 723, 61 N.W.2d 350 (1953); Kienzle v. Myers, 853 N.E.2d 1203 (Ohio App.2006). Cf. Vrazel v. Skrabanek, 725 S.W.2d 709 (Tex.1987) (landowner estopped to deny use of road, though he had made no oral agreement it could be used). But see Kitchen v. Kitchen, 465 Mich. 654, 641 N.W.2d 245 (license for use of land to allow irrigation system to cross land could not become irrevocable by estoppel alone, as this would create interest in land that could arise only in compliance with Statute of Frauds).

the oral grantor to renege would work a "fraud" on the grantee.[145] Not only is there seldom true fraud present, as Clark pointed out,[146] but even if the grantor did have fraudulent intent, the estoppel theory is as far as one needs to go to resolve the case. One should not waste a cannon to kill a rabbit.

The same facts that invoke the estoppel theory will usually support the equitable part performance theory. Here the reasoning is that the oral grantee's acts—making improvements of a kind one would make pursuant to an easement or profit—give tangible evidence, independent of the spoken words, that such an interest exists. The acts themselves "speak of" an easement or profit; the trier of fact need not rely on the oral statements alone.[147] Though Judge Clark preferred estoppel, some courts have adopted the part performance theory.[148] We do not need to make a choice between the two theories here; both are recognized equitable theories to excuse the operation of the Statute of Frauds upon oral conveyances.

§ 8.9   SCOPE OF EASEMENTS AND PROFITS

The "scope" of an easement or profit is what its holder may do with it—the purposes for which the holder may use it. As a general point of beginning, scope and location are determined by the express words of a deed creating an easement or by the events that create an easement by prescription or implication. Ideally, the words or events make the easement's scope or location perfectly clear;[149] problems arise when the operative words or events leave one of these matters unclear. Prescriptive and implied servitudes are always likely to present questions of scope or location, because the events giving rise to them are not communicative acts. Even with easements and profits created by direct verbal act, drafters have a deplorable tendency to be vague about scope and location.

As a general matter, when the scope of an easement is unclear, the courts often apply the "rule of reason" in interpreting the rights and obligations attendant to the easement. Unless the intentions of the parties (as determined by the express terms of the easement or the circumstances surrounding its creation) require a different result, the owner of the servient estate may make any use of the servient estate that does not unreasonably interfere with the holder's use and enjoyment of the easement. Likewise, the easement holder may make any use that is reasonably necessary to the enjoyment of the easement and does not unreasonably interfere with the servient owner's enjoyment of the servient estate.[150] The rest of this section explores the different issues that arise in scope disputes.

---

[145] E.g., Stoner v. Zucker, 148 Cal. 516, 83 P. 808 (1906); Mueller v. Keller, 18 Ill.2d 334, 164 N.E.2d 28 (1960); Prospect Dev. Co. v. Bershader, 515 S.E.2d 291 (Va.1999).

[146] Clark, supra note 143.

[147] The classic exposition of this theory is by Justice Cardozo in Sleeth v. Sampson, 237 N.Y. 69, 142 N.E. 355 (1923).

[148] E.g., Camp v. Milam, 291 Ala. 12, 277 So.2d 95 (1973) ("executed license" and also "estoppel"); Buckles-Irvine Coal Co. v. Kennedy Coal Corp., 134 Va. 1, 114 S.E. 233 (1922).

[149] See Wilson v. Abrams, 1 Cal.App.3d 1030, 82 Cal.Rptr. 272 (1969); Tooker v. Feinstein, 131 Or.App. 684, 886 P.2d 1051 (1994) (clear metes and bounds description located easement).

[150] Lazy Dog Ranch v. Telluray Ranch Corp., 965 P.2d 1229 (Colo.1998); Restatement (Third) of Property-Servitudes § 4.9 (2000) ("Except as limited by the terms of the servitude . . . , the holder of the servient estate is entitled to make any use of the servient estate that does not unreasonably interfere with enjoyment of the servitude."); § 4.10 ("Unless authorized by the terms of the servitude, the holder is not entitled to cause unreasonable damage to the servient estate or interfere unreasonably with its enjoyment.").

Location. The drafter should describe the location of an easement or profit so that a surveyor can run out the location on the ground by reference to the document alone. Expressions like "over the south 20 feet of Lot 2" or a metes and bounds description are best. In a pinch, such as when the parties will not pay for a survey of a sinuous roadway, it may be necessary to refer to an existing road or other feature, describing its general location as accurately as possible. Incorporation by reference of a recorded plat may help. When the grant is entirely vague, such as "a roadway [how wide?] across Blackacre from the county road to Whiteacre [what route?]," many decisions hold that a way that is reasonable and convenient for both parties is implied. The grantor has the power in the first instance to fix a reasonable and convenient location. If the grantor fails to act, the grantee may fix the location. If the parties establish an easement on the ground by use and acquiesce in it, this will fix the location and extent of the use.[151] What is a reasonable and convenient location is a judicial question, so that a court will have to fix it if the parties disagree.[152]

Often, utility companies have service easements that have arisen by prescription, and over time, the companies may understandably wish to replace the prescriptive easement (and its somewhat uncertain scope) with a new, well-drafted express easement clearly delineating its scope. If the servient owner refuses to grant an express easement, is the refusal an unreasonable interference with the utility's exercise of its prescriptive easement? Where a servient owner refused because the requested express easement covered a larger area in a different location on the servient tract, one recent court held that the servient owner's refusal was not an unreasonable interference with the prescriptive easement.[153]

Relocation. Imagine a scenario in which the owner wants to subdivide the servient estate into residential building lots, but needs to relocate the existing easement road by a small amount (say 15 feet) to make it possible to divide the lots into the ideal configuration for development purposes. The servient owner proposes to pay all costs of relocation, and the relocation will not inconvenience the holder of the easement or diminish the usefulness of the easement. In these circumstances, relocation would appear to maximize the utility of the parcels. But suppose that the holder refuses to consent unless the owner of the servient land pays the holder $10,000. Can the owner of the servient estate seek court approval to move the easement to facilitate the redevelopment of the servient estate?

Under the traditional common law rule, once the location of an easement is established, the owner of the servient estate cannot compel the easement holder to accept a substitute location.[154] This result may make sense if the language of the easement

---

[151] E.g., Rye v. Tahoe Truckee Sierra Disposal Co., Inc., 222 Cal.App.4th 84, 170 Cal.Rptr.3d 275 (2013). In *Rye*, the parcel in question was subject an easement for access, parking, storage, and utilities, which the parties had for many years located in the paved portion of the parcel. The court rejected an argument that Tahoe Truckee had a right to park trucks and store equipment throughout the entire area, concluding that this would have effectively granted Tahoe Truckee an exclusive easement, which the court would not infer from the general language in the easement document.

[152] See Ingelson v. Olson, 199 Minn. 422, 272 N.W. 270 (1937); Alban v. R.K. Co., 15 Ohio St.2d 229, 239 N.E.2d 22 (1968); Clearwater Realty Co. v. Bouchard, 146 Vt. 359, 505 A.2d 1189 (1985); 2 Am. Law of Prop. § 8.66 (1952); Annot., 110 A.L.R. 174 (1937).

[153] Zonnebloem, LLC v. Blue Bay Holdings, LLC, 200 Wash.App. 178, 401 P.3d 468 (2017).

[154] E.g., Sakansky v. Wein, 86 N.H. 337, 169 A. 1 (1933); McNaughton Props., LP v. Barr, 981 A.2d 222 (Pa.Super.2009); AKG Real Estate, LLC v. Kosterman, 296 Wis.2d 1, 717 N.W.2d 835 (2006). Perhaps not surprisingly, the common law also held that the owner of the dominant estate could not unilaterally relocate the easement onto a different portion of the servient estate absent the consent of the servient owner. E.g.,

expressly requires the holder's consent to any relocation. But what if the terms of the easement are silent on the point? Under the traditional rule, this did not matter. Section 4.8(3) of the Restatement of Servitudes breaks with the traditional rule and provides that "the owner of the servient estate is entitled to make reasonable changes in the location or dimensions of an easement, at the servient owner's expense, to permit normal use or development of the servient estate, but only if the changes do not (a) significantly lessen the utility of the easement, (b) increase the burdens on the owner of the easement in its use and enjoyment, or (c) frustrate the purpose for which the easement was created."[155] Under the Restatement, our servient owner would be able to relocate the easement despite the holder's objection, assuming that the servient owner can prove to the court's satisfaction that the 15-foot relocation will not lessen the utility of the easement or increase the burden on the holder in using the easement.[156]

Restatement § 4.8(3) has proven controversial in the courts since its promulgation. Several courts have cited it approvingly in allowing the servient owner to relocate an easement over the holder's objection, even when the easement terms provided a specific location for the easement.[157] Other courts have cited it as authority for relocation, but only when the creating instrument did not define the easement through specific reference to its location or dimensions.[158] Still other courts have explicitly rejected Section 4.8(3) and continue to adhere to the traditional rule, often citing the benefits of stability, predictability, and the desire not to encourage litigation.[159]

Koeppen v. Bolich, 318 Mont. 240, 79 P.3d 1100 (2003); Kave v. McIntosh Ridge Primary Rd. Ass'n, 198 Wash.App. 812, 394 P.3d 446 (2017).

In a few states, court decisions have given the servient owner somewhat more flexibility to relocate a prescriptive easement. E.g., Soderberg v. Weisel, 455 Pa.Super. 158, 687 A.2d 839 (1997) (no per se rule against relocation of prescriptive easement; relocation permissible if it is minor and does not unreasonably interfere with easement holder's right of use and enjoyment); Umphres v. J.R. Mayer Enters., 889 S.W.2d 86 (Mo.App.1994) (servient owner unilaterally relocated easement; court held this action was illegal, but refused equitable relief and awarded relatively nominal damages because relocation did not seriously harm enjoyment of easement holder).

[155] Restatement (Third) of Property-Servitudes § 4.8(3) (2000). Section 4.8(3) adopts the rule in effect in Louisiana and in jurisdictions following civil law traditions. La.Civ.Code art. 748 (express easements); La.Civ.Code art. 695 (easements of necessity); French Civ.Code art. 701. See generally Lovett, A New Way: Servitude Relocation in Scotland and Louisiana, 9 Edin.L.Rev. 352 (2005).

[156] Additional utilitarian arguments for the Restatement rule are that it (a) "will encourage the use of easements and lower their price by decreasing the risk the easements will unduly restrict future development of the servient estate," and (b) "provides a fair trade-off for the vulnerability of the servient estate to increased use of the easement to accommodate changes in technology and development of the dominant estate." Restatement (Third) of Property-Servitudes § 4.8 cmt. f (2000).

[157] E.g., Roaring Fork Club, L.P. v. St. Jude's Co., 36 P.3d 1229 (Colo.2001) (servient owner trespassed by relocating ditch without court order; however, court refused to order ditch restored to original location where relocation did not diminish the benefit of the easement to the dominant owner); McGoey v. Brace, 395 Ill.App.3d 847, 918 N.E.2d 559 (2009); M.P.M. Builders, LLC v. Dwyer, 442 Mass. 87, 809 N.E.2d 1053 (2004); Carlin v. Cohen, 73 Mass.App. 106, 895 N.E.2d 793 (2008); R & S Invsts. v. Auto Auctions, Ltd., 15 Neb.App. 267, 725 N.W.2d 871 (2006).

[158] For example, New York courts have held that unilateral relocation is not permissible where the easement was described by metes and bounds, but that relocation is permissible where the original terms described the easement as being over an "existing road" or an "existing driveway." Marsh v. Hogan, 56 A.D.3d 1090, 867 N.Y.S.2d 786 (2008); Mackinnon v. Croyle, 72 A.D.3d 1356, 899 N.Y.S.2d 422 (2010); Green v. Blum, 13 A.D.3d 1037, 786 N.Y.S.2d 839 (2004). Courts in South Dakota and Nevada take a similar approach. E.g., Stanga v. Husman, 694 N.W.2d 716 (S.D.2005); St. James Village, Inc. v. Cunningham, 125 Nev. 211, 210 P.3d 190 (2009).

[159] E.g., Alligood v. Lasaracina, 122 Conn.App. 473, 999 A.2d 836 (2009); Herrin v. Pettergill, 273 Ga. 122, 538 S.E.2d 735 (2000); A. Perin Dev. Co., LLC v. Ty Par Realty, Inc., 193 N.C.App. 450, 667 S.E.2d 324 (2008); McNaughton Props., LP v. Barr, 981 A.2d 222 (Pa.Super.2009); Sweezy v. Neal, 179 Vt. 507, 904 A.2d 1050 (2006); MacMeekin v. Low Income Hous. Inst., 111 Wash.App. 188, 45 P.3d 570 (2002); AKG Real Estate,

Purposes; uses; maintenance. Just as drafters are often lax in describing location, so too they frequently fail to describe the scope or purposes of an easement or profit with sufficient particularity.[160] For example, the instrument might merely create a "driveway easement" or a "pipeline easement," when more precise drafting could and should spell out the kind, maximum weight, and number per day of vehicles on the driveway or the maximum number and size of pipes to be installed. In some cases, the grantor may wish to limit the uses by reference to specific activities on the dominant estate that the easement may serve, e.g., "for vehicles to serve one single-family residence only."

An easement carries with it what might be called "secondary easements," allowing the easement holder to make such improvements and maintenance that are reasonable in the circumstances to make the easement serve its intended purposes.[161] When details about "secondary easements" are not spelled out, the general principle is that "reasonable" uses are implied. What is reasonable depends upon the surrounding circumstances; the most important of these circumstances, in the case of an easement appurtenant, are the activities that one might expect to conduct on the dominant estate.[162] Thus, for example, an easement of access to land to be developed for residential purposes would likely be construed to include a secondary easement for the installation of utility lines for utilities customarily serving a home, and a utility service easement would likely be construed to include a secondary easement permitting the utility to trim trees to protect power lines (assuming the instrument did not state such a right expressly).[163] Likewise, courts have interpreted easements for transmission of electricity to permit the utility to install fiber-optic cable for the utility's internal communications purposes.[164] Court opinions have split, however, on whether the utility could use the capacity of such a fiber-optic cable to operate commercial communications such as providing broadband.[165] Drafters of easement deeds and agreements chronically fail to

---

LLC v. Kosterman, 296 Wis.2d 1, 717 N.W.2d 835 (2006). Some courts have also rejected attempts by the servient owner to relocate the easement, but without specific reference to the Restatement. E.g., Rogers v. P-M Hunter's Ridge, LLC, 407 Md. 712, 967 A.2d 807 (Md.2009); Shooting Point, LLC v. Wescoat, 265 Va. 256, 576 S.E.2d 497 (2003); R.C.R., Inc. v. Rainbow Canyon, Inc., 978 P.2d 581 (Wyo.1999).

[160] Compare Criterion Interests, Inc. v. Deschutes Club, 136 Or.App. 239, 902 P.2d 110 (1995), modified, 137 Or.App. 312, 903 P.2d 421 (1995) (access easement described in general terms could be used for recreational purposes, though intent was to provide agricultural access) with Steil v. Smith, 901 P.2d 395 (Wyo.1995) (road easement limited to "agricultural related purposes" could not be used for big game hunting). Cf. Wendy's of Fort Wayne, Inc. v. Fagan, 644 N.E.2d 159 (Ind.App.1994) (access easement could not be used to place utility lines); Payne v. Rutledge, 391 S.W.3d 875 (Ky.App.2013) (where easement allowed "rebuilding" or "repair" of dirt driveway, easement holder could not pave driveway without consent of servient owner).

[161] See, e.g., Bilello v. Pacella, 223 A.D.2d 522, 636 N.Y.S.2d 112 (1996) (road easement holder has right to maintain it in reasonable condition); Shanak v. City of Waupaca, 185 Wis.2d 568, 518 N.W.2d 310 (Wis.App.1994) (easement holder has duty as well as right to maintain).

[162] See, e.g., Caldwell v. Cometto, 151 Idaho 34, 253 P.3d 708 (2011) (mature trees permissible within three-foot secondary easement alongside roadway); Grider v. Tingle, 325 S.W.3d 437 (Mo.App.2010) (easement for access to lake did not include right to build dock); Musselshell Ranch Co. v. Seidel-Joukova, 362 Mont. 1, 261 P.3d 570 (2011) (installation of bridge and culvert across water ditch unreasonably interfered with easement holder's right to repair and maintain ditch).

[163] Such an implied power to trim trees away from utility lines, however, would be subject to the rule of reason discussed supra note 150. E.g., Larew v. Monongahela Power Co., 199 W.Va. 690, 487 S.E.2d 348 (1997) (remanding for determination of reasonableness of trimming); Branson West, Inc. v. City of Branson, 980 S.W.2d 604 (Mo.App.1998) (city could not clear-cut all trees from 60-foot wide sewer easement, but could cut trees only to extent reasonably necessary to facilitate sewer installation).

[164] E.g., Barfield v. Sho-Me Power Elec. Coop., 852 F.3d 795 (8th Cir.2017) (Missouri law).

[165] The result in the cases tends to turn on the breadth of the language in the easement document. Compare Barfield v. Sho-Me Power Elec. Coop., 852 F.3d 795 (8th Cir.2017) (use of excess capacity in fiber-optic cable for commercial communications business was expanded use beyond scope of easement, where language did not expressly authorize that use) with CenterPoint Energy Houston Elec. LLC v. Bluebonnet

spell out the rights referred to here as "secondary easements." While no agreement written by finite human hands can anticipate every possible contingency, more thoughtful and complete drafting would prevent many disputes that end up in litigation.

In the absence of a contrary agreement, the owner of the servient estate has no duty to maintain the easement; that burden rests on the easement holder.[166] It should also follow that the easement holder is liable to third persons for injuries caused by lack of maintenance.[167] An exception applies in cases where the easement holder and the servient landowner share the use of improvements (e.g., where the holder has the right to cross a road on the servient owner's farm but the servient owner also uses that road in farming the parcel); in such cases, absent contrary agreement, the parties have a shared obligation to contribute to the repair and maintenance of the easement improvements.[168]

Changes in use or intensity of use. As suggested above, when the creating language is general, the holder may use an appurtenant easement to support not only the uses made of the dominant estate at the time of creation, but to a certain extent changing future uses. The permitted purposes are subject to a degree of change or growth; the question is, how much? Perhaps the best formula is that the purposes may keep up with those changes that might be reasonably anticipated for the dominant estate— evolutionary but not revolutionary changes.[169] So, for instance, a general access easement permits gradually changing uses to correspond with normal changes in modes of transportation and normal development of the dominant estate.[170] Likewise, an easement originally granted to a utility for telephone service likely permits the utility to provide cable television or fiber optic internet service, even though such services may not have existed at the time the easement first arose.[171] Much interest has focused on the "rails to trails" question: when a railroad abandons a rail line, can its "railroad" easement be used as a public recreational trail? While there is limited authority

---

Drive, Ltd., 264 S.W.3d 381 (Tex.App.2008) (terms of easement allowed installation of "desirable appurtenances" including "telephone and telegraph wires," which was interpreted to permit use of fiber-optic cable for both internal utility communications and licensing Sprint to provide commercial communications services).

[166] E.g., Page v. Bloom, 223 Ill.App.3d 18, 584 N.E.2d 813 (1991); Raksin v. Crown-Kingston Realty Assocs., 254 A.D.2d 472, 680 N.Y.S.2d 265 (1998); Tanglewood Prop. Owners' Ass'n, Inc. v. Isenhour, 803 S.E.2d 453 (N.C.App.2017). Where multiple holders use the same easement improvements (e.g., a shared road), each holder has a duty of contribution to the reasonable costs of maintenance and repair. Restatement (Third) of Property-Servitudes § 4.13(4) (2000); Brentwood Subdivision Rd. Ass'n v. Cooper, 461 N.W.2d 340 (Iowa App.1990).

[167] See Reyna v. Ayco Dev. Corp., 788 S.W.2d 722 (Tex.App.1990).

[168] Restatement (Third) of Property-Servitudes § 4.13(3) (2000); McDonald v. Bemboom, 694 S.W.2d 782 (Mo.App.1985).

[169] See, e.g., Petersen v. Friedman, 162 Cal. App.2d 245, 328 P.2d 264 (1958); Birdsey v. Kosienski, 140 Conn. 403, 101 A.2d 274 (1953); Cameron v. Barton, 272 S.W.2d 40 (Ky.1954); Restatement (Third) of Property-Servitudes § 4.10 (2000) ("The manner, frequency, and intensity of the use may change over time to take advantage of developments in technology and to accommodate normal development of the dominant estate or enterprise benefited by the servitude.").

[170] See e.g., Birdsey v. Kosienski, 140 Conn. 403, 101 A.2d 274 (Conn.1953) (access easement allowed removal and cartage of sand and gravel operations begun after grant of easement); Cameron v. Barton, 272 S.W.2d 40 (Ky.1954); Miller v. Street, 663 S.W.2d 797 (Tenn.App.1983) (right to take water from spring, originally by bucket, could change to allow piping of water); Palmer v. R.A. Yancey Lumber Corp., 294 Va. 140, 803 S.E.2d 742 (2017) (holder could widen easement of necessity as needed to accommodate larger trucks needed in timbering operation).

[171] E.g., Mumaugh v. Diamond Lake Area Cable TV Co., 183 Mich.App. 597, 456 N.W.2d 425 (1990); Henley v. Continental Cablevision of St. Louis Cty., Inc., 692 S.W.2d 825 (Mo.App.1985); Centel Cable Television Co. of Ohio, Inc. v. Cook, 58 Ohio St.3d 8, 567 N.E.2d 1010 (1991).

permitting such use,[172] the weight of recent authority concludes that a recreational trail is not within the scope of a railroad easement.[173]

Similar principles govern growth and changes in easements created by prescription or by implication, but the manner of creation poses special problems in applying the principles. These problems lie more in defining the purposes originally permitted than in determining the permissible degree of change or growth after that point. With an easement created by implication from prior use, one can typically determine the originally permitted uses by what they were when the two parcels were severed.[174] When the implied easement is a way of necessity, one must determine the original location and scope from what was then necessary, which may be a difficult task factually.[175] The original scope and location of a prescriptive easement is determined by the kind of adverse use made during the prescriptive period, allowing for some flexibility of use. Once the original scope and location of an easement created by implication or prescription is ascertained, it should be subject to change and growth in the same way as would a granted easement of the same original description.[176]

Scope of the dominant estate. Unless the terms of the easement provide otherwise, the holder of an easement appurtenant may use it to serve only the land to which it is appurtenant. The holder may not use it to pass over the dominant estate to reach another adjoining parcel.[177] Nor may the holder use it to serve integrated, inseparable activities

---

[172] See, e.g., Romanoff Equities, Inc. v. United States, 119 Fed.Cl. 76 (2014) (under New York law, railroad easement encompassed use for elevated park and recreational trail); State, by Washington Wildlife Preservation, Inc. v. State, 329 N.W.2d 543 (Minn.1983); Moody v. Allegheny Valley Land Trust, 601 Pa. 655, 976 A.2d 484 (2009) (railbanking of railroad right-of-way was within intended use and purposes of original easement).

[173] See, e.g., Harley-White v. United States, 129 Fed.Cl. 548 (2016) (under Maine law, recreational trail not within scope of railroad easement); Longnecker Prop. v. United States, 105 Fed.Cl. 393 (2012) (under Washington law, recreational trail was not within "railroad purposes"); Biery v. United States, 99 Fed.Cl. 565 (2011) (under Kansas law, conversion to recreational trail use and railbanking exceeded scope of easement for railroad purposes); Jenkins v. United States, 102 Fed.Cl. 598 (2011) (under Iowa law, railroad easement deeds were limited to railroad purposes only; recreational trail use fell outside scope of easements); Glosemeyer v. United States, 45 Fed.Cl. 771 (2000) (under Missouri law, railbanking fell outside scope of easement for railroad purposes); Presault v. United States, 100 F.3d 1525 (Fed.Cir.1996) (under Vermont law, recreational trail use not within scope of railroad purposes easement); Toews v. United States, 376 F.3d 1371 (Fed.Cir.2004) ("in California a public transportation easement defined as one for railroad purposes is not stretchable into an easement for a recreational trail"). See also Howard v. United States, 964 N.E.2d 779 (Ind.2012); Michigan Dept. of Natural Resources v. Carmody-Lahti Real Estate, Inc., 472 Mich. 359, 699 N.W.2d 272 (2005); Moore v. Missouri Friends of the Wabash Trace Nature Trail, Inc., 991 S.W.2d 681 (Mo.App.1999); Lawson v. State, 107 Wash.2d 444, 730 P.2d 1308 (1986).

[174] See Fristoe v. Drapeau, 35 Cal.2d 5, 215 P.2d 729 (1950).

[175] See Soltis v. Miller, 444 Pa. 357, 282 A.2d 369 (1971).

[176] See, e.g., Gutcheon v. Becton, 585 A.2d 818 (Me.1991) (increase in vehicular traffic on prescriptive easement due to residential development did not unreasonably burden servient estate); Mahoney v. Devonshire, Inc., 587 A.2d 1146 (Md.App.1991) (prescriptive easement holder had the right to repair, maintain, and improve easement where improvements resulted from evolution of dominant estate and did not unreasonably burden servient estate); Baldwin v. Boston & Maine R.R., 181 Mass. 166, 63 N.E. 428 (1902) (prescriptive easement). See generally 2 Am. Law of Prop. §§ 8.68, 8.69 (1952), and Restatement (Third) of Property-Servitudes §§ 4.1, 4.10 (2000).

Some courts have manifested greater reluctance to expand the scope of prescriptive easements. E.g., Jackson v. City of Auburn, 971 So.2d 696 (Ala.App.2006) (scope of prescriptive easement for power utility service did not encompass stringing of cable television wires); Ogg v. Mediacom, LLC, 142 S.W.3d 801 (Mo.App.2004) (same). But see Heydon v. Mediaone, 275 Mich.App. 267, 739 N.W.2d 373 (2007) (permitting use for cable television wires under facts similar to *Jackson* and *Ogg*); Centel Cable Television Co. of Ohio, Inc. v. Cook, 567 N.E.2d 1010 (Ohio 1991) (same).

[177] Restatement (Third) of Property-Servitudes § 4.11 (2000); Crimmins v. Gould, 149 Cal.App.2d 383, 308 P.2d 786 (1957); Kircheimer v. Carrier, 446 S.W.3d 224 (Ky.2014) (developer of subdivision could not grant

conducted in a building that sits astride the dominant estate and an adjoining parcel. As long as the usage cannot be separated, a court will enjoin any use of the easement.[178] While the appurtenant easement may serve only the dominant estate, it may serve all parts of that estate unless limited by its creating language. The question usually arises when the owner subdivides the dominant estate into lots or parcels after the easement is granted. In such cases the usual result is that subdivision does not per se prevent the easement from serving the divided lots.[179] However, if development of the subdivided land will cause the easement to be surcharged—used in ways or at an intensity that might not have been reasonably anticipated—then a court will enjoin the excessive use.[180]

---

easement rights for beach access to buyers within nearby developments, as doing so would enlarge dominant estate); Taylor v. Martha's Vineyard Land Bank Comm'n, 475 Mass. 682, 60 N.E.3d 319 (2016); State ex rel. Fisher v. McNutt, 73 Ohio App.3d, 597 N.E.2d 539 (1992); Kanefsky v. Dratch Constr. Co., 376 Pa. 188, 101 A.2d 923 (1954); Boerschig v. Southwestern Holdings, Inc., 322 S.W.3d 752 (Tex.App.2010); Grygiel v. Monches Fish & Game Club, Inc, 328 Wis.2d 436, 787 N.W.2d 6 (2010). But see Newmyer v. Parklands Ranch, LLC, 137 Cal.App.4th 1063, 40 Cal.Rptr.3d 801 (2006) (where owner of dominant estate holds access easement that expressly includes "the further right . . . to grant easements for like purposes to others to be appurtenant to other lands," owner of dominant estate could grant easement right over servient land to owner of adjoining parcel).

In a few cases, the owner of the dominant estate has tried to get around this rule by fractionalizing the ownership of the dominant estate, and then conveying a fraction of that ownership to the owner of an adjacent parcel, in an attempt to argue that the adjacent owner is now benefited. This effort should fail, as the rule presumes that the easement was intended to benefit only a specific parcel of land. See, e.g., Nettesheim v. S.G. New Age Prods., Inc., 285 Wis.2d 663, 702 N.W.2d 449 (App.2005). Nevertheless, the Alabama Supreme Court allowed such machinations, holding that it did not constitute overburdening of the servient estate as a matter of law, but recognizing that the servient owner could still enjoin the use if it could show the use constituting overburdening in fact. Perdido Place Condo. Owners Ass'n, Inc. v. Bella Luna Condo. Owners' Ass'n, Inc., 43 So.3d 1201 (Ala.2009).

[178] Penn Bowling Recreation Ctr., Inc. v. Hot Shoppes, 179 F.2d 64 (D.C.Cir.1949); McCullough v. Broad Exch. Co., 101 A.D. 566, 92 N.Y.S. 533 (1905), aff'd, 184 N.Y. 592, 77 N.E. 1191 (1906). Accord Brown v. Voss, 38 Wash.App. 777, 689 P.2d 1111 (1984), rev'd, 105 Wn.2d 366, 715 P.2d 514 (1986) (easement appurtenant could not be used to serve house that sat astride property line between dominant estate and another parcel, but injunction denied on equitable grounds). In the Penn Bowling case, the court held that if the inseparable use is permanent, the court would declare the easement extinguished rather than simply issue a permanent injunction against the use.

There is some limited authority to the contrary. Courts in Connecticut have held that "the mere addition of other land to the dominant estate does not constitute an overburden or misuse of the easement." Carbone v. Vigliotti, 222 Conn. 216, 610 A.2d 565 (1992). In Carbone, as in Brown v. Voss, the easement holder built a house on property that straddled the boundary line between the original dominant parcel and an adjacent lot that the holder subsequently acquired. In a later opinion, the Connecticut Supreme Court stated that Carbone did not in fact reject the traditional common law rule, but merely recognized that "in some circumstances, the parties at the time of the creation of an easement may be found to have contemplated, as a matter of law, that its benefits might accrue to adjacent property that was not formally within the terms of the agreement." Abington Ltd. Partn. v. Heublein, 246 Conn. 815, 717 A.2d 1232 (1998). Likewise, the New Hampshire Supreme Court ruled that an appurtenant parking easement could be used to benefit a third-party owner of land adjacent to the dominant estate, because the deed language allowed use of the easement "for all times and for all purposes." Heartz v. City of Concord, 148 N.H. 325, 808 A.2d 76 (2002). The Heartz court suggested that its result was consistent with the Restatement, but the result seems quite hard to reconcile with Section 4.11.

[179] Restatement (Third) of Property-Servitudes § 5.7 (2000); Moylan v. Dykes, 181 Cal.App.3d 561, 226 Cal.Rptr. 673 (1986) (appurtenant roadway easement serves both halves of land after dominant tenement is divided); Martin v. Music, 254 S.W.2d 701 (Ky.1953); Mularoni v. Bing, 306 Mont. 405, 34 P.3d 497 (2001); Cox v. Glenbrook Co., 78 Nev. 254, 371 P.2d 647 (1962); Cushman Virginia Corp. v. Barnes, 204 Va. 245, 129 S.E.2d 633 (1963).

[180] Mularoni v. Bing, 306 Mont. 405, 34 P.3d 497, 502–503 (2001) (on subdivision of dominant estate, "each grantee acquires a right to use easements appurtenant to the dominant estate, provided the easements can be enjoyed as to the separate parcels without any additional burden on the servient tenement.").

Rights of the servient owner. Because an easement or profit gives only limited uses of the servient land, the owner of a possessory estate in the servient land may make all other uses that do not unreasonably interfere with the easement or profit.[181] But the owner of the servient estate may not make a use that unduly interferes with the easement rights.[182] If the easement holder is not at the time using a certain part of the easement area, the owner of the servient estate may use that area, subject to the easement holder's right to use it later.[183] The owner may transfer its concurrent rights to third persons.[184]

§ 8.10 TRANSFER OF EASEMENTS AND PROFITS

The word "appurtenant" signifies that an easement appurtenant attaches to and is a part of the right of possession of the dominant estate. Use of the easement is one of the incidents of ownership of the dominant estate, even though this incident is enjoyed on other land. Therefore, any act that is sufficient to transfer title or even rightful possession of the dominant estate will carry the easement rights with it. The deed transferring the dominant estate need not mention the easement; it goes along like a dog's tail goes along with a sale of the dog. Nor may the holder transfer the easement separately from the dominant estate, for "appurtenant" also signifies that the easement serves only the dominant estate.[185]

Easements in gross present a different problem. Because there is no dominant estate, they could pass only by an independent act of transfer of the easement itself. Though easements in gross exist freely and in large numbers in America, there has been question about their transferability,[186] perhaps because English law traditionally questioned their existence.[187] It is clear that easements in gross for commercial purposes

---

[181] Marshall v. Blair, 130 Idaho 675, 946 P.2d 975 (1997) (owner may install gate that does not block intended access); Minneapolis Athletic Club v. Cohler, 287 Minn. 254, 177 N.W.2d 786 (1970); Messer v. Leveson, 23 A.D.2d 834, 259 N.Y.S.2d 662 (1965) (locked gate reasonable); Shingleton v. State, 260 N.C. 451, 133 S.E.2d 183 (1963) (locked gate reasonable); Energy Transp. Systems, Inc. v. Kansas City So. Rwy. Co., 638 P.2d 459 (Okla.1981). See Borrowman v. Howland, 119 Ill. App.3d 493, 75 Ill.Dec. 313, 457 N.E.2d 103 (1983) (owner of servient tenement could not maintain shed over area of drainage ditch easement because it would interfere with the right to maintain the easement). Even if the easement is described as "exclusive," the owner of the servient estate may still make uses of the easement area that do not interfere with the easement. Walton v. Capital Land, Inc., 252 Va. 324, 477 S.E.2d 499 (1996); Wilkoske v. Warren, 875 P.2d 1256 (Wyo.1994). But see Gray v. McCormick, 167 Cal.App.4th 1019, 84 Cal.Rptr.3d 777 (2008) (excluding servient owner from making shared use of driveway where easement language made clear that dominant owner's use was to be completely exclusive).

[182] Compare Louis W. Epstein Family Partn. v. Kmart Corp., 13 F.3d 762 (3d Cir.1994) (traffic control devices that would alter easement forbidden) and Riddell v. Ewell, 929 P.2d 30 (Colo.App.1996) (owner could not block driveway easement with curbing) with Scruby v. Vintage Grapevine, Inc., 37 Cal.App.4th 697, 43 Cal.Rptr.2d 810 (1995) (owner could partially block as long as easement holder had enough access).

[183] City of Pasadena v. California-Michigan Land & Water Co., 17 Cal.2d 576, 110 P.2d 983 (1941); Alban v. R.K. Co., 15 Ohio St.2d 229, 239 N.E.2d 22 (1968); Thompson v. Smith, 59 Wash.2d 397, 367 P.2d 798 (1962).

[184] City of Pasadena v. California-Michigan Land & Water Co., 17 Cal.2d 576, 110 P.2d 983 (1941).

[185] 2 Am. Law of Prop. § 8.71 (1952); Restatement (Third) of Property-Servitudes § 5.1 (2000); Fruth Farms v. Village of Holgate, 442 F.Supp.2d 470 (N.D.Ohio 2006).

[186] E.g., Tupper v. Dorchester County, 487 S.E.2d 187 (S.C.1997) (easement in gross is a mere personal privilege to use land of another and thus is incapable of transfer); Maw v. Weber Basin Water Conservancy Dist., 436 P.2d 230 (Utah 1968); Note, The Easement in Gross Revisited: Transferability and Divisibility Since 1945, 39 Vand.L.Rev. 109 (1986).

[187] See Colin Sara, Boundaries and Easements 161–162 (Sweet & Maxwell 1991) (noting easement must have a dominant estate under English law).

are alienable.[188] Any other rule would be disastrous for a public utility company that sought to transfer its utility easements to another company. The word "commercial" here does not refer only to easements held for use in a business, but also to easements held by private persons that have economic value as contrasted with a purpose of the holder's personal pleasure. Such "personal" easements in gross, e.g., an easement for the holder's recreation, are probably not alienable, though authority for the proposition seems to be speculative discussion more than case law.[189] Behind the commercial-personal dichotomy is the principle of intent, that the grantor would not intend the holder to transfer an easement that was for the limited purpose of serving the holder personally. Indeed, the Restatements suggest that an easement in gross should be alienable unless the circumstances indicate that the parties creating it would not have expected it to be alienable,[190] and there is case authority allowing the transfer of an easement in gross where the easement's express terms so permit.[191]

In contrast with easements in gross, profits a prendre in gross are freely alienable. This has been clear since at least *Mountjoy's Case* in 1583.[192] Because nearly all profits are in gross, nearly all are separately alienable. As the next section indicates, there may be questions about the divisibility or apportionability of profits in gross, but not about their alienability per se.

§ 8.11 DIVISIBILITY OR APPORTIONABILITY OF EASEMENTS AND PROFITS

As noted above, an easement appurtenant generally continues to serve a dominant estate that is divided into parcels.[193] For an easement or profit in gross, which has no dominant estate, the corresponding question is whether the holder may divide or apportion it among multiple persons. An easement or profit that may be so divided was traditionally called "admeasurable." The underlying problem is that to allow more than one person to use an easement or to exploit a profit—when it was created for only one—

---

[188] Restatement of Property § 489 (1944); Restatement (Third) of Property-Servitudes § 4.6(2) (2000); Johnston v. Michigan Consolidated Gas Co., 337 Mich. 572, 60 N.W.2d 464 (1953); Geffine v. Thompson, 76 Ohio App. 64, 62 N.E.2d 590 (1945); Miller v. Lutheran Conference & Camp Ass'n, 331 Pa. 241, 200 A. 646 (1938); Douglas v. Medical Invs., Inc., 256 S.C. 440, 182 S.E.2d 720 (1971).

[189] See 2 Am. Law of Prop. §§ 8.75–8.83 (1952); Restatement of Property § 491 (1944). See also Simes, Assignability of Easements in Gross in American Law, 22 Mich.L.Rev. 521 (1924); Note, 40 Dick.L.Rev. 46 (1935); and Comment, 32 Yale L.J. 813 (1923), all of which advocate assignability of easements in gross without making the commercial-personal distinction.

[190] Restatement of Property § 491 (1944) ("The alienability of noncommercial easements in gross is determined by the manner or terms of their creation."); Restatement (Third) of Property-Servitudes § 4.6(1) (2000) (easement in gross is transferable unless "personal"); id. § 4.6(2) (benefit is "personal" if "the relationship of the parties, consideration paid, nature of the servitude, or other circumstances indicate that the parties should not reasonably have expected that the servitude benefit would pass to a successor to the original beneficiary). See also Borek Cranberry Marsh, Inc. v. Jackson County, 773 N.W.2d 522 (Wis.App.2009) (easement in gross transferable unless creating deed shows intent to limit transferability).

[191] E.g., O'Donovan v. McIntosh, 728 A.2d 681 (Me.1999); Farmer's Marine Copper Works, Inc. v. City of Galveston, 757 S.W.2d 148 (Tex.App.1988).

[192] Earl of Huntington v. Lord Mountjoy, 1 And. 307, 123 Eng.Rep. 488, Godb. 17, 78 Eng.Rep. 11 (C.P. 1583). Accord: Loch Sheldrake Assocs. v. Evans, 306 N.Y. 297, 118 N.E.2d 444 (1954); Stanton v. T.L. Herbert & Sons, 141 Tenn. 440, 211 S.W. 353 (1919); Co.Litt. *164b (analyzing *Mountjoy's Case*).

[193] Restatement (Third) of Property-Servitudes § 5.7 (2000); Moylan v. Dykes, 181 Cal.App.3d 561, 226 Cal.Rptr. 673 (1986) (appurtenant roadway easement serves both halves of land after dominant tenement is divided); Martin v. Music, 254 S.W.2d 701 (Ky.1953); Mularoni v. Bing, 306 Mont. 405, 34 P.3d 497 (2001); Cox v. Glenbrook Co., 78 Nev. 254, 371 P.2d 647 (1962); Cushman Virginia Corp. v. Barnes, 204 Va. 245, 129 S.E.2d 633 (1963).

may work a surcharge or additional burden on the servient estate.[194] The key to solving the problem is to determine the appropriate "measure" of the easement or profit.

When the grantee received an "exclusive" easement or profit—the right to make sole use of the easement or to take all of a substance from the land—then the grantee may transfer to as many other persons as the grantee wishes.[195] No surcharge results, because any number of grantees cannot use any more than what was granted. Similarly, if the creating instrument established an absolute measure less than all, e.g., so many passages per day or so many tons of rock per day, the grantee may divide the right.

Divisibility problems are acute when the easement or profit is not exclusive and does not contain an absolute measure. Examples are "an easement of passage" or "a right to remove rock." Courts sometimes say flatly that a non-exclusive easement or profit is not divisible.[196] It seems more accurate to say that whether a non-exclusive easement or profit may be divided depends ultimately upon the grantor's intent. If the creating instrument contains language that shows the grantor anticipated or was willing that the easement or profit might be divided, then it may be;[197] some decisions have found such a willingness when the right was granted to the grantee and "its successors and assigns."[198] The fact that an easement or profit is non-exclusive is a powerful factor tending to show, or even raising a presumption, that divisibility was not intended, but it is not always conclusive.[199] Note that no "division" occurs when there is a transfer of an easement or profit to two or more persons who will use it "as one stock."[200] Persons who act "as one stock" are usually partners, joint venturers, or a corporation.

§ 8.12 TERMINATION OF EASEMENTS AND PROFITS

Release. The most obvious way to terminate an easement or profit is by the holder's express release to the owner of the servient estate. This occurs through an instrument executed with the same formalities required to grant an easement or profit, generally a deed in the form required to convey an estate in land.[201]

---

[194] See Jolliff v. Hardin Cable Television Co., 26 Ohio St.2d 103, 269 N.E.2d 588 (1971); Hinds v. Phillips Petroleum Co., 591 P.2d 697 (Okla.1979); Stanton v. T.L. Herbert & Sons, 141 Tenn. 440, 211 S.W. 353 (1919).

[195] E.g., Zhang v. Communications Enters., Inc., 272 Conn. 627, 866 A.2d 588 (Conn.2005) (power company could partially assign easement rights to wireless telephone provider to extent wireless provider's use was consistent with purposes for which easement was granted); Abbott v. Nampa School Dist. No. 131, 119 Idaho 544, 808 P.2d 1289 (1991); Hoffman v. Capitol Cablevision System, Inc., 52 A.D.2d 313, 383 N.Y.S.2d 674 (1976); Hinds v. Phillips Petroleum Co., 591 P.2d 697 (Okla.1979); Stanton v. T.L. Herbert & Sons, 141 Tenn. 440, 211 S.W. 353 (1919); Restatement of Property § 493, Comment b (1944); Restatement (Third) of Property-Servitudes § 5.9 (2000) ("Transferable benefits in gross may be divided unless contrary to the terms of the servitude, or unless the division unreasonably increases the burden on the servient estate.").

[196] E.g., Jolliff v. Hardin Cable Television Co., 22 Ohio App.2d 49, 258 N.E.2d 244 (1970), rev'd, 26 Ohio St.2d 103, 269 N.E.2d 588 (1971); Stanton v. T.L. Herbert & Sons, 141 Tenn. 440, 211 S.W. 353 (1919).

[197] Hoffman v. Capitol Cablevision System, Inc., 52 A.D.2d 313, 383 N.Y.S.2d 674 (1976); Jolliff v. Hardin Cable Television Co., 26 Ohio St.2d 103, 269 N.E.2d 588 (1971); Orange County v. Citgo Pipeline Co., 934 S.W.2d 472 (Tex.App.1996) ("exclusive" easement in gross for pipeline could be partially alienated when no burden beyond what grantor contemplated); Restatement of Property § 493, Illus. 4 (1944); Restatement (Third) of Property-Servitudes § 5.9 (2000).

[198] Hoffman v. Capitol Cablevision System, Inc., 52 A.D.2d 313, 383 N.Y.S.2d 674 (1976); Jolliff v. Hardin Cable Television Co., 26 Ohio St.2d 103, 269 N.E.2d 588 (1971).

[199] 2 Am. Law of Prop. § 8.84 (1952); Restatement of Property § 493, Comment d (1944); Restatement (Third) of Property-Servitudes § 5.9 Comment b (2000).

[200] Earl of Huntington v. Lord Mountjoy, 1 And. 307, 123 Eng.Rep. 488, Godb. 17, 78 Eng.Rep. 11 (C.P.1583); Miller v. Lutheran Conference & Camp Ass'n, 331 Pa. 241, 200 A. 646 (1938).

[201] 2 Am. Law of Prop. § 8.95 (1952); 3 H. Tiffany, Real Property § 824 (3d ed. 1939).

Expiration. Like other interests in land, easements may be limited to a definite time by their creating language. A servitude not so limited will have the duration of the estate of its creator, usually a fee simple estate. But an owner can expressly grant a servitude for the duration of a lesser estate, such as a defeasible fee, a life estate, or an estate for years.[202] Express time limits do not seem very common, but can be useful in appropriate circumstances.

A servitude's duration may be limited by implication as well as by express language. An implied easement of necessity expires when the necessity for it ends.[203] With other kinds of easements, termination most likely occurs when an easement or profit was created for a certain limited purpose, but can no longer serve that purpose.[204] The broader the purposes, the less likely the servitude will end, for all its purposes must have permanently ended.[205] There may be sharp debate over the facts, as to both the scope of the servitude and whether it can no longer serve any intended purpose.

Another way some easements may impliedly terminate is by the destruction of a structure on the servient estate. The cases involve either an easement of passage through a building that is destroyed, or an easement in a party wall that is altered or destroyed. With easements through buildings, the general rule is that they are limited to the life of the building, whose destruction terminates the easement.[206] A replacement building does not revive the easement unless the court finds the parties intended revival.[207] There is a split of authority over whether the owner of the servient estate may voluntarily raze the building or must suffer the easement to continue until the building's destruction from natural causes.[208] In the case of party walls, most decisions hold that

---

[202] See Miller v. City of New York, 15 N.Y.2d 34, 255 N.Y.S.2d 78, 203 N.E.2d 478 (1964); Thar v. Edwin N. Moran Revocable Trust, 905 P.2d 413 (Wyo.1995) (easement created in lease expires when leasehold ends); 2 Am. Law of Prop. § 8.87 (1952).

[203] Restatement (Third) of Property-Servitudes § 4.3(1) (2000); Hereford v. Gingo-Morgan Park, 551 So.2d 918 (Ala.1989); Moores v. Walsh, 38 Cal.App.4th 1046, 45 Cal.Rptr.2d 389 (1995) (termination when it became possible for holder of easement to condemn another access road); Enzor v. Rasberry, 648 So.2d 788 (Fla.App.1994) (no termination because new roadway did not provide "reasonable and practical" alternative access).

[204] Restatement (Third) of Property-Servitudes § 7.10 (2000); Pavlik v. Consolidation Coal Co., 456 F.2d 378 (6th Cir.1972) (under language of easement deed, cessation of coal slurry triggered termination clause); Grider v. Tingle, 325 S.W.3d 437 (Mo.App.2010) (severance of dominant estate into lakefront parcel and higher-elevation parcel terminated appurtenant lakebed easement as to higher-elevation parcel which was no longer contiguous to lakefront); Olson v. H & B Props., Inc., 118 N.M. 495, 882 P.2d 536 (1994) (ditch easement limited to irrigation purposes ended). As discussed in Section 8.9 supra, there is a division of authority on whether cessation of railroad operations will terminate an easement granted for railroad purposes, or whether railroad purposes would permit use of the easement as a recreational trail.

[205] See First Nat'l Bank v. Konner, 373 Mass. 463, 367 N.E.2d 1174 (1977); First Nat'l Trust & Sav. Bank v. Raphael, 201 Va. 718, 113 S.E.2d 683 (1960); Hopkins the Florist v. Fleming, 112 Vt. 389, 26 A.2d 96 (1942) (narrow purpose; easement terminated).

[206] E.g., Rothschild v. Wolf, 20 Cal.2d 17, 123 P.2d 483 (1942); Union Nat'l Bank v. Nesmith, 238 Mass. 247, 130 N.E. 251 (1921); Rudderham v. Emery Brothers, 46 R.I. 171, 125 A. 291 (1924) (destruction terminates easement unless express terms manifest otherwise); Annot., 34 A.L.R. 606 (1925), Supp., 154 A.L.R. 82 (1945). See also Amlea (Florida), Inc. v. Smith, 567 So.2d 981 (Fla.App.1990) (destruction of building extinguishes parking easement in gross). But see Nicol v. Gonzales, 127 S.W.3d 390 (Tex.App.2004) (destruction of garage did not terminate easement "for ingress and egress to a garage or outbuilding" where a separate toolshed still remained on servient estate).

[207] See Rudderham v. Emery Brothers, 46 R.I. 171, 125 A. 291 (1924) (not revived); Annot., 34 A.L.R. 606 (1925) Supp., 154 A.L.R. 82 (1945).

[208] Compare Rothschild v. Wolf, 20 Cal.2d 17, 123 P.2d 483 (1942) (owner may not raze) with Union Nat'l Bank v. Nesmith, 238 Mass. 247, 130 N.E. 251 (1921) (owner may raze). Even in states that say the owner may not voluntarily raze the building, one might argue there should be an implied outer limit to how

destruction of both buildings and the wall terminates each adjoining owner's easement.[209] Destruction of one building has been held to terminate the party wall easement for that building but not for the remaining building.[210] Party walls may also terminate by implication when they become inadequate or dangerous to support the original buildings or to support larger buildings that changed conditions make it appropriate to build.[211]

Merger. When an easement or profit holder acquires an interest in the servient estate, the easement or profit terminates to the extent the acquired estate allows the same use as the easement or profit did.[212] The servitude merges into the estate, which simply means an owner may not twice have the same rights of use in the same land. By the strong majority position, the easement is not automatically revived if its former holder later transfers the estate;[213] however, nothing precludes the former holder from creating a comparable new easement in a later transfer.[214] A few jurisdictions, notably Pennsylvania, allow revival in certain circumstances.[215] The merger rule will not terminate the easement where an intervening interest exists. For example, where owners of the dominant estate hold title to it subject to a mortgage, their subsequent acquisition of the servient estate will not extinguish the easement by merger; the easement would continue to benefit the mortgagee after acquiring the dominant estate through foreclosure.[216]

Abandonment. As a general rule, easements (and perhaps profits) may be terminated by abandonment, which requires two elements: a cessation of use and an

---

long the owner must maintain an old building for the sake of an easement. Good drafting can avoid the problem by establishing some limit on the easement's life.

[209] E.g., Salvation Army v. Kyle, 18 Neb.App. 19, 778 N.W.2d 485 (2009).

[210] Annot., 85 A.L.R. 288 (1933); 3 H. Tiffany Real Property, § 818 (3d ed.1939).

[211] S.S. Kresge Co. v. Garrick Realty Co., 209 Wis. 305, 245 N.W. 118 (1932); Annot., 85 A.L.R. 288, 293 (1933).

[212] Restatement of Property §§ 497, 499 (1944); Restatement (Third) of Property-Servitudes § 7.5 (2000); Danforth v. Groom, 2014 WL 316487 (Mass. Land Ct.2014); Witt v. Reavis, 284 Or. 503, 587 P.2d 1005 (1978); DWG Oil & Gas Acquisitions, LLC v. Southern Country Farms, Inc., 238 W.Va. 414, 796 S.E.2d 201 (2017); 2 Am. Law of Prop. §§ 8.90, 8.93 (1952).

In a recent Massachusetts decision, the court ruled that a registered easement (i.e., an easement benefitting a registered Torrens title) was terminated by merger when the registered title came into common ownership with the unregistered title to the servient estate. Williams Bros. Inc. of Marshfield v. Peck, 81 Mass.App. 682, 966 N.E.2d 860 (2012). This decision somewhat compromises the reliability of a registered title. The court also noted that a registered easement could likewise be abandoned, but that it could not be extinguished by prescription. See also Lasell College v. Leonard, 32 Mass.App. 383, 589 N.E.2d 342 (1992).

[213] E.g., Elrod v. Elrod, 272 Ga. 188, 526 S.E.2d 339 (2000); Pergament v. Loring Props. Ltd., 599 N.W.2d 146 (Minn.1999); Witt v. Reavis, 284 Or. 503, 587 P.2d 1005 (1978); 2 Am. Law of Prop. § 8.91 (1952); Restatement (Third) of Property-Servitudes § 7.5 (2000). Resumption of the legal use would require re-creation of the easement under the rules discussed in Section 8.3.

[214] For example, in Shah v. Smith, 181 Ohio App.3d 264, 908 N.E.2d 983 (2009), the Shahs acquired two adjacent parcels that shared a driveway, and their acquisition resulted in the termination by merger of an express recorded easement in favor of one of the parcels. The Shahs later sold the formerly burdened parcel to the Smiths, by a deed that stated that title was subject to the prior recorded easement. The court's opinion suggests that the deed was sufficient to create a new express easement similar to the one previously terminated by merger.

[215] Schwoyer v. Smith, 388 Pa. 637, 131 A.2d 385 (1957).

[216] E.g., Pergament v. Loring Props., Ltd., 599 N.W.2d 146 (Minn.1999); Cowan v. Carnevale, 300 A.D.2d 893, 752 N.Y.S.2d 737 (2002); Heritage Communities of N.C., Inc. v. Powers, Inc., 49 N.C.App. 656, 272 S.E.2d 399 (1980). This exception protects the mortgagee of the dominant estate from losing the value of its interest in an otherwise-extinguished easement. E.g., Duval v. Becker, 81 Md. 537, 32 A. 308 (1895) (allowing extinguishment of the mortgagee's interest "would jeopardize, if not wholly destroy the stability of every mortgage as security").

intent to relinquish.[217] This is a strange doctrine. Our law knows no doctrine of abandonment of estates in land; we do not conceive of unowned land. Abandonment of chattels is well recognized; they may become unowned, available for new ownership by whoever takes them into possession with intent to own. Abandonment of servitudes cannot result in their being unowned in this way, but must operate as a release to the owner of the servient estate. In this sense, there are some decisions in which courts have held that an abandonment occurred.[218] Far more decisions, however, recognize the possibility of abandonment but conclude that it did not occur,[219] or recite facts that permit termination on some other theory.[220] Many of these decisions find that while the easement holder ceased to use the easement, mere nonuse was not sufficient to establish abandonment; instead, the party seeking to terminate must prove the holder had the intent to abandon the easement.[221] Most courts have held that the use of another equally convenient way of access does not create an inference of abandonment,[222] though there is limited contrary authority. In sum, while our law recognizes a doctrine of abandonment of easements, it is not a judicial favorite, and intent to abandon is difficult to establish.

Prescription. Servitudes may terminate by adverse possession or prescription by the owner of the servient estate or by a third person. To be adverse, the possession or use must be adverse, actual, open, notorious, hostile or nonpermissive, and continuous, for the period of the statute of limitations.[223] Mere non-use by the easement holder will not

---

[217] 2 Am. Law of Prop. §§ 8.96–8.98 (1952); Restatement of Property § 504 (1944); Restatement (Third) of Property-Servitudes § 7.4 (2000); Annot., 25 A.L.R.2d 1265, 1272–1322 (1952).

[218] E.g., D.C. Transit Sys., Inc. v. State Roads Comm'n, 265 Md. 622, 290 A.2d 807 (1972); Carr v. Bartell, 305 Mich. 317, 9 N.W.2d 556 (1943); TMD of Chester, LLC v. Asdal Dev., LLC, 2006 WL 3408178 (N.J.Super.2006) (easement granted in conjunction with redevelopment plan; when plan was abandoned after failure to obtain necessary approvals, easement deemed abandoned); Hatcher v. Chesner, 422 Pa. 138, 221 A.2d 305 (1966); Graves v. Dennis, 691 N.W.2d 315 (S.D.2004).

[219] E.g., Rutland v. Mullen, 798 A.2d 1104 (Me.2002); Florian v. Cooper, 89 Mass.App. 1112, 46 N.E.3d 600 (2016) (removal of part of driveway within easement area to expand lawn did not manifest intention to abandon easement); Leisz v. Avista Corp., 356 Mont. 259, 232 P.3d 419 (2010) (nonuse following construction of other access did not constitute abandonment); Lambright v. Trahan, 322 S.W.3d 424 (Tex.App.2010); Spencer v. Kosir, 301 Wis.2d 521, 733 N.W.2d 921 (App.2007) (70 years of nonuse did not result in abandonment).

[220] See Simonton, Abandonment of Interests in Land, 25 Ill.L.Rev. 261 (1930). For example, some decisions finding abandonment present facts that would more readily justify a conclusion that the easement had terminated by prescription. E.g., Bank of Fayetteville, N.A. v. Matilda's, Inc, 304 Ark. 518, 803 S.W.2d 549 (1991) (stairway easement held abandoned where stairway had not been used for 15 and had been sealed for 29 years); Hickerson v. Bender, 500 N.W.2d 169 (Minn.App.1993) (access easement abandoned after two decades of nonuse and the erection without objection of numerous obstacles in easement's path).

[221] E.g., Luciani Realty Partners v. North Haven Academy, LLC, 119 Conn.App. 522, 988 A.2d 930 (2010) (abandonment requires "unequivocal and decisive acts clearly indicating an intent on the part of the owner of the easement to abandon use of it"); Smith v. Muellner, 283 Conn. 510, 932 A.2d 382 (Conn.2007); Pencader Assocs., Inc. v. Glasgow Trust, 446 A.2d 1097 (Del.1982) (mere non-use of easement for 170 years did not constitute abandonment); Kurz v. Blume, 407 Ill. 383, 95 N.E.2d 338 (1950); McCoy v. Barr, 47 Kan.App.2d 285, 275 P.3d 914 (2012); First Nat'l Bank v. Konner, 373 Mass. 463, 367 N.E.2d 1174 (1977); Leisz v. Avista Corp., 356 Mont. 259, 232 P.3d 419 (2010); Hillary Corp. v. U.S. Cold Storage, Inc., 250 Neb. 397, 550 N.W.2d 889 (1996) (mere non-use not abandonment); Sabados v. Kiraly, 258 Pa.Super. 532, 393 A.2d 486 (1978); Spangler v. Schaus, 106 R.I. 795, 264 A.2d 161 (1970); Miller v. Street, 663 S.W.2d 797 (Tenn.App.1983); Cushman Virginia Corp. v. Barnes, 204 Va. 245, 129 S.E.2d 633 (1963).

[222] E.g., Smith v. Muellner, 283 Conn. 510, 932 A.2d 382 (2007); Leisz v. Avista Corp., 356 Mont. 259, 232 P.3d 419 (2010).

[223] 2 Am. Law of Prop. § 8.102 (1952); Restatement of Property § 506 (1944); Restatement (Third) of Property-Servitudes § 7.7 (2000); Kurz v. Blume, 407 Ill. 383, 95 N.E.2d 338 (1950); Faulconer v. Williams, 327 Or. 381, 964 P.2d 246 (1998); Annot., 25 A.L.R.2d 1265, 1322–37 (1952).

suffice for adverse possession or use, just as it will not alone suffice for abandonment. Rather, the adverse claimant must do something that wrongfully and physically prevents the use of the easement—i.e., something that is inconsistent with the easement's existence.[224] Particularly when the adverse claimant is the servient owner, this may imply severe interference, because of the principle that the owner may make any use not inconsistent with the easement.[225] For example, it is usually rightful for the owner to maintain a reasonable gate across a roadway easement.[226] With an access easement, there is no absolute rule that the interference must be by a solid object such as a building or wall, but that type of interference is involved in most cases of extinguishment by prescription.[227] Opinions have differed on whether trees alone are a sufficient interference, though there is significant authority that they are not.[228]

Misuse or surcharge? Though the owner of the servient estate can enjoin the holder's misuse, overuse, or surcharge of an easement, misuse does not normally terminate the easement.[229] In a few decisions, however, courts have stated that an easement may be terminated if the misuse was under such circumstances that the court felt it appropriate to grant a permanent injunction to forbid use of the easement.[230] These cases are often

---

An implied easement of necessity cannot be terminated by prescription as long as the necessity exists. E.g., Hinrichs v. Melton, 11 Cal.App.5th 516, 218 Cal.Rptr.3d 13 (2017) (holding five-year statutory prescription period under California law "does not apply to an easement by necessity").

[224] If the interference meets this standard, the weight of authority and the better view suggests that the interference is hostile even if the claimant's interference originated due to a mistake as to location of the easement. E.g., Vieira Enters., Inc. v. McCoy, 8 Cal.App.5th 1057, 214 Cal.Rptr.3d 193 (2017); Faulconer v. Williams, 327 Or. 381, 964 P.2d 246 (1998).

[225] Compare Sabino Town & Country Estates Ass'n v. Carr, 186 Ariz. 146, 920 P.2d 26 (Ariz.App.1996) (no extinguishment when fencing did not prevent easement holder's needed use) with Faulconer v. Williams, 147 Or.App. 389, 936 P.2d 999 (1997) (fencing and trees that blocked easement extinguished it by adverse possession). The *Sabino* decision is subject to some question, because the easement was for both driving and walking; while the holder of the easement currently used it only for walking, the fencing apparently prevented both uses. The fact that an easement is not currently being used for its purpose should not prevent prescription against it if the possession would prevent the use for that purpose. Perhaps the court felt that the fencing was too insignificant to be adverse to driving.

[226] E.g., Hutter v. Medlock, 29 Ark.App. 122, 777 S.W.2d 869 (1989); Gandy Co. v. Freuer, 313 N.W.2d 576 (Minn.1981); Halverson v. Turner, 268 Mont. 168, 885 P.2d 1285 (1994). But see Strahan v. Bush, 237 Mont. 265, 773 P.2d 718 (1989) (locked gate may be unreasonable interference in some circumstances).

[227] Some courts have regarded fences, especially wire fences, as too insubstantial of an impediment to extinguish an access easement adversely. See, e.g., Annot., 25 A.L.R.2d 1265, 1325–32 (1952). Nevertheless, if the fence is a substantial enough interference to prevent use of the easement, it should be sufficient. See, e.g., Bennett v. Bowditch, 163 Conn.App. 750, 137 A.3d 81 (2016) (chain link and razor wire fence that completely blocked easement sufficient to commence running of prescriptive period).

[228] Compare Simpson v. Fowles, 272 Or. 344, 536 P.2d 499 (1975) (easement extinguished by maintenance of filbert orchard obstructing easement) with Smith v. Muellner, 283 Conn. 510, 932 A.2d 382 (2007) (ancient chestnut tree in middle of easement did not constitute adverse use sufficient to extinguish easement). The reasoning of the *Smith* decision is somewhat curious. The court reasoned that because the servient owner had no duty to maintain the easement, the servient owner's failure to remove the tree was not actionable. As a result, the court reasoned, the presence of the tree could not be considered adverse. See also Desotell v. Szczygiel, 338 Mass. 153, 154 N.E.2d 698 (presence of wild trees and brush not adverse use by servient tenant); Armour v. Marino, 140 A.D.2d 752, 527 N.Y.S.2d 632 (garden, trees not sufficiently adverse).

[229] Restatement (Third) of Property-Servitudes § 8.3 Comment c (2000) ("In the absence of an express provision allowing termination of an easement or profit for excessive use, a court order of forfeiture for excessive use is warranted only if injunctive relief cannot practicably be used to prevent excessive or unauthorized use of the servitude."); Schwartz v. Castleton Christian Church, 594 N.E.2d 473 (Ind.App.1992); Gagnon v. Carrier, 96 N.H. 409, 77 A.2d 868 (1951); Nishanian v. Sirohi, 243 Va. 337, 414 S.E.2d 604 (1992); Annot., 16 A.L.R.2d 609 (1951).

[230] E.g., Penn Bowling Recreation Ctr. v. Hot Shoppes, Inc., 179 F.2d 64 (D.C.Cir.1949); Crimmins v. Gould, 149 Cal.App.2d 383, 308 P.2d 786 (1957); Leasehold Estates, Inc. v. Fulbro Holding Co., 47 N.J.Super. 534, 136 A.2d 423 (1957) (court speaks of "abandonment").

ones in which the owner of an appurtenant access easement has built a permanent structure that sits astride both the dominant estate and another adjoining parcel. It seems clear that, for termination, the misuse must be more than only minor or technical.[231] Some courts are unwilling to declare termination, even when they will issue a permanent injunction.[232]

B. RUNNING COVENANTS (CONTRACTUAL SERVITUDES)

§ 8.13 INTRODUCTION AND OVERVIEW

A "covenant" is a promise by one person to another to do (or to refrain from doing) something, which promise the covenantee may enforce legally against the covenantor. The covenants we consider here have the peculiar quality of "running with land," i.e., they bind not only the covenantor and the covenantee, but also persons who subsequently acquire an interest in a parcel or parcels of land previously owned by the covenantor or covenantee. One should appreciate that a covenant has two "sides" to it. The covenantor's side (the "burden" side) is a duty to do or to refrain from doing, as promised. The covenantee's side (the "benefit" side) is the right to have the duty performed.

By nature, running covenants are first cousins to appurtenant easements. The burdened land corresponds to a servient estate and the benefited land to a dominant estate. In concept, the main difference between easements and covenants is that an easement allows its holder to enter and to do something on the servient estate; by contrast, the beneficiary of a covenant typically may not enter the burdened land, but may have a remedy if the owner of that land does (or fails to do) something in violation of the covenant. The performance of this covenant is regarded by the parties as benefitting the beneficiary's land. Because of the functional similarities between easements and restrictive covenants, restrictive covenants are sometimes called "negative easements."[233] Recognizing these similarities, the Restatement of Servitudes has attempted to reconcile much of the law of easements and covenants under the unified label of "servitude."[234] While restrictive covenants and negative easements are functionally similar, they nevertheless developed from different legal origins, and even today—despite the Restatement—many courts continue to subject easements and covenants to different legal standards regarding their enforceability. For this reason, for clarity's sake, this treatise does not use the term "negative easement" to apply to a running covenant, even if this terminology sometimes appears in the case law.

Our question in the ensuing sections is whether the burden or the benefit of a covenant has the quality of running with land to burden or benefit successors. The law

---

[231] E.g., Paul v. Blakely, 243 Iowa 355, 51 N.W.2d 405 (1952); Vieth v. Dorsch, 274 Wis. 17, 79 N.W.2d 96 (1956).

[232] E.g., McCullough v. Broad Exch. Co., 101 A.D. 566, 92 N.Y.S. 533 (1905), aff'd, 184 N.Y. 592, 77 N.E. 1191 (1906); Deavitt v. Washington Cty., 75 Vt. 156, 53 A. 563 (1903) ("forfeiture is not the remedy" for misuse).

[233] See, e.g., City of Olympia v. Palzer, 107 Wash.2d 225, 728 P.2d 135 (1986) (stating that in subdivisions, "restrictive covenants are the same as negative easements because they curtail the rights of the owner of the servient tenement in favor of the owners of all of the dominant tenements").

[234] Restatement (Third) of Property-Servitudes § 1.1(2) (2000) (defining "servitude" to include easements, profits, and covenants).

of real property has always controlled this question,[235] because a "running" covenant is connected with the acquisition of some sort of interest in land; the benefit or burden is said to "run with" land or with an estate in land. In the law of contracts, the original parties may assign rights or benefits and delegate duties or burdens consistent with their agreement and the law of contracts. Under real property law and the law of running covenants, express assignment or delegation does not occur. Rather, remote persons are benefited or burdened because they acquire an interest in land that carries the benefit or burden along with it, provided the covenant meets certain legal requirements. The ensuing sections define and explain the requirements that must be present for running to occur.

By convention and history, running covenants are of two kinds. Covenants that run under doctrine developed in the English common law courts of Common Pleas and King's Bench are known as covenants running "at law" or "real covenants."[236] The second kind of covenant runs under doctrine originating in the English Chancery Court in the 1848 decision in Tulk v. Moxhay.[237] We refer to them as covenants running in equity, "equitable restrictions," or "equitable servitudes." The ensuing sections will discuss the law of real covenants and the law of equitable servitudes separately; the rules governing their enforcement developed distinctly, and thus somewhat different rules developed for whether a covenant ran at law as contrasted with whether it ran in equity. Many of these distinctions will seem unnecessarily complex and bizarre—in fact, many of them are. As we will see, recent law reform has attempted to bring greater coherence to the law of running covenants; there has been progress, but the jury remains out on how successful these efforts will ultimately be.

While the ensuing sections will discuss real covenants and equitable servitudes separately, it is important at the inception to start with an admitted—but we think nevertheless useful—oversimplification. A running covenant is almost always created by virtue of explicit language in a deed or other instrument of conveyance. The drafter of the deed containing the covenant did not label it as a "real covenant" or as an "equitable servitude." Instead, the instrument simply expressed a contractual promise that either the grantor, the grantee, or both would do (or refrain from doing) something on a parcel of land—e.g., A conveyed part of Blackacre to B by deed that said "Grantee covenants that neither the Grantee, nor the Grantee's heirs, successors, or assigns, will use the land hereby conveyed for any purpose other than single-family residential purposes." If B later sells that parcel to C, C opens a restaurant, and A sues C for violating the covenant, how a court will label the covenant—and thus which rules the court will apply—depend on the remedy A seeks. To the extent A seeks to recover damages from C, the court will ask whether the covenant is a "real covenant," i.e., whether it ran with the land at law (where, historically, damages was the primary legal remedy) to bind C once C bought the land from B. To the extent that A seeks an

---

[235] Bordwell, The Running of Covenants—No Anomaly, 36 Iowa L.Rev. 1, 1–8 (1950); Stoebuck, Running Covenants: An Analytical Primer, 53 Wash.L.Rev. 861 (1977). Portions of the text in many of the ensuing sections derive, to varying degrees, from Prof. Stoebuck's article.

[236] "Real covenants" are assumed here to trace back to Spencer's Case, 5 Co. 16a, 77 Eng.Rep. 72 (Q.B.1583).

[237] 2 Phil. 774, 41 Eng.Rep. 1143 (Ch. 1848). For the view that, before Tulk v. Moxhay, American courts developed indigenous theories that subsumed both *Spencer's Case* and *Tulk,* see Reichman, Toward a Unified Concept of Servitudes, 55 S.Cal.L.Rev. 1179, 1188–1211 (1982).

injunction to prevent *C's* future violation of the covenant, the court will evaluate whether the covenant is an "equitable servitude," i.e., whether it runs with the land in equity.

§ 8.14   REAL COVENANTS—INTRODUCTION

For convenience and to promote analysis, the ensuing sections organize the discussion of real covenants according to their elements. These elements include: (1) the form of the covenant; (2) whether the covenanting parties intended the covenant to run with land; (3) whether the covenant touches and concerns land; (4) whether there is privity between one or both of the covenanting parties and the remote party or parties sought to be benefited or burdened (called "vertical privity"); and (5) whether there is privity between the original covenanting parties (called "horizontal privity"). After we explore these elements, we will address certain questions relating generally to real covenants.

§ 8.15   FORM OF REAL COVENANTS

For a covenant to be enforceable by or against a remote party, it must have been enforceable between the original covenanting parties as a matter of contract law. In this section, we focus on whether a real covenant must be in such a form as to satisfy the Statute of Frauds regulating transfer of interests in land.[238] Underlying this issue is the fundamental question whether real covenants are interests in land or merely contract rights that run by their connection with estates in land. If they are interests in land, it should follow that they must arise in a document that satisfies the Statute of Frauds or by some recognized exception to its operation.[239] The same issue arises in connection with equitable servitudes; courts usually make no distinction between legal and equitable restrictions in discussing the Statute of Frauds, though perhaps they have tended to excuse the statute more readily with equitable servitudes. In any event, it seems valid for purposes of the Statute of Frauds to discuss both legal and equitable restrictions collectively as "running covenants."

Most writers and the Restatements of Property concur that the Statute of Frauds applies to the creation of running covenants.[240] Some older decisions have held that the Statute of Frauds does not apply to running covenants because they are not interests in land,[241] but nearly all modern decisions agree with the approach of the Restatements.[242]

---

[238] The question becomes important in determining whether running covenants are a form of "property" for which eminent domain compensation must be paid in certain situations. A majority of the courts that have considered that question have resolved it affirmatively. See Palm Beach Cty. v. Cove Club Invs., Ltd., 734 So.2d 379 (Fla.1999); Dible v. City of Lafayette, 713 N.E.2d 269 (Ind.1999); Mercantile-Safe Deposit & Trust Co. v. Mayor & City Council, 308 Md. 627, 521 A.2d 734 (1987); Stoebuck, Condemnation of Rights the Condemnee Holds in Lands of Another, 56 Iowa L.Rev. 293, 301–10 (1970); Restatement (Third) of Property-Servitudes § 2.18, Comment h (2000).

[239] See Miller v. Lawlor, 245 Iowa 1144, 66 N.W.2d 267 (1954).

[240] C. Clark, Real Covenants and Other Interests Which "Run With Land" 94 (2d ed.1947); R. Powell & P. Rohan, Real Property ¶ 672 (abr. ed.1968); Restatement of Property § 522 (1944); Restatement (Third) of Property-Servitudes § 2.7 (2000).

[241] Johnson v. Mt. Baker Park Presbyterian Church, 113 Wash. 458, 194 P. 536 (1920); Sims, The Law of Real Covenants: Exceptions to the Restatement of the Subject by the American Law Institute, 30 Cornell L.Q. 1 (1944) (noting cases from fourteen states holding running covenants were not property interests).

[242] Adaman Mut. Water Co. v. United States, 278 F.2d 842 (9th Cir.1960); Palm Beach Cty. v. Cove Club Invs. Ltd., 734 So.2d 379 (Fla.1999) (right to collect fees under assessment covenant is property right); Dible v. City of Lafayette, 713 N.E.2d 269 (Ind.1999); Mercantile-Safe Deposit & Trust Co. v. Mayor and City Council of Baltimore, 308 Md. 627, 521 A.2d 734 (1987); Carolina Mills v. Catawba County Bd. of Educ., 27 N.C.App. 524, 219 S.E.2d 509 (1975); Horst v. Housing Auth., 184 Neb. 215, 166 N.W.2d 119 (1969); Inwood North

The modern approach coincides better with the concept that proprietary interests in land are the total bundle of rights that the holder enjoys. One who restricts previously enjoyed rights by covenanting not to exercise some of them (for instance, by covenanting not to build certain kinds of structures or make certain uses) has certainly diminished their quantum of ownership in the affected land.[243]

As a practical matter, the Statute of Frauds seldom proves an insurmountable obstacle to establishing a running covenant. Nearly all covenants for which enforcement is sought are created in a writing that satisfies the Statute, such as a deed, easement agreement, or lease.[244] Even if the formalities have not been observed, the covenant may be saved via estoppel or part performance.[245]

§ 8.16 REAL COVENANTS MUST TOUCH AND CONCERN

Whatever other attributes a real covenant may have, unless its benefit "touches and concerns" some estate in land, the benefit cannot run to the covenantee's successor. Similarly, unless the burden "touches and concerns" some estate in land, the burden cannot run to bind the covenantor's successor. To emphasize the point, suppose that in a valid written lease, the tenant covenanted to paint the landlord's portrait. Suppose further the parties expressly agreed that "this covenant shall be a covenant running with the land, binding and benefiting the parties' grantees and assigns forever." A court should not enforce this covenant to bind the tenant's assignee, because painting a portrait has nothing to do with the land, the leasehold, or being a tenant.[246] Nor would

---

Homeowners Ass'n v. Harris, 736 S.W.2d 632 (Tex.1987); R. Powell & P. Rohan, Real Property ¶ 672 (abr. ed.1968); Restatement of Property § 522 (1944).

[243] Likewise, running covenants are similar in their nature to easements, which must be created in compliance with the Statute of Frauds. See § 8.3 supra.

[244] With most of today's modern residential development occurring in common interest communities and the increasing comprehensiveness and standardization of common interest documentation, disputes involving covenant compliance with the Statute are rare. E.g., Forrest Constr., Inc. v. Milam, 345 Ark. 1, 43 S.W.3d 140 (2001) (covenant purporting to bind co-owned land, but signed by only one co-owner, held invalid); Dickson v. Kates, 132 Wash.App. 724, 133 P.3d 498 (2006) (restrictive covenant held invalid because it lacked sufficient legal description of burdened estate).

Courts have demonstrated a relaxed approach to the Statute in connection with the creation and enforcement of covenants. For one example, in evaluating whether the grantor intended to create a covenant, courts have tended to look at the four corners of the instrument rather than requiring the intent to be expressed in a specific part of the deed. E.g., 328 Owners Corp. v. 330 W. 86 Oaks Corp., 8 N.Y.3d 372, 865 N.E.2d 1228 (2007) (covenant valid even though it was expressed in deed recitals rather than in habendum clause). For another example, the Statute typically requires the signature of the person sought to be bound, but most covenants are created in deeds, and customarily only the grantor signs the deed. If the deed creates a covenant that burdens the land conveyed, and the grantee accepts the deed, courts typically deem that the grantee accepted title subject to the burden of the covenant—and the benefited party may enforce the covenant against the grantee despite the fact that the grantee did not sign the deed. See, e.g., C. Clark, Real Covenants and Other Interests Which "Run With Land" 94 (2d ed.1947); Brendonwood Common v. Franklin, 403 N.E.2d 1136 (Ind.App.1980); Sanborn v. McLean, 233 Mich. 227, 206 N.W. 496 (1925); Vogeler v. Alwyn Improvement Corp., 247 N.Y. 131, 159 N.E. 886 (1928); Rodruck v. Sand Point Maintenance Comm'n, 48 Wash.2d 565, 295 P.2d 714 (1956). However, where a deed containing a restrictive covenant provided a signature line for the grantee but the grantee failed to sign the deed, one court held that it was ambiguous as to whether the grantee had agreed to take subject to the covenant, and that this problem prevented the covenant from running with the land. See Jeremiah 29:11, Inc. v. Seifert, 284 Kan. 468, 161 P.3d 750 (2007).

[245] See 4 H. Tiffany, Real Property §§ 1235, 1236 (3rd ed.1975); Sleeth v. Sampson, 237 N.Y. 69, 142 N.E. 355 (1923).

[246] E.g., Giuffrida v. High Country Investor, Inc., 73 Mass.App. 225, 897 N.E.2d 82 (2008) (covenant in commercial lease granting no-cost dining privileges to family members of shareholder of corporate lessor did not touch and concern land).

the benefit be enforceable by the landlord's grantee, who would have no interest unique to owning the reversion in having the landlord's (or the grantee's) portrait done.

Touch and concern is a concept more easily understood through exploration than by simple definition. The clearest example of a covenant that meets the requirement is one calling for the doing of a physical thing to land. The tenant's covenant to build a wall in *Spencer's Case* was of this sort; so is a covenant to repair. Covenants to refrain from doing a physical thing to land—such as covenants not to build a structure or to make only single-family residential use—fit this category too. Courts have no difficulty finding that such covenants touch and concern the land.[247]

The meaning of "touch and concern" tends to become less clear as the covenant's physical impact becomes less direct. One problem area has involved affirmative covenants, particularly covenants to pay a sum of money.[248] For example, consider covenants to purchase insurance for a parcel of land. Under the old case of Masury v. Southworth[249] and decisions following it, a "bare" covenant to insure does not touch and concern; however, if the covenant to insure is coupled with a covenant to invest the insurance proceeds in restoring the damaged premises, the covenant does touch and concern.[250] Under this traditional view, the investment of proceeds provides a kind of indirect physical connection between the insurance and the land.[251]

---

[247] Barton v. Fred Netterville Lumber Co., 317 F.Supp.2d 700 (S.D.Miss.2004) (prohibiting operation of "hardwood sawmill"); Thruston v. Minke, 32 Md. 487 (1870) (building height restriction); Newman v. Wittmer, 277 Mont. 1, 917 P.2d 926 (1996) (prohibiting house trailers); Farmington Woods Homeowners Ass'n v. Wolf, 284 Neb. 280, 817 N.W.2d 758 (2012) (prohibiting business activities); Cobb v. Gammon, 389 P.3d 1058 (N.M.App.2016) (restricting lot size to five-acre minimum); Pocono Summit Realty, LLC v. Ahmad Amer, LLC, 52 A.3d 261 (Pa.Super.2012) (prohibiting operation of grocery store); Albright v. Fish, 136 Vt. 387, 394 A.2d 1117 (1978) (prohibiting subdivision into lots smaller than ten acres); Mains Farm Homeowners Ass'n v. Worthington, 121 Wash.2d 810, 854 P.2d 1072 (1993) (restricting use to single-family residential purposes).

[248] See, e.g., Vulcan Materials Co. v. Miller, 691 So.2d 908 (Miss.1997) (promise to pay royalty on minerals from land did not touch and concern); Pagano Co. v. 48 South Franklin Turnpike, LLC, 198 N.J. 107, 965 A.2d 1172 (2009) (covenant to pay brokerage commissions did not touch and concern land); Wayne Harwell Props. v. Pan American Logistics Ctr., 945 S.W.2d 216 (Tex.App.1997) (covenant to pay part of cash proceeds from developments on land did not run).

Much of the difficulty with affirmative covenants derives from New York case law, which reflected a historical hostility to affirmative covenants that surely influenced courts in other states. In 1913, the New York Court of Appeals held in Miller v. Clary, 210 N.Y. 127, 103 N.E. 1114 (1913), that a covenant to provide power to neighboring land via a turning shaft did not run because affirmative covenants did not touch and concern. For years, New York courts weakened the case by chipping away at it—most notably in Neponsit Prop. Owners' Ass'n, Inc. v. Emigrant Indus. Sav. Bank, 278 N.Y. 248, 15 N.E.2d 793 (1938), which held that a covenant imposing lot assessments in a residential subdivision for the benefit of maintaining common amenities touched and concerned all lots within the subdivision despite its affirmative character. Finally, in Nicholson v. 300 Broadway Realty Corp., 7 N.Y.2d 240, 164 N.E.2d 832 (1959), the court allowed the running of a covenant to supply steam heat to neighboring land, limiting *Miller v. Clary* so disingenuously as to render it a dead letter. Since then, affirmative covenants have fared better in New York courts, with occasional exceptions. See Eagle Enterprises, Inc. v. Gross, 39 N.Y.2d 505, 349 N.E.2d 816 (1976) (affirmative covenant to pay for water did not touch and concern because covenant's benefit was personal).

[249] 9 Ohio St. 340 (1859).

[250] E.g., International Interests, LP v. Mt. Hawley Ins. Co., 2012 WL 3776483 (S.D.Tex.2012); Spillane v. Yarmalowicz, 252 Mass. 168, 147 N.E. 571 (1925); Burton v. Chesapeake Box & Lumber Corp., 190 Va. 755, 57 S.E.2d 904 (1950); Rollman Corp. v. Goode, 400 A.2d 968 (Vt.1979).

[251] By contrast, Judge Clark advocated that a "bare" covenant to insure should run, though there is not much case authority for his position. See Northern Trust Co. v. Snyder, 76 F. 34 (7th Cir. 1896); St. Regis Restaurant Inc. v. Powers, 219 App.Div. 321, 219 N.Y.S. 684 (1927) (dictum); C. Clark, Real Covenants and Other Interests Which "Run With Land" 98–100 (2d ed.1947); Bigelow, The Content of Covenants in Leases, 12 Mich.L.Rev. 639, 644 (1914).

As to other forms of covenants to pay money, there is little doubt that they touch and concern when the payment is for the use of land or for improvements. A number of decisions so hold with respect to a landowner's promise to repay a neighbor for a portion of the cost of a party wall if, in the future, the landowner erects a building that uses the wall.[252] Controversy has existed over whether covenants to pay real estate taxes and assessments touch and concern, but the better view (and probably the trend) is that they do.[253] There is no longer much controversy over whether covenants to pay homeowners association assessments touch and concern; the overwhelming weight of modern authority holds that they do, at least where (as is typically the case) the assessments fund the construction or maintenance of common amenities which would serve to preserve or enhance lot values.[254] Leading cases are split over whether a landlord's covenant to repay the tenant's security deposit touches and concerns.[255] Courts uniformly hold that the covenant to pay rent in a lease touches and concerns.[256]

---

[252] Mackin v. Haven, 187 Ill. 480, 58 N.E. 448 (1900); Conduitt v. Ross, 102 Ind. 166, 26 N.E. 198 (1885); Bennett v. Sheinwald, 252 Mass. 23, 147 N.E. 28 (1925). Where the promise is to pay for a portion of a wall being built regardless of future use, courts have usually held the covenant not to run, though more because the parties did not intend it to run than because it does not touch and concern. Gibson v. Holden, 115 Ill. 199, 3 N.E. 282 (1885); Sebald v. Mulholland, 155 N.Y. 455, 50 N.E. 260 (1898). But see King v. Wight, 155 Mass. 444, 29 N.E. 644 (1891).

[253] Security System Co. v. S.S. Pierce Co., 258 Mass. 4, 154 N.E. 190 (1926) (dictum); Maher v. Cleveland Union Stockyards Co., 55 Ohio App. 412, 9 N.E.2d 995 (1936); C. Clark, Real Covenants and Other Interests Which "Run With Land" 98–100 (2d ed.1947).

[254] See, e.g., In re Foster, 435 B.R. 650 (9th Cir.2010); Boyle v. Lake Forest Prop. Owners Ass'n, Inc., 538 F.Supp. 765 (S.D.Ala.1982); Timberstone Homeowners' Ass'n v. Summerlin, 266 Ga. 322, 467 S.E.2d 330 (1996); Stream Sports Club, Ltd. v. Richmond, 99 Ill.2d 182, 457 N.E.2d 1226 (1983); In re County Treasurer and ex Officio County Collector, 373 Ill.App.3d 679, 869 N.E.2d 1065 (2007); Griffin v. Tall Timbers Dev., Inc., 681 So.2d 546 (Miss.1996); Neponsit Prop. Owners' Ass'n, Inc. v. Emigrant Industrial Sav. Bank, 278 N.Y. 248, 15 N.E.2d 793 (1938); Inwood North Homeowners' Ass'n v. Harris, 736 S.W.2d 632 (Tex.1987).

There is some uncertainty about whether covenants to pay dues for golf course memberships and other forms of social or recreational club memberships touch and concern. If the dues maintain amenities which are available for the use of lot owners within a community—and thus which potentially preserve or enhance the value of lots within the community—such dues should properly be viewed as touching and concerning land. See, e.g., Nickerson v. Green Valley Recreation, Inc., 228 Ariz. 309, 265 P.3d 1108 (App.2011); Dye v. Diamante, 510 S.W.3d 759 (Ark.2017); Anthony v. Brea Glenbrook Club, 58 Cal.App.3d 506, 130 Cal.Rptr. 32 (1976); Lend A Hand Charity, Inc. v. Ford Plantation Club, Inc., 338 Ga.App. 594, 791 S.E.2d 180 (2016); Regency Homes Ass'n v. Egermayer, 243 Neb. 286, 498 N.W.2d 783 (1993). Nevertheless, some decisions hold that such covenants are personal covenants that do not touch and concern. E.g., Chesapeake Ranch Club, Inc. v. C.R.C. United Members, Inc., 60 Md.App. 609, 483 A.2d 1334 (1984) (social and recreational club membership dues); Raintree Corp. v. Rowe, 38 N.C.App. 664, 248 S.E.2d 904 (1978). A more recent North Carolina decision has ruled that covenants to pay dues for golf course memberships do not touch and concern land where the lot owners would have only a license to use the golf course amenities rather than an easement. See Midsouth Golf, LLC v. Fairfield Harbourside Condo. Ass'n, Inc., 187 N.C.App. 22, 652 S.E.2d 378 (2007). An Oregon court held that a covenant to pay a golf club initiation fee required of initial lot purchasers did not touch and concern where there was no obligation on successor owners to become members and nonmember successor owners acquired no right to enjoy the golf course. Ebbe v. Senior Estates Golf & Country Club, 61 Or.App. 398, 657 P.2d 696 (1983).

[255] Compare Moskin v. Goldstein, 225 Mich. 389, 196 N.W. 415 (1923) (yes) with Richards v. Browning, 214 A.D. 665, 212 N.Y.S. 738 (1925), Castlebrook, Ltd. v. Dayton Props. Ltd. Partn., 78 Ohio App. 340, 604 N.E.2d 808 (1992), and Mullendore Theatres, Inc. v. Growth Realty Invs. Co., 39 Wash.App. 64, 691 P.2d 970 (1984) (no)). See C. Clark, Real Covenants and Other Interests Which "Run With Land" 98–100 (2d ed.1947).

[256] See, e.g., Excel Willowbrook, L.L.C. v. JP Morgan Chase Bank, N.A., 758 F.3d 592 (5th Cir.2014); Essex Co. v. Goldman, 357 Mass. 427, 258 N.E.2d 526 (1970); Riverbend Invs. v. Progressive Surface Preparation, L.L.C., 255 Mich.App. 327, 660 N.W.2d 373 (2003); Abbott v. Bob's U-Drive, 222 Or. 147, 352 P.2d 598 (1960); 2 Am. Law of Prop. § 9.4, at 351 n.55 (1952); 1 H. Tiffany, Real Property § 126, at 207 (3d ed.1939); Annot., 41 A.L.R. 1363, 1370 (1926); Annot., 102 A.L.R. 781, 784 (1936). On what basis does the covenant to pay rent touch and concern land? It is tempting to say that the covenant to pay rent touches the leasehold estate because the tenant must pay rent to preserve the tenant's estate, but this is bootstrapping—on this theory, any covenant (even a clearly personal one) would touch and concern as long as the lease permitted the

A recent and controversial example of a covenant to pay money is the "transfer fee covenant." In some residential developments, developers may impose on each lot or unit a covenant requiring its owner to pay a fee (say, 1% of the purchase price) every time the lot or unit is resold for the duration of the covenant. If these fees are payable to the owners association to fund the construction or maintenance of community facilities, the covenant to pay them should touch and concern in the same way as a covenant to pay periodic assessments.[257] But what if the covenant instead states that the fee is payable to the original developer (e.g., a "private" transfer fee covenant)? In this situation, continued enforcement of the covenant provides no benefit to any lot within the community; the benefit of the covenant is "in gross," purely personal to the developer. Traditionally, where the benefit of a covenant was in gross, the first Restatement of Property and many courts held that the burden of the covenant would not run with the land to bind successors.[258] Under this approach, a court should refuse to enforce a purely private transfer fee covenant against successors.[259]

Another source of controversy has involved covenants restricting certain types of business activity on a described parcel of land. Frequently, these covenants are intended to protect another existing business from competition. For many years, Massachusetts followed Holmes' decision in Norcross v. James[260] that such covenants do not touch and concern because they regulate the personal conduct of business only.[261] But

---

landlord to terminate the leasehold estate on the covenant's breach. One might instead analogize to covenants to pay owners association assessments, and argue that tenant's payment of rent provides landlord with the funds needed to fulfill landlord's lease obligations, thereby preserving to tenant the anticipated value of possession of the premises. This seems satisfactory in a modern residential lease in which the landlord has the burden of an implied warranty of habitability, but does not well fit as applied to a commercial "triple net" lease under which tenant takes on all maintenance and repair responsibilities. In any event, as noted in the text, there is judicial consensus that the covenant to pay rent touches and concerns.

Occasionally one sees the argument that a tenant's covenant, though seemingly personal in nature, touches and concerns because it was bargained for, has value, and thus is a covenant for "additional rent." E.g., St. Regis Restaurant Inc. v. Powers, 219 A.D. 321, 219 N.Y.S. 684 (1927). This argument proves too much; on this theory, every one of the tenant's covenants will run, even the covenant to paint the landlord's portrait mentioned at the beginning of this section.

[257] In fact, the documents creating New York cooperative apartment associations often impose such a transfer fee covenant (sometimes called a "flip tax"), and such a covenant is generally enforceable against successor owners. E.g., Mayerson v. 3701 Tenants Corp., 123 Misc.2d 235, 473 N.Y.S.2d 123 (Sup.1984) (upholding transfer fee of 7.5% of resale proceeds to fund cooperative association's operations).

[258] E.g., Restatement of Property § 537 (1944); Caullett v. Stanley Stilwell & Sons, Inc., 67 N.J.Super. 111, 170 A.2d 52 (1961) (covenant requiring lot owner to use specific builder for building first structure on land); Garland v. Rosenshein, 420 Mass. 319, 649 N.E.2d 756 (1995) (covenant reserving development control to grantor who retained no interest in affected land and did not own adjoining land); Bremmeyer Excavating, Inc. v. McKenna, 44 Wash.App. 267, 721 P.2d 567 (1986) (covenant requiring owner to use specific company to provide fill services).

[259] In the case of a private transfer fee covenant, this is the appropriate result as a matter of policy. If the covenant was enforceable, its effect would be to reduce the value of each affected lot—because any buyer of the lot will reduce their offer price by the expected cost of the obligation to pay the transfer fee upon resale. Enforcement of private transfer fee covenants as running covenants would thus incrementally lower a city's tax base—diminishing that city's ability to fund public services without increasing tax rates—but with that benefit entirely diverted into the pockets of private developers. See generally Freyermuth, Private Transfer Fee Covenants: Cleaning Up the Mess, 45 Real Prop., Tr. & Est. L.J. 421 (2010). Perhaps for this reason, legislatures in numerous states have enacted statutes explicitly prohibiting private transfer fee covenants from binding successors. E.g., Fla.Stat.Ann. § 689.28; Iowa Code § 558.48; Kan.Stat. § 58–3821; Mo.Rev.Stat. § 442.558; Utah Code Ann. § 57–1–46.

[260] 140 Mass. 188, 2 N.E. 946 (1885) (benefit of covenant did not add to "quiet enjoyment" of land).

[261] Shell Oil Co. v. Henry Ouellette & Sons, 352 Mass. 725, 227 N.E.2d 509 (1967); Shade v. M. O'Keeffe, Inc., 260 Mass. 180, 156 N.E. 867 (1927).

Massachusetts overruled *Norcross* in Whitinsville Plaza, Inc. v. Kotseas.[262] Today, American courts generally hold that covenants restricting the conduct of business on specified land touch and concern.[263] Typically, such a covenant—if properly drafted— will read that a parcel will not be used for a particular business. When the covenant refers to identifiable land, it is hard to escape the conclusion that it touches and concerns, because it certainly restricts the use of that land.[264]

Finally, one should appreciate the extent to which courts have used the touch and concern requirement to regulate a widely diverse range of covenants. For example, while there was formerly some doubt about purchase options in a lease, the weight of authority holds that they touch and concern land.[265] Courts have split on the question whether a covenant not to sue touches and concerns land,[266] and likewise disagree as to whether a tenant's covenant to indemnify the landlord touches and concerns.[267] Most courts have concluded that a covenant to arbitrate lease disputes touches and concerns the premises.[268] At least one decision found the touch and concern requirement satisfied by a covenant not to seek rezoning of a parcel.[269] Covenants placing restrictions on the future development of land have also produced some confusion. Certainly, a covenant restricting the use of land to certain purposes or to certain kinds of buildings touches and concerns the burdened land, and poses no conceptual problem where the covenant clearly benefits another parcel.[270] But courts have refused to enforce covenants as running covenants despite a clear physical impact on one parcel of land where the covenant did not provide an apparent benefit to other land. For example, a Washington court refused to allow an excavation company to enforce a covenant to fill a parcel of land

---

[262] 378 Mass. 85, 390 N.E.2d 243 (1979).

[263] E.g., Dick v. Sears-Roebuck & Co., 115 Conn. 122, 160 A. 432 (1932); Natural Prods. Co. v. Dolese & Shepard Co., 309 Ill. 230, 140 N.E. 840 (1923); Farmington Woods Homeowners Ass'n, Inc. v. Wolf, 284 Neb. 280, 817 N.W.2d 758 (2010); Davidson Bros., Inc. v. D. Katz & Sons, Inc., 121 N.J. 196, 579 A.2d 288 (1990) (prohibiting use as a grocery store); Pocono Summit Realty, LLC v. Ahmad Amer, LLC, 52 A.3d 261 (Pa.Super.2012) (prohibiting operation of grocery store); Ehler v. B.T. Suppenas, Ltd., 74 S.W.3d 515 (Tex.App.2002) (prohibiting use of land for retail alcohol sales). But see Hyde v. Liebelt, 394 N.W.2d 888 (N.D.1986) (covenant that buyer would not operate motel did not touch and concern because it benefited seller's business, not the land; wrongly decided).

[264] This type of covenant is distinguishable from a promise that the covenantor as an *individual* will not engage in a particular business; the latter covenant does not touch and concern because it does not relate to specific land. E.g., Savings, Inc. v. City of Blytheville, 240 Ark. 558, 401 S.W.2d 26 (1966); Hebert v. Dupaty, 42 La.Ann. 343, 7 So. 580 (1890).

[265] H.J. Lewis Oyster Co. v. West, 93 Conn. 518, 107 A. 138 (1919); Keogh v. Peck, 316 Ill. 318, 147 N.E. 266 (1925); C. Clark, Real Covenants and Other Interests Which "Run With Land" 98–100 (2d ed.1947).

[266] Compare 1515–1519 Lakeview Blvd. Condo. Ass'n v. Apartment Sales Corp., 146 Wash.2d 194, 43 P.3d 1233 (2002) (covenant releasing claims against the city relating to soil movement in a potential slide area held to touch and concern) with In re El Paso Refinery, LP, 302 F.3d 343 (5th Cir. 2002) (covenant not to assert claims for contribution or indemnity against refinery owner did not touch and concern) and Meritage Homeowners' Ass'n v. Bank of New York Mellon, 2018 WL 1787183 (D.Or.2018) (covenant not to sue owners' association in window-related disputes did not touch and concern).

[267] Compare Atwood v. Chicago, Milwaukee & St. Paul Rwy. Co., 313 Ill. 59, 144 N.E. 351 (1924) (no) with Northern Pac. Rwy. v. McClure, 9 N.D. 73, 81 N.W. 52 (1899) (yes).

[268] Kelly v. Tri-Cities Broadcasting, Inc., 147 Cal.App.3d 666, 195 Cal.Rptr. 303 (1983); Abbott v. Bob's U-Drive, 222 Or. 147, 352 P.2d 598 (1960). See also Baker v. Conoco Pipeline Co., 280 F.Supp.2d 1285 (N.D.Okla.2003) (covenant to arbitrate easement disputes touched and concerned). See generally Freyermuth, Foreclosure by Arbitration?, 37 Pepperdine L.Rev. 459 (2010). Cf. Waldrop v. Town of Brevard, 233 N.C. 26, 62 S.E.2d 512 (1950) (covenant not to sue neighbor for nuisance); Muldawer v. Stribling, 243 Ga. 673, 256 S.E.2d 357 (1979) (covenant not to apply for rezoning).

[269] Muldawer v. Stribling, 243 Ga. 673, 256 S.E.2d 357 (1979).

[270] E.g., City of Bowie v. MIE, Props., Inc., 398 Md. 657, 922 A.2d 509 (2007) (covenant restricting land to use as science and technology park).

against a successor to the covenantor on the ground that the covenant did not touch and concern any benefited parcel of land.[271] A New Jersey court held that a covenant ostensibly entitling a developer to build the first structure on the lot did not touch and concern land.[272] In a notorious Massachusetts decision, the court held that a deed covenant restricting development of a parcel in conjunction with neighboring land could not be enforced against the grantee's successor where the grantor-covenantee no longer owned any interest in the parcel or the neighboring land following the conveyance.[273]

A final context in which to discuss the "touch and concern" requirement involves covenants that purport to limit or prohibit an owner's ability to transfer the land. The building and use restrictions discussed above involve only indirect restraints on alienation, and thus courts typically conclude that they touch and concern land without evaluating whether enforcement is reasonable under the circumstances. But restrictions on the owner's ability to transfer are direct restraints on alienation. For this reason, decisions evaluating such covenants often do not use the language of "touch and concern" but instead evaluate whether the covenant imposes an unreasonable restraint on alienation of the land. Consider, for example, a covenant in a condominium or cooperative apartment project that requires that the owner of a unit cannot sell the unit without the prior consent of the owners association. On its face, such a covenant can be said to "touch and concern" the land—its enforcement certainly could benefit the community by assuring that owners within the community have the financial resources to pay the assessments needed to maintain the project's common elements and amenities. But the facial rationality of such a covenant is not a sufficient justification to give the association *carte blanche* to reject any proposed transfer. Thus, courts have held that covenants imposing direct restraints on alienation can be enforced, but only where enforcement would be reasonable under the circumstances.[274] Where the covenants prohibit leasing, courts have been more liberal in permitting enforcement, at least where the prohibition is unambiguous.[275]

To sum up, the trend in American courts has been and is to move away from any requirement of physical touching. In this process, courts have been influenced heavily by the views of Dean Harry Bigelow and by Judge Charles E. Clark on the touch and concern requirement. In an article on lease covenants, Bigelow advocated that the covenant's burden side should run if it limited the covenantor's rights, privileges, or powers as a tenant or landowner, and that the covenant's benefit should run if it made the rights, privileges, or powers of the covenantee's leasehold or reversion more valuable

---

[271] Bremmeyer Excavating, Inc. v. McKenna, 44 Wash.App. 267, 721 P.2d 567 (1986).

[272] Caullett v. Stanley Stilwell & Sons, Inc., 67 N.J.Super. 111, 170 A.2d 52 (1961). The decision was questionable because the covenantor still owned the lot and thus there was no need for the court to consider whether the covenant would run with the land.

[273] Garland v. Rosenshein, 420 Mass. 319, 649 N.E.2d 756 (1995). The covenant in *Garland* did not generally restrict development of the burdened parcel or benefit another parcel owned by the covenantee; it merely gave the covenantee a "veto" of any development of the parcel in conjunction with the neighboring parcel—owned at the time by a third party—without the covenantee's consent. The court held that the covenant did not touch and concern as the benefit of the covenant was purely personal to the covenantee.

[274] E.g., Laguna Royale Owners Ass'n v. Darger, 119 Cal.App.3d 679, 174 Cal.Rptr. 136 (1981) (association can withhold approval only for reasons rationally related to the protection, preservation, and proper operation of the property; rejection of creditworthy transferees whose single-family residential use would be consistent with other owners was unreasonable); Iglehart v. Phillips, 383 So.2d 610 (Fla.1980) (covenant creating option or first refusal right establishing price based on market value was reasonable, but option based on fixed-price unreasonable).

[275] E.g., Seagate Condo. Ass'n, Inc. v. Duffy, 330 So.2d 484 (Fla.App.1976).

or relieved all or part of the covenantee's duties.[276] Clark, endorsing the Bigelow test, restated it as follows:

> If the promisor's legal relations in respect to the land in question are lessened—his legal interest as owner rendered less valuable by the promise—the burden of the covenant touches or concerns that land; if the promisee's legal relations in respect to that land are increased—his legal interest as owner rendered more valuable by the promise—the benefit of the covenant touches or concerns that land.[277]

Observe two things about this formulation: (1) it relates benefit and burden to the estates instead of to physical land, and (2) it measures benefit and burden by economic impact. If the Bigelow-Clark test is vague,[278] it has still influenced the way courts have applied the touch and concern concept.

It should also be obvious that to a significant extent, courts have used (and continue to use) the "touch and concern" concept as a context-specific application of the general policy against unreasonable restraints on alienation of land. This is particularly clear when one considers the cases involving covenants that create benefits in gross; the "if the benefit is in gross, the burden won't run" rule operates as a particularized—if possibly overbroad—application of this principle. If the benefit of the covenant was in gross, the burden of the covenant would not bind successors even if the covenant's actual impact on the alienability of land was *de minimis*.[279] As Professors Cribbet and Johnson have explained, courts may have found this approach appealing because "it spared [them] the difficult task of evaluating the worth of an infinite variety of benefits and interests that imaginative drafters might seek to advance through covenants burdening land."[280]

Despite touch and concern's long heritage, Section 3.2 of the Restatement of Servitudes purports to abolish the concept.[281] In its place, the Restatement provides that a recorded servitude is valid unless it "violates public policy," which it does if it (1) is arbitrary, spiteful, or capricious, (2) unreasonably burdens fundamental constitutional rights, (3) imposes an unreasonable restraint on alienation,[282] (4) imposes an unreasonable restraint on trade or competition, or (5) is unconscionable.[283] Influences for this approach included California's Davis-Stirling Act, which provides that recorded

---

[276] Bigelow, The Content of Covenants in Leases, 12 Mich.L.Rev. 639, 645 (1914).

[277] C. Clark, Real Covenants and Other Interests Which "Run With Land" 97 (2d ed.1947).

[278] The *Neponsit* decision, which famously embraced the Bigelow-Clark formulation, explicitly acknowledged its elusive quality, noting that "whether a particular covenant is sufficiently connected with the use of land to run with the land, must be in many cases a question of degree." *Neponsit*, 278 N.Y. at 258, 15 N.E.2d at 796.

[279] Bremmeyer Excavating, Inc. v. McKenna, 44 Wash.App. 267, 721 P.2d 567 (1986), provides an excellent example; the covenant in that case had only a five-year duration, so it could have had no practical long-term impact on the parcel's alienability. Nevertheless, the court held that the covenant did not touch and concern absent a benefited parcel of land

[280] Cribbet & Johnson, Principles of the Law of Property 384 (3d ed.1989).

[281] Restatement (Third) of Property-Servitudes § 3.2 (2000) ("Neither the burden nor the benefit of a covenant is required to touch or concern land in order for the covenant to be valid as a servitude.").

[282] Consistent with prior case law, the Restatement distinguishes between covenants imposing a direct restraint on alienation and those imposing merely indirect restraints. The former covenants are valid if reasonable under the circumstances, i.e., if the utility of enforcing the covenant outweighs the "injurious consequences" of enforcement. Restatement (Third) of Property-Servitudes § 3.4 (2000). The latter covenants are valid if facially reasonable, i.e., they are invalid only if they lack a rational justification. Id. § 3.5.

[283] Restatement (Third) of Property-Servitudes § 3.1 (2000).

use restrictions for a common interest development are "enforceable equitable servitudes, unless unreasonable,"[284] and the decision of the New Jersey Supreme Court in Davidson Bros. v. D. Katz & Sons, Inc.,[285] where the court stated:

> The time has come to cut the Gordian knot that binds this state's jurisprudence regarding covenants running with the land. Rigid adherence to the 'touch and concern' test as a means of determining the enforceability of a restrictive covenant is not warranted. *Reasonableness*, not esoteric concepts of property law, should be the guiding inquiry into the validity of covenants at law."[286]

The comments to the Restatement justify this choice, suggesting that "[a]lthough courts still use the rhetoric of touch or concern, they increasingly determine the validity of servitudes on the basis of the rules stated in this [Restatement]."[287]

The Restatement's rejection of "touch and concern" has provoked some criticism,[288] for it is only that a covenant somehow concerns an interest in land that justifies our enforcing it against the covenantor's successor. But further reading of the integrated sections of the Restatement shows that it retains, if in different language, a requirement that appears at least as restrictive as the Bigelow-Clark test. Section 5.2 would have only "appurtenant benefits and burdens" run to successors."[289] In turn, section 1.5 defines "appurtenant" to mean "that the rights or obligations of a servitude are tied to ownership or occupancy of a particular unit or parcel of land," and further provides that "appurtenant" burdens and benefits are those that affect persons in their capacities as owners or occupiers of the unit or parcel.[290] Finally, section 4.5 further ties "appurtenant" benefits and burdens to interests in land by effectively limiting them to ones that will benefit or burden successors more than they will continue to benefit or burden the original parties after the latter have transferred their interests.[291] Courts firmly wedded to touch and concern are likely to reach the same results under the Restatement of Servitudes, despite its ostensible rejection of the concept.[292]

---

[284] Cal. Civ. Code § 5975(a) (2014) (formerly Cal. Civ. Code § 1354(a)).

[285] 579 A.2d 288 (1990). At the time of the decision, the Restatement was in preparation but had not been approved, so the court's references to the Restatement are to tentative discussion drafts of the Restatement.

[286] *Davidson Bros.*, 579 A.2d at 295 (emphasis added).

[287] Restatement (Third) of Property-Servitudes § 3.2, Comment b (2000).

[288] E.g., Tarlock, Touch and Concern Is Dead, Long Live the Doctrine, 77 Neb.L.Rev. 804 (1998) (criticizing the Restatement "for jettisoning a vague, but useful, doctrine in favor of more unworkable and redundant invalidation standards"). For other discussions of the potential efficiency value associated with the touch and concern doctrine, see Stake, Toward an Economic Understanding of Touch and Concern, 1988 Duke L.J. 925; Sterk, Freedom from Freedom of Contract: The Enduring Value of Servitude Restrictions, 70 Iowa L. Rev. 615 (1985); Reichman, Toward a Unified Concept of Servitudes, 55 S. Cal. L. Rev. 1177 (1982).

[289] Restatement (Third) of Property-Servitudes § 5.2 (2000).

[290] Restatement (Third) of Property-Servitudes § 1.5(1) (2000).

[291] Restatement (Third) of Property-Servitudes § 4.5 (2000).

[292] See Singer, The Rule of Reason in Property Law, 46 U.C. Davis L. Rev. 1369, 1416 (2013) (arguing that "the Restatement abolishes the touch and concern requirement only to reintroduce it through the backdoor"); Winokur, Ancient Strands Rewoven, or Fashioned Out of Whole Cloth?: First Impressions of the Emerging Restatement of Servitudes, 27 Conn.L.Rev. 131 (1994) ("contrasts between the old touch and concern rule and the new Restatement's replacement sections fade a bit upon closer examination"); Allen, Comment, A Touchy Subject: Has the Restatement Replaced the Touch and Concern Doctrine with an Equally Troublesome Test?, 65 Bay.L.Rev. 1034 (2013) ("[T]he Restatement makes no substantive impact on the law regarding the validity of servitudes because it replaces the vague touch and concern with an equally vague test for the courts

§ 8.17 INTENT TO BIND SUCCESSORS TO REAL COVENANTS

The main issue in *Spencer's Case*[293] was whether a covenantor's successors could be bound by the covenant unless the covenanting parties agreed that the covenant should bind "assigns," *using that precise word.* The court held that the word "assigns" had to be used if the covenant related to a thing not in existence, stating in dictum that the word was unnecessary if the covenant concerned a thing already existing. This distinction does not exist in American decisions, where courts have not required that a covenant use the express word "assigns."[294] Instead, American courts look for the covenanting parties' "intent" that the covenant shall run.[295] Intent is found from all the circumstances surrounding the covenant, including its language and intended purpose.[296] For example, one court held an agreement to "permanently maintain" a tile drain on a parcel reflected an intent to bind both the covenantor and later grantees of the parcel.[297] Obviously, the use of the word "assigns" is highly persuasive of an intent to bind successors.[298] The thorough drafter will use language to the effect that "this covenant is intended to be a running covenant, burdening and benefiting the parties' heirs, successors and assigns."

Few recent decisions contain much discussion of the intent element; rather, the courts tend to conclude that it is or is not present from the nature of the covenant. If a covenant is of a "personal" kind, such as one owner's promise to pay a neighbor for something the neighbor has already done, courts are likely to say the parties did not

---

to employ. Thus, even if Texas courts began adopting the approach of the Restatement, the detrimental remnants of the touch and concern doctrine will remain.").

The Restatement also purports to reject the "if the benefit is in gross, the burden won't run" rule, and to permit the running of the burden in that circumstance where enforcement would not create an unreasonable restraint on alienation. Massachusetts has refused to adopt this approach, e.g., Garland v. Rosenshein, 420 Mass. 319, 649 N.E.2d 756 (1995). The New York Court of Appeals has held that the city can enforce covenants restricting the use of land and designed to preserve its use as affordable housing against successors of the burdened parcel. 328 Owners Corp. v. 330 W. 86 Oaks Corp., 8 N.Y.3d 372, 865 N.E.2d 1228 (2007). See also Alfaro v. Community Hous. Improvement Sys. & Planning Ass'n, Inc., 171 Cal.App.4th 1356, 124 Cal.Rptr.3d 271 (2009). While the result in *328 Owners Corp.* would be impossible under the "if the benefit is in the gross, the burden won't run" rule, it is clearly the right result; a city should have the ability to enforce contractual restrictions designed to protect the investment the city has made in affordable housing even if the city does not own a parcel benefited by the covenant. But where a covenant provides an in gross benefit to a private party, such as in the case of the private transfer fee covenant discussed earlier in this section, the case for tying the burden of that covenant to ownership of land becomes more tenuous.

[293] 5 Co. 16a, 77 Eng.Rep. 72 (Q.B.1583).

[294] E.g., Wykeham Rise, LLC v. Federer, 305 Conn. 448, 52 A.3d 702 (2012) (presence or absence of express words of succession such as "heirs" or "assigns" offers evidence of parties' intent, but that evidence is not conclusive; intent can be found from circumstantial evidence); Montfort v. Trek Resources, Inc., 198 S.W.3d 344 (Tex.App.2006) (deed covenant to furnish water was intended to run with land despite fact that deed did not contain specific language indicating covenant would run to "successors and assigns" of the grantee). But see Charping v. J.P. Scurry & Co., Inc., 296 S.C. 312, 372 S.E.2d 120 (App.1988) (court refused to enforce covenant where deed lacked express statement of intent to run).

[295] Masury v. Southworth, 9 Ohio St. 340 (1859); C. Clark, Real Covenants and Other Interests Which "Run With Land" 95–96 (2d ed.1947); Williams, Restrictions on the Use of Land: Covenants Running with the Land at Law, 27 Tex.L.Rev. 419, 423–24 (1949); Restatement (Third) of Property-Servitudes § 2.2 (2000) ("The intent to create a servitude may be express or implied. No particular form of expression is required."). England has expressly abolished the rule in *Spencer's Case* about the word "assigns," first by decision and then by statute. See Law of Property Act, 1925, 15 & 16 Geo. 5, c. 20, § 79 (1925).

[296] PCS Phosphate Co. v. Norfolk Southern Corp., 559 F.3d 212 (4th Cir.2009); Columbia Club, Inc. v. American Fletcher Realty Corp., 720 N.E.2d 411 (Ind.App.1999).

[297] Moseley v. Bishop, 470 N.E.2d 773 (Ind.1984).

[298] E.g., Wykeham Rise, LLC v. Federer, 305 Conn. 448, 52 A.3d 702 (2012); County Comm'rs v. St. Charles Assocs. Ltd. Partn., 366 Md. 426, 784 A.2d 545 (2001); Net Realty Holding Trust v. Franconia Props., Inc., 544 F.Supp. 759 (E.D.Va.1982).

intend it to run.[299] Conversely, when the covenanted performance is not merely personal but is connected with land, courts tend to conclude that the parties intended it to run absent a clear indication to the contrary.[300]

Note that the parties may intend the burden side of a covenant to run but not the benefit side, or vice versa. A common example occurs when the covenantor makes a promise that clearly burdens one parcel, e.g., a building restriction, but the covenantee does not own other land or owns only land situated so far away that it cannot benefit from enforcement of the restriction. In this situation, a court might simply conclude that the covenant's benefit does not touch and concern—and therefore does not run with—any benefited parcel. Another analysis leading to the same result is that the parties would not, in the absence of express words to the contrary, intend for the benefit to run.

§ 8.18 VERTICAL PRIVITY WITH REAL COVENANTS (A BIRD ON A WAGON)

Real covenants run with *estates* in land. The burden passes with a transfer of the estate the covenantor held in the burdened land; the benefit passes with a transfer of the estate that the covenantee held in the benefited land, or at least some lesser estate carved out of that estate. It is therefore more precise to say that the respective *estates* are benefited and burdened.[301] As the quaint phrase puts it, real covenants run along with estates as a bird rides on a wagon.[302]

The obvious implication of this principle is that one can enforce the burden of a real covenant against a remote party only when that party has succeeded to the covenantor's estate in the burdened land. Such a party stands in privity of estate—to be precise, vertical privity—with the covenantor.[303] Thus, for example, a landlord may enforce a covenant to pay rent against the tenant's assignee, because the landlord and the assignee stand in vertical privity; by contrast, a landlord may not enforce a covenant to pay rent against the tenant's sublessee—who does not succeed to the tenant's entire estate—unless the sublessee expressly assumes that obligation.[304] Likewise, a grocery tenant could not recover damages against another tenant for violating an exclusive clause in

---

[299] Gibson v. Holden, 115 Ill. 199, 3 N.E. 282 (1885); Suttle v. Bailey, 68 N.M. 283, 361 P.2d 325 (1961); Sebald v. Mulholland, 155 N.Y. 455, 50 N.E. 260 (1898); Meado-Lawn Homes v. Westchester Lighting Co., 171 Misc. 669, 13 N.Y.S.2d 709 (1939), aff'd, 259 A.D. 810, 20 N.Y.S.2d 396 (1940), aff'd, 284 N.Y. 667, 30 N.E.2d 608 (1940); Wal-Mart Stores, Inc. v. Ingles Markets, Inc., 158 N.C.App. 414, 581 S.E.2d 111 (2003) (radius restriction on landlord's future leasing activity was personal to landlord and did not run to bind landlord's transferee with respect to other parcels that it owned within the radius).

[300] See Keogh v. Peck, 316 Ill. 318, 147 N.E. 266 (1925); King v. Wight, 155 Mass. 444, 29 N.E. 644 (1892); Musgrave v. Brookhaven Lake Prop. Owners Ass'n, 990 S.W.2d 386 (Tex.App.1999). But see Charping v. J.P. Scurry & Co., Inc., 296 S.C. 312, 372 S.E.2d 120 (App.1988) (court apparently required express statement of intent to run).

[301] Amco Trust, Inc. v. Naylor, 159 Tex. 146, 317 S.W.2d 47 (1958); C. Clark, Real Covenants and Other Interests Which "Run With Land" 93–94 (2d ed.1947); Bordwell, The Running of Covenants—No Anomaly, 36 Iowa L.Rev. 1, 3 (1950).

[302] The Powell treatise used the phrase "bird on a wagon," but did not attribute the source. 5 R. Powell, Real Property ¶ 670 (1990).

[303] Restatement of Property § 535 (1944).

[304] E.g., Abernathy v. Adous, 85 Ark.App. 242, 149 S.W.3d 884 (2004); Fields v. Conforti, 868 N.E.2d 507 (Ind.App.2007); Riverbend Invs. v. Progressive Surface Preparation, L.L.C., 255 Mich.App. 327, 660 N.W.2d 373 (2003); Southcross Commerce Ctr., LLP v. Tupy Props., LLC, 766 N.W.2d 704 (Minn.App.2009).

the grocery tenant's lease, because vertical privity was lacking because the other tenant held only a lease and did not succeed to the landlord's entire estate.[305]

The first Restatement of Property and traditional case authority relaxed the rule for the running of a covenant benefit, however. A successor grantee can enforce a benefit if that grantee succeeds to "some interest" of the promisee in the affected land, i.e., either the promisee's entire estate or a lesser estate carved out of that estate.[306] Thus, for example, a tenant of the original promisee-landlord may enforce against the promisor a covenant against business operations on the promisor's land, even though the tenant did not succeed to the landlord's entire estate.[307] By contrast, even under this relaxed approach, the benefit did not run to a person holding paramount title to the promisee or holding possession adversely to the promisee.[308] Perhaps not surprisingly, most courts have allowed a homeowners association to enforce subdivision restrictive covenants on behalf of a landowner who succeeded to the benefited estate—even though the association technically did not own any legal interest in that estate—on the theory that if the declaration designates the association as having the power to enforce the covenant, the association acts as agent for the benefited landowners.[309]

The benefited and burdened estates can be in the same land as well as in separate parcels. The most common example of the former arrangement occurs when the covenant is between landlord and tenant. Running covenants in a lease usually run with the leasehold and the reversion in the demised parcel, though it is possible to have either side of the covenant relate to an estate in other land.[310]

In truth, the vertical privity requirement is less than ideal as a constraint on the running of covenants. For example, suppose that all lots in a covenant-restricted subdivision are subject to a covenant that requires each lot owner to place their trash in uniform pet-proof containers (and authorizes fines for violations). Gotberg owns a home in the subdivision which she leases for one year to a tenant, Dean. Dean places his trash on the street in paper bags in violation of the covenant. If the law requires vertical privity for the burden to run, the owners association could not collect a fine from Dean for violating the covenant, because Dean did not succeed to Gotberg's entire estate. But this result makes little sense—as the possessor of the lot, Dean is in the best position to

---

[305] Winn-Dixie Stores, Inc. v. Dolgencorp, LLC, 746 F.3d 1008 (11th Cir.2014) (Mississippi courts would require strict vertical privity to enforce the burden of a real covenant).

[306] Restatement of Property § 547 (1944); Alexander's Dept. Stores of N.J., Inc. v. Arnold Constable Corp., 105 N.J.Super. 14, 250 A.2d 792 (1969); 2 Am. Law of Prop. § 9.20 (1952). The statement in the text assumes that the covenant meets the other requirements for running, i.e., that the parties intended the covenant to run and that the covenant touches and concerns land.

[307] Restatement of Property § 547 Comment c, Illus. 1 (1944).

[308] Restatement of Property § 547 Comment c, Illus. 2 & 3 (1944).

[309] Conestoga Pines Homeowners' Ass'n v. Black, 689 P.2d 1176 (Colo.App.1984); Merrionette Manor Homes Improvement Ass'n v. Heda, 11 Ill.App.2d 186, 136 N.E.2d 556 (1956); Conlin v. Upton, 313 Mich.App. 243, 881 N.W.2d 511 (2015); Neponsit Prop. Owners' Ass'n v. Emigrant Indus. Sav. Bank, 278 N.Y. 248, 15 N.E.2d 793 (1938); SPUR at Williams Brice Owners Ass'n, Inc. v. Lalla, 415 S.C. 72, 781 S.E.2d 115 (App.2015); Musgrave v. Brookhaven Lake Prop. Owners Ass'n, 990 S.W.2d 386 (Tex.App.1999). But see Palm Point Owners' Ass'n v. Pisarski, 626 So.2d 195 (Fla.1993) (refusing to recognize association's standing); Nieto v. Mobile Gardens Ass'n of Englewood, Inc., 130 So.3d 236 (Fla.App.2013) (association lacks standing to enforce covenants unless it is an assignee of developer's right or is the direct successor of developer's interest).

[310] For example, if a shopping center landlord covenanted that the tenant would have an exclusive right to operate a certain type of business in the center, the benefit would attach to the tenant's leasehold estate, while the burden would attach to the landlord's other parcels in the center.

perform the obligation of the covenant, and his failure to do so poses the precise harms the covenant sought to avoid.

The Restatement of Servitudes has rejected the vertical privity requirement, stating that "[l]ack of privity . . . between the originally burdened party and the person against whom enforcement is sought does not prevent enforcement by a remedy traditionally classified as a legal remedy."[311] In its place, the Restatement provides a general rule that appurtenant burdens and benefits run automatically with the estates to which they are appurtenant,[312] and to "all subsequent owners and possessors of the benefited and burdened property, including a lessee, life tenant, adverse possessor, and person who acquired title through a lien-foreclosure proceeding."[313] This general rule, however, is subject to the following qualifications:

- the burden of a covenant does not run to a person holding paramount title to that of the promisor;[314]

- the burden of an *affirmative* covenant runs to the lessee only if "it can be more reasonably performed by a person in possession than by the holder of a reversion in the burdened property;"[315]

- the benefit of an affirmative covenant runs to a lessee only if (a) the covenant is one to repair, maintain, or render services to the property; or (b) the lessee can enjoy the benefit without diminishing its value to the lessor and without materially increasing the burden on the person obligated to perform the covenant;[316]

- a life tenant's liability for performance of an affirmative covenant is limited to the value of the life estate;[317] and

- the benefit of an affirmative covenant runs to an adverse possessor (even one who has not yet acquired title) only if (a) the covenant is one to repair, maintain, or render services to the property; or (b) the possessor can enjoy the benefit without diminishing its value to the owner and without materially increasing the burden on the person obligated to perform the covenant.[318]

---

[311] Restatement (Third) of Property-Servitudes § 8.2 (2000).

[312] Restatement (Third) of Property-Servitudes § 5.1 (2000).

[313] Restatement (Third) of Property-Servitudes § 5.2 (2000).

[314] Restatement (Third) of Property-Servitudes § 5.2(1) (2000).

[315] Restatement (Third) of Property-Servitudes § 5.3(2), (3) (2000). Under this rule, for example, a covenant to pay a homeowners association assessment on a lot would not run with the lot to bind a tenant who leased that lot, as the tenant and the landlord are equally well-suited to pay the assessment. Id. Comment d, Illus. 5. By contrast, a covenant that obligated each lot owner to recycle using special containers would run with the lot to bind a tenant who leased that lot; as the party in possession, only the tenant can reasonably perform the covenant. Id. Comment d, Illus. 7.

[316] Restatement (Third) of Property-Servitudes § 5.3(1), (3) (2000). Under the latter qualification, a tenant could enforce an affirmative covenant by a neighboring landowner to trim trees that would otherwise block a protected view, but could not enforce an affirmative covenant to pay royalties from oil wells located on the property. Id. Comment c, Illustrations 2 & 3.

[317] Restatement (Third) of Property-Servitudes § 5.4 (2000).

[318] Restatement (Third) of Property-Servitudes § 5.5 (2000). Under the latter qualification, an adverse possessor could enforce an affirmative covenant by a neighboring landowner to trim trees that would otherwise block a protected view, but could not enforce an affirmative covenant to pay royalties from oil wells located on the property. Id. Comment b, Illus. 2 & 3.

It remains to be seen whether courts will embrace the Restatement's rejection of the vertical privity requirement. In one notable recent decision, a federal court of appeals acknowledged the Restatement yet nevertheless held that under Mississippi law, the lack of vertical privity prevented a tenant from enforcing a lease exclusive clause against another tenant.[319] Note that the Restatement's scope provision arguably preserves the privity concept within the context of lease covenants, and thus does not appear to have any intended effect on the traditional distinction between assignments and subleases.[320]

§ 8.19 HORIZONTAL PRIVITY WITH REAL COVENANTS

By contrast to vertical privity as discussed in the preceding section, "horizontal privity" refers to a relationship between the original parties to the covenant. Horizontal privity exists when the covenant is made in the context of a transaction in which one of the parties transfers some interest in the affected land to the other. This section will discuss whether the law does or should require horizontal privity for the running of covenants and, if so, under what circumstances horizontal privity exists.

There is some authority for saying that horizontal privity is not required for the *benefit* side of a covenant to run, but is necessary to the running of the *burden* side.[321] Some writers deny that such a distinction does or should exist.[322] The usual justification for the distinction lies in the broad policy against encumbering land titles; a burden is an encumbrance, while a benefit is not. Thus, on this argument, the law should impose tighter restrictions on the running of burdens than of benefits. This argument is unsatisfactory, for it does not explain why the presence or absence of horizontal privity serves to distinguish "useful" burdens that should run from "objectionable" ones that should not. Others have suggested that the horizontal privity requirement insures that a covenant will be contained in a document that is clearly recordable and that will thereby give notice of the potential burden to successors.[323] Despite somewhat shaky underpinnings in either theory or authority for treating horizontal privity differently on the burden and benefit sides, we will consider them separately.

When does horizontal privity exist for the burden to run? In American law, the most restrictive form of horizontal privity is commonly called "Massachusetts privity." This

---

[319] Winn-Dixie Stores, Inc. v. Dolgencorp, LLC, 746 F.3d 1008 (11th Cir.2014) (noting Mississippi courts would require strict vertical privity to enforce the burden of a real covenant).

[320] Restatement (Third) of Property-Servitudes § 1.1(2) (2000) (lease covenants are not within scope of Restatement to the extent that "special rules and considerations" apply to them). The comments to Section 1.1 indicate that "the law of lease covenants is covered in the Restatement Second of Property (Landlord and Tenant)," id. Comment e, and that Restatement (though two decades previously) did preserve the privity requirement as applicable to the running of lease covenants. Restatement (Second) of Property-Landlord & Tenant § 16.1 (1977).

[321] Restatement of Property § 548 (1944); City of Reno v. Matley, 79 Nev. 49, 378 P.2d 256 (1963); 3 H. Tiffany, Real Property § 849 (3d ed.1939) (suggesting that "authorities are about equally divided upon the question"); Walsh, Covenants Running with the Land, 21 N.Y.U.L.Q.Rev. 28, 31 (1946); Williams, Restrictions on the Use of Land: Covenants Running with the Land at Law, 27 Tex.L.Rev. 419, 429–30 (1949).

[322] C. Clark, Real Covenants and Other Interests Which "Run With Land" 131 (2d ed.1947); 5 R. Powell, Real Property ¶ 673 (1990).

[323] See Browder, Running Covenants and Public Policy, 77 Mich.L.Rev. 12, 25–26 (1978); Reichman, Toward a Unified Concept of Servitudes, 55 S.Cal.L.Rev. 1177, 1219–21 (1982). This theory also fails to provide a rational justification for a horizontal privity requirement; today, each American jurisdiction has a recording statute under which a purchaser for value would take land free of the burden of an unrecorded covenant of which the purchaser lacked notice.

term refers to Hurd v. Curtis,[324] an 1837 decision which established the rule that a covenant would not run unless it was made in a transaction that left the original covenanting parties holding simultaneous (or "mutual") interests in the same parcel of land. Strictly speaking, this would mean the covenanting parties would create a relationship in which one held a lesser estate carved out of the other's larger estate in the same land, i.e., a tenurial relationship. In modern terms, this generally means a landlord-tenant relationship. However, in Morse v. Aldrich,[325] decided the same year, the Massachusetts court held that the burden of a covenant made to settle a dispute over use of an easement also ran with the land. The doctrine as set forth in these cases still controls in Massachusetts, was adopted in Nevada in Wheeler v. Schad,[326] and has been cited with approval by a few courts in other states.[327]

The next most restrictive approach is that the burden will run only if the covenant was made in connection with the transfer of some interest in land between covenantor and covenantee (other than the covenant itself). This includes both leaseholds and easements, but also conveyances in fee which created "successive" interests in the affected land.[328] The Restatement of Property took the position that this was the American rule on horizontal privity.[329] The third view, Judge Clark's, is that horizontal privity was not necessary for the running of the burden of a real covenant. Several states have adopted this position,[330] which writers on the subject tend to favor.[331]

To compare these positions, consider a scenario in which Henning conveys part of Blueacre to Dean by a deed containing a covenant that neither Dean nor Dean's successors would use the land for other than residential purposes. Under the Massachusetts rule, Henning could not enforce the covenant in an action for damages

---

[324] 36 Mass. (19 Pick.) 459 (1837). The result in *Hurd* was consistent with English law, under which horizontal privity of estate existed only in the context of lease covenants under *Spencer's Case.*

[325] 36 Mass. (19 Pick.) 449 (1837).

[326] 7 Nev. 204 (1871). Nevada courts have limited *Wheeler* to the running of burdens and not the running of benefits. City of Reno v. Matley, 79 Nev. 49, 378 P.2d 256 (1963).

[327] E.g., Moseley v. Bishop, 470 N.E.2d 773 (Ind.App.1984); Flying Diamond Oil Corp. v. Newton Sheep Co., 776 P.2d 618 (Utah 1989).

[328] E.g., Winn-Dixie Stores, Inc. v. Dolgencorp, LLC, 746 F.3d 1008 (11th Cir.2014) (Mississippi law); H.J. Lewis Oyster Co. v. West, 93 Conn. 518, 107 A. 138 (1919); Muldawer v. Stribling, 243 Ga. 673, 256 S.E.2d 357 (1979); Natural Prods. Co. v. Dolese & Shepard Co., 309 Ill. 230, 140 N.E. 840 (1923); Runyon v. Paley, 416 S.E.2d 177 (N.C.1992); BM-Clarence Cardwell, Inc. v. Cocca Dev., Ltd., 65 N.E.3d 829 (Ohio App.2016); Clear Lake Apts., Inc. v. Clear Lake Utilities Co., 537 S.W.2d 48 (Tex.Civ.App.1976), modified on different grounds, 549 S.W.2d 385 (Tex.1977); Sonoma Dev., Inc. v. Miller, 515 S.E.2d 577 (Va.1999); Bremmeyer Excavating, Inc. v. McKenna, 721 P.2d 567 (Wash.App.1986); Newman & Losey, Covenants Running with the Land, and Equitable Servitudes: Two Concepts, or One?, 21 Hastings L.J. 1319, 1328–29 (1970); Sims, The Law of Real Covenants: Exceptions to the Restatement of the Subject by the American Law Institute, 30 Cornell L.Q. 1, 30–33 (1944); Williams, Restrictions on the Use of Land: Covenants Running with the Land at Law, 27 Tex.L.Rev. 419, 440–43 (1949).

[329] Restatement of Property § 534 (1944).

[330] E.g., Sea Watch Stores Ltd. Liability Co. v. Council of Unit Owners of Sea Watch Condo., 115 Md.App. 5, 691 A.2d 750 (1997); Neponsit Prop. Owners' Ass'n v. Emigrant Indus. Sav. Bank, 278 N.Y. 248, 15 N.E.2d 793 (1938); Matter of Parcel of Land Located on Geneva Lake, Town of Linn, Walworth Cty., 165 Wis.2d 235, 477 N.W.2d 333 (App.1991).

[331] Besides Clark, see 3 H. Tiffany, Real Property § 851, at 452 (3d ed.1939); French, Servitudes Reform and the New Restatement of Property: Creation Doctrines and Structural Simplification, 73 Cornell L.Rev. 928 (1988); French, Toward a Modern Law of Servitudes: Reweaving the Ancient Strands, 55 S.Cal.L.Rev. 1261 (1982); Newman & Losey, Covenants Running with the Land, and Equitable Servitudes: Two Concepts, or One?, 21 Hastings L.J. 1319, 1331 (1970); Sims, The Law of Real Covenants: Exceptions to the Restatement of the Subject by the American Law Institute, 30 Cornell L.Q. 1, 30–33 (1944); Walsh, Covenants Running with the Land, 21 N.Y.U.L.Q.Rev. 28, 41–44 (1946).

against a successor to Dean because horizontal privity was lacking (i.e., Henning and Dean had no mutual interest in the burdened parcel). By contrast, Henning could enforce the covenant at law against Dean's successor under the Restatement position (under which horizontal privity existed because Henning and Dean held a successive interest in the burdened parcel) or under the Clark position (under which horizontal privity is unnecessary). By contrast, consider an alternative scenario in which Henning and Dean are owners of neighboring parcels and enter into an agreement that neither would use their respective parcels for other than residential purposes. Here, horizontal privity would be lacking under the Massachusetts and Restatement approaches (Henning and Dean have neither a mutual nor successive interest, but are merely neighbors), but enforcement would be permissible under the Clark position.

Logic and sound policy justify the Clark position. The initial justification for the horizontal privity requirement was the concern that the burden of running covenants could have an undue impact on the alienation of affected land parcels, such that covenants should be allowed to run only if created in very limited contexts. But the presence or absence of horizontal privity does not rationally distinguish useful covenants (ones that should run) from burdensome covenants (ones that should not). In the example above, the enforcement of Dean's covenant would be equally beneficial to ownership of Henning's parcel without regard to how it arose, i.e., whether it arose in the deed by which Henning conveyed part of his land to Dean, or in an agreement between Henning and Dean after they had already become neighbors. Stated differently, the horizontal privity requirement provides no useful policy-based "check" on running covenants that is not already served by the "touch and concern" requirement. In addition, the horizontal privity requirement is a somewhat silly "check" given how easily prudent parties can manufacture horizontal privity. In the above example, if Henning and Dean are already neighbors, they could create horizontal privity by having Dean convey the parcel to Henning and having Henning reconvey the parcel back to Dean by a deed creating the covenant. It serves no point (other than enriching lawyers) to force the parties to jump through such formalistic hoops.[332] Consistent with the Clark position, the Restatement of Servitudes has abandoned the horizontal privity requirement for the running of a covenant.[333]

Horizontal privity and the running of the benefit. As noted previously, there is some authority for the view that even if horizontal privity is required for the running of burdens, it is not required for the running of benefits side. The original Restatement took the position that horizontal privity is not an element for the running of benefits,[334] and here Clark agreed in the sense that he rejected the horizontal privity requirement

---

[332] In this respect, it may be useful to analogize the horizontal privity requirement to training wheels on a bicycle. When a child is learning to ride a bike, a parent concerned about the child's lack of balance may install training wheels on the bike to protect against the harm the child might suffer from falling. But once a child has learned to ride a bike safely, the continued presence of training wheels becomes a hindrance to the child's ability to handle the bike, and possibly even a safety hazard. The horizontal privity requirement may have seemed an appropriate "check" by early judges concerned about the potential impacts of running covenants, but as the law and practice of running covenants evolved—and it became clear that horizontal privity served no purpose not already better served by other legal requirements—courts should have removed the training wheels and done away with the horizontal privity requirement.

[333] Restatement (Third) of Property-Servitudes § 2.4 (2000) ("No privity relationship between the parties is necessary to create a servitude."); id. § 8.2 ("Lack of privity between the parties who created the servitude . . . does not prevent enforcement by a remedy traditionally classified as a legal remedy.").

[334] Restatement of Property § 548 (1944).

entirely.[335] Case authority on the precise issue is slight. Nevada, which had required Massachusetts privity for the running of a burden,[336] has expressly held that no horizontal privity is needed on the benefit side.[337] The policy against encumbrances, which has traditionally made courts disfavor and impose restrictions upon the running of burdens, does not extend to the running of benefits. Further, as noted above, the Restatement of Servitudes entirely rejects the horizontal privity requirement. On balance, it seems justifiable to conclude that horizontal privity is not required for the running of the benefit side of a real covenant.

§ 8.20   NOTICE/VALUE AND THE RUNNING OF REAL COVENANTS

Under the traditional English rule for the running of real covenants, there was no requirement that the successor take the affected estate with notice of the covenant.[338] Under American law, however, real estate recording statutes exist in all jurisdictions and generally provide that an unrecorded interest in land is invalid against certain good faith purchasers for value without notice.[339] If an instrument creating a covenant is not recorded, a potential purchaser of the land otherwise burdened by that covenant may not discover the covenant in a title search—and thus may complete a purchase wrongly believing the land is free of the encumbrance that the unknown covenant would otherwise create. For this reason, a subsequent purchaser of the land for value will take free of an unrecorded covenant of which the purchaser lacked notice.[340] This principle has the practical effect of making notice an additional element for the running of a real covenant. We will further explore the meaning and implications of the notice requirement in Section 8.31.

§ 8.21   SEPARATE RUNNING OF BENEFIT AND BURDEN

We have suggested that one should consider separately the running of the benefit and the burden of a covenant. However, almost any case on real (or equitable) covenants will find the court speaking of the running of "the covenant." Usually nothing turns on this and no harm is done, for the question before the court will be whether a successor is liable for the burden or is entitled to assert the benefit. Occasionally both parties to a dispute are successors, so that there are really questions of the running of both sides.

Occasionally it matters to be precise in thinking separately of benefit and burden. The Nevada Supreme Court did so when, as noted above, it distinguished the benefit from the burden side as to the relevance of horizontal privity.[341] Another example of when the distinction matters occurs when the burden side of a covenant touches and concerns land, but the benefit side does not—i.e., when the benefit of the covenant is "in

---

[335] C. Clark, Real Covenants and Other Interests Which "Run With Land" 94 (2d ed.1947).

[336] Wheeler v. Schad, 7 Nev. 204 (1871).

[337] City of Reno v. Matley, 79 Nev. 49, 378 P.2d 256 (1963).

[338] Effectively, given how English law defined horizontal privity, real covenants could run under English law only in the context of lease covenants. In the typical assignment of a tenant's leasehold estate, of course, the assignee knows of the existence of the lease and its terms, so a specific "notice" requirement in that context may have seemed unnecessary.

[339] See generally §§ 11.9 to 11.11 infra.

[340] Restatement of Property § 539, Comments l and m (1944); Restatement (Third) of Property-Servitudes § 7.14 (2000) (benefit of an unrecorded servitude is subject to extinguishment under the recording statute).

[341] Wheeler v. Schad, 7 Nev. 204 (1871).

gross." As noted previously, many courts have held that when the benefit of a covenant does not touch and concern land, the burden of that covenant will not run with the land.[342] In the strictest sense this does not deny the existence of separate sides—it explicitly recognizes them—but it does tie them together.[343]

§ 8.22 INTERPRETATION OF REAL COVENANTS

Because running covenants impose restrictions on the use and enjoyment of the burdened land, they are "clouds" on title to that land. In theory they make title less marketable, in tension with the law's long-established policy in favor of land's alienability. Hence, traditionally courts took the view that covenants burdening title, if ambiguous in their language, will be interpreted narrowly in favor of "free use" (i.e., in favor of the owner of the burdened parcel).[344] Courts still sometimes assert and apply this traditional rule to give a narrow application to the language creating a covenant and conclude that no violation of the covenant has occurred. For example, courts have cited this narrow construction principle to conclude that:

- A covenant prohibiting "business or trade" does not prevent an owner's children from giving swimming lessons (even for pay) in the family pool;[345]

- A covenant prohibiting "livestock" does not prevent an owner from keeping a Vietnamese potbellied pig as a pet;[346]

- A covenant requiring "residential use" did not prevent an owner from keeping adult cougars and mountain lions as pets;[347]

- A covenant prohibiting a "trailer" or a "structure of a temporary character" did not prevent an owner from occupying a mobile home with its wheels and axles removed;[348]

- A covenant prohibiting any "dwelling . . . which exceeds two stories in height" was so indefinite as to be void, and thus did not prohibit a three-story residence;[349]

---

[342] E.g., Garland v. Rosenshein, 649 N.E.2d 756 (Mass.1995); Caullett v. Stanley Stilwell & Sons, Inc., 67 N.J.Super. 111, 170 A.2d 52 (1961); Bremmeyer Excavating, Inc. v. McKenna, 721 P.2d 567 (Wash.App.1986).

[343] For an argument that courts should not mechanically refuse to let the burden side run when the benefit is in gross, see Roberts, Promises Respecting Land Use—Can Benefits Be Held in Gross?, 51 Mo.L.Rev. 933 (1986). The Restatement (Third) of Property-Servitudes takes the view that a servitude burden may run (assuming the servitude is not contrary to public policy) even if the benefit of the servitude is in gross. See supra note 292.

[344] In some cases, the language of the covenant may be so ambiguous that the court treats it as being altogether void for vagueness. See, e.g., Hiner v. Hoffman, 90 Haw. 188, 977 P.2d 878 (1999) (covenant prohibiting dwellings more than "two stories in height" held indefinite and void); Fong v. Hashimoto, 92 Haw. 568, 994 P.2d 500 (2000) (same).

[345] Gabriel v. Cazier, 130 Idaho 171, 938 P.2d 1209 (1997).

[346] Gebauer v. Lake Forest Prop. Owners Ass'n, Inc., 723 So.2d 1288 (Ala.App.1998) ("doubts and ambiguities [as to the meaning of livestock] must be resolved against the party seeking enforcement"). See also, e.g., Eldorado Community Improvement Ass'n, Inc. v. Billings, 374 P.3d 737 (N.M.App.2016) (construing covenant allowing "recognized household pets" to permit hens).

[347] Turudic v. Stephens, 176 Or.App. 175, 31 P.3d 465 (2001).

[348] Holtmeyer v. Roseman, 731 S.W.2d 484 (Mo.App.1987).

[349] Hiner v. Hoffman, 90 Haw. 188, 977 P.2d 878 (1999). See also Fong v. Hashimoto, 92 Haw. 568, 994 P.2d 500 (2000) (applying same reasoning). The unique facts of *Hiner* may explain the result; the parcels in question were on a hillside, and the uphill owner—looking to maximize its ocean view—asserted that the downhill owner's three-level home would violate the covenant even though only two of the levels would be

- A covenant limiting the use of a lot to a "single family residence" was not violated by occupancy by three unrelated college students;[350]

- A covenant prohibiting the owner from building "any building intended for any purpose except a one family private residence" did not prevent the owner from building a parking lot to serve an adjacent commercial parcel not subject to the covenant;[351] and

- A covenant requiring use of subdivision lots for "residential purposes" did not preclude an owner that had constructed a home on one of three lots from building a lighted little league practice field on the other two lots.[352]

The foregoing are examples of the wide range of circumstances in which courts narrowly construed a covenant—ostensibly vindicating the expectations of the owner of the burdened parcel as to its permissible uses. But the traditional approach is dubiously one-sided—covenants are bilateral, after all, and reflexively construing them in favor of the owner of the burdened parcel fails to credit appropriately the expectations of the owners of the benefited parcels. While subdivision covenants do burden legal title, modern thinking focuses on their effect on use, enjoyment, and value of land in the marketplace. Many home buyers regard a tight system of restrictive covenants as desirable; they are willing to pay more for homes protected by such covenants than for homes not so protected—and may find that expected value destroyed if a court adopts a crabbed interpretation of the covenant that permits an unexpected, undesired, and harmful use.

Recognizing the reciprocal benefits of covenant enforcement in the common interest community context, many courts today are inclined to construe covenants expansively to carry out their intended purpose. Consistent with this recognition, the Restatement of Servitudes has rejected the traditional narrow rule of construction in favor of an explicitly intent-based approach. In Section 4.1, the Restatement provides that "[a] servitude should be interpreted to give effect to the intention of the parties ascertained from the language used in the instrument, or the circumstances surrounding creation of the servitude, and to carry out the purpose for which it was created."[353] Courts in several

---

above ground on the uphill side, with all three being above grade only on the downhill side. Still, the term hardly seems so ambiguous as to be entirely void; the court could have upheld the covenant generally and still concluded that the home satisfied it because it had only two visible stories as viewed from the benefited parcel. Note that courts in other states have concluded that similar restrictions are not ambiguous. E.g., Pool v. Denbeck, 196 Neb. 27, 241 N.W.2d 503 ("two stories"); Dickstein v. Williams, 93 Nev. 605, 571 P.2d 1169 (1977) ("one story from ground level"); King v. Kugler, 197 Cal.App.2d 651, 17 Cal.Rptr. 504 (1981) ("one story in height"). Nevertheless, the lawyering lesson should be clear—if the goal of the covenant is to impose a height restriction for aesthetic or view purposes, the drafter of the covenant should express that restriction in feet rather than "stories."

[350] South Kaywood Community Ass'n v. Long, 208 Md.App. 135, 56 A.3d 365 (2012) (noting that unrelated persons could constitute a "family" if they functioned as "a single housekeeping unit"). By contrast, see Danaher v. Joffe, 184 N.C.App. 642, 646 S.E.2d 783 (2007) (occupancy of home by seven college students, all teammates on college baseball team, violated "single family residential purposes" covenant).

[351] Dierberg v. Wills, 700 S.W.2d 461 (Mo.App.1985). Applying a narrow construction, the court held that the covenant only restricted the use to which a building could be put, and thus did "not restrict the use of the land if no building has been erected thereon." The Dierberg case nicely illustrates the absurdity of the strict-construction approach; clearly, while the covenant was inartfully drafted, its intent to restrict the lot to residential use is clear enough.

[352] Bagko Dev. Co. v. Damitz, 640 N.E.2d 67 (Ind.App.1994).

[353] Restatement (Third) of Property-Servitudes § 4.1(1) (2000).

states have explicitly adopted Section 4.1[354] and many others have adopted a similar intent-based approach, either prior to the Restatement's promulgation in 2000 or without explicit citation or adoption of Section 4.1.[355] Under this approach, courts have concluded that, for example:

- A covenant requiring use of a home for "residential purposes" precluded the developer from selling interval ownership ("time-share") interests in an unsold home in a subdivision;[356]

- A covenant requiring that "only private homes . . . are to be built" precluded the construction of a condominium or other multi-family dwelling;[357]

- A covenant prohibiting buildings other than one single-family dwelling, a two-car garage, and other buildings "incidental" to residential use precluded the lot owner from building a 30-foot tall "shop" building in which he parked a church bus and a "party barge" that he was rebuilding;[358]

- A covenant prohibiting "any commercial or business activity" within a residential subdivision precluded a lot owner with a trucking business from parking his trucks on the lot when not in use and using the garage to service the trucks;[359] and

- A covenant prohibiting "trade or business of any kind" did not preclude a homeowner who also operated a food-related products sales business from listing the home as the business's headquarters and using the home for communication and administrative tasks associated with his work, where

[354] E.g., Powell v. Washburn, 211 Ariz. 553, 125 P.3d 373 (2006); Lynch v. Town of Pelham, 167 N.H. 14, 104 A.3d 1047 (2014); Agua Fria Save the Open Space Ass'n v. Rowe, 149 N.M. 812, 255 P.3d 390 (2011).

[355] E.g., Lookout Mtn. Paradise Hills Homeowners' Ass'n v. Viewpoint Assocs., 867 P.2d 70 (Colo.App.1993); Highbaugh Enters. Inc. v. Deatrick & James Constr. Co., 554 S.W.2d 878, 879 (Ky.App.1977) (restrictive covenants are "to be regarded more as a protection to the property owner and the public rather than as a restriction on the use of property . . . the old-time doctrine of strict construction no longer applies"); Markey v. Wolf, 92 Md.App. 137, 607 A.2d 82 (1992) (tracing evolution of rule from strict construction to reasonable construction to give effect to purpose of restrictive covenants); Griffin v. Tall Timbers Dev., Inc., 681 So.2d 546, 551 (Miss.1996) ("In construing covenants imposing restrictions and burdens on use of land, the language used will be read in its ordinary sense, and the restriction and burden will be construed in light of the circumstances surrounding its formulation, with the idea of carrying out its object, purpose and intent, and the restrictions and burdens should be fairly and reasonably interpreted according to their apparent purpose."); Joslin v. Pine River Dev. Corp., 116 N.H. 814, 367 A.2d 599, 601 (1976) ("The former prejudice against restrictive covenants which led courts to strictly construe them is yielding to a gradual recognition that they are valuable land use planning devices."); Riss v. Angel, 131 Wash.2d 612, 934 P.2d 669 (1997); Wallace v. St. Clair, 147 W.Va. 377, 127 S.E.2d 742, 751 (1962) (noting that traditional justifications for rule of strict construction "do not obtain with full force" in context of modern reciprocal subdivision covenants).

[356] O'Connor v. Resort Custom Builders, Inc., 459 Mich. 335, 591 N.W.2d 216 (1999). In this decision, the court reversed a decision of the court of appeals that adopted a strict construction and concluded that the covenant was not violated because the time-share purchasers would be using the home for residential purposes.

[357] Stolba v. Vesci, 909 S.W.2d 706 (Mo.App.1995) (upholding trial court's conclusion that "private home" was intended to restrict each lot to a single-family residence). Similarly, courts taking this more liberal interpretational approach have concluded that covenants prohibiting "mobile homes" also preclude manufactured homes (even with wheels and axles removed). E.g., Toavs v. Sayre, 281 Mont. 243, 934 P.2d 165 (1997); Halls v. White, 715 N.W.2d 577 (2006); Albert v. Orwige, 731 S.W.2d 63 (Tenn.App.1987).

[358] Cochran v. Bentley, 369 Ark. 159, 251 S.W.3d 253 (2007).

[359] Smart v. Carpenter, 139 N.M. 524, 134 P.3d 811 (App.2006).

the owner's activities were not discernable to the public at large or to other residents and did not create any increase in traffic.[360]

Another complication for covenant interpretation is the occasional willingness of some courts either to invalidate restrictive covenants on the ground that they violate public policy[361] or to use public policy concerns as a basis to construe the covenant to avoid a violation (perhaps even relying on the traditional "narrow construction" approach to do so). Unless a covenant's enforcement would violate an explicit state or federal statute, courts typically do not second-guess the reasonableness or prudence of that covenant if it satisfies the standard for a running covenant.[362] But policy concerns can (and sometimes do) influence courts in interpreting an ambiguous covenant. Explicitly acknowledging this, the Restatement of Servitudes provides:

> Unless the purpose for which the servitude is created violates public policy, and unless contrary to the intent of the parties, a servitude should be interpreted to avoid violating public policy. Among reasonable interpretations, that which is more consonant with public policy should be preferred.[363]

In recent years, this tension has been most notable in the context of covenants that restrict land to "residential use" or "single-family residential use" but which do not provide detailed definitions of those terms. For example, consider the situation posed in the Michigan dispute in Terrien v. Zwit,[364] where a homeowner attempted to operate a home-based day care; would this violate a "residential use" covenant? On the one hand, where the owner is living in the home, the home's primary use remains residential. Likewise, a child being cared for is using the home as a temporary residence just as if the child was being cared for in the child's own home. Finally, construing such a use as

---

[360] 9394 LLC v. Farris, 10 A.D.3d 708, 782 N.Y.S.2d 281 (2004).

[361] E.g., Greenfield v. Mandalay Shores Community Ass'n, 21 Cal.App.5th 896, 230 Cal.Rptr.3d 827 (2018) (HOA rules prohibiting owners from entering into short term rentals violated state coastal protection act, which required HOA to obtain coastal development permit); McMillan v. Iserman, 120 Mich.App. 785, 327 N.W.2d 559 (1982) (deed restriction prohibiting use of lot for licensed group home for mentally impaired persons was unenforceable on public policy grounds); Davidson Bros., Inc. v. D. Katz & Sons, Inc., 274 N.J.Super. 159, 643 A.2d 642 (1994) (covenant prohibiting grocery store void on ground that it was against public policy favoring groceries in inner-city areas).

[362] Thus, for example, covenants imposing clear prohibitions on signs are generally enforceable, despite their impact on a lot owner's potential freedom of speech, even if a similar restriction imposed by a city or state government would violate the first amendment. E.g., Godley Park Homeowners Ass'n, Inc. v. Bowen, 286 Ga.App. 21, 649 S.E.2d 308 (2007) (upholding covenant prohibiting display of "for sale" sign). Likewise, courts have upheld condominium covenants prohibiting unit owners from keeping personal pets in their units. E.g., Nahrstedt v. Lakeside Village Condo. Ass'n, Inc., 8 Cal.4th 361, 878 P.2d 1275 (1994).

In many states, legislatures have reacted to notorious cases like *Nahrstedt* by enacting statutes explicitly limiting the ability of an owners association to enforce certain restrictions perceived as too intrusive on personal liberties. See, e.g., Ariz.Rev.Stat.Ann. § 33–441(A) (covenant cannot be applied to prohibit the display of a for-sale sign of 18" × 24" or smaller); Cal.Civ.Code § 4715 ("No governing documents shall prohibit the owner of a separate interest within a common interest development from keeping at least one pet within the common interest development, subject to reasonable rules and regulations of the association."); S.C. Code § 27–1–60(B) (restrictive covenant may not preclude display of one portable, removable U.S. flag on the property). Further, the federal Fair Housing Act would prohibit the enforcement of any restrictive covenant that precluded occupancy or use of land based upon race, color, religion, sex, familial status or national origin. 42 U.S.C.A. § 3604(b).

[363] Restatement (Third) of Property-Servitudes § 4.1(2) (2000). See, e.g., Chambers v. Old Stone Hill Rd. Assocs., 1 N.Y.3d 424, 806 N.E.2d 979 (2004) (enforcing covenant limiting development to single-family homes to require removal of cell tower antenna; public policy in favor of allowing residents to preserve residential character of subdivision not outweighed by public policy against limiting the provision of wireless communication services).

[364] 238 Mich.App. 412, 605 N.W.2d 681 (1999), rev'd, 467 Mich. 56, 648 N.W.2d 602 (2002).

residential would help satisfy the strong market demand for home-based day care. On the other hand, a day-care is a business operation typically requiring a license, and with each child being cared for, the operation may present neighboring homeowners with noise, traffic, and safety concerns—the very potential problems the covenant sought to avoid. In *Terrien*, the Michigan Court of Appeals held the operation would not violate the covenant, holding the day care was no more obtrusive than homes occupied by large families and that "the public policy in favor of family day care homes" justified its interpretation.[365] In a 4–3 decision, the Michigan Supreme Court reversed, holding the day care operation was a prohibited commercial activity.[366] The court held that even if the state's public policy was supportive of home day care, nothing in the state's existing statutes explicitly precluded the covenant's enforcement and thus nothing justified a conclusion that the covenant was contrary to public policy.[367] Other states have likewise confronted the issue, with most concluding that the covenant prohibited a day care operation;[368] a few states have reacted by enacting statutes limiting or prohibiting covenant enforcement against home day care operations.[369]

Likewise, many cases have addressed whether group homes for physically or mentally disabled persons violate "residential use" or "single-family residential use" covenants. Some courts have given a broad, liberal application to the covenant to restrict the operation of such group homes, though individual cases turn to some extent upon the precise language of the covenant and the precise nature of the group home.[370] Other courts have construed the covenant narrowly to allow a group homes, concluding that the use comported with "residential" or "single-family residential" use or that the covenant applied to the home's physical configuration and not the nature of its occupants.[371] Still others have concluded that a group home violates the covenant, but

---

[365] *Terrien*, 238 Mich.App. at 419–420, 605 N.W.2d at 685.

[366] *Terrien*, 467 Mich. at 63–65, 648 N.W.2d at 606–607.

[367] *Terrien*, 467 Mich. at 66–73, 648 N.W.2d at 608–611.

[368] Precluding day-care operation: Benjamin Crossing Homeowners' Ass'n, Inc. v. Heide, 961 N.E.2d 35 (Ind.App.2012); Southwind Homeowners Ass'n v. Burden, 283 Neb. 522, 810 N.W.2d 714 (2012); Walton v. Carignan, 103 N.C.App. 364, 407 S.E.2d 241 (1991); Hill v. Lindner, 769 N.W.2d 427 (N.D.2009); Martellini v. Little Angels Day Care, Inc., 847 A.2d 838 (R.I.2004); Peckham v. Milroy, 104 Wash.App. 887, 17 P.3d 1256 (2001). Allowing day-care operation: Stewart v. Jackson, 635 N.E.2d 186 (Ind.App.1994) (unlicensed home day care did not violate covenant); Quinones v. Board of Mgrs. of Regalwalk Condo. I, 242 A.D.2d 52, 673 N.Y.S.2d 450 (1998) (enforcement of residential-use-only covenant to prohibit group day care operation was barred by public policy); Khamnei v. Coven, 2007 WL 5313377 (Vt.2007).

[369] Statutes in California and Hawaii prohibit the enforcement of covenants to prohibit home day care. Cal.Health & Safety Code § 1597.40; Haw.Rev.Stat.Ann. § 501–231(a). Maryland's statute establishes a constructional rule that home-based child care is "residential activity," but allows covenants that explicitly prohibit the use of a home as a family child care home. Md.Real Prop. Code § 11B–111.1(c), (d). New Jersey's statute does not prohibit enforcement, but places on the owners association the burden of proof to demonstrate on a case-by-case basis that prohibiting the day care operation in question is "reasonably related to the health, safety, and welfare" of the unit owners. N.J.Stat.Ann. § 40:55D–66.5b.

[370] See, e.g., Shaver v. Hunter, 626 S.W.2d 574 (Tex.App.1981) (construing "family" to include only related persons); Omega Corp. of Chesterfield v. Malloy, 228 Va. 12, 319 S.E.2d 728 (1984) (supervision of residents by governmental employees made building "facility," not single-family home); Mains Farm Homeowners Ass'n v. Worthington, 121 Wash.2d 810, 854 P.2d 1072 (1993) (group home was not "residential purpose"). Cf. Parkwood Ass'n v. Capital Health Care Invs., 133 N.C.App. 158, 514 S.E.2d 542 (1999) (use of home as shelter for delinquent children violated covenant prohibiting "houses of detention").

[371] See Beverly Island Ass'n v. Zinger, 113 Mich.App. 322, 317 N.W.2d 611 (1982) (group home met "residential purposes" as restriction required); Blevins v. Barry-Lawrence Cty. Ass'n for Retarded Citizens, 707 S.W.2d 407 (Mo.1986) (applying both rationales described in text); Knudtson v. Trainor, 216 Neb. 653, 345 N.W.2d 4 (1984) (same); Beres v. Hope Homes, Inc., 6 Ohio App.3d 71, 453 N.E.2d 1119 (1982) (occupants were "single family unit" within meaning of covenant); Jackson v. Williams, 714 P.2d 1017 (Okla.1985) (group home constituted "single-family dwelling"); Gregory v. State, Dept. of Mental Health, Retardation & Hospitals, 495

nevertheless refused to enjoin its operation based on public policy as reflected in a federal or state civil rights statute.[372]

While courts are moving to embrace an intent-based construction approach generally, one context in which courts have clung to the strict construction rule involves short-term rentals. In the wake of the housing crisis of the late 2000s, many homeowners took advantage of internet sites such as Airbnb to offer short-term rentals of their homes (or rooms within their homes), often as a way to help make ends meet. Neighbors—who may not have expected a steady stream of strangers coming and going next door—often object that this conduct is commercial in nature and violates covenants requiring residential use or prohibiting commercial use. The weight of case authority has taken a narrow construction and concluded that such conduct does not violate a "residential use" or "no commercial use" covenant,[373] at least where the covenant does not explicitly prohibit short-term rentals.[374] In this situation, judicial willingness to apply strict construction presumably reflects a conclusion that the neighbors are not using the covenant to regulate use but to restrict the owner's ability to transfer an interest in the land.[375]

One final point regarding covenant interpretation bears mention. In many common interest communities, covenants often establish an "architectural review committee" that must approve all building plans before construction can commence on any lot.[376]

A.2d 997 (R.I.1985) (group home was within definitional scope of "single-family dwelling"); Permian Basin Centers for Mental Health & Mental Retardation v. Alsobrook, 723 S.W.2d 774 (Tex.App.1986) (covenant regulated structures, not use).

[372] See Westwood Homeowners Ass'n v. Tenhoff, 155 Ariz. 229, 745 P.2d 976 (App.1987); Dornbach v. Holley, 854 So.2d 211 (Fla.App.2002) (action to enforce residential purposes covenant against group home impermissibly discriminatory under federal and state fair housing acts); Hill v. Community of Damien of Molokai, 121 N.M. 353, 911 P.2d 861 (1996) (enforcement of single-family residence covenant to prevent siting of group home for disabled individuals violated Fair Housing Act); Hedingham Community Ass'n v. GLH Builders, Inc., 178 N.C.App. 635, 634 S.E.2d 224 (2006) (family care home protected from enforcement of residential purposes covenant under statutory exclusion). See also Crane Neck Ass'n, Inc. v. New York City/ Long Island Cty. Servs. Group, 61 N.Y.2d 154, 460 N.E.2d 1336 (1984) (group home violated covenant, but injunction denied; court exercised equitable discretion to deny injunction).

[373] E.g., Slaby v. Mountain River Estates Residential Ass'n, Inc., 100 So.3d 569 (Ala.App.2012); Vera Lee Angel Revocable Trust v. Jim O'Bryant & Kay O'Bryant Joint Revocable Trust, 537 S.W.3d 254 (Ark.2018); Houston v. Wilson Mesa Ranch Homeowners Ass'n, Inc., 360 P.3d 255 (Colo.App.2015); Santa Monica Beach Prop. Owners Ass'n, Inc. v. Acord, 219 So.3d 111 (Fla.App.2017); Applegate v. Colucci, 908 N.E.2d 1214 (Ind.App.2009); Lowden v. Bosley, 395 Md. 58, 909 A.2d 261 (2006); Mullin v. Silvercreek Condo Owner's Ass'n, Inc., 195 S.W.3d 484 (Mo.App.2006); Estates at Desert Ridge Trails Homeowners' Ass'n v. Vazquez, 300 P.3d 736 (N.M.App.2013); Russell v. Donaldson, 222 N.C.App. 702, 731 S.E.2d 535 (2012); Yogman v. Parrott, 325 Or. 358, 937 P.2d 1019 (1997); Community Servs. Assocs., Inc. v. Wall, 421 S.C. 575, 808 S.E.2d 831 (App.2017); Garrett v. Sympson, 532 S.W.3d 862 (Tex.App.2017); Scott v. Walker, 274 Va. 209, 645 S.E.2d 278 (2007); Wilkinson v. Chiwawa Communities Ass'n, 180 Wash.2d 241, 327 P.3d 614 (2014); Forshee v. Neuschwander, 381 Wis.2d 757, 914 N.W.2d 643 (2018). Contrary decisions: Eager v. Presley, 322 Mich.App. 174, 911 N.W.2d 470 (2017).

[374] New common interest community documents today typically do prohibit owners from leasing their lots or units on a short-term basis, usually prohibiting terms of less than 90 days or 180 days. Courts generally uphold such provisions. See also, e.g., South Ridge Homeowners' Ass'n v. Brown, 226 P.3d 758 (Utah App.2010) (owner's weekly rentals violated covenant prohibiting "nightly rentals" and "timeshares").

[375] In other words, courts seem to be imposing greater scrutiny to the covenants to the extent they are operating as a direct restraint on alienation (a transfer restriction) rather than an indirect restraint (a use restriction). As noted in Section 8.16 supra, courts tend to subject covenants imposing a direct restraint on alienation to more searching scrutiny.

[376] Owners within such a community ignore the approval requirement at their extreme peril. E.g., Heath v. Uraga, 106 Wash.App. 506, 24 P.3d 413 (2001) (owner built home that violated covenant as to roof pitch without obtaining consent of building review committee as covenants required; court upheld order requiring home to be razed!).

Sometimes, these architectural review covenants do not provide explicit standards to guide the decisionmaking of the committee in granting or withholding consent. Courts have generally refused to invalidate the covenants for this reason, instead implying a standard that the committee must act reasonably or in good faith in exercising its judgment.[377] To establish a violation, the disappointed proponent must establish that the association withheld its consent arbitrarily and capriciously[378] or in a manner that was procedurally inappropriate.[379]

§ 8.23 TERMINATION AND AMENDMENT OF REAL COVENANTS

Termination by expiration. As with other interests in land, a real covenant may terminate at a fixed time if the parties creating it so intend.[380] The clearest manifestation of their intent is express language in the instrument creating the covenant, e.g., "Grantee covenants that, for a period of 25 years from the date hereof . . . ." Some states have statutes that limit the duration of restrictive covenants in some circumstances. For example, Rhode Island and Massachusetts have statutes limiting the duration of certain restrictions to 30 years if the instrument creating the restriction does not express a specific duration.[381] Georgia provides that covenants restricting land uses shall not run for more than 20 years in municipalities that have adopted zoning laws, though it provides that most residential subdivision covenants renew for another 20-year term automatically unless terminated by action of the majority of lot owners.[382] In most planned residential development today, the covenants applicable to each lot or unit are given a fixed duration (ranging commonly from 5 to 25 years), and by their terms automatically renew for an additional term of the same duration unless a specified percentage of the owners takes sufficient action to terminate or modify them.[383] We will return to discuss modification of covenants later in this section.

---

[377] E.g., Grovenburg v. Rustle Meadow Assocs., LLC, 174 Conn.App. 18, 165 A.3d 193 (2017); Cypress Gardens, Ltd. v. Platt, 124 N.M. 472, 952 P.2d 467 (App.1997); Hoffman v. Gould, 714 A.2d 1071 (Pa.Super.1998).

[378] E.g., Gleneagle Civic Ass'n v. Hardin, 205 P.3d 462 (Colo.App.2008); Sierra Crest Homeowners Ass'n, Inc. v. Villalobos, 527 S.W.3d 235 (Tex.App.2016). See also Mack v. Armstrong, 147 Wash.App. 522, 195 P.3d 1027 (2008) (covenant imposing specific 30-foot height limit, as specific restriction of an aspect of design, prevailed over general consent provision; thus, rejection of plans for home less than 30 feet based on height violated covenant).

Riss v. Angel, 131 Wash.2d 612, 934 P.2d 669 (1997), provides an object lesson for owners serving on architectural review committees. In that case, the association was unincorporated and the association board, acting as an architectural committee, withheld permission for a new home based upon erroneous information. The court held that the rejection was unreasonable, and that the individual board members were jointly and severally liable for nearly $104,000 in damages and $102,000 in costs and attorney fees. The case is "Exhibit A" for why owners associations should be incorporated.

[379] E.g., DuTrac Community Credit Union v. Radiology Group Real Estate, L.C., 891 N.W.2d 210 (Iowa 2017) (control covenant could not be enforced where it required two-member committee, specifically named the members without any mechanism for succession, and where one member had died and the other had resigned or refused to act); Hartstene Pt. Maintenance Ass'n v. Diehl, 95 Wash.App. 339, 979 P.2d 854 (1999) (decision of five-member committee was invalid under covenant that required committee of three members).

[380] Restatement of Property § 554 (1944); Restatement (Third) of Property-Servitudes § 7.2 (2000).

[381] Mass.Gen. Laws Ann. ch. 184, § 23; R.I.Gen. Laws § 34–4–21. These statutes do not prevent someone from creating a covenant for a longer term than 30 years; the party creating the covenant must simply specify the precise duration.

[382] Ga.Code Ann. § 44–5–60(b), (d).

[383] An example of such a provision appears in Boyles v. Hausmann, 246 Neb. 181, 517 N.W.2d 610 (1994): "These covenants, restrictions and conditions shall run with the land and continue until January 1, 1983, after which time they shall be automatically extended for successive periods of five years, unless an

Termination by release. The person having the benefit of a real covenant may extinguish it by a formal release, which should be in deed form.[384] Release is a practical method of terminating a covenant when the covenant exists only between the owners of a discrete small number of parcels (e.g., two or three). It is not practical in a subdivision or condominium project with dozens or hundreds of owners, however, because the covenants reciprocally benefit all lot or unit owners. In that context, 100% of the owners would have to release the covenants to extinguish them, and 100% of the owners in a large subdivision or condominium are unlikely to agree on anything. For this reason, as noted above, modern subdivision or condominium covenants usually provide that the covenants can be terminated by action by a majority or supermajority of the owners.

Termination by merger. If ownership of the benefited parcel and the burdened parcel comes into the same person (or "merges") without any intervening interests, this extinguishes the covenant.[385] A subsequent transfer of one of the parcels by the common owner does not revive the covenant unless the covenant is re-created under the rules discussed in Section 8.3.[386] Note that in the context of a common interest community, termination by merger would not occur unless *all* of the lots or units within the community came into common ownership.[387]

Termination by waiver or abandonment. A covenant may terminate if the party entitled to enforce the benefit abandons the covenant or waives the benefit of its enforcement.[388] Abandonment can occur through an explicit statement by the benefited party, although in such circumstances the owner of the burdened parcel should insist that the intent to abandon be memorialized in a formal written release. More frequently, disputes arise in which the owner of the burdened parcel asks the court to imply that waiver or abandonment has occurred, typically due to the presence of obvious violation and nonenforcement of the covenant. Before a court will imply abandonment of a covenant, it must find clear and convincing evidence of general and substantial noncompliance.[389] In making this determination, courts will evaluate not only the

---

instrument signed by a majority of the then owners of said land shall have been recorded in the office of the County Clerk of Washington County, Nebraska, agreeing to change same in whole or in part." While the provision in *Boyles* allowed for termination or modification by action of a majority of owners, such provisions more commonly require a supermajority of owners (i.e., two-thirds or three fourths).

In Hardy v. Aiken, 369 S.C. 160, 631 S.E.2d 539 (2006), the covenants had a twenty-five year term and a majority amendment provision, but without an automatic renewal. Construing the covenant narrowly, the court held that an amendment to extend the duration of the covenants would require unanimous consent.

[384] Restatement of Property § 556 (1944); Restatement (Third) of Property-Servitudes § 7.3 (2000).

[385] Restatement of Property § 555 (1944); Restatement (Third) of Property-Servitudes § 7.5 (2000); Pollock v. Ramirez, 117 N.M. 187, 870 P.2d 149 (App.1994). Merger does not occur when there is an intervening interest in the affected parcel. For example, suppose Lots A and B are each burdened by a reciprocal covenant restricting each lot to residential use only, and Bank holds an unsatisfied mortgage on Lot B. The owner of Lot A then acquires Lot B. As long as the mortgage remains unsatisfied, the covenant would not terminate by merger absent the Bank's effective consent. Restatement (Third) of Property-Servitudes § 7.5 Comment d (2000).

[386] Restatement (Third) of Property-Servitudes § 7.5 (2000).

[387] E.g., Pollock v. Ramirez, 117 N.M. 187, 870 P.2d 149 (App.1994); Restatement (Third) of Property-Servitudes § 7.5 Comment c (2000).

[388] Restatement of Property § 558 (1944); Restatement (Third) of Property-Servitudes § 7.4 (2000).

[389] E.g. Blue Ridge Bank & Trust Co. v. Trosen, 309 S.W.3d 812 (Mo.App.2010) (association and members waived covenant providing right of first refusal to the extent association repeatedly refused to assert the right as to intra-family transfers for over four decades); Fink v. Miller, 896 P.2d 649 (Utah App.1995) (widespread violation of covenant requiring shake roofs). More frequently, the court notes the high standard required in the process of concluding that the party seeking abandonment failed to meet that standard. For example, where an owner of a 20-acre lot had committed violations of several covenants regarding animals and

number, nature, and severity of violations, but also the existence of prior enforcement efforts and whether it remains possible to realize the benefits of the covenant through future enforcement efforts.[390]

A common fact pattern in the cases involves a residential subdivision in which one owner starts making a business use (such as a home-based day care or catering service) in violation of a residential-use-only covenant, another owner (or the association) takes action to enjoin the violation, and a waiver or abandonment claim is asserted based on other owners also making business-related uses. Courts rarely find abandonment or waiver in this situation, given that such a finding would effectively destroy the residential character of the neighborhood.[391]

Apparent violations can present a dilemma in common interest communities, because a potential purchaser of a lot might see visible violations of a covenant and infer on that basis that the neighbors have abandoned the covenant. Such an inference is problematic and usually unjustified. First, the documents creating covenants in common interest communities often include "nonwaiver" provisions designed to rebut or negate any inference of waiver or abandonment.[392] Second, while the violation of a covenant

---

fences, this did not preclude the benefited landowner from enforcing a covenant restricting the lot to one single-family dwelling where the violations did not "radically and permanently change[ ] the overall neighborhood." Wimer v. Cook, 369 P.3d 210 (Wyo.2016). See also, e.g., Citizens Voices Ass'n v. Collings Lakes Civic Ass'n, 396 N.J.Super. 432, 934 A.2d 669 (2007); Swenson v. Erickson, 998 P.2d 807 (Utah 2000); Moore v. Wolititch, 341 P.3d 421 (Wyo.2015).

[390] E.g., Myers v. Armstrong, 324 P.3d 388 (N.M.App.2014); Vance v. Popkowski, 534 S.W.3d 474 (Tex.App.2017); Moran v. Memorial Pt. Prop. Owners Ass'n, Inc., 410 S.W.3d 397 (Tex.App.2013) ("severe and pervasive pattern of violations" necessary); Fink v. Miller, 896 P.2d 649 (Utah App.1995); Green v. Normandy Park, 137 Wash.App. 665, 151 P.3d 1038 (2007) (few violations found not sufficiently "habitual and substantial" to support finding of abandonment). Some of the cases can be somewhat difficult to reconcile factually. Compare Fink, supra (wood-shingle roofing covenant held abandoned where 23 of 81 lots were in violation) with Swenson v. Erickson, 998 P.2d 807 (Utah 2000) (small storage sheds on 19 of 52 lots in violation of covenant did not constitute abandonment so as to permit building of large workshop). See also Shader v. Hampton Improvement Ass'n, Inc. 443 Md. 148, 115 A.3d 185 (2015) (covenant precluded any building other than one single-family dwelling per lot, but numerous violations occurred such as gazebos, sheds, and poolhouses; court held association waived right to enforce covenant to prevent other auxiliary structures, but did not waive general benefit of covenant so as to preclude building of multiple dwellings per lot).

[391] For example, in Moore v. Wolititch, 341 P.3d 421 (Wyo.2015), Moore attempted to start a home-based day care for up to 15 children. When other owners in the subdivision sued to enforce the covenant, Moore claimed abandonment, noting other business-related activities being carried on by the plaintiffs, including babysitting (for compensation), operation of an identity-theft-victim assistance business, use of a home address as the business address for a landscaping business, and the parking of trailers and other equipment used in off-site business activity. The court rejected the abandonment claim and enforced the covenant, noting that Moore failed to show sufficient evidence of impact to justify a conclusion that the violations had radically changed the character of the subdivision. Likewise, in Roberts v. Lee, 289 Ga.App. 714, 658 S.E.2d 258 (2008), one owner attempted to enforce a covenant prohibiting commercial use of lots within a residential subdivision against a neighbor who was parking commercial vehicles in his driveway. The court enforced the covenant, rejecting an argument that the plaintiff had lacked "clean hands" because she typed transcripts for her job as a court reporter on her home computer in the evenings and received business mail at home, and noting that her actions had no effect on the value or residential character of her home or others in the subdivision. See also Pietrowski v. Dufrane, 247 Wis.2d 232, 634 N.W.2d 109 (App.2001).

[392] For example, consider the following nonwaiver provision at issue in Vance v. Popkowski, 534 S.W.3d 474 (Tex.App.2017): "No act or omission by any party hereto or any person hereafter acquiring any interest in said subdivision through or under same shall ever be constructed a waiver of the right to enforce any of these covenants, either against such person or against any other person." As the court explained in Vance, such nonwaiver provisions are generally enforceable, but they do not preclude waiver or abandonment claims as a matter of law. A court could conclude an entire covenant regime (including the nonwaiver provision) had been waived or abandoned if "there is evidence of violations so pervasive that they have destroyed the fundamental character of the neighborhood." Vance, 534 S.W.3d at 480. Likewise, a court could also conclude that a party had waived the nonwaiver provision itself, by having "intentionally engaged in conduct inconsistent with claiming the right to enforce" the provision. Vance, 534 S.W.3d at 480–481; see also College Book Centers, Inc.

may be visually obvious, whether the neighbors intend to enforce the covenant (or are enforcing it) typically is not. An owners association might have imposed fines or filed litigation to enforce the covenant, but this enforcement action would not be apparent based on a visual inspection of the land alone. A prudent buyer in this circumstance would engage in further investigation ("due diligence") of the owners association to ascertain facts relevant to past, present, and future enforcement of the covenant before drawing any inference that abandonment had occurred. Further, a truly prudent buyer would not rely on even a well-founded inference of abandonment, but would insist on an "estoppel letter" from the owners association stating that it would not take any enforcement action against the buyer based on the existing violation of the covenant, if the buyer completed the purchase. If the association will not provide this assurance, a buyer should assume that the association may attempt to enforce the covenant in the future.

Termination by changed circumstances. Over time, circumstances can change surrounding the covenant itself or the parcels burdened or benefited by it. If the changes are so significant that continued enforcement of the covenant would be oppressive or no longer serve the covenant's intended purposes, a court may declare the covenant is terminated (under one theory) or may refuse to enforce it (under a second theory).[393] The change must be substantial;[394] courts look for a change that affects the general vicinity and not merely a few parcels.[395] When the restrictions in question cover all land within a common interest community, courts frequently say that the changes must have occurred within the bounds of the community (as contrasted with changes occurring on land located outside the community).[396] The fact that the local municipality has rezoned the burdened parcel may be evidence of changed circumstances, but is not sufficient by

v. Carefree Foothills Homeowners' Ass'n, 225 Ariz. 533, 241 P.3d 897 (App.2010) (applying nonwaiver provision to defeat claim of waiver of specific covenant where facts did not justify finding waiver of entire covenant regime or of nonwaiver provision itself).

[393] See Bueno v. Firgeleski, 180 Conn.App. 384, 183 A.3d 1176 (2018); Osborne v. Hewitt, 335 S.W.2d 922 (Ky.1960); Chevy Chase Village v. Jaggers, 261 Md. 309, 275 A.2d 167 (1971); Jackson v. Stevenson, 156 Mass. 496, 31 N.E. 691 (1892); Birt v. Ratka, 66 A.D.3d 1363, 886 N.Y.S.2d 293 (2009); Chesterfield Meadows Shopping Ctr. Assocs., L.P. v. Smith, 264 Va. 350, 568 S.E.2d 676 (2002) (covenant prohibiting shopping center use, originally imposed to protect historic home, terminated by changed circumstances where historic home had since been relocated and surrounding area was entirely commercial in nature); N.Y.Real Prop. Law § 1951; 2 Am. Law of Prop. § 9.22 (1952); Restatement of Property § 564 (1944); Restatement (Third) of Property-Servitudes § 7.10(1) (2000); 3 H. Tiffany, Real Property § 875 (3d ed.1939).

[394] See, e.g., Bueno v. Firgeleski, 180 Conn.App. 384, 183 A.3d 1176 (changes must be "so great as clearly to neutralize the benefits of the restrictions to the point of defeating the object and purpose of the covenant"); River Heights Assocs. Ltd. Partn. v. Batten, 267 Va. 262, 591 S.E.2d 683 (2004) (changes must be "so radical as practically to destroy the essential objects and purposes" of the covenant); Restatement of Property § 564 (1944); Restatement (Third) of Property-Servitudes § 7.10(1) (2000) (change must make it "impossible as a practical matter to accomplish the purpose for which the servitude was created").

[395] E.g., Chevy Chase Village v. Jaggers, 261 Md. 309, 275 A.2d 167 (1971); Pearson v. DMH 2 Ltd. Liability Co., 449 N.J.Super. 30, 155 A.3d 17 (2016) (party seeking nonenforcement must show "pervasive transformation of the entire neighborhood"); Cilberti v. Angilletta, 61 Misc.2d 13, 304 N.Y.S.2d 673 (1969).

[396] E.g., West Alameda Heights Homeowners Ass'n v. Board of County Comm'rs, 458 P.2d 253 (Colo.1969); Marco Island Civic Ass'n, Inc. v. Mazzini, 881 So.2d 99 (Fla.App.2004); Osborne v. Hewitt, 335 S.W.2d 922 (Ky.1960); Country Club Dist. Homes Ass'n v. Country Club Christian Church, 118 S.W.3d 185 (Mo.App.2003); Western Land Co. v. Truskolaski, 88 Nev. 200, 495 P.2d 624 (1972); Cilberti v. Angilletta, 61 Misc.2d 13, 304 N.Y.S.2d 673 (1969); Vernon Township Volunteer Fire Dept., Inc. v. Connor, 579 Pa. 364, 855 A.2d 873 (2004); River Heights Assocs. Ltd. Partn. v. Batten, 267 Va. 262, 591 S.E.2d 683 (2004); 3 H. Tiffany, Real Property § 875 (3d ed.1939). But see El Di, Inc. v. Town of Bethany Beach, 477 A.2d 1066 (Del.1984) (change of restricted area from residential to commercial and violation of no-liquor restriction, to some extent within restricted area and moreso outside it, justified termination of no-liquor restriction).

itself to justify application of the doctrine.[397] Likewise, the impact of enforcement on the value or utility of the burdened parcel may be evidence of changed circumstances, but does not alone justify termination or nonenforcement.[398] One situation that has produced significant recent litigation involves residential subdivisions built around golf courses, where the operation of the golf course has become unprofitable and the owner of the golf course parcel (who wants to convert the course into new building lots and sell them) seeks to terminate the covenant requiring use of that parcel as a golf course. In most of these cases, the courts have refused to terminate the covenant—one Florida court noted that despite the economic impact on the golf course parcel, the course "preserve[d] the character of the community and provide[d] residents with a pleasant view" and thus continued enforcement of the covenant remained a benefit of "substantial value" to the residents.[399]

The extent to which changed circumstances doctrine should apply to real covenants depends on the theory upon which it operates. Courts have sometimes advanced the theory that changed circumstances is an equitable defense to an action to enforce the burden of the covenant—essentially, a form of balancing the equities. When the suit is to enforce a covenant in an action at law, this begs a question: to what extent may a defendant raise an equitable defense to a common-law cause of action? If the plaintiff seeks an equitable remedy—an injunction—the plaintiff may be denied that specific relief. However, the plaintiff would still theoretically have the ordinary common-law remedy of damages; moreover, the covenant itself would still exist. This was in fact the position adopted by the original Restatement, and some cases support it.[400] This result is awkward and unsatisfactory. Today most writers, most courts, and the Restatement of Servitudes conclude that sufficiently changed circumstances justify termination of the

---

[397] E.g., Goodman v. Superior Court, 137 Ariz. 348, 670 P.2d 746 (App.1983); West Alameda Heights Homeowners Ass'n v. Board of County Comm'rs, 169 Colo. 491, 458 P.2d 253 (1969); Essenson v. Polo Club Assocs., 688 So.2d 981 (Fla.App.1997); Highland Springs South Homeowners Ass'n, Inc. v. Reinstatler, 907 N.E.2d 1067 (Ind.App.2009); Gambrell v. Nivens, 275 S.W.3d 429 (Tenn.App.2008).

[398] Goodman v. Superior Court, 137 Ariz. 348, 670 P.2d 746 (App.1983); Shalimar Ass'n v. D.O.C. Enters., Ltd., 142 Ariz. 36, 688 P.2d 682 (App.1984) (enforcement of restrictive covenant may make use of restricted premises unprofitable, but this alone does not terminate covenant); Victorville West Ltd. Partn. v. Inverrary Ass'n, Inc., 226 So.3d 888 (Fla.App.2017); Osborne v. Hewitt, 335 S.W.2d 922 (Ky.1960); Dumbarton Improvement Ass'n, Inc. v. Druid Ridge Cemetery Co., 434 Md. 37, 73 A.3d 224 (2013) (increased value of land for residential development in high demand did not justify termination of covenant limiting land to cemetery use); Country Club Dist. Homes Ass'n v. Country Club Christian Church, 118 S.W.3d 185 (Mo.App.2003); Western Land Co. v. Truskolaski, 88 Nev. 200, 495 P.2d 624 (1972); Cilberti v. Angilletta, 61 Misc.2d 13, 304 N.Y.S.2d 673 (1969). See also Schuring v. Fosters Mill Village Community Ass'n, 396 S.W.3d 73 (Tex.App.2013) (cost of installing compliant metal roof was not so disproportionate to benefit of enforcing covenant as to justify nonenforcement).

[399] Victorville West Ltd. Partn. v. Inverrary Ass'n, Inc., 226 So.3d 888 (Fla.App.2017). See also Heatherwood Holdings, LLC v. First Commercial Bank, 61 So.3d 1012 (Ala.2010); New Castle Cty. v. Pike Creek Recreational Servs., LLC, 82 A.3d 731 (Del.Ch.Ct.2013); Skyline Woods Homeowners Ass'n, Inc. v. Broekemeier, 276 Neb. 792, 758 N.W.2d 376 (2008); Fairfield Harbour Prop. Owners Ass'n, Inc. v. Midsouth Golf, LLC, 215 N.C.App. 66, 715 S.E2d 273 (2011). For this reason, the covenants applicable to many golf course communities may require owners to maintain club memberships to assure the financial viability of the golf course and other recreational amenities. Cf. In re Heatherwood Holdings, LLC, 746 F.3d 1206 (11th Cir.2014) (restrictive covenant requiring use as golf course survived bankruptcy sale of golf course parcel and could be enforced against buyer).

[400] Restatement of Property § 564 (1944); Jackson v. Stevenson, 156 Mass. 496, 31 N.E. 691 (1892); Pearson v. DMH 2 Ltd. Liability Co., 449 N.J.Super. 30, 155 A.3d 17 (2016); McClure v. Leaycraft, 183 N.Y. 36, 75 N.E. 961 (1905) (dictum); Moseley v. Arnold, 486 S.W.3d 656 (Tex.App.2016); 2 Am. Law of Prop. § 9.22 (1952).

covenant.[401] An appropriate analogue exists in the doctrine that an easement terminates when the purpose for which it was created comes to an end.[402]

Amendment or modification of covenants. Over time, parties to a covenant may conclude that it is no longer optimal and may wish to modify or amend it to meet with their current expectations or desires. As with any covenant under contract law, the parties bound by a covenant can act to modify or amend it, although the modification or amendment of a running covenant would require compliance with statute of frauds. In the common interest community context, however, modification or amendment of a covenant is complicated by a "numbers" problem. If, for example, there are reciprocal covenants affecting 100 different lots, amendment or modification of the covenant would require the agreement of the owner of every lot.[403] But experience tells us that unanimity among large groups is impossible to achieve in practical terms. For this reason, common interest community covenants typically contain amendment provisions which allow the owners of a majority of the lots or units in the community (or a specified supermajority of such owners) to take certain specified action to amend the covenants.[404]

When an amendment occurs, a dissenting owner may object to the validity of the amended covenant, particularly if the amendment would increase the dissenting owner's financial obligation (e.g., an amendment imposing mandatory assessments where none existed previously) or result in a change that the dissenting owner considers drastic and unexpected (e.g., an amendment imposing a covenant prohibiting keeping of pets or rental of units, where the covenant initially contained no such prohibition). In a number of cases, courts have refused to enforce a covenant amendment—despite the requisite

---

[401] Restatement (Third) of Property-Servitudes § 7.10(1) (2000); 2 Am. Law of Prop. § 9.22 (1952); C. Clark, Real Covenants and Other Interests Which "Run With Land" 184–86 (2d ed.1947); 3 H. Tiffany, Real Property § 875 (3d ed.1939). The Restatement suggests the court has the authority to modify a servitude based on changed circumstances if modification would permit the purpose of the servitude to be accomplished; where modification is not practicable or would be ineffective, the court may terminate the servitude. Restatement (Third) of Property-Servitudes § 7.10(1) (2000).

This approach carries out a theory suggested by Dean Roscoe Pound: "It is submitted that the sound course is to hold that when the purpose of the restrictions can no longer be carried out the servitude comes to an end; that the duration of the servitude is determined by its purpose." Pound, The Progress of the Law, 1918–1919, Equity, 33 Harv.L.Rev. 813, 821 (1920). Pound was writing specifically of equitable servitudes, but the theory applies equally well to real covenants. The basic mechanism is a judicial inference that the covenanting parties intended the covenant to last only so long as it served their purpose. Because the covenant itself ends, both right and remedy are barred.

[402] See § 8.12 supra; Union Nat'l Bank v. Nesmith, 238 Mass. 247, 130 N.E. 251 (1921); 3 H. Tiffany, Real Property § 817 (3d ed.1939).

[403] E.g., Van Loan v. Heather Hills Prop. Owners Ass'n, Inc., 216 So.3d 18 (Fla.App.2017) (declaration of covenants did not expressly delegate authority to association to amend covenants, so amendments required unanimous consent).

[404] Many early subdivisions that did not involve common amenities did not provide for active homeowners associations, and in many of these subdivisions, the amendment covenant typically permitted amendments by a written instrument signed by the requisite majority or supermajority of the lot owners. For an example of this form of covenant, see, e.g., Boyles v. Hausmann, 246 Neb. 181, 517 N.W.2d 610 (1994). This type of provision would permit an amendment without an actual meeting of owners and without a formal vote; in fact, the amendment litigated in *Boyles* happened without a meeting, a vote, or the knowledge of the plaintiff! In more modern common interest developments in which active owners associations are common, amendment covenants more commonly require that proposed amendments be discussed and voted on at an owners association meeting.

In some circumstances, an amendment covenant may provide for majority approval but an applicable state statute may require a supermajority for approval of certain amendments. In these situations, the statutory supermajority requirement would control. See, e.g., Filmore LLLP v. Unit Owners Ass'n of Centre Pointe Condo., 183 Wash.App. 328, 333 P.3d 498 (2014) (90% supermajority requirement specified under Washington's version of Uniform Condominium Act).

majority or supermajority approval—on the ground that the covenant is not an authorized "change" or "amendment" but is instead the adoption of a "new" covenant that requires unanimous approval.[405] Courts commonly justify this result as an application of the "narrow construction in favor of free use" rule discussed in Section 8.22, and often express a concern that the dissenting owner could not have expected such a change. For example, in Boyles v. Hausmann,[406] the Nebraska Supreme Court refused to enforce an amendment imposing a 120-foot building setback restriction on all lots, stating that "none of the existing covenants involved setbacks" and "nothing in the existing covenants . . . would have put [the dissenting owners] on notice that their land would one day be subject to a setback limit."[407]

On its face, this argument is ridiculous. First, if the original recorded covenants contained an amendment provision, a buyer of an affected parcel takes it with constructive notice that majority or supermajority amendment is possible—thus, the argument that "I never thought it possible that the covenants might change" is empty and self-serving.[408] Second, as noted in Section 8.22, a principle of broad construction is more sensible in the modern common interest community than a narrow construction. If an original neighborhood covenant did not address trash containers, but a supermajority of residents decides to impose a restriction requiring animal-proof trash containers because of trash problems caused by animals, why should courts prevent that by absurdly construing the amendment covenant as inapplicable (and thus requiring unanimous, and unobtainable, approval)? Increasingly, many courts have rejected the narrow construction approach and have enforced covenant amendments against dissenting owners even where the original covenants did not address the subject of the amendment.[409]

---

[405] See, e.g., Dreamland Villa Community Club, Inc. v. Raimey, 224 Ariz. 42, 226 P.3d 411 (App.2010) (imposition of mandatory association membership); Lakeland Prop. Owners Ass'n v. Larson, 121 Ill.App.3d 805, 459 N.E.2d 1164 (1984) (imposition of mandatory assessments); Webb v. Mullikin, 142 S.W.3d 822 (Mo.App.2004) (addition of tennis club and imposition of mandatory assessments); Boyles v. Hausmann, 246 Neb. 181, 517 N.W.2d 610 (1994) (imposition of 120-foot setback restriction on lots where original covenants contained no setback); Caughlin Ranch Homeowners Ass'n v. Caughlin Club, 109 Nev. 264, 849 P.2d 310 (1993) (imposition of assessments against commercial parcels); Wilkinson v. Chiwawa Communities Ass'n, 180 Wash.2d 241, 327 P.3d 614 (2014) (imposition of prohibition on short-term vacation rentals where original covenants did not prohibit leasing); Grace Fellowship Church, Inc. v. Harned, 5 N.E.3d 1108 (Ohio App.2013) (imposition of covenant restricting nonresidential use where original covenants contained no such prohibition). See also Mackey v. Armstrong, 705 So.2d 1198 (La.App.1997) (amendment provision contemplates amendments that lift rather than add restrictions on use of land, so amendment that added restrictions required unanimous consent).

[406] 246 Neb. 181, 517 N.W.2d 610 (1994).

[407] *Boyles*, 246 Neb. at 191, 517 N.W.2d at 617.

[408] Other less sympathetic courts have so noted. E.g., Villa De Las Palmas Homeowners Ass'n v. Terifaj, 33 Cal.4th 73, 90 P.3d 1223 (2004) (buyer in condominium with recorded covenants containing amendment provision "accepts the risk that the power may be used in a way that benefits the community but harms the individual"); Cape May Harbor Village & Yacht Club Ass'n, Inc. v. Sbraga, 421 N.J.Super. 56, 22 A.3d 158 (2011) (because recorded covenants authorized amendments, "any purchaser was on notice that the provisions . . . were not immutable").

[409] Many of the cases involve associations that initially did not have mandatory assessments, but later voted to amend the covenants to impose mandatory assessments to address important financial needs of the association. E.g., Evergreen Highlands Ass'n v. West, 73 P.3d 1 (Colo.2003); Zito v. Gerken, 225 Ill.App.3d 79, 587 N.E.2d 1048 (1992); Windemere Homeowners Ass'n, Inc. v. McCue, 297 Mont. 77, 990 P.2d 769 (1999); Sunday Canyon Prop. Owners Ass'n v. Annett, 978 S.W.2d 654 (Tex.App.1998). See also Villa De Las Palmas Homeowners Ass'n v. Terifaj, 33 Cal.4th 73, 90 P.3d 1223 (2004) (upholding amendment prohibiting pets against existing dissenting owner); Lee v. Puamana Community Ass'n, 109 Haw. 561, 128 P.3d 874 (2006) (upholding amendment effecting transfer of common elements to private use); Hughes v. New Life Dev. Corp.,

There is an alternative satisfactory explanation for the result in *Boyles*. In *Boyles*, the 120-foot setback restriction would have had no practical impact on other lots, as all existing buildings already complied with it. However, according to the attorney for the dissenting owner, an existing pipeline easement on the dissenting owner's undeveloped lot—when combined with the setback—would have effectively prevented the dissenting owner from building on the lot.[410] In other words, even though the amendment ostensibly applied uniformly to everyone, in reality its impact was not uniform. Under the weight of authority, a covenant may not be amended by majority or supermajority vote where the amendment would not have uniform effect; such an amendment requires unanimity.[411]

Likewise, one can imagine a scenario in which a court might appropriately refuse to enforce a covenant amendment that sought to impose mandatory assessments. For example, imagine that Gotberg buys a home in a 20-lot subdivision that has no common amenities and recorded covenants that impose only modest use restrictions and contain a majority amendment provision. Several years later, 11 of her neighboring owners sign an amendment under which the owners would incur significant debt to purchase an adjoining golf course and impose mandatory assessments to fund maintenance of the course. In this situation, a court might reasonably characterize such a covenant as

---

387 S.W.3d 453 (Tenn.2012) (upholding supermajority amendment removing designation of certain areas within community as forest preserve).

Many courts have upheld amendments that imposed leasing restrictions, even though leasing was permissible to some extent under the original covenants. E.g., Woodside Village Condo Ass'n, Inc. v. Jahren, 806 So.2d 452 (Fla.2002); Apple II Condo. Ass'n v. Worth Bank & Trust Co., 277 Ill.App.3d 345, 659 N.E.2d 93 (1995); Cape May Harbor Village & Yacht Club Ass'n, Inc. v. Sbraga, 421 N.J.Super. 56, 22 A.3d 158 (2011) (subjecting amendment to reasonableness analysis but upholding it as reasonable against dissenting owners); McElveen-Hunter v. Fountain Manor Ass'n, Inc., 96 N.C.App. 627, 386 S.E.2d 435 (1989); Worthinglen Condo. Unit Owners' Ass'n v. Brown, 57 Ohio App.3d 73, 566 N.E.2d 1275 (1989) (subjecting amendment to reasonableness analysis but upholding it as reasonable against dissenting owners); North Country Props., LLC v. Lost Acres Homeowners Ass'n of Burnett Cty., 369 Wis.2d 74, 879 N.W.2d 810 (Table) (2016). In these cases, because the original covenants often referenced leasing in some respect, courts less commonly address arguments that the covenant is a "new" one. Still, other courts have refused to apply such an amendment retroactively against existing owners. E.g., Breene v. Plaza Tower Ass'n, 310 N.W.2d 730 (N.D.1981).

Where the declaration does not prohibit leasing and has not been amended, the association cannot impose a leasing restriction by the adoption of rules or bylaws without also amending the declaration. E.g., Stobe v. 842–848 W. Bradley Place Condo. Ass'n, 48 N.E.3d 310 (Ill.App.2016); Kiekel v. Four Colonies Homes Ass'n, 38 Kan.App.2d 102, 162 P.3d 57 (2007); Matter of Olszewski v. Cannon Pt. Ass'n, Inc. 148 A.D.3d 1306, 49 N.Y.S.3d 571 (2017); Strathmore Ridge Homeowners Ass'n, Inc. v. Mendicino, 63 A.D.3d 1038, 881 N.Y.S.2d 491 (2009); Shorewood West Condo. Ass'n v. Sadri, 140 Wash.2d 47, 992 P.2d 1008 (2000); Va.Code § 55–343.

[410] Further, a neighbor had wanted to buy the dissenting owner's lot to preserve a view, but the dissenting owner had refused to sell. In response, the neighbor obtained the necessary signatures to amend the covenant to impose the setback—and thus to prevent the dissenting owner from building so as to interfere with the neighbor's view—without the knowledge of the dissenting owner. Why the court's decision refers to none of this is an unexplained mystery!

[411] E.g., Camelback Del Este Homeowners Ass'n v. Warner, 156 Ariz. 21, 749 P.2d 930 (App.1987); Walton v. Jaskiewicz, 317 Md. 264, 563 A.2d 382 (1989); Maatta v. Dead River Campers, Inc., 263 Mich.App. 604, 689 N.W.2d 491 (2004); Montoya v. Barreras, 81 N.M. 749, 473 P.2d 363 (1970). But see Giguere v. SJS Family Enters., Ltd., 155 P.3d 462 (Colo.App.2006) (noting Colorado's version of Uniform Common Interest Ownership Act allows certain amendments to apply to less than all lots).

This expectation makes perfect sense in any common interest community; unless the covenants explicitly make it possible for owners to receive differential treatment, owners should reasonably expect that benefits and burdens will fall on a shared basis. E.g., Francis v. Aspen Mtn. Condo Ass'n, Inc. 401 P.3d 125 (Colo.App.2017) (where condominium declaration requires unanimous consent to reallocate common interest shares, association cannot use majority or supermajority voting to reallocate common interest shares); Watson v. Village at Northshore I Ass'n, Inc., 184 A.3d 1133 (Vt.2018) (airspace was common element; authorization of dormer expansions into community's airspace required unanimous consent of all unit owners).

sufficiently "new" or unexpected as to require unanimous consent.[412] But this should not preclude a majority of owners from amending a covenant to impose the assessments needed to properly maintain already-existing common elements.

There is one final situation in which courts have been solicitous of existing unit owners with respect to unexpected changes. Developers frequently reserve the right to make unilateral changes to the covenants during the early stages of development, and sometimes exercise this right if the developer's early marketing efforts are disappointing. For example, a developer that initially marketed a project as exclusively single-family residences—but whose initial marketing efforts produced few sales—might try to modify the covenants to permit townhome or multi-family development, or even commercial uses. Such a change might come as a very unwelcome surprise to the unit owners that had already purchased homes. In these cases, courts have generally allowed the developer to make such amendments, but only so long as the developer exercised this right in a reasonable manner consistent with the general scheme or plan of development.[413]

§ 8.24 REMEDIES FOR BREACH OF REAL COVENANTS

If a person liable to perform the burden of a real covenant has breached it, the person entitled to enforce it may recover for any damages resulting from the breach. The covenant is a common law creation and damages are the common law remedy. As a practical matter, the beneficiary often prefers an injunction against future breach of the covenant, together with any damages caused by past breaches. Although injunction is an equitable remedy and may once have been thought of as extraordinary, it is today routinely available on the theory that the legal remedy is inadequate to prevent future injury to unique property interests.[414] As an equitable remedy, a court may deny an injunction in a particular case because of an equity defense such as laches, unclean hands, or balancing of hardships.[415]

Even though a covenantor has conveyed the burdened land to a grantee who becomes liable for performing the burden of the covenant, in some cases the original covenantor may remain liable. The promise had a dual nature: as a contract, it bound the promisor personally; as a covenant it bound successors in privity. In theory, then, if the burdened estate has been conveyed but the benefited estate is still held by the original covenantee, the covenantee should be able to pursue both the grantee on the running covenant and the original promisor under "privity of contract." This is typically the result in the courts in actions by landlords to enforce lease covenants.[416] Between

---

[412] E.g., Armstrong v. Ledges Homeowners Ass'n, Inc., 360 N.C. 547, 633 S.E.2d 78 (2006) (striking down amended covenant for mandatory membership and assessments for expanded amenities; agreement in original covenant to pay pro rata share of cost of lighting subdivision entrance sign—at the time, the only common element—was not intended to confer unlimited powers of assessment on owners association).

[413] E.g., Miller v. Miller's Landing, L.L.C., 29 So.3d 228 (Ala.App.2009). See also Dunne v. Shenandoah Homeowners Ass'n, Inc., 12 P.3d 340 (Colo.App.2000) (developer cannot unilaterally revoke covenants without consent of already-existing lot owners if covenants are silent as to modification or revocation).

[414] See Cross, Interplay Between Property Law Change and Constitutional Barriers to Property Law Reform, 35 N.Y.U.L.Rev. 1317, 1325–26 (1960). See also W.F. White Land Co. v. Christenson, 14 S.W.2d 369 (Tex.Civ.App.1928) (court enforces a "covenant" by injunction).

[415] See Gaskin v. Harris, 82 N.M. 336, 481 P.2d 698 (1971) (injunction granted); Crowell v. Shelton, 948 P.2d 313 (Okla.1997).

[416] See § 6.68 supra.

themselves the covenantor and the grantee stand in a suretyship relation, the grantee being primarily liable and the covenantor only secondarily so.[417]

However, when the covenant is contained in a conveyance in fee, many decisions refuse to hold the original covenantor liable after the conveyance to a successor grantee. This makes sense when the covenant is to be performed upon the burdened land, such as a covenant to repair or to refrain from making certain uses; one can reason that the original parties intended the covenant to be performed only by the person in possession of the land (and thus in the position to perform).[418] Continued liability on the part of covenantor following conveyance of the burdened parcel should arise only where the covenanting parties intended that result.[419] Where the original covenantee has conveyed the benefited land, there is general agreement that the original covenantee loses the right to enforce the covenant.[420]

Today, covenants commonly arise in conjunction with common interest communities such as subdivisions or condominiums (such as covenants requiring owners to pay assessments,[421] limiting use to certain purposes, or requiring permission to erect buildings[422]). Frequently, when these covenants are violated, it is the owners association that takes action to enforce the covenants. Under a true running covenant theory, the benefit of a covenant should be enforceable only by one who owns land benefited by the covenant. In some subdivisions, the owners association may own land within the development that may be benefited by the covenant, such as a clubhouse or recreational facility. By contrast, in a condominium, the owners association typically does not own these amenities, which are instead concurrently owned by the unit owners themselves as tenants in common. Despite this technicality, courts typically permit the owners association to enforce the covenants, either as a successor to the rights of the developer or (perhaps more satisfactorily) as an agent or representative of the owners.[423]

---

[417] Gerber v. Pecht, 15 N.J. 29, 104 A.2d 41 (1954).

[418] E.g., Waikiki Malia Hotel, Inc. v. Kinkai Props. Ltd. Partn., 75 Haw. 370, 862 P.2d 1048 (1993); Paniaguas v. Endor, Inc., 847 N.E.2d 967 (Ind.App.2006) (original developer who sold partially completed subdivision owed no duty to lot owners to ensure successor's compliance with covenants); 2 Am. Law of Prop. § 9.18 (1952); Restatement of Property § 538, Comment c, Illus. 2 (1944) (covenant to maintain dam located on B's parcel no longer binds B upon conveyance of parcel); Restatement (Third) of Property-Servitudes § 4.4(1) (2000) (covenant running with benefited estate burdens covenantor only for obligations accruing during time covenantor holds burdened estate).

[419] Ideally, the parties would express this intent explicitly in the language of the covenant. In appropriate cases, a court might infer this intent from the nature of the act promised and circumstances tending to show that the covenantee was relying upon the personal credit of the covenantor. E.g., Restatement of Property § 538, Comment c & Illus. 1 (1944).

Where the burden of the covenant is in gross (i.e., where the covenantor's promise does not relate in any way to the covenantor's ownership of a parcel of land), questions regarding whether that burden is delegable and whether such a delegation relieves the covenantor of its obligation are governed by the law of contract. Restatement (Third) of Property-Servitudes § 4.4(3) (2000).

[420] Restatement of Property §§ 549, 550 (1944); Restatement (Third) of Property-Servitudes § 4.4(2) (2000).

[421] Rodruck v. Sand Point Maintenance Comm'n, 48 Wash.2d 565, 295 P.2d 714 (1956).

[422] See Hannula v. Hacienda Homes, 34 Cal.2d 442, 211 P.2d 302 (1949); Jones v. Northwest Real Estate Co., 149 Md. 271, 131 A. 446 (1925); Normandy Square Ass'n, Inc. v. Ells, 213 Neb. 60, 327 N.W.2d 101 (1982); Whiteco Metrocom, Inc. v. Industrial Props. Corp., 711 S.W.2d 81 (Tex.App.1986); Heath v. Uraga, 106 Wash.App. 506, 24 P.3d 413 (2001).

[423] See, e.g., Merrionette Manor Homes Improvement Ass'n v. Heda, 11 Ill.App.2d 186, 136 N.E.2d 556 (1956); Griffin v. Tall Timbers Dev., Inc., 681 So.2d 546 (Miss.1996); Harbor Village Homeowners Ass'n, Inc. v. Waldenberg, 369 P.3d 353 (Mont.2016); Neponsit Property Owners Ass'n v. Emigrant Industrial Sav. Bank,

§ 8.25 EQUITABLE RESTRICTIONS—INTRODUCTION

Covenants that run in equity—sometimes referred to here by the neutral name "equitable restrictions"—are today usually known as "equitable servitudes." They became recognized in 1848 as a result of Lord Chancellor Cottenham's decision in Tulk v. Moxhay.[424] One must realize that the equity chancellors were completely independent of the common law courts, literally a law unto themselves.[425] The decision in Tulk v. Moxhay was precisely contrary to English common law of real covenants, which did not allow the running of burdens that originate in a conveyance in fee.[426]

Tulk v. Moxhay concerned a covenant in a deed whereby the grantee of Leicester Square promised for himself, his heirs, and assigns, to maintain the square as a pleasure garden for the benefit of dwelling lots around the square. Owners of surrounding lots, upon payment of a fee, were to have access to the garden. By a series of conveyances from the grantee, the defendant became the owner of the square; the defendant knew fully of the covenant, but still intended to build houses upon the square. The plaintiff (the original covenantee) sought to enjoin the defendant's intended conduct as a violation of the covenant. At common law, the burden of this covenant would not have run to bind defendant because horizontal privity did not exist between the original covenantor and covenantee.[427] In Equity, though, Lord Cottenham concluded that there was "an equity attached to the property" which bound anyone who took the property with notice of it.[428] It would be "inequitable," Cottenham said, for the original covenantor to shed the burden simply by selling the land.

What was the mechanism underlying the decision? The question caused much debate among scholars, for Tulk v. Moxhay did not resolve the question clearly. Some have argued that equitable restrictions run under a contract theory, in which the promise is enforced against third persons. For example, Professor James Barr Ames thought prevention of unjust enrichment was the basis.[429] Dean Harlan F. Stone favored a variant of specific performance,[430] as does Tiffany's treatise.[431] Language in Tulk v. Moxhay about a "contract" tends to support a contract theory, and in certain situations such a theory works well. By contrast, others have considered equitable restrictions as creating servitudes on the burdened land, similar to easements; hence the name

---

15 N.E.2d 793 (N.Y.1938); Glenhurst Homeowners Ass'n, Inc. v. XI Family Trust, 330 P.3d 494 (Okla.2014); SPUR at Williams Brice Owners Ass'n v. Lalla, 781 S.E.2d 115 (S.C.App.2015).

[424] 2 Phil. 774, 41 Eng.Rep. 1143 (Ch. 1848). But cf. Reichman, Toward a Unified Concept of Servitudes, 55 S.Cal.L.Rev. 1177, 1188–1211 (1982), which presents evidence that American courts enforced the equivalent of equitable restrictions prior to Tulk v. Moxhay.

[425] If there had ever been any doubt of this, it had long ago been settled in one of the famous constitutional struggles of English history. At the beginning of the 17th century, Lord Coke, Chief Justice of King's Bench, had taken on both Chancery and King James, claiming in essence that the law courts could control decisions of equity. Coke lost the battle, lost his job, and was lucky not to lose his neck; after that, until Parliament established a unified court system in 1875, the chancellor's independence was assured.

[426] See supra § 8.19.

[427] Recall from Section § 8.19 that under English law, horizontal privity existed only where the covenantor and covenantee stood in a landlord-tenant relationship.

[428] 2 Phil. at 778, 41 Eng.Rep. at 1144.

[429] Ames, Specific Performance For and Against Strangers to the Contract, 17 Harv.L.Rev. 174, 177–79 (1904).

[430] Stone, The Equitable Rights and Liabilities of Strangers to a Contract, 18 Colum.L.Rev. 291, 294–96 (1918).

[431] 3 H. Tiffany, Real Property § 861, at 489 (3d ed.1939).

"equitable servitudes." Under this theory, the land itself—as distinct from an estate in the land—becomes burdened with the covenant; the servitude "sinks its tentacles into the soil." As one might suppose, real property teachers tend to favor this theory. Adherents include Judge Clark,[432] Dean Roscoe Pound,[433] Professor Richard R. Powell,[434] Professor William F. Walsh,[435] and the Restatements of Property.[436] Not only the recent writers but also the recent case law tends strongly to employ the equitable servitude theory.[437] It has become the accepted doctrine in England.[438] As with the contract theory, the servitude theory creates problems in certain situations, as we will see later in this Chapter. While neither theory can completely explain the operation of equitable restrictions as they have developed in the courts, the servitude theory has by far the better of it.

As was done with real covenants, the following sections divide the discussion of equitable restrictions according to their elements. These are: (1) the form of the covenant; (2) intent of the covenanting parties that the covenant shall run; (3) the requirement of touch and concern; (4) the (non)relevance of horizontal privity between the covenanting parties; (5) the running of the benefit or burden to successors of the covenanting parties; and (6) notice. The Chapter ends with discussion of the rules governing termination of equitable restrictions,[439] an overview of the manner in which a developer can properly create a set of reciprocal running covenants in the context of modern real estate development,[440] and an explanation of the legal theories upon which courts have enforced equitable servitudes despite the developer's failure to follow the proper procedures.[441]

One final observation: equitable servitude doctrine has generally surpassed real covenant doctrine in significance in the courts today. Because the plaintiff typically seeks to enforce the covenant through the equitable remedy of an injunction, recent court decisions rarely turn upon real covenant doctrine. To the extent the distinction between real covenants and equitable servitudes remains meaningful,[442] the standards for real

---

[432]   C. Clark, Real Covenants and Other Interests Which "Run With Land" 94 (2d ed.1947).

[433]   Pound, The Progress of the Law, 1918–1919, Equity, 33 Harv.L.Rev. 813–15 (1920).

[434]   5 R. Powell, Real Property ¶ 670 (1990) (the contract theory is "historically correct, but presently inadequate").

[435]   Walsh, Equitable Easements and Restrictions, 2 Rocky Mtn.L.Rev. 234, 236 (1930).

[436]   Restatement of Property § 539, Comment a (1944). The Restatement of Servitudes likewise embraces this approach, explicitly subsuming the concepts of "real covenant" and "equitable servitude" within the unified concept of "servitude." Restatement (Third) of Property-Servitudes § 1.4 (2000).

[437]   2 Am. Law of Prop. § 9.24 (1952); 5 R. Powell, Real Property ¶ 670 (1990) ("the great weight of authority"); L. Simes & C. Taylor, The Improvement of Conveyancing by Legislation 219 (1960).

[438]   London County Council v. Allen, [1914] 3 K.B. 642 (C.A.); Hayton, Restrictive Covenants as Property Interests, 87 L.Q.Rev. 539, 540–41 (1971).

[439]   See § 8.30 infra.

[440]   See § 8.32 infra, notes 479–480.

[441]   See § 8.32 infra, notes 481–496.

[442]   The Restatement of Servitudes essentially rejects any distinction between "real covenants" and "equitable servitudes," subsuming them under the unified term "servitudes" and thus generally applying the same elements for servitude enforcement regardless of the remedy sought. Restatement (Third) of Property-Servitudes § 1.4 (2000) ("The terms 'real covenant' and 'equitable servitude' describes servitudes encompassed within the term 'covenant that runs with land' and are not used in this Restatement except to describe the evolution of servitudes law."). Nevertheless, most courts have continued to treat real covenant and equitable servitude doctrines as distinct despite the promulgation of the Restatement of Servitudes, and for this reason this treatise continues its traditional approach of describing each doctrine distinctly. However, a reader cannot help but to note that many of the ensuing sections simply make reference to the corresponding section in the

covenant enforcement retain vitality only where the plaintiff is seeking a judgment for damages (e.g., a judgment for unpaid rent in a lease, or for unpaid fines imposed by an owners association)—as equity ordinarily will not grant such a remedy—and perhaps in a few situations in which courts will not enforce affirmative covenants in equity.

§ 8.26 FORM OF THE COVENANT IN EQUITY

The discussion of the form of real covenants in Section 8.15 generally applies to the form of covenants running in equity. We assume here that there is a covenant that is binding between covenantor and covenantee under the rules of contract law. Historically, scholars and courts diverged on the question whether equitable restrictions had to arise by virtue of an instrument that complied with the Statute of Frauds. Some suggested that the statute does not apply at all, because equitable restrictions are contract rights and not interests in land.[443] The opposing view—that equitable restrictions are interests in land and hence must comply with the Statute of Frauds—was adopted in the Restatements[444] and by leading American treatises.

As a practical matter, the application of the Statute of Frauds does not serve to invalidate many ostensible covenants. The large majority of covenants are created in instruments that comply with every required formality. Exceptions to the applicability of the Statute save most of the rest.[445]

§ 8.27 EQUITABLE RESTRICTIONS MUST TOUCH AND CONCERN

To run, equitable restrictions must touch and concern benefited and burdened land, and the requirement is essentially the same as for real covenants.[446] Thus, the prior discussion in section 8.16 generally applies and we do not repeat it all here.

---

prior discussion of real covenant doctrine. For example, the analysis of whether a covenant "touches and concerns" land does not differ analytically whether the covenant is being enforced at law or in equity.

[443] Johnson v. Mt. Baker Park Presbyterian Church, 113 Wash. 458, 194 P. 536 (1920); C. Clark, Real Covenants and Other Interests Which "Run With Land" 178 (2d ed.1947); Sims, The Law of Real Covenants: Exceptions to the Restatement of the Subject by the American Law Institute, 30 Cornell L.Q. 1, 27–28 (1944) (counting fourteen states adopting this position, against nine that had done otherwise). See also 3 H. Tiffany, Real Property § 860 (3d ed.1939) (agreeing with approach of Sims).

[444] Restatement of Property § 539, Comment j (1944); Restatement (Third) of Property-Servitudes § 2.1(1) (2000).

[445] See generally § 8.15 supra. Today, many equitable restrictions arise in connection with common interest development such as subdivisions or condominiums. Section 8.32 discusses the proper procedure by which a developer should create a set of reciprocal restrictions that benefit and burden every lot or unit within the development. When the developer follows the proper procedure described there, no Statute of Frauds problem arises. Problems can arise, however, when the developer fails to follow the proper procedure, such as (for example) by conveying one lot or unit to a buyer without creating a reciprocal burden on the developer's retained land. In these situations, a dispute may later arise in which the plaintiff argues that the court should nevertheless enforce the covenant as a reciprocal restriction, based on evidence that the developer intended to create reciprocal restrictions as reflected by extrinsic evidence of a "common plan of development" (which might include representations made by the developer orally or in written sales literature). In appropriate cases, courts have recognized such reciprocal restrictions by implication or under third-party-beneficiary theories. These theories are discussed in greater depth in Section 8.35.

[446] See 2 Am. Law of Prop. § 9.28 (1952); 5 R. Powell, Real Property ¶ 673 (1990). Treatises treat the touch and concern element the same for both real covenants and equitable restrictions, and the Restatement of Property (Servitudes) § 1.4 (2000) rejects any distinction between real covenants and equitable covenants.

As discussed in Section 8.16, there has been some question whether affirmative covenants meet the touch and concern standard so as to run at law. Most courts have held that affirmative equitable restrictions can touch and concern. E.g., Everett Factories & Terminal Corp. v. Oldetyme Distillers Corp., 300 Mass. 499, 15

Can an equitable restriction burden land the covenantor does not now own, but acquires at a later date? For example, suppose *A* conveys or leases Blackacre to *B* for *B*'s use for a certain business, and *A* covenants in the deed or lease that *A* will not operate a similar business on any land which *A* now or hereafter occupies or owns within a radius of two miles of Blackacre. Shopping center landlords sometimes make such covenants, typically called "radius" clauses, in tenant leases. Presumably the covenant cannot bind other land within the radius until *A* acquires it,[447] but once *A* does acquire such land, a valid equitable servitude should arise. The weight of authority supports this conclusion.[448]

§ 8.28 INTENT TO BIND SUCCESSORS BY EQUITABLE RESTRICTIONS

For the burden and benefit of an equitable restriction to run, the parties must have intended that the restriction would bind successors. This intent is commonly expressed overtly in the instrument creating the restriction; no particular form of expression is required.[449] As with real covenants, as discussed in Section 8.17, intent may be implied from the circumstances surrounding the creation of the restriction.[450]

N.E.2d 829 (1938) (holding that although promise in deed to pay one-third of track maintenance expenses and taxes was not a "covenant" because deed was not signed by promisor-grantee, promise bound grantee in equity, even though it called for the payment of money); Annot., 41 A.L.R. 1363, 1364 (1926); Annot., 102 A.L.R. 781, 784 (1936); Newman & Losey, Covenants Running with the Land, and Equitable Servitudes: Two Concepts, or One?, 21 Hastings L.J. 1319, 1339 (1970). But the theoretical justification for this result is complicated. If one accepts that equitable restrictions are interests in land similar to easements, how is it possible to have an easement requiring the owner of the servient estate to do affirmative acts? Puzzled by this dilemma, Judge Clark concluded in his treatise that the law should allow negative equitable restrictions, but that recognition of affirmative ones should "wait upon the development of a more enlightened policy." C. Clark, Real Covenants and Other Interests Which "Run With Land" 180–81 (2d ed.1947). The answer, enlightened or not, is that equitable restrictions are not easements; perhaps it is better to say only that they are both interests in land of the same general family (i.e., servitudes). Most equitable covenants today are negative, such as covenants limiting parcels to single-family residential use. But there is no question that covenants to join homeowners' associations and to support them and pay their dues—all affirmative undertakings—will run in equity as well. E.g., Kell v. Bella Vista Village Prop. Owners Ass'n, 258 Ark. 757, 528 S.W.2d 651 (1975); Alpenwald Village, Inc. v. Town of Readsboro, 166 Vt. 28, 687 A.2d 481 (1996); Rodruck v. Sand Point Maintenance Comm'n, 48 Wash.2d 565, 295 P.2d 714 (1956).

[447] See Hazen v. Mathews, 184 Mass. 388, 68 N.E. 838 (1903).

[448] E.g., Lewis v. Gollner, 129 N.Y. 227, 29 N.E. 81 (1891); 2 Am. Law of Prop. § 9.35 (1952). There is another theoretical barrier to the enforcement of such a servitude. Suppose that *A* acquires Whiteacre, a parcel within the radius, but sells Whiteacre two years later to *C*, who lacks actual knowledge of the radius clause. The question is whether the recording of the deed containing the radius clause is sufficient to give constructive notice of the radius clause to *C*. Under some authority, the answer is no, unless the radius clause appears in a deed within the chain of title to Whiteacre. For further discussion, see infra § 11.11.

[449] Restatement (Third) of Property-Servitudes § 2.2 (2000). With real covenants, *Spencer's Case* held that a covenant relating to a thing not then in existence would run only if the parties used the word "assigns." Because equitable restrictions have never been controlled by *Spencer's Case*, courts have not developed a rule requiring use of the word "assigns" or other "magic" words to create an equitable servitude. Nevertheless, as discussed in Section 8.17, any well-drafted covenant typically makes clear that it is intended to bind both the parties and their heirs, successors, and assigns.

[450] Restatement (Third) of Property-Servitudes § 2.2 (2000). For example, suppose *A* covenants with *B* not to build certain kinds of structures on *A*'s land. *B* owns adjacent land that will be greatly benefited by the covenant, but the language of the covenant does not expressly refer to *B*'s land. Courts may infer that such a benefit was intended to attach to and run with *B*'s adjacent land. Bauby v. Krasow, 107 Conn. 109, 139 A. 508 (1927); Waikiki Malia Hotel, Inc. v. Kinkai Props. Ltd. Partn., 75 Haw. 370, 862 P.2d 1048 (1993); Clem v. Valentine, 155 Md. 19, 141 A. 710 (1928); Peck v. Conway, 119 Mass. 546 (1876); Nature Conservancy v. Congel, 253 A.D.2d 248, 689 N.Y.S.2d 317 (1999); 2 Am. Law of Prop. § 9.29, at 417 (1952). But cf. Dennison v. Rubatino, 2003 WL 22996113 (Wash.App.2003) (not allowing adjacent owner to enforce height-restriction covenant absent evidence covenant was intended to benefit adjacent owner).

When we consider the benefit side, we find statements that the benefit of an equitable restriction will run only if the covenanting parties intend it.[451] This means only that the benefit side may not run to anyone if the thing to be done (or not to be done) by the covenantor is for the covenantee's personal benefit only, i.e., if it does not benefit some parcel of land.[452] This is obvious; a benefit cannot run with any land if it is in gross.

In some decisions, statements about intent deal with the issue of whose land is intended to be benefited by a covenant (assuming the covenant touches and concerns land). If a court is willing to employ third-party-beneficiary theory, it is possible for the parties to attach the benefit to a third person's land by an express statement.[453] In addition, courts have allowed third parties to enforce a covenant when the covenant is part of a common plan of development and they have land within the area covered by this plan. In substance, the court infers that, because the covenant was part of the common plan for the area, the covenant was intended to benefit (and also burden) all parcels within the area.[454] Some courts employ a different theory, known as "implied reciprocal servitudes," for making common-plan covenants attach; a comparison of these theories appears in Section 8.35.

§ 8.29 HORIZONTAL PRIVITY NOT REQUIRED WITH EQUITABLE RESTRICTIONS

A major difference between real covenants and equitable restrictions is that the latter may run even if they are not created in connection with the transfer of an interest in land. Horizontal privity, as explained in Section 8.18, is not necessary for the running of equitable restrictions.[455] In practice, equitable restrictions are usually made in an instrument of conveyance, which would satisfy the horizontal privity requirement in most American states. But the presence or absence of horizontal privity is irrelevant, and the reason is obvious enough: equitable restrictions are self-contained equitable interests in land that do not ride along on any other interest or estate.[456]

§ 8.30 EQUITABLE RESTRICTIONS RUN WITH BURDENED LAND (SINK THEIR ROOTS INTO THE SOIL)

This section corresponds to the discussion of the "vertical privity" requirement for real covenants in Section 8.17. We saw that real covenants run with estates in land;

---

[451] See 2 Am. Law of Prop. § 9.29 (1952).

[452] Stegall v. Housing Auth., 278 N.C. 95, 178 S.E.2d 824 (1971); Clark v. Guy Drews Post of Amer. Legion, 247 Wis. 48, 18 N.W.2d 322 (1945).

[453] E.g., Nature Conservancy v. Congel, 253 A.D.2d 248, 689 N.Y.S.2d 317 (1999). Cf. Hazen v. Mathews, 184 Mass. 388, 68 N.E. 838 (1903) (where the court refused to apply third-party beneficiary theory).

[454] Rodgers v. Reimann, 227 Or. 62, 361 P.2d 101, 103–04 (1961) (dictum); 2 Am. Law of Prop. § 9.29, at 417–18 (1952); 5 R. Powell, Real Property ¶ 673 (1990).

[455] E.g., Excel Willowbrook, L.L.C. v. JP Morgan Chase Bank, N.A., 758 F.3d 592 (5th Cir.2014) (Texas law); Desai v. OK Oil, Inc., 233 Ga.App. 855, 505 S.E.2d 271 (1998); St. Clair v. Krueger, 115 Idaho 702, 769 P.2d 579 (1989); Well-Built Homes, Inc. v. Shuster, 64 Mass.App. 619, 834 N.E.2d 1213 (2005); Pratte v. Balatsos, 99 N.H. 430, 113 A.2d 492 (1955); Lewis v. Gollner, 129 N.Y. 227, 29 N.E. 81 (1891); Bald Eagle Valley R.R Co. v. Nittany Valley R.R. Co., 171 Pa. 284, 33 A. 239 (1895); Stern v. Metropolitan Water Dist. of Salt Lake & Sandy, 274 P.3d 935 (Utah 2012); Lake Limerick Country Club v. Hunt Mfg. Homes, Inc., 120 Wash.App. 246, 84 P.3d 295 (2004). See 2 Am. Law of Prop. § 9.26 (1952); 5 R. Powell, Real Property ¶ 673 (1990); Restatement of Property § 539, Comment a (1944); Restatement (Third) of Property-Servitudes § 2.4 (2000).

[456] This point should not be confused with the requirement that equitable restrictions must either conform to the Statute of Frauds or fall within one of its exceptions. See § 8.26 supra.

hence, the simile that they ride with estates "like a bird on a wagon." The corresponding simile for equitable covenants is that they "sink their roots into the soil." By this we mean the land itself—more precisely, every possessory interest in it—is bound by the covenant in equity.[457] Any person who succeeds the covenantor as possessor of the burdened land may be bound, whether or not the person happens to hold the covenantor's precise estate. Thus, a tenant[458] or a contract purchaser who does not have title[459] may be bound, as well as an adverse possessor.[460] Whether vertical privity (as discussed in Section 8.18) exists between the party sought to be bound and that party's predecessor is irrelevant. The underlying theory should be obvious by now; equitable servitudes are equitable interests in land in the same family as easements.[461] As the original Restatement explained:

> The burden of this equitable interest binds all those having interests in the land subordinate to or arising posterior to that of the promisor who possesses the land without defense to it regardless of whether they have the same estate the promisor had or whether they succeeded [the promisor] in anything other than possession.[462]

§ 8.31 NOTICE/VALUE AND THE RUNNING OF EQUITABLE RESTRICTIONS

"[F]or if an equity is attached to the property by the owner," said the court in Tulk v. Moxhay,[463] "no one purchasing with notice of that equity can stand in a different situation from the party from whom he purchases." In *Tulk*, the purchaser who was bound by the covenant had "actual notice," i.e., actual subjective knowledge of the covenant. It is clear that actual notice is sufficient to fasten an equitable restriction upon a successor to the burdened land, provided the other elements for running are present.[464]

Typically, successors today receive "constructive notice" of an equitable covenant through the operation of recording acts. One who acquires an interest in land is charged with notice of an equitable restriction contained in a duly recorded instrument within the chain of title to that land.[465] Some doubt exists about constructive notice, however, when the prior instrument is outside the direct chain of title. Suppose *A,* who owns both Blackacre and Whiteacre, conveys Whiteacre to *B* and covenants in the deed that nothing but a single-family dwelling will be built on Blackacre. In this situation, the deed is

---

[457] 2 Am. Law of Prop. § 9.27 (1952); C. Clark, Real Covenants and Other Interests Which "Run With Land" 93–94 (2d ed.1947); Restatement of Property § 539, Comment i (1944); Restatement (Third) of Property-Servitudes § 5.2 & Comment b (2000); Bordwell, The Running of Covenants—No Anomaly, 36 Iowa L.Rev. 1, 3 (1950).

[458] Oliver v. Hewitt, 191 Va. 163, 60 S.E.2d 1 (1950).

[459] Huber v. Guglielmi, 29 Ohio App. 290, 163 N.E. 571 (1928).

[460] See Restatement (Third) of Property-Servitudes § 5.2 (2000); Restatement of Property § 539 Comment i, Illus. 3 (1944).

[461] See § 8.25 supra.

[462] Restatement of Property § 539, Comment i (1944).

[463] 2 Phil. 774, 778, 41 Eng.Rep. 1143, 1144 (Ch. 1848).

[464] E.g., Desai v. OK Oil, Inc., 233 Ga.App. 855, 505 S.E.2d 271 (1998).

[465] Wiegman v. Kusel, 270 Ill. 520, 110 N.E. 884 (1915); Everett Factories & Terminal Corp. v. Oldetyme Distillers Corp., 300 Mass. 499, 15 N.E.2d 829 (1938); Oliver v. Hewitt, 191 Va. 163, 60 S.E.2d 1 (1950); 2 Am. Law of Prop. § 9.24 (1952); C. Clark, Real Covenants and Other Interests Which "Run With Land" 183–84 (2d ed.1947); 5 R. Powell, Real Property ¶ 670 (1990); Restatement of Property § 539, Comments l, m (1944); Restatement (Third) of Property-Servitudes § 7.14 (2000) (benefit of an unrecorded servitude is subject to extinguishment under the recording statute); 3 H. Tiffany, Real Property § 863 (3d ed.1939).

conveying title to Whiteacre, but Blackacre is the burdened land. Assume the deed is properly recorded at once. Will C, a subsequent purchaser of Blackacre who has no other notice of the covenant, be deemed to have constructive notice of it by virtue of the recorded A-to-B deed? One line of cases, represented by Finley v. Glenn,[466] says yes; another line, represented by Glorieux v. Lighthipe,[467] says no. *Finley* holds that, because recorded deeds are indexed under the name of the grantor in the typical grantor-grantee index, and because C must search the index under the name of the prior grantor, A, C is thus charged with discovering the A-to-B deed. *Glorieux* holds it to be an unacceptable burden to require C to examine deeds that A has given to land other than Blackacre itself.[468]

Some decisions suggest that there is a kind of constructive notice besides record notice, sometimes called "inquiry notice." Sanborn v. McLean,[469] a leading and instructive if perhaps extreme equitable restriction case, held that because of the uniform appearance of the subdivision, a purchaser of a lot in the subdivision was charged with knowledge that all lots were restricted to private dwellings. The court said that anyone purchasing would thereby have either constructive notice of the uniform restriction or at least inquiry notice to make a further investigation to determine if the restriction existed.[470]

Even if a person acquires land burdened by an equitable restriction without notice of that restriction, the person will take the land free of the burden only if the person gave value for the land.[471] To state the proposition conversely, the equitable restriction binds any successor to the burdened land who is not a bona fide purchaser. As against a bona fide purchaser for value, the equitable interests cease to be effective.[472] There are indeed other kinds of equitable interests in land, of which the most frequent examples are equitable liens and beneficial interests in trust. And there is an established doctrine that such equitable interests are ineffective against a subsequent grantee who is innocent of their existence and purchases for value, i.e., is a bona fide purchaser.[473]

---

[466] 303 Pa. 131, 154 A. 299 (1931). See also Sanborn v. McLean, 233 Mich. 227, 206 N.W. 496 (1925).

[467] 88 N.J.L. 199, 96 A. 94 (1915).

[468] In other words, *Glorieux* suggests that a reasonable person in C's position (someone buying Blackacre) would see that the A-to-B deed conveys fee title to Whiteacre and would ignore it or fail to read it in detail—when a careful reading of the deed would reveal that it may also impose a covenant upon Blackacre. By contrast, *Finley* suggests that a reasonable searcher would read every recorded deed ever executed by A before concluding that A never imposed a covenant upon Blackacre.

In truth, the actual burden of the search required by *Finley* will vary depending on the volume of past land transactions in the county and the commonness of the grantor's name. If the grantor is named John Smith (there could be hundreds of John Smiths in a large county), or is a developer that has engaged in hundreds or thousands of prior transactions, the burden of searching every recorded deed under that name for covenants affecting the parcel being purchased could be quite significant. By contrast, if the land is located in a small rural county and the grantor's name is not common, the burden of the search required by *Finley* may be insubstantial.

[469] 233 Mich. 227, 206 N.W. 496 (1925).

[470] See, e.g., Shalimar Ass'n v. D.O.C. Enters., Ltd., 142 Ariz. 36, 688 P.2d 682 (App.1984) (notice of restrictive covenant exists if reasonably careful inspection of premises would disclose need for inquiry); Hagan v. Sabal Palms, Inc., 186 So.2d 302 (Fla.App.1966); Turner v. Brocato, 206 Md. 336, 111 A.2d 855 (1955).

[471] C. Clark, Real Covenants and Other Interests Which "Run With Land" 183 (2d ed.1947); Restatement of Property § 539, Comment *l* (1944); 3 H. Tiffany, Real Property § 861 (3d ed.1939).

[472] Restatement of Property § 539, Comment *l* (1944); Restatement (Third) of Property-Servitudes § 7.14 (2000). See also Murphy v. City of Seattle, 32 Wash.App. 386, 647 P.2d 540 (1982) (no notice of restrictive covenant that was contained in court records but not recorded in land records).

[473] Martin v. Bowen, 51 N.J.Eq. 452, 26 A. 823 (1893); 4 A. Scott, Trusts §§ 284, 287–289 (4th ed.1989).

§ 8.32 SEPARATE RUNNING OF BENEFIT AND BURDEN

This section parallels part of the discussion in Section 8.21. The general issue that has concerned courts is whether the benefit side and the burden side of an equitable restriction should be considered to exist separately. We have consistently spoken of them separately, and the decisions generally consider them separately. The more precise issue is whether both sides of the restriction must touch and concern and otherwise meet the requirements for running for either side to run. More specifically, some decisions have raised the question whether the burden side will run if the benefit side is "in gross," i.e., if the benefit side does not touch and concern any land. In England it has been held that the burden side cannot run in this situation, supposedly pursuant to the English rule against easements in gross. American decisions have split on the point, some allowing the burden side to run and some not.[474]

§ 8.33 TERMINATION, MODIFICATION, AND INTERPRETATION OF EQUITABLE RESTRICTIONS

The discussions of interpretation of running covenants in Section 8.22 and termination and amendment of running covenants in Section 8.23 generally apply equally to equitable restrictions. We repeat one matter for emphasis. In discussing the changed circumstances doctrine, we saw that most courts hold that a sufficient change in circumstances operates to terminate the covenant, not merely bar a remedy. However, some courts have followed a "balancing of the equities" approach under which equitable remedies (usually an injunction) are barred. When this latter doctrine is applied to a real covenant, the benefited party cannot have an injunction but perhaps might still recover damages. As explained below, equity courts have traditionally been reluctant to award money damages. With the merger of law and equity in American courts, this traditional reluctance has diminished; nevertheless, in theory it may be more difficult to persuade the equity court to award damages in this situation than to get damages at law upon a real covenant.[475]

§ 8.34 REMEDIES FOR BREACH OF EQUITABLE RESTRICTIONS

General principles distinguishing the equity/common law systems of relief[476] support some basic propositions. First, the equitable remedy of an injunction is generally

---

[474] See supra notes 342–343.

[475] See Jackson v. Stevenson, 156 Mass. 496, 31 N.E. 691 (1892); McClure v. Leaycraft, 183 N.Y. 36, 75 N.E. 961 (1905) (dictum); 2 Am. Law of Prop. § 9.39 (1952); 5 R. Powell, Real Property ¶ 676 (1990); Restatement of Property § 564, Comment d (1944). Under the Restatement of Servitudes, which rejects any distinction between real covenants and equitable servitudes, a court that determined not to grant an injunction based on a balancing of the equities could nevertheless award damages even if the covenant would not have run at law under the traditional common law rules.

[476] Equity, as a separate, coordinate system, had (and still has) two functions; the remedial (fashioning remedies) and the substantive (originating theories of recovery). Its remedial side has been the more important and receives the most attention in law schools; we are especially familiar with injunctions and specific performance. On its substantive side, equity's great contributions were the trust, the equity of redemption in mortgages, and the equitable restrictions we discuss here. Equitable remedies were available in chancery to vindicate equitable substantive claims, but equity never gave common law remedies as such, though certain equitable remedies paralleled the legal ones. For their part, the common law courts neither recognized equitable causes of action nor gave equitable relief, though law, too, developed a few theories of recovery and a few remedies similar to those in equity. In equity, however, it was not only possible but the ordinary course

available to prevent future breach of an equitable restriction. Conversely, the fact that damages are granted does tell us, under traditional equity and common law principles, that the covenant is probably a real covenant. Note the word "probably" must be inserted because equity occasionally would give money damages if for some reason its preferred specific remedy, injunction, could not be given. This has been called equity's "cleanup" jurisdiction.[477] An example might arise when the plaintiff sued to enjoin breach of an equitable restriction but during the pendency of the action the defendant sold the land to a bona fide purchaser to whom the restriction did not run and against whom the court could not issue an injunction. In such a case, an equity court might decree that the plaintiff was entitled to equitable damages for the defendant's past breaches. Such cases are rare.

The situation is more complex in America today, because most states have merged the functions of law and equity into unified court systems. Many of the historical distinctions between law and equity have broken down. Still, judges and lawyers have a notion of the differences between equitable and legal courses of action; there must be a general awareness of the origins of real covenants and equitable restrictions. It would be fairly novel for a merged court to grant damages for breach of an equitable restriction, though there is perhaps some indication of movement in that direction.[478] Of course an injunction is usually the preferred remedy.

§ 8.35 IMPLIED RECIPROCAL SERVITUDES

Despite the widespread use of covenants, the theoretical mechanism by which such restrictions arise and operate is complex and poorly understood. In this section, we begin with a discussion of how a developer properly creates the reciprocal covenant relationships on which the modern common interest development depends. We will then discuss various theories of how equitable servitudes might arise by implication, even when the developer fails to create the covenant regime properly. This section requires a firm working grasp on principles discussed in the preceding sections, and should help to synthesize those principles.

Creating an Effective Express Servitude Regime

A common interest community involves a set (or "regime") of servitudes which a developer establishes by preparing and recording a written instrument typically called a "declaration." This document sets forth the intended servitudes, often called "conditions, covenants, and restrictions" or "CC&Rs," and states that the CC&Rs are intended to burden and benefit the owner of each lot or unit covered by the declaration and the owner's heirs, successors, and assigns. The developer prepares the CC&Rs in conjunction with a plat (a form of map) that depicts the land within the community as divided into lots (or units) and common areas. By the terms of the declaration, the CC&Rs create reciprocal restrictions and obligations, burdening each lot or unit within the community for the benefit of every other lot or unit. The developer then records the declaration and the plat in the appropriate public land records before the developer sells

---

to give equitable forms of relief on a common law cause of action, provided the chancellor was convinced the remedy available in law was "inadequate." D. Dobbs, Remedies §§ 2.1–2.5 (1973).

[477] See D. Dobbs, Remedies § 2.7 (1973).

[478] Miller v. McCamish, 78 Wash.2d 821, 479 P.2d 919 (1971).

any lots or units. This places the CC&Rs in the "chain of title" for each lot or unit, so that anyone buying a lot or unit will be deemed to have constructive notice of the CC&Rs.

The recording of the declaration and plat also creates certain efficiencies for the developer as the developer begins conveying lots or units. For example, the plat typically assigns a number to each lot or unit depicted on it. When lot or unit sales commence, this permits the developer to describe each lot or unit by that assigned number in the deed of conveyance, rather than having to describe the lot or unit by a full metes and bounds legal description. Further, each deed of conveyance need not re-recite each and every covenant expressed in the CC&Rs; the deed can merely recite that the grantee's title to the lot or unit is subject to all covenants and restrictions of record.[479] This saves the developer (and the lot buyer) some transaction costs; it is cheaper to record a one-page deed that incorporates the CC&Rs by reference than it is to record a deed that takes ten to thirty pages or more to recite all of the applicable covenants. This also permits the developer to avoid potential problems that might arise if the developer attempted to re-recite all of the covenants in every conveyance deed, but inadvertently or negligently omitted one or more of the covenants from one or more of the conveyance deeds.

Suppose Developer follows the procedure described above for a simple subdivision of fifty lots, and that the CC&Rs include a covenant that each lot will be used for single-family purposes only. Developer then sells Lot 1 to Gotberg, executing and delivering to Gotberg a deed conveying fee title to Lot 1. The acceptance of this deed will impose reciprocal benefits and burdens on all fifty lots. As the owner of Lot 1, Gotberg enjoys the benefit of the covenants and may enforce them against the owner of each of Lots 2 through 50 (who, at this point, is still Developer). Gotberg also takes title to Lot 1 subject to the burden of the same covenants, which reciprocally benefit the owner of each of Lots 2 through 50 (again, at this point, still Developer). Now suppose Developer sells Lot 2 to Strong via the same process, and Strong later begins operating a restaurant on Lot 2. Developer clearly may enforce the covenant against Strong (there is a direct contract between them). But can Gotberg enforce the covenant against Strong? Yes, if the burden of the covenant affecting Lot 2 ran with Lot 2 from Developer to Strong.

Applying the standards established in the earlier sections, it is obvious that the single-family residential covenant ran with Lot 2 so as to permit Gotberg to enforce it against Strong. First, the covenant arose in the original transaction in which Developer conveyed Lot 1 to Gotberg and reciprocally restricted Lots 2 through 50, and it was enforceable between Developer and Gotberg as a contractual promise. Second, the covenant touches and concerns land, as it restricts the use of Lot 2 for the benefit of the other 49 lot owners in the community. Third, the original parties intended the covenant to bind successors, as indicated in the "heirs, successors, and assigns" language in the CC&Rs. Fourth, horizontal privity existed between Developer and Gotberg (the original parties), who stood in a grantor-grantee relationship by virtue of the deed conveying title to Lot 1. Fifth, vertical privity existed between Developer and Strong, who succeeded to Developer's entire fee estate in Lot 2. Sixth and finally, Strong has constructive notice of the covenant by virtue of the recorded declaration. The covenant thus satisfies the standard for a real covenant that runs to bind Strong at law, and Gotberg (as owner of

---

[479] At one time, some states (such as California) did not permit the developer to "pre-record" the CC&Rs in this way, but required the developer to recite them in each conveyance deed. Thankfully, California changed its mind and validated the method described in the text in Citizens for Covenant Compliance v. Anderson, 906 P.2d 1314 (Cal.1995).

Lot 1 and a beneficiary of the covenant) could enforce the covenant in an action against Strong for damages. For the same reasons, the covenant would satisfy the standard for a covenant running to bind Strong in equity—although the presence of horizontal and vertical privity would not be relevant to whether the covenant runs in equity—and Gotberg could obtain an injunction against Strong's future violation of the covenant.

Now consider the same series of events, but suppose that Gotberg (the owner of Lot 1) attempts to open the restaurant rather than Strong. Because Gotberg is still the original grantee of Lot 1, she remains bound as covenantor, and the benefit of the covenant that attached to Lot 2 will have run from Developer to Strong when Strong received title to Lot 2. Strong can thus enforce the covenant against Gotberg, either at law or in equity. By contrast, if Gotberg had previously conveyed Lot 1 to Bailey and it is Bailey that is now operating a restaurant in violation of the covenant, Strong (who is entitled to the benefit of the covenant as the successor to Lot 2) can enforce the covenant against Bailey at law or in equity as long as the burden of the covenant ran to bind Bailey as the successor owner of Lot 1. Assuming that Gotberg conveyed Lot 1 to Bailey in fee, the burden of the covenant would run to bind Bailey by the same rationale expressed in the previous paragraph.

One could work through the foregoing analysis as the Developer continues with the sale of Lots 3 through 50, with the same result. As the Developer delivers a deed to each lot, the buyer accepting that deed takes title to that lot subject to the burden of the covenants (which arose reciprocally on all lots when Developer first sold Lot 1 to Gotberg), and likewise takes title with the reciprocal benefit of those same covenants as they burden every other lot. We thus have a complete regime of reciprocal and mutually enforceable covenants, which will run under both real covenant doctrine (at least to possessors who succeed to the fee title to the affected lots)[480] and as equitable servitudes.

Implied Reciprocal Servitude Theory

Unfortunately, developers have not always established covenant regimes in the careful fashion described above. Suppose that in the previous example, Developer did not prepare and record a declaration containing reciprocal CC&Rs. Instead, suppose that Developer planned to insert into the deed for each lot (as each lot is sold) a uniform set of covenants binding the grantee and the grantee's heirs and assigns, including a covenant limiting use of the land to single-family residential purposes. Now assume that our sloppy Developer sells Lot 1 to Gotberg and Lot 2 to Strong, in that order—each time delivering a deed containing the uniform covenants.

Can Strong enforce the single-family residential use covenant against Gotberg if Gotberg opens a restaurant? Yes. The deed to Lot 1 created a burden on Lot 1 that Developer (as the owner of Lot 2 and grantor of the deed) could enforce against Gotberg

---

[480] Frequently, when an owner within the community violates a covenant, it is the owners association (rather than a specific neighbor) that takes action to enforce the covenants. Under a true running covenant theory, the benefit of a covenant is enforceable only by one who owns land benefited by the covenant. In some subdivisions, the owners association may own land within the development that may be benefited by the covenant, such as a clubhouse or recreational facility. By contrast, in a condominium, the owners association typically does not own these "common elements," which are concurrently owned by the unit owners themselves as tenants in common. Despite this technicality, courts typically permit the owners association to enforce the covenants, either as a successor to the rights of the developer or (perhaps more satisfactorily) as an agent of the owners. See, e.g., Merrionette Manor Homes Improvement Ass'n v. Heda, 11 Ill.App.2d 186, 136 N.E.2d 556 (1956); Griffin v. Tall Timbers Dev., Inc., 681 So.2d 546 (Miss.1996); Harbor Village Homeowners Ass'n, Inc. v. Waldenberg, 383 Mont. 543, 369 P.3d 353 (Table) (2016); Neponsit Property Owners Ass'n v. Emigrant Industrial Sav. Bank, 15 N.E.2d 793 (N.Y.1938).

as an enforceable contract. For the reasons explained earlier, the benefit of that covenant then ran to Strong when Developer conveyed Lot 2 to Strong. Further, the burden of the covenant would run with Lot 1 if Gotberg later sold it to Bailey. In effect, any fee owner of Lot 2 can enforce the covenant against any fee owner of Lot 1 that violates the covenant.

But now assume that Strong opens a restaurant on Lot 2, and Gotberg brings an action to enforce the covenant against Strong. We now have a conceptual problem. Developer may have *intended* that the series of deeds conveying each lot would create reciprocal restrictions benefiting and burdening each lot. *But each deed, on its face, burdened only the grantee.* Thus, when Developer deeded lot 1 to Gotberg, the covenant in that deed certainly burdened Lot 1 and correspondingly benefited Lots 2 through 50, which Developer still owned at the time—but it did not explicitly create any burden on Lots 2 through 50 (Developer's retained land) for Gotberg's benefit as owner of Lot 1! And although Developer's deed conveying Lot 2 to Strong also contains covenants binding the grantee (Strong) and successors, the covenants by their terms benefit only Developer (as grantor) and Developer's successors. But by now, Developer owns only Lots 3 through 50; Developer no longer owns Lot 1. Further, the covenant in Strong's deed does not explicitly benefit Gotberg—who is not a party to that deed and who cannot literally be a "successor" of Developer at this point, having previously acquired Lot 1. Oops! Developer's sloppiness has created a problem; giving the deeds their literal reading, purchasers of the later lots will be able to enforce the covenant against purchasers of the earlier lots (i.e., Strong can enforce against Gotberg or Gotberg's successors), but early purchasers seemingly cannot enforce the covenant against later ones (i.e., Gotberg cannot enforce the covenant against Strong or her successors). Almost certainly, this is not what either Developer, Gotberg, or (in all likelihood) Strong expected; the likely intent was that each lot in the neighborhood would be reciprocally bound for the benefit of every other lot in the neighborhood. As noted, the problem is that Developer's deed of Lot 1 to Gotberg did not expressly burden Developer's retained lots (Lots 2–50) for the benefit of Lot 1. Is it possible that a court will *imply* that the covenants in the deed to Lot 1 also burdened Developer's retained lots on a reciprocal basis, i.e., that the deed to Lot 1 created an *implied reciprocal servitude* over Lots 2–50 in favor of Lot 1?

Some courts have done so where the facts and circumstances demonstrate a "common plan" of development for all of the relevant land. For example, suppose that when Developer sold Lot 1 to Gotberg, Developer represented to Gotberg through agents and sales literature that "all fifty lots of this subdivision are going to be exclusively single-family homes." Suppose further that the layout of the lots and, to the extent homes may have been built in advance of sales, the overall appearance of the neighborhood is consistent with these representations. Based on these facts, a court may conclude that Developer impliedly covenanted to Gotberg (the grantee of Lot 1) that Lots 2–50 were also burdened by the covenants expressed in the deed.[481] If so, then as between Developer (as the owner of Lots 2–50) and Gotberg (as grantee of Lot 1), Developer is impliedly bound to the covenants as well. As Developer sells those lots, the buyer of each lot takes

---

[481] See Warren v. Detlefsen, 281 Ark. 196, 663 S.W.2d 710 (1984) (though deeds limited use to "residential purposes," restriction was to single-family residences because of developer's oral representations); Johnson v. Mt. Baker Park Presbyterian Church, 113 Wash. 458, 194 P. 536 (1920).

it subject to that burden for the benefit of Lot 1, provided the recording act and notice requirements are met. This a difficult problem that requires us to pause.

Because the covenant burdening the Developer's retained lots—we will use Lot 25 here as an example—was made only impliedly by Developer, a buyer of Lot 25 from Developer will not find a covenant expressly burdening Lot 25 in any prior deed from the Developer (i.e., the deeds that conveyed title to Lots 1–24), even if a buyer is charged with constructive notice of the contents of those deeds. If a common plan of development exists, though, this does not matter. The leading case is Sanborn v. McLean, a 1925 Michigan decision.[482] The court ruled that the defendant, a subsequent lot buyer, did have notice of the implied restriction based on a combination of factors demonstrating a "common plan" of development. The defendant could see that twenty prior recorded deeds from the developer all bound the grantees of those lots to a more or less uniform single-family-dwelling restriction, and could also see from a visual inspection that the subdivision was in fact developing in that uniform way. From these facts, the court held that the defendant was charged as a matter of law with sufficient information to conclude that the developer, in the deeds of conveyance to previously sold lots, had impliedly burdened all lots still remaining in the developer's hands—and thus that the defendant took its lot subject to the burden of that implied restriction.[483]

Implied servitude arguments also can arise in a different type of "sloppy developer" case, where a developer delivers one or more deeds that omit one or more covenants. For example, suppose that our Developer plans to sell all fifty lots and to insert a set of uniform grantee covenants into each deed, including a covenant prohibiting the installation of a mobile home. By mistake, however, Developer omits the no-mobile-home covenant from the deeds to Lots 1–5 as they are sold, but then catches the error and inserts the covenant correctly in the deeds to Lots 6–50 as they are sold. If Gotberg attempts to install a mobile home on Lot 1, can the other owners prohibit her from doing so? Gotberg's deed does not express a covenant prohibiting installation of a mobile home on Lot 1, but could this restriction be implied into the deed for the benefit of the remaining owners, based on a common plan of development contemplating that restriction?

The answer depends on the circumstances. First, an easy case: suppose that despite omitting the no-mobile-home covenant from the deed to Gotberg, the Developer had nevertheless recorded a plat that had included *all* of the restrictions, including the no-mobile-home restriction, and the deed to Gotberg referred to the plat. Here, a court will overlook the omission of the covenant from the deed to Lot 1 as an unintended mistake and imply the covenant based on the plan reflected by the plat.[484] Next, an easy case the

---

[482] 233 Mich. 227, 206 N.W. 496 (1925). See also § 8.28 supra. Accord, Turner v. Brocato, 206 Md. 336, 111 A.2d 855 (1955).

[483] Note that a "common plan of development" is not necessarily one that calls for every lot to be developed identically. For instance, suppose the developer's original plan called for several hundred lots to be restricted to single-family dwellings, but for four lots at the entrances to the subdivision to permit a school, a fire station, and a certain number of businesses. As long as these uses were part of the developer's plan for the development, the presence of these different uses would not preclude a court from implying a residential servitude as to the lots intended for dwellings under the plan.

[484] E.g., Hollis v. Garwall, Inc., 137 Wash.2d 683, 974 P.2d 836 (1999) (implication of residential servitude appropriate, despite lack of explicit covenant in deed to grantee, where subdivision plat was recorded with residential restriction expressed on plat and where grantee's deed contained reference to the plat). Another circumstance in which a court might imply a servitude would be if a neighbor could prove that Gotberg knew of the no-mobile-home plan and made an oral promise to comply. E.g., Johnson v. Mt. Baker Park Presbyterian Church, 113 Wash. 458, 194 P. 536 (1920).

other way: suppose that there was no recorded plat, and the Developer's sales materials did not state *anywhere* that mobile homes would be prohibited. In this case, no implied servitude arises; it is doubtful that the neighboring owners can prove that at the time of her purchase, Gotberg had notice of a general plan to prohibit mobile homes.[485] An intermediate case might involve facts in which Developer had prepared sales materials stating that no mobile homes would be permitted; again, this would be some evidence of a general plan of development, but the party seeking to enforce the covenant would have to prove that Gotberg saw the sales material and thus had reason to appreciate the intent to prohibit mobile homes within the neighborhood.

Now suppose that Developer included the no-mobile-home covenant in the deeds to Lots 1–20, but omitted it from the deed to Lot 21 when Developer conveyed Lot 21 to Wells. Here, owners seeking to enforce an implied covenant against Wells might offer proof of a general plan of development. The plan would appear not only through the explicit statements in sales materials that mobile homes would be prohibited, but also through the consistent incorporation of the covenant into the deeds to Lots 1–20,[486] and through the visible lack of any mobile homes on Lots 1–20—altogether placing Wells on inquiry notice of an implied servitude burdening Lot 21. In appropriate cases, courts have given significant weight to the existence of a common plan as manifest by a common visible pattern of development.[487] Note that courts generally do not regard a visible

---

[485] The inclusion of the restriction in the deeds to Lots 6–50 may provide some evidence of a general plan—but not necessarily of one that existed at the time that Gotberg purchased Lot 1, which is the time at which the restriction must be implied. E.g., Collins v. Rodgers, 938 So.2d 379 (Ala.2006). In *Collins*, the court refused to imply a 100-foot building setback based on the absence of sufficient evidence of a common plan of development including such a setback. The court pointed to several factors, including (a) the fact that the developer had omitted a setback covenant from several deeds, up to and including the one delivered to the defendants, (b) the fact that the developer had not filed a plat of the development reflecting a setback covenant, and (c) the absence of any evidence or general visible compliance within the neighborhood or of actual knowledge and acceptance of the setback by the owners whose deeds omitted the setback.

[486] By contrast, courts have been more reluctant to find a common plan of development from a series of deeds that contained sets of covenants that varied in significant ways. E.g., Creed v. Clogston, 176 Vt. 436, 852 A.2d 577 (2004) (no general plan for mobile-home-free community established where deeds to some lots prohibited mobile homes and deeds to others did not). See also Khan v. Alpine Haven Prop. Owners' Ass'n, Inc., 203 Vt. 251, 153 A.3d 1218 (2016) (series of deeds did not constitute declaration of a common interest community that would obligate owners to pay mandatory assessments under Vermont's enactment of Uniform Common Interest Ownership Act).

[487] In this example, where development has occurred on twenty lots already, a buyer may reasonably have notice of a general plan by virtue of consistent development in conformance with that plan. By contrast, in the prior example in which Gotberg was the first purchaser of Lot 1, Gotberg could not have inquiry notice of a general plan when no visible development had yet occurred. See, e.g., Buckley v. Mooney, 339 Mich. 398, 63 N.W.2d 655 (1954) (no implied servitude precluded grantee from erecting church building).

Note that courts generally do not regard a visible pattern of consistent development *alone* to establish a common plan. Hamlen v. Keith, 171 Mass. 77, 50 N.E. 462 (1898). Instead, it must be accompanied by other evidence of an intended general plan (e.g., a consistent pattern of restrictions in other deeds, a reference to the restriction in a recorded plat, and/or sales materials identifying the restriction sought to be implied). E.g., In re Heatherwood Holdings, LLC, 454 B.R. 495 (Bankr.N.D.Ala.2011) (common plan found in original developer's marketing materials, signage, street names, plat maps, and visible development resulted in implied servitude restricting parcel to use as a golf course); Heatherwood Holdings, LLC v. First Commercial Bank, 61 So.3d 1012 (Ala.2010) (same); Ward v. Prudential Ins. Co. of Am., 299 Mass. 559, 13 N.E.2d 411 (1938) (restriction reflected in recorded plat and visible consistent development); Skyline Woods Homeowners Ass'n, Inc. v. Broekemeier, 276 Neb. 792, 758 N.W.2d 376 (2008) (residents could demonstrate common plan for use of parcel as golf course where developer made express and implied representation to initial buyers that development was and would continue to be a golf course community); Riverview Community Group v. Spencer & Livingston, 181 Wash.2d 888, 337 P.3d 1076 (2014) (same).

pattern of consistent development *alone* to establish a common plan.[488] Instead, it must be accompanied by other evidence of an intended general plan (e.g., a consistent pattern of restrictions in other deeds, a reference to the restriction in a recorded plat, and/or sales materials identifying the restriction sought to be implied).[489]

For a parcel to be burdened or benefited by an implied reciprocal servitude, it is clear that the parcel must be within the particular area covered by the common plan of development.[490] Problems can arise when the owner of a large parcel of land develops a portion of it and then later attempts to develop the rest in a different manner. For example, suppose Developer carves a 30-lot development out of a larger parcel of land and sells all of the lots subject to uniform covenants that prohibit mobile homes. Several years later, Developer then attempts to develop the adjacent portion of the parcel for a mobile home park, only to have owners in the 30-lot development sue for an injunction that the Developer's parcel is reciprocally subject to an implied restriction prohibiting mobile homes. Here, the neighbors may be able to establish a common plan of development for the original subdivision, but that alone does not establish that the Developer's adjacent land is also part of that common plan. Absent proof that the entire parcel was part of the common plan, no implied servitude will arise to prevent the Developer's mobile home park.[491] In this situation, some courts hold that if a parcel of land has been restricted through a recorded declaration of CC&Rs and that declaration does not include adjacent property, the doctrine of implied reciprocal servitude categorically cannot apply to restrict the adjacent land.[492] Others have rejected a categorical rule, but hold that the recorded declaration creates a strong presumption that the doctrine will not extend beyond the scope of the declaration.[493]

Courts sometimes refer to an implied reciprocal servitude as an "implied reciprocal negative easement," demonstrating the conceptual similarity between easements and covenants. The implied servitude theory can fit both real covenant doctrine as well as equitable restriction doctrine though, as the phrase "reciprocal servitude" implies, the courts seem predominantly to contemplate the equitable doctrine.

---

[488] E.g., Hamlen v. Keith, 171 Mass. 77, 50 N.E. 462 (1898); Essex Cty. V. DMH 2 Ltd. Liability Co., 449 N.J.Super. 30, 155 A.3d 17 (2016) (common plan "must be rooted in actual restrictions on record, not in an incidental pattern of development").

[489] E.g., Ward v. Prudential Ins. Co. of Am., 299 Mass. 559, 13 N.E.2d 411 (1938) (restriction reflected in recorded plat and visible consistent development).

[490] E.g., Tibbetts v. Michaelides, 190 Vt. 520, 24 A.3d 581 (parcels subject to burden of covenant limiting total number of homes did not create reciprocal benefits among different owner of burdened parcels, but instead benefited grantor's retained adjacent land; no common plan covered all of the parcels in question).

[491] E.g., Olson v. Albert, 523 A.2d 585 (Me.1987); Chase v. Burrell, 474 A.2d 180 (Me.1984); Long Meadow Homeowners' Ass'n, Inc. v. Harland, 89 So.3d 573 (Miss.2012) (residential-only restrictions in first and second phases of development did not impliedly restrict land in third phrase from being used as church); Patch v. Springfield School Dist., 187 Vt. 21, 989 A.2d 500 (2009) (no common plan existed to subject school district to residential-use restrictions in adjacent development; neither plat nor declaration covered adjacent property and no subsequent agreement extended applicability of covenants to school district parcel).

[492] E.g., Walters v. Colford, 297 Neb. 302, 900 N.W.2d 183 (2017) ("A buyer of property has no reasonable expectation that neighboring property will be restricted as part of a plan of development where the entire development has been restricted through a declaration of restrictions that does not include that neighboring property."), citing Restatement (Third) of Property-Servitudes § 2.14, Comment i (2000). See also Save Sea Lawn Acres Ass'n v. Mercer, 140 Wash.App. 411, 166 P.3d 770 (2007).

[493] E.g., Roper v. Camuso, 376 Md. 240, 829 A.2d 589 (2003); Schovee v. Mikolasko, 356 Md. 93, 737 A.2d 578 (1999). See also New Castle County v. Pike Creek Recreational Servs., LLC, 82 A.3d 731 (Del.Ch.Ct.2013) (original declaration set aside 130 acres for golf course; only that area was restricted by express servitude, and no implied servitude arose over 47 additional acres even though portion of golf course was situated on additional acreage at time of course's closure).

Third-Party-Beneficiary Theory

Instead of the implied reciprocal servitude theory, some courts employ what is known as the "third-party-beneficiary" theory when faced with the "sloppy developer" problems discussed above. The original Restatement of Property adopted this approach for the implication of servitude restrictions.[494] Earlier, we explained that using the implied reciprocal servitude theory to make the benefit run "backward" (i.e., from a later purchaser to an early purchaser) can prove awkward. The third-party-beneficiary doctrine is easier to apply in this situation; however, it is subject to the fundamental objection that it supposes equitable restrictions, at least on the benefit side, to be contract rights rather than interests in land.

A previous example illustrates how the third-party-beneficiary theory operates. Suppose again that Developer sells fifty lots using deeds that contain uniform grantee covenants restricting use of the affected lot to single-family residential purposes only, and that the covenants do not contain express language reciprocally restricting Developer's retained lots. Further, suppose that Gotberg, as buyer of Lot 1, is now trying to enforce the covenant against Smith, a successor owner of Lot 20 who wishes to open a restaurant. A court that permitted enforcement under the implied reciprocal servitude theory would be enforcing the covenant expressed in the deed to Lot 1 (the Developer-to-Gotberg deed), on the theory that it reciprocally restricted Lot 20 (at that time part of Developer's retained land). By contrast, a court allowing Gotberg to enforce under third-party-beneficiary theory would be allowing her to enforce the grantee covenant in the deed conveying Lot 20 to Smith. The theory is that while Gotberg was not a party to that deed—the parties were the Developer as grantor and Smith as grantee of Lot 20— Gotberg was nevertheless an intended beneficiary of that covenant because it was intended to benefit the owners of all 50 lots within the development (i.e., all lots covered by the common plan of development). A court accepting this theory will permit Gotberg to enforce the covenant if she can prove that it was part of a common plan of development that covered both lots.[495] Whether a common plan exists is a question of fact, which a court would resolve by reference to the same types of factors mentioned in the prior discussion of implied reciprocal servitude theory.[496]

§§ 8.36–9.0 ARE RESERVED FOR SUPPLEMENTAL MATERIAL.

---

[494] Restatement of Property § 541 (1944).

[495] E.g., Wiegman v. Kusel, 270 Ill. 520, 110 N.E. 884 (1915); Snow v. Van Dam, 291 Mass. 477, 197 N.E. 224 (1935); Evans v. Foss, 194 Mass. 513, 80 N.E. 587 (1907); Nature Conservancy v. Congel, 253 A.D.2d 248, 689 N.Y.S.2d 317 (1999); Booth v. Knipe, 225 N.Y. 390, 122 N.E. 202 (1919).

[496] E.g., King v. Ebrens, 804 N.E.2d 821 (Ind.App.2004) (owner of land adjacent to covenant-restricted subdivision could not enforce subdivision covenants to require resident to remove noncompliant pole barn; no common plan existed to demonstrate covenants were intended to benefit adjacent land).

Chapter 9

GOVERNMENTAL REGULATION OF LAND USE

Table of Sections

A. THE POWER TO REGULATE: SOURCES AND CONSTITUTIONAL LIMITATIONS

§ 9.1   WHAT ARE LAND USE REGULATIONS?

"There is nothing which so generally strikes the imagination, and engages the affections of mankind, as the right of property; or that sole and despotic dominion which one man claims and exercises over the external things of the world, in total exclusion of the right of any other individual in the universe."[1] These famous words by Blackstone are not true today and were not true when written. Blackstone's words have to be understood in a special sense, referring to the pure concept of "property." Of course he knew well, as we know today, that there are many legal limitations upon the actual use and enjoyment of property rights in land. Many of these limitations have been highlighted in prior chapters of this treatise. The doctrines of nuisance, of lateral support, and of the sharing of riparian rights are examples of constraints the law imposes on landowners. Many owners have voluntarily limited their ownership rights, for instance, by granting easements or profits or by fragmenting their ownership into present and future estates, including leaseholds. Persons who choose thus to fragment ownership invoke special limitations on the estates they create; the rules against waste and much of the law of landlord and tenant are examples. Our rigid system of estates limits the permissible forms of ownership. The law of conveyancing forces transfers of interests in land into prescribed modes. Most of what we call the "law of property" limits the ways in which persons may use and deal with land.

This chapter focuses "land use regulations"—government-imposed restrictions on the use of land use. Building codes and zoning codes are the most common types of land use regulations, but descriptions of multiple other types follow in the coming pages. Like the restrictions highlighted in the preceding paragraph, building and zoning codes limit the ways landowners may use and enjoy their land. However, land use regulations also differ from those examples in some important ways. First, these regulations originate from legislative or administrative actions by federal, state, or (most often) local governments. They are not part of the common law, though much case law has grown emanated them in the form of judicial interpretation. Second, they restrict the ways land may be used or developed, including the physical activities owners or occupiers may engage in, but they do not regulate other incidents of ownership such as conveyances. Third, whereas the limitations referred to in the preceding paragraph relate to the rights and duties of private persons, arising out of their specific relationships to land, land use regulations create duties that owners or occupiers of land owe to the general public. In this sense, land use regulations play a role somewhat like the doctrine of public nuisance (even though land use regulations are generally categorized as "public law" and public nuisance law grew up as part of the "private" common law). Fourth, once established by legislative action, public land use regulations are generally administered by governmental agencies that may have both rule-making and quasi-judicial functions.

---

[1]   2 Blackstone, Commentaries, *2.

Indeed, the rules relating to these agencies and their activities are themselves a substantial part of land use regulation law. And fifth, land use regulations are rarely enforced by private persons in civil actions (though such actions are sometimes possible) and are generally enforced instead by governmental attorneys in either civil or criminal actions.

It is worth noting that the regulations examined in this chapter are imposed by governmental entities upon land owned by parties other than the governmental entity that imposes the regulation. It is true that vast amounts of land in America are owned by the Federal Government, by state governments, and by governmental entities created by the states, such as cities and counties. Of course a governmental entity may, as owner, control the uses of land it owns. However, this kind of control does not come within the definition of "land use regulation"; we are discussing only regulations imposed by governmental entities upon land owned by someone else. Such regulations usually restrict land owned by private persons, although sometimes one governmental entity may regulate land owned by another governmental entity. For instance, a county may attempt to impose its zoning regulations upon state- or city-owned land owned within the county. These cases pose difficult legal questions that are beyond the scope of this treatise.[2] Accordingly, this chapter considers only land use regulations that are imposed upon privately owned land.

In America today land use regulations are imposed by all levels of government, incorporated villages, cities, counties, state governments, and the Federal Government. These regulations take many forms. Safety, fire, health, and building codes control the erection and maintenance of structures in all but the most sparsely settled corners of the country. In most areas, zoning ordinances control the uses owners may make of their land and also such other matters as maximum percentages that may be covered by structures and their minimum distances from lot lines. Sensitive-area restrictions, such as wetlands, shorelands, and greenbelt ordinances, may severely restrict or even effectively prohibit the development of land parcels that happen to be in areas they protect. Land uses that cause air or water pollution may violate the Federal Clean Water Act or Clean Air Act or state statutes or local ordinances that serve similar purposes. In certain burgeoning localities, growth control statutes or ordinances may place limits on the total amount of permissible development and where it may occur. A parcel that has been designated a historic site or that lies within a historic preservation district or zone may have to be maintained as such. These are only some familiar examples of many kinds of governmental regulations that can restrict the use and enjoyment of privately-owned American land.

§ 9.2   SOURCE OF GOVERNMENT'S POWER TO REGULATE

Land use regulations are generally imposed by governments under the "police power" or "regulatory power," which, broadly defined, is the power to regulate human activity so as to promote citizens' general health and welfare.[3] One might reasonably question how useful it is to silo various powers of government into, say, the power to tax, to appropriate property (eminent domain), or the power to regulate since such categories

---

[2]   See D. Mandelker, Land Use Law §§ 4.26–4.41 (4th ed. 1997), for discussion of cases in which one governmental entity seeks to regulate the use of land owned by another such entity.

[3]   If authority is needed for this statement, see the United States Supreme Court's original zoning case, Village of Euclid v. Ambler Realty Co., 272 U.S. 365, 47 S.Ct. 114, 71 L.Ed. 303 (1926).

are artificial and sometimes overlap. Moreover, the police power in particular is extremely broad and supports a diverse array of laws ranging from traffic regulations to the entire criminal code. Police power-based land use regulations alone cover a lengthy list of matters, from abatement of nuisances to zoning. Still, warrants stating here at the outset that the particular regulations covered in this chapter are generally exercises of the police power that regulate human activities on privately owned land.

Most of the land use regulations described in this chapter are immediately imposed and enforced by local units of government—usually cities or counties. In our federal system of government, the power to impose regulations on land use must ultimately originate from either the Federal Government or a state government. Since this chapter does not attempt to cover federal schemes of land use regulation, we will simply note that, because the Federal Government is (at least in political theory) a government of "limited" powers, its power to regulate must be traceable to some delegation of power in the United States Constitution. So, for instance, the Federal Clean Air Act is founded upon the power of the national government to control the quality of moving masses of air, which of course do not respect state boundaries and are thus inherently "interstate."[4] The National Environmental Policy Act can likewise come into operation when a private landowner requires the permission of or seeks some action by a federal agency in connection with a use of land.[5] In that manner, chains of authority for federal environmental regulations begin with some power granted the Government by the United States Constitution and continue through acts of Congress that create specific regulatory programs.

State governments are governments of "inherent" powers; they have all traditional powers of government except as those powers may be limited by the United States Constitution or their own state constitutions. The Tenth Amendment to the Federal Constitution guarantees to the states "the powers not delegated to the United States by the Constitution, nor prohibited by it to the States." In the field of land use regulation, this means that state governments have the inherent power to impose such regulations and to enforce them directly. Moreover, and of particular importance here, state governments have the power to delegate their regulatory powers to local governmental units they create. These are mostly cities and counties, though in some instances so-called "regional" agencies have been created with powers of land use regulation. There are also other specialized local agencies, such as independent school districts and fire protection districts, but this chapter focuses primarily on local entities that land use regulatory authority.

Local governments are truly "creatures" of their state governments—organs whose powers and functions are confined to those delegated them by their state constitutions and statutes. State enabling acts authorize local governments to form themselves and define their general powers. A general grant of police power is made to them in language such as the classic phrase, "to provide for the public health, safety, and general welfare." It has often been held that a generic grant of police power, such as that quoted above, does not empower a city or county to enact zoning ordinances.[6] However, when a city or

---

[4] See 42 U.S.C.A. § 7401, which evinces a purpose to control air pollution that may affect more than one state.

[5] See 42 U.S.C.A. § 4332, which says, in effect, that the operation of the Act is triggered by actions of "agencies of the Federal Government."

[6] 1 R. Anderson, American Law of Zoning § 2.20 (3d ed. 1986).

county has enlarged powers, known as "home rule" powers, it may have the power to zone under those powers, especially when home rule is authorized by the state constitution and not merely by statute.[7] Typically, though, local governments enact zoning and other land use regulations under the authority of a specific state enabling act.

The most famous such enabling act is the Standard Zoning Enabling Act (SZEA). This was promulgated in several versions, beginning in the mid-1920s, by the United States Department of Commerce, not as a federal statute, but as a model act for state governments to consider as they wished. It happened that all or nearly all states responded by adopting the SZEA in some form as their original zoning enabling acts in the 1920s and 1930s. Through the years, though the original state acts have been amended and often replaced by more sophisticated new statutes, the basic framework of the SZEA still is present.[8] We therefore have in American zoning law an interesting phenomenon. Even though zoning law is grounded primarily in individual state statutes, in both statutory and judge-made law there is significant homogeneity among the states so it is possible to study an American law of zoning. Later portions of this chapter that consider specific statutory zoning provisions use the SZEA as their example. Indeed, at least half of this chapter focuses on the basics of zoning and at the body of law that has grown up around it. This approach is warranted for two reasons. First, despite a multiplicity of other more recent land use regulatory schemes, such as those for air and water quality, wetlands, and historic sites, zoning still remains the most pervasive system of land use regulation. Second, to a considerable extent the newer regulatory schemes have borrowed techniques that were pioneered in zoning, such as variances and the role of local administrative bodies. A lawyer who is a specialist in zoning law can thus adapt relatively easily to work within the other systems.

There are certainly limits on the power of all governmental units to regulate land use. Local governments' powers are obviously limited by the scope of delegations to them under state statutes. But the powers of the state governments themselves, as well as of local governments, are also limited by certain provisions in both state constitutions and the United States Constitution (which also limits the land use regulatory powers of the Federal Government). This chapter concentrates on the limitations contained in the first ten amendments to the United States Constitution, called the Bill of Rights. These directly limit the power of the Federal Government, and most of them also limit state and local governments by United States Supreme Court decisions that have incorporated them into the Due Process Clause or Equal Protection Clause of the 14th Amendment. Federal and state power to regulate land use is limited most broadly by constitutional guarantees contained in the Fifth and 14th Amendments of due process under the law, equal protection under the law and protection against the taking of property without compensation. The Constitutional guarantees of free speech and of free exercise of religion of the First Amendment will also be covered in this chapter to the extent they protect those certain citizens whose lands are primarily used for "religious" or "speech" activities.

---

[7]   See Id. at §§ 2.16, 2.17; D. Mandelker, Land Use Law § 4.41 (4th ed. 1997).

[8]   See D. Mandelker, Land Use Law § 4.15 (4th ed. 1997); Cunningham, Land-Use Control—The State and Local Programs, 50 Iowa L. Rev. 367 (1965). New York City is generally credited with adopting the first integrated zoning ordinance in 1916, under authority of a state statute special to the city. Shortly after that, the state enacted a general city zoning enabling act. Some early state statutes were patterned after this New York State act.

State constitutions usually contain guarantees that are similar to those of the Federal Constitution, though their wording often differs more or less. Of course a given state constitution limits only the actions of the state and local governments of that state and not of the United States Government. The final interpreter of a state constitution is the highest court of that state, not the United States Supreme Court.[9] We will mention state constitutions only incidentally here, since it would be impossible to cover all 50 in a treatise of this size.

§ 9.3   RELATIONSHIP OF REGULATIONS TO NUISANCE AND RUNNING COVENANTS

Nuisance law is covered in chapter 7 of this treatise and running covenants are covered in chapter 8. Both of these areas of law have close similarities to land use regulations. Although they differ from zoning regulations in that they are mostly judge-made laws and are not rooted in federal or state statutes, they serve a similar purpose of restricting landowners in the uses of their lands to promote certain broader interests. In practice, both nuisance law and private restrictive covenants sometimes supplement and even to duplicate or obviate zoning and other public land use regulations.

Running covenants share many similarities with zoning ordinances. Covenants differ in that they are privately-formed and originate in contractual agreements that become binding upon successors in land ownership, but they can restrict land use in ways that closely resemble zoning ordinance provisions.[10] Restrictive covenants often supplement zoning by adding to or tightening restrictions on land use. However, a subdivision in an area that has no public zoning could conceivably impose subdivision covenants extensive enough to duplicate the restrictions that typical zoning ordinances would have imposed. If there was a homeowners' association that the covenants required all owners in the subdivision to join, obey, and support, it could have mechanisms to enforce the covenants through an architectural review committee, board of directors, and ultimately homeowner-members in ways that also mimicked the enforcement of many zoning laws. Moreover, private covenants can give the homeowners' association powers beyond general land use regulation, such as to maintain privately owned streets, maintain a private water system, and guard certain shared amenities. Such master-planned, "gated communities" in fact exist and continue to grow in number.[11] The possibility, and indeed existence, of such communities illustrates the point that restrictive covenants and zoning are capable of serving remarkably similar functions.

In fact, the entire city of Houston, Texas, relies primarily on a network of private restrictive covenants instead of zoning, to regulate land uses. Houston does have building and housing codes, and minimum dimensions for single-family-dwelling lots are controlled by a subdivision ordinance, but it has no zoning code. Instead, Houston has long had extensive subdivision restrictive covenants, which the city, in an unusual

---

[9]   PruneYard Shopping Center v. Robins, 447 U.S. 74, 100 S.Ct. 2035, 64 L.Ed.2d 741 (1980).

[10]   Unless otherwise supported, statements in this section about running covenants are drawn from chapter 8 of this treatise.

[11]   The seminal article on the subject was Reichman, Residential Private Governments, 43 U. Chi. L. Rev. 253 (1976). There has been much theoretical writing on the subject and much practical writing. For a couple of short articles that tend to be practical, but that cite some of the theoretical writing, see Schwartz, Public Gated Residential Communities: The Rosemont, Illinois Approach and Its Constitutional Implications, 29 Urb. Law. 123 (1997), and Smith, Ross, et al., Gated Communities: Private Solution or Public Dilemma?, 29 Urb. Law. 413 (1997).

practice, has been enforcing since 1965. Professor Bernard Siegan, in his well-known study of the Houston system, concluded that the lack of zoning had not made the city's appearance noticeably different from other large American cities, nor had it depressed home values. He also concluded that the lack of zoning controls had produced more apartments, with affordable rents, than in zoned cities.[12] However, although Houston's experience illustrates how systems of running covenants can approximate zoning, there are definite limits to their actual use for that purpose. One major limitation is that it would be practically impossible except in the rarest instances to impose restrictive covenants on an existing and well-established neighborhood. Integrated schemes of covenants are in practice imposed by developers of new subdivisions, who put the covenants in place before lots are sold.[13] In any event, as interesting as the Houston experience is in theory, other major cities have not seen fit to emulate it.

Nuisance law also serves some zoning-like purposes but cannot be said to be of the same "stuff" as zoning. Nor is there any example, such as Houston, in which nuisance law alone has produced effects comparable to those of zoning, despite Professor Robert C. Ellickson's claim that this was a possibility and might actually promote economic efficiency. In a 1973 article, Professor Ellickson proposed fundamental changes to nuisance law, including allowing a plaintiff to make out a prima facie case of nuisance by showing the defendant's activities violated "contemporary community standards," rather than the traditional test of "unreasonable use that causes the plaintiff substantial harm." To implement his changes, he had to propose public enforcement by "metropolitan Nuisance Boards."[14]

Despite Professor Ellickson's provocative argument, American nuisance law has continued to employ the traditional definitional test and to rely mainly upon private suits for enforcement, as we saw in chapter 7, supra. The general purpose of nuisance law—to prevent uses of land that unreasonably disturb other landowners—is also one of the chief purposes of zoning. However, because of the traditional test for a nuisance, many, probably most, uses that are forbidden by zoning would not be serious enough disturbances to cause a nuisance. For instance, if a landowner builds and rents out a two-unit residential duplex in a zone that is strictly zoned for single-family dwellings, this use would clearly violate the zoning ordinance but would hardly amount to a nuisance. On the other hand one Massachusetts court famously held that a large pig farm whose stench greatly disturbed the residents of a nearby subdivision was an actionable nuisance even though it did not violate a zoning ordinance.[15] Because zoning ordinances establish fixed zone lines, activities conducted in a zone in which they are permitted sometimes have "spillover" effects that cause a nuisance in adjacent zones in which that activity is not permitted.[16] Although some courts have held that nothing

---

[12]   Siegan, Non-Zoning in Houston, 13 J. L. & Econ. 71 (1970).

[13]   See Ellickson, Alternatives to Zoning: Covenants, Nuisance Rules, and Fines as Land Use Controls, 40 U. Chi. L. Rev. 681, 711–19 (1973). Subdivision covenants, especially elaborate schemes of them that could approximate zoning, are associated with exclusive subdivisions of expensive homes. They do nothing for below-average-income persons except to keep them out of such subdivisions.

[14]   See Id., at 719–81.

[15]   Pendoley v. Ferreira, 345 Mass. 309, 187 N.E.2d 142 (1963). See also Mathewson v. Primeau, 64 Wn.2d 929, 395 P.2d 183 (1964), which held the stench from a pig farm was a nuisance to neighbors, but refused to so hold as to an unsightly junk pile.

[16]   See, e.g., Weltshe v. Graf, 323 Mass. 498, 82 N.E.2d 795 (1948) (all-night truck loading dock caused nuisance to nearby hotel).

permitted by zoning can be a nuisance,[17] a number of decisions have held otherwise. More accurately, whether a complained-of land use violates a zoning ordinance is a relevant factor to help a court determine if it is a nuisance but is not conclusive.

Nuisance law is not likely to ever replace zoning or replicate its effects, but it does function as a valuable supplementary and complementary system of land use control. Moreover, nuisance law has some distinct advantages over zoning. Among other things, private nuisance enforcement is generally in the hands of the private persons who are most directly affected by the disturbance. While those persons sometimes have standing to sue for zoning violations, their capacity to do so is limited and public prosecutors who are not directly affected and whose agendas may be different are more likely to bring such claims. Also, as highlighted above, nuisance law reaches some activities that zoning does not forbid and is no respecter of zone lines.

§ 9.4   WHAT IS A "REGULATORY TAKING"?

Section 9.2 alluded briefly to constitutional limitations on the power of governments, federal, state, and local, to impose land use regulations. Among them are limits under the "Takings Clause" of the Fifth Amendment. Over the past half-century, the Takings Clause has emerged as an important constraint on governments' ability to regulate uses of land. Regulatory takings law has accordingly developed into a subject of intense interest among lawyers and others. It has been called the most important issue in land use law, perhaps in all the law of real property. Yet, despite all its attention, confusion and uncertainty continue to plague this mystifying area of the law.

Distinguishing Regulatory Takings from Exercises of Eminent Domain

Understanding the constitutional origins of regulatory takings law and of how this area differs from eminent domain law is prerequisite to grasping the basics of this important and complex body of law. Regulatory takings law originates from the Takings Clause" of the Fifth Amendment to the United States Constitution. Although the Takings Clause originally applied only the United States Government, it has long been clear that the Takings Clause also restricts the states and their subdivisions through the Due Process Clause of the 14th Amendment.[18] The Takings Clause reads: ". . . nor shall private property be taken for public use without just compensation." Two distinct bodies of law have emerged from The Takings clause: [1] eminent domain law and [2] regulatory takings law.

Eminent domain law, which is not the focus of this chapter, governs situations in which government entities seek to unilaterally acquire property interests from private individuals. The Takings Clause does prohibit governments from taking private property. In fact, the clause has long been interpreted to authorize the Federal Government, state governments, most municipal governments, and some other quasi-governmental entities with delegated eminent domain authority to take private property under certain prescribed conditions described below.[19] When government entities "take"

---

[17]   E.g., this was stated in Bove v. Donner-Hanna Coke Corp., 236 App.Div. 37, 258 N.Y.S. 229 (1932), a classic zoning decision that is in many casebooks.

[18]   Pennsylvania Coal Co. v. Mahon, 260 U.S. 393 (1922); Chicago B. & Q. Railroad v. Chicago, 166 U.S. 226 (1897) (strong dictum).

[19]   Kohl v. United States, 91 U.S. 367 (1875), established that the Federal Government, in its own right, had power to condemn land, for the Government's custom had previously been to have the states condemn land for it. Thus, there was no question that state governments had the power.

interests in real or personal property by eminent domain, they literally compel a private owner to transfer those interests to them. In England this is called "compulsory purchase" or "appropriation." American law calls it by its Continental civil law name, "eminent domain." In most instances, the property interests taken through exercises of eminent domain authority are fee simple title or some lesser real property interest such as an easement or leasehold. For example, a state transportation department might exercise its eminent domain power to "condemn" or take title to specific tracts of land for use in building a new public highway. Such condemnations of land are effectuated through an actual conveyance of the interest from the landowner to the governmental entity, just as if the owner had given a deed. In fact, governmental entities and landowners often opt to avoid potentially costly condemnation actions by using a deed or other instrument to voluntarily convey the property interest to the government for a negotiated price.

Even in most contested eminent domain proceedings, the government openly admits its intention to acquire the private property interests involved. Accordingly, the legal issues adjudicated in eminent domain proceedings are generally focus solely on whether the government's intended use of the property is a sufficiently "public use" or whether the compensation amount offered to the private property owner is "just." Legal questions about which types of uses may satisfy the "public use" requirement and thereby authorize governments to condemn private property are captivating but are outside the scope of this chapter. Those interested in examining these issues should begin by studying the now-infamous 2005 U.S. Supreme Court case of Kelo v. City of New London. *Kelo* and the state-level legislative backlash that followed it epitomize the contentious and complex nature of the "public use" debate.[20]

Unlike eminent domain law, "regulatory takings" law governs situations in which a government entity merely imposes a law restricting the use of private property and insists it is not attempting to take any private property interest. In regulatory takings cases, private property owners (usually landowners) assert that a new government regulation is so restrictive that it *effectively* takes property interests from them. Accordingly, regulatory takings cases center on whether some new law restricts the use of certain private property so much that the government entity imposing it must compensate the property owner for its loss of those property rights. In discussing and thinking about the regulatory taking issue, it is helpful to consider two questions: (1) When does a regulation cause a taking: what is the substantive test for a taking? (2) If a court determines that a land use regulation has caused a taking, what is the landowner's remedy? The present section is about the first question; the next section, section 9.5, deals with the second question.

Some government actions occupying the middle ground between takings by eminent domain and regulatory takings help to illustrate how governments can effectively take private property rights even without ever touching the condemnee's land or acquiring title or other legal interests in it. Suppose that a city, without commencing any court proceedings and without the landowner's consent, totally or seriously blocks a private landowner's access onto the abutting public street with a physical barrier. The owner

---

[20]   545 U.S. 469, 125 S.Ct. 2655 162 L.Ed.2d 439 (2005); see also Ilya Somin, The Limits of Backlash: Assessing the Political Response to Kelo, 93 Minn. L. Rev. 2100 (2009) (discussing the "massive backlash" the *Kelo* decision generated); Charles E. Cohen, Eminent Domain After Kelo v. City of New London: An Argument for Banning Economic Development Takings, 29 Harv. J.L. & Pub. Pol'y 491 (2006) (providing an in-depth discussion of the *Kelo* decision).

does not like this, but courts generally will not enjoin the governmental entity from doing it. Has the owner lost any "property" right? Yes, for, according to a universal rule of judge-made law, an owner whose land abuts upon a "land-service" street or road has a "reasonable right of ingress and egress" to and from that public way—and let us agree that in our example "reasonable" or "substantial" access was lost.[21] This right of access is a form of easement that benefits (is appurtenant to) the owner's land and that burdens the city's property rights in the street. Accordingly, the owner has lost a valuable property right and the city has gained a correlative property right in that a burden has been removed from its street: at a fairly high level of abstraction, we can say there has been a transfer of property rights from owner to government without the owner's consent. The city could have brought a court action to condemn and pay for the owner's access rights, but instead it did not come forward as plaintiff in such an action. Though there once was a serious question about it, courts today will allow the landowner to come forward and, as plaintiff, commence the condemnation action that the city should have brought. Since the parties are reversed from the sides they usually have in a condemnation action, it is called "inverse condemnation." And, in the example just given, if the court concludes that the owner has been totally or (most courts say) "substantially" deprived of access, the court will award the owner just compensation for the diminution in land value caused by the loss of access on the theory that an "inverse taking" has occurred. This is one form of a "nontrespassory taking" since the city has not invaded and will not invade or make any physical use of the owner's land.

Regulatory Takings: A Dubious Beginning

Most modern regulatory takings claims involve even less governmental interference with property use than was present in the physical barrier example in the preceding paragraph. These regulatory takings claims assert simply that some new regulation has so severely restricted an owner's use of private property that the regulation has effectively taken the property. Accordingly, private owners who bring these claims generally seek compensation from the government entity that imposed the new law, even though that entity might never go near the property involved.

A simple example highlights the nature of regulatory takings cases and how they can arise. Suppose a city, again without commencing a condemnation action, imposes a coconut agriculture zoning ordinance on a hypothetical landowner that prohibits use of the land for anything except the growing and harvesting of coconuts. Assume further that the regulated land is in northern Minnesota where climate characteristics make coconut farming effectively impossible. For all practical purposes, the ordinance thus forbids any profitable or reasonable use of the land. The landowner can still access the property, walk across it, and exclude others from trespassing on it but can do little else with it. Under this a set of facts, has the owner lost anything we can call "property rights in land"? Rights of use and enjoyment "property," important and valuable sticks in the bundle, so in that sense the owner has lost a great deal of what we call "property." If we are also looking for a transfer of property rights to the city, what correlative rights has the city gained? It may be, if there is some advantage to them of having our owner's land lie fallow, that other landowners, chiefly those who live nearby, have gained property

---

[21] See, e.g., Garrett v. City of Topeka, 259 Kan. 896, 916 P.2d 21 (Kan. 1996) ("substantial," though not complete denial of access was a taking); Iowa State Highway Comm'n v. Smith, 248 Iowa 869, 82 N.W.2d 755 (1957) (leading case, similar to *Garrett*). See generally Stoebuck, The Property Right of Access Versus the Power of Eminent Domain, 47 Texas L. Rev. 733 (1969).

rights that are analogous to their burdening the owner's land with a coconuts-only restrictive covenant. At a high level of generality, we can perhaps synthesize a gain to them corresponding to the owner's loss and so a transfer of property rights from owner to neighbors. The city has imposed something like a restrictive covenant on the owner's land, which presumably benefits the other landowners. But it is pretty hard to see that there is any sort of transfer from owner to the governmental entity, the city. Can we possibly say, then, that a mere land use regulation is a compensable taking?

The United States Supreme Court first considered this question in the important case of Mugler v. Kansas.[22] Mr. Mugler owned a brewery in a newly and specially constructed building that had little value for any other purpose. Then Kansas went "dry"—its legislature enacted a statute enacted that forbade the production of alcoholic beverages, including beer. Mugler not only had to shut down his business; he also substantially lost the use and value of his land. He challenged the statute, both on the ground that it denied him substantive due process (which is addressed later in this chapter) and that it amounted to a taking of his real property rights. In a famous passage that it still quotes, the Supreme Court held: "prohibition simply upon the use of property for purposes that are declared, by *valid* legislation, to be injurious to the *health, morals, or safety* of the community, cannot, in any just sense, be deemed a taking or appropriation of property." (Emphasis added.)[23] Precisely what the Court meant is still a matter of some controversy today. Indeed, the Supreme Court itself has sometimes shifted what seemed to be the original meaning.[24] In essence, however, the Court appeared to be declaring that a land use regulation may be invalid because it denies due process but that no such regulation can trigger a compensable taking.

For a number of years, Supreme Court decisions were consistent with Mugler v. Kansas. The best known of these decisions are Hadacheck v. Sebastian[25] and Reinman v. City of Little Rock, both handed down in 1915.[26] In *Hadacheck* a Los Angeles ordinance had compelled Hadacheck to close down a brick kiln he had long operated on a parcel of land that contained valuable clay deposits, causing an alleged loss of value of over 90 percent. The plaintiff asserted regulatory taking, denial of due process, and denial of equal protection as constitutional objections to the ordinance. Without any overt discussion of the taking issue, the Court upheld the ordinance, explaining at length why it did not deny due process or equal protection. *Reinman* upheld a city ordinance that compelled the owner of a livery stable to cease the business, at least within the district in which it had operated. If the plaintiff raised the taking issue, the Court ignored it, deciding the case on rather vague due process and procedural grounds. Neither *Hadacheck* nor *Reinman* cited Mugler v. Kansas. They were consistent with *Mugler* in that they discussed only due process and equal protection, which must have led contemporary lawyers to suppose that regulatory takings were not a viable argument.

---

    [22]   123 U.S. 623, 8 S.Ct. 273, 31 L.Ed. 205 (1887).

    [23]   123 U.S. at 657.

    [24]   See especially the treatment of *Mugler* in Keystone Bituminous Coal Association v. DeBenedictis, 480 U.S. 470 (1987).

    [25]   239 U.S. 394, 36 S.Ct. 143, 60 L.Ed. 348 (1915).

    [26]   237 U.S. 171, 35 S.Ct. 511, 59 L.Ed. 900 (1914).

Regulatory Takings: New Era, New Doctrine

In 1922, the Supreme Court's unwillingness to embrace the possibility of a regulatory taking suddenly changed in Justice Holmes's majority opinion for the Court in Pennsylvania Coal Co. v. Mahon.[27] This famous decision is the cause of all the material in this section of the book and the next; it was "the source," sudden and unexpected, of the regulatory taking doctrine.[28] The coal company had conveyed a surface estate in land to the Mahons or their predecessors, severing and reserving for the coal company rights in the land's subsurface coal. In the deed, the company had also reserved the right to cause subsidence of the surface if necessary to mine the coal.—However, Pennsylvania's Kohler Act—a police power regulation for public protection—forbade the mining of coal in any location where mining would cause subsidence of soil under a house. Because the Mahons' house was on the surface, the effect of the statute was to prevent the coal company from making any profitable use of its property in this location. Justice Holmes' short, almost cryptic, opinion contains some oft-quoted, enigmatic phrases that still cause debate: "This is a case of a single private house. . . . If we were called upon to deal with the plaintiffs' position alone we should think it clear that the statute does not disclose a public interest sufficient to warrant so extensive a destruction of the defendant's constitutionally protected rights."[29] As we will see later in this chapter, a regulation that serves no public purpose is void because it denies due process. Was this the basis for the decision?[30]

Justice Holmes' most important statement from the *Mahon* opinion was that, "while property may be regulated to a certain extent, if regulation goes too far it will be recognized as a taking."[31] This simple declaration still captures the essence of the regulatory taking doctrine—the famous "too far" test. As it suggests, regulatory takings jurisprudence centers on whether challenged regulations destroy a landowner's rights of use and enjoyment so much that they amounts to a taking and entitle the owner to just compensation. Perhaps recognizing the implications of this newfound doctrine, Justice Holmes warned elsewhere in opinion that "[g]overnment could hardly go on if to some extent values incident to property could not be diminished without paying for every such

---

[27]   260 U.S. 393, 43 S.Ct. 158, 67 L.Ed. 322 (1922).

[28]   Countless subsequent decisions have recognized *Mahon* as "the source." See, e.g., Lucas v. South Carolina Coastal Council, 505 U.S. 1003, 112 S.Ct. 2886, 120 L.Ed.2d 798 (1992), and First English Evangelical Lutheran Church v. County of Los Angeles, 482 U.S. 304, 107 S.Ct. 2378, 96 L.Ed.2d 250 (1987). However, Justice Holmes had apparently been shaping the taking doctrine in his mind for some time. There are hints of this in Block v. Hirsh, 256 U.S. 135 (1921) and even as far back as Rideout v. Knox, 148 Mass. 368, 19 N.E. 390 (1889), when he was on the Massachusetts Supreme Judicial Court.

[29]   260 U.S. 393, 413–14, 43 S.Ct. 158–59.

[30]   This is not a frivolous question. Justice Stevens, writing for the Court, in effect so charged many years later in Keystone Bituminous Coal Ass'n v. DeBenedictis, 480 U.S. 470, 107 S.Ct. 1232, 94 L.Ed.2d 472 (1987). He labeled the part of *Mahon* that established the regulatory taking doctrine, an "advisory opinion"—dictum. But, as if nothing had happened, the Court was soon again calling *Mahon* the source of the taking doctrine and continues to do so to this day. See Lucas v. South Carolina Coastal Council, 505 U.S. 1003, 112 S.Ct. 2886, 120 L.Ed.2d 798 (1992), and First English Evangelical Lutheran Church v. County of Los Angeles, 482 U.S. 304, 107 S.Ct. 2378, 96 L.Ed.2d 250 (1987). Others have made the argument that Holmes was really thinking of a denial of due process, that the famous "too far" phrase really meant, "a regulation that goes too far denies due process unless the government offers eminent domain compensation." See especially Fred F. French Investing Co. v. City of New York, 39 N.Y.2d 587, 385 N.Y.S.2d 5, 350 N.E.2d 381 (1976), where the New York Court of Appeals was so bold as to say that *Mahon's* use of the word "taking" was a "metaphor" for denial of due process.

[31]   260 U.S. 393, 415, 43 S.Ct. 158, 160.

change in the general law."[32] This truthful observation highlights the potential dangers of regulatory takings doctrine and has long served as a reminder that confining the doctrine to a narrow sphere of circumstances is crucial to preserving governments' valuable regulatory power.

In discussing a similar statute that required pillars of coal to be maintained between adjacent coal mines and whose constitutionality had been sustained, Holmes made one other statement that continues to significantly impact regulatory takings law. He noted that the statute upheld in the other case "secured an average reciprocity of advantage that has been recognized as the justification of various laws."[33] He seemed to be emphasizing that each mine in that jurisdiction received reciprocal benefits from the fact that all other mines were also being regulated under the statute. This rationale similarly helps to justify zoning since all owners in a zone are presumably benefitted by everyone else being restricted. These reciprocal benefits may "soften the blow" for a landowner—provide a kind of offset against loss—and thereby make a taking less likely.

Despite the novelty and importance of *Mahon*, for 50 years after the decision the vitality of regulatory takings doctrine (though it was frequently applied in state courts) was clouded in the Supreme Court.[34] In 1926, in the Court's original zoning case, Village of Euclid v. Ambler Realty Co.,[35] where the owner suffered as much as a 75 percent value loss and the trial court had used the taking doctrine, the Supreme Court virtually ignored the doctrine and Justice Holmes signed the opinion without murmur. The next Supreme Court case in which the taking question was seriously raised was Goldblatt v. Town of Hempstead in 1962, where zoning caused a landowner loss in an unstated amount, but which seemingly was from 80 to 90 percent of land value.[36] Again the Court held there was no taking.

However, in 1978, in Penn Central Transportation Co. v. City of New York, the Court returned to the regulatory taking issue in a major way.[37] In the decades that have followed, regulatory takings doctrine has been among the most actively-developing and controversial areas of real property law. The claimants in *Penn Central* were the railroad company that controlled New York's iconic rail station building, Grand Central Terminal. In the late 1960s, recognizing that enormous skyscrapers had sprouted up on most of the Manhattan city blocks surrounding the terminal and hoping to capitalize the area's increasingly-valuable prime location for high-rise development, the railroad executed a long term lease agreement for erection of a 55-story office tower immediately above the terminal. Unfortunately, the city's Landmarks Preservation Commission had previously designated the terminal site as an historic landmark and refused to approve the office tower project on the theory that it would too severely disrupt various historic attributes of the site. Angered by this rejection, the railroad filed a claim against the

[32] 260 U.S. 393, 413, 43 S.Ct. 158, 159.

[33] 260 U.S. 393, 415, 43 S.Ct. 158, 160.

[34] A sampling of many state decisions includes Corthouts v. Town of Newington, 140 Conn. 284, 99 A.2d 112 (1953); Morris County Land Imp. Co. v. Parsippany-Troy Hills Tnp., 40 N.J. 539, 193 A.2d 232 (1963); and especially Arverne Bay Constr. Co. v. Thatcher, 278 N.Y. 222, 15 N.E.2d 587 (1938). *Arverne Bay* became itself a leading case. For more citations, see Stoebuck, Police Power, Takings, and Due Process, 37 Wash. & Lee L. Rev. 1057, 1063–64 (1980).

[35] 272 U.S. 365, 47 S.Ct. 114, 71 L.Ed. 303 (1926).

[36] 369 U.S. 590, 82 S.Ct. 987, 8 L.Ed.2d 130 (1962). The town's ordinance compelled Goldblatt to quit extracting gravel from a profitable gravel pit.

[37] 438 U.S. 104, 98 S.Ct. 2646, 57 L.Ed.2d 631 (1978), rehearing denied 439 U.S. 883, 99 S.Ct. 226, 58 L.Ed.2d 198 (1978).

City of New York and the suit ultimately made its way to the U.S. Supreme Court. The Court's now-notorious 1978 majority opinion in the case has become the subject of countless law review articles and other legal publications in the decades that have followed.

Although the Supreme Court appeared in *Penn Central* to squarely consider what constitutes a compensable regulatory taking, it arguably did more to obfuscate than to clarify its regulatory takings doctrine. Rather than setting forth a clear and workable test for determining which regulatory actions trigger takings and which do not, Justice Brennan's *Penn Central* opinion identifies three ambiguous factors and suggests that courts must apply these factors on an ad hoc basis to determine whether to find a taking in any given context. Specifically, Brennan explained:

> In engaging in these essentially ad hoc, factual inquiries, the Court's decisions have identified several factors that have particular significance. The *economic impact of the regulation* on the claimant and, particularly, the *extent to which the regulation has interfered with distinct investment-backed expectations* are, of course, relevant considerations. So, too, is the *character of the governmental action*. A "taking" may more readily be found when the interference with property can be characterized as a physical invasion by government, than when interference arises from some public program adjusting the benefits and burdens of economic life to promote the common good.[38]

After analyzing the facts of *Penn Central* under this newly-minted and confusing set of ad hoc factors, the Court essentially held that the railroad was not entitled to just compensation from the City for the loss of its rights to build an office tower above the terminal. Frustratingly, it was not even clear in the opinion how the Court had applied the new test to reach this conclusion. A chorus of criticism from lawyers and legal academics followed. Most of this negative attention was directed at the vague, unworkable and indeterminate nature of the Court's new ad hoc test, which seemed to raise more questions than it answered. Specifically, how are courts supposed to determine whether the adverse "economic impact" of a land use regulation on a given claimant is severe enough to trigger a compensable taking? How much must a new government restriction "interfere" with landowners' "investment-backed expectations" to necessitate that the government compensate them for those losses? Exactly how does the "character of the governmental action" at issue impact the analysis? And how are courts supposed to weigh and balance this disparate set of factors?

In addition to laying down a novel analytical test for taking claims, *Penn Central* accelerated the development of regulatory takings law. The case prompted many more private property holders to bring takings claims and, as those additional claims arose, the Supreme Court—perhaps recognizing the perceived deficiencies of its approach in *Penn Central*—gradually built upon it through a series of subsequent decisions. The first such decision came in 1982 in Loretto v. Teleprompter Manhattan CATV Corp.[39] The plaintiff in *Loretto* was a residential landlord who was challenging a New York statute requiring her to allow the installation of cable television wires and equipment on her building. After a cable company installed a single cable wire and two small cable boxes on the exterior of her building, she filed a claim alleging that the application of the

---

[38]   438 U.S. 104, 124, S.Ct. 2646, 2659 (emphasis added).

[39]   458 U.S. 419, 102 S.Ct. 3164, 73 L.Ed.2d 868 (1982).

statute to her property amounted to a compensable regulatory taking. Based on the ad hoc factors had laid down in *Penn Central* just a few years earlier, the plaintiff in *Loretto* appeared to have at best a questionable chance of prevailing in the case. Among other things, the small cable equipment installed on Ms. Loretto's building had a little or no adverse economic impact on her and did not significantly interfere with her investment-backed expectations in connection with the property. Nonetheless, the U.S. Supreme Court held in favor of Ms. Loretto and established a new "per se" takings rule. Specifically, the Court held that any law requiring a landowner to accommodate a "permanent physical occupation" of private land categorically triggered a taking entitling the landowner to just compensation. In the Court's words:

> Property rights in a physical thing have been described as the rights "to possess, use and dispose of it." To the extent that the government permanently occupies physical property, it effectively destroys each of these rights. First, the owner has no right to possess the occupied space himself, and also has no power to exclude the occupier from possession and use of the space. The power to exclude has traditionally been considered one of the most treasured strands in an owner's bundle of property rights. Second, the permanent physical occupation of property forever denies the owner any power to control the use of the property; he not only cannot exclude others, but can make no nonpossessory use of the property. . . . Finally, even though the owner may retain the bare legal right to dispose of the occupied space by transfer or sale, the permanent occupation of that space by a stranger will ordinarily empty the right of any value, since the purchaser will also be unable to make any use of the property.[40]

By establishing the per se or "categorical" takings rule for permanent physical occupations of private property in *Loretto*, the Court added some small measure of clarity to takings law in the wake of *Penn Central* and its much-criticized ad hoc test. Unfortunately, laws that require permanent physical occupations of private land comprise only a small fraction of the types of cases that might give rise to takings claims. In other words, an abundance of ambiguity and uncertainty about takings law remained.

In 1987, the Court seemingly added a bit more detail with its holding in Keystone Bituminous Coal Association v. DeBenedictis.[41] Though it did not answer *Mahon's* intractable question of "how far is 'too far'" or provide significant guidance to courts regarding *Penn Central*'s mushy factors, *Keystone* did involve an application of takings doctrine. *Keystone* involved a Pennsylvania statute intended to prevent subsidence in bituminous coal mines that was superficially like the Kohler Act in *Mahon*. However, upon closer analysis, the facts of the two cases were quite different. *Mahon* was site-specific to one location, while *Keystone's* plaintiff was an association of many coal companies, with many regulated mines. In summarizing the facts, the Court minimized the regulation's impact, saying at one point that the act would require the 13 mines to leave in place only two percent more coal than they already have to leave to support the mines and to satisfy other statutes. Accordingly, the Court held that *Mahon* did not control, and that there was no taking. But the Court did not let it go at that; they developed what amounted to an alternative ground of decision, one that cut deeply into *Mahon* and added a new dimension to this area of jurisprudence.

---

[40] 458 U.S. 419, 435–36, 102 S.Ct. 3164, 3176.
[41] 480 U.S. 470, 107 S.Ct. 1232, 94 L.Ed.2d 472 (1987).

Justice Stevens' opinion for the *Keystone* Court said, in effect, that that regulations that prohibit or forbid a "nuisance" have never been thought to cause a taking, a proposition that has never been doubted. Then he extended the "nuisance exception," saying that regulations that prevent activities "akin to a nuisance" are cannot possibly cause a taking. In his dissenting opinion, Chief Justice Rehnquist complained that Justice Stevens's phrase "akin to a nuisance" had too much "insulated" land use regulations from causing a taking. Thus came into being the "insulation doctrine," which might be loosely stated as, "regulations that protect certain particularly critical public interests cannot possibly cause a taking." In that sense, Keystone Bituminous Coal Association v. DeBenedictis seemed to marginalize *Mahon* and to restrict its doctrine.

The Supreme Court made a clearer and more sizable contribution to the further development of takings law in its 1992 decision in Lucas v. South Carolina Coastal Council.[42] Mr. Lucas had purchased two beachfront lots on the Isle of Palms, South Carolina, for $975,000 in 1986. At that time, the state's Beachfront Management Act would have allowed him to develop them with dwellings, but in 1988 the Act was amended and made more restrictive. The trial court had found as facts that the amendments had prevented any permanent habitable structures and had actually rendered the lots "valueless": zero use, zero value, a "zero-zero" case. These facts the South Carolina Supreme Court had accepted, but had nevertheless held that the Act did not cause a taking because it "prevented serious public harm."[43] In effect, South Carolina had invoked a form of "insulation" doctrine, that a total loss of use and value would not cause a taking if it prevented serious public harm.

Justice Scalia's majority opinion for the Supreme Court reversed South Carolina and held that there was a taking, for which compensation was due. He said that total denials of use and value were "categorical" takings, which was of course as far as the assumed facts in *Lucas* required the Court to go. But the opinion went on to lay down a more general test of when a land use regulation becomes so severe as to cause a taking variously stated as "no economically viable use," "all economically beneficial or productive use," and "all economically beneficial use." This refinement of *Mahon's* "too far" test, though still an imprecise, fact-laden test, is somewhat more usable. For instance, there is an indication in the opinion that value loss must be quite high to reach the threshold. Footnote 7 of the majority opinion involves an example of a 90 percent value loss, and footnote 8 uses an example of a 95 percent loss. Footnote 7 more or less says that a 90 percent loss might or might not cause a taking, and footnote 8 suggests that 95 percent would more likely cause a taking, but still might not in all cases.

Of course state governments and courts are bound by the *Lucas* decision in the sense that they cannot afford landowners less protection than the decision requires. State court decisions, as well as lower federal court decisions, since *Lucas*, and even some previous to it, have used its "viable-use" or "economically-beneficial-use" test.[44] Though the *Lucas* test is the standard judicial formula and is more usable than "too far," it still is far too

---

[42]   505 U.S. 1003, 112 S.Ct. 2886, 120 L.Ed.2d 798 (1992).

[43]   Lucas v. South Carolina Coastal Council, 304 S.C. 376, 404 S.E.2d 895 (1991).

[44]   See, e.g., among many, New Port Largo, Inc. v. Monroe County, 95 F.3d 1084 (11th Cir.1996) (no taking found); Cannone v. Noey, 867 P.2d 797 (Alaska 1994) (no taking found); Ramona Convent of Holy Names v. City of Alhambra, 21 Cal.App.4th 10, 26 Cal.Rptr.2d 140 (Cal.App. 1993) (no taking found); Moroney v. Mayor and Council of Borough of Old Tappan, 268 N.J.Super. 458, 633 A.2d 1045 (App. Div. 1993) (taking found); Sintra, Inc. v. City of Seattle, 119 Wn.2d 1, 829 P.2d 765 (1992) (taking found); Orion Corp. v. State, 109 Wn.2d 621, 747 P.2d 1062 (1987) ("all profitable use"; remanded).

imprecise to allow either land use regulators or landowners to predict the limits of regulation; it is a breeder of litigation. If degree of value loss were to be the determinant, what would be needed is a test that turns on a stated percentage of loss, whether it is 51 percent or 90 percent or something in between. Of course even that would not prevent all litigation since many factual disputes will arise about the amount of loss in a given case but it would go as far as a rule of law can go in that direction. Unfortunately, there is no reason to believe that such a test will emerge from courts or legislatures anytime soon.

After *Lucas*, there seemed to be three primary tests for finding a regulatory taking: the *Loretto*, *Penn Central*, and *Lucas* tests. The *Lucas* and *Loretto* tests are each per se takings tests; the *Penn Central* test is an ad hoc test. The U.S. Supreme Court helpfully confirmed this status of regulatory takings law in its majority opinion in *Lingle v. Chevron U.S.A., Inc.* in 2005.[45] *Lingle* involved the challenge of a Hawaii statute that limited the rent oil companies could charge dealers who leased company-owned gas stations. In addition to abrogating a takings analysis factor discussed in *Agins v. City of Tiburon*,[46] the *Lingle* court succinctly listed the three tests just described and affirmed their relevance. In the Court's words:

> Regulatory actions generally will be deemed per se takings for Fifth Amendment purposes (1) where government requires an owner to suffer a permanent physical invasion of her property, see *Loretto v. Teleprompter Manhattan CATV Corp* . . . , or (2) where regulations completely deprive an owner of "all economically beneficial us[e]" of her property, *Lucas v. South Carolina Coastal Council*, . . . Outside these two categories (and the special context of land-use exactions . . .), regulatory takings challenges are governed by *Penn Central Transp. Co. v. New York City*. . . . *Penn Central* identified several factors—including the regulation's economic impact on the claimant, the extent to which it interferes with distinct investment-backed expectations, and the character of the government action—that are particularly significant in determining whether a regulation affects a taking.[47]

Unfortunately, these three tests—the product of the U.S. Supreme Court's decades-long effort to clarify federal regulatory takings doctrine after *Penn Central*—leave myriad unanswered questions that continue to muddle this challenging area of the law.

A handful of subsidiary regulatory-taking questions remain at least somewhat unanswered. For instance, one minor question is whether Lucas v. South Carolina Coastal Council modified the "insulation" doctrine the Court announced in Keystone Bituminous Coal Association v. DeBenedictis. It will be recalled that Justice Stevens' majority opinion in *Keystone* said—though perhaps it was technically dictum—that regulations that prevented activities "akin to a nuisance" were, as Chief Justice Rehnquist termed them in his dissent, "insulated" from causing takings, no matter how severely they impacted the landowner. What then did Justice Scalia's majority decision in *Lucas* do to the insulation doctrine? Did he repudiate it entirely? No, but he certainly circumscribed it from *Keystone's* phrase, "akin to a nuisance." It is clear that Justice Scalia said that regulations that prevent nuisances as defined by common law are

---

[45] 544 U.S. 528, 125 S.Ct. 2074, 161 L.Ed.2d 876 (2005).
[46] 447 U.S. 255, 100 S.Ct. 2138, 65 L.Ed.2d 106 (1980).
[47] 544 U.S. 528, 529, 125 S.Ct. 2074, 2076.

"insulated."And, indeed, Chief Justice Rehnquist, who signed the majority opinion in *Lucas*, had admitted that in his dissent in *Keystone*. But Justice Scalia also said something broader, thoudgh there is debate about exactly what he meant. He said that when the state deprives an owner of all economically beneficial use of land, "we think it may resist compensation only if the logically antecedent inquiry into the nature of the owner's *estate* shows that the proscribed use interests were not part of his *title* to begin with."[48] (Emphasis added.) He offered nuisance, i.e., that an owner of an estate in land is never privileged to commit a common-law nuisance, as an example. Accordingly, although some may try to argue otherwise, it appears most likely that the only kinds of regulations insulated under this sub-doctrine are those that simply repeat and reinforce common-law restrictions that already exist.

The Lucas *Rule's Lingering "Denominator Problem"*

The most important and controversial set of unresolved questions in regulatory takings law centers on how courts should define the "denominator" or underlying property interest when applying the *Lucas* rule. Courts must first define the relevant property at issue when considering whether a challenged regulation has triggered a compensable *Lucas* taking by denying a property owner "all" economically viable use of it. Identifying the relevant property was relatively straightforward for the *Lucas* court because the claimant in that case held an undivided fee simple interest in a single, clearly-defined parcel and the challenged regulation precluded economically viable use of all of it.[49] Unfortunately, identifying the relevant property or "denominator" is not always so easy. Justice Scalia himself famously conceded in the *Lucas* majority opinion:

> Regrettably, the rhetorical force of our "deprivation of all economically feasible use" rule is greater than its precision, since the rule does not make clear the "property interest" against which the loss of value is to be measured. . . Unsurprisingly, this uncertainty regarding the composition of the denominator in our "deprivation" fraction has produced inconsistent pronouncements by the Court.[50]

In his dissenting opinion in *Lucas*, Justice Blackmun unsurprisingly latched on to this problem as a major weakness in the majority's holding. In his words:

> The threshold inquiry for imposition of the Court's new rule, "deprivation of all economically valuable use," itself cannot be determined objectively. As the Court admits, whether the owner has been deprived of all economic value of his property will depend on how "property" is defined. The "composition of the denominator in our 'deprivation' fraction" is the dispositive inquiry. Yet there is no "objective" way to define what that denominator should be.[51]

The set of unresolved issues regarding how to define the appropriate "denominator" for *Lucas* takings analysis have collectively become known as the "denominator problem" and have inspired volumes of commentary and criticism from legal scholars in recent

---

[48]   505 U.S. at 1027, 112 S.Ct. at 2899.

[49]   See 505 U.S. at 1017 n. 7, 112 S.Ct. at 2894 (noting that the court was able to circumvent the difficult task of the identifying relevant property "in the present case, since the 'interest in land' that Lucas has pleaded (a fee simple interest) is an estate with a rich tradition of protection at common law").

[50]   505 U.S. at 1017 n. 7, 112 S.Ct. at 2894.

[51]   505 U.S. at 1054, 112 S.Ct. at 2913.

decades[52] Despite the Supreme Courts' efforts to address these questions, they continue to inject ambiguity and controversy into takings analyses under the *Lucas* rule.

The denominator problem involves two primary sub-issues that can arise when courts attempt to define the relevant parcel for *Lucas* takings analysis. One of these sub-issues centers on whether courts may find a taking of "all" economically viable use by conceptually severing a narrower spatial property interest from an interest in an entire parcel and making that narrower interest the "denominator." The U.S. Supreme Court has confronted this issue of conceptual severance in various forms over the years and added some clarity to the debate, but unanswered questions surrounding it still remain. It seems settled that courts cannot apply *Lucas* by considering the impact a regulation has on only a part of the regulated land and must instead consider its impact on the whole parcel. Even prior to *Lucas*, in Penn Central Transportation Co. v. City of New York, the Court rejected the idea that a landowner could conceptually severe a parcel to spatially isolate a selected portion of it and thereby make the magnitude of a regulation's impact seem more severe. The *Penn Central* court refused to find a compensable taking based on the historic-site designation's impacts on air rights above the roof of Grand Central Station, focusing instead on the regulation's impact on the "parcel as a whole."[53]

Keystone Bituminous Coal Association v. DeBenedictis,[54] which also preceded the *Lucas* case, similarly held that such "piecemealing" is not permitted and seemed to require treatment of the denominator as the entire parcel. Though the facts of the case were not fully developed, it appeared that, of the 13 mines upon which the facts did focus, the subsidence statute required that 27 million tons of coal out of a total of over 1.46 billion tons in those mines, not be removed. The owners' association argued that there was a total taking of those 27 million tons, but the Court's majority opinion effectively held instead that the prohibition affected just a fraction of the mine assets having a numerator of 27 million and a denominator of 1.46 billion, which calculates out to an insignificant 1.849 percent. In his dissent Chief Justice Rehnquist, joined by three other justices, argued that the majority should have considered the 27 million tons as "a separate segment of property for takings purposes." Thus, it is clear that the question was treated as an issue and decided by the Court. Since *Keystone*, state courts have accordingly assumed that this piecemealing approach to takings analysis is not allowed and have so held.[55]

---

[52] See, e.g., John E. Fee, Unearthing the Denominator in Regulatory Taking Claims, 61 U. Chi. L. Rev. 1535, 1538 (1994) (suggesting that courts apply an "independent economic viability" standard for defining the denominator in regulatory takings cases); Marc R. Lisker, Regulatory Takings and the Denominator Problem, 27 Rutgers L.J. 663 (1996) (favoring a rule that "if the state law applicable to the property at issue recognizes the separate and distinct existence of the estate that one of the litigants seeks to sever (in making the denominator determination), then such severance is appropriate"); Lynn E. Blais, The Total Takings Myth, 81 86 Fordham L. Rev. 47, 76 (2017) (asserting that "[b]y far the biggest challenge to implementing the Lucas total takings rule in the lower courts is the denominator dilemma"); Danaya C. Wright, A New Time for Denominators: Toward a Dynamic Theory of Property in the Regulatory Takings Relevant Parcel Analysis, 34 Envt'l L. 175, 180 (2004) (calling the Supreme Court's "current approach to the denominator issue . . . incoherent and illogical.").

[53] 438 U.S. 104, 130–131, 98 S.Ct. 2646, 2663, 57 L.Ed.2d 631 (1978), rehearing denied 439 U.S. 883, 99 S.Ct. 226, 58 L.Ed.2d 198 (1978).

[54] 480 U.S. 470, 107 S.Ct. 1232, 94 L.Ed.2d 472 (1987).

[55] See Quirk v. Town of New Boston, 140 N.H. 124, 663 A.2d 1328 (N.H. 1995); Presbytery of Seattle v. King County, 114 Wn.2d 320, 787 P.2d 907 (1990), citing *Keystone* and expressly overruling Allingham v. City of Seattle, 109 Wn.2d 947, 749 P.2d 160 (1988), which had allowed piecemealing; Zealy v. City of Waukesha, 201 Wis.2d 365, 548 N.W.2d 528 (Wis. 1996).

Though *Keystone* and *Penn Central* appeared to have somewhat settled the piecemealing issue, some uncertainty about the issue remains. In footnote 7 in the majority opinion in Lucas v. South Carolina Coastal Council, Justice Scalia said that the Court's prior decisions, including *Keystone* and *Penn Central*, did not "make clear the 'property interest' against which the loss of value is to be measured."[56] He found an inconsistency in several of the Court's former decisions on that point. Of course it is debatable how much weight a footnote in a majority opinion signed by five justices carries.[57] However, as Professor Carol M. Rose has noted, a principled argument may be made that not to allow piecemealing can work injustice among owners of parcels of land of varying sizes or values. For instance, suppose there are two landowners—one who owns 100 acres of land and another who own 10 acres of the same quality of land. If piecemealing were not allowed, the owner of the 100 acres would receive no compensation if 10 (or probably even more) acres were put into an unusable land reserve, but the owner of the 10 acres would be compensated if his 10 acres were similarly restricted. Rose argues that to require the large landowner to bear the uncompensated loss and the small landowner to be compensated is an application of the "deep pocket" doctrine.[58] A handful of cases decided in the years after *Lucas,* have brought to life some of the unjust hypothetical scenarios highlighted in Rose's article, generating results that seem at least somewhat arbitrary.[59]

After more than two decades of scholarly criticism and court confusion surrounding conceptual severance and how to define the relevant property at issue in takings cases, the U.S. Supreme Court attempted to squarely address this issue again in the 2017 case of Murr v. Wisconsin.[60] The landowners in *Murr* owned two contiguous parcels of land— Lots E and F—abutting the St. Croix River. A cabin was situated on Lot F, but Lot E was undeveloped. Although both lots were over one acre in size, a steep embankment traversing both lots made less than one acre of each lot to be suitable for development. Under the St. Croix County's lot merger ordinance, this meant that the Murrs—as common owners of both lots—were prohibited from separately selling or developing Lot E. When the St. Croix County Board of Adjustment refused to grant a variance to the Murrs to do either of these things with Lot E, they challenged the Board's enforcement of the lot merger ordinance provisions as a regulatory taking.

Justice Kennedy, who wrote the five-justice majority opinion in *Murr*, acknowledged near the outset that the case sought to address an issue that was critically important to regulatory takings law. In his words:

> This case presents a question that is linked to the ultimate determination whether a regulatory taking has occurred: What is the proper unit of property

---

[56] Lucas v. South Carolina Coastal Council, 505 U.S. 1003, 112 S.Ct. 2886, 120 L.Ed.2d 798, n. 7 (1992).

[57] Justice Kennedy also joined in the decision, but in a separate concurring opinion.

[58] Rose, *Mahon* Reconstructed: Why the Takings Issue is Still a Muddle, 57 S. Cal. L. Rev. 561, 566–69 (1984).

[59] See, e.g., Palazzolo v. Rhode Island, 533 U.S. 606, 121 S.Ct. 2448, 150 L.Ed.2d 592 (2001) (holding that a regulation that caused a 93 percent diminution in the value of the claimant's private land did not trigger a compensable *Lucas* taking because the claimant could still make some economically viable use of portions of the land); Forest Properties, Inc. v. United States, 177 F.3d 1360 (1999) (declining to find a compensable taking of 9.4 acres of lake-bottom land based on a finding that owner also owned 53 contiguous acres so the relevant parcel was the entire 62 acres); Lost Tree Village Corp. v. United States, 707 F.3d 1286 (2013) (holding that a total prohibition on the use of 4.99 out of a landowner's contiguous1300 acres was a *Lucas* total taking, in part because the 4.99 was a separate parcel).

[60] 137 S.Ct. 1933, 198 L.Ed.2d 497 (2017).

against which to assess the effect of the challenged governmental action? Put another way, "[b]ecause our test for regulatory taking requires us to compare the value that has been taken from the property with the value that remains in the property, one of the critical questions is determining how to define the unit of property 'whose value is to furnish the denominator of the fraction.' "[61] Keystone Bituminous Coal Assn. v. DeBenedictis, 480 U.S. 470, 497, 107 S.Ct. 1232, 94 L.Ed.2d 472 (1987) (quoting Michelman, *Property, Utility, and Fairness*, 80 Harv. L. Rev. 1165, 1992 (1967)).

The Murrs argued in the case that state property law—which delineates between parcels based on lot lines—should govern the definition of the "relevant property" for takings analysis. Under that approach, since Lot E was an entirely separate parcel, the county ordinance provisions prohibiting any separate sale or development of it would seemingly constitute a *Lucas* taking. Ironically, Wisconsin also sought to have state law govern definition of the relevant parcel, albeit in a different way. Wisconsin argued that the two lots at issue should be treated as a single lot because of the effect of the lot merge ordinance provisions, which were enforceable under state law. As Wisconsin's lawyers pointed out, the approach of using state law to determine the relevant parcel seemed at least somewhat supported by the court's own prior takings jurisprudence. Indeed, language from a footnote in the *Lucas* majority opinion expressly stated that such determinations might be based on landowners' expectations as "shaped by the State's law of property—i.e., whether and to what degree the State's law has accorded legal recognition and protection to the particular interest in land with respect to which the takings claimant alleges a diminution in (or elimination of) value."[62]

In a somewhat surprising move, the *Murr* court rejected the state law-focused arguments of the Murrs and of the state of Wisconsin, even though embracing either might have provided at least some additional clarity regarding how the relevant property is defined under *Lucas* taking analysis. Again, quoting Justice Kennedy:

> [N]o single consideration can supply the exclusive test for determining the denominator. Instead, courts must consider a number of factors. These include the treatment of the land under state and local law; the physical characteristics of the land; and the prospective value of the regulated land. The endeavor should determine whether reasonable expectations about property ownership would lead a landowner to anticipate that his holdings would be treated as one parcel, or, instead, as separate tracts. The inquiry is objective, and the reasonable expectations at issue derive from background customs and the whole of our legal tradition.[63]

With that single paragraph, the *Murr* court obliterated all hope for a new, clearer rule for defining the relevant property under takings analysis. Rather than helping to clarify a notoriously uncertain aspect of takings jurisprudence, the Court further muddied the waters. Instead of prescribing reliance on state property law or on some other relatively objective means to define the unit of property that comprises the denominator in these cases, the Murr court embraced an ambiguous and difficult-to

---

[61] 137 S.Ct. 1933, 1944 (quoting Keystone Bituminous Coal Assn. v. DeBenedictis, 480 U.S. 470, 497, 107 S.Ct. 1232, 94 L.Ed.2d 472 (1987) and Michelman, Property, Utility, and Fairness, 80 Harv. L. Rev. 1165, 1992 (1967)).

[62] 137 S.Ct. 1933, 1946 (quoting Lucas 505 U.S., at 1017, n. 7, 112 S.Ct. 2886).

[63] 137 S.Ct. 1933, 1945.

apply multi-factor test. The *Murr* test for defining the relevant parcel treats state and local law as just one relevant factor and requires courts also consider a handful of others—specifically the "physical characteristics of the land", the "prospective value of the regulated land" and whether "reasonable expectations" would cause a landowner to anticipate treatment of the subject land as a separate parcel.[64]

Writing for the three dissenting justices in *Murr*, Justice Roberts sharply criticized the majority's disposition of the case. Among other things, Roberts' dissent characterized the majority's holding as an unjustifiable rejection of past precedent and as the creation of an unworkable rule what eroded landowners' rights under the Takings Clause. Roberts asserted that the Court's "decisions have, time and again, declared that the Takings Clause protects private property rights as state law creates and defines them", suggesting that the new *Murr* test deviates from that longstanding approach.[65] Roberts then added:

> Put simply, today's decision knocks the definition of "private property" loose from its foundation on stable state law rules and throws it into the maelstrom of multiple factors that come into play at the second step of the takings analysis. The result: The majority's new framework compromises the Takings Clause as a barrier between individuals and the press of the public interest.[66]

Almost immediately after the Court released the *Murr* opinion, legal scholars and other commentators began bemoaning it as an unnecessary injection of additional confusion into the already-frustrating field of regulatory takings law.[67] Although only time will tell whether the *Murr* decision further complicates "relevant parcel" analysis as much as its critics claim it does, the decision certainly did not make the process of defining the denominator in these cases any more predictable.

Another regulatory-taking issue related to the denominator problem is that of whether it is possible to have a "temporary taking." If a regulation were to deprive a landowner of all economically viable use of a parcel of land *for 20 years*, would that trigger a compensable taking? The U.S. Supreme Court provided some limited guidance on this question in First English Evangelical Lutheran Church v. County of Los Angeles.[68] In that case a floodplain ordinance had prevented the plaintiff from developing land for four or five years while the plaintiff challenged and litigated the alleged total denial of use. Chief Justice Rehnquist's majority opinion held that compensation would be due for the period of such a "temporary" taking. However, he added that "quite different questions . . . would arise in the case of normal delays in obtaining building permits, changes in zoning ordinances, variances, and the like which are not before us." This holding raised important questions above how long a temporary a denial of use has to be to trigger a viable takings claim. In his dissent, Justice Stevens also found an inconsistency in the majority's suggestion that some "temporary" denials of use would cause a taking but other less temporary denials would not. He added the

---

[64]   137 S.Ct. 1933, 1945.

[65]   137 S.Ct. 1933, 1950.

[66]   137 S.Ct. 1933, 1956.

[67]   See, e.g., Lynn E. Blais, The Total Takings Myth, 86 Fordham L. Rev. 47 (2017); Maureen E. Brady, Penn Central Squared: What the Many Factors of Murr v. Wisconsin Mean for Property Federalism, 166 U. PA. L. Rev. Online 53 (2017); Nicole Stelle Garnett, From a Muddle to a Mudslide: Murr v. Wisconsin, 2017 Cato Sup. Ct. Rev. 131 (2017).

[68]   482 U.S. 304, 107 S.Ct. 2378, 96 L.Ed.2d 250 (1987).

intriguing proposition that "regulations are three dimensional; they have depth, width, and length." In determining the degree of an owner's loss, which we know is measured by loss of value, why should we not consider the time span of a restriction as well as the amount of restriction at a given moment in time?

The U.S. Supreme Court's most direct examination of the temporal dimension of property in the takings law context came in 2002 in the landmark case, *Tahoe-Sierra Preservation Council, Inc. v. Tahoe Regional Planning Agency*.[69] The claimants in *Tahoe-Sierra* were owners of land near Lake Tahoe, a mountain lake bordering California and Nevada that has long attracted tourists and recreationalists. In August of 1981, the Tahoe Regional Planning Agency (TRPA)—a government agency created to help protect the lake and conserve natural resources in the area—imposed a moratorium that temporarily prohibited development in much of the Lake Tahoe area. According to the TRPA, the moratorium was necessary to bide some time for the agency while it finalized a more permanent regional development plan. The TRPA was somewhat delayed in finalizing the plan so it ended up issuing a second moratorium and the combined duration of the two moratoria extended until the agency adopted its plan in April of 1984. Soon thereafter, a group of landowners sued the agency claiming that the combined 32-month building moratoria triggered a *per se* compensable taking under the Fifth Amendment. The case gradually wound its way through the courts and finally arrived at the U.S. Supreme Court in 2002. In a 6–3 decision, the Court dismissed the landowners' takings claim, holding that the temporary moratoria did not trigger a categorical per se taking entitling the landowners to just compensation.

Writing for the majority in *Tahoe-Sierra*, Justice Stevens explained that a categorical takings rule entitling property holders to just compensation whenever a regulation temporarily deprives them of all economically viable use of property would severely constrain valuable regulatory activity. Stevens stated that "the extreme categorical rule that any deprivation of all economic use, no matter how brief, constitutes a compensable taking surely cannot be sustained" because it would "undoubtedly require changes in numerous practices that have long been considered permissible exercises of the police power."[70] Instead, the court concluded that the "the concepts of 'fairness and justice' that underlie the Takings Clause [would] be better served" if courts analyzed these temporary moratoria and the like under the ad hoc, fact-specific *Penn Central* test.[71] Justice Stevens added later in the opinion that the duration of such moratoria is "one of the important factors that a court must consider in the appraisal of a regulatory takings claim" but that the Court needed to resist the temptation to embrace a categorical rule involving that factor.[72] In summary, *Tahoe-Sierra* partially addressed takings law's denominator problem by making clear that courts would not permit claimants to temporally sever an interest in property as a means of showing a categorical *Lucas* taking.

Can Court Decisions Trigger Judicial Takings?

In addition to the "denominator"-related issues just highlighted, one other noteworthy takings question remains somewhat unresolved: whether it is possible for a court's adjudication of a case to trigger a compensable taking. Regulatory takings cases

---

[69]　535 U.S. 302, 122 S.Ct. 1465, 152 L.Ed.2d 517 (2002).

[70]　535 U.S. 302, 335, 122 S.Ct. 1465, 1486.

[71]　535 U.S. 302, 334, 122 S.Ct. 1465, 1486.

[72]　535 U.S. 302, 342, 122 S.Ct. 1465, 1489.

typically involve challenges to legislative or possibly administrative actions. However, it is also conceivable that a court could rule in a way that effectively takes property from a private party and redistributes it to a government entity. For instance, suppose hypothetically that the Texas Supreme Court were to somehow interpret the state's common law as prohibiting private parties from holding title to severed oil and gas rights and to provide that all such rights were actually vested in the state government. Might such a court action entitle private holders of oil and gas rights in the state to just compensation under the Takings Clause? More generally, could it even be possible for a state court ruling to trigger a compensable taking? The U.S. Supreme Court encountered this question in the case of Stop the Beach Renourishment, Inc. v. Florida Department of Environmental Protection.[73]

A bit of background information about the common law rights of beachfront landowners is needed to fully understand how the government activities at issue in *Stop the Beach* allegedly affected landowners' property rights. In Florida and most other states, "littoral" owners—owners of land that abuts an ocean or lake—have special rights of "accretion", meaning that if sand or other sediment gradually deposits along their beachfront parcels over time and causes the acreage of their parcels to grow they get title to that increased acreage.[74] In contrast, a beachfront parcel owner generally does not take title to new dry land resulting from "avulsions"—sudden and perceptible events affecting the water line on beachfront property. Consequently, when an avulsion event creates a new strip of land between the ocean and a formerly-beachfront parcel, the owner of that parcel ceases to be a littoral owner and loses rights to future accretions.[75]

The petitioner in *Stop the Beach* was a nonprofit corporation formed by owners of joining Florida beachfront land parcels. The City of Destin and Walton County had applied to the Florida Department of Environmental Protection for permits and funding under Florida's Beach and Shore Preservation Act to "restore" about 6.9 miles of beach following a series of hurricanes by adding roughly 75 feet of land "seaward of the main high-water line."[76] Because it would partially involve filling previously submerged lands, the project likewise required authorization from Florida's Board of Trustees of the Internal Improvement Trust Fund. Importantly, upon completion of the project, the Board would replace each beachfront parcel's former high-water line with a new "erosion control line." This designation would insert a new strip of state-owned land between the landowners' private parcels and the ocean such that the landowners were no longer littoral owners and held no accretion rights. The petitioner in the case argued, among other things, that this destruction of the landowners' accretion rights amounted to a compensable taking.[77] The issue eventually reached the Florida State Supreme Court, which held that accretion rights were merely "future contingent interest, not a vested property right" and that "there is no littoral right to contact with the water independent of the littoral right of access, which the Act does not infringe."[78]

---

[73]   560 U.S. 702, 130 S.Ct. 2592, 177 L.Ed.2d 184 (2010).

[74]   Littoral landowners also generally have rights of reliction, which can expand the acreage of their parcels in instances when ocean or lake waters recede and thereby expose more land that was formerly covered by water. The majority purposely consolidates rights of accretion and reliction in the case and refers to them simply as accretion rights.

[75]   See 560 U.S. 702, 709, 130 S.Ct. 2592, 2599.

[76]   560 U.S. 702, 711, 130 S.Ct. 2592, 2600.

[77]   560 U.S. 702, 710–712, 130 S.Ct. 2592, 2599–2600.

[78]   560 U.S. 702, 712, 130 S.Ct. 2592, 2600.

Convinced that the Florida Supreme Court's holding was a misapplication of well-established legal rules that effectively eliminated landowners' littoral rights, the petitioner appealed the case to the United States Supreme Court on a theory that the holding affected a judicial taking of property in violation of the Takings Clause.

The eight U.S. Supreme Court justices who heard the *Stop the Beach* case unanimously agreed that the Florida Supreme Court's decision did not trigger a compensable taking.[79] The Court essentially held that the state court's ruling, which characterized the beach restoration project as an avulsion event that could thus create a new state-owned strip of land, was "consistent with . . . background principles of state property law" governing rights of accretion and avulsion and thus didn't affect a taking.[80] However, the justices had somewhat divergent views regarding whether to clarify through the case that it was possible to have a judicial taking. Four of the eight justices joined onto those portions of Justice Antonin Scalia's majority opinion wrote the *Stop the Beach* majority opinion stating that judicial takings were entirely possible. In the opinion, Scalia argues that the Takings Clause is "not addressed to the action of a specific branch or branches" and is "concerned simply with the act" of taking private property for public use, "not with the governmental actor" involved.[81] He goes on to argue:

> There is no textual justification for saying that the existence or the scope of a State's power to expropriate private property without just compensation varies according to the branch of government effecting the expropriation. Nor does common sense recommend such a principle. It would be absurd to allow a State to do by judicial decree what the Takings Clause forbids it to do by legislative fiat.[82]

Ultimately, Scalia's opinion concludes:

> [T]he Takings Clause bars *the State* from taking private property without paying for it, no matter which branch is the instrument of the taking . . . [T]he particular state *actor* is irrelevant. If a legislature *or a court* declares that what was once an established right of private property no longer exists, it has taken that property, no less than if the State had physically appropriated it or destroyed its value by regulation.[83]

It is worth noting that even the four justices who opted not to join in the portions of the Scalia opinion emphasizing the real possibility of judicial takings did not dismiss the idea. Instead, they generally argued (in the two concurring opinions filed in the case) that the facts at hand did "not require the Court to determine"[84] whether a judicial action can trigger a compensable taking and that this question is "better left for another day."[85] These justices did, however, point out some potentially significant challenges with the enforcement of a judicial takings doctrine. Among other things, such a doctrine could require federal courts to interpret thorny questions of state law—a task that they arguably are not as well-suited as state courts to do. Moreover, if a court's decision were

[79] Justice Stevens, who owned beachfront property in Florida, recused himself from the case.
[80] 560 U.S. 702, 731, 130 S.Ct. 2592, 2612.
[81] 560 U.S. 702, 713–714, 130 S.Ct. 2592, 2601.
[82] 560 U.S. 702, 714, 130 S.Ct. 2592, 2601.
[83] 560 U.S. 702, 715, 130 S.Ct. 2592, 2602.
[84] 560 U.S. 702, 733–734, 130 S.Ct. 2592, 2613.
[85] 560 U.S. 702, 742, 130 S.Ct. 2592, 2618.

held to be trigger judicial taking, would the court—which likely has relatively modest financial resources—to pay just compensation? In the plurality portions of the opinion, Scalia dismisses both of these arguments. He argues that federal courts are routinely called upon to interpret state laws so it would not be too burdensome or unreasonable to expect the same in the narrow context of judicial takings cases.[86] He likewise argues that courts whose decisions were held to trigger takings could simply reverse the decisions and thereby avoid having to pay out compensation as a remedy.[87] Regardless, at this point only time will tell whether judicial takings doctrine ultimately developers into another relevant area of takings law.

§ 9.5   REGULATORY TAKINGS: REMEDY

If a court holds that a land use regulation has caused a taking, what is the landowner's remedy? When governmental entities exercise their eminent domain authority and condemn land for a public building, the private property holder receives monetary compensation. The amount of this compensation is generally based on the owner's loss—the fair market value of the land—and is a question of fact based on submitted evidence. Similarly, if a government condemns a roadway easement, compensation is determined based on the diminution in value of the land caused by the burden of the easement.[88] In contrast, without the slightest allusion to the question of remedy, Pennsylvania Coal Co. v. Mahon simply assumed and held that the remedy for the regulatory taking in that case was to void the Kohler Act.[89] Strangely, for many years decisions in state and lower federal courts raised few questions about the nature of the remedy for a regulatory taking, apparently assuming that the proper remedy was invalidation of the offending land use regulation. On the few occasions when courts offered a rationale for this approach, they tended to emphasize that the federal or state constitution in question required compensation for a taking and, since the regulation offered none, the regulation violated the constitution and was void.[90]

Beginning with dictum in Turner v. County of Del Norte[91] in 1972, several decisions in the California Court of Appeals and in the Federal Northern District of California began to question whether invalidation was the correct or sole remedy. They either held or said in dictum that compensation, not invalidation, was the constitutionally required remedy.[92] They based this determination on the rationale that constitutions do not forbid governmental entities to condemn land but simply require payment as a condition to taking. If compensation is the remedy for all other kinds of takings, why not in a

---

[86]   560 U.S. 702, 726, 130 S.Ct. 2592, 2609.

[87]   560 U.S. 702, 723, 130 S.Ct. 2592, 2607.

[88]   The owner may also be entitled to an element of compensation called "severance damages" if the taking of the easement causes harm to the remaining land. For instance, if a road bisects a farm that was used as a unit or if the traffic disturbances from the road will diminish the value of the land not touched by the road, the owner may receive additional compensation for loss of value of the untouched land.

[89]   260 U.S. 393, 43 S.Ct. 158, 67 L.Ed. 322 (1922).

[90]   The best known of the few decisions that explained this rationale were Pamel Corp. v. Puerto Rico Highway Authority, 621 F.2d 33 (1st Cir.1980), and Maryland-National Capital Park & Planning Comm'n v. Chadwick, 286 Md. 1, 405 A.2d 241 (1979).

[91]   24 Cal.App.3d 311, 101 Cal.Rptr. 93 (1972).

[92]   In addition to the *Turner* decision, see also Arastra Limited Partnership v. City of Palo Alto, 401 F.Supp. 962 (N.D.Cal. 1975), vacated 417 F.Supp. 1125 (N.D.Cal. 1976); Dahl v. City of Palo Alto, 372 F.Supp. 647 (N.D.Cal.1974); Eldridge v. City of Palo Alto, 57 Cal.App.3d 613, 129 Cal.Rptr. 575 (1976). The Palo Alto cases involved a regulation that kept an outlying area of the city, known as the "foothills" area, in an open-space land reserve.

regulatory taking case, too? However, the California Supreme Court flatly disapproved of these decisions and of the compensation remedy in its 1979 decision in Agins v. City of Tiburon, where the court essentially indicated that the only available remedy for a regulatory taking would be invalidation of the ordinance.[93] Though the United States Supreme Court reviewed the *Agins* case, it affirmed the decision on a procedural ground and thus did not reach the taking question.[94]

California's decision in *Agins* drew attention to, and demonstrated the importance of, the question of the remedy for a regulatory taking. If the remedy for an overly strict land use regulation is invalidation of the offending ordinance or statute, then, after perhaps years of litigation, the landowner is likely to win only a Pyrrhic victory. The offending regulation becomes unenforceable, but the governmental entity may, and is likely to, enact another similar, slightly milder, one—in which case the lengthy, expensive process of challenge starts over again.[95] Meanwhile, because of disrupted plans, loss of financing, or perhaps changes in the real estate market, the owner's project may well have become infeasible by that time. On the other hand, if, after several years of administrative procedures and litigation, the governmental entity must pay compensation to one or more landowners, then the entity suffers a real penalty for miscalculating the legal effect of its regulation that can have a powerful deterring effect. The possibility of compensation also gives the plaintiff landowner more bargaining leverage than if the only available remedy were invalidation.

In 1981, the compensation question drew significant attention with the Supreme Court's decision in San Diego Gas & Electric Co. v. City of San Diego.[96] The case came on direct appeal from a division of the California Court of Appeals, which had found that a kind of open-space zoning had caused a taking and had thus awarded the landowner a large amount of compensation. Five justices, including Justice Rehnquist, voted to dismiss the appeal on the ground that it was premature so the Court never reached the merits in the case. However, Justice Brennan, joined by three justices, wrote a lengthy, scholarly, ringing dissent in which he argued that the case was not premature, that the Court should decide it on the merits, and that if the zoning regulation were found to have caused a taking the remedy should be compensation. In graphic terms, he described the plight of the landowner who wins the "Pyrrhic victory" mentioned above when a court merely invalidates the regulation. Justice Rehnquist, in a separate opinion, after engaging in a palpable struggle with himself on the prematurity issue, finally concurred with the Court's opinion that the appeal was premature. But in the course of his opinion he commented that he agreed with "much of what is said in the dissenting opinion." Immediately some courts and many commentators on the law assumed the "much" to which he referred was the part about the compensation remedy and that therefore a majority of the Supreme Court favored that remedy. The law reviews came alive with

---

[93]   24 Cal.3d 266, 157 Cal.Rptr. 372, 598 P.2d 25 (1979). The ultimate holding was that a zoning ordinance had not caused a taking.

[94]   Agins v. City of Tiburon, 447 U.S. 255, 100 S.Ct. 2138, 65 L.Ed.2d 106 (1980).

[95]   For how a regulating governmental entity can "start all over again" with a slightly milder regulation, see Justice Brennan's graphic description in his dissent in San Diego Gas & Elec. Co. v. City of San Diego, 450 U.S. 621, 101 S.Ct. 1287, 67 L.Ed.2d 551 (1981).

[96]   450 U.S. 621, 101 S.Ct. 1287, 67 L.Ed.2d 551 (1981).

articles on the subject.[97] Some courts, including some federal courts, began to award compensation when they found regulatory takings had occurred.[98]

For several years, however, the Supreme Court was in a "holding pattern" on the compensation question. After *San Diego Gas* was dismissed for prematurity, Williamson County Regional Planning Commission v. Hamilton Bank[99] was decided in 1985, and MacDonald, Sommer & Frates v. Yolo County,[100] in 1986. Each of these cases attracted national attention as the cases that might settle the compensation question, but they each suffered the same fate as *San Diego Gas*, prematurity or that they were not "ripe" for decision on the merits. Finally, in June 1987, a divided Court decided the compensation question in First English Evangelical Lutheran Church v. County of Los Angeles.[101] With Chief Justice Rehnquist writing the opinion and five other justices, including Justice Brennan, concurring, the Court held six-to-three that compensation is a potential remedy when a land use regulation has caused a taking.

The Court's reasoning in *First English* was straightforward: the Fifth Amendment does not forbid governmental condemnation of interests in land; it merely imposes the condition that compensation must be paid. While the rule of the case is starkly simple, the decision left unanswered the question of whether, when measuring a regulated owner's loss, courts may deduct from loss the value of offsetting benefits the governmental entity offers the owner. The question has arisen in cases in which government regulation causes a value loss, which we may assume is a severe loss, but the governmental entity allows the owner transferable development rights ("TDR's").[102] Penn Central Transportation Co. v. City of New York contains dictum that TDR's may be considered, first, to ameliorate the owner's value loss on the question whether there is a taking and, second, if a taking is nevertheless found, to be counted as part of the owner's compensation.[103] In 1997 the Supreme Court held that, in a case in which a regulatory agency offered the regulated owner TDR's, she could proceed with her taking claim (her claim was "ripe" for determination) without her having yet sold the TDR's.[104] The Court reasoned that the value of her TDR's could be factored in because they had a market value that could be determined without actual sale and that, indeed, the federal

---

[97]   See, e.g., Bauman, The Supreme Court, Inverse Condemnation and the Fifth Amendment: Justice Brennan Confronts the Inevitable in Land Use Controls, 15 Rutgers Law J. 15 (1983); Blume & Rubinfeld, Compensation for Takings: An Economic Analysis, 72 Cal. L. Rev. 569 (1984); Cunningham, Inverse Condemnation as a Remedy for "Regulatory Takings," 8 Hastings Const. L.Q. 517 (1981); Johnson, Compensation for Invalid Land-Use Regulations, 15 Ga. L. Rev. 559 (1981); Mandelker, Land Use Takings: The Compensation Issue, 8 Hastings Const. L.Q. 491 (1981); Williams, Smith, Siemon, Mandelker & Babcock, The White River Junction Manifesto, 9 Vt. L. Rev. 193 (1984).

[98]   See, e.g., Hamilton Bank of Johnson City v. Williamson County Regional Planning Comm'n, 729 F.2d 402 (6th Cir.1984), reversed on other grounds, 473 U.S. 172, 105 S.Ct. 3108, 87 L.Ed.2d 126 (1985); Amen v. City of Dearborn, 718 F.2d 789 (6th Cir.1983).

[99]   473 U.S. 172, 105 S.Ct. 3108, 87 L.Ed.2d 126 (1985).

[100]   477 U.S. 340, 106 S.Ct. 2561, 91 L.Ed.2d 285 (1986).

[101]   482 U.S. 304, 107 S.Ct. 2378, 96 L.Ed.2d 250 (1987).

[102]   Transferable development rights, commonly called "TDR's," allow the owner to build on another site, or to sell to another owner of such a site, a governmental permission to develop that site more fully than the regulations in effect on that site would normally allow. The other site must be in an area designated as a "transfer zone." If the regulated owner owns the transfer-zone site, then the opportunity to "overdevelop" it presumably adds value to it. And of course if our regulated owner sells the TDR's to a third person who owns the other site, then the regulated owner has cash in hand that offsets the loss on the regulated site.

[103]   438 U.S. 104, 98 S.Ct. 2646, 57 L.Ed.2d 631 (1978), rehearing denied 439 U.S. 883, 99 S.Ct. 226, 58 L.Ed.2d 198 (1978).

[104]   Suitum v. Tahoe Regional Planning Agency, 520 U.S. 725, 117 S.Ct. 1659 (1997).

district court had "considerable evidence" of their value. Though the narrow question before the Court was only whether her taking claim was ripe for determination, the implication is that the value of TDR's should be factored in, in determining value loss on the taking issue. That, of course, lends support to the dictum in *Penn Central*, though the Court has not squarely made a holding on the question whether TDR's must be factored in. And before we say conclusively that they must be factored in, we need to bear in mind that the Supreme Court has not addressed some significant issues that would be argued upon full consideration of the question. For instance, there is a general principle in eminent domain law that an owner is entitled to receive compensation in money, i.e., may not be compelled against his or her wishes to accept an exchange of land as compensation. On that principle, the Arizona Supreme Court has held that an owner may not be compelled to accept TDR's as part compensation for a regulatory taking.[105] On the other hand, a Florida Court of Appeals decision approved the use of TDR's and held that a land use regulation did not cause a taking, though it is not clear whether the court concluded that no taking would have occurred even without the TDR's.[106]

While initially landowners and land developers may have welcomed the compensation remedy because it would have a "chilling effect" on land use regulatory bodies and would give owners and developers bargaining leverage, it seems quite possible that *First English* produced an "overkill" that has made some courts less willing to find that regulations have caused takings. In other words, courts that are concerned with the "chilling effect" may have reacted by increasing the degree of loss of use and value before a taking occurs.[107] As suggested in the discussion of *Lucas v. South Carolina Coastal Council* in the preceding section 9.4, it seems that the Supreme Court itself looks for a quite high percentage loss of value for a taking to occur.

§ 9.6   DENIAL OF DUE PROCESS

The 14th Amendment to the United States Constitution provides states in part: "nor shall any State deprive any person of life, liberty, or property, without due process of law. . . ." By its own terms, the Due Process Clause is directly binding upon the states and their political subdivisions. State constitutions contain similar language or language that their courts of last resort have interpreted to have the same effect.[108] The notion that all persons should be treated with basic fairness by their sovereigns is deeply ingrained in our history. It dates back at least as far as clause 39 in King John's Magna Carta of 1215 A.D., which guaranteed that, "No free man shall be taken or imprisoned

---

[105] Corrigan v. City of Scottsdale, 149 Ariz. 538, 720 P.2d 513 (1986).

[106] City of Hollywood v. Hollywood, Inc., 432 So.2d 1332 (Fla.App.1983); see also Suitum v. Tahoe Reg'l Planning Agency, 117 S.Ct. 1659, 1667 (1997) (Scalia, J., concurring) (explaining that TDRs' relevance in takings analysis concerns only that of just compensation because if TDRs are used to determine whether a taking has occurred, then there is a possibility of abuse); William Hadley Littlewood, Transferable Development Rights, TRPA, and Takings, the Role of TDRs in the Constitutional Takings Analysis, 30 McGeorge L. Rev. 201 (1998) (explaining some of the policy considerations behind allowing TDRs in takings analysis).

[107] See especially Presbytery of Seattle v. King County, 114 Wn.2d 320, 787 P.2d 907 (1990), where the court explicitly tightened the threshold for a taking, to avoid the "chilling effect."

[108] A formulation that does not use the words "due process" occurs especially in the constitutions of some of the original states of the Union. For example, N.J. Const., Art. I, par. 1, reads: "All persons are by nature free and independent, and have certain natural and unalienable rights, among which are those of enjoying and defending life and liberty, of acquiring, possessing, and protecting property, and of pursuing and obtaining safety and happiness." The New Jersey Supreme Court has called this a "due process" clause. See Southern Burlington County NAACP v. Township of Mount Laurel, 67 N.J. 151, 336 A.2d 713 (1975).

or disseised . . . nor will we go upon nor send upon him, except by the lawful judgment of his peers or by the law of the land." In law French, the then language of the courts, "law of the land" translates *"par due process de ley."* Dr. Bonham's Case,[109] coming in 1610 at the beginning of English settlement in America, deeply impressed our ancestors. It struck down an act of Parliament that allowed the censors of the College of Physicians to punish Dr. Bonham, one of their members, on the ground that it was "against common right and reason" for them to be judges in a case in which they were also parties. Today this would most likely be labeled a violation of due process of law.

Due process rights under the Constitution are widely interpreted to be both "procedural" and "substantive." Procedural due process is the more tangible kind and is easier to define. It is the notion that a governmental entity may not deprive a person of life, liberty, or property unwillingly except by procedures that are regularly established and fair. For instance, a person is entitled to reasonable notice of a proceeding that could deprive him or her of a protected interest, to a reasonable opportunity to defend in that proceeding, to a chance to present witnesses and other evidence, and to cross-examine the opponent's witnesses. A landowner certainly may be denied procedural due process in an action to enforce a land use regulation, just as in the enforcement of any statute or ordinance.[110] Of much more interest, however, in the field of land use regulation is the other kind of due process: substantive due process. Substantive due process is more amorphous and more difficult to define than procedural due process. Numerous state court decisions considering whether a land use regulation violates substantive due process have simply asked if the regulation is "unreasonable, arbitrary, or capricious," or some similarly ambiguous standard.

The classic test for applying substantive due process to the protection of property rights, including interests in land, is contained in Lawton v. Steele,[111] which involved New York State's seizure of some illegal fishing nets. In the *Lawton* court's words, "It must appear, first that the interests of the public . . . require such interference; and, second that the means are reasonably necessary for the accomplishment of the purpose, and not unduly oppressive upon individuals." As applied to a land use regulation, this may be rephrased to require that (1) there be some public problem that the regulation is intended to address; (2) it does in fact tend to alleviate that problem; and (3) balancing the public's benefit against the imposition on the regulated landowner, the regulation is not "unduly oppressive" on the owner. Since the range of public problems that is within the power of government to address (i.e., not ultra vires) is exceedingly large, and since regulations usually have at least a modest tendency to alleviate the problems to which they are supposedly addressed, the third, "unduly oppressive," category is by far the most frequent battleground.

The following three related, fictional examples help to illustrate the three requirements just enumerated. Suppose first that a city council were to adopt an ordinance that forbids any landowner from having a pet cat. When an owner who has a cat challenges the ordinance, there is simply no credible testimony that pet cats are causing any significant problem in town; it turns out that several members of the city

---

[109] 8 Co.Rep. 113b, 77 Eng.Rep. 638 (1610).

[110] See, e.g., Blanchard v. City of Ralston, 4 Neb.App. 692, 549 N.W.2d 652 (Neb. App. 1996), where the city condemned and demolished the plaintiff's house without giving the owner a statutory 60-day notice of the pending action.

[111] 152 U.S. 133, 137 (1894).

council merely had an irrational fear of cats. The second and third examples do involve a serious public problem: in a certain tenement-house section of town there is an infestation of large, vicious rats that breed in and around the buildings. Suppose that, to hopefully alleviate this problem, the city council were to enact a second ordinance forbid anyone from keeping a cat in that area. There is a public problem in this second example, but the ordinance does not tend to alleviate it. If anything, the prohibition on cats aggravates the problem so the ordinance is void. Suppose instead that a third ordinance required all landowners in the rat-infested district to burn their buildings to the ground. Such an ordinance would certainly addresses the public problem, but it (literally and figuratively) takes an overkill approach, so a court applying Lawton v. Steele would likely declare the ordinance "unduly oppressive" and void on that ground.

In federal jurisprudence, it remains somewhat unclear the extent to which the Due Process Clause limits economic and property regulation, including land use regulation. A brief historical sketch helps explain how and why this is so. There was a time, around the turn of the 20th century, when the Court used the Due Process Clause in a free-wheeling way to strike down economic and property regulations. The leading case was Lochner v. New York,[112] in which the Court struck down a New York statute that, for health reasons, limited the number of hours bakers could work, with little more than the laconic statement that it violated due process. This decision gave its name to the "*Lochner* era," which more or less lasted until the New Deal days of the 1930s, during which the Court supposedly was willing to strike down regulations on property and commerce on the vague ground of due process. However, it should be noted that, even during the "*Lochner* era," there was a current of Supreme Court decisions that tended to be contrary to *Lochner*. For instance, Muller v. Oregon,[113] upholding a statute that restricted women's hours of work, and Bunting v. Oregon,[114] upholding a statute that restricted factory working hours, were essentially contrary. The truth is that the balance of power in the Court see-sawed between groups with differing philosophies about economic and property rights.

Lochner v. New York has never been formally overruled, but West Coast Hotel Co. v. Parrish,[115] which upheld a state statute fixing minimum wages for women, is considered to mark the end of the "*Lochner* era." A new era, and an opposite philosophy about commercial and property regulations, was signaled by Justice Stone's famous footnote 4 in United States v. Carolene Products Co.[116] In it he suggested that legislation that was "within a specific prohibition of the Constitution, such as those of the first ten amendments" would be subjected to "more exacting judicial scrutiny" than legislation that was attacked "under the general prohibitions of the Fourteenth Amendment." In time it became clear, especially in Williamson v. Lee Optical Co.,[117] that, whatever else *Carolene Products* signified, it meant that the Court was taking a much, much more benign view of economic and property regulations than of laws restricting so-called "personal" rights and privileges. Realistically, the Court has employed a double

---

[112] 198 U.S. 45, 25 S.Ct. 539, 49 L.Ed. 937 (1905).

[113] 208 U.S. 412, 28 S.Ct. 324, 52 L.Ed. 551 (1908).

[114] 243 U.S. 426, 37 S.Ct. 435, 61 L.Ed. 830 (1917).

[115] 300 U.S. 379, 57 S.Ct. 578, 81 L.Ed. 703 (1937).

[116] 304 U.S. 144, 58 S.Ct. 778, 82 L.Ed. 1234 (1938).

[117] 348 U.S. 483, 75 S.Ct. 461, 99 L.Ed. 563 (1955).

standard, in which substantive due process is hardly ever used to invalidate an economic or property regulation, but in which personal liberties are subjected to close scrutiny.

For years it has been evident that the Supreme Court has no interest in applying the Due Process Clause generally to land use regulations. This is most evident in the fact that the Court, preferring the "regulatory taking" doctrine covered earlier in this chapter, has ignored due process. Perhaps the leading example of this is Penn Central Transportation Co. v. City of New York,[118] which upheld the city's designation of Grand Central Station as a historic site. New York's Court of Appeals had also upheld the designation but had considered the case as a due process case. Without even acknowledging New York's analysis, the Supreme Court treated *Penn Central* as strictly a "taking" case.

It is possible that one form of substantive due process may still be arguable in the Supreme Court. Recall Lawton v. Steele's categories, particularly the one in which a regulation on property rights is void if it does not advance any public interest or alleviate any public problem. In 1928, Nectow v. City of Cambridge[119] invalidated a city zoning ordinance on substantive due process grounds though the Court later wrongly cited *Nectow* as a taking case.[120] A zone line split the owner's land into residential and industrial zones, so that it could not be used for industrial purposes as neighboring land was. Some language in *Nectow* suggests that the ordinance was void because it imposed too harsh a burden on the owner—*Lawton*'s "unduly oppressive" rationale. However, other language suggests the problem was that it did not matter to the public whether the zone line had been drawn through the Nectow land or had avoided the land and gone down the middle of an adjacent street. If the latter was true, then it fell into *Lawton*'s category of regulations that serve no public purpose or alleviate no problem. Many years later, Justice Brennan cited *Nectow* approvingly for this latter category in his dissent in San Diego Gas & Electric Co. v. City of San Diego.[121] Particularly because Justice Brennan was not noted for his extensive protection of property rights, it may well be that a majority of the Supreme Court would be willing to strike down, on substantive due process grounds, a land use regulation if they were convinced it served no significant public purpose. Of course, such regulations are rare.

There are, however, certain instances when economic or property rights are intermixed with "personal" rights in which the Court has struck down regulations on due process grounds. Sniadach v. Family Finance Corporation,[122] and Fuentes v. Shevin,[123] declared unconstitutional the garnishment (*Sniadach*) or pre-judgment attachment (*Fuentes*) of wages without a hearing. We should note that these are procedural, not substantive, due process cases. Of more direct interest, Moore v. City of East Cleveland,[124] held void a zoning ordinance that forbade family members from living in the same home unless they were within certain close degrees of relationship. The Court emphasized that the ordinance was objectionable because it intruded too deeply into family relationships. And Justice Powell's majority opinion assured us rather

---

[118]   438 U.S. 104, 98 S.Ct. 2646, 57 L.Ed.2d 631 (1978).
[119]   277 U.S. 183, 48 S.Ct. 447, 72 L.Ed. 842 (1928).
[120]   See, e.g., Agins v. City of Tiburon, 447 U.S. 255, 100 S.Ct. 2138, 65 L.Ed.2d 106 (1980).
[121]   450 U.S. 621, 101 S.Ct. 1287, 67 L.Ed.2d 551 (1981).
[122]   395 U.S. 337, 89 S.Ct. 1820, 23 L.Ed.2d 349 (1969).
[123]   407 U.S. 67, 92 S.Ct. 1983, 32 L.Ed.2d 556 (1972).
[124]   431 U.S. 494, 97 S.Ct. 1932, 52 L.Ed.2d 531 (1977).

nervously that the Court was not returning to the "*Lochner* era." That much is certainly clear. Of course it is always possible that in time the Supreme Court might be willing to extend some degree of substantive due process limitation to ordinary land use regulations, but there is no evidence of it yet, even among members of the Court who are relatively protective of property rights.

Among state courts and some of the lower federal courts, it is a quite different story. Multitudes of their decisions test land use regulations under substantive due process. Often the analysis is very imprecise—some formulation such as "unreasonable, arbitrary, or capricious" being a favorite test. To avoid citation of hundreds of decisions (not to mention the unprofitable research to dig them out), this book cites only some representative due process decisions that have appeared in some casebooks on land use planning.[125] Sometimes a court will add the word "confiscatory," which, if used in any precise way (which it probably is not), is a synonym for a "taking."[126] Whatever the exact wording, it is a rough approximation of Lawton v. Steele's "unduly oppressive" category and affords significant discretion to courts to strike down a regulation. On the other hand, court wishing to spare a governmental action usually emphasize either or both of two related principles, both traceable back to the American concept of separation of powers of government. The first such principle is the presumption that legislative acts (including legislative acts of local governments) are valid. The second principle is that, in instances where there is evidence for and against the validity of a legislative act, it is not the function of a court to substitute its judgment for that of the legislative body.[127]

Many land use regulations have been struck down on such due process grounds by state courts. Many others have met the test and been upheld. With such flexible, manipulable judicial principles at work, it is easy to find decisions from different jurisdictions, or sometimes even within the same jurisdiction, that reach contrary results on similar facts. That, of course, makes it difficult for land use regulators and landowners to predict how a court will react to a regulation whose validity is in anywise doubtful. But that is a problem with many fact-laden legal doctrines, such as the test for negligence in tort law. And the very vagueness and flexibility of a substantive due

---

[125] Lingle v. Chevron U.S.A. Inc., 544 U.S. 528, 125 S.Ct. 2074, 161 L.Ed.2d 876 (2005) (explaining that if government regulation is found to be "so arbitrary as to violate due process[,]" that ends the constitutional inquiry); Crown Point Dev., Inc. v. City of Sun Valley, 506 F.3d 851, 852 (9th Cir. 2007) (considering a developer's substantive due process claim for the "alleged arbitrary and irrational denial of a permit application"); Marks v. City of Chesapeake, 883 F.2d 308 (4th Cir.1989) (city's refusal to grant permit for palmistry studio "arbitrary and capricious" because based upon irrational neighborhood objections); Dooley v. Town of Fairfield, 151 Conn. 304, 197 A.2d 770 (1964) (floodplain zoning, which prevented any profitable use, was "unreasonable and confiscatory"); La Salle Nat'l Bank v. City of Chicago, 5 Ill.2d 344, 125 N.E.2d 609 (1955) (downzoning that caused one-third value loss was "arbitrary and unreasonable"); Krause v. City of Royal Oak, 11 Mich.App. 183, 160 N.W.2d 769 (1968) (city's refusal to rezone for apartments was not "unreasonable and arbitrary"); Southern Burlington County NAACP v. Township of Mount Laurel, 67 N.J. 151, 336 A.2d 713 (1975) (exclusionary zoning void because it did not serve "public welfare"); Nova Horizon, Inc. v. City Council of Reno, 105 Nev. 92, 769 P.2d 721 (1989) (city's refusal to rezone land to permit large hotel "abuse of discretion" because based only upon campaign promises against new casinos); Karches v. City of Cincinnati, 38 Ohio St.3d 12, 526 N.E.2d 1350 (1988) (city's refusal to grant application for rezoning was "unreasonable and does not substantially advance legitimate government interests"). Sometimes state courts do use more precise tests for denials of due process, more along the lines urged in this treatise. See, e.g., Guimont v. Clarke, 121 Wn.2d 586, 854 P.2d 1 (1993).

[126] See, e.g., Krause v. City of Royal Oak, 11 Mich.App. 183, 160 N.W.2d 769 (1968); Karches v. City of Cincinnati, 38 Ohio St.3d 12, 526 N.E.2d 1350 (1988).

[127] See, e.g., Lockard v. City of Los Angeles, 33 Cal.2d 453, 202 P.2d 38, cert. denied, 337 U.S. 939 (1949) (valid unless "clearly and palpably wrong"); Krause v. City of Royal Oak, 11 Mich.App. 183, 160 N.W.2d 769 (1968) (landowner's evidence "insufficient to rebut the presumption of validity" of zoning ordinance).

process attack invites the land owner or developer who wishes to attack a land use regulation to throw in a claim of denial of due process, even though the main attack may be on another theory. In that sense, substantive due process can be a wild card.

§ 9.7 DENIAL OF EQUAL PROTECTION OF LAW

In several ways the study of "equal protection of law" parallels the study of due process of law, which was covered in the preceding section. Both guarantees are contained in clauses in section 1 of the 14th Amendment to the United States Constitution. The Equal Protection Clause reads: "No State shall . . . deny to any person within its jurisdiction the equal protection of the laws." As highlighted in the materials on due process, the 14th Amendment directly limits the actions of state governments and their local instrumentalities. Likewise, just as state constitutions contain guarantees that more or less replicate the Due Process Clause, so they generally contain clauses that operate similarly to the Equal Protection Clause. Moreover, there is in practice considerable overlap in the operation of the due process and equal protection clauses: state action that denies equal protection can often be said to be "fundamentally unfair" and thereby violate due process.

The United States Supreme Court has described the Equal Protection Clause as "essentially a direction that all persons similarly situated should be treated alike."[128] In this description the key words are "similarly situated." It is not wrong for law to treat different persons differently; that is what law is all about. Indeed, so-called rules of law are nothing more or less than statements that certain persons are to be treated differently than other persons. For instance, if A trespasses upon B's land, A will be treated less favorably than all other persons who did not similarly trespass. Or if a landlord fails to maintain residential premises in "habitable" condition in a state with a clear habitability requirement, the law will treat the landlord less favorably than other landlords. In these cases and thousands of others, courts would agree that the quality of trespassing or the quality of not maintaining justifies this disparate treatment. But suppose instead that new legislation required all persons with purple automobiles to pay an extra tax not charged to owners of autos of other colors. Unless a court were convinced there was some reason that purple autos were causing a special problem or imposing costs on society that cars with other colors were not, which is hard to imagine, then the court would strike down the statute as denying equal protection. Or, to take an actual case as an example, suppose a town were to allow plaintiff landowners to use their 450-foot-deep parcel for commercial purposes to a depth of only 150 feet back from the street (requiring that the remaining 300 feet be used for less-valuable residential uses) but allowed neighbors in the same block to make commercial uses for their full 450-foot depth? Might not the plaintiffs in this situation rightfully complain they were denied equal protection? In striking down the restriction, New York's Appellate Division gave us this pithy description of equal protection: " 'When Tweedledee is granted, and Tweedledum is denied [relief] suspicion ripens into certainty that Tweedledum has been denied justice.' "[129]

As the law of equal protection has developed, however, analysis under the doctrine has obviously become somewhat more complicated than the core concept just described. Some refinements have been added, which are expressed in terms of standards of proof.

---

[128] City of Cleburne v. Cleburne Living Center, 473 U.S. 432, 105 S.Ct. 3249, 87 L.Ed.2d 313 (1985).

[129] Jurgens v. Town of Huntington, 53 App.Div.2d 661, 384 N.Y.S.2d 870 (1976).

If a statute or ordinance treats persons differently based upon their race, religion, alienage, or national origin, the legislative act is "suspect" and is subjected to "strict judicial scrutiny." It is sustained only if the state shows it serves a "compelling state interest." As a practical matter, it is quite difficult for a state will carry this burden of proof, so statutes or ordinances falling within this category are fairly likely to be deemed unconstitutional. If a statute or ordinance classifies persons upon the basis of gender or legitimacy of birth, it is subjected to "heightened" or "intermediate" judicial scrutiny. In more recent years, a growing number of courts have also applied intermediate scrutiny to statutes and ordinances discriminating on the basis of sexual orientation.[130] Laws analyzed under this level of scrutiny can be sustained only if a court concludes they are "substantially related to an important state interest." Statutes or ordinances distinguishing among persons upon bases other than those just described are generally said to be subject to the much less demanding "rational basis" test: are they "a rational means to serve a legitimate end"? Importantly, there is no presumption that this third category of laws denies equal protection and the burden is on the party attacking them to convince the court that they do. Economic and commercial statutes and ordinances, including regulations on the use of land, are generally tested under the permissive "rational basis" test. They usually survive, but not always.[131]

Judges are seriously divided over whether heightened levels of scrutiny should be extended to new kinds of specially protected classes of persons. Or, more precisely, should new kinds of special classes of persons be given the enhanced protection of heightened scrutiny? Also, are there actually sub-levels within the general level of heightened scrutiny? So, for instance, should laws that distinguish persons on the basis of age be subjected to "heightened" ("somewhat heightened"?) scrutiny? This difference in judicial values was perhaps most evident in City of Cleburne v. Cleburne Living Center, which among the leading equal-protection-land use regulation decisions from the United States Supreme Court.[132] Sponsors of the Living Center, a home for mildly handicapped persons, sought to locate it in a zone in which certain similar uses, such as general hospitals, nursing homes for the elderly, fraternity houses, and apartment houses were allowed without a special permit. However, under the zoning ordinance, the siting of a "hospital for the feeble minded" within the zone required a special permit. When the Living Center applied for this special permit, the city denied it.

The Court's majority opinion, written by Justice White, struck down either the ordinance on its face or the denial of the permit (one can debate which), on the ground that it denied the applicant equal protection, in violation of the 14th Amendment. Justice White said his opinion applied merely the "rational basis" test; the majority evinced a

---

[130] See, e.g., Windsor v. U.S., 699 F.3d 169 (2012), aff'd 570 U.S. 744, 133 S.Ct. 2675, 186 L.Ed.2d 808 (2013) (holding that laws that classify individuals based on sexual orientation receive intermediate scrutiny); SmithKline Beecham Corp. v. Abbott Laboratories, 740 F.3d 471 (2014) (holding that heightened scrutiny applies to law that classify individuals based on sexual orientation).

[131] In support of the general statements in this paragraph, see City of Cleburne v. Cleburne Living Center, 473 U.S. 432, 105 S.Ct. 3249, 87 L.Ed.2d 313 (1985) (Court purported to apply "rational basis" test, but still struck down city's action); Thorp v. Town of Lebanon, 235 Wis. 2d 610 612 N.W.2d 59 (2000) (explaining that an ordinance rezoning the plaintiffs' property to an agricultural classification may not have met the rational basis test); J. Juergensmeyer & T. Roberts, Land Use Planning and Control Law § 10.14 (1998); D. Mandelker, Land Use Law §§ 2.49–2.51 (4th ed. 1997). See also Village of Belle Terre v. Boraas, 416 U.S. 1, 94 S.Ct. 1536, 39 L.Ed.2d 797 (1974), in which a zoning ordinance survived a shotgun attack on various grounds, including denial of equal protection; the Court applied the Equal Protection Clause in a much more relaxed fashion than later in *Cleburne*. We will discuss *Cleburne* and *Belle Terre* in detail later.

[132] 473 U.S. 432, 105 S.Ct. 3249, 87 L.Ed.2d 313 (1985).

fear of opening up "heightened scrutiny" protection, not only to developmentally disabled persons, but to other special groups, particularly the elderly. But in a separate opinion concurring in the result but dissenting as to the reasoning, Justice Marshall, joined by justices Blackmun and Brennan, argued tellingly that, whatever the majority said, its result was to afford some kind of heightened scrutiny to the ordinance, a more searching inquiry than in other cases involving commercial and property regulations. At the other end of the scale, Justice Stevens, joined by Chief Justice Burger, wrote a concurring opinion in which he argued that the entire notion of levels of scrutiny was wrong—that there should be only one test: whether there was a "rational basis" for the classification at issue. For the record, then, the Supreme Court applied the "rational basis" test, and the Court has not subsequently clarified the application of the Equal Protection Clause to land use regulations.

One other United States Supreme Court decision needs to be specially mentioned on the equal protection question: Village of Belle Terre v. Boraas, written by Justice Douglas in 1974.[133] The decision was a controversial one that suffered criticism from legal scholars and has met a mixed reception in the courts, but it introduced a feature of some zoning ordinances that tends to raise an equal protection challenge. The village, home to a New York state college, not only had zoning for single-family dwellings, but defined a "family" to consist of only related persons or not more than two unrelated adults. Obviously, the ordinance was directed against student group houses, of the kind occupied by the six unrelated students who were plaintiffs. They attacked the ordinance on myriad theories—not only denials of due process and of equal protection, but even on the theory that it tended to inhibit a constitutional right to travel. Justice Douglas's opinion for the Court replied at least as broadly, upholding the ordinance in cursory fashion, on the general rationale that "fraternity houses and the like" present problems such as noise and traffic that conventional family homes do not. The opinion is more noted for its sonorous phrases than for its extended reasoning, extolling the virtues of "a quiet place where yards are wide, people few, and motor vehicles restricted" and "zones where family values, youth values, and the blessings of quiet seclusion, and clean air make the area a sanctuary for people." The decision was not precise on whether it was directed toward due process or equal protection, though the thrust of the plaintiffs' complaint seems to be that they were denied equal protection.

Restrictive definitions of "family" or "single family" in zoning ordinances have produced a number of cases in which denial of equal protection has been argued. The argument, of course, is that there is no rational basis, as far as the purposes of zoning are concerned, to distinguish between households of persons who are related by blood or marriage and comparable households of persons who are not so related. Some of the cases have involved group homes, more or less similar to the one in the Cleburne case. Though of course the wording of different zoning ordinances and the facts of the cases vary, state courts remain somewhat split on the equal protection issue in such cases. Some decisions uphold the zoning, taking an approach like Belle Terre, but a growing number find denials of equal protection, sometimes explicitly criticizing that Supreme Court decision.[134] Moreover, that decision was narrowly limited by the Supreme Court's

---

[133] 416 U.S. 1, 94 S.Ct. 1536, 39 L.Ed.2d 797 (1974).

[134] See, e.g., City of Santa Barbara v. Adamson, 27 Cal.3d 123, 610 P.2d 436, 164 Cal.Rptr. 539 (1980) (leading case, striking down ordinance on state constitutional ground); College Area Renters and Landlord Ass'n v. City of San Diego, 43 Cal. App.4th 677, 50 Cal.Rptr.2d 515 (1996) (ordinance denied equal protection); Stegeman v. City of Ann Arbor, 213 Mich.App. 487, 540 N.W.2d 724 (1995) (upholding ordinance that

own 1977 decision in Moore v. City of East Cleveland, in which the Court struck down a zoning ordinance that defined "family" so as to exclude from residence in a home certain blood relatives of the owner, while permitting other blood relatives.[135] The ordinance, said the Court, was an "intrusive regulation of the family." In summary, zoning ordinances that define "family" so as to exclude certain classes or groups of persons who might live together clearly invite challenge on the ground that they deny the excluded persons equal protection. Whether an ordinance will survive depends not only upon the detailed language of the ordinance but upon the attitude of a particular court. As a postscript, it is worth noting that zoning ordinances that exclude mobile homes from zones that otherwise permit single-family dwellings have caused similar equal protection problems in the courts. Without delving into the subject further, suffice it to say that courts generally will allow a community to exclude mobile homes from a reasonable number of zones, or to require special permits for them, but will no longer allow their total exclusion from a community.[136]

When a zoning ordinance, or perhaps a community's refusal to amend its zoning, has the effect of denying equal protection to certain racial groups, special considerations apply. The definitive decision on this topic is the United States Supreme Court's 1977 decision in Village of Arlington Heights v. Metropolitan Housing Development Corporation.[137] The corporation (MHDC), a developer of low-income housing, acquired a 99-year lease on a vacant tract of land in Arlington Heights, Illinois, near Chicago, where it proposed to build 190 units of low- and moderate-income apartments. However, since the area was zoned for single-family dwellings, MHDC petitioned the village for a zoning amendment to permit its project. After a number of public hearings before the local planning commission, attended by many persons, the village board of trustees denied the petition. On trial it was established that, had the zoning been amended and the project completed, it would have attracted as tenants a larger number of minority persons, especially blacks, from the Chicago area than it would have persons of the majority white race. But it was also accepted as a fact by the Supreme Court that the village's refusal to rezone was not motivated by racial considerations, but by legitimate planning factors, chiefly that the tract of land had always been zoned single-family residential and that adjacent land was both zoned for and developed with such residences. The Court suggested that, had the village amended the zoning from a zone

distinguished families of related persons from groups of unrelated persons); State v. Baker, 81 N.J. 99, 405 A.2d 368 (1979) (explicitly rejecting *Belle Terre*, finding violation of state constitution); Armstrong v. Mayor and City Council of Baltimore, 410 Md. 426 (2009) (four unrelated individuals formed a "single housekeeping unit" that comprised a "family" under a city zoning code); Unification Theological Seminary v. City of Poughkeepsie, 201 A.D.2d 484 607 N.Y.S.2d 383 (1994) (upholding presumption that unrelated groups of over four unrelated persons were not a "family"). See generally, J. Juergensmeyer & T. Roberts, Land Use Planning and Control Law § 10.14 (1998); D. Mandelker, Land Use Law §§ 5.02, 5.03 (4th ed. 1997).

[135] 431 U.S. 494, 97 S.Ct. 1932, 52 L.Ed.2d 531 (1977). *Moore* went on the ground of denial of due process, not of equal protection. But, because of the narrow distinction between its facts and those of *Belle Terre*, the result was to weaken or limit the force of that decision.

[136] See, e.g., J. Juergensmeyer & T. Roberts, Land Use Planning and Control Law § 6.5 (1998); Robinson Township v. Knoll, 410 Mich. 293, 302 N.W.2d 146 (1981) (unconstitutional to confine mobile home parks; leading case); Collins v. Upper Salford Township Board, 162 Pa. Commw. 403, 639 A.2d 861 (1994) (total exclusion of mobile home parks unconstitutional); and the comprehensive notes following the *Robinson Township* case in the casebook, D. Mandelker, R. Cunningham & J. Payne, Planning and Control of Land Development, 302–06 (4th ed. 1995). Mobile-home-park decisions, such as *Knoll* and *Collins*, may turn on a due process analysis, as well as on equal protection grounds, or on a mixture of the two. Over the years, as modern, safe, comfortable "mobile homes" have replaced the older disfavored "trailer houses," courts have become much more favorable to them; it is a classic example of changing conditions producing changing law.

[137] 429 U.S. 252, 97 S.Ct. 555, 50 L.Ed.2d 450 (1977).

that permitted apartments to single-family-dwelling zoning, or had there been a pattern of discriminatory zoning in the town, or had there been discriminatory statements by the members of the village board, then intent to discriminate might have been found. Thus, the issue was whether a refusal to rezone that is not intended to be racially discriminatory, but has that effect, violates the Equal Protection Clause of the 14th Amendment.[138] Relying by analogy mainly upon its prior decision in Washington v. Davis,[139] an employment discrimination case, the Court held that, to establish that a land use action or non-action violates the Equal Protection clause on the basis of racial discrimination, one must show, not only that it had that effect, but that it was so intended.

Though it goes beyond the precise subject of this section, a discussion of the Equal Protection Clause, it must be noted that racially discriminatory land use decisions and regulations may also be challenged under the Federal Fair Housing Act, Title VIII of the 1968 Civil Rights Act.[140] In fact, such a challenge was made in *Arlington Heights* in the lower federal courts and was the basis for the decision of the United States Seventh Circuit Court on remand from the Supreme Court. The circuit court held that the village's refusal to rezone violated the Fair Housing Act, because there was "some evidence" of intent to discriminate, and the discriminatory effect was substantial.[141] Decisions from several other federal circuit courts have held that, under the Fair Housing Act, discriminatory intent need not be shown, i.e., that discriminatory effect is sufficient. However, the doctrines or formulas employed by these courts differ.[142] The United States Supreme Court has all but, though not quite, adopted the position of these circuit courts. It denied certiorari in two of the cases just cited, and in a third, Huntington Branch, NAACP v. Town of Huntington, the Court affirmed the decision, but in a per curiam decision that, on technical grounds, did not quite hold that discriminatory effect was sufficient to make out a case under the Fair Housing Act.

§ 9.8   DENIAL OF FREEDOM OF SPEECH

The First Amendment to the United States Constitution, adopted in 1791, reads in part: "Congress shall make no law . . . abridging the freedom of speech, or of the press. . . ." Originally, as with the rest of the first 10 amendments that comprised the Bill of Rights, the "Free Speech Clause" restricted only the Federal Government. But after the 14th Amendment was adopted following the Civil War, the Supreme Court recognized freedom to speak as one of the fundamental rights guaranteed by that

---

[138] By way of explanation, in the lower federal courts in *Arlington Heights*, there was both an issue whether the village's decision violated the Equal Protection Clause and whether it violated Title VIII of the Federal Civil Rights Act of 1968, the Fair Housing Act, 42 U.S.C.A. §§ 3601–3617. But the Title VIII question had been excluded procedurally when the case reached the Supreme Court. So, that Court's opinion did not reach Title VIII.

[139] 426 U.S. 229, 96 S.Ct. 2040, 48 L.Ed.2d 597 (1976).

[140] 42 U.S.C.A. §§ 3601–3617.

[141] Metropolitan Housing Development Corp. v. Village of Arlington Heights, 558 F.2d 1283 (7th Cir.1977), certiorari denied 434 U.S. 1025, 98 S.Ct. 752, 54 L.Ed.2d 772 (1978). On remand back down to the Northern District of Illinois, the parties worked out a settlement, which the court accepted, thus avoiding a judgment on the merits. Metropolitan Housing Dev. Corp. v. Village of Arlington Heights, 469 F.Supp. 836 (N.D.Ill.1979), affirmed 616 F.2d 1006 (7th Cir.1980).

[142] Metropolitan Housing Development Corp. v. Village of Arlington Heights, 558 F.2d 1283 (7th Cir.1977), certiorari denied 434 U.S. 1025, 98 S.Ct. 752, 54 L.Ed.2d 772 (1978); Huntington Branch, NAACP v. Town of Huntington, 844 F.2d 926 (2d Cir. 1988), affirmed per curiam 488 U.S. 15, 109 S.Ct. 276, 102 L.Ed.2d 180 (1988); United States v. City of Parma, 661 F.2d 562 (6th Cir.1981); United States v. City of Black Jack, 508 F.2d 1179 (8th Cir.1974), certiorari denied 422 U.S. 1042, 95 S.Ct. 2656, 45 L.Ed.2d 694 (1975).

amendment. Since the 14th Amendment applies expressly to the states, the federal constitutional guarantee limited the activities of state governments and local governments. For a time, the Court seemed not to read the First Amendment clause directly into the 14th Amendment and only seemed to recognize a general concept of free speech. For nearly a century now, however, courts have generally recognized that the Due Process Clause incorporates the Free Speech Clause, much like it incorporates the Takings Clause of the Fifth Amendment.[143] Modern free speech decisions do not even discuss whether the 14th Amendment incorporates the Free Speech Clause; they simply assume it.

The Free Speech Clause extends its protections not just to verbal speech but to nearly all means of expression or communication, including printed matter, such as newspapers.[144] Signboards, such as large billboards, small political signs, and yard signs are protected speech.[145] Motion pictures, indoors or outdoors, constitute speech.[146] Even activities such as nude dancing have been held to be expressions amounting to "speech" that are protected by the first and 14th amendments.[147] These examples will give you an idea of the broad constitutional meaning of "speech."

Because the First Amendment says Congress shall make "no" law "abridging" free speech, some earlier members of the Supreme Court argued that the right was absolute and subject to no governmental restriction. This view was espoused most notably by the late justices Hugo Black and William O. Douglas.[148] More broadly, the Supreme Court determined long ago that free speech, along with freedom of press and free exercise of religion, enjoyed a "preferred position" and thus some degree of increased protection.[149] However, the prevailing view in the Supreme Court has always been that the right of free speech is not absolute and must instead be balanced against the interests of the public.[150] Moreover, the Supreme Court has imposed some limits on free speech. Among them is Justice Holmes's "clear and present danger" doctrine, which, with some evolution through the years, still has vitality, though it originated in 1919 in Schenck v. United States.[151] In that decision, Holmes famously declared that "free speech would not protect a man in falsely shouting fire in a theater and causing panic." The Supreme Court has likewise held that communications that are "obscene" are "not within the area of constitutionally protected speech or press."[152] The problem, of course, is defining the subset of explicit or edgy speech that qualifies as being "obscene." This challenge led to

---

[143] See Gitlow v. New York, 268 U.S. 652 (1925).

[144] E.g., New York Times v. Sullivan, 376 U.S. 254 (1964) (libel case).

[145] E.g., Metromedia, Inc. v. City of San Diego, 453 U.S. 490 (1981) (advertising billboards); Members of City Council v. Taxpayers for Vincent, 466 U.S. 789 (1984) (political signs on city's electric poles); City of Ladue v. Gilleo, 512 U.S. 43, 114 S.Ct. 2038, 129 L.Ed.2d 36 (1994) (yard sign addressing public issue); City of Antioch v. Candidates' Outdoor Graphic Service, 557 F.Supp. 52 (N.D.Cal.1982) (political candidate's yard signs).

[146] E.g., City of Renton v. Playtime Theatres, Inc., 475 U.S. 41 (1986) (indoor "adult" movies); Erznoznik v. City of Jacksonville, 422 U.S. 205 (1975) (outdoor "adult" movies).

[147] See Schad v. Borough of Mt. Ephraim, 452 U.S. 61 (1981) (coin-operated live nude peepshow).

[148] See, e.g., the dissenting opinions in Konigsberg v. State Bar, 366 U.S. 36 (1961); and Barenblatt v. United States, 360 U.S. 109 (1959). Saxer, Zoning Away First Amendment Rights, 53 Wash. U. J. Urb. & Contemp. L. 1 (1998), advocates a position close to that of justices Black and Douglas. She advocates that "speech" activities be regulated, not by zoning, but merely by nuisance law. The article also is valuable because it gives a complete review of Supreme Court zoning-free speech jurisprudence.

[149] Murdock v. Pennsylvania, 319 U.S. 105 (1943).

[150] See especially the majority opinion in Konigsberg v. State Bar, 366 U.S. 36 (1961).

[151] 249 U.S. 47 (1919).

[152] Roth v. United States, 354 U.S. 476 (1957).

another famous phrase, by Justice Potter Stewart, who noted that while he couldn't objectively define obscenity, "I know it when I see it."

How can a regulation on the use of land restrict free speech? In short, a land use regulation potentially restrains free expression whenever land that is used for some activity that substantially involves protected free speech is regulated in ways that prohibit or seriously curtail that speech. Obviously, this relatively narrow set of contexts limits free speech claims to a comparatively small group of landowners. The constitutional free speech limitation is not a protection as broadly applicable as those related to takings, due process, or equal protection. In fact, a landowner who is able to establish a free speech claim can often also assert one or more of the other three protections just mentioned.

It is possible for an ordinary zoning ordinance to restrict free speech, as might be alleged when an ordinance does not permit theaters in a certain zone or is amended to require existing theaters to close down. This was essentially the problem in Schad v. Borough of Mt. Ephraim, in which the plaintiff complained that there was no zone in the borough that permitted his kind of live nude dancing peepshows.[153] In practice, most land use regulations that have given rise to free speech challenges have not been ordinary zoning ordinances but have been special ordinances that applied to and restricted only the particular activity in question. In the leading case of Metromedia v. City of San Diego, the regulation was one that dealt specifically with billboards and that, with some listed exceptions, prohibited them all over the city.[154] In another leading example, the regulation that was challenged in City of Renton v. Playtime Theatres was one that applied only to "adult" movie theaters and restricted and required the spacing of them throughout the city.[155]

The fact patterns in land use regulation free speech cases tend to feature certain recurring types of free speech issues. For instance, in adult-theater cases such as *Renton*, a key issue is whether the challenged regulation controls only the "time, place, and manner" of the speech activity, which is more likely to be upheld than a prohibition on speech. Restrictions on expression that are categorized as "prior restraints" are presumptively invalid. Because certain types of fact patterns in this area tend to present its own particular free speech issues, the balance of this section will discuss the leading cases, mostly United States Supreme Court decisions, by fact patterns.

Among the adult activity cases, the one law students are most likely to encounter in their casebooks is City of Renton v. Playtime Theatres, cited above. The city adopted an ordinance prohibiting "adult motion picture theaters" (defined in the ordinance) within 1,000 feet of any residential zone, dwelling, church, school, or park. Plaintiff Playtime Theatres, wishing to locate an adult theater in Renton and finding no suitable site, challenged the ordinance in federal court on the ground that it was a prior restraint on protected free speech. When the case reached the Supreme Court, a seven-justice majority upheld the ordinance. Although the Court admitted it was arguable whether the ordinance imposed a presumptively void prior restraint on speech or was acceptable as a time-place-and-manner restriction, the Court held it was of the latter kind. The Court also placed emphasis on the fact that the ordinance was directed not merely at

---

[153] 452 U.S. 61 (1981) (coin-operated live nude peepshow).
[154] 453 U.S. 490, 101 S.Ct. 2882, 69 L.Ed.2d 800 (1981).
[155] 475 U.S. 41, 106 S.Ct. 925, 89 L.Ed.2d 29 (1986).

theaters or their movies but at controlling secondary activities that tend to be attracted to adult theaters, such as prostitution and other illegal or "gray-area" activities. *Renton* was decided on the authority of an earlier decision with somewhat similar that the majority regarded as controlling, Young v. American Mini Theatres.[156] *Young* arose in Detroit, which had an ordinance somewhat similar to Renton's requiring the spacing of adult theaters 1,000 feet from certain other activities (including, for some reason, secondhand stores and shoeshine parlors). As in *Renton*, the Court upheld the ordinance as a time-place-and-manner restriction designed to prevent secondary effects of adult movie houses. Because Renton was a smaller city, even if the ordinance challenged in the *Renton* case did not make it impossible to locate a theater, as Playtime contended, it certainly had a more restrictive effect than did the Detroit ordinance. In that sense, *Renton* goes further than does *Young*.

Supreme Court free speech jurisprudence abounds in shadowy distinctions and decisions one must read very narrowly, else they seem contrary. A decision that is hard to reconcile with *Renton* and *Young* is Erznoznik v. City of Jacksonville,[157] which struck down a local ordinance that prohibited outdoor theaters' showing of films that displayed nudity if their screens were visible from a public street. Reading the opinion, one would think the fatal flaw in the ordinance was that "nudity" was over-broad; it would, the Court said, prevent showing a "baby's bottom." But the Court's decision in *Renton* said the "fatal" flaw was that no undesirable secondary effects existed in *Erznoznik*. Another decision that is narrowly distinguishable from *Renton* and *Young* is Schad v. Borough of Mount Ephraim, cited above. The plaintiff in that case challenged the borough's zoning ordinance, which prohibited the operation of coin-operated live nude dancing establishments in any zone in the municipality. While the United States Supreme Court held that the ordinance violated the plaintiff's free speech rights, no majority signed any of the several opinions in the case and the plurality decision was published as the Court's decision. Some language in it seems to indicate that it is a denial of free speech for a municipality completely to zone out "adult activities." *Schad* could be fitted together with *Renton* and *Young* by saying that adult activities may be restricted as to location, perhaps severely, but not totally forbidden in any single municipality. It has been suggested that *Schad* supports such a rule,[158] but a statement in a decision without a majority opinion seems a weak reed upon which to hang so mechanical a rule. Moreover, in *Renton* the Court suggested that the problem in *Schad*, as in *Erznoznik*, was that the borough's failure to show "secondary effects" from the establishment proved "fatal to the regulations."

Cases involving ordinances that restrict advertising billboards and signboards tend to present a somewhat different free speech issue: whether the Free Speech Clause protects so-called "commercial" speech. Before the mid-1970s, there was substantial doubt that the United States Supreme Court would extend the protection of that clause

---

[156] 427 U.S. 50, 96 S.Ct. 2440, 49 L.Ed.2d 310 (1976). For recent decisions that are generally in accord with *Renton* and *Young*, see North Avenue Novelties, Inc. v. City of Chicago, 88 F.3d 441 (7th Cir.1996), cert. denied 519 U.S. 1056, 117 S.Ct. 684, 136 L.Ed.2d 609 (1997); Stringfellow's of New York, Ltd. v. City of New York, 171 Misc.2d 376, 653 N.Y.S.2d 801 (Sup. Ct. 1996), aff'd 241 A.D.2d 360, 663 N.Y.S.2d 812 (1997) (emphasizing that ordinance protected against "secondary effects"). But see World Wide Video v. City of Tukwila, 117 Wn.2d 382, 816 P.2d 18 (1991), cert. denied 503 U.S. 986, 112 S.Ct. 1672 (1992), where the court struck down an ordinance that zoned out an adult bookstore, distinguishing *Renton* on the ground that the bookstore did not cause undesirable "secondary effects."

[157] 422 U.S. 205, 95 S.Ct. 2268, 45 L.Ed.2d 125 (1975).

[158] See D. Mandelker, J. Gerard & T. Sullivan, Federal Land Use Law § 8.02[4] (1986).

to commercial forms of speech.[159] However, Bigelow v. Virginia,[160] in 1975, and Bates v. State Bar of Arizona,[161] in 1977, made it clear that there is at least some protection of commercial speech. Those decisions held state governments and state bar associations cannot forbid attorneys from advertising. In between these decisions, in 1976, Virginia Pharmacy Board v. Virginia Citizens Consumer Council held that a state cannot completely suppress truthful advertising about pharmaceutical products.[162] A definitive decision on commercial advertising came down in 1980 in Central Hudson Gas & Electric Corporation v. Public Service Commission.[163] The Supreme Court essentially laid down a four-part test for protected commercial speech in that case. Basically if advertising deals with a lawful activity and is truthful, restrictions on it are valid only if they directly advance a substantial governmental interest and restrain the speech no more than is necessary to do so.

Of course, the aforementioned decisions did not deal with land use regulations restricting commercial speech. In that area, the leading case is Metromedia v. City of San Diego,[164] in which a billboard company challenged a city ordinance that forbade the large majority of billboards in San Diego and would eventually destroy the commercial billboard industry in the city. The city asserted the purposes of the ordinance were to eliminate traffic hazards and to improve the city's appearance. The ordinance included 12 specific exceptions such things as religious symbols, governmental signs, signs of historical societies, "temporary political signs," and "on-site" signs—signs advertising goods or services offered on the premises where the sign was located. The 1981 decision of the United States Supreme Court was fragmented and featured no majority opinion, but Justice White's four-justice plurality opinion has been treated as authoritative. A majority of the justices agreed that the ordinance was wholly or partially invalid on free speech grounds. The plurality opinion bifurcated the ordinance, declaring it valid to the extent it proscribed all commercial billboards except on-site signs and invalid insofar as it applied to noncommercial signs. The proffered reasons for the bifurcation are what make the plurality opinion important. Relying on *Central Hudson,* cited above, the opinion noted that, while commercial speech is entitled to some degree of free speech protection, the city's stated public purposes justified a ban on off-site commercial signs. The plurality suggested that the ordinance's exception for on-site commercial signs was also justified because the city could conclude that persons who had on-site activities had a stronger claim than persons who advertised off-site matters. In contrast, the plurality asserted that non-commercial advertising, such as political advertising, had a stronger claim to protection than any kind of commercial advertising. Because there could be no such thing as on-site advertising of some types of non-commercial activities—signs conveying political messages, a most sensitive kind of speech, come especially to mind— the ordinance invidiously operated to treat non-commercial signs less favorably than

---

[159] See especially Valentine v. Chrestensen, 316 U.S. 52, 62 S.Ct. 920, 86 L.Ed. 1262 (1942).

[160] 421 U.S. 809, 95 S.Ct. 2222, 44 L.Ed.2d 600 (1975).

[161] 433 U.S. 350, 97 S.Ct. 2691, 53 L.Ed.2d 810 (1977). However, an attorney's constitutional right to promote his or her services is not unlimited. Ohralik v. Ohio State Bar Ass'n, 436 U.S. 447, 98 S.Ct. 1912, 56 L.Ed.2d 444 (1978), upheld a bar association's power to sanction an attorney for some blatant face-to-face solicitation of business.

[162] 425 U.S. 748, 96 S.Ct. 1817, 48 L.Ed.2d 346 (1976).

[163] 447 U.S. 557, 100 S.Ct. 2343, 65 L.Ed.2d 341 (1980).

[164] 453 U.S. 490, 101 S.Ct. 2882, 69 L.Ed.2d 800 (1981). The California Supreme Court had treated the case as a due process case, not a free speech case, and had upheld the ordinance. See Metromedia, Inc. v. City of San Diego, 26 Cal.3d 848, 164 Cal.Rptr. 510, 610 P.2d 407 (1980).

commercial ones. Moreover, by permitting some kinds of non-commercial signs among the 12 exceptions but forbidding other kinds, the ordinance was impacting which non-commercial subjects citizens could discuss. For these reasons the Court sent the ordinance back to the California Supreme Court with directions to bifurcate the ordinance if it could. Unable to bifurcate it, the California Supreme Court simply struck down the entire ordinance.[165]

Three years after the Supreme Court's decision in *Metromedia*, in the Court heard another signboard case, Members of City Council of Los Angeles v. Taxpayers for Vincent involving a free speech issue. The primary issue in *Vincent* was whether all public areas are forums for speaking.[166] The issue was presented in the case in acute form because the signs carried political messages—the most sensitive kind of speech. The city ordinance in question in the case required city employees to remove all kinds of private advertising signs from city property, making no exception for political signs. Campaign workers for Mr. Vincent, a city council candidate, had placed signs on electric poles on public property and city employees had dutifully cleaned the signs off. The evidence showed that the employees had not concentrated upon Mr. Vincent's signs and that they had indeed removed far more nonpolitical than political signs. In upholding the ordinance and the city employees' actions under it, the Court acknowledged that some public places, such as sidewalks and the soapbox in the park, are traditional places where citizens have the right freely to engage in speech activities. However, public utility infrastructure and buildings (and presumably most public buildings) are not such places. Freedom to speak is not absolute. The city's interest in maintaining its property outweighed Mr. Vincent's claim to post his campaign signs in that particular location, especially given that many other locations were available for the purpose.

In contrast to its treatment of signs in *Vincent*, the Supreme Court and other courts have treated political signs on private property more deferentially. One case illustrating this difference is the Supreme Court's 1994 decision in City of Ladue v. Gilleo.[167] The claimant in the case, Mrs. Gilleo, had placed a small sign opposing American participation in the 1990 Persian Gulf War in the front yard and later in the front window of her home in violation of an ordinance of the City of Ladue—and exclusive suburb of St. Louis, Missouri. To preserve the town's neat appearance, the Ladue ordinance prohibited all yard signs in residential areas except for "residence identification," for-sale, and safety-hazard signs. Despite its acknowledging that the city had an interest in preserving its appearance and that the ordinance was content-and view-point-neutral, the Court held, as the federal district and circuit courts had held, that the ordinance denied Mrs. Gilleo her right of free speech. The opinion emphasized that home yard signs are a "venerable" and "unique" means of communication, especially on matters of politics and public interest, and held that they may not be completely

---

[165] Metromedia, Inc. v. City of San Diego, 32 Cal.3d 180, 185 Cal.Rptr. 260, 649 P.2d 902 (1982).

[166] 466 U.S. 789, 104 S.Ct. 2118, 80 L.Ed.2d 772 (1984). Accord, Grossbaum v. Indianapolis-Marion County Building Auth., 100 F.3d 1287 (7th Cir.1996), cert. denied 520 U.S. 1230, 117 S.Ct. 1822, 137 L.Ed.2d 1030 (1997), holding that the building authority might prohibit private persons and groups from posting displays in the lobby of a city-county building.

[167] 512 U.S. 43, 114 S.Ct. 2038, 129 L.Ed.2d 36 (1994). City of Rochester Hills v. Schultz, 224 Mich.App. 323, 568 N.W.2d 832 (1997), is consistent with *Gilleo*; it struck down an ordinance that prohibited yard signs advertising home businesses, but which merely regulated, but did not prohibit, other forms of commercial advertising. Also consistent is State v. Miller, 83 N.J. 402, 416 A.2d 821 (1980), which held void, as denying free speech, a city ordinance whose effect was to prohibit a yard sign that proclaimed a position on a matter of local public interest.

banned, though the Court suggests some slight limitations might be placed upon them. Generally consonant with *Gilleo* are several decisions from other courts that uniformly strike down local ordinances that limit the time political signs may be posted, the period of 60 days before an election being a common time limit.[168] These decisions, though acknowledging a municipality's interests in preventing clutter and causing traffic hazards, emphasize that such ordinances single out and regulate only political signs and that these signs are a cheap way for candidates, especially under-funded ones running against stronger opponents, to campaign. Among other things, a ban of 60 days or such may prevent a candidate who prevails in a primary election from keeping his or her signs up until the general election.

§ 9.9   VIOLATIONS OF RELIGION CLAUSES

The First Amendment to the United States Constitution begins with the phrase, "Congress shall make no law respecting an establishment of religion, or prohibiting the free exercise thereof. . . ." Two distinct constitutional clauses have emerged from these words: the "Establishment" Clause, which this book will only lightly cover, and the "Free Exercise" Clause, which is the main subject of this section. Like the Free Speech Clause, the Free Exercise Clause applies not only to actions of the Federal Government but, through the 14th Amendment Due Process Clause, to state and local governments as well.[169] Moreover, as with the other constitutional limitations covered in this chapter, state constitutions contain guarantees that more or less parallel the Free Exercise Clause and that may be interpreted by state courts to give more protection than does the First Amendment. Indeed, far more regulations have been struck down on the authority of state constitutional provisions than have been under the First Amendment.

Unquestionably, the most significant development over the past few decades relating to the protection of constitutional religious rights in land use regulation has been Congress' enactment of the Religious Land Use and Institutionalized Persons Act of 2000 (RLUIPA).[170] The RLUIPA reshaped how courts and stakeholders approach religious freedom issues in the land use context, so many cases decided in this area prior to the statute's enactment now have minimal precedential value. To keep some order on this subject, the section first discusses Free Exercise Clause issues in land use law prior to enactment of the RLUIPA and then focuses on the growing body of case law interpreting this influential statute.

Religious Free Exercise and Land Use Law Before Enactment of the RLUPIA

Prior to Congress' enactment of the RLUIPA in 2000, the rules and standards protecting free exercise rights in the land use context were relatively difficult to articulate. State-court free exercise decisions almost defied analysis; it was extremely difficult to make accurate generalizations about them, sometimes even within a given jurisdiction.[171] They tended to be fact-intensive, they sometimes turned upon the

---

[168] See, e.g., City of Antioch v. Candidates' Outdoor Graphic Service, 557 F.Supp. 52 (N.D.Cal.1982) (60 days); Orazio v. Town of North Hempstead, 426 F.Supp. 1144 (E.D.N.Y.1977) (six weeks); Collier v. City of Tacoma, 121 Wn.2d 737, 854 P.2d 1046 (1993) (60 days).

[169] E.g., Cantwell v. Connecticut, 310 U.S. 296 (1940).

[170] 42 U.S.C. § 2000cc (2006).

[171] New York, which has many religious zoning cases, is a leading example of a state whose decisions are often difficult to distinguish from each other, to determine if they are contrary or if their different facts account for different results. E.g., compare Jewish Reconstructionist Synagogue v. Incorporated Village of Roslyn Harbor, 38 N.Y.2d 283, 342 N.E.2d 534, 379 N.Y.S.2d 747 (1975), with Matter of Westchester Reform

language of a particular local ordinance. Moreover, many of these older state decisions would analyze a religious institution's challenge to a land use regulation as a question of denial of due process or possibly of a regulatory taking rather than of denial of free exercise.[172]

Not surprisingly, most of the free exercise land use cases in the pre-RLUIPA era involved zoning regulations. To be clear: it was doubtful that any state court would uphold a total ban on churches from an entire community.[173] In fact, the great majority of state decisions likewise held that zoning could not even totally exclude churches from a given residential zone.[174] A common practice, especially in residential zoning, is for churches to be permitted but only upon receipt of a special permit such as a special exception or a conditional-use permit. When this approach was used, it was historically quite difficult to make categorical statements about how denial of such permit to churches would fare in court. The best general statement that could be made is that this technique was generally permissible and that whether denial of the permit violated the free exercise clause depended upon the facts of the case. Many courts, however, seemed to reverse the normal presumption that a local government's denial of such a permit was valid—or at least the church seemed to "have something going for it" that another applicant would not.[175]

An important threshold question has always been whether a given structure or the activity at a given location amounts to an "exercise of religion" entitled to protection under a constitutional free exercise clause. Obviously, a traditional church, synagogue,

Temple v. Brown, 22 N.Y.2d 488, 239 N.E.2d 891, 293 N.Y.S.2d 297 (1968). Moreover, since the date of those decisions, Cornell University v. Bagnardi, 68 N.Y.2d 583, 503 N.E.2d 509, 510 N.Y.S.2d 861 (1986), is generally believed to have marked a general trend for the New York Court of Appeals to be less favorable than formerly to religious institutions in zoning cases. *Bagnardi* involved an educational institution, but the court discussed educational and religious institutions interchangeably. See Rice, Re-Evaluating the Balance Between Zoning Regulations and Religious and Educational Uses, 8 Pace L. Rev. 1 (1988).

[172] See, e.g., Lutheran Church in America v. City of New York, 35 N.Y.2d 121, 316 N.E.2d 305, 359 N.Y.S.2d 7 (1974) (regulatory taking); J. Juergensmeyer & T. Roberts, Land Use Planning and Control Law § 4.28 (1998); D. Mandelker, R. Cunningham & J. Payne, Planning and Control of Land Development 337 (4th ed. 1995); Note, 84 Colum. L. Rev. 1562, 1568–70 (1984) (many courts ignore free exercise clause); Annot., 74 A.L.R.2d 377, 380–81 (1960). However, when courts treat claims of religious institutions as claims of denial of due process, they are likely to reverse the usual presumption that the regulation is valid. See, e.g., Jehovah's Witnesses Assembly Hall v. Woolwich Tnp., 220 N.J.Super. 381, 532 A.2d 276 (L.Div. 1987); State ex rel. Lake Drive Baptist Church v. Bayside Board of Trustees, 12 Wis.2d 585, 108 N.W.2d 288 (1961).

[173] J. Juergensmeyer & T. Roberts, Land Use Planning and Control Law § 4.28 (1998).

[174] Ibid.; Annot., 74 A.L.R.2d 377, 380–81 (1960). It should be added that these decisions tended to be older ones and a few states, notably California, were contrary. See, e.g., Seward Chapel, Inc. v. City of Seward, 655 P.2d 1293 (Alaska 1982); Corporation of Presiding Bishop v. City of Porterville, 90 Cal.App.2d 656, 203 P.2d 823 (1949) (leading case).

[175] For examples of decisions holding that permits were wrongfully denied, see, e.g., Jehovah's Witnesses Assembly Hall v. Woolwich Tnp., 220 N.J.Super. 381, 532 A.2d 276 (L.Div. 1987); Jewish Reconstructionist Synagogue v. Incorporated Village of Roslyn Harbor, 38 N.Y.2d 283, 342 N.E.2d 534, 379 N.Y.S.2d 747 (1975); Holy Spirit Ass'n v. Rosenfeld, 91 A.D.2d 190, 458 N.Y.S.2d 920 (1983); City of Sumner v. First Baptist Church, 97 Wn.2d 1, 639 P.2d 1358 (1982) (city could not enforce fire code against church, but had to be "flexible" with church); State ex rel. Lake Drive Baptist Church v. Bayside Board of Trustees, 12 Wis.2d 585, 108 N.W.2d 288 (1961). For examples of decisions that allow permits to be denied when church activities would pose serious public problems, see Cornell University v. Bagnardi, 68 N.Y.2d 583, 503 N.E.2d 509, 510 N.Y.S.2d 861 (1986) (dictum); Matter of Westchester Reform Temple v. Brown, 22 N.Y.2d 488, 239 N.E.2d 891, 293 N.Y.S.2d 297 (1968); Milwaukie Company of Jehovah's Witnesses v. Mullen, 214 Ore. 281, 330 P.2d 5 (1958), cert. denied 359 U.S. 436, 79 S.Ct. 940, 3 L.Ed.2d 932 (1959). Note the New York decisions that tend to be inconsistent. See generally, J. Juergensmeyer & T. Roberts, Land Use Planning and Control Law § 4.28 (1998); D. Mandelker, Land Use Law § 5.57 (4th ed. 1997) (when churches do not have extreme impact on residential areas, courts tend to favor conditional use permits for them).

or mosque that is regularly used for worship qualifies, but even before the RLUIPA the definition of "religious activities" was generally considered to be much broader than that. For instance, the term was interpreted to encompass such land uses as a university students' religion and recreational center, a recreational complex on the grounds of a church, a convent, a lay spiritual retreat center, and a 53-acre bible camp.[176] On the other hand, activities that failed to get classification as religious activities included camp meetings on church grounds, a mikvah for ritualistic bathing, a religious organization's radio station, a child care facility operated by a minister and his wife at their personal residence, and a Jewish foundation's educational, religious, and recreational center.[177] Courts' generally liberal interpretation of what was a religious activity seemed to largely flow from their reluctance to intrude into the content of religious belief and inclination to give religious institutions much leeway regarding their religious beliefs are and what they require.[178]

A comparison of some leading cases historic preservation cases involving religious land uses shows the range of judicial treatment of Free Exercise Clause issues prior to the RLUIPA. Lutheran Church in America v. City of New York[179] struck down the landmark designation of a denomination's national headquarters in a historic brownstone mansion, not on the ground of denial of free exercise, but as a regulatory taking. However, the New York Court of Appeals accepted as a fact that the building was used for religious purposes and may have given some weight to that fact. In contrast, in a somewhat similar case arising in New York, a federal district court held that the landmark designation of a church-owned building used for some worship and other multiple purposes did not deny free exercise.[180] In First Covenant Church v. City of Seattle, the Supreme Court of Washington struck down the landmark designation of a church on the express ground that it so burdened the church as to deny it free exercise of religion.[181] Then the United States Supreme Court granted certiorari and, in a brief per curiam opinion, remanded the case to Washington with instructions indicating that the federal Supreme Court wanted Washington to reverse itself.[182]

In the decades preceding the RLUIPA's enactment, the United States Supreme Court managed to avoid a direct holding on the application of the Free Exercise Clause to land use regulations on religious institutions. However, the Court's decisions in some analogous cases, as well as its remand in the *First Covenant* case just discussed,

---

[176] Annot., 62 A.L.R.3d 197, 202–03 (1975).

[177] As to the Jewish center last mentioned in text, Munns v. Martin, 131 Wn.2d 192, 930 P.2d 318 (1997), seems contrary. It held that a "pastoral center" that was used as an educational and social center, as well as for some worship services and religious instruction, was a religious use.

[178] 35 N.Y.2d 121, 316 N.E.2d 305, 359 N.Y.S.2d 7 (1974)

[179] 35 N.Y.2d 121, 316 N.E.2d 305, 359 N.Y.S.2d 7 (1974).

[180] Rector, Wardens, and Members of the Vestry of St. Bartholomew's Church v. City of New York, 728 F.Supp. 958 (1989, 1990), aff'd 914 F.2d 348 (2d Cir.1990), cert. denied 499 U.S. 905, 111 S.Ct. 1103, 113 L.Ed.2d 214 (1991).

[181] First Covenant Church v. City of Seattle, 114 Wn.2d 392, 787 P.2d 1352 (1990), vacated and remanded, 499 U.S. 901 (1991).

[182] City of Seattle v. First Covenant Church, 499 U.S. 901 (1991). The Supreme Court instructed Washington to reconsider its decision "in light of *Employment Division, Department of Human Resources of Oregon v. Smith*, 494 U.S. 872, 110 S.Ct. 1595, 108 L.Ed.2d 876 (1990)." In *Smith* the Court had held that two men who had used peyote in Native American religious ceremonies might be discharged from employment under a state statute that prohibited the use of hallucinogenic drugs. Despite the claim of denial of free exercise, the Court upheld the application of the statute because it did not target religion, but was "neutral and of general applicability." We will analyze United States Supreme Court decisions in a moment.

indicated pretty strongly that it was willing to tolerate land use regulations that many courts have stricken down. In remanding *First Covenant*, the Court directed Washington to reconsider the case "in the light of Employment Division, Department of Human Resources of Oregon v. Smith," a 1990 Supreme Court decision.[183] In that decision the Court held that the Free Exercise Clause did not prevent application of Oregon's controlled-substance laws to the use of peyote in Native American religious ceremonies. The rationale was that the statute did not single out religious activities but was "neutral and of general applicability." The Court applied the same test, though a local ordinance was invalidated under it, in a 1993 case analogous to a land use case, Church of the Lukumi Babalu Aye v. City of Hialeah.[184] A city ordinance, though it permitted the killing of animals for food, expressly prohibited it if done for religious purposes. Because the latter feature of the ordinance was not neutral, but applied especially to religion, the Court struck it down. Relying on, though distinguishing, that decision, First Assembly of God of Naples v. Collier County, an 11th Circuit Court decision, upheld a local zoning ordinance that prevented a church from conducting a homeless shelter, even though the church said its beliefs required it to operate the shelter. Since the zoning ordinance did not specifically single out churches, it was deemed neutral and of general applicability. The United States Supreme Court refused to review the 11th Circuit decision.[185]

Though it is not directly applicable, we should also note the Supreme Court's disposition of the case in City of Boerne v. Flores, a 1997 decision.[186] When the city designated a church a historic landmark, the church attacked the validity of the designation, arguing that it violated the Religious Freedom Restoration Act, which Congress had enacted in 1993. Roughly stated, this statute required governmental entities to show a "compelling" public interest to regulate religious activities.[187] The Supreme Court held against the church, not by direct application of the Free Exercise Clause, but by declaring the Religious Freedom Restoration Act beyond the power of Congress and void. The decision indicated in a general way that the justices were not inclined to be overly protective of religious institutions and activities. It seemed likely that, when the Court did hand down a definitive decision on free exercise, it would employ the test of "neutral and of general applicability." Under that test, if it were taken literally, it seemed that churches and religious activities would receive no special treatment under zoning and other land use regulations—that regulations could be applied to a church the same as to a grocery store—as long as the ordinance itself did not set it apart.

Religious Free Exercise and Land Use Law Under the RLUPIA

The *Smith* and *Boerne* cases described above generated frustration among religious and civil rights advocates, who feared that these cases had excessively weakened constitutional free exercise protections in the land use regulatory context. At least partly fueled by this frustration, and after roughly three years of lengthy hearings on these issues, Congress finally enacted the RLUIPA in September of 2000. Although the

---

[183] 494 U.S. 872, 110 S.Ct. 1595, 108 L.Ed.2d 876 (1990).

[184] 508 U.S. 520, 113 S.Ct. 2217, 124 L.Ed.2d 472 (1993).

[185] 20 F.3d 419, modified 27 F.3d 526 (11th Cir.1994), cert. denied 513 U.S. 1080, 115 S.Ct. 730, 130 L.Ed.2d 634 (1995).

[186] 521 U.S. 507, 117 S.Ct. 2157, 138 L.Ed.2d 624 (1997).

[187] 42 U.S.C.A. § 2000bb et seq.

RLUIPA also created important new protections or institutionalized individuals, its greatest impacts since its enactment have been in the field of land use law.

The RLUIPA uses four main statutory provisions to protect religious institutions against excessive land use regulation. The first such provision, known generally as the "substantial burden" provision, requires courts to use a "strict scrutiny" test when analyzing land use regulations that "substantially burden" the free exercise of religion: courts must ask whether the challenged regulation is the "least restrictive means" of serving a "compelling government interest."[188] The second relevant RLUIPA provision, the "equal terms" provision, prohibits government entities from treating "a religious assembly or institution on less than equal terms with a nonreligious assembly or institution."[189] A third RLUIPA provision, commonly labeled the "nondiscrimination" provision, prohibits governments from "impos[ing] or implement[ing] a land use regulation that discriminates against any assembly or institution on the basis of religion or religious denomination."[190] And the fourth main RLUIPA land use provision, the "exclusion" provision, forbids local governments from geographically excluding or unreasonably limiting "religious assemblies, institutions, or structures" within their jurisdiction.[191]

In the years since the RLUIPA's enactment, countless legal scholars and commentators have elaborated on the RLUIPA, its impacts, and its shortcomings.[192] Numerous unresolved questions about the statute remain, but most seem to agree that the statute has led to an overall increase in protection for religious institutions against land use regulations that might otherwise limit their free exercise rights. Although other statutory language places limits on its applicability,[193] the "substantial burden" provision's strict scrutiny standard affords significantly greater protection for religious exercise in land use settings than under the rational basis standard the United States Supreme Court held was applicable in *Smith*. The statute's other provisions have added substantial additional protections for religious institutions as well. However, the RLUIPA has still generated plenty of controversy and some uncertainty remains regarding the interpretation of some of its provisions.

One significant source of uncertainty related to the RLUIPA is the lack of a clear definition for the term "substantial burden." The RLUIPA requires courts to apply its strict scrutiny standard for land use regulations only when the regulation imposes a "substantially burdens" on citizens' free exercise of religion. However, the statute intentionally failed to specify what constitutes a "substantial burden" capable of

---

[188] 42 U.S.C. § 2000cc(a)(1) (2006).

[189] 42 U.S.C. § 2000cc(b)(1) (2006).

[190] 42 U.S.C. § 2000cc(b)(2) (2006).

[191] 42 U.S.C. § 2000cc(b)(3)(A) (2006).

[192] See, e.g., Douglas Laycock & Bruce W. Goodrich, RLUIPA: Necessary, Modest, and Under-Enforced, 39 Fordham Urb. L.J. 1021, 1023 (2012) (categorizing the RLUIPA's land use provisions as the "substantial-burden", "non-discrimination", "equal terms", and "exclusion-and-limitations" provisions); Zachary Bray, RLUIPA and the Limits of Religious Institutionalism, 2016 Utah L. Rev. 41 (2016) (characterizing to the RLUIPA as a "deeply flawed statute" that has "been a magnet for controversy since its passage"); Kellen Zale, God's Green Earth? The Environmental Impacts of Religious Land Use, 64 Me. L. Rev. 207 (2011) (arguing that, by "allowing religious entities to use their property in ways that no other land users can," the RLUIPA "threatens to undermine local environmental protection efforts nationwide").

[193] See 42 U.S.C. §§ 2000cc(a)(2)(B)–(C) (2006) (requiring additional showings that the regulation at issue affects interstate commerce and authorizes regulators to make "individualized assessments of the proposed uses for the property involved").

triggering strict scrutiny analysis.[194] Many have bemoaned this approach, which appears to be a source of ongoing legal uncertainty. Some commentators have suggested that many courts have interpreted "substantial burden" too narrowly and thereby limited the efficiency of the statute. For instance, on commentator who reviewed RLUIPA "substantial burden" cases from 2001 to 2009 found that landowners were able to meet their burden of establishing a "substantial burden" in only 18 out of 83 reported decisions.[195] In contrast, at least one other commentator has argued that Congress' decision not to define "substantial burden" under the RLUIPA has led many courts to interpret the phrase too loosely in potentially unconstitutional ways.[196]

Legal uncertainty also continues to surround the "equal terms" provision of the RLUIPA. Under the equal terms provision, "no government shall impose or implement a land use regulation in a manner that treats a religious assembly or institution on less than equal terms with a nonreligious assembly or institution."[197] Questions regarding this provision have tended to center primarily on the question of what constitutes "less than equal terms." For example, in the Ninth Circuit held in *Centro Familiar Cristiano Buenas Nuevas v. City of Yuma* in 2011 that a city ordinance requiring religious institutions to secure conditional use permits but not requiring the same from non-religious landowners who were "similarly situated" as to the ordinance's regulatory purpose violated the RLUIPA's equal terms provision.[198] In contrast, the Eleventh Circuit has interpreted the provision to not require courts to make comparisons to "similarly situated" secular landowners. In Midrash Sephardi, Inc. v. Town of Surfside in 2004, that court held that even though the equal terms provision "has the 'feel' of an equal protection law, it lacks the 'similarly situated' requirement usually found in equal protection analysis."[199]

Land Use Regulation and the Establishment Clause

This section has said almost nothing about the "Establishment Clause" of the First Amendment, which states that there shall be no law "respecting the establishment of religion." Only in rare instances do land use regulations implicate this clause, but a United States Supreme Court decision, Larkin v. Grendel's Den, illustrates that it is possible.[200] A local zoning ordinance provided that an applicant for a liquor license could not operate if there was a "church" within 500 feet that objected; i.e., the church had a veto power. This ordinance the Court held void, on the ground that it violated the First Amendment Establishment Clause. Interestingly, shortly after its enactment some

---

[194] Language in the RLUIPA's legislative history states that the statute's sponsors purposely opted not to define "substantial burden', intending instead for courts to interpret the phrase "by reference to Supreme Court jurisprudence" and not make "any broader interpretation than the Supreme Court's articulation of the concept of substantial burden or religious exercise." 146 Cong. Rec. S7774–01, S7776 (daily ed. July 27, 2000) (joint statement of Senator Hatch and Senator Kennedy).

[195] See Lora A. Lucero, The Eleventh Commandment: Thou Shalt Not Burden Religious Land Use Applicants, 33 No. 4 Zoning and Planning Law Report 1 (April 2010).

[196] See generally Marci A. Hamilton, RLUIPA is a Bridge Too Far: Inconvenience is Not Discrimination, 39 Fordham Urb. L.J. 959 (2012).

[197] 42 U.S.C. § 2000cc(b)(1) (2006).

[198] 651 F.3d 1163 (2011).

[199] 366 F.3d 1214 (2004).

[200] 459 U.S. 116, 103 S.Ct. 505, 74 L.Ed.2d 297 (1982). But cf. Cohen v. City of Des Plaines, 8 F.3d 484 (7th Cir.1993), which upheld an ordinance that allowed churches to operate day-care centers outright, but required others to obtain a special permit. The court upheld the distinction, reasoning that it was justified to prevent governmental interference with religious activities.

argued that certain provisions of the RLUIPA itself might violate the Establishment Clause by excessively favoring religious land users over secular ones. However, the United States Supreme Court upheld the RLUIPA against an Establishment Clause-based challenge in Cutter v. Wilkinson in 2005.[201] Today most seem to recognize that the statute's drafters intended for it to be interpreted and applied so as not to violate the Establishment Clause.[202]

B. THE SYSTEM OF PLANNING AND ZONING

§ 9.10 OVERVIEW OF PLANNING AND ZONING

This section 9.10 provides a very basic primer for those who have never worked in or with a local system of planning and zoning. Persons who are generally knowledgeable about the structure and workings of such a system may thus find it worthwhile to skip forward to the next section. For purposes of illustration, this section describes how a newly-incorporated hypothetical suburban city might create its planning-zoning system and agencies to administer it. Since this section is only descriptive and simply foretells matters that are discussed with supporting citations in subsequent sections, it is written without footnotes.

Land use planning and zoning are a relatively novel type of regulatory tool. New York City is generally credited with adopting the first zoning ordinances in 1916, and the period of the 1920s and 1930s was the time when zoning spread to all states. The vast majority of the nation's cities and counties now have zoning ordinances, although comprehensive planning has been somewhat slower coming along. Cities get their general power to establish systems of zoning by delegation under state "zoning enabling acts," of which each state now has at least one. These delegations of state authority are necessary because the general grant of police power to cities and counties—to provide for the public welfare—is generally not sufficient to enable them to zone land.

Even though all 50 states have individually enacted their own 50 zoning enabling acts, it is still possible to state general principles of American planning and zoning law. There is actually much commonality from state to state, thanks to the "Standard Zoning Enabling Act" (SZEA). This model state statute was promulgated in several versions by the United States Department of Commerce for states to consider enacting as a means of authorizing their local governments to engage in zoning. Every one of the early state zoning enabling acts was based upon the SZEA, with only some minor variation across jurisdictions. Although many states have replaced their early enabling acts with more sophisticated (and longer) statutes, the SZEA's basic pattern is fortunately still in them. Accordingly, this chapter uses the SZEA as its example when referring to some feature of a zoning enabling act. Court decisions interpreting these similar enabling acts have also developed an American common law of zoning, so the descriptions in this section tell a fairly typical American story.

Suppose that the hypothetical suburban city of Greenlawns has just become an incorporated small city in the State of Franklin, carved out of an unincorporated area of Jefferson County, and a suburb of nearby Big Town. Suppose further that the city's first

---

[201] 544 U.S. 709, 125 S.Ct. 2113, 161 L.Ed.2d 1020 (2005).

[202] See, e.g., Lisa Mathews, Hobby Lobby and Hobbs to the Rescue: Clarifying RLUIPA's Confusing Substantial Burden Test for Land-Use Cases, 24 Geo. Mason L. Rev. 1025 (2017) (noting that the "RLUIPA was intended to protect churches to the full extent allowed without violating the Establishment Clause").

election has been held and that the city has elected a city council and mayor. If the city is large enough it will likely hire a city attorney and possibly even a full-time "planning department" director. But if the city is quite small, it may have no planning department and instead engage a planning firm on a contract basis to assist the city attorney in the planning-zoning process. Assuming that Jefferson County already had a zoning ordinance in place, one of the city council's first tasks will be to adopt a resolution continuing that zoning as the city's interim zoning until the new planning director or planning firm can complete studies to recommend what changes the city should make.

Though the city council must ultimately adopt any zoning ordinance or changes in zoning laws, the planning director or planning firm typically works with and presents its proposals to another official city body—usually called a "planning commission"—that then makes recommendations to the city council. The work of this council-appointed administrative body is discussed in more detail in section 9.15. Although planning commissions adopt motions by vote, their resolutions are merely recommendations that the city council may vote to adopt, reject, adopt with modifications, or return for further study and recommendation. In some localities, planning commissions study and recommend an original "comprehensive [or master] plan" (which is defined below) that the city council may adopt or merely allow the planning commission to use as an internal document to aid it in recommending zoning ordinances. In practice, the bulk of a commission's continuing work involves the consideration of applications from landowners for the "rezoning" of specific parcels of land.

The first step a new city typically takes to commence its regulation of land use is to prepare a comprehensive (or master) plan. In the early twentieth century, the making of a "comp plan" usually did not precede the adoption of zoning ordinances even though the SZEA said zoning had to be "in accordance with a comprehensive plan." Courts interpreted this not to require that a formal comp plan precede the adoption of zoning ordinances or even to come into being later on the theory that a zoning ordinance could itself form a "comprehensive" pattern. However, most modern cities and counties that wishes to adopt an initial zoning ordinances tend to first establish a formal comp plan. This begins with a series of studies of different "elements" of land use in the community, usually including studies of transportation routes, public utility and communications systems, public areas, areas for different kinds of private land uses, and optional elements such as recreational areas or conservation. These studies yield various descriptive documents, maps, diagrams, and charts. A comp plan does not merely show existing development; it usually looks at least one or two decades into the future and may include outlying areas that are not even presently within city limits.

Comp plans tend to be less detailed than zoning ordinances and maps in their descriptions of boundaries and identification of various locations and elements. The most important difference between a comp plan and the zoning ordinance that follows is that the plan itself does not impose any restrictions on the use of any land. It is merely a resource for the planning commission to resort to when crafting the original zoning ordinance and later making amendments to it. However, comp plans often do control the freedom of the planning commission and the city council to adopt or change zoning ordinances. When the planning commission is satisfied with the original comp plan, the group adopts it by vote. As noted above, in some states and localities, the city council also adopts the comp plan by resolution but even then the plan itself does not impose any restrictions on land use.

Once a city's planning commission (and sometimes its city council) has adopted a comp plan, the planning commission begins preparing the city's original zoning ordinance. American zoning laws generally divide cities and counties into fixed geographical areas called "zoning districts" or "zones" for short. These zones have fixed boundary lines and are usually shown on a city map. Cities and counties usually have several different, the number depending upon the size of the municipality and the sophistication of its zoning code. The zones differ in that they allow different land uses, set different height limits, and have different "bulk" restrictions. "Bulk" restrictions include such requirements as minimum building parcel sizes, minimum amounts of open space on a parcel, and minimum distances that structures may be set back from the boundaries of a parcel. Typical zoning ordinances feature several different kinds of zones for residential use, for commercial use, for industrial use, and for agricultural use and open space.

Most zoning codes describe each zone by a designation that is suggestive of the principal types of uses that are permitted in it. for example, a zone that permits one single-family residence per building lot as its principal use (but which often permits a few other supporting uses, such as "accessory" uses for dwellings and possibly churches and some home occupations), is frequently labeled an "R-1" or "RS-1" zone. An R-2 zone usually suggests duplexes as the principal use, R-4 apartment buildings, C-1 light commercial, C-3 heavier commercial, I-1 light industry, I-6 heavy industry, and so forth. A city or county generally has a number of locations for each of its zones, pursuing an optimal balance of diversity and uniformity.

Typically, a zoning ordinance or "zoning code" comprises a title in a city's city code and is divided into chapters. Many chapters establishing a type of zone and describing the uses permitted in that zone. Many zoning ordinances are "cumulative," meaning that the uses permitted in the lighter zones (such as residential zones) are generally also permitted in the heavier zones (such as commercial or industrial zones). For instance, in jurisdictions with cumulative zoning ordinances, single-family residences are traditionally permitted throughout the other types of residential zones and in the commercial and industrial zones. However, zoning is sometimes "non-cumulative," meaning that at least some of the lighter uses are not permitted in at least some of the heavier zones. Other sections of the code chapter for each zone generally contain height and bulk requirements and perhaps other requirements, such as those for off-street parking. A landowner who proposes to use land as expressly permitted under the code does not need any special zoning permission, though of course he or she must comply with local building and health codes. In addition to describing uses permitted "outright," code chapters for most zones also list uses that are permitted only upon the receipt of a "special exception" or "conditional use" permit—a topic discussed in more detail below. Other chapters in the zoning code deal with the administration of the system and the roles of the city council, planning commission, and board of adjustment. Others outline the penalties for violations of the zoning code, which usually constitute misdemeanors requiring involvement of the local prosecutor. When the planning commission has finalized and approved its draft of the original zoning code, it recommends the draft to the city council. The council may adopt, amend, or reject it or send it back to the commission for further study before finally adopting it.

As mentioned above, the zoning code typically establishes a third body called the "board of adjustment" or "board of zoning appeals." Thus, the three bodies that operate a system of planning and zoning are the city council, the planning commission, and the board of adjustment. In some small towns, the planning commission also performs the functions of a board of adjustment. Whereas the planning commission is part of the legislative process, making recommendations to the local legislative body, the board of adjustment is a quasi-judicial body. It considers and grants or denies applications from landowners for individual relief from the normal requirements of the zoning code. It also has limited powers to grant permits to do what the zoning of their land would not normally allow them to do. These are flexibility devices that allow departures from rigid zoning restrictions and are discussed in more detail in section 9.15.

It is worth emphasizing again that the members of a typical planning commission comprise a permanent body whose ongoing work continues as long as the city exists. Among other things, local zoning codes generally contain regularized procedures for citizens to petition the planning commission to consider and recommend changes in the zoning code to the city council. City councils may, unless restrained by state law, amend any city ordinance, such as ordinances governing speed limits or the building code. However, there usually are no regularized procedures for citizens to petition for such amendments, making the planning commission's role a relatively unique one. The zoning code typically also directs the commission to conduct ongoing studies and to recommend on its own proposed changes to the comp plan and the zoning code, but in reality the commission is usually so occupied with specific citizen petitions and matters that it has scant time to initiate studies of its own.

City councils can make two basic types of amendments to the zoning code: "text" amendments and "map" amendments. A text amendment changes the wording of some part of the code itself. For instance, a text amendment might expressly add rooftop solar panels arrays to the list of uses permitted within R-1 zones. Such an amendment would not change the location of any of the R-1 areas but would allow the new use in every existing R-1 zone. In contrast, map amendments do not change the text of the code but change instead the zoning designation of a particular area of land and thus change the city's zoning map. For instance, a city council might adopt an ordinance changing the zoning designation of a certain area or parcel of land from R-1 to R-2 to permit more dense residential uses.

Most zoning codes establish regular procedures through which citizens may petition the planning commission to recommend map amendments such as in the example above. Most commonly, these petitioners seek to have land "upzoned." For example, landowners might seek a map amendment to change their R-1 land to R-4 land capable of hosting apartments rather than just single-family homes—a type of change that usually increases the value of the land. In contrast, neighbors or other stakeholders occasionally petition to have someone else's land "downzoned" from, say, R-4 to R-1, to prevent its intensive development. In either case, zoning enabling acts and local codes typically require such interested persons to file application with the planning commission and pay an application fee. This starts a process that includes at least one public hearing before the commission upon advance notice, often by newspaper publication and posting on the subject land and also by notices mailed to nearby owners. Applications of this sort are often bitterly fought and highly charged because much is at stake for the owner and for residents of the area. At the end of the hearings process, the planning commission generally recommends to the city council that the application for rezoning be granted, denied, or granted with modifications. In the city council, the matter is placed on the agenda of a council meeting for discussion and vote. Further hearings allowing the applicant and other interested persons to address the council are not usually required by law but are often granted. Ultimately, the council votes to adopt the planning commission's recommendation, modify it, reject it, or return it to the commission for further study and a later recommendation.

The consideration of planning commission applications usually ends before the city council. Most board of adjustment matters similarly end with that board, although some end with the city council. Wherever a given matter finally ends within the city government, the next step is a petition for review to the local court of general jurisdiction. When an applicant for relief who seeks court review, opponents sometimes raise the defense of "failure to exhaust administrative remedies." This generally means that the applicant has not gone through all the steps in the zoning process that the city's procedures allow that might have given the applicant the desired relief. Obviously, a local government may raise this defense if an applicant has not carried an application through to the city body, such as the city council, that, under the city ordinances, is the "end of the line." In most jurisdictions, an applicant for rezoning whose application is denied has likewise failed to exhaust administrative remedies if the city code allowed a variance that could have potentially given the applicant relief.

Assuming that the procedures allowed by the city have been fully completed and exhausted, a losing party who believes those procedures were somehow flawed can seek review by the local court of general jurisdiction. There are obviously many grounds for asking a court to reverse or modify a city's land use regulatory decision. For instance, perhaps the city has failed to follow the zoning code's prescribed procedures, such as those for notice of hearings. Minor failures may not bring reversal, but ones that cause substantial prejudice will. Or, perhaps the code provision at issue is unconstitutional or contradicts or goes beyond the authority granted by the state's zoning enabling act. One common grounds is that a particular rezoning constituted "spot zoning"—a claim with constitutional underpinnings that is discussed later in this chapter.

§ 9.11 HISTORY AND PURPOSES OF ZONING

In urban areas, zoning is typically the most important form of governmental land use control based upon the police power.[203] It has been said that "[t]he essence of zoning is territorial division in keeping with the character of the lands and structures and their peculiar suitability for particular uses, and uniformity of use within the division."[204] Zoning is essentially an extension of the common law concept of public nuisance by legislation. The London fire code of the pre-colonial era, which banned wooden buildings in the central part of the city, is a famous early example. During the colonial period preceding the formation of the United States, many municipalities in the British colonies likewise enacted regulatory ordinances banishing slaughter houses, gunpowder mills, and similar "noisome" activities to the outskirts of the municipality.[205] In 1889, a Wisconsin statute authorized cities to create districts with building regulations that differed from district to district according to the fire risks involved.[206] In the same year, building height restrictions were enacted in Washington, D.C. Similar restrictions

---

[203] The most useful multi-volume treatises are R. Anderson, American Law of Zoning (5 vols., 2d ed. 1976 and annual supplements); and N. Williams, American Land Planning Law (5 vols., 1975 and annual supplements). Recommended single-volume texts are J. Juergensmeyer & T. Roberts, Land Use Planning and Control Law (West "Hornbook" 1998); and D. Mandelker, Land Use Law (4th ed. Michie 1997.)

[204] Katobimar Realty Co. v. Webster, 20 N.J. 114, 118 A.2d 824 (1955).

[205] E.g., Acts & Resolves of the Province of Massachusetts Bay 1692–93, ch. 23.

[206] See Solberg, Rural Zoning in the United States (Ag.Info.Bull. 59, U.S.D.A. 1952).

adopted in Boston were held constitutional in 1909.[207] Of course, American municipalities still have specific regulations of these sorts in the form of fire, building and health codes. However, modern zoning goes beyond these kinds of regulations in several ways. The "evils" it seeks to prevent are less pressing than preventing city fires or contagion. Zoning seeks to prevent incompatible uses of land from neighboring each other and to promote pairings of synergistic ones to create attractive and desirable communities. One reason early zoning ordinances raised the constitutional issues discussed in earlier sections of this chapter was that its public purposes are more amorphous and less obvious than those of early health and safety regulations.

Modern urban planning and zoning grew out of the City Beautiful Movement that began in America in the 1890s. During this era, "village improvement associations" were formed in villages and towns across the country. The aim of these voluntary citizens' movements was to improve the appearance and comfort of communities by agitating to get streets and sidewalks paved, private yards and alleys cleaned up, attractive vegetation planted, and public parks established. Formed in 1901, the American League for Civic Improvement lobbied for and secured local expenditures in many communities for attractive architecture and other municipal improvements. They also promoted the formation of voluntary citizens' advisory planning commissions that were precursors of the governmental planning commissions described above.[208]

New York City was the first American municipality to adopt a comprehensive scheme of building and land use regulations based upon the creation of a number of districts or zones. The Building Zone Resolution adopted by New York City in 1916 established three separate classes of districts and delineated restrictions for each on the use of land and buildings, heights of buildings, and land coverage.[209] "Use" districts were classified either as residence, business, or unrestricted. In residence districts, trade and industry of every kind were prohibited. In business districts, specified trades and industries—mainly nuisance-creating industries such as boiler-making, ammonia manufacturing, and the like—were prohibited but residences and all other kinds of trade and industry were permitted. In unrestricted districts, any kind of land use was permitted. The regulations were prospective in their operation and sought to supply a sensible framework for future building development in New York City.

Although the 1916 New York City Building Zone Resolution was adopted under the authority of a special enabling act, the New York Legislature shortly thereafter adopted a general zoning enabling act for cities within that state. As zoning spread to other states, state legislatures' enactment of general zoning enabling legislation generally preceded the adoption of local zoning ordinances. By 1926, all but five of the then forty-eight states had adopted zoning enabling legislation and some 420 municipalities had enacted zoning ordinances. Until 1923, most of the new state zoning enabling acts were modeled on the New York zoning enabling statute. In January of 1923, the United States Department of Commerce published the first draft of a Standard State Zoning Enabling Act that departed in some respects from the New York zoning enabling legislation. The Standard Act, revised and republished in 1924 and again in 1926, was the model for

---

[207]　Welch v. Swasey, 214 U.S. 91, 29 S.Ct. 567, 53 L.Ed. 923 (1909).

[208]　The history of the City Beautiful Movement and its successors is described in J. Juergensmeyer & T. Roberts, Land Use Planning and Control Law §§ 2.3, 2.4 (1998).

[209]　For a discussion of the 1916 New York City Building Zone Resolution and its drafting, see E. Bassett, Zoning 7–8, 20–29 (1940); McGoldrick, et al., Building Regulations in New York City 91–95 (1944); S. Toll, Zoned American 78–187 (1969).

most of the zoning enabling legislation adopted after 1923.[210] Eventually, all fifty states enacted zoning enabling legislation for municipalities, and most states also enacted zoning enabling legislation for counties.[211] Although the state zoning enabling legislation currently in force throughout the country often embodies very substantial changes from the enabling acts originally adopted, probably a majority of the current statutes still retain the substance of the New York or Standard Act models. For instance, most of the current zoning enabling acts still contain, either in identical or substantially similar language, the basic grant of power included in Sections 1 through 3 of the Standard Act, as follows:

> Sec. 1.   For the purpose of promoting health, safety, morals, or the general welfare of the community, the legislative body of cities and incorporated villages is hereby empowered to regulate and restrict the height, number of stories, and size of buildings and other structures, the percentage of lot that may be occupied, the size of yards, courts, and other open spaces, the density of population, and the location and use of buildings, structures, and land for trade, industry, residence, or other purposes.

> Sec. 2.   For any or all of said purposes the local legislative body may divide the municipality into districts of such number, shape, and area as may be deemed best suited to carry out the purposes of this act; and within such districts it may regulate and restrict the erection, construction, reconstruction, alteration, repair, or use of buildings, structures, or land. All such regulations shall be uniform for each class or kind of buildings throughout each district, but the regulations in one district may differ from those in other districts.

> Sec. 3.   Such regulations shall be made in accordance with a comprehensive plan and designed to lessen congestion in the streets; to secure safety from fire, panic, and other dangers; to promote health and the general welfare; to provide adequate light and air; to prevent the overcrowding of land; to avoid undue concentration of population; to facilitate the adequate provision of transportation, water, sewerage, schools, parks, and other public requirements. Such regulations shall be made with reasonable consideration, among other things, to the character of the district and its peculiar suitability for particular uses, and with a view to conserving the value of buildings and encouraging the most appropriate use of land throughout such municipality.

Prior to 1926, this relatively new strategy of using zoning to regulate land use in urban areas had survived constitutional attack in a majority of the jurisdictions in which its constitutionality had been challenged.[212] However, zoning had been held

---

[210] The Standard State Zoning Enabling Act (hereafter "Standard Act" in text and "SSZEA" in footnotes) is no longer in print in its original form as a publication of the U.S. Dept. of Commerce, but is reprinted in full, with the draftsmen's footnotes, as Appendix A, Am.L.Inst., A Model Land Development Code, Tent. Draft 1, p. 210 (1968). It is also reprinted, without the footnotes, in D. Mandelker, R. Cunningham & J. Payne, Planning and Control of Land Development, 197–201 (4th ed. 1995).

[211] Cunningham, Land-Use Control—The State and Local Programs, 50 Iowa L.Rev. 367, 368 (1965).

[212] These jurisdictions were California, Illinois, Kansas, Louisiana, Massachusetts, Minnesota, New York, Ohio, Oregon, and Wisconsin. See Brief *amicus curiae* filed by A. Bettman, as counsel for the Nat. Conf. on City Planning, the Nat. Housing Ass'n, and the Mass. Fed. of Town Planning Boards, in Euclid v. Ambler Realty Co., 272 U.S. 365, 47 S.Ct. 114, 71 L.Ed. 303 (1926). This brief is reprinted in A. Bettman, City and Regional Planning Papers 157 (1946).

unconstitutional in several states.[213] If the United States Supreme Court had held zoning to be unconstitutional, local governments obviously would have had to abandon the practice. Fortunately, in Village of Euclid v. Ambler Realty Co.,[214] the Court held that zoning ordinances on their face did not violate the Due Process Clause of the Fourteenth Amendment. The plaintiff alleged that Euclid's zoning ordinance reduced the value of its land by about seventy-five percent. However, the *Euclid* court did not directly address this substantive due process argument seemingly premised on the "not-unduly-oppressive" branch of Lawton v. Steele's[215] substantive due process test. Instead, the Court considered only the "facial" validity of the zoning ordinance itself—its "general scope and dominant features"[216]—and concluded that the reasons urged in support of the ordinance were "sufficiently cogent to preclude" the Court from determining that the ordinance was "clearly arbitrary and unreasonable, having no substantial relationship to the public health, safety, morals, or general welfare."[217]

In reaching this conclusion, the *Euclid* Court found that the Euclid ordinance's general exclusion of "all industrial establishments" from all but two of the ordinance's six "use" districts was clearly a reasonable exercise of the police power. The court relied heavily on analogies to the law of nuisance, although it also acknowledged that "some industries of an innocent character might fall within" a proscribed class" and thereby be unnecessarily prohibited in certain areas.[218] The Court had somewhat greater difficulty in upholding the validity of "the provisions of the ordinance excluding from residential districts apartment houses, business houses, retail stores and shops, and other like establishments," which it characterized as "really the crux of the more recent zoning legislation."[219] The Court ultimately decided, however, that such provisions were justifiable based on studies indicating that the segregation of one- and two-family dwellings from both businesses and apartments had a rational basis. Specifically, the Court noted that this

> will make it easier to provide fire apparatus suitable for the character and intensity of the development of each section; * * * will increase the safety and security of home life, greatly tend to prevent accidents, especially to children, by reducing the traffic and resulting confusion in residential sections, decrease noise and other conditions which produce or intensify nervous disorders, preserve a more favorable environment in which to rear children, etc.[220]

The *Euclid* opinion closed with a warning that "when, if ever, the provisions set forth in the ordinance in tedious and minute detail, come to be concretely applied to particular premises, * * * or to particular conditions, or to be considered in connection

---

[213] These jurisdictions were Delaware, Georgia, Maryland, Missouri, and New Jersey. See A. Bettman, Brief, Id.

[214] 272 U.S. 365, 47 S.Ct. 114, 71 L.Ed. 303 (1926).

[215] 152 U.S. 133, 14 S.Ct. 499, 38 L.Ed. 385 (1894). See discussion supra § 9.6.

[216] The Bettman Brief *amicus curiae,* supra note 212, asked the Court to limit its review of "comprehensive zoning" in this way, instead of considering "the contentions of the parties" as to "the reasonableness or arbitrariness of the Euclid Village ordinance itself in its districting of the particular property of the appellee."

[217] 272 U.S. at 395, 47 S.Ct. at 121. The Court employed the "deferential" standard of review and, in substance, recognized a presumption that the zoning ordinance was valid.

[218] See 272 U.S. at 388, 47 S.Ct. at 119.

[219] See 272 U.S. at 390, 47 S.Ct. at 119.

[220] See 272 U.S. at 394, 47 S.Ct. at 120.

with specific complaints, some of them, or even many of them, may be found to be clearly arbitrary and unreasonable."[221] This dictum—which uses substantive due process rather than "taking" language—seemed to foreshadow a continuing "watchdog" role for the Supreme Court in zoning cases. In the first few years after *Euclid*, the Supreme Court did review some additional zoning cases. Perhaps most significantly, in the 1928 case of Nectow v. City of Cambridge[222] the court held that a residential use classification as applied to a small part of the plaintiff's land violated substantive due process.[223] However, the Supreme Court generally refused to review zoning cases from 1928 through the 1960s and did not again become active in reviewing zoning cases until the mid-1970s. Consequently, for almost half a century state courts were primarily responsible for developing the law of zoning. During this period, with the general validity of zoning established by *Euclid*,[224] state courts reached varying conclusions as to the applicability of the substantive due process and "taking" tests to zoning cases.[225]

§ 9.12 PLANNING: RELATIONSHIP TO ZONING

Section 3 of the Standard Zoning Enabling Act, quoted in the preceding section, began with the words, "Such [zoning] regulations shall be made in accordance with a comprehensive plan. . . ." In the early years of American zoning, questions lingered about the meaning of this phrase. Did it mean that localities needed to create and adopt a formal comprehensive plan, such as those described in section 9.10 above, before the municipality could adopt its first zoning ordinance? If so, then most American zoning at that time would have been invalid because in those early days most cities and counties adopted zoning ordinances before crafting any formal comp plan. Fortunately, courts eventually affirmed that formal plans did not need to precede zoning. Instead, if there is no formal plan the phrase "in accordance with" merely required that zoning regulations be "comprehensive" and form a rational pattern.[226] The corollary, of course, remains true: if the zoning of a certain area is seriously out of whack with that rational pattern, it violates the state zoning enabling act and is invalid.

Today, most local governments or their planning commissions have adopted a formal comp plan. Generally, this plan itself does not restrict the use of any land—that is the role of zoning ordinances.[227] But to what extent must zoning ordinances be "in

---

[221] See 272 U.S. at 395, 47 S.Ct. at 121.

[222] 277 U.S. 183, 48 S.Ct. 447, 72 L.Ed. 842 (1928).

[223] The Court relied on the finding of a master appointed by the state trial court to the effect that "the districting of the plaintiff's land in a residence district would not promote the health, safety convenience and general welfare of the inhabitants of that part of the defendant city." Although the Court concluded that "because of the industrial and railroad purposes to which the immediately adjoining lands * * * have been devoted and for which they are zoned, the locus is of comparatively little value for the limited uses permitted by the zoning ordinance," the Court did *not* hold that the ordinance amounted to a *de facto* "taking" nor did it cite Pennsylvania Coal Co. v. Mahon, 260 U.S. 393, 43 S.Ct. 158, 67 L.Ed. 322 (1922), discussed in § 9.5, supra.

[224] In some states where comprehensive zoning was held to violate the state constitutions—e.g., Georgia and New Jersey—constitutional amendments were required to legalize the comprehensive zoning technique.

[225] In many cases it is not clear whether the courts are applying a constitutional or a statutory test (i.e., are the zoning regulations *ultra vires*). Even where a court bases its decision on constitutional grounds it is often unclear whether the court is relying on the state or the federal constitution, or both, perhaps because the courts assume that it makes no difference.

[226] Still the leading decision is Kozesnik v. Township of Montgomery, 24 N.J. 154, 131 A.2d 1 (1957). For a critical analysis, see Haar, In Accordance With a Comprehensive Plan, 68 Harv. L. Rev. 1154 (1955).

[227] Holmgren v. City of Lincoln, 199 Neb. 178, 256 N.W.2d 686 (1977); Ford v. Board of County Comm'rs, 924 P.2d 91 (Wyo.1996); J. Juergensmeyer & T. Roberts, Land Use Planning and Control Law § 2.10 (1998).

accordance with" that plan? In most states, zoning ordinances need not slavishly conform to the comp plan but that the plan is a general "guide" or "blueprint" for the actual zoning.[228] Courts have not always invalidated zoning regulations that are somewhat inconsistent with the plan,[229] although some courts place more emphasis on consistency with the comp plan than others.[230] A minority of states require zoning ordinances to strictly comply with the applicable comp plan.[231]

In a number of states the relationship between planning and zoning has undergone substantial change over time. The Oregon Supreme Court held, *inter alia,* in Fasano v. Board of County Commissioners of Washington County[232] that rezoning decisions must be based on the comprehensive land use plan previously adopted by the county planning commission. However, *Fasano* was applicable only to rezoning decisions. Two years after *Fasano,* the same court held, in Baker v. City of Milwaukie,[233] that existing zoning regulations must be changed to conform to a subsequently adopted comprehensive land use plan. However, a later intermediate appellate court decision interpreted *Baker* to mean that zoning ordinances need not conform when they are more restrictive than the plan requires.[234] Though these Oregon decisions of the 1970s evoked considerable scholarly comment at the time, they had little or no following in the appellate decisions of other states.[235]

What did ultimately emerge, however, is legislation in several states making local comprehensive plans mandatory and possibly also requiring that zoning be "consistent" with such plans. Shortly after the *Baker* decision, the Oregon legislature enacted legislation requiring local governments within the state to adopt comprehensive land use plans based upon the state Land Conservation and Development Commission's (LCDC's) statewide planning goals and to make all zoning and other land use regulations conform to the local comprehensive plan.[236] The Oregon planning legislation, which provides for state-level review of all local plans and regulatory ordinances to determine whether they comply with the statewide planning goals, survived multiple attempts at repeal through statewide voter referenda.[237]

But see Board of County Comm'rs v. Conder, 927 P.2d 1339 (Colo. 1996), in which subdivision approval was denied because a county ordinance said that "consideration should be given" to the county comprehensive plan.

[228] See, e.g., Smith v. City of Little Rock, 279 Ark. 4, 648 S.W.2d 454 (1983); Manning v. Boston Redevelopment Auth., 400 Mass. 444, 509 N.E.2d 1173 (1987).

[229] E.g., Rosenberg v. Planning Bd., 155 Conn. 636, 236 A.2d 895 (1967); Cascio v. Town Council, 158 Conn. 111, 256 A.2d 685 (1969); Nottingham Village, Inc. v. Baltimore County, 266 Md. 339, 292 A.2d 680 (1972); Miller v. Abrahams, 239 Md. 263, 211 A.2d 309 (1965); Ward v. Knippenberg, 416 S.W.2d 746 (Ky.1967); Biske v. City of Troy, 381 Mich. 611, 166 N.W.2d 453 (1969) (plan adopted by planning comm'n but not by governing body); Cheney v. Village 2 at New Hope, Inc., 429 Pa. 626, 241 A.2d 81 (1968); Barrie v. Kitsap County, 93 Wn.2d 843, 613 P.2d 1148 (1980) (comp plan is "guide").

[230] E.g., Scull v. Coleman, 251 Md. 6, 246 A.2d 223 (1968); Norbeck Village Joint Venture v. Montgomery County Council, 254 Md. 59, 254 A.2d 700 (1969).

[231] See, e.g., City of Cape Canaveral v. Mosher, 467 So. 2d 468 (Fla. Dist. Ct. App. 1985); HNS Dev., LLC v. People's Counsel for Baltimore Cty., 200 Md. App. 1, 15, 24 A.3d 167, 176 (2011).

[232] 264 Or. 574, 507 P.2d 23 (1973).

[233] 271 Or. 500, 533 P.2d 772 (1975).

[234] Pohrman v. Klamath County Comm'rs, 25 Or.App. 613, 550 P.2d 1236 (1976).

[235] D. Mandelker, Land Use Law § 3.15 (4th ed. 1997).

[236] See Or.Rev.Stat. ch. 197.

[237] See 49 Planning, No. 1, January 1983, p. 7.

California was one of the first states to make local comprehensive planning mandatory.[238] The state's comprehensive planning legislation is quite detailed and sets out both mandatory and optional plan elements for inclusion in local comprehensive plans. The California zoning enabling statute requires all local zoning ordinances to be consistent with the local comprehensive land use plan and defines "consistent" to mean that "[t]he various land uses authorized by the ordinance are [to be] compatible with the objectives, policies, general land uses and programs specified in [the] plan."[239] This statutory definition of "consistent" was later amplified by a Guideline issued by the California Office of Planning and Research, which provides that the consistency requirement is satisfied if local regulatory ordinances "will not inhibit or obstruct the attainment of" the policies articulated in the local comprehensive plan. Compliance with the consistency requirement can be enforced by court action.[240]

The Florida Local Government Comprehensive Planning Act of 1975,[241] like the California comprehensive planning legislation, mandates planning by all Florida counties, municipalities, and special districts.[242] County plans are controlling in municipalities and special districts that fail to prepare comprehensive plans, and the state may impose its own plan on any county that fails to prepare a comprehensive plan. Both mandatory and optional elements of the local comprehensive plan are set out in great detail in the statute.[243] Among the mandatory elements is a "housing element" requiring provision for low- and moderate-income housing needs.[244] The statute includes the following "consistency" provision: "After a comprehensive plan * * * has been adopted * * * all development undertaken by, and all actions taken in regard to development orders by, government agencies in regard to land covered by such plan * * * shall be consistent with such plan. * * * All land development regulations enacted or amended shall be consistent with the adopted comprehensive plan[.]"[245] This requirement is reinforced by a statement that the intent of the planning act is that local land development regulations shall implement the comprehensive plan, and a provision for judicial review of the consistency of governmental actions or land development regulations with the plan.[246]

In 1989 the State of Washington adopted its Growth Management Act, somewhat like the Oregon legislation, requiring its more populous counties and others that elect to join in to have county comprehensive plans and comp plans for each city within those counties. A state agency, the Department of Ecology, reviews these plans, with the power

[238] See West's Ann.Cal.Gov.Code § 65300 et seq. for the current planning legislation.

[239] West's Ann.Cal.Gov.Code § 65860(a)(iii). There is a comparable requirement for local and subdivision regulations; see id. § 66473.5.

[240] Id. § 65750; see, e.g., Orange Citizens for Parks & Recreation v. Superior Court, 2 Cal. 5th 141, 385 P.3d 386 (2016) (rejecting the City of Orange's determination that a residential development was "consistent" with its General Plan).But see Kennedy Com. v. City of Huntington Beach, 16 Cal. App. 5th 841, 843, Cal. Rptr. 3d 665 (Ct. App. 2017) (holding that charter cities are exempt from the statutory requirement that specific plans and zoning ordinances be consistent with the cities' general plan).

[241] Local Government Comprehensive Planning Act of 1975, West's Fla.Stat.Ann. §§ 163.3161–163.3211.

[242] See, e.g., Nassau County v. Willis, 41 So. 3d 270 (Fla. 1st DCA 2010) (the comprehensive plan is similar to a constitution for all development within the governmental boundary).

[243] Id. § 163.3177.

[244] Id. § 163.3177(6)(f).

[245] Id. § 163.3194(1)(a).

[246] Id. § 163.3201.

to make them conform to its requirements. An important feature of the Act is that "growth areas" must be established, generally around existing urbanized areas, and urban growth confined to those areas. "Development regulations," which includes zoning, must be "consistent" with the comprehensive plan. The state may invoke financial sanctions against a county or city whose comp plan or regulations are found to be in violation of the Act.[247] At least nine states, in addition to the states discussed above, have also passed legislation requiring preparation and adoption of local comprehensive plans and consistency of zoning regulations with the adopted land use plan.[248]

Those who advocate mandatory comprehensive planning and consistency of land use regulations with comprehensive plans[249] obviously tend to favor state legislation like that described above. However, in much of the country local governments remain relatively free to determine for themselves how closely their zoning ordinances will follow their comprehensive plans.

§ 9.13   ROLE OF THE STATE LEGISLATURE

Since zoning is carried on by local governments, those governments must obtain their power to zone by grant or delegation under state legislation. Statutes that authorize the formation of cities and counties always contain a general grant of the "police power," typically expressed as the power to provide for the "public health, safety, [morals,] and welfare." However, except in a very few states, this general grant has been held not to cover the power to zone land. Instead, a specific zoning enabling act akin to the Standard Zoning Enabling Act (SZEA) is required.[250] Although that basic question is now moot because every state has at least one zoning enabling act, some subsidiary questions still remain. One is whether a city or county that has home-rule powers may choose to zone under those powers instead of under the otherwise applicable zoning enabling act. This is not the place to attempt a full delineation of home-rule powers, but in general they are powers granted by the statutes or constitutions of most states to their larger cities or counties, which grant them enhanced powers of self-government, beyond those enjoyed by other cities or counties. The scope of home-rule powers differs among the states. However, where these powers exist most courts that have addressed the question have decided that home-rule cities and counties may zone under their special powers at least somewhat free of the restraints of the ordinary zoning enabling acts. However, some states limit the power to zone under home rule may be limited as to certain subject matter and many states seem to limit it on the theory that such home rule-empowered zoning may not be in conflict with state law.[251]

---

[247] See Wash. Rev. Code Ch. 36.70A, especially §§ .040, .110, .120, .302–.345.

[248] E.g., Ariz.Rev.Stat. § 9–462.01E (municipalities); Del. Code. Ann. tit. ix, § 2653(b), § 2656; Ky. Rev. Stat. Ann. § 100.187; Me. Rev. Stat. Ann. tit. 30–A, § 4352.2; Neb. Rev. Stat. § 23–114.03; Nev. Rev. Stat. Ann. 278.150, 278.160(1)(e), 278.250(2); N.J. Stat. Ann. § 40:55D–62(a); R.I. Gen. Laws § 45–22.2–2; Wis. Stat. § 66.0295(2). For a general analysis of how different states view comprehensive plans, see Edward J. Sullivan & Michael J. Michel, Ramapo Plus Thirty: The Changing Role of the Plan in Land Use Regulation, 35 Urb. Law. 75, 86 (2003).

[249] For early advocacy of these requirements, see Haar, In Accordance with a Comprehensive Plan, 68 Harv.L.Rev. 1154 (1955); Haar, The Master Plan: An Impermanent Constitution, 20 L. & Contemp. Prob. 353 (1955). For more recent support of these requirements, see Report of ABA's Advisory Comm'n on Housing and Urban Growth, Housing for All under Law 408–410 (R. Fishman ed. 1978); D. Mandelker, The Role of the Local Comprehensive Plan in Land Use Regulation, 74 Mich. L.Rev. 900, 944–973 (1976).

[250] J. Juergensmeyer & T. Roberts, Land Use Planning and Control Law § 3.5 (1998).

[251] See Id. at § 3.7; D. Mandelker, Land Use Law § 4.25 (4th ed. 1997).

When a city or county zones under the authority of a state zoning enabling act, its local ordinances and procedures must be within the authority thus granted and must not be contrary to the enabling act. The actions taken in a given case, such as actions on an application for rezoning or a variance, must likewise be in conformity with both the enabling act and the local zoning code. For example, if the enabling act or the local code requires a certain form of notice of a hearing before the planning commission or the board of adjustment, then a failure to give such notice is a ground for reversal if the failure causes substantial prejudice.[252] As implied in the discussion of due process earlier in this chapter, a procedural defect that serious can also be the basis for a constitutional claim of denial of due process.[253] In fact, claims of statutory violations are often joined with claims of constitutional violations such as regulatory takings and denials of due process and of equal protection. If the statutory claim has merit it can be quite powerful because of the well-known judicial principle to avoid deciding constitutional questions if a case can be disposed of on another ground. Also, the result on the statutory claim may be more predictable because it may turn on positive language of the statute rather than upon such ambiguous constitutional law concepts as "unreasonable" or "no economically viable use."

Of course, claims of statutory violations arise based on not just procedural issues but on substantive issues as well. For instance, to obtain a variance a landowner applicant typically must establish under section 7 of the SZEA that, "owing to special conditions, a literal enforcement of the provisions of the ordinance will result in unnecessary hardship. . . ." The key word in this provision is "hardship", as covered later in this chapter, and many local zoning codes contain identical language. Suppose a landowner applies for a variance and is not granted it on the ground of no "hardship." Upon appeal of the decision to the local court of general jurisdiction, courts are likely to look to a vast repertoire of appellate cases in which that word was interpreted in factual situations as near as may be found to the case at hand. The question is usually a mixed question of fact and law, but at bottom it is a question of interpretation of the state enabling act.

§ 9.14   ROLE OF THE LOCAL LEGISLATIVE BODY

The local legislative body, usually the city council in a city or the board of county commissioners in a county, is the keystone of local zoning. Section 1 of the original SZEA authorized "the legislative body of cities and incorporated villages" to engage in zoning. As described earlier in this chapter it is typically up to the local legislative body to make the first move, to appoint a planning commission, to direct it or a hired planning consultant to draft the initial zoning ordinances and comprehensive plan, and to adopt the initial zoning code. Section 4 of SZEA empowers the legislative body to amend or supplement the initial code when it sees fit, including final action on the many individual applications for changes in zoning designation. It usually receives a recommendation for action or inaction from the planning commission, but the legislative body may entirely reject the recommendation if it chooses. However that body acts, its decision is of course legislative in nature and reviewed as such by a court, which will accord the action a

---

[252] See, e.g., American Oil Corp. v. City of Chicago, 29 Ill.App.3d 988, 331 N.E.2d 67 (1975) (lack of notice of hearing fatal); Bowen v. Story County Bd. of Supvrs., 209 N.W.2d 569 (Iowa 1973) (failure to provide statutory notice of hearing fatal).

[253] See, American Oil Corp. v. City of Chicago, 29 Ill.App.3d 988, 331 N.E.2d 67 (1975) (lack of notice of hearing denied due process).

presumption of validity. As vacancies occur in the membership of the planning commission, their replacements must be appointed by the local legislative body. If the municipality is large enough to have a professional planning director, he or she is usually hired by the legislative body, which exercises general oversight over the conduct of the planning department.

The local legislative body also appoints the initial board of adjustment and fills vacancies as they occur in that body. Under the classic pattern set out in section 7 of the SZEA, decisions of the board of adjustment may be reviewed directly by the local court of general jurisdiction; they do not pass through the local legislative body first. However, in states in which the enabling act does not require direct judicial review, municipalities are allowed to have board of adjustment decisions, or certain kinds of them, finally determined by the local legislative body.[254] Though boards of adjustment are administrative bodies and their decisions quasi-judicial, there is a divergence of opinion among courts whether a local legislative body that takes final action in such a matter acts in a legislative or administrative capacity.[255] Because of the judicial presumption that legislative acts are valid, the answer to that question may affect the scope of judicial review.

§ 9.15   LOCAL ADMINISTRATIVE BODIES

The two local administrative bodies involved in the planning-zoning process are usually called the planning commission or planning board and the board of adjustment or board of zoning appeals. This section 9.15 first describes the functions of the planning commission and then discusses the board of adjustment.

Sections 1 and 2 of the Standard Zoning Enabling Act authorized "the local legislative body" to regulate land uses and to divide the municipality into zoning districts with different regulations. Section 4 generally allowed the same body to determine "the manner" for adopting the original zoning ordinance, and section 5 permitted the same body to make "changes" to the original ordinance.[256] Section 6 is of particular interest as it relates to planning commissions. It required the legislative body to appoint a "zoning commission" whose duties were to hold public hearings and to "recommend" zoning regulations and districts to the legislative body. However, the SZEA seemingly contemplated that the "zoning commission" would exist only to recommend the adoption of the original zoning ordinances and not that it would be a continuing body after that point.[257] As zoning laws actually developed, that "zoning commission" dropped out of the

---

[254] E.g., Kotrich v. County of DuPage, 19 Ill.2d 181, 166 N.E.2d 601 (1960), appeal dismissed, 364 U.S. 475, 81 S.Ct. 243, 5 L.Ed.2d 221 (1960); Corporation Way Realty Trust v. Building Comm'r, 348 Mass. 732, 205 N.E.2d 718 (1965).

[255] See Wheeler v. Gregg, 90 Cal.App.2d 348, 203 P.2d 37 (1949) (administratively); Kotrich v. County of DuPage, 19 Ill.2d 181, 166 N.E.2d 601 (1960), appeal dismissed, 364 U.S. 475, 81 S.Ct. 243, 5 L.Ed.2d 221 (1960) (legislatively); Osius v. City of St. Clair Shores, 344 Mich. 693, 75 N.W.2d 25 (1956) (administratively); Green Point Sav. Bank v. Board of Zoning App., 281 N.Y. 534, 24 N.E.2d 319 (1939), appeal dismissed 309 U.S. 633, 60 S.Ct. 719, 84 L.Ed. 990 (1940) (legislatively).

[256] The full text of SZEA is reprinted in some of the casebooks in national use, e.g., D. Mandelker, R. Cunningham & J. Payne, Planning and Control of Land Development, 197–201 (4th ed. 1995). However, the cited casebook merely summarizes section 6.

[257] The full text of section 6 is reprinted in 1 R. Anderson, American Law of Zoning § 4.09 (3d ed. 1986).

picture. In nearly all communities with zoning, it has been replaced by the "planning commission" or "planning board," a similar body that has somewhat broader functions.[258]

The planning commission, typically comprised of seven to nine members, is appointed by the local legislative body. It is essentially an administrative body that exists to make recommendations to the local legislative body for ordinances. Planning commissioners are not professional planners like the planning department or planning firms. In most localities, their members are citizens who have some familiarity with real estate such as architects, engineers, officers of lending institutions, real estate brokers, an occasional lawyer, and perhaps an ordinary homeowner or two for balance. They are citizen volunteers, usually unpaid, who meet perhaps once or twice a month. Though the commission is a separate entity from the legislative body, its functions are similar to those that might be performed by a committee of that body. Like the SZEA's zoning commission, the planning commission generally conducts studies, holds hearings, and recommends the original zoning ordinances to the legislative body. If a comprehensive plan is to be adopted before or concurrently with the original zoning ordinances, the commission also usually drafts it and at least adopts it as a working document to guide changes to the zoning ordinances. In some communities, the planning commission also recommends the comprehensive plan for adoption by the local legislative body to serve as a non-binding guide for zoning changes. Especially in small communities, the planning commission may be advised by hired professional planning consultants in formulating the original comprehensive plan and zoning ordinances.

Modern planning commissions differ from the SZEA's zoning commission in that they are permanent bodies whose functions continue after the initial adoption of zoning and a comp plan. Planning commissions are charged with the duty to conduct continuing studies and to recommend amendments to the comp plan and to the zoning ordinances. However, in practice those duties are often overshadowed by the commission's charge to handle the steady stream of citizen applications for changes in zone designations of particular parcels of land known as "rezonings" or "map amendments". The applicants for these changes are usually the owners of the subject land seeking "upzoning"—to have the land rezoned for a more intensive and valuable use than present zoning allows. On rare occasions, applicants may be nearby owners who seek to have someone else's land "downzoned" to a "lighter" zone. Regular procedures are set up for parties to file such applications with the planning commission directly or through a municipality's professional planning department.

State zoning enabling acts and local zoning codes require planning commissions to hold a public hearing on each application. Notice of the hearing is generally by publication in a local newspaper and sometimes also by the posting of notice on the subject land and mailing to landowners in the vicinity.[259] Some hearings go smoothly with little opposition, but many become quite adversarial with large numbers of opponents attending to protest intrusions of what they insist are incompatible uses into their neighborhoods. In these spirited hearings, proponents and opponents are often represented by attorneys. Hearings are conducted informally, as administrative bodies usually conduct their hearings, with about the only rule of evidence observed being a

---

[258] See 1 R. Anderson, American Law of Zoning §§ 4.08, 4.09 (3d ed. 1986); D. Mandelker, R. Cunningham & J. Payne, Planning and Control of Land Development, 198 (4th ed. 1995).

[259] For details on notice and other planning commission procedures, see 1 R. Anderson, American Law of Zoning §§ 4.11–4.14 (3d ed. 1986).

notion that evidence received must have some general relevancy to the application. For instance, planning commissions often receive, consider, and perhaps even read at their hearings, letters from interested persons, commenting on the matter at hand—a practice that would be a serious error for a court. Individuals are also allowed to speak at the hearings who may have only tangential personal interests in the application under consideration and who may ramble on about matters that are only remotely relevant.[260] However, the decision of the planning commission can have real legal consequences because its recommendation may carry great weight with the local legislative body empowered to grant or deny the application.

The board of adjustment is similar to the planning commission in some respects, but it performs quite different functions. In some small communities the planning commission may also perform the duties of a board of adjustment, but the classic pattern is for both administrative bodies to exist. Like the planning commission, the board of adjustment is a zoning administrative agency appointed by the local legislative body and usually has a similar number of members whose backgrounds are similar to those described above for members of that commission. However, while the planning commission is part of the legislative process, the board of adjustment is a quasi-judicial administrative body. Its function is to consider applications from individual landowners for permission to do things on their land that the zoning code ordinarily does not allow. Usually, a board of adjustment considers two kinds of such applications: "special exception" or "conditional use permit" applications and "variance" Applications. These are important features of zoning described briefly here and in detail in later sections of this chapter that allow departures from rigid zoning restrictions. Under the classic form of zoning code, a board of adjustment's decisions are appealable directly to the county court of general jurisdiction. However, some zoning codes make the board's decisions or certain classes of them appealable to the local legislative body before they can be appealed to the court.

Special exceptions and conditional use permits add flexibility to zoning codes. Typical zoning codes list two kinds of permitted uses for each zone: "regularly" permitted uses and "specially" or "conditionally" permitted uses." Landowners need no special zoning permission for regularly permitted uses, but they must apply to the board of adjustment for special permits for specially or conditionally permitted uses. Specially permitted uses are ones that are generally desirable but could disturb regular permitted uses if conducted in the wrong place or under wrong conditions within a zone. Classic examples are utility substations, churches, and schools in residential zones or gas stations in some commercial zones. The ordinance for a given zone generally lists the specially permitted uses and prescribes some conditions for them beyond those normally required. Though boards of adjustment have some discretion to deny conditional use applications, they will nearly always be granted if the applicant meets the special conditions of the ordinance and perhaps some further conditions the board imposes. Special exceptions and conditional use permits are discussed in more detail in section 9.28, infra.

---

[260] The description of the conduct of planning commission proceedings is based upon the author's own observation of a number of such meetings. W. Stoebuck. But if you do not believe me, read the observations of the "dean" of American planning attorneys, the late Richard Babcock. See his delicious description of those proceedings in R. Babcock, The Zoning Game, Ch. 9, "The Interested Parties," pp. 138–52 (1966).

The other main job of a board of adjustment is to consider applications for variances. Decisions on these are far more discretionary than those for special exceptions and are thus more likely to lead to litigation. Most state zoning enabling acts and local zoning codes grant boards of adjustment the power to "vary" or waive any provision of the zoning code if, in the peculiar circumstances of a given case, the literal application of the code would cause an owner undue "hardship." "Hardship" is usually defined to mean that, unless the variance is granted, the owner can make no profitable use of the land—a standard that obviously has constitutional overtones. Variances fall into two general categories: "bulk" variances and "use" variances. Bulk variances waive physical requirements such as building setback lines or lot coverage limits and usually make up the largest percentage of variances granted. Use variances permit owners to make some use of land that is not normally permitted within the zone as a regularly or specially permitted use. Use variances are forbidden by law in several states or by ordinance in a number of communities, and where they are permitted they tend to require a stronger showing of hardship than for bulk variances. Use variance applications are also more likely to end up in litigation. Variances are discussed in detail later in section 9.29 of this chapter.

§ 9.16 ORIGINAL ZONING

As a starting point, it is worthwhile to briefly describe how communities originally adopt zoning ordinances. When a new city is formed out of a previously unincorporated area of a county, one of the first steps for the new town's city council is likely to be the adoption of a resolution continuing the county's zoning as an interim, temporary measure. Then, the city's planning commission develops the city's own zoning code and recommends it to the city council for adoption. The following paragraphs provide a basic overview of the general characteristics of the simple zoning code that cities in these situations might adopt.[261]

After some preliminary provisions reciting that the city establishes this zoning code for the general welfare, better governance of the city, rational use and development of land, etc., a zoning code then gets down to business. It often comprises a lengthy "title" in the overall city code. Various "chapters" within that title each describe different kinds of zones, typically including several types of residential zones, commercial zones, and industrial zones. Each such chapter is then divided into "sections" that describe the regularly permitted uses, the specially permitted uses, bulk restrictions, height restrictions, perhaps off-street parking requirements, and so forth. The chapters that provide for the several kinds of commercial and industrial zones usually have analogous kinds of descriptions and restrictions. Some modern zoning ordinances may prescribe specific "performance standards" within certain commercial and industrial zones, such as requirements that industrial enterprises keep noise or pollution below certain technically described levels.

In areas of the new city that are already fully developed or nearly so, the new zoning designations usually conform to the existing uses. As discussed in the next section of this chapter, when a new zoning code imposes restrictions that are inconsistent with existing

---

[261] The material in this section, which is mostly descriptive, is common knowledge to anyone who has worked with zoning. Further elaboration of the matters described here will be found in 2 R. Anderson, American Law of Zoning §§ 9.02–9.79 (3d ed. 1986); and D. Mandelker, R. Cunningham & J. Payne, Planning and Control of Land Development (casebook), 204–11 (4th ed. 1995), which, along with descriptive text, contains a "typical zoning ordinance."

land uses those existing uses are typically allowed to continue anyway as "preexisting nonconforming uses." Zone lines are generally drawn to follow the centers of streets or at least boundaries of land ownership, at least partly because of the influence of the United States Supreme Court's 1928 decision in Nectow v. City of Cambridge.[262] New zoning codes tend to have their greatest effects in undeveloped or lightly developed areas of new cities, where they can shape development yet to come.

When a newly-formed city has a formal comprehensive plan, the zoning code usually has a chapter describing it, including such elements as transportation, land use, public areas, and open space. The comp plan's time span and geographic reach are also often described.

Other chapters of a typical new city's zoning ordinance will establish the planning commission and board of adjustment. These provisions will describe their numbers of members, their qualifications, their terms of office, and the manner of their appointment by the city council. For the planning commission, its duties in formulating and maintaining the comp plan and zoning ordinances and making recommendations to the city council will be delegated. For the board of adjustment, its duties in processing special exceptions or conditional-use permits and variances will be outlined. If hearing examiners are to handle some kinds of applications, they will be provided for and their relationships to the planning commission or board of adjustment described.

Very importantly, somewhere in the zoning code detailed procedures must be spelled out for the making and processing of applications for rezonings, special exceptions, variances, and any other kinds of special permits. The requirements that applicants must satisfy to obtain any such form of zoning relief, such as the definition of a "hardship" for a variance, will be set forth. The conduct of hearings and especially the manner of notice is likewise carefully described. Particularly in connection with these matters, scrupulous attention must be paid to the state zoning enabling act.

§ 9.17 NONCONFORMITIES

Obviously, when the first zoning ordinances were adopted in the 1920s and 1930s there were many parcels of land being used in ways that did not conform to the new zoning requirements. For instance, many established commercial land uses such as neighborhood grocery stores were already operating in newly-designated single-family residential zones. In other instances, buildings were situated closer to lot boundary lines than the new zoning allowed. Similar situations can still arise today when a new cities is carved out of unincorporated parts of a county and the city then adopts its own zoning code. Amendments to existing zoning ordinances can also give rise to these situations. These instant violations resulting from new or amended zoning codes are commonly known as "preexisting nonconforming uses." However, since that phrase technically describes only uses that violate use restrictions this section instead uses the term "nonconformities," which also encompasses bulk and height violations. Local governments naturally had to determine what to do with such nonconformities. Should

---

[262] 277 U.S. 183, 48 S.Ct. 447, 72 L.Ed. 842 (1928). The Court held that zoning of Nectow's land was invalid, as a violation of substantive dues process. It is debatable whether the due process was denied because the zoning ordinance served no public purpose or because it was "unduly oppressive" on the landowner. But it is clear that the critical factual problem was that the city drew the zone line down the middle of Nectow's parcel of land, rather than drawing down adjacent Francis Street. Planners have kept that fact in mind ever since.

they require them to cease immediately or "grandfather" them in and allow them to continue?

The draftsmen of the Standard State Zoning Enabling Act omitted any reference to nonconformities, and most early zoning enabling legislation was also silent with respect to the subject. Courts and local governments interpreted this silence to mean that nonconformities could continue indefinitely despite their inconsistency with new or amended zoning provisions. Many early planners surely would have preferred to abolish preexisting nonconformities, but they seemingly feared that eliminating them without compensation could spur due process or regulatory takings claims. Decisions such as the California Supreme Court's decision in Jones v. City of Los Angeles made this more than an idle threat.[263] The Supreme Court's 1978 decision in Penn Central Transportation Co. v. City of New York likewise made clear that the destruction of "investment-backed expectations" was a factor that disposes toward a land use regulation's being declared unconstitutional.[264] Moreover, the early planners feared that legislatures would hesitate to enact zoning enabling legislation that they felt courts would strike down.[265]

A few states enacted enabling acts expressly providing that nonconformities could not be eliminated without payment of compensation.[266] And in cases where the zoning enabling act was silent as to nonconformities, early zoning ordinances almost invariably contained express provisions authorizing their continuance. Accordingly, preexisting nonconformities are not illegal and are often expressly allowed. However, since nonconformities were allowed to continue only grudgingly many early zoning ordinances also imposed various restrictive regulations designed to hasten their ultimate demise. Such provisions are still a standard feature of many local zoning ordinances. One such restriction prohibits or severely limits the physical extension or expansion of nonconforming uses—a provision that has caused no end of litigation.[267] Other familiar provisions impose restrictions on the repair, alteration, or reconstruction of

---

[263] 211 Cal. 304, 295 P. 14 (1930). *Jones* invalidated, on due process grounds, a zoning ordinance that would have compelled a private hospital to close down. But cf. DeKalb Stone, Inc. v. County of DeKalb, 106 F.3d 956 (11th Cir.1997), which held that, since the right to continue a nonconforming use is a state-created property right, it is not entitled to protection under the Due Process Clause of the 14th Amendment to the U.S. Constitution.

[264] 438 U.S. 104, 98 S.Ct. 2646, 57 L.Ed.2d 631 (1978). Justice Brennan's phrase in that opinion, "investment backed expectations," is a fancy way of saying, "uses in which the landowner has already made an investment."

[265] See Comment, 39 Yale L.J. 735, 737 (1930); E. Bassett, Zoning 108, 112 (1940); Note, 35 Va.L.Rev. 348, 352 (1949).

[266] E.g., Mich.Comp.Laws Ann. § 125.583a.

[267] E.g., see and compare the following decisions. Hansen Bros. Enterprises v. Board of Supervisors, 12 Cal.4th 533, 907 P.2d 1324, 48 Cal.Rptr.2d 778 (1996) (increase of mining operation from smaller to larger area was allowable intensification, not expansion), reversing a California Appeals Court decision; Anderson v. Board of Adjustment, 931 P.2d 517 (Colo.App.1996) (unauthorized "enlargement" of nonconforming use for service station to add automated auto wash); Campbell v. Rose, 221 A.D.2d 527, 634 N.Y.S.2d 137 (1995) (unauthorized expansion of greeting card business to add business of compiling mailing lists); Waukesha County v. Pewaukee Marina, Inc., 187 Wis.2d 18, 522 N.W.2d 536 (1994) (existing nonconforming use, a marina, might add dockage space but could not add retail sales). Generally, see 4 N.Williams, Am.Land Planning Law ch. 113 (1975 and Supp.1982).

nonconforming structures[268] and prohibit the resumption of nonconforming uses after "abandonment" or "discontinuance."[269]

One reason early planners allowed nonconformities to continue was that they believed the passage of time would take care of the matter and these nonconformities would eventually wither away. In practice, however, nonconformities, especially nonconforming uses, have tended not to disappear as the zoning pioneers expected they would. In some cases—for example, where there is a neighborhood grocery store or gas station in a residence district—nonconforming uses enjoy a monopoly position that only helps to prolong its continuance. Consequently, beginning in the 1950s, a growing number of local governments began adopting zoning ordinance amendments that required termination of nonconformities—mostly nonconforming uses—within some specified time. Such provisions came to be known as "amortization" provisions, apparently because it was thought that the owner of a nonconforming use could recover, or "amortize," all or a major part of his investment in the use during the period during which it was authorized to continue. The types of nonconforming uses required to be terminated upon "amortization" vary widely across jurisdictions. Some ordinances only require termination of particular uses such as billboards, garages, gas stations, and junk yards. Others require termination of substantially all nonconforming uses. Many ordinances also usually provide different periods of "amortization" for different types of non-conforming uses. In general, short periods such as one or two years are provided for "open land" uses or nonconforming uses in conforming structures. Much longer periods— often as much as ten or twenty years—are provided for nonconforming structures which cannot be brought into conformance with the zoning ordinance at reasonable expense.[270]

A few early cases sustained zoning ordinance provisions requiring termination of nonconforming uses either immediately or after a relatively short time.[271] Since 1950, the cases have been in conflict but a majority of the cases sustain mandatory termination requirements where the "amortization" period is found to be "reasonable." Courts seldom attempt any precise measurement of the life of the use or of the value loss when amortization terminates it before the end of that life. Instead, they tend to simply wet their judicial fingers and hold them to the wind to determine what is "reasonable."[272] In

---

[268] See, e.g., Application of O'Neal, 243 N.C. 714, 92 S.E.2d 189 (1956); Granger v. Board of Adjustment, 241 Iowa 1356, 44 N.W.2d 399 (1950). Generally, see 4 N.Williams, Am.Land Planning Law ch. 114 (1975 and Supp.1982).

[269] See Annot., 56 A.L.R.3d 14, 43–46 (1974); 4 N. Williams, Am.Land Planning Law ch. 115 (1975 and Supp.1982). "Abandonment" is frequently defined to mean the non-use of a nonconforming use for some specific period of time, such as one year.

[270] Generally, see R. Scott, the Effect of Nonconforming Land-Use Amortization (Am.Soc. of Planning Officials, Planning Advis.Serv.Report 280, May 1972); 4 N.Williams, Am.Land Planning Law ch. 116 (1975 and Supp.1982).

[271] E.g., Reinman v. City of Little Rock, 237 U.S. 171, 35 S.Ct. 511, 59 L.Ed. 900 (1914); Hadacheck v. Sebastian, 239 U.S. 394, 36 S.Ct. 143, 60 L.Ed. 348 (1915); State ex rel. Dema Realty Co. v. McDonald, 168 La. 172, 121 So. 613 (1929), appeal dismissed 280 U.S. 556, 50 S.Ct. 16, 74 L.Ed. 612 (1929); State ex rel. Dema Realty Co. v. Jacoby, 168 La. 752, 123 So. 314 (1929); Standard Oil Co. v. City of Tallahassee, 87 F.Supp. 145 (N.D.Fla.1949), affirmed 183 F.2d 410 (5th Cir.1950), cert. denied 340 U.S. 892, 71 S.Ct. 208, 95 L.Ed. 647 (1950).

[272] E.g., Livingston Rock & Gravel Co. v. County of Los Angeles, 43 Cal.2d 121, 272 P.2d 4 (1954); City of Los Angeles v. Gage, 127 Cal.App.2d 442, 274 P.2d 34 (1954); Spurgeon v. Board of Commissioners of Shawnee County, 181 Kan. 1008, 317 P.2d 798 (1957); Grant v. Mayor & City Council of Baltimore, 212 Md. 301, 129 A.2d 363 (1957); Stoner McCray System v. City of Des Moines, 247 Iowa 1313, 78 N.W.2d 843 (1956); Harbison v. City of Buffalo, 4 N.Y.2d 553, 176 N.Y.S.2d 598, 152 N.E.2d 42 (1958); Hatfield v. City of Fayetteville, 278 Ark. 544, 647 S.W.2d 450 (1983); New Castle v. Rollins Outdoor Advertising, Inc., 475 A.2d 355 (Del.1984). See especially Justice Van Voorhis's scathing dissent in the *Harbison* case, in which he

most of the cases where the "amortization" technique has been sustained the nonconforming use required to be terminated has been nuisance-like and has not involved a large capital investment by the landowner.[273]

Though "amortization" continues to be a feature of many if not most zoning codes in larger cities and counties, over the years some local zoning administrators have expressed their disenchantment with the technique.[274] The American Law Institute's position as of the 1970s is expressed in the following excerpt from its Commentary to Article 4 of the Model Land Development Code:[275]

> [T]he existing law of nonconforming uses consists of ineffective or unenforced regulations that seek to promote a poorly-defined concept—conformity—the value of which seems increasingly questionable. Considerable confusion has resulted. * * * The difference between a nonconforming building and a building constructed in violation of law becomes increasingly fuzzy, and boards of adjustment regularly grant variances from any attempt by the zoning officials to limit the expansion of nonconforming uses. * * * Nuisance-type ordinances are likely to be more effective means of eliminating noxious uses than any regulations artificially based on the desire to promote homogeneous land uses.

§ 9.18 BULK AND HEIGHT REGULATIONS

The Standard State Zoning Enabling Act expressly empowered local governments "to regulate and restrict the height, number of stories, and size of buildings and other structures, the percentage of lot that may be occupied, the size of yards, courts, and other open spaces, [and] the density of population."[276] Current zoning enabling acts contain substantially the same grant of power to regulate the height and bulk of structures, the relation between structures and the open space surrounding them, lot sizes, and the density of population.

Restrictions on the height of buildings are among the oldest forms of land use control in the United States. In New York, Boston, and Baltimore, such restrictions were adopted long before there were any comprehensive zoning ordinances in an attempt to deal with the problem of growing congestion in urban areas in the late nineteenth

---

condemns "amortization" as "a catch phrase," an "empty shibboleth," which has "not the same meaning which it carries in law or accounting."

Recent cases upholding required amortization of nonconforming uses include the following: Tahoe Regional Planning Agency v. King, 233 Cal.App.3d 1365, 285 Cal.Rptr. 335 (1991) (5 year amortization period reasonable); Metromedia, Inc. v. City of San Diego, 26 Cal.3d 848, 164 Cal.Rptr. 510, 610 P.2d 407 (1980), reversed on other grounds 453 U.S. 490, 101 S.Ct. 2882, 69 L.Ed.2d 800 (1981) (upholding amortization schedule requiring nonconforming signs to be removed within one to five years); Lone v. Montgomery County, 85 Md.App. 477, 584 A.2d 142 (1991) (ten year amortization period was reasonable on the facts).

Contra: Art Neon Co. v. City & County of Denver, 488 F.2d 118 (10th Cir.1973), cert. denied 417 U.S. 932, 94 S.Ct. 2644, 41 L.Ed.2d 236 (1974) (requiring removal of signs over a five year period was invalid); O'Connor v. City of Moscow, 69 Idaho 37, 202 P.2d 401, 9 A.L.R.2d 1031 (1949); Ailes v. Decatur County Area Planning Commission, 448 N.E.2d 1057 (Ind.1983); City of Akron v. Chapman, 160 Ohio St. 382, 116 N.E.2d 697, 42 A.L.R.2d 1140 (1953).

[273] See R. Scott, the Effect of Nonconforming Land-Use Amortization (Am.Soc. of Planning Officials, Planning Advis.Serv.Report 280, May 1972); Am.L.Inst., Model Land Development Code, Commentary to Art. 4 (1976).

[274] See R. Scott, the Effect of Nonconforming Land-Use Amortization (Am.Soc. of Planning Officials, Planning Advis.Serv.Report 280, May 1972).

[275] Am.L.Inst., Model Land Development Code at 150–158 (1976).

[276] SZEA § 1 (1926).

century. The constitutionality of municipal regulations fixing maximum building heights and creating different districts with different maximum height limits was established when challenged as a violation of the Fourteenth Amendment in Welch v. Swasey.[277] Nonetheless, the reasonableness of particular height limits is always subject to judicial review. Likewise, although maximum height limits in both business and residence districts have generally been sustained,[278] courts have uniformly held minimum height limits to be invalid.[279]

The 1916 New York City Building Zone Resolution included height and land coverage regulations primarily designed to assure adequate light and air and based on "light angles." The theory of the "light angle" was that building walls must stay behind an inclined plane which rose from the center of the street and, by "leaning" against buildings fronting on the street, defined an angle of light coming down into the street.[280] The 1916 New York Resolution also included requirements for yards and courts in its land coverage regulations. The general validity of land coverage regulations as against challenges based on the Fourteenth Amendment was established by Gorieb v. Fox,[281] which sustained regulations requiring that all new buildings should be set back from the street a distance as great as the setbacks of 60 percent of the existing houses in a block.

Many present-day zoning ordinances seek to control the bulk of structures and the relationship between structures and open spaces around them in urban central business districts through the use of "floor area ratios" and "open space ratios."[282] A "floor area ratio" (FAR) regulates the amount of permitted floor space on a given lot by specifying a mathematical relationship between the area of the lot and the floor space area allowed on the lot. The FAR is equal to the height of the building in stories times the percentage of the lot covered. Thus, for example, a FAR of 1.0 would permit either a one-story building covering the entire lot or a ten-story building covering ten percent of the lot. An "open space ratio" is the mathematical ratio between the amount of floor space on a lot and the area left open, including parking areas. Open space ratio restrictions are often coupled with "bonuses" for additional open space at ground level provided by relaxation of the applicable FAR.[283]

In residential zones for single-family and small multi-family dwellings, the building lot is the starting point for bulk regulations. Most zoning ordinances try to control lot coverage and density of population by the use of front, side, and rear setbacks, minimum lot frontage requirements, restrictions on the percentage of a lot that may be covered by

---

[277] 214 U.S. 91, 29 S.Ct. 567, 53 L.Ed. 923 (1909).

[278] E.g., La Salle National Bank of Chicago v. City of Evanston, 57 Ill.2d 415, 312 N.E.2d 625 (1974); Loyola Federal Savings & Loan Association v. Buschman, 227 Md. 243, 176 A.2d 355 (1961); William C. Haas & Co. v. City and County of San Francisco, 605 F.2d 1117 (9th Cir.1979), cert. denied 445 U.S. 928, 100 S.Ct. 1315, 63 L.Ed.2d 761 (1980); see also Penn Central Transportation Co. v. City of New York, 438 U.S. 104, 98 S.Ct. 2646, 57 L.Ed.2d 631 (1978), rehearing denied 439 U.S. 883, 99 S.Ct. 226, 58 L.Ed.2d 198 (1978). Contra: La Salle National Bank of Chicago v. City of Chicago, 5 Ill.2d 344, 125 N.E.2d 609 (1955).

[279] See, e.g., City of N. Miami v. Newsome, 203 So. 2d 634 (Fla. Dist. Ct. App. 1967); 122 Main Street Corp. v. City of Brockton, 323 Mass. 646, 84 N.E.2d 13 (1949); Brookdale Homes v. Johnson, 123 N.J.L. 602, 10 A.2d 477 (N.J. Sup. Ct. 1940); Brown v. Board of Appeals of City of Springfield, 327 Ill. 644, 159 N.E. 225, 56 A.L.R. 242 (1927).

[280] See 1 N. Williams, Am.Land Planning Law § 35.09 (1974); 3 id. §§ 70.02, 70.06 (1975). See also Toll, Zoned American 163–164 (1969).

[281] 274 U.S. 603, 47 S.Ct. 675, 71 L.Ed. 1228 (1927).

[282] See 1 N. Williams, Am.Land Planning Law ch. 37 (1974 and Supp.1982); 3 id. ch. 70 (1975 and Supp.1982).

[283] 3 id. §§ 70.10, 70.11 (1975 and Supp. 1982).

structures, and minimum lot size requirements.[284] The density of population restrictions in zones that permit apartment developments usually limit the number of dwelling units that may be built upon an acre of land. And suburban communities in some parts of the United States have imposed minimum single-family dwelling floor area requirements.

Except for minimum single-family dwelling floor area requirements—which courts have often held invalid as lacking a substantial relationship to public health, safety, morals, or welfare[285]—zoning regulations of the types listed in the preceding paragraph have generally been sustained in principle against challenges based on the Fourteenth Amendment. However, particular regulations have sometimes been held to be "unreasonable" and therefore invalid. Minimum lot size requirements have been challenged more frequently than any other types of area or density restrictions and they have generally been sustained by state courts on the ground that they protect or promote public health, safety, or general welfare in one or more of the following ways: (1) preserving the semi-rural character and appearance of suburban communities by assuring sufficient open space around buildings;[286] (2) preservation of specific historic sites and buildings in their historic settings;[287] (3) permitting low-density development of sites not easily buildable at higher densities because of their topography;[288] (4) providing large enough building sites to assure a safe water supply and safe on-site sewage disposal in areas without a public water supply or without public sanitary sewers;[289] (5) maintaining the natural capacity of the soil to absorb rainfall by limiting the area built upon, thus protecting land and buildings against flooding and soil erosion;[290] (6) controlling the rate and pattern of suburban growth to assure orderly, efficient, and economical expansion of necessary public facilities such as sewers, water mains, and schools;[291] (7) implementing specific planning principles of the proper

---

[284] See 1 id. ch. 37 (1974 and Supp. 1982); 2 id. ch. 38 (1974 and Supp.1982).

[285] E.g., Builders League of S. Jersey v. Westampton Twp., 188 N.J. Super. 559, 457 A.2d 1252 (Law. Div. 1983); Home Builders League of South Jersey, Inc. v. Township of Berlin, 81 N.J. 127, 405 A.2d 381 (1979), overruling Lionshead Lake, Inc. v. Wayne Township, 10 N.J. 165, 89 A.2d 693 (1952) (the leading case sustaining minimum floor area requirements); Appeal of Medinger, 377 Pa. 217, 104 A.2d 118 (1954); Northwood Properties Co. v. Perkins, 325 Mich. 419, 39 N.W.2d 25 (1949); Builders Service Corp. v. Planning and Zoning Comm'n, 208 Conn. 267, 545 A.2d 530 (1988) (zoning regulations establishing different minimum floor areas for single-family houses in different districts, not tied to occupancy, are invalid because they serve no legitimate zoning purpose other than "conserving the value of buildings"). But see Gackler Land Co. v. Yankee Springs Twp., 427 Mich. 562, 398 N.W.2d 393 (1986) (upholding minimum floor-area requirements) Rumson Estates, Inc. v. Mayor & Council of Borough of Fair Haven, 828 A.2d 317 (N.J. 2003) (upholding cap on floor-area for single-family dwellings because the developer failed to show the cap was unreasonable).

[286] E.g., Senior v. Zoning Comm'n of New Canaan, 146 Conn. 531, 153 A.2d 415 (1959), appeal dismissed 363 U.S. 143, 80 S.Ct. 1083, 4 L.Ed.2d 1145 (1960) (4 acres); Fischer v. Bedminister Township, 11 N.J. 194, 93 A.2d 378 (1952) (5 acres); Flora Realty & Investment Co. v. City of Ladue, 362 Mo. 1025, 246 S.W.2d 771 (1952), appeal dismissed 344 U.S. 802, 73 S.Ct. 41, 97 L.Ed. 626 (1952) (3 acres); Levitt v. Incorporated Village of Sands Point, 6 N.Y.2d 269, 189 N.Y.S.2d 212, 160 N.E.2d 501 (1959) (2 acres).

[287] E.g., County Comm'rs v. Miles, 246 Md. 355, 228 A.2d 450 (1967) (5 acres). See § 9.33, infra, for detailed discussion of historic zoning and landmark designation.

[288] E.g., Metropolitan Homes, Inc. v. Town Plan & Zoning Comm'n, 152 Conn. 7, 202 A.2d 241 (1964) (30,000 sq. ft.). See also Senior v. Zoning Comm'n of New Canaan, supra note 286; Honeck v. County of Cook, 12 Ill.2d 257, 146 N.E.2d 35 (1957) (5 acres); Flora Realty & Investment Co. v. City of Ladue, 362 Mo. 1025, 246 S.W.2d 771 (1952), appeal dismissed 344 U.S. 802, 73 S.Ct. 41, 97 L.Ed. 626 (1952).

[289] De Mars v. Zoning Comm'n, 142 Conn. 580, 115 A.2d 653 (1955) (1 acre); Zygmont v. Planning & Zoning Comm'n, 152 Conn. 550, 210 A.2d 172 (1965) (4 acres); Salamar Builders Corp. v. Tuttle, 29 N.Y.2d 221, 325 N.Y.S.2d 933, 275 N.E.2d 585 (1971) (2 acres).

[290] Bogert v. Washington Township, 25 N.J. 57, 135 A.2d 1 (1957) (1 acre).

[291] Flora Realty & Investment Co. v. City of Ladue, supra note 286; Rockaway Estates v. Rockaway Township, 38 N.J.Super. 468, 119 A.2d 461 (App.Div.1955).

organization of residential areas and location of public schools;[292] (8) promoting community identity by providing predominantly open areas ("green belts") between suburban communities;[293] (9) maintaining a community tax base and community balance by intermixing expensive, low-density housing with more modest homes in developing areas;[294] and (10) protecting the value of existing houses on large lots against the depreciation that would result "if sections here and there are developed with smaller lots."[295]

The validity of restrictions requiring minimum lot sizes larger than one acre is questionable in some states. For example, the Pennsylvania supreme court has invalidated two, three-, and four-acre lot minimums on the ground that, when the asserted justifications are balanced against the loss in value suffered by the landowner and the exclusionary effect of large lot minimums on less-than-affluent home buyers, large minimum-lot-size requirements violate the constitutional guarantee of substantive due process.[296] However, Pennsylvania has sustained minimum lot size requirements where they were not shown to be unreasonable or arbitrary.[297] In Massachusetts, the action of a suburban community in zoning one-third of its area for lots with a minimum size of two and one-half acres was held to be confiscatory and to be an improper attempt to use zoning as a substitute for condemnation in order to preserve open space.[298] And drastic "downzoning" amendments that increased the minimum lot size to five or ten acres in order to prevent development of open space have been held to constitute a *de facto* "taking" in California.[299]

Even in states where large-lot zoning has withstood constitutional challenge, the courts in recent years have viewed it as one factor that, along with other factors such as total or near-total exclusion of mobile homes and apartments, may lead to the conclusion that an entire municipal zoning ordinance is so "exclusionary" as to violate constitutional

[292] Padover v. Farmington Township, 374 Mich. 622, 132 N.W.2d 687 (1965) (20,000 sq. ft.).

[293] Norbeck Village Joint Venture v. Montgomery County Council, 254 Md. 59, 254 A.2d 700 (1969) (2 acres).

[294] Clary v. Borough of Eatontown, 41 N.J.Super. 47, 124 A.2d 54 (1956) (1/2 acre).

[295] Flora Realty & Investment Co., supra note 286.

[296] See National Land & Investment Co. v. Kohn, 419 Pa. 504, 215 A.2d 597 (1965) (4 acres, invalid); Concord Township Appeal, 439 Pa. 466, 268 A.2d 765 (1970) (2 acres, invalid; reported in A.2d sub nom. Appeal of Kit-Mar Builders, Inc.). One-acre minimums were sustained in Bilbar Construction Co. v. Easttown Township, 393 Pa. 62, 141 A.2d 851 (1958). *Concord Township Appeal* may have been qualified by subsequent Pennsylvania Commonwealth Court cases such as DeCaro v. Washington Township, 21 Pa.Cmwlth. 252, 344 A.2d 725 (1975), and Delaware County Investment Corp. v. Zoning Hearing Bd., 22 Pa. Cmwlth. 12, 347 A.2d 513 (1975), which have sustained lot minimums of more than one acre where the zoning ordinance, as a whole, was found not to be "exclusionary."

[297] See, e.g., Caste v. Zoning Hearing Bd. of Whitehall Borough, 70 Pa. Commw. 368, 453 A.2d 69 (1982) (upholding a 10-acre minimum lot requirement).

[298] Aronson v. Town of Sharon, 346 Mass. 598, 195 N.E.2d 341 (1964). One-acre lot minimums were sustained in Simon v. Town of Needham, 311 Mass. 560, 42 N.E.2d 516 (1942), probably the first "acreage zoning" case.

[299] Arastra Limited Partnership v. City of Palo Alto, 401 F.Supp. 962 (N.D.Cal. 1975), vacated after an out-of-court monetary settlement, 417 F.Supp. 1125 (1976) ("downzoning" from 1-acre to 5-acre lot minimums found to be a "taking"); see also San Diego Gas & Electric Co. v. City of San Diego, 81 Cal.App.3d 844, 146 Cal.Rptr. 103 (1978), reversed on remand from Calif.Sup.Ct., in an unpublished opinion, and appeal dismissed 450 U.S. 621, 101 S.Ct. 1287, 67 L.Ed.2d 551 (1981) (state appellate court sustained trial court's finding that rezoning land from industrial to agricultural classification and "downzoning" some agriculturally zoned land from 1-acre to 10-acre lot minimums amounted to a *de facto* "taking").

guarantees of substantive due process and equal protection.[300] "Exclusionary" zoning and other "exclusionary" land use controls are considered in a later section of this chapter.

§ 9.19 DEFINITIONS OF "FAMILY"

Since much zoning is for single-family homes, a well drafted zoning ordinance must define "single-family". The simplest and most conventional definition is that a "family" is a group of persons "living together as a single housekeeping unit." This definition causes no difficulty, of course, when a home is occupied by a traditional family of married parents and their children, nor should it cause a problem when other blood relatives live there as part of the family unit since the language does not put a limit on the number of persons in the unit. The purpose of the term "single-family" is to prevent a multi-family dwelling. But the term might also permit a fairly large number of unrelated persons, such as a group of college students, to live in a dwelling, at least if they share meals and some facilities. And that is where the rub begins.[301]

Many communities do not want communal units such as boarding houses or student group houses to be regarded as "single-families" under zoning laws. In the earlier decades of zoning, these concerns seemed to sometimes be partly based on a community's desire to preserve the sanctity of the traditional marital unit. More often, however, the concern seems to be that group homes disproportionately cause disturbances such as noise, congestion, traffic, and a careless use of property that are sometimes associated with temporary residents. Accordingly, some zoning ordinances have defined "family" so as to exclude such group homes. The most famous case involving such an ordinance is the Supreme Court decision in Village of Belle Terre v. Boraas.[302] The formula employed in the Belle Terre ordinance was to define "family" to include two categories of persons, first any number of persons related by blood or marriage and, second, a group of not over two unrelated persons. The ordinance was challenged by a group of six unrelated students at Stony Brook State College who occupied a group home on a broad range of constitutional grounds, including denial of due process. A divided Court upheld the ordinance, Justice Douglas's majority opinion finding that it protected community values such as "the blessings of quiet seclusion" and did not violate the plaintiffs' fundamental rights.

The *Belle Terre* decision was controversial, particularly among legal commentators but also in state courts. A number of state-court decisions have tested the validity of ordinances that use essentially the Belle Terre two-category formula (though some ordinances may also have other categories, too). These decisions are split in their results, some agreeing with *Belle Terre* and some reaching a contrary result on the basis of state constitutions or statutes.[303] Of course, the Supreme Court decision is normative as far

---

[300] The leading examples of anti-exclusionary-zoning cases are a number of decisions from the New Jersey Supreme Court, the most celebrated of which are Southern Burlington County NAACP v. Township of Mt. Laurel, 67 N.J. 151, 336 A.2d 713 (1975) (Mt. Laurel I); and Ditto, 92 N.J. 158, 456 A.2d 390 (1983) (Mt. Laurel II).

[301] See Borough of Glassboro v. Vallorosi, 117 N.J. 421, 568 A.2d 888 (1990), where the ordinance allowed "families" only, and the court held that 10 college students living together in a group home constituted "the functional equivalent of a family."

[302] 416 U.S. 1, 94 S.Ct. 1536, 39 L.Ed.2d 797 (1974).

[303] Examples of decisions that are generally in accord with *Belle Terre*, though their precise facts may somewhat differ, include Stegeman v. City of Ann Arbor, 213 Mich. App. 487, 540 N.W.2d 724 (1995) (group home of six college students did not qualify as "functional family" under university city ordinance); Unification

as the United States Constitution is concerned but, as that Court itself has recognized, state courts are free to interpret their own constitutions to give more, though not less, protection to personal rights than that Court does under the Federal Constitution.[304] One form of ordinance that is likely to be struck down on constitutional grounds is one that attempts to exclude certain persons who are in fact related by blood or marriage from the definition of "family." In Moore v. City of East Cleveland, a decision that followed only three years after *Belle Terre*, the United States Supreme Court held that an ordinance that so excluded certain family members violated the Due Process Clause.[305] In distinguishing *Belle Terre*, the Court said the East Cleveland ordinance cut too deeply into the family itself. One effect of *Moore* is that it drew such a fine line in distinguishing *Belle Terre* as to raise a question about the viability of that decision; it certainly is safe to say it limited *Belle Terre*. In any event, *Moore* erects a federal constitutional barrier to any ordinance that has the effect of the one in that case.

Another kind of case that has in recent years tested the meaning of "single family" in zoning ordinances is a case in which the owner of a structure that has the general configuration of a single-family dwelling wishes to use it for what might generically be called a "group home for special persons." These types of uses might include home child care (including foster homes), home care for elderly and infirm adults, group homes for physically and mentally disabled persons, drug and alcohol rehabilitation centers, or even halfway houses for felons. This section does not attempt a full discussion of the legal problems that arise when the sponsors of such a group home propose to locate it in a "residential" or "single-family-residential" zone as it would be far beyond the scope of this book. However, some similar issues are touched upon later in this chapter in section 9.27's discussion of the Federal Fair Housing Act.

One influential group-home decision is City of Cleburne v. Cleburne Living Center, the United States Supreme Court's leading equal-protection-land use regulation decision discussed previously in section 9.7 of this chapter.[306] Sponsors of the Living Center, a home for mildly handicapped persons, desired to locate it in a zone in which certain similar uses—such as general hospitals, nursing homes for the elderly, fraternity houses, and apartment houses—were allowed without a special permit but in which a "hospital for the feeble minded" required a special permit. The city denied the Living Center's application for the special permit. The Court's majority opinion, written by Justice

---

Theological Seminary v. City of Poughkeepsie, 201 A.D.2d 484, 607 N.Y.S.2d 383 (1994) (ordinance might create presumption that unrelated groups of over four persons do not comprise a family); City of Brookings v. Winker, 554 N.W.2d 827 (S.D.1996) (city ordinance that limited number of unrelated persons who could live as a family was constitutional). Examples of decisions that, more or less, reject *Belle Terre* and strike down similar ordinances on state constitutional or statutory grounds include City of Santa Barbara v. Adamson, 27 Cal.3d 123, 164 Cal.Rptr. 539, 610 P.2d 436 (1980) (city ordinance that limited to five the number of unrelated persons who could comprise "family" violated Cal. Const., Art. I's, guarantee of right of privacy); College Area Renters and Landlord Assoc. v. City of San Diego, 43 Cal.App.4th 677, 50 Cal.Rptr.2d 515 (1996) (ordinance that restricted number of unrelated adults who could occupy single-family house but exempted home owners, violated California's equal protection clause); State v. Baker, 81 N.J. 99, 405 A.2d 368 (1979) (ordinance that prohibited more than four unrelated persons to comprise "family" violated due process clause of N.J. constitution).

[304] PruneYard Shopping Center v. Robins, 447 U.S. 74, 100 S.Ct. 2035, 64 L.Ed.2d 741 (1980) (California Supreme Court could grant more, but not less, protection of free speech under its constitution than U.S. Supreme Court did under U.S. Constitution).

[305] 431 U.S. 494, 97 S.Ct. 1932, 52 L.Ed.2d 531 (1977). The ordinance allowed Mrs. Moore to have living with her one of her sons and that son's son, but it prohibited her housing the son of another son who did not live with her.

[306] 473 U.S. 432, 105 S.Ct. 3249, 87 L.Ed.2d 313 (1985).

White, either struck down the ordinance on its face or struck down the denial of the permit (one can debate which) on the ground that it denied the applicant equal protection, in violation of the 14th Amendment. Justice White said his opinion applied merely the "rational basis" test, though Justice Marshall in a separate opinion argued that the majority had applied that test unusually favorably to the Living Center.

Most state decisions on "group homes for special persons" do not rise to the level of constitutional cases but involve simply the interpretation and application of local zoning ordinances. But some, like the *Cleburne* decision, do turn on constitutional principles—usually questions of due process or equal protection—or upon an application of the Federal Fair Housing Act. An attempt to state general principles in this area almost defies analysis. However, there seems to be a growing tendency to broaden the definition of "single family" to include group homes for special persons. If an ordinance defines "family" to include not only related persons but a certain number of unrelated persons, such as six, and the group home will not house more than that number, then generally the use is allowed. If they exceed that number, then many courts will broaden the meaning to include group homes, and some will not. Some kinds of group homes seem to be treated less favorably than others for reasons that lie more in public policy or public concern than in legal theory. For example, halfway houses for felons tend to be relatively disfavored uses but home day care centers for a few children are a generally favored kind of group home. In fact, several state statutes expressly require that the latter be allowed in single-family zones.[307]

§ 9.20　ZONING FOR AESTHETIC PURPOSES

Despite Justice Sutherland's litany of possible evils listed in Village of Euclid v. Ambler Realty Co.[308] from the introduction of apartment houses into single-family-residence zones—traffic, noise, congestion, children run over in the street, etc.—the main reasons for zoning are less tangible and more tinged with aesthetic considerations. Many citizens seek a community that is well-balanced, harmonious, and attractive. It is clear that aesthetic considerations influence traditional zoning.[309] However, references to "aesthetic zoning," refer to certain kinds of zoning that are more expressly based upon, and tend to focus on, aesthetic considerations. Leading examples are anti-billboard ordinances, architectural-design restrictions, and zoning for historic preservation purposes. Such land use controls have been more difficult for the courts to deal with than have ordinary zoning ordinances.[310]

The earliest aesthetic zoning cases involved the regulation or total prohibition of advertising signs in urban areas. At first, the courts generally invalidated such regulatory measures on the ground that aesthetic considerations were not within the police power so regulation for aesthetic purposes violated substantive due process.[311] Since aesthetics is inherently subjective—some persons dote on modern art, but others

---

[307]　See Hawaii Code §§ 46–15.35, 501–231, 502–111; Md. Real Prop. Code Ann. § 2–121; N.C. Gen. Stat. § 168–22; Wash. Rev. Code §§ 35.63.185, 35A.63.215, 36.70A.450; Wis. Stat. §§ 50.01 et seq.

[308]　272 U.S. 365, 47 S.Ct. 114, 71 L.Ed. 303 (1926).

[309]　In Pearson v. City of Grand Blanc, 756 F.Supp. 314 (E.D.Mich.1991), affirmed 961 F.2d 1211 (6th Cir.1992), it was held that aesthetic considerations may properly be taken into account in denying an application to rezone from a residential to a commercial classification.

[310]　See, generally, D. Mandelker, Land Use Law §§ 11.01–11.05 (4th ed. 1997); Costonis, Law and Aesthetics: A Critique and a Reformulation of the Dilemmas, 80 Mich.L.Rev. 361 (1982).

[311]　E.g., City of Passaic v. Paterson Bill Posting, Etc. Co., 72 N.J.L. 285, 62 A. 267 (Err. & App.1905).

can neither stand nor understand it—any statute or ordinance that favors or disfavors anything on aesthetic grounds invites a claim that it is "arbitrary." Mere mention of the word "arbitrary" can trigger thoughts about possible denial of substantive due process, as covered in section 9.6.[312] After the earliest decisions, however, urban sign controls were sustained on the basis of asserted non-aesthetic considerations such as safety and morals.[313] Still later, courts began to hold that urban sign controls could be sustained where aesthetic considerations were just one of multiple factors justifying such controls. Other factors commonly invoked include traffic safety, protection of economic interests such as tourism, and preservation of property values.[314] However, over the years judicial attitudes have become increasingly accepting of aesthetic regulations. A 1954 "watershed" decision that helped to drive this gradual change in judicial attitudes is Berman v. Parker, which upheld an urban renewal project in Washington, D.C.[315] Justice Douglas's opinion for the Court contained the oft-repeated phrase that Congress might make the city "beautiful as well as healthy, spacious as well as clean, well-balanced as well as carefully patrolled." Some writers and a few courts have said they accept aesthetic considerations standing alone as sufficient justification for urban advertising sign controls, but it is difficult to find a decision that does not also throw in something about other more tangible factors such as economic advantages or safety considerations.[316]

In the real world, aesthetic considerations never "stand alone" and the validity of comprehensive billboard-banning ordinances remains at least somewhat subject to doubt on the basis of First Amendment "free speech" considerations. The leading case is the

---

[312] See, e.g., Anderson v. City of Issaquah, 70 Wn.App. 64, 851 P.2d 744 (1993), where city design controls that turned on the words "interesting" versus "monotonous" and "harmonious" with a nearby valley and mountains were held to be unconstitutionally vague.

[313] E.g., St. Louis Gunning Advertisement Co. v. City of St. Louis, 235 Mo. 99, 137 S.W. 929 (1911), appeal dismissed 231 U.S. 761, 34 S.Ct. 325, 58 L.Ed. 470 (1913). This decision is famous because it described advertising billboards as hiding places for "the lowest form of prostitution."

[314] E.g., Opinion of the Justices, 333 Mass. 773, 128 N.E.2d 557 (1955) (upholding historic zoning on Nantucket because it promoted tourism); United Advertising Corp. v. Borough of Metuchen, 42 N.J. 1, 198 A.2d 447 (1964).

[315] 348 U.S. 26, 75 S.Ct. 98, 99 L.Ed. 27 (1954).

[316] E.g., Metromedia, Inc. v. San Diego, 26 Cal.3d 848, 164 Cal.Rptr. 510, 610 P.2d 407 (1980), reversed on other grounds 453 U.S. 490, 101 S.Ct. 2882, 69 L.Ed.2d 800 (1981); City of Lake Wales v. Lamar Advertising Association of Lakeland, 414 So.2d 1030 (Fla.1982). See also State v. Jones, 305 N.C. 520, 290 S.E.2d 675 (1982) (junkyard regulation). State v. Diamond Motors, Inc., 50 Haw. 33, 429 P.2d 825 (1967), is often cited as standing on aesthetics alone, but a careful reading will show the court spoke also of "promoting the tourist trade." Donrey Communications Co. v. City of Fayetteville, 280 Ark. 408, 660 S.W.2d 900 (1983), a case involving an anti-signboard ordinance, has been cited as relying on aesthetics alone, but in fact the court also relied upon "economic development," "tourist industry," and "hazardous" signboards. State v. Miller, 83 N.J. 402, 416 A.2d 821 (1980), also cited as a "pure aesthetics" decision made statements that aesthetics alone could sustain an ordinance, but it was dictum, since the court struck down the ordinance in question. It is difficult to find decisions whose holdings support Professor Mandelker's statement that "a clear majority of courts hold that aesthetics alone is a legitimate government purpose in land use regulation." See D. Mandelker, Land Use Law § 11.05 (4th ed. 1997). Professor Mandelker apparently argues that "the additional governmental purposes that courts require to support an aesthetic regulation *derive from* its aesthetic purposes." (Emphasis added.) Id. at § 11.04. That is a nice point; it has a chameleon-like aspect as to some such "governmental purposes" and is false as to other purposes. When signboards are said to be safety hazards, that is a fact that operates independently of whether they are ugly or beautiful; they block drivers' lines of sight. When it is said that architectural-conformity ordinances enhance property values, viewed one way, this does depend upon an implied underlying assumption that the required designs are aesthetically pleasing; but even here, if the chameleon is looked at from another angle, one could argue that testimony by expert appraisers that a pyramid-shaped house in a neighborhood of traditional homes (see State ex rel. Stoyanoff v. Berkeley, 458 S.W.2d 305 [Mo. 1970]) lowers property values, is an independent evidentiary fact, perhaps based upon "comparable sales."

Supreme Court's decision in Metromedia, Inc. v. City of San Diego, which we analyzed previously under the heading of Denial of Freedom of Speech in section 9.8 of this chapter.[317] However, the scope of the plurality opinion in *Metromedia* was somewhat limited by the Court's later decision in City Council of the City of Los Angeles v. Taxpayers for Vincent.[318] Among courts, a number of decisions leave the force of *Metromedia* in doubt; a large number might be classified as tending to agree, but a number of more recent cases have tended to disagree, though of course their varied facts make those generalizations somewhat spongy.[319] Also relevant here are another class of decisions covered in section 9.8, of which the best known is City of Ladue v. Gilleo, which have invalidated ordinances whose effect is to prohibit or unduly restrict yard signs and candidates' signs that carry political messages.[320]

---

[317] For a fuller discussion, see § 9.8 of this chapter, where we discussed a number of decisions that have struck down different kinds of sign and billboard ordinances on the ground that they denied freedom of speech. The leading case is Metromedia, Inc. v. City of San Diego, 453 U.S. 490, 101 S.Ct. 2882, 69 L.Ed.2d 800 (1981). There the United States Supreme Court invalidated a city-wide ban on "off premises" billboards contained in a comprehensive sign control ordinance on First Amendment grounds, because it would have the effect of permitting some commercial signs but of banning all signs expressing beliefs on matters of political or social interest. The San Diego city council then sought to salvage its sign ordinance by repealing all the provisions dealing with noncommercial billboards—which would have satisfied the objections of the United States Supreme Court plurality—but the California Supreme Court then struck down the entire ordinance, as revised, on the ground that the provisions relating to commercial and noncommercial billboards were not severable. Metromedia, Inc. v. City of San Diego, 32 Cal.3d 180, 185 Cal.Rptr. 260, 649 P.2d 902 (1982).

[318] 466 U.S. 789, 104 S.Ct. 2118, 80 L.Ed.2d 772 (1984), on remand 738 F.2d 353 (9th Cir.1984), where the Supreme Court sustained an ordinance prohibiting the posting of public property of any signs, including political campaign posters.

[319] For decisions that tend to agree closely with *Metromedia*'s invalidation of a comprehensive sign ordinance like the San Diego ordinance, see National Advertising Co. v. Town of Niagara, 942 F.2d 145 (2d Cir.1991) (ordinance provision that allows only on-site commercial advertising signs is invalid, and the entire ordinance must be invalidated because, under state law, the different provisions of the ordinance are not severable); National Advertising Co. v. Town of Babylon, 900 F.2d 551 (2d Cir. 1990), cert. denied 498 U.S. 852, 111 S.Ct. 146, 112 L.Ed.2d 112 (1990) (an ordinance that prohibits all signs except those advertising on-site business is unconstitutional because it favors commercial over non-commercial speech); Tahoe Regional Planning Agency v. King, 233 Cal.App.3d 1365, 285 Cal.Rptr. 335 (1991) (ordinance banning all off-site non-commercial signs except temporary political signs was facially invalid as a violation of First Amendment free speech rights).

Decisions that tend in some general way to agree with *Metromedia* are Adams Outdoor Advertising of Atlanta, Inc. v. Fulton County, 738 F.Supp. 1431 (N.D.Ga.1990) (failure of ordinance to state explicitly what governmental interest was sought to be advanced made ordinance invalid on First Amendment free speech grounds); City of Lakewood v. Colfax Unlimited Association, Inc., 634 P.2d 52 (Colo.1981) (invalid); Kevin Gray-East Coast Auto Body v. Village of Nyack, 171 A.D.2d 924, 566 N.Y.S.2d 795 (1991) (ordinance that prohibited change in content of nonconforming signs invalid); Norton Outdoor Advertising, Inc. v. Village of Arlington Heights, 69 Ohio St.2d 539, 433 N.E.2d 198 (1982) (invalid).

For decisions that tend generally to disagree with *Metromedia*, see Advantage Media, L.L.C. v. City of Eden Prairie, 456 F.3d 793 (8th Cir. 2006); Lavey v. City of Two Rivers, 171 F.3d 1110, 1114 (7th Cir. 1999); Cleveland Area Bd. of Realtors v. City of Euclid, 88 F.3d 382 (6th Cir. 1996); Advantage Media, LLC v. City of Eden Prairie, 405 F.Supp.2d 1037, 1044 (D. Minn. 2005); Maurice Callahan & Sons, Inc. v. Outdoor Advertising Bd., 12 Mass.App.Ct. 536, 427 N.E.2d 25 (1981) (valid); Singer Supermarkets, Inc. v. Zoning Bd. of Adjustment, 183 N.J.Super. 285, 443 A.2d 1082 (App.Div.1982) (valid).

[320] City of Ladue v. Gilleo, 512 U.S. 43, 114 S.Ct. 2038, 129 L.Ed.2d 36 (1994). City of Rochester Hills v. Schultz, 224 Mich.App. 323, 568 N.W.2d 832 (1997), is consistent with *Gilleo;* it struck down an ordinance that prohibited yard signs advertising home businesses, but which merely regulated, but did not prohibit, other forms of commercial advertising. Also consistent is State v. Miller, 83 N.J. 402, 416 A.2d 821 (1980), which held void, as denying free speech, a city ordinance whose effect was to prohibit a yard sign that proclaimed a position on a matter of local public interest. See also Beaulieu v. City of Alabaster, 454 F.3d 1219 (11th Cir.2006) (finding ordinance that limited display of political signs to residential areas invalid); City of Antioch v. Candidates' Outdoor Graphic Service, 557 F.Supp. 52 (N.D.Cal.1982); Sugarman v. Village of Chester, 192 F.Supp.2d 282 (S.D. N.Y. 2002) (finding ordinance invalid that treated political signs different than other signs); Orazio v. Town of North Hempstead, 426 F.Supp. 1144 (E.D.N.Y.1977); McFadden v. City of Bridgeport,

Since World War II, many urban and suburban communities have adopted architectural design regulations for new residential structures.[321] These regulations, which may be separately enacted or enacted as part of the local zoning ordinance, usually create a design review board with relatively broad power to approve or reject designs of proposed structures. The architectural design regulations generally include standards governing the exterior features of structures covered by the regulations and often include "anti-look-alike" provisions—to prevent developers from building large numbers of almost identical structures—or a "design compatibility" provisions that prevent construction of new buildings that are too dissimilar to the existing buildings in the neighborhood.

Architectural design regulations have been tested in a relatively small but growing number of appellate court decisions. Most of these cases came from residential suburbs and were decided before courts had generally accepted aesthetic considerations as a proper stand-alone basis for exercises of the zoning power. In a few early cases, architectural design regulations were held invalid on the ground that promotion of aesthetic values was not a proper zoning purpose. In other cases, the courts struck down design review requirements on the ground that they improperly delegated the zoning power. However, most cases now uphold architectural design regulations requiring new residential structures to be approved by a design review board. In two of the leading cases, State ex rel. Saveland Park Holding Corp. v. Wieland[322] and Reid v. Architectural Board of Review,[323] the courts sustained ordinances requiring that the design of new houses should be sufficiently compatible with existing houses in the immediate neighborhood so as not to cause substantial depreciation in property values in the neighborhood. And in State ex rel. Stoyanoff v. Berkeley,[324] the court sustained a design control ordinance that contained both "anti-look-alike" and "design-compatibility" standards.

All three of the decisions just cited relied largely on a protection of property values rather than a pure aesthetics-based rationale. Of course, the protection-of-property-values rationale may prove inadequate in light of the facts in a particular case. In Hankins v. Borough of Rockleigh,[325] for example, the New Jersey intermediate appeals court found the design requirements invalid "in light of the actual physical development of the community." Specifically, a prohibition of flat roofs was unreasonable because there were several flat-roofed buildings and buildings with flat-roofed extensions in the vicinity of the proposed new flat-roofed house so the regulation did not protect property values as alleged.

---

422 F.Supp.2d 659 (N.D. W. Va. 2006) (finding ordinance prohibiting posting of political signs for more 30 days before an event invalid).

[321] Generally, see J. Juergensmeyer & T. Roberts, Land Use Planning and Control Law § 12.5 (1998); D. Mandelker, Land Use Law §§ 11.22, 11.23 (4th ed. 1997).

[322] 269 Wis. 262, 69 N.W.2d 217 (1955), certiorari denied 350 U.S. 841, 76 S.Ct. 81, 100 L.Ed. 750 (1955).

[323] 119 Ohio App. 67, 192 N.E.2d 74 (1963).

[324] 458 S.W.2d 305 (Mo.1970). See also Novi v. City of Pacifica, 169 Cal.App.3d 678, 215 Cal.Rptr. 439 (1985) (ordinance requiring "variety in architectural design" is valid under "general welfare" standard and is not void for vagueness).

[325] 55 N.J.Super. 132, 150 A.2d 63 (App.Div.1959).

§ 9.21 ZONING AMENDMENTS: THE PROCESS

All the zoning enabling acts authorize the local governing body to change zoning regulations and district boundaries by amending zoning ordinances.[326] Although not expressly stated in the early New York zoning enabling legislation or in the Standard State Zoning Enabling Act, the generally-accepted basis for any amendment to a zoning ordinance mirrors that for enacting an original zoning ordinance—the promotion of health, safety, morals, or the general welfare. Under many early zoning ordinances, established communities were protected against frequent or whimsical changes to zoning by provision requiring a three-fourths vote of the entire membership of the local legislative body to enact a rezoning amendment over the written protest of the owners of twenty percent of the land most directly affected by the amendment.[327] Though not all states have continued to employ this technique, a number still do. Where it is used, the percentage of persons who must sign petitions, the specific area in which they must live (which was not provided for in SZEA), and the percentage vote by which the local legislative body may override their veto varies from state to state.[328]

The expectation of some zoning pioneers that original zoning regulations would be stable and seldom amended has proven untrue in actual experience. Many early planners seemingly believed that most zoning amendments would be general amendments to zoning designations of whole zones or of whole parts of the city or county based on the planning commission's own studies. Obviously, it has not turned out that way. The vast majority of zoning amendments relate to specific parcels of land owned by the party seeking the amendment. Such amendments are a species of "map" amendments—seeking a redrawing of the local zoning map by changing the designation of a certain area or parcel—rather than "text" amendment that change certain text in a zoning ordinance. Even before World War II, some local legislative bodies had adopted the practice of enacting frequent rezoning amendments in response to specific requests from landowners or developers to rezone specific land to allow for some type of new

---

[326] SZEA § 5 (1967) provided for amendments of the zoning "regulations, restrictions, and boundaries," subject to the same provisions "relative to public hearings and official notice" as were applicable to enactment of an original zoning ordinance.

[327] SSZEA § 5 (1926). The validity of the "protest" provision was settled in early cases in New York and elsewhere. E.g., Morrill Realty Corp. v. Rayon Holding Corp., 254 N.Y. 268, 172 N.E. 494 (1930); Russell v. Murphy, 177 Okla. 255, 58 P.2d 560 (1936); Rhode Island Episcopal Convention v. Providence City Council, 52 R.I. 182, 159 A. 647 (1932); Holzbauer v. Ritter, 184 Wis. 35, 198 N.W. 852 (1924). See also Northwood Properties Co. v. Perkins, 325 Mich. 419, 39 N.W.2d 25 (1949); Leighton v. City of Minneapolis, 16 F.Supp. 101 (D.Minn.1936). *Caveat:* One must distinguish between a protest petition that is a *condition* to a zoning amendment that has been *adopted by the local legislative body* becoming effective (which courts have approved, as just stated) and a zoning code that would purport to *require* the local legislative body *to enact* a zoning amendment that has been *initiated by a petition of a certain percentage of residents of a neighborhood.* The former technique gives the petitioners a *veto* over local legislation, and was approved by the United States Supreme Court in Thomas Cusack Co. v. Chicago, 242 U.S. 526, 37 S.Ct. 190, 61 L.Ed. 472 (1917). But the latter technique in effect gives a small group of citizens, less than the whole body of voters of the governmental entity, the *initiative to enact* local legislation. That technique was held unconstitutional many years ago by the United States Supreme Court in Eubank v. City of Richmond, 226 U.S. 137, 33 S.Ct. 76, 57 L.Ed. 156 (1912). Also, one must distinguish petitions by relatively small neighborhood groups from zoning actions that may be initiated or vetoed by *all the voters* of the political entity by the *referendum* process. That process, if allowed by state and local law, has been approved by the Supreme Court and will be discussed in § 9.23, infra. See City of Eastlake v. Forest City Enterprises, 426 U.S. 668, 96 S.Ct. 2358, 49 L.Ed.2d 132 (1976); James v. Valtierra, 402 U.S. 137, 91 S.Ct. 1331, 28 L.Ed.2d 678 (1971).

[328] See 1 R. Anderson, American Law of Zoning §§ 4.35–4.37 (3d ed. 1986), which fully discusses protest petitions and also consent requirements.

development[329] After World War II, some localities combined this practice with "wait-and-see" zoning, which involves zoning most of the undeveloped land in a suburban community what are effectively "holding zones" subject to use density restrictions that do not permit any profitable development. Within these holding zones, very little development can occur without an amendment that rezones the land to a classification that permits some proposed development.[330] In making the decision to rezone or not, the local authorities making use of this approach usually take into account—contrary to formal zoning theory—the "personal" characteristics of each developer with respect to "financial capacity, reputation for quality, and record of good management."[331]

Local governments' reliance on rezoning procedures as a flexible planning tool has caused much of planning commissions' time and energy to be spent considering applicant rezoning requests. Routine administrative procedures exist in every community for the reception and processing of rezoning petitions. Although the procedural details for addressing these petitions vary somewhat from jurisdiction to jurisdiction, some generalizations can be made about the basic steps involved.[332] In almost all cases, the applicant must file a petition with the planning commission and pay a fee. If the community has a professional planning department, the petition will be filed with it and then forwarded to the planning commission, which schedules a time for a public hearing upon advance notice. Forms of notice vary but must include personal notice to the applicant and usually include posting of notices on the subject land, perhaps mailing of notice to nearby landowners, and generally publication of notice in a local newspaper since zoning amendments are viewed as affecting the entire community. Because the planning commission is an administrative body and not a court, hearings are much less formal than in court, with the only rule of evidence being a loose notion that evidence considered must bear some relevance to the application. Commissions regularly consider hearsay, including letters received from persons who are not at the hearing. Applicants are usually represented by an attorney. If there is serious opposition, the opponents may similarly have representation and the hearing may take on a distinct adversary nature. A hearing may be continued to a later date if the commission deems it necessary. When the process is finished, the commission must render some form of report and recommendation to the city council or county commission. The degree to which a commission must record the evidence it receives and the findings and conclusions that support its recommendations varies widely from state to state. Simple narrative summaries are sufficient in some jurisdictions, but other states go so far as to require verbatim transcripts and formal findings if the local legislative body's decision is reviewed by a court.[333]

---

[329] See, e.g., Mueller v. C. Hoffmeister Undertaking & Livery Co., 343 Mo. 430, 121 S.W.2d 775 (1938); Linden Methodist Episcopal Church v. Linden, 113 N.J.L. 188, 173 A. 593 (1934).

[330] See, e.g., Krasnowiecki, Abolish Zoning, 31 Syracuse L.Rev. 719, 734–741 (1980), using the term "short zoning" rather than "wait and see zoning"). Cf. D. Mandelker, Land Use Law §§ 4.15, 6.01 (4th ed. 1997). To some extent, of course, development may be "licensed" by approval of a "variance" or "special exception." See §§ 9.28, 9.29, infra.

[331] See Krasnowiecki, Abolish Zoning, 31 Syracuse L.Rev. 719, 729–31 (1980).

[332] The material in this paragraph is mostly drawn from 1 R. Anderson, American Law of Zoning §§ 431–433 (3d ed. 1986), and J. Juergensmeyer & T. Roberts, Land Use Planning and Control Law § 5.6 (1998), as well as the author's personal experience. The treatises cited give details, and cover some matters, not discussed here.

[333] E.g., Parkridge v. City of Seattle, 89 Wn.2d 454, 573 P.2d 359 (1978), and other Washington decisions require that a reviewing court have a verbatim transcript.

§ 9.22 ZONING AMENDMENTS: APPLICATIONS BY OWNERS, CHALLENGES BY THIRD PERSONS

Applications by Landowners and Remedies for Denials

Landowners' applications for rezonings of their land nearly always involve a request by a landowner or developer to make some more intensive and more lucrative use of his or her land. For instance, suppose an owner of land zoned for residential use has sought a rezoning of it to allow the development of a shopping center—a distinctly commercial use. When such applicants are developers who presently hold only an option or contract to purchase the subject land, questions can arise regarding the applicants' standing to seek zoning amendments. However, let's assume that the applicant addressed any such issues by requiring the title holder to join in all proceedings respecting zoning.[334] Assume further that the applicant has determined that a special exception or conditional use permit or a variance (both to be discussed in later sections of this chapter) would not allow for the desired development so an application for rezoning is the only recourse. Moreover, assume that the applicant has pursued the rezoning procedures described in the previous section of this chapter and been denied rezoning by the local legislative body. At that point, an applicant's next step is to bring an action in the local court of general jurisdiction challenging the denial of the rezoning application.

The first thing applicants who end up in these circumstances must do is determine the proper form of action. Technically, their action is not an "appeal" since that term refers to a higher court's review of a decision of a lower court. Instead, the rezoning applicant is complaining about an action or inaction by a local legislative body so the action is one for "review."[335] Importantly, claimants' remedial options in these proceedings are limited by the general "separations of power" principle that courts will not order legislative bodies to enact legislation. This principle precludes the use of a writ of mandamus or a mandatory injunction to compel a city council to grant a rezoning application.[336] Accordingly, the owner must attack the *existing zoning ordinance* on some ground or other unless the owner can find some procedural or mechanical ground to attack the refusal to rezone. Although the precise forms of such actions vary from state to state, the most common actions appear to be requests for injunctions against the enforcement of the existing ordinance. Certiorari is used in some states, declaratory judgment actions are possible others, and a few states have special statutory forms of action that may be called "appeals."[337]

---

[334] 4 R. Anderson, American Law of Zoning § 27.12 (3d ed. 1986), says that contract vendees and optionees generally have standing, but to avoid the issue, the drafter of an option or contract to purchase should insert a clause requiring the vendor or optionor to lend his or her name to, and fully to cooperate in the prosecution of, any proceeding to obtain zoning relief of any kind for the vendee's or optionee's intended use of the land.

[335] See Copple v. City of Lincoln, 210 Neb. 504, 315 N.W.2d 628 (1982).

[336] See 4 R. Anderson, American Law of Zoning §§ 28.09, 29.04 (3d ed. 1986); J. Juergensmeyer & T. Roberts, Land Use Planning and Control Law § 5.33 (1998); D. Mandelker, Land Use Law § 8.13 (4th ed. 1997). Anderson indicates that mandamus may be used to order a local board of adjustment, a quasi-judicial body, to do a certain act; but he distinguishes mandamus to that body from mandamus to the local legislative body. Also, Juergensmeyer and Roberts note that courts will sometimes order a legislative body *to act*, e.g., to order a city council that has refused even to consider a rezoning application to do so, but they will not order the council *how to decide* the application.

[337] See authorities cited in preceding note.

The substantive grounds upon which rejected applicants may seek to have the existing zoning set aside were covered in earlier sections of this chapter. For example, the planning commission or local legislative body may have simply failed to follow the requirements of the local zoning code (see § 9.14) in refusing to rezone. The central issues in many other zoning cases focus simply on the interpretation of some term or phrase of the local zoning code such as whether the right to have a "home occupation" in a residential zone encompasses rights to conduct a machine shop from an residential owner's garage. Another ground of attack may be that the existing zoning is not "in accordance with the comprehensive plan" (see § 9.12). On other occasions, landowners may contend that the existing zoning code or the local legislative body's refusal to rezone go beyond the authority granted by or somehow violate the state zoning enabling act (see § 9.13). And landowners may obviously challenge existing zoning provisions under constitutional theories such as regulatory takings doctrine, denial of due process, denial of equal protection of law, denial of free speech, or denial of free exercise of religion (see §§ 9.4 through 9.9).

Rezoning applicants who bring an action challenging an existing zoning ordinance are sometimes met with the defense that they have "failed to exhaust administrative remedies." In general, this means that a court action to have the ordinance set aside is premature because the zoning code provides some administrative procedure whereby the owner might have otherwise circumvented the zoning code's restrictions on the subject land. The typical alternative procedures cited in these defenses are petitions to the board of adjustment for variances or for special exceptions or conditional use permits. In some localities, boards of adjustment are also empowered to render administrative interpretations of the zoning ordinance. If such an administrative procedure was available and the owner failed to apply for it, that may be a defense to the court action.[338] One possible exception to the "exhaustion of remedies" defence is a showing that it would have been "futile" to pursue one of those alternative procedures. Unfortunately, judicial decisions on the meaning of "futility" span a range that goes from "extremely unlikely" to "absolutely impossible."[339] A failure to exhaust all administrative remedies may also be excused in cases in which an owner makes a "facial" constitutional attack on a zoning ordinance. Since facial attacks differ from "as applied" attacks in that the former do not

---

[338] See, e.g., Ben Lomond, Inc. v. Municipality of Anchorage, 761 P.2d 119 (1988) (variance); Johnson County Memorial Gardens, Inc. v. City of Overland Park, 239 Kan. 221, 718 P.2d 1302 (1986) (special exception); Poe v. City of Baltimore, 241 Md. 303, 216 A.2d 707 (1966) (special exception); Paragon Properties Co. v. City of Novi, 452 Mich. 568, 550 N.W.2d 772 (1996) (dissent argues variance was futile because it could not possibly have been granted because no "hardship"); Lange v. Town of Woodway, 79 Wn.2d 45, 483 P.2d 116 (1971) (variance); J. Juergensmeyer & T. Roberts, Land Use Planning and Control Law § 5.36 (1998); D. Mandelker, Land Use Law §§ 8.08, 8.09 (4th ed. 1997).

[339] See, e.g., Karches v. City of Cincinnati, 38 Ohio St.3d 12, 526 N.E.2d 1350 (1988) (city code did not allow use variances); Orion Corp. v. State, 109 Wn.2d 621, 747 P.2d 1062 (1987) (multiplicity of permits required made it extremely unlikely owner could get all of them). Compare Orion with Estate of Friedman v. Pierce County, 112 Wn.2d 68, 768 P.2d 462 (1989) (fact that city officials had stated opposition to intended development did not excuse application for variance). See generally J. Juergensmeyer & T. Roberts, Land Use Planning and Control Law § 5.36 (1998). For a nice puzzle, see also the dissent in Paragon Properties Co. v. City of Novi, 452 Mich. 568, 550 N.W.2d 772 (1996), which makes the interesting argument that if, in the court's judgment, the landowner could not have shown a "hardship," and therefore could not legally have obtained a variance, that established "futility." The problem is, boards of adjustment frequently do grant variances when no true "hardship" is shown, i.e., when, if appealed to a court, the variance would not stand up. Should the court, in the rezoning action, consider the practical possibility that the board of adjustment would violate legal principles?

focus on a particular parcel, facial attacks involve no specific land as to which an administrative remedy might have been granted.[340]

Because land development projects have generally become larger in scope through the years and required ever more time for completion, zoning changes increasingly affect developments in progress when the zoning changes are made. In such cases, the developer often argues that he is entitled to proceed with the development as planned either because he has acquired a "vested right" in the prior zoning or on the ground that the municipality is "estopped" from applying the zoning change to the development in progress.[341] The "vested rights" argument is based on the theory that the developer has acquired constitutionally protected property rights in the development in progress. The "estoppel" theory is based on the equitable doctrine protecting good faith changes of position in reliance upon some act or omission of a municipality. These theories are quite distinct doctrinally but many courts have nonetheless failed to distinguish clearly between them when considering whether a developer has a right to proceed under pre-amendment zoning regulations. Under the "vested rights" theory, a developer's right to proceed may date either from the time he or she applies for the first "permit" required by the applicable regulations—usually a building permit, a site plan approval, or a subdivision approval—or the actual issuance of the required "permit," provided the issuance of the "permit" is not illegal.[342] Under the "estoppel" theory, the developer's right to proceed is protected only when, after obtaining the required "permit," he or she takes action pursuant to the "permit" resulting in "substantial" detrimental reliance.[343]

In practice, the "vested rights" and "estoppel" theories tend to blend together. In some sense, the labels given to these theories are not as important as the factors courts look to when determining whether a given landowner is entitled to develop under original regulations. Most courts require that developers seeking to apply either theory have been granted some kind of governmental permission to proceed, which usually means a building permit. When required, that fixes a date after which changes in land use regulations may not apply to the development. Beyond that, courts may or may not consider such other factors as the magnitude of the developer's financial investment in the project, the project's progress to date, or whether the owner proceeded reasonably and in "good faith," under the circumstances. If a developer reasonably should have anticipated the change in regulations but nonetheless proceeded, this is generally a showing bad faith. Most courts require that the developer or owner have already performed some physical work on the project. However, some will accept preliminary actions such as site preparation while others want to see substantial work on structures. Usually, if a project has been fully completed then rights are vested. Unfortunately,

---

[340] Poe v. City of Baltimore, 241 Md. 303, 216 A.2d 707 (1966) (dictum); Golden v. Planning Board of Town of Ramapo, 30 N.Y.2d 359, 334 N.Y.S.2d 138, 285 N.E.2d 291 (1972) (application for special permit); D. Mandelker, Land Use Law § 8.10 (4th ed. 1997).

[341] The discussion of these topics is based largely on the discussion in D. Mandelker, Land Use Law §§ 6.11 through 6.22 (2d ed. 1988).

[342] D. Mandelker, Land Use Law §§ 6.15–6.17 (4th ed. 1997). If development occurs on a single lot, the first "permit" required will ordinarily be a building permit, although in some cases it will be "site plan approval." When development requires approval of a subdivision plat, "subdivision approval" is the "first permit." See, e.g., Western Land Equities, Inc. v. City of Logan, 617 P.2d 388 (Utah 1980); Littlefield v. Inhabitants of Town of Lyman, 447 A.2d 1231 (Me.1982). Subdivision and review procedure is considered in § 9.30, infra.

[343] D. Mandelker, Land Use Law §§ 6.19–6.21 (4th ed. 1997).

because of the flexibility of the various factors when applied to widely varying facts, predicting the outcome of a given case on these issues is extremely difficult.[344]

Because of substantial confusion in many jurisdictions as to the standards to be applied under either the "vested rights" or the "estoppel" theory, some states have added provisions to their enabling acts and some municipalities have added provisions to their land use ordinances designed to clarify these issues.[345] Some states protect developers by authorizing the execution of development agreements between a developer and municipalities with respect to permitted uses and densities, maximum height and size of buildings, reservation or dedication of land for public use or payment of fees in lieu thereof, the allocation of responsibility for the timing and construction of public facilities, and similar questions.[346] In addition, a few courts have abandoned the "vested rights" and "estoppel" theories in favor of a much simpler rule. Under the common law "vested right doctrine" in the state of Washington, rights vest simply upon a "fully complete" application for a building permit or for subdivision approval.[347] However, the continued validity of the doctrine has been called into question in a series of relatively recent cases.[348] A few other states have adopted a modified version of the Washington approach, some adding the proviso that the rule applies only if no zoning amendment is pending when the developer applies for the building permit.[349]

Challenges by Third Persons

Many amendments to rezone a single tract of land in response to an owner's or developer's request are likely to provoke challenges in court from unhappy persons in the vicinity whom this section generically calls "the neighbors." The first question the neighbors in these situations must consider is whether they have standing to maintain such an action. Rules on standing vary widely from state to state, but typically a

---

[344] For supporting discussion and much more detail, see J. Juergensmeyer & T. Roberts, Land Use Planning and Control Law §§ 5.27–5.29 (1998); D. Mandelker, Land Use Law §§ 6.12–6.21 (4th ed. 1997). See also Sycamore Realty v. People's Counsel, 344 Md. 57, 684 A.2d 1331 (1996) (rights do not "vest" if owner has not obtained permit or commenced construction; court rejects "estoppel" theory); Town of Orangetown v. Magee, 88 N.Y.2d 41, 665 N.E.2d 1061, 643 N.Y.S.2d 21 (1996) (rights vested when developer had obtained building permit and spent substantial money to prepare for development); Lake Bluff Housing Partners v. City of South Milwaukee, 197 Wis.2d 157, 540 N.W.2d 189 (1995) (owner must submit application for building permit that conforms to zoning and building code for rights to vest); Knight & Schoettle, Current Issues Related to Vested Rights and Development Agreements, 25 Urb. Law. 779 (1993).

[345] D. Mandelker, Land Use Law § 6.22 (4th ed. 1997).

[346] D. Mandelker, Land Use Law § 6.23 (4th ed. 1997), citing West's Ann.Cal.Gov't Code §§ 65864–65869.5, West's Fla.Stat. Ann. §§ 163.3220–163.3243, Hawaii Rev. Stat.Ann. §§ 46–121 through 46–132, and Nev.Rev.Stat.Ann. §§ 278.0201–278.0207.

[347] Wash. Rev. Code 19.27.095 (building permit); Wash. Rev. Code 58.17.033 (subdivision application); Allenbach v. City of Tukwila, 101 Wn.2d 193, 676 P.2d 473 (1984) (building permit); Town of Woodway v. Snohomish County, 180 Wash. 2d 165, 173, 322 P.3d 1219 (2014); Noble Manor Co. v. Pierce County, 133 Wn.2d 269, 943 P.2d 1378 (1997) (application for subdivision approval that discloses homes to be built vests not only that application but also right to build the homes).

[348] See Alliance Inv. Group of Ellensburg, LLC v. City of Ellensburg, 189 Wash. App. 763, 768, 358 P.3d 1227 (Div. 3 2015); Potala Village Kirkland, LLC v. City of Kirkland, 183 Wash. App. 191, 334 P.3d 1143 (Div. 1 2014). For an in-depth discussion of Washington's vested rights doctrine, see Roger D. Wynne, Washington's Vested Rights Doctrine: How We Have Muddled A Simple Concept and How We Can Reclaim It, 24 Seattle U. L. Rev. 851 (2001).

[349] Ben Lomond, Inc. v. City of Idaho Falls, 92 Idaho 595, 448 P.2d 209 (1968); Gallagher v. Building Inspector, 432 Pa. 301, 247 A.2d 572 (1968); Boron Oil Co. v. Kimple, 445 Pa. 327, 284 A.2d 744 (1971) (adding proviso that no zoning amendment is pending); Western Land Equities, Inc. v. City of Logan, 617 P.2d 388 (Utah 1980) (with provisos that no zoning amendment is pending, that developer proceeds with reasonable diligence, and that there is no "compelling, countervailing public interest"); McKee Family I, LLC v. City of Fitchburg, 374 Wis. 2d 487, 893 N.W.2d 12 (2017).

challenger must be an "aggrieved" or "interested" person. Usually, the rezoning must have caused a third-party challenger a loss that is at least somewhat different from that suffered by the public. However, a few states will allow any taxpayer of the local zoning entity to have standing.[350] Landowners who adjoin the subject land nearly always have standing.[351] Beyond that, the only safe general statement in most states is that as a challenger's land gets farther and farther away from the parcel involved in the rezoning application the chances of having standing diminish. Of course, distance is not the ultimate question and the inquiry focuses more acutely on the impact the proposed rezoning is likely to have on the challengers' land. In summary, one must look at the statutes and case law of each jurisdiction and even then it may be difficult to articulate a very reliable test.[352]

One special standing question that may arise is whether residents of areas beyond the city or county line have standing to challenge rezoning actions, assuming they are close enough and affected enough that they would have otherwise had standing. While earlier decisions tended to deny standing to such outsiders, the trend of more recent decisions, and now probably the prevailing rule, is that such persons do have standing.[353] A second special standing question, increasingly frequent in recent years, is the extent to which an association such as a neighborhood community association or environmental group has standing. Some courts deny standing to such organizations, but other courts follow the federal rule that an organization generally has standing if it represents the interests of one or more of its members who have standing.[354] Of course, if the state were to deny such an organization standing, one or more of its members who had standing could still bring the action.

---

[350] This wants a bit of explanation. Article 7 of the Standard Zoning Enabling Act allowed not only any "person aggrieved," but also any "taxpayer" to appeal decisions of the *board of adjustment*, but there was no comparable provision for appeals from rezoning actions by the local legislative body. Nevertheless, some states have allowed third persons standing as taxpayers to challenge rezoning actions. 4 R. Anderson, American Law of Zoning § 27.16 (3d ed. 1986); J. Juergensmeyer & T. Roberts, Land Use Planning and Control Law § 5.34, p. 249 (1998).

[351] See J. Juergensmeyer & T. Roberts, Land Use Planning and Control Law § 5.34, p. 248 (1998); D. Mandelker, Land Use Law § 8.04 (3d ed. 1993). But see 222 East Chestnut Street Corp. v. Board of Appeals, 14 Ill.2d 190, 152 N.E.2d 465 (1958), an unusual decision in which the court denied standing to an adjoining owner who failed specifically to prove economic loss.

[352] See especially Anderson v. Island County, 81 Wn.2d 312, 501 P.2d 594 (1972), where the court held that "neighboring land owners" and "residents of the larger zoning area" (whatever that means) had standing. The court even opined that "there may be something to be said" for allowing "a citizen, a resident, or a taxpayer" to have standing. And *Anderson* is the State of Washington's most definitive decision on third-party standing to challenge rezonings!

[353] See Scott v. City of Indian Wells, 6 Cal.3d 541, 99 Cal.Rptr. 745, 492 P.2d 1137 (1972) (leading case); Smith v. City of Papillion, 270 Neb. 607, 705 N.W.2d 584 (2005) (finding adjacent landowner have standing); Reed v. Vill. of Philmont Planning Bd., 34 A.D.3d 1034, 825 N.Y.S.2d 284 (2006) (finding adjacent landowners have standing); Save a Valuable Environment v. City of Bothell, 89 Wn.2d 862, 576 P.2d 401 (1978); J. Juergensmeyer & T. Roberts, Land Use Planning and Control Law § 5.34; D. Mandelker, Land Use Law § 8.05 (4th ed. 1997). See also Town of Mesilla v. City of Las Cruces, 120 N.M. 69, 898 P.2d 121 (N.M.App.1995) (neighboring town has standing to challenge zoning decision of adjoining city).

[354] See Hunt v. Washington State Apple Advertising Comm'n, 432 U.S. 333, 97 S.Ct. 2434, 53 L.Ed.2d 383 (1977) (state commission had standing to defend for its members who would have standing); Sierra Club v. Morton, 405 U.S. 727, 92 S.Ct. 1361, 31 L.Ed.2d 636 (1972) (organization did not have standing to contest action of federal agency when it did not represent members who were allegedly injured by such action); Save a Valuable Environment v. City of Bothell, 89 Wn.2d 862, 576 P.2d 401 (1978) (citizens' group had standing when members had standing); J. Juergensmeyer & T. Roberts, Land Use Planning and Control Law § 5.34 (1998).

Assuming that a third party who sues to challenge a rezoning has standing, the suit may be predicated upon a number of grounds that have been covered in prior sections of this chapter. Of course, a regulatory taking argument (see sections 9.4, 9.5) is not available since that argument may generally be made only by the landowner under a claim that zoning had diminished his or her property rights. The third party would similarly be unable to make out a claim of denial of free speech (section 9.8) or of free exercise of religion (section 9.9). However, third parties may and frequently do base their challenges upon one or more of the other grounds for invalidity that have already been discussed. They are: denial of substantive due process (section 9.6); "reverse denial of equal protection" when third parties allege that a rezoning has discriminated against them because they received less favorable regulatory treatment (section 9.7); claims that a rezoning was not "in accordance with" the comprehensive plan (section 9.12); or claims that a rezoning action was in contravention of the state zoning enabling act (section 9.13) or local zoning code (section 9.14).

A fairly frequent third-party challenge to a rezoning is that the rezoning constitutes illegal "spot zoning."[355] The phrase "spot zoning" is itself only a label. The only absolute certainty related to this doctrine is that if a court labels a particular zoning action "spot zoning" the action will is void. However, it is possible to describe the type of factual pattern that gives rise to a suspicion of spot zoning and to ferret out some legal underpinnings for the label. At the factual level, two factors seem to be at work: (1) that the rezoned area is small and (2) that the uses permitted by the rezoning are inconsistent with the zoning and the actual uses of the surrounding area.[356] It is the combination of both factors that counts. The smaller the area and the more out of keeping it is, the more likely a court is to label it spot zoning. Though spot zoning cases usually involve uses that are at least substantially inconsistent with the surrounding area, courts may strike down the rezoning of quite large areas as spot zoning when the permitted use involved is jarringly out of place (e.g., the rezoning for heavy industrial use in a lightly developed residential area).[357] As the example in the preceding sentence suggests, in most spot zoning cases the rezoned area is reclassified for more intensive uses than are permitted in the surrounding area. However, in a few cases courts have held that rezonings for less intensive uses than in the areas surrounding them have constituted spot zoning.[358]

Though the courts frequently do not articulate their reasons for labeling a rezoning "spot zoning," it is possible to glean several legal bases from the case law. First, when a landowner gets his or her land rezoned for more intensive—and therefore more valuable—uses than allowed for neighboring owners, the neighbors have a basis to contend that the rezoned owner has been given special privileges denied to them and have thus been discriminated against. Accordingly, one type of legal argument against

---

[355] Generally, as to "spot zoning," see D. Mandelker, Land Use Law §§ 6.28–6.32 (4th ed. 1997); 1 N. Williams, Am.Land Planning Law ch. 27 (1974 and Supp.1982); 2A Rathkopf, Law of Zoning and Planning ch. 26 (1983).

[356] A classic case in which both factors were at work is Fritts v. City of Ashland, 348 S.W.2d 712 (Ky.1961), in which the city rezoned a four-acre tract in the middle of a surrounding residential area and near a new high school as an industrial zone, to accommodate a garment factory that threatened to leave town unless it was given a new site.

[357] See, e.g., Smith v. Skagit County, 75 Wn.2d 715, 453 P.2d 832 (1969), which held that the rezoning of over 400 acres was "spot zoning." But of course the rezoning was to permit an ocean-front aluminum smelter on a somewhat remote, and scenic, island that was rural residential, with many recreational homes. Another Washington decision is similar, holding that the rezoning of 635 acres for industrial use (oil refinery) in a semi-rural area was spot zoning. Chrobuck v. Snohomish County, 78 Wn.2d 858, 480 P.2d 489 (1971).

[358] See J. Juergensmeyer & T. Roberts, Land Use Planning and Control Law § 5.10 (1998).

spot zoning is denial of equal protection.[359] Second, a rezoning that creates an island that stands out in contrast to the surrounding area may be challengeable as "unreasonable", or "irrational" or "arbitrary," in violation of substantive due process. Third—and this is the most specific and probably the most frequent argument against spot zoning— singling out small parcels and affording them quite different regulatory treatment may not be "in accordance with a comprehensive plan" as required under the Standard Zoning Enabling Act and most state zoning enabling acts. If the municipality has a formal comprehensive plan, then the rezoning may be compared with the uses the plan calls for in the area. Even if there is no formal plan, the neighbors can still try to argue that the rezoning is not consistent with the municipality's "comprehensive" zoning plan in the sense that it is a break in the pattern formed by the general uses and zoning in the area.[360] (See section 9.12 for discussion of "in accordance.")

When neighbors challenge a rezoning as "spot zoning" based on an assertion that the action is not "in accordance with a comprehensive plan," a municipality may be able to ward off the challenge by modifying its formal comprehensive plan. The origins of this stratagem are found in the comparison of two old Connecticut decisions that have been in many casebooks: Bartram v. Zoning Commission of Bridgeport and Kuehne v. Town Council of East Hartford.[361] In *Bartram,* Bridgeport rezoned a small one-third-acre parcel for commercial use in an area that was zoned as a residential area but was on an arterial street that had some other retail commercial establishments. The key factor in the court's decision to uphold the rezoning against the charge of spot zoning was a city official's testimony stating that the city had a "policy"—not a formal comprehensive plan at all—of scattering zoning for retail businesses along arterial streets in residential areas. The court seized on this scrap of evidence to conclude that the rezoning was "comprehensive" because it coincided with a city-wide pattern. A year later, in *Kuehne,* a nearly identical set of facts was presented to the same court: rezoning of a (slightly larger) parcel of land for commercial use along an arterial street in a developing area. However, this time the court struck down the rezoning action as "spot zoning." Making a narrow distinction that must have dismayed Connecticut lawyers, the court distinguished *Bartram* rezoning on the assertion that it was justified by the city-wide policy whereas there was no evidence of such a policy in *Kuehne.*

Seeking to deal with cases where a rezoning amendment is attacked as illegal "spot zoning"[362] or as not "in accordance with a comprehensive plan", a number of state courts have adopted the rule that rezoning amendments affecting relatively small parcels can be sustained only if the local government shows they were justified by "changed

---

[359] Kuehne v. Town of East Hartford, 136 Conn. 452, 461, 72 A.2d 474, 478 (1950), is the early leading case, saying that spot zoning is intended to benefit "a particular individual or group of individuals." See also, e.g., Appeal of Mulac, 418 Pa. 207, 210, 210 A.2d 275, 277 (1965) (spot zoning is a "singling out of one lot or a small area for different treatment from that accorded to similar surrounding land indistinguishable from it in character, for the economic benefit of the owner or to his economic detriment").

[360] J. Juergensmeyer & T. Roberts, Land Use Planning and Control Law § 5.10 (1998); D. Mandelker, Land Use Law § 6.29 (4th ed. 1997).

[361] Citations for the two decisions are, in the order cited in text, 136 Conn. 89, 68 A.2d 308 (1949), and 136 Conn. 452, 72 A.2d 474 (1950).

[362] Jacobs, Visconsi & Jacobs Co. v. City of Lawrence, 927 F.2d 1111 (10th Cir. 1991) (refusal to rezone area outside central business district for a shopping mall does not violate due process or equal protection when comprehensive plan provides that central business district shall be the region's only retail business center).

conditions"[363] or an "original mistake" in zoning the tract in question.[364] Even in states where the "change of condition or original mistake" rule is not rigidly applied, proof of either a "change of condition" or "original mistake" may be given substantial weight when a rezoning amendment is attacked as illegal "spot zoning."[365]

In their early spot zoning jurisprudence, Oregon courts tended to give significant weight to "change of condition" and "original mistake" in cases where rezoning amendments were challenged as illegal "spot zoning" and they largely treated rezoning amendments as "legislative acts" entitled to a presumption of validity.[366] In Fasano v. Board of County Commissioners of Washington County,[367] however, the Oregon Supreme Court held that an applicant rezoning should henceforth be treated as a "quasi-judicial" rather than a "legislative" act. In theory, this meant that rezoning amendments would be subject to a much stricter standard of judicial review than under the conventional approach. . This is because appellate courts simply consider whether the lower court has committed an error of law and never ask whether it has acted in an "unconstitutional" manner. In contrast judicial reviews of zoning legislation most frequently consider whether the legislation at issue is inconsistent with the state or federal constitution. Also, if applicant rezonings are "quasi-judicial" acts, then the burden of proof is upon the applicant to show that the original zoning was mistaken or that conditions had changed.[368]

In actual practice, the main practical effects of the *Fasano* doctrine seem to be that (1) it signifies a disposition of a court to keep a tight rein on local governments in their land use decisions and (2) if the process is quasi-judicial planning commissions must keep verbatim hearing records and enter formal findings of fact that are more detailed than many states require.[369] In any event, the *Fasano* doctrine, though it attracted much attention from legal scholars, seems not to have caught on much in the courts. For several years after *Fasano* came down, it looked like it might catch on; several states went to that position.[370] However, more recent decisions have shied away from doing so

---

[363] William S. Hart Union High School District v. Regional Planning Com'n, 226 Cal.App.3d 1612, 277 Cal.Rptr. 645 (1991).

[364] Generally, see D. Mandelker, Land Use Law § 6.31 (4th ed. 1997); 1 N. Williams, American Land Planning Law § 32.01 (1974 and Supp.1982). Although the "change or mistake" rule seems to have originated in Maryland, it was also adopted in Connecticut, Mississippi, New Mexico, and Washington, at least in modified form. See, e.g., MacDonald v. Board of County Comm'rs, 238 Md. 549, 210 A.2d 325 (1965); Zoning Comm'n v. New Canaan Building Co., 146 Conn. 170, 148 A.2d 330 (1959); Lewis v. City of Jackson, 184 So.2d 384 (Miss.1966); Miller v. City of Albuquerque, 89 N.M. 503, 554 P.2d 665 (1976); Hayden v. City of Port Townsend, 93 Wn.2d 870, 613 P.2d 1164 (1980). The rule is now codified in Maryland Code Art. 66B, § 4.05(a).

[365] E.g., King's Mill Homeowners Association v. City of Westminster, 192 Colo. 305, 557 P.2d 1186 (1976); Lanner v. Board of Appeal, 348 Mass. 220, 202 N.E.2d 777 (1964). The "change or mistake" rule has been expressly rejected in some states. E.g., Dye v. City of Phoenix, 25 Ariz.App. 193, 542 P.2d 31 (1975); Conner v. Shellburne, Inc., 281 A.2d 608 (Del.1971), on remand 315 A.2d 620 (Del.Ch.1974) affirmed 336 A.2d 568 (1975); Oka v. Cole, 145 So.2d 233 (Fla.1962), conformed to 145 So.2d 900 (Fla.App.1962).

[366] E.g., Roseta v. County of Washington, 254 Or. 161, 458 P.2d 405, 40 A.L.R.3d 364 (1969).

[367] 264 Ore. 574, 507 P.2d 23 (1973).

[368] This was stated explicitly in Parkridge v. City of Seattle, 89 Wn.2d 454, 573 P.2d 359 (1978), in which Washington formally adopted the *Fasano* "quasi-judicial" view.

[369] In formally adopting the *Fasano* position, Parkridge v. City of Seattle, 89 Wn.2d 454, 573 P.2d 359 (1978), emphasized the keeping of a verbatim record and of explicit findings by the planning commission. However, this marked no change in Washington law, because those formalities were already required in hearings before planning commissions and also boards of adjustment.

[370] E.g., Snyder v. City of Lakewood, 189 Colo. 421, 542 P.2d 371 (1975); Golden v. City of Overland Park, 224 Kan. 591, 584 P.2d 130 (1978); Lowe v. City of Missoula, 165 Mont. 38, 525 P.2d 551 (1974);

and the doctrine's limited momentum seems to have largely petered out.[371] By the mid-1990s, several states had outright rejected the *Fasano* doctrine.[372] At least two states repudiated the doctrine after it had been previously adopted.[373] Also, while the United States Supreme Court has not had occasion to pass upon the doctrine itself, the Court's characterization of the applicant rezoning process as "legislative" in another context has thrown cold water on *Fasano*.[374]

§ 9.23 ZONING BY REFERENDUM AND INITIATIVE

A "referendum" is a vote of the people of a state, city, or county that has the effect of ratifying or setting aside a piece of legislation that has been previously adopted by the legislative body of the governmental entity. In other words, the legislation is "referred" to the voters, either by the legislative body itself or upon a petition signed by some required number of persons. An "initiative" is a piece of legislation not previously enacted by the legislative body that is adopted as a new measure by direct vote of the people. In essence, it is direct legislation by the people. Initiatives are generally put on the ballot by a petition signed by some required number of persons. As of the mid-1990s, "almost all states ha[d] constitutional provisions authorizing the referendum at the state and local level, while about half the states ha[d] constitutional provisions authorizing the initiative at both governmental levels. Initiatives and referenda may also be authorized by statute or by local charters."[375] Within the study of planning and zoning law, one interesting issue centers on the extent to which referenda or initiatives may ratify, set aside, or adopt zoning ordinances. Because the considerations for referenda and initiatives are or may be different, these materials consider first the referendum process and then the initiative process.

On at least two occasions, the United States Supreme Court has held that the United States Constitution does not forbid the use of the referendum process for local

---

Parkridge v. City of Seattle, 89 Wn.2d 454, 573 P.2d 359 (1978); Tate v. Miles, 503 A.2d 187 (Del.1986). Some of these decisions applied the *Fasano* rule to denials of rezoning applications as well as to approvals.

[371] Wait v. City of Scottsdale, 127 Ariz. 107, 618 P.2d 601 (1980); Arnel Development Co. v. City of Costa Mesa, 28 Cal.3d 511, 169 Cal.Rptr. 904, 620 P.2d 565 (1980); Florida Land Co. v. City of Winter Springs, 427 So.2d 170 (Fla.1983); Hall Paving Co. v. Hall County, 237 Ga. 14, 226 S.E.2d 728 (1976); Pemberton v. Montgomery County, 275 Md. 363, 340 A.2d 240 (1975); Kirk v. Tyrone Township, 398 Mich. 429, 247 N.W.2d 848 (1976); State v. City of Rochester, 268 N.W.2d 885 (Minn.1978); Quinn v. Town of Dodgeville, 122 Wis.2d 570, 364 N.W.2d 149 (1985) (exercise of town's veto power over county zoning decision changing district boundaries within town was a "legislative" act and was entitled to a presumption of validity). For the background of Kirk v. Tyrone Township, see Cunningham, Reflections on Stare Decisis in Michigan: The Rise and Fall of the "Rezoning as Administrative Act" Doctrine, 75 Mich.L.Rev. 983 (1977). West's Ann.Cal.Gov.Code § 65301.5 now provides expressly that adoption of a rezoning amendment is a "legislative" act.

[372] See, e.g., Cabana v. Kenai Peninsula Borough, 21 P.3d 833 (Alaska 2001); Wait v. City of Scottsdale, 127 Ariz. 107, 618 P.2d 601 (1980); Arnel Development Co. v. City of Costa Mesa, 28 Cal. 3d 511, 169 Cal. Rptr. 904, 620 P.2d 565 (1980); Hall Paving Co. v. Hall County, 237 Ga. 14, 226 S.E.2d 728 (1976).

[373] Colorado, which had previously adopted the *Fasano* doctrine, has since eviscerated, if not actually repudiated, it in Margolis v. District Court, 638 P.2d 297 (Colo.1981). And Greens at Fort Missoula, LLC v. City of Missoula, 271 Mont. 398, 897 P.2d 1078 (1995), expressly overruled Lowe v. City of Missoula, 165 Mont. 38, 525 P.2d 551 (1974), which had adopted the *Fasano* doctrine.

[374] The *Fasano* concept, if not the actual doctrine, was rejected in City of Eastlake v. Forest City Enterprises, Inc., 426 U.S. 668, 96 S.Ct. 2358, 49 L.Ed.2d 132 (1976), on remand 48 Ohio St.2d 47, 356 N.E.2d 499 (1976), sustaining an ordinance requiring a referendum, with a favorable vote of 55%, to give effect to any zoning change adopted by the city council. Accord: R.G. Moore Bldg. Corp. v. Committee for Repeal of Ordinance, 239 Va. 484, 391 S.E.2d 587 (1990) (rezoning is "legislative," and hence subject to referendum).

[375] D. Mandelker, Planning and Control of Land Development, 231 (8th ed. 2011).

zoning or rezoning ordinances.[376] In the later of the two decisions just cited, City of Eastlake v. Forest City Enterprises, the Court cited Federalist Paper Number 39 for the Lockean proposition that free to reserve a part of the legislative power to themselves since our system of government supposes that they originally delegated a part of that power to their elected representatives, they are. Of course, as the Court said, legislative acts by the people are subject to the usual constitutional limitations on such acts, such as regulatory takings or denials of due process. Note, however, that the Court did not require state or local governments to reserve this power and only authorized it if a state or local government has chosen to do so. Even in states in which the referendum power generally exists, state courts seem divided as to whether that power extends to local zoning or rezoning ordinances. The question is whether something about zoning and rezoning ordinances makes them distinct from other kinds of actions that may be taken by local legislative bodies.

In states that follow the *Fasano* doctrine that applicant rezonings are quasi-judicial and not legislative acts, one would expect courts to not allow such rezoning ordinances to be subjected to the referendum process. The reason is plain: the people may not be judges, even if they may be legislators. In *Fasano* states, judicial decisions seem to bear out this conclusion.[377] In the large majority of other states which do not follow the *Fasano* doctrine, judicial decisions are split over the use of referenda of rezoning ordinances.[378] States that have allowed it tend to mirror the Supreme Court's reasoning in *Eastlake*. But other states, in which referenda are generally allowed, have not approved its use for zoning and rezoning ordinances. They usually reason that the nature of the zoning process differentiates it from other kinds of legislation. Unlike ordinary legislation, zoning enabling acts and local ordinances generally require public hearings and at least some findings of fact by planning commissions and perhaps local legislative bodies. Zoning and rezoning is supposed to be based upon a certain measure of administrative expertise. However, these safeguards and principles may be nullified if the voters have the final word in an election in which a zoning action may be turned into a popularity contest in the political arena.[379]

There are fewer judicial decisions considering zoning through initiatives than those focused on the referendum process, but the decisions that courts have reached have leaned against the use of initiatives. The best known decision upholding the initiative process in principle is Arnel Development Co. v. City of Costa Mesa, from California, though the particular rezoning ordinance in that case was, in a later decision, struck

---

[376] City of Eastlake v. Forest City Enterprises, 426 U.S. 668, 96 S.Ct. 2358, 49 L.Ed.2d 132 (1976) (approving a city charter provision that required that proposed land-use amendments be ratified by a 55% vote of the people); James v. Valtierra, 402 U.S. 137, 91 S.Ct. 1331, 28 L.Ed.2d 678 (1971) (approving California's requirement that required a referendum vote on all local public housing projects).

[377] E.g., Leonard v. City of Bothell, 87 Wn.2d 847, 557 P.2d 1306 (1976). Cf. Greens at Fort Missoula, LLC v. City of Missoula, 271 Mont. 398, 897 P.2d 1078 (1995), in which the court approved of the referendum process and in doing so expressly overruled Lowe v. City of Missoula, 165 Mont. 38, 525 P.2d 551 (1974), which had adopted the *Fasano* doctrine.

[378] See discussion and review of decisions in J. Juergensmeyer & T. Roberts, Land Use Planning and Control Law § 5.5 (1998); and in D. Mandelker, Land Use Law § 6.82 (4th ed. 1997).

[379] See, e.g., Township of Sparta v. Spillane, 125 N.J.Super. 519, 312 A.2d 154 (1973), cert. denied 64 N.J. 493, 317 A.2d 706 (1974); see also Marcilynn A. Burke, The Emperor's New Clothes: Exposing the Failures of Regulating Land Use Through the Ballot Box, 84 Notre Dame L. Rev. 1453 (2009); Kenneth A. Stahl, The Artifice of Local Growth Politics: At-Large Elections, Ballot-Box Zoning, and Judicial Review, 94 Marq. L. Rev. 1 (2010).

down on constitutional grounds as "arbitrary and discriminatory."[380] Elsewhere, courts addressing the issue have overwhelmingly held that the initiative process may not be used to adopt or amend zoning ordinances.[381] In a few states with especially broad constitutional initiative provisions, however, courts have held that the people have the power to both amend and enact zoning ordinances.[382] Still, the primary objection made to use of the referendum process—that it nullifies the special safeguards of hearings and planning expertise—may be made more strongly against the initiative process. At least with the referendum process these special safeguards have been met in the planning commission and local legislative body before the voters get hold of the ordinance. In contrast, with the initiative process the safeguards are never applied. One gets the distinct impression from their decisions that courts are concerned that initiatives will be used to rezone land to stop unpopular projects such as commercial uses or low-income-housing developments.

§ 9.24 FLOATING ZONES AND PLANNED UNIT DEVELOPMENTS

Floating zoning and planned unit developments are so interconnected that it is difficult to define one without referring to the other. Some treatises do not separate the definitions,[383] but we shall try. A "floating" zone ordinance is one that gives owners of land within certain zones an explicit option to apply to have it placed down in certain existing "regular" zones. For instance, the ordinance might allow a landowner to have land rezoned for multi-family dwellings in the middle of single-family-residence zones, provided the applicant meets certain special conditions. Apparently to protect against charges of spot zoning, such options are almost always conditioned on a requirement that the land be a certain minimum size, such as 10 acres or 25 acres Perhaps the difference between that traditional approach to rezoning and this "floating zoning" approach is merely one of degree in that the latter more specifically invites the rezoning and provides special guidelines for it.

In "real life," floating zoning provisions nearly always requires as one of the conditions to the rezoning that the landowner accompany the rezoning application with a specific detailed plan for an integrated development of the area to be rezoned. Developments approved pursuant to these plans are often called "planned unit developments" or "PUDs." The kinds of developments that are permitted under PUD

---

[380] The *Arnel* case took a rather strange trip through the California courts. After the trial judge upheld the use of the initiative process, a division of the California Court of Appeals reversed, on the general ground that the initiative process could not be used. Arnel Development Co. v. City of Costa Mesa, 98 Cal.App.3d 567, 159 Cal.Rptr. 592 (1979). On appeal to the California Supreme Court, that court reversed the decision, holding that the initiative process was a proper method to amend the existing zoning ordinance. But that court transferred the case back to the court of appeal, to determine whether this particular rezoning ordinance was valid on its merits. Ditto, 28 Cal.3d 511, 620 P.2d 565, 169 Cal.Rptr. 904 (1980). Finally the court of appeal struck down the rezoning on the ground that the ordinance was "arbitrary and discriminatory" against the landowner. The court said that the ordinance would have been invalid on that ground even if it had been enacted by the city council. Ditto, 126 Cal.App.3d 330, 178 Cal.Rptr. 723 (1981). A reading of the latter opinion makes it pretty clear that the rezoning was struck down because it prevented the development of a moderate-income housing development.

[381] J. Juergensmeyer & T. Roberts, Land Use Planning and Control Law § 5.5 (1998); D. Mandelker, Land Use Law § 6.83 (4th ed. 1997).

[382] See, e.g., Staudenmaier v. Municipality of Anchorage, 139 P.3d 1259 (Alaska 2006); City of Colorado Springs v. Bull, 143 P.3d 1127 (Colo. Ct. App. 2006); City of Seattle v. Yes for Seattle, 93 P.3d 176 (Wash. Ct. App. Div. 1 2004).

[383] E.g., J. Juergensmeyer & T. Roberts, Land Use Planning and Control Law § 4.16 (1998).

provisions vary by jurisdiction. Some ordinances may permit only planned residential developments (PRD's). Others may be tailored to permit other kinds of PUD's such as for shopping centers, office parks, or industrial parks. Still other ordinances may be so generally drawn as to permit any of the above.[384] Since the submission and approval of the PUD is a condition to obtaining the rezoning, a floating-zoning-PUD ordinance has some of the characteristics of the special exception (conditional use permit) that are discussed in a later section of this chapter.

The PUD plan itself is somewhat akin to a subdivision plat, which is also discussed later. For instance, a residential PUD plan typically shows streets (generally artistically curving), the locations of buildings and descriptions of their designs (*e.g.,* six-unit apartment, etc.), open spaces and recreational areas, and other physical features of the whole integrated planned area in some detail. "Cluster zoning" provisions, in which there are no fixed setbacks for individual buildings but buildings are allowed or required to be clustered with ample open spaces among them, are a characteristic feature of floating-zoning-PUD ordinances. Such ordinances generally allow a mix of uses, such as—in our residential PUD example—single-family homes, multi-family dwellings of various sizes, and perhaps even some supporting retail commercial uses. Both the application for rezoning and the PUD plan will be submitted to the planning commission, and the approval of each one depends upon the approval of the other: it is a "package deal." The planning commission acts as a clearinghouse, distributing copies of the submitted plan to other interested municipal departments such as the building, engineering, and health departments, and receiving their input. This results in negotiations with the applicant that usually result in modifications of the plan. Of course, as with any rezoning there must be public hearings on the plan as well. If agreement is reached on the final plan and on the rezoning itself, the planning commission recommends the rezoning and the plan to the local legislative body.

The floating-zoning-PUD concept was an innovation that came into American land use planning in the 1950s. As has happened repeatedly in zoning law, some courts were wary of the entire idea when it was new. A famous early decision disapproving of the technique was the Pennsylvania case of Eves v. Zoning Board of Adjustment of Lower Gwynedd Township, in which the floating zoning would have allowed industrial uses in a 103-acre tract carved out of a residential area.[385] On the other hand, New York had previously approved a floating rezone for a 10-acre parcel for multi-family dwellings in a single-family zone in its famous decision in Rodgers v. Village of Tarrytown.[386] Today, however, the floating-zoning-PUD technique has become generally accepted and is a standard feature of many, if not most, zoning ordinances. Even Pennsylvania has

---

[384] Will you pardon a personal anecdote? A few years ago, after examining his city's then very general PUD ordinance, it seemed to the writer that it might be used for at least commercial uses, such as a shopping center, and perhaps for industrial or business parks, as well as for residential PUD's. So, he called the local planning department and asked if, in their opinion, it might be used for a shopping center. Their reply was, yes, they thought so—and they would welcome such an application, though so far it had been used only for residential PUD's.

[385] 401 Pa. 211, 164 A.2d 7 (1960). The court's objections were rather diffuse, but spot zoning was the most clearly articulated objection. Professor Charles M. Haar, a leading pioneer in teaching land-use planning, was critical of the *Eves* decision in his article, Haar & Hering, The *Lower Gwynedd Township* Case: Too Flexible Zoning or an Inflexible Judiciary?, 74 Harv. L. Rev. 1552 (1961). See also Reno, Non-Euclidean Zoning: The Use of the Floating Zone, 23 Md. L. Rev. 105 (1963).

[386] 302 N.Y. 115, 96 N.E.2d 731 (1951). Huff v. Board of Zoning Appeals, 214 Md. 48, 133 A.2d 83 (1957), is another early decision that approved of floating zoning.

effectively bypassed, if not literally overruled, its decision in *Eves*.[387] Where PUD ordinances exist, formal comprehensive plans generally provide for them to be scattered throughout the municipality, thus addressing the spot zoning objection.

None of this is to say that every proposed PUD gets approved. As already suggested above, the developer and the municipality may not be able to agree on the development plan. Moreover, it is still possible that a given floating-zoning application may be struck down as spot zoning or on the ground that the ordinance lacks specific enough guidelines.[388] That problem may be exacerbated by inadequacies in the local comprehensive plan. Some courts may also be wary of the "dealmaking" that goes on in the negotiations over PUD plans, fearing that they invite corruption even more than straight rezonings.[389] Nevertheless, the floating-zoning-PUD technique has become a familiar feature and important flexibility device in American zoning law.

§ 9.25 CONTRACT AND CONDITIONAL ZONING

In pure theory, when a landowner applies for a rezoning, the planning commission and local legislative body should not take into account the particular use to which the owner proposes to put the land. Theoretically, they should consider only whether the rational development of the area, the comprehensive plan if there is one, and the public good justify rezoning as outlined in the proposal. However, in practice applicants often do disclose the particular use they want to make and local authorities do take this into account. Such an approach is sometimes called "project rezoning" and is contrasted with "non-project rezoning" in which owners seeking rezoning does not disclose any particular development plan. When the owner applies for a project rezone, local authorities often want to "tailor" the regulations applicable to the proposed rezoned tract so as to (1) protect neighboring land from negative externalities from the proposed development and (2) preclude the developer from submitting plants for a very different type of development after securing a desired rezoning action. For example, suppose that a planning commission and city council is willing to rezone certain land from residential to commercial so long as the project that results is a quiet professional office building that serves the community. On the other hand, suppose the commission does not want a gas station developed on the parcel even though that is also a permitted use in commercial zones. The "tailoring" needed to achieve these narrow goals might be achievable by creating in advance "a whole range of much more sophisticated districts than are generally found in zoning ordinances, so that local authorities can "pick the district that is closest to the particular proposal made by the developer."[390] The special exception (conditional use permit) might sometimes accomplish the purpose, too. But many local governing bodies want greater flexibility than would be possible with "preset" classifications and therefore resort to what is termed either "conditional" or "contract" zoning.[391]

---

[387] See Cheney v. Village 2 at New Hope, Inc., 429 Pa. 626, 241 A.2d 81 (1968), in which the court approved a PUD and indicated that the problem in *Eves* was that the rezoning there would have allowed incompatible industrial uses in a residential area.

[388] See J. Juergensmeyer & T. Roberts, Land Use Planning and Control Law § 4.16 (1998).

[389] This is suggested in R. Ellickson & D. Tarlock, Land-Use Controls, 236–38 (1981).

[390] Krasnowiecki, Abolish Zoning, 31 Syracuse L.Rev. 719, 741 (1980).

[391] See generally 2 R. Anderson, American Law of Zoning § 9.21 (3d ed. 1986); J. Juergensmeyer & T. Roberts, Land Use Planning and Control Law § 5.11 (1998); D. Mandelker, Land Use Law §§ 6.64–6.67 (4th

There is some inconsistency in land use law with respect to contract or conditional zoning, in part because of conflicting judicial attitudes and the fact that jurisdictions have used these terms to describe several different techniques. Rightly used, at least to the author, "contract" zoning should mean that the municipality rezones pursuant to some type of contractual agreement between owner and municipality. This agreement could take the form of a "bilateral" contract or a "unilateral" contract. In a bilateral contract, a city promises to rezone in exchange for the owner's promise to, say, build the professional office building described above and nothing else. In case it isn't obvious: that form of contract zoning is unenforceable and against public policy because legislative bodies may not contractually bind themselves to enact specific legislation. The city's promise under such an agreement is illusory, so the owner's promise is also unenforceable for lack of consideration.[392]

A "unilateral" contract is one in which a landowner promises to build only the professional office building *if* the city rezones. Some courts might call this "conditional" zoning because the city's performance is a condition to the owner's. Since the city does not attempt to contract away its legislative discretion, it seems in theory that the owner's promise should be enforceable if the city does in fact choose to rezone. But at this point some courts raise other objections that cause them to hold such contracts, and the rezoning adopted pursuant to them, invalid. The general nature of objections in these courts is that it is not the business of the city council to contract for the control of land uses and that only zoning is authorized for that purpose.[393]

A safer—though by no means acceptable in all jurisdictions—technique is what one might call "true conditional zoning." This technique comes in several variants. For instance, a city council might insert into its rezoning ordinance the use limitations it wishes. Alternatively, a city council might require as a condition to a rezoning that the applicant to place restrictive covenants on the land constraining it to develop only in the way the city desires. Third, a city council could both insert the limitations it wishes into its rezoning ordinance and require the applicant to record the same limitations in a running restrictive covenant on the land. (See chapter 8, part B, of this Hornbook, for the principles of "running covenants" that will be invoked in the present discussion without specific attribution.) With all three of these techniques there are generally negotiations with the developer before the city acts, although in theory the city could act without prior negotiations.

"Conditional" zoning techniques have generally been sustained against attacks by neighboring landowners and by developers hoping not to have to comply with agreed-upon conditions after their land is rezoned.[394] Indeed, the general trend over the last

ed. 1997); Kramer, Contract Zoning—Old Myths and New Realities, 34 Land Use L. & Zoning Dig. 4 (1982); Comment, Contract and Conditional Zoning: A Tool for Zoning Flexibility, 23 Hastings L.J. 825 (1972).

[392] Hartnett v. Austin, 93 So.2d 86 (Fla. 1956), is a leading early contract zoning case that held such an agreement to be void. There were several problems in the *Hartnett* case, but the bilateral nature of the agreement was the most critical problem. See also dictum in Collard v. Incorporated Village of Flower Hill, 52 N.Y.2d 594, 421 N.E.2d 818, 439 N.Y.S.2d 326 (1981). See 2 R. Anderson, American Law of Zoning § 9.21, n. 75 (3d ed. 1986); D. Mandelker, Land Use Law § 6.65 (4th ed. 1997).

[393] See 2 R. Anderson, American Law of Zoning § 9.21, esp. notes 96, 97 (3d ed. 1986).

[394] E.g., Scrutton v. County of Sacramento, 275 Cal.App.2d 412, 79 Cal.Rptr. 872 (1969); Cross v. Hall County, 238 Ga. 709, 235 S.E.2d 379 (1977); Sylvania Electric Products, Inc. v. City of Newton, 344 Mass. 428, 183 N.E.2d 118 (1962); Bucholz v. City of Omaha, 174 Neb. 862, 120 N.W.2d 270 (1963); Church v. Town of Islip, 8 N.Y.2d 254, 203 N.Y.S.2d 866, 168 N.E.2d 680 (1960); Collard v. Incorporated Village of Flower Hill, 52 N.Y.2d 594, 439 N.Y.S.2d 326, 421 N.E.2d 818 (1981); Gladwyne Colony, Inc. v. Township of Lower Merion, 409 Pa. 441, 187 A.2d 549 (1963); State ex rel. Myhre v. City of Spokane, 70 Wn.2d 207, 422 P.2d 790 (1967);

half-century has been toward increasing judicial approval.[395] However, the analysis in judicial opinions on this topic has not been particularly clear and often turns on issues that seem relatively unimportant. Moreover, courts in both Connecticut and Pennsylvania still do not approve of either "contract" or "conditional" zoning.[396] Objections these courts most frequently raise are that the rezoning is "spot zoning," that it violates the requirements that zoning be "comprehensive" and "uniform," and that it is a "bargaining away" of the local government's police power.[397]

Although some scholarly commentators disapprove of "conditional" or "contract" zoning,[398] it is hard to see why this zoning technique is any more objectionable than the well-accepted practices of imposing *ad hoc* conditions when a variance or a special exception (or special use or conditional use) is approved[399] or imposing conditions not expressly set out in the subdivision regulations when new subdivision developments are approved.[400] In all these cases the additional protective conditions imposed by the municipality obviously benefit neighboring landowners. A rezoned area is arguably no more a "spot" under a conditional zoning approach than if the municipality had rezoned it to the same zone without conditions and the developer had freely chosen to develop it in the same way. The "bargaining away" argument has some slight force if, by it, the court is expressing concern about possible corrupt "dealmaking". However, that concern is arguably no greater in this context than with the negotiating that goes into planned-unit-developments or the formulation of *ad hoc* conditions attached to special exceptions and variances.

Because of the division of judicial opinion on this issue from state to state, or lack of any decision in some states, it behooves any developer's attorney to search a state's decisions carefully before taking actions that might implicate these issue. If the highest court of the state has a decision approving a certain technique, the safe course is to use that technique. It follows, of course, that if the state is one that seems to have foreclosed the use of any such technique, none may safely be tried. In the many states in which there is no answer or no clear answer, the safest course may be to impose the restrictions the municipality desires by way of running restrictive covenants of the kind described in chapter 8, part B, of this treatise and not to put parallel restrictions into the rezoning ordinance. This is contrary to the opinion of the authors of another leading treatise, who

---

Housing and Redevelopment Authority v. Jorgensen, 328 N.W.2d 740 (Minn.1983). Contra: Hartnett v. Austin, 93 So.2d 86 (Fla.1956); Cederberg v. City of Rockford, 8 Ill.App.3d 984, 291 N.E.2d 249 (1972); Carlino v. Whitpain Investors, 499 Pa. 498, 453 A.2d 1385 (1982). But see Broward County v. Griffey, 366 So.2d 869 (Fla.App.1979), cert. denied 385 So.2d 757 (Fla.1980), as to Florida law.

[395] See especially the well-known decisions in Sylvania Electric Products, Inc. v. City of Newton, 344 Mass. 428, 183 N.E.2d 118 (1962), Bucholz v. City of Omaha, 174 Neb. 862, 120 N.W.2d 270 (1963), and Church v. Town of Islip, 8 N.Y.2d 254, 203 N.Y.S.2d 866, 168 N.E.2d 680 (1960), in which courts that had previously had decisions disapproving "contract" zoning approved forms of "conditional" zoning. See generally 2 R. Anderson, American Law of Zoning § 9.21 (3d ed. 1986); J. Juergensmeyer & T. Roberts, Land Use Planning and Control Law § 5.11 (1998).

[396] See, e.g., Kaufman v. Zoning Comm'n, 653 A.2d 798, 812 (Conn. 1995); Carlino v. Whitpain Investors, 499 Pa. 498, 453 A.2d 1385 (1982). See generally, 2 R. Anderson, American Law of Zoning § 9.21 (3d ed. 1986); D. Mandlker, Land Use Law § 6.66 (4th ed. 1997).

[397] Kaufman v. Zoning Comm'n, 653 A.2d 798, 812 (Conn. 1995); Carlino v. Whitpain Investors, 499 Pa. 498, 453 A.2d 1385 (1982); see also Collard v. Incorporated Village of Flower Hill, 52 N.Y.2d 594, 421 N.E.2d 818, 439 N.Y.S.2d 326 (1981), identifies and, by implication rejects, all these arguments.

[398] E.g., D. Mandelker, Land Use Law § 6.64 (4th ed. 1997); Krasnowiecki, Abolish Zoning, 31 Syracuse L.Rev. 719, 741 (1980).

[399] See §§ 9.28, 9.29, infra.

[400] See §§ 9.30, 9.32, infra.

fear the "uncertainty" of restrictive covenants—even though they are placed of public record—feeling that the restrictions should be placed in the rezoning ordinance where "one expects to find" them.[401] However, a recorded covenant, if properly done and recorded, is an enforceable running restriction on the land and one that, indeed, cannot be undone by some later city council. It would show up in the title examination whenever the developer or any successor sold the land.

§ 9.26 EXCLUSIONARY ZONING: CONSTITUTIONAL OBJECTIONS

All zoning is exclusionary in that it excludes certain uses and thereby excludes certain classes of persons from residing or working in certain parts of a community—a fact that has been understood from the beginning of zoning.[402] However, the term "exclusionary zoning" has come to refer to zoning that has a pronounced effect of excluding persons of low or moderate income from a whole town or from an area within the town. Zoning techniques that tend to do this include large-lot and wide-frontage requirements (big lots usually mean big, expensive homes); exclusions of multi-family dwellings (apartments tend to be affordable housing); restrictions on the number of bedrooms in multi-family dwellings (keeping out families with lots of children); exclusions of mobile homes; and the over-zoning of undeveloped land for industrial or commercial rather than residential use (to limit population growth and hopefully improve the tax base). Courts in several states have recognized that zoning that is "exclusionary" in the narrower sense described above may be invalid on constitutional grounds. Likewise, the United States Supreme Court has recognized the possibility that such zoning may also violate the Equal Protection Clause of the United States Constitution. This section first describes state decisions involving these issues then highlights some from the Supreme Court.

Exclusionary Zoning Activities at the State Level

Exclusionary zoning decisions in which state appellate courts have been willing to grant relief have nearly all come from New Jersey, Pennsylvania, New York, and New Hampshire. In California and Oregon, the state legislatures have passed statutes intended to fight exclusionary zoning.[403] However, in most other states local conditions have not produced true exclusionary zoning cases or courts and legislatures have generally not been willing to grant relief.[404] In New Jersey, exclusionary zoning litigation has been facilitated by much more relaxed "standing" rules than those applied in the federal courts. New Jersey has thus permitted nonresidents to initiate exclusionary zoning cases[405] and generally has not required that the plaintiffs have an interest in a

---

[401] See J. Juergensmeyer & T. Roberts, Land Use Planning and Control Law § 5.11 (1998).

[402] In striking down the zoning ordinances that the Supreme Court later upheld in the *Euclid* case, Judge D. C. Westenhaver, judge of the District Court for the Northern District of Ohio, wrote these oft-quoted words: "In the last analysis, the result to be accomplished is to classify the population and segregate them according to their income or situation in life." Ambler Realty Co. v. Village of Euclid, 297 Fed. 307, 316 (N.D.Ohio 1924).

[403] Cal. Gov't Code § 65583 (West 2018); Or. Rev. Stat. Ann. § 197.005 (2018).

[404] See, e.g., Johnson v. Town of Edgartown, 425 Mass. 117, 680 N.E.2d 37 (1997) (three-acre minimum size for residential lots not exclusionary); Countrywalk Condominiums, Inc. v. City of Orchard Lake Village, 221 Mich.App. 19, 561 N.W.2d 405 (1997); see generally Prentiss Dantzler, Exclusionary Zoning: State and Local Reactions to the Mount Laurel Doctrine, 48 Urb. Law. 653 (2016).

[405] E.g., Southern Burlington County NAACP v. Township of Mount Laurel, 67 N.J. 151, 336 A.2d 713 (1975), appeal dismissed and certiorari denied 423 U.S. 808, 96 S.Ct. 18, 46 L.Ed.2d 28 (1975), hereafter

site-specific low-or moderate-income housing project as a condition of bringing suit.[406] Though some of the plaintiffs in the cases in the four states have been minority persons, the courts have not required any showing of racially discriminatory zoning as a condition of granting relief.[407] State legislatures in a few states and some local governmental units have adopted statutes or ordinances that address exclusionary zoning. However, these efforts have attracted less attention than have the decisions from New Jersey, New York, Pennsylvania, and New Hampshire so the following materials discuss the leading decisions first and then briefly describe statutes and ordinances.

The leading state exclusionary zoning case is Southern Burlington County NAACP v. Township of Mt. Laurel, which was twice reviewed by the New Jersey Supreme Court—first in 1975 (*Mt. Laurel I*) and then again in 1983 (*Mt. Laurel II*).[408] In *Mt. Laurel I,* the New Jersey court concluded that the township had over-zoned for industry—preventing any development of a large amount of vacant land—and that the residential zoning classifications placed upon the rest of the township's undeveloped land would "realistically allow only homes within the financial reach of persons of at least middle income" and would exclude "low and moderate income families."[409] On the basis of New Jersey's state constitutional provision guaranteeing to all persons the "natural and unalienable" right "of acquiring, possessing, and protecting property"[410]—which the court viewed as incorporating "requirements of substantive due process and equal protection of the laws"—the court held the Mt. Laurel zoning ordinance invalid to the extent that it failed, "to make realistically possible the opportunity for an appropriate variety and choice of housing for all categories of people who may desire to live there, * * * including all those of low and moderate income."[411] On this basis, the court found that the ordinance failed to promote the general welfare. More specifically, the court held that Mount Laurel "must permit multi-family housing, without bedroom or similar restrictions, as well as small dwellings on very small lots, low cost housing of other types and, in general, high density zoning."[412] The court noted further that "[t]he amount of land removed from residential use by allocation to industrial and commercial purposes must be reasonably related to the present and future potential for such purposes."[413]

---

referred to as *Mount Laurel I*; Home Builders League v. Township of Berlin, 81 N.J. 127, 405 A.2d 381 (1979). *Mount Laurel I* is particularly notable on the standing issue, since all the plaintiffs were individuals, home building contractors, or organizations representing them who were "outsiders" who sought to have the township zone more land for multi-family use, so that they could "get into the township." Essentially contrary is the United States Supreme Court's decision in Warth v. Seldin, 422 U.S. 490, 95 S.Ct. 2197, 45 L.Ed.2d 343 (1975), which denied standing to similar "outsiders" on the ground that they could show no "injury in fact."

[406] E.g., *Mount Laurel I,* ibid. But exclusionary zoning cases may well arise from municipal refusals to rezone a specific site to permit construction of low-or moderate income housing. E.g., Oakwood at Madison, Inc. v. Township of Madison, 72 N.J. 481, 371 A.2d 1192 (1977).

[407] See, e.g., decisions cited in two preceding notes.

[408] Southern Burlington County NAACP v. Township of Mount Laurel, 67 N.J. 151, 336 A.2d 713 (1975), appeal dismissed and certiorari denied 423 U.S. 808, 96 S.Ct. 18, 46 L.Ed.2d 28 (1975), hereafter referred to as *Mount Laurel I*. The second *Mount Laurel* appeal, along with 7 companion cases, is Southern Burlington County NAACP v. Township of Mount Laurel, 92 N.J. 158, 456 A.2d 390 (1983), hereafter referred to as *Mount Laurel II.*

[409] See 67 N.J. at 161–173, 336 A.2d at 718–724.

[410] N.J.S.A. Const. Art. 1, par. 1, quoted in 67 N.J. at 175 n. 11, 336 A.2d at 725 n. 11.

[411] 67 N.J. at 179–188, 336 A.2d at 727–731. The decision was expressly based on the New Jersey Constitution in order to preclude review by the United States Supreme Court.

[412] 67 N.J. at 187, 336 A.2d at 732.

[413] Id.

Since it was obvious that not every New Jersey "developing" municipality could be required to accommodate all the low- and moderate-income persons who might wish to reside in it, the *Mount Laurel* opinion purported to provide a general formula to measure compliance with the court's mandate. This became known as the famous "*Mount Laurel* doctrine." Specifically: (1) every "developing" municipality (2) must zone in such a way as to accommodate" the municipality's (3) "fair share of the present and prospective (4) regional need" for (5) low- and moderate-income housing.[414] The numbers we inserted into the preceding sentence emphasize the elements of the *Mt. Laurel* doctrine. First, the court stated that the doctrine applied only to those municipalities that were near enough to a large city that its centrifugal population pressures created a demand for housing in the municipality. Mt. Laurel Township was described as being within a semicircle that had a radius of about 20 miles from the heart of Camden, New Jersey. It was also slightly over 10 miles from Philadelphia, Pennsylvania. Subsequent New Jersey decisions made clear that the *Mount Laurel* doctrine does not apply to communities that are already fully developed or are beyond the zone of population pressures from a large city.[415] "Fair share" is difficult to define, but *Mount Laurel* and subsequent New Jersey decisions made clear that it cannot be satisfied by showing that other municipalities within the region have provided more than their fair share of zoning for low- and moderate-income housing. The words "regional need" introduced into the *Mount Laurel* decision the concept into planning and zoning law that zoning should be on a regional basis. And the decision obviously focused upon housing needs for low- and moderate-income families, not upon zoning for other purposes. As already noted, it did not focus on housing for minority groups, though it has historically been generally recognized that minority groups tend to have a disproportionately greater need for low-cost housing.

In *Mt. Laurel II,*[416] the New Jersey Court reaffirmed and extended its *Mt. Laurel I* holdings. The first feature of *Mt. Laurel II* that strikes the reader is the court's disclosure of the tumultuous reception *Mt. Laurel I* had received in New Jersey. It is no exaggeration to say that, while the decision had been welcomed by many and had tended to receive approval by legal scholars, there had been massive resistance to it in New Jersey. The state supreme court had been accused of invading the province of the legislature and engaging in social engineering in the guise of legal reasoning. *Mt. Laurel II* gives evidence that many towns had either refused to comply or had dragged their feet. Even many lower courts in New Jersey had not applied the *Mount Laurel* doctrine with the rigor that the supreme court had intended. Indeed, after *Mt. Laurel I* was remanded to the trial court, even Mount Laurel Township had only superficially complied with the supreme court's intent and the trial judge who was reversed in *Mt. Laurel II* had approved its efforts. One positive response was that the state legislature, which the court had prodded in *Mt. Laurel I,* had adopted the New Jersey Fair Housing Act establishing a Council on Affordable Housing.[417] The Council had promulgated its State Development Guide Plan (SDGP), which partially addressed the problems with which the court had grappled. Unfortunately, *Mt. Laurel I* had not produced any appreciable amount of low- and moderate-income housing *on the ground,* The court saw

---

[414] See 67 N.J. at 188, 336 A.2d at 732.

[415] See especially Pascack Ass'n, Ltd. v. Mayor and Council of Township of Washington, 74 N.J. 470, 379 A.2d 6 (1977); Fobe Assocs. v. Board of Adjustment, 74 N.J. 519, 379 A.2d 31 (1977).

[416] Southern Burlington County N.A.A.C.P. v. Township of Mount Laurel, 92 N.J. 158, 456 A.2d 390 (1983).

[417] N.J. Stat. §§ 52:27D–301, et seq.

that it could not because, the court said in *Mt. Laurel II,* it was one thing for zoning to *allow* the development of the desired housing, but it was another for developers to actually *produce* it. In *Mt. Laurel II,* the Supreme Court of New Jersey thus attempted to fashion devices that would not only halt the resistance to *Mt. Laurel I* but would induce developers to build on the ground. With a steely resolve and an exercise of judicial activism rarely seen, the court undertook to implement the housing goals it had had in *Mt. Laurel I.*

The most straightforward way to explain *Mt. Laurel II* and its significance is to enumerate and highlight is main features. First, since the court found that since the "growth areas" defined in the SGDP were similar to the "developing" communities the court had defined in *Mt. Laurel I* but covered even broader areas, the court substituted the SDGP definition. Second, the court established that challengers in exclusionary zoning litigation can make a *prima facie* case for invalidity by proving that a zoning ordinance in fact substantially limits construction of low- and moderate-income housing. Third, the case established that a municipality must introduce "numerical" evidence of the number of units needed immediately and within a reasonable time in the future, to rebut the *prima facie* case and cannot satisfy its burden simply by showing it has made a "bona fide effort" to eliminate exclusionary land use regulations. Fourth, the court determined that it would name three trial judges to hear all *Mt. Laurel* cases for the entire state as a way of taking foot-dragging local judges out of this type of litigation. Fifth, the court held that if removal of exclusionary land use regulations did not independently provide a "reasonable opportunity" for construction of low- and moderate-income housing a municipality must cooperate with the attempts of land developers to obtain federal housing subsidies and undertake various forms of "inclusionary zoning." Finally, if all else fails and a trial court finds that a municipality has not met its *Mt. Laurel* obligation, the court must appoint a master to advise on the needed zoning revisions and issue mandatory orders to the local legislative body to enact specific remedial ordinances. If the plaintiff is a developer, the court may grant what New Jersey calls the "builder's remedy"—a judicial grant of permission to the builder to proceed with a proposed development.

An important sub-feature of *Mt. Laurel II* is the court's rather complete "catalog" of possible "inclusionary zoning" devices. The court's list of these devices includes (a) density bonuses to developers who voluntarily provide units for low- and moderate-income households; (b) mandatory provisions requiring developers to set aside some dwelling units for low- and moderate-income households ("mandatory set-asides"); (c) over-zoning for low- and moderate-income housing in some zones; and (d) allowing mobile homes in residential zones.

The only other court that has substantially approached the New Jersey decisions on the topic of fair housing is the Supreme Court of New Hampshire. In its 1991 decision in Britton v. Town of Chester, that court struck down a town zoning ordinance that effectively limited "affordable" housing to only 1.7 percent of the town's areas and required developers to pay for experts to assist the town in assessing the impact of proposed planned unit developments.[418] The court also awarded a "builder's remedy" to

---

[418] Britton v. Town of Chester, 134 N.H. 434, 595 A.2d 492 (1991). The term "affordable" is now in common use to describe what was called "low- and moderate-income" housing in *Mount Laurel II*. The *Britton* decision, unlike the two *Mount Laurel* decisions, was not constitutionally based; instead it was based entirely on the New Hampshire court's holding that the town's existing zoning ordinance did not promote "the health,

the plaintiff developer but, unlike New Jersey, made the granting of that remedy always discretionary with trial courts. The New Hampshire court did not impose a *Mount Laurel II* duty with respect to accommodation of a "fair share of the regional need for low- and moderate-income housing" as a basis for calculating how many new housing units a municipality should seek to accommodate. However, the New Hampshire regional planning process established relatively soon after the *Britton*[419] has produced "fair share" numbers for each municipality in each planning region.[420] Today, most New Hampshire courts are likely to require municipalities to use these "fair share" numbers as a basis for rezoning land for the construction of "affordable housing."

Pennsylvania courts encountered some of the earliest exclusionary zoning-type decisions in the mid-1960s, although those cases merely invalidated large-lot residential zoning. The best known of these was National Land and Investment Co. v. Kohn, which invalidated a four-acre residential zoning ordinance.[421] A few years later, in Township of Williston v. Chesterdale Farms,[422] the Pennsylvania Supreme Court seemed to adopt the New Jersey "fair share" rule. However, shortly after that, the court held in Surrick v. Zoning Hearing Board[423] that the "fair share" doctrine stated only a "general precept" and proceeded to apply a substantive due process test instead. The court held that the proper inquiry is "whether the zoning formulas fashioned by [local government] entities reflect a balanced and weighted consideration of the many factors that bear upon local and regional housing needs and development"[424] and applied that test to invalidate the almost total exclusion of apartments from a Philadelphia suburb. For the benefit of Pennsylvania trial courts, the supreme court further stated that, if a trial court determines that a particular municipality is a logical place for high-density housing development because it is part of a growing metropolitan area and has land available for such development, the court should apply an "exclusionary impact" test to determine whether the zoning ordinance denies substantive due process. Accordingly, a zoning ordinance that zones a disproportionately small portion of the municipal area for multifamily development may be invalid even though it does not totally exclude such development.[425]

---

safety, or the general welfare of the community" and hence was *ultra vires* because it did not advance the purposes set forth in New Hampshire's zoning enabling act.

[419] Statutory provisions authorizing creation of regional planning commissions and defining their powers are contained in N.H.Rev.Stat.Ann. §§ 36.45 through 36.58 (1986 and 1991 Cum.Supp.). Id. § 36.47, Para. 1, provides (*inter alia*) that "[a] regional planning commission's powers shall be advisory, and shall generally pertain to the development of the region within its jurisdiction as a whole. * * * The area of jurisdiction of a regional planning commission shall include the areas of the respective municipalities within the delineated planning region." In *Britton,* the court made no attempt to delineate the "region" of which Chester was a part. It was, in fact, located within the Southern New Hampshire Planning Commission Region, for which the Southern New Hampshire Planning Commission had (in June, 1988) completed the "housing element of the Land Use Plan 2010" which identified a total "affordable housing" need for the region of 8,322 units based on the 1980 census. Chester's adjusted "fair share" allocation was 90 units. Chester's own master plan, which assumed the relevant region to be Rockingham County, called for 67 units of "affordable housing." Amicus Curiae Brief in Britton v. Town of Chester, reprinted in 40 Wash.U.J. of Urban & Contemp.Law 3, at 20, n. 50.

[420] Payne, Exclusionary Zoning and the "Chester Doctrine," 20 Real Est.L.J. 366, at 327 (1992).

[421] 419 Pa. 504, 215 A.2d 597 (1965). See also Appeal of Kit-Mar Builders, Inc., 439 Pa. 466, 268 A.2d 765 (1970) (two-acre residential zoning invalid).

[422] 462 Pa. 445, 341 A.2d 466 (1975).

[423] 476 Pa. 182, 382 A.2d 105 (1977).

[424] 476 Pa. at 191, 382 A.2d at 109–110.

[425] 476 Pa. at 194–195, 382 A.2d at 111.

In general, Pennsylvania's fair housing decisions do not show the judicial activism that characterizes the New Jersey decisions reviewed above. Also, the plaintiffs in the Pennsylvania cases have been "insiders"—owners or developers in the towns—and not "outsiders" as in the New Jersey cases. Therefore, Pennsylvania courts have not been called upon to grant standing in the very liberal way New Jersey has. When existing zoning regulations are invalidated in Pennsylvania, the "builder's remedy"—granting permission for his proposed development—is practically assured by statutes (codifying prior case law) providing for that remedy if the developer's site is suitable for the proposed development and public facilities available at that site are adequate.[426]

In New York, the leading 1972 decision in Golden v. Town of Ramapo upheld the validity of an 18-year, phased-growth plan that limited housing starts.[427] Legal commentators sometimes classify the *Ramapo* decision as a "phased-growth" one, but the majority opinion recognized that an exclusionary-zoning issue was present and Judge Breitel's dissenting opinion reads much like Justice Hall's decision in *Mt. Laurel I* was to read in 1975. In that same year, the New York Court of Appeals also handed down an exclusionary-zoning decision in Berenson v. Town of New Castle, in which it fashioned a doctrine to restrict exclusionary zoning that was considerably milder than New Jersey's *Mt. Laurel I* (and certainly *Mt. Laurel II*).[428] Also, as in the Pennsylvania decisions just reviewed, the plaintiff was not an "outsider" but was merely a landowner seeking rezoning to allow a condominium development. The New York court adopted a two-tiered test of validity: (1) does the challenged zoning ordinance "provide for the development of a balanced, cohesive community which will make efficient use of the town's available land" and (2) does the ordinance enable the municipality to accommodate otherwise unmet regional housing needs for county and metropolitan area residents to live near their places of employment? The court's second element certainly falls far short of New Jersey's "fair-share" mandate because it refers to a region around the city in question but does not require that city to provide low- and moderate-income housing if the needs are met elsewhere in the region. The New York court also made it clear that it was not mandating "a certain relative proportion between various types of development."[429]

In a later case,[430] the New York Court of Appeals seemingly modified its *Berenson* ruling somewhat, holding that a zoning ordinance alleged to be "exclusionary" is still entitled to the traditional presumption of validity unless it shows on its face that it was enacted for an impermissible purpose. This presumption can be rebutted only by showing that the ordinance was, in fact, enacted for an impermissible purpose or "without proper regard to local and regional housing needs and has an exclusionary effect."[431] On the facts, the court held that a five-acre minimum lot size requirement "within a coherent area characterized by estate-type development * * * and generally bounded by properties developed on a large lot basis" was valid. The court said the large lot zoning was not facially invalid because such zoning may have legitimate purposes—e.g., preservation of

[426] 53 Penn.Stat. §§ 10609.1, 11004(1)(c), 11011(2).

[427] 30 N.Y.2d 359, 334 N.Y.S.2d 138, 285 N.E.2d 291 (1972), appeal dismissed 409 U.S. 1003, 93 S.Ct. 436, 34 L.Ed.2d 294 (1972).

[428] 38 N.Y.2d 102, 378 N.Y.S.2d 672, 341 N.E.2d 236 (1975).

[429] 38 N.Y.2d at 109, 378 N.Y.S.2d at 679–680, 341 N.E.2d at 241.

[430] Kurzius, Inc. v. Incorporated Village of Upper Brookville, 51 N.Y.2d 338, 434 N.Y.S.2d 180, 414 N.E.2d 680 (1980), cert. denied 450 U.S. 1042, 101 S.Ct. 1761, 68 L.Ed.2d 240 (1981).

[431] 51 N.Y.2d at 344–345, 434 N.Y.S.2d at 182–183, 414 N.E.2d at 683–684.

open space. And the court found insufficient proof of either an improper purpose or of exclusionary effect—e.g., "no proof that persons of low or moderate incomes were foreclosed from housing in the general region because of the unavailability of properly zoned land."[432]

As noted above, New York's decision in Golden v. Town of Ramapo is sometimes classified as a "phased-growth" case. The "Ramapo Plan" and other elaborate "growth management" programs are likely to have a substantial "exclusionary" effect. However, the leading decisions upholding such programs while recognizing their "exclusionary" potential conclude that the particular "growth management" programs before the court were not actually "exclusionary." Issues related to "growth-management" plans are covered in more detail in section 9.31 of this chapter.

Several states have statutes that are at least somewhat designed to require local governments to provide for low- and moderate-income housing. As early as 1969, Massachusetts adopted its "anti-snob zoning act," which gives building-permit preference to developers of such housing. California, Florida, and Washington require local governments to include a housing element in their comprehensive plans, and Connecticut and Rhode Island have statutes that include elements of the statutes of all of the three states just named. Local governments tend to resist compliance with such state-mandated requirements, just as municipalities in New Jersey have resisted the mandates of the *Mt. Laurel* decisions. Widespread local violations of the state statutes just mentioned have been reported. In New Jersey, a 1996 study estimated that that state's exertions had produced some 13,000 units of affordable housing.[433] This is a reminder that other forces in society—including economic, social, and political ones—are often more powerful than the force of law. Perhaps Solon was right in declaring that ultimately "laws are like cobwebs."[434]

Exclusionary Zoning Activities at the Federal Level

This subsection covers only a couple of the leading United States Supreme Court decisions considering whether zoning that tended to be "exclusionary" violated the Equal Protection Clause of the 14th Amendment: Warth v. Seldin[435] and Village of Arlington Heights v. Metropolitan Housing Development Corporation.[436] The next subsection focuses on the question of whether zoning ordinances that tend to exclude classes of persons protected by the Federal Fair Housing Act violate that Act.

Warth v. Seldin[437] was an exclusionary zoning case, but the Supreme Court's decision never reached the merits because the plaintiffs were denied standing to

---

[432] 51 N.Y.2d at 345–347, 434 N.Y.S.2d at 183–185, 414 N.E.2d at 684–685.

[433] The material in this paragraph was drawn from J. Juergensmeyer & T. Roberts, Land Use Planning and Control Law § 6.6 (1998). Those authors do not mention Washington State, but the state's Growth Management Act requires counties and cities that are subject to the Act, which are most of them, to include "housing for low-income families" as an element of their comprehensive plans. Wash. Rev. Code § 36.70A.070(2).

[434] "[L]aws were like cobwebs—for that if any trifling or powerless thing fell into them, they held it fast; but if a thing of any size fell into them, it broke the meshes and escaped." 1 Diogenes Laertius, The Lives and Opinions of Eminent Philosophers, p. 28 (C.D. Yonge trans. 1901) (Solon).

[435] 422 U.S. 490, 95 S.Ct. 2197, 45 L.Ed.2d 343 (1975).

[436] 429 U.S. 252, 97 S.Ct. 555, 50 L.Ed.2d 450 (1977), on remand 558 F.2d 1283 (7th Cir.1977), certiorari denied 434 U.S. 1025, 98 S.Ct. 752, 54 L.Ed.2d 772 (1978), on remand 469 F.Supp. 836 (N.D.Ill. 1979), affirmed 616 F.2d 1006 (7th Cir. 1980).

[437] 422 U.S. 490, 95 S.Ct. 2197, 45 L.Ed.2d 343 (1975).

maintain the action. As the Court explained in *Warth,* its "standing" rules generally require plaintiffs to show that the local zoning regulations challenged on "equal protection" grounds have caused them to suffer "injury in fact" and to show that they would be personally benefitted if the court granted the relief sought. In *Warth* a number of non-resident plaintiffs (mainly non-profit organizations) challenged an ordinance zoning practically all of Penfield, New York, for single-family dwellings only. The Court held that neither standing requirement was met, stating that there must be proof of "specific, concrete facts demonstrating" harm to the plaintiffs caused by the zoning and proof that they "personally would benefit from the court's intervention." In a footnote,[438] the Court added that "usually the initial focus should be on a particular project."

A second Supreme Court decision, Village of Arlington Heights v. Metropolitan Housing Development Corporation,[439] somewhat relaxed *Warth's* standing requirements but erected another barrier to Equal Protection exclusionary zoning cases. Metropolitan Housing Development Corporation, a provider of low-income housing in the Chicago area, had a contract to purchase a tract of vacant land in suburban Arlington Heights from a Catholic order. However, to build its desired apartment complex on the land the corporation needed the village council to amend the zoning ordinance to permit multi-family housing. After extended hearings before the local planning commission and village council, the council denied the rezoning application. The corporation and some individual plaintiffs—including an African American man who worked in Arlington Heights but lived some 20 miles away and testified he would probably move to apartments if it were developed—challenged the rezoning denial. On the standing issue, distinguishing *Warth*, the Court held that this individual man and the corporation both had standing to maintain the 14th-Amendment challenge. *Warth* can narrowly be distinguished because, unlike in that case, *Arlington Heights* was site-specific for a certain project the corporation wanted to build, and the individual plaintiff's interest was more specific than that of the plaintiffs in *Warth*.

However, the plaintiffs in *Arlington Heights* ultimately lost on the merits. The Court accepted as a fact that the denial of the zoning and the defeat of the project had a racially discriminatory *effect:* it excluded blacks and other minority persons more than "majority" persons. However, the Court found insufficient evidence that the village had an *intent* to discriminate. Relying on its decision in Washington v. Davis[440] (a 14th-Amendment employment discrimination case), the Court held that an allegedly exclusionary zoning ordinance cannot be struck down on "equal protection" grounds unless there is proof of actual racially discriminatory intent on the part of local officials. In an extended dictum,[441] the Court discussed the kinds of evidence that might tend to show discriminatory intent—evidence of "a clear pattern unexplainable on grounds other than race" and of substantive departures from an established zoning policy in reaching the zoning decision that barred the proposed site-specific project. Having concluded that the evidence was insufficient to "warrant overturning the concurrent findings of both courts below" that discriminatory intent was not proved in *Arlington Heights,* the Court remanded the case for further consideration of plaintiffs' claims that the rezoning denial

---

[438]   422 U.S. at 508 n. 18, 95 S.Ct. at 2210 n. 18.

[439]   429 U.S. 252, 97 S.Ct. 555, 50 L.Ed.2d 450 (1977), on remand 558 F.2d 1283 (7th Cir.1977), certiorari denied 434 U.S. 1025, 98 S.Ct. 752, 54 L.Ed.2d 772 (1978), on remand 469 F.Supp. 836 (N.D.Ill. 1979), affirmed 616 F.2d 1006 (7th Cir. 1980).

[440]   426 U.S. 229, 96 S.Ct. 2040, 48 L.Ed.2d 597 (1976).

[441]   429 U.S. at 266, 97 S.Ct. at 564.

constituted a violation of the federal Fair Housing Act (Title VIII of the Civil Rights Act of 1968). That leads us to the next section of this chapter, which considers the effect of that Act on zoning that discriminates against groups the Act specially protects.

§ 9.27 EXCLUSIONARY ZONING: FEDERAL FAIR HOUSING ACT

As noted in the preceding paragraph, the United States Supreme Court remanded the *Arlington Heights* case[442] to the Seventh Circuit for further consideration under the Federal Fair Housing Act, which is Title VIII of the Civil Rights Act of 1968.[443] The specific section of that Act that was to be considered reads in pertinent part that "it shall be unlawful . . . to make unavailable or deny . . . a dwelling to any person because of race, color, religion, or national origin."[444] Housing discrimination actions under the Act have nearly always been brought by persons of minority races, though a 1997 federal district court decision held that a white couple were protected against "reverse discrimination" in favor of minority persons.[445] Since *Arlington Heights* held that intent to discriminate must be shown for zoning to be found discriminatory on the grounds of race or color, the issue before the Seventh Circuit on remand was whether such intent must also be shown to establish a violation of Title VIII. The Seventh Circuit held that discriminatory effect alone may establish a violation and set out a formula or test to determine when such a violation occurs. Other federal circuit court decisions have since similarly held that effect alone may constitute a violation of the Act, but some have applied somewhat different formulas or tests. To give a view of the range of these tests, the following materials review the Seventh Circuit decision and some other leading federal decisions.

On the remand of *Arlington Heights,* the Seventh Circuit laid down a four-part test for determining whether a local decision not to rezone to permit construction of a site-specific housing project constitutes a violation of the Fair Housing Act. The test considers: (1) whether there is "some evidence" of discriminatory intent (though not sufficient to amount to a denial of equal protection); (2) the magnitude of the racially discriminatory effect; (3) whether the municipality acted within the scope of its statutory authority; and (4) whether the plaintiff seeks to compel the defendant to construct integrated housing or to take affirmative steps to insure that integrated housing is built. Under the fourth part of the test, if a plaintiff is seeking to compel construction courts should be less willing to grant relief than if "the plaintiff only wish[es] to build integrated housing on his own land and to enjoin the defendant from interfering with that construction". In *Arlington Heights*, the Seventh Circuit ultimately concluded that items (1) and (3) weighed in favor of the defendant, that item (4) weighed in favor of the plaintiff, and that item (2) should be decisive.

After reviewing the evidence, the court held that the plaintiff was entitled to the relief sought—rezoning the proposed project site to permit the proposed development—unless the defendant could identify a parcel of land within Arlington Heights both properly zoned and suitable for low-cost housing under federal standards. According to

---

[442] Metropolitan Housing Development Corp. v. Village of Arlington Heights, 558 F.2d 1283 (7th Cir.1977), certiorari denied 434 U.S. 1025, 98 S.Ct. 752, 54 L.Ed.2d 772 (1978), on remand 469 F.Supp. 836 (N.D.Ill. 1979), affirmed 616 F.2d 1006 (7th Cir. 1980).

[443] 42 U.S.C.A. §§ 3601–3617.

[444] 42 U.S.C.A. § 3604(a).

[445] Jordan v. Khan, 969 F.Supp. 29 (N.D.Ill.1997). The case did not involve zoning, but white leasehold tenants who claimed their landlord discriminated in favor of tenants of Asian or Middle Eastern ancestry.

the court, if the defendant failed to satisfy this burden "the district court should conclude that the Village's refusal to rezone effectively precluded plaintiffs from constructing low-cost housing within Arlington Heights and should grant plaintiffs the relief they seek."

In a pre-*Arlington Heights* case, United States v. City of Black Jack,[446] the Eighth Circuit took an even more expansive view of the application of the Fair Housing Act to racially discriminatory exclusionary zoning. The *Black Jack* court held that proof of a total exclusion of multifamily housing created a *prima facie* case of racial discrimination, shifting to the defendant the burden of showing a "compelling governmental interest" that would justify such exclusionary zoning. This approach to litigation under the Fair Housing Act is obviously similar to the United States Supreme Court's "strict scrutiny" approach to racial discrimination cases under the equal protection clause of the Fourteenth Amendment. The Eighth Circuit concluded that the defendant's evidence as to the adverse effect of multifamily housing development on property values, road and traffic problems, and school overcrowding did not establish a "compelling government interest" and held the Black Jack zoning ordinance invalid insofar as it excluded all multifamily housing development.

The Supreme Court denied certiorari in *Black Jack*. On the facts, the court seemingly could have applied *Arlington Heights* analysis and found racially discriminatory intent on the basis of the "substantive departure" from prior zoning policy in the newly incorporated City of Black Jack's actions zoning out all multifamily housing. Notably, there was no standing problem in *Black Jack* because the suit was brought by the United States on the basis of an express statutory provision authorizing suits by the United States to enforce the Fair Housing Act of 1968. Such suits may be the best method of challenging racially discriminatory zoning because the Federal Government clearly has standing and no proof of discriminatory intent is required.

One of the most famous large-scale fair housing suits brought by the Federal Government is United States v. City of Parma.[447] In *City of Parma*, the Sixth Circuit Court of Appeals sustained a sweeping district court finding that Parma, Ohio, was guilty of racial discrimination in violation of the 1968 Fair Housing Act. The *City of Parma* finding of racial discrimination was based on an entire "pattern and practice" of racially discriminatory conduct, rather than the local zoning ordinance alone. Although the Supreme Court's holding in *Arlington Heights* would seem to have made it unnecessary, both the district and circuit courts found that Parma's land use regulations and municipal conduct in general were both motivated by a racially discriminatory intent and produced a racially discriminatory effect. Among the Parma ordinances that both the district and circuit courts struck down was an ordinance requiring a public referendum on all proposals for construction of low-income housing. This is particularly noteworthy because, as discussed in section 9.23 of this chapter, the United States Supreme Court has twice upheld the use of zoning referenda.[448]

---

[446] 508 F.2d 1179 (8th Cir.1974), certiorari denied 422 U.S. 1042, 95 S.Ct. 2656, 45 L.Ed.2d 694 (1975), rehearing denied 423 U.S. 884, 96 S.Ct. 158, 46 L.Ed.2d 115 (1975).

[447] 661 F.2d 562 (6th Cir.1981); see also U.S. v. Yonkers Bd. of Educ., 927 F.2d 85 (2d Cir. 1991).

[448] See City of Eastlake v. Forest City Enterprises, 426 U.S. 668, 96 S.Ct. 2358, 49 L.Ed.2d 132 (1996) (approving a city charter provision that required that proposed land-use amendments be ratified by a 55% vote of the people); James v. Valtierra, 402 U.S. 137, 91 S.Ct. 1331, 28 L.Ed.2d 678 (1971) (approving California's requirement that required a referendum vote on all local public housing projects).

An important aspect of *City of Parma* is that the court of appeals approved most of the extensive district court remedial order requiring affirmative action by the city. This order included requirements that Parma adopt an educational program for city officials and employees responsible for carrying out the order, adopt a resolution welcoming all persons of good will to the city, set up a fair housing committee to develop plans and to monitor compliance with the order, and participate in a variety of public housing and housing subsidy programs. On the other hand, the court of appeals set aside those portions of the district court's order requiring the city to make all efforts to ensure that at least 133 units of low- and moderate-income housing are constructed each year and appointing a special master to oversee the city's compliance with the order.

A more recent federal Fair Housing Act case is Huntington Branch, N.A.A.C.P. v. Town of Huntington,[449] in which the Second Circuit adopted a somewhat different approach to the problem of racial discrimination in housing. That court held that a plaintiff need not prove discriminatory intent in cases brought under the Fair Housing Act but may rely upon proof of discriminatory impact—as in cases brought under the federal Equal Employment Opportunity Act—to establish that a facially neutral policy such as a refusal to rezone violates the Fair Housing Act. The court held that the plaintiff had established a prima facie case by showing that the town's refusal to rezone land in a white neighborhood for federally subsidized multifamily housing had a discriminatory effect on black persons and that a larger proportion of blacks than whites needed affordable housing.[450] The town had failed to justify this discriminatory impact by showing (1) that there was no feasible alternative that would be less discriminatory and (2) that there were bona fide and legitimate reasons for the town's refusal to rezone. The second prong of the court's holding was based on its conclusion that the town had failed to show a "substantial" government concern that would justify a decision not to rezone by a "reasonable" town official. The court granted site-specific relief to the plaintiff to remedy the Fair Housing Act violation.

The judgment of the court of appeals in *Huntington Branch* was affirmed by the United States Supreme Court in a per curiam opinion[451] stating that the court was satisfied on [the] record that disparate impact was shown, and the justification proffered to rebut the *prima facie* case was inadequate." Although the town argued that proof of "disparate impact," without proof of actual "discriminatory intent," should not justify a finding that the Fair Housing Act was violated, the Supreme Court refused, on technical grounds, to address this argument.[452] Following *Huntington Branch*, the validity of disparate impact claims remained uncertain for nearly two decades. But in 2015, the Supreme Court held in Texas Department of Housing and Community Affairs v. Inclusive Communities Project that disparate impact claims are cognizable under the

---

[449] 844 F.2d 926 (2d Cir.1988), affirmed per curiam, 488 U.S. 15, 109 S.Ct. 276, 102 L.Ed.2d 180 (1988).

[450] Rezoning of the land in question was sought by plaintiff because privately constructed multi-family housing was limited by the Huntington zoning ordinance to an urban renewal area largely occupied by racial minorities.

[451] Town of Huntington v. Huntington Branch, N.A.A.C.P., 488 U.S. 15, 109 S.Ct. 276, 102 L.Ed.2d 180 (1988).

[452] The grounds for refusal to address the issue were (1) the court of appeals' holding that the town's refusal to rezone violated the Fair Housing Act should have been challenged by petition for certiorari rather than by appeal, and (2) that the town had "conceded the applicability of the disparate impact test under Title VIII"—the Fair Housing Act—in a facial challenge to the zoning ordinance itself.

Fair Housing Act, regardless of whether discriminatory intent is shown.[453] In doing so, the Court also imposed important limitations on the theory. Specifically, the Court explained that a racial imbalance, without more, cannot sustain a disparate impact claim. Rather, the plaintiff must show "robust" causal connection between the challenged practice and the alleged disparities.

§ 9.28 SPECIAL EXCEPTIONS AND CONDITIONAL USES

This section builds upon those portions of section 9.15 of this chapter describing the functions of the board of adjustment or board of zoning appeals. The consideration of applications for special exceptions—called "conditional uses" or "special uses" in some states—is normally one of that board's chief functions, as provided for in Section 7 of the Standard Zoning Enabling Act (SZEA). In some localities, however, the function may be performed by the planning commission, a hearing examiner, or even the local legislative body. Some localities also have somewhat different procedures, such as initial consideration by a hearing examiner of appeals to the board of adjustment, or perhaps an initial decision by that board with an appeal of all or certain classes of special exceptions to the legislative body.

The special exception is one of zoning law's traditional "flexibility devices," together with applicant rezonings and variances. A special exception is a "permitted" use but not a "regularly permitted" use. Zoning ordinance sections governing a particular zone often contain two lists of permitted uses: one list of uses that require no special zoning permission, and a second list of uses that are allowed only upon the board of adjustment's issuance of an individualized permit. Section 7 of the SZEA specifically empowered the board of adjustment "[t]o hear and decide special exceptions to the terms of the ordinance upon which such board is required to pass under such ordinance." Since this language resembles the earlier 1917 statutory language authorizing New York City's governing body to empower a board of appeals "to determine and vary" the zoning regulations "in accordance with general or specific rules therein contained,"[454] it's hardly surprising to find that early courts often had difficulty distinguishing "variances" from "special exceptions."[455] Because this confusion still lingers in the minds of some persons who do not regularly work in the planning and zoning field, the following quotation from Zylka v. City of Crystal, a 1969 Minnesota Supreme Court decision, is included to make the distinction clear:

> Provisions such as the one contained in defendant city's ordinance providing for special-use permits, sometimes called 'special exception permits' or 'conditional use permits,' were introduced into zoning ordinances as flexibility devices. They are designed to meet the problem which arises where certain uses, although generally compatible with the basic use classification of a particular zone, should not be permitted to be located as a matter of right in every area included within the zone because of hazards inherent in the use itself or special problems which its proposed location may present. By this

---

[453] 135 S.Ct. 2507, 192 L.Ed.2d 514 (2015); see also Robert G. Schwemm, Fair Housing Litigation After Inclusive Communities: What's New and What's Not, 115 Colum. L. Rev. Sidebar 106 (2015) (providing an in-depth discussion of the case).

[454] Substantially similar language is still found in New York. McKinney's Town Law § 267 (5); McKinney's Village Law § 7–712 (2)(c).

[455] The Rhode Island courts seem to have had unusual difficulty in making the distinction. See 5 N. Williams, Am.Land Planning Law § 139.02 (1975).

device, certain uses (e.g., gasoline service stations, electric substations, hospitals, schools, churches, country clubs, and the like) which may be considered essentially desirable to the community, but which should not be authorized generally in a particular zone because of considerations such as current and anticipated traffic congestion, population density, noise, effect on adjoining land values, or other considerations involving public health, safety, or general welfare, may be permitted upon a proposed site depending upon the facts and circumstances of the particular case. Unlike a variance provision which permits particular property to be used in a manner forbidden by the ordinance by varying the terms of the ordinance, a special-use provision permits property, within the discretion of the governing body, to be used in a manner expressly authorized by the ordinance. In theory, if not in practice, provisions authorizing the issuance of special-use permits are intended to provide more flexibility in land use control than provisions authorizing a variance.[456]

The following hypothetical example of a special exception in action helps to further clarify the nature of this important zoning tool. Utility substations, such as an electric transformer stations or water pumping stations, are typical special exceptions in residential zones. These stations are necessary in residential areas, but one does not want them located indiscriminately. Accordingly, developers of utility substations within residential zones typically must meet special conditions that do not apply to regularly permitted dwellings, such as minimum distances from residential lots and requirements for screening and noise reduction devices. If it believes a proposed substation would meet those special requirements, the utility company seeking to develop it must first apply to the board of adjustment for a special exception permit. The board is almost certain to grant the permit, though boards are allowed to add further conditions that the local situation requires. For instance, the board might require a special kind of fencing to protect neighborhood children or might require site's access gate to face a certain direction to reduce disturbance to neighbors. In practice, the applicant is usually willing to meet any special requirements and the permit is granted and accepted without problems. Zoning ordinances, in setting out the requirements for special exceptions, generally contain a catch-all phrase that requiring the proposed use not "be inimical to the public interest." Materials found later in this section describe just how much power this gives the board to deny an otherwise deserved permit.

As noted in the above quotation from Zylka v. City of Crystal, in some states the term "special use" or "conditional use" is employed instead of "special exception."[457] In states where the enabling act still retains the Standard Act language delegating the power to grant special exceptions to the board of adjustment, attempted delegation of the "special exception" approval power to the local planning commission or governing body has generally been held invalid.[458] However, some New Jersey courts have upheld

[456] Zylka v. City of Crystal, 283 Minn. 192, 195–96, 167 N.W.2d 45, 48–49 (1969).

[457] The term "conditional use" is employed, e.g., in West's Ann.Cal.Gov.Code § 65901. That "special exception" and "special use" are identical, see Depue v. City of Clinton, 160 N.W.2d 860 (Iowa 1968).

[458] E.g., Langer v. Planning & Zoning Commission, 163 Conn. 453, 313 A.2d 44 (1972); Franklin County v. Webster, 400 S.W.2d 693 (Ky.1966) (planning commission); Swimming River Golf & Country Club, Inc. v. Borough of New Shrewsbury, 30 N.J. 132, 152 A.2d 135 (1959) (same); Depue v. City of Clinton, 160 N.W.2d 860 (Iowa 1968) (governing body); State ex rel. Skelly Oil Co. v. Common Council, 58 Wis.2d 695, 207 N.W.2d 585 (1973) (same).

zoning ordinances providing that the board of adjustment must merely recommend approval or disapproval of a "special exception" request, with the final decision reserved to the local governing body.[459] In states where the enabling act does not specifically delegate the power to approve "special exceptions," "special uses," or "conditional uses" to the board of appeals (or adjustment), a reservation of that power to the local governing body has generally been upheld.[460] And in some states the enabling act authorizes delegation of that power to either of two or more local bodies.[461]

Courts are divided on whether a local legislative body acts "administratively" or "legislatively" when it approves or disapproves rules on an application for a special exception, special use, or conditional use.[462] However, when the board of adjustment is the body acting on a special exception application, it is clear that that body acts "administratively." It is a truism that local "administrative" action must be restrained by standards designed to prevent an arbitrary exercise of discretion by the administrative agency.[463] Hence, the courts have generally struck down delegations to zoning boards of appeal (or adjustment) of the power to consider applications for special exceptions, special uses, or conditional uses when the zoning ordinance provides no review standards.[464] On the other hand, the courts have almost uniformly sustained simple "nuisance" standards—i.e., negatively phrased provisions prohibiting approval of proposed uses if they would create substantial negative externalities such as increased traffic congestion, increased noise, or increased air pollution.[465] Courts are somewhat divided as to the adequacy of simple "general welfare" standards—i.e., provisions authorizing approval of requests for special exceptions, special uses, or conditional uses when this will protect or promote "public health, safety, or general welfare."[466] Some courts that have held such standards to be inadequate have reasoned that it is

[459] See Schmidt v. Board of Adjustment, 9 N.J. 405, 88 A.2d 607 (1952).

[460] E.g., Kotrich v. County of DuPage, 19 Ill.2d 181, 166 N.E.2d 601 (1960), appeal dismissed 364 U.S. 475, 81 S.Ct. 243, 5 L.Ed.2d 221 (1960); Corporation Way Realty Trust v. Building Commissioner of Medford, 348 Mass. 732, 205 N.E.2d 718 (1965); Detroit Osteopathic Hospital Corp. v. City of Southfield, 377 Mich. 128, 139 N.W.2d 728 (1966) (but note that governing body is authorized to serve as "zoning board of appeals" in Michigan).

[461] E.g., West's Ann.Cal.Gov.Code §§ 65901–65904 allows delegation to either a zoning administrator, a planning commissioner, or a board of appeals, or retention of the power by the local governing body.

[462] That it acts "administratively," see, e.g., Wheeler v. Gregg, 90 Cal.App.2d 348, 203 P.2d 37 (1949); Osius v. City of St. Clair Shores, 344 Mich. 693, 75 N.W.2d 25 (1956); State ex rel. Ludlow v. Guffey, 306 S.W.2d 552 (Mo.1957). But see, holding that it acts "legislatively," Kotrich v. County of DuPage, supra note 460; Green Point Savings Bank v. Board of Zoning Appeals, 281 N.Y. 534, 24 N.E.2d 319 (1939), appeal dismissed 309 U.S. 633, 60 S.Ct. 719, 84 L.Ed. 990 (1940).

[463] Generally, see D. Mandelker, Land Use Law § 6.02 (3d ed. 1993).

[464] E.g., City of St. Petersburg v. Schweitzer, 297 So.2d 74 (Fla.App.1974), certiorari denied 308 So.2d 114 (Fla.1975); Smith v. Board of Appeals of Fall River, 319 Mass. 341, 65 N.E.2d 547 (1946); Ostrand v. Village of North St. Paul, 275 Minn. 440, 147 N.W.2d 571 (1966); State ex rel. Humble Oil & Refining Co. v. Wahner, 25 Wis.2d 1, 130 N.W.2d 304 (1964).

[465] E.g., Certain-Teed Products Corp. v. Paris Township, 351 Mich. 434, 88 N.W.2d 705 (1958); Ours Properties, Inc. v. Ley, 198 Va. 848, 96 S.E.2d 754 (1957). Contra: Kenville Realty Corp. v. Board of Zoning Appeals, 48 Misc.2d 666, 265 N.Y.S.2d 522 (1965). Cases holding the "nuisance" standard adequate are based on the presumption that special exceptions, special uses, or conditional uses are compatible with other uses allowed in the district in which they may be authorized by the administrative decision.

[466] *Adequate:* E.g., Napleton v. Village of Hinsdale, 229 Ill. 2d 296, 322 Ill. Dec. 548, 891 N.E.2d 839 (2008); Schultz v. Board of Adjustment, 258 Iowa 804, 139 N.W.2d 448 (1966); Mobil Oil Corp. v. City of Clawson, 36 Mich.App. 46, 193 N.W.2d 346 (1971); Nash-Rocky Mount Bd. of Educ. v. Rocky Mount Bd. of Adjustment, 169 N.C. App. 587, 610 S.E.2d 255, 196 Ed. Law Rep. 709 (2005); Peachtree Development Co. v. Paul, 67 Ohio St.2d 345, 423 N.E.2d 1087 (1981). *Inadequate:* E.g., Redwood City Co. of Jehovah's Witnesses v. City of Menlo Park, 167 Cal.App.2d 686, 335 P.2d 195 (1959); Clark v. Board of Appeals, 348 Mass. 407, 204 N.E.2d 434 (1965); Osius v. City of St. Clair Shores, 344 Mich. 693, 75 N.W.2d 25 (1956).

inappropriate to allow an unelected administrative agency to make zoning policy on the basis of the general standard applicable to legislative bodies.

Some zoning ordinances contain quite specific and detailed standards for approving or disapproving requests for special exceptions, special uses, or conditional uses. Some ordinances also reserve discretion to disapprove an application on grounds that it will cause substantial negative externalities or will not promote the general welfare. Such standards are almost always sustained when challenged as insufficient.[467] Indeed, at least where there is no residual discretion to disapprove on nuisance or general welfare grounds, courts have sometimes held that compliance with all the specific standards in the zoning ordinance entitles an applicant as a matter of right to approval of his request for a special exception, special use, or conditional use.[468] However, where there is a residual discretion to disapprove—i.e., where, after listing specific conditions that must relate to the applicant's land, the ordinance adds language such as, "and shall not be inimical to the public welfare"—there is a question of the board's authority to deny an application solely on the grounds of the quoted language. Based on limited case law examining this question, it appears that the board generally cannot deny a permit as "inimical to the public welfare" unless it enters findings stating how it is "inimical," because the proposed use would cause described disturbances to nearby landowners. A reviewing court must likewise be convinced that the reasons given are sufficient to justify the denial.[469] The Standard Act[470] and most current zoning enabling acts expressly authorize the imposition of ad hoc conditions when special exceptions, special uses, or conditional uses are approved. The courts generally insist that such conditions relate to the use of the land as to which approval is granted.[471]

The draftsmen of the Standard Act clearly intended that large-scale changes in the municipal zoning pattern be effected by amendment of the zoning ordinance rather than by means of "special exceptions."[472] Although the "special exception" has sometimes been

---

[467] E.g., St. John's Roman Catholic Church Corp. v. Town of Darien, 149 Conn. 712, 184 A.2d 42 (1962); Mirschel v. Weissenberger, 277 App.Div. 1039, 100 N.Y.S.2d 452 (1950); Kline v. Louisville & Jefferson County Board of Zoning Adjustment & Appeals, 325 S.W.2d 324 (Ky.1959).

[468] E.g., Lazarus v. Village of Northbrook, 31 Ill.2d 146, 199 N.E.2d 797 (1964); C.R. Investments, Inc. v. Village of Shoreview, 304 N.W.2d 320 (Minn.1981); Verona, Inc. v. West Caldwell, 49 N.J. 274, 229 A.2d 651 (1967). See generally D. Mandelker, Land Use Law § 6.57 (4th ed. 1997).

[469] See Zylka v. City of Crystal, 283 Minn. 192, 167 N.W.2d 45 (1969) (city council erroneously denied permit when it gave no reasons); D. Mandleker, Land Use Law § 6.57 (4th ed. 1997). See also Evans v. Shore Communications, Inc., 112 Md.App. 284, 685 A.2d 454 (1996) (board erroneously denied permit for antenna tower when it found there were too many in area, but ordinance allowed them to determine whether tower was in harmony with neighborhood and with comprehensive plan); Hansen v. Chelan County, 81 Wn.App. 133, 913 P.2d 409 (1996) (error to deny permit for golf course as inconsistent with comprehensive plan when zoning permitted uses outright that were more intensive than golf course). Compare, Chambers v. Kootenai County Bd. of Comm'rs, 125 Idaho 115, 867 P.2d 989 (1994) (error for board to grant permit based upon information not part of record at hearing).

[470] SSZEA & 7 (1926).

[471] E.g., Middlesex & Boston Street Railway Co. v. Board of Aldermen, 371 Mass. 849, 359 N.E.2d 1279 (1977); Exxon, Inc. v. City of Frederick, 36 Md.App. 703, 375 A.2d 34 (1977); Mechem v. City of Santa Fe, 96 N.M. 668, 634 P.2d 690 (1981). But see Cupp v. Board of Supervisors of Fairfax County, 227 Va. 580, 318 S.E.2d 407 (1984), holding that conditions such as required land donations and off-site improvements cannot be imposed when a special use permit is sought because such conditions are *ultra vires* and were unrelated (in this case) to any problem generated by the proposed use of the property in question. The court clearly adopted, as the second ground for its decision, what is generally termed the "rational nexus" doctrine in subdivision exaction cases.

[472] See SCIT, Inc. v. Planning Bd. of Braintree, 19 Mass.App.Ct. 101, 472 N.E.2d 269 (1984), holding that a zoning bylaw making all uses in a business district subject to issuance of a special permit violated two provisions of the zoning enabling act: (1) that zoning regulations should be uniform for each class of building

misused to effect large-scale rezonings without a formal amendment, most large-scale (as well as many small-scale) zoning changes are brought about by the amendment process. In two states, however, zoning enabling act provisions governing "special exceptions" and "variances" appear to practically allow municipalities to establish land use licensing systems. In Rhode Island, the statute authorizes the "board of review" to "make special exceptions to the terms of the ordinance * * * where such exception is reasonably necessary for the convenience or welfare of the public."[473] In New Jersey, the statute authorizes the governing body to grant what is misleadingly called a "variance" on recommendation of the board of adjustment "in particular cases and for special reasons" if "such relief can be granted without substantial detriment to the public good and will not substantially impair the intent and purpose of the * * * zoning ordinance."[474] These statutory provisions appear to authorize the local zoning board to permit any use whatever in any district, without proof of hardship to the landowner, on the basis of extremely vague and general standards.[475] New Jersey courts have not been notably successful in articulating more specific standards for "special reasons" variances.[476] However, the New Jersey Supreme Court has made it clear that municipalities may not establish a system in which nearly all uses are allowable only by special exception rather than by a spectrum of different kinds of zones.[477]

§ 9.29 VARIANCES

The preceding section on special exceptions included a lengthy quotation from Zylka v. City of Crystal[478] that described special exceptions, which are sometimes called special permits or conditional use permits. Because special exceptions are often confused with the zoning device discussed in this section—the "variance"—it may be useful to compare that quotation with the description of variances given here. Special exceptions and variances are both zoning flexibility devices, and both are generally considered by a local government's board of adjustment. As previously mentioned, the board of adjustment is

---

or use within a district; and (2) that special permits shall be issued only for "specific types of uses." The court said that the enabling act does not contemplate the "conferral on local zoning boards of a roving and virtually unlimited power to discriminate as to uses between landowners similarly situated."

[473] Rhode Island Gen.Laws 1956, § 45–24–13, which is derived from the original Rhode Island zoning enabling act (Rhode Island Laws 1923, c. 430, § 2).

[474] New Jersey Stat.Ann. 40:55–39(d). This provision authorizes "use" variances, and empowers the local governing body to make the final decision after receiving a recommendation from the board of adjustment. The New Jersey "special reasons" variance is really a "special use permit" that is not limited as to the kinds of nonconforming uses that may be authorized, rather than a true "variance." The broad authorization to grant "special reasons" variances would seem largely to emasculate the rather strict standards for granting "conditional uses * * * according to definite specifications and standards" imposed on the planning board by New Jersey Stat. Ann. 40:55D–67.

[475] See 5 N. Williams, Am.Land Planning Law §§ 149.16–149.20 (1975 and Supp.1982).

[476] See, e.g., Ward v. Scott, 11 N.J. 117, 93 A.2d 385 (1952); Andrews v. Board of Adjustment, 30 N.J. 245, 152 A.2d 580 (1959); Black v. Town of Montclair, 34 N.J. 105, 167 A.2d 388 (1961); Yahnel v. Board of Adjustment, 79 N.J.Super. 509, 192 A.2d 177 (App.Div.1963), certification denied 41 N.J. 116, 195 A.2d 15 (1963); Kramer v. Board of Adjustment, 45 N.J. 268, 212 A.2d 153 (1965); Brown Boveri, Inc. v. Township Committee of North Brunswick, 160 N.J.Super. 179, 389 A.2d 483 (App.Div. 1978); Castroll v. Township of Franklin, 161 N.J.Super. 190, 391 A.2d 544 (App.Div. 1978). But see Medici v. BPR Co., 107 N.J. 1, 526 A.2d 109 (1987) (statutory policy favors "zoning by ordinance rather than by variance" in absence of "hardship"; this policy requires applicant to show "special reasons," including proof that the site in question is specially suited for the proposed use, when no "hardship" is shown).

[477] Rockhill v. Chesterfield Township, 23 N.J. 117, 128 A.2d 473 (1957) (township entirely zoned for agriculture and single-family dwellings "as of right," with almost all other uses to be allowed by special permit pursuant to broad, general standards; held invalid as the "antithesis" of zoning).

[478] Zylka v. City of Crystal, 283 Minn. 192, 195–96, 167 N.W.2d 45, 48–49 (1969).

sometimes called the board of zoning appeals but the term "board of adjustment" is used here. A variance comes to the board upon the application of a landowner. Requirements for hearings and notice are usually the same for both special exceptions and variances, and the board's decision in either case is typically appealable to the local court of general jurisdiction. However, beyond that a special exception is entirely different from a variance. A variance is essentially a waiver of some restriction that the zoning ordinance normally imposes. Zoning ordinances generally contain no list of variances akin to the lists of special exceptions found in many zoning codes. Instead, the ordinance empowers the board to grant waiver from zoning restriction whenever an applicant convinces the board that, without the waiver, the zoning would cause the applicant "hardship" in the use of his or her land. Variances are divided into two basic types: "use" variances (which permit an applicant to make a use the zoning normally does not allow) and "bulk" or "dimension" variances (which relax area or dimension restrictions to allow an owner to build in ways not normally allowed).

A simple example of a bulk variance helps to illustrate how this type of variance works. Suppose that houses in a hypothetical single-family-residence zone must be set back 35 feet from the curb line, 25 feet from the back line of the lot, and 10 feet from each side line. However, suppose further that on a particular lot has a large boulder on one rear corner that would make it practically impossible to build a normal house on the lot that complied with the normal setback and side lines. In such an instance, the board of adjustment is likely to grant the owner variances narrowing the front setback and one of the side lot line distances so the owner can build a normal home on the lot.

Requests for use variances tend to be more controversial and litigious than bulk variances. Usually, a landowner's argument in favor of a use variance relates to some off-site problem, such as a disruptive commercial use already occurring next to a lot zoned residential. Boards of adjustment are less likely to grant use variances than bulk variances and, when they grant them, courts tend to reverse their decisions. Many local governments, and two or three states, flatly forbid use variances by statute or ordinance. In jurisdictions where use variances are permitted, there are usually far fewer applications for them than for bulk variances. Moreover, local boards of adjustment often grant bulk variances even when there is no real showing of hardship but these cases are seldom appealed because nearby owners often do not object.

In most variance applications and in judicial review of board decisions, the central issue is whether the applicant has presented adequate evidence of a "hardship." Section 7 of the Standard Zoning Enabling Act (SZEA) empowered the board of adjustment to:

> authorize, upon appeal in specific cases, such variance from the terms of the ordinance as will not be contrary to the public interest where, *owing to special conditions,* a literal enforcement of the provisions of the ordinance will result in *unnecessary hardship,* and so that the spirit of the ordinance shall be observed and substantial justice done. (Emphasis added.)

The SZEA formulation still seems to reflect the language in most state zoning enabling acts. However, in a number of states, following New York's lead, the zoning enabling acts contain a different formulation. As amended in 1920, the New York act authorized the board of appeals, where:

> there are *practical difficulties or unnecessary hardship* in the way of carrying out the strict letter of [the zoning ordinance], to vary or modify any of its rules,

regulations or provisions relating to the construction, structural changes in, equipment, or alteration of buildings or structures, or the use of land, buildings or structures, so that the spirit of the ordinance shall be observed, public safety secured and substantial justice done.[479] (Emphasis added.)

This section calls the phrase "practical difficulties or unnecessary hardship" the "double language," On its face, it allows variances not only in cases of "unnecessary hardship," as did the SZEA, but also in cases of "practical difficulties," which seems to indicate less pressing circumstances. However, New York and states that have its "double language" have generally held that an owner must establish "unnecessary hardship" to obtain a use variance, but only "practical difficulties" to obtain a bulk variance.[480]

In a few early cases, the variance clause of section 7 of the SZEA was held unconstitutional because it did not provide an adequate standard to guide the board of appeals in the exercise of its discretionary power to grant variances.[481] The "unnecessary hardship" standard is now generally held to be constitutionally adequate, but there is no uniformity in the interpretation of this standard across states. The strictest interpretation, adopted in several of the states where zoning litigation is very common, is that laid down by the New York Court of Appeals in the ever-leading case of Otto v. Steinhilber:[482]

> Before the Board may exercise its discretion and grant a variance upon the ground of unnecessary hardship, the record must show that (1) the land in question *cannot yield a reasonable return* if used only for a purpose allowed in that zone; (2) that the plight of the owner is due to *unique circumstances* and not to the general conditions in the neighborhood which may reflect the unreasonableness of the zoning ordinance itself; and (3) that the use to be authorized by the variance will not alter the essential character of the locality. (Emphasis added.)

This interpretation of the "unnecessary hardship" standard has constitutional overtones. It suggests that, unless the owner is granted the variance, he or she might be able to maintain an action for a regulatory taking (see section 9.4, supra) or a denial of

---

[479] Substantially identical language is still contained in New York-McKinney's Town Law § 267(5) and in New York-McKinney's Village Law § 7–712(2)(c). The 1917 General City Zoning Enabling Act merely provided that a zoning board of appeals should be created with the power to "vary the application of zoning regulations in harmony with their general purpose and intent and in accordance with the general or specific rules contained therein."

[480] See, e.g., Puritan-Greenfield Improvement Association v. Leo, 7 Mich.App. 659, 153 N.W.2d 162 (1967); Otto v. Steinhilber, 282 N.Y. 71, 76, 24 N.E.2d 851, 853 (1939) (perennially the classic, leading case).

[481] Welton v. Hamilton, 344 Ill. 82, 176 N.E. 333 (1931), overruled in Heft v. Zoning Board of Appeals, 31 Ill.2d 266, 201 N.E.2d 364 (1964); Jack Lewis, Inc. v. Mayor & City Council of Baltimore, 164 Md. 146, 164 A. 220 (1933), appeal dismissed 290 U.S. 585, 54 S.Ct. 56, 78 L.Ed. 517 (1933).

[482] 282 N.Y. 71, 76, 24 N.E.2d 851, 853 (1939). This standard, which was applied by the New York courts until 1966, was also, in substance, adopted in Massachusetts, Pennsylvania, Michigan, and, with respect to one type of variance, New Jersey. See 5 N. Williams, Am. Land Planning Law chaps. 134 (Massachusetts) and 136 (Pennsylvania), and, as to Michigan law, Puritan-Greenfield Improvement Association v. Leo, 7 Mich.App. 659, 153 N.W.2d 162 (1967). The New Jersey law as to variances is summarized in 5 N. Williams, Am. Land Planning Law § 138.03, as follows:

> "[The] two types of so-called variances in New Jersey are strikingly different: in fact, the second one * * * is not a variance at all but a type of special permit without standards [allowing relaxation of use restrictions] * * *. The first type, dealing with bulk variances, has strict standards, and the local board of adjustment has the power to grant these. The other type * * * has very loose standards; the board of adjustment may recommend these, but they must actually be granted by the governing body."

substantive due process (see section 9.6 supra). This is consistent with the view that the authority to grant variances was given to the zoning board of appeals (or adjustment) to provide a safety valve in cases where the application of zoning regulations to a particular parcel of land impose so great a hardship on the landowner as to invite a constitutional attack. Under this view, the safety valve of variance helps to prevent owners from otherwise chopping up zoning ordinances by getting them declared unconstitutional here and there.

To justify a variance, a hardship must be one that would affect any owner of the particular land involved and not relate solely to difficulties unique to the current owner. For instance, the fact that a particular applicant wishes to establish a certain kind of business but cannot secure any land for it in the community does not justify the granting of a variance. That is a problem unique to the applicant and not unique to the land.[483]

Self-created hardships also do not justify a variance: a variance should not be granted if the applicant has created his or her own hardship even when it relates to the land. For example, suppose that an applicant owns a parcel of land that, pursuant to the zoning ordinance's minimum-lot-size restriction, is large enough to be subdivided into nine lots, but not quite large enough for ten lots. If the owner applies for a variance to allow 10 slightly undersized lots rather than simply dividing the land into nine slightly oversized lots, that application should be denied. A landowner who seeks a variance after already developing land in violation of the law—for example, by building closer to the lot line than the zoning ordinance allows—should also have their applications denied rather than being "bailed out" of the violation.[484]

In states that have New York's double language, the *Steinhilber* formula has generally been applied only to use variances.[485] Without direct statutory support, New York decisions have established different standards for granting what they call "area" variances, holding that "[a]n applicant for an area variance need not establish special hardship" and should be granted an area variance "on the ground of practical difficulties alone."[486] The reason given is that "[w]hen the variance is one of area only, there is no change in the character of the zoned district and the neighborhood considerations are not as strong as in [the case of] a use variance."[487] But in states whose enabling acts use only the SZEA's "unnecessary hardship" language, the *Steinhilber* formula is likely to control if the courts in that state have adopted that formula. On the other hand, in some states the strict *Steinhilber* rule has not been adopted and the courts have held that a variance may be granted almost as a matter of course where zoning regulations are particularly restrictive.[488] And in many states the cases dealing with the question of

---

[483] See Appeal of the Catholic Cemeteries Ass'n, 379 Pa. 516, 109 A.2d 537 (1954) (cemetery could not find another suitable location); J. Juergensmeyer & T. Roberts, Land Use Planning and Control Law § 5.17 (1998).

[484] J. Juergensmeyer & T. Roberts, Land Use Planning and Control Law § 5.17.

[485] See, e.g., Puritan-Greenfield Improvement Association v. Leo, 7 Mich.App. 659, 153 N.W.2d 162 (1967); Otto v. Steinhilber, 282 N.Y. 71, 76, 24 N.E.2d 851, 853 (1939).

[486] Matter of Hoffman v. Harris, 17 N.Y.2d 138, 144, 269 N.Y.S.2d 119, 123, 216 N.E.2d 326, 330 (1966); Otto v. Steinhilber, 282 N.Y. 71, 76, 24 N.E.2d 851, 853 (1939) (dictum).

[487] Id., 17 N.Y.2d at 144, 269 N.Y.S.2d at 123, 216 N.E.2d at 330.

[488] E.g., Nelson v. Board of Zoning Appeals of Indianapolis, 240 Ind. 212, 162 N.E.2d 449 (1959); Kessler-Allisonville Civic League, Inc. v. Marion County Board of Zoning Appeals, 137 Ind.App. 610, 209 N.E.2d 43 (1965). But see The Light Co. v. Houghton, 141 Ind.App. 93, 226 N.E.2d 341 (1967).

standards for granting a variance leave the law in such confusion as to make useful generalization impossible.[489]

Unfortunately, the New York courts have not clearly defined what they mean by "area" variances or "practical difficulties," although it is clear that the latter standard is much less strict than the "unnecessary hardship" standard for "use" variances. It seems likely that the term "area" variance is intended to include "bulk" and "density" variances. In Wilcox v. Zoning Board of Appeals,[490] the New York Court of Appeals sustained a variance allowing an increase in density in an apartment development as an "area" variance, despite the fact that this variance would arguably change "the character of the zoned district" substantially. In other states where the zoning enabling act provides for granting variances in cases of "practical difficulties" as well as "unnecessary hardship," at least four states, in addition to New York, follow the "area" variance rule.[491]

Section 7 of the SZEA and zoning enabling acts and ordinances in general require that the circumstances that justify the granting of a variance be "unique." The hypothetical case offered earlier in this section involving a large boulder on a particular parcel certainly involves a unique condition. However, to be sufficient the condition need not be strictly unique to the applicant's parcel of land and may exist on a few other parcels. At the very least, the term "unique" in this context requires that the conditions affecting the parcel not be "general" to the area. As stated in *Steinhilber*, "general conditions in the neighborhood ... may reflect the unreasonableness of the zoning ordinance itself."[492] In other words, if the condition is "general," then the proper avenue for zoning relief is an amendment of the ordinance and not a variance. For instance, if an owner seeks a variance based on a given parcel's rugged topography even though such topography is common to the area, a court will likely find that the circumstances are not unique.[493] One fact pattern that often justifies a use variance is that the applicant's parcel of land is "under the shadow of" incompatible uses, such as a residential home that is substantially surrounded by commercial uses.[494] On the other hand, courts usually deny variances when the ground advanced is simply that the land lies on a zone line and is adjacent to a different kind of use in another zone since zone lines must stop somewhere.[495]

---

[489] New York now falls in this category. See 5 N. Williams, Am. Land Planning Law §§ 135.04, 135.05. Connecticut also seems to fall into this category, but for different reasons than New York. See Ibid. § 136.02, pointing out that, "so far as both the language and most of the holdings go, there is no appreciable difference between the Connecticut law on variances and that of Massachusetts, or New York before 1967. The problem is that there is a separate line of Connecticut cases, which say more or less the opposite." (Id. § 136.02.) A "clear break in the direction of tightening up on variances (and particularly on use variances) in Connecticut" in a 1965 case, along with more recent Connecticut cases, has left the Connecticut standard for variances uncertain. (Id. § 136.04.)

[490] 17 N.Y.2d 249, 270 N.Y.S.2d 569, 217 N.E.2d 633 (1966).

[491] Use and Area Variances, 2 Am. Law. Zoning § 13:9 (5th ed.) (listing Indiana, Maine, Michigan, Rohde Island, and New York as following some form of the area variance rule).

[492] 282 N.Y. 71, 76, 24 N.E.2d 851, 853 (1939).

[493] See, e.g., Topanga Ass'n for a Scenic Community v. County of Los Angeles, 11 Cal.3d 506, 113 Cal.Rptr. 836, 522 P.2d 12 (1974). See generally, J. Juergensmeyer & T. Roberts, Land Use Planning and Control Law § 5.20; D. Mandelker, Land Use Law § 6.46 (3d ed. 1993).

[494] E.g., Sherwood v. Grant County, 40 Wn.App. 496, 699 P.2d 243 (1985) (residential zone that did not permit mobile homes surrounded on three sides by mobile homes in zone that permitted them). See generally J. Juergensmeyer & T. Roberts, Land Use Planning and Control Law § 5.20.

[495] E.g., Puritan-Greenfield Improvement Association v. Leo, 7 Mich.App. 659, 153 N.W.2d 162 (1967). See generally J. Juergensmeyer & T. Roberts, Land Use Planning and Control Law § 5.20.

In a few states, courts have held that the board of adjustment has no power to grant "use" variances because they are tantamount to "rezoning" and thus require amendment of the zoning ordinance by the local governing body.[496] California and several other states have statutes that ban use variances state-wide.[497] Many local zoning ordinances also forbid use variances altogether.[498] Where use variances are permitted, it is generally understood that an owner may obtain a bulk variance upon a showing of a less pressing "hardship" than would be necessary to obtain a use variance. As a statistical matter, boards of adjustment receive far fewer applications for, and grant far fewer, use variances than they do bulk variances. Nonetheless, use variances tend to more easily raise the ire of neighboring landowners than do bulk variances and produce a majority of the variance litigation.

Most courts have held that boards of adjustment have power to attach appropriate conditions to the grant of any variance as necessary to protect the "essential character of the locality", although the enabling acts generally do not expressly confer such power on the board.[499] Municipal zoning ordinances often expressly authorize the board to impose conditions when a variance is granted, although this seems to be unnecessary. Courts have generally held that conditions attached to variances must relate to the use of the land itself rather than to the person who owns or occupies the land.[500] Conditions imposing requirements as to access, paving of access roads, and landscaping are generally upheld as valid.[501] Conditions limiting the hours of operation or imposing time limits on a variance are sometimes invalidated on the ground that they do not relate to land use.[502] In a few cases, conditions requiring dedication of land for street widening have been sustained where a proposed development will generate sufficient traffic to justify the requirement.[503]

If boards of adjustment had generally adhered to the statutory "unnecessary hardship" standard for granting variances (as expanded by judicial formulas like that in Otto v. Steinhilber),[504] the variance might have performed its intended function of relieving particularized hardships and protecting the zoning regulations from piecemeal challenge on constitutional grounds. However, in practice, many local zoning boards freely grant variances (usually bulk variances) simply to enable individual landowners

---

[496] E.g., Josephson v. Autrey, 96 So.2d 784 (Fla.1957); Bray v. Beyer, 292 Ky. 162, 166 S.W.2d 290 (1942); Lee v. Board of Adjustment, 226 N.C. 107, 37 S.E.2d 128 (1946).

[497] Ariz. Rev. Stat. Ann. § 9–462.06; West's Ann.Cal.Gov. Code § 65906; Ind. Code Ann. § 36–7–4–918(d); Minn. Stat. Ann. § 394.27(7); Va. Code Ann. § 15:1–431(p); see also J. Juergensmeyer & T. Roberts, Land Use Planning and Control Law § 5.15 (1998).

[498] J. Juergensmeyer & T. Roberts, Land Use Planning and Control Law § 5.15 (1998).

[499] See, generally, 3 A. Rathkopf, Law of Zoning and Planning ch. 40 (4th ed. 1983). Some current zoning enabling acts do specifically authorize imposition of conditions when variances are granted. E.g., West's Ann.Cal.Gov.Code § 65906; Mass. Gen.Laws Ann. c. 40A, § 10.

[500] 3 A. Rathkopf, Law of Zoning and Planning § 40.02 (4th ed. 1983).

[501] E.g., Wright v. Zoning Bd. of Appeals, 174 Conn. 488, 391 A.2d 146 (1978); Nicholson v. Zoning Bd. of Adjustment, 392 Pa. 278, 140 A.2d 604 (1958).

[502] E.g., Bora v. Zoning Bd. of Appeals, 161 Conn. 297, 288 A.2d 89 (1972) (hours of operation); Huntington v. Zoning Bd. of Appeals, 12 Mass.App.Ct. 710, 428 N.E.2d 826 (1981) (time limit).

[503] E.g., Bringle v. Board of Supervisors, 54 Cal.2d 86, 4 Cal.Rptr. 493, 351 P.2d 765 (1960); Alperin v. Mayor & Township Comm., 91 N.J.Super. 190, 219 A.2d 628 (Ch.Div.1966). Cf. Scrutton v. County of Sacramento, 275 Cal.App.2d 412, 79 Cal. Rptr. 872 (1969).

[504] 282 N.Y. 71, 24 N.E.2d 851 (1939).

to convert land to a more profitable use.[505] This seems to be a result of various factors, including heavy caseloads, a lack of expertise among local officials, political influence, and outright bribery. Aggrieved parties may appeal the grant of a variance and courts can reverse the board of adjustment on the ground that a variance was improperly granted, but typically there is no appeal and no opportunity for judicial review. In some urban areas, the frequent and indiscriminate granting of variances without proof of "unnecessary hardship" has substantially eroded the uniformity of the zoning regulations applicable in particular districts.[506]

When courts review decisions of the zoning board of appeals (or adjustment) on variance applications, the board's actions have consistently been characterized by the courts as "administrative" or "quasi-judicial" or "adjudicative."[507] Accordingly, courts have often imposed procedural due process requirements on these proceedings such as a requirement that the board shall create a written record and make findings of fact as a basis for its decision.[508] Many courts have likewise overturned board decisions on the ground that they are not based upon substantial evidence contained in the record and (where required) the board's findings.[509] On the other hand, in Shelton v. City of College Station, the United States Court of Appeals for the Fifth Circuit held in 1986 that decisions of the zoning board of appeals should be considered "quasi-legislative" and that the board's decision must be sustained if there is any rational basis for its decision even though it may not be supported by evidence in the record.[510] Since the characterization of board action as "quasi-legislative" and the application of a substantive due process test appropriate in judicial review of legislative action is contrary to the uniform state court approach, the Fifth Circuit's decision seems to be designed to discourage resort to the federal courts (in the 5th Circuit, at least) when the action of a zoning board of appeals on a variance application is challenged.

---

[505] See Dukeminier & Stapleton, The Zoning Board of Adjustment: A Case Study in Misrule, 50 Ky.L.J. 273 (1962); Comment, 50 Calif.L.Rev. 101 (1962).

[506] See Am.L.Inst., Model Land Development Code, Art. 4 Commentary (1976), for discussion of the relation between nonconforming uses and the practice of granting variances without regard to the statutory criteria.

[507] For a good general discussion of the distinction between policy-making and policy-application, with particular reference to the functions of zoning agencies, see Mandelker, Delegation of Power and Function in Zoning Administration, 1963 Wash. U.L.Q. 60.

[508] See Topanga Ass'n for a Scenic Community v. Los Angeles County, 11 Cal.3d 506, 113 Cal.Rptr. 836, 522 P.2d 12 (1974). Some state zoning enabling acts expressly require findings. E.g., Ill.—Smith-Hurd Ann. ch. 24, ¶ 11–13–11.

[509] See D. Mandelker, Land Use Law § 6.52 (4th ed. 1997), which also notes that the SSZEA § 7 authorizes the court to take additional evidence, and that some courts interpret this as authorizing a *de novo* trial, with appellate review based on the trial court record rather than the board proceedings.

[510] 780 F.2d 475 (5th Cir.1986) (en banc), certiorari denied 477 U.S. 905, 106 S.Ct. 3276, 91 L.Ed.2d 566 (1986). The majority relied, in support of its decision, entirely on cases characterizing zoning amendments enacted by the local legislative body as "legislative"—where the amendment changed the zoning classification of a substantial area—or "quasi-legislative"—where the amendment rezoned a single property. The majority opinion was concurred in by nine judges; one judge concurred only in the result; and five judges dissented on the ground that the majority's characterization of the action of a zoning board of appeals in variance cases as "quasi-legislative" was erroneous and, consequently, that the majority had applied the wrong standard of judicial review in the case at hand.

C. NON-ZONING LAND USE CONTROLS

§ 9.30 SUBDIVISION CONTROLS AND SITE PLAN REVIEW

Residential Subdivision Controls

Land subdivision controls are an important type of governmental land use regulation that is separate from but closely related to zoning. Raw land that is used for agriculture or other non-urban purposes is usually held in relatively large tracts. To be suitable for single-family residential development, it must first be divided into parcels that are appropriate as sites for residential structures. In a traditional subdivision that is large enough to have internal streets, the areas between the streets are called "blocks", which are divided into building "lots" or "tracts."[511] Originally, the main purpose of subdividing land was to provide a method of land description that is more convenient than metes and bounds description. Once a subdivision has been approved by the local government, the original subdivision map or "plat" is recorded in the county land records. Thereafter, land within that subdivision may be described by the name of the subdivision and the designation of the particular block and lot. However, as described later in this section, the subdivision process has increasingly been used as a means of controlling the development of subdivided land. The subdivision of raw land provides a strategic point at which local governments may intervene to control the pattern of future urban land development.

The regulation of land subdivision began in the United States long before 1900. Indeed, the rectangular survey of the public domain of the United States, carried out pursuant to the Northwest Ordinance of 1785, constituted a rudimentary framework for controlling the subdivision of land because subsequent transfers of surveyed farm land usually involved survey "sections" or some fraction thereof. After 1844, so-called "town site laws" were passed to regulate the division of public domain lands for town development. However both the federal statutes dealing with the public domain and the early state statutes regulating land subdivision were primarily designed to assure that parties supplied adequate engineering data and that recorded subdivision plats were as accurate as possible. As late as 1928, only a few states had legislation imposing any substantial design or infrastructure requirements upon subdividers.[512]

Drawing on existing New York land planning and subdivision control legislation, a committee appointed by the United States Department of Commerce published the Standard City Planning Enabling Act in 1928.[513] Title I of the Standard Act focused on planning in the literal sense and authorized municipalities to create and empower planning commissions "to make and adopt a master plan for the physical development of the municipality, including any areas outside of its boundaries which, in the commission's judgment, bear relation to the planning of such municipality." Title II of the Standard Act authorized municipal planning commissions, after "adopting a major street plan of the territory within its subdivision jurisdiction or part thereof," to "adopt

---

[511] Subdivision of a tract may also be required in some cases when a large-scale industrial or commercial development is contemplated—e.g., when a developer initiates an "industrial village" development.

[512] Generally, see Melli, Subdivision Control in Wisconsin, 1953 Wis.L.Rev. 389.

[513] The Standard Act (hereafter termed SCPEA) is no longer in print in its original form as a publication of the U.S. Dept. of Commerce, but it is reprinted in full, with the draftsmen's footnotes, as Appendix B in Am.L.Inst., Model Land Development Code, Tentative Draft 1 (1968).

regulations governing the subdivision of land within its jurisdiction." Commissions were to provide for "the proper arrangement of streets in relation to other existing streets and to the master plan, for adequate and convenient open spaces for traffic, utilities, access of fire-fighting apparatus, recreation, light and air, and for the avoidance of congestion of population, including minimum width and area of lots."[514]

The Standard Act defined the "subdivision jurisdiction" of a municipal planning commission as all land within the corporate limits of a municipality and "within 5 miles of the corporate limits of the municipality and not located in any other municipality."[515] Within this jurisdiction, a municipal planning commission was essentially a legislative body enacting subdivision regulations and an administrative body applying the regulations to individual applications for subdivision plat approval. Some current enabling statutes also provide for extraterritorial exercise of the subdivision control power.[516] Although rarely challenged, such grants of extra-territorial jurisdiction have generally been sustained.[517]

The Standard Act substantially restricted the power of municipalities to accept or improve new streets, install or authorize installations of utility lines in new streets, or issue permits for building construction on new streets after the municipal planning commission adopted a major street plan unless the new streets were within a commission-approved subdivision.[518] The Standard Act further provided that, where a major street plan had been adopted, "no plat of a subdivision * * * [could] be filed or recorded until it [had] been approved by such planning commission."[519] The Act even authorized the imposition of a civil penalty or issuance of an injunction whenever a subdivider "transfers or sells or agrees to sell or negotiates to sell any land by reference to or exhibition of or by other use of a plat of a subdivision, before such plat has been approved by the planning commission and recorded," even if the land is sold or conveyed by "metes and bounds."[520]

Most current subdivision control enabling legislation can be traced back either to Title II of the Standard City Planning Act or to one of the Model Municipal Subdivision Regulation Acts published in the Harvard City Planning Series in the mid-1930s.[521] The latter were principally drafted by persons who had participated in drafting the Standard Act[522] and did not differ substantially from it. Many current subdivision control enabling statutes authorize local agencies to require subdividers to install an even wider range of infrastructure "improvements" than did the Standard Act;[523] to require subdividers to dedicate land to the local government or to a school district for use as parks, playgrounds,

[514] SCPEA §§ 13, 14 (1928). Although minimum lot width and area requirements are usually contained in the local zoning ordinance, they are sometimes included in the subdivision regulations. See also Town of Sun Prairie v. Storms, 110 Wis.2d 58, 327 N.W.2d 642 (1983), holding that municipalities may enforce a state statute fixing minimum lot sizes, although the requirements have not been incorporated into their local zoning ordinances.

[515] SCPEA § 12 (1928).

[516] At least 19 states have such provisions.

[517] See, e.g., Petterson v. City of Naperville, 9 Ill.2d 233, 137 N.E.2d 371 (1956).

[518] SCPEA § 15 (1928).

[519] SCPEA § 13 (1928).

[520] SCPEA § 16 (1928).

[521] E.g., A. Bettman, Municipal Subdivision Regulation Act, in E. Bassett, A. Bettman, F. Williams & Whitten, Model Laws for Planning Cities, Counties and States (Harvard City Planning Series 1935).

[522] The draftsmen were Edward Bassett and Alfred Bettman.

[523] E.g., West's Ann.Cal.Gov.Code § 66419.

or school sites;[524] require approval of subdivisions by specified local and state agencies such as health departments, water departments, and highway commissions;[525] and authorize local or state agencies to refuse subdivision approval entirely in certain instances.[526] In some jurisdictions, the enabling statutes require local subdivision regulations to be adopted by the local governing body[527] and/or require individual subdivision plats to be approved by the local governing body as well as by the planning commission.[528]

Some current subdivision control enabling statutes expressly require that land subdivisions comply with local zoning regulations,[529] and in the few cases where the issue has been litigated courts have generally held that local subdivision agencies have the power to deny approval of subdivision plats when the subdivision does not comply with the local zoning ordinance.[530] In a few states, land subdivisions are expressly required to be consistent with the local comprehensive plan. In these states subdivision approval generally must be withheld if the subdivision is inconsistent with the plan, even if it fully complies with the local zoning and subdivision regulations.[531]

The Standard City Planning Enabling Act defined "subdivision" as "the division of a lot, tract, or parcel of land into two or more lots, plats, sites, or other divisions of land for the purpose, whether immediate or future, of sale or of building development."[532] However, most current subdivision statutes either exempt, authorize the local authorities to exempt, or allow abbreviated approval procedures for subdivisions of less than a specified number of new lots (*e.g.,* four lots) or that create only lots larger than a specified size (*e.g.,* five acres) or do not require creation of a new street.[533]

The subdivision control enabling acts generally authorize the local subdivision control agency to disapprove proposed subdivisions if they fail to comply with local subdivision regulations with respect to street, block, and lot layout, improvement of internal subdivision streets, and installation of utility lines.[534] Modern enabling acts also often authorize the rejection of proposed subdivisions on the ground that they would cause serious traffic problems due to inadequate existing public road access, or on the ground that the topography or soil conditions of the site make it unsuitable for development until public water, sewer, or drainage facilities have been extended to the

---

[524] E.g., West's Ann.Cal.Gov.Code §§ 66477, 66478; Wash. Rev. Code § 58.17.110.

[525] E.g., Mich.Comp.Laws Ann. §§ 560.114–560.119.

[526] E.g., Ariz. Rev. Stat. § 9–463.01(C)(4); N.H. Rev .Stat. Ann. 36:21.

[527] E.g., West's Ann.Cal.Gov.Code § 66411; Wash. Rev. Code § 58.17.100.

[528] E.g., Mich.Comp.Laws Ann. §§ 560.120, 560.167.

[529] E.g., New Jersey Stat.Ann. 40:55D–38(d). West's Ann.Cal.Gov.Code § 66473.5 requires compliance with local general plans.

[530] See, e.g., People v. City of Park Ridge, 25 Ill.App.2d 424, 166 N.E.2d 635 (1960).

[531] E.g., West's Ann.Cal.Gov.Code § 66473.5.

[532] SCPEA § 1 (1928).

[533] E.g., West's Ann.Cal.Gov.Code § 66426; Mich.Comp.Laws Ann. § 560.102(d); New Jersey Stat.Ann. 40:55D–7; Wash. Rev. Code § 58.17.060 (abbreviated procedures for "short plats" of 4 or less lots); Wash. Rev. Code § 58.17.040(2) (exemption for parcels 5 acres or larger).

[534] E.g., West's Ann.Cal.Gov.Code §§ 66474–66474.2; Mich.Comp.Laws Ann. §§ 560.105–560.106.

site.[535] Rejection of proposed subdivisions on such grounds, when authorized by statute has generally been sustained.[536]

Site Plan Review

Because subdivision controls are applicable only to land development projects involving subdivisions of substantial tracts into smaller parcels ("lots"), local governments eventually realized they could not rely on their delegated subdivision control powers to regulate many apartment or industrial projects or other large-scale developments that required no subdividing of land. To address this problem, "site plan" review procedures were established by many communities during the 1960s without any express statutory authorization.[537] A few early cases held that site plan review procedures were impliedly authorized by the zoning enabling acts, in connection with applications for variances, special exceptions (or special uses or conditional uses) or rezoning amendments.[538] Today, a number of states have adopted enabling legislation expressly authorizing site plan review procedures.[539] In some states, however, the scope of the local power to impose site plan review requirements is still unclear.

Although site plan review procedures were originally designed to give local governments additional control over land developments that did not require subdivisions of the land, some states' enabling statutes now permit local governments to require submission of site plans even where the land is to be subdivided.[540] The purpose of these statutory provisions is apparently to enable local governments to get an advance look at an applicant's proposed development project when a request for rezoning is submitted. Local governments have also used the site plan review procedure to impose requirements for "[p]reservation of existing natural resources on the site; * * * [s]afe and efficient vehicular and pedestrian circulation, parking and loading; * * * [s]creening, landscaping and location of structures; * * * [e]xterior lighting needed for safety reasons in addition to any requirements for street lighting; and * * * [c]onservation of energy and use of

---

[535] See, e.g., West's Ann.Cal.Gov.Code § 66474(c), (d), (f); Mich.Comp.Laws Ann. §§ 560.105(g), 560.114, 560.117, 560.118.

[536] See, e.g., Garipay v. Town of Hanover, 116 N.H. 34, 351 A.2d 64 (1976) (inadequate public access road); Hamilton v. Planning Board, 4 Mass.App.Ct. 802, 345 N.E.2d 906 (1976); Christianson v. Gasvoda, 242 Mont. 212, 789 P.2d 1234 (1990) (flooding problems).

[537] Generally, see D. Mandelker, Land Use Law § 6.68 (4th ed. 1997); 5 N. Williams, American Land Planning Law § 152.01 (1975 and Supp.1982).

[538] See, e.g., McCrann v. Town Plan and Zoning Commission, 161 Conn. 65, 282 A.2d 900 (1971); Sun Oil Co. v. Zoning Board of Adjustment, 403 Pa. 409, 169 A.2d 294 (1961); Wilson v. Borough of Mountainside, 42 N.J. 426, 201 A.2d 540 (1964). Contra: Coolidge v. Planning Board of North Andover, 337 Mass. 648, 151 N.E.2d 51 (1958).

[539] E.g., Mich.Comp.Laws Ann. § 125.584d; New Jersey Stat.Ann. 40:55D–14 through 40:55D–44, 40:55D–46, 40:55D–46.1; Wash. Rev. Code §§ 58.17.020(7), 58.17.040(4). New Jersey Stat.Ann. 40:55D–7 defines "site plan" as follows:

 a development plan of one or more lots on which is shown (1) the existing and proposed conditions of the lot, including but not necessarily limited to topography, vegetation, drainage, flood plains, marshes and waterways, (2) the location of all existing and proposed buildings, drives, parking spaces, walkways, means of ingress and egress, drainage facilities, utility services, landscaping, structures and signs, lighting, and screening devices, and (3) any other information in order to make an informed determination pursuant to an ordinance requiring review and approval of site plans by the planning board * * *.

[540] See New Jersey's definition of "site plan," preceding note.

renewable energy sources,"[541] as well as monetary contributions for off-tract water, sewer, drainage, and street improvements,[542] and reservations of land for public use.[543]

Subdivision and Site Plan Review Procedures

Local subdivision regulations usually outline the review procedure a local government must follow when considering a proposed subdivision. The initial stage in many localities is an informal "pre-application review" of the proposed subdivision based on a sketch map of the tract and a location map showing the relationship of the proposed subdivision to existing development and the community facilities required to service the subdivision.[544] The sketch map and location map are generally reviewed by the professional planning staff and other local officials such as the municipal engineer to determine whether the proposed subdivision is consistent with the local comprehensive land use plan (if any), whether it satisfies municipal subdivision design standards and improvement requirements, and whether the site is suitable with respect to topography, drainage, etc. The results of this informal review are then discussed with the subdivider, who is informed of any changes necessary to comply with the subdivision regulations and the comprehensive plan. Even when a subdivider and the local authorities do not engage in the "pre-application review" just described, the subdivider or his advisers often seek informal guidance from local officials on questions they might have. Suggestions for improvement of the subdivision design are often made and discussed at this stage.

After the "pre-application" review, if any, the subdivider must usually submit a "tentative" or "preliminary" plat of the proposed subdivision to the planning commission.[545] While the name suggests that approval of the plat and accompanying documents, such as subdivision restrictive covenants, is only "tentative" or "preliminary," that is not the case. Approval of the "tentative" or "preliminary" plat authorizes the laying out and improvement of streets, installation of sewer and utility lines and, in some cases, construction of houses.[546] Because the decision to approve or deny approval of the preliminary plat is so important, the subdivision regulations generally set out in considerable detail the information the plat must include.[547] The plat must be submitted in sufficient time to allow for consideration and recommendations by a variety of local agencies such as the municipal engineer, the public works department, the school board, and the health department.[548] Recommendations from all these

---

[541] New Jersey Stat.Ann. 40:55D–7.

[542] N.J. Stat. Ann. 40:55D–42. Cf. N.Y.-McKinney's Town Law § 274, held not to authorize monetary exactions in Riegert Apartments Corp. v. Planning Bd. of Clarkstown, 57 N.Y.2d 206, 455 N.Y.S.2d 558, 441 N.E.2d 1076 (1982); Wash. Rev. Code § 58.17.110 held not to authorize monetary exactions in Hillis Homes, Inc. v. Snohomish County, 97 Wn.2d 804, 650 P.2d 193 (1982).

[543] N.J. Stat. Ann. 40:55D–44.

[544] This "pre-application" review is often not expressly authorized by the enabling act. See generally, Green, Land Subdivision, in Principles and Practice of Urban Planning 443, 449–454 (W. Goodman & E. Freund eds. 1968).

[545] E.g., West's Ann.Cal.Gov.Code § 66426 ("tentative map"); Mich.Comp. Laws Ann. § 560.105 ("preliminary plat"); New Jersey Stat.Ann. 40:55D–48 ("preliminary * * * subdivision approval"); Wash. Rev. Code § 58.17.020(4) (" 'preliminary plat' " is a "neat and approximate drawing").

[546] See Green, Land Subdivision, in Principles and Practice of Urban Planning 443, 449–454 (W. Goodman & E. Freund eds. 1968). Improvements that may be made, upon the posting of a completion bond, between the time the preliminary plat is approved and the final plat is approved may be limited to improvements required in the approval of the preliminary plat, which usually means infrastructure improvements such as streets, curbs, gutters, etc. See, e.g., Wash. Rev. Code § 58.17.130.

[547] E.g., Mich.Comp.Laws Ann. § 560.111.

[548] E.g., West's Ann.Cal.Gov.Code §§ 66453–66455.7; Mich.Comp.Laws Ann. §§ 560.113–560.119.

agencies are usually received by the planning commission or local governing body before the public hearing on the proposed subdivision.[549] Before approval is granted, there is often a good deal of discussion and negotiation between the subdivider and the local authorities involved in subdivision review, and the parties often agree on modifications of the subdivision design and/or the physical improvements required to be installed before final plat approval will be granted.

As previously indicated, "tentative" or "preliminary" plat approval usually authorizes the subdivider to proceed with installation of required utility lines and street improvements. The subdivision control statutes almost always require the subdivider to complete certain required public improvements prior to approval of the final plat or to post a bond or other security guaranteeing completion of these improvements.[550] Some statutes also authorize alternatives to construction of improvements by the subdivider, such as construction by the local government on the basis of its usual procedures for local improvements and the levying of a special assessment against the subdivision lots to recover the cost. Statutes may likewise authorize the formation of a new special local improvement district with power to issue bonds, make the required improvements, and recover the cost by levying a special assessment against the subdivision lots.[551]

Local subdivision regulations often authorize subdivision developers to obtain building permits for dwellings after their "tentative" or "preliminary" plat is approved and they have posted the required security for installation of all required utility lines and street improvements.[552] Residential subdivision developers typically sell either unimproved lots upon which purchasers build their own "custom" homes) or sell lots with completed "spec" homes on them. Regardless, subdividers usually want assurances that they will not be required to make costly modifications due to changes in zoning or subdivision regulations applicable to their developments before proceeding with construction of houses and/or required street improvements. In a number of states, the subdivision control enabling statutes expressly provide that, after "tentative" or "preliminary" approval, the subdivider is protected for a stated period from any substantial change in subdivision or zoning regulations.[553]

At any time within the period for which the "tentative" or "preliminary" subdivision approval has been granted, subdividers may submit their "final" subdivision plat for approval provided that installation of the required utility lines and street improvements is complete. Subdividers are usually allowed to submit different parts of their tract for final approval at different times so that they can initially build houses on only part of

---

[549] The planning commission hearing must, of course, satisfy both statutory and constitutional due process requirements as to notice and opportunity of interested parties to be heard. Thus in Mutton Hill Estates, Inc. v. Town of Oakland, 468 A.2d 989 (Me.1983), appeal after remand 488 A.2d 151 (1985), the board's action in denying subdivision approval was vacated because the planning board had invited opponents of the proposed subdivision to assist in preparation of the findings of fact necessary to support the board's decision. Neither the developer nor any representative of the developer was given notice of or attended the meetings in which the findings were prepared; the board's decision was later announced at an open meeting attended by the developer's representative. The court also held that the developer was unlikely ever to receive a fair and expeditious hearing from the planning board and remanded the case to the trial court to determine whether the proposed subdivision should be approved.

[550] E.g., West's Ann.Cal.Gov.Code §§ 66499 through 66499.10; Mich.Comp. Laws Ann. § 560.182(1)(e); New Jersey Stat.Ann. 40:55D–53; Wash. Rev. Code § 58.17.130.

[551] E.g., West's Ann.Cal.Gov.Code § 66499.5.

[552] See Green, Land Subdivision, in Principles and Practice of Urban Planning 443, 449–454 (W. Goodman & E. Freund eds. 1968).

[553] E.g., Mich.Comp.Laws Ann. § 560.120 (2 years); New Jersey Stat.Ann. 40:55D–49 (3 years).

the tract and thus reduce the amount they must initially borrow to finance construction.[554] This is called development "in stages." Some municipalities actually require two "final" plats—an "engineering" plat setting out details of the construction and location of subdivision utility lines and street improvements and a plat "for record" containing primarily land title information such as precise lot lines, street boundaries, utility easement locations, and the like.[555] Local subdivision regulations usually provide for submission and approval of the "final" plat in substantially the same manner as the "tentative" or "preliminary" plat. The primary concern of local authorities at the "final" plat stage is to be sure that the "final" plat is in conformity with the "tentative" or "preliminary" plat and that all required improvements have been properly completed.[556] Some subdivision ordinances provide for approval of the "final" plat by the local governing body even though the planning commission has authority to approve the "tentative" or "preliminary" plat.[557]

In instances where subdividers have not yet obtained building permits for all planned housing construction prior to receiving "final" plat approval, they need assurance—which is provided by some current subdivision control statutes—that there will be no substantial change in the zoning or subdivision regulations applicable to his subdivision for a reasonable period of time. Many subdivision control enabling acts now so provide.[558] Even in the absence of a protective statutory provision, a substantial change of position by the subdivider in reliance on his "final" plat approval may estop the municipality from substantially changing the zoning or subdivision regulations applicable to the subdivision.[559] However, it is generally difficult to convince a court that the subdivider has substantially changed position unless he has actually started construction of houses before the regulations are changed.[560]

Some subdivision control enabling statutes authorize local governing bodies to classify certain types of subdivisions—e.g., subdivisions that require creation of no new streets, do not involve a planned unit development, and do not require extension of any off-site improvements—as "minor" subdivisions.[561] The review procedures for these "minor" subdivisions are substantially simpler and more expeditious than those required for "major" subdivisions.[562]

In states where a statute authorizes local governments to require site plan review and approval, site plan review procedures generally resemble subdivision review

---

[554] E.g., West's Ann.Cal.Gov.Code § 66456; New Jersey Stat.Ann. 40:55D–49(b).

[555] See Green, Land Subdivision, in Principles and Practice of Urban Planning 443, 449–454 (W. Goodman & E. Freund eds. 1968).

[556] E.g., New Jersey Stat.Ann. 40:55D–50. But see West's Ann.Cal.Gov.Code § 66464 as to agreements relating to improvements not completed when a final map is approved.

[557] See, e.g., West's Ann.Cal.Gov.Code §§ 66452, 66457, 66458.

[558] E.g., New Jersey Stat.Ann. 40:55D–52 (2 years, with possible 1-year extensions up to a maximum of 3 years); 53 Penn.Stat. § 10508(4) (3 years).

[559] E.g., Ward v. City of New Rochelle, 20 Misc.2d 122, 197 N.Y.S.2d 64 (1959), affirmed 9 A.D.2d 911, 197 N.Y.S.2d 128 (1959), motion denied 7 N.Y.2d 1026, 200 N.Y.S.2d 68, 166 N.E.2d 859 (1960), affirmed 8 N.Y.2d 895, 204 N.Y.S.2d 144, 168 N.E.2d 821 (1960).

[560] E.g., Elsinore Property Owners Association v. Morwand Homes, 286 App.Div. 1105, 146 N.Y.S.2d 78 (1955); Telimar Homes, Inc. v. Miller, 14 A.D.2d 586, 218 N.Y.S.2d 175 (1961), appeal denied 14 A.D.2d 701, 219 N.Y.S.2d 937 (1961); Garvin v. Baker, 59 So.2d 360 (Fla.1952); Blevens v. City of Manchester, 103 N.H. 284, 170 A.2d 121 (1961).

[561] See New Jersey Stat.Ann. 4:55D–5.

[562] See, e.g., New Jersey Stat.Ann. 40:55D–47.

procedures.[563] In states where local governments may require review and approval of both site plans and subdivision plans, there is a considerable overlap. In at least one state, the statute expressly authorizes the local planning board "to review and approve or deny conditional uses or site plans simultaneously with review for subdivision approval without the developer being required to make further application to the planning board, or the planning board being required to hold further hearings.[564] The effect of preliminary and final site plan approval is the same, with respect to protection of a land developer, as the effect of "preliminary and final approval of a subdivision."[565]

Once approved, a site plan is treated like an approved subdivision plat. Compliance with the plan as approved is usually enforced by suspension of building permits and/or refusal to permit connection with public water and sewer systems.

§ 9.31 GROWTH CONTROL PLANS

Suburban growth management became an issue in the 1960s because the pace of residential development often threatened to outrun the capacity of local governments to provide the needed new infrastructure of arterial roads, schools, water and sewage treatment plans, and parks. Before suburban communities began to exact "impact fees" or "impact taxes,"[566] these centralized public facilities had to be funded out of general tax revenues that often did not grow as rapidly as the demand for new facilities. Hence, many suburban communities adopted various land use-control techniques to try to slow and efficiently manage efficiently the rush to the suburbs.

Low-Density Residential Zoning

Beginning in the 1950s, some suburban communities began zoning most of their outlying undeveloped acreage exclusively for single-family dwellings at very low densities. Older suburban communities that were already "overzoned" for high-or medium-density residential development similarly "downzoned" large areas to permit only low-density single-family dwellings. The purpose in both cases was to direct growth to the undeveloped areas closest to the existing built-up portions of the community so that residential development in outlying areas proceeded slowly and the demand for and cost of new public facilities was minimized. As already highlighted, the initial zoning of large portions of suburban communities for single-family dwellings at low densities (i.e., with large minimum-lot-size requirements) was generally upheld when challenged by

---

[563] See, e.g., N.J. Stat. Ann. 40:55D–41, authorizing "standards and requirements" relating to the following: a. Preservation of existing natural resources on the site; b. Safe and efficient vehicular and pedestrian circulation parking and loading; c. Screening, landscaping and location of structures; d. Exterior lighting needed for safety reasons in addition to any requirements for street lighting; and e. Conservation of energy and use of renewable energy sources.

N.J. Stat.Ann. 40:55D–5 authorizes the local governing body to create a "minor" site plan classification when a new development "does not involve planned development, any new street or extension of any off-tract improvement." The approval procedure for "minor" site plans under id. 40:55D–46.1 are simpler than that for approval of other site plans under id. 40:55D–46 and 40:55D–50, which require both "preliminary" and "final" approval.

See also Wesley Investment Co. v. County of Alameda, 151 Cal.App.3d 672, 198 Cal. Rptr. 872 (1984), holding that a county may reject a proposed development through its site plan review procedure where the development contemplated a land use (a "7–11" convenience store) permitted by the county zoning ordinance, but the county site plan ordinance authorized an administrative denial of that use.

[564] See, N.J Stat.Ann. 40:55D–51.

[565] See, e.g., N.J. Stat.Ann. 40:55D–49, 40:55D–52.

[566] See § 9.32, infra.

landowners and developers in the 1950s and 1960s.[567] Courts have also largely sustained extensive "downzonings" to lower densities so long as they are consistent with or pursuant to a comprehensive and carefully worked-out growth management plan.[568]

Moratoria on Suburban Growth

In suburban communities where uncontrolled growth had already overtaxed public facilities such as sewage treatment plants and schools, local governments in the late 1960s and early 1970s began resorting to temporary moratoria on land development, subdivision approvals, building permits, or utility hook-ups. The United States Supreme Court's decision in Lucas v. South Carolina Coastal Council makes it clear that a total and *permanent* ban on all profitable use of land that has value for development is a "taking" in violation of the Fifth and Fourteenth Amendments to the Federal Constitution.[569] However, that is not necessarily true for *temporary* bans on development such as moratoria on subdivision approvals, building permits, or utility hook-ups. These moratoria have sometimes been struck down but have usually been sustained if a court is persuaded that certain elements are present. First, there must be some pressing and temporary situation or condition that justifies the moratorium. Certainly a potential health hazard, such as might result from inadequate existing sewage treatment infrastructure, satisfies this requirement. However, this inquiry is sometimes more debatable, such as when a city seeks to halt development white it overhauls zoning ordinances to cope with too-rapid growth.[570] Second, the local government must have a plan for coping with the temporary situation that drives the moratoria and be actually implementing the plan in good faith.[571] Third, the moratorium must not violate constitutional guarantees of equal protection.[572] Fourth, the moratorium must be "temporary" and be no longer than is reasonably necessary to correct the pressing situation that justifies it. It is impossible to state any flat time as an outside limit. A justifiable time limit of a year "or so" is likely void, and a federal district court in Smoke

---

[567] See § 9.18, supra, for discussion of large-lot zoning.

[568] E.g., Carty v. City of Ojai, 77 Cal. App.3d 329, 143 Cal.Rptr. 506 (1978); Norbeck Village Joint Venture v. Montgomery County Council, 254 Md. 59, 254 A.2d 700 (1969).

[569] 505 U.S. 1003, 112 S.Ct. 2886, 120 L.Ed.2d 798 (1992). See generally, § 9.4, supra. A "taking" would, of course, require compensation. See First English Evangelical Lutheran Church v. County of Los Angeles, 482 U.S. 304, 107 S.Ct. 2378, 96 L.Ed.2d 250 (1987); § 9.5, supra.

[570] Kaplan v. Clear Lake City Water Auth., 794 F.2d 1059 (5th Cir.1986) (water and sewer connections); Ocean Acres Ltd. Partnership v. Dare County Bd. of Health, 707 F.2d 103 (4th Cir.1983) (septic tanks); Smoke Rise, Inc. v. Washington Suburban Sanitary Com'n, 400 F.Supp. 1369 (D.Md. 1975) (sewer hook-up moratorium); Gilbert v. State of California, 218 Cal.App.3d 234, 266 Cal.Rptr. 891 (1990) (moratorium on water service construction during period of water shortage); Williams v. City of Central, 907 P.2d 701 (Colo.App.1995) (10-month moratorium while city changed zoning ordinance); DeKalb County v. Townsend Associates, Inc., 243 Ga. 80, 252 S.E.2d 498 (1979) (necessity for sewer moratorium not proved); Belle Harbor Realty Corp. v. Kerr, 35 N.Y.2d 507, 364 N.Y.S.2d 160, 323 N.E.2d 697 (1974) (moratorium on building until inadequacy of sewerage was corrected); Sun Ridge Development, Inc. v. City of Cheyenne, 787 P.2d 583 (Wyo.1990) (construction moratorium to enforce drainage regulations).

[571] E.g., Associated Home Builders of Greater Eastbay, Inc. v. City of Livermore, 18 Cal.3d 582, 135 Cal.Rptr. 41, 557 P.2d 473 (1976) (instructions on remand that trial court must find city has plan to complete needed improvements and when they will be completed); Westwood Forest Estates, Inc. v. Village of South Nyack, 23 N.Y.2d 424, 297 N.Y.S.2d 129, 244 N.E.2d 700 (1969) (sewage problem due to longstanding inadequacy of village's central treatment facilities, and village had no clear plan to correct problem). See generally J. Juergensmeyer & T. Roberts, Land Use Planning and Control Law § 9.5 (1998); D. Mandelker, Land Use Law § 6.10 (4th ed. 1997).

[572] E.g., Pritchett v. Nathan Rodgers Const. & Realty Corp., 379 So.2d 545 (Ala. 1979) (invalid because sewer tap-ins were denied on an arbitrary, case-by-case basis). Generally, see J. Juergensmeyer & T. Roberts, Land Use Planning and Control Law § 9.5 (1998); D. Mandelker, Land Use Law § 6.10 (4th ed. 1997).

Rise, Inc. v. Washington Suburban Sanitary Commission upheld a five-year moratorium.[573] On the other hand, First English Evangelical Lutheran Church v. County of Los Angeles suggested that a complete moratorium on construction that amounted to some eight years could cause a "taking."[574] For a more detailed discussion on regulatory takings issues and temporary moratoria, see Section 9.4, infra.

Local Growth Management Programs

Some local governments have adopted rather elaborate growth management programs.[575] Such programs usually specify some limited set of areas in which new development will be allowed to occur and may also indicate the sequence in which these areas will be permitted to develop. Some such programs establish an "urban growth boundary" beyond which urban development will not be permitted at all, unless and until the local government extends the boundary. Where the local government unit adopting the program is a county or a regional authority, the program may drastically limit the growth of existing municipalities and provide for dispersal of new development in outlying areas.

Most suburban growth control programs link the approval of new development to the availability of essential public facilities ("infrastructure") and prohibit new development not served by adequate facilities. However, the extension of certain kinds of public facilities such as public water supply may be subject to cross-cutting statutory or case law rules under which municipal utility departments may have a duty to extend services to growing suburban and exurban areas. The imposition of such a duty can thus undercut growth management programs that limit public utility extensions in order to control new development.[576]

---

[573] 400 F.Supp. 1369 (D.Md.1975) (sewer hook-up moratorium). See also Williams v. City of Central, 907 P.2d 701 (Colo.App. 1995) (10-month moratorium upheld); J. Juergensmeyer & T. Roberts, Land Use Planning and Control Law § 9.5 (1998) (of "limited" and "reasonable" duration). Several states have adopted statutes that limit the times moratoria may exist while an interim zoning ordinance is in effect. E.g., Minn. Stat. Ann. § 394.34 (one year); Mont. Code Ann. § 76–2–206 (one year); Utah Code Ann. § 10–9–18 (six months).

[574] 482 U.S. 304, 107 S.Ct. 2378, 96 L.Ed.2d 250 (1987). However, the Court's decision was predicated upon the supposition that the moratorium, in the form of a floodplain ordinance, prohibited all use from the time it went into effect until the Court's decision some eight years later. Upon remand, the California courts found that the ordinance had not in fact prohibited the use of all parts of the plaintiff's land and that there was no "taking." First English Evangelical Lutheran Church v. County of Los Angeles, 210 Cal.App.3d 1353, 258 Cal.Rptr. 893 (1989), cert. den., 493 U.S. 1056, 110 S.Ct. 866, 107 L.Ed.2d 950 (1990). For full discussion of *First English,* see § 9.5, supra.

[575] See, generally, J. Juergensmeyer & T. Roberts, Land Use Planning and Control Law §§ 9.1–9.4, 9.7, 9.8 (1998); D. Mandelker, Land Use Law §§ 10.01–10.09 (4th ed. 1997); D. Godschalk, D. Brower, L. Bennett & B. Vestal, Constitutional Issues of Growth Management 8–10 (1977).

Local governments also occasionally attempt to control regional growth by limiting utility extensions outside municipal limits, with varying results. See, e.g., Dateline Builders, Inc. v. City of Santa Rosa, 146 Cal.App.3d 520, 194 Cal.Rptr. 258 (1983) (valid); Robinson v. City of Boulder, 190 Colo. 357, 547 P.2d 228 (1976) (invalid); Delmarva Enterprises, Inc. v. Mayor and Council of City of Dover, 282 A.2d 601 (Del.1971) (invalid).

[576] See, e.g., Robinson v. City of Boulder, 190 Colo. 357, 547 P.2d 228 (1976); Reid Development Corp. v. Parsippany-Troy Hills Township, 31 N.J.Super. 459, 107 A.2d 20 (App.Div.1954); Corcoran v. Village of Bennington, 128 Vt. 482, 266 A.2d 457 (1970). Cf. Westminster, Colorado, Growth Control cases discussed in 34 Land Use Law & Zoning Digest, March 1982, at pp. 15–16. See also Note, Control of Timing and Location of Government and Utility Extensions, 26 Stan.L.Rev. 945 (1974).

Full-fledged growth management programs have been challenged and upheld several cases.[577] One of the earliest leading cases is Golden v. Town of Ramapo, where the New York Court of Appeals sustained an elaborate program against challenges that the program was ultra vires, resulted in a "taking" of private property without "just compensation," and violated substantive due process .[578] Similarly, in Construction Industry Association v. City of Petaluma, the Ninth Circuit Court of Appeals sustained an elaborate growth control program that placed annual quotas building permits[579] against a substantive due process challenge and a claim that the program infringed the ill-defined constitutional "right to travel" and interfered unduly with interstate commerce.[580]

The Ramapo growth management program was keyed to an ambitious capital improvement program. The program was designed to assure that land development would go hand-in-hand with extension of essential public services and would proceed in an orderly and efficient manner outward from existing developed areas.[581] To implement its growth management program, Ramapo adopted an amendment to its zoning ordinance requiring all new residential development (except for single-family homes) to proceed on the basis of a special permit from the governing body. Permits were to be granted only if a developer had acquired a specified number of points. Points were awarded on the basis of proximity of a proposed development to each of five specified public facilities, up to a stated maximum for each. Until a developer obtained a special permit was obtained the developer could not get subdivision approval. Variances were authorized in narrow cases where developers had acquired almost the number of required points, and developers could acquire points by providing some of specified facilities on their own. Landowners could also obtain reductions in property tax assessments on land where the growth management plan prohibited development for a substantial period. And the plan itself required that all undeveloped land in Ramapo be available for development within the eighteen-year period adopted for completion of the town's capital facilities program.

The New York court first rejected an argument that Ramapo's growth management ordinance was *ultra vires*. More specifically, the court held that New York's zoning enabling legislation included, "by way of necessary implication, the authority to direct the growth of population for the purposes indicated"[582] and that delaying approval of residential subdivisions pending accumulation of the required number of points was justified under the New York subdivision control law.[583] The court further held that delaying land development, even as much as eighteen years in some cases, did not

---

[577]   See, e.g., City of West Linn v. Land Conservation and Development Com'n, 201 Or. App. 419, 119 P.3d 285 (2005); Manzo v. Mayor and Tp. Council of Tp. of Marlboro, 365 N.J. Super. 186, 838 A.2d 534 (Law Div. 2002); Faben Point Neighbors v. City of Mercer Island, 102 Wash. App. 775, 11 P.3d 322 (Div. 1 2000).

[578]   30 N.Y.2d 359, 334 N.Y.S.2d 138, 285 N.E.2d 291 (1972), appeal dismissed 409 U.S. 1003, 93 S.Ct. 436, 34 L.Ed.2d 294 (1972).

[579]   Although there was no express statutory authorization for a "quota system," the Petaluma program was not attacked as *ultra vires,* perhaps because Petaluma as a home-rule city enjoyed a very broad delegation of police power under its charter.

[580]   522 F.2d 897 (9th Cir.1975), certiorari denied 424 U.S. 934, 96 S.Ct. 1148, 47 L.Ed.2d 342 (1976).

[581]   The Ramapo ordinance is set out in full in 24 Zoning Dig. 68 (1972). See also Emanuel, Ramapo's Managed Growth Program, 4 Planner's Notebook, No. 5, at p. 5 (Am.Inst. of Planners 1974).

[582]   30 N.Y.2d at 371, 334 N.Y.S.2d at 146, 285 N.E.2d at 297.

[583]   30 N.Y.2d at 374, 334 N.Y.S.2d at 148–149, 285 N.E.2d at 298.

amount to a *de facto* "taking" rendering the Ramapo ordinance as "facially" invalid[584] even though the constitutionality of the ordinance as applied to individual properties might be challenged in a later proceeding.[585] The court likewise rejected the "exclusionary" zoning challenge.[586]

The *Ramapo* case was both praised[587] and criticized.[588] Critics argued that the Ramapo growth management program effectively perpetuated an underlying low-density zoning pattern that was clearly "exclusionary". They asserted that much of Ramapo's land might ultimately go undeveloped for more than the projected eighteen years under the plan because of delays in making the capital improvements necessary to make outlying areas eligible for development. They likewise opposed the notion that individual communities should be permitted to promote their own "general welfare" at the expense of the broader "general welfare" of the region or state. In light of the subsequent condemnation of exclusionary zoning in the *Berenson* case,[589] it seems clear that future New York courts will look more carefully at allegations that growth management programs like Ramapo's are really a device to exclude low- and moderate-income households. And Ramapo itself decided in March, 1983, to drop its famous point system because it proved to be impossible to provide public facilities on schedule.[590]

In *Petaluma,*[591] the courts considered a local growth management program based on an explicit annual quota of building permits for residential development. Like Ramapo,[592] Petaluma had experienced explosive growth during the 1960s. Much of Petaluma's growth took the form of single-family residential development in the eastern part of the city, contributing to a shortfall in moderately priced multi-family dwellings in this area. The growth management program adopted in 1972 limited residential growth in the 1972–1977 period to 500 dwelling units per year but exempted housing projects with four units or less. To allocate the 500 building permits available each year, the program established a "point system" modeled on Ramapo's point system but somewhat more elaborate. Unlike Ramapo's system, the Petaluma point system awarded points for good environmental and architectural design, for provision of recreational facilities, and for provision of low- and moderate-income housing in compliance with the city's housing policy. Among the stated objectives of the Petaluma growth management system were the prevention of "urban sprawl," creation of an urban growth boundary

---

[584] 30 N.Y.2d at 380, 334 N.Y.S.2d at 153–154, 285 N.E.2d at 304.

[585] 30 N.Y.2d at 382, 334 N.Y.S.2d at 155–156, 285 N.E.2d at 304.

[586] The court said, "far from being exclusionary, the present [zoning] amendments merely seek, by the implementation of sequential development and time growth, to provide a balanced community dedicated to the efficient utilization of land" on the basis of a "comprehensive plan" designed "to maximize population density consistent with orderly growth." Compare Associated Home Builders v. City of Livermore, 18 Cal.3d 582, 135 Cal.Rptr. 41, 557 P.2d 473 (1976), where the court upheld moratorium on issuance of building permits, saying that the Livermore ordinance "impartially bans all residential construction, expensive or inexpensive" and thus avoided "any claim that the ordinance discriminates on a basis of race or wealth."

[587] E.g., Freilich, Comment, 24 Zoning Dig. 72 (1972).

[588] E.g., H. Franklin, Controlling Urban Growth—But for Whom? (Potomac Inst. 1973); Scott, Comment, 24 Zoning Dig. 75 (1972); Bosselman, Can the Town of Ramapo Pass a Law to Bind the Rights of the Whole World?, 1 Fla.St.U.L.Rev. 234 (1973).

[589] Berenson v. Town of New Castle, 38 N.Y.2d 102, 378 N.Y.S.2d 672, 341 N.E.2d 236 (1975).

[590] See 49 Planning, June 1983, p. 8.

[591] Construction Industry Association v. City of Petaluma, 522 F.2d 897 (9th Cir. 1975), certiorari denied 424 U.S. 934, 96 S.Ct. 1148, 47 L.Ed.2d 342 (1976).

[592] For more detail on the Petaluma program, see McGivern, Putting a Speed Limit on Growth, 38 Planning 263 (1972).

and a circumferential "greenbelt," and correction of the imbalances between the growth of the eastern and western parts of the city and between new single-family and multi-family residential development.

The United States District Court for the Northern District of California invalidated the Petaluma growth management system. The court more specifically held that, by substantially interfering with the growth which Petaluma would have experienced as a result of market forces, the program violated the constitutional "right to travel"—an intensely undefined right not expressed anywhere in the United States Constitution.[593] However, the Ninth Circuit Court of Appeals reversed, holding that none of the plaintiffs had standing to raise the "right-to-travel" issue.[594] The court then rejected the plaintiffs' substantive due process and right-to-travel arguments.

The court of appeals took the traditional deferential approach to the *Petaluma* plaintiffs' substantive due process argument, which was based on the alleged exclusionary effect of the growth management program and its supposed failure to further any "legitimate governmental interest." The court pointed out that all kinds of land use controls have some exclusionary effect and that the Petaluma program's low- and moderate-income housing policy made the program "inclusionary" rather than "exclusionary" with respect to lower income households. In any case, the court said held that the exclusionary effect of the program could be justified because it bore a "rational relationship to a *legitimate state interest*"—i.e., "the preservation of Petaluma's small town character and the avoidance of the social and environmental problems caused by an uncontrolled growth rate."[595] The court relied heavily on the Supreme Court's decision in Village of Belle Terre v. Boraas[596] and its own prior decision in Ybarra v. Town of Los Altos Hills.[597]

Perhaps the most significant passage in Judge Choy's majority opinion for the Ninth Circuit was his response to the argument that the Petaluma program violated substantive due process because it did not promote the "general welfare of the region or entire state":

> We agree with appellees that unlike the situation in the past most municipalities today are neither isolated nor wholly independent from neighboring municipalities and that, consequently, unilateral land use decisions by one local entity affect the needs and resources of an entire region. * * * It does not necessarily follow, however, that the *due process* rights of builders and landowners are violated merely because a local entity exercises in its own self-interest the police power lawfully delegated to it by the state. * * *

---

[593] Construction Industry Association v. City of Petaluma, 375 F.Supp. 574 (N.D.Cal.1974), reversed 522 F.2d 897 (9th Cir.1975), cert. denied 424 U.S. 934, 96 S.Ct. 1148, 47 L.Ed.2d 342 (1976). A constitutional right to travel across state boundaries was found to exist in Edwards v. California, 314 U.S. 160 (1941), which struck down a State of California depression-era statute that penalized the bringing of "indigent" persons into the state. Some of the justices based the right to travel upon the constitutional right to travel across state lines to meet with federal governmental officials, and some based it upon the Commerce Clause. The trial court in *Petaluma* adopted the "growth center" theory developed by economic consultants to the plaintiffs. See Gruen, The Economics of Petaluma: Unconstitutional Regional Socio-Economic Impacts, in II Management and Control 173. The right-to-travel argument was effectively killed in Village of Belle Terre v. Boraas, 416 U.S. 1, 94 S.Ct. 1536, 39 L.Ed.2d 797 (1974), where the Court simply ignored it.

[594] 522 F.2d at 904.

[595] Id. at 906.

[596] 416 U.S. 1, 94 S.Ct. 1536, 39 L.Ed.2d 797 (1974).

[597] 503 F.2d 250 (9th Cir.1974) (one-acre lot minimums and exclusive single-family zoning upheld).

If the present system of delegated zoning power does not effectively serve the state interest in furthering the general welfare of the region or entire state, it is the state legislature's and not the federal courts' role to intervene and adjust the system. * * * [T]he federal court is not a super zoning board and should not be called on to mark the point at which legitimate local interests in promoting the welfare of the community are outweighed by legitimate regional interests.[598]

Several observations may be drawn from the *Ramapo* and *Petaluma* decisions. First, there is some obvious tension between decisions upholding staged-growth plans and exclusionary-zoning decisions such as New Jersey's *Mt. Laurel* decision.[599] Hidden within the folds of the staged-growth cases were certainly some concerns about exclusionary effects. Second, both *Ramapo* and *Petaluma* seem to suggest that "scientific" studies can do much to enhance the survival of otherwise questionable land use regulation or plans. Many courts have seemed favorably impressed by such studies, especially when made by independently-hired consultants. Third, Judge Choy's strong statement that a federal court "is not a super zoning board" for state local governments seemingly signals that federal courts are generally reluctant to enter local zoning frays and prefer to leave the field to the state courts. As previously mentioned when discussing the United States Supreme Court's decision in Village of Belle Terre v. Boraas, there is reason to believe that Court may feel the same reluctance.[600]

Statewide Statutory Growth Management Systems

Several states that have experienced significant population growth over the past few decades have adopted statutory systems to control urban growth.[601] For Example, Indiana, Florida, Maine, Maryland, Minnesota, New Hampshire, Oregon, South Dakota, Hawaii, Washington, and Vermont all have growth management systems for all or parts of their counties that employ various techniques for population control. The Oregon, Maryland, and Washington statutes are certainly among the most complete systems. Below is a brief summary of some of the key features contained in state growth management statutes.

Local comprehensive plans. Nearly every state with a statutory growth management system requires county comprehensive plans within areas of the state covered by their statutes.[602] The statutes provide for "elements" that are mandatory or optional for the comprehensive plans. These elements generally list those similar to the elements for traditional comprehensive plans described in section 9.12, supra. However,

---

[598] 522 F.2d at 908.

[599] Southern Burlington County NAACP v. Township of Mount Laurel, 67 N.J. 151, 336 A.2d 713 (1975), appeal dismissed and certiorari denied 423 U.S. 808, 96 S.Ct. 18, 46 L.Ed.2d 28 (1975) was the first *Mount Laurel* appeal; and the second *Mount Laurel* appeal, along with seven companion cases, is Southern Burlington County NAACP v. Township of Mount Laurel, 92 N.J. 158, 456 A.2d 390 (1983). For full discussion of exclusionary-zoning decisions from New Jersey and Pennsylvania, see § 9.26, supra.

[600] 416 U.S. 1, 94 S.Ct. 1536, 39 L.Ed.2d 797 (1974). See § 9.19, supra, for full discussion of *Belle Terre* and related decisions.

[601] See generally Ed Bolen, Kara Brown, David Kiernan, Kate Konschnik, Smart Growth: A Review of Programs State by State, 8 Hastings W.-N.W. J. Envtl. L. & Pol'y 145 (2002) (providing a comprehensive state-by-state review of growth management statutes and cases).

[602] See, e.g., Ariz. Rev. Stat. § 37–102; Fla. Stat. Ann. § 163.3180; Ind. Code § 36–7–4–202(a–c); Haw. Rev. Stat. § 279E–1; Vt. Stat. Ann. tit.10, §§ 6081(a), 6001(3); Wash. Rev. Code § 36.70A.170(1)(d) & (2).

some growth management plans include more innovative elements, such as those for low- and moderate-income housing in "growth" areas.

Urban growth "areas" or "boundaries". At the heart of a true urban growth statute is an effort to channel "urban-type" growth into areas described as "urban" and to discourage or forbid such growth in "non-urban" or "rural" areas. Most statutory schemes speak of either "urban areas" or "urban boundaries."[603] The concept of "urban growth boundaries" appears, especially in the Oregon statute, to be more restrictive than the concept of "urban growth areas." "Boundaries" are defined as lines on maps, surrounding areas already marked by "urban-type" development, within which that type of development is to be channeled and encouraged and beyond which such development is to be discouraged or forbidden.

"Consistency" requirement. As suggested in section 9.12, supra, traditional planning and zoning ordinances typically require that zoning be "in accordance with" a comprehensive plan. Some of the statutes reviewed here (and likely some other statutes, too) similarly contain requirements that zoning and other land use regulations be "consistent with" the mandatory comprehensive plans.[604] The avowed intent of "consistency" language is to require that land use regulations conform more closely to the comprehensive plan than has been true historically under the "in-accordance-with" language. However, there is some reason to doubt that courts are applying that "consistency" concept, shall we say, consistently.[605]

"Concurrency" requirement. Some state growth management statutes have "concurrency" requirements, which essentially require that public infrastructure improvements such as streets, transportation systems, and public utilities keep up with land development. Conversely, these requirements effectively prohibit land development in a given area unless the infrastructure is already in place or is put in concurrently with the development. Some state statutes and local ordinances contain such "concurrency" requirements for at least some types of the infrastructure.[606]

Sanctions for violations. If a growth-management statute is to have "teeth," it must contain a system of sanctions for local governments that fail to comply. Sanctions that appear in the state statutes tend to come in two varieties: (1) the withholding of state funds from local governments that fail to comply and (2) a state agency's bringing of an action in court against such a local government. For example, growth management statutes in Oregon and Washington provide for one or both of these kinds of sanctions.[607]

---

[603] See, e.g., Minn. Stat. Ann. § 473.859 ("urbanization and redevelopment areas"); Or. Rev. Stat. § 197.296 (urban growth boundaries mandatory); Wash. Rev. Code § 36.70A.110 (urban growth areas mandatory).

[604] See, e.g., Fla. Stat. Ann. § 163.3194 (a); Me. Rev. Stat. Ann., Tit. 30–A, § 4314 (2) (3); Wash. Rev. Code § 36.70A.040 (3).

[605] See, e.g., Haines v. City of Phoenix, 151 Ariz. 286, 727 P.2d 339 (1986) (court butchered "consistency" requirement); Citizens for Mount Vernon v. City of Mount Vernon, 133 Wn.2d 861, 947 P.2d 1208 (1997) (court ignored word "consistent" in Growth Management Act and said that, in cases of conflict, zoning "controlled" GMA comprehensive plan).

[606] See, e.g., Fla. Stat. Ann. § 163.3177(5) (requiring concurrence); Wash. Rev. Code § 36.70A.070(6)(a) (iii) (transportation concurrent).

[607] Or. Rev. Stat. Ann. § 197.320 (authorizing state agency to "issue an order requiring a local government . . . to take action necessary to bring its comprehensive plan, land use regulation, limited land use decisions or other land use decisions into compliance"); Wash. Rev. Code Ann. § 36.70A.250 (loss of state funds and court review of "hearings boards" decisions).

System statewide or only in selected areas? Most state statutes require all counties to have comprehensive plans, and to coordinate with a state agency. For example, the Florida statute applies to all cities and counties in those states.[608] However, some statutes are more limited in their application. For example, the Minnesota statute applies only to its seven most populous counties.[609]

§ 9.32 DEVELOPMENT EXACTIONS

One of the most increasingly important ways that governmental entities affect the development of land today is through the imposition of "development exactions." Development exactions are government-imposed requirements that developers dedicate land to the public, install public improvements, or help to fund various public purposes as conditions of development permission. Few subjects are more difficult to comprehend and accurately described in the short space that can be devoted to it in a one-volume treatise on property law.

The law governing development exactions has evolved in stages through the years that correspond to various historical forces and events. Accordingly, the clearest way to describe this area of law is to do so chronologically. Over time, monetary exactions have gradually been added to physical ones and used to fund improvements that are increasingly distant from the land being developed.

Learning some basic definitions and distinctions is key to understanding development exactions law. "Exactions in kind" are dedications of interests in land, such as titles or easements, to the public and often include installations of physical improvements upon the areas so dedicated. Examples are streets, curbs, sidewalks, public utilities, public parks, and school grounds. Exactions in kind were the earliest forms of exactions, with the dedications of the lesser areas tending to come earlier than of larger areas, such as parks and school grounds. They are mostly associated with residential subdivision approvals, though developers of other land improvements, such as shopping centers, industrial parks, and office buildings, may also be required to make in-kind dedications. In contrast, "Monetary exactions" is the umbrella term used here to refer to required contributions of money to governmental entities in place of exactions in kind when the latter are not feasible or desired. In the evolution of exactions law, monetary exactions tended to come along later than in-kind exactions and have been the cause of much more litigation.

Monetary exactions come in several kinds and go by several names, with much imprecision and overlap in the use of their names. "In-lieu" exactions, which are usually associated with subdivision development, were the earliest form of monetary exaction. An example would be a monetary exaction for development of a public park, not on the land being subdivided but near enough to it that it would specially serve the persons who were to live in the subdivision (as well as other members of the public). "Impact fees," which tended to come along next in time, are to generate capital funds for public purposes that are less closely or directly related to the proposed land development project in question but as to which the development creates part of the need. Examples include

---

[608] Fla. Stat. Ann. §§ 163.3167, –.3177, –.3184 ("each local government," meaning cities and counties); Or. Rev. Stat. §§ 197.175, –.225, –.250 ("each city and county in this state"). In those states the named local governments must submit their comprehensive plans to a state agency for approval.

[609] The Minnesota statute names seven counties (with a few towns excepted) as the "Metropolitan Area" covered by the statute. Enforcement in those counties is not by the state government, but by a "Metropolitan Council." Minn. Stat. Ann. § 473.121, –.123, –.145, –.146, –.175.

fees for parks, streets, schools, sewer treatment plants, and public buildings throughout an entire city or county. Obviously, the line between "in-lieu" fees and "impact" fees blurs at the margins. Historically, both are associated with the post-World-War-II period when the rapid development of residential subdivisions and of supporting commercial developments placed heavier demands upon municipal governments than their ordinary tax revenues could cover. A more recent form of monetary exaction is the "linkage" fee, which some local governments impose on developers of office or commercial buildings for general public purposes that are only tangentially related to the development. Examples might include fees to support low-income housing, day-care centers, city beautification, or environmental protection programs. Again, the line between "impact" and "linkage" fees is very blurred. One example of this type of fee was highlighted in Russ Building Partnership v. City and County of San Francisco, in which a court upheld a "linkage" fee imposed on developers of new office buildings for maintenance of Muni, the San Francisco transit system.[610] "Impact" fees and "linkage" fees both began to increase in popularity in the 1980s when a decline in federal matching funds for municipal projects forced cities and counties to scrabble for funds.

Section 14 of the Standard City Planning Act authorized local governments to require subdividers to dedicate land to the public for and install the basic subdivision infrastructure—i.e., improved streets, water, sewer, and other utility mains and piping, and other facilities—at their own expense as a condition precedent to subdivision approval.[611] As long as local governments require only dedications and improvements of the kinds just described, subdividers have little objection. After all, lots in a subdivision cannot be sold unless the purchasers have street access to get into them and access to utilities usually enhances lot sales. However, after World War II, as the American middle class began its migration to the suburbs, many suburban communities—in an effort to make new residential subdivisions "pay their way"—enacted subdivision regulations that imposed requirements far beyond those authorized by the Standard Act. For instance, some imposed requirements for dedication and/or improvement of off-site land, dedication of subdivision land for recreational or school use, or for cash payments into a park or school fund in lieu of land dedication.[612] Under state enabling acts identical with or similar to the Standard Act, developers challenged these heavier exactions. They have often been held to be beyond the authority granted by the Act,[613] although language

---

[610] 199 Cal.App.3d 1496, 246 Cal.Rptr. 21 (1987) (the fee was calculated at five dollars per square foot of office space, on the theory that more office workers would, in general, impose more traffic on the transit system). Another well-known California Appeals decision, Terminal Plaza Corp. v. City and County of San Francisco, 177 Cal. App.3d 892, 223 Cal.Rptr. 379 (1986), involved, and upheld, a less "blurry" form of linkage fee, charged against hotel owners who wished to convert their low-income-residential hotels to hotels for travelers.

[611] SCPEA § 14 (1928). This section also authorizes provision in the regulations for "adequate and convenient open spaces for * * * recreation."

[612] Provisions for "in lieu" cash payments are desirable where a subdivision is too small to justify requiring the subdivider to donate the necessary land within the subdivision, or where the local park or school plans call for a particular new subdivision to be served by a park or school located outside that subdivision.

[613] E.g., Briar West, Inc. v. City of Lincoln, 206 Neb. 172, 291 N.W.2d 730 (1980); Hylton Enterprises, Inc. v. Board of Supervisors, 220 Va. 435, 258 S.E.2d 577 (1979); Admiral Development Corp. v. City of Maitland, 267 So.2d 860 (Fla.App.1972); Rosen v. Village of Downers Grove, 19 Ill.2d 448, 167 N.E.2d 230 (1960); Arrowhead Development Co. v. Livingston County Road Commission, 413 Mich. 505, 322 N.W.2d 702 (1982) (off-site improvements); West Park Avenue, Inc. v. Ocean Township, 48 N.J. 122, 224 A.2d 1 (1966); Haugen v. Gleason, 226 Or. 99, 359 P.2d 108 (1961). Contra: Divan Builders, Inc. v. Planning Board of Wayne Township, 66 N.J. 582, 334 A.2d 30 (1975) (off-site improvements); Hylton Enterprises, Inc. v. Board of Supervisors of Prince William County, 220 Va. 435, 258 S.E.2d 577 (1979) (off-site improvement requirement was *ultra vires*).

slightly more specific than the Standard Act language has sometimes been held to authorize park and school dedication requirements or even "in-lieu" charges.[614] In some cases, "in-lieu" charges have been held invalid as unauthorized taxes.[615] However, in more recent years a number of states have adopted new enabling legislation that expressly authorizes subdivision exactions that go beyond those authorized by the Standard Act.[616]

The most serious question concerning the validity of exactions is a constitutional one. Why should not these required dedications require the exercise of eminent domain and the payment of compensation? As a basic principle of eminent domain law, if a governmental entity demands the dedication of an interest in land and the owner is unwilling to dedicate it as a gift, the governmental entity must condemn the interest and pay for it. As described in section 9.4 of this chapter, the Takings Clause of the Fifth Amendment to the United States Constitution (applicable to the states through the Due Process Clause of the 14th Amendment) and state constitutions require "just compensation" for a "taking." Accordingly, the most difficult and important legal question related to exactions is how far governments may go in imposing them before they trigger a compensable taking. An early decision addressing this question was the California Supreme Court's decisions in Ayres v. City Council of City of Los Angeles.[617] In upholding the validity of certain mandatory subdivision exactions, that court laid down a baseline test of validity that formed a general foundation for later decisions: a mandatory dedication is not a taking if it is "reasonably required by the subdivision type and use" and will benefit the residents of the new development, even though it will also "incidentally" benefit the "city as a whole."[618] Of course, subsequent decisions have modified *Ayres*'s core concept in greater or lesser ways.

Mandatory dedications of land for larger areas such as parks and schools and in-lieu fees for such purposes tend to be more controversial than dedications for streets, etc., but usually have been upheld. Along the lines of the *Ayres* concept, courts usually reason that subdividers profit when subdivision plats are approved because home sites sell for more than unplatted property. In return, the municipality may require a dedication of land "to meet a demand to which the municipality would not have been put but for the influx of people into the community to occupy the subdivision lots."[619] In-lieu fees, if the assessment formula is accurate, can allow for treatment of developers who are required to dedicate park land that is equivalent to that of those who are assessed fees in lieu of land.[620] Not all exactions, either exactions in kind or in-lieu exactions, have

[614] E.g., Jordan v. Menomonee Falls, 28 Wis.2d 608, 137 N.W.2d 442 (1965), appeal dismissed 385 U.S. 4, 87 S.Ct. 36, 17 L.Ed.2d 3 (1966); Jenad, Inc. v. Village of Scarsdale, 18 N.Y.2d 78, 271 N.Y.S.2d 955, 218 N.E.2d 673 (1966).

[615] E.g., Haugen v. Gleason, 226 Or. 99, 359 P.2d 108 (1961); Hillis Homes v. Snohomish County, 97 Wn.2d 804, 650 P.2d 193 (1982).

[616] E.g., Ariz.Rev.Stat. § 9–463.01(D) to (F); West's Ann.Cal.Gov.Code §§ 66477, 66478; Colo.Rev.Stat.1973, 30–28–133(4)(a); New Jersey Stat.Ann. 40:55D–42; 24 Vermont Stat.Ann. § 4417; Wash. Rev. Code § 82.02.020 (voluntary in-lieu fees). It is important that local governments follow the statutory procedural requirements, which may be strictly interpreted. See, e.g., Arnett v. City of Mobile, 449 So.2d 1222 (Ala. 1984); New Jersey Builders Ass'n v. Bernards Tp., 108 N.J. 223, 528 A.2d 555 (1987).

[617] 34 Cal.2d 31, 207 P.2d 1 (1949).

[618] Id. at 5–7.

[619] See especially the leading decision, Jordan v. Village of Menomonee Falls, 28 Wis.2d 608, 137 N.W.2d 442, 448 (1965), appeal dismissed, 385 U.S. 4 (1966).

[620] See Associated Home Builders v. City of Walnut Creek, 4 Cal.3d 633, 94 Cal.Rptr. 630, 484 P.2d 606, appeal dismissed, 404 U.S. 878 (1971).

been upheld, however. The history of exaction law since *Ayres* is first complicated by the fact that state courts have developed at least three more or less different doctrines. And, second, since its celebrated 1987 decision in Nollan v. California Coastal Commission,[621] followed by its equally celebrated 1994 decision in Dolan v. City of Tigard,[622] the United States Supreme Court's decisions have overshadowed the state decisions. We will trace these developments, with special emphasis on the Supreme Court decisions.

Among state courts, the California Supreme Court and California courts of appeals have arguably given the most liberal treatment to exactions. In Associated Home Builders v. City of Walnut Creek, the California Supreme Court extended the *Ayres* formula to in-lieu fees.[623] The court upheld a statute and ordinance requiring residential developers to pay into a fund to acquire park and recreation land in amounts that "bear a reasonable relationship to the use of the facilities by the future inhabitants of the subdivision." Since open land was being consumed for residential property, the court held it was not necessary that a municipality prove that a particular subdivider would increase the need for recreational facilities. Under this reasoning, in-lieu fees could theoretically be assessed very broadly. Several decisions of divisions of the California Court of Appeals went even further than *Walnut Creek*. Russ Building Partnership v. City and County of San Francisco upheld a "linkage fee" of five dollars per square foot of floor space in new office buildings, to be used for the municipal transit system, on the theory that more office space meant more employees to use public transit.[624] Grupe v. California Coastal Commission[625] and Remmenga v. California Coastal Commission.[626] even apparently took the position that public need for a dedication justifies it, regardless of whether the development in question adds to that need. However, the deferential standard of review for land use exactions that was applied in *Grupe* and *Remmenga* was quickly overcome by the stricter standard articulated by the United States Supreme Court in Nollan v. California Coastal Commission, discussed below.

Unlike California courts, Illinois courts proved reluctant to liberally validate exactions imposed by local governments in that state. This hesitance was in full display in Pioneer Trust and Savings Bank v. Village of Mt. Prospect.[627] In *Pioneer Trust,* the Illinois Supreme Court held that the Village of Mt. Prospect could not require a developer to dedicate land (or pay an in-lieu fee) for a school because the overcrowding problem driving the exaction was not "specifically and uniquely attributable" to the development. However, the Illinois formula was apparently followed only by Illinois and Rhode Island and is only followed in Illinois today.[628]

Between the California and Illinois extremes, prior to the *Nollan* and *Dolan* decisions described below virtually all states that addressed the question employed a "rational nexus" test that was perhaps first described by the Supreme Court of New

[621] 483 U.S. 825, 107 S.Ct. 3141 (1987).
[622] 512 U.S. 374, 114 S.Ct. 2309 (1994).
[623] 4 Cal.3d 633, 94 Cal.Rptr. 630, 484 P.2d 606, appeal dismissed, 404 U.S. 878 (1971).
[624] 234 Cal.Rptr. 1 (1987).
[625] 166 Cal.App.3d 148, 212 Cal.Rptr. 578 (1985).
[626] 163 Cal.App.3d 623, 209 Cal.Rptr. 628 (1985).
[627] 22 Ill.2d 375, 176 N.E.2d 799 (1961).
[628] See Northern Illinois Home Builders Ass'n v. County of Du Page, 165 Ill.2d 25, 208 Ill.Dec. 328, 649 N.E.2d 384 (1985); see also Callies and Grant, Paying for Growth and Planning Gain: An Anglo-American Comparison of Development Conditions, Impact Fees and Development Agreements, 23 Urban Lawyer 221, 233 (1991).

Jersey in Longridge Builders, Inc. v. Planning Board. Specifically, the *Longridge Builders* court held that "the subdivider could be compelled only to bear that portion of the cost which bears a *rational nexus* to the needs created by, and benefits conferred upon, the subdivision."[629] (Emphasis added.) In another influential decision, Jordan v. Village of Menomonee Falls, the Supreme Court of Wisconsin held that Illinois' *Pioneer Trust* decision was a good yardstick "provided the words 'specifically and uniquely attributable. . . .' are not so restrictively applied as to cast an unreasonable burden of proof upon the municipality. . . ."[630] The Wisconsin court did not "consider the fact that other residents of the village as well as residents of the subdivision may make use of a public site required to be dedicated by subdivider for school, park or recreational purposes [to be] particularly material to the constitutional issue."[631] Because of the qualifications the Wisconsin court put upon *Pioneer Trust,* the *Jordan* decision seemed close to the "rational nexus" test.

In 1987 the United States Supreme Court eclipsed all the prior state decisions, making the validity of development exactions a question of federal constitutional law. Nollan v. California Coastal Commission[632] addressed the validity of conditions imposed on those seeking a building permit. Although the development in question was only a single home, the constitutional principles unquestionably apply to larger developments. The Nollans sought two permits: one to demolish their old home near a beach and one to construct a new larger home. The California Coastal Commission, which considered the permits, required as a condition of approval that the Nollans grant an easement across the ocean side of their lot. The purpose of the proposed easement was to allow people to travel along the beachfront between two public parks located some distances north and south of the Nollans' property. The Commission asserted it sought to protect the public's ability to see the beach, to assist the public in overcoming the "psychological barrier" to using the beach created by the Nollans' new, larger home, and to prevent congestion on public beaches.

The Supreme Court held that the condition was unwarranted. In an opinion by Justice Scalia, the Court did hold that conditions may be placed on the granting of a permit. In the Court's words, "the Commission's assumed power to forbid construction of the house in order to protect the public's view of the beach must surely include the power to condition construction upon some concession by the owner, even a concession of property rights, that serves the same end."[633] However, the Court further held that there must be a "nexus" between the condition sought and the problem to be alleviated: the prohibition must "further the end advanced as the justification for the prohibition."[634] The Court reasoned that the proposed easement—whose proposed area would have run parallel to the beach—did not further the end advanced as the justification because such an easement would not reduce the obstacles to viewing the beach created by the Nollans' new house. An overlook providing the public an uninterrupted view of the ocean would

---

[629] 52 N.J. 348, 245 A.2d 336, 337 (1968).

[630] Jordan v. Village of Menomonee Falls, 28 Wis.2d 608, 137 N.W.2d 442, 447 (1965), appeal dismissed, 385 U.S. 4 (1966).

[631] Jordan v. Village of Menomonee Falls, 28 Wis.2d 608, 137 N.W.2d 442, 448 (1965), appeal dismissed, 385 U.S. 4 (1966).

[632] 483 U.S. 825, 107 S.Ct. 3141 (1987).

[633] 483 U.S. 825, 836, 107 S.Ct. 3141 (1987).

[634] 483 U.S. 825, 836, 837, 107 S.Ct. 3141 (1987).

have addressed the problems cited by the Coastal Commission, but a walkway easement along the beach did not.

Nollan seemed to outlaw so-called "naked linkage" programs in which cities exact money or land for unrelated projects from developers in need of a permit. The positions of the California Court of Appeals on this issue in Russ Building Corporation v. City and County of San Francisco, Grupe v. California Coastal Commission, and Remmenga v. California Coastal Commission (cited above in this section) thus appeared untenable. Even the California Supreme Court's decision in the *Walnut Creek* case, supra, was put in doubt.[635] However, *Nollan* also left a lot of questions unanswered. First, it is not always clear whether a state court particular decision is applying state or federal constitutional law since courts often speak simply of "constitutional" questions. A state is allowed to be more, but not less, protective of private property rights under its state constitution than the Supreme Court requires under the Federal Constitution.[636] Neither *Nollan* nor Dolan v. City of Tigard,[637] is (discussed below) control how much additional constitutional protection a state court may afford a landowner under a state constitution.

Second, *Nollan* did not adopt any of the tests used by state courts. The opinion did not cite *Ayres v. Los Angeles,* supra, even though the "nexus" rule's ancestry back to *Ayres* is plain. However, *Nollan* did cite with approval a long string of state decisions that follow either the rational nexus test or the more stringent "specifically and uniquely attributable" test. The Court's language appeared closest to the rational nexus test highlighted above. However, the rational nexus test requires that exactions reasonably benefit the development and *Nollan* did not deal with the issue of benefits to the development

In summary, *Nollan* provided some valuable new guidance on how to analyze the constitutionality of exactions but still left multiple important issues unsettled. The case established that a development exaction—at least an exaction of an interest in the developer's land as opposed to a monetary exaction—is void as an uncompensated taking unless there is a "nexus" between the thing to be exacted and some public impact or problem the development will cause. "Nexus" means that exaction and impact must be of the same kind or quality; the exaction must go to alleviate that particular impact or problem. It is not enough that the exaction benefits the public in some other way. For instance, in *Nollan* it was not sufficient that the public would gain a walkway easement parallel to the beach because the problem created by the Nollans' new house involved something quite different—perceptions of the beach from up above. This did not involve a tight enough fit between problem and benefit. However, while *Nollan* told us that problem and benefit must be of the same *quality,* it created an obvious and important further question: how close must the *quantitative* relationship be between problem and benefit? The *Nollan* decision shed little light on this subject. In particular, if a proposed development would have a minimal adverse impact on the public, may the governmental entity require the developer to dedicate something, which, though of the same kind, would benefit the public many times over the amount of impact? And who has the burden

---

[635] See Callies and Grant, Paying for Growth and Planning Gain: An Anglo-American Comparison of Development Conditions, Impact Fees and Development Agreements, 23 Urban Lawyer 221, 236 (1991).

[636] PruneYard Shopping Center v. Robins, 447 U.S. 74 (1980).

[637] 512 U.S. 374, 114 S.Ct. 2309 (1994).

of establishing these matters? Fortunately, the Supreme Court's 1994 decision in Dolan v. City of Tigard[638] helped to address these issues.

Dolan v. City of Tigard, like *Nollan,* involved dedications of interests in land, exacted as a condition for development permission. Ms. Dolan, who owned a plumbing and electrical supply store, sought to raze her existing store, replace it with one nearly twice as large, and pave and enlarge her off-street parking lot. Her site lay along Fanno Creek, and part of her land was within the creek's 100-year floodplain. It was obvious that the increased impervious surface area resulting from the project would cause some increase in the rate and amount of stormwater drainage from her site into the creek. It was also obvious that her larger store would cause some increase in traffic in the area. However—a critical aspect of the case—in the various hearings and appeals on her application, the city did not quantify the increase in traffic or the increased drainage or relate quantities to the dedications required. When she applied for a redevelopment permit, the city was willing to grant it but only upon the condition that she: (1) dedicate to the city title to the portion of her land that lay within the floodplain and (2) dedicate title to an adjoining 15-foot strip of land for a public bicycle path. Altogether, the required dedications amounted to approximately 7,000 square feet or 10 percent of her land.

In addition to making a rhyme, *Dolan/Nollan* make a legal pair. *Dolan* extended *Nollan,* picked up where *Nollan* left off, and put teeth in it. *Nollan* requires that there be *some* degree of qualitative identity between the exaction demanded and the public problem or adverse impact the development would cause. In *Dolan,* the Court had no doubt that there was a nexus. Obviously, the increased impervious surfaces would affect drainage and dedicating the land along the creek to be kept in vegetation would alleviate that problem. Likewise, the larger store would attract more customers and increased traffic and the bicycle path could at least slight alleviate that problem by inducing travelers to substitute bicycles for automobiles. But in each of these respects, how much would the impact be, and how much the alleviation? Neither the city nor Ms. Dolan had presented evidence to quantify these matters.

Reversing the Supreme Court of Oregon, the United States Supreme Court determined based on the record in *Dolan* that the city's imposition of its conditions was void as an uncompensated taking. On the merits, the Court established two important propositions. First, the burden of proof is on the governmental entity to establish by evidence that a sufficient "nexus" exists between a problem or impact caused by the proposed development and the property interests exacted.[639] This the city had not done, having shown only that dedication of the floodplain open space would in some degree alleviate flooding and that a bicycle path "could" alleviate traffic problems. Second, the Court adopted a test it called "rough proportionality": the governmental entity must "demonstrate 'rough proportionality' between the harm caused by the new land use and the benefit obtained by the condition." In adopting this formula, the Court reviewed and rejected the tests employed by various state courts.

---

[638] 512 U.S. 374, 114 S.Ct. 2309 (1994).

[639] In his dissenting opinion in *Dolan,* Justice Stevens, joined by justices Blackmun and Ginsburg, objected to placing the burden of proof on the governmental entity, on the ground that it violated the "traditional presumption of constitutionality." But in defense of the burden shifting, it may be said to be consonant with the principle of evidence law that a party who bears the general burden of proof, does not have to prove a negative. It is very difficult to prove that a thing did not exist because, theoretically, one would have to disprove all the possible ways in which it might have existed.

As illuminating as *Nollan* and *Dollan* were in clarifying the constitutional standards for development exactions, these landmark cases still left multiple questions unanswered. Fortunately, in 2013 the United States Supreme Court addressed two of these previously unanswered questions in Koontz v. St. John River Water Management District.[640] One important question *Dolan* failed to address was whether the Nollan/Dolan doctrine applied equally to monetary exactions. Both *Nollan* and *Dolan* involved exactions in kind of interests in land. In neither case did the governmental entity seek to require any kind of monetary fee, whether called an in-lieu fee, impact fee, linkage fee, or other. Nor did the Supreme Court offer any dictum on whether their "nexus" doctrine applies to monetary exactions. Accordingly, both decisions left that question unanswered. The potential appeal to municipalities of imposing monetary exactions in lieu of or as an alternative to in-kind of exactions is obvious than land exactions. Among other things, when money can be substituted for land, it may be easier to quantify an amount of money in relation to the impact of the development—to establish the "rough proportionality" of money to impact—than to quantify a land exaction in relation to impact.

The Supreme Court did seem to give some limited indirect direction on the monetary-exaction question in Ehrlich v. Culver City.[641] That case, which came to the Supreme Court from California in 1996, involved a monetary exaction imposed upon a land development. Remanding the case to the California Supreme Court, the United States Supreme Court directed that court to reconsider the case in light of Dolan v. City of Tigard. Upon reconsideration, the California Supreme Court did apply *Dolan,* holding that the evidence was insufficient to show that the monetary exaction was "roughly proportional" to the alleged impact of the development. The Federal Supreme Court refused to review this decision, creating at least an inference that the test applied.[642]

However, in *Koontz* the United States Supreme Court gave even clearer guidance on the question of whether the Takings Clause and Nollan/Dollan test applied to monetary exactions. The claimant in Koontz filed a permit application with the St. Johns River Water Management District to develop portions of his Florida land. Recognizing that much of the land was classified as wetlands under state law, in his permit application Koontz offered to mitigate the adverse environmental impacts of his proposed development by granting a conservation easement to the District that covered roughly three quarters of his land. Koontz expected that these mitigation efforts would be sufficient under the applicable state statutes to enable him secure his development permit. However, the District rejected his permit and notified him that it would grant him the permit only if he granted a conservation easement over an even greater proportion of his land and also funded the improvement of some other, District-owned wetlands at a different site. Concluding that these conditions were "excessive" in light of the nature of his development project, Koontz sued under a state statute that entitles citizens to collect money damages for any "unreasonable exercise of the state's police power constituting a taking without just compensation."[643] One of the more controversial issues analyzed by lower courts that heard the case was whether the Nollan/Dollan test applied to monetary exactions in the same basic ways that it applied to in-kind exactions.

---

[640] 570 U.S. 595, 133 S.Ct. 2586, 186 L.Ed.2d 697 (2013).

[641] 512 U.S. 1231, 114 S.Ct. 2731, 129 L.Ed.2d 854 (1994).

[642] Ehrlich v. Culver City, 12 Cal.4th 854, 50 Cal.Rptr.2d 242, 911 P.2d 429 (1996), cert. denied, 519 U.S. 929, 117 S.Ct. 299, 136 L.Ed.2d 218 (1996).

[643] 570 U.S. 595, 602, 133 S.Ct. 2586, 2593 (2013).

The district court argued it did not, citing language in concurring and dissenting opinions in an earlier Supreme Court case for the notion that an "obligation to spend money can never provide the basis for a takings claim."[644]

In a 5–4 decision, the United States Supreme Court held that monetary exactions could potentially provide the basis for takings claims and that the Nollan/Dollan test did indeed apply to these exactions. Writing for the majority, Justice Alito reasoned that, in the absence of such a rule, localities could potentially circumvent constitutional constraints on exactions by merely giving citizens an option to pay money in lieu of dedicating easements or other requested in-kind contributions in exchange or permit approvals. Finding such in-lieu monetary exactions to be the "functionally equivalent to other types of land use exactions", the court resolved a lower-court split on this issue by holding that such monetary conditions are subject to the same Nollan/Dollan standard.[645]

Koontz also provided additional clarity on the issue of whether a city must formally grant a permit and attach exaction conditions to it before the Nollan/Dollan test can apply. The St. Johns River Water Management District had only informally suggested to Koontz that he would have to convey the larger conservation easement and fund other offsite wetlands improvements to win permit approval. This posture was certainly different from other previous exactions cases in which the government agency had formally granted a permit with the challenged conditions attached to it—situations that clearly implicated the unconditional conditions doctrine. Given that the District had not formally imposed is approval conditions in an issued permit, could Koontz still bring his takings claim? The majority held that Koontz could still bring his claim, even though the District had issued no formal permit featuring the controversial conditions. Justice Alito noted that and other approach "would enable the government to evade the limitations of *Nollan* and *Dolan* simply by phrasing its demands for property as conditions precedent to permit approval." By doing so, the majority added a bit more clarity to the murky and still-evolving field of land use exactions law.

Of course, even after *Koontz,* multiple other unresolved questions continue to infuse uncertainty into the Nollan/Dolan test. For instance, there is still some uncertainty as to what "rough proportionality" really means. *Dolan*'s phrase "rough proportionality" or "roughly proportional," is essentially the Court's attempt to define how close *Nollan*'s "nexus" must be. Though the Court disavowed that it wanted any "precise mathematical calculation," *Dolan*'s test does imply that a governmental entity must in some degree quantify the public impact or harm a development will do and compare it to the public benefit that will be conferred by the land or monetary exaction imposed. A kind of balance sheet must be drawn up, but the figures in it, and so the balance struck, may all be approximate: the expression "ballpark figure" comes to mind.

The problem in *Dolan* was that, although Ms. Dolan's hard surfaces would almost certainly increase runoff into the creek and her store's larger size would increase traffic, it was totally unclear how much more water or traffic would flow. Similarly, although the greenbelt would almost certainly slow or decrease runoff and the bicycle path "could" relieve some of the street traffic problem, it was unclear how much decrease or relief there would be. The Court wanted the city to carry the burden to show harm and benefit

[644] 570 U.S. 595, 612, 133 S.Ct. 2586, 2598 (2013) (citing Eastern Enterprises v. Apfel, 524 U.S. 498, 118 S.Ct. 2131, 141 L.Ed.2d 451 (1998)).

[645] 570 U.S. 595, 612, 133 S.Ct. 2586, 2598 (2013).

were proportional in some degree, and, searching for an apt phrase, the Court formulated "roughly proportional." What the Court really wanted was that governmental entities should make some calculations, based upon factual data, before they even ask for development exactions. Calculations should be "individualized," said the Court.

As with any flexible legal test, "roughly proportional" can never be an infallible predictor for every case. The term is no more imprecise or difficult than the many legal tests that turn upon the word "reasonable" or, for that matter, than the "rational nexus" test. Accordingly, it seemed that the Court did not mean to impose a very high burden on local governments.[646] The problem, in the Court's view, was that Tigard had made *no attempt* to quantify impacts and benefits by showing how much runoff would be caused by the hard surfaces or alleviated by the greenbelt or how much new traffic the new store would cause or the bicycle path divert. Had the city, for instance, generated scientifically-generated qualitative estimates of impacts on stormwater drainage, traffic congestion, and the like and of how extending the greenbelt or floodplain area would address those impacts, that could have potentially satisfied the Court. This type of evidence may be particularly difficult to generate in certain cases, as when harmful impacts are the cumulative result of several developments. However, that is true of any adjudicative process—a problem the phrase "roughly proportional" seems to encompass.

Another open question following *Nollan*, *Dolan* and *Koontz* is whether the Nollan/Dolan test applies to legislative as well as adjudicative proceedings. Footnote 8 of Chief Justice Rehnquist's majority opinion in *Dolan* raises, somewhat obliquely, the question of whether a municipality has the burden to establish "rough proportionality" in its actions that are essentially legislative instead of "adjudicative." The Chief Justice seemingly assumed that an individualized decision to impose a development exaction, such as occurred in *Dolan*, was an "adjudicative" governmental act. He used the enactment of a zoning ordinance as the example of a different kind of process, that one might call "legislative"). In cases involving such an action, footnote 8 suggests that the governmental entity would not have the burden of proving "rough proportionality" but that the burden would instead "rest[ ] on the party challenging the regulation," the note said.

It seems in line with accepted principles that no burden should be on a legislative body to justify its legislative acts. The presumption is that they are valid. That was the position of the Supreme Court of Arizona in Homebuilders Association v. City of Scottsdale, which held that *Dolan* did not apply to the imposition of a water fee that was imposed according to a formula set out in a city ordinance that was generally applicable to developers.[647] Nonetheless, the question cannot always turn on the nature of the body that takes the governmental action. Bodies that are in general legislative, usually local legislative bodies, sometimes have the final say in granting individual land use permits. In such cases, they act in a quasi-judicial or administrative way, and *Dolan* should apply if the local body seeks to impose exactions.[648] Also, in *Homebuilders Association*, the

---

[646] For a decision that appears to support this view, see Sparks v. Douglas County, 127 Wn.2d 901, 904 P.2d 738 (1995).

[647] 187 Ariz. 479, 930 P.2d 993 (1997) (alternative holding). For an analysis of *Homebuilders Ass'n* and its relationship to *Ehrlich v. Culver City*, which was discussed earlier in text in this section, see Davidson & Lindgren, Exactions and Impact Fees—*Nollan/Dolan*: Show Me the Findings!, 29 Urban Lawyer 427, 432–37 (1997).

[648] So-called "applicant rezonings" pose an interesting question. Most states consider them "legislative" acts, because they are acts of the local legislative body. Yet, they are actions that relate to specific parcels of

Arizona court suggested that even a legislative act might be subject to *Dolan* if it was "individually tailored" to a particular landowner and not of general applicability.

One final question about both *Nollan* and *Dolan* is whether they involve the same "taking" question as do the regulatory "taking" cases in the *Mahon-to-Lucas* line of cases or whether they are of a distinct species. Knowledgeable lawyers and scholars who are versed in takings jurisprudence still sometimes disagree on this question. Indeed, the Supreme Court itself cited some of this line of decisions in *Dolan* and *Nollan,* though not in the critical parts of its reasoning. This is mostly an academic question but it has some bearing on the resolution of actual cases. Regardless, one can certainly argue that the cases that involve development exactions and the cases that involve land use regulations are two fundamentally different kinds of cases.

Briefly stated, without going deeply into underlying theory, there seem to be at least three significant differences between land use exactions cases and more conventional regulatory takings cases. First, *Nollan/Dolan* and *Mahon/Lucas* (to refer to the lines of cases by shorthand expressions) involve substantially different fact patterns. In *Nollan/Dolan,* the governmental entity demands the transfer of an interest in land, or of a monetary fee in lieu of such an interest, from the landowner to the governmental entity. The governmental entity does not precisely restrict what the owner may do and instead allows it to be done, exacting property in land or money as a condition. An actual transfer to government is demanded, as in ordinary eminent domain cases. By contrast, in *Mahon/Lucas* the government seeks no transfer to itself of any property in either land or money and simply restricts what the owner may do. Second, in *Mahon/Lucas* the question whether the regulation amounts to a "taking" is a matter of degree: does the regulation go "too far" or deprive the owner of "all economically viable use"? By contrast, the question of degree is far less prominent in *Nollan/Dolan.* If there is no "roughly proportional nexus" between the negative externalities a development will impose upon the public and the land or money exacted, then there is an uncompensated taking regardless if the owner's degree of loss. An exaction of one square foot is as bad as the exaction of an acre or 10 acres if the "nexus" is missing. Third, the *Nollan/Dolan* line of decisions has historically developed separately from, and without direct reference to, the *Mahon/Lucas* line. This section of this book traced how *Nollan* and *Dolan* were in a line of many state decisions, long strings of which the Supreme Court cited and relied upon in analyzing those two decisions. Those state decisions developed entirely separately from either the Supreme Court or the state court decisions that form the *Mahon/Lucas* lineage.

The United States Supreme Court's 1999 decision in City of Monterey v. Del Monte Dunes at Monterey[649] seemingly validates the argument that the Nollan/Dollan line and Mahon/Lucas line of cases are distinct. *Del Monte Dunes* was a "Section-1983" (420 U.S.C.A. § 1983) case, brought on the theory that land use regulations had caused a Fifth-Amendment "taking" by repeatedly blocking a land development project. The Court's majority held a regulatory "taking" had occurred, but four justices dissented on the merits. An issue in the case was whether decisions both in the Mahon/Lucas line and in the Nollan/Dolan line were precedential or only in the Mahon/Lucas line. All members

---

land. The question is especially interesting in the few states that follow the position of Fasano v. Board of County Comm'rs of Washington County, 264 Ore. 574, 507 P.2d 23 (1973). That position is that applicant rezoning actions are not "legislative," but "quasi-judicial." See generally § 9.22, supra.

[649] 526 U.S. 687, 119 S.Ct. 1624, 143 L.Ed.2d 882 (1999).

of the Court, majority and dissent, agreed that the two lines were essentially different and that only the Mahon/Lucas line was applicable to a regulatory "taking."

The relationship between what government does in the regulatory cases and what it does in the exaction cases is analogous to the relationship between an easement and a restrictive covenant. These latter relationships are also closely related and often confused. However, their essential difference is that the holder of an easement has an affirmative right to make some use of the servient tenement. By contrast, the holder of a restrictive covenant has a negative right that the owner of the burdened land shall do or not do certain things on that land but has no right to make any affirmative use of the land. An analogous distinction separates land use regulations from governmental exactions. In the former, the owner is forbidden to make certain uses of the land; in the latter, the owner's property (whether it be land or money) is transferred to the government.

§ 9.33 HISTORIC DISTRICT AND LANDMARK CONTROLS

An "historic district" is an area having special historic characteristics in which the design of buildings is regulated by law to maintain appearances that exemplify those characteristics. For instance, a city may designate the original section and old village green of a New England town that was founded in colonial times to be a historic district and thus require that buildings within it preserve their exterior colonial appearance.[650] Often, new structures within historic districts must be designed to have the appearance of old historic buildings. Historic districts are designated by zoning ordinances, usually in the form of an overlay ordinance that is superimposed upon the underlying zoning. A "landmark" or "historic site" is a single building that is designated as such for its historic value or unique architectural or cultural features. Parcels of land that are designated as landmarks or historic sites are generally scattered throughout a municipality. Like owners of land included within historic districts, owners of historic sites or landmarks must generally maintain the design of such sites in their traditional state. Most historic-district and landmark ordinances require maintenance of the exterior of buildings, but ordinances sometimes apply to interiors as well. Interior restrictions may be viewed somewhat more warily by courts than exterior restrictions, although in a 19932 case of first impression the New York Court of Appeals upheld the interior regulation of a restaurant.[651] The procedure through which a site becomes designated is typically fairly straightforward: a municipality's appointed "landmarks commission" nominates historic sites to the local legislative body, and then that body approves the designation. A famous example of this is New York City's designation of Grand Central Station as a landmark,

---

[650] The example was drawn from Figarsky v. Historic District Comm'n, 171 Conn. 198, 368 A.2d 163 (1976), which arose in Norwich, Connecticut. Another famous, and earlier, example is found in Opinion of the Justices to the Senate, 333 Mass. 773, 128 N.E.2d 557 (1955), in which the Senate of the Commonwealth of Massachusetts had established two historic districts on Nantucket Island.

[651] See Teachers Insurance and Annuity Ass'n v. City of New York, 82 N.Y.2d 35, 623 N.E.2d 526, 603 N.Y.S.2d 399 (1993). Unfortunately, the opinion does not contain a lengthy or well-reasoned justification for the regulation of interiors as opposed to exteriors. There is an implication in the opinion that the interior of a building may be regulated only if it is customarily open to the public; at least, the court discussed at length whether the restaurant was so open. But cf. Society of Jesus v. Boston Landmarks Comm'n, 409 Mass. 38, 564 N.E.2d 571 (1990), which struck down an ordinance that regulated the interior design of a church. However, the ground of decision was that the ordinance violated free exercise of religion because the interior design of a church is an expression of religious belief.

which gave rise to the important United States Supreme Court "taking" decision in Penn Central Transportation Co. v. City of New York.[652]

Local historic district and landmark regulations are enacted under the authority of state statutes. State governments themselves may also establish historic areas and sites. By 1965, every state had enacted some form of historic preservation legislation.[653] The Federal Government has also long been active in the field of historic preservation. State programs of historic preservation go back into the 1930s, the most notable examples being a historic district in Charleston, South Carolina, the Vieux Carre district in New Orleans, Louisiana, and Beacon Hill in Boston, Massachusetts.[654] However, the Federal Government enacted the Antiquities Act long before those designations in 1906 and enacted the Historic Sites Act in 1935.[655] Currently, several federal programs of historic preservation are carried on under the National Historic Preservation Act of 1966.[656] However, these federal and state programs are mentioned only as background and the discussion in the remainder of this section focuses on problems arising out of local historic zoning and landmark designation.

Citizens do not always welcome designations of their property as landmarks or as being within historic districts. Such designations may bring new opportunities for tax-favored renovations, but they can also impose unwanted maintenance costs on owners and may freeze their lands from being developed for more profitable use. Historic zoning and landmark designations bear much resemblance to "aesthetic" regulations. They consequently present the general types of legal problems highlighted in section 9.20, entitled "Zoning for Aesthetic Purposes." As described in that section, landowners whose properties become subject to these restrictions may challenge them on due process grounds by arguing that is the restrictions do not promote the general welfare or are so subjective that governmental choices involving them are vague or inherently "arbitrary and capricious. In cases, such as *Penn Central,* in which owners feel particularly burdened by not being able to make profitable uses of their land or by having to spend excessive amounts to maintain property in its required historic condition, such regulations can potentially trigger a regulatory taking claims. Some religious groups have likewise challenged designations of their houses of worship as landmarks on the ground that the burdens thereby imposed upon them have denied them free exercise of religion. And of course challenges may be based upon such prosaic factual questions as whether the district is truly "historic" or the building truly a significant landmark as defined in an ordinance.

The most basic question concerning historic preservation laws is one of due process. Specifically, some have challenged whether certain such laws serve a valid public purpose, or are within the power of government. If this question were answered in the negative, there would obviously be no use asking any further questions. However, if there was ever a serious issue on the point, the answer has been "yes" at least since 1896

---

[652] 438 U.S. 104, 98 S.Ct. 2646, 57 L.Ed.2d 631 (1978), rehearing den. 439 U.S. 883, 99 S.Ct. 226, 58 L.Ed.2d 198 (1978). The Court's opinion noted that some 400 sites had been designated as landmarks in New York City at the time the case arose. See § 9.4, supra, for discussion of the *Penn Central* decision.

[653] See J. Morrison, Supplement to Historic Preservation Law 1 (1972).

[654] See J. Juergensmeyer & T. Roberts, Land Use Planning and Control Law § 12.8 (1998).

[655] 16 U.S.C.A. §§ 431, et seq., and 461, et seq., respectively. An earlier effort by the Federal Government was the purchase of Civil War battlefield sites. However, this was not by regulating the owners, but by purchase, including compulsory purchase by condemnation.

[656] 16 U.S.C.A. § 470 et seq.

when the United States Supreme Court held in United States v. Gettysburg Electric Railway Co. that the federal eminent domain power could be used to acquire land to preserve the Gettysburg battlefield.[657] More modernly, but still at an early date in state historic preservation efforts, the Massachusetts Supreme Judicial Court held in 1955 in Opinion of the Justices to the Senate that the police power included the power to establish historic districts on Nantucket Island.[658] Other well-known decisions of somewhat later date that are in accord with these earlier decisions include Maher v. City of New Orleans[659] and A-S-P Associates v. City of Raleigh.[660] In the decisions cited and in other similar decisions, as in the aesthetic zoning cases we saw in section 9.20, courts often fall back on the argument that such regulations need not be upheld simply because they promote certain values but also because they also have a beneficial economic impact. In any event, there is no serious question left that historic preservation ordinances are in general valid; they are viewed today as a form of zoning overlay ordinance.[661]

Local legislation that establishes either historic zoning or historic site designation generally also establishes a historical preservation commission or landmarks commission to administer such laws. One question is whether the local legislative body may delegate to its historic preservation commission the power to define the boundaries of historic districts or whether the legislative body must do that itself.[662] Once the boundaries of historic districts are established, the local historic preservation commission may be delegated the power to determine which structures are "historic" in appearance and how they must be maintained to keep that appearance. In the case of site designations, the landmarks commission is given the power to identify sites, though final approval usually lies with the local legislative body. The ordinance must give the commission sufficient guidelines to make the determinations is must make, in keeping with the principle of delegation of legislative authority to administrative bodies. A-S-P Associates v. City of Raleigh, cited above, contains one of the most thorough discussions of such guidelines. The city council involved in that case had fixed the boundaries of the historic Oakwood District—an area that contained many Victorian homes—and established a historic district commission to designate whether and how new and existing structures could be built, restored, or altered. The general guideline for the board, copied from the language in the statute, was that structures should not "be

---

[657] 160 U.S. 668, 16 S.Ct. 427, 40 L.Ed. 576 (1896).

[658] 333 Mass. 773, 128 N.E.2d 557 (1955). In a companion case handed down the same day, the Massachusetts court upheld the creation of a historic district to preserve Beacon Hill in Boston. Opinion of the Justices to the Senate, 333 Mass. 783, 128 N.E.2d 563 (1955). See also the earlier decision in City of New Orleans v. Impastato, 198 La. 206, 3 So.2d 559 (1941), which upheld a New Orleans city ordinance that granted to a commission the power to regulate the historic appearance of buildings in the Vieux Carre section of that city. However, *Impastato* did not technically involve a constitutional question, because the Louisiana constitution had specifically authorized the creation of the Vieux Carre historic district.

[659] 516 F.2d 1051 (5th Cir.1975) (Vieux Carre district in New Orleans).

[660] 298 N.C. 207, 258 S.E.2d 444 (N.C. 1979) (historic district to preserve area of "great variety" of "predominantly" Victorian homes).

[661] J. Juergensmeyer & T. Roberts, Land Use Planning and Control Law § 12.10 (1998).

[662] See South of Second Assocs. v. Georgetown, 196 Colo. 89, 580 P.2d 807 (1978). However, a close reading of the decision leaves it somewhat unclear whether the court meant to say a local commission could never be granted power to define the boundaries or whether the particular ordinance in question did not contain sufficient guidelines to direct the commission and to advise individual landowners when their lands might be included within a historic district. The city council's ordinance declared the entire city a historic district. Dictum in A-S-P Assocs. v. City of Raleigh, 298 N.C. 207, 258 S.E.2d 444 (1979), indicates that the local legislative body must define the boundaries of historic districts.

incongruous with the historic aspects of the district." However, the ordinance also contained the following "safeguards" that influenced the court to uphold the delegation of discretion to the commission. First, the commission's decisions were appealable to the local board of adjustment. Second, "architectural guidelines and standards" that the local planning commission had adopted for Victorian styles were incorporated into the ordinance. Third, the members of the commission were required to be persons who had special expertise in architecture or history. All the "safeguards" just listed don't necessarily have to be present to satisfy a court, but *A-S-P Associates* contains a rather complete listing. Some courts have been satisfied with less detailed guidelines, such as that structures in their design must have significant historical and architectural value in relation to the prevailing architecture or styles of the area.[663]

When the owner of a specific parcel of land included in a historic zone or designated as a landmark challenges the restriction, a typical legal argument is that it denies due process or amounts to a "regulatory taking." These challenges have been unsuccessful in a great majority of the cases. Some of the early decisions, while not fully embracing the "aesthetic" rationale, gave it considerable weight as a basis for regulation. Other decisions have emphasized more purely "historical" values. For instance, in the *A-S-P* case (cited above) the court sustained an historic district designation of the "only intact nineteenth century neighborhood remaining in Raleigh * * * composed predominantly of Victorian houses." *A-S-P* also sustained the denial of a certificate of appropriateness for construction of a new office building in the Raleigh historic district on the ground that this was necessary to prevent the intrusion of an architecturally incompatible structure in an area with a unifying architectural theme. The court also held that the property owner's inability to develop land in the historic district for its most profitable use did not result in a *de facto* "taking."

Rebman v. City of Springfield[664] went even further than *A-S-P*, rejecting a taking claim in a case where a four-block historic district was created simply to preserve the noncommercial surroundings of an important historic building—Abraham Lincoln's house in Springfield, Illinois. The court found it "clear that the use of the [plaintiff's] property not in conformity with the existing [historic district] zoning would be detrimental to the Lincoln Home area and the planning concept of the community."[665] The court also stated that the creation of the historic district had enhanced the value of the plaintiff's property rather than depreciating it. The Connecticut case of Figarsky v. Historic District Commission[666] reached a similar conclusion in a case in which the owners of a house on the edge of a historic district were required to make extensive repairs instead of demolishing it as they wished. Though built in the 18th century, the house had little historic value itself and merely shielded other historic buildings from the view of buildings outside the district. The court concluded that the owner had failed to show the house would be without some value if repaired.

---

[663] See, e.g., Figarsky v. Historic District Comm'n, 171 Conn. 198, 368 A.2d 163 (1976) ("historical and architectural value and significance, architectural style, general design, arrangement"); State ex rel. Stoyanoff v. Berkeley, 458 S.W.2d 305 (Mo.1970) (architectural-conformity zoning; "unsightly, grotesque and unsuitable structures . . . be avoided"). See also Teachers Insurance and Annuity Ass'n v. City of New York, 82 N.Y.2d 35, 623 N.E.2d 526, 603 N.Y.S.2d 399 (1993), where the court said that courts should "defer to the expertise" of a landmarks commission on the question whether a site was of "special historical or aesthetic interest."

[664] 111 Ill.App.2d 430, 250 N.E.2d 282 (1969).

[665] 111 Ill.App.2d at 412, 250 N.E.2d at 288.

[666] 171 Conn. 198, 368 A.2d 163 (1976).

On the taking issue, the leading decision by far is Penn Central Transportation Co. v. City of New York, which is previously examined at length in section 9.4.[667] The United States Supreme Court in *Penn Central* upheld the action of the New York City Landmarks Preservation Commission in refusing to approve an elaborate Penn Central proposal to construct a 50-plus-story office building behind and above the existing Grand Central Terminal, which had been given landmark status. This structure, the commission concluded, would be destructive of the Terminal's historic and aesthetic features as a prime example of neoclassic Beaux Arts design. The plaintiff conceded that "New York City's objective of preserving structures and areas with special historic, architectural, or cultural significance is an entirely permissible governmental goal" and that "the restrictions imposed on its parcel are appropriate means of securing the purposes of the New York City law," so that only the "taking" issue was before the Court.

Penn Central had practically precluded itself from challenging the specific application of the New York City Landmark Law to the Grand Central Terminal site by conceding that the Terminal site "must, in its present state, be regarded as capable of earning a reasonable return," and that the transferable development rights available to Penn Central by virtue of the site's designation as a landmark "are valuable, even if not as valuable as the rights to construct above the Terminal." Moreover, Penn Central had not sought approval for the construction of a smaller structure. Accordingly, the court was not prepared to assume that Penn Central would be denied all use of the airspace above the Terminal—especially since "nothing the Commission has said or done suggests an intention to prohibit *any* construction above the Terminal." Having made these concessions, Penn Central was effectively limited to arguing that all landmark preservation ordinances amount to a *de facto* taking or violate substantive due process. The Court's holding there was no taking in the particular case thus arguably extended more broadly to landmark designations as a general land use regulatory approach.

As described in section 9.4, the Supreme Court's 1978 decision in *Penn Central* marked the beginning of a period in which the Court had an intense interest in regulatory takings doctrine. Subsequent decisions, including Lucas v. South Carolina Coastal Council,[668] have provided somewhat greater clarity than *Penn Central* did about how restrictive a land use regulation must be to cause a taking. It is obvious that the plaintiff in *Penn Central* did not come close to meeting the *Lucas* test. Indeed, under the United States Constitution, an historic district or landmark designation would have to cause a very substantial value loss before it might trigger a compensable taking.

Other decisions have considered the difficult issues arising when the owner of a landmark structure or a building in a historic district desires to demolish the structure and put up a more profitable building on the site. In Maher v. City of New Orleans,[669] the Fifth Circuit Court of Appeals rejected the owner's taking claim in such a case on the ground that the owner had failed to show that all reasonable uses of its property were precluded unless demolition was allowed. However, in Lafayette Park Baptist Church v. Scott,[670] it was held that a historic district ordinance "must be interpreted to authorize demolition when the condition of the structure is such that the economics of restoration

---

[667]   438 U.S. 104, 98 S.Ct. 2646, 57 L.Ed.2d 631 (1978) rehearing den. 439 U.S. 883, 99 S.Ct. 226, 58 L.Ed.2d 198 (1978).

[668]   505 U.S. 1003, 112 S.Ct. 2886, 120 L.Ed.2d 798 (1992).

[669]   516 F.2d 1051 (5th Cir.1975), certiorari denied 426 U.S. 905, 96 S.Ct. 2225, 48 L.Ed.2d 830 (1976).

[670]   553 S.W.2d 856 (Mo.App.1977).

preclude the landowner from making any reasonable economic use of the property."[671] Other courts have applied the *Lafayette* holding to landmark structures not located in historic districts. A leading New York case, Lutheran Church in America v. City of New York,[672] overturned, as a taking, the Landmark Preservation Commission's refusal to allow demolition of a landmark structure used as an office building, on a showing that the building had become inadequate for its office use. But *Lutheran Church* has been heavily criticized, and seems to have been substantially qualified by Society for Ethical Culture v. Spatt.[673] In *Spatt,* the court did not discuss the "enterprise" theory of taking[674] which was a partial basis for the decision in *Lutheran Church,* and held that a taking did not result from the mere fact that the landmark designation "stands as an effective bar against putting the property to its most lucrative use."[675]

Penn Central was appealed to the Supreme Court from a decision by the New York Court of Appeals. The latter court's decision is an important landmark-designation due process decision.[676] Whereas the United States Supreme Court treated *Penn Central* as a taking case, the New York court analyzed it as a due process case and considered whether Penn Central's loss was so great, when balanced against the public benefit from the designation, as to deny it due process. Upon that analysis, the New York court reached the same end result as would the Supreme Court: that the landmark designation was valid. While, as described in section 9.6, the United States Supreme Court has seemed unwilling for many years to test land use regulations of any kind under the Due Process Clause of the 14th Amendment, state courts often do so test regulations under their state constitutions.

Some of the more important post-*Penn Central* "historic landmark" cases have involved both "taking" and "free exercise of religion" issues. In St. Bartholomew's Church v. City of New York,[677] the Church challenged (on Fifth and Fourteenth Amendment grounds and on First Amendment grounds) the New York Landmarks Commission's refusal to grant a permit to demolish the Church's seven-story "community house" and erect a high-rise office tower in its place. The federal district court found no merit in the church's claim that the Landmarks Law was invalid on its face as a violation of the First Amendment's Free Exercise and Establishment Clauses. After trial, the district court also denied the church's claims that, "as applied," the commission's refusal to permit demolition of the "community house" amounted to a "taking" and also violated the church's First Amendment rights. The district court held that the same test was applicable to both the "taking" and the First Amendment claims—the test being whether the church could "no longer carry out its religious mission in its existing facilities"—and concluded that the church failed to carry its burden of proof under this test. On appeal, the Second Circuit affirmed[678] but used a somewhat different analysis. The Second Circuit's "taking" test was "[whether] the landmark designation would prevent or

[671] Id. at 862.

[672] 35 N.Y.2d 121, 359 N.Y.S.2d 7, 316 N.E.2d 305 (1974).

[673] 51 N.Y.2d 449, 434 N.Y.S.2d 932, 415 N.E.2d 922 (1980).

[674] This theory is advanced in Sax, Takings and the Police Power, 74 Yale L.J. 36 (1964).

[675] 51 N.Y.2d at 456, 434 N.Y.S.2d at 936, 415 N.E.2d at 926.

[676] Penn Central Transportation Co. v. City of New York, 42 N.Y.2d 324, 397 N.Y.S.2d 914, 366 N.E.2d 1271 (1977).

[677] 728 F.Supp. 958 (S.D.N.Y.1989), affirmed 914 F.2d 348 (2d Cir.1990), cert. denied 499 U.S. 905, 111 S.Ct. 1103, 113 L.Ed.2d 214 (1991).

[678] 914 F.2d 348 (2d Cir.1990), cert. denied 499 U.S. 905, 111 S.Ct. 1103, 113 L.Ed.2d 214 (1991).

seriously interfere with the carrying out of the charitable purpose of the institution"—a test identical in substance with the test applied by the district court. Applying the test, the Second Circuit concluded that the Landmarks Law was "a facially neutral regulation of general applicability within the meaning of Supreme Court decisions."[679] Accordingly, the Court held that the law did not violate the Free Exercise clause, absent a showing of discriminatory motive, coercion with respect to religious practice, or deprivation of the church's ability to carry out its religious mission in its existing facilities.[680]

The saga of First Covenant Church v. City of Seattle,[681] which extended from 1990 to 1993 in the Supreme Court of Washington and the United States Supreme Court, was another leading historic landmark free exercise case. Seattle designated the church building as a historic site, under authority of the city's historic preservation ordinance. This designation prohibited the church from altering the building's exterior facade without applying to, and receiving permission from, the city's Landmarks Preservation Board. However, some special procedures were built into the ordinance that, if pursued by the church, would have allowed the church to escape orders of the board if they would impose a heavy burden on the church. When the case was before the state supreme court the first time, the court struck down the ordinance on the ground that it violated First Covenant Church's right to free exercise of religion.[682] The court held the ordinance caused a "substantial infringement" of that right, which could be justified only by a "compelling governmental interest." The preservation of "aesthetic and cultural features of a community" was held not to be such a "compelling interest." After granting certiorari, the United States Supreme Court vacated the Washington judgment in a one-paragraph opinion and remanded. The Court tersely instructed Washington to reconsider in light of its 1990 decision in Employment Division, Department of Human Resources v. Smith,[683] in which the Court held that employees who used peyote in Native American religious ceremonies were subject to an Oregon statute forbidding use of peyote. This statute was upheld because it was "neutral [toward religion] and of general applicability." Though the Supreme Court did not reverse Washington, the language on remand certainly suggested Washington should uphold the application of the landmark ordinance to the church.

In its second decision, after remand from the United States Supreme Court, the Washington Supreme Court once again struck down the historic preservation ordinance in an opinion that was even more lengthy, elaborate, and far-reaching than its first one.[684] After distinguishing *Smith,* the Washington court offered multiple grounds for its decision, based upon the free exercises clauses of both the United States and Washington constitutions. By basing its decision in the alternative on the Washington

---

[679] Id. at 355–56.

[680] Id. at 354, relying on Employment Division v. Smith, 494 U.S. 872, 110 S.Ct. 1595, 108 L.Ed.2d 876 (1990), where the Court said, "The critical distinction is thus between a neutral, generally applicable law that happens to bear on religiously motivated action, and a regulation that restricts certain conduct because it is religiously oriented."

[681] 114 Wn.2d 392, 787 P.2d 1352 (1990), remanded, 499 U.S. 901 (1991), 120 Wn.2d 203, 840 P.2d 174 (1992), 61 U.S.L.W. 2334 (1993).

[682] 114 Wn.2d 392, 787 P.2d 1352 (1990).

[683] 494 U.S. 872, 110 S.Ct. 1595, 108 L.Ed.2d 876 (1990), where the court said, "The critical distinction is thus between a neutral, generally applicable law that happens to bear on religiously motivated action, and a regulation that restricts certain conduct because it is religiously oriented."

[684] First Covenant Church v. City of Seattle, 120 Wn.2d 203, 840 P.2d 174 (1992), 61 U.S.L.W. 2334 (1993).

Constitution, the state supreme court effectively put it beyond the power of the United States Supreme Court to reverse. That Court declined to review the second Washington decision.[685] The most novel basis for Washington's second decision, and one that received much emphasis, was that the architectural features of the outside of the church building were expressions of religious belief—a means of communicating the content of First Covenant's religious tenets.[686] An ordinance that regulated those features was an attempt to regulate the content of religious belief, almost as if the city were to control the content of the church's preaching and teaching. The ordinance was also held to restrict free exercise, including the imposition of burdensome financial costs.

Today, challenges to historic landmark or district designations affecting church buildings are most likely to center on claims under the Religious Land Use and Institutionalized Persons Act (RLUIPA), which is discussed in significant detail in section 9.9 of this chapter. As described in that section, the RLUIPA is federal legislation enacted in 2000 that increases protections for religious land uses. To successfully challenge a landmark designation based on the RLUIPA, a church would need to satisfy one of the specific tests outlined in section 9.9. Readers interested in such tests are encouraged to refer back to that section for those details.

§ 9.34 WETLANDS AND BEACHFRONT REGULATIONS

The Federal Government plays an important role in the protection of water quality and wetlands under authority of the Federal Water Pollution Control Act Amendments of 1972,[687] which were supplemented by amendments known as the Clean Water Act of 1977,[688] and the Water Quality Act of 1987.[689] The Pollution Control Act with these amendments is also called the "Clean Water Act." Of special interest to developers of land is Section 404 of the Act, which gives the Army Corps of Engineers jurisdiction to grant permits for the discharge of dredged or filled material.[690] Ordinarily, one thinks of the Corps of Engineers as having control over activities that affect navigable waters. However, under Section 404 developers of land not only on navigable waters but on wetlands far removed from navigable waters may have to obtain permits from the Corps. Further discussion of the Federal Government regulations that affect wetlands is beyond the scope of this treatise. A full discussion of those regulations is set forth in Professor William H. Rodgers's authoritative Hornbook, *Environmental Law.*[691]

In the last couple of decades of the twentieth century, many states on the Atlantic, Pacific, and Gulf coasts enacted statutes specifically designed to protect coastal wetlands[692] and several states in the Midwest and elsewhere enacted statutes designed

---

[685] 61 U.S.L.W. 2334 (1993).

[686] On this point, see also Society of Jesus v. Boston Landmarks Comm'n, 409 Mass. 38, 564 N.E.2d 571 (1990), which struck down a landmark ordinance that regulated the *interior* design of a church, on the ground that interior design was an expression of religious belief.

[687] 33 U.S.C.A. §§ 1251–1376.

[688] Pub.L. No. 95–217, 91 Stat. 1566 (1977).

[689] Pub.L. No. 100–4 (Feb. 4, 1987), 100th Cong., 1st Sess., 101 Stat. 7.

[690] 33 U.S.C.A. § 1344.

[691] W. Rodgers, Environmental Law §§ 4.1–4.6 (2d ed. 1994).

[692] E.g., Calif. Coastal Act of 1976, Cal. Pub. Res. Code Ann. § 30000 et seq.; Conn. Gen.Stat.Ann. § 22a–28 et seq.; 7 Del.Code § 6601 et seq.; Georgia Code, § 43–2601 et seq.; 38 Maine Rev.Stat.Ann. § 471 et seq.; Mass.Gen.Laws Ann. c. 130, § 105; New Hamp.Rev.Stat.Ann. 483–A:1 et seq.; New Jersey Stat.Ann. 13:9A–1 et seq.; Rhode Island Gen.Laws 1956, § 2–10–14; N.Y. Envtl. Conserv. Law §§ 25–0101 to 25–0601, 71–2501 to 71–2507.

to protect inland wetlands.[693] Typically, these statutes authorize a designated state agency to map wetland areas and to regulate their use and development. Such statutes generally require that a permit be obtained for any substantial new development within a wetland area or for dredging and filling of wetlands, which are preliminary steps in most wetlands development.[694] The statutes usually contain quite restrictive standards for evaluation of permit applications and set out procedures for obtaining permits (including appeal procedures) and penalties for violations of the statute.

In some states, local government regulation of wetlands is also specifically authorized.[695] Even where it is not specifically authorized, it has been held that authority may be implied from the language of traditional zoning enabling statutes derived from the Standard Act.[696] On the other hand, state environmental protection legislation does not unconstitutionally infringe on local home rule powers.[697] Indeed, in some cases such state legislation may be found to pre-empt the environmental protection field.[698]

Challenges by land developers to state and local wetlands protection statutes and ordinances have generally been based on the contention that the restriction of use and development results in a regulatory "taking" of private property without "just compensation." In several early cases, the "taking" challenge was successful in state courts. In its 1963 decision in Morris County Land Improvement Co. v. Township of Parsippanny-Troy Hills,[699] the New Jersey court held a local wetland ordinance unconstitutional both because the purpose of the ordinance was to acquire a public benefit by preserving the wetland as a flood retention basin and because the effect was to deprive the landowner of any reasonable use of the land. Connecticut reached a similar result in 1964 in Dooley v. Town of Fairfield.[700] As late as 1970, in State v. Johnson,[701] the Maine court also held a wetlands protection statute unconstitutional as applied to the facts of the case, on the ground that the landowners' "compensation by sharing in the benefits which this restriction [on filling a wetland area] is intended to secure is so disproportionate to their deprivation of reasonable use that such exercise of the State's police power is unreasonable."[702]

---

[693] E.g., Wis.Stat.Ann. 59.971, 144.26.

[694] The Massachusetts statute, supra note 692, is an exception; it authorizes the state agency to adopt protective orders "regulating, restricting or prohibiting dredging, filling, removing or otherwise altering, or polluting, coastal wetlands." A "plan" of the lands affected as well as the order must be recorded in the local land title registry. See F. Bosselman & D. Callies, The Quiet Revolution in Land Use Control, 205–34 (1971), for a discussion of the administration of the Massachusetts statute.

[695] E.g., Wash. Rev. Code Ann., Ch. 90.58; Wis.Stat.Ann. 59.971, 144.26. The Washington statute, known as the "Shoreline Management Act," requires local governments to adopt "master plans" that regulate shorelines and associated "wetlands" within 200 feet of shorelines. Wash. Rev. Code 36.70.350, a zoning enabling act, authorizes counties to designate "water sheds, soils, rivers and other waters" in their comprehensive plans. Wash. Rev. Code 36.70A.170, known as the Growth Management Act, requires cities and counties that are subject to the Act (29 of the state's 39 counties as of 1998) to designate "critical areas," which includes wetlands.

[696] E.g., Morland Development Co., Inc. v. City of Tulsa, 596 P.2d 1255 (Okl.1979).

[697] E.g., CEEED v. California Coastal Zone Conservation Commission, 43 Cal. App.3d 306, 118 Cal.Rptr. 315 (1974).

[698] E.g., Lauricella v. Planning & Zoning Board, 32 Conn.Sup. 104, 342 A.2d 374 (1974). Contra: Golden v. Board of Selectmen, 358 Mass. 519, 265 N.E.2d 573 (1970).

[699] 40 N.J. 539, 193 A.2d 232 (1963).

[700] 151 Conn. 304, 197 A.2d 770 (1964).

[701] 265 A.2d 711 (Me.1970).

[702] Id. at 716.

In subsequent years, both the New Jersey and the Maine courts seemingly changed their views on the constitutionality of wetlands protection programs that make substantial private use or development impossible.[703] The period of the early 1970s seemed to mark a turning point at which courts became more accepting of wetlands and beachfront regulations than they had earlier. It is no coincidence, of course, that this was also the time period in which the environmental movement gathered force in America. Of particular interest was Just v. Marinette County,[704] in which the Wisconsin court sustained a wetlands zoning ordinance enacted pursuant to a state wetlands protection statute against attack on the ground that it resulted in a regulatory "taking." The plaintiff alleged, and the court apparently accepted as a fact, that the designation of a wetland prevented all development. It distinguished wetlands regulations from other forms of land use regulation on the theory that the filling in and development of wetlands is not a reasonable use of land. Although it cited Pennsylvania Coal Co. v. Mahon[705] for the proposition that when a regulation goes too far it must be recognized as a "taking," the court effectively announced that development of land was not a right of property.[706] This remarkable statement attracted much attention, though it seems to have had little if any subsequent effect in Wisconsin.[707]

Nevertheless, Wisconsin's decision in Just v. Marinette County did seemingly have some influence on wetlands decisions in several other states. *Just* was expressly relied upon in Graham v. Estuary Properties, Inc.[708] In that case, a Florida court sustained the denial of a permit for a major residential and commercial development in a coastal wetland area on the ground that the proposed development would destroy a large stand of mangroves, which in turn would have an adverse impact on water quality in the adjacent coastal bay.[709] Reasoning similar to that in *Just* underlies New Hampshire's decision in Claridge v. New Hampshire Wetlands Board, though the court did not cite *Just*.[710] And in other states where the issue has been raised, wetlands-protection regulations have generally been sustained.[711]

---

[703] See New Jersey Builders Association v. Department of Environmental Protection, 169 N.J.Super. 76, 404 A.2d 320 (App. Div.1979), cert. denied 81 N.J. 402, 408 A.2d 796 (1979); Sands Point Harbor, Inc. v. Sullivan, 136 N.J.Super. 436, 346 A.2d 612 (App.Div.1975); In re Spring Valley Development, 300 A.2d 736 (Me.1973).

[704] 56 Wis.2d 7, 201 N.W.2d 761 (1972).

[705] 260 U.S. 393, 43 S.Ct. 158, 67 L.Ed. 322 (1922).

[706] The court's actual statement was that it was not a taking to limit the use of private property to its natural uses. In the *Just* case, this meant that there was no taking of Mr. and Mrs. Just's property if the county required them to keep it as bare land.

[707] See Bryden, A Phantom Doctrine: The Origins and Effects of *Just v. Marinette County,* 1978 Am. Bar Foundation Res. J. 397, 443–44.

[708] 399 So.2d 1374 (Fla.1981), certiorari denied sub nom. Taylor v. Graham, 454 U.S. 1083, 102 S.Ct. 640, 70 L.Ed.2d 618 (1981).

[709] 399 So.2d 1374 (Fla.1981), certiorari denied sub nom. Taylor v. Graham, 454 U.S. 1083, 102 S.Ct. 640, 70 L.Ed.2d 618 (1981). In turn, Graham v. Estuary Properties influenced the decision in Glisson v. Alachua County, 558 So.2d 1030 (Fla.App. 1990), where the court upheld some "resource protection" regulations that included wetlands regulations against a "facial" challenge by 18 landowners. See also Lee County v. Morales, 557 So.2d 652 (Fla.App. 1990), review denied 564 So.2d 1086 (Fla. 1990).

[710] 125 N.H. 745, 485 A.2d 287 (1984), where the court sustained very restrictive wetland regulations.

[711] E.g., Manor Development Corp. v. Conservation Comm'n, 180 Conn. 692, 433 A.2d 999 (1980); Santini v. Lyons, 448 A.2d 124 (R.I.1982); Nelson v. Conservation Com'n of Wayland, 90 Mass. App. Ct. 133, 56 N.E.3d 889 (2016); Moskow v. Commissioner of Dep't of Environmental Management, 384 Mass. 530, 427 N.E.2d 750 (1981); Sibson v. State, 115 N.H. 124, 336 A.2d 239 (1975); Chokecherry Hills Estates, Inc. v. Deuel County, 294 N.W.2d 654 (S.D.1980); Olympic Stewardship Found. v. State Envtl. & Land Use Hearings Office through W. Washington Growth Mgmt. Hearings Bd., 199 Wash. App. 668, 399 P.3d 562 (2017). See also

However, as courts have come to give their general approval to such regulations, specific issues have emerged. Often, when an owner owns a sizable parcel of land, wetlands comprise only part of that parcel and although substantial development may be prohibited on that part the rest of the parcel is left free for development. This can raise the "denominator" issues discussed earlier in section 9.4 of this chapter. When development permit approvals are conditioned on an applicant's preservation of specific wetlands areas or contribution of funds to promote such preservation, such situations can also raise exaction law issues, as described in connection with Koontz v. St. Johns River Water Management District in section 9.32 above. One other wetlands-related issue that has been litigated centers upon language often found in wetlands ordinances providing that a wetland area may be developed only if a wetlands agency finds that "a feasible and prudent alternative does not exist." In Samperi v. Inland Wetlands Agency of West Haven,[712] the Supreme Court of Connecticut held that such an agency does not have to eliminate every imaginable "alternative" to satisfy this standard. As long as there is evidence that several suggested alternatives are not feasible, the agency may find that no feasible alternative exists. The court in that case was moved by the practical consideration that it would be impossible for an applicant to eliminate a potentially infinite number of alternatives.

§§ 9.35–10.0 ARE RESERVED FOR SUPPLEMENTAL MATERIAL.

Candlestick Properties, Inc. v. San Francisco Bay Conservation and Dev. Comm'n, 11 Cal.App.3d 557, 89 Cal.Rptr. 897 (1970); Potomac Sand & Gravel Co. v. Governor of Maryland, 266 Md. 358, 293 A.2d 241 (1972), Cert. Den. 409 U.S. 1040, 93 S.Ct. 525, 34 L.Ed.2d 490 (1972); Presbytery of Seattle v. King County, 114 Wn.2d 320, 787 P.2d 907 (1990).

[712] 226 Conn. 579, 628 A.2d 1286 (1993).

Chapter 10

CONTRACTS FOR THE SALE OF LAND

Table of Sections

§ 10.1 SALES CONTRACTS AND THE STATUTE OF FRAUDS

Nearly every real estate transfer by sale is preceded by a sales contract. Such contracts may have various names, such as "earnest money agreement," "offer and acceptance," or "deposit receipt," depending on local tradition and the nature of the transaction. Most commonly the buyer submits an offer of purchase to the seller, and the seller's acceptance transmutes the offer into a contract. The offer is usually accompanied by an earnest money deposit, although such a deposit is not essential to the validity of the offer or the resulting contract.

There is, of course, no legal requirement that a contract precede a conveyance, and occasionally sales occur with no prior contractual relationship. Gifts of real estate rarely involve contracts, since by definition no consideration is to be paid by the recipient. But in sale transactions the contract is highly useful, since it allows each party to obtain various items of information and make various arrangements with the assurance that the other party is obligated to complete the transaction. For example, the buyer can confidently apply for the necessary financing to complete the purchase, arrange to sell other real estate, and obtain moving services. He or she can also investigate such matters as the title, zoning and other land use controls affecting the property, the physical condition of any improvements, the presence of hazardous waste, and the land's boundaries, topography, and other features. The contract "ties up" the land, making the time and money spent in these endeavors justifiable. The seller may have similar arrangements to make. Of course, if the parties wish to have the right to be excused from performance of the contract if they are dissatisfied with the results of their "due diligence," they will need to so provide in the contract, and this is very frequently done.

It may seem peculiar to include a chapter on contract law in a book about property. Real estate sales contracts are subject to most of the same legal rules that govern other contracts. Offer, acceptance, and consideration are still essential, and the concepts of misconduct or mistake, illegality, and the like also apply.[1] But numerous special rules govern land sale contracts, especially in the areas of formation, conditions, and remedies. Many of these rules grew out of the special solicitude which the English equity courts showed for land sellers and purchasers; even today, equitable remedies play an important role in land contract litigation, and equitable concepts sometimes control results even in cases in which no equitable remedy is sought. This chapter is concerned with the special contractual rules and principles (often termed the law of "vendor and purchaser") that apply to real estate contracts, and with the relationship of the seller and purchaser up to the time legal title is transferred.

In principle, it should be possible to state with some precision just what matters must be agreed to by the parties in order to have an enforceable real estate sales contract. Unfortunately, there is little basis in the decided cases for determining what those elements are. The reason, peculiarly, is the existence and importance of the statute of frauds. The statute requires a writing for the enforceability of a contract, and a large number of cases deal with the elements which the writing must contain to satisfy the statute. It is often impossible to determine whether a court is enumerating the essential ingredients of the agreement itself (under the common law of contracts) or the necessary elements of the writing (as a matter of judicial interpretation of the statute of frauds.) Hence, as a practical matter the two sets of elements are indistinguishable, and they will be treated as such here.[2]

One further preliminary point is important. Real estate sales contracts are often employed as financing devices. For example, the purchaser may go into possession under a contract which requires a small initial down payment and regular periodic payments, say, monthly for twenty years. The purchaser receives a deed only when the final installment is paid. Interest is usually computed and paid on the unpaid balance of the purchase price in the same fashion as is common on mortgage loans. This type of contract, often called an installment contract or a "contract for deed," is obviously the functional and economic equivalent of a purchase-money mortgage, although its legal consequences may be somewhat different.[3] The point is that it is not the sort of contract with which we are concerned here.

Instead, our focus is on what might be termed the "earnest money contract" or "marketing contract"—one whose function is to obligate the parties to engage in an immediate transfer of title, with financing (if any) provided either by the seller or by a

---

[1]   See Durham v. Smith, 2010 Ark. App. 329, 374 S.W.3d 799 (2010) (contract of sale could be set aside for fraud, misrepresentation, or gross mistake); Steiner v. Thexton, 48 Cal. 4th 411, 226 P.3d 359 (2010) (where one party could withdraw at will, contract was illusory and unenforceable); Morrison v. Trust Company Bank, 229 Ga.App. 145, 493 S.E.2d 566 (Ga.App. 1997) (no contract formed where acceptance did not agree precisely with offer); Thor Properties, LLC v. Willspring Holdings LLC, 118 A.D.3d 505, 988 N.Y.S.2d 47 (2014) (offer was not accepted, so no contract was formed).

[2]   Occasionally a court will explicitly recognize the distinction; see, e.g., Lexington Heights Dev., LLC v. Crandlemire, 140 Idaho 276, 92 P.3d 526 (2004) (issue was not whether parties had agreed to exact description of land, but whether their writing contained it so as to satisfy Statute of Frauds).

[3]   See Nelson, Whitman, Burkhart & Freyermuth, Real Estate Finance Law, §§ 3.26–3.37 (6th ed. 2014) for a detailed consideration of real estate installment contracts.

third party lender under other documents. Such contracts are usually expected to be performed within a fairly short term—say, a matter of a few months—and they usually do not authorize the buyer to take possession until legal title has passed by delivery of a deed. Thus, the seller is not financing the buyer's occupancy of the property and the contract is not a substitute for mortgage financing. Most of the issues we will consider here are also applicable in some degree to installment or other financing contracts, but they raise many additional problems that are outside the scope of this book.

The Statute of Frauds. The notion that land sale contracts should be evidenced by a writing is an ancient one. Even before the enactment in 1677 of the English Statute of Frauds, Stat. 29 Car. II, c. 3, the courts of equity generally required a writing before granting specific performance of a real estate contract.[4] But the statute solidified and broadened the requirement. Its purpose, of course, was to prevent fraud—in particular, fraud perpetrated by someone might claim to have entered into a land sale contract that was in fact fictitious or that differed in its terms from those averred. It sought to make more difficult the task of those who might lie about the contract or attempt to produce false evidence of its existence or terms.

Whether the statute has produced the desired results is not so easy to say. The nature of a writing requirement is to protect the sophisticated, sometimes at the expense of the naive. There is obviously some number of contracts, otherwise fully valid and relied upon, which are unenforceable simply because the party wishing to enforce them did not realize the necessity of procuring a writing from the other. Does this disadvantage of the statute outweigh its plain advantage of making the prospective defrauder's task more onerous? Perhaps not in the current age, when surely nearly everyone recognizes that the law of real estate contracts demands a writing. But the question may be a close one, and it is worth serious consideration whether the statute facilitates as much or more fraud than it prevents.[5]

As it applied to real estate contracts, the text of the English statute was concise:

> * * * no action shall be brought * * * upon any contract or sale of lands, tenements or hereditaments or any interest in or concerning them * * * unless the agreement upon which such action shall be brought or some memorandum or note thereof shall be in writing, and signed by the party to be charged therewith, or some other person thereunto by him lawfully authorized.[6]

Other clauses of the statute applied to conveyances of title to land (a matter discussed later in this book) and to matters not uniquely related to real estate, such as contracts not to be performed within a year and agreements in consideration of marriage. On its face, the statute's effect seems simple, but virtually every word has been the subject of extensive judicial construction, often with results one would never surmise from a mere

---

[4]   See Kepner, Part Performance in Relation to Parol Contracts, 35 Minn.L.Rev. 1 (1950).

[5]   See Braunstein, Remedy, Reason, and the Statute of Frauds: A Critical Economic Analysis, 1989 Utah L.Rev. 383, suggesting that the statute is unnecessary and sometimes a hindrance to efficient contract enforcement; James J. O'Connell, Jr., Boats Against the Current: The Courts and the Statute of Frauds, 47 Emory L.J. 253 (1998), suggesting that the courts are so "flexible" in applying the statute that results are essentially unpredictable. There is indeed a suggestion in some cases that, where a party's own fraud has been sufficiently egregious, she or he will not be permitted to raise a defense based on the Statute of Frauds; see Warren v. Merrill, 143 Cal. App. 4th 96, 49 Cal. Rptr. 3d 122 (2006).

[6]   Stat. 29 Car. II, c. 3, § 4 (1677).

reading of the text itself. Hence, a study of the statute really becomes a study of the jurisprudence of its interpretation as represented by a massive body of decisions.

Every American state has a statute of frauds. Many are virtually verbatim copies of the English statute above, while others contain only minor variations. Moreover, even what seem to be significant modifications of the traditional language have had, for the most part, little or no effect on the opinions of the courts. A good illustration is found in the phrase "no action shall be brought" at the beginning of the statute. Perhaps ten or so states have chosen instead to provide that a contract lacking the necessary writing is "void," a term which certainly sounds much more far-reaching than the original language. But the decisions in these states usually reach the same results as would be expected in the "no action shall be brought" jurisdictions on similar facts.[7]

What, then, is the meaning of the phrase "no action shall be brought?" Plainly it means that a plaintiff cannot maintain a successful action to enforce the contract, either at law for damages or in equity for specific performance,[8] if the required writing was not made. Equally plainly, the contract is not "void" in an absolute sense. On the contrary, it has considerable legal significance. This is perhaps most obvious from the fact that the defendant in the enforcement action has, in effect, a power to validate the contract and thereby to make it fully enforceable merely by signing an appropriate writing; surely this power could not exist if the contract itself were deemed never to have existed.

The contract is significant in other ways as well despite the absence of a writing. For example, if both parties fully perform, the resulting legal relationships are precisely the same as those that would have existed if the statute had been fully complied with.[9] Neither party can thereafter rescind or recover what he or she had before by claiming that the contract is a nullity. As we will see in the next section, even partial performance by a party may make the contract enforceable, at least in equity, under certain circumstances, although the rules are more complex and less certain than those that pertain to full performance.[10] In addition, a party who relies upon a misrepresentation in, or in connection with, an oral contract may recover damages[11] and a purchaser under an oral contract who defaults may be able to recover in an action for restitution of the funds paid, and perhaps other out-of-pocket expenses in reliance on the contract, insofar

---

[7]   See 3 Am.L.Prop. § 11.3 (1952); Guerin v. Smith, 2012 WL 6827056 (N.Y. S.Ct. 2012) (failure to comply with the statute renders contract unenforceable, though statute says "void").

[8]   See, e.g., Ravosa v. Zais, 40 Mass. App.Ct. 47, 661 N.E.2d 111 (Mass.App.Ct. 1996). In theory the statute applies equally to enforcement in law or equity, although the courts have been somewhat more inclined to circumvent its technical requirements in equitable actions; see Kepner, Part Performance in Relation to Parol Contracts for the Sale of Land, 35 Minn.L.Rev. 1 (1951); Barkho v. Ready, 523 S.W.3d 37 (Mo. Ct. App. 2017) (noncompliant contract is not enforceable at law, but may be enforceable in equity under part performance theory). Regarding part performance, see § 10.2, infra.

[9]   See In re Garcia, 465 B.R. 181 (Bankr. D. Idaho 2011); Don King Equip. Co. v. Double D Tractor Parts, Inc., 115 S.W.3d 363 (Mo. Ct. App. 2003); McMahon v. Poisson, 99 N.H. 182, 107 A.2d 378 (1954); Denney v. Teel, 688 P.2d 803 (Okl. 1984) (Ky. law); Cash v. Granite Springs Retreat Ass'n, Inc., 2011 Wyo. 25, 248 P.3d 614, 621 (2011). Full performance by only one party is sometimes held to permit enforcement by that party; see Ala v. Chesser, 5 So. 3d 715 (Fla. Dist. Ct. App. 2009); Fox v. Bechthold, 2001 Ok. Civ. App. 151, 37 P.3d 966 (2001); Parthenon Const. & Design, Inc. v. Neuman, 166 Or. App. 172, 999 P.2d 1169 (2000).

[10]   See § 10.2 infra.

[11]   Foster Rd. Assocs. v. NJM Realty Ltd. P'ship, 1996 WL 532502 (Conn. Super. Ct. 1996); Guest v. Claycomb, 932 So. 2d 567 (Fla. Dist. Ct. App. 2006); Burgdorf v. Weston, 259 Or.App. 755, 316 P.3d 303 (2013); Fericks v. Lucy Ann Soffe Tr., 2004 Utah 85, 100 P.3d 1200 (2004). See also Guest v. Claycomb, 932 So. 2d 567 (Fla. Dist. Ct. App. 2006) (court may recognize a constructive trust and equitable lien in connection with oral contract of sale).

as they exceed the seller's actual damages.[12] The contract is valid as against third parties despite the absence of a writing, and one who attempts to interfere with it tortiously may be liable for doing so.[13] In all of these senses the contract subsists even though the statute of frauds bars its enforcement by one or both of the parties.

Writings that satisfy the statute. It is often loosely said that the statute requires the contract to be written, but that is plainly not the case; a written contract is only one way to meet the statute's demands. A written offer, accepted by a separate writing, is equally acceptable. Indeed, either an offer or an acceptance alone in writing will do if it contains the necessary elements, including an appropriate signature.[14] More surprisingly, a writing which forms no part of the contract itself may also suffice as a "memorandum", as the statute uses the term.[15] Moreover, the writing need not have existed when the contract was formed, but may have been created later.[16] A series of letters between the parties,[17] a letter to a third party[18], a deed[19], a check[20], an affidavit in a separate lawsuit[21], or a set of escrow instructions[22] may do quite well. Even a deed or will prepared pursuant to the oral contract has been held sufficient.[23] It is not necessary that the

---

[12]   See, e.g., Rich v. Gulliver, 564 So.2d 578 (Fla.App. 1990); Osage Energy Res., LLC v. Pemco, LLC, 2016 Okl. Civ App. 70, 394 P.3d 265 (2016) (even if contract is unenforceable, purchaser may assert vendee's lien to recover outlays); L.Q. Development, Oreg. v. Mallory, 98 Or.App. 121, 778 P.2d 972 (1989) (despite conclusion by court that contract was "null and void," vendor could still be liable under restitution theory); Firetree, Ltd. v. Dep't of Gen. Servs., 978 A.2d 1067 (Pa. Commw. Ct. 2009). See Comment, Need for Uniformity in Statute of Frauds and Suggested Remedy: Recoupment in Real Estate Transactions, 49 Marq.L.Rev. 419 (1963). Restitution of deposit and out-of-pocket expenses will be denied to a purchaser who raises a Statute of Frauds defense when the vendor is ready, willing, and able to perform; see Thompson v. Selvidge, 2000 WL 284076 (Ark. Ct. App. 2000) (unpublished); Kellogg v. Shushereba, 194 Vt. 446, 82 A.3d 1121 (2013); Kofmehl v. Baseline Lake, LLC, 177 Wash. 2d 584, 305 P.3d 230 (2013).

[13]   Daugherty v. Kessler, 264 Md. 281, 286 A.2d 95 (1972).

[14]   Mor v. Fastow, 32 A.D.3d 419, 819 N.Y.S.2d 560 (2006). But see Anderson v. Garrison, 402 P.2d 873 (Okl.1965), requiring both offer and acceptance to be in writing; see Annot., 1 A.L.R.2d 841 (1948).

[15]   Sterling v. Taylor, 40 Cal. 4th 757, 152 P.3d 420 (2007); Jacobson v. Gulbransen, 2001 S.D. 33, 623 N.W.2d 84 (2001).

[16]   Elec. Wholesalers, Inc. v. M.J.B. Corp., 99 Conn. App. 294, 912 A.2d 1117 (2007); Royal Inv. Grp., LLC v. Wang, 183 Md. App. 406, 436, 961 A.2d 665, 682 (2008).

[17]   Ellison v. Town of Yorktown, 47 N.E.3d 610, 620 (Ind. Ct. App. 2015); Varoz v. Varoz, 144 N.M. 7, 183 P.3d 151 (2008).

[18]   D'Angelo v. Schultz, 306 Or. 504, 760 P.2d 866 (1988), appeal after remand 110 Or.App. 445, 823 P.2d 997 (1992) (delivery of the writing not essential to satisfaction of statute); Smith v. McClam, 289 S.C. 452, 346 S.E.2d 720 (1986) (letter may satisfy statute even if not delivered to other contracting party).

[19]   Sloop v. Kiker, 2016 Ark. App. 125, 484 S.W.3d 696 (2016) (deed supplied an adequate description of land to satisfy statute of frauds).

[20]   A.B.C. Auto Parts, Inc. v. Moran, 359 Mass. 327, 268 N.E.2d 844 (1971). See Annot., 9 A.L.R.4th 1009 (1981).

[21]   Roberts v. Karimi, 79 F.Supp.2d 174 (E.D.N.Y. 1999), rev'd on other grounds, 251 F.3d 404 (2d Cir. 2001).

[22]   Shepard v. Fid. Nat. Title Co. of California, 2004 WL 2406627 (Cal. Ct. App. 2004) (unpublished); T.D. Dennis Builder, Inc. v. Goff, 101 Ariz. 211, 418 P.2d 367 (1966).

[23]   Carolina Builders Corp. v. Howard-Veasey Homes, Inc., 72 N.C.App. 224, 324 S.E.2d 626 (1985), review denied 313 N.C. 597, 330 S.E.2d 606 (1985) (deed); Southern States Development Co., Inc. v. Robinson, 494 S.W.2d 777 (Tenn. App. 1972) (undelivered deed); Collins v. Morris, 122 Md.App.764, 716 A.2d 384 (Md. App. 1998) (will); In re Beeruk's Estate, 429 Pa. 415, 241 A.2d 755 (1968) (will). Often a will or deed will not contain a sufficient reference to the existence of a contract and will fail to satisfy the statute for this reason. See generally 10 Williston on Contracts § 29:21 (4th ed. 2018 update). It is logically irrelevant whether the deed or will is itself operative as a conveyance or not.

Other unusual illustrations satisfying the memorandum requirement include Richardson v. Schaub, 796 P.2d 1304 (Wyo. 1990) (property report filed with the United States Department of Housing and Urban Development); Timberlake v. Heflin, 180 W.Va. 644, 379 S.E.2d 149 (1989) (former wife's divorce complaint).

writing have been intended to satisfy the statute, if it does so in fact.[24] Indeed, some courts will disregard the lack of writing if the defendant admits the existence of the contract in pleadings, deposition, or sworn testimony at trial; the cases are divided on this matter.[25] It is not even necessary that the writing be introduced as evidence; if it has been destroyed or is otherwise unavailable, its contents may be proved by parol or other evidence.[26]

The necessary writing may be composed of more than one piece of paper. As we will see below, certain minimum elements must be present, but they need not all be contained in the same writing. Many courts are quite liberal in permitting two or more documents to be employed together to provide the necessary elements.[27] This approach is likely to be successful only if there is sufficient oral evidence tying the documents together and showing that they relate to the same transaction, but this is frequently easy to prove.[28]

Electronic communications. Until fairly recently, it was controversial whether electronic communications could satisfy the "writing" requirement of the statute. That issue has been put to rest by the adoption of the Electronic Records in Global and National Commerce Act[29] ("E-Sign") by Congress in 2000, and the roughly simultaneous adoption by nearly all states of the Uniform Electronic Transactions Act (UETA). Both acts contain substantially the same language; here is the E-Sign version:

---

[24] See Fleckenstein v. Faccio, 619 P.2d 1016 (Alaska 1980); 3 Am.L.Prop. § 11.5 n. 3 (supp. 1977), citing numerous cases. The writing will usually be considered sufficient despite the fact that the parties intended to enter into a more complete or formal contract later; see, e.g., McCarthy v. Tobin, 429 Mass. 84, 706 N.E.2d 629 (Mass. 1999); Sabetfard v. Djavaheri Realty Corp., 18 A.D.3d 640, 795 N.Y.S.2d 643 (2005). But if the parties believed that they were merely in the negotiating stage, and had not yet reached an agreement, a writing reflecting their negotiations will not bind them; see Von Papen v. Rubman, 18 F.Supp.3d 77, 85 (D. Mass. 2014); Carruthers v. Flaum, 450 F.Supp.2d 288 (S.D.N.Y. 2006); Beazer Homes Corp. v. VMIF/Anden Southbridge Venture, 235 F.Supp.2d 485 (E.D. Va. 2002); Mohrenweiser v. Blomer, 573 N.W.2d 704 (Minn.Ct.App. 1998). Thus, both a "meeting of the minds" and a sufficient writing must be shown.

[25] See Peter J. Shedd, The Judicial Admissions Exception to the Statute of Frauds in Real Estate Transactions, 19 Real Est. L.J. 232 (1991). Most recent cases accept judicial admissions as satisfying the statute; see Gibson v. Arnold, 288 F.3d 1242 (10th Cir. 2002) (Okl. law); Sutton v. Culver, 204 F.Supp.2d 20 (D. Me. 2002); In re Peter Peter Cottontail, LLC, 498 B.R. 242 (Bkrtcy. 2013); Roti v. Roti, 364 Ill. App. 3d 191, 845 N.E.2d 892 (2006); Davis v. Roberts, 563 N.W.2d 16, 21 (Iowa Ct. App. 1997); In re Marriage of Takusagawa, 38 Kan. App. 2d 401, 166 P.3d 440 (2007); Grisham v. Grisham, 289 P.3d 230, 234 (Nev. 2012). Refusing to treat judicial admissions as satisfying the statute, see Losh Family, LLC v. Kertsman, 155 Wash.App. 458, 228 P.3d 793 (2010); Darby v. Johnson, 477 So.2d 322 (Ala. 1985). See also Hickey v. Green, 14 Mass.App.Ct. 671, 442 N.E.2d 37 (1982), review denied 388 Mass. 1102, 445 N.E.2d 156 (1983), which reads Restatement (Second) Contracts § 129, comment d (1981) as endorsing enforcement of the contract if the defendant fails to deny its existence. An admission by the defendant may also help the plaintiff enforce the contract under the part performance doctrine, discussed in the next section of this book; see Martin v. Scholl, 678 P.2d 274 (Utah 1983); Sutton v. Warner, 12 Cal.App.4th 415, 15 Cal.Rptr.2d 632 (Cal.Ct.App. 1993).

In contracts for the sale of goods, U.C.C. § 2–201(3)(b) provides an exception to the statute of frauds for judicial admissions; see Baker v. Jim Walter Homes, Inc., 438 F.Supp.2d 649 (W.D. Va. 2006).

[26] Reed v. Hess, 239 Kan. 46, 716 P.2d 555 (1986).

[27] Cohen Dev. Co. v. JMJ Properties, Inc., 317 F.3d 729 (7th Cir. 2003); Von Papen v. Rubman, 18 F.Supp.3d 77 (D. Mass. 2014); Young v. Hefton, 38 Kan. App. 2d 846, 173 P.3d 671 (2007).

[28] St. John's Holdings, LLC v. Two Elecs., LLC, 2016 WL 1460477 (Mass. Land Ct. 2016); In re Estate of Looney, 975 S.W.2d 508 (Mo.Ct.App. 1998); Pee Dee Oil Co. v. Quality Oil Co., 80 N.C.App. 219, 341 S.E.2d 113 (1986), review denied 317 N.C. 706, 347 S.E.2d 438 (1986). The predominant view is that the documents need not refer internally to one another, provided that sufficient external evidence links them to one another and to the transaction in question; see Sackett v. Wilson, 258 Ga. 612, 373 S.E.2d 10 (1988); Dobbs v. Vornado, Inc., 576 F.Supp. 1072 (E.D.N.Y. 1983). But some courts require internal references in the signed document to the unsigned ones; Green v. Interstate United Management Services Corp., 748 F.2d 827 (3d Cir.1984) (Pa. law); Hoffman v. S V Co., Inc., 102 Idaho 187, 628 P.2d 218 (1981).

[29] 15 U.S.C. § 7001.

Notwithstanding any statute, regulation, or other rule of law, * * * with respect to any transaction in or affecting interstate or foreign commerce—

(1)   a signature, contract, or other record relating to such transaction may not be denied legal effect, validity, or enforceability solely because it is in electronic form; and

(2)   a contract relating to such transaction may not be denied legal effect, validity, or enforceability solely because an electronic signature or electronic record was used in its formation.

Thus, the statute of frauds is as readily satisfied by electronic writings and signatures[30] as by those on paper or other media. This includes, for example, facsimile transmissions,[31] e-mail,[32] and SMS text messages.[33]

The writing's content. What are the minimum elements that the writing must contain? The statute itself gives no clue except for its mention of the signature, and the other requirements mentioned below are entirely the product of case adjudication. The decisions are not easy to harmonize, although there is a basic core of requirements which are quite uniformly agreed upon. Some of the cases stop there, while others mention further matters (such as the selling price)[34] whose absence is fatal, making generalization difficult. It is reasonably clear that not every term orally agreed upon by the parties must be included in the writing, although some cases go so far in demanding detail as almost to make this the rule.[35]

The essential matters required in virtually all jurisdictions include identification of the parties and of the land, some words indicating an intention to sell or buy, and a signature.[36] Each of these items warrants some discussion here. The parties are usually identified by name, of course,[37] but there seems no reason in principle to object to other forms of identification, such as "parents of John Jones" or the like. The cases appear to follow a rather odd distinction to the effect that a reference to a party as "owner" or "proprietor" is sufficient but a reference to "seller" or "vendor" is not, presumably because ownership can be determined from the public records while one's status as a seller

---

[30]   However, the mere fact that a party's name appears in the communication does not make it a signature unless the party placed it there or adopted it with intent to authenticate the writing; see J.B.B. Inv. Partners, Ltd. v. Fair, 232 Cal. App. 4th 974, 182 Cal. Rptr. 3d 154 (2014); SN4, LLC v. Anchor Bank, FSB, 848 N.W.2d 559 (Minn. Ct. App. 2014); Vista Developers Corp. v. VFP Realty LLC, 17 Misc. 3d 914, 847 N.Y.S.2d 416 (Sup. Ct. 2007). A name that is appended automatically by the e-mail or facsimile system, as distinguished from a hand-typed name, is unlikely to qualify. See Sigg v. Coltrane, 45 Kan. App. 2d 65, 253 P.3d 781 (2010).

[31]   Parma Tile Mosaic & Marble Co., Inc. v. Estate of Short, 87 N.Y.2d 524, 640 N.Y.S.2d 477, 663 N.E.2d 633 (1996).

[32]   McClare v. Rocha, 86 A.3d 22 (Me. 2014); Naldi v. Grunberg, 80 A.D.3d 1, 908 N.Y.S.2d 639 (2010); Waddle v. Elrod, 367 S.W.3d 217 (Tenn. 2012).

[33]   St. John's Holdings, LLC v. Two Elecs., LLC, 2016 WL 1460477 (Mass. Land Ct. 2016).

[34]   See, e.g., Sterling v. Taylor, 40 Cal. 4th 757, 152 P.3d 420 (2007).

[35]   See, e.g., Troj v. Chesebro, 30 Conn. Sup. 30, 296 A.2d 685 (1972); Note, 24 Baylor L.Rev. 406 (1972).

[36]   Sterling v. Taylor, 40 Cal. 4th 757, 152 P.3d 420 (2007); Application of Sing Chong Co., Limited, 1 Hawaii App. 236, 617 P.2d 578 (1980); Williamson v. United Farm Agency of Alabama, Inc., 401 So.2d 759 (Ala. 1981); Higbie v. Johnson, 626 P.2d 1147 (Colo. App. 1980); Moorman v. Blackstock, Inc., 276 Va. 64, 661 S.E.2d 404 (2008). See Dixon v. Hill, 456 So.2d 313 (Ala.Civ.App. 1984) (under Alabama statute, when land is sold at auction, memorandum may be prepared by auctioneer and parties' signatures are unnecessary).

[37]   Gabriele v. Brino, 85 Conn. App. 503, 858 A.2d 273 (2004).

depends on the enforceability of the very contract that the memorandum is supposed to reflect.[38]

The writing must identify the land to be sold with reasonable certainty,[39] but this does not require a formal legal description by metes and bounds or by reference to a recorded map or subdivision plat.[40] The courts are fairly lenient, often accepting a street address, for example, if it is unambiguous.[41] But it is difficult to reconcile the cases entirely. If a street address does not include the city and state, some cases hold it insufficient[42] while others deem it acceptable if the vendor owns only one parcel of land bearing that address or if the context of the negotiations makes it clear which land was the subject of the agreement[43]; this is surely the more reasonable approach.

If the written description of the land is ambiguous, the courts will usually admit extrinsic evidence as to the precise boundaries of the parcel to be conveyed.[44] A

---

[38]   See 10 Williston, Contracts § 29:9 (4th ed. 2018 update).

[39]   Rogers v. United States, 109 Fed. Cl. 280 (2013) (description could be modified in the future and was therefore ambiguous); Redevelopment Agency of City of Stockton v. BNSF Ry. Co., 643 F.3d 668 (9th Cir. 2011) (exact boundaries of land were not described; conveyance was ineffective); Knapp v. Estate of Wright, 76 N.E.3d 900 (Ind. Ct. App. 2017) (contract referred to map in an attached exhibit, but no exhibit was attached). Cf. Stubler v. Ross, 325 F. App'x 68 (3d Cir. 2009) (reference to tax parcel map was sufficient); Nicholson v. Coeur D'Alene Placer Mining Corp., 161 Idaho 877, 392 P.3d 1218 (2017) (description too ambiguous to be enforced).

[40]   See, e.g., Nguyen v. Yovan, 317 S.W.3d 261 (Tex. App. 2009). A few courts are much more demanding, actually insisting on a full and formal legal description. Washington is notorious for inflexibility in this respect; see, e.g., Home Realty Lynnwood, Inc. v. Walsh, 146 Wash. App. 231, 189 P.3d 253 (2008). Idaho may be similar; see In re McMurdie, 448 B.R. 826 (Bankr. D. Idaho 2010) (Idaho law); Ray v. Frasure, 146 Idaho 625, 200 P.3d 1174 (2009). See 73 A.L.R.4th 135.

Description of the land as a certain number of acres out of a larger parcel, without explicating the shape of the carveout, are usually held insufficient. See Nix v. Wick, 66 So. 3d 209 (Ala. 2010); Dev. & Const. Mgmt., Inc. v. City of N. Little Rock, 83 Ark. App. 165, 119 S.W.3d 77 (2003); O'Dell v. Pine Ridge Investments, LLC, 293 Ga. App. 696, 667 S.E.2d 912 (2008); Doss & Harper Stone Co. v. Hoover Bros. Farms, 191 S.W.3d 59 (Mo. Ct. App. 2006); Reeder v. Curry, 426 S.W.3d 352 (Tex. App. 2014); 303, LLC v. Born, 344 Wis. 2d 364, 823 N.W.2d 269 (2012). A description based on a survey to be conducted later is unlikely to be acceptable; see Min Quin Shao v. Corley, 95 So. 3d 14 (Ala. Civ. App. 2012).

[41]   See, e.g., Price v. Willbanks, 2009 Ark. App. 849, 374 S.W.3d 28 (2009); Sterling v. Taylor, 40 Cal. 4th 757, 152 P.3d 420 (2007); Jernas v. Gumz, 53 N.E.3d 434 (Ind. Ct. App. 2016); Qutifan v. Shafiq, 70 N.E.3d 43 (Ohio Ct. App. 2016); Burrus v. Reyes, 516 S.W.3d 170 (Tex. App. 2017); Timberlake v. Heflin, 180 W. Va. 644, 379 S.E.2d 149 (1989). Compare Salim v. Solaiman, 302 Ga. App. 607, 691 S.E.2d 389 (2010) (address insufficient, where no evidence was offered linking it to a parcel description); Sieger v. Prehay, 16 A.D.3d 575, 791 N.Y.S.2d 657 (2005) ("the house" at a certain street corner was an insufficient description); Ukkestad v. RBS Asset Fin., Inc., 235 Cal. App. 4th 156, 185 Cal. Rptr. 3d 145 (2015) (trust instrument describing "all of [the trustor's] real property wherever situated" was enforceable).

[42]   See Jones v. Riley, 471 S.W.2d 650 (Tex.Civ.App.1971), refused n.r.e.; Hertel v. Woodard, 183 Or. 99, 191 P.2d 400 (1948); Pardee v. Jolly, 163 Wash. 2d 558, 182 P.3d 967 (2008).

[43]   Maccioni v. Guzman, 145 A.D.2d 415, 535 N.Y.S.2d 96 (1988) (address and tax numbers of property were sufficient where subject property was only property owned by vendor at that address); Garner v. Redeaux, 678 S.W.2d 124 (Tex.App. 1984) (parol evidence admitted to show circumstances before and after agreement, and thus to supply county and state); Seabaugh v. Sailer, 679 S.W.2d 924 (Mo.App. 1984) ("my farm" is sufficient description, where vendor owned only one farm); Guel v. Bullock, 127 Ill.App.3d 36, 468 N.E.2d 811 (1984) (street address without city or state is sufficient, where vendor owned property at such address in only one city); Taefi v. Stevens, 53 N.C.App. 579, 281 S.E.2d 435 (1981). Compare Coulter & Smith, Ltd. v. Russell, 976 P.2d 1218 (Utah Ct.App.1999) ("vendor's lots west of" a certain intersection was sufficient, although the land had not yet been subdivided into lots) with Berg v. Ting, 125 Wn.2d 544, 551, 886 P.2d 564 (1995) (reference to lots not yet subdivided was insufficient). See also Lafayette Place Assocs. v. Boston Redevelopment Auth., 427 Mass. 509, 694 N.E.2d 820 (1998) (contract was enforceable, though price and exact land description were to be determined by future arbitration); Rhodes v. Dep't of Transp., 2008 Utah App. 374, 196 P.3d 632 (Utah Ct. App. 2008) (contract was enforceable where one party was given authority to select the precise land to be conveyed in the future).

[44]   Thornhill, Inc. v. NVR, Inc., 422 F.Supp.2d 646 (N.D.W. Va. 2006); Prezioso v. Aerts, 358 Wis. 2d 714, 858 N.W.2d 386 (2014); Sperling v. Marler, 963 P.2d 577 (Ok. 1998). Cf. Lynn v. Wade Stuart Family

distinction is usually drawn between evidence which merely clarifies a written description and evidence which supplies a description not found in the writing.[45] Obviously this sort of legal formulation is subject to considerable manipulation by the courts, and cases which reject descriptions as inadequate may sometimes reflect a court's unstated reluctance, on other grounds, to enforce the contract. In the main, however, it is fair to say that descriptions which would be far too loose to give adequate guidance to a surveyor on the ground are often deemed adequate for purposes of the statute of frauds when supplemented by further evidence of negotiations and intent.[46]

Beyond the identification of the parties and the land, the signature, and some words indicating a sale, there is little agreement on the essential content of the memorandum. Much controversy has occurred over the price term. It seems fairly clear that if the parties did not agree on a price, no mention of the fact need be made in the writing and the court will assume that a reasonable price was to be paid.[47] But if a price was agreed to, the cases are badly divided as to whether the writing must include it.[48] Alternatively, it is sufficient for the writing to contain a method of arriving at a price.[49]

There is considerable variation among the courts as to the necessity of further elements in the memorandum. The only general statements that can be made are virtually useless; as the Second Restatement of Contracts puts it:

Enterprises, L.P., 3 So. 3d 866 (Ala. Civ. App. 2008) (extrinsic evidence may be considered only if referred to in the writing). See generally 3 Am.L.Prop. § 11.5 (1952).

[45]　See Gagne v. Stevens, 696 A.2d 411(Me. 1997) ("a piece of lot #58 on property map of the Town of Belgrade, in the approximate size of 30 [acres]+-" was ambiguous; parol evidence not admissible to clarify); Calvary Temple Assembly of God v. Lossman, 200 Ill.App.3d 102, 146 Ill.Dec. 122, 557 N.E.2d 1309 (1990) (writing alone was insufficient as description of property; parol evidence not admitted to attain sufficiency). See generally Annots., 30 A.L.R.3d 935 (1970); 46 A.L.R.2d 894 (1956). A subsequent survey is no substitute for an adequate description in the writing; McCumbers v. Trans-Columbia, Inc., 172 Ga.App. 275, 322 S.E.2d 516 (1984).

[46]　See C-470 Joint Venture v. Trizec Colorado, Inc., 176 F.3d 1289 (10th Cir. 1999); Boyd v. Mercantile-Safe Deposit & Trust Co., 28 Md.App. 18, 344 A.2d 148 (1975); Bliss v. Rhodes, 66 Ill.App.3d 895, 384 N.E.2d 512 (1978).

[47]　Qutifan v. Shafiq, 70 N.E.3d 43 (Ohio Ct. App. 2016); 3 Am. L.Prop. § 11.5 n. 25 (1952). Contra, see In re Cameron, 452 B.R. 754 (Bankr. E.D. Ark. 2011) (where parties did not agree upon price, contract is unenforceable).

[48]　A few states' statutes insist on a memorandum "expressing the consideration", while a few others provide that no such expression is necessary; see Restatement (Second) of Contracts § 131, Reporter's Note, Comment a (1981). But Professor Corbin pointed out that the "consideration" and the price are two quite different things, since in a bilateral contract the consideration given by the buyer is literally the promise to pay the price and not the price itself; see 2 Corbin, Contracts § 501 (1950); Peterson Homes, Inc. v. Johnson, 691 So.2d 563 (Fla.App.1997). Recent cases seem to display an increasing tendency to regard the price as an essential term of the writing; see, e.g., Sterling v. Taylor, 40 Cal. 4th 757, 152 P.3d 420 (2007) (contract was unenforceable because price term was ambiguous); Fruin v. Colonnade One at Old Greenwich Ltd. Partnership, 38 Conn.App. 420, 662 A.2d 129 (Conn.App.1995), certification granted on other grounds, 235 Conn. 916, 665 A.2d 607 (1995) (price term required, but making price "contingent" on subsequent events was acceptable); Piazza v. Combs, 226 S.W.3d 211 (Mo. Ct. App. 2007); Maalin Bakodesh Soc'y, Inc. v. Lasher, 301 A.D.2d 634, 754 N.Y.S.2d 331 (2003); Trowbridge v. McCaigue, 2010 Pa. Super. 50, 992 A.2d 199 (2010).

[49]　WBT, L.L.C. v. A.B./Wildwood Ltd. P'ship, 793 So. 2d 779 (Ala. Civ. App. 1999), rev'd on other grounds, 793 So.2d 784 (Ala. 2000) (formula for determining price was acceptable); Schreck v. T & C Sanderson Farms, Inc., 37 P.3d 510 (Colo. App. 2001) (determination of price by future appraisal was acceptable); Wakelam v. Hagood, 151 Idaho 688, 263 P.3d 742 (2011) (writing may contain "a definite method to determine the purchase price, such as being established by an appraiser, by arbitrators, or by the successful bidder at an absolute auction"); Pino v. Harnischfeger, 42 A.D.3d 980, 840 N.Y.S.2d 504 (2007) (writing must contain price or a method of determining price); Coulter & Smith, Ltd. v. Russell, 976 P.2d 1218 (Utah Ct. App. 1999) (city annexation and zoning requirements would determine price).

The "essential terms of unperformed promises" must be stated; "details or particulars" need not. What is essential depends on the agreement and its context and also on the subsequent conduct of the parties, including the dispute which arises and the remedy sought.[50]

One area of particular confusion involves the financing of the sale. If the buyer is to pay all cash or obtain financing from external sources, there is generally no necessity for those arrangements to be mentioned in the writing.[51] However, if the seller is to finance the purchase, as by taking back a note and mortgage for part of the price, many courts are much more strict in demanding that the detailed terms (interest rate, maturity, type of security instrument, frequency and amount of payments, etc.) be mentioned.[52] This approach seems justified, since there can be serious unfairness in imposing financing terms to which the seller did not agree. Courts are also more likely to insist on specificity in the financing terms when specific performance rather than damages is sought.[53]

There are, of course, numerous other terms to which parties often agree in oral contracts: the time of performance, relinquishment of possession, the quality of the title to be conveyed, the risk of loss during the contract's executory period, and so on.[54] The courts typically take the view that these and similar matters are sufficiently minor or nonessential that their absence from the writing is not fatal,[55] although one finds occasional cases to the contrary.

The signature. The English version of the statute followed by most American jurisdictions requires the writing to be signed by "the party to be charged or his agent."

---

[50] Restatement (Second) of Contracts § 131 Comment g (1981); see Burgess v. Arita, 5 Hawaii App. 581, 704 P.2d 930 (1985). New York courts hold that the contract must contain "those terms customarily encountered in" a particular transaction, which sometimes leads to requiring many additional elements, including the price, the closing date, quality of title, tax and insurance adjustments, risk of loss, and other elements. See, e.g., Saul v. Vidokle, 151 A.D.3d 780, 56 N.Y.S.3d 230 (2017); Simmonds v. Marshall, 292 A.D.2d 592, 740 N.Y.S.2d 362 (2002). Most other courts would not require a statement of the closing date; see, e.g., Zurcher v. Herveat, 238 Mich. App. 267, 605 N.W.2d 329 (1999).

[51] Compare Cone v. Abood, 238 So.2d 169 (Fla.App. 1970), cert. denied 240 So.2d 813 (Fla. 1970), in which the contract was enforced although the writing merely said "subject to long term loan", with Fox v. Sails at Laguna Club Development Corp., 403 So.2d 456 (Fla.App. 1981), refusing specific performance because the contract made no statement about the method of payment of the price. See Busching v. Griffin, 465 So.2d 1037 (Miss. 1985), appeal after remand 542 So.2d 860 (1989) (price is essential term of writing, but will be presumed cash where no terms of payment are set out).

[52] A.S. Reeves & Co. v. McMickle, 270 Ga. App. 132, 605 S.E.2d 857 (2004); Ashkenazi v. Kelly, 157 A.D.2d 578, 550 N.Y.S.2d 322 (1990); 3 Am.L.Prop. § 11.5 n. 31 (Supp.1977). Cf. Booras v. Uyeda, 295 Or. 181, 666 P.2d 791 (1983) (financing terms not stated with enough specificity to grant specific performance, but since purchaser could have prepaid financing without penalty, he could tender cash and have specific performance). See generally Note, 24 Baylor L.Rev. 406 (1972).

[53] See Genest v. John Glenn Corp., 298 Or. 723, 696 P.2d 1058 (1985); § 10.5 infra at note 213.

[54] An excellent discussion of real estate contract drafting and the wide variety of clauses which should be considered is found in Friedman & Smith, Contracts and Conveyances of Real Property (8th ed. 2017).

[55] See Kane v. McDermott, 191 Ill. App.3d 212, 138 Ill.Dec. 541, 547 N.E.2d 708 (1989) (terms relating to apportionment of taxes, closing date, and type of deed to be conveyed were not essential to enforcement); Lafayette Place Associates v. Boston Redevelopment Authority, 427 Mass. 509, 694 N.E.2d 820 (1998), cert. denied 525 U.S. 1177, 119 S.Ct. 1112 (1999). The time of performance is rarely considered an essential ingredient of the contract; see, e.g., Patel v. Liebermensch, 45 Cal. 4th 344, 86 Cal.Rptr.3d 366 (2008); 160 Chambers St. Realty Corp. v. Register of the City of New York, 226 A.D.2d 606, 641 N.Y.S.2d 351 (1996); Meyer v. Kesterson, 151 Or.App. 378, 950 P.2d 896 (1997). But see Kemp Const. v. Landmark Bancshares Corp., 784 S.W.2d 306 (Mo.App. 1990) (complexity of the transaction required that closing date, default events, payment terms, insurance, etc. should be included).

The party referred to is the person resisting the contract;[56] ordinarily it is the defendant in the litigation, but it may be the plaintiff if the contract is asserted as the basis for a counterclaim. Of course, at the time the writing is made it is generally impossible to predict which of the parties will be "charged," so good practice dictates signing by both. Perhaps half a dozen statutes substitute "the vendor" or a similar term for "the party to be charged."[57] Such provisions seem anomalous, since they appear to permit an unscrupulous seller to make up the necessary writing, sue the purchaser, and force the writing upon him or her. In reality, however, the courts are most unlikely to countenance such a result; it is usually held under such language that the purchaser-defendant must at least have seen and assented to the writing in order to be bound by it.[58]

The nature of the signature requirement is such that contracts are not always mutually enforceable. If the writing has been signed by only one party to the agreement, only that party is bound by it, and the other may escape its enforcement.[59] Such a result may seem odd, but it follows from the basic policy of compelling performance only from those whose assent to the contract takes the form of a written signature, and it is by no means novel in the law of contracts.[60] The point is that the *plaintiff's* assent to the bargain need not appear in the form of a written signature, but may be proved by oral testimony.[61] Note well that a signed writing is no substitute for the basic elements of the law of contracts; offer, acceptance, and consideration must still be proved whether the writing discloses them or not (although it commonly will do so).[62]

---

[56]   Jernas v. Gumz, 53 N.E.3d 434 (Ind. Ct. App. 2016); Ayalla v. Southridge Presbyterian Church, 37 Kan. App. 2d 312, 152 P.3d 670 (2007).

[57]   See, e.g., Ariz.Rev.Stat. § 33–301. A few cases have reached the same result by judicial construction of the "party to be charged" language, but they seem plainly wrong; see 10 Williston, Contracts § 29:38 (4th ed. 2018 update).

[58]   Schwinn v. Griffith, 303 N.W.2d 258 (Minn. 1981), noted 8 Wm.Mitch.L.Rev. 991 (1982) (where statute requires only vendor's signature, a plaintiff-vendor must prove that the purchaser accepted delivery of the contract); 300 West End Avenue Corp. v. Warner, 250 N.Y. 221, 165 N.E. 271 (1928); National Bank v. Louisville Trust Co., 67 F.2d 97 (6th Cir.1933), certiorari denied 291 U.S. 665, 54 S.Ct. 440, 78 L.Ed. 1056 (1934). The New York Statute was subsequently amended to require signing by the "party to be charged."

[59]   Sun Kyung Ahn v. Merrifield Town Ctr. Ltd. P'ship, 584 F.Supp.2d 848, 861 (E.D. Va. 2008); Passero v. Siciliano, 37 A.D.3d 1048, 829 N.Y.S.2d 321 (2007); Heritage Bldg. Prop., LLC v. Prime Income Asset Mgmt., Inc., 43 So. 3d 1138 (Miss. Ct. App. 2009).

[60]   See Restatement (Second) of Contracts § 135 (1981); 25 Williston, Contracts § 67:45 (4th ed. 2018 update).

[61]   Lilling v. Slauenwhite, 145 A.D.2d 471, 535 N.Y.S.2d 428 (1988) (memorandum signed only by purchaser not enforceable against seller, the party charged in the suit); Jolly v. Kent Realty, Inc., 151 Ariz. 506, 729 P.2d 310 (1986) (contract enforceable against vendor who signed writing despite absence of purchaser's signature); Annot., 30 A.L.R.2d 972 (1953).

[62]   See Board of Education v. James Hamilton Constr. Co., 119 N.M. 415, 891 P.2d 556 (N.M.App. 1994).

A party's agent may sign on his or her behalf, but it is necessary to show that the agent was authorized to do so.[63] Under most formulations of the statute, the agent's authorization must also be in writing.[64]

The courts are remarkably liberal with respect to the nature of the signature. Its form is not of critical importance. It may be in ink, pencil, or rubber stamp, and may even be typed or printed. It may be the signatory's full name, initials, an arbitrary mark, or "any symbol made or adopted with an intention, actual or apparent, to authenticate the writing as that of the signer."[65] The location of the signature on the page is ordinarily irrelevant, although a few statutes require the document to be "subscribed"—a term sometimes construed to mean signed at the end.[66]

Rescission and modification. If the parties become dissatisfied with their agreement, they may decide either to rescind it or to modify its terms in some way. If such actions are accomplished without a writing, even though the original contract was supported by a memorandum satisfying the statute, what is their effect? The usual statement is that an oral rescission is enforceable,[67] while an oral modification is not and leaves the original contract in force.[68] The first part of the statement is pretty clearly

---

[63] See, e.g., B & F Slosman v. Sonopress, Inc., 148 N.C. App. 81, 85, 557 S.E.2d 176, 179 (2001); Bowling v. Pedzik, 302 A.D.2d 343, 754 N.Y.S.2d 653 (2003) (brokerage agreement did not authorize broker to sign contract of purchase). There is no automatic agency between co-owners, and one cannot bind another without an express grant of authority; see Kwang Hee Lee v. ADJMI 936 Realty Assocs., 46 A.D.3d 629, 847 N.Y.S.2d 234 (2007); Parker v. Glosson, 182 N.C. App. 229, 641 S.E.2d 735 (2007); Gajovski v. Estate of Philabaun, 192 Ohio App. 3d 755, 950 N.E.2d 595 (2011); Verdi Energy Grp., Inc. v. Nelson, 2014 Utah App. 101, 326 P.3d 104 (2014); Moorman v. Blackstock, Inc., 276 Va. 64, 661 S.E.2d 404 (2008). However, each co-owner may bind his or her own share of ownership without the joinder of other co-owners; Franklin Credit Mgmt. Corp. v. Hanney, 2011 Utah App. 213, 262 P.3d 406 (2011).

[64] See, e.g., N.Y.-McKinney's Gen.Obl.Law § 5–703(2); Ruggieri-Lam v. Oliver Block, LLC, 120 F.Supp.3d 400 (D. Vt. 2015); In re Cohen, 422 B.R. 350 (E.D.N.Y. 2010); Garrett v. S. Health Corp. of Ellijay, 320 Ga. App. 176, 191, 739 S.E.2d 661, 672 (2013); Ogden v. Griffith, 149 Idaho 489, 236 P.3d 1249 (2010); Williams v. Singleton, 723 P.2d 421 (Utah 1986). Contra, see The Currituck Assocs. v. Hollowell, 166 N.C. App. 17, 601 S.E.2d 256 (2004), aff'd 360 N.C. 160, 622 S.E.2d 493 (2005) (agent's authority need not be in writing). See also Behniwal v. Mix, 133 Cal. App. 4th 1027, 35 Cal. Rptr. 3d 320 (2005) (where party ratifies the signature of an unauthorized agent, the ratification must be in writing); Gresser v. Hotzler, 604 N.W.2d 379 (Minn. Ct. App. 2000) (same); Leist v. Tugendhaft, 64 A.D.3d 687, 882 N.Y.S.2d 521 (2009) (real estate agent had no authority to sign on behalf of sellers).

[65] Restatement (Second) of Contracts § 134 (1981); Durham v. Harbin, 530 So.2d 208 (Ala. 1988) (writing including only vendor's typewritten notation and letterhead is insufficient to bind him, absent showing that vendor intended to authenticate the agreement by such inscriptions); Hansen v. Hill, 215 Neb. 573, 340 N.W.2d 8 (1983) (telegram sent by party is sufficient signature).

[66] See, e.g., Commercial Credit Corp. v. Marden, 155 Or. 29, 62 P.2d 573 (1936); Annot. 112 A.L.R. 937 (1938). It is doubtful that "subscribed" need be taken so literally, and some decisions treat the term as the equivalent of "signed"; Butler v. Lovoll, 96 Nev. 931, 620 P.2d 1251 (1980); Radke v. Brenon, 271 Minn. 35, 134 N.W.2d 887 (1965). See also 26 Beverly Glen, LLC v. Wykoff Newberg Corp., 334 F. App'x 62 (9th Cir. 2009) (initials on each page did not satisfy signature requirement, where signature line at foot of document was left blank).

[67] Ionian Corp. v. Country Mut. Ins. Co., 836 F.Supp.2d 1173, 1190 (D. Or. 2011) (Oregon law); Dolansky v. Frisillo, 92 A.D.3d 1286, 939 N.Y.S.2d 210 (2012); Smith v. Mohan, 723 S.W.2d 94, 98 (Mo. Ct. App. 1987). See also Rosepark Properties, Ltd. v. Buess, 167 Ohio App. 3d 366, 855 N.E.2d 140 (2006) (attempted oral revival of oral rescission was unenforceable; rescission acted to terminate contract, after which statute of frauds barred enforcement of new oral contract).

[68] In re A & M Florida Properties II, LLC, 435 B.R. 9 (Bankr. S.D.N.Y. 2010); Miller v. Neil, 2010 Ark. App. 555, 377 S.W.3d 425 (2010); Bradley v. Sanchez, 943 So. 2d 218 (Fla. Dist. Ct. App. 2006); Needham v. Fannie Mae, 854 F.Supp.2d 1145, 1153 (D. Utah 2012); Prue v. Royer, 193 Vt. 267, 282, 67 A.3d 895, 906 (2013); Roussalis v. Wyoming Med. Ctr., Inc., 4 P.3d 209, 242 (Wyo. 2000); Restatement (Second) of Contracts §§ 148–49 (1981).

correct; the theoretical explanation is that the statute applies to contracts for the sale of land but not to contracts that rescind other contracts.[69]

The situation with respect to oral modifications is more complex. A modification obviously results in the formation of a new contract whose terms consist partly of the old contract and partly of the agreement which modifies it. The test is whether this new contract would fall within the statute of frauds if it were the only contract the parties had made. With the great majority of real estate sales contracts the answer is plainly affirmative, and the conclusion reached is that the new contract cannot be enforced.[70] What, then, is the parties' relationship? The standard answer is that the original contract (assuming it was supported by an adequate writing) is still in effect.[71]

In practice, however, oral modifications are very frequently given effect by the courts under principles of estoppel. Most oral modifications can fairly be described as reducing the difficulty of one party's performance or of eliminating or making less onerous a condition upon which a party's duties depend. In either case, the modification amounts to a waiver which, if detrimentally relied upon by the party whom it benefits, will be treated as estopping the other party from enforcing the contract's original terms.[72] Perhaps the most common illustration involves the time of performance. Even if the parties have agreed on a specific date for settlement and the passage of legal title, and even if they have agreed that this time is "of the essence," an oral statement by one

---

[69]   Frank v. Motwani, 513 So.2d 1170 (La. 1987); Favre Prop. Mgmt., LLC v. Cinque Bambini, 863 So. 2d 1037 (Miss. Ct. App. 2004); Smith v. Mohan, 723 S.W.2d 94 (Mo.App. 1987); Niernberg v. Feld, 131 Colo. 508, 283 P.2d 640 (1955), noted 28 Rocky Mt.L.Rev. 268 (1956); 42 A.L.R.3d 242 (1972). There are contrary decisions, sometimes based on the highly artificial notion that under the doctrine of equitable conversion the purchaser has "equitable title" during the executory period of the contract, and that a rescission conveys this interest back to the vendor and hence must be in writing under the provisions of the statute dealing with conveyances. See Reyes v. Smith, 288 S.W.2d 822 (Tex.Civ.App. 1956); Annot., 38 A.L.R. 294 (1925).

[70]   Davis v. Patel, 32 Ark.App. 1, 794 S.W.2d 158 (1990); Walden v. Smith, 249 Ga. App. 32, 546 S.E.2d 808 (2001); Player v. Chandler, 299 S.C. 101, 382 S.E.2d 891 (1989); Dickinson, Inc. v. Balcor Income Properties, 12 Kan. App.2d 395, 745 P.2d 1120 (1987) (requiring "substantial" modifications to be in writing); Eldridge v. Farnsworth, 2007 Ut. App 243, 166 P.3d 639 (2007); Restatement (Second) of Contracts § 149 (1981). If the modification deals with a term so incidental or nonessential that it would not have been required to be mentioned in the original writing, there is a good deal of authority that the contract as orally modified should be enforced. See, e.g., McKinley Investments, Inc. v. Middleborough Land, LLC., 62 Mass. App. Ct. 616, 818 N.E.2d 627 (2004) (change in time of performance and price were incidental); Stegman v. Chavers, 704 S.W.2d 793 (Tex.App. 1985) (change in who earnest money would be delivered to was incidental). In substance, these cases hold that the original memorandum is a sufficient writing to support the modified contract as well. But other cases hold that any modification, however minor, requires a written memorandum; see 10 Williston on Contracts § 29:49 (4th ed. 2018 update).

[71]   Restatement (Second) of Contracts § 149(2) (1981); Note, 24 Baylor L.Rev. 406 (1972); Note, 44 Iowa L.Rev. 693 (1959). But even this result may not follow if the court can characterize the modification as a rescission followed by a new oral contract; under this view the rescission alone would be effective, and the parties would have no contractual relationship at all. See Burnford v. Blanning, 33 Colo.App. 444, 525 P.2d 494 (1974), reversed on the basis of part performance, 189 Colo. 292, 540 P.2d 337 (1975).

[72]   The classic statement is Judge Cardozo's concurring opinion in Imperator Realty Co. v. Tull, 228 N.Y. 447, 127 N.E. 263 (1920), in which the parties to a real estate exchange orally agreed that a cash bond would be acceptable in lieu of clearing certain city ordinance violations, as required by the original contract. When one party, relying on the modification, failed to clear the violations, the other refused to perform; the court held him liable in damages, in effect enforcing the modification. Cardozo's opinion suggests that the defendant could have withdrawn the modification, even "at the very hour of the closing," if he had been willing to grant reasonable additional time for the other to perform. See also Huber v. Hamilton, 33 N.E.3d 1116, 1124 (Ind. Ct. App.), reh'g denied (Aug. 14, 2015), transfer denied, 41 N.E.3d 690 (Ind. 2015); Richey v. Olson, 709 P.2d 963 (Colo.App.1985); Restatement (Second) of Contracts § 150 (1981); Gold Coast Homes at Evert St., Inc. v. Cannuscio, 62 A.D.3d 748, 879 N.Y.S.2d 514 (2009) (rejecting the claimed estoppel because the acts were not unequivocally referable to the contract). Contra, see DK Arena, Inc. v. EB Acquisitions I, LLC, 112 So. 3d 85, 97 (Fla. 2013), rejecting the use of estoppel in this context.

that the other may have additional time will very often be given effect.[73] In such a case, the reliance may consist simply of delaying beyond the originally agreed time before performing.[74] The party who agreed to accept late performance may reconsider and revoke the waiver by notifying the other party soon enough that the revocation causes no significant hardship;[75] but if the notice is given too late to meet this test, the waiver will be binding despite its oral character.

While the great majority of estoppel cases involve waivers of time deadlines, waivers of other conditions or of various aspects of contract performance are also possible.[76] The effect of this sort of waiver is clearly not the same as a true modification of the contract, since the waiving party is permitted to revoke the waiver and reinstate the original contract terms if this can be done before the other party has detrimentally relied.[77] Cases of waivers of time are unique in this respect, since the very fact of the passage of the originally-agreed time establishes the detrimental reliance and makes a revocation of the waiver unconscionable and hence impermissible.

In addition to waiver and estoppel, oral modifications of written contracts may be upheld by the courts on other theories, such as part performance, discussed in the next section as exceptions to the statute's operation.

§ 10.2 PART PERFORMANCE

Like any rule that exalts formality over intention, the statute of frauds sometimes leaves courts feeling acutely uncomfortable. Two factors frequently combine to produce this discomfort. The first is a sense that, despite the absence of a suitable writing, the parties' conduct is strong evidence that they really did enter into the sort of contract the plaintiff alleges. The second is the court's observation that, due to actions taken or investments made by the plaintiff in reliance on the contract, serious and unrecompensed harm may result if it is held unenforceable on account of the statute of frauds.

It is not surprising that the desire to avoid the evident injustice created by these factors has manifested itself in the cases, mainly through the development of the doctrine of part performance. What is surprising is the ease with which courts apply this doctrine, overtly contradicting the literal terms of the statute to enforce contracts where no written memorandum has been made. Part performance is simply a judicially-created exception to a legislative rule * * * an idea which at first seems shocking.[78] Yet the

---

[73] Kammert Brothers Enterprises, Inc. v. Tanque Verde Plaza Co., 4 Ariz.App. 349, 420 P.2d 592 (1966), transferred to 102 Ariz. 301, 428 P.2d 678 (1967); Taylor v. Eagle Ridge Developers, LLC, 71 Ark. App. 309, 29 S.W.3d 767 (2000); McGuire v. Norris, 180 Ga.App. 383, 349 S.E.2d 261 (1986); In re Estate of Yates, 368 N.J. Super. 226, 236, 845 A.2d 714 (App. Div. 2004) (oral extension enforceable only if time is not of the essence); Fracassa v. Doris, 814 A.2d 357 (R.I. 2003); Cooper Valves, LLC v. ValvTechnologies, Inc., 531 S.W.3d 254 (Tex. App. 2017); Iota, LLC v. Davco Mgmt. Co., LC, 2012 Ut. App 218, 284 P.3d 681 (2012). See also Johnson v. Sellers, 2011 S.D. 24, 798 N.W.2d 690 (2011), not requiring a showing of reliance.

[74] But see Best v. Edwards, 217 Ariz. 497, 176 P.3d 695 (Ariz. Ct. App. 2008), rejecting this argument.

[75] See Imperator Realty Co. v. Tull, supra note 72.

[76] See 10 Williston on Contracts § 29:48 (4th ed. 2018 update).

[77] See Restatement (Second) of Contracts § 150 Comment c (1981); Imperator Realty v. Tull, supra note 72.

[78] A few states expressly recognize the part performance doctrine in statute; see, e.g., Idaho Code § 9–504; Official Code Ga. Ann. § 20–402; (Mich.Stat.Ann. § 26.910; Mont.Code Ann. § 70–20–101, construed in Orlando v. Prewett, 218 Mont. 5, 705 P.2d 593 (1985); McKinney's N.Y. Gen. Obl. L § 5–703(4); N.D. Cent. Code § 47–10–01. See also Ala.Code § 8–9–2 (requiring partial payment plus possession), applied in Swain v. Terry, 454 So.2d 948 (Ala.1984).

doctrine has existed for so long, and is so well established in so many jurisdictions, that it is far too late to complain that the statute itself mentions no such exception. Note, however, that part performance is a substitute for the absent writing, and not for the contract itself, which must still be proved.[79] When applying the part performance doctrine, courts often require an exceptionally high standard of proof of the contract's terms, such as "clear and convincing" or the like.[80]

The doctrine of part performance is a misnomer, for the term seems to suggest that performance by a party of some duties under the contract will substitute for the absent memorandum. The reality is somewhat different; some of the acts which may be shown are not necessarily required by the contract at all.[81] The three traditional types of acts acceptable to courts are (1) payment of all or part (sometimes, a "substantial" part)[82] of the purchase price; (2) taking of possession (a few courts require "open and notorious possession"[83]) of the property; and (3) the making of substantial improvements on the land.[84] Note that in all three cases these acts are those of the purchaser. Only the first, payment of the price, can fairly be regarded as performance by the buyer of a contractual obligation; indeed, payment may well be the buyer's only obligation. Possession and improvements may occur pursuant to the contract in the sense that they would not have taken place if no contract existed, but they can hardly be viewed as performances under it; the vendor typically has little or no interest in whether the purchaser takes possession or improves the property.

The three types of acts mentioned above must appear in various combinations, depending on the jurisdiction, in order to qualify as "part performance." One, two, or all three may be required. Rarely will a court accept partial payment by itself,[85] but some

---

[79]   See In re Galbreath, 286 B.R. 185 (Bankr. S.D. Ga. 2002) (Georgia law); Bauchman-Kingston Partnership, LP v. Haroldsen, 149 Idaho 87; 233 P.3d 18 (2008); In re Estate of Thompson, 752 N.W.2d 624 (N.D. 2008); Verdi Energy Group, Inc. v. Nelson, 2014 Utah App. 101, 326 P.3d 104 (2014).

[80]   See Peterson v. Petersen, 355 N.W.2d 26 (Iowa 1984); Darsaklis v. Schildt, 218 Neb. 605, 358 N.W.2d 186 (1984).

[81]   However, a few courts refuse to recognize a party's acts if they were not required by the contract. See, e.g., Payne v. Warren, 282 Ga. App. 524, 639 S.E.2d 528 (2006) (purchaser's wetlands study and interest rate negotiation with bank not required by contract); Moorman v. Blackstock, Inc., 276 Va. 64, 661 S.E.2d 404 (2008) (purchaser's engineering work on land not required by contract).

[82]   A very small payment may be insufficient. See Boesiger v. Freer, 85 Idaho 551, 381 P.2d 802 (1963).

[83]   See, e.g., Beverly Enterprises, Inc. v. Fredonia Haven, Inc., 825 F.2d 374 (11th Cir. 1987) ("possession must be clear and definite" so that it would reasonably appear to an outsider that the alleged contract existed); Rebel Van Lines v. City of Compton, 663 F.Supp. 786 (C.D.Cal. 1987) (storage of material on subject land insufficient to meet "open and notorious possession" as required by California law). If the purchaser was already in possession under a lease or other arrangement when the contract of sale was formed, the court may refuse to find the "possession" element satisfied; see United States v. 29.16 Acres of Land, 496 F.Supp. 924 (E.D.Pa. 1980); Rentz v. Grant, 934 So. 2d 368 (Ala. 2006); Rose v. Cain, 247 Ga. App. 481, 544 S.E.2d 453 (2001); Yarto v. Gilliland, 287 S.W.3d 83 (Tex. App. 2009).

[84]   Not all improvements will satisfy the demands of part performance. See Bradshaw v. Ewing, 297 S.C. 242, 376 S.E.2d 264 (1989) (improvements directed by a third party are irrelevant to this requirement; improvements by the party to the alleged contract must be permanent or substantially increase the value of the land); Rebel Van Lines v. City of Compton, 663 F.Supp. 786 (C.D.Cal. 1987) (improvements required by a local zoning ordinance are merely performance of pre-existing legal duty and are insufficient to meet requirement).

[85]   Payment alone not enough; see In re Nation's Capital Child and Family Development, Inc., 457 B.R. 142 (2011); Sutton v. Warner, 12 Cal.App.4th 415, 15 Cal. Rptr.2d 632 (Cal.Ct.App. 1993); Cain v. Cross, 293 Ill.App.3d 255, 227 Ill.Dec. 659, 687 N.E.2d 1141 (Ill.Ct.App. 1997); Piazza v. Combs, 226 S.W.3d 211 (Mo. Ct. App. 2007); Tikvah Realty, LLC v. Schwartz, 43 A.D.3d 909, 841 N.Y.S.2d 616 (2007); Bradshaw v. Ewing, 297 S.C. 242, 376 S.E.2d 264 (1989) Messer v. Runion, 210 W. Va. 102, 556 S.E.2d 69 (2001); Firth v. Lu, 103 Wash. App. 267, 12 P.3d 618 (2000). Iowa Code Ann. § 622.33 recognizes partial payment or the taking of possession by the purchaser standing alone as sufficient; see Peterson v. Petersen, 355 N.W.2d 26 (Iowa 1984). Also

will treat the taking of possession[86] or the making of substantial improvements[87] as sufficient standing alone. More commonly, a combination of payment plus one of the other factors must be shown,[88] and a few jurisdictions require all three.[89] Four states— Kentucky, Mississippi, North Carolina, and Tennessee—do not recognize the part performance doctrine at all.[90]

The Second Restatement of Contracts takes the view that the acts of reliance are not limited to the traditional three (payment, possession, and improvements), but may encompass other acts of reliance by either party if "injustice can be avoided only by specific enforcement" of the contract.[91] This broadening of the part performance concept seems highly desirable, and a number of courts (though not all) have been eager to adopt it.[92]

---

recognizing payment alone, see Greene v. Scott, 3 Conn. App. 34, 484 A.2d 474 (1984); Greene v. McLeod, 156 N.H. 724, 942 A.2d 1254 (2008) (payment of price plus 30 years of taxes was sufficient); Spears v. Warr, 2002 Utah 24, 44 P.3d 742 (2002).

[86]   See, e.g., In re Paro, 362 B.R. 419 (Bankr. E.D. Ark. 2007); Saints in Christ Temple of Holy Ghost v. Fowler, 448 So.2d 1158 (Fla. App. 1984); Harrison v. Oates, 234 Ark. 259, 351 S.W.2d 431 (1961); Sullivan v. Porter, 2004 Me. 134, 861 A.2d 625 (2004) (payment plus possession and repairs). Chaffee and Re, Cases and Materials on Equity 609 (4th ed. 1958), lists 14 states as accepting possession alone. Compare Pate v. Billy Boyd Realty Constr., Inc. 699 So.2d 186 (Ala.Civ.App. 1997) (proof of possession is essential) with Johnson Farms v. McEnroe, 586 N.W.2d 920 (N.D. 1997) (possession is not essential).

[87]   Strandberg v. Lawrence, 216 N.Y.S.2d 973 (1961). Pure improvement cases are rare, since the improver generally goes into possession as well. There is a large body of cases finding possession plus improvements sufficient. See Montoya v. New Mexico Human Services Dept., 108 N.M. 263, 771 P.2d 196 (1989); Crossroads Church of Prior Lake MN v. Cty. of Dakota, 800 N.W.2d 608 (Minn. 2011) (possession plus either payment or improvements sufficient).

[88]   Recognizing part payment plus possession, see Beverly Enterprises, Inc. v. Fredonia Haven, Inc., 825 F.2d 374 (11th Cir. 1987); Gartman v. Hill, 874 So. 2d 555 (Ala. Civ. App. 2003); Forsberg v. Day, 127 Ariz. 308, 620 P.2d 223 (App. 1980); Johnston v. Curtis, 70 Ark. App. 195, 16 S.W.3d 283 (2000). The first Restatement of Contracts took the view that possession plus either improvements or part payment would be sufficient; Restatement, Contracts § 197. See also Hoke v. Neyada, Inc., 161 Idaho 450, 387 P.3d 118 (2016) (possession plus improvements are "most important"); Wood v. Anderson, 2017 Mt. 180, 399 P.3d 304 (2017) (payment plus surveying of land); Powers v. Hastings, 93 Wn.2d 709, 612 P.2d 371 (1980) (any two of the three elements sufficient); 20 Suffolk U.L.Rev. 400 (1986) (Rhode Island survey; possession plus improvements required).

[89]   See, e.g., United States v. Capital Tax Corp., 545 F.3d 525 (7th Cir. 2008) (Illinois law). Cases in which all three requirements were met include Moraitis v. Galluzzo, 487 So.2d 1151 (Fla.App. 1986), appeal after remand 511 So.2d 427 (1987); Bear v. Troyer, 2016 Ohio 3363, 2016 WL 3219711 (2016) (unpublished); Zaragoza v. Jessen, 511 S.W.3d 816 (Tex. App. 2016); Losh Family, LLC v. Kertsman, 155 Wash.App. 458, 228 P.3d 793 (2010). Some Washington authority suggests that any two of the three factors will suffice; see Berg v. Ting, 125 Wash. 2d 544, 886 P.2d 564 (1995). Cf. Pickett v. Keene, 47 S.W.3d 67 (Tex. App. 2001) (possession is not always strictly required).

[90]   See Chaffee and Re, note 86 supra; Williams v. Mason, 556 So.2d 1045 (Miss. 1990) (contract not enforced despite proof that it existed and compliance with it by promisee for 20 years); Miller v. Russell, 217 N.C. App. 431, 720 S.E.2d 760 (2011). Even in those states not recognizing part performance as such, sufficient proof of a representation and reliance may allow a party to employ the contract, at least defensively, under an estoppel theory. See, e.g., Logan v. Estate of Cannon, 2016 WL 5344526, at *10 (Tenn. Ct. App. 2016) (unpublished); Note, 10 Mem.St. U.L.Rev. 107 (1979).

[91]   See Restatement (Second) of Contracts § 129 (1981); Annot., Promissory Estoppel as Basis for Avoidance of Statute of Frauds, 56 A.L.R.3d 1037 (1974). Cases adopting the broader view under Restatement § 129 but finding acts of reliance insufficient include Spring Hill Developers, Inc. v. Arthur, 879 N.E.2d 1095 (Ind. Ct. App. 2008); Ayalla v. Southridge Presbyterian Church, 37 Kan. App. 2d 312, 152 P.3d 670 (2007); Schmidt v. White, 43 S.W.3d 871 (Mo. Ct. App. 2001). See also Young v. Moore, 663 P.2d 78 (Utah 1983) (part performance not "confined to a fixed, inflexible formula").

[92]   Typical "other acts" by purchasers include investing in a business on the property, installing fixtures, arranging for financing, and selling other real estate. Typical "other acts" by sellers include making modifications to suit the new purchaser, evicting tenants, and arranging to buy other real estate. See Rutt v. Roche, 138 Conn. 605, 87 A.2d 805 (1952); Hernandez v. Carnes, 290 Ga. App. 730, 659 S.E.2d 925 (2008) (purchaser hired lawyer to carry out modification of contract); Hickey v. Green, 14 Mass.App.Ct. 671, 442

If the part performance doctrine is satisfied, the result is that the contract will be enforced in equity (normally by means of a decree of specific performance) notwithstanding the lack of a written memorandum. The courts often say that part performance "takes the contract out of the statute of frauds," but such terminology is a bit misleading; technically, the only contracts which are "out of" the statute are those not covered by its terms in the first place because, for example, they do not involve agreements to buy and sell real estate. It is more accurate to characterize the part performance doctrine simply as an exception to the statute. It is not easy to explain why the exception should operate only in equity and not at law, although this is usually said to be the case.[93] The reason is more historical than logical, and is related to the greater flexibility traditionally exercised by courts of equity, and perhaps to the notion, now discredited in its overt form, that the statute of frauds was not intended to apply to equitable proceedings in the first place.[94] In terms of modern policy, there appears to be no reason to deny the legal remedy of damages once part performance is shown,[95] but only a few cases can be found that grant it.[96]

Two main rationales for the doctrine of part performance are asserted by the courts; they correspond to the two reasons for judicial uneasiness with the statute of frauds mentioned at the beginning of this section. The first might be termed the evidentiary theory. Courts that follow it regard the statute's function as evidentiary in nature. If a writing had been made, it would be excellent evidence that a contract existed, but it is not the only satisfactory evidence. These courts treat acts of part performance as a substitute for the written evidence, and deem them to justify enforcement of the contract, at least in equity. Because they are concerned with the potential unreliability of such unwritten evidence, they often say that the part performance must be "unequivocally referable" to the contract—that is, that the acts cannot be explainable on any other plausible ground.[97]

N.E.2d 37 (1982); Piazza v. Combs, 226 S.W.3d 211 (Mo. Ct. App. 2007); Mazza v. Scoleri, 304 N.J.Super. 555, 701 A.2d 723 (N.J.Super.A.D. 1997); Capital Mortg. Holding v. Hahn, 101 Nev. 314, 705 P.2d 126 (1985); Jacobson v. Gulbransen, 2001 S.D. 33, 623 N.W.2d 84 (2001); Gillespie v. Dunlap, 125 Wis.2d 461, 373 N.W.2d 61 (App. 1985), review denied 126 Wis.2d 520, 378 N.W.2d 293 (1985). Compare Moorman v. Blackstock, Inc., 276 Va. 64, 661 S.E.2d 404 (2008), refusing to consider purchaser's engineering work because it was not part of performance of the contract of sale, with Harley v. Indian Spring Land Co., 123 Conn. App. 800, 827, 3 A.3d 992, 1011 (2010) (purchaser's expenditures on design of house and submission of plans to review committee were sufficient part performance). See also Zier v. Lewis, 352 Mont. 76, 218 P.3d 465 (2009) (purchaser's sale of other property was not sufficient part performance); Lovett v. Lovett, 283 S.W.3d 391 (Tex. App. 2008) ("improvement" element may be substituted by other acts of reliance).

[93] See Lance J. Marchiafava, Inc. v. Haft, 777 F.2d 942 (4th Cir.1985) (Virginia law); In re Peter Peter Cottontail, LLC, 498 B.R. 242 (Bkrtcy. D. Ariz. 2013); Robert Phillips v. Britton, 162 Ill. App.3d 774, 114 Ill.Dec. 537, 516 N.E.2d 692 (1987); Zito v. County of Suffolk, 106 A.D.3d 814, 964 N.Y.S.2d 644 (2013); Harmon & Bore, Inc. v. Jenkins, 282 S.C. 189, 318 S.E.2d 371 (S.C. Ct. of App. 1984); Winters v. Alanco, Inc., 435 So.2d 326 (Fla.App.1983); Annot., 59 A.L.R. 1305 (1929).

[94] See Costigan, Interpretation of the Statute of Frauds, 14 Ill.L.Rev. 1 (1919); cf. Pound, Progress of the Law, 33 Harv.L.Rev. 936 (1920).

[95] See, e.g., Wolfe v. Wallingford Bank & Trust Co., 122 Conn. 507, 191 A. 88 (1937), granting damages.

[96] Among them are Miller v. McCamish, 78 Wn.2d 821, 479 P.2d 919 (1971); White v. McKnight, 146 S.C. 59, 143 S.E. 552, 59 A.L.R. 1297 (1928). By contrast, the Restatement (Second) of Contracts limits its version of part performance (expanded in other respects) to decrees of specific performance; Restatement (Second) of Contracts § 129 (1981).

[97] The classic case is Burns v. McCormick, 233 N.Y. 230, 135 N.E. 273 (1922). More recent holdings to the same effect include In re Nation's Capital Child and Family Development, Inc., 457 B.R. 142 (Bkrtcy. 2011); Wolske Brothers, Inc. v. Hudspeth Sawmill Co., 116 Idaho 714, 779 P.2d 28 (1989); Blackwell v. Mahmood, 120 Conn.App. 690, 992 A.2d 1219 (2010); Matthews v. Matthews, 215 Neb. 744, 341 N.W.2d 584 (1983); Buettner v. Nostdahl, 204 N.W.2d 187 (N.D. 1973); Burgdorf v. Weston, 259 Or.App. 755, 316 P.3d 303 (2013);

Under this theory, little or no attention is paid to the harshness to the plaintiff of refusal to enforce the contract. The emphasis is on whether the acts are adequate evidence that a contract existed. Unfortunately, the "unequivocal referability" test is far too stringent to be practical. It is almost inconceivable that a case can arise in which no other explanation than a contract of sale can be given for a party's payment, possession, and improvements to real estate. For example, the acts might as well be motivated by a landlord-tenant relationship as by a sale in most cases.[98] Since the test is impractical, many courts simply do not apply it literally, and they often assert that the acts are explainable only by a contract of sale when an objective observer could easily think of other explanations.[99] Hence the test is imprecise in operation and subject to considerable manipulation. Realistically, the question asked by most courts following the evidentiary theory is a fairly lenient one: if the acts are not *unequivocally* referable, do they nonetheless point with reasonable clarity to the presence of a contract?[100]

The other main theoretical explanation for the part performance doctrine is much like equitable estoppel. Indeed, some courts call it that (or sometimes, "promissory estoppel"), while others show a wondrous ability to write entire opinions adopting the estoppel concept without using that term. Like estoppel in other contexts, it proceeds from the view that when a plaintiff has reasonably relied to his or her substantial detriment on the defendant's representations (here, that there is a binding contract), the defendant ought not to be permitted to disaffirm those representations even if some

---

Thomas v. Miller, 500 S.W.3d 601 (Tex. Ct. App. 2016). See also Merchants National Bank v. Steiner, 404 So.2d 14 (Ala.1981) ("indisputably related to the contract"). Many jurisdictions use somewhat weaker language, as that the acts of part performance must be "clear and convincing evidence" of a contract. See Smith v. Smith, 466 So.2d 922 (Ala. 1985); Greene v. Scott, 3 Conn.App. 34, 484 A.2d 474 (1984); Gegg v. Kiefer, 655 S.W.2d 834 (Mo.App. 1983).

The "unequivocal referability" element often is found lacking, with the result that the contract is not enforced. See Herrera v. Herrera, 126 N.M. 705, 974 P.2d 675 (N.M.App. 1999); Klein v. Sletto, 2017 N.D. 26, 889 N.W.2d 918 (2017); In re Estate of Conkle, 982 S.W.2d 312 (Mo.App. 1998); Hall v. Hall, 222 Cal.App.3d 578, 271 Cal.Rptr. 773 (1990); Mann v. White Marsh Properties, Inc., 321 Md. 111, 581 A.2d 819 (1990); Nat'l Prop. Holdings, L.P. v. Westergren, 453 S.W.3d 419 (Tex. 2015) (payment was made in settlement of suit for breach of contract, and hence not pursuant to performance of contract).

[98] New York courts, which take "unequivocal referability" quite seriously, have frequently found that a landlord-tenant relationship could explain the purchaser's acts; see, e.g., Bohensky v. 3912 NU Rainspring, LLC, 148 A.D.3d 666, 48 N.Y.S.3d 481 (N.Y. App. Div. 2017); McCormick v. Bechtol, 68 A.D.3d 1376, 891 N.Y.S.2d 188 (2009); Congdon v. Everett, 63 A.D.3d 1541, 879 N.Y.S.2d 873 (2009); Lebowitz v. Mingus, 100 A.D.2d 816, 474 N.Y.S.2d 748 (1984); Wilson v. La Van, 22 N.Y.2d 131, 291 N.Y.S.2d 344, 238 N.E.2d 738 (1968). The New York view is perhaps the most rigid in the nation on this point, and makes a purchaser's efforts to show part performance exceedingly difficult. See also Coleman v. Dillman, 624 P.2d 713 (Utah 1981). Purchasers have a much easier time in some other states; see Collins v. Morris, 122 Md.App. 764, 716 A.2d 384 (Md.Ct.App.1998); Tzitzon Realty Co. v. Mustonen, 352 Mass. 648, 227 N.E.2d 493 (1967); Burgdorf v. Weston, 259 Or.App. 755, 316 P.3d 303 (2013).

[99] See, e.g., Shaughnessy v. Eidsmo, 222 Minn. 141, 23 N.W.2d 362 (1946). The formal test purports to consider *possible* rather than *actual* explanations of the acts of the putative purchaser, but cases often seem to turn on whether there is any real evidence of an alternate explanation; if there is none, the courts are much more willing to find that the acts are "unequivocally referable" to a sale contract. See, e.g., Ward v. Ladner, 322 S.W.3d 692, 701 (Tex. App. 2010).

[100] See Johnson Farms v. McEnroe, 568 N.W.2d 920 (N.D. 1997) (the test is whether the acts are "consistent only with the existence of the alleged oral contract"); Hinkle v. Winey, 126 Idaho 993, 895 P.2d 594 (Id.Ct.App.1995) (payments were equally consistent with lease or purchase contract; part performance argument rejected); Perkins v. Owens, 721 N.E.2d 289 (Ind. Ct. App. 1999) (no unequivocal referability, where purchasers' acts on the land began before contract was formed); Beaver v. Brumlow, 148 N.M. 172, 231 P.3d 628 (2010) (the test is whether an outsider would "naturally and reasonably conclude that the contract alleged actually exists").

technical requirement for their enforcement (here, a writing) is unmet.[101] This approach is sometimes termed the "fraud" theory, with the courts observing that they should not allow the use of the statute of frauds to perpetrate a fraud.[102] But the word fraud is an unfortunate misnomer here, for fraud usually connotes a representation made by one who presently intends not to fulfill it, while under part performance most courts regard it as irrelevant whether the defendant *intended* to disaffirm the oral contract at the time it was formed.[103] Almost equally misleading is the tendency of the courts to say that this theory depends on a showing that the plaintiff would suffer "irreparable injury" if the contract were not specifically enforced.[104] Such a statement is too strong, for no rigorous inquiry is generally made into the reparability of the injury. Still, it correctly suggests that the courts are concerned with the magnitude of the harm that unenforceability would inflict on the plaintiff, and that a slight or modest hardship will not suffice.[105]

In principle, a court following the evidentiary theory of part performance would be unconcerned with the gravity of the hardship to the plaintiff, while a jurisdiction which adopted the estoppel approach would have little interest in whether the acts were "unequivocally referable" to a contract. In practice, however, it is not unusual for courts to discuss both theories or implement both tests in the same opinion[106] or to switch between them in successive opinions.[107] No criticism of a combined approach is intended,

---

[101] See, e.g., Kolkman v. Roth, 656 N.W.2d 148 (Iowa 2003); Swartzfager v. Saul, 213 So. 3d 55 (Miss. 2017). Note that estoppel here is employed as a substitute for a writing, and hence is distinguishable from the "promissory estoppel" of Restatement (Second) of Contracts § 90, which serves as a substitute for consideration. Of course, the same acts might suffice for both purposes. The version of estoppel applicable to part performance cases is often a narrow one, with some courts recognizing only three types of detrimental reliance—payment, taking of possession, and making of improvements.

[102] See Darby v. Johnson, 477 So.2d 322 (Ala. 1985) (court would enforce oral contract despite insufficient part performance, in the form of payment and possession, if there was actual fraud in the sense of defendant's intent from the outset not to perform the contract); Fannin v. Cratty, 331 Pa.Super. 326, 480 A.2d 1056 (1984) (innocent party may recover loss of bargain damages on oral contract if actual fraud is shown); Shaughnessy v. Eidsmo, 222 Minn. 141, 23 N.W.2d 362 (1946).

[103] See, e.g., Wood v. Anderson, 2017 Mt. 180, 399 P.3d 304 (2017); Sullivan v. Porter, 2004 Me. 134, 861 A.2d 625 (2004) (finding vendor's silence in the face of purchaser's acts of part performance to be a misrepresentation); Kaslauskas v. Emmert, 248 Or. App. 555, 275 P.3d 171 (2012) ("avoidance of unjust enrichment or relief from fraud"). Contra, see Moorman v. Blackstock, Inc., 276 Va. 64, 661 S.E.2d 404 (2008), refusing to find estoppel because the defendant sellers made no false statement or concealment. Note that if an actual fraud grows out of an oral contract, the court may provide a remedy entirely independently of the part performance doctrine. See Davis v. Barnfield, 833 So. 2d 58 (Ala. Civ. App. 2002); § 10.1 n. 11 supra.

[104] Id.; see Winters v. Alanco, Inc., 435 So.2d 326 (Fla. Ct. App.1983) (specific performance not granted where plaintiff's acts are "capable of adequate pecuniary measurement and compensation"); In re Deppe, 215 B.R. 743 (Bkrtcy. D. Minn. 1997) (specific performance granted if plaintiff provided personal services "not subject to pecuniary measure"); 3 Am.L.Prop. § 11.10 (1952).

[105] See, e.g., Gabriele v. Brino, 85 Conn.App. 503, 858 A.2d 273 (2004) (purchaser's application for a bank loan was insufficient reliance); Church Yard Commons Ltd. P'ship v. Podmajersky, Inc., 2017 Ill. App. 161152, 76 N.E.3d 96 (2017) (purchaser had already been fully compensated for his acts of reliance in managing property); O'Farrill Avila v. Gonzalez, 974 S.W.2d 237 (Tex.Ct.App. 1998); Gegg v. Kiefer, 655 S.W.2d 834 (Mo.App. 1983). Some cases, especially in Massachusetts, emphasize the question whether the plaintiff could be adequately compensated by money, i.e., by restitution; if that is possible, no decree of specific performance is available. See, e.g., Hazleton v. Lewis, 267 Mass. 533, 166 N.E. 876 (1929). The amount of the plaintiff's expenditure on improvements is commonly a decisive factor in such cases.

[106] See, e.g., Owens v. M.E. Schepp Ltd. Partnership, 216 Ariz. 273, 165 P.3d 674 (2007) (following estoppel theory but requiring unequivocal referability); Blackwell v. Mahmood, 120 Conn.App. 690, 992 A.2d 1219 (2010); In re Guardianship of Huesman, 354 N.W.2d 860 (Minn.App. 1984), appeal after remand 381 N.W.2d 73 (1986); Martin v. Scholl, 678 P.2d 274 (Utah 1983); H. Pearce Real Estate Co., Inc. v. Kaiser, 176 Conn. 442, 408 A.2d 230 (1979).

[107] See, e.g., the Minnesota case development described in Shaughnessy v. Eidsmo, 222 Minn. 141, 23 N.W.2d 362 (1946).

for there may be considerable sense in demanding both strong referability to a contract and a showing of serious harm to the plaintiff.

Another difference in principle might be expected to flow from the theory selected by the court. Since the traditional acts of part performance (payment, possession, and improvements) are by definition acts of the purchaser, one might expect only purchasers to be permitted to take advantage of them in jurisdictions which follow the estoppel approach, since only purchasers could engage in the relevant acts of reliance.[108] On the other hand, in states that use the evidentiary theory, either party should logically be allowed to assert part performance, since once the evidence of the contract's existence is deemed acceptable, both parties should be able to employ it. This distinction is indeed followed in some cases.[109]

§ 10.3 REMEDIES FOR CONTRACT BREACH—DAMAGES

Since parties often fail to fully perform their obligations under contracts of sale, it is important to understand the range of remedies available to the nonbreaching party. They are discussed in this and the succeeding sections. The main remedy at law is, of course, damages, and the most-used equitable remedy is specific performance. Restitution may be available as an alternative equitable remedy. Each of these remedies is generally available to both vendors and purchasers. Likewise, either party may assert a lien on the land, either as an aid to recovery of the price owed (for the vendor) or restitution of payments made (for the purchaser). The vendor may also have a self-help "remedy" which has no analogue favoring the purchaser: "forfeiture" or retention of payments received, without any corresponding obligation to convey the land.

We do not deal with all possible remedies here. The material in this chapter discusses only remedies for contract breach. Such other legal wrongs as fraud, mistake, concealment, and the like are beyond our scope.[110] Moreover, once the contract has been performed by the vendor's delivery of the deed, breaches by the vendor of contract terms relating to the property's title generally cannot be the subject of an action on the contract, and the purchaser's suit must instead be based on the deed's covenants of title, if any; this topic is discussed later in this book.[111]

We exclude here remedies for breach of long-term installment contracts, which are in reality security instruments and are analogous to mortgages. In such cases, the courts sometimes borrow from the short-term marketing-type contract concepts discussed here,

---

[108] In re Winstar Commc'ns, Inc., 348 B.R. 234, 270 (Bankr. D. Del. 2005) (only the party doing acts of reliance may argue for part performance), aff'd in part, modified in part, 554 F.3d 382 (3d Cir. 2009); St. Germain v. St. Germain, 135 Conn. App. 329, 41 A.3d 1126 (2012) (vendor could assert part performance, where court was willing to consider vendor's acts of reliance).

[109] Compare Pearson v. Gardner, 202 Mich. 360, 168 N.W. 485 (1918) (evidentiary theory; vendor may assert) with Palumbo v. James, 266 Mass. 1, 164 N.E. 466 (1929) (estoppel theory; vendor may not assert). See also Chotkowski v. Downey, 2015 WL 4775968 (Conn. Super. Ct. 2015) (landlord could enforce oral lease based on tenant's acts of part performance). But it is perhaps equally common for courts to permit the vendor to employ the doctrine without any serious discussion of the theory being used; see, e.g., Hayes v. Hartelius, 215 Mont. 391, 697 P.2d 1349 (1985) (vendor may assert part performance, where he gave up possession of property to purchasers and withheld it from market for four years); Wiggins v. White, 157 Ga.App. 49, 276 S.E.2d 104 (1981).

[110] See, e.g., Dobbs, Hayden, and Bublick, Torts and Compensation, Personal Accountability and Social Responsibility for Injury, ch. 34 (8th ed. 2017). The same facts might give rise to both breach of contract and fraud liability. See, e.g., Terry v. Panek, 631 P.2d 896 (Utah 1981) (false representation in contract that property had two wells.)

[111] The contract provisions as to title are said to be "merged into the deed." See § 10.12 at note 474 infra.

but they are best treated separately.[112] Even with these exclusions, the discussion of remedies in this section is relatively brief. For a treatment in greater depth, the reader is referred to any of the several excellent treatises on remedies.[113]

Finally, we note that the recovery of damages for contract breach may be limited or barred by language in the contract itself. In general, clauses limiting or prohibiting particular remedies are enforceable.[114] However, if the limitation on the purchaser's remedies is so broad that the only remaining remedy is a return of the purchaser's earnest money, it is arguable that the vendor's duties are illusory and hence that the contract is unenforceable.[115]

Damages. The standard measure of general "loss-of-bargain" (or "expectation") damages for a total breach is the difference between the agreed contract price and the market value of the land on the date of breach.[116] Thus, if the parties contracted for a $100,000 price and the land's value had risen to $120,000 when the breach occurred, the purchaser could recover $20,000 if the vendor breached, while the vendor could recover no general damages if the purchaser breached. Conversely, if the value of the land had declined to $80,000, the vendor could recover $20,000 and the purchaser nothing. In a rough sense, general damages represent the non-breaching party's lost profit on the transaction. The measure is somewhat artificial, since no account is taken of further market fluctuations which might occur after the breach, which is typically deemed to occur on the date set for delivery of the deed in an "earnest money" type contract.[117] Thus

---

[112] Nelson, Whitman, Burkhart & Freyermuth, Real Estate Finance Law, §§ 3.25–3.32 (6th ed. 2014); Lee, Remedies for Breach of the Installment Land Contract, 19 U.Miami L.Rev. 550 (1965).

[113] E.g., Dobbs and Roberts, Remedies, Damages, Equity, Restitution (3d ed. 2018); Ames, Chafee, and Re, Remedies (2012); Weaver, Shoben, and Kelly, Principles of Remedies Law (3d ed. 2016).

[114] Stein v. Paradigm Mirasol, LLC, 586 F.3d 849 (11th Cir. 2009) (Florida law); Seybold v. Nicholson USA Properties, LTD., 890 So. 2d 351, 353 (Fla. Dist. Ct. App. 2004) (prohibition of recovery of damages by purchaser did not bar damages for vendor's failure to provide promised landscaping); Frostar Corp. v. Malloy, 63 Mass. App. Ct. 96, 823 N.E.2d 417 (2005); Arker Companies v. State Urban Dev. Corp., 47 A.D.3d 739, 849 N.Y.S.2d 660 (2008); Cameron Gen. Contractors, Inc. v. Kingston Pike, LLC, 370 S.W.3d 341 (Tenn. Ct. App. 2011) (upholding prohibition on recovery of damages). New York holds that, even if the contract purports to bar both damages and specific performance, a purchaser may have specific performance if the vendor has acted in bad faith; see Naso v. Haque, 289 A.D.2d 309, 734 N.Y.S.2d 214 (2001).

[115] Ocean Dunes of Hutchinson Island Dev. Corp. v. Colangelo, 463 So.2d 437 (Fla. Dist. Ct. App. 1985).

[116] The cases are legion. See, e.g., Radetic v. Murphy, 71 So. 3d 642 (Ala. 2011) (breach by purchaser); Macal v. Stinson, 468 N.W.2d 34 (Iowa 1991) (breach by purchaser); Dorsett v. Johnson, 786 So. 2d 897 (La. Ct. App. 2001) (breach by purchaser); Ours v. City of Rolla, 14 S.W.3d 627 (Mo. Ct. App. 2000); White v. Farrell, 20 N.Y.3d 487, 987 N.E.2d 244 (2013) (breach by purchaser; declining to depart from common-law rule); Hickey v. Griggs, 106 N.M. 27, 738 P.2d 899 (1987) (breach by vendor); Landers v. Biwer, 2006 N.D. 109, 714 N.W.2d 476 (2006) (breach by vendor; no damages awarded because land value was found to be less than contract price); Sorenson v. Connelly, 36 Colo.App. 168, 536 P.2d 328 (1975) (breach by purchaser). See also Nieto v. Kezy, 846 N.E.2d 327 (Ind. Ct. App. 2006) (purchaser provided no evidence of value at date of breach, and hence could recover no damages). Value is usually established by appraisal testimony; see, e.g., Manson v. Kejo Enterprises, LLC, 145 A.D.3d 994, 44 N.Y.S.3d 167 (N.Y. App. Div. 2016) (appraisal based on comparable sales approach); Friebe v. Supancheck, 98 Wn. App. 260; 992 P.2d 1014 (1999) (appraisal based on capitalization of income for rental property). See also Decision One Mortg. Co., LLC v. Victor Warren Properties, Inc., 304 Ga. App. 423, 696 S.E.2d 145 (2010) (where plaintiff fails to provide any evidence of fair market value, court will assume it is the same as contract price); Shirley's Realty, Inc. v. Hunt, 160 S.W.3d 804 (Mo. Ct. App. 2005) (where value and contract price are the same, vendor can recover only nominal damages for breach); Reese v. Wong, 93 Cal. App. 4th 51, 112 Cal. Rptr. 2d 669 (2001) (value as of time of trial is an incorrect standard).

[117] See 25 Williston on Contracts § 66:80 n.20 (4th ed. 2018 update); Vines v. Orchard Hills, Inc., 181 Conn. 501, 435 A.2d 1022 (1980); Royer v. Carter, 37 Cal.2d 544, 233 P.2d 539 (1951); Wolf v. Cohen, 379 F.2d 477 (D.C.Cir. 1967); Goldman v. Olmstead, 414 S.W.3d 346 (Tex. Ct. App. 2013) (denying recovery to vendor for expenditures on property after date of breach). Sometimes a later date, such as the date of trial, is used on the ground that the contract provided for no specific closing date (see Sullivan v. Esterle, 268 S.W.2d 919 (Ky. 1954)) or that the plaintiff originally sought specific performance and did not give up that claim in favor of

in the first illustration above, the purchaser in an inflating market may ultimately have to pay $130,000 for a comparable piece of real estate, but his or her damages will still be limited to $20,000.

However, further transactions after the breach are not necessarily irrelevant. If the vendor, following the purchaser's breach, soon resells the property in an arms-length transaction, the courts will often treat the resale price as strong evidence of the value at the date of breach.[118] Indeed, some cases go so far as to treat the two figures as identical.[119] No analogous argument can be made by an innocent purchaser whose vendor has breached, since it is literally impossible for the purchaser to buy an exactly identical piece of land. But if the purchaser has in fact already arranged an advantageous resale of the property by the time the vendor breaches, the resale price

---

damages until trial (see Cameron v. Benson, 295 Or. 98, 664 P.2d 412 (1983)); Dunning v. Alfred H. Mayer Co., 483 S.W.2d 423 (Mo.App. 1972)). If a party commits an anticipatory breach prior to the agreed closing date, the earlier date of breach will be used to fix damages; see Jenkins v. Brice, 231 Ga.App. 843, 499 S.E.2d 734 (Ga.App. 1998). The use of the closing date has been criticized on the ground that it may leave an innocent seller with the risk of declining land value between the date of breach and the date of a later disposition of the land; see Askari v. R & R Land Co., 179 Cal.App.3d 1101, 225 Cal.Rptr. 285 (1986), holding that if the purchaser breaches and the land thereafter declines in value, and the vendor is prevented from remarketing it during the period of decline by the purchaser's having clouded the title or refusing to relinquish possession, the vendor can recover damages in the amount of the decline; Note, 26 Okla.L.Rev. 277 (1973). The problem of further value declines after the scheduled closing or settlement date is also mitigated by the courts' common reliance on the ultimate resale price as evidence of value; see cases cited in the following footnote.

[118] Cases approving the use of resale price as evidence of value at the time of breach include Cedar Point Apartments, Ltd. v. Cedar Point Inv. Corp., 756 F.2d 629 (8th Cir. 1985) (resale six months later); Widener v. Ashkouti, 239 Ga. App. 530, 521 S.E.2d 215 (1999) (resale price is evidence of value if resale is relatively close to the date of breach); 1472 N. Milwaukee, Ltd. v. Feinerman, 2013 Ill. App. 121191, 996 N.E.2d 652 (2013) (resale 8 months later); Ner Tamid Congregation of N. Town v. Krivoruchko, 638 F.Supp.2d 913 (N.D. Ill. 2009) (offer to purchase 3 to 4 months later); Burson v. Simard, 424 Md. 318, 35 A.3d 1154 (2012) (resale price may be used if resale was "fairly made within a reasonable time after breach"); Williams v. Ubaldo, 670 A.2d 913 (Me. 1996) (resale prior to trial); Crabby's, Inc. v. Hamilton, 244 S.W.3d 209, 217 (Mo. Ct. App. 2008) (resale 11½ months after breach); 12 Baker Hill Rd., Inc. v. Miranti, 130 A.D.3d 1425, 14 N.Y.S.3d 787 (N.Y. App. Div. 2015) (resale price may be used as value at date of breach if time to resale is short and market is stable); Spalla v. Fransen, 188 Ohio App. 3d 658, 936 N.E.2d 552 (2010) (resale 1½ years later); Benya v. Gamble, 282 S.C. 624, 321 S.E.2d 57 (App. 1984), cert. dismissed 329 S.E.2d 768 (1985) (resale 18 months later); Piroschak v. Whelan, 2005 Wyo. 26, 106 P.3d 887 (Wyo. 2005). Contra, see Radetic v. Murphy, 71 So. 3d 642, 651 (Ala. 2011) (use of resale price 8 months after breach was improper); Kirkpatrick v. Strosberg, 385 Ill. App. 3d 119, 894 N.E.2d 781 (2008) (appraisal testimony based on value seven years after breach was improperly admitted); Teachout v. Wilson, 376 N.W.2d 460 (Minn.App. 1985) (sale 2½ years later was insufficient evidence of value at time of breach); Jones v. Lee, 971 P.2d 858 (N.M. App. 1998) (use of resale price 4 months later was improper); Chris v. Epstein, 113 N.C.App. 751, 440 S.E.2d 581 (N.C.App.1994) (resale price 1 year later was too remote to measure damages); Barry v. Jackson, 309 S.W.3d 135 (Tex. App. 2010) (resale 1 year later was not good measure of damages, where there was no evidence of lack of market fluctuations). See also Martinez v. River Park Place, LLC, 2012 Ill. App 111478, 980 N.E.2d 1207 (2012) (higher price which vendor demanded purchasers pay was not evidence of higher market value at time of vendor's breach); Dunn v. Venture Bldg. Grp., Inc., 283 Ga. App. 500, 642 S.E.2d 156 (2007) (offer to buy property 3 weeks prior to breach was not satisfactory evidence of value on date of breach). Of course, the vendor can recover damages whether he or she actually resells the property at all; see Gilmartin Bros. v. Kern, 916 S.W.2d 324 (Mo.App. 1995).

Evidence of subsequent *exchanges* for other realty may be inadmissible on the issue of value, since the value of the land taken in trade is fixed only by the agreement of the parties to the exchange; Jackson v. Raisor, 248 S.W.2d 905 (Ky. 1952). See generally Annot., 85 A.L.R.2d 116 (1962). But see Iowa-Mo Enterprises, Inc. v. Avren, 639 F.2d 443 (8th Cir. 1981).

[119] There is a modest trend toward legitimizing the use of the resale price to measure damages. See, e.g., Middelthon v. Crowder, 563 So.2d 94 (Fla.App. 1990); Theobald v. Nosser, 752 So. 2d 1036 (Miss. 1999); Cohen v. Kranz, 15 A.D.2d 938, 226 N.Y.S.2d 509 (1962), affirmed 12 N.Y.2d 242, 238 N.Y.S.2d 928, 189 N.E.2d 473 (1963); Kuhn v. Spatial Design, Inc., 245 N.J.Super. 378, 585 A.2d 967 (App.Div. 1991), discussed in Gerald Korngold, Seller's Damages from a Defaulting Buyer of Realty: The Influence of the Uniform Land Transactions Act on the Courts, 20 Nova L.Rev. 1069 (1996); Spurgeon v. Drumheller, 174 Cal.App.3d 659, 220 Cal.Rptr. 195 (1985) (if vendor in fact resells property before trial for more than contract price, he cannot recover loss of bargain damages).

may well be considered strong evidence of value.[120] On the other hand, proof that the purchaser's lost value is less than would be indicated by the market value at breach (for example, because she or he had contracted to resell at a below-market price or intended to hold the property for a long term, and the market subsequently declined in fact) will convince at least a minority of courts to award the purchaser less than full loss-of-bargain damages. This result is based on the notion that damages should merely compensate for the plaintiff's actual loss, a view that has been severely criticized.[121]

In one situation—where the vendor who has acted in good faith but cannot convey satisfactory title[122]—the courts divide sharply as to whether the purchaser can recover loss-of-bargain damages. Nearly half of the cases limit the purchaser on these facts to a restitutionary remedy—return of earnest money or other payments made with interest, plus such incidental expenses as abstract, title examination, and loan application costs.[123] Under this view, the vendor will be liable for loss of bargain only if acting in bad faith, as by intentionally impairing his or her own title,[124] selling the property to a third

---

[120] See George E. Shepard, Jr., Inc. v. Kim, Inc., 52 N.C.App. 700, 279 S.E.2d 858 (1981), review denied 304 N.C. 392, 285 S.E.2d 831 (1981).

[121] Simon & Novack, Limiting the Buyer's Market Damages to Lost Profits: A Challenge to the Enforceability of Market Contracts, 92 Harv.L.Rev. 1395 (1979). It is well established that the purchaser cannot recover more than loss-of-bargain damages by showing that he or she had an unusually advantageous resale opportunity, unless this fact was within the contemplation of the vendor when the contract was made. See Wolf v. Cohen, 379 F.2d 477 (D.C.Cir. 1967); Annot., 11 A.L.R.3d 719 (1967). But see Foster v. Bartolomeo 581 N.E.2d 1033, 31 Mass.App.Ct. 592 (1991) (where land was being purchased for subdivision and development, measure of damages suffered by purchaser was lost development profits, rather than loss of bargain).

[122] Ordinarily "satisfactory" means marketable title, but the parties may fix the quality of title the purchaser must accept by contract language. See § 10.12 infra. The definition of "good faith" is open to debate. The Kentucky court, for example, held that good faith did not exist where the vendor knew that an interest in the land was held by a third party, even though he reasonably expected that party to cooperate in signing a deed; Raisor v. Jackson, 311 Ky. 803, 225 S.W.2d 657 (1949); Gassner v. Lockett, 101 So. 2d 33 (Fla. 1958) ("where the vendor had no title but acting on the supposition that he might acquire title," he is liable for loss-of-bargain damages).

[123] E.g., In re Standard Jury Instructions—Contract & Bus. Cases, 116 So. 3d 284, 338 (Fla. 2013), In re Shelbyville Rd. Shoppes, LLC, 775 F.3d 789, 797 (6th Cir. 2015) (Kentucky law); Large v. Gregory, 417 N.E.2d 1160 (Ind. Ct. App. 1981) (Indiana rule is uncertain); Walch v. Crandall, 164 Mich. App. 181, 416 N.W.2d 375 (1987); Wolofsky v. Behrman, 454 So.2d 614 (Fla.App. 1984); Hoang v. Hewitt Ave. Assocs., LLC, 177 Md. App. 562, 596, 936 A.2d 915, 935 n.7 (2007); Long v. Brown, 593 S.W.2d 371 (Tex.Civ. App. 1979); Eurovision 426 Dev., LLC v. 26–01 Astoria Dev., LLC, 80 A.D.3d 656, 915 N.Y.S.2d 288 (2011); Khanjani v. Schreiber, 104 A.D.3d 1181, 960 N.Y.S.2d 771 (2013) (purchaser may not recover for loss of bargain if vendor has disclosed his title is deficient); Seidlek v. Bradley, 293 Pa. 379, 142 A. 914, 68 A.L.R. 134 (1928). Some formulations of the rule extend it to nontitle-related breaches by a good faith vendor; see Charles County Broadcasting Co., Inc. v. Meares, 270 Md. 321, 311 A.2d 27 (1973); Shepherd v. Davis, 265 Va. 108, 574 S.E.2d 514 (2003). Statutes adopting the rule are found in Montana, South Dakota, and Oklahoma. West's Ann.Cal.Civ.Code § 3306 was amended in 1983 to permit the purchaser to recover loss of bargain damages whether the vendor's breach was in good or bad faith. See Hartley, New Remedies for Seller's Breach of a Contract to Convey Real Property, 2 Cal.Real Prop.J. 22 (Fall 1984). See also Burgess v. Arita, 5 Hawaii App. 581, 704 P.2d 930 (1985) granting loss of bargain damages irrespective of the vendor's good faith.

Even in a jurisdiction that does not restrict the purchaser's recovery of loss-of-bargain damages, the parties may do so by their agreement. The New York courts have held that this sort of clause is effective only if the vendor has acted in good faith; see Progressive Solar Concepts, Inc. v. Gabes, 161 A.D.2d 752, 556 N.Y.S.2d 105 (1990).

[124] Hupp v. George R. Rembold Bldg. Co., 279 Md. 597, 369 A.2d 1048 (1977). For more elaborate discussion and examples of bad faith on the part of the vendor, see Key v. Alexander, 91 Fla. 975, 108 So. 883 (1926); Williams v. Snider, 190 Va. 226, 56 S.E.2d 63 (1949).

party,[125] knowingly contracting to convey a better title than he or she had,[126] refusing to cure a readily curable title defect, or simply refusing to convey.[127] In effect, this approach makes the contract's provisions regarding title into conditions rather than covenants.[128] No satisfactory justification for limiting a good-faith vendor's liability in this fashion can be stated. The rule originated in the 1776 English case of Flureau v. Thornhill,[129] and may have stemmed from the notion that English land titles of that day were so uncertain that it was unreasonable to subject a vendor to substantial liability for the title's failure. Such an explanation should have little credibility in modern America, where a vendor generally knows the state of the title or can ascertain it with little expense or difficulty.

The rule limiting the purchaser's recovery to restitution of payments plus expenses is sometimes explained on the ground that to award loss-of-bargain damages would be inconsistent with the measure of recovery under title covenants in deeds, which is generally limited to the consideration paid. But contracts and deed covenants are fundamentally different;[130] the contract purchaser has usually not yet had an opportunity to make his or her own independent examination of title, while the deed grantee has done so. Moreover, the risk to the vendor of a major increase in market value (and hence of loss-of-bargain damages) is not very great in a short-term executory contract of sale, but would be far larger (and arguably quite unmanageable) in a deed covenant for title which might be the basis of a suit many years after the deed was delivered.[131] Thus it may be rational to limit the vendor's liability for title defects in the case of a long-term installment sale contract,[132] but such a limitation makes no sense in

---

[125] In re Besade, 76 B.R. 845 (Bankr. M.D. Fla. 1987); Coppola Enterprises, Inc. v. Alfone, 531 So. 2d 334 (Fla. 1988) (irrespective of bad faith, vendor who sells to a third party is liable to purchaser for loss of bargain damages); Soloman v. W. Hills Dev. Co., 110 Mich. App. 257, 312 N.W.2d 428 (1981). Compare Shakeshober v. Florida Resort Dev. Corp., 492 So. 2d 816 (Fla. Dist. Ct. App. 1986) (no bad faith existed, where vendor erroneously but negligently sold to third party).

[126] Mickam v. Joseph Louis Palace Trust, 849 F.Supp. 516 (E.D.Mich. 1993) (Michigan law); Masini v. Quilici, 67 Nev. 333, 371, 218 P.2d 946, 964 (1950); Mokar Properties Corp. v. Hall, 6 A.D.2d 536, 179 N.Y.S.2d 814 (1958); Carson v. Isabel Apartments, Inc., 20 Wn.App. 293, 579 P.2d 1027 (1978). See also Narendra v. Thieriot, 41 A.D.3d 442, 838 N.Y.S.2d 131 (2007) (vendor who failed in bad faith to convey good title could not rely on contract provision limiting her liability to return of purchaser's earnest money).

A few courts have recognized a further situation in which the purchaser's remedy is limited to restitution: the case in which the purchaser knows full well when entering into the contract that the vendor's title is defective and does not expect the vendor to cure it. See Madison v. Marlatt, 619 P.2d 708 (Wyo.1980); Kessler v. Rae, 40 A.D.2d 708, 336 N.Y.S.2d 680 (1972). On these facts the purchaser's knowledge arguably makes the vendor's behavior tantamount to good faith.

[127] In re Waldron, 36 B.R. 633 (Bankr. S.D. Fla. 1984); Beard v. S/E Joint Venture, 321 Md. 126, 581 A.2d 1275 (1990).

[128] See § 10.12 infra for a discussion of title covenants in sales contracts.

[129] 2 W.Bl. 1078, 96 Eng.Rep. 635 (C.P. 1776). Lord Westbury is quoted as having said that title deeds of that day were "difficult to read, disgusting to touch, and impossible to understand." See Donovan v. Bachstadt, 91 N.J. 434, 453 A.2d 160 (1982); Oakley, Pecuniary Compensation for Failure to Complete a Contract for the Sale of Land, 39 Camb.L.J. 58, 69 (1980).

[130] See Dobbs, Remedies § 12.8 (2d ed. 1992).

[131] On the measure of damages for breach of deed covenants of title, see § 11.13, infra. Note that the return-of-purchase-price ceiling on the grantor's liability under a deed covenant does not depend on his or her good faith.

[132] But see Missouri Slope Livestock Auction, Inc. v. Wachter, 107 N.W.2d 349 (N.D.1961) in which the court (strongly guided by statute) refused to limit the vendor's liability even under a long-term installment contract.

a short-term earnest-money contract. Hence many courts, probably a majority, refuse to insulate even a good-faith vendor from loss-of-bargain liability.[133]

If the vendor breaches or the contract fails for other reasons (for example, a failure of conditions) without the purchaser's fault, the purchaser may obtain, in addition to any applicable loss-of-bargain damages, restitution of any earnest money payments made.[134] The purchaser's right to recover the deposit is not regarded as a species of damages, but as restitution to prevent unjust enrichment of the vendor.[135] This right is subject to modification by the terms of the contract of sale; this is commonly done by making part of all of the earnest money "nonrefundable."[136]

In addition to "general" loss-of-bargain damages, two categories of "special" damage may be recovered by the non-breaching party to the contract.[137] The first might be termed expenses made in reliance on the contract, and the second is lost profits which the plaintiff would have earned in other transactions if the contract had been performed. Both of these categories are subject to the foreseeability[138] rule of Hadley v.

---

[133] Donovan v. Bachstadt, 91 N.J. 434, 453 A.2d 160 (1982); Forbes v. Wells Beach Casino, Inc., 409 A.2d 646 (Me. 1979); Widebeck v. Sullivan, 327 Mass. 429, 99 N.E.2d 165 (1951); Hartzell v. Crumb, 90 Mo. 629, 3 S.W. 59 (1886). See Comment, 26 Okla. L.Rev. 277 (1973); 3 Am.L.Prop. § 11.67; Annot., 48 A.L.R. 12 (1927); Annot., 68 A.L.R. 137 (1930). There is no discernible trend toward or away from the rule limiting the vendor's liability.

[134] Addie v. Kjaer, 737 F.3d 854, 861 (3d Cir. 2013) (Puerto Rico law; neither party tendered performance); In re Decker Oaks Dev. II, Ltd., 415 B.R. 239 (S.D. Tex. 2009); Rutherford Holdings, LLC v. Plaza Del Rey, 223 Cal. App. 4th 221, 166 Cal. Rptr. 3d 864 (2014); Motherway v. Geary, 82 Conn. App. 722, 846 A.2d 909 (2004); In re Standard Jury Instructions—Contract & Bus. Cases, 116 So. 3d 284, 337 (Fla. 2013); Am. Nat. Bank & Tr. Co. v. Bentley Builders, Inc., 308 Ill. App. 3d 246, 719 N.E.2d 360 (1999); St. Louis Title, LLC v. Talent Plus Consultants, LLC, 414 S.W.3d 24 (Mo. Ct. App. 2013); Lamini v. Baroda Properties, Inc., 128 A.D.3d 910, 11 N.Y.S.3d 608 (N.Y. App. Div. 2015); Skyline Restoration, Inc. v. Roslyn Jane Holdings, LLC, 95 A.D.3d 1203, 944 N.Y.S.2d 643 (2012); Jipac, N.V. v. Silas, 174 Vt. 57, 800 A.2d 1092 (2002) (contract failed due to vendor's not obtaining subdivision permit); G.D. Holdings, Inc. v. H.D.H. Land & Timber, L.P., 407 S.W.3d 856 (Tex. App. 2013) (purchaser breached obligations based on promissory estoppel, restitution of earnest money refused). See § 10.7 infra at note 267.

[135] Rutherford Holdings, LLC v. Plaza Del Rey, 223 Cal. App. 4th 221, 166 Cal. Rptr. 3d 864 (2014). Note that the purchaser cannot have restitution if vendor is ready, willing and able to perform, even if the contract is unenforceable under the statute of frauds; see Kellogg v. Shushereba, 194 Vt. 446, 82 A.3d 1121 (2013); Kofmehl v. Baseline Lake, LLC, 177 Wash. 2d 584, 305 P.3d 230 (2013).

[136] See, e.g., Prime Income Asset Mgmt. Inc. v. One Dallas Ctr. Assocs. LP, 358 F. App'x 569 (5th Cir. 2009) (Texas law); Demattia v. Mauro, 86 Conn. App. 1, 860 A.2d 262 (2004). But see Kuish v. Smith, 181 Cal. App. 4th 1419, 105 Cal. Rptr. 3d 475 (2010) (breaching purchaser can obtain restitution of deposit if vendor has no damages, even if deposit is designated nonrefundable).

[137] A third category, damages for delay in performance, is treated at § 10.9, infra. Georgia appears to refuse to award any special damages unless specifically authorized in the contract of sale; see Roba v. Dotson, 315 Ga. App. 721, 727 S.E.2d 542 (2012).

[138] Restatement (Second) of Contracts § 351 (1981).

Baxendale,[139] and thus can be the basis of recovery only if they were within the contemplation of the parties when the contract was made.[140]

Expenditures in reliance on the contract are of various types. Some may be in the course of actual performance of the contract, such as the vendor's eviction of an existing tenant[141] or refurbishment of the premises so they will meet the contract's specifications.[142] Others are simply the ordinary expenses of sale, such as brokers' commissions, title search and examination fees, surveys, document drafting expenses, appraisals, and the like.[143] The foreseeability requirement is obviously no major barrier to recovery here, since the items in question are usually customary and common, and may even have been mentioned in the contract. Finally, there may be expenses which are not in pursuance of the contract's performance at all, but are nonetheless made in reliance on it, such as travel[144] or commuting costs,[145] preparations for moving onto or off of the land,[146] expenses of arranging financing,[147] and so on.[148] Here foreseeability may be a serious question, turning on the defendant's knowledge or reasonable

---

[139] 9 Exch. 341, 156 Eng.Rep. 145 (1854). Cases refusing, on the basis of lack of foreseeability, to allow various elements of consequential damages to non-breaching purchasers, include Danburg v. Keil, 235 Va. 71, 365 S.E.2d 754 (1988) (expenditures made by purchaser in renovating and altering the premises prior to the closing, which never occurred as a result of vendor's breach); Lotito v. Mazzeo, 132 A.D.2d 650, 518 N.Y.S.2d 22 (1987) (increase in mortgage interest rates occurring after vendors' breach); Wall v. Pate, 104 N.M. 1, 715 P.2d 449 (1986) (loss of opportunity to assume an exceptionally low-interest mortgage on the premises). But see Crown Life Ins. Co. v. American Nat'l Bank, 35 F.3d 296 (7th Cir.1994) (vendor awarded damages resulting from foreclosure of mortgage on shopping center, where vendor's loan default was caused by purchaser's breach of contract to purchase part of shopping center): Soloway v. Malibu Highlands 30, Ltd., 2002 WL 31831687 (Cal. Ct. App. 2002) (purchaser could recover present value of higher mortgage interest rate resulting from vendor's delay); Morrow v. Jones, 165 S.W.3d 254 (Tenn. Ct. App. 2004) (allowing vendor's recovery of late fees and attorneys fees incident to vendor's mortgage default caused by purchaser's breach of contract). See also Lawson v. Menefee, 132 S.W.3d 890 (Ky. Ct. App. 2004) (vendor's consequential damages were offset by vendor's resale of property at a higher price).

[140] See, e.g., Ash v. N. Am. Title Co., 223 Cal. App. 4th 1258, 168 Cal. Rptr. 3d 499 (2014) (failure of purchaser's property exchange intermediary, and consequent loss of tax-free exchange opportunity, were not foreseeable elements of damage); St. Lawrence Factory Stores v. Ogdensburg Bridge & Port Auth., 121 A.D.3d 1226, 994 N.Y.S.2d 704 (2014) (purchaser's claimed damages in preparing to build mall were not recoverable, where feasibility of mall's success was too speculative).

[141] McKinley v. Lagae, 207 Cal.App.2d 284, 24 Cal.Rptr. 454 (1962).

[142] Aliferis v. Boudreau, 1 Mass.App.Ct. 845, 301 N.E.2d 688 (1973).

[143] Missouri Slope Livestock Auction, Inc. v. Wachter, 107 N.W.2d 349 (N.D. 1961) (purchaser can recover title examination expense); Harris v. Shell Development Corp., Nevada, Inc., 95 Nev. 348, 594 P.2d 731 (1979) (vendor can recover for appraisal and other miscellaneous expenses.) It seems clear that the relevant expenses are those actually incurred on the first (abortive) sale, not those which might be incurred on resale; see Royer v. Carter, 37 Cal.2d 544, 233 P.2d 539 (1951). Courts sometimes use the latter figure, but properly speaking, it is only a proxy for the former. The better practice is to use the actual expenses of the first sale. See also Kooloian v. Suburban Land Co., 873 A.2d 95 (R.I. 2005) (purchaser could recover costs of obtaining property at foreclosure sale after vendor breached).

[144] Fountain v. Mojo, 687 P.2d 496 (Colo.App. 1984); Meyer v. Furgat, 133 Vt. 265, 336 A.2d 169 (1975).

[145] Jensen v. Dalton, 9 Cal.App.3d 654, 88 Cal.Rptr. 426 (1970).

[146] Missouri Slope Livestock Auction, Inc. v. Wachter, note 143 supra; Loveday v. Barnes, 909 S.W.2d 448 (Tenn.App.1995) (moving expense); Bush v. Cathey, 598 S.W.2d 777 (Tenn.App. 1979).

[147] St. Lawrence Factory Stores v. Ogdensburg Bridge & Port Auth., 13 N.Y.3d 204, 918 N.E.2d 124 (2009) (approving recovery by purchaser of money spent to arrange financing and secure tenants for the property).

[148] See, e.g., Schellinger Bros. v. Cotter, 2 Cal. App. 5th 984, 207 Cal. Rptr. 3d 82 (2016) (approving recovery by purchaser of $2.8 million for site preparation and governmental permits); Ruble v. Reich, 259 Neb. 658, 611 N.W.2d 844 (2000) (approving recovery by purchasers of costs of hotel rooms, house rental fees (less payments they would have made on mortgage if sale had closed), loan and inspection fees, and truck rental).

expectations about the plaintiff's preparations.[149] Further, courts may refuse to grant damages for expenditures incurred after the breach, on the ground that they were avoidable.[150] They may also refuse to allow full recovery for expenditures which have residual value to the plaintiff despite the breach, such as those of the vendor which can be applied to reduce the costs of resale.[151] For example, a seller who obtains a survey of pays to have an abstract brought up to date in preparation for the aborted sale may be able to use those documents to facilitate a subsequent sale.[152]

One other argument may persuade a court to deny recovery of expenses. The non-breaching party who is awarded loss-of-bargain damages or specific performance has in effect been given the same economic benefit which would have resulted from performance of the contract; hence the court may deny recovery for that party's incidental expenses on the ground that he or she would not have expected reimbursement for them if actual performance had occurred.[153] By contrast, if the plaintiff is the purchaser and the rule of Flureau v. Thornhill limits recovery to a restitution of the payments made, the result is more analogous to rescission than to

---

[149] See, e.g., Bakken Residential, LLC v. Cahoon Enterprises, LLC, 154 F.Supp.3d 812 (D.N.D. 2015) (purchaser who was unable to complete purchase may not recover engineering and permit expenses on theories of quantum meruit or unjust enrichment); Ranch Homes, Inc. v. Greater Park City Corp., 592 P.2d 620 (Utah 1979) (purchaser may not recover for expense of incorporating, corporate legal services, or fees to officers for management, architectural, or engineering services.) When the purchaser breaches, many cases permit recovery of the vendor's interest, taxes, insurance, and other carrying costs which accrue for a reasonable time after breach while he attempts to resell; see Jones v. Lee, 126 N.M. 467, 971 P.2d 858 (N.M.App. 1998) (mortgage interest allowed); Van Moorlehem v. Brown Realty Co., 747 F.2d 992 (10th Cir. 1984) (property taxes until vendor resumed residency of house allowed, but prejudgment interest and mortgage interest disallowed on the ground that since she had possession, interest would constitute a double recovery); Turner v. Benson, 672 S.W.2d 752 (Tenn. 1984) (allowing insurance, utilities, and repairs to property while attempting to remarket property after purchaser's breach); Askari v. R & R Land Co., 179 Cal.App.3d 1101, 225 Cal.Rptr. 285 (1986) (same, but vendor must offset his claim by any increase in property's value prior to trial); Jones v. Lee, 971 P.2d 858 (N.M. App. 1998); Taefi v. Stevens, 53 N.C.App. 579, 281 S.E.2d 435 (1981); Higbie v. Johnson, 626 P.2d 1147 (Colo.App. 1980). But see Johnston v. Curtis, 338 Ark. 752, 16 S.W.3d 283 (2000) (disapproving vendor's recovery of real estate commission, monthly house payments, and utilities); Buschman v. Clark, 583 So.2d 799 (Fla.App. 1991) (disapproving vendor's recovery of mortgage payments, insurance, and association dues for period following purchaser's breach); Macal v. Stinson, 468 N.W.2d 34 (Iowa 1991) (disapproving vendor's recovery of interest on loan they had to obtain when purchasers breached contract of sale); Quigley v. Jones, 255 Ga. 33, 334 S.E.2d 664 (1985) (disapproving vendor's recovery for taxes, insurance, utilities, repairs, or loss of use of sales proceeds during time he attempted to remarket property); Zipper v. Affordable Homes, Inc., 461 So.2d 988 (Fla. App.1984), review dismissed 469 So.2d 748 (Fla. 1985) (disapproving prejudgment interest to vendor); Morrow v. Jones, 165 S.W.3d 254 (Tenn.Ct.App. 2004) (disapproving vendor's recovery of mortgage payments but allowing recovery of late fees and attorneys fees incident to vendor's mortgage default). See Annot., 17 A.L.R.2d 1300 (1951).

[150] Restatement (Second) of Contracts § 1350 (1981). Plainly this argument ought not to apply to the carrying costs incurred by the vendor while attempting to remarket the property; these costs are generally unavoidable. Nonetheless, recovery for them is usually denied, See, e.g., Oltman Homes, Inc. v. Mirkes, 2008 Okl. Civ. App. 64, 190 P.3d 1182 (2008).

[151] See Aliferis v. Boudreau, 1 Mass. App.Ct. 845, 301 N.E.2d 688 (1973) (vendor can recover for costs of renovating and equipping beauty school, less fair resale value of equipment).

[152] If the court uses the actual expenses of resale as a proxy for the damages on the breached contract, this factor is taken into account automatically; see note 143 supra. No law requires the vendor to resell; if he or she does not, the expenditures will have little or no value, and the vendor should recover their full cost. A purchaser's incidental expenditures will seldom have any residual value after the vendor breaches, since they generally relate to the specific parcel of land which was the subject of the breached contract.

[153] Soffe v. Ridd, 659 P.2d 1082 (Utah 1983); Higbie v. Johnson, 626 P.2d 1147, 1151 (Colo.App. 1980); Mahoney v. Tingley, 10 Wn.App. 814, 520 P.2d 628 (1974), reversed 85 Wn.2d 95, 529 P.2d 1068 (1975). See D. Dobbs, Remedies § 12.3(2) (2d ed. 1993); C. McCormick, Damages § 186 nn. 144–45 (1935); Restatement of Contracts § 333, comment a (1933).

performance; the foregoing argument does not apply, the purchaser is out-of-pocket the expenses and can recover them.[154]

The actual results with respect to claims for expenses of sale, over and above loss-of-bargain damages, seem to be extraordinarily variable and inconsistent. For example, one can easily find cases both allowing[155] and denying[156] the vendor's claim for a real estate broker's commission paid. But the inconsistencies may be apparent rather than real, and may turn on what the court means by "market value" in the standard loss-of-bargain formula. For example, suppose V contracts to sell land to P for $100,000. V spends $10,000 on brokerage commissions, abstracts, and other fees, none of which will be refunded to V by the broker, title company, etc., despite P's breach of the contract, and none of which will have any value in facilitating a subsequent resale. Assume the land's value has declined by $5,000, so its gross market value is $95,000. If this figure is used to compute V's loss-of-bargain damages, V will get only $5,000 of recovery. V will presumably place the land back on the market, sell it for $95,000, and pay a new commission and other expenses on the resale of about $10,000. Plainly V has been undercompensated in damages unless the court also awards V the unrecoverable expenses of the first sale.[157] On the other hand, if V's loss-of-bargain damages are computed on the basis of the land's net market value at the time of breach, or $85,000, the resulting damage figure of $15,000 will fully compensate V without any further award for incidental expenses. The cases seldom mention whether the market value "found" by the court is gross or net of expenses, but the point is crucial in judging whether additional expenses of sale should be awarded. A few cases recognize this definition problem explicitly,[158] but all ought to do so.

In many cases, the purchaser under a land sale contract will have in mind some further use or disposition of the land. If that use would have produced profits over and above the land's fair market value, the buyer may be able to recover those profits, in addition to loss-of-bargain damages and expenses, from the breaching vendor. But he or she will have several hurdles to overcome. The first, if the vendor's breach was due to a good-faith lack of title, is the doctrine of Flureau v. Thornhill, discussed above. If the purchaser would be denied loss-of-bargain damages on this ground, loss of profits will be denied *a fortiori*.[159] Second, the profit opportunity which the purchaser lost must have been "foreseeable" or "within the contemplation of the parties" under Hadley v. Baxendale. This point is often hotly controverted, and the cases produce varying results, depending on the facts.[160] The final barrier is the requirement that the lost profits be

---

[154] See note 123 supra.

[155] Gordon v. Pfab, 246 N.W.2d 283, 289 (Iowa 1976); Warner v. Wilkey, 2 Mass. App.Ct. 798, 307 N.E.2d 847 (1974); Popwell v. Abel, 226 So.2d 418 (Fla.App. 1969); Jensen v. Dalton, 9 Cal.App.3d 654, 88 Cal. Rptr. 426 (1970).

[156] Mahoney v. Tingley, note 153 supra.

[157] See note 143 supra.

[158] Stephenson v. Butts, 187 Pa.Super. 55, 142 A.2d 319 (1958); Royer v. Carter, 37 Cal.2d 544, 233 P.2d 539 (1951), in which the court seemed to feel bound by statute (West's Ann.Cal.Civ.C. § 3307) to measure the vendor's loss-of-bargain damages based on "gross" market value, and hence properly awarded additional damages for his expenses.

[159] Surprisingly, this point has not often been explicitly discussed in the cases. Cf. Rea v. Ford Motor Co., 355 F.Supp. 842, 852 (W.D.Pa.1972), vacated 497 F.2d 577 (3d Cir.1974), certiorari denied 419 U.S. 868, 95 S.Ct. 126, 42 L.Ed.2d 106 (1974), on remand 406 F.Supp. 271 (W.D.Pa.1975), vacated 560 F.2d 554 (3d Cir.1977), certiorari denied 434 U.S. 923, 98 S.Ct. 401, 54 L.Ed.2d 281 (1977).

[160] Finding foreseeability: Republic National Life Insurance Co. v. Red Lion Homes, Inc., 704 F.2d 484 (10th Cir. 1983); C. & C. Blaschka, Inc. v. Frazer, 32 A.D.2d 774, 302 N.Y.S.2d 443 (1969), affirmed 30 N.Y.2d

proved with reasonable (although not total) certainty, and here most purchasers' claims founder.[161] In general, the courts quite naturally tend to view claims of lost profits somewhat cynically, as representing only the extravagant hopes of the plaintiff rather than realistic opportunities. But if the proof is strong, recovery is possible.[162]

The discussion above has centered on the problem of the total breach. However, partial breaches are also common. A vendor, for example, may be unable to convey all of the land promised; the title may be subject to some outstanding claim or interest (such as a right of surface entry in favor of the owner of a mineral estate) which is at variance with the seller's duty under the contract; or the property may have physical defects which violate the contract. In such cases the purchaser has the right (if the breach is material) to avoid the contract and claim damages for a total breach. However, the purchaser may regard the land as essentially satisfactory notwithstanding the shortage or defect, and hence may wish to proceed with the transaction, at the same time claiming damages (or, what amounts to the same thing, an abatement of the price) to compensate for the partial breach.[163]

The courts are divided as to the proper measure of such damages or abatement, with the division following the same basic lines as the *Flureau* controversy discussed above. About half of the cases measure the damages by the price of the land as fixed in the contract,[164] while the remainder measure them by the land's market value at the date of

---

645, 331 N.Y.S.2d 669, 282 N.E.2d 623 (1972); Caughey v. Ames, 315 Mich. 643, 24 N.W.2d 521 (1946). Finding no foreseeability: Susi v. Simonds, 147 Me. 189, 85 A.2d 178 (1951); Merritt v. Adams County Land & Investment Co., 29 N.D. 496, 151 N.W. 11 (1915). See generally Annot., 11 A.L.R.3d 719 (1967); Ehly v. Cady, 212 Mont. 82, 687 P.2d 687 (1984) (breaching vendor held liable for purchaser's loss of investment tax credit under federal income tax law, which loss was reasonably foreseeable). See also Community Dev. Service, Inc. v. Replacement Parts Mfg., Inc., 679 S.W.2d 721 (Tex. App.1984) awarding lost profits to a *vendor* which was selling a large number of lots as a real estate dealer.

[161] The usual holding is that either the occurrence or the amount of the expected profits is too speculative and uncertain. See, e.g., Atias v. Sedrish, 133 F. App'x 759 (2d Cir. 2005); Gilmore v. Cohen, 95 Ariz. 34, 386 P.2d 81, 11 A.L.R.3d 714 (1963); Greenwich S.F., LLC v. Wong, 190 Cal. App. 4th 739, 118 Cal. Rptr. 3d 531 (2010) (describing many other California cases denying recovery of lost profits); McGehee v. Elliott, 849 N.E.2d 1180 (Ind. Ct. App. 2006); St. Lawrence Factory Stores v. Ogdensburg Bridge & Port Auth., 13 N.Y.3d 204, 918 N.E.2d 124 (2009); CFJ Assocs. of New York Inc. v. Hanson Indus., 294 A.D.2d 772, 742 N.Y.S.2d 433 (2002); Shepherd v. Davis, 265 Va. 108, 574 S.E.2d 514 (2003). The uncertainty issue is particularly acute in the case of a new business with no record of profitability; see Guard v. P & R Enterprises, Inc., 631 P.2d 1068 (Alaska 1981). See Note, The Requirement of Certainty in the Proof of Lost Profits, 64 Harv.L.Rev. 317 (1950).

[162] Hoang v. Hewitt Ave. Assocs., LLC, 177 Md. App. 562, 610, 936 A.2d 915, 944 (2007) (where purchaser intended to develop and sell town houses on the property, had a strong track record and experience, and presented expert testimony on expected costs and profits, lost profits were recoverable). See also Home Depot U.S.A., Inc. v. Cytec Indus., Inc., 2009 WL 4915278 (Conn. Super. Ct. 2009), approving in principle the awarding of lost profits. However, the purchaser was unable to provide any proof at trial of such loss; see Home Depot USA, Inc. v. Cytec Indus., Inc., 2013 WL 388202 (Conn. Super. Ct. 2013).

[163] Wooten v. Lightburn, 579 F.Supp.2d 769 (W.D. Va. 2008), aff'd, 350 F. App'x 812 (4th Cir. 2009); Specific performance with abatement will generally be ordered against the vendor in these situations; see Chesapeake Builders, Inc. v. Lee, 254 Va. 294, 492 S.E.2d 141 (Va.1997); Moser v. Thorp Sales Corp., 334 N.W.2d 715 (Iowa 1983); Greene v. Jones, 377 So.2d 947 (Ala.1979); Ga.Code Ann. § 44–5–35, construed in McIntyre v. Varner, 156 Ga.App. 529, 275 S.E.2d 90 (1980). A court may decline to order specific performance if the defect or shortage is so great, and hence the abatement so large, that it virtually eats up the contract price, thus radically altering the parties' original agreement. See Merritz v. Circelli, 361 Pa. 239, 64 A.2d 796 (1949); § 10.5 infra.

[164] Kleiner v. Randall, 72 Or.App. 465, 696 P.2d 556 (1985), opinion clarified 74 Or.App. 27, 701 P.2d 458 (1985); Kuhlman v. Grimminger, 213 Neb. 64, 327 N.W.2d 104 (1982); Hardin v. Hill, 149 Mont. 68, 423 P.2d 309 (1967); Queen v. Sisk, 238 N.C. 389, 78 S.E.2d 152 (1953). See also Cantor v. Hotchkiss, 465 So.2d 614 (Fla. App. 1985) (where vendor was ordered to convey *more* land than contract provided, in order to cure an encroachment, purchasers were required to *increase* purchase price pro rata).

breach.[165] To illustrate, suppose the contract provides for the sale of 10 acres at a price of $5,000 per acre. A subsequent survey discloses that the tract contains only 9 acres. At the date of settlement the land's value has risen to $6,000 per acre. Under the former rule mentioned, the purchaser's damages are $5,000, the pro-rata contract price of the shortage. The latter rule bases recovery on the value of the land, and would result in a damage award of $6,000, in effect giving the purchaser the benefit of the bargain. The analogy to the *Flureau* controversy is obvious. If the contract provides for the sale of the land "in gross" (by stating only a total price rather than a price per acre or other area measure), the courts are much more reluctant to award damages for shortages of area, but they will generally do so if the deficiency is great or the vendor has affirmatively misrepresented the area to be conveyed; again, the measure may be based on either market value or contract price.[166] Other elements of damage are also conceivable; one purchaser was awarded $3,000 to cover the expense of redesigning a construction project to fit within the remaining land.[167]

Deficiencies that constitute contract breaches are not necessarily shortages in area. The vendor may tender the property in a damaged or defective condition, or may remove from it some fixtures or improvements of value. It may be encumbered with title defects that depreciate its value. In these cases, the courts often adopt damage measurements similar to the benefit-of-bargain approach discussed above: an abatement based on the diminished market value of the property,[168] or (where feasible) damages equal to the cost of remedying or correcting the defect.[169] It is less common in these situations to measure damages by a pro-rata reduction in the price, since there is usually no obvious way of

---

[165] Weinstein v. Sprecher, 2 Wn.App. 325, 467 P.2d 890 (1970); Emery v. Medal Building Corp., 164 Colo. 515, 436 P.2d 661 (1968); Fant v. Howell, 547 S.W.2d 261 (Tex. 1977).

[166] See Parcel v. Myers, 214 Mont. 225, 697 P.2d 92 (1985) (no abatement where sale was in gross); Snow's Auto Supply, Inc. v. Dormaier, 108 Idaho 73, 696 P.2d 924 (App. 1985) (even if sale was in gross, purchaser was entitled to relief if vendor made fraudulent misrepresentation); Hodecker v. Butler, 64 Or.App. 167, 667 P.2d 540 (1983); Hardin v. Hill, supra note 164; Flygare v. Brundage, 76 Wyo. 350, 302 P.2d 759 (1956). Courts sometimes refuse to grant modifications of the price in sales in gross despite great acreage discrepancy; see Perfect v. McAndrew, 798 N.E.2d 470 (Ind.App. 2003) (18.7 percent acreage overage); Bridgewater v. Adamczyk, 421 S.W.3d 617, 628 (Tenn. Ct. App. 2013) (20 percent acreage deficiency); Cedar Lane Ranch v. Lundberg, 991 P.2d 440 (Mont. 1999) (85% acreage overage); Branton v. Jones, 222 Va. 305, 281 S.E.2d 799 (1981) (60 percent acreage overage).

[167] Pareira v. Wehner, 133 Vt. 74, 330 A.2d 84 (1974).

[168] See, e.g., Cooper v. Burson 521 So.2d 745 (La.App. 1988); Harris v. Adame, 2015 Ill. App. (1st) 123306, 43 N.E.3d 1050, 1064, appeal denied, 48 N.E.3d 1092 (Ill. 2016) (where one of two joint tenants lacked capacity to convey his interest, purchaser received one-half interest and was entitled to abatement of one-half of price paid); Nugent v. Beckham, 37 N.C.App. 557, 246 S.E.2d 541 (1978) (abatement for title defects based on diminution in market value); Wilkinson Homes, Inc. v. Stewart Title Guar. Co., 271 Ga. App. 577, 610 S.E.2d 187 (2005). A few jurisdictions will grant specific performance with abatement only for title defects or land shortages, and not for physical defects; see Ide v. Joe Miller & Co., 703 P.2d 590 (Colo. App. 1984) (where well had much lower capacity than contract required, but contract price was already lower than market value, court refused to order abatement; purchasers given election to purchase "as is" at contract price, or to rescind). Note that the parties may contract against any abatement of the price for title defects; see Highbridge House Ogden LLC v. Highbridge Entities LLC, 48 Misc. 3d 976, 989, 16 N.Y.S.3d 669, 679 (N.Y. Sup. 2015), aff'd, 145 A.D.3d 487, 43 N.Y.S.3d 291 (N.Y. App. Div. 2016).

[169] Tennant v. Lawton, 26 Wn.App. 701, 615 P.2d 1305 (1980) (damages based on reduction in market value). Cf. Sallinger v. Mayer, 304 So.2d 730 (La.App. 1974) (damages based on cost of repairs.) Some cases indicate that the cost-of-repair measure should be employed if the defects can be readily remedied without destruction of any part of the building, and the market value measure if correction of the defects would involve substantial demolition; see Coley v. Eudy, 51 N.C.App. 310, 276 S.E.2d 462 (1981). See generally Annot., Measure of Damages Where Vendor, After Execution of Contract of Sale but before Conveyance of Property, Removes Part of Property Contracted For, 97 A.L.R.3d 1220 (1980). If the defect is one of title, and can be cured by a liquidated sum, the typical practice is to give the purchaser an abatement of the price in an amount necessary to clear the title; see, e.g., Streater v. White, 26 Wn. App. 430, 613 P.2d 187 (1980).

allocating the price among various features of the improvements or title; hence, the purchaser is more likely to be awarded the full benefit of his or her bargain.[170]

§ 10.4 REMEDIES FOR CONTRACT BREACH— LIQUIDATED DAMAGES

Without question the most controversial issue involving realty contract damages is the validity and scope of the vendor's asserted right to retain, as liquidated damages, money which the breaching purchaser has paid toward the price. In nearly every transaction the purchaser will hand some "earnest money" to the seller (or the seller's lawyer or real estate broker) at the time the contract is entered into. In some areas of the country the amount is customarily ten percent of the full price, while in other places it is commonly much less; the exact amount is subject to negotiation between the parties. Sometimes further payments are made by the buyer prior to settlement. If the buyer subsequently defaults, the seller very often takes the position that all such payments are forfeited as damages for the breach, while the purchaser claims the funds under the general principles of restitution discussed later in this chapter.

Such attempted forfeitures raise a variety of legal questions. The most obvious is simply whether the seller can keep the money if it exceeds the seller's actual damages as measured by the general principles discussed in the preceding section. It is of critical importance here to distinguish between long-term installment contracts which serve to secure a purchase-money debt and short-term marketing or "earnest money" contracts. Only the latter are dealt with here; cases involving the former are legion, but the principles involved are different because of their close analogy to mortgage law.[171]

The seller's right to forfeiture of earnest money is often mentioned in a contract clause, and its wording may be of great significance, but numerous states permit a forfeiture even in the absence of any clause.[172] That right is usually explained on the grounds (1) that the seller could always seek specific performance and hence is only retaining a portion of the entire price which a court of equity would award him, or (2) that the buyer, being in breach, has no standing to assert any rights under the contract.[173] There is little logic in these statements. At the point at which the forfeiture occurs, there is no judicial finding that specific performance is available to the vendor,

---

[170] See Dobbs, Remedies § 12.11(1) (2d ed. 1993).

[171] See Nelson, Whitman, Burkhart & Freyermuth, Real Estate Finance Law, §§ 3.28 (6th ed. 2014), for an extended discussion of forfeitures in installment contracts; see also § 10.7 note 269 infra.

[172] The classic case is Lawrence v. Miller, 86 N.Y. 131 (1881). See Uzan v. 845 UN Ltd. P'ship, 10 A.D.3d 230, 778 N.Y.S.2d 171 (2004); Northern Ill. Const. Co. v. Zale, 136 Ill.App.3d 822, 483 N.E.2d 1013 (1985); Halldorson v. Gunderson, 401 N.W.2d 519, 522 (N.D. 1987). If the parties are sophisticated, there seems to be no limit on the amount New York courts will allow to be forfeited; see Vitolo v. O'Connor, 223 A.D.2d 762, 636 N.Y.S.2d 163 (1996).

In theory there is no necessary connection between the amounts of earnest money and liquidated damages; the liquidated sum might be more than or less than the earnest money deposit, and a liquidated damages clause might be included in a contract which provides for no earnest money at all. But in the vast majority of all sale contracts, the deposit and the liquidated sum are identical.

[173] See, e.g., Bruce Builders, Inc. v. Goodwin, 317 So.2d 868 (Fla.App.1975); Wasserman v. Steinman, 304 Pa. 150, 155 A. 302 (1931). See Friedman & Smith, Contracts and Conveyances of Real Property § 12.1(c) (7th ed. 2005). Friedman and Smith argue that the vendor is well-advised not to include a liquidated damages clause, and can thus avoid the risk that a court will construe it as limiting other remedies the vendor might later wish to pursue. See also S. Goldberg, Sales of Real Property 494 (1971). A numerical count of the cases bears out this advice, but it is questionable whether practitioners ought to rely on a rule of such doubtful fairness and analytic soundness. See Annot., 4 A.L.R.4th 993, 1025ff (1981).

who in any event usually does not seek it. A seller who in fact sought specific performance would have to tender a conveyance of the land, while the seller who seeks a forfeiture has no intention of doing so. Moreover, courts generally do not make the validity of forfeiture turn on whether the vendor still has the property or has resold it;[174] yet the vendor obviously could not have specific performance if he or she had parted with the title. Finally, the buyer who seeks a refund of earnest money is arguably not relying on contract rights, but is merely asking relief from the seller's unjust enrichment. For all these reasons it is very doubtful that courts should impute an automatic right of forfeiture in every realty sale contract, and some refuse to do so.[175]

But even if a specific clause is included in the contract, the major question remains: will a court enforce the forfeiture of the buyer's money? The issue is typically phrased in terms of whether the retention represents a valid liquidation of damages or an invalid penalty. Most modern cases purport to follow the First Contracts Restatement[176] and hold that forfeiture is permissible only if (1) the seller's actual damages are difficult or impossible to measure and (2) the amount of the liquidated sum to be retained appeared, when the contract was entered into, to be a reasonable estimate of the actual damages. These requirements obviously suffer a bit from internal inconsistency, since if the damages are so hard to measure, almost any estimate of them might be considered reasonable. In practice, the "difficult to measure" standard has been largely assumed or ignored, and most of the cases have focused on the reasonableness of the figure.[177] A minority of decisions refuses forfeiture entirely and permits the buyer to recover so much of the deposit as exceeds the vendor's actual damages.[178]

The traditional view called for testing the reasonableness of the liquidated damages clause as of the time the contract was formed. Courts have often felt uncomfortable with this approach in cases in which the property's market value has risen sharply after contracting and before breach, so that the seller has little actual damages or none at all;

---

[174] See Pruett v. La Salceda, Inc., 45 Ill.App.3d 243, 359 N.E.2d 776 (1977); Gaynes v. Allen, 116 N.H. 469, 362 A.2d 197 (1976).

[175] See Kutzin v. Pirnie, 124 N.J. 500, 591 A.2d 932 (1991) (overruling prior common law rule, and holding that retention of deposit exceeding the vendor's actual damages would not be permitted in absence of clause so providing); Frank v. Jansen, 303 Minn. 86, 226 N.W.2d 739 (1975).

[176] Restatement of Contracts § 339 (1933); Rumsey v. Gillis, 329 Ga. App. 488, 765 S.E.2d 665 (2014). The second Restatement continues to use both of the tests mentioned, but places the emphasis on reasonableness "in light of the anticipated or actual harm * * * and the difficulties of proof of loss." Restatement (Second) of Contracts § 356 (1981). Comment b indicates that the greater the difficulty of proof of loss, the greater the latitude which should be allowed in the setting of liquidated damages. See Shallow Brook Associates v. Dube, 135 N.H. 40, 599 A.2d 132 (1991); Preferred Sav. Bank, Inc. v. Elkholy, 303 S.C. 95, 399 S.E.2d 19 (1990); Clarkson, Miller & Muris, Liquidated Damages v. Penalties: Sense or Nonsense?, 1978 Wisc.L.Rev. 351. See Judge Posner's attack on the penalty concept in XCO Int'l Inc. v. Pac. Sci. Co., 369 F.3d 998 (7th Cir. 2004).

[177] See, e.g., Orr v. Goodwin, 157 N.H. 511, 953 A.2d 1190 (2008). A third factor sometimes mentioned is the intention of the parties to provide for liquidated damages rather than a penalty whose purpose is to compel performance. Yet it is clear that the label the parties placed on the clause is not controlling, and in practice little attention is usually paid to intention. See generally Perillo, Contracts § 14–31(a) (7th ed. 2014). But see Hanson Dev. Co. v. East Great Plains Shopping Center, Inc., 195 Conn. 60, 485 A.2d 1296 (1985), in which both majority and dissenting opinions purport to analyze the intent question; Benya v. Gamble, 282 S.C. 624, 321 S.E.2d 57 (S.C.App. 1984), cert. dismissed 329 S.E.2d 768 (1985) (reasonableness in light of damages which were either anticipated or were actually suffered was a jury question.

[178] See, e.g., Wilkins v. Birnbaum, 278 A.2d 829 (Del. 1971). See also Walker v. Graham, 706 P.2d 278 (Wyo. 1985), seeming to take the position that damages for breach of a real estate sale contract are per se not difficult to measure (under the first Restatement test), so that forfeiture of the purchaser's deposit is never appropriate; Reid v. Auxier, 690 P.2d 1057 (Okl.App. 1984) (same, although contract recited that it would be "impractical and extremely difficult" to determine actual damages).

an estimate of damages that was reasonable when made may sometimes turn out to be a gross exaggeration of actual damages. Some recent cases display a willingness to take this factor into account, and to take a "second look," refusing enforcement of the forfeiture if it would result in a substantial windfall to the vendor based on his or her actual damages at the time of breach.[179] Others, more logically, hold that a deposit that was reasonable when made can be retained even if the vendor has much smaller damages or none at all.[180] Note that the very fact that issues of reasonableness of amount, difficulty of estimation, and the like are pertinent and litigable in itself destroys much of the supposed advantage of liquidated damages clauses—their extra-judicial operation. With respect to the question of how great a gap the courts will tolerate between actual damages and the liquidated amount, the cases are much too variable to generalize, but unusually large earnest money deposits are commonly recoverable by purchasers.[181] The ironic result is that the vendor who was piggish may end up with only actual damages, and only after being put to the trouble of proving them in court.

---

[179] Kuish v. Smith, 181 Cal. App. 4th 1419, 105 Cal. Rptr. 3d 475 (2010) (a case in which Cal. Civ. Code § 1675, discussed below, was inapplicable); Vines v. Orchard Hills, Inc., 181 Conn. 501, 435 A.2d 1022 (1980); Peterson v. McAndrew, 160 Conn.App. 180, 125 A.3d 241 (2015) (vendor must prove some actual damage in order to retain deposit); Shanghai Inv. Co. v. Alteka Co., 92 Haw. 482, 993 P.2d 516 (2000); Strouse v. Starbuck, 987 S.W.2d 827 (Mo. Ct. App. 1999); Nohe v. Roblyn Dev. Corp., 296 N.J. Super. 172, 686 A.2d 382 (App. Div. 1997); Guiliano v. Cleo, Inc., 995 S.W.2d 88 (Tenn. 1999); Wheeling Clinic v. Van Pelt, 192 W.Va. 620, 453 S.E.2d 603 (W.Va. 1994).

In order to circumvent the possibility that the liquidated damages clause might not survive a "second look," a vendor might be tempted to recast the transaction as an option to purchase with a substantial option fee. But courts can be expected to scrutinize such fakery very carefully; see Allen v. Smith, 94 Cal. App. 4th 1270, 114 Cal. Rptr. 2d 898 (2002).

[180] Kelly v. Marx, 428 Mass. 877, 705 N.E.2d 1114 (Mass. 1999); Woodhaven Apartments v. Washington, 942 P.2d 918, 921 (Utah 1997); Tardanico v. Murphy, 983 F.Supp. 303 (D.P.R. 1997); Watson v. Ingram, 124 Wn.2d 845, 881 P.2d 247 (Wash. 1994). The cases are about evenly divided. The Restatement (Second) of Contracts § 356 (1981) seems to give equal weight to both anticipated and actual reasonableness.

The California case law development was short-circuited as to owner-occupied residential property in 1978 by the passage of West's Ann.Cal.Civ.Code § 1675, which presumes the validity of liquidated damages up to 3 percent of the purchase price, and presumes invalidity if an amount exceeding 3 percent is paid; both presumptions may be rebutted by proof of unreasonableness in the first situation and reasonableness in the second. Reasonableness is assessed by considering circumstances at the time the contract was made as well as any subsequent transactions which occur within 6 months of the buyer's breach. The statute does not call for any consideration of intention, mutual negotiation, or difficulty of proof of actual damages. See Ben Hamburg, Liquidated Damages Provisions In Real Estate Sales Contracts, 16 Cal. Real Prop. J. No. 2, at 12 (1998); Allen v. Smith, 94 Cal.App.4th 1270, 114 Cal.Rptr.2d 898 (2002), holding that substantial compliance with the statute actuates it, and that the vendors were entitled to retain so much of the breaching purchaser's deposit as did not exceed 3 percent of the purchase price.

See also West's Rev.C.Wash. Ann. § 64.04, conclusively sustaining forfeiture of earnest money in real estate sale contracts if the amount forfeited does not exceed 5% of the purchase price and the contract expressly makes forfeiture the vendor's sole remedy; Chrisp v. Goll, 126 Wash. App. 18, 104 P.3d 25 (2005), holding that substantial compliance does not actuate the statute.

[181] See Annot., 4 A.L.R.4th 993 (1981); Annot., 6 A.L.R.2d 1401, at § 9–10 (1949); Uzan v. 845 UN Ltd. P'ship, 10 A.D.3d 230, 778 N.Y.S.2d 171 (2004) (upholding retention of more than $8 million); Hauppauge Country Club Assoc. v. Kabro of Hauppauge, Inc., 226 A.D.2d 186, 640 N.Y.S.2d 529 (App.Div.1996) (upholding retention of $2 million); Thanksgiving Tower Partners v. Anros Thanksgiving Partners, 64 F.3d 227 (5th Cir.1995) (upholding retention of $5 million). Some cases rather illogically focus on the size of the deposit in relation to the total price, a ratio which may have little to do with the vendor's prospective or actual damages. Ten percent is often used as a rule of thumb; see Tsiropoulos v. Radigan, 163 Conn. App. 122, 133 A.3d 898 (2016); Lefemine v. Baron, 556 So.2d 1160 (Fla.App. 1990); Krupnick v. Guerriero, 247 N.J.Super. 373, 589 A.2d 620 (N.J.Super. 1990); Olcott Lakeside Devel., Inc. v. Krueger, 207 A.D.2d 1032, 616 N.Y.S.2d 841 (App.Div. 1994). Cf. Weber v. Rivera, 255 Mont. 195, 841 P.2d 534 (Mont. 1992), refusing to enforce retention of a 10% deposit. See also Shanghai Inv. Co. v. Alteka Co., 92 Haw. 482, 993 P.2d 516 (2000) (retention of $5 million deposit was not permitted, where deposit bore no reasonable relationship to actual damages); Olmo v. Matos, 439 Pa.Super. 1, 653 A.2d 1 (Pa.Super. 1994) (retention of deposit of 60% of price was an unconscionable penalty and unenforceable); Magill v. Watson, 409 S.W.3d 673 (Tex. App. 2013) (clause providing liquidated

The other principal issue raised by liquidated damages clauses is whether they preclude the vendor's assertion of other remedies, especially actual damages and specific performance. (Of course the vendor cannot both retain the deposit as liquidated damages and at the same time get actual damages or specific performance.[182]) One might expect the recovery of actual damages to be foreclosed almost automatically by the presence of a liquidated damage clause; after all, the evident purpose of the clause is to fix the vendor's damages recovery at the agreed amount. Indeed, many cases do take this view,[183] although it sometimes gives rise to the bizarre spectacle of a vendor's attempting to convince a court that the clause, obviously inserted for his or her own benefit, is invalid so that a larger sum can be recovered in actual damages![184] Surprisingly, numerous cases permit the seller to disregard the liquidated damages clause and seek actual damages if the wording of the clause plainly makes retention of the deposit optional with the seller.[185] Such an approach lets the seller have his or her cake and eat it too, gaining a windfall if the deposit exceeds the damages, while preserving an action against the buyer if the deposit is inadequate to cover the damages.[186] This collection of rights has been too much for some courts to swallow.[187] In jurisdictions where it works, a large premium is placed on careful drafting to make it clear that retention of the deposit is an optional and not an exclusive remedy.[188]

---

damages equal to four times earnest money deposit was unenforceable penalty). The fact that the liquidated amount is unreasonably *small* is not usually a basis for refusal to enforce the clause; see Bodin v. Butler, 338 F. App'x 448 (5th Cir. 2009) (Louisiana law); Roscoe-Gill v. Newman, 188 Ariz. 483, 937 P.2d 673 (Ariz.App. 1996).

[182] Outrigger Resort Corp. v. L & E. Corp., 611 So.2d 1358 (Fla.App. 1993) (actual damages); Handex of Carolinas, Inc. v. Cty. of Haywood, 168 N.C. App. 1, 607 S.E.2d 25 (2005) (actual damages); Perroncello v. Donahue, 448 Mass. 199, 859 N.E.2d 827 (2007) (specific performance).

[183] Lefemine v. Baron, 573 So. 2d 326 (Fla. 1991); Rumsey v. Gillis, 329 Ga. App. 488, 765 S.E.2d 665 (2014); Grimsley v. Lenox, 643 So.2d 203 (La.App. 1994), writ denied 647 So.2d 1117 (La. 1994); Warstler v. Cibrian, 859 S.W.2d 162 (Mo.App.1993); Orr v. Goodwin, 157 N.H. 511, 953 A.2d 1190 (2008); Mahoney v. Tingley, 85 Wn.2d 95, 529 P.2d 1068 (1975); City of Kinston v. Suddreth, 266 N.C. 618, 146 S.E.2d 660 (1966). Contra, allowing election by the vendor of retention of the deposit or a suit for actual damages where the contract was silent with respect to a right of election, see Shull v. Walcker, 2009 ND 142, 770 N.W.2d 274 (2009). See Comment, Liquidated Damages: A Comparison of the Common Law and the Uniform Commercial Code, 45 Fordham L.Rev. 1349, 1367–68 (1977).

[184] See Universal Builders, Inc. v. Moon Motor Lodge, Inc., 430 Pa. 550, 244 A.2d 10 (1968) (construction contract); Community Dev. Service, Inc. v. Replacement Parts Mfg., Inc., 679 S.W.2d 721 (Tex.App. 1984); City of Kinston v. Suddreth, id. (vendor's argument rejected).

[185] Ravenstar, LLC v. One Ski Hill Place, LLC, 2017 Co. 83, 401 P.3d 552 (2017); Sheffield v. Paul T. Stone, Inc., 98 F.2d 250 (D.C. Cir. 1938); Frasier v. Schauweker, 915 S.W.2d 601 (Tex.App. 1996); Margaret H. Wayne Trust v. Lipsky, 123 Idaho 253, 846 P.2d 904 (Idaho 1993); Sampson v. McAdoo, 47 Md.App. 602, 425 A.2d 1 (Md. Ct. Spec. App. 1981); Bannon v. Knauss, 282 S.C. 589, 320 S.E.2d 470 (S.C.App. 1984); G.H. Swope Bldg. Corp. v. Horton, 207 Tenn. 114, 338 S.W.2d 566 (1960); Noble v. Ogborn, 43 Wn.App. 387, 717 P.2d 285 (1986). Cf. Harris v. Dawson, 479 Pa. 463, 388 A.2d 748 (1978), noted at 52 Temp.L.Rev. 829 (1979) (clause construed to make retention of $100 deposit the sole remedy at law, precluding recovery of actual damages).

[186] See, e.g., Avery v. Hughes, 661 F.3d 690 (1st Cir. 2011), allowing the vendor to elect liquidated or actual damages and recognizing the potential windfall under N.H. law.

[187] See Ner Tamid Congregation of N. Town v. Krivoruchko, 2010 WL 391611 (N.D. Ill. 2010) (unpublished); Hanson Dev. Co. v. East Great Plains Shopping Center, Inc., 195 Conn. 60, 485 A.2d 1296 (1985); Lefemine v. Baron, 573 So.2d 326 (Fla. 1991); Grossinger Motorcorp, Inc. v. American Nat'l Bank, 240 Ill.App.3d 737, 607 N.E.2d 1337 (1992); Jarro Building Industries Corp. v. Schwartz, 54 Misc.2d 13, 281 N.Y.S.2d 420 (Sup.Ct. 1967). The matter was well put by Mr. Justice Van Brunt, dissenting in Caesar v. Rubinson, 71 App. Div. 180, 185, 75 N.Y.S. 544, 547 (1902), reversed 174 N.Y. 492, 67 N.E. 58 (1903): "I am unable to comprehend how the amount fixed in an agreement can, by its terms, be both liquidated and unliquidated." See also Ropiza v. Reyes, 583 So.2d 400 (Fla.App. 1991) (clause providing vendor the options of deposit retention, actual damages, and specific performance was unenforceable as a matter of law).

[188] See Annot., Provision in Land Contract for Liquidated Damages upon Default of Purchaser as Affecting Right of Vendor to Maintain Action for Damages for Breach of Contract, 39 A.L.R.5th 33 (1996);

If liquidated and actual damages seem obviously inconsistent, the same is not true of liquidated damages and specific performance. In general, the courts have no difficulty awarding specific performance (if the other necessary elements are present) despite the presence of a liquidated damages clause.[189] In contrast to the question of actual damages discussed above, the opposite presumption applies here; specific performance is denied only if the clause makes it very clear that damages was intended to be the sole remedy.[190]

Courts often enforce forfeiture-of-deposit clauses only grudgingly. Since they seem obviously designed to protect the vendor, they are construed against him or her in cases of ambiguity.[191] Moreover, some jurisdictions impose rather severe time limits and election-of-remedies concepts on vendors. For example, the Utah courts require the seller to make an immediate refund of the deposit if he or she wishes to seek damages or specific performance; if the seller retains it for an appreciable period, it becomes the only remedy.[192] In the District of Columbia, case law requires the seller to make an affirmative election to forfeit the deposit, without waiting to see whether liquidated or actual damages would be greater before doing so.[193] Yet despite these and comparable limitations in other states, the concept of forfeiture of the deposit is built into the vast majority of real estate sale contracts, probably due to its ability to reduce litigation in the general run of cases.

Catholic Charities of Archdiocese of Chicago v. Thorpe, 318 Ill. App. 3d 304, 741 N.E.2d 651 (2000), where the drafting failed to achieve that objective.

[189] Specific performance allowed: Bell v. Alsip, 435 So.2d 840 (Fla.App. 1983) (contract specifically reserved all remedies of both parties); Laseter v. Brown, 251 Ga. 179, 304 S.E.2d 72 (1983); Miller v. United States Naval Institute, 47 Md.App. 426, 423 A.2d 283 (1980). See also Houston v. Willis, 24 So. 3d 412 (Miss. Ct. App. 2009) (deposit not identified as liquidated damages; specific performance ordered).

[190] Specific performance denied: Seabaugh v. Keele, 775 S.W.2d 205 (Mo.App. 1989) (vendors' actions demonstrated that they considered liquidated damages their only remedy); Gulf City Body & Trailer Works, Inc. v. Phoenix Properties Trust, Inc., 531 So.2d 870 (Ala. 1988) (contract made forfeiture vendor's sole remedy). Specific performance granted, because clause did not make it sufficiently clear that forfeiture was the sole remedy: Conner v. Auburn Partners, L.L.L. 852 So. 2d 755 (Ala. Civ. App. 2002).

Several Florida cases deal with condominium purchase agreements which purported to limit the purchaser's sole remedy for vendor breach to a return of earnest money. The courts rejected this language as "antithetical to fair dealing in the marketplace" and awarded purchasers loss of bargain damages, see Blue Lakes Apartments, Ltd. v. George Gowing, Inc., 464 So.2d 705 (Fla. App. 1985); Clone, Inc. v. Orr, 476 So.2d 1300 (Fla.App. 1985); and specific performance, see Ocean Dunes of Hutchinson Island Dev. Corp. v. Colangelo, 463 So.2d 437 (Fla.App. 1985). They also refused to enforce the vendor's claim for forfeiture of deposit under such a clause; see IDEVCO v. Hobaugh, 571 So.2d 488 (Fla.App. 1990). Contra, see Bailey v. CitiMortgage, Inc., 13 F.Supp.3d 29 (D. D.C. 2014); Simpson Dev. Corp. v. Herrmann, 155 Vt. 332, 583 A.2d 90 (1990) (similar clause upheld, where issue had not been properly preserved on appeal); Mancini-Ciolo, Inc. v. Scaramellino, 118 A.D.2d 761, 500 N.Y.S.2d 276 (1986) (such clause valid unless vendor acts in bad faith). Clauses excluding damages, but allowing rescission and specific performance, have been sustained; see Leet v. Totah, 329 Md. 645, 620 A.2d 1372 (1993).

[191] See, e.g., Giomona Corp. v. Dawson, 568 S.W.2d 954 (Mo.App. 1978).

[192] McKeon v. Crump, 2002 Utah App. 258, 53 P.3d 494 (2002). See also Orr v. Goodwin, 157 N.H. 511, 953 A.2d 1190 (2008) (retention by vendors constitutes an election of remedies); Heflin v. Brackelsberg, 2010 Ark. App. 261, 374 S.W.3d 755 (2010) (whether retention of deposit by vendors for one year was an election of remedies was a material issue of fact); Whitman v. Knapp, 285 Ala. 57, 228 So. 2d 814 (1969) (vendor's agent's statement to purchaser that vendor would retain deposit and seek no other remedies was not a binding election of remedies); Calvetti v. Crismore, 176 Ill. App. 3d 260, 530 N.E.2d 581 (1988) (vendor's entry on property to collect rents from tenants to be applied toward purchasers' liability was not an election of remedies).

[193] Sampson v. McAdoo, 47 Md.App. 602, 425 A.2d 1 (1981) (D.C. law); Sheffield v. Paul T. Stone, Inc., 98 F.2d 250 (D.C.Cir. 1938). Cf. Erwin v. Scholfield, 416 So.2d 478 (Fla.App. 1982), rejecting the argument that a complaint by the vendor praying for actual damages or specific performance was an election of remedies, and allowing the vendor's amended complaint for liquidated damages; Avery v. Hughes, 661 F.3d 690 (1st Cir. 2011) (vendor must elect within a reasonable time after breach).

§ 10.5 REMEDIES FOR CONTRACT BREACH—
SPECIFIC PERFORMANCE

Both the vendor and purchaser are generally entitled to bring a suit in equity and obtain a decree of specific performance, compelling the other party to complete the contract. The court's order is backed by the threat of a civil contempt citation if the defendant is able but unwilling to perform.[194] The traditional bromide tells us that specific performance should be ordered only when the remedy at law is inadequate.[195] When the purchaser seeks specific performance, this test is automatically deemed satisfied; each parcel of land is unique, and no other parcel can possibly be an exact substitute for the one the purchaser bargained to buy.[196] Hence, damages are inadequate per se. This notion is generally accepted as a truism, and the courts impose no duty on the purchaser to prove the unique qualities of the land for which he or she contracted.[197]

It is not so easy to apply this reasoning when the vendor seeks specific performance. After all, if the contract were performed, the vendor would receive only money—hardly a unique commodity. Yet the courts routinely award specific performance to vendors.[198] One explanation, now thoroughly discredited, is that some principle of contract law requires mutuality of remedy, so that each party's remedies are a mirror image of the other's. There is no such operative principle, and situations in which the parties' remedies differ sharply are common.[199] Mutuality of remedy is probably a misguided extension of the quite proper notion of mutuality of obligation, which holds that each party is bound to a bilateral contract only if the other is also obligated. But mutuality of

---

[194] Hampton Island, LLC v. HAOP, LLC, 317 Ga. App. 80, 731 S.E.2d 71 (2012); Wilson v. Fenton, 312 N.W.2d 524 (Iowa 1981); Boudreaux v. Vankerkhove, 993 So. 2d 725 (La. Ct. App. 2008); Ash Park, LLC v. Alexander & Bishop, Ltd., 324 Wis. 2d 703, 783 N.W.2d 294 (2010).

[195] Restatement (Second) of Contracts § 359 (1981); Kronman, Specific Performance, 45 U.Chi.L.Rev. (1978); Perillo, Contracts § 16.1 (7th ed. 2014). The requirement of uniqueness is vigorously criticized in Schwartz, The Case for Specific Performance, 89 Yale L.J. 271 (1979).

[196] Vincent v. Vits, 208 Ill.App.3d 1, 152 Ill.Dec. 941, 566 N.E.2d 818 (1991); Schumacher v. Ihrke, 469 N.W.2d 329 (Minn. App. 1991); Broad St. Energy Co. v. Endeavor Ohio, LLC, 975 F.Supp.2d 878 (S.D. Ohio 2013), aff'd, 806 F.3d 402 (6th Cir. 2015); Friendship Manor, Inc. v. Greiman, 244 N.J.Super. 104, 581 A.2d 893 (1990); Allegheny Country Farms, Inc. v. Huffman, 237 W. Va. 355, 787 S.E.2d 626 (2016). See West's Ann.Cal.Civil Code § 3387, as amended in 1984 to provide that damages are conclusively inadequate to compensate a purchaser of a single-family dwelling who intends to occupy it, but in other cases of vendor breach are merely presumed inadequate. Cf. Straisa Realty Corp. v. Woodbury Associates, 154 A.D.2d 453, 546 N.Y.S.2d 19 (1989), appeal after remand 185 A.D.2d 96, 592 N.Y.S.2d 745 (1993) (specific performance of a contract to lease real estate to a tenant will not be awarded as a matter of course, despite physical uniqueness of the property).

[197] Treasure Valley Bank v. Long, 92 Or. App. 598, 759 P.2d 1108 (1988); O'Halloran v. Oechslie, 402 A.2d 67 (Me. 1979); Restatement (Second) of Contracts § 374 comment e. But see Perron v. Hale, 108 Idaho 578, 701 P.2d 198 (1985) (implying that court might require proof of actual uniqueness even from a purchaser).

[198] See, e.g., Abatti v. Eldridge, 103 Cal.App.3d 484, 163 Cal.Rptr. 82 (1980); Metro Holdings One, LLC v. Flynn Creek Partner, LLC, 25 N.E.3d 141 (Ind. Ct. App. 2014); Lane v. Associated Housing Developers, 767 S.W.2d 640 (Tenn.App. 1988); Thompson v. Kromhout, 413 N.W.2d 884 (Minn.App. 1987); Barker v. Francis, 741 P.2d 548 (Utah App. 1987); Steiner v. Wisconsin Am. Mut. Ins. Co, 281 Wis. 2d 395, 697 N.W.2d 452 (2005). Some Pennsylvania decisions speak of a vendor's "action for the price," but recognize that this is essentially identical to specific performance; Trachtenburg v. Sibarco Stations, Inc., 477 Pa. 517, 384 A.2d 1209 (1978).

[199] For example, a written contract signed by only one of the parties may be enforceable against only that party under the statute of frauds. On the demise of the doctrine of mutuality of remedy, see Restatement of Contracts § 372(1) and comment a (1933); 67 Williston, Contracts § 67:39 (4d ed. 2017 update); Bleecher v. Conte, 29 Cal.3d 345, 213 Cal.Rptr. 852, 698 P.2d 1154 (1981) (purchaser may obtain specific performance although vendor has waived it); Jonmil, Inc. v. McMerty, 265 N.W.2d 257 (N.D. 1978); Saliterman v. Bigos, 352 N.W.2d 494 (Minn.App. 1984).

obligation offers no explanation for the practice of awarding specific performance to sellers.

A better reason lies in the cramped definition of loss-of-bargain damages and the uncertainties of collecting consequential damages, both of which we have discussed above.[200] Because damages are measured on the date of breach, if the purchaser breaches, the vendor is left with the task of disposing of the land. This forces the vendor to pay the holding costs of the property for an unknown period and to take the risk that a falling market will result in an ultimate sale at a price well below the market value on the date of breach. Resale of the property may be further delayed by the existence of the old contract, which clouds the title until the matter has been resolved by settlement or a court decision.[201] All of these are risks that the vendor thought she or he had gotten rid of under the original contract of sale. A decree of specific performance will put them back on the purchaser, where they belong.

Still, the question remains whether specific performance for vendors should be granted automatically, as most courts do, or whether it ought to depend on a showing of actual, and not merely conceivable, risks of the type described above, as is the rule with respect to non-realty contracts.[202]

Only a few cases have taken the view that actual uniqueness must be proved. The most notable is Centex Homes Corporation v. Boag,[203] in which the developer of a 3600-unit luxury condominium housing project sought specific performance against a breaching purchaser of one of the apartment units. The Chancery Division of the New Jersey Superior Court relegated the seller to money damages,[204] emphasizing the absence of any unique qualities in a condominium unit in such a large project containing many virtually identical units. The lack of uniqueness *per se* seems somewhat irrelevant where it is the vendor who seeks specific performance. More to the point is the fact that the vendor's large pool of units and its extensive sales experience with them would probably make its proof of damages very straightforward and accurate. Hence, damages are an entirely satisfactory remedy and specific performance is unnecessary. Such a conclusion might as easily be reached in many other cases, not necessarily limited to those involving condominiums or other large developments with many similar parcels.[205]

---

[200] See supra § 10.3.

[201] Restatement (Second) of Contracts § 360, Comment e (1981). See also Tombari v. Griepp, 55 Wn.2d 771, 350 P.2d 452 (1960); Comment, 48 Temp.L.Q. 847 (1975). Further arguments for the inadequacy of damages in real estate contracts are made in Kronman, Specific Performance, 45 U.Chi.L.Rev. 351, 355–64 (1978).

[202] See Ash Park, LLC v. Alexander & Bishop, Ltd., 324 Wis. 2d 703, 783 N.W.2d 294 (2010) (specific performance for vendor may be granted or denied in trial court's discretion); Restatement (Second) of Contracts §§ 359–60 (1981).

[203] 128 N.J.Super. 385, 320 A.2d 194 (Ch.Div. 1974), noted 48 Temp.L.Q. 847 (1975); 43 U.Cin.L.Rev. 935 (1974). See Pruitt v. Graziano, 215 N.J.Super. 330, 521 A.2d 1313 (1987) and Giannini v. First Nat. Bank, 136 Ill.App.3d 971, 91 Ill.Dec. 438, 483 N.E.2d 924 (1985), awarding condominium unit *purchasers* specific performance despite the vendor's assertion that it had many similar units on the market, rendering the real estate non-unique.

[204] Since the contract contained a liquidated damages clause which the court construed as limiting damages to the amount paid at the time of the breach, the vendor was permitted to retain the $525 earnest money deposit but denied any further recovery.

[205] The Idaho Supreme Court reached a similar conclusion in Suchan v. Rutherford, 90 Idaho 288, 410 P.2d 434 (1966), but it was also influenced by the fact that the sales contract contemplated the execution, at closing, of an 18-year installment contract; the court was reluctant to attempt enforcement *in specie* of such a contract which, it thought, might subsequently appear inequitable or involve further defaults. See also Manning v. Bleifus, 166 W.Va. 131, 272 S.E.2d 821 (1980) (dictum). The Idaho courts subsequently adopted a

The *Centex* court's emphasis on lack of uniqueness suggests a more unorthodox question: should *purchasers* of real estate automatically be permitted to treat damages as inadequate, particularly in situations in which many substantially similar properties are readily obtainable? Thus far no American court has seen fit to depart from the traditional view on this point.

There are several situations in which a court will not grant specific performance. Obviously, if the plaintiff is in material breach,[206] or there are unfulfilled conditions, imposed by the terms of the contract, that were intended to protect the defendant's interests, the plaintiff cannot prevail.[207] As we have already seen, a liquidated damage clause may be construed to exclude other remedies including specific performance;[208] likewise, a clause in the contract may expressly deny specific performance.[209] Obviously no remedy *in specie* can be ordered if the vendor has already transferred the land to a bona fide purchaser,[210] or if for other reasons the vendor has no (or defective) title.[211] A few courts have rejected specific performance as a remedy for purchasers who were buying only for immediate resale, on the grounds that their damages were readily

---

policy which permits one resisting specific performance to adduce evidence that rebuts the general presumption that the land is unique; see Wood v. Simonson, 108 Idaho 699, 701 P.2d 319 (App. 1985); Perron v. Hale, 108 Idaho 578, 701 P.2d 198 (1985).

[206] The plaintiff must be ready, willing, and able to perform; see Frumento v. Mezzanotte, 192 Conn. 606, 473 A.2d 1193 (1984); B.A.G. Investments, Inc. v. Victoria Apartments Partnership, 2002 WL 31888209 (Cal. Super. Ct. 2002) (unpublished).

[207] See, e.g., Blackmore v. Honnas, 141 Ariz. 354, 687 P.2d 362 (App. 1984) (purchaser who abandoned contract by taking no action for $6\frac{1}{2}$ months after vendors' breach cannot obtain specific performance); Henderson v. Winkler, 454 So.2d 1358 (Ala. 1984) (after mutual rescission, purchaser may not obtain specific performance); Cohen v. Rasner, 97 Nev. 118, 624 P.2d 1006 (1981); Annot., 55 A.L.R.3d 10 (1974). Cf. Baugh v. Johnson, 6 Ark.App. 308, 641 S.W.2d 730 (1982) (vendor can get specific performance despite minor deficiency in land area).

[208] See the discussion at § 10.4 note 190 supra and accompanying text; Kohrs v. Barth, 212 Ill.App.3d 468, 156 Ill.Dec. 551, 570 N.E.2d 1273 (1991); Seabaugh v. Keele, 775 S.W.2d 205 (Mo.App. 1989); Gulf City Body & Trailer Works, Inc. v. Phoenix Properties Trust, Inc., 531 So.2d 870 (Ala. 1988); In re Columbus Plaza, Inc., 79 B.R. 710 (Bkrtcy.S.D.Ohio 1987). But see Logue v. Seven-Hot Springs Corp., 926 F.2d 722 (8th Cir. 1991) (liquidated damages not intended to be vendor's exclusive remedy); Saliterman v. Bigos, 352 N.W.2d 494 (Minn. App. 1984) (even though contract limits *vendor's* remedy to rescission, *purchaser* may obtain specific performance; mutuality of remedy is not required).

[209] Bailey v. CitiMortgage, Inc., 13 F.Supp.3d 29 (D. D.C. 2014); Kessler v. Tortoise Devel., Inc., 130 Idaho 105, 937 P.2d 417 (Idaho 1997); S.E.S. Importers, Inc. v. Pappalardo, 53 N.Y.2d 455, 442 N.Y.S.2d 453, 425 N.E.2d 841 (1981); Bleecher v. Conte, 29 Cal.3d 345, 213 Cal.Rptr. 852, 698 P.2d 1154 (1981). However, the mere mention in the contract that particular remedy is available is not enough to exclude other remedies; see Dean V. Kruse Foundation, Inc. v. Gates, 973 N.E.2d 583 (Ind. Ct. App. 2012).

[210] Allegheny Country Farms, Inc. v. Huffman, 237 W. Va. 355, 787 S.E.2d 626 (2016). If the vendor does so, frustrating the purchaser's specific performance claim, the court may award the purchaser damages; UFG, LLC v. Southwest Corp., 848 N.E. 2d 353 (Ind. App. 2006). Damages may be measured by the vendor's price from the sale to the third party, thus forcing the vendor to disgorge any profit; Schachter v. Krzynowek, 958 So.2d 1061 (Fla. Ct. App. 2007). Contra, limiting damages to a measure based on value at the time of breach, see Reese v. Wong, 93 Cal. App. 4th 51, 112 Cal. Rptr. 2d 669 (2001).

[211] Barnes v. McKellar, 434 Pa.Super. 597, 644 A.2d 770 (Pa.Super. 1994); Canton v. Monaco Partnership, 156 Ariz. 468, 753 P.2d 158 (1987); Smith v. Hooker/Barnes, Inc., 253 Ga. 514, 322 S.E.2d 268 (1984); Carson v. Isabel Apartments, Inc., 20 Wn. App. 293, 579 P.2d 1027 (1978). But see Giannini v. First Nat. Bank, 136 Ill.App.3d 971, 91 Ill.Dec. 438, 483 N.E.2d 924 (1985), granting specific performance of sale of a condominium unit despite the fact that the vendor had not yet converted the building into a condominium. If the vendor's title or interest is only partially deficient, the purchaser can generally get specific performance with abatement of the price; see § 10.3 supra at note 163. If the vendor has transferred title to one with notice of the contract, specific performance will lie against the title-holder; Hallmark Builders, Inc. v. Hickory Lakes of Brandon, Inc., 458 So.2d 45 (Fla.App. 1984); Dean Operations, Inc. v. Pink Hill Associates, 678 S.W.2d 897 (Mo.App. 1984); Glynn v. Marquette, 152 Cal.App.3d 277, 199 Cal.Rptr. 306 (1984). Cf. E.G. Realty, Inc. v. Nova-Park New York, Inc., 176 A.D.2d 680, 575 N.Y.S.2d 481 (1991).

computable and that the land's unique qualities were irrelevant to them except as reflected in their prospective profits.[212] Finally, many courts require a higher degree of specificity for enforcement of contracts at equity than in law;[213] hence, damages may be available even though the contract's language is too vague to warrant specific performance.[214]

An interesting question arises when specific performance is sought against the purchaser who claims it is impossible for him or her to raise the funds to pay the purchase price. It is theoretically possible to prevail with this defense, but the courts are extremely reluctant to deny the vendor specific performance on grounds that it is impossible for the purchaser to perform.[215]

Perhaps the most important and least predictable barrier to specific performance is the notion that the remedy is inherently discretionary and should not be ordered where it would lead to an unjust result. Obviously this concept includes such matters as the plaintiff's fraud, deception, undue influence, concealment of material facts, or the like, even if the misbehavior is not so serious as to deny remedies at law or to make the plaintiff liable for damages; equity is more vigilant than the law.[216] It also encompasses cases involving no misbehavior *per se* in which specific enforcement would produce hardship to the defendant or to third parties.[217] The most variable results are found

---

[212] Watkins v. Paul, 95 Idaho 499, 511 P.2d 781 (1973); Schmid v. Whitten, 114 S.C. 245, 103 S.E. 553 (1920). Contra, see Chan v. Smider, 31 Wn.App. 730, 644 P.2d 727 (1982); Justus v. Clelland, 133 Ariz. 381, 651 P.2d 1206 (App. 1982).

[213] Barkho v. Ready, 523 S.W.3d 37, 43 (Mo. Ct. App. 2017).

[214] Povey v. Clow, 146 Or.App. 760, 934 P.2d 528 (Or.App. 1997); Sayer v. Bowley, 243 Neb. 801, 503 N.W.2d 166 (Neb. 1993); Honolulu Waterfront Ltd. Partnership v. Aloha Tower Development Corp., 692 F.Supp. 1230 (D.Hawai'i 1988), affirmed 891 F.2d 295 (9th Cir. 1989); Note, 5 U.C.L.A.-Alaska L.Rev. 112 (1975). If the contract requires the vendor to subordinate a purchase-money mortgage to a future construction loan, specific performance may be denied if the latter loan is not fully described in the contract; see Farrell v. Phillips, 414 So.2d 1119 (Fla.App.1982); Nelson, Whitman, Burkhart & Freyermuth, Real Estate Finance Law § 12.9 (6th ed. 2014). But see Marder's Nurseries, Inc. v. Hopping, 171 A.D.2d 63, 573 N.Y.S.2d 990 (1991) (contract was specifically enforceable despite its lack of statement of interest rate on purchase-money mortgage, where purchaser had the option of paying all cash); White Hen Pantry, Inc. v. Cha, 214 Ill.App.3d 627, 158 Ill.Dec. 310, 574 N.E.2d 104 (1991) (contract was specifically enforceable despite lack of reference to type of deed, apportionment of taxes, closing date, and other minor matters).

[215] Hampton Island, LLC v. HAOP, LLC, 306 Ga. App. 542, 702 S.E.2d 770 (2010); Fazzio v. Mason, 150 Idaho 591, 249 P.3d 390 (2011); Ash Park, LLC v. Alexander & Bishop, Ltd., 324 Wis. 2d 703, 783 N.W.2d 294 (2010). "[L]imited financial resources sometimes may be a defense to contempt, but only when it is proved that the person to be held in contempt has exhausted all of the resources and assets available to him, has made a diligent and good faith effort to comply;" Hampton Island, LLC v. HAOP, LLC, 317 Ga. App. 80, 731 S.E.2d 71 (2012).

[216] Decisions denying specific performance on grounds of the plaintiff's inequitable conduct include Dergo v. Kollias, 567 N.W.2d 443 (Iowa App. 1997) (purchaser failed to disclose identity of true buyer); Lincoln-Mercury Inc. v. J & H Landfill, Inc., 493 N.W.2d 375 (Wis.App. 1992) (sale would violate subdivision ordinance); Estate of Younge v. Huysmans, 127 N.H. 461, 506 A.2d 282 (1985) (purchaser's laches); Nahn v. Soffer, 824 S.W.2d 442 (Mo.App.1991) (purchaser's laches); Cimina v. Bronich, 349 Pa.Super. 399, 503 A.2d 427 (1985) (tenant-purchaser failed to pay taxes as required by lease); In re Estate of Mihm, 345 Pa.Super. 1, 497 A.2d 612 (1985) (purchasers breached a confidential relationship with vendor); Barnard & Son, Inc. v. Akins, 109 Idaho 466, 708 P.2d 871 (1985) (both parties breached contract); Kauffmann v. Baker, 392 So.2d 13 (Fla.App.1980) (both parties conspired to inflate the price and deceive the lender). But see Oneida City School Dist. v. Seiden & Sons, Inc., 177 A.D.2d 828, 576 N.Y.S.2d 442 (1991) (vendor awarded specific performance despite its knowledge that the purchaser would not be able to get zoning approval for its intended use of the land); Kessler v. Tortoise Dev., Inc., 134 Idaho 264, 1 P.3d 292 (2000) (court ordered specific performance for purchaser on condition that purchaser paid certain costs of vendor incurred to prepare for quick closing).

[217] See Kilarjian v. Vastola, 379 N.J. Super. 277, 877 A.2d 372 (N.J. Super. Ct. 2004) (court refused to order specific performance because of increased severity of vendor wife's debilitating illness); Citrone v. SNJ Assoc., 682 A.2d 92 (R.I. 1996) (purchaser's development of land would be delayed eight years by unexpected regulatory proceedings); Bailey v. Musumeci, 134 N.H. 280, 591 A.2d 1316 (1991) purchaser acted under a

when the hardship is simply an unfair price—too high if the vendor is the plaintiff, or too low if the purchaser is seeking enforcement. The answer here depends on numerous factors, some of which may be unarticulated: the size of the mismatch between price and value, the relative sophistication and bargaining power of the parties, and the adequacy of other remedies.[218]

Finally, note that specific performance does not always provide a full remedy for the plaintiff's harm, since the decree is almost invariably delayed beyond the date fixed by the contract. Hence, incidental damages may be awarded along with the order compelling performance.[219] An excellent example is Godwin v. Lindbert,[220] in which the purchaser obtained an order of specific performance but found that as a result of rising interest rates, the financing of the purchase would be much more costly than anticipated when the contract was formed. The court agreed and awarded damages to reflect the higher cost of mortgage funds. A similar argument can be made by a purchaser whose possession of the property is delayed during the prosecution of a specific performance action, and who seeks to recover the fair rental value of the property from the date agreed for performance until the actual performance.[221] However, in most cases the purchaser has also been spared the necessity of investing cash in the property during the same period—except perhaps an earnest money deposit. In addition, the vendor may have paid the carrying costs of the property—property taxes, insurance premiums, costs of security, and the like—during the period of delay. These factors tend to offset the purchaser's rental-value claim, often leaving the purchaser with little or no net damages.[222]

---

unilateral mistake); Herzog v. Belizario, 52 Misc. 3d 583, 28 N.Y.S.3d 822 (N.Y. Sup. 2016); Anderson v. Onsager, 155 Wis.2d 504, 455 N.W.2d 885 (1990); Dawdy v. Sample, 178 Ill.App.3d 118, 127 Ill.Dec. 299, 532 N.E.2d 1128 (1989), appeal denied 125 Ill.2d 564, 130 Ill.Dec. 479, 537 N.E.2d 808 (1989); Thompson v. Kromhout, 413 N.W.2d 884 (Minn.App. 1987); Maggs, Remedies for Breach of Contract Under Article Two of the U.L.T.A., 11 Ga.L.Rev. 275 (1977).

[218] Numerous cases deny specific performance where the price is grossly unfair; see, e.g., Wagner v. Estate of Rummel, 391 Pa.Super. 555, 571 A.2d 1055 (1990), appeal denied 527 Pa. 588, 588 A.2d 510 (1991) (chancellor should consider unfairness, where testimony indicated land was worth 100 times contract price); Jensen v. Southwestern States Management Co., 6 Kan. App.2d 437, 629 P.2d 752 (1981); Official Code Ga.Ann. § 37–805. Cf. Giannini v. First Nat. Bank, 136 Ill.App.3d 971, 91 Ill. Dec. 438, 483 N.E.2d 924 (1985), holding "there is no hardship in compelling the seller to do what he agreed to do when he thought it was to his advantage;" Resource Management Co. v. Weston Ranch and Livestock Co., 706 P.2d 1028 (Utah 1985); Seabaugh v. Sailer, 679 S.W.2d 924 (Mo. App. 1984). Denial of specific performance due to unfairness of price is strongly criticized by Schwartz, supra note 195, at 299–301.

[219] See Restatement (Second) of Contracts § 358, Comment c (1981); Annot., 11 A.L.R. 4th 891 (1981); III Lounge, Inc. v. Gaines, 227 Neb. 585, 419 N.W.2d 143 (1988) (where vendor had possession during period of delay, he was liable for taxes, repairs, utilities and insurance accruing during that time); Cooperstein v. Patrician Estates, 117 A.D.2d 774, 499 N.Y.S.2d 423 (1986) (purchaser granted specific performance of contract to convey, plus damages due to vendor's failure to complete construction of house on the land).

[220] 101 Mich.App. 754, 300 N.W.2d 514 (1980); see also Housing Authority of Monterey County v. Monterey Senior Citizen Park, 164 Cal.App.3d 348, 210 Cal.Rptr. 497 (1985); Amick v. Hagler, 286 S.C. 481, 334 S.E.2d 525 (App .1985). But see Wall v. Pate, 104 N.M. 1, 715 P.2d 449 (1986) (where vendor breaches and no sale occurs, purchaser may not recover damages for loss of opportunity to assume advantageous mortgage); Smith v. Stout, 40 Wn.App. 646, 700 P.2d 343 (1985) (same). See generally Garland, Purchaser's Interest Rate Increase: Caveat Venditor, 27 N.Y.L.Sch. L.Rev. 745 (1982).

[221] But see Marshall v. Bare, 107 Idaho 201, 687 P.2d 591 (App. 1984) (vendor may not recover rental value where purchaser went into possession prior to passage of title).

[222] Dillingham Commercial Co., Inc. v. Spears, 641 P.2d 1 (Alaska 1982); B.A.G. Investments, Inc. v. Victoria Apartments Partnership, 2002 WL 31888209 (Cal. Ct. App. 2002) (unpublished); Futernick v. Trushina, 207 So.3d 329 (Fla. Ct. App. 2016); Bohlin v. Jungbauer, 615 N.E.2d 438 (Ind. Ct. App. 1993); Rekhi v. Olason, 28 Wn.App. 751, 626 P.2d 513 (1981). A similar analysis can be applied when the vendor seeks specific performance; the vendor has typically lost the interest which could have been earned on the purchase

As already noted, specific performance and general damages are alternative remedies, and a contracting party cannot obtain both.[223] However, if the vendor is unable to supply the full land area contracted for, or if the property has other deficiencies, the purchaser may still obtain a decree of specific performance, but with an abatement of the price to reflect the property's insufficiency.[224]

§ 10.6 REMEDIES FOR CONTRACT BREACH—VENDOR'S LIEN

Courts of equity generally recognize an implied lien, much like a mortgage on the land, in favor of the vendor for the amount of the unpaid purchase price.[225] Prior to the transfer of legal title by deed, the purchaser has an equitable title to the property under the doctrine of equitable conversion.[226] The vendor's lien exists on this equitable interest,[227] although as a practical matter it usually has little significance, since the vendor who has not conveyed legal title at the time the purchaser defaults will ordinarily seek either damages or specific performance, or even more commonly will attempt to terminate purchaser's rights under the contract and forfeit the payments made to date.[228] Thus, efforts to foreclose formally on the vendor's lien are rare when the default has occurred before title has passed at the closing or "settlement."[229]

After legal title has been transferred to the purchaser, the vendor's (perhaps more aptly, "grantor's") lien is imposed on that interest and is of much greater practical importance, since retention of title is no longer an option open to the seller. Even here,

---

price, but at the same time has had the use or rental value of the property from the agreed closing date. See Kassir v. Zahabi, 164 Cal. App. 4th 1352, 80 Cal. Rptr. 3d 1 (2008); Paris v. Allbaugh, 41 Wn.App. 717, 704 P.2d 660 (1985) (where specific performance is ordered against vendor in default, he is entitled to interest on the price only to the extent that it is offset against rents and profits from the property during the period of delay); Shelter Corp. v. Bozin, 468 So.2d 1094 (Fla.App. 1985) (same).

[223] McMaster v. Strickland, 322 S.C. 451, 472 S.E.2d 623 (1996).

[224] See § 10.3 notes 168–170 supra.

[225] See Golden v. Woodward, 15 So. 3d 664 (Fla. Dist. Ct. App. 2009); Krajcir v. Egidi, 305 Ill.App.3d 613, 238 Ill.Dec. 813, 712 N.E.2d 917 (Ill. App. 1999); In re Butler, 552 N.W.2d 226, 229 (Minn. 1996); Rader v. Dawes, 651 S.W.2d 629 (Mo.App. 1983); Easterling v. Ferris, 651 P.2d 677 (Okl. 1982); McGoodwin v. McGoodwin, 671 S.W.2d 880 (Tex. 1984). A number of states recognize the lien by statute; see, e.g., Idaho Code § 45–801, discussed in Estates of Somers v. Clearwater Power Co., 107 Idaho 29, 684 P.2d 1006 (1984) (judgment lien against vendor does not attach to vendor's lien); Mont.Code Ann. § 71–3–1301; Ohio Rev.Code § 5301.26; 42 Okla. Stat.1981, § 26; South Dakota Compiled Laws 44–6–1. The lien is confined to the purchase price of the land; the price of personal goods or sums owing on other debts cannot be included; Inwood North Homeowners' Ass'n v. Harris, 707 S.W.2d 127 (Tex.App. 1986), judgment reversed on other grounds 736 S.W.2d 632 (Tex.1987) (vendor's lien does not include amount owing on assessments by owners association in subdivision); Lessard v. Lessard Acres, Inc., 349 So.2d 293 (La. 1977); Grace Development Co., Inc. v. Houston, 306 Minn. 334, 237 N.W.2d 73 (1975). But see Krone v. McCann, 219 Mont. 353, 711 P.2d 1367 (1986) (vendor's lien may include attorneys' fees, where contract so provides). The lien attaches only to the land sold (or to be sold), and not to personal property; see First Const. Credit, Inc. v. Simonson Lumber of Waite Park, Inc., 663 N.W.2d 14 (Minn. Ct. App. 2003).

[226] The concept of equitable conversion is discussed at § 10.13 infra.

[227] See Huffman v. Foreman, 163 Ind. App. 263, 323 N.E.2d 651 (1975); Butler v. Wilkinson, 740 P.2d 1244 (Utah 1987); D. Dobbs, Remedies § 12.12(4) (2d ed. 1993). Professor Pomeroy argued that the term "vendor's lien" was a misnomer. He urged that while prior to the passage of legal title the vendor had the rights mentioned in the text, they in no sense constituted a lien. After title was conveyed, he conceded that a lien existed, but preferred to term it the "grantor's lien" J. Pomeroy, Equity Jurisprudence §§ 1249, 1260 (Symonds ed. 1941). This usage, however, has not generally been followed by the courts.

[228] Indeed, this right is sometimes itself termed a vendor's lien; see Stagg v. Van Sant, 390 So.2d 620 (Ala.1980); Dobbs, supra note 227.

[229] But see Sebastian v. Floyd, 585 S.W.2d 381 (Ky.1979), in which the court held that forfeiture was unavailable to an installment contract vendor and relegated him to an action to foreclose the lien by judicial sale.

however, the assertion of the vendor's lien is not very common. One reason is that in many transactions the contract provides for full payment of the price in cash at settlement. Even when payment is deferred, most vendors obtain and enforce the more specific type of security represented by a recorded purchase-money mortgage or deed of trust. In such cases the vendor's lien seems irrelevant, and some courts hold that it is waived by the taking of other security.[230] In any event, neither the parties nor their lawyers are likely to realize that it exists.[231]

The vendor's lien is an invention of the equity courts. As an "implied" lien it does not depend on any specific language in the sale contract or the deed, although it certainly may be mentioned therein and in some jurisdictions it is customary to do so.[232] It will be subordinate in priority to a mortgage given contemporaneously by the purchaser to a third-party lender, unless it is memorialized by a written and recorded document (rarely the case except in Texas[233]) or the lender has actual knowledge of it.[234]

The vendor's lien is commonly foreclosed by the same sort of judicial action in equity by which mortgages are foreclosed.[235] The term "foreclosed" is quite appropriate, since if the purchaser fails to pay the remaining balance of the price before foreclosure is decreed, the purchaser's opportunity to acquire the land is permanently lost. Foreclosure may be by judicially-supervised sale, typically conducted by the sheriff, with the highest bidder taking the land.[236] The proceeds are paid first to the vendor in the amount of the

---

[230] Wartux Assocs. v. Kings Coll., 161 Misc. 2d 733, 616 N.Y.S.2d 417 (Sup. Ct. 1994). Contra, recognizing the validity of the lien even though express security has been taken, see Goidl v. North American Mortgage Investors, 564 S.W.2d 493 (Tex.Civ. App. 1978); Rader v. Dawes, 651 S.W.2d 629 (Mo.App. 1983).

[231] One may well have a vendor's lien without realizing it, much less mentioning it in the contract of sale or other documents; see Maroney v. Boyle, 141 N.Y. 462, 36 N.E. 511, 38 Am.St.Rep. 821 (1894).

[232] See, e.g., Arkansas State Highway Commission v. First Pyramid Life Insurance Co., 265 Ark. 417, 579 S.W.2d 587 (1979); R & P Enterprises v. LaGuarta, Gavrel & Kirk, Inc., 596 S.W.2d 517 (Tex. 1980). Professor Pomeroy pointed out that where the lien is reserved by express language, especially in a recorded deed, it becomes a more powerful tool for the vendor in several respects. Courts are much less likely to find a waiver through the taking of other security; the recordation will give notice of the lien to all subsequent takers, precluding their assertion of BFP status; and there is no doubt (as there sometimes is with respect to a purely implied lien) of its assignability by the vendor to another. See J. Pomeroy, Equity Jurisprudence §§ 1257–59 (Symonds ed. 1941).

Texas is unique in the use of vendors' liens. If the grantor is financing the sale, the customary warranty deed includes an express reservation of a vendor's lien to the grantor. If the purchaser is financing the property with a loan from a third party lender, a clause will also be included in the deed assigning the vendor's lien to the lender. This is done even though the lender (or the grantor, in the case of seller financing) will also take a separate deed of trust on the property; the two forms of security exist side-by-side. The principal benefit of the separate vendor's lien from the lender's viewpoint is that it permits repossession of the property without the necessity of foreclosure of the deed of trust; Glenn v. Lucas, 376 S.W.3d 268, 275 (Tex. App. 2012). See Nixon, A Review of Texas Real Property Liens 9–10, available at http://www.ccsb.com/Publications/Texas_Property_Liens.pdf; McGlinchey, Stafford & Youngblood, The Importance of Lender-Counsel's Review of the Deed in a Texas Purchase-Money Loan Transaction (2010); Norvell, The Vendor's Lien and Reservation of the Paramount Legal Title et al., 44 Tex.L.Rev 22 (1965). While vendor's liens are customarily documented in Texas as explained above, an implied equitable lien will arise even without any documentation; Skelton v. Washington Mut. Bank, F.A., 61 S.W.3d 56, 60 (Tex. App. 2001).

[233] See the preceding footnote.

[234] Sunnyside Feedyard, L.C. v. Metro. Life Ins. Co., 106 S.W.3d 169 (Tex. App. 2003).

[235] See Quintana v. Anthony, 109 Idaho 977, 712 P.2d 678 (App. 1985) (vendor's lien is not technically a mortgage, but courts of equity enforcing such liens should generally follow mortgage law concepts of debtor protection, including Idaho's "one-action" or "security first" rule, its fair value limitation on deficiency judgments, and its statutory post-foreclosure redemption); Sewer v. Martin, 511 F.2d 1134 (3d Cir. 1975); 3 Am. L.Prop. § 11.74 (1952).

[236] See Annot., 77 A.L.R. 270 (1932). In some states if the vendor obtains a decree for specific performance and the purchaser refuses to pay the price, the court can order the property sold at a public sale

unpaid portion of the contract price; any surplus proceeds are distributed to the contract vendee or to others who claim through or under him or her.[237] If the proceeds are insufficient to cover the remaining sale price, many jurisdictions will give the vendor a personal judgment for the deficiency.[238]

An alternative to foreclosure by judicial sale is strict foreclosure, a procedure under which the court gives the purchaser a specific time period within which to pay the remaining price.[239] If the purchaser fails to do so, the court decrees that full title is in the vendor, and the purchaser's rights are cancelled. In cases in which legal title by deed has not yet been conveyed, the result of strict foreclosure is not materially different than if the vendor had simply retained title and obtained a court decree forfeiting the purchaser's rights. There is ordinarily no possibility of the purchaser's recovering any of the payments made on the contract, a fact which obviously leads to potential injustice to the purchaser whenever strict foreclosure is ordered. In many jurisdictions statutes or court decisions prohibit the strict foreclosure of ordinary mortgages, and instead require foreclosure by sale.[240] Whether similar rules will or should be applied to the foreclosure of vendor's liens is often hard to tell, although they present a similar risk of unfairness.[241] Since forfeiture of earnest money deposits is so widely accepted in American courts,[242] it is hard to see any reason for denying strict foreclosure of vendors' liens unless the result would be inequitable on the facts of the case.

Ordinarily the vendor's lien is asserted only when the vendor has not taken back some specific type of security interest in the land by way of mortgage or deed of trust. Indeed, many cases treat the taking of a purchase-money mortgage as inherently inconsistent with the equitable lien, and hence as waiving it, unless it is expressly reserved.[243] But if an express reservation is made in the documents, a purchase-money

---

and the proceeds applied against the purchase obligation. In effect, this procedure converts specific performance into a judicial foreclosure of the vendor's lien. See Clements v. Leonard, 70 So.2d 840 (Fla. 1954).

[237] On judicial foreclosure of mortgages, see generally, Nelson, Whitman, Burkhart & Freyermuth, Real Estate Finance Law § 7.16 (6th ed. 2014).

[238] See Quintana v. Anthony, 109 Idaho 977, 712 P.2d 678 (App. 1985); Carman v. Gibbs, 220 Neb. 603, 371 N.W.2d 283 (1985); Ricard v. Equitable Life Assur. Soc., 462 So.2d 592 (Fla.App. 1985); R & P Enterprises v. LaGuarta, Gavrel & Kirk, Inc., 596 S.W.2d 517 (Tex. 1980). A jurisdiction which by statute limits or prohibits deficiency judgments after mortgage foreclosures is likely to take a similar position with respect to deficiency judgments following vendor's lien foreclosures; see Nevin v. Salk, 45 Cal. App.3d 331, 119 Cal.Rptr. 370 (1975).

[239] See Zumstein v. Stockton, 199 Or. 633, 264 P.2d 455 (1953); Walton v. First Nat. Bank of Trenton, Trenton, Tex., 956 S.W.2d 647, 652 (Tex. App. 1997); 3 Am.L.Prop. § 11.75. On strict foreclosure of mortgages, see generally, Nelson, Whitman, Burkhart & Freyermuth, Real Estate Finance Law § 7.9 (6th ed. 2014).

[240] Nelson, Whitman, Burkhart & Freyermuth, id.

[241] In Sebastian v. Floyd, 585 S.W.2d 381 (Ky. 1979), the court held that the vendor's lien was analogous to a mortgage and hence must be foreclosed as one—by judicial sale rather than strict foreclosure or forfeiture.

It is arguable that strict foreclosure never disadvantages the purchaser, since if the land had substantial value in excess of the balance owing on the contract the purchaser would resell or refinance it and pay the debt; see Dieffenbach v. Attorney General of Vermont, 604 F.2d 187 (2d Cir. 1979). But this view disregards the expenses of sale or refinancing, as well as the very real possibility that these actions may be entirely impractical in periods of market weakness or high interest rates. Many courts will refuse strict foreclosure in any case in which the value of the land substantially exceeds the unpaid portion of the price; see, e.g., Riffey v. Schulke, 193 Neb. 317, 227 N.W.2d 4 (1975); Marquardt v. Fisher, 135 Or. 256, 295 P. 499, 77 A.L.R. 265 (1931). Such an approach roughly parallels the minority doctrine which refuses to permit forfeiture of the purchaser's interest in the contract when it would be unconscionable to do so. See text at § 10.4 notes 176–181 supra.

[242] See text at § 10.4 notes 176–177 supra.

[243] Back v. Union Life Insurance Co., 5 Ark.App. 176, 634 S.W.2d 150 (1982); Edwards-Town, Inc. v. Dimin, 9 Cal. App. 3d 87, 87 Cal. Rptr. 726 (Ct. App. 1970); Oliver v. Mercaldi, 103 So.2d 665, 67 A.L.R.2d 1089 (Fla.App. 1958); Finlayson v. Waller, 64 Idaho 618, 134 P.2d 1069 (1943); Stump v. Swanson Dev. Co.,

mortgage and a vendor's lien can exist side by side. The lien could have significant consequences if, for example, the vendor subordinated the mortgage to other claims on the land but did not mention the vendor's lien when doing so.[244]

In general, the lien remains on the property even if the purchaser makes a further transfer. But if (as very often happens) the original purchaser makes a resale to a bona fide purchaser for value, the new subpurchaser takes free of the lien.[245] This result is usually explained on the ground that the lien is equitable in origin, and that equity will not impose the lien on an innocent party; as it is often put, the legal interest acquired by a BFP will prevail over a prior equity.[246] Even if the lien were conceived as growing out of the contract, one would usually reach the same result by the operation of the recording acts; if the contract is unrecorded (as is usually the case with short-term earnest money agreements), the lien would be void as against subsequent BFP's (who record first, if the jurisdiction has a notice-race recording statute.)[247] The choice between these two rationales could be highly important, however, in a notice-race state if the BFP failed to record his or her conveyance. Most of the decisions merely state the BFP's protected position without bothering to explain its theoretical basis.

Since the question whether the subsequent purchaser has notice of the lien is a crucial one, it is necessary to consider what will give notice. If the subpurchaser knows or has reason to know that the full purchase price on the prior contract is still unpaid, that is surely enough.[248] On the other hand, it is very doubtful whether mere knowledge that a prior contract existed will deny BFP status;[249] after all, a very large proportion of land transfers are preceded by sales contracts. But if the contract or deed recites that part of the price will be paid after settlement, and if it is recorded or the subpurchaser has other notice of it, he or she should be bound by the lien.[250]

LLC, 2014 Ill. App. 3d 110784, 5 N.E.3d 279, 298 (2014); Buhecker v. R. B. Petersen & Sons Constr. Co., 112 Nev. 1498, 929 P.2d 937 (Nev. 1996); Wartux Associates v. Kings College, 161 Misc.2d 733, 616 N.Y.S.2d 417 (N.Y.Sup. 1994). This result follows from statute in Ohio; see Ohio Rev.Code § 5301.26; Summer & Co. v. DCR Corp., 47 Ohio St.2d 254, 351 N.E.2d 485 (1976). In Oklahoma a statute apparently restricts the vendor's lien to cases in which the debt is otherwise unsecured; 42 Okla.Stat. § 26. Cases permitting the vendor's lien to coexist with express security include Whelan v. Midland Mortgage Co., 591 P.2d 287 (Okl. 1978); In re Midwestern Companies, Inc., 49 B.R. 98 (Bkrtcy. W.D.Mo. 1985); Graves v. Joyce, 590 So.2d 1261 (La.App. 1991); Rader v. Dawes, 651 S.W.2d 629 (Mo.App. 1983).

[244] Goidl v. North American Mortgage Investors, 564 S.W.2d 493 (Tex.Civ.App. 1978); Rader v. Dawes, id.

[245] AgriBank FCB v. Maxfield, 316 Ark. 566, 873 S.W.2d 514 (Ark. 1994); Stanovsky v. Group Enterprise & Const. Co., 714 S.W.2d 836 (Mo.App. 1986); Anjo Restaurant Corp. v. Sunrise Hotel Corp., 98 Misc.2d 597, 414 N.Y.S.2d 265 (1979). Typically judgment creditors are not treated as bona fide purchasers, since they do not give consideration contemporaneously with their acquisition of an interest in the land. But at least one state by statute protects even them from vendor's liens of which they have no notice; Ohio Rev.Code § 5301.26.

[246] See 2 Pomeroy, Equity Jurisprudence §§ 413, 1253 (Symonds ed. 1941). The prevailing view is that the lien is implied in law and not derived from the contract; Weaver v. Blake, 300 N.W.2d 52 (S.D. 1980); Old First National Bank & Trust Co. v. Scheuman, 214 Ind. 652, 13 N.E.2d 551, 119 A.L.R. 1165 (1938).

[247] See the discussion of recording acts, § 11.9 infra at note 471ff. In Brock v. First South Sav. Ass'n, 8 Cal.App.4th 661, 10 Cal.Rptr.2d 700 (Cal.App. 1992), the court held that a purchase-money mortgage to a third-party lender prevailed over the vendor's lien for the unpaid purchase price, irrespective of the operation of the recording acts and irrespective of the mortgagee's knowledge of the vendor's lien.

[248] See, e.g., Edwards-Town, Inc. v. Dimin, 9 Cal.App.3d 87, 87 Cal.Rptr. 726 (1970) (subpurchaser had notice from actual reading of prior contract); 21 West, Inc. v. Meadowgreen Trails, Inc., 913 S.W.2d 858 (Mo.Ct. App. 1995) (transferee had notice that contract had been breached and suit had been filed); Rader v. Dawes, 651 S.W.2d 629 (Mo. Ct. App. 1983) (mortgage lender had knowledge that vendors had not been paid in full).

[249] Stump v. Swanson Development Co., LLC, 2014 Ill. App. 3d 110784, 5 N.E.3d 279, 301 (2014).

[250] If a deed in the chain of title recites the fact that payment of the price is deferred, it will give notice of the lien to the subpurchaser whether it is recorded or not, since one is presumed to have examined one's

Vendors can waive their liens, and courts often find such waivers by examining their behavior.[251] Since a waiver can be inferred from any act which suggests an intent not to rely on the lien, the waiver cases are somewhat unpredictable and suggest that considerable judicial manipulation may be occurring to reach conclusions which are in reality supported by general considerations of fairness or other unstated reasons.[252] As noted above, in numerous jurisdictions the vendor's taking of a purchase-money mortgage or other express security will act as a waiver of the lien.[253]

§ 10.7   REMEDIES FOR CONTRACT BREACH—RESTITUTION

Restitution suggests the returning, by a party to a contract, of the performance he or she has received from the other party.[254] It makes sense only if for some reason the contract will not be performed in accordance with its original terms. While it is quite possible for a party to make restitution voluntarily, our concern here is with judicially-ordered restitution as a remedy for contract breach. It can be a much more attractive remedy than damages to a party who has made an unfavorable bargain. For example, a vendor whose land was worth $100,000 when he agreed to sell it for that amount, and worth the same at the time of breach, but which has risen in value to $120,000 by the time of trial, might be delighted to have restitution if the purchaser has committed a breach.

The terms restitution and rescission are frequently used together, sometimes as if they were synonymous. This usage is potentially confusing, and it is helpful to distinguish the two words.[255] Restitution refers to a judicial order compelling the defendant to return to the plaintiff the value of the performance the defendant has received, thus returning the plaintiff to his or her position before the contract was formed.[256] Rescission has at least two meanings, similar but distinct. One meaning is a mutual agreement between the parties to a contract to cancel it and excuse one another from performance, at the same time making restitution to each other of the values of performances made to date.[257] In this sense, rescission is not a judicial remedy at all, but

---

chain of title. Lindsey v. Thornton, 234 Ala. 109, 173 So. 500 (1937); C.D. Shamburger Lumber Co. v. Holbert, 34 S.W.2d 614 (Tex.Civ.App. 1931). If the vendor's deed recites the existence of the lien and is recorded, it is all the more clear that the subpurchaser cannot be a BFP; Cooksey v. Sinder, 682 S.W.2d 252 (Tex. 1984); In re Hercules Machine Co., 51 B.R. 530 (Bkrtcy. E.D.Tenn. 1985).

[251] Courts often say that they are reluctant to find waivers except on very clear evidence; see Colquette v. Forbes, 680 S.W.2d 536 (Tex.App. 1984); Edwards-Town, Inc. v. Dimin, 9 Cal.App.3d 87, 87 Cal.Rptr. 726 (1970). Nevertheless, waivers are sometimes found; see Pelican Homestead and Savings Association v. Royal Scott Apartments Partnership, 541 So.2d 943 (La.App.1989), writ denied 543 So.2d 9 (La. 1989) (act of sale recited receipt of full cash price and granted "full acquittance and discharge therefor"); Lincoln National Life Insurance Company v. Overmyer, 530 N.E.2d 784 (Ind.App. 1988) (grantors intentionally conveyed property free and clear in order to permit purchasers to obtain first mortgage from bank; vendor's lien was waived as to real estate, but would attach to any surplus remaining after mortgage foreclosure by bank).

[252] See, e.g., DeVenney v. Hill, 918 So.2d 106 (Ala. 2005) (waiver inferred from vendor's acceptance of post-dated check at closing, indicating vendor was relying on purchaser's personal responsibility to pay remainder of price); Russo v. Cedrone, 118 R.I. 549, 375 A.2d 906 (1977) (waiver inferred from vendor's delay in asserting lien and his assignment of his interest before assertion of the lien).

[253] See text supra at note 243.

[254] See Perillo, Contracts § 15.2 (7th ed. 2014).

[255] To escape this confusion the Restatement (Second) of Contracts carefully avoids the use of the term rescission in its discussion of restitutionary remedies; see, e.g., Restatement (Second) of Contracts § 370ff (1981).

[256] See Lee v. Thunder Dev., Inc., 77 Or.App. 7, 711 P.2d 978 (1985); Perillo, note 254 supra.

[257] See Bazurto v. Burgess, 136 Ariz. 397, 666 P.2d 497 (App. 1983) (if parties to mutual rescission do not expressly reserve their claims to damages, such claims are impliedly waived); Esecson v. Bushnell, 663

merely an agreed relationship between the parties. The term rescission is also used to describe cases in which a single party unilaterally treats his or her duty of performance under the contract as excused and ended, and who then seeks judicial confirmation of this position.[258] Such a person will often demand restitution from the other party; hence, unilateral rescission and a claim for restitution frequently go hand in hand. This sort of rescission may be grounded on one or more of a number of legal doctrines, such as mutual mistake,[259] misrepresentation,[260] duress,[261] undue influence, non-occurrence of a condition, impracticability, or frustration.[262] Since our present concern is with rescission based on the opposing party's breach of contract, the other grounds mentioned will not be discussed further here.[263]

There are important practical differences between mutual and unilateral rescission. When the former occurs, there is usually no need for judicial intervention if the parties' intent is clear. Unilateral rescission, on the other hand, often gives rise to litigation; the aggrieved party may find it necessary to resort to the court for a determination that a good ground for rescission exists. Here the terminology becomes increasingly confused, with some courts saying that they are confirming the rescission that has already occurred, while others state that they are "rescinding" or "granting a rescission" of the contract.[264]

P.2d 258 (Colo.App. 1983) (mutual rescission may be inferred from parties' conduct, if sufficiently clear); Henderson v. Winkler, 454 So.2d 1358 (Ala. 1984) (after a mutual agreement to rescind, neither party may obtain damages or specific performance); Preheim v. Ortman, 331 N.W.2d 62 (S.D. 1983); Perillo, note 254 supra. The Uniform Commercial Code uses the term rescission exclusively in this sense; see U.C.C. § 2–209 comment 3.

[258] See Demattia v. Mauro, 86 Conn. App. 1, 860 A.2d 262 (2004); Humphrey v. Camelot Retirement Community (Tex.App.1994). Professor Corbin argued that the use of the term rescission in this context was improper and undesirable, although he conceded that it was well-ingrained in the language of the courts; he preferred to say that the party was legally permitted to abandon the contract. 5 Corbin, Contracts §§ 1104–05 (1964). The two uses of the term rescission are discussed in Brannock v. Fletcher, 271 N.C. 65, 155 S.E.2d 532 (1967).

[259] See, e.g., D'Agostino v. Harding, 217 A.D.2d 835, 629 N.Y.S.2d 524 (App.Div. 1995); Grahn v. Gregory, 800 P.2d 320 (Utah App. 1990); Lundeen v. Lappi, 361 N.W.2d 913 (Minn.App. 1985); Berry v. Romain, 194 Mont. 400, 632 P.2d 1127 (1981). Unilateral mistake is not usually enough; see, e.g., C.B. & T. Co. v. Hefner, 98 N.M. 594, 651 P.2d 1029 (App. 1982). See Note, 29 Wayne L.Rev. 1433 (1983).

[260] See Mulle v. Scheiler, 484 So.2d 47 (Fla.App. 1986) (where purchasers were defrauded, they may have restitution of the price paid even though changes in the property made it impossible to restore it to vendors in exactly the form conveyed); Bogosian v. Bederman, 823 A.2d 1117 (R.I. 2003) (purchasers entitled to rescission and restitution, where vendor had sold the land to another party); Gray v. Baker, 485 So.2d 306 (Miss. 1986) (vendor may rescind, if purchaser conceals his intention to resell land to a subpurchaser who he knows is obnoxious to vendor, and to whom vendor would have been unwilling to sell directly); MacCurrach v. Anderson, 678 S.W.2d 459 (Mo.App. 1984); Ballard v. Carroll, 2 Ark.App. 283, 621 S.W.2d 484 (1981).

[261] See, e.g., Wolf v. Marlton Corp., 57 N.J.Super. 278, 154 A.2d 625 (1959).

[262] Restatement (Second) of Contracts § 377 (1981).

[263] See Humphrey v. Camelot Retirement Community, 893 S.W.2d 55 (Tex.App. 1994); Breuer-Harrison, Inc. v. Combe, 799 P.2d 716 (Utah App.1990); Cooper v. Peoples Bank, 725 P.2d 78 (Colo.App. 1986); Metcalfe v. Talarski, 213 Conn. 145, 567 A.2d 1148 (1989). Sometimes a breach which justifies unilateral rescission is termed, quite inappropriately, a "failure of consideration"; see Ragen v. Weston, 191 Mont. 546, 625 P.2d 557 (1981), applying Mont.Code Ann. 28–2–1711; Royal v. Parado, 462 So.2d 849 (Fla.App.1985) (rescission not available for mere "failure of consideration," but only for fraud, accident, or mistake).

[264] Countless examples could be given. See Dewey v. Arnold, 159 Ariz. 65, 764 P.2d 1124 (App. 1988) (rescission occurs by party's action, notwithstanding later assistance by the courts). The confusion is often illustrated by inconsistent phrases in the same judicial opinion; see, e.g., Berry v. Romain, 194 Mont. 400, 632 P.2d 1127 (1981) ("A party to a contract may rescind * * *"; "The trial court was urged to rescind * * *"). See also Halvorson v. Birkland, 84 S.D. 328, 171 N.W.2d 77 (1969).

Whether one conceives of unilateral rescission as an act of the aggrieved party or of the court, it is typically unsatisfactory in the plaintiff's eyes without a further granting of restitution, damages, or both. As we have already seen, the usual claim for damages by a purchaser is accompanied by rescission and restitution: if the vendor breaches, the purchaser is entitled to (1) treat the contract as ended (rescission), (2) recover the earnest money already paid (restitution), and have a judgment for loss of bargain damages if they can be proved.[265] Properly understood, there is no inconsistency or duplicative recovery in this result, and no election of remedies is involved.[266]

In general, one who seeks restitution must also give restitution. Even a party in breach is entitled to a return of that which has been given when compelled to return that which has been received.[267] Of course, the breaching party usually will owe loss-of-bargain or other damages; hence, his or her recovery in restitution will be reduced by that amount. The Restatement (Second) of Contracts aptly illustrates this concept: A enters into a contract to sell land to B for $100,000. B pays $30,000 toward the price, but then refuses to make further payments. A resells the land to another buyer for $95,000. B is entitled to restitution, despite the breach, but B's restitutionary recovery will be reduced by the damages for which B is liable. Here the damages are $5,000 (assuming the resale price is the equivalent of fair market value), so B can recover only $25,000 in restitution.[268] It is also quite possible, depending on the contract language and judicial attitudes, that B's payments or some portion of them can be treated by A as liquidated damages under principles we have discussed earlier, thus permitting A to retain most or all of the $30,000 rather than giving restitution of the $25,000 figure based on actual damages.[269]

---

[265] See supra § 10.3 at notes 134–135. There is no serious doubt that the purchaser can in fact recover both payments made and loss-of-bargain damages, subject to the Flureau v. Thornhill limitation; see Mazzochetti v. Cassarino, 49 A.D.2d 695, 370 N.Y.S.2d 765 (1975); Horner v. Holt, 187 Va. 715, 47 S.E.2d 365 (1948).

[266] There is a good deal of rather unfortunate and nonsensical dicta in the cases to the effect that rescission and damages cannot coexist; see Canady v. Mann, 107 N.C.App. 252, 419 S.E.2d 597 (N.C.App. 1992); Shoreham Developers, Inc. v. Randolph Hills, Inc., 269 Md. 291, 305 A.2d 465 (1973); Jennings v. Lee, 105 Ariz. 167, 461 P.2d 161 (1969); Perillo, Contracts § 15.7 (7th ed. 2014).

[267] Restatement (Second) of Contracts § 374 (1981). See Ben Lomond, Inc. v. Allen, 758 P.2d 92 (Alaska 1988) (defaulting buyer entitled to restitution of value of lot she transferred to builder, less damages incurred by builder); Blair v. Boulger, 358 N.W.2d 522 (N.D.1984), appeal dismissed, certiorari denied 471 U.S. 1095, 105 S.Ct. 2314, 85 L.Ed.2d 834 (1985) (vendor may not have rescission of contract unless she offers to make restitution of everything of value she has received from purchaser); see North Dak.Cent.Code § 9–09–04; Lancellotti v. Thomas, 341 Pa.Super. 1, 491 A.2d 117 (1985) (sale of business).

See Gegan, In Defense of Restitution: A Comment on Mather, Restitution as a Remedy for Breach of Contract: The Case of the Partially Performing Seller, 57 So.Cal. L.Rev. 723 (1984).

[268] Restatement (Second) of Contracts § 374, Comment a, Illustration 1.

[269] Section 10.4 supra. See the excellent discussion in Vines v. Orchard Hills, Inc., 181 Conn. 501, 435 A.2d 1022 (1980). The question has arisen frequently in installment sales of land in which the purchaser goes into possession, makes payments, and then defaults. The classic work is Corbin, The Right of a Defaulting Vendee to the Restitution of Installments Paid, 40 Yale L.J. 1013 (1931). While some courts continue to uphold forfeiture clauses which permit the vendor to treat the amount paid as liquidated damages, there is a discernible trend toward requiring the vendor to make restitution of the payments received insofar as they exceed the vendor's actual damages. Such damages may be measured by the traditional loss-of-bargain formula or by the loss of rental value due to the purchaser's possession of the land. See Honey v. Henry's Franchise Leasing Corp., 64 Cal.2d 801, 52 Cal.Rptr. 18, 415 P.2d 833 (1966); Johnson v. Carman, 572 P.2d 371 (Utah 1977); Brannock v. Fletcher, 271 N.C. 65, 155 S.E.2d 532 (1967); Chace v. Johnson, 98 Fla. 118, 123 So. 519 (1929); Annot., 4 A.L.R.4th 993 (1981). Whether restitution is ordered in these cases sometimes depends on the "wilfullness" of the default or other rather intangible considerations. But see Freedman v. Rector, 37 Cal.2d 16, 230 P.2d 629, 31 A.L.R.2d 1 (1951), ordering restitution for a wilfully defaulting purchaser. See generally Nelson, Whitman, Burkhart & Freyermuth, Real Estate Finance Law § 3.29 (6th ed. 2014).

Damages caused by one's own breach are not the only possible offset against one's restitutionary recovery. If the breaching purchaser has made valuable improvements on the land, the restitution owed to the vendor may be reduced by their value. Similarly, if the vendor has held the purchaser's earnest money or other payments for an appreciable period, the interest that was or might have been earned on the funds may offset the vendor's recovery in restitution. On the other side, a purchaser who has benefitted from possession of the property during the contract's executory period may have his or her restitutionary recovery reduced by the rental value of that possession.[270] These offsets are highly discretionary; some courts seem to disregard them entirely, and others deal with them in only a rough or approximate manner. For example, the rental value of the purchaser's possession and the interest value of the payments held by the vendor may be deemed by the court to be equivalent, and hence to cancel one another, without any serious effort to analyze them.[271] Given the amounts involved and the cost and complexity of expert testimony and proof on such points, this sort of judicial looseness may be quite appropriate when the time between contract formation and breach is short. When long times elapse, however, neglect or approximation of these amounts (which in reality represent the time value of money) can produce bizarre and unfair results.[272]

Restitution is an appropriate remedy for breach only if the breach is "vital" or "total."[273] These terms are not as absolute as they seem; they are intended to indicate simply that the breach must be a serious and important one, not minor or trivial.[274] The test is whether the breach is sufficiently material to excuse the aggrieved party from any further duty of performance.[275] Where the defendant makes an anticipatory repudiation

---

[270] MCC Investments v. Crystal Properties, 451 N.W.2d 243 (Minn.App. 1990) (vendor entitled to actual rent received, rather than reasonable rental value); Metcalfe v. Talarski, 213 Conn. 145, 567 A.2d 1148 (1989) (same); Kracl v. Loseke, 236 Neb. 290, 461 N.W.2d 67 (1990); Barnard & Son, Inc. v. Akins, 109 Idaho 466, 708 P.2d 871 (1985); Heifner v. Hendricks, 13 Ark.App. 217, 682 S.W.2d 459 (1985); Boegner v. Olivares, 429 S.W.2d 692 (Tex. Civ. App. 1968); Busch v. Nervik, 38 Wn.App. 541, 687 P.2d 872 (1984) (vendor ordered to return purchase price plus interest and value of improvements made by purchasers, less reasonable rental value for period of purchasers' possession). The rental value is normally computed only for the time the purchaser has actual possession; if the purchaser makes an appropriate offer to return the property and abandons it, he or she is not responsible for any further rental value, even if the purchaser does not immediately resume possession. Miller v. Sears, 636 P.2d 1183 (Alaska 1981); Limoli v. Accettullo, 358 Mass. 381, 265 N.E.2d 92 (1970); Restatement of Restitution § 67, Comment a (1937).

[271] See Lane v. Unger, 599 F.Supp. 63 (E.D.Mo.1984), affirmed in part and reversed in part without opinion 786 F.2d 1171 (8th Cir.1986) (vendors are entitled to compensation for purchasers' 8 months use of the property, and may retain purchasers' down payment for this purpose); Willcox Clinic, Ltd. v. Evans Products Co., 136 Ariz. 400, 666 P.2d 500 (App. 1983) (restitution to purchaser of payments made must be reduced by any claim paid to purchaser by its title insurer). Compare the treatment of incidental damages in an action for specific performance, § 10.5 notes 219–222 supra.

[272] See Kim v. Conway & Forty, Inc., 772 S.W.2d 723 (Mo.App. 1989) (rescinding purchasers awarded prejudgment interest from date of vendor's breach); Brunner v. LaCasse, 234 Mont. 368, 763 P.2d 662 (1988), appeal after remand 241 Mont. 102, 785 P.2d 210 (1990) (same); Restatement of Restitution § 156, Comment a (1937), approving interest on the purchaser's payment from the date made. An illustration of the importance of considering the time value of money in a restitution action is found in Nelson, Whitman, Burkhart & Freyermuth, Real Estate Finance Law § 3.29 (6th ed. 2014).

[273] See Cady v. Burton, 257 Mont. 529, 851 P.2d 1047 (Mont. 1993); Folkers v. Southwest Leasing, 431 N.W.2d 177 (Iowa App. 1988) (rescission available as a matter of right if damages cannot be ascertained with reasonable certainty); Beefy Trail, Inc. v. Beefy King International, Inc., 267 So.2d 853 (Fla.App. 1972); Perillo, Contracts § 15.5 (7th ed. 2014).

[274] See, e.g., Smith v. Continental Bank, 130 Ariz. 320, 636 P.2d 98 (1981) (no rescission for construction defects which could be remedied for $2,235 in a house sold for $33,000); Kohenn v. Plantation Baking Co., Inc., 32 Ill.App.3d 231, 336 N.E.2d 491 (1975) (no rescission for minor defects in industrial plant building.)

[275] To say that the breach is material is equivalent to saying that substantial performance has not been rendered when due. Since each party's substantial performance is a constructive condition of the other party's duty to perform, a material breach excuses the other's performance. The aggrieved party is therefore permitted

of the contract, there is no doubt that the breach is sufficiently vital.[276] In other cases, the availability of restitution may depend on the quantitative degree of breach, the breaching party's willfulness or bad faith, the length of time the breach continues, and other factors.[277]

Several doctrines impose further limitations on the availability of restitution. Suppose the vendor has fully performed the contract, so that the purchaser is obligated to pay the full purchase price. If the purchaser at that point commits a material breach or repudiation, the vendor may seek restitution. In general, such a vendor has a choice of demanding a return of the land itself or of its value.[278] But if the vendor seeks the money value of the land, the maximum recovery will be the agreed contract price. In effect, the parties' agreement fixes this value for the property, and the vendor cannot be heard to say that a higher amount should be set.[279] This rule is a salutary one, for there is little justification for consuming judicial time and energy in determining the value of land the parties have already evaluated to their satisfaction.[280]

If the vendor elects to seek a return of the land in specie, or if the purchaser's demand for restitution makes it necessary to give the vendor restitution as well, other problems arise. Some cases dogmatically assert that, once a deed transferring title has been delivered and accepted, cancellation of the deed and restitution of the land in specie cannot be ordered at the behest of either party.[281] Where it is the purchaser who seeks restitution, and where the breach consists of a defect in the title conveyed, these cases are merely illustrative of the general notion that once a purchaser has accepted a deed, the purchaser's remedies under the contract for title-related breaches are "merged" into the deed—a matter discussed in a later section.[282] But the cases denying restitution are broader than this.[283]

The courts' reluctance to set aside or cancel deeds is understandable, for to do so may cause serious title problems or result in unfair loss to a purchaser who has spent money in moving costs or improvements. But many courts today would probably be more flexible, and would order specific restitution if no bona fide third party had relied on the conveyance,[284] the time elapsed since the conveyance was relatively brief, the breach was

---

to rescind and to seek restitution and/or damages. See Dunham v. Belinky, 248 Ga. 479, 284 S.E.2d 397 (1981); Restatement (Second) of Contracts § 237 (1981).

[276] An anticipatory repudiation is nearly always deemed a "total" breach; see ULTA § 2–404; Juarez v. Hamner, 674 S.W.2d 856 (Tex.App. 1984) (one of two co-owners signed a written statement refusing to convey).

[277] Restatement (Second) of Contracts § 241 (1981).

[278] See Restatement (Second) of Contracts § 371–72 (1981).

[279] Restatement (Second) of Contracts § 373, Comment b (1981).

[280] This is not to say that further recovery is unavailable to the plaintiff, who may be able to show numerous forms of incidental or consequential damage. As the text above suggests, restitution should not be treated as excluding such further damages. See Perillo, Contracts § 15.7 (7th ed. 2014).

[281] See Suburban Properties, Inc. v. Hanson, 234 Or. 356, 382 P.2d 90 (1963); McMillan v. American Suburban Corp., 136 Tenn. 53, 188 S.W. 615 (1916). Cf. Early v. Street, 192 Tenn. 463, 241 S.W.2d 531 (1951). These cases generally preclude restitution only when breach of contract, rather than some other ground such as misrepresentation, is asserted.

[282] See, e.g., Jolley v. Idaho Securities, Inc., 90 Idaho 373, 414 P.2d 879 (1966); Annots., 50 A.L.R. 180 (1927); 65 A.L.R. 1142 (1930); § 10.12, infra.

[283] See, e.g., Carter v. Barclay, 476 S.W.2d 909 (Tex.Civ.App. 1972), relying on the "merger" concept to deny restitution of the land in specie. The grantor sought restitution because the grantee's bank had refused payment of his check for the purchase price; merger seems a particularly inappropriate explanation of such a decision.

[284] See Restatement (Second) of Contracts § 372 Illustration 4 (1981). If the purchaser wishes to seek (and must therefore make) restitution, he or she may find it necessary to secure the release of the interests

a serious one,[285] and the plaintiff's alternate remedies seemed inadequate or uncertain.[286]

§ 10.8   REMEDIES FOR CONTRACT BREACH—VENDEE'S LIEN

In general, restitution is available to both vendors and purchasers under the principles discussed in the preceding section. Where the purchaser demands restitution of money paid toward the contract of sale,[287] courts generally recognize an equitable lien on the property in favor of the purchaser as an aid to his or her recovery.[288] The lien is based on the assumption that the vendor holds the legal title, either because it has never been conveyed or because the vendor has committed some act which justifies the purchaser's rescission.[289] The vendee's lien, like the vendor's lien discussed in Section 10.6, is a creation of equity and need not grow out of any specific language in the contract.[290] Foreclosure is by judicial sale.[291]

The lien is usually of serious value to the purchaser only if it has a priority higher than those of competing interests, such as mortgages or mechanics liens on the land or the rights of subsequent purchasers from the vendor. If there are no competing interests, the vendee hardly needs the lien, for he or she can simply get a personal judgment against the vendor and satisfy it by execution on the real estate. If such competing interests are created prior to the entering of the contract of sale, and if they are properly recorded or the vendee has other notice of them, the vendee's lien will be inferior.[292] On the other hand, the lien will have priority over interests created after the sales contract is signed unless the holders of those interests establish that they took in good faith, for

---

acquired by any subsequent takers, such as mortgagees; see ULTA § 2–402, Comment 3. Alternatively, the purchaser may return the value of the land rather than its actual title; see Lumsden v. Lawing, 117 N.C.App. 514, 451 S.E.2d 659 (N.C.App. 1995).

[285] See Easterling v. Ferris, 651 P.2d 677 (Okl. 1982).

[286] See Benassi v. Harris, 147 Conn. 451, 162 A.2d 521 (1960). Where the breaching purchaser is paying by means of a promise of support or care of the vendor or by other services rather than money, it is often held that the vendor can get restitution and cancellation of the deed because of the difficulty of proving damages; see, e.g., Huntley v. Dubois, 129 Vt. 389, 278 A.2d 750 (1971); Myers v. Diehl, 365 P.2d 717 (Okl. 1961).

[287] The lien is generally limited to the payments made to the vendor; it is sometimes extended to other expenditures made in reliance on the contract, such as expenditures by the purchaser for improvements, but clearly does not include recovery of loss-of-bargain damages. See Warner v. Peterson, 234 Mont. 319, 762 P.2d 872 (1988); Annot., 43 A.L.R.2d 1384 (1954).

[288] Sparks v. Charles Wayne Group, 568 So.2d 512 (Fla.App. 1990); Stanovsky v. Group Enterprise & Const. Co., 714 S.W.2d 836 (Mo.App.1986); Gribble v. Stearman & Kaplan, Inc., 249 Md. 289, 239 A.2d 573 (1968); Wayne Building & Loan Co. v. Yarborough, 11 Ohio St.2d 195, 228 N.E.2d 841 (1967); Cole v. Haynes, 216 Miss. 485, 62 So.2d 779 (1953); Elterman v. Hyman, 192 N.Y. 113, 84 N.E. 937, 127 Am.St.Rep. 862 (1908). Some cases award the lien only if the vendee is not guilty of any breach of the contract; see, e.g., Tuttle v. Ehrehart, 102 Fla. 1129, 137 So. 245 (1931).

[289] In Davis v. William Rosenzweig Realty Operating Co., 192 N.Y. 128, 84 N.E. 943, 127 Am.St.Rep. 890 (1908), the New York Court of Appeals refused to recognize the vendee's lien where the vendee sought to rescind the contract for fraud, reasoning that the lien depended on the continued existence of the contract. This distinction was abrogated by the legislature in 1947 in N.Y.-McKinney's Civ.Prac.Law & Rules 3002(f), which recognizes the lien even if the contract is rescinded. Other jurisdictions also recognize the lien when rescission is sought; see, e.g., Reed v. Sixth Judicial District Court, 75 Nev. 338, 341 P.2d 100 (1959); Mihranian, Inc. v. Padula, 70 N.J. 252, 359 A.2d 473 (1976).

[290] See In re Oligbo, 328 B.R. 619 (Bankr. E.D.N.Y. 2005); First Banc Real Estate, Inc. v. Johnson, 321 S.W.3d 322, 334 (Mo. Ct. App. 2010). In Connecticut the common-law vendee's lien has been supplanted by a statute requiring that the contract of sale or a notice of the lien, with signatures witnessed and acknowledged, be recorded in the public records. See Conn. Gen. Stat. Ann. § 49–92a; Goebel v. Glover, 91 Conn. App. 442, 881 A.2d 493 (2005).

[291] Cox v. RKA Corp., 164 N.J. 487, 753 A.2d 1112 (2000).

[292] State Savings & Loan Association v. Kauaian Development Co., 50 Hawaii 540, 445 P.2d 109 (1968).

value, and without notice of the contract.[293] Even this priority may be lost if the contract of sale itself contains language waiving or subordinating the purchaser's rights to those of persons acquiring later interests. Such language is commonly used in pre-construction earnest money agreements on condominium units or subdivision houses in order to protect subsequent construction loan mortgage lenders.[294]

§ 10.9 TIME OF PERFORMANCE

Timing is often of great importance in a real estate sale. If performance is delayed beyond the date to which the parties agreed, either buyer or seller may incur significant and unexpected inconvenience and expense. On the other hand, sales transactions are often complex, with each party involved in a variety of detailed and sometimes unpredictable arrangements; hence, delays are common. Since one party's desire for promptness often conflicts with the other's need to extend the time for performance, litigation frequently results.

There is no rule requiring the parties to agree in the contract about the timing of their performances,[295] and if they do not do so the courts will simply infer that performance within a reasonable time was intended.[296] But in the great majority of cases

---

[293] In re Pearl, 40 B.R. 860 (Bkrtcy.D.N.J. 1984); In re Laketown Wharf Mktg. Corp., 433 B.R. 401 (Bankr. N.D. Fla. 2010); Benz v. D.L. Evans Bank, 152 Idaho 215, 268 P.3d 1167 (2012); Cole Taylor Bank v. Cole Taylor Bank, 224 Ill.App.3d 696, 166 Ill.Dec. 817, 586 N.E.2d 775 (Ill.App. 1992); Tile House, Inc. v. Cumberland Fed. Sav. Bank, 942 S.W.2d 904 (Ky. 1997) (subsequent mechanics lienors without notice of vendees' right prevailed over vendees' liens); Stahl v. Roulhac, 50 Md.App. 382, 438 A.2d 1366 (1982); Hembree v. Mid-America Federal S. & L. Ass'n, 64 Ohio App.3d 144, 580 N.E.2d 1103 (1989); Osage Energy Res., LLC v. Pemco, LLC, 2016 Okl. Civ. App. 70, 394 P.3d 265 (2016). See generally Annot., 82 A.L.R.3d 1040 (1978); South Carolina Fed. Sav. Bank v. San-A-Bel, 307 S.C. 76, 413 S.E.2d 852 (S.C.App. 1992) (same with respect to construction disbursements). Contra, and apparently wrong, see Nelson v. Great Northwest Federal Sav. & Loan Ass'n, 37 Wn.App. 316, 679 P.2d 953 (1984). The notice which disqualifies the subsequent taker may be actual, or it may be constructive notice from the recorded contract; see Lockie v. Cooperative Land Co., 207 Cal. 624, 279 P. 428 (1928). The notice need not include information as to the vendee's identity or the amount of the lien; knowledge that a prior contract of sale existed is sufficient to place the later taker on inquiry notice; South Carolina Fed. Sav. Bank v. San-A-Bel, supra.

The foregoing may be subject to an exception if the lien competing with that of the purchaser is itself a purchase-money mortgage, since such mortgages are presumed to take priority over all other liens created in the same transaction. See BancFlorida v. Hayward, 689 So.2d 1052 (Fla. Ct. App. 1997); Nelson, Whitman, Burkhart & Freyermuth, Real Estate Finance Law §§ 9.1–9.2 (6th ed. 2014).

[294] Posnansky v. Breckenridge Estates Corp., 621 So.2d 736 (Fla.App. 1993). In Arundel Fed. Sav. & Loan Ass'n v. Lawrence, 65 Md.App. 158, 499 A.2d 1298 (1985), the purchase contract provided that "the buyers understand and consent to the seller placing a construction mortgage on the property." This language was held sufficient to subordinate the vendee's lien to the construction mortgage, despite the court's observation that subordinations will "not be lightly implied." The court thought the language must have had some purpose, and could think of none except subordination. Cf. Rigoli v. 44 Monroe Mktg., LLC, 236 Ariz. 112, 336 P.3d 745 (Ct. App. 2014) (language limiting purchaser's remedies did not act as waiver of vendee's lien). See also State Savings & Loan Association v. Kauaian Development Co., 50 Hawaii 540, 445 P.2d 109 (1968). The problem is discussed in Nelson, Whitman, Burkhart & Freyermuth, Real Estate Finance Law § 12.9 (6th ed. 2014), questioning the enforceability of a vague, general subordination clause in a contract signed by an unsophisticated vendee.

The subordination concept can cut both ways. In State Savings & Loan Association v. Kauaian Development Co., 62 Hawaii 188, 613 P.2d 1315 (1980), the above-cited case was reconsidered by the court. The construction loan mortgage recited that it was "subject to" the condominium declaration, and from that language the court inferred that the mortgage was intended to be subordinate to all of the vendees' equitable liens, whether their contracts were entered into before or after the mortgage was made and recorded.

[295] Even if an agreement is reached as to the time of performance, most jurisdictions construe their statutes of frauds as not requiring that the time be included in the written memorandum; see Park v. Acierno, 160 Ohio App. 3d 117, 826 N.E.2d 324 (2005); § 10.1 note 54 supra.

[296] See, e.g., Angle v. Marco Builders, Inc., 128 Ariz. 396, 626 P.2d 126 (1981); Gwinnett Cty. v. Old Peachtree Partners, LLC, 329 Ga. App. 540, 764 S.E.2d 193 (2014); Yale Development Co. v. Aurora Pizza Hut,

the parties do agree, at least concerning the time of "settlement" or "closing," which ordinarily means the date on which legal title is to be transferred by deed.[297] It is more common for the parties to fail to specify the time limits on various conditions which must be met, such as the purchaser's obtaining of a mortgage loan commitment; again, a reasonable time will be allowed by the courts.[298]

If a party does not perform within the agreed time, what legal consequences follow? Perhaps surprisingly, the results are often rather trivial. Unless time has been made "of the essence," it is usually said that failure of timely performance will be considered a breach of contract only at law, and that in equity no breach will be deemed to occur until the performance becomes unreasonably late. In other words, time is always of the essence at law (unless the parties expressly agree otherwise), but it is not of the essence in equity unless made so by the contract or surrounding circumstances.[299]

These statements are unsatisfactory as they stand and need further analysis, for the precise position of a late-performing party where time is not "of the essence" is more complex. First, it is clear that the late party has committed a breach, albeit a nonmaterial breach, and is liable at law for damages.[300] These may be expanded to include loss-of-bargain damages if the delinquent party never performs, but if his or her performance is ultimately tendered within a reasonable time, the damages owed will be limited to harms resulting from the delay *per se.* Thus, a tardy seller might be liable for lost rents or profits which the buyer was forced to forego,[301] and conceivably for higher interest on the buyer's mortgage loan if rates have risen during the delay,[302] while a late buyer might be compelled to reimburse the seller for interest and taxes paid during the

---

Inc., 95 Ill.App.3d 523, 51 Ill.Dec. 409, 420 N.E.2d 823 (1981); Prestenbach v. Collins, 159 So. 3d 531 (Miss. 2014); Clements v. 201 Water St. LLC, 157 A.D.3d 615, 70 N.Y.S.3d 4 (N.Y. App. Div. 2018); Earls v. Corning, 207 Or. App. 706, 143 P.3d 243 (2006); New York Ave. LLC v. Harrison, 2016 Utah App. 240, 391 P.3d 268 (2016); Sisters & Bros. Inv. Grp. v. Vermont Nat. Bank, 172 Vt. 539, 773 A.2d 264 (2001). The principle is enshrined in California statute; West's Ann.Cal.Civ.Code § 1657; Patel v. Liebermensch, 45 Cal. 4th 344, 197 P.3d 177 (2008). If the contract states no time, either party may send the other a notice fixing a reasonable time for performance; see Schneider v. Warner, 69 Wis.2d 194, 230 N.W.2d 728 (1975). See also Peak-Las Positas Partners v. Bollag, 172 Cal. App. 4th 101, 90 Cal. Rptr. 3d 775 (2009) (vendor had duty to act reasonably in granting time extension for closing).

[297] In some areas of the nation it is fairly common, if the vendor agrees to finance the purchase by means of an installment sale contract, to initialize the transaction with an earnest money agreement which calls for execution of the installment contract at the time of "closing." While legal title will not pass at this "closing", it is functionally analogous to the more common sort of transaction described in the text, and will be treated similarly for present purposes.

[298] If times for such conditions are set, but are not made essential, a reasonable delay is allowed; Harris v. Stewart, 193 N.C. App. 142, 666 S.E.2d 804 (2008).

[299] For typical statements, see Hamilton v. Bradford, 502 F.Supp. 822 (S.D.Miss. 1980); Kaiman Realty, Inc. v. Carmichael, 2 Hawaii App. 499, 634 P.2d 603 (1981), amended 650 P.2d 609 (Hawai'i App. 1982); 3 Am.L.Prop. § 11.45 (1952). Courts usually accept without question contractual language that time is essential, but occasionally a court will conclude that the parties didn't really mean it, or that it does not apply to some particular performance under the contract. See Royal Dev. & Management Corp. v. Guardian 50/50 Fund V, Ltd., 583 So.2d 403 (Fla.App. 1991); cases cited at notes 318–320, infra.

[300] See, e.g., Richardson v. Van Dolah, 429 F.2d 912 (9th Cir. 1970); McPherson v. Dauenhauer, 187 Or. App. 551, 69 P.3d 733 (2003); 15 Williston on Contracts § 46:1 (4th ed. 2018 update); Restatement (Second) of Contracts § 242, Illustrations 4 & 5 (1981).

[301] In re Tribby, 241 B.R. 380 (E.D. Va. 1999) (purchaser may recover damages after closing for vendor's delay in closing).

[302] See Donovan v. Bachstadt, 91 N.J. 434, 453 A.2d 160 (1982). For cases awarding loss-of-financing damages as an adjunct to specific performance, see § 10.5, supra, at note 220.

delay.[303] But a delay in closing often results in savings as well as costs to the aggrieved party, and the courts will usually offset these savings against the damages, a process which may reduce the net recovery very materially.[304] As a result, recoveries may be small or nominal and are rarely sought.

A second aspect of the late-performing party's position, where time is not of the essence, is the ability to enforce the contract by a decree of specific performance if the delinquent party tenders performance, though late, within a reasonable time.[305] One party's tardiness (unless it is unreasonable) does not excuse the other party from performance. The delay in performance is a nonmaterial breach, one which is not deemed sufficiently "total" to permit the aggrieved party to rescind or abandon the contract.[306] In other words, strict performance on time is a covenant, but it is not a condition of the other party's duty to perform. The underlying policy viewpoint here is simply that moderate delays are common in real estate sales, and are rarely so harmful to the aggrieved party as to justify discharging him or her from the contract's duties.[307]

Suppose time is not of the essence and one party is late in performing (though not unreasonably so), but the other then repudiates the contract entirely. The first can plainly get specific performance as discussed above, but if he or she prefers damages for total breach instead there seems no reason to deny them. There is little authority on the point, but the few cases dealing with the issue award the late party damages,[308] and they

---

[303] These damages are essentially the same as are sometimes awarded incidentally to a grant of specific performance; see § 10.5 notes 219–222 supra.

[304] For example, the buyer may lose rents or other revenues from the property, but may also save the taxes, utilities, maintenance expenses, and mortgage loan interest which would have begun to accrue as of the agreed closing date, as well as the investment earnings on the purchase price in excess of the earnest money. See § 10.5 notes 219–222 supra. The Restatement indicates that for a breach which prevents the buyer's use of property for some period of time, "* * * the loss in value to the injured party is based on the profits that he would have made during that period." Restatement (Second) of Contracts § 348 Comment b (1981). "Profits" here presumably means net profits. The Restatement suggests alternative measures based on interest value or rental value if profits cannot be proved with reasonable certainty, but it is unclear as to whether the sorts of "savings" mentioned above would be deducted from this recovery; see id. at § 348 Comment b; § 352. Clearly such offsets are appropriate. See Walker v. Benton, 407 So.2d 305 (Fla.App. 1981); Ellis v. Mihelis, 60 Cal.2d 206, 32 Cal.Rptr. 415, 384 P.2d 7 (1963).

[305] In re Mona Lisa at Celebration, LLC, 436 B.R. 179, 209 (Bankr. M.D. Fla. 2010) (Florida law); Osborn ex rel. Osborn v. Kemp, 991 A.2d 1153 (Del. 2010); Lee v. Schneider, 822 So. 2d 311 (Miss. Ct. App. 2002) (3 year delay to resolve title defects was reasonable); Frenzen v. Taylor, 232 Neb. 41, 439 N.W.2d 473 (1989); In re Estate of Yates, 368 N.J. Super. 226, 845 A.2d 714 (App. Div. 2004) (2 year delay was reasonable); Litvak v. Smith, 180 N.C. App. 202, 636 S.E.2d 327 (2006); Empire Acquisition Grp., LLC v. Atl. Mortg. Co., 35 A.3d 878 (R.I. 2012) (delay of two months after latest date mutually agreed by parties was unreasonable); Colony Park Associates v. Gall, 154 Vt. 1, 572 A.2d 891 (1990); Bernardi Bros. v. United States, 47 Fed. Cl. 708 (2000) (delay of 3½ years was reasonable while waiting for county to vacate alley); Hugg v. Kastner, 314 Wis. 2d 506, 758 N.W.2d 224 (2008) (purchaser's delay of 7 years was reasonable, where it was caused by vendor's failure to remediate contamination). See also Pines Plaza Ltd. P'ship v. Berkley Trace, LLC, 431 Md. 652, 66 A.3d 720 (2013) (delay may be excused only if it is not wilful and does not harm the other party). What is a reasonable time may be influenced by the needs of the party from whom an extension is requested; see Jaramillo v. Case, 100 Conn. App. 815, 919 A.2d 1061 (2007) (vendor was justified in refusing to extend time, where vendor faced the prospect of making payments on two properties and was concerned about damage to the property under contract from coming winter weather).

[306] See American Somax Ventures v. Touma, 547 So.2d 1266 (Fla.App. 1989); Restatement (Second) of Contracts § 242(c) and Illustrations 4 & 5 (1981).

[307] See Lajayi v. Fafiyebi, 860 A.2d 680 (R.I. 2004).

[308] Tanenbaum v. Sears, Roebuck & Co., 265 Pa.Super. 78, 401 A.2d 809 (1979); Davis v. Lacy, 121 F.Supp. 246 (E.D.Ky. 1954).

are likely to be followed.[309] To do so runs counter to the axiom that time is always of the essence at law; on this point, the axiom is simply overbroad and inaccurate.

If time is made of the essence, much of the foregoing discussion is reversed. If late performance is tendered and voluntarily accepted, and the contract completed, the late party is still liable for damages for the delay as above. But the tender of strict performance on time is now treated as a condition, failure of which will be deemed a total breach and will fully discharge the other party.[310] Thus one who is late cannot enforce the contract judicially, in law or equity, unless the other party is willing to waive the right to timely performance.[311] Some cases are exceptionally rigid on this point; in Doctorman v. Schroeder,[312] the New Jersey Court of Errors and Appeals refused to grant the buyers specific performance where they were only thirty minutes late. Other cases are somewhat more lenient, particularly if it is the purchaser who is late and he or she stands to forfeit a large earnest money deposit.[313] But it is clear that significant tardiness will result in loss of the right to enforce the contract.

If the time set for closing arrives and neither party tenders performance, what is their legal posture? If time is not of essence, neither is in material breach and the closing is automatically extended until one sets a new date and provides notice to the other a reasonable time in advance of that date.[314] If time is of the essence, the problem is more complex, and a court might either follow the automatic extension approach above,[315] or it might treat both parties as discharged on the ground that a condition to each's

---

[309] Restatement (Second) of Contracts § 242, Illustrations 4 & 5 (1981) expressly approves the late party's recovery for total breach both in law and equity.

[310] Benedict v. Snead, 271 Ga. 585, 519 S.E.2d 905 (1999); Thor Properties, LLC v. Willspring Holdings LLC, 118 A.D.3d 505, 988 N.Y.S.2d 47 (2014); Lewis v. Muchmore, 26 S.W.3d 632 (Tenn. Ct. App. 2000). Occasionally a court will exercise its equitable discretion and grant enforcement of the contract to a party who tenders late even though time is of the essence; see Postregna v. Tanner, 903 So. 2d 219 (Fla. Dist. Ct. App. 2005); Scotella v. Osgood, 4 Haw. App. 20, 659 P.2d 73 (1983).

[311] Schneider v. Dumbarton Developers, Inc., 767 F.2d 1007 (D.C.Cir. 1985); Fogarty v. Saathoff, 128 Cal.App.3d 780, 180 Cal.Rptr. 484 (1982); Department of Community Affairs v. Atrium Palace Syndicate, 247 N.J.Super. 511, 589 A.2d 1046 (1991), cert. denied 126 N.J. 338, 598 A.2d 895 (1991); Fairview Developers, Inc. v. Miller, 187 N.C. App. 168, 652 S.E.2d 365 (2007). See also Lafayette Place Associates v. Boston Redevelopment Authority, 427 Mass. 509, 694 N.E.2d 820 (Mass. 1998) (party's refusal to waive time deadline was not a breach the duty of good faith). With respect to waiver, see text at notes 327–333 infra.

[312] 92 N.J.Eq. 676, 114 A. 810 (1921). See also F.J. Miceli v. Dierberg, 773 S.W.2d 154 (Mo.App. 1989), denying enforcement to a purchaser who was 3¹/₂ hours late, but who did not inform the vendor of the delay; Kulanski v. Celia Homes, Inc., 7 App. Div. 2d 1006, 184 N.Y.S.2d 234 (1959), denying enforcement to a vendor who tendered one day late, even though the date scheduled for closing was a legal holiday.

[313] PR Pension Fund v. Nakada, 8 Haw.App. 480, 809 P.2d 1139 (Haw.App. 1991); Williams Plumbing Co. v. Sinsley, 53 Cal.App.3d 1027, 126 Cal.Rptr. 345 (1975); Lance v. Martinez-Arango, 251 So.2d 707 (Fla.App. 1971); Rymland v. Berger, 242 Md. 260, 219 A.2d 7 (1966). See also In re Johnson, 379 B.R. 150 (Bankr. N.D. Ill. 2007) (under Illinois law, strict enforcement of time-of-essence clause depends on parties' intent). There is some tendency for courts to resort to a reinterpretation of time-of-the-essence doctrine to avoid forfeitures of purchasers' payments, a problem which could better be dealt with directly; see § 10.4 supra.

[314] Fletcher v. Jones, 314 N.C. 389, 333 S.E.2d 731 (1985) (tender seven weeks after opposing party indicated readiness to close sale was reasonable); Johnson v. Morris, 645 P.2d 51 (Utah 1982); Limpus v. Armstrong, 3 Mass.App.Ct. 19, 322 N.E.2d 187 (1975); Luna v. Atchafalaya Realty, Inc., 325 So.2d 835 (La.App.1976); 3 Am. L.Prop. § 11.44 (1952).

[315] Life Sav. & Loan Ass'n of America v. Bryant, 125 Ill.App.3d 1012, 467 N.E.2d 277 (1984); Dullanty v. Comstock Devel. Corp., 25 Wn.App. 168, 605 P.2d 802 (1980).

obligation to perform has failed.[316] Their intent, as gleaned from their actions and surrounding circumstances, may be a helpful guide.[317]

What facts will make time of the essence? Most commonly the determination follows from language in the contract itself. A mere statement that performance shall occur on a given date is plainly not enough, but the phrase "time is of the essence of this contract" or words of similar import are usually sufficient.[318] However, such language can be seen as ambiguous where the contract calls for (and gives dates or time periods for) numerous performances or conditions in addition to the closing itself. Are all of these times of the essence?[319] It is a better practice to state explicitly which times mentioned in the contract are considered essential.[320]

Even if the contract does not expressly make time essential, the surrounding circumstances may convince a court that the parties intended it to be such.[321] Typical evidence in this respect might include the fact that one party was very concerned about a prompt settlement, and the other knew of this concern;[322] that land values were

---

[316] Pittman v. Canham, 2 Cal.App.4th 556, 3 Cal.Rptr.2d 340 (Cal.App. 1992); Goldston v. AMI Investments, Inc., 98 Nev. 567, 655 P.2d 521 (1982); Devine v. Williams Brothers, Inc., 4 Mass.App.Ct. 816, 348 N.E.2d 445 (1976); Mid Town Ltd. Partnership v. Preston, 69 Wash.App. 227, 848 P.2d 1268 (1993).

[317] See Matter of Mastapeter, 56 B.R. 413 (Bkrtcy.D.N.J. 1985) (where both parties act as if contract is still in full force despite passing of closing date, they have waived time-of-essence clause and purchaser may obtain specific performance); Smith v. Crissey, 478 So.2d 1181 (Fla.App. 1985) (intent is question of fact, precluding summary judgment). See also 15 Williston on Contracts § 47:2 (4th ed. 2–18 update).

[318] Compare Shumaker v. Lear, 235 Pa.Super. 509, 345 A.2d 249 (1975) (provision that contract would be "null and void" if time deadline was not met made time of the essence) and Jannetti v. Whelan, 131 App. Div. 3d 1209, 17 N.Y.S.3d 455 (2015) (same) with Kakalik v. Bernardo, 184 Conn. 386, 439 A.2d 1016 (1981) (contract "null and void" if financing condition not met by specified date; held time not of the essence) and Walker v. Weaver, 23 N.C.App. 654, 209 S.E.2d 537 (1974) (provision that sale was "to be definitely closed within a period of 30 days" did not make time of the essence.) See also Johnson v. Mark, 2013 N.D. 128, 834 N.W.2d 291 (2013) ("Final Pay Will be 2003" made time essential); Demattia v. Mauro, 86 Conn. App. 1, 860 A.2d 262 (2004); Dominion Investments v. Yasechko, 767 F.Supp. 1460 (N.D.Ind. 1991); Twin Towers Dev., Inc. v. Butternut Apartments, L.P., 257 Neb. 511, 599 N.W.2d 839 (1999) (contract statement that it would expire and purchaser's rights would terminate on closing date made time of the essence).

The fact that time is of the essence in a option does not make it such in a contract of sale growing out of the option; see Bethlehem Christian Fellowship, Inc. v. Planning & Zoning Comm'n of Town of Morris, 58 Conn. App. 441, 755 A.2d 249 (2000); Blum v. Kenyon, 29 Mass. App.Ct. 417, 560 N.E.2d 742 (1990); In re Estate of Heyl, 42 S.W.3d 19 (Mo. Ct. App. 2001); CDC Nassau Associates v. Fatoullah, 163 A.D.2d 227, 558 N.Y.S.2d 946 (1990).

[319] See Nacoochee Corp. v. Pickett, 948 So. 2d 26 (Fla. Dist. Ct. App. 2006) (time of essence clause applied to date deposit was due); Tantillo v. Janus, 87 Ill.App.3d 231, 408 N.E.2d 1000 (1980) (court assumed time of essence clause applied to all times mentioned in contract); Sherman v. Real Source Charities, Inc., 41 A.D.3d 946, 837 N.Y.S.2d 432 (2007) (time of essence statement in brokerage commission clause applied to all time deadlines in contract); Faulkner v. Millar, 319 S.C. 216, 460 S.E.2d 378 (S.C. 1995) (time for fulfillment of mortgage loan condition was not essential); Keliher v. Cure, 534 N.E.2d 1133 (Ind.App. 1989) (same).

[320] See Jim Lorenz, Inc. v. O'Haire, 212 N.C.App. 648, 711 S.E.2d 820 (2011).

[321] See Joseph v. MTS Inv. Corp., 964 So. 2d 642 (Ala. 2006); Woodhull Corp. v. Saibaba Corp., 234 Ga.App. 707, 507 S.E.2d 493 (1998); Menke v. Foote, 199 Neb. 800, 261 N.W.2d 635 (1978); Mercury Gas & Oil Corp. v. Rincon Oil & Gas Corp., 79 N.M. 537, 445 P.2d 958 (1968); Barker v. Francis, 741 P.2d 548 (Utah App.1987); Restatement (Second) of Contracts § 242(c) (1981) ("the circumstances . . . indicate that performance . . . by that day is important.")

[322] See, e.g., Kipahulu Investment Co. v. Seltzer Partnership, 4 Hawaii App. 625, 675 P.2d 778 (1983); Gunn v. Heggins, 964 So. 2d 586 (Miss. Ct. App. 2007); Builders Sand, Inc. v. Turtur, 678 S.W.2d 115 (Tex.App. 1984). Cf. Henry v. Sharma, 154 Cal. App.3d 665, 201 Cal.Rptr. 478 (1984) (one party's need for prompt closing does not make time essential, where other party is unaware of the need).

changing rapidly;[323] or that the property involved was a wasting asset, such as a producing mine or oil well or a short-term leasehold.[324]

Even if the contract contains no language making time essential, either party can make it such by notice to the other.[325] The notice can make the originally-agreed date strictly binding if it is given within a reasonable time prior to that date; otherwise, the notice can set a new and later date on which strict performance must be made, again provided that a reasonable time is granted between the notice and the date it fixes.[326] This looks suspiciously like a power to make a unilateral modification of the contract, but it is very widely recognized. Once the notice has been given, it binds both parties and neither can revert to the former situation, in which time was not essential, without the other's consent.[327]

The cases suggest that courts are often hostile to strict application of time clauses in contracts. They frequently find waivers of the essentiality of time, both from written or oral statements of waiver[328] and from the surrounding circumstances,[329] as when the parties continue to communicate with each other as if the contract is still in force even

---

[323] Lexington Ins. Co. & Chartis v. S. Energy Homes, Inc., 101 So. 3d 1190 (Ala. 2012); Kersch v. Taber, 67 Cal.App.2d 499, 154 P.2d 934 (1945); Thlocco Oil Co. v. Bay State Oil & Gas Co., 207 Okl. 83, 247 P.2d 740 (1952); Local 112, I.B.E.W. Bldg. Ass'n v. Tomlinson Dari-Mart, Inc., 30 Wn.App. 139, 632 P.2d 911 (1981).

[324] Herber v. Sanders, 336 S.W.2d 783 (Tex.Civ.App. 1960).

[325] 11–01 36 Ave. LLC v. Quamar, 54 Misc. 3d 622, 41 N.Y.S.3d 684 (N.Y. Sup. Ct. 2016). In New York the notice must clearly state that failure to comply with the given time will be a breach of contract); Nehmadi v. Davis, 63 A.D.3d 1125, 882 N.Y.S.2d 250 (2009).

[326] Fowler v. Ross, 142 Cal.App.3d 472, 191 Cal.Rptr. 183 (1983); Merry v. A.W. Perry, Inc., 18 Mass.App.Ct. 628, 469 N.E.2d 73 (1984); Miller v. Almquist, 241 A.D.2d 181, 671 N.Y.S.2d 746 (1998) (14 days notice unreasonable); Revital Realty Grp., LLC v. Ulano Corp., 112 A.D.3d 902, 978 N.Y.S.2d 77 (2013) (16 days notice unreasonable); 2626 Bway LLC v. Broadway Metro Assocs., LP, 85 A.D.3d 456, 925 N.Y.S.2d 437 (2011) (3 weeks notice reasonable). In New York, the reasonableness of the notice may depend on "the presence or absence of good faith, the experience of the parties and the possibility of prejudice or hardship to either one;" see Mills v. Chauvin, 103 A.D.3d 1041, 962 N.Y.S.2d 412 (2013). See also Latora v. Ferreira, 102 App. Div. 3d 838, 958 N.Y.S.2d 727 (2013) (letter from purchaser's attorney demanding that vendor fix a closing date was ineffective to make time of the essence); Marioni v. 94 Broadway, Inc., 374 N.J.Super. 588, 866 A.2d 208 (2005) (notice was ineffective because party giving notice was already in anticipatory breach); Eichengrun v. Matarazzo, 136 A.D.3d 1184, 25 N.Y.S.3d 431 (2016) (notice was ineffective because it failed to comply with the notice provisions of the contract).

A similar approach is generally followed if the contract sets no date for performance; an appropriate notice can both fix a reasonable date and make it "of the essence." See Schneider v. Warner, 69 Wis.2d 194, 230 N.W.2d 728 (1975); Annot., Necessity and Reasonableness of Vendor's Notice to Vendee of Requisite Time of Performance of Real Estate Sales Contract After Prior Waiver or Extension of Original Time of Performance, 32 A.L.R. 4th 8 (1984).

When giving a notice that sets a new time of performance and makes time of the essence, a party must not attempt to unilaterally modify the contract in other respects, or to add conditions that were not in the original contract. Such actions are likely to be deemed an anticipatory breach; see Demattia v. Mauro, 86 Conn. App. 1, 860 A.2d 262 (2004).

[327] Jahnke v. Palomar Financial Corp., 22 Ariz.App. 369, 527 P.2d 771 (1974); Wyatt v. Bergen, 2 N.J. Misc. 1169, 98 N.J.Eq. 502, 130 A. 595 (1924), affirmed 98 N.J.Eq. 738, 130 A. 597 (1925).

[328] See, e.g., Cedar Point Apartments, Limited v. Cedar Point Investment Corp., 693 F.2d 748 (8th Cir.1982), cert. denied 461 U.S. 914, 103 S.Ct. 1893, 77 L.Ed.2d 283 (1983); Oceania Joint Venture v. Trillium, Inc., 681 So.2d 881 (Fla.App.1996); Frank v. Fleet Finance, Inc., 227 Ga.App. 543, 489 S.E.2d 523 (Ga. App. 1997); Soliz v. Jimenez, 222 Or. App. 251, 193 P.3d 34 (2008). Cf. Uznay v. Bevis, 139 Wash. App. 359, 161 P.3d 1040 (2007) (no waiver found). See generally 15 Williston, Contracts § 46:11 (4th ed. 2018 update); 3 Am.L.Prop. § 11.46 (1952).

[329] Owen v. Kessler, 56 Mass. App. Ct. 466, 778 N.E.2d 953 (2002); BOB Acres, LLC v. Schumacher Farms, LLC, 797 N.W.2d 723 (Minn. Ct. App. 2011). But see Miami Child's World, Inc. v. City of Miami Beach, 688 So.2d 942 (Fla. Ct. App. 1997) (repeated granting of time extensions did not waive time of the essence); Ash Park, LLC v. Alexander & Bishop, Ltd., 317 Wis. 2d 772, 767 N.W.2d 614, aff'd, 324 Wis. 2d 703, 783 N.W.2d 294 (2010) (vendor's willingness to consider time extension did not waive time of the essence).

though the time set for performance has passed.[330] The statute of frauds is typically held no barrier to such waivers.[331] Even silence or failure to demand strict performance may be construed as a waiver, particularly where the opposing party is under the reasonable impression that timely performance will not be insisted upon.[332] Acceptance without objection of late performance of some of the other party's obligations may be taken to waive late performance of the remainder.[333] Once a waiver has been made, the waiving party can reinstate the essentiality of time only by notifying the other party of the intention to do so and stating a reasonable time for the latter to come into compliance.[334] Because the courts so readily find waivers, a clause making time essential often turns out to be less effective than one would expect.

The concept of reasonableness adds to the uncertainty of judicial enforcement of time clauses. We have seen that in several situations a court may be called upon to determine what is a reasonable time; perhaps the most common is the case in which time is not of the essence and one party delays closing the sale beyond the agreed date.[335] Such determinations are scarcely predictable in advance of litigation. What is a reasonable time depends on the parties' expectations, the nature of the transaction, and

---

[330] Galdjie v. Darwish, 113 Cal. App. 4th 1331, 7 Cal. Rptr. 3d 178 (2003); McCarthy v. Tobin, 429 Mass. 84, 706 N.E.2d 629 (1999); 17090 Parkway, Ltd. v. McDavid, 80 S.W.3d 252 (Tex. App. 2002).

[331] See § 10.1 supra at notes 72–77; Tiedemann v. Cozine, 297 N.J.Super. 579, 688 A.2d 1056 (1997); Thompson v. McCann, 762 A.2d 432 (R.I. 2000). Likewise, a contract provision that all changes must be in writing will not preclude a waiver arising from the parties' conduct; see Miller v. Coleman, 284 Ga. App. 300, 643 S.E.2d 797 (2007).

[332] Northeast Land Dev., LLC v. City of Scranton, 728 F.Supp.2d 617, 625 (M.D. Pa. 2010) (both parties treated time as not being essential); Turley v. Staley, 2009 Ark. App. 840, 372 S.W.3d 821 (2009); Galdjie v. Darwish, 113 Cal. App. 4th 1331, 7 Cal. Rptr. 2d 178 (2004) (despite time-of-essence clause, vendor continued to cooperate with purchaser in arranging financing after closing date had passed); Peachstate Developers, LLC v. Greyfield Res., Inc., 284 Ga. App. 501, 644 S.E.2d 324 (2007); Stevens v. Cliffs at Princeville Associates, 67 Hawaii 236, 684 P.2d 965 (1984) (despite time-of-essence language in financing condition, vendors did not object to purchasers' delay in seeking financing, and thus waived clause by their conduct); Goldstein v. Hanna, 97 Nev. 559, 635 P.2d 290 (1981) (vendor's agent advised purchaser that time would be extended; vendor was bound by waiver, since he did nothing to correct purchaser's impression); Phoenix Ltd. P'ship of Raleigh v. Simpson, 201 N.C. App. 493, 688 S.E.2d 717 (2009). But silence is not necessarily deemed a waiver; see Schulze v. Kwik-Chek Realty Co., 212 Va. 111, 181 S.E.2d 629 (1971).

[333] Leiter v. Eltinge, 246 Cal.App.2d 306, 54 Cal.Rptr. 703 (1966); Holverson v. Lundberg, 2016 N.D. 103, 879 N.W.2d 718 (2016); Restatement (Second) of Contracts § 247 and Illustration 2 (1981). Many of the cases involve installment sales contracts requiring a series of regular payments by the purchaser. If a pattern of acceptance of late payments by the vendor is established, a finding of waiver will frequently follow; see Nelson, Whitman, Burkhart & Freyermuth, Real Estate Finance Law 75–77 (6th ed. 2014); Legg v. Allen, 72 Or.App. 351, 696 P.2d 9 (1985). But refusing to find waivers, see Jones v. Clark, 418 P.2d 792 (Wyo. 1966); Perroncello v. Donahue, 64 Mass. App. Ct. 564, 835 N.E.2d 256 (2005), rev'd in part, 448 Mass. 199, 859 N.E.2d 827 (2007); Hunt v. Estate of Hunt, 348 S.W.3d 103 (Mo. Ct. App. 2011).

[334] In re Simpson, 7 B.R. 41 (Bkrtcy. D.Ariz.1980); Ashworth v. Hankins, 248 Ark. 567, 452 S.W.2d 838 (1970); Church of God in Christ, Inc. v. Congregation Kehillath Jacob, 370 Mass. 828, 353 N.E.2d 669 (1976); Clifton Park Affiliates, Inc. v. Howard, 36 A.D.2d 984, 320 N.Y.S.2d 981 (1971);. If the waiver itself is verbal, it may include the necessary statement as to when strict performance will be required; if it did not, or if the waiver was by conduct rather than words, an appropriate notice must be given to reinstate the essentiality of time.

[335] See text at note 300 supra.

the surrounding circumstances.[336] In the ordinary case a few weeks will be considered a reasonable delay,[337] but special facts may extend the time much more.[338]

§ 10.10 CONCURRENT CONDITIONS AND TENDER

The word "condition," in its technical sense, refers to contract language, or a contractual provision supplied by the court, that makes a party's duty of performance depend on some event that must occur or some fact that must exist. If the condition has not been met, no performance is due and a court will not order performance or hold the party liable for its failure.[339] Real estate sales contracts often contain numerous conditions. Some may be events entirely outside the control of the parties: "I am obligated to sell you this land only if the federal estate tax is repealed by August 15," or "I will buy your house only if Mount St. Helens does not erupt before the closing date." Other conditions may intimately involve the behavior of the parties themselves: "I am obligated to buy this land only if I am able to sell my farm in Iowa by June 1."

Where a condition is partially or entirely within the control, or dependent upon the actions or efforts, of a party to the contract, it is common to include in the contract a promise by that party that he or she will try (or use "good faith," "reasonable efforts," or the like) to accomplish it. For example, the contract in the preceding illustration might include a promise by the purchaser to attempt in good faith to sell the Iowa farm.[340] Even if no such promise is spelled out, courts will likely read it into the contract, construing the language as a covenant as well as a condition.[341] If this were not done, there would be a serious risk that a court might find that the party whose duty depends on the condition has, in effect, the power to turn the duty on or off at will. Such a power would

---

[336] Safeway System, Inc. v. Manuel Brothers, Inc., 102 R.I. 136, 228 A.2d 851 (1967).

[337] Henry v. Sharma, 154 Cal.App.3d 665, 201 Cal.Rptr. 478 (1984); Fletcher v. Jones, 314 N.C. 389, 333 S.E.2d 731 (1985) (seven weeks reasonable); Johnson v. Smith, Scott & Associates, Inc., 77 N.C.App. 386, 335 S.E.2d 205 (1985) (two weeks reasonable); Safeway System, Inc. v. Manuel Bros., supra note 336 (6 days reasonable); Freeman v. Boyce, 66 Hawaii 327, 661 P.2d 702 (1983) (4 months reasonable); Hicks v. Bridges, 580 So.2d 743 (Miss. 1991) (11 months reasonable); Kaiser v. Crouch, 504 P.2d 429 (Okl.1972) (120 days reasonable where contract required purchasers to build a house on the property). But see Woodhull Corp. v. Saibaba Corp., 234 Ga.App. 707, 507 S.E.2d 493 (Ga.App. 1998) (8 month delay unreasonable, where it caused vendor to make large payments to lender); Johnson v. Gregg, 807 S.W.2d 680 (Mo.App. 1991) (25 months unreasonable).

[338] FDIC v. Slinger, 913 F.2d 7 (1st Cir.1990) (3½ year delay reasonable, where lis pendens that prevented closing was not removed for 3 years); Yale Development Co. v. Aurora Pizza Hut, Inc., 95 Ill.App.3d 523, 51 Ill.Dec. 409, 420 N.E.2d 823 (1981) (17 months delay reasonable, where closing was conditioned on rezoning); Krotz v. Sattler, 586 N.W.2d 336 (Iowa 1998) (ten years' delay reasonable, in contract to sell abandoned railroad right-of-way, where neither party tendered earlier); Barber v. Fox, 36 Mass.App.Ct. 525, 632 N.E.2d 1246 (Mass.App. 1994) (in intrafamily sale, 20 year delay reasonable).

[339] See Restatement (Second) of Contracts § 224ff (1981); 13 Williston, Contracts § 38:1 (4th ed. 2018 update); Perillo, Contracts § 11.5 (7th ed. 2014).

[340] See, e.g. Head v. Sorensen, 220 So. 3d 569 (Fla. Dist. Ct. App. 2017); Mann v. Addicott Hills Corp., 238 Va. 262, 384 S.E.2d 81 (1989). No such duty will be implied (and even an express duty will be excused) if the effort would have been futile; Waksman Enterprises, Inc. v. Oregon Properties, Inc., 862 So.2d 35 (Fla. Dist. Ct. App. 2003).

[341] See Restatement (Second) of Contracts § 225 Comment d (1981); Emmert v. O'Brien, 72 Or.App. 752, 697 P.2d 222 (1985) (where contract contained condition that zoning use permit would be obtained, vendor had implied obligation to refrain from frustrating its issuance, and possibly an affirmative obligation to use reasonable efforts to bring it about; Moreland Dev. Co. v. Gladstone Holmes, Inc., 135 Cal.App.3d 973, 186 Cal.Rptr. 6 (1982) (condition that purchaser's board of directors approve contract did not make obligation illusory, as directors had duty to act in good faith); Galasso v. Ferraro, 280 A.D.2d 450, 720 N.Y.S.2d 518 (2001) (purchaser's efforts satisfied duty to seek mortgage loan); Perillo, Contracts § 11.11 (7th ed. 2014); Annot., Sufficiency of Real-estate Buyer's Efforts to Secure Financing upon which Sale Is Contingent, 78 A.L.R.3d 880 (1977).

render the obligation illusory, and might lead a court to deny entirely enforcement of the contract.[342] For present purposes, however, the point is simply that contract language may at the same time comprise both a promise or covenant, obligating a party to take certain actions, and a condition to one of the parties' performance of other duties.[343] Thus a vendor may provide, "I promise to obtain a report from a licensed pest inspector on the house, and you are obligated to buy only if it shows no infestation by termites."

Many conditions in sales contracts, such as those in the illustrations above, are conditions precedent, in the sense that some further duty of performance will become due only after they are satisfied.[344] However, consider the essential core of such a contract: the buyer's promise to pay the purchase price and the seller's promise to convey the land: "V agrees to deed Blackacre to P on June 1, for which P agrees to pay $50,000 cash." These words obviously represent covenants by each party, but because they contemplate a simultaneous exchange of performances, they will also be construed as concurrent conditions.[345] Thus, the substantial performance, or at least the tender of such performance, by each party is treated as a constructive[346] condition of the other party's duty to perform. If V does not tender a deed, P has no duty to pay the price; if P does not tender the price, V has no duty to deliver a deed.[347] If both parties fail to tender, neither is in breach.[348]

---

[342] See, e.g., Gerruth Realty Co. v. Pire, 17 Wis.2d 89, 115 N.W.2d 557 (1962). But see Steiner v. Thexton, 48 Cal. 4th 411, 226 P.3d 359 (2010) (once purchaser had expended money and effort in subdividing land, contract was not illusory despite purchaser's right to withdraw at will); Vohs v. Donovan, 322 Wis. 2d 721, 777 N.W.2d 915 (2009) (contract "subject to sellers obtaining home of their choice" was not illusory). Where the condition is "satisfaction" by a party or his attorney with some report or information, the courts will usually enforce the contract, subject to an obligation of good faith by the party who asserts dissatisfaction; see Nalley v. Harris, 176 Ga.App. 553, 336 S.E.2d 822 (1985) (satisfaction of structural inspector); Smith v. Crimson Ridge Development, LLC, 410 S.W.3d 619 (Ky. 2013) (buyer satisfaction with survey); Trenta v. Gay, 191 N.J.Super. 617, 468 A.2d 737 (1983) (attorney review clause permitting party's attorney to reject contract for any reason); Omni Group, Inc. v. Seattle-First National Bank, 32 Wn.App. 22, 645 P.2d 727 (1982) (buyer satisfaction with feasibility report on property); 13 Williston, Contracts § 38:21 (4th ed. 2018 update).

[343] See First National Bank of DeKalb County v. National Bank of Georgia, 249 Ga. 216, 290 S.E.2d 55 (1982); Restatement (Second) of Contracts § 225 Comment d; § 227 Comment d (1981); Perillo, Contracts §§ 11.8–11.11 (7th ed. 2014).

[344] See the discussion at § 10.11, infra.

[345] Bell v. Elder, 782 P.2d 545 (Utah App.1989); Esplendido Apartments v. Olsson, 144 Ariz. 355, 697 P.2d 1105 (App. 1984); Ball v. Maynard, 184 N.C. App. 99, 645 S.E.2d 890 (2007); Kossler v. Palm Springs Developments, Limited, 101 Cal.App.3d 88, 161 Cal.Rptr. 423 (1980); 3 Am.L.Prop. § 11.44 (1952); 3A Corbin, Contracts § 663 (1960); Restatement (Second) of Contracts § 238 (1981). Express language in the contract may make a party's tender a precedent rather than a concurrent condition; see Roberts v. Clark, 188 S.W.3d 204 (Tex. App. 2002) (tender of purchase price was a condition precedent to execution of deed).

[346] The condition is "constructive" simply because in the usual contract no language specifies that a condition exists; the language is, in effect, supplied by the court. See note 340 supra.

[347] See Carpenter v. Parsons, 186 Ga. App. 3, 366 S.E.2d 367 (1988); Prestenbach v. Collins, 159 So. 3d 531 (Miss. 2014) (tender is not required until closing); Deckert v. McCormick, 2014 N.D. 231, 857 N.W.2d 355 (2014) (tender required to exercise option); Shaw v. Ferguson, 767 P.2d 1358 (Okl.App. 1986). The discussion in the text refers to cash sales. If the contract calls for the price to be paid in installments, with conveyance of title upon payment of the last installment—a common arrangement—the tender of all installments except the last is obviously a condition precedent to the vendor's duty to convey; Hensley v. Williams, 726 P.2d 90 (Wyo. 1986); Church of God in Christ, Inc. v. Congregation Kehillath Jacob, 370 Mass. 828, 353 N.E.2d 669 (1976). And the vendor may sue for the unpaid installments without tendering a deed. But payment of the last installment and conveyance of the title are usually treated as concurrent conditions; see Sharbono v. Darden, 220 Mont. 320, 715 P.2d 433 (1986); Ideal Family and Youth Ranch v. Whetstine, 655 P.2d 429 (Colo.App. 1982); 3 Am.L.Prop. § 11.44 (1952).

[348] Addie v. Kjaer, 60 V.I. 881, 737 F.3d 854 (3d Cir. 2013); Rutherford Holdings, LLC v. Plaza Del Rey, 223 Cal.App.4th 221, 166 Cal.Rptr.3d 864 (2014).

These conclusions may seem too elementary to be worth stating; to the modern mind it would seem absurd to compel V to hand over a deed if V is not getting his or her money, or vice versa. But the doctrine of constructive concurrent conditions was not always accepted by the courts[349] and it has important modern consequences. The most significant is the requirement of tender: one may not treat the other party as in breach of the promises of the contract which contemplate simultaneous performance—payment of the price and transfer of the title—until one has performed or tendered one's own performance.[350] In general, the tendered performance need only be substantial and not perfect;[351] as we saw in the preceding section, for example, a tender later than the agreed date is sufficient if it is not unreasonably late and time is not essential.[352] But the parties may contract for a strict rather than a substantial performance, as illustrated by the "time of the essence" clause discussed in the preceding section.[353] And if the performance is only substantial rather than full, the other party (although obligated to perform) is entitled to damages or, in the case of the purchaser, an abatement of the price, to reflect the deficiency.[354]

A party who fails to tender is denied damages,[355] restitution,[356] and usually specific performance.[357] Professor Corbin pointed out that specific performance may well be granted despite the plaintiff's failure to tender, since the tender is implicit in the filing of the action itself, and since the court can make its decree conditional on the plaintiff's actual delivery into court of the necessary documents or funds.[358] In theory this is correct, but as a practical matter the action often will be filed so long after the agreed closing date that the passage of time will prevent the ostensible tender from complying with the contract.[359]

---

[349] See, e.g., Pordage v. Cole, 1 Wms. Saund. 319 (Kings Bench 1669), discussed in 15 Williston, Contracts § 44:1 (4th ed. 2018 update).

[350] In re Conservatorship and Estate of Buchenau, 127 Cal.Rptr.3d 109, 196 Cal.App.4th 1031 (2011); McGee v. V.T. Pierret Realty & Construction Co., Inc., 407 So.2d 1288 (La.App. 1981); Frostar Corp. v. Malloy, 63 Mass. App. Ct. 96, 823 N.E.2d 417 (2005); Cobb v. Cougle, 351 A.2d 110 (Me. 1976); Gunn v. Heggins, 964 So.2d 586 (Miss. Ct. App. 2007).

[351] See Schneider v. Dumbarton Developers, Inc., 767 F.2d 1007 (D.C.Cir. 1985); Hausam v. Wodrich, 574 P.2d 805 (Alaska 1978); Kofmehl v. Baseline Lake, LLC, 177 Wash. 2d 584, 305 P.3d 230 (2013); § 10.12, infra.

[352] See § 10.9 supra at note 299.

[353] Id. at note 310.

[354] Kossler v. Palm Springs Developments, Limited, 101 Cal.App.3d 88, 161 Cal. Rptr. 423 (1980).

[355] Ching-Ming Chen v. Advantage Co., 713 S.W.2d 79 (Tenn.App. 1986); Daybreak Const. Specialties, Inc. v. Saghatoleslami, 712 P.2d 1028 (Colo.App. 1985); Hellrung v. Hoechst, 384 S.W.2d 561 (Mo. 1964).

[356] Pelletier v. Dwyer, 334 A.2d 867 (Me. 1975); Cohen v. Kranz, 12 N.Y.2d 242, 238 N.Y.S.2d 928, 189 N.E.2d 473 (1963).

[357] Nix v. Clary, 640 P.2d 246 (Colo.App. 1981); MasTec, Inc. v. TJS, LLC, 979 So. 2d 285 (Fla. Dist. Ct. App. 2008); Green, Inc. v. Smith, 40 Ohio App.2d 30, 317 N.E.2d 227 (1974); Tamuno Ifiesimama v. Haile, 522 S.W.3d 675, 686 (Tex. App. 2017); Johnson v. Morris, 645 P.2d 51 (Utah 1982). But see Passehl Estate v. Passehl, 712 N.W.2d 408 (Iowa 2006) (where both parties failed to tender, neither was in breach but contract remained in force).

[358] 3A Corbin, Contracts § 663, at 179–180; § 1175 at 298–99 (1960). See Fleenor v. Church, 681 P.2d 1351 (Alaska 1984); Goldston v. AMI Investments, Inc., 98 Nev. 567, 655 P.2d 521 (1982).

[359] See § 10.9, supra. This is particularly true if time is of the essence, but even if it is not, an unreasonable time will often have elapsed. See also Crow v. Bertram, 725 S.W.2d 634 (Mo.App. 1987) (purchaser's long delay in tendering constituted abandonment of the contract, depriving him of right to specific performance). But see Wilhorn Builders, Inc. v. Cortaro Management Co., 82 Ariz. 48, 308 P.2d 251 (1957), permitting the vendor to tender after filing an action to enforce the contract; Restatement (Second) of Contracts § 238 Comment c and Illustration 5 (1981).

What is a tender? The term conjures a picture of a vendor with a deed in outstretched hand or a purchaser holding out a cashier's check. Such actions may once have been required and are certainly acceptable, but the modern notion of tender is more relaxed. What is required is a clear offer to perform, coupled with the present ability to do so.[360] Increasingly the courts have dropped the use of the term "tender" in recent years, employing instead such phrases as "ready, willing, and able to perform" which denote a more lenient attitude.[361] But these cases do not eliminate the need to communicate the offer of performance to the other party; it is not enough to be secretly willing and able.[362] It is permissible to condition the offer on the opposing party's tender of his or her own due performance[363], but if it is accompanied by further conditions not found in the contract, it is not a valid tender.[364]

Under some circumstances tender is excused and a party who does not tender is nonetheless entitled to full remedies. This is so if the opposing party has repudiated the contract[365] or if other circumstances make plain his or her unwillingness or inability to perform.[366] Moreover, one need not tender if the other side's performance has become impossible. For example, a purchaser is excused from tender if the vendor has sold the

---

[360] Acme Inv., Inc. v. Southwest Tracor, Inc., 105 F.3d 412 (8th Cir. 1997); Schellinger Bros. v. Cotter, 2 Cal. App. 5th 984, 207 Cal. Rptr. 3d 82 (Ct. App. 2016); Tamuno Ifiesimama v. Haile, 522 S.W.3d 675, 687 (Tex. App. 2017). Restatement (Second) of Contracts § 238 requires that the party must, "with manifested present ability to do so, offer performance of his part of the simultaneous exchange." It avoids the use of the word "tender."

[361] Gaggero v. Yura, 108 Cal. App. 4th 884, 134 Cal. Rptr. 2d 313 (Cal. Ct. App. 2003); Kottis v. Cerilli, 526 A.2d 506 (R.I. 1987); Harrison v. Baker, 402 So.2d 1270 (Fla.App. 1981); Chandler v. Independent School District No. 12, 625 P.2d 620 (Okl. 1981); Danforth v. More, 129 A.3d 63 (R.I. 2016). See also Hutton v. Gliksberg, 128 Cal.App.3d 240, 180 Cal.Rptr. 141 (1982) (letter from mortgage lender to escrow officer, committing to make loan, was sufficient tender by purchaser; actual cash deposit into escrow was not customary and not required.) But see Kuderer v. United States, 739 F.Supp. 1422 (D.Or. 1990) (a draft drawn on an unincorporated business trust is not the equivalent of cash, and is not a proper tender); Carr v. Enoch Smith Co., 781 P.2d 1292 (Utah App. 1989) (a letter expressing an intent to pay was not a proper tender).

[362] See, e.g., Nix v. Clary, 640 P.2d 246 (Colo.App. 1981) ("must give unequivocal notice of an unconditional commitment to be bound by the contract.") The communication may be to the other party's attorney or some other appropriate agent; see Parks Enterprises, Inc. v. New Century Realty, Inc., 652 P.2d 918 (Utah 1982) (title company held not to be vendor's agent); Cobb v. Cougle, 351 A.2d 110 (Me. 1976); Trapuzzano v. Lorish, 467 Pa. 27, 354 A.2d 534 (1976).

[363] See Pond v. Lindell, 194 Mont. 240, 632 P.2d 1107 (1981) (purchasers placed $9,600 contract balance in escrow with instructions that it be released only upon issuance of title policy showing vendor's merchantable title; held a valid tender); Restatement (Second) of Contracts § 238 Comment b (1981).

[364] Schneider v. Dumbarton Developers, Inc., 767 F.2d 1007 (D.C.Cir. 1985); Flynn v. Korneffel, 451 Mich. 186, 547 N.W.2d 249 (Mich. 1996); Mayer v. Boston Metropolitan Airport, Inc., 355 Mass. 344, 244 N.E.2d 568 (1969); New York Ave. LLC v. Harrison, 2016 Ut. App. 240, 391 P.3d 268 (Utah 2017).

[365] In re Canyon Group, LLC, 242 B.R. 136 (D. Vt. 1999) (Utah law); McClure v. Gower, 259 Ga. 678, 385 S.E.2d 271 (1989); Stauffer v. Benson, 288 Neb. 683, 850 N.W.2d 759 (2014); Princes Point LLC v. Muss Development L.L.C., 138 A.D.3d 112; 24 N.Y.S.3d 292 (2016); Pee Dee Oil Co. v. Quality Oil Co., 80 N.C.App. 219, 341 S.E.2d 113 (1986), review denied 317 N.C. 706, 347 S.E.2d 438 (1986); Jitner v. Gersch Dev. Co., 101 Or.App. 220, 789 P.2d 704 (1990); Internacional Realty, Inc. v. 2005 RP W., Ltd., 449 S.W.3d 512 (Tex. App. 2014).

[366] See Sterling Devel. Co. v. Collins, 309 S.C. 237, 421 S.E.2d 402 (S.C. 1992); Tower v. Halderman, 162 Ariz. 243, 782 P.2d 719 (1989); Kessler v. Tortoise Dev., Inc., 134 Idaho 264, 1 P.3d 292 (2000); Meunier v. Liang, 521 So.2d 475 (La.App. 1988); Kopp v. Boyango, 67 A.D.3d 646; 889 N.Y.S.2d 200 (2009); Anderson v. Meador, 56 A.D.3d 1030, 869 N.Y.S.2d 233 (2008); Spalla v. Fransen, 188 Ohio App.3d 658; 936 N.E.2d 552 (2010); Lee v. Thunder Development, Inc., 77 Or.App. 7, 711 P.2d 978 (1985). Tender will be excused where the other party fails to appear at the closing; see SG/IP Ltd. v. Centers, 121 F. App'x 546 (5th Cir. 2004); Johnson v. Moore, 931 S.W.2d 191, 195 (Mo. Ct. App. 1996).

property to another,[367] or if the title is subject to such defects that the vendor cannot reasonably expect to cure them by the time he or she must close.[368]

§ 10.11 PRECEDENT CONDITIONS

As the preceding section suggests, a condition may be precedent to a party's duty to perform rather than concurrent.[369] If a condition precedent does not occur, no duty of performance arises and no tender is required, and if the party who is benefitted by the condition fails to perform he or she is not in breach of the contract.[370] Both vendors and purchasers frequently insert a variety of conditions in sales contracts so that they will not be bound to proceed with the sale if various investigations or arrangements prove disappointing. A seller may not wish to go forward if the buyer's credit references are unsatisfactory[371] or if the seller is unable to acquire certain other real estate. The purchaser may condition the duty to buy on the completion of certain improvements on the land, the production of suitable investigative reports on structural quality or lack of contamination, or the availability of local governmental approvals such as rezonings, building permits, or sewer connections. As we will see in the next section, the courts will infer a covenant by the vendor to provide a title of acceptable quality, and will also treat the existence of such a title as a condition precedent to the buyer's duty to purchase.[372] Courts often say that conditions precedent are disfavored, and that a condition will not be found in the absence of clear language showing that a condition was intended.[373]

---

[367] Robert Lawrence Associates, Inc. v. Del Vecchio, 178 Conn. 1, 420 A.2d 1142 (1979).

[368] Spagat v. Schak, 130 Ill.App.3d 130, 85 Ill.Dec. 389, 473 N.E.2d 988 (1985); Martocci v. Schneider, 119 A.D.3d 746, 990 N.Y.S.2d 240 (2014); Langston v. Huffacker, 36 Wn.App. 779, 678 P.2d 1265 (1984). If it feasible for the vendor to cure the defects, the purchaser must give notice of them and a reasonable time to cure; see *Martocci*, supra; § 10.12 infra.

[369] § 10.10 supra at note 346. See generally Bowman, Escrow Agreements: How Enforceable Are They?, 34 L.A.Bar.Bull. 41 (No. 2, 1958), for an able discussion of common conditions precedent.

[370] Cate v. Woods, 299 S.W.3d 149 (Tex. Ct. App. 2009); Arthur Rutenberg Corp. v. Pasin, 506 So.2d 33 (Fla.App. 1987); M & M Grp., Inc. v. Holmes, 379 S.C. 468, 666 S.E.2d 262 (Ct. App. 2008); Salvo v. Thatcher, 128 Wash.App. 579, 116 P.3d 1019 (2005).

In principle, a condition can be subsequent rather than precedent or concurrent. A condition subsequent is one which, if it occurs, will discharge a contractual duty that has already arisen. Such conditions are not commonly found in real estate sales contracts. See Southport Congregational Church—United Church of Christ v. Hadley, 320 Conn. 103, 128 A.3d 478 (2016) (financing condition was subsequent, not precedent); 3A Corbin, Contracts § 628 (1960); Perillo, Contracts § 11.7 (5th ed. 2014). The Second Restatement does not employ the term "condition subsequent," but instead treats such an occurrence under its provisions on discharge of contractual duties; see Restatement (Second) of Contracts § 224 Comment e, § 230 (1981). It also states a preference for interpreting conditions as precedent rather than as discharging duties which have already matured; id, at § 227(3). The Missouri cases seem consistently to term conditions "subsequent" when all other courts would call them "precedent"; see Maynard v. Bazazzadegan, 732 S.W.2d 950 (Mo.App. 1987).

[371] The seller would ordinarily be concerned with the buyer's credit only if the seller were financing all or part of the price by way of a purchase-money mortgage or an installment sale contract. Such transactions are common.

[372] See § 10.12 infra.

[373] Davis v. Woodlake Partners, LLC, 230 N.C. App. 88, 748 S.E.2d 762 (2013). Despite this supposed preference, courts sometimes find conditions from contract language that is far from clear. See, e.g., Binford v. Shicker, 553 N.E.2d 845 (Ind.App. 1990) (buyers' promise to apply for mortgage loan held to be a condition precedent); Armstrong v. Berco Res., LLC, 752 F.3d 716 (8th Cir. 2014) ("subject to title review" made compliance with attorney's curative requirements a condition precedent); Sabatine BK Dev., LLC v. Fitzpatrick Enterprises, Inc., 2017 Ohio 805, 85 N.E.3d 1127 (Ohio Ct. App. 2017) ("subject to a mutually agreeable replat of the property" held to be a condition precedent). Contra, see Magnani v. Cuggino, 57 Misc. 3d 1, 55 N.Y.S.3d 585 (N.Y. App. Term. 2017) (covenant requiring removal of equipment from sold premises was not a condition precedent); Coldwell v. Moore, 2017 Ohio 526, 85 N.E.3d 262 (Ohio Ct. App. 2017) (purchaser's covenants to perform contract were not conditions precedent).

Contracts of sale commonly set dates by which their conditions precedent must be fulfilled. Ordinarily, fulfillment of the condition within a reasonable time after the date fixed is considered acceptable unless time has expressly been made of the essence as to the condition.[374]

Perhaps most common condition found in sales contracts is one based on the availability of new mortgage financing to enable the buyer to purchase. Such clauses have been in use for many decades, yet continue to be very widely litigated. During the 1970s and 1980s, as a consequence of relatively high and volatile interest rates, large numbers of real estate sales were financed by the purchaser's assumption of or taking subject to a preexisting mortgage, typically carrying an interest rate lower than current rates. This technique raised the need for a different kind of financing condition, since the approval of the existing mortgage holder was usually needed under a "due-on-sale" clause in the mortgage,[375] in order for the transaction to proceed. Under these circumstances a well-advised purchaser would make such approval a condition of the duty to close the sale;[376] surprisingly, the point was often overlooked.[377]

As we have already seen,[378] a condition which is entirely under the control of the party whose performance depends on it has the effect of letting him or her out of the contract at will. In such a contract there is no mutuality of obligation, and hence under the orthodox view neither party can enforce the contract.[379] The courts dislike this result, and very often avoid it by construing the contract in a manner that denies the party in question unfettered discretion as to whether the condition will be met. Most often this is accomplished by reading the condition as containing an implicit covenant to use "good faith", "reasonable efforts", or the like to make the condition occur.[380] Thus the language

---

[374] Vanbuskirk v. Nakamura, 2016 WL 2985026 (Nev. 2016) (unreported); Harris v. Stewart, 193 N.C. App. 142, 666 S.E.2d 804 (2008); § 10.9 supra.

[375] See generally Nelson, Whitman, Burkhart & Freyermuth, Real Estate Finance Law §§ 5.21–5.26 (6th ed. 2014). See Maxwell, The Due-on-Sale Clause: Restraints on Alienation and Adhesion Theory in California, 28 U.C.L.A.L.Rev. 197 (1981); § 341 of the Garn-St. Germain Depository Institutions Act of 1982, 12 U.S.C.A. § 1701j–3, generally making due-on-sale clauses enforceable as a matter of preemptive federal law. See also Investors Savings & Loan Association v. Ganz, 174 N.J.Super. 356, 416 A.2d 918 (1980), upholding a clause which permitted the lender to demand repayment of the loan if the borrower moved out of the house.

[376] See Zavradinos v. Lund, 741 S.W.2d 863 (Mo. Ct. App. 1987); Wendy's of Montana v. Larsen, 196 Mont. 525, 640 P.2d 464 (1982); McDaniel v. Kudlik, 598 S.W.2d 350 (Tex. Ct. Civ. App. 1980).

[377] See Wallstreet Properties, Inc. v. Gassner, 53 Or.App. 650, 632 P.2d 1310 (1981). If there is no condition, and the lender's refusal to consent to the sale makes it impossible to proceed under the original contractual terms, a court asked to order specific performance for the vendor is faced with a difficult problem. Compare Barry M. Dechtman, Inc. v. Sidpaul Corp., 178 N.J.Super. 444, 429 A.2d 411 (1981), reversed 89 N.J. 547, 446 A.2d 518 (1982) (contract too uncertain to be enforced), with Schrader v. Benton, 2 Hawaii App. 564, 635 P.2d 562 (1981) (contract enforced with court restructuring the transaction).

[378] § 10.10 supra at note 342.

[379] Allentown Patriots, Inc. v. City of Allentown, 162 A.3d 1187 (Pa. Commw. Ct. 2017); Resource Management Co. v. Weston Ranch & Livestock Co., 706 P.2d 1028 (Utah 1985); Long Investment Co. v. O'Donnel, 3 Wis.2d 291, 88 N.W.2d 674 (1958); Restatement (Second) of Contracts § 226 Illustration 4 (1981); Perillo, Contracts § 4.12(4) (5th ed. 2014); 1 Corbin, Contracts § 149 (1960). Courts frequently attempt to construe contract provisions so as to narrow the unfettered discretion of the party who appears to have control of the condition, thereby making that party's obligation meaningful and enforcing the contract. See, e.g., Hunt v. Shamblin, 179 W.Va. 663, 371 S.E.2d 591 (1988).

[380] See, e.g., Bunnell v. Haghighi, 661 F. App'x 110 (2d Cir. 2016) (New York law); General Inv. & Devel. Co. v. Guardian Sav. and Loan Ass'n, 862 F.Supp. 153 (S.D.Tex. 1994); Bryant v. City of Atlantic City, 309 N.J.Super. 596, 707 A.2d 1072 (N.J.Super. 1998); Wooten v. DeMean, 788 S.W.2d 522 (Mo. Ct. App. 1990) ("reasonable efforts"). Cf. Anzalaco v. Graber, 970 N.E.2d 1143 (Ohio Ct. App. 2012) (making of repairs was condition precedent, but vendor had no duty to make them); Temkin, Too Much Good Faith in Real Estate Purchase Agreements? Give Me an Option, 34 Kan.L.Rev. 43 (1985).

of the condition is treated as a covenant as well. A party who has failed to make the good faith effort required is liable for breach of that covenant, even though the duty to perform the main body of the contract has not arisen. The breach is typically treated as a material or total one, much as if the defaulting party had refused to complete the sale itself.[381] On the other hand, if the condition is unfulfilled despite the exertion of good faith efforts, the party protected by the condition is excused from further performance and can get restitution of any payments made to date.[382]

Most of the cases employing this judicial technique involve conditions of financing; it is nearly always held that the buyer (the only party who *can* apply for mortgage financing) has a duty to make good faith efforts to arrange it.[383] A similar approach is often used with other types of conditions, such as the sale by the buyer of another house[384] or the approval by a lender of a loan assumption.[385] Often a question arises as to whether the party with the duty to use good faith efforts has tried hard enough. For example, in a contract involving a condition of financing, is it sufficient for the buyer to apply for a loan with only a single lending institution? Results in such cases vary,[386] with

---

A fortiori, the party benefitted by the condition may not rely upon it if she or he has exercised bad faith by obstructing or preventing its occurrence; see Wells Fargo Bank, NA v. SBC IV REO, LLC, 318 Mich. App. 72, 896 N.W.2d 821 (2016); Bunnell v. Haghighi, 661 F. App'x 110 (2d Cir. 2016).

A party with a duty to make the condition occur will be excused from doing so if the opposing party commits an anticipatory breach; see Princes Point LLC v. Muss Dev. L.L.C., 138 A.D.3d 112, 24 N.Y.S.3d 292 (2016), rev'd on other grounds, 30 N.Y.3d 127, 87 N.E.3d 121, 65 N.Y.S.3d 89 (2017).

[381] In the typical case, the purchaser is seeking restitution of an earnest money deposit, and the claim is rejected due to his or her lack of good faith; see, e.g., Price v. Bartkowiak, 729 F.Supp. 14 (S.D.N.Y.1989) (purchasers acted in bad faith, where they rejected a loan commitment that met the terms of the condition and continued to search for better terms); Schollian v. Ullo, 558 So.2d 776 (La.App. 1990), writ denied 564 So.2d 324 (La. 1990) (purchasers did not make application for mortgage loan until date it was to have been approved, according to contract; their tardiness was held to constitute bad faith).

[382] Weaver v. Hilzen, 147 A.D.2d 634, 538 N.Y.S.2d 40 (1989); Storen v. Meadors, 295 S.C. 438, 369 S.E.2d 651 (1988); Ide v. Joe Miller & Co., 703 P.2d 590 (Colo.App. 1984); Teachout v. Wilson, 376 N.W.2d 460 (Minn.App. 1985); Brown v. Matton, 406 So.2d 1269 (Fla.App. 1981); Mobil Oil Corp. v. V.S.H. Realty, Inc., 408 So.2d 585 (Fla.App. 1981); Management, Inc. v. Mastersons, Inc., 189 Mont. 435, 616 P.2d 356 (1980).

[383] Century 21 Acadia Realty & Development Co., Inc. v. Brough, 393 So.2d 287 (La.App. 1980); Bushmiller v. Schiller, 35 Md.App. 1, 368 A.2d 1044 (1977); Stackhouse v. Gaver, 19 Neb. App. 117, 801 N.W.2d 260 (2011); Manning v. Bleifus, 166 W.Va. 131, 272 S.E.2d 821 (1980). See Perillo, Contracts § 4.12(6) (5th ed. 2014); Restatement (Second) of Contracts § 225 Illustration 8 (1981); Delsack, The Mortgage Contingency Clause: A Trap for the Residential Real Estate Purchaser Using a Mortgage Broker, 17 Cardozo L.Rev. 299 (1995); Aiken, "Subject to Financing" Clauses in Interim Contracts for Sale of Realty, 43 Marq.L.Rev. 265 (1960). The duty extends to good faith in actions taken after the loan application has been made that might jeopardize its approval; see Bruyere v. Jade Realty Corp., 117 N.H. 564, 375 A.2d 600 (1977). On financing conditions generally, see Annot., 81 A.L.R.2d 1338 (1962); 30 A.L.R.4th 474 (1984).

[384] Cox v. Funk, 42 N.C.App. 32, 255 S.E.2d 600 (1979). See also Friend v. McGarry, 141 Misc.2d 479, 533 N.Y.S.2d 357 (1988) (purchaser required to use good faith efforts to sell his old house even where contract was not explicitly conditioned on such sale, where new loan commitment required sale of the house).

[385] Farahzad v. Monometrics Corp., 119 A.D.2d 721, 501 N.Y.S.2d 136 (1986); Dawson v. Malloy, 428 So.2d 297 (Fla.App. 1983); McDaniel v. Kudlik, 598 S.W.2d 350 (Tex.Civ.App. 1980).

[386] Grossman v. Melinda Lowell, P.A., 703 F.Supp. 282 (S.D.N.Y. 1989) (contract required "best efforts," which means more than mere good faith; three phone calls and one written application not sufficient); In re Kirkbride, 409 B.R. 354 (Bankr. E.D.N.C. 2009) (application with one mortgage broker sufficient); McCoy v. Brown, 130 Conn. App. 702, 24 A.3d 597 (2011) (purchaser had duty to pursue other financing options when first application was rejected because he had lost his job); Hoelscher v. Schenewerk, 804 S.W.2d 828 (Mo.App. 1991) (one application insufficient, where contract clause called for three); Gast v. Miller, 44 Ohio Misc.2d 15, 541 N.E.2d 497 (1988) (one application sufficient); Stevens v. Cliffs at Princeville Associates, 67 Hawaii 236, 684 P.2d 965 (1984) (one application sufficient, where neither party knew of any other institution which would have approved the loan); Weger v. Silveria, 460 So.2d 49 (La.App. 1984) (one application sufficient). See Annot., 78 A.L.R.3d 880 (1977).

appellate courts often presuming to decide the question themselves despite its factual aspects.

Clauses expressing financing conditions are often remarkably vague; it is not unusual to see "Contract subject to financing" or "Contingent on buyer obtaining loan."[387] At the other extreme, carefully-drawn clauses sometimes spell out the minimum amount, maximum interest rate and whether fixed or adjustable, minimum term, type of institutional lender, type of loan (FHA, VA, privately-insured or conventional), and even set out the number of applications which must be made.[388] Vague clauses are an invitation to litigate. If the court finds the language too indefinite, the entire contract will usually be treated as a nullity which neither party can enforce.[389] The buyer may argue that the contract gives him or her the power to fill in the missing terms, but such a power would quite arguably make the obligation to buy illusory, and the contract would be unenforceable for that reason.[390]

Most courts, however, are quite willing to supply the missing terms in a financing condition by referring to reasonable expectations and practices in the locality. Even clauses which include no details about the loan at all are frequently upheld.[391] There can

---

[387] Or worse yet, fails to make financing a condition at all; see Hoecher v. Runyan, 21 P.3d 339 (Wyo. 2001). See Raushenbush, Problems and Practices with Financing Conditions in Real Estate Contracts, 1963 Wis.L.Rev. 566. Suppose a lender gives a loan commitment, but later revokes it through no fault of the purchaser. Does the condition require merely that a commitment be issued, or that the loan actually be available at closing? Holding that the condition was not satisfied where the commitment was revoked, see Carter v. Cline, 2011 Ark. 474, 385 S.W.3d 745 (2011); Rosen v. Empire Valve & Fitting, Inc., 381 Pa.Super. 348, 553 A.2d 1004 (1989); Northeast Custom Homes, Inc. v. Howell, 230 N.J.Super. 296, 553 A.2d 387 (1988). Contra, see Malus v. Hager, 312 N.J.Super. 483, 712 A.2d 238 (App.Div. 1998). See the thorough discussion in Chaplick for Canal Vista Tr. v. Jeng Fen Mao, 215 F.Supp.3d 470, 484 (D. Md. 2016). A well-drafted clause (from the purchaser's viewpoint) will require the actual availability of funds at the closing as a condition. Note also that a court may distinguish between the "ability" to obtain a loan commitment and actually obtaining one. See Khalidi v. Weeks Family Partnership, 912 So.2d 256 (Ala. Civ. App. 2005); Wyda Assoc. v. Merner, 50 Cal.Rptr.2d 323 (Cal.App. 1996). In Carter v. Cline, 2011 Ark. 474, 385 S.W.3d 745 (2011), the court construed the contract to require actual availability of financing at the closing, and excused the purchasers from performance when it was not available.

[388] For an exceptionally thorough clause, see Feldman v. Oman Associates, Inc., 20 Ill.App.3d 436, 314 N.E.2d 338 (1974). For an equally lengthy but very poorly drafted clause which the court held violated the New Jersey "Plain Language" Act, see Wheatly v. Myung Sook Suh, 217 N.J. Super. 233, 525 A.2d 340 (App.Div. 1987).

A wise seller will include an obligation on the purchaser to give notice if the mortgage commitment has (or has not) been obtained by a fixed date; otherwise, the seller may be unaware of the purchaser's intentions with respect to performance of the contract. See Howard v. Youngman, 81 S.W. 3d 101 (Mo. Ct. App. 2002); Bellon v. Acosta, 10 So. 3d 1165 (Fla. Dist. Ct. App. 2009) (purchasers were in breach of contract due to their failure to notify vendor of status of loan commitment as required by financing condition); Humble v. Wyant, 2014 S.D. 4, 843 N.W.2d 334 (2014) (same).

[389] The courts of Georgia, Maryland, New York, and Wisconsin have been notably stringent in rejecting conditions as too indefinite. See, e.g., Parks v. Thompson Builders, Inc., 296 Ga.App. 704, 675 S.E.2d 583 (2009) (amount and interest rate must be specified); Imas Gruner & Associates, Limited v. Stringer, 48 Md.App. 364, 427 A.2d 1038 (1981) (amount, interest rate, and term must be specified); Nodolf v. Nelson, 103 Wis.2d 656, 309 N.W.2d 397 (1981); Perkins v. Gosewehr, 98 Wis.2d 158, 295 N.W.2d 789 (1980) (amount of loan is an insufficient description, with court mentioning numerous other factors as desirable additions); Gerruth Realty Co. v. Pire, 17 Wis.2d 89, 115 N.W.2d 557 (1962) (amount of loan must be stated); Neiss v. Franze, 101 Misc.2d 871, 422 N.Y.S.2d 345 (1979) (amount, interest rate, and term must be specified.) See Conn.Stat. § 49–5b, requiring at a minimum the principal amount, the time within which a commitment must be obtained, and the term of the loan. But see Channawood Holdings, LLC v. 1209 Washington, LLC, 333 S.W.3d 480, 486 (Mo. Ct. App. 2010) (upholding a condition requiring obtaining of "satisfactory" financing).

[390] See Gerruth Realty Co. v. Pire, id.

[391] See Gildea v. Kapenis, 402 N.W.2d 457 (Iowa App. 1987) ("subject to buyer obtaining suitable financing interest rate no greater than $12^3/_4\%$" was sufficient description of financing); Wiggins v. Shewmake,

be no sound objection to this practice, for if the purchaser has not taken the trouble to spell out the protection in detail, it is eminently sensible for the court to give only "reasonable" protection, while to deny enforcement in this setting is an unnecessary frustration of the parties' agreement.

Changes in the financial markets in recent decades have made the drafting of a comprehensive condition-of-financing clause quite challenging. A wide array of mortgage loan formats has become available, characterized by adjustable interest rates, flexible payment schedules, and options to convert from adjustable to fixed rates.[392] Borrowers are also faced with a broad range of possible mortgage clauses dealing with such matters as prepayment fees, late charges, and provisions for acceleration upon future sale of the property.[393] Few printed form contracts of sale contain financing clauses which deal with all of these financing issues, and even fewer lay parties or real estate agents are likely to insert language covering them. Good practice undoubtedly would require mention of these factors in the contract, but most courts would not insist on it as a prerequisite to judicial enforcement. Instead the cases tend to regard mortgages with any reasonable or common terms as satisfying the condition, even if they include fairly burdensome provisions of the type mentioned above.[394]

Even if a condition is too indefinite to be enforced, the actual behavior of the parties may supply sufficient additional information to warrant enforcement. For example, if the buyer proceeds to apply for and obtain a mortgage loan commitment on terms which are reasonable and satisfactory to him or her, that action may be sufficient to give the requisite content to an otherwise vague financing condition.[395]

---

374 N.W.2d 111 (S.D.1985) ("13% conventional loan" was sufficient); Manning v. Bleifus, 166 W.Va. 131, 272 S.E.2d 821 (1980); Restatement (Second) of Contracts § 204 (1981).

[392] See generally Nelson, Whitman, Burkhart & Freyermuth, Real Estate Finance Law § 11.4 (6th ed. 2014); Thomas, Alternative Residential Mortgages for Tomorrow, 26 Prac.Law. 55 (Sept. 1980); Hyer & Kearl, Legal Impediments to Mortgage Innovation, 6 Real Est. L.J. 211 (1978). In Zepfler v. Neandross, 497 So.2d 901 (Fla.App. 1986), the financing condition called for an interest rate "not to exceed 13.5%," but did not specify whether a fixed-rate or adjustable-rate loan was intended. The buyers obtained a commitment for an adjustable rate loan at 13% with a 2.5% cap on future rate increases. The court held that this commitment did not satisfy the condition.

[393] See Nelson, Whitman, Burkhart & Freyermuth, id., at §§ 5.21–23, 6.1–.3, 6.6.

[394] The condition was silent on the particular loan provision in question, but was held to have been satisfied by a loan containing the provision, in the following cases: Gaynes v. Allen, 116 N.H. 469, 362 A.2d 197 (1976) (prepayment penalty and variable interest rate); Yasuna v. National Capital Corp., 273 Md. 617, 331 A.2d 49 (1975) (action for commission by mortgage loan broker; condominium construction loan procured, but required progress fees, 50 percent presale of units, and other "common and predictable" features of construction loans). Contra, see Woodland Realty, Inc. v. Winzenried, 82 Wis.2d 218, 262 N.W.2d 106 (1978), noted 62 Marq.L.Rev. 123 (1978). Where a loan commitment is obtained, but it contains unusual conditions that were not mentioned in the financing clause of the contract of sale, it is usually held that the commitment does not satisfy the contract. A typical example is a condition that the purchaser sell an existing house to qualify for the new mortgage loan. See, e.g., Kressel, Rothlein & Roth v. Gallagher, 155 A.D.2d 587, 547 N.Y.S.2d 653 (1989); Farrell v. Janik, 225 N.J. Super. 282, 542 A.2d 59 (1988); Educational Placement Service, Inc. v. Watts, 789 S.W.2d 902 (Tenn.App. 1989). Contra, see Rousset v. Smith, 176 So. 3d 632, 648 (La. Ct. App. 2015) (loan commitment was valid despite containing condition of sale of home, and purchasers were discharged from contract when home sale failed).

[395] See Highlands Plaza, Inc. v. Viking Investment Corp., 2 Wn.App. 192, 467 P.2d 378 (1970); 1 Corbin, Contracts § 101 (1960). But see Thomas v. Harris, 127 Ga. App. 361, 193 S.E.2d 260 (1972), holding that lack of mutuality may be cured by subsequent performance, but that indefiniteness cannot; Nodolf v. Nelson, 103 Wis.2d 656, 309 N.W.2d 397 (1981). An alternative approach to saving a contract with an indefinite condition is the waiver of the condition by the party it protects; see cases cited at note 399 infra.

A financing condition which is sufficiently detailed to be enforced may still produce questions of interpretation.[396] One common problem arises when the buyer cannot obtain institutional financing on qualifying terms; the seller, to avoid losing the sale, may then offer to provide the financing by taking back a purchase-money mortgage, or may attempt to arrange financing through private sources such as friends or relatives. If the buyer demurs to such an offer, the court may have to determine whether the clause contemplates only institutional financing.[397] If the terms of the private mortgage offer meet the specifications of the condition, the case should turn on whether some other legitimate objective of the condition would be frustrated by forcing the buyer to accept a non-institutional loan.[398]

If it becomes difficult or impossible to fulfill a condition, a contracting party may purport to waive the condition and seek enforcement of the contract despite its failure. If the condition was inserted for the sole benefit of the waiving party, the waiver will be effective.[399] However, if the condition was intended to benefit the other party, or both of them, enforcement will be denied.[400] The difficulty arises in deciding for whose benefit

---

[396] Thus, a condition which does not specify the time within which the buyer must obtain financing will be construed to allow a reasonable time; see Bradford v. Alvey & Sons, 621 P.2d 1240 (Utah 1980); see § 10.9 supra. See also Clarke v. Hartley, 7 Ohio App.3d 147, 454 N.E.2d 1322 (1982); Meaux v. Adams, 456 So.2d 670 (La.App. 1984).

[397] These cases often depend on the precise language of the condition. Cases holding that the condition contemplated only institutional financing, and that the purchaser had no duty to proceed with vendor financing, include Gardner v. Padro, 164 Ill.App.3d 449, 115 Ill.Dec. 445, 517 N.E.2d 1131 (1987); Macho Assets, Inc. v. Spring Corp., 128 A.D.2d 680, 513 N.Y.S.2d 180 (1987), appeal denied 69 N.Y.2d 609, 516 N.Y.S.2d 1025, 509 N.E.2d 360 (1987); Biersbach v. Landin, Ltd., 454 So.2d 779 (Fla.App. 1984). Cf. Kovarik v. Vesely, 3 Wis.2d 573, 89 N.W.2d 279 (1958) (specific bank mentioned in the condition, but held not to be a material factor; financing offered by vendor held to satisfy the condition). See also Peterson v. Wirum, 625 P.2d 866 (Alaska 1981). Restatement (Second) of Contracts § 226 Illustration 6 (1981) indicates that where the condition mentions a specific lender, it is not satisfied by an offer of an equivalent loan from the vendor. See Harrington v. Norris B. Strickland & Associates, Inc., 161 Ga.App. 518, 289 S.E.2d 17 (1982); Smalley v. Layne, 428 So.2d 298 (Fla.App. 1983).

[398] When the courts hold that private financing fails to satisfy the condition, they may emphasize the advantage to the purchaser of obtaining the results of the institutional lender's appraisal as a check on whether the property was overpriced. If there is evidence that this was an important objective of the buyer, the courts are justified in letting the buyer reject non-institutional financing. A carefully structured condition of financing can provide the buyer a very effective hedge against overpricing. The court upheld the purchaser's right to rescind and recover his earnest money on such facts in Thaly v. Namer, 496 So.2d 1211 (La.App. 1986). Of course, a more direct approach for the purchaser is simply to condition the obligation to buy on the property's appraising for at least the contract price; see, e.g., Connor v. Cal-Az Properties, Inc., 137 Ariz. 53, 668 P.2d 896 (App. 1983), upholding such a condition.

[399] Virginia Oak Venture, LLC v. Fought, 448 S.W.3d 179 (Tex. App. 2014).

[400] See generally 13 Williston on Contracts § 39:17 (4th ed. 2018 update); Pelligreen v. Wood, 111 S.W.3d 446 (Mo. Ct. App. 2003) (condition was for benefit of vendor, and purchaser could not waive it). Cases holding waivers effective include Widener v. Ashkouti, 239 Ga. App. 530, 521 S.E.2d 215 (Ga.App. 1999); Harper v. Gibson, 284 S.C. 274, 325 S.E.2d 586 (1985); Bossi v. Whalen, 19 Mass.App. Ct. 966, 473 N.E.2d 1167 (1985); Defreitas v. Holley, 93 A.D.2d 852, 461 N.Y.S.2d 351 (1983). Contrary cases, finding the condition for mutual benefit and denying a party a unilateral right of waiver, include Oak Bee Corp. v. N.E. Blankman & Co., Inc., 154 A.D.2d 3, 551 N.Y.S.2d 559 (1990), appeal denied 76 N.Y.2d 713, 563 N.Y.S.2d 769, 565 N.E.2d 518 (1990); Poquott Dev. Corp. v. Johnson, 104 A.D.2d 442, 478 N.Y.S.2d 960 (1984); Arata v. Shefco, Ltd., 2014 Utah App. 148, 330 P.3d 115 (2014). See Romm v. Flax, 340 Md. 690, 668 A.2d 1 (Md.Ct.App. 1995) (statutory requirement for seller's disclosure statement was for benefit of buyer and could be waived only by buyer). A party who renders performance that was conditioned upon some event, without waiting for that event to occur, may be held to have waived the condition; see, e.g., Field v. Perry, 564 So.2d 504 (Fla.App.1990), review denied 576 So.2d 290 (Fla. 1991). Oral waivers, and waivers inferred from a party's conduct, are widely upheld, even in the face of contract language requiring modifications to be in writing; see Crabby's, Inc. v. Hamilton, 244 S.W.3d 209 (Mo. Ct. App. 2008); Dellicarri v. Hirschfeld, 210 A.D.2d 584, 619 N.Y.S.2d 816 (1994); Williams v. Ubaldo, 670 A.2d 913 (Me. 1996).

the condition was inserted. Financing conditions are nearly always viewed as benefitting only the buyer, so that he or she can waive them unilaterally.[401] This seems generally correct, although an exception should be recognized where the seller is also taking back a subordinated purchase-money mortgage and is therefore vitally concerned that the buyer deal with a reputable primary lender on terms which will not endanger the buyer's ability to pay the debt.[402]

With other types of conditions, it is not always easy to identify the beneficiary. Where the condition is based on approvals of rezonings, building permits, utility connections, or the like by a local government agency, and where the obvious purpose is to protect the buyer's right to construct certain improvements on the land, unilateral waiver by the buyer is usually allowed.[403] Here again, however, the seller may have an interest in fulfillment of the condition if he or she is taking back a secured purchase-money obligation, since the land's value as security may well be dependent on issuance of the approvals.[404] One may imagine other equally compelling arguments for the seller;[405] it is simply a question of fact whether he or she has a genuine interest in the realization of the condition.[406]

A similar but less common occurrence is the elimination of a condition by estoppel. The distinction between waiver and estoppel is that only the waiving party's action is necessary to a waiver, while an estoppel involves the detrimental reliance of the other party on the first's representations. See, e.g., NGA #2 Limited Liability Co. v. Rains, 113 Nev. 1151, 946 P.2d 163 (Nev. 1997); Gorzelsky v. Leckey, 402 Pa.Super. 246, 586 A.2d 952 (1991), appeal denied 528 Pa. 630, 598 A.2d 284 (1991); Dziadiw v. 352 State Street Corp., 107 A.D.2d 1003, 484 N.Y.S.2d 727 (1985); Alliance Financial Services, Inc. v. Cummings, 526 So.2d 324 (La.App. 1988).

[401] Watson v. Gerace, 175 F. App'x 528 (3d Cir. 2006); Crabby's, Inc. v. Hamilton, 244 S.W.3d 209 (Mo. Ct. App. 2008); Xhelili v. Larstanna, 150 A.D.2d 560, 541 N.Y.S.2d 132 (1989); Friedman v. Chopra, 220 N.J.Super. 546, 533 A.2d 48 (1987), cert. denied 110 N.J. 164, 540 A.2d 165 (1988) (purchaser is free to accept a mortgage loan for a lower amount than specified in condition clause). See also Garnot v. LaDue, 45 A.D.3d 1080, 845 N.Y.S.2d 555 (2007) (purchaser could waive inspection condition). But see Lajayi v. Fafiyebi, 860 A.2d 680 (R.I. 2004). If the contract provides that failure of the condition makes the contract "null and void", a court may hold that it cannot be waived; see Ormond Realty v. Ninnis, 341 Pa.Super. 101, 491 A.2d 169 (1985); Keller v. Reich, 646 S.W.2d 141 (Mo.App. 1983); Dvorak v. Christ, 692 N.E.2d 920 (Ind. Ct. App. 1998) (contract provided "agreement shall terminate" if financing was not obtained; contract terminated automatically although purchaser desired to enforce it); Davies, Some Thoughts on the Drafting of Conditions in Contracts for the Sale of Land, 15 Alberta L.Rev. 422 (1977). Cf. McCain v. Cox, 531 F.Supp. 771 (N.D.Miss. 1982), affirmed 692 F.2d 755 (5th Cir. 1982) ("null and void" means voidable at the election of the non-defaulting party).

[402] Fleischer v. McCarver, 691 S.W.2d 930 (Mo.App. 1985). But see Highlands Plaza, Inc. v. Viking Investment Corp., 2 Wn.App. 192, 467 P.2d 378 (1970).

[403] W.W.W. Associates, Inc. v. Giancontieri, 152 A.D.2d 333, 548 N.Y.S.2d 580 (1989) (termination of certain litigation involving vendors); Berryhill v. Hatt, 428 N.W.2d 647 (Iowa 1988) (availability of adjacent property to purchaser); Regional Gravel Products, Inc. v. Stanton, 135 A.D.2d 1079, 524 N.Y.S.2d 114 (1987), appeal dismissed 71 N.Y.2d 949, 528 N.Y.S.2d 827, 524 N.E.2d 147 (1988) (land use approvals); Schreiber v. Karpow, 290 Or. 817, 626 P.2d 891 (1981) (septic tank and building permits); Prestige House, Inc. v. Merrill, 51 Or.App. 67, 624 P.2d 188 (1981) (building permits); Eliason v. Watts, 615 P.2d 427 (Utah 1980) (septic tank permit; held not to benefit seller although he owned nearby land). Cf. Epstein Hebrew Academy v. Wondell, 327 S.W.2d 926 (Mo. 1959). On rezoning conditions generally, see Annot., 76 A.L.R.2d 1195 (1961).

[404] Cf. Prestige House, Inc. v. Merrill, id., in which the vendor was providing financing for the sale, but never indicated that it was concerned about the issuance of the building permits from a security viewpoint. The argument in the text was considered but rejected in Major v. Price, 196 Va. 526, 84 S.E.2d 445 (1954).

[405] For example, the rezoning of the land being sold might enhance the value of nearby land retained by the vendor. See LaGrave v. Jones, 336 So.2d 1330 (Ala. 1976), accepting a similar argument in principle but rejecting it on the facts for lack of convincing evidence.

[406] Hing Bo Gum v. Nakamura, 57 Hawaii 39, 549 P.2d 471 (1976).

§ 10.12 TITLE QUALITY

A real estate title is not a piece of paper. It is an abstract concept which represents the legal system's conclusions as to how the interests in a parcel of realty are arranged and who owns them. As we have already seen, interests in land can be divided along numerous dimensions, including both time and space,[407] and among numerous persons.[408] Nearly all of these interests are capable of being transferred individually, but in most real estate sales the buyer intends to get, at a minimum, a presently possessory fee simple absolute, subject only to encumbrances that the buyer is aware of and finds acceptable.

A lay person might suppose that whether this is the sort of title contracted for, and whether the vendor can in fact convey it in conformity to the contract, are rather simple questions; after all, the vendor either does or does not own the land. Unfortunately, the American system of proof of title does not lend itself well to such straightforward thinking. There is generally no mechanism for discovering with absolute certitude the state of the title to land.[409] The recording system, contrary to popular conception, does not provide a title searcher with a statement as to who has the title; rather, it serves merely as a depository or library for copies of documents which have been recorded by parties to prior transactions affecting the land.[410] The searcher is invited to sift through these papers and decide the condition of the title by reconstructing its history. There is no guarantee that all relevant instruments are present, that those which are present are authentic and valid, or that the title is free of claims based on such doctrines as adverse possession that may give rise to no documentation at all.[411]

But even if one disregards these deficiencies of the recording system, one rarely finds perfect titles in the records. All too commonly prior conveyances, especially those from many decades ago, are marred by inconsistent and confusing legal descriptions, missing signatures, erratic spellings of names, absent notarial acknowledgements, and the like. One encounters unsatisfied mortgages made so long ago that they are probably (but not certainly) barred by the statute of limitations; grants of easements whose location on the land is given only in vague or general terms; and spouses who probably had marital rights that they did not relinquish when the property was sold. The list of possible defects is much longer than suggested here, but the point should be clear: without knowledge of extrinsic facts now lost and unrecoverable, a searcher can often make only an educated guess about the condition of title. Title is a matter of judgment, and a searcher's judgment is seldom incontrovertible.

For these reasons the concept of marketability of title has developed. In a way, marketability is defined circularly: a marketable title is one which a court will force upon an unwilling contract purchaser.[412] But more broadly, the concept reflects a compromise

---

[407] See Ch. 3 supra.

[408] See Ch. 5 supra.

[409] The exception is the "Torrens" or title registration system, available in eight states plus Guam and Puerto Rico, but little used in most of them. Even in this system there are serious inadequacies in the averment made to the public; see § 11.15 infra.

[410] The recording system is discussed in § 11.9–11.11 infra.

[411] These deficiencies of the recording system are discussed in § 11.9 infra.

[412] See, e.g., Lake Forest, Inc. v. Bon Marche Homes, Inc., 410 So.2d 362 (La. App. 1982). The statement in the text, while suggesting that equity will not order a purchaser to take an unmarketable title, should not

with the view that buyers want, and sellers should convey, perfect titles. Since perfect titles are rare and hard to identify, the law instead holds the vendor to a lesser standard. It infers in every realty sale contract, unless a contrary intent appears, a covenant that the title transferred will be free of all reasonable risk of attack—in other words, that it will be marketable.[413] The key is reasonableness. The title need not be perfect, but if it is sufficiently doubtful or risky that a reasonable buyer (or a buyer's reasonable counsel) would object to it, the vendor has not fulfilled his or her contractual duty.[414] In a sense, it is the reasonable reaction of the marketplace for land that decides the question.[415]

Both a covenant and a condition are involved here. The law reads into the contract a promise by the vendor to convey marketable title. The concept of marketable title is similar to that of substantial performance,[416] and a failure to tender marketable title is thus deemed a material breach; this breach, in turn, constitutes the nonoccurrence of a constructive condition.[417] Hence, the buyer is both discharged from further performance and given remedies for breach, including specific performance with abatement,[418]

---

be taken to imply that a different standard applies at law; in fact, the standards at law and in equity are identical.

The marketable title concept may even have criminal law consequences. See Fraidin v. State, 85 Md.App. 231, 583 A.2d 1065 (1991), cert. denied 322 Md. 614, 589 A.2d 57 (1991), in which a foreclosure trustee was convicted of theft by deception. He had conducted a sale at which he stated the land's title was clear, when he knew that it was encumbered by a mortgage, and subsequently attempted to conceal the mortgage for three months thereafter.

[413] See generally 3 Am.L.Prop. § 11.47 (1952); 17 Williston on Contracts § 50:1 (4th ed. 2018 update); Annot., Marketable Title, 57 A.L.R. 1253 (1928). The concept originated in England in Marlow v. Smith, 2 P.Will. 198 (1723). Prior to that time, a purchaser could escape the contract only by proving that the title was in fact defective. This is clearly no longer the case; see, e.g., Stover v. Whiting, 157 Mich.App. 462, 403 N.W.2d 575 (1987) ("* * * it is not necessary that the title actually be bad in order to render it unmarketable"). See also Stapylton v. Scott, 16 Vesey 272 (Ch. 1809).

[414] Hundreds of cases state this test of reasonableness in similar terms. See, e.g., Regan v. Lanze, 40 N.Y.2d 475, 481–482, 387 N.Y.S.2d 79, 83, 354 N.E.2d 818, 822 (1976):

"A marketable title * * * is one which can be readily sold or mortgaged to a person of reasonable prudence, the test of the marketability of a title being whether there is an objection thereto such as would interfere with a sale or with the market value of the property. The law assures to a buyer a title free from reasonable doubt, but not from every doubt, and the mere possibility or suspicion of a defect, which according to ordinary experience has no probable basis, does not demonstrate an unmarketable title. If 'the only defect in the title' is 'a very remote and improbable contingency,' a 'slender possibility only,' a conveyance will be decreed."

See also Sanders v. Coastal Capital Ventures, Inc., 296 S.C. 132, 370 S.E.2d 903 (1988), cert. denied 298 S.C. 204, 379 S.E.2d 133 (1989); Degueyter v. First Am. Title Co., 230 So. 3d 652 (La. Ct. App. 2017); Denton v. Browntown Valley Assoc., Inc., 294 Va. 76, 803 S.E.2d 490 (2017); Liberty Lake Sewer Dist. v. Liberty Lake Utilities Co., 37 Wn. App. 809, 683 P.2d 1117 (1984); Ehlers, What Constitutes Marketable Title in Oregon, 33 Ore.L.Rev. 77 (1953). Local custom plays a role; see Coe v. Hays, 105 Md.App. 778, 661 A.2d 220 (Md.App. 1995) (missing conveyance 90 years earlier did not render title unmarketable, where customary title search was only 60 years in length).

[415] But note well that marketability of title is not directly related to value; land with marketable title may be essentially worthless, while land with unmarketable title may still be highly valuable. See Mortg. Assocs., Inc. v. Fid. & Deposit Co. of Maryland, 105 Cal. App. 4th 28, 129 Cal. Rptr. 2d 365 (2002).

[416] See ULTA § 2–301 Comment 3.

[417] See § 10.10 supra at notes 340–341. The contract may, however, excuse performance by both parties without further liability if the vendor is unable to perfect title. See, e.g., CHG International, Inc. v. Robin Lee, Inc., 35 Wn.App. 512, 667 P.2d 1127 (1983). Of course, the purchaser may waive fulfillment of the condition and go forward with the purchase notwithstanding unmarketability of title; see In re Will of Wilcher, 994 So. 2d 170 (Miss. 2008); Beagle Developers, LLC v. Long Island Beagle Club # II, Inc., 63 A.D.3d 607, 882 N.Y.S.2d 79 (2009).

[418] See, e.g., Satterly v. Plaisted, 52 A.D.2d 1074, 384 N.Y.S.2d 334 (1976), affirmed 42 N.Y.2d 933, 397 N.Y.S.2d 1008, 366 N.E.2d 1362 (1977); Lawton v. Byck, 217 Ga. 676, 124 S.E.2d 369 (1962). Cf. Barnes v. Sind, 341 F.2d 676 (4th Cir.1965), rehearing denied 347 F.2d 324 (1965), certiorari denied 382 U.S. 891, 86

rescission and restitution,[419] reimbursement for out-of-pocket expenses, and possibly loss-of-bargain damages. This last remedy is subject to the limitation of Flureau v. Thornhill, discussed earlier.[420]

All of this assumes that the contract itself either makes no mention of the quality of title or merely repeats the general legal mandate that the title must be marketable. In their agreement the parties are free to vary this standard by express language, and may make it either more or less rigorous.[421] They might, for example, provide that the vendor will convey "whatever title I have, but with no promise that I have any;" or on the other hand, "I promise to convey a perfect title, subject to no risks or defects whatever." This sort of phraseology is not very common, but would probably be construed at face value by the courts. Less forceful statements, however, are often construed as not departing from marketability at all.[422] The marketability standard is a magnet, drawing the courts toward it unless the parties make their contrary wishes exceptionally clear.

In modern cases the most frequent contractual variant of marketable title is "insurable title": a title which a "reputable title company would approve and insure," or the like.[423] Such language usually imposes a more lenient standard than marketable title, since title insurers are often willing to disregard minor or remote defects which

---

S.Ct. 183, 15 L.Ed.2d 149 (1965) (no abatement allowed under Maryland law.) See generally Note, 24 Okla.L.Rev. 495 (1971).

[419] This is doubtless the most common remedy sought. See, e.g., In re Cantin, 114 B.R. 339 (Bkrtcy.D.Mass. 1990); Regency Highland Associates v. Sherwood, 388 So.2d 271 (Fla.App. 1980); Harrodsburg Indus. Warehousing, Inc. v. MIGS, LLC, 182 S.W.3d 529 (Ky. Ct. App. 2005) (rescission was sole remedy under parties' agreement); Holoubek v. Romshek, 16 Neb. App. 677, 749 N.W.2d 901 (2008); § 10.7, supra. But see Man Ngok Tam v. Hoi Hong K. Luk, 154 Wis.2d 282, 453 N.W.2d 158 (App.1990), refusing to grant rescission where the vendor breached the covenant of marketable title by conveying subject to a mortgage, but then discharged the mortgage before the purchaser was harmed by it.

[420] See § 10.3 supra at note 129. In general, the condition that title must be marketable is viewed as protecting only the purchaser, and the vendor cannot use his or her lack of title to discharge his own duties; see Edisto Island Historical Soc'y, Inc. v. Gregory, 354 S.C. 198, 580 S.E.2d 141 (2003). But if the contract provides that it shall become "null and void" or "terminate" if title is unmarketable, the vendor may well assert the clause to avoid liability in a purchaser's action for damages or specific performance with abatement. To do so, however, the vendor will probably be required to show good faith. See Wolofsky v. Waldron, 526 So.2d 945 (Fla.App. 1988); Trabucco v. Nelson, 8 Mass.App.Ct. 641, 396 N.E.2d 466 (1979) (vendor in good faith; specific performance denied); Karl v. Kessler, 47 A.D.3d 681, 850 N.Y.S.2d 164 (2008). Cf. Space Center, Inc. v. 451 Corp., 298 N.W.2d 443 (Minn. 1980) (failure to cure title defect was vendor's fault, so vendor could not rely on "null and void" language); Hastings v. Gay, 55 Mass. App. Ct. 157, 161, 770 N.E.2d 11, 15 (2002) (vendor could not rely on escape clause where inability to convey good title was the result of his own fault or collusion). See generally Annot., 13 A.L.R.4th 927 (1982).

[421] Alcan Aluminum Corp. v. Carlsberg Financial Corp., 689 F.2d 815 (9th Cir. 1982); Ayers v. Hodges, 517 S.W.2d 589 (Tex.Civ.App. 1974).

[422] See, e.g., Shannon v. Mathers, 271 Or. 148, 531 P.2d 705 (1975) (contract made obligation to buy conditional upon purchasers' approval of title report; held, they could reject title only if it was unmarketable); Bull v. Weisbrod, 185 Iowa 318, 170 N.W. 536 (1919) (vendor agreed to sell all his right, title, and interest, but to convey by warranty deed; held, title must be marketable). An "as is" clause does not excuse the vendor's duty to convey marketable title; see 325 Schermerhorn, LLC v. Nevins Realty Corp., 76 A.D.3d 625, 906 N.Y.S.2d 339 (2010); Azat v. Farruggio, 162 Md. App. 539, 875 A.2d 778 (2005). On the other hand, such seemingly strong language as "good title" or even "indisputable title" is commonly held to require only a marketable title; see Holoubek v. Romshek, 16 Neb. App. 677, 749 N.W.2d 901 (2008), equating "good," "clear," "marketable," and "merchantable" title; Jones v. Hickson, 204 Miss. 373, 37 So. 2d 625 (1948), equating "good," "perfect," and "marketable" title; 3 Am. L.Prop. § 11.47 nn. 7–10 (1952). Contra, see Mid-State Homes v. Moore, 515 So.2d 716 (Ala.Civ.App. 1987). Title subject to a "cloud" is not marketable; see Stump v. Cheek, 2007 Okl. 97, 179 P.3d 606 (2007).

[423] The language is taken from Laba v. Carey, 29 N.Y.2d 302, 327 N.Y.S.2d 613, 277 N.E.2d 641 (1971). Note that the title policy itself may or may not insure that the title is marketable; see Annot., Defects Affecting Marketability of Title Within Meaning of Title Insurance Policy, 18 A.L.R.4th 1311 (1982).

might nonetheless make a title technically unmarketable.[424] As a consequence of careless drafting, it is often debatable whether the parties intended to substitute insurability for marketability as a standard, or whether they intended to require the vendor to meet both standards; the latter is the preferred construction unless the language plainly adopts insurability as the sole test.[425] Another problem with the insurability standard arises because of the fact that title insurance policies always contain printed lists of "general exceptions"—matters which the company does not insure against, and for which it may not even search. Policies and companies vary, and some employ much broader lists of general exceptions or exclusions than others.[426] Suppose a particular title defect is within the standard exceptions used by some but not all local title companies in some but not all types of policies; does the title comply with the contract or not?[427] Careful drafting is essential to avoid this sort of dispute.

A purchaser cannot object to the taking of a title which is subject only to defects mentioned and agreed to in the contract itself.[428] Hence, if the parties are familiar with the title, or if a current title report or abstract is at hand, they can list the specific encumbrances which are acceptable to the buyer; this is an excellent practice. However, printed form contracts often contain broad clauses, such as "title will be subject to easements and restrictions of record." The buyer may have no idea at the time the contract is signed what easements or restrictions exist, and may be surprised and disappointed when a subsequent search discloses very burdensome or inconvenient matters, but the clause will probably be upheld.[429] Obviously purchasers should avoid general contract clauses of this kind. They are, fortunately, typically construed quite narrowly against the vendor; for example, "subject to restrictions" generally does not

---

[424] See, e.g., Kipahulu Investment Co. v. Seltzer Partnership, 4 Hawaii App. 625, 675 P.2d 778 (1983), cert. denied 67 Hawaii 685, 744 P.2d 781 (1984) (contract called for both marketable and insurable title; actual title satisfied the title insurer, but was still unmarketable); Holmby, Inc. v. Dino, 98 Nev. 358, 647 P.2d 392 (1982). But see Aronoff v. Lenkin Co., 618 A.2d 669 (D.C.App. 1992) (title may have been marketable but did not satisfy insurer). On the operations of title insurers generally, see § 11.14, infra.

[425] Hudson-Port Ewen Associates, L.P. v. Kuo, 165 A.D.2d 301, 566 N.Y.S.2d 774 (1991), affirmed 78 N.Y.2d 944, 573 N.Y.S.2d 637, 578 N.E.2d 435 (1991) (where contract provided title would be insurable and also in fee simple free of encumbrances, purchaser was entitled to insist that both standards be satisfied); Brown v. Yacht Club of Coeur d'Alene, Ltd., 111 Idaho 195, 722 P.2d 1062 (App. 1986) (contract required title to be both marketable and insurable; these standards are distinct and both must be met); Regency Highland Associates v. Sherwood, 388 So.2d 271 (Fla.App. 1980), review denied 397 So.2d 778 (Fla. 1981). See Goldberg, Sales of Real Property 420 (1971); Comment, Title Insurance and Marketable Title, 31 Ford.L.Rev. 559 (1963).

[426] See § 11.14 infra at notes 766–770. Among the common exclusions are claims in eminent domain and matters of governmental regulation. Some policies have much longer lists, including rights of parties in possession, encroachments, unrecorded easements and liens, and reserved rights under federal or state patents. See Nelson, Whitman, Burkhart & Freyermuth, Real Estate Transfer, Finance, and Development (6th ed. 2014) at ch. 2, for reproductions of illustrative policies.

[427] See Laba v. Carey, 29 N.Y.2d 302, 327 N.Y.S.2d 613, 277 N.E.2d 641 (1971): "* * * the title company's approval must be unequivocal unless the exceptions are those contemplated by the contract." See also Eurovision 426 Dev., LLC v. 26–01 Astoria Dev., LLC, 80 A.D.3d 656, 915 N.Y.S.2d 288 (2011) (title company must insure title "unconditionally and without exception" unless parties have agreed otherwise). One court observed that virtually any title could be considered insurable if the company added enough exceptions or the insured were willing to pay a high enough premium; see Hebb v. Severson, 32 Wn.2d 159, 201 P.2d 156 (Wash. 1948).

[428] See, e.g., Stauffer v. Benson, 288 Neb. 683, 850 N.W.2d 759 (2014).

[429] See McCain v. Cox, 531 F.Supp. 771 (N.D.Miss. 1982), affirmed 692 F.2d 755 (5th Cir. 1982); Kirkwall Corp. v. Sessa, 48 N.Y.2d 709, 422 N.Y.S.2d 368, 397 N.E.2d 1172 (1979).

require the buyer to take the property if there are existing *violations* of restrictive covenants.[430]

Another factor which might be thought to vary the standard of title quality is the type of deed to be used for conveyance, a matter usually dealt with in the contract itself. Deeds generally may contain extensive covenants of title (a "full warranty" deed), more limited covenants (a "special warranty" deed), or no covenants at all (a "quitclaim deed"). There is no intrinsic link between the deed and the quality of the title it passes; a quitclaim deed can convey a perfect title, while a warranty deed may transmit a title which is severely defective. The distinction lies only in the nature of the seller's liability under the deed if defects exist.[431] Yet because quitclaim deeds are commonly used where the seller's title is doubtful, one might argue that a contract calling for a quitclaim deed should not be construed to promise marketable title. The New York Court of Appeals, however, reached a contrary result in Wallach v. Riverside Bank,[432] holding that the type of deed called for was irrelevant so long as the contract contemplated sale of the land itself rather than merely some limited interest in it. This is the view of the Uniform Land Transactions Act[433] and would probably be followed by most courts today.[434]

A marketable title is one that is held as an indefeasible fee simple.[435] But what sorts of defects can make a title unmarketable? The list is lengthy, with manifold variations. It can conveniently be divided into three types of imperfections: (1) those attributable to some flaw in the vendor's chain of ownership, so that vendor might never have had fee title at all; (2) those resulting from encumbrances—rights of others in the land, even though they do not negate the vendor's fee title; and (3) events which have deprived the vendor of title, such as the adverse possession of another or governmental action in eminent domain.[436] We will not attempt here to list and provide authority for every possible kind of defect which renders title unmarketable; the cases tend to turn on factual variations that raise few questions of theoretical importance, and rather complete lists are found in other works.[437] But the next few paragraphs will illustrate some of the more controversial issues of marketable title.

---

[430] See Lohmeyer v. Bower, 170 Kan. 442, 227 P.2d 102 (1951); Hebb v. Severson, supra note 427. But see Camp v. Commonwealth Land Title Ins. Co., 787 F.2d 1258 (8th Cir. 1986) (breach of existing restrictive covenant is not a title defect; title is marketable).

[431] See § 11.13 infra for a discussion of deed warranties.

[432] 206 N.Y. 434, 100 N.E. 50 (1912). See also Hirlinger v. Hirlinger, 267 S.W.2d 46 (Mo.App. 1954) (contract called for executor's deed with no warranties, but title must still be marketable.) Similarly, a contract clause calling for marketable title does not require the vendor to convey by warranty deed; see Department of Public Works and Buildings v. Halls, 35 Ill.2d 283, 220 N.E.2d 167 (1966); Tymon v. Linoki, 16 N.Y.2d 293, 266 N.Y.S.2d 357, 213 N.E.2d 661 (1965); Boekelheide v. Snyder, 71 S.D. 470, 26 N.W.2d 74 (1947).

[433] ULTA § 2–304(d). However, if the contract provides for a quitclaim deed, the buyer is limited to a restitutionary remedy in the event title is unmarketable, and may not recover loss-of-bargain damages or (presumably) specific performance with abatement.

[434] Contra, see Industrial Partners Ltd. v. CSX Transportation, Inc., 974 F.2d 153 (11th Cir. 1992) (Alabama law).

[435] Mills v. Parker, 253 Ga. App. 620, 560 S.E.2d 42 (2002); Real Estate Bar Ass'n for Massachusetts, Inc. v. Nat'l Real Estate Info. Servs., 459 Mass. 512, 534, 946 N.E.2d 665, 685 (2011).

[436] A similar taxonomy was followed by R.G. Patton in 3 Am.L.Prop. § 11.49 (1952).

[437] Lengthy citations can be found in 3 Am.L.Prop. § 11.49 (1952); Friedman & Smith, Contracts and Conveyances of Real Property ch.14 (8th ed. 2017).

Chain of title problems which can affect marketability include the vendor's never having held title to part or all of the land,[438] conveyances in the chain that are simply missing,[439] or were forged, undelivered, procured by fraud or duress, or executed by a minor.[440] A title traced through a judicial or other legal proceeding may be unmarketable if it was conducted without jurisdiction or without compliance with statute. A fiduciary's deed will not convey a marketable title if he or she acted beyond authority or in violation of duty.[441] Perhaps the most interesting chain of title issue is raised by the vendor who claims title by adverse possession. If the contract requires a title "of record," adverse possession alone obviously fails to qualify,[442] but if it does not the courts have had difficulty deciding whether the title is marketable. Such a title may be perfectly good, of course, but its validity depends on the existence of extrinsic facts: Was the possession open and notorious, continuous, hostile, and so on?[443] Unless the vendor or a predecessor in title has already established these issues in litigation with the record owner, they might be raised in a later action brought against the purchaser. Such a risk of litigation might well be thought unreasonably burdensome, and hence deemed to make the vendor's title unmarketable. The question is likely to turn on the court's assessment of the practical probability that an attack will be made or will succeed, and unless that risk is very low,[444] the title is likely to be held unmarketable until the vendor establishes the necessary facts in a forum that will bind the record owner.[445]

---

[438] Chicago Title Ins. Co. v. Arkansas Riverview Dev., LLC, 573 F.Supp.2d 1152 (E.D. Ark. 2008) (vendor did not own air rights occupied by existing building); Bermont Lakes, LLC v. Rooney, 980 So. 2d 580 (Fla. Dist. Ct. App. 2008) (vendor did not own 40 acres of 160-acre parcel described in contract of sale); Holoubek v. Romshek, 16 Neb. App. 677, 749 N.W.2d 901 (2008) (vendor did not own 27-foot-wide portion of land described in contract of sale); Scalise Dev., Inc. v. Tidelands Investments, LLC, 392 S.C. 27, 707 S.E.2d 440 (Ct. App. 2011) (vendor did not own portion of the land below mean high water mark).

[439] Davis v. St. Romain, 222 So. 3d 793 (La. Ct. App. 2017); Quarter Dev., LLC v. Hollowell, 96 So. 3d 49 (Miss. Ct. App. 2012); Scalise Dev., Inc. v. Tidelands Investments, LLC, 392 S.C. 27, 707 S.E.2d 440 (Ct. App. 2011).

[440] See also Mattson Ridge, LLC v. Clear Rock Title, LLP, 824 N.W.2d 622 (Minn. 2012) (ambiguous land description in deed in chain of title rendered title unmarketable).

[441] Slomkowski v. Levitas, 109 N.J.L. 545, 162 A. 530 (1932).

[442] Babo v. Bookbinder Financial Corp., 27 Ariz.App. 73, 551 P.2d 63 (1976) (dictum). The reason is that the adverse possessor has no document to record. An exception exists in a few states which by statute permit one who has acquired title by adverse possession, and has then relinquished possession, to file for record a sworn statement of the claim. See, e.g., 68 Penn.Stat. §§ 81–88. A similar result follows where the contract requires the vendor to show marketable title by an abstract, since there will usually be no document in the abstract reflecting the adverse possession. See TriState Hotel Co. v. Sphinx Investment Co., Inc., 212 Kan. 234, 510 P.2d 1223 (1973); Hillebrenner v. Odom, 237 Ark. 720, 375 S.W.2d 664 (1964). See Annot., 46 A.L.R.2d 544 (1956).

[443] The elements of adverse possession are discussed at § 11.7, infra.

[444] One formulation states that an adverse possession title will be marketable if the court finds "(1) that the outstanding claimants could not succeed were they in fact to assert a claim, and (2) that there is no real likelihood that any claim will ever be asserted"; Conklin v. Davi, 76 N.J. 468, 388 A.2d 598 (1978). Compare Simis v. McElroy, 160 N.Y. 156, 54 N.E. 674, 73 Am.St.Rep. 673 (1899) ("the proof must * * * exclude to a moral certainty any right or claim * * *" by the record owner), with Rehoboth Heights Development Co. v. Marshall, 15 Del.Ch. 314, 137 A. 83 (1927) (doubt of the validity of vendor's title "* * * appears to rest on mere speculation, conjecture, and imagination.") See also Barter v. Palmerton Area School Dist., 399 Pa.Super. 16, 581 A.2d 652 (1990) (lengthy adverse possession may give rise to a marketable title); Kipahulu Investment Co. v. Seltzer Partnership, 4 Hawaii App. 625, 675 P.2d 778 (1983), cert. denied 67 Hawaii 685, 744 P.2d 781 (1984) (title based on adverse possession was unmarketable, where there was no proof that adverse possessor had given its cotenants notice as required to begin running of statutory period).

[445] The court in which the vendor and purchaser litigate the marketability of the title cannot bind the record owner or cut off his or her rights unless the latter is a party to the action, not a common situation. Hence, the vendor must ordinarily pursue a separate action against the record owner if the court determines that the vendor's adverse possession title is too risky to force upon the purchaser. Cf. Bartos v. Czerwinski,

A broader question is whether the title must be fully deducible from the public records to be marketable, assuming that the contract itself is silent on the point.[446] The cases are fairly evenly divided, but perhaps the majority of courts have not required that every link in the chain be of record; missing transfers can, for example, be explained by affidavits or other evidence, provided that the result is not to impose unreasonable risks on the purchaser.[447]

Even if a vendor's chain of title to land is complete and unobjectionable, the title itself may still be unmarketable as a result of encumbrances in favor of other parties.[448] A wide variety of encumbrances may be found, including leases, covenants,[449] mineral reservations, mortgages, easements,[450] party wall agreements, marital rights, contracts, options, and various types of liens.[451] Any such encumbrances will make title unmarketable unless the buyer contracted to accept them or they are so minor or so unlikely to be asserted as to be *de minimis*.[452] A question often arises as to whether the

---

323 Mich. 87, 34 N.W.2d 566 (1948); Lynbrook Gardens v. Ullmann, 291 N.Y. 472, 53 N.E.2d 353 (1943), certiorari denied 322 U.S. 742, 64 S.Ct. 1144, 88 L.Ed. 1575 (1944). If the action brought by the vendor is a general one to quiet the title, and service is only by publication, it may be subject to collateral attack, but most courts would probably hold that it nonetheless makes the vendor's title marketable. See Note, Enhancing the Marketability of Land: The Suit to Quiet Title, 68 Yale L.J. 1245 (1959).

[446] The contract, of course, can provide for a "marketable record title," and can thereby foreclose the issue. See, e.g., Lucas v. Independent School District No. 284, 433 N.W.2d 94 (Minn. 1988); Gaines v. Dillard, 545 S.W.2d 845 (Tex.Civ.App. 1976) (title by accretion does not meet contract's requirement of title shown by abstract); Hurley v. Werly, 203 So.2d 530 (Fla. App. 1967).

[447] See Annot., 57 A.L.R. 1253, 1324 (1928); 3 Am.L.Prop. § 11.48 nn. 16–23 (1952); Brown v. Kelly & Picerne, Inc., 518 F.Supp. 730 (D.Mass. 1981), affirmed 676 F.2d 682 (1st Cir. 1982) (a merchantable title must be of record); Chavez v. Gomez, 77 N.M. 341, 423 P.2d 31 (1967) (same); Douglass v. Ransom, 205 Wis. 439, 237 N.W. 260 (1931). But see In re Governor's Island, 45 B.R. 247 (Bkrtcy.E.D.N.C. 1984) (a 60-year chain of recorded conveyances is not necessary for a title to be marketable); Meeks v. Romen Petroleum, Inc., 452 So.2d 1191 (La.App. 1984) (title need not be entirely of record to be marketable).

[448] Occasionally a court will apply some doctrine other than marketable title to permit a buyer to rescind a purchase contract for a defective title. See, e.g., Ger v. Kammann, 504 F.Supp. 446 (D.Del. 1980) (neither party knew of sewer easement running under house; purchaser could rescind for mutual mistake); Dover Pool & Racquet Club, Inc. v. Brooking, 366 Mass. 629, 322 N.E.2d 168 (1975) (zoning ordinance prohibited purchaser's intended use; held, mutual mistake.)

[449] Little v. Stogner, 162 N.C. App. 25, 592 S.E.2d 5 (2004); Bankers Tr. Co. of California v. Bregant, 261 Wis. 2d 855, 661 N.W.2d 498 (2003).

[450] Haisfield v. Lape, 264 Va. 632, 570 S.E.2d 794 (2002); Turner v. Taylor, 268 Wis. 2d 628, 673 N.W.2d 716 (2003).

[451] KJB Vill. Prop., LLC v. Craig M. Dorne, P.A., 77 So. 3d 727 (Fla. Dist. Ct. App. 2011); Humphries v. Ables, 789 N.E.2d 1025 (Ind. Ct. App. 2003); West v. Club at Spanish Peaks, L.L.C., 343 Mont. 434, 186 P.3d 1228 (2014) (recording of notice of lis pendens impairs marketability of title); Ward v. Yokley, 338 S.W.3d 912 (Tenn. Ct. App. 2010); Town & Country Bank v. Stevens, 2014 Utah App. 172, 332 P.3d 387 (2014); Wharton v. Tri-State Drilling & Boring, 175 Vt. 494, 824 A.2d 531 (2003) (mechanics' lien). Cf. Carr v. Acacia Country Club Co., 2012 Ohio 1940, 970 N.E.2d 1075 (2012) (pending shareholder's derivative suit against vendor did not make vendor's title unmarketable); Ensberg v. Nelson, 178 Wash. App. 879, 320 P.3d 97 (2013) (possible future assessment by HOA against dwelling unit was not an encumbrance making title unmarketable).

[452] See, e.g., G/GM Real Estate Corp. v. Susse Chalet Motor Lodge, Inc., 61 Ohio St.3d 375, 575 N.E.2d 141 (1991) (lapsed memorandum of lease in public records was trivial defect; title was marketable); Caselli v. Messina, 193 A.D.2d 775, 598 N.Y.S.2d 265 (1993) (buyer must accept title despite existence of an unviolated restrictive covenant, where contract stated buyers would take subject to covenants that did not render title unmarketable; a dubious result); Lovell v. Jimal Holding Corp., 127 A.D.2d 747, 512 N.Y.S.2d 138 (1987) (prior mortgage, barred by the statute of limitations, did not impair marketability); Camp v. Commonwealth Land Title Ins. Co., 787 F.2d 1258 (8th Cir. 1986) (breach in existing restrictive covenant was not a title defect; title was marketable).

Numerous cases have considered and rejected the argument that the presence of hazardous waste on land, in violation of state or federal environmental statutes, constitutes a failure of marketable title. See, e.g., In re Country World Casinos, Inc., 181 F.3d 1146 (10th Cir.1999); HM Holdings, Inc. v. Rankin, 70 F.3d 933 (7th Cir. 1995); Vandervort v. Higginbotham, 222 A.D.2d 831, 634 N.Y.S.2d 800 (N.Y. 1995); Donahey v. Bogle,

purchaser must accept a title subject to an encumbrance that was readily visible when the contract was signed, was in fact known to the purchaser,[453] or is beneficial to the land. On each of these points the courts are divided, and cases can be found favoring the vendor because of the presence of one, two, or all three of the factors mentioned.[454] The theoretical justification for compelling the buyer to take the land is that he or she must have recognized and planned for the encumbrance. Hence, the purchaser is treated as if it had been specifically agreed to in the contract. This result is nearly always followed where the encumbrance is an easement for a visible public road or street along one edge of the property.[455]

There are several situations in which the courts find title to be unmarketable even though the alleged "encumbrance" does not literally affect title at all. For example, land which has no public access, or to which access is severely limited, may be treated as having unmarketable title until the vendor provides a suitable easement or a public way is created.[456] Encroachments of significant dimensions are regarded as making title unmarketable, whether they involve an improvement on the subject property which encroaches on a neighboring parcel[457] or vice versa.[458] This result follows whether or not the statute of limitations or prescriptive period has run on the trespass. Unresolved boundary disputes likewise can make title unmarketable.[459]

---

987 F.2d 1250 (6th Cir. 1993); Lick Mill Creek Apartments v. Chicago Title Ins. Co., 231 Cal.App.3d 1654, 283 Cal.Rptr. 231 (1991). Contra, see Jones v. Melrose Park Nat'l Bank, 228 Ill.App.3d 249, 170 Ill.Dec. 126, 592 N.E.2d 562 (Ill. App. 1992) (vendor expressly warranted that no notice of health violations had been received, and in fact had been notified of cleanup liability by EPA). If a lien has actually been imposed on the property for payment of cleanup costs, title is obviously unmarketable unless the lien is removed.

[453] But see 325 Schermerhorn, LLC v. Nevins Realty Corp., 76 A.D.3d 625, 906 N.Y.S.2d 339 (2010) (purchaser's knowledge of encumbrance did not excuse vendor's duty to convey marketable title).

[454] Cases requiring the buyer to accept the encumbrance include In re Ilana Realty, 154 B.R. 21 (S.D.N.Y. 1993) (New York law); Egeter v. West & North Properties, 92 Or. App. 118, 758 P.2d 361 (1988); Alcan Aluminum Corp. v. Carlsberg Financial Corp., 689 F.2d 815 (9th Cir. 1982); Alumni Association of University of North Dakota v. Hart Agency, Inc., 283 N.W.2d 119 (N.D. 1979). Contrary cases include Patten of New York Corp. v. Geoffrion, 193 A.D.2d 1007, 598 N.Y.S.2d 355 (1993); Waters v. North Carolina Phosphate Corp., 310 N.C. 438, 312 S.E.2d 428 (1984); Gossels v. Belluschi, 4 Mass.App.Ct. 810, 348 N.E.2d 115 (1976). A similar line of reasoning may be adopted by courts with reference to other types of title "defects." See, e.g., Hall v. Fitzgerald, 671 P.2d 224 (Utah 1983) (where purchaser under installment contract knows that vendor is acquiring the land under a prior installment contract, the "equitable title" of the vendor is a sufficient form of marketable title).

[455] Tabet Lumber Co. v. Golightly, 80 N.M. 442, 457 P.2d 374 (1969) (public highway); Eaton v. Trautwein, 288 Ky. 97, 155 S.W.2d 474 (1941) (sidewalk); Annot., 64 A.L.R. 1477 (1929). See also Stone Inv. Co. v. Estate of Robinson, 82 So. 3d 631, 643 (Miss. Ct. App. 2011) (known public sewer easement did not make title unmarketable). But see Create 21 Chuo, Inc. v. Southwest Slopes, Inc., 81 Hawai'i 512, 918 P.2d 1168 (1996) (native trails and footpaths).

[456] Barasky v. Huttner, 210 A.D.2d 367, 620 N.Y.S.2d 121 (App.Div. 1994); Wilfong v. W.A. Schickedanz Agency, Inc., 85 Ill. App.3d 333, 406 N.E.2d 828 (1980). Contra, see Campbell v. Summit Plaza Assocs., 192 P.3d 465 (Colo. App. 2008) (title was marketable although parcel was landlocked); Sinks v. Karleskint, 130 Ill.App.3d 527, 474 N.E.2d 767 (1985) (title was marketable despite lack of legally assured access, where purchasers had notice of problem at the inception of the contract); Bob Daniels and Sons v. Weaver, 106 Idaho 535, 681 P.2d 1010 (App.1984) (similar).

[457] DeJong v. Mandelbaum, 122 A.D.2d 772, 505 N.Y.S.2d 659 (1986) (encroachment on adjacent land does not render title unmarketable if adjacent owner has given an easement legalizing the encroachment); Zatzkis v. Fuselier, 398 So.2d 1284 (La.App. 1981); Sydelman v. Marici, 56 A.D.2d 866, 392 N.Y.S.2d 333 (1977).

[458] Mid-State Homes, Inc. v. Brown, 47 Ala.App. 468, 256 So.2d 894 (1971); Mellinger v. Ticor Title Ins. Co. of California, 93 Cal. App. 4th 691, 113 Cal. Rptr. 2d 357 (2001). See generally Annot., 47 A.L.R.2d 331 (1956); 3 Am.L.Prop. § 11.49 nn. 93–97 (1952).

[459] Denton v. Browntown Valley Associates, Inc., 294 Va. 76, 803 S.E.2d 490 (2017); Latter & Blum, Inc. v. Ditta, 223 So. 3d 54 (La. Ct. App. 2017).

These latter situations illustrate an important point: to make title unmarketable, it is not essential that the defect in the title chain or the existence of the offending encumbrance be established with certainty. If the matter in question raises a substantial risk of litigation with a third party, title will be deemed unmarketable on the ground that no purchaser should be compelled to buy a lawsuit.[460]

Local government ordinances affecting land use present another interesting problem. Obviously title and use are distinct concepts, and it is very widely held that the presence, or even the violation, of subdivision, housing, or building codes does not constitute an encumbrance on title.[461] Zoning is treated differently, perhaps on the ground that it is easier for the vendor to become aware of violations of zoning ordinances, and thus that he or she should be responsible for them. The presence of a zoning ordinance itself is not deemed an encumbrance, but an existing violation is generally treated as making title unmarketable.[462] If the zoning will seriously frustrate the buyer's planned use of the property, even an unviolated ordinance will often justify avoidance of the contract, albeit on grounds other than unmarketability of title. Such grounds include

---

[460] Degueyter v. First Am. Title Co., 230 So. 3d 652 (La. Ct. App, 2017); Sonido, LLC v. Arcadia Enterprises, LLC, 3 So. 3d 1273 (Fla. Dist. Ct. App. 2009); Ferrara v. Walters, 919 So. 2d 876 (Miss. 2005) (risk of litigation because heirship of prior owner had never been adjudicated). But the risk of litigation must be substantial and not merely a bare assertion; see Saxon Mortg. Servs., Inc. v. Coakley, 145 A.D.3d 699, 43 N.Y.S.3d 97 (N.Y. App. Div. 2016). See also Princeton S. Inv'rs, LLC v. First Am. Title Ins. Co., 437 N.J. Super. 283, 97 A.3d 1190 (App. Div. 2014) (municipal tax appeal is not litigation that renders title unmarketable); Booth v. Attorneys' Title Guar. Fund, Inc., 2001 UT 13, 20 P.3d 319 (2001) (vendor's bankruptcy does not make title unmarketable if bankruptcy court has authorized sale of property).

[461] Haw River Land & Timber Co., Inc. v. Lawyers Title Ins. Corp. 152 F.3d 275 (4th Cir. 1998) (ordinance prohibiting cutting of timber); Hocking v. Title Insurance & Trust Co., 37 Cal.2d 644, 234 P.2d 625 (1951) (subdivision ordinance violation); Elysian Inv. Grp. v. Stewart Title Guar. Co., 105 Cal. App. 4th 315, 129 Cal. Rptr. 2d 372 (2002) (notice of building code violations); McCrae v. Giteles, 253 So.2d 260 (Fla.App. 1971) (housing code); Ellison Heights Homeowners Ass'n, Inc. v. Ellison Heights LLC, 112 A.D.3d 1302, 978 N.Y.S.2d 481 (2013) (density and open space restrictions); Seth v. Wilson, 62 Or.App. 814, 662 P.2d 745 (1983) (subdivision ordinance); Truck S., Inc. v. Patel, 339 S.C. 40, 528 S.E.2d 424 (2000) (wetlands designation). See Note, 1958 Wis.L.Rev. 128. Cf. Henley v. MacDonald, 971 So. 2d 998 (Fla. Dist. Ct. App. 2008) (unpaid fines for code violations subject purchaser to risk of future litigation and hence make title unmarketable); Brunke v. Pharo, 3 Wis.2d 628, 89 N.W.2d 221 (1958), noted 1958 Wis.L.Rev. 640 (housing code violations constitute breach of deed covenant against encumbrances if enforcement action is under way.) Contra, see Voorheesville Rod & Gun Club, Inc. v. E.W. Tompkins Co., 158 A.D.2d 789, 551 N.Y.S.2d 382 (1990), appeal dismissed 76 N.Y.2d 888, 561 N.Y.S.2d 550, 562 N.E.2d 875 (1990) (failure of vendor to subdivide land into legal lots rendered title unmarketable); Shinn v. Thrust IV, Inc., 56 Wn. App. 827, 786 P.2d 285 (1990), review denied 114 Wn.2d 1023, 792 P.2d 535 (1990) (replatting of subdivision by vendor caused potential violation of earlier restrictive covenants, and thus rendered title unmarketable). See generally Freyfogle, Real Estate Sales and the New Implied Warranty of Lawful Use, 71 Cornell L.Rev. 1 (1985), advocating adoption by the courts of an implied warranty protecting purchasers against both public and private restrictions that make use of the property illegal.

[462] Radovanov v. Land Title Co. of America, 189 Ill.App.3d 433, 136 Ill.Dec. 827, 545 N.E.2d 351 (1989); Venisek v. Draski, 35 Wis.2d 38, 150 N.W.2d 347 (1967); Lohmeyer v. Bower, 170 Kan. 442, 227 P.2d 102 (1951); Moyer v. De Vincentis Construction Co., 107 Pa.Super. 588, 164 A. 111 (1933). New York has consistently refused to follow this view; see Cone v. Stranahan, 44 A.D.3d 1145, 843 N.Y.S.2d 717 (2007); Voorheesville Rod and Gun Club, Inc. v. E.W. Tompkins Co., 82 N.Y.2d 564, 606 N.Y.S.2d 132, 626 N.E.2d 917 (1993). See Note, 1958 Wis. L.Rev. 128; Dunham, Effect on Title of Violation of Building Covenants and Zoning Ordinances, 27 Rocky Mt.L.Rev. 255 (1955); Annot., 39 A.L.R.3d 362, 370 (1971). The effect of zoning changes during the executory period of the contract is discussed in § 10.13 infra at note 524.

Likewise, a violation of an existing restrictive covenant will often be held to make title unmarketable, even if the existence of the covenant does not; see Nelson v. Anderson, 286 Ill. App. 3d 706, 676 N.E.2d 735 (1997).

misrepresentation, excessive hardship, breach of express warranty,[463] and mutual or unilateral mistake.[464]

At what point in time must the vendor's title be marketable or otherwise in compliance with the contract? The question sometimes arises when the land is subject to mortgages or liens which the vendor plans to discharge out of the proceeds of the sale. So long as the sale price is sufficient to accomplish this, and reasonable precautions have been taken to prevent release of the purchaser's funds until it is clear that good title will be transferred, the purchaser has no ground to object; the closing will make the title marketable.[465] A more serious timing question arises if the defect is not merely a lien which can be paid off, but some encumbrance which may be difficult to cure or even a complete absence of title. The traditional view is that the vendor need not have marketable title until the closing,[466] but some recent cases have given the purchaser a right of immediate rescission if it appears very unlikely that the vendor can cure the title problems.[467] The question is particularly acute in long term installment contracts which might place the buyer in the position of paying for many years with no assurance of ever getting a good title.[468]

The law imposes no duty to examine the title on either party, but as a practical matter the buyer is expected to do so,[469] since he or she will otherwise have no basis for rejecting it as unmarketable. Of course, the contract may obligate the seller to pay some of the buyer's search expenses, as by furnishing a preliminary title report from a title

---

[463] See Scharf v. Tiegerman, 166 A.D.2d 697, 561 N.Y.S.2d 271 (1990); Sachs v. Swartz, 233 Ga. 99, 209 S.E.2d 642 (1974).

[464] Schultz v. County of Contra Costa, 157 Cal.App.3d 242, 203 Cal.Rptr. 760 (1984); Dover Pool & Racquet Club, Inc. v. Brooking, 366 Mass. 629, 322 N.E.2d 168 (1975); Gardner Homes, Inc. v. Gaither, 31 N.C.App. 118, 228 S.E.2d 525 (1976), review denied 291 N.C. 323, 230 S.E.2d 675 (1976). See generally Annot., 39 A.L.R.3d 362 (1971). See also the discussion of zoning and equitable conversion, § 10.13 infra at note 524.

[465] See Bakken Residential, LLC v. Cahoon Enterprises, LLC, 154 F.Supp.3d 812 (D.N.D. 2015); In re Wolfe, 378 B.R. 96 (Bankr. W.D. Pa. 2007); George v. Nevett, 462 So.2d 728 (Ala. 1984); Open Permit Servs. of Florida, Inc. v. Curtiss, 15 So. 3d 822 (Fla. Dist. Ct. App. 2009); Auclair v. Thomas, 39 Mass. App.Ct. 344, 656 N.E.2d 321 (Mass.App. 1995). Cf. Rankin v. McFerrin, 626 P.2d 720 (Colo. App. 1980) (title not marketable if balance on outstanding liens exceeds sale price.) The buyer is entitled to reasonable assurances that the discharge of the encumbrances will occur; see Kaiser v. Wright, 629 P.2d 581 (Colo. 1981); First National Bank of Nevada v. Ron Rudin Realty Co., 97 Nev. 20, 623 P.2d 558 (1981). See In re Aman, 492 B.R. 550 (Bankr. M.D. Fla. 2010), where the vendor concealed a mortgage lien and it was not paid off at closing.

[466] Luette v. Bank of Italy, 42 F.2d 9 (9th Cir. 1930), certiorari denied 282 U.S. 884, 51 S.Ct. 87, 75 L.Ed. 779 (1930); In re Ricks, 433 B.R. 806 (Bankr. D. Idaho 2010); Ballew v. Charter Realty ERA, 603 So.2d 877 (Ala. 1992); Trinity Quadrille, LLC v. Opera Place, LLC, 42 So. 3d 884 (Fla. Dist. Ct. App. 2010); Warner v. Denis, 84 Hawai'i 338, 933 P.2d 1372 (Haw.App. 1997); Powell v. Bagley, 862 S.W.2d 412 (Mo.App. 1993); Parker v. Byrne, 996 A.2d 627 (R.I. 2010); Rusch v. Kauker, 479 N.W.2d 496 (S.D. 1991); 3 Am.L.Prop. § 11.15 (1952), Hence, there is nothing wrong with a vendor's entering into a contract to sell land she does not own, but hopes to acquire before the closing of the sale; Douglas v. Lyles, 841 A.2d 1 (D.C. 2004); Weeks v. Rowell, 289 Ga. App. 507, 657 S.E.2d 881 (2008).

[467] Risse v. Thompson, 471 N.W.2d 853 (Iowa 1991); Breuer-Harrison, Inc. v. Combe, 799 P.2d 716 (Utah App. 1990); MidState Homes, Inc. v. Moore, 460 So.2d 172 (Ala.Civ.App. 1984). The buyer who has legitimate doubts about the vendor's title is entitled to demand reasonable assurances that they will be resolved, and to treat the vendor as in breach if such assurances are not forthcoming; see Shaffer v. Earl Thacker Co., 3 Hawaii App. 81, 641 P.2d 983 (1982), appeal after remand 6 Haw.App. 188, 716 P.2d 163 (1986); Restatement (Second) of Contracts § 251, Illustrations 3, 5 (1981).

[468] See Yellowstone II Dev. Grp., Inc. v. First Am. Title Ins. Co., 304 Mont. 223, 20 P.3d 755 (2001), overruled on other grounds by Mary J. Baker Revocable Tr. v. Cenex Harvest States, Cooperatives, Inc., 338 Mont. 41, 164 P.3d 851 (2007).

[469] Bruzzese v. Chesapeake Expl., LLC, 998 F.Supp.2d 663 (S.D. Ohio 2014).

insurer or providing to the buyer a current abstract.[470] This is a common practice in the western and midwestern United States, but not on the East Coast.[471] The buyer who discovers defects that make the title objectionable must notify the seller of them with specificity and allow the seller a reasonable time to cure them; only if the vendor fails to do so may the buyer avoid the contract,[472] or if the contract permits it, sue for damages. The time to cure may well extend the agreed closing date, and this will probably follow even if time was made of the essence.[473]

If the purchaser accepts a deed, a doctrine known as merger[474] limits any claims based on title matters to those which can be brought under the deed's title covenants; the contract's covenants of title, whether express or implied, are said to be "merged into the deed" and can no longer be the basis of legal action.[475] This doctrine is not a popular one with modern courts,[476] since it can readily defeat meritorious claims. There was once

[470] In most jurisdictions the seller has no affirmative duty to disclose title defects to the purchaser. But Massachusetts so requires by statute, if the matter is an "encumbrance" and the seller has knowledge of it; see Mass.Gen.Laws Ann. c. 184, § 21; Security Title and Guaranty Co. v. Mid-Cape Realty, Inc., 723 F.2d 150 (1st Cir. 1983), holding this statute inapplicable where the title defect in question is not merely an encumbrance but a total failure of title.

[471] See generally Payne, Ancillary Costs in the Purchase of Homes, 35 Mo.L.Rev. 455 (1970); Annot., 52 A.L.R. 1460 (1928).

[472] Nielson v. Benton, 903 P.2d 1049 (Alaska 1995), appeal after remand 957 P.2d 971 (Alaska 1998); Schreck v. T & C Sanderson Farms, Inc., 37 P.3d 510 (Colo. App. 2001); Reid v. Landsberger, 123 Conn. App. 260, 1 A.3d 1149 (2010); Point S. Land Tr. v. Gutierrez, 997 So. 2d 967 (Miss. Ct. App. 2008) (defects cured); Gentile v. Kim, 101 A.D.2d 939, 475 N.Y.S.2d 631 (1984); Houston v. Whitworth, 444 So.2d 1095 (Fla.App. 1984). The notice must be specific and demand a cure of the defects; see Real Estate World, Inc. v. Southeastern Land Fund, Inc., 137 Ga.App. 771, 224 S.E.2d 747 (1976), affirmed in part, reversed in part 237 Ga. 227, 227 S.E.2d 340 (1976). But in the absence of a contract term so providing, the vendor has no affirmative duty to attempt to cure; see In re Air Nail Co., Inc., 329 B.R. 512 (Bankr. W.D. Pa. 2005), aff'd sub nom. Alameda Produce Mkt., Inc. v. Air Nail Co., 348 B.R. 39 (W.D. Pa. 2006). For a contract so providing, see Castigliano v. O'Connor, 911 So. 2d 145 (Fla. Dist. Ct. App. 2005). The buyer can place the seller in breach without such notification or time allowance where the defect is plainly incurable; see Bertrand v. Jones, 58 N.J.Super. 273, 156 A.2d 161 (1959), cert. denied 31 N.J. 553, 158 A.2d 452 (1960) (public sewer easement); Siegel v. Shaw, 337 Mass. 170, 148 N.E.2d 393 (1958) (public sewer easement); Oppenheimer v. Knepper Realty Co., 50 Misc. 186, 98 N.Y.S. 204 (1906) (party wall).

[473] See O'Hara Group Denver, Limited v. Marcor Housing Systems, Inc., 197 Colo. 530, 595 P.2d 679 (1979) (time probably of the essence); compare Sugden, Vendors 408 (1873 ed.). As a matter of policy, if the buyer waits until just prior to closing to notify the seller of the title defects, a reasonable extension of time ought to be available for cure even if this means postponing an essential closing date; see Martocci v. Schneider, 119 A.D.3d 746, 990 N.Y.S.2d 240 (2014); Klaiber, LLC v. Coon, 48 A.D.3d 856, 851 N.Y.S.2d 667 (2008) (vendor who took one year to clear title defects did not act within reasonable time). Compare the closely analogous situation of the buyer who enters into an oral modification making the vendor's performance easier, and who then disavows the modification on the eve of the closing, relying on the statute of frauds. The buyer cannot hold the seller in breach of the original contract without allowing an additional time for performance, even if time was of the essence. See Imperator Realty Co. v. Tull, 228 N.Y. 447, 127 N.E. 263 (1920), discussed in § 10.1 supra at note 72.

[474] Professor Corbin suggested that merger is a poor description of this process, which is in reality similar to an accord and satisfaction; 6 Corbin, Contracts § 1319 (1962), followed in Pryor v. Aviola, 301 A.2d 306 (Del.Super. 1973).

[475] See, e.g., Bennett v. Behring Corp., 466 F.Supp. 689, 701–702 (S.D.Fla. 1979); Knudson v. Weeks, 394 F.Supp. 963 (W.D.Okl. 1975); Russell v. Mullis, 479 So.2d 727 (Ala. 1985) (if the contractual provisions are incorporated into the deed, they survive to confer an independent cause of action); Colorado Land & Resources, Inc. v. Credithrift of America, Inc., 778 P.2d 320 (Colo.App. 1989); Gloucester Landing Assocs. Ltd. P'ship v. Gloucester Redevelopment Auth., 60 Mass. App. Ct. 403, 802 N.E.2d 1046 (2004). Contractual clauses dealing with the issue are discussed in Friedman & Smith, Contracts and Conveyances of Real Property § 7:11.2 (8th ed. 2017). On deed covenants, see generally § 11.13, infra.

[476] Krajcir v. Egidi, 305 Ill.App.3d 613, 712 N.E.2d 917 (1999). See also Czarobski v. Lata, 227 Ill. 2d 364, 882 N.E.2d 536 (2008) (merger does not bar claim based on mutual mistake regarding taxes owed on property).

considerable authority that it applied to all contractual covenants,[477] but it has been persistently narrowed and limited, mainly by holdings that it is inapplicable to matters which are "collateral" to or not ordinarily mentioned in the deed.[478] Hence, it is now largely limited to the title provisions of the contract.[479] Hence, covenants relating to the physical condition of the property, improvements to be built, and the like are not subject to merger.[480]

Merger is subject to judicial manipulation in several ways. It is said to be inapplicable to cases of fraud or mistake.[481] Thus, a buyer of the "Brooklyn Bridge" has a remedy on the contract even if only a quitclaim deed was delivered. Merger may also be rejected on a showing of the parties' contrary intent, which may be inferred from contract language or the parties' behavior and circumstances.[482]

Despite its weakening in recent years, merger is still an unruly horse. It is generally confined to title matters, but exactly what a court will deem related to title is hard to predict.[483] The Uniform Land Transactions Act rejects the merger doctrine entirely

[477] See 3 Am.L.Prop. § 11.65 (1952). Some courts continue to adhere to this broader construction of the doctrine; see AEP Indus., Inc. v. B.G. Properties, Inc., 533 S.W.3d 674 (Ky. 2017).

[478] Cases finding no merger include Lasher v. Paxton, 956 P.2d 647 (Colo.App. 1998) (attorneys' fee clause); Empire Mngmt & Devel. Co. v. Greenville Assoc., 255 Va. 49, 496 S.E.2d 440 (Va. 1998) (rent guaranty agreement); In re Tribby, 241 B.R. 380 (E.D. Va. 1999) (time clause); Hammerquist v. Warburton, 458 N.W.2d 773 (S.D. 1990) (covenant regarding use of land); Colorado Land & Resources, Inc. v. Credithrift of America, Inc., 778 P.2d 320 (Colo.App. 1989); Durden v. Century 21 Compass Points, Inc., 541 So.2d 1264 (Fla.App .1989) (warranties and indemnities of personal representative of vendor); G.G.A., Inc. v. Leventis, 773 P.2d 841 (Utah App. 1989) (purchaser's right of first refusal); Reeves v. McClain, 56 Wn. App. 301, 783 P.2d 606 (1989) (covenant to furnish title insurance); Sullivan v. Cheshire, 190 Ga.App. 763, 380 S.E.2d 294 (1989) (covenant regarding condition of ponds on the premises); American National Self Storage, Inc. v. Lopez-Aguiar, 521 So.2d 303 (Fla.App. 1988), review denied 528 So.2d 1182 (Fla.1988) (covenant to extend utilities to site).

[479] See James v. McCombs, 936 P.2d 520 (Alaska 1997); Beal v. Schewe, 291 Ill. App.3d 204, 225 Ill.Dec. 516, 683 N.E.2d 1019 (Ill.App. 1997); Rojas v. Paine, 101 A.D.3d 843, 956 N.Y.S.2d 81 (2012); Maynard v. Wharton, 912 P.2d 446 (Utah 1996); Annot., 38 A.L.R.2d 1310 (1954); Annot., 52 A.L.R.2d 647 (1957). Cf. Johnson Farms v. McEnroe, 568 N.W.2d 920 (N.D. 1997) (claim based on shortage of acreage not merged). Judge Seldin said it well in Burwell v. Jackson, 9 N.Y. 535 (1854), quoted in Wallach v. Riverside Bank, 206 N.Y. 434, 100 N.E. 50 (1912): "* * * there is an implied warranty on the part of the vendor that he has a good title which continues until merged in the deed of conveyance." It is doubtful than any more should ever have been made of the merger doctrine than this. See Secor v. Knight, 716 P.2d 790 (Utah 1986).

[480] Lanterman v. Edwards, 294 Ill. App.3d 351, 689 N.E.2d 1221 (Ill.App. 1998) (warranty of heating system); Davis v. Tazewell Place Assoc., 254 Va. 257, 492 S.E.2d 162 (Va. 1997) (warranty of quality of house); Greco v. Vollmer, 890 S.W.2d 307 (Mo.App. 1994) (septic system warranty); Clackamas County Service Dist. v. American Guaranty Life Ins. Co., 77 Or.App. 88, 711 P.2d 980 (1985) (contractual provisions dealing with provision of sewage treatment); Annot., 25 A.L.R.3d 383, 432 (1969) (warranties of quality not merged). But see Gordon v. Bartlett, 452 So.2d 1077 (Fla.App. 1984) (contractual provision for attorneys fees merged into deed).

[481] West v. Bowen, 127 Idaho 128, 898 P.2d 59 (Idaho 1995); Bryan v. Breyer. 665 A.2d 1020 (Me. 1995); Newton v. Brown, 222 Neb. 605, 386 N.W.2d 424 (1986); Schultz v. Contra Costa County, 157 Cal.App.3d 242, 203 Cal.Rptr. 760 (1984); Southpointe Development, Inc. v. Cruikshank, 484 So.2d 1361 (Fla.App.1986).

[482] Hanneman v. Downer, 110 Nev. 167, 871 P.2d 279 (Nev. 1994); Reed v. Hassell, 340 A.2d 157 (Del.Super. 1975); Webb v. Graham, 212 Kan. 364, 510 P.2d 1195 (1973); Vaughey v. Thompson, 95 Ariz. 139, 387 P.2d 1019 (1963). It is clear that a stipulation against merger in the contract will be sustained; see Gray v. Lynch Contractors, Inc., 156 Ga.App. 473, 274 S.E.2d 614 (1980); Randolph Hills, Inc. v. Shoreham Developers, Inc., 266 Md. 182, 292 A.2d 662 (1972). From the purchaser's viewpoint, such a clause is nearly always desirable. Of course, the parties may also provide expressly *for* merger, and their agreement will be given effect; see Jones v. Dearman, 508 So.2d 707 (Ala. 1987); Rivietz v. Wolohojian, 38 A.D.3d 301, 832 N.Y.S.2d 505 (2007).

[483] See, e.g., Opler v. Wynne, 402 So.2d 1309 (Fla.App. 1981) (contract clause guaranteeing access to land not merged into deed); Bakken v. Price, 613 P.2d 1222 (Wyo. 1980) (contract covenant to provide a title insurance policy held to be merged into deed; a vigorous dissent); Miles v. Mackle Brothers, 73 Wis.2d 84, 242 N.W.2d 247 (1976) (contract covenant that vendor would pay future taxes, held merged into deed which contained clause stating that title was subject to the lien of current taxes).

unless the parties agree in the contract that acceptance of a deed will terminate the purchaser's contractual claims.[484] A more moderate judicial approach would limit the application of merger to cases in which the proof affirmatively showed the intent of the parties to discard claims based on the contract and to rely exclusively on the deed.[485] Such cases are probably rare.

§ 10.13 THE EXECUTORY PERIOD AND EQUITABLE CONVERSION

Nearly all American jurisdictions agree that after a contract for the sale of real estate becomes enforceable, a shift occurs in the nature of the parties' interests.[486] The purchaser is now regarded in substance, for many purposes, as the owner of the property, even though she or he does not yet have legal title. At the same time, the vendor's interest is now considered to have two aspects. First, the vendor has "bare" legal title to the land, which will not be relinquished until the vendor delivers a deed to the purchaser. Second, the vendor holds a security interest in the land and the legal title, as we have discussed previously, in the form of a vendor's lien, analogous to a mortgage on the land.[487]

During the period between formation and performance of a land sale contract, a variety of events may occur which raise questions about the contract's significance. Some of them have their principal effect on only one of the parties: the death of a party, a judgment obtained against him or her, or the like. Such events may trigger the operation of legal rules, such as an intestate succession statute or a judgment lien act, which depend on *characterization* of the party's interest as real or personal property. In most American jurisdictions, this characterization is made on the basis of the theory of equitable conversion, which holds that once the parties have entered into a contract that equity would specifically enforce, the buyer's interest in the contract is converted into real estate and the seller's interest into personal property. This result is said to follow from the view that equity regards as having been done that which ought to be done, and which equity would order done—namely, the conveyance of the title to the buyer and payment of the price to the seller.[488]

---

[484] See ULTA § 1–309, abolishing merger; ULTA § 2–402, permitting the purchaser to revoke the contract in some circumstances even after accepting a deed. For a case in which the contract expressly called for merger, see Ballard v. Walsh, 353 Mass. 767, 233 N.E.2d 926 (1968).

[485] See the heavy emphasis on intent in Szabo v. Superior Court, 84 Cal.App.3d 839, 148 Cal.Rptr. 837 (1978).

[486] These concepts are well explained in In re Blanchard, 819 F.3d 981 (7th Cir. 2016), holding that a real estate mortgage can attach to the vendor's interest, even though it is for most purposes regarded as personal property. See also Rogers v. United States, 109 Fed. Cl. 280 (2013); United States v. Singer, 950 F.Supp.2d 930 (W.D. Mich. 2013); Southport Congregational Church—United Church of Christ v. Hadley, 320 Conn. 103, 128 A.3d 478 (2016); Batton-Jajuga v. Farm Bureau Gen. Ins. Co. of Michigan, 322 Mich. App. 422, 913 N.W.2d 351 (2017); Relling v. Khorenian, 261 Or. App. 1, 323 P.3d 293 (2014). The equitable conversion doctrine's application is not mandatory, and the parties are free to modify or eliminate it by agreement; see Noor v. Centreville Bank, 193 Md. App. 160, 996 A.2d 928 (2010). Wyoming has rejected the application of equitable conversion in numerous contexts, while applying it in others; see Bentley v. Dir. of Office of State Lands & Investments, 2007 Wyo. 94, 160 P.3d 1109, 1118 (Wyo. 2007). Massachusetts does not follow equitable conversion; In re Pina, 363 B.R. 314 (Bankr. D. Mass. 2007).

[487] See § 10.6; In re Coffelt, 395 B.R. 133, 139 (Bankr. D. Kan. 2008) (vendor's interest is an "equitable mortgage"); Bolen v. Bolen, 169 S.W.3d 59 (Ky. Ct. App. 2005) (vendor's lien must be foreclosed by judicial sale).

[488] The doctrine's modern form originated with Lord Eldon's opinion in Seaton v. Slade, 7 Ves.Jun. 265 (1802); see Davis, The Origin of the Doctrine of Equitable Conversion by Contract, 25 Ky.L.Rev. 58 (1936). See

Events during the executory period of the contract may bring the parties into conflict with one another, usually because they involve a loss in value of the property. Some such events cause physical damage: fire, windstorm, flood, frost damage to crops, and so on. Other risks flow from changes in the land's legal status: an amendment to a zoning ordinance, the imposition of new housing code requirements, or a taking by eminent domain, for example. Here the issue is *allocation of the risk* between vendor and purchaser. Typically the buyer surveys the loss and decides that he or she no longer wants the property, or is willing to take it only with an abatement of the purchase price. Can the vendor enforce the contract on its original terms, notwithstanding the loss? Again, most American courts turn to the doctrine of equitable conversion and conclude that because the realty is already owned by the purchaser "in equity", the purchaser also has the risk of loss and must pay the full purchase price.

In both its characterization and risk aspects, equitable conversion might strike the objective observer as a grand *non-sequitur*. To say that equity will specifically enforce the contract certainly does not compel one to disregard reality and view the contract as already performed. Yet enforceability of the contract in equity is commonly treated as a talisman, employed to decide cases for which it has no practical relevance at all. The decisions often seem adamant in their unwillingness to discuss the underlying policy issues; equitable conversion almost becomes a substitute for thinking about the real questions in the case.[489] As Professor Dobbs said, it is an example of a "moral principle * * * carried to the limit of its logic, rather than to the limit of its morality."[490]

Characterization of the parties' property interests. The most common characterization issue arises because of the death of a contracting party. Consider first the vendor's death. If equitable conversion has occurred, the vendor's interest is considered personal property. True, the "bare" legal title descends to the vendor's heirs or devisees,[491] but they hold it subject to an obligation (sometimes termed a "trust"[492]) to convey to the purchaser under the contract. The proceeds of the sale will go to the decedent's personal representative (the administrator or executor), and after the usual expenses, taxes, and debts are paid, will be distributed to the takers of the decedent's personal property, the legatees or next-of-kin. Thus, if the real property and personal

---

generally 3 Am.L.Prop. §§ 11.22–.35 (1952); Simpson, Legislative Changes in the Law of Equitable Conversion by Contract: I, 44 Yale L.J. 559 (1935); 17 Williston on Contracts § 50:47 (4th ed. 2018 update).

Equitable conversion is often employed by the courts as an adjunct to the resolution of ordinary priority and recording issues. See, e.g., In re Estate of Clark, 447 N.W.2d 549 (Iowa App. 1989) (under equitable conversion, purchasers' interest is not impaired by vendor's deed to a third party during contract's executory period); Lincoln Park Federal Sav. & Loan Ass'n v. DRG, Inc., 175 Ill.App.3d 176, 529 N.E.2d 771 (1988) (contract purchasers have an equitable title that is protected by recording act from a prior unrecorded mortgage); Cox v. RKA Corp., 164 N.J. 487, 753 A.2d 1112 (2000) (purchasers have an equitable title, enforceable by way of a vendee's lien). On vendee's liens, see § 10.8 supra.

[489] Consider Bleckley v. Langston, 112 Ga.App. 63, 143 S.E.2d 671 (1965), in which the court followed equitable conversion despite its own conclusion that a contrary rule would be "* * * more expedient, and more in accord with practical common sense and business practices."

[490] Dobbs, Remedies 40 (1973).

[491] A review of terminology may be helpful here. "Heirs" are the persons who take the decedent's real estate under the relevant succession statute if he or she dies intestate. If the decedent dies testate as to real estate, it passes to the "devisees" under the will. Personal property passes to "next-of-kin" if the decedent is intestate, or to "legatees" if disposed of by the will.

[492] Mackiewicz v. J.J & Assoc., 245 Neb. 568, 514 N.W.2d 613 (1994); Griggs Land Co. v. Smith, 46 Wash. 185, 89 P. 477 (1907).

property takers are different individuals, the heirs or devisees receive nothing in return for conveying legal title.[493]

In most states this set of rules is unimportant if the vendor dies intestate, since the heirs and the next-of-kin are typically the same persons taking the same shares in the property; whether it is viewed as realty or personalty is irrelevant unless the personal property must be used first to pay debts and taxes. But when the decedent dies testate, and the will identifies different persons as devisees of the land and legatees of personalty, equitable conversion assumes great importance. The principles outlined above are usually followed in cases in which the will was made before the contract. The courts tend to see the contract as the equivalent of an outright conveyance of title; if such a conveyance had occurred, it would have left the decedent's estate bereft of the land in question. The gift would be adeemed, the will clause would be ineffective, and the proceeds of the sale would be part of the residuary estate.[494] The devisees would be disappointed, but could hardly complain, since the result would presumably be consistent with the decedent's wishes. The same logic applies where the decedent has entered into an enforceable contract of sale, even if the will contains a specific devise of the same property.[495] This is the prevailing view in the absence of a contrary statute, at least if the contract was formed after the will was executed.[496]

However, if the will is made after the contract is formed, and yet it specifically identifies and devises the land, it is much harder to believe that the decedent did not wish to have the devisees receive the land's value. Some cases have awarded the purchase price to them, rejecting the logic of equitable conversion in favor of a construction which seems to follow the grantor's intent.[497] Even when the will predates the contract, it is by no means obvious that the decedent intended to disfavor the devisee and favor the residuary legatees when he or she contracted to sell the land, The Uniform Probate Code reverses the logic of equitable conversion; it gives the specific devisee not

---

[493] In re Estate of Line, 122 Ohio App.3d 387, 701 N.E.2d 1028 (1997); Estate of Everhart, 226 A.D.2d 892, 640 N.Y.S.2d 621 (App.Div.1996), Coe v. Hays, 328 Md. 350, 614 A.2d 576 (Md. 1992), appeal after remand 105 Md. App. 778, 661 A.2d 220 (1995); Matter of Hills' Estate, 222 Kan. 231, 564 P.2d 462 (1977). Cf. Estate of Atkinson, 19 Wis.2d 272, 120 N.W.2d 109 (1963), discussed in Church, Equitable Conversion in Wisconsin, 1970 Wis.L.Rev. 404, 410–14. See generally Hermann, The Doctrine of Equitable Conversion: I, Conversion by Contract, 12 DePaul L.Rev. 1, 27–35 (1962). If the conversion was in effect at the time of death, the fact that the contract was subsequently rescinded or terminated is irrelevant; the legatees get the land itself. See Clapp v. Tower, 11 N.D. 556, 93 N.W. 862 (1903).

[494] The loss to the heirs or devisees is similar to that resulting from ademption—the disposition by the decedent before death of property which the will purports to convey; see Stanford v. Paris, 209 N.C. App. 173, 703 S.E.2d 488 (2011); Righter v. First Reformed Church of Boonton, 17 N.J.Super. 407, 86 A.2d 305 (1952).

[495] Southport Congregational Church—United Church of Christ v. Hadley, 320 Conn. 103, 128 A.3d 478 (2016).

[496] See In re Sweet's Estate, 254 So. 2d 562 (Fla. Dist. Ct. App. 1971) (overruled by Fla. Stat. § 732.606); In re Estate of Pickett, 879 So. 2d 467 (Miss. Ct. App. 2004); Mattlage v. Mattlage, 243 S.W.3d 763 (Tex. App. 2007). See also Kelley v. Neilson, 433 Mass. 706, 745 N.E.2d 952 (2001), reaching the same result on the ground that it conformed with the testator's intent, without using the logic of equitable conversion.

[497] Father Flanagan's Boys' Home v. Graybill, 178 Neb. 79, 132 N.W.2d 304 (1964). The same conclusion may be reached even under a general devise of "all my lands" or the like, if the decedent in fact had no land other than that under contract of sale, so that equitable conversion would render the devise meaningless; see Covey v. Dinsmoor, 226 Ill. 438, 80 N.E. 998 (1907). Cf. In re McDonough's Estate, 113 Ill.App.2d 437, 251 N.E.2d 405 (1969), in which the decedent owned other land as well, so that the general devise still had some effect notwithstanding the operation of equitable conversion.

only the naked legal title but also the right to enforce the contract in equity and get the remaining purchase money.[498]

If it is the purchaser who dies, the result is a mirror image of the principles discussed above. The purchaser's interest descends as realty to the heirs or devisees, while the purchase price must be paid by the personal representative out of the personalty assets of the estate, and thus reduces the amount passing to the legatees or next-of-kin.[499] The land passes free and clear of the indebtedness. This result is an application of the doctrine of exoneration, which is more familiarly employed to require the personal representative to satisfy mortgages on the decedent's realty at no expense to the heirs or devisees.[500] Whether the decedent would have wanted this to occur is often doubtful, and England and many American states have eliminated or weakened the doctrine of exoneration.[501]

On the whole, following equitable conversion probably does little harm in the context of devolution upon the death of the vendor or purchaser. Certainly the decedent's intent is the most desirable guide to such cases,[502] but all too often that intent is opaque. So long as equitable conversion does not distract the courts from their primary task of assessing intent where possible, it is a reasonably satisfactory method of determining the property's course.

A second characterization issue which equitable conversion is often called upon to resolve is the amenability of the contracting parties' interests to the claims of judgment creditors.[503] In most states a judgment becomes, by statute, a lien on the defendant's real property in the county where it is docketed. If the judgment is against a vendor who has already contracted to sell certain land, the vendor may argue that under equitable conversion his or her interest is no longer real property, and hence that the lien does not attach. This view is supported by the argument that the vendor's position is similar to

---

[498] Uniform Probate Code § 2–606, which also gives the devisee any unpaid condemnation award, casualty insurance premiums, foreclosure proceeds, and any property acquired by the decedent in replacement of the specifically devised property. It also authorizes the courts to give the devisee the full value of the property sold if that result is determined to correspond to the testator's intent. See Rowe v. Newman, 290 Ala. 289, 276 So.2d 412 (1972), construing Ala. Code § 13, tit. 61; Melican v. Parker, 289 Ga. 420, 711 S.E.2d 628 (2011), construing Fla. Stat. § 732.606(2)(a); Douglas v. Newell, 719 P.2d 971 (Wyo. 1986), applying the UPC approach to a case arising before it was enacted. See also Funk v. Funk, 563 N.E.2d 127 (Ind.App.1990), in which the contract was entered into by the vendor's attorney in fact while the vendor was in a coma. The court concluded that there was insufficient evidence that the vendor intended to deprive his devisees under his previously-executed will of the benefit of the land, and refused to apply equitable conversion.

[499] This result follows with both general and specific devises; see Timberlake v. Heflin, 180 W.Va. 644, 379 S.E.2d 149 (1989); First Camden National Bank v. Broadbent, 66 N.J.Super. 199, 168 A.2d 677 (1961); In re Reid's Estate, 26 Cal.App.2d 362, 79 P.2d 451 (1938); Cutler v. Meeker, 71 Neb. 732, 99 N.W. 514 (1904); Palmer v. Morrison, 104 N.Y. 132, 10 N.E. 144 (1887).

[500] See generally Johnson, Executor or Heir: Who Pays the Mortgage?, 113 Trusts & Estates 244 (1974); McGovern, Kurtz & English, Wills, Trusts & Estates § 8.4 (2d ed. 2011); 3 Am.L.Prop. §§ 11.27, 14.25 (1952); Note, 40 Harv.L.Rev. 630 (1927).

[501] See, e.g., Vernon's Ann. Missouri Stat. § 474.450 (exoneration only when property encumbered after will executed, and even then only when no contrary intent appears); Goodfellow v. Newton, 320 Mass. 405, 69 N.E.2d 569 (1946); In re Estate of Riddle, 2018 WL 1465198 (Pa. Super. Ct. 2018). See 3 Am. L.Prop. § 11.27 (1952). Uniform Probate Code § 2–609 (1969 version) abolishes the doctrine of exoneration. The English abrogation of the doctrine is found in 17 & 18 Vict., c. 113 (1854), and 40 & 41 Vict., c. 34 (1877), with the latter applying specifically to unpaid purchase money.

[502] See Church, Equitable Conversion in Wisconsin, 1970 Wis.L.Rev. 404.

[503] It seems obvious that under equitable conversion, both vendor and purchaser have interests in the property, and that a judgment that creates a lien on the vendor's interest will not affect the purchaser's; see SMS Fin., LLC v. CBC Fin. Corp., 2017 UT 90, 417 P.3d 70 (2017).

that of an ordinary mortgagee who holds an interest in the land only as security for payment of the remainder of the purchase price. The cases are nearly evenly divided, with a slight majority rejecting equitable conversion and recognizing the lien.[504] Where this result is reached, there is some indication in the cases that once notified of the lien, the purchaser must make any further payments on the contract to the judgment creditor rather than the vendor.[505] The purchaser does not, however, have any obligation to examine the vendor's title and discover newly filed judgments before making each contract payment; the burden of doing so would be unreasonable, and the purchaser is protected in making payments to the vendor until receiving actual notice.[506] Provided he or she pays the appropriate person, the purchaser's essential right to enforce the contract is otherwise unaffected by the judgment against the vendor.[507]

A creditor who obtains a judgment against the purchaser, on the other hand, will argue for equitable conversion since it would characterize the purchaser's interest as real estate and thus subject it to the judgment lien statute. While the results in the decided cases often turn on precise statutory language (most notably whether the statute stipulates that equitable interests are lienable), conversion is usually followed in this context, thus subjecting the purchaser's interest to the lien.[508] If the vendor terminates

---

[504] See the discussion of Michigan law in In re Vandenbosch, 405 B.R. 253 (Bankr. W.D. Mich. 2009). Recognizing lien: Schleuter Co. v. Sevigny, 564 N.W.2d 309 (S.D. 1997); Bedortha v. Sunridge Land Co., 312 Or. 307, 822 P.2d 694 (1991); Monroe v. Lincoln City Employees Credit Union, 203 Neb. 702, 279 N.W.2d 866 (1979); First Security Bank v. Rogers, 91 Idaho 654, 429 P.2d 386 (1967); United Cmty. Bank v. Prairie State Bank & Tr., 2012 Ill. App 4th 110973, 972 N.E.2d 324, 332 (2012) (recognizing lien on ground that prior sale contract was unrecorded and, under recording act, judgment lienor had no notice of it); Walker v. Fairbanks Investment Co., 268 F.2d 48 (9th Cir. 1959) (Alaska law). Not recognizing lien: Cannefax v. Clement, 818 P.2d 546 (Utah 1991); Bank of Hawaii v. Horworth, 71 Haw. 204, 787 P.2d 674 (1990); Grant v. Kahn, 198 Md. App. 421, 18 A.3d 91 (2011); Marks v. City of Tucumcari, 93 N.M. 4, 595 P.2d 1199 (1979); Mueller v. Novelty Dye Works, 273 Wis. 501, 78 N.W.2d 881 (1956). See generally Lacy, Creditors of Land Contract Vendors, 24 Case W.Res.L.Rev. 645 (1973); 3 Am. L.Prop. § 11.29 n. 20 (1952). Note that the denial of a judgment lien is not necessarily a disaster for the creditor, who can seek garnishment of the debt owed to the vendor by the purchaser; see, e.g., Rural Acceptance Corp. v. Pierce, 157 Ind.App. 90, 298 N.E.2d 499 (1973). Some courts might reject this approach because the debt is conditional upon marketability of the vendor's title, but all would probably recognize a creditor's bill in equity to collect the payments owed by the purchaser. See Lacy, supra, at 665–81.

[505] Heider v. Dietz, 234 Or. 105, 380 P.2d 619 (1963). This gives the creditor an immediate right to the future payments without the need to go through an execution sale, a result which is very hard to justify; it may put the purchaser to a difficult choice in determining to whom the payments are legally owed. It seems preferable to require the creditor to employ a sale, garnishment, or equitable process to implement his or her claim to the payments. See Lacy, id., at 658–65.

[506] Burke v. Johnson, 37 Kan. 337, 15 P. 204 (1887); Filley v. Duncan, 1 Neb. 134 (1871); cf. Wehn v. Fall, 55 Neb. 547, 76 N.W. 13 (1898) (no constructive notice if purchaser has gone into possession.) See Church, supra note 502, at 418 n. 66. Cf. Lang v. Klinger, 34 Cal.App.3d 987, 110 Cal.Rptr. 532 (1973).

[507] Stephens v. Jenkins, 312 S.C. 233, 439 S.E.2d 849 (S.C. 1994); Hogan v. Weeks, 178 A.D.2d 968, 579 N.Y.S.2d 777 (1991); Clarence M. Bull, Inc. v. Goldman, 30 Md. App. 665, 353 A.2d 661 (1976); Wenzel v. Roberts, 236 Wis. 315, 294 N.W. 871 (1940). This is usually so even if the contract is unrecorded and the vendor's creditor has no other notice of it, since generally the recording acts do not protect judgment creditors; they are thought not to be "for value." See § 11.10 infra at notes 530–533. If the purchaser is in possession of the land, that possession will usually constitute constructive notice to the judgment creditor, obviating the latter's BFP claim; see Cook v. City of Indianapolis, 559 N.E.2d 1201 (Ind.App. 1990).

[508] In re Griffin, 397 B.R. 356 (Bankr. W.D. Va. 2008); Hannah v. Martinson, 232 Mont. 469, 758 P.2d 276 (1988); Butler v. Wilkinson, 740 P.2d 1244 (Utah 1987); Fulton v. Duro, 107 Idaho 240, 687 P.2d 1367 (1984), affirmed 108 Idaho 392, 700 P.2d 14 (1985); Farmers State Bank v. Slaubaugh, 366 N.W.2d 804 (N.D.1985). See also Cascade Security Bank v. Butler, 88 Wn.2d 777, 567 P.2d 631 (1977), holding the purchaser's interest lienable but without expressly adopting the theory of equitable conversion. For a thorough analysis of Washington law, see Hume, Real Estate Contracts and the Doctrine of Equitable Conversion in Washington: Dispelling the *Ashford* Cloud, 7 U. Puget Sound L.Rev. 233 (1984). Cases rejecting equitable conversion and holding the purchaser's interest not subject to the judgment lien include Matter of Estate of Ventling, 771 P.2d 388 (Wyo. 1989); Stanley v. Velma A. Barnes Real Estate, Inc., 571 P.2d 871 (Okl.App.

the contract because of the purchaser's default, the creditor's rights will also be cut off,[509] but the creditor can assert whatever theories would have been available to the purchaser to reinstate or enforce the contract.[510]

Beyond the matters of devolution on death and rights of creditors, equitable conversion has been used to resolve numerous other characterization questions, including the meaning of "owner" or some similar term under various contracts[511] and statutes.[512] Lien and mortgage priority issues are often decided on the basis of equitable conversion.[513] The construction of state inheritance or estate tax statutes that operate on real property has also been determined by reference to equitable conversion in a

---

1977) (purchaser has no lienable interest until purchase is price paid in full.) See 3 Am.L.Prop. § 11.29 nn. 1–15 (1952); Annot., 1 A.L.R.2d 727 (1948).

[509] See Welling v. Mount Si Bowl, Inc., 79 Wn.2d 485, 487 P.2d 620 (1971).

[510] Jahnke v. Palomar Financial Corp., 22 Ariz.App. 369, 527 P.2d 771 (1974). Cf. Warren v. Rodgers, 82 N.M. 78, 475 P.2d 775 (1970). A similar result is reached in the case of an assignment or mortgage of the purchaser's interest; see Murray First Thrift & Loan Co. v. Stevenson, 534 P.2d 909 (Utah 1975); Fincher v. Miles Homes of Missouri, Inc., 549 S.W.2d 848 (Mo. 1977), noted 43 Mo.L.Rev. 371 (1978).

[511] See, e.g., Stapley v. American Bathtub Liners, Inc., 162 Ariz. 564, 785 P.2d 84 (App. 1989) (purchaser who took possession during executory period with consent of vendor owed no rent); Cote v. A.J. Bayless Markets, Inc., 128 Ariz. 438, 626 P.2d 602 (App. 1981) (purchaser was successor in interest of original landlord, and could maintain action against tenant for breach of lease covenants); In re Dwyer's Estate, 159 Cal. 664, 115 P. 235 (Cal. 1911) (grant of authority to executor of vendor's estate to sell estate's real estate did not apply to property that was subject to a contract of sale by vendor prior to his death); Salce v. Wolczek, 314 Conn. 675, 104 A.3d 694 (2014) (vendor's entering into contract of sale was a "transfer" under previous agreement); Bayer v. Showmotion, Inc., 292 Conn. 381, 973 A.2d 1229 (2009) (tenant who exercised option to purchase could not be held liable for further rent). Contra, see Carollo v. Irwin, 2011 Ill. App 1st 102765, 959 N.E.2d 77 (2011) (contract for sale of real estate was not a "sale" under prior settlement agreement).

[512] See, e.g., United States v. Capital Tax Corp., 545 F.3d 525, 532 (7th Cir. 2008) (liability for cleanup of hazardous waste); United States v. Ben-Hur, 20 F.3d 313 (7th Cir.1994) (forfeiture of property for criminal acts); Dominion Bank v. Wilson, 867 F.2d 203 (4th Cir. 1989) (optionee's interest in option to purchase land, once exercised, was real property and not subject to a personal property security agreement under UCC Art. 9); United States v. 74.05 Acres of Land, 428 F.Supp.2d 57(D. Conn. 2006) (purchaser had standing to contest civil forfeiture); United States v. Holthaus, 437 F.Supp.2d 932 (N.D. Iowa 2006), aff'd, 486 F.3d 451 (8th Cir. 2007) (criminal fraud in bankruptcy); In re Guerrero, 536 B.R. 817 (Bankr. E.D. Wis. 2015) (vendor's interest was not an executory contract under Bankruptcy Code § 365); In re Beery, 295 B.R. 385 (Bankr. D.N.M. 2003) (purchaser's interest was part of his bankruptcy estate); First Nat. Bank v. McGinnis, 819 P.2d 1080 (Colo.App. 1991) (purchaser had a sufficient interest to maintain a quiet title action); Steward v. Panek, 251 Mich. App. 546, 652 N.W.2d 232 (2002) (same); Graham v. Claypool, 26 Kan. App. 2d 94, 978 P.2d 298 (1999) (vendor not liable for tort to injured tenant of purchaser); DeShields v. Broadwater, 338 Md. 422, 659 A.2d 300 (Md. 1995) (lis pendens filed against vendor was not effective against purchaser under prior contract); Jock v. Zoning Bd. of Adjustment of Twp. of Wall, 184 N.J. 562, 878 A.2d 785 (2005) (merger of lots under zoning ordinance); State v. Earp, 326 P.3d 491 (N.M. 2014) (contract purchaser could not be held criminally responsible for damaging property); Greenwood Gaming & Entm't, Inc. v. Pennsylvania Gaming Control Bd., 609 Pa. 368, 15 A.3d 884 (2011) (purchaser was eligible for gaming license); Commonwealth v. Inv. Res. Holding, Inc., 2017 Pa Super 251, 168 A.3d 225 (2017) (purchaser was responsible under municipal ordinance requiring safe upkeep of property); Pioneer Builders Co. of Nevada v. K D A Corp., 2012 Utah 74, 292 P.3d 672, 692 (2012) (purchaser's interest was protected by the recording act).

Contra, see Bank of Commerce v. Breakers, L.L.C., 2011 Okl. Civ App. 45, 256 P.3d 1053 (2011) (equitable conversion did not give contract purchasers standing to intervene in mortgage foreclosure action); Burke v. State ex rel. Dep't of Land Conservation & Dev., 352 Or. 428, 290 P.3d 790 (2012) (vendor was "owner" under statute giving relief from land use ordinances).

[513] In re Blanchard, 819 F.3d 981 (7th Cir. 2016); In re Restivo Auto Body, Inc., 772 F.3d 168 (4th Cir. 2014); Trustee 1245 13th St., NW No. 608 Trust v. Anderson, 905 A.2d 181 (D.C. 2006).

number of cases,[514] as has the meaning of other tax code provisions.[515] The doctrine has sometimes been applied in deciding whether a sale contract by a co-owner works a severance of a joint tenancy, although this seems a singularly inappropriate use of equitable conversion.[516]

Risk of loss. Equitable conversion treats the purchaser as the owner of the land during the contract's executory period. Hence, the purchaser is obliged to complete the contract and pay the remaining price even if some unforeseen event, not the fault of the vendor, causes a major loss in value before the closing. This is the majority view.[517] Yet it is subject to strong criticism on both theoretical and practical grounds. As Dean Stone observed long ago, the doctrine is theoretically objectionable because it is circular: Since the contract is specifically enforceable in equity, the buyer is treated as the owner; and since the buyer is deemed the owner, equity will impose the loss on the buyer and compel him or her to complete the contract.[518]

Equitable conversion as a risk-allocation tool for short-term earnest money contracts is equally questionable in practical terms, at least in cases of physical damage occurring while the vendor is in possession. First, it rarely comports with lay parties' expectations; they generally assume the risk is on the vendor.[519] Second, the vendor is far more likely than the purchaser to carry insurance against the loss, since the vendor has usually owned the land for some time, while the buyer thinks of his or her ownership as not yet having begun. Third, until the purchaser takes possession the vendor is in the

---

[514] In re Highberger's Estate, 468 Pa. 120, 360 A.2d 580 (1976); In re Ryan's Estate, 102 N.W.2d 9 (N.D.1960); In re Briebach's Estate, 132 Mont. 437, 318 P.2d 223 (1957). But see Matter of Houghton's Estate, 147 N.J.Super. 477, 371 A.2d 735 (1977), affirmed 75 N.J. 462, 383 A.2d 713 (1978) (state agency regulation adopting equitable conversion held invalid); Connell v. Crosby, 210 Ill. 380, 71 N.E. 350 (1904) (equitable conversion inappropriate for resolution of tax cases).

[515] McPherson v. United States, 673 F.Supp.2d 1167 (D. Mont. 2009) (standing to bring wrongful levy claim against IRS); Benedict v. U.S., 881 F.Supp. 1532 (D.Utah 1995) (deductibility of interest and property taxes); Ocean Ave. LLC v. Cty. of Los Angeles, 227 Cal. App. 4th 344, 173 Cal. Rptr. 3d 445 (2014) (equitable conversion did not trigger property tax reassessment).

[516] See Yannopoulos v. Sophos, 243 Pa.Super. 454, 365 A.2d 1312 (1976); Gustin v. Stegall, 347 A.2d 917 (D.C.App. 1975), certiorari denied 425 U.S. 974, 96 S.Ct. 2174, 48 L.Ed.2d 798 (1976); In re Estate of Fischer, 22 Wis.2d 637, 126 N.W.2d 596 (1964); Tingle v. Hornsby, 111 So.2d 274 (Fla.App. 1959). A severance is ordinarily thought to occur when the co-owners no longer have unity of time, title, interest, or possession; see § 5.4 supra. If all co-owners execute the contract as vendors, the unities among them are obviously not disturbed and no severance should be deemed to occur unless there is other evidence that they wish to terminate the right of survivorship. The characterization of their interest as realty or personalty is irrelevant. See In re Estelle's Estate, 122 Ariz. 109, 593 P.2d 663 (1979); Yannopoulos v. Sophos, supra (concurring opinion).

[517] See, e.g., Brush Grocery Kart, Inc. v. Sure Fine Mkt., Inc., 47 P.3d 680 (Colo. 2002) (applying equitable conversion only if purchaser has possession); Bleckley v. Langston, 112 Ga.App. 63, 143 S.E.2d 671 (1965); Ridenour v. France, 442 N.E.2d 716 (Ind.App. 1982); Ambrose v. Harrison Mutual Insurance Association, 206 N.W.2d 683 (Iowa 1973); Northwest Kansas Area Vocational-Technical School v. Wolf, 6 Kan.App.2d 817, 635 P.2d 1268 (1981); Duhon v. Dugas, 407 So.2d 1334 (La.App. 1981) (under Louisiana statute); Graham v. Kim, 111 Nev. 1039, 899 P.2d 1122 (Nev. 1995) (without mentioning equitable conversion); Midfirst Bank v. Graves, 399 N.J. Super. 228, 943 A.2d 923 (Ch. Div. 2007) (foreclosure sale). See generally 17 Williston on Contracts § 50:46 (4th ed. 2018 update); Fineberg, Risk of Loss in Executory Contracts for the Sale of Real Property, 14 Colum.J.L. & Soc. Prob. 453 (1979); Note, 22 Drake L.Rev. 626 (1973); Hirshler & Fleischer, Risk of Loss in Executory Contracts for the Purchase of Lands, 34 Va.L.Rev. 965 (1948); Annot., 27 A.L.R.2d 444 (1953).

[518] Stone, Equitable Conversion by Contract, 13 Colum.L.Rev. 369, 386 (1913), quoted at length in Skelly Oil Co. v. Ashmore, 365 S.W.2d 582 (Mo.1963).

[519] The writers know of no systematic study of this point, but one of them has surveyed his first-year law students for many years; a large majority of them invariably express the view that the vendor probably has the risk.

better position to take whatever precautions might prevent the occurrence of the loss.[520] For these reasons, equitable conversion's broad imposition of risk on the buyer has been resoundingly condemned by nearly all academic writers who have considered it.[521] In practice it causes much less trouble than one might expect, mainly because of the prevalence of casualty insurance and the fact that the parties have the power to make their own agreement in contradiction of equitable conversion's rule.[522] Nearly all printed form sale contracts do so, usually imposing the risk on the vendor until closing of the sale. Thus, equitable conversion is primarily a trap for amateur conveyancers.

Losses due to changes in the property's legal status are often imposed on the purchaser under equitable conversion.[523] The property's value may fall, for example, due to a rezoning or loss of benefits under a zoning ordinance,[524] a change in a building code,[525] or an eminent domain action.[526] In these cases the arguments against equitable conversion in the previous paragraph lose much of their force. One cannot insure against a zoning change or a condemnation suit, and there may be little one can do to prevent the loss that ensues. It is also much more debatable whether the usual expectation of the parties would favor the purchaser.[527]

A number of jurisdictions have modified or rejected equitable conversion as an allocator of risk. A few place the risk on the purchaser only if he or she has taken

---

[520] See the discussion in Appleton Electric Co. v. Rogers, 200 Wis. 331, 228 N.W. 505 (1930); Church, Equitable Conversion in Wisconsin, 1970 Wis.L.Rev. 404, 421–22.

[521] See articles cited in notes 517, 518 & 520 supra.

[522] See In re Nickels Midway Pier, LLC, 452 B.R. 156 (D.N.J. 2011); Munshower v. Martin, 641 So.2d 909 (Fla.App.1994), appeal after remand 660 So.2d 794 (Fla. App. 1995); Winterchase Townhomes, Inc. v. Koether, 193 Ga.App. 161, 387 S.E.2d 361 (1989), cert. vacated 260 Ga. 152, 392 S.E.2d 533 (1990); Holscher v. James, 124 Idaho 443, 860 P.2d 646 (Idaho 1993); White v. Simard, 152 Md. App. 229, 831 A.2d 517 (2003), aff'd, 383 Md. 257, 859 A.2d 168 (2004); Smith v. Mohan, 723 S.W.2d 94 (Mo.App. 1987); Hans v. Lucas, 270 Neb. 421, 703 N.W.2d 880 (2005); Marion Family YMCA v. Hensel, 897 N.E.2d 184 (Ohio Ct. App. 2008). See generally J. Pomeroy, Equity Jurisprudence § 1159ff (5th ed. 1941).

[523] See, e.g., Latipac Corp. v. BMH Realty LLC, 93 A.D.3d 115, 938 N.Y.S.2d 30 (2012) (purchaser bore risk of change in judicial interpretation of rent control law).

[524] Mohave County v. Mohave-Kingman Estates, Inc., 120 Ariz. 417, 586 P.2d 978 (1978); Alhambra Redevelopment Agency v. Transamerica Financial Services, 212 Cal. App.3d 1370, 261 Cal. Rptr. 248 (1989); J.C. Penney Co. v. Koff, 345 So.2d 732 (Fla.App. 1977); DiDonato v. Reliance Standard Life Insurance Co., 433 Pa. 221, 249 A.2d 327 (1969). See also La Rosa Del Monte Express, Inc. v. G.S.W. Enterprises Corp., 483 So.2d 472 (Fla.App.1986) (lease may be rescinded for total failure of consideration, where zoning ordinance prevents use for which property was leased). See generally Annot., 39 A.L.R.3d 362 (1971). Note that if the zoning is changed so as to make the existing use of the property a violation of the ordinance, the title may unmarketable under the principles discussed in § 10.12, supra, and the purchaser will usually have the power to avoid the contract. In addition, the doctrine of commercial frustration may sometimes operate to discharge the purchaser from the contract; see Felt v. McCarthy, 130 Wash.2d 203, 922 P.2d 90 (1996).

[525] Cox v. Supreme Savings & Loan Association, 126 Ill.App.2d 293, 262 N.E.2d 74 (1970).

[526] Hauben v. Harmon, 605 F.2d 920 (5th Cir. 1979) (applying Florida law); Arko Enterprises, Inc. v. Wood, 185 So.2d 734 (Fla.App. 1966); Annot., 27 A.L.R.3d 572 (1969). If the event which causes the loss also imposes an encumbrance on the vendor's title, the contract's title covenants may well give the purchaser a right of rescission; see, e.g., Byrne v. Kanig, 231 Pa.Super. 531, 332 A.2d 472 (1974) (imposition by city of lien for sewer improvement assessment). Note that an eminent domain action may possibly produce a windfall—that is, an award in excess of the contract price—and that the purchaser will be entitled to it under equitable conversion. See Alhambra Redevelopment Agency v. Transamerica Financial Services, 212 Cal.App.3d 1370, 261 Cal.Rptr. 248 (1989).

[527] The vendor was denied specific performance after a rezoning diminished the property's value for the purchaser's intended use in Clay v. Landreth, 187 Va. 169, 45 S.E.2d 875, 175 A.L.R. 1047 (1948); Anderson v. Steinway & Sons, 178 App.Div. 507, 165 N.Y.S. 608 (1917), affirmed 221 N.Y. 639, 117 N.E. 575 (1917). The rationale of both decisions was that specific enforcement would be inequitable in light of the loss it would impose on the buyer.

possession of the property.[528] There is considerable sense to this; the purchaser in possession probably expects to have responsibility for the property, and is normally in a good position to insure and protect against loss. Several other courts have rejected equitable conversion entirely and placed the loss on the vendor irrespective of possession.[529] Both of these categories of decisions generally distinguish between "substantial" or "material" losses and those which are not so severe. If the vendor has the risk and the loss is substantial, the vendor cannot enforce the contract at all, and must return the buyer's payments. If the loss is insubstantial, the vendor may have specific performance, but must allow an abatement against the price to account for the damage.[530] This approach causes at least two difficulties. First, it is not necessarily easy to determine whether a given loss is "substantial;" the term is not self-defining, and litigation may be necessary.[531] Second, it is often unclear whether, in the case of a substantial loss, the *purchaser* may insist upon specific performance with abatement if the vendor wishes to treat the contract as terminated. If one thinks of the continued and unimpaired existence of the improvements on the land as an implied condition precedent to the duty to complete the contract, the question is whether the condition is for the benefit of both parties or only the buyer.[532] In the usual case the answer should rather obviously be the latter.[533]

There have been two major statutory attempts to resolve the question of risk of loss. The first, the Uniform Vendor and Purchaser Risk Act (UVPRA), was drafted by Professor Williston and promulgated by the Commissioners on Uniform State Laws in 1935; it has been adopted in ten states.[534] The second is Section 2–406 of the Uniform

---

[528] Brush Grocery Kart, Inc. v. Sure Fine Mkt., Inc., 47 P.3d 680 (Colo. 2002); Smith v. Warth, 483 S.W.2d 834 (Tex.Civ.App. 1972) (risk on party having "beneficial interest", which the court apparently deemed indicated by possession); Potwin v. Tucker, 128 Vt. 142, 259 A.2d 781 (1969); Briz-Ler Corp. v. Weiner, 39 Del. Ch. 578, 171 A.2d 65 (1961); Appleton Electric Co. v. Rogers, 200 Wis. 331, 228 N.W. 505 (1930) (rendered obsolete by passage of the Uniform Vendor and Purchaser Risk Act, discussed infra).

[529] Skelly Oil Co. v. Ashmore, 365 S.W.2d 582 (Mo. 1963), noted at 1964 Wash. U.L.Q. 128; Lampesis v. Travelers Insurance Co., 101 N.H. 323, 143 A.2d 104 (1958); Anderson v. Yaworski, 120 Conn. 390, 181 A. 205 (1935); Ashford v. Reese, 132 Wash. 649, 233 P. 29 (1925); Libman v. Levenson, 236 Mass. 221, 128 N.E. 13 (1920); Kelley v. Neilson, 433 Mass. 706, 745 N.E.2d 952 (2001). See also Tate v. Wood, 169 W.Va. 584, 289 S.E.2d 432 (1982), suggesting in dictum that the destruction of the improvements on land might "void the contract" on grounds of impossibility of performance. The foregoing cases do not discuss the significance of possession; some of the jurisdictions cited might shift the risk to a purchaser in possession, aligning themselves with the states mentioned in note 528 supra.

[530] See, e.g., Hawkes v. Kehoe, 193 Mass. 419, 79 N.E. 766 (1907).

[531] Perhaps the most intriguing case is Skelly Oil Co. v. Ashmore, supra note 529, in which the purchaser had planned to demolish the building which was destroyed by fire before the closing. The court found the loss material, but the dissent argued that the fire had actually saved the buyer money.

[532] See § 10.11, supra, at notes 399–401. The condition might be thought for the benefit of both parties if the vendor were taking back a purchase money mortgage or for other reasons had a continuing interest in the presence of the improvements on the land.

[533] See Skelly Oil Co. v. Ashmore, supra note 529, granting the purchaser specific performance with abatement for a material loss; Bornemann v. Richards, 245 La. 851, 161 So.2d 741 (1964) (same result under La. statute); Phinizy v. Guernsey, 111 Ga. 346, 36 S.E. 796 (1900). See also Laurin v. DeCarolis Construction Co., 372 Mass. 688, 363 N.E.2d 675 (1977) (willful destruction by vendor, but court implied same result would follow an innocent loss). See generally 3 Am.L.Prop. § 11.30 (1952). The purchaser can have specific performance if he or she is willing to pay the full price without abatement; see Stapper v. Rusch, 127 Tex. 151, 92 S.W.2d 431 (1936).

[534] The UVPRA is the law in California, Hawaii, Illinois, Michigan, New York (with significant changes), North Carolina, Oklahoma, Oregon, South Dakota, and Wisconsin. See generally Pusateri, Risk of Loss After Contract to Sell Real Property: Adoption of Uniform Vendor and Purchaser Risk Act in Illinois, 52 Ill.B.J. 464 (1964); Lacy, The Uniform Vendor and Purchaser Risk Act and the Need for a Law-Revision Commission in Oregon, 36 Or.L.Rev. 106 (1957). See Unger v. Nunda Township Rural Fire Protection Dist., 135 Ill.App.3d

Land Transactions Act (ULTA), adopted by the Commissioners in 1975 but not enacted by any legislature. Both take the same basic approach, leaving the risk of loss on the vendor until possession or legal title is transferred to the purchaser. They deny the vendor the right to enforce the contract and compel him to return the buyer's deposit if a material loss occurs while he has the risk. Yet both acts leave the law in an uncertain state on several points. They appear to apply only to physical damage[535] and to takings in eminent domain; whether they would influence a court in a case of loss by zoning amendment or other change of legal status is unclear. Both employ the concept of materiality of loss[536] without attempting to define it in dollar or percentage terms. For example, it is by no means obvious whether a $1000 fire in a single-family home would qualify. The UVPRA is also deficient in failing to indicate whether, after a material loss, the purchaser may nonetheless specifically enforce the contract with abatement of the price,[537] and whether, if the loss is non-material and the contract is enforced against the purchaser, the latter is entitled to a price abatement for the damage.[538] The ULTA answers both of these questions affirmatively.[539] The inadequacies of both of these model acts suggest that neither is an adequate substitute for a competently-drafted contract clause which deals explicitly with all of the matters discussed above.[540]

The legal rules governing risk of loss are complicated when the loss is covered by a casualty insurance policy. If there is only one policy and it insures the party on whom the law or the contract imposes the risk of loss, the problems are minimal.[541] But all too often the logic of equitable conversion puts the risk on the buyer when the seller is the only party insured. If the seller recovers the full price for the land and also collects from his insurer, he or she seems to receive an unwarranted stroke of good fortune. The seller may argue that there is no reason to give the buyer any benefit from the insurance,

---

758, 90 Ill. Dec. 416, 482 N.E.2d 123 (1985) (purchaser with legal right of possession, who had been removing trees from it, had sufficient possession to have risk of loss under UVPRA).

[535] UVPRA speaks of the "subject matter" being "destroyed"; ULTA speaks of "casualty loss."

[536] UVPRA is triggered if a "material part" is destroyed; ULTA operates if there is a "substantial failure of the real estate to conform to the contract." See National Factors, Inc. v. Winslow, 52 Misc.2d 194, 274 N.Y.S.2d 400 (1966) (loss of $10,000 on $180,000 property was not material, where purchaser had planned to rebuild on the site.)

[537] The New York cases permit the purchaser to enforce with abatement under the UVPRA despite the statute's silence on the point; Kendle v. Town of Amsterdam, 36 A.D.3d 985, 828 N.Y.S.2d 620 (2007); Jewell v. Rowe, 119 A.D.2d 634, 500 N.Y.S.2d 787 (1986) (purchaser may have rescission or specific performance with abatement); Lucenti v. Cayuga Apartments, Inc., 59 A.D.2d 438, 400 N.Y.S.2d 194 (1977), appeal after remand 66 A.D.2d 928, 410 N.Y.S.2d 928 (1978); Burack v. Tollig, 10 N.Y.2d 879, 223 N.Y.S.2d 505, 179 N.E.2d 509 (1961). Contra, see Dixon v. Salvation Army, 142 Cal.App.3d 463, 191 Cal.Rptr. 111 (1983).

[538] The New York version of UVPRA, unlike the official version, explicitly provides for abatement on these facts; see N.Y.-McKinney's Gen.Obl.Law § 5–1311, applied in National Factors, Inc. v. Winslow, 52 Misc.2d 194, 274 N.Y.S.2d 400 (1966).

[539] ULTA § 2–406(1), (2).

[540] See Friedman & Smith, Contracts and Conveyances of Real Property § 18:1.4 (8th ed. 2017). Ordinarily the parties can vary existing law at their pleasure by appropriate contract language. See Caulfield v. Improved Risk Mutuals, Inc., 66 N.Y.2d 793, 497 N.Y.S.2d 903, 488 N.E.2d 833 (1985) (contract clause controls over UVPRA).

[541] The principal difficulty is simply that the insurance may be inadequate in amount. Many casualty policies contain "coinsurance clauses." A typical clause provides that if the policy's face amount is not at least 80% of the property's replacement cost, the insurer's liability for any loss is limited to the fraction of the loss which the policy amount bears to 80% of the property's replacement cost. For example, suppose the replacement cost of the improvements is $100,000 and the policy amount $60,000. If a $1000 loss occurs, the insurer will pay only 60/80, or $750.

which is, after all a personal contract of indemnity between insurer and insured.[542] But such a seller's windfall has been too much for most modern courts to swallow, and the cases generally permit the seller to enforce the contract only if he or she is willing to abate the price to the extent of the insurance recovery.[543] This result, which is often explained as the imposition of a constructive trust on the insurance funds in favor of the purchaser, greatly mitigates the original unfairness of equitable conversion.[544]

Occasionally a case arises in which the positions of the parties are reversed: the purchaser has insurance, but the risk is on the vendor. Here again is an opportunity for a windfall, this time to the purchaser. Can the purchaser collect the insurance proceeds and at the same time escape the contract or buy the land at an abated price? To do so the purchaser must meet several objections. First, if he or she refuses to complete the contract (plainly a permissible course of action on these facts), the insurer may argue that no loss at all has occurred, and hence that no claim can be made on the insurance policy.[545] This argument has considerable force. Even if the purchaser proceeds with the contract and buys with an abatement of price, the insurer can take much the same position. Moreover, if the insurer pays the claim, the vendor may argue that the insurance was intended for his or her benefit as well, despite the fact that the policy did

---

[542] Such an argument has succeeded in a few courts; see Long v. Keller, 104 Cal. App.3d 312, 163 Cal.Rptr. 532 (1980) (purchaser was in possession; had risk under UVPRA); Whitley v. Irwin, 250 Ark. 543, 465 S.W.2d 906 (1971); Twin City Fire Insurance Co. v. Walter B. Hannah, Inc., 444 S.W.2d 131 (Ky. 1969) (construing statute); Brownell v. Board of Education, 239 N.Y. 369, 146 N.E. 630, 37 A.L.R. 13, 19 (1925). These cases generally follow Rayner v. Preston, 18 Ch. Div. 1 (1881). Note also the possibility that the insurer will attempt to deny the vendor's claim on the ground that he or she has no loss, and therefore nothing to indemnify, if the risk is on the buyer. This argument has usually been rejected; see Kintzel v. Wheatland Mutual Insurance Association, 203 N.W.2d 799 (Iowa 1973); cases cited note 545 infra.

[543] See, e.g., Hillard v. Franklin, 41 S.W.3d 106 (Tenn. Ct. App. 2000); Hendricks v. M.C.I., Inc., 152 Wis.2d 363, 448 N.W.2d 289 (1989); Alabama Farm Bureau Mut. Ins. Co. v. Meyers, 516 So.2d 661 (Ala.Civ. App.1987); Wood v. Donohue, 136 Ohio App. 3d 336, 736 N.E.2d 556 (1999) (purchaser entitled to credit for amount of settlement vendor reached with uranium plant for damage to property); New Hampshire Ins. Co. v. Vetter, 326 N.W.2d 723 (S.D. 1982); Berlier v. George, 94 N.M. 134, 607 P.2d 1152 (1980); Cheatwood v. De Los Santos, 561 S.W.2d 273 (Tex.Civ.App. 1978), refused n.r.e. See also Petrie v. LeVan, 799 S.W.2d 632 (Mo. App. 1990); Estes v. Thurman, 192 S.W.3d 429 (Ky. Ct. App. 2005), where the court awarded the full amount of the insurance proceeds to the purchaser even though they exceeded the price the purchaser had agreed to pay! Even the New York Court of Appeals, which has generally denied the purchaser the benefit of the vendor's insurance, granted that privilege to a purchaser who had paid the insurance premiums; Raplee v. Piper, 3 N.Y.2d 179, 164 N.Y.S.2d 732, 143 N.E.2d 919, 64 A.L.R.2d 1397 (1957). Several of the foregoing cases indicate that the abatement in favor of the purchaser should be reduced by the amount of premiums paid by the vendor while the purchaser had the risk of loss. See generally Davis v. Skinner, 474 So.2d 1136 (Ala.Civ. App. 1985). Annot., 64 A.L.R.2d 1402 (1959).

[544] See In re Nickels Midway Pier, LLC, 452 B.R. 156 (D.N.J. 2011). Perhaps surprisingly, the ULTA does not address the question of disposition of the proceeds of the seller's insurance where the purchaser has the risk of loss. It does, however, allow the purchaser credit for the proceeds as an alternate measure of abatement of price if the risk is on the seller; ULTA § 2–406(b)(1), (2). See text at note 543 supra. The tentative draft of the UVPRA prepared by Professor Williston gave the purchaser a clear right to enforce the contract with abatement of price in the amount of insurance proceeds received by the seller, but this language was not included in the Commissioners' official version; see O. Browder, et al., Basic Property Law 1089 (3d ed. 1979).

[545] Sanford v. Breidenbach, 111 Ohio App. 474, 173 N.E.2d 702 (1960); Phillips v. Bacon, 245 Ga. 814, 267 S.E.2d 249 (1980). For an analogous case in which the insurance company successfully defended a suit by its insured vendor on the ground that the purchaser had paid him the full price, and thus that he had no loss, see Westfall v. American States Insurance Co., 43 Ohio App.2d 176, 334 N.E.2d 523 (1974). See also Paramount Fire Insurance Co. v. Aetna Casualty & Surety Co., 163 Tex. 250, 353 S.W.2d 841 (1962), noted 17 Sw.L.J. 334 (1963), which may be explainable on the ground that the purchaser was in possession when the loss occurred. Contra, and probably the majority view, see Wolf v. Home Insurance Co., 100 N.J.Super. 27, 241 A.2d 28 (1968), affirmed 103 N.J.Super. 357, 247 A.2d 345 (1968); Vogel v. Northern Assurance Co., 219 F.2d 409 (3d Cir.1955). See generally Fineberg, Risk of Loss in Executory Contracts for the Sale of Real Property, 14 Colum.J.L. & Soc.Prob. 453, 478–82 (1979).

not name the vendor as an insured; this argument is likely to succeed only if the contract stipulated that the purchaser would carry insurance.[546] The vendor may then insist that the abatement of price owing to the loss be reduced by the insurance proceeds, or if the purchaser defaults on the contract the vendor may seek to recover the insurance proceeds.

Time of conversion. Both the characterization and risk cases seem to assume that it is easy to tell when equitable conversion has occurred. But that is not always so. It is clear enough that there must be a fully formed contract of sale; an unexercised option, for example, is not enough.[547] Moreover, the contract must be enforceable in equity.[548] Hence, an oral contract which has not been the subject of part performance[549] or a contract which is so unjust as to be unenforceable[550] will not work a conversion. If the seller's title is so defective that it does not comply with the contract's specifications, no conversion occurs, at least for purposes of shifting away the risk of loss, until the defects are cured.[551] Note that conversion does not depend on actual enforcement of the contract; if it is enforceable at the critical time (the loss, death of a party, etc.), the fact that it is later rescinded or abandoned is immaterial.[552]

If none of the barriers mentioned above is present, conversion is generally assumed to occur the moment the contract of sale is signed.[553] But occasionally a court has seized on the presence of unfulfilled conditions in the contract as a basis for denying that there has been a conversion,[554] and dictum is fairly common to the effect that the contract

---

[546] See Kintzel v. Wheatland Mutual Insurance Association, 203 N.W.2d 799 (Iowa 1973) (vendor identified as such on the face of policy insuring purchaser); Kindred v. Boalbey, 73 Ill.App.3d 37, 29 Ill.Dec. 77, 391 N.E.2d 236 (1979); Nevada Refining Co. v. Newton, 88 Nev. 333, 497 P.2d 887 (1972); Marbach v. Gnadl, 73 Ill.App.2d 303, 219 N.E.2d 572 (1966). Cf. Phillips v. Bacon, id. (no contract clause; purchaser's insurer not liable to vendor.) See generally 5 Couch, Insurance § 68:10 (3d ed. 2018 update).

[547] See County of San Diego v. Miller, 13 Cal.3d 684, 119 Cal.Rptr. 491, 532 P.2d 139 (1975); Brush Grocery Kart, Inc. v. Sure Fine Mkt., Inc., 47 P.3d 680 (Colo. 2002); Eddington v. Turner, 27 Del.Ch. 411, 38 A.2d 738, 155 A.L.R. 562 (1944); Riddle, ex rel. Riddle v. Elk Creek Salers, Ltd., 52 S.W.3d 644 (Mo. Ct. App. 2001); Moncrief v. Louisiana Land & Exploration Co., 861 P.2d 500 (Wyo.1993); Bauserman v. Digiulian, 224 Va. 414, 297 S.E.2d 671 (Va.1982); Am. Canadian Expeditions, Ltd. v. Gauley River Corp., 221 W. Va. 442, 655 S.E.2d 188 (2007) See 3 Am.L.Prop. § 11.23 (1952); Annot., 172 A.L.R. 438 (1948). See also LaSalle Bank, N.I. v. First Am. Bank, 316 Ill. App. 3d 515, 736 N.E.2d 619 (2000) (contract of sale entered into by land trust beneficiary does not actuate equitable conversion, since legal title is held by trustee of land trust).

[548] Lindsey v. Prillman, 921 A.2d 782 (D.C. 2007); Lewis v. Muchmore, 26 S.W.3d 632 (Tenn. Ct. App. 2000) (no equitable conversion existed after contract expired).

[549] Guzman v. Acuna, 653 S.W.2d 315 (Tex.App.1983) (part of contract was so illegible as to be unenforceable; no equitable conversion occurred). See § 10.2, supra.

[550] See § 10.5 supra at notes 216–218; 3 Am.L.Prop. § 11.24 (1952). See also Metz v. United States, 933 F.2d 802 (10th Cir. 1991), cert. denied 502 U.S. 957, 112 S.Ct. 416, 116 L.Ed.2d 436 (1991) (under Kansas law, a contract to devise property by will is not specifically enforceable, and hence gives rise to no equitable conversion).

[551] Coe v. Hays, 328 Md. 350, 614 A.2d 576 (Md.1992), appeal after remand 105 Md.App. 778, 661 A.2d 220 (1995); Sharbono v. Darden, 220 Mont. 320, 715 P.2d 433 (1986). But see Life Sav. & Loan Ass'n v. Bryant, 125 Ill.App.3d 1012, 81 Ill.Dec. 577, 467 N.E.2d 277 (1984) (conversion occurred when contract was signed, despite vendor's lack of title; but case involved purchaser's priority as against vendor's mortgagee, not risk of loss); Northwest Kansas Area Vocational-Technical School v. Wolf, 6 Kan.App.2d 817, 635 P.2d 1268 (1981); Phillips v. Bacon, 245 Ga. 814, 267 S.E.2d 249 (1980); Amundson v. Severson, 41 S.D. 377, 170 N.W. 633 (1919).

[552] Frietze v. Frietze, 78 N.M. 676, 437 P.2d 137 (1968); Clapp v. Tower, 11 N.D. 556, 93 N.W. 862 (1903).

[553] See Shay v. Penrose, 25 Ill.2d 447, 185 N.E.2d 218 (1962).

[554] The best-known example is Sanford v. Breidenbach, 111 Ohio App. 474, 173 N.E.2d 702 (1960). See also Rodisch v. Moore, 266 Ill. 106, 107 N.E. 108 (1914); Tollefson Dev., Inc. v. McCarthy, 668 N.W.2d 701 (Minn. Ct. App. 2003); Jacobs v. Great Pacific Century Corp., 197 N.J.Super. 378, 484 A.2d 1312 (1984), affirmed 204 N.J.Super. 605, 499 A.2d 1023 (1985) (dictum); Frankiewicz v. Konwinski, 246 Mich. 473, 224 N.W. 368 (1929); See Re, Equity and Equitable Remedies 585 (1975); Annot., 27 A.L.R.2d 444, 453 (1953).

must be "unconditional" to effect a conversion.[555] The basis of this language is presumably that equity will not enforce the contract until the conditions have been met, but this reasoning is too broad. If the condition in question is also a covenant—that is, if a party has promised to fulfill it—the parties properly consider themselves bound by the contract, and equity will enforce it.[556] Certainly such common conditions as the mutual tender of the deed and the price or the completion of promised repairs by the vendor should not defeat equitable conversion. Only if the condition is dependent on the actions of a third party, as in conditions of financing or rezoning, can one logically deny that conversion has occurred until the third party has acted.[557] Unfortunately, there is little helpful discussion of this distinction in the cases.[558]

§ 10.14　OPTIONS AND PREEMPTIVE RIGHTS

A real estate option consists of two concepts linked together: first, an offer to sell property on certain defined terms; and second, a contractual undertaking to leave that offer open for a period of time. Ordinarily an offeror may revoke an offer to sell at will before it has been accepted, but in an option the optionor suspends the power to revoke by contracting not to do so.[559] If consideration is paid for the option, the promise to hold the offer of sale irrevocable is specifically enforceable, and the offer cannot be withdrawn

---

[555] See, e.g., Hall v. Pioneer Crop Care, Inc., 212 Kan. 554, 512 P.2d 491 (1973); Greenwood Gaming & Entm't, Inc. v. Pennsylvania Gaming Control Bd., 609 Pa. 368, 15 A.3d 884 (2011).

[556] See § 10.11, supra.

[557] See Lincoln Park Federal Sav. & Loan Ass'n v. DRG, Inc., 175 Ill.App.3d 176, 124 Ill.Dec. 790, 529 N.E.2d 771 (1988) (conversion occurred when enforceable contract was entered into, even though price had not yet been paid). Cf. United Bank of Bismarck v. Trout, 480 N.W.2d 742 (N.D. 1992) (where purchaser did not pay earnest money, no enforceable contract was formed and no equitable conversion occurred). Compare In re Governor Mifflin Joint School Authority Petition, 401 Pa. 387, 164 A.2d 221 (1960) (unfulfilled condition of rezoning; no equitable conversion), and Simmons v. Krall, 201 Ga.App. 893, 412 S.E.2d 559 (1991) (unfulfilled condition that vendor cover land and sow grass; no equitable conversion) with Filsam Corp. v. Dyer, 422 F.Supp. 1126 (E.D.Pa. 1976) (unfulfilled condition that vendor make repairs; conversion occurred.) See also Southport Congregational Church—United Church of Christ v. Hadley, 320 Conn. 103, 128 A.3d 478 (2016), avoiding the issue by construing a financing contingency as a condition subsequent rather than precedent, so that it did not preclude the application of equitable conversion. There is some suggestion in the cases that, where the condition is for the benefit of only one party, that party may take advantage of equitable conversion while the other may not. See Grant v. Kahn, 198 Md. App. 421, 18 A.3d 91 (2011); Northern Texas Realty & Construction Co. v. Lary, 136 S.W. 843 (Tex.Civ.App. 1911). Cf. Re, Equity and Equitable Remedies 585 (1975), suggesting that, for purposes of devolution upon death, if only one party can enforce the contract there is no equitable conversion on either side.

[558] See, however, the good discussions in Matter of Estate of Clark, 447 N.W.2d 549 (Iowa App. 1989) and Filsam Corp. v. Dyer, id.

[559] Sutton Place Dev. Co. v. Bank of Commerce, 149 Ill.App.3d 513, 103 Ill.Dec. 122, 501 N.E.2d 143 (1986); In re Smith Tr., 480 Mich. 19, 745 N.W.2d 754 (2008).

during the option period.[560] If and when the offer is accepted, the option is said to be exercised and a contract of sale is formed.[561]

As a practical matter, an optionor must take the property off the market for the period of the option, or must at least warn interested potential buyers that any transaction with them is subject to being preempted by the exercise of the option. Since this means that the optionor may be forced to forego acceptance of other, potentially more attractive offers, the optionor ordinarily demands a significant price for the option.

In many situations the option is an attractive and convenient technique for acquiring land, especially for future development. For example, a subdivision builder may identify a tract of land which seems suitable for development, but only after many conditions are satisfied. Rezoning may be needed, approval of the subdivision by the local planning authorities may be necessary, soil tests must be made, surveys must be obtained, and the builder must arrange land acquisition and construction financing. In theory the land seller and the builder could enter into a "firm" contract in which each of these matters was recited in detail as a condition precedent to the builder's obligation to proceed with the sale. As more and more conditions were added that give the purchaser a potential "out," the contract would approach in practical effect an option (except that it might provide for return of the earnest money if the conditions were not met). But the drafting of such conditions is complex and their subsequent interpretation is open to dispute. An option is a more efficient approach. It is a much simpler document, and it permits the builder to become fully satisfied with all of the matters mentioned, as well as any others that arise in the course of investigation, with no obligation to purchase the land unless all of these concerns are met.[562]

In the context just described, an option typically stands alone. But options are often included in leases as well, giving the tenant the right to extend the lease term, to purchase the premises, or both. If the tenant is in default under the terms of the lease, or the lease has been terminated prematurely because of the tenant's default, controversy often arises as to the continued viability of the option. The cases are divided on these issues.[563]

---

[560] Polk v. BHRGU Avon Properties, LLC, 946 So. 2d 1120 (Fla. Dist. Ct. App. 2006); McLellan v. Charly, 313 Wis. 2d 623, 758 N.W.2d 94 (2008). If no consideration is paid by the optionee, the optionor may withdraw the offer at any time; see Crowley v. Bass, 445 So.2d 902 (Ala. 1984); Steiner v. Thexton, 163 Cal.App.4th 359, 77 Cal.Rptr.3d 632 (2008); LaRoche v. Nehama, 979 So. 2d 1021 (Fla. Dist. Ct. App. 2008); Allison v. Agribank, 949 S.W.2d 182 (Mo.App. 1997); Board of Education v. James Hamilton Constr. Co., 119 N.M. 415, 891 P.2d 556 (N.M.App. 1994); Pifer v. McDermott, 836 N.W.2d 432 (N.D. 2013); Property Assistance Corp. v. Roberts, 768 P.2d 976 (Utah App. 1989); RSD AAP, LLC v. Alyeska Ocean, Inc., 190 Wash. App. 305, 358 P.3d 483 (2015); Restatement (Second) of Contracts § 25 (1981); Murray, Options and Related Rights with Respect to Real Estate: An Update, 47 Real Prop. Tr. & Est. L.J. 63 (2012); Brown, Real Estate Purchase Options, 12 Nova L.Rev. 147 (1987); Gosfield, A Primer on Real Estate Options, 35 Real Prop. Prob. & Tr. J. 129 (2000). The consideration need not be in cash; see Guthmiller Farms, LLP v. Guthmiller, 840 N.W.2d 636 (N.D. 2013). See also Garcia v. Sonoma Ranch E. II, LLC, 298 P.3d 510 (N.M. 2013) (optionee who does not exercise option has no obligation to pay for it). Whether a refundable deposit paid by the optionee is sufficient consideration is disputed; compare McLamb v. T.P. Inc., 173 N.C. App. 586, 619 S.E.2d 577 (2005) with Benson v. Chalfonte Dev. Corp., 348 So. 2d 557 (Fla. Dist. Ct. App. 1976).

[561] A purported exercise by the optionee that changes the terms of the option is ineffective; see Sung v. Hamilton, 676 F.Supp.2d 990 (D. Haw. 2009); Elderkin v. Carroll, 403 Md. 343, 941 A.2d 1127 (2008); Zafarani v. Gluck, 40 A.D.3d 1082, 837 N.Y.S.2d 252 (2007).

[562] See Temkin, Too Much Good Faith in Real Estate Purchase Agreements? Give Me an Option, 34 Kan.L.Rev. 43 (1985).

[563] See § 6.65, supra; Pack 2000, Inc. v. Cushman, 311 Conn. 662, 89 A.3d 869 (2014) (in order to exercise option, tenant must be in substantial compliance with lease); Bayer v. Showmotion, Inc., 292 Conn. 381, 973

An option is not a contract of sale, since it does not impose any duty on the purchaser to buy the property.[564] However, some purported contracts of sale are in fact options. If the contract provides that, in the event of the purchaser's breach, the vendor's sole remedy is the retention of the earnest money or some other sum as liquidated damages,[565] the practical effect is to render the contract nothing more than an option.[566]

The drafting of options is a more exacting process than the parties sometimes realize. There is a temptation to think of the option as a short, simple document that merely describes the land and the parties and sets forth the method of exercising the option and the selling price.[567] However, if the option is exercised it will become a binding contract of sale. Hence it should contain provisions dealing with every matter that would be included in a well-drawn contract; this may be conveniently done by attaching the form of contract as an appendix to the option.[568] It must at a minimum contain the elements essential to satisfy the statute of frauds,[569] for while the option itself may not be within the coverage of the statute, the contract that results from its exercise surely

A.2d 1229 (2009) (once option is exercised, lease is extinguished and tenant owes no more rent); King v. Conley, 87 N.E.3d 1146 (Ind. Ct. App. 2018) (tenant validly exercised option before landlord declared an event of default); Ebrecht v. Ponchatoula Farm Bureau Ass'n, 498 So.2d 55 (La.App. 1986) (right of first refusal in lease is limited to the term of the lease); Moosavideen v. Garrett, 300 S.W.3d 791 (Tex. App. 2008) (option is exercisable irrespective of tenant's default); Luccia v. Ross, 274 S.W.3d 140 (Tex. App. 2008) (tenant could exercise option a second time after first sale failed to close).

[564] N. Shore Energy, L.L.C. v. Harkins, 501 S.W.3d 598 (Tex. 2016); A contract of sale is formed only when the option is exercised; see Am. Canadian Expeditions, Ltd. v. Gauley River Corp., 221 W. Va. 442, 655 S.E.2d 188 (2007). See also Robinson v. Gwinnett Cty., 290 Ga. 470, 722 S.E.2d 59 (2012) (holder of unexercised right of first refusal had no right to any part of condemnation award).

[565] Ordinarily the mere presence of a liquidated damages clause does not preclude the vendor from claiming non-damage remedies, such as specific performance. However, an express preclusion of such remedies will be given effect. See § 10.4 note 162 supra.

[566] See, e.g., Cutter Dev. Corp. v. Peluso, 212 Conn. 107, 561 A.2d 926 (1989) (concurring opinion); Dodek v. CF 16 Corp., 537 A.2d 1086 (D.C.App. 1988); Pace v. Garcia, 631 F.Supp. 1417 (W.D.Tex. 1986). In some contexts the distinction between an option and a contract limiting the vendor to liquidated damages may be significant. See Pollard v. City of Bozeman, 228 Mont. 176, 741 P.2d 776 (1987) (if document is a contract, purchaser is responsible for property taxes); Interactive Properties Corp. v. Blue Cross & Blue Shield of Greater New York, 114 Misc.2d 255, 450 N.Y.S.2d 1001 (1982) (if document is a contract, real estate broker has earned a commission); Ziegler Furniture & Funeral Home, Inc. v. Cicmanec, 709 N.W.2d 350 (S.D. 2006) (document was a firm contract, though labeled an option).

[567] Compare Busching v. Griffin, 542 So.2d 860 (Miss. 1989) (option failed to mention the type of deed, the quality of the title, taxes, or the method by which the purchase price would be paid, but court nonetheless found option enforceable) with Christmas v. Turkin, 148 Ariz. 602, 716 P.2d 59 (1986) (option failed to state manner in which purchase price would be paid; held too indefinite to be enforced) and Mukilteo Ret. Apartments, L.L.C. v. Mukilteo Inv'rs L.P., 176 Wash. App. 244, 310 P.3d 814 (2013) (option must contain a method of determining the sale price).

[568] F & S Pharmacy, Inc. v. Dandra Realty Corp., 302 A.D.2d 204, 754 N.Y.S.2d 256 (2003) (optionor demanded that optionee accept vendor financing, a term not included in the option); Guthmiller Farms, LLP v. Guthmiller, 2013 N.D. 248, 840 N.W.2d 636 (2013) (after exercise, parties may negotiate nonessential terms of contract of sale); Kruse v. Hemp, 121 Wn.2d 715, 853 P.2d 1373 (Wash. 1993) (form of contract must be attached to option).

[569] Cases finding options unenforceable include Drost v. Hill, 639 So.2d 105 (no purchase price stated); Patellis v. 100 Galleria Parkway Assoc., 214 Ga.App. 154, 447 S.E.2d 113 (Ga. App.1994) (no rent stated in option to renew lease); Jones v. Consolidated Rail Corp., 33 Mass.App.Ct. 918, 597 N.E.2d 1375 (Mass.App. 1992) (description of land insufficient). Cf. Carolan v. Nelson, 226 S.W.3d 923, 926 (Mo. Ct. App. 2007) (option was enforceable despite omitting to state a closing date for the sale). The option itself is not a contract for the sale of land, and hence is outside the statute; see W.M., R.W., and T.R. Bowler v. TMG Partnership, 357 N.W.2d 109 (Minn.App. 1984); cf. Trear v. Chamberlain, 53 Kan. App. 2d 385, 388 P.3d 607 (2017). There is no requirement that the option must be exercised in writing, provided that other writings exist to satisfy the statute; Kaplan v. Lippman, 75 N.Y.2d 320, 552 N.Y.S.2d 903, 552 N.E.2d 151 (1990).

will be.[570] It is also important that the precise manner of exercise of the option be spelled out; countless disputes have occurred over this matter.[571]

The optionee generally pays cash for the option itself. In the simplest case there is only a single payment at the time the option is entered into. Other, more complex, arrangements are possible, under which the optionee pays additional amounts at prescribed intervals in order to extend the option's life.[572]

The sale price is a particularly critical feature of an option, and may be handled in one of several ways. Many options are for a stated price. Alternatively, the option may describe a method of arriving at the price, as by an appraisal to be conducted in the future[573] or by the application of an external index such as the Consumer Price Index to an initially stated amount.[574] In no event should the price be left to future agreement of the parties.[575] The consideration paid for the option itself may or may not be credited against the price if the option is exercised. Likewise, if the option is contained in a lease, a provision may be included crediting the rental payments against the selling price.[576]

Time is considered essential in the exercise of an option even if it is not stated to be such; hence, the optionee who is even slightly tardy loses the power to exercise.[577] The courts are also quite rigorous in enforcing the option's terms with respect to the place and manner of exercise; substantial performance is usually not enough.[578] Thus it is well for the drafter to specify these matters with great precision.

---

[570] Old Quarry Ass'n v. Hickey, 659 F.Supp. 1064 (D.Conn. 1986); Prestenbach v. Collins, 159 So. 3d 531 (Miss. 2014); McCormick v. Bechtol, 68 A.D.3d 1376, 891 N.Y.S.2d 188 (2009).

[571] Karakehian v. Boyer, 900 P.2d 1273 (Colo.App. 1994), affirmed 915 P.2d 1295 (Colo. 1996) (where no method of exercise is specified, any clear manifestation of intent to exercise by optionee is sufficient).

[572] See, e.g., U.S. Gen., Inc. v. Jenson, 128 P.3d 56 (Utah Ct. App. 2005).

[573] Wells v. Gootrad, 112 Idaho 912, 736 P.2d 1366 (App. 1987) (where parties did not follow option's procedure for obtaining appraisal, court had authority to appoint appraiser); Castrucci v. Young, 33 Ohio Misc.2d 41, 515 N.E.2d 658 (1986) (option to purchase for "reasonable market value" was enforceable, since the value was readily ascertainable).

[574] Southeast Cinema Entm't, Inc. v. P.B. Realty, Inc., 585 F.Supp.2d 754 (D.S.C. 2008). If the option itself fails to establish the price or a mechanism for determining it, the court may fix the price as the current market value; Kaufman v. Lassiter, 520 So.2d 692 (Fla.App. 1988), appeal after remand 563 So.2d 209 (1990).

[575] Abbott v. Abbott, 2016 WL 3976760 (Tenn. Ct. App. 2016).

[576] See Conner v. Alvarez, 285 S.C. 97, 328 S.E.2d 334 (1985).

[577] Finkle v. Gulf & Western Mfg. Co., 744 F.2d 1015 (3d Cir. 1984); Rice v. Wood, 91 N.C.App. 262, 371 S.E.2d 500 (1988); TST, Ltd. v. Houston, 256 Ga. 679, 353 S.E.2d 26 (1987); Lewis v. Chase, 23 Mass.App. 673, 505 N.E.2d 211 (1987); Martin v. Williams, 172 So. 3d 782 (Miss. Ct. App. 2013); Richmond v. Miele, 30 A.D.3d 575, 817 N.Y.S.2d 157 (2006); Probus Properties v. Kirby, 200 S.W.3d 258 (Tex. App. 2006); Otis Hous. Ass'n, Inc. v. Ha, 140 Wash. App. 470, 164 P.3d 511 (2007), aff'd on other grounds, 165 Wash. 2d 582, 201 P.3d 309 (2009); Annot., 87 A.L.R.3d 805 (1978); Annot., 72 A.L.R.2d 1127 (1960). Contra, where the option was "buried" in a lease and stated ambiguously, see Taylor v. Carbajal, 304 S.W.3d 585 (Tex. App. 2010). New York is the only jurisdiction consistently indicating a willingness to give the optionee relief from tardy exercise where the optionor has not been prejudiced and the optionee would otherwise suffer a loss out of proportion to his or her fault; see Tritt v. Huffman & Boyle Co., 121 A.D.2d 531, 503 N.Y.S.2d 842 (1986), appeal denied 68 N.Y.2d 611, 510 N.Y.S.2d 1025, 502 N.E.2d 1007 (1986). See also Pardee v. Jolly, 163 Wash. 2d 558, 182 P.3d 967 (2008). In most jurisdictions the "mailbox rule" followed in contract acceptance cases is not applicable to an option; unless the parties specifically agree to exercise by deposit in the mails, actual receipt of the notice of exercise within the allotted time is necessary. See Velez Santiago v. United States, 642 F.Supp. 267 (D.P.R. 1986); Musgrove v. Long, 248 Ga. 902, 287 S.E.2d 23 (1982).

[578] Best v. Miranda, 229 Ariz. 246, 274 P.3d 516 (App. 2012) (exercise required payment of purchase price); Stratman v. Dietrich, 765 P.2d 603 (Colo.App. 1988); Howard-Arnold, Inc. v. T.N.T. Realty, Inc., 315 Conn. 596, 109 A.3d 473 (2015); Pack 2000, Inc. v. Cushman, 311 Conn. 662, 676, 89 A.3d 869, 879 (2014) (exercise required payment of a portion of purchase price); Metro Dev. Grp., L.L.C. v. 3D-C & C, Inc., 941 So. 2d 11 (Fla. Dist. Ct. App. 2006); Estate of Collins v. McKinney, 936 N.E.2d 252 (Ind. Ct. App. 2010) (exercise did not require payment of purchase price); Duffy v. Casady, 29 Kan. App. 2d 549, 28 P.3d 1040 (2001); Brick

When an optionor transfers optioned property, the option remains effective against the land if the transferee has actual or constructive notice of it.[579] In most jurisdictions the recording acts apply to options, so that recordation will provide constructive notice.[580] This result is perhaps surprising, since under the doctrine of equitable conversion, an unexercised option is not yet, for most purposes, an interest in real property.[581] But applicability of the recording acts is obviously of immense practical utility.[582]

Preemptive rights. The most common preemptive right is a right of first refusal. Such a right is a conditional option; the holder can exercise it only if the seller first decides to accept some other person's offer to buy the property.[583] The holder of the preemptive right then has the option to purchase the property, typically at the same price and on the same terms as the third party's offer.[584] If the holder declines to exercise the right, the owner is free to sell to the third party.[585] Less commonly, the holder may have the right to buy at a fixed price or at some percentage of the third party's offering

---

Plaza, Inc. v. Humble Oil & Ref. Co., 218 N.J. Super. 101, 526 A.2d 1139 (App. Div. 1987); Master Builders, Inc. v. Cabbell, 95 N.M. 371, 622 P.2d 276 (1980); Miller v. Russell, 217 N.C. App. 431, 720 S.E.2d 760 (2011); Deckert v. McCormick, 2014 N.D. 231, 857 N.W.2d 355 (2014). Occasionally a court will give relief for an optionee's late or improper exercise, particularly if the infraction is minor and inadvertent, and nonenforcement would impose significant financial loss; see, e.g., Brunswick Hills Racquet Club, Inc. v. Route 18 Shopping Ctr. Assocs., 182 N.J. 210, 864 A.2d 387 (2005); P.L. Dev., Inc. v. Fetterman, 293 A.D.2d 657, 740 N.Y.S.2d 634 (2002); Cornish Coll. of the Arts v. 1000 Virginia Ltd. P'ship, 158 Wash. App. 203, 242 P.3d 1 (2010); Annot., 27 A.L.R. 4th 266 (1984). Where the option does not state the method of exercise, it can be exercised by tender of the purchase price; Tristram's Group, Inc. v. Morrow, 22 Mass.App.Ct. 980, 496 N.E.2d 176 (1986); Petition of Hilltop Development, 342 N.W.2d 344 (Minn. 1984). Once the option is exercised, the parties have a duty to close the sale within a reasonable time unless otherwise stated; Meccariello v. DiPasquale, 35 A.D.3d 678, 826 N.Y.S.2d 702 (2006).

[579] Spokane School Dist. No. 81 v. Parzybok, 96 Wn.2d 95, 633 P.2d 1324 (1981); Dunlap v. Fort Mohave Farms, Inc., 89 Ariz. 387, 363 P.2d 194 (1961). See generally Annot., 17 A.L.R.2d 331 (1951). A transfer of the land does not relieve the optionor of liability for performance of the option, and if the transferee refuses to perform, the optionor may be liable in damages; Martinesi v. Tidmore, 158 Ariz. 53, 760 P.2d 1102 (App. 1988).

[580] See § 11.9 n. 508 infra; Wachovia Bank v. Lifetime Indus., Inc., 145 Cal. App. 4th 1039, 52 Cal. Rptr. 3d 168 (2006) (purchaser's priority under contract of sale may relate back to date of recording of option).

[581] See Niagara Falls Redevelopment, LLC v. Cerrone, 28 A.D.3d 1138, 814 N.Y.S.2d 427 (2006); Bauserman v. Digiulian, 224 Va. 414, 297 S.E.2d 671 (1982); Eddington v. Turner, 27 Del.Ch. 411, 38 A.2d 738 (1944). See generally § 10.13 supra.

[582] See, e.g., Wachovia Bank v. Lifetime Indus., Inc., 145 Cal. App. 4th 1039, 52 Cal. Rptr. 3d 168 (2006).

[583] Keeper's, Inc. v. ATGCKG Realestate, LLC, 146 Conn. App. 789, 80 A.3d 88 (2013). All of the essential terms of the third party's offer must be communicated to the right-holder; see Roeland v. Trucano, 214 P.3d 343 (Alaska 2009); T.W. Nickerson, Inc. v. Fleet Nat. Bank, 73 Mass. App. Ct. 434, 898 N.E.2d 868 (2009), rev'd in part, 456 Mass. 562, 924 N.E.2d 696 (2010).

[584] Mamo v. Skvirsky, 960 A.2d 595 (D.C. 2008); Walters v. Sporer, 298 Neb. 536, 905 N.W.2d 70 (2017) (right of first refusal may be reserved in a deed); Advanced Recycling Sys., LLC v. Southeast Properties Ltd. P'ship, 2010 S.D. 70, 787 N.W.2d 778 (2010); See also FWT, Inc. v. Haskin Wallace Mason Prop. Mgmt., L.L.P., 301 S.W.3d 787 (Tex. App. 2009) (right holder must meet all conditions of third party's offer except those that were "not commercially reasonable, were imposed in bad faith, or were specifically designed to defeat" the right); St. George's Dragons, L.P. v. Newport Real Estate Grp., L.L.C., 407 N.J. Super. 464, 971 A.2d 1087 (App. Div. 2009) (same). The owner and the third party may not change the terms of the offer while the right-holder's decision is pending; see In re Smith Trust, 480 Mich. 19, 745 N.W.2d 754 (2008). Similarly, the right-holder may not elect to buy on terms that differ materially from the third party's offer. See Jones v. Stahr, 16 Neb. App. 596, 746 N.W.2d 394 (2008); Fienberg v. Hassan, 77 Mass. App. Ct. 901, 928 N.E.2d 356 (2010) (holder of right must match closing date in third party's offer); Hicks v. Castille, 313 S.W.3d 874 (Tex. App. 2010); Bischoff v. Bletz, 188 Vt. 47, 998 A.2d 705 (2010).

[585] Mercy Hosp. v. McNulty, 2015 WL 576016 (Iowa Ct. App. 2015) (unpublished). Like ordinary options, rights of first refusal must be exercised strictly according to their terms; Richmond v. EBI, Inc., 53 So. 3d 859 (Miss. Ct. App. 2011).

price.[586] Where the holder must match a third party's offer, the holder obviously has a right to be informed clearly of the terms of that offer.[587] Rights of first refusal are frequently given to tenants under leases, and among tenants in common.[588]

Under a similar but less commonly used type of preemptive right, termed a "right of first offer," the holder of the right can buy the property at the fixed price at which the owner offers it for sale, whether a third party has offered to buy it or not.[589]

Rights of first refusal are problematic in many ways.[590] Where the price is fixed by the third party's offer, the implicit assumption is that the third party will wish to buy exactly the land subject to the right. But difficult problems of construction arise if the third party's offer is to purchase a larger parcel that includes the subject property,[591] or to purchase only a part of the subject property. Similarly, if the third party's offer is an exchange of land rather than money, or is somehow unique in financing or other terms, and consequently is difficult or impossible for the holder of the right to match, is the right lost, or should the court consider "commercial realities" and allow the holder to tender a reasonable approximation of the third party's offer?[592] Is the right triggered by

---

[586] Shaffer v. Bellows, 260 P.3d 1064 (Alaska 2011). If the method of determining the price is stated ambiguously, the court may conclude that the right is unenforceable; see Crestview Builders, Inc. v. Noggle Family Ltd. P'ship, 352 Ill. App. 3d 1182, 816 N.E.2d 1132 (2004); Doyle v. McNulty, 478 A.2d 577 (R.I. 1984).

[587] Hancock v. Dusenberry, 110 Idaho 147, 715 P.2d 360 (App. 1986); Jarvis v. Peltier, 400 S.W.3d 644 (Tex. App. 2013).

[588] See, e.g., LEG Investments v. Boxler, 183 Cal. App. 4th 484, 107 Cal. Rptr. 3d 519 (2010) (rights of first refusal between cotenants did not preclude them from seeking partition); Kozak v. Porada, 154 A.D.3d 1242, 63 N.Y.S.3d 594 (2017) (rights of first refusal among cotenants violated Rule Against Perpetuities).

[589] See Bill Signs Trucking, LLC v. Signs Family Ltd. P'ship, 157 Cal. App. 4th 1515, 69 Cal. Rptr. 3d 589 (2007); Eastbanc, Inc. v. Georgetown Park Assocs. II, L.P., 940 A.2d 996 (D.C. 2008); Constellation Development, LLC v. Western Trust Co., 2016 N.D. 141, 882 N.W.2d 238 (2016); Kelly v. Ammex Tax & Duty Free Shops W., Inc., 162 Wash. App. 825, 256 P.3d 1255 (2011). See also Stephens v. Trust For Pub. Land, 475 F.Supp.2d 1299 (N.D. Ga. 2007) (right of first offer for a price to be determined by future appraisal was valid).

[590] However, creation of a right of first refusal in a third party does not rule afoul of the rule against a reservation of an interest in land to a stranger; Peters v. Smolian, 154 A.D.3d 980, 63 N.Y.S.3d 436 (N.Y. App. Div. 2017); § 11.1 infra at notes 57–58.

[591] Holding that the right to purchase is triggered by a third party offer to buy a larger parcel, see Tiger, Inc. v. Time Warner Entertainment Co., 26 F.Supp.2d 1011 (N.D. Ohio 1998); Waste Connections of Kansas, Inc. v. Ritchie Corp., 296 Kan. 943, 971, 298 P.3d 250, 269 (2013); Stuart v. Stammen, 590 N.W.2d 224 (N.D. 1999); Boyd & Mahoney v. Chevron U.S.A., 419 Pa.Super. 24, 614 A.2d 1191 (Pa.Super. 1992); Dowling Family P'ship v. Midland Farms, 865 N.W.2d 854 (S.D. 2015); Landa v. Century 21 Simmons & Co., 237 Va. 374, 377 S.E.2d 416 (1989). Contra, see Crow-Spieker No. 23 v. Helms Const. & Dev. Co., 103 Nev. 1, 731 P.2d 348 (1987) (right to purchase is not triggered by a third party offer to buy a larger parcel, provided the sale is not "engineered" to avoid the right; the right continues to be held in an unripened or suspended state until an offer for the subject land alone is received); Rome Sav. Bank v. B.W. Husted & Son, Inc., 171 A.D.2d 1048, 569 N.Y.S.2d 236 (1991) (same); Raymond v. Steen, 882 P.2d 852 (Wyo. 1994) (same). Cf. Sawyer v. Firestone, 513 A.2d 36 (R.I. 1986) (preemptive right to purchase is not triggered by a proposed sale of a larger parcel to a third party, but the holder of the right can enjoin the sale). See Annot., 34 A.L.R.4th 1217 (1984); Daskal, Rights of First Refusal and the Package Deal, 22 Ford. Urb. L.J. 461 (1995).

[592] See Hewatt v. Leppert, 259 Ga. 112, 376 S.E.2d 883 (1989) (giving an option to purchase to a third party does not trigger a right of first refusal, but nonetheless breaches it, since it takes the property off the market); Vincent v. Doebert, 183 Ill. App.3d 1081, 132 Ill.Dec. 293, 539 N.E.2d 856 (1989) (third party's offer was accompanied by a guaranty by a guarantor with a net worth of $10 million; while holder of the right of first refusal could not match this precisely, his offer was sufficiently close to be enforceable); Ellis v. Chevron, U.S.A., Inc., 201 Cal.App.3d 132, 246 Cal. Rptr. 863 (1988) (third party offered to lease the subject property and additional land, and to build a large retail store on both parcels; when holder of right declined to match the offer to acquire the additional property or to build the building; owner had no duty to accept holder's offer). The problem was well described in C. Robert Nattress & Associates v. CIDCO, 184 Cal.App.3d 55, 229 Cal.Rptr. 33, 43 (1986):

> If the literal matching of terms were required, a triggering offeror could by offering some unique consideration such as existing trust deed notes, a bag of diamonds or a herd of Arabian horses,

a foreclosure or other judicially-ordered sale,[593] a gift,[594] a restructuring among related corporations,[595] or a testamentary transfer[596] to a third party? What about a long-term lease to a third party?[597] If the holder of the right declines to exercise it when a third-party offer is made, but that offer does not result in a sale, is the right still exercisable when the owner subsequently wishes to sell to a different third party?[598] Careful drafting (something rarely found in rights of first refusal) is necessary to resolve these questions.

If the owner of property subject to a right of first refusal sells to a third party who has notice of the right, without giving the holder of the right appropriate notice and an opportunity to exercise the right, the right will typically survive the sale and continue to be exercisable against the third party.[599] The owner may also be held liable for damages

---

effectively defeat the lessee's right of first refusal. How would the holder of the right of first refusal in such a case make an offer to exercise the right of first refusal on the same terms and conditions as in the triggering offer?

The court concluded that only a reasonable economic equivalence, and not a precise matching of terms, was required. See also Castle Properties, Inc. v. Wasilla Lake Church of the Nazarene, 347 P.3d 990 (Alaska 2015); Arden Group, Inc. v. Burk, 45 Cal.App.4th 1409, 53 Cal.Rptr.2d 492 (Cal.App. 1996). But see Matson v. Emory, 36 Wn.App. 681, 676 P.2d 1029 (1984).

[593] Finding the right of first refusal was not triggered, see Tadros v. Middlebury Medical Center, Inc., 263 Conn. 235, 820 A.2d 230 (2003) (foreclosure sale); Pecora v. Berlin, 62 So. 3d 28, 31 (Fla. Dist. Ct. App. 2011) (sale by court-appointed receiver); Royal Oldsmobile Co. v. Heisler Props. L.L.C., 58 So.3d 483 (La. Ct. App. 2010) (involuntary bankruptcy sale); Huntington Nat. Bank v. Cornelius, 80 A.D.3d 245, 914 N.Y.S.2d 327 (2010) (foreclosure sale); Tuminno v. Waite, 110 A.D.3d 1456, 972 N.Y.S.2d 775 (2013) (partition); Wells Fargo Bank, N.A. v. Michael, 993 N.E.2d 786 (Ohio Ct. App. 2013) (foreclosure sale). Finding the right of first refusal was triggered, see Hornsby v. Holt, 257 Ga. 341, 359 S.E.2d 646 (1987) (foreclosure by trustee under power of sale); Cities Serv. Oil Co. v. Estes, 208 Va. 44, 155 S.E.2d 59 (1967) (estate sale).

[594] Park Station Ltd. P'ship, LLLP v. Bosse, 378 Md. 122, 835 A.2d 646 (2003) (right not triggered by gift to charity); Christ Holdings, L.L.C. v. Schleappi, 67 N.E.3d 47 (Ohio Ct. App. 2016) (right could be triggered by gifts, leases, or licenses); Mericle v. Wolf, 386 Pa.Super. 82, 562 A.2d 364 (1989) (same); Blue Ridge Bank & Tr. Co. v. Trosen, 309 S.W.3d 812 (Mo. Ct. App. 2010) (right not triggered by intrafamily transfer). See also Kowalsky v. Familia, 71 Misc. 2d 287, 336 N.Y.S.2d 37 (Sup. Ct. 1972) (right not triggered by a sale to county under threat of condemnation).

[595] Evans v. SC Southfield Twelve Assocs., LLC, 208 F. App'x 403 (6th Cir. 2006) (transfer by owners to LLC formed by them did not trigger right of first refusal); Texaco Antilles Ltd. v. Creque, 273 F.Supp.2d 660 (D.V.I. 2003) (transfer of assets in connection with a corporate restructuring did not trigger right of first refusal).

[596] Smith v. Estate of La Tray, 161 A.D.2d 1178, 555 N.Y.S.2d 968 (1990) (testamentary transfer did not trigger right of first refusal); Brooks v. Terteling, 107 Idaho 262, 688 P.2d 1167 (1984) (same).

[597] Wilson v. Whinery, 37 Wn.App. 24, 678 P.2d 354 (1984) (long-term lease to third party triggered right of first refusal). See also Rollins v. Stokes, 123 Cal.App.3d 701, 176 Cal.Rptr. 835, 840 (1981) (granting of option to purchase to a third party triggered right of first refusal).

[598] See Meridian Bowling Lanes, Inc. v. Meridian Athletic Ass'n, Inc., 105 Idaho 509, 670 P.2d 1294 (1983). If the holder declines to exercise the right and the property is sold to a third party, the right will probably be construed as expiring; see MS Real Estate Holdings, LLC v. Donald P. Fox Family Tr., 362 Wis. 2d 258, 285, 864 N.W.2d 83, 96 (2015).

[599] This assumes, of course, that the third party purchaser has notice of the right, and hence is not a bona fide purchaser under the applicable recording act. Briggs v. Sylvestri, 49 Conn.App. 297, 714 A.2d 56 (Conn.App. 1998); Hornsby v. Holt, 257 Ga. 341, 359 S.E.2d 646 (1987); Hongsermeier v. Devall, 16 Neb. App. 379, 744 N.W.2d 481 (2008); Legacy Vulcan Corp. v. Garren, 222 N.C. App. 445, 731 S.E.2d 223 (2012); Stuart v. Stammen, 590 N.W.2d 224 (N.D. 1999); Sorrell v. Micomonaco, 89 N.E.3d 21, 32 (Ohio Ct. App. 2017); McCullough v. Silverfield, 215 S.W.3d 356 (Tenn. Ct. App. 2006). See also Natl. City Bank v. Welch, 188 Ohio App. 3d 641, 936 N.E.2d 539 (2010) (right continued to be enforceable against mortgagee who obtained title to land through foreclosure, under principles of covenants running with land); Jewish Ctr. for Aged v. BSPM Trustees, Inc., 295 S.W.3d 513 (Mo. Ct. App. 2009) (similar). But see Belton Chopper 58, LLC v. N. Cass Dev., LLC, 496 S.W.3d 529 (Mo. Ct. App. 2016) (foreclosure sale did not trigger, but terminated right of first refusal).

for breaching the right of first refusal, and if a sufficient degree of culpability is shown, punitive damages may be assessed.[600]

Restraints on alienation. A right of first refusal is inevitably, by its nature, a drag on the property's marketability, since any prospective third party purchaser must recognize that the time and effort to prepare an offer to purchase may be wasted if the holder exercises the right. Nonetheless, courts generally hold rights of first refusal to be restraints on alienation and strike them down only if they contain unreasonable terms.[601] Three terms in particular are usually analyzed.[602] First, is the right's duration reasonable?[603] Second, is the price a reasonable reflection of market value? A price that must match a third-party offer is not a problem.[604] However, in an inflationary market, almost all fixed-price rights of first refusal will eventually become unreasonably low and are likely to be held unenforceable if the right has a long or unlimited duration.[605] Note that ordinary options as well as rights of first refusal may be struck down on the first and second grounds.[606] Third, the party holding the right of first refusal must be limited to a reasonable time in exercising it after receiving notice of the third party's offer.[607] Unless a reasonable limitation is imposed, the holder of the right can effectively tie up the property and kill any prospective sale simply by delaying his or her response until the prospective purchaser becomes tired of waiting and withdraws the offer.

Rule against Perpetuities. The application of the Rule against Perpetuities has raised persistent problems with options and rights of first refusal.[608] Cases that apply the Rule generally assume or argue that an option is similar to a springing executory

---

[600] Arlington State Bank v. Colvin, 545 N.E.2d 572 (Ind.App. 1989) (punitive damages based on proof of malice, fraud, gross negligence, or oppressive conduct).

[601] See Restatement (Third) of Property (Servitudes), § 3.3 cmt. b (2000).

[602] See Bortolotti v. Hayden, 449 Mass. 193, 204, 866 N.E.2d 882, 890 (2007); SKI, Ltd. v. Mountainside Properties, Inc., 198 Vt. 384, 114 A.3d 1169 (2015).

[603] See, e.g., Iglehart v. Phillips, 383 So. 2d 610 (Fla. 1980); Peavey v. Reynolds, 946 So. 2d 1125 (Fla. Dist. Ct. App. 2006) (two-year lease with option to renew indefinitely was invalid restraint on alienation); New Bar P'ship v. Martin, 221 N.C. App. 302, 729 S.E.2d 675 (2012) (right of first refusal extending beyond 21-year perpetuities period was an unreasonable restraint and void). But see Smurfit-Stone Container Enterprises, Inc. v. Zion Jacksonville Ltd. P'ship, 52 So. 3d 55 (Fla. Dist. Ct. App. 2010), upholding a right of first offer with unlimited duration. See also Randolph v. Reisig, 272 Mich. App. 331, 727 N.W.2d 388 (2006), limiting a preemptive right to the lifetimes of the parties unless by express terms it had a longer life.

[604] Bortolotti v. Hayden, id.; Stephens v. Trust for Pub. Land, 475 F.Supp.2d 1299 (N.D. Ga. 2007) (price to be determined by appraisal upheld). But see Uno Restaurants, Inc. v. Boston Kenmore Realty Corp., 441 Mass. 376, 805 N.E.2d 957 (2004) (holder was required to match third party's offer made in good faith, even though it was higher than market value).

[605] Zecco v. Hess Corp., 777 F.Supp.2d 207, 216 (D. Mass. 2011); Mr. Sign Sign Studios, Inc. v. Miguel, 877 So. 2d 47 (Fla. Dist. Ct. App. 2004); Iglehart v. Phillips, 383 So. 2d 610 (Fla. 1980); Urquhart v. Teller, 288 Mont. 497, 958 P.2d 714 (Mont.1998); Herrmann v. AMD Realty, Inc., 8 A.D.3d 619, 779 N.Y.S.2d 560 (2004); Kowalsky v. Familia, 71 Misc. 2d 287, 290, 336 N.Y.S.2d 37, 40 (Sup. Ct. 1972); Taylor v. Miller, 215 N.C. App. 558, 715 S.E.2d 643 (2011); Laska v. Barr, 2018 S.D. 6, 907 N.W.2d 47 (2018).

[606] Sander v. Ball, 781 So.2d 527 (Fla. Ct. App. 2001) (court refused to reform option by providing a time limit); Allentown Patriots, Inc. v. City of Allentown, 162 A.3d 1187 (Pa. Commw. Ct. 2017) (option without stated time limit will be limited by court to a reasonable time); S.C. Elec. & Gas Co. v. Hartough, 375 S.C. 541, 654 S.E.2d 87 (Ct. App. 2007) (same). Cf. Bakken v. Duchscher, 827 N.W.2d 17 (N.D. 2013) (option without stated time limit could be exercised beyond 10-year period).

[607] Hare v. McClellan, 234 Conn. 581, 662 A.2d 1242 (Conn. 1995); Navasota Res., L.P. v. First Source Texas, Inc., 249 S.W.3d 526 (Tex. App. 2008); Girard v. Myers, 39 Wn.App. 577, 694 P.2d 678 (1985). See also McNabb v. Barrett, 257 S.W.3d 166, 174 (Mo. Ct. App. 2008) (response by right holder must be made within a reasonable time). The negative impact on marketability can be minimized by giving the holder of the right a very short time period (e.g., 24 or 48 hours) to exercise, but this is often not done.

[608] On the operation of the Rule, see generally §§ 3.17–.18 supra.

interest, and hence is void unless it must be exercised or expire no later than 21 years after some life in being at its creation.[609] Since no human life is usually involved in measuring an option's duration,[610] in most cases an option that can be exercised more than 21 years after the date of its creation will be declared void. However, if the option states no time limit at all, some courts are willing to construe it as requiring exercise within a reasonable time (which surely must be less than 21 years), and hence as valid.[611] Moreover, the Rule is not applied to an option granted to a tenant under a lease, to renew the term or buy the property, and exercisable only within the term of the lease, even if the term is longer than 21 years.[612]

Whether the Rule should be applied to options at all is open to very serious doubt on both theoretical and practical grounds, and a number of courts have rejected its application.[613] An option is merely an irrevocable offer to sell, and until exercised creates no present or future interest in the land.[614] Moreover, even options for very long terms do not appear to raise serious problems of practical inalienability of land titles. Land subject to an option may be "off the market" in the sense that the owner is not actively attempting to sell it, but it is not, strictly speaking, inalienable, since a conveyance executed by both the optionor and the optionee will pass good title. The necessity of the buyer's negotiating with both and getting both signatures may be somewhat burdensome, but hardly more so than, for example, obtaining the signatures of two

---

[609] This notion apparently originated with London & S.W. Ry. Co. v. Gomm, 20 Ch. 562 (1882). See, e.g., Nash v. Scott, 62 Ark.App. 8, 966 S.W.2d 936 (1998); Fallschase Devel. Corp. v. Blakey, 696 So.2d 833 (Fla.App. 1997); Schafer v. Deszcz, 120 Ohio App.3d 410, 698 N.E.2d 60 (1997); Symphony Space, Inc. v. Pergola Properties, Inc., 88 N.Y.2d 466, 646 N.Y.S.2d 641, 669 N.E.2d 799 (1996); Buck v. Banks, 668 N.E.2d 1259 (Ind.App. 1996). See also Selig v. State Highway Admin., 383 Md. 655, 861 A.2d 710 (2004) (Rule against Perpetuities did not apply to right of first refusal mandated by statute).

[610] Kozak v. Porada, 154 A.D.3d 1242, 63 N.Y.S.3d 594 (2017), pointing out that the right of first refusal before the court was not intended to terminate at the deaths of any of the parties. But a court may be able to construe the right as limited to the lifetimes of the holders, and thus to escape the Rule Against Perpetuities; see In re Estate of Owen, 855 N.E.2d 603 (Ind. Ct. App. 2006); Nickels v. Cohn, 764 S.W.2d 124 (Mo.App. 1989); Firebaugh v. Whitehead, 263 Va. 398, 559 S.E.2d 611 (2002).

[611] See, e.g., Kellner v. Bartman, 250 Ill.App.3d 1030, 620 N.E.2d 607 (1993) (limited to lifetimes of the parties); Pinewood Rd., Inc. v. Kuntz, 2017 WL 361172 (Mass. Land Ct. 2017); Coulter & Smith, Ltd. v. Russell, 966 P.2d 852 (Utah 1998).

[612] Shaver v. Clanton, 26 Cal.App.4th 568, 31 Cal. Rptr.2d 595 (Cal.App. 1994); Venture Stores, Inc. v. Pacific Beach Co. Inc., 980 S.W.2d 176 (Mo.App. 1998); Bleecker St. Tenants Corp. v. Bleeker Jones LLC, 16 N.Y.3d 272, 945 N.E.2d 484 (2011); Moosavideen v. Garrett, 300 S.W.3d 791 (Tex. App. 2008) (option exercisable 70 years into 99-year lease); Citgo Petroleum Corp. v. Hopper, 245 Va. 363, 429 S.E.2d 6 (Va. 1993). See Berg, Long-Term Options and the Rule Against Perpetuities, 37 Cal L Rev 1, 22 (1949). The exemption for options appurtenant to leases originated in Bridges v Hitchcock, 5 Bro PC 6, 2 ER 498 (House of Lords 1715).

[613] Weber v. Texas Co., 83 F.2d 807, 808 (5th Cir.), cert. denied, 299 U.S. 561, 57 S.Ct. 23, 81 L.Ed. 413 (1936) (rights to purchase oil not within traditional purpose of rule); Greenshields v. Warren Petroleum Corp., 248 F.2d 61, 71 (10th Cir.), cert. denied, 355 U.S. 907, 78 S.Ct. 334 (1957); Shaver v. Clanton, 26 Cal. App. 4th 568, 31 Cal. Rptr. 2d 595 (1994); Pathmark Stores, Inc. v. 3821 Assocs., L.P., 663 A.2d 1189 (Del. Ch. 1995); Old Port Cove Holdings, Inc. v. Old Port Cove Condo. Assoc. One, Inc., 986 So.2d 1279 (Fla. 2008); Randolph v. Reisig, 272 Mich. App. 331, 727 N.W.2d 388 (2006); Hartnett v. Jones, 629 P.2d 1357, 1363 (Wyo. 1981). Restatement (Third) of Prop. (Servitudes) § 3.3 cmt. b (2000) takes this position. See also Unif. Statutory Rule Against Perpetuities § 4 (1990), enacted in about half of the states, which adopts a 90-year "wait and see" alternative to the common law RAP. As a practical matter, this statutory rule would effectively validate most options. However USRAP § 2–904 exempts most nondonative transactions, such as options, from the statutory rule. See, e.g., New Bar P'ship v. Martin, 221 N.C. App. 302, 729 S.E.2d 675 (2012) (preemptive right in lease was exempt from USRAP and was void under common law RAP). Care must be exercised, for numerous states modified the Uniform Act when adopting it. See, e.g., Mass. Gen. L. c. 184A, making options and rights of first refusal void if not exercised within 30 years after their creation.

[614] Some courts have taken this view; see Pathmark Stores, Inc. v. 3821 Assoc. L.P., 663 A.2d 1189 (Del.Ch. 1995); Gartley v. Ricketts, 107 N.M. 451, 760 P.2d 143 (1988); Robroy Land Co. v. Prather, 95 Wn.2d 66, 622 P.2d 367 (1980); Mercer v. Lemmens, 230 Cal.App.2d 167, 40 Cal.Rptr. 803 (1964).

tenants in common.[615] Nonetheless the Rule against Perpetuities is widely applied to options and preemptive rights.[616] This is unfortunate; the doctrine of restraints on alienation provides a much more effective tool for invalidating unreasonable options and rights of first refusal.[617]

Assignment of options and preemptive rights. Ordinary options are routinely considered assignable by their holders and are frequently assigned. An objection to assignability would be countenanced only if the option itself prohibited assignment,[618] or the circumstances indicated that the optionor relied on some special qualities of the optionee.[619] An option contained in a lease is typically presumed not to be assignable apart from the leasehold, although the parties can contract for a different result.[620] If the leasehold itself is assigned, the option is generally deemed to run with it to the assignee.[621]

The assignability of preemptive rights to purchase is much more in doubt, and is usually said to depend on whether the parties intended the right to be assignable or merely personal.[622] If the terms of the right are not clear on the point, the decision is difficult and unpredictable, but the courts seem to lean toward nonassignability.[623] For example, a preemptive right is commonly granted because the optionee has an interest in other nearby land which would be augmented in value if the land in question were purchased. Under these circumstances, a court may suppose that an assignment of the

---

[615] See Atl. Richfield Co. v. Whiting Oil & Gas Corp., 2014 Colo. 16, 320 P.3d 1179, 1191 (2014).

[616] See, e.g., In re Restaurant Assocs., L.L.C., No. 1, 2007 WL 951849 (N.D.W. Va. 2007) (West Virginia law, not reported in F.Supp.2d); Welsh v. Heritage Homes of Delaware, Inc., 2008 WL 442549 (Del. Ch. 2008) (unreported); Viola E. Buford Family Ltd. P'ship v. Britt, 283 Ga. App. 676, 642 S.E.2d 383 (2007) (Delaware law); Wedel v. American Electric Power, 681 N.E.2d 1122 (Ind. App. 1997); The Arundel Corp. v. Marie, 383 Md. 489, 860 A.2d 886 (2004); Hensley-O'Neal v. Metropolitan Nat. Bank, 297 S.W. 3d 610 (Mo. Ct. App. 2009); Kozak v. Porada, 154 A.D.3d 1242, 63 N.Y.S.3d 594 (2017) (holding "commercial" transactions exempt from the Rule, but finding the exemption inapplicable); New Bar P'ship v. Martin, note 613 supra; Allegheny Country Farms, Inc. v. Huffman, 237 W. Va. 355, 787 S.E.2d 626 (2016).

[617] See Heather M. Marshall, Instead of Asking "When," Ask "How": Why the Rule Against Perpetuities Should Not Apply to Rights of First Refusal, 44 New Eng. L. Rev. 763 (2010). Further discussion is found in the section of this book that deals with those concepts. See § 3.18 supra notes 291–297.

[618] See, e.g., Cass Atl. Dev. Corp. v. Pellett, 725 N.W.2d 658 (Iowa Ct. App. 2006); Megargel Willbrand & Co., LLC v. FAMPAT Ltd. P'ship, 210 S.W.3d 205, 211 (Mo. Ct. App. 2006) (prohibition on assignment of lease by tenant also prohibits assignment of preemptive right in lease).

[619] Melrose Enterprises, Inc. v. Pawtucket Form Const. Co., 550 A.2d 300 (R.I. 1988); Stuart v. Ennis, 482 So.2d 1168 (Ala. 1985) (option between close personal friends held not assignable). See also Shower v. Fischer, 47 Wn.App. 720, 737 P.2d 291 (1987) (option presumed nontransferrable).

[620] Gilbert v. Van Kleeck, 284 A.D. 611, 132 N.Y.S.2d 580 (1954); Bewick v. Mecham, 26 Cal.2d 92, 156 P.2d 757 (1945).

[621] See § 6.65 supra.

[622] See Mitchell, Can A Right of First Refusal Be Assigned? 68 U. Chi. L. Rev. 985 (2001). The decision may be strongly influenced by whether the document refers to the heirs and assigns of the original parties. The right was held to be personal and to expire at the owner's death in Ryan v. Lawyers Title Ins. Corp., 959 N.E.2d 870 (Ind. Ct. App. 2011); Anderson v. Parker, 351 S.W.3d 827 (Mo. Ct. App. 2011); Gilmore v. Jordan, 132 A.D.3d 1379, 17 N.Y.S.3d 545 (N.Y. App. Div. 2015).

[623] Matter of Wauka, Inc., 39 B.R. 734 (Bankr. N.D. Ga. 1984); Old Nat. Bank of Washington v. Arneson, 54 Wash. App. 717, 776 P.2d 145 (1989). Note that if the right is nonassignable and is held by a natural person, it will expire at the holder's death, thus validating it under the Rule against Perpetuities; see Park Station Ltd. P'ship, LLLP v. Bosse, 378 Md. 122, 835 A.2d 646 (2003); Firebaugh v. Whitehead, 263 Va. 398, 559 S.E.2d 611 (2002).

preemptive right to someone who holds no interest in the nearby land would be contrary to the original parties' intent and unenforceable.[624]

§§ 10.15–11.0 ARE RESERVED FOR SUPPLEMENTAL MATERIAL.

---

[624] HSL Linda Gardens Properties, Ltd. v. Seymour, 163 Ariz. 396, 788 P.2d 129 (1990) (where two tenants in common give each other preemptive rights, either may enforce the right, so long as each owns his or her interest, against the successors of the other); Old Nat. Bank of Washington v. Arneson, 54 Wn.App. 717, 776 P.2d 145 (1989) (right of first refusal is presumed nontransferrable, but may be assigned if parties so intended).

Chapter 11

CONVEYANCES AND TITLES

Table of Sections

---

§ 11.1   DEEDS

The American legal system recognizes a variety of methods of transferring interests in land, but the deed is unquestionably the most common. Other transfer devices include wills, intestate succession, adverse possession and prescription[1], dedication[2], legislative acts of transfer[3], and various court decrees such as removal of clouds on title and judgments in eminent domain. In nearly all sales of real property, the deed is the instrument used to effect the ultimate transfer of legal title.[4] Hence it is of vast practical importance.

Historical background of the modern deed. In early English history, conveyances of possessory freehold interests in land did not depend on written instruments. Instead, a

---

[1]   Technically, adverse possession and prescription do not result in a transfer, but rather a new right or title arising in the adverse user. See § 11.7, infra. But the practical effect is similar to a transfer.

[2]   See § 11.6, infra.

[3]   These include both acts which grant government land to private parties, see 2 Patton and Palomar, Land Titles § 292 (3d ed. 2017 update), and acts which acquire private land for public use, see Nichols, Eminent Domain.

[4]   It is possible for the parties to contract that title will be passed by will; see, e.g., Larkins v. Howard, 252 Ala. 9, 39 So.2d 224, 7 A.L.R.2d 541 (1949), holding that a devisee was a bona fide purchaser for purposes of the recording act. But such transactions are rare, mainly because of the inherent uncertainty as to when the testator will die and legal title will pass.

method known as feoffment with livery of seisin was employed.[5] The parties met on, or in sight of, the land in the presence of witnesses.[6] The feoffor announced orally the transfer of the land to the feoffee, and handed over a twig or clump of earth to symbolize the conveyance. It was sometimes customary to prepare a written "charter of feoffment" memorializing the livery of seisin, but this was not considered essential and was merely evidence of the transfer, not an instrument of transfer itself.[7]

By contrast, interests other than possessory freeholds, such as leaseholds, easements, and future interests, were not conveyed by livery but by means of a grant. The grant was originally an oral conveyance, but at a very early date it became obligatory to make it by a written deed—that is, an instrument under seal. Thus, the grant was the first direct ancestor of the modern deed.[8] Since the grant was not seen as conveying seisin, it was not necessary for the delivery of the deed to take place on the land itself.

Livery of seisin was often inconvenient, since it required the parties to travel to the location of the land. The common law conveyancers soon developed a technique for transferring a possessory fee simple while circumventing this disadvantage. The conveyor would first grant a lease to the conveyee with a duration of, say, one year, leaving the conveyor with a reversion. As soon as the conveyee had entered upon the land, the conveyor would transfer the reversion to the conveyee by means of a second grant, termed a "release." The two interests would merge, giving the grantee a fee simple absolute. Since the first interest was not a freehold and the second was a future interest, livery was not necessary to transfer either of them.[9]

With the enactment of the Statute of Uses in 1536,[10] several new types of conveyances that avoided the need for livery of seisin came into use. The statute, in substance, converted equitable interests in land into legal interests. While most of the affected equitable interests arose in the form of "uses," or explicit arrangements under which one person held title for the benefit of another, the statute also applied to the sort of equitable interest, an ancestor of the doctrine of equitable conversion discussed in the previous chapter[11], which arose in the purchaser under a land sale contract—provided the contract recited the payment of consideration. Thus a document which employed contract-like language, reciting that the vendor "has bargained and sold" the land to the purchaser, was treated under the statute as recognizing that the vendor's legal title was held merely as a trustee, and hence as immediately vesting that title in the purchaser.

---

[5] The seisin, which was intangible but was treated virtually as a tangible object, represented in a rather mystical sense the right of possession of the land. See generally Payne, The English Theory of Conveyancing Prior to the Land Registration Acts, 7 Ala.L.Rev. 227 (1955); Thorne, Livery of Seisin, 52 L.Q.Rev. 345 (1936); Holdsworth, An Historical Introduction to the Land Law 113 (1927); 2 Pollock & Maitland, History of English Law 182 (1895).

[6] The purpose of the witnesses was to create a general public awareness of the transfer so that jurors would remember it if it were later challenged. In the Teutonic law, which followed the same general method of conveyance, it was customary to assemble a group of small boys from the neighborhood, compel them to watch the livery of seisin, and then to give each a sharp clout on the head so that the occasion would be impressed on his memory. See J. Lawler & G. Lawler, A Short Historical Introduction to the Law of Real Property 41–42 (1940).

[7] The charters were made after the fact, and hence described the livery in the past tense. Some modern deeds continue to follow this usage with such terminology as "I have this day granted and conveyed * * *" See 2 Patton and Palomar on Land Titles § 343 (3d ed. 2017 update); Pierson v. Armstrong, 1 Iowa 282 (1855).

[8] Payne, supra note 5, at 243–44.

[9] See 1 Patton and Palomar, Land Titles § 3 (3d ed. 2017 update).

[10] 27 Hen. VIII, Ch. 10 (1536). See generally § 3.11, supra; 3 Am.L.Prop. § 12.12 (1952).

[11] See the discussion of equitable conversion, § 10.13 supra.

It became known as a "bargain and sale deed," and was required to be in writing only if it conveyed a freehold. No entry on the land was necessary.[12] A similar process of reasoning was applied to the "covenant to stand seized", a promise by which a person owning land agreed to hold it for the use of another to whom he or she was related by blood or marriage. The familial relationship was enough to supply the needed consideration, and the courts applied the Statute of Uses to "execute" the use and place legal title in the hands of the relative. No writing was necessary.[13]

Parliament recognized the potential of the Statute of Uses for facilitating secret conveyances, and thus defeating the crown's collection of the feudal incidents at which the Statute was aimed. Hence it enacted the Statute of Enrollments[14], which required the public registration of all conveyances of freeholds by bargain and sale deeds. But the land owners and their lawyers found that they could avoid enrollment by employing the lease and release; since the lease component was not a freehold and the release could be made by grant rather than bargain and sale, both parts were outside the Statute of Enrollments. Moreover, the lease could now be made by bargain and sale, avoiding even the need for the lessee to enter on the land.[15] The lease and release enjoyed a vast expansion of popularity as a result.

Thus, up to the time of the enactment of the Statute of Frauds in 1676[16], some types of conveyances, including "bargains and sales" of freeholds and grants were required to be by written deed, while others, including livery of seisin and covenants to stand seised, were not.[17] Writings were by then very usual even for transactions in which they were not legally essential. The Statute of Frauds, in substance, insisted that every conveyance of an interest in land except short-term leases be written. This requirement has been carried over into every American jurisdiction[18], and is of great modern importance.[19]

As we will see below, the American approach to conveyancing has been far less technical than the traditional English.[20] American courts have shown little interest in classifying deeds as bargain-and-sale, lease and release, or the like, and they generally

---

[12]   Sargent v. Coolidge, 399 A.2d 1333 (Me.1979), appeal after remand 433 A.2d 738 (1981); 1 Patton and Palomar, Land Titles § 3 (3d ed. 2017 update).

[13]   3 Am.L.Prop. § 12.12 (1952). The covenant to stand seized was recognized by the New Hampshire Supreme Court in French v. French, 3 N.H. 234 (1825).

[14]   27 Hen. VIII, Ch. 16 (1536); see id.

[15]   Lutwitch v. Minton, Cro.Jac. 604, 79 Eng.Repr. 516 (1620), holding that when a leasehold was created by bargain and sale deed, the tenant was deemed immediately in possession without any necessity for entry on the land. See T. Bergin & P. Haskell, Preface to Estates in Land and Future Interests 108 (1966); Payne, supra note 5, at 261.

[16]   29 Car. II, Ch. 3 (1676).

[17]   See Goodwin, Before the Statute of Frauds, Must An Agreement to Stand Seised Have Been in Writing?, 7 Harv. L.Rev. 464 (1894).

[18]   See 1 Patton and Palomar on Land Titles § 3 (3d ed. 2017 update). A few cases have recognized oral gifts of land, where the grantee has taken possession and made improvements or done other acts in reliance on the gift; see Gillis v. Buchheit, 232 Ga.App. 126, 500 S.E.2d 38 (1998); Lynch v. Lynch, 239 Iowa 1245, 34 N.W.2d 485 (1948); Mertz v. Arendt, 564 N.W.2d 294 (N.D.1997); Ohmer v. Ohmer, 149 Ohio Misc.2d 60; 898 N.E.2d 106 (2008) (recognizing the application of the doctrine of part performance to an oral gift of land but finding it inapplicable); Troxel v. Bishop, 201 S.W.3d 290 (Tex. Ct. App. 2006); McFadden, Oral Transfers of Land in Illinois, 1988 U.Ill.L.Rev. 667.

[19]   The importance is well explained in In re Gonzalez, 456 B.R. 429 (Bankr. C.D. Cal. 2011), rev'd on other grounds, 2012 WL 8262445 (C.D. Cal. June 14, 2012).

[20]   See generally 3 Am.L.Prop. § 12.13 (1952). The British, too, have become much less technical. The Real Property Act of 1845, 8 & 9 Vict. Ch. 106, § 2, made a simple deed of grant sufficient to convey any interest, whether possessory or not.

try diligently to give effect to the grantor's intention irrespective of the choice of conveying language. Yet the early English history remains pervasive, manifesting itself in the language commonly employed in printed deed forms and in the requirement of delivery. Modern quitclaim deeds often use the term "release" and warranty deeds in many states still have the grantor "bargain and sell" the land. A few states still follow the common law in requiring private seals for the validity of deeds.[21] A number of statutes have been enacted authorizing the use of a particular phrase, such as "grants" or "bargains and sells" and imputing certain warranties of title when the statutory phrase is used.[22] The recitation of consideration, plainly unnecessary in modern times[23], remains customary as a holdover from the days of the Statute of Uses and the bargain and sale deed. In sum, the common law's technicality is no longer with us, but much of its phraseology remains.

At common law, it was necessary to name the grantee and add the phrase "and his heirs" or the like in order to pass a fee simple estate. This technical requirement has been abandoned by statute in nearly all American jurisdictions.[24] Modern deeds will pass a fee simple absolute to the grantee if that is what the grantor holds, unless the grantor specifies a lesser estate, whether words of inheritance are used or not.[25] Obviously a deed cannot convey more than the grantor owns,[26] but if a deed describes a greater estate than the grantor actually holds, the lesser estate actually held by the grantor will pass unless it is excepted or reserved by the deed's language.[27] For example, a deed purporting to convey a fee simple will actually convey a life estate if that is all the grantor holds,[28] and a deed by a 50% tenant in common will convey that tenant's interest, even though the deed purports to convey a 100% fee simple.[29]

Novices frequently confuse deeds and titles. A deed is a written document—a tangible piece of paper (or an electronic record, which under both federal and state law is fully acceptable as a substitute for a paper document).[30] A title is an intangible legal construct; it represents the law's conclusion as to ownership of an interest in land. The

---

[21] See, e.g., Williams v. North Carolina State Board of Education, 284 N.C. 588, 201 S.E.2d 889 (1974).

[22] 2 Patton and Palomar on Land Titles § 331 (3d ed. 2017 update).

[23] In most states, neither actual consideration nor its recitation is necessary to validity of the deed; see note 62 infra.

[24] See, e.g., Ala.Code § 35–4–2; Kan.Stat.Ann. § 58–2202; Wyo. Stat. Ann. § 34–2–101.

[25] See § 2.2 infra; In re Estate of Roloff, 36 Kan. App. 2d 684, 143 P.3d 406 (2006) (deed conveyed growing crops); Stone v. Washington Reg'l Med. Ctr., 2017 Ark. 90, 515 S.W.3d 104 (2017) (deed conveyed grantors' reversionary interest); 2 Patton and Palomar, Land Titles § 345 (3d ed. 2017 update). See Denny v. Regions Bank, 527 S.W.3d 920 (Mo. Ct. App. 2017) (deed reserved life estate in grantors). An exception is widely recognized for deeds of timber rights, which are construed as lasting for only a reasonable time unless expressly made perpetual; see Marrujo v. Sanderson, 144 N.M. 730, 191 P.3d 588 (2008).

[26] Hinote v. Owens, 2017 WL 3929005 (Ala. 2017) (unpublished); Kafka v. Hess, 2017 WL 2439142 (D. Md. 2017) (unpublished). This principle is susceptible to modification by the doctrine of estoppel by deed; see § 11.5 infra.

[27] Estate of Haan v. Haan, 237 S.W.3d 231 (Mo. Ct. App. 2007); Combest v. Mustang Minerals, LLC, 502 S.W.3d 173, 179 (Tex. App. 2016).

[28] Dixon v. Dixon, 2017 N.D. 174, 898 N.W.2d 706 (2017). See also Cavazos v. Cavazos, 246 S.W.3d 175 (Tex. App. 2007) (deed will convey grantor's future interest or expectancy if that is all the grantor has).

[29] Ka'Upulehu Land LLC v. Heirs & Assigns of Pahukula, 136 Haw. 123, 358 P.3d 692 (2015); Deckoff v. W. Manning Family Ltd. P'ship, 59 Misc. 3d 1207(A) (N.Y. Sup. Ct. 2018).

[30] Both federal and state law authorize use of electronic means of communication and electronic signatures in lieu of paper documents for deeds and other transactions. See eSign, the Electronic Signatures in Global and National Commerce Act', 15 U.S.C. § 7001 (2019). UETA, the Uniform Electronic Transactions Act, approved by the Uniform Laws Commission in 1999, has been adopted in all states except Illinois, New York, and Washington, all of which have similar legislation.

purpose of a deed is to convey or transfer title. Unlike a paper deed, a title cannot be seen or touched. The two concepts are distinct, and care should be taken to use both terms accurately.[31]

One other nicety must be explained. A deed is not a contract, despite overenthusiastic judicial statements sometimes so stating.[32] It is a conveyance. However, a deed may well contain a contract if appropriate language is used or incorporated by reference into the deed.[33] For example, restrictive covenants in the nature of contracts are often incorporated into deeds.

Elements of a deed. What must a deed contain? The list of essential elements is strikingly similar to that which governs contracts for the sale of land.[34] It includes identification of the parties, description of the land, some words indicating a present intent to convey, and the grantor's signature.[35] The signature alone is not generally considered a sufficient identification of the grantor.[36] However, the identification of the parties need not appear in any particular clause[37] and need not be precisely accurate.[38] Several states have statutes which regulate the naming of the parties to a deed, sometimes requiring full names, both previous and present names, addresses, or marital status.[39] In the absence of such a statute the courts tend to be very liberal in accepting identifying language.[40]

In lieu of a signature by the grantee, a deed may be executed by the grantee's attorney-in-fact. The power of attorney, like the deed itself, is typically required by the

---

[31] See In re Skidmore, 2011 IL App (2d) 100730, 953 N.E.2d 981, 991 (2011).

[32] E.g., Estate of Stephens, 28 Cal. 4th 665, 49 P.3d 1093 (2002); Hamlet HMA, Inc. v. Richmond Cty., 138 N.C. App. 415, 531 S.E.2d 494 (2000).

[33] See, e.g., Dep't of Transp. v. Meadow Trace, Inc., 274 Ga. App. 267, 617 S.E.2d 246 (2005), aff'd, 280 Ga. 720, 631 S.E.2d 359 (2006) (deed incorporated plat). A deed containing mutual contract terms is sometimes called an "indenture;" see K & K Food Servs., Inc. v. S & H, Inc., 2000 Okl. 31, 3 P.3d 705 (2000).

[34] See § 10.1 supra at note 36.

[35] Greer v. Kooiker, 312 Minn. 499, 253 N.W.2d 133 (1977). See Rekis v. Lake Minnewaska Mountain Houses, Inc., 170 A.D.2d 124, 573 N.Y.S.2d 331 (1991), appeal dismissed 79 N.Y.2d 851, 580 N.Y.S.2d 201, 588 N.E.2d 99 (1992) (deed with no description of property is void, but if description is later filled in, grantor may be estopped to challenge its validity, as against a subsequent bona fide purchaser). See generally 3 Am.L.Prop. § 12.38 (1952); 2 Patton & Palomar, Land Titles §§ 331–365 (3d ed. 2017 update).

There is no requirement that the conveyance be called a deed; see, e.g., Adams v. Anderson, 142 Idaho 208, 127 P.3d 111 (2005) (recorded survey adjusting boundary, signed by the parties, was effective to change boundary).

[36] See, e.g., Christian v. Johnson, 556 S.W.2d 172 (Ky.App.1977) (deed by corporation is void where signed by president who is identified as such on signature line, but where corporation is not otherwise identified). There is little to commend such a rigid approach. Compare Milstid v. Pennington, 268 F.2d 384 (5th Cir.1959) (deed was signed by both husband and wife, but granting clause named wife twice and omitted husband; held, deed conveyed husband's interest.) See generally 2 Patton & Palomar, Land Titles § 335 (3d ed. 2017 update).

[37] St. Michael and Archangel Russian Orthodox Greek Catholic Church v. Uhniat, 451 Pa. 176, 301 A.2d 655 (1973).

[38] Shulansky v. Michaels, 14 Ariz.App. 402, 484 P.2d 14 (1971); Barton v. Baptist General Convention, 477 P.2d 679 (Okl. 1970). The name given in the deed may be an alias or an assumed name; see Roeckl v. FDIC, 885 P.2d 1067 (Alaska 1994); Marky Investments, Inc. v. Arnezeder, 15 Wis.2d 74, 112 N.W.2d 211 (1961); Gallagher v. Girote, 23 Ill.2d 170, 177 N.E.2d 103 (1961).

[39] See generally 6A Powell, Real Property ¶ 886 (1980).

[40] For numerous cases upholding deeds in which the grantee's name was not given, but in which the grantee was described as someone's child, heir, trustee, or the like, see 2 Patton & Palomar, Land Titles § 338 n. 4 (3d ed. 2017 update). See also 3 Am.L.Prop. § 12.40 (1952). See Garraway v. Yonce, 549 So.2d 1341 (Miss.1989) (upholding deed naming trustees of school district and their successors as grantees).

Statute of Frauds to be in writing.[41] However, a deed may also be executed by an amanuensis—someone who performs the mechanical act of signing the grantor's name because the grantor is unable to do so. The authority to act in this way need not be in writing; an oral request by the grantor will suffice.[42]

An interesting problem arises if a deed is delivered with the grantee's name left blank, but the grantor expects or authorizes the person to whom delivery is made to fill in his own name or that of someone he chooses. Plainly the deed is void until a grantee's name is actually inserted.[43] But once this is done the majority of the cases sustain the deed, often implying authority from the grantor's acquiescence even if none was given explicitly.[44] One might expect the authority to expire if the grantor died before the name was written in, but even that sequence of events has been held to result in a valid deed on the ground that the grantee's agency was "coupled with an interest" and thus was irrevocable.[45]

A deed to a nonexistent grantee is said to be void. Examples include a deed to a deceased grantee, to the heirs of a living grantee, or to a corporation which has not yet been formed or has been dissolved.[46] Yet the courts are generally quite willing to reform such deeds if by doing so they can carry out the grantor's intent.[47]

---

[41] The relevant statute may also require recording of the power of attorney; see, e.g., N.M. Stat.Ann. § 47–1–7 (2018).

[42] Estate of Stephens, 28 Cal. 4th 665, 674, 49 P.3d 1093, 1098 (2002) (amanuensis' signature was effective, although she signed outside grantor's presence); Estate of Bronson, 2017 S.D. 9, 892 N.W.2d 604 (2017).

[43] Myers v. Francis, 548 So.2d 833 (Fla.App.1989); Karlen v. Karlen, 89 S.D. 523, 235 N.W.2d 269 (1975). See also McCormick v. Brevig, 294 Mont. 144, 164, 980 P.2d 603, 616 (1999) (if grantee is authorized to fill in blank legal description, the authority must be given in writing).

[44] Mehus v. Thompson, 266 N.W.2d 920 (N.D.1978); Gajewski v. Bratcher, 221 N.W.2d 614 (N.D.1974), appeal after remand 240 N.W.2d 871 (1976). The deed is void where there is a clear absence of authorization from the grantor; see Rice v. Rice, 499 F.Supp.2d 1245 (M.D. Fla. 2007); Robinson v. Bascom, 85 N.M. 453, 513 P.2d 190 (App. 1973); West v. Witschner, 482 S.W.2d 733 (Mo.1972); Application of County Collector, 1 Ill.App.3d 707, 274 N.E.2d 164 (1971). See generally 2 Patton & Palomar, Land Titles § 338 n.2 (3d ed. 2017 update); 4 Tiffany, Real Property § 969 (3d ed. 2017 update). See also McCormick v. Brevig, 980 P.2d 603 (Mont. 1999), construing the Statute of Frauds to require the authority of the grantor's agent to be in writing.

[45] Kindred v. Crosby, 251 Iowa 198, 100 N.W.2d 20 (1959); Womack v. Stegner, 293 S.W.2d 124 (Tex.Civ.App. 1956). These cases also refer to the deliveree of the deed as having "equitable title," but this apparently means nothing more than that a court of equity would sustain the deed, giving a decree of reformation if necessary.

[46] Oregon v. Bureau of Land Management, 876 F.2d 1419 (9th Cir.1989); Haney's Chapel United Methodist Church v. United Methodist Church, 716 So.2d 1156 (Ala.1998), appeal after remand 1999 WL 778572 (Ala. 1999); Buckeye Ret. Co., LLC., LTD v. Walter, 2012 Ark. App. 257, 404 S.W.3d 173 (2012); Stone v. Jetmar Properties, LLC, 733 N.W.2d 480 (Minn. Ct. App. 2007); House Rescue Corp. v. Thomas, 328 S.W.3d 267 (Mo. Ct. App. 2010); Gifford v. Linnell, 157 N.C. App. 530, 579 S.E.2d 440 (2003); Cohen v. Tour Partners, Ltd., 2017 WL 1528776 (Tex. App. 2017). Compare Sharp v. Riekhof, 747 P.2d 1044 (Utah 1987) (a trust, as distinct from a trustee, cannot hold property, and a deed conveying property to a trust is void) with Luna v. Brownell, 185 Cal. App. 4th 668, 110 Cal. Rptr. 3d 573 (2010) (deed to trustee of trust not yet formed was valid). See Annot., 148 A.L.R. 252 (1944). In the case of a conveyance of a future interest, it is sufficient if the takers will be ascertainable when the interest becomes possessory. A deed to one's self is obviously void; see Elk Park Ranch, Inc. v. Park County, 282 Mont. 154, 935 P.2d 1131 (1997).

[47] See, United States v. Stubbs, 776 F.2d 1472 (10th Cir. 1985) (deed to estate of deceased person was valid, where grantor intended that result); John Davis & Co. v. Cedar Glen No. Four, Inc., 75 Wn.2d 214, 450 P.2d 166 (1969) (corporation not organized when deed delivered, but takes title when subsequently organized); Haile v. Holtzclaw, 414 S.W.2d 916 (Tex. 1967) (deed to "the W.B. Haile Estate" sustained as conveyance to heirs of the decedent); Wilson v. Dearing, Inc., 415 S.W.2d 475 (Tex. Civ.App. 1967) (deed to deceased grantee may be treated as to his heirs or assigns to carry out grantor's intent). See generally 3 Am.L.Prop. § 12.40 (1952); Annot., 148 A.L.R. 252, 257 (1944).

Some words indicating an intent to make a present transfer of the title must be included in the deed.[48] This requirement is not construed technically, and nearly any appropriate words, such as "give," "transfer,"[49] "deed over," or the like will suffice.[50] But the words must indicate an intent to make a present conveyance,[51] and difficulty is encountered with such words as "I will to * * *"[52], which suggest an intent that the conveyance operate at death rather than immediately. Words which merely covenant or warrant the title, rather than purporting to transfer it, will not suffice.[53] The title of the document is not controlling, and if it contains words of grant and the other necessary elements it will be treated as a deed whether it is labelled as one or not.[54]

The remaining essential elements of the deed are the land description and the grantor's signature. Descriptions are of such importance that they are discussed separately in the next section.[55] The signature requirement is liberally construed,[56] and need not necessarily be met by the grantor's writing his or her name. Virtually any mark or writing which is intended to serve as the grantor's approval of the instrument will do,[57] and the grantor's agent may sign if the grantor is present or the agent has previously been given a power of attorney.[58]

---

[48] This is not to say that the interest conveyed must be a present interest. For example, the grantor may reserve a life estate, and thus convey only a future interest; see Lanford v. Cornett, 1966 Okl. 112, 415 P.2d 984 (1966).

[49] Matter of Estate of White, 234 So. 3d 1210 (Miss. 2017).

[50] Saltzman v. Ahern, 306 So.2d 537 (Fla.App. 1975); Bonkowski v. Commissioner, 458 F.2d 709 (7th Cir.1972), certiorari denied 409 U.S. 874, 93 S.Ct. 121, 34 L.Ed.2d 127 (1972). See also Harris v. Strawbridge, 330 S.W.2d 911 (Tex.Civ.App. 1959), upholding a deed whose only words of conveyance were "to have and to hold"; Veltmann v. Damon, 696 S.W.2d 241 (Tex.App. 1985) (same), affirmed in part and reversed in part 701 S.W.2d 247 (Tex. 1985).

[51] Smith v. Smith, 892 So. 2d 384 (Ala. Civ. App. 2003); Masgas v. Anderson, 310 S.W.3d 567 (Tex. App. 2010).

[52] Caldwell v. Caldwell, 140 Ga. 736, 79 S.E. 853 (1913); Lemus v. Aguilar, 491 S.W.3d 51 (Tex. App. 2016).

[53] See, e.g., Lilly v. Earl, 463 So.2d 143 (Ala.1984) (where deed omitted words of grant, although it contained warranty of title, and where grantees named in granting clause were not same as those in habendum clause, deed was void); Raley v. Raley, 121 Miss. 555, 83 So. 740 (1920); Hummelman v. Mounts, 87 Ind. 178 (1882).

[54] See Berry v. Berry, 32 Ill.App.3d 711, 336 N.E.2d 239 (1975); Hinchliffe v. Fischer, 198 Kan. 365, 424 P.2d 581 (1967); Mountain Properties, Inc. v. Tyler Hill Realty Corp., 2001 Pa. Super 45, 767 A.2d 1096 (2001); Warburton v. Virginia Beach Fed. Sav. & Loan Ass'n, 899 P.2d 779 (Utah App.1995); Petersen v. Schafer, 42 Wn.App. 281, 709 P.2d 813 (1985). Cf. Performance Constr., LLC v. Glenn, 195 Wash. App. 406, 380 P.3d 618 (2016) (unacknowledged assignment of post-foreclosure redemption rights did not transfer title to real estate).

[55] See § 11.2, infra.

[56] Lane v. Spriggs, 71 S.W.3d 286 (Tenn. Ct. App. 2001) (where failure to sign was a mere oversight, could would reform deed to add signature). But see In re Evans, 397 B.R. 744 (Bankr. W.D. Pa. 2008) (mortgage on entireties property signed by only one spouse was void).

[57] See Runge v. Moore, 196 N.W.2d 87 (N.D.1972); J.D. Loizeaux Lumber Co. v. Davis, 41 N.J.Super. 231, 124 A.2d 593 (1956), cert. denied 22 N.J. 269, 125 A.2d 753 (1956). Cf. Walker v. Walker, 485 S.W.3d 403 (Mo. Ct. App. 2016) (where signature was not genuine, deed was invalid).

[58] Hildebrandt v. Hildebrandt, 9 Kan. App.2d 614, 683 P.2d 1288 (1984) (if agent has previously been given power of attorney, she may sign the grantor's name and bind him whether or not he is present and without stating in the deed that she is acting as an agent); Haffa v. Haffa, 115 Ill.App.2d 467, 253 N.E.2d 507 (1969). The signature of a purported agent or corporate officer who lacks authority is ineffective; see Catawba County Horsemen's Ass'n v. Deal, 107 N.C.App. 213, 419 S.E.2d 185 (1992); Rice v. Hill City Stock Yards Co., 121 Idaho 616, 826 P.2d 1328 (App.1990).In some jurisdictions, if there are multiple grantors and fewer than all sign the deed, it is ineffective even as to those who sign; Wachter Development, L.L.C. v. Gomke, 579 N.W.2d 209 (N.D. 1998).

The traditional deed contained several formal parts.[59] The "premises" included the parties' names, the recitation of consideration, a description of the land, and the granting clause. The "habendum" clause, so called because in medieval times it began with the Latin phrase "habendum et tenendum" ("to have and to hold") followed, and limited the estate being granted if, for example, only a life tenancy was being conveyed. A "reddendum" clause might then follow if the grantor wished to make a reservation of some part of the interest conveyed. The deed would conclude with the warranties of title, a formal reference to the execution and date, and the signature lines. A certificate of acknowledgement by a notary public would be added and in several states, lines for the signatures of attesting witnesses.

Today, although printed forms of deeds commonly follow the outline above, it is clear that no such formality is necessary;[60] in fact, as noted above, there is no requirement that the deed be called a "deed" at all.[61] Only the basic elements discussed in the preceding paragraphs are essential. For example, in most states no consideration need be recited or paid.[62] No habendum nor reddendum clauses are required, although of course the grantor must say so if he or she wishes to limit the estate to something less than a fee simple or to make a reservation. The grantee's signature is not necessary, and it is not customary for grantees to sign deeds.[63] Including a date is customary but not essential.[64]

---

[59] See 3 Am.L.Prop. § 12.39 (1952); 4 Tiffany, Real Property § 966 (3d ed. 2017 update). See also Kipp v. Estate of Chips, 169 Vt. 102, 732 A.2d 127 (1999) (no part of deed should be given constructional priority over any other part).

[60] See, e.g., Masgas v. Anderson, 310 S.W.3d 567 (Tex. App. 2010).

[61] See Ex parte Rucker, 702 So.2d 456 (Ala. 1997), on remand 702 So.2d 458 (Ala. Civ.App.1997); Matter of Estate of White, 234 So. 3d 1210 (Miss. 2017); Kindred v. City of Smithville, 292 S.W.3d 420 (Mo. Ct. App. 2009); Franklin Park Plaza, LLC v. V & J Nat. Enterprises, LLC, 57 A.D.3d 1450, 870 N.Y.S.2d 193 (2008) (contract of sale held to convey easement, although it was inadvertently omitted from description in deed); Harris v. Strawbridge, 330 S.W.2d 911 (Tex.Civ.App. 1959).

[62] Sintz v. Stone, 562 So.2d 228 (Ala. 1990), appeal after remand 572 So.2d 1270 (1990); United States v. Porath, 764 F.Supp.2d 883, 898 (E.D. Mich. 2011), aff'd, 490 F. App'x 789 (6th Cir. 2012); Black v. Duffie, 2016 Ark. App. 584, 508 S.W.3d 40 (2016); Chase Federal Sav. & Loan Ass'n v. Schreiber, 479 So.2d 90 (Fla.1985) (rejecting the doctrine, derived from the Statute of Uses, that valuable consideration, consanguinity, or marital relation is necessary to a valid deed), certiorari denied 476 U.S. 1160, 106 S.Ct. 2282, 90 L.Ed.2d 723; City of Virginia v. Mitchell, 991 N.E.2d 936 (Ill. App. 2013); Smith v. Vest, 265 S.W.3d 246 (Ky. Ct. App. 2007); Holmes v. O'Bryant, 741 So. 2d 366 (Miss. Ct. App. 1999); Basile v. Rose, 127 A.D.3d 1444, 7 N.Y.S.3d 664 (N.Y. App. Div. 2015); Barlow Society v. Commercial Security Bank, 723 P.2d 398 (Utah 1986); Kelley v. Tonda, 198 Wash. App. 303, 316, 393 P.3d 824, 832 (2017). See 4 Tiffany, Real Property § 984 (3d ed. 2017 update). In a few states, a statement of the consideration is required for recordation; see, e.g., Ky. Rev. Stat. Ann. § 382.135, construed in Smith v. Vest, 265 S.W.3d 246, 252 (Ky. Ct. App. 2007); Mass.Gen.L.Ann. ch.183 § 6. Recitation of consideration may raise a rebuttable presumption that consideration was paid in fact, and this in turn may be helpful in a grantee's attempt to rely on the recording acts as a bona fide purchaser. See J.C. Vereen & Sons, Inc. v. City of Miami, 397 So.2d 979 (Fla.App.1981); Estate of Fallon v. Fallon, 30 So. 3d 1281 (Miss. Ct. App. 2010); § 11.10, infra; 3 Am.L.Prop. § 12.43 (1952). Consideration may be relevant in other ways; see, e.g., Connolly v. Knight, 95 A.D.3d 926, 943 N.Y.S.2d 602 (2012) (deed in contemplation of expected marriage could be rescinded when marriage did not take place).

[63] Kindred v. City of Smithville, 292 S.W.3d 420 (Mo. Ct. App. 2009). If there are covenants or other terms in the deed binding the grantee, the grantee's asset will be inferred from acceptance of the deed's delivery; see Great Water Lanier, LLC v. Summer Crest at Four Seasons on Lanier Homeowners Ass'n, Inc., 344 Ga. App. 180, 811 S.E.2d 1 (2018).

[64] Gregg v. Georgacopoulos, 990 S.W.2d 120 (Mo. Ct. App. 1999).

Except in a few states no seal is necessary.[65] A certificate of acknowledgement by a notary or other officer is required for recordation in nearly all states,[66] and attestation by one or more witnesses is also needed for recording in several jurisdictions[67], but except in a few states neither item is essential to the deed's validity as between the parties themselves.[68] Likewise, recording in the public records is extremely useful and advantageous to the grantee,[69] but is not at all essential for the deed's validity as between its parties.[70] The deed may be either a warranty or a quitlclaim deed, and either will pass whatever title the grantor holds.[71]

Construction of deeds. When the language of a deed is ambiguous or confusing, judicial construction may be necessary to determine the parties' intent.[72] Of course, there are countless types of possible ambiguities that may be introduced by thoughtless drafting, but some common patterns emerge from the cases and will be discussed here. We must first deal with a preliminary question: should a court consider "extrinsic" evidence—that is, facts which do not appear on the face of the document—in construing a deed? Relevant facts might include the parties' statements at the time the deed was given, the nature of the land and surrounding circumstances, and the prior or subsequent behavior of the parties. An old bromide states that if the ambiguity is "patent", or apparent on the face of the deed, no extrinsic evidence may be considered, while if the confusion is "latent," or discernible only in the light of outside facts, further extrinsic proof can be introduced to explain the deed.[73] This quite irrational distinction has now been very widely abandoned, and most courts freely admit testimony which will

---

[65]   See note 21 supra.

[66]   See 2 Patton & Palomar, Land Titles § 356 (3d ed. 2017 update); In re David Buchholz, 224 B.R. 13 (D. N.J. 1998); McElwain v. Wells, 174 W.Va. 61, 322 S.E.2d 482 (1984) (acknowledgement required for recording of deed, but not for validity); Abraham v. Mihalich, 330 Pa.Super. 378, 479 A.2d 601 (1984) (same). But see Saunders v. Callaway, 42 Wn.App. 29, 708 P.2d 652 (1985) (acknowledgement is necessary to validity of deed or of lease exceeding one year).

[67]   3 Am.L.Prop. § 12.59 n. 4 (1952) lists 18 states as requiring at least one witness. See, e.g., In re Ryan, 851 F.2d 502 (1st Cir.1988) (two witnesses required for valid recordation); Leasing Enterprises, Inc. v. Livingston, 294 S.C. 204, 363 S.E.2d 410 (App.1987) (same); Earp & Shriver, Inc. v. Earp, 466 So.2d 1225 (Fla.App.1985) (witnesses required, but deed lacking witnesses is not void, and under curative statute, becomes fully valid five years after recording); Sweat v. Yates, 463 So.2d 306 (Fla.App. 1984) (witnesses need not sign in presence of grantor or each other, nor sign prior to delivery); Ala. Code § 35–4–20 (2018) (one witness required).

[68]   Requirements of acknowledgment for validity of a deed are reflected in Hout v. Hout, 20 Ohio St. 119 (1870); Lewis v. Herrera, 10 Ariz. 74, 85 P. 245 (1906), affirmed 208 U.S. 309, 28 S.Ct. 412, 52 L.Ed. 506 (1908); Selene RMOF II REO Acquisitions II, LLC v. Ward, 189 Wash. 2d 72, 399 P.3d 1118 (2017).

[69]   See §§ 11.9–11.11 infra.

[70]   In re Smith, 469 B.R. 198 (Bankr. S.D.N.Y. 2012); In re Caldwell, 457 B.R. 845, 852 (Bankr. M.D. Fla. 2009); Lumpkins v. CSL Locksmith, LLC, 911 A.2d 418, 425 (D.C. 2006); Patterson v. Seavoy, 822 N.E.2d 206, 211 (Ind. Ct. App. 2005); In re Humann, 136 A.D.3d 1036, 26 N.Y.S.3d 304 (N.Y. App. Div. 2016); Nevitt v. Robotham, 235 N.C. App. 333, 762 S.E.2d 267 (2014). But see Le Gault v. Erickson, 70 Cal. App. 4th 369, 82 Cal. Rptr. 2d 692 (1999) (deed of land not in compliance with subdivision map act is voidable by grantee).

[71]   Cooper v. Cano, 72 Cal. App. 4th 672, 84 Cal. Rptr. 2d 922 (1999) (quitclaim deed is effective to discharge and release deed of trust). Of course, if the title is not as purported, the grantee will have a damages remedy against the grantor only if the deed contains warranties of title; See § 11.13 infra.

[72]   If the deed is unambiguous, neither construction nor the consideration of extrinsic evidence is said to be necessary. See, e.g., O'Brien v. Village Land Co., 794 P.2d 246 (Colo.1990); Cole v. Minor, 518 So.2d 61 (Ala.1987); Ouellette v. Butler, 125 N.H. 184, 480 A.2d 76 (1984).

[73]   See In re Thompson, 799 S.E.2d 658 (N.C. Ct. App. 2017); MacKay v. Breault, 121 N.H. 135, 427 A.2d 1099 (1981); McBane, The Rule Against Disturbing Plain Meaning of Writings, 31 Cal.L.Rev. 145 (1943); Annot., 68 A.L.R. 12 (1930).

help resolve the ambiguity without bothering to classify it as latent or patent.[74] There is also some tendency to resolve ambiguities against the deed's drafter, which is usually the grantor.[75]

One common ambiguity arises from the use of language which seems to suggest that only an easement rather than a possessory estate is being granted or reserved.[76] For example, a deed reference to a "right of way" for road or railway purposes is usually construed as conveying only an easement, since most rights of way are indeed easements.[77] On the other hand "a parcel of land" or "a strip of land" for a right of way is more likely to be deemed to convey possessory title, with the language identifying the use to be made of the strip treated as merely precatory and nonbinding.[78] The cases are not particularly consistent, and the wise drafter will make clear what sort of interest is intended.

Another familiar constructional problem arises from the use of reservations and exceptions in deeds. In theory, a reservation gives the grantor a new interest in the land which did not exist before the delivery of the deed, such as a life estate or a new easement across the land conveyed. An exception, by comparison, denotes the retention by the grantor of some previously existing interest in or portion of the land granted, as "I hereby grant all of Lot 6 except the north 50 feet thereof."[79] There is little practical difference between the two terms and nearly all modern cases regard them as interchangeable,

---

[74] City of Manhattan Beach v. Superior Court, 13 Cal.4th 232, 52 Cal.Rptr.2d 82, 914 P.2d 160 (1996); Bledsoe v. Hill, 747 P.2d 10 (Colo.App. 1987); Boardwalk at Daytona Dev., LLC v. Paspalakis, 220 So. 3d 457 (Fla. Dist. Ct. App. 2016); R.C. Acres, Inc. v. Cambridge Faire Properties, LLC, 331 Ga. App. 762, 771 S.E.2d 444 (2015); Nationsbanc Mortg. Corp. v. Cazier, 127 Idaho 879, 908 P.2d 572 (App. 1995); Stockstill v. Gammill, 943 So. 2d 35 (Miss. 2006); Ouellette v. Butler, 125 N.H. 184, 480 A.2d 76 (1984); 3 Am.L.Prop. § 12.91 (1952). Cf. The David & Marvel Benton Tr. v. McCarty, 161 Idaho 145, 384 P.3d 392 (2016) (extrinsic evidence may be considered only if it is referenced in the deed itself); Morris v. Byrd, 338 Ga. App. 540, 790 S.E.2d 556 (2016) (same). If the court is unable to determine the intent even with the aid of extrinsic evidence, the deed may simply be held void for ambiguity. See Myers v. Francis, 548 So.2d 833 (Fla.App. 1989) ("hopelessly confused" deed is totally void); Minor v. Neely, 247 Ga. 253, 275 S.E.2d 333 (1981); Schade v. Stewart, 205 Cal. 658, 272 P. 567 (1928); The David & Marvel Benton Tr. v. McCarty, supra.

[75] See, e.g., United States v. Stearns Co., 595 F.Supp. 808 (E.D.Ky. 1984), affirmed 816 F.2d 279 (6th Cir.1987), cert. denied 484 U.S. 953, 108 S.Ct. 344, 98 L.Ed.2d 370 (1987); In re Benton, 563 B.R. 113 (Bankr. D. Mass. 2017); Harrison v. Loyd, 87 Ark. App. 356, 192 S.W.3d 257 (2004); Sally-Mike Properties v. Yokum, 175 W.Va. 296, 332 S.E.2d 597 (1985).

[76] The issue may be important because of the discovery of oil or other valuable subsurface rights, or because an easement can be lost by abandonment while a possessory estate cannot. The cases often describe the question as "easement versus fee simple," but this is inaccurate since the term "fee simple" indicates the duration of the interest rather than denoting it as possessory or as an easement. Easements can be (and usually are) of perpetual duration and are therefore held in "fee simple." See generally § 8.1, supra.

[77] Crum v. Butler, 601 So.2d 834 (Miss.1992); Robert Jackson Real Estate Co. v. James, 755 S.W.2d 343 (Mo.App. 1988); International Paper Co. v. Hufham, 81 N.C.App. 606, 345 S.E.2d 231 (1986), review denied 318 N.C. 506, 349 S.E.2d 860 (1986). Cf. Rogers v. United States, 184 So.3d 1087 (Fla. 2015). See Annot., 6 A.L.R.3d 973 (1966).

[78] Severns v. Union Pac. R.R. Co., 101 Cal. App. 4th 1209, 125 Cal. Rptr. 2d 100 (2002); Grill v. West Virginia R.R. Maintenance Auth., 188 W.Va. 284, 423 S.E.2d 893 (1992); Safeco Title Ins. Co. v. Citizens & Southern Nat. Bank, 190 Ga. App. 809, 380 S.E.2d 477 (1989). Cf. Bumgarner v. Bumgarner, 124 Idaho 629, 862 P.2d 321 (App.1993).

[79] See Dept. of Transportation v. First Interstate Commercial Mortg. Co., 881 P.2d 473 (Colo.App. 1994); Piper v. Mowris, 466 Pa. 89, 351 A.2d 635 (1976); In re Estate of Harding, 178 Vt. 139, 878 A.2d 201 (2005); Comment, 36 Calif.L.Rev. 470 (1948); Bigelow & Madden, Exception and Reservation of Easements, 38 Harv.L.Rev. 180 (1924); 2 Patton and Palomar, Land Titles § 346 (3d ed. 2017 update); Annot., 34 A.L.R. 698 (1930).

with no penalty attaching to an incorrect usage.[80] A more serious problem is the old English rule that neither a reservation nor an exception can be made in favor of a person other than the grantor; thus, "I hereby reserve an easement in favor of my next-door neighbor" is ineffective. The supposed difficulty is the absence of any granting language running to the third party.[81] But this conclusion stems from an unduly technical construction of the words "reserve" or "except," and several recent cases have rejected it and recognized that the third party receives the interest in question.[82]

A final constructional issue derives from the common law rule that no subsequent language in a deed would be permitted to derogate from the estate conveyed in the granting clause.[83] This "repugnancy" rule (so-called because words repugnant to the granting clause are disregarded) has been increasingly discredited, and most modern cases either reject it entirely[84] or give only a rather mild priority to the granting clause.[85] The touchstone today is the intent of the parties as discerned from the "four corners" of the document and appropriate extrinsic evidence.

Defects in deeds. Two types of deed defects may be considered. The first is an error, usually inadvertent, which causes the deed to reflect inaccurately the intention of at least one of the parties[86], even though there is nothing amiss in its essential formalities. Here reformation of the deed in equity is available to the aggrieved plaintiff if the

---

[80]　Campbell v. Johnson, 87 Ohio App.3d 543, 622 N.E.2d 717 (1993); O'Brien v. Village Land Co., 794 P.2d 246 (Colo. 1990); Russell v. Garver, 55 Wn.App. 175, 777 P.2d 12 (1989); Sally-Mike Properties v. Yokum, 175 W.Va. 296, 332 S.E.2d 597 (1985).

[81]　Cayce v. Carter Oil Co., 618 F.2d 669 (10th Cir. 1980); In re Fraley, 2018 WL 1568527 (Bankr. W.D. Va. 2018); Estate of Thomson v. Wade, 69 N.Y.2d 570, 516 N.Y.S.2d 614, 509 N.E.2d 309 (1987); Windham v. Riddle, 381 S.C. 192, 672 S.E.2d 578 (2009); Pitman v. Sweeney, 34 Wn.App. 321, 661 P.2d 153 (1983); Tallarico v. Brett, 137 Vt. 52, 400 A.2d 959 (1979); Shirley v. Shirley, 259 Va. 513, 525 S.E.2d 274 (2000). See Peters v. Smolian, 154 A.D.3d 980, 63 N.Y.S.3d 436 (N.Y. App. Div. 2017), affirming the rule but finding that it did not apply to a right of first refusal. Cf. Johnson v. Republic Steel Corp., 262 F.2d 108 (6th Cir.1958), holding the words "excepted and conveyed" to be a sufficient grant to a third party.

[82]　Nelson v. Parker, 687 N.E.2d 187 (Ind.1997); In re Marriage of Wade, 20 Kan. App.2d 159, 884 P.2d 736 (1994); Simpson v. Kistler Inv. Co., 713 P.2d 751 (Wyo. 1986); Katkish v. Pearce, 490 A.2d 626 (D.C.App. 1985); Jakobson v. Chestnut Hill Properties, Inc., 106 Misc.2d 918, 436 N.Y.S.2d 806 (1981) (same); Mott v. Stanlake, 63 Mich.App. 440, 234 N.W.2d 667 (1975); Willard v. First Church of Christ, Scientist, Pacifica, 7 Cal.3d 473, 102 Cal. Rptr. 739, 498 P.2d 987 (1972), noted 61 Calif.L.Rev. 548 (1973). See Comment, 60 N.D.L.Rev. 317 (1984), commenting on Malloy v. Boettcher, 334 N.W.2d 8 (N.D.1983); Lasater, Reservations in Favor of Strangers to the Title: California Abandons the Common Law Rule, 24 Hast.L.J. 469 (1973); Harris, Reservations in Favor of Strangers to the Title, 6 Okla.L.Rev. 127 (1953); Note, 52 S.C. L.Rev. 269 (2000). Rather nonsensically, the *Willard* case, supra, upholds a reservation to a third party but states in dictum that a contrary result would follow with an exception! *Willard*, supra, at n. 35.

[83]　See In re Fleck's Estate, 261 Iowa 434, 154 N.W.2d 865 (1967); Herd, Deed Construction and the "Repugnant to the Grant" Doctrine, 21 Tex.Tech.L.Rev. 635 (1990); Annot., 84 A.L.R. 1054 (1930); 4 Tiffany, Real Property § 980 (3d ed. 2017 update).

[84]　Smith v. Nugget Exploration, Inc., 857 P.2d 320 (Wyo.1993), appeal after remand 896 P.2d 769 (Wyo. 1995); Turner v. Lassiter, 484 So.2d 378 (Ala. 1985); Heyen v. Hartnett, 235 Kan. 117, 679 P.2d 1152 (1984); Smith v. Graham, 705 S.W.2d 705 (Tex.App. 1985). But see Hornets Nest Girl Scout Council v. Cannon Foundation, Inc., 79 N.C.App. 187, 339 S.E.2d 26 (1986), applying the "repugnancy" rule despite acknowledgment that it has been criticized as harsh, technical, and tending to frustrate the grantor's intent.

[85]　Lusk v. Broyles, 694 So.2d 4 (Ala. Civ.App. 1997); Premier Bank v. Bd. of Cty. Comm'rs of Cty. of Bent, 214 P.3d 574 (Colo. App. 2009); Elliott v. Cox, 100 N.C.App. 536, 397 S.E.2d 319 (1990); Knell v. Price, 318 Md. 501, 569 A.2d 636 (1990); Kerr-McGee Corp. v. Henderson, 763 P.2d 92 (Okl.1988); Goodson v. Capehart, 232 Va. 232, 349 S.E.2d 130 (1986). See Healy, Conflict Between the Granting and Habendum Clauses, 11 N.Y.U.Intra.L.Rev. 201 (1965).

[86]　Either grantor or grantee may seek reformation. It is usually said that the mistake must be one of fact and not of law; see Paradise Hills Church, Inc. v. International Church, 467 F.Supp. 357 (D.Ariz. 1979); Lea v. Byrd, 242 Ark. 673, 415 S.W.2d 336 (1967); but see Grossman Furniture Co. v. Pierre, 119 N.J.Super. 411, 291 A.2d 858 (1972).

defendant was also under a mistake or was guilty of fraud or other inequitable conduct[87]; even the defendant's silence in the face of knowledge of the error is often enough.[88] The proof to support reformation must be "clear and convincing,"[89] and the equitable nature of the action precludes reformation against a bona fide purchaser who has relied on the face of the deed.[90]

The second type of defect is one which affects the essential formalities of the deed's execution and delivery or which casts doubt on the grantor's capacity. In cases of this type the grantor or his successors typically rely on the defect in an effort to have the deed cancelled or set aside. A variety of such defects is possible, and the courts generally label the deed as "void" or "voidable," depending on which particular defect exists. These labels are somewhat misleading, since they seem to suggest that a void deed is automatically nugatory, while a voidable deed will be set aside only upon the grantor's request. In fact they have no such meaning; in either case a court will cancel the deed at the grantor's instance if the grantee has made no further conveyance. The distinction between void and voidable deeds arises only if the grantee has retransferred the land to a bona fide purchaser for value.[91] If the defect is regarded as making the deed void, even a BFP will have no title, but if the deed is merely voidable the title will be unassailable in the hands of a BFP.[92]

The defect which most clearly will make a deed void, and thus defeat even a BFP, is forgery—for example, a false signature or an attempt to enlarge the scope of a deed by an addition, alteration, or deletion after it is signed but before delivery.[93] The ground for

---

[87] See In re Huskey, 479 B.R. 827 (Bankr. E.D. Ark. 2012); In re Pak Builders, 284 B.R. 663 (Bankr. C.D. Ill. 2002); Groff v. Kohler, 922 P.2d 870 (Alaska 1996); In re Estate of Munawar, 981 A.2d 584 (D.C. 2009); Ceasar v. Wells Fargo Bank, N.A., 322 Ga. App. 529, 744 S.E.2d 369 (2013); Carla Realty Co. v. County of Rockland, 222 A.D.2d 480, 635 N.Y.S.2d 67 (1995); Twin Forks Ranch, Inc. v. Brooks, 120 N.M. 832, 907 P.2d 1013 (App. 1995), appeal after remand 125 N.M. 674, 964 P.2d 838 (App. 1998); Drake v. Hance, 195 N.C. App. 588, 673 S.E.2d 411 (2009); Hoffman v. Kaplan, 875 S.W.2d 948 (Mo.App.1994); 4 Tiffany, Real Property § 985 (3d ed. 2017 update). If the defendant was not at fault nor under a mistake, no reformation will be ordered; McKee v. Douglas, 362 S.W.2d 870 (Tex.Civ.App. 1962).

[88] See Paradise Hills Church, Inc. v. International Church, supra note 86; Demetris v. Demetris, 125 Cal.App.2d 440, 270 P.2d 891 (1954).

[89] Bourne v. Lajoie, 149 Vt. 45, 540 A.2d 359 (1987); Gasaway v. Reiter, 736 P.2d 749 (Wyo. 1987); Praggastis v. Sandner, 40 Or.App. 477, 595 P.2d 520 (1979); LeMehaute v. LeMehaute, 585 S.W.2d 276 (Mo.App.1979); Lazenby v. F.P. Asher, Jr. & Sons, Inc., 266 Md. 679, 296 A.2d 699 (1972); Galyen v. Gillenwater, 247 Ark. 701, 447 S.W.2d 137 (1969).

[90] In re R & J Construction Co., 43 B.R. 29 (Bkrtcy.E.D.Mo. 1984); United States v. LaRosa, 765 F.2d 693 (7th Cir. 1985); Touchstone v. Peterson, 443 So.2d 1219 (Ala. 1983); Jones v. Carrier, 473 A.2d 867 (Me. 1984). But see Bailey v. Ewing, 105 Idaho 636, 671 P.2d 1099 (App. 1983) (reformation may be ordered against a bona fide purchaser if he is fully and fairly compensated for the loss).

[91] In one situation the term "voidable" generally does indicate that the deed may be set aside, even against a BFP, by the grantor's disaffirmance; that is the case of a minor grantor who seeks to set aside the deed after reaching majority. If the grantor remains in possession, his or her presence on the land will usually impart inquiry notice to any subsequent purchaser, precluding BFP status. See Stevens v. American Savings Institution, Inc., 289 Or. 349, 613 P.2d 1057 (1980); Houston v. Mentelos, 318 So.2d 427 (Fla.App. 1975).

[92] See, e.g., Bennion Ins. Co. v. 1st OK Corp., 571 P.2d 1339 (Utah 1977). When farm foreclosures are rampant, farmers sometimes try to ward off foreclosure by recording bogus "land patents" purporting to represent transfers of original title from the federal government. They have mainly succeeded in arousing the ire of the courts. See, e.g., Wisconsin v. Glick, 782 F.2d 670 (7th Cir. 1986). Yet the Iowa Supreme Court held that county recorders have no authority to reject such bogus instruments; see Proctor v. Garrett, 378 N.W.2d 298 (Iowa 1985) (recorder has no discretion to reject a proffered filing of a "common law lien" which is a legal nullity); § 11.9 infra at note 463.

[93] La Jolla Grp. II v. Bruce, 211 Cal. App. 4th 461, 149 Cal. Rptr. 3d 716 (2012); Upson v. Goodland State Bank, 823 P.2d 704 (Colo. 1992); M.M. & G. Inc. v. Jackson, 612 A.2d 186 (D.C.App. 1992) (forged deed void, but innocent purchaser may have equitable lien to recover cost of improvements made in good faith);

this rule is surely not that the BFP could have prevented the loss by using greater care; in many cases a forgery is entirely undetectable by untrained persons.[94] Rather, the rule is based on the innocence and lack of complicity of the true owner, who is favored by the law simply because he or she is entirely blameless.[95]

Fraud in the execution is usually treated like forgery, making the deed absolutely void.[96] It exists when the grantor is tricked into signing a deed in the mistaken belief that it is some other document, as when the grantee slips the deed in among other papers the grantor is signing.[97] The conclusion that the deed is void is particularly probable if the grantor is elderly, illiterate, ill, confused, or has particular reason to trust the grantee.[98] By comparison, if a deed's signing is induced by the grantee's fraudulent representations, such as a bad check or a false financial statement, but the grantor understands the nature of the deed, the document is usually regarded as only voidable rather than void.[99] The distinction again is placed on the ground of the grantor's culpability; with fraud in the execution the grantor is regarded as blameless while with fraud in the inducement, the courts feel he or she could and should have been more careful. This rationale is an overgeneralization, since the degree of blame varies with a wide spectrum of additional facts. The cases are not wholly consistent in following this distinction or in their classification of the two kinds of fraud.[100]

Zurstrassen v. Stonier, 786 So.2d 65 (Fla. Ct. App. 2001); Vatacs Grp., Inc. v. U.S. Bank, N.A., 292 Ga. 483, 738 S.E.2d 83 (2013); Morris v. Wells Fargo Bank, N.A., 334 S.W.3d 838, 841 (Tex. App. 2011); Scott D. Erler, D.D.S. Profit Sharing Plan v. Creative Finance & Inv., LLC, 349 Mont. 207, 203 P.3d 744 (2009) (forged deed is void but may be ratified by grantor). The principle applies as well to other forms of conveyance, such as mortgages; see Bierman v. Hunter, 190 Md. App. 250, 988 A.2d 530 (2010). Contra, finding a forged deed merely voidable, see Treglia v. Zanesky, 67 Conn. App. 447, 788 A.2d 1263 (2001); Bank of New York v. Langman, 2013 Ill. App. 2d 120609, 986 N.E.2d 749 (2013) (forged mortgage release valid in hands of BPF). If the alteration is an addition of a grantee's name, the deed will still be effective in favor of the original grantees; see Donovan v. Kirchner, 100 Md. App. 409, 641 A.2d 961 (Md.Spec.App. 1994). Note that a grantee under a forged deed may nonetheless get title by adverse possession by remaining in possession long enough under appropriate conditions; see Bergesen v. Clauss, 15 Ill.2d 337, 155 N.E.2d 20 (1958); § 11.7, infra. An alteration after the deed is delivered is simply irrelevant and has no legal significance; see Lindley v. Lindley, 961 P.2d 202 (Okla. 1998); Julian v. Petersen, 966 P.2d 878 (Utah App. 1998).

[94] Consider, for example, the battle of expert witnesses over the authenticity of the signature on the widely-publicized "Mormon will" attributed to Howard Hughes; see Rhoden v. First National Bank of Nevada, 96 Nev. 654, 615 P.2d 244 (1980).

[95] See Harding v. Ja Laur Corp., 20 Md.App. 209, 315 A.2d 132 (1974). Of course the BFP is blameless too, but the courts will not disturb the status quo of the putative grantor's ownership where both parties are innocent.

[96] Upson v. Goodland State Bank & Trust Co., 823 P.2d 704 (Colo.1992); Cumberland Capital Corp. v. Robinette, 57 Ala. App. 697, 331 So.2d 709 (1976); Annot., 11 A.L.R.3d 1074 (1967). This sort of fraud is also known as "fraud in the factum." If "extrinsic" fraud is practiced on the court in a proceeding leading to a judicial sale, the sheriff's deed or other conveyance is void even against a BFP; see Groves v. Witherspoon, 379 F.Supp. 52 (E.D.Tenn. 1974).

[97] See Sheffield v. Andrews, 679 So.2d 1052 (Ala. 1996), cert. denied 519 U.S. 1041, 117 S.Ct. 610 (1996); Bennion Ins. Co. v. 1st OK Corp., 571 P.2d 1339 (Utah 1977).

[98] Houston v. Mentelos, 318 So.2d 427 (Fla.App. 1975) (limited to cases of fraud in the execution by McCoy v. Love, infra note 100); Hoffer v. Crawford, 65 N.W.2d 625 (N.D. 1954).

[99] Compass Bank v. Petersen, 886 F.Supp.2d 1186 (C.D. Cal. 2012); Malcom v. Wilson, 534 So.2d 241 (Ala.1988); Schiavon v. Arnaudo Brothers, 100 Cal.Rptr.2d 801, 84 Cal.App.4th 374 (2000); Dines v. Ultimo, 532 So.2d 1131 (Fla.App.1988); Blaise v. Ratliff, 672 S.W.2d 683 (Mo.App. 1984); Hill v. Watts, 801 S.W.2d 176 (Tex. App. 1990).

[100] If the grantor realizes that the document is a deed, but is duped as to its coverage or details, it is generally held merely voidable; see McCoy v. Love, 382 So.2d 647 (Fla. 1979) (grantee prepared deed, informed elderly illiterate grantor that it conveyed much less land than it in fact described; held, fraud in the inducement; deed voidable); Grube v. Bessenger, 259 Mich. 57, 242 N.W. 837 (1932) (grantor's husband told her he would fill in description of his land, but filled in her land instead; deed voidable). But if the grantor is

One other common defect, lack of delivery, is generally held to make the deed void; it is discussed in a subsequent section.[101] A deed executed by a minor is said to be "voidable," but most of the cases permit the grantor to disaffirm it even as against a BFP by acting within a reasonable time after reaching majority.[102] Virtually all other defects result in only a finding of voidability and not outright voidness.[103] They include insanity or lack of capacity[104], duress[105], undue influence[106], mistake[107] and breach of fiduciary duty.[108] For a discussion of the substantive legal rules governing these defects the reader is referred to other sources.[109]

Beneficiary (transfer on death) deeds. An ordinary deed's transfer of title is effective as of the time of its delivery; indeed, as we shall see, that is the essence of delivery.[110] But beginning with a Missouri statute in 1989, a new form of deed has arisen, termed a "beneficiary deed" or "transfer on death deed."[111] Such a deed is executed while the

---

tricked into believing the deed is some other sort of document, it is usually held void; see 11 A.L.R.3d 1074 (1967).

[101] See § 11.3, infra.

[102] See Searcy v. Hunter, 81 Tex. 644, 17 S.W. 372 (1891); Annot., 16 A.L.R.2d 1420, 1421 n. 1 (1951); 2 Patton & Palomar, Land Titles § 336 (3d ed. 2017 update); Burby, Real Property § 119 (3d ed. 1965). See note 92 supra and accompanying text respecting the use of the term "voidable." The cases regard the minor as innocent per se, and thus protect him or her even against a BFP. The underlying policy is of dubious merit. A few states follow an even more extreme rule, holding a minor's deed absolutely void even without his or her disaffirmance; see Sparks v. Sparks, 101 Cal. App.2d 129, 225 P.2d 238 (1950), based on West's Ann.Cal.Civ. Code § 33. A minor who has misrepresented his or her age is considered by some jurisdictions estopped to disaffirm the deed; see Lewis v. Van Cleve, 302 Ill. 413, 134 N.E. 804 (1922); Annot., 29 A.L.R.3d 1270 (1970).

[103] First Fiduciary Corp. v. Blanco, 276 N.W.2d 30 (Minn.1979). Many possible defects not mentioned in the text may be conceived. See, e.g., Mason v. Pitt, 21 Mo. 391 (1855) (property sold without compliance with platting law; BFP protected). As to the validity of deeds executed without compliance with platting and subdivision ordinances, see generally Annot., 77 A.L.R.3d 1058 (1977).

[104] Go-Mart, Inc. v. Olson, 198 W.Va. 559, 482 S.E.2d 176 (1996); Hall v. Financial Enterprises Corp., 188 B.R. 476 (Bkrtcy.D.Mass. 1995); Matter of LeBovici, 171 Misc. 2d 604, 655 N.Y.S.2d 305 (Sup. Ct. 1997); Simon v. Marlow, 515 F.Supp. 947 (W.D.Va. 1981). A contrary rule, treating the deed as void, is usually followed if the grantor has been placed under a guardianship, since a title examination will disclose the proceedings and hence the grantor's incapacity; see Scott v. Nelson, 820 So. 2d 23 (Miss. Ct. App. 2002); O'Neal by & through Small v. O'Neal, 803 S.E.2d 184 (N.C. Ct. App. 2017); Patton & Palomar, Land Titles § 336 (3d ed. 2017 update). Judicial opinions sometimes state that a deed from an incompetent is void, but almost invariably the statements are dictum since no BFP was involved; see, e.g., Runge v. Moore, 196 N.W.2d 87 (N.D. 1972); McCutcheon v. Brownfield, 2 Wn.App. 348, 467 P.2d 868 (1970).

[105] Goodwin v. City of Dallas, 496 S.W.2d 722 (Tex.Civ.App.1973); Campbell v. Genshlea, 180 Cal. 213, 180 P. 336 (1919).

[106] First Interstate Bank v. First Wyoming Bank, 762 P.2d 379 (Wyo.1988); United Companies Financial Corp. v. Wyers, 518 So.2d 700 (Ala.1987). See 4 Tiffany, Real Property § 988 (3d ed. 2018 update). See also Stewart v. Dickerson, 455 So.2d 809 (Ala. 1984), appeal after remand 473 So.2d 1078 (Ala.Civ.App. 1985), applying Ala.Code 1975, § 8–9–12, which permits a grantor to disaffirm (except as against a BFP) a deed given in consideration of a promise to support the grantor for life.

[107] See Tilbury v. Osmundson, 143 Colo. 12, 352 P.2d 102 (1960). Cancellation of the deed is ordinarily the appropriate remedy if the grantor was mistaken about the fact that the document was a deed, see Felonenko v. Siomka, 55 Or.App. 331, 637 P.2d 1338 (1981), while reformation is proper if the mistake related to the precise contents of the deed; see 3 Am.L.Prop. § 12.86 at nn. 26–31 (1952); text at notes 86–90, supra.

[108] See Daughton v. Parson, 423 N.W.2d 894 (Iowa App.1988); Loftis v. Eck, 288 S.C. 154, 341 S.E.2d 641 (App.1986).

[109] See 5 Williston on Contracts § 9:1 (4th ed. 2017 update); Bogart, Trusts § 543 (2018 update).

[110] See § 11.3 infra.

[111] See Stephanie Emrick, Transfer on Death Deeds: It Is Time to Establish the Rules of the Game, 70 Fla. L. Rev. 460 (2018); Susan N. Carey, Transfer on Death Deeds: The Non-Probate Revolution Continues, 41 Real Prop. Prob. & Tr. J. 539 (2006); John M. Gradwold, Legislative Enactment of Standard Forms, 91 Neb. L. Rev. 273 (2012).

grantor is living, but does not transfer title until his or her death.[112] A beneficiary deed, like a will, is "ambulatory"—that is, it can be modified or revoked as long as the grantor is still alive.[113] But it need not be executed with the formalities of a will.[114] Instead, the usual formalities of deed execution, including signing, acknowledgment, and recording,[115] are sufficient. In effect, recording substitutes for delivery, and no other delivery is necessary. There is no necessity for the grantee to sign, or even to be informed, of the deed.

Beneficiary deeds are now authorized by statute in more than half of the states and have proven highly popular.[116] Like transfer-on-death bank accounts and securities, they serve as simple will substitutes and require no probate proceedings.[117] But they share with wills the characteristic that, because they speak at death of the donor, it is likely that the donor will be unable to testify in any litigation questioning the validity of the instrument. This fact his been the traditional justification for the increased formality of execution required of wills. Yet strangely, there seems to be little concern about doing away with such formality in the case of beneficiary deeds.

§ 11.2   LAND DESCRIPTIONS

Both real estate contracts of sale and deeds, to be valid, must describe or otherwise identify the land affected.[118] The Statute of Frauds insists on a written identification; physical markers on the earth's surface or such other sources as maps or surveyor's notes are not enough unless they are identified or referred to in the instrument.[119] The

---

[112] Because passage of title occurs at the grantor's death, perforce the grantor must be a natural person; see Fischbach v. Holzberlein, 215 P.3d 407 (Colo. App. 2009) (beneficiary deed executed by trust was void because trust was not a natural person). If there are multiple owners, the deed may designate passage of title at the death of the last to die. But see Delcour v. Rakestraw, 340 S.W.3d 320 (Mo. Ct. App. 2011) (deed designating passage of title at date of death of last to die of an owner and a nonowner was not a valid beneficiary deed); Bohr v. Nodaway Valley Bank, 411 S.W.3d 352, 359 (Mo. Ct. App. 2013) (grantor who held a life estate with power to dispose of the remainder was an "owner" and could validly execute a beneficiary deed).

[113] A subsequent inter vivos transfer of the same property by the grantor has the effect of revoking the beneficiary deed; see Jennings v. Atkinson, 456 S.W.3d 461 (Mo. Ct. App. 2014).

[114] Wills typically require two or three witnesses, who must see the testator sign and who must sign in the presence of the testator and each other. See, e.g., 9 Tex. Prac., Texas Law Of Wills § 18:11 (4th ed. 2018 update).

[115] Recording is, of course, usual but not essential to the validity of an ordinary deed. But recording *is* required by statute for validity of beneficiary deeds. See, e.g., Mo. Rev. Stat. § 461.025; Estate of Dugger v. Dugger, 110 S.W.3d 423 (Mo. Ct. App. 2003) (unrecorded beneficiary deed is void). Likewise, any modification or revocation must be recorded.

[116] See Patton & Palomar, Land Titles § 333 (3d ed. 2017). In 2011 the Uniform Law Commission approved the Uniform Real Property Transfer on Death Act, which has been adopted by 16 states at this writing.

[117] See Grayson M.P. McCouch, Probate Law Reform and Nonprobate Transfers, 62 U. Miami L. Rev. 757 (2008). But see In re Estate of Carlson, 2016 Okl. 6, 367 P.3d 486 (2016) (where realty was transferred by beneficiary deeds subject to existing mortgages, clause in decedent's will directing that her debts be paid by her estate included debts secured by the mortgages).

[118] The description is ordinarily included in the deed itself, but may be placed in an appendix if the appendix is incorporated by reference into the body of the deed; see Field v. Mednikow, 279 Ga. App. 380, 631 S.E.2d 395 (2006); Maurice v. Maurice, 131 A.D.3d 454, 15 N.Y.S.3d 133 (N.Y. App. Div. 2015).

[119] A deed lacking a sufficiently definite description is void; see Modern, Inc. v. Fla., 444 F.Supp.2d 1234 (M.D. Fla. 2006); Lake Canal Reservoir Co. v. Beethe, 227 P.3d 882 (Colo. 2010); Lord v. Holland, 282 Ga. 890, 655 S.E.2d 602 (2008); Plano Petroleum, LLC v. GHK Expl., L.P., 2011 Okl. 18, 250 P.3d 328 (2011); Patton & Palomar, Land Titles § 81 (3d ed. 2017). The description may, of course, incorporate or refer to other sources of information outside the document itself; see Brasher v. Tanner, 256 Ga. 812, 353 S.E.2d 478 (1987); Stauth

doctrines of practical location of boundaries, discussed later, may result in modification of a boundary without a writing, and a court may reform a writing which does not comport with the parties' intent,[120] but in general a written description is essential.[121]

Methods of describing land. A land description is a statement defining a series of boundary lines on the earth's surface which delineate a two-dimensional geometric figure. The parcel of land thus described is bounded horizontally on the surface by this figure and extends vertically from the earth's center to the "sky,"[122] unless by its terms it is more limited.[123] A wide variety of methods of specifying boundary lines is possible. Some of these methods involve an "official" determination of the location and extent of parcels of land, physically marked by monuments on the land and shown on a map maintained in a government office. Two systems for doing this, the Government Survey system and the subdivision plat, are discussed below.[124] The written description of a parcel in these systems may consist simply of a reference to an appropriate parcel on the official map.[125]

But there are many areas of the nation not covered by either of these systems, and even where they are available the parties may wish to carve out and transfer only a portion of an official parcel. In such cases the parties must describe the land conveyed without governmental assistance or review. They do so by writing a "metes and bounds" description which begins at some geographic "point of beginning" and specifies or "calls" each boundary line in turn, until the last line described returns to the point of

---

v. Brown, 241 Kan. 1, 734 P.2d 1063 (1987) Dickson v. Kates, 132 Wash. App. 724, 133 P.3d 498 (2006). See generally Annot, 73 A.L.R.4th 135 (1989).

[120] Torrao v. Cox, 26 Mass.App.Ct. 247, 525 N.E.2d 1349 (1988). See § 11.8, infra (boundaries by practical location); Palmer, Reformation and the Statute of Frauds, 65 Mich.L.Rev. 421 (1967).

[121] A special rule applies to the grant or reservation of an easement: the servient land must be identified in the deed's description, but the precise location of the easement on the servient land need not be shown. See Vinson v. Brown, 80 S.W.3d 221 (Tex. App. 2002); Maier v. Giske, 254 Wash. App. 6, 223 P.3d 1265 (2010).

[122] The Latin phrase was "cujus est solum ejus est usque ad coelum." As to subsurface rights, see Edwards v. Sims, 232 Ky. 791, 24 S.W.2d 619 (1929), holding that a surface owner also owns the portions of a valuable cave which run under his land. The "ad coelum" (to the sky) phrase not taken literally in modern cases. Aircraft overflights above a reasonable altitude are not considered trespassory. The Restatement (Second) of Torts § 159 (1965) regards an overflight as a trespass only if it interferes substantially with the landowner's use and enjoyment and enters the "immediate reaches" of the land. 500 feet is presumptively not "immediate," and 50 feet presumptively is, with distances between 50 and 500 feet presenting a question of fact.

[123] A "land" parcel may also be explicitly limited in the third dimension, consisting of specific regions above or below the surface, such as mining rights between given depths or air rights between given heights or altitudes. But even this sort of parcel must be defined by the sort of two-dimensional figure in the horizontal plane discussed in the text as well.

[124] See text at notes 132–137 infra.

[125] Sometimes careless or hurried drafters use a much more convenient but less accurate parcel designator, the street address. It does not really locate the land's boundaries, but many courts will uphold it, using extrinsic evidence to identify the boundaries. See French v. Bank of New York Mellon, 729 F.3d 17 (1st Cir. 2013) (N.H. law); DTND Sierra Investments LLC v. Bank of New York Mellon Tr. Co., 958 F.Supp.2d 738 (W.D. Tex. 2013); In re Gresham, 373 B.R. 914 (Bankr. W.D. Mo. 2007); Western World Inc. v. Dansby, 566 So.2d 866 (Fla.App.1990), appeal after remand 603 So.2d 597 (Fla. App. 1992); City of Virginia v. Mitchell, 991 N.E.2d 936 (Ill. App. 2013); City of St. Louis v. Parcel 107 of Land, 702 S.W.2d 123 (Mo.App.1985); Park West Village, Inc. v. Avise, 714 P.2d 1137 (Utah 1986). Holding street addresses insufficient, see In re Brandt, 434 B.R. 493 (W.D. Mich. 2010) (construing Michigan statute); Gateway Family Worship Centers, Inc. v. H.O.P.E. Found. Ministries, Inc., 244 Ga. App. 286, 535 S.E.2d 286 (2000); The David & Marvel Benton Tr. v. McCarty, 161 Idaho 145, 384 P.3d 392 (2016); Martin v. Seigel, 35 Wn.2d 223, 212 P.2d 107 (1949). See also Sieger v. Prehay, 16 A.D.3d 575, 791 N.Y.S.2d 657 (2005) ("house at a" specified street corner was an insufficient description).

beginning.[126] These descriptions are often lengthy, cumbersome, and rife with potential for mistranscription and other errors; they must be used with the greatest care.[127]

The earliest metes and bounds descriptions relied heavily on natural monuments. In older deeds, references such as "beginning at the great white oak tree," "along Mill Creek 50 chains," or the like were very common. The lack of permanence of these monuments sometimes created severe problems for later buyers and their counsel; if the tree were removed or the creek changed course, it might be virtually impossible to locate the boundaries.[128] Artificial or manmade monuments, such as roads, bridges, fences, stakes, and posts are more widely used today, but are subject to the same objection to some degree. Modern surveying instruments using global positioning satellite technology can achieve acceptable accuracy without monuments under good conditions,[129] but some use of artificial monuments continues to be made.[130] It is also common for a metes and bounds description to refer to the boundaries of adjoining land, as in "west 20 chains, more or less, to the land of Mary Jones." The adjoining land may be thought of as analogous to an artificial monument.

Many modern metes and bounds descriptions make no reference to either natural or artificial monuments except to establish a point of beginning. Instead, they employ successive calls of courses and distances, with the first call starting at the point of beginning and the last call returning to it. A course is a statement of direction, and is usually expressed as some number of degrees, minutes, and seconds east and west of due north or south. By convention, north or south is first specified, and the numbers and words which follow indicate how far the course differs from due north or south. Thus a course in a northeasterly direction would be stated as "North 45 degrees East," while a course directly west could be written either as "North 90 degrees West" or "South 90 degrees West."[131] If a particular boundary is not a straight line, it can be described as an arc or a series of arcs by specifying the center and the radius of each.

In each call a distance must be stated together with the course. Thus, a complete call might read "North 37° 40′ 35″ East 29.55 feet." Most descriptions in American deeds give the distances in feet, rods, or chains. Table 1 provides the information necessary to convert distances from any of the common units to other units.

---

[126] See Ault v. Holden, 2002 UT 33, 44 P.3d 781 (2002), upholding a deed despite the fact that the final call did not return to the point of beginning, where surveyors were able to extrapolate the correct call.

[127] See, e.g., Reverse Mortg. Sols., Inc. v. Rahman, 2017 Ill. App. (1st) 161035, 82 N.E.3d 578 (2017) (upholding a metes and bounds description despite the fact that several lines were omitted). This does not imply that descriptions based on the Government Survey system or officially-approved subdivision plats are always perfect. See, e.g., Pierce v. Sanderlin, 460 S.W.3d 9 (Mo. Ct. App. 2014) (upholding deed despite use of incorrect range number); Van Deven v. Harvey, 9 Wis.2d 124, 100 N.W.2d 587 (1960), involving serious discrepancies in a plat. Moreover, even an error-free description can give rise to severe title problems; see Howard v. Kunto, 3 Wn. App. 393, 477 P.2d 210 (1970), in which each of a series of neighboring lot owners had occupied (and in some cases built houses upon) the lot next door to the one she or he owned; Gilmore v. M&B Realty Co., 895 So. 2d 200 (Ala. 2004) (similar).

[128] A description which raises these problems is reprinted and commented upon in Cunningham, Making Land Surveys and Preparing Descriptions to Meet Legal Requirements, 19 Mo.L.Rev. 234 (1954).

[129] Accuracies of better than 1 centimeter are usually achievable, but accuracy may be degraded by the presence of nearby buildings, mountains, or other obstructions that impair the instruments' view of the sky. See David DiBiase, The Nature of Geographic Information, Ch. 5, available at https://www.e-education.psu.edu/natureofgeoinfo/.

[130] See, e.g., Zerafa v. Montefiore Hosp. Hous. Co., 403 F.Supp.2d 320 (S.D.N.Y. 2005).

[131] See Brown, Boundary Control and Legal Principles 5–9 (1957).

Table 1

Units	Inches	Links	Feet	Yards	Rods	Chains	Miles	Meters
1 inch	1	0.126 263	0.083 333 3	0.027 777 8	0.005 050	0.001 262	0.000 015 783	0.025 400.05
1 link	7.92	1	0.66	0.22	0.04	0.01	0.000 125	0.201 168 4
1 foot	12	1.515 152	1	0.333 333	0.060 606	0.015 151	0.000 189 394	0.304 800 6
1 yard	36	4.545.45	3	1	0.181 818	0.045 454	0.000 568 182	0.914 401 8
1 rod	198	25	16.5	5.5	1	0.25	0.003 125	5.029 210
1 chain	792	100	66	22	4	1	0.0125	20.116 84
1 mile	63 360	8 000	5 280	1 760	320	80	1	1 609.347 2
1 meter	39.37	4.970 960	3.280 833	1.093 611 1	0.198 838	0.049 710	0.000 621 370	1

Two systems provide for governmental recognition of "official" land parcels. The first, the Government Survey system (also termed the "public land survey system" or "rectangular survey system"), was devised by Thomas Jefferson and adopted by the Continental Congress in 1785. Most of the land added to the United States since that time has been surveyed under the system, with Texas being the notable exception. Thus, it is generally available throughout the country except along the Atlantic seaboard and in Kentucky, Tennessee, and West Virginia. The system is based on the establishment of sets of Principal Meridians and intersecting Base Lines; there are 36 such sets in the contiguous 48 states.[132] The Principal Meridians run north-south and the Base Lines run east-west. Spaced out parallel to each Base Line at intervals of approximately six miles and running east-west are additional lines dividing the land into "Townships." Similarly, spaced parallel to each Principal Meridian at six-mile intervals are north-south lines which divide the land into "Ranges." Thus, one may describe a parcel of land in the form of a square about six miles on a side by stating both a Township number and a Range number. These numbers are counted from the intersection of the Principal Meridian and the Base Line, as in "Township 2 North, Range 6 West, Cimmaron Base and Meridian." Often such a description will be abbreviated to "T 2 N, R 6 W, C.B. & M."

The six-mile square defined in this way is, rather confusingly, also called a "Township." The term thus refers to both the north-south divisions along the Principal Meridian and to the square land areas which they help to identify. Note that these townships are not political or governmental subdivisions, but merely land descriptions. Each township is divided into thirty-six "sections" about one mile square.[133] The sections are numbered consecutively, starting with Section 1 in the northeast corner of the township and running back and forth to Section 36 in the southeast corner. A section, being an approximate square mile, contains about 640 acres. The corners of the sections and townships are marked with monuments on the ground.[134]

Each section may be further divided into halves, quarters, and so on, so that one might own "the North half of the Southwest quarter of Section 21." If this parcel were in

---

[132] See generally Grants pursuant to United States survey, 1 Patton and Palomar, Land Titles § 116 (3d ed. 2017 update). A high-resolution map locating and identifying the Principal Meridians and Base Lines is available at https://en.wikipedia.org/wiki/Public_Land_ Survey_System#/media/File:Meridians-baselines.png See also Article, The Public Land Survey System, in NationalAtlas.gov.

[133] The dimensions given in the text are approximate, mainly because the curvature of the earth requires that all north-south lines (such as the Principal Meridians and their fellows) must converge toward the North Pole; hence they are not precisely parallel, and the resulting townships are not precisely square.

[134] The Government Survey system is far from perfect; the original surveyors made many errors. See, e.g., Rivers v. Lozeau, 539 So.2d 1147 (Fla.App. 1989) (the true location of a government section is where the original surveyor established it, regardless of whether subsequent surveys show it as erroneous); Helehan v. O.M. Ueland, 223 Mont. 228, 725 P.2d 1192 (1986) (same); Patton & Palomar, note 132 supra.

the township described in the example above, its full description would be abbreviated as "N ½ of SW ¼, Sec. 21, T 2 N, R 6 W, C.B. & M." A half of a quarter section, as described here, would contain about 80 acres.

The other principal system of officially recognized land descriptions, available in every state, is the plat. A plat is a map, usually showing several new lots, which meets certain standards of format and accuracy. In many localities a plat is a legal prerequisite to every subdivision of land. It must be approved by some agency of city or county government, such as a planning commission or city council, and is filed for permanent record with the county recorder or other recording office. The plat differs from the Government Survey system in important ways. It is not prepared by government employees, but rather by the landowner or an engineer or surveyor hired by the owner. The parcels it creates are not generally of identical shape or uniform size, but are laid out by the developer to make them attractive in the market. However, the subdivider does not have carte blanche, for governmental approval of the plat is usually conditioned upon compliance with a "subdivision ordinance" imposing requirements regarding lot size, street width and curvature, monumentation of lots on the ground, and the like.[135]

The plat must of necessity contain one or more references to known monuments external to the subdivision itself, so that it can be located in relation to its environment. Once it has been approved and recorded, it can form the basis for legal descriptions of its individual lots.[136] Such descriptions are usually brief and convenient, as in "Lot 3, Block D, Ridgefield Acres Subdivision as shown in Plat Book B, page 23, Official Records of Orange County, California." No detailed recitation of the boundaries of the lot is needed, since they are shown on the plat.[137] Nearly all modern residential subdivisions are platted, and plats are commonly employed for land that has been assembled for commercial projects, such as shopping centers and industrial parks, as well.[138]

Beyond the Government Survey and plat systems, other governmentally-approved land description systems are available in some localities. These include "official maps" prepared by city or county engineers or surveyors, records of survey maps prepared and filed for record by individual surveyors, maps prepared by highway departments or other public agencies, and maps produced by property tax assessors.[139] These maps vary in accuracy, and it may or may not be considered good practice to use them as the basis for

---

[135] See §§ 9.15–.16 supra; 4 Anderson, American Law of Zoning § 25.13 (4th ed. 2011); Melli, Subdivision Control in Wisconsin, 1953 Wis.L.Rev. 389; 1 Patton & Palomar, Land Titles § 119 (3d ed. 2018 update). The plat may be the basis of a valid conveyance of a parcel of land even though the plat has not been approved by the local government; see Nejati v. Stageberg, 286 Va. 197, 747 S.E.2d 795 (2013).

[136] See Davis v. Hall, 365 Mont. 216, 280 P.3d 261 (2012) (deed and plat, read together, comprised adequate description). References to plats are often used to create and convey easements shown thereon, but the plat must make clear what parcels comprise the dominant and servient land; see Blazer v. Wall, 343 Mont. 173, 183 P.3d 84 (2008).

[137] Fox v. Norfolk Southern Corp., 342 Ga. App. 38, 802 S.E.2d 319 (2017). But see Rogers v. United States, 109 Fed. Cl. 280, 286 (2013) (plats and surveys did not identify common areas of the project, and hence references to plats and surveys were inadequate descriptions of common areas).

[138] Urban Land Institute, Shopping Center Development Handbook 59–67 (3d ed. 1999). References to other sorts of maps, such as tax maps prepared by assessors, may also form the basis of valid descriptions; see Haney v. Molko, 123 Idaho 132, 844 P.2d 1382 (App.1992).

[139] See, e.g., Firma, Inc. v. Twillman, 126 S.W.3d 790, 794 (Mo. Ct. App. 2004) (reference to tax assessor's map was ambiguous and insufficient description); Hahn v. Love, 394 S.W.3d 14, 25 (Tex. App. 2012) (reference to county appraisal district map was sufficient description).

a land description.[140] Tax maps, for example, are mainly concerned with identifying each parcel in general terms, and not with fixing accurate boundaries.

The metes and bounds, Government Survey, and plat systems are not mutually exclusive. A plat, for example, may be created within a given section of land in the Government Survey system and located by reference to a section corner. An owner may employ a metes and bounds description to carve out and convey a portion of a platted lot or a part of a section in the Government Survey system. Indeed, both plats and the Government Survey system often provide convenient references to points of beginning of metes and bounds descriptions.

Other descriptive techniques may also be used. One which is both common and dangerous is to specify a quantitative part of a larger parcel which is already described, such as "the West 50 feet of Lot 13." This is satisfactory if Lot 13 is precisely rectangular and its boundaries run exactly north-south and east-west, but if this is not so the description is ambiguous. Is the 50 feet measured along the northerly boundary or the southerly boundary (which may not be parallel to each other); is it measured at right angles to the westerly boundary; or is it measured due east from the westernmost point of the lot?[141] Fractional parts of larger parcels can also be troublesome, as in "the West half of Lot 13." Should the new boundary run exactly north-south or should it be parallel to the existing westerly boundary? Most courts would probably hold the latter.[142] Other forms of quantity or fractional description may be so unclear as to force a court to declare the conveyance void for vagueness: for example, a statement of acreage, unaccompanied by any indication of the shape of the land conveyed.[143] If a conveyance uses a fractional description (e.g., "one-fourth of my farm"), but contains no clue as to which geographic portion of the land is intended, it may be construed as an undivided tenancy in common.[144]

A final type of description is one which depends entirely on extrinsic information about the grantor's land ownership. One form is the "omnibus" or "Mother Hubbard" clause: "I hereby grant all of my land in Adams County," or the like. Another is the "after-acquired property" clause sometimes found in mortgages: "This mortgage shall bind all of the land which I may acquire in Adams County until the debt secured hereby is repaid." As between the original parties to the instrument, these sorts of descriptions

---

[140] See, e.g., Favre Prop. Mgmt., LLC v. Cinque Bambini, 863 So. 2d 1037 (Miss. Ct. App. 2004) (descriptions in general and sectional land indexes for each county are often incomplete or conflicting).

[141] See Walters v. Tucker, 281 S.W.2d 843 (Mo. 1955) (perpendicular to westerly boundary, so as to produce a strip of 50-foot width); Fears v. Texas Bank, 247 S.W.3d 729 (Tex. Ct. App. 2008) ("20 acres off of the West end" of a described parcel was ambiguous; deed held void).

[142] See 1 Patton & Palomar, Land Titles § 149 n. 9 (3d ed. 2017 update).

[143] Mobley v. Evans, 2009 Ark. App. 348, 308 S.W.3d 165 (2009); Strickland v. CMCR Investments, LLC, 279 Ga. 112, 610 S.E.2d 71 (2005); McDonald v. Jones, 258 Mont. 211, 852 P.2d 588 (1993); Haines v. Mensen, 233 Neb. 543, 446 N.W.2d 716 (1989); Lewis v. Adams, 979 S.W.2d 831 (Tex. App. 1998). But see Kauka Farms, Inc. v. Scott, 256 Ga. 642, 352 S.E.2d 373 (1987) (20 acres "surrounding" an existing home was sufficient to describe a circle centered on the home); Stephenson v. Rowe, 315 N.C. 330, 338 S.E.2d 301 (1986) (30 acres "surrounding" an existing home; court allowed devisee to make reasonable choice of land, with home near center). See also Bybee v. Hageman, 66 Ill. 519 (1873), upholding "one acre and a half in the northwest corner of section five." The court noted that Illinois was a Government Survey state and that square parcels were very common, and concluded that a square shape was intended.

[144] Mounce v. Coleman, 133 Ariz. 251, 650 P.2d 1233 (App.1982) (20 acres out of 160-acre parcel gives fractional interest); Aspen-Western Corp. v. Bd. of Cty. Comm'rs of Pitkin Cty., 661 P.2d 1175 (Colo. App. 1982); Morehead v. Hall, 126 N.C. 213, 35 S.E. 428 (1900). But see Ellett v. Liedtke, 668 S.W.2d 880 (Tex.App. 1984), noted 37 Baylor L.Rev. 1059 (1985) (conveyance of "one-half of an undivided interest" was void, since there was no method of determining the fractional size of the undivided interest).

are generally upheld.[145] But they are very difficult for a subsequent title examiner to find, since the examiner usually cannot tell by looking at the recorder's index entry for a document whether it affects the land one is now searching. Hence, instruments using descriptions of this kind are sometimes treated as unrecorded for purposes of the recording acts.[146]

Monuments. Monuments having significant width raise interesting problems. For example, public streets and highways are usually easements in favor of some public body, such as a city or county, with the so-called "underlying fee" remaining in private ownership. Where this is so, the usual rule of construction is that a conveyance describing lan262550d with a call "to Main Street" will actually convey title to the center of the street, subject to the street easement.[147] The policy ground for the rule is obvious; if the street easement is someday vacated, it makes little sense to hold that some former owner or developer can take possession of a strip of land 20 or 30 feet wide. The rule is sometimes applied, although not as consistently, even if the instrument describes the boundary as running along one side or edge of the street.[148] A very clear expression of intention is necessary for the grantor to exclude the street from the document's coverage.[149] A similar rule making the center line the boundary is applied to railroad and other rights of way, and to the thread of rivers or streams, provided, of course, that the title to the bed is in fact in private ownership and held by the grantor.[150]

---

[145] In re Hard Rock Expl., Inc., 580 B.R. 202 (Bankr. S.D.W. Va. 2017) (both after-acquired property and Mother Hubbard clauses upheld); Whitehead v. Johnston, 467 So.2d 240 (Ala.1985), noted at 37 Ala.L.Rev. 699 (1986); Ukkestad v. RBS Asset Finance, Inc., 235 Cal.App.4th 156, 185 Cal.Rptr.3d 145 (2015); Partnership Properties Co. v. Sun Oil Co., 552 So.2d 246 (Fla.App.1989) (specific description of parcel controls over "Mother Hubbard" clause); Matter of Estate of White, 234 So. 3d 1210 (Miss. 2017); Davis v. Mueller, 528 S.W.3d 97 (Tex. 2017); Roeder Co. v. Burlington Northern, Inc., 105 Wn.2d 567, 716 P.2d 855 (1986); 1 Patton and Palomar, Land Titles § 125 (3d ed. 2017 update). Cf. Dickson v. Kates, 132 Wash.App. 724, 133 P.3d 498 (2006) ("the land immediately to the west" was ambiguous and an insufficient description).

[146] In re Cornerstone E & P Company, L.P., 435 B.R. 390 (N.D. Tex. 2010); Luthi v. Evans, 223 Kan. 622, 576 P.2d 1064 (1978); See Nelson, Whitman, Burkhart & Freyermuth, Real Estate Finance Law § 9.3 (6th ed. 2014); 3 Glenn, Mortgages § 418 (1943). See the discussion of the chain of title concept, § 11.11 infra at note 615.

[147] See Haggart v. United States, 108 Fed. Cl. 70 (2012) (Washington law); Cottonwood/Verde Valley Chamber of Commerce, Inc. v. Cottonwood Professional Plaza I, 183 Ariz. 121, 901 P.2d 1151 (Ariz. App. 1994); Near v. Calkins, 946 P.2d 537 (Colo.App. 1997); Mierzejewski v. Laneri, 130 Conn. App. 306, 23 A.3d 82 (2011); Carney v. Heinson, 133 Idaho 275, 985 P.2d 1137 (1999); Pluimer v. City of Belle Fourche, 549 N.W.2d 202 (S.D.1996); 1 Patton and Palomar, Land Titles § 146 (3d ed. 2017 update); Annot., 49 A.L.R.2d 982 (1956). Cf. City of Albany v. State of New York, 28 N.Y.2d 352, 321 N.Y.S.2d 877, 270 N.E.2d 705 (1971). The same principle is applied when the property is described by reference to a recorded map or plat showing the street; see Baker v. Ramirez, 190 Cal.App.3d 1123, 235 Cal.Rptr. 857 (1987). The presumption is not usually applied if the easement has already been vacated or abandoned by the time the conveyance is made; see Note, 5 Ariz.L.Rev. 143 (1963); Morrissey v. Achziger, 147 Colo. 510, 364 P.2d 187 (1961).

[148] See Greenberg v. L.I. Snodgrass Co., 161 Ohio St. 351, 119 N.E.2d 292 (1954); cf. 3 Am.L.Prop. § 12.112 n. 17 (1952).

[149] See Bowers v. Atchison, Topeka, & Santa Fe Railway Co., 119 Kan. 202, 237 P. 913, 42 A.L.R. 228 (1925).

[150] United States v. Goodrich Farms Partnership, 753 F.Supp. 879 (D.Colo. 1991), affirmed 947 F.2d 906 (10th Cir. 1991) (deed conveys to thread of nonnavigable stream); Oppliger v. Vineyard, 19 Neb. App. 172, 803 N.W.2d 786 (2011); Padilla v. City of Santa Fe, 107 N.M. 107, 753 P.2d 353 (App.1988); State v. Hardee, 259 S.C. 535, 193 S.E.2d 497 (1972); Annot., 78 A.L.R.3d 604 (1977). The thread of a stream is the last part to dry up, and not necessarily the geographic center line; see Wilson v. Lucerne Canal & Power Co., 150 P.3d 653 (Wyo. 2007); Edlund v. 4-S, LLC, 13 Neb. App. 800, 702 N.W.2d 812 (2005). The rationale here is that ownership of the stream bed is of little practical value in light of the rights of the various riparian owners to the water itself, and hence the grantor is unlikely to have intended to reserve the bed. Again, as with roadways, the presumption may be rebutted by a description which expressly runs to or along the bank of the stream; see Glover v. Giraldo, 824 P.2d 552 (Wyo.1992); Knutson v. Reichel, 10 Wn.App. 293, 518 P.2d 233, 78 A.L.R.3d

Rivers and streams that serve as boundaries pose additional problems because they can and do change course.[151] When such changes are slow and imperceptible, the law's policy is to treat the legal boundary as changing with the stream itself, whether the boundary is the stream's border or its thread. In this way, the upland owner's adjacency to the stream is preserved.[152] Where the stream's edge is the boundary, if accretion (a gradual buildup of alluvial soil on the bank) or reliction (a gradual recession of water from the bank) occurs, the additional area automatically becomes the property of the abutting littoral landowner.[153] Similarly, if slow erosion results in the wearing away of soil on the stream's bank, the littoral owner loses title to the affected area.[154] If the parcel's boundary is the thread of the stream or some other line rather than its edge, and the result of accretion, reliction, or erosion is to shift the line, the practical consequences

---

598 (1973). As to private ownership of river and stream beds generally, see 1 Patton and Palomar, Land Titles §§ 129–145 (3d ed. 2017 update).

Note that the thread boundary principle discussed here applies to watercourses, but not to static bodies of water such as lakes; see Eifling v. Southbend, Inc., 2016 Ark. App. 393, 500 S.W.3d 756 (2016) (where lake is designated as boundary, property runs to ordinary high water mark of lake); Walton Cty. v. Stop Beach Renourishment, Inc., 998 So. 2d 1102 (Fla. 2008), aff'd sub nom. Stop the Beach Renourishment, Inc. v. Fla. Dep't of Envtl. Prot., 560 U.S. 702, 130 S.Ct. 2592, 177 L.Ed.2d 184 (2010) (where ocean beach is boundary, property extends to mean high water line).

[151] The principles of accretion and reliction discussed here apply only when the body of water is itself the boundary, and not when the boundary is fixed by a metes and bounds description that happens to coincide with the water's edge; see Norby v. Estate of Kuykendall, 2015 N.D. 232, 869 N.W.2d 405 (2015).

[152] There is a strong presumption that a riparian or littoral owner does not intend to separate the land from access to the water; see, e.g., Haynes v. Carbonell, 532 So.2d 746 (Fla.App.1988). See Board of Trustees of Internal Improvement Trust Fund v. Medeira Beach Nominee, Inc., 272 So.2d 209 (Fla.App. 1973), for a further discussion of the policies underlying the rules mentioned in the text. See also Lundquist, Artificial Additions to the Riparian Land: Extending the Doctrine of Accretion, 14 Ariz.L.Rev. 315 (1972); Potomac Shores, Inc. v. River Riders, Inc., 219 Md. App. 29, 55, 98 A.3d 1048, 1064 (2014), applying the principles of accretion and reliction to the Potomac River, which serves as the boundary between Maryland and Virginia.

[153] United States v. Byrne, 291 F.3d 1056 (9th Cir. 2002); United States v. Pappas, 814 F.2d 1342 (9th Cir.1987); Devon Energy Prod. Co., L.P. v. Norton, 685 F.Supp.2d 614 (W.D. La. 2010); Spottswood v. Reimer, 41 So. 3d 787 (Ala. Civ. App. 2009); State v. Hatchie Coon Hunting & Fishing Club, Inc., 372 Ark. 547, 279 S.W.3d 56 (2008) (title to accreted land subsequently lost by adverse possession); Accardi v. Regions Bank, 201 So. 3d 743 (Fla. Dist. Ct. App. 2016); Bruce v. Garges, 259 Ga. 268, 379 S.E.2d 783 (1989); Walker Lands, Inc. v. E. Carroll Par. Police Jury, 871 So. 2d 1258 (La. App. 2004); Stidham v. City of Whitefish, 229 Mont. 170, 746 P.2d 591 (1987); Martin v. Bay, 400 S.C. 140, 732 S.E.2d 667 (Ct. App. 2012); Turner v. Mullins, 162 S.W.3d 356 (Tex. App. 2005). The addition of accreted land to the upland owner's title applies to ocean-front property as well; see Sea River Properties, LLC v. Parks, 355 Or. 831, 333 P.3d 295 (2014); Maunalua Bay Beach Ohana 28 v. State, 122 Haw. 34, 222 P.3d 441 (Ct. App. 2009) (accretion doctrine modified by statute); Stop the Beach Renourishment, Inc., supra note 150. See also Brown v. Kalicki, 90 Mass. App. Ct. 534, 62 N.E.3d 71 (2016), applying the principle to land registered under the Torrens system. But see Bayview Land, Ltd. v. State ex rel. Clark, 950 So.2d 966 (Miss. 2006) (artificial accretions to oceanfront property belonged to the state by statute). See Annot., 54 A.L.R.2d 643 (2004); Note, Accretion and Severed Mineral Estates, 53 U.Chi. L.Rev. 232 (1985); 1 Patton and Palomar, Land Titles §§ 144. 300 (3d ed. 2017 update). A similar concept may be applied to a deed which employs a "meander line" of a body of water as a boundary. See Thomas v. Nelson, 35 Wn.App. 868, 670 P.2d 682 (1983). Subsequent conveyances of the upland property are presumed to include the accretions, but the presumption may be overcome; see In re Estate of Rosenbaum, 2001 S.D. 44, 624 N.W.2d 821 (S.D. 2001).

[154] 101 Ranch v. United States, 714 F.Supp. 1005 (D.N.D. 1988), affirmed 905 F.2d 180 (8th Cir.1990); Wyatt v. Griffin, 242 Ark. 562, 414 S.W.2d 377 (1967); Borough of Wildwood Crest v. Masciarella, 92 N.J.Super. 53, 222 A.2d 138 (1966), affirmed 51 N.J. 352, 240 A.2d 665 (1968). If the process of erosion goes on long enough, an owner can lose his or her entire land, and the next adjacent owner will then become a littoral owner. If this occurs and the bank subsequently begins to accrete, the courts are divided as to whether the new littoral owner remains such even if the soil added is in the same physical location as the lost land of the original littoral owner. Compare Winkle v. Mitera, 195 Neb. 821, 241 N.W.2d 329 (1976) and Kruse v. Grokap, Inc., 349 So.2d 788 (Fla.App. 1977) (title to accreted land belongs to new owner), with United States v. 1,629.6 Acres of Land, More or Less, in Sussex County, Delaware, 503 F.2d 764 (3d Cir.1974) and Mikel v. Kerr, 499 F.2d 1178 (10th Cir.1974) (title to accreted land restored to former owner).

are much the same; the littoral owners gain or lose useable land.[155] If the change is gradual, it is generally immaterial whether it results from natural causes or some construction project,[156] although one owner is not allowed to acquire another's land by causing accretion to occur.[157]

If a stream suddenly shifts course, or soil is added to or removed from its bank rapidly rather than gradually, the process is known as avulsion and the boundaries of the littoral owners are not affected. The stream's original thread, bank, or other previous boundary line remains such despite the change of course.[158] This distinction between quick and slow changes obviously requires resolution of close questions of fact in particular cases.[159] It does not appear to be relevant whether the change was natural or man-made[160], but the character of the river or stream itself may be important; if the stream is one which frequently undergoes fairly major changes in course, it is more likely that such changes will be considered accretive rather than avulsive.[161]

Resolving discrepancies. Since metes and bounds descriptions are often long and complicated, it is easy for a drafter or copyist to make an error in them. Sometimes the mistake and the needed correction are obvious, but if they are not the courts often resort to a list of priorities which have been developed over the years to resolve inconsistencies in descriptions. They are based on common-sense assumptions about the relative probability of error in various types of descriptive statements. While they are not carved in stone and are sometimes disregarded in light of extrinsic evidence of a contrary intent[162], they are nonetheless useful. The following are the priorities, listed in descending order with the highest and most reliable first:

[155] Curry v. Furby, 20 Neb. App. 736, 832 N.W.2d 880 (2013).

[156] Wilson v. Lucerne Canal & Power Co., 150 P.3d 653 (Wyo. 2007).

[157] State Department of Natural Resources v. Pankratz, 538 P.2d 984 (Alaska 1975); United States v. Robertson Terminal Warehouse, Inc., 575 F.Supp.2d 210 (D.D.C. 2008), aff'd sub nom. United States v. Old Dominion Boat Club, 630 F.3d 1039 (D.C. Cir. 2011) (fill added by wharf owners was not accretion); H.K. Porter Co., Inc. v. Board of Supervisors, 324 So.2d 746 (Miss. 1975); Borough of Wildwood Crest v. Masciarella, supra note 154; Littlefield v. Nelson, 246 F.2d 956 (10th Cir. 1957). Cf. State ex rel. State Lands Commission v. Superior Court, 11 Cal.4th 50, 44 Cal.Rptr.2d 399, 900 P.2d 648 (1995), distinguishing between natural and artificial accretion. See Lundquist, Artificial Additions to Riparian Land: Extending the Doctrine of Accretion, 14 Ariz. L.Rev. 315 (1972); Smith, Right of Riparian Owner to Artificial Accretion, 25 Miss.L.J. 174 (1954); Annots., 134 A.L.R. 467 (1941); 63 A.L.R.3d 249 (1975); 3 Am.L.Prop. § 15.29 n. 8 (1952).

[158] Walton Cty. v. Stop the Beach Renourishment, Inc., 998 So. 2d 1102, 1117 (Fla. 2008), aff'd sub nom. Stop the Beach Renourishment, Inc. v. Fla. Dep't of Envtl. Prot., 560 U.S. 702, 130 S.Ct. 2592, 177 L.Ed.2d 184 (2010) (avulsive addition of sand to beach by state agency); Bobo v. Jones, 364 Ark. 564, 222 S.W.3d 197 (2006); Osterloh v. Idaho, 105 Idaho 50, 665 P.2d 1060 (1983); Longabaugh v. Johnson, 163 Ind.App. 108, 321 N.E.2d 865 (1975); Cox v. F-S Prestress, Inc., 797 So. 2d 839 (Miss. 2001); City of Long Branch v. Jui Yung Liu, 203 N.J. 464, 4 A.3d 542 (2010); City of Long Beach v. Mansell, 3 Cal.3d 462, 91 Cal.Rptr. 23, 476 P.2d 423 (1970).

[159] See Anderson-Tully Co. v. Franklin, 307 F.Supp. 539 (D.Miss. 1969) (avulsion must be so rapid as to be distinctly perceptible or measurably visible at the time of its progress); Sieck v. Godsey, 254 Iowa 624, 118 N.W.2d 555 (1962).

[160] The California cases generally treat all man-made changes as avulsive and as not modifying existing boundaries; see City of Long Beach v. Mansell, supra note 158. Dicta to this effect can be found in occasional cases from other jurisdictions; see, e.g., Trustees of Internal Improvement Fund v. Sutton, 206 So.2d 272 (Fla.App. 1968), requiring "natural and actual continuity of accretion" to the land of the riparian owner.

[161] See Sieck v. Godsey, supra note 159; Beck, The Wandering Missouri River, A Study in Accretion Law, 43 N.D.L.Rev. 429 (1967).

[162] See Cities Service Oil Co. v. Dunlap, 115 F.2d 720 (5th Cir. 1940), rehearing denied 117 F.2d 31 (1941), certiorari denied 313 U.S. 566, 61 S.Ct. 940, 85 L.Ed. 1525 (1941); Bernier v. Fredette, 85 Mass. App. Ct. 265, 8 N.E.3d 769 (2014); Grondin v. Hanscom, 2014 ME 148, 106 A.3d 1150 (2014); Sacrison v. Evjene, 388 Mont. 144, 398 P.3d 273 (2017).

1. natural monuments

2. artificial monuments and marked or surveyed lines

3. adjacent tracts or boundaries

4. courses or directions

5. distances

6. area or quantity.[163]

The operation of the priorities may be illustrated by a deed describing a boundary as "105 feet to the Southeast corner of the Cassady Tract," when in fact the distance to the Cassady Tract is 150 feet. Since a call to an adjacent tract controls over a call of distance, the court will treat the distance as 150 feet.[164] In addition, if there is a discrepancy between a deed's metes and bounds description and a plat referred to in the deed, the plat will control.[165]

§ 11.3 DELIVERY AND ACCEPTANCE

A deed is effective only when it is delivered, and an undelivered deed passes no title.[166] Ordinarily delivery involves a physical transfer of possession of the deed from the grantor to grantee,[167] but this is not essential.[168] Delivery is a question of the grantor's intent to pass present title,[169] and many cases hold that evidence of intent that the deed be presently operative will suffice, even if the grantor retains the deed itself and has done no other overt act indicating delivery.[170] At the same time, a line of seemingly inconsistent cases holds that, to consummate a delivery, the deed must be

---

[163] See, e.g., Wyatt v. Arkansas Game & Fish Comm'n, 360 Ark. 507, 202 S.W.3d 513 (2005); Bodiford v. Spanish Oak Farms, Inc., 317 S.C. 539, 455 S.E.2d 194 (App. 1995); Grubbs v. Crosson, 634 So.2d 593 (Ala.Civ.App.1994); DD & L, Inc. v. Burgess, 51 Wn.App. 329, 753 P.2d 561 (1988); 1 Patton & Palomar, Land Titles § 151 et seq. (3d ed. 2017 update); McCarver, Legal Principles for Determining Boundary Lines, J.Mo.Bar, April-May 1987, at 147. There are hundreds of cases illustrating these principles. See, e.g., Nourachi v. United States, 655 F.Supp.2d 1215 (M.D. Fla. 2009); Harmon v. Ingram, 572 So.2d 411 (Ala. 1990); Sun Valley Shamrock Resources, Inc. v. Travelers Leasing Corp., 118 Idaho 116, 794 P.2d 1389, 1392 (1990); Larsen v. Richardson, 361 Mont. 344, 260 P.3d 103 (2011). See Comment, Boundary Law: The Rule of Monument Control in Washington, 7 U.P.S.L.Rev. 355 (1983).

[164] Quality Plastics, Inc. v. Moore, 131 Ariz. 238, 640 P.2d 169 (1981).

[165] McClendon v. Thomas, 768 So. 2d 261 (La. Ct. App. 2000).

[166] Robinson v. Williams ex rel. Estate of Dunn, 280 Ga. 877, 635 S.E.2d 120 (2006); Jorgensen v. Crow, 466 N.W.2d 120 (N.D.1991); Cavazos v. Cavazos, 246 S.W.3d 175 (Tex. Ct. App. 2007); Winegar v. Froerer Corp., 813 P.2d 104 (Utah 1991). See generally 3 Am. L.Prop. § 12.64 (1952).

[167] E.g., Wood v. Wood, 284 Ill.App.3d 718, 672 N.E.2d 385 (1996)

[168] Abraham v. Mihalich, 330 Pa. Super. 378, 479 A.2d 601 (1984); Jones v. Innkeepers, Inc., 12 Ark.App. 364, 676 S.W.2d 761 (1984); B-T Limited v. Blakeman, 705 P.2d 307 (Wyo.1985). As Lord Coke's famous dictum put it, "As a deed may be delivered to the party without words, so may a deed be delivered by words without any act of delivery;" 1 Co.Litt. 36A. See Boohaker v. Brashier, 428 So.2d 627 (Ala.1983); Gonzales v. Gonzales, 267 Cal.App.2d 428, 73 Cal.Rptr. 83 (1968).

[169] Estate of Mendelson v. Mendelson, 2016 Ill. App. 2d 150084, 48 N.E.3d 891 (2016); Gheen v. State ex rel. Dep't of Health, Div. of Healthcare Fin./EqualityCare, 2014 Wy. 70, 326 P.3d 918 (Wyo. 2014).

[170] See, e.g., Evans v. Waddell, 689 So.2d 23 (Ala. 1997); Kerr v. Fernandez, 792 So.2d 685 (Fla. Ct. App. 2001); In re Van Houten, 56 B.R. 891 (Bkrtcy. W.D.Mich. 1986); In re Estate of Lloyd, 676 S.W.2d 889 (Mo.App.1984); In re Estate of Plance, 175 A.3d 249, 260 (Pa. 2017); Lemus v. Aguilar, 491 S.W.3d 51 (Tex. Ct. App. 2016). If the grantor is incapacitated or cannot speak, nods or gestures can constitute a delivery; see Arwe v. White, 117 N.H. 1025, 381 A.2d 737 (1977). But delivery must occur while the grantor is living; see Sargent v. Baxter, 673 So.2d 979 (Fla.App.1996); Robinson v. Williams ex rel. Estate of Dunn, 280 Ga. 877, 635 S.E.2d 120 (2006). See generally Annot., 87 A.L.R.2d 787 (1963); Note, The Issue of Delivery Raised by "Dispositive" Conveyances, 18 Drake L.Rev. 67 (1968).

placed within the control of the grantee, or outside the control of the grantor.[171] In any event, a manual handing over of the deed to the grantee is not necessarily a delivery if it is not accompanied by the requisite intent, although it generally raises a strong presumption of delivery,[172] while nondelivery is presumed if the grantor retains possession of the deed.[173]

Delivery is seldom an issue in arms-length sales of real estate, since the grantor's intention to make an immediate transfer is usually perfectly clear. The problems generally arise in gratuitous intra-family transfers. Here the grantor's intent, perhaps cloudy and imperfectly formed, is often to make a disposition of the property which will take effect only at death, but which will avoid the formality, publicity, and expense of probate of a will. To accomplish this, the grantor executes a deed but does not make an immediate manual delivery to the grantee; indeed, the grantee is often told nothing of the arrangement. The deed may be retained by the grantor in his or her home or office, or it may be placed in a safety deposit box which is held in the grantor's name, the grantee's name, or held jointly by both of them.[174] These acts may be accompanied by a variety of more or less explicit statements of intent. Typically the grantee obtains the deed after the grantor's death, and then engages in a title dispute with the grantor's heirs or residuary devisees who claim that the deed was never delivered. From a planning viewpoint this is a sorry affair and constitutes a virtual invitation to litigation.

The essential problem is that the grantor has attempted to use the deed as a will. An intent that the instrument take effect at the maker's death is perfectly appropriate to a will, but it will not do for a deed at all; what is required for delivery of a deed is intent that an interest in land be transferred *immediately*. Much of the controversy would be swept away if the requisite formalities for deeds and wills were the same. It would then make little difference, in terms of ultimate validity, whether or not the grantor intended an immediate transfer, for the courts could enforce the deed as a will.[175]

---

[171] In re Gomez, 388 B.R. 279 (Bankr. S.D. Tex. 2008); In re Ragsdel, 414 B.R. 515 (Bankr. E.D. Mo. 2009); Johnson v. Johnson, 327 Ga.App. 604, 760 S.E.2d 618 (2014). See also Temple v. Temple, 2015 Ohio 2311, 38 N.E.3d 342 (Ohio App. 2015) (grantor's retention of deed was evidence of lack of intent to deliver it).

[172] S & S Servs., Inc. v. Rogers, 35 F.Supp.2d 459 (D.V.I. 1999) (accidental manual delivery was not legally effective absent intent); Patterson v. Seavoy, 822 N.E.2d 206 (Ind. Ct. App. 2005); Walls v. Click, 209 W. Va. 627, 550 S.E.2d 605 (2001). For example, the grantor may hand the deed to the grantee to inspect it or for other reasons, but without intending a present transfer. See, e.g., James v. Mabie, 819 So. 2d 795 (Fla. Dist. Ct. App. 2002); Riley v. W.R. Holdings, LLC, 143 Idaho 116, 138 P.3d 316 (2006); Associated Financial Services Co. v. Bennett, 611 So.2d 973 (Miss. 1992); Walter v. Grover, 540 A.2d 120 (Me. 1988). But if the grantee proceeds wrongfully to convey title to a bona fide purchaser, a court may hold the grantor estopped to deny that a delivery occurred, notwithstanding lack of intent; see Webb v. Stewart, 255 Or. 523, 469 P.2d 609 (1970); text at notes 187 & 204 infra.

[173] See In re Estate of Wittmond, 314 Ill. App. 3d 720, 732 N.E.2d 659 (2000); Hans v. Hans, 482 So.2d 1117 (Miss.1986); Sofsky v. Rosenberg, 76 N.Y.2d 927, 563 N.Y.S.2d 52, 564 N.E.2d 662 (1990); Cusick v. Meyer, 124 Or.App. 515, 863 P.2d 486 (1993); In re Estate of Plance, 175 A.3d 249, 260 (Pa. 2017); Hanson v. Harding, 245 Va. 424, 429 S.E.2d 20 (1993). This presumption is inapplicable if the grantor is retaining a life estate; see Estate of Sabbs v. Cole, 57 Ark. App. 179, 944 S.W.2d 123 (1997).

[174] See, e.g., Robinson v. Williams ex rel. Estate of Dunn, 280 Ga. 877, 635 S.E.2d 120 (2006) (deed retained in grantor's safe deposit box deemed undelivered). Another possibility is the "death escrow," created by handing the deed to a third party to deliver upon the grantor's death; it is discussed in § 11.4, infra.

[175] This would not solve all problems, for there might still be a dispute between the "grantee" under the putative deed and the devisees under a subsequent formal will's residuary clause, with the latter arguing that the will revoked the former deed even if it is regarded as a will. In addition, a document which is in form of a deed but in substance a will would have to be probated and would be subject to related rules and procedures. But see Noble v. Fickes, 230 Ill. 594, 82 N.E. 950 (1907), in which the court denied probate of a deed on the ground that the testamentary intent must appear on the face of the document and not from extrinsic evidence. It is hardly conceivable that such reasoning would be followed today.

But the formalities do differ rather drastically. In particular, deeds require no attestation by witnesses in most states, while wills require attestation of a particular and rigorous kind.[176] Hence an instrument which fails as a deed for lack of delivery can seldom be treated as a valid will even if the grantor's intent would be carried out by doing so.

Courts sometimes overcome these difficulties by finding the requisite intent to make an immediate transfer in the face of such seemingly contrary facts as the grantor's continued possession of both the deed and the land, particularly if the grantee or some other person has been told about the deed.[177] It is difficult to generalize, since the cases tend to turn on the grantor's precise words and actions, and perhaps on the court's view of the grantee's worthiness as against competing claimants.[178] For example, placing the deed in a jointly-held safety deposit box may or may not be a sufficient delivery.[179] Recording of the deed, although not common in these cases, may be influential, for there is a presumption that a deed that has been recorded has been delivered.[180] Where the grantor remains in possession of the property, receives income from it, pays taxes on it, or the like, the courts sometimes find that the "immediate" transfer was subject to a retained life estate in the grantor despite the fact that neither the document nor the

---

[176] See, e.g., Lemus v. Aguilar, 491 S.W.3d 51 (Tex. Ct. App. 2016). As to deeds, see § 11.1 supra at note 67. As to wills, see Horton, Partial Harmless Error for Wills: Evidence from California, 103 Iowa L. Rev. 2027, 2031 n. 23 (2018) (wills require at least two witnesses, who must sign in the presence of the testator and each other).

[177] See, e.g., Evans v. Waddell, 689 So.2d 23 (Ala.1997) (delivery of photocopy sufficient); Ferrell v. Stinson, 233 Iowa 1331, 11 N.W.2d 701 (1943). In theory, continued possession of the land by the grantor is not necessarily inconsistent with delivery; see Richardson v. Kelley Land & Cattle Co., 504 F.2d 30 (8th Cir.1974); Hartley v. Stibor, 96 Idaho 157, 525 P.2d 352 (1974); Hackett v. Hackett, 429 P.2d 753 (Okl.1967). But if the deed purports to convey a possessory fee simple and there is no reservation of a leasehold or life estate to the grantor, it is difficult to imagine that the grantor actually intends a present transfer; see Den-Gar Enterprises v. Romero, 94 N.M. 425, 611 P.2d 1119 (App. 1980), cert. denied 94 N.M. 628, 614 P.2d 545 (1980); Avery v. Lillie, 260 Iowa 10, 148 N.W.2d 474 (1967).

[178] See, e.g., the court's comments about the grantor's fondness for the grantees in Ferrell v. Stinson, id.; Chillemi v. Chillemi, 197 Md. 257, 78 A.2d 750 (1951), in which the court severely disapproved of the grantee wife's profligate behavior.

[179] Finding no delivery, see Estate of Dittus, 497 N.W.2d 415 (N.D.1993); Lenhart v. Desmond, 705 P.2d 338 (Wyo.1985); Bennion v. Hansen, 699 P.2d 757 (Utah 1985). Finding delivery, see McMahon v. Dorsey, 353 Mich. 623, 91 N.W.2d 893 (1958).

[180] See Baldridge v. Baldridge, 100 Ark. App. 148, 265 S.W.3d 146 (2007); Brown v. Board of County Com'rs, 720 P.2d 579 (Colo.App.1985); Mattox v. Mattox, 777 So.2d 1041 (Fla. Ct. App. 2001) (recording is delivery *per se*); Giefer v. Swenton, 23 Kan. App.2d 172, 928 P.2d 906 (1996); Estate of Dykes v. Estate of Williams, 864 So.2d 926 (Miss. 2003); Gross v. Gross, 239 Mont. 480, 781 P.2d 284 (1989); Myers v. Key Bank, 68 N.Y.2d 744, 506 N.Y.S.2d 327, 497 N.E.2d 694 (1986). See also Morrow v. Morrow, 129 So. 3d 142 (Miss. 2013) (deeds were presumed to have been delivered on recording dates). The presumption (which, like that arising from possession, see note 171 supra, is better described as an inference which shifts the burden of going forward with evidence) is rebuttable; see Matter of Snaza Family Tr., 2018 S.D. 23, 909 N.W.2d 719 (2018); Odom v. Forbes, 500 So.2d 997 (Miss. 1987). In Massachusetts the presumption is conclusive, a rule which is greatly advantageous to title examiners; see Mass. Gen.L.Ann., c. 183, § 5. The presumption does not apply if the deed is recorded after the grantor's death; Estate of Mendelson v. Mendelson, 2016 Ill. App. 2d 150084, 48 N.E.3d 891 (2016). Lack of recording ordinarily raises no presumption of nondelivery; see In re Humann, 136 A.D.3d 1036, 26 N.Y.S.3d 304 (N.Y. App. Div. 2016); Estate of Blettell v. Snider, 114 Or.App. 162, 834 P.2d 505 (1992); Cantrell v. Henry, 696 S.W.2d 12 (Tenn.App. 1985). But see In re Estate of Plance, 175 A.3d 249, 260 (Pa. 2017), where grantor and grantee were same person (with grantee acting in the capacity of a trustee), failure to record indicated nondelivery.

grantor said anything about such a life estate.[181] There is often an air of artificiality about all discussion of the grantor's intent, if the grantor is dead and cannot testify.[182]

The traditional view is that a delivery to a grantee cannot pass title conditionally; if the grantor delivers the deed to the grantee but orally states that no title shall pass unless or until some future event occurs, the condition is not legally binding. As it is sometimes put, the grantee cannot be his or her own escrow holder.[183] But the courts divide as to where this leaves the deed itself. Where the condition is simply the grantor's death, the deed is usually held void because the underlying intent is testamentary.[184] This result makes little sense in light of the fact, discussed in the next section, that a delivery to a third person for delivery upon the grantor's death is usually held to vest an immediate future interest in the grantee.

Other types of conditions, unrelated to the grantor's death, are more troublesome. The majority of the cases probably hold that the deed is valid and the condition is disregarded,[185] despite the inconsistency of this approach with the basic axiom that delivery must convey title unconditionally. A growing minority view enforces the condition and gives the grantee title only if it has been fulfilled.[186] There is little to commend the majority approach. It has the advantage of protecting subsequent bona fide purchasers from the grantee, but it is unlikely that any court following the minority view would apply it against a BFP.[187]

The rule against conditional delivery does not make it impossible for a grantor to defer the grantee's possession until a future date or to make it conditional upon a future event. This objective can be accomplished simply by drafting the deed so as to convey a future interest, such as a springing executory interest contingent on the event's occurrence. The concept of delivery is not offended in the slightest by doing so. The key,

---

[181] See, e.g., Agrelius v. Mohesky, 208 Kan. 790, 494 P.2d 1095 (1972); Berigan v. Berrigan, 413 Ill. 204, 108 N.E.2d 438 (1952). Contra, see First Union Nat'l Bank v. Shealy, 325 S.C. 351, 479 S.E.2d 846 (App.1996). See the discussion at § 11.4 infra nn. 235–243.

[182] Lenhart v. Desmond, 705 P.2d 338 (Wyo.1985) (grantor's testimony accepted). If the grantor is alive and is the plaintiff, his testimony as to his own intent may or may not be persuasive; compare Havens v. Schoen, 108 Mich.App. 758, 310 N.W.2d 870 (1981) with Controlled Receivables, Inc. v. Harman, 17 Utah 2d 420, 413 P.2d 807 (1966).

[183] A true escrow—a delivery to an independent third party to be delivered to the grantee on certain conditions—is entirely permissible, but seldom used in interfamily transfers; see § 11.4 infra.

[184] See Raim v. Stancel, 339 N.W.2d 621 (Iowa App. 1983); First National Bank v. Bloom, 264 N.W.2d 208 (N.D. 1978); Broomfield v. Broomfield, 242 Ark. 355, 413 S.W.2d 657 (1967); Mueller v. Marshall, 166 Cal.App.2d 367, 333 P.2d 260 (1958). A few cases are contrary, holding the deed valid and the condition ineffective; see Rausch v. Devine, 80 P.3d 733 (Alaska 2003); Takacs v. Takacs, 317 Mich. 72, 26 N.W.2d 712 (1947); Ritchie v. Davis, 26 Wis.2d 636, 133 N.W.2d 312 (1965).

[185] State, by Pai v. Thom, 58 Hawaii 8, 563 P.2d 982 (1977) (condition that purchaser pay the agreed price); Bolyea v. First Presbyterian Church, 196 N.W.2d 149 (N.D. 1972); Paoli v. Anderson, 208 So.2d 167 (Miss. 1968) (condition that grantee survive grantor); DiMaio v. Musso, 2000 Pa. Super. 326, 762 A.2d 363 (2000); Walls v. Click, 209 W. Va. 627, 550 S.E.2d 605 (2001); Wynhoff v. Vogt, 2000 Wis. App. 57, 608 N.W.2d 400 (Wis. Ct. App. 2000); West's Ann.Cal.Civ.Code § 1056. The rule originated in Whyddon's Case, Cro.Eliz. 520, 78 Eng.Repr. 769 (1596). See generally Turner, Conditional Delivery of a Deed to the Grantee, 44 Ky.L.Rev. 218 (1956); Gavit, The Conditional Delivery of Deeds, 30 Colum.L.Rev. 1145 (1930); 3 Am. L.Prop. § 12.66 (1952).

[186] See Blancett v. Blancett, 102 P.3d 640 (N.M. 2004); United States v. 222.0 Acres of Land, 306 F.Supp. 138 (D.Md. 1969), adhered to, 324 F.Supp. 1170 (1971); Chillemi v. Chillemi, 197 Md. 257, 78 A.2d 750 (1951), noted 31 B.U.L.Rev. 437 (1951) and 12 Md.L.Rev. 248 (1951).

[187] See Kitchens v. Kitchens, 142 So.2d 343 (Fla.App. 1962). Note that the law of delivery theoretically has little solicitude for BFP's; an undelivered deed is simply void, no matter into whose hands the putative title may later pass. See the discussion of void and voidable deeds, § 11.1 supra at notes 91–109.

however, is to express the condition in the deed itself rather than merely to make it as an oral statement accompanying the delivery. The most common illustration is the reservation in the deed of a life estate in the grantor. The delivery is perfectly satisfactory, since an interest in the land (in this case a future interest) is *presently* transferred by the deed.[188]

A more challenging issue is posed if the grantor reserves not only a life estate but also a power to revoke the future interest or to dispose of the property in the future in fee simple. This combination of continued possession and the power of revocation seem to put the grantor in a position practically identical to that of a testator under a will. There is, of course, the technical distinction that the deed presently conveys an interest, subject to later divestment, while a will conveys nothing at all until death. Numerous cases, probably a majority, uphold the arrangement on this quite unsatisfying ground.[189] Perhaps the courts have been influenced by the ease with which a grantor may accomplish the same thing through the alternative means of a revocable inter vivos trust, which has the ambulatory characteristics of a will without its formality.[190] If this is so, logic suggests carrying the analogy further and forsaking the line of authority which now strikes down deeds intended to take effect at the grantor's death, at least if the intention is expressed in writing or otherwise proved by suitably convincing evidence.[191]

Delivery may be made to the grantee's agent rather than to the grantee personally.[192] In practice the difficulty is determining whose agent the recipient is. The question is one of fact, and can become exceedingly perplexing where the parties and the agent are members of the same family, or where the agent is the attorney of one or both parties.[193] If there are several grantees, as cotenants or as holders of present and future interests, delivery to any one of them is sufficient.[194]

---

[188] See, e.g., Smith v. Trinity United Methodist Church of Springfield, 47 Conn.Supp. 618, 821 A.2d 291 (2002); Russell v. Walz, 458 N.E.2d 1172 (Ind.App.1984); Parramore v. Parramore, 371 So.2d 123 (Fla.App.1978); Branton v. Martin, 243 S.C. 90, 132 S.E.2d 285 (1963); Thomas v. Williams, 105 Minn. 88, 117 N.W. 155 (1908); York v. Boatman, 487 S.W.3d 635, 641 (Tex. App. 2016); 3 Am.L.Prop. § 12.65 (1952).

[189] See, e.g., Harris v. Neely, 257 Ga. 361, 359 S.E.2d 885 (1987); St. Louis County National Bank v. Fielder, 364 Mo. 207, 260 S.W.2d 483 (1953); Tennant v. John Tennant Memorial Home, 167 Cal. 570, 140 P. 242 (1914). Contra, see Woods v. United States, 77 A.F.T.R.2d 96–2320 (W.D.Mich. 1996); Peebles v. Rodgers, 211 Miss. 8, 50 So.2d 632 (1951). See generally Garvey, Revocable Gifts of Legal Interests In Land, 54 Ky.L.Rev. 19 (1965).

[190] See generally McGovern et al., Principles of Wills, Trusts and Estates 420 (2d ed. 2011). Other types of non-will transfers at death which are both revocable and relatively informal include life insurance, transfer-on-death beneficiary designations of securities, and joint bank accounts.

[191] This appears to be precisely the step taken in Estate of O'Brien v. Robinson, 109 Wn.2d 913, 749 P.2d 154 (1988). The court conceded that the grantor's intent was not to pass title until her death, but nonetheless upheld the delivery.

[192] Hamilton v. United States, 806 F.Supp. 326 (D.Conn. 1992); United States v. Capobianco, 652 F.Supp. 325 (E.D.Pa. 1987); In re Craddock, 403 B.R. 355 (Bankr. M.D.N.C. 2009); Fike v. Harshbarger, 20 Md.App. 661, 317 A.2d 859 (1974), affirmed 273 Md. 586, 332 A.2d 27 (1975).

[193] See, e.g., Chapman v. Chapman, 473 So.2d 467 (Miss. 1985) (where deed was retained by grantor husband's attorney, there was no delivery to co-grantee wife); Stout v. Clayton, 674 S.W.2d 821 (Tex.App.1984) (deed retained by attorney employed by one of the grantees; court upheld jury finding of delivery); Gilmer v. Anderson, 34 Mich.App. 6, 190 N.W.2d 708 (1971) (handing deed to grantor's attorney not a delivery; he was exclusively grantor's agent).

[194] See Perkins v. Kerby, 308 So.2d 914 (Miss. 1975); Kresser v. Peterson, 675 P.2d 1193 (Utah 1984); Controlled Receivables, Inc. v. Harman, 17 Utah 2d 420, 413 P.2d 807 (1966). However, the grantor may present evidence that delivery to only some and not all grantees was intended; see West v. West, 620 So.2d 640 (Ala.1993).

Once a deed has been delivered, what happens to it is largely irrelevant. Its loss or destruction will not take away the grantee's title.[195] If the grantee redelivers it to the grantor, no retransfer of title takes place.[196] If someone alters the deed, the act has no legal significance.[197] If the grantor later executes a "correction deed" that reduces the rights granted by the original deed, the correction deed is ineffective.[198] Once delivered, a deed cannot be rescinded unless there is proof of mutual mistake, fraud, undue influence, or a scrivener's error.[199] Deeds are usually retained by their grantees following delivery, but they have only evidentiary value and even that is relatively unimportant if the deed is recorded.

Delivery is not complete without the grantee's acceptance of the deed,[200] but the concept of acceptance is a highly artificial one. Acceptance is presumed if the conveyance would be beneficial to the grantee,[201] and some cases hold it is not even necessary to show that the grantee knew of the deed or its delivery.[202] As a practical matter the role of the doctrine of acceptance is mainly to allow the grantee to disclaim the conveyance if it is not wanted.[203]

In theory, failure of either delivery or acceptance makes the deed void, and not even a subsequent bona fide purchaser can take title through such a deed.[204] This rule is a harsh one, for there is obviously no way a title examiner who inspects a deed on record

---

[195] Miami Holding Corp. v. Matthews, 311 So.2d 802 (Fla.App. 1975), cert. denied 325 So.2d 8 (Fla.1975); Capozzella v. Capozzella, 213 Va. 820, 196 S.E.2d 67 (1973); Newell v. Edwards, 7 N.C.App. 650, 173 S.E.2d 504 (1970). See also Caruso v. Parkos, 262 Neb. 961, 637 N.W.2d 351 (2002) (once deed is delivered, grantor cannot retain title by changing her mind).

[196] In re Baldridge, 256 B.R. 284 (Bankr. E.D. Ark. 2000); Payne v. Carver, 534 So.2d 566 (Ala. 1988); In re Estate of Bright, 215 N.W.2d 253 (Iowa 1974); Gonzales v. Gonzales, 267 Cal.App.2d 428, 73 Cal.Rptr. 83 (1968). See also Buckley v. Chevron, U.S.A., Inc., 149 Misc.2d 476, 565 N.Y.S.2d 419 (1991) (delivery was not impaired by grantee's handing deed to his attorney after receiving it). See also the remarkable English case, Sen v. Headley, [1991] Ch. 425, [1991] 2 All E.R. 636, holding in apparent disregard of the Statute of Frauds that a delivery of the *prior* title deeds was an effective conveyance of land as a gift *causa mortis*.

[197] Perry v. Perry, 234 Ark. 1066, 356 S.W.2d 419 (1962); Hansen v. Walker, 175 Kan. 121, 259 P.2d 242 (1953); Julian v. Peterson, 966 P.2d 878 (Utah Ct. App. 1998).

[198] Knapp v. Hughes, 25 A.D.3d 886, 808 N.Y.S.2d 791 (2006); Hilterbrand v. Carter, 175 Or. App. 335, 27 P.3d 1086 (2001); Myrad Properties, Inc. v. LaSalle Bank Nat. Ass'n, 300 S.W.3d 746 (Tex. 2009). If corrective deed takes away rights granted by the original deed, but the grantee signs it, it will be effective as a reconveyance from the grantee to the grantor; Knapp v. Hughes, id.

[199] Ward v. Ward, 70 Mass. App. Ct. 366, 874 N.E.2d 433 (2007) (mistake of law by grantor is not ground for rescission); Benton v. Harkins, 800 So.2d 1186 (Miss.App. 2001).

[200] Bercot v. Velkoff, 111 Ind. App. 323, 41 N.E.2d 686 (1942); Salmon v. Thompson, 391 So.2d 984 (Miss.1980); Kirkman v. Faulkner, 524 P.2d 648 (Colo.App.1974); Fritz v. Fritz, 479 S.W.2d 198 (Mo.App.1972). See Annot., 74 A.L.R.2d 992 (1960); 3 Am.L.Prop. § 12.70 (1952). Cf. Halleck v. Halleck, 216 Or. 23, 337 P.2d 330 (1959), adopting the English rule that acceptance is unnecessary.

[201] Collins v. Columbia Gas Transmission Co., 188 W.Va. 460, 425 S.E.2d 136 (1992); In re Van Houten, 56 B.R. 891 (Bkrtcy.W.D.Mich.1986). The presumption is rebuttable, see State v. Thomason, 2014 S.D. 18, 845 N.W.2d 640 (2014), and is not applied if receipt of the land would be burdensome to the grantee; see CUNA Mortgage v. Aafedt, 459 N.W.2d 801 (N.D. 1990); Messer v. Laurel Hill Associates, 93 N.C.App. 439, 378 S.E.2d 220 (1989), appeal after remand 102 N.C.App. 307, 401 S.E.2d 843 (1991); County of Worth v. Jorgenson, 253 N.W.2d 575 (Iowa 1977). Recording of the deed, particularly if done by the grantee, also raises a presumption of acceptance; see Smith v. Trinity United Methodist Church of Springfield, 47 Conn.Supp. 618, 821 A.2d 291 (2002); Panhandle Baptist Found., Inc. v. Clodfelter, 54 S.W.3d 66, 73 (Tex. App. 2001).

[202] See In re Gorenflo, 351 B.R. 64, 67 (Bankr. W.D.N.Y. 2006); Williams v. Herring, 15 N.C. App. 642, 190 S.E.2d 696 (1972). But see the contrary view expressed in In re Ragsdel, 414 B.R. 515 (Bankr. E.D. Mo. 2009); Blankenship v. Myers, 97 Idaho 356, 544 P.2d 314 (1975); Caron v. Wadas, 1 Mass. App.Ct. 651, 305 N.E.2d 853 (1974).

[203] See, e.g., Underwood v. Gillespie, 594 S.W.2d 372 (Mo.App. 1980); Hood v. Hood, 384 A.2d 706 (Me.1978); Jenkins v. Miller, 2008 Wyo. 45, 180 P.3d 925 (2008).

[204] See text, § 11.1 supra at notes 91–109.

can tell whether it was delivered or not. The presumption of delivery which flows from recording is obviously helpful here, but in most states it can be rebutted.[205] If the grantor has voluntarily permitted the deed to leave his or her hands or has been negligent in allowing the grantee to obtain or record it, a court will probably be eager to hold the grantor estopped to deny delivery as against a subsequent bona fide purchaser.[206] And the purchaser may get notice of the grantor's claim from the latter's continued possession. But there remains a residual risk to later purchasers that delivery will be found not to have occurred and that the grantor will be found to have engaged in no behavior on which to predicate notice or an estoppel.

§ 11.4 ESCROWS

An escrow is an instrument deposited[207] by its maker with a custodian with instructions that it be delivered to another party on the occurrence of one or more future conditions. In most cases the instrument is a deed deposited by the grantor. In a colloquial sense, the escrow is the entire arrangement under which such a deed is deposited and delivered. Thus, one speaks of "opening an escrow," and the deed is said to be "in escrow." Recording or delivery of the deed is referred to as the "close of escrow." Since the escrow is a particular means of delivering a deed, it is logically related to the general discussion of delivery in the preceding section. While money or other documents may be held and delivered through escrow, the discussion here is focused solely on deeds.[208]

There are two principal types of real estate escrows, and both raise interesting legal issues. One is the commercial or sales escrow,[209] handled by a lending institution, attorney, title insurance company, or professional escrow company and widely employed, especially in the western United States and in many urban areas elsewhere, to "settle" or "close" all types of real estate sales. The other is the "death escrow," in which a grantor deposits a deed with a custodian (usually a friend or relative) accompanied by instructions to deliver it to the grantee upon the grantor's death; in substance, it is a substitute for a will, and raises delivery problems similar to those discussed in the preceding section. The treatment here will focus first on the sales escrow, and will then compare with it the death escrow.

---

[205] See cases cited at note 180 supra.

[206] Webb v. Stewart, 255 Or. 523, 469 P.2d 609 (1970); Tutt v. Smith, 201 Iowa 107, 204 N.W. 294, 48 A.L.R. 394 (1925), discussed in W. Burby, Real Property 297 (3d ed. 1965). See 3 Am.L.Prop. § 12.68 n. 17 (1952).

[207] In an escrow the delivery to the custodian must be of physical possession of the document, and mere intent to deliver will not suffice. See 4 Tiffany, Real Property § 1049 (3d ed. 2017 update); Rundell, Delivery and Acceptance of Deeds in Wisconsin, 1 Wis.L.Rev. 65 (1921), at nn. 41–43. This rule is unlike that for delivery directly to the grantee discussed in § 11.3 supra at note 170.

[208] The escrow concept originally applied to deeds, but is now employed with other sorts of instruments as well; see Norwich Lumber Co. v. Yatroussis, 5 Conn.Cir. 95, 243 A.2d 311 (1967). In California, for example, a liquor license must be transferred by escrow; West's Ann.Cal.Bus. & Prof.Code § 24074. Computer source code is often put in escrow when a software developer is transferring it to another party; see 2 E-Commerce and Internet Law 18.03[3] (2017 update). Money may also be the subject of an escrow; see Edward Rose Sales Co. v. Shafer, 41 Mich.App. 105, 199 N.W.2d 655 (1972). For example, casualty insurance proceeds are often held in escrow pending completion of repairs on the property; see, e.g., Avila v. CitiMortgage, Inc., 801 F.3d 777 (7th Cir. 2015).

[209] See Comment, The Independent Escrow Agent: The Law and the Licensee, 38 So.Cal.L.Rev. 289 (1965); Lowe & Bothel, Escrow and Closing the Sale, in California Real Property Sales Transactions Ch. 15 (2018); Johnson v. Schultz, 195 N.C.App. 161, 671 S.E.2d 559 (2009), discussing use of both escrow and nonescrow closings in North Carolina.

Sales escrows. The use of an escrow agent or "escrowee" to consummate a real estate sale has several advantages.[210] The escrowee can compute the various charges and credits to each party and handle the mailing of checks, recording of documents, and other administrative aspects of the transfer. The parties may hand the escrowee their papers and funds at any convenient time, and need not meet together for a formal closing. This is particularly helpful in transactions involving numerous parties. In some areas of the nation, escrow companies work hand-in-hand with title insurers. The insurer will check the public records at the end of the business day prior to the closing of the escrow, and will report to the escrowee if no instruments have been recorded that might impair the title being transferred. The escrowee can then close the escrow and record the deed and other documents at the beginning of the next business day, virtually eliminating the possibility that closing could occur without knowledge of some adverse recorded instrument.[211]

A further advantage of the escrow is the legal rule that, when the stated conditions are satisfied and the custodian delivers the deed to the grantee, the delivery "relates back" to the date the deed was handed to the custodian, at least for some purposes.[212] Thus, the closing can occur and the deed can be validly delivered by the escrowee even if the grantor dies or becomes incapacitated after placing the deed in escrow.[213] This is an extremely useful feature of escrows, and can save vast time and effort that might otherwise be expended in having guardians appointed, locating heirs or devisees, persuading them to execute deeds, and so on. It is particularly desirable from the purchaser's viewpoint to employ an escrow if the sale is by long-term installment

---

[210]   See generally, Mann, Escrows—Their Use and Value, 1949 U.Ill.L.F. 398. See also Walker & Eshee, The Safeguards and Dilemmas of Escrows, 16 Real Est.L.J. 45 (1987); Young, Escrow Agreements: Bridges Over Troubled Closings, 58 Wis.Bar.Bull. 9 (Sept. 1985).

[211]   But the procedure is not problem-free, for it is possible that two competing instruments will both be recorded in the same batch at the beginning of the same day, and thus both bear identical recording dates and times. See First Bank v. E. W. Bank, 199 Cal. App. 4th 1309, 132 Cal. Rptr. 3d 267 (2011), holding in such a case that the two deeds of trust have equal priority. A better solution would be to hold the recording act inapplicable, since neither instrument was recorded before the other, and thus to base priority on the order of delivery of the instruments.

See Ferguson v. Caspar, 359 A.2d 17, 21 n. 9 (D.C.App.1976). An alternative approach is reported to be used in Cook County, Illinois, where title searches cannot be made up to the current date because of backlogs in the recorder's office. The escrowee records the deed as soon as the purchase money is deposited, and then searches the title to the date of recording. If an adverse conveyance is discovered, the escrowee records a quitclaim deed, previously executed by the purchaser for this purpose, to return title to the grantor. See Mann, id, at 404–05.

[212]   Hartman v. Wood, 436 N.W.2d 854 (S.D. 1989). See generally Annot., 117 A.L.R. 69 (1938); Jackson v. Jackson, 67 Or. 44, 135 P. 201 (1913). The "relation back" feature will prevail as against the grantor's death or insanity, against spousal rights which accrue at death, and against the rights of subsequent takers from the grantor who are not bona fide purchasers for value; see DeBoer v. Oakbrook Home Ass'n, Inc., 218 Neb. 813, 359 N.W.2d 768 (1984); First National Bank & Trust Co. v. Scott, 109 N.J.Eq. 244, 156 A. 836 (1931); Chaffin v. Harpham, 166 Ark. 578, 266 S.W.2d 685 (1924). The doctrine is flexible, and is unlikely to be applied to other issues, such as rights to rents and profits or liability for taxes as between the grantor and grantee. See Vierneisel v. Rhode Island Ins. Co., 77 Cal. App. 2d 229, 175 P.2d 63 (1946) (vendor remained covered by fire insurance for fire after deed deposited in escrow); Dixon v. O'Connor, 180 Neb. 427, 143 N.W.2d 364 (1966); Mohr v. Joslin, 162 Iowa 34, 142 N.W. 981 (1913); Larry D. Simons & Rina Welles, Is It In Or Is It Out? Determining the Operative Transfer Date for Escrow Accounts in Preference Litigation, 28 Cal. Bankr. J. 574 (2006); Annot., id., at 81–82.

[213]   Fuqua v. Fuqua, 528 S.W.2d 896 (Tex.Civ.App. 1975), refused n.r.e.; Donnelly v. Robinson, 406 S.W.2d 595 (Mo. 1966); Davis v. Stegall, 246 Miss. 593, 151 So.2d 813 (1963); Masquart v. Dick, 210 Or. 459, 310 P.2d 742 (1957).

contract, since the risk of the grantor's death or incapacity before completion of the contract is more substantial.[214]

Two requirements must be met for the doctrine of relation back to operate. The first is that there must be an enforceable contract of sale between the grantor and grantee,[215] and the second is that the grantor must have reserved no legal power to recall the deed from the custodian.[216] The genesis of both of these requirements is in the ancient law of delivery of deeds, and in particular the notion that a delivery must place the deed beyond the grantor's control. It makes some sense to demand that the grantor have no power to retrieve the deed, since such a power strongly suggests that the grantor has not yet formed a firm intention to deliver it. But the insistence on an enforceable contract of sale has been strongly criticized[217] and seems to serve little purpose, especially in light of the courts' willingness to admit oral testimony of intent when considering the validity of a direct delivery from grantor to grantee and the fact that no contract is needed in such cases.[218] In sale transactions there is ordinarily a contract, but if it is not embodied in a writing sufficient to satisfy the statute of frauds,[219] the relation back effect of the escrow may be defeated.[220] There is no legal requirement that the escrow instructions themselves be written,[221] although all professional escrowees insist on a writing for obvious practical reasons. If the instructions are written they will often contain all of the elements required to resolve the statute of frauds problem even if the contract of sale is oral.[222] There is authority that even the deed itself may provide sufficient a sufficient writing to make an oral contract of sale enforceable.[223]

---

[214] The escrow arrangement has a further advantage if the installment contract sale is subject to (or "wraps around") a prior mortgage or other lien which is not discharged when the contract is signed, but the future payments on which are to be made by the vendor. The escrowee can be instructed to collect the contract purchaser's payments each month and to disburse the appropriate amount to the holders of the prior lien. This obviates the risk that the contract vendor will fail to make the payments on the prior encumbrances and will abscond with the funds. On wrap-around encumbrances, see generally Note, 10 Pac.L.J. 932 (1979); Note, 1972 Duke L.J. 785; Nelson, Whitman, Burkhart & Freyermuth, Real Estate Finance Law § 9.8 (6th ed. 2014).

[215] See Penick v. May, 240 So.2d 461 (Miss. 1970); Merry v. County Board of Education, 264 Ala. 411, 87 So.2d 821 (1956), noted 9 Ala.L.Rev. 130 (1956); Johnson v. Wallden, 342 Ill. 201, 173 N.E. 790 (1930). A few cases do not require an underlying contract; see, e.g., Calbreath v. Borchert, 248 Iowa 491, 81 N.W.2d 433 (1957). Note that the contract requirement is inapplicable to death escrows; see text at note 234, infra.

[216] Donovan v. Kirchner, 100 Md.App. 409, 641 A.2d 961 (1994); Sargent v. Baxter, 673 So.2d 979 (Fla.App.1996); Brandt v. Schucha, 250 Iowa 679, 96 N.W.2d 179 (1959). Whether the right of recall or control is actually exercised by the grantor is irrelevant for this purpose.

[217] See, e.g., 4 Tiffany, Real Property § 1052 (3d ed. 2017 update); Ballentine, Delivery in Escrow, 29 Yale L.J. 831 (1920); Aigler, Is a Contract Necessary to Create an Effective Escrow? 16 Mich.L.Rev. 569 (1918); Tiffany, Conditional Delivery of Deeds, 14 Colum.L.Rev. 389 (1914).

[218] See § 11.3 supra at note 169ff.

[219] See § 10.1 supra.

[220] West Federal Savings & Loan Association v. Interstate Investment, Inc., 57 Wis.2d 690, 205 N.W.2d 361 (1973).

[221] In re Nealon, 532 B.R. 412 (Bankr. D. Mass. 2015); Bentz v. Wallowa Title Co., 93 Or. App. 27, 761 P.2d 10 (1988); Lewis v. Shawnee State Bank, 226 Kan. 41, 596 P.2d 116 (1979); Kennedy v. District-Realty Title Insurance Corp., 306 A.2d 655 (D.C.App. 1973); Young v. Bishop, 88 Ariz. 140, 353 P.2d 1017 (1960); Osby v. Reynolds, 260 Ill. 576, 103 N.E. 556 (1913); Johnson v. U.S. Title Agency, Inc., 91 N.E.3d 76 (Ohio App. 2017). See generally Earl L. Segal, Working with Escrow Agreements (with Form), Prac. Real Est. Law., January 2000, at 35.

[222] T.D. Dennis Builder, Inc. v. Goff, 101 Ariz. 211, 418 P.2d 367 (1966); Wood Building Corp. v. Griffitts, 164 Cal.App.2d 559, 330 P.2d 847 (1958).

[223] Southern States Development Co., Inc. v. Robinson, 494 S.W.2d 777 (Tenn. App. 1972); but see Baker v. Glander, 32 Mich.App. 305, 188 N.W.2d 263 (1971); Main v. Pratt, 276 Ill. 218, 114 N.E. 576 (1916). In many cases the deed will not contain all of the necessary contractual elements; see § 10.1 supra at note 34ff.

If the requirements of the preceding paragraph are not met, and there is consequently no "true" escrow, two conclusions follow. First, the grantor has a legal power to recall the deed at any time before the escrowee actually delivers it.[224] Second, if the grantor remains alive and competent and does not recall the deed, the conditions set out in the escrow instructions are met, and the escrowee delivers the deed to the grantee, there will be no relation back.[225] Such a delivery is itself perfectly good, however, as of the time it occurs.[226]

In the "true" escrow, a dispute sometimes arises as to when the second delivery occurs. The cases are not entirely consistent, but there is considerable authority that the deed is deemed delivered out of escrow when all conditions have occurred,[227] even if manual delivery or recording is delayed.[228] This view coincides with the general theory that delivery is a matter of the grantor's intent; the escrow instructions presumably reflect the grantor's desire that title should pass as soon as all conditions have been met. Often the final condition is the transfer of the purchaser's funds, representing the full purchase price, to the escrow holder. Many states have "good funds" statutes that specify the form this transfer of money must take.[229]

It is fundamental to the escrow concept that title cannot pass until all conditions have been fulfilled.[230] Suppose, however, the grantee bribes or connives with the escrowee to get hold of the deed even though some condition, such as full payment of the purchase price, remains unmet. As between grantor and grantee, all courts would agree that no title has passed.[231] But the problem is more difficult if the grantee records the deed and then sells the land to a bona fide purchaser for value. In some cases the grantor's continued possession may give the purchaser notice that something is amiss, but if that is not so the purchaser may have no clue that the delivery out of escrow was wrongful; indeed, it may not even be apparent to the grantee that an escrow was involved in the prior transfer. Rather surprisingly, most of the decisions hold that title is still in the grantor as against the bona fide purchaser.[232] This result, which has been severely

---

[224] See Chaffin v. Harpham, 166 Ark. 578, 266 S.W. 685 (1924); Eaton v. Eaton, 336 P.3d 921 (Kan. Ct. App. 2014); Jozefowicz v. Leickem, 174 Wis. 475, 182 N.W. 729 (1921). This right of recall presumably exists whether the grantor expressed it when depositing the deed in escrow or not.

[225] See cases cited at note 212 supra.

[226] Campbell v. Thomas, 42 Wis. 437 (1877).

[227] See Boatmen's Nat. Bank v. Dandy, 804 S.W.2d 783 (Mo.App.1990); Sturgill v. Industrial Painting Corp., 82 Nev. 61, 410 P.2d 759 (1966); McLoughlin v. McLoughlin, 237 A.D.2d 336, 654 N.Y.S.2d 407 (1997); Whitehead v. Hartford Fire Ins. Co., 278 S.W. 959 (Tex. Civ. App. 1926). The variety of theories which may be employed is discussed in Roberts v. Osburn, 3 Kan.App.2d 90, 589 P.2d 985 (1979). See also Andover Land Co. v. Hoffman, 264 Cal.App.2d 87, 70 Cal.Rptr. 38 (1968) (when all conditions are met, purchaser has "equitable title.")

[228] Recording will almost surely be treated as the equivalent of manual delivery by the escrowee; see § 11.3 supra at note 180.

[229] See, e.g., Col. Rev. Stat. § 38–35–125; Ga. Code Ann. § 44–14–13; Mass. Gen. L. c. 183. § 63B; Minn. Code Ann. § 82.176; Mo. Rev. Stat. § 381.410–.412; N.D. Gen. Stat. ch. 47–34; Va. Code § 6.1–2.10 to § 6.1–2.15; Wash. Rev. Code § 18.44.070.

[230] See Ferguson v. Caspar, 359 A.2d 17 (D.C.App. 1976); Dixon v. O'Connor, 180 Neb. 427, 143 N.W.2d 364 (1966).

[231] See, e.g., Laolagi v. First Am. Title Ins. Co., 2009 WL 2351607 (Cal. Ct. App. 2009) (unpublished); Allen v. Allen Title Co., 77 N.M. 796, 427 P.2d 673 (1967).

[232] See Watts v. Archer, 252 Iowa 592, 107 N.W.2d 549 (1961); Clevenger v. Moore, 126 Okl. 246, 259 P. 219, 54 A.L.R. 1237 (1927); Everts v. Agnes, 6 Wis. 453 (1858). See 3 Am.L.Prop. § 12.68 n. 19 (1952); Roberts, Wrongful Delivery of Deeds in Escrow, 17 Ky.L.Rev. 31 (1928); Annots., 48 A.L.R. 405 (1927), 54 A.L.R. 1246 (1928). The BFP will prevail if the deed was obtained from the escrowee by fraud rather than by knowing participation in the grantee's scheme; see Clevenger v. Moore, supra. The Florida Supreme Court held the

criticized by scholars,[233] is certainly objectionable if the escrowee was at fault in any degree; the grantor should in fairness bear responsibility for selecting and employing the escrowee as an agent, as opposed to a subsequent bona fide purchaser who had no dealings with the escrowee at all. Even in states following the majority rule, the grantor may be estopped to deny the delivery if he or she was negligent in selecting the escrowee or failed to assert title within a reasonable time after learning of the purchaser's claim.[234]

Death escrows. Many of the concepts discussed above in connection with sales escrows are equally applicable to cases in which the grantor hands a deed to a custodian for delivery upon the grantor's death. There are, however, some important differences. Most death escrows are gratuitous, and there is no underlying contract. But no contract is required for a valid death escrow; all that is necessary is that the grantor place the deed beyond his or her control, reserving no power over it once it has been deposited.[235] Moreover, to defeat the escrow a power to recall the deed must be fairly explicit; it is not enough that the custodian testifies he or she would hypothetically have returned the deed to the grantor upon request.[236]

The rule that enforces death escrows without underlying contracts seems to be based, not altogether logically, on the fact that the only condition in a death escrow, namely the death of the grantor, is *certain* to occur; thus, it is in a sense not a condition at all. From this premise the courts reason that no further legal element (other than the absence of a power of recall) is necessary to commit the grantor irrevocably to the transaction, and thus to constitute a delivery.[237] This reasoning may help to explain why some (although not all) courts have refused to enforce death escrows involving a more elaborate condition, such as the survival of the grantor by the grantee.[238] Such courts seem to view the possibility that the condition will fail as giving the grantor a fatal measure of additional control. From a policy standpoint, this distinction has no more to

---

contrary in Houston v. Adams, 85 Fla. 291, 95 So. 859 (1923), but that holding was limited to fraud in the execution by McCoy v. Love, 382 So.2d 647 (Fla. 1979).

[233] See Mann, supra note 210, at 417–18, quoting 4 Thompson, Real Property §§ 3954–55 (1924).

[234] In a subsequent appeal of Clevenger v. Moore, supra note 232, the court found that the grantor had indeed estopped herself to attack the BFP's title by her own failure to assert her claim expeditiously; 126 Okl. at 361, 298 P. at 299.

[235] See, e.g., Chandler v. Chandler, 409 So. 2d 780 (Ala. 1981); Taylor v. Welch, 609 So.2d 1225 (Miss. 1992); Albrecht v. Brais, 324 Ill.App.3d 188, 754 N.E.2d 396 (2001); Blackmer v. Blackmer, 165 Mont. 69, 525 P.2d 559 (1974); Daugherty v. DeWees, 172 W.Va. 553, 309 S.E.2d 52 (1983). Since nonprofessionals are commonly employed in death escrows, they are frequently attacked on the ground that the escrowee is merely the grantor's agent, and not an escrowee at all. In most jurisdictions this is a question of fact, but the Georgia courts appear to have entirely rejected the validity of death escrows, reasoning that the agent's authority must expire upon the principal's death; see Stinson v. Gray, 232 Ga. 542, 207 S.E.2d 506 (1974).

[236] See Herron v. Underwood, id; Chandler v. Chandler, 409 So.2d 780 (Ala. 1981); Brown v. Hutch, 156 So.2d 683 (Fla.App. 1963), cert. denied 162 So.2d 665 (Fla. 1964). On the other hand, the testimony of the grantor herself that she intended to have continuing control over the deed may be quite persuasive; see Cain v. Morrison, 212 Kan. 791, 512 P.2d 474 (1973).

[237] See cases cited note 235 supra.

[238] See Raim v. Stancel, 339 N.W.2d 621 (Iowa App. 1983) (oral condition that grantee care for grantor until his death renders delivery after grantor's death invalid); Atchison v. Atchison, 198 Okl. 98, 175 P.2d 309 (1946); Stanforth v. Bailey, 344 Ill. 38, 175 N.E. 784 (1931). Cases upholding death escrows which incorporated additional conditions include Videon v. Cowart, 241 So.2d 434 (Fla.App.1970), cert. denied 245 So.2d 88 (Fla.1971) (condition that grantee ask for the deed); Smith v. Fay, 228 Iowa 868, 293 N.W. 497 (1940) (condition that grantee survive grantor.)

commend it than the contract requirement in sales escrows; it is hard to see any good reason to deny enforcement to a death escrow which includes further conditions.[239]

The notion that the condition in a simple death escrow is certain to occur has another potentially important consequence. It leads most courts to treat the delivery *to the custodian* as immediately passing title to the grantee. The interest thus conveyed is deemed a future interest to become possessory on the grantor's death—presumably a springing executory interest, although most cases do not bother to identify it—with the grantor retaining what is usually termed a life estate,[240] although it is technically a fee simple subject to an executory limitation. As thus interpreted, such a conveyance is entirely valid.[241] This result commonly follows despite the fact that none of the parties has said anything whatever about a future interest. Such a construction seems bizarre but it has a certain logic, for death is indeed inevitable and by hypothesis no act of the grantor can retrieve the deed prior to his death. The relation back doctrine which governs sales escrows is wholly inapplicable under this view of death escrows, for the first delivery is legally the only delivery![242] The doctrine that the grantee immediately receives a future interest, rather than having a mere expectancy until the grantor's death, may have significant consequences in terms of such doctrines as waste, liability of third parties for damage to the land, gift and inheritance taxes, and the grantee's ability to make conveyances while the grantor remains alive, but these issues are seldom discussed in the cases.[243]

Duties of escrowees. The escrowee is an agent of both parties until the close of the escrow,[244] and thereafter the grantor's agent with respect to the purchase money and the grantee's agent with respect to the deed.[245] The agent's fundamental duty is to comply

---

[239] See 2 Walsh, Real Property § 214 nn. 7, 17 (1947), discussed in 3 Am. L.Prop. 321 (1952); 4 Tiffany, Real Property § 1054 nn. 26–27 (3d ed. 2017 update).

[240] Rausch v. Devine, 80 P.3d 733 (Alaska 2003); Garrett v. Garrett, 154 Idaho 788, 302 P.3d 1061 (2013); Pipes v. Sevier, 694 S.W.2d 918 (Mo.App. 1985); Annot., 52 A.L.R. 1222. See cases cited note 235 supra; Mann, supra note 210, at 420–22. But see Herron v. Underwood, 152 Ill.App.3d 144, 105 Ill.Dec. 105, 503 N.E.2d 1111 (1987) (in death escrow, no title passes until grantor's death). In a few states, statutes explicitly describe the grantor's retained interest as a "life estate." On springing executory interests, see § 3.12 supra.

[241] See, e.g., Callaghan v. Reed, 44 Or. App. 489, 605 P.2d 1382 (1980); Rothrock v. Rothrock, 104 S.W.3d 135 (Tex. App. 2003); Vasquez v. Vasquez, 973 S.W.2d 330 (Tex. App. 1998); § 11.3 supra at note 189.

[242] Masquart v. Dick, 210 Or. 459, 310 P.2d 742 (1957); In re Bell's Will, 161 Pa. Super. 3, 54 A.2d 79 (1947).

[243] See 4 Tiffany, Real Property § 1054 n. 5 (3d ed. 2017 update).

[244] Bob Daniels and Sons v. Weaver, 106 Idaho 535, 681 P.2d 1010 (App. 1984). But a party may unilaterally and effectively amend the instructions to change the method of disbursement of his or her own funds from the escrow; see Contemporary Investments, Inc. v. Safeco Title Ins. Co., 145 Cal.App.3d 999, 193 Cal.Rptr. 822 (1983); Maganas v. Northroup, 135 Ariz. 573, 663 P.2d 565 (1983). The escrowee's agency is limited to acts authorized by the agent's instructions, and does not extend to other matters, such as interpreting the parties' contract or giving consents or waivers in their behalf; see Bell v. Safeco Title Ins. Co., 830 S.W.2d 157 (Tex.App. 1992); Barr v. Pratt, 105 Or.App. 220, 804 P.2d 496 (1991). It is a dangerous practice for a lawyer who represents one of the parties to serve as escrowee; see Patel v. Gannaway, 726 F.2d 382 (8th Cir.1984); Collins v. Norton, 136 Ga. App. 105, 220 S.E.2d 279 (1975). Connecticut does not allow the practice; see Galvanek v. Skibitcky, 55 Conn. App. 254, 738 A.2d 1150 (1999).

[245] Ferguson v. Caspar, 359 A.2d 17 (D.C.App.1976); Edward Rose Sales Co. v. Shafer, 41 Mich.App. 105, 199 N.W.2d 655 (1972). Thus, if the agent decamps with the funds before the closing, the loss is the buyer's, but if afterward, the seller's; see GE Capital Mortg. Services, Inc. v. Avent, 114 N.C.App. 430, 442 S.E.2d 98 (1994); Lawyers Title Insurance Corp. v. Edmar Construction Co., Inc., 294 A.2d 865 (D.C.App.1972); Pagan v. Spencer, 104 Cal. App.2d 588, 232 P.2d 323 (1951); Bio-Electronics v. C & J Partnership, 268 Neb. 252, 682 N.W.2d 248 (2004), Noted 84 Neb. L. Rev. 1266 (2004). See Flores, A Comparison of the Rules and Rationales for Allocating Risks Arising in Realty Sales Using Executory Sale Contracts and Escrows, 59 Mo.L.Rev.307 (1994). See also Johnson v. Schultz, 195 N.C.App. 161, 671 S.E.2d 559 (2009) and In re Brown, 28 Fed.Appx. 725 (9th Cir. 2002) (rule allocating loss on basis of which party is entitled to the funds is

strictly with the escrow instructions,[246] and not to do anything contrary to them which might damage either of the parties.[247] He or she is held to a duty of reasonable care and skill[248] which, depending on the court and the facts, may or may not be relievable by exculpatory language in the escrow instructions.[249] The cases often describe the escrowee as a fiduciary, but this must be understood as limited to the context of the escrow instructions received;[250] the agent is not required to give the parties legal or financial advice or to correct errors in documents drawn by the parties or their advisors.[251] The cases reflect no clear rule as to the escrowee's duty to divulge to the parties information about the transaction that may be important to them.[252]

inapplicable if one party is at fault in the loss). If an attorney handles the closing, the loss may be allocated on the basis of which party the attorney represents; Johnson v. Schultz, id.

[246] Kirk Corp. v. First American Title Co., 220 Cal. App.3d 785, 270 Cal.Rptr. 24 (1990); H.B.I. Corp. v. Jimenez, 803 S.W.2d 100 (Mo.App. 1990); Cash v. Titan Fin. Servs., Inc., 58 A.D.3d 785, 873 N.Y.S.2d 642 (2009); Lacy v. Ticor Title Ins. Co., 794 S.W.2d 781 (Tex.App. 1990).

[247] See, e.g., Miller v. Craig, 27 Ariz. App. 789, 558 P.2d 984 (1976). When faced with a dispute between the parties, the escrowee will often file an interpleader action, but may not be required to do so; see Takayama v. Schaefer, 240 A.D.2d 21, 669 N.Y.S.2d 656 (1998), noted 76 Siegel's Prac. Rev. 3 (Oct. 1998); For an illustration of a case in which interpleader would have been most helpful to the escrowee, see Int'l Capital Corp. v. Moyer, 347 Ill. App. 3d 116, 806 N.E.2d 1166 (2004).

The escrowee generally owes no duty to nonparties to the escrow; Luce v. State Title Agency, Inc., 190 Ariz. 500, 950 P.2d 159 (Ariz. App. 1997); Summit Fin. Holdings, Ltd. v. Continental Lawyers Title Co., 27 Cal.4th 705, 41 P.3d 548 (2002), Noted 23 No. 3 Cal. Tort Rep. 90 (2002); Markowitz v. Fid. Nat. Title Co., 142 Cal. App. 4th 508, 48 Cal. Rptr. 3d 217 (2006); Mark Properties v. National Title Co., 14 P.3d 507 (Nev. 2000).

[248] See, e.g., Perkins v. Clinton State Bank, 593 F.2d 327 (8th Cir. 1979); Buffington v. Title Insurance Co. of Minnesota, 26 Ariz.App. 97, 546 P.2d 366 (1976) ("scrupulous honesty, skill and diligence"); Woodworth v. Redwood Empire Savings & Loan Association, 22 Cal.App.3d 347, 99 Cal.Rptr. 373 (1971) ("ordinary skill and diligence"); Meridian Title Corp. v. Pilgrim Fin., LLC, 947 N.E.2d 987 (Ind. Ct. App. 2011) ("due care"); Zimmerman v. First American Title Ins., 790 S.W.2d 690 (Tex.App. 1990) ("a high degree of care"); Reeves v. McClain, 56 Wn.App. 301, 783 P.2d 606 (1989).

[249] Selby v. Burtch, 193 Cal.App.3d 147, 238 Cal.Rptr. 212 (1987); Akin v. Business Title Corp., 264 Cal.App.2d 153, 70 Cal. Rptr. 287 (1968). Contra, enforcing exculpatory language, see Rooz v. Kimmel, 55 Cal.App.4th 573, 64 Cal.Rptr.2d 177 (1997); Baquerizo v. Monasterio, 90 A.D.3d 587, 933 N.Y.S.2d 869 (2011); Lynch v. Santa Fe Nat'l Bank, 627 P.2d 1247 (N.M. 1981), noted 12 N.M. L. Rev. 821 (1982). For illustrations of typical exculpatory language, see Heminway & McLemore, Acquisition Escrows in Tennessee: An Annotated Model Tennessee Acquisition Escrow Agreement, 7 Transactions: Tenn. J. Bus. L. 273 (2006); A New York Real Estate Escrow Agreement with Consumer Protection Ingredients, 27 Ariz. J. Int'l & Comp. L. 465 (2010).

[250] Baquerizo v. Monasterio, id.; Wandler v. Lewis, 567 N.W.2d 377 (S.D.1997). See generally Barlow Burke, The Law of Title Insurance § 13.03 (2018 supp.).

[251] Patel v. Gannaway, 726 F.2d 382 (8th Cir. 1984); Schaefer v. Manufacturers Bank, 104 Cal.App.3d 70, 163 Cal.Rptr. 402 (1980); Gebrayel v. Transamerica Title Ins. Co., 132 Or.App. 271, 888 P.2d 83 (1995); Denaxas v. Sandstone Court of Bellevue, L.L.C., 148 Wash.2d 654, 63 P.3d 125 (2003) (no duty to correct erroneous legal description). See Templeton, Escrow Obligations and Liabilities, Title News, Mar.-Apr. 1986, at 9, available at https://www.alta.org/title-news/1986/v65i01.pdf for a wry description of some of the dilemmas of serving as an escrowee. An escrowee who undertakes to prepare documents or give advice that amounts to the practice of law may be held to the professional standards of the legal profession; see Bishop v. Jefferson Title Co., 107 Wash. App. 833, 28 P.3d 802 (2001) (escrowee added incorrect language to standard form document); Bowers v. Transamerica Title Ins. Co., 100 Wn.2d 581, 675 P.2d 193 (1983).

[252] Plaza Home Mortg., Inc. v. N. Am. Title Co., 184 Cal. App. 4th 130, 109 Cal. Rptr. 3d 9 (2010) (duty to inform lender of kickback to purchaser); Triple A Management Co., Inc. v. Frisone, 69 Cal.App.4th 520, 81 Cal.Rptr.2d 669 (1999) (duty to inform buyer of seller's prior sham transactions to inflate price); Styrk v. Michie, 61 Wn.App. 463, 810 P.2d 1366 (1991), review denied 117 Wn.2d 1020, 818 P.2d 1098 (1991) (duty to inform seller that the loan-to-value ratio for her subordinated purchase-money mortgage exceeded the amount agreed to by the parties); Kitchen Krafters, Inc. v. Eastside Bank, 242 Mont. 155, 789 P.2d 567 (1990) (duty to inform contract purchaser that prepayment had been sent directly to vendor, rather than applied on preexisting mortgage); Home Loan Corp. v. Texas Am. Title Co., 191 S.W.3d 728 (Tex. App. 2006) (duty to inform lender of suspicious acts of borrower). The escrow agent has a duty to disclose to one party any known fraud that the other party intends to commit; see Manley v. Ticor Title Ins. Co. of Cal., 168 Ariz. 568, 816 P.2d 225 (1991); Mark Properties v. National Title Co., 14 P.3d 507 (Nev, 2000); Butko v. Stewart Title Co., 99 Wash.App. 533, 991 P.2d 697 (2000); Jacobsen, California Escrow Agents: A Duty to Disclose Known Fraud?,

An escrowee who breaches his or her duties is liable in damages for the loss thus caused.[253] Consequential damages may be included,[254] as may punitive damages if the escrowee's default was reckless or willful.[255]

§ 11.5   ESTOPPEL BY DEED

A deed may be executed and delivered by a person who has no title to the described land, or who has a lesser interest than the deed purports to convey. Such a grantor may be subject to liability for breach of covenants relating to title in an earlier contract of sale[256] or in the deed itself.[257] But our concern in this section is not with the grantor's liability in damages. Instead, we consider what legal results follow if the grantor later acquires part or all of the very title the previous deed described.[258]

The law's response to this situation is to deny to the grantor the right, as against the grantee and his or her successors, to assert the title thus acquired. The theory is estoppel: if the grantor, by language in the deed, represents to the grantee that title of a certain quality is being conveyed, the grantor is estopped to deny later that such title has passed to the grantee.[259] This theory is sensible only if the deed does in fact make a representation about the quality of the title it conveys; not all deeds do so. Older cases often distinguished between warranty and quitclaim deeds on this score. But that approach can be misleading, for language of warranty may really represent nothing (e.g., "I hereby warrant whatever title I may have at this time, if any,") while a quitclaim deed

---

17 Pac.L.J. 309 (1985). But there is no duty to facilitate business communications between the parties; Bowles v. Key Title Company, 163 Or.App. 9, 986 P.2d 1236 (1999).

[253] Lawyers Title Ins. Corp. v. Pokraka, 595 N.E.2d 244 (Ind.1992); Chicago Title Agency v. Schwartz, 109 Nev. 415, 851 P.2d 419 (1993); Banville v. Schmidt, 37 Cal. App.3d 92, 112 Cal.Rptr. 126 (1974).

[254] Wade v. Lake County Title Co., 6 Cal. App. 3d 824, 86 Cal. Rptr. 182 (1970).

[255] Edwards v. Stewart Title & Trust, 156 Ariz. 531, 753 P.2d 1187 (Ariz. App. 1988); Sanders v. Park Towne, Limited, 2 Kan.App.2d 313, 578 P.2d 1131 (1978); Toro Petroleum Corp. v. Newell, 33 Ill. App. 3d 223, 338 N.E.2d 491 (1974); Giddens Const. Co., Inc. v. Fickling & Walker Company, 258 Ga. 891, 376 S.E.2d 655 (1989); Eastern Atlantic Transp. and Mechanical Engineering, Inc. v. Dingman, 727 S.W.2d 418 (Mo. App.1987).

[256] On covenants of title in contracts, see generally § 10.12 supra. In many cases the doctrine of merger will preclude the grantee's assertion of any claim based on the contract's covenants once he or she has accepted the deed; see § 10.12, supra, at note 474.

[257] Gilstrap v. June Eisele Warren Tr., 2005 WY 21, 106 P.3d 858 (Wyo. 2005). See § 11.13 infra.

[258] The operation of the doctrine is limited to the quantum of estate that the original deed, if fully valid, would have conveyed; see Reece v. Smith, 276 Ga. 404, 577 S.E.2d 583 (2003); F.D.I.C. v. Taylor, 2011 Ut. App 416, 267 P.3d 949, 959 (2011); Gilstrap v. June Eisele Warren Tr., 2005 WY 21, 106 P.3d 858, 866 (Wyo. 2005). The discussion in the text deals with deeds, but it is clear that the same principles apply to mortgages, leases, or other conveyances which purport to transfer interests in land. See, e.g., Southland Corp. v. Shulman, 331 F.Supp. 1024 (D. Md. 1971) (lease); Alabama Home Mortg. Co. v. Harris, 582 So.2d 1080 (Ala. 1991) (mortgage); BMCL Holding LLC v. Wilmington Tr., N.A., 201 So. 3d 109 (Fla. Dist. Ct. App. 2015) (mortgage); Guess v. Gathings, 728 So. 2d 1038 (La. App. 1999) (mortgage); Hardigan v. Kimball, 553 A.2d 1265 (Me.1989) (contract of sale); McLaughlin v. Lambourn, 359 N.W.2d 370 (N.D. 1985) (contract for deed); Wood v. Sympson, 833 P.2d 1239 (Okla. 1992) (mortgage); IDC Properties, Inc. v. Goat Island S. Condo. Ass'n, Inc., 128 A.3d 383 (R.I. 2015) (condominium declaration). Cf. Hall v. Malloy, 2015 N.D. 94, 862 N.W.2d 514 (2015) (after-acquired title doctrine did not apply to divorce judgment).

[259] Crowder v. Avelo Mortg., LLC, 2015 WL 5331761 (E.D. Mo. 2015) (unpublished); Barris v. Keswick Homes, L.L.C., 268 Va. 67, 597 S.E.2d 54 (2004). See generally 3 Am.L.Prop. §§ 15.19–15.24 (1952); 1 Patton & Palomar, Land Titles § 219 (3d ed. 2017 update); Note, Estoppel by Deed, 37 Baylor L.Rev. 1059 (1985). In general, it makes no difference by what route or method the grantor subsequently acquires the title. But acquisition from the grantee himself is an exception, and no estoppel against the grantor will arise in such a case, since there is no inconsistency with the purport of the original deed; see, e.g., Sorenson v. Wright, 268 N.W.2d 203 (Iowa 1978); Turner v. Miller, 276 So.2d 690 (Miss. 1973); 4 Tiffany, Real Property § 1233 (3d ed. 2017 update).

may assert that title of a certain quality is being conveyed (e.g., "I hereby set over and quitclaim a fee simple absolute.")[260] The modern trend is simply to look for language in the deed which fairly constitutes an assertion about the title's quality; if it is found, estoppel by deed will operate. The ordinary warranty deed will nearly always be sufficient, and most quitclaims will not.[261]

In its bare form, this doctrine of estoppel would merely permit the grantee to sue the grantor and compel the delivery of a new conveyance. But most modern courts take the doctrine a step further, and treat the title as passing automatically to the grantee as soon as the grantor gets it.[262] This simplifies title examinations, since a searcher who discovers a situation raising an estoppel by deed can simply assume that the grantee got the title without being concerned with whether any judicial action was taken to obtain it. Under this view it is sometimes picturesquely said that the belated title obtained by the grantor "feeds the estoppel."[263]

Estoppel ordinarily presupposes reasonable reliance by the innocent party on the other's representations; the one who relies must be ignorant of the true facts.[264] The cases are divided as to whether this concept applies to estoppel by deed.[265] But even if

---

[260] See, e.g., Schaeffer v. Maddox, 794 So. 2d 1139 (Ala. Civ. App. 2000); Taitano v. Lujan, 2005 Guam 26; Guess v. Gathings, 728 So.2d 1038 (La.App.1999); Zayka v. Giambro, 32 Mass.App.Ct. 748, 594 N.E.2d 894 (1992); White v. Ford, 124 N.H. 452, 471 A.2d 1176 (1984); Stevens v. Stevens, 10 Wn.App. 493, 519 P.2d 269 (1974); Kennedy Oil v. Lance Oil & Gas Co., Inc., 2006 WY 9, 126 P.3d 875, 884 (Wyo. 2006). North Carolina courts have been particularly willing to construe quitclaim deeds as making a sufficient averment of title to actuate estoppel by deed; see Tunnell v. Berry, 73 N.C. App. 222, 326 S.E.2d 288 (1985). For the traditional view that a quitclaim does not trigger an estoppel, see Barlow Soc. v. Commercial Security Bank, 723 P.2d 398 (Utah 1986); Idaho ex rel. Moore v. Scroggie, 109 Idaho 32, 704 P.2d 364 (1985); Van Pelt v. Estate of Clarke, 476 So.2d 746 (Fla.App. 1985). Some states have statutes expressly applying the doctrine to any deed "purporting to convey an estate in fee simple absolute;" see notes 281–283 infra and accompanying text.

A court may view the jurisdiction's fee simple presumption statute as imputing to even a quitclaim deed a sufficient representation of title to make the deed effective to pass an after-acquired title; see Crowder v. Avelo Mortg., LLC, 2015 WL 5331761 (E.D. Mo. 2015) (unpublished, dictum); Taitano v. Lujan, 2005 Guam 26. But this seems quite a stretch.

[261] See Harkins & Co. v. Lewis, 535 So.2d 104 (Ala.1988); Richards v. Tibaldi, 272 Mich. App. 522, 726 N.W.2d 770 (2006) (quitclaim deed will never actuate estoppel by deed); Webster Oil Co. v. McLean Hotels, Inc., 878 S.W.2d 892 (Mo.App. 1994); Premier Bank v. Bd. of Cty. Comm'rs of Cty. of Bent, 214 P.3d 574 (Colo. App. 2009) (construing granting language of deed of trust as a quitclaim); Walliker v. Escott, 608 P.2d 1272 (Wyo. 1980); See generally Annots., 58 A.L.R. 345 (1929); 144 A.L.R. 554 (1943). It is not necessary that all possible covenants of title be present in the deed to create an estoppel; generally any one of them is sufficient; see Gutierrez v. Rodriguez, 30 S.W.3d 558 (Tex. App. 2000) (either general or special warranty deed will suffice).

[262] See, e.g., Fadili v. Deutsche Bank Nat. Tr. Co., 772 F.3d 951 (1st Cir. 2014) (N.H. law); Turner v. Lassiter, 484 So.2d 378 (Ala.1985); Schwenn v. Kaye, 155 Cal. App.3d 949, 202 Cal.Rptr. 374 (1984); Douglas v. Lyles, 841 A.2d 1 (D.C. 2004); Hughes v. Insley, 155 Md. App. 608, 845 A.2d 1 (2003); Southern Missouri Sav. & Loan v. Thomas, 754 S.W.2d 937 (Mo. App. 1988); Rendleman v. Heinley, 140 N.M. 912, 149 P.3d 1009 (2007); Campbell v. Butler, 770 P.2d 7 (Okl. 1988). See generally 3 Am.L.Prop. § 15.21 (1952). Sometimes automatic inurement of after-acquired title is explained on the basis of theories other than estoppel. For example, the grantor's conveyance may be treated as the equivalent of a contract to convey, which the courts will specifically enforce when the grantor acquires title. See G. Osborne, Mortgages § 37 (2d ed. 1970), for a discussion of this and other, more obscure theories in the context of mortgages.

[263] Perkins v. Coleman, 90 Ky. 611, 14 S.W. 640 (1890).

[264] See, e.g., United States v. Ruby Co., 588 F.2d 697 (9th Cir.1978), certiorari denied 442 U.S. 917, 99 S.Ct. 2838, 61 L.Ed.2d 284 (1979).

[265] Ignorance of true facts required: Shell Oil Co. v. Trailer & Truck Repair Co., 828 F.2d 205 (3d Cir.1987) (N.J. law); Hilco Prop. Servs., Inc. v. United States, 929 F.Supp. 526, 546 (D.N.H. 1996); McLaughlin v. Lambourn, 359 N.W.2d 370 (N.D. 1985). Estoppel applied even though grantee had notice of true facts: Brown v. Baldi, 2017 WL 3016768 (D.N.H. 2017); Ayer v. Philadelphia & Boston Face Brick Co., 159 Mass. 84, 34 N.E. 177 (1893); Shedden v. Anadarko E. & P. Co., L.P., 635 Pa. 381, 136 A.3d 485 (2016). See Burby, Real Property 320 (3d ed. 1965).

the original grantee must believe the deed is good, it makes no sense to demand good faith reliance on the part of those who take in later succession from the grantee. In most cases they will search the title and will discover that the grantor gave a deed before obtaining title. If they are penalized for that knowledge, the principal value of estoppel by deed to title examiners is lost. Plainly title should inure to such remote grantees whether they have become aware of their need for the inurement or not. This point seems to be assumed without discussion in the cases.

The notion of automatic inurement is obviously very convenient to subsequent grantees and their title examiners, but it also raises several important questions. One is whether it is an exclusive remedy. Suppose the grantee, upon discovering that the grantor had no title, brings an action based on the deed's title covenants. Can the grantor, by acquiring the title and permitting it to inure to the grantee, cure the breach of covenant and defeat the suit? The modern cases are fairly uniform in holding that the grantee has a choice of accepting the title or pursuing the action for damages, since the inurement doctrine is intended for the grantee's benefit.[266]

The inurement theory may also influence the resolution of the claims of competing grantees. If the grantor, after acquiring the belated title, purports to deed it to a second grantee, which of the two grantees will have the title? If the second pays no value or has notice of the claim of the first, plainly the first will prevail.[267] But if the second is an innocent purchaser for value, the cases divide.[268] Some courts emphasize the notion of automatic inurement and recognize title in the original grantee on the ground that it passed to the grantee the instant the grantor acquired it; thus, the grantor had nothing to pass by a second deed.[269] Other cases, probably more numerous, focus on the estoppel concept and give priority to the bona fide purchaser, reasoning that only the grantor and not the innocent second grantee is estopped.[270]

But this debate is largely irrelevant unless the recording acts are taken into account. The first deed is recordable, and if the grantee does not in fact record it, it will be void as against subsequent good faith purchasers for value who (in notice-race jurisdictions) record their own deeds.[271] But if the first deed is recorded, its grantee will argue that the recording acts cannot divest the interest it grants, and further that no

---

[266] Resser v. Carney, 52 Minn. 397, 54 N.W. 89 (1893); 3 Am.L.Prop. § 15.23 (1952).

[267] BMCL Holding LLC v. Wilmington Tr., N.A., 201 So. 3d 109 (Fla. Dist. Ct. App. 2015); Dillard v. Brannan, 217 Ga. 179, 121 S.E.2d 768 (1961); Lucus v. Cowan, 357 P.2d 976 (Okl.1960); Duke v. Hopper, 486 S.W.2d 744 (Tenn.App.1972).

[268] See 4 Tiffany, Real Property § 1234 nn. 11–12 (3d ed 2017 update); W. Burby, Real Property § 128 (2d ed. 1965); Lawler, Estoppel to Assert an After-Acquired Title in Pennsylvania, 3 U.Pitt.L.Rev. 165, 176–77 (1937).

[269] See Annot., 25 A.L.R. 83 (1923); Tiffany, supra note 268, at nn. 5–8. Clear holdings are sparse, and cases cited for rejecting the subsequent BFP's claim often do not make it clear whether he was in fact a BFP; see, e.g., Letson v. Roach, 5 Kan.App. 57, 47 P. 321 (1896), affirmed 58 Kan. 817, 50 P. 1101 (1897).

[270] Builders Sash & Door Co. v. Joyner, 182 N.C. 518, 109 S.E. 259 (1921); Gallagher v. Stern, 250 Pa. 292, 95 A. 518 (1915); See Annot., supra note 269.

[271] Life Sav. & Loan Ass'n v. Bryant, 125 Ill.App.3d 1012, 81 Ill.Dec. 577, 467 N.E.2d 277 (1984) (where second grantee had notice of first conveyance, and hence was not a BFP, estoppel worked to give title to first grantee, whose claim was not divested by operation of the recording act). In a pure "notice" jurisdiction, the second grantee who lacks notice need not even record. See generally § 11.9 infra at note 474. If the second interest is not created by deed, but is a judgment lien, the matter is more complex. In a number of states the recording acts do not protect judgment creditors, usually on the ground that they have not paid contemporaneous value; see § 11.10 infra at notes 530–535. But such a creditor might still be regarded on equitable grounds as having priority over the grantee under the deed. See Swenson, Statutory Estoppel by Deed, 1950 Wash.U.L.Q. 361, 375–76; 4 Tiffany, Real Property § 1234 nn. 13–16 (3d ed. 2017 update).

later grantee can be a good faith purchaser, since the recordation of the first deed will give constructive notice. The second grantee's response is that the first deed cannot be deemed *properly* recorded, since it is outside the "chain of title."

In a jurisdiction in which title searches are based on indexes of grantors' and grantees' names, this is a fairly persuasive argument for the following reason. Once the searcher has constructed a chain of conveyances backward in time from the present, using the grantee index, he or she will then employ the grantor index to discover whether any prior owner made a conveyance which was adverse to the chain.[272] The first deed in the illustration above is such a conveyance. The difficulty is that it was recorded prior to the time the grantor obtained the land. Searchers ordinarily look for adverse conveyances under each prior owner's name only during the time that owner appears to have held title.[273] To search earlier years is not impossible, but it is a great deal of additional effort, since in theory such a conveyance could have been recorded many decades earlier, and to be entirely safe one would have to search under each prior owner's name back in time to the beginning of the records. Thus, the argument is that the law should not impose such a burden, and hence that BFPs and their searchers should not be held to a duty to find the first deed

The majority of courts, especially in recent years, have held that because the first deed is recorded so early, and out of time sequence, a searcher has no duty to find it. From this premise they reason that it gives no constructive notice to a later purchaser, who will therefore prevail over the first deed[274] either (1) because of the general principle favoring BFP's discussed above,[275] or (2) because the first deed must be treated as if it were unrecorded, so that subsequent BFP's may regard it as void under the normal operation of the recording acts.[276] The cases often do not bother to distinguish these two rationales, and the distinction is usually of little importance.[277]

---

[272] On title search procedures, see § 11.11 infra at notes 601 et seq.

[273] See Philbrick, Limits of Record Search and Therefore of Notice, Part I, 93 U.Pa.L.Rev. 125, 177–186 (1944). As one author described it:

> Do conveyancers do this [search each owner's name back to the beginning of the records]? They do not. The cost of such examination would exceed the value of the land. Perhaps they hope that by ignoring the specter of estoppel by deed, they can prevent it from materializing.

R. Swain, 1949 Supplement to Crocker's Notes on Common Forms, Sixth (Conveyancers') Edition 95–96 (1949), quoted in Harr & Liebman, Property and Law 527 (1977).

[274] Far West Sav. & Loan Ass'n v. McLaughlin, 201 Cal.App.3d 67, 246 Cal. Rptr. 872 (1988); Schuman v. Roger Baker & Associates, Inc., 70 N.C.App. 313, 319 S.E.2d 308 (1984); Security Pacific Finance Corp. v. Taylor, 193 N.J.Super. 434, 474 A.2d 1096 (1984). Contra, see Lucus v. Cowan, 357 P.2d 976 (Okl.1960), in which the court may have been influenced by the use in Oklahoma of abstracts based on tract indexes, see text at note 278 infra; Ayer v. Philadelphia & Boston Face Brick Co., 159 Mass. 84, 34 N.E. 177 (1893); Tefft v. Munson, 57 N.Y. 97 (1875); Dalessio v. Baggia, 57 Mass. App. Ct. 468, 783 N.E.2d 890 (2003). See Johanson, Estoppel by Deed and the Recording System: The "Ayer Rule" Re-examined, 43 B.U.L.Rev. 441 (1963) (collecting the cases on both sides at nn. 83 and 91); Cross, The Record "Chain of Title" Hypocrisy, 57 Colum.L.Rev. 787, 793 (1957). For a discussion of other "chain of title" problems, see § 11.11 infra at notes 606–617.

[275] See text at notes 268–270 supra.

[276] Perhaps the clearest decision to this effect is Sabo v. Horath, 559 P.2d 1038 (Alaska 1976). holding that the first deed cannot be deemed "duly recorded." See also Schuman v. Roger Baker & Associates, Inc., supra note 274; Southeastern Sav. & Loan Ass'n v. Rentenbach Constructors, Inc., 114 B.R. 441 (E.D.N.C. 1989) (deed has "same effect on notice as no registration").

[277] The distinction could be important if the second grantee is a BFP but fails to record in a notice-race jurisdiction, and thus is disqualified from the protection of the recording act.

The "chain of title" reasoning reflected in these holdings is sensible only if searches are performed in a grantor-grantee index system. If the public records are maintained on a tract index basis, the early-recorded deed presents no inconvenience for searchers, for it will appear (albeit out of chain-of-title order) on the same page of the index book which lists all other instruments affecting the parcel in question. Hence, it will give constructive notice to later purchasers.[278] The same is true in jurisdictions that have adopted computerized indexes, since such indexes usually permit searches both by the names of the parties and by tract or parcel.

Perhaps the most interesting question is raised in areas of the nation where the official records employ only name indexes but where searches are ordinarily performed by private title or abstract companies in their own private "plants" equipped (as they almost invariably are) with tract indexes.[279] There is no reason in good policy to apply "chain of title" thinking in such a context; if the searching firm in fact has the early-recorded deed in its records, and could have found it in the ordinary course of its tract-index search, then the firm (and arguably its customer, the purchaser, as well) should be held to have notice of it.[280]

About twenty states have statutes relating to estoppel by deed.[281] They vary widely in content, but many of them contain language adopting the automatic inurement theory. Since most of these statutes say nothing about the rights of subsequent bona fide purchasers from the grantor,[282] some courts have construed them as mechanically favoring the estoppel grantee against such purchasers, and thus as rejecting the "chain of title" reasoning discussed above.[283] Such a construction seems both unwarranted and undesirable.

The statutes vary the law in other ways as well. Some of them explicitly recognize that a deed with no warranties will raise an estoppel, provided that it purports to convey some particular quantum of title.[284] Some provide that only a purported conveyance of a fee simple absolute will estop the grantor, while others recognize an estoppel from the

---

[278] Balch v. Arnold, 9 Wyo. 17, 59 P. 434 (1899).

[279] See Whitman, Optimizing Land Title Assurance Systems, 42 Geo.Wash.L.Rev. 40, 58 (1973); Erskine Florida Properties, Inc. v. First American Title Ins. Co., 557 So.2d 859 (Fla.1989) (title company was negligent in failing to search in official tract index); Cipriano v. Tocco, 772 F.Supp. 344 (E.D.Mich. 1991) (indexing only in tract index was sufficient to give constructive notice, although statute required indexing in grantor-grantee index as well).

[280] There is no discussion of this point in the published decisions, but at least one court has implicitly rejected the argument in the text. See In Ryczkowski v. Chelsea Title & Guaranty Co., 85 Nev. 37, 449 P.2d 261 (1969) and Snow v. Pioneer Title Insurance Co., 84 Nev. 480, 444 P.2d 125 (1968).

[281] The development and content of the statutes is thoroughly examined in Swenson, Statutory Estoppel by Deed, 1950 Wash.U.L.Q. 361.

[282] One exception is Virginia Code § 55–105, which provides that a subsequent purchaser is "not affected" by a deed recorded before its grantor has acquired legal or record title. This language is apparently intended to adopt the chain of title reasoning.

[283] Compare Bernardy v. Colonial & United States Mortgage Co., 17 S.D. 637, 98 N.W. 166 (1904) (estoppel grantee prevails), with Ford v. Unity Church Society, 120 Mo. 498, 25 S.W. 394 (1893) (subsequent BFP prevails). See Swenson, supra note 281, at 372–75.

[284] See, e.g. Colo.Rev.Stat.1973, § 38–30–104; 765 Ill. Comp. Stat. Ann. 5/7; Miss. Code 1972, § 89–1–39. The same result is generally reached under court-made law; see cases cited at note 260 supra. See also Stevens v. Stevens, supra note 260, construing West's Rev.Code Wash.Ann. 64.04.070 as permitting after-acquired title to pass under a quitclaim which specifically stated that such title would pass. Cf. South Dakota Codified Laws 43–25–8 (after-acquired title does not pass under statutory form of quitclaim deed.)

purported conveyance of any interest in the land.[285] Some exclude from the effects of the estoppel a spouse who signs the deed only to waive a dower, curtesy, homestead, or other similar claim.[286] In most cases in which the facts would raise an estoppel under court-made principles but not under the narrower statute, the courts have felt free to treat the statute as not preempting the field.[287]

§ 11.6 DEDICATION

A dedication is a transfer of an interest in land from a private owner to the public generally or to a public body, such as a municipal corporation.[288] Such a transfer might, of course, be made by deed,[289] and many dedications are effected in this manner. But dedications are flexible and may be made in a variety of ways, including acts of an owner which would by no means constitute valid deeds under the statute of frauds.

Offers of dedication. A valid dedication requires both an offer to dedicate by the owner and an acceptance by the public. The offer must comprise some words or acts on the part of the owner evincing an intent to turn the property over to the public. A clear oral statement will suffice, for compliance with the statute of frauds is unnecessary.[290] If a writing is used, it need not be executed with any particular formality.[291] Words written on a document used for some other purpose, such as a plat or map of the land, will often do,[292] as when sales of lots are made by reference to a map which shows streets

---

[285] Ark.Stat. § 50–404 (applies to any estate); Iowa Code Ann. § 557.4. Cf. West's Ann.Cal.Civ.Code § 1106 (fee simple); Colo. Rev. Stat. § 38–30–104 (fee simple absolute); Idaho Code § 55–605 (fee simple); Kan.Stat.Ann. § 67–207 (indefeasible fee simple absolute).

[286] See Iowa Code Ann. § 557.4. Cf. Virginia Code § 55–52 (if spouse joins in estoppel deed, it will bar dower or curtesy claim to after-acquired title).

[287] Robben v. Obering, 279 F.2d 381 (7th Cir. 1960); Barberi v. Rothchild, 7 Cal.2d 537, 61 P.2d 760 (1936). But see Schultz v. Cities Service Oil Co., 149 Kan. 148, 86 P.2d 533 (1939), refusing to go beyond the statute and apply the doctrine of inurement to a mineral deed.

[288] There is authority in some jurisdictions recognizing dedications to churches or other religious bodies, but the point of these cases seems to be simply to uphold a gift to an organization which is not yet in existence. See, e.g., Atkinson v. Bell, 18 Tex. 474 (1857); Boyce v. Kalbaugh, 47 Md. 334 (1877); Beatty v. Kurtz, 27 U.S. (2 Pet.) 566, 7 L.Ed. 521 (1829). See Tigner, Dedication–Part I, 15 Baylor L.Rev. 179, 179–80 (1963); 4 Tiffany, Real Property § 1098 (3d ed. 2017 update). This objective may be desirable enough, but it is doubtful whether extending the doctrine of dedication in this way is necessary to achieve it, and modern cases seldom do so.

[289] In its earliest meaning, a dedication was a conveyance to the general public, and not to a particular governmental agency. Hence, it could have no specific grantee, and could not be accomplished by deed; see Lander v. Village of South Orange, 58 N.J. 509, 279 A.2d 633 (1971); 4 Tiffany, Real Property § 1099 (2017 update). But this usage is now obsolete, and dedications to municipal corporations and other agencies, including those made by express deeds, are generally recognized. See, e.g., Williams v. City of Kuttawa, 466 S.W.3d 505 (Ky. Ct. App. 2015); Koch v. St. Louis Cty., 527 S.W.3d 189 (Mo. Ct. App. 2017); Bolinger v. City of Bozeman, 158 Mont. 507, 493 P.2d 1062 (1972). See also McCarrey v. Kaylor, 301 P.3d 559 (Alaska 2013) (federal land patents dedicated roads to local governments).

[290] Friends of Martin's Beach v. Martin's Beach 1 LLC, 246 Cal. App. 4th 1312, 201 Cal. Rptr. 3d 516 (2016), review denied and ordered not to be officially published (July 20, 2016); 2000 Baum Family Tr. v. Babel, 488 Mich. 136, 793 N.W.2d 633 (2010); Greenco Corp. v. City of Virginia Beach, 214 Va. 201, 198 S.E.2d 496 (1973).

[291] Benjamin v. City of Norwalk, 170 Conn. App. 1, 153 A.3d 669 (2016); Cooper v. City of Great Bend, 200 Kan. 590, 438 P.2d 102 (1968). See generally 3 Am.L.Prop. § 12.133 (1952).

[292] See Town of Gilbert v. Fruehauf, 2013 Ark. App. 17, 425 S.W.3d 816 (2013); Town of Granby v. Feins, 154 Conn. App. 395, 105 A.3d 932 (2014); Republic Bank of Chicago v. Vill. of Manhattan, 2015 Ill. App 3d 130379, 32 N.E.3d 1141 (Ill. App. 2015); Doyle v. Lowrey, 698 S.W.2d 56 (Mo.App. 1985); Winnie Dev. LLLP v. Reveling, 2018 N.D. 47, 907 N.W.2d 413 (2018); Dept. of Transportation v. Haggerty, 127 N.C.App. 499, 492 S.E.2d 770 (1997); Haven Chapel United Methodist Church v. Leebron, 496 S.W.3d 893 (Tex. App. 2016). Cf. Muzzy v. Wilson, 259 Or. 512, 487 P.2d 875 (1971), in which the term "alley" was held insufficient evidence of intent to dedicate. Compare Mobile County v. Isham, 695 So.2d 634 (Ala.App. 1996) (word "park" was sufficient

DEDICATION

or other public areas.[293] Many states have formal statutory procedures under which the submission to and approval of a subdivision plat by a local government acts as an offer and acceptance of dedication of any public areas, such as streets and parks, shown on the plat.[294] But the existence of these procedures generally does not eliminate the possibility of a common law dedication as well; hence the two procedures usually coexist.[295]

An implied common law dedication may be accomplished without any statement, written or spoken, for one who invites or merely permits the public to use his or her land for a long period may be held to have made an offer of implied dedication.[296] Some courts rationalize implied dedications on the theory that the owner, having admitted the public to use of the land over a long time, is estopped to deny permanent public access.[297]

Traditionally, proof of the owner's intent to dedicate has been an essential element in an implied dedication,[298] but some courts have virtually eliminated the need for actual intent. In these jurisdictions an implied dedication may result despite the owner's stout protestations of objection to the public use, if it actually occurred nonetheless. A well-

---

evidence of dedication) with Emalfarb v. Krater, 266 Ill.App.3d 243, 203 Ill.Dec. 666, 640 N.E.2d 325 (1994) (word "park" insufficient).

[293] Clarke v. Tannin, Inc., 301 F.Supp.3d 1150 (S.D. Ala. 2018) (Alabama law) (marking strip of land "beach access" did not sufficiently indicate intent to dedicate strip as public road); Bonifay v. Dickson, 459 So.2d 1089 (Fla.App. 1984); Morse v. Colitti, 317 Mich. App. 526, 896 N.W.2d 15 (2016); Village of Climax Springs v. Camp, 681 S.W.2d 529 (Mo.App. 1984); Friends of Crooked Creek, L.L.C. v. C.C. Partners, Inc., 802 S.E.2d 908 (N.C. Ct. App. 2017); Mid-Valley Res., Inc. v. Foxglove Properties, LLP, 280 Or. App. 784, 381 P.3d 910 (2016); Kilmartin v. Barbuto, 158 A.3d 735 (R.I. 2017); Town of Kingstree v. Chapman, 405 S.C. 282, 311, 747 S.E.2d 494, 508 (Ct. App. 2013); Baywood Estates Prop. Owners Ass'n, Inc. v. Caolo, 392 S.W.3d 776 (Tex. App. 2012); Island Inn, Inc. v. City of Virginia Beach, 216 Va. 474, 220 S.E.2d 247 (1975).

[294] See, e.g., Laughlin v. Morauer, 849 F.2d 122 (4th Cir. 1988) (Virginia law); Harshbarger v. County of Jerome, 107 Idaho 805, 693 P.2d 451 (1984); J & A Cantore, LP v. Vill. of Villa Park, 2017 IL App (2d) 160601, 79 N.E.3d 800 (2017); Nettleton Church of Christ v. Conwill, 707 So.2d 1075 (Miss.1997); Town of Clifton Park v. Boni Builders, Inc., 156 A.D.3d 1035, 66 N.Y.S.3d 550 (N.Y. App. Div. 2017); Donald v. City of Vancouver, 43 Wn.App. 880, 719 P.2d 966 (1986). But see Cavin v. Ostwalt, 76 N.C.App. 309, 332 S.E.2d 509 (1985) (under statute, N.C.Gen. Stat. 153A–333, approval of plat by county does not automatically constitute acceptance of dedicated streets shown thereon); Tupper v. Dorchester County, 326 S.C. 318, 487 S.E.2d 187 (1997) (same).

[295] Arnold v. United States, 137 Fed.Cl. 524 (2018) (Kansas law); Pleak v. Entrada Prop. Owners' Ass'n, 207 Ariz. 418, 87 P.3d 831 (2004); Friends of Denver Parks, Inc. v. City & Cty. of Denver, 327 P.3d 311 (2013) (city ordinance restricted dedication of parks to statutory procedure); Pelican Creek Homeowners, LLC v. Pulverenti, 243 So.3d 467 (Fla. Dist. Ct. App. 2018); Rowley v. Ada Cty. Highway Dist., 156 Idaho 275, 322 P.3d 1008 (2014); City of Covington v. Glockner, 486 So.2d 837 (La.App. 1986); McBroom v. Jackson Cty., 154 So. 3d 827 (Miss. 2014); McConiga v. Riches, 40 Wn.App. 532, 700 P.2d 331 (1985). One exception is Mass.Gen. Laws Ann. c. 84, § 4 et seq., applied in Uliasz v. Gillette, 357 Mass. 96, 256 N.E.2d 290 (1970).

[296] Templeman v. Resmondo, 507 So.2d 494 (Ala. 1987); Moreland v. Henson, 256 Ga. 685, 353 S.E.2d 181 (1987); Smith v. Sponheim, 399 N.W.2d 899 (S.D. 1987); McCulloch v. Brewster Cty., 391 S.W.3d 612 (Tex. App. 2012); 3232 Page Ave. Condo. Unit Owners Ass'n v. City of VA. Beach, 284 Va. 639, 735 S.E.2d 672 (2012). Under some authorities, the period must be "long", but may be shorter than the statute of limitations for adverse possession or prescription: see Cole v. Dych, 535 S.W.2d 315 (Tenn.1976). Contra, requiring public use for at least the adverse possession period, see Gold Coast Neighborhood Ass'n v. State, 140 Haw. 437, 403 P.3d 214 (2017). Texas has abolished implied dedication for counties of 50,000 population or less; see Tex. Code Ann., Transportation Code § 281.003; Mitchell v. Ballard, 420 S.W.3d 122 (Tex. App. 2012).

[297] See CRW, Inc. v. Twin Lakes Property Owners Ass'n, Inc., 521 So.2d 939 (Ala. 1988); Ellington v. Becraft, 534 S.W.3d 785 (Ky. 2017); Swift v. Kniffen, 706 P.2d 296 (Alaska 1985); Agnew v. Haskell, 71 Or.App. 357, 692 P.2d 650 (1984); Niemi v. Fredlund Twp., 2015 S.D. 62, 867 N.W.2d 725 (2015). A classic statement of this theory is McCormick v. Baltimore, 45 Md. 512 (1877).

[298] See Clarke v. Tannin, Inc., 301 F.Supp.3d 1150 (S.D. Ala. 2018) (Alabama law); Stone v. International Paper Co., 293 S.C. 138, 359 S.E.2d 83 (App. 1987); Star Island Associates v. City of St. Petersburg Beach, 433 So.2d 998 (Fla.App. 1983); Somers USA, LLC v. State of Wisconsin Dep't of Transp., 361 Wis. 2d 807, 864 N.W.2d 114 (2015).

known illustration is Gion v. City of Santa Cruz,[299] in which the general public had used a privately-owned beach for many years despite the owners' half-hearted and ineffectual efforts to stop the use. The California Supreme Court held that a dedication had occurred, with intent to dedicate being inferred as a matter of law from public use for the prescriptive period and the inadequacy of the owners' attempts to halt it. The "intent" thus found is obviously highly artificial.[300] The decision seems to be based on dedication by prescription, similar to an ordinary prescriptive easement[301] except that the adverse use is by the public generally rather than by any identifiable person or group.[302] Moreover, the *Gion* court presumed, from the long public use, the hostility required for prescription.[303] Thus the decision represents a sort of amalgam of two distinct concepts, implied dedication and prescriptive easements. From the viewpoint of the local government, this approach combines the most advantageous features of prescription and "standard" implied dedication, eliminating the need to prove explicitly either intent or hostility. Most courts today continue to insist that the public body satisfy in full the elements of dedication or prescription, rather than merging the two concepts.[304]

An effective express dedication can be made only by the owner of the land; one cannot transfer more rights than one has. If a possessory estate in fee simple is to be dedicated, it is necessary for the holders of all private interests, such as mortgagees,

---

[299] 2 Cal.3d 29, 84 Cal.Rptr. 162, 465 P.2d 50 (1970), noted in 18 U.C.L.A.L.Rev. 795 (1971); 44 So.Cal.L.Rev. 1092 (1971); 4 Loyala L.A.L.Rev. 438 (1971). See also Friends of Martin's Beach v. Martin's Beach 1 LLC, 246 Cal. App. 4th 1312, 201 Cal. Rptr. 3d 516 (2016), review denied and ordered not to be officially published (2016) (finding an implied dedication of coastal property); City of Los Angeles v. Venice Peninsula Properties, 205 Cal.App.3d 1522, 253 Cal.Rptr. 331 (1988) (distinguishing *Gion* on the ground that the lagoon in question was neither a "beach or shoreline" nor a public road, and that there was no evidence of public use which even approximated the extent of the public use in *Gion*); Lincoln Parish Police Jury v. Davis, 559 So.2d 935 (La.App.1990) (relaxing the intent requirement); Seaway Co. v. Attorney General, 375 S.W.2d 923 (Tex.Civ.App.1964), refused n.r.e. The reasoning of the *Gion* case was rejected in Department of Natural Resources v. Mayor & Council of Ocean City, 274 Md. 1, 332 A.2d 630 (1975), and Automotive Products Corp. v. Provo City Corp., 28 Utah 2d 358, 502 P.2d 568 (1972). See generally Note, 48 N.Y.U.L.Rev. 369 (1973).

[300] After *Gion* was decided, the California legislature amended West's Ann.Cal. Civ.Code § 813 to permit an owner to record a notice giving the public permission to use his or her land and thereby conclusively rebutting prescription; it also enacted Civil Code § 1009 to prohibit all dedications arising out of public use (whether or not a notice under § 813 has been recorded) unless the owner makes an express written offer of dedication. The statute was construed to bar all dedications implied from public use of noncoastal property, whether for recreational or nonrecreational purposes; see Scher v. Burke, 3 Cal. 5th 136, 395 P.3d 680 (2017).

[301] See generally § 8.7, supra; Thomas v. City of Rainsville, 502 So.2d 346 (Ala. 1987).

[302] See Clarke v. Tannin, Inc., 301 F.Supp.3d 1150 (S.D. Ala. 2018); Weidner v. Department of Transportation, 860 P.2d 1205 (Alaska 1993); Warner v. Richardson, 2016 WL 675825 (Ky. Ct. App. 2016) (not reported in S.W.3d); Department of Natural Resources v. Mayor and Council of Ocean City, 274 Md. 1, 332 A.2d 630 (1975).

[303] Most cases take the opposite tack, presuming permission rather than hostility from the public use in the absence of any specific evidence; see e.g., Ford v. Alabama By-Products Corp., 392 So.2d 217 (Ala. 1980); Daytona Beach v. Tona-Rama, Inc., 294 So.2d 73 (Fla.1974). But there is some authority favoring the *Gion* court's position; see Daytona Beach v. Tona-Rama, Inc., supra, at 9 (Boyd, J., dissenting).

[304] Hardy v. Smith, 148 So. 3d 64 (Ala. Civ. App. 2013); State ex rel. Haman v. Fox, 100 Idaho 140, 594 P.2d 1093 (1979); Daytona Beach v. Tona-Rama, Inc., supra note 303; Department of Natural Resources v. Mayor and Council of Ocean City, supra note 302. The difficulty of showing hostility under a prescription theory is illustrated by Waterway Drive Prop. Owners' Ass'n, Inc. v. Town of Cedar Point, 224 N.C. App. 544, 737 S.E.2d 126 (2012). Cf. Nature Conservancy v. Machipongo Club, Inc., 419 F.Supp. 390 (E.D.Va. 1976), affirmed in part, reversed in part on other grounds 571 F.2d 1294 (4th Cir. 1978), in which the court concluded that there was no meaningful distinction between implied dedication and prescription; Luevano v. Maestas, 117 N.M. 580, 874 P.2d 788 (App. 1994) (elements of dedication and prescription largely overlap).

Landowners often attempt to forestall prescriptive dedication of private streets normally open to the public by closing them off with barriers for one day each year, thus interrupting the running of the prescriptive period. Whether this will work is debatable; see, e.g., Wasatch Cty. v. Okelberry, 357 P.3d 586 (Ut. 2015) (under statute, use must be "interrupted to a degree that reasonably puts the traveling public on notice").

lessees, easement holders, and the like to join.[305] However, if only an easement is dedicated, the joinder of those whose rights are not inconsistent with the easement is unnecessary. For example, a public easement may be dedicated along the route of a preexisting nonexclusive private easement without creating any conflict between the two.[306]

A dedicator need not necessarily transfer all that he or she has, and controversy sometimes develops as to precisely what rights have been dedicated.[307] The donor can, of course, explicitly specify the interest being dedicated;[308] if this is not done, the courts are likely to examine the nature of the expected public use and infer from it the probable intent of the parties. Thus, roads and streets are commonly deemed to be easements,[309] particularly if acquired by common-law dedication, while park and school sites are somewhat more likely to be considered possessory estates in the absence of evidence of a contrary intent.[310] Many jurisdictions regard dedications under statutory procedures, even of roads and streets, to give the public possessory estates in fee simple, while common law dedications for these purposes are regarded as conveying only easements.[311]

---

[305] Lane Title & Trust Co. v. Brannan, 103 Ariz. 272, 440 P.2d 105 (1968) (mortgagee must join); Lexington-Fayette County Planning & Zoning Commission v. Levas, 504 S.W.2d 685 (Ky. 1973) (tenant cannot dedicate without landlord's joinder); Fla. Stat. Ann. § 177.081, requiring joinder of mortgagees.

[306] See Jennings v. High Farms Corp., 28 A.D.2d 693, 281 N.Y.S.2d 110 (1967). If the public easement involves construction of improvements which would interfere with the private easement, the private easement-holder will have an action for removal of the improvements or for compensation; see Sargent v. Brunner Housing Corp., 31 A.D.2d 823, 297 N.Y.S.2d 879 (1969), affirmed 27 N.Y.2d 513, 312 N.Y.S.2d 993, 261 N.E.2d 105 (1970).

[307] Jacobs v. Lyon Township, 181 Mich. App. 386, 448 N.W.2d 861 (1989), judgment vacated, case remanded for further findings of fact, 434 Mich. 922, 455 N.W.2d 715 (1990) (dedication of public streets which terminate at the edge of navigable water inherently implies a right to public access to water); City of Evanston v. Robinson, 702 P.2d 1283 (Wyo. 1985) (statutory street dedication, although in "fee simple," did not convey underlying mineral rights to city).

[308] See, e.g., Park County Rod and Gun Club v. Department of Highways, 163 Mont. 372, 517 P.2d 352 (1973); Rainier Avenue Corp. v. City of Seattle, 80 Wn.2d 362, 494 P.2d 996 (1972), certiorari denied 409 U.S. 983, 93 S.Ct. 321, 34 L.Ed.2d 247 (1972); City of Bartlesville v. Ambler, 499 P.2d 433 (Okl. 1971), construing wording on plat to dedicate only an easement.

[309] Waterway Drive Prop. Owners' Ass'n, Inc. v. Town of Cedar Point, 224 N.C. App. 544, 737 S.E.2d 126 (2012); Jones v. Deeter, 152 Cal.App.3d 798, 199 Cal.Rptr. 825 (1984); Village of Kalkaska v. Shell Oil Co., 433 Mich. 348, 446 N.W.2d 91 (1989); Erickson Bushling, Inc. v. Manke Lumber Co., 77 Wn.App. 495, 891 P.2d 750 (1995); Town of Moorcroft v. Lang, 761 P.2d 96 (Wyo. 1988). See 3 Am.L.Prop. § 12.132 nn. 10–12 (1952). Cf. Jasinski v. Hudson Pointe Homeowners Ass'n, Inc., 124 A.D.3d 978, 1 N.Y.S.3d 487 (N.Y. App. Div. 2015) (dedication by deed conveyed fee simple estate); Landis v. Limbaugh, 282 Or. App. 284, 385 P.3d 1139 (2016); Falula Farms, Inc. v. Ludlow, 866 P.2d 569 (Utah App. 1993). A contrary result, treating roads and street as fee estates, is often reached if the dedication is pursuant to a statutory procedure.

If only an easement is dedicated, the donor continues to hold the servient estate or so-called "underlying fee," and may use it for in any way which does not interfere with the public easement; see, e.g., Arnold v. United States, 137 Fed.Cl. 524 (2018) (Kansas law); City of Daytona Beach v. Tona-Rama, 294 So.2d 73 (Fla.1974). Where the road or street abuts private land, the private owner is usually held to own to the center line of the street, subject to the public easement; see, e.g., Pub. Lands Access Ass'n v. Bd. of Cty. Comm'rs of Madison Cty., 373 Mont. 277, 321 P.3d 38 (2014); Town of Clifton Park v. Boni Builders, Inc., 156 A.D.3d 1035, 66 N.Y.S.3d 550 (N.Y. App. Div. 2017).

[310] See Sutton v. United States, 107 Fed. Cl. 436 (2012) (California law); Gion v. City of Santa Cruz, supra note 299, at n. 3; Verizon Wireless Pers. Commc'ns, L.P. v. Sanctuary at Wulfert Point Cmty. Ass'n, Inc., 916 So. 2d 850 (Fla. Dist. Ct. App. 2005) (dedication of wastewater treatment plant was fee estate, not easement). But see Rainier Avenue Corp. v. City of Seattle, supra note 308, presuming a dedication for a park gave only an easement.

[311] See, e.g., Arnold v. United States, supra note 309; Moeur v. City of Tempe, 3 Ariz.App. 196, 412 P.2d 878 (1966); Pelican Creek Homeowners, LLC v. Pulverenti, 243 So.3d 467 (Fla. Dist. Ct. App. 2018); Chesapeake Operating, Inc. v. City of Shreveport, 132 So. 3d 537 (La. App. 2014) (statutory dedication conveys fee simple unless dedicator expressly reserves fee); Gunn v. Delhi Township, 8 Mich.App. 278, 154 N.W.2d 598

Whatever the interest conveyed, the donor may impose restrictions on the use of the dedicated land, either by way of covenants running with the land or more commonly by the granting of a defeasible interest which leaves a reversionary right in the grantor, to become possessory if the restrictions are ever violated.[312] For example, land dedicated as a school site may be explicitly restricted to use for school purposes. The public body is bound by such restrictions unless it employs its power of eminent domain to enlarge its rights, in which event payment of compensation may well be necessary.[313] Moreover, courts and statutes often infer and enforce a use restriction merely from the fact that a particular use was mentioned or contemplated at the time of the dedication.[314]

Acceptance. A dedication, like an ordinary conveyance by deed, must be accepted to be complete. But dedications impose practical burdens of maintenance and supervision on local governments which they may not wish to assume. For this reason, acceptance is not presumed as it is for deeds between private parties;[315] instead, affirmative proof of acceptance is necessary.[316] The acceptance may take one of several forms. A formal resolution of the local government's legislative body or some similar action will certainly suffice.[317] Much less formal behavior can also constitute an acceptance: taking over of

(1967); McBroom v. Jackson Cty., 154 So. 3d 827 (Miss. 2014); Winnie Dev. LLLP v. Reveling, 2018 N.D. 47, 907 N.W.2d 413 (2018); Horsham Township v. Weiner, 435 Pa. 35, 255 A.2d 126 (1969). Even if the local government has only an easement, it includes not only public passage on the surface but also the right to grade and improve the surface and to lay subsurface sewers, drains, and pipes for various utilities; Arthur E. Selnick Assocs., Inc. v. Howard Cty. Maryland, 206 Md. App. 667, 51 A.3d 76 (2012).

[312] Historic Licking Riverside Civic Ass'n v. City of Covington, 774 S.W.2d 436 (Ky. 1989); Coral Gables v. Old Cutler Bay Homeowners Corp., 529 So.2d 1188 (Fla. App. 1988); Donald v. City of Vancouver, 43 Wn.App. 880, 719 P.2d 966 (1986). Cf. Neighbors and Friends of Viretta Park v. Miller, 87 Wn.App. 361, 940 P.2d 286 (1997) (insufficient evidence of intent to restrict right-of-way to pedestrian use).

[313] See, e.g., State of Louisiana v. Richardson, 453 So.2d 572 (La.App. 1984); Burns v. Board of Supervisors, 226 Va. 506, 312 S.E.2d 731 (1984); Ink v. City of Canton, 4 Ohio St.2d 51, 212 N.E.2d 574 (1965); Comment, The Effect of Condemnation Proceedings by Eminent Domain upon a Possibility of Reverter or Power of Termination, 19 Vill.L.Rev. 137 (1973); Annot., 60 A.L.R.3d 581 (1974). The requirement that the public body observe the original restrictions on use is sometimes referred to as a "public trust;" see note 327 infra.

[314] See, e.g., Ackerman v. Steisel, 104 A.D.2d 940, 480 N.Y.S.2d 556 (1984), affirmed 66 N.Y.2d 833, 498 N.Y.S.2d 364, 489 N.E.2d 251 (1985); Lord v. City of Wilmington, 332 A.2d 414 (Del.Ch. 1975), affirmed 378 A.2d 635 (Del. 1977). Cf. Timberlake Plantation Co. v. County of Lexington, 314 S.C. 556, 431 S.E.2d 573 (1993) (county could use dedicated roads for cable TV installation).

[315] See § 11.3 supra at note 201. Of course, acceptance of a deed is a perfectly satisfactory method of accepting the dedication of the land it conveys; see Rolleston v. Sea Island Properties, Inc., 254 Ga. 183, 327 S.E.2d 489 (1985), cert. denied 474 U.S. 823, 106 S.Ct. 77, 88 L.Ed.2d 63 (1985).

[316] Burgess v. United States, 109 Fed. Cl. 223 (2013) (Iowa law); Hardy v. Smith, 148 So. 3d 64, 70 (Ala. Civ. App. 2013); Orange County v. Chandler-Sherman Corp., 54 Cal.App.3d 561, 126 Cal.Rptr. 765 (1976); Stafford v. Klosterman, 134 Idaho 205, 998 P.2d 1118 (2000); Dotson v. Payne, 71 N.C.App. 691, 323 S.E.2d 362 (1984); Chandler v. Independent School District, 625 P.2d 620 (Okl. 1981); Brown v. Moore, 255 Va. 523, 500 S.E.2d 797 (1998); Hayes v. Mountain View Estates Homeowners Ass'n, 188 A.3d 678 (Vt. 2018); Somers USA, LLC v. State of Wisconsin Dep't of Transp., 361 Wis. 2d 807, 864 N.W.2d 114 (2015). In some jurisdictions statutes require acceptance within a fixed time; but see Twp. of Middletown v. Simon, 193 N.J. 228, 937 A.2d 949 (2008), recognizing acceptance many decades after the offer of dedication.

[317] See, e.g., Coppinger v. Rawlins, 239 Cal. App. 4th 608, 191 Cal. Rptr. 3d 414 (2015) (resolution of county board of supervisors required); Delta County Board of Commissioners v. Sherrill, 757 P.2d 1085 (Colo.App. 1987); Worley Highway District v. Yacht Club, 116 Idaho 219, 775 P.2d 111 (1989); Edwards v. Blackman, 2015 Me. 165, 129 A.3d 971 (2015); White v. Nw. Prop. Grp.-Hendersonville No. 1, LLC, 225 N.C. App. 810, 739 S.E.2d 572 (2013) (adoption of zoning map operated to accept dedication of street).

maintenance or construction of improvements,[318] cessation of property taxation,[319] or any other acts indicating the government's assumption of control over the land. If the dedication is made under a statutory procedure, approval of the donor's plat is generally considered a sufficient acceptance of areas marked on the plat for public use.[320] Finally, long and substantial public use of land offered for dedication will constitute an acceptance even in the absence of any action by the local government.[321]

Some sort of acceptance must occur within a "reasonable" time after the offer of dedication is made, but very long time periods have often been approved.[322] The donor may withdraw the offer of dedication at any time prior to acceptance, and withdrawal may be inferred from acts of the donor which are inconsistent with the dedication, such as selling the subject land or fencing it to keep the public out.[323] However, a sale of land by reference to a plat showing public streets is generally held to create private easements for access in favor of the lot owners as well as to constitute a public dedication.[324] The

---

[318] Mathers v. Wakulla Cty., 219 So. 3d 140 (Fla. Dist. Ct. App. 2017); Bryant v. Kern & Co., Inc., 196 Ga.App. 165, 395 S.E.2d 620 (1990); Pierce v. McCoy, 207 So. 3d 1069 (La. App. 2016) (width of public roadway was determined by extent of maintenance by local government); Haynes v. Vill. of Beulah, 308 Mich. App. 465, 865 N.W.2d 923 (2014) (entire platted width of roadway was dedicated to the public, even though only part of width was actually maintained); State v. NICO-WF1, L.L.C., 384 S.W.3d 818 (Tex. 2012) (same); Favre v. Jourdan River Estates, 148 So. 3d 361 (Miss. 2014) (entire length of roadway was accepted for dedication by paving part of roadway); Concerned Citizens v. Holden Beach Enterprises, Inc., 95 N.C.App. 38, 381 S.E.2d 810 (1989); Gensburg v. Clark, 2017-Ohio-7967; Baugus v. Wessinger, 303 S.C. 412, 401 S.E.2d 169 (1991). Several states have statutes providing that public use or maintenance for some period of years will make a roadway public; see Hillelson v. Grover, 105 A.D.2d 484, 480 N.Y.S.2d 779 (1984) (10 years use and maintenance); Wilson v. Seminole Coal, Inc., 175 W.Va. 518, 336 S.E.2d 30 (1985) (10 years use and maintenance).

[319] LaSalle National Bank v. City of Chicago, 19 Ill.App.3d 883, 312 N.E.2d 322 (1974); United States v. 329.22 Acres of Land, 307 F.Supp. 34 (M.D.Fla. 1968), affirmed 418 F.2d 551 (5th Cir. 1969).

[320] Moeur v. City of Tempe, 3 Ariz.App. 196, 412 P.2d 878 (1966); see Annot., 11 A.L.R.2d 524, 574 (1950). Cf. Thompson v. Town of Portland, 159 Conn. 107, 266 A.2d 893 (1970) (approval by planning commission was insufficient acceptance, where statute required an "official layout" of streets by the town.)

[321] San Juan Cty., Utah v. United States, 754 F.3d 787 (10th Cir. 2014) (under Utah law, 10 years continuous public use constituted both offer and acceptance of dedication); Laughlin v. Morauer, 849 F.2d 122 (4th Cir.1988) (under Virginia law. 70 years public use constituted acceptance); Hays v. Vanek, 217 Cal.App.3d 271, 266 Cal.Rptr. 856 (1989); Hughes v. Town of Mexico Beach, 455 So.2d 566 (Fla.App. 1984); Moreland v. Henson, 256 Ga. 685, 353 S.E.2d 181 (1987); Gold Coast Neighborhood Ass'n v. State, 140 Haw. 437, 403 P.3d 214 (2017); Lagro Twp. v. Bitzer, 999 N.E.2d 902 (Ind. Ct. App. 2013) (burials in public cemetery may serve as acceptance of dedication); Ellington v. Becraft, 534 S.W.3d 785 (Ky. 2017); Matter of Request of Lafayette Devel. Corp., 567 N.W.2d 743 (Minn.App. 1997), affirmed 576 N.W.2d 740 (Minn. 1998). Limited or sporadic public use may not suffice; see, e.g., Vestavia Hills Board of Education v. Utz, 530 So.2d 1378 (Ala. 1988); Luchetti v. Bandler, 108 N.M. 682, 777 P.2d 1326 (App. 1989), cert. denied 108 N.M. 681, 777 P.2d 1325 (1989). See also Pleak v. Entrada Prop. Owners' Ass'n, 207 Ariz. 418, 87 P.3d 831 (2004) (sale of lots pursuant to plat constituted acceptance of dedicated road).

[322] See, e.g., Town of Glenarden v. Lewis, 261 Md. 1, 273 A.2d 140 (1971) (48 years). Kraus v. Gerrish Tp., 205 Mich.App. 25, 517 N.W.2d 756 (1994) (90 years); Osborne v. Town of North Wilkesboro, 280 N.C. 696, 187 S.E.2d 102 (1972) (limited to 15 years by statute); Zalman v. City of Chester, 165 A.3d 82 (Pa. Commw. Ct. 2017) (limited to 21 years by statute). See also City of Ozark, Arkansas v. Union Pac. R.R. Co., 149 F.Supp.3d 1107 (W.D. Ark. 2015), rev'd in part, on other grounds, 843 F.3d 1167 (8th Cir. 2016) (doctrine of laches does not apply to city in accepting a dedication). But see Estojak v. Mazsa, 522 Pa. 353, 562 A.2d 271 (1989) (21 years delay deemed excessive; dedication failed).

[323] See Vivian v. Roscommon County Board of Road Commissioners, 433 Mich. 511, 446 N.W.2d 161 (1989) (landowner's erection of fence blocking road site operated to withdraw offer of dedication); Cavin v. Ostwalt, 76 N.C.App. 309, 332 S.E.2d 509 (1985). See generally Annot., 36 A.L.R.4th 625 (1985). A revocation of the offer of dedication must be by all those having an interest in the land in question; Soldatenko v. Vill. of Scarsdale, 138 A.D.3d 975, 31 N.Y.S.3d 117 (N.Y. App. Div. 2016).

[324] Bonifay v. Dickson, 459 So.2d 1089 (Fla.App. 1984); Price v. Walker, 95 N.C.App. 712, 383 S.E.2d 686 (1989); Foreal Homes, Inc. v. Incorporated Village of Muttontown, 128 A.D.2d 585, 512 N.Y.S.2d 849

donor's later withdrawal of the dedication cannot affect these private rights, which can only be given up by the lot owners themselves.[325] The same principle applies if, after dedication, the local government vacates the dedicated land; the private easements remain in effect unless released by their owners.[326]

Relinquishment of dedicated land. After a dedication has been accepted, the donor cannot take the land back unilaterally, and the local government is obligated by the "public trust" doctrine to keep the property open to the public for the uses specified in the original dedication.[327] However, the local government may give up its rights by a formal resolution vacating the property,[328] or by abandonment.[329] Mere nonuse, even for a very long time, will not constitute an abandonment unless it is accompanied by some further evidence that the local government no longer intends to assert rights in the land.[330] When public land is vacated or abandoned, a dispute often arises as to who is entitled to it. If the public's interest was only an easement, the land is simply freed of the servitude and the owners of the servient estate (usually those who own the abutting lots) now have unencumbered possession.[331] But if the public interest was a possessory fee simple, the cases are divided as between the original donor and the owners of the abutting land. The donor will usually prevail if he or she expressly reserved a reversionary interest.[332] If this was not done, the courts often find a way to award the

---

(1987); Dayton v. Jordan, 279 Or. App. 737, 381 P.3d 1031 (2016); Gooldy v. Storage Ctr.-Platt Springs, LLC, 422 S.C. 332, 811 S.E.2d 779 (2018). On the scope of the implied easement, see § 8.6 supra.

[325] Rudisill v. Icenhour, 92 N.C.App. 741, 375 S.E.2d 682 (1989); Riek v. Binnie, 352 Pa.Super. 246, 507 A.2d 865 (1986); Bond v. Dunmire, 129 Ill.App.3d 796, 84 Ill.Dec. 862, 473 N.E.2d 78 (1984); Carolina Land Co., Inc. v. Bland, 265 S.C. 98, 217 S.E.2d 16 (1975); Feldman v. Monroe Township Board, 51 Mich.App. 752, 216 N.W.2d 628 (1974). See 3 Am.L.Prop. § 12.134 n. 12 (1952).

[326] McPhillips v. Brodbeck, 289 Ala. 148, 266 So.2d 592 (1972); Potter v. Citation Coal Corp., 445 S.W.2d 128 (Ky.1969); Highway Holding Co. v. Yara Engineering Corp., 22 N.J. 119, 123 A.2d 511 (1956); Town of Kingstree v. Chapman, 405 S.C. 282, 747 S.E.2d 494 (Ct. App. 2013); Oak Lane Homeowners Ass'n v. Griffin, 2011 UT 25, 255 P.3d 677 (2011). Cf. Williams Place, LLC v. State ex rel. Dep't of Transp., 187 Wash. App. 67, 348 P.3d 797 (2015).

[327] Palmer v. City of Phoenix, 242 Ariz. 158, 393 P.3d 938 (Ct. App. 2017); Glick v. Harvey, 25 N.Y.3d 1175, 36 N.E.3d 640 (2015); In re Borough of Downingtown, 639 Pa. 673, 161 A.3d 844 (2017); Town of Kingstree v. Chapman, 405 S.C. 282, 311, 747 S.E.2d 494, 508 (Ct. App. 2013); Friends of N. Spokane Cty. Parks v. Spokane Cty., 184 Wash. App. 105, 130, 336 P.3d 632, 643 (2014). See also Wibby v. Boulder Cty. Bd. of Cty. Commissioners, 409 P.3d 516 (Colo. 2016) (subdivision owners have no standing to demand good maintenance of public streets by county).

[328] See, e.g., Etzler v. Mondale, 266 Minn. 353, 123 N.W.2d 603 (1963). In some jurisdictions a court order approving the vacation is necessary; see Bangle v. Green, 34 Mich.App. 287, 191 N.W.2d 160 (1971); In re Borough of Downingtown, 639 Pa. 673, 161 A.3d 844 (2017).

[329] See Burke Cty. v. Askin, 327 Ga. App. 116, 755 S.E.2d 602 (2014); Palmer v. City of Phoenix, note 327 supra. North Carolina presumes abandonment if the dedicated property is not opened and used by the public within 15 years after dedication; see Waterway Drive Prop. Owners' Ass'n, Inc. v. Town of Cedar Point, 224 N.C. App. 544, 737 S.E.2d 126 (2012).

[330] Miller v. Hoskinson, 189 W.Va. 189, 429 S.E.2d 76 (1993); Cruz v. City of Coral Gables, 560 So.2d 1196 (Fla.App.1990); Worley Highway District v. Yacht Club, 116 Idaho 219, 775 P.2d 111 (1989); Raftopoulos v. Farrow, 691 P.2d 1160 (Colo.App.1984). Cf. Real Progress, Inc. v. City of Seattle, 91 Wn.App. 833, 963 P.2d 890 (1998) (under statute, five years of nonuse accomplished vacation).

[331] Iowa State Highway Commission v. Dubuque Sand & Gravel Co., 258 N.W.2d 153 (Iowa 1977); State ex rel. State Highway Commission v. Johns, 507 S.W.2d 75 (Mo.App.1974); Potter v. Citation Coal Co., supra note 326. Note, however, that existing private easements in favor of other surrounding owners may continue to exist despite the vacation by the public; see note 326 supra.

[332] Trustees of Howard College v. McNabb, 288 Ala. 564, 263 So.2d 664 (1972); Peninsular Point, Inc. v. South Georgia Dairy Co-op., 251 So.2d 690 (Fla. App. 1971); Grant v. Koenig, 67 Misc.2d 1028, 325 N.Y.S.2d 428 (1971), affirmed 39 A.D.2d 1000, 333 N.Y.S.2d 591 (1972).

land to the abutting owners.[333] This result is sometimes hard to explain in theoretical terms, but it generally represents sounder policy, particularly in the case of a long, thin strip of land created by the vacation of a street.

Compelled dedications. Perhaps the most controversial aspect of dedications is the extent to which local governments can force developers to donate land for various public purposes by conditioning the granting of building permits or other development approvals on such dedications. Generally developers have little objection to dedicating streets and storm and sanitary sewers to the public, since maintenance of these facilities would be a financial burden on the lot owners if they remained private. But many local governments also demand dedications of land for school and park purposes, and cash fees in lieu of land, ostensibly covering the cost of current or projected expansion of water and sewerage treatment facilities or other public works, have also become common. These demands are costly, and are often resisted by developers. In general, the courts have approved such compulsory dedications only if the facilities thus provided have some reasonable nexus with the expected burdens on public services imposed by the new residents of the development. Judicial formulations of this test vary widely,[334] and statutes may also play a role.[335] More extended discussion is found in another section of this book.[336]

§ 11.7 ADVERSE POSSESSION

Adverse possession is a strange and wonderful system under which the occupation of another's land gains the occupier title[337]—but only if the occupation is indeed wrongful. To gain title the wrongful occupant must be in "adverse possession" for at least the statutory period of limitation on the owner's action to recover possession. So, there

---

[333] Falula Farms, Inc. v. Ludlow, 866 P.2d 569 (Utah App.1993); Christian v. Purdy, 60 Wn.App. 798, 808 P.2d 164 (1991); Tidewater Area Charities, Inc. v. Harbour Gate Owners Association, Inc., 240 Va. 221, 396 S.E.2d 661 (1990); Glass v. Carnes, 260 Ga. 627, 398 S.E.2d 7 (1990). Absent a statute, the same result might be reached by construing the original donor/developer's deeds of the lots as implicitly conveying the right to abutting dedicated streets if they are ever vacated.

[334] Compare Krughoff v. City of Naperville, 68 Ill.2d 352, 12 Ill.Dec. 185, 369 N.E.2d 892 (1977), with Associated Home Builders of Greater East Bay, Inc. v. City of Walnut Creek, 4 Cal.3d 633, 94 Cal.Rptr. 630, 484 P.2d 606 (1971), appeal dismissed 404 U.S. 878, 92 S.Ct. 202, 30 L.Ed.2d 159 (1971). See Annot., 43 A.L.R.3d 862 (1972).

[335] See, e.g., West's Rev.Code Wash. Ann. §§ 35.21.710, 82.02.020, limiting local governments to a 0.25% excise tax in lieu of all other fees, but still permitting certain dedications of land; West's Ann.Cal.Gov't Code § 65995, construed in Shapell Industries, Inc. v. Governing Bd. of Milpitas Unified School Dist., 1 Cal.App.4th 218, 1 Cal. Rptr.2d 818 (1991).

[336] See § 9.32 supra.

[337] See, e.g., West v. Hogan, 88 A.D.3d 1247, 930 N.Y.S.2d 708 (2011), aff'd, 19 N.Y.3d 1073, 979 N.E.2d 802 (2012) (successful adverse possessor can maintain action against trespasser); Nat. Gas Pipeline Co. of Am. v. Pool, 124 S.W.3d 188 (Tex. 2003) (severed mineral interest may be adversely possessed); Scott v. Burwell's Bay Imp. Ass'n, 281 Va. 704, 708 S.E.2d 858 (2011) (riparian rights to water may be adversely possessed). Though the adverse possessor gains legal title, it is not likely to be "marketable" title from the viewpoint of subsequent purchasers. This is because, first, the title is subject to litigation and, second, conveyancers generally have the notion that title must be marketable of record, and adverse possession gives rise to no recordable document. See Rehoboth Heights Development Co. v. Marshall, 15 Del.Ch. 314, 137 A. 83 (1927) (adverse possession title may be certain enough to be marketable); Simis v. McElroy, 160 N.Y. 156, 54 N.E. 674 (1899) (not marketable). The only sure way to make the title marketable is to establish a paper record by a favorable court decision, such as a quiet title action, to which the record owner is a party. See Beach v. Twp. of Lima, 489 Mich. 99, 802 N.W.2d 1 (2011); § 10.12, infra.

Because title by adverse possession need not be reflected in any document, a bona fide purchaser might purchase the land from the record owner, but the adverse possessor title-holder will prevail over the BFP. See Faloon v. Simshauser, 130 Ill. 649, 22 N.E. 835 (1889); Lacy v. Adams, 256 S.W.3d 610 (Mo. App. 2008); Mugaas v. Smith, 33 Wash. 2d 429, 206 P.2d 332 (1949).

are two aspects, the statutory limitations period—typically 5 to 20 years—and the doctrine of adverse possession, which is a judicial gloss on the statute. In most cases if an owner has a possessory action, the defendant's possession will be "adverse," but there can be exceptions.[338] Title gained is usually in fee simple absolute, but in cases when the fee is divided between a present possessory and future estates, the adverse possessor will get only the possessory title—that is, title replacing that of the party who had a possessory action.[339]

Adverse possession title is not derived from the former owner but begins a new chain of title. Thus, adverse possession provides a rare instance in which an original title may arise in a mature society. The concept of adverse possession stems, at least in part, from the ancient concept that possession, in and of itself, is a form of title, and can be asserted as such against all except the true owner of the land in question. Thus an adverse possessor may make such an assertion, even though his or her claim has not yet matured through the running of the statute of limitations.[340]

Few adverse possession cases deal with the statute of limitations itself, but an adverse possessor cannot gain title if the owner is one against whom the statute will not run. For this reason, title cannot be gained to land owned by the United States government, the states, and, at least as to land held for public use, by local governments.[341] Some states add churches, other charitable institutions, and utility companies to this list of owners who are exempt from losing their land to adverse possessors.[342] The statutes also contain various tolling conditions which prevent the statutory period from running against owners who are insane, infants, imprisoned, absent from the state, or in military service when the cause of action first accrues.[343]

---

[338] For instance, a holdover tenant or tenant at sufferance may be dispossessed, but his possession is not considered adverse. And, because, as we will see, adverse possession must be "open and notorious," one whose occupancy is underground or otherwise hidden is not in adverse possession.

[339] Adverse possession will not begin to run against the future interest until it becomes possessory. See Schaeffer v. Maddox, 794 So. 2d 1139 (Ala. Civ. App. 2000); Heath v. Turner, 309 N.C. 483, 308 S.E.2d 244 (1983); Miller v. Leaird, 307 S.C. 56, 413 S.E.2d 841 (1992); Annot., 58 A.L.R.2d 299, 302–05 (1958); Restatement of Property § 222, Comment f (1944). The adverse possessor will take free of other interests in the land, such as easements and mortgages, only if the possessor acts antagonistically to them; see Faulconer v. Williams, 327 Or. 381, 964 P.2d 246 (1998) (easement); Stat-o-matic Retirement Fund v. Assistance League of Yuma, 189 Ariz. 221, 941 P.2d 233 (App. 1997) (mortgage).

[340] Lensky v. DiDomenico, 2016 COA 89, 409 P.3d 457 (Colo. 2016).

[341] See Tadlock v. United States, 774 F.Supp. 1035 (S.D.Miss. 1990); Aaron v. Boston Redevelopment Auth., 850 N.E.2d 1105 (Mass.App.Ct. 2006); Houck v. Bd. of Park Commrs. of the Huron Cty. Park Dist., 116 Ohio St. 3d 148, 876 N.E.2d 1210 (2007); Nyman v. Anchor Dev., L.L.C., 2003 UT 27, 73 P.3d 357 (2003); Kiely v. Graves, 173 Wash. 2d 926, 271 P.3d 226 (2012); Annot., 55 A.L.R.2d 554 (1957). Compare Gorman v. City of Woodinville, 175 Wash. 2d 68, 283 P.3d 1082 (2012) (purported transfer of title by the disseisee to the government after adverse possession is completed has no effect on the adverse possessor) with Burke v. Pierro, 159 N.H. 504, 986 A.2d 538 (2009) (transfer by disseisee to government during adverse possession period prevents statute from running).

Maryland, Connecticut, and New Jersey have held adverse possession applies to land held by state government and its agencies if not held for a public use; see Devins v. Borough of Bogota, 124 N.J. 570, 592 A.2d 199 (N.J.App.Div. 1991), containing a discussion of the law nationwide. Of course, a governmental entity may *acquire* title by adverse possession; see Tanner v. Brasher, 254 Ga. 41, 326 S.E.2d 218 (1985); City of Gainesville v. Morrison Fertilizer, Inc., 158 S.W.3d 872 (Mo. Ct. App. 2005).

[342] MacDonough-Webster Lodge No. 26 v. Wells, 175 Vt. 382, 834 A.2d 25 (2003) (fraternal organization was not a charity exempt from adverse possession). See also Montgomery Cty. v. Bhatt, 446 Md. 79, 130 A.3d 424 (2016) and Mississippi Exp. R. Co. v. Rouse, 926 So. 2d 218 (Miss. 2006) (railroad property is immune from adverse possession unless railroad use has been discontinued).

[343] See, e.g., Ill.—S.H.A. ch. 83, ¶ 9; New Jersey Stats.Ann. 2A:14–21; West's Rev. Code Wash.Ann. 4.16.080, 4.16.090.

Such tolling provisions may delay the inception of statute's time period, and hence delay acquisition of title.[344]

Most of the judicial decisions deal, not with the terms of the statute itself, but with the definition and application of the judicial doctrine of adverse possession. A typical formulation, abstracted from the opinions cited below, is that possession, to be adverse, must be: (1) actual, (2) open and notorious, (3) hostile, (4) exclusive, and (5) continuous. Sometimes courts add a couple of other troublesome elements, probably subsets of "hostile," such as (6) claim of right or claim of title and (7) good faith. Statutes, often special ones that shorten the normal limitation period, sometimes require "color of title" or payment of taxes, perhaps combined with good faith.[345] The balance of this section will be organized under the main elements just listed.

Actual. With an important exception to be noted, adverse possession must be "actual." This requires some degree of physical occupation, but how much is the subject of many, many cases. Because the question is one of mixed fact and law, we simply have to reconcile ourselves to a wide range of judicial results. Of course the clearest case is one who fences a parcel, puts substantial structures on it, and maintains visible marks of use all over it. However, fences or walls are not essential, though courts are sensitive to some marks that show the boundaries of possession, such as partial fence lines, mowed grass, cultivation lines, trees or shrubs, paved areas, or other objects or improvements so located as to suggest boundaries.[346] Possessory acts must be substantial and must leave some physical evidence, not only to be actual but also to meet the overlapping requirement that they be "open and notorious." If a court concludes the acts are too

---

[344] See, e.g., Rehoboth Heights Development Co. v. Marshall, 15 Del.Ch. 314, 137 A. 83 (1927).

[345] Cowan v. Yeisley, 255 P.3d 966 (Alaska 2011) (color of title or good faith required by statute); First Nat'l Bank of Wray v. McGinnis, 819 P.2d 1080 (Colo.App. 1991) (contract of sale constituted color of title); Slemmons v. Massie, 102 N.M. 33, 690 P.2d 1027 (1984) (mortgage did not constitute color of title). Several states require payment of taxes by all adverse possessors; see Whispell Foreign Cars, Inc. v. United States, 106 Fed. Cl. 777 (2012) (Florida law); Ark. Code Ann. § 18–11–106 (payment of taxes and color of title required), discussed in Morrison v. Carruth, 2015 Ark. App. 224, 459 S.W.3d 317 (2015); Gilardi v. Hallam, 30 Cal.3d 317, 178 Cal.Rptr. 624, 636 P.2d 588 (Cal. 1981); Cumulus Broad., Inc. v. Shim, 226 S.W.3d 366 (Tenn. 2007) (payment of taxes is normally required, but not for small boundary adjustments); Lindgren v. Martin, 130 Idaho 854, 949 P.2d 1061 (Idaho 1997); Tungsten Holdings, Inc. v. Parker, 305 Mont. 329, 27 P.3d 429 (2001); Martin v. Kearl, 917 P.2d 91 (Utah App. 1996). See Annot., Presumptions and Evidence Respecting Identification of Land on which Property Taxes Were Paid to Establish Adverse Possession, 36 A.L.R.4th 843 (1985). Compare Hagman v. Meher Mount Corp., 215 Cal. App. 4th 82, 155 Cal. Rptr. 3d 192 (2013) (payment of taxes not required, where owner was a tax-exempt religious organization) and United States v. Stubbs, 776 F.2d 1472 (10th Cir. 1985) (payment of taxes not required, where adverse possessor was tax-exempt) with State v. Serowiecki, 892 N.E.2d 194 (Ind. Ct. App. 2008) (state could not comply with requirement to pay taxes, where state was tax-exempt, and therefore could not acquire title by adverse possession).

[346] E.g., Ewing's Lessee v. Burnet, 36 U.S. (11 Pet.) 41, 9 L.Ed. 624 (1837) (jury question; unfenced); Morrison v. Boyd, 475 So.2d 509 (Ala. 1985); Peters v. Juneau-Douglas Girl Scout Council, 519 P.2d 826 (Alaska 1974); Bryan v. Reifschneider, 181 Neb. 787, 150 N.W.2d 900 (1967); McGarry v. Coletti, 33 A.3d 140 (R.I. 2011); Krona v. Brett, 72 Wn.2d 535, 433 P.2d 858 (1967). Compare Walker v. Murphree, 722 So.2d 1277 (Miss.App. 1998), Machholz-Parks v. Suddath, 884 S.W.2d 705 (Mo.App. 1994), Crown Credit Co. v. Bushman, 170 Ohio App. 3d 807, 869 N.E.2d 83 (2007), and Blaylock v. Holland, 396 S.W.3d 720 (Tex. App. 2013) (mowing lawn insufficient) with Brennan v. Manchester Crossings, Inc., 708 A.2d 815 (Pa.Super. 1998) (mowing lawn sufficient). See Littleton v. Saline Lakeshore, LLC, 178 So. 3d 274 (La. App. 2015) (campsite suspended on ropes above island that was sporadically submerged was sufficient possession). But see Moore v. Stills, 307 S.W.3d 71 (Ky. 2010) (hunting, fishing and one-time removal of timber were insufficient). The 2008 amendments to New York's statute disallow mowing and similar maintenance activity, as well as non-structural encroachments, including fences, hedges, shrubbery, plantings, sheds and non-structural walls; see N.Y. Real Prop. Act. & Proc. L. § 522. In Franza v. Olin, 73 A.D.3d 44, 897 N.Y.S.2d 804 (2010), the court held application of the new statute to one who had already completed adverse possession when it was enacted would be unconstitutional. See Greenberg, note 369 infra.

insubstantial or temporary, there is no actual possession.[347] Seasonal or sporadic use of unenclosed land gives rise to many difficult questions of actual possession, as well as of open and notorious and continuous possession. Most such cases involve grazing animals, cutting timber, or harvesting natural crops. Some decisions seem to adopt a rule that these activities cannot be sufficient for adverse possession of unenclosed land, but others make the issue turn on whether the acts were normal and appropriate use of land so situated.[348] Enclosure of the land, or use of it up to some natural physical boundary, is not mandatory but is a factor favorable to the possessor.[349] Adverse possession on the surface of the earth is normally possession of the underlying earth, but this is generally not so as to underground minerals that, by previous severance, are owned by someone other than the surface owner.[350] The best test of actual possession, increasingly recognized in the courts, is whether the acts of possession are such as would be normal for an owner to make of land situated such as this in all the circumstances?[351]

An important exception to the requirement of actual possession is the doctrine of "constructive adverse possession." One who is in actual adverse possession of *part* of a parcel of land and who holds a "colorable" document of title to the entire parcel is, with qualifications to be noted, regarded as being in adverse possession of the *whole* parcel.[352] Colorable title, or "color of title," is usually defined as a document that appears to give title but, for some reason not apparent on its face, does not.[353] Typical examples are deeds derived from tax sales, sheriffs' deeds, and other deeds from public sales that are void for some reason, such as improper sale procedures.[354] The adverse possessor's acquisition of title under this doctrine is limited to the land area described in the

---

[347] Compare Monroe v. Rawlings, 331 Mich. 49, 49 N.W.2d 55 (1951) and Kenney v. Bridges, 123 Mont. 95, 208 P.2d 475 (1949) (sufficient acts) with Lilly v. Markvan, 563 Pa. 553, 763 A.2d 370 (2000), Rayburn v. Coffelt, 153 Or.App. 76, 957 P.2d 580 (1998), and Harkins v. Fuller, 652 A.2d 90 (Me. 1995) (acts not sufficient). See Double "D" Bar "C" Ranch v. Bell, 283 Ga. 386, 658 S.E.2d 635 (2008).

[348] Compare Crowley v. Whitesell, 702 S.W.2d 127 (Mo.App. 1985) (fencing "wild" land, selling some timber, running cattle on it, and clearing brush were sufficient acts to constitute adverse possession); Alaska National Bank v. Linck, 559 P.2d 1049 (Alaska 1977); Peters v. Juneau-Douglas Girl Scout Council, 519 P.2d 826 (Alaska 1974); Monroe v. Rawlings, 331 Mich. 49, 49 N.W.2d 55 (1951). A few statutes specifically require enclosure, cultivation, or improvement by the adverse possessor; see Lindgren v. Martin, 130 Idaho 854, 949 P.2d 1061 (Idaho 1997); Schultz v. Dew, 564 N.W.2d 320 (S.D. 1997); Yamin v. Daly, 205 A.D.2d 870, 613 N.Y.S.2d 300 (App.Div. 1994). See generally Annot., 48 A.L.R.3d 818 (1973).

[349] Whittemore v. Amator, 148 Ariz. 173, 713 P.2d 1231 (1986) (fence helpful in establishing extent of adverse possession); Brumagim v. Bradshaw, 39 Cal. 24 (1870) (natural boundary); Miceli v. Foley, 83 Md. App. 541, 575 A.2d 1249 (Md.App. 1990) ("visible boundary," a fence, marked extent of adverse possession).

[350] Spurlock v. Santa Fe Pacific Railroad Co., 143 Ariz. 469, 694 P.2d 299 (App. 1984), certiorari denied 472 U.S. 1032, 105 S.Ct. 3513, 87 L.Ed.2d 642 (1985); Failoni v. Chicago & North Western Railway Co., 30 Ill.2d 258, 195 N.E.2d 619 (1964); Stoebuck, Adverse Possession of Severable Minerals, 68 W.Va.L.Rev. 274 (1966).

[351] See Ewing's Lessee v. Burnet, 36 U.S. (11 Pet.) 41, 9 L.Ed. 624 (1837); Alaska National Bank v. Linck, 559 P.2d 1049 (Alaska 1977); Monroe v. Rawlings, 331 Mich. 49, 49 N.W.2d 55 (1951); Krona v. Brett, 72 Wn.2d 535, 433 P.2d 858 (1967).

[352] Lott v. Muldoon Road Baptist Church, Inc., 466 P.2d 815 (Alaska 1970); Monroe v. Rawlings, 331 Mich. 49, 49 N.W.2d 55 (1951); Cobb v. Spurlin, 73 N.C.App. 560, 327 S.E.2d 244 (1985); Taylor v. Brittain, 76 N.C.App. 574, 334 S.E.2d 242 (1985), modified and affirmed 317 N.C. 146, 343 S.E.2d 536 (1986). See also New York-Kentucky Oil & Gas Co. v. Miller, 187 Ky. 742, 220 S.W. 535 (1920).

[353] Foreman v. Sholl, 113 N.C.App. 282, 439 S.E.2d 169 (N.C.App.1994); Lott v. Muldoon Road Baptist Church, Inc., 466 P.2d 815 (Alaska 1970); Monroe v. Rawlings, 331 Mich. 49, 49 N.W.2d 55 (1951); 3 Am.L.Prop. § 15.11 (1952); Annot., 38 A.L.R.2d 986, 991 (1954).

[354] E.g., New York-Kentucky Oil & Gas Co. v. Miller, 187 Ky. 742, 220 S.W. 535 (1920) (private deeds); Mullins v. Colbert, 898 So. 2d 1149 (Fla. Dist. Ct. App. 2005) (tax deed); Monroe v. Rawlings, 331 Mich. 49, 49 N.W.2d 55 (1951) (tax deed); Annot., 71 A.L.R.2d 404 (1960) (judgment or decree); Annot., 38 A.L.R.2d 986 (1954) (tax deed).

colorable instrument.[355] There also must be some limit to how large a parcel may be constructively possessed; presumably it would have to be reasonably related in size to the area actually possessed.[356] Some decisions have imposed a requirement that the possessor have a good faith belief that the instrument is valid, which is also required by a number of special adverse possession statutes.[357]

Open and notorious. This usually means possession that gives visible evidence to one on the surface of the possessed land. The purpose of this element is to afford the owner opportunity for notice. The owner need not actually have seen evidence of the adverse occupation, but is charged with notice of what a reasonable inspection would disclose.[358] Possession that is "actual" is very likely to be open and notorious unless it is hidden in some unusual way. For example, when possession is of a cave, with no entrance apparent from the disseisee's land, it is not open and notorious.[359] One might also imagine a strange case in which possessory acts were carried out only under cover of darkness. The nature of the acts on the ground usually determines if they are notorious, but in some instances courts have given weight also to the possessor's reputation as owner or his having public records evidencing ownership.[360]

Hostile. "Hostility" is the very marrow of adverse possession; it has even redundantly been called adversity. The term is a bit misleading, for it does not refer to animus or enmity.[361] Properly understood, it means nothing more than that the possession is without permission of the one legally empowered to give possession, usually the owner.[362] Any kind of permissive use, as by a tenant, licensee, contract purchaser in possession, or easement holder is rightful, not hostile.[363] The better view is that unexplained possession is presumed hostile, so that it is up to the one who wishes to do so to establish that it is rightful.[364] Permission is usually by the owner's express act, but there are some cases in which it is proper to infer permission, as when an owner might

---

[355] Bryan v. Reifschneider, 181 Neb. 787, 150 N.W.2d 900 (1967); Jackson ex dem. Gilliland v. Woodruff, 1 Cow. 276 (N.Y. 1823).

[356] Jackson ex dem. Gilliland v. Woodruff, id. (dictum).

[357] Annot., 71 A.L.R.2d 404, 408 (1960); Annot., 38 A.L.R.2d 986, 1032–87 (1954) (statutes reviewed). See Lott v. Muldoon Road Baptist Church, Inc., 466 P.2d 815 (Alaska 1970).

[358] See Alaska National Bank v. Linck, 559 P.2d 1049 (Alaska 1977); Kenney v. Bridges, 123 Mont. 95, 208 P.2d 475 (1949); McGarry v. Coletti, 33 A.3d 140 (R.I. 2011).

[359] Marengo Cave Co. v. Ross, 212 Ind. 624, 10 N.E.2d 917 (1937). See also Edwards v. Sims, 232 Ky. 791, 24 S.W.2d 619 (1929) (cave); Silipigno v. F.R. Smith & Sons, Inc., 71 A.D.3d 1255, 896 N.Y.S.2d 261 (2010) (buried fuel tank).

[360] Alaska National Bank v. Linck, 559 P.2d 1049 (Alaska 1977) (paying taxes); Kenney v. Bridges, 123 Mont. 95, 208 P.2d 475 (1949) (colorable recorded deed, paying taxes). The New Jersey court, in a dubious decision, held that an encroachment of 15 inches by a stairway was too slight to be "open and notorious;" Mannillo v. Gorski, 54 N.J. 378, 255 A.2d 258 (1969). See Stump v. Whibco, 314 N.J. Super. 560, 715 A.2d 1006 (App. Div. 1998), limiting the scope of *Mannillo.*

[361] Estate of Becker v. Murtagh, 19 N.Y.3d 75, 968 N.E.2d 433 (2012); Villarreal v. Guerra, 446 S.W.3d 404 (Tex. App. 2014).

[362] Nevells v. Carter, 122 Me. 81, 119 A. 62 (1922); Ottavia v. Savarese, 338 Mass. 330, 155 N.E.2d 432 (1959); Mellenthin v. Brantman, 211 Minn. 336, 1 N.W.2d 141 (1941) (recommended reading); Krona v. Brett, 72 Wn.2d 535, 433 P.2d 858 (1967); Lanham v. Marley, 475 N.E.2d 700 (Ind. App.1985); 3 Am.L.Prop. § 15.4 (1952). Permission given to a prior possessor will continue to bind a successor possessor unless the later commits new and different acts of hostility; see Barrow v. D & B Valley Assocs., LLC, 22 A.3d 1131 (R.I. 2011).

[363] Ruhland v. Elliott, 302 Kan. 405, 353 P.3d 1124 (2015) (if grantor continues to possess the land after deeding it away, grantor's possession is presumed permissive).

[364] But many jurisdictions presume permissiveness if the land is open, unfenced, unimproved, in its natural state, or some combination of the foregoing factors; see, e.g., Breeding v. Koste, 443 Md. 15, 115 A.3d 106 (2015).

customarily allow others to make light use of vacant land.[365] Any time an adverse possessor and owner have discussed the adverse possession, permissive agreement may have occurred. However, the owner's mere knowledge of the possession, his demands upon the possessor to leave the property,[366] or, by the better view, even the latter's offer to compromise, do not destroy hostility.[367]

This brings us to the most difficult, thoroughly maddening, question in adverse possession law: whether an adverse possessor's subjective state of mind, imprecisely often called "intent," can destroy hostility. It is our view, as of nearly all scholars, that what the possessor believes or intends should have nothing to do with it.[368] This is indeed probably the majority view today.[369] Yet two minority positions, pointing is diametrically opposite directions, continue to persist in the case law. At one extreme view is the view that an adverse possessor must be acting in good faith, and have "a bona fide claim * * * that he has got a right as owner."[370] At the other extreme is the view that the possessor

[365] Permission may be inferred if the possessor and true owner are members of the same family or otherwise have a close and cooperative relationship; see Jaffer v. Hirji, 887 F.3d 111 (2d Cir. 2018) (New York law). But see Totman v. Malloy, 431 Mass. 143, 725 N.E.2d 1045 (2000) (no presumption of permission among family members); Larsen v. The Arlington Condo. Owners Ass'n, Inc., 795 S.E.2d 435 (N.C. Ct. App. 2016) (condominium unit owner may adversely possess parking space against owners' association).

If the possession is initially permissive, it can become hostile only by virtue of an ouster, "a distinct and open disavowal of the title of the owner, brought home to the owner"; Hillard v. Marshall, 888 P.2d 1255 (Wyo. 1995); Ropitzky v. Hungerford, 27 A.D.3d 1031, 812 N.Y.S.2d 682 (2006); 1525 Highland Assocs., LLC v. Fohl, 62 Conn. App. 612, 772 A.2d 1128 (2001). Most cases involve claims by one cotenant against another; see, e.g., Center Line Enterprises, Inc. v. Washington, 465 So.2d 1129 (Ala. 1985); Preciado v. Wilde, 139 Cal. App. 4th 321, 42 Cal. Rptr. 3d 792 (2006); O'Connor v. Larocque, 302 Conn. 562, 31 A.3d 1 (2011); DeFoor v. DeFoor, 290 Ga. 540, 722 S.E.2d 697 (2012); Pioneer Mill Co. v. Dow, 90 Haw. 289, 978 P.2d 727 (1999) (cotenant's administrator); Dyer v. Cotton, 333 S.W.3d 703 (Tex. App. 2010). See also Estate of Wells v. Estate of Smith, 576 A.2d 707 (D.C.App. 1990) (holdover by leasehold tenant after lease expiration); Hutchinson v. Taft, 2010 WY 5, 222 P.3d 1250 (Wyo. 2010) (same); Berg v. Fairman, 107 Idaho 441, 690 P.2d 896 (1984) (occupation by blood relative of owner); Sugarman v. Malone, 30 A.D.3d 197, 816 N.Y.S.2d 453 (2006) (occupation by owner's daughter-in-law and sister-in-law); McDaniel v. Kendrick, 386 S.C. 437, 688 S.E.2d 852 (Ct. App. 2009) (occupation by owner's stepmother).

[366] Such a demand, far from interrupting the running of the statute, is actually evidence of hostility or nonpermissiveness, and thus strengthens the adverse possessor's case. But if the owner files a suit to eject the possessor, or physically removes the possessor from the land, the continuity of the owner's possession is interrupted; see Crone v. Nuss, 46 Kan. App. 2d 436, 263 P.3d 809 (2011).

[367] Some decisions take the position that if the possessor, in offering a compromise, admits the owner's title, this destroys hostility. Preciado v. Wilde, 139 Cal. App. 4th 321, 42 Cal. Rptr. 3d 792 (2006); Bowen v. Serksnas, 121 Conn. App. 503, 997 A.2d 573 (2010); Mann v. La-Salle Nat. Bank, 205 Ill.App.3d 304, 150 Ill.Dec. 230, 562 N.E.2d 1033 (1990), appeal denied 136 Ill.2d 545, 153 Ill.Dec. 375, 567 N.E.2d 333 (1991). The better view is that the possessor's knowledge or offer has nothing to do with hostility. Warren v. Bowdran, 156 Mass. 280, 31 N.E. 300 (1892); Patterson v. Reigle, 4 Pa. 201 (1846).

[368] See Peters v. Juneau-Douglas Girl Scout Council, 519 P.2d 826 (Alaska 1974); Ottavia v. Savarese, 338 Mass. 330, 155 N.E.2d 432 (1959); Mellenthin v. Brantman, 211 Minn. 336, 1 N.W.2d 141 (1941); Norgard v. Busher, 220 Or. 297, 349 P.2d 490 (1960); City of Rock Springs v. Sturm, 39 Wyo. 494, 273 P. 908 (1929); 3 Am. L.Prop. § 15.4 (1952); Annot., 80 A.L.R.2d 1171, 1183 (1961). The *Norgard* decision cites a string of leading secondary authorities on the point.

[369] Evanich v. Bridge, 119 Ohio St. 3d 260, 893 N.E.2d 481 (2008); Chaplin v. Sanders, 100 Wn.2d 853, 676 P.2d 431 (1984). See Smith, Neighboring Property Owners § 6:8 (2017 update); Greenberg, Reasonableness Is Unreasonable: A New Jurisprudence of New York Adverse Possession Law, 31 Cardozo L. Rev. 2491 (2010); Stake, The Uneasy Case for Adverse Possession, 89 Geo. L.J. 2419, 2426–2432 (2001).

[370] Prax v. Zalewski, 400 P.3d 116 (Alaska 2017), based on Alaska Stat. Ann. § 09.45.052; Thompson v. Cent. of Georgia R.R., 282 Ga. 264, 646 S.E.2d 669 (2007), based on Ga. Code Ann. § 44–5–161(a); LeGardeur v. Coleman, 131 So. 3d 1035 (La. App. 2013); Clark v. Ranchero Acres Water Co., 198 Or. App. 73, 108 P.3d 31 (2005); Harsha v. Anastos, 693 P.2d 760 (Wyo. 1985). Contra, see Walling v. Przybylo, 7 N.Y.3d 228, 851 N.E.2d 1167 (2006) (good faith not required); Chaplin v. Sanders, supra note 369 (good faith and bad faith irrelevant). The *Walling* case was reversed by New York's 2008 statutory amendments, which now require a showing of good faith. See N.Y. Real Prop. Act. & Proc. L. § 501(3); Hogan v. Kelly, 86 A.D.3d 590, 927 N.Y.S.2d 157 (2011) (statute did not apply retroactively to titles vested before its enactment. See Helmholtz, Adverse Possession

must be in bad faith; thus, a belief that the possessor is on his or her own land will be fatal.[371] Under this position, if the possessor admits (probably during clever cross-examination) that she or he intended to claim only to wherever the true boundary was, the courts will deny hostility and defeat the possessor's claim.[372] Presumably, then, a possessor who said he knew he was occupying his neighbor's land and intended to get it if he could would be better off. Both of these extremes are unfortunate and ought to be done away with; a requirement of a particular state of mind is highly subject to manipulation, and reduces the capacity of adverse possession to quiet titles in mistaken-boundary cases.

Notions about state of mind and intent apparently came into adverse possession law through use of the phrases "claim of right" or "claim of title."[373] Perhaps these phrases would cause no harm if they could be strictly limited to mean that the adverse possessor's use and possession must be of a character an owner would make. But because the phrases have no clear fixed meaning and cause much trouble, it would be better if they, and the notions they have spawned, were forgotten.

Some question has existed whether possession that began as permissive or rightful may, without a break in physical possession, become adverse.[374] Most of the cases involve lessees who enter permissively or co-tenants whose entry is rightful under the principle that each co-tenant is entitled to full possession. The answer is that such continuing possession may become adverse to the landlord or other co-tenants only if the element of hostility is supplied by an "ouster," which means the true owner's or the possessor's repudiation of the original rightful possession. A clear case would be the lessee or co-tenant who expressly notified his landlord or co-tenants that he denied their interests and was holding possession in his own right alone.[375] Many courts require that the disseisee be aware of the words or act of ouster. But the ouster need not be, and in most cases is not, by express words but by circumstances showing clearly that the possessor now claims in repudiation of the true owner's rights. Courts give weight to colorable title documents; the possessor's purporting to give conveyances, leases, and mortgages; his paying taxes; long-continued possession; intensive use of the land; community

---

and Subjective Intent, 61 Wash.U.L.Q. 331 (1983), suggesting that even though most courts formally reject good faith as a requirement for adverse possession, they frequently manipulate the other elements of the doctrine in order to rule against bad faith claimants. See also Merrill, Property Rules, Liability Rules, and Adverse Possession, 79 Nw.U.L.Rev. 1122 (1985), commenting on this thesis.

[371] Hollander v. World Mission Church, 255 Va. 440, 498 S.E.2d 419 (Va. 1998) (will not); Brown v. Gobble, 196 W.Va. 559, 474 S.E.2d 489 (W.Va. 1996) (will not); Predham v. Holfester, 32 N.J.Super. 419, 108 A.2d 458 (1954) (will); Krona v. Brett, 72 Wn.2d 535, 433 P.2d 858 (1967) (will not); Annot., 80 A.L.R.2d 1171, 1173–74 (1961).

[372] E.g. Price v. Whisnant, 236 N.C. 381, 72 S.E.2d 851 (1952); Brown v. Hubbard, 42 Wn.2d 867, 259 P.2d 391 (1953); Wilcox v. Estate of Hines, 355 Wis. 2d 1, 849 N.W.2d 280 (2014) (subjective intent not to claim title will defeat adverse possession); Annot., 80 A.L.R.2d 1171, 1174–81 (1961). Contra, see Henninger v. Brewster, 357 S.W.3d 920 (Ky. Ct. App. 2012); Evanich v. Bridge, 119 Ohio St. 3d 260, 893 N.E.2d 481 (2008).

[373] Carpenter v. Coles, 75 Minn. 9, 77 N.W. 424 (1898).

[374] See Annot., Adverse Possession under Parol Gift of Land, 43 A.L.R.2d 6.

[375] Glover v. Glover, 92 P.3d 387 (Alaska 2004); Williams v. White, 207 So. 3d 59 (Ala. Civ. App. 2016); Johnson v. James, 237 Ark. 900, 377 S.W.2d 44 (1964) (dictum); Adams v. Johnson, 271 Minn. 439, 136 N.W.2d 78 (1965) (dictum); Villarreal v. Guerra, 446 S.W.3d 404 (Tex. App. 2014); 3 Am.L.Prop. §§ 15.6, 15.7; Annot., 82 A.L.R.2d 5, 21–25, 104–06 (1962). In New York, a cotenant is regarded as hostile to other cotenants only after holding exclusively for ten years; see Myers v. Bartholomew, 91 N.Y.2d 630, 674 N.Y.S.2d 259, 697 N.E.2d 160 (N.Y 1998). See also Mauna Kea Agribusiness Co. v. Nauka, 105 Haw. 252, 96 P.3d 581 (2004) (ouster unnecessary, where adverse possessor did not realize that a cotenant held ownership).

reputation; and so forth.[376] Naturally courts are reluctant to find an ouster if the evidence of it is incomplete or ambiguous or if the disseised owner may have given permission,[377] but in practice it is not rare.

Exclusive. The requirement that adverse possession must be "exclusive" embodies two related concepts. First, possession must not be shared with the disseised owner.[378] Thus, if the true owner is in possession of the entire land, an adverse possessor can never succeed in acquiring title. Of course, the adverse possessor may be in exclusive possession of part of a parcel of land and the owner in possession of another part; that is usually so in mistaken boundary cases.

Second, exclusivity means that if two or more competing adverse possessors are on the same land, none of them can acquire title.[379] On the other hand, if multiple adverse possessors are cooperating or working together, they can acquire title (when the other elements are satisfied) as tenants in common.[380] By the same token, one may be in adverse possession through another whom he or she has put in possession as a tenant; the tenant's possession inures to the benefit of the putative landlord.[381]

Continuous. The final element, that adverse possession must be "continuous," means that it must continue without significant interruption for a solid block of time at least as long as the statutory period of limitation. What is a significant interruption depends upon the nature of the land. Brief and ordinary absences, while the possessor goes to town, is gone overnight, or is away working or on vacation, for instance, would surely not break any adverse possession.[382] With land that is, by its nature, suitable and normally used for seasonal pursuits, then seasonal adverse possession is usually

---

[376] See Wheeling Dollar Bank v. Delray Beach, 639 So.2d 113 (Fla.App. 1994); Johnson v. James, 237 Ark. 900, 377 S.W.2d 44 (1964); Adams v. Johnson, 271 Minn. 439, 136 N.W.2d 78 (1965); Annot., 82 A.L.R.2d 5, 64–217 (1962). But see Olwell v. Clark, 658 P.2d 585 (Utah 1982) (one co-tenant's payment of taxes for about 40 years was not ouster of other co-tenants); Wright v. Wright, 270 Ga. 530, 512 S.E.2d 618 (Ga. 1999) (purported sale by adverse possessor signified an ouster and ended permission).

[377] See Estate of Wells v. Estate of Smith, 576 A.2d 707 (D.C.App. 1990) (court reluctant to find ouster by holdover tenant); Denton v. Denton, 627 S.W.2d 124 (Tenn.App. 1981) (one co-tenant's purchase of tax title is for benefit of all co-tenants and is not adverse to them unless they are aware of the co-tenancy); Mercer v. Wayman, 9 Ill.2d 441, 137 N.E.2d 815 (1956); Smith v. Tremaine, 221 Or. 33, 350 P.2d 180 (1960).

[378] Parker v. Rhoades, 225 So. 3d 642 (Ala. Civ. App. 2016); Crone v. Nuss, 46 Kan. App. 2d 436, 263 P.3d 809 (2011); Akin v. Castleberry, 2012 Okl. 79, 286 P.3d 638 (2012). Occasional use by other trespassers or even the true owner will not usually defeat exclusivity; see Estate of Becker v. Murtagh, 19 N.Y.3d 75, 968 N.E.2d 433 (2012); Georgia Power Co. v. Irvin, 267 Ga. 760, 482 S.E.2d 362 (Ga. 1997); Nevells v. Carter, 122 Me. 81, 119 A. 62 (1922); Brasher v. Craig, 483 S.W.3d 446 (Mo. Ct. App. 2016); Apperson v. White, 950 So. 2d 1113 (Miss. Ct. App. 2007); Russell v. Gullett, 285 Or. 63, 589 P.2d 729 (1979); Bryant v. Palmer Coking Coal Co., 86 Wn.App. 204, 936 P.2d 1163 (1997).

[379] Malone v. Smith, 355 Ill. App. 3d 812, 823 N.E.2d 1158 (2005); Ortmeyer v. Bruemmer, 680 S.W.2d 384 (Mo.App. 1984); Tran v. Macha, 213 S.W.3d 913 (Tex. 2006); ITT Rayonier, Inc. v. Bell, 51 Wash. App. 124, 129, 752 P.2d 398, 401 (1988), aff'd in part, rev'd in part, 112 Wash. 2d 754, 774 P.2d 6 (1989).

[380] Preston v. Smith, 41 Tenn.App. 222, 293 S.W.2d 51 (1955) (husband and wife acquired title as tenants in common, not by entirety); 4 Tiffany, Real Property § 1141 (3d ed. 2017 update).

[381] Dickinson v. Suggs, 196 So. 3d 1183 (Ala. Civ. App. 2015); Berryhill v. Moore, 180 Ariz. 77, 881 P.2d 1182 (Ariz.App. 1994); Gurley v. E. Atlanta Land Co., 276 Ga. 749, 583 S.E.2d 866 (2003); Nevells v. Carter, 122 Me. 81, 119 A. 62 (1922); Allred ex rel. Jensen v. Allred, 2008 UT 22, 182 P.3d 337 (2008); 4 Tiffany, Real Property § 1146 (3d ed. 2017 update). But see Norris v. Cox, 860 So. 2d 319 (Miss. Ct. App. 2003) (adult children's possession did not count in favor of parents' possession).

[382] Parker v. Potter, 2014 VT 109, 197 Vt. 577, 109 A.3d 406 (2014) (foreclosure of adversely possessed property and sale by foreclosing bank did not break continuity of possession).

continuous enough.[383] Again, the test should be whether the adverse possessor used the land as a true owner would. But if the possessor's occupation is only intermittent or sporadic, a court will likely find that continuity of possession is missing.[384]

Tacking. An interesting question within the subject of continuity is "tacking," the adding together of periods of possession that are continuous but by different persons. This is allowed, provided there is a sufficient nexus, often called "privity," between the successors. This nexus is provided if the earlier possessor gives the next one a colorable title document that describes the area possessed or if the next one is the heir of the first.[385] And tacking may occur, without any formal or even express transfer, simply by the earlier possessor's turning over possession to his successor. This may occur when an adversely possessed strip is turned over in connection with the conveyance of adjoining land the possessor owns or by a pointing out of boundaries or by other acts or oral statement that evince a turning over.[386] The idea of an informal transfer is easy enough to justify in theory, though, because a possessory "title" should be transferable by a transfer of possession.

Consider the case in which, midway through the period of limitations, the true owner sells or give the property to another. Must the adverse possessor start over again in order to acquire title against the new owner? The answer is no. Once the adverse possession has commenced, a transfer of title by the true owner will have no effect at all on the running of the statute in favor of the possessor.[387] The same is generally true of other types of title manipulations by the true owner, such as dividing the title into present and future interests, placing a mortgage on the property, severing a mineral estate, or becoming subject to a legal disability.[388]

Is the doctrine of adverse possession justified? Some decisions smack of a desire to punish the landowner who is not diligent or to award the possessor who is. Diligence is a quality society might promote, though hardly at the expense of the owner's title. But other broader reasons exist: that after a long time uncertain boundaries should be stabilized; that persons who have taken interests in the land or dealt with the adverse possessor in reliance upon his or her apparent ownership should be protected; and that those who will keep land productive by using it should be given permanence. Adverse

---

[383] Alaska National Bank v. Linck, 559 P.2d 1049 (Alaska 1977) (vacant land, seasonal use); Manderscheid v. Dutton, 193 Or. App. 9, 88 P.3d 281 (2004) (seasonal grazing); Howard v. Kunto, 3 Wn.App. 393, 477 P.2d 210 (1970) (summer home).

[384] Dzuris v. Kucharik, 164 Colo. 278, 434 P.2d 414 (1967); Miceli v. Foley, 83 Md.App. 541, 575 A.2d 1249 (1990) (entry to make survey did not break continuity); Mendonca v. Cities Service Oil Co., 354 Mass. 323, 237 N.E.2d 16 (1968); Ortmeyer v. Bruemmer, 680 S.W.2d 384 (Mo.App. 1984).

[385] Catawba Indian Tribe v. South Carolina, 978 F.2d 1334 (4th Cir. 1992), cert. denied 507 U.S. 972 (1993); Water Works & Sanitary Sewer Bd. of City of Montgomery v. Parks, 977 So. 2d 440 (Ala. 2007); Bryan v. Reifschneider, 181 Neb. 787, 150 N.W.2d 900 (1967) (dictum); Stump v. Whibco, 314 N.J. Super. 560, 715 A.2d 1006 (App. Div. 1998); Murdock v. Zier, 2006 WY 80, 137 P.3d 147 (Wyo. 2006); Annot., 43 A.L.R.2d 1061 (1955).

[386] White v. Matthews, 506 S.W.3d 382 (Mo. Ct. App. 2016); Brand v. Prince, 35 N.Y.2d 634, 364 N.Y.S.2d 826, 324 N.E.2d 314 (1974); Howard v. Kunto, 3 Wn.App. 393, 477 P.2d 210 (1970); Brown v. Gobble, 196 W.Va. 559, 474 S.E.2d 489 (W.Va. 1996). Contra, see Baylor v. Soska, 540 Pa. 435, 658 A.2d 743 (Pa.1995) (tacking may occur only by written deed describing the adversely-possessed land).

[387] Compart v. Wolfstellar, 906 N.W.2d 598 (Minn. Ct. App. 2018); 1148 Davol St. LLC. v. Mech.'s Mill One LLC, 86 Mass. App. Ct. 748, 21 N.E.3d 547 (2014).

[388] Berryhill v. Moore, 180 Ariz. 77, 881 P.2d 1182 (Ariz.App. 1994) (mortgage); Battle v. Battle, 235 N.C. 499, 70 S.E.2d 492 (1952) (disability); Miller v. Leaird, 307 S.C. 56, 413 S.E.2d 841 (S.C. 1992) (disability). Even a temporary transfer to the government will merely toll, but not reset, the statutory period; Weible v. Wells, 2017 PA Super 49, 156 A.3d 1220 (2017).

possession is best explained as a doctrine of repose. Perhaps, too, the mystical connection between possession and title is worth something. Title by possession, along with prescription, is an old subject in English law; it had its counterparts in Roman law.[389] If we had no doctrine of adverse possession, we should have to invent something very much like it.

§ 11.8 PRACTICAL LOCATION OF BOUNDARIES

It often happens that a landowner is uncertain of the precise location on the ground of the parcel's boundaries. This uncertainty may result from an ambiguous or confusing description in the deed or other documents,[390] but it is not always easy to locate boundaries even if the written description is clear. A survey may be obtained, but it can be very costly, especially if the parcel is large, its terrain is uneven, or it is overgrown with vegetation. In some states it is possible to bring an equitable or statutory proceeding for judicial determination of the boundaries,[391] but that course is likely to be even more expensive. To avoid these costs, abutting owners frequently enter into informal relationships which fix the boundaries between them. In general the law tends to uphold these determinations, even though they often have the effect of placing a boundary somewhere other than at its "true" location as a surveyor would fix it by following the written description.

At least four fairly distinct doctrines fit this general discussion: (1) boundaries by agreement; (2) boundaries by acquiescence; (3) boundaries by estoppel; and (4) boundary determinations by a common grantor. Each of these doctrines is a type of "practical location" of boundaries[392] and is discussed in this section. Discussion of them is hampered by the inconsistency, overlap, and uncertainty which characterizes their treatment in the courts. They are, however, doctrinally distinct from the concept of adverse possession, covered in the preceding section, which also operates to adjust boundary locations in many cases.

None of the doctrines discussed here require a writing satisfying the statute of frauds,[393] yet all of them have the effect of reducing the size of one owner's parcel while enlarging another's—a process any lay person would surely describe as a transfer of land. The courts do *not* consider a transfer to take place; instead, they hold that boundary in question has simply been redefined or reconstrued by the parties' actions.[394] This

---

[389] Taylor ex dem. Atkyns v. Horde, 1 Burr. 60, 97 Eng.Rep. 190 (K.B.1757); Stokes v. Berry, 2 Salk. 421, 91 Eng.Rep. 366 (K.B. 1699); Britton 250–51 (Nichols transl. 1901); Buckland, A Manual of Roman Private Law §§ 47–49 (1925); Walsh, Title by Adverse Possession, 16 N.Y.U.L.Q.Rev. 532 (1939).

[390] On construction of ambiguous descriptions, see § 11.2 supra at notes 163–165.

[391] See, e.g., Shirk v. Schmunk, 192 Neb. 25, 218 N.W.2d 433 (1974) applying Neb. Rev.Stat. § 34–301; Curtis Fishing & Hunting Club, Inc. v. Johnson, 214 Va. 388, 200 S.E.2d 542 (1973), applying what is now Virginia Code § 8.01–179. See generally 2 Tiffany Real Prop. § 652 (3d ed. 2017 update).

[392] See Browder, The Practical Location of Boundaries, 56 Mich.L.Rev. 487 (1958); Lamm v. McTighe, 72 Wn.2d 587, 434 P.2d 565 (1967).

[393] This is usually explained by the fiction that the doctrines do not involve a transfer of land, but merely a redefinition of the parcels; see Spivey v. Smith, 303 Ga. App. 469, 693 S.E.2d 830 (2010); Goodman v. Lothrop, 143 Idaho 622, 151 P.3d 818 (2007). A few courts have rejected one or more of the doctrines mentioned because they operate without compliance with the statute of frauds. See, e.g., Andrews v. Andrews, 252 N.C. 97, 113 S.E.2d 47 (1960), refusing to enforce oral boundary line agreements.

[394] E.g., Hoyer v. Edwards, 182 Ark. 624, 32 S.W.2d 812 (1930); Fischer v. Croston, 163 Idaho 331, 413 P.3d 731 (2018); Garrett v. Spear, 998 N.E.2d 297 (Ind. Ct. App. 2013); DeWitt v. Lutes, 581 S.W.2d 941 (Mo.App.1979); 1 Patton and Palomar, Land Titles § 162 (3d ed. 2017 update); 2 Tiffany, Real Property § 653 n. 79 (3d ed. 2017 update). The party whose land area is reduced by the boundary change is not entitled to compensation or damages; see Gabler v. Fedoruk, 756 N.W.2d 725 (Minn. Ct. App. 2008). The concept that a

highly artificial viewpoint has a practical advantage: it avoids the need for a writing, and in effect rewrites the documents of title by operation of law to reflect the change the parties have wrought.[395] Thus, if the distance call in the deed is "500 feet," it may henceforth be treated as if it read "517 feet" or "483 feet," and every future deed of the land which copies or incorporates the original description will also be so read.[396]

Two underlying policies justify this seemingly bizarre disregard for the statute of frauds and the literal meaning of the written word. One is repose: the notion that the law ought not to tinker with the well-settled and long-held understanding of the people involved, even if it does not comport with their documents.[397] The other is estoppel: if one reasonably relies on another's representations (even those arising from conduct rather than words), the law should not allow the representations to be withdrawn or denied.[398] These two ideas, repose and estoppel, mixed together in varying proportions and recognized at varying levels of consciousness, form the policy underpinnings of the cases we now consider.

Agreement. To establish a boundary by agreement, it must first be shown either that the parties were uncertain or unaware of the correct location, or that a dispute as to the true location existed between them.[399] Some courts recognize only uncertainty or only dispute, while others, probably the majority, recognize both. If the basis of the agreement is uncertainty, it is usually said that both owners must be uncertain,[400] while if the

---

boundary agreement is not a transfer can be traced back to an agreement between William Penn and Lord Baltimore resolving a dispute over the boundary between Pennsylvania and Maryland; see Penn v. Lord Baltimore, 1 Ves.Sr. 444, 27 Eng.Repr. 1132 (1750); Browder, supra note 392, at n. 43.

[395] Browder, supra note 392, at 497–98. As one court put it, "the new boundary effectively attaches to the respective deeds and, in legal effect, becomes the true dividing line between the parties." Duncan v. Peterson, 3 Cal.App.3d 607, 83 Cal.Rptr. 744 (1970). Mineral rights underlying the strip also become the property of the new owner; Sachs v. Board of Trustees, 89 N.M. 712, 557 P.2d 209 (1976), appeal after remand 92 N.M. 605, 592 P.2d 961 (1978).

[396] But if, after a boundary adjustment, the owner of the parcel that is reduced in size sells the property by warranty deed containing the original written description, at least one court has held the grantor liable for breach of the warranty, apparently irrespective of whether the grantees were bona fide purchasers; see Nielson v. Talbot, 163 Idaho 480, 415 P.3d 348 (2018). As to the binding effect on future owners, see text at notes 447–450 infra.

[397] See Sachs v. Board of Trustees, 89 N.M. 712, 557 P.2d 209 (1976), appeal after remand 92 N.M. 605, 592 P.2d 961 (1978); Finley v. Yuba County Water District, 99 Cal.App.3d 691, 160 Cal.Rptr. 423 (1979); Baldwin v. Brown, 16 N.Y. 359 (1857); Browder, supra note 392, at 511.

[398] See Sceirine v. Densmore, 87 Nev. 9, 479 P.2d 779 (1971); Buza v. Wojtalewicz, 48 Wis.2d 557, 180 N.W.2d 556 (1970); Browder, supra note 392, at 498. In many situations to be discussed infra the estoppel appears in a rather diluted form, and little is required in the way of detrimental reliance; Wisconsin takes the reliance element more seriously than most courts; see, e.g., Northrop v. Opperman, 331 Wis. 2d 287, 795 N.W.2d 719 (2011); Chandelle Enterprises, LLC v. XLNT Dairy Farm, Inc., 282 Wis. 2d 806, 699 N.W.2d 241 (2005). See also the California decisions which permit "substantial loss" to substitute for a holding for the statute of limitations period in boundary line agreement cases; Note, 9 Loy. L.A.L.Rev. 637, 654–57 (1976).

[399] Connell v. Moody, 98 So. 3d 549 (Ala. Civ. App. 2012); Miller v. Neil, 2010 Ark. App. 555, 377 S.W.3d 425 (2010); Gillis v. Buchheit, 232 Ga.App. 126, 500 S.E.2d 38 (Ga.App. 1998); Fischer v. Croston, 163 Idaho 331, 413 P.3d 731 (2018). In California it is necessary to show that the boundary is unclear in the public records; see Bryant v. Blevins, 9 Cal.4th 47, 36 Cal.Rptr.2d 86, 884 P.2d 1034 (Cal. 1994). The doctrine is inapplicable where the same party owns both parcels; see Grappo v. Mauch, 110 Nev. 1396, 887 P.2d 740 (Nev.1994); Terry v. Salazar, 892 P.2d 391 (Colo.App. 1994), affirmed Salazar v. Terry, 911 P.2d 1086 (Colo. 1996). It is likewise inapplicable where one party owns both parcels and sells one parcel to the other; see Baraban v. Hammonds, 49 Kan. App. 2d 530, 312 P.3d 373 (2013). See generally Annots., 69 A.L.R. 1430 (1930), 113 A.L.R. 421 (1938).

[400] Kendall v. Lowther, 356 N.W.2d 181 (Iowa 1984); Martin v. Lopes, 28 Cal.2d 618, 170 P.2d 881 (1946); Lenn v. Bottem, 221 Or. App. 241, 190 P.3d 399 (2008). The uncertainty need not originate in or be apparent from the deeds, and the owners need not have had a survey made or gone to any other efforts to resolve the uncertainty; Ekberg v. Bates, 121 Utah 123, 239 P.2d 205 (1951). But see Mehdizadeh v. Mincer,

agreement is based on a dispute it appears to be no objection that one party is both certain and correct. The insistence of the courts on uncertainty or a dispute is deeply embedded, and springs from a conviction that if the parties *know* that their agreement will shift the boundary, they are doing nothing less than conveying land from one to another, and hence must employ a written conveyance to satisfy the statute of frauds.[401] A related rule, widely but not universally followed, holds the agreement unenforceable if the parties mistakenly thought they were actually identifying the true boundary rather than merely selecting a line (which they understood might or might not be the true boundary) as a way of settling their uncertainty or compromising their dispute.[402] The point is to bind the parties only if they recognized the risk they were taking by entering into the agreement.[403] Unfortunately, these rules concerning uncertainty, dispute, and mistake leave enormous latitude for judicial discretion and manipulation, and as Professor Browder put it, "reduce the predictability of decision on the effect of such agreements almost to zero."[404]

A second fundamental requirement is the agreement itself. Since no particular formality is necessary, agreements can be found from a wide variety of types of communication. Yet it is common for a court to reject the proffered boundary because no agreement has been adequately proved.[405]

The final element in establishment of a boundary by agreement is the taking (and relinquishing) of possession by the parties to the agreed line.[406] Possession serves an evidentiary purpose here, and is roughly analogous to the part performance doctrine in land sale contracts.[407] There is considerable confusion as to how long the possession must continue in order to finalize the boundary change. Some cases, probably a majority, seem

---

46 Cal. App.4th 1296, 54 Cal.Rptr.2d 284 (Cal.App. 1996) (boundary may be established by agreement only when existing legal records do not locate boundary clearly).

[401] Madsen v. Clegg, 639 P.2d 726 (Utah 1981); United States v. Williams, 441 F.2d 637, 648–649 (5th Cir.1971); Thompson v. Bain, 28 Wn.2d 590, 183 P.2d 785 (1947); 2 Tiffany, Real Property § 653 n. 80 (3d ed. 2017 update).

[402] Goff v. Lever & Hood, 566 So.2d 1274 (Miss.1990); Powers Ranch Co. v. Plum Creek Mktg., Inc., 243 Or. App. 371, 258 P.3d 1275 (2011); Sceirine v. Densmore, 87 Nev. 9, 479 P.2d 779 (1971); 2 Tiffany, Real Property § 653 n. 83 (3d ed. 2017 update); Browder, supra note 392, at 498–504. The "mistake rule" was rejected in Martin v. Lopes, 28 Cal.2d 618, 170 P.2d 881 (1946) and Schlender v. Maretoli, 140 Kan. 533, 37 P.2d 993 (1934).

[403] See Short v. Mauldin, 227 Ark. 96, 296 S.W.2d 197 (1956).

[404] Browder, supra note 392, at 504.

[405] E.g., Martin v. Van Bergen, 209 Cal. App. 4th 84, 146 Cal. Rptr. 3d 667 (2012); Cecil v. Gagnebin, 146 Idaho 714, 202 P.3d 1 (2009); Martin v. Hinnen, 3 Kan.App.2d 106, 590 P.2d 589 (1979); Embry v. Turner, 185 S.W.3d 209 (Ky. Ct. App. 2006); Slindee v. Fritch Investments, LLC, 760 N.W.2d 903 (Minn. Ct. App. 2009); Huggans v. Weer, 189 Mont. 334, 615 P.2d 922 (1980); Robert v. Shaul, 62 A.D.3d 1127, 879 N.Y.S.2d 240 (2009); Gibbons v. Lettow, 180 Or. App. 37, 42 P.3d 925 (2002). See Huskinson v. Nelson, 152 Idaho 547, 272 P.3d 519 (2012) (fence built while both parcels were held by common owner could not be a boundary by agreement). Cf. Capps v. Abbott, 897 N.E.2d 984 (Ind. Ct. App. 2008) (agreement proved). Absent an express agreement, a court may find an implied one if the elements of a boundary by acquiescence are present; see Cameron v. Neal, 130 Idaho 898, 950 P.2d 1237 (Idaho 1997); text at notes 414–416, infra.

[406] See Humphrey v. Futter, 169 Cal. App.3d 333, 215 Cal.Rptr. 178 (1985), questioning whether California law requires actual occupation to the agreed line. Browder, supra note 392, at 493–94. The actual possession required may be quite minimal if the terrain is rough and difficult; see Aborigine Lumber Co. v. Hyman, 245 Cal.App.2d 938, 54 Cal.Rptr. 371 (1966).

[407] See § 10.2 supra.

to require no particular period,[408] while others demand a "long" period[409] or one equal to the statute of limitations for adverse possession.[410] A few courts also require the parties to mark their new boundary on the ground with a fence or monuments,[411] and at least one jurisdiction has accepted such markings as a substitute for actual possession.[412]

Acquiescence. Even if there is no explicit agreement between abutting owners, their long recognition and acceptance of a particular line as their boundary may make it so.[413] Many courts treat boundaries by acquiescence as a species of agreed boundaries, with the lengthy acquiescence "constituting" or creating a "conclusive presumption" of an agreement[414] even though there is no evidence whatever of any agreement in fact.[415] Other courts regard agreement and acquiescence as separate but parallel doctrines.[416] Because of the affinity of the two theories, courts often do not clearly distinguish the

---

[408] Campbell v. Noel, 490 So.2d 1014 (Fla.App. 1986); Wells v. Williamson, 118 Idaho 37, 794 P.2d 626 (1990); Bahr v. Imus, 2011 UT 19, 250 P.3d 56 (2011) (overruling prior Utah case law); Piotrowski v. Parks, 39 Wn.App. 37, 691 P.2d 591 (1984). In many cases long possession to the agreed line has occurred in fact, and it is difficult to tell whether the court believes a shorter period would have produced a different result.

[409] See, e.g., Seddon v. Edmondson, 411 So.2d 995 (Fla.App.1982) ("occupation * * * for a period of time sufficient to show a settled recognition of the line as the permanent boundary."); Lake for Use and Benefit of Benton v. Crosser, 202 Okl. 582, 216 P.2d 583 (1950).

[410] Bearden v. Ellison, 560 So.2d 1042 (Ala. 1990) (10 years required); Herrmann v. Woodell, 107 Idaho 916, 693 P.2d 1118 (App. 1985); Humphrey v. Futter, 169 Cal. App.3d 333, 215 Cal.Rptr. 178 (1985) (acceptance of the line must continue for the adverse possession period, or until there has been such reliance that alteration of the boundary would result in substantial loss).

[411] New Hampshire Dep't of Res. & Econ. Dev. v. Dow, 148 N.H. 60, 803 A.2d 581 (2002); Osberg v. Murphy, 88 S.D. 485, 221 N.W.2d 4 (1974); Piotrowski v. Parks, 39 Wn.App. 37, 691 P.2d 591 (1984). The agreed boundary must be an exact and precise line; see Slindee v. Fritch Investments, LLC, 760 N.W.2d 903 (Minn. Ct. App. 2009). A physical marker or set of monuments might be very significant in giving notice to subsequent purchasers of the land, see text at notes 447–450 infra, but it is hard to see why it should be essential as between the parties to the agreement. The Utah court agreed; see Bahr v. Imus, 2011 UT 19, 250 P.3d 56 (2011).

[412] Cothran v. Burk, 234 Ga. 460, 216 S.E.2d 319 (1975).

[413] Fletcher v. Stewart, 2015 Ark. App. 105, 456 S.W.3d 378 (2015). The acquiescence in the line as a boundary must be by both parties, not just one; see Heriot v. Lewis, 35 Wn.App. 496, 668 P.2d 589 (1983). See generally 2 Tiffany, Real Property § 654 (3d ed. 2017 update); Browder, supra note 392, at 504–19. Acquiesence is based on the behavior of the parties; their subjective belief or mental state is not in issue; see Essential Botanical Farms, LC v. Kay, 2011 UT 71, 270 P.3d 430 (2011).

[414] See, e.g., Clark v. Caughron, 2017 Ark. App. 409, 526 S.W.3d 867 (2017); Boyd-Davis v. Baker, 157 Idaho 688, 339 P.3d 749 (2014); Garrett v. Spear, 998 N.E.2d 297 (Ind. Ct. App. 2013); Evans v. Wittorff, 869 S.W.2d 872 (Mo.App.1994); Stone v. Rhodes, 107 N.M. 96, 752 P.2d 1112 (N.M.App. 1988). Utah and California merged the two theories in a series of confusing and ambiguous cases, so that it was hard to judge whether an agreement, a long acquiescence, or both were required. See Madsen v. Clegg, 639 P.2d 726 (Utah 1981); Comment, Boundaries by Agreement and Acquiescence in Utah, 1975 Utah L.Rev. 221; Armitage v. Decker, 218 Cal.App.3d 887, 267 Cal.Rptr. 399 (1990); Comment, Agreed Boundaries and Boundaries by Acquiescence: The Need for a Straight Line from the Courts, 9 Loy.L.A.L.Rev. 637 (1976). But Utah reversed this trend and clarified the law in Anderson v. Fautin, 2016 UT 22, 379 P.3d 1186 (2016), and no longer requires long acquiescence for a boundary by agreement, see Bahr v. Imus, 2011 UT 19, 250 P.3d 56 (2011).

[415] See Broadhead v. Hawley, 109 Idaho 952, 712 P.2d 653 (App.1985) (neither actual dispute nor agreement is required). It is generally unclear whether these courts would refuse to find a boundary by acquiescence if they were presented with direct evidence that no agreement had ever been made. The Utah court seems to have done so in Madsen v. Clegg, supra note 414, but Utah's boundary adjustment cases have been unusually murky and inconsistent. See Browder, supra note 392, at 507.

[416] E.g., Seddon v. Edmondson, 411 So.2d 995 (Fla.App.1982).

elements of each.[417] For example, the cases are seriously split as to whether a boundary by acquiescence must originate from uncertainty or dispute as to the true location.[418]

It is clear that the period of acquiescence must be lengthy; some courts, probably the majority, have "borrowed" the period of the adverse possession statute (typically 5 to 20 years) and apply it here,[419] while others require only a reasonably long time.[420] A few follow more complex or ambiguous rules with respect to time,[421] or have special statutes governing the period of acquiescence.[422] Whatever the time period, title to the adjusted land vests automatically (as with adverse possession) when the time has run.[423]

The nature of "acquiescence" is also controversial. For example, if one owner puts up a fence and the other simply makes no objection, has the latter acquiesced? Most of the cases hold that silence is enough,[424] but a few require some overt words or actions

---

[417] But see Whitecotton v. Owen, 2016 Ark. App. 120, 487 S.W.3d 380 (2016), distinguishing the two theories.

[418] Requiring uncertainty or dispute: Sanders v. Thomas, 821 So. 2d 1214 (Fla. Dist. Ct. App. 2002); Flying Elk Inv., LLC v. Cornwall, 149 Idaho 9, 232 P.3d 330 (2010); Gibbons v. Lettow, 180 Or. App. 37, 42 P.3d 925 (2002); Clair W. & Gladys Judd Family Ltd. Partnership v. Hutchings, 797 P.2d 1088 (Utah 1990). Not requiring doubt or dispute: Whitecotton v. Owen, 2016 Ark. App. 120, 487 S.W.3d 380 (2016); Tresemer v. Albuquerque Public School District, 95 N.M. 143, 619 P.2d 819 (1980); Salinas v. Sheets, 2018 OK CIV APP 21, 413 P.3d 890 (2018). See 2 Tiffany, Real Property § 654 nn. 93–94 (3d ed. 2017 update). In Halladay v. Cluff, 685 P.2d 500 (Utah 1984), the Utah Supreme Court adopted a much more restrictive requirement of "objective uncertainty," in the sense of actual difficulty in locating the boundary, rather than mere lack of knowledge or difference of opinion. This change proved unsatisfactory, and the same court abandoned it six years later in Staker v. Ainsworth, 785 P.2d 417 (Utah 1990).

[419] Lee v. Konrad, 337 P.3d 510 (Alaska 2014) (7 years); Sanlando Springs Animal Hospital, Inc. v. Douglass, 455 So.2d 596 (Fla.App.1984); LeeJoice v. Harris, 404 N.W.2d 4 (Minn. App.1987) (15 years); Allred v. Reed, 362 N.W.2d 374 (Minn.App.1985) (15 years); Lounsbury v. Yeomans, 139 A.D.3d 1230, 32 N.Y.S.3d 671 (N.Y. App. Div. 2016) (10 years); Sauter v. Miller, 2018 ND 57, 907 N.W.2d 370 (2018) (20 years); Salinas v. Sheets, 2018 OK CIV APP 21, 413 P.3d 890 (2018) (15 years); Long Run Timber Co. v. Dep't of Conservation & Nat. Res., 145 A.3d 1217 (Pa. Commw. Ct. 2016) (21 years); Jacobs v. Hafen, 917 P.2d 1078 (Utah 1996) (20 years, court-made rule). See Backman, The Law of Practical Location of Boundaries and the Need for an Adverse Possession Remedy, 1986 B.Y.U.L.Rev. 957.

[420] Clark v. Caughron, 2017 Ark. App. 409, 526 S.W.3d 867 (2017) ("many years"); Stith v. Williams, 227 Kan. 32, 605 P.2d 86 (1980); Tresemer v. Albuquerque Public School District, 95 N.M. 143, 619 P.2d 819 (1980); Dodds v. Lagan, 595 P.2d 452 (Okl.App .1979); Jordan v. Judy, 413 S.C. 341, 776 S.E.2d 96 (Ct. App. 2015) (period may be short, much less than for adverse possession); Parsons v. Anderson, 690 P.2d 535 (Utah 1984) (absent unusual circumstances, 20 years required; 15 years in instant case was too short). Idaho abandoned strict adherence to the statute of limitations in Paurley v. Harris, 75 Idaho 112, 268 P.2d 351 (1954).

[421] See, e.g., McGee v. Eriksen, 51 Mich.App. 551, 215 N.W.2d 571 (1974) (period must exceed statute of limitations unless line is a product of a "bona fide controversy."); Amato v. Haraden, 280 Minn. 399, 159 N.W.2d 907 (1968) (long period, "usually" time prescribed in statute of limitations); Anderson v. Fautin, 2016 UT 22, 379 P.3d 1186 (2016) (20 years required, although statute of limitations is only 7 years); Minson Co. v. Aviation Finance, 38 Cal.App.3d 489, 113 Cal. Rptr. 223 (1974) (limitations period normally required, but shorter time is sufficient if to deny the new boundary would result in substantial loss); see Comment, 9 Loy.L.A.L.Rev. 637, 654–57 (1976).

[422] Colo.Rev.Stat. § 38–44–109 (20 years); Official Code Georgia Ann. § 44–4–6 (7 years); Iowa Code Ann. § 650.6 (10 years). See Albert v. Conger, 886 N.W.2d 877 (Iowa Ct. App. 2016).

[423] Hence, the vesting of title is not dependent on a judicial decree; Sauter v. Miller, 2018 ND 57, 907 N.W.2d 370 (2018); Q-2 L.L.C. v. Hughes, 2016 UT 8, 368 P.3d 86 (2016).

[424] Stevenson v. Prairie Power Co-op., Inc., 118 Idaho 52, 794 P.2d 641 (Idaho App. 1989), affirmed 118 Idaho 31, 794 P.2d 620 (1990); Albert v. Conger, 886 N.W.2d 877 (Iowa Ct. App. 2016); Sauter v. Miller, 2018 ND 57, 907 N.W.2d 370 (2018); Carter v. Hanrath, 925 P.2d 960 (Utah 1996) (silence is acquiescence unless silent owner has no access to disputed area). It is clear that where one owner objects overtly to the other's claimed boundary, there is no acquiescence; see Waters v. Spell, 190 Ga.App. 790, 380 S.E.2d 55 (1989); Brown v. McDaniel, 261 Iowa 730, 156 N.W.2d 349 (1968).

which indicate acceptance or at least recognition of the fence as a boundary.[425] Certain other elements are more clearly required by the decisions. The asserted boundary must be marked physically on the ground,[426] usually by a fence or other barrier, which must be put in place with the intention of marking a boundary and not for some other purpose, such as containing livestock[427] or complying with a city ordinance.[428] Its presence must be known to both adjoining owners,[429] and they must take (and relinquish) possession to the marked line.[430]

There is no necessity that the adjoining parcels be held by the same owners for the entire period of acquiescence. If either tract is transferred and the acquiescence continues, the time periods of the successive owners will be tacked together.[431] Since the deed given by the owner whose land is enlarged by the new boundary is unlikely to describe the added strip explicitly, one might argue that there is no privity between the grantor and grantee. But the argument is irrelevant, for here (unlike adverse possession) privity is unnecessary to the tacking of ownerships.[432]

Estoppel. The doctrines of agreement and acquiescence discussed above are based in part on rather loose notions of estoppel.[433] But when an estoppel can be made out with greater specificity, the owner who claims land beyond his or her paper boundary may prevail without meeting such requirements as an agreement, a marking on the ground, or the long passage of time. A boundary by estoppel arises when one owner erroneously represents to the other that the boundary between them is located along a certain line; the second, in reliance on the representations, builds improvements which encroach on

---

[425] See, e.g., Kiker v. Anderson, 226 Ga. 121, 172 S.E.2d 835 (1970) ("acts and declarations of adjoining landowners"); Downey v. Vavold, 144 Idaho 592, 166 P.3d 382 (2007); Britney v. Swan Lake Cabin Corp., 795 N.W.2d 867 (Minn. Ct. App. 2011) ("passive consent" not enough).

[426] Vella v. Ratto, 17 Cal. App.3d 737, 95 Cal.Rptr. 72 (1971); Sille v. Shaffer, 297 N.W.2d 379 (Iowa 1980); Lounsbury v. Yeomans, 139 A.D.3d 1230, 32 N.Y.S.3d 671 (N.Y. App. Div. 2016) (line of grass); Knutson v. Jensen, 440 N.W.2d 260 (N.D. 1989); Dodds v. Lagan, 595 P.2d 452 (Okl.App. 1979); Banville v. Brennan, 84 A.3d 424 (R.I. 2014) (tree line); Jordan v. Judy, 413 S.C. 341, 776 S.E.2d 96 (Ct. App. 2015) (dike built by Dept. of Transportation); Englert v. Zane, 848 P.2d 165 (Utah App. 1993) (river). If a court concludes that a boundary by acquiescence has been established, it is very helpful for the court to provide a written legal description of the boundary; see Cross v. Cross, 2016 Ark. App. 327, 497 S.W.3d 712 (2016).

[427] Boyd-Davis v. Baker, 157 Idaho 688, 339 P.3d 749 (2014); Stone v. Turner, 106 N.M. 82, 738 P.2d 1327 (App. 1987); Sauter v. Miller, 2018 ND 57, 907 N.W.2d 370 (2018); Francis v. Rogers, 2001 OK 111, 40 P.3d 481 (2001); Brunswick v. Rundell, 126 Or.App. 582, 869 P.2d 886 (Or.App. 1994); Roderick v. Durfey, 746 P.2d 1186 (Utah App. 1987). But a fence will qualify if erected both to contain livestock and to mark the boundary; Wright v. Wells, 231 Or. App. 349, 218 P.3d 569 (2009). Cf. Grondin v. Hanscom, 2014 ME 148, 106 A.3d 1150 (2014) (blaze markings on trees insufficient); Hoskins v. Cook, 239 Ark. 285, 388 S.W.2d 914 (1965) (fence nailed to existing trees insufficient). See generally Annot., 7 A.L.R.4th 53, 92 (1981).

[428] Dooley's Hardware Mart v. Trigg, 270 Cal.App.2d 337, 75 Cal.Rptr. 745 (1969). See also Dean v. Kang Sik Park, 2012 UT App 349, 293 P.3d 388 (2012) (fence was for privacy, not to mark boundary).

[429] Sille v. Shaffer, supra note 426; Dodds v. Lagan, supra note 426; Parr v. Worley, 93 N.M. 229, 599 P.2d 382 (1979); Fuoco v. Williams, 18 Utah 2d 282, 421 P.2d 944 (1966); Hakanson v. Manders, 158 Neb. 392, 63 N.W.2d 436 (1954).

[430] Hodges v. Gravel Hill Cemetery Comm., 2016 Ark. App. 360, 498 S.W.3d 746 (2016); Pratt Inv. Co. v. Kennedy, 636 N.W.2d 844 (Minn. Ct. App. 2001); Anderson v. Fautin, 2016 UT 22, 379 P.3d 1186 (2016) (only occupation to marked line by claimant gaining land is required). The extent of required acts of possession depends on the nature of the property and the uses to which it is suited, and may be quite limited; see Little v. Gray, 137 Vt. 569, 409 A.2d 574 (1979).

[431] Cornelison v. Flanagan, 198 Okl. 593, 180 P.2d 823 (1947); Renwick v. Noggle, 247 Mich. 150, 225 N.W. 535 (1929).

[432] Siegel v. Renkiewicz' Estate, 373 Mich. 421, 129 N.W.2d 876 (1964) (privity not required); Corbin v. Cowan, 716 A.2d 614, 618 (Pa. Super. Ct. 1998) (privity seemingly required). Cf. § 11.7 supra at notes 385–386.

[433] See Elsea v. Day, 448 S.W.3d 259 (Ky. Ct. App. 2014); text at note 398 supra.

the true boundary or takes other detrimental actions. The party who made the representations is then estopped to deny them, and the boundary is in effect shifted accordingly.[434]

The cases are divided as to the knowledge which the person making the representation must possess. Most indicate that the representer must know that the true boundary is not where he or she says it is,[435] and a few take the rather extreme position that the representer must have intended to deceive the other owner, or must at least have been grossly negligent in making the representations.[436] But a substantial minority of cases disregard lack of knowledge and estop the representer anyway.[437] There must, of course, be a representation made,[438] although a surprising number of cases find it from an owner's silence in the face of knowledge that the neighbor is building an encroaching structure.[439] But if the party being encroached upon issues a warning or protest, estoppel is obviously defeated.[440]

An owner who claims estoppel must have relied reasonably on the other's representations. If the claimant's actions were induced by other factors,[441] or if the claimant knew the true location of the boundary,[442] there is no basis for estoppel. The reliance must lead to a substantial and costly change of position; the most common is the construction of improvements,[443] but a prospective buyer who purchases land in reliance on an erroneous statement of the boundary by an adjoining owner may also assert estoppel.[444] There is no requirement that the reliance continue for any particular period of time.[445]

Common grantor. It is plain that a line established or marked by a common grantor may form the basis for a boundary by agreement or acquiescence between two abutting

[434] See Lilly v. Lynch, 88 Wash. App. 306, 945 P.2d 727 (1997); Browder, supra note 392, at 519–25; 2 Tiffany, Real Property § 656 (3d ed. 2017 update). Cf. Desruisseau v. Isley, 27 Ariz.App. 257, 553 P.2d 1242 (1976), rejecting the doctrine of estoppel in boundary disputes.

[435] LeeJoice v. Harris, 404 N.W.2d 4 (Minn.App. 1987); Wojahn v. Johnson, 297 N.W.2d 298 (Minn. 1980); Summers v. Holder, 254 Or. 180, 458 P.2d 429 (1969). Where both parties acted under a mistake as to the true location, one court ordered the land conveyed to the encroaching party upon his payment of its reasonable value; see Faulkner v. Lloyd, 253 S.W.2d 972 (Ky. 1952).

[436] Production Credit Association v. Terra Vallee, Inc., 303 N.W.2d 79 (N.D. 1981); Dodds v. Lagan, 595 P.2d 452 (Okl. App. 1979); Roman v. Ries, 259 Cal.App.2d 65, 66 Cal.Rptr. 120 (1968). See generally 2 Tiffany, Real Property § 656 n. 11 (3d ed. 2017 update).

[437] Bahr v. Imus, 2011 UT 19, 250 P.3d 56 (2011); Burkey v. Baker, 6 Wn.App. 243, 492 P.2d 563 (1971); see Browder, supra note 392, at 521 n. 147.

[438] Keel v. Covey, 206 Okl. 128, 241 P.2d 954 (1952).

[439] Wojahn v. Johnson, supra note 435; Amato v. Haraden, 280 Minn. 399, 159 N.W.2d 907 (1968); Hansen v. Pratt, 240 Ark. 746, 402 S.W.2d 108 (1966); Kennedy v. Oleson, 251 Iowa 418, 100 N.W.2d 894 (1960).

[440] Dart v. Thompson, 261 Iowa 237, 154 N.W.2d 82 (1967); Dye v. Ebersole, 218 Ark. 97, 234 S.W.2d 376 (1950).

[441] Thomas v. Harlan, 27 Wn.2d 512, 178 P.2d 965, 170 A.L.R. 1138 (1947); Aransas Properties, Inc. v. Brashear, 410 S.W.2d 934 (Tex.Civ.App. 1967).

[442] See State v. Hall, 244 Mont. 161, 797 P.2d 183 (1990). One opinion suggests the claimant will be disqualified if he or she had the means of learning the truth (as by obtaining a survey), but this is an extreme position; Gilbertson v. Charlson, 301 N.W.2d 144 (N.D. 1981).

[443] Dunn v. Fletcher, 266 Ala. 273, 96 So.2d 257 (1957); Kincaid v. Morgan, 188 W.Va. 452, 425 S.E.2d 128, 133 (1992). Cf. Dart v. Thompson, supra note 440 (trenches & footings not sufficient expenditure); Downing v. Boehringer, 82 Idaho 52, 349 P.2d 306 (1960) (small irrigation ditch not sufficient expenditure).

[444] Clark v. Moru, 19 Wis.2d 503, 120 N.W.2d 888 (1963); Frericks v. Sorensen, 113 Cal.App.2d 759, 248 P.2d 949 (1952); 2 Tiffany, Real Property § 656 n. 10 (3d ed. 2017 update).

[445] Mahrenholz v. Alff, 253 Iowa 446, 112 N.W.2d 847 (1962); Browder, supra note 392, at 523 n. 161.

owners. However, a separate legal doctrine may make such a line their boundary even though the elements of agreement or acquiescence are not present. This doctrine operates only if the common grantor marks the line on the ground and sells both parcels by reference to it. Moreover, the deeds employed must not use metes and bounds descriptions, but must mention only lot numbers; otherwise, the deed descriptions and not the marked line will control.[446]

Subsequent purchasers. All four of the modes of practical location discussed above act to shift boundaries so that they do not coincide with the literal language of the relevant deeds. Once this shift has occurred, the cases generally assume that it is binding on all future owners of both parcels involved.[447] One who buys the enlarged parcel is unlikely to complain about this assumption, but a subsequent purchaser of the diminished parcel may be shocked to discover that he or she does not own as much land as the deed described. A purchaser who has no notice of the change of boundary will be protected according to some decisions,[448] while others refuse to do so.[449] But purchasers without notice are rare, since the presence of a fence or other physical marker, or the visible extent of the existing owners' possession, will usually give the purchaser actual or constructive notice of the boundary's changed location.[450]

Adverse possession distinguished. Adverse possession often operates to adjust boundaries with much the same effects as do the doctrines of practical location discussed above.[451] But adverse possession has its own set of required elements, discussed in the preceding section; they differ from the elements of practical location in several important ways.[452] The most obvious is hostility: an adverse possessor's claim will be defeated if he or she acted with the true owner's permission, and in some states the possessor must also know that the land being encroached upon does not belong to him or her.[453] No such

---

[446] Huffman v. Peterson, 272 Neb. 62, 718 N.W.2d 522 (2006); Arnold v. Robbins, 209 Wis.2d 428, 563 N.W.2d 178 (Wis.App.1997); Pendergrast v. Matichuk, 186 Wash. 2d 556, 379 P.3d 96 (2016); Miller v. Stovall, 717 P.2d 798 (Wyo.1986). The seminal case is Herse v. Questa, 100 App.Div. 59, 91 N.Y.S. 778 (1904).

[447] Garrett v. United States, 407 F.2d 146 (8th Cir.1969); Roberts v. Feitz, 933 N.E.2d 466 (Ind. Ct. App. 2010); Goff v. Lever, 566 So.2d 1274 (Miss. 1990); Huntington v. Riggs, 862 N.E.2d 1263 (Ind. Ct. App. 2007); Lakeview Farm, Inc. v. Enman, 166 Vt. 158, 689 A.2d 1089 (1997). See 2 Tiffany, Real Property § 653 n. 87 (3d ed. 2017 update). Some courts seem to assume that the written descriptions in future deeds should be treated as if they had been automatically revised to reflect the change. But others hold that, unless the legal description of the reduced-size parcel in a future warranty deed has actually been revised to reflect the boundary adjustment, the grantor may be held liable for breach of the title covenants in that deed. See Nielson v. Talbot, 163 Idaho 480, 415 P.3d 348 (2018); Egli v. Troy, 602 N.W.2d 329 (Iowa 1999); Mason v. Loveless, 2001 UT App 145, 24 P.3d 997 (2001).

[448] Weitz v. Green, 148 Idaho 851, 230 P.3d 743 (2010); United States v. Williams, 441 F.2d 637 (5th Cir. 1971); Proctor v. Libby, 110 Me. 39, 85 A. 298 (1912).

[449] Dahl Inv. Co. v. Hughes, 2004 UT App 391, 101 P.3d 830 (2004). See Browder, supra note 392, at 530 n. 188.

[450] Schultz v. Plate, 48 Wn.App. 312, 739 P.2d 95 (1987); Duff v. Seubert, 110 Idaho 865, 719 P.2d 1125 (1985); Sanlando Springs Animal Hospital, Inc. v. Douglass, 455 So.2d 596 (Fla.App. 1984).

[451] Roy v. Woodstock Cmty. Tr., Inc., 195 Vt. 427, 94 A.3d 530 (2014) (statute exempting charitable property from adverse possession also applies to boundaries by acquiescence).

[452] See Moody v. Sundley, 2015 ND 204, 868 N.W.2d 491 (2015); O'Hearne v. McClammer, 163 N.H. 430, 42 A.3d 834 (2012); Britney v. Swan Lake Cabin Corp., 795 N.W.2d 867 (Minn. Ct. App. 2011) (practical adjustment of boundaries applies to land registered under the Torrens system, but adverse possession does not). But courts are prone to confusing boundaries by acquiescence with adverse possession; see Fischer v. First Am. Title Ins. Co., 388 S.W.3d 181 (Mo. Ct. App. 2012).

[453] See Stasher v. Perry, 217 So. 3d 765 (Miss. Ct. App. 2017); Stroem v. Plackis, 96 A.D.3d 1040, 948 N.Y.S.2d 90 (2012); § 11.7 at notes 361–377 supra.

hostility is necessary for a boundary by practical location.[454] Indeed, agreement or permission is presumed or inferred in the case of a boundary by acquiescence[455] and is literally present in the other three modes of practical location.

A second distinction involves notice. In all forms of practical location, including acquiescence, the owner encroached upon must have actual knowledge of the encroachment.[456] On the other hand, adverse possession must be merely "open and notorious," and it is unnecessary to show that the owner had actual knowledge of the encroachment.[457] The time periods required for a successful boundary shift may also be different. While adverse possession always requires occupancy for the full period of the statute of limitations, the cases are divided as to whether boundaries by acquiescence[458] or agreement[459] do so, and boundaries fixed by a common grantor or by estoppel require no specific time period at all.

Despite these distinctions, it is entirely conceivable that the same factual evidence may give rise to a boundary change either by adverse possession or by acquiescence if all of the elements of both are present. The only apparently irreconcilable inconsistency between them is that of hostility versus permission, and if the party who is encroached upon is simply silent, either conclusion might easily be reached.[460]

§ 11.9 THE RECORDING SYSTEM—INTRODUCTION

Ownership of land can exist only because it is recognized and enforced by the legal institutions of the state. Hence, it is not surprising that virtually all modern governments have developed and operate systems of records designed to permit interested persons to discover who owns any parcel. In most countries, these systems are constructed and organized in a way that allows the government to make affirmative statements to the inquirer about the condition of the title; thus, one who requests the information might be told by a governmental official that "This land is owned by A, subject to a one-year lease to B, an easement held by C, and a mortgage to the D Bank." Copies of the documents which created the lease, easement, and mortgage might also be given to the searcher for his or her scrutiny.

In America, each state is responsible for the records of title to land within its borders, usually on a county-by-county basis (although the systems in Alaska and Hawaii are administered state-wide). The Federal Government operates no general title records system. Nine states have systems like the paradigm described above which makes affirmative statements respecting the title, although these systems are little used in most of them. These so-called title *registration* or "Torrens" systems are described in

---

[454] Agrons v. Strong, 250 Or. App. 641, 282 P.3d 925 (2012); Chandelle Enterprises, LLC v. XLNT Dairy Farm, Inc., 282 Wis. 2d 806, 699 N.W.2d 241 (2005); LeBleu v. Aalgaard, 193 Wash. App. 66, 371 P.3d 76 (2016); One opinion argues that the doctrine of boundary by acquiescence was developed by the courts precisely to alleviate the difficulty of proving hostility in adverse possession; Buza v. Wojtalewicz, 48 Wis.2d 557, 180 N.W.2d 556 (1970). See also Morton v. Hall, 239 Ark. 1094, 396 S.W.2d 830 (1965).

[455] See text at notes 414–415 supra.

[456] See text at note 413 supra.

[457] See, e.g., Hakanson v. Manders, 158 Neb. 392, 63 N.W.2d 436 (1954), comparing the two theories; § 11.7 at notes 358–360 supra.

[458] See text at notes 408–410 supra.

[459] See text at notes 419–421 supra.

[460] See, e.g., Clark v. Caughron, 2017 Ark. App. 409, 526 S.W.3d 867 (2017); Salazar v. Terry, 911 P.2d 1086 (Colo. 1996); Waisanen v. Superior Twp., 305 Mich. App. 719, 854 N.W.2d 213 (2014); Ferguson v. Hoffman, 462 S.W.3d 776 (Mo. Ct. App. 2015).

a later section.[461] But every state maintains a *recording* system, far more widely used, which functions on very different principles. The recording system comprises the only publicly-maintained set of title records in most states, and it is the predominant system even in states which also operate a registration system.[462] Recording systems are complex and have many inadequacies, but their use is so widespread that an understanding of them is essential to real estate law practice.

In fundamental concept, a recording system is much like a library of title-related documents. These documents include all of the instruments which have been employed in prior legal transactions affecting the land, and which someone has taken the trouble to "record," or add to the library's collection. The searcher is expected to visit the library, use its official index system to identify and read the documents which relate to the land in question, and then to decide, by the application of his or her knowledge of real estate law and practice, who owns the land and to what encumbrances it is subject. This system is frugal in its expenditure of public funds and personnel. The government employees' only tasks are to receive, copy, index, and return the documents and to maintain the collection.[463] The more demanding work of searching, analyzing, and reaching of legal conclusions from the instruments is left to private users. The government makes no averment as to the state of the title. In this way the recording system differs markedly from "registration" systems of the kind described in the first paragraph of this section.[464]

Unfortunately, the recording system is seriously deficient with respect to the reliability of the information it yields to searchers. The unreliability stems from several sources, summarized here and discussed in greater length below: (1.) The recorded documents may appear to be valid and enforceable, yet may turn out to be fatally defective for reasons which cannot be detected by reading them.[465] (2.) Land titles may

---

[461] See § 11.15 infra.

[462] Discussing the two systems, see Wells Fargo Bank, N.A. v. Omiya, 420 P.3d 370 (Haw. 2018); In re Mbazira, 518 B.R. 11, 21 (Bankr. D. Mass. 2014); In re Mortg. Elec. Registration Sys., Inc., 835 N.W.2d 487 (Minn. Ct. App. 2013); Garro, Recording of Real Estate Transactions in Latin America: A Comparison with the Recording System in the United States, 1984 Ariz.J.Int.L. 90. Note carefully the distinction between the terms "registration," referring to a Torrens-type system that makes affirmative statements about titles, discussed in § 11.15 infra, and "recording," referring to the predominant American system described in this section. Unfortunately, this terminology is not always followed; for example, in a few states conventional recording is called "registration" and the official whose duty is to maintain the recording system is called the "register of deeds" or some similar term. See, e.g., North Carolina Gen.Stat. § 47–17.1.

[463] For commentary on the skill and knowledge of recording personnel, see Charles Szypszak, Local Government Registers of Deeds and the Enduring Reliance on Common Sense Judgment in a Technocratic Tide, 44 Real Est. L.J. 351 (2015). Ordinarily the recorder's personnel pay little attention to whether a proffered document is legally valid; see Proctor v. Garrett, 378 N.W.2d 298 (Iowa 1985) (recorder has no discretion to reject a proffered filing of a "common law lien" although it is a legal nullity). But the 1990s and 2000s saw the recording of a spate of plainly invalid documents for purposes of harassment. For an illustration involving a well-known stadium, see Garrick, Bogus Title Transfer Clouds Petco Ownership, San Diego Union-Tribune, Dec. 24, 2015. Some states adopted statutes intended to stop this practice. See, e.g., Kester v. CitiMortgage, Inc., 709 F. App'x 869 (9th Cir. 2017) (Arizona law, discussing Ariz. Rev. Stat. § 33–420, prohibiting knowing recording of document that is "forged, groundless, contains a material misstatement or false claim or is otherwise invalid"); Minn. Stat. Ann. § 514.99.

[464] See Whitman, Optimizing Land Title Records Systems, 42 Geo.Wash.L.Rev. 40, 63 (1973). Registration systems also incorporate provisions for indemnifying those injured by errors in the system to a much greater extent than do recording systems; see id. For a good discussion of the recorder's "archivist" role, see Woodward v. Bowers, 630 F.Supp. 1205 (M.D.Pa.1986) (recorder's action in accepting a deed containing a racially restrictive covenant did not violate federal civil rights legislation). See also S & H Petroleum Corp., Inc. v. Register of Deeds for County of Bristol, 46 Mass.App.Ct. 535, 707 N.E.2d 843 (Mass.App. 1999) (recorder has no duty to give legal advice).

[465] See text at notes 512–516 infra.

be affected by a variety of events and claims which are outside the coverage of the recording system, and thus are binding despite the fact that nothing appears in the public records concerning them.[466] (3.) A full search of the records requires tracing the chain of title instruments back to a grant from a sovereign; yet in many cases such a search would be prohibitively time-consuming and difficult, and searchers commonly limit their searches to, say, 40 to 60 years. Hence there is a residual risk that earlier, unexamined documents could adversely affect the title. (4.) Finally, there is the possibility that the searcher may make a clerical error in the search (the process of assembling the relevant instruments) or a mistake in the examination (the process of reading and analyzing the instruments found in the search), and consequently reach an incorrect conclusion as to the state of the title.[467]

These inadequacies in the recording system have led to the development by private industry of two devices which supplement the public records: abstracts and title insurance. An abstract is a commercially-prepared set of copies or summaries of all of the documents in the public records affecting a particular parcel of land. One who obtains an abstract can "examine" the title without the need to visit the courthouse, and the risk of missing a relevant document lies with the abstract company, not the examiner. Title insurance goes further; the insurance company or its agents perform both the search and the examination, and issue an insurance policy promising to indemnify the insured if the title turns out to be defective except in the specific ways noted in the policy itself. Neither abstracts nor title insurance are perfect solutions to the problems of the recording system, but they are helpful and are widely used. They are discussed in detail in a later section.[468]

Recording and priorities. If the owner of land purports to make two competing or inconsistent conveyances their priority, in the absence of a recording system, is determined by the chronological order of their delivery. To illustrate, assume that in a hypothetical jurisdiction without a recording system O, who owns land, delivers a deed to A. The next day O delivers another deed of the same land to B. A will have the title to the land and B will have nothing except a possible claim against O for tort, contract, or on any covenants of title in the O-B deed.[469] The same principles apply if O delivers leases, grants of easements, or any other sorts of conveyances. For example, if O gives mortgages to both A and B, the first mortgage delivered will have priority, and the second in time will be subordinate to it. If O conveys an easement to A and a deed

---

[466] See Stroup, The Unreliable Record Title, 60 N.D.L.Rev. 203 (1984); text at notes 490–505 infra.

[467] An error may also be made by the public employees who operate the system. If negligence is proved, they are liable; see, e.g., Baccari v. DeSanti, 70 A.D.2d 198, 431 N.Y.S.2d 829 (1979); Ralston Purina Co. v. Cone, 344 So.2d 95 (La.App. 1977); Maddox v. Astro Investments, 45 Ohio App.2d 203, 343 N.E.2d 133, 74 O.O.2d 312 (1975). In most states recording officials are required by law to be bonded, but the bond is often for a limited amount, usually considerably less than the value of the average parcel of real estate. Recovery against the local government itself may be barred by sovereign immunity, and courts will obviously be reluctant to levy large personal judgments against public officials in their individual capacities. For all of these reasons, negligence suits against recorders often result in inadequate recovery. See Badger v. Benfield, 78 N.C.App. 427, 337 S.E.2d 596 (1985), review denied 316 N.C. 374, 342 S.E.2d 890 (1986).

[468] See § 11.14 infra.

[469] See text at notes 487–488 supra; Berger, An Analysis of the Doctrine that "First in Time is First in Right," 64 Neb.L.Rev. 349, 364–65 (1985); § 11.13 infra on covenants of title.

purporting to convey full title to B, B will hold title subject to A's easement. Thus, first in time is first in right.[470]

The recording system's purpose is to determine the priority of potentially competing conveyances.[471] It has the rather extraordinary ability to reverse, in some situations, the chronological priorities described above. The recording acts give O and his or her successors a power, under certain circumstances, to give B a conveyance which has priority over A's. If both conveyances are deeds, this means that B will own the land and A will have nothing.[472] For this surprising result to occur, two factors must be present. First, A must have failed to record the first deed; a conveyance which is properly recorded can never be divested by subsequent conveyances under the recording acts.[473] Second, B's behavior must qualify for the protection of the particular act. On this point there is a good deal of variation among the states, but their statutes can be divided into three general groups.[474] About half of the statutes protect B if he or she is a bona fide purchaser for value; they are usually called "notice" statutes, although the term is somewhat misleading since both lack of notice and payment of value are usually essential to B's qualifying for the act's protection. When or whether B records B's conveyance is irrelevant under this approach. Roughly the other half of the statutes impose the same bona fide purchaser qualification, but add to it the further requirement that B record before A's deed is recorded. Since this conjures a mental picture, wholly fictitious, of A

---

[470] See, e.g., U.S. Bank Nat. Ass'n v. Grant, 180 So. 3d 1092 (Fla. Dist. Ct. App. 2015); The Pennington Grp., LLC v. PriorityOne Bank, 228 So. 3d 880 (Miss. Ct. App. 2017); Windham v. Citizens Nat. Bank, 105 S.W.2d 348 (Tex. Civ. App. 1937).

[471] Klein v. Oakland/Red Oak Holdings, LLC, 294 Neb. 535, 883 N.W.2d 699 (2016).

[472] Selene RMOF II REO Acquisitions II, LLC v. Ward, 189 Wash. 2d 72, 399 P.3d 1118 (2017).

[473] The first-recorded instrument will be immune from attack under the recording act, even though its competitor instrument is filed very soon thereafter; see Daughters v. Preston, 131 Ill.App.3d 723, 86 Ill.Dec. 944, 476 N.E.2d 445 (1985) (filed deed prevails over subsequent deed filed 75 minutes later); Prochaska v. Midwest Title Guarantee Co. of Florida, 85 Wn.App. 256, 932 P.2d 172 (1997), opinion withdrawn & vacated upon joint motion of the parties, 950 P.2d 497 (Wash.App.1997) (filed judgment lien prevails over deed filed nine minutes later); Little v. Duncombe, 143 B.R.243 (Bankr.C.D.Cal.1992) (bankruptcy filing prevails over deed filed one hour later). But see In re Berkley Multi-Units, Inc., 91 B.R. 150 (Bkrtcy.M.D.Fla.1988), refusing to give priority to a mortgage that was recorded one minute before competing mortgages; "no reasonable definition of 'constructive notice' would contemplate a literal one minute's difference in recordation time as notice of a prior recorded mortgage." See also NYCTL 1998–1 Tr. & the Bank of New York v. Ibrahiem, 15 Misc. 3d 294, 832 N.Y.S.2d 767 (Sup. Ct. 2007) (document was deemed recorded, for timing purposes, when submitted to recording office, rather than at the time the recorders' personnel entered it into the system). See also cases cited infra notes 604–605.

There are situations in which a conveyance is recorded at a time or in a manner which make it very difficult or impossible for a searcher to locate; some courts treat such conveyances as unrecorded even though they have literally been recorded. See § 11.11 infra at notes 606–618. Moreover, in some recording systems it is possible for two documents to be recorded simultaneously; see First Bank v. East West Bank, § 11.4 n. 211 supra; Borrenpohl v. DaBeers Properties, LLC, 276 Neb. 426, 755 N.W.2d 39 (2008) (where deed of trust and notice of commencement of construction were recorded simultaneously, parties' intention determined priority); N. C. Gen. Stat. § 47–18(a) (order of page numbers or document numbers controls, unless parties have otherwise stated in a recorded document). If a document has been presented to the recording office, but the public officials have failed to index it properly, the cases divide as to whether it has been "recorded." See § 11.11 infra at notes 604–605.

[474] See generally the discussions in Mattis, Recording Acts: Anachronistic Reliance, 25 Real Prop.Prob. & Tr.J. 17 (1990); Ray E. Sweat, Race, Race-Notice and Notice Statutes: The American Recording System, Probate & Property, May-June 1989, at 27 (listing 21 pure notice jurisdictions, 26 race-notice jurisdictions and 3 pure race jurisdictions); Baird & Jackson, Information, Uncertainty, and the Transfer of Property, 13 J. Legal Studies 299 (1984); 1 Patton & Palomar, Land Titles § 5 (3d ed. 2017 update); 4 Am.L.Prop. § 17.5 (1952). The Uniform Simplification of Land Transfers Act adopts a notice-race approach; see USLTA § 3–202. See also Note, Recording Statutes: Their Operation and Effect, 17 Washb.L.J. 615 (1978); Johnson, Purpose and Scope of Recording Acts, 47 Iowa L.Rev. 231 (1962).

and B racing one another to the court-house, this second group of statutes is usually called "notice-race." A third type of statute pays no attention to B's BFP status, but simply defeats A if B records first.[475] Only three states, Delaware, Louisiana and North Carolina, have acts applying this pure "race" approach to the general run of conveyances, although a few others employ it for mortgages or other special types of conveyances.

In general, no one is obliged to record anything, and there is no direct penalty if a conveyance goes unrecorded. As between its original parties, an instrument is fully binding whether it is recorded or not.[476] But the recording acts provide a strong incentive for every grantee to record, for one who fails to do so is taking the risk that his or her grantor will make a subsequent conveyance that will diminish or destroy the efficacy of the prior transfer. This principle is well recognized by people in the real estate and lending business, and the vast majority of conveyances today are immediately and properly recorded. Hence, litigation concerning the recording system's operation is not very common.

The discussion above oversimplifies the categorization of recording acts somewhat. A good deal can be learned by examining their language in more detail. Perhaps the most common form runs along these lines:

> Every conveyance not recorded is void as against any subsequent purchaser or mortgagee in good faith and for valuable consideration * * * whose conveyance is first duly recorded.[477]

This statute is of the "notice-race" type, since the subsequent purchaser, to prevail, must both be a BFP and record first. It could easily be modified to make it a pure "notice" type statute by deleting the last phrase quoted, "* * * whose conveyance is first duly recorded." Many "notice" statutes follow this form.[478] An alternative form of "notice" statute, found in many states, is as follows:

> No instrument affecting real estate is of any validity against subsequent purchasers for a valuable consideration, without notice, unless filed in the office of the recorder.[479]

---

[475] Under the Louisiana statute, the subsequent purchaser who records first is protected only if she or he is not guilty of fraud or bad faith; see Davis v. St. Romain, 222 So. 3d 793 (La. App. 2016).

[476] Union Cty., Ill. v. MERSCORP, Inc., 735 F.3d 730 (7th Cir. 2013); Waxler v. Waxler, 699 A.2d 1161 (Me. 1997); Markham v. Markham, 80 Hawai'i 274, 909 P.2d 602 (App. 1996); Burris v. McDougald, 832 S.W.2d 707 (Tex.App. 1992). See also Horman v. Clark, 744 P.2d 1014 (Utah App. 1987) (grantor is not liable for failing to record contract giving parking rights to grantee). One rather peculiar exception is Ariz.Rev.Stat. § 33–411.01, which requires the transferor to record within 60 days of the transfer, and in lieu of doing so makes him or her liable to indemnify the transferee in any action in which the latter's interest is at issue. Another anomaly is Md. Real Prop. Code § 3–101, which requires recording for validity of a transfer of legal title, even as between the immediate parties to the instrument.

[477] See, e.g., N.Y.-McKinney's Real Prop. Law § 291; N.J.Stat.Ann. § 46:22–1; Utah Code Ann. § 57–3–103; West's Rev. Code of Wash.Ann. 65.08.070. The race-notice concept is expressed in somewhat more confusing terms in 33 Me. Rev. Stat. § 201, discussed in Spickler v. Ginn, 2012 Me. 46, 40 A.3d 999 (2012). A slightly different form, in which the protected parties are described in an "exception" clause, is represented by West's Ann.Cal.Civ.Code § 1007:

> Every grant * * * is conclusive against the grantor, also against everyone subsequently claiming under him, except a purchaser or incumbrancer who in good faith and for a valuable consideration acquires a title or lien by an instrument that is first duly recorded.

[478] See Ark.Stat. § 16–115.

[479] See Ala.Code § 35–4–90; Ariz. Rev. Stat. § 33–412; Iowa Code Ann. § 558.41. Classification of statutes as "notice" or "notice-race" can sometimes be difficult. See Szypszak, note 482 infra. The Colorado statute was formerly the subject of considerable confusion on this score; see Fees-Krey, Inc. v. Page, 42 Colo. App. 8, 591

The wording of the "race" type statutes is also instructive. The North Carolina[480] and Louisiana[481] statutes are similar, and can be paraphrased as follows:

No conveyance shall be valid, as against [N.C.: purchasers for valuable consideration] [La.: third parties] until it is recorded.

Under both versions above, having notice of the prior conveyance will not disqualify a subsequent purchaser who records first.[482] But under the North Carolina version, in order to prevail the subsequent purchaser must have paid value for the land,[483] while there seems to be no "value" requirement in Louisiana.[484]

Delaware's statute,[485] while worded differently, presumably has the same effect as Louisiana's in permitting the subsequent purchaser who records first to prevail without paying value. Slightly simplified, it reads, "A deed shall have priority from the time that it is recorded."[486]

An interesting question arises when an unrecorded prior grantee is deprived of title by virtue of the grantor's making a subsequent, conflicting conveyance to one who qualifies for the protection of the recording act, either by recording first, being a BFP, or both. Does the first grantee have an action in damages against the grantor for behaving in a way that "pulls the rug out" from under the grantee? There is not much authority, but several cases recognize that such an action is justified on a variety of contract, tort,

---

P.2d 1339 (1978), reversed on other grounds 617 P.2d 1188 (Colo.1980). It was amended in 1984 to state "this is a race-notice recording statute;" West's Colo. Rev.Stat.Ann. § 38–35–109. See Reeves, The Colorado Recording Act, Part I: History and Character of the Act, 24 Colo.Lawyer 1329 (1995); Cottonwood Hill, Inc. v. Ansay, 782 P.2d 1207 (Colo.App.1989). See also State Street Bank v. Heck's, Inc. 963 S.W.2d 626 (Ky.1998), incorrectly describing Kentucky's notice-type statute as race-notice; Leasing Enterprises, Inc. v. Livingston, 294 S.C. 204, 363 S.E.2d 410 (1987) (amendment in 1958 changed S.C. statute from "notice" to "race-notice"); Utah Farm Production Credit Ass'n v. Wasatch Bank, 734 P.2d 904 (Utah 1986) (statute is "notice-race" despite prior case suggesting it was pure "race").

[480] N.C.Gen.Stat. § 47–18, discussed in Department of Transportation v. Humphries, 496 S.E.2d 563 (N.C. 1998).

[481] La. Stat. Ann.-R.S. § 9:2721.

[482] See New Bar P'ship v. Martin, 221 N.C. App. 302, 729 S.E.2d 675 (2012), Rowe v. Walker, 114 N.C.App. 36, 441 S.E.2d 156 (N.C.App.1994), affirmed 340 N.C. 107, 455 S.E.2d 160 (1995) (with a fascinating dissent arguing that the N.C. statute is really "race-notice"); Avenue Plaza, L.L.C. v. Falgoust, 654 So.2d 838 (La.App.1995). But see Arnette v. Morgan, 88 N.C. App. 458, 363 S.E.2d 678 (1988), using the equitable principle of constructive trust to introduce a "notice" element into the North Carolina statute. See Charles Szypszak, Real Estate Records, the Captive Public, and Opportunities for the Public Good, 43 Gonz. L. Rev. 5, 25–26 (2008).

[483] Chrysler Credit Corp. v. Burton, 599 F.Supp. 1313 (M.D.N.C. 1984).

[484] The Louisiana cases consistently refer to the act's protection to "third parties," with no reference to whether such parties have paid value. See Hargrave, Public Records and Property Rights, 56 La. L. Rev. 535 (1996).

[485] 25 Del.Code § 153. The equivalent section for mortgages, containing virtually identical language, is 25 Del.Code § 2106. That statute was amended in 1968 to make it pure "race," but it was not construed by the Delaware courts until the 1980s; see N & W Dev. Co. v. Carey, 1983 WL 17997 (Del.Ch.1983) (unpublished).

[486] See Cravero v. Holleger, 566 A.2d 8 (Del.Ch.1989), describing the statute as "pure race." There is no indication that the Delaware courts would read a "value" requirement into the statute, but they might read in a "notice" requirement. Delaware has a separate recording statute for mortgages, 25 Del. C. § 2106; see E. Sav. Bank, FSB v. Cach, LLC, 124 A.3d 585 (Del. 2015), describing this statute as also pure "race," but it has been construed to deny priority to a recorded mortgage if the mortgagee had notice (actual or constructive) of a prior equitable mortgage that was not properly recorded; see Handler Const., Inc. v. CoreStates Bank, N.A., 633 A.2d 356 (Del. 1993). This adds a "notice" element to the statute that is not present in the text. See Szypszak, note 482 supra.

or equity theories.[487] In addition, if the first grantee's deed contains the "future" covenants of warranty or quiet enjoyment, an action on the deed covenants is possible.[488]

Interests and conveyances outside the acts. From the description of recording acts above one might imagine that all types of interests, created in all possible ways, are within the coverage of the acts. However, this is not the case. As we will see, several types of interests in land are excluded from the acts by statutory or constitutional provisions. Other interests are excluded if they are created or transferred in certain specific ways. The priority of interests which are outside the scope of the acts is determined by common-law rules, and the usual rule is that first in time is first in right, whether recorded or not.[489] The result is that the records are less reliable than they might be; one cannot be fully confident of the results of one's search, for some interests in the land may be legally recognized despite the fact that the records make no reference at all to them.

The most commonly-encountered exclusion from the operation of the recording acts is the short-term lease. Nearly all of the statutes protect leases of one to three years' duration without the necessity of recording them,[490] perhaps in recognition of the fact that they are not customarily recorded and that the tenant's possession will usually (though not always) give subsequent purchasers notice of the lease.

Unfiled mechanics' and materials suppliers' liens are usually excluded from the operation of the recording acts for some period after they arise. The lien acts typically provide that if a notice of lien is recorded within, say, 60 to 120 days after the right to payment arises, the lien's priority relates back to the date the work was commenced. Hence a purchaser may be bound by the lien despite the fact that a record search during this "relation back" period would have revealed nothing.[491]

Spousal rights arising from common-law dower and curtesy and from similar statutory schemes are valid without recording, and indeed do not give rise to any recordable document. It is common to recite the grantor's marital status in a deed, but

---

[487] Madden v. Caldwell Land Co., 16 Idaho 59, 100 P. 358 (1909) (constructive fraud); Niles v. Groover, 3 S.E. 899 (Ga. 1887) (unjust enrichment); Bardwell v. White, 762 So.2d 778 (Miss. Ct. App. 2000) (unjust enrichment); Jones v. Garden Park Homes Corp., 393 S.W.2d 501 (Mo. 1965) (contract or tort); Hilligas v. Kuns, 86 Neb. 68, 124 N.W. 925 (1910) (tort); Patterson v. Bryant, 216 N.C. 550, 5 S.E.2d 849 (1939) (quasi-contract); Talman v. Dixon, 253 N.C. 193, 116 S.E.2d 338 (1960) (no recovery, where first grantee's contract provided that grantor would convey only such title as grantor had).

[488] Curtis v. Deering, 12 Maine 499 (1835); § 4.13 infra.

[489] An exception exists with respect to the set of interests created in equity by way of resulting and constructive trusts, equitable liens, rights to reform or set aside conveyances, and the like. Such rights are not ordinarily reflected in recorded documents, and they may indeed take priority over persons whose claims are recorded. However, a rule of equity nearly always subordinates them to the rights of subsequent bona fide purchasers for value; see, e.g., § 11.1 supra at notes 91–92 (rights to set aside deeds); Scott & Ascher, Trusts (5th ed. 2017) (resulting and constructive trusts); Osin v. Johnson, 243 F.2d 653 (D.C.Cir.1957); In re Harrison, 503 B.R. 835 (Bankr. N.D. Okla. 2013) (resulting trust); Hunnicutt Constr., Inc. v. Stewart Title & Trust of Tucson Trust No. 3496, 187 Ariz. 301, 928 P.2d 725 (Ariz.App. 1996) (equitable lien); Hocking v. Hocking, 137 Ill. App.3d 159, 484 N.E.2d 406 (1985) (resulting trust). The net result of this rule of equity is much like that of a notice-type recording act.

[490] See In re Fry Brothers, 52 B.R. 169 (Bkrtcy.S.D.Ohio 1985) (under Ohio law, lease exceeding 3 years is within recording act); Reeves v. Alabama Land Locators, Inc., 514 So.2d 917 (Ala.1987) (20 year lease is within recording act); 4 Am.L.Prop. § 17.8 n. 10 (1952).

[491] See generally Nelson, Whitman, Burkhart & Freyermuth, Real Estate Finance Law § 12.4 (6th ed. 2014). In some jurisdictions the lien relates back only if the work of the lienor is "visible," thus providing some limited degree of protection to bona fide purchasers; see Riverview Muir Doran, LLC v. JADT Dev. Grp., LLC, 790 N.W.2d 167 (Minn. 2010).

in general an incorrect or missing recitation is not binding against an undisclosed spouse.[492] Since it is virtually impossible for a grantee to know with certainty that a grantor is unmarried, some decisions have refused to enforce such spousal rights as against bona fide purchasers.[493]

Finally, conveyances made by[494] or to[495] the Federal government cannot be defeated by state recording acts. The reason lies in the Supremacy Clause of the U.S. Constitution, which makes Federal law preemptive of state law. In general, Federal agencies voluntarily record conveyances of land they acquire, but in the absence of a specific congressional act requiring recordation[496] they incur no legal risk if they fail to do so.

In addition to the types of interests discussed above which are outside the recording acts, there are numerous other claims which will prevail without recording because of the specific manner in which they are created. In some cases these claims can be discovered, at least in theory, by searching in places other than the recording office. For example, wills and transfers by intestate succession need not be recorded,[497] but can ordinarily be found in the records of the appropriate probate court. Takings by eminent domain are sometimes held not subject to the recording acts, but some record of them is usually maintained by the government agency doing the taking.[498] The assets of a bankrupt are transferred to the trustee in bankruptcy by virtue of federal statute, and no indication of the transfer need appear in the local real estate records, although the docket of the bankruptcy court will reflect the action. A purchaser who has no knowledge of the bankruptcy can claim title as against the trustee only by paying the "present fair equivalent value," a higher standard than the recording acts normally impose.[499] A purchaser who pays less has only a lien on the property to aid in recovery of the payment.

---

[492] The recital creates, at most, a presumption of its truthfulness which can be rebutted; see Uniform Simplification of Land Transfers Act (USLTA) § 2–305(a)(8).

[493] See Petta v. Host, 1 Ill.2d 293, 115 N.E.2d 881 (1953). USLTA continues to follow the traditional rule favoring the undisclosed spouse as against even a bona fide purchaser; USLTA § 3–202(a)(3). But see State v. Pettis, 149 Wis.2d 207, 441 N.W.2d 247 (App.1989), review denied 439 N.W.2d 144 (1989), based on Wisconsin statute which extinguishes claims based on homestead rights if an otherwise valid conveyance has been recorded for five years and if the conveyance fails to indicate marital status.

[494] Thus one who takes land by a Federal patent need not record it to be protected from subsequent BFP's from the government, United States v. Schurz, 102 U.S. (12 Otto) 378, 26 L.Ed. 167 (1880); Rankin v. Miller, 43 Iowa 11 (1876).

[495] See United States v. Snyder, 149 U.S. 210, 13 S.Ct. 846, 37 L.Ed. 705 (1893) (federal tax lien); Norman Lumber Co. v. United States, 223 F.2d 868 (4th Cir. 1955), certiorari denied 350 U.S. 902, 76 S.Ct. 181, 100 L.Ed. 792 (1955) (federal eminent domain taking).

[496] See, e.g., the Federal Tax Lien Act, 26 U.S.C.A. § 6323, which requires the Internal Revenue Service to record notices of liens it claims; see also United States v. Union Central Life Insurance Co., 368 U.S. 291, 82 S.Ct. 349, 7 L.Ed.2d 294 (1961); Haye v. United States, 461 F.Supp. 1168 (N.D. Cal. 1978); Plumb, Federal Tax Liens, ch. 2, § 2 (1972).

[497] See 4 Am.L.Prop. § 17.8 (1952), at nn. 21–28. Cf. Koschler v. Dean, 642 So.2d 1119 (Fla.App.1994) (records of probate division of court give no constructive notice).

[498] See, e.g., Norman Lumber Co. v. United States, 223 F.2d 868 (4th Cir. 1955), certiorari denied 350 U.S. 902, 76 S.Ct. 181, 100 L.Ed. 792 (1955); Smirlock Realty Corp v. Title Guarantee Co., 418 N.E.2d 650, 437 N.Y.S.2d 57 (N.Y. 1981); State ex rel. State Highway Commission v. Meeker, 75 Wyo. 210, 294 P.2d 603 (1956). But see Alabama v. Abbott, 476 So.2d 1224 (Ala. 1985) (order of condemnation in favor of state is a conveyance subject to recording act; if unrecorded, a subsequent BFP will prevail over it); Devine v. Town of Nantucket, 449 Mass. 499, 870 N.E.2d 591 (2007) (condemnation order was not properly recorded and conferred no constructive notice, where it listed owner as "unknown.")

[499] See 11 U.S.C.A. § 549. The purchaser is protected only if the land is located in a different county than the bankruptcy court; purchasers are expected to check the federal court docket in the county where the land is situated. The cited section also authorizes the trustee to record a copy of the bankruptcy petition in the relevant county's land records; if this is done, no subsequent purchaser is protected. With respect to the amount

Note that the ability of a searcher to locate documents which are maintained outside the recording system may be more theoretical than real. In the case of eminent domain, for example, there may be dozens of state and local agencies with the power, and it is hardly practical for a searcher to check with them all as part of the ordinary title search process. It is similarly not feasible for a purchaser to check the records of all bankruptcy courts. In many jurisdictions a variety of agencies, including welfare, taxing, utility, and corporation departments, can acquire liens on real estate in the course of their operations. Where they maintain their own records rather than filing their claims of liens in the recording system, title searches are made more complex and much more subject to possible error.[500]

Other claims are outside the recording acts because they are created by a process which does not involve a document; hence there is literally nothing to record. Illustrations include acquisition of title by adverse possession,[501] creation of easements by prescription, implication, and necessity,[502] some forms of dedication,[503] and adjustments of boundaries by the various techniques of practical location.[504] In most cases these modes of creating interests are incomplete until the claimant takes possession or makes use of the land, so one might suppose that a searcher could discover the claim by a physical inspection of the land. But this is by no means always the case, for the possession or use may have both begun and been completed long before the title

---

of value which a purchaser must pay to receive protection, compare § 11.10 infra at notes 520–522 on the more lenient requirements of the recording acts.

[500] This fragmentation of sources of title records is a severe problem in some jurisdictions. One compilation for Cleveland, Ohio listed 76 types of records in 16 different public offices which might contain land title data, and hence which should be checked in a thorough title search; Johnstone & Hopson, Lawyers and Their Work 274–75 (1967). It is widely held that public records in a variety of governmental offices give constructive notice to title searchers. See, e.g., Pelfresne v. Village of Williams Bay, 917 F.2d 1017 (7th Cir.1990), appeal after remand 965 F.2d 538 (7th Cir. 1992) (judgment docket card); Citizens for Covenant Compliance v. Anderson, 12 Cal.4th 345, 47 Cal. Rptr.2d 898, 906 P.2d 1314 (Cal.1995) (filed subdivision plat); South Creek Associates v. Bixby & Associates, 781 P.2d 1027 (Colo. 1989) (municipal government's adoption of planned unit development zoning); City of Lakewood v. Mavromatis, 817 P.2d 90 (Colo. 1991) (road petition in county clerk's "road book"); Haugh v. Smelick, 126 Idaho 481, 887 P.2d 26 (1993) (filed subdivision plat). Contra, finding that records do not impart constructive notice, see Story Bed & Breakfast v. Brown County Area, 794 N.E. 2d 519 (Ind.App. 2003) (planned unit development statement filed in county plan dep't office); Miller v. Title Ins. Co. of Minnesota, 296 Mont. 115, 987 P.2d 1151 (1999) (records of city engineer and water department); Ioannou v. Southold Town Planning Bd., 304 A.D.2d 578, 758 N.Y.S.2d 358 (2003) (covenant filed with town planning board); First Am. Title Ins. Co. v. J.B. Ranch, Inc., 966 P.2d 834 (Utah 1998) (road maps in county clerk's office).

[501] See § 11.7, supra.

[502] See §§ 8.4–8.5, 8.7, supra. Restatement (Third) of Property (Servitudes) § 7.14 takes the view that easements by prescription, implication, and estoppel are subject to the recording acts and may be extinguished by a subsequent conveyance to a qualified subsequent purchaser. However, the case law is mixed on the point. See Reporter's Note, id.; McKeon v. Brammer, 238 Iowa 1113, 29 N.W.2d 518, 174 A.L.R. 1229 (1947). The problem is acute with hidden or underground easements. See Bush v. Duff, 754 P.2d 159 (Wyo.1988) (unrecorded easement of necessity gives no constructive notice to foreclosing mortgagee, and foreclosure destroys easement even though easement's owner is not made a party to the foreclosure). Unwritten easements are generally held extinguished in favor of subsequent BFPs, but it is often unclear whether the court is applying the recording act or an equitable principle; see Tiller v. Hinton, 19 Ohio St.3d 66, 482 N.E.2d 946 (1985); Gill Grain Co. v. Poos, 707 S.W.2d 434 (Mo.App. 1986). See Eichengrunn, The Problem of Hidden Easements and the Subsequent Purchaser Without Notice, 40 Okla.L.Rev. 34 (1987).

[503] Dedications may result from oral statements and accompanying actions, with no writing involved; see § 11.6 supra at notes 296–297. Cf. Board of County Commissioners v. White, 547 P.2d 1195 (Wyo. 1976), refusing to recognize a prescriptive dedication of a public road because the statutory procedures, including recordation of a certificate declaring the existence of the road, were not met; Nohowel v. Hall, 218 Md. 160, 146 A.2d 187 (1958), protecting a subsequent bona fide purchaser against a prior unrecorded common law dedication.

[504] See § 11.8, supra.

search in question is made, so that the claimant's interest is fully protected even though no further trace of it appears on the ground.[505]

Occasionally controversy develops as to whether a particular instrument is entitled to be recorded. The statutes usually speak in terms of "conveyances of interests in real estate" or similar language. There is no question that any document conveying a legal, as opposed to an equitable, interest is recordable, provided it includes the notarial acknowledgment usually required by statute.[506] Moreover, contracts of sale and other papers creating equitable interests are now very widely considered recordable.[507] Option agreements are somewhat more problematic, since it can be argued that they create no interest in real estate, but only a right to accept an offer and form a contract. Yet treating them as granting interests in land has obvious practical advantages, and most modern decisions regard them as recordable.[508]

A grantor who does not want his or her conveyance recorded may try to achieve this objective by refusing to appear before a notary for the necessary acknowledgment. This is a common practice when a long-term installment contract is executed, since the vendor may anticipate that in the event of a default, it will be easier to terminate the contract and resell the land if the record title is not clouded by the contract.[509] The purchaser, in turn, may attempt to get on record anyway, either by persuading the recorder to accept the instrument despite the absence of an acknowledgment or by executing, acknowledging, and recording some new document, perhaps termed a "notice of interest," which recites the existence of the previous contract. Such a paper is not a conveyance and may well be held legally unrecordable. Whichever technique is used, it is probable that the courts will hold the recorded instrument to give no constructive notice to future purchasers.[510] But as a practical matter, the purchaser will still have largely achieved

[505] See Mugaas v. Smith, 33 Wn.2d 429, 206 P.2d 332, 9 A.L.R.2d 846 (1949) (adverse possession completed prior to title search; no visible evidence of adverse claim); Otero v. Pacheco, 94 N.M. 524, 612 P.2d 1335 (App.1980), cert. denied 94 N.M. 674, 615 P.2d 991 (1980) (purchasers held to have constructive notice of implied easement from "visibility" of a buried sewer line); Carter v. Helmsley-Spear, Inc., 861 F.Supp. 303 (S.D.N.Y.1994) (artist could enjoin owner from demolishing murals and sculptures in building under Visual Artists Rights Act of 1990, 17 U.S.C. § 106(a)).

[506] If an instrument is not acknowledged, it is usually deemed unrecorded even though the recording officials actually accepted it and placed it in the records. See Summa Investing Corp. v. McClure, 569 So.2d 500 (Fla.App. 1990); Maxwell, The Hidden Defect in Acknowledgment and Title Security, 2 U.C.L.A.L.Rev. 83 (1954). Moreover, such an instrument is typically held to give no constructive notice to searchers; see notes 510–511 infra.

[507] See, e.g., West v. Bowen, 127 Idaho 128, 898 P.2d 59 (1995); Hawthorne Trust v. Maine Sav. Bank, 136 N.H. 533, 618 A.2d 828 (N.H. 1992); Tomlinson v. Clarke, 118 Wn.2d 498, 825 P.2d 706 (1992); Leman v. Quinn, 170 A.D.2d 452, 565 N.Y.S.2d 541 (1991); Annot., 26 A.L.R. 1546 (1923). Note that many types of equitable interests can be created without a writing, and these are usually held to be outside the recording system; in general, however, the equitable doctrine of bona fide purchaser will operate, much like a notice-type recording act, to protect later buyers without notice of the equitable interest. See note 489 supra; Barrish v. Flitter, 715 F.Supp. 692 (E.D.Pa. 1989); Annot., 87 A.L.R. 1505 (1933).

[508] Province v. Johnson, 894 P.2d 66 (Colo.App. 1995); Matter of Berge, 39 B.R. 960 (Bkrtcy. W.D.Wis. 1984); Daniel v. Kensington Homes, Inc., 232 Md. 1, 192 A.2d 114 (1963). Cf. Wetzel v. Mortg. Elec. Registration Sys., Inc., 2010 Ark. 242 (2010) (affidavit of lost mortgage was not entitled to be recorded). The USLTA imposes no limits whatever on the sorts of documents which can be recorded, taking the view that "* * * the decision as to what to record is a private rather than a public one." USLTA § 2–301, Comment 1.

[509] See Nelson, Whitman, Burkhart & Freyermuth, Real Estate Finance Law § 3.30 (6th ed. 2014).

[510] See Phipps v. CW Leasing, 186 Ariz. 397, 923 P.2d 863 (Ariz. Ct. App. 1996); Department of Banking and Finance v. Davis, 227 Neb. 172, 416 N.W.2d 566 (1987); Spady v. Graves, 307 Or. 483, 770 P.2d 53 (1989); In re Crim, 81 S.W.3d 764 (Tenn. 2002). See generally Annots., 3 A.L.R.2d 577 (1949), 59 A.L.R.2d 1299 (1958). Contra, see Cipriano v. Tocco, 772 F.Supp. 344 (E.D.Mich. 1991); In re Casbeer, 793 F.2d 1436 (5th Cir. 1986).

the objective, for the instrument will give actual notice to those who in fact search the records and discover it, and thus will preclude them from using the recording acts to defeat it.[511]

The discussion above suggests that title searches may give an incomplete and unreliable picture because the law recognizes and protects numerous types of instruments and interests that are unrecorded. A further source of unreliability arises from the fact that the instruments in the records may not be legally efficacious. A recorded deed, for example, may be a forgery,[512] procured by fraud in the execution,[513] executed by a minor,[514] or never delivered.[515] Any one of these defects will make the deed void, and the fact that it is recorded in no sense enhances its validity. Such defects are virtually impossible for a title searcher to detect, yet they can have a devastating effect on title.[516] In sum, even a complete and careful title search may produce seriously incomplete or legally erroneous results and may subject the buyer of land to risks of major dimensions.[517]

§ 11.10   THE RECORDING SYSTEM— BONA FIDE PURCHASER STATUS

Payment of value. Nearly all of the recording acts protect subsequent conveyees only if they are bona fide purchasers. This status has two elements: paying value and taking in good faith with no notice of the prior conveyance. We first consider the value requirement. Obviously donees do not qualify, nor do heirs or devisees[518] except in the very unusual cases in which they have bargained and paid for their reward.[519] There is considerable disagreement as to how much a grantee must pay. A few cases seem to

---

In Utah the "notice of interest" is widely used and provides constructive notice; see Morris v. Off-Piste Capital LLC, 2018 UT App 7, 418 P.3d 66 (2018).

[511] See Metropolitan Nat. Bank v. United States, 901 F.2d 1297 (5th Cir. 1990) (defectively acknowledged deed of trust gave no constructive notice, but might have given actual notice if subsequent lienor had in fact searched the records; but there was no evidence that lienor had done so); Annot., 3 A.L.R.2d 577, 589 (1949).

[512] See Lloyd v. Chicago Title Ins. Co., 576 So.2d 310 (Fla.App. 1990); Weiss v. Phillips, 157 A.D.3d 1, 65 N.Y.S.3d 147 (N.Y. App. Div. 2017); Dyson Descendant Corp. v. Sonat Exploration Co., 861 S.W.2d 942 (Tex. App. 1993); Fidelity & Deposit Co. v. Ticor Title Insur. Co., 88 Wn.App. 64, 943 P.2d 710 (1997); § 11.1 supra at note 93. USLTA § 3–202(a)(5)(i) retains this rule.

[513] § 11.1 supra at note 96. USLTA § 3–202(a)(5)(iii) retains this rule.

[514] § 11.1 supra at note 102. USLTA § 3–202(a)(5)(ii) apparently retains this rule.

[515] § 11.3 supra at note 166; Stone v. French, 37 Kan. 145, 14 P. 530 (1887). USLTA § 2–202 reverses this rule and upholds the innocent third party who relied on the putative delivery, but permits the victimized grantor to record an affidavit that there was no delivery, and thus to prevent BFP rights from arising. See also Mass.Gen.Laws Ann. c. 183, § 5, making recording conclusive evidence of delivery.

[516] A variety of other defects, such as fraud in the inducement and most types of incapacity, make the instrument voidable rather than void, and thus will not defeat a bona fide purchaser; see § 11.1 supra at notes 99, 104–108. Yet if they exist they put the purchaser to the risk of proving his or her BFP status, perhaps in expensive litigation.

[517] See Andersen, Conveyancing Reform: A Great Place to Start, 25 Real Prop. Prob. & Tr.J. 333 (1990); Stroup, The Unreliable Record Title, 60 N.D.L.Rev. 203 (1984); Fiflis, Land Transfer Improvement: The Basic Facts and Two Hypotheses for Reform, 38 U.Colo.L.Rev. 431, 453–54 (1966); Straw, Off-Record Risks for Bona Fide Purchasers of Interests in Real Property, 72 Dick.L.Rev. 35 (1967).

[518] Texas Eastern Transmission Corp. v. Garza, 894 F.Supp. 1055 (S.D.Tex. 1995); Jordan v. Copeland, 545 So.2d 27 (Ala. 1989); Gregg v. Link, 774 S.W.2d 174 (Tenn.App. 1988); Gullett v. Burton, 176 W.Va. 447, 345 S.E.2d 323 (1986); Bagwell v. Henson, 124 Ga.App. 92, 183 S.E.2d 485 (1971).

[519] See Horton v. Kyburz, 53 Cal.2d 59, 346 P.2d 399 (1959), permitting the devisee to prevail, as a BFP, over a prior constructive trust.

accept any amount, however nominal,[520] but most require an amount which is substantial in relation to the property's value and not grossly inadequate.[521] There is general agreement, on the other hand, that the full market value need not be paid.[522] The payment need not be in the form of money, but can be represented by goods or services instead.[523] Love and affection or familial relationship are usually held insufficient.[524]

The grantee who gives a promise to pay, as distinct from an actual payment, is not considered to have given value;[525] nor is the giving of a mortgage or other lien to secure a future payment.[526] However, an exception is made for a mortgage securing a negotiable instrument given by the grantee which is in fact negotiated to a holder in due course.[527] The reason for different treatment is based on the severe limitations which the law imposes upon the maker's defenses on the note in the latter case, so that the grantee is very likely to be legally compelled to pay it even if the title to the land turns out to be defective.[528] Observe also that the payment need not be an irrevocable transfer; it is universally agreed that a lender who takes a mortgage on land to secure a contemporaneous loan has given value despite the fact that the money advanced is expected to be repaid.[529]

Judgment creditors. There is much more controversy over the status of judgment creditors. In most states a judgment becomes a lien on the defendant's land in the county where the judgment is docketed. If the defendant appears to have record title, but in fact has made an unrecorded conveyance prior to the entry of the judgment, will the subsequent plaintiff's lien prevail over the non-recording grantee? A substantial

---

[520] See, e.g., Walters v. Calderon, 25 Cal. App.3d 863, 102 Cal.Rptr. 89 (1972), finding nominal consideration sufficient to confer BFP status as against a prior constructive trust.

[521] Anderson v. Anderson, 435 N.W.2d 687 (N.D. 1989) (recitation of $10 and other good and valuable consideration was nominal, and insufficient to establish BFP status); Phillips v. Latham, 523 S.W.2d 19 (Tex.Civ.App. 1975), refused n.r.e., appeal after remand 551 S.W.2d 103 (Tex.Civ.App. 1977), refused n.r.e.; United States v. West, 299 F.Supp. 661 (D.Del. 1969).

[522] Cheatham v. Gregory, 227 Va. 1, 313 S.E.2d 368 (1984) ($400 paid for 2.5 acres in 1973 was "value;" recording acts do not require fair and adequate consideration); Asher v. Rader, 411 S.W.2d 477 (Ky. 1967). See generally 4 Am.L.Prop. § 17.10 nn. 8–9 (1952).

[523] Lundgren v. Lundgren, 245 Cal. App.2d 582, 54 Cal.Rptr. 30 (1966).

[524] Hanscome-James-Winship v. Ainger, 71 Cal. App. 735, 236 P. 325 (1925); Town House Dep't Stores, Inc. v. Ahn, 2000 Guam 32 (2000); Baker National Bank v. Lestar, 153 Mont. 45, 453 P.2d 774 (1969). But see Strong v. Whybark, 204 Mo. 341, 102 S.W. 968 (1907). A promise of marriage may be valuable consideration; see Berge v. Fredericks, 95 Nev. 183, 591 P.2d 246 (1979).

[525] Lattin v. Gray, 75 Nev. 128, 335 P.2d 778 (1959); Bell v. Pierschbacher, 245 Iowa 436, 62 N.W.2d 784 (1954). USLTA § 1–201(31)(iv) following U.C.C. § 1–201(44)(d), takes the opposite approach; it provides that one pays value if he or she gives "any consideration sufficient to support a simple contract."

[526] South Carolina Tax Commission v. Belk, 266 S.C. 539, 225 S.E.2d 177 (1976); Chevron Oil Co. v. Clark, 291 F.Supp. 552 (S.D.Miss. 1968), reversed in part 432 F.2d 280 (5th Cir. 1970); Alden v. Trubee, 44 Conn. 455 (1877). See 4 Am.L.Prop. § 17.10 n. 10 (1952).

[527] Dunn v. Stack, 418 So.2d 345 (Fla. App.1982), quashed 444 So.2d 935 (Fla. 1984); Donalson v. Thomason, 137 Ga. 848, 74 S.E. 762 (1912); Davis v. Ward, 109 Cal. 186, 41 P. 1010 (1895). In Middlemas v. Wright, 493 S.W.2d 282 (Tex.Civ.App. 1973), the grantee's personal check (a negotiable instrument) was regarded as valuable consideration despite the fact that it was never presented for payment.

[528] The holder in due course is subject only to so-called "real defenses," which include infancy, incapacity, duress, fraud in the execution, and discharge in insolvency proceedings. See U.C.C. § 3–305(a)(1).

[529] Some of the acts include "mortgagees" or "creditors" as protected parties, but even if there is no such reference, mortgagees who make contemporaneous loans are invariably protected. See Sun Valley Land and Minerals, Inc. v. Burt, 853 P.2d 607 (Idaho App. 1993); Washington Mut. Bank v. Homan, 186 Md. App. 372, 974 A.2d 376 (2009); Nev.Rev.Stat. § 111.320; Wyo.Stat. § 34–1–101.

minority of the acts contain language explicitly protecting the judgment creditor,[530] but absent such language the usual answer is no.[531] Often this conclusion is based on the literal language of the pertinent judgment lien statute, which typically imposes the lien on "the defendant's real property"—not the record property, the courts frequently hold, but the actual property as depleted by unrecorded conveyances.[532] An alternative basis for the same result is that the creditor is simply not a "purchaser" in the sense used by the recording statute.[533]

In reality, these cases require reconciliation of an ambiguity in the interaction of the recording act and the judgment lien act, although the decisions do not always explicitly recognize that fact. From a policy viewpoint, it is hard to envision a sound basis for denying protection to the judgment creditor, who has usually gone to the trouble and expense of filing and prosecuting a lawsuit in reliance on the state of the record title. For the law to inform such a person, at the conclusion of this perilous course, that the judgment is uncollectible despite the record's indication to the contrary, is a cruel trick. The winner in such a case is the prior grantee (often another creditor of the defendant) who was too careless or devious to record. Such a result is pernicious, but is widely reached. However, if the creditor completes the collection process by foreclosing the lien or holding an execution sale, the buyer at that sale is uniformly held protected by the recording act.[534] This usually follows even if the creditor purchases at his or her own sale.[535]

Preexisting debt. A common problem is raised by the creditor who takes a mortgage or other interest in land as further security for a pre-existing debt. For example, a bank may make an unsecured loan and later ask the debtor to give it a mortgage as security. Unless the bank somehow changes its position detrimentally in return for the mortgage, as by granting an extension of time for repayment, agreeing to forbear bringing suit, or giving some other concession such as a reduction in interest rate, it will by the large majority of cases be deemed not to have given value under the recording acts.[536] Hence, the bank's mortgage will be subordinate to any prior unrecorded conveyances the debtor

---

[530] See, e.g., West's Ann. Cal.Civ.Code § 1214; Nelson v. Barnett Recovery Corp., 652 So.2d 279 (Ala.Civ.App. 1994); United Cmty. Bank v. Prairie State Bank & Tr., 2012 IL App (4th) 110973, 972 N.E.2d 324 (2012); Solans v. McMenimen, 80 Mass. App. Ct. 178, 951 N.E.2d 999 (2011) (creditor obtaining order of attachment is protected by recording act); Nussbaumer v. Fetrow, 556 N.W.2d 595 (Minn.App. 1996); Schleuter Co. v. Sevigny, 564 N.W.2d 309 (S.D. 1997); 21 Pa.Stat. § 351. See generally 4 Am.L.Prop. § 11.29 n. 1 (1952).

[531] In re Brosnahan, 312 B.R. 220 (Bankr.W.D.N.Y. 2004) (N.Y. law); In re Tanner, 145 B.R. 672 (Bankr.W.D.Wash. 1992) (Washington law); Siegel Mobile Home Group, Inc. v. Bowen, 114 Idaho 531, 757 P.2d 1250 (Idaho App. 1988); ABN AMRO Mortg. Grp., Inc. v. Am. Residential Servs., LLC, 845 N.E.2d 209 (Ind. Ct. App. 2006); Washington Mut. Bank v. Homan, 186 Md. App. 372, 974 A.2d 376 (2009). See generally Note, Status of Judgment Creditors under the Recording Acts, 32 N.Dame L.Rev. 471 (1957).

[532] Garland v. Fleischmann, 831 P.2d 107 (Utah 1992); Wilson v. Willamette Industries, Inc., 280 Or. 45, 569 P.2d 609 (1977); Oklahoma State Bank v. Burnett, 65 Okl. 74, 162 P. 1124, 4 A.L.R. 430 (1917); Holden v. Garrett, 23 Kan. 98 (1879).

[533] See Davis v. Johnson, 241 Ga. 436, 246 S.E.2d 297 (1978); Wilson v. Willamette Industries, Inc., supra note 532.

[534] Keefe v. Cropper, 196 Iowa 1179, 194 N.W. 305 (1923); Sternberger & Willard v. Ragland, 57 Ohio St. 148, 48 N.E. 811 (1897); Note, 24 Minn.L.Rev. 807 (1940).

[535] Hansen v. G & G Trucking Co., 236 Cal.App.2d 481, 46 Cal.Rptr. 186 (1965). Even if the creditor merely bids the amount of the judgment debt, so that no money changes hands, he or she has in substance paid value by giving up the claim on the judgment in return for the land. See 4 Am.L.Prop. § 17.30 n. 9 (1952).

[536] In re Fair Oaks, Ltd., 168 B.R. 397 (9th Cir. BAP 1994) (California law); In re Kraft, LLC, 429 B.R. 637, 664 (Bankr. N.D. Ind. 2010); Manufacturers & Traders Trust Co. v. First National Bank, 113 So.2d 869 (Fla.App. 1959). The USLTA takes the contrary position, treating a pre-existing claim as value for recording act purposes; USLTA § 1–201(31), following U.C.C. § 1–201(44).

has made. A similar result follows with respect to mechanics lien claimants; since they originally perform their work without taking any interest in the land, and since they give no further value in return for the lien, an earlier conveyance, even though unrecorded, will have priority.[537]

The rule, then, is that the "value" must be paid contemporaneously with or subsequent to the conveyance to be protected; otherwise the conveyee is not "out" anything in reliance on the records. But consider the case of the creditor who has previously made an unsecured loan, and who later takes a deed of the land in full or partial satisfaction of the debt. The creditor's position here is superficially similar to one who takes a mortgage to secure an antecedent debt, as discussed in the previous paragraph. Yet there is a vast difference, for here the creditor has detrimentally changed legal position by treating the debt as satisfied, typically by cancelling the debtor's promissory note and thereby giving up all further claim against the debtor. Surprisingly, a number of courts have misunderstood this distinction, and have found no value to have been paid.[538] This is plainly incorrect; the creditor should be protected, and most recent decisions adopt this view.[539]

Taking without notice. The second aspect of bona fide purchaser status is lack of notice of the prior unrecorded conveyance.[540] Thus it is necessary to consider what sorts of notice might be imputed to a purchaser of real estate. Three main types of notice are discussed in the cases: (1) actual knowledge, gained from whatever source; (2) constructive notice of facts which would be apparent upon a visual inspection of the property and an interrogation of those in possession of it;[541] and (3) constructive notice of information found in the public records.

---

[537] See Stout v. Lye, 103 U.S. (13 Otto) 66, 26 L.Ed. 428 (1880). Contra, see Shade v. Wheatcraft Industries, Inc., 248 Kan. 531, 809 P.2d 538 (1991) (mortgage loses priority to mechanics lien that attaches after mortgage is given but before it is recorded, if lien claimant has no actual knowledge of mortgage). In many cases, the "relation back" feature of mechanics liens provides the lien claimant with a better priority than he or she would gain through the recording acts; see, Nelson, Whitman, Burkhart & Freyermuth, Real Estate Finance Law § 12.4 (6th ed. 2014).

[538] See 4 Am.L.Prop. § 17.10 n. 29 (1952), citing numerous cases refusing to treat the creditor as a BFP.

[539] Fox v. Templeton, 229 Va. 380, 329 S.E.2d 6 (1985); Wight v. Chandler, 264 F.2d 249 (10th Cir. 1959); Orphanoudakis v. Orphanoudakis, 199 Va. 142, 98 S.E.2d 676 (1957); Reserve Petroleum Co. v. Hutcheson, 254 S.W.2d 802 (Tex.Civ.App. 1952).

[540] The date when the existence of notice is evaluated is the date that the purported BFP acquired his or her own interest, and that is ordinarily the date of delivery of his or her deed. See Washington Mut. Bank v. Homan, 186 Md. App. 372, 974 A.2d 376 (2009); Kourt Sec. Partners, LLC v. Judy's Locksmiths, Inc., 239 W. Va. 757, 806 S.E.2d 188 (2017). Cf. Hongsermeier v. Devall, 16 Neb. App. 379, 744 N.W.2d 481 (2008) (to be a BFP, one must have no notice as of date purchase price is paid).

As we have already seen, under all recording acts except the pure "race" type, a subsequent purchaser who has notice of the prior conveyance will not be protected by the recording act against it. In the absence of the act's protection, priority between competing conveyances is ordinarily determined by the dates of their delivery. However, in the case of competing and essentially simultaneous mortgages, one of which is a purchase-money mortgage to a vendor, a common-law principle grants priority to the vendor over mortgages to third parties. See, e.g., ALH Holding Co. v. Bank of Telluride, 18 P.3d 742 (Colo. 2000); Furnari v. Wells Fargo Bank N.A., 2006 WL 664843 (Mich. Ct. App. 2006) (unpublished); Nelson, Whitman, Burkhart & Freyermuth, Real Estate Finance Law § 7.13 (6th ed. 2014); Restatement (Third) of Property (Mortgages) § 7.2.

[541] In Massachusetts the recording act refers to "actual notice" and the concept of constructive notice from possession of the land is not recognized. See Mass.Gen. Laws Ann. c. 183, § 4; In re Dlott, 43 B.R. 789 (Bkrtcy. D.Mass. 1983); Toupin v. Peabody, 162 Mass. 473, 39 N.E. 280 (1895). Several other states' acts use the phrase "actual notice" or similar terminology, but nonetheless recognize constructive notice of more or less the conventional type described in the text. See Bowen v. Perryman, 256 Ark. 174, 506 S.W.2d 543 (1974); Lane v. Courange, 187 Kan. 645, 359 P.2d 1115 (1961); Swift v. Fed. Home Loan Mortg. Corp., 417 S.W.3d 342

Overlying all of these is the doctrine of "inquiry notice", which holds that one who has information from any source suggesting the existence of a prior conveyance must make a reasonable investigation of it; a purchaser who fails to do so will be held to the knowledge that such an investigation would have disclosed.[542] In such cases, an inquiry of one's own grantor is prima facie insufficient, for that is the very person who has the strongest incentive to conceal the prior conveyance.[543] Incidentally, the term "constructive notice," as used in the recording act cases, refers generically to any notice which is imputed by legal rules. Thus, notice growing out of the fact of an adverse claimant's possession, from the public records, or from the doctrine of inquiry notice is "constructive" if the purchaser does not in fact make the necessary search or investigation; the law simply imputes the knowledge to the purchaser anyway.[544]

Actual notice. Actual notice may come from a variety of sources. For example, the grantor may inform the purchaser of a preexisting encumbrance, such as a lease or easement.[545] A conveyee under the prior instrument or others in the locality may also do so.[546] The purchaser may have learned of the conveyance in the course of business dealings or personal relationships.[547] It may be discovered during a visit to the property or an examination of public or proprietary records.[548] Actual notice of facts which suggest the existence of third parties' interests in the land may form the basis for a duty to make

---

(Mo. Ct. App. 2013); Taylor v. Hanchett Oil Co., 37 N.M. 606, 27 P.2d 59 (1933); Johnson v. Bell, 666 P.2d 308 (Utah 1983). See 4 Am.L.Prop. § 17.12 n. 3 (1952).

[542] See In re Brannon, 584 B.R. 417 (Bankr. N.D. Ga. 2018); In re Jones, 573 B.R. 665 (Bankr. N.D. Tex. 2017); Methonen v. Stone, 941 P.2d 1248 (Alaska 1997); In re Marriage of Cloney, 91 Cal. App. 4th 429, 110 Cal. Rptr. 2d 615 (2001); Goodman Assocs., LLC v. Winter Quarters, LLC, 292 P.3d 1060 (Colo. Ct. App. 2012); Guthrie v. National Advertising Co., 556 N.E.2d 337 (Ind. Ct. App. 1990); Miller v. Hennen, 438 N.W.2d 366 (Minn. 1989); Sundance Oil & Gas, LLC v. Hess Corp., 2017 ND 269, 903 N.W.2d 712 (2017); Gorzeman v. Thompson, 162 Or. App. 84, 986 P.2d 29 (1999); Richart v. Jackson, 171 Vt. 94, 758 A.2d 319 (2000). Massachusetts, in reliance on the "actual notice" language of its recording act, has virtually eliminated the doctrine of inquiry notice; see supra note 541.

[543] See Berge v. Fredericks, 95 Nev. 183, 591 P.2d 246 (1979).

[544] See 5 Tiffany, Real Property § 1284 (3d ed. 2017 update), arguing that inquiry notice is a species of actual, rather than constructive notice. The distinction is not of any great importance, and the cases are not entirely consistent, but it seems more sensible to regard all legally-imputed notice, including inquiry notice, as "constructive." When a trustee in bankruptcy acts under the "strong-arm" powers of Bankruptcy Code § 544, the trustee's actual knowledge is irrelevant, but she or he is bound by constructive and inquiry notice; see, e.g., In re Thulis, 474 B.R. 668 (Bankr. W.D. Wis. 2012).

[545] Massey v. Wynne, 302 Ark. 589, 791 S.W.2d 368 (1990); McDonald v. McGowan, 402 So.2d 1197 (Fla.App. 1981); Guthrie v. National Advertising Co., 556 N.E.2d 337 (Ind.App. 1990); Spickler v. Ginn, 2012 Me. 46, 40 A.3d 999 (2012); Hunt Trust Estate v. Kiker, 269 N.W.2d 377 (N.D. 1978).

[546] First Alabama Bank v. Key, 394 So.2d 67 (Ala.Civ.App. 1981); Swanson v. Swanson, 2011 ND 74, 796 N.W.2d 614 (2011). Cf. Levine v. Bradley Real Estate Trust, 457 N.W.2d 237 (Minn.App. 1990) (where easement claimant stated that an easement might be granted, but did not state that it actually existed, the statement did not give notice of the easement).

[547] First Alabama Bank v. Brooker, 418 So.2d 851 (Ala. 1982); Caruso v. Parkos, 262 Neb. 961, 637 N.W.2d 351 (2002); Chisholm v. Mid-Town Oil Co., 57 Tenn.App. 434, 419 S.W.2d 194 (1966); Pioneer Builders Co. of Nevada v. K D A Corp., 2012 UT 74, 292 P.3d 672 (2012) (appraisal report may have given actual notice). Cf. Durden v. Hilton Head Bank & Trust Co. N.A., 198 Ga.App. 232, 401 S.E.2d 539 (1990) (purchaser not held to notice of prior deed, even though his attorney had prepared it some months earlier for another client); First of America Bank v. Alt, 848 F.Supp. 1343 (W.D.Mich. 1993) (IRS not bound by actual knowledge of prior unrecorded mortgage).

[548] Metropolitan Nat. Bank v. Jemal, 2013 WL 5299489 (N.J. Super. Ct. App. Div. 2013) (unpublished) (cryptic notation on credit report did not give notice of prior unrecorded mortgage).

a further reasonable investigation under the doctrine of "inquiry notice," although the purchaser need not pursue rumors or ambiguous statements.[549]

Notice of possessors. A purchaser who buys property in the possession of someone other than the grantor will be held to constructive notice of the rights which an inquiry of the possessor would have disclosed.[550] Moreover, the inquiry must be a rather direct one; a mere casual conversation with the possessor may not be enough.[551] If the possessor is also a former record owner, about half the cases excuse the purchaser from making an inquiry, at least if the possessor has been there only for a relatively short time since the conveyance; the holdover's presence is supposedly explainable by the notion that the present owner has merely allowed the predecessor to remain on the land temporarily.[552] But since there are so many possible alternate explanations for the former owner's continued possession, the more sensible rule is to require an inquiry in all cases.[553]

It seems simple to expect the purchaser to inquire of the possessor, but in practice several tricky problems arise. They stem mainly from the rule that no inquiry is necessary if the seller personally is in possession, since such possession is consistent with the record title and an inquiry would presumably be redundant.[554] Suppose there are two or more people in possession, and one of them is the record owner. Is a prospective purchaser bound to inquire of the other possessors, or can it simply be assumed that they are licensees of the record owner who will have to vacate the property when the sale is completed? The latter inference is a particularly natural one when all of the possessors are members of the same family; if a mother and father contract to sell their house, it hardly seems necessary to make an inquiry of their children! The bulk of the cases agree, holding that no inquiry need be made of those who possess along with

[549] Kabayan v. Yepremian, 116 F.3d 1295 (9th Cir. 1997); Friendship Manor, Inc. v. Greiman, 244 N.J.Super. 104, 581 A.2d 893 (1990).

[550] In re Fibison, 474 B.R. 864 (Bankr. W.D. Wis. 2011); American Nat'l Bank v. Vinson, 273 Ill.App.3d 541, 210 Ill.Dec. 426, 653 N.E.2d 13 (Ill.App. 1995); Claflin v. Commercial State Bank, 487 N.W.2d 242 (Minn.App. 1992); Willett v. Centerre Bank, 792 S.W.2d 916 (Mo.App. 1990); Williston Co-op. Credit Union v. Fossum, 459 N.W.2d 548 (N.D. 1990); Grose v. Sauvageau, 942 P.2d 398 (Wyo. 1997). USLTA § 3–202 follows the rule. The rights to be inquired about are those of the possessor, and there is no duty to inquire about unrecorded mortgages on the property; see In re Thulis, 474 B.R. 668 (Bankr. W.D.Wis. 2012).

[551] See, e.g., Webb v. Stewart, 255 Or. 523, 469 P.2d 609 (1970), in which the plaintiff, a prior record owner, remained in possession. The purchaser's agent remarked to him, "Well, it looks like you've sold your house." Plaintiff confirmed that he had done so, but was permitted by the court to show that no proper delivery of the deed had ever occurred. The agent's inquiry was held insufficient. See also Willis v. Stager, 257 Or. 608, 481 P.2d 78 (1971). On the other hand, there is no need to inquire of the possessor about the rights of other persons to whom the possessor might have made conveyances; see Mellon National Mortgage Co. v. Jones, 54 Ohio App.2d 45, 374 N.E.2d 666 (1977).

[552] Buhecker v. R.B. Petersen & Sons Const. Co., Inc., 112 Nev. 1498, 929 P.2d 937 (Nev. 1996); Vann v. Whitlock, 692 P.2d 68 (Okl.App. 1984); Raub v. General Income Sponsors of Iowa, Inc., 176 N.W.2d 216 (Iowa 1970); Annot., 105 A.L.R. 845 (1936); 4 Am.L.Prop. § 17.14 (1952). Cf. Martinez v. Affordable Hous. Network, Inc., 123 P.3d 1201 (Colo. 2005), holding subsequent purchaser to duty of inquiry of former owner still in possession.

[553] See Holleran v. Cole, 200 W.Va. 49, 488 S.E.2d 49 (W.Va. 1997); In re Weisman, 5 F.3d 417 (9th Cir. 1993); Perimeter Development Corp. v. Haynes, 234 Ga. 437, 216 S.E.2d 581 (1975); Webb v. Stewart, supra note 551; 5 Tiffany, Real Property § 1292 (3d ed. 2017 update).

[554] In re Henshaw, 585 B.R. 605 (D. Haw. 2018); Kane v. Huntley Financial, 146 Cal. App.3d 1092, 194 Cal.Rtpr. 880 (1983); Valley National Bank v. Avco Development Co., 14 Ariz.App. 56, 480 P.2d 671 (1971). See 4 Am.L.Prop. § 17.14 (1952).

the record owner;[555] but one finds occasional contrary decisions.[556] Some cases only eliminate the need to inquire of other possessors if the record owner appears to be "in control" and the others "subordinate;"[557] but this seems a slender thread on which to hang a purchaser's title.

A similar problem is raised by the possession of a tenant of the record owner. If the lease is recorded or the purchaser is given a copy of it, he or she might assume that there is no need for a further inquiry of the tenant. Such an assumption can be dangerous, for the great majority of the cases hold the purchaser to inquiry notice of any option to purchase, lease extension, or other rights of the tenant even if they were negotiated after the original lease was signed and do not appear in it.[558] Thus, one cannot safely fail to inquire of the tenant even though her or his possession is "consistent with the record." A careful purchaser will insist that all tenants execute "estoppel statements" which set out the status of their leases in detail with the understanding that the purchaser is relying on them.

What sort of possession will place a purchaser on inquiry notice? The courts commonly say it must be visible, open, exclusive, and unambiguous.[559] Yet one can find cases imputing notice from very limited and ambiguous acts of possession. In Miller v. Green[560] a landlord sold farm land to his tenant. The tenant, who failed to record, did not reside on the land, and his only acts there were to plow two of a total of 63 acres and to have his father haul a number of loads of manure onto the land. The Wisconsin Supreme Court thought this sufficient to give notice to a subsequent purchaser who was in fact entirely unaware of this limited activity. A more sensible case is Wineberg v. Moore,[561] in which the prior purchaser of the property, which consisted of 880 acres of timber land with a residential cabin, did not reside there. However, there were personal possessions of his in the cabin, and he had posted several "no trespassing" signs which

---

[555] See Kane v. Huntley Financial, id.; Yancey v. Harris, 234 Ga. 320, 216 S.E.2d 83 (1975) (dictum); Tompkins Cty. Tr. Co. v. Talandis, 261 A.D.2d 808, 690 N.Y.S.2d 330 (1999); Triangle Supply Co. v. Fletcher, 408 S.W.2d 765 (Tex.Civ.App.1966). See 4 Am.L.Prop. § 17.13 (1952).

[556] J.C. Else Coal Co. v. Miller and Banker, 45 Ill.App.2d 475, 196 N.E.2d 233 (1964).

[557] See 5 Tiffany, Real Property § 1290 (3d ed. 2017 update).

[558] Janss v. Pearman, 863 S.W.2d 643 (Mo.App. 1993); Dahari v. Villafana, 2016 WL 5816207 (N.Y. Sup. Ct. 2016) (unreported); Grosskopf Oil, Inc. v. Winter, 156 Wis.2d 575, 457 N.W.2d 514 (1990). See Annots., 37 A.L.R.2d 1112 (1953); 74 A.L.R. 350 (1931); 4 Am.L.Prop. § 17.12 n. 12. There is a small minority view; see Gates Rubber Co. v. Ulman, 214 Cal.App.3d 356, 262 Cal.Rptr. 630 (1989); Stumph v. Church, 740 P.2d 820 (Utah App. 1987); Scott v. Woolard, 12 Wn.App. 109, 529 P.2d 30 (1974). In a similar vein, the possession of a tenant will give notice of the landlord's interest even if it is not of record, at least if an inquiry of the tenant would have disclosed it in fact; see In re Fletcher Oil Co., 124 B.R. 501 (Bkrtcy. E.D.Mich. 1990) (Michigan law). Cf. Madison v. Gordon, 39 S.W.3d 604 (Tex. 2001) (possession as apparent tenant in four-plex apartment building did not give constructive notice of possessor's claim of ownership of building because possession was not exclusive). Compare Mazza v. Realty Quest Brokerage Corp., 185 Misc. 2d 162, 712 N.Y.S.2d 288 (Civ. Ct. 2000) (possession of apparent tenant in two-family house gave constructive notice).

[559] Lamb v. Lamb, 569 N.E.2d 992 (Ind. App.1991) (clearing of underbrush does not impart constructive notice of contract purchaser's claim); Ames v. Brooks, 179 Kan. 590, 297 P.2d 195 (1956); Pioneer Builders Co. of Nevada v. K D A Corp., 2012 UT 74, 292 P.3d 672 (2012) (observation of recreational vehicles on some sites on the property did not give constructive notice of unrecorded leases on other sites).

[560] 264 Wis. 159, 58 N.W.2d 704 (1953). Compare Bradford v. Kimbrough, 485 So.2d 1114 (Ala. 1986), in which the jury found that farming and bulldozing operations by prior claimant were insufficient to impart constructive notice, with White v. Boggs, 455 So.2d 820 (Ala. 1984), in which maintaining a grove of trees on the land and using it as a driveway were found sufficient.

[561] 194 F.Supp. 12 (N.D.Cal. 1961); see also Foster v. Piasecki, 259 A.D.2d 804, 686 N.Y.S.2d 184 (App.Div. 1999). Cf. Nussbaumer v. Fetrow, 556 N.W.2d 595 (Minn.App. 1996) (house under construction and "for sale signs" gave no notice of owner's identity).

gave his name and address. The court found these acts sufficient to give notice to a later purchaser, although it conceded that they did not "present the strongest case possible."

Even if there is no human occupancy of the land, structures on it may be enough to give notice. The signs in Wineberg v. Moore furnish one illustration. Similarly, a prospective purchaser who observes a driveway running across the subject property to a neighboring house should inquire of the neighbor about whether an easement is claimed.[562] A structure on adjacent land which encroaches on the subject property also gives notice of the adjoining owner's rights.[563] But many types of improvements, unlike those just mentioned, furnish no clue as to the identity of the person who erected them, and thus provide no starting point for an inquiry; this is generally so of buildings, growing crops, and the like. Cases can be found which impute constructive notice on such facts,[564] but they are analytically unsound.[565]

Notice from public records. The third principal source of notice is that given by the records themselves.[566] At first blush this statement seems irrelevant; if the earlier conveyance is recorded, a subsequent purchaser cannot take priority over it, whether he or she has notice of it or not; that is a fundamental premise of all recording acts.[567] But the idea that the records give constructive notice is nonetheless important, for a recorded document in the chain of title to the land may describe or make reference to another, unrecorded one, and thus give notice of the latter.[568] This is a highly useful concept in

---

[562] Gill Grain Co. v. Poos, 707 S.W.2d 434 (Mo.App.1986); Dana Point Condominium Ass'n, Inc. v. Keystone Service Co., 141 Ill.App.3d 916, 96 Ill.Dec. 249, 491 N.E.2d 63 (1986); Otero v. Pacheco, 94 N.M. 524, 612 P.2d 1335 (App.1980), cert. denied 94 N.M. 674, 615 P.2d 991 (1980); Fenley Farms, Inc. v. Clark, 404 N.E.2d 1164 (Ind. App.1980).

[563] Nikas v. United Construction Co., 34 Tenn.App. 435, 239 S.W.2d 41 (1950) (encroachment by party wall). Compare Levien v. Fiala, 79 Wn.App. 294, 902 P.2d 170 (1995) (encroachment of 5-foot × 70-foot triangle by fence was too slight and did not give notice of encroacher's claim) with Bank of Mississippi v. Hollingsworth, 609 So.2d 422 (Miss. 1992) (fence enclosing 18-acre tract gave notice of encroacher's claim).

[564] See Vandehey Development Co. v. Suarez, 108 Or.App. 154, 814 P.2d 1094 (1991), review denied 312 Or. 235, 819 P.2d 731 (1991) (prior grantees camped on land from time to time, improved roof of building on it, cut the grass, and placed lawn furniture on it; constructive notice found); Harker v. Cowie, 42 S.D. 159, 173 N.W. 722 (1919) (growing crops); Carnes v. Whitfield, 352 Ill. 384, 185 N.E. 819 (1933).

[565] See Bearden v. John Hancock Mut. Life Ins. Co., 708 F.Supp. 1196 (D.Kan. 1987); W.I.L.D. W.A.T.E.R.S., Ltd. v. Martinez, 152 A.D.2d 799, 543 N.Y.S.2d 579 (1989); Burnex Oil Co. v. Floyd, 106 Ill. App.2d 16, 245 N.E.2d 539 (1969), appeal after remand 4 Ill.App.3d 627, 281 N.E.2d 705 (1971); 4 Am.L.Prop. § 17.15 (1952).

[566] Union Cty., Ill. v. MERSCORP, Inc., 735 F.3d 730 (7th Cir. 2013); Deutsche Bank Nat'l Tr. Co. v. Pyle, 13 Cal. App. 5th 513, 220 Cal. Rptr. 3d 691 (Ct. App. 2017), Compare In re El-Erian, 512 B.R. 391 (Bankr. D.D.C. 2014) and In re Ibach, 399 B.R. 61 (Bankr. D. Minn. 2008) (prior recorded instrument gave constructive notice despite defective legal description) with In re Couillard, 486 B.R. 481 (Bankr. W.D. Wis. 2012) (prior recorded deed with defective legal description gave no constructive notice) and Keybank Nat. Ass'n v. NBD Bank, 699 N.E.2d 322 (Ind. Ct. App. 1998) (same).

[567] In a few states, a "notice of interest" which is not a conveyance of any interest in land may be recorded and will impart constructive notice; see, e.g., Morris v. Off-Piste Capital LLC, 2018 UT App 7, 418 P.3d 66 (2018).

[568] In re Colon, 563 F.3d 1171 (10th Cir. 2009); Municipal Trust & Sav. Bank v. United States, 114 F.3d 99 (7th Cir. 1997); In re Jones, 580 B.R. 916 (Bankr. M.D. Ga. 2017); O'Connell v. JPMorgan Chase Bank Nat. Ass'n, 2012 WL 6151972 (E.D.N.Y. 2012) (unpublished) (recorded second mortgage made reference to unrecorded first mortgage); AHF-BAY Fund, LLC v. City of Largo, 227 So. 3d 740 (Fla. Dist. Ct. App. 2017); Kalange v. Rencher, 136 Idaho 192, 30 P.3d 970 (2001); Camino Real Enterprises, Inc. v. Ortega, 107 N.M. 387, 758 P.2d 801 (1988); Gerow v. Sinay, 28 Misc. 3d 990, 905 N.Y.S.2d 827 (Sup. Ct. 2010); Ford v. Baska, 2017-Ohio-4424, 93 N.E.3d 195 (2017); Waggoner v. Morrow, 932 S.W.2d 627 (Tex. App. 1996). The scope of the "chain of title" is discussed in § 11.11 infra. If the instrument containing the reference is itself not entitled to be recorded or is defectively acknowledged, most cases hold that it gives no constructive notice of its contents; see § 11.9 notes 506–508 supra and accompanying text. Cf. Connecticut Nat'l Bank v. Lorenzato, 221 Conn. 77, 602 A.2d 959 (Conn. 1992) (recorded but unsigned mortgage gives constructive notice); In re Barnacle, 623

cases in which the parties do not want to record the full text of the granting instrument. A "short form" or "memorandum" of the instrument, typically only a page or two, can be recorded, identifying the parties and describing the land, but omitting the details of the transaction.[569] This serves the parties' desire for privacy and saves on recording costs.

However, the courts have had considerable difficulty in dealing with broad and ambiguous references in recorded documents. Suppose a prior deed recites that title is conveyed "subject to an easement in favor of Mary Jones." Unfortunately the easement's location is not given, its scope is not indicated, and a title searcher may have no idea which Mary Jones is involved or where she may be found. If a court imputes inquiry notice on such facts, the investigative burden it imposes can be a very heavy one. The test should be whether a reasonable inquiry has been made.[570] If the reference is quite indefinite, it may provide no starting point for an investigation at all, and hence it may be reasonable to make none. In a few states statutes have been enacted to limit the searcher's duty of inquiry to cases in which the prior conveyance referred to is itself recorded.[571] But in all cases, the lesson of this doctrine is that a searcher must read *in full* all recorded documents in the chain of title, in order to discover any information they contain about other documents or rights outside the recorded chain.

The concept of constructive notice from public records operates to expand the scope of title searches, for many types of records besides those in the recorder's office are often deemed to give notice. Property tax, special assessment, and court records are commonly included, as are various sorts of liens or claims of local government agencies.[572] The common law doctrine of lis pendens has a similar effect. It holds that the commencement of any judicial action which may affect a land title, and in which the land is specifically described, acts as constructive notice of the action's pendency, so that a purchaser who buys thereafter will be bound by the court's decree as fully as the original parties.[573] In

---

A.2d 445 (R.I. 1993). See also Statler Mfg., Inc. v. Brown, 691 S.W.2d 445 (Mo.App. 1985) (building contractor had no reason to search the records, and hence no constructive notice of their contents).

[569] See, e.g., Winn-Dixie Stores, Inc. v. Big Lots Stores, Inc., 886 F.Supp.2d 1326 (S.D. Fla. 2012), aff'd in part, rev'd in part sub nom. Winn-Dixie Stores, Inc. v. Dolgencorp, LLC, 746 F.3d 1008 (11th Cir. 2014).

[570] See Smith v. F.D.I.C., 61 F.3d 1552 (11th Cir. 1995); Slachter v. Swanson, 826 So. 2d 1012 (Fla. Dist. Ct. App. 2001); Deljoo v. SunTrust Mortg., Inc., 284 Ga. 438, 668 S.E.2d 245 (2008); Miller v. Alexander, 13 Kan.App.2d 543, 775 P.2d 198 (1989). Cf. Camp Clearwater, Inc. v. Plock, 52 N.J.Super. 583, 146 A.2d 527 (1958), affirmed 59 N.J.Super. 1, 157 A.2d 15 (1959); Fertitta v. Bay Shore Development Corp., 252 Md. 393, 250 A.2d 69 (1969); Chadwell v. Wojtaszek, 2004 WL 950056 (Mich. Ct. App. 2004) (unpublished) (reference to "seller's existing driveway," with no indication of easement's location, gave no constructive notice).

[571] See Colo.Rev.Stat.1973, § 38–35–108, construed in Swofford v. Colorado National Bank, 628 P.2d 184 (Colo.App. 1981); Mass.Gen.Laws Ann. c. 184, § 25; New Jersey Stat.Ann. 46:22–2; N.Y.-McKinney's Real Property Law § 291–e, applied in L.C. Stroh & Sons, Inc. v. Batavia Homes & Development Corp., 17 A.D.2d 385, 234 N.Y.S.2d 401 (1962). The Uniform Simplification of Land Transfers Act takes an additional step, providing that a reference to another instrument gives no notice unless the latter is recorded and the reference includes its "record location", such as a book and page number in the official records; see USLTA § 3–207. See generally L. Simes and C. Taylor, The Improvement of Conveyancing by Legislation 101–06 (1960).

[572] See § 11.9 note 500 supra. But see Noble Mortg. & Investments, LLC v. D & M Vision Investments, LLC, 340 S.W.3d 65 (Tex. App. 2011) (judgment lien confers no constructive notice until recorded in real estate records system).

[573] See In re Land, 980 F.2d 601 (9th Cir. 1992); Chrysler Corp. v. Fedders Corp., 670 F.2d 1316 (3d Cir. 1982); Tikhomirov v. Bank of New York Mellon, 223 So. 3d 1112 (Fla. Dist. Ct. App. 2017); Partlow v. Clark, 295 Or. 778, 671 P.2d 103 (1983); Fishman v. Murphy ex rel. Estate of Urban, 433 Md. 534, 72 A.3d 185 (2013); Jones v. Jones, 249 Miss. 322, 161 So.2d 640 (1964); Nelson, Whitman, Burkhart & Freyermuth, Real Estate Finance Law § 7.13 (6th ed. 2014); White, Lis Pendens in the District of Columbia: A Need for Codification, 36 Cath. U.L.Rev. 703 (1987); Janzen, Texas Statutory Notice of Lis Pendens: A Deprivation of Property Interest Without Due Process, 19 St. Mary's L.J. 377 (1987); Notes, 47 Harv.L.Rev. 1023 (1934); 25 Cal.L.Rev. 480

some states statutes provide for recordation of notices of lis pendens in the land records system,[574] but most of these statutes are not exclusive and leave some room for the operation of the doctrine even when no notice is recorded.[575] The result is that a searcher must check the relevant court dockets as a part of every title examination.

Quitclaim deeds. There are a number of cases holding that one who takes by quitclaim deed cannot be a bona fide purchaser. The theory seems to be that a grantor who refuses to give any covenants of title in effect admits, or at least creates a strong suspicion, that the title is defective.[576] The clear majority of modern cases reject this rule,[577] and for good reason. There are many factors other than a questionable title which may cause sellers to use quitclaims; indeed, in some areas of the nation they are the typical mode of transfer. Moreover, the fact that a quitclaim deed is employed provides no specific information about earlier title defects which the purchaser can investigate. Hence, to say that it is constructive notice begs the question: notice of what, precisely? There is no sound basis for denying the protection of the recording acts to purchasers who take by quitclaim.

Muniments of title. Obviously one acquiring an interest in land is held to have notice of the contents of all of the documents in the land parcel's recorded chain of title. Perhaps surprisingly, it is also widely held that one has notice of matters recited in the documents in one's own chain of title even if they are *not* recorded. The basis of this rule is simply that purchasers can reasonably be expected to, and ordinarily do, examine their own muniments of title.[578] A more extreme and debatable position is represented by several cases holding that a subsequent purchaser gets no protection from the recording acts if there are earlier links in his or her own chain of title that are unrecorded.[579] Under a

---

(1937). But see 139 Lefferts, LLC v. Melendez, 156 A.D.3d 666, 67 N.Y.S.3d 240 (N.Y. App. Div. 2017) (lis pendens is not a substitute for actual recording of one's contract or conveyance).

[574] See, e.g., Sommers for Alabama & Dunlavy, Ltd. v. Sandcastle Homes, Inc., 521 S.W.3d 749 (Tex. 2017); Belleville State Bank v. Steele, 117 Wis. 2d 563, 345 N.W.2d 405 (1984).

[575] Belleville State Bank v. Steele, id.; Note, Statutory Lis Pendens, 20 Iowa L.Rev. 476 (1934); West's Ann.Cal.Code Civ.Proc. § 409. A few statutes require recordation of a notice in the land records in all cases; see West's Fla.Stat.Ann. § 48.23; Mich.Comp.Laws Ann. § 600.2701; Virginia Code 1950, §§ 8.01–268, 8.01–269.

[576] See Polhemus v. Cobb, 653 So.2d 964 (Ala. 1995), opinion after remand 671 So.2d 1379 (Ala. 1995); Pankins v. Jackson, 891 S.W.2d 845 (Mo.App. 1995); Bright v. Johnson, 302 S.W.3d 483 (Tex. App. 2009). A few decisions deny the present purchaser BFP status when there is a quitclaim anywhere in the chain of title, a truly bizarre position; see Schwalm v. Deanhardt, 21 Kan.App.2d 667, 906 P.2d 167 (Kan.App. 1995). There is also considerable debate as to exactly what language will take the deed out of the quitclaim classification. See 4 Am.L.Prop. § 17.16 (1952); 5 Tiffany, Real Property § 1277 (3d ed. 2017 update). There is a little authority for a similar rule which would deny BFP status to one who purchases for a grossly inadequate price; see Jordan v. Warnke, 205 Cal.App.2d 621, 23 Cal.Rptr. 300 (1962); Asisten v. Underwood, 183 Cal. App.2d 304, 7 Cal.Rptr. 84 (1960). See also Jenner v. Bloomington Cellular Servs., Inc., 77 N.E.3d 1232 (Ind. Ct. App. 2017) (buyer at tax sale cannot be BFP).

[577] Miller v. Hennen, 438 N.W.2d 366 (Minn. 1989); Palamarg Realty Co. v. Rehac, 80 N.J. 446, 404 A.2d 21 (1979); Sabo v. Horvath, 559 P.2d 1038 (Alaska 1976). See Note, 28 Ore.L.Rev. 258 (1949); Annot., 162 A.L.R. 556 (1946). A few states have adopted the majority rule by statute; see, e.g., Minn.Stat.Ann. § 507.34. USLTA § 3–203(c) specifically permits one who takes a quitclaim to be a purchaser for value, and § 1–201(31)(iv) defines "value" to include any consideration sufficient to support a simple contract.

[578] In re Adams, 583 B.R. 541 (Bankr. N.D. Ga. 2018); In re TMH Corp., 62 B.R. 932 (Bkrtcy. S.D.N.Y. 1986) (tenant held to knowledge of landlord's muniments); Burlington Northern, Inc. v. Hall, 322 N.W.2d 233 (N.D. 1982); Hughes v. North Carolina State Highway Commission, 275 N.C. 121, 165 S.E.2d 321 (1969); 2327 Manana LLC v. Summit Elec. Supply Co., 316 S.W.3d 241 (Tex. App. 2010). See 5 Tiffany, Real Property § 1293 nn. 63–64 (3d ed. 2017 update).

[579] Zimmer v. Sundell, 237 Wis. 270, 296 N.W. 589 (1941), noted 1942 Wis.L.Rev. 127; Annot., 133 A.L.R. 886 (1941); Miller v. Hennen, 438 N.W.2d 366 (Minn. 1989). For the purchaser to lose protection, the

notice-race statute, this position can be supported (although rather weakly) by arguing that to "record first", one must record not only one's own deed but also those of one's predecessors in title.[580] In a sense, it is both illogical and impractical to treat a purchaser whose predecessor is unrecorded as lacking bona fide purchaser status; after all, the presence of unrecorded links in one's title chain gives one no indication that there are also prior adverse conveyances and provides no starting point for an inquiry into such conveyances. On the other hand, the rule stated provides a strong incentive to make the public records complete.[581] Perhaps the most extreme illustration of this sort of reasoning is found in Messersmith v. Smith,[582] in which a recorded deed in the purchaser's chain of title had been acknowledged by its grantor over the telephone rather than by personal appearance. The court held that since this acknowledgement was improper, the deed should be deemed unrecorded. This deprived the purchaser of BFP status and subordinated him to the rights of a claimant under an earlier, unrecorded, and entirely unrelated adverse deed made by a predecessor in title. The case is doubly objectionable, since the purchaser had neither a way of detecting the faulty acknowledgement nor, even if he had known of it, of determining from it that there was a prior unrecorded adverse deed.[583]

The shelter principle. Once a bona fide purchaser has perfected title by operation of the recording acts, he or she can pass that perfected status along to a chain of future grantees even if they do not qualify as BFPs.[584] This "shelter" principle means that even one who has actual knowledge of an adverse conveyance can have, in an indirect sense, the protection of the recording acts. If this principle were not followed, the results could be disastrous. Imagine a case in which, after a BFP bought land, information about a prior adverse conveyance was widely disseminated in the press. The BFP would own the land in theory, but as a practical matter it would be unmarketable because so few other BFP's would exist to purchase it. Thus the shelter principle is essential to protect the BFP's market. It is not applied to a former non-BFP owner who reacquires the land after

---

unrecorded deed must be in the portion of the title chain which is between the purchaser and the most recent grantor who is common to the present purchaser and the adverse claimant.

[580] 4 Am.L.Prop. § 17.10 n. 31. Cf. Quinn v. Johnson, 117 Minn. 378, 135 N.W. 1000 (1912), in which the court seemed to place emphasis on the notice-race nature of the statute; but the purchasers in fact recorded the previously-unrecorded deed in their chain at the same time they recorded their own deed, and the court found them fully qualified for protection under the act.

[581] See Note, 1942 Wis.L.Rev. 127. It is fairly common for courts to hold that if a recorded document has a defective acknowledgment, it confers no constructive notice; see In re BowlNebraska, L.L.C., 447 B.R. 597 (B.A.P. 8th Cir. 2010) (Nebraska law); In re Trujillo, 378 B.R. 526 (B.A.P. 6th Cir. 2007) (Kentucky law); In re Stewart, 422 B.R. 185 (Bankr. W.D. Ark. 2009); In re Nowak, 414 B.R. 269 (Bankr. S.D. Ohio 2009); In re Shannon, 343 B.R. 585 (Bankr. E.D. Ky. 2006); Bank of Am., N.A. v. Casey, 474 Mass. 556, 52 N.E.3d 1030 (2016). Cf. In re Androes, 382 B.R. 805 (Bankr. D. Kan. 2008) (if acknowledgment defect is latent and not apparent on face of document, it will confer constructive notice).

[582] 60 N.W.2d 276 (N.D.1953). In *Messersmith,* as in *Zimmer,* the adverse claimant was prior, not subsequent, to the holder under the defectively-recorded chain. Thus, standard chain-of-title reasoning is in no sense served by the decision; Cf. § 11.11 infra at notes 601–608.

[583] Moreover, the decision does not serve the objective, mentioned above, of giving the purchaser an incentive to make the records more complete; the purchaser had no way of knowing that they were "incomplete," and indeed they were only in the most narrow and technical sense. See generally Maxwell, The Hidden Defect in Acknowledgment and Title Security, 2 U.C.L.A.L.Rev. 83 (1954). USLTA § 2–301(b) entirely does away with the requirement for an acknowledgment.

[584] Strekal v. Espe, 114 P.3d 67 (Colo. App. 2004); Hoggarth v. Somsen, 496 N.W.2d 35 (N.D.1993); Corey v. United Savings Bank, Mutual, 52 Or.App. 263, 628 P.2d 739 (1981); Hendricks v. Lake, 12 Wn.App. 15, 528 P.2d 491 (1974). See generally 1 Patton & Palomar, Land Titles § 13 (3d ed. 2017 update).

it has passed through the hands of a BFP, for to do so would permit the former owner to "cleanse" the title unjustly.[585]

Timing of notice. The discussion above assumes that the purchaser either has or does not have notice of a prior adverse conveyance. But buying land is a process which may occur over a span of time; the buyer enters into a contract of purchase, pays the price (perhaps in installments), receives a deed, and records it. If he or she receives notice at some point in this process, will it vitiate the protection of the recording acts? It seems clearly established that at a minimum the buyer, to be protected, must make payment before receiving notice.[586] Some cases go farther and insist on receipt of a conveyance as well,[587] and a few notice-race jurisdictions even require that it be recorded before notice is received.[588] The better view is to require only payment, since it is at that point that the buyer incurs an irrevocable detriment and thereby earns the act's protection. The buyer who gains notice prior to payment can simply assert the adverse conveyance as a defense to the contract of sale and refuse to pay.[589]

The problem is more complex when the land is being purchased on a long-term installment contract. Suppose the owner deeds the land to John, who fails to record, and then purports to sell it to Mary on an installment contract calling for payments of $1,000 per year for 20 years. Assume that Mary examines title when the contract is signed, but discovers no title defects. She then makes a down payment, records the contract, and takes possession. After she has made regular installment payments for ten years, John, who holds the prior adverse conveyance, records it. Does she have constructive notice from this recording? To so hold would in effect compel her to re-examine the records before making each payment—an "intolerable burden."[590] The great majority of the cases would continue her protection unless she received actual notice.[591]

[585] Chergosky v. Crosstown Bell, Inc., 463 N.W.2d 522 (Minn. 1990); Walker v. Wilson, 469 So.2d 580 (Ala. 1985); Murray v. Johnson, 222 Ga. 788, 152 S.E.2d 739 (1966). The shelter principle is also said to be inapplicable to a grantee who has himself been guilty of a violation of a trust or duty with respect to the property; see Sun Valley Land & Minerals, Inc. v. Burt, 123 Idaho 862, 853 P.2d 607 (Ct. App. 1993).

[586] See Sams v. McCaskill, 282 S.C. 481, 319 S.E.2d 344 (Ct. App. 1984); Doane Agricultural Service, Inc. v. Neelyville Grain Co., Inc., 516 S.W.2d 788 (Mo.App. 1974); Black River Associates, Inc. v. Koehler, 126 Vt. 394, 233 A.2d 175 (1967); Annot., 109 A.L.R. 163 (1937). See also Lewis v. Superior Court, 30 Cal.App.4th 1850, 37 Cal. Rptr.2d 63 (1994).

[587] Mills v. Damson Oil Corp., 686 F.2d 1096 (5th Cir. 1982) (Mississippi law); South Carolina Tax Commission v. Belk, 266 S.C. 539, 225 S.E.2d 177 (1976). This is evidently the approach of USLTA § 3–202(a)(3), which protects the purchaser only if he had no knowledge of the adverse claim "at the time his interest was created."

[588] See 1 Patton and Palomar, Land Titles § 11 n. 22 (3d ed. 2017 update). This view can be reached as a construction of the "who records first" language in the typical notice-race statute, which arguably implies that recording is an integral part of the behavior which must be completed while lacking notice. It is unlikely that any pure "notice" jurisdiction would take this view; see, e.g., Hemingway v. Shatney, 152 Vt. 600, 568 A.2d 394 (1989), rejecting it under a "notice" statute.

[589] See 5 Tiffany, Real Property § 1304 (3d ed. 2017 update); Goldstein v. Gold, 106 A.D.2d 100, 483 N.Y.S.2d 375 (1984), affirmed 66 N.Y.2d 624, 495 N.Y.S.2d 32, 485 N.E.2d 239 (1985).

[590] The phrase is from J. Cribbet, Property 287 n. 67 (2d ed. 1975). See also Lown v. Nichols Plumbing and Heating, Inc., 634 P.2d 554 (Alaska 1981) (Rabinowitz, C.J., dissenting: "unduly burdensome"). Note, however, that the purchaser may still have to examine the title before the first payment is made, even if he or she previously received a conveyance and examined the title at that time; see note 586 supra.

[591] Henson v. Wagner, 642 S.W.2d 357 (Mo.App. 1982); Giorgi v. Pioneer Title Insurance Co., 85 Nev. 319, 454 P.2d 104 (1969); Dame v. Mileski, 80 Wyo. 156, 340 P.2d 205 (1959); Lowden v. Wilson, 233 Ill. 340, 84 N.E. 245 (1908). The principal contrary case, widely criticized, is Alexander v. Andrews, 135 W.Va. 403, 64 S.E.2d 487 (1951).

But actual notice is quite possible; John may visit Mary, exhibit his conveyance, and insist that he owns the land. If this occurs, she would plainly be foolish to make any further payments to her (presumably crooked) grantor.[592] Equally plainly, she ought to be protected to the extent of the payments she has already made while in good faith, and the cases uniformly do so. There are at least three methods that courts have developed to achieve this *pro tanto* protection.[593] The most common is to award the land to the prior claimant, but to give the contract purchaser a right to recover the payments she has made with interest, usually with a lien on the land to assist in that recovery.[594] A second approach is to give the contract purchaser a fractional interest as a tenant in common based on the portion of the total price which she has paid prior to receiving notice; the adverse claimant would hold the remaining fractional share.[595] The third method is to permit the contract buyer to complete the purchase simply by paying the remaining installments to the adverse claimant.[596] Only this method gives the purchaser the full benefit of her bargain, certainly a desirable objective in light of her innocence. Courts exercise considerable latitude in these cases, taking into account the relative equities of the parties and the value of the property. If the contract purchaser has made improvements on the land, she will generally be compensated for them.[597]

§ 11.11   THE RECORDING SYSTEM—INDEXES, SEARCH METHODS, AND CHAIN OF TITLE

The previous discussion has indicated that a purchaser of land has constructive notice of matters in the public records only if they are in the chain of title. Indeed, instruments which are recorded but are outside the chain of title may be treated as if they were not recorded at all. The term "chain of title" is a shorthand way of describing the collection of documents which one can find by the use of the ordinary techniques of title search. Hence, it can be understood only through comprehension of the way the records are indexed and searched.

Since the typical recorder's office may contain thousands of volumes and millions of documents, some form of index is essential so that searchers can locate instruments that affect the land whose title is being searched. Thus the office contains two types of volumes: index books and books which hold the actual copies of the legal instruments. The latter are sometimes called "deed books," even though they include other types of

---

[592]   See Black River Associates, Inc. v. Koehler, 126 Vt. 394, 233 A.2d 175 (1967). The New York recording statute, unusual in this respect, protects the purchaser for payments made both before and after notice if he or she was in good faith at the time of contracting; see N.Y.-McKinney's Real Prop.Law § 294, subd. 3; La Marche v. Rosenblum, 82 Misc.2d 1046, 371 N.Y.S.2d 843 (1975), affirmed 50 A.D.2d 636, 374 N.Y.S.2d 443 (1975).

[593]   See generally Perry v. O'Donnell, 749 F.2d 1346 (9th Cir. 1984); Daniels v. Anderson, 162 Ill.2d 47, 204 Ill.Dec. 666, 642 N.E.2d 128 (Ill. 1994); Tomlinson v. Clarke, 60 Wn. App. 344, 803 P.2d 828 (1991); Annot., 109 A.L.R. 163 (1937). A lessee is protected in the same general way as a contract purchaser—that is, only to the extent of rental payments made prior to receipt of notice. See Egbert v. Duck, 239 Iowa 646, 32 N.W.2d 404 (1948). Hence a long-term lease may be terminated prematurely, with great hardship to the lessee. See Johnson, Purpose and Scope of Recording Statutes, 47 Iowa L.Rev. 231, 235 (1962).

[594]   In a similar context, see Hocking v. Hocking, 137 Ill.App.3d 159, 91 Ill.Dec. 847, 484 N.E.2d 406 (1985) (installment contract purchaser held entitled to reimbursement of portion of the price he paid before gaining notice that the land was subject to a resulting trust); Scult v. Bergen Valley Builders, Inc., 76 N.J.Super. 124, 183 A.2d 865 (1962), affirmed 82 N.J.Super. 378, 197 A.2d 704 (1964).

[595]   It is hard to find any modern authority which actually applies this approach.

[596]   Sparks v. Taylor, 99 Tex. 411, 90 S.W. 485 (1906); Green v. Green, 41 Kan. 472, 21 P. 586 (1889).

[597]   See Henry v. Phillips, 163 Cal. 135, 124 P. 837 (1912) (dictum); 5 Tiffany, Real Property § 1305 n.44 (3d ed. 2017 update).

documents, such as leases, mortgages, and releases in addition to deeds. We use the term "books" here, but many recording offices, particularly in more populous jurisdictions, have shifted to computer-based records, so that the "deed books" are actually files in an electronic data base and the index books are computerized indexes to those files.[598]

There are two dominant methods of indexing. The oldest and most common is based on the names of the parties to each instrument. Under this "name index" system, two separate alphabetical indexes are maintained: one by the names of the grantors or other persons against whom the document operates, and the other by the names of the grantees or other persons in whose favor it operates. A separate set of these indexes is typically constructed each year, and they may be consolidated periodically into index books covering, say, 5-year or 10-year time spans. A few counties employ computers to produce and regularly update a consolidated set of grantor and grantee indexes for the entire time covered by the records.

An alternative and far superior approach to indexing is the tract or parcel index, but it is available statewide in only a handful of states.[599] Here a separate page or set of pages in the index books is devoted to each tract of land, such as a quarter-quarter section, a specific block in a subdivision, or even an individual parcel of land. This page reflects the history of the tract's title from the time of the original conveyance from the sovereign. In jurisdictions where computerized recording has been implemented, tract indexing has become much more common.[600]

In both name and tract index systems, the index books do not contain copies of the actual documents. Instead, they merely give the names of the parties, the recording date, the book and page number of the deed book in which the full copy of each instrument is to be found, and sometimes a brief legal description of the land affected. The searcher must jot down the book and page number and must then pull down and open the relevant deed book (or in a computerized system, simply click on the record in the index) to read the instrument itself.

In a name index system the search procedure is generally as follows.[601] The searcher begins by looking for the name of the putative present owner in the grantee index, working backward from the present date. When it is found, the searcher notes the name of the corresponding grantor of that instrument, and then seeks his or her name in the grantee index. This process is repeated until the searcher has worked backward in time

---

[598] See text at notes 625–634 infra.

[599] States having tract indexes in all counties include Nebraska, North Dakota, Oklahoma, South Dakota, Utah, and Wyoming. States which permit tract indexing on a county option basis include Kansas, Ohio, Wisconsin and Minnesota. See In re Arnette, 584 B.R. 304 (Bankr. W.D. Wis. 2018) (even if document was not indexed in tract index, indexing in name index imparted constructive notice). New York City and Washington D.C. have "block index" systems. Some counties in other states may operate non-required tract indexes, but their information imparts no constructive notice; see In re Bruder, 207 B.R. 151 (N.D.Ill. 1997) (Illinois law). See generally Note, The Tract and Grantor-Grantee Indices, 47 Iowa L.Rev. 481 (1962). See Maggs, Land Records of the Uniform Simplification of Land Transfers Act, 1981 So.Ill.U.L.J. 491, 500–01.

[600] See text infra at notes 625–634.

[601] See generally Behringer & Altergott, Searching Title and Clearing Away What You Find, 4 Prac.Real Est.Law. 11 (No. 6, Nov. 1988); Berryhill, Title Examination in Virginia, 17 U.Rich.L.Rev. 229 (1983); Johnson, Title Examination in Massachusetts, reproduced as chapter 39, J. Casner & B. Leach, Cases & Text on Property (2d ed. 1969). In most jurisdictions, the doctrine of "idem sonans" requires the searcher to examine not only documents indexed under the precise name of the apparent owner, but also those indexed under similar-sounding names; Franklin Bank, N.A. v. Bowling, 74 P.3d 308 (Colo. 2003); In re Thibault, 518 B.R. 698 (Bankr. D. Mass. 2014). See also Bilden Properties, LLC v. Birin, 165 N.H. 253, 75 A.3d 1143 (2013) (title examiner held to search under trade name of owner entity as well as official name).

through a chain of successive conveyances extending back, in theory, to the sovereign, or in practice some predetermined number of years.[602] The second phase of the search is to look up the name of each of the prior owners, as discovered by the foregoing process, in the grantor index to determine whether any of them made an "adverse" conveyance—that is, one to a person outside the chain of title. In the third phase, the searcher must pull down the relevant deed books and read carefully each instrument which has been identified from both the grantee and grantor indexes, to determine that it is in regular order, is properly executed, and purports to transfer the land in question. Finally, the searcher must check whatever public records are maintained separately from the indexes to the deed books, such as court dockets and probate indexes, tax and assessment records, and the like.

A search in a jurisdiction using a tract index is much simpler, since all instruments affecting a given parcel will be indexed on a single page or a set of consecutive pages in the index book, or in a computerized system on a single screen or set of consecutive screens. It is easy to construct the chain of title and to identify potentially adverse conveyances merely by running one's eye down the appropriate column.[603] Of course, the instruments themselves must still be read and other relevant public records checked.

Whether a name or a tract index is used, the accuracy of the index is obviously crucial; an instrument which is copied into the deed books, but is unindexed or erroneously indexed as a result of carelessness by the recording personnel, is as impossible to find as a needle in a haystack. Should such a document be considered as "recorded" in litigation between its grantee and a later grantee from a common grantor who seeks the protection of the recording act? The cases are divided, and often turn on the specific language of the act. The majority regard mere copying of the instrument into the deed book as a sufficient recording to protect its proponent,[604] but many recent cases treat unindexed or misindexed instruments as unrecorded.[605] Both the earlier and later

---

[602] In many jurisdictions it is common to extend the search back only some fixed number of years, rather than all the way to a conveyance from the sovereign. Sixty years is a common standard; see In re Taneja, 427 B.R. 109 (Bankr. E.D. Va. 2010) (Virginia); Coe v. Hays, 105 Md.App. 778, 661 A.2d 220 (Md. 1995) (Maryland); Whitman, Transferring North Carolina Real Estate, Part I: How the Present System Functions, 49 N.C.L.Rev. 413, 425–26 (1971).

[603] This assumes, of course, that the document contains an intelligible description to guide the indexer. But see In re Rivera, 513 B.R. 742 (Bankr. D. Colo. 2014) (document with only a street address and no legal description was deemed validly recorded).

[604] See, e.g., Hanafy v. United States, 991 F.Supp. 794 (N.D.Tex. 1998); United States v. Lomas Mortgage, USA, Inc., 742 F.Supp. 936 (W.D.Va. 1990); In re Schmiel, 362 B.R. 802 (Bankr. E.D. Mich. 2007) (document deemed recorded if delivered to recorder in proper form with fee paid, even if not placed in entry book or indexed); Mayfield v. First City Bank of Fla., 95 So. 3d 398 (Fla. Dist. Ct. App. 2012) (document deemed recorded though removed from index); Leeds Bldg. Products, Inc. v. Weiblen, 267 Ga. 300, 477 S.E.2d 565 (Ga.1996), appeal after remand 225 Ga. App. 806, 488 S.E.2d 131 (1997); Miller v. Simonson, 140 Idaho 287, 92 P.3d 537 (2004); First Citizens Nat. Bank v. Sherwood, 583 Pa. 466, 879 A.2d 178 (2005); Annot., 63 A.L.R. 1057 (1929); Cross, The "Record Chain of Title" Hypocrisy, 57 Colum.L.Rev. 787, 790 n. 15 (1957); R. Bernhardt, Misindexed Documents, The Abstract, Fall 2006, at 16; 1 Patton and Palomar, Land Titles § 68 (3d ed. 2017 update); 4 Am.L.Prop. § 17.31 (1952). The Sherwood case was reversed by statute in 2006; see 21 Penn. Stat. § 358, providing that a document confers constructive notice only when it is "indexed properly as to the party in all alphabetical indices."

[605] See In re Gordon Duane Nowlin, 558 B.R. 907 (Bankr. C.D. Cal. 2016); Bank of E. Asia (U.S.A.) N.A. v. Javaherian, 2013 WL 206127 (Cal. Ct. App. 2013) (unpublished); Dyer v. Martinez, 147 Cal. App. 4th 1240, 54 Cal. Rptr. 3d 907 (2007); Waicker v. Banegura, 357 Md. 450, 745 A.2d 419 (2000); Coco v. Ranalletta, 189 Misc. 2d 535, 733 N.Y.S.2d 849 (Sup. Ct. 2001); Howard Savings Bank v. Brunson, 244 N.J.Super. 571, 582 A.2d 1305 (1990). See also Cipriano v. Tocco, 772 F.Supp. 344 (E.D.Mich. 1991) (indexing in tract index was sufficient to give constructive notice, although statute required indexing in grantor-grantee index as well). In jurisdictions where proper indexing is necessary to treat a document as recorded, an attorney for a grantee

grantees are innocent in this situation, but the former could at least have discovered the error by returning to the recorder's office a few days after the recording to check the indexing. The latter, on the other hand, would have had no basis for suspicion that the earlier document even existed, and could not possibly have corrected the indexing error. The losing party may, of course, have an action against the recorder or its bonding company.

Chain of title problems. Because of the way titles are searched in name-index records systems, certain types of adverse conveyances are difficult or impossible to find even though they are extant in the deed books and are accurately indexed. There are four generic types of such problems, discussed below.[606] The courts have tended to protect searchers in these cases by treating the conveyances in question as if they were unrecorded and as giving no constructive notice.[607] The treatment here focuses on name-index systems, since most of these difficulties do not arise in the less-common tract-index systems. The illustrations below are based on an assumed chain of deeds from the sovereign to A, from A to B, and from B to C in succession, and an adverse conveyance by one of them, unknown to the searcher, to X.

The wild deed. The first problem is the "wild" deed. Assume that B, a former owner who is in the chain of title and is readily identifiable by a searcher, made an unknown and unrecorded deed, adverse to the chain of title, to X. Further assume that X then deeded to Y, and that deed was regularly recorded. A searcher may check the grantor index under B's name but will find nothing, since the B-X deed is unrecorded. The X-Y deed is recorded, but it is impossible for the searcher to discover from the index books, since neither X's nor Y's name is known to the searcher. It can be found only by browsing through all of the deed books themselves, a task which might take several years! The cases uniformly treat the X-Y deed, contrary to literal fact, as if it were unrecorded and as imparting no constructive notice.[608] If they did not do so, the result would be an unconscionable burden on title examiners and a severe flaw in the system's basic operation. Observe that in a tract index system the wild deed is perfectly easy for the searcher to find, since it is indexed on the same page or pages as all other instruments affecting the parcel in question; hence it should be considered to be properly recorded, and there is no need for any special rule governing it.[609]

---

may be held liable for negligence for not verifying, after submitting a document, that it has been indexed correctly; see Antonis v. Liberati, 821 A.2d 666 (Pa. Commw. Ct. 2003).

[606] The classic discussion is Cross, The Record Chain of Title Hypocrisy, 57 Colum.L.Rev. 787 (1957).

[607] The opinions are often sloppy on this matter, concluding merely that the instrument gives no constructive notice. But to protect the subsequent searcher and his client, it is necessary both to treat it as giving no constructive notice and to deem it unrecorded; obviously, if it is regarded as "recorded," no subsequent conveyee can prevail against it under the recording acts. A good example of a more careful statement is found in Sabo v. Horvath, 559 P.2d 1038 (Alaska 1976).

[608] In re Bruder, 207 B.R. 151 (N.D.Ill. 1997); Ranch O, LLC v. Colorado Cattlemen's Agric. Land Tr., 2015 COA 20, 361 P.3d 1063 (Colo. Ct. App. 2015); Mederos v. Selph (L.T.), Inc., 625 So.2d 894 (Fla.App. 1993). See 4 Am.L.Prop. § 17.17 (1952); 1 Patton & Palomar, Land Titles § 69 n. 5 (3d ed. 2017 update).

[609] Miller v. Hennen, 438 N.W.2d 366 (Minn. 1989); Utah Farm Production Credit Ass'n v. Wasatch Bank, 734 P.2d 904 (Utah 1986); Andy Associates, Inc. v. Bankers Trust Co., 49 N.Y.2d 13, 424 N.Y.S.2d 139, 399 N.E.2d 1160 (1979) (under New York City block index). But see Pioneer Builders Co. of Nevada v. K D A Corp., 2012 UT 74, 292 P.3d 672, 685 (2012) (notwithstanding Utah's tract index system, a grantee taking under a wild deed cannot be a bona fide purchaser). It can be argued that the tract index system, with its greater power to disclose out-of-chain documents, is actually disadvantageous in the sense that it brings to light "wild" and other types of difficult-to-find instruments discussed in the text which impair the marketability of titles, and which would be cut off by chain-of-title reasoning in a name index system. See L. Simes, Handbook for More Efficient Conveyancing 93–94 (1961).

The late-recorded deed. A second chain-of-title problem is raised by the conveyance which is recorded too late. Again, assume B is a former owner in the regular chain of title who makes an adverse conveyance to X. X fails to record at that time. B thereafter conveys to C in the chain of title. C records C's deed, but is not a BFP, perhaps because C does not pay value or has knowledge of the adverse conveyance to X. (This assumption is necessary, since if C were a BFP the "shelter" principle discussed earlier would protect any later grantee from C.)[610] Some time after C records, X finally records the old deed from B. The problem is this: if C now contracts to sell the land to D, is D's title searcher expected to find the B-X deed? If so, the searcher must search in the grantor index for adverse conveyances by B, not only during the period B owned the land, but on up to the present date as well—thus taking account of the fact that someone like X might have recorded a deed long after receiving it. It is not impossible for a searcher to do this, but it adds very considerably to the time and expense of the search. The cases are fairly evenly divided, with somewhat more than half treating X's later-recorded deed as unrecorded; the minority deem it recorded, thus requiring the more extensive search effort.[611] The problem does not arise in a tract index system, since the B-X deed is easy to spot on the index page for the parcel even though it is recorded out of time sequence.

The early-recorded deed. The third problem is raised by the deed which is recorded too early. Imagine that B purports to deed the land to X before B has any title, and X immediately records the deed. Later B acquires the title from A. The doctrine of estoppel by deed is usually held to pass title to X instantly on these facts, at least if the B-X deed contained warranties or represented that title was being conveyed.[612] But if B later purports to convey to C, the question is raised whether C's title searcher can be expected to find the B-X deed. This is not impossible, but to do so the searcher must examine the grantor index under B's name not only during the time B owned the land, but for a lengthy and burdensome prior period as well,[613] in order to account for the possibility that B made an adverse conveyance before acquiring title. Most of the recent cases have

  [610] See § 11.10 supra at notes 584–585.

  [611] See generally Perry v. O'Donnell, 749 F.2d 1346 (9th Cir. 1984); Rolling "R" Construction, Inc. v. Dodd, 477 So.2d 330 (Ala. 1985). Treating the late-recorded deed as unrecorded and as imparting no constructive notice, see Jefferson County v. Mosley, 284 Ala. 593, 226 So.2d 652 (1969); McLeod v. Clements, 297 Ga. 371, 774 S.E.2d 102 (2015); Residents of Green Springs Valley Subdivision v. Town of Newburgh, 168 Ind. App. 621, 344 N.E.2d 312 (1976); Morse v. Curtis, 2 N.E. 929 (1885); Fekishazy v. Thomson, 204 A.D.2d 959, 612 N.Y.S.2d 276 (App.Div. 1994). See In re Dlott, 43 B.R. 789 (Bkrtcy.D.Mass. 1983), questioning the continuing vitality of Morse v. Curtis based on current Massachusetts practice. Treating the late-recorded deed as properly recorded, see Woods v. Garnett, 72 Miss. 78, 16 So. 390 (1894); Angle v. Slayton, 102 N.M. 521, 697 P.2d 940 (1985); Spaulding v. H.E. Fletcher Co., 124 Vt. 318, 205 A.2d 556 (1964). See Cross, supra note 606, at nn. 25–26.

  [612] See § 11.5, supra.

  [613] To be safe, the searcher would need to look under B's name in the grantor index books for about 80 years prior to the B-C deed, since this would be a reasonable estimate of B's maximum "conveyancing life." Some states follow a doctrine of lineal warranty which would bind a descendant to a warranty deed made by his or her ancestor, so that one could not safely stop even at 80 years! The same is true if B is a corporation or other entity with unlimited life. See In re Taneja, 427 B.R. 109 (Bankr. E.D. Va. 2010) (under Virginia law, searcher is held to examine each owner's name for adverse conveyances for at least 60 years, even if that predates an owner's acquisition of title); Johnson, Title Examination in Massachusetts, reproduced as chapter 39, J. Casner & B. Leach, Cases & Text on Property (2d ed. 1969), at 903. Johnson reports that despite the searcher's rather clear legal duty to examine for early-recorded deeds in Massachusetts, most searchers in fact do not do so.

excused the searcher from this obligation, holding that the B-X deed must be regarded as unrecorded.[614] As before, the problem does not exist in a tract-index system.[615]

The conveyance of one parcel that affects another. The final chain-of-title problem involves a common owner of two or more parcels who includes, in a conveyance of one parcel, language purporting to encumber the title to one or more other parcels retained. To illustrate, assume that A owns adjacent parcels 1 and 2, and sells parcel 1 to X, including in the deed a covenant promising to restrict parcel 2 to single-family residential use. X records the deed. Later A sells parcel 2 to B without mentioning the restriction. Is B bound by it?

Consider the difficulty which B will face in discovering that the A-X deed exists and affects parcel 2. In many states which use name indexes, the index books include a "brief description" column which indicates in summary form what land is affected by each indexed document. Some statutes mandate that this column be included in the index books, while in other states it is maintained by the recorder voluntarily as a convenience to searchers. If the column exists, it is by no means certain that the recording office personnel will fill it in correctly in the present situation, marking entry for the A-X deed as affecting both parcel 1 and parcel 2. They will probably do so only if the deed's impact on parcel 2 is very obvious or they read it very carefully; neither of these is likely.

Arguably, a searcher is entitled to rely on the "brief description" column only if it is legally mandated; failing that, the searcher's only alternative is to read every conveyance by A in the county during the time A owned parcel 2, no matter what land the "brief description" entry for each of them mentions, and to see whether any of them affect parcel 2. Such a task can be monumental if B is an active real estate dealer or subdivider who has sold hundreds of land parcels.

Unlike the other chain of title problems, this one does not necessarily disappear in a tract index system or a computerized system that is searchable by tract. The question simply becomes whether the recording personnel are sophisticated enough to recognize that the A-X deed affects both parcels 1 and 2, and thus should be indexed under both tracts. Moreover, the problem is not limited to restrictive covenants; it can arise any time a deed of one parcel contains language imposing any encumbrance—an easement, a lease, or a lien, for example—on another parcel. In name-index jurisdictions the cases are about evenly divided as to whether the "buried" language creating the encumbrance is regarded as properly recorded;[616] they usually contain little or no analysis of the role

---

[614] Treating the early-recorded deed as if it were unrecorded, see Southeastern Sav. & Loan Ass'n v. Rentenbach Constructors, Inc., 114 B.R. 441 (E.D.N.C. 1989), affirmed 907 F.2d 1139 (4th Cir. 1990); Far West Sav. & Loan Ass'n v. McLaughlin, 201 Cal.App.3d 67, 246 Cal. Rptr. 872 (1988); Schuman v. Roger Baker & Associates, Inc., 70 N.C.App. 313, 319 S.E.2d 308 (1984); Security Pacific Finance Corp. v. Taylor, 193 N.J.Super. 434, 474 A.2d 1096 (1984). Cf. Collins v. Scott, 943 P.2d 20 (Colo.App.1996). See § 11.5 supra at notes 273–280, for a more complete discussion and citations to contrary cases.

[615] See Balch v. Arnold, 9 Wyo. 17, 59 P. 434 (1899). In addition to the early-recorded deed problem discussed in the text, see the treatment of "omnibus" or "Mother Hubbard" legal descriptions and after-acquired property clauses, § 11.2 supra at note 143, which raise similar problems. Note that a tract index is of no use in searching for these sorts of documents, since they contain no tract descriptions; hence, only a cumbersome name index search, using the procedure described in the text, will locate them. This becomes especially burdensome if some parties in the chain of title were real estate developers or speculators who entered into large numbers of deeds or mortgages.

[616] Protecting the searcher, see Dunlap Investors Limited v. Hogan, 133 Ariz. 130, 650 P.2d 432 (1982); Krueger v. Oberto, 309 Ill. App. 3d 358, 724 N.E.2d 21 (1999); Oliver v. Schultz, 885 S.W.2d 699 (Ky. 1994); Basore v. Johnson, 689 S.W.2d 103 (Mo.App. 1985); Witter v. Taggart, 78 N.Y.2d 234, 573 N.Y.S.2d 146, 577 N.E.2d 338 (N.Y. 1991); Glorieux v. Lighthipe, 88 N.J.L. 199, 96 A. 94 (1915); Dickson v. Kates, 132 Wash.

of the "brief description" column in the searcher's task. In a state with official tract indexes, there is a stronger argument for protecting the searcher, since tract indexes are inherently predicated on the notion that the recorder's staff can and should discover what land is affected by every document they index.[617]

On the whole, the chain of title problems illustrate well the deficiencies of the recording system, especially in its use of name indexes. In many areas of the United States few title searches are conducted in the public records. Instead, title insurance and abstract companies have created sets of private records, called "title plants," in which they do their searches. Since the plants are invariably arranged on a tract-index basis, most of the chain-of-title problems discussed above are of no practical importance in these areas of the nation. It would make little sense for a court to adopt the sorts of rules described above for the protection of name-index searchers in a case in which the actual search was made in a private tract index which contained and properly indexed the out-of-chain documents. Since the whole chain-of-title concept is a judicially-created exception to the literal language of the recording acts, made in recognition of the practical difficulty of finding out-of-chain documents through use of the official indexes, there seems to be no reason to extend it to situations where that difficulty does not exist.[618]

Computerized recording. The statutes of frauds in the United States have traditionally required hard-copy signed writings for both contracts of sale[619] and deeds[620] of land. But in the late 1990s, as the use of electronic documentation became common in many other types of business transactions, the recognition grew that electronic contracts of sale and deeds of land should also be legitimized. This was accomplished at both the state and federal levels, roughly simultaneously and with similar statutory language. The Uniform Law Commission promulgated the Uniform Electronic Transactions Act (UETA) in 1999, and it was enacted by the states nearly universally.[621] The following year Congress passed the Electronic Signatures in Global and National Commerce Act (ESIGN).[622] Both acts apply to both "records" (documents) and signatures, and provide that they may not be denied legal effect, validity, or enforceability solely because they

App. 724, 133 P.3d 498 (2006). Finding the encumbrance validly recorded, see Szakaly v. Smith, 544 N.E.2d 490 (Ind. 1989); Hi-Lo Oil Co. v. McCollum, 38 Ohio App.3d 12, 526 N.E.2d 90 (1987); Stegall v. Robinson, 81 N.C.App. 617, 344 S.E.2d 803 (1986), review denied, stay denied 317 N.C. 714, 347 S.E.2d 456 (1986); Guillette v. Daly Dry Wall, Inc., 367 Mass. 355, 325 N.E.2d 572 (1975); Finley v. Glenn, 303 Pa. 131, 154 A. 299 (1931). See also In Genovese Drug Stores, Inc. v. Connecticut Packing Co., 732 F.2d 286 (2d Cir. 1984).

[617] In a tract-index system, then, the question is essentially one of official misindexing; see text at note 605 supra. By contrast, the court in the *Guillette* case, supra note 616, specifically rejected the searcher's defense of reliance on the "brief legal description" entry, observing that such entries were not required by law in Massachusetts.

[618] Surprisingly, none of the decisions from states where private-plant searches predominate have given this issue any discussion. For example, the court applied chain-of-title reasoning despite evidence that the title insurer had actual knowledge of the out-of-chain encumbrance in Dunlap Investors Limited v. Hogan, supra note 616. See also Far West Sav. & Loan Ass'n v. McLaughlin, 201 Cal.App.3d 67, 246 Cal. Rptr. 872 (1988), in which the court applied standard chain of title reasoning to a "wild deed" transaction in southern California, where virtually every title search is performed by title companies in tract-indexed private plants. The same is probably true of Snow v. Pioneer Title Ins. Co., 84 Nev. 480, 444 P.2d 125 (1968). Such decisions make little sense.

[619] See § 10.1 supra.

[620] See § 11.1 supra.

[621] Only Illinois, New York, and Washington have not adopted UETA, and each of them has similar legislation in place.

[622] 15 U.S.C. § 7001.

are in electronic form.[623] While contracts of sale and deeds initially created in electronic form are not yet common,[624] this legislation assures their legitimacy.

However, it was debatable whether eSign and UETA contained adequate language to authorize local real estate recorders' office to accept electronic instruments, and the acts said nothing about electronic indexes or document standards.[625] Thus it became apparent that separate legislation was needed to pave the way for electronic recording. The Uniform Law Commission's answer was the Uniform Real Property Electronic Recording Act (URPERA), promulgated in 2005. URPERA authorizes the recorders in a state adopting it, on a local option basis, to accept electronic documents for recordation. Such a document might have been electronic in its origin, or it might have been a paper document that has been electronically scanned.[626] There is no requirement that a physical or electronic image of a stamp, impression, or seal accompany an electronic signature.[627]

The act also provides for creation of a state agency (generically termed the Electronic Recording Commission) to establish statewide standards for recordable electronic documents.[628] Recorders are authorized to create electronic indexes, although nothing is said about whether the indexes should be based on names, tracts, or both.[629] Collection of recording fees by electronic means is also authorized.[630] Recorders are permitted to do retrospective conversion of existing recorded paper documents to electronic form.[631]

URPERA must be accounted a striking success. It has been enacted in more than 30 states, and some of the remaining states have adopted analogous but non-uniform legislation. Electronic recording is now available in more than half of the recording offices in the nation. In eight states—Alaska, Arizona, Delaware, District of Columbia, Hawaii, Iowa, Massachusetts and Oregon—all recording offices in the state provide for electronic recording. The early adopters have tended to be in larger-population areas, and it is estimated that at this writing 82 percent of the U.S. population lives where electronic recording is enabled.[632] The records are generally available on-line to title examiners, and in most cases, to the public as well, either free or at a nominal charge.

Electronic recording has important implications for the chain-of-title issues discussed above. Even in states which do not mandate tract indexes for paper records, electronic recording is almost always implemented with indexes based on both names

---

[623] 15 U.S.C. § 7001(a)(1); UETA § 7(a).

[624] See Edgar Snow, Having Your Electronic Signatures and Inking Them Too: Thoughts on Continuing Reluctance to Closing Commercial Loans Solely by Electronic Means, 135 Bank. L.J. 75 (2018).

[625] David E. Ewan, John A. Richards, Margo H. K. Tank, It's the Message, Not the Medium! Electronic Record and Electronic Signature Rules Preserve Existing Focus of the Law on Content, Not Medium of Recorded Land Title Instruments, 60 Bus. Law. 1487 (2005).

[626] URPERA § 3(a).

[627] URPERA § 3(c).

[628] URPERA § 4(b)(1), § 5. See David Ewan & Mark Ladd, Race to the (Virtual) Courthouse: How Standards Drive Electronic Recording of Real Property Documents, 22 Probate & Property, Jan-Feb. 2008, at 8.

[629] URPERA § 4(b)(2), (3).

[630] URPERA § 4(b)(7).

[631] URPERA § 4(b)(6).

[632] Current information on adoption of electronic recording throughout the nation can be found on the web site of the Property Records Industry Association (PRIA), www.pria.us.

(grantor and grantee) and tracts. While the period of retrospective conversion of paper records to electronic form has varied from one recording office to another, it is clear that the time will come (and has already come in some offices) when, as a practical matter, electronic tract indexes will be sufficient in their coverage to accommodate most title searches. In Washington DC, for example, the electronic indexes extend back to 1921, allowing nearly 100-year searches by tract.

This sort of effective search period in electronic tract indexes means that most of the chain-of-title issues—the wild deed, the early-recorded deed, and the late-recorded deed—simply cease to exist in any practical sense. However, it is unclear whether the courts will recognize this state of affairs, particularly in light of the fact that these new tract indexes are not mandated by statute in most states.[633] No case has yet considered this question.[634]

§ 11.12 CURATIVE AND MARKETABLE TITLE ACTS

Under the conventional recording system, a purchaser of land must obtain an historical search of the records back to a conveyance from the sovereign in order to be certain that the record title is good. This sort of complete search is expensive and time-consuming. Moreover, in most cases it has little practical value, since most titles which are good "of record" for the past several decades are good in fact, and nothing recorded in more remote times casts any serious doubt on them. Nevertheless, one cannot be certain that no old documents create title defects until one has looked at them; the searcher who limits his or her search to a shorter period than the entire chain of title is taking a distinct and significant risk.

At least four types of legislation have been enacted in various states which reduce this risk. The oldest and most widespread is the statute of limitations in an action to recover possession of land,—the basis of the doctrine of adverse possession.[635] There is no doubt that adverse possession has cured millions of title defects; indeed, that is probably the main justification for the doctrine. But the title examiner who relies on adverse possession as a substitute for a full historical search is merely exchanging one significant risk for another. The problem is that successful adverse possession depends on the concurrence of a set of facts which usually do not appear of record, which the searcher probably does not know are true, and which even if true may be hard to prove in court. Have the owners in the record chain of title been in possession which was actual, open, hostile, exclusive, and continuous for the statutory period? Has the statute's running been tolled by the infancy, imprisonment, or insanity of the holder of paramount title?[636] Is that paramount title held by a governmental body or a charity against which the statute will not run?[637] Is it a future interest, against which the limitations period does not commence until it becomes possessory?[638] To learn the answers to these

---

[633] Bayer-Pacht, Note, The Computerization of Land Records: How Advances in Recording Systems Affect the Rationale Behind Some Existing Chain of Title Doctrine, 32 Cardoza L. Rev. 337 (2010); 3 Patton and Palomar, Land Titles § 705 (3d ed. 2017 update).

[634] A Pennsylvania Superior Court held that where computerized indexes were available, searchers were held to constructive notice of their contents; see First Citizens Nat. Bank v. Sherwood, 2003 PA Super 47, 817 A.2d 501 (2003), rev'd on other grounds, 583 Pa. 466, 879 A.2d 178 (2005).

[635] See generally § 11.7 supra.

[636] See § 11.7 supra at notes 343–344; Saint-Paul, Clearing Land Titles § 4:4 (3d ed. 2017 update).

[637] See § 11.7 supra at notes 341–342; Saint-Paul, id., at § 4:3.

[638] See § 11.7 supra at note 339; Saint-Paul, id., at § 4:2.

questions is generally far more effort than a full historical search of the records! Yet without clear answers, a searcher who relies on adverse possession is taking a serious risk.

Another type of legislation, the curative act, dates back to colonial times in some states and has become quite widespread. Curative acts attempt to make prior conveyances, typically those more than two or three years old, valid and recordable despite some minor defects they may contain.[639] Among the kinds of defects often dealt with are improper executions, acknowledgments, recordings, exercises of powers of attorney and appointment, parties, and judicial proceedings. Of course, there are plenty of other types of defects which may arise in conveyances and which the acts do not affect; they are no panacea.[640] Not all states have curative statutes, and some have acts of very limited scope. From the viewpoint of a title searcher, the acts have little impact on the need for a full historical search. They merely permit an examiner to have greater confidence in the validity of conveyances found in the title chain which might otherwise be considered ineffective or dubious. The result is to make a somewhat greater proportion of titles marketable.

The next step in the development of legislation to improve the title search process has been the enactment of special statutes which bar certain specific types of very old but apparently valid claims to land. The most common types of such claims are "ancient" mortgages[641] and some varieties of future interests, such as rights of entry and possibilities of reverter.[642] The interest being cut off must be quite old, commonly thirty to fifty years. In the case of mortgages the period is typically measured from the due date of the debt if stated in the mortgage, and otherwise from its execution date. Provision is usually made for the recording of a notice periodically as a means of keeping the old claim alive if its owner desires. The constitutionality of the statutes barring old future interests has been attacked frequently on the ground that they constitute takings of property without due process of law, but most of the decisions have upheld them.[643]

---

[639] The best and most comprehensive treatment is Saint-Paul, id., at chapters 12–20. A Model Curative Act is presented and discussed in L. Simes & C. Taylor, The Improvement of Conveyancing by Legislation 17–27 (1960).

[640] Crotts Andrews v. All Heirs & Devisees of Bellis, 297 Ark. 3, 759 S.W.2d 532 (1988) (curative statute did not validate a certificate of acknowledgment which was not signed by a notary).

[641] One might imagine that the running of the statute of limitations on the underlying note or other indebtedness would be a sufficient protection against the enforceability of the mortgage, but in most states the mortgage can be foreclosed even if the debt is barred; Phinney v. Levine, 116 N.H. 379, 359 A.2d 636 (1976); Nelson, Whitman, Burkhart & Freyermuth, Real Estate Finance Law § 6.9 (6th ed. 2014).

[642] See, e.g., The Indiana Dormant Mineral Interest Act, West's Ann.Ind.Code 32–5–11; Ohio Dormant Mineral Act, Ohio Rev. Code Ann. § 5301.56 (West), construed in Corban v. Chesapeake Expl., L.L.C., 149 Ohio St. 3d 512, 76 N.E.3d 1089 (2017); Md. Code Ann., Real Prop. § 6–102 (West); Mich. Comp. Laws Ann. § 554.61 et. seq. (West); Minn. Stat. Ann. § 500.20 (West). See Simes & Taylor, supra note 639, at 201–17; Saint-Paul, supra note 636, at § 9:15.

[643] Severns v. Union Pac. R.R. Co., 101 Cal. App. 4th 1209, 125 Cal. Rptr. 2d 100 (2002); Cline v. Johnson County Board of Education, 548 S.W.2d 507 (Ky. 1977); Presbytery of Southeast Iowa v. Harris, 226 N.W.2d 232 (Iowa 1975), certiorari denied 423 U.S. 830, 96 S.Ct. 50, 46 L.Ed.2d 48 (1975); Short v. Texaco, Inc., 273 Ind. 518, 406 N.E.2d 625 (1980), affirmed 454 U.S. 516, 102 S.Ct. 781, 70 L.Ed.2d 738 (1982); Hiddleston v. Nebraska Jewish Education Society, 186 Neb. 786, 186 N.W.2d 904 (1971); Town of Brookline v. Carey, 355 Mass. 424, 245 N.E.2d 446 (1969); Trustees of Schools of Township No. 1 v. Batdorf, 6 Ill.2d 486, 130 N.E.2d 111 (1955). Contra, see Girl Scouts of S. Illinois v. Vincennes Indiana Girls, Inc., 988 N.E.2d 250 (Ind. 2013) (retroactive application of statute held unconstitutional); Board of Education of Central School District No. 1 v. Miles, 15 N.Y.2d 364, 259 N.Y.S.2d 129, 207 N.E.2d 181 (1965), noted 51 Corn.L.Q. 402 (1966); Biltmore Village v. Royal Biltmore Village, 71 So.2d 727 (Fla. 1954).

These statutes, like the curative acts, help make some titles marketable, but they do not eliminate the need for a full historical search of the records, for there are too many other possible types of defects that they do not affect. A more ambitious attempt to shorten search periods is represented by the "marketable record title" acts.[644] These acts, which exist in 18 states,[645] simply make void most types of claims to land if they are not reflected in the records between the date of the "root of title" and the present. The root of title is defined as the most recent deed or other title transaction recorded in an unbroken chain of title at least some specified number of years in the past—typically 20 to 40 years.[646] For example, if the statute specified 30 years and a search were being made in 2020, a deed recorded in 1995 could not be the root of title, but one recorded in 1985 could be. If there were no exceptions to the coverage of the acts, it would be entirely unnecessary to search earlier than the root of title, since nothing found there could affect the present title.

Marketable title acts are in a sense both more and less powerful than the specialized statutes dealing with ancient reversionary interests described earlier. The latter cut off all such interests which are sufficiently old unless some formal notice of them is recorded in the more recent records. Marketable title acts, on the other hand, will not affect ancient rights if a specific reference to them is made in any document recorded in the chain of title within the appropriate time period following the root. But marketable title acts are far more potent, in that they terminate not merely reversionary future interests but also most other types of pre-root claims[647] unless they are preserved by one of the

---

[644] See generally Saint-Paul, supra note 636, at Chapter 5; Simes & Taylor, supra note 639, at 295; Halligan, Marketable Title and Stale Records: Clearing Exceptions and Closing Deals, 59 Wis.Bar.Bull. 23 (No. 5, May 1986); Comment, The Nebraska Marketable Title Act: Another Tool in the Bag, 63 Neb.L.Rev. 124 (1983); Barrett, Marketable Title Acts—Panacea or Pandemonium, 53 Corn L.Rev. 45 (1967); Swenson, Marketable Title Acts, 6 Utah L.Rev. 472 (1959). The constitutionality of the Acts has been uniformly upheld despite the fact that they provide for no notice to the holders of old interests being cut off. See Bennett v. Whitehouse, 690 F.Supp. 955 (W.D.Okl. 1988); Wichelman v. Messner, 250 Minn. 88, 83 N.W.2d 800 (1957); Pindar, Marketability of Titles—Effect of Texaco, Inc. v. Short, 34 Mercer L.Rev. 1005 (1983); Aigler, Constitutionality of Marketable Title Acts, 50 Mich.L.Rev. 185 (1951); Aigler, A Supplement to "Constitutionality of Marketable Title Acts"—1951–1957, 56 Mich. L.Rev. 225 (1957).

[645] States with marketable title statutes (with year of enactment) are California (1982), Connecticut (1967), Florida (1963), Illinois (1941), Indiana (1941), Iowa (1919), Kansas (1973), Michigan (1945), Minnesota (1943), Nebraska (1947), North Carolina (1973), North Dakota (1951), Ohio (1961), Oklahoma (1961), South Dakota (1947), Utah (1963), Vermont (1969), Wisconsin (1941), and Wyoming (1975). The Uniform Simplification of Land Transfers Act (USLTA) also contains a marketable title act as Art. 3, Part 3. See Curtis, Simplifying Land Transfers: The Recordation and Marketable Title Provisions of the Uniform Simplification of Land Transfers Act, 62 Or.L.Rev. 363 (1983).

[646] The root itself must be a recorded document; see City of Marquette v. Gaede, 672 N.W.2d 829 (Iowa 2003). See also Stecklein v. City of Cascade, 693 N.W.2d 335 (Iowa 2005) (present claimant lacked unbroken chain of title back to root); Fowler v. Doan, 261 Mich. App. 595, 683 N.W.2d 682 (2004). The most common period in existing acts is 40 years; USLTA § 3–301(4) adopts a 30-year period. Several decisions hold that the root of title must purport to convey some specific interest in the land; hence, a quitclaim deed would not ordinarily do. See Wilson v. Kelley, 226 So.2d 123 (Fla.App. 1969); Obermiller v. Baasch, 284 Neb. 542, 823 N.W.2d 162 (2012). The fact that a deed in the chain prior to the root of title is a complete forgery or is otherwise defective does not prevent the operation of the acts; see Marshall v. Hollywood, Inc., 236 So.2d 114 (Fla.1970), certiorari denied 400 U.S. 964, 91 S.Ct. 366, 27 L.Ed.2d 384 (1970); Harrell v. Wester, 853 F.2d 828 (11th Cir. 1988). But see Il Giardino, LLC v. Belle Haven Land Co., 254 Conn. 502, 757 A.2d 1103 (2000). However, if the root contains defects which are obvious on its face or if it specifically refers to some prior adverse claim, the searcher will take subject to these matters; see ITT Rayonier, Inc. v. Wadsworth, 346 So.2d 1004 (Fla. 1977); Reid v. Bradshaw, 302 So.2d 180 (Fla.App. 1974). See also Weber v. Eisentrager, 498 N.W.2d 460 (Minn. 1993) (root must be followed by a later conveyance to another person).

[647] See Rush v. Sterner, 143 Mich.App. 672, 373 N.W.2d 183 (1985) (interests originating by way of exception or reservation are cut off by the Act); Spellman Outdoor Advert. Servs., LLC v. Ohio Tpk. & Infrastructure Comm., 2016-Ohio-7152, 72 N.E.3d 229 (Ohio 2016).

methods described in the next paragraph. Hence forgeries, gaps in the chain of title, and technical defects in conveyances are simply irrelevant if they are prior to the root of title. Even interests not based on recordable documents, such as adverse possession titles and prescriptive easements, are barred if they were perfected before the root.

There are several ways in which pre-root interests can be preserved as against the operation of a marketable title act. One mentioned above is a specific timely reference to such an interest in a post-root document in the chain of title.[648] Another is the timely re-recording, during the post-root statutory period, of a pre-root instrument which creates or refers to the interest, or of a notice (specifically authorized by most of the acts) of a claim arising under a pre-root instrument.[649] The recording during the post-root statutory period of a conveyance of the adverse interest has much the same effect. Finally, a person who is occupying the land may, under some of the acts, have possession treated as the equivalent of notice of his or her claim.[650]

A person need not be a bona fide purchaser to be protected from pre-root claims by a marketable title act, and under most of the acts need not take possession of the land.[651] A few acts limit their protection to persons who acquire fee simple interests,[652] but under most of the statutes any sort of interest or claim is protected.

The usefulness of marketable title acts is impaired by the fact that they contain a number of exceptions—lists of various types of pre-root claims that the acts do not eliminate. At least one exception, for interests of the United States government, is inevitable, since it is plain that state law cannot divest federal land interests without the government's consent. Exceptions for rights of parties in possession[653] and for

---

[648] See Kirkman v. Wilson, 98 N.C.App. 242, 390 S.E.2d 698 (1990); Blakely v. Capitan, 34 Ohio App.3d 46, 516 N.E.2d 248 (1986). A vague or general reference will not do; see Johnson v. Sourignamath, 90 Conn. App. 388, 877 A.2d 891 (2005); Martin v. Town of Palm Beach, 643 So.2d 112 (Fla.App. 1994); Swaby v. N. Hills Reg'l R.R. Auth., 2009 S.D. 57, 769 N.W.2d 798 (2009). But see Mannweiler v. LaFlamme, 65 Conn. App. 26, 781 A.2d 497 (2001). See also McBurney v. Cirillo, 276 Conn. 782, 809, 889 A.2d 759, 776 (2006) (reference in post-root deed to 1885 map was sufficient to preserve implied easement disclosed by map); Berger v. Riverwind Parking, LLP, 842 So. 2d 918 (Fla. Dist. Ct. App. 2003) (amendment to CC&Rs recorded after root was insufficient to preserve pre-root CC&Rs).

[649] See, e.g., Strong v. Detroit & Mackinac Ry. Co., 167 Mich.App. 562, 423 N.W.2d 266 (1988) (railroad easement was preserved by filing of notice). Cf. Cunningham v. Haley, 501 So.2d 649 (Fla.App. 1986) (restrictive covenants cut off by act, where no notice was filed within the statutory period).

[650] Under the USLTA version, it is necessary only that the possession have existed at the time the title search was made, assuming a reasonable inquiry would have revealed it; USLTA § 3–306(2). Under the Model Act, on the other hand, the possession must have continued by the record owner continuously for more than 40 years with no transactions on record affecting her interest; Model Act § 4(b), reprinted in Simes & Taylor, supra note 639, at 8. See State v. Cox Corp., 29 Utah 2d 127, 506 P.2d 54 (1973).

[651] See Merritt v. Merritt, 146 Vt. 246, 500 A.2d 534 (1985), in which the court appears to have required BFP status for one to claim the protection of the Vermont marketable title act. However, the prior claim against which protection was sought was simply an *unrecorded post-root deed,* and hence would properly have been avoided by the court under the normal operation of the recording acts, but only, of course, as against a BFP. Thus, the case suggests that the presence of a marketable title act did not eliminate the usual BFP requirement of the recording act.

[652] See the construction of the Minnesota act in Wichelman v. Messner, 250 Minn. 88, 83 N.W.2d 800 (1957). Some of the statutes require the root of title itself to be a purported conveyance of fee simple title; see, e.g., Town of Belle Prairie v. Kliber, 448 N.W.2d 375 (Minn.App. 1989). See also Hersh Properties, LLC v. McDonald's Corp., 588 N.W.2d 728 (Minn. 1999) (marketable title act applies to land registered under Torrens system).

[653] See Village Apartments, LLC v. Ward, 169 Conn. App. 653, 152 A.3d 76 (2016) (fence was insufficient to give notice of easement); Sampair v. Village of Birchwood, 784 N.W.2d 65 (Minn. 2010) (use of easement must be sufficient to put a prudent person on inquiry); Zimmerman v. Cindle, 48 Ohio App.3d 164, 548 N.E.2d 1315 (1988) (possession must be "clearly observable"); City of Jacksonville v. Horn, 496 So.2d 204 (Fla.App. 1986); Rush v. Sterner, 143 Mich.App. 672, 373 N.W.2d 183 (1985); Kraft v. Town of Mt. Olive, 183 N.C. App.

observable easements and use restrictions are common, and may be justified on the ground that any reasonably thorough title examination will include an inspection of the property, which indeed is necessary under ordinary recording act principles.

But almost as common, and much more disruptive, are exceptions for a variety of "special interest" claims which have been lobbied into the statutes of many states; they include public easements and rights of way, mineral interests, water rights, utility easements, railroad easements, and the like.[654] The exceptions usually apply whether the claim is physically observable or not. The holders of these claims—utility and mining companies and city and county governments, for example—wish to avoid the burden of rerecording their rights periodically, and sometimes argue that their records are so incomplete or complex that rerecording would be impractical. Yet the exceptions tend to defeat the very purpose of the marketable title acts: to limit the title search period. A searcher must go back beyond the root of title at least carefully enough to determine whether any of the pre-root documents involve interests that the acts recognize as exceptions. If there are many such documents, this effort is tantamount to performing a full historical search.[655]

Perhaps the most intriguing problem with marketable title acts arises because of the possibility that two conflicting chains of title can exist simultaneously. This can occur because an owner delivers two deeds of the same property to two grantees; because a forger with no title starts a new paper chain with a "wild" deed; or, perhaps most commonly, because an owner delivers two deeds which inadvertently contain overlapping land descriptions. To illustrate, assume a marketable title act with a 40-year period. O owns land in fee simple, and in 1910 delivers a deed to A. A in turn deeds

---

415, 645 S.E.2d 132 (2007); TJ Auto LLC v. Mr. Twist Holdings LLC, 355 Wis. 2d 517, 851 N.W.2d 831 (2014) (act cuts off easement even if purchaser has notice of it). If the mineral estate has been severed from the surface estate, possession of the surface estate is not possession of the minerals; Sickler v. Pope, 326 N.W.2d 86 (N.D. 1982); Kriss v. Mineral Rights, Inc., 911 P.2d 711 (Colo. App. 1996); XTO Energy Inc. v. Nikolai, 357 S.W.3d 47 (Tex. App. 2011). Thus, to acquire title to the mineral estate, the mineral claimant must explore for or produce the minerals.

[654] State sovereignty lands are exempt from the acts in some states; see Coastal Petroleum Co. v. American Cyanamid Co., 492 So.2d 339 (Fla. 1986), cert. denied 479 U.S. 1065, 107 S.Ct. 950, 93 L.Ed.2d 999 (1987); Dennison v. N. Dakota Dep't of Human Servs., 2002 ND 39, 640 N.W.2d 447 (2002). Contra, see N. Carolina by & through N. Carolina Dep't of Admin. v. Alcoa Power Generating, Inc., 853 F.3d 140 (4th Cir. 2017). See Powell, Unfinished Business—Protecting Public Rights to State Lands from Being Lost under Florida's Marketable Record Title Act, 13 Fla.St. U.L.Rev. 599 (1985). Florida also held a restrictive covenant imposed pursuant to local zoning approval was not cut off by the act; Save Calusa Tr. v. St. Andrews Holdings, Ltd., 193 So. 3d 910 (Fla. Dist. Ct. App. 2016). Cf. H & F Land, Inc. v. Panama City–Bay County Airport & Industr. Dist., 736 So.2d 1167 (Fla. 1999) (no exception for easements of necessity); Springer v. Cahoy, 2013 S.D. 86, 841 N.W.2d 15 (2013) (same); Martin v. Town of Palm Beach, 643 So.2d 112 (Fla.App. 1994) (no exception for interests owned by charities); King Assocs., LLP v. Bechtler Dev. Corp., 179 N.C. App. 88, 632 S.E.2d 243 (2006) (exception for railroad rights of way did not preserve underlying landowners' possibilities of reverter); State v. Hess, 684 N.W.2d 414 (Minn. 2004) (same); Swaby v. N. Hills Reg'l R.R. Auth., 2009 S.D. 57, 769 N.W.2d 798 (2009) (conditions subsequent are not cut off by act); In re Estate of Hord, 836 N.W.2d 1 (Iowa 2013) (future interests arising prior to root of title are cut off); Mitchell v. Redvers, 130 Conn. App. 100, 22 A.3d 659 (2011) (same). Compare W. Lakes Properties, L.C. v. Greenspon Prop. Mgmt., Inc., 908 N.W.2d 883 (Iowa Ct. App. 2017) (preemptive rights are subject to termination by act) with Hempel v. Creek House Tr., 743 N.W.2d 305, 312 (Minn. Ct. App. 2007) (preemptive rights not subject to termination). Restatement (Third) of Property (Servitudes) § 7.16 takes the view that a variety of easement types are not subject to termination under marketable title acts unless the specific act requires a different result.

[655] See Note, Property Law—North Carolina's Marketable Title Act—Will the Exceptions Swallow the Rule?, 52 N.C.L.Rev. 211 (1973). Even Simes and Taylor conceded that their Model Act, which had very few exceptions, would not "usher in an era of forty year abstracts of title," but they argued that the task of the title examiner would "definitely be lightened." Simes & Taylor, supra note 639, at 5.

the land to B in 1920. Then, in 1930, X (a forger) purports to deed the same land to Y. A diagram may help:

```
        1910        1920
O ------------> A ------------> B

        1930
X ------------> Y
                          [C7686]
```

In 1980, who owns the land? The answer is Y, based on the typical statutory language which provides that one's title is subject to any "interest arising out of a title transaction recorded after the root of title."[656] The 1930 deed to Y is a root of title, and from the viewpoint of Y or anyone who might buy from Y, there is no document recorded after that root of title which reflects the existence of any conflicting interest. One might argue that the A-B deed in 1920 is also a root of title, and indeed it is. However, the title which the act confirms in B through that root is subject to Y's interest under the language of the act quoted above, since the X-Y deed was recorded in 1930, later than the 1920 A-B root of title. In summary, B's title is subject to Y's but Y's is not subject to B's; hence, Y prevails.[657]

Note that the result would be different if B had conveyed to C in, say, 1935, so that the chains of title were as follows:

```
        1910        1920        1935
O ------------> A ------------> B ------------> C

        1930
X ------------> Y
                          [C7687]
```

The B-C deed is a root of title (since it is more than 40 years old) and C's claim would be superior to that of Y, which arose prior to 1935. Indeed, the result would also be reversed if B had conveyed to C, not in 1935, but in, say, 1960. Such a conveyance is too recent to be a root of title, but it will still act to preserve C's claim under the language quoted in the preceding paragraph. On these facts, the marketable title act would make both C's claim and Y's claim "subject to" one another. In effect, the act would not resolve the conflict between the two, and general principles of deeds, recording and priorities would

---

[656] The quoted language is from USLTA § 3–303(3); see also Model Act § 2(d), reprinted in Simes & Taylor, supra note 639, at 7. The idea that claims are preserved by the recording of more recent instruments conveying or referring to them can be troublesome. In Kittrell v. Clark, 363 So.2d 373 (Fla.App. 1978), certiorari denied 383 So.2d 909 (Fla. 1980), the more recent instrument was a will which was probated. Neither the will nor the probate inventory gave any legal description of the land, but the court nonetheless found the will sufficient to preserve the devisee's claim; there was a vigorous dissent from the Florida Supreme Court's denial of certiorari.

[657] The result reached in the text is supported by Lehmann v. Cocoanut Bayou Ass'n, 157 So. 3d 289 (Fla. Dist. Ct. App. 2014) and Whaley v. Wotring, 225 So.2d 177 (Fla. Dist. Ct. App. 1969). Compare Exchange National Bank v. Lawndale National Bank, 41 Ill.2d 316, 243 N.E.2d 193 (1968), in which the Illinois Supreme Court held that the act was not intended to be applied where there were two competing chains of title, or to confirm a chain from a root of title which was "wild" or forged. There seems no warrant in the statutory language for this conclusion, and the drafters of the Model Act plainly disagreed with it; see Simes & Taylor, supra note 639, at 13–14. It is likely that under most of the acts a wild or forged deed can be a root of title; see City of Miami v. St. Joe Paper Co., 364 So.2d 439 (Fla. 1978), appeal dismissed 441 U.S. 939, 99 S.Ct. 2153, 60 L.Ed.2d 1040 (1979); Hyland v. Kirkman, 204 N.J. Super. 345, 498 A.2d 1278 (Ch. Div. 1985); Esterholdt v. PacifiCorp, 2013 WY 64, 301 P.3d 1086 (Wyo. 2013).

be called upon to do so. Since the X-Y deed was a forgery (and out of the chain of title of C as well), C should prevail.[658]

Finally, assume that the conveyance from B to C was made and recorded, not in 1935 or 1960, but in 1975. It is obviously too recent to be a root of title as of 1980. Moreover, it will not be effective to preserve C's claim from the competing X-Y title chain. The reason is that in 1970, 40 years after the X-Y deed was recorded, the act confirmed the title in Y. A conveyance in a competing chain recorded later than 1970 will not revive that previously extinguished interest.[659]

All of the early marketable title statutes were adopted in states which employed either official or unofficial (abstract company or title plant) parcel indexes. The problem of two conflicting chains of title is trivial in a parcel index system, since an examination of the relevant index page or pages will immediately reveal both chains. More recently states such as North Carolina, Connecticut, and Vermont, where official name indexes are widely used by searchers, have enacted marketable title legislation. In such a state, consider the facts raised in the latter diagram above, with B conveying to C in either 1935 or 1960. A searcher who examines Y's title will conclude that the act makes it good, having no reason to suspect the existence of the competing A-B-C chain; a searcher examining C's title will similarly discover no clue that the X-Y deed exists. In this setting the legal rules discussed in the preceding paragraphs, particularly when they give viability to a chain of title originating in a forged deed, are intolerable, since they operate to defeat purchasers who have reasonably relied on the records.[660]

Several methods of resolving this dilemma have been employed. Under a few of the acts, only grantees who take possession are protected.[661] They will doubtless discover the existence of a competing chain if claimants under it are already in possession. Another possibility is simply to add language excepting from the act's operation the rights of all parties in possession.[662] But the drafters of the Model Act rejected these approaches on the ground that they were only partial solutions, since they did not deal with vacant land, and since they required reference to facts outside the record.[663] USLTA from the statute's termination effects the rights of persons in possession, and also incorporates a provision, borrowed from Florida, preserving the rights of anyone whose name is carried on the real property tax rolls within three years of the time marketability is determined; thus, inspecting the land and checking the tax records will nearly always disclose any competing chain.[664]

[658] See Minnich v. Guernsey Sav. & Loan Co., 36 Ohio App.3d 54, 521 N.E.2d 489 (1987), finding that the Act did not resolve the competing chains, and resorting to construction of an 1883 deed to do so; Heath v. Turner, 309 N.C. 483, 308 S.E.2d 244 (1983); Holland v. Hattaway, 438 So.2d 456 (Fla.App. 1983); Medway Assocs. v. Shoneck, 1992 WL 156142 (Conn. Super. Ct. 1992) (unreported).

[659] See Simes & Taylor, supra note 639, at 13–14.

[660] See Webster, The Quest for Clear Land Titles—Making Land Title Searches Shorter and Surer in North Carolina via Marketable Title Legislation, 44 N.C.L.Rev. 89, 108–110 (1965).

[661] North Dakota Cent.Code 47–19.1–01.

[662] See USLTA § 3–306(2); Webster, supra note 660, at 109.

[663] See Simes & Taylor, supra note 639, at 353. The drafters did, however, include a provision preserving the rights of a record owner who has been in continuous possession for 40 years or more down to the date marketability is being determined; Model Act § 4(b), reprinted in Simes & Taylor, supra note 639, at 8.

[664] USLTA § 3–306(3); see West's Fla. Stat.Ann. § 712.03(6). A related problem arises from the fact that a claimant can preserve his or her interest by recording a notice of the claim periodically; see, e.g., USLTA § 3–305; Model Act § 4(a). If there is no tract index, such a notice may be "wild" in relation to the record chain of title and impossible to find. This problem can be resolved by requiring a separate tract index for such notices,

§ 11.13   COVENANTS OF TITLE IN DEEDS

The law does not generally read into a deed a representation or promise that it conveys any title, or title of any particular quality. Sometimes the grantor will wish to exclude any such promise quite expressly, and hence will employ the term "quitclaim" or similar language to indicate that no covenants as to title are being made. Quitclaim deeds are commonly used when there is a serious doubt as to whether the grantor has title at all, when the conveyance is gratuitous, or when the grantor is a person of so little financial substance that a claim on a title covenant could not be collected. A quitclaim deed will, of course, convey whatever interest the grantor has in the described land.[665]

However, it is customary in most areas of the nation for the grantor in an ordinary sale transaction to include covenants regarding the title. A deed containing such covenants is loosely termed a "warranty deed," although this term is somewhat misleading since a technical covenant of warranty is only one of the six types of common covenants found in deeds.

Deed covenants of title are not a highly effective means of title assurance. They depend on the covenantor's continued solvency and availability for suit, and recovery under them is seriously limited by the doctrines discussed in this section. Most grantees rely on additional modes of title assurance, such as examination of public records under the recording system and the purchase of title insurance. Yet deed covenants remain important, and continue to form the basis of suits, both by disappointed grantees and by their title insurers, with the latter acting under their right of subrogation after indemnifying insured grantees for their losses.[666]

Deed covenants for title are conceptually similar to the implied (and sometimes express) covenant of marketable title found in real estate sales contracts. Yet there are several major differences. One is difference is the fact that with deeds, unlike contracts of sale, there is no implied covenant concerning the quality of the title; deed covenants of title must be express. Another difference is the doctrine of merger by deed, which disallows any recovery on the contract covenants of title once the grantee accepts a deed, so that the deed's covenants (if any) take up just when the contract's leave off.[667] There is also a difference in the standards of acceptable title. The concept of marketable title which applies to contracts requires substantial but not perfect performance;[668] thus a title is objectionable only if it poses significant risks, while a title which is good in fact may be deemed unmarketable if it presents a risk of litigation which the court feels a

---

see, e.g., Iowa Code Ann. § 614.18, or by requiring the claimant to record the notice under the name of the person who has record title at the time the notice is recorded; see Simes & Taylor, supra note 639, at 358.

[665] Reid v. Southeastern Materials, 396 So.2d 667 (Ala.1981) (quitclaim deed conveyed grantor's title, even if grantor was not aware of holding title); Eastbrook Homes, Inc. v. Treasury Dep't, 296 Mich. App. 336, 820 N.W.2d 242 (2012); Jackson v. Wildflower Prod. Co., Inc., 505 S.W.3d 80 (Tex. App. 2016).

Deeds derived from sheriffs' sales, mortgage and deed of trust foreclosure sales, partition sales, and other "forced" sales are nearly always made without any covenants of title; see, e.g., Outback Properties, LLC v. Johnson, 225 Or. App. 366, 201 P.3d 246 (2009).

[666] See, e.g., Midfirst Bank v. Abney, 365 Ill. App. 3d 636, 850 N.E.2d 373 (2006); § 11.14 infra at note 776.

[667] See Weiss v. Old Republic Nat. Title Ins. Co., 262 Ga. App. 120, 584 S.E.2d 710 (2003); Warner v. Estate of Allen, 776 N.E.2d 422 (Ind. Ct. App. 2002); West 90th Owners Corp. v. Schlechter, 165 A.D.2d 46, 565 N.Y.S.2d 9 (1991); Simpson v. Johnson, 100 Idaho 357, 597 P.2d 600 (1979); § 10.12 supra at notes 474–485. The Uniform Land Transactions Act rejects the merger doctrine entirely; ULTA § 1–309.

[668] See ULTA § 2–301 comment 3.

purchaser should not be forced to accept.[669] No such notions apply to deed covenants for title. They are deemed violated only if the title is actually bad or defective, not merely risky or in doubt.[670] From the purchaser's perspective, the contract approach is usually more attractive and flexible, but the merger doctrine requires that the contract-based claim must be asserted before the deed is delivered.

A final distinction between contract and deed covenants relates to the available remedies. Under the contract, the purchaser may get specific performance with abatement for the title defect, rescission and restitution, or damages.[671] In about half the states damages may include the loss of bargain, while in the other half recovery is limited to restitution plus out-of-pocket expenses if the vendor acted in good faith.[672] A claim based on deed covenants, other than the covenant of further assurances, can give rise only to damages, and recovery is nearly always limited to the amount the grantor received for the property, plus interest and in some cases attorneys' fees.[673] Specific performance is technically denied except for the covenant of further assurances. However, if the grantor has subsequently acquired the title which the deed covenants promised, the doctrine of estoppel by deed will vest it in the grantee automatically unless the latter rejects it in preference to damages.[674]

American law generally recognizes six distinct types of title covenants in deeds. In many areas it is customary to spell them out in detail on the face of the deed, but some states have statutes which impose certain of the covenants whenever specific words, such as "grant," "convey and warrant," or the like are used in a deed.[675] A grantor may also use express words to limit the coverage of the covenants. For example, it is common in some areas for grantors to give a full set of covenants, but to limit their application to title defects caused or created by the grantor personally, and not those created by his or her predecessors in title. Such a deed is usually termed a "special warranty deed."[676] It

---

[669] See § 10.12 supra at note 412.

[670] James v. McCombs, 936 P.2d 520 (Alaska 1997); House v. First Am. Title Co., 883 N.E.2d 197 (Ind. Ct. App. 2008); Stevenson v. Ecklund, 263 Mont. 61, 865 P.2d 296 (Mont.1993); Roper v. Elkhorn at Sun Valley, 100 Idaho 790, 605 P.2d 968 (1980). But see the contrary dictum in Fechtner v. Lake County Savings & Loan Association, 66 Ill.2d 128, 5 Ill.Dec. 252, 361 N.E.2d 575 (1977); Frimberger v. Anzellotti, 25 Conn. App. 401, 594 A.2d 1029 (1991).

[671] See § 10.12 supra at note 418.

[672] See § 10.3 supra at notes 122–129.

[673] See text at note 719 infra.

[674] See § 11.5 supra at notes 262–263.

[675] See, e.g., Ala.Code § 35–4–271 ("grant," "bargain," or "sell"); West's Ann.Cal.Civ.Code § 1113 ("grant"); 765 Ill. L. Comp. Stat. 5/9, applied in In re Terranova, 301 B.R. 509 (Bankr. N.D.Ill. 2003); Miss. Code Ann. § 89–1–33 ("warrants"); N.D. Cent.Code § 47–10–19 ("grant"); Ore.Rev.Stat. 93.850 ("conveys and warrants"); Vernon's Ann. Tex.Civ.Stat. art. 1297 ("grant" or "convey"); Utah Code Ann.1953, 57–1–12 ("conveys and warrants"); West's Rev.Code Wash.Ann. 64.04.030 ("conveys and warrants"); id. at 64.04.040 ("bargains, sells, and conveys"), applied in Edmonson v. Popchoi, 172 Wash. 2d 272, 256 P.3d 1223 (2011); Winn v. Mannhalter, 708 P.2d 444 (Alaska 1985) (in absence of words "conveys and warrants" no covenants of title are implied in conveyance of real estate); Annot., Right of Purchaser at Execution Sale, Upon Failure of Title, to Reimbursement or Restitution from Judgment Creditor, 33 A.L.R.4th 1206. ULTA § 2–306 imputes in every deed, unless there is an expression to the contrary, title warranties of right to convey, against encumbrances, of quiet enjoyment, and to defend the title; there are no implied covenants of seisin or further assurances. By ULTA § 2–304, every land sale contract is presumed to call for a deed containing these covenants unless the contrary is agreed.

[676] See Woolf v.1417 Spruce Associates, 68 F.Supp.2d 569 (E.D. Pa. 1999); Ochse v. Henry, 202 Md. App. 521, 33 A.3d 480 (2011); Morello v. Land Reutilization Comm'n of Cty. of Douglas, 265 Neb. 735, 659 N.W.2d 310 (2003); Greenberg v. Sutter, 173 Misc.2d 774, 661 N.Y.S.2d 933 (N.Y.S.Ct. 1997); Tanglewood Land Co., Inc. v. Wood, 40 N.C.App. 133, 252 S.E.2d 546 (1979); State Bank & Trust of Kenmare v. Brekke, 602 N.W.2d 681 (N.D. 1999); Mason v. Loveless, 24 P.3d 997 (Utah App. 2001); Chicago Title Ins. v. Aurora Loan Servs.,

is also common to list in the deed, as exceptions to the covenants, any specific encumbrances that the grantee has agreed to accept.[677] Examples might include a mortgage which the grantee is assuming, a recorded declaration of use restrictions, or an existing easement for utility lines.[678] Such a listing is very desirable, for it avoids any subsequent dispute as to whether such matters were intended to be within the coverage of the covenants.

The six traditional title covenants[679] may be used separately or together in any combination the parties agree upon. The first three are known as "present" covenants, and the latter three as "future" covenants, for reasons explained below. The basic coverage of each covenant is as follows.

Seisin. The medieval notion of seisin connoted possession, and a few jurisdictions today simply treat this covenant as promising that the grantor is in possession of the land, whether that possession is legal or wrongful.[680] In most states, however, the covenant of seisin is in substance a promise that the grantor both owns and holds possession of the estate in the land that the deed purports to convey.[681] On the other hand, it is usually held that the existence of an outstanding encumbrance, such as an easement or mortgage, is not a breach of this covenant.[682]

LLC, 2013 IL App (1st) 123510, 996 N.E.2d 44 (2013). See also Egli v. Troy, 602 N.W.2d 329 (Iowa 1999) (special warranty deed covered grantor's acquiescence as well as affirmative acts); Greenberg v. Sutter, 661 N.Y.S.2d 933 (S.Ct. 1997) (special warranty deed covered loss to title to adverse possessor during grantor's holding period).

[677] The exceptions to coverage are commonly listed in a "subject to" clause; see McCormick v. Crane, 2012 ME 20, 37 A.3d 295 (2012); Rubel v. Johnson, 2017-Ohio-9221. 101 N.E.3d 1092 (Ohio Ct. App. 2017). See also Collins v. Overstreet, 959 So. 2d 102 (Ala. Civ. App. 2006) (grantor reserved hunting rights).

[678] The exceptions may also be stated in more general terms, such as "* * * subject to any and all easements appearing of record." See Pruitt v. Meadows, 393 So.2d 986 (Ala.1981); Bennett v. Inv'rs Title Ins. Co., 370 S.C. 578, 635 S.E.2d 649 (Ct. App. 2006); Elk Ridge Lodge, Inc. v. Sonnett, 2011 WY 106, 254 P.3d 957 (Wyo. 2011). This is a less desirable practice from the grantee's viewpoint, since it does not call clearly to the attention of the grantee the specific existing encumbrances. Moreover, if not carefully worded, such a general listing may not be broad enough to fully protect the grantor; see, e.g., JV Properties, LLC v. SMR7, LLC, 2014 WL 7277393 (Nev. 2014) (unpublished) (exclusion for "reservations, restrictions, conditions, rights, rights of way and easements, if any of record" did not exclude liability for mortgage encumbrance); Foxley & Co. v. Ellis, 2009 WY 16, 201 P.3d 425 (Wyo. 2009).

[679] See Levin, Warranties of Title—A Modest Proposal, 29 Vill.L.Rev. 649 (1984), recommending legislation to eliminate distinctions between the two classes of covenants, present and future, described in the text. The full gamut of covenants is discussed in Rowe v. Klein, 409 P.3d 1152 (Wash. Ct. App. 2018).

[680] See, e.g., Baughman v. Hower, 56 Ohio App. 162, 10 N.E.2d 176 (1937); 4 Tiffany, Real Property § 1000 (3d ed. 2017 update). The covenant is usually regarded as promising both possession and title; see Bernklau v. Stevens, 150 Colo. 187, 371 P.2d 765 (1962). The presence of an adverse possessor on the land breaches the covenant of seisin, even if the possessor has not yet acquired title; Double L. Properties, Inc. v. Crandall, 51 Wn.App. 149, 751 P.2d 1208 (1988). Cf. Utah Stat.Ann. § 57–1–1.

[681] Wyatt v. Arkansas Game & Fish Comm'n, 360 Ark. 507, 202 S.W.3d 513 (2005) (where sale was "in gross," discrepancy in acreage as described in deed did not breach covenant of seisin); Ives v. Real-Venture, Inc., 97 N.C.App. 391, 388 S.E.2d 573 (1990) (a deed purports to convey both surface and mineral estates to the land described unless its terms limit the conveyance; grantor who delivers an unrestricted deed, but who lacks title to mineral estate, has breached covenant of seisin); Riddle v. Nelson, 84 N.C.App. 656, 353 S.E.2d 866 (1987) (grantee is entitled, under covenant of seisin, to the precise land described in the deed and not merely an equivalent amount of land); Knudson v. Weeks, 394 F.Supp. 963 (W.D.Okl. 1975); Allard v. Al-Nayem Int'l, Inc., 59 So. 3d 198 (Fla. Dist. Ct. App. 2011); Thompson v. Thomas, 499 S.W.2d 901 (Tenn.App. 1973); Reyes v. Booth, 2003 WL 21663708 (Tex. App. 2003) (unpublished) (conveyance of only one-half interest breached covenant of seisin); Rowe v. Klein, 409 P.3d 1152 (Wash. Ct. App. 2018).

[682] See Cochran Investments, Inc. v. Chicago Title Ins. Co., 550 S.W.3d 196 (Tex. App. 2018); 3 Am.L.Prop. § 12.127 nn. 22–26 (1952). Cf. Thompson v. Thomas, 499 S.W.2d 901 (Tenn. App. 1973), noted in 4 Memphis St.L.Rev. 650 (1974) (public easement for flooding violates covenant of seisin); United States v. Lacy, 234 F.R.D. 140 (S.D. Tex. 2005) (federal tax lien violates covenant of seisin).

Right to convey. In most cases, the covenants of seisin and right to convey are virtually synonymous,[683] but there can be differences, at least theoretically. For example, a grantor who owned land subject to a valid restraint on alienation might satisfy the covenant of seisin but not the right to convey.[684] It is also possible for one to have a right to convey but lack seisin, as in the case of a grantor acting under a power of appointment or serving as attorney in fact for the owner; in theory such a conveyance might breach the covenant of seisin, although damages would be only nominal.[685]

Against encumbrances. An encumbrance is some outstanding right or interest in a third party which does not totally negate the title which the deed purports to convey.[686] Typical encumbrances include mortgages, liens, easements, leases, and restrictive covenants.[687] In general, the principles that define encumbrances in the context of the marketable title concept, discussed earlier,[688] apply equally to deed covenants against encumbrances. One problem that arises frequently is the encumbrance that is not expressly excepted in the deed, but that is either plain and obvious or is well-known to the grantee. The cases are badly divided;[689] some of them distinguish between the grantee's knowledge in fact (which is no defense to a claimed breach) and the open

---

[683] Knudson v. Weeks, 394 F.Supp. 963 (W.D.Okl.1975); Howard v. Clanton, 481 So. 2d 272 (Miss. 1985); Cochran Investments, Inc. v. Chicago Title Ins. Co., 550 S.W.3d 196 (Tex. App. 2018); Holmes Dev., LLC v. Cook, 2002 UT 38, 48 P.3d 895 (2002).

[684] In theory, seisin and right to convey are also distinct in the case of land occupied by an adverse possessor, who has (wrongful) seisin, but no right to convey.

[685] But see Avery v. McHugh, 423 S.W.2d 17 (Mo.App. 1967), finding no breach of the covenant of seisin where the grantor had no title but acted under authority of a valid trust agreement.

[686] See Fahmie v. Wulster, 81 N.J. 391, 408 A.2d 789 (1979); Aczas v. Stuart Heights, Inc., 154 Conn. 54, 221 A.2d 589 (1966).

[687] Contamination by hazardous chemicals is not an encumbrance and does not affect title unless a lien to enforce cleanup or other costs has been imposed; see Holly Hill Holdings v. Lowman, 30 Conn.App. 204, 619 A.2d 853 (Conn.App. 1993); Cameron v. Martin Marietta Corp., 729 F.Supp. 1529 (E.D.N.C. 1990); U.S. v. Allied Chemical Corp., 587 F.Supp. 1205 (N.D.Cal. 1984). Encroachments from or onto the subject property are usually considered encumbrances; see Bryant v. Moritz, 97 Or.App. 481, 776 P.2d 1299 (1989), review denied 308 Or. 465, 781 P.2d 1214 (1989); In re Meehan's Estate, 30 Wis.2d 428, 141 N.W.2d 218 (1966). Contra, see Commonwealth Land Title Ins. Co. v. Stephenson, 101 N.C.App. 379, 399 S.E.2d 380 (1991). See also Fid. Nat. Title Ins. Co. v. Captiva Lake Investments, LLC, 941 F.Supp.2d 1121 (E.D. Mo. 2013) (right to file a mechanics lien was an encumbrance, although claim of lien had not yet been filed); Regan v. Jeff D., 157 Idaho 758, 339 P.3d 1162 (2014) (easement that was beneficial to the land was not an encumbrance); Kelly v. Nat'l Attorneys Title Assur. Fund, 955 N.E.2d 224, 227 (Ind. Ct. App. 2011) (unrecorded federal tax lien was an encumbrance); Ensberg v. Nelson, 178 Wash. App. 879, 320 P.3d 97 (2013) (HOA's judgment, which might become a lien on land in the future, was not an encumbrance).

[688] See § 10.12 supra.

[689] Grantee's knowledge of encumbrance is a defense: Ludke v. Egan, 87 Wis.2d 221, 274 N.W.2d 641 (1979); Marathon Builders, Inc. v. Polinger, 263 Md. 410, 283 A.2d 617 (1971) (dictum). Grantee's knowledge is no defense; grantor liable: Fidelity Nat. Title Ins. Co. v. Miller, 215 Cal.App.3d 1163, 264 Cal. Rptr. 17 (1989); Etheridge v. Fried, 183 Ga.App. 842, 360 S.E.2d 409 (1987); Midfirst Bank v. Abney, 365 Ill. App. 3d 636, 850 N.E.2d 373 (2006); Tammac Corp. v. Miller-Meehan, 643 A.2d 370 (Me. 1994); Webster v. Ragona, 40 A.D.3d 1360, 836 N.Y.S.2d 381 (2007). It is obvious that knowledge of the encumbrance should be no defense where the parties agreed or clearly contemplated that the grantor would remove it; see, e.g., Dillard v. Earnhart, 457 S.W.2d 666 (Mo. 1970).

visibility of the encumbrance (which is a defense).[690] Public road, street, and sidewalk rights of way, if visible, are nearly always held not to violate the covenant.[691]

Another common point of controversy is the existence of violations of building, housing or similar municipal codes. Technically, such matters do not affect title at all, and the great bulk of the cases hold that they do not breach the covenant against encumbrances.[692] One widely cited case recognizes an exception if the violation has already become the subject of enforcement proceedings by local government officials at the time the covenant is given.[693] A similar issue is raised by existing violations of zoning ordinances. They are often held to make titles unmarketable in the context of executory contracts.[694] As to whether this concept should be extended to deed covenants of title, the cases are about evenly divided.[695] A comparable question arises if the property being conveyed has been included in a local improvement district for, say, street paving or sewer line installation. If the district has already imposed assessments secured by liens on the properties it covers, these are plainly encumbrances. However, there is no breach of the covenant against encumbrances if the district merely plans or expects to impose such liens in the future.[696]

Warranty and quiet enjoyment. These two covenants are usually considered identical in their coverage.[697] They have much the same practical effect as the three

---

[690] Leach v. Gunnarson, 290 Or. 31, 619 P.2d 263 (1980). Cf. Gill Grain Co. v. Poos, 707 S.W.2d 434 (Mo.App. 1986) (visible appearance of prescriptive easement is no defense to action on covenant of title); Northrip v. Conner, 107 N.M. 139, 754 P.2d 516 (1988) (unrecorded easement, visible on the ground, violated covenant against encumbrances, where deed excepted from the covenant only "easements of record"); Leach v. Gunnarson, 290 Or. 31, 619 P.2d 263 (1980) (exception to liability for open and notorious "public highways, powerlines, railroads and the like").

[691] See Richitt v. Southern Pine Plantations, Inc., 228 Ga.App. 333, 491 S.E.2d 528 (Ga.App. 1997); Webster v. Ragona, 40 A.D.3d 1360, 836 N.Y.S.2d 381 (2007); McKnight v. Cagle, 76 N.C.App. 59, 331 S.E.2d 707 (1985). Contra, see Campagna v. Parker, 116 Idaho 734, 779 P.2d 409 (1989) (public road easement breached covenants of title, where it did not provide the sole access to the property and did not enhance its value); Commissioner, Department of Highways v. Rice, 411 S.W.2d 471 (Ky. 1966).

[692] Domer v. Sleeper, 533 P.2d 9 (Alaska 1975) (fire code); Elysian Inv. Grp. v. Stewart Title Guar. Co., 105 Cal. App. 4th 315, 129 Cal. Rptr. 2d 372 (2002) (notice of code violation); McCrae v. Giteles, 253 So.2d 260 (Fla.App. 1971) (housing code); Fahmie v. Wulster, 81 N.J. 391, 408 A.2d 789 (1979) (regulation of stream culvert size); Seth v. Wilson, 62 Or.App. 814, 662 P.2d 745 (1983) (ordinance prohibiting subdivision of land); Stone v. Sexsmith, 28 Wn.2d 947, 184 P.2d 567 (1947) (electrical code). Vermont is contra, see Bianchi v. Lorenz, 166 Vt. 555, 701 A.2d 1037 (Vt. 1997) (non-code-complying septic system and no certificate of occupancy); Hunter Broadcasting, Inc. v. City of Burlington, 164 Vt. 391, 670 A.2d 836 (Vt. 1995) (lack of subdivision approval).

[693] Brunke v. Pharo, 3 Wis.2d 628, 89 N.W.2d 221 (1958), noted 1958 Wis.L.Rev. 640.

[694] See § 10.12 supra at note 462; Annot., 39 A.L.R.3d 362 (1971); Oatis v. Delcuze, 226 La. 751, 77 So.2d 28 (1954).

[695] Zoning violation held to be an encumbrance: Seymour v. Evans, 608 So.2d 1141 (Miss. 1992); Feit v. Donahue, 826 P.2d 407 (Colo.App. 1992); Lohmeyer v. Bower, 170 Kan. 442, 227 P.2d 102 (1951); Moyer v. De Vincentis Constr. Co., 107 Pa.Super. 588, 164 A. 111 (1933); War Eagle, Inc. v. Belair, 204 N.C. App. 548, 694 S.E.2d 497 (2010). Zoning violation held not an encumbrance: Barnett v. Decatur, 261 Ga. 205, 403 S.E.2d 46 (1991); Frimberger v. Anzellotti, 25 Conn.App. 401, 594 A.2d 1029 (1991) (illegal filling of wetlands without permit was not a breach of covenants of title); Hoffer v. Callister, 137 Idaho 291, 47 P.3d 1261 (2002); Arnell v. Salt Lake County Bd. of Adjustment. 2005 UT App 165, 112 P.3d 1214 (Utah App. 2005). See also Favero Farms, LC v. Baugh, 2015 UT App 182, 356 P.3d 188 (2015) (federal wetlands regulations did not constitute an encumbrance, but an existing violation of those regulations did).

[696] Brewer v. Peatross, 595 P.2d 866 (Utah 1979); Wells v. DuRoss, 54 Ohio App.2d 50, 374 N.E.2d 662 (1977). But see First American Federal Sav. & Loan Ass'n v. Royall, 77 N.C.App. 131, 334 S.E.2d 792 (1985).

[697] See Clarke v. Tannin, Inc., 301 F.Supp.3d 1150 (S.D. Ala. 2018); Brown v. Lober, 75 Ill.2d 547, 27 Ill.Dec. 780, 389 N.E.2d 1188 (1979); Spiegle v. Seaman, 160 N.J.Super. 471, 390 A.2d 639 (1978); Fritts v. Gerukos, 273 N.C. 116, 159 S.E.2d 536 (1968); 4 Tiffany, Real Property § 1010 (3d ed. 2017 update); 3 Am.L.Prop. § 12.129 (1952).

present covenants just discussed, for they obligate the grantor to indemnify the grantee for any loss resulting from an "eviction" or disturbance of the grantee due either to an absence of title to all or part of the land, or to an outstanding encumbrance.[698] They include an obligation on the grantor's part to defend against any legal attack on the grantee's title or possession.[699]

Further assurances. This is a promise by the grantor to execute any additional documents that may be needed in the future to perfect the title which the original deed purported to convey. It is the only one of the six standard covenants that can be enforced by specific performance as well as damages.[700] In most cases a grantor's after-acquired title will inure to the grantee automatically[701] and no further instrument is needed, so this covenant is not asserted very frequently.

Timing of breach. The three "present" covenants (seisin, right to convey, and against encumbrances) are so called because they are breached, if at all, the moment the deed is delivered and accepted; the grantor either has or does not have seisin and the right to convey, and encumbrances either do or do not exist.[702] The statute of limitations begins to run against the grantee at that time,[703] and thus may bar any claim before the grantee even discovers that the title is defective. Moreover, the present covenants are usually held not to "run with the land" and hence do not benefit remote grantees who trace their title through the covenantee.[704] This view is a relic of the common-law notion that a cause of action was not assignable. Since the present covenants are breached when made,

---

[698] See George v. Hercules Real Estate Servs., Inc., 339 Ga. App. 843, 795 S.E.2d 81 (2016); Booker T. Washington Const. & Design Co. v. Huntington Urban Renewal Authority, 181 W.Va. 409, 383 S.E.2d 41 (1989); Fechtner v. Lake County Savings & Loan Association, 66 Ill.2d 128, 5 Ill.Dec. 252, 361 N.E.2d 575 (1977).

[699] Kitchen v. Schmedeman, 31 Kan. App. 2d 694, 71 P.3d 486 (2003); Dillon v. Morgan, 362 So.2d 1130 (La.App. 1978); Choquette v. Roy, 167 N.H. 507, 114 A.3d 713 (2015); Hull v. Federal Land Bank, 134 Vt. 201, 353 A.2d 577 (1976); Edmonson v. Popchoi, 172 Wash. 2d 272, 256 P.3d 1223 (2011) (grantor has duty to actively defend the title against a third party's attack, and not merely to settle without a defense). The grantor is also precluded by the covenant of quiet enjoyment from personally attacking the grantee's title or asserting title by adverse possession against the grantee or the grantee's successors; see Carrozza v. Carrozza, 944 A.2d 161, 166 (R.I. 2008). But see Sharpton v. Lofton, 721 S.W.2d 770 (Mo.App. 1986) (grantor's action to set deed aside is not precluded by covenant of warranty in deed).

[700] See Spiegle v. Seaman, 160 N.J.Super. 471, 390 A.2d 639 (1978); 4 Tiffany, Real Property § 1015 (3d ed. 2017 update). The other covenants can give rise only to an action for damages; see Forrest v. Hanson, 424 S.W.2d 899 (Tex. 1968).

[701] See generally § 11.5 supra.

[702] S. Utsunomiya Enterprises, Inc. v. Moomuku Country Club, 75 Haw. 480, 866 P.2d 951 (Haw. 1994); Brown v. Lober, 75 Ill.2d 547, 27 Ill.Dec. 780, 389 N.E.2d 1188 (1979); Double L. Properties, Inc. v. Crandall, 51 Wn.App. 149, 751 P.2d 1208 (1988); Holmes Dev., LLC v. Cook, 2002 UT 38, 48 P.3d 895 (2002). No eviction is necessary to constitute a breach of the present covenants, but in the absence of an eviction, the grantee's damages may be only nominal; see text at note 728 infra; Holmes Dev., LLC v. Cook, id.

[703] Brown v. Lober, id.; Cape Co. v. Wiebe, 196 Neb. 204, 241 N.W.2d 830 (1976); Bernklau v. Stevens, 150 Colo. 187, 371 P.2d 765, 95 A.L.R.2d 905 (1962). ULTA § 2–521 applies the same rule to its six-year statute of limitations. Contra, see Christiansen v. Utah-Idaho Sugar Co., 590 P.2d 1251 (Utah 1979). If the covenant is statutory, it may be unclear whether the limitations period commences when the deed is delivered; compare Cecil Lawter Real Estate School, Inc. v. Town & Country Shopping Center Co., 143 Ariz. 527, 694 P.2d 815 (Ariz.App. 1984) with HSL Linda Gardens Properties, Ltd. v. Freeman, 176 Ariz. 206, 859 P.2d 1339 (Ariz.App. 1993).

[704] Colonial Capital Corp. v. Smith, 367 So.2d 490 (Ala.Civ.App. 1979); S. Utsunomiya Enterprises, Inc. v. Moomuku Country Club, 76 Hawai'i 396, 879 P.2d 501 (Haw. 1994); Bridges v. Heimburger, 360 So.2d 929 (Miss. 1978); Rich, Rich & Nance v. Carolina Const. Corp., 153 N.C. App. 149, 570 S.E.2d 212 (2002). ULTA § 2–312 provides that all title covenants will run with the land unless there is a contrary agreement; so does Colo.Rev.Stat. § 118–1–21. See generally Comment, Covenants of Title Running with the Land in California, 49 Cal.L.Rev. 931 (1961); Comment, 7 U.Miami L.Rev. 378 (1953).

the grantee has only a cause of action and not a continuing covenant. Causes of action generally are now freely assignable, and there seems to be no sound objection to treating the grantee's subsequent deed as implying an assignment, thus permitting remote grantees to sue on present covenants. This is a reasonable construction of the parties' probable intent, but only a few courts have been willing to take this step.[705]

The treatment of the three "future" covenants (warranty, quiet enjoyment, and further assurances) is quite different. They are breached only when the covenantee is actually disturbed by one with paramount title, an event termed an "eviction"[706] even though it does not necessarily signify actual loss of possession. The statute of limitations commences only from the date of the eviction,[707] so there is little risk of the grantee's being barred without awareness of the claim. And since no cause of action accrues until an eviction occurs, the unbreached covenant is held to run with the land and to benefit remote grantees.[708] For all of these reasons, future covenants are often much more advantageous to covenantees than are present covenants.

Since the future covenants are breached only by an eviction, the grantee who is not disturbed in any way has no action on them.[709] On the other hand, a serious physical interference with the grantee's possession by the holder of paramount title will obviously suffice;[710] so will a court decree ordering the grantee off the land or decreeing that he or she has no title.[711] An eviction may also be "constructive," operating without a physical disturbance.[712] Thus, if the grantee voluntarily surrenders possession to one who has

---

[705] Schofield v. Iowa Homestead Co., 32 Iowa 317 (1871). See 3 Am.L.Prop. § 12.127 n. 11 (1952).

[706] Colonial Capital Corp. v. Smith, 367 So.2d 490 (Ala.Civ.App. 1979); Brown v. Lober, 75 Ill.2d 547, 27 Ill.Dec. 780, 389 N.E.2d 1188 (1979); Bridges v. Heimburger, 360 So.2d 929 (Miss. 1978); Omega Chemical Co. v. Rogers, 246 Neb. 935, 524 N.W.2d 330 (Neb. 1994); Wells v. Tennant, 180 W.Va. 166, 375 S.E.2d 798 (1988).

[707] Self v. Petty, 469 So.2d 568 (Ala. 1985); Brown v. Lober, id.

[708] Weiss v. Old Republic Nat. Title Ins. Co., 262 Ga. App. 120, 584 S.E.2d 710 (2003); Bridges v. Heimburger, 360 So.2d 929 (Miss. 1978); Marathon Builders, Inc. v. Polinger, 263 Md. 410, 283 A.2d 617 (1971). See generally 3 Am.L.Prop. § 12.131 (1952). If the grantor had no title whatever, it might be argued that there is no "land" with which the covenant can run. But this argument is usually rejected on the ground that a delivery of possession, actual or constructive, establishes the necessary succession, see Solberg v. Robinson, 34 S.D. 55, 147 N.W. 87 (1914), or that the covenantor is estopped to deny that he or she passed some estate, see Wead v. Larkin, 54 Ill. 489 (1870). It is clear that there must be "privity" between the original covenantee and remote plaintiffs, and that an adverse possessor cannot recover on the covenant; see Deason v. Findley, 145 Ala. 407, 40 So. 220 (1906). See generally 4 Tiffany, Real Property § 1022 nn. 4–8 (3d ed. 2017 update).

[709] Elliott v. Elliott, 252 Ark. 966, 482 S.W.2d 123 (1972) (mere filing of suit against grantee is not an eviction); Veterans' Land Board v. Akers, 408 S.W.2d 795 (Tex.Civ.App. 1966), refused n.r.e. (land office's issuance of prospecting permit to third party is not an eviction). An exception exists if the paramount title is in the government; no further eviction is necessary. See Thompson v. Dildy, 227 Ark. 648, 300 S.W.2d 270 (1957). If the grantee already owns the interest which the grantor has failed to convey, it is impossible for the grantee to suffer an eviction; see Gibson v. Turner, 156 Tex. 289, 294 S.W.2d 781 (1956); Gilstrap v. June Eisele Warren Tr., 2005 WY 21, 106 P.3d 858 (Wyo. 2005).

Occasionally a court will construe the covenant of warranty to encompass the present covenants as well, thus allowing immediate recovery for an encumbrance without an eviction. See the thorough discussion in Greggory G. v. Burlington Res. Oil & Gas, Co., LP, 2011 WL 2600458 (D.N.D. 2011) (unpublished).

[710] McCleary v. Bratton, 307 S.W.2d 722 (Mo.App. 1957). If the holder of paramount title is already in possession when the deed containing the covenant is delivered, an eviction occurs upon delivery; see Hull v. Federal Land Bank, 134 Vt. 201, 353 A.2d 577 (1976); Haas v. Gahlinger, 248 S.W.2d 349 (Ky. 1952).

[711] Foley v. Smith, 14 Wn.App. 285, 539 P.2d 874 (1975); Schneider v. Lipscomb County National Farm Loan Association, 146 Tex. 66, 202 S.W.2d 832 (1947).

[712] See generally Annot., 172 A.L.R. 18 (1948); Booker T. Washington Const. & Design Co. v. Huntington Urban Renewal Auth., 181 W.Va. 409, 383 S.E.2d 41 (1989) (when grantee who holds under warranty deed is sued by a prospective contract purchaser because the grantee's title is unmarketable, the grantee has suffered an eviction and the warranty is breached).

paramount title[713] or buys that title from its holder,[714] an eviction has occurred. And if a grantor pays damages on a deed covenant to a grantee, the former has been constructively evicted for purposes of an action against an earlier grantor on the covenant of warranty in a prior deed.[715]

Note, however, that there is no eviction in any case unless the interference is by one who *in fact* has a title superior to the grantee's; it is not enough that the grantee believes that a third party has legal grounds for the eviction.[716] For this reason, it is usually wise for the grantee to notify the grantor of any litigation with a party claiming paramount title and to invite the grantor to defend it. Unless the grantor has an opportunity to intervene and participate in the lawsuit, he or she will not be bound by *res judicata* and may later make an independent attack, in an action against the grantor on the covenant, on the validity of the asserted paramount title.[717] Rather ironically, a grantee who is successful in resisting the claim of a third party has obviously not been evicted and can recover nothing on the deed covenants, even though the grantee may have a significant outlay for costs and attorneys' fees.[718]

Damages. Perhaps the broadest principle governing the recovery of damages on deed covenants is that the covenantor cannot be made to pay more than the price received for the land.[719] This rule, which applies no matter which covenants are involved, is obviously harsh in some applications. If the land's value has risen sharply or if it was originally worth more than the grantee paid for it, the recovery on the covenant may pay only a small fraction of the actual loss, particularly if there is a total failure of title. The same is true if the grantee has built valuable buildings on the land, although the loss of an improver who acted in good faith will usually be mitigated by statutes or judicial doctrines relating to mistaken improvements.[720] The limitation of damages to the price

---

[713] Weiss v. Old Republic Nat. Title Ins. Co., 262 Ga. App. 120, 584 S.E.2d 710 (2003); Green Harbour Homeowners Ass'n, Inc. v. Ermiger, 72 A.D.3d 1186, 898 N.Y.S.2d 302 (2010); Brewster v. Hines, 155 W.Va. 302, 185 S.E.2d 513 (1971), noted at 74 W.Va. L.Rev. 415 (1972).

[714] Greenwood v. Robbins, 108 N.J.Eq. 122, 154 A. 333 (1931); Kramer v. Dunn, 2000 PA Super 101, 749 A.2d 984 (2000); Morgan v. Haley, 107 Va. 331, 58 S.E. 564 (1907).

[715] Kramer v. Carter, 136 Mass. 504 (1884).

[716] See Roper v. Elkhorn at Sun Valley, 100 Idaho 790, 605 P.2d 968 (1980); Garcia v. Herrera, 125 N.M. 199, 959 P.2d 533 (N.M.App. 1998); Green v. Ayres, 272 Or. 117, 535 P.2d 762 (1975); Mastro v. Kumakichi Corp., 90 Wn.App. 157, 951 P.2d 817 (1998).

[717] Holzworth v. Roth, 78 S.D. 287, 101 N.W.2d 393 (1960); May v. Loeb, 57 Ga. App. 788, 196 S.E. 268 (1938), affirmed 186 Ga. 742, 198 S.E. 785 (1938). See generally 3 Am.L.Prop. § 12.131 nn. 19–27 (1952).

[718] Elliott v. Elliott, 252 Ark. 966, 482 S.W.2d 123 (1972); McDonald v. Delhi Sav. Bank, 440 N.W.2d 839 (Iowa 1989); Chaney v. Haeder, 90 Or.App. 321, 752 P.2d 854 (1988); Jarrett v. Scofield, 200 Md. 641, 92 A.2d 370 (1952). There is some thought in the cases that the grantee who litigates the title successfully might recover costs and attorneys' fees if the grantor has "thrust him into litigation" with the third party; see First Fiduciary Corp. v. Blanco, 276 N.W.2d 30 (Minn. 1979).

[719] See Teems v. City of Forest Park, 137 Ga.App. 733, 225 S.E.2d 87 (1976); Woods v. Schmitt, 439 N.W.2d 855 (Iowa 1989); Holmes Dev., LLC v. Cook, 2002 UT 38, 48 P.3d 895 (2002); MGIC Financial Corp. v. H.A. Briggs Co., 24 Wn.App. 1, 600 P.2d 573 (1979); Annots., 100 A.L.R. 1194 (1937); 61 A.L.R. 127 (1929). Consequential damages, such as lost profits on a prospective resale of the property, are not recoverable; Clark v. Cypress Shores Development Co., 516 So.2d 622 (Ala. 1987); Bridges v. Heimburger, 360 So.2d 929 (Miss. 1978).

[720] Lockhart v. Phenix City Investment Co., 549 So.2d 48 (Ala. 1989). Contra, allowing damages for improvements, see Finucane v. Prichard, 811 S.W.2d 348 (Ky.App. 1991). The holder of the paramount title is usually given an option to sell the land to the mistaken improver at its unimproved value, or to purchase the improvements at an amount equal to the value they add to the property. See, e.g., Madrid v. Spears, 250 F.2d 51 (10th Cir. 1957); State Mutual Insurance Co. v. McJenkin Insurance & Realty Co., 86 Ga.App. 442, 71 S.E.2d 670 (1952); Brunt v. McLaurin, 178 Miss. 86, 172 So. 309 (1937); D. Dobbs, Remedies § 5.8(3) (Practitioner 2d ed. 1992).

received by the covenantor has been criticized,[721] and a few New England states have adopted a contrary rule allowing recovery of the property's value as of the time of eviction.[722] But that approach opens the grantor to liability for an amount which may be many times the price received and which may extend, under the "future" covenants, for many decades into the future. Given the wide availability of title insurance as an alternative form of protection for the grantee which can, in theory, be increased in dollar coverage whenever he or she desires, it is very doubtful that the law should place such a vast and uncertain potential burden on the grantor in the absence of fraud or a very clear promise to assume it.[723]

A further limitation is usually applied if there is only a partial breach of the covenants of title. Suppose there is a shortage in the land owned by the grantor, so that the deed conveys only 80 percent (in terms of value, not necessarily acreage) of the land it describes. If the price paid for the whole was $100,000, but it would be worth much more at the time of the eviction or the trial, most cases nevertheless limit the grantee's recovery to the pro-rata share of the shortage in the original price, or $20,000.[724] Whether this sort of constraint on damages is necessary to fair treatment of the grantor is very much open to doubt.

Where the breach is not a deficiency in land area, but instead the property is subject to an encumbrance such as an easement or restrictive covenant that has not been removed by the grantee, the cases allow recovery for the diminution in value of the land, subject to the absolute limitation that damages may not exceed the total price received. But by analogy to the area-deficiency cases mentioned above, the reduction in value is generally measured as of the date of the sale rather than the time of eviction.[725] If the grantee actually purchases the outstanding encumbrance at a reasonable price, the amount thus spent is the measure of damages,[726] although again capped by the total

---

[721] See Groetzinger, Breach of the Warranty Covenants in Deeds and the Allowable Measure of Damages, 17 N.H. Bar J. 1 (1975); Hymes v. Esty, 133 N.Y. 342, 31 N.E. 105 (1892).

[722] Connecticut, Maine, Massachusetts, and Vermont do not limit recovery to the amount the covenantor received; see Annot., 61 A.L.R. 10, 31–32 (1929) for extensive quotations from the cases. See also Bridwell v. Gruner, 212 Ark. 992, 209 S.W.2d 441 (1948), which is ambiguous but may be a departure from the majority rule.

[723] See Gray v. Paxton, 662 P.2d 1105 (Colo.App. 1983). ULTA § 2–513 retains the majority rule.

[724] Griggs v. Driftwood Landing, Inc., 620 So.2d 582 (Ala. 1993); Hillsboro Cove, Inc. v. Archibald, 322 So.2d 585 (Fla.App. 1975); McClure v. Turner, 165 Ga.App. 380, 301 S.E.2d 304 (1983); Patrick v. Meachum, 2007 WL 286712 (Ky. Ct. App. 2007) (unpublished) (title lacked mineral rights; damages computed on basis of ratio of values of mineral and surface rights); Grey v. Konrad, 133 Vt. 195, 332 A.2d 797 (1975). Cf. Gonzales v. Garcia, 89 N.M. 337, 552 P.2d 468 (1976) (grantor can recover full value of the deficiency). See Annot., 94 A.L.R.3d 1091 (1979).

[725] See, e.g., Gill Grain Co. v. Poos, 707 S.W.2d 434 (Mo.App. 1986); Yonkers City Post No. 1666, Veterans of Foreign Wars of the United States, Inc. v. Josanth Realty Corp., 67 N.Y.2d 1029, 503 N.Y.S.2d 321, 494 N.E.2d 452 (1986), on remand 143 A.D.2d 267, 532 N.Y.S.2d 169 (1988); Ellison v. F. Murray Parker Builders, Inc., 573 S.W.2d 161 (Tenn.App. 1978); East Montpelier Development Corp. v. Barre Trust Co., 127 Vt. 491, 253 A.2d 131 (1969); Reed v. Rustin, 375 Mich. 531, 134 N.W.2d 767 (1965); Evans v. Faught, 231 Cal.App.2d 698, 42 Cal.Rptr. 133 (1965). See also In re Meehan's Estate, 30 Wis.2d 428, 141 N.W.2d 218 (1966). For earlier cases, see Annot., 61 A.L.R. 10, 90 n. 71 (1929). In a state like Connecticut, which generally follows the minority rule measuring damages at the time of eviction, the reduction in market value resulting from an easement would also be measured as of the eviction; but the only modern case found dealing with the question is ambiguous as to the date of measurement of damages. See Aczas v. Stuart Heights, Inc., 154 Conn. 54, 221 A.2d 589 (1966).

[726] Neil v. Phillips, 2009 Ark. App. 827 (2009) (not published in S.W.3d); Loveland Essential Grp., LLC v. Grommon Farms, Inc., 251 P.3d 1109 (Colo. App. 2010); Skipper v. McMillan, 349 So.2d 808 (Fla.App. 1977); Bryant v. Moritz, 97 Or.App. 481, 776 P.2d 1299 (1989); Creason v. Peterson, 24 Utah 2d 305, 470 P.2d 403 (1970).

price. Note that if the property's market value is significantly higher than the price paid, the latter can be a much more attractive strategy, since the grantee's recovery is not subject to any limitation based on a pro-rata portion of the original price paid. Finally, if the encumbrance in question is one which can be removed for a liquidated amount, such as a mortgage or a mechanics lien, that amount is the measure of damages (again, capped by the original price the grantor received).[727]

Damage claims raise several other interesting issues. The "present" covenants are breached when the deed is delivered, if at all, but that does not mean substantial damages can be collected immediately. The grantee must show actual harm, which practically amounts to requiring an eviction; otherwise one can have only nominal damages.[728] Yet if the grantee waits for an eviction before suing on the covenants, there is a considerable risk that any substantial recovery will be barred by the statute of limitations. Another problem arises if the deed containing the covenants was a gift, with no dollar consideration received by the covenantor. Some authority permits recovery on the covenant, with the upper limit fixed by the land's value at the time of the conveyance.[729] Finally, note that if the grantee recovers damages equal to the full price paid for the land, the grantee will be obliged to reconvey to the grantor upon request any interest which was in fact received by the original deed; otherwise, it is reasoned that the grantee would be unjustly enriched.[730]

Since the "future" covenants run with the land and can be asserted by remote grantees, the question arises whether the upper limit of damages is the price the covenantee paid for the land or the amount the covenantor received. The two figures may well be different. Suppose A sells land to B with a covenant of warranty for $10,000. Later B sells the same land to C for $15,000. If C brings an action against A on the covenant, there is wide agreement that C's recovery will be limited to the $10,000 A received.[731] However, if B sells to C for only $5,000, the cases are seriously divided as to whether C can recover the full $10,000 A received or only the $5,000 C paid.[732] The

---

[727] Again, the recovery is limited to the price the covenantor received. See Ticor Title Ins. Co. v. Graham, 576 N.E.2d 1332 (Ind.App. 1991); Forrer v. Sather, 595 P.2d 1306 (Utah 1979); Evans v. Faught, 231 Cal.App.2d 698, 42 Cal.Rptr. 133 (1965); Wolff v. Commercial Standard Insurance Co., 345 S.W.2d 565 (Tex.Civ.App. 1961).

[728] Fong v. Batton, 214 So.2d 649 (Fla. App. 1968); Dillard v. Earnhart, 457 S.W.2d 666 (Mo. 1970); Fisk v. Powell, 349 Mich. 604, 84 N.W.2d 736 (1957); Annot., 61 A.L.R. 10, 76 n. 27 (1929). But see Fechtner v. Lake County Savings & Loan Association, 66 Ill.2d 128, 5 Ill.Dec. 252, 361 N.E.2d 575 (1977), approving recovery of substantial damages for judgment liens on the land although the plaintiff/grantee had not discharged them and they had not been foreclosed.

[729] Smith v. Smith, 243 Ga. 56, 252 S.E.2d 484 (1979); Annot., 61 A.L.R. 10, 150 n. 89 (1929). But see Ragsdale v. Ragsdale, 172 S.W.2d 381 (Tex.Civ.App. 1943), affirmed 142 Tex. 476, 179 S.W.2d 291 (1944), allowing no recovery where no price was paid. If the transaction was an exchange rather than a sale, there may be no explicit dollar price stated; the value of the land which the covenantee gave up will be the upper limit of the recovery. See Maxwell v. Redd, 209 Kan. 264, 496 P.2d 1320 (1972); 61 A.L.R. 10, 150 (1928).

[730] Fong v. Batton, 214 So.2d 649 (Fla. App. 1968). In some jurisdictions it is customary for the court to order or decree a reconveyance as a condition of entering judgment in damages for the covenantee; see, e.g., Wood v. Setliff, 232 Ark. 233, 335 S.W.2d 305 (1960). The same principle applies when there is a total failure of title to a physical portion of the land; that portion must be reconveyed; id.

[731] Smith v. Smith, 243 Ga. 56, 252 S.E.2d 484 (1979); Bridges v. Heimburger, 360 So.2d 929 (Miss. 1978). ULTA § 2–513(2) agrees. However, if C has only a partial loss of value, say, one-half, the cases allow him to measure his damages as of the date of the deed to himself, rather than the earlier deed given by A; thus he could recover $7,500, since that would not exceed the total consideration received by A. See ULTA § 2–513 comment 2.

[732] Compare Brooks v. Black, 68 Miss. 161, 8 So. 332 (1890) (remote grantor liable for amount received) with Taylor v. Wallace, 20 Colo. 211, 37 P. 963 (1894) (recovery limited to amount grantee paid). Modern

argument for the latter figure is based on the notion that C should not recover more than actual damages, but inflation or improvements built by C may well make C's damages exceed the price paid. It is hard to see how A can reasonably complain about reimbursing C's actual damages up to the amount A received.

In addition to the measures of damages discussed above, two other factors often form a basis for damage claims: interest and litigation costs, including attorneys' fees. Both are widely recognized as proper.[733] However, there is a good deal of confusion about the basis and measurement of interest. One common approach allows interest only for the period, if any, that the plaintiff has been denied actual possession or use of the property as a result of the title defect.[734] This same idea is embodied in decisions which allow interest only from the date of the grantee's eviction.[735] Another view holds that even if the plaintiff has had possession for the entire time since taking the deed, he or she may be liable as a trespasser to the holder of paramount title for so-called mesne profits, and hence should get interest for the full period as an approximate way of compensating for that liability.[736] Arguably this idea breaks down if the grantee purchases the paramount title, since he or she obviously cannot then be sued for mesne profits; but it might be assumed that the price paid for the outstanding interest must have included a factor representing the mesne profits the true owner could otherwise have collected.[737]

Perhaps surprisingly, the majority of cases allow the grantee to recover the court costs and attorneys' fees expended in litigating the title with a third party who turns out to hold a paramount interest.[738] It does not matter whether the grantee was the plaintiff or the defendant in that action, so long as the grantee pursued it in good faith and lost, and the fees are reasonable.[739] Attorneys' fees for negotiating to acquire the outstanding title without litigation can also be recovered.[740] However, somewhat ironically, if the

---

authority on the point is very scant. See Annot., 61 A.L.R. 10, 120–24 (1929); J. Cribbet, Real Property 276–77 (2d ed. 1975).

[733] Koelker v. Turnbull, 127 Idaho 262, 899 P.2d 972 (Idaho 1995); Foley v. Smith, 14 Wn.App. 285, 539 P.2d 874 (1975). But see Maxwell v. Redd, 209 Kan. 264, 496 P.2d 1320 (1972), where the court refused to allow interest because the transaction had been an exchange of land rather than a sale, and the parties had never agreed to any specific price or value for the parcels exchanged.

[734] See Yonkers City Post No. 1666, Veterans of Foreign Wars of the United States, Inc. v. Josanth Realty Corp., 104 A.D.2d 980, 481 N.Y.S.2d 95 (1984), reversed on other grounds 67 N.Y.2d 1029, 503 N.Y.S.2d 321, 494 N.E.2d 452 (1986), on remand 143 A.D.2d 267, 532 N.Y.S.2d 169 (1988); Hillsboro Cove, Inc. v. Archibald, 322 So.2d 585 (Fla.App. 1975); Forrest v. Hanson, 424 S.W.2d 899 (Tex. 1968). See generally Annot., 61 A.L.R. 10, 174–82 (1929).

[735] See, e.g., Tucker v. Walker, 246 Ark. 177, 437 S.W.2d 788 (1969).

[736] Davis v. Smith, 5 Ga. 274 (1848). Some cases consider the actual liability of the grantee for mesne profits. If, for example, the grantee is insulated by the statute of limitations from such liability for a portion of the time he or she has been in possession, interest is computed only for the remaining time. See Smith v. Nussbaum, 71 S.W.2d 82 (Mo.App. 1934); Hilliker v. Rueger, 228 N.Y. 11, 126 N.E. 266 (1920); Curtis v. Brannon, 98 Tenn. 153, 38 S.W. 1073 (1897).

[737] See Harding v. Larkin, 41 Ill. 413 (1866).

[738] The fees must be both actual and reasonable; see Liddycoat v. Ulbricht, 276 Or. 723, 556 P.2d 99 (1976); Morgan v. Haley, 107 Va. 331, 58 S.E. 564 (1907), discussing but rejecting the majority view; cases cited at note 733 infra. See 4 Tiffany, Real Property § 1020 (3d ed. 2017 update). Cf. Elliott v. Elliott, 252 Ark. 966, 482 S.W.2d 123 (1972) (under Texas law, no recovery for attorneys' fee in absence of agreement to pay them).

[739] Nelson v. Growers Ford Tractor Co., 282 So.2d 664 (Fla.App. 1973); Louisville Public-Warehouse Co. v. James, 139 Ky. 434, 56 S.W. 19 (1900); Annot., 61 A.L.R. 10, 167 n. 28 (1929).

[740] Mastro v. Kumakichi Corp., 90 Wn. App. 157, 951 P.2d 817 (1998); Creason v. Peterson, 24 Utah 2d 305, 470 P.2d 403 (1970).

grantee litigates the validity of the title and prevails, so that the court determines that the grantee's title was not defective, the grantee's attempt to recover attorneys' fees and costs (or for that matter, damages for breach) from the grantor will be disallowed—simply because the court's decision establishes that the grantor did not breach the title covenants.[741]

At one time it was generally held that a grantee could not get attorneys' fees without first giving the grantor notice of the litigation and requesting him or her to represent the grantee,[742] but most of the recent cases do not impose this requirement. Note carefully that only attorneys' fees in the action against the third party can be recovered; fees in the action against the grantor on the title covenants themselves are not collectable, at least in the absence of fraud or bad faith.[743]

§ 11.14   TITLE INSURANCE

As the preceding sections have shown, the recording system is imperfect in its ability to warn prospective purchasers of land that title defects are present. The risk of such defects can be reduced by curative statutes and marketable title acts, but it is still great enough to be a serious concern. Title insurance has arisen as a way of compensating for this risk.[744]

A title insurance policy is a contract of indemnity. It states the name of the person or persons in whom the title is vested, and it lists all significant[745] encumbrances or other title defects which the insurer knows are present, ordinarily through a title search, and for which it therefore assumes no liability. If it later develops that the title was differently vested or was subject to other defects or encumbrances on the date of the policy, the insurer is obligated to indemnify the insured for any losses caused by the discrepancy.[746]

---

[741] Outcalt v. Wardlaw, 750 N.E.2d 859 (Ind. Ct. App. 2001); RAMA Operating Co. v. Barker, 47 Kan. App. 2d 1020, 286 P.3d 1138 (2012); Seratt v. Liberty State Bank, 816 P.2d 584 (Okl. App. 1991); Nunes v. Meadowbrook Dev. Co., 24 A.3d 539 (R.I. 2011); Black v. Patel, 357 S.C. 466, 594 S.E.2d 162 (2004); Stumhoffer v. Perales, 459 S.W.3d 158 (Tex. App. 2015). But see Coco v. Jaskunas, 159 N.H. 515, 523, 986 A.2d 531, 538 (2009) (grantee need only show potential liability to third party in order to establish grantor's duty to provide or pay for defense of title).

[742] See Bloom v. Hendricks, 111 N.M. 250, 804 P.2d 1069 (1991); Mellor v. Chamberlin, 100 Wn.2d 643, 673 P.2d 610 (1983); Smith v. Nussbaum, 71 S.W.2d 82 (Mo.App. 1934); 61 A.L.R. 10, 162 n. 16 (1929). Even if notice is not a prerequisite to recovery of attorneys' fees, it is still a wise precaution, since it will bind the covenantor to a judicial determination that the third party in fact has paramount title; see text at note 741 supra. See also Rowe v. Klein, 409 P.3d 1152 (Wash. Ct. App. 2018) ("warranty to defend" the title is breached only if grantee tenders defense to grantor and grantor refuses to defend); Buck Mountain Owner's Ass'n v. Prestwich, 174 Wash. App. 702, 308 P.3d 644 (2013) (to validly tender defense to grantor, grantee must inform grantor that if she refuses to defend she will be bound by the outcome of litigation between grantee and third party).

[743] Skipper v. McMillan, 349 So.2d 808 (Fla.App. 1977); Wilkinson Homes, Inc. v. Stewart Title Guar. Co., 271 Ga. App. 577, 610 S.E.2d 187 (2005); Bridges v. Heimburger, 360 So.2d 929 (Miss. 1978); Forrer v. Sather, 595 P.2d 1306 (Utah 1979); Barber v. Peringer, 75 Wn.App. 248, 877 P.2d 223 (1994). But see Flynn v. Allison, 97 Idaho 618, 549 P.2d 1065 (1976).

[744] The mortgage crisis of the late 2000s was difficult for the title industry and caused considerable contraction. At this writing (2018) there remain only seven national title insurance underwriters.

[745] If the title insurer is aware of an encumbrance but considers it trivial or unlikely to be asserted, the insurer may intentionally omit it from the list in the title policy of matters not insured against (usually in Schedule B of the policy). This is known as "insuring over" the particular risk.

[746] See generally Palomar, Title Insurance Law (2017); Gosdin, Title Insurance: A Comprehensive Overview (1996); Burke, Law of Title Insurance (3d ed. 2018). Some title insurance policies (but not all) insure not only against defects of title, but also that title is marketable; see Annot., Defects Affecting Marketability

There are two general kinds of title insurance policies, insuring respectively mortgage lenders and owners. Lenders' policies are more widely used, and nearly all commercial lenders insist upon them (usually at the borrower's expense) in every mortgage loan. Likewise, virtually all secondary market purchasers of mortgages require lender's title insurance, a fact which largely explains the explosive growth of the title industry since World War II. Owners' policies are nearly universally employed in real estate sales in the western United States, where it is customary for the seller to pay for an owner's policy for the buyer. They are less common in the midwest and east, where buyers are usually expected to pay for their own title insurance.[747]

Title insurance differs from most other insurance lines in important ways. It is paid for by a single premium, and the coverage under an owner's policy lasts indefinitely so long as the owner or his or her heirs, devisees, or corporate successors continue to hold the land.[748] It covers the condition of the title only as of the policy's date, and defects

---

of Title Within Meaning of Title Insurance Policy, 18 A.L.R.4th 1311 (1982). Defects in title arising after the policy is issued are generally not covered; see BV Jordanelle, LLC v. Old Republic Nat'l Title Ins. Co., 830 F.3d 1195 (10th Cir. 2016); Rosen v. Nations Title Ins. Co., 56 Cal. App.4th 1489, 66 Cal.Rptr.2d 714 (Cal.App. 1997); Woodle v. Commonwealth Land Title Ins. Co., 287 Neb. 917, 844 N.W.2d 806 (2014); Vestin Mortg., Inc. v. First Am. Title Ins. Co., 2006 UT 34, 139 P.3d 1055 (2006). The public regulation of the title insurance industry is beyond the scope of the present discussion. See generally Note, The Title Insurance Industry and Government Regulation, 53 Va.L.Rev. 1523 (1967). For additional information on the title insurance market, see Gov't Account. Off., Title Insurance: Preliminary Views and Issues for Further Study, GAO-06-568 (Apr. 2006).

[747] See generally B. Burke, American Conveyancing Patterns (1978); U.S. Department of Housing and Urban Development & Veterans Administration, Report on Mortgage Settlement Costs (1972); Payne, Ancillary Costs in the Purchase of Homes, 35 Missouri L.Rev. 455 (1970).

[748] The American Land Title Association (ALTA), the title industry's trade and lobbying organization, issues standard forms that are widely used by title insurers. At this writing the most recent ALTA forms for general use are the Owner's Policy and Loan Policy approved in 2006. A "plain language" Owner's Policy for residential use was approved in 2013. The 2006 forms are referred to here.

Inter vivos transferees of the insured are not covered by an owner's title insurance policy; see, e.g., Fid. Nat'l Title Ins. Co. v. Butler, 2017 WL 2774337 (Cal. Ct. App. 2017) (unpublished). However, the original insured under an owner's policy continues to be protected if he or she conveys the land away and is later sued on a title covenant in the deed; see 2006 ALTA Owners Policy, Condition 2, Termination of Insurance; Stewart Title Guaranty Co. v. Lunt Land Corp., 162 Tex. 435, 347 S.W.2d 584 (1961). But if the title defect is one created by the insured, coverage will be denied; see ASK Realty II Corp. v. First Am. Title Ins. Co., 2004 WL 1254005 (D. Md. 2004) (unpublished); Gebhardt Family Inv., L.L.C. v. Nations Title Ins. of New York, Inc., 132 Md. App. 457, 752 A.2d 1222 (2000); note 767 infra. Further, an insured owner who sells the property and takes back a purchase-money mortgage continues to be covered with respect to the mortgage; see Condition 2, id.

The notion that owner's policy coverage terminates if the insured transfers the property has proven troublesome in cases where, for example, the transfer is to the insured's wholly-owned LLC or family trust. Under traditional policy language even these transfers cause a termination of coverage; see, e.g., Kwok v. Transnation Title Ins. Co., 170 Cal. App. 4th 1562, 89 Cal. Rptr. 3d 141 (2009); Point of Rocks Ranch, L.L.C. v. Sun Valley Title Ins. Co., 143 Idaho 411, 146 P.3d 677 (2006); Butera v. Attorneys' Title Guar. Fund, Inc., 321 Ill. App. 3d 601, 747 N.E.2d 949 (2001); Shotmeyer v. New Jersey Realty Title Ins. Co., 195 N.J. 72, 948 A.2d 600 (2008). Cf. N. Fork Land & Cattle, LLLP v. First Am. Title Ins. Co., 2015 WY 150, 362 P.3d 341 (Wyo. 2015). The 2013 ALTA Homeowner's Policy, Conditions, par. 2, loosens this rule considerably, providing coverage to the insured's heirs, devisees, spouse in the event of marriage dissolution, family trust, and trust beneficiaries. The 2006 ALTA Owner's Policy, Conditions, par. 1(d), provides similar protection to heirs, devisees, trusts and trust beneficiaries, and also to wholly-owned business entities if the transfer is without consideration. See also Kan. Stat. Ann. § 58a–1107, providing for the continuation of title insurance coverage after a transfer to an inter vivos trust.

A loan policy protects not only the original mortgagee, but also corporate successors, secondary market assignees of the note and mortgage, and any government agency insuring or guaranteeing the loan; it continues in effect if the insured lender buys the property at a foreclosure sale or takes a deed in lieu of foreclosure. See 2006 ALTA Loan Policy, Conditions and Stipulations par. 1(a), par. 2. But if the lender forecloses the mortgage and a third party buys at the sale, coverage under the policy terminates; see Hovannisian v. First Am. Title Ins. Co., 14 Cal. App. 5th 420, 221 Cal. Rptr. 3d 883 (Ct. App. 2017).

arising afterward cannot be the basis of a claim.[749] It indemnifies only for losses that result from title matters; other problems, such as physical defects or government regulations which inhibit the use of the property, do not bring the policy into play.[750]

Unlike other insurance carriers, whose level of risk is largely a function of the characteristics and behavior of the persons and property they insure, title insurers have considerable control of the risk they undertake. By a careful examination of the record title (and in some cases a physical inspection of the land) before issuance of each policy, the company can identify most types of defects and encumbrances which might pose unacceptable risks, and can list them in the policy as exceptions to coverage. In some areas of the nation, the companies employ staff members to do searches, usually in the companys' own private "title plants" which duplicate the public records but are organized on the basis of parcel indexes. In other areas the companies use agents or "approved attorneys" who make their examinations from commercial abstracts or directly from the public records and whose findings form the basis for issuance of policies on behalf of the title insurance company.[751] Where company staff performs the search, the premium charged is usually an "all-inclusive rate" which covers both the search and insurance functions. A "preliminary title report," a "commitment," or a "binder" is generally sent to the proposed insureds prior to the closing of the transaction; it lists the significant encumbrances and defects the search has disclosed, and constitutes the company's commitment to issue a policy with no further exceptions.[752]

It might be considered foolish for a title company to issue policies without procuring a careful search of the records first, since such a practice will obviously lead to larger claims in the long run. But is a search legally required?[753] Most binders and policies contain no explicit statement that a search has been made, although prospective insureds routinely treat the binder as a report of a search, and hence as a summary of the title defects disclosed by it. Several cases have held that there is an implied duty to make a reasonable search, and a number of states have adopted statutes to the same effect. If one grants that there is a duty to search, it follows that there is likewise a duty

---

[749] See, e.g., Safeco Title Insurance Co. v. Moskopoulos, 116 Cal.App.3d 658, 172 Cal.Rptr. 248 (1981); National Mortgage Corp. v. American Title Insurance Co., 299 N.C. 369, 261 S.E.2d 844 (1980).

[750] Sec. Serv. Fed. Credit Union v. First Am. Title Ins. Co., 585 F. App'x 591 (9th Cir. 2014) (failure to obtain state approval of subdivision); Allison v. Ticor Title Ins. Co., 907 F.2d 645 (7th Cir. 1990), appeal after remand 979 F.2d 1187 (7th Cir.1992) (securities law violation); Nishiyama v. Safeco Title Insurance Co., 85 Cal.App.3d Supp. 1, 149 Cal.Rptr. 355 (1978) (illegal subdivision); Somerset Sav. Bank v. Chicago Title Ins. Co., 420 Mass. 422, 649 N.E.2d 1123 (Mass.1995) (land use regulation); Sonnett v. First Am. Title Ins. Co., 2013 WY 106, 309 P.3d 799 (Wyo. 2013) (master plan amendment). A loan policy does not cover the non-title risk of failure of payment on the secured debt; see Lawyers Title Ins. Corp. v. JDC (America) Corp., 52 F.3d 1575 (11th Cir. 1995).

[751] See In re Evans, 464 B.R. 272 (Bankr. S.D. Miss. 2011) (title company had no duty to supervise approved attorneys); First American Title Ins. Co. v. First Title Service Co., note 754 infra; Brohman, Has Title Insurance Changed the Attorney's Role in Real Estate Transactions?, 60 Fla.B.J. 47 (Feb.1986); Annot., Title Insurance Company's Rights in Title Information, 38 A.L.R.4th 968 (1985). On methods of title search by title insurers, see Whitman, Optimizing Land Title Assurance Systems, 42 G.Wash.L.Rev. 40 (1973).

[752] If a preliminary report is issued, the title insurer is probably under no legal duty to follow through and issue a policy; see, e.g., Abikasis v. Provident Title Co., 2016 WL 3611016 (Cal. Ct. App. 2016) (unpublished). On the other hand, a "binder" or "commitment" does impose such a legal duty.

[753] See Comment, Title Insurance: The Duty to Search, 71 Yale L.J. 1161 (1962). In a few states, statutes specifically mandate that a search be made; see, e.g., Ariz.Rev. Stat. § 20–1567; Colo. Rev .Stat. § 10–11–106; West's Fla. Stat. Ann. § 627.7845; N.H. Rev. Stat. § 416–A:6; N.C. Gen. Stat. § 58–132. These statutes make no reference to any duty to disclose search results to the insured; however, such a duty might be inferred. See also Erskine Florida Properties, Inc. v. First American Title Ins. Co. of St. Lucie County, Inc., 557 So.2d 859 (Fla. 1989) (title company acting as abstractor has duty to search all relevant public records).

to disclose the search's results to the customer. From there, it is a short step to treating the title insurer much like an abstractor,[754] liable on the basis of negligence if a search is not done and reported with ordinary care and skill.[755] On the other hand, there are many jurisdictions that find no duty at all to provide title information, do not treat the insurance company as an abstractor, and impose no liability outside the scope of the insurance policy itself.[756]

An insured might attempt to use tort rather than contract principles in an action against a title insurer for several reasons. The prospective insured may have received a title report or commitment, but never ordered an actual policy.[757] Some policies contain clauses requiring the insured to report all claims within a very short period—typically 60 or 90 days—after the insured discovers the loss; a tort theory might permit the insured to evade this time limit.[758] The insured may have reconveyed the property, causing the coverage of the policy to terminate.[759] The plaintiff might attempt to use tort theories to recover amounts greater than the policy limits,[760] or measures of damage which would be difficult or impossible to sustain under contract law, such as lost business profits caused by delayed construction due to a title defect.[761] The insured may

---

[754] Abstractors are liable for ordinary negligence; see, e.g., First American Title Ins. Co. v. First Title Service Co., 457 So.2d 467 (Fla.1984), on remand 458 So.2d 822 (Fla.App.1984); Williams v. Polgar, 391 Mich. 6, 215 N.W.2d 149 (1974); Annot., Negligence in Preparing Abstract of Title as Ground of Liability to One Other than Person Ordering Abstract, 50 A.L.R.4th 314 (1986).

[755] See MacDonald v. Old Republic Nat. Title Ins. Co., 882 F.Supp.2d 236 (D. Mass. 2012); Parker v. Ward, 614 So.2d 975 (Ala. 1992); Breck v. Moore, 910 P.2d 599 (Alaska 1996); 100 Investment Ltd. Partnership v. Columbia Town Ctr. Title Co., 430 Md. 197, 60 A.3d 1 (2013) (title agent was liable for negligence in search, but underwriter's liability was limited to the title insurance policy); Tess v. Lawyers Title Ins. Corp., 251 Neb. 501, 557 N.W.2d 696 (Neb. 1997); Sears Mortg. Corp. v. Rose, 134 N.J. 326, 634 A.2d 74 (N.J. 1993) (duty to warn insured if insurer is not providing the usually-expected coverage); Cottonwood Enterprises v. McAlpin, 111 N.M. 793, 810 P.2d 812 (1991); Moore v. Title Ins. Co. of Minnesota, 148 Ariz. 408, 714 P.2d 1303 (App. 1985); Davis, More Than They Bargained For: Are Title Insurance Companies Liable in Tort for Undisclosed Title Defects?, 45 Cath.U.L.Rev. 71 (1995).

[756] See Focus Investments Associates, Inc. v. American Title Insurance Co., 992 F.2d 1231 (1st Cir. 1993); Chicago Title Ins. Co. v. Commonwealth Forest Inv., Inc., 494 F.Supp.2d 1332 (M.D.Fla. 2007); Mickam v. Joseph Louis Palace Trust, 849 F.Supp. 516 (E.D.Mich. 1993); Cummings v. Stephens, 157 Idaho 348, 336 P.3d 281 (2014); Centennial Dev. Grp., LLC v. Lawyer's Title Ins. Corp., 233 Ariz. 147, 310 P.3d 23 (Ct. App. 2013) (based on Ariz. Rev. Stat. § 20–1562); Pearman v. Stewart Title Guar. Co., 2018 WL 3132451 (Ind. Ct. App. 2018) (unpublished); First Midwest Bank, N.A. v. Stewart Title Guar. Co., 218 Ill. 2d 326, 843 N.E.2d 327 (2006); Walker Rogge, Inc. v. Chelsea Title & Guar. Co., 116 N.J. 517, 562 A.2d 208 (1989), appeal after remand 254 N.J.Super. 380, 603 A.2d 557 (1992); Citibank v. Chicago Title Ins. Co., 214 A.D.2d 212, 632 N.Y.S.2d 779 (App. Div. 1995); Chapman v. Uintah Cty., 2003 UT App 383, 81 P.3d 761 (2003); Barstad v. Stewart Title Guar. Co., 145 Wash. 2d 528, 39 P.3d 984 (2002); Greenberg v. Stewart Title Guar. Co., 171 Wis.2d 485, 492 N.W.2d 147 (Wis. 1992); Hulse v. First Am. Title Co. of Crook Cty., 2001 WY 95, 33 P.3d 122 (Wyo. 2001). See also Stewart Title Guar. Co. v. Becker, 930 S.W.2d 748 (Tex.App. 1996) (statute imposes duty to search, but provides no private remedy to insured).

[757] See, e.g., Marcantel v. Stewart Title Guar. Co., 2018 WL 1621498, ___ F.Supp.2d ___ (D. Utah 2018) (rejecting liability based on commitment).

[758] The 2006 ALTA Owner's Policy, Conditions, par. 3 does not fix a definite time within which a claim must be made, but instead requires notification "promptly" after the insured learns of an adverse title matter. See Countrywide Home Loans, Inc. v. First Am. Title Ins. Co., 2012 WL 516824 (Cal. Ct. App. 2012) (unpublished).

[759] See note 748 supra. This was the case in 100 Investment Ltd. Partnership v. Columbia Town Ctr. Title Co., 430 Md. 197, 60 A.3d 1 (2013); see the opinion of the court in the insured's litigation on his policy claim, Chicago Title Ins. Co. v. 100 Inv. Ltd. P'ship, 355 F.3d 759, 766 (4th Cir. 2004).

[760] Southland Title Corp. v. Superior Court, 231 Cal. App.3d 530, 282 Cal.Rptr. 425 (1991), Russo v. PPN Title Agency, LLC, 2017 WL 3081709 (N.J. Super. Ct. App. Div. 2017) (unpublished).

[761] See text at notes 772–776 infra.

wish to claim punitive damages, which of course are not permitted under the policy.[762] In a rather celebrated case, a California Court of Appeal awarded $200,000 in tort damages for the insureds' mental distress; the title insurer had failed to find and report an easement, and then refused for three years to pay for the loss or eliminate the easement![763]

But all told, the courts have increasingly rejected the concept that an insured party under a title policy or title commitment can recover in tort.[764] This conclusion is strongly reinforced by language like the following in most modern policies: "Any claim of loss or damage that arises out of the status of the Title or by any action asserting such claim shall be restricted to this policy."[765]

Most title policies contain a number of more-or-less standard exclusions for matters which are not insured against. They include laws and governmental ordinances[766] and exercises of eminent domain rights unless appearing in the public records. It is nearly universal to exclude title matters "created, suffered, assumed, or agreed to" by the insured,[767] and off-record matters which the insured knows about at the date of the policy or the date the insured acquires his or her interest, and of which the insurer has not been notified.[768] Less widespread, but quite common, are boiler-plate exceptions for various types of title claims if they are not shown by the public records; these often

---

[762] Lawyers Title Ins. Corp. v. Vella, 570 So.2d 578 (Ala. 1990); Red Lobster Inns of America, Inc. v. Lawyers Title Insurance Corp., 492 F.Supp. 933 (E.D.Ark. 1980), affirmed 656 F.2d 381 (8th Cir. 1981).

[763] Jarchow v. Transamerica Title Insurance Co., 48 Cal.App.3d 917, 122 Cal. Rptr. 470 (1975), noted 8 Sw.U.L.Rev. 203 (1976); 1976 B.Y.U.L.Rev. 895. The policy limit in the case was only $75,000. Ordinarily, lost profits are not recoverable under a title insurance policy; see Lawyers Title Ins. Co. v. Synergism One Corp., 572 So.2d 517 (Fla.App. 1990). See also Southland Title Corp. v. Superior Court, 231 Cal. App.3d 530, 282 Cal.Rptr. 425 (1991), where the tort liability claim simply represented the insured's attempt to get a recovery larger than the policy limit.

[764] See cases cited note 756 supra.

[765] See, e.g., 2006 ALTA Owners Policy, Conditions, par. 15. Relying on the quoted or similar language, see Bank of California v. First American Title Ins. Co., 826 P.2d 1126 (Alaska 1992); Reflections Townhomes v. First Am. Title Ins. Co., 2010 WL 445521 (Ariz. Ct. App. 2010) (unpublished); White v. Western Title Ins. Co., 40 Cal.3d 870, 221 Cal.Rptr. 509, 710 P.2d 309 (Cal. 1985); Country Home Loans, Inc. v. First Am. Title Ins. Co., 2012 WL 516824 (Cal. Ct. App. 2012) (unpublished); 100 Investment Ltd. Partnership v. Columbia Town Ctr. Title Co., 430 Md. 197, 60 A.3d 1 (2013); Express Fin. Servs. Inc. v. Gateway Abstract Inc., 71 Pa. D. & C.4th 344, 350 (Com. Pl. 2004), aff'd sub nom. Express Fin. Servs. v. Gateway Abstract, 897 A.2d 525 (Pa. Super. Ct. 2006).

[766] These are probably not technically title matters, and thus would not be covered in any event; see text at note 750 supra.

[767] 2006 ALTA Owners Policy, Exclusions from Coverage 3(a). See First Am. Title Ins. Co. v. Lane Powell PC, 764 F.3d 114 (1st Cir. 2014) (lender which was fully aware of prior mortgages held to have "assumed" and "agreed" to them); First Am. Title Ins. Co. v. Action Acquisitions, LLC, 218 Ariz. 394, 187 P.3d 1107 (2008); Schuman v. Investors Title Ins. Co., 78 N.C.App. 783, 338 S.E.2d 611 (1986), review denied 316 N.C. 554, 344 S.E.2d 9 (1986); Keown v. West Jersey Title & Guaranty Co., 161 N.J.Super. 19, 390 A.2d 715 (1978), certification denied 78 N.J. 405, 396 A.2d 592 (1978); Annot., 87 A.L.R.3d 515 (1978); Fifth Third Mortg. Co. v. Chicago Title Ins. Co., 692 F.3d 507 (6th Cir. 2012) (lender did not "create" title defect by its careless underwriting of mortgage loan). In BB Syndication Servs., Inc. v. First Am. Title Ins. Co., 780 F.3d 825 (7th Cir. 2015), the court held that a construction lender that cut off loan disbursements (as a result of which mechanics' liens were filed) because the project was over budget had "created" the liens by its actions, and thus could not claim indemnification for the liens from its title insurer. Contra, see Home Fed. Sav. Bank v. Ticor Title Ins. Co., 695 F.3d 725 (7th Cir. 2012).

[768] 2006 ALTA Owners Policy, Exclusions from Coverage 3(b). See Lawyers Title Ins. Corp. v. First Federal Sav. Bank & Trust, 744 F.Supp. 778 (E.D.Mich. 1990); Southern Title Insurance Co. v. Crow, 278 So.2d 294 (Fla.App.1973), cert. denied 284 So.2d 221 (Fla. 1973); C 1031 Properties, Inc. v. First Am. Title Ins. Co., 175 Wash. App. 27, 301 P.3d 500 (2013); Annot., 75 A.L.R.3d 600 (1977). A similar duty exists under common law principles even if not spelled out in the contract; see Collins v. Pioneer Title Insurance Co., 629 F.2d 429 (6th Cir. 1980).

include rights of persons in possession, property taxes and assessments, matters which a survey would disclose, public rights-of-way, easements, water and mining rights, and mechanics liens.[769] Policy coverages vary considerably, and owners' policies are usually weaker than lenders' policies; some contracts contain so many exceptions and exclusions that there is very little protection against off-record risks.[770]

The insurer has three related duties under a title insurance policy: to indemnify the loss by payment of damages, to defend the insured in the event of a legal attack on the title, and (under one view) to take affirmative action to cure the title defects if feasible.[771] Damages are calculated in much the same manner as for breach of title covenants in deeds, although the insured need not show an eviction.[772] If there is no loss to the insured, nothing can be recovered on the policy.[773] For a complete failure of title, the insured under an owner's policy can recover the value of the land so long as it does not exceed the policy limit.[774] If an encumbrance exists which can be paid off by a liquidated sum, that amount is the recovery on the policy.[775] For other types of encumbrances, such as easements or restrictive covenants that cannot be removing by paying money, the measure of recovery is the difference in value of the land with and without the encumbrance, provided the policy limit is not exceeded.[776] Under a lender's policy, the

---

[769] Disputes over the construction of these exceptions abound; see, e.g., Oak Park Trust & Sav. Bank v. Intercounty Title Co., 287 Ill.App.3d 647, 222 Ill.Dec. 851, 678 N.E.2d 723 (Ill.App. 1997); Transamerica Title Ins. Co. v. Northwest Bldg. Corp., 54 Wn.App. 289, 773 P.2d 431 (1989), review denied 113 Wn.2d 1008, 779 P.2d 727 (1989); Walker Rogge, Inc. v. Chelsea Title & Guar. Co., 116 N.J. 517, 562 A.2d 208 (1989); Annot., 98 A.L.R. 537 (1964). See also Pedowitz, Title Insurance: Non-Coverage of Hazardous Waste Super-Liens, 13 Probate & Property no. 4, p. 46 (Spring 1985).

[770] On the other hand, residential owner's policies often include coverages that are unavailable, or available only under extra-cost endorsements, on other policies. For example, the 2013 ALTA Homeowner's Policy covers damage from entry by mineral rights owners (Covered Risks 25), costs of removing encroaching structures (Covered Risks 21), zoning preventing single-family residence use (Covered Risks 19, 20), and violations of subdivision regulations (Covered Risks 16). Many companies will waive the usual exceptions or issue endorsements overriding them, and some companies will also issue affirmative coverage of such matters as zoning, usury, and truth-in-lending compliance, if an additional fee is paid and the company is furnished with added information which satisfies it that the risk is acceptable; see the lengthy list of ALTA-approved endorsements at https://www.alta.org/policy-forms/.

[771] See cases cited note 782 infra. Title matters outside the coverage of the policy are also outside the insured's duty to defend; see Bidart v. American Title Ins. Co., 103 Nev. 175, 734 P.2d 732 (1987).

[772] See § 11.13 supra at note 709; Securities Service, Inc. v. Transamerica Title Insurance Co., 20 Wn.App. 664, 583 P.2d 1217 (1978); Southern Title Guaranty Co. v. Prendergast, 494 S.W.2d 154 (Tex. 1973).

[773] Karl v. Commonwealth Land Title Ins. Co., 60 Cal.App.4th 858, 70 Cal.Rptr.2d 374 (Cal.App. 1997) (loan policy); Youngblood v. Lawyers Title Ins. Corp., 923 F.2d 161 (11th Cir. 1991) (owner's policy). Note that even if an asserted title defect turns out not to exist, the insurer may still be liable if it breaches its duty to defend; see notes 781–784 infra and accompanying text.

Ordinarily a claim on a loan policy may not be made until the lender forecloses the mortgage; the foreclosure proceeds thus determine the amount of the lender's loss. See 2006 ALTA Loan Policy, Conditions, par. 9(b). But this "foreclosure first" rule does not apply if insurer concedes that the mortgage is defective and cannot be foreclosed; see First Citizens Bank & Tr. Co. v. Stewart Title Guar. Co., 2014 Colo. App. 1, 320 P.3d 406 (2014).

[774] See Aja v. Appleton, 86 Nev. 639, 472 P.2d 524 (1970); Gray v. Commonwealth Land Title Ins. Co., 162 N.H. 71, 27 A.3d 852 (2011); Annot., 60 A.L.R.2d 977 (1958).

[775] Arizona Title Insurance & Trust Co. v. Smith, 21 Ariz.App. 371, 519 P.2d 860 (1974); Caravan Products Co. v. Ritchie, 55 N.J. 71, 259 A.2d 223 (1969). Virtually all policies provide that any payment of a claimed loss for less than the full policy amount operates to reduce the remaining coverage to the extent of the payment; see, e.g., 2006 ALTA Owner's Policy, Conditions, par. 10. However, payments for litigation and other related expenses do not count against the policy limit; id.

[776] Swanson v. Safeco Title Ins. Co., 186 Ariz. 637, 925 P.2d 1354 (Ariz.App. 1995); Aboussie v. Chicago Title Ins. Co., 949 S.W.2d 207 (Mo.App. 1997); Miller v. Ticor Title Ins. Co., 194 Or. App. 17, 93 P.3d 88 (2004); Stewart Title Guaranty Company v. Cheatham, 764 S.W.2d 315 (Tex.App. 1988).

insurer can always discharge its duty fully by paying the mortgagee the loan balance with accrued interest and costs; upon doing so, the insurer is entitled to an assignment of the note and mortgage.[777]

When a title insurer pays a claim to its insured, it is subrogated to the insured's rights against others who would be liable to pay the insured for the loss.[778] The most common illustration is that of a grantor or mortgagor who is liable to the grantee or mortgagee under a covenant of title in the deed or mortgage. Many, perhaps most, of the claims on deed warranties in modern times are brought by title insurers under their right of subrogation.[779] Moreover, because mortgages invariably contain covenants of title, title insurers who pay off mortgages under lenders' policies are subrogated against the borrowers unless the latter   are also covered by owner's policies.[780]

The insurer's duties to attempt to cure title defects and to defend the title are closely allied. Most policies mention only the latter,[781] but a significant number of cases also recognize an affirmative obligation to make a good faith effort to bring the title into compliance with the policy, provided this can be done by an expenditure within the policy limits.[782] The duty to defend likewise includes a good faith element, and the insurer cannot escape its obligations by asserting that the attack on the title is ill-founded or

---

[777] See 2006 ALTA Loan Policy, Conditions, par. 7(a)(ii); Paramount Properties Co. v. Transamerica Title Insurance Co., 1 Cal.3d 562, 83 Cal.Rptr. 394, 463 P.2d 746 (1970). Subrogation may or may not be denied if the title insurer was negligent in conducting its search; compare American Title Ins. Co. v. M-H Enterprises, 815 P.2d 1219 (Okl.App. 1991) (subrogation denied) with Wilkinson Homes, Inc. v. Stewart Title Guar. Co., 271 Ga. App. 577, 610 S.E.2d 187 (2005) and Romero v. Stewart Title Guar., 2015 WL 348870 (Tex. App. 2015) (unpublished) (subrogation allowed). If title insurer pays a claim for which it has no liability, it cannot claim subrogation; see Rainier Nat'l Bank v. Wells, 65 Wn.App. 893, 829 P.2d 1168 (1992).

[778] See, e.g., Wilkinson Homes, Inc. v. Stewart Title Guar. Co., 271 Ga. App. 577, 610 S.E.2d 187 (2005). The title insurer also has a claim against an abstract company that has negligently provided it with incorrect information, but this is not based on subrogation; see Fidelity Nat. Title Ins. Co. v. Tri-Lakes Title Co., Inc., 968 S.W.2d 727 (Mo.App. 1998).

[779] See, e.g., Weiss v. Old Republic Nat. Title Ins. Co., 262 Ga. App. 120, 584 S.E.2d 710 (2003); Chicago Title Ins. v. Aurora Loan Servs., LLC, 2013 IL App (1st) 123510, 996 N.E.2d 44 (2013).

[780] Puente v. Beneficial Mortg. Co. of Indiana, 9 N.E.3d 208 (Ind. Ct. App. 2014). Because of the subrogation principle, an owner-mortgagor who fails to obtain an owner's policy is taking a double risk; the owner not only gets no protection from the lender's policy, but may be sued by the title insurer, as subrogee or assignee of the lender, on the note or the covenants of title in the mortgage. This may occur even though the owner paid the title insurance premium for the lender's policy! See, e.g., Title Insurance Company of Minnesota v. Costain Arizona, Inc., 791 P.2d 1086, 164 Ariz. 203 (App. 1990); Midfirst Bank v. Abney, 365 Ill. App. 3d 636, 850 N.E.2d 373 (2006).

[781] See 2006 ALTA Owner's Policy, Conditions, par. 5(a); Fifth Third Mortg. Co. v. Chicago Title Ins. Co., 692 F.3d 507 (6th Cir. 2012); Davis v. Stewart Title Guaranty Co., 726 S.W.2d 839 (Mo.App. 1987); Lambert v. Commonwealth Land Title Ins. Co., 53 Cal.3d 1072, 282 Cal.Rptr. 445, 811 P.2d 737 (1991).

[782] See Ticor Title Ins. Co. v. University Creek, Inc., 767 F.Supp. 1127 (M.D.Fla. 1991); Jarchow v. Transamerica Title Insurance Co., supra note 763; Shada v. Title & Tr. Co. of Fla., 457 So. 2d 553 (Fla. Dist. Ct. App. 1984); Summonte v. First American Title Ins. Co., 180 N.J.Super. 605, 436 A.2d 110 (N.J.Super. 1981); Lawyers Title Insurance Corp. v. McKee, 354 S.W.2d 401 (Tex.Civ.App. 1962); Universal Holdings II Ltd. P'ship v. Overlake Christian Church, 115 Wash. App. 59, 60 P.3d 1254 (2003). Contra, finding no affirmative duty to eliminate title defects, see Eliopoulos v. Nation's Title Ins. of New York, Inc., 912 F.Supp. 28 (N.D.N.Y. 1996); Childs v. Mississippi Title Ins. Co., 359 So.2d 1146 (Ala. 1978); U.S. Bank, N.A. v. Stewart Title Guar. Co., 2014 WL 1096961 (D. Colo. 2014) (unpublished); Childs v. Mississippi Valley Title Ins. Co. 359 So.2d 1146 (Ala. 1978); Thurlow v. Ticor Title Ins. Co., 2009 WL 2358307 (Conn. Super. Ct. 2009) (unpublished); Ruger v. Funk, 1996 WL 110072 (Del. Super. Ct. 1996) (unpublished); Schwartz v. Stewart Title Guar. Co., 134 Ohio App. 3d 601, 731 N.E.2d 1159 (1999); OPY I, L.L.C. v. First Am. Title Ins. Co., 2015 OK CIV APP 49, 350 P.3d 163 (2015). The 2006 ALTA Owner's Policy describes elimination of title defects as the insurer's right, but not as a duty; see Conditions, par. 5(b).

will be unsuccessful.[783] If the insurer wrongfully refuses to defend when called upon by the insured, it will be liable for the insured's costs and reasonable attorney's fees expended in the defense of the title.[784] On the other hand, the insured is usually denied recovery of attorney's fees expended in an action against the title insurer itself.[785]

§ 11.15　TITLE REGISTRATION

The conventional recording system makes no averments to the public about the state of the title to any parcel of land. Instead, it simply invites searchers to inspect the copies of instruments which it contains and to draw their own conclusions as to title.[786] However, an alternative method of maintaining land records in which government assumes a far larger role, termed the Torrens or title registration system, is available in eight states[787] and in Guam and Puerto Rico. It is named for Richard Robert Torrens, who became the first premier of the state of South Australia in the 1850s. He was experienced in the English system for registration of title to merchant ships, and devised a system of land title registration based on similar concepts; it began operation in 1858. Torrens' ideas became popular in many countries of the British Commonwealth and Europe, and were the inspiration for statutes enacted in about twenty American states, beginning with Illinois in 1895.[788]

Despite this fairly widespread legal adoption, the Torrens system is actually implemented in America with significant numbers of land parcels in only a few locales. Its use is voluntary, not legally mandated; it is up to each owner whether or not to register his or her land, or to permit it to continue under the recording system instead. Most of the American Torrens statutes have been repealed,[789] and important activity

---

[783] Home Fed. Sav. Bank v. Ticor Title Ins. Co., 695 F.3d 725 (7th Cir. 2012); Jesko v. American-First Title & Trust Co., 603 F.2d 815 (10th Cir. 1979); Jarchow v. Transamerica Title Insurance Co., supra note 763. See Hosack & O'Connor, Handling Bad Faith Claims Against Title Insurers, 5 Cal.Law. 31 (Jun. 1985).

[784] National Heat & Power Corp. v. City Title Insurance Co., 57 A.D.2d 611, 394 N.Y.S.2d 29 (1977), appeal denied 42 N.Y.2d 811, 399 N.Y.S.2d 1027, 369 N.E.2d 1193 (1977); Foremost Construction Co. v. Killam, 399 S.W.2d 593 (Mo.App. 1966). If the coverage of the policy is uncertain or disputed, the insurer must defend if the claim is potentially or arguably covered by the policy; see Ticor Title Ins. Co. of California v. American Resources, Ltd., 859 F.2d 772 (9th Cir. 1988) (Hawaii law); Israelsky v. Title Insurance Company of Minnesota, 212 Cal.App.3d 611, 261 Cal.Rptr. 72 (1989). See also Schneider v. Commonwealth Land Title Ins. Co., 17 Misc. 3d 552, 844 N.Y.S.2d 657 (Sup. Ct. 2007) (duty to defend includes duty to appeal adverse trial ruling).

[785] Eureka Investment Corp. v. Chicago Title Ins. Co., 743 F.2d 932 (D.C.Cir. 1984); Espinoza v. Safeco Title Insurance Co., 598 P.2d 346 (Utah 1979); Securities Service, Inc. v. Transamerica Title Insurance Co., supra note 772; Jesko v. American-First Title & Trust Co., supra note 783. But see Tumwater State Bank v. Commonwealth Land Title Ins. Co., 51 Wn.App. 166, 752 P.2d 930 (1988).

[786] See § 11.9 supra at note 463.

[787] Official Code Georgia Ann. tit. 60; Haw.Rev.Stat. Ch. 501; Mass.Gen.Laws Ann. c. 185; Minn.Stat.Ann. § 508.01 et seq.; North Carolina Gen.Stat. c. 43; Ohio Rev.Code § 5309; Va.Code 1950, § 55–112; West's Rev.Code Wash.Ann. 65.12. See generally Greg Taylor, Torrens' Contemporaneous Antipodean Simulacrum, 49 Am. J. Legal Hist. 392 (2007); McCormack, Torrens and Recording: Land Title Assurance in the Computer Age, 18 Wm. Mitchell L. Rev. 61 (1992); Comment, The Torrens System of Title Registration: A New Proposal for Effective Implementation, 29 U.C.L.A.L.Rev. 661 (1982); B. Shick & I. Plotkin, Torrens in the United States (1978); T. Mapp, Torrens' Elusive Title (Alberta L.Rev.Book Series No. 1, 1978). See also Batalov, The Russian Title Registration System for Realty and its Effect on Foreign Investors, 73 Wash.L.Rev. 989 (1998); Bostick, Land Title Registration: An English Solution to an American Problem, 63 Ind. L.J. 55 (1988).

[788] The major incentive for the Illinois statute's passage was the destruction of the Cook county official land records in the Chicago fire of 1871. The original act was held unconstitutional because it provided for administrative rather than judicial determination of title in People v. Chase, 165 Ill. 527, 46 N.E. 454 (1897). A new version correcting this defect was immediately passed.

[789] The former edition of Professor Powell's treatise estimated that some 10,000 titles were registered in four Southern California counties prior to 1937, and related the story of a single claim of $48,000 which

under the system occurs today only in Hawaii, Cook County (Chicago) Illinois, some counties in Minnesota, and selected areas of Ohio and Massachusetts. A casual observer might conclude that Torrens is an idea whose time has come—and gone. Yet academic writers continue to advance the thesis that Torrens, at least in some revised form, has intrinsic superiority over the recording/title insurance system which is far more widely used today.[790]

The essence of the system is the certificate of title—a document issued by an official of state or local government that states the identity of the owners of the title, which may be numerous if there are cotenants or present and future interests. It also lists as "memorials" all encumbrances (easements, liens, mortgages, leases, restrictive covenants, and the like) to which that title is subject. With certain exceptions discussed below, the certificate's statement as to the vesting of the title is, in theory, conclusive;[791] that is, it is legally impossible for it to be incorrect. Of course, the responsible officials may make an error, vesting title in the wrong person or failing to include a valid encumbrance as a memorial. But the certificate is still legally binding; one who is the victim of such a mistake loses his or her interest in the land, and has recourse only by way of a claim for monetary compensation against the indemnity fund that the system maintains for that purpose.

The official certificate is retained by the registrar, although in most of the systems a duplicate copy is issued to the owner as well. If encumbrances are added or removed, appropriate notations are made on the official certificate. If an owner transfers his or her land, the deed (and the owner's duplicate, if applicable) are brought to the registry and a new certificate is issued in the name of the new owner. Thus in principle the certificate is always up-to-date and always reliable. No historical search of the chain of title is ever necessary or relevant. A title examiner who represents a prospective

---

entirely wiped out the assurance fund of the California system in that year. See Gill v. Johnson, 21 Cal.App.2d 649, 69 P.2d 1016 (1937); R. Powell, Real Property ¶ 921 n. 40 (1968). The California statute was immediately repealed. The most recent casualties of the repeal movement were the Torrens systems of Colorado (no new registrations after Jan, 1, 2018), Illinois (no new registrations after Jan.1, 1992), and New York (no new registrations after Jan.1, 1997). See Colo. Rev. Stat. Ann. § 38–36–101(2); Ill.—S.H.A. ch. 30, § 1201 et seq.; N.Y. Real Prop. Law art. 12, § 436. In Ohio, county commissioners may abolish the Torrens system on a county option basis; see Ohio Rev. Code Ann. § 5310.32ff. One survey indicated that, of the 88 Ohio counties, 48 counties never had registered land, and of the remaining 40, 26 counties had abolished the system. See https://fiscalofficer.cuyahogacounty.us/en-US/Torrens-RegisteredLand.aspx. See John V. Orth, Torrens Title in North Carolina–Maybe A Hundred Years Is Long Enough, 39 Campbell L. Rev. 271 (2017), recounting the history of the North Carolina Torrens system and recommending its repeal.

[790] See Comment, supra note 787; Lobel, A Proposal for a Title Registration System for Realty, 11 U.Rich.L.Rev. 501 (1977); Whitman, Optimizing Land Title Assurance Systems, 42 Geo.Wash.L.Rev. 40 (1973); Cribbet, Conveyancing Reform, 35 N.Y.U.L.Rev. 1291, 1303 (1960). The most notable recent attack on the Torrens concept is that of Shick & Plotkin, supra note 787; but the authors were consultants to the title insurance industry, a dedicated foe of Torrens, making their objectivity questionable. Moreover, they made no effort to suggest improvements that could make the system more efficient and functional.

[791] See generally Wells Fargo Bank, N.A. v. Omiya, 142 Haw. 439, 420 P.3d 370 (2018). The degree of conclusiveness is actually somewhat variable; see Petition of Mill City Heating & Air Conditioning Co. v. Nelson, 351 N.W.2d 362 (Minn.1984) (a mechanics' lienor is entitled to rely on the certificate of title to registered land, and need not give the usual pre-lien notice to a party who has an unregistered contract to buy the land, unless the lienor has actual knowledge of the contract or the purchaser is in possession); In re Cuzco Dev. U.S.A., LLC, 574 B.R. 724 (D. Haw. 2017) (subsequent purchaser would be bound by unregistered lease, where it was referred to in notice of pending foreclosure action). Compare Tetrault v. Bruscoe, 398 Mass. 454, 497 N.E.2d 275 (1986) (all easements not shown as memorials are cut off by registration) with Henmi Apartments, Inc. v. Sawyer, 3 Hawaii App. 555, 655 P.2d 881 (1982) (a valid implied easement can arise over land registered under the Torrens system). See also Williams Bros. Inc. of Marshfield v. Peck, 81 Mass. App. Ct. 682, 966 N.E.2d 860 (2012) (merger of dominant and servient estates terminated easement, although it was shown on Torrens certificate).

purchaser of the land need only inspect the current certificate and read and evaluate the documents referred to in the current memorials.[792] The title examination process is vastly simplified and duplication of searches as successive transfers of the same land occur is eliminated.

The public employees of the Torrens registry must make decisions on a day-to-day basis as to how the state of the title to each parcel changes. For example, assume one of the memorials on a certificate of title represents a lien on the land. If a release of the lien is presented at the registry and deemed to be authentic by the appropriate official, the lien itself will be marked cancelled on the certificate;[793] moreover, the next time a certificate for that parcel is issued (for example, when the fee title is next transferred), the lien will be omitted entirely. Overall, much of the work of data retrieval and evaluation which is done by private attorneys or title insurers in the conventional recording system is handled by public employees in the Torrens system.

The biggest barrier to the large-scale success of Torrens systems in the United States has been the cost and difficulty of initial registration. None of the American statutes makes registration compulsory. An owner who wishes to register land must file a petition in an *in rem* judicial or quasijudicial proceeding much like a quiet title action. An official title examiner or, under some systems, an approved private attorney investigates the title and reports to the court. Notice is given by mail, posting, and publication to all persons having any interest in the land. In some systems, such as that of Massachusetts, an official survey is made of the land parcel, and the boundaries are registered; in other systems, registration of the boundaries is optional.[794] A hearing is scheduled, and if there is no persuasive contrary evidence, the owner's petition is granted and a certificate of registration is issued, bringing the land within the system. This procedure is time-consuming, probably taking at least six to eight months, with significant costs in attorney's fees and official fees.[795]

Except in special cases, the registering owner does not get much direct return for this investment. The costs of future title examinations may be lower as a result of registration,[796] but those will be expenses of future owners and may not be reflected in

---

[792] See, e.g., Hickey v. Pathways Ass'n, Inc., 472 Mass. 735, 37 N.E.3d 1003 (2015) (purchasers of registered land took subject to easements shown on plan referred to in certificate of title). The registrar maintains files or books containing the originals or copies of all documents referred to in the memorials so that an examiner can review them. These files or books are usually indexed by tract or parcel, permitting easy location. The Torrens system obviously lends itself to computer production of certificates and indexing of files; see McCormack, supra note 787.

[793] See, e.g., In re Tyrell, 528 B.R. 790 (Bankr. D. Haw. 2015) (land court has power to reinstate on the certificate a mortgage that was cancelled by error).

[794] See In re Petition of Geis, 576 N.W.2d 747 (Minn.App. 1998).

[795] See the estimates given by Shick & Plotkin, supra note 787, at 89, of $550 to $750 for the Twin Cities area, which probably has the best-functioning Torrens system in the nation. The authors estimate time of one year to 18 months, and costs of $1,500 to $2,100 in Massachusetts, where the official examiner's fee is much higher than in Minnesota and where a survey is a required part of every initial registration; id. at 115. They estimate the time and cost in Cook County, Illinois to be similar to those of the Twin Cities; id. at 135. All of these estimates assume an uncontested proceeding, as is usually the case. Attorneys' fees in a contested registration could be much higher.

[796] Shick and Plotkin argue that these future savings may be small or non-existent; id. at 65. However, this is in part attributable to the hostility with which the title insurance industry views Torrens and its consequent maintenance of pricing policies for Torrens land that do not reflect the actual cost savings that flow from avoidance of historical searches. To some extent attorneys who examine titles reflect the same bias; see id. at 68–69. One study of the Cook County, Illinois system estimated that the average cost savings per parcel was about $100 in 1967 prices, and that the present value of aggregate savings from a total conversion to

the market price of the property when it is resold. Unless a judicial proceeding is needed to clear up clouds on the property's title anyway, it is difficult to convince a landowner that the expenditure of time and money is worthwhile.[797] For this reason, there are relatively few new registrations even in areas of the nation in which the system is well-known and well-regarded.[798]

In principle, a Torrens certificate offers an owner a far more impregnable form of assurance of title than a search in the conventional recording system, even if the latter is augmented by title insurance. However, existing American Torrens systems are characterized by numerous features which make their protection of the certificate-holder less than ideal. All of the statutes contain lists of exceptions—types of interests which can exist in the land even though they are unmentioned in the certificate. These lists are much like those found in marketable title acts[799] and title insurance policy exceptions,[800] and exist for much the same reasons. The "overriding interests" typically include such matters as claims of the United States,[801] rights of parties in possession under short-term leases, property tax and special assessment liens, mechanics liens, and public rights-of-way.[802]

Other factors also militate against the Torrens certificate's conclusiveness and reliability. One is the possibility that, at the time of initial registration, some person

---

Torrens in Cook County would be $76 million in 1976 prices. Janczyk, An Economic Analysis of the Land Title Systems for Transferring Real Property, 6 J. Legal Studies 213 (1977).

[797] Some additional owners might be willing to stand the cost of initial registration in order to forestall adverse possessors, since adverse possession will not run against Torrens land under the American statutes (although Torrens land is subject to practical location of boundaries in Minnesota). See Minn. Stat. Ann. § 508.02; Hebert v. City of Fifty Lakes, 744 N.W.2d 226 (Minn. 2008); Ruikkie v. Nall, 798 N.W.2d 806 (Minn. Ct. App. 2011). Likewise, registered land is not subject to the acquisition of prescriptive easements; Calci v. Reitano, 66 Mass. App. Ct. 245, 846 N.E.2d 1164 (2006). In addition, Torrens can be a convenient way of "cleaning up" overlapping or inconsistent parcels for a larger project; see Brian Peterson, Not All Work is Finished at New Target Field, Minneapolis Star Tribune (Apr. 25, 2010). Finally, Torrens can be an effective way to consolidate the ownership of property held by large numbers of heirs; see Meghan E. B. Pridemore, Tides, Torrens, and Family Trees: Heirs Property Preservation Challenges, Prob. & Prop., May/June 2009, at 24.

[798] For example, in Hennepin County, Minnesota, with something over one-third of the parcels registered under the Torrens system, and with deeds being recorded at the rate of about 25,000 to 30,000 per year, applications for new registrations were typically between 100 and 200 per year during the mid-1970s. Shick & Plotkin, supra note 787, at 87–88.

[799] See § 11.12 supra, text at notes 653–654.

[800] See § 11.14 supra, text at notes 769–770.

[801] In general, the United States government cannot be compelled to participate in the registration process against its will. See Johnson, Rights Arising Under Federal Law Versus the Torrens System, 9 Miami L.Q. 258 (1955). The government's cooperation has been quite limited. For example, Federal law gives priority to a federal tax lien only from the time the notice of lien is filed by the IRS "in one office within the county * * * as designated by the laws of such state;" 26 U.S.C.A. § 6323(f)(1). But the statute has been held not to mandate registration as a memorial on a certificate of title if the land has been Torrenized; see United States v. Rasmuson, 253 F.2d 944 (8th Cir. 1958). The real objection of the IRS to Torrens memorialization is that it requires the inclusion of a legal description of the land in the notice of lien, a step the IRS sees as excessively burdensome; see United States v. Union Central Life Insurance Co., 368 U.S. 291, 82 S.Ct. 349, 7 L.Ed.2d 294 (1961).

[802] See, e.g., Henmi Apartments, Inc. v. Sawyer, 3 Hawaii App. 555, 655 P.2d 881 (1982) (implied easement may arise against land registered under the Torrens system). The Minnesota courts have been quite protective of the Torrens system in that state. See, e.g., Petition of Willmus, 568 N.W.2d 722 (Minn. Ct. App. 1997) (estoppel by deed does not apply to Torrens land); Phillips v. Dolphin, 776 N.W.2d 755 (Minn. Ct. App. 2009) (boundaries of registered land may not be modified by arbitration); Hersh Properties, LLC v. McDonald's Corp., 588 N.W.2d 728 (Minn. 1999) (marketable title act applies to Torrens land, but an encumbrance that is memorialized on an owner's certificate of title issued within past 40 years is binding and is not cut off by the act), noted 26 Wm. Mitchell L. Rev. 601 (2000).

whose rights in the land would have been disclosed by a careful search was missed or ignored and received no notice of the proceeding. The order registering the land is, of course, subject to any appeal filed by a party to the proceeding within the usual brief period. But a claimant who was reasonably discoverable but received no notice may also have the power to attack the registration collaterally, perhaps years afterward, on the ground that the court lacked jurisdiction and that it would be unconstitutional to impose its judgment on him or her.[803] Most of the existing statutes place time limits, typically several years in length, on collateral attacks, but it is doubtful that they would control an attack based on constitutional grounds.[804] No case yet decided seems to present this problem where the registered land has passed to a good faith purchaser. A similar problem exists if some third party claims that the original decree was procured by fraud. It is unlikely that a court would set aside a registration on this ground if the property had passed to a good faith purchaser for value, but there is some risk of this result.[805]

Subsequent transfers that involve fraud or forgery are also problematic. It is generally conceded that, if the registrar is duped by the wrong-doer and actually issues a new certificate, it will be conclusive in favor of a subsequent good faith purchaser for value, and the party whose interest has been cut off will be left only with a claim against the indemnity fund.[806] But good faith status can be elusive. For example, in Hoffman v. Schroeder[807] a forger executed a mortgage to a lending institution and the registrar issued a mortgagee's duplicate certificate to the lender. The court found that the lender was not in good faith because its employee, a notary public who took the forger's acknowledgment on the documents, did not demand identification of the forger as notaries are normally expected to do. The mortgage was held invalid despite the issuance of the certificate.[808]

---

[803]   Francisco v. Look, 537 F.2d 379 (9th Cir. 1976); Lobato v. Taylor, 70 P.3d 1152 (Colo. 2003); Konantz v. Stein, 283 Minn. 33, 167 N.W.2d 1 (1969); Couey v. Talalah Estates Corp., 183 Ga. 442, 188 S.E. 822 (1936); Sheaff v. Spindler, 339 Ill. 540, 171 N.E. 632 (1930). See Todd Barnet, Lobato v. Taylor: Torrens Title Lost to Legal Fictions, 15 Mo. Envtl. L. & Pol'y Rev. 309 (2008). See also Mason v. Wailea Resort Co., 79 Hawai'i 56, 897 P.2d 983 (Haw.App. 1995) (owners of registered land are entitled to notice and hearing before change is made in restrictive covenants affecting their land). See Note, Konantz, Koester, McCrossan, and Title to Torrens Property, 4 Wm.Mitch.L.Rev. 59 (1978).

[804]   See In re Hauge, 766 N.W.2d 50 (Minn. Ct. App. 2009); Couey v. Talalah Estates Corp., id.; Sheaff v. Spindler, id.

[805]   R.G. Patton argued that there was no ultimate danger to a good faith purchaser for value from a collateral attack based on fraud in registration; see 4 Am.L.Prop. § 17.47 (1952). The cases seem to bear this out; several decisions recognize collateral attacks and set aside registrations for fraud, but emphasize that no rights of good faith purchasers had intervened. See McDonnell v. Quirk, 22 Mass.App.Ct. 126, 491 N.E.2d 646 (1986) (fraud in registration of title may not be asserted against a BFP who has relied upon the registration); Petition of Brainerd National Bank, 383 N.W.2d 284 (Minn. 1986) (court will not set aside a Torrens title decree on grounds of excusable neglect of counsel for a party whose interest was cut off by the decree); Kozdras v. Land/Vest Properties, Inc., 382 Mass. 34, 413 N.E.2d 1105 (1980); Note, Forgeries and Land Registration, 101 Law Q.Rev. 79 (1985).

[806]   Eliason v. Wilborn, 281 U.S. 457, 50 S.Ct. 382, 74 L.Ed. 962 (1930); Fialkowski v. Fialkowski, 1 W.W.R. 216 (Alberta 1911). Note that forgeries are rare, since the registry will not issue a new certificate in the ordinary course of business unless the old owner's duplicate is presented for cancellation. In addition, the registries in some states maintain files of signature cards against which purported conveyances are checked.

[807]   38 Ill.App.2d 20, 186 N.E.2d 381 (1962). The lender lost its mortgage on the land, but was given a claim against the assurance fund. See also In re Collier, 726 N.W.2d 799 (Minn. 2007) (one who takes registered land with knowledge of an unregistered mortgage is bound by it); Imperial Developers, Inc. v. Calhoun Dev., LLC, 790 N.W.2d 146 (Minn. 2010) (mortgage is "registered" when placed with registrar).

[808]   The opinion seems to offer as an alternative holding the rather shocking notion that the lender was not protected by the Torrens Act because it was "not a registered owner in the sense that it did not obtain its registration as a result of a transfer from the true registered owner, but from one who impersonated her." In substance, the Illinois court followed the English decisions, represented by Gibbs v. Messer, [1891] A.C. 248,

To the extent that the Torrens system adopts the concepts of actual and constructive notice which apply in the traditional recording system,[809] the certificate itself is made less reliable. Yet the courts have been reluctant to abandon these concepts. It is fairly clear that a purchaser who has actual knowledge of some adverse claim to the land will take subject to it, even though the certificate fails to memorialize it.[810] Some of the statutes incorporate the notion of constructive notice by making the certificate subject to the rights of certain categories of persons in possession. Where there is no clear statutory statement, the cases are divided as to whether possession will give constructive notice to a Torrens purchaser who has no actual knowledge; the majority of decisions refuse to do so.[811] To some extent the cases turn on the language of the specific statute, and on whether the adverse claim existed before initial registration of the land or was created later.[812]

On the whole, it is doubtful that Torrens has a bright future in America. In several respects it is theoretically superior to the recording system, but the latter is strongly supported by a network of title insurers and attorneys whose livelihood would be jeopardized by any radical change. The criticisms of Torrens are valid enough: slow and expensive original registration, indemnity funds of doubtful adequacy, and gaps in the conclusiveness of the certificate. In areas having few registered parcels consumers, lenders, and real estate brokers find the system unfamiliar, confusing, irritating, and error-prone. In addition, title insurers are fond of pointing out that the Torrens system makes no provision for payment of the litigation expenses of one whose land interests are erroneously terminated by the system or who must make a claim on the assurance fund.[813] Finally, the Torrens systems typically ensure that mortgages shown on the certificate are *valid,* but do not ensure their *priority*—a fatal oversight from the viewpoint of lenders.[814]

---

which had held that the direct recipient of a defective transfer under the registration system is not protected from the defects in question, even if he or she is a bona fide purchaser. Under this view, only later BFP transferees who are not parties to the defective transaction are protected. See Mapp, supra note 787, at 131.

[809] See § 11.10 supra at notes 550–575.

[810] In re Mbazira, 518 B.R. 11 (Bankr. D. Mass. 2014); In re Collier, supra note 807; Butler v. Haley Greystone Corp., 347 Mass. 478, 198 N.E.2d 635 (1964); Taylor Bros. v. Boyce, 190 Ohio App. 3d 189, 941 N.E.2d 114 (2010); Annot., 42 A.L.R.2d 1387 (1955). But see Knaefler v. Mack, 680 F.2d 671 (9th Cir. 1982) (under Hawaii law, certificate is conclusive even if holder has actual knowledge of adverse claim).

[811] Constructive notice not recognized, see Wells v. Lizama, 396 F.2d 877 (9th Cir. 1968); Commonwealth Elec. Co. v. MacCardell, 450 Mass. 48, 876 N.E.2d 405 (2007); In re Juran, 178 Minn. 55, 226 N.W. 201 (1929); Abrahamson v. Sundman, 174 Minn. 22, 218 N.W. 246 (1928). Contra, see Follette v. Pacific Light and Power Corp., 189 Cal. 193, 208 P. 295 (1922) (constructive notice imputed, where possession existed before original registration). See also Francisco v. Look, 537 F.2d 379 (9th Cir. 1976), which seems to rely on both actual and constructive notice; In re Woodman, 497 B.R. 668, 674 (Bankr. D. Mass. 2013) (under Massachusetts law, subsequent purchasers are held to inquiry notice of matters shown on the face of the certificate of title, but not constructive notice of documents in the conventional recording system).

[812] See Konantz v. Stein, 283 Minn. 33, 167 N.W.2d 1 (1969), drawing this distinction. If the claim predated the original registration and was reasonably discoverable, the claimant may have a constitutional right to attack the registration collaterally; see notes 802–803 supra and accompanying text.

[813] Moreover, most of the existing Torrens systems require claimants to exhaust their remedies against other parties (e.g., forgers) before presenting claims to the assurance fund. Compare the duties of title insurers, discussed in § 11.14 supra at notes 771–777. Given the frequency with which title insurers seem to refuse to defend their insureds and to resist payment of claims, this may be a less significant difference between title insurance and Torrens than it first appears, but the basic criticism is correct.

[814] See In re Ocwen Fin. Servs., Inc., 649 N.W.2d 854, 858 (Minn. Ct. App. 2002) (mortgage priority is determined by order of registration of mortgages).

But it is probable that all of these difficulties could be cured if any state legislature had the will to undertake the task.[815] One of the most attractive proposals, advocated by several writers,[816] is the introduction of a procedure for registering "possessory titles"— that is, registration on only a "day forward" basis with no attempt, or only a very inexpensive effort, to identify and memorialize preexisting claims. Each parcel would be registered on a mandatory basis when it was next transferred. This approach, which has been widely used in England,[817] has the effect of placing land within the system gradually and cheaply. Over a period of years, unidentified claims can then be cut off by a statute similar to marketable title legislation, eventually making the certificate conclusive. A form of possessory title registration operates successfully in Hennepin County, Minnesota.[818] Such a statute was drafted in Colorado under the support of a federal grant and would have operated on a test basis in a single county. But the vehement opposition of the title insurance industry defeated the bill in 1980 and 1981. Future experiments along these lines in states in which Torrens is not now popular seem unlikely. The opponents of Torrens clearly have no interest in seeing it improved.

§ 11.16 SELLER LIABILITY FOR PHYSICAL QUALITY

Under the traditional common law notion of *caveat emptor,*[819] a seller of real estate is generally not liable for failure to disclose to a prospective buyer defects in the property or facts that affect its value. In recent years, however, this rule has broken down in a number of important respects, and purchasers are often successful in suits against their sellers based on failure to reveal defective conditions. It is convenient to discuss these developments under two main headings: first, principles generally applicable to all properties, and second, special rules that are imposed on builders of new housing.

Duty of disclosure. Courts often continue to give lip service to *caveat emptor,* but in a number of situations they are apt to disregard it and impose liability for a seller's nondisclosure of defects. Most obviously, the vendor who makes an affirmative misrepresentation about the property, relied upon by the purchaser, can be held liable for fraud.[820] Even in the absence of a false statement, if the vendor has a fiduciary or other special relationship of trust or confidence with the purchaser, a court may impose a duty of candor and complete disclosure.[821] Such a duty may arise simply from the purchaser's asking the vendor a question, a candid and full response to which would

---

[815] See McCormack, Torrens and Recording: Land Title Assurance in the Computer Age, 18 Wm.Mitch.L.Rev. 61 (1992), arguing that as conventional recording systems are computerized, they approach the advantages of Torrens systems without the corresponding disadvantages.

[816] See Comment, supra note 787; Whitman, supra note 790.

[817] See Fiflis, English Registered Conveyancing: A Study in Effective Land Transfer, 59 Nw.U.L.Rev. 468 (1964).

[818] Minn.Stat.Ann. ch. 508A. The registration in Minnesota, unlike that in England, is optional with the landowner and not automatic. Five years after registration, the possessory title certificate can be converted into a regular Torrens certificate. See Note, Possessory Title Registration: An Improvement of the Torrens System, 11 Wm.Mitch.L.Rev. 825 (1985); Sclar, Minnesota Simplifies Land Registration, 11 Real Est.L.J. 258 (1983); Kimball Foster, Certificates of Possessory Title: A Sensible Addition to Minnesota's Successful Torrens System, 40 Wm. Mitchell L. Rev. 112 (2013).

[819] The first prominent case adopting the principle was Moore v. Hussey, Hobart 93, 80 Eng. Rep. 243 (1601).

[820] See, e.g., Brooks v. Bankson, 248 Va. 197, 445 S.E.2d 473 (Va. 1994).

[821] See, e.g., Mackintosh v. California Fed. Sav. & Loan Ass'n, 113 Nev. 393, 935 P.2d 1154 (1997) (lender that both sold foreclosed house and lent purchase money had a duty to disclose basement flooding problem to its purchaser).

have required disclosure of the defect.[822] Although merely failing to disclose defects in the property is generally not actionable, there is a strong trend toward holding sellers accountable for not disclosing material defects that are not readily discoverable by the purchaser's inspection of the property,[823] usually under the rubric of negligent misrepresentation or fraudulent concealment.

Formulations of the pertinent legal rules vary somewhat from jurisdiction to jurisdiction, but they generally share the following features. First, the defect must be material, generally defined as something that would substantially affect the value of the property if it were known.[824] Second, the vendor must have actual knowledge of the defect;[825] it is not enough that the vendor should have known of it. Third, the purchaser must not have knowledge of the defect from the vendor's disclosure or other sources.[826] Many courts add a fourth element: that the defect must be latent, in the sense that the purchaser could not discover it by an ordinary (or perhaps even a very careful) inspection of the property.[827]

A number of additional factors make the imposition of liability more probable. They include the facts that the property was residential and was being purchased by an unsophisticated purchaser;[828] the defect in the property posed a danger to health or safety;[829] the defect was created personally by the seller;[830] the seller gave reassurances to the purchaser about the quality of the property;[831] or the vendor intentionally covered up the defect.[832] If the purchaser did not obtain an expert inspection of the property, the

---

[822] See Gaulden v. Mitchell, 849 So. 2d 192 (Ala. Civ. App. 2002); Fimbel v. DeClark, 695 N.E.2d 125 (Ind.App. 1998); Ries v. Shoemake, 359 S.W.3d 137 (Mo. Ct. App. 2012).

[823] See, e.g., Haney v. Castle Meadows, Inc., 839 F.Supp. 753 (D.Colo. 1993); Layman v. Binns, 35 Ohio St.3d 176, 519 N.E.2d 642 (1988); Gaito v. Auman, 313 N.C. 243, 327 S.E.2d 870 (1985); Hill v. Jones, 151 Ariz. 81, 725 P.2d 1115 (Ariz. App. 1986). Cf. M & D, Inc. v. W.B. McConkey, 231 Mich.App. 22, 585 N.W.2d 33 (1998).

[824] Spitale v. Smith, 721 So. 2d 341 (Fla. Dist. Ct. App. 1998); Young v. Vista Homes, Inc., 243 S.W.3d 352 (Ky. Ct. App. 2007); Barylski v. Andrews, 439 S.W.2d 536 (Mo. App. 1969).

[825] Cook's Pest Control, Inc. v. Rebar, 28 So. 3d 716 (Ala. 2009); Lewis v. Chevron U.S.A., Inc. 119 Cal. App. 4th 690, 14 Cal. Rptr. 3d 636 (2004); Jensen v. Bailey, 76 So. 3d 980 (Fla. Dist. Ct. App. 2011); Addison v. Distinctive Homes, Ltd., 359 Ill. App. 3d 997, 836 N.E.2d 88 (2005); Li-Conrad v. Curran, 2016-Ohio-1496, 50 N.E.3d 573 (2016); Gallagher v. Ruzzine, 147 A.D.3d 1456, 46 N.Y.S.3d 323 (2017); Parmely v. Hildebrand, 630 N.W.2d 509 (S.D. 2001); Anderson v. Kriser, 266 P.3d 819 (Utah 2011). Cf. Iowa Code Ann. § 558A.6 (liability may be based on actual knowledge or on failure to use ordinary care).

[826] Preston v. Goldman 42 Cal. 3d 108, 227, Cal. Rptr. 817 (1986).

[827] Pressman v. Wolf, 732 So.2d 356 (Fla.App. 1999); Hudson v. Pollock, 267 Ga. App. 4, 598 S.E.2d 811 (2004); Brennan v. Kunzle, 37 Kan. App. 2d 365, 154 P.3d 1094 (2007); Behar v. Glickenhaus Westchester Dev., Inc., 122 A.D.3d 784, 996 N.Y.S.2d 678 (2014); Everts v. Parkinson, 147 N.C. App. 315, 555 S.E.2d 667 (2001); Roberts v. McCoy, 2017-Ohio-1329, 88 N.E.3d 422 (2017); Mitchell v. Christensen, 2001 UT 80, 31 P.3d 572 (2001); Jackowski v. Borcheit, 151 Wash.App. 1, 209 P.3d 514 (2009).

[828] Transcapital Bank v. Shadowbrook at Vero, LLC, 226 So. 3d 856 (Fla. Dist. Ct. App. 2017).

[829] See, e.g., Roberts v. C & S Sovran Credit Corp., 621 So.2d 1294 (Ala. 1993); Alejandre v. Bull, 159 Wash. 2d 674, 153 P.3d 864 (2007).

[830] See, e.g., Stambovsky v. Ackley, 169 A.D.2d 254, 572 N.Y.S.2d 672 (1991); Anderson v. Harper, 424 Pa.Super. 161, 622 A.2d 319 (1993).

[831] See, e.g., Brewer v. Brothers, 82 Ohio App.3d 148, 611 N.E.2d 492 (1992) ("as is" clause does not waive liability for misrepresentation).

[832] Rhee v. Highland Dev. Corp., 182 Md. App. 516, 958 A.2d 385 (2008); Borgschulte v. Bonnot, 285 S.W.3d 345 (Mo. Ct. App. 2009); Newman v. Arenstein, 2006 WL 561072 (N.J. Super. Ct. App. Div. 2006) (unpublished); Pesce v. Leimsider, 59 Misc. 3d 23, 72 N.Y.S.3d 760 (N.Y. App. Term 2018); Van Deusen v. Snead, 247 Va. 324, 441 S.E.2d 207 (Va. 1994). See Restatement (Second) of Contracts § 160 (1979).

case for liability is weakened.[833] A seller may also be liable to remote purchasers, those who buy the real estate from the party to whom the seller sold it, despite lack of privity between the parties, if the seller had "reason to expect" that the nondisclosure would affect subsequent purchasers.[834] On the other hand, if the purchaser became aware of the defects from an inspection or other sources of information prior to the purchase,[835] or if such information was readily available to the purchaser,[836] liability is unlikely to be imposed. The fact that the defect is reflected in a publicly-recorded document will likely exculpate the seller from liability.[837]

While the defects in these cases have usually been problems with the land or structures, an increasing number of cases have imposed liability for nondisclosure of off-site "neighborhood" problems.[838] For example, in Shapiro v. Sutherland,[839] the seller was held liable for failing to reveal that the next-door neighbors had been a long-time source of noise, commotion, loud arguments, and late-night music.

Disclosure statutes. In recent years nearly all states have adopted statutes requiring home sellers to disclose specific property information to their purchasers.[840] The statutes typically apply to existing (but not newly constructed) one- to four-family homes and require that, before a contract of sale is signed, the seller must either give a disclaimer of all warranties and representations, or a disclosure of any defects of which the seller has knowledge in a "laundry list" of the house's systems and features. Failure of the seller to provide the disclosures in a timely manner usually gives rise to a right of the purchaser to rescind the contract,[841] and under many of the statues this is the sole remedy stated. Under others, a knowingly false disclosure statement is grounds for damages or rescission.[842] But even if there are no other statutory remedies, a seller who

---

[833] Gaulden v. Mitchell, 849 So. 2d 192 (Ala. Civ. App. 2002); Alires v. McGehee, 277 Kan. 398, 85 P.3d 1191 (2004).

[834] See Geernaert v. Mitchell, 31 Cal. App.4th 601, 37 Cal.Rptr.2d 483 (1995); Mallin v. Good, 93 Ill.App.3d 843, 49 Ill.Dec. 168, 417 N.E.2d 858 (1981); Lempke v. Dagenais, 130 N.H. 782, 547 A.2d 290 (1988); Oates v. Jag, Inc., 314 N.C. 276, 333 S.E.2d 222 (1985); Richards v. Powercraft Homes, Inc., 139 Ariz. 242, 678 P.2d 427 (1984).

[835] Lambert v. Hein, 218 Wis.2d 712, 582 N.W.2d 84 (Wis.App. 1998).

[836] See cases cited note 827 supra.

[837] Finding no liability where the defect was discoverable in public records, see Norris v. Mitchell, 255 Va. 235, 495 S.E.2d 809 (1998); Khindri v. Getty Petroleum Mktg., Inc., 33 Misc. 3d 1208(A), 2011 WL 4904403 (N.Y. Sup. 2011) (unreported); Bianchi v. Lorenz, 166 Vt. 555, 701 A.2d 1037 (1997) (liability based on deed covenant of title).

[838] See, e.g., Strawn v. Canuso, 140 N.J. 43, 657 A.2d 420 (1995) (hazardous waste dump-site within a half-mile); Van Camp v. Bradford, 63 Ohio Misc.2d 245, 623 N.E.2d 731 (1993) (rapes occurring recently both on and near the property); Timm v. Clement, 574 N.W.2d 368 (Iowa Ct. App. 1997) (leaking underground petroleum tank on adjacent property also owned by the seller). Cf. Blaine v. J.E. Jones Constr. Co., 841 S.W.2d 703 (Mo.Ct.App. 1992) (subdivision developer had no duty to disclose his intention to build an apartment complex nearby). See Annot., 41 A.L.R.5th 157 (1996); Roberts, Off-Site Conditions and Disclosure Duties: Drawing the Line at the Property Line, 2006 B.Y.U. L. Rev. 957 (2006).

[839] 64 Cal.App.4th 1534, 76 Cal.Rptr.2d 101 (1998). The sellers had checked "no" on a disclosure form question asking, "Are you aware of any neighborhood noise problems or other nuisances?" See also Alexander v. McKnight, 7 Cal.App.4th 973, 9 Cal.Rptr.2d 453 (1992).

[840] See, e.g., Md. Real Prop. Code Ann. § 10–702; Johnson, An Economic Analysis of the Duty to Disclose Information: Lessons Learned From the Caveat Emptor Doctrine, 45 San Diego L. Rev. 79 (2008); Crowfoot, "Seller Beware!": Making Necessary Revisions to the South Carolina Seller Disclosure Statement and South Carolina Residential Property Condition Disclosure Act, 6 Charleston L. Rev. 599 (2012).

[841] Little v. Stogner, 162 N.C.App. 25, 592 S.E.2d 5 (N.C.App. 2004).

[842] See Woods v. Pence, 303 Ill. App. 3d 573, 708 N.E.2d 563 (1999); Bohm v. DMA P'ship, 8 Neb. App. 1069, 607 N.W.2d 212 (2000); Engelhart v. Kramer, 570 N.W.2d 550 (S.D. 1997); Murvin v. Cofer, 968 S.W.2d 304 (Tenn.App. 1997); Iadanza v. Mather, 820 F.Supp. 1371 (D. Utah 1993). Cf. Brasier v. Sparks, 17 Cal. App.

checks "no" or "no knowledge" when the seller in fact does know of a defect is providing documentary proof of his or her concealment. Such proof may provide the evidence necessary to establish a fraudulent misrepresentation claim.[843]

New York's disclosure statute, which was not adopted until 2002, has an unusual feature. It allows a seller to opt out of all disclosure obligations by crediting the buyer with $500 toward the selling price.[844] If this is done, the seller can be held liable only for common law fraud (not fraudulent concealment). However, in the absence of any other affirmative disclosures or representations, fraud will be very difficult to prove.[845]

In addition to the general disclosure statement described above, individual states may require other specific disclosures. For example California, something of a champion in this arena, requires the vendor to give the purchaser disclosures or warnings concerning earthquake fault zones, earthquake hazards, flood zones, fire hazards, home environmental hazards, lead-based paint, home energy rating, and the presence of nearby registered sex offenders.[846]

The principal proponent of disclosure statement statutes for residential properties has been the real estate brokerage industry. Brokers have been (understandably) worried about their liability for failure to disclose material facts, and statutes such as this are designed to relieve them of that liability.[847] Many of the statutes provide that brokers have a duty to inform buyers and sellers of their rights and obligations under the statute, and that if a broker does so, he or she "shall have no further duties under this section to the parties to a residential real estate transaction; and is not liable to any party to a residential real estate transaction for a violation of this section."[848]

Stigmatized property. Numerous suits have been generated by "psychologically impacted" or "stigmatized" property, which has no observable physical defects but is considered undesirable as a result of its past history or reputation. One of the earliest cases was Reed v. King,[849] in which the house had been the scene of a gruesome multiple homicide. The court held that the purchaser could recover upon a showing that this fact negatively impacted the house's value. Sellers and their agents have also worried about whether they must disclose the fact that a former owner died of AIDS or some other

---

4th 1756, 22 Cal. Rptr. 2d 1 (1993) (finding no liability where the disclosure statement expressly recited that "it is not a warranty of any kind by the sellers * * * and is not intended to be part of any contract between the buyer and seller"). Perhaps surprisingly, several courts have granted damages in such cases even when the buyer had actual knowledge of the falsity of the disclosure. See, e.g., Woods v. Pence, 303 Ill. App. 3d 573, 236 Ill. Dec. 977, 708 N.E.2d 563 (1999); Bohm v. DMA Partnership, id.

[843] Vanderwier v. Baker, 937 N.E.2d 396 (Ind. Ct. App. 2010).

[844] N.Y. Real Prop. Code § 465.

[845] See, e.g., Hecker v. Paschke, 133 A.D.3d 713, 19 N.Y.S.3d 568 (N.Y. App. Div. 2015); Bishop v. Graziano, 10 Misc. 3d 342, 804 N.Y.S.2d 236 (Dist. Ct. 2005).

[846] Most of these requirements appear in Cal. Civ. Code §§ 2079–2079.24. In addition, there are the usual disclosures relating to the duties of real estate salespersons. Salespersons are required "to conduct a reasonably competent and diligent visual inspection of the property offered for sale and to disclose to that prospective purchaser all facts materially affecting the value or desirability of the property that an investigation would reveal"); Cal. Civ. Code 2079(a).

[847] See Lefcoe, Property Condition Disclosure Forms: How the Real Estate Industry Eased the Transition from Caveat Emptor to "Seller Tell All", 39 Real Prop. Prob. & Tr. J. 193 (2004).

[848] Md. Code Ann., Real Prop. § 10–702(m)(3). Similarly, see Cal. Civ. Code § 1102 et seq.; Ill. Stat. Ch. 765 § 77/1 et seq.; R.I. Gen. L. § 5–20.8–1 et seq. See Miceli, Pancak & Sirmans, Evolving Property Condition Disclosure Duties: Caveat Procurator?, 39 Real Est. L.J. 464 (2011).

[849] 145 Cal.App.3d 261, 193 Cal.Rptr. 130 (1983).

illness,[850] that the property was at one time contaminated with hazardous waste or is located near such waste,[851] that a registered sex offender resides nearby,[852] that there is a nearby high-voltage power line that is thought to induce cancer,[853] or that the property is in a project with a history of construction litigation.[854]

In one of the most amusing cases, Stambovsky v. Ackley,[855] the property had been widely publicized by the seller as haunted by ghosts. The New York Appellate Division did not decide whether the ghosts were real, but focused instead on the seller's activities in creating the perception that the house was haunted, and thus impairing the house's value as an ordinary residence without disclosing that fact to the purchaser. The court permitted rescission of the contract.

A large number of states have adopted statutes in recent years denying the purchaser of a house a remedy on account of at least some of the attributes mentioned above, such as the property's having been occupied by an AIDS patient or having been the scene of a crime.[856] South Carolina, for example, has adopted legislation stating:

> the fact or suspicion that property may be or is psychologically impacted, as a result of facts or suspicions that the death of an occupant of the real property has occurred or may have occurred upon the real property, or the manner of death where the death has occurred, or that an occupant was inflicted with or died from [HIV] . . . or any other disease [highly unlikely to be transmitted by occupancy]

---

[850] Goldberg, Disclosing the Inevitable: Reconciling the Varied Requirements for the Disclosure of Death on Real Property, 32 Notre Dame J.L. Ethics & Pub. Pol. 183 (2018); Edmiston, Secrets Worth Keeping: Toward A Principled Basis for Stigmatized Property Disclosure Statutes, 58 UCLA L. Rev. 281 (2010); Williams, Stigmatized Property Law, 85 Mich. B. J. 34 (Feb. 2006); Fisk, Stigma Damages in Construction Defect Litigation: Feared by Defendants, Championed by Plaintiffs, Awarded by (Almost) No Courts—What Gives?, 53 Drake L. Rev. 1029 (2005). If the underlying claim is in nuisance, no stigma damages are allowed in the absence of physical injury; see Cook v. Rockwell Int'l Corp., 618 F.3d 1127 (10th Cir. 2010); McCormick v. Halliburton Co., 2014 WL 1328352 (W.D. Okla. 2014) (unpublished); Smith v. Kansas Gas Serv. Co., 285 Kan. 33, 169 P.3d 1052 (2007).

[851] See Walker Drug Co. v. La Sal Oil Co., 972 P.2d 1238 (Utah 1998), approving damages for stigma attached to property that had been invaded by leaking gasoline, despite the fact that the leakage had been remediated; Lewsky, Recovery for Market Stigma Damages May Be Allowed for Environmental Pollution, 7 S.C.Envtl.L.J. 104 (1998); Geisinger, Nothing but Fear Itself: A Social-Psychological Model of Stigma Harm and its Legal Implications, 76 Neb. L. Rev. 452 (1997).

[852] See Saxer, "Am I My Brother's Keeper?": Requiring Landowner Disclosure of the Presence of Sex Offenders and Other Criminal Activity, 80 Neb. L. Rev. 522 (2001); Van Camp v. Bradford, 63 Ohio Misc.2d 245, 623 N.E.2d 731 (Ohio Com.Pl. 1993) (duty to disclose previous rapes in neighborhood); Cal.Civ.Code § 2079.10a, which requires real estate brokers to give purchasers a generic explanation of how to learn about the presence of sex offenders, but does not make it clear whether a more specific warning should be given if the seller or agent knows of an actual sex offender.

[853] See Sick & Bolton, Power Lines and Property Values: The Good, the Bad, and the Ugly, 31 Urb. Law. 331 (1999); Criscuola v. Power Authority of State of New York, 81 N.Y.2d 649, 602 N.Y.S.2d 588, 621 N.E.2d 1195 (1993) (awarding eminent domain damages).

[854] Aas v. Superior Court, 75 Cal. Rptr.2d 581 (Cal.App. 1998) (declining to permit recovery for stigma); Stott, Stigma Damages: The Case for Recovery in Condominium Construction Defect Litigation, 25 Cal.W.L.Rev. 367 (1988).

[855] 169 A.D.2d 254, 572 N.Y.S.2d 672 (1991). See Murray, AIDS, Ghosts, Murder: Must Real Estate Brokers and Sellers Disclose?, 27 Wake For.L.Rev. 689 (1992).

[856] See, e.g., Cal.Civ.Code § 1710.2; Nev. Rev. Stat. Ann. § 40.770; McEvoy, Stigmatized Property: What a Buyer Should Know, 48 J.Mo.Bar 57 (1992). These statutes usually authorize silence by the seller, but often do not make it clear whether liability will ensue (for example, under fair housing legislation) if the seller in fact discloses that an AIDS patient has occupied the property.

is not a material fact and does not have to be disclosed by the seller.[857] These statutes were largely a result of lobbying by real estate brokers, who were concerned about possible liability for failure to disclose. But for other types of stigma, outside the scope of the relevant statute, the risk of liability for nondisclosure still exists.[858]

Disclaimers of liability. There is little doubt that a seller may effectively disclaim the duty to disclose defects if the disclaimer is sufficiently clear and specific.[859] However, the courts often refuse to enforce simple "as is" clauses' or similar general disclaimers,[860] holding that such a clause does not bar an action by the purchaser alleging either positive misrepresentation or fraudulent concealment.[861]

Disclaimers of liability for remediation of hazardous waste under CERCLA[862] have frequently been a point of contention. No clause in a purchase contract can eliminate the purchaser's cleanup liability,[863] but it is possible for the purchaser to obtain an effective indemnity from the seller. However, that indemnity must be very clearly and specifically expressed, and a simple "as is" clause will almost certainly be insufficient to accomplish it if the purchaser has no actual knowledge of the contamination.[864] Indeed, vendors' attempts at disclaimers for all sorts of defects are much more likely to be sustained by the courts if they are explicitly bargained for and specifically identify the types of defects for which the seller is not to be liable.[865]

Builder's liability for sale of new housing. The doctrine of caveat emptor has been almost entirely abolished in sales of new houses by their builders[866] to owner-occupants.

---

[857] S. Carolina Stat. § 40–57–270. See also Idaho Code § 55–2801; Milliken v. Jacono, 96 A.3d 997 (Pa. 2014) (previous murder/suicide held not a material fact).

[858] But see White v. Mock, 140 Idaho 882, 886, 104 P.3d 356, 360 (2004) (stigma damages for mold, while not an enumerated risk under statute, were not recoverable).

[859] See, e.g., Tyus v. Resta, 328 Pa.Super. 11, 476 A.2d 427 (1984) (warranties may be limited or disclaimed only by clear and unambiguous language in a written contract between the builder-vendor and the home purchaser); Rice v. Patterson Realtors, 857 P.2d 71 (Okl. 1993); and G-W-L, Inc. v. Robichaux, 643 S.W.2d 392 (Tex. 1982). For an illustration of a sufficiently clear and detailed disclaimer, see Alires v. McGhehee, 85 P.3d 1191 (Kan. 2004).

[860] See, e.g., Pitre v. Twelve Oaks Trust, 818 F.Supp. 949 (S.D.Miss. 1993); Loughrin v. Superior Court, 15 Cal.App.4th 1188, 19 Cal.Rptr.2d 161 (1993); and Stemple v. Dobson, 184 W.Va. 317, 400 S.E.2d 561 (1990).

[861] Fimbel v. DeClark, 695 N.E.2d 125 (Ind. Ct. App. 1998); Wagner v. Cutler, 232 Mont. 332, 757 P.2d 779 (1988); Newman v. Arenstein, 2006 WL 561072 (N.J. Super. Ct. App. Div. 2006) (unpublished); Montgomery v. Vargo, 2016-Ohio-809, 60 N.E.3d 709 (2016); Ingram v. Cendant Mobility Fin. Corp., 215 S.W.3d 367 (Tenn. Ct. App. 2006); Limoge v. People's Trust Co., 719 A.2d 888 (Vt. 1998).

[862] Comprehensive Environmental Response, Compensation, and Liability Act, 42 U.S.C. § 9601–9675. See Johnson, For Real Estate Lawyers: A Practical Guide to Identifying and Managing Potential Environmental Hazards and Conditions Affecting Commercial Real Estate, 32 Real Prop., Prob. & Tr.J. 619 (1998); Boyce, As Is, Where Is—Where Are We?, Probate & Property, May/June 1997, at 26; Bonnieview Homeowners Ass'n v. Woodmont Builders, L.L.C., 655 F.Supp.2d 473 (D.N.J. 2009) (no recovery by purchasers in the absence of expenditure of cleanup costs).

[863] California Fin., LLC v. Perdido Land Dev. Co., 303 F.Supp.3d 1306 (M.D. Fla. 2017).

[864] See M & M Realty Co. v. Eberton Terminal Corp., 977 F.Supp. 683 (M.D.Pa. 1997); Southland Corp. v. Ashland Oil, Inc., 696 F.Supp. 994 (D.N.J. 1988); Car Wash Enterprises, Inc. v. Kampanos, 74 Wn.App. 537, 874 P.2d 868 (1994). For an illustration of an effective clause shifting the cost of environmental remediation to the purchaser, see Western Ohio Pizza, Inc. v. Clark Oil & Refining Corp., 704 N.E.2d 1086 (Ind.App. 1999). Cf. Prudential Ins. Co. v. Jefferson Assoc., Ltd., 896 S.W.2d 156 (Tex. 1995) ("as is" clause was sufficient to avoid seller liability for asbestos remediation under Texas Deceptive Trade Practices Act).

[865] Olmsted v. Mulder, 72 Wn.App. 169, 863 P.2d 1355 (1993).

[866] Only builders, and not other vendors, are typically subject to the implied warranty. See, e.g., Paden v. Murray, 240 Ga.App. 487, 523 S.E.2d 75 (Ga.App. 1999) (vendor was not liable as a builder, although he supervised the subcontractors who performed the construction); Choung v. Iemma, 708 N.E.2d 7 (Ind.App. 1999) (vendor who relocated house onto new foundation was not liable as a builder). On the other hand, the

By virtue of both statutes and judicial rulemaking, builders are widely regarded as similar to manufacturers of articled of personal property, and are held to have legal responsibility for the quality of the property. Courts have adopted at least three theories of recovery for purchasers; the most common by far is implied warranty,[867] but there is also authority for negligence actions in tort[868] and for strict liability in tort.[869] The theory employed by the plaintiff may affect the facts that must be pleaded and proved, and the remedies available.[870] In many states the warranties are court-created, but some states have embodied them in state statutes.[871] Unlike the fraudulent concealment and related doctrines discussed above, these warranties do not depend on proof of the vendor's knowledge or concealment, although they are usually conditioned on proof that the defect was "latent"—that is, the purchaser was unaware of it and could not readily have discovered it.[872]

There are wide variations in the standard to which the builder is held under these implied warranties and related theories. Perhaps the most common formulation is that the residence must be designed and constructed in a workmanlike manner and fit for habitation or the like.[873] But at one extreme, some courts will permit recovery for rather minor or temporary defects;[874] at the other are courts that recognize a violation only if the problems are so severe that living in the house is a practical impossibility[875] or that the structure itself is unstable or unsafe.[876] The courts have generally been willing to extend recovery to defective conditions in the lot or land parcel, not merely the

---

builder need not be a professional or construct houses in large volume to be liable; see Rogers v. Lewton, 570 N.E.2d 133 (Ind.App. 1991); Hoke v. Beck, 224 Ill.App.3d 674, 167 Ill.Dec. 122, 587 N.E.2d 4 (1992).

[867] Evans v. J. Stiles, Inc., 689 S.W.2d 399 (Tex. 1985); Crites & Blanner, Builders Beware: Strict Liability for Hidden Defects in New Homes, 72 J. Mo. B. 12 (2016); Sovern, Toward a Theory of Warranties in Sales of New Homes: Housing the Implied Warranty Advocates, Law and Economics Mavens, and Consumer Psychologists under One Roof, 1993 Wis. L. Rev. 13; O'Brien, Note, Caveat Venditor: A Case for Granting Subsequent Purchasers a Cause of Action Against Builder-Vendors for Latent Defects in the Home, 20 J. Corp. L. 525, 529 (Spring 1995). Depending on the facts, a variety of other theories may also be available against builders, including fraud and concealment as discussed earlier in this section, mutual or unilateral mistake, breach of express warranty, and violation of fraudulent trade practices statutes.

[868] Oates v. Jag, Inc., 314 N.C. 276, 333 S.E.2d 222 (1985).

[869] Patitucci v. Drelich, 153 N.J.Super. 177, 379 A.2d 297 (1977); Gay v. Cornwall, 6 Wn.App. 595, 494 P.2d 1371 (1972); Kriegler v. Eichler Homes, Inc., 269 Cal.App.2d 224, 74 Cal.Rptr. 749 (1969). See generally McKernan, Strict Liability Against Homebuilders for Material Latent Defects: It's Time, Arizona, 38 Ariz. L.Rev. 373 (1996).

[870] A negligence theory, of course, requires pleading and proof of the builder's failure to use reasonable care; see Cosmopolitan Homes, Inc. v. Weller, 663 P.2d 1041 (Colo. 1983). On the other hand, a remote subpurchaser who has no privity with the builder may find it easier to prevail on a tort rather than a warranty theory.

[871] See, e.g., Conn. Gen. Stat. § 47–121; Minn. Stat. § 327A.02; N.Y. Gen. Bus. Law § 777–b.4. Compare Fumarelli v. Marsam Devel., Inc., 92 N.Y.2d 298, 680 N.Y.S.2d 440, 703 N.E.2d 251 (1998) (statute provides sole remedy against builder) with Thorn v. Caskey, 745 So.2d 653 (La.App. 1999) (common law remedies coexist with statute).

[872] See, e.g., Kirk v. Ridgway, 373 N.W.2d 491 (Iowa 1985).

[873] Sirrah Enterprises, LLC v. Wunderlich, 242 Ariz. 542, 399 P.3d 89 (2017); Fattah v. Bim, 2016 IL 119365, 52 N.E.3d 332 (2016); Davencourt at Pilgrims Landing Homeowners Ass'n v. Davencourt at Pilgrims Landing, LC, 2009 UT 65, 221 P.3d 234 (2009); Rogers v. Wright, 2016 WY 10, 366 P.3d 1264 (Wyo. 2016).

[874] Roper v. Spring Lake Dev. Co., 789 P.2d 483 (Colo. App. 1990) (foul odor in garage); Deisch v. Jay, 790 P.2d 1273 (Wyo. 1990) (damp basement).

[875] Samuelson v. A.A. Quality Constr., Inc., 230 Mont. 220, 749 P.2d 73 (1988) (defects must preclude use of the dwelling as a residence).

[876] Stuart v. Coldwell Banker Commercial Group., Inc., 109 Wn.2d 406, 745 P.2d 1284 (1987) (defects must "profoundly compromise" the structure). See the critique of this narrow approach in Hansen v. Residential Dev., Ltd., 128 Wash. App. 1066, 2005 WL 1871127 (2005) (unpublished).

structures.[877] Some courts limit recovery against builders to the first owner of the new house,[878] on the ground that the warranty is contractual in nature and hence requires privity of contract, while others will permit subsequent subpurchasers to recover, particularly if the defects were latent and not reasonably discoverable at the time of the subpurchaser's acquisition of the property.[879]

If the courts overcome the privity problem and permit remote grantees to sue the builder or contractor, the period of potential liability lasts for a much longer time, on the average, than under the older cases that required direct privity between the plaintiff and the builder or contractor who performed the work. One way to limit this liability is to require that the suit be brought within a "reasonable time,"[880] but this is a highly subjective and elastic standard. To make the expiration of liability more predictable, a number of states have adopted special statutes of repose. These are distinct from statutes of limitation, which are usually are construed as incorporating a "discovery rule," meaning that their time periods do not begin to run until the injury was or should have been discovered.[881] A statute of repose fixes a time period (usually commencing from the date construction is completed or the house is sold to the first occupant) after which claims are cut off, irrespective of the date of discovery.[882] Note that a statute of repose (which disregards the discovery rule) and a statute of limitations (which incorporates the discovery rule) can operate side by side.[883] Typically, however, the period of a statute of repose is much longer (5 to 10 years) than a statute of limitation (2 to 5 years).

In the 1990s and 2000s about thirty states adopted "NOR" (short for "notice and opportunity to repair") statutes in an attempt to quell what seemed to be a tide of residential construction defect litigation.[884] These statutes require property owners to put builders on notice of construction defect claims and give them an opportunity to cure the defects.[885] Such statutes, which were vigorously supported by builder groups, usually

---

[877] Andrulis v. Levin Const. Corp., 331 Md. 354, 628 A.2d 197 (1993) (retaining wall in yard); Buchanan v. Scottsdale Environmental Constr. & Devel. Co., 163 Ariz. 285, 787 P.2d 1081 (Ariz.App. 1989) (settlement of soil). See French, Florida's Implied Warranty of Habitability: How Far Does A Homebuyer's Protection from A Developer's Ticky Tacky Construction Extend?, 44 Stetson L. Rev. 925, 926 (2015).

[878] Maack v. Resource Design & Constr., Inc., 875 P.2d 570 (Utah App. 1994); Foxcroft Townhome Owners Ass'n v. Hoffman Rosner Corp., 96 Ill.2d 150, 70 Ill.Dec. 251, 449 N.E.2d 125 (1983); Tereault v. Palmer, 413 N.W.2d 283 (Minn. App. 1987); Conway v. Cutler Group, Inc., 99 A.3d 67 (Pa. 2014). Speight v. Walters Devel. Co., Ltd., 744 N.W.2d 108 (Iowa 2008) lists 17 jurisdictions taking this view.

[879] Speight v. Walters Devel. Co., Ltd., id, lists 19 jurisdictions allowing actions by successor owners. See, e.g., Briggs v. Riversound Ltd. Partnership, 942 S.W.2d 529 (Tenn.App. 1996); Barlage v. Key Bank, 892 P.2d 124 (Wyo. 1995); Oates v. Jag, Inc., 314 N.C. 276, 333 S.E.2d 222 (1985).

[880] Bankston v. Pulaski County School District, 281 Ark. 476, 665 S.W.2d 859 (1984); Redarowicz v. Ohlendorf, 92 Ill. 2d 171, 65 Ill. Dec. 411, 441 N.E.2d 324 (1982).

[881] See, e.g., 328 Barry Avenue v. Nolan Properties Group, 871 N.W.2d 745 (Minn. 2016), noted 43 Mitchell Hamline L. Rev. 224 (2017); Haidar v. Nortey Foundation Designs, Inc., 239 S.W.3d 924 (Tex. App. 2007).

[882] See Albano v. Shea Homes Ltd. P'ship, 227 Ariz. 121, 254 P.3d 360 (2011); Petrus Family Tr. Dated May 1, 1991 v. Kirk, 163 Idaho 490, 415 P.3d 358 (2018); Alsenz v. Twin Lakes Village, Inc., 108 Nev. 1117, 843 P.2d 834 (1992).

[883] See, e.g., Gomez v. David A. Williams Realty & Const., Inc., 740 N.W.2d 775 (Minn. App. 2007) (2-year statute of limitations, 10-year statute of repose).

[884] Noble-Allgire, Notice and Opportunity to Repair Construction Defects: An Imperfect Response to the Perfect Storm, 43 Real Prop. Tr. & Est. L.J. 729 (2009).

[885] Baeza v. Superior Court, 201 Cal. App. 4th 1214, 135 Cal. Rptr. 3d 557 (2011); Davison v. Debest Plumbing, Inc., 163 Idaho 571, 416 P.3d 943 (2018). See Sandberg, Under Construction: The California Appellate Court's Misguided Decision in Liberty Mutual v. Brookfield Crystal Cove and the Legislature's

prohibit the filing of a suit until some fixed time (e.g., 60 days) after the builder is given notice, and they require the builder to respond to the notice either by disputing it, inspecting the property, or making a cash offer of settlement.[886]

§§ 11.17–12.0 ARE RESERVED FOR SUPPLEMENTAL MATERIAL.

Blueprint to Reconstruct the Right to Repair Act, 36 Whittier L. Rev. 485 (2015); Lutz, Restore Colorado's Repair Doctrine for Construction-Defect Claims, 83 U. Colo. L. Rev. 875 (2012).

[886] See Standard Pacific Corp. v. Superior Court, 98 Cal. Rptr. 3d 295 (Cal. App. 2009) (homeowners must give builder notice and opportunity to cure, as a prerequisite to filing suit, unless builder has failed to give them proper documentation); Hoch, The Kansas Residential Construction Defect Act: A Schematic Blueprint for Repairs, 74 J. Kan. Bar Assn. 20 (Mar. 2005).

Table of Cases

Index

References are to Pages

DRAINAGE
Water rights, 345–346

EASEMENTS AND PROFITS A PRENDRE
Generally, 350–387
Apportionability, 381–382
Appurtenant easements and profits, 354–356
Conveyance of easements or profits, 356–357
Deeds for railroad right of way, 356
Distinctions, 350–352
Divisibility, 381–382
Drafting express easements, 356–358
Estoppel, easement by, 371–373
Express easements, 356–358
Implied easements, 358–365
Necessity, 358–361
Plat, 364–365
Prior use, 361–364
In gross easements and profits, 354–356
Incorporeal hereditaments, history, 350
Leases distinguished, 350–351
License distinguished, 352
Nature of easements and profits, 350–354
Necessity, implied easements, 358–361
Negative easement, defined, 353–354
Part performance creating, 372–373
Plat, implied easements, 364–365
Prescriptive easements, 366–371
Prior use, implied easements, 361–364
Running covenants compared, 354
Scope of easements or profits, 373–380
Terminating easements or profits, 382–387
Transfers of easements or profits, 380–381
Use or possession, generally, 350–353

ELECTION REFERENDA
Zoning, 528–530

EMBLEMENTS IN CROPS
Life tenants and remainder holders inter se, 135–136

EMINENT DOMAIN
Compelled dedication, 572, 747
Leasehold, 231–232
Regulatory taking. See Government Land Use Regulation

ENABLING ACTS
Zoning, 442–443

ENCUMBRANCES
Covenant against, in deed, 804
Liens. See Liens
Mortgage interest, life tenants, 107–109
Mortgagee in possession, 200

ENJOINING WASTE
Life tenants and remainder holders inter se, 130–132

EQUITABLE CONVERSION DOCTRINE
Sales and conveyances, 675 et seq.

EQUITABLE INTERESTS DISTINGUISHED
Legal property, 7–8

EQUITABLE SERVITUDES
Covenants. See Running Covenants

ESCROW
Rent withholding, habitability breach, 259–260

ESTATES IN REALTY
Generally, 15–62
See also Title
Condition subsequent, fee subject, 32–39
Defeasible fee simple, 27 et seq.
Determinable fee, 30–32
Executory limitation, fee subject, 38
Fee simple absolute, 22–27
Fee simple determinable, 30–32, 42–46
Fee tail, 43–46
Future estates. See Future Estates or Interests
Leaseholds. See Landlord and Tenant
Seisin, covenant, 803

ESTOPPEL BY DEED
Deeds, 735

EVICTION
See Landlord and Tenant

EXCLUSIONARY ZONING
Zoning, 535–546

EXCLUSIVITY
Private property indicia, 2

EXECUTION OF INSTRUMENTS
Easement, 356–358
Equitable servitude, 424
Lease, 206–207
Running covenant, 389–390

EXECUTORY CONTRACTS OR INTERESTS
Fee estates, 39–43
Future interests
Alternative contingent remainders or vested remainders, 86–88
Shifting executory interests, 82–84
Springing executory interests, 85
Risk of loss, 681
Sales and conveyances, 595 et seq.

FAIR HOUSING ACT
Zoning, exclusionary, 543–546

FAMILY
Zoning, definitions, 512–514

FEE INTERESTS
See Estates in Realty

FIDUCIARY DUTIES
Cotenancy and joint ownership, 166–169

FINAL ACCOUNTING
Cotenancy and joint ownership, 173–174

FIRST REFUSAL RIGHTS
Sales and conveyances, 691

FITNESS FOR INTENDED USE
Leaseholds. See Landlord and Tenant

FIXTURES
Landlord and tenant, 279–281
Life tenants and remainder holders inter se, 135–136